DIRECTORY OF PENNSYLVANIA FOUNDATIONS

SEVENTH EDITION

Researched, compiled
and edited by
S. Damon Kletzien

TRIADVOCATES PRESS
SPRINGFIELD, PENNSYLVANIA

Published by
TRIADVOCATES PRESS
Post Office Box 336
Springfield, Pennsylvania 19064
Telephone: 610-544-6927
    FAX: 610-328-2805
    E-mail: PaFoundations@aol.com

Ordering information: See the Flyer/Order Form on page 623 or send a check for $88.50 (which includes shipping) *plus* Pa. Sales Tax of $5.30—unless exempt to the publisher at the address above.

Library of Congress Cataloging in Publication Data

Kletzien, S. Damon
        Directory of Pennsylvania foundations.
        Includes index.
        1. Endowments—Pennsylvania—Directories.
        I.Title
HV98.P4K53 2003 361.7'632'025748 86–050426

ISBN 0–9616806–4–4

Cover design by First Impressions Design Group, Inc.
Printed and bound in the United States of America

TABLE OF CONTENTS

Foreword & Dedication

Dare I say, 'twas <u>only</u> 25 years ago that I was midpoint in compiling the First Edition of the ***Directory of Pennsylvania Foundations***, working then under the aegis of The Free Library of Philadelphia . . . and what an interesting personal and technological journey it's been since that time!

That inaugural edition—cobbled together before personal computers revolutionized our world and lives—was handwritten on special forms, typed, with the final paste-up using rubber cement! Just preparing indexes required 10,000+ index cards, sorting, then typing! Sounds much closer to Gutenberg's era than 1977/78! Each subsequent edition (1981, 1986, 1991, 1995, 1998) embraced technology's newest "new thing" of the time: databases, desktop publishing, laser printers . . . The 7th Edition heads to the printer as a digital PDF file and it will not be long before that sounds quaint!

Over this quarter century, Pennsylvania's Foundation Universe itself has undergone remarkable change; aggregated assets have leapt from under $3 Billion to nearly $25 Billion, not to mention the hundreds and hundreds of newly-created foundations. The 7th Edition, I'd judge, has five times as much grants data as the First Edition! That's a whole lot of data to compile and keep up to date, so the future certainly involves developing web-based ways to access the directory's empowering cache of comprehensive grantsmanship information. Stay logged on/tuned in!

●

It's fair to say that all seven editions of the directory have been, in large measure, labors of love, usually much longer in duration than expected.

But, it's given me immense satisfaction over the years for countless non-profit-world friends and acquaintances to have affirmed the directory's importance in ensuring their organization's present and future. I salute all of you, your caring commitments, and the love you bring to your work.

And, on the home front, the directory owes bundles of love to my most wonderful spouse and best friend of 35 years, Sharon Benge Kletzien. It is unlikely that without her critical moral and material support the seven editions would ever have happened! Thank you, my dearest!

S. Damm Kletzien

PENNSYLVANIA'S FOUNDATIONS: A BRIEF OVERVIEW

Over 60,000 grant-making foundations in the United States hold about $480 Billion in assets according to *The Foundation Directory* (2002 Edition) and annually award over $27 Billion in grants. About one-third of this philanthropic wealth is held by foundations in six mid-Atlantic states—New York, New Jersey, Pennsylvania, Delaware, Maryland, and the District of Columbia.

Foundation Assets in Pennsylvania

As the keystone state of this "foundation belt," Pennsylvania hosts a diverse foundation community with assets exceeding $24.8 Billion (2000 or 2001 data). This places Pennsylvania as the nation's #4 Foundation State, behind New York ($83 Billion), California ($64 Billion), Washington State ($27 Billion) and ahead of Illinois, Indiana, Michigan, and Texas (all around $20 Billion).

The Commonwealth's 100 largest foundations account for 82% of the state's foundation wealth and, indeed, just the largest dozen foundations comprise 57% of total assets! Table V (pp. viii-x) lists Pennsylvania's top 214 foundations—those with assets over $15 Million *and/or* awarding $750,000 or more in grants, listed by *descending assets*. Table VI (pp. xi-xiii) lists these same foundations by *descending grant totals*. At the other/lower end of the assets spectrum are 1,400 smaller foundations whose assets comprise only 11.7% of the total.

The bulk of Pennsylvania's foundation wealth is concentrated in the highly urbanized and industrialized Southwestern (SW) and Southeastern (SE) regions (see map below) centering on Pittsburgh and Philadelphia, respectively. Together the SW and SE regions account for 91.6% of the state's foundation assets even though only 56.3% of Pennsylvanians reside in the 19 counties comprising these regions.

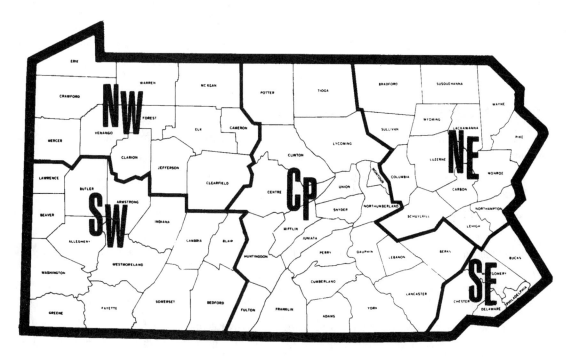

Table I (next page) details the regional distribution of assets of foundations profiled in the 7th Edition which account for nearly all discretionary giving by Pennsylvania foundations.

Table I
REGIONAL DIVISION OF 1,614 PROFILED FOUNDATIONS WITH
DISTRIBUTION OF ASSETS IN COMPARISON TO POPULATION

	SW	NW	CP	NE	SE	STATE-WIDE
Number of Foundations	399	79	231	155	750	1,614
Assets	$8,763,582,911	$421,123,923	$1,070,538,202	$594,756,857	$14,015,765,679	$24,865,767,572
% of Total Assets	35.2%	1.7%	4.3%	2.4%	56.4%	100%
% of PA Population ‡	25.0%	7.5%	22.4%	13.8%	31.3%	100%

‡ Pennsylvania's population: 12,281,054 per 2000 census

Table II
ASSET CATEGORIES OF 1,614 PROFILED FOUNDATIONS, BY REGION

	SW	NW	CP	NE	SE	STATE-WIDE
Assets over $100 Million	14	1	1	1	13	30
Assets $25—$100 Million	25	3	10	3	26	67
Assets $7.5—$25 Million	58	8	26	11	84	187
Assets $1—$7.5 Million	152	32	82	63	269	598
Assets under $1 Million	150	35	112	77	358	732

Foundation Definition and Criteria for Inclusion

For a foundation to be profiled in the 7th Edition it had to meet two fiscal criteria based on the foundation's most recent year of record (2001 or 2000 with few exceptions):

- **Assets at Market Value were $250,000 or more,** *and/or*
- **Total grant support exceeded $10,000**

In addition, a foundation had to meet (in most cases) The Foundation Center's definition of a Private Foundation:

...a nongovernmental, nonprofit organization, with funds (usually from a single source, either an individual, a family or corporation) and program managed by its own trustees or directors, and established to maintain or aid social, educational, charitable, religious, or other activities serving the common welfare, primarily through the making of grants. Charitable trusts are included as well as community foundations (which receive funds from many sources).

Profile-entries were **not** prepared for the following: (1) private operating foundations which administer their own programs directly and generally make no discretionary grants; (2) charitable organizations which bear the name "Foundation" but whose primary purpose is not awarding grants; and, (3) charitable trusts, typically managed by a bank trust department, which restrict grants—generally under the terms of a Will or Trust Instrument—grants to designated beneficiary institutions or to a narrowly defined group of beneficiaries.

Grant Support by Pennsylvania Foundations

The 7th Edition's 1,614 profiled foundations awarded over 80,000 grants totaling over $1.51 Billion, representing a payout rate of 6.0% on the foundations' aggregated assets. Table III details the regional spread of grant support and grant-dollars per capita.

TABLE III
GRANT SUPPORT AND GRANT-DOLLARS PER CAPITA, BY REGION, OF 1,614 PROFILED FOUNDATIONS

	S W	N W	C P	N E	S E	STATE-WIDE
Total Grant Support	$512,296,457	$22,487,345	$69,393,673	$34,966,707	$874,248,206	$1,513,392,388
Percentage of Total	33.9%	1.5%	4.6%	2.3%	57.7%	100%
Grant-Dollars per capita ‡	$167	$24	$25	$21	$227	$123

‡ Based on County Population Data from the 2000 Decennial Census

It is estimated that about three-fourths of the Pennsylvania's top 214 foundations (see Table VI on the following pages) awarded at least $500,000 in grants to organizations or institutions *within* the Commonwealth. An estimated 70% of all grant support by Pennsylvania foundations goes to Pennsylvania organizations or institutions, yet there are notable variances in regional giving. Foundations in the CP, NE and NW regions likely award over 90% of their support to Pennsylvania, whereas the figure for the SE and SW regions is about two-thirds, largely because of significant, nationwide giving by Pittsburgh-based corporate foundations, or nationally-oriented foundations such as Philadelphia's Pew Charitable Trusts and The Annenberg Foundation.

Non-Profiled Foundations

Table IV below details the categories of 2,100+ Pennsylvania foundations or charitable trusts which did **not** meet the criteria to be profiled in the 7th Edition. For grantseekers, the 371 foundations classified as "Limited Assets/Giving" (generally assets under $250,000 and $10,000 or less in discretionary grants) may be of possible interest. Definitions of Non-Profiled Foundation categories can be found in the **User's Guide to the Directory** chapter.

Table IV
STATUS OF THE 2,181 NON-PROFILED FOUNDATIONS

	S W	N W	C P	N E	S E	STATE-WIDE
Limited Assets/Giving	101	14	59	27	170	371
Operating Foundation	32	7	51	14	78	182
Restricted Giving	196	114	340	89	429	1,168
Inactive	14	4	8	9	45	80
"Non-PA" Foundations	41	2	9	5	143	200
Terminated/Uncertain Status	55	8	22	8	87	180
TOTALS	439	149	489	152	952	2,181

Table V

PENNSYLVANIA'S TOP 214 FOUNDATIONS
LISTED BY DESCENDING ASSETS
Assets exceed $15,000,000 — *or* — Total Grants $750,000 or more

Assets at Market Value	Fiscal Year Ending	Foundation Name	Regional Profile Number	County	Total Grant Support
$4,338,580,605	12-01	Pew Charitable Trusts, The	SE-513	Philadelphia	$230,135,400
$2,932,205,767	6-01	Annenberg Foundation, The	SE-022	Delaware	$136,895,959
$1,661,919,000	12-01	Mellon (Richard King) Foundation	SW-243	Allegheny	$77,054,950
$1,047,720,982	12-01	Penn (William) Foundation	SE-505	Philadelphia	$64,193,032
$912,613,000	12-01	Heinz (Howard) Endowment	SW-160	Allegheny	$41,100,027
$733,997,000	12-01	Board of City Trusts, City of Philadelphia	SE-071	Philadelphia	$72,060,000
$564,173,106	9-01	McCune Foundation	SW-231	Allegheny	$27,858,921
$519,616,368	12-01	Pittsburgh Foundation, The	SW-284	Allegheny	$25,539,949
$468,932,000	12-01	Heinz (Vira I.) Endowment	SW-161	Allegheny	$18,501,097
$410,121,949	12-01	Alcoa Foundation	SW-004	Allegheny	$21,284,785
$364,327,000	12-00	Scaife (Sarah) Foundation	SW-329	Allegheny	$25,785,000
$346,406,822	12-00	Benedum (Claude Worthington) Foundation	SW-021	Allegheny	$16,668,604
$298,126,612	12-00	Templeton (John) Foundation	SE-688	Delaware	$13,417,578
$263,595,333	12-00	Connelly Foundation	SE-145	Montgomery	$14,008,662
$237,865,221	12-00	Carpenter (E. Rhodes & Leona B.) Foundation, The	SE-116	Philadelphia	$10,626,224
$234,656,940	12-01	Grable Foundation, The	SW-145	Allegheny	$10,984,014
$195,278,685	11-00	Oberkotter Foundation	SE-493	Philadelphia	$21,334,724
$195,134,000	12-01	Philadelphia Foundation, The	SE-515	Philadelphia	$18,605,408
$194,219,827	12-00	Eden Hall Foundation	SW-097	Allegheny	$9,765,730
$180,910,159	11-00	McCune (John R.) Charitable Trust	SW-232	Allegheny	$8,563,359
$159,631,581	6-01	Smith (W.W.) Charitable Trust, The	SE-642	Montgomery	$7,606,465
$157,410,225	6-01	Lenfest Foundation, The	SE-406	Montgomery	$6,635,656
$132,594,674	12-01	Hillman Foundation, Inc., The	SW-164	Allegheny	$6,462,400
$131,761,086	12-01	Independence Foundation	SE-337	Philadelphia	$8,973,778
$119,803,018	12-01	Jewish Healthcare Foundation	SW-186	Allegheny	$6,000,000
$119,632,864	3-01	Trexler Trust	NE-142	Lehigh	$4,924,674
$118,790,818	6-00	Philadelphia Health Care Trust	SE-516	Philadelphia	$4,300,000
$108,063,816	12-00	Scaife Family Foundation	SW-328	Allegheny	$7,710,135
$102,870,466	6-01	Degenstein Foundation, The	CP-045	Northumberland	$6,370,352
$100,900,000	12-01	Erie Community Foundation, The	NW-019	Erie	$6,933,853
$95,065,725	5-01	Hunt (Roy A.) Foundation, The	SW-175	Allegheny	$3,644,131
$93,167,985	12-01	Scaife Charitable Foundation	SW-327	Allegheny	$4,319,431
$89,438,347	12-00	Hillman (Henry L.) Foundation, The	SW-165	Allegheny	$4,098,150
$87,823,863	12-01	First Union Regional Foundation	SE-225	Philadelphia	$4,575,000
$85,335,916	12-00	McKenna (Katherine Mabis) Foundation	SW-238	Westmoreland	$3,717,750
$80,664,699	6-01	Buhl Foundation, The	SW-047	Allegheny	$4,396,118
$80,438,412	12-00	Trees (Edith L.) Charitable Trust	SW-368	Allegheny	$4,245,258
$76,299,076	12-00	Heinz Family Foundation	SW-158	Allegheny	$6,375,393
$70,609,602	12-00	Measey (Benjamin & Mary Siddons) Foundation	SE-448	Delaware	$2,910,094
$68,435,515	12-01	Pool (Dorothy Rider) Health Care Trust	NE-113	Lehigh	$6,127,613
$65,116,758	12-00	Mellon Financial Corporation Foundation	SW-241	Allegheny	$4,300,349
$62,681,937	12-01	Oxford Foundation	CP-146	Lancaster	$3,010,843
$61,905,075	12-00	Davenport Family Foundation, The	SE-161	Chester	$2,600,729
$58,243,872	6-01	Presser Foundation, The	SE-532	Montgomery	$2,180,348
$55,058,475	6-01	Allerton Foundation, The	SE-017	Montgomery	$596,985
$54,500,983	12-00	Barra Foundation, The	SE-045	Montgomery	$3,966,213
$54,459,134	12-00	Bayer Foundation	SW-018	Allegheny	$4,573,274
$52,783,731	12-01	Grundy Foundation, The	SE-289	Bucks	$1,275,915
$52,209,245	4-00	Perelman (Raymond & Ruth) Education Foundation	SE-510	Montgomery	$2,056,200
$51,265,949	12-01	Claneil Foundation, The	SE-130	Montgomery	$3,718,604
$49,843,763	12-00	Jennings (Mary Hillman) Foundation	SW-184	Allegheny	$3,408,000
$49,733,968	9-01	Arcadia Foundation, The	SE-025	Montgomery	$7,955,744
$48,999,555	12-00	Hamilton Family Foundation	SE-302	Delaware	$4,247,185
$48,385,944	12-00	Williamsport-Lycoming Foundation	CP-221	Lycoming	$883,090
$47,200,000	12-01	McLean Contributionship, The	SE-446	Montgomery	$2,269,240
$47,197,631	12-00	Staunton Farm Foundation	SW-356	Allegheny	$1,171,699
$47,114,633	12-01	Fels (Samuel S.) Fund	SE-215	Philadelphia	$2,368,036
$46,340,891	12-00	Wyss Foundation, The	SE-747	Chester	$2,225,732
$44,080,889	6-00	National City Foundation	SW-260	Allegheny	$17,127,194
$42,948,724	12-00	Laurel Foundation	SW-205	Allegheny	$1,895,045
$42,098,138	12-00	Allegheny Foundation	SW-006	Allegheny	$1,582,500
$41,303,651	12-00	Huston Foundation, The	SE-332	Montgomery	$2,059,741
$40,380,930	6-01	Ellis (Charles E.) Grant & Scholarship Fund	SE-196	Philadelphia	$1,815,869

Assets at Market Value	Fiscal Year Ending	Foundation Name	Regional Profile Number	County	Total Grant Support
$39,571,913	12-01	Mellon (R.K.) Family Foundation	SW-242	Allegheny	$1,944,550
$38,433,065	12-01	Massey Charitable Trust	SW-227	Allegheny	$1,926,580
$38,400,376	6-01	FISA Foundation	SW-117	Allegheny	$1,557,330
$37,820,880	12-00	Wyomissing Foundation, The	CP-228	Berks	$1,566,636
$36,600,192	12-00	Century Fund Foundation	NE-032	Lehigh	$2,407,527
$36,066,807	4-00	Perelman (Raymond & Ruth) Judaica Foundation	SE-511	Montgomery	$1,556,980
$35,322,721	12-00	Community Foundation of Warren County	NW-009	Warren	$1,172,800
$34,340,737	4-02	Lancaster County Foundation, The	CP-115	Lancaster	$1,046,750
$33,935,480	12-01	Morris (Charles M.) Charitable Trust, The	SW-254	Allegheny	$1,412,854
$33,667,953	12-00	Carnegie Hero Fund Commission	SW-056	Allegheny	$685,312
$33,632,347	12-00	Comcast Foundation, The	SE-142	Philadelphia	$1,925,198
$33,451,568	7-00	Whitaker (Helen F.) Fund, The	CP-219	Cumberland	$4,458,007
$33,133,071	6-01	Phoenixville Community Health Foundation	SE-518	Chester	$1,723,337
$32,129,985	12-00	PNC Foundation	SW-287	Allegheny	$10,440,079
$31,585,289	12-00	Hopwood (J.M.) Charitable Trust	SW-169	Allegheny	$1,418,354
$30,949,523	12-00	Steinman (John Frederick) Foundation, The	CP-194	Lancaster	$1,429,549
$29,782,462	12-01	First Hospital Foundation	SE-222	Philadelphia	$682,123
$29,628,164	12-01	Kind (Patricia) Family Foundation	SE-372	Montgomery	$2,427,600
$29,326,754	12-01	Gibson (Addison H.) Foundation	SW-138	Allegheny	$1,720,092
$29,306,760	12-00	Frick (Helen Clay) Foundation, The	SW-128	Allegheny	$943,719
$29,226,273	12-00	Strauss Foundation	SE-667	Montgomery	$1,607,325
$29,078,518	12-00	Wyss (Hansjoerg) AO Medical Foundation	SE-748	Chester	$4,132,010
$28,780,800	12-00	Steinman (James Hale) Foundation, The	CP-193	Lancaster	$1,203,230
$28,057,800	12-00	Nelson (Grace S. & W. Linton) Foundation, The	SE-480	Chester	$1,435,055
$27,154,326	12-00	Stackpole-Hall Foundation, The	NW-070	Elk	$1,454,463
$26,415,852	6-00	Maplewood Foundation	SW-222	Allegheny	$1,420,312
$26,060,615	7-01	Pine Tree Foundation	SE-522	Montgomery	$1,255,000
$25,814,260	12-00	Berwick Health & Wellness Foundation	NE-017	Columbia	$1,550,571
$25,687,346	6-00	Graham Foundation, The	CP-070	York	$476,020
$25,650,712	12-00	Kline (Josiah W. & Bessie H.) Foundation	CP-109	Dauphin	$1,287,628
$25,529,464	12-01	York Foundation	CP-231	York	$1,427,579
$25,463,758	12-00	Stine (James M. & Margaret V.) Foundation	SE-665	Philadelphia	$724,800
$25,322,284	12-00	Hirtzel (Orris C. & Beatrice Dewey) Memorial Foundation	NW-027	Erie	$1,572,074
$25,013,090	12-00	Colcom Foundation	SW-067	Allegheny	$882,000
$24,919,606	12-00	PPG Industries Foundation	SW-295	Allegheny	$4,896,746
$24,862,046	6-01	Lenfest (Brook J.) Foundation, The	SE-405	Montgomery	$95,000
$24,565,077	12-00	Carthage Foundation, The	SW-057	Allegheny	$627,500
$24,509,682	9-00	Clapp (Anne L. & George H.) Charitable & Educational Trust	SW-062	Allegheny	$1,244,000
$24,357,558	12-00	Janssen (Henry) Foundation, The	CP-101	Berks	$1,131,500
$23,940,213	12-00	Huston (Stewart) Charitable Trust, The	SE-333	Chester	$1,989,454
$23,273,641	7-00	Kimmel (Sidney) Foundation	SE-371	Philadelphia	$5,134,100
$23,190,175	12-01	Lindback Foundation, The	SE-416	Philadelphia	$1,255,804
$22,929,184	12-00	Warwick Foundation, The	SE-719	Philadelphia	$1,220,000
$22,910,847	6-01	Berks County Community Foundation	CP-014	Berks	$2,579,801
$22,752,064	12-00	Stein (Louis & Bessie) Foundation	SE-655	Montgomery	$1,199,817
$22,725,979	10-00	Brossman (William & Jemima) Charitable Foundation	CP-025	Lancaster	$1,002,720
$22,649,023	12-01	Greater Harrisburg Foundation, The	CP-073	Dauphin	$5,086,523
$22,584,306	12-00	Fourjay Foundation, The	SE-236	Montgomery	$1,257,270
$22,277,793	8-00	Schwartz Foundation, The	SE-609	Montgomery	$2,674,780
$22,000,000	12-00	Justus (Samuel) Charitable Trust	NW-032	Venango	$563,934
$21,761,406	12-01	Snee-Reinhardt Charitable Foundation	SW-342	Allegheny	$831,298
$21,564,546	6-01	Birmingham Foundation, The	SW-032	Allegheny	$1,035,175
$21,357,108	12-00	Kelly (Paul E.) Foundation	SE-367	Montgomery	$795,850
$21,167,233	12-00	Eberly Foundation, The	SW-095	Fayette	$18,799,868
$21,166,973	12-00	Rossin Foundation	SW-314	Washington	$1,896,470
$21,078,824	12-00	Hall (Edwin), 2nd Charitable Trust	SE-300	Delaware	$795,981
$20,910,497	12-01	McFeely-Rogers Foundation	SW-233	Westmoreland	$894,245
$20,502,961	6-01	1957 Charity Foundation	SE-001	Montgomery	$1,325,562
$20,391,968	11-00	Roberts (Ralph & Suzanne) Foundation, The	SE-558	Philadelphia	$1,018,349
$20,143,787	12-00	Tyco Electronics Foundation, The	CP-206	Dauphin	$1,182,596
$20,106,487	9-01	Eustace Foundation, The	SE-204	Montgomery	$1,436,350
$19,682,099	12-00	McKenna (Philip M.) Foundation	SW-239	Westmoreland	$1,234,495
$19,605,844	12-00	Cornerstone Foundation	SE-151	Chester	$1,182,120
$19,482,390	8-00	Giant Eagle Foundation	SW-137	Allegheny	$2,624,913
$19,382,601	12-00	Dietrich (William B.) Foundation, The	SE-176	Philadelphia	$1,038,135
$19,302,601	6-01	West Family Foundation, The	SE-723	Chester	$332,212
$19,047,068	3-00	McKinney (William V. & Catherine A.) Charitable Foundation	SW-240	Allegheny	$591,500
$18,910,873	12-00	Crels Foundation	CP-040	Lancaster	$841,500
$18,667,825	12-01	Genuardi Family Foundation	SE-255	Montgomery	$72,500
$18,197,264	4-00	Beneficia Foundation	SE-056	Montgomery	$1,377,000
$18,197,000	12-01	Scranton Area Foundation	NE-133	Lackawanna	$530,758
$17,992,785	12-00	Saligman (Robert) Charitable Trust	SE-590	Montgomery	$879,685
$17,669,254	12-00	Williams (C.K.) Foundation, The	SE-729	Philadelphia	$546,100
$17,559,288	8-01	Falk (Maurice) Medical Fund	SW-107	Allegheny	$520,578
$17,532,231	5-01	Smith (Ethel Sergeant Clark) Memorial Fund	SE-640	Philadelphia	$938,299
$17,423,906	12-00	Scholler Foundation, The	SE-605	Philadelphia	$766,762

Assets at Market Value	Fiscal Year Ending	Foundation Name	Regional Profile Number	County	Total Grant Support
$17,412,426	12-00	Glencairn Foundation	SE-271	Montgomery	$882,265
$17,377,122	11-00	Neubauer Foundation, The	SE-481	Philadelphia	$704,800
$17,372,207	3-01	Palumbo (A.J. & Sigismunda) Charitable Trust	SW-269	Allegheny	$934,000
$17,256,590	9-00	Colonial Oaks Foundation	CP-038	Berks	$799,220
$17,255,427	12-00	Mandell (Samuel P.) Foundation	SE-431	Philadelphia	$1,574,635
$17,106,068	12-00	Donley Foundation	SE-181	Montgomery	$1,071,300
$16,903,144	9-01	Dolfinger-McMahon Foundation	SE-180	Philadelphia	$1,026,187
$16,779,084	12-00	Stuart (G.B.) Charitable Foundation	CP-196	Cumberland	$619,198
$16,699,340	7-01	Sherrerd Foundation	SE-621	Montgomery	$780,124
$16,551,801	9-00	Phillips (Dr. & Mrs. Arthur William) Charitable Trust	NW-058	Venango	$695,623
$16,529,137	4-00	Perelman (Raymond & Ruth) Community Foundation	SE-509	Montgomery	$826,350
$16,423,745	12-00	Rockwell Foundation, The	SW-311	Allegheny	$1,001,500
$16,416,630	12-00	Posner Foundation of Pittsburgh	SW-294	Allegheny	$169,815
$16,357,483	6-01	Community Foundation for the Alleghenies, The	SW-069	Cambria	$1,179,225
$15,985,266	12-00	Weisbrod (Robert & Mary) Foundation	SW-385	Allegheny	$746,818
$15,600,000	6-02	Chester County Community Foundation, The	SE-125	Chester	$1,100,000
$15,529,312	12-00	Kavanagh (T. James) Foundation	NW-035	Mercer	$303,101
$15,528,555	12-00	Ressler Mill Foundation	CP-165	Lancaster	$212,295
$15,147,312	6-00	de Mazia (Violette) Trust	SE-164	Montgomery	$1,074,764
$14,952,727	12-00	Shenango Valley Foundation	NW-065	Mercer	$1,048,997
$14,757,262	12-00	Bozzone Family Foundation	SW-039	Westmoreland	$1,330,242
$14,729,203	12-00	Sordoni Foundation, Inc.	NE-140	Luzerne	$941,165
$14,506,787	12-00	FirstFruits Foundation	SE-226	Chester	$1,007,500
$14,029,867	4-01	Betz (Theodora B.) Foundation	SE-066	Philadelphia	$1,279,615
$13,544,203	6-01	Willis (Hilda M.) Foundation #2	SW-391	Allegheny	$1,078,264
$13,520,743	10-01	Hoyt Foundation, The	SW-173	Lawrence	$1,019,021
$13,236,055	4-00	Snider Foundation, The	SE-645	Philadelphia	$1,364,350
$12,415,464	12-00	Berkman (Sybiel B.) Foundation	SW-026	Allegheny	$1,078,220
$11,112,402	12-00	Simmons (Richard P.) Family Foundation	SW-336	Allegheny	$6,251,234
$10,855,972	11-00	Rangos (John G.), Sr. Charitable Foundation, The	SW-300	Allegheny	$1,633,765
$10,694,682	12-00	Bitz Foundation	SW-034	Beaver	$936,524
$10,511,365	11-01	United States Steel Foundation, Inc.	SW-371	Allegheny	$6,505,023
$10,478,636	7-00	Field (Joseph & Marie) Foundation	SE-218	Montgomery	$760,000
$10,383,872	11-00	Buncher Family Foundation	SW-048	Allegheny	$808,055
$9,912,479	11-00	Garfield (Eugene) Foundation, The	SE-248	Montgomery	$1,098,909
$9,734,607	6-01	Sedwick Foundation	SW-330	Butler	$1,830,527
$9,244,598	12-00	Strawbridge (Maxwell) Charitable Trust	SE-670	Philadelphia	$1,096,400
$9,061,280	6-01	Community Foundation of Westmoreland County, The	SW-073	Westmoreland	$945,990
$9,050,954	11-00	RAF Foundation, The	SE-544	Montgomery	$3,680,000
$8,775,067	12-00	Harsco Corporation Fund	CP-083	Cumberland	$1,153,080
$8,749,092	12-00	Foster (John H.) Foundation, The	SE-235	Montgomery	$1,441,000
$8,300,476	12-00	Widener Memorial Foundation in Aid of Handicapped Children	SE-728	Montgomery	$832,495
$8,048,954	12-00	Dominion Foundation	SW-087	Allegheny	$4,084,563
$7,801,846	12-00	Ametek Foundation	SE-021	Chester	$984,155
$7,591,198	7-01	Maple Hill Foundation	SE-432	Montgomery	$1,275,100
$7,408,291	10-00	Arronson Foundation	SE-030	Philadelphia	$847,140
$5,604,872	6-01	Donnelly (Mary J.) Foundation	SW-090	Allegheny	$1,454,500
$5,469,760	12-00	Hamer Foundation, The	CP-080	Centre	$919,750
$5,321,168	4-01	Sylvan Foundation, The	SE-678	Delaware	$1,155,000
$5,284,419	12-00	Brickman Foundation	SE-083	Montgomery	$6,878,701
$5,044,791	12-01	Armstrong Foundation	CP-010	Lancaster	$2,121,985
$4,915,356	12-00	Cardone (Michael) Foundation	SE-112	Philadelphia	$765,750
$4,639,358	12-00	Hooker (Janet Annenberg) Charitable Trust	SE-326	Philadelphia	$5,455,500
$3,846,048	12-00	Vanguard Group Foundation, The	SE-706	Chester	$2,322,504
$3,654,550	12-00	Donahue Family Foundation	SW-088	Allegheny	$2,664,836
$3,547,861	6-00	Hooper (Elizabeth S.) Foundation	SE-327	Chester	$761,100
$3,401,675	12-00	GlaxoSmithKline Foundation	SE-270	Philadelphia	$3,525,509
$3,333,657	12-00	Byers Foundation, The	SE-103	Bucks	$1,414,705
$3,266,430	12-00	Eglin (Meyer & Stephanie) Foundation	SE-192	Philadelphia	$1,798,000
$2,934,548	12-00	Allegheny Technologies Charitable Trust	SW-007	Allegheny	$1,475,840
$2,602,725	12-00	Rock (Milton L. & Shirley) Foundation	SE-560	Philadelphia	$1,067,208
$2,100,814	6-00	Charlestein (Julius & Ray) Foundation, Inc.	SE-124	Montgomery	$1,682,711
$2,098,809	12-00	Fox (Richard J.) Foundation, The	SE-238	Delaware	$1,069,350
$1,909,221	12-00	Susquehanna Foundation	SE-676	Montgomery	$1,790,585
$1,383,359	12-00	Donnell (Richard H.) Foundation	SW-089	Washington	$775,137
$1,121,024	12-00	CIGNA Foundation	SE-129	Philadelphia	$5,799,574
$1,100,436	12-00	Good (Richard & Annetta) Foundation	CP-068	Lancaster	$980,884
$892,746	12-00	First Union Foundation	SE-224	Philadelphia	$23,933,599
$872,327	12-00	CMS Foundation	SE-135	Philadelphia	$823,575
$753,778	12-00	Heinz (H.J.) Company Foundation	SW-159	Allegheny	$6,494,241
$719,289	12-00	Miller (Marlin), Jr. Family Foundation	CP-134	Berks	$2,514,078
$396,781	12-00	Green (Mayer A.) Allergy Foundation	SW-148	Allegheny	$1,173,904
$238,957	12-00	Bethlehem Steel Foundation	NE-018	Lehigh	$1,580,013
$59,661	12-00	Safeguard Scientifics Foundation	SE-586	Chester	$2,929,806
$2,155	12-00	Jomar Foundation	SE-349	Bucks	$2,714,704

Table VI

PENNSYLVANIA'S TOP 214 FOUNDATIONS
LISTED BY DESCENDING GRANT TOTALS
Total Grants of $750,000 or more — *or* — Assets exceed $15,000,000

Total Grant Support	Fiscal Year Ending	Assets at Market Value	Foundation Name	County	Regional Profile Number
$230,135,400	12-01	$4,338,580,605	Pew Charitable Trusts, The	Philadelphia	SE-513
$136,895,959	6-01	$2,932,205,767	Annenberg Foundation, The	Delaware	SE-022
$77,054,950	12-01	$1,661,919,000	Mellon (Richard King) Foundation	Allegheny	SW-243
$72,060,000	12-01	$733,997,000	Board of City Trusts, City of Philadelphia	Philadelphia	SE-071
$64,193,032	12-01	$1,047,720,982	Penn (William) Foundation	Philadelphia	SE-505
$41,100,027	12-01	$912,613,000	Heinz (Howard) Endowment	Allegheny	SW-160
$27,858,921	9-01	$564,173,106	McCune Foundation	Allegheny	SW-231
$25,785,000	12-00	$364,327,000	Scaife (Sarah) Foundation	Allegheny	SW-329
$25,539,949	12-01	$519,616,368	Pittsburgh Foundation, The	Allegheny	SW-284
$23,933,599	12-00	$892,746	First Union Foundation	Philadelphia	SE-224
$21,334,724	11-00	$195,278,685	Oberkotter Foundation	Philadelphia	SE-493
$21,284,785	12-01	$410,121,949	Alcoa Foundation	Allegheny	SW-004
$18,799,868	12-00	$21,167,233	Eberly Foundation, The	Fayette	SW-095
$18,605,408	12-01	$195,134,000	Philadelphia Foundation, The	Philadelphia	SE-515
$18,501,097	12-01	$468,932,000	Heinz (Vira I.) Endowment	Allegheny	SW-161
$17,127,194	6-00	$44,080,889	National City Foundation	Allegheny	SW-260
$16,668,604	12-00	$346,406,822	Benedum (Claude Worthington) Foundation	Allegheny	SW-021
$14,008,662	12-00	$263,595,333	Connelly Foundation	Montgomery	SE-145
$13,417,578	12-00	$298,126,612	Templeton (John) Foundation	Delaware	SE-688
$10,984,014	12-01	$234,656,940	Grable Foundation, The	Allegheny	SW-145
$10,626,224	12-00	$237,865,221	Carpenter (E. Rhodes & Leona B.) Foundation, The	Philadelphia	SE-116
$10,440,079	12-00	$32,129,985	PNC Foundation	Allegheny	SW-287
$9,765,730	12-00	$194,219,827	Eden Hall Foundation	Allegheny	SW-097
$8,973,778	12-01	$131,761,086	Independence Foundation	Philadelphia	SE-337
$8,563,359	11-00	$180,910,159	McCune (John R.) Charitable Trust	Allegheny	SW-232
$7,955,744	9-01	$49,733,968	Arcadia Foundation, The	Montgomery	SE-025
$7,710,135	12-00	$108,063,816	Scaife Family Foundation	Allegheny	SW-328
$7,606,465	6-01	$159,631,581	Smith (W.W.) Charitable Trust, The	Montgomery	SE-642
$6,933,853	12-01	$100,900,000	Erie Community Foundation, The	Erie	NW-019
$6,878,701	12-00	$5,284,419	Brickman Foundation	Montgomery	SE-083
$6,635,656	6-01	$157,410,225	Lenfest Foundation, The	Montgomery	SE-406
$6,505,023	11-01	$10,511,365	United States Steel Foundation, Inc.	Allegheny	SW-371
$6,494,241	12-00	$753,778	Heinz (H.J.) Company Foundation	Allegheny	SW-159
$6,462,400	12-01	$132,594,674	Hillman Foundation, Inc., The	Allegheny	SW-164
$6,375,393	12-00	$76,299,076	Heinz Family Foundation	Allegheny	SW-158
$6,370,352	6-01	$102,870,466	Degenstein Foundation, The	Northumberland	CP-045
$6,251,234	12-00	$11,112,402	Simmons (Richard P.) Family Foundation	Allegheny	SW-336
$6,127,613	12-01	$68,435,515	Pool (Dorothy Rider) Health Care Trust	Lehigh	NE-113
$6,000,000	12-01	$119,803,018	Jewish Healthcare Foundation	Allegheny	SW-186
$5,799,574	12-00	$1,121,024	CIGNA Foundation	Philadelphia	SE-129
$5,455,500	12-00	$4,639,358	Hooker (Janet Annenberg) Charitable Trust	Philadelphia	SE-326
$5,134,100	7-00	$23,273,641	Kimmel (Sidney) Foundation	Philadelphia	SE-371
$5,086,523	12-01	$22,649,023	Greater Harrisburg Foundation, The	Dauphin	CP-073
$4,924,674	3-01	$119,632,864	Trexler Trust	Lehigh	NE-142
$4,896,746	12-00	$24,919,606	PPG Industries Foundation	Allegheny	SW-295
$4,575,000	12-01	$87,823,863	First Union Regional Foundation	Philadelphia	SE-225
$4,573,274	12-00	$54,459,134	Bayer Foundation	Allegheny	SW-018
$4,458,007	7-00	$33,451,568	Whitaker (Helen F.) Fund, The	Cumberland	CP-219
$4,396,118	6-01	$80,664,699	Buhl Foundation, The	Allegheny	SW-047
$4,319,431	12-01	$93,167,985	Scaife Charitable Foundation	Allegheny	SW-327
$4,300,349	12-00	$65,116,758	Mellon Financial Corporation Foundation	Allegheny	SW-241
$4,300,000	6-00	$118,790,818	Philadelphia Health Care Trust	Philadelphia	SE-516
$4,247,185	12-00	$48,999,555	Hamilton Family Foundation	Delaware	SE-302
$4,245,258	12-00	$80,438,412	Trees (Edith L.) Charitable Trust	Allegheny	SW-368
$4,132,010	12-00	$29,078,518	Wyss (Hansjoerg) AO Medical Foundation	Chester	SE-748
$4,098,150	12-00	$89,438,347	Hillman (Henry L.) Foundation, The	Allegheny	SW-165
$4,084,563	12-00	$8,048,954	Dominion Foundation	Allegheny	SW-087
$3,966,213	12-00	$54,500,983	Barra Foundation, The	Montgomery	SE-045
$3,718,604	12-01	$51,265,949	Claneil Foundation, The	Montgomery	SE-130
$3,717,750	12-00	$85,335,916	McKenna (Katherine Mabis) Foundation	Westmoreland	SW-238
$3,680,000	11-00	$9,050,954	RAF Foundation, The	Montgomery	SE-544
$3,644,131	5-01	$95,065,725	Hunt (Roy A.) Foundation, The	Allegheny	SW-175
$3,525,509	12-00	$3,401,675	GlaxoSmithKline Foundation	Philadelphia	SE-270

Total Grant Support	Fiscal Year Ending	Assets at Market Value	Foundation Name	County	Regional Profile Number
$3,408,000	12-00	$49,843,763	Jennings (Mary Hillman) Foundation	Allegheny	SW-184
$3,010,843	12-01	$62,681,937	Oxford Foundation	Lancaster	CP-146
$2,929,806	12-00	$59,661	Safeguard Scientifics Foundation	Chester	SE-586
$2,910,094	12-00	$70,609,602	Measey (Benjamin & Mary Siddons) Foundation	Delaware	SE-448
$2,714,704	12-00	$2,155	Jomar Foundation	Bucks	SE-349
$2,674,780	8-00	$22,277,793	Schwartz Foundation, The	Montgomery	SE-609
$2,664,836	12-00	$3,654,550	Donahue Family Foundation	Allegheny	SW-088
$2,624,913	8-00	$19,482,390	Giant Eagle Foundation	Allegheny	SW-137
$2,600,729	12-00	$61,905,075	Davenport Family Foundation, The	Chester	SE-161
$2,579,801	6-01	$22,910,847	Berks County Community Foundation	Berks	CP-014
$2,514,078	12-00	$719,289	Miller (Marlin), Jr. Family Foundation	Berks	CP-134
$2,427,600	12-01	$29,628,164	Kind (Patricia) Family Foundation	Montgomery	SE-372
$2,407,527	12-00	$36,600,192	Century Fund Foundation	Lehigh	NE-032
$2,368,036	12-01	$47,114,633	Fels (Samuel S.) Fund	Philadelphia	SE-215
$2,322,504	12-00	$3,846,048	Vanguard Group Foundation, The	Chester	SE-706
$2,269,240	12-01	$47,200,000	McLean Contributionship, The	Montgomery	SE-446
$2,225,732	12-00	$46,340,891	Wyss Foundation, The	Chester	SE-747
$2,180,348	6-01	$58,243,872	Presser Foundation, The	Montgomery	SE-532
$2,121,985	12-01	$5,044,791	Armstrong Foundation	Lancaster	CP-010
$2,059,741	12-00	$41,303,651	Huston Foundation, The	Montgomery	SE-332
$2,056,200	4-00	$52,209,245	Perelman (Raymond & Ruth) Education Foundation	Montgomery	SE-510
$1,989,454	12-00	$23,940,213	Huston (Stewart) Charitable Trust, The	Chester	SE-333
$1,944,550	12-01	$39,571,913	Mellon (R.K.) Family Foundation	Allegheny	SW-242
$1,926,580	12-01	$38,433,065	Massey Charitable Trust	Allegheny	SW-227
$1,925,198	12-00	$33,632,347	Comcast Foundation, The	Philadelphia	SE-142
$1,896,470	12-00	$21,166,973	Rossin Foundation	Washington	SW-314
$1,895,045	12-00	$42,948,724	Laurel Foundation	Allegheny	SW-205
$1,830,527	6-01	$9,734,607	Sedwick Foundation	Butler	SW-330
$1,815,869	6-01	$40,380,930	Ellis (Charles E.) Grant & Scholarship Fund	Philadelphia	SE-196
$1,798,000	12-00	$3,266,430	Eglin (Meyer & Stephanie) Foundation	Philadelphia	SE-192
$1,790,585	12-00	$1,909,221	Susquehanna Foundation	Montgomery	SE-676
$1,723,337	6-01	$33,133,071	Phoenixville Community Health Foundation	Chester	SE-518
$1,720,092	12-01	$29,326,754	Gibson (Addison H.) Foundation	Allegheny	SW-138
$1,682,711	6-00	$2,100,814	Charlestein (Julius & Ray) Foundation, Inc.	Montgomery	SE-124
$1,633,765	11-00	$10,855,972	Rangos (John G.), Sr. Charitable Foundation, The	Allegheny	SW-300
$1,607,325	12-00	$29,226,273	Strauss Foundation	Montgomery	SE-667
$1,582,500	12-00	$42,098,138	Allegheny Foundation	Allegheny	SW-006
$1,580,013	12-00	$238,957	Bethlehem Steel Foundation	Lehigh	NE-018
$1,574,635	12-00	$17,255,427	Mandell (Samuel P.) Foundation	Philadelphia	SE-431
$1,572,074	12-00	$25,322,284	Hirtzel (Orris & Beatrice Dewey) Memorial Foundation	Erie	NW-027
$1,566,636	12-00	$37,820,880	Wyomissing Foundation, The	Berks	CP-228
$1,557,330	6-01	$38,400,376	FISA Foundation	Allegheny	SW-117
$1,556,980	4-00	$36,066,807	Perelman (Raymond & Ruth) Judaica Foundation	Montgomery	SE-511
$1,550,571	12-00	$25,814,260	Berwick Health & Wellness Foundation	Columbia	NE-017
$1,475,840	12-00	$2,934,548	Allegheny Technologies Charitable Trust	Allegheny	SW-007
$1,454,500	6-01	$5,604,872	Donnelly (Mary J.) Foundation	Allegheny	SW-090
$1,454,463	12-00	$27,154,326	Stackpole-Hall Foundation, The	Elk	NW-070
$1,441,000	12-00	$8,749,092	Foster (John H.) Foundation, The	Montgomery	SE-235
$1,436,350	9-01	$20,106,487	Eustace Foundation, The	Montgomery	SE-204
$1,435,055	12-00	$28,057,800	Nelson (Grace S. & W. Linton) Foundation, The	Chester	SE-480
$1,429,549	12-00	$30,949,523	Steinman (John Frederick) Foundation, The	Lancaster	CP-194
$1,427,579	12-01	$25,529,464	York Foundation	York	CP-231
$1,420,312	6-00	$26,415,852	Maplewood Foundation	Allegheny	SW-222
$1,418,354	12-00	$31,585,289	Hopwood (J.M.) Charitable Trust	Allegheny	SW-169
$1,414,705	12-00	$3,333,657	Byers Foundation, The	Bucks	SE-103
$1,412,854	12-01	$33,935,480	Morris (Charles M.) Charitable Trust, The	Allegheny	SW-254
$1,377,000	4-00	$18,197,264	Beneficia Foundation	Montgomery	SE-056
$1,364,350	4-00	$13,236,055	Snider Foundation, The	Philadelphia	SE-645
$1,330,242	12-00	$14,757,262	Bozzone Family Foundation	Westmoreland	SW-039
$1,325,562	6-01	$20,502,961	1957 Charity Foundation	Montgomery	SE-001
$1,287,628	12-00	$25,650,712	Kline (Josiah W. & Bessie H.) Foundation	Dauphin	CP-109
$1,279,615	4-01	$14,029,867	Betz (Theodora B.) Foundation	Philadelphia	SE-066
$1,275,915	12-01	$52,783,731	Grundy Foundation, The	Bucks	SE-289
$1,275,100	7-01	$7,591,198	Maple Hill Foundation	Montgomery	SE-432
$1,257,270	12-00	$22,584,306	Fourjay Foundation, The	Montgomery	SE-236
$1,255,804	12-01	$23,190,175	Lindback Foundation	Philadelphia	SE-416
$1,255,000	7-01	$26,060,615	Pine Tree Foundation	Montgomery	SE-522
$1,244,000	9-00	$24,509,682	Clapp (Anne & George) Charitable & Educational Trust	Allegheny	SW-062
$1,234,495	12-00	$19,682,099	McKenna (Philip M.) Foundation	Westmoreland	SW-239
$1,220,000	12-00	$22,929,184	Warwick Foundation, The	Philadelphia	SE-719
$1,203,230	12-00	$28,780,800	Steinman (James Hale) Foundation, The	Lancaster	CP-193
$1,199,817	12-00	$22,752,064	Stein (Louis & Bessie) Foundation	Montgomery	SE-655
$1,182,596	12-00	$20,143,787	Tyco Electronics Foundation, The	Dauphin	CP-206
$1,182,120	12-00	$19,605,844	Cornerstone Foundation	Chester	SE-151
$1,179,225	6-01	$16,357,483	Community Foundation for the Alleghenies, The	Cambria	SW-069

Total Grant Support	Fiscal Year Ending	Assets at Market Value	Foundation Name	County	Regional Profile Number
$1,173,904	12-00	$396,781	Green (Mayer A.) Allergy Foundation	Allegheny	SW-148
$1,172,800	12-00	$35,322,721	Community Foundation of Warren County	Warren	NW-009
$1,171,699	12-00	$47,197,631	Staunton Farm Foundation	Allegheny	SW-356
$1,155,000	4-01	$5,321,168	Sylvan Foundation, The	Delaware	SE-678
$1,153,080	12-00	$8,775,067	Harsco Corporation Fund	Cumberland	CP-083
$1,131,500	12-00	$24,357,558	Janssen (Henry) Foundation, The	Berks	CP-101
$1,100,000	6-02	$15,600,000	Chester County Community Foundation, The	Chester	SE-125
$1,098,909	11-00	$9,912,479	Garfield (Eugene) Foundation, The	Montgomery	SE-248
$1,096,400	12-00	$9,244,598	Strawbridge (Maxwell) Charitable Trust	Philadelphia	SE-670
$1,078,264	6-01	$13,544,203	Willis (Hilda M.) Foundation #2	Allegheny	SW-391
$1,078,220	12-00	$12,415,464	Berkman (Sybiel B.) Foundation	Allegheny	SW-026
$1,074,764	6-00	$15,147,312	de Mazia (Violette) Trust	Montgomery	SE-164
$1,071,300	12-00	$17,106,068	Donley Foundation	Montgomery	SE-181
$1,069,350	12-00	$2,098,809	Fox (Richard J.) Foundation, The	Delaware	SE-238
$1,067,208	12-00	$2,602,725	Rock (Milton L. & Shirley) Foundation	Philadelphia	SE-560
$1,048,997	12-00	$14,952,727	Shenango Valley Foundation	Mercer	NW-065
$1,046,750	4-02	$34,340,737	Lancaster County Foundation, The	Lancaster	CP-115
$1,038,135	12-00	$19,382,601	Dietrich (William B.) Foundation, The	Philadelphia	SE-176
$1,035,175	6-01	$21,564,546	Birmingham Foundation, The	Allegheny	SW-032
$1,026,187	9-01	$16,903,144	Dolfinger-McMahon Foundation	Philadelphia	SE-180
$1,019,021	10-01	$13,520,743	Hoyt Foundation, The	Lawrence	SW-173
$1,018,349	11-00	$20,391,968	Roberts (Ralph & Suzanne) Foundation, The	Philadelphia	SE-558
$1,007,500	12-00	$14,506,787	FirstFruits Foundation	Chester	SE-226
$1,002,720	10-00	$22,725,979	Brossman (William & Jemima) Charitable Foundation	Lancaster	CP-025
$1,001,500	12-00	$16,423,745	Rockwell Foundation, The	Allegheny	SW-311
$984,155	12-00	$7,801,846	Ametek Foundation	Chester	SE-021
$980,884	12-00	$1,100,436	Good (Richard & Annetta) Foundation	Lancaster	CP-068
$945,990	6-01	$9,061,280	Community Foundation of Westmoreland County, The	Westmoreland	SW-073
$943,719	12-00	$29,306,760	Frick (Helen Clay) Foundation, The	Allegheny	SW-128
$941,165	12-00	$14,729,203	Sordoni Foundation, Inc.	Luzerne	NE-140
$938,299	5-01	$17,532,231	Smith (Ethel Sergeant Clark) Memorial Fund	Philadelphia	SE-640
$936,524	12-00	$10,694,682	Bitz Foundation	Beaver	SW-034
$934,000	3-01	$17,372,207	Palumbo (A.J. & Sigismunda) Charitable Trust	Allegheny	SW-269
$919,750	12-00	$5,469,760	Hamer Foundation, The	Centre	CP-080
$894,245	12-01	$20,910,497	McFeely-Rogers Foundation	Westmoreland	SW-233
$883,090	12-00	$48,385,944	Williamsport-Lycoming Foundation	Lycoming	CP-221
$882,265	12-00	$17,412,426	Glencairn Foundation	Montgomery	SE-271
$882,000	12-00	$25,013,090	Colcom Foundation	Allegheny	SW-067
$879,685	12-00	$17,992,785	Saligman (Robert) Charitable Trust	Montgomery	SE-590
$847,140	10-00	$7,408,291	Arronson Foundation	Philadelphia	SE-030
$841,500	12-00	$18,910,873	Crels Foundation	Lancaster	CP-040
$832,495	12-00	$8,300,476	Widener Memorial Fdn in Aid of Handicapped Children	Montgomery	SE-728
$831,298	12-01	$21,761,406	Snee-Reinhardt Charitable Foundation	Allegheny	SW-342
$826,350	4-00	$16,529,137	Perelman (Raymond & Ruth) Community Foundation	Montgomery	SE-509
$823,575	12-00	$872,327	CMS Foundation	Philadelphia	SE-135
$808,055	11-00	$10,383,872	Buncher Family Foundation	Allegheny	SW-048
$799,220	9-00	$17,256,590	Colonial Oaks Foundation	Berks	CP-038
$795,981	12-00	$21,078,824	Hall (Edwin), 2nd Charitable Trust	Delaware	SE-300
$795,850	12-00	$21,357,108	Kelly (Paul E.) Foundation	Montgomery	SE-367
$780,124	7-01	$16,699,340	Sherrerd Foundation	Montgomery	SE-621
$775,137	12-00	$1,383,359	Donnell (Richard H.) Foundation	Washington	SW-089
$766,762	12-00	$17,423,906	Scholler Foundation, The	Philadelphia	SE-605
$765,750	12-00	$4,915,356	Cardone (Michael) Foundation	Philadelphia	SE-112
$761,100	6-00	$3,547,861	Hooper (Elizabeth S.) Foundation	Chester	SE-327
$760,000	7-00	$10,478,636	Field (Joseph & Marie) Foundation	Montgomery	SE-218
$746,818	12-00	$15,985,266	Weisbrod (Robert & Mary) Foundation	Allegheny	SW-385
$724,800	12-00	$25,463,758	Stine (James M. & Margaret V.) Foundation	Philadelphia	SE-665
$704,800	11-00	$17,377,122	Neubauer Foundation, The	Philadelphia	SE-481
$695,623	9-00	$16,551,801	Phillips (Dr. & Mrs. Arthur William) Charitable Trust	Venango	NW-058
$685,312	12-00	$33,667,953	Carnegie Hero Fund Commission	Allegheny	SW-056
$682,123	12-01	$29,782,462	First Hospital Foundation	Philadelphia	SE-222
$627,500	12-00	$24,565,077	Carthage Foundation, The	Allegheny	SW-057
$619,198	12-00	$16,779,084	Stuart (G.B.) Charitable Foundation	Cumberland	CP-196
$596,985	6-01	$55,058,475	Allerton Foundation, The	Montgomery	SE-017
$591,500	3-00	$19,047,068	McKinney (William & Catherine) Charitable Foundation	Allegheny	SW-240
$563,934	12-00	$22,000,000	Justus (Samuel) Charitable Trust	Venango	NW-032
$546,100	12-00	$17,669,254	Williams (C.K.) Foundation, The	Philadelphia	SE-729
$530,758	12-01	$18,197,000	Scranton Area Foundation	Lackawanna	NE-133
$520,578	8-01	$17,559,288	Falk (Maurice) Medical Fund	Allegheny	SW-107
$476,020	6-00	$25,687,346	Graham Foundation, The	York	CP-070
$332,212	6-01	$19,302,601	West Family Foundation, The	Chester	SE-723
$303,101	12-00	$15,529,312	Kavanagh (T. James) Foundation	Mercer	NW-035
$212,295	12-00	$15,528,555	Ressler Mill Foundation	Lancaster	CP-165
$169,815	12-00	$16,416,630	Posner Foundation of Pittsburgh	Allegheny	SW-294
$95,000	6-01	$24,862,046	Lenfest (Brook J.) Foundation, The	Montgomery	SE-405
$72,500	12-01	$18,667,825	Genuardi Family Foundation	Montgomery	SE-255

USERS' GUIDE TO THE DIRECTORY

Criteria for Inclusion and Regional Organization of the Directory

The 7th Edition includes 1,614 detailed profile-entries of grant-making foundations in Pennsylvania. Each of these foundations held assets of at least $250,000 and/or awarded grants on a discretionary basis which totaled $10,000 or more in the most recent year of record. In addition, over 2,100 foundations which did not meet these criteria are listed in brief; see the "Non-profiled Foundations" paragraph on the next page.

Since the great majority of foundations direct their grant support primarily to organizations or institutions in their own geographic area, the profile-entries are organized into five regions: Central Pa. (CP), Northeastern (NE), Northwestern (NW), Southeastern (SE), and Southwestern (SW). Pennsylvania's 67 counties are listed below with the regional section of the Directory under which each appears.

Adams — CP	Cumberland — CP	Lycoming — CP	Venango — NW
Allegheny — SW	Dauphin — CP	McKean — NW	Warren — NW
Armstrong — SW	Delaware — SE	Mercer — NW	Washington — SW
Beaver — SW	Elk — NW	Mifflin — CP	Wayne — NE
Bedford — SW	Erie — NW	Monroe — NE	Westmoreland — SW
Berks — CP	Fayette — SW	Montgomery — SE	Wyoming — NE
Blair — SW	Forest — NW	Montour — CP	York — CP
Bradford — NE	Franklin — CP	Northampton — NE	
Bucks — SE	Fulton — CP	Northumberland — CP	
Butler — SW	Greene — SW	Perry — CP	
Cambria — SW	Huntingdon — CP	Philadelphia — SE	*Note*
Cameron — NW	Indiana — SW	Pike — NE	*A map of Pennsylvania*
Carbon — NE	Jefferson — NW	Potter — CP	*showing the bounda-*
Centre — CP	Juniata — CP	Schuylkill — NE	*ries of the five regions*
Chester — SE	Lackawanna — NE	Snyder — CP	*appears in the pre-*
Clarion — NW	Lancaster — CP	Somerset — SW	*vious chapter.*
Clearfield — NW	Lawrence — SW	Sullivan — NE	
Clinton — CP	Lebanon — CP	Susquehanna — NE	
Columbia — NW	Lehigh — NE	Tioga — CP	
Crawford — NW	Luzerne — NE	Union — CP	

Informational Sources & Research Procedure

Compiling, editing and verifying data for the 7th Edition consumed 3,000+ hours of work over a 12 month period. The principal source of information was the Forms 990-PF (primarily for 2000 and 2001), the "tax return" which foundations file annually with IRS. Additional information was gleaned from countless web searches and many other sources: Guidestar's online collection of Form 990-PFs; foundation annual reports; published statements of program policy or grant application guidelines; Triadvocates Press' extensive research archives; CD-ROMs of business/residential telephone listings and corporate databases; online databases such as Hoovers; publications of The Foundation Center [New York City]; the Council for Advancement & Support of Education's listings of matching gift programs; and some corporate annual reports.

Perhaps most importantly, there were several thousand mail, FAX, E-mail, or telephone communications with virtually all profiled foundations, mostly regarding the draft profile-entries which were mailed/faxed to the foundations. In most cases a Triadvocates Press questionnaire accompanied the draft profile-entry and which requested information about grant application policies/procedures, website, fax number, e-mail, giving limitations/restrictions, special program interests/emphases, preferred manner and months for submission of grant applications, deadlines, board meeting schedule, and other information useful to grant applicants. Nearly 500 foundations replied with additions or corrections to the draft profile-entry, providing vital information of interest to grantseekers.

SAMPLE FOUNDATION PROFILE & KEY TO DATA

CP-077 George (Max) Foundation, The
101 West Avenue
Reading 19604   (Berks County)

AMV $3,128,395   **FYE** 12/01   **(Gifts Received** $0)

MI-11-15-18-19-41-42-52
Phone 610-555-1234 FAX 610-555-1235
EIN 23-6247000 **Year Created** 1992
14 **Grants totaling** $85,250

GRANTS SUMMARY: Mostly local/Pa. giving. High local grant of $51,500 to Reading Symphony. $10,000 each to United Way of Berks County and Caron Foundation. $6,500 to Foundation for Independent Colleges/Pa. $1,000 each Alvernia College, Cornwall Manor, Planned Parenthood of Northeast Pa., and Reading Music Foundation. Other smaller local contributions. Out-of-state giving includes **$2,000** to Harvard U. [MA]. **PUBLICATIONS:** application guidelines. **WEBSITE:** None **E-MAIL:** tothemax@msn.com **APPLICATION POLICIES & PROCEDURES:** The Foundation reports that with limited exceptions, grants are restricted to Berks County and mostly for special projects, building funds, capital needs, and scholarships. Grant requests may be submitted in a letter (2 pages maximum) during April-May (deadline is June 1st); include the amount requested and intended use of funds, and IRS tax-exempt status documentation.

O+D+T Paul B. George (P+D+Con) — Lawrence B. George (VP+S+F) Maximilian George [MA] (Donor)

- **CP-077** is the **Regional Profile Number**. These sequentially-assigned reference numbers are based on region and are used in all six indexes. The directory is divided into five regions: CP, NE, NW, SE and SW.

- **Telephone & Fax numbers:** These may be at the Foundation office, a bank's trust department, law firm, brokerage firm, or accountant (if acting as trustee or manager), or at the Contact Person's home.

- **MI** or Major Interest Codes. There are 52 possible Major Interest Codes which are assigned based on the largest grants awarded or on a general weighting of aggregated giving. Generally, a maximum of 24 MI Codes are assigned to any one foundation. Refer to the *Key to Major Interest Codes and O+D+T Titles* (next page or inside the back cover) for an annotated listing of all Major Interest Codes.

- **EIN** or Employer Identification Number (Federal ID) assigned by Internal Revenue Service; can be useful in locating a foundation which may be called by different names.

- **Year Created** generally is the year in which the foundation was formed, although in some instances is the year in which tax-exempt status was received or was incorporated.

- **AMV** or Assets at Market Value, as of the end of the fiscal year indicated (see next item).

- **FYE** or Fiscal Year Ending: month/year

- **Gifts Received** is the "new money" added to the corpus of the foundation during that fiscal year; it does not include interest on or earnings from existing foundation assets.

- **Grants Totaling:** the number of grants awarded and the dollar total of those grants for the fiscal year. When the number of grants is not shown, an explanation is usually provided under the Grants Summary.

- **Grants Summary** usually begins with a geographical focus of grants activity followed by a detailed listing of all grants, generally $1,000 or larger, awarded to Pennsylvania organizations. The grants are listed by descending size to provide an overall "framework" of giving priorities. Some of the larger foundations also may have their grants clustered in overall Major Interest categories, e.g. Human Services. Significant out-of-state grants typically follow the Pennsylvania grants listing.

- **Publications** may include a foundation's published annual report, statement of program policies, application guidelines, etc. If any of these are available a grantseeker should *first* request (and review) a copy before submitting any request.

- **Website & E-mail Address**: If the foundation has a website, check it out for up-to-date information on grants, application guidelines, etc. If you have short inquiries, contact the foundation by e-mail but follow proper netiquette! Remember that very few foundations are prepared to accept grant requests electronically.

- **Application Policies & Procedures** includes, *when available*, stated giving priorities and restrictions, the preferred means of submitting a grant request, required information and documentation, deadlines, and other information of interest to grantseekers.

- **O+D+T** (Officers, Directors & Trustees). The first person listed is generally the Contact Person, or the person to whom grant requests should be sent. The *Key to Major Interest Codes and O+D+T Titles* (next page or inside the back cover) details the title abbreviations. When an individual's city/town location is known (including those resident outside Pennsylvania) that is listed in brackets, e.g. [Williamsport] -or- [NJ].

Non-profiled Foundations

About 60% of Pennsylvania's foundations did not meet required criteria to be profiled in the 7th Edition. However, these foundations are listed by Name, Address and Status Code in regional "Non-profiled Foundations" sections. On the first page of these regional sections is a Status Code Key as to why foundations did not qualify to be profiled.

KEY TO MAJOR INTEREST CODES and O+D+T TITLES

HUMAN SERVICES

11 United Ways
(federated community campaigns, community chests)

12 Child & Family Welfare
(daycare centers, foster care, family counseling)

13 Youth
(Y's, Scouts, PAL, Big Brothers/Big Sisters)

14 Disabled/Handicapped
(blind, deaf, crippled, vocational rehabilitation)

15 Aged/Senior Citizens
(retirement homes, hospices, planning/service agencies)

16 Minorities/Race Relations
(African-American/Hispanic organizations,
gay/lesbian groups)

17 Women/Girls
(counseling services, shelters, rape crisis/prevention
agencies, Women's Way, advocacy groups)

18 Family Planning
(Planned Parenthood, pregnancy counseling, adoption)

19 Alcohol/Drug Abuse
(treatment programs, special hospitals and services)

20 Crime/Justice
(crime prevention, ex-offender, parole and
court improvement programs)

21 Community Service Clubs
(Rotary, Kiwanis, Golden Slipper,
Jaycees, Junior League, veterans groups)

22 Religion-related Agencies/Services
(Catholic Charities, federated Jewish appeals, Salvation
Army, sectarian human service agencies)

23 Direct Assistance to Needy Individuals

24 Neighborhood Organizations

25 Housing & Homeless Programs

29 Other Human Services
(multi-purpose agencies, volunteerism, Red Cross)

HEALTH/MEDICAL

31 Hospitals/Medical Centers

32 Medical Research
(national/local health funds, research grants)

33 Mental Health
(community MH/MR centers, psychiatric
hospitals, special programs)

34 Medical Education
(schools of medicine, dentistry, nursing
and veterinary medicine)

35 Public Health
(visiting nurse services, health education programs)

39 Other Health
(health planning agencies, para-medic/ambulance corps)

EDUCATION

41 Primary & Secondary Education
(public, private and parochial schools, IUs)

42 Colleges & Universities

43 Scholarships & Fellowships

44 Libraries

45 Community Education & Literacy

49 Other Education
(economic education, Junior Achievement,
educational research)

ARTS/CULTURE

51 Theatre & Dance
(performing arts companies and schools)

52 Music
(orchestras, music schools, and concert series)

53 Visual Arts
(art exhibitions, galleries, art schools)

54 Museums
(all types)

55 Community Arts
(urban art programs, festivals and special
arts events, arts councils and federations)

56 Historical
(historical restoration/preservation, historical
societies, celebrations)

57 Public Broadcasting
(public radio/TV, program underwriting)

RELIGION

61 Catholic Churches & Missions

62 Jewish Synagogues & Charities

63 Protestant Churches & Missions

64 Theological Education

65 Ecumenical Programs & Organizations

69 Other Religions
(Islam, Eastern religions, etc..)

ENVIRONMENTAL

71 Conservation & Ecology
(parks, protected lands, arboreta, nature centers,
conservation groups, horticultural societies)

72 Zoos/Animal Humane/Wildlife
(zoological parks, SPCAs,
international wildlife funds)

79 Other Environmental
(special environmental or recycling
programs, advocacy organizations)

MISCELLANEOUS

81 International
(international exchange, hospitality or
education programs; refugee services)

82 Overseas Institutions & Programs

83 Good Government
(Pa. Economy League, League of Women Voters,
public interest organizations, watchdog groups)

84 Sports & Camps
(community sports/recreation programs
camping programs, Little League)

85 Economic Development
(public and private economic or
community development organizations)

86 Public Policy Research

88 Matching Gift Programs
(corporate grants matching employee gifts)

89 Other Miscellaneous
(fire companies, local government projects, etc.)

99 Mixed Charitable Giving
(Assigned only to foundations in the non-profiled
Limited Assets/Giving category)

Con = Contact Person
PO = Principal Officer
P = President
VP = Vice President

C = Chairman
VC = Vice Chairman
D = Director
T = Trustee

Co-T = Co-Trustee
F = Treasurer/Financial Officer
S = Secretary
Preface of **A** = Assistant

B-r-o-a-d-e-n-i-n-g Your Foundation Search

Hopefully, the *Directory of Pennsylvania Foundations* will greatly assist you in identifying the Pennsylvania foundations whose grantmaking activities have supported organizations like yours, or will help you locate a foundation director or trustee who you know (or have heard about) is interested in your type of program. In short, we hope this directory may lead to many new, happy "partnerships" between grantors and grantees (you)!

Yet, inevitably, a conscientious and resourceful grantseeker will need more current information on Pennsylvania's foundations, or wish to explore funding prospects outside of Pennsylvania. So, where do you turn?

Step 1:
Visit Your Nearest
Regional Foundation Center

Pennsylvania is fortunate in having ten valuable, specialized collections of information on foundations, corporate giving, fundraising techniques, and much more. These Centers, all affiliated with The Foundation Center in New York, are strategically located throughout the state: Bethlehem, Erie, Harrisburg, Lancaster, Philadelphia, Pittsburgh, Pittston (between Wilkes-Barre and Scranton), Reading, Williamsport, and York. Each of these Regional Foundation Centers, because of their affiliation with The Foundation Center, has a "core collection" of The Foundation Center's publications as well as other valuable resources for fundraising and nonprofit management; each Center is described below.

So, if your fundraising research needs go beyond what the *Directory of Pennsylvania Foundations* offers, visit your nearest Foundation Center Collection. Plan to spend several hours exploring the very wide world of philanthropy in and beyond Pennsylvania. If you expect an orientation to the Collection or some consultative advice from the Center's supervising librarian, make sure you call the Center in advance,

» BETHLEHEM

Northampton Community College, Foundation Center Collection, Mack Library, 3835 Green Pond Road, Bethlehem, PA 18020; Telephone: 610-861-5359; FAX: 610-861-5373; E-mail: reference-desk@northampton.edu. When the College is in session the Collection is available Monday-Thursday, 8 am to 10 pm; Friday, 8 am to 5 pm; Saturday, 8:30 am to 4:30 pm; and Sunday 1 pm to 8 pm. Call for the hours during college vacations and semester breaks. Available for reference use are publications of The Foundation Center and the *Directory of Pennsylvania Foundations* as well as annual reports of selected foundations, some monographs, and periodicals. Quick reference information questions (not involving searching) are handled by telephone, FAX, e-mail, or mail.

» ERIE

Erie County Public Library, Raymond Blasco Memorial Library, Foundation Center Collection/Reference Room, 160 East Front Street, Erie, PA 16507; Telephone: 814-451-6927; FAX: 814-451-6907; E-mail: reference@erielibrary.org. The Collection is open Monday-Thursday, 9 am to 8:30 pm; Friday, 9 am to 6 pm; Saturday, 9 am to 5 pm; and Sunday,1 pm-5 pm. The Collection includes The Foundation Center's major reference publications and *FC Search: The Foundation Centers Database on CD-ROM*, the *Directory of Pennsylvania Foundations*, annual reports of selected Pennsylvania and out-of-state foundations, and many other standard foundation or government funding reference resources. Quick reference questions only (not involving searching) are accepted by telephone, e-mail, or mail.

» HARRISBURG

Dauphin County Library System, East Shore Area Library, Grants Information Center, 4501 Ethel Street, Harrisburg, PA 17109; Telephone: 717-652-9380, x-4; FAX: 717-652-5012; website: www.dcls.org. E-mail: wzimmerman@dcls.org. Supervisor: Walter B. Zimmerman. The Center is open Monday-Friday , 9:30 am to 9 pm; Saturday, 9:30 am to 5 pm, and Sunday, 1pm-5pm. An available flyer, *Pathfinder for Grants Information* lists many of the reference books or other available information in the Center, e.g. publications of The Foundation Center including *FC Search: The Foundation Centers Database on CD-ROM*, the *Directory of Pennsylvania Foundations*, and directories from The Taft Group and other publishers. In addition, annual reports of some foundations and corporations, monographs, videos and journals dealing with grantsmanship are available. Funding workshops and orientations are arranged by the Center. Quick reference questions (not involving searching) are accepted by telephone, e-mail, fax or mail.

» LANCASTER

Lancaster Public Library, Reference Department/Foundation Collection, 125 North Duke Street, Lancaster, PA 17602; Telephone: 717-394-2651 x-105; FAX: 717-394-3083; E-mail: administration@lancaster.lib.pa.us. Supervisor: Lesley Sprute. The Collection is open Monday-Thursday, 9 am to 9 pm and Friday-Saturday, 9 am to 5:30 pm. Most major publications of The Foundation Center, the *Directory of Pennsylvania Foundations*, as well as other selected materials are available for reference use. Quick reference questions (not involving searching) are accepted by telephone, fax, e-mail, or mail.

» PHILADELPHIA

The Free Library of Philadelphia, Regional Foundation Center/Social Science & History Department, 1901 Vine Street at Logan Square, Philadelphia, PA 19103; Telephone: 215-686-5423; FAX: 215-563-3628. Website: www.library.phila.gov/rfc/rfcabout.htm. To e-mail questions, visit the library's Web Site at www.library.phila.gov and click on the question mark icon "Ask the Librarian." Collection Supervisor: Gloria D. Hibbett. Full service is available Monday-Friday, 9 am to 5 pm, and the first Saturday of each month from 1pm to 5 pm. A Fact Sheet about the Center is available. Two-hour orientation sessions to the Collection, for individuals or small groups, are held on selected Tuesday or Saturday morningsfrom 9-11 am; call in advance for exact dates and times and to make a reservation. The Center's extensive collection of materials on fundraising and philanthropy includes The Foundation Center's publications and *FC Search: The Foundation Center's Database on CD-ROM*. Both print and computerized versions of the *Directory of Pennsylvania Foundations* are available together with other computerized grants information databases. In addition, directories from Gale Research/The Taft Group, Aspen Publishers, Jossey-Bass, Council on Foundations, Independent Sector, and others are available. The Center's computers may also be used to search The Foundation Center's website, Guidestar, and other on-line nonprofit resources. The Center subscribes to several dozen fundraising journals/periodicals. Also available are annual reports of selected foundations, monographs on government program resources, corporate funding, managing/organizing nonprofit organizations, and writing grant proposals. Most materials are for reference use only in the Center, but photocopy machines are available for use (25 cents per copy). Quick reference information questions (not involving searching) are accepted by telephone or mail.

» PITTSBURGH

The Carnegie Library of Pittsburgh, downtown Library Center (Lower Level), The Foundation Center, 414 Wood Street, Pittsburgh, PA 15222; Telephone: 412-281-7143. Website: http://www.carnegielibrary.org/foundation. E-mail: foundation@carnegielibrary.org. Supervisor: Jim Lutton. The Center is open Monday-Thursday, 8:30 am to 6 pm; Friday, 8:30 am to 5 pm; and Saturday, 10 am to 4:00 pm; Sundays closed. A Fact Sheet on the Center's collection is available. Patrons needing a librarian's assistance are advised to call ahead for an appointment. The Center's extensive reference collection has all major publications of The Foundation Center including *FC Search: The Foundation Center's Database on CD-ROM*. Other available computerized databases include *Directory of Pennsylvania Foundations*, Grants Select, and Prospector's Choice. The computers also may be used to access Guidestar (for viewing Form 990-PFs), the Foundation Directory on-line, and other on-line resources. Other materials available are many specialized funding directories, fundraising periodicals and materials, foundation management publications, and annual reports of selected foundations. Public programs sponsored on a regular basis include Orientation Sessions to the Center's collection and Computer Resources for Nonprofits. Other programs sponsored periodically include Basic Proposal Writing, Fundraising 101, Marketing Your Nonprofit, Meet the Grantmakers, and Meet the Consultants. Programs are announced through Center's quarterly newsletter, *Charitable Reminders*; contact the Center to be added to the mailing list at no charge. Patrons may check out selected books/audiovisuals about philanthropy, government/foundation grantsmanship, proposal writing, nonprofit management, fundraising, and volunteerism from a circulating collection. Quick reference questions (not involving searching) are accepted by telephone, mail, E-mail, or in person.

» PITTSTON

Pocono Northeast Development Fund, Nonprofit Organization Assistance Center (NOAC), James Pettinger Memorial Library, 1151 Oak Street, Pittston, PA 18640; Telephone: 570-655-5581, x-238; FAX: 570-654-5137; Website: www.pndf.org. E-mail: smp@nepa-alliance.org. Managing Director: Shirley Perhalla. The Library is open Monday-Friday, 8 am to 5 pm. but appointments are required to use the reference collection. The Center has an annual membership fee of $35. NOAC's collection has *FC Search: The Foundation Center's Database on CD-ROM* as well as The Foundation Center's core collection of directories and other publications. Also available are the *Directory of Pennsylvania Foundations* and annual reports of selected foundations, monographs, etc. A bi-monthly newsletter on foundation basics is published. Free orientation sessions are held on How to Use The Library, Direct Mail Fundraising, Board Development, and Grantwriting, for individuals, small groups, or at agencies for a minimum of ten persons. NOAC also sponsors regional workshops on grant writing, strategic planning and board development. One-on-one consultation is available. Each fall NOAC sponsors the Pocono Northeast Community Awards Program to honor exemplary projects and organizations which improve communities and the quality of life in the seven-county region. Quick reference research questions (no involving searching) are accepted by telephone, fax, e-mail or mail.

» READING

Reading Public Library, Foundation Center Collection/Reference Department, 100 South 5th Street, Reading, PA 19602; Telephone: 610-655-6355, FAX: 610-655-6609; E-mail: rplref@reading.lib.pa.us. Supervisor: Krista Graser. Open to the public during regular library hours: Monday-Wednesday, 8:15 am to 9 pm; Thursday-Friday, 8:15 am to 5:30 pm; and Saturday, 8:45 am to 5:00 pm. The Center's collection includes the *Directory of Pennsylvania Foundations*, a core collection of The Foundation Center's publications, *FC Search: The Foundation Center's Database on CD-ROM*, and other funding directories. In addition, general information on foundations and philanthropy, grants to special interests and individuals, proposal writing, nonprofit theory and management, fundraising, and government funding and agencies is available. Public access computers may be used for access to Guidestar, and other on-line grantsmanship resources. Some of the Collection's materials may be checked out by patrons. Quick reference questions only (not involving searching) are answered by telephone, fax, e-mail or mail.

» WILLIAMSPORT

James V. Brown Library, Nonprofit Resources Center, 19 East Fourth Street, Williamsport, PA 17701; Telephone: 570-326-0536; FAX: 570-323-6938; E-mail: ask@jvbrown.edu. Supervisor: Wanda Bower. The Center's collection is available to the public during all regular library hours: Monday-Thursday, 9 am to 9 pm; Friday, 9 am to 6 pm; Saturday, 9 am to 5 pm, and Sunday 1pm-5 pm. The collection includes the Foundation Center's core collection, *FC Search: The Foundation Center's Database on CD-ROM*, the *Directory of Pennsylvania Foundations*, various grant resource guides, and nonprofit management materials. Some of the Collection's materials may be checked out by patrons. In addition, two computers are available for patron use to access Guidestar and other on-line resources. Quick reference questions only (not involving searching) are accepted by telephone, fax. E-mail, or mail.

» YORK

Martin Library, 2nd Floor, The Grants Resource Center, 159 East Market Street, York, PA 17401; Telephone: 717-846-5300, ext. 226; FAX: 717-848-1496; E-mail: malib@yorklibraries.org. Supervisor: Dottie Fitton, Director of Information Services. Voluntary annual membership contributions ranging from $25 to $150 are requested, depending upon a nonprofit organization's size. The Center's collection is available to the public during regular library hours: Monday-Thursday, 9 am to 9 pm; Friday, 9 am to 5:30 pm; Saturday, 9 am to 5 pm except during July-August when the library closes at 1 pm. The Center includes The Foundation Center's core collection of directories and publications, including *FC Search: The Foundation Center's Database on CD-ROM*. Also available are *Directory of Pennsylvania Foundations*, subject guides to specific grant support, proposal-writing guides, materials/periodicals on philanthropy and grantsmanship, and the "Association of Fundraising Professional's Heritage Collection of Fundraising & Nonprofit Management Resources Materials." Public access computers are available for accessing Guidestar and other on-line resources. Some of the Center's materials are available for check-out by patrons. The Center periodically publishes a newsletter and arranges workshops on fund development and nonprofit management. Quick reference questions (not involving searching) are accepted by telephone, fax, e-mail, or mail.

Step 2: Now that I'm "Here" How Do I Find What I'm Looking For?

Good! You've made the trip to a Regional Foundation Center and now you can plunge into The Foundation Center's many publications—not to mention lots of other funding directories and fundraising materials. You may be overwhelmed, so where do you begin your research?

Following are five of the most commonly asked questions about funding research" which have been adapted for Pennsylvania researchers from a Foundation Center handout and, naturally, most of the reference sources cited are Foundation Center publications. However, not all Regional Foundation Collections have all the publications mentioned, e.g. *FC Search: The Foundation's Center's Database on CD-ROM* is available only at some of the Collections described above.

Here are the questions!

1. WHICH FOUNDATIONS MAKE GRANTS FOR PROGRAMS LIKE MINE?

- see SUBJECT INDEX, TYPES OF SUPPORT INDEX in *The Foundation Directory*, *The Foundation Directory/Part 2* and Supplement, *The Foundation 1000*, or, if applicable, one of nine publications entitled *National Guide to Funding in . . . Aging . . . AIDS . . . Arts & Culture . . . Environment & Animal Welfare . . . Health . . . Higher Education . . . International & Foreign Programs . . . Libraries & Information Services . . . Religion*

- see FIELD OF INTEREST INDEX in *FC Search: The Foundation Center's database on CD-ROM*

- see RECIPIENT INDEX in *Grant Guides series*—see next page for a listing of the 15 separate volumes)

2. WHERE CAN I FIND OUT WHICH FOUNDATIONS MAKE GRANTS TO A PARTICULAR CITY OR STATE?

- see GEOGRAPHIC INDEX in: *The Foundation Directory*, *The Foundation Directory/Part 2*, and *The Foundation 1000*

- see GRANTMAKER STATE INDEX or GEOGRAPHIC FOCUS INDEX in *FC Search (CD-ROM)*

3. WHERE DO I LOCATE A SPECIFIC FOUNDATION?

- see FOUNDATION NAME INDEX in *Guide to U.S. Foundations, their Trustees, Officers & Donors*

- see GRANTMAKER NAME INDEX in *FC Search (CD-ROM)*

4. WHAT ARE THE MOST DETAILED SOURCES OF INFORMATION ON PRIVATE FOUNDATIONS THAT ARE *OUTSIDE* PENNSYLVANIA?

- request Annual reports from those foundations that publish them or see *The Foundation 1000*

- review the IRS Form 990-PFs which foundations must file with IRS and which now are available online at www.guidestar.org

5. WHERE CAN I FIND INFORMATION ON CORPORATE GIVING?

- see *National Directory of Corporate Giving, Corporate Foundation Profiles, FC Search (CD-ROM), or Taft's Corporate Giving Directory*.

●

The Foundation Center also offers online subscription access to most of their publications; monthly subscriptions run from $19.95 to $149.95 per month, depending upon the depth of information you wish to access. For more information, log on to http://fdncenter.org. In addition, the website has numerous links to the vast world of funding resources and is an excellent place to start your online research!

In you cannot access the web, call 1-800-424-9836 to request a catalog of The Foundation Center's publications.

The 15 volumes in the GRANT GUIDES series provide descriptions of hundreds (often thousands) of grants $10,000 or larger awarded by the nation's largest 1,000 foundations including fewer than 100 Pennsylvania foundations. Each volume has three indexes: Key Word/Subject, Geographic, and Grant Recipient. Most volumes are 200-500 pages. ($75 each)

ARTS, CULTURE & THE HUMANITIES — Grants to arts and cultural organizations, historical societies and historic preservation, media, visual arts, performing arts, music, and museums.

CHILDREN & YOUTH — Grants for neonatal care, child welfare, adoption, foster care, services for abused children, research on child development, pregnancy prevention and counseling, rehabilitation of juvenile delinquency, and youth clubs.

ELEMENTARY & SECONDARY EDUCATION — Grants for academic programs, scholarships, counseling, educational testing, dropout prevention, teacher training and education, salary support, student activities, and school libraries.

ENVIRONMENTAL PROTECTION & ANIMAL WELFARE — Grants for pollution abatement and control, conservation, and environmental education; and for animal protection and welfare, zoos, botanical gardens, and aquariums.

FILM, MEDIA & COMMUNICATIONS — Grants for film, video, documentaries, radio, television, printing, publishing, and censorship issues.

FOREIGN & INTERNATIONAL PROGRAMS — Grants to domestic and foreign organizations for development and relief, peace and security, arms control, human rights, conferences and research.

HIGHER EDUCATION — Grants to higher education including graduate and professional schools, for programs in all disciplines, and to academic libraries and student services.

LIBRARIES & INFORMATION SERVICES—Grants for public, academic, research, special, and school libraries; for archives and information centers; and for consumer information, and philanthropy information centers.

MENTAL HEALTH, ADDICTIONS & CRISIS SERVICES — Grants to hospitals, health centers, residential treatment facilities, group homes, and mental health associations for addiction prevention and treatment; for addiction prevention and treatment, hotline/crisis intervention services; and for public education and research.

MINORITIES — Grants for ethnic groups and minority populations, including African-Americans, Hispanics, Asian Americans, Native Americans, gays and lesbians, and immigrants and refugees.

PHYSICALLY & MENTALLY DISABLED — Grants to hospitals, schools, and primary care facilities for research, medical and dental care, employment and vocational training, education, diagnosis and evaluation, recreation and rehabilitation, legal aid, and scholarships.

RELIGION, RELIGIOUS WELFARE & RELIGIOUS EDUCATION — Grants to churches, synagogues, missionary societies, and religious orders; and to associations and organizations concerned with religious welfare and education.

SCHOLARSHIPS, STUDENT AID & LOANS — Grants to organizations that provide scholarships and student aid, including undergraduate colleges and universities, medical and dental schools, law schools, nursing schools, music and art schools, cultural organizations, vocational and technical schools, and social service organizations.

SOCIAL SERVICES — Grants to human service organizations for a broad range of services, including children and youth services, family services, personal social services, emergency assistance, residential! custodial care; and services to promote the independence of specific population groups such as the homeless and developmentally disabled.

WOMEN & GIRLS — Grants for education, career guidance, vocational training, equal rights, rape prevention, shelter programs for victims of domestic violence, health programs, abortion rights, pregnancy programs, athletics and recreation, arts programs, and social research.

THE
FOUNDATIONS
OF
PENNSYLVANIA

Central Region / CP

covers the following 22 counties
Adams - Berks - Centre - Clinton - Cumberland - Dauphin - Franklin - Fulton
Huntingdon - Juniata - Lancaster - Lebanon - Lycoming - Mifflin - Montour
Northumberland - Perry - Potter - Snyder - Tioga - Union - York

---

CP-001 Abrams (Samuel L.) Foundation, The MI-43
c/o Consolidated Scrap Resources, Inc.
2301 North 3rd Street, P.O. Box 3053 **Phone** 717-233-7927 **FAX** None
Harrisburg 17105 (Dauphin County) **EIN** 23-6408237 **Year Created** 1965
AMV $2,732,916 **FYE** 12-00 **(Gifts Received** $2,500) 53 **Grants totaling** $128,550

All grants are interest-free loans for graduates of certain Harrisburg-area public, private and parochial high schools (listed below) to complete a specific course of study at a college, university or technical school; loans are mostly **$2,000-$4,000,** some higher or lower. In addition, interest-free loans are available to Harrisburg School District teachers to further their education with the proviso that they must continue teaching in the District for at least two years after completing the course/s for which the loans were made.■**PUBLICATIONS:** statement of program policy and application guidelines ■**WEBSITE:** www.slabramsfounda-tion.org ■**E-MAIL:** support@slabramsfoundation.org ■**APPLICATION POLICIES & PROCEDURES:** Only graduates of the following secondary schools are eligible to apply: all public/parochial high schools within the City of Harrisburg, The Harrisburg Academy, and the following high schools: Camp Hill, Cedar Cliff, Central Dauphin, Central Dauphin East, Cumberland Valley, Lower Dauphin Senior, Mechanicsburg, Middletown Area, Red Land, Steelton-Highspire, Susquehanna Township, Susquenita, and Trinity. Scholarship-loans are awarded based on need and other qualifications. Prospective applicants should telephone the Foundation to discuss the feasibility of submitting an application. An Application & Statement of Financial Need, available on the website or from the Foundation, must be completed and submitted during January-May; the deadline is May 30th; letters of recommendation, transcripts, SAT scores, and applicant's and parents' income tax returns must accompany the completed form. The Selection Committee meets to interview candidates and makes awards in July. The loans are to be repaid over five years following graduation.

O+D+T Richard E. Abrams (P+D+Donor+Con) — Ruth Abrams Gonzalez (S+D+Donor) — James R. Reeser (F+D) — Beryl A. Abrams (D+Donor) — Dr. Raphael Aronson (D) — James W. Evans, Esq. (D) — Dr. Thomas Holtzman (D) — Hon. William W. Lipsitt (D) — Dr. Ruth Leventhal (D) — Dr. George Love (D) — Katherine McCorkle (D) — Gerald K. Morrison, Esq. (D) — Mellon Bank N.A. (Agent)

CP-002 Adams County Foundation MI-12-13-25-29-32-45-55-71
101 West Middle Street **Phone** 717-337-3353 **FAX** 717-337-1080
Gettysburg 17325 (Adams County) **EIN** 22-5144001 **Year Created** 1985
AMV $397,217 **FYE** 3-01 **(Gifts Received** $5,531) **Grants totaling** $9,296

As a Community Foundation all discretionary giving is restricted to organizations serving Adams County. Details on recent grants are unavailable. In prior years, grants of **$1,000-$3,000** (mostly) were awarded to Adams County Arts Council, Adams County Habitat for Humanity, Adams County Literacy Council, American Cancer Society, Children's Aid Society, Community Center, Gettysburg YWCA, Land Conservancy of Adams County, Littlestown Food Pantry, Penn Laurel Girl Scout Council, South Central Community Action Programs, and others. ■**PUBLICATIONS:** Annual Report; informational brochure with application guidelines ■**WEBSITE:** None ■**E-MAIL:** None ■**APPLICATION POLICIES & PROCEDURES:** Only organizations serving Adams County are eligible to apply. Funding preference is given to start-up costs, projects with potential to generate additional funding, one-time only grants, and for projects/capital needs supporting direct human services. As a rule, favor is given to supporting one-time/short-term needs vs. operating support. Prospective applicants should make an initial telephone inquiry about the feasibility of submitting an application. Grant requests may be submitted in a letter-proposal well before January 30th and July 30th deadlines; describe the organization's purpose/activities, state a clear need for the proposed project and how the requested funds would be used; also include organization and project budgets, list of major funding sources, and a Board member list. Grants are awarded at February and August meetings.

O+D+T Distribution Committee members: John W. Phillips, Esq. (Acting Director+S+Con) — C.K. Roulette (C) — Gary H. Bechtel — E.C. Grim — Joan M. Miller — George M. Peters — Charles E. Ritter — Thomas A. Ritter — Caroline Smith

---

CP-003 Adams (James K. & Arlene L.) Foundation MI-43
c/o Cherewka & Radcliff
624 North Front Street **Phone** 717-236-9318 **FAX** None
Wormleysburg 17043 (Dauphin County) **EIN** 25-1665127 **Year Created** 1992
AMV $291,050 **FYE** 12-00 **(Gifts Received** $48,000) 17 **Grants totaling** $26,500

All giving for scholarships for graduates of high schools in Eastern Cumberland County; awards ranged from **$1,250** to **$2,500**
■**PUBLICATIONS:** None ■**WEBSITE:** None ■**E-MAIL:** None ■**APPLICATION POLICIES & PROCEDURES:** Only graduates of Eastern Cumberland County high schools are eligible to apply for scholarship awards. Submit requests in a letter before the December 31st deadline.
O+D+T David H. Radcliff, Esq. (T+Con) — James K. Adams, II [Mechanicsburg] (T+Donor)

CP-004 Alexander (H.B.) Foundation, The
16 Wagner Street
Hummelstown 17036   (Dauphin County)
AMV $1,010,121   FYE 12-00   (**Gifts Received** $0)

MI-12-15-41-42-52-54-55
Phone 717-566-3029 **FAX** 717-566-1494
EIN 23-6242501   **Year Created** 1962
14 **Grants totaling** $166,725

Most giving to Cumberland and Dauphin counties. High grant of **$128,000** to Susquehanna Art Museum. **$10,000** to Penn State U./Harrisburg. **$5,000** to Allied Arts Fund. **$2,000-$2,500** each to Bethany Village (Care Assurance Fund), Fund for the Advancement of the State System of Higher Education, and Heinz Harrisburg Senior Center. **$1,000** each to Harrisburg Symphony, Pa. Partnership for Children, Sylvan Heights Science Center, U. of Pittsburgh, and Whitaker Center for Science. Other smaller local contributions. **Out-of-state** grant: **$11,500** to Wilderness Education Institute [CO]. — Major grants approved for future payment: **$131,000** to Whitaker Center for Science; **$15,000** to Harrisburg Area Community College; and **$10,000** to Penn State U./Harrisburg. ■**PUBLICATIONS:** None ■**WEBSITE:** None ■**E-MAIL:** None ■**APPLICATION POLICIES & PROCEDURES:** The Foundation reports that giving is limited to Dauphin and Cumberland counties and only to organizations/activities in which Alexander Family members actively participate. Most grants are for capital campaigns. Prospective applicants initially should make a telephone inquiry about the feasibility of submitting a request. Grant requests may be submitted in any form at any time; describe the purpose of the request, state an amount requested, and include a project budget and IRS tax-exempt status documentation. Grants are awarded at a meeting in February.
O+D+T William H. Alexander (VC+S+Con) — Marion C. Alexander (C+F) — Dianne L. Fairall (AS) — Hershey Trust Company (Trustee) — Corporate donor: Alexander Enterprises, Inc.

CP-005 Allergy & Asthma Foundation of Lancaster County
c/o Allergy & Asthma Center
2445 Marietta Ave.
Lancaster 17603   (Lancaster County)
AMV $379,750   FYE 12-00   (**Gifts Received** $0)

MI-31-32-34-35-43
Phone 717-393-1365 **FAX** None
EIN 23-6424184   **Year Created** 1991
4 **Grants totaling** $20,000

All local giving. High grant of **$10,000** to Franklin & Marshall College (scholarship). **$7,000** to Lancaster General Nursing School (scholarship). **$2,000** to Pa. Allergy Education & Research Trust [Harrisburg] (program). **$1,000** to Lancaster General Hospital Foundation (program). ■**PUBLICATIONS:** None ■**WEBSITE:** None ■**E-MAIL:** None ■**APPLICATION POLICIES & PROCEDURES:** The Foundation reports all giving is limited to Pa. No grants awarded to individuals.
O+D+T Stephen D. Lockey, III, M.D. (VP+D+Con) — Doris Lockey Geier [MD] (P+D) — James E. Lockey, M.D. [OH] (S+D) — Susan Lockey Hawkins [MD] (F+D) — Paul L. Geier [MD] (D) — Sarah R. Landis [East Petersburg] (D) — Anna F. Lockey (D) — Brian Lockey [NJ] (D) — Catherine A. Lockey [York] (D) — Richard F. Lockey, M.D. [FL] (D) — Elizabeth J. Lockey [OH] (D) — Napoleon Monroe [MD] (D)

CP-006 Alley (Albert A.) Family Foundation
1510 Cornwall Road
Lebanon 17042   (Lebanon County)
AMV $493   FYE 12-00   (**Gifts Received** $31,900)

MI-11-13-14-22-63-71-82
Phone 717-273-0662 **FAX** None
EIN 23-6862791   **Year Created** 1986
32 **Grants totaling** $31,631

Mostly local/Pa. giving. High grants of **$5,000** each to Friendship Ministries, Lebanon Valley Family YMCA, and Lehigh Valley Rails to Trails. **$2,500** to Religious Society of Friends/Lancaster. **$2,000** to Salvation Army (Operation Santa). **$1,000-$1,500** each to Developmental & Disability Services of Lebanon Valley, Boy Scouts/Lancaster-Lebanon Council, Keystone Roundball Classic, St. Joseph's Center Foundation [Scranton], Susquehanna Assn. for the Blind, and United Way of Lebanon County. **$850** to Avon Zion United Methodist Church. Other local contributions **$50-$500** for various charities. **Out-of-state** grant: **$1,000** to B.T.L. Foundation for International Services [DE]. ■**PUBLICATIONS:** None ■**WEBSITE:** None ■**E-MAIL:** None ■**APPLICATION POLICIES & PROCEDURES:** Information not available.
O+D+T Albert A. Alley, M.D. (T+Donor+Con) — Richard Alley, M.D. (T)

CP-007 Angela Foundation, The
c/o Auntie Anne's, Inc.
160-A Route 41, P.O. Box 529
Gap 17527   (Lancaster County)
AMV $794,704   FYE 12-00   (**Gifts Received** $722,170)

MI-12-13-14-15-22-31-41-63
Phone 717-442-4766 **FAX** 717-442-4139
EIN 23-2985480   **Year Created** 1998
38 **Grants totaling** $511,121

Mostly local giving. High grant of **$303,290** to Family Resource & Counseling Center. **$43,990** to The Worship Center. **$7,500** to Auntie Anne's, Inc./CARES Community. **$6,900** to Task Force. **$5,000** to Newsong Fellowship Church. **$2,400** to Victory Chapel. **$1,700-$2,000** to Dayspring Christian Academy, Freedom Life Christian Center, Pa. Family Institute, and Teen Challenge Training Center. Other smaller local contributions. **Out-of-state** giving includes **$96,000** to Emerge Ministries [OH]; **$7,200** to Focus on the Family [CO]; **$4,800** to Wycliffe Associates [CA]; and other smaller grants/contributions to church-related or mission organizations, particularly Assemblies of God. ■**PUBLICATIONS:** None ■**WEBSITE:** None ■**E-MAIL:** None ■**APPLICATION POLICIES & PROCEDURES:** Grant requests may be submitted in any form at any time; provide information on the organization and the reason for requesting support.
O+D+T Samuel Beiler (P+Con) — Jonas Beiler (C+Donor) — Doris Swaim (S) — Ronald Risser (F) — Anne Beiler (Donor)

CP-008 **Anselmo (Joseph J.), Sr. Charitable Trust**

MI-11-44-52-71-84

c/o Northumberland National Bank
245 Front Street
Northumberland 17857 (Northumberland County)

Phone 570-473-3531 **FAX** 570-473-9697
EIN 23-7898558 **Year Created** 1998

AMV $770,387 **FYE** 12-99 (**Gifts Received** $0) 6 **Grants totaling** $35,800

All locally restricted giving. High grant of **$15,450** to United Way of Susquehanna Valley. **$7,500** each to C.W. Rice Middle School (computers). Point Township (park improvements). **$3,000** to Shikellamy Band Assn. (uniforms). **$1,500** to Northumberland Midget Football (uniforms). **$850** to Norry Flash ASA Girls Softball (uniforms and fees). — Giving in prior years for a library, church, and sports. ■**PUBLICATIONS:** None ■**WEBSITE:** None ■**E-MAIL:** None ■**APPLICATION POLICIES & PROCEDURES:** All giving is restricted to organizations serving youths in the Borough of Northumberland and Point Township; most grants are for general support, special projects, or building funds. Prospective applicants should make an initial telephone inquiry about the feasibility of submitting a request. Grant requests must be submitted on a formal application form, available from the Bank, together with organization and project budgets, Board member list, and IRS tax-exempt status documentation; requests may be submitted at any time. Site visits sometimes are made to organizations being considered for a grant. Grants are awarded at meetings in January, April, July, and October.

O+D+T Stephen A. Hafer (Trust Officer at Bank+Con)

CP-009 **Apple (Benjamin & Lillie E.) Foundation**

MI-13-14-56-63-64

c/o Butter Krust Baking Co.
249 North 11th Street, P.O. Box 705
Sunbury 17801 (Northumberland County)

Phone 570-286-5845 **FAX** None
EIN 24-6014088 **Year Created** 1963

AMV $455,993 **FYE** 7-00 (**Gifts Received** $0) 6 **Grants totaling** $19,675

All Central Pa. giving. High grant of **$5,675** to Gettysburg Lutheran Theological Seminary. **$5,000** each to Central Susquehanna Sight Services and Christ Evangelical Church of Lewisburg. **$2,500** to Boy Scouts/Susquehanna Council. **$1,250** to Packwood House Museum. One smaller contribution. ■**PUBLICATIONS:** None ■**WEBSITE:** None ■**E-MAIL:** None ■**APPLICATION POLICIES & PROCEDURES:** The Foundation reports that giving is limited to Pa.

O+D+T John B. Apple (T+Con) — James G. Apple (T) — Joan Apple Zimmerman (T)

CP-010 **Armstrong Foundation**

MI-11-13-25-29-42-43-52-55-56-71-81-83-85-88-89

c/o Armstrong World Industries, Inc.
2500 Columbia Ave., P.O. Box 3001
Lancaster 17604 (Lancaster County)

Phone 717-396-5536 **FAX** 717-396-6133
EIN 23-2387950 **Year Created** 1985

AMV $5,044,791 **FYE** 12-01 (**Gifts Received** $50,000) 750+ **Grants totaling** $2,121,985

About 40% local giving. High grant of **$536,800** to United Way of Lancaster County. **$50,000** to Lancaster Area Habitat for Humanity. **$43,800** to Millersville University. **$40,000** to Lancaster Country Day School. **$35,000** to Thaddeus Stevens Foundation. **$30,000** to Eisenhower Exchange Fellowship [Philadelphia]. **$26,000** to Salvation Army. **$25,000** to Lancaster Alliance. **$13,713** to Franklin & Marshall College. **$11,625** to Elizabethtown College. **$10,000** each to Celebrate Lancaster! 2001, Lancaster Campaign, and Linden Hall. **$7,407** to School District of Lancaster. **$5,490** to Lancaster Bible College. **$5,000** each to Bucknell U., Lancaster Chamber Foundation and Rocky Springs Carousel Assn. **$2,000-$2,500** each to American Cancer Society, Boy Scouts/Pa. Dutch Council, Heritage Center Museum, Lancaster County Academy, Leadership Lancaster, Maytown/East Donegal Fire Company, Susquehanna Assn. for the Blind, and West Lancaster Fire Company #1. **$1,000-$1,600** each to Community Action Program, Hempfield Fire Company, Hospice of Lancaster County, Janus School, Lancaster Theological Seminary, Lancaster Recreation Commission, Make-A-Wish Foundation, Maytown/East Donegal Ambulance Assn., Neffsville Community Fire Company, Pioneer Fire Company, and West End Ambulance Assn. Other contributions **$350-$500** for local community organizations. **Out-of-state** giving includes **$200,000** to American Forests Global Releaf [DC]; **$100,000** to National Arbor Day Foundation [NE]; **$55,000** to Hardwood Forestry Fund [VA]; and many other grants/contributions in 38 corporate operating locations nationwide. ■**PUBLICATIONS:** None ■**WEBSITE:** www.armstrongfoundation.com ■**E-MAIL:** contact@armstrongfoundation.com ■**APPLICATION POLICIES & PROCEDURES:** The Foundation reports that support focuses on improving the quality of life in communities where Armstrong employees live and work through general grant requests, employee choice matching gifts and higher education matching gifts ($50 minimum, $250 maximum/year/employee), and scholarships for employee dependents. No grants are awarded for—and no grant money may be used for—political or lobbying purposes. Guidelines and applications for all programs are available on the website. Grant requests **must** be submitted electronically on the Foundation's website; documents may be attached. The deadline for applications is July 1st for grants that are awarded the following year. Site visits sometimes are made to organizations being considered for a grant. — In addition, the Foundation awards $250 to nonprofit organizations in which an Armstrong employee has volunteered at least 36 hours in a calendar year during nonscheduled work hours. — Formerly called Armstrong World Industries Foundation.

O+D+T All Officers & Directors are Armstrong employees: Debra J. Brooks (Foundation Coordinator+AS+Con) — Debra L. Miller (P+D) — David Frank (S) — Barry Sullivan (F) — Walter Gangl, Esq. (AS+Legal Counsel) — Matt J. Angello (D) — John N. Rigas, Esq. (D) — Stephen Senkowski (D) — April L. Thornton (D) — Corporate donor: Armstrong World Industries, Inc.

CP-011 **Ashland Foundation, The**

MI-15-18-19-21-22-24-29-32-34-56-61-63

645 Willow Valley Square, #J-305
Lancaster 17602 (Lancaster County)

Phone 717-464-6326 **FAX** None
EIN 23-6245778 **Year Created** 1949

AMV $3,475,288 **FYE** 10-00 (**Gifts Received** $0) 128 **Grants totaling** $151,810

Mostly local/regional giving. High grant of **$43,525** to Schuylkill Area Community Foundation. **$25,000** to Masonic Charities. **$7,500** each to Thomas Jefferson U. [Philadelphia] and Willow Valley Manor North. **$6,000** to Supreme Council Benevolent Fund. **$5,000** each to Good Shepherd Lutheran Church [Ashland], Heritage Society (Helping Hand), Schuylkill Lodge H-138, and Willow Valley North Gift Fund. **$3,600** to Penn State U. **$1,000-$1,250** each to American Cancer Society, Drug & Alcohol Rehabilitation Services, Planned Parenthood, Red Cross, St. Anne's Center, St. Paul's Church, St. Philip the Apostle Church, and Urban Promise [St. David's]. Numerous other contributions to eastern Pa., **$50-$750** each, for community organizations and purposes. **Out-of-state** giving to NC and NY. ■**PUBLICATIONS:** None ■**WEBSITE:** None ■**E-MAIL:** None ■**APPLICATION POLICIES & PROCEDURES:** Most giving focuses on Schuylkill or Lancaster counties. Grant requests may be submitted in a letter at any time. The Board meets in mid-January.

O+D+T Paul G. Reidler (VP+Donor+Con) — Carl J. Reidler [Klingerstown] (P) — Helen Reidler (S) — Diane K. Reidler [Klingerstown] (F) — Corporate donors: Reidler's Inc.; Ashland Knitting Mills, Inc.

CP-012 **Barsumian (Jane B.) Memorial Fund**

c/o First Union/Wachovia - PA 6497
600 Penn Street, P.O. Box 1102
Reading 19603 (Berks County)

MI-31-32-34

Phone 610-655-3148 **FAX** None
EIN 23-6492481 **Year Created** 1997

AMV $3,942,280 **FYE** 12-00 **(Gifts Received** $0) 3 **Grants totaling** $167,400

Mostly local giving. High grant of **$74,400** to Penn State College of Medicine. **$65,000** to Lancaster Heart Foundation. **Out-of-state** grant: **$27,500** to Arnold P. Gold Foundation [NJ]. — Giving in the prior year included **$56,915** to St. Joseph's Hospital & Care Center; **$49,125** to Penn State College of Medicine; and **$20,000** to Lancaster Heart Foundation. ■**PUBLICATIONS:** None ■**WEBSITE:** None ■**E-MAIL:** None ■**APPLICATION POLICIES & PROCEDURES:** The Fund reports that giving focuses on medical research with first preference given to institutions in the Lancaster-Hershey area. Submit grants requests in a proposal before the September 30th deadline. An outside committee makes decisions on grants which are disbursed in December.

O+D+T Hans Hass (Assistant VP at Bank+Con) — John May, Esq. (Co-T) — First Union/Wachovia (Corporate Trustee)

CP-013 **Bartlett Foundation**

c/o First Union/Wachovia - PA 6497
600 Penn Street, P.O. Box 1102
Reading 19603 (Berks County)

MI-12-13-17-19-25-29-32-35-72

Phone 610-655-3135 **FAX** None
EIN 23-6567275 **Year Created** 1972

AMV $2,438,185 **FYE** 12-00 **(Gifts Received** $0) 21 **Grants totaling** $134,850

Mostly local giving. High grant of **$22,500** to Olivet Boys & Girls Club of Reading/Berks. **$18,400** to Police Athletic League of Greater Reading. **$17,000** to Reading Berks Emergency Shelter. **$16,750** to Caron Foundation. **$12,000** to Camp Fire Boys & Girls/Adahi Council. **$5,000** each to Bethany Children's Home and Make-A-Wish Foundation of Berks County. **$4,000-$4,200** each to Berks Visiting Nurse Assn., GPU Project Good Neighbor, Salvation Army, and YMCA of Reading & Berks. **$3,000-$3,350** each to Animal Rescue League of Berks County, Humane Society of Berks County, Pa. Special Olympics, and St. Joseph Health Ministries. **$1,000** to Red Cross. **$1,450** to Planned Parenthood of NE Pa. **Out-of-state** giving includes **$4,000** to Covenant House [NY] and **$1,000** each to Alzheimer's Disease Research [MD], American Cancer Society [AZ], and The Gideons International [AZ]. ■**PUBLICATIONS:** grant proposal guidelines ■**WEBSITE:** None ■**E-MAIL:** None ■**APPLICATION POLICIES & PROCEDURES:** The Foundation reports that support focuses primarily on Berks County, especially programs dealing with at-risk youth and alcohol/drug abuse; also low-income families, single parents, or the elderly; scholarship programs at local educational institutions are supported. Support for cultural organizations will be considered but is not a primary interest. Strong consideration is given to organizations that offer the broadest benefit to the community, particularly those programs dealing with youth and the elderly. Capital improvement grants have a lower priority and are only considered when a specific project and a clear need are demonstrated. No grants are awarded for endowment, political support, fundraising dinners, athletic events, medical research, fellowships/scholarships, or to individuals or for loans. Grant requests must be submitted on the requesting organization's letterhead (5 pages or less on 8 1/2 x 11 sheets, single-sided) and signed by an officer on behalf of the governing board. The proposal must include (a) Project title and purpose of the grant request including the expected outcome of the project; (b) A problem statement documenting the needs to be met or problems to be solved by the project; (c) A plan of action for how the purposes will be achieved; (d) The budget request which outlines program elements in budgetary terms; (e) A statement describing the project's duration; if an ongoing project, include anticipated long-term funding requirements. In addition, include organizational background information; list of current Board members; immediate past and present major funding sources; current organizational budget; bound audited financial statement; and IRS tax-exempt status documentation. Also, the applicant organization must complete and file a First Union National Bank Charitable Funds Services Common Grant Application with the proposal. Grant requests must be received by the April 30th and November 15th deadlines. Incomplete proposals will not be considered.

O+D+T Andrew C. Meltzer (VP at Bank+Con) — First Union/Wachovia (Trustee)

CP-014 **Berks County Community Foundation**

501 Washington Street, Suite 801
P.O. Box 212
Reading 19603 (Berks County)

MI-11-12-13-14-20-22-25-29-35-42-43-44-51
55-56-71-85
Phone 610-685-2223 **FAX** 610-685-2240
EIN 23-2769892 **Year Created** 1994

AMV $22,910,847 **FYE** 6-01 **(Gifts Received** $3,750,100) 340+ **Grants totaling** $2,579,801

As a Community Foundation all discretionary giving is limited to organizations serving Berks County; 28 grants from discretionary funds totaled about **$185,000.** High grant of **$25,000** to Police Athletic League of Reading (arts programming). **$20,000** each to Goodwill Industries of Mideastern Pa. (Wheels 4 Work) and Mt. Penn Volunteer Fire Dept. (rapid intervention team). **$12,500** each to Center for Community Leadership and Reading Community Players (operating-production support). **$10,000** each to CONCERN (foster/adopt program) and United Way of Berks County (child care initiative). **$9,000** to Community Works (Labor Festival). **$8,000** to Greater Berks Food Bank (Kids' Cafe). **$7,630** to Berks County District Attorney's Office (law enforcement equipment). **$4,700-$5,000** each to Crime Alert Bucks County (community awareness program), Pa. Partnerships for Children (Pa. Child Advocacy Network-capacity building), Reading & Berks County Visitors Bureau (heritage development), and Reading

Downtown Improvement District (downtown renewal). **$3,000-$3,600** each to Community Alliance & Reinvestment Endeavor (Y.E.S. program), Easter Seals/Eastern Pa. (feeding management clinic), and Reading-Berks Conference of Church (summer interns). **$2,000-$2,500** each to Berks Arts Council (Arts Tool Kit), Berks County Community & Economic Development (industrial site assessment), and Berks County Conservancy (Centre Township Land Preservation Project). Six other grants/contributions of **$1,000** or less awarded for various purposes. Other grants were awarded from donor-advised or restricted funds, and from scholarship funds for students graduating from (or attending) designated educational institutions or pursuing special courses of study. ■**PUBLICATIONS:** Annual Report; Newsletter; Information for Grant Seekers brochure ■**WEBSITE:** www.bccf.org ■**E-MAIL:** info@bccf.org ■**APPLICATION POLICIES & PROCEDURES:** The Foundation reports that all discretionary giving is restricted to organizations serving Berks County; preference is given to proposals which: (a) improve and strengthen existing organizations' capacities to reach a broader community; (b) provide innovative responses to recognized community needs and not duplicate existing efforts; (c) encourage interagency cooperation and collaboration; (d) have multiple funding sources and able to leverage other financial support (normally the Foundation will not be the only source of support); (e) have a long-term, identifiable and measurable impact on community; and (f) Foundation Board/staff are knowledgeable about. Generally, no grants will be awarded for the following: recurring requests for the same program, routine operating expenses, endowment, annual appeals, membership drives, benefit events, or capital campaigns (unless compelling evidence shows it is vital to meeting a priority community need). Refer to the website for details on the Foundation's Demonstration Grants Program and the Community Investment Grant Program. Prospective applicants initially should make a telephone inquiry about the feasibility of submitting a request. If encouraged by Foundation staff, a Letter of Intent (2 pages maximum) then should be submitted before the late January and mid-July deadlines (call for exact dates); describe your organization (mission, history, and who you serve); describe the project idea (its importance, intended beneficiaries, anticipated results, and the total cost); and state how much funding is requested. After thorough review, Foundation staff will advise if a full application may be submitted and will provide complete application materials, as well as the deadline. Organizations being considered for a grant usually will be visited or interviewed by telephone. The Board awards grants at April and October meetings.

O+D+T Kevin K. Murphy (P+D+Con) — Robert W. Cardy (C+D) — Sidney D. Kline, Jr. (VC+D) — J. William Widing, III, Esq. (S) — Andrew Maier, II (F+D) — Jan Armfield (D) — Thomas A. Beaver (D) — Mary M. Bertolet, Esq. (D) — G. Walton Cottrell (D) — Dennis M. Draeger (D) — Ronald Foy (D) — T. Jerome Holleran (D) — Julia H. Klein (D) — Samuel A. McCullough (D) — William M. Moeller (D) — Glen E. Moyer (D) — Leon S. Myers (D) — Paul R. Roedel (D) — David L. Thun (D) — Ramona D. Turpin (D) — Col. Harry D. Yoder (D)

CP-015 **Berks County Tuberculosis Society, The**
151 Leisure Court
Reading   19610   (Berks County)

MI-12-15-17-25-29-31-35-42
Phone 610-374-4951 **FAX** None
EIN 23-1409703   **Year Created** 1965

AMV $32,731   **FYE** 12-00   (**Gifts Received** $45,718)   11 **Grants totaling** $34,500

All giving restricted to Berks County. High grant of **$11,000** to Visiting Nurse Assn. **$9,000** to Reading Hospital. **$4,000** to St. Joseph Hospital. **$2,500** to Reading Emergency Center. **$2,000** to Greater Reading Food Bank. **$1,000** each to Albright College, Chit Chat Foundation, Rainbow Home, Threshold, United Labor Food Pantry, and Women in Crisis. ■**PUBLICATIONS:** None ■**WEBSITE:** None ■**E-MAIL:** None ■**APPLICATION POLICIES & PROCEDURES:** Only Berks County organizations providing direct patient care or support are eligible to apply. Prospective applicants initially should make a telephone inquiry about the feasibility of submitting a grant request. Written requests should be submitted in August; describe the organization and proposed use of requested funds, and include IRS tax-exempt status documentation. Site visits sometimes are arranged to organizations being considered for a grant. The Board of Directors meets in September, December, March and June.

O+D+T R. William Alexander, M.D. (P+Con) — Jerome A. LaManna (VP) — Eric C. Jaxheimer, M.D. [Wyomissing] (F)

CP-016 **Berks Products Foundation**
c/o Berks Products Company
726 Spring Street, P.O. Box 421
Reading   19603   (Berks County)

MI-11-12-15-19-22-41-42-54-56
Phone 610-374-5131 **FAX** None
EIN 23-6396201   **Year Created** 1965

AMV $581,241   **FYE** 12-00   (**Gifts Received** $0)   48 **Grants totaling** $77,027

All local/Pa. giving. High grant of **$16,000** to Historical Society of Berks County. **$10,000** each to Albright College and Reading Fair. **$6,667** to Caron Foundation. **$5,500** to Independent Colleges of Pa. **$5,000** to Bethany Children's Home. **$4,000** to United Way of Berks County. **$3,000** to Salvation Army. **$2,000** each to Oley Valley School District and Reading Public Museum. **$1,000-$1,500** each to Alvernia College, Lutheran Home at Topton, and Make-A-Wish Foundation of Lancaster. Other contributions **$50-$500** for various purposes. ■**PUBLICATIONS:** None ■**WEBSITE:** None ■**E-MAIL:** None ■**APPLICATION POLICIES & PROCEDURES:** The Foundation reports that giving is limited primarily to Berks County. Grant requests may be submitted at any time in a letter (2 pages maximum); include IRS tax-exempt documentation.

O+D+T Anne Fehr Neilsen (Administrator+Con) — Allfirst Trust Co. of Pa. N.A. (Trustee) — Corporate donor: Berks Products Co.

CP-017 **Bishop (Vernon & Doris) Foundation, The**
1616 Fieldcrest Road
Lebanon   17042
                                  (Lebanon County)

MI-11-13-15-22-31-41-42-44-49-52-55-56-61
63-64-71
Phone 717-273-1462 **FAX** None
EIN 23-6255835   **Year Created** 1957

AMV $5,062,858   **FYE** 12-00   (**Gifts Received** $0)   42 **Grants totaling** $308,219

Mostly local giving; grants are for general purposes except as noted. High grant of **$100,000** to Penn Laurel Girl Scout Council. **$97,000** to Good Samaritan Health Services Foundation (hospital TV project). **$30,000** to Lebanon Valley Rails to Trails. **$14,169** to Lebanon Valley College. **$10,500** to United Way of Lebanon County. **$10,000** to Pa. Historic Dramas. **$4,400** to St. Andrews Presbyterian Church. **$4,250** to Boy Scouts/Pa. Dutch Council. **$3,000** to Lebanon Community Library. **$2,000** each to Avon Zion United Methodist Church and Church Farm School. **$1,000-$1,100** each to American Cancer Society, Chemical Heritage Foundation, Cornwall Manor, David Broderic Memorial Foundation, Development & Disability Service of Lebanon, Evangelical School of Theology, Gretna Theatre, Lebanon Catholic High School, Lebanon Christian Academy, Lebanon County Historical Society, Lebanon Valley Family YMCA, Lebanon Valley Youth for Christ, New Covenant Christian School, Our Lady of the Valley Development Fund, Philhaven, Rotary Foundation/Lebanon, Rotary Youth Fund, and WITF. Other local contributions **$100-$500** for various purposes. **Out-of-state** giving includes **$3,500** to The Heritage Foundation [DC]; **$2,000** to Phi Gamma Delta Educational Foundation [KY]; and smaller grants for schools/universities in CT, MD, and MI. ■**PUBLICATIONS:** None ■**WEBSITE:** None ■**E-MAIL:** None ■**APPLICATION POLICIES & PROCEDURES:** Written grant requests may be submitted at any time. No grants awarded to individuals.

O+D+T Vernon Bishop (T+Con) — Doris Bishop (T) — Corporate donor: Lebanon Chemical Corporation

---

CP-018 **Blue Mountain Foundation**

1015 Penn Ave., Suite 202
Wyomissing   19610

(Berks County)

MI-11-12-13-17-18-25-29-42-44-45-52-53-54
55-56-71
Phone 610-376-1595 **FAX** None
EIN 23-2586321   **Year Created** 1989

AMV $1,742,983	**FYE** 12-00	**(Gifts Received** $533,167)	29 **Grants totaling** $68,000

All local/Pa. giving; grants are for general support except as noted. High grant of **$13,500** to Performing Arts Center (campaign fund). **$10,000** to Historical Society of Berks County (endowment fund). **$6,500** to Berks County Conservancy. **$3,000-$3,500** each to Rocky Springs Carousel Assn., Lancaster Day Care Center, Pine Creek Valley Watershed Assn., and Wyomissing Public Library. **$2,000** each to Olivet Boys & Girls Club, Pa. School of Art, United Way of Berks County (endowment fund), and Wilson College. **$1,000-$1,500** each to Berks Talkline, Berks Women in Crisis, Fulton Opera House, Greater Berks Food Bank, Heritage Center Museum of Lancaster County, Literacy Council of Lancaster-Lebanon, Literacy Council of Reading/Berks County, Planned Parenthood of NE Pa., Planned Parenthood of Susquehanna Valley, Police Athletic League of Reading, Reading Public Museum, Schuylkill River Greenway Assn., South Mountain Camps Foundation, and Teen Challenge. **Out-of-state** grants: **$1,000** each to Chewonki Foundation [ME] and Deerwood Foundation [NH], and Popcorn Park Zoo [NJ]. ■**PUBLICATIONS:** None ■**WEBSITE:** None ■**E-MAIL:** None ■**APPLICATION POLICIES & PROCEDURES:** The Foundation reports that giving is limited to Berks & Lancaster counties, mostly for special projects, building funds, and capital drives. Grant requests may be submitted in writing at any time.

O+D+T Thomas A. Beaver, CPA (S+F+D+Con) — Lynda Overly Levengood [Lancaster] (P+D) — Anne Overly Moll (VP+D) — Thomas P. Handwerk, CPA (AS+AF+D) — Donor: Estate of Olive D. Overly Cook

---

CP-019 **Bon-Ton Stores Foundation, The**

c/o Bon-Ton Stores, Inc.
2801 East Market Street, P.O. Box 2821
York   17405

(York County)

MI-11-12-13-14-15-25-31-35-41-44-45-51-52
55-88
Phone 717-757-7660 **FAX** 717-751-3196
EIN 23-2656774   **Year Created** 1988

AMV $259,452	**FYE** 1-01	**(Gifts Received** $116,850)	140+ **Grants totaling** $148,663

About four-fifths local/Pa. giving in communities with company stores (see list of Pa. county locations below). High grant of **$10,000** to Cultural Alliance of York County. **$8,000** to United Disabilities Services [Lancaster]. **$5,000** each to Pa. Breast Cancer Coalition [Ephrata] and United Way of York County (Focus on Our Future). **$3,900** to Boy Scouts/York. **$3,000** each to Fulton Opera House and Strand-Capitol Performing Arts Center. **$2,800** to Agape Residential Ministries [Dillsburg]. **$2,500** to Allied Arts Fund. **$2,300** to March of Dimes/Reading. **$1,000-$1,750** each to Alzheimer's Assn./Pittsburgh, ARC-York, Assn. of Independent Colleges & Universities of Pa., Butler Health System Foundation, Celtic Fest [Bethlehem], Center for Family Life [Indiana], Community Services for Children [Bethlehem], Easter Seals [Monroe County], Elizabethtown Public Library, Health Education Center, Jewish Community Center of York, Logos Academy, Miller Memorial Blood Center, Penn Laurel Girl Scout Council, South George St. Community Partnership, Stepping Stone Counseling & Education Services, Wyomissing Institute for Fine Arts [Berks County], York Chorus, York Country Day School, York County Literacy Council, York Foundation, York Habitat for Humanity, York Little Theatre, YWCA of Carlisle, and YWCA of York. **$850** to Salvation Army/West Pittston. **$800** to Historic York. Other local/Pa. contributions **$50-$500** for civic, cultural, educational, health, human service, and other purposes. **Out-of-state** giving to MD, WV, CT, NH, NJ, and NY State in vicinity of store locations. Also, matching gift donations totaled **$15,853.** ■**PUBLICATIONS:** Grant Application packet; Primary Aims, Guidelines & Procedures brochure ■**WEBSITE:** www.bonton.com/careerops/communityinvolvement.htm ■**E-MAIL:** None ■**APPLICATION POLICIES & PROCEDURES:** The Foundation reports that primary consideration is given to communities served by Bon-Ton Department Stores in the following Pa. counties: Berks, Butler, Chester, Columbia, Cumberland, Dauphin, Fayette, Lackawanna, Lancaster, Lehigh, Lycoming, Mifflin, Monroe, Montour, and Westmoreland; as well as in New England, NY and MD. Its present targeted areas of interest of Community Health, Youth, and serving the needs of the Economically Disadvantaged. Most grants are for general support, special projects, capital drives, scholarships and matching grants; multiple-year grants are awarded. Applicant organizations must be soundly managed with responsible fiscal management practices, have a method for evaluating its programs/activities, and have an active Board with policy-making authority. No support is given to individuals or for mass-mailing requests, religious activities, political groups/activities, fraternal orders, labor groups, or organizations that discriminate. Also, the Foundation discourages requests for the following: operating expenses, capital campaigns, equipment, publications, films or radio-TV programs, research, endowment, or conferences. Grant requests from York area organizations may be submitted at any time on a formal Grant Application form which is available on request. Organizations located elsewhere, e.g. Bon-Ton communities, should contact their local Bon-Ton General Manager as other guidelines apply (based on the amount of funding requested) and are detailed in the *Primary Aims, Guidelines & Procedures* brochure. Applications are reviewed about four times annually and the initial review may take up to three months; the Foundation may request additional information. Notifications on declined requests, however, are sent within one month. — Additional support may be available through Bon-Ton's Retail Associate Volunteerism Outreach Program and Matching Gift program. — Formerly called SGS Foundation.

O+D+T Christine DeJuliis (Foundation Administrator+Con) — Ryan J. Sattler (P+D) — Melinda A. Shue (S+F+D) — Ken Heitz (D) — Mary Kerr (D) — Joseph L. Leahy (D) — James Volk (D) — Susan M. Wolfe (D) — Corporate donor: Bon-Ton Stores, Inc.

CP-020 Bowman (Anne L. & Robert K.) Family Foundation, The
436 Ringneck Lane
Lancaster   17601   (Lancaster County)

MI-42-44-56-71-89
Phone 717-392-1211 **FAX** None
EIN 23-7850323   **Year Created** 1997

AMV $297,809   **FYE** 12-99   **(Gifts Received** $45,000)   7 **Grants totaling** $18,000

Mostly local/Pa. giving. High grants of **$5,000** each to Penn State U. (endowment) and Trinity Lutheran Church (AV equipment). **$3,000** to Lancaster County Conservancy (operating). **$1,000** each to The Demuth Foundation (capital campaign), Lancaster County Library System (operating), and Lancaster Police Horse Fund (capital campaign). **Out-of-state** grant: **$3,000** to Wake Forest U. [NC] (endowment). — Other giving in prior years included **$10,000** to Bucknell U. (capital campaign) and **$4,000** to Samaritan Counseling Center (building fund). ■**PUBLICATIONS:** None ■**WEBSITE:** None ■**E-MAIL:** None ■**APPLICATION POLICIES & PROCEDURES:** The Foundation reports that unsolicted requests are not accepted; all grants are Trustee-directed.

O+D+T Robert K. Bowman (C+Con) — Anne L. Bowman (S) — Mark W. Bowman [CT] (T) — Susan E. Bowman [MA] (T)

CP-021 Boyd (Alexander & Jane) Foundation
c/o Union Deposit Corporation
750 East Park Drive, P.O. Box 4153
Harrisburg   17111   (Dauphin County)

MI-13-14-15-18-22-25-31-32-41-61

Phone 717-564-0832 **FAX** 717-564-4759
EIN 23-2251378   **Year Created** 1983

AMV $667,284   **FYE** 12-00   **(Gifts Received** $0)   36 **Grants totaling** $38,300

Mostly local giving. High local grants of **$2,000** each to Ecumenical Relief Fund and PinnacleHealth Foundation. **$1,000-$1,500** each to Big Brothers/Big Sisters, Bethesda Mission, Cystic Fibrosis Foundation of Central Pa., Dauphin County ARC, Feed My Sheep of Dauphin County, Gaudenzia, Harrisburg Academy, Harrisburg Area YMCA, Hereditary Disease Foundation, Hershey Medical Center (cancer research), The Hill School, Holy Name of Jesus, Hospice of Central Pa., Kidney Foundation, Pa. State YMCA (Youth in Government), Planned Parenthood of Susquehanna Valley, South Central Pa. Food Bank, St. Francis of Assisi Food Kitchen, St. Stephen's School, and Villa Teresa Nursing Home. Other smaller local contributions. **Out-of-state** giving includes high grant of **$3,000** to Woodberry Forest School [VA]. ■**PUBLICATIONS:** None ■**WEBSITE:** None ■**E-MAIL:** None ■**APPLI-CATION POLICIES & PROCEDURES:** The Foundation reports that giving is primarily restricted to charities in Lower Paxton Township, Swatara Township and Susquehanna Township—all in Dauphin County, and scholarships are limited to high school graduates in those townships. Organizational grant requests may be submitted at any time in the form of a letter (3 pages maximum); include an organizational budget, project budget, audited financial statement, and IRS tax-exempt status documentation. Scholarship applicants should contact local high school guidance departments for more information. Decisions on organizational grants are made at a December meeting.

O+D+T Paul L. Mahoney (Co-T+Donor+Con) — Robert S. Jones (Co-T) — Sherill T. Moyer (Co-T) — Henry W. Rhoads (Co-T) — John P. Trach (Co-T) — Alexander Boyd (Donor) — Allfirst Trust Co. of Pa. N.A. (Co-Trustee) — Corporate donor: Union Deposit Corporation

---

CP-022 Boyer (James K.) Family Foundation
2201 Ridgewood Road, #180
Wyomissing   19610   (Berks County)

MI-13-18-44-71-79
Phone 610-372-6414 **FAX** None
EIN 23-7788030   **Year Created** 1994

AMV $409,529   **FYE** 12-00   **(Gifts Received** $0)   4 **Grants totaling** $20,154

All local/regional giving. High grant of **$5.154** to James F. Boyer Library. **$5,000** each to 10,000 Friends of Pa., Planned Parenthood, and YMCA. — In prior years, giving included three grants totaling **$30,000** to Boyertown Community Library; **$14,903** to The Hill School; and **$4,000** to Boyertown Ambulance. ■**PUBLICATIONS:** None ■**WEBSITE:** None ■**E-MAIL:** None ■**AP-PLICATION POLICIES & PROCEDURES:** Information not available.

O+D+T Nancy Lang Boyer (P+Donor+Con) — Walter Lang Boyer (S) — James K. Boyer, Jr. (F) — Mary Ann Boyer (D) — Patricia Lang Boyer (D)

CP-023 Brenneman (J.P. & M.H.) Fund, The
c/o Blakey, Yost, Bupp & Schauman
17 East Market Street
York   17401   (York County)

MI-43
Phone 717-845-3674 **FAX** None
EIN 23-7850463   **Year Created** 1996

AMV $1,704,971   **FYE** 12-00   **(Gifts Received** $0)   95 **Grants totaling** $96,827

All grants are post-secondary scholarships, mostly **$900-$1,200** each, for York County residents attending colleges, universities or technical schools in the U.S. ■**PUBLICATIONS:** None ■**WEBSITE:** None ■**E-MAIL:** None ■**APPLICATION POLICIES & PROCEDURES:** Only residents of York County are eligible to apply for financial aid at universities, colleges, or technical schools in the U.S. Contact the Fund in February to request a formal application form. The deadline for applications is May 1st.

O+D+T Robert O. Beers, Esq. (Manager+Con) — Mellon Bank N.A. (Trustee)

CP-024 Broadbent Foundation, The
1 Chestnut Hill Drive
Mohnton   19540   (Berks County)

MI-43-49
Phone 610-796-7682 **FAX** 610-796-7683
EIN 23-2703271   **Year Created** 1992

AMV $977,948   **FYE** 6-00   **(Gifts Received** $0)   9 **Grants totaling** $46,657

All local giving. High grant of **$8,676** to Berks County Intermediate Unit (Economic America Program). All other grants are scholarships, ranging from **$3,100** to **$5,000** for graduates of Gov. Mifflin High School. ■**PUBLICATIONS:** scholarship application guidelines and form ■**WEBSITE:** None ■**E-MAIL:** None ■**APPLICATION POLICIES & PROCEDURES:** The Foundation reports its major interest is in economic education programs which train elementary/secondary school teachers, primarily in Berks County or other areas selected by the Trustees. Prospective applicants should make an initial telephone call to inquire about the feasibility of submitting a request. Also, proposals may be solicited from organizations deemed to be cost-effective education providers. Grant requests may be submitted in a letter (2 pages maximum), preferably during May-July; include organization and project budgets, list of major funding sources, and IRS tax-exempt status documentation—other materials subsequently may be requested. Site visits sometimes are made to organizations being considered for a grant. Scholarships are awarded only Gov. Mifflin High School graduates.

O+D+T John H. Broadbent, Jr. (T+Donor+Con) — Richard L. Broadbent [Reading] (T) — Dana L. Bunting [NJ] (T)

CP-025 **Brossman (William & Jemima) Charitable Foundation**
c/o Ephrata National Bank
31 East Main Street, P.O. Box 457
Ephrata   17522   (Lancaster County)

MI-11-13-14-22-25-29-41-42-43-44-49-51-52
53-54-55-56-57-64-71-72-89
Phone 717-733-6576 **FAX** 717-733-2097
EIN 23-6087844   **Year Created** 1987

AMV $22,725,979   **FYE** 10-00   **(Gifts Received** $0)   102 **Grants totaling** $1,002,720

Mostly Central Pa. giving; grants are for annual/general support except as noted; some grants represent multiple payments. High grants of **$50,000** each to Ephrata Area Community Theatre and Lutheran Theological Seminary [Gettysburg]. **$41,000** to Ephrata Public Library (mostly children's collection endowment). **$38,000** to Red Cross/Susquehanna Valley Chapter. **$30,000** each to Franklin & Marshall College and Thaddeus Stevens Foundation. **$25,000** each to Linden Hall (Project Beyond One Classroom), Pa. Academy of Music, and Whitaker Center. **$20,000** to Boy Scouts/Dutch Council (general support/benefit event). **$14,000** to Junior Achievement of Central Pa. (general support/golf benefit). **$13,000** to Penn Laurel Council Girl Scouts. **$12,500** to Lancaster County Historical Society. **$10,000** each to Lancaster Theological Seminary, Lititz Public Library, Philadelphia Zoo, United Way of Lancaster County, and WITF (documentary). **$9,500** to Lancaster Symphony Orchestra (sponsorship). **$7,000-$7,500** each to Fulton Opera House (Shakespeare productions), Hands On House (capital campaign), and Millersville U. (Brossman Science Lectureship). **$6,000** each to Big 33 Scholarship Inc. and Family Service. **$5,000** each to Ephrata TRACK, Lincoln Fire Company #1, Lititz Fire Company #1, Pa. Breast Cancer Coalition, Pa. School of Art & Design, and Salvation Army. **$4,000** each to Central Pa. Symphony, Ephrata Community Hospital (indigent care), and St. Anne's Home for the Aged. **$3,500** to Music at Gretna. **$3,000** to Big Brothers Big Sisters of Lancaster. **$2,000-$2,500** each to Berks County Conservancy, Bethany Christian Services, Demuth Foundation (garden tour), Kutztown U. Foundation, Lancaster Museum of Art (exhibit sponsorship), and Lancaster YWCA. **$1,000-$1,500** each to Adamstown Area Library, American Heart Assn. (benefit event), Central Pa. Food Bank, Children's Playroom Inc. (benefit event), Cocalico School District (alumni assn.), Goodwill Industries of SE Pa., Lancaster Day Care Center, Lebanon Valley College (memorial scholarship), Mennonite Home, Mental Health Assn. Lancaster County, The Second Mile [State College], and Susquehanna Waldorf School. Other smaller local contributions for various purposes. Also, **$396,000** transferred to Brossman Scholarship Foundation. **Out-of-state** grant: **$50,000** to Rider U. [NJ] (annual leadership gift). ■**PUBLICATIONS:** None ■**WEBSITE:** None ■**E-MAIL:** None ■**APPLICATION POLICIES & PROCEDURES:** The Foundation reports giving is limited to South Central Pa.; most grants are for general support, special projects, capital campaigns, building/renovations, or scholarships that are restricted to high school graduates (or equivalent) of Ephrata High School or residents in the Denver & Ephrata Telephone Company franchise service area. Multiyear grants are awarded. Grant requests may be submitted in a letter (3 pages maximum) at any time; include organizational and project budgets, an audited financial statement, and IRS tax-exempt status documentation. Site visits sometimes are made to organizations being considered for a grant. Grants are awarded at meetings in April, August, and October.

O+D+T Carl L. Brubaker (VP at Bank+Con) — Ephrata National Bank (Trustee)

CP-026 **Brougher (W. Dale) Foundation**
1200 Country Club Road
York   17403   (York County)

MI-11-13-17-35-41-49-52-55-56-63-71
Phone 717-845-2959 **FAX** None
EIN 52-1499358   **Year Created** 1986

AMV $4,718,613   **FYE** 12-00   **(Gifts Received** $799,707)   40 **Grants totaling** $264,900

About two-thirds local giving. High grant of **$100,000** to Strand Capitol Performing Arts Center. **$25,000** to United Way of York County. **$10,000** each to Historic York and Penn Laurel Girl Scouts. **$5,000** each to Byres Health Education Center and Dreamwrights Youth & Family Theatre. **$3,500** to Planned Parenthood of York County. **$1,000-$1,750** each to Cultural Alliance of York, Farm & Natural Lands Trust, First Presbyterian Church of York, Junior Achievement of York County, Pa. National Horse Show, York Catholic High School, YMCA of York & York County, and YWCA of York. **$850** to York Murals. Other smaller local contributions for various purposes. Our-of-state giving includes **$35,000** to The Peddie School [NJ]; **$25,800** to Adopt a Family [FL]; and **$11,000** to Society of Four Arts [FL]. ■**PUBLICATIONS:** None ■**WEBSITE:** None ■**E-MAIL:** None ■**APPLICATION POLICIES & PROCEDURES:** Information not available.

O+D+T W. Dale Brougher (P+F+Donor+Con) — Nancy M. Brougher (VP+S) — Louis F. Friedman, Esq. [MD] (AS)

CP-027 **Browning (Ida W.) Audio-Visual Trust**
c/o First Union/Wachovia
30 North 3rd Street, P.O. Box 1071
Harrisburg   17108   (Dauphin County)

MI-17-22-44-57-63
Phone 717-234-2757 **FAX** 717-234-2756
EIN 23-6271540   **Year Created** 1952

AMV $1,154,380   **FYE** 9-00   **(Gifts Received** $0)   15 **Grants totaling** $35,529

Giving is restricted to the greater Harrisburg area (geograpical specifics below) for audio-visual materials for religious, educational, and character-building purposes. High grant of **$21,000** to WITF-TV (underwrite children's programs). **$2,500** to Dauphin County Library System. **$3,000** to Jewish Community Center of Harrisburg. **$2,500** to West Shore Public Library. **$1,500** to Domestic Violence Services. **$900** to Bethesda Mission. **$800** to Wesley United Methodist Church. Other contributions **$130-$600,** mostly to churches or church-related organizations. ■**PUBLICATIONS:** application guidelines ■**WEBSITE:** None ■**E-MAIL:** brenton.hake@wachovia.com ■**APPLICATION POLICIES & PROCEDURES:** Only churches, schools, or educational groups located in Dauphin County or parts of Cumberland County and within 10-15 miles of the center of Harrisburg are eligible to apply; preference is given to religious institutions. Prospective applicants initially should make a telephone inquiry about the feasibility of submitting a grant request. Requests may be submitted at any time on a formal application form (provided by the Trust) before the June 30th deadline; include IRS tax-exempt status documentation. Grants are awarded at a late summer meeting.

O+D+T Distribution Committee Members: Brenton Hake (Regional Trust Officer+VP at Bank+Con) — James C.V. Lehr — Miriam G. Menaker — Henry W. Rhoads, Esq. — Jacqueline Rucker — First Union/Wachovia (Trustee)

CP-028 **Butz (William B.) Memorial Fund**

220 Long Lane
Oley 19547   (Berks County)
AMV $4,624,392   **FYE** 12-00   **(Gifts Received** $0)

MI-12-31-52-56-86
Phone 610-987-6582 **FAX** None
EIN 23-6259515   **Year Created** 1956
7 **Grants totaling** $270,000

One Pa. grant: **$50,000** to Lockridge Furnace Historical Society [Alburtis] (historic preservation). **Out-of-state** giving includes **$65,000** to Metropolitan Opera [NY]; **$50,000** each to New York Community Trust and Young Concert Artist, Inc. [NY]. **$30,000** to New York Downtown Hospital; **$15,000** to Center for Speech & Language Disorders [IL]; and **$10,000** to Institute for Visual Science [NY] (research). ■**PUBLICATIONS:** None ■**WEBSITE:** None ■**E-MAIL:** None ■**APPLICATION POLICIES & PROCEDURES:** Grant requests may be submitted in any form at any time. — Formerly William & Alice Butz Memorial Trust.
O+D+T Ingrid E. Morning (T+Con) — Ober Morning (T) — Scott Stoneback [Alburtis] (T)

CP-029 **Cantwell (Arthur T.) Charitable Foundation**

c/o Citizens Trust Company
10 North Main Street
Coudersport 16915   (Potter County)
AMV $1,167,322   **FYE** 12-00   **(Gifts Received** $0)

MI-31-32-34
Phone 814-274-9150 **FAX** 814-274-0401
EIN 25-1643251   **Year Created** 1990
3 **Grants totaling** $52,000

High grant of **$37,900** to Charles Cole Memorial Hospital (medical education). **$13,100** to Guthrie Research Institute [Sayre]. **$3,610** to Research to Prevent Blindness [NY]. — For several years these same institutions have been the only grantees. ■**PUBLICATIONS:** None ■**WEBSITE:** None ■**E-MAIL:** None ■**APPLICATION POLICIES & PROCEDURES:** The Foundation reports that giving is restricted to primary medical research. A formal application form available from the Bank must be completed and submitted prior to the September 1st deadline; include IRS tax-exempt status documentation. Grants are awarded at a Trustees' meeting in early September.
O+D+T Justin F. Krellner (VP at Bank+Con) — Citizens Trust Company (Trustee)

CP-030 **Caplan (Julius H.) Charity Foundation**

c/o Keystone Weaving Mills
1349 Cumberland Street., P.O. Box 208
Lebanon 17042   (Lebanon County)
AMV $7,802,002   **FYE** 12-00   **(Gifts Received** $0)

MI-11-13-14-15-22-25-31-32-42-55-62-71
Phone 717-272-4665 **FAX** 717-272-4240
EIN 13-6067379   **Year Created** 1944
88 **Grants totaling** $325,141

Mostly local/Pa. giving, including Philadelphia area and York County. High grant of **$36,000** to Temple U. (Program for Actuarial Science). **$25,000-$25,360** each to Good Samaritan Hospital, Hershey Medical Center, Penn State U. (professorship), and U. of Pa. Medical Center [Philadelphia]. **$20,525** to Franklin & Marshall College. **$18,000** to Jewish Home of Greater Harrisburg. **$16,500** to Auerbach Central Agency for Jewish Education [Melrose Park]. **$16,000** to Jewish Federation of Greater Philadelphia. **$10,000** to Temple Shalom [Philadelphia] (Mitzvah Food Pantry). **$9,000** to Jewish Outreach Partnership [Melrose Park]. **$7,500** to Gratz College [Melrose Park]. **$6,658** to Congregation Beth Israel. **$6,000** to Philadelphia U. **$5,000** to Fox Chase Cancer Center. **$3,000-$3,600** each to Four Diamonds Research Institute, Hadassah/Lebanon Chapter, Lebanon Valley Rails to Trails, and United Way of York County. **$1,900-$2,000** each to Allied Arts Fund [Harrisburg], Lebanon Rotary Club, Salvation Army [Philadelphia], World Blindness Outreach, and YMCA of Greater Harrisburg. **$1,000** each to Avon Zion Methodist Church, Harrisburg Area Community College, Lebanon Valley Educational Partnership, Lebanon YMCA, and Pa. School of Art & Design. Other local contributions **$50-$750** for various purposes. **Out-of-state** giving includes **$18,000** to Israel Colloquium [NY]; **$5,000** to Village Temple [NY]; and **$1,800** to U.S. Holocaust Museum [DC]. ■**PUBLICATIONS:** None ■**WEBSITE:** None ■**E-MAIL:** None ■**APPLICATION POLICIES & PROCEDURES:** Grant requests may be submitted in any form may at any time.
O+D+T Eli Caplan (S+D+Con) — Perry C. Caplan [York] (VP+D) — Helen Caplan (D) — Corporate donor: Keystone Weaving Mills

---

CP-031 **Carpenter (J. Donald) Foundation, The**

21 Cumberland Road
Lemoyne 17043   (Cumberland County)
AMV $49,290   **FYE** 12-00   **(Gifts Received** $20,364)

MI-44-57
Phone 717-761-6606 **FAX** None
EIN 23-7866406   **Year Created** 1997
1 **Grant of** $20,000

Sole grant to West Shore Public Library (building fund). — Giving in prior years to West Shore Public Library and WITF-TV/FM. ■**PUBLICATIONS:** None ■**WEBSITE:** None ■**E-MAIL:** None ■**APPLICATION POLICIES & PROCEDURES:** Information not available.
O+D+T Isabel C. Masland (T+Donor+Con) — Carol Masland Gleeson [Manheim] (T) — John C. Masland [Camp Hill] (T) — Leslie Masland [Carlisle] (T)

CP-032 **Center for Research on Women & Newborn Health**
1059 Columbia Ave.
Lancaster 17604 (Lancaster County)

MI-12-31-32
Phone 717-393-1338 **FAX** 717-293-4146
EIN 23-2744470 **Year Created** 1994

AMV $965,131 **FYE** 8-00 **(Gifts Received** $0) 3 **Grants totaling** $49,096

All giving to Pa. for medical research affecting women/newborns; all grants were to individual researchers, as three institutions: **$27,161** to Penn State/Geisinger-Hershey; **$18,165** to Thomas Jefferson U.; and **$3,770** to Penn State U. College of Medicine. ■**PUBLICATIONS:** application guidelines ■**WEBSITE:** None ■**E-MAIL:** None ■**APPLICATION POLICIES & PROCEDURES:** The Foundation reports that giving is restricted to Central/Eastern Pa. for clinical medical research which benefits women and infants. Submit grant requests on a formal application form which the Foundation will provide on request; application deadlines are June 30th and December 31st. Grantee investigators are expected to publish their research results in a peer-reviewed professional journal. Grants are awarded at meetings in January, April and July. **O+D+T** Daniel P. Kegel, M.D. (T+D+Con) — Dianne M. Nast, Esq. (P+D) — Dale Matt, CPA (VP+D) — Mark Regan, M.D. (S+D) — William Haggerty, Esq. (D) — H. Carol Lebischak, M.D. (D) — Donor: Settlement from Norelco litigation

---

CP-033 **Centre County Community Foundation, Inc.**
2013 Sandy Drive, P.O. Box 824
State College 16804
(Centre County)

MI-12-13-14-20-25-29-35-39-34-52-54-56-65
71-84-89
Phone 814-237-6229 **FAX** 814-237-2624
EIN 25-1782197 **Year Created** 1981

AMV $8,968,647 **FYE** 12-00 **(Gifts Received** $2,609,025) 200+ **Grants totaling** $457,687

As a Community Foundation all discretionary giving is limited to organizations in (or serving) Centre County. Forty grants totaling **$120,550** awarded from Discretionary Funds; some grants comprised multiple payments: **$12,500** to Logan Fire Company #1. **$10,000** each to Child Development & Family Council and Moshannon Valley Citizens. **$7,000** to Clearwater Conservancy. **$5,000** each to Bellefonte Museum, CentrePeace, Inc., House of Care, National Assn. for Public Interest Law, and State College Baseball. **$4,000-$4,500** each to AIDS Project of Centre County, Borough of State College, Leadership Centre County, Tri-County Habitat for Humanity. **$3,300** to The Music Academy. **$3,000** to Historic Bellefonte. **$2,000-$2,500** each to Alpha Ambulance, Community Academy for Lifelong Learning, Family Connection, Pa. Centre Chamber Chamber Orchestra Society, Pa. Partnerships for Children, PASA, Pa. Special Olympics, State College Area Interfaith Mission, and Sun Home Health Systems. **$1,000-$1,500** each to Boalsburg Heritage Museum, Centre County Historical Society, First Book of Central Pa., Food Bank of State College, Pa. Chamber Chorale, State College YMCA, and Volunteer Center of Centre County. **$750** to Centre Community Hospital. Other local contributions **$250-$500** for various purposes. All other giving, including scholarships, was from donor-advised or restricted funds. ■**PUBLICATIONS:** Annual Report; Guidelines for Grants from Discretionary Funds; grant application forms; Ways We Can Help Organizations brochure ■**WEBSITE:** www.centrecountycf.org ■**E-MAIL:** rpotter@centrecountycf.org ■**APPLICATION POLICIES & PROCEDURES:** Only nonprofit organizations serving Centre County residents/communities are eligible to apply. Giving focuses on Health/Social Services, The Arts, Education, and The Environment. Most grants are to support programs and capital equipment needs related to a particular program, and normally are for one year although multi-year commitments can be made. The Foundation gives priority to projects/programs which (a) have potential for long-term impact, (b) have been planned in light of overall community needs, (c) do not duplicate existing services, and (d) help those not adequately served by existing community resources. No grants from discretionary funds are awarded for sectarian religious purposes or for travel/accommodations; normally no support is given to government entities that have taxing authority. Grant requests must be submitted on an application form available from the Foundation; a Short Form Grant Application is used for grants up to $1,000 and full Grant Application Form for larger grants; application deadlines are March 1st, June 1st, September 1st, and December 1st. Site visits or meetings sometimes are arranged with organizations being considered for a grant. Grants are awarded at meetings in January, April, July and October. **O+D+T** Robert W. Potter (P+Con) — Martha L. Starling (C+D) — Richard L. Kalin (1st VC+D) — Jeffrey M. Bower (2nd VC+D) — Frances E. Mason (S+D+VC, Grants Committee) — Robert McNichol (F) — Milton J. Bergstein (D) — Richard L. Campbell (D) — Charles J. Curley (D+C, Grants Committee) — Edward A. Friedman (D) — Stanley L. Goldman (D) — Henry B. Haitz, III (D) — Donald W. Hamer (D) — Gerald C. Hartman (D) — Bruce K. Heim (D) — William D. Karch (D) — Norman K. Lathbury (D) — Eileen W. Leibowitz (D) — Robert N. Levy (D) — John P. Mandryk (D) — William H. Martin (D) — James M. Rayback (D) — Charles W. Rohrbeck (D) — Helen Dix Steward (D) — Eloise Dunn Stuhr (D) — Dolores Taricani (D) — Ellie Beaver (Ex Officio) — Trustee banks: Mellon Bank N.A., Mid-State Bank, Omega Bank

---

CP-034 **Children's Home Foundation**
P.O. Box 11537
Harrisburg 17108 (Dauphin County)

MI-12-13-14-16-22-25-41-55-71
Phone 717-255-2174 **FAX** 717-231-2636
EIN 23-1352079 **Year Created** 1965

AMV $1,455,467 **FYE** 11-00 **(Gifts Received** $2,731) 13 **Grants totaling** $64,550

All giving generally limited to/for Dauphin, Perry and Cumberland counties; grants are unrestricted support. High grants of **$10,000** each to Harrisburg Parks Partnership and Hemlock Girl Scouts Council. **$8,000** to Central Pa. Food Bank. **$7,500** to Baptist Children's Mission. **$6,000** each to Bethesda Mission and Urban League of Metropolitan Harrisburg. **$4,000** to YWCA of Greater Harrisburg. **$3,500** to Second Mile. **$3,000** to Big Brothers/Big Sisters of Capital Region. **$2,800** to Council for Public Education. **$2,250** to Rejoice! Inc. **$1,000** to Perry County Council for the Arts. **$500** to Pa. Assn. for the Blind. ■**PUBLICATIONS:** application guidelines ■**WEBSITE:** None ■**E-MAIL:** joe.macri@allfirst.com ■**APPLICATION POLICIES & PROCEDURES:** The Foundation reports that only child-related projects in Dauphin, Cumberland, and Perry counties are eligible to apply. Most grants are for special projects, building funds, capital drives, publications, or matching grants; multi-year grants are awarded. Grant requests must be submitted during January, April, July, or October on a formal application form available from the foundation (deadlines for receipt are the 15th of those months); provide an organizational budget, project budget, audited financial statement, Board member list, and IRS tax-exempt status documentation. Site visits sometimes are made to organizations being considered for a grant. The Board awards grants at meetings held in late January, April, July or October.

O+D+T Joseph A. Macri (F+D+Con) — Charles H. Fromer (P+D) — Dean Weidner (VP+D) — Sheila M. Ross (S+D) — Kara Arnold (D) — Joyce Bolden (D) — Cathy Jones [Camp Hill] (D) — Paul L. Mahoney (D) — Christopher Markley (D) — Sandy Pepinsky (D) — Alice Ann Schwab (D)

CP-035 **Clark (Charles H.) Foundation, The**

206 Farmers Trust Building
1 West High Street
Carlisle   17013   (Cumberland County)

MI-11-31-42-63

Phone 717-249-1019 **FAX** None
EIN 23-6243797   **Year Created** 1957

AMV $222,197   **FYE** 12-00   (**Gifts Received** $0)   **Grants totaling** $11,575

About half local giving. High Pa. grant of **$1,525** to United Way of Carlisle. **$1,000** each to Alison United Methodist Church and Dickinson College. **$700** to Medical Care Foundation. Other smaller local contributions for various purposes. **Out-of-state** grant: **$6,000** to Lakeland Volunteers in Medicine [FL]. ■**PUBLICATIONS:** None ■**WEBSITE:** None ■**E-MAIL:** None ■**APPLI-CATION POLICIES & PROCEDURES:** Information not available.

O+D+T Robert W. Chilton (P+Con) — Virginia C. Chilton (VP) — Evelyn C. Craig (VP) — Mary C. McKnight [FL] (VP) — John H. McKnight [FL] (F) — Jeffrey R. Boswell, Esq. (S) — Mary Chilton Foote (AS)

CP-036 **Clinton County Community Foundation**

c/o Lugg and Lugg
350 East Water Street, P.O. Box 905
Lock Haven   17745   (Clinton County)

MI-12-13-14-41-43-44-51-52-54-56-71-84-89

Phone 570-748-6751 **FAX** 570-748-7368
EIN 25-6093782   **Year Created** 1968

AMV $3,849,199   **FYE** 12-00   (**Gifts Received** $165,360)   **Grants totaling** $105,627

As a Community Foundation all discretionary giving is limited to organizations serving Clinton County; grants information for 2000 is unavailable. In prior years, grants **$5,000-$13,000** awarded to Clinton County Camp Cadet Program, Friends of Community Pool, Infant Development Program, Millbrook Playhouse, Piper Museum, Western Clinton County Recreational Authority, and Woodward Township Recreational Authority. Other smaller grants/contributions to other local organizations and for scholarships. ■**PUBLICATIONS:** Annual Report (published in local newspapers), application form ■**WEBSITE:** None ■**E-MAIL:** wmarino@eagle.lhu.edu ■**APPLICATION POLICIES & PROCEDURES:** Only Clinton County organizations are eligible to apply. Most grants are for special projects, building funds, capital funds, or matching grants. Single and multiyear grants are awarded, and grants over $5,000 are mostly for capital purposes; those less than $5,000 generally are for operating support. A formal application form, available from the Foundation, should be submitted during December-January (deadline is January 15th); include a project budget and list of other funding sources. The Board meets annually in late January.

O+D+T William Marino (C+D+Con) — John J. Helbley (S+D) — Jocelyn Harltey (D) — John Lipez (D) — Robert Lugg, Esq. (D) — Gerald J. Rosamilia (D) — Lewis G. Steinberg (D) — Darlene Weaver (D) — Mellon Bank N.A. (Trustee) — First Union/Wachovia (Trustee)

CP-037 **Cole Foundation**

c/o Owlett, Lewis & Ginn P.C.
1 Charles Street, P.O. Box 878
Wellsboro   16901   (Tioga County)

MI-17-22-31-63

Phone 570-723-1451 **FAX** None
EIN 25-6339152   **Year Created** 1989

AMV $2,872,034   **FYE** 12-00   (**Gifts Received** $15,725)   **4 Grants totaling** $145,350

Mostly Lancaster County giving. High grant of **$115,600** to The Worship Center [Lancaster] (programs for youth/business community). **$16,900** to Loving & Caring [Lancaster] (support for women). **Out-of-state** grants: **$6,500** to Memorial Sloan Kettering Cancer Center [NY] (cancer research) and **$6,350** to Campus Crusade for Christ [FL] (Jesus film project). ■ **PUBLICATIONS:** application guidelines ■**WEBSITE:** None ■**E-MAIL:** None ■**APPLICATION POLICIES & PROCEDURES:** The Foundation reports that most grants are for special projects or matching grants, both to organizations and individuals. No grants awarded to individuals. Grant requests may be submitted at any time on the Application for Charitable Funds form, available from the Foundation; include an organizational budget, list of major funding sources, Board member list, and IRS tax-exempt status documentation. Site visits sometimes are made to organizations being considered for a grant. Grants are awarded at meetings in January and October.

O+D+T Edward H. Owlett, Esq. (T+Con) — Bruce F. Eilenberger [FL] (T+Donor) — Vickie L. Eilenberger [FL] (T+Donor)

CP-038 **Colonial Oaks Foundation**

P.O. Box 5936
Wyomissing   19610   (Berks County)

MI-12-13-17-19-22-25-29-31-41-42-61-71
Phone 610-988-2400 **FAX** 610-988-2416
EIN 23-2705277   **Year Created** 1992

AMV $17,256,590   **FYE** 9-00   (**Gifts Received** $0)   **76 Grants totaling** $799,220

Mostly local/SE Pa. giving; grants are annual giving/general support except as noted otherwise. High grant of **$145,000** to Holy Name High School (capital campaign/fundraiser). **$60,000** to Caron Foundation (capital campaign). **$40,000** to Dayspring Homes (renovations). **$35,000** to Reading-Berks Emergency Shelter. **$30,000** to Reading Hospital & Medical Center. **$25,000** each to Alvernia College (building campaign) and Save-A-Life Fund (AEDs purchase). **$20,500** to Boy Scouts/Hawk Mountain Council (facility improvements). **$20,000** to John Paul II Center for Special Learning. **$18,500** to St. Ignatius Roman Catholic church (parish expenses). **$18,480** to Red Cross (disaster relief). **$15,000** to Betsy King Classic Charities [Kutztown], Blue Spruce Foundation (post-high school student support), Breast Cancer Support Services, and Wood-to-Wonderful (toys for needy children). **$12,000** to Schuylkill River Greenway Assn. (land acquisition). **$10,000** each to Berks Community Television (capital campaign), Central Catholic High School, Jewish Community Center (renovation/expansion), Police Athletic League, Sacred Heart Roman Catholic School (computer/language programs), St. Joseph Medical Center Foundation, United Way of Berks County. and Wyomissing Public Library (building campaign). **$8,800** to Mary's Shelter. **$7,000-$7,840** each to Greater Berks Food Bank, Habitat for Humanity, Jesuit Center for Spiritual Growth, Multiple Sclerosis Society, and The Second Mile [Camp Hill] (Berks County programs). **$6,000-$6,500** each to Olivet Boys & Girls Club, Reading Musical Foundation (school performances), and Sisters of St. Joseph-Chestnut Hill [Philadelphia]. **$5,000** each to Albright College, Beacon House, Berks County Conservancy, Berks County Senior Citizens Council, Berks Women in Crisis, Bethany Children's Home, Children's Home of Reading, Diocese of Allentown (Bishops Annual Appeal), Historical Society of Berks County, Humane Society of Berks County (spay/neuter clinic), Missionary Sisters of the Sacred Heart, Reading Urban Ministries (child abuse prevention programs), Sisters of Christian Charity [Philadelphia], and St. Veronica Roman Catholic Church [Hawley]. **$2,000-$2,500** each to Cystic Fibrosis Foundation, Hawk Mountain Sanctuary Assn. (education center), Hill School, Penn State Catholic Community [University Park] (women's programs), and Wyomissing Institute of Fine Arts (building campaign). **$1,000-$1,500** each to American Diabetes Assn., American Heart Assn. (school health programs), Berks Classical Children's Chorus, Friends in Action [Wayne], Junior Achievement of Berks, Literacy Council of Reading-Berks, Lower Heidelberg Fire Company, St. Joseph's U. [Philadelphia] (campus ministry), and Tafton Fire Company. Other smaller contributions for various purposes. **Out-of-state** giving includes **$12,500** to U. of Notre Dame [IN]; **$10,000** each to Cleveland Clinic Foundation [OH] and Congregation of the Holy Cross [IN] (renovations); and **$8,000** to Committee of A Thousand [FL] (philharmonic/arts center). ■**PUBLICATIONS:** None ■**WEBSITE:** None ■**E-MAIL:** None ■**APPLICATION POLICIES & PROCEDURES:** The Foundation reports giving primarily to Berks County for operating support, program development, and capital campaigns. No grants are awarded to individuals. Grant requests may be submitted in a letter (2 pages maximum) at any time; include organization and project budgets, board member list, list of major funding sources, audited financial statement, and IRS tax-exempt status documentation. Site visits sometimes are made to organizations being considered for a grant.

O+D+T Kristin E. McGlinn [Reading] (Co-Executive Director+Con) — Christine McGlinn Auman (Co-Executive Director+S+T) — Terrence J. McGlinn, Sr. [Sinking Spring] (P+D+Donor) — Margaret McGlinn Shields (F+T) — Barbara T. McGlinn, II [Sinking Spring] (AS+T) — John F. McGlinn, II [Wayne] (AF+T) — Terrence J. McGlinn, Jr. [Reading] (T)

CP-039 **Common Sense for Drug Policy Foundation**

1377-C Spencer Ave.	**MI**-19
Lancaster 17603 (Lancaster County)	**Phone** 717-393-0463 **FAX** None
	EIN 23-2792942 **Year Created** 1995
AMV $222,756 **FYE** 12-0 (Gifts Received $194,075)	1 **Grant of** $50,000

Sole grant to Central Pa. Syringe Exchange Foundation. — In the prior year one grant, **$114,900,** to the same grantee. ■**PUBLICATIONS:** None ■**WEBSITE:** None ■**E-MAIL:** None ■**APPLICATION POLICIES & PROCEDURES:** Information not available.

O+D+T Robert E. Field (C+F+T+Donor+Con) — Kevin Zeese [VA] (P+T) — Melvin R. Allen [Millersville] (S+T) — Foundation donor: Open Society Institute [NY]

CP-040 **Crels Foundation**

c/o Melbert Associates	**MI**-14-15-22-31-41-42-63-64-71
5917 Main Street	
East Petersburg 17520 (Lancaster County)	**Phone** 717-581-8130 **FAX** 717-581-8132
	EIN 23-6243577 **Year Created** 1953
AMV $18,910,873 **FYE** 12-00 (Gifts Received $0)	103 **Grants totaling** $841,500

All giving is limited to Lancaster County; grants are for general support except as noted. **RELIGIOUS GRANTS:** High grant of **$100,000** to Weaverland Conference Mennonite Church. **$10,000** to Home Messenger Literature Service. **$7,500** to Parish Resource Center. **$6,000** to Eastern Mennonite Missions. **$5,000** to New Holland Evangelical Methodist Church. **MEDICAL GRANTS:** **$50,000** each to Fairmount Homes (caring fund/general support). **$35,000** to Ephrata Community Hospital Foundation. **$20,000** each to Lancaster Health Alliance and Philhaven Hospital. **$12,500** each to Fairview Reception Center and Hospice of Lancaster County. **$10,000** each to Welsh Mountain Home and Welsh Mountain Medical & Dental Center. **$7,500** to Landis Homes. **$6,000** to Mennonite Home. **$5,000** each to Lancaster Cleft Palate Clinic and Visiting Nurse Assn./Lancaster. **$3,500** to Brethren Village. **$2,500** to Valley View Retirement Community. **EDUCATION GRANTS:** **$50,000** to Weaverland Mennonite Schools. **$15,000** to Gehmans Mennonite School (special matching fund). **$10,000** each to Ephrata Mennonite School, Faith Mennonite High School, Hinkletown Mennonite School, Kraybill Mennonite School, Lititz Area Mennonite School, Locust Grove Mennonite School, New Danville Mennonite School, and Terre Hill Mennonite High School. **$7,000-$8,000** each to Hillside Special Education Parochial School, Lancaster Bible College, and Lancaster Mennonite High School. **$5,000** to Elizabethtown College. **$4,000** each to 58 Mennonite schools located in Denver, East Earl, Ephrata, New Holland, Leola, Lititz, Manheim, Narvon, Reinholds, and Stevens. **$1,000** to Ursinus College. **HUMAN SERVICES/OTHER GRANTS:** **$30,000** to United Way of Lancaster County. **$20,000** to Water Street Rescue Mission. **$15,000** each to Light House Rehabilitation Center and Susquehanna Assn. for the Blind. **$7,500** to Lancaster Farmland Trust. **$5,000** each to Occupational Development Center, Support of Prison Ministries, and Upward Call Counseling Services. **$3,500** to Goodwill Industries of SE Pa. **$2,000** to Lancaster Mennonite Historical Society. ■**PUBLICATIONS:** None ■**WEBSITE:** None ■**E-MAIL:** None ■**APPLICATION POLICIES & PROCEDURES:** The Foundation reports that giving is limited to Lancaster County; medical institutions receive preference and only schools conducted in the Mennonite tradition are considered for support. Grant requests may be submitted in a letter at any time (deadline is September 15th); include an annual report, organization budget, project budget, audited financial statement, and IRS tax-exempt status documentation. Grants are awarded at a November meeting or as required.

O+D+T Kenneth N. Burkholder [Gordonville] (C+T+Con) — Clarence J. Nelson [New Holland] (S+T) — Eugene N. Burkholder [New Holland] (T) — Leon Ray Burkholder [Ephrata] (T) — J. Michael Melbert (AS)

CP-041 **Danowsky-Reeds Memorial Fund** MI-22-29-43-56-63
c/o First Union/Wachovia - PA 6612
12 East Market Street **Phone** 717-852-9648 **FAX** None
York 17401 (York County) **EIN** 23-6829035 **Year Created** 1998
AMV $1,598,942 **FYE** 12-01 (**Gifts Received** $0) 43 **Grants totaling** $88,350

Mostly Central Pa. giving, particularly to Union County. High grant of **$37,200** to Mazeppa Union Church [Lewisburg]. **$6,000** each to Evangelical Lutheran Church of America/Upper Susquehanna Synod and United Methodist Church/Penn Central Conference. **$3,000** to Evangelical Hospice. **$2,400** to Slifer House [Lewisburg]. Other local and **Out-of-state** contributions **$100-$1,500** for various community organizations, churches, scholarships, and other purposes. ■**PUBLICATIONS:** None ■**WEBSITE:** None ■**E-MAIL:** brenton.hake@wachovia.com ■**APPLICATION POLICIES & PROCEDURES:** Information not available.

O+D+T Brenton Hake (Regional Trust Officer+VP at Bank+Con)

CP-042 **Dearden (William E.C. & Mary) Foundation** MI-11-12-13-22-25-29-41-42-49-63
26 Franklin Drive **Phone** 717-361-5197 **FAX** None
Elizabethtown 17022 (Lancaster County) **EIN** 23-6814400 **Year Created** 1986
AMV $429,024 **FYE** 12-00 (**Gifts Received** $0) 24 **Grants totaling** $35,500

About two-thirds local giving; all grants are for general purposes. High grants of **$5,000** each to Family & Children Services and First United Methodist Church of Hershey. **$2,500** to Masonic Charities. **$1,000-$1,500** each to Albright College, Boy Scouts/Keystone Area Council, Heritage Building Endowment, Milton Hershey School Alumni Assn., Pa. Partnership for Economics Education, Red Cross, and United Way of the Capital Region. Other smaller local contributions. **Out-of-state** giving includes **$3,000** to Crystal Cathedral [CA]; **$2,000-$2,500** each to Horatio Alger Assn. [VA] and Tom Harrai & Associates Foundation [NC]; **$1,500** to Blanton-Peale Institute [NY]; and **$1,000** each to Food Industry Crusade Against Hunger [MO] and Ocean City Tabernacle Assn. [NJ]. ■**PUBLICATIONS:** None ■**WEBSITE:** None ■**E-MAIL:** None ■**APPLICATION POLICIES & PROCEDURES:** Grant requests may be submitted in a letter at any time; describe fully the intended use of the requested funds.

O+D+T William E.C. Dearden (C+Donor+Con) — Mary Dearden (P) — Hershey Trust Company (Trustee)

CP-043 **Degenstein (Charles B.) Foundation, The** MI-12-13-14-18-22-29-31-35-41-54-55-57-84-89
Refer to The Degenstein Foundation entry.
(Northumberland County) **EIN** 23-6971532 **Year Created** 1989
AMV $2,578,408 **FYE** 9-01 (**Gifts Received** $0) 30 **Grants totaling** $301,713

All local/NE Pa. giving; some grants comprise multiple awards. High grant of **$32,500** to Americus Hose Company (hovercraft purchase/pledge payment). **$25,000** to City of Sunbury (swimming pool restoration/medical equipment-supplies/ice skates purchase). **$20,000** each to Children's Home of Easton (pledge payment) and Lehigh Valley Family & Counseling Service. **$15,000** to Weller Health Education Center [Easton] (substance abuse programs). **$13,325** to Selinsgrove Area Recreation Assn. (pool restoration-lighting). **$12,555** to Mifflinburg Hose Company (thermal imager). **$10,000** each to Donald Heiter Community Center (pledge payment), Evangelical Community Hospital (pledge payment), Packwood House Museum (maintenance-renovations), Pa. Special Olympics, Ronald McDonald House/Danville (pledge payment), and Sunbury Community Hospital (capital campaign). **$5,000** each to ARC of Lehigh-Northampton Counties (advisory program), The Growing Center (horticultural therapy program), Hemlock Girl Scout Council (pledge payment), Lewisburg Elementary School (handicapped accessible swing), St. Rose of Lima School [Montgomery County] (computers), Shikellamy School District (wrestling scholarship), and Sun Home Health Services (retire debt). **$4,000** each to Family Planning Services of SUN County (HIV-AIDS services) and Red Cross/Sunbury (blood/community services). **$1,000** each to Central Susquehanna Interfaith Council (prison chaplain), Sunbury Softball Assn., and Union-Snyder Office of Human Resources (youth shooting sports program). — In the prior year, major grants included **$25,000** each to Camp Victory (dining hall construction), Fort Discovery (playground), and Sunbury YMCA (job skill training); **$20,000** each to United Cerebral Palsy (van), and Snyder-Union-Mifflin Child Development (program development); and **$10,000** each to Central Susquehanna Sight Services (new building), Donald Heiter Community Center (pledge payment), Evangelical Community Hospital (emergency room study and systems development), Mental Health Assn./Compeer (local programs), Ronald McDonald House of Danville (pledge payment), Sunbury YMCA (van), Tact the Actors [NY] (production at Susquehanna U.), WVIA-TV (central Susquehanna Valley programming), and YMCA of Milton (feasibility study). ■**APPLICATION POLICIES & PROCEDURES:** All requests for support from this Foundation must be directed to The Degenstein Foundation.

CP-044 **Degenstein (Charles & Betty) Foundation** MI-11-12-13-14-15-20-22-29-35-41-71-84-89
Refer to The Degenstein Foundation entry.
(Northumberland County) **EIN** 23-6661599 Year Created 1977
AMV $1,964,757 **FYE** 12-01 (**Gifts Received** $0) 32 **Grants totaling** $80,200

All giving restricted to Snyder, Union or Northumberland counties. High grant of **$18,000** to Action Health. **$6,000** to Red Cross/Sunbury Chapter. **$5,700** to City of Sunbury. **$4,500-$5,000** each to Lewisburg Area Recreation Authority, Pa. Special Olympics, and Selinsgrove Area Recreational Assn. **$3,500** each to Salvation Army/Sunbury, Shikellamy School District (High School/Peer Leadership Program), and Susquehanna Valley Chorale. **$1,000-$3,000** each to Albright Care Services, American Legion Post #841/Marine Corps League, Americus Hose Company, Central Susquehanna Valley Interfaith Council (Meals on Wheels/Prison Ministry Program), Emmanuel Lutheran Pre-Kindergarten, Mifflinburg Hose Company, North Penn Legal Services, Northumberland County Conservation District, Rainbow Connection, Red Cross/Sunbury, Selinsgrove Are School District (Peer Leadership Program), Selinsgrove Meals on Wheels, Shikellamy Youth Football Club, Snyder-Union-Mifflin Child Development,

SRI for Litefest, Sunbury Quadraleague, United Way of Central Susquehanna Valley, United Way of Union County, and West Snyder Recreation Assn. Other smaller local contributions for similar purposes. ■**APPLICATION POLICIES & PROCEDURES:** All requests for support from this Foundation must be directed to The Degenstein Foundation.

O+D+T Kathryn Pakuta (C+D) — Rev. Jonathan Albright (D) — Jeffrey Apfelbaum, Esq. (D) — Michael M. Apfelbaum, Esq. (D) — Sidney Apfelbaum, Esq. (D) — Belle Kamsler (D) — Fred Kelley, Jr. [Selinsgrove] (D) — Helen Nunn [Selinsgrove] (D) — Carl Rohrbach [Selinsgrove] (D) — First National Trust Bank (Trustee)

CP-045 **Degenstein Foundation, The**	MI-11-12-13-14-15-25-29-31-32-33-35-41-42
c/o Apfelbaum, Apfelbaum & Apfelbaum	43-44-52-54-55-56-57-65-84-89
43 South 5th Street	**Phone** 570-286-1582 **FAX** 570-286-5349
Sunbury 17801 (Northumberland County)	**EIN** 23-7792979 **Year Created** 1994

AMV $102,870,466   **FYE** 6-01   **(Gifts Received** $13,137,204)   107 **Grants totaling** $6,370,352

Mostly local/Pa. giving within 75 miles of Sunbury; grants are for general purposes except as noted, and some comprise multiple payments. High grant of **$3,681,250** to Susquehanna U.; other Susquehanna U. grants totaled **$245,000+** (basic skills training center, scholarship funds, outing club/outdoors equipment, performance by a NY theatre company, SU4U program, and discretionary support). **$488,142** to United Way of Central Susquehanna Valley (new giving initiative, contractors-electricians payment, equipment, summer day camp). **$228,540** to City of Sunbury (pool renovations, skating rink equipment, porch renovation project, Quadraleague, discretionary support). **$185,000** to Red Cross/Sunbury (medical-dental clinic building purchase, van, general support). **$150,000** to Concerned Citizens Day Care (leasehold improvements). **$115,000** to Mifflinburg Buggy Museum (challenge grant). **$101,340** to Wyoming Seminary [Luzerne County]. **$100,000** each to Milton YMCA (library renovations), Shamokin Area Community Hospital (pledge payment). **$52,000** to Northumberland Habitat for Humanity (storage building/home construction/demolition). **$48,000-$50,000** each to Camp Victory (pledge payment), Donald Heiter Community Center (matching grant), Lower Mahanoy Township (recreational facility), and Priestly-Forsyth Memorial Library (building improvements/horticultural therapy program). **$45,000** to Central Susquehanna Sight Services (building improvements/eye equipment). **$29,000** to West Snyder Recreation Assn. (Beaver Springs center). **$23,000-$25,000** each to Bloomsburg U. (Mowad scholarship fund), Bucknell U. (biomedical engineering program/Quest program), Children's Hospital of Philadelphia (oncology dept.), Daily Item Combined Community Fund (Christmas Fund), Danville School District (psychologist services), and WVIA-TV (broadcast of local performances/regional arts calendar). **$20,000-$20,8980** each to Action Health (Pagana Clinic equipment), Union County West End Fire Company (thermal imaging system), and Union & Snyder County Habitat for Humanity. **$12,500** to Central Pa. Forum. **$10,000** to Friendship Fire Station #10/Danville (aerial platform truck) and The Growing Center (additional equipment). **$7,500** each to Allied Council for the Arts and Northumberland County Historical Society (five walking tours). **$4,500-$5,000** each to American Cancer Society (5K Run), Bloomsburg Theatre Ensemble (Project Discovery), Evangelical Community Hospital (community health education endowment), Lewisburg Borough (4th of July celebration), and West Shore Public Library (new Cumberland County library). **$1,000-$3,000** each to B.P.O.E. Sunbury (construction-remodeling), Daily Item Combined Community Fund (newspapers for schools), Lewisburg Elementary PSA (obstacle course/equipment), and Susquehanna Valley Chorale (student scholarships). Also, about **$140,000** total awarded to 30+ local nonprofit organizations/government units under the Degenstein Summer Jobs Program. **Out-of-state** grant: **$100,000** to Friends of the Jewish Chapel/U.S. Naval Academy [MD]. In the prior year, major grants included **$1,350,000** to Penn State-Geisinger Foundation (women's facility/cardiac rehab center/palliative care program), **$787,790** to Susquehanna U. (sports fitness center/summer theatre); **$450,000** to Kaufmann Public Library (building project challenge grant); and **$400,000** to Penn Valley Airport. ■**PUBLICATIONS:** application guidelines; Grant Application Form ■**WEBSITE:** www.deg-fdn.org ■**E-MAIL:** None ■**APPLICATION POLICIES & PROCEDURES:** All giving by the three Degenstein foundations (includes The Charles B. Degenstein Foundation and the Charles & Betty Degenstein Foundation, listed above) is restricted to nonprofit organizations or municipal government units, with priority given to those within a 75 mile radius of Sunbury or to others providing a unique benefit to residents within that geographical area. Special consideration is given to unique, innovative, and creative projects which will benefit children, promote education, improve health care, encourage business and culture, conserve natural resources, and protect the environment. Most grants are for program development, special projects, capital campaigns, or equipment providing new organizational capabilities. Organizational applicants must demonstrate clear statements of purpose, well defined programs and competent leadership. Because the Foundation favors broad-based community support (through local contributions and volunteer support), grants covering the full cost of a project are rarely awarded. Projects of special interest to the Foundation occasionally will be initiated and funded by the Foundation. No grants are awarded for annual campaigns, general endowment, operating budgets, religious or political activities, mass mailings, or to individuals for any purpose. Prospective applicants first must secure the very explicit, detailed application guidelines and a copy of the formal Grant Application Form; both are available *only on the website*. While inquiries/grant requests are accepted throughout the year, personal visits to the Foundation office are discouraged. If a grant is awarded, a complete funds accounting must be provided upon the project's completion. — Also known as 1994 Charles B. Degenstein Foundation.

O+D+T Jeffrey Apfelbaum, Esq. (Con) — Michael M. Apfelbaum, Esq. (Con) — Sidney Apfelbaum, Esq. (Co-T) — Mellon Bank (Corporate Co-Trustee)

CP-046 **Dentsply International Foundation, The**	MI-11-12-14-16-25-35-42-49
c/o Dentsply International	
570 West College Ave.	**Phone** 717-845-7511 **FAX** None
York 17405 (York County)	**EIN** 23-6297307 **Year Created** 1955

AMV $35,864   **FYE** 12-00   **(Gifts Received** $125,000)   33 **Grants totaling** $122,500

About one-fifth local giving. High local grant of **$13,000** to United Way of York County. **$3,500** to Make-A-Wish Foundation of York County. **$2,500** to Junior Achievement of York. **$1,500** to Penn State U./Hershey (Four Diamonds). **$1,000** each to Central Pa. Health Education Center, Community Progress Council, Easter Seals, Spanish Community Assn. of Central Pa., and York

Union Rescue Mission. **Out-of-state** giving includes high grant of **$85,500** to Oral Health America [IL] and **$300-$2,000** for community service organizations in corporate operating locations in DE and NJ. ■**PUBLICATIONS:** None ■**WEBSITE:** None ■**E-MAIL:** None ■**APPLICATION POLICIES & PROCEDURES:** Prospective applicants should initially telephone the foundation to inquire about the feasibility of submitting a request. Submit grant requests in a letter in September, October, or November for consideration at a Board meeting in January or February.

O+D+T Brian M. Addison (S+Con) — William R. Jellison (T) — John C. Miles, II (T) — Mellon Bank N.A. (Custodian) — Corporate donor: Dentsply International, Inc.

CP-047 **Dixon (Francis J.) Foundation**   MI-12-22-42-43-44-63-71
c/o Brandywine Recyclers, Inc.
328 North 14th Street   **Phone** 717-272-4655 **FAX** None
Lebanon 17046   (Lebanon County)   **EIN** 25-1600852   **Year Created** 1989
AMV $1,617,832   **FYE** 12-00   (**Gifts Received** $365,704)   36 **Grants totaling** $82,850

All local/Harrisburg-area giving. High grant to Harrisburg Area Community College Foundation (Lebanon Campus). **$10,000** to In The Light Ministries. **$5,350** to Lebanon Rescue Mission. **$2,500** to West Shore Library [Camp Hill]. **$2,000** to Philhaven Child & Adolescent Day Hospital. **$1,000** each to Bethesda Mission, DDS Foundation, Lebanon Rails to Trails, and Lebanon Valley College (educational partnership). Other contributions **$500** each, including 25 individual merit scholarships for local students at colleges in many states. ■**PUBLICATIONS:** None ■**WEBSITE:** None ■**E-MAIL:** None ■**APPLICATION POLICIES & PROCEDURES:** Information not available.

O+D+T Francis J. Dixon [NJ] (P+D+Donor+Con) — Timothy J. Huber (D) — Christine Dixon Rathborn (D) — Richard P. Scott (D+Donor) — Thomas I. Siegel (D) — Joanne Dixon White (D) — Corporate donors: Dixon-Scott Investment Partnership; Dixon Properties

---

CP-048 **Dunitz (Michael) Crisis Foundation**   MI-12-13-31-35-42
c/o Bauscher, 127 Main Street   **Phone** 610-589-5201 **FAX** None
Stouchsburg 19567   (Berks County)   **EIN** 23-2195430   **Year Created** 1982
AMV $451,863   **FYE** 6-01   (**Gifts Received** $0)   6 **Grants totaling** $19,317

Mostly local giving. High grant of **$7,817** to Reading Hospital & Medical Center (books for Dunitz Library). **$4,500** to Camp Can Do (overnight camp). **$1,500** to St. Joseph Medical Center (educational materials for families). **$1,000** to Berks AIDS Network (general support). **$500** to Rainbow Home. **Out-of-state** grant: **$4,000** to Wish Friends [MD] (ill children's wishes). ■**PUBLICATIONS:** None ■**WEBSITE:** None ■**E-MAIL:** None ■**APPLICATION POLICIES & PROCEDURES:** No grants are awarded to individuals.

O+D+T Roberta Dunitz (P+Con) — Jay Dunitz [CA] (VP) — Debra Dunitz Greenblatt [MD] (F)

CP-049 **Einstein (Richard E.) Trust**   MI-12
c/o Allfirst Trust Co. of Pa. N.A.
213 Market Street, P.O. Box 2961   **Phone** 717-255-2174 **FAX** 717-231-2636
Harrisburg 17105   (Dauphin County)   **EIN** 23-6216029   **Year Created** 1945
AMV $957,537   **FYE** 12-00   (**Gifts Received** $0)   1 **Grant of** $47,000

All giving restricted to Dauphin County. Sole grant to Salvation Army. — In prior years support awarded to Dauphin County Social Services for Children & Youth, Spanish Speaking Center, and other organizations. ■**PUBLICATIONS:** None ■**WEBSITE:** None ■ **E-MAIL:** joe.macro@allfirst.com ■**APPLICATION POLICIES & PROCEDURES:** Only Dauphin County agencies which distribute toys or clothing to needy children, 16 years or under, are eligible to apply. Submit grant requests in any form at any time; include a project outline, financial statement and copy of the IRS tax-exempt status documentation. Grants are awarded at an October meeting.

O+D+T Joseph A. Macri (VP & Trust Officer at Bank+Con) — Allfirst Trust Co. of Pa. N.A. (Trustee)

CP-050 **Elizabethtown Historical Society**   MI-44-85
P.O. Box 301   **Phone** 717-361-9382 **FAX** None
Elizabethtown 17602   (Lancaster County)   **EIN** 23-1993908   **Year Created** 1976
AMV $922,693   **FYE** 12-00   (**Gifts Received** $2,434)   7 **Grants totaling** $10,960

All local giving. High grant of **$10,000** to Elizabethtown Public Library. **$500** to Elizabethtown Economic Development. Other small contributions to local charities. ■**PUBLICATIONS:** None ■**WEBSITE:** None ■**E-MAIL:** None ■**APPLICATION POLICIES & PROCEDURES:** Information not available.

O+D+T Margaret Gable (P+Con) — Dr. Richard McMaster (VP) — Anna Ruth Hess (S) — Dr. Carl Shull (F)

CP-051 **Engle (Alvin S.) Foundation**   MI-12-22-41-63-64
c/o Engle Printing & Publishing Company, Inc.
1425 West Main Street, P.O. Box 500   **Phone** 717-653-1833 **FAX** 717-653-6198
Mount Joy 17552   (Lancaster County)   **EIN** 23-2747886   **Year Created** 1993
AMV $216,681   **FYE** 12-00   (**Gifts Received** $250,000)   8 **Grants totaling** $280,000

All local giving; all grants are unrestricted contributions. High grant of **$110,000** to Mt. Calvary Christian School. **$50,000** to Lancaster Mennonite High School. **$35,000** to Pa. Family Institute. **$25,000** each to Lancaster Bible College and Locust Grove Mennonite School. **$20,000** to Pocket Testament League. **$10,000** to The Navigators. **$5,000** to Center for Parent/Youth Understanding. ■**PUBLICATIONS:** None ■**WEBSITE:** None ■**E-MAIL:** None ■**APPLICATION POLICIES & PROCEDURES:** Information not available.

O+D+T Charles A. Engle (P+Donor+Con) — Dennis L. Engle [Manheim] (VP+Donor) — Pauline H. Engle [Hershey] (VP+Donor) — Audrey Engle Rutt (S+F+Donor) — Corporate donor: Engle Printing & Publishing Company, Inc.

CP-052   Eve (Edith Davis) Foundation   MI-43
c/o Mellon Private Wealth Management
2 North Second Street, 12th Floor, P.O. Box 1010   **Phone** 717-780-3037 **FAX** None
Harrisburg 17108   (Dauphin County)   **EIN** 23-6235141   **Year Created** 1979
AMV $1,139,742   **FYE** 12-00   **(Gifts Received** $0)   **Grants totaling** $59,000

All grants are scholarships for Blair County residents with families unable to provide adequate financial support for students to attend any U.S. college/university. Scholarship disbursements paid directly to Juniata College, Mt. Aloysius College, Penn State U./Altoona Campus, St. Francis College, State System of Higher Education, and U. of Pittsburgh/Johnstown. ■**PUBLICATIONS:** None ■**WEBSITE:** None ■**E-MAIL:** None ■**APPLICATION POLICIES & PROCEDURES:** Only residents of and graduates of Blair County high schools are eligible for scholarships. The schools determine finanancial need with awards being made based on the number of students attending.

O+D+T Distribution Committee members: Cindy Semic (Trust Officer at Bank+Con) — Richard A. Carothers, Esq. — Bernard Dembert, CPA — Thomas Martin — Dr. Dennis Murray — Mellon Private Wealth Management (Trustee)

CP-053   Ferguson Foundation   MI-12-13-14-15-18-22-29-31-41-55-63
110 Regent Court, Suite 202   **Phone** 814-238-0760 **FAX** None
State College   16801   (Centre County)   **EIN** 25-1728428   **Year Created** 1994
AMV $904,642   **FYE** 12-00   **(Gifts Received** $0)   16 **Grants totaling** $386,875

Most giving restricted to Centre County. High grant of **$100,000** to Operation Safety Net. **$92,500** to Centre Community Hospital. **$25,000** to Centre County Community Foundation. **$23,000** to Stand Together, Inc. (single parent education). **$20,000** to The Second Mile (youth program). **$18,000** to University Baptist & Brethren Church. **$15,000** each to Make-A-Wish Foundation of Western Pa. and Penn's Valley Area School District. **$13,375** to Centre County Office of Aging. **$10,000** to State College Area YMCA. **$5,000** each to Centre Peace, Heart to Heart Adoption Services, Interfaith Mission, Volunteer Center [Pittsburgh], and Youth Service Bureau. **Out-of-state** grant: **$30,000** to Barrier Island Group (arts appreciation) [FL]. ■**PUBLICATIONS:** None ■**WEBSITE:** None ■**E-MAIL:** None ■**APPLICATION POLICIES & PROCEDURES:** No grants awarded to individuals.

O+D+T Fredrick Farber (S+F+Con) — Wallace C. Snipes [Pine Grove Mills] (P+Donor) — Roberta Snipes [Pine Grove Mills] (D+Donor)

CP-054   Fogelsonger (G. Leonard) Foundation, The   MI-11-42-85
c/o Orrstown Bank, Trust Dept.
77 East King Street, P.O. Box 250   **Phone** 717-530-2608 **FAX** None
Shippensburg 17257   (Cumberland County)   **EIN** 22-2599260   **Year Created** 1985
AMV $313,676   **FYE** 5-00   **(Gifts Received** $0)   6 **Grants totaling** $25,750

All local giving. High grant of **$11,500** to Main Street Non-Profit Redevelopment. **$10,000** to Shippensburg University Foundation. **$2,000** to Shippensburg United Way. **$1,000** each to Downtown Organizations Investing Together nad Shippensburg Public Library. Other smaller contributions. ■**PUBLICATIONS:** None ■**WEBSITE:** None ■**E-MAIL:** None ■**APPLICATION POLICIES & PROCEDURES:** Submit grant requests in a letter before the September 30th deadline; state the purpose of the project, and include a financial statement and IRS tax-exempt status documentation.

O+D+T Members of the Distribution Committee: Phyllis Nye (Trust Officer at Bank+Con) — Peggy Boinis — Forest Myers — Kenneth Shoemaker — Orrstown Bank (Trustee)

CP-055   Fowler (Robert H. & Beverly U.) Foundation Trust   MI-12-18-10-44-56-57-63
1728 Cushing Greene   **Phone** 717-774-4401 **FAX** None
Camp Hill 17011   (Cumberland County)   **EIN** 25-6578901   **Year Created** 1998
AMV $515,618   **FYE** 12-00   **(Gifts Received** $241,455)   1 **Grant of** $1,000

Sole grant to Perry County Library. — Giving in the prior year included **$3,000** to Africa U. Development Center [TN]; **$2,500** each to Children's Playroom, Goodwill Industries, and Perry County Literacy Council; **$1,500** to Neighborhood Center of Harrisburg; and **$1,000** to Cumberland County 250th Celebration Committee. ■**PUBLICATIONS:** None ■**WEBSITE:** None ■**E-MAIL:** None ■**APPLICATION POLICIES & PROCEDURES:** The Foundation reports that giving focuses on Central Pa. with most grants for special projects, research, or matching grants. No grants awarded for building funds or scholarships. Prospective applicants should make an initial telephone inquiry regarding the feasibility of submitting a request. Grant requests may be submitted in any form at any time. Grants are awarded at July and December meetings.

O+D+T Wade U. Fowler (P+T+Con) — Beverly U. Fowler (T+Donor) — Robert H. Fowler (T+Donor)

CP-056   Freas Foundation   MI-12-13-14-22-25-29-31-35-41-42-44-45-55
11912 Lebanon Church Road   56-63-64-71
Felton 17322   **Phone** 717-246-1515 **FAX** None
                                    (York County)   **EIN** 22-1714810   **Year Created** 1953
AMV $8,983,465   **FYE** 12-00   **(Gifts Received** $0)   76 **Grants totaling** $439,804

About one-half Central Pa./Centre County giving. High grant of **$34,105** to Strand-Capitol Performing Arts Center. **$16,027** to York County Heritage Trust. **$13,666** to Access York. **$11,750** to York College of Pa. **$8,000** each to York Rescue Mission and York YMCA. **$7,000-$7,500** each to Bucknell U. , Children's Home of York, and Penn Laurel Girl Scout Council. **$5,000-$5,500** each to Martin Library, Historic York, Susan Byrnes Health Education Center, York Benevolent Assn., York County Literacy Council, and York's Helping Hand for the Homeless. **$4,000-$4,800** each to Jewish Community Center of York, Unitarian

Church of Harrisburg, and York Catholic High School. **$3,000-$3,500** each to Lancaster Theological Seminary, State College Area Family YMCA, and York Arts. **$2,000-$2,700** each to Bell Socialization Services, Easter Seals/South Central Pa., Huston Township Park & Recreation Center, Jewish Family Services of York, Kaltreider-Benfer Library, Salvation Army, York County Blind Center, and York Health System. **$1,000-$1,750** each to Bald Eagle Area High School, Capital Area Greenbelt Assn., Centre County Law Enforcement Camp, Charlton Play School, Children's Aid Society, Contact York, Schlow Memorial Library, and Spiritual Frontiers Fellowship International. **Out-of-state** giving primarily to CT where trustees reside. ■**PUBLICATIONS:** None ■ **WEBSITE:** None ■**E-MAIL:** None ■**APPLICATION POLICIES & PROCEDURES:** Information not available.

O+D+T Arthur K. Freas (Manager+Con) — Margery H. Freas (Manager) — David M. Trout, Jr. [CT] (Manager) — Rebecca Freas Trout [CT] (Manager) — First Union/Wachovia (Trustee)

CP-057 Freedom Forge Corporation Foundation
c/o Freedom Forge Corporation
500 North Walnut Street
Burnham 17009 (Mifflin County)
AMV $1,464,289 **FYE** 12-00 **(Gifts Received** $0)

MI-11-13-21-31-41-43-44-52-55-71-72-85

Phone 717-248-4911 **FAX** None
EIN 34-6516721 **Year Created** 1956
42 **Grants totaling** $137,237

Mostly local giving. High grant of **$37,500** to United Way of Mifflin-Juniata. **$31,486** to Juniata Valley YMCA. **$5,000** each to Belleville Mennonite School, Downtown Lewistown, Mifflin County Library, and the Unimart Golf Classic. **$3,300** to Nittany Valley Symphony. **$2,000-$2,500** each to Boy Scouts and five scholarships. **$1,000-$1,750** each to 2001 Student Government Seminar, Centre County Hospital, Juniata County Food Pantry, Kiwanis of Juniata County, La Vie, Lewistown Healthcare Foundation, Mifflin-Juniata Arts Council, National MS Society, Penn State U./Center for the Performing Arts, and Western Pa. Conservancy. **Out-of-state** giving includes **$5,000** to Forging Industry Education & Research Foundation [OH]; **$2,500** to American Museum of Fly Fishing [VT]; and **$2,000** to Atlantic Salmon Federation [ME]. ■**PUBLICATIONS:** None ■**WEBSITE:** None ■**E-MAIL:** None ■**APPLICATION POLICIES & PROCEDURES:** Grant requests may be submitted in a letter at any time; include appropriate supporting documentation.

O+D+T Joseph Wapner (S+Con) — Corporate donor: Freedom Forge Corporation — Kish Bank Asset Management (Trustee)

CP-058 Frey (Charles F. & Anna E.) Foundation
259 Willow Valley Drive
Lancaster 17602 (Lancaster County)
AMV $178,246 **FYE** 12-00 **(Gifts Received** $46,599)

MI-13-18-19-22-25-41-56-63-82

Phone 717-464-0350 **FAX** None
EIN 23-2189219 **Year Created** 1982
60+ **Grants totaling** $295,988

About three-quarters local/Pa. giving; some grants comprise multiple awards. High grant of **$38,000** to Manor Brethren In Christ Church. **$25,650** to Teen Haven. **$25,000** each to Brethren in Christ World Ministries [Grantham] and Kenbrook Bible Camp [Lehman]. **$22,530** to Water Street Rescue Mission. **$20,000** to International Health Services [Chester County]. **$10,000** each to Action Impact [Chester County], Lancaster Mennonite School, and Yost Evangelistic Ministry [Berwick] **$5,000** each to Brethren in Christ Historical Society [Grantham], Light House Rehab Center, and Teen Challenge Training Center. **$4,000** to Naaman Center [Elizabethtown]. **$3,000** to Rivers of Living Waters. **$2,000-$2,500** each to Ambassadors for Christ, Coalition for Christian Outreach [Pittsburgh], and New Hope Ministries. **$1,000** each to Circle Venture [Philadelphia], Friendship Ministries, Joni & Friends [Lancaster], and Lancaster United for Life. Other local contributions **$22-$500** for similar purposes. **Out-of-state** giving includes **$27,000** to Freedom Village USA [NY]; **$25,000** to Sandy Cove [MD]; **$10,000** to Jesus Film Project [CA]; and **$5,000** to Calvary Tabernacle [NJ]. ■**PUBLICATIONS:** None ■**WEBSITE:** None ■**E-MAIL:** None ■**APPLICATION POLICIES & PROCEDURES:** Grant requests may be submitted in a letter at any time.

O+D+T Charles F. Frey (P+Donor+Con) — Anna E. Frey (Donor) — Corporate donor: Turkey Hill Dairy and related companies

---

CP-059 Friendship Foundation, Inc.
c/o Fisher Development Company
2101 Oregon Pike, Suite 300
Lancaster 17601 (Lancaster County)
AMV $219,722 **FYE** 6-00 **(Gifts Received** $152,400)

MI-22-41-63

Phone 717-399-5220 **FAX** None
EIN 23-2474740 **Year Created** 1976
30+ **Grants totaling** $61,551

About four-fifths local/Pa. giving; all grants are to promote religious awareness. High grant of **$11,205** to Middle Creek Bible Conference. **$10,000** to BCM International [Upper Darby]. **$5,405** to Christian & Missionary Alliance. **$5,161** to No Longer Alone Ministries. **$2,000-$2,571** each to Lancaster United for Life, National Day of Prayer, Neighbors Who Care, and Pa. Family Institute. **$1,000** each to Child Evangelism Fellowship, Dayspring Christian Academy, and Lancaster Youth for Christ. Other smaller local contributions for similar purposes. **Out-of-state** giving includes **$10,000** to Ravi Zacharias International Ministry [GA]. -- **Note:** In addition to its grantmaking activities, the Foundation presents programs and concerts. ■**PUBLICATIONS:** None ■**WEBSITE:** www.friendshipfoundation.org ■**E-MAIL:** None ■**APPLICATION POLICIES & PROCEDURES:** The Foundation reports that it assists Christian-based organizations in proclaiming the Good News through community Bible studies, concerts, luncheons, and executive dinner parties where individuals are presented with the opportunity to grow in their relationship with God. Also individuals are financially aided in obtaining counseling and other supportive services from various organizations. Grant requests may be submitted in a letter at any time; fully describe the proposed project and include a copy of the IRS tax-exempt status documentation.

O+D+T J. Herbert Fisher, Jr. (P+F+Donor+Con) — Dona L. Fisher (VP+S)

CP-060 **Fuller (Glenwood A.) Foundation**

11 Almond Drive
Hershey 17033   (Dauphin County)

MI-63
Phone 717-533-6743 **FAX** None
EIN 23-2227958   **Year Created** 1984

AMV $767,598   **FYE** 12-99   (**Gifts Received** $4,500)   10 **Grants totaling** $4,235

Three-fourths local giving. High grant of **$2,800** to Evangelical Free Church of Hershey. Small contributions to Child Evangelism Fellowship and BCM International [Delaware County]. Small **Out-of-state** contributions to evangelical churches in several states. ■**PUBLICATIONS:** None ■**WEBSITE:** None ■**E-MAIL:** None ■**APPLICATION POLICIES & PROCEDURES:** Giving is restricted to "charities or ministries that are faithful to and support the World of God as inerrant and infallible in the original manuscripts in total and which are not charismatic or pentecostal and are not members of the National Council of Churches or World Council of Churches or similar ecumenical associations." Grantees must also subscribe to Mt. Calvary Church of Elizabethtown Statement of Faith which will be supplied by the Foundation. No grants awarded to individuals. Grant requests in any form may be submitted at any time.

O+D+T Glenwood A. Fuller (T+Donor+Con) — Jean Fuller (T+Donor)

CP-061 **Gamber Foundation**

c/o Dutch Gold Honey, Inc.
2220 Dutch Gold Drive
Lancaster 17601   (Lancaster County)

MI-12-14-19-22-25-43-71
Phone 717-393-1716 **FAX** None
EIN 23-2331958   **Year Created** 1984

AMV $1,452,848   **FYE** 9-00   (**Gifts Received** $124,000)   21 **Grants totaling** $79,500

Mostly local giving; grants are general support except as noted. High grant of **$25,000** to Water Street Rescue Mission. **$8,500** to S. June Smith Center. **$8,000** to Lancaster Cleft Palate Clinic. **$5,000** to Salvation Army (capital/general support). **$4,000** to Hospice of Lancaster (endowment). **$2,000-$2,500** each to Friendship Community Ministries (capital), Habitat for Humanity/Lancaster Area, HARB-Adult, Lynsey House, Susquehanna Assn. for the Blind (capital/general support), and The Second Mile (summer camp). **$1,500** to Occupational Development Center. **$1,000** to United Support Group. Also, three scholarships (**$2,000** or **$3,000**) for local students. **Out-of-state** grants: **$2,500** to Foundation for the Preservation of Honey Bees [GA] and **$2,000** to U. of Vermont (maple research). ■**PUBLICATIONS:** None ■**WEBSITE:** None ■**E-MAIL:** None ■**APPLICATION POLICIES & PROCEDURES:** Grant requests may be submitted in any form at any time; include all necessary and pertinent information.

O+D+T William R. Gamber, II (P+D+Con) — Marianne M. Gamber (S+D) — Nancy J. Gamber (F+D) — W. Ralph Gamber (D+Donor) — Luella M. Gamber (D+Donor) — Kitty L. Gamber (D) — Robert D. Garner (D) — Julie A. Good [Manheim] (D) — Michael T. Kane [Clarks Summit] (D) — W. Scott Stoner (D) — Corporate donors: Dutch Gold Honey, Inc.; Gamber Glass Container Company

CP-062 **Garver (David B.) Charity Fund**

c/o Bellefonte Elks Lodge #1094
120 West High Street
Bellefonte 16823   (Centre County)

MI-12-13-29-32-41-43-44-52-56-71-84-89
Phone 814-383-2453 **FAX** None
EIN 25-6212802   **Year Created** 1979

AMV $1,018,851   **FYE** 1-01   (**Gifts Received** $0)   31 **Grants totaling** $69,300

All giving restricted to/for the Bellefonte, Penns Valley or Bald Eagle areas in Centre County. High grant of **$7,000** to Undine Fire Company. **$5,000** each to Centre County Library and Snow Shoe Borough Fire Company. **$4,200** to Central Pa. Community Action. **$3,000-$3,500** each to Bellefonte Education Foundation, Bellefonte Wrestling Assn., Centre County Historical Society, Happy Valley Pride, and St. John the Evangelist Catholic School. **$2,000-$2,500** each to American Cancer Society, Bellefonte Cemetery Assn., Bellefonte Youth Football Assn., Boy Scout Troop 381, Citizens Hook & Ladder, Historic Bellefonte, Milesburg Historical Society, Pigskin Parents, and Pleasant Gap Fire Co. **$1,000-$1,650** each to Bald Eagle School District (scholarships), Bellefonte Community Band, Bellefonte Historical & Cultural Assn., Benner Township Parks & Recreation, Church of the Good Shepherd, Infant Evaluation Program, and Red Cross. Other small contributions, mostly for scholarships. ■**PUBLICATIONS:** application guidelines ■**WEBSITE:** None ■**E-MAIL:** None ■**APPLICATION POLICIES & PROCEDURES:** The Fund reports that only civic projects or needy persons in the Bellefonte, Penns Valley, or Bald Eagle areas are eligible to apply. Prospective applicants initially should make a telephone inquiry about the feasibility of submitting a request. Grant requests are accepted at any time but must be submitted on a formal application form available from the Fund; describe/justify the request, and include supporting information and IRS tax-exempt status documentation. The Trustees award grants at quarterly meetings. — Formerly called the Garver Trust for BPOE #1094.

O+D+T Distribution Committee members: James Hoy (S+Con) — Jack Kelley (T) — Richard Sager (T) — Donald Zook (T) — Mellon Bank (Agent)

CP-063 **German (Sgt. Philip) Memorial Foundation**

c/o Allfirst Trust Co. of Pa. N.A.
213 Market Street, P.O. Box 2961
Harrisburg 17105   (Dauphin County)

MI-43
Phone 717-255-2174 **FAX** 717-231-2636
EIN 23-6745697   **Year Created** 1986

AMV $1,838,192   **FYE** 12-00   (**Gifts Received** $0)   33 **Grants totaling** $83,700

All giving restricted to scholarships, usually **$2,500** each per year, for veterans' children in Cumberland or Dauphin counties; students attended colleges, universities, or specialized schools in many states. ■**PUBLICATIONS:** application guidelines ■**WEBSITE:** None ■**E-MAIL:** joe.macri@allfirst.com ■**APPLICATION POLICIES & PROCEDURES:** Only children of veterans from Cumberland or Dauphin counties are eligible to apply. A formal scholarship application form, available from the Bank, most be completed and submitted during April-May; the deadline is June 10th.

O+D+T Joseph A. Macri (VP & Trust Office at Bank+Con) — Allfirst Trust Co. of Pa. N.A. (Co-Trustee)

CP-064   Gibbel Foundation   **MI**-11-12-15-22-35-42-63-64
c/o Lititz Mutual Insurance Co.
2 North Broad Street   **Phone** 717-626-4751 Ext. 226 **FAX** None
Lititz   17543   (Lancaster County)   **EIN** 23-6402619   **Year Created** 1965
AMV $2,009,807   **FYE** 12-00   (**Gifts Received** $0)   60 **Grants totaling** $105,134

About three-fourths local/Pa. giving; grants are annual support except as noted. High grant of **$30,500** to Juniata College. **$14,750** to Lititz Church of the Brethren. **$6,500** to Camp Swatara (capital). **$3,150** to Brethren Village. **$3,000** to Elizabethtown College (capital). **$1,000-$2,300** each to ACTS Covenant Fellowship, Brethren Church/Susquehanna Valley Satellite, Brethren Encyclopedia, Inc. [Montgomery County], COBYS Family Services, Lancaster Health Alliance, and United Way of Lancaster County. Other local contributions **$35-$600** for various purposes. **Out-of-state** giving includes **$10,600** to Bethany Theological Seminary [IN]; **$9,125** to Church of the Brethren General Board [IL]; **$3,200** to On Earth Peace Assembly [MD]; and **$2,500** to Goshen College [IN]. ■**PUBLICATIONS:** None ■**WEBSITE:** None ■**E-MAIL:** None ■**APPLICATION POLICIES & PROCEDURES:** Grant requests may be submitted in a letter at any time.

O+D+T Henry H. Gibbel (P+F+Donor+Con) — James C. Gibbel (VP+Donor) — John R. Gibbel (S+Donor) — Corporate donor: Gibbel Enterprises, Inc.

CP-065   Gilbert (Mary R.) Memorial Fund   **MI**-31-32-34
c/o First Union/Wachovia - PA 6497
600 Penn Street, P.O. Box 1102   **Phone** 610-655-3148 **FAX** None
Reading   19603   (Berks County)   **EIN** 23-7879665   **Year Created** 1997
AMV $1,103,454   **FYE** 12-99   (**Gifts Received** $0)   3 **Grants totaling** $59,945

Mostly local giving. High grants of **$25,000** each to Lancaster Heart Foundation and Penn State/Harrisburg. **$9,945** to Thomas Jefferson U. [Philadelphia]. — Giving in the prior year to the same institutions and **$10,000** to Lancaster Heart Assn. ■**PUBLICATIONS:** None ■**WEBSITE:** None ■**E-MAIL:** None ■**APPLICATION POLICIES & PROCEDURES:** The Fund reports that giving focuses on medical research with first preference given to institutions in the Lancaster-Hershey area. Submit grants requests in a proposal before the September 30th deadline. An outside committee makes decisions on grants which are disbursed in December.

O+D+T Hans Hass (Assistant VP at Bank+Con) — Charles Rohr (Co-T) — First Union/Wachovia (Corporate Trustee)

CP-066   Gilmore-Hoerner Endowment Fund   **MI**-51-52-55
P.O. Box 6010   **Phone** 717-263-2917 **FAX** None
Chambersburg   17201   (Franklin County)   **EIN** 25-6084059   **Year Created** 1967
AMV $611,399   **FYE** 12-00   (**Gifts Received** $0)   3 **Grants totaling** $11,000

All giving restricted to subsidizing musical, theatrical, or special performances in Chambersburg. **$5,000** to Chambersburg Area Council for the Arts. **$3,500** to Cumberland Valley Chamber Players. **$2,500** to Cumberland Valley School of Music. — Grants awarded in the prior year: **$45,000** to Baltimore Symphony (local performances) and **$2,500** each to Chambersburg Area Council for the Arts and Cumberland Valley School of Music. ■**PUBLICATIONS:** application guidelines ■**WEBSITE:** None ■**E-MAIL:** None ■**APPLICATION POLICIES & PROCEDURES:** Only non-profit organizations serving Chambersburg residents are eligible to apply. Prospective applicants initially should make a telephone inquiry about the feasibility of submitting a request. Submit grant requests at any time on a formal application form available from the Fund; include a list of Board members and IRS tax-exempt status documentation.

O+D+T Ruth J. Harrison (P+D+Con) — Frank Rhodes (F+D) — Joan Applegate (D) — George S. Glen, Esq. (D) — Lisbeth Luka (D) — Farmers & Merchants Trust Co. (Trustee)

CP-067   Gitt (Elizabeth) Foundation, The   **MI**-12-13-16-17-18-22-29-35-42-44-65-71-83
P.O. Box 693   **Phone** 717-632-2245 **FAX** None
Hanover   17331   (York County)   **EIN** 23-2790834   **Year Created** 1995
AMV $1,817,121   **FYE** 5-01   (**Gifts Received** $0)   33 **Grants totaling** $96,000

About two-thirds local/Pa. giving. High grant of **$30,000** to Hanover Day Nursery. **$8,000** to YWCA of Hanover (Early Childhood Education/Safe Home). **$4,000** to Planned Parenthood of Central Pa. **$3,000** to HART Center. **$2,000** each to Hanover Council of Churches, Hanover Public Library, Hanover Wellness Connection, Hoffman Homes for Youth, and Operation to Help the Children [Chester County]. **$1,000** each to Adams-Hanover Counseling Services, Hawk Mountain Sanctuary Assn. [Berks County], Health Education Center, Lifeskills Unlimited, and Salvation Army. Other smaller local contributions. **Out-of-state** giving includes **$5,000** to United Negro College Fund [NY]; **$4,000** to Center to Prevent Handgun Violence [DC]; **$3,000** each to Berea College [KY], Center for Constitutional Rights [NY], and NAACP Legal Defense Fund [NY]; and other smaller grants for cancer research and several progressive causes. ■**PUBLICATIONS:** None ■**WEBSITE:** None ■**E-MAIL:** None ■**APPLICATION POLICIES & PROCEDURES:** The Foundation reports that giving is primarily to organizations which Elizabeth M. Gitt supported during her lifetime, and other organizations are not encouraged to apply. No grants are awarded to individuals. Grant requests may be submitted in a letter during January-February—the deadline is February 28th deadline; include an annual report, audited financial statement, and IRS tax-exempt status documentation. Grants are awarded at a meeting in April or May.

O+D+T Marian Gitt Rebert (F+D+Con) — Susan Gitt Gordon [NY] (P+D) — Cynthia Gitt [CA] (S+D) — Forrest R. Schaeffer [Kutztown] (D) — Carson G. Taylor, Esq. [MT] (D) — M&T Trust Company (Trustee)

CP-068   Good (Richard & Annetta) Foundation
275 Edgemere Drive
Lancaster   17801   (Lancaster County)
AMV $1,100,436   **FYE** 12-00   **(Gifts Received** $301,590)

MI-17-22-25-18-31-63-64
Phone 717-397-5331   **FAX** None
EIN 23-2869865   **Year Created** 1996
14 **Grants totaling** $980,884

Mostly local giving; grants are for programs except as noted. Two grants totaling **$745,000** to Lancaster Bible College (chapel building and scholarship/graduates fund). **$78,824** to Grace Baptist Church of Lancaster (building fund). **$25,000** each to Lancaster Health Alliance (women/babies hospital) and Mennonite Central Committee (A Welcoming Place). **$20,000** each to Jessica & Friends and Sunnyside Housing. **$12,100** to Ephrata Church of the Brethren. **$4,000** each to Bridge of Hope [Coatesville] and Samaritan Counseling Center. **Out-of-state** giving includes **$24,000** to South America Mission [FL] (Cienaga project); and **$10,000** each to Amazing Grace Adoptions [NC] and Paideia Academy [NC]. ■**PUBLICATIONS:** None ■**WEBSITE:** None ■ **E-MAIL:** None ■**APPLICATION POLICIES & PROCEDURES:** The Foundation reports that giving is limited to local Christian charities or organizations personally known by the trustees. Grant requests may be submitted in any form at any time. Site visits sometimes are made to organizations being considered for a grant.

O+D+T Richard W. Good (P+F+Donor+Con) — Annetta B. Good (S+Donor)

CP-069   Gooding Group Foundation
c/o Gooding, Simpson & Mackes, Inc.
345 South Reading Road
Ephrata   17522   (Lancaster County)
AMV $384,209   **FYE** 12-00   **(Gifts Received** $10,150)

MI-11-13-29-42-44-49-55-56
Phone 717-733-1241   **FAX** 717-733-0037
EIN 23-2516754   **Year Created** 1988
98 **Grants totaling** $32,342

Mostly local giving; all grants are for general support. High grant of **$2,000** to Millersville U. **$1,000-$1,100** each to Boy Scouts/Dutch Council, Elizabethtown College, Franklin & Marshall College, Lancaster Foundation for Education Enrichment, Thaddeus Stevens College of Technology, and United Way of Lancaster County. **$600-$750** each to Ephrata Public Library, Fulton Opera House, Historic Preservation Trust of Lancaster County, Junior Achievement, Mom's House, and S. June Smith Center. Other local and **Out-of-state** contributions, **$50-$500** each, for various community organizations/purposes. ■**PUBLICATIONS:**|None ■**WEBSITE:** None ■**E-MAIL:** None ■**APPLICATION POLICIES & PROCEDURES:** The Foundation reports that giving generally is for communities where their companies are located; no grants awarded to individuals. Grant requests may be submitted in a letter during April-June (deadline is June 30th); include IRS tax-exempt status documentation. Site visits sometimes are made to organizations being considered for a grant. Grants are awarded at meetings in July/August.

O+D+T John S. Gooding [Lancaster] (P+Con) — James K. Towers, III [Lititz] (VP) — Robert E. Burkholder [Lititz] (S+F) — Corporate donors: GSM Industrial, Inc.; Gooding, Simpson & Mackes, Inc.; Gooding Delaware, Inc.

CP-070   Graham Foundation, The
c/o The Graham Companies
1420 Sixth Ave., P.O. Box 1104
York   17405   (York County)
AMV $25,687,346   **FYE** 6-00   **(Gifts Received** $30,000)

MI-13-14-22-31-35-41-42-43-49-52-55-56
Phone 717-848-3755   **FAX** None
EIN 23-6805421   **Year Created** 1986
47 **Grants totaling** $476,020

About one-third local/Pa. giving; grants are for general purposes except as noted. High Pa. grant of **$43,000** to United Way of York County. **$40,000** to Penn State U./York (scholarship fund). **$12,000** to ARC of York County. **$10,300** to Junior Achievement of South Central Pa. **$10,000** each to Pa. Heritage Society (preservation campaign) and YMCA of York & York County (capital campaign). **$6,000** to Penn Laurel Girl Scout Council (capital campaign). **$5,000** each to Salvation Army (capital campaign), York Foundation (revitalization fund), York Health Systems (uninsured children's fund), and York Little Theatre (capital campaign). **$4,840** to Strand-Capital Performing Arts Center. **$4,000** to Historic York (capital campaign). **$2,000** each to Jewish Community Center, Maryland & Pa. Railroad Preservation Society, and York College of Pa. (nursing building). **$1,000-$1,750** each to American Heart Assn., Atkins House, Bryne Health Education Center (scholarship fund), Make-A-Wish Foundation, Penn-Mar Organization, Pa. Wildlife Federation, York Arts (capital campaign), York Day Nursing (building campaign), York Habitat for Humanity, York Mothers' Center, and York VNA Home Care (hospice). **Out-of-state** giving includes **$177,000** to Burke Mountain Academy [VT]; **$105,000** to U. of Michigan School of Engineering (Virtual Reality Fund/Graham Endowment Fund); and **$5,000** to Somerset County Historical Trust [MD]. ■**PUBLICATIONS:** None ■**WEBSITE:** None ■**E-MAIL:** None ■**APPLICATION POLICIES & PROCEDURES:** The Foundation reports that giving focuses on the York area. No grants awarded to individuals. Submit grant requests in a letter at any time. The Trustees award grants at March, June, September, and December meetings. — Formerly known as The Graham Family Foundation.

O+D+T William H. Kerlin, Jr. (T+Con) — Donald C. Graham (T+Donor) — Corporate donor: The Graham Companies

CP-071   Grass Family Foundation
4025 Crooked Hill Road
Harrisburg   17110   (Dauphin County)
AMV $11,420,854   **FYE** 11-00   **(Gifts Received** $200,000)

MI-15-22-41-52-57-62-82
Phone 717-652-5211   **FAX** None
EIN 23-7218002   **Year Created** 1972
17 **Grants totaling** $699,000

About two-thirds local giving; grants are for general purposes except as noted. High grant of **$325,000** to United Jewish Community of Greater Harrisburg (capital campaign/annual support). **$155,000** to The Whitaker Center for Science & the Arts. **$50,000** to Temple Ohev Sholom. **$15,000** to Concertante Chamber Players. **$5,000** to Harrisburg Academy. **Out-of-state** giving includes **$30,000** to The Park School of Baltimore [MD]; **$25,000** each to The Peabody Preparatory [MD] and Israel Education Fund; **$20,000** to Jewish Community Center of Baltimore; **$10,000** each to Medical Development for Israel [NY] and Associated Jewish Community Foundation of Baltimore [MD]; and other smaller grants for the arts in FL, MD, and NY. ■**PUBLI-**

CATIONS: None ■**WEBSITE:** None ■**E-MAIL:** None ■**APPLICATION POLICIES & PROCEDURES:** Most grants are for operating budgets or special projects. No grants awarded to individuals. Grant requests may be submitted in a letter at any time; include an organizational budget, project budget, and IRS tax-exempt status documentation. Site visits sometimes are made to organizations being considered for a grant.

O+D+T Alex Grass (C+D+Donor+Con) — Linda Grass Shapiro [MD] (S+D+Donor) — Elizabeth Grass Weese [MD] (D+Donor)

CP-072 **Grass (Lois Lehrman) Foundation**
P.O. Box 593
Harrisburg 17108   (Dauphin County)
AMV $4,074,235   **FYE** 11-00   **(Gifts Received** $1,000)

MI-22-25-32-52-54-55-57-62
Phone 717-737-7231 **FAX** None
EIN 23-7218005   Year Created 1972
10 **Grants totaling** $208,375

All local giving; some grants comprise multiple payments. High grant of **$115,000** to Temple Ohev Sholom (capital campaign). **$32,000** to Susquehanna Art Museum (salary/catalog). **$18,500** to Market Square Concerts. **$10,000** each to American Cancer Society, The Whitaker Center for Science & the Arts (Green Room art), and WITF (annual gift). **$6,875** to Temple Ohev Sholom (lecture series/reception). **$5,000** to Delta Housing, Inc. **$1,000** to Harrisburg Opera Assn. (Opera in the Park). ■**PUBLICATIONS:** None ■**WEBSITE:** None ■**E-MAIL:** None ■**APPLICATION POLICIES & PROCEDURES:** The Foundation reports that giving is generally restricted to the Harrisburg area for The Arts or Jewish interests; most grants are for annual/general support, building/renovations, capital campaigns, or endowment. No grants awarded to individuals. Grant requests may be submitted in any form at any time; include a project budget and IRS tax-exempt status documentation. Site visits sometimes are made to organizations being considered for a grant. — Formerly known as the Lois F. Grass Foundation.

O+D+T Lois Lehrman Grass (C+D+Donor+Con) — Linda Grass Shapiro [MD] (S+D+Donor) — Elizabeth Grass Weese [MD] (D)

CP-073 **Greater Harrisburg Foundation, The**
200 North 3rd Street, 8th Floor
P.O. Box 678
Harrisburg 17108   (Dauphin County)
AMV $22,649,023   **FYE** 12-01   **(Gifts Received** $6,543,828)

MI-12-13-14-15-16-17-22-25-29-35-41-42-43-
44-45-51-52-53-54-55-56-57
Phone 717-236-5040 **FAX** 717-231-4463
EIN 23-6294219   **Year Created** 1920
449 **Grants totaling** $5,086,523

As a Community Foundation all discretionary giving is limited to organizations serving the Greater Harrisburg area; nearly 10% of giving is from unrestricted/area-of-interest funds. Most of the following grants are from unrestricted funds but some of the larger ones are in part from restricted funds. High grant of **$71,741** to Whitaker Center for Science & the Arts. **$37,393** to Harrisburg Academy. **$20,163** to Susquehanna Art Museum. **$17,003** to AIDS Community Alliance. **$12,100** to September 11th Fund. **$11,079** to Harrisburg Symphony. **$7,000-$8,800** each to Capital Area Coalition on Homelessness, Community First Fund, Cumberland County Historical Society, Danzante, Gaudenzia, Institute for Cultural Partnerships, Mechanicsburg Area Public Library, Open Stage of Harrisburg, Perry County Council of the Arts, Tri-County Assn. for the Blind, and Urban League of Metropolitan Harrisburg. **$5,000-$6,900** each to AHEDD, Concertante Chamber Players, Domestic Violence Services of Cumberland & Perry Counties, EGAL Partnership Fund, Escape Parent-Child Center of Franklin County, Financial Counseling Services, Greater Harrisburg AIDS Fund, Harrisburg School District (Health Services), Interfaith Center for Homeless Families, Keystone Family & Children Services, Metro Arts, New Hope Ministries (community program), WITF, and Women's Enrichment Center. **$3,000-$4,600** each to American Literacy Corp., Art Center School & Galleries, Harrisburg Area YMCA/Camp Curtin, Harrisburg Community & Economic Affairs, Jump Street, Lebanon Family Health Services, Market Square Concerts, Messiah Village Adult Day Center, Mifflin County Library, Mt. Pleasant Hispanic Center, Parentworks, Inc., Susquehanna Housing Initiatives, Tressler Lutheran Church (community program), and Wesley Union Community Development Corp. **$1,000-$2,800** each to African American Museum of Harrisburg, Alzheimer's Assn., Cantate Carlisle, Capital Region Health System at HHC, Center for Independent Living, Center for Women's Creative Expression, Central Pa. Friends of Jazz, Collaborative Ministry Project/Join Hands, Common Roads, Common Sense Adoption Services, Community Library of Western Perry County, Compeer of Lebanon County, Creative Planning, Inc., Cumberland Dance Company, Family Health Services of South Central Pa., Habitat for Humanity of Perry County, Halifax Area Historical Society, Harrisburg Opera Assn., Healthy Communities Partnership of Greater Franklin County, Historical Society of Perry County, Holy Spirit Hospital, Keystone Rural Health Center, Kittochtinny Historical Society, Marysville-Rye Library Assn., New Baldwin Corridor Coalition, Opera Outreach, Parents Anonymous of Central Pa., Pa. Academy of Family Physicians Foundation, Philhaven, Perry County Literacy Council, Shalom House, Susquehanna Chorale, Susquehanna Service Dogs, Susquenita Education Foundation, UCP of Central Pa., and Wordsworth. Other smaller local discretionary contributions for similar purposes. All other grants (including religion grants and the 145 scholarships totaling $280,000) are made from donor-advised or other restricted funds. — **THE WHITAKER FOUNDATION REGIONAL PROGRAM GRANTS** — *Math & Science Program Recipients*: **$500,000** to Whitaker Center for Science & the Arts. **$275,000** to Gettysburg College. **$261,390** to Council for Public Education. **$150,000** to Wilson College. **$90,000** to The Janus School. **$84,040** to Lebanon Valley College. **$83,160** to Penn State/Hershey Medical Center. **$20,000** to Harrisburg Area YMCA. **$9,250-$10,200** each to Junior Achievement of Central Pa., St. Theresa School, and YWCA of Greater Harrisburg. **$5,000** to Byrnes Health Education Center. **$2,460** to The Eagle Foundation. — *Economic Self-Sufficiency Program Recipients*: **$61,952** to Geisinger Health System (Living Unlimited Program). **$61,200** to YWCA of Greater Harrisburg. **$50,000** each to Brethren Community Ministries, Goodwill Industries of Central Pa., and Keystone Service Systems. **$43,450** to Community Action Commission. **$36,800** to Loveship, Inc. **$28,000** to New Baldwin Corridor Coalition. **$25,000** to Channels Food Rescue. **$22,500** to Brethren Housing Assn. **$20,485** to Program for Female Offenders. **$18,113** to Volunteers of America. **$15,000** to Delta Housing. **$10,000** to Teen Challenge. **$7,500** to Pa. Assn. for the Blind.— Also, **FOUR REGIONAL FOUNDATIONS** (Camp Hill Community Foundation, Franklin County Foundation, Mechanicsburg Area Foundation, and Perry County Community Foundation) are component funds of The Greater Harrisburg Foundation but grant decisions are made by independent, local advisory boards; refer to the website for more details on addresses, board members, and grants awarded. ■**PUBLICATIONS:** Annual Report with application guidelines; The Whitaker Foundation Regional Program Guidelines & Application Procedure booklet ■**WEBSITE:** www.ghf.org ■**E-MAIL:** info@ghf.org

■**APPLICATION POLICIES & PROCEDURES:** Only organizations which directly serve residents of Dauphin, Cumberland, Franklin, Lebanon, or Perry counties are eligible to apply for discretionary support; grants generally range from $2,500-$5,000 with a maximum of $10,000. The Foundation is interested in supporting innovative activities that (a) empower the disadvantaged or underserved, (b) are collaborative efforts, (c) have the potential to become solutions to problems, and (d) respect and involve diverse citizens while making positive changes in the local community. Grants may be made for operating expenses, new or ongoing projects, replacement of government funding cuts, capital costs, and equipment purchase. Grants from discretionary funds may be renewable for up to three years. No discretionary grants are awarded for sectarian religious purposes, endowment drives, annual fund drives of umbrella fundraising agencies, underwriting or capital for fundraising events, activities or performances; advertising; scholarships, internships or awards; retroactive expenses (project or operating); projects that would be completed by grant approval date; budgetary deficits; or projects/programs outside the five stipulated counties. Also, it is unlikely that discretionary grants will be awarded to/for private or parochial schools, travel/conferences, or brochures/publications. Grant requests (one original and 12 collated copies) must include the following: (1) a completed Application Cover Sheet, available on the website or from the Foundation; (2) a Letter of Interest (3 pages maximum) which describes the applicant organization, the proposed project and its expected results; documents the need for the project; gives a timeline for implementation; estimates the cost of the project; and states a specific amount requested; (3) a completed project budget using the Project Budget form (also available on the website); (4) a statement indicating whether the organization ended its last fiscal year with a surplus or deficit; (5) a complete Board member list, and (6) a list of all grants received by The Greater Harrisburg Foundation for up to three years from date of the application. Optionally, up to three letters of endorsement from collaborating organizations may be submitted; include one original and 12 copies collated with each packet. In addition, submit one copy each of the following: a Cover Letter addressed to the Program Officer; copy of most recent organizational budget; most recent financial statement prepared by an accountant; copy of the Certificate of Registration from the Pa. Bureau of Charitable Organizations; and IRS tax-exempt status documentation. Deadlines for receiving Letters of Interest are mid-January, mid-April, mid-July, and mid/late-September—consult the website or contact the Foundation for exact dates. After reviewing the preliminary material, the Foundation may decline the request, award a grant, conduct a site visit, and/or request additional information. — **THE WHITAKER FOUNDATION REGIONAL PROGRAM** (administered by The Greater Harrisburg Foundation) generally restricts grants to Dauphin, Cumberland, and Perry counties for two programmatic objectives: (a) improvement in science-math education, from elementary school through higher education, by way of curriculum change, and (b) support of eligible organizations which assist economically disadvantaged persons in removing themselves from economic dependency. Prospective applicants should first review the The Whitaker Foundation Regional Program Guidelines & Application Procedure booklet (available on the website or from the Program Officer) which contains more details on programmatic objectives, eligibility requirements/restrictions, and the application procedure. In brief, applicants must submit a preliminary letter (4 pages maximum) before the February 15th, April 15th, July 15th, or November 15th deadlines which includes (1) a brief history of the organization, (2) a clear statement of the proposed program's objectives, (3) a brief description of the proposed program; (4) proposed timetable for the program; (5) estimated budget for the program and the amount requested; (6) name/title of the organization's contact person; (7) brief resume of the qualification of the person responsible for implementing the program; and (8) criteria for measuring the project's success or failure. Submit one original and nine copies of the preliminary letter. After Foundation staff review the preliminary letter, a full application may be invited at which time the required form/content of the full proposal and deadline will be stipulated.

O+D+T Janice R. Black (President/CEO+S+Con) — William Lehr, Jr. (C) — Jonathan Vipond, III Esq. (VC) — John S. Oyler, Esq. (S) — Dorothea Aronson (AS+F) — Raymond L. Gover — Leonardo Herreda — Linda A. Hicks — Joan R. Holman — Ellen Brody Hughes — Harold A. McInnes — Velma A. Redmond, Esq. — David Schankweiler — Hasu Shah — Kathleen Smarilli — John Synodinos, L.H.D. — Mary Webber Weston — Robert G. Zullinger

---

CP-074 Green Clover Foundation   MI-11-13-19-31-41-42-61-84-89
  c/o Hofmann Industries, Inc.
  3145 Shillington Road   **Phone** 610-678-8051 **FAX** None
  Sinking Spring 19608   (Berks County)   **EIN** 23-6264992   **Year Created** 1953
AMV $251,539   **FYE** 12-00   **(Gifts Received** $0)   27 **Grants totaling** $10,646

All local giving. High grant of **$4,500** to Penn State U./Berks-Lehigh Campus (capital campaign). **$1,000** each to Caron Foundation and Liberty Fire Company #1. **$785** to Wilson High School (athletic dept.). Other local contributions **$50-$350** for various purposes. ■**PUBLICATIONS:** None ■**WEBSITE:** None ■**E-MAIL:** None ■**APPLICATION POLICIES & PROCEDURES:** The Foundation reports that giving is restricted to recognized charitable organizations in the Berks County area or known Catholic charities. Most grants are for general support, special projects, capital drives, and matching grants; multiyear grants are awarded. No grants are awarded to individuals. Prospective applicants should make an initial telephone inquiry regarding the feasibility of submitting a request. Grant requests may be submitted in one-page letter during January-early February; deadline is February 15th; include IRS tax-exempt status documentation. Site visits sometimes are made to organizations being considered for a grant. Decisions on grants are made at a February meeting.

O+D+T Bernard Hofmann (T+Con)

CP-075 Grumbacher Family Foundation, The   MI-11-12-13-14-15-18-22-41-42-55-56-62-71
  c/o The Bon-Ton Stores, Inc.
  2801 East Market Street, P.O. Box 2821   **Phone** 717-751-3106 **FAX** 717-751-3015
  York 17405   (York County)   **EIN** 23-2524417   **Year Created** 1988
AMV $536,250   **FYE** 1-01   **(Gifts Received** $1,550)   17 **Grants totaling** $91,935

Mostly local giving. High grant of **$28,602** to York Council of Jewish Charities. **$12,000** to Mercersburg Academy. **$10,000** to United Way of York County. **$6,000** to York JCC Childcare Initiative. **$5,000** each to Salvation Army and YMCA of York. **$4,000** to ARC of York County. **$3,000** each to Planned Parenthood of York County and York Arts. **$2,500** to Margaret Moul Home.

$2,000 to York JCC Annual Fund. **$1,700** to Temple Beth Israel. **$1,000** each to Historic York and York County Parks Foundation. Other smaller local contributions. **Out-of-state** grant: **$6,333** to Dartmouth College Alumni Fund [NH]. ■**PUBLICATIONS:** None ■**WEBSITE:** None ■**E-MAIL:** None ■**APPLICATION POLICIES & PROCEDURES:** Grant requests may be submitted in a letter at any time; include an annual report, organization budget, project budget, list of major funding sources, audited financial statement, list of Board members, and IRS tax-exempt status documentation. No grants awarded to individuals. — Formerly called Nancy & Tim Grumbacher Family Foundation

O+D+T M.T. Grumbacher (P+D+Con) — David R. Glyn, Esq. [Philadelphia] (S+D)

CP-076   Grumbacher (M.S.) Foundation, The   MI-13-14-15-18-16-31-32-41-42-43-44-55-57
c/o S. Grumbacher & Son
2801 East Market Street, P.O. Box 2821   **Phone** 717-757-2606 **FAX** None
York   17405   (York County)   **EIN** 23-2697348   **Year Created** 1958
AMV $7,628,004   **FYE** 8-00   (**Gifts Received** $0)   33 **Grants totaling** $335,650

About four-fifths local/Pa. giving. High grant of **$130,000** to Penn State U./York (scholarship endowment fund). **$40,000** to Alzheimer's Assn. of South Central Pa. **$25,000** to Margaret Moul Home. **$10,000** each to Easter Seals and YMCA of York County. **$6,000** to Mercersburg Academy. **$5,000** each to Cultural Alliance of York County, Martin Library, NAACP [Philadelphia], Wyoming Seminary [Luzerne County], WITF, York Arts, York College of Pa. (annaul fund), and York Hospital (annual giving). **$3,000** to American Heart Assn. (Operation Heart Beat). **$2,500** to Planned Parenthood of Central Pa. **$1,000** to Penn State U./York (annual fund). Smaller local contributions for various purposes. **Out-of-state** giving includes **$20,000** to GEO-Global Enviornmental Options; **$15,000** to Greater Miami Jewish Federation; and **$5,000** each to American Civil Liberties Union [NY], National Urban League [NY], and several organizations in CA. ■**PUBLICATIONS:** None ■**WEBSITE:** None ■**E-MAIL:** None ■**APPLICATION POLICIES & PROCEDURES:** The Foundation reports that most giving is limited to Pa., principally the York area. Grant requests may be submitted in a letter between November 1st and the deadline of April 30th; include all pertinent information.

O+D+T M.S. Grumbacher (C+Donor+Con) — Richard Grumbacher [MD] (D) — David J. Kaufman, Esq. [Philadelphia] (D) — Joshua Schultz [CA] (D) — Corporate donor: S. Grumbacher & Son

---

CP-077   Guyer (G. Scott & Bessie K.) Foundation   MI-13-17-18-22-23-25-31-35-41-42-56-89
c/o Apfelbaum, Apfelbaum & Apfelbaum
43 South 5th Street   **Phone** 570-286-1582 **FAX** 570-286-5349
Sunbury   17801   (Northumberland County)   **EIN** 23-7413781   **Year Created** 1975
AMV $833,427   **FYE** 12-00   (**Gifts Received** $0)   36 **Grants totaling** $38,165

All giving limited to within 10 miles of Shamokin Dam—in Snyder, Union, or Northumberland counties; grants are for general purposes except as noted. High grant of **$4,000** to Sunbury Community Hospital (capital campaign). **$3,000** each to Hemlock Girl Scout Council and Kauffman Public Library (construction). **$2,500** each to Central Susquehanna Sight Services (renovations), Fort Discovery (construction), and Northumberland County Historical Society (collection). **$1,000-$1,500** each to Central Susquehanna Valley Interfaith Council (meals on wheels), City of Sunbury (sports activities), Concerned Citizens for Child Care (daycare), Daily Item Christmas Fund, In Transition, Milton YMCA (renovations), New Berlin Recreation (parks), Northumberland Pine Knotter Midget Football (field improvements), Packwood House Museum (exhibitions), Priestly House Museum, Selinsgrove Community Center Library, Snyder County Children & Youth (sports programs/special needs), Susquehanna Valley Choral (concert), and Union County Library. Smaller contributions for other local community organizations or to assist needy individuals. ■**PUBLICATIONS:** application guidelines; application form ■**WEBSITE:** www.guyer-fdn.org ■**E-MAIL:** None ■**APPLICATION POLICIES & PROCEDURES:** The Foundation reports that only organizations or municipal agencies within a 10 mile radius of Shamokin Dam (Snyder County) are eligible to apply. Most grants are for program development, special projects, equipment providing new organizational capabilities, and capital campaigns. Rarely are grants awarded to cover all costs of a project; broad-based community support through contributions from local citizenry and volunteerism is viewed favorably. No funding is given for annual campaigns, general endowment, operating budgets, religious or political activities, mass mailings, or to individuals for any purpose. Occasionally the Foundation may initiate and fund projects of special interest to the Foundation. Since grant application guidelines are quite explicit and detailed, and a formal grant application form must be completed, prospective applicants must first secure these as posted on the website. Personal visits to the Foundation are discouraged. Inquiries/grant requests are accepted throughout the year. Grants are awarded at quarterly meetings.

O+D+T Jeffrey Apfelbaum, Esq. (Con) — Michael M. Apfelbaum, Esq. (Con) — Sidney Apfelbaum, Esq. (D) — Margaret Chubb [Port Trevorton] (D) — Thurston S. Fulmer [Northumberland] (D) — Donald P. Micozzi [Selinsgrove] (D) — Mary Jane Mitterling [Selinsgrove] (Bank Representative) — George A. Park [Selinsgrove] (D) — Martha Zeller [Lewisburg] (D) — Sun Bank (Trustee)

CP-078   Hall Foundation, The   MI-11-12-13-14-15-25-29-31-32-41-42-44-51
P.O. Box 1200   52-54-55-56-63-72-84
Camp Hill   17011   **Phone** 717-761-1057 **FAX** None
                                     (Cumberland County)   **EIN** 23-6243044   **Year Created** 1952
AMV $9,197,239   **FYE** 12-00   (**Gifts Received** $0)   158 **Grants totaling** $357,968

Mostly local/Pa. giving. High grant of **$40,000** to United Way of the Capital Region. **$38,200** to Penn State U. **$15,675** to Keystone Partnership, Inc. **$15,000** to The Second Mile [State College]. **$12,000** to Pinnacle Health Foundation. **$11,900** to Hospice of Central Pa. **$10,000-$10,600** each to Big 33 School Foundation, Harrisburg Area YMCA, and Harrisburg Symphony. **$7,500** to Exchange Club of Harrisburg. **$7,200** to Elegant Processions. **$5,833** to Harrisburg Community Theatre. **$5,000** each to American Cancer Society, Susquehanna Art Museum, and Trinity Lutheran Church of Camp Hill. **$4,715** to World Mission of Central Pa. **$3,000** each to Channels, Holy Spirit Hospital, Humane Society of Harrisburg, National MS Society/Central Pa. Chapter, and Share Our Strength. **$2,000-$2,500** each to Council of Public Education, Harrisburg Area Community College,

Lebanon Valley College, Leukemia & Lymphoma Society, Red Cross, and Susquehanna U. **$1,000-$1,600** each to Children's Hospital of Pittsburgh, The Harrisburg Singers, Historical Society of Dauphin County, Make-A-Wish Foundation, March of Dimes [State College], Metro Arts of the Capital Region, National AIDS Marathon, New Home Ministries [Dillsburg], Salvation Army, South Central Pa. Food Bank, The Wednesday Club, West Shore Public Library, The Wildcat Foundation, and WXPN-FM [Philadelphia]. Other smaller contributions for various purposes. In addition, 100 scholarships of **$1,000** each were awarded for students attending colleges/universities in many states. **Out-of-state** giving primarily to CT where a trustee resides. ■**PUBLICATIONS:** None ■**WEBSITE:** None ■**E-MAIL:** None ■**APPLICATION POLICIES & PROCEDURES:** The Foundation reports its primary objective is educating youth for the future with about one-third of giving for college scholarships. Organizational Grants: Grant requests from organizations should be submitted in a one-page letter three calendar months prior to the date of the requested grant; provide supporting documentation. Scholarship Awards: Scholarships of $1,000 each are awarded to four categories of students: (1) graduating seniors (one male, one female) from school districts that sponsor Harrisburg Area Community College; (2) first and second year students who attend Harrisburg Area Community College; (3) first and second year students selected by P.H.E.A.A. officials; and (4) participants in local charitable or sporting events in which the Foundation is involved. Complete scholarship guidelines are available at schools or colleges. Recipients are selected by the officials at the schools/institutions and are based on financial need, meritorious academic achievement, leadership qualities, and personal service to others through contributions to school or community. The school/institution must submit the applications directly to the Foundation by May 1st; no applications are accepted directly from students. The Trustees meet as necessary, usually quarterly, to award organizational grants.

O+D+T Gerald N. Hall (Executive Director+T+Con) — Robert E. Hall [Harrisburg] (S+F+T) — Shirley Hall Carr [CT] (T) — Gerald N. Hall, Jr. [Harrisburg] (T) — LeRoy S. Zimmerman, Esq. (T)

CP-079 **Hambay (James T.) Foundation**		MI-12-13-14-17-23
P.O. Box 6361		**Phone** 717-652-7911 **FAX** 717-231-2636
Harrisburg 17112	(Dauphin County)	**EIN** 23-6243877 **Year Created** 1941
AMV $3,425,572 **FYE** 12-00	(**Gifts Received** $0)	30 **Grants totaling** $177,313

All giving is restricted to the Harrisburg area to aid crippled, blind or indigent children under 18 years of age. High grant of **$42,425** to Goodwill Industries. **$18,661** to Keystone Service Systems. **$10,000** to UCP of the Capital Area. **$5,000** to ARC of Dauphin County. **$3,906** to Escape Center. Other disbursements were primarily to doctors, dentists, opticians, or organizations providing health services to individuals. ■**PUBLICATIONS:** None ■**WEBSITE:** None ■**E-MAIL:** joe.macro@allfirst.com ■**APPLICATION POLICIES & PROCEDURES:** All giving restricted to Dauphin, Cumberland, or Perry counties to aid crippled, blind or indigent children under 18 years of age; some grants directly support organizations and others aid individuals indirectly. No grants awarded for operating budgets, building, or endowment funds. Prospective applicants (individuals or organizations) initially should telephone regarding the procedure for submitting a request. A formal application form provided by the Foundation must be completed and submitted with documentation as stipulated. The Trustees Committee meets monthly.

O+D+T Delores P. Macri (Executive Director+Con) — Joseph A. Macri (Trust Officer at Bank) — Worthington C. Flowers (Co-T) — Allfirst Trust Co. of Pa. N.A. (Co-Trustee)

CP-080 **Hamer Foundation, The**		MI-12-13-16-17-22-25-31-42-43-71
c/o State of the Art, Inc.		
2470 Fox Hill Road		**Phone** 814-355-8004 **FAX** None
State College 16803	(Centre County)	**EIN** 25-1610780 **Year Created** 1989
AMV $5,469,760 **FYE** 12-00	(**Gifts Received** $1,040,440)	19 **Grants totaling** $919,750

Mostly local/Pa. giving; grants are for operating support except as noted. High grant of **$822,500** to Penn State U. (capital fund). **$12,500** to Centre County Community Foundation (distribution fund). **$10,000** each to Centre County Hospital (building fund) and Centre County Parks & Recreation Nature Center (capital fund). **$6,500** to Temporary Housing, Inc. **$5,000** each to Penn State U. (Renaissance Scholarship Fund) and The Second Mile. **$4,000** each to The Nature Conservancy-Pa. Chapter [Montgomery County] and Western Pa. Conservancy [Pittsburgh]. **$3,500** to Food Bank of State College. **$3,000** to Interfaith Mission. **$2,500** each to Hemlock Council Girl Scouts (building fund) and Women's Resource Center (building fund). **$1,000** each to Conservation Fund [Harrisburg] and Family Health Services [Bellefonte]. **Out-of-state** giving includes **$12,500** to The Nature Conservancy; **$10,000** to U. of Chicago School of Business [IL] (capital fund); and **$3,000** to United Negro College Fund [NY]. ■**PUBLICATIONS:** None ■**WEBSITE:** None ■**E-MAIL:** None ■**APPLICATION POLICIES & PROCEDURES:** The Foundation reports its primary focus is organizations benefiting Centre County citizens, or educational or environmental organizations. Most grants are for annual campaigns, general support, building/renovations, or capital campaigns; no grants are awarded to individuals. Grant requests may be submitted in a proposal at any time. The Board meets as needed.

O+D+T Diane M. Kerly (T+Con) — Donald W. Hamer [Bellefonte] (T+Donor) — Edward J. Matosziuk, Jr. [Altoona] (T)

CP-081 **Hanford (Aubrey L.) Memorial Fund**		MI-13-41-63-64
c/o Textile Printing & Finishing Co.		
1601 Elm Street, P.O. Box 746		**Phone** 717-272-0805 **FAX** None
Lebanon 17042	(Lebanon County)	**EIN** 23-7041851 **Year Created** 1972
AMV $887,348 **FYE** 5-01	(**Gifts Received** $0)	22 **Grants totaling** $43,380

Limited local giving. High Pa. grant of **$1,000** to Evangelical School of Theology. Other smaller local contributions, mostly **$25-$150.** for various purposes. **Out-of-state** high grant to **$40,000** to First Baptist Church of Marco Island [FL]. — In 1999, local grants included **$10,000** to Lebanon YMCA and **$1,000** to Lebanon Christian Academy. ■**PUBLICATIONS:** None ■**WEBSITE:** None ■**E-MAIL:** None ■**APPLICATION POLICIES & PROCEDURES:** Grant requests may be submitted in any form at any time; the deadline is December 31st.

O+D+T A.L. Hanford, Jr. (Donor+Con) — A.L. Hanford, III (Donor) — Corporate donors: Textile Printing & Finishing Company; Valley Screen Printing Company; Fine-Tex Company; Textile Chemical Company

CP-082 Hanover Shoe Farms Foundation
c/o Hanover Shoe Farms, Inc.
Route 194 South, P.O. Box 339
Hanover 17331   (York County)
AMV $2,260,853   **FYE** 11-00   **(Gifts Received** $0)

MI-12-13-14-32-41-43-63-72

Phone 717-637-8931 **FAX** None
EIN 23-2647725   **Year Created** 1991
24 **Grants totaling** $66,750

Mostly local giving; grants are for general fund purposes except as noted. High Pa. grants of **$5,000** each to Delone Catholic High School and Hanover-Adams Habilitation & Training Center. **$4,000** each to Adams Cran & Natural Service Center and Hoffman Homes for Youth. **$3,000** each to Hanover Area YMCA, Hanover High School (scholarship fund), Littlestown YMCA, Make-A-Wish Foundation of York County, and Sacred Heart School. **$2,000** each to American Cancer Society, and Hanover Public Library. **$1,000-$1,500** each to Adams-Hanover Counseling Service, Christ United Church of Christ, Easter Foundation, Hanover Area Family Center, Hanover High School (relays), Horses for Humanity, Lost & Found Horse Rescue, and The Second Mile. **Out-of-state** giving includes high grant of **$7,500** to Harness Racing Museum [IN]; **$4,000** to Standardbred Retirement Foundation [NJ]; and **$3,500** to Harness Horse Youth Foundation [IN]. ■**PUBLICATIONS:** None ■**WEBSITE:** None ■**E-MAIL:** None ■**APPLICATION POLICIES & PROCEDURES:** The Foundation reports that giving is restricted to local organizations or those related to standardbred horses. Grant requests should be submitted in a one-page letter, preferably in September (deadline is October 31st); describe the nature of the request, state a specific amount requested, and include IRS tax-exempt status documentation. Site visits sometimes are made to organizations being considered for a grant. Grants are awarded at a November meeting.
O+D+T Russell C. Williams (P+D+Con) — James W. Simpson (VP+D) — Shawn R. Eisenhauer (S+D) — Shirley J. Kuhn (F+D) — Patricia Eisenhauer (D) — Sharon Young (D) — Corporate donor: Hanover Shoe Farms, Inc.; Foundation donor: Lawrence B. Sheppard Foundation

---

CP-083 Harsco Corporation Fund
c/o Harsco Corporation
350 Poplar Church Road, P.O. Box 8888
Camp Hill 17001   (Cumberland County)
AMV $8,775,067   **FYE** 12-00   **(Gifts Received** $0)

MI-11-13-14-22-25-29-35-41-42-45-51-52-54
55-81-86-88
Phone 717-763-7064 **FAX** None
EIN 23-6278376   **Year Created** 1956
240+ **Grants totaling** $1,153,080

About two-thirds local/Pa. giving in corporate operating locations (Allegheny, Butler, Cumberland, Dauphin, Monroe, Philadelphia, and Washington counties). High Pa. grant of **$158,000** to Messiah College. **$70,000** to Eisenhower Exchange Fellowships [Philadelphia]. **$58,333** to Harrisburg Community Theatre. **$50,550** to United Way of the Capital Region. **$50,000** to Fund for the Advancement of the State System of Higher Education. **$35,650** to Harrisburg Symphony. **$25,000** each to Allied Arts Fund and Council for Public Education. **$20,000** to Susquehanna Valley Center for Public Policy.**$15,000** each to Big Brothers/Big Sisters of the Capital Region and Dickinson School of Law. **$11,000** each to Harrisburg Opera Assn. and World Mission of Central Pa. **$10,000** each to Butler County Community College, Pa. Breast Cancer Coalition [Ephrata], and Red Cross/Susquehanna Valley. **$7,000-$7,550** each to Capital Center for the Arts, Science & Education, MetroArts of the Capital Region, and Open Stage of Harrisburg. **$5,000-$5,800** each to ARC of Dauphin County, Central Pa. Literacy Council, City of Harrisburg/National Civil War Museum, Finnegan Foundation [Reading], Goodwill Industries of Central Pa., Harrisburg YMCA, and Penn State U. **$3,000-$3,750** each to Easter Seals, Harrisburg Shakespeare Festival, Hemlock Girl Scout Council, Muscular Dystrophy Assn., Share Our Strength, and South Central Pa. Food Bank. **$1,000-$2,500** each to Bob Burgess Memorial Foundation, Boy Scouts/Keystone Council, Burnley Workshop of the Poconos, Butler Memorial Hospital, Chamber Singers of Harrisburg, Children's Play Room, Church of the Holy Spirit [Palmyra], Eagle Foundation, Harrisburg Parks Partnership, Harrisburg YWCA, Leadership-Harrisburg Area, Lebanon Catholic High School, Marywood U. [Scranton], Mental Health Assn., Mount Gretna Productions, National MS Society, Pinnacle Health Auxiliaries, Pocono Medical Center [Monroe County], UCP of the Capital Area, United Way of Allegheny County, United Way of Butler County, United Way of Monroe County, and United Way of Washington County. Other smaller Pa. contributions for similar purposes. **Out-of-state** giving, primarily to corporate operating locations in over 30 states, included many grants to United Ways. In addition, 53 matching gifts totaling **$49,345** were disbursed to/for colleges/universities, cultural/arts organizations, libraries, or public broadcasting. Also, scholarships awarded to dependents of company employees. ■**PUBLICATIONS:** statement of program policy ■**WEBSITE:** None ■**E-MAIL:** None ■**APPLICATION POLICIES & PROCEDURES:** The Foundation reports that most grants are initiated by management personnel at local corporate plants/facilities who forward requests to the Foundation's central office for approval/disapproval; grants usually are for general operating support or matching gifts. No grants are awarded for special projects, endowment, building funds, research, or to individuals. Scholarships are awarded only to dependents of company employees. Grant requests may be submitted in a letter at any time; describe the organization's charitable activities and provide IRS tax-exempt status documentation. Matching gifts for higher educational institutions, performing arts groups, libraries, and public broadcasting stations have a $25 minimum, $1,000 maximum/employee/institution/year for educational institutions and $100 maximum for non-educational organizations. The Board meets in April and as necessary.
O+D+T Robert G. Yocum (C+T+Con (Charitable Requests)) — Salvatore D. Fazzolari (S+F+T) — P.C. Coppock (T) — Derek C. Hathaway (T) — Corporate donor: Harsco Corporation

---

CP-084 Health Alliance Charitable Foundation, The
c/o Health Alliance of Pennsylvania
4750 Lindle Road
Harrisburg 17111   (Dauphin County)
AMV $1,943,325   **FYE** 12-00   **(Gifts Received** $0)

MI-12-31-35-39

Phone 717-564-9200 **FAX** 717-561-5333
EIN 25-1642600   **Year Created** 1990
6 **Grants totaling** $191,755

All Pa. giving. High grant of **$100,000** to Pa. Partnerships for Children (enrollment of children in government health insurance programs). **$50,000** to Free Health Clinic of Montgomery County (provide access to prenatal care for low-income residents). **$12,500** to Montgomery Health Foundation (provide healthcare to uninsured residents). **$10,000** each to Hershey Medical

Center (computer-based follow-up care network for religious congregations) and Lancaster Healthy Communities (develop electronic community network for tracking, mapping, analysis). **$9,255** to Pocono Medical Center (violence prevention facilitator training for schools) ■ **PUBLICATIONS:** statement of program policy; application guidelines ■ **WEBSITE:** None ■ **E-MAIL:** None ■ **APPLICATION POLICIES & PROCEDURES:** The Foundation reports that only Pa. organizations/partnerships dealing with community health or quality of life issues are eligible to apply. Prospective applicants initially should make a telephone inquiry about the feasibility of submitting a request. Grant requests may be submitted in a letter (3 pages maximum) at any time; include a project budget and IRS tax-exempt status documentation. Site visits sometimes are made to organizations being considered for a grant. The Board of Directors meets as necessary. — Formerly called Hospital Association Trust.

O+D+T Michael A. Suchanick (Executive Director+S+FCon) — Msgr. Andrew J. McGowan [Scranton] (C+D) — Carolyn F. Scanlan (VC+D) — William A. Alexander (D) — Clifford L. Jones [Mechanicsburg] (D) — Rodrique Mortel, M.D. [Hershey] (D) — JoAnn K. Mower [NJ] (D) — Robert F. Nation [Camp Hill] (D) — H. Sheldon Parker, Jr. [Hershey] (D) — Linda W. Rhodes, Ed.D. (D) — Organizational donors: Capital Blue Cross; Independence Blue Cross; Pa. Assn. of Non-Profit Homes for the Aging; and other undesignated donors.

CP-085	**Heim (Joseph A. & Clara S.) Foundation**	**MI**-13-41-56-84-89
	c/o Woodlands Bank	
	2450 East 3rd Street	**Phone** 570-320-2468 **FAX** None
	Williamsport 17701 (Lycoming County)	**EIN** 23-2528851 **Year Created** 1990
AMV $610,982	**FYE** 12-00 (Gifts Received $0)	10 **Grants totaling** $25,668

All local giving; grants are for general purposes except as noted. Three grants totaling **$11,366** to Borough of Montoursville (smoke detectors/pool repairs/park project). **$5,625** to Montoursville Little League. **$3,000** to Montoursville Area High School (art dept./scholarships). **$2,577** to Lycoming County Historical Society. **$1,500** to Montoursville Library. **$1,000** to Hemlock Girl Scout Council. **$600** to Montoursville Cemetery. ■ **PUBLICATIONS:** None ■ **WEBSITE:** None ■ **E-MAIL:** None ■ **APPLICATION POLICIES & PROCEDURES:** The Foundation reports that giving is restricted to/for Montoursville Borough. Grant requests may be submitted in any form at any time.

O+D+T Thomas B. Burkholder (VP+Trust Officer+Con) — Richard W. DeWald [Montoursville] (T) — Maryanne W. Freeman [MD] (T) — Constance L. Metherall [UT] (T)

CP-086	**Henderson (Bruce) Trust**	**MI**-13-14-15-22-31-33-35-44
	c/o Allfirst Trust	
	55 South Main Street, P.O. Box 459	**Phone** 717-261-2833 **FAX** 717-263-1630
	Chambersburg 17201 (Franklin County)	**EIN** 23-6262592 **Year Created** 1949
AMV $423,621	**FYE** 12-01 (Gifts Received $0)	12 **Grants totaling** $23,040

All giving restricted to Chambersburg. Grants of **$1,920** each awarded to 12 local organizations, for for operating support or special projects; other details are unavailable. In prior years grantees included Chambersburg Hospital, Coyle Free Library, Home Care Services Agency, Mental Health Center of Franklin-Fulton Counties, Occupational Services, Inc., and Pa. Assn. of Retarded Citizens. ■ **PUBLICATIONS:** None ■ **WEBSITE:** None ■ **E-MAIL:** None ■ **APPLICATION POLICIES & PROCEDURES:** Only the neediest charities located in Chambersburg are eligible to apply. Grant requests may be submitted in any form before the March 31st deadline; include an annual report and IRS tax-exempt status documentation. Grants are designated by the Bank's Board of Directors at a May meeting and then approved by the Orphans Court Division, Court of Common Pleas.

O+D+T Jacquline L. Hill (Trust Officer at Bank+Con) — Allfirst Trust Bank of Pa. (Trustee)

CP-087	**Herman (Oliver Reeder) Memorial Trust**	**MI**-15-63
	10790 Ross Valley Road	**Phone** 570-368-3130 **FAX** None
	Trout Run 17771 (Lycoming County)	**EIN** 23-7899364 **Year Created** 1997
AMV $421,061	**FYE** 4-00 (Gifts Received $0)	8 **Grants totaling** $30,000

Nearly half local/Pa. giving. Four grants totaling **$7,800** to Christian Church of Cogan Station (construction, mission work, and building loan). **$4,200** to Montrose Broadcasting Corp. [Susquehanna County] (Christian programs). **$2,400** to Masonic Home of Pa. [Montgomery County] (nursing home services). **Out-of-state** grants, mostly for Christian radio broadcasting, to organizations in several states. ■ **PUBLICATIONS:** None ■ **WEBSITE:** None ■ **E-MAIL:** None ■ **APPLICATION POLICIES & PROCEDURES:** Information not available.

O+D+T Edward J. Conover (T+Con)

CP-088	**Herr (Irvin E.) Foundation**	**MI**-43
	c/o Allfirst Trust Co. of Pa. N.A.	
	213 Market Street, P.O. Box 2961	**Phone** 717-255-2174 **FAX** 717-231-2636
	Harrisburg 17105 (Dauphin County)	**EIN** 22-2550087 **Year Created** 1983
AMV $558,707	**FYE** 12-00 (Gifts Received $0)	28 **Grants totaling** $28,000

All grants are scholarships, **$1,000** each, for graduating high school seniors from Cumberland, Dauphin, Northumberland, and Perry counties who can attend a college/university in any state. ■ **PUBLICATIONS:** None ■ **WEBSITE:** None ■ **E-MAIL:** joe.macro@all-first.com ■ **APPLICATION POLICIES & PROCEDURES:** Only graduating seniors from high schools in the four Central Pa. counties listed above are eligible to apply for scholarships; the application deadline is April 1st.

O+D+T Joseph A. Macri (VP & Trust Officer at Bank+Con) — Allfirst Trust Co. of Pa. N.A. (Trustee)

CP-089 **Hess (Albert T.) Foundation, The**
6543 Fairway Drive West
Fayetteville 17222 (Franklin County)
AMV $314,564 **FYE** 9-00 **(Gifts Received** $0)

MI-11-13-14-22-32-39-72-89
Phone 717-352-4733 **FAX** None
EIN 23-6272406 **Year Created** 1953
12 **Grants totaling** $8,950

All local giving; all grants are unrestricted support. **$1,000** each to American Cancer Society, Antietam Humane Society, ATH&L Fire & Ambulance Company, Easter Seals, Salvation Army, United Way of Franklin County, Waynesboro Advanced Life Support, and Waynesboro YMCA. Other smaller local contributions. ■**PUBLICATIONS:** None ■**WEBSITE:** None ■**E-MAIL:** None ■**APPLICATION POLICIES & PROCEDURES:** Grant applicants should send an brief, initial letter outlining a proposed request; if the Foundation is interested, a proposal may be requested. Grants generally are awarded in December.

O+D+T Donald L. Walters (S+F+Con) — A. Tracy Hess-King (P) — Ruth Grundy (VP) — Corporate donor: Hess Manufacturing Company

---

CP-090 **Hess Trust, The**
170 Ridge Ave.
Ephrata 17522 (Lancaster County)
AMV $290,324 **FYE** 6-00 **(Gifts Received** $119,474)

MI-22-34-63-65-82
Phone 717-738-4819 **FAX** None
EIN 23-2112168 **Year Created** 1979
2 **Grants totaling** $2,000

All Pa. giving. **$1,000** each to Highland Presbyterian Church [Lancaster] and Jefferson Medical College [Philadelphia]. Major giving in prior years to Mennonite Central Committee and several international Christian organizations.
■**PUBLICATIONS:** None ■**WEBSITE:** None ■**E-MAIL:** None ■**APPLICATION POLICIES & PROCEDURES:** The Foundation reports that preference is given organizations which focus on relief efforts, education, or life enhancement opportunities for youth. Submit grant requests at any time which is signed and dated by the requesting person. The application should (a) describe organizational purpose and general activities, (b) state a specific amount of funding requested, how it will be used, and describe the intended beneficiaries, (3) provide the name, address and title of all Board members, and (4) include IRS tax-exempt status documentation. If applicable, identify any organization which controls, is related to, or sponsors the applicant organization.

O+D+T Kenneth E. Hess (T+Donor+Con) — J. Clair Hess [Lancaster] (T+Donor)

CP-091 **High Foundation, The**
c/o High Industries, Inc.
1853 William Penn Way, P.O. Box 10008
Lancaster 17605 (Lancaster County)
AMV $4,083,007 **FYE** 8-00 **(Gifts Received** $30,000)

MI-13-17-19-22-29-33-41-42-43-49-51-63-71
Phone 717-293-4498 **FAX** 717-293-4451
EIN 23-2149972 **Year Created** 1980
29 **Grants totaling** $150,000

Mostly South Central Pa. giving; grants are for general purposes except as noted. High grant of **$25,000** to Thaddeus Stevens Foundation (capital campaign). **$20,000** to Salvation Army (capital campaign). **$15,000** each to Arbor Place Christian Community Center (capital campaign) and Penn Laurel Girl Scout Council (capital campaign). **$8,000** to Locust Grove School (capital campaign). **$7,000** to Samaritan Counseling Center. **$5,000** each to Drug & Alcohol Rehab Services, Mennonite Central Committee (capital campaign), and Milagro House. **$4,000-$4,500** each to Lancaster Partnership Program, Mom's House, Neffsville Mennonite Church, and Theatre of the Seventh Sister. **$2,000** to New School of Lancaster. **$1,000-$1,500** each to ASSETS Lancaster, Bridge of Hope [Coatesville] (capital campaign), Contact Lancaster, Junior Achievement, Lebanon Valley College, Rails to Trails Conservancy of Pa., and St. Peter's Evangelical Lutheran Church of Lancaster. Also, seven scholarships, **$2,000** or **$3,000**, for dependent children of company employees, or of related companies ■**PUBLICATIONS:** None ■**WEBSITE:** None ■**E-MAIL:** None ■**APPLICATION POLICIES & PROCEDURES:** The Foundation reports that giving is largely limited to South Central Pa. organizations located in company operating areas; most grants are for special projects, building funds, and capital drives. Prospective applicants initially should submit basic information concerning a request; the Foundation then may request a formal application (deadline December 1st) together with an annual report, organizational budget, project budget, audited financial statement, Board member list, and IRS tax-exempt status documentation. Only rarely are site visits made to organizations being considered for a grant. Grants are awarded at a late January/early February meeting.

O+D+T Robin D. Stauffer (S+Con) — Sadie H. High (C+T) — Richard L. High (F+T) — Calvin G. High (T+Donor) — Gregory A. High (T) — Janet C. High (T) — S. Dale High (T+Donor) — Steven D. High (T) — Chester A. Raber (T) — Corporate donor: High Industries, Inc.

CP-092 **Hoffman (Bob) Foundation**
c/o York Bar Bell Company
3300 Board Road, P.O. Box 1707
York 17405 (York County)
AMV $2,123,781 **FYE** 3-00 **(Gifts Received** $21,706)

MI-13-14-29-35-42-49-84
Phone 717-767-6481 **FAX** 717-764-0044
EIN 23-6298674 **Year Created** 1964
26 **Grants totaling** $79,229

Mostly local giving. High grant of **$20,000** each to Penn State U.-York and York YMCA. **$8,500** to Health Education Center. **$10,690** to Hoffman Terpak Meet. **$5,000** each to East Coast Gold Weighlifting and Penn Laurel Girl Scout Council. **$2,500** to York YWCA. **$1,200** to Junior Achievement of York County. **$1,000** to Pa. Special Olympics. **$900** to York College of Pa. Other smaller local contributions for various purposes. **Out-of-state** grant: **$1,000** to National Strength & Conditioning Assn. [CO]. ■**PUBLICATIONS:** application guidelines ■**WEBSITE:** None ■**E-MAIL:** None ■**APPLICATION POLICIES & PROCEDURES:** The Foundation reports that Pa. giving is limited to York and Lancaster counties with priority interest in physical fitness or athletic purposes; grants are mostly for general support, special projects, building funds, or capital drives. Grant requests may be submitted in a letter (2 pages maximum) in March, June, September, or December (deadlines are March 31st, June 30th, September 30th, and December 31st); include organizational/project budgets and IRS tax-exempt status documentation. Grants are awarded at meetings in January, April, July, and October.

O+D+T David J. Fortney (D+Con) — Alda M. Ketterman [Dover] (D) — George E. McDonald, Esq. (D) — Paul Stombaugh (D) — J.B. Terpak, Jr. (D) — Corporate donors: York Bar Bell Company; Swiss Automatics Division; U.S. Lock & Hardware Company

CP-093   Hofmann (Catherine V. & Martin W.) Foundation   MI-11-13-31-41-42-53-61
c/o Hofmann Industries, Inc.
3145 Shillington Road   **Phone** 610-678-8051 **FAX** 610-670-2221
Sinking Spring 19608   (Berks County)   **EIN** 23-6447843   **Year Created** 1968
AMV $747,667   **FYE** 12-01   **(Gifts Received** $0)   57 **Grants totaling** $38,550

Mostly local giving. High grant of **$12,010** to Boy Scouts/Hawk Mountain Council. **$7,500** to United Way of Berks County. **$1,000-$4,000** each to Holy Name High School, Jesuit Center for Spiritual Growth, John Paul II Center for Special Learning, Missionary Sisters of Precious Blood, St. Joseph's Medical Center, St. Joseph's U. Other local and **Out-of-state** contributions **$25-$900** for Catholic and other purposes. ■**PUBLICATIONS:** None ■**WEBSITE:** None ■**E-MAIL:** None ■**APPLICATION POLICIES & PROCEDURES:** The Foundation reports that giving is generally limited to recognized charitable organizations in the Berks County area or to known Catholic charities; most grants are for general support, special projects, capital drives, or matching grants; multiple-year grants are awarded. Prospective applicants should make an initial telephone inquiry about the feasibility of submitting a request. Grant requests should be submitted in a one-page letter in January-February; include IRS tax-exempt status documentation. Site visits sometimes are made to organizations being considered for a grant. Grants are awarded at a February meeting.

O+D+T Bernard M. Hofmann (T+Con) — Martin J. Hofmann (T)

CP-094   Holmes (Charles A. & Elizabeth Guy) Foundation   MI-13-29-41-51-52-57-63
c/o Mellon Private Wealth Management
2 North Second Street, 12th Floor, P.O. Box 1010   **Phone** 717-780-3034 **FAX** None
Harrisburg 17108   (Dauphin County)   **EIN** 23-6807649   **Year Created** 1986
AMV $400,000 est.   **FYE** 12-01   **(Gifts Received** $0)   13 **Grants totaling** $28,500

All local giving. High grant of **$6,000** to Harrisburg Symphony. **$3,750** to Camp Hill Presbyterian Church. **$3,000** to WITF. **$2,000** to Boys & Girls Club of Harrisburg. **$1,500** each to Camp Hill High School, Cantata Carlisle, and Christ Episcopal Church. **$1,000** each to East Pennsboro, Susquehanna Chorale, and Wednesday Club. **$500** each to Harrisburg Singers and Harrisburg Opera Assn. **Out-of-state** giving to Columbia, MD. ■**PUBLICATIONS:** None ■**WEBSITE:** None ■**E-MAIL:** None ■**APPLICATION POLICIES & PROCEDURES:** The Foundation reports that priority is given to organizations which the late Mrs. Holmes supported during her lifetime. Grant requests should be submitted in a letter in March, before the April 1st deadline; describe the need/purpose and include IRS tax-exempt status documentation. Grants are awarded at a May meeting.

O+D+T Angela R. Thompson (Trust Officer at Bank+Con) — Mellon Private Wealth Management (Trustee)

CP-095   Horn (Russell & Eleanor) Foundation   MI-12-14-22-25-29-35-45-63
c/o Pace Resources
40 South Richland Ave.   **Phone** 717-699-0023 **FAX** None
York 17404   (York County)   **EIN** 22-2663207   **Year Created** 1985
AMV $1,824,892   **FYE** 12-00   **(Gifts Received** $34,943)   36 **Grants totaling** $75,903

All Central Pa. giving. High grant of **$22,100** to York Habitat for Humanity. **$6,885** to The Well. **$6,625** to Access-York. **$5,000** each to Bell Socialization Services, York County Literacy, and York Union Rescue Mission. **$4,000** to New Hope Ministries. **$3,000** to Our Daily Bread. **$2,000-$2,500** each to Contact-York, Health Education Center, and Salvation Army. **$1,000-$1,500** each to Agape Residential Ministries & Services, Calvary United Methodist Church, Easter Seals, The Lehman Center, Southern York County Food Bank, and York Day Nursery & Kindergarten. Other local contributions **$25-$700** for various purposes, some as matching gifts of Pace Resources, Inc. employees. ■**PUBLICATIONS:** application guidelines ■**WEBSITE:** None ■**E-MAIL:** None ■**APPLICATION POLICIES & PROCEDURES:** The Foundation reports that giving focuses on agencies in or serving York County with priority for matching charitable contributions of Pace Resources, Inc. employees. Every fall the Board of Directors determines an area of special need and supports local organizations addressing that need. Most grants are for general support, special projects, building funds, capital drives, endowment, and research. No grants are awarded to United Way, Planned Parenthood, or for church budgets. Grant requests should be submitted in early November (deadline is November 15th) on a formal application form available from the Foundation; include organization and project budgets (including future years' budgets for a continuing project), a Board member list, list of other funding sources, and IRS tax-exempt status documentation. Site visits sometimes are made to organizations being considered for a grant. The Board awards grants at a December meeting.

O+D+T Rosalind H. Kunkel (P+D+Con) — Russell E. Horn, Sr. (S+D+Donor) — William H. Kiick [Hanover] (F+D) — Carole D. Horn (D) — Ralph E. Horn, Jr. (D) — Russell E. Horn, III (D) — Rev. Owen Walter (D) — Corporate donor: Pace Resources, Inc.

CP-096   Horner (Daniel M. & Wilma T.) Foundation   MI-43-53
c/o Allfirst Trust Co. of Pa. N.A.
213 Market Street, P.O. Box 2961   **Phone** 717-255-2174 **FAX** None
Harrisburg 17105   (Dauphin County)   **EIN** 23-6242523   **Year Created** 1956
AMV $827,471   **FYE** 12-00   **(Gifts Received** $0)   5 **Grants totaling** $42,567

One Pa. grant: **$30,000** to Lehigh U. **Out-of-state** giving, all to Charlottesville, VA, includes **$5,000** each to Second Street Gallery and U. of Va./Bayly Art Museum. — In prior years several Central Pa. organizations were supported. ■**PUBLICATIONS:** None ■**WEBSITE:** None ■**E-MAIL:** None ■**APPLICATION POLICIES & PROCEDURES:** Grant requests may be submitted in a letter (3 pages maximum) at any time; include a project outline and budget, financial statement, Board member list, and IRS tax-exempt status documentation. Send requests directly to Edith B. Warner, P.O. Box 186, Free Union, VA 22940.

O+D+T Edith B. Warner [VA] (Co-T+Con) — Joseph A. Macri (VP & Trust Officer at Bank+Manager) — Allfirst Trust Co. of Pa. N.A. (Co-Trustee)

CP-097 Horst (Abram & Marian R.) Foundation
2060 Waterford Drive
Lancaster 17601 (Lancaster County)

MI-41-64
Phone 717-581-9853 **FAX** None
EIN 23-2968157 **Year Created** 1998

AMV $64,934 **FYE** 12-00 **(Gifts Received** $152,800) 2 **Grants totaling** $105,000

High grant of **$90,000** to Lancaster Bible College. **$15,000** to Lancaster Christian School. ■**PUBLICATIONS:** None ■**WEBSITE:** None ■**E-MAIL:** None ■**APPLICATION POLICIES & PROCEDURES:**

O+D+T Marian R. Horst (P+D+Donor+Con) — William R. Horst (S+D) — Robert L. Horst (F+D) — Barbara J. Hess (D) — Judi E. Martin [New Holland] (D) — Marilou Horst Schaffer [Willow Street] (D)

CP-098 Hosfeld (Richard & Mary K.) Memorial Trust #1
c/o Mellon Private Wealth Management
28 Penn Square
Lancaster 17603 (Lancaster County)

MI-11-13-42-56-71-84-89
Phone 717-295-3214 **FAX** None
EIN 25-6377613 **Year Created** 1991

AMV $1,085,924 **FYE** 4-01 **(Gifts Received** $0) 8 **Grants totaling** $32,000

All giving to Shippensburg area. High grant of **$8,000** to Shippensburg U. **$7,000** to Shippensburg Area United Way. **$5,000** each to Friends of Memorial Park Pool and Shippensburg Area Recreation & Parks Commission. **$4,000** to Shippensburg Historical Society. **$1,000** each to Penn Laurel Girl Scout Council, Vigilant Hose Company, and West End Fire & Rescue Company. ■**PUBLICATIONS:** None ■**WEBSITE:** None ■**E-MAIL:** None ■**APPLICATION POLICIES & PROCEDURES:** Only Shippensburg-area organizations are eligible to apply. Grant requests must be submitted on an application form available from the Bank; deadline for applications is January 1st.

O+D+T Charles Hiestand (Trust Officer at Bank+Con) — Mellon Private Wealth Management (Trustee)

CP-099 Hoverter (Lawrence L. & Julia Z.) Charitable Foundation
c/o Goldberg, Katzman & Shipman
320 Market Street, P.O. Box 1268
Harrisburg 17108 (Dauphin County)

MI-31-89
Phone 717-234-4161 **FAX** 717-234-6808
EIN 23-2944271 **Year Created** 1998

AMV $1,348,829 **FYE** 12-00 **(Gifts Received** $0) 1 **Grant of** $25,000

Sole grant to Millerstown Fire Company. — In the prior year, one grant: $25,000 to Perry County Health Center. ■**PUBLICATIONS:** None ■**WEBSITE:** None ■**E-MAIL:** None ■**APPLICATION POLICIES & PROCEDURES:** Information not available.

O+D+T Ronald M. Katzman, Esq. (S+Con) — Lawrence Hoverter [Millerstown] (P+Donor) — Julia Hoverter [Millerstown] (VP+Donor) — Joe Ceceri [Hummelstown] (T) — Amos Miller [Millerstown] (T) — H. Craig Watkins [Camp Hill] (T)

CP-100 Hughes (W. Marshall), Jr. Scholarship Foundation
2201 Ridgewood Road, Suite 180
Reading 19610 (Berks County)

MI-43
Phone Unlisted **FAX** None
EIN 23-6934996 **Year Created** 1988

AMV $278,743 **FYE** 12-00 **(Gifts Received** $0) 4 **Grants totaling** $6,750

All grants are college scholarships—three **$2,000** awards and one **$750** award—for Berks County students pursuing a major in architecture, literature, music, or theatre. ■**PUBLICATIONS:** application guidelines ■**WEBSITE:** None ■**E-MAIL:** None ■**APPLICATION POLICIES & PROCEDURES:** Only students/graduates of a public/private high school in Berks County are eligible to apply; scholarships must be to pursue a major in architecture, literature, music or theatre. Applications must be submitted before the April 15th deadline on a Grant Application form available from the Foundation or from a local high school guidance office; interviews are required as well as auditions, when applicable.

O+D+T W. Marshall Hughes, Jr. (T+Con) — Thomas K. Williams (T) — C. Thomas Work (T)

CP-101 Janssen (Henry) Foundation, The
c/o Tulpehocken Ltd.
2650 Westview Drive
Wyomissing 19610 (Berks County)

MI-11-13-15-19-22-25-31-32-35-41-42-44-45 49-52-53-54-55-56-57-71
Phone 610-678-2426 **FAX** None
EIN 23-1476340 **Year Created** 1931

AMV $24,357,558 **FYE** 12-00 **(Gifts Received** $0) 47 **Grants totaling** $1,131,500

About three-fourths local/Eastern Pa. giving. High grant of **$250,000** to Performing Arts Center. **$124,000** to United Way of Berks County. **$65,000** each to Historical Society of Berks County and Reading-Berks Emergency Shelter. **$60,000** to Berks County Conservancy. **$57,000** to Wyomissing Public Library. **$35,000** to Berks Business Education Coalition. **$30,000** to Reading Public Museum Foundation. **$22,500** to Reading Hospital & Medical Center. **$16,000** to Wyomissing Institute of Fine Arts. **$15,000** each to Lehigh U. and Mercersburg Academy. **$12,000** each to Historic Preservation Trust of Berks County, Reading Symphony Orchestra, and South Mountain YMCA. **$10,000** each to Albright College, Berks County Senior Citizens Council, Caron Foundation, Elizabethtown College, Keystone Arts & Theatre School, Literacy Council of Reading-Berks, Police Athletic League of Reading, Salvation Army/Reading, and WHYY. **$6,500** to Reading Musical Foundation. **$5,000** each to American Cancer Society, Berks Visiting Nurse Assn., Old Dry Road Farm, Pine Creek Valley Watershed Assn., Star Series, and Tulpehocken Settlement Historical Society. **$3,000** to Beacon House. **$2,000** to Reading Choral Society. **Out-of-state** giving includes **$50,000** to Miss Hall's School [MA]; **$20,000** each to Belgrade Regional Conservation Alliance [ME] and Wells College [NY]; **$15,000** each to Belgrade Regional Health Center [ME], Dartmouth College [NH], and Roanoke Valley Speech Center [VA]; and smaller grants to New England and VA for colleges, conservation organizations, or human service agencies. ■**PUBLICATIONS:** None ■**WEBSITE:** None ■**E-MAIL:** None ■**APPLICATION POLICIES & PROCEDURES:** No grants are awarded to individuals.

O+D+T Elroy P. Master (P+T+Con) — John W. Bowman, Jr. (VP+T) — Elizabeth B. Rothermel (S+T) — Elsa M. Hoppman (F+T) — David F. Rick (AF+T) — Sandra M. Keppley (AS)

CP-102 **Jerlyn Foundation**
1170 Cedar Hill Drive
Reading 19605
(Berks County)

MI-12-13-15-16-17-19-22-25-29-41-42-44-52
53-54-57-63-71
Phone 610-378-1606 **FAX** None
EIN 23-2699256 **Year Created** 1992

AMV $2,355,543 **FYE** 12-00 (**Gifts Received** $0) 73 **Grants totaling** $270,451

Mostly local or Pittsburgh giving. Four grants totaling **$46,088** to Carnegie Mellon U. [Pittsburgh] (general support/Trustee pledge/professorship/GSIA pledge). 32,613 to Alvernia College. **$10,000** to Berks County Conservancy. **$8,300** to Wyomissing Institute of Fine Arts. **$6,000** each to Caron Foundation and Red Cross/Reading. **$5,000-$5,500** each to Berks County Senior Citizens Center, Bethany Children's House, Hispanic Center of Reading, Holy Name High School, Lauer's Park School, Olivet Boys & Girls Club, Reading Public Museum, Trinity Lutheran Church of Reading, Wyomissing Area Education Foundation, and Wyomissing Public Library. **$3,000** each to Berks Community TV, Berks County Community Foundation, Central Catholic High School [Pittsburgh], and Police Athletic League of Reading (arts program). **$2,000-$2,500** each to CARE, Concerned Brothers, Great Valley Girl Scout Council, Holy Name High School (scholarship), Lifeline of Berks County, Women's Counseling Services. **$1,000-$1,500** each to American Heart Assn., Beacon House, Berks Women in Crisis, Boy Scouts/Hawk Mountain Council, Children's Home of Reading, Hawk Mountain Sanctuary, Historical Society of Berks County, Holy Rosary Church of Reading, Jesuit Center for Spiritual Growth, Kutztown U. Foundation, Lancaster Country Day School, Mary's Shelter, Mentors for Berks Youth, Rainbow Home, Reading-Berks Habitat for Humanity, Reading Emergency Shelter, Reading Music Foundation, Reading Symphony Orchestra, and St. Monica School [Sunbury]. Other smaller local contributions for similar purposes. **Out-of-state** giving includes **$50,000** to Connecticut College and **$2,000** to a VA church. ■**PUBLICATIONS:** None ■**WEBSITE:** None ■**E-MAIL:** None ■ **APPLICATION POLICIES & PROCEDURES:** The Foundation reports giving primarily to Berks County area organizations;most grants are for annual/operating support, program development or capital campaigns. No grants awarded to individuals. Grant requests may be submitted in a letter at any time; the deadlines are May and November.

O+D+T T. Jerome Holleran (P+Donor+Con) — Carolyn R. Holleran (S+F+Donor)

CP-103 **John Family Foundation**
RR #1, Box 452
Winfield 17889 (Union County)

MI-12-13-14-17-22-25-29-31-32-35-41-42-63
Phone 570-743-7549 **FAX** None
EIN 23-2616038 **Year Created** 1990

AMV $3,635,882 **FYE** 12-00 (**Gifts Received** $209,689) 29 **Grants totaling** $125,000

Mostly local giving; all grants are for general purposes. High grant of **$50,000** to Susquehanna U. **$20,000** to Sunbury Community Hospital. **$10,000** each to Red Cross and Salvation Army. **$5,000** to Evangelical Community Hospital. **$2,000-$3,000** each to Boy Scouts Troop **$533**, Forum for the Future, Make-A-Wish Foundation/Selinsgrove, Second Chance Ministries of Pa. [Camp Hill], Shamokin Area High School Alumni Assn., Sun Home Health Services, and Susquehanna Valley Women in Transition. **$1,000** each to American Heart Assn., Center for Parent-Youth Understanding, Central Pa. Youth Ministries, Fort Discovery, Pa. Partnership for Economic Education, Pa. Special Olympics, Ronald McDonald House [Danville], Tuzzolino Memorial Fund, Watsontown Christian Academy, and Youth Challenge/International Bible Institute. Other smaller local contributions. **Out-of-state** giving: **$1,000** each to Habitat for Humanity [GA] and National Neurofibromatosis Foundation [NY]. ■**PUBLICATIONS:** None ■**WEBSITE:** None ■**E-MAIL:** None ■**APPLICATION POLICIES & PROCEDURES:** Grant requests may be submitted in a letter at any time; detail the purpose of the request.

O+D+T Paul R. John (P+F+Donor+Con) — Mildred D. John (VP+S+Donor) — Robert L. Shangraw [Williamsport] (D)

CP-104 **Jones (Wilbur K.) Foundation**
c/o Allfirst Trust Co. of Pa. N.A.
213 Market Street, P.O. Box 2961
Harrisburg 17105 (Dauphin County)

MI-41-61
Phone 717-255-2174 **FAX** 717-231-2636
EIN 23-6291359 **Year Created** 1963

AMV $539,680 **FYE** 12-00 (**Gifts Received** $0) 4 **Grants totaling** $12,500

No Pa. giving. High grant of **$10,500** to Pope John Paul II High School [FL]. **$500-$1,000** each for religious purposes in AL and CA. — In prior years Pa. grants awarded to George Junior Republic [Mercer County] and Our Lady of Czestochowa Shrine [Bucks County]. ■**PUBLICATIONS:** None ■**WEBSITE:** None ■**E-MAIL:** joe.macro@allfirst.com ■**APPLICATION POLICIES & PROCEDURES:** Grant requests may be submitted at any time in a letter (3 pages maximum); include a project outline and budget, audited financial statement, and IRS tax-exempt status documentation. No grants awarded to individuals.

O+D+T Joseph A. Macri (VP & Trust Officer at Bank+Con) — Loretta K. Press [FL] (P+Co-T) — Allfirst Trust Co. of Pa. N.A. (Co-Trustee)

CP-105 **Jordan (Richard E. & Louise K.) Foundation**
4 Foxtail Court
Mechanicsburg 17055 (Cumberland County)

MI-41-44
Phone Unlisted **FAX** None
EIN 31-1559400 **Year Created** 1997

AMV $416,579 **FYE** 12-00 (**Gifts Received** $6,154) 2 **Grants totaling** $25,100

All local giving. High grant of **$25,000** to West Shore Public Library (capital campaign). **$100** to The Eagle Foundation. — Major grant in the prior year: **$5,000** to The Eagle Foundation (math program). ■**PUBLICATIONS:** None ■**WEBSITE:** None ■**E-MAIL:** None ■**APPLICATION POLICIES & PROCEDURES:** Information not available.

O+D+T Richard E. Jordan, II (P+F+D+Donor+Con) — Louise K. Jordan (VP+D+Donor) — Barbara Jordan Schenck (VP+D) — Sharon N. Jordan (S+D) — Robert C. Sherwood (D) — Richard E. Jordan, III (D) — Clark B. Schenck, III [Lancaster] (D)

CP-106 **Judson (Arthur) Foundation**   MI-52-55
c/o Stevens & Lee
111 North 6th Street, P.O. Box 679   **Phone** 610-478-2000 **FAX** 610-376-5610
Reading 19603   (Berks County)   **EIN** 23-7411037   **Year Created** 1959
AMV $1,273,808   **FYE** 5-01   (**Gifts Received** $0)   16 **Grants totaling** $52,500

Over half SE Pa. giving, mostly to Philadelphia; grants are for general support/expanded operations. High grant of **$7,500** to Philomel Concerts. **$5,000** to Philadelphia Chamber Music Society. **$3,000** each to Art Growth 2000 [Melrose Park], Painted Bride Art Center, and Sylvan Opera. **$2,500** each to Asociacion de Musicos Latino Americanos, Astral Artistic Services, and Orchestra 2001. **$2,000** to Concerto Soloists Chamber Orchestra. **$1,500** to Music Group of Philadelphia. **Out-of-state** giving includes **$5,000** to String Orchestra of New York City and Westfield Symphony Orchestra [NJ] and smaller grants for similar purposes in NJ and NY. ■**PUBLICATIONS:** statement of program policy; application guidelines ■**WEBSITE:** None ■**E-MAIL:** jww@stevenslee.com ■**APPLICATION POLICIES & PROCEDURES:** The Foundation reports that giving focuses on supporting instrumental and/or vocal performances by professional musicians, especially for large audience/mass media performances. Most grants are for general operations, specific programs, or endowment. No grants are ever awarded for bricks & mortar, purchase of musical instruments, or other tangible property. Only rarely do grants exceed $7,500 and generally no multiyear grants are awarded. Prospective applicants initially should make a telephone inquiry about the feasibility of submitting a request. Grant requests should be submitted in a letter or proposal in August (deadline is August 31st) with a detailed description of the project and amount of funding requested; include an annual report, brief history of the organization, organizational and project budgets, audited financial statements for the two most recent complete fiscal years, list of other funding sources, Board members/officers list, and IRS tax-exempt status documentation. Site visits sometimes are made to organizations being considered for a grant. The Board meets in April and September, but most grants are awarded at the Fall meeting.
O+D+T J. William Widing, III, Esq. (S+D+Con) — Alex L. Rosenthal [Elkins Park] (F+D) — Arthur Judson, III [King of Prussia] (D) — Bright Miller Judson [Philadelphia] (D) — Frances Judson Kennedy [UT] (D+Donor) — James S. Kennedy [OR] (D) — Ann St. George [CT] (D) — Bradway G. Widing [TX] (D) — Helen Judson Widing [MA] (D) — Laura Collings Widing [TX] (D)

CP-107 **Key Foundation**   MI-15-16-22-25-32-41-42-62-71-79-83
345 Quarry Road   **Phone** 717-737-7231 **FAX** None
Wellsville 17365   (York County)   **EIN** 23-2894154   **Year Created** 1997
AMV $1,957,419   **FYE** 12-00   (**Gifts Received** $0)   41 **Grants totaling** $105,000

Limited local/Pa. giving; all grants are unrestricted support. High Pa. grants of **$5,000** each to Jewish Home of Harrisburg and U. of Pa. [Philadelphia]. **$2,000** to Temple Beth Shalom. **$1,000** each to Harrisburg Academy, Jewish Family Service, and South Central Pa. Food Bank. Other contributions **$150-$500** for various purposes. **Out-of-state** giving includes **$25,000** to New Israel Fund [DC]; **$10,000** each to American Jewish World Service [NY] and Givat Haviva [NY]; **$5,000** to American Foundation for AIDS Research [NY] and Southern Poverty Law Center [AL]; **$2,000-$2,500** each to American Friends of Peace Now [DC], Earthjustice Legal Defense Fund [CA], National AIDS Fund [DC], Native American Rights Fund [CO], Natural Resources Defense Fund [NY], and Rainforest Action Network [CA]. ■**PUBLICATIONS:** None ■**WEBSITE:** None ■**E-MAIL:** None ■**APPLICATION POLICIES & PROCEDURES:** Grants requests may be submitted in any form at any time. No grants awarded to individuals.
O+D+T Martin Margolis (P+Donor+Con) — Joelle Margolis (S+Donor)

CP-108 **Kinsley Family Foundation**   MI-11-13-14-15-25-35-41-44-55-56-71
RD #1, Box 131AA   **Phone** 717-741-8407 **FAX** None
Seven Valleys 17360   (York County)   **EIN** 23-2870170   **Year Created** 1997
AMV $5,181,177   **FYE** 12-00   (**Gifts Received** $663,010)   44 **Grants totaling** $518,920

Mostly local giving. High grant of **$375,000** to Gettysburg National Battlefield Museum Foundation. **$15,000** to Cultural Alliance of York County. **$10,000-$10,600** each to ARC Foundation of York County, Dreamwrights, and Penn Laurel Girl Scout Council. **$8,500** to United Way of York County. **$5,000** each to Brethren Home Foundation, Boy Scouts/York-Adams Council, Christian School of York, Easter Seals, Farm & Natural Lands Trust, Hanover YMCA, and York Habitat for Humanity. **$4,400** to Strand-Capitol Performing Arts Center. **$4,000** each to Historic York and York Country Day School. **$3,350** to YMCA of York. **$2,500** each to Friends of the Village Library [Jacobus], Golden Vision Foundation, and Susan Byrnes Health Education Center. **$1,000** to Pa. Wildlife Federation. Other local contributions **$100-$500** for various purposes. **Out-of-state** giving includes **$10,000** to Land Preservation Trust [MD]; **$9,000** to St. Paul's School [MD]; and **$5,000** to The Holderness Challenge [NH].
■**PUBLICATIONS:** None ■**WEBSITE:** None ■**E-MAIL:** None ■**APPLICATION POLICIES & PROCEDURES:** Grant requests may be submitted in a letter at any time; give a detailed description of the project, state the funding requested and how it will be utilized, and provide descriptive organizational literature.
O+D+T Anne W. Kinsley (VP+Donor+Con) — Robert A. Kinsley (P+Donor) — Timothy J. Kinsley (S) — Christopher A. Kinsley (F) — Corporate donor: Kinsley Construction, Inc.; Walton & Co.; Gettle, Inc.; I.B. Abel, Inc.

CP-109 **Kline (Josiah W. & Bessie H.) Foundation**   MI-11-13-14-15-22-25-42-44-52-53-54-55-63
c/o Wildeman & Obrock CPAs   72-84
515 South 29th Street   **Phone** 717-561-4373 **FAX** 717-561-0826
Harrisburg 17104   (Dauphin County)   **EIN** 23-6245783   **Year Created** 1952
AMV $25,650,712   **FYE** 12-00   (**Gifts Received** $0)   41 **Grants totaling** $1,287,628

All South Central Pa. giving; grants are for general purposes except as noted. High grants of **$100,000** each to Bethesda Mission (men's center), Dauphin County Library System (relocate Kline Village library), and West Shore Public Library (new construction). **$75,000** each to Harrisburg Area YMCA (facility improvements) and YWCA of Greater Harrisburg (Camp Reily improvements). **$50,000** each to Boy Scouts/Keystone Area Council (camp improvements), Gaudenzia (expansion/renovation), Goodwill Industries of Central Pa. (building program), Lebanon Valley College (classroom/laboratory), United Way of the Capital Region, and Wilson College (library automation). **$40,000** each to Agape Residential Ministries & Services (home for disabled adults), Dickinson College (planetarium/lecture hall construction), Elizabethtown College (information technology in education underwriting), Gettysburg College (Carlisle House renovation), Harrisburg Area Community College Foundation (library automation), Messiah College (Kline Hall of Science improvements), and Susquehanna U. (business building construction). **$33,000** to Paxton Ministries (new furnace). **$26,000** to Boys & Girls Club of Central Pa. (roof replacement). **$25,000** each to Carlisle Family YMCA (camp capital campaign), Harrisburg Symphony Orchestra (concerts/bassoon position sponsorship). Mechanicsburg Area Meals on Wheels (freezer), and Susquehanna Art Museum (Kunkel Building renovations). **$20,000** to Channels Food Rescue. **$12,750** to WITF-TV (program underwriting). **$10,000** each to Music at Gretna (concerts), Neighborhood Center of the United Methodist Church (new roof), and Setebait Services/Harrisburg Diabetic Youth Camp. **$5,000-$5,900** each to Art Assn. of Harrisburg (equipment), Harrisburg Opera Assn. (production support), Humane Society of Harrisburg Area (exterior signage), and Linking Individuals with Non-Medical Congregational Support Services [Hershey] (program seed money). **$2,000-$3,500** each to Gretna Productions/Theatre (performances), Leukemia Society of America/Central Pa. Chapter (project), Marysville-Rye Library Assn. (heating-cooling replacement), National MS Society/Central Pa. Chapter (educational program), and The Second Mile (summer camp scholarships). ■**PUBLICATIONS:** application guidelines; Application for Consideration of Grant Request Form ■**WEBSITE:** None ■**E-MAIL:** None ■**APPLICATION POLICIES & PROCEDURES:** The Foundation reports that all giving is limited to the South Central Pa. area for (a) private colleges and universities, (b) hospitals or institutions for crippled children, (c) other benevolent or charitable institutions, and (d) scientific or medical research performed by scientists in colleges, universities, or research institutions. Most grants are for building or capital funds, special projects, research, scholarship funds, or matching funds; multiyear awards are made. No grants are awarded to individuals, and generally not for regular operations of established programs, to campaigns of national organizations, or for religious programs. Normally grants are not awarded to State-affiliated schools, colleges or universities. Also, no loans are made. Grant requests may be submitted at any time but must be on the Application for Consideration of Grant Request Form, available from the Foundation. Site visits sometimes are made to organizations being considered for a grant. The Board of Directors awards grants May and November meetings.

O+D+T John A. Obrock, CPA (S+Con) — Robert F. Nation [Camp Hill] (P+D) — William J. King [Dauphin] (VP+F+D) — Derek C. Hathaway [Camp Hill] — Samuel D. Ross, Jr. [Carlisle (D) — John A. Russell [Hershey] (D) — James E. Marley [Elliottsburg] (D) — David A. Smith, M.D. [New Cumberland] (D)

CP-110 Kozloff Family Charitable Trust
c/o Northeastern Distributing Company
1150 Bern Road
Wyomissing 19610   (Berks County)

MI-11-13-22-25-32-41-62

Phone 610-374-2242 **FAX** None
EIN 23-7680042   **Year Created** 1991

AMV $1,726,343   **FYE** 12-00   (**Gifts Received** $20,000)   48 **Grants totaling** $138,613

About four-fifths local giving. High grant of **$30,350** to Jewish Federation of Reading. **$30,000** to Jewish Community Center of Reading. **$23,100** to Lancaster Country Day School. **$10,150** to Reform Congregation Oheb Sholom. **$7,500** to United Way of Berks County. **$1,930** to Boy Scouts/Hawk Mountain Council. **$1,600** each Olivet Boys & Girls Club. **$1,000** to Reading-Berks Emergency Shelter. **$800** to Easter Seals. Other local contributions **$100-$450** for various purposes. **Out-of-state** giving includes **$9,200** to Jewish Federation of Palm Beach [FL]; **$5,000** to Dana Farber Cancer Institute [MA]; and **$3,850** to Angels of Charity [FL]. ■**PUBLICATIONS:** None ■**WEBSITE:** None ■**E-MAIL:** None ■**APPLICATION POLICIES & PROCEDURES:** Grant requests may be submitted in writing at any time.

O+D+T Paul J. Kozloff (D+Con) — Allen Kozloff (D) — Lauren Kozloff Sinrod (D) — Corporate donor: Northeastern Distributing Co.

CP-111 Kuentzel (Agnes Douglas) Foundation
1113 Nissley Road
Lancaster 17601   (Lancaster County)

MI-14-16-22-31-42-43-82

Phone 717-560-8387 **FAX** None
EIN 23-2895347   **Year Created** 1997

AMV $366,993   **FYE** 12-00   (**Gifts Received** $0)   7 **Grants totaling** $23,000

No Pa. giving. **Out-of-state** giving includes **$5,000** each to Davidson College [NC] (scholarship) and Lakeland College [WI] (scholarship). **$4,000** to Rehabilitation Institute of Chicago (support medically indigent musicians); **$3,000** each to Church World Service [IN] (disaster relief) and Southern Poverty Law Center [AL]; **$2,000** to Committee for Racial Justice [OH]; and **$1,000** to Presbyterian Peacemaking [MO] (land mines removal). ■**PUBLICATIONS:** None ■**WEBSITE:** None ■**E-MAIL:** None ■**APPLICATION POLICIES & PROCEDURES:** Information not available.

O+D+T Agnes Douglas Kuentzel (P+S+T+Donor+Con) — John D. Kuentzel [NJ] (T) — P. Craig Kuentzel [WI] (T) — Walter F. Kuentzel [VT] (T)

CP-112 Kunkel (John Crain) Foundation
1010 Brentwater Road, P.O. Box 658
Camp Hill 17011   (Cumberland County)

MI-13-15-31-41-44-51-55-71-89

Phone 717-763-1284 **FAX** None
EIN 23-7026914   **Year Created** 1965

AMV $13,890,362   **FYE** 12-00   (**Gifts Received** $0)   13 **Grants totaling** $626,800

All local giving; grants are for general purposes except as noted. High grant of **$200,000** to Homeland Center. **$150,000** to YWCA of Harrisburg. **$100,000** to Whitaker Center for the Arts. **$50,000** to West Shore Public Library (building fund). **$25,000** each to Allied Arts Fund, and Harrisburg Academy. **$20,000** to Friends of Wildwood Lake Park. **$17,800** to Keystone Partnership. **$15,000** to Camp Hill Borough. **$10,000** to Camp Hill Fire Company #1. **$5,000** each to Popcorn Hat Players and

Ned Smith Center. **$4,000** to Harrisburg Housing Authority. — Grants approved for future payment: **$600,000** to Pinnacle-Health Foundation and **$200,000** to Fredrickson Public Library (building fund). ■ **PUBLICATIONS:** None ■ **WEBSITE:** None ■ **E-MAIL:** None ■ **APPLICATION POLICIES & PROCEDURES:** Written grant requests for a specific project may be submitted in any form at any time.

O+D+T Nancy Wright Bergert (Executive Trustee+Con) — Elizabeth Kunkel Davis (T) — Deborah L. Facini (T) — John C. Kunkel, II (T) — Paul A. Kunkel (T) — John K. Stark (T) — Jay W. Stark (T) — William T. Wright (T)

CP-113   Lamade (Howard J. & George R.) Foundation   MI-14-22-29-31-42-44
c/o Lamco Communications, Inc.
460 Market Street, Suite 310
Williamsport 17701   (Lycoming County)   **Phone** 570-323-2252 **FAX** 570-323-2298
                                                                   EIN 24-6012802   **Year Created** 1958
AMV $413,821   **FYE** 12-00   (**Gifts Received** $0)   13 **Grants totaling** $17,000

All local giving. High grants of **$2,500** each to American Rescue Workers and Red Cross. **$2,000** each to Lycoming College and Williamsport Hospital. **$1,500** to James V. Brown Library. **$1,000** each to Hope Enterprises, Salvation Army, North Central Sight Services, and Williamsport Library. Other contributions **$500** each for various purposes. ■ **PUBLICATIONS:** None ■ **WEBSITE:** None ■ **E-MAIL:** None ■ **APPLICATION POLICIES & PROCEDURES:** The Foundation reports that most giving is limited to Lycoming and nearby counties. Grant requests may be submitted in writing at any time; provide a detailed description of the project and amount of funding requested, and include a project budget, listing of other funding sources, and IRS tax-exempt status documentation. Site visits sometimes are made to organizations being considered for a grant.

O+D+T Advisory Committee members: Andrew W. Stabler, Jr. (C+Con) — James S. Lamade — Howard J. Lamade, Jr. — J. Robert Lamade — M&T Bank (Trustee)

CP-114   LAMCO Foundation   MI-13-22-42-56-84
c/o Lamco Communications, Inc.
460 Market Street, Suite 310
Williamsport 17701   (Lycoming County)   **Phone** 570-323-2252 **FAX** 570-323-2298
                                                                   EIN 24-6012727   **Year Created** 1958
AMV $499,652   **FYE** 12-00   (**Gifts Received** $0)   4 **Grants totaling** $13,733

About two-thirds local giving. High grant of **$5,000** to Little League Baseball. **$3,333** to Lycoming County Historical Society. **$400** to Shepherd of the Streets. **Out-of-state** grant: **$5,000** to The Campaign for King College [IN]. — In prior years other local giving for cultural and civic purposes. ■ **PUBLICATIONS:** None ■ **WEBSITE:** None ■ **E-MAIL:** None ■ **APPLICATION POLICIES & PROCEDURES:** The Foundation reports that most giving is limited to Lycoming and nearby counties. No grants awarded to individuals. Grant requests may be submitted in writing at any time; provide a detailed description of the project and amount of funding requested, and include a project budget, listing of other funding sources, and IRS tax-exempt status documentation. Site visits sometimes are made to organizations being considered for a grant. — Formerly called The Grit Foundation.

O+D+T Advisory Committee members: Andrew W. Stabler, Jr. (C+Con) — James S. Lamade — Howard J. Lamade, Jr. — J. Robert Lamade — M&T Bank (Trustee)

CP-115   Lancaster County Foundation, The   MI-12-13-14-15-16-17-25-31-33-35-39-41-43
29 East King Street, Suite 221   44-45-49-52-53-54-55-56-71-85
P.O. Box 1745   **Phone** 717-397-1629 **FAX** 717-397-6877
Lancaster 17608   (Lancaster County)   **EIN** 23-6419120   **Year Created** 1924
AMV $34,340,737   **FYE** 4-02   (**Gifts Received** $2,042,717)   78 **Grants totaling** $1,046,750

As a Community Foundation all discretionary giving is limited to organizations serving Lancaster County; 64 grants awarded from unrestricted/discretionary funds. **ARTS & CULTURE GRANTS:** **$16,800** to Lancaster Opera Company (costume shop renovation/inventory). **$16,000** to Fulton Opera House (Youtheatre for disadvantaged-disabled teens). **$10,362** to Long's Park Amphitheater Foundation (sound system enhancement). **$10,000** to Pa. Academy of Music (public awareness/outreach program). **$6,000-$7,500** each to Demuth Foundation (art-in-a-box program), Hands-On House Children's Museum (family workshop), Historic and Preservation Trust of Lancaster County (Stevens-Smith historic site educational program). **$3,750-$5,000** each to Heritage Center Museum of Lancaster (phone system), James Buchanan Foundation-Wheatland (document preservation-cataloging), Lancaster Museum of Art (educational materials for exhibit), Lancaster Summer Arts Festival (children's summer series), Landis Valley Associates (educational materials/museum programs), and Memorial Park Assn.-Reamstown (improve band shell). **$2,500** to Gretna Music (computer). **EDUCATION GRANTS:** **$12,000** to Janus School (science program greenhouse). **$9,000** to Lancaster County Historical Society (day camps on Underground Railroad). **$8,800** to North Museum (natural history collection upgrading). **$7,000** to Pa. School of Art & Design (new website design curriculum). **$5,250-$5,665** each to 32nd Degree Masonic Learning Centers for Children (video monitoring equipment), Junior Achievement of Central Pa. (recruitment equipment), and Literacy Council of Lancaster/Lebanon (volunteer recruitment brochure). **$4,114** to Lititz Public Library (electronic magnifier). **$2,500-$3,605** each to Leadership Lancaster (youth program), Linden Hall School for Girls (link historic records with local libraries), and Parish Resource Center (scholarship fund for needy churches). **$645** to Mount Joy Area Historical Society (security system). **ECONOMIC DEVELOPMENT GRANTS:** **$50,000** to Community First Fund (start-up assistance for minority/women-owned businesses). **$36,400** to SACA Development (home rehabilitation for low-income families). **$5,600** to Lancaster Housing Opportunity Partnership (community education materials). **ENVIRONMENT GRANTS:** **$20,000** to Lancaster Farmland Trust (Leacock Township land preservation). **$7,000** to Strasburg Community Parks (open air amphitheater). **$5,100** to Lancaster County Conservancy (outdoor education interns). **$3,850** to Furnace Run/Segloch Run Watershed (high school ecology program materials). **HUMAN SERVICES & HEALTH GRANTS:** **$50,000** to SouthEast Lancaster Health Services (van for preventive dental care in schools). **$30,000** to Milagro House (transitional house purchase). **$25,000** each to Schreiber Pediatric Rehab Center (recreational therapy satellite program) and YWCA of Lancaster (programs expansion). **$22,500** to Clare House (children's study-play center). **$20,000** to Tabor Community Services (homeownership training). **$19,000** to Ephrata Area Social Services (van). **$16,000** to Willow Street Lions Club (install kitchen). **$14,000-$15,000** each to ICAN/Involved Consumer Action Network (van), Lancaster Emergency Medical Services Assn. (CPR/other equipment), Phil-haven (recreation room furnishing), Red Cross/Susquehanna Valley Chapter (CPR/Safety training for Amish workers), Visiting Nurse Assn. (training updates), and YMCA of Lancaster (camp program for at-risk youth). **$12,000-$12,737** each to Lancaster Mediation Center (volunteer training materials), Light House Rehabilitation Center/Vocational (client transportation), Partners Achieving Independence (expanded adult day care program), and Salvation Army (latchkey program equipment). **$10,000-$10,904** each to CAP-Head Start (handicapped-accessible playground), CAP-Lancaster Shelter for Abused Women (child care for residents' children), Lancaster Crime Commission (citywide conference), Special Olympics/Lancaster County (modified bowling alleys), and Urban League of Lancaster County (on-site access to CareerLinks). **$6,000-$7,200** each to Lancaster Day Care Center (classroom flooring), Lancaster Cleft Palate Clinic (parent education), The Lodge of Pa. (financial services for disabled residents), and United Disabilities Services (respite apartment). **$4,000-$5,500** each to Boys & Girls Club of Lancaster (employment readiness program), Contact-Lancaster Helpline (telephone equipment), East Side Athletic Club (equipment), Family Service (thera-play program), Lancaster Heart Foundation (prescription assistance for needy clients), Long Home (telephone system upgrading), Mental Health Assn. in Lancaster County (mental health care seminar), Partners for a Healthier Tomorrow (training/peer mediation materials), and Pinnacle Health Hospital/Childhood Lead Poisoning Prevention Program (program promotion/supplies). **$3,000-$3,500** each to MidPenn Legal Services (program for families transitioning from welfare), Planned Parenthood of the Susquehanna Valley (glucose monitor), Southern End Community Assn. (handicapped-assessible restrooms), and Susquehanna Assn. for the Blind & Vision Impaired (summer program). **$1,400-$2,500** each to Boy Scouts/Pa. Dutch Council (anti-drug brochure), Hospice of Lancaster County (schools program), Lancaster Area Victim Offender Reconciliation Program (volunteer training materials), New Hope Community Life Ministry (book/video library for counseling clients). **$905** to Lititz Community Center (children's play area). All other grants and scholarships were awarded from donor-advised, donor-designated, or otherwise restricted funds. ■**PUBLICATIONS:** Annual Report; How To Apply For A Grant brochure; grant application form ■**WEBSITE:** www.lancastercountyfoundation.org ■**E-MAIL:** info@lancastercountyfoundation.org ■**APPLICATION POLICIES & PROCEDURES:** Only Lancaster County organizations are eligible for support from unrestricted/discretionary funds. The Foundation encourages requests for new programs, new dimensions of existing programs, seed monies for new services, equipment integral to new programs, new capital facilities or expansion of services, and proposals for matching grants. Generally no grants are awarded directly to individuals, or for projects outside Lancaster County (unless in collaboration with the Foundation); sectarian religious programs; government/tax-supported agencies; endowment; building funds; budget deficits; routine operating expenses, including salaries; retroactive project expenses; or more than one project of an agency. Beginning 2003, grants will be awarded semiannually, and a two-step application process initiated: (1) Submit a Letter of Interest before the early January or mid-June deadlines; and then (2) about five or six weeks later, submit a formal application form with supporting documentation. For detailed application instructions, required forms, and specific deadlines, contact the Foundation or consult the website. Also, prospective grant applicants may attend the Foundation's annual grantseekers workshop for guidance/information. Site visits sometimes are made to organizations being considered for a grant. Grant awards are announced in April and October.

O+D+T Deborah B. Schattgen (Executive Director+Con) — Rev. John R. Baldwin (C+D) — Rev. David L. Gockley (VC+D) — Carol Gundel Falk (D) — William D. Fisher (D) — S. Dale High (D) — Dawn K. Johnston (D) — J. Roger Moyer, Jr. (D) — Bruce P. Ryder, Esq. (D) — W. Jeffrey Sidebottom, Esq. (D) — representatives of 12 local banks comprise the Bank Trustees Committee

---

CP-116   **Laverty (George W.) Foundation**   MI-31-32
c/o Allfirst Trust Co. of Pa. N.A.
213 Market Street, P.O. Box 2961   **Phone** 717-255-2174   **FAX** 717-231-2636
Harrisburg   17105   (Dauphin County)   **EIN** 23-2102516   **Year Created** 1980
AMV $1,229,439   **FYE** 3-01   **(Gifts Received** $0)   3 **Grants totaling** $33,962

All giving restricted to medical/surgical research. High grant of **$17,912** to York Health System. **$10,500** to Penn State Geisinger System. **$5,500** to PinnacleHealth System. ■**PUBLICATIONS:** None ■**WEBSITE:** None ■**E-MAIL:** joe.macro@allfirst.com ■**APPLICATION POLICIES & PROCEDURES:** The Foundation reports that all giving is limited to medical/surgical research to prevent disease with preference given to local medical institutions. No grants awarded to individuals. Submit grant requests in a letter between January and April (deadline is May 31st); include a project budget, Board member list, and list of other funding sources. Decisions on grants are made at a June meeting.

O+D+T Joseph A. Macri (VP & Trust Officer at Bank+Con) — Allfirst Trust Co. of Pa. N.A. (Co-Trustee)

CP-117   **Lavin (Katharine Masland) Foundation**   MI-12-13-41-63-84
497 Orlando Avenue   **Phone** 814-238-1547   **FAX** None
State College   16803   (Centre County)   **EIN** 23-6296612   **Year Created** 1955
AMV $348,560   **FYE** 12-00   **(Gifts Received** $0)   12 **Grants totaling** $21,000

About half local/Pa. giving. **$3,000** to State College Assembly of God (youth football program and children's ministry). **$2,000** each to Centre County Youth Service Bureau (Big Brother/Big Sister Program) and Chi Alpha Christian Fellowship (university student outreach). **$1,500** to Church Farm School [Chester County]. **$1,000** to Child Evangelism Fellowship [Boalsburg]. **Out-of-state** giving includes **$2,000** for evangelical Christian organizations in several states. ■**PUBLICATIONS:** None ■**WEBSITE:** None ■**E-MAIL:** None ■**APPLICATION POLICIES & PROCEDURES:** The Foundation reports that unsolicited requests are not accepted; grants are made on the recommendation of individual trustees and approval by the Board.

O+D+T Peter Masland Lavin (F+T+Con) — Cynthia Lavin Hurley [MA] (T) — Michael B. Hurley [MA] (T) — Ruth Ann Lavin (T)

CP-118 **Lebanon Mutual Foundation**
c/o Lebanon Mutual Insurance Company
137 West Penn Ave., P.O. Box 2005
Cleona   17042   (Lebanon County)

MI-11-13-31-32-35-41-42-71

Phone 717-272-6655   **FAX** 717-274-1746
EIN 23-2521649   **Year Created** 1984

AMV $304,264   **FYE** 12-00   (**Gifts Received** $0)   14 **Grants totaling** $16,025

All local giving; grants are for general purposes except as noted. High grant of **$5,000** to Lebanon Valley College (Heilman Center for Physical Therapy). **$3,000** to Harrisburg Area Community College. **$2,500** to United Way of Lebanon County. **$1,000-$1,500** each to American Cancer Society, Good Samaritan Hospital (emergency room), Lebanon Valley Educational Partnership, and Lebanon Valley Rails to Trails. **$500** to Lebanon Valley YMCA. Other local contributions **$25-$250**. ■**PUBLICATIONS:** None ■**WEBSITE:** www.lebins.com/ [Corporate info only] ■**E-MAIL:** None ■**APPLICATION POLICIES & PROCEDURES:** The Foundation reports that giving focuses on the Lebanon area with most grants for building/renovations or general operating support. No grants awarded to individuals. Grant requests may be submitted in a letter, preferably in May or November; detail the proposed use of funds and include IRS tax-exempt status documentation. Grants are awarded at June and December meetings.
O+D+T Rollin Rissinger, Jr. (P+D+Con) — Darwin Glick (VP+D) — Keith A. Ulsh (F+D) — Milton Garrison (D) — Mark J. Keyser (D) — S. Bruce Kurtz (D) — Joseph Lauck (D) — Warren Lewis (D) — William Schadler (D) — Corporate donor: Lebanon Mutual Insurance Co.

CP-119 **Levan Family Foundation, The**
c/o Levan Family LLC
1094 Baltimore Pike
Gettysburg   17325   (Adams County)

MI-13-25-32-41-55-84-85

Phone Unlisted   **FAX** None
EIN 23-2899050   **Year Created** 1997

AMV $1,465,761   **FYE** 12-00   (**Gifts Received** $0)   5 **Grants totaling** $124,000

All local/Pa. giving. High grant of **$100,000** to Main Street Gettysburg. **$10,000** each to Adams County Homeless Shelter and Gettysburg Recreation Dept (building fund). **$2,000** to Adams County Art Council. **$1,000** each to American Cancer Society and Houston School [Montgomery County]. ■**PUBLICATIONS:** None ■**WEBSITE:** None ■**E-MAIL:** None ■**APPLICATION POLICIES & PROCEDURES:** Grant requests may be submitted at any time, but must be on an application form available from the Foundation; include a copy of the IRS tax-exempt status documentation.
O+D+T David M. Levan (C+P+D+Donor+Con) — Todd M. Levan [Philadelphia] (VP+D) — Jennifer S. Levan (S+F+D) — Burton K. Stein [West Conshohocken] (D)

CP-120 **Light of the World Foundation**
260 North Jackson Street, P.O. Box 310
Strasburg   17579   (Lancaster County)

MI-22-63

Phone 717-687-4220   **FAX** None
EIN 23-2871256   **Year Created** 1996

AMV $1,043,070   **FYE** 12-00   (**Gifts Received** $0)   4 **Grants totaling** $49,500

Mostly local giving. High grant of **$36,500** to Worship Center Ministries. **$10,000** to James S. Herr Foundation [Chester County]. **$2,500** to National Day of Prayer. **$500** to Mission Aviation Fellowship [CA]. ■**PUBLICATIONS:** None ■**WEBSITE:** None ■**E-MAIL:** None ■**APPLICATION POLICIES & PROCEDURES:** Information not available.
O+D+T Glenn Eshelman (P+D+Donor+Con) — Shirley R. Eshelman (S+F+D+Donor)

CP-121 **Long (Andrew C.) Foundation**
c/o John Woytowich & Company
101 West Independence Street
Shamokin   17872   (Northumberland County)

MI-11-13-14-21-43-44-61

Phone 570-644-0341   **FAX** None
EIN 22-2807255   **Year Created** 1986

AMV $201,240   **FYE** 12-00   (**Gifts Received** $0)   9 **Grants totaling** $22,000

All local giving; all grants are unrestricted support. High grants of **$5,000** each Our Lady of Lourdes (development fund) and United Way of Shamokin. **$4,000** to Shamokin/Coal Township Public Library. **$2,000** each to ARC Northumberland County and Hope Springs Equestrian Therapy. **$1,500** to Coal Township High School Scholarship Fund. **$1,000** to Shamokin Lodge F&AM 255. **$750** each to Boy Scouts/Williamsport and Girl Scouts/Shamokin. ■**PUBLICATIONS:** None ■**WEBSITE:** None ■**E-MAIL:** None ■**APPLICATION POLICIES & PROCEDURES:** The Foundation reports giving primarily to/for the Shamokin area; no grants awarded to individuals.
O+D+T John Woytowich, CPA (T+Con) — Community Banks N.A. (Corporate Trustee)

CP-122 **Long (Robert F.) Foundation**
300 Belvedere Street, P.O. Box 39
Carlisle   17013   (Cumberland County)

MI-11-13-14-41-42
Phone 717-243-7995   **FAX** None
EIN 22-2719260   **Year Created** 1985

AMV $276,684   **FYE** 12-00   (**Gifts Received** $0)   7 **Grants totaling** $25,500

All local giving. High grant of **$10,000** to Trinity High School. **$5,000** each to Center for Industrial Training and Carlisle YMCA. **$3,000** to United Way of Carlisle. **$1,000** each to Dickinson College and FOCUS. **$500** to Assn. of Independent Colleges & Universities of Pa. ■**PUBLICATIONS:** None ■**WEBSITE:** None ■**E-MAIL:** None ■**APPLICATION POLICIES & PROCEDURES:** No grants awarded to individuals.
O+D+T Robert F. Long (P+T+Con) — Benjamin James (T) — Katherine Long (T)

CP-123 Lowengard (Leon) Scholarship Foundation
c/o Harrisburg Area Community College
Financial Aid Office, One HACC Drive
Harrisburg 17110   (Dauphin County)

MI-43

Phone 717-780-2330 **FAX** None
EIN 23-6236909   **Year Created** 1937

AMV $4,303,335   **FYE** 9-00   **(Gifts Received** $0)   22 **Grants totaling** $127,087

All giving limited to scholarships for Greater Harrisburg area high school graduates. The tuition-only awards—ranging from about **$1,500** to **$21,000**—are for undergraduate or graduate study at any college/university, not just H.A.C.C. ■**PUBLICATIONS:** None ■**WEBSITE:** www.hacc.edu/services/finaid/pdfs/lowengrd_app.pdf ■**E-MAIL:** admit@hacc.edu ■**APPLICATION POLICIES & PROCEDURES:** Only high school graduates from Greater Harrisburg are eligible to apply with clear preference given to applicants of the Jewish faith. A formal application form, available from the Foundation (or on the website), must be submitted during January-March; the deadline is April 1st. State the amount of support needed and include personal and financial data, and a copy of the latest high school or college transcript. Decisions on awards are made in June.

O+D+T Director of Financial Aid (Con) — David Sanchez (D) — Mellon Bank N.A. (Trustee)

CP-124 Mann Family Foundation, The
c/o Donsco, Inc.
North Front Street, P.O. Box 2001
Wrightsville 17638   (Lancaster County)

MI-41-63-71-85

Phone 717-252-1561 **FAX** None
EIN 23-2683304   **Year Created** 1992

AMV $557,338   **FYE** 12-00   **(Gifts Received** $0)   2 **Grants totaling** $101,000

All local giving. High grant of **$100,000** to Hourglass Foundation. **$1,000** to Lancaster Foundation for Educational Enrichment. — Giving in the prior year included **$9,000** to The Pasadena Symphony [CA]; **$5,000** to First Presbyterian Church of Lancaster; and **$1,000** to Lancaster Farmland Trust. ■**PUBLICATIONS:** None ■**WEBSITE:** None ■**E-MAIL:** None ■**APPLICATION POLICIES & PROCEDURES:** No grants awarded to individuals.

O+D+T Arthur K. Mann, Sr. (P+D+Con) — Arthur K. Mann, Jr. (VP+D)

CP-125 Masland (Charles H. & Annetta R.) Foundation
497 Orlando Avenue
State College 16803   (Centre County)

MI-13-14-22-29-31-41-42-43-63

Phone 814-238-1547 **FAX** None
EIN 23-6296887   **Year Created** 1948

AMV $1,183,713   **FYE** 12-00   **(Gifts Received** $0)   13 **Grants totaling** $80,000

About one-third Pa. giving. High Pa. grant of **$9,000** to Wilson College [Franklin County] (annual giving). **$8,000** to Abington Friends School [Montgomery County] (scholarships). **$6,000** to Carlisle YMCA [Cumberland County] (general support). **$2,000** to Associated Services for the Blind [Philadelphia] (Braille production/custom services). **Out-of-state** giving includes **$10,000** to Healthcare Ministries [MO] (medical team support); **$8,000** to Mission Viejo Christian School [CA] (scholarships); **$7,000** each to Red Cross [DC] (international relief) and Victorious Living Ministries [NY] (AIDS children orphanage/scholarships); and smaller grants, mostly for Christian-mission-related projects. ■**PUBLICATIONS:** None ■**WEBSITE:** None ■**E-MAIL:** pml4@psu.edu ■**APPLICATION POLICIES & PROCEDURES:** The Foundation reports that unsolicited requests are not accepted; grants are made on the recommendation of individual trustees and approval by the Board.

O+D+T Peter Masland Lavin (S+F+T+Con) — David M. McCoy [NC] (C+T) — Cynthia M. Lavin [MA] (T) — Frank E. Masland, III [Carlisle] (T) — Christopher H. Stetser [FL] (T) — Virginia Stetser [FL] (T)

CP-126 McCormick (Anne) Trust
c/o Allfirst Trust, M.C. 001-02-05
213 Market Street, P.O. Box 2961
Harrisburg 17105   (Dauphin County)

MI-11-12-13-14-29-31-42-51-52-54-55

Phone 717-255-2045 **FAX** 717-231-2636
EIN 23-6471389   **Year Created** 1969

AMV $9,225,658   **FYE** 12-00   **(Gifts Received** $0)   19 **Grants totaling** $447,500

All giving restricted to Dauphin, Cumberland, Lancaster, Lebanon, Perry and York counties. High grant of **$250,000** to Pinnacle-Health System. **$50,000** to United Way of the Capital Region. **$31,000** to Goodwill Industries of Central Pa. **$25,000** to Susquehanna Art Museum. **$15,000** each to Allied Arts Fund and Theatre Harrisburg. **$10,000** each to Dickinson College and Perry County Council of the Arts. **$7,500** to Carlisle Family YMCA. **$5,000** each to Big Brothers & Big Sisters of the Capital Region, Harrisburg Opera, and Red Cross. **$4,000** to Ronald McDonald House Charities. **$3,000** each to ARC of Dauphin County and Art Assn. of Harrisburg. **$2,000-$2,500** each to Area M Special Olympics, Gaudenzia, Opera Outreach, and Tri-County Assn. for the Blind. ■**PUBLICATIONS:** None ■**WEBSITE:** None ■**E-MAIL:** larry.hartman@allfirst.com ■**APPLICATION POLICIES & PROCEDURES:** Only organizations in Dauphin, Cumberland, Lancaster, Lebanon, Perry and York counties are eligible to apply. No grants are awarded to individuals. Grant requests may be submitted in a full proposal at any time; include an organizational budget, project budget, audited financial statement, and IRS tax-exempt status documentation. Site visits sometimes are made to organizations being considered for a grant.

O+D+T Larry A. Hartman (Senior VP at Bank+Con) — Allfirst Trust (Trustee)

CP-127 McCormick (Anne) Trust for Charitable Purposes
c/o Allfirst Trust, M.C. 001-02-05
213 Market Street, P.O. Box 2961
Harrisburg 17105   (Dauphin County)

MI-14-15-32-52-54-71

Phone 717-255-2045 **FAX** 717-231-2636
EIN 23-6508184   **Year Created** 1967

AMV $245,791   **FYE** 12-00   **(Gifts Received** $0)   1 **Grant of** $13,500

All giving limited to Dauphin, Cumberland and Perry counties. Sole grant to Hospice of Central Pa. — Grants awarded in prior years included: **$5,000** to Susquehanna Art Museum; **$3,500** to Friends of Wildwood Lake Nature Center; and **$2,000** each to Music at Gretna and United Cerebral Palsy of the Capital Area. ■**PUBLICATIONS:** None ■**WEBSITE:** None ■**E-MAIL:** larry.hartman@allfirst.com■**APPLICATION POLICIES & PROCEDURES:** Only organizations in Dauphin, Cumberland, or Perry counties are eligible to apply. Submit requests in a full proposal at any time; include an organizational budget, project budget, audited financial report, annual report, and IRS tax-exempt status documentation. Site visits sometimes are made to organizations being considered for a grant.
O+D+T Larry A. Hartman (Senior VP at Bank+Con) — Allfirst Trust (Trustee)

CP-128 McCormick (Margaret T. Ogilvie) Charitable Trust
c/o Allfirst Trust, M.C. 001-02-05
213 Market Street, P.O. Box 2961
Harrisburg 17105   (Dauphin County)

MI-14-31-32-42-51-52-55-57

Phone 717-255-2045 **FAX** 717-231-2636
EIN 25-6407465   **Year Created** 1987

AMV $4,034,156   **FYE** 12-00   **(Gifts Received** $0)   11 **Grants totaling** $212,500

All giving limited to Greater Harrisburg. High grant of **$75,000** to Strand-Capitol Performing Arts Center. **$62,000** to Messiah College. **$26,250** to PinnacleHealth System (Camp Dragonfly). **$20,000** to Harrisburg Symphony. **$10,000** to WITF-TV. **$5,000** each to Elizabethtown College and Metro Arts of the Capital Region. **$3,250** to Mt. Gretna Theatre. **$3,000** to Area M Special Olympics. **$2,000** to Kidney Foundation of Central Pa. **$1,000** to Harrisburg Cemetery Assn. ■**PUBLICATIONS:** None ■**WEBSITE:** None ■**E-MAIL:** larry.hartman@allfirst.com ■**APPLICATION POLICIES & PROCEDURES:** The Trust reports that giving is restricted to religious, charitable, scientific, literary, or educational purposes in the City of Harrisburg and vicinity. Submit requests in a letter at any time; state the purpose, scope of the project, and the amount of funding requested.
O+D+T Larry A. Hartman (Senior VP at Bank+Con) — Allfirst Trust (Trustee)

CP-129 McCormick (Vance) Trust for Local Charities
c/o Allfirst Trust, M.C. 001-02-05
213 Market Street, P.O. Box 2961
Harrisburg 17105   (Dauphin County)

MI-13-15-19-32-41-52-57-63

Phone 717-255-2045 **FAX** 717-231-2636
EIN 23-6508188   **Year Created** 1946

AMV $653,735   **FYE** 12-00   **(Gifts Received** $0)   8 **Grants totaling** $36,000

All giving limited to Greater Harrisburg. High grant of **$12,500** to Paxton Ministries. **$5,000** each to Gaudenzia, Jake Gittlen Memorial Golf Tournament, and WITF-TV. **$1,500-$2,500** each to Council for Public Education, Harrisburg Cemetery Assn., Hospice of Central Pa., and Music at Gretna. ■**PUBLICATIONS:** None ■**WEBSITE:** None ■**E-MAIL:** larry.hartman@allfirst.com ■**APPLICATION POLICIES & PROCEDURES:** Only organizations located in City of Harrisburg or vicinity are eligible to apply. No grants awarded to individuals. Submit grant requests in a full proposal at any time; include both organizational and project budgets, audited financial statement, and IRS tax-exempt status documentation. Site visits sometimes are made to organizations being considered for a grant.
O+D+T Larry A. Hartman (Senior VP at Bank+Con) — Allfirst Trust (Trustee)

CP-130 McDowell (S. Ira) Foundation Trust
c/o Mellon Bank/Private Asset Mgmt. Group
204 North George Street, Suite 290
York 17401   (York County)

MI-12-13-14-15-22-29-31-34-35-44-55-63-64

Phone 717-846-4075 **FAX** 717-843-0072
EIN 23-6465481   **Year Created** 1969

AMV $580,553   **FYE** 11-00   **(Gifts Received** $0)   42 **Grants totaling** $95,000

Most giving limited to the City of York/York County; all grants are for operating support. High grant of **$23,000** to St. Paul's United Church of Christ [Dallastown]. **$8,000** each to Bethany United Methodist Church and Hoffman Homes for Youth. **$5,000** each to Jefferson Medical College [Philadelphia] and York Health Foundation. **$3,000** each to Salvation Army and York Rescue Mission. **$2,000** each to Access York, Boy Scouts/York-Adams Area Council, Margaret E. Moul Home, Penn-Mar Organization, and St. John's Blymire Church of Christ. **$1,000** each to Agape Residential Ministries & Service, Atkins House, Bell Socialization Services, Susan P. Byrnes Health Education Center, Children's Home of York, Community Progress Council, Contact York, Crispus Attucks Assn., Easter Seals, Family Service of York/York County, Good News Counseling, Leave A Legacy, Lancaster Theological Seminary, Lehman Center, Martin Library, New Life for Girls, OPEN, Pa. Special Olympics, Penn Laurel Girl Scout Council, Planned Parenthood of Central Pa., Strand Capital Performing Arts Center, Summit Grove Christian Conference Center, Visiting Nurse Assn. of York, York Benevolent Assn., York Catholic High School, York County Council of Churches, York Hospital (Growth & Development Center), York YMCA, and York YWCA. ■**PUBLICATIONS:** None ■**WEBSITE:** None ■**E-MAIL:** None ■**APPLICATION POLICIES & PROCEDURES:** The Trust reports York County/City organizations receive primary consideration. Grant requests may be submitted in a letter during August-September—deadline is October 1st; clearly state the purpose and amount of funding requested, and include IRS tax-exempt status documentation. The Trustees award grants at a November meeting.
O+D+T Angela R. Thompson (Trust Officer at Bank+D+Con) — Paula Belt (D) — John Herzog (D) — Pauline K. Lecrone (D) — Mellon Bank N.A. (Trustee)

CP-131 **Mellinger (R. & R.) Medical Research Memorial Fund**   MI-32
c/o Fulton Financial Advisors N.A.
One Penn Square, P.O. Box 3215   **Phone** 717-291-2523 **FAX** None
Lancaster 17604   (Lancaster County)   **EIN** 23-2823954   **Year Created** 1995
AMV $287,666   **FYE** 2-01   **(Gifts Received** $0)   2 **Grants totaling** $12,330

All local giving for medical research. High grant of **$9,864** to Penn State College of Medicine/Hershey Medical Center. **$2,466** to Lancaster Heart Foundation. ■**PUBLICATIONS:** None ■**WEBSITE:** None ■**E-MAIL:** None ■**APPLICATION POLICIES & PROCEDURES:** The Foundation reports that only requests from Pa. residents for medical research are accepted. Grant requests may be submitted in a letter at any time; provide details of the proposed medical research program.

O+D+T Vincent J. Lattanzio (Trust Officer at Bank+Con) — John S. May, Esq. (Co-T) — Fulton Financial Advisors N.A. (Co-Trustee)

CP-132 **Miller (Edwill B.) Trust**   MI-13-31-42-63
c/o Allfirst Trust Co. of Pa. N.A.
21 East Market Street - MC 402-120   **Phone** 717-852-3068 **FAX** 717-852-3050
York 17401   (York County)   **EIN** 23-6657558   **Year Created** 1977
AMV $3,561,456   **FYE** 3-01   **(Gifts Received** $0)   14 **Grants totaling** $235,053

All local giving; 95% of annual income is disbursed to designated organizations, primarily Protestant churches, hospitals, youth agencies and colleges in Central Pa., and the remaining 5% (**$12,662**) was awarded on a discretionary basis to non-profit organizations in South Central Pa., as follows: **$2,500** to YWCA of York. **$1,500** each to Mental Health Assn. of York and York Literacy Council. **$1,000** each to Access-York, The Lehman Center, Make-A-Wish Foundation, Strand-Capitol Performing Arts Center, and York Health Foundation (Wellspan). **$912** to Leadership York. **$750** to Martin Library. **$500** to Penn-Mar Organization. ■ **PUBLICATIONS:** None ■**WEBSITE:** None ■**E-MAIL:** arlene.lapore@allfirst.com ■**APPLICATION POLICIES & PROCEDURES:** The Trust reports that York County organizations receive first preference in discretionary giving. Grant requests may be submitted in a letter (2 pages maximum) in January or August; include an annual report, organizational/project budgets, list of Board members, and IRS tax-exempt status documentation. Decisions on discretionary grants are made by the Bank's Trust Committee in March and September.

O+D+T Arlene C. Lapore (VP & Trust Officer at Bank+Con) — Allfirst Trust Co. of Pa. N.A. (Trustee)

CP-133 **Miller (Henry M. & Beatrice B.) Foundation**   MI-18-22-29-72
4708 Galen Road   **Phone** See below **FAX** None
Harrisburg 17110   (Dauphin County)   **EIN** 23-6282470   **Year Created** 1954
AMV $259,786   **FYE** 12-00   **(Gifts Received** $0)   9 **Grants totaling** $14,000

Two Pa. grants: **$2,000** to American Friends Service Committee [Philadelphia] (Haiti Fund). **$300** to Hadassah/Harrisburg. **Out-of-state** giving includes **$3,000** to Poor People's Fund [MA]; and **$2,000-$2,500** each to International Planned Parenthood [NY], Massachusetts SPCA, and Partners in Health [MA]. ■**PUBLICATIONS:** None ■**WEBSITE:** None ■**E-MAIL:** None ■ **APPLICATION POLICIES & PROCEDURES:** Grant requests may be submitted in any form at any time to Linda Miller, 2284 Maple Hill Road, Shaftsbury, VT 05262; telephone 802-375-6773. No grants awarded to individuals.

O+D+T Linda Miller [MA] (VP+S+F+Con) — Beatrice B. Miller (P)

CP-134 **Miller (Marlin), Jr. Family Foundation**   MI-12-13-18-25-42-45-54
211 North Tulpehocken Road   **Phone** 610-777-5159 **FAX** None
Reading 19601   (Berks County)   **EIN** 23-2591890   **Year Created** 1989
AMV $719,289   **FYE** 12-00   **(Gifts Received** $0)   17 **Grants totaling** $2,514,078

About half local/Pa. giving; grants are annual fund gifts except as noted. High Pa. grant of **$739,672** to Foundation for the Reading Public Museum. **$511,406** to Carnegie Mellon U. **$108,500** to Boy Scouts/Hawk Mountain Council (mostly capital campaign). **$25,000** to Berks County Emergency Shelter. **$10,000** to Planned Parenthood of NE Pa./Berks County. **$5,000** each Penn State U. (capital campaign). **$2,500** to Children's Home of Reading. **$2,000** to Literacy Council of Reading. **$1,000** to Albright College (Freedman Gallery). **Out-of-state** giving includes **$1,069,000** to Alfred U. [NY]; **$15,000** to WXXI-TV [NY]; and five **$5,000** grants to New England for cultural, historical and conservation purposes. ■**PUBLICATIONS:** None ■**WEBSITE:** None ■**E-MAIL:** None ■**APPLICATION POLICIES & PROCEDURES:** Grant requests may be submitted in a letter at any time; describe in detail the proposed project and state an amount requested. No grants awarded to individuals.

O+D+T Marlin Miller, Jr. (T+Donor+Con) — Douglas Miller (T) — Eric Miller (T) — James H. Miller [NY] (T) — Regina Miller (T)

CP-135 **Motter Foundation, The**   MI-11-12-16-22-25-29-31-32-41-42-55-56-89
c/o KBA North America
3900 East Market Street   **Phone** 717-505-1150 **FAX** 717-505-1165
York 17402   (York County)   **EIN** 23-6280401   **Year Created** 1961
AMV $1,094,278   **FYE** 2-01   **(Gifts Received** $0)   42 **Grants totaling** $61,000

All local giving. High grant of **$25,000** to Strand-Capitol Performing Arts Center. **$4,500** to United Way of York County. **$5,500** to Red Cross. **$3,000** each to Janus School and York College of Pa. **$2,000** each to Bill Goodling Teacher Scholarship Foundation, York County Day, and York Day Nursery & Kindergarten. **$1,000** each to American Heart Assn., Crispus Attucks Center, Memorial Health Systems Corp., Springetts Fire Company, York Habitat for Humanity, York Health System Children's Fund, York Health Systems, York Heritage Trust, and York Rescue Mission. Other local contributions **$100-$500** for various community organizations. ■**PUBLICATIONS:** None ■**WEBSITE:** None ■**E-MAIL:** None ■**APPLICATION POLICIES & PROCEDURES:** The Foundation reports all giving limited to the York area; most grants are for annual or general, operating support. No grants awarded to individuals. Grant requests may be submitted in a letter at any time.

O+D+T Frank Motter (C+T+Con) — Edward L. Motter (S+T) — Corporate donor: Motter Printing Press Company

CP-136 **Moyer Memorial Foundation**
c/o Apfelbaum, Apfelbaum & Apfelbaum
43 South 5th Street
Sunbury   17801   (Northumberland County)

MI-12-13-22-25-41-42-44-55-84-89

Phone 570-286-1582 **FAX** 570-286-5349
EIN 23-2689605   **Year Created** 1992

AMV $1,171,426   **FYE** 12-00   **(Gifts Received** $0)   34 **Grants totaling** $36,447

All giving restricted to organizations serving children/youth in Snyder and Northumberland counties; grants are for general purposes except as noted. High grant of **$3,000** to City of Sunbury (ice rink/children's skates). **$1,000-$1,500** each to Kauffman Public Library (acquisitions), Priestly Forsyth Memorial Library (acquisitions), Snyder County Historical Society (youth program computers), Snyder County Library (acquisitions), and Susquehanna U. (science dept.). **$800** to Haven Ministries (shelter supplies for children). **$750** to Music Gazebo Program of Selinsgrove. Other contributions **$50-$700** to local organizations, schools, or local government agencies serving children/youth, or for scholarships. Other grants are disbursed as directed under terms of the donor's will. ■**PUBLICATIONS:** application guidelines; application form ■**WEBSITE:** www.moyer-fdn.org ■**E-MAIL:** None ■**APPLICATION POLICIES & PROCEDURES:** The Foundation reports that only Snyder or Northumberland County organizations (or municipal units) aiding children 18 years and under are eligible for support. Most grants are for program development, special projects, equipment providing new organizational capabilities, and capital campaigns. Rarely are grants awarded to cover all costs of a project; broad-based community support through contributions from local citizenry and volunteerism is viewed favorably. No funding is given for annual campaigns, general endowment, operating budgets, religious or political activities, mass mailings, or to individuals for any purpose. Occasionally the Foundation may initiate and fund projects of special interest to the Foundation. Since application guidelines are quite explicit and detailed, and a formal grant application form must be completed, prospective applicants must first secure these, as posted on the website. Personal visits to the Foundation are discouraged. Inquiries and grant requests are accepted throughout the year. — Formerly called Fern & Gladys Moyer Foundation

O+D+T Distribution Committee members: Jeffrey Apfelbaum, Esq. (Con) — Michael M. Apfelbaum, Esq. (Con) — Sidney Apfelbaum, Esq. (Co-T) — Jill Fecker — Scott A. Heintzelman [Selinsgrove] — Margaret Keller [Port Trevorton] — Mary Jane Mitterling [Selinsgrove] — Sun Bank (Co-Trustee)

CP-137 **Murry (E.E.) Foundation**
c/o E.E. Murry Realty, Inc.
1899 Lititz Pike
Lancaster   17601   (Lancaster County)

MI-11-12-13-14-15-17-22-25-29-39-63-89

Phone 717-569-0495 **FAX** None
EIN 23-1948416   **Year Created** 1974

AMV $4,375,566   **FYE** 12-00   **(Gifts Received** $1,036,060)   30 **Grants totaling** $547,200

Limited local giving. High Pa. grant of **$15,000** to Milagro House (capital expenditure). **$5,000** each to United Way of Lancaster County. **$2,000-$2,500** each to COBYS Youth Services, HARB-Adult, Schreiber Pediatric Rehabilitation, and Water Street Rescue Mission. **$1,000** each to Grandview Heights Methodist Church, Hospice of Lancaster County, Lancaster County Opportunity Partnership, Pa. Special Olympics, Rotary Foundaiton, Salvation Army, Mom's House, and United Disabilities Services. Also,11 grants/contributions **$250-$1,000** to local fire departments or ambulance corps, and other local contributions for various purposes. **Out-of-state** grants: **$500,250** to Hillcrest Home [AR] and **$1,000** to Johns Hopkins Oncology Center [MD]. ■**PUBLICATIONS:** None ■**WEBSITE:** None ■**E-MAIL:** None ■**APPLICATION POLICIES & PROCEDURES:** The Foundation reports that grants are mostly for annual campaigns, capital campaigns, or building/renovation. Grant requests may be submitted in a letter at any time; describe the organization and purpose of the requested funding, and include IRS tax-exempt status documentation.

O+D+T Emanuel E. Murry (T+Con) — Barbara K. Demchyk (T) — William E. Murry (T) — Corporate donors: E.E. Murry Construction Company; Murry Development Corporation; Wm. Murry & Son; Wheatland Arms

---

CP-138 **Naugle (Carl & Nellie) Foundation**
c/o Allfirst Trust Co. of Pa. N.A.
55 South Main Street, P.O. Box 459
Chambersburg   17201   (Franklin County)

MI-11-32-34-42-44-57-63-72-84-85-89

Phone 717-261-2822 **FAX** 717-263-1630
EIN 23-6266566   **Year Created** 1955

AMV $637,963   **FYE** 12-00   **(Gifts Received** $0)   16 **Grants totaling** $31,600

Most giving limited to the Shippensburg area. High grant of **$4,000** to Shippensburg United Way. **$3,000-$3,700** each to Grace United Church of Christ, Shippensburg Borough Park & Recreation Dept., and Shippensburg U. Foundation. **$2,000** each to Cumberland Valley Animal Hospital, Kings Kettle, and Shippensburg Little League. **$1,000-$1,500** each to Chambersburg Hospital, Cumberland Valley Hose Co., D.O.I.T., Penn State College of Medicine, Shippensburg Borough Industrial Development, Shippensburg Public Library, Vigilant Hose Co., West End Fire & Rescue Co., and WITF-TV. ■**PUBLICATIONS:** None ■**WEBSITE:** None ■**E-MAIL:** None ■**APPLICATION POLICIES & PROCEDURES:** The Foundation reports that giving is generally restricted to the Shippensburg area; most grants are for general operating support, special projects or building funds of local organizations. Submit grant requests at any time in a letter which outlines the proposed project; and include a financial statement. Grant decisions are made monthly.

O+D+T Alan B. Rhinehart (Trust Officer at Bank+Con) — Elmer E. Naugle (P) — Nellie I. Naugle (Donor) — Allfirst Trust Co. of Pa. N.A. (Trustee)

CP-139 **Naugle (Elmer E.) Foundation**
c/o Allfirst Trust Co. of Pa. N.A.
55 South Main Street, P.O. Box 459
Chambersburg   17201   (Franklin County)

MI-11-31-42-44-84-89

Phone 717-261-2822 **FAX** 717-263-1630
EIN 23-6853070   **Year Created** 1986

AMV $535,145   **FYE** 7-00   **(Gifts Received** $39,750)   18 **Grants totaling** $26,900

All giving limited to Shippensburg area. High grant of **$7,200** to Shippensburg Borough Park & Recreation Dept. **$3,000** to Shippensburg United Way. **$2,500** to Shippensburg U. Foundation. **$1,200-$1,400** each to Carlisle Hospital, Chambersburg

Hospital, Cumberland Valley Hose Company, Shippensburg Public Library, Vigilant Hose Company, and West End Fire & Rescue Company. **$600-$800** to other community organizations for animal welfare, sports, history, education, youth, and family services. ■**PUBLICATIONS:** None ■**WEBSITE:** None ■**E-MAIL:** None ■**APPLICATION POLICIES & PROCEDURES:** Only organizations serving the Shippensburg area are eligible to apply. Grant requests may be submitted in a letter at any time—deadline is September 15th; outline the proposed project and include financial statements and IRS tax-exempt status documentation.

O+D+T Alan B. Rhinehart (Trust Officer at Bank+Con) — Elmer E. Naugle (P+Donor) — Allfirst Trust Co. of Pa. N.A. (Trustee)

CP-140 **Neag (Ray & Lynn Wood) Charitable Foundation**
1216 Old Mill Road
Wyomissing 19610   (Berks County)
AMV $685,596   **FYE** 6-00   (**Gifts Received** $0)

MI-11-42-54-63
Phone 610-478-3115 **FAX** None
EIN 23-2712023   **Year Created** 1992
3 **Grants totaling** $141,702

Mostly local/Pa. giving; all grants were in the form of securities. High grant of **$25,588** to Trinity Church (parish fund). **$18,518** to Penn State U. **Out-of-state** grant: **$$11,165** to Yale U. [CT]. — Grants awarded in the prior year: **$105,110** to United Way of Berks County; **$91,651** to U. of Connecticut; **$30,834** to Penn State U.; and **$5,000** to Reading Museum (DaVinci service). ■**PUBLICATIONS:** None ■**WEBSITE:** None ■**E-MAIL:** None ■**APPLICATION POLICIES & PROCEDURES:** The Foundaiton reports that most grants are for operating support or scholarship funds. No grants awarded to individuals.

O+D+T Ray Neag (T+Donor+Con) — Harriet H. Lawson [CT] (T) — Nancy Neag Satalino [CT] (T)

CP-141 **Nestor Charitable Foundation**
c/o Reiff and Nestor Company
Reiff & West Streets, P.O. Box 147
Lykens 17048   (Dauphin County)
AMV $590,770   **FYE** 6-01   (**Gifts Received** $0)

MI-13-23-41-42-44-61-63-84
Phone 717-453-7113 **FAX** None
EIN 23-6255983   **Year Created** 1952
51 **Grants totaling** $31,064

All local/Pa. giving. High grant of **$3,000** each to Our Lady Help of Christians Church, Upper Dauphin Area School District, and Williams Valley School District. **$2,000-$2,500** each to Dauphin County Library System/Northern Dauphin, Lykens & Wiconisco Baseball Assn., Lykens & Wiconisco Softball Assn., Northern Dauphin County YMCA, and Upper Dauphin Area Legion Baseball. **$900** to Assn. of Independent Colleges & Universities of Pa. **$1,250** for food certificates for local needy families. **$600** to St. John's Lutheran Church of Berrysburg. Other contributions **$50-$500** for various Central Pa. and **Out-of-state** organizations. ■**PUBLICATIONS:** None ■**WEBSITE:** None ■**E-MAIL:** None ■**APPLICATION POLICIES & PROCEDURES:** Grant requests from local organizations may be submitted in a letter at any time; include any necessary descriptive background information.

O+D+T Donald E. Nestor (P+Con) — Robin M. Nestor (S) — Corporate donor: Reiff & Nestor Company

---

CP-142 **Nestor (Mary Margaret) Foundation**
c/o Reiff & Nestor Company
Reiff & West Streets, P.O. Box 147
Lykens 17048   (Dauphin County)
AMV $134,717   **FYE** 6-01   (**Gifts Received** $0)

MI-43
Phone 717-453-7113 **FAX** None
EIN 23-6277570   **Year Created** 1953
45 **Grants totaling** $20,500

All grants are scholarships, **$250, $500** or **$750** each, for Dauphin County residents. ■**PUBLICATIONS:** None ■**WEBSITE:** None ■**E-MAIL:** None ■**APPLICATION POLICIES & PROCEDURES:** Scholarship awards are restricted to Dauphin County residents. Submit applications in a letter at any time for scholarship support and to request a resume for detailing academic/personal achievements.

O+D+T Donald E. Nestor (P+F+Con) — Robin M. Nestor (S) — Corporate donor: Reiff & Nestor Co.

CP-143 **Nitterhouse (William K.) Charitable Foundation**
c/o Nitterhouse Concrete Products
2655 Molly Pitcher Highway, P.O. Box N
Chambersburg 17201   (Franklin County)
AMV $507,998   **FYE** 6-01   (**Gifts Received** $32,200)

MI-11-42-54-63-85
Phone 717-264-6154 **FAX** 717-267-4549
EIN 23-2493715   **Year Created** 1987
49 **Grants totaling** $34,352

Mostly local giving. High grant of **$15,000** to Central Presbyterian Church. **$2,500** to Shippensburg U. **$1,000** each to Messiah College, Renfrew Museum, and United Way of Franklin County. **$667** to Chambersburg Chamber of Commerce Foundation. **$600** to American Cancer Society. Other local contributions **$25-$500** for various community organizations. **Out-of-state** grant: **$5,000** to World Center for Concrete Technology [MI]. ■**PUBLICATIONS:** None ■**WEBSITE:** None ■**E-MAIL:** None ■ **APPLICATION POLICIES & PROCEDURES:** The Foundation reports that requests are accepted only from Franklin County organizations; most grants are for general support, special projects, building funds, and capital drives. No grants awarded to individuals.

O+D+T William K. Nitterhouse (T+Donor+Con) — Karen Nitterhouse Diller (T) — Diane R. Nitterhouse (T) — Corporate donors: Nitterhouse Concrete Products; WCN Properties

---

CP-144 **North American Railway Foundation**
105 North Front Street, Suite 307
P.O. Box 867
Harrisburg 17108   (Dauphin County)
AMV $13,305,563   **FYE** 9-00   (**Gifts Received** $3,131,742)

MI-54-56-85
Phone 717-232-8696 **FAX** 717-232-0982
EIN 25-1801614   **Year Created** 1996
Grants totaling $0

Nationwide giving is limited to railway safety/technology projects and preservation of railroad history. Foundation-supported projects in recent years have included the following: construction of a 'hands on learning' educational center at the Railroad Museum of Pa. [Altoona]; a 'Crossing Safely' program to promote public awareness of the dangers of railroad crossings; restoration of railroad photographs, negatives and artifacts in several museum collections; a documentary video about the technological advancements of high speed trains in Europe and how they could benefit North American transportation; and a campaign to promote high speed rail in the United States. ■**PUBLICATIONS:** None ■**WEBSITE:** www.narfoundation.org/ ■**E-MAIL:** narf00@earthlink.net ■**APPLICATION POLICIES & PROCEDURES:** The Foundation's mission is to explore, nurture and support railway safety, efficiency and technology and to educate about and preserve the history of railroads in the United States and Canada. As an Operating Foundation, it works actively and directly with coordinators of projects it has selected to support. Outright grants are awarded only infrequently and, therefore, unsolicited grant requests are not encouraged. However, prospective applicants may make an initial telephone inquiry to discuss a project's feasibility. Grant requests must be submitted on letterhead paper and signed by the organization's CEO on behalf of its governing body; briefly describe the purpose of the project with a specific dollar amount stated; include background information on the organization, project/organizational budgets, Board member list, audited financial statement, and IRS tax-exempt status documentation.

O+D+T Philip J. Sullivan, II (Executive Director+Con) — Richard J. Myers (C+D) — Thomas W. Jackson (VC+D) — Mark Robb [Canada] (S+D) — O.J. Foisy [Canada] (D) — K.L. Mayle [CA] (D) — P.L. Wingo, Jr. [TN] (D) — M.A. Wofford [IN] (D) — Donor: Brotherhood's Relief & Compensation Fund

---

CP-145 **Ortenzio Family Foundation, The**
 4718 Old Gettysburg Road, Suite 405
 Mechanicsburg   17055   (Cumberland County)
AMV $4,253,020   **FYE** 12-00   (**Gifts Received** $56,403)

MI-13-22-41-42-43-61
Phone 717-972-1305   **FAX** None
EIN 23-6805409   **Year Created** 1986
17 **Grants totaling** $215,000

All local/Pa. giving; many grants comprise multiple payments. High grant of **$92,100** to Bishop McDevitt High School (tuition assistance/gym renovations). **$55,300** to Prince of Peace Elementary School [Steelton] (tuition assistance/computers). **$30,000** to Diocese of Harrisburg (classroom expansion). **$10,000** each to Dickinson School of Law (endowment), and St. Patrick's Cathedral School (tuition assistance). **$5,000** each to Catholic Charities (Lourdes House/memorial gift). CURE International [Lemoyne], and West Chester U. (football scholarship/CLIMT project/annual fund). **$1,000** each to Cathedral Parish of St. Patrick and Harrisburg YMCA (annual support). Other smaller contributions. ■**PUBLICATIONS:** None ■**WEBSITE:** None ■**E-MAIL:** None ■**APPLICATION POLICIES & PROCEDURES:** The Foundation reports that giving focuses on Roman Catholic educational institutions (tuition, scholarships, or other assistance) for qualified, financially-needy students; first preference is given to students who are members of St. Ann's Church, Steelton. Grant requests may be submitted in a letter at any time; describe the need and state the funding needed.

O+D+T Robert A. Ortenzio [Camp Hill] (T+Con) — John M. Ortenzio (T) — Martin J. Ortenzio [MD] (T) — Rocco A. Ortenzio [Lemoyne] (T+Donor)

CP-146 **Oxford Foundation**
 125-D Lancaster Ave.
 Strasburg   17579
        (Lancaster County)
AMV $62,681,937   **FYE** 12-01   (**Gifts Received** $122,498)

MI-12-13-21-22-25-29-31-32-35-39-41-42-43
44-52-54-55-56-71-63-64-71-81-89
Phone 717-687-9335   **FAX** 717-687-9336
EIN 23-6278067   **Year Created** 1947
187 **Grants totaling** $3,010,843

About four-fifths Central/SE Pa. giving; grants are for general operations/annual giving except as noted; many grants comprise multiple awards. High grant of **$485,516** to U. of Pa. Medical Center (John H. Ware, III Chair in Alzheimer's Research). **$315,000** to Swarthmore College (mostly Parrish Hall renovations). **$132,857** to U. of Pa. (nursing gerontology chair/scholarships). **$105,000** to Southern Chester County YMCA (mostly capital campaign). **$75,000** to Fund for Capitol Visitors Center [Harrisburg] (general operations/capital campaign). **$60,000** to Upland Country Day School (campaign fund). **$50,000** each to Lancaster Country Day School (endowment/capital campaign), Regional Performing Arts Center (endowment), and YWCA of Chester. **$45,000** each to Chester County Historical Society (general support/education/endowment) and Union Fire Co. #1/Fire Division (mostly endowment). **$43,750** to Brandywine Conservancy (mostly for farmland preservation program). **$38,000** to Oxford Area Civic Assn. (endowment/annual fund). **$37,100** to Pa. Academy of Music (property acquisition/program sponsorship/annual fund). **$36,333** to Thaddeus Steven Foundation (mostly campaign fund). **$36,000** to Silvan S. Tompkins Institute [Philadelphia] (equipment). **$34,084** to Oxford Borough Office & Public Works Dept. (gift fund). **$30,000-$31,000** each to Mercersburg Academy (capital campaign/annual fund), Oxford Educational Foundation (endowment/annual fund), Sacred Heart Church of Oxford (capital campaign), and YWCA of Lancaster (mostly capital campaign). **$28,000-$29,000** each to Boy Scouts/Pa. Dutch Council (endowment/general support), City of Chester (school resource officer program), North Museum of Natural History & Science (science education program), and Oxford Library. **$25,000** each to Capitol Ministries [Harrisburg] (capital ministry program), Coatesville Center for Community Health (new center), Eisenhower Exchange Fellowships [Philadelphia] (fellowships), Franklin & Marshall College (research/annual fund), Russell Byers Charter School Fund [Philadelphia], and Union Fire Co. #1/Ambulance Division (mostly endowment). **$22,000** each to Boys Club & Girls Club of Lancaster (mostly for clubhouse), Janus School (mostly restaffing costs), and Samaritan Counseling Center (mostly neuropsychology program/development program). **$20,000** each to Lancaster Theological Seminary (building renovations), Penn State U./School of Forest Resources (Goddard Chair), Pa. School of Art & Design (facility acquisition), Philadelphia Museum of Art (challenge grant), and Rocky Springs Carousel Assn. (carousel restoration/utilization). **$17,800** to Octorara Watershed Assn. (matching fund/general operations). **$17,000** to Ware Presbyterian Village. **$15,000-$16,000** each to Canine Partners for Life (security system/annual fund), Chester County Children's Service, Chester County Community Foundation (public education programs/women's fund), Chester County Dept. of Aging (emergency fund), Chester County Futures (Oxford portion), Family Service of Lancaster (house renovation), HDC3 Corporation (fair housing development), Lancaster Museum of Art (expansion project), Pa. Ballet (Lancaster performance), Red Cross/SE Pa. Chapter (mostly for earthquake relief), and United Disabilities Services [Lancaster] (PR/marketing). **$13,000** to Hospital of the U. of Pa. (nurse training/annual fund). **$12,000** to Salvation Army/Lancaster (Chapel/multipurpose room/annual fund). **$9,000-$10,000** each to 4-H Center of Chester County (indoor horse ring), Alliance Project of Lebanon (children's health facility), Lancaster County Foundation (Afghan U.), Lancaster Family

YMCA (capital campaign readiness), Lancaster General Hospital Foundation (osteoporosis center), Library System of Lancaster (African-American literary program), Neighborhood Services Center for Oxford, Oxford Presbyterian Church, Penn State College of Medicine [Hershey] (clinical research), Please Touch Museum, Stroud Water Research Center, Susquehanna Assn. for the Blind & Vision Impaired (building), United Way of Lancaster County, and Vantage/Gaudenzia (capital campaign). **$7,500-$8,000** each to Boy Scouts/Cradle of Liberty Council (programs), Delaware County Board of Fire & Life Safety (honor guard), Milagro House, and Women's Way. **$4,900-$6,000** each to Children's Hospital of Philadelphia (vaccine education center), Deaf & Hard of Hearing Services of Lancaster, FatherBirth [Uwchlan] (publication), HARB-Adult (drug testing kits), Lancaster Farmland Trust, Parish Resource Center of Lancaster (Forward in Faith campaign), Pa. Partnerships for Children (mostly endowment), Providence Forum [Bryn Mawr] (Liberty Bell project), Strasburg Community Parks Foundation (park construction), Tabor Community Services (case management support), and Widener U. **$3,000-$4,000** each to Bournelyf Special Camp (pool), Boy Scouts/Chester County Council, Friends Assn. for Care & Protection of Children, Heritage Center Museum of Lancaster County (regional history day competition), Lancaster Crime Commission, Lancaster Heart Foundation (film documentary), Lighthouse Youth Center, Neighborhood Services Center of Lancaster, Oxford Area Civic Assn., PennPIRG Education Fund (Preserving Pa. project), WITF-TV, and YWCA of Coatesville. Also, 62 other local grants/contributions **$500-$2,500** for similar purposes. **Out-of-state** giving includes **$75,000** to American Enterprise Institute [DC] (capital fund); **$25,000** each to The Conservation Fund [VA] (Lancaster activity) and Vice President's Residence Foundation [DC] (rehabilitation); **$15,000** to Beth Israel Deaconess Medical Center [MA] (spine fellowship program); **$10,000** to West Nottingham Academy [MD] (computer lab/library); and other smaller grants for conservation and other purposes. ■**PUBLICATIONS:** None. ■**WEBSITE:** www.oxfordfoundation.org ■**E-MAIL:** pcalhoun@oxfordfoundation.org ■**APPLICATION POLICIES & PROCEDURES:** The Foundation reports priority interests as health, early childhood development, education, youth programs, arts/culture, and public policy planning with giving focused on Lancaster and Chester counties and Philadelphia; most grants are for specific projects, endowments and, occasionally, general operations. No grants are awarded to individuals or for loans. Grant applicants must submit a brief Letter of Inquiry which includes a description of the organization, its mission and history, and a 1-page summary of the the proposed project with approximate budget, a list of other possible funding sources, and expected project accomplishments and how they will be achieved. All inquiries are acknowledged, either with an explanation of a denial or a request for a full proposal which must be submitted before the September 15th deadline; the required proposal format/elements are available on the website or available on request. Only one grant application per year may be submitted for any given project. When appropriate, Foundation staff will arrange for a meeting or an informal site visit.

O+D+T Philip L. Calhoun (Executive Director+Con) — Paul W. Ware [Lancaster] (C+P+D) — John H. Ware, IV [Oxford] (VP+D) — Marilyn Ware (S+D) — Carol Ware Gates [Christiana] (F+D) — Marian S. Ware (Chairman Emeritus)

CP-147 **Packer (Horace B.) Foundation**
c/o Carson Consumer Discount Company
70 Main Street, P.O. Box 732
Wellsboro 16901 (Tioga County)

MI-12-13-17-29-31-41-42-43-44-51-52-55
84-89
Phone 570-724-1800 **FAX** 570-724-1661
EIN 23-6390932 **Year Created** 1940

AMV $5,076,293 **FYE** 12-00 **(Gifts Received** $0) 36 **Grants totaling** $244,520

All giving restricted to Tioga County; grants are for general purposes except as noted. High grant of **$78,571** to Mansfield U. Foundation (scholarships). **$30,000** to Borough of Mansfield (swimming facilities). **$20,000** to Pa. College of Technology (scholarships). **$10,000** to His Thousand Hills (challenge course). **$8,000** to Valley Nypum Children (building interior). **$6,000** each to Knoxville Library System (computer services), Northern Tioga School District (school band) and Wellsboro Little League (field improvements). **$5,000-$5,400** each to Franciscan Health Center (new equipment), Girl Scouts (center renovations), Hamilton Gibson Productions (theater production), Martha Lloyd Community Services (renovations), Tioga County 4-H Clubs (show ring renovations), Tioga County Human Services Agency (greenhouse), and Wellsboro Cemetery Co. (site improvements). **$4,000-$4,700** each to Partners in Progress (summer camp), Southern Tioga School District (scholarships), Tioga County FIT (health risk appraisals), Tioga County Women's Coalition (house upgrading), Trinity Lutheran School (basketball court), and Wellsboro Area School District (scholarships). **$3,094** to Borough of Wellsboro (street beautification). **$3,000** to Wellsboro Parks & Recreation (football equipment/uniforms). **$2,000** each to Big Brothers Big Sisters (local startup costs) and Tioga County Leadership Foundation. Other local grants/contributions **$500-$1,800** for similar purposes. ■**PUBLICATIONS:** application guidelines; application form ■**WEBSITE:** None ■**E-MAIL:** None ■**APPLICATION POLICIES & PROCEDURES:** The Foundation reports that only organizations serving Tioga County citizens are eligible to apply. Most grants are for special projects, building funds, matching grants, and scholarships. Prospective applicants initially should make a telephone inquiry about the feasibility of submitting a request. Grant requests must be submitted on an Application for Charitable Funds form, available from the Foundation; completed applications must include a Board member list, financial statements and IRS Form 990s for the three prior fiscal years, and IRS tax-exempt status documentation. Requests should be submitted in April or September (deadlines are May 1st and October 1st). Site visits sometimes are made to organizations being considered for a grant. The Trustees award grants at May and October meetings.

O+D+T Carl E. Carson (P+D+Con) — Edward H. Owlett, Esq. (VP+D) — Hon. Robert M. Kemp (S+D) — David Kupinsky, Esq. [Williamsport] (F+D) — R. James Dunham (D) — Rev. Gregory P. Hinton (D) — Rhonda Litchfield (D) — Harold D. Hershberger, Jr. [Williamsport] (Co-T) — M&T Bank (Corporate Trustee)

CP-148 **Pennsylvania Dutch Company Foundation, The**
c/o The Pennsylvania Dutch Company
366 Belvedere Street
Carlisle 17013 (Cumberland County)

MI-42-43-56-57-84-86

Phone 717-761-5440 **FAX** None
EIN 23-2022526 **Year Created** 1976

AMV $1,268 **FYE** 10-00 **(Gifts Received** $41,400) 18 **Grants totaling** $42,800

About two-thirds local giving; grants are for general purposes except as noted. High Pa. grants of **$5,000** each to Military Heritage Foundation [Carlisle], Penn State U. (scholarship fund), Schuylkill Valley Center for Public Policy (education services), and

WITF-TV. **$1,000-$1,500** each to Bubbler Foundation (athletic scholarships), Cumberland County Historical Society (religious heritage brochure), and Messiah College. Other local contributions **$100-$500** for various purposes. **Out-of-state** giving includes high grant of **$16,000** to Brian Bex Report [IN]. ■**PUBLICATIONS:** None ■**WEBSITE:** None ■**E-MAIL:** None ■**APPLICATION POLICIES & PROCEDURES:** Generally no grants are awarded to individuals.

O+D+T Lincoln A. Warrell (S+Manager+Con) — Corporate donors: Pennsylvania Dutch Company, Inc.; The Warrell Corp.

CP-149 **Pennsylvania Environmental Defense Foundation**   MI- 71-79
P.O. Box 371   **Phone** 717-761-3883 **FAX** None
Camp Hill 17001   (Cumberland County)   **EIN** 23-2425827 **Year Created** 1994
AMV $324,515   **FYE** 5-01   (**Gifts Received** $82,109)   **Grants totaling** $0

No grants awarded in 2001, but in prior years the Foundation has assisted watershed associations, land conservancies, chapters of Trout Unlimited, and—where groups do not exist—facilitate the creation of an organization. Since 1996, the Foundation has pursued environmental action throughout Pa., in 15+ counties (see website for details). ■**PUBLICATIONS:** Annual Report ■**WEBSITE:** www.pedf.org [organizational activity info] ■**E-MAIL:** None ■**APPLICATION POLICIES & PROCEDURES:** The Foundation's mission is to advocate for and to help enforce citizen rights to a clean environment, especially water quality. When environmental laws give citizens the right to enforcement through litigation, the Foundation advises/assists environmental organizations, watershed associations, and educational institutions (as well as individual litigants) of their rights and enables them to pursue legal action against polluters. Other grant assistance is available for special projects or research. Grant requests may be submitted in any form at any time; describe fully how the requested funds will be used. Site visits sometimes are made to organizations being considered for a grant.

O+D+T Ronald G. Evans (C+Con) — Frederick W. Johnson [Harrisburg] (VC-Central) — Letitia M. Ryan [Schwenksville] (VC-East) — Vinnedge Lawrence [Washington] (VC-West) — James P. LaLumia [New Wilmington] (S) — Averill Shepps [Mechanicsburg] (F) — Elizabeth Leary [Gouldsboro] (T) — Charles Marshall [Paoli] (T) — Jerry McAllister [Perkiomenville] (T) — Robert L. Petrie [IL] (T) — Pete Retzlaff [Gilbertsville] (T) — Stan M. Stein, Esq. [Pittsburgh] (T) — Edward J. Zygmunt [Laceyville] (T) — John E. Childe, Jr., Esq. [Palmyra] (Chief Counsel)

CP-150 **Philips (Thomas E. & Marcia W.) Family Foundation**   MI-11-15-22-42-54-55-62
4737 Rock Ledge Drive   **Phone** 717-234-3115 **FAX** None
Harrisburg 17110   (Dauphin County)   **EIN** 23-6982149 **Year Created** 1990
AMV $354,335   **FYE** 12-00   (**Gifts Received** $0)   19 **Grants totaling** $13,465

About two-thirds local giving. High Pa. grant of **$2,000** to Jewish Community Center. **$1,400** to United Way of the Capital Region. **$1,250** to Susquehanna Art Museum. **$1,000** each to Way Point and Whitaker Center. **$500** to Guild for the Jewish Home. Other local contributions **$25-$250** for various purposes. **Out-of-state** grant: **$5,000** to Northwestern U. [IL]. ■**PUBLICATIONS:** None ■**WEBSITE:** None ■**E-MAIL:** None ■**APPLICATION POLICIES & PROCEDURES:** The Foundation reports that giving focuses on the Harrisburg area; no grants awarded to individuals.

O+D+T Thomas E. Philips (T+Donor+Con) — Marcia W. Philips (T+Donor)

CP-151 **Pierce (Allen F.) Foundation**   MI-12-13-17-39-44-54-55-56-63-72-84-89
c/o First Union/Wachovia
33 West 3rd Street, Suite 580   **Phone** 570-327-5075 **FAX** None
Williamsport 17703   (Lycoming County)   **EIN** 23-2044356 **Year Created** 1977
AMV $2,025   **FYE** 12-00   (**Gifts Received** $0)   19 **Grants totaling** $91,240

All giving to/for Bradford County; all grants are for general support. High grant of **$15,000** to Martha Lloyd Community Services. **$10,000** to Pierce Free Library. **$7,000** to Wyalusing Public Library. **$5,000** each to Bradford County Regional Arts Council, First Baptist Church of Troy, French Azilum, Rainbow Riders, Oscoluwa Engine #7 Hose Company, Seven Lakes Girl Scout Council, and Windfall United Methodist Church. **$4,000** to Green Free Library. **$3,000-$3,500** each to Alparon Park Swimming Pool, Bradford County Humane Society, Home Textile Tool Museum, and Troy Swimming Pool. **$2,740** to Western Alliance Emergency Services. **$2,000** each to The Main Link and Tioga Point Museum. **$1,000** to Bradford County Heritage Assn. ■**PUBLICATIONS:** None ■**WEBSITE:** None ■**E-MAIL:** brenton.hake@wachovia.com ■**APPLICATION POLICIES & PROCEDURES:** The Foundation reports all giving is restricted to/for Bradford County. Grant requests may be submitted in any form at any time to Mrs. Jean M. Elfvin, 33 Gates Circle - #4, Buffalo, NY 14209.

O+D+T Brenton Hake (Regional Trust Officer+VP at Bank+Con) — Jean Margaret Elfvin [NY] (D+Con) — Carole DeLauro [Troy] (D) — Ann D. DiLaura [FL] (D) — Hon. John T. Elfvin [NY] (D) — Janet A. Knapp [NY] (D) — Donor: Beatrice Pierce Trust

---

CP-152 **Piper Foundation**   MI-13-17-18-22-35-42-43-52-53-54
P.O. Box 227   **Phone** 570-748-7472 **FAX** 781-235-4982
Lock Haven 17745   (Clinton County)   **EIN** 24-0863140 **Year Created** 1957
AMV $1,292,036   **FYE** 9-01   (**Gifts Received** $0)   29 **Grants totaling** $105,000

About four-fifths local giving. High grant of **$10,000** to Piper Aviation Museum Foundation. **$8,000** to Lock Haven YMCA. **$5,000** to Clinton County United Way. **$6,000** each to Community Nursing Service of Clinton County, Family Planning Clinic of Lock Haven, Lock Haven U. Foundation, and Salvation Army. **$4,000** each to Clinton County Women's Center and Ross Library. **$3,000** to Mill Brook Playhouse. **$2,000** to Lock Haven U. Community Chorus. Other local contributions **$550-$600** for human service organizations, and eight scholarships, **$2,500** each, for Keystone Central School District graduates. **Out-of-state** grant: **$20,000** to Ute Distribution Corp. [UT] (scholarship fund for Ute Indians). ■**PUBLICATIONS:** None ■**WEBSITE:** None ■**E-MAIL:** None ■**APPLICATION POLICIES & PROCEDURES:** The Foundation reports giving is limited almost entirely to the Lock Haven/Clinton County area but no applications are accepted except for college scholarship applications from graduating seniors of Keystone Central School District, or from descendants of Ute Indians.

O+D+T William T. Piper, Jr. (P+F+Con) — Patricia Piper-Smyer [MA] (VP+F) — Betsy Barrett [NJ] (S) — Corporate donor: Piper Aircraft Corporation

---

CP-153   Plankenhorn (Harry) Foundation, The   MI-12-13-14-15-22-25-29-35-43-44-65-84
c/o New Covenant United Church of Christ
202 East 3rd Street   **Phone** 570-326-3308 **FAX** 570-320-7252
Williamsport 17701   (Lycoming County)   **EIN** 24-6023579   **Year Created** 1959
AMV $9,387,213   **FYE** 12-00   (**Gifts Received** $50,100)   24 **Grants totaling** $467,308

All local giving; grants are for general support except as noted and some grants comprise multiple payments. **$65,000** to American Rescue Workers (disaster relief/workshops). **$62,500** to Williamsport YMCA (remodeling/building fund). **$57,500** to Salvation Army (mostly emergency aid). **$50,000** to Habitat for Humanity. **$39,900** to North Central Sight Services. **$32,000** to Williamsport YWCA (pool remodeling for handicapped). **$25,000** each to James V. Brown Library (large-print books/bookmobile) and Volunteers of America (parents networking program). **$21,066** to Emergency Aid Fund. **$20,000** to St. Anthony's Center. **$15,000** each to Jersey Shore YMCA (building remodeling) and Shepherd of the Streets. **$12,000** to Lycoming County Community Care Facility (handicap-accessible vehicle). **$10,000** each to Sun Home Health Services (telehome care services) and United Churches of Lycoming County. **$6,842** to Lycoming County Crippled Children Society (clinical equipment). **$2,500** each to Camp Cadet, Camp Kiwanis for Underprivileged Children, and Camp Susque (all for campership sponsorships), Lycoming County 4H (scholarship program), and Pa. Special Olympics. ■**PUBLICATIONS:** None ■**WEBSITE:** None ■**E-MAIL:** None ■ **APPLICATION POLICIES & PROCEDURES:** The Foundation reports that giving is limited to the Lycoming County area, mainly to benefit the disabled; most grants are for general support, special projects, or building funds; multiyear awards are made. No grants awarded to individuals. Grant requests for less than $5,000 may be made verbally to any director. Larger grant requests must be submitted in a letter (4 pages maximum), preferably in January, April, September, or November; include an annual report, project budget, Board member list, and IRS tax-exempt status documentation. Site visits sometimes are made to organizations being considered for a grant. Grants are awarded at meetings in January, April, September, and November.

O+D+T Charles F. Greevy, III, Esq. (P+D+Con) — Abram M. Snyder [Cogan Station] (VP+D) — W. Herbert Poff, III (S+D) — Fred A. Foulkrod (F+D) — Eleanor W. Whiting (AF+D) — Rev. Bruce Druckenmiller [Cogan Station] (D) — Barbara Ertel (D) — Carol O. Hieber (D) — Bob Hively (D) — Robert M. Reeder (D) — Carolyn Seifert [South Williamsport] (D) — Nancy Stearns [Cogan Station] (D)

CP-154   Pollock (S. Wilson & Grace M.) Foundation   MI-11-12-14-32-42-44-63-89
c/o Keefer, Wood, Allen & Rahal
210 Walnut Street, P.O. Box 11963   **Phone** 717-255-8011 **FAX** 717-255-8050
Harrisburg 17108   (Dauphin County)   **EIN** 23-7889770   **Year Created** 1997
AMV $10,741,185   **FYE** 4-01   (**Gifts Received** $0)   14 **Grants totaling** $596,284

Mostly local giving. High grant of **$317,000** to West Shore Public Library. **$75,000** to United Way of the Capital Region. **$70,000** to Cumberland-Perry Assn. for Retarded Citizens. **$21,500** to Borough of Camp Hill (police dept./general support). **$10,000** each to Camp Hill Presbyterian Church and Escape Center/ParentWorks. **$7,500** to Camp Hill Fire Dept. (ambulance). #1. **$5,000** each to Sunshine Foundation [Philadelphia] and Susquehanna U. **$4,000** to Center for Advancement in Cancer Research [Wynnewood]. **$1,000** to Greater Harrisburg Foundation. **Out-of-state** giving includes **$50,000** to U. of Washington and **$20,284** to Mission at the Eastward Capital Area [ME]. — Local grants in the prior year included **$350,000** to West Shore Public Library; **$10,000** to United Cerebral Palsy/Capital Area; and **$3,000** to Susquehanna U. ■**PUBLICATIONS:** None. ■ **WEBSITE:** None ■**E-MAIL:** hallen@keeferwood.com ■**APPLICATION POLICIES & PROCEDURES:** Grant requests in any form may be submitted at any time; include the most recent annual report, audited financial statement, and Form 990. No grants awarded to individuals.

O+D+T Heath L. Allen, Esq. (Con) — Grace M. Pollock [Camp Hill] (Donor) — S. Wilson Pollock [Camp Hill] (Donor) — Allfirst Bank (Corporate Trustee)

CP-155   Powder Mill Foundation   MI-13-41-56-63-64-71
c/o Susquehanna-Pfaltzgraff Company
140 East Market Street   **Phone** 717-848-5500 **FAX** 717-852-2594
York 17401   (York County)   **EIN** 23-7751589   **Year Created** 1993
AMV $1,134,615   **FYE** 12-00   (**Gifts Received** $6,991)   **Grants totaling** $31,764

Information on grants awarded in 2000 is not available, but in 1999 seven grants totaling **$31,000** were awarded: **$8,000** to Penn Laurel Girl Scout Council; **$5,000** each to Historic York, Lancaster Theological Seminary, and Preservation Pa.; **$4,500** to Trinity United Church of Christ; **$3,000** to York Country Day School; and **$500** to Bible Tabernacle Youth Development Center. ■**PUBLICATIONS:** None ■**WEBSITE:** None ■**E-MAIL:** None ■**APPLICATION POLICIES & PROCEDURES:** The Foundation reports that giving is limited to the York area. Grant requests may be submitted in a letter at any time; outline the need for the funding.

O+D+T John L. Finlayson (T+F+Con) — Louis J. Appell, Jr. (P+Donor+T) — Josephine S. Appell (T)

CP-156   **Price (William F.) Foundation**
50 Linree Ave.
Reading   19606   (Berks County)

MI-34-44-53-61-72
Phone 610-927-1240 **FAX** None
EIN 23-6243630   **Year Created** 1959

AMV $301,648   **FYE** 11-00   (**Gifts Received** $0)   38 **Grants totaling** $36,190

Limited local giving. High Pa. grant of **$2,700** to Sacred Heart Church [West Reading]. **$1,000** to Bishop's Annual Appeal. **$500** each to Humane Society of Berks County, Wyomissing Public Library and Wyomissing Institute of Fine Arts. Other local contributions **$100-$300** for various purposes. **Out-of-state** giving includes **$5,000** each to Canterbury Towers [FL], Medical College of Virginia Foundation, and VOF Foundation College of Nursing; and **$3,390** to St. Williams Church of Naples [FL]. ■ **PUBLICATIONS:** None ■ **WEBSITE:** None ■ **E-MAIL:** None ■ **APPLICATION POLICIES & PROCEDURES:** Grant requests may be submitted in a letter at any time.

O+D+T Patricia Ann Restrepo (T+Con) — William F. Price [FL] (T) — Michael J. Restrepo (T)

CP-157   **Progress Education Foundation, The**
c/o Daily Express, Inc.
1076 Harrisburg Pike, P.O. Box 810
Carlisle   17013   (Cumberland County)

MI-11-13-14-15-16-17-22-25-29-55-57-63

Phone 717-243-7812 **FAX** None
EIN 23-2053536   **Year Created** 1978

AMV $916,577   **FYE** 12-00   (**Gifts Received** $0)   35 **Grants totaling** $322,500

About two-thirds local giving. High grant of **$79,000** to United Way of Carlisle. **$25,000** to Second Presbyterian Church of Carlisle. **$20,000** each to Carlisle Family YMCA and Cumberland-Perry ARC. **$15,000** each to Carlisle Area OIC, Habitat for Humanity of Cumberland County, and YWCA of Carlisle. **$4,500** to Salvation Army/Carlisle. **$4,000** to Hospice of Central Pa. **$1,000-$3,000** each to Carlisle Arts Learning Center, Domestic Violence of Cumberland-Perry, Junior Achievement of South Central Pa., Meals on Wheels of Carlisle, Pa. Special Olympics, Project Share Food Bank, Red Cross, Safe Harbor of Carlisle, and WITF. Other smaller local contributions for various purposes. **Out-of-state** giving includes **$50,000** to Unity Church of Naples [FL]; **$10,000** each to Professional Givers Anonymous [FL] and Fresh Start Endowment [FL]; and **$5,000** each to Foundation for Conscious Evolution [CA] and Institute of Noetic Sciences [CA]. ■ **PUBLICATIONS:** None ■ **WEBSITE:** None ■ **E-MAIL:** None ■ **APPLICATION POLICIES & PROCEDURES:** The Foundation reports giving focuses on the Carlisle area. No grants awarded to individuals. Grant requests may be submitted in any form at any time; describe the organization's charitable activities and state the amount and proposed use of the requested funding.

O+D+T C. Marius Haayen (Grant Manager+T+Con) — David E. Lutz [FL] (T+Donor) — June B. Lutz [FL] (T+Donor)

CP-158   **Pronio (Vincent A.) Charitable Trust**
401 Douglas Road
Hummelstown   17036   (Dauphin County)

MI-13-41-42-63-65
Phone 717-566-0484 **FAX** None
EIN 23-7880699   **Year Created** 1997

AMV $222,362   **FYE** 12-00   (**Gifts Received** $0)   16 **Grants totaling** $11,800

All local giving. High grant of **$2,000** to St. Joan of Arc Church. **$1,000-$1,500** each to Boy Scouts/Keystone Area Council, Catholic Charities, Hershey Ministerium, Holy Name of Jesus Church, Lebanon Valley College, and St. Joan of Arc School. Other local contributions **$200-$500** each for various purposes. ■ **PUBLICATIONS:** None ■ **WEBSITE:** None ■ **E-MAIL:** None ■ **APPLICATION POLICIES & PROCEDURES:** Information not available.

O+D+T Vincent A. Pronio (Advisory Committee+Con) — Victoria Pronio (Advisory Committee) — Hershey Trust Company (Trustee)

CP-159   **Property Management, Inc. Charitable Foundation**
c/o Rhodes Development Group, Inc.
1300 Market Street, #307, P.O. Box 622
Lemoyne   17043   (Cumberland County)

MI-12-13-14-17-19-31-35-45-57

Phone 717-730-7055 **FAX** 717-730-7056
EIN 25-1721134   **Year Created** 1994

AMV $210,777   **FYE** 12-00   (**Gifts Received** $25,000)   10 **Grants totaling** $13,916

All local giving. High grant of **$2,316** to Parent Works (Brazelton Program). **$2,000** each to Penn State-Geisinger Health System (Friends of Women's Health), Penn State U./Harrisburg (program for incarcerated men), Volunteers of America (literacy program), and WITF-TV/FM (festival sponsorship). **$1,000-$1,500** each to Domestic Violence Service of Cumberland-Perry Counties (training/direct services), Hemlock Girl Scout Council (leader mentoring), and The Second Mile (dinner sponsorship). ■ **PUBLICATIONS:** statement of program policy; application guidelines ■ **WEBSITE:** None ■ **E-MAIL:** None ■ **APPLICATION POLICIES & PROCEDURES:** The Foundation reports that giving is limited to Central Pa.; no grants awarded to individuals. Prospective applicants initially should make a telephone inquiry about the feasibility of submitting a request. Grant requests should be submitted during March or October (deadlines are March 31st and October 31st) on a formal application form available from the Foundation; include an annual report, organizational/project budgets, Board member list, list of major funding sources, audited financial statement, and IRS tax-exempt status documentation. Site visits sometimes are made to organizations being considered for a grant. Grants are awarded at meetings in April and November.

O+D+T John H. Rhodes (P+D+Donor+Con) — Bonnie F. Rhodes (Executive Director+D+Donor) — Lawrence M. Means (VP+D) — Dianne L. Fairall (S+D) — Jeffrey D. Billman (F+D) — David E. Dyson (D) — Gail R. Siegel (D+Donor) — Thomas R. Wenger (D) — Corporate donors: Harrisburg Hotel Corp.; Rhodes Development Group, Inc.

CP-160 **Proserpi (Sergio V. & Penelope Pattrill) Foundation**
1906 Philadelphia Ave.
Reading 19607   (Berks County)

MI-42-52-54-55
Phone 610-373-8258 **FAX** None
EIN 23-7849593   **Year Created** 1996

AMV $88,797   **FYE** 12-00   **(Gifts Received** $0)   15 **Grants totaling** $25,930

About three-fourths local/Pa. giving. High grant of **$7,000** to Alvernia College. **$3,000** to Reading Symphony Orchestra. **$2,500** to Reading Public Museum. **$2,000** to Friends of Chamber Music. **$1,400** to Wyomissing Institute. **$1,000** to Beaver College. Smaller local contributions. **Out-of-state** giving includes **$5,250** to Metropolitan Opera [NY] and **$2,500** to The Ravenna Festival [Italy]. ■**PUBLICATIONS:** None ■**WEBSITE:** None ■**E-MAIL:** None ■**APPLICATION POLICIES & PROCEDURES:** Information not available.

O+D+T Sergio V. Proserpi (P+Donor+Con) — Penelope Pattrill Proserpi (S+F)

CP-161 **Raub Foundation**
630 Oakwood Lane
Lancaster 17603   (Lancaster County)

MI-13-15-18-31-35-41-42-52-63
Phone 717-291-1833 **FAX** None
EIN 22-2743870   **Year Created** 1986

AMV $561,630   **FYE** 12-00   **(Gifts Received** $2,600)   18 **Grants totaling** $22,550

All local/Pa. giving. High grant of **$3,500** to Boys & Girls Club of Lancaster. **$2,500** each to St. James Episcopal Church and Widener U. [Chester]. **$2,000** each to Janus School, Lancaster Country Day School, and YWCA of Lancaster. **$1,000** to Lancaster Health Alliance. **$750-$900** each to Deb's House, Fulton Opera House Foundation, Hospice of Lancaster, Penn Laurel Girl Scout Council, and Planned Parenthood of the Susquehanna Valley. Other local contributions **$500** each for various purposes. ■**PUBLICATIONS:** None ■**WEBSITE:** None ■**E-MAIL:** None ■**APPLICATION POLICIES & PROCEDURES:** The Foundation reports that giving is primarily to the Lancaster area. Grant requests may be submitted in a letter at any time; describe in detail the proposed project and state the funding requested.

O+D+T Stuart H. Raub, Jr. (T+Con) — Marie T. Raub (T)

CP-162 **Reese Foundation**
c/o Fulton Financial Advisors N.A.
One Penn Square, P.O. Box 3215
Lancaster 17604   (Lancaster County)

MI-12-14-17-22-25-32-63-64-65
Phone 717-291-2523 **FAX** None
EIN 23-2349281   **Year Created** 1985

AMV $4,883,955   **FYE** 5-00   **(Gifts Received** $0)   11 **Grants totaling** $250,000

About three-fourths local giving. High grant of **$55,000** to Salvation Army/Lancaster. **$40,000** to Christ's Home for Children. **$24,000** to Bethany Christian Services. **$20,000** each to Mennonite Central Committee and Water Street Rescue Mission. **$10,000** to Mom's House/Lancaster. **$5,000** to Parish Resource Center. **$2,000** to St. Joseph Hospital Foundation. **Out-of-state** giving: **$32,000** to Christ Chapel Bible Church of Ft. Worth [TX]; **$22,000** to Covenant Theological Seminary [MO]; and **$20,000** to Westminster Theological Seminary [CA]. ■**PUBLICATIONS:** None ■**WEBSITE:** None ■**E-MAIL:** None ■**APPLICATION POLICIES & PROCEDURES:** Grant requests may be submitted in a letter at any time; describe the purpose and state the amount of funding requested.

O+D+T Vincent J. Lattanzio (Trust Officer at Bank+Con) — Harry A. Blank (D) — Dr. I. Philip Reese [TX] (D)

CP-163 **Reese (Ralph C. & Dorothy C.) Foundation**
P.O. Box 736
Hershey 17033   (Dauphin County)

MI-32-63
Phone 717-534-1357 **FAX** None
EIN 23-7931814   **Year Created** 1997

AMV $185,038   **FYE** 12-00   **(Gifts Received** $0)   21 **Grants totaling** $11,105

Mostly local giving. High grant of **$10,400** to Derry Presbyterian Church. Other local and **Out-of-state** contributions, **$15-$125,** for health charities and other purposes. ■**PUBLICATIONS:** None. ■**WEBSITE:** None ■**E-MAIL:** None ■**APPLICATION POLICIES & PROCEDURES:** Information not available.

O+D+T Ralph C. Reese (C+T+Donor+Con) — Dorothy C. Reese (T+Donor) — Patricia Reese Foltz (T) — Hershey Trust Company (Corporate Trustee)

CP-164 **Rehmeyer (Herbert M.) Trust**
c/o Stock and Leader
35 South Duke Street, P.O. Box 5167
York 17405   (York County)

MI-12-13-14-18-25-29-31-33-44-45-51-55-56-85
Phone 717-843-7841 **FAX** None
EIN 23-6708035   **Year Created** 1981

AMV $1,110,306   **FYE** 4-01   **(Gifts Received** $0)   30 **Grants totaling** $98,500

All giving restricted to the York area. High grants of **$10,000** each to York Little Theatre and YWCA of York. **$7,500** each to Child Care Consultants and Focus on Our Future. **$5,000** each to ARC of York County, Historic York, Penn Laurel Girl Scout Council, Planned Parenthood of Central Pa., South George Street Community Partnership, York Foundation, York Murals, and YMCA of York/York County. **$2,000-$2,500** each to Kaltreider-Benfer Library, Mental Health Assn. of York, York County Audit of Human Rights, and York County Heritage Trust. **$1,000-$1,500** each to Access-York, Atkins House, Children's Home of York, Contact York, Crispus Attucks Assn., Easter Seals, H.O.P.E., Martin Library, York Arts/The Art Center, York County Bar Foundation, York Hospital (Children's Growth & Development Center), York County Literacy Council, and York Habitat for Humanity. Other smaller contributions. ■**PUBLICATIONS:** None ■**WEBSITE:** None ■**E-MAIL:** None ■**APPLICATION POLICIES & PROCEDURES:** The Foundation reports that only York-area organizations are eligible to apply; most grants are for general/operating support, program expenses, capital campaigns/improvements, equipment, or scholarship funds. Grant requests must be submitted on a a formal application form, available from the Trust, in August-September (deadline is October 1st); include organizational/project budgets, Board member list, and IRS tax-exempt status documentation. Site visits occasionally are made to organizations being considered for a grant. Decisions on grants are made at a meeting in November and as needed.

O+D+T Henry B. Leader, Esq. (Co-T+Con) — Allfirst Trust (Co-Trustee)

CP-165 **Ressler Mill Foundation**　　　　　　　　　　　MI-12-13-14-35-42-44-45-52-53-54-55-56-71
29 East King Street, Room 14　　　　　　　　　　　　**Phone** 717-481-7702　**FAX** 717-481-7702
Lancaster　17602　　　　　　(Lancaster County)　　　**EIN** 23-6430663　　**Year Created** 1967
AMV $15,528,555　　**FYE** 12-00　　(**Gifts Received** $1,892)　　40+ **Grants totaling** $212,295

Mostly Lancaster County giving. High grant of **$50,000** to Lancaster County Foundation (promotion of charitable activities in eastern Lancaster County). **$17,832** to Friends of Leola Library (furnishings). **$10,000** each to Library System of Lancaster County (computers/foreign language bookmobile books) and Pa. School of Art & Design (library books). **$9,651** to Lancaster County Historical Society (local newspaper microfilm). **$8,050** to Penn Laurel Girl Scout Council (event). **$7,835** to Lancaster Mennonite Historical Society (microfilm printer). **$5,000** each to Advantage Ephrata Task Force (educational videos), Contact Lancaster Helpline (promotion of services), The Factory (tutoring/parent training), and Samaritan Counseling Center (child/adolescent program). **$4,000-$4,600** each to Christ's Home for Children (parent training), Lancaster Day Care Center (materials/literacy equipment), Partners in Achieving Independence (professional lending library), and Trout Unlimited (stream bank project equipment). **$3,488** to YWCA of Lancaster (summer program). **$3,000** each to Boys Club & Girls Club of Lancaster (program supplies), Lancaster Theological Seminary (underground railroad programs), Mom's House of Lancaster (playground improvements), and Musical Art Society of Lancaster (artist-in-residence program). **$2,000-$2,800** each to Elizabethtown Preservation Associates (camera/preschool materials), HARB-Adult (program), Lancaster Farmland Trust (farmers' educational booklet), Lancaster Heart Assn. (instructional booklets), Lancaster Museum of Art (artist-in-residence project), Milagro House (GED testing/books), Pequea Mill Creek Project (stream bank fencing), Quarryville Library (reference materials), Southeast Lancaster Health Services (books/teaching handouts), and UCP of Lancaster County (classrooms/supplies). Other smaller local grants/contributions for arts/cultural, historical, and health/human service programs which are educational in nature. **Out-of-state** grants: **$6,000** to T.I.M.S./The International Molinilogical Society-America [IA] and **$5,400** to Danish Windmill Corp. [IA] (apprentice millwright position). ■**PUBLICATIONS:** Grant Program Packet; Grant Application Form ■**WEBSITE:** www.resslermill.com/pages/foundation.html ■**E-MAIL:** None ■**APPLICATION POLICIES & PROCEDURES:** The Foundation's new guidelines (2002) focus support on a wide variety of educational activities in Lancaster County, including preschool education, daycare for children from low-income families, libraries, museums, adult education, essay contests, science fairs, fellowships for college students, health education, and apprenticeships. In addition, the Foundation continues to support mill preservation projects nationwide. Rarely are grants awarded for general operating support, endowment, building campaigns, personnel, or budgeted support. Prospective applicants initially must request a Grant Program Packet (includes complete guidelines and a formal Grant Application Form). Completed applications should be submitted with required supporting documentation during July-December; the deadline for requests is mid-January (call for exact date). Site visits sometimes are made to organizations being considered for a grant. Only one request per year may be submitted by an organization. Grants are disbursed after a June-July Board meeting.

O+D+T Donald B. Hostetter (Executive Director, Grants Program+Con) — Gloria Patterson (Administrative Assistant, Grants Program) — Stephen J. Kindig [Oley] (P+D) — Mary L. Clinton (VP+D) — W. James Morton, Jr. [Akron] (S+D) — Richard P. Heilig (F+D) — Reynold A. Schenke [Paradise] (AS+D) — Ralph J. Homsher [Paradise] (D)

CP-166 **Richmond (William R. & Esther) Foundation, The**　　　MI-15-22-29-42-55-62-85
c/o PNC Advisors
4242 Carlisle Pike, P.O. Box 308　　　　　　　　　　**Phone** 717-730-2382　**FAX** 717-730-2254
Camp Hill　17011　　　　　　(Cumberland County)　　**EIN** 23-7918063　　**Year Created** 1999
AMV $626,495　　**FYE** 11-01　　(**Gifts Received** $0)　　9 **Grants totaling** $28,872

Mostly local giving. High grant of **$7,500** to Allied Arts Fund. **$5,000** each to David L. Silver Yeshiva Academy and Temple Beth El. **$2,500** to Shippensburg U. **$2,000** to United Way of the Capital Region Foundation. **$1,000-$1,500** each to Contact Helpline, Gretna Theatre, Jewish Home of Greater Harrisburg, and Midtown Market District. Other smaller local contributions. ■ **PUBLICATIONS:** None ■**WEBSITE:** None ■**E-MAIL:** None ■**APPLICATION POLICIES & PROCEDURES:** Information not available.

O+D+T David A. Brown (VP at Bank+Con) — PNC Advisors (Trustee)

CP-167 **Ritchie (Lt. Robert B.) Memorial Fund**　　　　　　MI-43
c/o First Union/Wachovia - PA 6497
600 Penn Street, P.O. Box 1102　　　　　　　　　　　**Phone** 610-655-3135　**FAX** None
Reading　17604　　　　　　(Berks County)　　　　　　**EIN** 23-6718706　　**Year Created** 1980
AMV $1,070,728　　**FYE** 12-00　　(**Gifts Received** $0)　　16 **Grants totaling** $62,333

All grants are scholarships for Lancaster City/County public high school graduates attending colleges/universities in many states; awards generally were **$4,000** or less. ■**PUBLICATIONS:** Brochure ■**WEBSITE:** None ■**E-MAIL:** None ■**APPLICATION POLICIES & PROCEDURES:** Only Lancaster City/Lancaster County high school graduates are eligible to apply; a descriptive brochure and formal application form are available from guidance counselors in the county's high schools. Applicants must be nominated by one's own high school officials who must submit applications before the February 28th deadline. Awards are made at an April meeting.

O+D+T Andrew C. Meltzer (VP at Bank+Con) — First Union/Wachovia (Trustee)

CP-168   Ritter Foundation
c/o Ritter Brothers, Inc.
1511 N. Cameron Street, P.O. Box 1577
Harrisburg   17105   (Dauphin County)

MI-12-41-56-85

Phone 717-234-3061 **FAX** None
EIN 23-6290484   **Year Created** 1949

AMV $4,117   **FYE** 12-00   **(Gifts Received** $0)   7 **Grants totaling** $11,870

All local giving. High grant of **$10,000** to Harrisburg Area Community College Foundation. **$1,000** to Children's Playroom. Other local contributions **$100-$250** for various purposes. — Grants awarded in the prior year included **$10,000** to Harrisburg Area Community College Foundation; **$2,000** to Historic Harrisburg Assn.; and **$1,000** to African-American Chamber of Commerce of Harrisburg. ■**PUBLICATIONS:** None ■**WEBSITE:** None ■**E-MAIL:** None ■**APPLICATION POLICIES & PROCEDURES:** Grant requests may be submitted in a letter at any time; describe in detail the proposed project and funding requested, and include an audited financial statement and IRS tax-exempt status documentation. No grants awarded to individuals.

O+D+T William R. Brightbill (P+F+Con) — Steven L. Daniels (VP+S) — Corporate donor: Ritter Brothers, Inc.

CP-169   Sachs (Mary) Trust
c/o Keefer, Wood, Allen & Rahal
210 Walnut Street
Harrisburg   17101   (Dauphin County)

MI-11-13-15-22-31-41-42-44-57-62-82

Phone 717-255-8000 **FAX** None
EIN 23-6239669   **Year Created** 1999

AMV $3,892,013   **FYE** 12-99   **(Gifts Received** $0)   57 **Grants totaling** $158,700

Mostly local giving. High grant of **$75,000** to United Jewish Appeal of Harrisburg. **$13,000** to Harrisburg Area Community College. **$10,000** to Jewish Community Center of Harrisburg. **$5,000** to YWCA of Harrisburg. **$3,500** each to Penn State and Yeshiva Academy (scholarship). **$3,000** each to Franklin & Marshall College, United Jewish Appeal of Lancaster, and United Way of Capital Region. **$2,500** each to Boy Scouts and WITF. **$1,500** each to Holy Spirit Hospital and Milton Eisenhower Library. **$1,000** each to Dickinson College, Elizabethtown College, Gettysburg College, Hadassah-Harrisburg, Harrisburg Academy, Hope Lodge of Central Pa., Jewish Home of Greater Harrisburg, Lebanon Valley College, Messiah College, and Polyclinic Medical Center. Other local giving **$100-$500** for various organizations and purposes. **Out-of-state** giving includes **$5,000** each to Hadassah College of Technology [Israel] and Hadassah Ein Karem Hospital [Israel]. ■**PUBLICATIONS:** None ■**WEBSITE:** None ■**E-MAIL:** None ■**APPLICATION POLICIES & PROCEDURES:** Information not available.

O+D+T Thomas E. Wood, Esq. (Co-T+Con) — First Union/Wachovia (Co-Trustee)

CP-170   Saltsgiver Family Foundation
694 Ganderback Road
Hughesville   17737   (Lycoming County)

MI-18-22-41-63

Phone 570-546-5444 **FAX** None
EIN 23-2803397   **Year Created** 1995

AMV $5,228,954   **FYE** 12-00   **(Gifts Received** $1,001,819)   15 **Grants totaling** $243,000

About one-quarter local/Pa. giving. High Pa. grant of **$25,000** to Watsontown Christian Academy. **$10,000** each to American Rescue Workers, Pregnancy Care Center of the Susquehanna Valley, Red Cross, and Salvation Army. **$5,000** to Faith Alive [York]. **$2,000** to Faith Broadcasting Network Corp. [Luzerne County]. **Out-of-state** giving includes **$100,000** to Acts 29 Ministries [GA]; **$25,000** each to Prison Fellowship Ministries [VA] and Samaritan's Purse [NC]; and other grants for similar purposes. in FL, MO, VA, and WA. ■**PUBLICATIONS:** None ■**WEBSITE:** None ■**E-MAIL:** None ■**APPLICATION POLICIES & PROCEDURES:** No grants awarded to individuals.

O+D+T Thomas M. Saltsgiver (P+Donor+Con) — Joann Saltsgiver (S+F+Donor)

CP-171   Schaefer Foundation
161 Hardt Hill Road
Bechtelsville   19505   (Berks County)

MI-42-52-56-71

Phone 610-845-7955 **FAX** None
EIN 22-6042871   **Year Created** 1957

AMV $362,913   **FYE** 12-00   **(Gifts Received** $0)   19 **Grants totaling** $7,510

Limited local contributions under **$100** for historical and conservation purposes. **Out-of-state** giving includes **$3,000** to Sonoma State U. [CA]; and **$1,000** each to Daughters of Wisdom [NY], Symphony of the Lakes [MN], and Williams College Alumni Fund [MA]. ■**PUBLICATIONS:** None. ■**WEBSITE:** None ■**E-MAIL:** None ■**APPLICATION POLICIES & PROCEDURES:** Information not available.

O+D+T Dr. Joseph B. Schaefer, Jr. (P+Con) — William C. Schaefer [FL] (S+F) — Mrs. Robert Hamlin [CA] (T) — Sue M. Larson [CA] (T) — Herbert S. Meeker [NY] (T) — Margaret T. Schaefer [CA] (T) — Terry A. Thompson [NJ] (T)

CP-172   Schmidt (John) Foundation
511 Shady Dell Road
York   17403   (York County)

MI-13-15-22-29-31-44-45-49-52-55-56-57

Phone 717-854-6402 **FAX** None
EIN 23-6298307   **Year Created** 1952

AMV $1,772,730   **FYE** 12-00   **(Gifts Received** $0)   16 **Grants totaling** $62,750

All local giving; all grants are for general support. High grants of **$10,000** each to Strand-Capital Performing Arts Center and York Murals, Inc. **$9,500** to Cultural Alliance of York County. **$5,000** each to Margaret Moul Home, Salvation Army, and York Health Foundation. **$4,000** each to Red Cross and York County Heritage. **$2,500** to Junior Achievement of South Central Pa. **$2,000** to YMCA of York County. **$1,000-$1,500** each to Access York, Martin Memorial Library, WITF and a scholarship. **$750** to Contact York. **$500** to York County Literacy Council. ■**PUBLICATIONS:** None ■**WEBSITE:** None ■**E-MAIL:** None ■**APPLICATION POLICIES & PROCEDURES:** The Foundation reports that only organizations serving the greater York County area are

eligible for support. No grants awarded to individuals. Grant requests may be submitted in a letter at any time; state the name/purpose of organization, geographic area and population served, and include income/expense statements for the prior year.
O+D+T John C. Schmidt (Co-T+Con) — D. Duncan Schmidt [MD] (Co-T) — Dana E. Schmidt [CA] (Co-T) — Allfirst Trust Co. of Pa. (Agent)

CP-173 **Schoffstall Family Foundation, The**
    1818 Signal Hill Road
    Mechanicsburg 17055   (Cumberland County)
AMV $352,564   **FYE** 12-00   (**Gifts Received** $100,000)

MI-13-22-41-63-64
Phone 717-728-9090 **FAX** None
EIN 23-2872636   **Year Created** 1997
3 **Grants totaling** $76,000

All local giving. High grant of **$55,000** to Harrisburg Christian School (capital campaign). **$11,000** to Evangelical School of Theology [Myerstown] (computer technology). **$10,000** to Bethesda Mission (New Life campaign). — Grants awarded in recent years included **$10,000** to Boy Scouts/Keystone Area Council (capital campaign) and **$5,000** to The Youth Network (general support). ■**PUBLICATIONS:** None ■**WEBSITE:** None ■**E-MAIL:** None ■**APPLICATION POLICIES & PROCEDURES:** Grant requests may be submitted in a letter prior a mid-November deadline.
O+D+T Martin L. Schoffstall [Harrisburg] (C+D+Donor+Con) — Louann Martin [Harrisburg] (D) — Brenda Pinckney [Maytown] (D) — Marvin L. Schoffstall (D) — Stephen A. Schoffstall [Camp Hill] (D)

CP-174 **Schwab-Spector-Rainess Foundation**
    c/o Credential Leasing Corporation
    2525 North 7th Street, P.O. Box 5967
    Harrisburg 17105   (Dauphin County)
AMV $4,122,815   **FYE** 12-00   (**Gifts Received** $64,362)

MI-11-22-31-32-41-42-52-54-55-57-62
Phone 717-255-7803 **FAX** 717-255-7879
EIN 23-6401901   **Year Created** 1965
66 **Grants totaling** $153,422

About two-thirds local/Pa. giving. High grant of **$42,220** to United Jewish Community of Greater Harrisburg. **$17,025** to United Way of the Capital Region. **$10,000** to Penn State Alumni Center [University Park]. **$9,100** to Hadassah. **$5,000** to National Liberty Museum [Philadelphia]. **$3,000** to Theatre Harrisburg. **$2,800** to Allied Arts Fund. **$1,000-$2,000** each to American Cancer Society, Beth El Temple, Chisuk Emuna Congregation, Jewish Community Center of Harrisburg, MS Society of Central Pa., PinnacleHealth Foundation, WITF, and Yeshiva Academy. Other local contributions **$10-$500** for various purposes. **Out-of-state** giving includes **$30,000** to International Multiple Sclerosis Foundation [AZ] and **$4,300** to Associated Jewish Community Federation of Baltimore [MD]. — Major grants approved for future payment: **$20,000** each to Penn State Alumni Center, National Liberty Museum, and United Jewish Appeal of Harrisburg. ■**PUBLICATIONS:** None ■**WEBSITE:** None ■**E-MAIL:** None ■**APPLICATION POLICIES & PROCEDURES:** The Foundation reports that most grants are for general support, special projects, and building funds; multi-year grants are awarded. Grant requests may be submitted in a letter at any time; describe the project and the amount of funding requested.
O+D+T Morris Schwab (T+Donor+Con) — Israel Schwab (T+Donor) — Andrew E. Schwab (Donor) — Corporate donors: Credential Leasing Corporation; D&H Distributing Company

---

CP-175 **Seven Trees, The**
    3601 Gettysburg Road
    Camp Hill 17011   (Cumberland County)
AMV $1,708,138   **FYE** 12-00   (**Gifts Received** $725,000)

MI-13-41-42-44-51
Phone 717-975-3590 **FAX** None
EIN 23-6245788   **Year Created** 1953
17 **Grants totaling** $61,500

Mostly local/Pa. giving; grants are unrestricted support/annual giving except as noted. High grant of **$10,000** to Center for Industrial Training (capital campaign). **$5,000** each to Carlisle Family YMCA (Camp Thompson capital campaign), Linden Hall School for Girls (capital campaign), Mechanicsburg School District (Wildcat Foundation-capital campaign), Theatre Harrisburg (capital campaign), West Shore Public Library, and YMCA of Greater Harrisburg. **$3,000-$3,500** each to Hemlock Girl Scout Council (STAR Center), The Hill School, Messiah College, and Pa. Special Olympics (summer games). **$1,000** each to Central Pa. Conservancy and United Way of Greater Carlisle (endowment campaign). **$500** to Grove City College. **Out-of-state** giving includes **$3,000** to Princeton U. [NJ] and **$1,000** to a KS theatre group. ■**PUBLICATIONS:** None ■**WEBSITE:** None ■**E-MAIL:** None ■**APPLICATION POLICIES & PROCEDURES:** The Foundation reports that giving is chiefly to educational institutions and programs in Central Pa.; no grants are awarded to individuals. Prospective applicants initially should telephone the Foundation to inquire about the feasibility of submitting a request. Grant requests may be submitted in a letter at any time; include organizational/project budgets, list of major funding sources, Board member list, and IRS tax-exempt status documentation.
O+D+T Ernest S. Burch, Jr. (P+Con) — John L. Burch [KS] (VP) — Deanne M. Burch (S)

CP-176 **Sheary (Edna M.) for Charity**
    c/o Mellon Private Wealth Management
    2 North Second Street, 12th Floor, P.O. Box 1010
    Harrisburg 17108   (Dauphin County)
AMV $1,672,338   **FYE** 5-01   (**Gifts Received** $0)

MI-12-29-41-42-44-56-63-84
Phone 717-780-3037 **FAX** None
EIN 25-6368952   **Year Created** 1991
14 **Grants totaling** $397,983

All Central Pa. giving, primarily Northumberland, Snyder and Union counties; grants are for specific projects. High grant of **$200,000** to Christ Lutheran Church of Lewisburg. **$50,000** each to Susquehanna U. and Union County Public Library. **$30,000** to Mifflinburg Buggy Museum. **$20,000** to Kauffman Library. **$8,750** to Evangelical Lutheran Church/Upper Susquehanna Synod. **$8,000** to Lewisburg Elementary School. **$7,500** to New Berlin Recreation Assn. **$6,884** to Montandon Baptist

Church. **$5,642** to St. John's Nursery School. **$5,000** to Camp Mount Luther. **$1,000-$2,500** each to New Berlin Heritage Assn., Red Cross-Sunbury, and St. Paul's Daycare Center. ■**PUBLICATIONS:** application form ■**WEBSITE:** None ■**E-MAIL:** None ■**APPLICATION POLICIES & PROCEDURES:** Grant requets may be submitted on a formal application form, available from the Bank; include a proposal and IRS tax-exempt status documentation before the April 1st deadline.

O+D+T Cindy Semic (Trust Officer at Bank+Con) — Mellon Private Wealth Management (Trustee)

CP-177 Sheppard (Lawrence B.) Foundation
c/o Buchen Wise & Dorr
126 Carlisle Street
Hanover 17331 (York County)

MI-11-12-13-14-22-29-32-41-44-52-55-56-72-84

Phone 717-637-2160 **FAX** None
EIN 23-6251690 **Year Created** 1946

AMV $1,727,559 **FYE** 11-00 **(Gifts Received** $0) 32 **Grants totaling** $92,000

Mostly local giving; grants are for general support except as noted. High grant of **$6,000** to Community Health Services (uncompensated health care). **$5,000** each to Delone Catholic High School (scholarships/educational services), Hanover Area YMCA (endowment/general support), Littlestown Activity Center of Hanover YMCA, Red Cross/Hanover, and St. Vincent de Paul School (scholarships/endowment). **$4,000** to Hanover-Adams Rehabilitation & Training Center. **$3,000** each to American Cancer Society/Hanover, Hanover Area Historical Society, Hanover Area YWCA (Safe Home program), Harness Horse Retirement & Youth Assn. (animal care), Junior Achievement of South Central Pa. (schools program), Mt. Olivet Cemetery, Pa. Academy of Music [Lancaster] (scholarships), and Sacred Heart School (scholarships). **$2,000-$2,500** each to Adams-Hanover Counseling Services, Children's Aid Society, Hanover Public Library (children's section), Hanover Senior High School (physical education projects), Hoffman Home for Youth, Paradise School (care for adjudicated youth), UCP of South Central Pa., and United Way of York County. **$1,000-$1,500** each to Eichelberger Performing Arts Center, Hanover Area Needlework Assn. (clothing for indigent), Life Skills Unlimited, Make-A-Wish Foundation of York County, Strand-Capitol Performing Arts Center (student programs), and York County Special Olympics. **Out-of-state** giving includes **$5,000** to Harness Racing Museum & Hall of Fame [NY] and **$3,000** to AmeriCares Foundation [CT]. ■**PUBLICATIONS:** None ■**WEBSITE:** None ■**E-MAIL:** None ■**APPLICATION POLICIES & PROCEDURES:** The Foundation reports that giving focuses on local organizations, particularly schools and education projects, youth, and health. No grants are awarded to individuals. Grant requests should be submitted in a letter before the October 31st deadline; describe in detail the proposed project, state the amount requested, and include IRS tax-exempt status documentation.

O+D+T Donald W. Dorr, Esq. (S+D+Con) — Charlotte S. DeVan (P+D) — Dr. W. Todd DeVan (VP+D) — Lawrence Sheppard DeVan [CT] (F+D)

CP-178 Shoemaker (Ray S.) Scholarship Foundation
c/o Harrisburg Area Community College
Financial Aid Office, One HACC Drive
Harrisburg 17110 (Dauphin County)

MI-43

Phone 717-780-2330 **FAX** None
EIN 23-6237250 **Year Created** 1940

AMV $7,545,087 **FYE** 9-00 **(Gifts Received** $0) 150+ **Grants totaling** $319,788

All giving limited to scholarships for Greater Harrisburg area high school graduates. Tuition-only awards vary widely but generally range from **$500** to **$8,000** with students attending many colleges/universities in many states. ■**PUBLICATIONS:** None ■**WEBSITE:** www.hacc.edu/services/finaid/pdfs/shoemaker_app.pdf ■**E-MAIL:** admit@hacc.edu ■**APPLICATION POLICIES & PROCEDURES:** Only high school graduates from the Greater Harrisburg area are eligible to apply. A formal application form, available from the Foundation (or on the website), should be submitted during January-March (the deadline is April 1st); include high school or college transcripts, parents' financial information, and monetary needs. Decisions on awards are made in June. Scholarships are renewable.

O+D+T Director of Financial Aid (Con) — Benjamin Lowengard (D) — David Sanchez (D) — Karen Sebastian (D) — Mellon Bank N.A. (Trustee)

CP-179 SICO Foundation, The
c/o SICO Company
15 Mount Joy Street, P.O. Box 302
Mount Joy 17552 (Lancaster County)

MI-42-43

Phone 717-653-1411 **FAX** None
EIN 23-6298332 **Year Created** 1941

AMV $14,312,104 **FYE** 5-00 **(Gifts Received** $0) 9 **Grants totaling** $461,500

Grants ranging from **$36,000** to **$109,000** were awarded to nine designated colleges/universities in PA, DE, MD, and NJ to support 120 scholarships (**$3,000-$4,000** each) for students majoring in elementary education. Participating institutions are Cheyney U., Kutztown U., Millersville U., Shippensburg U., West Chester U., Delaware State U., U. of Delaware, Salisbury State College [MD], and Stockton State College. Rowan College [NJ] also is a participating institution. ■**PUBLICATIONS:** Scholarship Bulletin with application guidelines ■**WEBSITE:** www.sicoco.com/scholarships.htm ■**E-MAIL:** —see website ■**APPLICATION POLICIES & PROCEDURES:** The Foundation reports that scholarship applicants must reside in one of the following Pa. counties: (Adams, Berks, Chester, Cumberland, Dauphin, Delaware, Lancaster, Lebanon, or York) or in specified DE, MD, or NJ counties (see website for details). A formal application form is available from participating school guidance offices and must be submitted in duplicate with a letter explaining one's need for financial assistance; the deadline is February 15th. All scholarship awards are paid directly to the college or university.

O+D+T Dr. William H. Duncan (P+Con) — John N. Weidman (VP) — Darlene F. Halterman (S) — Franklin R. Eichler (F) — Charles Caputo (D) — Dr. Anthony F. Ceddia (D) — Harrison L. Diehl, Jr. (D) — Dr. Harry K. Gerlach (D) — Carl R. Hallgren, Esq. (D) — Dr. Joseph D. Moore (D) — Charles Ricedorf (D) — Dr. Forrest R. Schaeffer (D) — David F. Eichler (D) — Helen A. Stine (D) — Fred S. Engle (D) — Corporate donor: SICO Company

CP-180 **Simpson (Joseph T. & Helen M.) Foundation**
105 North Front Street, P.O. Box 1103
Harrisburg 17108   (Dauphin County)

MI-11-13-14-15-22-25-31-42-51-52-55-57-63
Phone 717-238-1171 **FAX** 717-238-1188
EIN 23-6242538   **Year Created** 1954

AMV $2,082,078   **FYE** 12-00   (**Gifts Received** $0)   116 **Grants totaling** $157,825

Mostly local/Pa. giving. High grants of **$20,000** each to Messiah College, United Way of the Capital Region, and Whitaker Center for Science & The Arts. **$12,500** to Bethesda Mission. **$4,000-$4,500** each to Allied Arts Fund, Boys & Girls Club of Harrisburg, Harrisburg Opera, and Silver Spring Presbyterian Church. **$3,000-$3,500** each to Goodwill Industries of Central Pa., Red Cross, and Salvation Army. **$2,000-$2,500** each to Harrisburg Symphony, Hospice of Central Pa., Leadership Institute, Lehigh U., Market Square Concerts, Sonshine Ministries, West Shore Public Library, and WITF-TV/FM. **$1,000-$1,500** each to Central Pa. Food Bank, Central Pa. Youth Ballet, Cumberland-Perry Assn. for Retarded Citizens, Greater Harrisburg Foundation (Simpson Scholarship/Boys Club), Harrisburg Community Theatre, Philadelphia Orchestra, PinnacleHealth Foundation, and United Methodist Home for Children. Other local contributions **$75-$750** for various purposes. **Out-of-state** giving includes **$1,000-$1,500** each to Metropolitan Opera Guild [NY], Vermont Academy, Western Maryland College, and WETA [DC]. ■**PUBLICATIONS:** Grant Request Guidelines; Grant Application Form ■**WEBSITE:** None ■**E-MAIL:** None ■**APPLICATION POLICIES & PROCEDURES:** The Foundation reports that giving focuses on Central Pa. for educational and health/human services purposes; national causes are occasionally supported. Prospective applicants should make an initial telephone call to inquire about the feasibility of submitting a request. Grant requests must be submitted on a formal application form provided by the Foundation, and are accepted at any time. Only one request per year is accepted from an organization. Site visits sometimes are made to organizations being considered for a grant. Grants are awarded at meetings three or four times annually.

O+D+T Mark Simpson (Executive Director+T+Con) — Jerry T. Simpson [Mechanicsburg] (C+T) — Rebecca Reese (T) — Helen M. Simpson (T) — Hilary M. Simpson [Mechanicsburg] (T) — Hugh T.J. Simpson [Mechanicsburg] (T) — Allfirst Bank (Corporate Trustee)

CP-181 **Smith (E.G. & Klara M.) Foundation**
c/o E.G. Smith Inc.
3333 Penn Ave.
West Lawn 19609   (Berks County)

MI-12-22-25-29-41-63
Phone 610-670-1000 **FAX** 610-670-1354
EIN 23-2494804   **Year Created** 1987

AMV $463,727   **FYE** 12-00   (**Gifts Received** $180,750)   71 **Grants totaling** $151,491

All local giving. High grant of **$101,813** to Glad Tidings Assembly of God Church. **$10,100** to Church of God Spring Valley. **$9,187** to Betsy King Classic Charity. **$5,000** each to Berks County Emergency Shelter and Berks County Learning Disabilities Assn. **$1,337** to Trinity United Church of Christ. **$1,000** to Make-A-Wish Foundation. **$930** to St. Mark's United Church of Christ. **$765** to Salvation Army. Other local contributions **$109-$733,** mostly local churches or church groups. ■**PUBLICATIONS:** None ■**WEBSITE:** None ■**E-MAIL:** None ■**APPLICATION POLICIES & PROCEDURES:** No grants awarded to individuals.

O+D+T Edwin G. Smith [Sinking Spring] (S+F+Donor+Con) — Klara M. Smith [Sinking Spring] (C+D+Donor) — Janis L. Weller (P) — John Glass (VP) — Corporate donors: Terre Hill Silo Company; Boyertown Oil Company; E.G Smith, Inc.

CP-182 **Smith Foundation, The**
c/o Stock & Leader
35 South Duke Street, P.O. Box 5167
York 17405   (York County)

MI-13-21-39-41-56-71-84-89
Phone 717-846-9800 **FAX** None
EIN 23-2633100   **Year Created** 1993

AMV $1,505,395   **FYE** 12-00   (**Gifts Received** $895,531)   13 **Grants totaling** $27,473

All giving generally restricted to parts of York County. High grants of **$5,000** each to Eastern York Schools (Dollars for Scholars) and Wrightsville Fire Company. **$3,000** each to Historic Wrightsville and Wrightsville Community Recreation Committee. **$2,000** each to Columbia Recreation Assn., Wrightsville Ambulance Assn. and Wrightsville Rotary Club. **$1,333** to Lancaster Preservation Trust. **$1,000** to Wrightsville 4th of July Celebration. Other smaller local contributions. **Out-of-state** grant to MA. ■**PUBLICATIONS:** None ■**WEBSITE:** None ■**E-MAIL:** None ■**APPLICATION POLICIES & PROCEDURES:** The Foundation reports that only organizations providing charitable services to residents of Wrightsville or Columbia boroughs [York County], or Eastern York County School District are eligible to apply. Grant requests may be submitted in any form at any time—deadline is November 1st; state the purpose of the grant and amount requested.

O+D+T W. Bruce Wallace, Esq. (Con) — Arthur K. Mann, Sr. (D) — Mary Elizabeth Mann (D) — Julianne Smith McNamara (D)

CP-183 **Smith (Marguerite Carl) Foundation**
c/o First Union/Wachovia
33 West 3rd Street, Suite 580
Williamsport 17703   (Lycoming County)

MI-43-44-56-63-71
Phone 570-327-5075 **FAX** None
EIN 23-2564406   **Year Created** 1989

AMV $3,107,715   **FYE** 5-00   (**Gifts Received** $0)   42 **Grants totaling** $116,541

All local giving for organizations and scholarships. High organizational grant of **$6,400** to James V. Brown Library. **$5,500** to Northcentral Pa. Conservancy. **$3,000** to First Baptist Church of Jersey Shore. **$2,500** to Trinity United Methodist Church. **$1,000** to Lycoming County Historical Society. **$500** to Jersey Shore YMCA. About 35 scholarships, mostly **$2,500** each—a few larger, were awarded to local students. ■**PUBLICATIONS:** None ■**WEBSITE:** None ■**E-MAIL:** brenton.hake@wachovia.com ■**APPLICATION POLICIES & PROCEDURES:** The Foundation reports giving is primarily to Lycoming county, especially to Jersey Shore. Grant requests may be submitted in a letter at any time.

O+D+T Brenton Hake (Regional Trust Officer+VP at Bank+Con) — Ralph Kuhns [Jersey Shore] (T) — Mrs. Ralph Kuhns [Jersey Shore] (T) — Shirley Loud [NJ] (T) — Mary Tuefel [Jersey Shore] (T) — Lee Smith [CT] (T)

CP-184   Snyder (Abram M.) Foundation
3791 Lycoming Creek Road
Cogan Station   17728   (Lycoming County)

MI-12-13-14-15-20-21-22-25-29-43-63
Phone 570-494-0465 **FAX** None
EIN 23-2746308   **Year Created** 1994

AMV $714,536   **FYE** 12-00   (**Gifts Received** $104,217)   27 **Grants totaling** $35,611

All local giving; grants are annual gifts except as noted. High grant of **$7,000** to Williamsport YMCA (Heritage Fund). **$5,121** to Habitat for Humanity (building materials). **$4,500** to American Rescue Mission (homeless services). **$2,750** for scholarships. **$2,600** to Crime Stoppers Program (children's program). **$2,000** to Williamsport YWCA (Wise Options/swimming pool). **$1,000-$1,600** each to Kiwanis Charities (youth camp/food for needy), New Covenant United Church of Christ (various purposes), North Central Sight Services (Christmas party), and Red Cross. **$750** each to Children's Development Center and Hospice. Other local contributions **$100-$700** for various community organizations. ■**PUBLICATIONS:** None ■**WEBSITE:** None ■**E-MAIL:** None ■**APPLICATION POLICIES & PROCEDURES:** The Foundation reports that giving is principally to Lycoming County. Grant requests may be submitted in person or a letter to any Foundation officer at any time. Site visits sometimes are made to organizations being considered for a grant.

O+D+T Abram M. Snyder (P+Donor+Con) — Lucinda A. Snyder [Montoursville] (VP+S) — Carl Snyder (VP+F) — Dorothy Snyder (VP+Donor)

CP-185   Snyder (Bruce R. & Madelyn G.) Foundation
c/o Security Fence Company
P.O. Box 395
Red Lion   17356   (York County)

MI-14-15-22-63

Phone 717-244-7653 **FAX** None
EIN 23-2706874   **Year Created** 1992

AMV $335,003   **FYE** 9-00   (**Gifts Received** $85,000)   8 **Grants totaling** $16,500

Nearly half local giving. High Pa. grant of **$3,500** to Salvation Army/York. **$1,000** each to Alzheimer's Assn. of South Central Pa., White Rose Hospice, and York County Blind Center. **Out-of-state** giving includes **$4,500** to Mission to Children Leprosy Fund [CA]; **$3,000** to Samaritan's Purse [NC]; and **$1,000** each to St. Paul's House [NY] and Son'Spot Ministries [NJ]. ■**PUBLICATIONS:** None ■**WEBSITE:** None ■**E-MAIL:** None ■**APPLICATION POLICIES & PROCEDURES:** Grant requests may be submitted in any form at any time.

O+D+T B. Robert Snyder (P+Donor+Con) — William Snyder (VP+Donor) — Carolyn Kline [Dallastown] (D) — Joann Seidenstricker [Dallastown] (D)

CP-186   Sovereign Bank Foundation, The
c/o Sovereign Bank
601 Penn Street, P.O. Box 12646
Reading   19612   (Berks County)

MI-11-12-13-14-15-16-17-18-25-29-35-42-44 54-55-71-85-88
Phone 610-378-6190 **FAX** None
EIN 23-2548113   **Year Created** 1988

AMV $0   **FYE** 12-00   (**Gifts Received** $338,778)   **109 Grants Totaling** $338,740

All giving limited to the Bank's trading area in SE Pa. and other states (see below); grants are for operating support except as noted and some are payments on multiyear pledges. High Pa. grant of **$30,000** to Delaware Valley Habitat for Humanity (pledge payment). **$16,667** to Reading-Berks Emergency Shelter (capital campaign). **$10,000** each to CACLV/Community Action Committee of the Lehigh Valley and Surrey Services for Seniors (multiyear pledge payment). **$7,000** to Neighborhood Housing Services of Reading (affordable housing services). **$5,000** each to Bethany Children's Home [Berks County] (pledge payment), Bucks County Funders Initiative (pledge payment), Fox Chase Cancer Center (research), Penn State U./Berks Campus (capital campaign), and Philadelphia Commercial Development Corp. **$4,000** each to Greater Philadelphia Food Bank (Kids' cafe) and Tabor Community Services [Lancaster] (pledge payment). **$3,000** each to Allentown Economic Development Corp. (membership), The Enterprise Center [Philadelphia], Greater Berks Food Bank (Kids Cafe program), Philadelphia Museum of Art (corporate partner), and Police Athletic League of Reading (teen center). **$2,000-$2,500** each to Advocate Community Development Corp., ASSETS [Lancaster], Camphill Village Kimberton Hills, Campus Boulevard Corp. (job training programs), Community First Fund [Lancaster], Community Women's Education Project (Teaching through Technology), Delaware County Community College Education Foundation (Chester County campus capital campaign), Eastern Pa. HOBY (sponsorship), Goodwill Employment Services-Berks County, Greater Philadelphia Urban Affairs Coalition, Harcum College (sponsored scholars program), Housing Assn. & Development Corp. [Allentown] (inner-city revitalization), Lutheran Home at Topton (New Century Fund), Mt. Airy USA (new programs), PACDC/Philadelphia Assn. of Community Development Corporations, Philadelphia Council for Community Advancement (housing counseling), ProJeCt of Easton, Reading-Berks Human Relations Council (capital campaign), and Spanish-Speaking Council of Reading & Berks County. **$1,000-$1,500** each to Albright College (local government program), ARC of Lehigh & Northampton Counties (Family Resource Center), Centro Pedro Claver, Habitat for Humanity of Susquehanna County, HARB-Adult [Lancaster] (adopt-a-room endeavor), IHM Center for Literacy & GED Programs (language education), Indian Valley Housing Corp., Lankenau Hospital, Lehigh Valley Child Care (high school center), Lock Haven U. Foundation, The Partnership Community Development Corp., Rainbow Home [Reading], Salvation Army/Allentown, Williamsport-Lycoming Foundation (Book of Dreams), Willow Grove Community Development Corp., Women's Christian Alliance [Philadelphia] (capital campaign). Other smaller local contributions. Out-of-state giving primarily to NJ. In addition, 14 matching gifts disbursed to colleges/universities. ■**PUBLICATIONS:** How To Apply for a Grant from Sovereign Bank Foundation brochure ■ **WEBSITE:** www.sovereignbank.com■**E-MAIL:** jschupp@sovereignbank.com■**APPLICATION POLICIES & PROCEDURES:** The Foundation reports that only organizations, projects, or concerns which directly affect communities in the Bank's trading area (SE Pa., NJ, and New England) are eligible for support. Grants are awarded primarily for Housing & Housing Advocacy, Health/Hunger Relief, Social Services, Community Culture, Development of Minority Populations, and Micro-business lending in Urban Environments. A major area of focus is housing and transitional housing for at-risk populations in the Bank's local communities; emergency sheltering, single family housing by nonprofits, and support services for these types of services are a high priority. Matching grants (up to **$500**) for employee donations are made to institutions of higher education. No grants are awarded to/for individuals, athletic, beauty or scholarships pageants, sectarian religious purposes, political candidates or parties, or fraternal or labor organizations. Local United Way agencies are ineligible for general support but will be considered for secondary campaigns. The Foundation encourages collaboration between agencies in addressing community needs. Most grants are for one year; multi-year funding is considered, particularly for capital fund campaigns, but must be specifically requested. Most giving is for (a) special programs not part of the ongoing maintenance or operation of an organization, (b) seed money for pilot programs of the potential to be self-sufficient, (c) programs and capital projects which stimulate or provide leverage for additional funding, and (d) capital and equipment needs. Prospective applicants initially should make a telephone inquiry about the feasibility of submitting a request. Grant requests may be submitted at any time in a proposal (on agency letterhead paper) which covers the following points: (1) Purpose of the grant and specific dollar amount being requested. (2) An itemized program budget. (3) Why this program is important and the population being served. (4) Why one's agency is the best sponsor of this program. If other agencies with similar programs exist in the area, discuss why this proposed project is not duplicative. (5)Is it a pilot program? Has it been tried elsewhere in the country and what were the results? (6) Qualifications of key personnel. (7) What other funding has been secured or requested? (8) How will the program be funded in future? (9) How will it be evaluated? (10) When are funds expected to be needed? (11) Documentation of endorsement by the Board of Directors. (12) Evidence of support (financial, volunteer work, etc.) by Board members. (13) If for equipment, how will it improve agency efficiency. (14) If for capital support, has the community been surveyed to see how the proposed project will be received? In addition, submit a current annual operating budget showing year-to-date income/expenditures by line item; the most recent audit including income statement and balance sheet; a list of Board members and principal occupations; and IRS tax-exempt status documentation. A cover letter on agency letterhead should provide the name, address and telephone number of the person who could be contacted for further information, if necessary, and a statement if the organization has received or been denied a grant in the past by the Foundation—give dates. Also, proposals which follow Delaware Valley Grantmakers' Common Grant Application Form are accepted. Incomplete applications will not be considered and will be returned. Do not use folders or plastic covers and do not submit videos. Site visits sometimes are made to organizations being considered for a grant. Grants are awarded at Directors' meetings held four times a year on an irregular basis.

O+D+T Joseph E. Schupp (Administrator+Assistant VP at Bank+Con) — Lawrence M. Thompson, Jr. (P+D) — John V. Killen (VP+D) — David A. Silverman (S+D) — Richard Kosak (F+D) — Stewart B. Kean (D) — Joseph E. Lewis (D) — F. Joseph Loeper (D) — Richard E. Mohn (D) — Rhoda S. Oberholzer (D) — Daniel K. Rothermel (D) — Elizabeth B. Rothermel (D) — Robert A. Sadler (D) — Jay S. Sidhu (D) — G. Arthur Weaver (D) — Corporate donor: Sovereign Bank

---

CP-187 **Sparr Foundation, The**
10 Lawndale Road, P.O. Box 6007
Wyomissing 19610   (Berks County)
AMV $294,904   **FYE** 6-01   **(Gifts Received** $0)

MI-13-34-41-43-84
Phone 610-374-3085 **FAX** None
EIN 22-2512696   **Year Created** 1984
14 **Grants totaling** $28,300

Mostly local giving. High organization grant of **$3,500** to Camp Mantawny (camp scholarships). **$2,000** for a humanitarian grant to an individual. **$1,500** to Coventry Christian School of Pottstown. **$1,300** to Carlson Prison Fellowship [DC]. Other grants are tuition payments (mostly **$650-$1,500**, some higher) to colleges in many states. ■**PUBLICATIONS:** None ■ **WEBSITE:** None ■**E-MAIL:** t.fowler@d-k.com ■**APPLICATION POLICIES & PROCEDURES:** The Foundation reports most giving for religion and ministerial assistance (especially Churches of Christ), education, and children's causes. Grant requests may be submitted in person or writing, preferably during January-April (deadline is June 1st); describe the organization and purpose of requested funding, and include an organizational budget. Grants are awarded at a June meeting.

O+D+T John A. Wiest (F+T+Con) — Joseph A. Bolognese (C+T) — John R. Allen [West Chester] (T) — Thomas B. Fowler (T) — Jeffrey J. Howell, Esq. [Reading] (T)

CP-188 **Sports Medicine Foundation**
c/o Orthopedic Surgery Institute, Inc.
1779 5th Ave.
York 17403   (York County)
AMV $3,368   **FYE** 6-01   **(Gifts Received** $14,401)

MI-43
Phone 717-846-7846 **FAX** None
EIN 23-2663406   **Year Created** 1992
15 **Grants totaling** $15,000

All awards are scholarships **$500-$3,500** each for York-area students. ■**PUBLICATIONS:** None ■**WEBSITE:** None ■**E-MAIL:** None ■**APPLICATION POLICIES & PROCEDURES:** The Foundation reports that scholarships are restricted to residents of Pa. Scholarship requests must be submitted on a application form, available from the Foundation, together with high school transcript and recommendation letters before the May 1st deadline; applicants must be accepted for full-time study as a freshman at an accredited college/university.

O+D+T Dean Nachtigall, D.O. (P+Donor+Con) — Corporate donor: Orthopedic Surgery Institute

---

CP-189 **Stabler (Donald B. & Dorothy L.) Foundation, The**
c/o Allfirst Trust, M.C. 001-02-05
213 Market Street, P.O. Box 2961
Harrisburg 17105   (Dauphin County)
AMV $14,217,135   **FYE** 12-00   **(Gifts Received** $51,500)

MI-11-13-14-15-22-25-29-31-32-35-41-42-43
44-52-55-61-63
Phone 717-255-2045 **FAX** 717-231-2636
EIN 23-6422944   **Year Created** 1966
75 **Grants totaling** $650,250

Mostly local/Eastern Pa. giving; grants are for general purposes except as noted. High grant of **$60,000** to Catholic Diocese of Allentown. **$50,000** each to Harrisburg Area Community College Foundation, Lehigh U. (Stabler Foundation Fund), Susquehanna U., and Wilson College (Curran Scholarships). **$45,000** to Catholic Diocese of Harrisburg. **$30,000** to United Way of Capital Region. **$25,000** to PinnacleHealth Foundation. **$15,000** each to Council for Public Education (Capital Region Plan) and Red Cross. **$11,500** to ARC of Dauphin & Lebanon Counties. **$11,250** to Harrisburg Area YMCA. **$10,000** each to Fredrickson Library [Camp Hill], Homeland Center (new building/renovations), Hospice of Central Pa. (facility enlargement), Memorial Hospital [Towanda], YMCA Camp Curtin Branch, and YMCA of Greater Harrisburg. **$7,500** each to Bethesda Mission and Boys & Girls Club of Harrisburg. **$5,000-$5,500** each to Allied Arts Fund, Big Brothers/Big Sisters of the Capital Region, Boy Scouts/Keystone Area Council (Camp Hidden Valley), Bucknell U. (student aid fund), Delta Housing, Discovery Center for Science & Technology [Bethlehem], Faith Presbyterian Church, Harrisburg Symphony, Hemlock Girl Scout Council (meditation areas), Lehigh U. (Excellence in Teaching Award), Messiah College, NAMI Pa., Pa. Assn. for the Blind/Tri-County Branch, PinnacleHealth System/Polyclinic Hospital (medical education & research), Salvation Army/Harrisburg, and Visiting Nurse Assn. of Harrisburg. **$3,750** to Paxton Ministries. **$2,500** to Goodwill Industries of Central Pa. and South Central Pa. Food Bank. **$2,000** to Volunteers of America. **$1,000-$1,500** each to Children's Playroom, Christian Churches United-Help Ministries, Cumberland Perry Association for Retarded Citizens, National MS Society, Dauphin County Library System, Downtown Daily Bread, Family & Children's Services of the Capital Region, Gaudenzia, Habitat for Humanity/Greater Harrisburg, Lycoming College (athletic facility), Mental Health Assn., Middletown Christian School, and Presbyterian Homes. Other local contributions **$500** or **$750**. Out-of-state giving includes **$35,000** to Johns Hopkins U. [MD] (rheumatic disease research) and **$10,000** to Miami Heart Research Institute [FL]. ■**PUBLICATIONS:** None ■**WEBSITE:** None ■**E-MAIL:** larry.hartman@allfirst.com ■**APPLICATION POLICIES & PROCEDURES:** The Foundation reports most grants for annual campaigns, continuing support, building funds, capital needs, endowment, scholarships, professorships, or matching funds. No grants are awarded for land acquisition, research, seed money, publications, conferences, deficit financing, or to individuals. Submit grant requests in a full proposal at any time; include an organizational budget, project budget, audited financial statement, and IRS tax-exempt status documentation. Deadlines for applications are one month prior to Board meetings held usually in May, August, and November. Site visits sometimes are made to organizations being considered for a grant. Applicants are notified of decisions within a month of the meetings.

O+D+T Larry A. Hartman (Senior VP at Bank+Con) — William J. King (C) — Frank A. Sinon, Esq. (S) — Cyril C. Dunmire, Jr. (D) — David H. Schaper (D) — Dorothy L. Stabler (D+Donor) — Richard A. Zimmerman [Hershey] (D) — Corporate donors: Eastern Industries, Inc.; State Aggregates; Stabler Development Company; Precision Solar Controls, Inc. [TX]; Protection Services, Inc.; Work Area Protection, Inc. [IL].

CP-190 Staiman (Marvin H.) Charitable Trust　　MI-11-13-22-42-62
c/o Woodlands Bank
2450 East 3rd Street　　　　　　　　　　**Phone** 570-320-2468 **FAX** None
Williamsport 17701　　　(Lycoming County)　**EIN** 23-6610250　**Year Created** 1974
AMV $30,156　　**FYE** 12-00　(**Gifts Received** $15,645)　8 **Grants totaling** $27,000
About half local/Pa. giving. High Pa. grant of **$5,000** to Lycoming College. **$3,600** to Ohev Shalom Synagogue. **$1,800-$2,000** each to Boy Scouts/Susquehanna Council, Hemlock Council Girl Scout Council, Lycoming United Way, and United Jewish Appeal of Williamsport. **Out-of-state** grants: **$10,000** to Orthodox Union [NY] and **$1,000** to National Jewish Committee on Scouting [TX]. ■**PUBLICATIONS:** None ■**WEBSITE:** None ■**E-MAIL:** None ■**APPLICATION POLICIES & PROCEDURES:** Grant requests may be submitted in any form at any time; describe the purpose, state an amount requested, and include IRS tax-exempt status documentation. — Formerly called Staiman Brothers Charities.

O+D+T Thomas B. Burkholder (VP+Trust Officer at Bank+Con) — Marvin H. Staiman (T+Donor) — Jeffrey W. Staiman (T) — Woodlands Bank (Corporate Trustee)

CP-191 Staples (P.A.) Testamentary Trust　　MI-11-12-13-15-22-32-41-44-52-54-71
c/o Hershey Trust Company
100 Mansion Road East, P.O. Box 445　　　　**Phone** 717-520-1130 **FAX** 717-520-1111
Hershey 17033　　　(Dauphin County)　**EIN** 23-6242753　**Year Created** 1956
AMV $244,805　　**FYE** 12-01　(**Gifts Received** $0)　20 **Grants totaling** $17,850
All local giving. High grant of **$1,600** to Boy Scouts/Keystone Area Council. **$1,000** each to American Cancer Society (Hope Lodge), Council for Public Education, Derry Township Social Ministry, Family & Children's Services, Greater Harrisburg Foundation, Hershey Gardens, Hershey Museum, Hershey Public Library, Hershey Symphony Orchestra, Palmyra Public Library, Ronald McDonald House of Hershey, Senior Citizens Center of Derry Township, and United Way of the Capital Region. Other local contributions **$250-$500** for various purposes. ■**PUBLICATIONS:** None ■**WEBSITE:** None ■**E-MAIL:** None ■**APPLICATION POLICIES & PROCEDURES:** The Trust reports that only Hershey-area organizations are eligible to apply. No grants are awarded to individuals. Grant requests may be submitted in a letter (2 pages maximum) before the September 30th deadline; describe the organization, its purpose and activities, and state the principal contact person; include an annual report and IRS tax-exempt status documentation.

O+D+T Raymond T. Cameron (VP/Trust Officer at Bank+Con) — Robert C. Vowler (C+P) — and a ten-member Board of Directors — Hershey Trust Company (Trustee)

CP-192 Stayman (Minnie Patton) Foundation　　MI-43
c/o Mellon Private Wealth Management
2 North Second Street, 12th Floor, P.O. Box 1010　**Phone** 717-780-3037 **FAX** None
Harrisburg 17108　　　(Dauphin County)　**EIN** 23-6235009　**Year Created** 1979
AMV $1,278,755　**FYE** 12-00　(**Gifts Received** $0)　6 **Grants totaling** $70,000
All grants are scholarships for Altoona-area residents whose parents cannot provide adequate financial support. Students may attend any college or university in the U.S. and the scholarships are disbursed directly to the institutions. ■**PUBLICATIONS:** None ■**WEBSITE:** None ■**E-MAIL:** None ■**APPLICATION POLICIES & PROCEDURES:** Only residents and graduates of Altoona-area high schools are eligible for scholarships. The schools determine finanancial need with awards being made based on the number of students attending.

O+D+T Distribution Committee members: Cindy Semic (Trust Officer at Bank+Con) — Richard A. Carothers, Esq. — Bernard Dembert, CPA — Thomas Martin — Dr. Dennis Murray — Mellon Private Wealth Management (Trustee)

CP-193 Steinman (James Hale) Foundation, The
c/o Lancaster Newspapers, Inc.
8 West King Street, P.O. Box 128
Lancaster 17608   (Lancaster County)

MI-11-12-13-14-15-16-19-22-25-29-31-32-41
42-43-51-52-55-56-71
Phone 717-291-8793 **FAX** 717-291-8728
EIN 23-6266377   **Year Created** 1952

AMV $28,780,800   **FYE** 12-00   (**Gifts Received** $1,000,000)   90+ **Grants totaling** $1,203,230

All local giving. High grant of **$420,580** to the J.H. Steinman Conestoga House Foundation. **$107,500** to Lancaster Boys & Girls Club. **$100,000** to Lancaster General Womens & Babies Hospital. **$85,000** to Pa. Academy of Music. **$57,500** to United Way of Lancaster County. **$52,000** to Linden Hall. **$50,000** to Lancaster Foundation for Educational Enrichment. **$25,000** to Salvation Army. **$20,000** to Community First Fund. **$15,000** to Historic Preservation Trust. **$12,000-$12,500** each to Lancaster Farmland Trust, Lancaster Housing Opportunity, Lancaster Partnership Program, and Manos House. **$10,000-$10,400** each to Family & Children's Services, Hands-On-House, Heritage Center of Lancaster, Lancaster Alliance, Penn State U./College of Communications, and UCP of Central Pa. **$7,500** each to Elizabethtown College, Milagro House, and Project Forward Leap. **$5,000** each to Bridge of Hope, Lancaster Campaign, Lancaster Country Day School, Lancaster County Conservancy, Long Home, Penn Laurel Girl Scout Council, and Strand-Capitol Performing Arts Center. **$4,000** to Clare House. **$2,000-$2,500** each to Chesapeake Bay Foundation, Demuth Foundation, Junior Achievement, Lancaster Cleft Palate Clinic, Lancaster Summer Arts Festival, Martin Luther King Scholarship, Mom's House, S. June Smith Center, St. James Church, and Theatre of the Seventh Sister. **$1,000-$1,750** each to Church Farm School [Chester County], Clinic for Special Children, Coby's Family Service, Contact Lancaster, Ephrata Area Community Theatre, Fulton Opera House, Historic Rock Ford/Foundation, Hospice of Lancaster County, Lancaster County Historical Society, Lancaster County Library, Lancaster Family YMCA, Lancaster Museum of Art, Lancaster Symphony Orchestra, MS Society, Next Generation Festival, Planned Parenthood of Lancaster County, Spanish America Civic Assn., Spina Bifida Assn., and Susquehanna Assn. for the Blind. **$750** to Junior Achievement/Lancaster. Other local contributions **$500** for various purposes. Also, **$48,000** for scholarships (**$1,000** or **$2,000** each) restricted to newspaper carriers or dependents of employees of companies listed below. ■**PUBLICATIONS:** application guidelines; grant application form; scholarship application form. ■**WEBSITE:** None ■**E-MAIL:** dgetz@lnpnews.com ■**APPLICATION POLICIES & PROCEDURES:** The Foundation reports that normally only Lancaster County organizations are eligible for support; United Way-supported organizations are ineligible for operating support and no grants are awarded to individuals. Grant requests from organizations must be submitted on a formal application form, available from the Foundation, prior to the October 1st deadline; include an audited financial statement, Board member list, and IRS tax-exempt status documentation. Decisions on organizational grants are made at a December Board meeting. Scholarships are restricted to newspaper carriers or employees' children of donor corporations listed below; applicants must request a formal application form during their senior year in high school; deadline is February 28th for scholarship applications.

O+D+T Dennis A. Getz (S+Con) — Caroline Steinman Nunan (C+T) — Beverly R. Steinman (VC+T) — Willis W. Shenk (F+T) — Corporate donors: Intelligencer Printing Company; Lancaster Newspapers, Inc.; Delmarva Broadcasting Company

CP-194 Steinman (John Frederick) Foundation, The
c/o Lancaster Newspapers, Inc.
8 West King Street, P.O. Box 128
Lancaster 17608   (Lancaster County)

MI-11-12-13-15-16-18-19-22-25-29-31-32-33
35-41-42-44-51-52-54-55-56-64-65-71-85
Phone 717-291-8793 **FAX** 717-291-8728
EIN 23-6266378   **Year Created** 1952

AMV $30,949,523   **FYE** 12-00   (**Gifts Received** $0)   114 **Grants totaling** $1,429,549

Mostly local giving. High grant of **$135,000** to Linden Hall. **$132,500** to Lancaster Boys & Girls Club. **$125,000** to Pa. Academy of Music. **$105,000** to Elizabethtown College. **$100,000** to Lancaster Womens & Babies Hospital. **$75,000** to Salvation Army/Lancaster. **$57,500** to United Way of Lancaster County. **$50,000** each to Lancaster Foundation for Educational Enrichment and Sunnyside Development Corp. **$35,000** to Community First Fund. **$31,000** to Ephrata Hospital. **$30,000** to Historic Preservation Trust. **$26,000** to Spanish American Civic Assn. **$25,000** to Habitat for Humanity/Lancaster. **$20,000** to Columbia Downtown Development. **$12,000-$12,500** each to Friendship Community, Lancaster Farmland Trust, Lancaster Housing Authority, Lancaster Partnership Program, Manos House, and Project Forward Leap. **$11,400** to UCP of Central Pa. **$10,000** each to Elizabethtown Public Library, Family & Children's Services, Franklin & Marshall College (Cultural Enrichment Program), Heritage Center of Lancaster, Hands-On-House, Jewish Community Center, Lancaster Campaign, Light House Rehabilitation Center [New Holland], Penn State U./College of Communications, and Quarryville Library. **$7,500** to Milagro House. **$6,000** to Lancaster Day Care Center. **$5,000** each to Bridge of Hope, Camp Andrews [Holtwood], Fulton Opera House Foundation, HARB Adult, Janus School, Junior Achievement/Lancaster, Lancaster Alliance, Lancaster Cleft Palate Clinic, Lancaster County Conservancy, Long Home, Parish Resource Center, Susquehanna Assn. for the Blind, and Tabor Community Services. **$4,100** to Samaritan Center. **$4,000** to Clare House. **$3,000-$3,500** each to Lancaster Country Day School, Lancaster Museum of Art, Planned Parenthood of Lancaster County, and The Second Mile. **$2,000-$2,500** each to Child Abuse Prevention, Church Farm School [Chester County], COBY's Family Service, Demuth Foundation, Lancaster Mental Health Assn., Lancaster Summer Arts Festival, Martin Luther King Scholarship Fund, Mom's House of Lancaster, Oasis Youth Services, PAI Corp., Pa. Breast Cancer Coalition, Pa. School of Art & Design, Philhaven Hospital, S. June Smith Center, Teen Haven, Theatre of the Seventh Sister, and Water Street Rescue Mission. **$1,000-$1,750** each to ARC of Lancaster County, Arch Street Center, ASSETS, Base, Inc., Boy Scouts/Lancaster, Citizens Scholarship Foundation, Clinic for Special Children, Contact Lancaster Hotline, Council on Drug & Alcohol Abuse, Betty Finney House, Hospice of Lancaster County, Lancaster County Art Assn., Lancaster Catholic High School, Lancaster County Council on Alcoholism, Lancaster County Council of Churches, Lancaster Family YMCA, Lancaster-Lebanon Literacy Council, Lancaster Mediation Center, Lancaster Symphony Orchestra, Lebanon Valley College, Mennonite Historical Society, Mid Atlantic Career Center, Moravian Church of Lancaster, Music at Gretna, North Museum, Occupational Development Center, Pa. Special Olympics, Sexual Assault & Prevention, Urban League of Lancaster, WITF (Next Generation Festival), and to 11 local chapters of national health/disease organizations. Also, **$58,299** was given in Fellowship Awards for graduate study in mental health or a related field. **Out-of-state** grants: **$2,500** to Chesapeake Bay Foundation [MD] and **$1,000** to Mennonite Economic Development Assn. [MO]. ■**PUBLICATIONS:** application guidelines ■**WEBSITE:** None ■**E-MAIL:** dgetz@lnpnews.com ■**APPLICATION POLICIES & PROCEDURES:** The Foundation reports that normally only Lancaster County organizations are eligible for support; United Way-supported organizations are ineligible for operating support and no grants are awarded to individuals, except as indicated below. Grant requests from organizations must be submitted on a formal application form, available from the Foundation, prior to the October 1st deadline; include an audited financial statement, Board member list, and IRS tax-exempt status documentation. Decisions on organizational grants are made at a December Board meeting. Individuals applying for a Fellowship Award—restricted to graduate study in mental health or a related field—must complete a formal application form available from Mary Knopp, Fellowship Program Secretary (e-mail: mknopp@lnpnews.com); February 1st is the deadline for Fellowship applications.

O+D+T Dennis A. Getz (S+Con) — Pamela M. Thye [CT] (C+T) — Willis W. Shenk (F+T) — Henry Pildner, Jr. [NY] (T) — Corporate donors: Intelligencer Printing Company; Lancaster Newspapers, Inc.; Delmarva Broadcasting Company

---

CP-195 Stewart Foundation
　　c/o York Building Products Company
　　1020 North Hartley Street
　　York 17404　　　　　　　　　　　(York County)

MI-11-12-13-14-15-29-35-41-49-55-56-63-71

Phone 717-854-9581　**FAX** 717-843-7207
EIN 22-2762903　　**Year Created** 1986

AMV $1,169,330　　**FYE** 12-00　　(**Gifts Received** $330,500)　　44 **Grants totaling** $220,239

Mostly local giving; grants are for general fund purposes except as noted. High grant of **$75,000** to York Catholic High School. **$30,000** to Strand-Capitol Performing Arts Center. **$20,000** to United Way of York County. **$17,342** to Holy Child Nursery. **$7,433** to Margaret Moul Home. **$5,833** to YMCA of York. **$5,000-$5,00** each to Better York, Inc., Children's Home of York, Cultural Alliance of York, Freedom Hills, and Red Cross/York. **$4,000** to Spring Grove Schools. **$2,000-$2,500** each to Easter Seals, Junior Achievement of South Central Pa., Union Lutheran Church, and York County Heritage Trust. **$1,000-$1,600** to Central Pa. MS Society, Family Services of York, Farm & Natural Lands Trust of York County, Historic York, Jewish Community Center of York, Make-A-Wish Foundation/York, Susan Byrnes Health Education Center, and YCIGA (scholarship fund), and York's Helping Hand. **$800** to The Lehman Center. Other local contributions **$100-$525** for various community purposes. **Out-of-state** grant: **$1,000** to Memorial Sloan Kettering Cancer Center [NY]. ■**PUBLICATIONS:** None ■**WEBSITE:** None ■**E-MAIL:** None ■**APPLICATION POLICIES & PROCEDURES:** The Foundation reports that only organizations in York County or Cecil County, MD are eligible to apply. Prospective applicants initially should make a telephone inquiry about the feasibility of submitting a request. Grant requests may be submitted in a full proposal with cover letter in January or June; include an annual report, organization budget, and Board member list.

O+D+T Gary A. Stewart (P+D+Con) — Karyl L. Gilbert (S+D) — Robert H. Stewart, Jr. (F+D) — Gary M. Gilbert (AS+D) — Mark A. Harrold (AF+D) — Terrence S. Stewart (D+Donor) — Dale C. Voorheis (D) — Corporate donors: Apple Chevrolet; Stewart & Tate, Inc.; York Building Products, Inc.

CP-196 Stuart (G.B.) Charitable Foundation
　　3 South Hanover Street
　　Carlisle 17013　　　　　　　　(Cumberland County)

MI-11-22-31-32-44-56-63-89

Phone 717-243-3737　**FAX** None
EIN 23-2042245　　**Year Created** 1977

AMV $16,779,084　　**FYE** 12-00　　(**Gifts Received** $137,352)　　32 **Grants totaling** $619,198

Mostly local giving; all grants are for public service activities except as noted. High grant of **$105,000** to Bosler Public Library. **$101,000** each to Carlisle Area Religious Council and United Way of the Greater Carlisle Area. **$80,400** to Dickinson Presbyterian Church (religious purposes). **$60,000** to The Great Conewago Presbyterian Church [Gettysburg] (repairs). **$35,050** to 250th C.A.C. 2000. **$25,823** to County of Cumberland. **$21,000** to Union Fire Company (fire engine restoration). **$20,000** to Dickinson Township. **$15,000** to First Presbyterian Church (maintenance/repairs). **$10,657** to Dickinson College (educational purposes). **$7,500** to Silver Spring Presbyterian Church (repairs). **$6,000** to Samaritan Fellowship. **$5,000** each to Historic Carlisle Celebration,Inc. and Messiah College (educational purposes). **$4,350** to Borough of Carlisle (public purposes). **$4,218** to Harrisburg Area Community College (educational purposes). **$2,000** each to Carlisle Meals-on-Wheels and Penn State U. (educational purposes). **$1,000** each to Arthritis Foundation/Central PA Chapter, Juvenile Diabetes Foundation, PA College of Technology [Williamsport], and Scheie Eye Institute [Philadelphia] (teaching/research). Other local grants/contributions, **$200-$500** each, mostly for health/human services. ■**PUBLICATIONS:** None ■**WEBSITE:** None ■**E-MAIL:** None ■**APPLICATION POLICIES & PROCEDURES:** The Foundation reports that organizations in the Carlisle/Cumberland County area receive preference. Prospective applicants initially should make a telephone inquiry about the feasibility of submitting a request. Grant requests may be submitted in a letter at any time—deadline is July 1st; state the purpose and amount of funds needed.

O+D+T Karen E. Faircloth (S+F+D+Con) — Barbara E. Falconer [MA] (P+D) — Victoria J. Macauley [NJ] (VP+D) — Keith D. Falconer [CT] (D) — Alison J. Brockmeyer [MA] (D) — Mellon Bank N.A. (Trustee) — M&T Investment Group (Trustee)

CP-197 Stuck (Clair E. & Flora E.) Foundation
　　7958 U.S. Highway 522 South
　　McVeytown 17051　　　　　　　(Mifflin County)

MI-43

Phone 717-248-8245　**FAX** None
EIN 25-1709803　　**Year Created** 1993

AMV $224,818　　**FYE** 12-00　　(**Gifts Received** $546)　　40 **Grants totaling** $30,000

All grants are college tuition scholarships, **$750** each, for Mifflin or Juniata County residents. ■**PUBLICATIONS:** application guidelines ■**WEBSITE:** None ■**E-MAIL:** None ■**APPLICATION POLICIES & PROCEDURES:** Only graduates of Mifflin or Juniata County high schools are eligible to apply; besides the residency requirement, an applicant must have maintained a 'C' average in high school and will attend an institution of higher education. An applicant is ineligible for support if scholarship support has been received from another foundation or endowment. Applicants must submit a Formal Application Form, available from the Foundation, before the school year ends. Awards are announced in July.

O+D+T Gloria J. Shank (P+F+T+Con) — Nevin L. Shank (VP+S) — Flora E. Stuck [Lewistown] (T+Donor) — Stephen P. Dalton [Lewistown] (T)

CP-198 **Susquehanna-Pfaltzgraff Foundation**
c/o Susquehanna-Pfaltzgraff Company
140 East Market Street, P.O. Box 2026
York 17405   (York County)

MI-11-12-13-14-15-25-29-33-35-41-42-44-55
-56-71-85
Phone 717-848-5500 **FAX** 717-771-1440
EIN 23-6420008   **Year Created** 1966

AMV $1,702,908   **FYE** 12-00   (**Gifts Received** $450,000)   41 **Grants totaling** $510,084

Mostly local/Central Pa. giving. High grant of **$200,000** to Strand-Capitol Performing Arts Center. **$66,700** to United Way of York County. **$22,500** to Focus on Our Future. **$20,000** to Penn State U. **$17,500** to York Habitat for Humanity. **$16,000** to Penn Laurel Girl Scout Council. **$15,000** each to Cultural Alliance of York County, Margaret Moul Home, and York County Blind Center. **$12,000** each to Historic York and Red Cross/York County. **$10,000** each to ARC Foundation-York County and Kaltreider-Benfer Library [Red Lion]. **$7,500** each to Boy Scouts/York-Adams Council and Brethren Home Foundation. **$5,000** each to Christian School of York, Health Education Center, Marantha Church (Nehemia Plan), Team Pa. Foundation [Harrisburg], and YMCA of York/York County. **$3,000-$3,400** each to Adams-Hanover Counseling Services, Easter Seals, and United Way of Lycoming County. **$1,000-$2,000** each to Adams County Agricultural & Natural Resource Center, Assn. of Independent Colleges & Universities in Pa., Eichelberger Performing Arts Center, James V. Brown Library [Williamsport], Lycoming College, Wind Ridge Farm Equine Sanctuary [Wellsport], and York Catholic High School (development fund). Other local contributions **$100-$600** for various purposes. **Out-of-state** giving to corporate operating locations in ME, IN, GA and SC. ■**PUBLICATIONS:** None ■ **WEBSITE:** None ■**E-MAIL:** None ■**APPLICATION POLICIES & PROCEDURES:** The Foundation reports that giving is primarily to York and other corporate operating locations. Prospective applicants initially should telephone the Foundation to inquire about the feasibility of submitting a request. Grant requests may be submitted in a letter at any time; include an annual report, organizational/project budgets, audited financial statement, Board member list, and IRS tax-exempt status documentation. The Board meets as necessary to act on grant applications.
O+D+T John L. Finlayson (Con) — Louis J. Appell, Jr. (P+F+D) — George N. Appell (VP+D) — Helen A. Norton (VP+D) — William H. Simpson (S) — Corporate donors: Cable TV of York; Susquehanna Radio Corporation; The Pfaltzgraff Company; and other related companies

---

CP-199 **Sweet (Ernest L. & Mildred Roberts) Foundation**
c/o Walrath & Coolidge
126 Main Street, P.O. Box 609
Wellsboro 16901   (Tioga County)

MI-13-29-39-41-71-84-85

Phone 570-724-3801 **FAX** None
EIN 22-6408974   **Year Created** 1985

AMV $2,775,158   **FYE** 12-00   (**Gifts Received** $0)   16 **Grants totaling** $92,194

All local giving. High grant to Wellsboro Foundation (downtown enhancement). **$18,500** to Wellsboro Area School District (athletic complex/reader program/equipment). **$16,666** to Partners in Progress. **$12,000** to Wellsboro Area Chamber of Commerce (downtown beautification). **$7,151** to Hamilton-Gibson Productions (lighting system). **$5,000** to Wellsboro Cemetery Company (repaving). **$1,500-$3,100** each to Red Cross (telephone system), Tioga County Cooperative Extension (4-H show ring), Tioga County Emergency Services (training), Wellsboro Shade Tree Commission (tree planting), and Wellsboro Small Fry Football (general support). ■**PUBLICATIONS:** None ■**WEBSITE:** None ■**E-MAIL:** None ■**APPLICATION POLICIES & PROCEDURES:** Only nonprofit organizations located in the Wellsboro Area School District are eligible to apply. No grants are awarded to individuals. Grant requests must be submitted in a letter before the deadlines of April 1st and September 1st; include IRS tax-exempt status documentation.
O+D+T Administrative Committee members: R. Lowell Coolidge, Esq. (Con) — Thomas L. Briggs — Rev. Robert K. Greer — Donna Mettler, Ed.D. — F. David Pennypacker — Citizens & Northern Bank (Trustee)

CP-200 **Tabor (Earl W. & Ina G.) Foundation, The**
c/o Owlett, Lewis & Ginn P.C.
1 Charles Street, P.O. Box 878
Wellsboro 16901   (Tioga County)

MI-12-13-21-41-42-84-89

Phone 570-723-1470 **FAX** None
EIN 25-1815106   **Year Created** 1998

AMV $3,417,213   **FYE** 12-00   (**Gifts Received** $0)   26 **Grants totaling** $141,200

All local giving; some grants comprise several payments. high grant of **$16,500** to Wellsboro Area School District (track repair/replacement). **$15,000** to Mansfield Borough (new pool/bathhouse). **$14,000** to Partners in Progress (building purchase/renovation). **$10,000** each to Tioga Borough (playground), Valley NYPUM Children & Youth Program (summer program building), Westfield Child Development Center (new construction). **$8,000** to Rainbow Riders Riding for Handicapped (expansion/new horses). **$4,000-$6,000** each to Blossburg Area Swimming Assn. (building improvements), Elkland Youth Baseball Assn. (girls program), Knoxville Youth Baseball Assn. (building improvements), Mansfield U. Foundation (camp programs), New Covenant Academy (music program), Tioga County Human Services Agency (support for foster care children), Tioga-Lawrenceville Little League (senior league field), Westfield Youth Baseball Assn. (field renovations). **$2,000-$3,000** each to Adventure Challenge Experience (equipment), American Youth Soccer Assn. (field improvements), Blossburg Kiwanis Club (building improvements), Southern Tioga Gridiron Club (summer football program), Tioga County 4-H Clubs (fairground renovations), and Tioga County Women's Coalition (house repairs). Other smaller contributions for similar purposes. ■**PUBLICATIONS:** Application for Charitable Funds ■**WEBSITE:** None ■**E-MAIL:** None ■**APPLICATION POLICIES & PROCEDURES:** The Foundation reports that most giving is to Tioga County organizations serving children. Grant requests may be submitted at any time on the Application for Charitable Funds available from the Foundation.
O+D+T Thomas W. Owlett, Esq. (T+Con) — Eric L. Beard [Elkland] (T) — Elinor Kantz [Mansfield] (T) — Richard H. Learn [Osceola] (T)

CP-201 **Tozier (Gladys) Memorial Scholarship Trust** MI-43
1400 Woodmont Avenue **Phone** 570-323-0320 **FAX** None
Williamsport 17701 (Lycoming County) **EIN** 23-2650705 **Year Created** 1991
AMV $550,193 **FYE** 12-00 **(Gifts Received** $0) 14 **Grants totaling** $29,000

All grants are scholarships (most range from **$1,500** to **$3,500**) for students from Lycoming, Elk, or Clearfield counties. ■**PUBLICATIONS:** None ■**WEBSITE:** None ■**E-MAIL:** None ■**APPLICATION POLICIES & PROCEDURES:** The Trust reports that only applicants residing in Lycoming, Elk, or Clearfield counties are eligible to apply. A formal scholarship application form, available from the Foundation, must be submitted with supporting academic documentation.

O+D+T Evan R. Rosser, Jr. (Co-T+Con) — Maj. G. Edwin Sinclair — Scott Williams — M&T Bank (Co-Trustee)

CP-202 **Triple H Foundation** MI-22-63
c/o Esbenshade's Greenhouses
619 East 28th Division Highway **Phone** 717-626-7000 **FAX** 717-626-7302
Lititz 17543 (Lancaster County) **EIN** 23-2986164 **Year Created** 1997
AMV $178,729 **FYE** 11-00 **(Gifts Received** $100,000) 6 **Grants totaling** $90,872

Nearly half local giving. High Pa. grant of **$15,000** to Dove Christian Fellowship International. **$10,000** to Abundant Living Ministries. **$8,372** to Dove Ephrata/Lititz. **$2,000** to Lititz Christian Church. **$500** to Tabor Community Service. **Out-of-state grant: $55,000** to Harvest Evangelism [CA]. ■**PUBLICATIONS:** None. ■**WEBSITE:** None ■**E-MAIL:** None ■**APPLICATION POLICIES & PROCEDURES:** The Foundation reports it is changing; no further information is available.

O+D+T Lamar R. Esbenshade (P+Con) — Nancy Jane Esbenshade (S) — Corporate donor: Esbenshade's Greenhouses

---

CP-203 **Trout (Alice Livingston) Family Memorial Fund** MI-32
c/o Fulton Financial Advisors N.A.
One Penn Square, P.O. Box 3215 **Phone** 717-291-2523 **FAX** None
Lancaster 17604 (Lancaster County) **EIN** 23-7660671 **Year Created** 1993
AMV $461,270 **FYE** 2-01 **(Gifts Received** $0) 2 **Grants totaling** $22,826

All local giving; all grants for medical research. High grant of **$18,261** to Penn State College of Medicine/Hershey Medical Center. **$4,565** to Lancaster Heart Foundation. ■**PUBLICATIONS:** None ■**WEBSITE:** None ■**E-MAIL:** None ■**APPLICATION POLICIES & PROCEDURES:** Grant requests may be submitted in a letter at any time; describe in detail the proposed medical research program.

O+D+T Vincent J. Lattanzio (Trust Officer at Bank+Con) — John S. May, Esq. (Co-T) — Fulton Financial Advisors N.A. (Co-Trustee)

CP-204 **Troutman (Paul A.) Foundation** MI-13-14-25-29-32-39-43-55-56-63-84-89
c/o Community Banks, N.A.
150 Market Square, P.O. Box 350 **Phone** 717-692-4781 **FAX** 717-692-5014
Millersburg 17061 (Dauphin County) **EIN** 23-2086508 **Year Created** 1978
AMV $884,138 **FYE** 11-00 **(Gifts Received** $0) 25 **Grants totaling** $40,800

All local giving; grants are unrestricted support except as noted. High grants of **$3,500** each to Millersburg Area Ambulance and Millersburg Fire Company. **$2,000** each Grace United Methodist Church and eight college scholarships for local students. **$1,700** to Millersburg Area Pool Assn. **$1,500** each to E.S.C.A.P.E., Ned Smith Center for Nature & Art, Red Cross/Capital Region Chapter, and YMCA/North Dauphin County (sustaining funds/annual drive). **$1,000** each to American Cancer Society, American Heart Assn., Arthritis Foundation, Delta Housing, Goodwill Industries of Central Pa., Millersburg Borough Christmas Lighting Fund, and Millersburg/Upper Paxton Township Historical Society. Other smaller local contributions. ■**PUBLICATIONS:** None ■**WEBSITE:** None ■**E-MAIL:** None ■**APPLICATION POLICIES & PROCEDURES:** Prospective applicants initially should telephone the Bank to inquire about the feasibility of submitting a request.

O+D+T Shirley G. Helwig (VP/Trust Officer at Bank+Con) — John A. Hayes [Hummelstown] (Co-T) — Community Banks N.A. (Co-Trustee)

CP-205 **Troutman (William C. & Dorothy T.) Foundation** MI-13-15-39-55-56-63-89
c/o Troutman's Chevrolet, Olds & Geo
640 State Street **Phone** 717-896-3903 **FAX** 717-692-3081
Millersburg 17061 (Dauphin County) **EIN** 25-1777792 **Year Created** 1996
AMV $261,905 **FYE** 7-01 **(Gifts Received** $0) 8 **Grants totaling** $15,000

All local giving. High grant of **$3,500** to Borough of Millersburg. **$3,000** each to Grace United Methodist Church and Ned Smith Center for Nature & Art. **$2,000** each to Millersburg Ferry Boat Assn. and Upper Dauphin County YMCA. **$1,000** to Boy Scouts/Troop 151. **$250** each to Millersburg Area Ambulance Assn. and Susquehanna Lutheran Village. ■**PUBLICATIONS:** None ■**WEBSITE:** None ■**E-MAIL:** None ■**APPLICATION POLICIES & PROCEDURES:** The Foundation reports that giving is generally restricted to organizations, public schools and municipalities for enhancing the well-being of northern Dauphin County and western Schuylkill County. Grant requests may be submitted in a letter at any time; state a specific request for funds, explaining the need.

O+D+T David A. Troutman (D+Con) — Dorothy T. Troutman (D+Donor) — Steven Shade

CP-206 **Tyco Electronics Foundation, The**
c/o Tyco Electronics Corporation
P.O. Box 3608, MS 140-10
Harrisburg   17105   (Dauphin County)
AMV $20,143,787   **FYE** 12-00   (**Gifts Received** $0)

MI-11-13-14-31-32-41-42-44-49-51-52-55-57-88

Phone 717-592-4869   **FAX** 717-592-4022
EIN 23-2022928   **Year Created** 1976
340+   **Grants totaling** $1,182,596

About three-fourths local/Pa. giving to corporate operating locations in the following counties: Adams, Cumberland, Dauphin, Franklin, Lancaster, Schuylkill, and York; some education grants are partly matching gifts. High grant of **$138,676** to United Way of the Capital Region. **$35,000** to Allied Arts Fund. **$32,250** to Lebanon County Career & Tech Center. **$30,000** to Council for Public Education [Harrisburg]. **$24,600-$25,950** each to Harrisburg Area Community College, Junior Achievement of Central Pa., Penn State U., and Whitaker Center for Science & The Arts. **$21,290** to Elizabethtown College. **$20,000** each to PinnacleHealth System and West Shore Public Library. **$17,910** to Gettysburg College. **$15,000-$15,860** each to Goodwill Industries of Central Pa., Messiah College, Pa. Assn. of Vocational Administrators, The Second Mile, and WITF. **$13,850** to Shippensburg U. Foundation. **$10,000** each to Big Brothers/Big Sisters of the Capital Region, Carlisle Performing Arts Center, Cultural Alliance of York County, and Harrisburg Symphony Assn. **$9,500** to United Way of Lancaster County. **$7,000-$8,383** each to American Cancer Society/Harrisburg, Thaddeus Stevens College of Technology, United Way of York County, and WHTM-TV. **$5,000-$5,500** each to Archbishop Wood High School [Bucks County], Boy Scouts/Keystone Area Council, Byrnes Health Education Center [York], Dreamwrights Youth & Family Theatre, Gretna Children's Theatre Program, Lebanon Community Theatre, Millersville U., Opera Outreach, YMCA of Carlisle, YWCA of Carlisle, and YWCA of Greater Harrisburg. **$4,400** each to United Way of Greater Carlisle and York College of Pa. **$3,000-$3,700** each to Fulton Opera House Foundation, Juniata College, United Way of Adams County, and United Way of Franklin County. **$2,000-$2,810** each to Archbishop McDevitt High School, Central Pa. Food Bank, Channels Food Rescue [New Cumberland], The Nature Conservancy/Pa. Chapter, Ned Smith Center for Nature & Art, SCORE [Camp Hill], Susquehanna Art Museum, United Disabilities Services [Lancaster], and United Way of Schuylkill County. **$1,800** to United Way of Lebanon County. Other smaller local grants/contributions, primarily for educational institutions. **Out-of-state** giving includes **$20,000** to National Engineers Week [VA] with other support to corporate operating locations primarily in MA, VA, NC, SC, and smaller amounts to other states, as well as for educational matching gifts nationwide. ■**PUBLICATIONS:** statement of program policy; application guidelines ■**WEBSITE:** www.tycoelectronics.com/about/foundation/ ■**E-MAIL:** mjrakocz@tycoelectronics.com ■**APPLICATION POLICIES & PROCEDURES:** The Foundation reports that giving focuses on geographic areas where Tyco Electronics has significant employee populations (Harrisburg/Central Pa. and locations in MA, NC, SC, MI, and TX) or for projects consistent with corporate objectives. Most grants are for specific projects or programs in two priority interest areas (1) Education—especially precollege math/science education, matching gifts, and programs that address a Tyco Electronics corporate concern/interest; and (2) Community Impact—especially United Ways and arts/cultural organizations. In addition, the Foundation gives preferential support to organizations where employees demonstrate a commitment through volunteering. Preference is given to organizations which Tyco Electronics Corp. employees support as volunteers. The Foundation generally does not support organizations in areas with few or no Tyco employees; individuals; private foundations; national organizations; service clubs; fraternal, social or labor/trade organization; churches/religious groups except if providing a nonsectarian service; organizations that discriminate; political campaigns; loans or investments; or programs that pose a potential conflict of interest. Grant requests may be submitted at any time in proposals which include the following: organization name, address, telephone and fax numbers, and name of organization's contact person; description of the organization and its purposes; list of governing board members; current operating budget and the organization's income sources; audited financial statement; most recent IRS Form 990; and IRS tax-exempt status documentation. The proposal should succinctly address the following questions: (a) Briefly describe the program, service or activity for which you funds are requested, how much is being requested, and the planned mode of delivery, including activities/goals. (b) Briefly describe the need for the program, service or activity proposed, how many people it may expect to reach, and what documentation can be provided that the program is needed? (c) Will you be collaborating with other organizations/agencies on this program and, if so, who are the likely collaborators and how will this be accomplished? (d) List any Tyco Electronics employees who volunteer with your organization, and their position if an officer or board member. (e) The estimated cost of the program and projected budget; list the sources of funding committed and proposed. (f) How will the program's success be evaluated? (g) If applicable, how has your organization used previous Tyco Electronics Foundation funding? Grant application deadlines are March 15th, June 15th, September 15th, and December 15th. Grants are awarded at meetings held quarterly. Matching gifts are limited to secondary schools, two-year and four-year colleges/universities, theological or graduate schools, and technical colleges; there is $25 minimum and $2,000 maximum/employee/organization/year with the first $100 matched 2:1, above that 1:1. — Formerly called The AMP Foundation.
O+D+T Mary Rakoczy (Director, Community Relations/Contributions+Con) — AllFirst Bank (Trustee) — Corporate donor: Tyco Electronics Corporation

---

CP-207 **Tyo (Ray)-St. Ferdinand Scholarship Foundation**
c/o Diocese of Harrisburg
4800 Union Deposit Road, P.O. Box 3553
Harrisburg   17105   (Dauphin County)
AMV $2,520,515   **FYE** 12-00   (**Gifts Received** $0)

MI-43

Phone 717-657-4804   **FAX** 717-657-3790
EIN 23-6508132   **Year Created** 1967
51   **Grants totaling** $109,650

All grants are scholarships, currently **$2,000** each for four years, for financially-needy graduates (male and female) of a Diocese of Harrisburg Catholic high school attending a Catholic college/university. ■**PUBLICATIONS:** application guidelines ■**WEBSITE:** None ■**E-MAIL:** None ■**APPLICATION POLICIES & PROCEDURES:** Only financially-needy graduates of the seven Diocese of Harrisburg Catholic high schools who are (or will be) attending a Catholic college/university are eligible to apply. Scholarship applications must be submitted on a formal application form available from the Foundation; applications should be submitted during March-early April (deadline is April 15th). Scholarships are awarded at a May meeting. Awards may be renewed for up to four years providing academic progress is satisfactory and other stipulations apply. — Formerly called King St. Ferdinand, III Scholarship Foundation.
O+D+T Rev. Edward Quinlan (Con) — Most Rev. Nicholas C. Dattilo (T) — George H. Holder (T) — Donald S. Santarelli, Esq. [DC] (T) — Allfirst Bank (Trustee)

CP-208 **Union County Foundation**
c/o Mifflinburg Bank & Trust Co.
250 East Chestnut Street
Mifflinburg 17844   (Union County)

MI-12-13-21

Phone 570-966-1041 **FAX** 570-988-4174
EIN 23-2742485   **Year Created** 1994

AMV $290,766   **FYE** 12-01   **(Gifts Received** $148,022)   **Grants totaling** $18,492

As a Community Foundation, all discretionary giving is limited to organizations serving Union County; information on 2001 grano grants was unavailable. In prior years, grant awarded included **$20,000** to Commonwealth Community Foundation [Harrisburg], **$6,152** to Lewisburg Rotary Golf Club, and support for children/youth programs/projects. ■**PUBLICATIONS:** application guidelines ■**WEBSITE:** None ■**E-MAIL:** jmensch@ptd.net ■**APPLICATION POLICIES & PROCEDURES:** Only Union County organizations are eligible to apply. Prospective applicants initially should make a telephone inquiry about the feasibility of submitting an application and to request a copy of the guidelines; the deadline for requests is April 1st.

O+D+T Patty Zimmerman (Trust Officer at Bank+F+D+Con) — Jeffrey L. Mensch, Esq. (P+D) — Robert Bausinger [New Columbia] (VP+D) — Ann Kaye [Milton] (S+D) — Sharon Cawley [New Columbia]' (D) — Lorraine Lenhart (D) — Carol Schwartz (D) — Graham S. Showalter [Lewisburg] (D) — Guy Temple [Lewisburg] (D)

CP-209 **United Services Foundation**
Post Office Box 36
New Holland 17557
                                                         (Lancaster County)

MI-12-13-14-16-19-22-25-29-32-41-51-63-81-82-84

Phone 717-354-2591 **FAX** 717-354-2481
EIN 23-7038781   **Year Created** 1969

AMV $12,925,158   **FYE** 12-00   **(Gifts Received** $0)   34 **Grants totaling** $676,040

About half local/Pa. giving; grants are for general operations except as noted. High Pa. grant of **$75,000** to Camp Hebron [Halifax] (computer/sewer project). **$50,000** to Philadelphia Mennonite High School. **$25,000** each to to Arbor Place and MEDA. **$20,000** to Ten Thousand Villages [Mechanicsburg] (computer system). **$15,040** to Milagro House. **$10,000** each to Cross Connection Youth, Global Disciples Network [Millersville], Harrisburg Teen Challenge, Lancaster Habitat for Humanity (housing), Samaritan Counseling Center, Student Mobilization Center [Harrisburg], and Water Street Rescue Mission (building repairs). **$5,000** each to ASSETS (training program), Beth Shalom, Diamond Street Early Child Center (scholarships), HARB-Adult, Joni & Friends of Eastern Pa. (conference), Lancaster Mennonite High School (philanthropy program), Theatre of the Seventh Sister (minority voices), and Tabor Community Services. **$3,000** to Music at Gretna. **Out-of-state** giving includes high grant of **$217,000** to Mennonite Foundation [IN]; **$25,000** each to Bethany Christian Community Center [IL] (senior projects) and Goodwill Industries/Michiana [IN] (equipment); **$20,000** each to Christian Peacemakers [IL] (training/equipment) and Duke U. AIDS Research Clinic [NC]; **$10,000** each to Body Wisdom, Inc. [CA] (capital campaign), Latino Union of Chicago [IL], and Metropolitan Community Fund of San Francisco [CA]. ■**PUBLICATIONS:** None ■**WEBSITE:** None ■**E-MAIL:** None ■**APPLICATION POLICIES & PROCEDURES:** Prospective applicants should make an initial telephone inquiry regarding the feasibility of submitting a request. Requests must be submitted on a formal application form which the Foundation will supply; requests should be submitted preferably in September-October. Site visits sometimes are made to organizations being considered for a grant. Decisions on grants are made at a December meeting.

O+D+T Dale M. Weaver (P+Donor+Con) — Edith M. Weaver (Donor)

CP-210 **Visiting Nurse Assn. Foundation of Lebanon County**
2015 Kline Ave.
Lebanon 17042   (Lebanon County)

MI-14-15-17-19-23-31-35
Phone 717-273-2846 **FAX** None
EIN 23-1365981   **Year Created** 1984

AMV $774,566   **FYE** 6-01   **(Gifts Received** $0)   12 **Grants totaling** $17,667

All giving limited to health care services in Lebanon County. High grant of **$6,367** to Lebanon Family Health Services (equipment/outreach/educational materials). **$2,820** to Red Cross (Life Line units). **$1,574** to Compeer of Lebanon County (program). **$1,000** to SARCC/Sexual Assault Resource & Counseling Center (counseling/educational services). Also, eight payments **($57-$3,654)** to provide medical services, insurance, or equipment for persons with disabilities or special needs. ■**PUBLICATIONS:** None ■**WEBSITE:** None ■**E-MAIL:** None ■**APPLICATION POLICIES & PROCEDURES:** Only organizations providing health care services in Lebanon County are eligible to apply. Grant requests may be submitted in a letter at any time; describe how the grant will benefit health care in Lebanon County. Applications for assistance to individuals are reviewed as received, but requests from organizations are reviewed only at an April meeting. Site visits sometimes are made to organizations being considered for a grant.

O+D+T Edgar J. Miller (P+Con) — Margaret Fava (VP) — Sandy Mesics (S) — Denise Johnson (F)

CP-211 **Warehime (A.K., H.V. & J. William) Foundation**
c/o Warehime Enterprises
305 Baltimore Street
Hanover 17331   (York County)

MI-29-33-63-89

Phone 717-632-7278 **FAX** None
EIN 31-1481509   **Year Created** 1996

AMV $353,030   **FYE** 12-00   **(Gifts Received** $0)   8 **Grants totaling** $16,647

Mostly local giving. High grant of **$15,000** to Adams-Hanover Counseling Services. Other local contributions **$100-$308** for various community organizations. — Giving in the prior year included **$284,165** to Borough of Hanover; **$15,000** to Adams-Hanover Counseling Services; and **$5,000** to Emmanuel United Church of Christ. ■**PUBLICATIONS:** None ■**WEBSITE:** None ■**E-MAIL:** None ■**APPLICATION POLICIES & PROCEDURES:** Information not available.

O+D+T J. William Warehime (P+Donor+Con) — Elizabeth Stick [York] (VP) — Linda A. Lohr (S+F) — Edward L. Geesaman [Waynesboro] (D)

CP-212 Warfel (J.R. & D.) Foundation
2001 Harrisburg Pike, P.O. Box 4488
Lancaster 17604   (Lancaster County)

MI-15-22-25-63
Phone 717-391-3640 **FAX** None
EIN 23-2788089   **Year Created** 1994

AMV $773,935   **FYE** 12-00   **(Gifts Received** $0)   40+ **Grants totaling** $36,848

Mostly local giving. High grant of **$19,479** to Grace Evangelical Congregational Church. **$2,000** to Water Street Rescue Mission. **$1,000** each to Evangelical Congregational Retirement Village and Salvation Army. **$750** to Coral Ridge Ministries. **$740** to Associates in Media. Other local and **Out-of-state** contributions **$10-$500** for various types of organizations. ■**PUBLICATIONS:** None ■**WEBSITE:** None ■**E-MAIL:** None ■**APPLICATION POLICIES & PROCEDURES:** No grants awarded to individuals. Grant requests may be submitted verbally or in writing at any time.
O+D+T J. Richard Warfel (P+D+Donor+Con) — Doreen Warfel (S+D+Con) — Derrick M. Warfel [CA] (F+D) — John S. Ross, Jr. CPA (D)

CP-213 Watchorn (Stephen) Foundation
c/o McNees Wallace & Nurick
100 Pine Street, P.O. Box 1166
Harrisburg 17108   (Dauphin County)

MI-33-42-63
Phone 717-232-8000 **FAX** None
EIN 23-7037270   **Year Created** 1969

AMV $512,446   **FYE** 8-00   **(Gifts Received** $0)   10+ **Grants totaling** $19,100

Nearly half local giving. High Pa. grant of **$3,200** to Franklin & Marshall College. **$2,000** to Wilson College. **$1,800** to Penn State U. **$500** to Trinity Evangelical Lutheran Church. Other smaller local contributions. **Out-of-state** giving, mostly where Trustees reside, includes **$4,000** to Episcopal Church of St. Paul & St. James [CT] and **$2,500** to Gestalt Institute of New England [MA]. ■**PUBLICATIONS:** None ■**WEBSITE:** None ■**E-MAIL:** None ■**APPLICATION POLICIES & PROCEDURES:** The Foundation reports that giving generally is limited to organizations that the directors know personally. Grant requests may be submitted in a letter (2 pages maximum) at any time.
O+D+T W. Jeffry Jamouneau, Esq. (S+Con) — Robert Watchorn, III (P+D) — Barbara Watchorn Fiddler [CT] (VP+F+D) — Kathryn Watchorn Hearn [MA] (VP+D)

CP-214 Waypoint/York Federal Foundation, Inc.
c/o Waypoint Bank
101 South George Street, P.O. Box 15068
York 17405   (York County)

MI-11-12-13-14-15-16-29-33-35-39-41-42-43
44-49-51-55-56-64-85
Phone 717-815-4502 **FAX** 717-699-2929
EIN 23-2111139   **Year Created** 1985

AMV $299,715   **FYE** 6-01   **(Gifts Received** $336,900)   75+ **Grants totaling** $289,840

All local/Pa. giving. **PLEDGE PAYMENTS** on multiyear grant commitments: **$81,250** to United Way of York County. **$27,500** to Cultural Alliance of York County. **$15,000** to York College of Pa. **$10,000** each to Focus on Our Future, Margaret Moul Home, Penn Laurel Girl Scout Council, and York County Alliance on Learning. **$5,000** each to ARC Foundation of York County (capital campaign), Better York, Inc., Historic York, Inc., Kaltreider-Benfer Library, Lancaster Theological Seminary (York Connection), York Arts, and York Murals, Inc. **$4,800** to Easter Seals of South Central Pa. **$3,333** to Dreamwrights Youth & Family Theatre. **$3,000** each to Boy Scouts/York-Adams Council and West York Area Dollars for Scholars. **$2,000** to Jacobus Lion's Ambulance Club. **$1,000** each to Adams Hanover Counseling Services, Penn State U. (Four Diamonds), Spring Grove Scholarship Fund, and Theatre Harrisburg (capital campaign). **OTHER GRANTS** (all for annual/general support except as noted): **$25,000** to Cultural Alliance of York County (A New Beginning campaign). **$5,000** to Junior Achievement of South Central Pa. **$3,500** to Allied Arts Fund. **$3,000** to Justice-Compassion-Community Campaign. **$2,500** each to to A-T Children's Project (walk sponsor) and Byrnes Health Education Center (Heartbeat Scholarship program). **$2,000** to Access York. **$1,000-$1,500** each to Dallastown Forensic Team Booster Club (tournament), Greater York Center for Dance Education (renovation), Historic York, Inc. (preservation program), Latin Voice of York (parade sponsorship), Leave A Legacy/York County, Optimist International Foundation (track-field event), Penn State/York Campus, Salvation Army (Coats for Kids program), SCORE, York Arts (ArtWorks program), York Spanish American Center (meeting sponsorship), York YMCA, York YWCA, and Young Life. **$900** to Christopher Columbus Scholarship Fund. Other local contributions **$100-$800** for various community organizations and activities. ■**PUBLICATIONS:** None ■**WEBSITE:** www.waypointbank.com [corporate info only] ■**E-MAIL:** robert.pullo@waypointbank.com ■**APPLICATION POLICIES & PROCEDURES:** Giving is generally limited to the Bank's marketing area. No grants are awarded to individuals. Prospective applicants initially should make a telephone inquiry about the feasibility of submitting a request. Grant requests may be submitted in a letter at any time; include an annual report, list of Board members, audited financial statement, and IRS tax-exempt status documentation. Site visits sometimes are made to organizations being considered for a grant. The Board of Directors awards grants at monthly meetings.
O+D+T Robert W. Pullo (P+T+Con) — James H. Moss (F) — Cynthia A. Dotzel, CPA (T) — Robert W. Erdos (T) — Randall A. Gross (T) — Byron M. Ream (T) — Robert L. Simpson (T) — Corporate donors: Waypoint Bank; York Federal Savings & Loan Assn.

CP-215 Weld Foundation, The
814 Willow Valley Lakes Drive
Willow Street 17583   (Lancaster County)

MI-13-14-15-22-41-44-52-56-71
Phone 717-291-8797 **FAX** None
EIN 23-2680871   **Year Created** 1992

AMV $2,335,545   **FYE** 12-00   **(Gifts Received** $16,287)   42 **Grants totaling** $86,750

About two-thirds local giving. High Pa. grants of **$10,000** to Linden Hall School (capital campaign) and Salvation Army (capital campaign). **$2,500** to Milagro House. **$1,500** to Gate House. **$1,000** each to Arch Street Center, Boys & Girls Club, Fulton Opera House, HARB-Adult, The Heritage Center, Historic Preservation Trust, Hospice, Janus School, Lancaster County Assn. for the Blind, Lancaster County Conservancy, Lancaster Farmland Trust, Library, Linden Hall, Parish Resource Center, Pa. Academy of Music, Salvation Army, and Water Street Rescue Mission. Other local contributions **$500** each for cultural, youth, human services, historic, environmental, and other purposes. **Out-of-state** grants include high grant of **$31,250** to Wilbraham & Monson Academy [MA] (mostly for capital campaign) and **$5,000** to Long Trail School [VT] (capital campaign). ■**PUBLICATIONS:** None ■ **WEBSITE:** None ■ **E-MAIL:** None ■**APPLICATION POLICIES & PROCEDURES:** Information not available. — An alternate contact address is J. David Shenk, P.O. Box 1092, Manchester Village, VT 05254.

O+D+T Willis W. Shenk (C+Donor+Con) — J. David Shenk [VT] (P+Donor) — Elsie S. Shenk (VP+S+Donor) — Mary Louise Shenk [VT] (F)

CP-216	**Wells (Franklin H. & Ruth L.) Foundation, The**		**MI**-12-22-25-31-39-41-42-43-44-51-52-55-56

4718 Old Gettysburg Road, Suite 209   **Phone** 717-763-1157   **FAX** 717-763-1832
Mechanicsburg 17055   (Cumberland County)   **EIN** 22-2541749   **Year Created** 1983

AMV $6,646,926   **FYE** 5-00   **(Gifts Received** $0)   37 **Grants totaling** $213,320

About three-fourths local/Pa. giving; grants are for annual support except as noted. High grants of **$25,000** each to Carlisle Hospital Medical Care (dental clinic/caring center) and River Rescue of Harrisburg (community life team/EMS unification project). **$20,000** to Cumberland Valley Habitat for Humanity (purchase land/materials). **$12,284** to Brethren Housing Assn. (expand transitional housing program). **$12,000** to Messiah College (nursing scholarships). **$11,000** to Legal Services, Inc. (child support project). **$10,000** each to Agape Residential Ministries (furnishings/appliances), Allied Arts Fund (administrative costs), and Susquehanna Housing Initiatives (matching grant). **$9,036** to The Greater Harrisburg Foundation (mostly early childhood training institute planning). **$5,000** to West Perry School District (careers program). **$1,000-$2,000** each to Central Pa. Friends of Jazz, Cumberland Dance Company, Cumberland Valley School District (buddy program), Danzante, Gretna Productions, Harrisburg Area Community College (cultural arts series), Harrisburg Opera Assn., Harrisburg Shakespeare Festival, Harrisburg Symphony, Market Square Concerts, MetroArts of the Capital Region, Music at Gretna, Theatre Harrisburg, United Negro College Fund, and The Wednesday Club. Other smaller local contributions, mostly for cultural purposes. **Out-of-state** giving includes **$25,000** to Tri-State U. [IN] (physics lab equipment) and **$16,000** to Monmouth College [IL] (technology equipment). ■**PUBLICATIONS:** None ■**WEBSITE:** None ■**E-MAIL:** None ■**APPLICATION POLICIES & PROCEDURES:** The Foundation reports that giving is generally limited to Cumberland, Dauphin, and Perry counties, mostly for special projects or seed money for new programs. Priority areas of interest are health/human services, education, and arts/culture; no grants are awarded for religious activities or endowments. Prospective applicants should initially telephone the Foundation to inquire about the feasibility of submitting a request. Submit grant requests in a letter or proposal at any time (deadlines are February 28th and August 31st); state the purpose/goals of the project and include an annual report, organizational/project budgets, audited financial statement, list of major funding sources, Board member list, and IRS tax-exempt status documentation. Site visits sometimes are made to organizations being considered for a grant. The Committee awards grants in April and October.

O+D+T Distribution Committee members: Miles J. Gibbons, Jr. (Executive Director+Con) — William Cramer [VA] — Julie Thomas [VA] — Allfirst Bank (Trustee)

CP-217	**Wettrick (Marian J.) Charitable Foundation**		**MI**-34-43

c/o Citizens Trust Company
10 North Main Street   **Phone** 814-274-9150   **FAX** 814-274-0401
Coudersport 16915   (Potter County)   **EIN** 25-6545149   **Year Created** 1996

AMV $1,950,045   **FYE** 12-00   **(Gifts Received** $9,000)   8 **Grants totaling** $87,500

Eight scholarships, ranging from **$10,000** to **$15,000**, were awarded to women attending medical school in Pa. ■**PUBLICATIONS:** Medical Internship Application Form ■**WEBSITE:** None ■**E-MAIL:** None ■**APPLICATION POLICIES & PROCEDURES:** The Foundation reports that scholarships are only for medical education and all applicants must meet the following criteria: (a) a female graduate of a Pa. college/university, (b) accepted to or attending a Pa. medical school or interning at an accredited medical teaching hospital in Pa., and (c) have an inclination to practice medicine at Charles Cole Memorial Hospital, Coudersport. Prospective applicants should contact a Financial Aid Officer at any Pa. medical school for a copy of the Foundation's Medical Internship Application Form or for additional information.

O+D+T Justin F. Krellner (VP at Bank+Con) — Citizens Trust Company (Trustee)

CP-218	**Whipple Sunbury Foundation**		**MI**-11-13-14-22-44-65

c/o Susquehanna Trust & Investment Co.
400 Market Street   **Phone** 570-863-6251   **FAX** None
Sunbury 17801   (Northumberland County)   **EIN** 23-6528682   **Year Created** 1973

AMV $353,497   **FYE** 12-00   **(Gifts Received** $0)   10 **Grants totaling** $12,250

All giving restricted to the Sunbury area. High grant of **$3,500** to Central Susquehanna Valley Interfaith Council (Meals on Wheels). **$2,750** to Greater Susquehanna Valley YMCA (financial assistance program). **$1,750** to Kauffman Public Library (book purchase). **$1,000** to Special Olympics. **$750** to Boy Scouts/Susquehanna Council (community scouting services). Other smaller contributions for various community organizations. ■**PUBLICATIONS:** Annual Report ■**WEBSITE:** None ■**E-MAIL:** None ■**APPLICATION POLICIES & PROCEDURES:** The Foundation reports that only Sunbury-area organizations are eligible to apply. Submit grant requests in any form at any time; include IRS tax-exempt status documentation. The Board meets in June and December to award grants.

O+D+T John Gallo, Jr. (Sr. VP+Sr. Regional Trust Officer at Bank+Con) — Susquehanna Trust & Investment Co. (Trustee)

CP-219   Whitaker (Helen F.) Fund, The   MI-52-55
4718 Old Gettysburg Road, Suite 209   **Phone** 717-763-1600 **FAX** 717-763-1832
Mechanicsburg   17055   (Cumberland County)   **EIN** 22-2459399   **Year Created** 1983
AMV $33,451,568   **FYE** 7-00   (**Gifts Received** $0)   61 **Grants totaling** $4,458,007

Nationwide giving for music-related purposes—about 10% local/Pa. giving; grants are for general operations/seasonal support except as noted. High Pa. grant of **$146,000** to Concerto Soloists [Philadelphia] (administrative/development costs). **$90,000** to Curtis Institute of Music (conducting program). **$50,000** each to Academy of Vocal Arts [Philadelphia] (oratorio training) and Pittsburgh Opera (Duquesne program). **$35,000** to Opera Company of Philadelphia (debut artists program). **$30,000** to Harrisburg Symphony (educational outreach programs/seasonal support). **$25,000** each to Market Square Concerts (summer festival/seasonal support), Philadelphia Chamber Music Society (emerging artists project), and Susquehanna Art Museum (building renovations). **$20,000** to Central Pa. Youth Ballet (new studio construction). **$11,000** to Harrisburg Opera Assn. (mostly production support). **$10,000** to Conductors Guild [Chester County] (conductor training workshops), **$5,000** each to Concertante Chamber Players [Wormleysburg], and MetroArts of the Capital Region (Arts for Change program). **$750-$2,000** each to Chamber Singers of Harrisburg, Gretna Productions, Harrisburg Choral Society, Harrisburg Singers, Music at Gretna, Open Stage of Harrisburg, Perry County Council of the Arts, Susquehanna Chorale, and Theatre Harrisburg. **Out-of-state** giving includes **$1,600,000** to Boston Symphony Orchestra (Tanglewood endowment); **$600,794** (4 grants) to Chamber Music America (programs/services and endowment match); **$190,000** to New World Symphony [FL] (musician development); **$155,000** to American Music Center [NY] (copying assistance program/seasonal support). **$115,000** to Chorus America [DC] (multiple purposes); **$105,000** to Assn. of Performing Arts Presenters (Classical Connections Project). **$100,000** each to Concert Artists Guild [NY], Meet the Composer [NY] (Commissioning Music), and San Diego Opera Assn. [CA] (education/outreach); and **$10,000-$90,000** each for musical organizations in CO, DC, FL, IL, MN, MO, NY, and SC. ■**PUBLICATIONS:** Brochure; Contents of Grant Application memorandum ■**WEBSITE:** None ■**E-MAIL:** paula@whitaker.org ■**APPLICATION POLICIES & PROCEDURES:** The Foundation reports that most giving is limited to national nonprofit organizations which (a) support advanced training or career development of classical musicians or (b) provide membership/support services for some aspect of classical music. Additional support is given to charitable organizations in the Harrisburg, Philadelphia, or Naples, FL areas which present classical music or provide other cultural activities. Most grants are for special projects or general support; multiyear grants are awarded. Grants for endowment are only considered in the context of special initiatives. No grants are awarded to individuals. Prospective grant applicants should first submit a preliminary letter (4 pages maximum) covering the following: brief history of organization; clear statement of proposed program's objectives; brief description/timetable of proposed program; summary budget for each year of the program and budget amount to be requested from The Whitaker Fund; criteria for measuring the program's success or failure; and name/statement of qualifications of the program's contact person. Do not include brochures, annual reports, printed materials, or recordings. Deadlines for receipt of the preliminary letter are March 1st, July 1st, and November 1st. The Fund, after review of the preliminary letter, may invite submission of a full proposal and will specify at that time its form/content and deadline. Site visits sometimes are made to organizations being considered for a grant. Grants are awarded at meetings in January, June and October. — **Note:** The Fund anticipates liquidating all assets and terminating operations by the end of 2006.

O+D+T Committee members: Miles J. Gibbons, Jr. (Executive Director+Con) — Ruth Whitaker Holmes, Ph.D. [FL] — Carmelita Biggie [Rosemont] — Chase Bank [NY] (Corporate Trustee)

CP-220   Williams (John G.) Scholarship Foundation   MI-43
c/o The American Group
3425 Simpson Ferry Road   **Phone** 717-763-1333 **FAX** 717-631-1336
Camp Hill   17011   (Cumberland County)   **EIN** 23-2329462   **Year Created** 1986
AMV $641,095   **FYE** 3-01   (**Gifts Received** $0)   17 **Grants totaling** $70,800

All disbursements are scholarship-loans ranging from **$1,000** to **$15,000** for Pa. residents attending colleges in many states. ■**PUBLICATIONS:** brochure with eligibility requirements ■**WEBSITE:** None ■**E-MAIL:** None ■**APPLICATION POLICIES & PROCEDURES:** The Foundation reports that applicants for scholarship-loans must: (1) be a resident of Pa.; (2) demonstrate financial need; and (3) have high academic standing. Applications may be submitted at any time on a formal application form available from the Foundation. Interest on a loan begins to accrue one year after completion of full-time study, and when repayment begins, continues for five years.

O+D+T Connie Williams-Jack (Executive Director)

CP-221   Williamsport-Lycoming Foundation   MI-12-14-15-17-25-31-35-41-42-43-44-51-52
220 West 4th Street, 3rd Floor, Suite C   56-71-72-84-85-89
Williamsport   17701   **Phone** 570-321-1500 **FAX** 570-321-6434
                        (Lycoming County)   **EIN** 24-6013117   **Year Created** 1916
AMV $48,385,944   **FYE** 12-00   (**Gifts Received** $4,247,203)   120+ **Grants totaling** $883,090

As a Community Foundation all discretionary giving is generally limited to organizations serving Lycoming County; about 50 grants from discretionary funds totaled **$200,231** of which some comprised multiple awards. High grant of **$30,200** to Community Arts Center (community outreach/annual support). **$17,500** to Sun Home Health Services (tele-homecare units). **$12,525** to Lycoming Mediation Project (volunteer training). **$12,500** to Lycoming Health Improvement Coalition (administrative support). **$10,500** to Williamsport-Lycoming Habitat for Humanity (home construction/community service award). **$10,000** to Gen. John Burrows Historical Society (facility renovation). **$9,075** to Jersey Shore YMCA (interior improvements). **$9,000** to Campbell Street Family Youth & Community Assn. (breaking-down-barriers program). **$8,500** to Muncy Historical Society (restoration/security system/program). **$7,500** to Evangelical Community Hospital (newborns testing). **$6,000** each to Meadows Assisted Living (handicapped accessible vehicle) and Muncy Pool Assn. (operating support). **$5,000-$5,559** each to Commonwealth Community Foundations [Harrisburg] (membership fee), Council on Foundations [DC] (membership fee), Lycoming United Way (annual giving), and St. Andrew Lutheran Church (replace carillon). **$4,000-$4,300** each to City of Williamsport (facade improvement project), Muncy Baptist Church (annual support), and St. Michael's School (adventure-based counseling). **$3,000** to American Lung Assn. (computer upgrades). **$2,500** each to Annunciation Church (community service award) and Muncy Public Library (annual support). **$1,000-$1,600** each to Leadership Lycoming (community forum), Muncy Pop Warner Football (equipment shed), Williamsport-Lycoming Arts Council (fundraising training), and Young Marines (uniforms/equipment). Also, six scholarships (**$3,000** or **$1,250** each) awarded to students of Muncy School District and Warrior Run High School. Other smaller local discretionary contributions **$49-$350** for various purposes. All other grants awarded from restricted or donor-advised funds. ■**PUBLICATIONS:** annual Report to Community; mission statement; Grant/Loan Guidelines memorandum ■**WEBSITE:** www.wlfoundation.org ■**E-MAIL:** wlf@wlfoundation.org ■**APPLICATION POLICIES & PROCEDURES:** The Foundation reports funding priorities of arts/culture, economic/community development, education, health/human Services, and recreation & the environment. Generally, only Lycoming County organizations are eligible to apply for discretionary funds which mostly are for seed money, special projects, capital projects—generally limited to 10%-30% of total, and matching grants; multiple-year awards are made but are discouraged. Generally no grants/loans are awarded for ongoing operational support (except for seed funding or special situations), annual campaigns, event sponsorships, debt reduction, sectarian religious purposes, clubs/organizations serving a select membership, sports teams, fire companies, individuals, highly-specialized research, endowment (unless created within the Foundation), or (except as provided by established funds managed by high schools/colleges) scholarships, fellowships, honorary awards, or travel grants. Prospective applicants initially should make a telephone inquiry about the feasibility of submitting a request. Grant requests must be submitted on the Grant/Loan Application form available from the Foundation; the form details many required attachments. Ten sets of the complete application/attachments packet must be submitted. Mini-grant requests—up to $10,000 are considered quarterly (deadlines for applications are March 1st, June 1st, September 1st and December 1st). Regular Grant Requests—over $10,000 are considered semi-annually (deadlines are March 1st and September 1st). Contact the Foundation for information about low- or no-interest loans. Site visits usually are made to organizations being considered for a grant. The Board of Directors awards grants at meetings about 8-10 weeks following each deadline. — Formerly called The Williamsport Foundation.

O+D+T Kimberley Pittman-Schulz (P+Con) — Ann M. Alsted [Montoursville] (C+D) — Thomas C. Raup (VC+D) — Daniel G. Fultz (S+F+D) — Robert E. Moore (D) — John C. Schultz (D) — Carol D. Sides (D) — John M. Young (D)

CP-222 **Winchester Foundation**		MI-42-43
c/o First Union/Wachovia - PA 6906		
P.O. Box 3226		**Phone** 717-295-3847 **FAX** None
Lancaster 17604	(Lancaster County)	**EIN** 23-6215528 **Year Created** 1934
AMV $448,227 **FYE** 9-00	**(Gifts Received** $0)	**4 Grants totaling** $17,500

All giving restricted to Philadelphia-area colleges/universities to provide financial assistance to students. High grant of **$6,000** to Eastern College, **$5,000** to LaSalle U. **$4,000** to Manor College. **$2,500** to Harcum College. ■**PUBLICATIONS:** None ■**WEBSITE:** None ■**E-MAIL:** None ■**APPLICATION POLICIES & PROCEDURES:** Only colleges and universities in the Delaware Valley are eligible to apply for scholarship funds; no awards are made directly to individuals. Grant requests should be submitted before the December 31st deadline. Grants are awarded at a January meeting.

O+D+T Richard Fritsch (Assistant VP at Bank+Con) — First Union/Wachovia (Trustee)

CP-223 **Wolf Foundation, The**		MI-11-13-14-15-16-25-29-31-42-44-45-51-55
c/o The Wolf Organization, Inc.		56-57-63-71-84
20 West Market Street, P.O. Box 1267		**Phone** 717-852-4800 **FAX** None
York 17405	(York County)	**EIN** 23-7028494 **Year Created** 1969
AMV $439,657 **FYE** 12-00	**(Gifts Received** $17,952)	**48 Grants totaling** $254,719

Mostly local giving. High grant of **$40,000** to Cultural Alliance of York County. **$25,600** to United Way of York County. **$23,334** to York Foundation. **$17,500** to York Habitat for Humanity. **$11,500** to Penn Laurel Girl Scout Council. **$10,000** each to ARC Foundation of York County, Red Cross/York County Chapter, York County Alliance for Learning, and York Little Theatre. **$5,000** each to Access York, Dreamwrights Youth & Family Theatre, Foundation of York County Chamber of Commerce, Historic York, Kaltreider Memorial Library, Margaret Moul Home, Otterbein United Methodist Church, Strand Capital Performing Arts Center, United Way of York Housing Initiatives, York Federal Savings & Loan Foundation, and Yorkarts. **$3,000** each to Friends of Scouting Dinner, YWCA of Gettysburg & Adams County, and YWCA of York. **$2,000-$2,500** each to Crispus Attucks Assn., Escape, Inc., Habitat for Humanity of Washington County [MD], and Mt. Wolf Athletic Assn. **$1,000-$1,500** each to Byrnes Health Education Center, Eagle Fire Company, Farm & Natural Land Trust, Home Partnership, Inc. [MD], Leadership York, Memorial Hospital, OPEN, WITF, YMCA of York & York County, York College of Pa., York County Engineering Fair, and York County Heritage Trust. **$750** to Stepping Stone Counseling & Education. Other contributions **$140-$500** for similar purposes. ■**PUBLICATIONS:** None ■**WEBSITE:** None ■**E-MAIL:** None ■**APPLICATION POLICIES & PROCEDURES:** Grant requests may be submitted in writing at any time; describe the organization's purpose and indicate how many persons will benefit from the funding requested. No grants awarded to individuals.

O+D+T William B. Zimmerman [Mt. Wolf] (C+Donor+Con) — Thomas W. Wolf [Mt. Wolf] (P+Donor) — George W. Hodges [Mt. Wolf] (S+F+Donor) — Corporate donors: Worco, Inc; The Lumber Yard companies; Wolf Distributing Company and related enterprises; Baublitz Advertising

CP-224 **Wolf (Thomas P. & Marian G.) Trust, The**

Carroll Valley, 33 Spring Trail

Fairfield   17320   (Adams County)

MI-31-42-55-63-84

Phone 717-642-8300 **FAX** None

EIN 13-6208693   **Year Created** 1966

AMV $68,378   **FYE** 4-01   (**Gifts Received** $0)   42 **Grants totaling** $16,955

About one-third local giving. High grant of **$3,775** to Prince of Peace Episcopal Church. **$1,350** to Adams County Art Council. **$1,250** to Gettysburg Area Health Care Foundation. Other local contributions **$25-$200** for various purposes. **Out-of-state** giving includes **$3,060** to Mount St. Mary's College [MD] and **$3,000** to Jackie Robinson Foundation [NY]. ■**PUBLICATIONS:** None ■**WEBSITE:** None ■**E-MAIL:** None ■**APPLICATION POLICIES & PROCEDURES:** The Foundation reports that grants generally are awarded to preselected charitable organizations but that unsolicited requests are funded occasionally.

O+D+T Thomas P. Wolf (T+Donor+Con) — Martin L. Edelman [NY] (T)

CP-225 **Wood (Charles O., III & Miriam M.) Foundation**

c/o Wood Holdings, Inc.

273 Lincoln Way East

Chambersburg   17201   (Franklin County)

MI-11-42-51-53-54-55-63

Phone 717-267-3174 **FAX** 717-267-2689

EIN 25-1568770   **Year Created** 1987

AMV $1,672,426   **FYE** 12-00   (**Gifts Received** $0)   55 **Grants totaling** $145,256

Limited local giving; grants are unrestricted support/annual giving except as noted. High Pa. grant of **$5,000** to Caledonia Theatre Company (Martha Walker Fund). **$2,000** to Chambersburg United Way. **$1,000** to Falling Spring Presbyterian Church. Other local contributions **$75-$250** for various purposes. **Out-of-state** giving includes **$37,000** to Harvard Graduate School of Education [MA]; **$18,000** to Addison Gallery of American Art [MA] (exhibition/acquistion); **$14,218** to Celebrity Series of Boston [MA]; **$12,000** to Boston Museum of Fine Arts [MA] (picture fund); **$11,000** to Harvard U. Art Museums [MA] (American Art fund); and other smaller grants, largely to the Boston area. ■**PUBLICATIONS:** None ■**WEBSITE:** None ■**E-MAIL:** None ■**APPLICATION POLICIES & PROCEDURES:** The Foundation reports that it does not respond to unsolicited requests; grants are awarded only to a selected list of charities.

O+D+T Charles O. Wood, III (T+Donor+Con) — Miriam M. Wood (T+Donor)

CP-226 **Wood Foundation of Chambersburg, The**

c/o Wood Holdings, Inc.

273 Lincoln Way East

Chambersburg   17201   (Franklin County)

MI-11-12-13-15-17-22-25-29-31-41-42-44-51

52-72

Phone 717-267-3174 **FAX** 717-267-2689

EIN 25-1607838   **Year Created** 1988

AMV $11,931,986   **FYE** 12-00   (**Gifts Received** $0)   55 **Grants totaling** $467,367

About one-third local/Pa. giving; grants are unrestricted support/pledge payments except as noted. High Pa. grant of **$29,187** to Financial Counseling Services. **$25,000** to Keystone Health Center. **$20,227** to Caledonia Theatre Group (Martha Walker Fund). **$15,000** to Chambersburg Area United Way. **$12,965** to Franklin County Learning Center (playground). **$10,000** each to Habitat for Humanity of Franklin County (two houses) and Legal Services (domestic violence services). **$7,500** to Cumberland Valley Animal Shelter. **$6,000** to BOPIC/Building Our Pride in Chambersburg. **$5,700** to Coyle Free Library. **$5,000** to Mercersburg Academy. **$4,500** to Salvation Army/Chambersburg (heat/rent/general support). **$4,000** to Quincy United Methodist Home (music therapy program). **$3,000-$3,500** each to E.S.C.A.P.E./Parent-Child Center of Franklin County (ADD initiative). Frances Leiter Centers (satellite expansion), Mothers Against Drunk Driving, and Scotland School Foundation (culinary arts center). **$2,000** each to Chambersburg YMCA, Cumberland Valley Chamber Players, Menno Haven, Occupational Services, Inc., Penn Laurel Girl Scout Council, and Shook Home for the Aged. **$1,000-$1,875** each to Chambersburg Area School District (endowment fund), Franklin County Shelter for the Homeless, HOSPICE (benefit event), Meals on Wheels, Pa. Special Olympics, Therapeutic Riding Center (sidewalk), Waynesboro Cares, and Women in Need. Other smaller local contributions for various purposes. **Out-of-state** giving includes high grant of **$85,000** to Boston Celebrity Series [MA]; **$65,000** to Isabella Stewart Gardner Museum [MA]; **$45,000** to Community Foundation of the Eastern Shore [MD]; **$20,000** to Winterthur Museum Garden & Library [DE]; **$15,000** to Azusa Christian Community [MA]; and **$10,000** each to Harvard Graduate School of Education [MA] and Cambridge School Volunteers [MA]. ■**PUBLICATIONS:** None ■**WEBSITE:** None ■**E-MAIL:** None ■**APPLICATION POLICIES & PROCEDURES:** The Foundation reports that organizations serving the Chambersburg-Franklin County area receive first consideration. Grant requests may be submitted in any form at any time; provide enough detail to enable a complete evaluation of the request.

O+D+T Charles O. Wood, III (T+Donor+Con) — Emilie Wood Robinson [MD] (T) — David S. Wood [CA] (T) — Miriam M. Wood (T)

CP-227 **Wright Family Charitable Foundation**

115 Mayer Street

Reading   19606   (Berks County)

MI-41-42-61

Phone 610-779-9040 **FAX** None

EIN 23-2967798   **Year Created** 1999

AMV $3,675   **FYE** 12-99   (**Gifts Received** $25,000)   10 **Grants totaling** $25,500

Mostly local/Pa. giving. High grant of **$9,000** to Alvernia College (mostly for capital campaign). **$5,000** to Central Catholic High School. **$3,500** to St. Catherine of Siena (sponsorship/general support). **$2,000** to LaSalle U. [Philadelphia] (annual gift). **$1,000** each for capital campaigns to Cardinal Brennan Jr./Sr. High School, Holy Family College [Philadelphia], and Holy Name High School. ■**PUBLICATIONS:** None. ■**WEBSITE:** None ■**E-MAIL:** None ■**APPLICATION POLICIES & PROCEDURES:** Information not available.

O+D+T Robert T. Wright (T+Donor+Con) — Catherine D. Wright (T+Donor)

CP-228   Wyomissing Foundation, The
12 Commerce Drive
Wyomissing   19610
                                                              (Berks County)

MI-11-12-13-16-18-19-29-35-42-44-52-55-57
71
Phone 610-376-7496 **FAX** 610-372-7626
EIN 23-1980570   **Year Created** 1929

AMV $37,820,880   **FYE** 12-00   (**Gifts Received** $0)   26 **Grants totaling** $1,566,636

Mostly local giving. Three grants totaling **$316,000** to Berks County Community Foundation (human services endowment and operating support). **$150,000** to Berks County Conservancy (transitional operating grant). **$111,000** to United Way of Berks County (annual campaign). **$110,000** to Berks County Childcare Initiative. **$66,000** to Penn State U./Reading Campus. **$50,000** to Wyomissing Public Library (building campaign). **$42,000** each, all for capital campaigns, to Boy Scouts/Hawk Mountain Council, Caron Foundation, and Reading-Berks Emergency Shelter. **$38,000** to Schuylkill River Greenway Assn. (transition grant). **$25,000** to Bethany Children's Home (capital campaign). **$22,500** to Spanish Speaking Council of Reading/Berks County (multi-service implementation study). **$20,000** to Berks Business Adventure (Kutztown Business Seminar). **$18,000** to Reading Musical Foundation (operating support). **$17,000** to Berks Community Television (program development). **$14,000** to Wyomissing Institute of Fine Arts (capital campaign). **$12,750** to Berks Visiting Nurse Assn. (healthy baby/adolescent program). **$4,600** to Planned Parenthood Center of Berks County (expanded educational services). **$2,000** each to Berks Talkline (operating support), Historical Society of Berks County (annual campaign) and Wood-to-Wonderful (toys for children). **$1,000** each to Jewish Federation of Reading (annual campaign) and Junior Achievement of Reading/Berks County. **Out-of-state** grant: **$37,500** to American Littoral Society [NJ] (Schuylkill Riverkeeper). — In 2001, major local grants awarded include: **$190,000** to Berks County Conservancy; **$176,074** to Berks County Community Foundation; **$130,000** to United Way of Berks County; **$125,000** to Trustees of Reservations; **$110,000** to Berks County Child Care Initiative; **$92,781** to Hispanic Center of Reading & Berks; **$85,500** to Boy Scouts/Hawk Mountain Council; **$85,000** to Performing Arts Center (capital campaign); and **$50,000** each to Police Athletic League and Schuylkill River Greenway. ■**PUBLICATIONS:** program policy statement; application guidelines ■**WEBSITE:** None ■**E-MAIL:** wfbbec@nnl.com ■**APPLICATION POLICIES & PROCEDURES:** The Foundation reports that giving focuses on Berks County with support for general operations, annual campaigns, emergency funding, building and capital campaigns/needs, matching funds, or seed money. No grants are awarded for endowment, land acquisition, publications, conferences, scholarships, fellowships, deficit financing, or to individuals. Prospective applicants should make an initial telephone inquiry regarding the feasibility of submitting a request. Grant requests may be submitted in a letter/proposal (2 pages maximum, excluding supporting materials) before the deadlines of March 25th, June 25th, August 25th, and December 25th; include organizational/project budgets, Board member list, list of major funding sources, audited financial statement, and IRS tax-exempt status documentation. Site visits sometimes are made to organizations being considered for a grant. The Trustees award grants at meetings in January, April, July, and October; applicants are notified of decisions within three months from date of application.
O+D+T Thomas A. Beaver [Sinking Spring] (P+T+Con) — David L. Thun [Sinking Spring] (VP+T) — Ned E. Diefenderfer (S) — Paul L. Roedel (F) — Robert W. Cardy (T) — Charlotte Cooper (T) — Antonia Lake [MA] (T) — Marlin Miller, Jr. [Reading] (T) — Cornelia St. John (T) — Peter Thun (T) — John P. Weidenhammer (T)

CP-229   York Container Foundation
c/o York Container Company
138 Mount Zion Road, P.O. Box 3008
York   17402   (York County)

MI-11-13-14-15-21-29-31-35-41-42-43-44-51
52-55-56-63-71-83-89
Phone 717-757-7611 **FAX** 717-755-8090
EIN 22-2473590   **Year Created** 1983

AMV $585,961   **FYE** 12-00   (**Gifts Received** $300,000)   135 **Grants totaling** $337,910

Mostly local/Pa. giving; grants are for general support except as noted; pledge payments are on multiyear grants. High grant of **$43,685** to Strand-Capitol Performing Arts Center (pledge payment/corporate membership). **$33,000** to Susquehanna U. (pledge payment/general support). **$22,000** to Aldersgate United Methodist Church (pledge payment/general support). **$20,000** to Red Cross (pledge payment). **$15,000** to Cultural Alliance of York County. **$13,500** to United Way of York County. **$12,500** to York College of Pa. **$13,000** to Christian School of York (pledge payment/general support). **$10,000** each to ARC Foundation of York County (pledge payment), Asbury United Methodist Church Building Fund (pledge payment), and Gretchen Wolf Schwartz Scholarship Fund. **$6,200** to York Country Day School (pledge payment/playground). **$5,000** each to Better York, Inc. (pledge payment), Farm & Natural Lands Trust of York County (guardian sponsorship), Historic York, Inc., Junior League of York (general support/lecture sponsorship), Margaret Moul Home (pledge payment), Northeastern School District Scholarship Fund, Union Fire Company #1 of Manchester (convention), York YMCA (pledge payment), and York YWCA (general support/program). **$4,000** to Dreamwrights Youth & Family Theatre. **$2,000-$2,500** each to Assn. of Independent Colleges & Universities of Pa., Crispus Attucks Community Center, Easter Seals, Kaltreider-Benfer Library, Otterbein United Methodist Church (operating fund), York Health Foundation (mother-child clinic), York Vo-Tech (flexo project), Young Life of York County (pledge payment), and York Symphony (general support/concert). **$1,000-$1,500** each to 10,000 Friends/Advocates of Pa. (host sponsorship), Boy Scouts/York-Adams Council, Susan Byrnes Health Education Center, Eagle Fire Company #1, Intervarsity Christian Fellowship [Lancaster], Junior Achievement of South Central Pa., Martin Library, Messiah College, Mt. Wolf Athletic Assn., National MS Society, Penn-Mar Organization, Pennsylvanians for Effective Government [Harrisburg] (education committee), Pennsylvanians for Right to Work [Harrisburg], Rohler's Assembly of God, Salvation Army/York, Springetts Fire Company, Tennis for Kids, Trinity United Church of Christ (piano fund), York Cancer Center (benefit sponsorship), York City Recreation & Parks, York County Blind Center (benefit walk), York County Council of Churches (Christmas festival), York Jewish Community Center, York County Literacy Council, and York Little Theatre. **Out-of-state** giving includes **$3,200** to Intercollegiate Prayer Fellowship [MD] and **$1,500** to SPORTworks Ministry [NC]. ■**PUBLICATIONS:** None ■ **WEBSITE:** www.yorkcontainer.com [corporate info only] ■**E-MAIL:** None ■**APPLICATION POLICIES & PROCEDURES:** The Foundation reports giving focuses on York County; most grants are for annual campaigns/general support, capital campaigns, building/renovations, or endowment. Prospective applicants should initially telephone the Foundation to inquire about the feasibility of submitting a request. Grant requests may be submitted in any form at any time; include organizational and project budgets, list of other funding sources, and IRS tax-exempt status documentation.
O+D+T Dennis E. Willman (P+D+Con) — Constance L. Wolf (S+D) — Charles S. Wolf, Jr. (F+D) — Corporate donor: York Container Co.

CP-230 York County Medical Society Educational Trust   MI-34-43
c/o York Hospital
1001 South George Street   **Phone** 717-843-6744 **FAX** None
York 17405   (York County)   **EIN** 23-6284266   **Year Created** 1963
AMV $349,495   **FYE** 12-00   (**Gifts Received** $0)   4 **Grants totaling** $30,000

All grants are scholarship-loans, **$7,500** each, for York county residents studying at qualified schools of medicine. ■**PUBLICA-TIONS:** None ■**WEBSITE:** None ■**E-MAIL:** None ■**APPLICATION POLICIES & PROCEDURES:** Only York County residents are eligible to apply for scholarship-loans. Applicants must submit a brief resume before the June 30th deadline together with copies of academic records; also, describe present status, financial needs, and intended goals to pursue and continue medical studies at a qualified school of medicine.

O+D+T Rhonda S. Renninger (Executive Secretary, Scholarship Committee+Con) — and a Scholarship Education Trust Committee of York County doctors — Allfirst Bank (Corporate Trustee)

CP-231 York Foundation   MI-12-13-14-15-16-17-18-22-24-29-35-41-52
First Floor   55-56-71-86
20 West Market Street   **Phone** 717-848-3733 **FAX** 717-854-7231
York 17401   (York County)   **EIN** 23-6299868   **Year Created** 1961
AMV $25,529,464   **FYE** 12-01   (**Gifts Received** $5,147,544)   160+ **Grants totaling** $1,427,579

As a Community Foundation all discretionary giving is limited to organizations serving York County; 28 Venture Grants—from discretionary funds—totaled nearly **$90,000.** High grants of **$5,000** each to Crispus Attucks Community Development Corp. (consultant costs for retail market study re community grocery store) and Penn Laurel Girl Scout Council (Teens Before Their Time conference). **$4,965** to York Jewish Community Center (child development classes for parents/childcare professionals). **$4,000-$4,500** each to Bell Socialization Services (launch income-producing retail outlet for recycled building materials—with York Habitat For Humanity), Byrnes Health Education Center (pilot learning labs in Dallastown & York City school districts), Crispus Attucks Assn. (research re strategic planning/marketing), Institute for Cultural Partnerships (collaboration with York Spanish American Center re Latino Arts in community program), York County Bar Foundation (strategic plan re Leave A Legacy program), York County Heritage Trust (exhibition on York County's agricultural heritage), York Spanish American Center (underwrite consulting services by Spanish American Civic Assn. of Lancaster re programs/operations), and York Symphony Assn. (develop/test market new marketing strategy). **$3,000-$3,500** each to Atkins House (develop strategic plan re women offenders), Family Service of York and York County (develop collaboration with other York County/Dauphin County family service organizations), Mediation Services for Conflict Resolution (underwrite staff support for conflict resolution training in schools), Pa. Immigration Resource Center (partner with International Friendship House to assist women asylum-seekers), Planned Parenthood of Central Pa. (evaluate HIV peer-to-peer education/prevention program re expansion), South George Street Community Partnership (train new TALL team members), York Benevolent Assn. (research re identifying collaboration possibilities for delivery of services), York County Area Agency on Aging (needs assessment re elderly Latino residents), and YWCA of York (collaboration with Penn State Cooperative Extension re strategies to reach/support grandparents raising grandchildren). **$2,700** to York County Parks Foundation Charitable Trust (Nixon Park environmental education program curriculum). **$2,250** to New Hope Ministries (research/design model for Life Skills program). **$1,250-$1,750** each to Community First Fund (develop small business training program in Hanover), Cultural Alliance of York County (strategic planning beyond start-up phase), Victim Assistance Center (strategic planning services), York Jewish Community Center (evaluation of diversity acceptance programs), York Murals (planning/preparation re partnering with William Penn Sr. High School students in murals project). **$500** to York County Bar Foundation (project with York County Chamber of Commerce re business support for youth in drug rehab). Other grants from discretionary (or semi-discretionary) funds (totaling **$333,917**) supported specific program strategies in particular fields of interest including agriculture and farmland preservation, energy conservation, management assistance to nonprofit organizations, as well as community-wide initiatives such as Focus On Our Future and YorkCounts; recipients were identified by advisory committees to the programs and/or funds. Grants awarded from donor-advised funds (totaling **$405,710**) were recommended by advisors to these funds, subject to Board approval. ■**PUBLICATIONS:** Annual Report with application guidelines ■**WEBSITE:** www.yorkfoundation.org ■**E-MAIL:** info@yorkfoundation.org ■**APPLICATION POLICIES & PROCEDURES:** Only organizations serving York County are eligible to apply for Venture Grants (up to $5,000 and from unrestricted, discretionary funds) which focus on two areas: Nonprofit Excellence—strengthen capacity/encourage excellence in program services, management and governance; and Collaborative Approaches to Community Problem Solving—program partnerships involving two or more organizations or community-wide initiatives. No grants are awarded to individuals or for scholarships, budget deficits, projects/programs which duplicate existing United Way-funded efforts, sectarian religious projects, or organizations that practice discrimination. Prospective applicants for Venture Grants should request/secure a copy of the detailed application guidelines and the required Grant Application Summary (available also on the website); deadlines for Venture Grant applications are the last business day of March and September. Informal site visits sometimes are made to organizations being considered for a grant. Venture Grants are awarded at spring and fall Board meetings. Inquiries about support from field-of-interest or donor-advised funds are accepted throughout the year.

O+D+T Richard H. Brown (Executive Director+Con) — William H. Kerlin, Jr. (P+D) — Cornelia W. Wolf (VP+D) — Michael L. Gleim (S+D) — Stephen H. Klunk (F+D) — D. Reed Anderson (D) — Louis J. Appell, Jr. (D) — C. Kim Brown (D) — Anthony P. Campisi (D) — R. Joe Crosswhite (D) — Edward L. Daisey (D) — Linda B. Davidson (D) — Donald B. Dellinger, Jr. (D) — Cynthia A. Dotzel (D) — Wanda D. Filer, M.D. (D) — George H. Glatfelter, II (D) — William F. Goodling (D) — Terrence L. Hormel (D) — David E. Kennedy (D) — Anne W. Kinsley (D) — Melanie A. Lehman (D) — David G. Meckley (D) — Larry J. Miller (D) — Michael F. O'Connor (D) — Robert W. Pullo (D) — Michael W. Rice (D) — Delaine A. Toerper (D) — Frederick Uffelman, II (D) — Ernest J. Waters (D) — Rose Marie Woodyard (D)

Central Pa. Region / CP
Non-profiled Foundations

*CP Region foundations which did **not** meet the criteria for profiling are listed here; the letter code in parentheses after the foundation name indicates its status, per the following key:*

L **Limited Assets/Giving**: The market value of assets was $250,000 or under and the total of grants awarded was less than $12,500 in the last year of record. If information about grants is available, up to three Major Interest (MI) Codes are listed; if no information on giving interests is available, the notation "N/R" (Not Reported) is shown.

O **Operating Foundation**: This special designation by IRS is for a foundation that operates its own program or institution and, generally, does not award grants to other organizations.

R **Restricted Trust/Foundation**: Grants are awarded only to designated organizations or beneficiaries, typically under the terms of a Will or Trust Instrument.

I **Inactive**: The assets, generally, are nominal (typically under $5,000) and there has been little or no grants activity within the last year or more.

NP **Non-Pennsylvania Foundation**: The foundation's connection to Pennsylvania is only incidental; typically these are trusts or foundations managed by a bank trust department or a lawyer located in Pennsylvania, but there are no Pennsylvania-based trustees/directors and no grants are awarded to Pennsylvania.

T **Terminated**: A final IRS Form 990-PF has been filed, or the foundation has provided notice of intended liquidation/termination.

U **Undetermined Status**: There is no record of Form 990-PFs being filed for the last three or more years and no other evidence of grant-making activity. In many cases the foundation may have terminated without giving formal notice or has been reclassified by IRS as a "public charity."

1144 OM Foundation (L) MI-29
  c/o Patel, Holiday Inn, 148 Sheraton Drive, New Cumberland 17070

1994 Degenstein (Charles B.) Foundation
  (Refer to Degenstein Foundation)

Abel (Roy) Trust (R)
  c/o Allfirst Trust, York 17401

AFR Foundation, Inc. (L) MI-15-22-99
  c/o Parthemer, 2 North 2nd Street, 7th Floor, Harrisburg 17101

Ahl (P. Vaughn) Trust for Helen R. Ahl Scholarship Fund (R)
  c/o Allfirst Bank, 2 West High Street, Carlisle 17013

Aikens (Woodrow U.) Family Foundation (R)
  1923 Holly Street, Harrisburg 17104

Allen (Thomas J. & Florence M.) Trust (R)
  c/o Citizens & Northern Bank, P.O. Box 58, Wellsboro 16901

Allentown Area Foundation (R)
  c/o First Union/Wachovia, Reading 19603

Althouse Foundation (R)
  c/o First Union/Wachovia, Reading 19603

Alwine (Harry K.) Trust for Elizabethtown H.S. Fund (R)
  c/o Hershey Trust Co., Hershey 17033

Alwine (Harry K.) Trust for Middletown H.S. Fund (R)
  c/o Hershey Trust Co., Hershey 17033

American Society for Hispanic Art Historical Studies (R)
  c/o Bucknell U./Art Department, Lewisburg 17837

AMP Foundation, The
  (New name: The Tyco Electronics Foundation)

Anderson (Chester) for Charity (R)
  c/o Mellon Bank N.A., Harrisburg 17108

Angle (Faerie L.) Educational Trust (U)

Animal Education Protection & Information Fund (O)
  180 Shannon Lane, York 17406

Apple (John A.) Foundation (L)
  249 North 11th Street, P.O. Box 705, Sunbury 17801

Arbee Foundation, The (T)

Area Scholastic Awards Trust Fund (R)
  c/o First Union/Wachovia, Reading 19603

Arnold (Suzanne H.) Foundation, The (L) MI-53-55-99
  136 Woodside Court, Annville 17003

Arnold (Teresa Youtz) Memorial Scholarship Fund (R)
  c/o Lebanon Valley National Bank, Lebanon 17042

Arnold Industries Scholarship Foundation (R)
  c/o New Penn Motor Express, P.O. Box 630, Lebanon 17042

Arrow International Inc. Scholarship Trust (R)
  c/o First Union/Wachovia, Reading 19603

Asbury Trust (L)
  3235 Glengreen Drive, Lancaster 17601

Auman Family Foundation, The (L) MI-53-54-63
  1968 Meadow Lane, Wyomissing 19610

Austin Foundation (L) MI-63
  660 Willow Valley Square, #M403, Lancaster 17602

Avery Foundation, The (O)
  P.O. Box 684, Philipsburg 16866

Bache (William) Memorial Fund (L) MI-52
c/o Robert C. Bair, West Avenue, Wellsboro 16901

Bare (John D.) Memorial Scholarship Fund (R)
c/o Allfirst Bank, Harrisburg 17105

Beattie (John J. & Mildred M.) Scholarship Fund (R)
c/o First Union/Wachovia, Reading 19603

Behney (Thomas H.), Jr. Memorial (R)
c/o Lebanon Valley National Bank, Lebanon 17042

Berg (Quentin) Trust, The (T)

Berger (Walter S.) Trust (R)
c/o First Union/Wachovia, Reading 19603

Bicksler & Greiner Memorial Scholarship Fund (R)
c/o Farmers Trust Bank, Lebanon 17042

Bighorn Nature Conservancy Charitable Trust (U)

Bingaman (Max E. & Martha E.) Charitable Foundation (L)
MI-22-41-63
P.O. Box 247, Kreamer 17833

BLAST Intermediate Unit 17 (I)
c/o Zeigler, 501 East 3rd Street, Williamsport 17701

Bloch-Selinger Educational Trust Fund (R)
c/o Danville Senior High School, Danville 1721

Bobb (E.G. & C.S.) Trust for Church of God (R)
c/o Mellon Bank N.A., Harrisburg 17108

Bobb (E.G. & Clara S.) Trust for Nason Hospital (R)
c/o Mellon Bank N.A., Harrisburg 17108

Boscov-Berk-Tek, Inc. Scholarship Fund (R)
c/o Styer, 132 White Oak Road, New Holland 17557

Boyer Foundation (T)
(Refer to Berks County Community Foundation)

Brady (Mary S.) Memorial Library Trust Fund (R)
c/o York Bank & Trust Co., York 17405

Bricker (Pearl M.) Trust (L) MI-13-44-63
c/o Eakin & Eakin, Market Square Building, Mechanicsburg 17055

Briggs (Chreston K.) Trust (R)
c/o Allfirst Bank, York 17405

Brose (Melvin F.) Memorial Fund (R)
c/o Allfirst Bank, York 17405

Brossman Family Charitable Trust for Scholarships (R)
130 Main Street, P.O. Box 458, Ephrata 17522

Bryant Family Foundation, The (L) MI-13-25
4232 Kota Avenue, Harrisburg 17110

Buchart (Lester & Anna) Trust for Christ U.M. Church (R)
c/o Allfirst Bank, York 17405

Buchart (Lester) Trust for St. John's Lutheran Church (R)
c/o Allfirst Bank, York 17405

Buchmiller (D.F.) Trust (R)
c/o Fulton Bank, Lancaster 17604

Buchmiller (D.F.) Trust for Buchmiller Park (R)
c/o Fulton Bank, Lancaster 17604

Bucktrout-Braithwaite Memorial Foundation (L) MI-99
c/o Bruce Cleveland, P.O. Box 271, State College 16804

Buckwalter (Beulah M.) Charitable Trust (T)

Bucs (George J.) Memorial Scholarship Fund (R)
396 Yorktown Road, Hershey 17033

Bush (Mamie B.) Trust (R)
c/o York Bank & Trust Co., York 17401

Butler (Beatrice M.) Trust for Methodist Home (R)
c/o Mellon Bank N.A., Harrisburg 17108

Camp Hill Community Foundation
(Refer to The Greater Harrisburg Foundation)

Camp Kanesatake Trust (R)
223 Washington Street, Huntingdon 16652

Carl (Dean R.) Memorial Fund (L) MI-43
1600 West Lynn Street, Coal Township 17166

Carosella Family Foundation (L) MI-31-41
100 Industrial Drive, Hamburg 19526

Carpenter Technology Corporation Foundation (T)

Cassel (Violette) Trust for Harrisburg Hospital (R)
c/o Mellon Bank N.A., Harrisburg 17108

Cassel (Violette) Trust for Holy Spirit Hospital (R)
c/o Mellon Bank N.A., Harrisburg 17108

Cassel (Violette) Trust for Osteopathic Hospital (R)
c/o Mellon Bank N.A., Harrisburg 17108

Cassel (Violette) Trust for Polyclinic Hospital (R)
c/o Mellon Bank N.A., Harrisburg 17108

Central & Southern Africa Legal Assistance Foundation (R)
One South Market Square, 12th Floor, Harrisburg 17101

Chi Psi Educational Trust, Alpha Psi of (O)
c/o McConnell, 1150 Ashley Hill Road, Mansfield 16933

Cobb (E.G. & S.C.) Trust for Nason Hospital (R)
c/o Mellon Bank N.A., Harrisburg 17108

Cohen (Irvin & Lois E.) Foundation (L) MI-12-17-99
1505 Lorraine Road, Reading 19604

Cohn (Benjamin) MC Fund (R)
c/o Mellon Bank N.A., Harrisburg 17108

Cohn (Benjamin) Trust for Altoona Foundation (R)
c/o Mellon Bank N.A., Harrisburg 17108

Cole Family Scholarship Trust (R)
c/o Danville Senior High School, Danville 17821

Coleman (Raymond J.) Scholarship Trust (R)
c/o Lebanon School District, Lebanon 17042

Columbus Chapel/Boalsburg Estate (O)
P.O. Box 116, Boalsburg 16827

Community Homes of Lebanon County (R)
800 Willow Street, Lebanon 17042

Cooper (Walter T. & Bessie H.) Charitable Trust (R)
c/o Allfirst Bank, York 17405

Cornelius (Clair) Clay Township Award (R)
c/o First Commonwealth Trust Company, Huntingdon 16652

Crimestoppers of Dauphin County (R)
Front & Market Streets, Harrisburg 17101

Cullier (Earl & Catherine) Memorial Fund (R)
c/o First Union/Wachovia, Reading 19603

Currens (Robert M. & Grace A.) Trust (L) MI-11-99
c/o Allfirst Bank, P.O. Box 459, Chambersburg 17201

Damico Family Foundation (L) MI-N/R
1588 Fairfield Road, Gettysburg 17325

Danner (George H.) Estate (O)
422 Orchard Lane, Manheim 17545

Danner (Norman S.) Scholarship Fund Trust (R)
c/o Allfirst Bank, 13 Baltimore Street, Hanover 17331

Daugherty (Frank L.) Trust (R)
c/o Gettysburg College/Student Aid Office, Gettysburg 17325

Deckard (Percy Edward) Trust (R)
c/o Allfirst Bank, Harrisburg 17105

Decker (Aimee Y.) Charitable Trust (R)
c/o Fulton Bank, Lancaster 17604

Desmond Foundation for Historic Preservation (O)
2705 Old Philadelphia Pike, Bird in Hand 17505

Dessem Honorary Trust (R)
c/o Mellon Bank N.A., Harrisburg 17108

Deutsch Family Mem'l Scholarship Fund for Geisinger Hospital (R)
c/o First National Bank of Danville, Danville 17821

Deutsch Family Memorial Scholarship Fund for Danville H.S. (R)
c/o First National Bank of Danville, Danville 17821

69

Dibeler (Minnie) Trust for Falmouth Cemetery (R)
c/o Mellon Bank N.A., Harrisburg 17108

Dilcher (Harry J. & Mollie S.) Student Loan Fund (R)
c/o First Union/Wachovia, Reading 19603

Dipple (Dora D.) Charitable Trust for Lewistown U.P.C. (R)
c/o The Russell National Bank, Lewistown 17044

Dipple (Dora D.) Char. Trust for Presbyterian Homes.. (R)
c/o The Russell National Bank, Lewistown 17044

Donegal School District Education Foundation (R)
366 South Market Street, Mount Joy 17552

Dreher (Grace) Memorial Scholarship Fund (R)
c/o First Union/Wachovia, Reading 19603

Dreibelbis Farm Historical Society (R)
53 Fox Road, Hamburg 19526

Drummeller-Swank, Keyser & Bargo Poor Fund (L) MI-23
c/o First Susquehanna Bank & Trust Co., Sunbury 17801

Dubbs (Alfred W.), M.D. Fellowship Fund (R)
c/o First Union/Wachovia, Reading 19603

Dubbs (Mignon W.) Fellowship Fund (R)
c/o First Union/Wachovia, Reading 19603

Dubbs (Sallie B.) Fellowship Fund (R)
c/o First Union/Wachovia, Reading 19603

Dubbs (Sallie) Scholarship Fund (R)
c/o First Union/Wachovia, Reading 19603

Duffy (Mary Louise) Trust (NP)
c/o Delaware Trust Capital Mgmt, P.O. Box 1102, Reading 19603

E.C.C. Homes, Inc. (O)
South Railroad Street, Myerstown 17067

Eagles Mere Foundation, The (R)
c/o JCL Realty, 25 West Third Street, Williamsport 17701

Earley (Israel) Trust for Bindnagles Lutheran Church (R)
c/o L.V.N.B., P.O. Box 448, Lebanon 17042

Earley (Myra) Trust for Bindnagles Lutheran Church (R)
c/o L.V.N.B., P.O. Box 448, Lebanon 17042

East Texas Media Assn. (NP)
6079 Wertztown Road, Narvon 17555

Ebert (Herman A. & Carrie S.) Trust (R)
c/o Allfirst Bank, York 17405

Ecumenical Community, The (O)
830 Cherry Drive, Hershey 17033

Edmondson (William & Lenore) Memorial Fund (R)
c/o First Union/Wachovia, Reading 19603

Eichelberger Family Foundation (I) MI-N/R
4 Barlow Circle, Dillsburg 17019

Eisenhauer (John Henry & Clarissa Arnold) Scholarship Fund (O)
347 North Sixth Street, Lebanon 17042

Elfner (Charlotte R. & Kermit H.) Trust (R)
c/o Allfirst Bank, York 17405

Epsilon Alumni Group (L) MI-43
800 Belvedere Street, Carlisle 17013

Evans (Pearle H.) Scholarship Fund (R)
c/o Probst, 14 North Main Street, Chambersburg 17201

Evergreen Foundation, The (L) MI-63
549 Carlisle Street, Hanover 17331

Everybody Ought to Know, Inc. (O)
c/o Martin, 12 Summit Drive, Dillsburg 17019

Evleth (Raymond C.) Trust for Goodwill Industries (R)
c/o Allfirst Bank, Harrisburg 17105

Family Information Center, Inc. (O)
P.O. Box 488, Gap 17527

Faust (Roscoe A.) & William C. Heller Family Trust (R)
c/o Guidance, Danville Senior High School, Danville 17821

Feagley (Frank H.) Trust (R)
c/o Mellon Bank N.A., Harrisburg 17108

Feigler (Ervin D.) Trust (R)
c/o York Bank & Trust Co., York 17405

Felding (Sara) Memorial Foundation (R)
c/o Mellon Bank N.A., Harrisburg 17108

Fellowship Center for Biblical Studies (R)
R.D. #1, Box 144, B4, Bainbridge 17502

Fetherston Foundation/Packard House Museum (R)
c/o First Union/Wachovia, Reading 19603

FGB Foundation (L) MI-31-63
81 Winged Foot Drive, Reading 19607

Fielding (Sara) Memorial Trust (R)
c/o Mellon Bank N.A., Harrisburg 17108

Firecon Institute for Research & Education (R)
P.O. Box 99, East Earl 17519

First United Methodist Church Nursery (R)
c/o Mellon Bank N.A., Harrisburg 17108

Fisher (George L.) Memorial Foundation (O)
c/o Mellon Bank N.A., Harrisburg 17108

Fisher (George L.) Trust (R)
c/o Mellon Bank N.A., Harrisburg 17108

Fitzpatrick (Rev. William J.) Memorial Scholarship Fund (R)
c/o York Bank & Trust Co., York 17401

Flegal (Donald L. & Bernice Durgin) Charitable Fdn. (R)
c/o Woodlands Bank, Williamsport 17701

Flexer (E. J.) Fund (R)
c/o First Union/Wachovia, Reading 19603

Fluhrer (Blanche S.) Trust (R)
c/o Mellon Bank N.A., Harrisburg 17108

Fluhrer (R.C.) for Salvation Army (R)
c/o Mellon Bank N.A., Harrisburg 17108

Fluhrer (R.C.) Trust for Charities (R)
c/o Mellon Bank N.A., Harrisburg 17108

Fohl (Walter D.), Jr. Medical Education Loan Fdn. (R)
c/o PNC Bank N.A., Gettysburg 17325

Frankhouser (Jame & Mary) Charitable Trust (R)
c/o Allfirst Bank, York 17401

Frankhouser (James & Mary) Charitable Trust (R)
c/o Allfirst Trust, York 17401

Franklin County Foundation
(Refer to The Greater Harrisburg Foundation)

Fredricksen Foundation, The (T)

French (William & Marion) Scholarship Fund (R)
c/o Fulton Financial Advisors, P.O. Box 215, Lancaster 17604

Frey (Robert A.) Trust for Jordan U.C.C. Cemetery Assn. (R)
c/o First Union/Wachovia, Reading 19603

Friedman (Nina & Philip) Memorial Scholarship Fund (R)
c/o Allfirst Bank, York 17405

Froelich (Edward) Charitable Trust (R)
c/o Fulton Bank, Lancaster 17604

FSL Scholarship Foundation, The (R)
c/o Reese, RD #2, Box 142, Douglassville 19519

Fulton Bank Scholarship Foundation (R)
c/o Fulton Bank, Lancaster 17604

Gale (William & L.R.) Community Foundation (L) MI-N/R
c/o Citizens & Northern Bank-Trust Division, Wellsboro 16901

Gentzler (W. Emerson) Residuary Trust (R)
c/o York Bank & Trust Co., York 17401

Gerber (John L.) Trust for Hoffman Orphanage (R)
c/o Drovers & Mechanics National Bank, York 17401

Gerber (K.A.) Trust for Hoffman Orphanage (R)
c/o Drovers & Mechanics National Bank, York 17401

Gerber (K.A.) Trust for Quincy Orphanage (R)
c/o Drovers & Mechanics National Bank, York 17401

Gerhart Foundation (U)

Gettig (William A. & Loene M.) Foundation (L) MI-12-43
P.O. Box 85, Spring Mills 16875

Gibbs (Florence Lauer) Trust (R)
c/o First Union/Wachovia, Reading 19603

Gibbs (Walter & Lila) Memorial Trust (R)
c/o Allfirst Bank, York 17405

Gift (Harold C.) Scholarship Trust (R)
c/o First Union/Wachovia, Reading 19603

Gitt (Josiah, Elizabeth & Charles) Memorial Library (O)
P.O. Box 303, Hanover 17331

Gitt-Moul Historic Properties (O)
120 Eichelenger Street, Hanover 17331

Glatfelter (Arthur J.) Foundation (I)
183 Leaders Heights Road, York 17402

Glatfelter Memorial Field Fund (R)
c/o First Union/Wachovia, Reading 19603

Glatfelter Memorial Field Trust (O)
951 Chestnut Street, Columbia 17512

Glatfelter Memorial Scholarship Trust (R)
c/o Drovers Bank, York 17401

Glazer (Charles C.) Scholarship Fund (R)
c/o Valley Bank & Trust Co., Chambersburg 17201

Global SourceNet, Inc. (R)
c/o Achenbach, 77 Cedar Ave., Hershey 17033

Good Hope Dam Association (R)
512 Woodcrest Drive, Mechanicsburg 17055

Goodwin (Howard D. & Rose E.) Scholarship Trust (R)
c/o First Union/Wachovia, Reading 19603

Gospel Ministries, Inc. (O)
435 Jordan Avenue, Montoursville 17754

Graham (Bessie S.) Trust for Allentown Hospital Assn. (R)
c/o First Union/Wachovia, Reading 19603

Graham (Bessie S.) Trust for Muhlenberg Hospital (R)
c/o First Union/Wachovia, Reading 19603

Greathead (Elsie S.) Trust/Student Loan Fund (R)
c/o Chambersburg Trust Company, Chambersburg 17201

Greencastle-Antrim Foundation (O)
P.O. Box 158, Greencastle 17225

Grimley (Isaac) Trust (R)
c/o First Union/Wachovia, Reading 19603

Groff (Dorothy S.) Scholarship Fund (R)
P.O. Box 47, Morgantown 19543

Groff (Mary S.) Scholarship Trust (R)
c/o First Union/Wachovia, Reading 19603

Groff Memorial Park Trust (R)
c/o Blue Ball National Bank, Blue Ball 17506

Grove (Robert & Esther) Family Foundation (O)
100 Oregon Street, Mercersburg 17236

Gruber (Leona) for Catholic & Community Charities (R)
c/o First Union/Wachovia, Reading 19603

Grumbacher (Nancy & Tim) Family Foundation
(New name: Grumbacher Family Foundation)

Grumbine (Harvey C.) Foundation (R)
c/o First Union/Wachovia, Lebanon 17042

Guyer (B.K.) Trust for Catherine Guyer Scholarship Fund (R)
c/o Snyder County Trust Company, Selinsgrove 17870

Hadley (Charles C.) Trust (R)
c/o First Union/Wachovia, Reading 19603

Hafer Foundation (O)
28 Warwick Street, Boyertown 19512

Hahn Home (O)
863 South George Street, York 17403

Hanover Area Historical Society History Scholarship Award (R)
21 East Market Street, York 17401

Harbaugh/Thomas Foundation (L) MI-N/R
4 South Main Street, Biglerville 17307

Harenza (Susan J. & Joseph M.) Foundation (T)

Harrison (Ann L.) Foundation (I)
P.O. Box 1166, Harrisburg 17108

Hartman (Marion M.) Trust for City of Lancaster (R)
c/o Fulton Bank, Lancaster 17604

Hartman (Marion M.) Trust for St. Joseph Ambulance Society (R)
c/o Fulton Bank, Lancaster 17604

Harvest Fields Ministry Center, Inc. (O)
P.O. Box 77, Boalsburg 16827

Haverstick Family Trust (R)
c/o Fulton Bank, Lancaster 17604

Hawbaker Nature Trust, Inc. (R)
4003 Mercersburg Road, Mercersburg 17236

Heckert (Oscar H.) Scholarship Fund (R)
c/o York Bank & Trust Co., York 17401

Heiney (Kenneth E.) Trust for Christ Lutheran Church (R)
c/o Drovers Bank, York 17401

Heintzelman (Marie) Memorial Music Award Fund (R)
c/o First Union/Wachovia, Reading 19603

Helfrick (E.W.) Senior Citizens Trust (L) MI-23
c/o Susquehanna Trust & Investment Co., Sunbury 17801

Hellenic Foundation
(Formerly of York, now located in UT)

Helwig (Bruce R.) Readng High School Scholarship Trust (R)
c/o Weiler, 1136 Penn Ave., Reading 19610

Hench (Louise C.) Trust for Bethany Children's Home (R)
3607 Derry Street, Harrisburg 17111

Hershey (Andrew J.) Memorial Scholarship Fund (R)
c/o York Bank & Trust Co., York 17405

Hershey (Jacob Reist) Trust (R)
c/o Farmers First Bank, Lititz 17543

Hershey (M.S.) Foundation (O)
c/o Hershey Trust Co., Hershey 17033

Hershey Food Corporation Fund (I)
100 Crystal A Drive, P.O. Box 810, Hershey 17033

Hertzler (E. & E.) Foundation (L) MI-63
2404 Main Street, Narvon 17553

Hill (Dorothy) Memorial Fund (R)
c/o 61 East High Street, Carlisle 17013

Hilton Charitable Trust (R)
c/o First Union/Wachovia, Reading 19603

Hinnershots (Louise) Trust for Scholarship Fund (R)
c/o Allfirst Bank, Harrisburg 17105

Hirschler (Albert) Trust (R)
c/o Mellon Bank N.A., Harrisburg 17108

Hoffert (Valeria B.) Scholarship Trust (R)
c/o Sprow, P.O. Box 2961, Harrisburg 17105

Hoffman Mills Scholarship Fund (R)
c/o Hoffman Mills, 120 North Seneca Street, Shippensburg 17257

Homiak (Walter M.) Scholarship Fund (R)
c/o Ezring, 309 Water Street, Danville 17821

Hoodner (Francis A.) Trust (R)
c/o York Bank & Trust Co., York 17405

Hoover (George & Anne) Scholarship Loan Fund (R)
c/o Snyder County Trust Company, Selinsgrove 17870

Hoover (H. Kathryn) Trust (R)
c/o Drovers & Mechanics National Bank, York 17401

Hosfeld (George W. & Marjorie E.) Memorial Fund (R)
c/o Mellon Bank N.A., Harrisburg 17108

Hosfeld (John & Clara) Memorial Fund (R)
c/o Mellon Bank N.A., Harrisburg 17108

Hosfeld (Richard & Mary K.) Memorial Trust #2 (T)

Hosfeld (Richard H.) Memorial Fund (R)
c/o Mellon Bank N.A., Harrisburg 17108

Hosfeld (Richard H.) Trust for Cumberland Valley Hose Co. (R)
c/o Mellon Bank N.A., Harrisburg 17108

Howe (Anna Verna) Trust (R)
c/o Allfirst Bank, York 17405

Hower (Geary C. & Mary B.) Memorial Fund (R)
c/o First Union/Wachovia, Reading 19603

Hoy (Clarence A.) Foundation (R)
c/o Mellon Bank N.A., Harrisburg 17108

Huber (Charles H.), Jr. Charitable Trust (U)
c/o Hulton, 88 Walker Ave., Gettysburg 17325

Hull (Ralph B.) Charitable Trust (R)
c/o Fulton Bank, Lancaster 17604

Human Ideas Ltd. (O)
2565 Spencer Road, Mansfield 16933

Institute of American Deltiology (R)
300 West Main Avenue, Myerstown 17067

Jacobus-Iacobucci Foundation (L) MI-31-42
450 Pinkerton Road, Mount Joy 17552

Jaynes (Ruth B.) Trust (R)
c/o Allfirst Bank, York 17405

Johnson (Eldridge Reeves) Memorial Trust (NP)
c/o Delaware Trust Capital Management, Reading 19603

Jones (Robert M. & Marion M.) Foundation (R)
c/o First Citizens National Bank, Mansfield 16933

Jones Family Foundation, The (NP)
c/o Monaghan Transportation, 106 Carpenter Street, Blossburg 16912

Jordan (John C.) Trust (R)
c/o York Bank & Trust Co., York 17401

Kable (Edgar P.) Foundation (R)
c/o First Union/Wachovia, Lancaster 17604

Keithan's Bluebird Garden Foundation (R)
c/o First National Trust Bank, Sunbury 17801

Keller (M.E.) Charitable Memorial Fund (R)
c/o First Union/Wachovia, Reading 19603

Keller (William E.) Charitable Foundation (L) MI-99
344 Campbell Road, York 17402

Keystone CDC, Inc. (R)
225 Market Street, 4th Floor, Harrisburg 17101

Keystone Mountain Park Trust (R)
P.O. Box 99, Muncy Valley 17758

Kidsbank.com Foundation (I)
1130 Berkshire Boulevard, Wyomissing 19610

Kiess (Emma) Award Trust (R)
c/o Williamsport Area High School, Williamsport 17701

Kimes (Maynard R.) Trust for Charities (R)
c/o Mellon Bank N.A., Harrisburg 17108

King Arthur Scouts (R)
1464 Queen Street, Annville 17003

Kirkwith (Mike) Trust for Post #386 (R)
c/o Hershey Trust Co., Hershey 17033

Klinger (Matthew P.) Memorial Trust (L) MI-63
P.O. Box 342, Millersburg 17061

Klumpp (M. Elizabeth) Trust (R)
c/o Fulton Bank, Lancaster 17604

Koons (Edna C.) Charitable Trust (R)
c/o First Union/Wachovia, Reading 19603

Kopp (J. Clifford & Ruth N.) Charitable Foundation (R)
c/o Lebanon Valley National Bank, Lebanon 17042

Kratz (J.W.) Trust (R)
c/o First Union/Wachovia, Reading 19603

Kravas Scholarship Foundation (L) MI-43
P.O. Box 766, Wellsboro 16901

Krumrine (G.D. & Mary J.) Foundation (L) MI-15-29-99
c/o Omega Bank, N.A., P.O. Box 298, State College 16801

Lambert-Tyson Foundation, The (L) MI-32-52
248 South Market Street, Williamsport 17701

Lancaster Alliance, The (R)
100 North Queen Street, Lancaster 17608

Lancaster County Council of Churches Foundation (R)
447 East King Street, Lancaster 17602

Lancaster Heart Association, Women's Auxiliary of the (R)
c/o Mellon Bank N.A., Harrisburg 17108

Lancaster Medical Society Foundation (L) MI-34-43
137 East Walnut Street, Lancaster 17602

Landis (Miriam G.) Trust (R)
c/o Mellon Bank N.A., Harrisburg 17108

Lapp (Christ G.) Foundation, The (L) MI-63
270 Brook Farms Road, Lancaster 17601

Larosh (Ralph) Church Flower Fund (R)
c/o First Union/Wachovia, Reading 19603

Larosh (Ralph) Trust (R)
c/o First Union/Wachovia, Reading 19603

Laudermilch (Harry A.) Trust, The (R)
c/o Lebanon Valley National Bank, Lebanon 17042

Leaman (Dorothy M.) Trust (R)
c/o Allfirst Bank, York 17405

Lebzelter (Charles) Residuary Trust (R)
c/o Mellon Bank N.A., Harrisburg 17108

Lehman (Frank H. & Julia R.) Educational Fund (L) MI-43
P.O. Box 3215, Lancaster 17604

Leibenguth (Albert) Charitable Trust (R)
c/o First Union/Wachovia, Reading 19603

Leidy-Rhoads Foundation Trust (R)
c/o Boyertown Area School District, 911 Montgomery Ave. Boyertown 19512

Leighow (Nellie E.) Scholarship Fund (R)
c/o Northumberland National Bank, Northumberland 17857

Leiphart (Luther S.) Evangelistic Assn. (R)
P.O. Box 484, Dallastown 17313

Lerew (Russell A. & Della C.) Memorial Trust (R)
c/o Allfirst Bank, Harrisburg 17105

Levan Memorial Scholarship Trust (NP)

Leydich Burial Grounds Assn. (O)
c/o Leidy, 42 East Third Street, Boyertown 19512

Lichtenwalner (Norton L.) Trust (R)
c/o First Union/Wachovia, Reading 19603

Lichty (Margaret M.) Charitable Trust (R)
c/o First Union/Wachovia, Reading 19603

Light, Inc./Green Hills Health Center (O)
2015 Morgantown Road, Reading 19607

Lincoln & Soldiers Institute (R)
233 North Washington Street, Gettysburg 17325

Little League Baseball Summer Camp (R)
c/o Northern Central Bank, Williamsport 17701

Long (Henry) Home (O)
200 West End Ave., Lancaster 17603

Lugar (Denise) Scholarship Fund (R)
c/o Hopewell Valley Regional High School, Reading 19601

Macklin (G. Howard & Helen S.) Trust (R)
c/o Mellon Bank N.A., Harrisburg 17108

Macklin (Helen S.) for Charity (R)
c/o Mellon Bank N.A., P.O. Box 19, State College 16804

Madeira (Ellen) Scholastic Award Fund (R)
c/o First Union/Wachovia, Reading 19603

Maggiaro (Judith M.) Memorial Scholarship Trust (R)
c/o Muhlenberg Senior High School, Reading 19605

Main Street Non-Profit Redevelopment Corp. (O)
53 West King Street, Shippensburg 17257

Manbeck (Annabelle M.) Trust (R)
c/o Fulton Bank, Lancaster 17604

Marks (Ellen) Trust for Hoffman Orphanage (R)
c/o Drovers & Mechanics National Bank, York 17401

Martin (Mary M.) Trust (R)
c/o Mellon Bank N.A., Harrisburg 17108

Martz (Dolly & George) Scholarship Fund (R)
c/o Fulton Bank, Lancaster 17604

Mase (Marsha Kay) Foundation (L) MI-12-13-22
c/o First Citizens National Bank, 15 South Main St., Mansfield 16933

Masland Conservancy Trust (L) MI-71
205 Heiser Lane, Carlisle 17013

Matthews (Harold & Evelyn) Scholarship Trust Fund (R)
c/o York Bank & Trust Co., York 17405

Mayr (Chrissie B.) Educational Trust Fund (R)
c/o Montoursville High School, Guidance Office, Montoursville 17754

McCarthy (Robert & Nina) Foundation, The (L) MI-72-89
100 Fellows Ave., Wellsboro 16901

McClain (Lena B.) Trust (R)
c/o Chambersburg Trust Company, Chambersburg 17201

McCloskey (Charles A.) Memorial Scholarship Fund (R)
c/o Austin Area School, Austin 16720

McCoy (J.) Trust for Duncannon United Church of Christ (R)
c/o Mellon Bank N.A., Harrisburg 17108

McGee (Charles M.) Scholarship Fund (R)
c/o Valley Bank & Trust Co., Chambersburg 17201

McInroy-Sheffer People Trust (U)

McMillan (Elsie Hilcker) Memorial Foundation
(Formerly of Lemoyne, now located in SD)

Mechanicsburg Area Foundation
(Refer to The Greater Harrisburg Foundation)

Mellinger Scholarship Fund (R)
c/o Ephrata National Bank, Ephrata 17522

Mentzer (Esther R.) Trust for St. Stephens U.C.C. (R)
c/o Allfirst Bank, York 17405

Metzger (Morris Witmer) Scholarship Fund (R)
c/o Superintendent, Hempfield School District, Landisville 17538

Metzger (Stella E.) Scholarship Fund (R)
c/o Lebanon School District, Lebanon 17042

Mid-State Private Industry Council (R)
105 South Spring Street, Bellefonte 16823

Miller (Daniel R.) Trust Fund for Education (R)
c/o First Union/Wachovia, Reading 19603

Miller (Edwill B. & Rachel H.) Trust (R)
c/o Allfirst Bank, York 17405

Miller (Rachel H.) Trust (R)
c/o Allfirst Bank, York 17405

Millport Conservancy, The (O)
741 East Millport Road, Lititz 17543

Miszkiewicz (Antoni) Foundation (O)
42 South Oak Street, Mount Carmel 17851

Moran (Edward & Suzan) Scholarship Trust (NP)
c/o Keystone Financial Bank, Williamsport 17701

Morris (Addie) Trust (R)
c/o Mellon Bank N.A., Harrisburg 17108

Morris (Lloyd M.) Trust Scholarship Fund (R)
c/o Mellon Bank N.A., Harrisburg 17108

Mortel Family Charitable Foundation (L) MI-41-42-61
1229 Sandy Hill Drive, Hummelstown 17036

Moul (Clara G.) Trust (R)
c/o York Bank & Trust Co., York 17401

Mountville Community Services Foundation (O)
P.O. Box 94, Mountville 17554

Moyer (Fern & Gladys) Foundation
(New name: Moyer Memorial Foundation)

Moyer-Longacre Scholarship Fund (R)
c/o Lebanon Valley National Bank, Lebanon 17042

Munro (Isabel W.) Trust for Methodist Church (R)
c/o Mellon Bank N.A., Harrisburg 17108

Murray (Geraldine M.) Foundation (L) MI-41-29
5020 Ritter Road, #211, Mechanicsburg 17055

Musselman (Emma G.) Foundation, The (T)

Myers (Clinton N.) Foundation
Formerly of Hanover; now located in MT)

Myers (Malcolm W. & Anna G.) Scholarship Fund (R)
c/o First Union/Wachovia, Reading 19603

Nelson (William H.) Educational Foundation (R)
c/o Nelson Real Estate, 1601 North Front Street, Harrisburg 17102

Neuber (Pryor & Arlene) Fund (R)
c/o Mellon Bank N.A., Harrisburg 17108

Noble (Ralph L.) Scholarship Fund (R)
c/o Penn Township P.T.A., 225 Bowman Road, Hanover 17331

North Central Pa. Golf Assn. Scholarship Trust (L) MI-43
c/o Post Office S, Hummels Wharf 17831

Noss (Charlotte L.) Trust (R)
c/o York Bank & Trust Co., York 17405

Nursing Foundation of Pennsylvania (O)
P.O. Box 8525, Harrisburg 17105

Oblender Foundation, The (L) MI-99
c/o Fulton Bank of Lancaster, Lancaster 17604

Ocean Mammal Institute, The (R)
175 Hawthorne Court, Wyomissing 19610

Open Door Youth Center (R)
P.O. Box 127, Leola 17540

Oritsky (Isadore & Anna) Foundation, The (T)

Palmer (Frank R.) Foundation (L) MI-11-42-63
1201 Reading Boulevard, Wyomissing 19610

Park Home (O)
800 West Fourth Street, Williamsport 17701

PARTS Scholarship Foundation - Pa. Automotive Recycling Trade Society (R)
c/o HACC/Financial Aid Office, 1 HACC Drive, Harrisburg

Patchett (Allan) Private Foundation (NP)
c/o Keystone Financial Bank, Williamsport 17701

Peckitt (Hattie M.) Trust (R)
c/o First Union/Wachovia, Reading 19603

Pennsylvania Children's Services, Inc. (U)
2909 North Front Street, Harrisburg 17110

Pennsylvania Dental Assn. Health & Well-Being Fdn. (O)
3501 North Front Street, Harrisburg 17110

Pennsylvania Dental Foundation (L) MI-43
3501 North Front Street, P.O. Box 3341, Harrisburg 17105

Pennsylvania District Attorneys Institute (R)
2101 North Front Street, Building 1, Suite 210, Harrisburg 17102

Pennsylvania Farmers' Assn. Legal Fund (R)
510 South 31st Street, Camp Hill 17011

Pennsylvania Poultry Federation Foundation (R)
500 North Progress Ave., Harrisburg 17109

Pennsylvania Public Education Foundation (R)
c/o P.S.B.A., 774 Limekiln Road, New Cumberland 17070

Pennsylvania State Park Memorial Fund Assn. (R)
40 Rocky Mountain Road, Fayetteville 17222

Pennsylvania State Police Camp Cadet Program - Lancaster County (U)

Pennsylvania Steel Foundry Foundation (R)
Hamburg 19526

Perry County Community Foundation
(Refer to The Greater Harrisburg Foundation)

Peters (C.E. & L.V.) Charitable Trust (R)
c/o Fulton Bank, Lancaster 17604

Plank (Elsie L.) Trust (R)
c/o Mellon Bank N.A., Harrisburg 17108

PMTA Student Award Fund (O)
413 South Cherry Street, Lititz 17543

Polish American Board of Education (R)
c/o Parker, 311 Mifflin Boulevard, Shillington 19607

Polk (Charles P. & Margaret E.) Foundation (O)
129 Market Street, Millersburg 17061

Post (Carl B.) Memorial Foundation (T)

Post (John R.) Charitable Foundation (I)
1133 Reading Boulevard, Wyomissing 19610

Potter County Historical Society (O)
308 North Main Street, Coudersport 16915

Project Forward Leap Foundation (R)
c/o Field, 1377-C Spencer Ave., Lancaster 17603

Rager (Martha A.) Trust (R)
c/o Mellon Bank N.A., Harrisburg 17108

Rappaport (Susan & Donald) Foundation (NP)
100 East Market Street, York 17401

Rappoport (Florence & Julian) Scholarships (R)
c/o York Catholic High School, York 17403

Rau (Alexander & Cassia) Trust (R)
c/o St. Mark's Lutheran Church, York 17403

Reading Blue Mountain & Northern Railroad Scholarship Fund (O)
1 Railroad Boulevard, Port Clinton 19549

Reagan (Marcella O'R.) Fund for Father Flanagan's Boys' Home (R)
c/o First Union/Wachovia, Reading 19603

Reagan (Marcella O'R.) Fund for Servants of Relief... (R)
c/o First Union/Wachovia, Reading 19603

Ream (Roy H.) Foundation (R)
c/o Mellon Bank N.A., Harrisburg 17108

Reber (Miriam L.) Trust for Bucknell U. (R)
c/o Allfirst Bank, Harrisburg 17105

Reber Foundation (R)
c/o First Union/Wachovia, Reading 19603

Reber Home (O)
c/o First Union/Wachovia, Reading 19603

Redner Foundation (L) MI-41-99
c/o Redner's Markets, 3 Quarry Road, Reading 19605

Reichert (Clint) Memorial Trust (L) MI-13-33
c/o Kline, 1140 Hoff Road, Hanover 17331

Reinhardt Foundation, The (L) MI-43
P.O. Box 577, Manchester 17345

Reitnauer (Henry K. & Evelyn) Scholarship Fund (R)
c/o Boyertown High School, Boyertown 19512

Reitz (William D.) Trust (R)
c/o Mellon Bank N.A., Harrisburg 17108

Revington Arthur Foundation (L) MI-53-54-55
809 Cornwall Road, State College 16803

RG Charitable Foundation, The (L) MI-11-87-99
c/o RG Industries, P.O. Box 2824, York 17405

Rhoads (T.L.) Foundation
(Refer to Leidy-Rhoads Foundation Trust)

Rhoneymeade, Inc. (R)
R.D. #1, Box 258, Centre Hall 16828

Rieders (Herbert) Fdn. for Recovery of Objects Judaica (L)
MI-62
161 West Third Street, P.O. Box 215, Williamsport 17703

Rissinger (R.W. & Shirley) Foundation (L) MI-63
900 Manor Drive, Millersburg 17061

Roche (Mary A.) #1 Trust for Charities (R)
c/o Drovers & Mechanics National Bank, York 17401

Rogers (Barbara Witman) Foundation (L)
RD4, Wooded Hills Road, Linglestown 17112

Rohrer (Anna M.) Trust (R)
c/o Allfirst Trust Company of Pa., York 17401

Roman Catholic Scholarship Fund (NP)
c/o Delaware Trust Capital Management, Reading 19603

Ross (Alice Nason) Charitable Trust (R)
c/o Mid-State Bank, Altoona 16603

Ross Loan Fund, The (R)
c/o Valley Bank & Trust Co., Chambersburg 17201

Roter, Inc. (R)
2354 Magnolia Road, Harrisburg 17104

Rouzer (D. Lyda) Foundation (L) MI-22-63-99
322 Gettys Street, Gettysburg 17325

Rowland Theatre, Inc. (O)
P.O. Box 56, Philipsburg 16866

Rudy (George B.), Jr. Trust (R)
c/o York Bank & Trust Co., York 17401

Russ (William) Trust Ice Fund (R)
c/o Mellon Bank N.A., Harrisburg 17108

Saint Andrews Educational Trust (R)
P.O. Box 167, Waynesboro 17268

Saint Thomas High School Alumni Assn. (R)
c/o Chambersburg Trust Company, Chambersburg 17201

Saylor (Melba M.) Trust for St. John's Parsonage Fund (R)
c/o Allfirst Bank, York 17405

Saylor (Melba M.) Trust for St. John's U.C.C. (R)
c/o Allfirst Bank, York 17405

Schafer (Gerber D.) Charities
(Formerly of Reading, now located in UT)

Scheetz (Elsie M.) Trust for Camp Conrad Weiser (R)
c/o Allfirst Bank, Harrisburg 17105

Scheetz (Elsie) Trust for Reading Hospital/Nursing (R)
c/o Allfirst Bank, Harrisburg 17105

Schoeneck Area Civic Association (R)
305 Gockley Road, Stevens 17578

Scoboria (C.P.), Jr. Athletic Scholarship Foundation (R)
403 Eisenbrown Street, Reading 19605

Seaman Scholarship Fund Trust (R)
c/o First Union/Wachovia, Reading 19601

Sechrist (Alverta) Trust (R)
c/o Mellon Bank N.A., Harrisburg 17108

Seebold (Donald J.) Scholarship Fund (R)
c/o Danville Senior High School, Danville 17821

Seibert (Anna) Trust for Steelton Welfare Assn. (R)
c/o Mellon Bank N.A., Harrisburg 17108

Sharing Cupboard (I)
c/o Floyd, 717 Claster Boulevard, Dauphin 17018

Sharp (Frances C.) Charitable Foundation (R)
c/o First Union/Wachovia, Reading 19603

Shaull (Clyde L. & Mary C.) Education Foundation (R)
94 Brindle Road, Mechanicsburg 17055

Shellenberger (Augustus) Memorial Fund (R)
c/o Mellon Bank N.A., Harrisburg 17108

Shippenhouse Trust (R)
c/o Mellon Bank N.A., Harrisburg 17108

Shoemaker (Robert E.) Charitable Trust (R)
c/o First Union/Wachovia, Reading 19603

Shrewsbury Housing, Inc. (R)
P.O. Box 167, Luther Road, Shrewsbury 17361

Smarsh (John & Blanch) Trust for Frey Village (R)
c/o Mellon Bank N.A., Harrisburg 17108

Smith (Fred G.) Golden Rule Trust Fund (R)
c/o National City Bank of Pa., Mount Carmel 17851

Smith (Paul L.) Charitable Foundation Trust (R)
c/o Allfirst Bank, York 17403

Smucker (Paul M.) Family Foundation (L) MI-41-42-63
c/o Smucker Mgmt. Corp., 2727 Old Philadelphia Pike,
Bird-in-Hand 17505

Snyder (Ruby F.) Trust for Bethany UMC (R)
c/o Allfirst Bank, York 17401

Snyder (Ruby F.) Trust for Martin Memorial Library (R)
c/o Allfirst Bank, York 17401

Snyder (Ruby F.) Trust for Quincy Methodist Church (R)
c/o Allfirst Bank, York 17401

Snyder (Ruby F.) Trust for St. Pauls U.M.C. (R)
c/o Allfirst Bank, York 17401

Society for the Preservation of the Gruber Wagon Works (R)
P.O. Box 486, Leesport 19533

South Mountain Camps Foundation, The (O)
P.O. Box 147, Wernersville 19565

Spangler (Edward S.) Memorial (O)
c/o Drovers & Mechanics National Bank, Chambersburg 17401

Spangler (H. Mary) Scholarship Trust (R)
c/o Valley Bank & Trust Co., Chambersburg 17201

Sparrow Foundation (T)

Spong (Harper W.) Family Scholarship Foundation (R)
c/o Allfirst Bank, Harrisburg 17111

Stager (Henry B. & Mary B.) Memorial Nursing Scholarship (R)
c/o Fulton Bank, Lancaster 17604

Stager Charitable Trust for Hospitals (R)
c/o Fulton Bank, Lancaster 17604

Stager Charitable Trust for Zion United Church of Christ (R)
c/o Fulton Bank, Lancaster 17604

Staiman Brothers Charities
(New name: Marvin H. Staiman Charitable Trust)

Starkey (Eleanor) Scholarship Foundation (R)
c/o First Union/Wachovia, Williamsport 17701

Stehman (John V. R.) Scholarship Fund (R)
c/o First Union/Wachovia, Reading 19601

Steinman (James Hale) Conestoga House Fdn. (O)
P.O. Box 128, Lancaster 17604

Stewart (A.)/Shippen House Trust (R)
c/o Mellon Bank N.A., Harrisburg 17108

Stine (Timothy M.) Memorial Foundation (T)

Stiteler (Leonore G.) Trust for Tri-County Assn. for Blind (R)
3607 Derry Street, Harrisburg 17111

Stoner (Katherine M.) Trust (R)
c/o Financial Trust Company, Chambersburg 17201

Stout (Florence M.) Trust for Charities (R)
c/o Allfirst Bank, Harrisburg 17105

Sunbury Kiwanis Foundation (U)

Sunderland (Klare S.) Foundation (L) MI-42-63
c/o Sun Enterprises, Inc. P.O. Box 367, Camp Hill 17011

Swartz (Elizabeth W.) Trust for First Pres. Church/York (R)
c/o Vaughn, 22 South Beaver Street, York 17401

Taylor (Frances E.) Scholarship Trust (R)
c/o Allfirst Bank, Harrisburg 17105

There's Room in The Inn, Inc. (R)
RR2, Box 1605, Warfordsburg 17267

Thoracic Surgical Educational & Research Trust Fund (O)
2 Bluejay Drive, Wyomissing 19610

Tioga County Foundation (L) MI-N/R
c/o Blair, 114 Main Street, Wellsboro 16901

Trexler (Dr. Ethan L. & Katherine) Scholarship Trust (R)
c/o First Union/Wachovia, Reading 19601

Trexler (John J.) Foundation (R)
c/o First Union/Wachovia, Reading 19603

Trissler (P.) Trust for Conestoga Church (R)
c/o Mellon Bank N.A., Harrisburg 17108

Trushell (Allene S.) Scholarship Trust (R)
c/o Oswayo Valley School District, Shinglehouse 16748

Unger (Guinn & Phyllis) Foundation (L) MI-41-52-63
c/o PNC Bank N.A., 545 West Middle Street, Gettysburg 17325

Usner (Gail L.) Memorial Scholarship (R)
c/o Ephrata High School - Guidance Dept., Ephrata 17522

Valero (Lucy A.) Memorial Scholarship Fund (R)
c/o P.S.E.A., 400 North Third Street, Harrisburg 17108

Vastine (Elizabeth B.) & K.V. Bernheimer Memorial Fund (R)
c/o First National Bank of Danville, Danville 17821

Viviano (Paulette) Foundation for the Performing Arts (O)
1051 Sand Hill Road, Hershey 17033

Von Hess (Louise Steinman) Foundation (O)
38 South Second Street, Columbia 17512

Von Hess (Louise) Foundation for Medical Education (O)
445 North Duke Street, Lancaster 17602

Von Hess (Richard C.) Foundation (R)
38 South Second Street, Box 68, Columbia 17512

VVV Athletic Association Sports Fund (R)
c/o First Union/Wachovia, Reading 19603

Wacker (Joseph) Family Foundation (R)
c/o Fulton Bank, Lancaster 17604

Walker (Edna & Frank) Trust (R)
c/o Allfirst Bank, Harrisburg 17105

Walker (Frank & Edna) Residuary Trust (R)
c/o Allfirst Bank, Harrisburg 17105

Walker (Joseph) Family Scholarship Fund (R)
c/o Fulton Bank, Lancaster 17604

Walnut Acres Foundation (R)
Penns Creek 17862

Warehime (Alan R.) Charitable Trust (R)
c/o Allfirst Bank, Harrisburg 17105

Waring (Tom L.) Trust Fund (R)
c/o Fulton Bank, Lancaster 17604

Warrell Family Historical Foundation (R)
c/o Financial Trust Services Company, Carlisle 17013

Watson (Albert) Trust (R)
c/o Mellon Bank N.A., Harrisburg 17108

Watson (Naomi) Trust (R)
c/o Mellon Bank N.A., Harrisburg 17108

Waynesboro Beneficial Fund Assn. (O)
13 West Main Street, Waynesboro 17268

Weber (Henry & Frances) Foundation (T)

Weeber (Cora M.) Trust (R)
3350 North Progress Ave., Harrisburg 17101

Weinrich (Jennie L.) Worthy Poor Coal Fund (R)
    c/o First National Trust Bank, Sunbury 17801

Weiser (Nettie S.) Trust (R)
    c/o Drovers & Mechanics National Bank, York 17401

Welch (Sara & Warren) Foundation (R)
    P.O. Box 125, Newville 17241

Welker (Robert J. 'Tag') Memorial Scholarship Trust (R)
    39 North Maple Street, Mount Carmel 17851

Wenger Foundation, The (O)
    P.O. Box 409, Myerstown 17067

Western Hemisphere Cultural Society, Inc. (O)
    P.O. Box 122, York 17405

Weyer (Albert S.) Trust for Hospital Fund (R)
    c/o First Union/Wachovia, Lancaster 17604

White (Susan K.) Charitable Trust (R)
    c/o Allfirst Bank, Harrisburg 17105

Whitaker Foundation, The
    (Formerly of Mechanicsburg, now located in VA)

Wildasin (George M. & Pauline F.) Trust (R)
    c/o Allfirst Bank, York 17405

Willard House & Clock Museum (O)
    514 Poplar Street, Columbia 17512

Williams (James T.) Scholarship Fund (R)
    360 Holiday Lane, Lewistown 17044

Wingaris Scholarship Fund (R)
    c/o First Union/Wachovia, Reading 19603

Winter (Charles R.) Foundation (R)
    c/o Fulton Bank, Lancaster 17604

Witmer (Ann C.) Home Trust (R)
    c/o First Union/Wachovia, Lancaster 17604

Witmer (John L. & Jeanette) Trust (R)
    c/o PNC Advisors, P.O. Box 308, Camp Hill 17011

Witmer (Mabel M.) Trust (R)
    c/o Chambersburg Trust Company, Chambersburg 17201

Witmer (Richard Howell) Foundation (R)
    c/o May & Metzger, 49 North Duke Street, Lancaster 17602

Wolf (Frances H.) Trust for Wolf Museum of Music & Art (O)
    c/o First Union/Wachovia, Lancaster 17604

Wolf Foundation for Education Trust (R)
    c/o Ephrata National Bank, Ephrata 17522

Woods (Elizabeth C.) Foundation (R)
    c/o First Union/Wachovia, Lancaster 17604

Woods (Valeria Walton) Scholarship Fund (R)
    c/o Danville Senior High School, Danville 17821

Worst (Raymond B.) Residuary Trust (R)
    c/o Fulton Bank, Lancaster 17604

Wright (Irene Mae) Charitable Trust (R)
    c/o Drovers & Mechanics National Bank, York 17401

Wunch (Edward R.P.) Trust (R)
    c/o First Union/Wachovia, Reading 19603

Yagel (Romaine H.) Trust (R)
    c/o York Bank & Trust Co., York 17401

Yellott (Anne J.) Foundation (L) MI-41-52-55
    c/o Rhoads & Sinon, 1 South Market Square, Harrisburg 17108

Yocum Family Perpetual Charitable Trust (R)
    920 Centre Ave., Reading 19601

Yoder (Leonard) Trust (R)
    c/o Allfirst Bank, Harrisburg 17101

Yohn (Eleanor B.) Medical Foundation (L)
    c/o May & Metzger, LLP, 49 North Duke Street, Lancaster 17602

York Catholic High School Student Aid & Endowment Fund (R)
    601 East Springettsbury Ave., York 17403

Zimmerman-Klinger Scholarship Fund (R)
    c/o Lebanon Valley National Bank, Lebanon 17042

Northeastern Region / NE

covers the following 14 counties

**Bradford - Carbon - Columbia - Lackawanna - Lehigh - Luzerne - Monroe
Northampton - Pike - Schuylkill - Sullivan - Susquehanna - Wayne - Wyoming**

NE-001   Amaranth Foundation
1751 Lehigh Parkway, North
Allentown 18103   (Lehigh County)
AMV $90,338   **FYE** 12-00   (**Gifts Received** $302,907)

MI-11-12-13-29-41-51-52-53-54-63-71-72-84
Phone 610-435-1492 **FAX** None
EIN 23-7743235   **Year Created** 1994
67 **Grants totaling** $247,550

Mostly local giving; grants are for general purposes except as noted. High grant of **$70,000** to Allentown Symphony Orchestra. **$25,220** to Cedar Crest College. **$15,000** to United Way of Greater Lehigh Valley. **$12,500** to St. John's United Church of Christ. **$12,430** to Wildlands Conservancy. **$10,000** to The Nature Conservancy. **$6,500** each to Bach Choir of Bethlehem and Touchstone Theatre. **$5,000** each to Allentown Art Museum, Banana Factory, Baum School of Art (building fund), Community Action Committee of the Lehigh Valley, Curtis Institute of Music [Philadelphia], and Girl Scouts/Great Valley Council. **$2,000-$3,500** each to Allentown YMCA/YWCA, Boys & Girls Club of Allentown, KidsPeace, Lehigh U., Lehigh Valley Chamber Orchestra, Little Pond Foundation, The Theatre Outlet, Unity of Lehigh Valley, and Valley Youth House (Project Child). **$1,000-$1,500** each to Adams International Tennis Academy, Community Music School, Hawk Mountain Sanctuary Assn., Parkettes National Gymnastic Training Center, and The Program for Women & Families. Other local/Eastern Pa. contributions, **$100-$700,** for similar purposes. **Out-of-state** giving includes **$5,000** each to Bread for the World Institute [MD] and Mount Holyoke College [MA]; **$2,500** each to Orangutan Foundation International [CA] and Sojourners [DC] and **$2,000** to Journey into Freedom [OR]. ■ **PUBLICATIONS:** None ■ **WEBSITE:** None ■ **E-MAIL:** None ■ **APPLICATION POLICIES & PROCEDURES:** The Foundation reports giving primarily to Pa., particularly Allentown, and that grant requests are not encouraged; no grants are awarded to individuals.
O+D+T Joan M. Moran (Manager+Donor+Con)

NE-002   Arnold Foundation
c/o Joseph J. Paciotti, CPA
Plaza 315, 1094 Route 315
Wilkes-Barre 18702   (Luzerne County)
AMV $1,255,035   **FYE** 3-01   (**Gifts Received** $0)

MI-42-43-61

Phone 570-823-8855 **FAX** None
EIN 23-6417708   **Year Created** 1966
15 **Grants totaling** $47,191

About half local giving. High grant of **$19,900** - scholarship for local student. **$3,000** to St. Ignatius Church. **$2,500** to Kings College. **$1,000** to Mercy Institute for Educational Development and for a scholarship. **Out-of-state** giving all to NC or SC for various purposes. ■ **PUBLICATIONS:** None ■ **WEBSITE:** None ■ **E-MAIL:** None ■ **APPLICATION POLICIES & PROCEDURES:** The Foundation reports that Luzerne County charitable organizations receive preference. Grant requests may be submitted at any time; individual scholarship applicants should submit a brief resume of academic qualifications.
O+D+T Arnold K. Biscontini [NC] (P+F+Donor+Con) — Cynthia W. Ross [NC] (S)

NE-003   Auto Racing Fraternity Foundation of America
c/o Pocono International Raceway
Long Pond Road, P.O. Box 500
Long Pond 18334   (Monroe County)
AMV $3,653,020   **FYE** 3-00   (**Gifts Received** $0)

MI-11-12-13-15-31-41-42-61-71-89

Phone 570-646-2300 **FAX** 570-643-1423
EIN 23-2136313   **Year Created** 1980
43 **Grants totaling** $117,175

About two-thirds local/Pa. giving. High grant of **$10,000** to United Way of Monroe County. **$8,000** to East Stroudsburg U. Foundation. **$5,000** each to Carnegie Mellon U., Elizabethtown U., Greater Nanticoke Area Schools, Temple U., and Times-Leader Newspapers in Education Program. **$3,000** each to Checkered Flag Fan Club [Kutztown], Kettle Creek Environmental Fund, and Pocono Friends of Scouting. **$2,000** each to Christ the King Church, Meals on Wheels/Stroudsburg, Pocono Medical Center, Pocono Service for Families, and St. Maria Goretti Church. **$1,000** each to Camp Cadet Troop N, Pocono Mountain Regional Police Assn., and Tunkhannock Township Volunteer Fire Dept. (scholarship fund). Other smaller local contributions for various purposes. **Out-of-state** giving includes **$6,000** to Elon College [NC]; **$5,000** each to CARE 2000 [NC], National Motorsports Press Assn. [NC], and Winston Cup Racing Wives Auxiliary [NC]; and other grants to FL and NC. ■ **PUBLICATIONS:** None ■ **WEBSITE:** www.poconoraceway.com [corporate information only] ■ **E-MAIL:** None ■ **APPLICATION POLICIES & PROCEDURES:** The Foundation reports that most giving is for special projects and that most grantees are selected by Board members.
O+D+T Dr. Joseph R. Mattioli (P+D+Con) — Joseph R. Mattioli, Jr. (VP+D) — Lovena Mattioli (S+D) — Michelle Mattioli (F+D)- Corporate donor: Pocono International Raceway

---

NE-004   AYSR Foundation   MI-23
        c/o JDK Management Company
        RD5, Box 290
        Bloomsburg 17815   (Columbia County)   **Phone** 570-784-0111 **FAX** 570-784-7950
                                                                     EIN 23-2966353   **Year Created** 1998
AMV $130,000 est.   **FYE** 12-01   (**Gifts Received** $30,000)   55 **Grants totaling** $32,000

All giving to assist needy individuals and families; most grants were **$1,000** or less. ■**PUBLICATIONS:** None ■**WEBSITE:** None ■**E-MAIL:** None ■**APPLICATION POLICIES & PROCEDURES:** Grant requests must be submitted on a formal application form, available from the Foundation, together with a statement on family income/expenses and the need for support. Requests may be submitted at any time. Grants are awarded at monthly meetings.

O+D+T John D. Klingerman (P+F+D+Con) — Richard Staber (VP+D) — Robyn Klingerman (S+D) — Janet Bachinger (D) — John Grabert (AS)

NE-005   Baker (Dexter F. & Dorothy H.) Foundation   MI-11-12-13-14-31-32-42-43-51-52-53-54-55
        c/o Air Products & Chemicals, Inc.   56-57-63
        7201 Hamilton Boulevard   **Phone** 610-481-4911 **FAX** None
        Allentown 18195   (Lehigh County)   **EIN** 23-2453230   **Year Created** 1986
AMV $13,831,310   **FYE** 12-00   (**Gifts Received** $452,577)   35 **Grants totaling** $661,185

Mostly local giving. High grant of **$180,000** to Muhlenberg College (artist in residence/arts scholarships/Baker Theatre campaign). **$153,000** to Lehigh U. (cultural activities/students abroad program/capital campaign). **$109,000** to First Presbyterian Church of Allentown (outreach/youth choir/shelter). **$75,000** to Lehigh Valley Hospital (intensive care unit research). **$15,000** to YMCA-YWCA Development Program (health center renovations). **$13,000** to Lehigh Valley Chamber Orchestra (1st violin underwriting). **$10,000** to United Way of the Greater Lehigh Valley (Boy Scouts/Minsi Trails Council). **$9,000** to Repertory Dance Theatre (dance scholarships/Regional Dance America). **$8,000** each to Allentown Art Museum (exhibition). **$7,500** to Lehigh Valley Public Telecommunications Corp. (closed captioning). **$4,000-$5,000** to Discovery Center of Science & Technology (outreach/Hall of Fame), Girls Club of Allentown (field trips), Koresh Dance Company (local concert), Lehigh Valley Arts Council (marketing support), and Mayfair (performance support). **$2,000-$3,000** each to The Bach Choir (schools program), Community Bike Works (after school program), Community Music School (student assistance), DeSales U. (Baker Performing Arts Scholarships), Lehigh County Council of Churches (daybreak program), Lehigh Valley Community Broadcasters (arts calendar), Lehigh Valley Parents Group for Hard of Hearing Children (program underwriting), Mock Turtle Marionette Theatre (technical assistance/support), Satori, Inc. (senior citizen programs), and Touchstone Theatre (teen troupe). **$1,000-$1,500** each to Ballet Guild of the Lehigh Valley (Nutcracker soloists), Baum School of Art (Good Shepherd Patrons art class), and Lehigh County Historical Society (student visit materials). **Out-of-state** giving includes **$10,385** to First Presbyterian Church of Bonita Springs [FL] (music instruction/radio ministry); **$10,000** to Johns Hopkins U. [MD] (robotic surgical ear tools); and smaller grants to NY and FL. ■**PUBLICATIONS:** statement of program policy; application guidelines, application form ■**WEBSITE:** None ■**E-MAIL:** None ■**APPLICATION POLICIES & PROCEDURES:** The Foundation reports that most giving is limited to the Lehigh & Northampton counties. No grants are awarded for endowment or to individuals. Prospective applicants must send a Letter of Intent before March 15th and request a copy of a formal application form. Completed grant applications must be submitted before the July 15th deadline; include an annual report, organizational/project budgets, Board member list, list of major funding sources, promotional materials, audited financial statement, and IRS tax-exempt status documentation. Site visits sometimes are made to organizations being considered for a grant. Grants are awarded at a November meeting.

O+D+T Ellen Baker Baltz [Center Valley] (Executive Director+T+Con) — Dexter F. Baker (C+T+Donor) — Dorothy H. Baker (T+Donor) — Carolyn J. Baker [CA] (T) — Leslie Baker Boris [Haverford] (T) — Susan Baker Royal [TX] (T) — Mellon Bank (Corporate Trustee)

NE-006   Baltimore Family Foundation   MI-11-12-13-22-32-42-44-62
        34 South River Street   **Phone** 570-823-2222 **FAX** None
        Wilkes-Barre 18702   (Luzerne County)   **EIN** 23-2308091   **Year Created** 1984
AMV $1,048,276   **FYE** 12-00   (**Gifts Received** $0)   32 **Grants totaling** $103,100

All local giving. High grant of **$50,000** to Jewish Federation of Greater Wilkes-Barre. **$15,000** to Temple B'nai B'rith Bimah Fund. **$12,500** to United Way of Wyoming Valley. **$9,200** to Osterhout Library (mostly for capital fund). **$3,000** to Wilkes-Barre YMCA. **$2,000** each to King's College (annual fund) and Wilkes College (annual fund). **$1,000** each to Family Service Assn. of the Wyoming Valley and Susan Komen Breast Cancer Fund. Other local contributions **$100-$750** for various community purposes. ■**PUBLICATIONS:** None ■**WEBSITE:** None ■**E-MAIL:** None ■**APPLICATION POLICIES & PROCEDURES:** The Foundation reports that only local organizations are supported.

O+D+T David M. Baltimore (P+Donor+Con) — Muriel Baltimore (S+Donor) — Terry S. Baltimore [Dallas] (D+Donor) — Lynn Baltimore [Kingston] (D+Donor) — Charles Baltimore [FL] (D+Donor)

NE-007   Banks (Joseph B. & Virginia H.) Foundation   MI-13-42-61
        c/o Banks Companies
        403 Coal Street   **Phone** 570-824-8264 **FAX** None
        Wilkes-Barre 18702   (Luzerne County)   **EIN** 23-2953650   **Year Created** 1998
AMV $1,135,649   **FYE** 12-00   (**Gifts Received** $0)   8 **Grants totaling** $91,500

All local giving. High grant of **$75,000** to College Misericordia (capital improvements). **$5,000** each to St. Joseph's Center Foundation [Scranton] and St. Therese's Church [Shavertown]. **$2,500** to Penn's Woods Girl Scouts Council. **$2,000** to The

Luzerne Foundation. **$1,000** to St. John the Evangelist Church [Pittston]. Other smaller contributions. — Grant approved for future payment: **$150,000** to College Misericordia (capital improvements). ■**PUBLICATIONS:** None ■**WEBSITE:** None ■**E-MAIL:** None ■**APPLICATION POLICIES & PROCEDURES:** Information not available.

O+D+T Advisory Board Members: Virginia H. Banks (T+Donor+Con) — J. Christopher Banks — J. Gregory Banks — Jennifer Banks — Lisa Banks — Margaret L. Banks

---

NE-008 Bastian (Walter & Alma) Foundation, The
　　c/o Tallman, Hudders & Sorrentino, P.C.
　　1611 Pond Road, Suite 300
　　Allentown 18104 (Lehigh County)
AMV $1,203,783 **FYE** 12-00 **(Gifts Received** $0)

MI-12-13-14-22-29-31-35-39-42-52-56-65
Phone 610-391-1800 **FAX** 610-391-1805
EIN 23-6278134 **Year Created** 1956
　22 **Grants totaling** $73,500

All giving to Lehigh County; all grants are for capital purposes with some as payments on multiyear pledges. High grant of **$10,000** to Lehigh County Historical Society. **$5,000** each to Allentown College, Child Advocacy Center of Lehigh County, Community Action Committee of Lehigh Valley, KidsPeace, and Sacred Heart Foundation. **$4,000** each to Community Bike Works and Fund to Benefit Children & Youth. **$3,000** each to Assn. for Blind & Visually Impaired, Miller Memorial Blood Bank, and Salvation Army/Allentown. **$2,000** each to Allentown Symphony, The ARC, Eastern Pa. Downs Syndrome Center, The Caring Place, Good Shepherd, and Weller Health Education Center. **$1,000-$1,500** each to Lehigh County Conference of Churches, Lehigh Valley Child Care, Inc., and Liberty Bell Shrine Museum. Other smaller contributions for similar purposes. ■**PUBLICATIONS:** None ■**WEBSITE:** None ■**E-MAIL:** None ■**APPLICATION POLICIES & PROCEDURES:** The Foundation reports that giving is limited to Lehigh Valley organizations. Grants are awarded for capital projects and operating support; an organization's size and the number of Lehigh County citizens who would benefit from support are taken into consideration. No grants awarded to individuals. Submit requests at any time in a letter-proposal; include an organizational and project budgets, a list of Board members, and IRS tax-exempt status documentation. Site visits and/or meetings sometimes are arranged with organizations being considered for a grant. The Board of Directors awards grants at meetings in February, May, August and November.

O+D+T Robert G. Tallman, Esq. (P+F+D+Con) — John B. Lizak [Northampton] (V+D) — Ray W. Biondi [Emmaus] (S+D)

NE-009 Behler (A. Donald & Mary G.) Foundation
　　333 Columbia Ave.
　　Palmerton 18071 (Carbon County)
AMV $1,017,643 **FYE** 12-00 **(Gifts Received** $0)

MI-11-14-29-31-44-55-57-63-71-84-89
Phone 610-377-2510 **FAX** None
EIN 23-2903583 **Year Created** 1997
　21 **Grants totaling** $45,500

Mostly local giving. High grant of **$20,500** to Palmerton Library (mostly building fund). **$5,000** each to ARC of Carbon County and Lehighton Borough (Memorial Park). **$1,000-$1,500** each to Caladium Arts & Crafts, First United Church of Christ, Mauch Chunk Historical Society, Palmerton Hospital Foundation, Palmerton Memorial Park Assn., Palmerton Wrestling Assn., Red Cross, United Way of Palmerton, and West End Fire Company #2. Other smaller contributions, many for local fire companies. **Out-of-state** grant: **$1,000** to Wentworth Institute of Technology [MA]. ■**PUBLICATIONS:** None. ■**WEBSITE:** None ■**E-MAIL:** None ■**APPLICATION POLICIES & PROCEDURES:** No grants to individuals.

O+D+T A. Donald Behler (P+F+D+Donor+Con) — Mary G. Behler (S+D) — Judith Ann Bartholmew [Lehighton] (D) — Andrew D. Behler (D) — Donna L. Correll (D) — Corporate donor: Blue Ridge Pressure Casting

---

NE-010 Beitel (Will R.) Children's Community Foundation
　　P.O. Box 292
　　Nazareth 18064 (Northampton County)
AMV $2,320,776 **FYE** 9-00 **(Gifts Received** $0)

MI-11-12-13-14-17-18-29-33-35-44
Phone 610-861-8929 **FAX** None
EIN 24-0800920 **Year Created** 1874
　30 **Grants totaling** $134,877

All local giving restricted to programs serving youth in Northampton County; grants are for general support except as noted. High grant of **$25,000** to Nazareth YMCA (debt reduction/operations). **$7,000-$7,500** each to Boys & Girls Club of Easton, Children's Home of Easton, Salvation Army/Bethlehem, Turning Point of Lehigh Valley, and Valley Youth House. **$6,097** to Visual Impairment and Blindness Services of Northampton County. **$6,000** each to Lehigh Valley Child Care, Inc. (Easton Teen Project/scholarships) and South Bethlehem Neighborhood Center. **$4,500-$5,000** each to Boys & Girls Club of Bethlehem, Memorial Library of Nazareth & Vicinity, Northeast Ministry, ProJeCt, and Third Street Alliance for Women & Children. **$2,000-$3,000** each to August Survivor's Center, Bethlehem YMCA, Center for Humanistic Change, Child Abuse Prevention Coalition, Northampton County 4-H Center, Pa. Youth Theater, The Program for Women & Children, Saucon Valley Community Center, and Sayre Child Center. **$1,000-$1,940** each to ARC of Lehigh & Northampton Counties, Easter Seals, Family & Counseling Services of the Lehigh Valley, Fund to Benefit Children & Youth, Planned Parenthood of NE Pa., and Special Olympics. ■**PUBLICATIONS:** Information for Applicants memorandum ■**WEBSITE:** None ■**E-MAIL:** None ■**APPLICATION POLICIES & PROCEDURES:** The Foundation reports that all giving is limited to organizations serving youth in Northampton County; services/programs which reach only a small area of the county also are eligible for support. Priority interests are (1) providing housing/maintenance for youths who are without family care, and (2) providing youths with a good non-sectarian influence. Most grants are for operating budgets, special projects, building funds, and capital needs. No grants are awarded to organizations which are tax-supported, educational, or affiliated with a specific church. Prospective applicants should initially request a copy of the detailed application guidelines and follow them explicitly. Submit grant requests in a letter during February-March (April 1st is the deadline); include an annual report, organizational/project budgets, Board member list, audited financial statement, and IRS tax-exempt status documentation. Site visits sometimes are arranged to organizations being considered for a grant. The Board of Directors awards grants at a June meeting with funds disbursed September 30th.

O+D+T Thomas C. Kelchner [Bethlehem] (S+AF+Con) — Robert C. Hoch [Pen Argyl] (P+D) — John M. Dusinski (VP+D) — Grant W. Walizer (F) — Stephen Bajan (D) — Elwood G. Buss, Sr. (D) — Phillip E. Molln, II (D)

NE-011 Benevento & Mayo Foundation

c/o Benevento & Mayo Partners
46 Public Square, Suite 500
Wilkes-Barre   18701   (Luzerne County)

MI-12-42-43

Phone 570-824-7895 **FAX** None
EIN 23-7880441   **Year Created** 1997

AMV $587,196   **FYE** 12-00   (**Gifts Received** $0)   1 **Grant of** $5,000

Sole grant to Kidsave International [DC]. — Grants awarded in 1998: **$175,000** to King's College (scholarship endowment) and **$12,500** to College Misericordia (library construction). ■**PUBLICATIONS:** None ■**WEBSITE:** None ■**E-MAIL:** None ■**APPLICATION POLICIES & PROCEDURES:** No grants awarded to individuals.

O+D+T John Parente [Tunhannock] (T+Con) — Brian J. Parente [FL] (T) — Charles E. Parente [FL] (T) — Charles E. Parente, Jr. [FL] (T) — Mary M. Parente [FL] (T) — Marla Parente Sgarlat [Harveys Lake] (T) –- Corporate donor: Benevento & Mayo Partners

NE-012 Benevolent Association of Pottsville

1632 Lightfoot Drive
Auburn   17922   (Schuylkill County)

MI-12-13-14-17-22-29-41-44-55-84
Phone 570-739-1288 **FAX** None
EIN 23-6279703   **Year Created** 1942

AMV $838,231   **FYE** 12-00   (**Gifts Received** $6,645)   21 **Grants totaling** $33,025

All giving restricted to charitable organizations in Schuylkill County. High grant of **$5,000** to Pottsville Library (capital campaign). **$3,000** each to Big Brothers/Big Sisters of Pottsville (One-to-one program) and Schuylkill County Women in Crisis (zero tolerance violence program). **$2,000-$2,650** each to St. Ambrose School (preschoolers club house), St. Joseph's Center (classroom equipment), Salvation Army (summer camp), and Schuylkill County Therapeutic Program (indoor arena). **$1,000-$1,859** each to Eastern Schuylkill Recreation Commission (basketball equipment), Friendship House (household provisions fund), Genesis (school programs), Penn's Woods Girl Scouts Council (capital campaign), Pottsville Lions Legion (baseball bats), and Schuylkill County Council of the Arts (arts education program). Other local grants **$400-$951** for similar purposes. ■**PUBLICATIONS:** None ■**WEBSITE:** None ■**E-MAIL:** None ■**APPLICATION POLICIES & PROCEDURES:** Only Schuylkill County organizations that serve youth are eligible to apply. A formal application form, available from the Association, must be completed and submitted by the August 1st deadline.

O+D+T Marian A. Yanaitis (S+Con) — William C. Schuettler [Pottsville] (P) — Frances Weiss [Pottsville] (VP) — Robert Yanaitis [Auburn] (F)

NE-013 Bergman Foundation, The

Suite 801,
67-69 Public Square
Wilkes-Barre   18701   (Luzerne County)

MI-11-12-13-14-22-29-41-42-44-51-52-55-56
61-62-63-65
Phone 570-823-6282 **FAX** 570-873-6282
EIN 24-6014771   **Year Created** 1950

AMV $2,849,402   **FYE** 9-00   (**Gifts Received** $21,227)   55 **Grants totaling** $137,900

Mostly local giving. High grant of **$26,430** to Temple B'nai B'rith. **$16,165** to St. Stephen's Church. **$11,000** to Jewish Federation of Wilkes-Barre. **$10,000** to United Way of Wyoming Valley. **$8,575** to Wyoming Valley Children's Assn. **$6,500** to Jewish Community Center. **$5,000** each to Camp Kresge for Handicapped Kids and McGlynn Learning Center. **$4,100** to Wilkes College (annual fund). **$3,000-$3,500** each to Back Mountain Memorial Library, Hoyt Library, Osterhout Free Library, Penn State U. (annual fund), Sisters of Mercy Institute of Education, and Wyoming Historical & Geological Society. **$2,000-$2,100** each to Allied Services Foundation, Red Cross, and St. Vincent de Paul Kitchen. **$1,000-$1,500** each to Greater Anthracite Scenic Trails, Family Service Assn. of Wilkes-Barre, First Presbyterian Church of Wilkes-Barre, Jewish Family Services of Wilkes-Barre, Kiwanis Wheelchair Club, NE Pa. Children's Theatre Festival, NE Pa. Philharmonic, Salvation Army, and Wilkes-Barre Assn. for the Blind. Other local and out-of-state contributions for similar purposes. ■**PUBLICATIONS:** None ■**WEBSITE:** None ■**E-MAIL:** None ■ **APPLICATION POLICIES & PROCEDURES:** The Foundation reports that giving focuses on the Wilkes-Barre area with most grants for general support, building funds, capital drives, or endowment. No grants are awarded to individuals. Grant requests may be submitted in a letter (3 pages maximum) at any time, but preferably in March; include a project budget, list of major funding sources, and IRS tax-exempt status documentation.

O+D+T Justin Bergman, Jr. (T+Donor+Con) — Cordelia Bergman (T) — Florence Shubilla (T)

NE-014 Berkheimer Foundation

c/o H.A. Berkheimer, Inc.
50 North 7th Street
Bangor   18013   (Northampton County)

MI-12-13-14-22-31-39-56-89
Phone 610-588-0965 **FAX** 610-863-1997
EIN 23-2582881   **Year Created** 1989

AMV $169,930   **FYE** 12-00   (**Gifts Received** $10,000)   9 **Grants totaling** $18,500

All local/regional giving; grants are for general purposes except as noted. High grant of **$3,000** to Pocono Medical Center. **$2,000-$2,500** each to Blue Valley Rescue Squad (truck fund), Burnley Workshop, Discovery Center, Salvation Army of Monroe County, Slate Belt Heritage Center, and Wilkes-Barre YMCA. **$1,000** each to Lehigh Valley Child Care (renovation/expansion) and Mount Pocono Borough (recreation complex). ■**PUBLICATIONS:** None ■**WEBSITE:** None ■**E-MAIL:** None ■**APPLICATION POLICIES & PROCEDURES:** The Foundation reports giving primarily to Pa. organizations and only for special projects, building funds, and capital drives. Grant requests may be submitted in a letter at any time; include an organizational budget, project budget, and IRS tax-exempt status documentation. Grants are awarded at meetings in January, April, July, and October.

O+D+T John D. Berkheimer (P+Con) — Henry U. Sandt, Jr. (S+F) — William Carson (D) — Dennis J. Harris (D) — Robert S. Pharo (D) — William Sykes (D) — David Gordon (AS) — Corporate donor: H.A. Berkheimer, Inc.

NE-015 Berman (Bernard & Audrey) Foundation
2830 Gordon Street
Allentown 18104   (Lehigh County)
AMV $1,525,773   **FYE** 12-00   **(Gifts Received** $0)

MI-11-22-41-42-52-54-62
Phone 610-435-2451 **FAX** None
EIN 23-6268670   **Year Created** 1960
25 **Grants totaling** $78,626

Mostly local giving. High grant of **$30,000** to Allentown Art Museum. **$23,000** to Jewish Federation of Lehigh Valley. **$7,900** to Moravian Academy. **$2,500** to Lehigh Valley Chamber Orchestra. **$1,000-$1,250** each to Beth Israel Temple, Cedar Crest College, Congregation Keneseth Israel, and United Way of the Greater Lehigh Valley. **$920** to Jewish Community Center of Allentown. Other contributions **$100-$500** for various purposes. **Out-of-state** giving includes **$3,000** to Metropolitan Opera [NY] and **$1,500** to World Jewish Congress [NY] ■**PUBLICATIONS:** None ■**WEBSITE:** None   ■**E-MAIL:** None ■**APPLICATION POLICIES & PROCEDURES:** Grant requests may be submitted in a letter at any time.

O+D+T Bernard Berman (P+Con) — Ann E. Berman (VP) — Eileen Berman Fischmann (S+F) — Corporate donors: Allentown Brake & Wheel Company; Parker Inc.

NE-016 Berman (Philip & Muriel) Foundation, The
2000 Nottingham Road
Allentown 18103   (Lehigh County)
AMV $240,433   **FYE** 5-00   **(Gifts Received** $130,000)

MI-42-62
Phone 610-433-7497 **FAX** 610-437-1435
EIN 23-6270983   **Year Created** 1960
2 **Grants totaling** $10,400

High grant of **$10,000** to Lehigh U. (Jewish studies program). **$400** to Jewish Funders Network [NY] (Jewish studies). — In the prior year, one grant of **$22,500** to Lehigh U. (Jewish studies program). ■**PUBLICATIONS:** None ■**WEBSITE:** None ■**E-MAIL:** murielberman@entermail.net ■**APPLICATION POLICIES & PROCEDURES:** The Foundation reports that it is presently not really active; historical priorities have been education and arts/culture with most grants for special projects, publication, research, or scholarships. Grant requests may be submitted in a letter (2 pages maximum) at any time; include an annual report, project budget, Board member list, list of major funding sources, and IRS tax-exempt status documentation. Site visits sometimes are made to organizations being considered for a grant.

O+D+T Nancy Berman Bloch [CA] (P+D+Con) — Muriel M. Berman (VP+F+Donor) — Jack Kushner (S)

NE-017 Berwick Health & Wellness Foundation
309 Vine Street
Berwick 18603
                                          (Columbia County)
AMV $25,814,260   **FYE** 12-00   **(Gifts Received** $557,644)

MI-12-13-14-15-17-19-25-29-31-33-41-43-44-55-84-85
Phone 570-752-3930 **FAX** 570-752-7435
EIN 23-2982141   **Year Created** 1998
43 **Grants totaling** $1,550,571

All local giving. High grant of **$850,000** to YMCA (recreational/therapeutic pool). Ten grants totaling **$195,500** to Berwick Area School District (for reading, parenting, drug-alcohol, sports, playground equipment, counseling, and other programs). **$100,000** to Beyond Violence (mortgage/salary). **$85,000** to Susquehanna Warrior Trail (construct exercise trail). **$35,000** to Nescopeck Area Playground (equipment). **$33,000** to Penn's Woods Girl Scouts (in-school program). **$30,000** to Boy Scouts-Columbia/Montour Council (camp improvements). **$24,000** to Women's Center (advocacy program re domestic violence). **$20,000** to American Cancer Society (van for patient transport). **$15,000** Women's Center (bridge housing - Berwick). **$20,500** to Habitat for Humanity (property renovations). **$12,000** each to Berwick Public Library (renovations/purchase books) and Mental Health Association (Compeer Mentoring program). **$11,660** to Peaceful Crossings (vehicle). **$10,696** to EOS Riding Center (indoor arena/session fees). **$10,225** to Your Loving Choices (office equipment). **$10,000** to Columbia/Montour Home-Health Hospice (pain medication). **$10,000** each to Bloomsburg Theatre Ensemble (Project Discovery) and Nicholas Wolff Foundation (special needs camping for kids). **$2,000-$4,000** each for Berwick Youth Soccer, Central Pa. Forum for Future (student attendance fees), Columbia/Montour Family Health (parent classes), Shickshinny Food Pantry, health-related scholarships for students from four local school districts, and defibrillators for five local police/fire/EMT. **$1,250** to Columbia Child Development (car seats for low income families). **$1,000** to Columbia/Montour Women's Conference (speaker fee).
■**PUBLICATIONS:** None ■**WEBSITE:** www.berwickfoundation.org ■**E-MAIL:** edewald@sunlink.net ■**APPLICATION POLICIES & PROCEDURES:** All giving restricted to the Berwick area—defined below—to (1) improve access to preventive health care, particularly dental and mental health care; (2) increase adult and youth participation in domestic abuse counseling, and (3) improve educational and recreational opportunities that enhance the area's welfare. Consideration is also given to programs dealing with cardiovascular disease, economic development, housing, nonprofit organization effectiveness, parenting, prescription drugs, safety, and transportation. The Foundation's Primary Service Area: Berwick Borough, Briar Creek Borough, Briar Creek Township, Hollenback Township, Huntington Township, Mifflin Township, Nescopeck Borough, Nescopeck Township, North Centre Township, Salem Township, Shickshinny Borough, South Centre Township, Union Township; Secondary Service Area: Benton Borough, Benton Township, Butler Township, Conyngham Borough, Conyngham Township, Fishing Creek Township, Hunlock Township, Sugarloaf Township. Only nonprofit organizations serving people in these areas are eligible to submit a Part I application; contact the Foundation for details on deadlines and to request a copy of the required forms; grants are awarded semi-annually.

O+D+T Eric DeWald (Executive Director+Con) — C. James Ferrigno, M.D. (P) — Emily Bittenbender (VP) — Herbert D. Woodeshick (S) — John E. DeFinnis, D.D.S. (F) — Rev. Frank Demmy — John Gordner — Sally Halbeleib — Kenneth Hart — James L. Hinckley, Jr. — Garry Kanouse, M.D. — Ferne Soberick Krothe — Debra Force Moore — Holly Morrison — Donald W. Shiner — Al Steward — Patricia Torsella, DNSc, R.N. — Lucille Whitmire — Foundation assets from sale of Berwick Hospital Center.

NE-018 **Bethlehem Steel Foundation**

c/o Bethlehem Steel Corporation
1711 Martin Tower, 1170 Eighth Avenue
Bethlehem   18016   (Lehigh County)

MI-11-13-1619-31-35-41-42-49-52-54-55-56
57-71-88
Phone 610-694-6940   **FAX** 610-694-1509
EIN 23-2709041   **Year Created** 1993

AMV $238,957   **FYE** 12-00   **(Gifts Received** $1,584,555)   272 **Grants totaling** $1,580,013

Nearly half local/Pa. giving in corporate operating locations (list of Pa. locations below); grants are for general operating support except as noted. High Pa. grant of **$237,500** to United Way of Greater Lehigh Valley. **$60,000** to United Way of Chester County. **$44,500** to United Way of the Capital Region [Harrisburg]. **$30,000** to Burn Prevention Foundation. **$28,000** to Graystone Society [Coatesville]. **$26,500** to Discovery Center for Science & Technology. **$25,000** to Thaddeus Stevens College of Technology [Lancaster] (operating support/capital). **$20,000** to Historic Bethlehem (capital). **$16,200** to United Way of SE Pa. [Philadelphia]. **$10,000** each to Bethlehem Steelworkers Memorial (capital), Enterprising Environmental Solutions [Philadelphia], Lafayette College (capital), Lehigh Valley Community Foundation, Nightingale Productions [Philadelphia], and Weller Health Education Center (capital). **$7,500** each to Coatesville YWCA and Historic Bethlehem Partnership. **$6,250** to Bach Choir of Bethlehem. **$6,000** to Allentown Art Museum. **$5,000** each to Bethlehem Musikfest Assn., Chester County Iron & Steel Heritage Region Initiative, Coatesville Area Senior High School, Drug Free Pa. [Harrisburg], St. Luke's Hospital (capital), Team Pennsylvania [Harrisburg], WLVT-TV, and YWCA of Bethlehem (capital). **$4,500** to Lehigh U. (economic education/fellowship). **$3,000-$3,500** each to Brandywine Valley Assn. [Chester County], Hispanic American Organization (capital), and The Philadelphia Foundation. **$2,000-$2,500** each to Boy Scouts/Minsi Trails Council, Brandywine YMCA [Coatesville], City of Coatesville, Fellowship House of Conshohocken, Lehigh Valley Legal Services, Lehigh Valley Summerbridge Program, The Nature Conservancy [Long Pond], Steelton Community Development Foundation, and Wildlands Conservancy. **$1,000-$1,700** each to ALERT Partnership for a Drug-Free Lehigh Valley, Commonwealth Foundation for Public Policy Alternatives [Harrisburg], First Night Bethlehem, Hugh Moore Historical Park & Museums, Junior Achievement of the Delaware Valley, Junior Achievement of the Lehigh Valley, Lehigh Valley Business-Education Partnership, Lehigh Valley Chamber Orchestra, Miller Memorial Blood Center, Montgomery Hospital Foundation [Norristown], Operation Christmas [Coatesville], Pa. Economy League, Schuylkill River Greenway Assn. [Berks County], State Theatre Center for the Arts, Touchstone Theatre, VICA/Vocational Industrial Clubs of America-Lehigh Valley, and WDIY-FM. Other local/Pa. contributions **$250-$750** for similar purposes. **Out-of-state** giving, mostly in corporate operating locations, includes high grant of **$250,000** to United Way of Central Maryland; **$127,450** to United Way of Porter County [IN]; **$75,000** to Economic Strategy Institute [DC]; **$26,850** to United Way of Greater LaPorte County [IN]; **$26,000** to United Way of Buffalo & Erie County [NY]; **$25,000** to World War II Memorial Fund [VA]; **$19,800** to Lake Area United Way [IN]; **$16,400** to CERES/Coalition for Environmentally Responsible Economies [MA]; **$12,500** to NACME, Inc. [NY]; **$11,500** to National Minority Suppliers Development Council [NY]; and smaller grants/contributions to organizations in many states, especially in locations of corporate operations. Also, **$45,650** in Matching Gifts for Education were paid to 98 colleges/universities. ■ **PUBLICATIONS:** Annual Report; detailed application guidelines ■ **WEBSITE:** www.bethsteel.com/about/foundation.shtml ■ **E-MAIL:** bsfoundation@bethsteel.com ■ **APPLICATION POLICIES & PROCEDURES:** The Foundation reports that giving focuses on organizations serving communities where Bethlehem Steel (or its divisions) operate or where a significant number of employees/their families live—Bethlehem, Pittsburgh, and the Pa. counties of Chester (especially Coatesville), Dauphin, Fayette, and Washington. The Foundation has five major objectives: (1) promote excellence in education; (2) enhance the quality of life in communities where the corporation has operations or other important interests, or where its employees/families live; (3) support improvements in the workplace environment and safety; (4) advance discussion and development of public policy; and (5) strengthen/sustain the economic, social and political environment necessary to nurture our free society. Most grants are for annual/general support, capital campaigns, endowment, matching/challenge grants, in-kind gifts, and employee matching gifts; multi-year grants are awarded. The Foundation does NOT support individuals, political organizations or those engaged in influencing legislation, sectarian religious purposes, foreign institutions/agencies, or non-501(c)(3) organizations. Submit grant requests in a brief letter and proposal, preferably in September; describe the organization and its objectives; explain the purpose/goals for which support is requested; describe how the grant would benefit the area being served; financial information, including an explanation of disbursements, contributions and other sources of revenue; plans for measuring results/reporting; and amount requested, justification for the request, and how the funding will be used. Also provide IRS tax-exempt status documentation. Grant requests from organizations in Bethlehem Steel communities outside the Lehigh Valley may be sent to the Community Relations Officers in those external locations for a local review. Site visits sometimes are made to organizations being considered for a grant. An initial response to a grant request is sent generally within four weeks. The Board meets annually in April.

O+D+T James F. Kostecky (Executive Director+Con) — Duane R. Dunham (C+D) — Stephen G. Donches (P+D) — Augustine E. Moffitt, Jr. (VP+D) — L.A. Arnett (Controller+D) — C.W. Campbell (S) — G.L. Millenbruch (F) — V.R. Reiner (D) — Frank L. Fisher (Administrator) — Corporate donor: Bethlehem Steel Corporation

---

NE-019 **Billera (Patsy & Rose H.) Foundation, The**

c/o Bell Sponging Company, Inc.
333 Court Street, P.O. Box 788
Allentown   18105   (Lehigh County)

MI-11-13-29-31-32-41-42-55-63-81

Phone 610-433-7501   **FAX** None
EIN 23-2184588   **Year Created** 1982

AMV $659,944   **FYE** 12-00   **(Gifts Received** $189,054)   60+ **Grants totaling** $77,515

About half local giving. High Pa. grant of **$4,675** to Cathedral St. Catherine of Siena. **$3,000** each to DeSales U./Allentown College and Villanova U. **$2,500** each to Northampton Recreation Center, Red Cross, and United Way of the Greater Lehigh Valley. **$1,000-$1,750** each to Good Shepherd Home, Jewish Federation of Allentown, Lehigh Valley Arts Council, Northampton School District (PP4NE), Sisters of St. Joseph [Philadelphia], St. Michael the Archangel School [Limeport], and St. Thomas More Parish. Other smaller local contributions for various purposes. **Out-of-state** giving includes high grant of **$10,000** to Fund for Johns Hopkins Medicine [MD]; **$7,500** to Excalibur Classic [FL]; **$7,000** to Boys Club of New York; and **$5,000** to Italian American Fund [NY].

■**PUBLICATIONS:** None ■**WEBSITE:** None ■**E-MAIL:** None ■**APPLICATION POLICIES & PROCEDURES:** Prospective applicants initially should make a telephone inquiry about the feasibility of submitting a request. Grant requests in any form may be submitted at any time.

O+D+T Patsy Billera (Manager+Donor+Con) — Joseph P. Billera [FL] (P+C+Donor) — Howard A. Wiener [FL] (S) — Corporate donor: Bell Sponging Company, Inc.

NE-020   **Biondo (Ingeborg A.) Memorial Trust**
4040 Somerset Court, Milford Landing
Milford   18337   (Pike County)
AMV $2,150,940   **FYE** 12-00   **(Gifts Received** $15,025)

MI-14-23-33
Phone 570-296-3925 **FAX** None
EIN 11-2801815   **Year Created** 1986
31 **Grants totaling** $4,400

All giving restricted to assisting orphans and/or physically, mentally, or emotionally handicapped individuals; most grants were Christmas Grants to 28 families with handicapped family members. In addition, the Foundation supported special programs at the Center for Developmental Disabilities, The Gait Program (therapeutic horseback riding), an adaptive swimming program at Delaware Valley School, and other activities for handicapped individuals. ■**PUBLICATIONS:** None ■**WEBSITE:** None ■**E-MAIL:** None ■**APPLICATION POLICIES & PROCEDURES:** Only local agencies (primarily Pike and surrounding counties) serving orphans or handicapped individuals are eligible to apply for assistance. Submit requests at any time on a formal application form, available from the Foundation. The Board meets monthly.

O+D+T Trudy Derse (T+Con) — Joseph R. Biondo [Matamoras] (C+T+Donor) — Marion Almquist (T) — Joseph P. Biondo [NY] (T) — Michael Dickerson [Dingmas Ferry] (T) — Elaine Greiner [NY] (T+Donor) — Robert Onofry [NY] (T) — Arthur K. Ridley (T) — Joyce Rocko [Matamoras] (T) — Walter Greiner [NY] (Donor)

NE-021   **Blackhorse Foundation, The**
c/o Petroleum Services, Inc.
454 South Main Street
Wilkes-Barre   18701   (Luzerne County)
AMV $1,751,471   **FYE** 12-00   **(Gifts Received** $63,709)

MI-15-22-41-42-56
Phone 570-822-1151 **FAX** None
EIN 23-2725907   **Year Created** 1993
5 **Grants totaling** $51,457

Mostly local giving. High grant of **$40,000** to Wilkes U. **$8,457** to Kings College. **$1,000** each to Little Flower Manor, Wyoming Seminary, and Colonial Williamsburg Foundation [VA]. ■**PUBLICATIONS:** None ■**WEBSITE:** None ■**E-MAIL:** None ■**APPLICATION POLICIES & PROCEDURES:** Information not available.

O+D+T A.L. Simms (P+Donor+Con) — Ronald Simms (VP+Donor) — Corporate donor: Petroleum Services, Inc.

NE-022   **Bloch (Leonard & Beverly) Foundation**
3346 Trexler Boulevard
Allentown   18104   (Lehigh County)
AMV $333,615   **FYE** 12-00   **(Gifts Received** $0)

MI-22-62
Phone 610-432-9808 **FAX** None
EIN 23-6779289   **Year Created** 1986
68 **Grants totaling** $14,850

Mostly local giving. High grant of **$3,098** to Temple Beth El. **$2,500** to Jewish Federation of Lehigh Valley. **$853** to Allentown Jewish Community Center. Other local contributions **$25-$800** for various local and out-of-state organizations. ■**PUBLICATIONS:** None ■**WEBSITE:** None ■**E-MAIL:** None ■**APPLICATION POLICIES & PROCEDURES:** Grant requests may be submitted in any form at any time.

O+D+T Leonard S. Bloch (T+Donor+Con) — Beverly Bloch (T+Donor)

NE-023   **Bloomsburg Area Community Foundation**
c/o Town Hall
301 East Main Street
Bloomsburg   17815   (Columbia County)
AMV $266,626   **FYE** 12-00   **(Gifts Received** $500)

MI-13-25-35-54-56
Phone 570-784-1660 **FAX** 570-784-3912
EIN 23-2843673   **Year Created** 1996
5 **Grants totaling** $7,500

As a Community Foundation all discretionary giving is limited to organizations serving the Bloomsburg area. High grant of **$2,500** to Bloomsburg Area YMCA. **$1,500** to Columbia-Montour Home Health Services and Habitat for Humanity of Columbia-Montour Counties. **$1,000** each to The Children's Museum and Columbia County Historical & Genealogical Society. ■**PUBLICATIONS:** None ■**WEBSITE:** None ■**E-MAIL:** None ■**APPLICATION POLICIES & PROCEDURES:** Information not available.

O+D+T John R. Thompson (F+D+Con) — Elwood Harding, Jr. (P+D) — Paul E. Reichard (VP+D) — Linda Bailey (S+D) — Ed Edwards (D) — Donna Kreisher (D) — Mary Lenzini-Howe (D) — Rev. Marjorie Mewaul (D) — Isabell Tarr (D)

NE-024   **Bohorad (Anna C.) Trust 'B'**
c/o M&T Bank
1 South Centre Street
Pottsville   17901   (Schuylkill County)
AMV $1,207,804   **FYE** 2-01   **(Gifts Received** $0)

MI-11-12-13-17-22-31-41-42-44-52-55-62-63-72-89
Phone 570-628-9309 **FAX** 570-622-1306
EIN 23-6627730   **Year Created** 1975
Grants totaling $62,946

Grant details for 2000 are unavailable. — In the prior year, 60 grants totaling **$60,140** were awarded, mostly local/Pa. High grant of **$6,070** to Pottsville Free Public Library. **$5,066** to Schuylkill Symphony Orchestra. **$3,900-$4,150** each to Oheb Zedeck Synagogue, Pottsville Hospital & Warne Clinic, and Schuylkill United Way. **$2,000** to Trinity Lutheran Church. **$1,000-$1,500** each to Boy Scouts/Hawk Mountain Council, Franklin & Marshall College, Hillside SPCA, Kline Township, Make-A-Wish Foundation of Mideastern Pa., Mercersburg Academy, Pottsville Area School District, Salvation Army/Pottsville, Schuylkill Council for the Arts, Schuylkill County Volunteer Fire Fighters, Schuylkill County VISION, Schuylkill Women in Crisis, U. of Pa., and Wyoming Seminary. **$700** to St. Richard's Church [Barnesville]. Other local contributions **$50-$600** for various community organizations. **Out-of-state** giving includes **$4,100** to Phillips Academy [MA] and **$2,600** to Widener U. School of Law [DE]. ■ **PUB-LICATIONS:** None ■ **WEBSITE:** None ■ **E-MAIL:** None ■ **APPLICATION POLICIES & PROCEDURES:** Grant requests may be submitted at any time in an informal letter; include an organizational budget, list of Board members, and IRS tax-exempt status documentation. Site visits sometimes are made to organizations being considered for a grant. The Trustees meet in November.

O+D+T (Mr.) Lynn Veach (VP at Bank+Con) — James Bohorad (Co-T) — Robert C. Bohorad (Co-T) — Robert N. Bohorad, Esq. (Co-T) — M&T Bank (Co-Trustee)

NE-025   Born (Ross J.) Family Charitable Trust
3571 Catherine Ave.
Allentown   18103
(Lehigh County)

MI-11-12-13-14-15-17-18-22-25-35-41-45-52-53-55-62-65
Phone 610-432-1608   **FAX** None
EIN 23-7653033   **Year Created** 1990

AMV $4,640,961   **FYE** 12-00   **(Gifts Received** $438,251)   52 **Grants totaling** $223,830

Mostly local giving; all grants are unrestricted support except as noted. High grant of **$138,000** to Jewish Federation of Lehigh Valley. **$32,000** to United Way of Greater Lehigh Valley. **$6,000** to Salvation Army. **$3,000** to Boys & Girls Club of Allentown. **$2,000-$2,500** each to Baum School of Art, King's Way Academy (scholarship), Lehigh Valley Conference of Churches, and Mercy Special Learning Center. **$1,000-$1,500** each to Adult Literacy Center of the Lehigh Valley, Assn. for the Blind, Boys & Girls Club of Bethlehem, Child Care Information Services, Children's Home of Easton, Community Music School, Easter Seals, Fund to Benefit Children & Youth, Good Shepherd Home, Habitat for Humanity, Hillside School, Institute for Jewish Christian Understanding, Lehigh Valley Center for Independent Living, Lehigh County Senior Citizens Center, Lehigh Valley Child Care, Lehigh Valley Hospital, New Bethany Ministries, Pinebrook Services for Children & Youth, Planned Parenthood of NE Pa., Program for Women & Families, Project of Easton, Red Cross, Second Harvest Food Bank, South Bethlehem Neighborhood Center, Third Street Alliance for Women & Children, Turning Point of Lehigh Valley, Valley Youth House, and VIA Foundation. Other contributions **$100-$750** for various purposes. **Out-of-state** giving includes **$1,800** to Yerushalagin College (scholarship fund) and **$1,000** to Jewish Theological Seminary [NY]. ■ **PUBLICATIONS:** None ■ **WEBSITE:** None ■ **E-MAIL:** None ■ **APPLICATION POLICIES & PROCEDURES:** The Foundation reports that giving focuses on the Lehigh Valley; most grants are for general support, special projects, or capital drives. Prospective applicants initially should make a telephone inquiry about the feasibility of submitting a request. Grant requests may be submitted in any form at any time; include an annual report, organization budget, project budget, list of major funding sources, audited financial statement, list of Board members, and IRS tax-exempt status documentation. Site visits sometimes are made to organizations being considered for a grant.

O+D+T Ross J. Born (T+Donor+Con) — Wendy G. Born (Donor)

NE-026   Brenner (Jeannette M. & Joseph F.) Foundation
217 Butler Street
Kingston   18704
(Luzerne County)

MI-22-62
Phone 570-288-3607   **FAX** None
EIN 23-6282254   **Year Created** 1954

AMV $296,779   **FYE** 12-00   **(Gifts Received** $0)   4 **Grants totaling** $9,955

All local/Pa. giving. High grant of **$5,025** to Temple Ohev Shalom [Berks County]. **$2,000** to Jewish Federation of Reading. **$1,750** to Jewish Federation of Wilkes-Barre. **$1,180** to Temple B'nai B'rith. ■ **PUBLICATIONS:** None ■ **WEBSITE:** None ■ **E-MAIL:** None ■ **APPLICATION POLICIES & PROCEDURES:** Information not available.

O+D+T Joseph M. Nelson (P+D) — Sue R. Viener [Reading] (VP+D) — Joseph Nelson (S+F+D) — George P. Viener [Reading] (D) — Louise B. Nelson (D)

NE-027   Briggs (Margaret) Foundation
c/o PNC Advisors/Northeast Pa.
201 Penn Ave., P.O. Box 937
Scranton   18501
(Lackawanna County)

MI-11-12-13-14-15-17-20-22-25-29-35-41-42-52-54-55-57-71
Phone 570-961-7149   **FAX** 570-961-7269
EIN 23-2719328   **Year Created** 1969

AMV $12,174,602   **FYE** 12-00   **(Gifts Received** $0)   43 **Grants totaling** $556,973

Mostly local/Pa. giving, grants are for general purposes except as noted. High grant of **$78,245** to Lackawanna County Human Services (co-parenting program). **$59,500** to United Way of Lackawanna County. **$53,929** (in five grants) to Scranton Area Foundation (Briggs Housing IMPAC, teacher mini-grants, equipment, Molly Fund, and Bovard Fund). **$43,000** to Scranton Tomorrow (arts/culture programs). **$40,000** to Boy Scouts/Northeast Pa. (urban scouting program). **$35,000** to Scranton Cultural Center (stories programs). **$25,000** each to Countryside Conservancy (greenway acquisition) and Telespond Senior Services (debt-reduction program). **$22,000** to United Neighborhood Center (violence intervention program). **$20,000** each to Everhart Museum (JC orientations/Star Lab purchase) and Teen Mercy (outreach program). **$15,000** to Johnson Technical Institute (equipment). **$14,150** to Habitat for Humanity of Lackawanna County (equipment/salary). **$10,832** to Cancer Patient Legal Advocacy Network. **$9,600** to Women's Resource Center (shelter renovation). **$8,947** to Northeast Pa. Philharmonic (young peoples concert). **$6,900** to Employment Opportunity & Training Center (parenting program). **$6,250** to Clarks Summit/Allied Services (equipment). **$5,000** each to Congregation I.H.M. (tutoring program), Mercy Hospital Hospice, VNA Foundation Hospice, WVIA-FM, and YMCA of Wilkes-Barre (Camp Kresge). **$4,600-$4,800** each to Church of the Epiphany (community programs), Lupus Foundation (outreach program) and Scranton Cultural Center/Allied Services (equipment/training program). **$2,500-$3,500** each to Lackawanna Pro Bono (unemployed workers advocacy), Scranton Community Concerts (evening program), Scranton-Lackawanna Jewish Federation (holocaust museum), and Waverly Community House (art for mentally disabled). **$1,000-$1,500** each to Christmas Holiday Bureau, Easter Seals, Junior Achievement of NE Pa., Northeast Pa. Race for the Cure, Robert Dale Chorale, Safety Net, and Scranton Lackawanna Human Services. **Out-of-state** giving: **$3,000** to Orbis [NY] (blindness prevention) and **$2,000** to Recording for the Blind [NJ] (audio outreach program). ■ **PUBLICATIONS:** statement of program policy; application guidelines, application form ■ **WEBSITE:** None ■ **E-MAIL:** None ■ **APPLICATION POLICIES & PROCEDURES:** The Foundation reports that giving focuses on Scranton/Lackawanna County for innovative programs/projects in health, education, arts, social welfare, environmental science, and institutional academic research which benefits local residents. Matching grants are awarded. Generally no support is given for annual/capital fund drives, operating expenses, multi-year awards, or grants less than $1,000 or greater than $25,000. A formal application form, available from the Bank, may be submitted at any time; include organizational and project budgets, a Board member list, and IRS tax-exempt status documentation. Grants are awarded at meetings in March, June, September and December. — Formerly called Walmar Foundation.

O+D+T Joanne Sabatella (VP at Bank+Con) — Matthew D. Mackie, Jr. [Clarks Summit] (C+D) — Thomas G. Gallagher (D) — Joseph C. Kreder, Esq. (D) — PNC Advisors/Northeast Pa. (Trustee)

NE-028 **Brown (Grant M.) Memorial Foundation**　　　　　　MI-12-13-41
　　　　　2200 Spyglass Hill　　　　　　　　　　　　　　　　**Phone** 610-882-0337 **FAX** None
　　　　　Center Valley　18034　　　　　　(Lehigh County)　　**EIN** 23-2805616　　**Year Created** 1994
AMV $813,472　　　　　**FYE** 8-01　　　　(**Gifts Received** $1,275)　　　7 **Grants totaling** $51,232

Mostly local giving. High grant of **$20,000** to Child Advocacy Council of Lehigh Valley. **$1,650** to Valley Youth House. **$1,000** to Upper Saucon Public Library. **$400** to DeSales U. **Out-of-state** grants include **$5,000** to Virginia Technical Institute and **$4,781** to Cal-Poly Institute [CA]. — Grants approved for future payment include **$14,801** to United Friends School and **$3,000** to Project Child-Prison Parenting Project. ■**PUBLICATIONS:** None ■**WEBSITE:** None ■**E-MAIL:** None ■**APPLICATION POLICIES & PROCEDURES:** Grant requests may be submitted in writing at any time. — **Note:** The Foundation reports that its assets will be turned over to the Lehigh Valley Community Foundation.

O+D+T Barbara Barker (Administrator+T+Donor+Con) — Ross Brown (Donor) — Corporate donors: Germinsky Group; Hussman Corporation

---

NE-029 **Brown-Daub Foundation**　　　　　　　　　　　MI-12-29-35-41-44-54-56-85
　　　　　c/o Brown-Daub Chevy-Olds
　　　　　819 Nazareth Pike, P.O. Box 265　　　　　　　　**Phone** 610-759-1000 **FAX** None
　　　　　Nazareth　18064　　　　　　(Northampton County)　**EIN** 23-2900410　　**Year Created** 1995
AMV $339,379　　　　　**FYE** 12-00　　　　(**Gifts Received** $77,825)　　11 **Grants totaling** $14,500

All local giving. High grant of **$5,000** to Easton Heritage Alliance. **$1,000** each to Children's Home of Easton, CACLV/Community Action Committee of the Lehigh Valley, Discovery Center of Science & Technology, Easton Area Public Library, Holy Family School (building fund), Hugh Moore Historical Park (restoration), Miller Memorial Blood Bank, ProJect, and Weller Center for Health Education. **$500** to Communities in Schools. ■**PUBLICATIONS:** None ■**WEBSITE:** None ■**E-MAIL:** None ■**APPLICATION POLICIES & PROCEDURES:** Information not available.

O+D+T L. Anderson Daub (P+D+Donor+Con) — William John Daub, III (S+D+Donor) — Elsie Louise Brown (Donor) — Corporate donors: Brown-Daub, Inc.; Nazareth Ford, Inc.; Solt Chevrolet-Oldsmobile

---

NE-030 **Butz Foundation**　　　　　　　　　　　　　　MI-31-42-64
　　　　　c/o Alvin H. Butz, Inc.
　　　　　1347 Hausman Road, P.O. Box 509　　　　　　　**Phone** 610-395-5100 **FAX** None
　　　　　Allentown　18105　　　　　　(Lehigh County)　　**EIN** 23-2940646　　**Year Created** 1997
AMV $617,941　　　　　**FYE** 6-00　　　　(**Gifts Received** $501,197)　　4 **Grants totaling** $152,500

All local/Pa. giving. High grant of **$70,000** to Lehigh Valley Hospital. **$50,000** to Muhlenberg College. **$20,000** to Sacred Heart Hospital. **$12,500** to Lutheran Theological Seminary. — In the prior year, grants of **$70,000** to Lehigh Valley Hospital and **$50,000** to Muhlenberg College. ■**PUBLICATIONS:** None ■**WEBSITE:** None ■**E-MAIL:** None ■**APPLICATION POLICIES & PROCEDURES:** Information not available.

O+D+T Lee A. Butz (CEO+VP+Donor+Con) — Greg L. Butz [Orefield] (P) — Eric R. Butz (VP) — Shari Buth McKeever [Whitehall] (VP) — Dolores A. Butz (S+Donor) — Corporate donor: Alvin H. Butz, Inc.

NE-031 **C&E Foundation**　　　　　　　　　　　　　　MI-12-43-63-89
　　　　　c/o Peil & Egan, P.C.
　　　　　4510 Bath Pike, Suite 100, P.O. Box 20467　　　**Phone** 610-691-8670 **FAX** None
　　　　　Lehigh Valley　18002　　　　　(Lehigh County)　　**EIN** 23-2929096　　**Year Created** 1997
AMV $4,990,742　　　　**FYE** 12-00　　　(**Gifts Received** $196,426)　　16 **Grants totaling** $186,485

All local/nearby NJ giving. High grant of **$65,000** to Good Shepherd Home. **$10,000** each to Bloomsbury United Methodist Church [NJ], Children's Home of Easton, Christ United Methodist Church, and Holland Township [NJ]. Other grants are college scholarships, mostly **$5,000** each, restricted to graduates of three designated high schools in Pa. and NJ—see below. ■**PUBLICATIONS:** None ■**WEBSITE:** None ■**E-MAIL:** None ■**APPLICATION POLICIES & PROCEDURES:** Grant requests from organizations may be submitted in a letter at any time. Scholarships for higher education are restricted to graduating students from Pleasant Valley High School [Brodheadsville], Delaware Valley Regional High School [NJ], and Phillipsburg High School [NJ]; scholarship requests must be submitted in a letter to Frank W. Stull, 806 Rugby Road, Phillipsburg, NJ 08865.

O+D+T Russell Singer (C+T+Donor+Con) — James R. Singer [NH] (S+T) — Norman A. Peil, Jr. Esq. (F+T) — Hazel Singer (T+Donor) — Frank W. Stull [NJ] (T+Scholarship Coordinator)

NE-032 **Century Fund Foundation**
462 West Walnut Street, Suite 202
Allentown 18102
(Lehigh County)

MI-12-13-14-15-16-17-18-22-24-25-29-41-42
49-52-54-56-65-71-72
Phone 610-434-4000 **FAX**|610-434-4316
EIN 22-6404912   **Year Created** 1985

AMV $36,600,192   **FYE** 12-00   (**Gifts Received** $24,850)   103 **Grants totaling** $2,407,527

All local/regional giving. High grants of **$500,000** each to Cedar Crest College and Muhlenberg College. **$125,000** to DeSales U. **$75,000** to Allentown YMCA-YWCA. **$57,500** to Child Advocacy Center. **$50,000** each to Baum School of Art, Communities in Schools and Salvation Army. **$40,000** to Cathedral Church of St. Catherine. **$36,000** to Pa. Community Learning & Information Network. **$35,000** to Phoebe Ministries. **$30,000** each to Lehigh County Conference of Churches and Second Harvest Food Bank. **$25,000** each to Allentown Art Museum, Allentown Public Library, America On Wheels, Boy Scouts/Minsi Trails Council, Boys & Girls Club of Allentown, CEO America, Discovery Center, Kidspeace, Lehigh Carbon Community College, Lehigh County Historical Society, Lehigh County Humane Society, Old Allentown Preservation Assn., and United Way of Greater Lehigh Valley. **$20,000** each to Alliance for Children & Families, Lehigh County Senior Citizens Center, and Pinebrook Services for Children. **$16,500** to Burn Prevention Foundation. **$15,000** each to Communities United for Neighborhood Action, Housing Assn. & Development Corp., Parkettes National Gymnastic Team, Program for Women & Families, and Weller Center for Health Education. **$10,000-$10,125** each to Allentown School District, Banana Factory, Camelot for Children, Red Cross, Fund to Benefit Children & Youth, Girls Club of Allentown, Habitat for Humanity, Lehigh Valley Center for Independent Living, Lehigh Valley Child Care, Liberty Bell Shrine, Lifepath, Mayfair, Meals on Wheels, The Nature Conservancy, New Bethany Ministries, Pa. Sinfonia Orchestra, South Mountain Middle School, Valley Youth House, and Youth Recreation Expansion Program. **$7,400** to Allentown Symphony. **$5,000-$5,600** each to Allentown Area Ecumenical Food Bank, Allentown Band, Bethlehem Area Public Library, Big Brothers & Big Sisters, Boys & Girls Club of Easton, The Caring Place, City of Allentown, Evangelical & Reformed Historical Society [Lancaster], Hawk Mountain Sanctuary Foundation, Lehigh Valley Christian School, Northeast Pa. Lions Eye Bank, Planned Parenthood of Northeast Pa., and Wildlife Information Center. **$4,000-$4,500** each to Alliance for Building Communities, Community Music School, Junior Achievement of Lehigh Valley, and Lehigh Valley Chamber Orchestra. **$1,500-$3,600** each to AIDS Service Center, Allentown Recreation Commission, ARC, Assn. for the Blind & Visually Impaired, Community Bike Works, Emanuel's Hands Post, Good Shepherd Home, Grace Community Foundation, Lehigh Valley Summerbridge, Marine Band of Allentown, Mauch Chunk Opera House, Mercy Special Learning Center, Mock Turtle Marionette Theater, Municipal Band, Municipal Opera Company, Museum of Indian Culture, Open Space Gallery, Pa. Shakespeare Festival, Pa. Youth Theatre, Pioneer Band, Police Athletic League, Repertory Dance Theater, Sharecare Interfaith Volunteers, Special Olympics, Touchstone Theatre, Union & West End Cemetery, Walnutport Canal Assn., and WDIY-FM. Other smaller contributions. — Major grants in the prior year include **$135,000** to Muhlenberg College; **$125,000** to Cedar Crest College; **$100,000** to YMCA/YWCA; **$75,000** to Alliance for Building Communities; **$50,000** each to Allentown Symphony and Baum School of Art. **$35,000** to Phoebe Ministries; **$30,200** to Allentown Economic Development Corporation; **$30,000** to Second Harvest Food Bank; and **$25,000** each to Allentown Art Museum, Allentown Public Library, America on Wheels, Boy Scouts/Minsi Trails Council, Boys & Girls Club of Allentown, and United Way. ■**PUBLICATIONS:** Grant Application Policy memorandum ■**WEBSITE:** None ■**E-MAIL:** centuryfund@aol.com ■**APPLICATION POLICIES & PROCEDURES:** The Trust reports that giving is limited to local organizations serving the Lehigh Valley. Most grants are for general support, special projects, capital campaigns, building funds, matching grants and scholarships. support; multiple-year grants are awarded. Grant requests may be submitted in a full proposal with cover letter (an original plus 5 copies)—deadlines are April 1st and October 1st; describe specifically how the funds will be used (including how the community will benefit and how many persons will be served) and state a specific dollar amount requested; include an audited financial statement, Board member list, and IRS tax-exempt status documentation. If fees are charged for client services, detail specifically what they are. Site visits sometimes are made to organizations being considered for a grant. Grants are awarded at meetings in April, May, October, and November.
O+D+T Lisa M. Curran (Con) — Alice Anne Miller (P+T) — Rev. Dr. Grant E. Harrity (S+T) — Richard J. Hummel (F+T) — John H. Leh, II (T) — David K. Bausch (T) — Donor: Estate of Donald P. Miller

NE-033 **Cohen (Martin D.) Family Foundation**
c/o Cohen & Feeley
2940 Wm. Penn Highway, P.O. Box 1127
Easton 18044
(Northampton County)

MI-11-12-13-22-29-35-42-43-51-52-53-62-84
Phone 610-258-4303 **FAX** None
EIN 23-2294358   **Year Created** 1984

AMV $1,817,656   **FYE** 12-00   (**Gifts Received** $175,395)   175+ **Grants totaling** $176,104

Mostly Lehigh Valley giving; grants are for general purposes except as noted. High grant of **$22,600** to Jewish Federation of Lehigh Valley. **$15,045** to United Way of Lehigh Valley. **$6,500** to Penn State U. (scholarship fund). **$8,320** to Bethlehem Musikfest Assn. **$5,000** to Moravian Academy (scholarship fund). **$3,000-$3,737** each to Allentown Symphony Assn., Family YMCA of Easton, Lehigh U. (athletic dept. scholarship fund), and Pa. Youth Theatre. **$2,025-$2,830** each to Boys & Girls Club of Easton, Lafayette College (scholarship fund), Northampton Community College (scholarship fund), Penn State U. (athletics dept.), ProJeCt of Easton, Temple U. (scholarship fund), and The Weller Center. **$1,900** to B'nai Abraham Synagogue. **$1,000-$1,675** each to Baum School of Art, Discovery Center, Lehigh U. (scholarship fund), Moravian College, Muhlenberg College, Northampton Community College, Pa. Bar Foundation [Harrisburg], Pinebrook Services for Children, South Bethlehem Neighborhood Center, S.T.A.R. Academy, Valley Youth House, and VIA of the Lehigh Valley. Other local contributions mostly **$100-$200,** some higher, for various community organizations and purposes. In addition, **$30,250** in college scholarship awards (**$250** or **$500** each) to 89 Lehigh Valley residents. ■**PUBLICATIONS:** application form ■**WEBSITE:** None ■**E-MAIL:** None ■**APPLICATION POLICIES & PROCEDURES:** The Foundation reports that only Lehigh Valley organizations are eligible to apply for support; most grants for general support or scholarships. Prospective applicants must complete an application form available from the Foundation; scholarship applicants must provide academic information and evidence of financial need. — Formerly called J&J Charitable Foundation.
O+D+T Martin D. Cohen, Esq. (P+Donor+Con) — Edward Rubin (VP)

NE-034 **Cohn (Hannah & Samuel A.) Memorial Foundation**

c/o Laputka, Bayless Ecker & Cohn P.C.

2 East Broad Street, 6th Floor

Hazleton   18201   (Luzerne County)

MI-11-22-29-32-41-52-57-62-82

Phone 570-455-4731 **FAX** 570-459-0729

EIN 23-2500519   **Year Created** 1987

AMV $5,858,462   **FYE** 3-00   **(Gifts Received** $106,708)   33 **Grants totaling** $231,783

About one-quarter local giving. High Pa. grant of **$36,196** to Agudas Israel Congregation. **$5,000** to Penn State/Hazleton. **$2,000** to Salvation Army/Hazleton. **$1,000-$2,000** each to American Cancer Society, Can Do Community Foundation, United Way of Greater Hazleton, and WVIA-TV. Other smaller local contributions. **Out-of-state** giving includes **$75,000** to Tibet Fund [NY]; **$25,000** to The Bridge Fund/The Philharmonic Collaborative [NY]; **$24,000** to Mayo Foundation for Medical Education & Research [MN]; **$11,000** to The Churchill School & Center [NY]; **$10,000** to Aleph Society [NY]; and smaller grants for synagogues, medical research and other purposes in NY, CA, IL and other states. ■**PUBLICATIONS:** None ■**WEBSITE:** None ■**E-MAIL:** None ■**APPLICATION POLICIES & PROCEDURES:** The Foundation reports that giving is allocated as follows: 60% to educational, religious, cultural, and humanitarian organizations which benefit the Jewish community; 30% to similar organizations benefiting Greater Hazleton residents; and 10% for other purposes. No grants awarded to individuals.

O+D+T Martin D. Cohn, Esq. (S+F+Donor+Con) — Gerald L. Cohn [FL] (P+Donor) — David Cohn (Donor) — Elsie Cohn (Donor) — Joseph S. Cohn (Donor) — Lawrence B. Cohn (Donor) — Sandra Cohn (Donor) — David Gilberg (Donor) — Judy Gilberg (Donor) — Thomas J. Pritzker (Donor)

NE-035 **Comerford (Mary B.) Charitable Trust**

c/o M&T Bank

1 South Centre Street

Pottsville   17901   (Schuylkill County)

MI-11-12-35-41-42-44-55-62-63

Phone 570-628-9309 **FAX** 570-622-1306

EIN 23-2193785   **Year Created** 1982

AMV $1,197,077   **FYE** 9-00   **(Gifts Received** $0)   39 **Grants totaling** $46,550

All local giving. High grant of **$6,000** to First United Methodist Church of Mahanoy City. **$4,800** to Schuylkill County Council for the Arts. **$4,500** to Pottsville Public Library. **$4,000** each to Trinity Lutheran Church and Oheb Zedeck Synagogue. **$3,000** to Make-A-Wish Foundation of Mideastern Pa. **$2,000-$2,700** each to All Saints School, Schuylkill Symphony Orchestra, and Schuylkill United Way. **$1,000** each to Mahanoy Area High School, Mahanoy City Public Library, Mahanoy City Visiting Nurses Assn., and Mary Queen of Peace Church. Other local contributions **$50-$500** for various purposes. ■**PUBLICATIONS:** None ■**WEBSITE:** None ■**E-MAIL:** None ■**APPLICATION POLICIES & PROCEDURES:** Most grants are for special projects or capital needs in Schuylkill County. No grants are awarded to individuals. Submit grant requests in a letter at any time; include an organizational budget, list of Board members, and IRS tax-exempt status documentation. Site visits sometimes are made to organizations being considered for a grant. The Trustees meet in November.

O+D+T (Mr.) Lynn Veach (VP at Bank+Con) — Robert N. Bohorad, Esq. (Co-T) — Lois Griffiths [Mahanoy City] (Co-T) — M&T Bank (Co-Trustee)

NE-036 **Conner (Robert B.) Foundation**

c/o Mauch Chunk Trust Company

1111 North Street, P.O. Box 289

Jim Thorpe   18229   (Carbon County)

MI-23

Phone 570-325-2721 **FAX** 570-325-5048

EIN 24-6024098   **Year Created** 1948

AMV $2,906,336   **FYE** 12-01   **(Gifts Received** $0)   150+ **Grants totaling** $155,140

All giving restricted to aiding deserving, needy persons in the Borough of Jim Thorpe, including payments on their behalf to local merchants/providers for fuel, food, utilities, health/medical services, drugs/prescriptions, eye glasses, hearing aids, and community nursing expenses. Also, in prior years some local organizations have received support, e.g. Palmerton Hospital, Dimmick Memorial Library, Shepherd Home, and Phoenix Hose Company. ■**PUBLICATIONS:** Application for Assistance form ■**WEBSITE:** None ■**E-MAIL:** None ■**APPLICATION POLICIES & PROCEDURES:** All giving is restricted to the Borough of Jim Thorpe to help deserving, needy individuals or organizations serving needy persons; direct assistance to individuals is restricted to those who have been borough residents for at least 10 years. Prospective applicants should initially telephone the Foundation to inquire about the feasibility of submitting a request. An Application for Assistance form, available from the Foundation, must be submitted between September15th and the October 15th deadline; individual applicants must provide verification of personal income from all sources. Decisions on grants are made at a November meeting.

O+D+T Linda L. Snyder (Trust Officer at Bank+Con) — Harold A. Queen (VC) — Mauch Chunk Trust Co. (Corporate Trustee)

NE-037 **Deutsch Family Foundation**

5 Sunset Terrace

Scranton   18505   (Lackawanna County)

MI-22-62

Phone 570-346-7561 **FAX** None

EIN 22-2783304   **Year Created** 1986

AMV $386,216   **FYE** 10-00   **(Gifts Received** $0)   32 **Grants totaling** $5,584

About half local giving. High grant of **$1,100** to Temple Israel. **$833** to Jewish Community Center of Scranton. **$600** to Scranton Hebrew Day School. Other smaller local contributions. **Out-of-state** small contributions to NY, MD, DC, CA, TN, and Israel. ■**PUBLICATIONS:** None ■**WEBSITE:** None ■**E-MAIL:** None ■**APPLICATION POLICIES & PROCEDURES:** The Foundation reports that grants are awarded to preselected charitable organizations only and unsolicited applications are not accepted.

O+D+T Ignatz Deutsch (P+S+F+Donor+Con) — Henri Deutsch, Ph.D. [Dalton] (VP+Donor)

NE-038   East Stroudsburg Savings Assn. Foundation   MI-12-13-14-19-22-25-31-42-52-54-89
c/o East Stroudsburg Savings Assn.
744 Main Street   **Phone** 570-421-0531 **FAX** 570-421-1625
East Stroudsburg   18360   (Monroe County)   **EIN** 23-2947729   **Year Created** 1998
AMV $84,436   **FYE** 12-00   (**Gifts Received** $296,200)   12 **Grants totaling** $294,849

All giving to/for Monroe County; all grants are for capital campaigns or capital equipment. High grant of **$85,000** to Pocono Medical Center. **$50,000** to Salvation Army. **$30,000** each to Northampton Community College and Pocono Services for Families & Children. **$25,000** to Pocono Family YMCA. **$22,000** to Quiet Valley Farm Museum. **$20,000** to Habitat for Humanity. **$10,000** each to Monroe County Drug Force and West End Fire Company. **$5,000** each to Burnley Workshop of the Poconos and Pleasant Valley Choral Society. **$2,849** to Pocono Township Volunteer Fire Co. — Grants approved for future payment, all for capital campaigns: **$200,000** to Salvation Army; **$165,000** to Pocono Medical Center; **$90,000** to Northampton Community College; and **$50,000** to Pocono Family YMCA. ■ **PUBLICATIONS:** application guidelines ■**WEBSITE:** None ■**E-MAIL:** None ■ **APPLICATION POLICIES & PROCEDURES:** The Foundation reports that all giving must be for the benefit of Monroe County residents. Grant requests may be submitted at any time on a predetermined form, available from the Foundation; provide a copy of the IRS determination letter.
O+D+T Richard E. Talbot [Stroudsburg] (Executive Trustee+Con) — John E. Burrus [Brodheadsville] (T) — W. Jack Wallie (T) — Corporate donor: East Stroudsburg Savings Assn.

NE-039   Evans (Annette) Foundation for the Arts & Humanities   MI-51-52-53-54-55
c/o President's Office, Wilkes University - Box 11   **Phone** 570-408-4000 **FAX** None
Wilkes-Barre   18702   (Luzerne County)   **EIN** 23-6498179   **Year Created** 1969
AMV $662,264   **FYE** 9-00   (**Gifts Received** $0)   4 **Grants totaling** $32,000

All giving to Wyoming Valley arts organizations; all grants are for operating support. High grant of **$16,000** to Wilkes U. (summer theatre). **$10,000** to Fine Arts Fiesta. **$5,000** to Northeastern Pa. Philharmonic. **$1,000** to Wilkes Little Theatre.
■**PUBLICATIONS:** None ■**WEBSITE:** None ■**E-MAIL:** None ■**APPLICATION POLICIES & PROCEDURES:** Giving is limited to special projects at non-profit, Wyoming Valley organizations which teach, encourage, develop, or present the arts, especially audio and visual arts. Grant requests may be submitted at any time in a letter (2 pages maximum); briefly describe the organizational purpose, state the amount of the request, and provide a project budget and copy of the IRS tax-exempt status documentation; other documentation subsequently may be requested. The Advisory Board of Trustees awards grants at meetings in June and December.
O+D+T Members of the Advisory Committee: Dr. Joseph E. Gilmour (Con) — Alfred S. Groh — Ruth B. Schooley — PNC Bank N.A. (Trustee)

NE-040   Faber (Eberhard L.) Foundation   MI-11-42-56
918 Mellon Bank Center   **Phone** 570-826-1712 **FAX** None
Wilkes-Barre   18701   (Luzerne County)   **EIN** 23-6292125   **Year Created** 1957
AMV $852,128   **FYE** 12-00   (**Gifts Received** $0)   14 **Grants totaling** $39,482

Mostly local giving. High grant of **$16,150** to Bear Creek Historical Society. **$15,307** to King's College (capital campaign). **$5,600** to United Way of Wyoming Valley. Other local and out-of-state contributions **$100-$500** for various purposes. ■**PUBLICATIONS:** None ■**WEBSITE:** None ■**E-MAIL:** None ■**APPLICATION POLICIES & PROCEDURES:** No grants awarded to individuals.
O+D+T Eberhard L. Faber [Bear Creek] (T+Con) — Mary Louise Faber [Bear Creek] (T) — John M. Randolph, Jr. [Dallas] (T)

NE-041   Feibus (Hilda) Foundation   MI-22-62
35 Oakford Glen   **Phone** 570-586-3968 **FAX** None
Clarks Summit   18411   (Lackawanna County)   **EIN** 23-7029768   **Year Created** 1969
AMV $320,005   **FYE** 12-00   (**Gifts Received** $0)   3 **Grants totaling** $20,860

Mostly local giving. High grant of **$16,000** to Scranton Jewish Federation. **$3,500** to Jewish Community Center of Scranton. **Out-of-state** grant: **$1,360** to Perrineville Jewish Center [NJ]. ■**PUBLICATIONS:** None ■**WEBSITE:** None ■**E-MAIL:** None ■ **APPLICATION POLICIES & PROCEDURES:** Grant requests may be submitted, preferably in July-August, in a full proposal with cover letter; describe the intended purpose of the grant and clearly state the funds requested; also include an annual report, organization and project budgets, Board member list, audited financial statement, list of major funding sources, and IRS tax-exempt status documentation.
O+D+T Shirley Feibus Alperin (P+D+Con) — Belle Estroff [NY] (D) — Rabbi David Geffen [Scranton] (D) — Corporate donors: Anthracite Plate Glass Company; Luster Life, Inc.

NE-042   First Federal Charitable Foundation   MI-12-13-14-15-25-29-32-41-42-43-44-51-52
c/o Northeast Pa. Financial Corp.   55-84
12 East Broad Street   **Phone** 570-459-3797 **FAX** None
Hazleton   18210   (Luzerne County)   **EIN** 06-1512796   **Year Created** 1998
AMV $5,287,358   **FYE** 9-00   (**Gifts Received** $0)   23 **Grants totaling** $254,000

All giving to the Bank's six-county business area. High grant of **$42,000** to Hazleton YMCA/YWCA (new heating system). **$25,000** each to Bishop Hafey High School (scholarship endowment) and Hazleton Area Public Library (capital fund). **$17,000** to Luzerne County Community College (Care Campaign for Children). **$15,000** each to Child Development of NE Pa. (renovations), College Misericordia (Women with Children program) and Housing Development Corp. of NE Pa. (single parents housing). **$10,000** each to American Cancer Society (Look Good/Feel Better program), Bloomsburg U. Foundation (community-based computer lab), Hazleton Community Concerts (program support), and United Rehabilitation Services (vehicle). **$7,000** each to

MMI Preparatory School (endowment) and Operation Overcome (van). **$5,000-$5,500** each to American Heart Assn. (defibrillators), Bloomsburg Theatre Ensemble (Project Discover), Danville Community Center (pool rehab), Kirby Library (children's books/materials), Northeast Pa. Philharmonic (young people's concerts), Panther Valley Library (new Lansford Branch), Sun Home Services (video equipment), and Wilkes-Barre YMCA (facility updating). **$3,000** to East Penn Elementary PTO Playground (pool rehabilitation). **$2,500** to Your Loving Voices (relocation/service expansion). ■**PUBLICATIONS:** Grant Application Guidelines & Application Form ■**WEBSITE:** www.1stfederalcharitable.com [application guidelines & appplication form] ■**E-MAIL:** ffedfoundation@1stfederalbank.com■**APPLICATION POLICIES & PROCEDURES:** The Foundation reports that only requests from nonprofit organizations in the bank's six-county business area (Carbon, Columbia, Luzerne, Montour, Monroe and Schuylkill counties) will be considered. Applicant organizations must demonstrate active board leadership, comprehensive resource development plans (including income generating activities), resource sharing, special support from individuals, and evidence of efficient and effective programmatic/financial administration. No support is given to (1) individuals, (2) religious programs of churches or other sectarian organizations, or (3) political parties, campaigns or candidates. Support generally is not available for fraternal organizations, attendance at seminars/conferences, specialized health campaigns, or programs/projects of statewide, national, or international organizations. Multiyear capital campaign grants, if approved, will preclude annual fund support. Grant requests must be submitted in writing on the formal Application Form (available from the Bank or on the website) and must include the attachments as stipulated on the form.

O+D+T Megan Kennedy (Con) — Thomas L. Kennedy (C) — Ms. E. Lee Beard (P) — Gary M. Gatski (S+F) — Anthony Cusatis (D) — Martin D. Cohn (D) — Corporate donor: Northeast Pa. Financial Corp.

NE-043 **Flach (Florence Y.) Allentown Area Music Appreciation Trust** MI-52-55
c/o First Union/Wachovia - PA 2106
640 Hamilton Street **Phone** 610-439-4686 **FAX** 610-740-1207
Allentown 18101 (Lehigh County) **EIN** 23-7711957 **Year Created** 1992
AMV $405,376 **FYE** 5-00 (**Gifts Received** $0) 10 **Grants totaling** $24,830

All giving restricted to musical/music appreciation purposes in the Allentown area. High grants of **$4,000** to Allentown Symphony Orchestra and Community Music School. **$3,000** each to Lehigh Valley Chamber Orchestra and Pa. Sinfonia Orchestra. **$2,000-$2,500** each to Allentown Art Museum, Allentown Band, and Camerata Singers. **$1,500** each to Good Shepherd Home (music appreciation fund) and Satori. ■**PUBLICATIONS:** None ■**WEBSITE:** None ■**E-MAIL:** None ■**APPLICATION POLICIES & PROCEDURES:** The Trust reports that only organizations/programs which stimulate a better understanding, appreciation, cultivation, advancement, or enjoyment of music by Allentown area residents are eligible to apply. Grants for these purposes are made to organizations and for individual music-education scholarships; no grants are awarded to/for general operating support, endowment, political activities, loans, fund-raising events or benefits. Submit complete, written requests in a letter (deadline is November 30th) on organization letterhead and signed by an officer of the Board; describe the purpose of the grant and the project/program time frame, and include a current Board list, the most recent financial statement, and IRS tax-exempt status documentation. Scholarship applicants must include a current transcript of grades with their application letter. The Trustees Committee awards grants at a December meeting. — **Note:** In Fall 2002, administration of this Trust will move to a First Union office in Reading; call 610-655-3148 for updated information.

O+D+T James A. Kressler (VP at Bank+Con) — Charles Noonan (Co-T) — First Union/Wachovia (Co-Trustee)

NE-044 **Fleming Foundation** MI-11-14-15-22-31-72
Windfields, 7661 Beryl Road **Phone** 610-966-2010 **FAX** None
Zionsville 18092 (Lehigh County) **EIN** 23-2585510 **Year Created** 1989
AMV $9,419,886 **FYE** 12-00 (**Gifts Received** $6,603,702) 25 **Grants totaling** $106,235

Mostly local/Pa. giving. High grant of **$80,000** to Lehigh Valley Hospital. **$10,000** to United Way of Greater Lehigh Valley. **$3,000** to Salvation Army. **$2,500** each to Allentown Rescue Mission and Good Shepherd Home. **$1,000-$1,500** each to Canine Partners for Life [Chester County], Leonard Pool Society/Lehigh Valley Hospital, and Red Cross. Other local contributions **$50-$500** for various purposes. **Out-of-state** giving includes **$1,000** to Guide Dog Foundation for the Blind [NY] and other smaller contributions. ■**PUBLICATIONS:** None ■**WEBSITE:** None ■**E-MAIL:** None ■**APPLICATION POLICIES & PROCEDURES:** The Foundation reports that giving is generally limited to the Allentown area; no grants awarded to individuals.

O+D+T Richard Fleming (T+Donor+Con) — Kathleen Arnold (T) — Roberta Fleming (T)

NE-045 **Fortinsky Charitable Foundation, Inc.** MI-11-13-14-17-22-29-31-32-35-41-42-62
c/o Fortune Fabrics, Inc.
315 Simpson Street **Phone** 570-288-3666 **FAX** None
Swoyersville 18704 (Luzerne County) **EIN** 23-2338218 **Year Created** 1985
AMV $788,832 **FYE** 12-00 (**Gifts Received** $111,000) 30 **Grants totaling** $95,565

Mostly local giving. High grant of **$12,646** to United Way of Wyoming Valley. **$11,000** to Temple Israel. **$9,500** to Jewish Federation of Wilkes-Barre. **$6,000-$7,000** each to Fred M. Kirby Center, Penn State U./Wilkes-Barre, United Hebrew Institute, and Wyoming Seminary. **$4,350** to Boy Scouts of NE Pa. **$2,000-$3,500** each to College Misericordia, Jewish Community Center, Luzerne Foundation, Wilkes-Barre YMCA, and Wilkes U. **$1,000-$1,500** each to Allied Services, Assn. for Retarded Citizens, Domestic Violence Center, Hoyt Library, Leadership of Wilkes-Barre, Luzerne County Community College, Penn State/Geisinger Foundation, Regis Elementary School, St. Jude's Children's Hospital, and St. Stephen's Episcopal Church. Other smaller local contributions. **Out-of-state** grant: **$5,000** to Cancer Research Institute [NY]. ■**PUBLICATIONS:** Annual Report ■**WEBSITE:** None ■**E-MAIL:** None ■**APPLICATION POLICIES & PROCEDURES:** The Foundation reports that most grants are for annual or general support or scholarship funds. No grants awarded to individuals.

O+D+T Robert A. Fortinsky (P+F+D+Donor+Con) — Jill F. Schwartz (S+D) — Corporate donor: Wyoming Weavers, Inc.

NE-046 Fox (Will S. & Anna S.) Foundation
c/o Lipkin, Marshall, Bohorad & Thornburg
One Norwegian Plaza, P.O. Box 1280
Pottsville 17901   (Schuylkill County)

MI-29-42-52-55-62-63-89

Phone 570-622-1811 **FAX** None
EIN 23-6395250   **Year Created** 1952

AMV $463,597   **FYE** 10-01   **(Gifts Received** $7,463)   95 **Grants totaling** $19,239

Mostly local/Pa. giving. High grant of **$1,100** to Borough of Frackville. **$960** to Schuylkill County Symphony. **$750** to Penn State U. **$693** to Oheb Zedek Synagogue. Other contributions **$10-$500** for human services, civic, cultural, and religious organizations. ■ **PUBLICATIONS:** None ■ **WEBSITE:** None ■ **E-MAIL:** None ■ **APPLICATION POLICIES & PROCEDURES:** The Foundation reports that grants are awarded to preselected charitable organizations only; unsolicited applications are not accepted.
O+D+T Alvin B. Marshall, Esq. (P) — Robert N. Bohorad, Esq. (VP) — Fred J. Boote, CPA (S) — Margaret A. Daniels (F)

NE-047 Gates Family Foundation, The
840 Yorkshire Drive
Bethlehem 18017   (Northampton County)

MI-11-12-41-42-49-52-63

Phone 610-865-1519 **FAX** None
EIN 23-7962091   **Year Created** 1998

AMV $49,216   **FYE** 12-00   **(Gifts Received** $97,120)   10 **Grants totaling** $56,725

Mostly local giving. High grants of **$16,000** each to DeSales U. and United Way of Greater Lehigh Valley. **$10,055** to The Lutheran Academy. **$7,500** to Allentown Symphony. **$2,620** to Concordia Lutheran Church. **$1,000** to Community Services for Children. Other smaller contributions. **Out-of-state** grant: **$2,050** to Vocational Industrial Clubs of America [VA].■ **PUBLICATIONS:** None ■ **WEBSITE:** None ■ **E-MAIL:** None ■ **APPLICATION POLICIES & PROCEDURES:** Information not available.
O+D+T Elmer D. Gates (T+Donor+Con) — Betty S. Gates (T+Donor) — Jodi A. Key (T) — Patti Gates Smith (T)

NE-048 Gelb Foundation
111 Pellar Ave.
Scranton 18515   (Lackawanna County)

MI-11-12-22-29-42-44-54-55-62

Phone 570-343-2524 **FAX** None
EIN 24-6018072   **Year Created** 1948

AMV $1,276,046   **FYE** 12-99   **(Gifts Received** $44,836)   85 **Grants totaling** $112,540

About two-thirds local/Pa. giving. High grant of **$22,500** to Jewish Campaign of Scranton. **$5,000** to Hadassah of Scranton/Philadelphia. **$6,000** to Scranton Cultural Center. **$5,000** to Elan Gardens. **$4,000** to United Jewish Appeal of Scranton. **$3,000-$3,500** each to Center for Leadership & Learning, Jewish Community Center, United Way of Lackawanna County, and U. of Scranton. **$1,900** to Jewish Home of Scranton. **$1,000-$1,200** each to Anne Frank Center [Philadelphia], Federation of Jewish Agencies [Philadelphia], Golden Slipper/24-Karat Club of Scranton, Jewish Foundation of Scranton, Keystone College, Kings College, Northeast Regional Cancer Center, Scranton Tomorrow, Temple Beth Am, and The Philadelphia Scholars. **$950** to Make-A-Wish Foundation of Scranton. Other local contributions **$50-$600** each for various purposes. **Out-of-state** giving includes **$8,000** to Connecticut College; **$6,000** to American Jewish Joint Distribution Committee [NY]; **$4,000** to New Israel Fund [CA]; **$2,000** to Anderson Ranch Arts Center [CO] and Holocaust Fund [DC]; and other smaller grants/contributions for cultural, health, educational, civic, and Jewish organizations in many states. ■ **PUBLICATIONS:** None ■ **WEBSITE:** None ■ **E-MAIL:** None ■ **APPLICATION POLICIES & PROCEDURES:** Grant requests may be submitted in a letter (on organizational letterhead) at any time.
O+D+T Beverly Gelb Klein (S+F+Donor+Con) — Mae S. Gelb (P+Donor) — Sondra Gelb Myers (VP+Donor) — Carol Kaplan (Donor) — Jerome A. Klein (Donor) — David Myers (Donor) — Jonathan Myers (Donor) — Morey M. Myers (Donor) — Judith Premselaar (Donor)

NE-049 Gibbs (C.E.) Memorial Trust
c/o Honesdale National Bank/Trust Dept.
733 Main Street, P.O. Box 350
Honesdale 18431   (Wayne County)

MI-23

Phone 570-253-3355 **FAX** 570-253-5263
EIN 23-6496941   **Year Created** 1971

AMV $335,872   **FYE** 12-00   **(Gifts Received** $0)   2 **Grants totaling** $5,155

All grants were disbursements on behalf of Wayne County residents for projected medical/drug expenses. ■ **PUBLICATIONS:** None ■ **WEBSITE:** www.hnbbank.com [bank info only] ■ **E-MAIL:** None ■ **APPLICATION POLICIES & PROCEDURES:** Only Wayne County residents/patients needing medical assistance are eligible to apply. Requests must be received prior to the actual need for assistance, and must be submitted in a letter which is certified by their doctor; provide the patient's name, address, telephone number, and a description of expected medical need/estimated cost, and include the applicant's most recent Form 1040 tax return. The Board or Directors meets semi-monthly.
O+D+T Mary T. McNichols (Trust Officer at Bank+Con)

NE-050 Gicking Family Foundation
130 Walnut Street
Sugarloaf 18249   (Luzerne County)

MI-11-13-29-31-42-44-63

Phone 570-788-7588 **FAX** None
EIN 23-6995405   **Year Created** 1990

AMV $343,858   **FYE** 12-00   **(Gifts Received** $0)   14 **Grants totaling** $25,750

Mostly local/Pa. giving; some grants are payments on multiyear pledges. High grants of **$5,000** each to Hazleton YMCA/YWCA and Susquehanna U. **$3,000** to St. Peter's Episcopal Church. **$2,000** each to Can Do Community Foundation and United Way of Greater Hazleton. **$1,000** to Hazleton Public Library. Other local **$500** contributions for various purposes. **Out-of-state** giving includes **$2,000** to Kartemquin Educational Foundation [IL] (educational films) and **$1,000** to Stonybrook Hospital [NY] (burn center). ■ **PUBLICATIONS:** None ■ **WEBSITE:** None ■ **E-MAIL:** None ■ **APPLICATION POLICIES & PROCEDURES:** The Foundationr reports most grants for annual giving or capital campaigns. Grant requests in any form may be submitted at any time.
O+D+T Jeffrey S. Gicking (S+Con) — Robert K. Gicking [Bethlehem] (C+Donor) — Linda M. Gicking [Bethlehem] (VC+Donor) — John M. Gicking [NY] (F)

NE-051 Graham Foundation, The
c/o Ad-Ease, Inc.
271 South Pine Street
Hazleton 18201   (Luzerne County)

MI-13-31-53-84

Phone 570-459-2670 **FAX** None
EIN 23-2505366   **Year Created** 1987

AMV $10,973   **FYE** 12-00   (**Gifts Received** $255,000)   3 **Grants totaling** $265,000

Mostly local giving. **$235,000** to Mount Laurel Pools. **Out-of-state** grants: **$25,000** to Children's National Medical Center [DC] and **$5,000** to Norwood Art Assn. [MA]. ■**PUBLICATIONS:** None ■**WEBSITE:** None ■**E-MAIL:** None ■**APPLICATION POLICIES & PROCEDURES:** Grant requests may be submitted in any form at any time.

O+D+T Evelyn Dennis (P+D+Donor+Con) — Russell Graham (VP+D) — Evelyn R. Dennis (S+D) — Martin D. Cohn (D) — Bradley Graham (D)

NE-052 Grossman (Irving & Edythe) Foundation
550 Clay Ave., Apt. 3A
Scranton 18510   (Lackawanna County)

MI-12-13-14-18-22-25-29-42-43-56-62-71
Phone Unlisted **FAX** None
EIN 23-2574759   **Year Created** 1988

AMV $1,261,052   **FYE** 12-00   (**Gifts Received** $0)   26 **Grants totaling** $64,000

All local giving. High grant of **$25,000** to United Jewish Appeal. **$5,000** to Penn State U./Dunmore (Atlas Scholarship Fund). **$4,000** to Allied Services. **$2,000** each to IHM Friends of the Poor, Lackawanna United Fund, Meals on Wheels, Pa. Assn. for the Blind, Red Cross, Salvation Army, Scranton-Lackawanna Jewish Foundation, and St. Joseph's Center. **$1,000** each to Catholic Social Services, Friendship House, Lackawanna Pro Bono, Lackawanna Historical Society, Lackawanna River Corridor Assn., Make-A-Wish Foundation, Penn State U./Dunmore, Planned Parenthood of NE Pa., St. Francis Kitchen, Temple Israel, United Neighborhood Center, Voluntary Action Center of NE Pa., and Women's Resource Center. Other contributions **$500** each for medical purposes. ■**PUBLICATIONS:** None ■**WEBSITE:** None ■**E-MAIL:** None ■**APPLICATION POLICIES & PROCEDURES:** No grants are awarded to individuals.

O+D+T Jeanne Atlas (VP+F+Con) — Irving Atlas (P) — Cynthia Atlas Gricus [VA] (T) — Judith Atlas Jackson [VA] (T)

NE-053 Gruber (Charles A. & Leona K.) Foundation
c/o First Union/Wachovia - PA 2106
640 Hamilton Street
Allentown 18101   (Lehigh County)

MI-12-13-14-34-35-42-43-52-54-65
Phone 610-439-4686 **FAX** 610-740-1207
EIN 23-2003708   **Year Created** 1975

AMV $532,881   **FYE** 3-01   (**Gifts Received** $0)   19 **Grants totaling** $30,230

All giving to Lehigh Valley. High grant of **$3,000** to DeSales U. **$2,000** each to Big Brothers & Big Sisters, Cedar Crest College, Lehigh Valley Child Care, Muhlenberg College, Pinebrook Services for Children & Youth, St. Luke's School of Nursing, and Weller Health Education Center. **$1,000-$1,500** each to Allentown Art Museum, Allentown Symphony, Fund to Benefit Children & Youth, Girls' Club of Allentown, Lafayette College, Lehigh County Conference of Churches, Mercy Special Learning Center, Moravian College, Turning Point of Lehigh Valley, and Valley Youth House. **$730** to ARC of Lehigh & Northampton Counties. ■**PUBLICATIONS:** Annual Report; application guidelines ■**WEBSITE:** None ■**E-MAIL:** None ■**APPLICATION POLICIES & PROCEDURES:** The Foundation reports that giving is limited to Lehigh Valley organizations which are meeting essential community needs. Most grants are for general support or special projects, as well as scholarships which are restricted to sophomores, juniors, or seniors residing in Northampton or Lehigh counties and who (preferably) are pursuing majors in mathematics, science or engineering. Submit grant requests in a letter (2 pages maximum) in early January (deadline is January 31st); state the amount of funding requested and how it will be used, and include an annual report, project budget, financial statement, and IRS tax-exempt status documentation. The Board of Directors awards grants at a March meeting. — **Note:** In Fall 2002, administration of this Foundation will move to a First Union office in Reading; call 610-655-3148 for updated information.

O+D+T James A. Kressler (VP at Bank+Con) — Andrew C. Melzer [Reading] (S+F at Bank) — Robin Crawford (D) — Kindra Brown (D) — John Labukas [Bethlehem] (D)

NE-054 Hanna Foundation
c/o M&T Bank
1 South Centre Street
Pottsville 17901   (Schuylkill County)

MI-12-42-63
Phone 570-628-9309 **FAX** 570-622-1306
EIN 23-6868675   **Year Created** 1986

AMV $862,009   **FYE** 11-00   (**Gifts Received** $90)   9 **Grants totaling** $38,480

One Pa. grant: **$5,000** to Chartiers Hill United Presbyterian Church [Washington County]. **Out-of-state** giving includes **$6,000** each to Rider U. [NJ] and The Children's Home [FL]; and smaller grants for various purposes in FL. ■**PUBLICATIONS:** None ■**WEBSITE:** None ■**E-MAIL:** None ■**APPLICATION POLICIES & PROCEDURES:** The Foundation reports that grants are awarded to preselected charitable organizations only.

O+D+T (Mr.) Lynn Veach (VP at Bank+Con) — Paul J. Hanna [FL] (C+Manager+D) — Lee E. Hanna [FL] (P+Manager+D) — Melinda M. Hanna [FL] (S+D) — Paul J. Hanna, II [FL] (F+D) — Deborah G. Hanna [Harrisburg] (AS+D) — M&T Trust Co. (Trustee)

NE-055 Heritage Helping Hand
RR #1, Box 48
Klingerstown 17941 (Schuylkill County)

MI-34-42-63-89
Phone 570-648-0082 **FAX** None
EIN 22-2456684 **Year Created** 1983

AMV $191,333 **FYE** 12-00 **(Gifts Received** $5,000) 11 **Grants totaling** $11,000

All local/Pa. giving. High grant of **$3,000** to Thomas Jefferson U. [Philadelphia]. **$2,000** each to St. Paul U.C.C. Church [Herndon] and U. of Pa. School of Veterinary Medicine. **$1,250** to Penn State U. Other local contributions **$150-$650** for local charities. ■**PUBLICATIONS:** None ■**WEBSITE:** None ■**E-MAIL:** None ■**APPLICATION POLICIES & PROCEDURES:** No grants awarded to individuals.

O+D+T Carl J. Reidler (Manager+Donor+Con) — Paul G. Reidler (Donor) — Summit Bank (Trustee)

NE-056 Hess (Elizabeth D.) Charitable Trust
c/o Buckno Lisicky & Company
1524 Linden Street
Allentown 18102 (Lehigh County)

MI-61-65

Phone 610-850-8580 **FAX** None
EIN 23-7927341 **Year Created** 1999

AMV $32,264 **FYE** 12-00 **(Gifts Received** $0) 3 **Grants totaling** $16,500

Two-thirds local giving. High grant of **$7,000** to National Coalition of Clergy & Laity [Whitehall]. **$4,500** to Veil of Innocence [Catasauqua]. **Out-of-state** grant: **$5,000** to Our Lady of the Prairies [ND]. ■**PUBLICATIONS:** None ■**WEBSITE:** None ■**E-MAIL:** None ■**APPLICATION POLICIES & PROCEDURES:** Information not available.

O+D+T Christopher D. Lloyd, CPA (T+Con)

NE-057 Hoch (Charles H.) Foundation
1825 Lehigh Parkway, North
Allentown 18103 (Lehigh County)

MI-12-13-14-15-17-22-25-35-41-42-43-44-51
52-54-55-56-57-63-71-72
Phone 610-435-5570 **FAX**|None
EIN 23-6265016 **Year Created** 1956

AMV $7,342,357 **FYE** 12-00 **(Gifts Received** $0) 72 **Grants totaling** $334,822

All giving limited to Lehigh and Northampton counties; grants are for general purposes except as noted. High grant of **$12,000** to Boys & Girls Club of Allentown (two projects). **$11,000** to Salvation Army (building/Christmas funds). **$10,000** each to Allentown Rescue Mission (homeless assistance), Cedar Crest College (scholarships), Lehigh County Meals on Wheels, Muhlenberg College (scholarships), and YMCA-YWCA of Allentown (youth programs). **$8,000** each to Boy Scouts/Minsi Trails Council, Lehigh County Historical Society (building fund), and Salem United Methodist Church (missions). **$7,500** to Lehigh County Senior Citizens Center (renovations). **$6,000** each to Allentown Art Museum, Assn. for the Blind & Visually Impaired of Lehigh Valley, Girls Club of Allentown (scholarship program), Great Valley Girl Scout Council (capital campaign), and Habitat for Humanity-Allentown (house rehabilitation). **$5,000** each to Allentown Area Ecumencial Food Bank, Allentown Symphony (school concerts), DeSales U., Grace Community Foundation (food bank), Hawk Mountain Sanctuary Assn. (educational programs), KidsPeace (therapeutic center), Lehigh Carbon Community College (scholarships), Lehigh Valley Christian High School (roof repairs), Northeast Pa. Lions Eye Bank (In-situ program), Parkette National Gymnastic Team (scholarships), Second Harvest Food Bank, Southern Lehigh Public Library (capital campaign), Volunteers of America Children's Center (building repairs), Weller Center for Health Education, West End Youth Center (capital campaign), Wildlands Conservancy (wildlife education center expansion), and WLVT-TV (Ready to Learn program). **$4,000-$4,500** each to Allentown Music Festival (aid crippled children), Community Bike Works (Earn-A-Bike program), Fund to Benefit Children & Youth (equipment), Hillside School (study equipment), Lehigh County Humane Society (building fund), Lehigh Valley Child Care (renovation project), Mercy Special Learning Center (tuition assistance), Milford Park Camp Meeting (programs), Phoebe Ministries (alternative program), Pinebrook Services (counseling), Program for Women & Families, and St. Stephen's Lutheran Church. **$3,000-$3,500** each to Allentown Band, Assn. for Retarded Citizens, Burn Prevention Foundation (children's fire safety program), Community in Schools (arts education), Community Music School (music instruction), Eastern Pa. Downs Syndrome Center, Junior Achievement of the Leigh Valley, Marine Band (concerts), Municipal Band (concerts), Pioneer Band (concerts), NAACP-Easton (scholarships), Police Athletic League (youth programs), Red Cross, and Sixth Street Shelter (homeless assistance). **$2,000-$2,500** each to Allentown College Theatre, Allentown Recreation Commission (playgrounds), Hellertown Library (middle school programs), InterVarsity Christian Fellowship, Liberty Bell Shrine, Macungie Bank (community concerts), Mock Turtle Marionette Theatre (residency), National Canal Museum (educational programs), and Open Space Gallery (scholastic art awards). Other smaller local grants/contributions for similar purposes. ■**PUBLICATIONS:** None ■**WEBSITE:** None ■**E-MAIL:** None ■**APPLICATION POLICIES & PROCEDURES:** Only organizations in Lehigh or Northampton counties are eligible to apply. Grant requests may be submitted in a letter (or verbally) at any time; describe the project in detail, state the funding requested, and include an annual report, project budget, Board member list, list of major funding sources, audited financial statement, and IRS tax-exempt documentation. Site visits sometimes are made to organizations being considered for a grant. Grants are awarded at meetings in May/June and November.

O+D+T Richard J. Hummel (P+F+D+Con) — James L. Weierbach, Esq. (S+D) — William Daniels (D) — Alfred E. DeMott (D) — Carol Feller (D) — The Trust Company of Lehigh Valley (Corporate Trustee)

NE-058 Holt Family Foundation
1611 Pond Road, Suite 300
Allentown 18104 (Lehigh County)

MI-11-13-31-41-42-51-52-53-54-56-63-65-71
Phone 610-391-0377 **FAX** None
EIN 23-6906143 **Year Created** 1987

AMV $5,026,638 **FYE** 12-00 **(Gifts Received** $142,814) 47 **Grants totaling** $218,050

Mostly local/Eastern Pa. giving; all grants are unrestricted support. High grant of **$60,000** to Allentown Art Museum. **$25,000** to U. of Pa. **$15,000** to Episcopal Church of the Mediator. **$10,000** each to Allentown Symphony, Discovery Center of Science & Technology, Lehigh U., Lehigh Valley Hospital, The Nature Conservancy [Philadelphia], and Wildlands Conservancy. **$5,000** each to Baum School of Art, Lehigh County Conference of Churches, and Lehigh County Historical Society. **$1,000-$2,500** each to 10,000 Friends of Pa., Ballet Guild of the Lehigh Valley, Community Bike Works, Community Music School, DeSales U./Allentown College, Episcopal Academy [Merion], Fund to Benefit Children & Youth, Girls Club of Allentown, Good Shepherd Home, The Hillside School, Lehigh Valley Chamber Orchestra, Leonardo DaVinci's Horse, Moravian Academy, Mock Turtle Marionette Theatre, Parkette National Gymnastic Training Center, Pa. Environmental Council, Repertory Dance Theatre, Shipley School [Bryn Mawr], and United Way of the Greater Lehigh Valley. Other smaller local contributions for various purpose. **Out-of-state** giving includes **$5,000** to Cornell U. [NY] and **$2,000** to Committee for Economic Development [NY]. ■**PUBLICATIONS:** Funding Guidelines brochure ■**WEBSITE:** None ■**E-MAIL:** None ■**APPLICATION POLICIES & PROCEDURES:** The Foundation reports that giving is primarily to the Lehigh Valley for educational, environmental protection, and arts/cultural purposes. Most grants are for one year only for general support, special projects, or capital drives. No support is given to/for political, fraternal, social or veterans organizations; lobbying to influence legislation; endowments; debt reduction; charitable/testimonial dinners; fundraising events or related advertising; religious/sectarian purposes; or individuals. Submit requests in a letter (3 pages maximum) during March-early April or August-early September (deadlines are April 15th and September 15th); give a brief overview of the organization, summarize the proposed program and state the amount requested; briefly describe the plan for accomplishing objectives and how results will be measured/evaluated. Also include organizational/project budgets, list of major funding sources, Board member list, and IRS tax-exempt status documentation. Site visits sometimes are made to organizations being considered for a grant. Grants are awarded at meetings in May and October-November.

O+D+T Leon C. Holt, Jr. (T+Donor+Con) — June W. Holt (T+Donor) — Richard W. Holt [Bethlehem] (T) — Deborah Holt Weil [Berwyn] (T)

NE-059 Hommer (Julius & Katheryn) Foundation
P.O. Box 8
Brodheadsville 18322   (Monroe County)
AMV $1,033,833   **FYE** 12-00   **(Gifts Received** $300,000)

MI-31-44-54-55
Phone Unlisted **FAX** None
EIN 23-2847257   **Year Created** 1996
1 **Grant of** $50,000

Sole grant to Palmerton Hospital Foundation. — In prior two years, grants only to same grantee. ■**PUBLICATIONS:** None ■**WEBSITE:** None ■**E-MAIL:** None ■**APPLICATION POLICIES & PROCEDURES:** The Foundation reports that Pa. and NJ organizations receive preference. Most grants are for general support, special projects, building funds, capital drives, and matching grants. Grant requests may be submitted at any time in a letter (2 pages maximum); include a project budget and IRS tax-exempt status documentation. Site visits sometimes are made to organizations being considered for a grant. Grants are awarded at June and November meetings.

O+D+T Peter L. Kern (C+T+Con) — Carol Hommer Kern (VC+T) — First Union/Wachovia (Corporate Trustee)

NE-060 Horsehead Community Development Fund
c/o Horsehead Resource Development Corp.
Central Laboratory Bldg., P.O. Box 351
Palmerton 18071   (Carbon County)
AMV $179,017   **FYE** 12-00   **(Gifts Received** $171,196)

MI-12-13-15-21-29-31-35-41-44-45-55-56-71
84-89
Phone 610-826-2239 **FAX** None
EIN 23-2588172   **Year Created** 1990
36 **Grants totaling** $131,737

All giving limited to Palmerton Borough and neighboring Carbon County communities; grants are for operating expenses except as noted. High grant of **$20,000** to Palmerton Library Assn. (improvements). **$15,000** each to Carbon County Lion/Lioness Fair Assn. and Palmerton Hospital (neonatal unit). **$11,000** to Palmerton Area Recreation Committee. **$5,000** each to Aquashicola Fire Company (apparatus), Carbon County Head Start (utilities), Carbon History Project (publication), East Penn Parent-Teacher Organization, Franklin Elementary School Parent-Teacher Organization, Lehigh Gap Historical Society (office equipment), and Palmerton Visiting Nurse Assn. (vehicle). **$3,500** to Palmerton Borough (park maintenance). **$3,000** to Palmerton Booster Club (helmets/uniforms). **$2,000-$2,800** each to Bowmanstown Fire Company (equipment), Diligence Fire Company, Panther Valley Renaissance Library Task Force (seed money), Sacred Heart Catholic Youth Organization, Volunteers for Literacy, and Walnutport Canal Assn. (improvements). **$1,000-$1,500** each to Laurel Festival of the Arts, Lutheran Welfare Services (home care), Northern Lehigh YAA, Soccer Palmerton Band, Palmerton Concourse Club Bandstand (concerts), Palmerton Midget Baseball (uniforms), Palmerton Over-60 Club, Palmerton Swim & Dive Team (programs), and Towamensing Soccer (field improvements).■**PUBLICATIONS:** Annual Report (lists grantees but not grant sizes); statement of program policy; application guidelines ■**WEBSITE:** None ■**E-MAIL:** None ■**APPLICATION POLICIES & PROCEDURES:** The Foundation reports that only organizations in and around the Borough of Palmerton [Carbon County] are eligible to apply. Most grants are for operating support, special projects, building funds, and matching grants; all funds must be used within one year. No grants awarded for start up or to individuals. Prospective applicants initially should make a telephone inquiry about the feasibility of submitting a request. Grant requests must be submitted in a letter (or formal proposal with cover letter) well in advance of the April 1st, July 1st, September 1st, and December 1st deadlines; include organizational/project budgets, Board member list, audited financial statement, and IRS tax-exempt status documentation. Site visits sometimes are made to organizations being considered for a grant. Grants are awarded at quarterly meetings.

O+D+T Michael Harleman (F+Con) — William Bechdolt (C+D) — Joseph Bechtel (VC+D) — Richard Hager (S+D) — Corporate Donor: Horsehead Resource Development Corp.

NE-061 Hughes Foundation
P.O. Box 149
Stroudsburg 18360   (Monroe County)
AMV $2,569,326   **FYE** 4-01   **(Gifts Received** $135,000)

MI-13-14-15-25-42-44-49-55
Phone 570-424-8654 **FAX** None
EIN 23-6298104   **Year Created** 1959
9 **Grants totaling** $120,550

All local giving. High grant of **$60,000** to Eastern Monroe Public Library. **$20,250** to Monroe County Home Assn. (Laurel Manor Nursing Home). **$15,000** each to Burnley Workshop of the Poconos and Pocono Area Transitional Housing. **$4,000** to

East Stroudsburg U. **$2,500** to Monroe County Arts Council. **$2,000** to Junior Achievement. **$1,500** to East Stroudsburg Youth Assn. Other smaller contributions.■**PUBLICATIONS:** None ■**WEBSITE:** None ■**E-MAIL:** None ■**APPLICATION POLICIES & PROCEDURES:** The Foundation reports that most giving is restricted to Stroudsburg or Monroe County area; no grants awarded to individuals. Most grants are for annual campaigns, general support, program development, or scholarship funds. Submit grant requests in a letter (2 pages maximum) during January-March (deadline is March 31st); include annual report, project budget, list of other funding sources, and IRS tax-exempt status documentation. Site visits sometimes are made to organizations being considered for a grant. The Board of Directors meets in April and October.

O+D+T R. Clinton Hughes, Jr. (P+D+Donor+Con) — R. Dale Hughes (VP+Donor+D) — Kevin Hughes (S+D) — Terry A. Cramer (F+D) — Bernie Billick (D) — Bryan Hughes (D) — Corporate donors: Hughes Printing Company; Science Press; Hughes Printing Company of Connecticut

---

NE-062   Hughes (R. Dale & Frances M.) Foundation   MI-22-25-31-42-43-44
131 Stoneleigh Drive   **Phone** 570-424-8654 **FAX** None
East Stroudsburg 18301   (Monroe County)   **EIN** 23-7914215   **Year Created** 1997
AMV $1,793,415   **FYE** 12-00   (Gifts Received $0)   2 **Grants totaling** $121,819

One Pa. grant: **$120,000** to Pocono Medical Center (cancer center). **Out-of-state** grant: **$1,819** to St. Petersburg Junior College [FL]. — Giving in prior years included **$25,000** to Eastern Monroe Public Library (general support/books purchase); **$5,000** to Northampton Community College (scholarships); and **$2,500** each to Pocono Area Transitional Housing (operating funds) and Salvation Army/Monroe County (operating funds). ■**PUBLICATIONS:** None ■**WEBSITE:** None ■**E-MAIL:** None ■ **APPLICATION POLICIES & PROCEDURES:** Information not available.

O+D+T R. Dale Hughes (T+Donor+Con) — Frances M. Hughes (T+Donor) — PNC Bank (Corporate Trustee)

NE-063   J.A. Foundation   MI-13-41-42-61-84
1 Amato Drive   **Phone** 570-655-4514, x-4252 **FAX** 570-655-4005
Moosic 18507   (Lackawanna County)   **EIN** 23-2883862   **Year Created** 1997
AMV $402,523   **FYE** 12-00   (Gifts Received $16,458)   6 **Grants totaling** $18,000

Mostly local giving. High grant of **$10,500** to Nativity of our Lord School [Scranton]. **$2,500** to St. Mary's Youth Basketball. **$2,000** to House of Prayer of Nanticoke. **$1,000** to Lehigh Carbon Community College Foundation. **$500** to Catherine McAuley Center. **Out-of-state** grant: **$1,500** to Racers for Christ [AZ]. ■**PUBLICATIONS:** None ■**WEBSITE:** None ■**E-MAIL:** None ■ **APPLICATION POLICIES & PROCEDURES:** Information not available.

O+D+T Joseph Amato (P+F+Donor+Con) — Donna Amato (S)

NE-064   Jaindl (Fred J.) Foundation, The   MI-12-13-14-31-32-41-61-71-89
c/o Jaindl's Turkey Farm
3150 Coffeetown Road   **Phone** 610-395-3333 **FAX** 610-395-8608
Orefield 18069   (Lehigh County)   **EIN** 23-2495124   **Year Created** 1988
AMV $2,862,164   **FYE** 12-00   (Gifts Received $0)   40 **Grants totaling** $186,933

All local giving. High grant of **$75,000** to Lehigh Valley Hospital. **$84,333** to St. Joseph the Worker Church. **$2,500** to Rodale Institute. **$2,000** to Boys & Girls Club of Allentown. **$1,700** to March of Dimes. **$1,000** each to ARC of Lehigh & Northampton Counties, Cystic Fibrosis Foundaiton, Dreams Come True, Easter Seals, Good Shepherd Home, Hillside School, Holy Infancy Parish, Lehigh Valley Child Care, Neffs Fire Company, Schnecksville Fire Company, and Tri-Clover Fire Company. **$900** to American Cancer Society. Other local contributions, mostly **$250** or **$500**, for various community organizations including several fire companies. ■**PUBLICATIONS:** None ■**WEBSITE:** None ■**E-MAIL:** None ■**APPLICATION POLICIES & PROCEDURES:** The Foundation reports that recognized charities in the Lehigh Valley receive preference. Grant requests should be submitted in writing 90 days before funding is needed; describe the proposed use of the requested funds.

O+D+T David Jaindl (T+Con) — Mark W. Jaindl (T) — Fred J. Jaindl (Donor) — PNC Advisors/Northeast Pa. (Trustee) — Corporate donor: Jaindl Turkey Farm

---

NE-065   Jerome (Ben) Charitable Testamentary Trust   MI-12-41-42-61-63
c/o Wallitsch & Figore
654 Wolf Ave.   **Phone** 610-250-6585 **FAX** None
Easton 18042   (Northampton County)   **EIN** 23-7984640   **Year Created** 1998
AMV $1,379,123   **FYE** 12-00   (Gifts Received $48,400)   7 **Grants totaling** $33,750

All local and Allegheny County giving. High grant of **$7,500** to Moravian Academy. **$6,250** to Mt. St. Peter's Church [New Kensington]. **$5,000** to Lehigh U. **$4,000** each to Children's Home of Easton, Day Spring Christian Church [Tarentum], and Grace Community Presbyterian Church [Lower Burrell]. **$3,000** to Our Lady of Perpetual Hope [Bethlehem]. ■**PUBLICATIONS:** None ■**WEBSITE:** None ■**E-MAIL:** None ■**APPLICATION POLICIES & PROCEDURES:** Grant requests may be submitted in any form at any time.

O+D+T Gary S. Figore, Esq. (T+Con) — Donor: Estate of Ben Jerome

NE-066 Jerome (Ben) Foundation
c/o Wallitsch & Figore
654 Wolf Ave.
Easton 18042   (Northampton County)
AMV $1,054,683   **FYE** 12-00   (**Gifts Received** $0)

MI-13-22-29-31-32-41-42-44

Phone 610-250-6585 **FAX** None
EIN 25-6066649   **Year Created** 1961
27 **Grants totaling** $49,300

All local or Allegheny County giving; all grants are for general support. High grant of **$10,000** to YMCA of New Kensington. **$6,0000** to Salvation Army [New Kensington]. **$5,000** each to Lehigh U., Magee-Women's Health Foundation [Pittsburgh], and Mt. St. Peters Church School [New Kensington]. **$4,000** to Moravian Academy. **$3,000** each to Day Spring Christian Church [Tarentum] and People's Library of New Kensington. **$1,000-$1,250** each to China Passage [Springdale], Suzanne G. Komen Breast Cancer Research Foundation [New Kensington], and Red Cross [New Kensington]. Other contributions **$100-$500** in both locations for various purposes. ■**PUBLICATIONS:** None ■**WEBSITE:** None ■**E-MAIL:** None ■**APPLICATION POLICIES & PROCEDURES:** Grant requests may be submitted in any form at any time. — Formerly called Jerome Foundation
O+D+T Gary S. Figore, Esq. (T+Con) — R. Jerry Little, Esq. [New Kensington] (T) — Donor: Estate of Ben Jerome

NE-067 Johnson (John A. & Wilhelmina S.) Foundation, The
5150 Hoffmansville Road
Orefield 18069   (Lehigh County)
AMV $1,437,735   **FYE** 12-00   (**Gifts Received** $0)

MI-14-31-32-72-89

Phone 610-395-1823 **FAX** None
EIN 23-2010791   **Year Created** 1978
2 **Grants totaling** $66,268

All local giving. High grant of **$41,268** to Lehigh Valley Hospital (oncology research). **$25,000** to Community Company of New Tripoli (general support). — Giving in two previous years included **$66,600** to Lehigh Valley Hospital (oncology research); **$53,646** to Red Cross/Lehigh Valley Chapter (disaster relief); and **$5,000** each to Greater Lehigh Valley Radio Reading Service for the Print Handicapped, and Kent County SPCA [DE]. ■**PUBLICATIONS:** None ■**WEBSITE:** None ■**E-MAIL:** None ■**APPLICATION POLICIES & PROCEDURES:** Grant requests may be submitted in any form at any time. No grants awarded to individuals.
O+D+T John A. Johnson, Jr. (P+D+Con) — Arthur W. Johnson (S+F+D) — Frank P. Johnson [DE] (T) — William G. Malkames [Allentown] (T) — Marian G. Wallsten [NJ] (T)

NE-068 Kairos Trust, The
6829 Sandy Court
New Tripoli 18066   (Lehigh County)
AMV $58,069   **FYE** 12-00   (**Gifts Received** $305,000)

MI-11-12-13-17-22-52-63-65-81-82

Phone 610-298-2149 **FAX** None
EIN 23-7743234   **Year Created** 1993
75 **Grants totaling** $249,000

About one-third local giving; all grants are for general purposes. High Pa. grant of **$15,000** to United Way of the Greater Lehigh Valley. **$12,100** to Unity of Lehigh Valley. **$10,500** to KidsPeace. **$10,000** to Allentown Symphony Orchestra. **$9,500** to St. John's United Church of Christ of Allentown. **$9,000** to Lehigh County Council of Churches. **$6,000** to Turning Point of Lehigh Valley. **$5,100** to Great Valley Girl Scout Council. **$4,000** to YMCA/YWCA of Allentown. **$3,300** to Bach Choir of Bethlehem. **$2,000** to Jesuit Spiritual Center. **$1,000-$1,600** each to Allentown Art Museum, Communities in Schools of the Lehigh Valley, and The Program for Women & Families. **$700** to Allentown Public Library. Other local contributions **$100-$500** for various purposes. **Out-of-state** giving includes **$18,000** each to Good Shepherd Ministries [DC] and Journey Into Freedom [OR]; **$15,900** to Festival Center [DC]; **$15,000** to Jubilee Jobs [DC]; **$14,200** to The Friends of Jesus Church [DC]; **$10,000** each to Bartimaeus Cooperative Ministries [CA], New Born Holistic Ministries [MD], and Pavilion Foundation [NC]; and **$5,000** each to Bread for the World Institute [MD], Samaritan Inns, Inc. [DC], Children of the Americas [DC], and Unity of Lebanon [NJ].■**PUBLICATIONS:** None ■ **WEBSITE:** None ■**E-MAIL:** None ■**APPLICATION POLICIES & PROCEDURES:** Information not available.
O+D+T Alice Anne Miller (T+Donor+Con) — Joan M. Moran [Allentown] (Donor)

NE-069 Kalmbach (Frederick) Charitable Trust
c/o Kalmbach Memorial Park
200 Cotton Street
Macungie 18062   (Lehigh County)
AMV $5,495,484   **FYE** 12-00   (**Gifts Received** $1,278)

MI-13-71-84

Phone 610-965-1140 **FAX** 610-966-2017
EIN 23-6742794   **Year Created** 1983
2 **Grants totaling** $15,600

All local giving. **$12,000** to Lehigh U. (Kalmbach Institute). **$3,600** to Roving Nature Center [Bath]. ■**PUBLICATIONS:** None ■ **WEBSITE:** www.kalmbachpark.com ■**E-MAIL:** mail@kalmbachpark.com ■**APPLICATION POLICIES & PROCEDURES:** The Trust reports that under current guidelines only charitable organizations in Macungie and the surrounding area are eligible to apply; most of the Trust's giving each year is for Kalmbach Memorial Park operations. Grant requests may be submitted at any time in a letter; describe the purpose of the proposed project/program and include IRS tax-exempt status documentation.
O+D+T Michael C. McCready (Administrator, Kalmbach Memorial Park+Con) — Robert C. Dorney [Emmaus] (Co-T) — Hon. Robert Young [Emmaus] (Co-T) — Fleet Bank (Corporate Co-Trustee)

NE-070 Kalnoski (William & Dora) Memorial Scholarship Fund
c/o First Columbia Bank & Trust Company
11 West Main Street, P.O. Box 240
Bloomsburg 17815   (Columbia County)
AMV $1,111,925   **FYE** 12-01   (**Gifts Received** $1,129,997)

MI-43

Phone 570-387-4609 **FAX** 570-387-2602
EIN 25-1882103   **Year Created** 2001
18 **Grants totaling** $54,000

All grants are scholarships of **$3,000** each awarded to Columbia and Schuylkill county students pursuing a college major of art, architecture, or related field of study. ■**PUBLICATIONS:** None ■**WEBSITE:** None ■**E-MAIL:** trustdpt@firstcolumbiabank.com ■ **APPLICATION POLICIES & PROCEDURES:** Only high school graduates of Columbia and Schuylkill counties are eligible to apply for scholarships when pursuing a major in art, architecture, or a related field. A formal application form, available from the Bank, should be submitted in April—the deadline is May 1st; include personal income tax returns. Awards are made at a May meeting.

O+D+T John Thompson (VP & Trust Officer at Bank+Con) — also a Scholarship Committee of Columbia and Schuylkill county residents

---

NE-071   Katz (David) Foundation
P.O. Box 247
Honesdale   18431   (Wayne County)

MI-12-13-15-22-29-31-44-62-79
Phone 617-223-1900 **FAX** None
EIN 22-2783266   **Year Created** 1987

AMV $903,138   **FYE** 12-00   **(Gifts Received** $0)   15 **Grants totaling** $38,392

About two-thirds local giving. High grant of **$5,302** to Beth Israel Congregation. **$5,000** to Wayne Memorial Health System. **$3,000** to Survivors Resources, Inc. **$2,000** each to Bill Bursis Foundation, Jewish Home of Scranton, Wayne County Historical Society, and Wayne County Public Library. **$1,000-$1,500** each to Enrichment Audio Research Services, Honesdale Communities That Care, and Wayne-Pike YMCA. **Out-of-state** giving includes **$5,000** each to National Coalition Against Misuse of Pesticides [DC] and National Coalition for Cancer Survivors [MD]; and **$2,000** to Brain Tumor Society [MA].   ■**PUBLICATIONS:** Guidelines/Procedures; Application Form ■**WEBSITE:** None ■**E-MAIL:** None ■**APPLICATION POLICIES & PROCEDURES:** The Foundation reports a preference for programs which directly benefit Honesdale residents, especially in health, the environment, education, and charities supporting NE Pennsylvania's Jewish community. Grant requests may be submitted at any time on an Application Form available from the Foundation.

O+D+T Sigmund J. Roos [MA] (P+F+D+Con) — William J. Roos [Honesdale] (VP+S+D) — Nathan Lewis [MD] (AS+D)

NE-072   Kazanjian (Calvin K.) Economics Foundation, The
P.O. Box 300
Dallas   18612   (Luzerne County)

MI-13-17-42-49
Phone 570-675-7074 **FAX** 570-675-8436
EIN 23-2847257   **Year Created** 1947

AMV $6,843,810   **FYE** 12-00   **(Gifts Received** $0)   14 **Grants totaling** $243,135

One Pa. grant: **$15,000** to U. of Scranton (detailed syllabus on how to teach economics to pre-service teachers). **Out-of-state** grants include: **$35,000** each to Foundation for Teaching Economics [CA] (lesson plans re the demise of the Soviet Union and US economic issues) and STRIVE of Fairfield County [CT] (basic work-entry skills program); **$22,700** to National Council of Economics Education [NY] (curriculum project); **$25,000** to U. of Kansas (economics institute for state judges); **$14,000-$15,000** each to American Women's Economic Development Corp. [NY] (business startup course for women with limited resources), Center for True Economic Progress [MN] (symposium on women's role in the economy), Harvard U. [MA] (support for book on the moral consequences of economic growth), and South End Community Services [CT] (materials development for inner-city youth program); and other smaller grants for similar purposes. ■**PUBLICATIONS:** informational brochure; application guidelines ■ **WEBSITE:** www.kazanjian.org ■**E-MAIL:** director@kazanjian.org ■**APPLICATION POLICIES & PROCEDURES:** The Foundation support economic research or economic education projects/programs of a national scope/impact that address one of the following issues: (1) Promotion of Economic Literacy—through programs that raise various public's participation in economic education and/or create a demand for greater economic literacy; (2) Effective Economics Education—through projects that are unique and present economics in an effective, thoughtful, and understandable way; (3) Testing the Impact of Economic Education—through projects, policy studies, or programs that encourage measurement of economic understanding more often, and/or more effectively; and (4) Economics Education for At-Risk Students—through programs for disenfranchised youth and/or adults to learn how to participate in our nation's free-enterprise economic system. Most grants are for curriculum or program development, conferences, seminars, or programmatic seed money. Usually the Foundation does not support regional or statewide programs. No grants are awarded to individuals, or for capital projects, endowment funds, operating budgets, continuing support, annual campaigns, emergency funds, deficit financing, matching gifts, scholarships, fellowships, or loans. Grant requests which address one of the four foundation priorities can be submitted in a letter which describes the applicant organization's background, the purposes and duration of the project, a detailed budget, and IRS tax-exempt status documentation. If the proposed project/program is complex, a full proposal may be submitted. Deadlines for requests are April 1st and October 1st; grants are awarded at meetings in May and November.

O+D+T Dr. Michael A. McDowell (Manager+Con) — Lloyd L. Elston [FL] (P+F) — Richard L. Elston [CT] (VP+T) — Joseph Kinsella [CT] (S+T) — Dr. John Clizbe [CT] (T) — George H. Hartman [RI] (T) — Worth Loomis [CT] (T) — Marnie W. Mueller [CT] (T) — John M. Sumansky (T)

NE-073   Keystone Savings Foundation
c/o Keystone Savings Bank
Rt. 512 & Highland Ave., P.O. Box 25012
Lehigh Valley   18002   (Northampton County)

MI-12-13-14-15-22-25-31-39-44-52-55-56-57
Phone 610-861-5000 **FAX** 610-861-5059
EIN 23-2407218   **Year Created** 1986

AMV $718,135   **FYE** 12-99   **(Gifts Received** $0)   20 **Grants totaling** $33,000

All giving limited to the Lehigh Valley. High grant of **$3,000** to ProJeCt. **$2,000-$2,500** each to Boys & Girls Club of Allentown, Caring Place, Catholic Social Agency, Community Bike Works, Lehigh Valley Summerbridge, Pinebrook Services for Children, and Salvation Army. **$1,000-$1,500** each to AIDS Service Center, Fund to Benefit Children, Girls Club of Allentown, Haven House, Holy Infancy Rectory, Lehigh Valley Child Care, Lehigh Valley Council of Churches, Liberty Bell Shrine, Miller Memorial Blood Bank, Muhlenberg Summer Music Festival, and Valley Health Foundation. ■**PUBLICATIONS:** Annual Report; application guidelines ■ **WEBSITE:** None ■**E-MAIL:** nbilliard@keystonesavingsbank.com ■**APPLICATION POLICIES & PROCEDURES:** Only organizations located in Keystone Savings Bank's general business area (the Lehigh Valley) are eligible to apply; priority giving interests are human services, health/medical and arts/culture, and most grants are for general support, capital campaigns, equipment, program development/evaluation, or scholarship funds. No grants are awarded to individuals. Prospective applicants should make an initial telephone inquiry about the feasibility of submitting a request. Grant requests must be submitted on a formal application form, available from the Bank; include an annual report, organization and project budgets, number of individuals being served, Board member list, list of major funding sources, audited financial statement, and IRS tax-exempt status documentation. Site visits sometimes are made to organizations being considered for a grant. The Board awards grants at meetings late in March, June, September, and December.

O+D+T Nancy A. Billiard (Con) — Jeffrey Feather (P) — R. Charles Stehly (VP) — Frederick E. Kutteroff (S+F) — Corporate donor: Keystone Savings Bank

---

NE-074   Kinney (Clair) Scholarship/Library Science Reference Fund   MI-43-44
c/o First Columbia Bank & Trust Company
11 West Main Street, P.O. Box 240   **Phone** 570-387-4609 **FAX** 570-387-2602
Bloomsburg   17815   (Columbia County)   **EIN** 23-6664657   **Year Created** 1977
AMV $204,632   **FYE** 12-01   (**Gifts Received** $24,513)   5 **Grants totaling** $34,303

All local giving. Four academic scholarships, **$3,000** each, awarded to Columbia and Montour county students. Also, a designated grant of **$22,303** to Bloomsburg Public Library (purchase books) as stipulated by the Fund's donor. ■**PUBLICATIONS:** None ■**WEBSITE:** None ■**E-MAIL:** trustdpt@firstcolumbiabank.com ■**APPLICATION POLICIES & PROCEDURES:** Only public high school graduates in Columbia and Montour counties are eligible to apply for scholarships. A formal application form, available from the Bank, should be submitted in April—the deadline is May 1st; include personal income tax returns. Awards are made at a May meeting. — Formerly called the Clair Kinney Trust.

O+D+T John Thompson (VP & Trust Officer at Bank+Con)

NE-075   Kiwanis Foundation of Allentown   MI-12-13-14-15-25-41-42-43-52-55-56
P.O. Box 4355   **Phone** 610-434-5191 **FAX** None
Allentown   18105   (Lehigh County)   **EIN** 25-6050029   **Year Created** 1952
AMV $480,808   **FYE** 9-01   (**Gifts Received** $1,446)   13 **Grants totaling** $63,266

Mostly local giving. High grant of **$40,000** to Salvation Army (new building). **$10,000** to Lehigh County Historical Society (new building). **$2,000-$2,500** each to Community in Schools (school enrichment program), Girls Club of Allentown (summer program), and Lehigh County Community College Computer Camp (for inner-city children). **$1,000-$1,166** each to Allentown Symphony (children's concert), Personalized Books Given to Children, Inc. (inner-city schools), and two scholarships. Other smaller local contributions. **Out-of-state** grant: **$1,000** to Kiwanis International [IN] (health initiative). ■**PUBLICATIONS:** None ■**WEBSITE:** None ■**E-MAIL:** None ■**APPLICATION POLICIES & PROCEDURES:** The Foundation gives preference to organizations serving Lehigh Valley. Submit requests in a letter at any time; describe the purpose of the requested funding, amount needed, when the funds will be used, and include IRS tax-exempt status documentation. The Trustees meet in February, April, June, August, and October.

O+D+T Chairperson, Service Committee (Con) — Tom Harp (P+T) — Enos Martin (VP+T) — James Snyder (S+T) — James Fronheiser (F+T) — Ann Bieber (T) — John Denuel (T) — Ron Lewis [Emmaus] (T) — John Stoffa [Northampton] (T) — Judy M. Wannemacher [Bethlehem] (T)

NE-076   Kiwanis Foundation of Easton   MI-12-13-14-22-29
1832 Washington Blvd.   **Phone** 610-258-7429 **FAX** None
Easton   18042   (Northampton County)   **EIN** 23-6299967   **Year Created** 1963
AMV $202,973   **FYE** 2-01   (**Gifts Received** $18,570)   22 **Grants totaling** $16,028

Mostly local giving; grants are for general program purposes except as noted. High grant of **$2,649** to Children's Home of Easton (improvements). **$2,011** to Easton YMCA. **$1,000-$1,250** each to Community Care Center [Reading], Shilo Baptist Church, Spring Garden Day Care Center, and Third Street Alliance. **$823** to Handicapped Children's Christmas Party. Other local contributions **$100-$500** for various community organizations/programs. **Out-of-state** grants: **$1,250** to Forth Youth Center of Phillipsburg [NJ] and **$1,000** to Kiwanis International Foundation [IN] (health initiative). ■**PUBLICATIONS:** None ■**WEBSITE:** None ■**E-MAIL:** None ■**APPLICATION POLICIES & PROCEDURES:** The Foundation reports that normally only Easton and Lehigh Valley-area organizations are eligible to apply. No grants awarded to individuals. Prospective applicants initially should make a telephone inquiry about the feasibility of submitting a request. Submit requests in a letter (2 pages maximum) at any time; describe the purpose of the organization and the project, and state a specific amount requested; include IRS tax-exempt status documentation. The Board awards grants at January, April, July, and September meetings.

O+D+T Roger J. Connors, II (VP+Con) — Rev. Charles L. Bomboy [NJ] (P) — Fred C. Finken, Jr. (S+F) — Thomas F. Barton, III (D) — Joanne Cappelano [Bangor] (D) — Victor Dennis (D) — Alvin Fairchild (D) — Thomas Malerba (D) — Elaine G.L. Rutherford (D) — Clarence Snyder (D) — Gary D. Tempest [Catasauqua] (D)

NE-077   Klemow (Sidney & Lillian) Foundation   MI-22-62
7 West Aspen Street   **Phone** 570-454-7842 **FAX** None
Hazleton   18201   (Luzerne County)   **EIN** 11-2729095   **Year Created** 1985
AMV $461,121   **FYE** 12-00   (**Gifts Received** $0)   25 **Grants totaling** $30,405

About four-fifths local giving. High grant of **$12,500** to Hazleton Federated Jewish Charities. **$4,470** to Agudas Israel Congregation. **$2,424** to Congregation B'nai Israel. **$1,100** to Jewish Home of NE Pa. Other local contributions **$25-$500** for various purposes. **Out-of-state** giving includes **$5,000** to Haifa Foundation [Israel] and **$1,000** to Jewish Federation of Pinellas County [FL]. ■**PUBLICATIONS:** None ■**WEBSITE:** None ■**E-MAIL:** None ■**APPLICATION POLICIES & PROCEDURES:** Grant requests may be submitted in any form at any time; clearly state the purpose of the request. No grants awarded to individuals.

O+D+T Sidney Klemow (P+Donor+Con) — Lillian Klemow (Donor)

NE-078 Kline (Charles & Figa) Foundation

626 North Main Street
Allentown 18104 (Lehigh County)

MI-11-13-14-22-31-41-42-54-62-65
Phone 610-437-4077 **FAX** None
EIN 23-6262315 **Year Created** 1955

AMV $9,080,259 **FYE** 10-00 (Gifts Received $0) 22 **Grants totaling** $411,348

Mostly local/Pa. giving. High grant of **$210,000** to Jewish Federation of Allentown. **$65,481** to Jewish Community Center of Allentown. **$31,000** to Jewish Day School of Allentown. **$22,000** to Congregation Sons of Israel. **$17,900** to Temple Beth El. **$10,447** to Jewish Family Services. **$10,000** to United Way of Greater Lehigh Valley. **$7,500** to Girls Club of Allentown. **$6,500** to Congregation Keneseth Israel [Montgomery County]. **$5,000** each to Anti-Defamation League and Sacred Heart Foundation. **$4,000** to Assn. for the Blind & Visually Impaired of Lehigh Valley. **$3,000** to Cedar Crest College. **$2,000-$2,500** each to Hadassah/Allentown Chapter, Hillside School, Jewish Family League, Lehigh U., and Muhlenberg College. **$1,000** each to Allentown Art Museum and Lehigh County Conference of Churches. Other smaller local contributions. ■ **PUBLICATIONS:** None ■ **WEBSITE:** None ■ **E-MAIL:** None ■ **APPLICATION POLICIES & PROCEDURES:** Grant requests may be submitted in any form at any time before the September 30th deadline.

O+D+T Fabian I. Fraenkel (VP+D+Con) — Leonard Rapoport (P+F+D) — Stewart Furmansky (D)

NE-079 Kotur (Eugene R.) Foundation

c/o Ukrainian Fraternal Assn.
1327 Wyoming Ave.
Scranton 18509 (Lackawanna County)

MI-43

Phone 570-342-0937 **FAX** 570-347-5649
EIN 25-6394138 **Year Created** 1997

AMV $406,836 **FYE** 12-00 (Gifts Received $0) 5 **Grants totaling** $7,000

All grants are scholarships for students of Ukrainian ancestry who attend one of the 31 designated universities/colleges in the United States and Canada. ■ **PUBLICATIONS:** Application Guidelines & Form ■ **WEBSITE:** None ■ **E-MAIL:** None ■ **APPLICATION POLICIES & PROCEDURES:** Only students of Ukrainian ancestry are eligible to apply; applicants must currently be enrolled in an undergraduate (freshman year excepted) or postgraduate program at one of 31 highly-competitive, designated universities/colleges in CA, CT, IL, IN, LA, MA, MD, MI, MO, NC, NH, NJ, NY, OH, PA, RI, TN, and WI; also Ontario and Quebec. Scholarship applications should be submitted on a formal application form (provided by the Foundation) in the six weeks before the June 15th deadline; the form also lists the 31 designated institutions. Transcripts must be sent directly to the Foundation by the institution. For detailed scholarship information contact Stephen M. Wichar, Sr., 39182 Aynesley Drive, Clinton Township, MI 48038; telephone 810-286-6490.

O+D+T Stephen M. Wichar, Sr. [MI] (Secretary, Scholarship Committee+Con) — PNC Advisors (Trustee)

NE-080 Lake Foundation Charitable Trust, The

P.O. Box 331
Lake Ariel 18436 (Wayne County)

MI-13-22-29-42-61

Phone 570-698-5902 **FAX** None
EIN 22-2816562 **Year Created** 1986

AMV $152,746 **FYE** 12-00 (Gifts Received $0) 22 **Grants totaling** $12,100

Mostly Lackawanna County giving. High grant of **$1,800** to St. Francis of Assisi Kitchen. **$1,300** each to Christmas Bureau and Salvation Army. **$550-$600** each to Boys & Girls Club of Scranton, Friends of the Poor, IHM Retirement Fund, Little Sisters of the Poor, Red Cross, U. of Scranton Campus School, and U. of Scranton International Service. Other contributions **$150-$400** for various purposes. ■ **PUBLICATIONS:** None ■ **WEBSITE:** None ■ **E-MAIL:** None ■ **APPLICATION POLICIES & PROCEDURES:** No grants awarded to individuals.

O+D+T Douglas M. Holcomb (T+Donor+Con) — Madge M. Holcomb (T+Donor)

NE-081 LaMel Garden Foundation

c/o First Union/Wachovia - PA 2106
640 Hamilton Street
Allentown 18101 (Lehigh County)

MI-12-13-14-15-22-31-33-41-84-89

Phone 610-439-4686 **FAX** 610-740-1207
EIN 23-6277099 **Year Created** 1956

AMV $489,059 **FYE** 12-00 (Gifts Received $6,365) 16 **Grants totaling** $11,411

All giving restricted to organizations serving the Perkasie, Bucks County community. No details on grant sizes, but the following received support: LIfePath, Inc., Lutheran Community at Telford, Nova Foundation, Penn Foundation for Mental Health, Pennridge FISH Organization, Pennridge Little League, Pennridge Senior Center, Perkasie Fire Company, Perkasie Garden Club, Salvation Army/Upper Bucks, Sellersville Fire Company, Special Equestrians, United Friends School, Upper Bucks YMCA, and Upper Bucks YWCA ■ **PUBLICATIONS:** None ■ **WEBSITE:** None ■ **E-MAIL:** None ■ **APPLICATION POLICIES & PROCEDURES:** The Foundation reports that only agencies serving Perkasie [Bucks County] residents are eligible to apply. Prospective applicants should initially telephone the foundation to inquire about the feasibility of submitting a request. Grant requests may be submitted in any form before the October 31st deadline. Site visits sometimes are made to organizations being considered for a grant. The Trustees award grants at a December meeting.

O+D+T James A. Kressler (VP at Bank+Con) — Russell Hollenbach (T) — Dr. William E. Keim (T) — First Union/Wachovia (Corporate Trustee)

NE-082 Langan (Manus & Laura Kelly) Educational Fund MI-43
c/o Director of Financial Aid
401 St. Thomas Hall, University of Scranton **Phone** 570-941-7700 **FAX** None
Scranton 18510 (Lackawanna County) **EIN** 23-6645283 **Year Created** 1977
AMV $1,338,545 **FYE** 12-00 (Gifts Received $0) 100+ **Grants totaling** $62,775

All grants are scholarship awards—typically **$200-$500** each, some larger—for Scranton-area students to pursue an undergraduate or vocational program at any college/university in the United States. ■**PUBLICATIONS:** statement of policy; application guidelines ■**WEBSITE:** None ■**E-MAIL:** finaid@uofs.edu ■**APPLICATION POLICIES & PROCEDURES:** Only Scranton-area students are eligible for apply. Applicants must request a formal grant application form, available from the Director of Financial Aid, U. of Scranton, and submit it with a a needs-analysis document to establish financial need; if a candidate has applied for a Federal Pell Grant then the Student Eligibility Report will meet that requirement. Completed applications must be received no later than the May 15th deadline; the Selection Committee makes awards in August.
O+D+T Director of Financial Aid (Con) — PNC Bank/Northeast Pa. (Corporate Trustee)

NE-083 Laros (R.K.) Foundation MI-12-13-14-16-34-35-41-42-51-54-56-71
4513 Virginia Drive **Phone** 610-867-8452 **FAX** None
Bethlehem 18017 (Northampton County) **EIN** 23-6207353 **Year Created** 1952
AMV $5,127,005 **FYE** 12-00 (Gifts Received $0) 18 **Grants totaling** $374,131

All local giving; many grants are payments on multiyear pledges. Two grants totaling **$40,000** to Council of Spanish Speaking Organizations (payments on two pledges). **$35,000** to YMCA of Bethlehem (Fountain Hill childcare site). **$30,000** to Community Action Committee of the Lehigh Valley (Forte Building restoration). **$26,331** to Lehigh Valley Child Care (center renovation). **$25,000** each to City of Bethlehem (Steel Workers Memorial Park), Moravian College, National Museum of Industrial History (preview museum), New Bethany Ministries (facility safety improvements), and Woodmere Art Museum [Philadelphia] (Museum Tower). **$20,000** each to Discovery Center, St. Luke's Hospital Nursing School (Latino student support), and Stephen's Place (building addition). **$14,000-$15,000** each to Good Shepherd (rehabilitation garden), KidsPeace (Washington School location improvements), and Pa. Youth Theatre (studio modifications). **$10,000** to Holy Infancy School (system upgrading). **$4,000** to Visiting Nurse Assn. of the Lehigh Valley (computerized drug module). ■**PUBLICATIONS:** None ■**WEBSITE:** None ■ **E-MAIL:** None ■**APPLICATION POLICIES & PROCEDURES:** The Foundation reports that giving is limited generally to community outreach organizations in Bethlehem and surrounding townships. Most grants are for special projects, building/renovations, capital campaigns, equipment, or seed money; multiple-year grants are awarded. No grants are awarded to individuals or for endowment. Prospective applicants initially should make a telephone inquiry about the feasibility of submitting a request. Submit eight copies of a full proposal (or a letter which fully describes the need) between January and the March 1st deadline; include a project budget. Trustees meet annually in late Spring/early Summer.
O+D+T Elizabeth C. Mowrer (AS+Con) — Russell K. Laros, Jr., M.D. [CA] (P+T) — Robert A. Spillman (S+T) — Ronald J. Donchez (T) — Laurie Gostley-Hackett (T) — Robert Huth, Jr. [VT] (T) — Russell K. Laros, III [HI] (T) — Gordon B. Mowrer (T) — Robert H. Young, Jr. [Merion] (T) — Nazareth National Bank (Corporate Trustee)

NE-084 Leavitt (Herbert M. & Naomi R.) Family Foundation MI-11-12-18-22-31-34-41-62-71-72
c/o Matus, 425 Dogwood Terrace **Phone** 610-253-7742 **FAX** None
Easton 18040 (Northampton County) **EIN** 23-7891877 **Year Created** 1997
AMV $406,480 **FYE** 12-00 (Gifts Received $125,000) 20 **Grants totaling** $24,000

About half local giving. High grants of **$2,000** each to Jewish Federation of the Lehigh Valley, Planned Parenthood of NE Pa., United Way of the Greater Lehigh Valley, and Valley Health Foundation. **$1,500** to Family & Counseling Services of the Lehigh Valley. **$1,000** each to Easton Area High School, Jewish Family Service of the Lehigh Valley, and Project of Easton. Other smaller local contributions for health/human services. **Out-of-state** giving includes **$2,000** to Dermatology Foundation [IL], Dolphin Institute [HI], and Marin Agricultural Land Trust [CA]; and **$1,000** to Warren Hospital Foundation [NJ]. ■**PUBLICATIONS:** None ■**WEBSITE:** None ■**E-MAIL:** None ■**APPLICATION POLICIES & PROCEDURES:** Grant requests may be submitted in any form at any time.
O+D+T Nancy R. Matus (T+Con) — Bernard T. Matus (S+Con) — Naomi R. Leavitt (T+Donor)

NE-085 Lebovitz Fund, The MI-12-13-22-41-42-51-52-54-55-62-71
3050 Tremont Street **Phone** 610-820-5053 **FAX** None
Allentown 18104 (Lehigh County) **EIN** 23-6270079 **Year Created** 1944
AMV $3,806,650 **FYE** 7-00 (Gifts Received $21,150) 76 **Grants totaling** $192,847

About one-quarter local/Pa. giving. High Pa. grant of **$18,500** to Allentown Art Museum. **$5,000** to Jewish Federation of Lehigh Valley. **$2,600** to Baldwin School [Bryn Mawr]. **$2,000** each to Touchstone Theatre and Wildlands Conservancy. **$1,000-$1,750** each to Beth David Reform Congregation [Gladwyne], Boys & Girls Club of Allentown, Child Care Information Services, Community Music School, Congregation Keneseth Israel, Fund to Benefit Children & Youth, Haverford School, and Lehigh Valley Arts Council. Other local contributions **$50-$650** for various purposes. **Out-of-state** giving includes high grant of **$70,000** to Columbia U. [NY]; **$15,000** to Dartmouth College/Tuck School of Business; **$10,000** each to The Outback [CT] and Wheaton College [MA]; **$8,000** to Federation of Jewish Services [MN]; and **$5,000** each to Nursing & Home Care [CT] and Salvation Army [MD]; and other grants/contributions, mostly where trustees reside. ■**PUBLICATIONS:** None ■**WEBSITE:** None ■**E-MAIL:** None ■**APPLICATION POLICIES & PROCEDURES:** Grant requests may be submitted in a letter at any time; include an annual report, organization and project budgets, Board member list, and IRS tax-exempt status documentation. Site visits sometimes are made to organizations being considered for a grant.

O+D+T Herbert C. Lebovitz (P+F+D+Con) — Beth Ann Segal [MN] (VP+S+D) — James Lebovitz [Bryn Mawr] (D) — Jonathan Javitch [NY] (D) — Peter Lebovitz (Donor)

NE-086 Lehigh Valley Community Foundation
Suite 300
961 Marcon Boulevard
Allentown 18109 (Lehigh County)

MI-12-13-15-17-18-19-22-29-31-41-42-43-51
52-54-55-56-57-65-71
Phone 610-266-4284 **FAX** 610-266-4285
EIN 23-1686634 **Year Created** 1967

AMV $8,307,913 **FYE** 6-01 **(Gifts Received** $542,169) 136 **Grants totaling** $530,394

As a Community Foundation all discretionary giving is limited to organizations serving Lehigh or Northampton counties except as noted below; 45 grants totaling **$213,479** were awarded from unrestricted or area-of-interest funds. High grant of **$20,000** to WLVT/Lehigh Valley PBS. **$11,800** to Valley Health Foundation for Easton Hospital. **$10,000** each to Easton Area School District/Day Care Center and Valley Youth House. **$9,872** to VIABL. **$6,256** to VIA of the Lehigh Valley. **$5,000-$6,000** each to Allentown Area Ecumenical Food Bank, Allentown Art Museum, Center for Humanistic Change, Communities in Schools of the Lehigh Valley, Community Bike Works, Fund to Benefit Children & Youth, LifePath, Inc., New Bethany Ministries, Northampton Community College, Palisades High School, Quakertown Alive!, Quakertown Christian School, Salvation Army/Allentown, and Touchstone Theatre. **$4,075-$4,874** each to Good Shepherd Home, Lehigh Valley Child Care/Fowler Center, and Meals on Wheels of Northampton County/Bethlehem. **$3,000-$3,500** each to Allentown Symphony Assn., Boys & Girls Club of Easton, Child Advocacy Center of Lehigh Valley, Girls' Club of Allentown, Lehigh County Conference of Churches, Main Street Theatre, Mercy Special Learning Center, Quakertown Community School District, Repertory Dance Theatre, Springfield Township Historical Commission, Third Street Alliance for Women & Children, Tinicum Elementary School, and YMCA of Upper Bucks. **$2,000-$2,500** each to Holland-Glen, Temple Covenant of Peace, and Weller Health Education Center. **$1,000-$1,200** each to Community Music School, Junior Achievement of Lehigh Valley, Planned Parenthood of NE Pa., and SE Pa. Resource Conservation & Development. Other grants awarded from donor-advised, donor-designated or other restricted funds. ■**PUBLICATIONS:** Annual Report; Grant Application Form ■**WEBSITE:** www.lehighvalleyfoundation.org ■**E-MAIL:** lvcf@lehighvalleyfoundation.org ■**APPLICATION POLICIES & PROCEDURES:** Only nonprofit organizations in Lehigh and Northampton counties are eligible to apply, with two exceptions: Monroe County agencies can apply for support from the Benjamin Franklin Trust Fund and Upper Bucks County organizations are eligible for support from the Neusch Fund. Giving focuses on the arts, education, environment, history & heritage, healthcare, human services, and science. Collaboration between agencies in addressing community needs is encouraged. The Foundation prefers (1) pilot programs requiring seed money but with the potential to be self-sufficient; (2) programs and capital projects which stimulate or provide leverage for additional funding; (3) programs which complement but do not duplicate United Way-funded services; and (4) organizations that collaborate with others to maximize community impact while drawing the community closer together. Grants from discretionary funds are not awarded for annual campaigns (local, state or national), sectarian religious purposes, operating/maintenance needs, or scholarships. Prospective applicants are requested to make an initial telephone call regarding the feasibility of submitting a request. Grant requests should be submitted beginning May 1st until the July 1st deadline; a formal application form, available on the website or from the Foundation, must be submitted together with the required documentation. Organizations may receive support for two consecutive years only, and may reapply after a one-year waiting period. Site visits sometimes are made to organizations being considered for a grant. The Board of Governors awards grants at a November meeting which are disbursed in January. — Formerly known as The Bethlehem Area Foundation.

O+D+T Board of Governors: Carol Dean Henn (Executive Director+S+Con) — Robert H. Littner, Sr., Esq. (C) — Patrick J. Connell (VC) — J. Marshall Wolff (F) — Joseph W. Boligitz — Llyena F. Boylan — Walter W. Buckley, Jr. — Lee A. Butz — Rev. Dr. Douglas Caldwell — Alvina L. Campbell — Hon. Maxwell Davison — Lesley H. Fallon — Robert Finn — Fr. Daniel Gambet, OSFS — Kostas Kalogeropoulos — Frederick E. Kutteroff — Hon. Cynthia A. Lambert — Richard G. Lang — Michael J. Lieberman — Stephen P. Link — Jack H. McNairy — Charles M. Meredith, III — William K. Murphy, Esq. — Betsy Roberts — Robert D. Romeril — Barbara Rothkopf — Barbara Tallman — Ferdinand Thun — John H. Updegrove, M.D. — Trustee banks: Summit Bank, First Union/Wachovia

---

NE-087 Levit Family Foundation, The
c/o Penn Treaty Network America Insurance Co.
3440 Lehigh Street
Allentown 18103 (Lehigh County)

MI-11-22-35-62

Phone 610-965-2222 **FAX** 877-582-3299
EIN 23-2792552 **Year Created** 1994

AMV $178,102 **FYE** 6-01 **(Gifts Received** $53,161) 8 **Grants totaling** $37,000

About half local giving; all grants are for general purposes. High grant of **$15,000** to Jewish Federation of the Lehigh Valley. **$1,000** each to Jason Goldenberg Memorial Fund and United Way of Greater Lehigh Valley. **$500** to Burns Memorial Award. **Out-of-state** giving includes **$15,000** to Friends' Health Connection [NJ]; **$3,000** to Standardbred Retirement Foundation [NJ]; and **$1,000** to Southern Poverty Law Center [AL]. ■**PUBLICATIONS:** None ■**WEBSITE:** www.penntreaty.com [corporate info only] ■**E-MAIL:** None ■**APPLICATION POLICIES & PROCEDURES:** No grants are awarded to individuals.

O+D+T Irving Levit (P+T+Donor+Con) — Judith M. Levit (VP+S)

NE-088 Linder (Albert A. & Bertram N.) Foundation
P.O. Box 681
Dalton 18414 (Lackawanna County)

MI-11-22-32-42-52-57-61-62-81

Phone See below **FAX** None
EIN 13-6100590 **Year Created** 1947

AMV $2,694,200 **FYE** 5-00 **(Gifts Received** $0) 192 **Grants totaling** $120,488

About one-fifth local/Pa. giving. High Pa. grant of **$10,000** to United Way of Lackawanna County. **$3,000** to United Jewish Appeal/Scranton. **$2,400** to U. of Pa. **$1,000-$1,200** each to Diocese of Scranton, Keystone College, Marywood College, Northeastern Pa. Philharmonic, and U. of Scranton. Other Pa. contributions **$50-$500** for various purposes. **Out-of-state** giving included **$16,000** to New York City Opera; **$11,700** to Chicago Council on Foreign Relations [IL]; **$5,050** to World Federalist Movement [DC]; **$4,700** to American Foundation for AIDS Research [NY]; **$3,100** to WNET-TV [NY]; and other smaller grants/contributions, primarily to NYC and DC. ■**PUBLICATIONS:** None ■**WEBSITE:** None ■**E-MAIL:** None ■**APPLICATION POLICIES & PROCEDURES:** The Foundation reports that most grants are for general support, special projects, capital drives, and research. No grants awarded for scholarships, loans, or to individuals. Grant requests may be submitted in a letter at any time to Mary Ellen Linder, 305 East 40th Street, New York, NY 10016, telephone 212-986-7983; include an organizational budget, list of major funding sources, and IRS tax-exempt status documentation. Site visits sometimes are made to organizations being considered for a grant.

O+D+T Mary Ellen Linder [NY] (VP+Con) — Bertram N. Linder (P+F+Donor)

NE-089 Link Family Foundation, The
HC 88, Box 404
Pocono Lake 18347   (Monroe County)
AMV $1,534,478   **FYE** 12-00   (**Gifts Received** $0)

MI-12-13-41-42-43-56
Phone 570-646-2657 **FAX** None
EIN 23-7647088   **Year Created** 1990
6 **Grants totaling** $73,000

Mostly local/Pa. giving. High grants of **$20,000** each to Drexel U. (scholarship fund) and Student Partner Alliance (at-risk children program). **$10,000** each to Boy Scouts/Cradle of Liberty Council [Valley Forge] (for boys at risk) and Monroe County Head Start (books/reading materials). **Out-of-state** grants: **$10,000** to The Oaks Academy [IN] (scholarships) and **$3,000** to Coastal Georgia Historical Society (school history programs). ■**PUBLICATIONS:** None ■**WEBSITE:** None ■**E-MAIL:** None ■**APPLICATION POLICIES & PROCEDURES:** The Foundation reports that primary consideration is given to supporting education of the young and/or needy, especially for scholarships. Prospective applicants initially should make a telephone inquiry about the feasibility of submitting a request. Grant requests may be submitted in a letter during January—June (deadline is June 30th); include organizational/project budgets and a Board member list. Site visits sometimes are made to organizations being considered for a grant. Grants are awarded at a July meeting.

O+D+T Alfred H. Link (S+F+Donor+Con) — Elizabeth P. Link (P+Donor) — Paul M. Hannan (T) — Bruce Link [Orefield] (T) — Gary C. Link [NJ] (T) — Stephen C. Link [IN] (T)

NE-090 Lutron Foundation, The
1506 Pleasant View Road
Coopersburg 18036
          (Lehigh County)
AMV $2,402,751   **FYE** 12-00   (**Gifts Received** $750,000)

MI-11-13-15-17-22-39-41-42-52-54-55-57-81
85-89
Phone 610-282-3800 **FAX** None
EIN 23-2322928   **Year Created** 1984
120+ **Grants totaling** $366,888

About half local/Pa. giving; grants are for general purposes except as noted and some grants represent multiple payments. High grant of **$34,970** to United Way of Greater Lehigh Valley. **$30,000** to Eisenhower Exchange Fellowships [Philadelphia]. **$7,500** to Community Music School. **$7,000** to Cybersonics Technology Team. **$5,000** each to Banana Factory Community Arts Center, Bethlehem Musikfest Assn., and Penn State U. (automotive technology education center). **$4,152** to Muhlenberg College (pavilion opening). **$3,000-$3,875** to Allentown Art Museum (corporate membership/benefit event), DeSales U. (annual fund/theatre/benefit event), Lehigh Valley Chamber Orchestra, Mayfair, Pa. and Sinfonia. **$2,000-$2,500** each to Boy Scouts/Minsi Trails Council, Coopersburg Ambulance, Discovery Center of Science & Technology, Good Shepherd (annual fund/celebrity classic), Lehigh County Community College Foundation, The Program for Women & Families, and WLVT. **$1,000-$1,500** each to Assn. of Independent Colleges & Universities in Pa., Boys & Girls Club of Allentown, Burn Prevention Foundation, Coopersburg Fire Dept., Jewish University Center [Pittsburgh] (capital campaign), Lehigh Valley Business Education Partnership, Northampton Community College Foundation, Penn State U./Lehigh Valley, Upper Saucon Ambulance, and Upper Saucon Volunteer Fire Company. Other local contributions **$100-$795** for arts/cultural, civic, health, human service, historic, scholarships, and other purposes. **Out-of-state** giving includes **$26,000** to Massachusetts Institute of Technology (Japan Design Workshop/Teaching Excellence program); **$20,000** each to Emory U./Dept. of Medicine [GA], Ohio U., and Wellesley College [MA]; **$19,560** each to City of Hope [CA] (various program support) and Rensselaer Polytechnic Institute [NY] (Lighting Research Center). **$9,000** to Cornell U. (faculty support/scholarships). **$5,000** to National Electrical Safety Foundation [VA], Purdue U. [IN] (physics dept./award); and other grants/contributions for similar purposes. ■**PUBLICATIONS:** None ■**WEBSITE:** None ■**E-MAIL:** None ■**APPLICATION POLICIES & PROCEDURES:** Grant requests may be submitted in any form at any time. No grants awarded to individuals.

O+D+T Joel S. Spira (T+Donor+Con) — Ruth R. Spira (T+Donor) — Corporate donor: Lutron Electronics Co., Inc.

NE-091 Luzerne Foundation, The
East Mountain Corporate Center
613 Baltimore Drive
Wilkes-Barre 18702   (Luzerne County)
AMV $4,744,928   **FYE** 12-00   (**Gifts Received** $462,689)

MI-12-13-15-19-29-35-41-43-49-55-56-71
Phone 570-822-5420 **FAX** 570-208-9145
EIN 23-2765498   **Year Created** 1994
160 **Grants totaling** $247,426

As a Community Foundation all discretionary giving is limited to organizations serving Luzerne County—19 grants totaling about **$26,000** were awarded from unrestricted or field-of-interest funds. High grant of **$8,600** to Celebrity Luncheon (program support). **$3,500** to Greater Hazleton YMCA & YWCA (youth program). **$2,000-$2,500** each to Commission on Economic Opportunity (Kids' Cafe), Greater Hazleton Area Civic Partnership (playground renovation), and Wyoming Valley Alcohol & Drug Services (educational materials for school-community programs). **$1,000-$1,050** each to Children's Services Center of Wyoming Valley (children's day partial hospitalization program), Committee for Economic Growth (Great Valley Alliance), Forty Fort Cemetery Assn. (meeting house repairs), and North Branch Land Trust (conservation easement project). **$500-$725** each to Beer Creek Historical Society (interpretive panels), Forty Fort Cemetery (holiday program), Little Theatre of Wilkes-Barre (new doors), Luzerne County SPCA (video), Pa. Partnership for Children (advocacy network), and Volunteers to America (parent network).

Other smaller discretionary contributions for community projects. All other grants or scholarships were awarded from donor-advised or pass-through funds. ■**PUBLICATIONS:** Annual Report; newsletter; brochure with application guidelines; application form ■**WEBSITE:** www.luzernefoundation.org ■**E-MAIL:** LuzerneFdn@aol.com ■**APPLICATION POLICIES & PROCEDURES:** The Foundation reports that discretionary giving is restricted to Luzerne County nonprofit organizations and municipalities, for health/human services, arts/humanities, education, and environmental beautification/enhancement. Grants are awarded for creative/innovative programs, current or emerging charitable opportunities, services not presently offered, and occasional capital projects. Projects proposed by coalitions of service providers and those likely to secure matching funding are of particular interest. No support is given to cover annual operating budgets. Prospective applicants initially should make a telephone inquiry about the feasibility of submitting a request. Grant requests are accepted at any time but must be submitted on a Formal Application Form, available from the Foundation or on the website; the required supporting documentation and selection criteria are detailed on the form/website. Site visits sometimes are made to organizations being considered for a grant.

O+D+T Charles M. Barber (Executive Director+Con) — Charles D. Flack, Jr. [Wyoming] (C+D) — Charie K. Aponick [Shavertown] (D) — Stuart M. Bell [Plains] (D) — Frank H. Bevevino [Shavertown] (D) — John R. Bevevino [Shavertown] (D) — Daylene T. Burnside [Shavertown] (D) — Joseph F. Butcher [Plymouth] (D) — Terrence W. Casey [Dallas] (D) — Sherry Davidowitz [Dallas] (D) — Philip G. Decker [Kingston] (D) — Louis F. Goeringer [Hanover] (D) — Thomas L. Kennedy [Hazleton] (D) — Joseph E. Kluger, Esq. [Kingston] (D) — Kenneth J. Krogulski [Dallas] (D) — Gary F. Lamont [Sugarloaf] (D) — Melanie Maslow Lumia [Dallas] (D) — Rev. Andrew J. McGowan [Scranton] (D) — Michael F. Morgan [Scranton] (D) — A. Edward Nork (D) — Donald M. Pachence [West Hazleton] (D) — Joseph L. Persico, Esq. [Dallas] (D) — Mary R. Siegel [Forty Fort] (D) — Rhea P. Simms [Kingston] (D) — John T. Yudichak [Nanticoke] (D)

NE-092 Magee Foundation, The
c/o Magee Industrial Enterprises, Inc.
480 West 5th Street
Bloomsburg 17815   (Columbia County)

MI-11-12-13-15-22-25-29-32-35-39-41-42-44 51-54-57-63-84-89
Phone 570-784-4100 **FAX** None
EIN 23-6398294   **Year Created** 1964

AMV $2,185,410   **FYE** 10-00   **(Gifts Received** $0)   50 **Grants totaling** $119,038

Mostly local/Central Pa. giving. High grant of **$34,000** to Columbia County United Way. **$10,000** to Wesley United Methodist Church. **$6,000** to Bloomsburg U. Foundation. **$5,500** to Bloomsburg Theatre Ensemble (Project Discovery). **$5,000** to Columbia-Montour Home Health Services. **$4,500** to Bloomsburg Library. **$4,000** to Volunteers in Medicine. **$3,000** each to Boy Scouts and Red Cross. **$2,000-$2,500** each to American Cancer Society, American Heart Assn., Bloomsburg U. Trust Fund, Camp Victory, Columbia Day Care Center, Danville Child Development Center, Foundation for Independent Colleges, Habitat in Bloom, and Salvation Army. **$1,000-$1,500** each to Bloomsburg Ambulance Assn., Bloomsburg Fire Dept., Bloomsburg Town Park, Camp Dost, Children's Museum, Danville Community Center, Greenwood Friends School, Mental Health Assn., Pinnacle Health Hospice, Ronald McDonald House, Women's Center, WVIA-TV, and YMCA. Other local and out-of-state contributions for similar purposes. ■**PUBLICATIONS:** None ■**WEBSITE:** None ■**E-MAIL:** None ■**APPLICATION POLICIES & PROCEDURES:** No grants awarded to individuals.

O+D+T Drue A. Magee (PO+T+Con) — Joanne Magee Katerman (T) — Audrey R Magee (T) — James A. Magee (T) — Barbara Paule (T) — Corporate donor: Magee Industrial Enterprises

---

NE-093 Margolies (Albert) Trust for Charities
c/o First Union/Wachovia - PA2106
640 Hamilton Street
Allentown 18101   (Lehigh County)

MI-14-22-31-62

Phone 610-439-4686 **FAX** 610-740-1207
EIN 23-7840492   **Year Created** 1996

AMV $974,584   **FYE** 4-01   **(Gifts Received** $0)   4 **Grants totaling** $59,200

All giving restricted to Scranton area; all grants are for general support. **$14,800** each to Geisinger Foundation, Jewish Community Center of Scranton, Pa. Assn. of the Blind/Lackawanna County, and Red Cross/Scranton. ■**PUBLICATIONS:** None ■**WEBSITE:** None ■ **E-MAIL:** None ■**APPLICATION POLICIES & PROCEDURES:** The Trust reports that only charities in the Scranton area are eligible to apply. Grant requests in any form may be submitted at any time. — **Note:** In Fall 2002, administration of this Trust will move to a First Union office in Reading; call 610-655-3148 for updated information.

O+D+T James A. Kressler (VP at Bank+Con) — Donor: Estate of Albert Margolis

---

NE-094 Marquardt (Richard C.) Family Foundation
BDA Building, Suite 102, Abington Executive Park
Clarks Summit 18411   (Lackawanna County)

MI-11-29-32-41-42-44-49-52-54-63-85
Phone 570-586-9237 **FAX** None
EIN 23-2896467   **Year Created** 1997

AMV $1,673,121   **FYE** 12-00   **(Gifts Received** $101,344)   47 **Grants totaling** $131,700

Mostly local giving. High grant of **$36,500** to Lehigh U. **$21,000** to Covenant Presbyterian Church of Scranton. **$15,000** to United Way of Lackawanna County. **$10,000** to The Hill School [Pottstown].**$7,000** to U. of Scranton. **$6,150** to Scranton Area Foundation. **$5,250** to Marywood U. **$5,000** to Scranton Tomorrow. **$3,000** to Penn State U. **$2,100** to Waverly Community House. **$1,000-$1,200** each to Abington Community Library, Allied Services Foundation, Everhart Museum, Johnston Technical Institute, Junior Achievement of NE Pa., Lackawanna Pro Bono, Lackawanna Junior College, NE Pa. Philharmonic, NE Regional Cancer Institute, Red Cross, and Scranton Preparatory School. Other smaller contributions for various purposes. **Out-of-state** giving primarily small contributions to FL. ■**PUBLICATIONS:** None ■**WEBSITE:** None ■**E-MAIL:** None ■**APPLICATION POLICIES & PROCEDURES:** Grant requests may be submitted at any time on organizational letterhead; include IRS tax-exempt status documentation.

O+D+T Richard C. Marquardt [Waverly] (P+F+Donor+Con) — Sarah W. Marquardt [Waverly] (VP+S) — Jeffrey W. Marquardt [MA] (D)

NE-095 **Martin Guitar Charitable Foundation**   **MI**-42-51-52-54-55-56-57
c/o C.F. Martin Guitar Company
510 Sycamore Street   **Phone** 610-759-2837   **FAX** 610-759-5757
Nazareth   18064   (Northampton County)   **EIN** 31-1483218   **Year Created** 1996
AMV $853,084   **FYE** 12-00   **(Gifts Received** $200,000)   7 **Grants totaling** $22,500

Mostly local/Pa. giving; all grants are general donations. High grants of **$5,000** each to Northampton Community College Foundation and Philadelphia Folk Festival. **$2,500** each to Godfrey Daniels, Sing Out Corp. of Bethlehem, State Center Theatre for the Arts, and WDIY-FM. **Out-of-state** grant: **$2,500** to Museum of Making Music [CA]. — In prior year, high grant of **$8,300** to Moravian Historical Society. ■**PUBLICATIONS:** None ■**WEBSITE:** www.cfmartin.com [corporate information only] ■**E-MAIL:** None ■**APPLICATION POLICIES & PROCEDURES:** Information not available.

O+D+T Christian F. Martin, IV (P+Con) — Diane S. Repyneck (S) — Sylvia Fehnel (F) — Corporate donor: C.F. Martin Guitar Company

---

NE-096 **Maslow Family Foundation**   **MI**-14-42-44-51-54-55-63
"Four Views," Huntsville Road, RR 4   **Phone** 570-674-6532   **FAX** None
Dallas   18612   (Luzerne County)   **EIN** 23-2791676   **Year Created** 1994
AMV $3,937,875   **FYE** 12-00   **(Gifts Received** $126,460)   8 **Grants totaling** $150,500

About one-third local giving. High Pa. grant of **$14,000** to Everhart Museum. **$10,000** each to College Misericordia, Greater Wilkes-Barre Association for the Blind, and F.M. Kirby Center for the Performing Arts. **$3,500** to First Presbyterian Church of Wilkes-Barre. **$2,000** to Little Theatre of Wilkes-Barre. **$1,000** to Back Mountain Library. **Out-of-state** grant: **$100,000** to Philo Center for Sensory-Based Evaluation & Treatment [VT]. ■**PUBLICATIONS:** None ■**WEBSITE:** None ■**E-MAIL:** None ■ **APPLICATION POLICIES & PROCEDURES:** The Foundation reports that giving generally focuses on the greater Wyoming Valley area. Most grants are for building/renovation, capital campaigns, general support, challenge grants, and seed money. No grants awarded to individuals. Grant requests may be submitted in a letter at any time.

O+D+T Richard Maslow (P+D+Donor+Con) — Douglas Maslow (VP+D) — Jennifer Maslow Holtzman [Shavertown] (S+D) — Melanie Maslow Lumia (F+D) — Allison Maslow [NY] (D) — Leslie Maslow [NY] (D) — Hilary Maslow Naud [VT] (D) — Eugene Roth, Esq. [Wilkes-Barre] (D)

NE-097 **McCole Foundation**   **MI**-11-13-22-29-32-41-42-44-52-55-61
c/o Kronick Kalda Berdy & Company
190 Lathrop Street   **Phone** 570-283-2727   **FAX** None
Kingston   18704   (Luzerne County)   **EIN** 23-2439590   **Year Created** 1986
AMV $1,588,420   **FYE** 12-00   **(Gifts Received** $33,398)   19 **Grants totaling** $113,453

Mostly local/Pa. giving; grants are for general operations except as noted and some comprise multiple payments. High grant of **$25,000** to Wyoming Seminary. **$20,204** to Wilkes U. (McCole House repairs/insurance premium). **$12,775** to College Misericordia (educational purposes/insurance premium). **$12,000** to YMCA of Wilkes-Barre (capital campaign/camperships). **$10,000** to King's College. **$5,000** to Catholic Youth Center (capital fund). **$3,699** to U. of Scranton (general operations/insurance premium). **$3,000** to Northeast Regional Cancer Institute. **$2,000-$2,500** each to The American College of Chartered Life Underwriters [Bryn Mawr], Junior Achievement of NE Pa., F.M. Kirby Center for the Performing Arts, Leadership Wilkes-Barre, Northeastern Pa. Philharmonic, Osterhout Free Library, United Way of Lackawanna County, and United Way of Wyoming Valley. **$1,000** each to Hoyt Library and St. Vincent DePaul Kitchen. **$500** to Luzerne Foundation (celebrity luncheon). ■**PUBLICA-TIONS:** None ■**WEBSITE:** None ■**E-MAIL:** None ■**APPLICATION POLICIES & PROCEDURES:** Contact the Foundation for application guidelines which are being developed.

O+D+T William R. Lazor, CPA (F+Con) — Dr. Cornelius E. McCole [MI] (C+VP) — Constance K. McCole [Clarks Summit] (P) — Allan M Kluger, Esq. [Wilkes-Barre] (S) — Donor: Estate of John A. McCole.

NE-098 **Miorelli (Robert J. & Louise P.) Foundation**   **MI**-61
c/o Fleet Bank, Trust Dept.
1 Bethlehem Plaza   **Phone** 610-997-7740   **FAX** 610-865-8636
Bethlehem   18018   (Lehigh County)   **EIN** 23-7816449   **Year Created** 1995
AMV $109,371   **FYE** 12-00   **(Gifts Received** $0)   1 **Grant of** $11,026

Sole grant to Our Lady of Mt. Carmel Church [Hazleton]. ■**PUBLICATIONS:** None ■**WEBSITE:** None ■**E-MAIL:** None ■**APPLI-CATION POLICIES & PROCEDURES:** Information not available.

O+D+T William Evans (VP at Bank+Con) — Louis J. Miorelli [Conyngham] (Co-T) — Robert Miorelli [CT] (Co-T) — Louise P. Miorelli (Donor) — Robert J. Miorelli (Donor) — Fleet Bank (Corporate Co-Trustee)

NE-099 **Mitrani Family Foundation**   **MI**-11-13-22-32-42-52-62-89
c/o Milco Industries, Inc.
550 East 5th Street, P.O. Box 568   **Phone** 570-784-0400   **FAX** 570-387-8433
Bloomsburg   17815   (Columbia County)   **EIN** 24-6018102   **Year Created** 1959
AMV $3,631,210   **FYE** 12-00   **(Gifts Received** $0)   200+ **Grants totaling** $295,387

About one-third local/Pa. giving; many grants comprise multiple payments. High grant of **$43,049** to Bloomsburg U. **$11,000** to Beth Israel Congregation. **$9,125** to U. of Pittsburgh. **$8,200** to United Way of Columbia County. **$8,000** to Bloomsburg U. Foundation. **$7,489** to Penn State U. **$5,612** to Indiana U. of Pa. **$4,000-$4,500** each to Clarion U., Pa. College of Technology, and York College of Pa. **$3,250-$3,800** each to American Cancer Society, Bloomsburg Theatre Ensemble, Lycoming College, and

Penn State U. (Levi Lamb Fund). **$2,000-$2,715** each to Berwick Area YMCA, Dickinson College, King's College, and Luzerne County Community College. **$1,000-$1,500** each to Bloomsburg Police Dept., Central Pa. Forum for the Future, First Night Bloomsburg, and Villanova U. Other grants/contributions to organizations and individuals for various purposes. **Out-of-state** giving, primarily to NY or for Israel, includes **$27,100** to American Technion Society; **$20,000** to American Friends of Ben Gurion U.; **$10,236** to American Sephardi Federation [NY]; **$10,000** each to Jupiter Symphony [NY] and Parsons Fashion Critics Award Benefit [NY]; **$5,000** each to Lincoln Center [NY] and Megiddo Expedition [Israel]. ■**PUBLICATIONS:** None ■**WEBSITE:** None ■**E-MAIL:** None ■ **APPLICATION POLICIES & PROCEDURES:** The Foundation reports that unsolicited requests for support are not accepted.

O+D+T Norman Belmonte (P+Con) — Leonard Comerchero [Berwick] (VP) — Corporate donor: Milco Industries, Inc.

NE-100   Mitrani (Jacques H.) Foundation

214 Elan Gardens		MI-15-22-34-62-82
		Phone 570-585-4475 **FAX** None
Clarks Summit 18411	(Lackawanna County)	**EIN** 23-7103779 **Year Created** 1969
AMV $343,389 **FYE** 7-00	**(Gifts Received** $0)	11 **Grants totaling** $2,850

Mostly local giving. High grant of **$1,000** to The Sephardic Home. **$500** to Anti-Defamation League. **$450** to Beth Israel Congregation. Other contributions **$50-$250** for various purposes. — In the prior year, major grants included **$100,000** to Misgav Hadack General Hospital [Jerusalem] and **$1,000** to The Sephardic Home. Also, in earlier years medical scholarships were awarded. ■**PUBLICATIONS:** None ■**WEBSITE:** None ■**E-MAIL:** None ■**APPLICATION POLICIES & PROCEDURES:** Scholarship applicants must be Columbia County residents pursuing medical studies; submit applications in a letter with high school scholastic records and SAT results before the May 15th deadline.

O+D+T Selma T. Mitrani (T+Donor+Con) — Leonard Comerchero (T) — Ralph Reissman [NY] (T)

NE-101   Moffat Charitable Trust

c/o PNC Advisors/Northeast Pa.		MI-12-15-22-31-32-35-56-63-72-84
201 Penn Ave., P.O. Box 937		**Phone** 570-961-7341 **FAX** 570-961-7269
Scranton 18501	(Lackawanna County)	**EIN** 23-6967783 **Year Created** 1989
AMV $580,666 **FYE** 12-00	**(Gifts Received** $0)	23 **Grants totaling** $29,050

Mostly local/Pa. giving. High grant of **$10,000** to Historical Society of Western Pa. [Pittsburgh]. **$2,500** to Presbyterian Church of Dunmore. **$2,000** each to Mercy Home Health & Hospice and St. Joseph's Hospital. **$1,000** each to Humane Society of Lackawanna County, Keystone Gymnastics, Salvation Army [Philadelphia], and St. Francis of Assisi Kitchen. Other smaller local contributions for health/human services and other purposes. **Out-of-state** giving includes **$3,000** to Shriners Hospitals for Children [FL] and **$2,200** to St. Jude Children's Research Hospital [TN]. ■**PUBLICATIONS:** None ■**WEBSITE:** None ■**E-MAIL:** None ■ **APPLICATION POLICIES & PROCEDURES:** Grant requests may be submitted in any form at any time.

O+D+T Joseph Paddock (VP at Bank+Con) — Robert Y. Moffat, Jr. [Moscow] (T+Donor) — PNC Advisors/Northeast Pa. (Trustee)

NE-102   Mooney (Michael J.) Charitable Trust

201 Bowman Street		MI-14-22-25-31-32-42-61
		Phone 570-822-5872 **FAX** None
Wilkes-Barre 18702	(Luzerne County)	**EIN** 23-7875628 **Year Created** 1997
AMV $334,620 **FYE** 12-00	**(Gifts Received** $0)	15 **Grants totaling** $15,075

Mostly local giving. High grant of **$2,500** to American Diabetes Assn. **$2,300** to Greater Wilkes-Barre Assn. of the Blind. **$1,000-$1,500** each to First United Methodist Church (Community Thanksgiving), Friendly Sons of St. Patrick, King's College (annual fund), Muscular Dystrophy Assn. of NE Pa., and St. Vincent DePaul Kitchen. Other smaller local contributions. **Out-of-state** giving includes **$1,500** to St. Jude Children's Research Hospital [TN] and **$1,000** to Little Sisters of the Poor [KY]. ■**PUBLICATIONS:** None ■**WEBSITE:** None ■**E-MAIL:** None ■**APPLICATION POLICIES & PROCEDURES:** No grants awarded to individuals.

O+D+T Joseph T. Coyne (T+Con)

NE-103   Morgan (John E.) Charitable Trust II

P.O. Box 349		MI-12-15-22-31-41-42-44-52-89
		Phone 570-386-3554 **FAX** None
Tamaqua 18252	(Schuylkill County)	**EIN** 52-1761389 **Year Created** 1992
AMV $6,258,802 **FYE** 12-01	**(Gifts Received** $4,250,000)	8 **Grants totaling** $320,500

Mostly local/NE Pa. giving. High grant of **$250,000** to Children's Home of Reading. **$32,000** to Tamaqua Public Library. **$12,500** to Schuylkill Symphony Orchestra. **$10,000** to Tamaqua High School. **$5,000** to Tamaqua Area Adult Day Care. Other local contributions **$500** each. **Out-of-state** grant of **$10,000** to Palm Beach Atlantic College [FL]. — Grants awarded in the prior year included **$1,500,000** each to Gnaden Huetten Hospital and Miners Medical Center; **$800,000** to Delaware Valley College; **$100,000** to Bethany Evangelical Congregational Church of Tamaqua; **$45,000** to West Penn Fire Company [New Ringgold]; **$40,000** to Salvation Army/Tamaqua; and **$12,000** to Tamaqua Public Library. ■**PUBLICATIONS:** None. ■ **WEBSITE:** None ■**E-MAIL:** None ■**APPLICATION POLICIES & PROCEDURES:** Information not available.

O+D+T Harry B. Loder (Executive Trustee+Con) — John Eddy [NJ] (F+T) — Dorothy Morgan [Andreas] (T+Donor) — Jay R. Wagner [Reading] (T) — James Zigmant [Tamaqua] (T)

NE-104 **Oppenheim Foundation**
718 Taylor Avenue
Scranton 18510   (Lackawanna County)

MI-11-14-15-22-29-42-52-54-62-85
Phone 570-344-4131 **FAX** None
EIN 23-6296919 **Year Created** 1946

AMV $1,689,553   **FYE** 12-01   (**Gifts Received** $0)   49 **Grants totaling** $101,925

About half local/Pa. giving. High Pa. grant of **$20,000** to Congregation Keneseth Israel [Allentown]. **$15,000** to Keystone College. **$12,000** to United Way of Lackawanna County. **$10,000** to U. of Scranton. **$6,500** to Jewish Federation of Wyoming Valley. **$5,000** each to Jewish Community Center and Volunteer Action Center. **$3,200** to Temple Hesed. **$1,000-$1,100** each to Allied Services for the Handicapped, Everhart Museum, Jewish Home of Eastern Pa., Marywood U., Northeastern Pa. Philharmonic, and Scranton Tomorrow. Other local contributions **$50-$550** for various community organizations. **Out-of-state** giving includes **$5,300** Union for American Hebrew Congresssions [NY]; **$2,800** to World Union for Progresssive Judaism; and **$2,000** to Hunter College [NY]. ■**PUBLICATIONS:** None ■**WEBSITE:** None ■**E-MAIL:** None ■**APPLICATION POLICIES & PROCEDURES:** The Foundation reports that giving generally focuses on the Scranton area. No grants awarded to individuals. Prospective applicants initially should make a telephone inquiry about the feasibility of submitting a request. Grant requests may be submitted in a letter (on organizational letterhead) at any time; state the amount requested and the purpose of the funds.

O+D+T Jane E. Oppenheim (P+F+Con) — Susan Dimond [Kingston] (S)

NE-105 **Overlook Estate Foundation**
P.O. Box 225
Dalton 18414   (Lackawanna County)

MI-13-42-55-71
Phone 570-563-1217 **FAX** None
EIN 16-1526226 **Year Created** 1997

AMV $937,934   **FYE** 12-00   (**Gifts Received** $52,278)   8 **Grants totaling** $43,362

Mostly local giving. High grant of **$30,000** to Countryside Conservancy (environmental acquisition). **$2,000-$2,600** each to Keystone College (environmental project), Marywood College (environmental project), Scranton Cultural Center (general support), Wilkes U. (graduate program). **$1,600** to U. of Scranton (university success program). **Out-of-state** giving includes **$1,162** to Olmstead Landscape Project [NY] and **$1,000** to Jon Bonaire Foundation [NY] (youth center improvements). ■**PUBLICATIONS:** None ■**WEBSITE:** None ■**E-MAIL:** None ■**APPLICATION POLICIES & PROCEDURES:** Grant requests in any form may be submitted at any time to Mortimer B. Fuller III, 71 Lewis Street, Greenwich, CT 06830.

O+D+T Frances Gunster (F+Con) — Mortimer B. Fuller, III [CT] (P) — Patricia A. Fuller [RI] (S+Donor) — Frances A. Fuller (Donor)

NE-106 **Passan (John J. & Marjorie M.) Foundation**
c/o Valley Distributing & Storage
1 Passan Drive
Wilkes-Barre 18702   (Luzerne County)

MI-11-22-32-41-42-62

Phone 570-654-2403 **FAX** 570-654-4206
EIN 23-2870593 **Year Created** 1997

AMV $713,978   **FYE** 9-00   (**Gifts Received** $0)   7 **Grants totaling** $69,400

Mostly local giving. High grant of **$50,000** to Wilkes U. **$10,000** to United Way of Wyoming Valley. **$5,000** to Temple Israel. **$1,000-$1,200** each to Jewish Federation of Greater Wilkes-Barre, Kings College, Michael Wolk Heart Foundation [NY], and Wyoming Seminary. ■**PUBLICATIONS:** None ■**WEBSITE:** None ■**E-MAIL:** None ■**APPLICATION POLICIES & PROCEDURES:** Information not available.

O+D+T John J. Passan [Laflin] (D+Con) — Michael O'Boyle [Jenkins Twp.] (D) — Ann Passan [Laflin] (D) — Corporate donor: Valley Distributing & Storage

---

NE-107 **Pearsall (Adrian M. & Doris K.) Family Foundation**
1950 Englewood Ave.
Forty Fort 18704   (Luzerne County)

MI-11-13-41-42-43-44-52-55-56-63
Phone 570-287-3141 **FAX** None
EIN 23-2963241 **Year Created** 1998

AMV $802,346   **FYE** 12-00   (**Gifts Received** $0)   24 **Grants totaling** $40,370

About one-third local giving. High Pa. grant of **$8,000** to Kirby Center for the Performing Arts. **$2,750** to United Way of Lackawanna County. **$2,250** to Church of Christ Uniting of Kingston. **$1,500** each to Family YMCA of Wilkes-Barre and Wyoming Seminary. **$500** to Dorranceton Methodist Church. Other local contributions **$10-$100** for various purposes. **Out-of-state** giving includes **$10,000** each to Ulysses Historical Society [NY] and Ulysses Philomathic Library [NY]; and **$2,500** to Ithaca College (scholarship fund). ■**PUBLICATIONS:** None ■**WEBSITE:** None ■**E-MAIL:** None ■**APPLICATION POLICIES & PROCEDURES:** No grants awarded to individuals.

O+D+T Adrian M. Pearsall (P+Donor+Con) — Doris K. Pearsall (VP+Donor) — Kenneth J. Krogulski (S+F)

NE-108 **Pearsall (Richard L. & Marion K.) Family Foundation**
Highland Acres, RR4
Dallas 18612   (Luzerne County)

MI-11-41-42-44-63-52-55-56-72
Phone 570-675-3127 **FAX** None
EIN 23-2954560 **Year Created** 1998

AMV $798,686   **FYE** 12-00   (**Gifts Received** $0)   9 **Grants totaling** $89,200

Mostly local giving; all grants are unrestricted support. High grant of **$52,500** to Wilkes U. **$6,200** to Church of Christ Uniting of Kingston. **$5,500** to Kirby Center for the Performing Arts. **$4,000** to Luzerne County SPCA. **$3,500** to United Way of Wyoming Valley. **$3,000** to Wyoming Seminary. **$2,500** to Kings College Library. **$2,000** to Back Mountain Library. **Out-of-state** grant: **$10,000** to Ulysses Historical Society Museum [NY]. ■**PUBLICATIONS:** None. ■**WEBSITE:** None ■**E-MAIL:** None ■**APPLICATION POLICIES & PROCEDURES:** No grants awarded to individuals.

O+D+T Richard L. Pearsall (P+Donor+Con) — Marion K. Pearsall (S+F)

NE-109 Penske (Richard & Patricia) Foundation
1851 Saucon Valley Road
Bethlehem 18015 (Northampton County)

MI-14-15-22-31-41-42-55-63
Phone 610-909-9393 **FAX** None
EIN 23-2858131 **Year Created** 1996

AMV $84,960 **FYE** 12-00 (**Gifts Received** $0) 22 **Grants totaling** $25,635

All local giving. High grant of **$11,125** to Lehigh U. **$3,000** each to Meals on Wheels/Lehigh Valley and New Bethany Ministries. **$2,000** to DeSales U. **$1,000** each to Banana Factory Community Arts Center, Moravian Academy, Recording for the Blind & Dyslexic, and St. Luke's Hospital. Other local contributions **$35-$500** for various community organizations. ■**PUBLICA-TIONS:** None ■**WEBSITE:** None ■**E-MAIL:** None ■**APPLICATION POLICIES & PROCEDURES:** No grants awarded to individuals.

O+D+T Richard H. Penske (P+Con) — Patricia L. Penske (VP) — Victoria L. Penske-Aitchinson (S) — Crislyn A. Penske [NY] (F)

NE-110 Perin (Ronald R. & Linda S.) Trust
c/o Parkhill Realty
818 Grand Central Road, P.O. Box 7
Pen Argyl 18072 (Northampton County)

MI-12-13-14-15-31-42-51-72

Phone 610-863-7070 **FAX** None
EIN 23-7895570 **Year Created** 1997

AMV $305,194 **FYE** 12-00 (**Gifts Received** $0) 12 **Grants totaling** $13,000

All local giving; all grants are for general operating support. High grants of **$2,500** each to Big Brothers/Big Sisters and Good Shepherd Home. **$1,000** each to Burnley Workshop, Guiding Eyes for the Blind, Lehigh Valley Hospice, Lehigh Valley Hospital, Northampton Community College, and State Theatre. Other local contributions **$500** each for animal humane and other purposes. ■**PUBLICATIONS:** None ■**WEBSITE:** None ■**E-MAIL:** None ■**APPLICATION POLICIES & PROCEDURES:** The Foundation reports that giving is limited to Lehigh Valley organizations. Grant requests may be submitted at any time in proposal; include IRS tax-exempt status documentation.

O+D+T Ronald R. Perin (T+Donor+Con) — Linda S. Perin (T+Donor+Con)

NE-111 Perkin (Sylvia) Perpetual Charitable Trust
2919 Tilghman Street
P.O. Box 443
Allentown 18105 (Lehigh County)

MI-12-13-14-15-17-18-22-41-42-51-52-54-56-57-62-65-85

Phone 610-776-0369 **FAX** None
EIN 23-6792999 **Year Created** 1986

AMV $8,230,405 **FYE** 4-01 (**Gifts Received** $0) 41 **Grants totaling** $455,200

All giving restricted to the Lehigh Valley; grants are for general purposes. High grant of **$60,000** to Jewish Family Service. **$45,000** to Muhlenberg College. **$40,000** each to Jewish Community Center and Jewish Federation of the Lehigh Valley. **$28,000** to Cedar Crest College. **$20,000** each to Allentown Art Museum, Allentown Economic Development Corp., America On Wheels, Lehigh Valley Child Care, Inc., and Lehigh Valley Public Telecommunications Corporation. **$15,000** to Congregation Keneseth Israel. **$10,000** to Lehigh County Historical Society. **$8,000** to Red Cross. **$7,500** each to Allentown Symphony. **$6,500** to Planned Parenthood of NE Pa. **$6,000** to Meals on Wheels. **$5,000** each to Allentown Public Library, Allentown YMCA-YWCA Council, Camelot for Children, Family & Counseling Services, Lehigh County Conference of Churches, Lehigh Valley Center for Independent Living, Lehigh Valley Community Broadcasters, LifePath, and Valley Youth House. **$4,500** to Program for Women & Families. **$4,000** to Repertory Dance Theatre. **$3,000-$3,500** each to Assn. for the Blind, Community Music School, Hillside School, and Union & West End Cemetery. **$2,000-$2,500** each to Ballet Guild of the Lehigh Valley, Boys Club of Allentown, Civic Theatre of Allentown, Community Bike Works, Community Services for Children, Good Shepherd, Pa. Assn. for Retarded Citizens, Phoebe-Devitt Homes, and Pinebrook Services for Children. **$1,500** to Girls Club of Allentown. ■**PUBLICATIONS:** None ■**WEBSITE:** None ■**E-MAIL:** None ■**APPLICATION POLICIES & PROCEDURES:** The Trust reports that only Lehigh Valley organizations are eligible to apply. Grant requests may be submitted in a letter during December-February—the deadline is February 28th; include descriptive literature about the organization and IRS tax-exempt status documentation. Grants are awarded at meetings in March and April.

O+D+T Hon. Arnold C. Rapoport, Esq. (Co-T+Con) — James D. Christie (Co-T) — First Union/Wachovia (Co-Trustee)

NE-112 Pharo Foundation
c/o Cempro, Inc.
298 Keystone Drive
Bethlehem 18017 (Northampton County)

MI-15-25-29-31-42-44-52-56-63

Phone 610-837-6719 **FAX** None
EIN 23-7376724 **Year Created** 1974

AMV $854,023 **FYE** 12-00 (**Gifts Received** $0) 21 **Grants totaling** $35,183

Mostly local giving. High grants of **$5,000** each to Community Action Committee of the Lehigh Valley and St. Luke's Hospital (in-patient hospice). **$4,700** to Central Moravian Church. **$3,000** to Advent Moravian Church. **$2,000-$2,500** each to Habitat for Humanity/Allentown, Moravian College Music Dept., Moravian Historical Society, and Northampton County Community College. **$1,000-$1,300** each to Kirkland Village, Memorial Library of Nazareth, and Moravian College. Other smaller local contributions for various purposes. **Out-of-state** grant: **$2,500** to Masterworks Chorale [MA].##### ■**PUBLICATIONS:** None ■
WEBSITE: None ■**E-MAIL:** None ■**APPLICATION POLICIES & PROCEDURES:** The Foundation reports that capital projects have priority over operating support. Prospective applicants initially should make a telephone inquiry about the feasibility of submitting a request. Grant requests may be submitted in a letter (2 pages maximum) at any time; include a project budget and IRS tax-exempt status documentation.

O+D+T John W. Pharo (S+Donor+Con) — Donald N. Pharo (P+Donor) — Robert S. Pharo (VP+Donor)

NE-113   Pool (Dorothy Rider) Health Care Trust   MI-12-31-32-34-35-39
Suite 202,
1050 South Cedar Crest Boulevard   **Phone** 610-770-9346 **FAX** 610-770-9361
Allentown 18103   (Lehigh County)   **EIN** 23-6627932   **Year Created** 1976
AMV $68,435,515   **FYE** 12-01   (**Gifts Received** $0)   21 **Grants totaling** $6,127,613

All giving restricted to the Lehigh Valley for improving the health of area residents. Twelve grants for Lehigh Valley Hospital &
Health Network were approved/appropriated for various departments or programs: **$2,700,000** (over 5 years) to Dept. of Medi-
cine/Program to Improve the Department of Medicine's Education/Residency Program. **$1,500,000** each (in perpetuity) to
Dept. of Family Practice/Leonard Parker Pool Chair and the Dept. of Medicine/Leonard Parker Pool Chair. **$375,000** (over 5
years) for Peggy Fleming Endowed Chair in Nursing. **$350,000** (over 6 months) for Health Studies Bridge Grant. **$225,000**
(over 3 years) to Dept. of Obstetrics & Gynecology/Chair's Discretionary Fund. **$200,000** (over 3 years) to Dept. of Medi-
cine/Anticoagulation Service. **$180,000** (over 3 years) to Dept. of Emergency Medicine/Emergency Medicine Residency Pro-
gram at LVH-Muhlenberg. **$150,000** (over 3 years) to Dept. of Emergency Medicine/Sexual Assault Response Team. **$120,000**
(over 3 years) to Physician Leaders in the Lehigh Valley. **$25,000** (over 1 year) for The Cycle of Life at Nite Lites. **$20,000** (over
3 years) to Dept. of Surgery (develop a Cardiac Surgery Database for Academic Research and Performance Analysis. **OTHER
GRANTS** to Lehigh Valley health service providers: **$100,000** to The Wellness Community of the Greater Lehigh Valley (general
operating support). **$90,000** Child Advocacy Center of Lehigh County (forensic interviewer support-3 years). **$50,000** to Good
Shepherd Rehabilitation Hospital (MS Day Hospital Wellness Program-2 years). **$30,000** each to City of Allentown (thermal im-
aging cameras) and DeSales University (Lehigh Valley Nursing Camp-3 years). **$11,211** to Jenn's Hospital Hospitality House
(matching grant). ■**PUBLICATIONS:** Annual Report; grant application guidelines ■**WEBSITE:** www.pooltrust.com ■**E-MAIL:**
drpool@ptd.net ■**APPLICATION POLICIES & PROCEDURES:** The Foundation reports that giving is restricted to the Lehigh Valley in six priority categories: Access to Care, Community Health, Health Studies, Medical Education, Clinical Innovation, and Re-
cruitment/Retention of Talented Persons at Lehigh Valley Hospital. Historically, the Trust's major beneficiary has been the Lehigh
Valley Hospital & Health Network (LVHHN), but other health service providers in the Lehigh Valley are eligible for support, including collaborative projects with LVHHN. Multiyear grants are awarded, but none for equipment or building funds. Applicants
with a proposed project matching one of the six priority categories above should submit a Letter of Intent (5 pages maximum)
covering very briefly the six Proposal Elements listed below; deadlines for Letters of Intent are March 1st and August 1st. If the
program proposed in the Letter of Intent is of interest to the Trustees (and the grant is large), a full proposal will be invited covering the following Proposal Elements: (1) Purpose: Provide a one page (or shorter) summary of the request's purpose, including
how it matches with one of the above identified priority areas, and an itemized list of concrete, measurable goals or expected outcomes. (2) Method: Describe the specific outcome indicators or measurable deliverables that will result directly from this proposed program/project. Provide a work plan, including time schedule and list those responsible for accomplishing the objectives.
(3) Leadership: List the qualifications, credentials or experience of the project leader and the responsible person relative to each
objective. (4) Measurement: Describe the method of evaluating progress and effectiveness, to determine if the intended goals are
being/will be met. (5) Budget: Attach a fully defined budget that includes total project costs, including a list of all committed and
projected sources of financial support. (6) Sustainability: If it is not a contained study, how will the program activity be continued
after the Trust's funding ends? (7) IRS tax-exempt status documentation must be provided. Site visits sometimes are made to organizations being considered for a grant.
O+D+T Ronald C. Dendas (Program Officer+Con) — Joseph J. Napolitano (Program Officer+Con) — Edward F. Meehan, MPH
(Executive Director) — H.A. Wagner (C+T) — S. Brooke Cheston [Philadelphia] (T) — Lawrence P. Levitt, M.D. (T) — Carol M.
McCarthy, Ph.D., J.D. [MD] (T) — Andrew G. Wallace, M.D. [NC] (T) — PNC Bank N.A. (Corporate Trustee)

NE-114   Quin (Robert D. & Margaret W.) Foundation   MI-11-12-13-23
c/o Northeast Pa. Trust Co.
31 West Broad Street   **Phone** 570-459-4240 **FAX** None
Hazleton 18201   (Luzerne County)   **EIN** 22-2439876   **Year Created** 1984
AMV $9,733   **FYE** 12-00   (**Gifts Received** $18,952)   40 **Grants totaling** $16,496

All local giving. High grant of **$3,000** to Greater Hazleton YMCA/YWCA (summer camp). **$1,500** to United Way of Greater
Hazleton (special programs). All other disbursements, mostly under **$700** each, are to assist local, needy individuals or families
with personal needs: day care, household furniture, medical/dental bills, medicine, tutoring, enrichment activities, etc. ■**PUBLI-
CATIONS:** Brochure and Application Form ■**WEBSITE:** None ■**E-MAIL:** None ■**APPLICATION POLICIES & PROCEDURES:**
The Foundation reports that assistance is restricted to individuals/families who are: (a) 19 years or younger, (b) living within 10
miles of Hazleton City Hall, (c) a resident for one year or more, and (d) meet financial requirements. A formal application form,
available from the Foundation, may be submitted at any time.
O+D+T Eugene F. Gallagher [Freeland] (P+Con) — Thelma Yuhas [Wilkes-Barre] (S+D) — Mary Ann Zubris (F+D) — Jane
Bartol [West Hazleton] (D) — Rev. Thomas Cvammen [Conyngham] (D) — Lori Roth [Drums] (D) — Beth M. Turnbach (D) — (D)

NE-115   Raymond-Cryder Foundation   MI-43-52
c/o Stitt & Cordts
101 South 3rd Street, P.O. Box 483   **Phone** 610-253-9111 **FAX** 610-258-3150
Easton 18044   (Northampton County)   **EIN** 23-2663528   **Year Created** 1991
AMV $772,230   **FYE** 12-00   (**Gifts Received** $0)   3 **Grants totaling** $17,000

All grants for are music scholarship funds. One Pa. grant: **$5,000** to West Chester U. **Out-of-state** grants: **$7,000** to Julliard
School [NY] and **$5,000** to Duke U. [NC]. ■**PUBLICATIONS:** None ■**WEBSITE:** None ■**E-MAIL:** None ■**APPLICATION**

POLICIES & PROCEDURES: The Foundation reports that giving is restricted to the education of adults/children in the instruction of music, literacy, and health. Scholarship funds are awarded only to institutions of higher education; no grants awarded to individuals.

O+D+T Thomas P. Stitt, Sr. Esq. (T+Con) — John D. Raymond [Bethlehem] (T+Donor) — Melinda M. Stitt (T)

NE-116   Reidler Foundation, The
    c/o Fleet Bank, Trust Dept.
    101 West Broad Street
    Hazleton   18201   (Luzerne County)

MI-11-13-18-25-29-31-35-41-42-43-44-53-55
56-57-63-71-82
Phone 570-459-4251 **FAX** None
EIN 24-6022888   **Year Created** 1944

AMV $10,288,676   **FYE** 10-00   **(Gifts Received** $30,984)   55 **Grants totaling** $465,000

Mostly local/NE Pa. giving; grants are for general contributions except as noted. High grant of **$59,500** to Bethlehem Area Public Library (renovations/improvements). **$41,500** to Schuylkill Area Community Foundation (memorial fund). **$40,000** each to Grace Episcopal Church (endowment/organ/building/general funds) and Wildlands Conservancy (Monocacy Creek restoration/rivers program). **$34,000** to Hazleton Area Public Library (endowment/capital/book funds). **$21,000** to WVIA (capital campaign/endowment). **$19,000** to Lebanon Valley College (capital campaign). **$18,000** each to Hazleton YMCA (capital project) and Hazleton YWCA (capital project). **$13,000** to Lehigh U. (mathematics dept.). **$10,000** each to Planned Parenthood of NE Pa. (security enhancements) and Trinity Evangelical Lutheran Church (endowment). **$9,500** each to Geisinger Foundation Health Care System Foundation (women's wellness programs) and MMI Preparatory School (scholarship/capital expenses). **$8,500** to Red Cross/Hazleton (disaster relief). **$7,000** to Greater Hazleton Historical Society & Museum. **$5,000** each to AIDS Outreach (capital fund/transportation), Baum School of Art (addition/renovations), The Can Do Foundation (capital campaign), Hazleton Community Concerts, Lafayette College, The Nature Conservancy (interns program), Ned Smith Center [Millersburg], Penn State U./Hazleton (scholarship), United Way of Greater Hazleton, and Wilson College [Chambersburg]. **$4,250** to Washington Crossing Foundation [Bucks County] (scholarship program). **$2,000-$2,750** each to Habitat for Humanity of the Lehigh Valley, Hawk Mountain Sanctuary, Helping Hands Society/Hazleton, St. Peter's Episcopal Church of Hazleton, and Visiting Nurse Assn./Home Health Service [Wilkes-Barre]. **$1,000-$1,500** each to Boy Scouts/Minsi Trails Council, Hazleton Animal Shelter, Hazleton Art League, Hazleton Cemetery Assn., Meals on Wheels of Greater Hazleton, NE Pa. Lions Eye Bank, Penn State U. (forage program), Penn Woods Girl Scout Council, St. Paul's United Church of Christ [Ashland], Shippensburg U. Foundation, U. of Pa. School of Veterinary Medicine, and two scholarships. Other smaller local contributions for various purposes. **Out-of-state** giving includes **$5,000** each to Oxfam America [MA], St. Catherine College Oxford Foundation [MA], and University Lutheran Church of Cambridge [MA]; and **$3,000** to Heifer Project International [AR]. ■**PUBLICATIONS:** None ■**WEBSITE:** None ■**E-MAIL:** None ■**APPLICATION POLICIES & PROCEDURES:** The Foundation reports giving focuses on Ashland, Hazleton and the Lehigh Valley, mostly for general/operating support, endowment, building/renovation, and capital campaigns. Grant requests may be submitted in a letter between October and March; grants are awarded in April, June, and October. No grants are awarded to individuals except for scholarships.

O+D+T Diana James (S+F+Con) — Ann B. Fegan [Bethlehem] (P+Donor) — Robert K. Gicking [Bethlehem] (VP) — Howard D. Fegan [Bethlehem] (D+Donor) — John H. Fegan [U.K.] (D) — Eugene C. Fish, Esq. [Rydal Park] (D) — Paul J. Reidler [Ashland] (D) — Paul G. Reidler [Ashland] (President Emeritus) — Fleet Bank (Corporate Trustee)

NE-117   Reynolds (Edith L.) Trust
    c/o Mellon Bank N.A./Trust Division
    8 West Market Street
    Wilkes-Barre   18711   (Luzerne County)

MI-17-22-31-32-44-52-53-55-56-63-71-72
Phone 570-826-2981 **FAX** 570-826-2892
EIN 23-6409220   **Year Created** 1973

AMV $497,383   **FYE** 12-00   **(Gifts Received** $0)   18 **Grants totaling** $41,272

All giving restricted to Luzerne County. High grant of **$5,000** to Wyoming Historical & Geological Society. **$4,772** to Fine Arts Fiesta. **$3,000** each to Hoyt Library, Northeastern Pa. Genealogical Society, Planned Parenthood of NE Pa., Victims Resource Center, and Wyoming Library. **$2,000-$2,500** each to Little Theatre of Wilkes-Barre, North Branch Land Trust, Osterhout Library, Pa. Environmental Council, and Wilkes-Barre YMCA. **$1,000-$1,500** each to Back Mountain Memorial Library, First Presbyterian Church of Wilkes-Barre, Luzerne County SPCA, Red Cross, and Salvation Army. **$500** to Wyoming Valley Art League. ■**PUBLICATIONS:** application form ■**WEBSITE:** None ■**E-MAIL:** None ■**APPLICATION POLICIES & PROCEDURES:** The Donor's will stipulates that the Selection Committee must award grants by June 30th, but if it does not act by that date grants in equal parts will be awarded to seven designated Luzerne County organizations. Other grants, special projects for Luzerne County organizations, are restricted to the following interest areas: environment, family services, federated giving programs, historic preservation/historical societies, hospitals, libraries, and the performing arts. Generally, no grants are awarded for purchase of real estate, equipment, or to individuals. Prospective applicants initially should make a telephone inquiry about the feasibility of submitting a request. Grant requests should be submitted in May (deadline is June 1st) on a formal Application Form available from the Bank; include a project budget, list of major funding sources, Board member list, and IRS tax-exempt status documentation.

O+D+T Selection Committee members: Ruth B. Schooley [Kingston] (C+Con) — Dorrance R. Belin, Esq. [Scranton] — Stephen B. Killian, Esq. [Kingston] — Mellon Bank N.A. (Corporate Trustee)

NE-118   Riddle (Mary Jane & Marvin) Foundation
    3635 Chapman Road
    Easton   18045   (Northampton County)

MI-11-31-41-42-63
Phone 610-258-3183 **FAX** None
EIN 23-2693114   **Year Created** 1993

AMV $468,696   **FYE** 12-00   **(Gifts Received** $31,065)   18 **Grants totaling** $23,305

Mostly local giving; all grants are unrestricted support. High grant of **$16,580** to Lafayette College. **$1,700** to College Hill Presbyterian Church. **$1,200** to United Way of the Greater Lehigh Valley. **$1,050** to Valley Health Foundation. Other local contributions **$25-$60**. **Out-of-state** grant: **$1,000** to Deerfield Academy [MA]. ■**PUBLICATIONS:** None ■**WEBSITE:** None ■

E-MAIL: None ■**APPLICATION POLICIES & PROCEDURES:** Grant requests may be submitted in a letter at any time; no grants awarded to individuals.

O+D+T H. Marvin Riddle (C+T+Donor+Con) — Deborah Riddle Bernier [MA] (T) — Mary Jane Riddle (T+Donor) — Sheila J. Riddle (T) — Stephen A. Riddle [NJ] (T)

NE-119 Rider-Pool Foundation
Suite 202,
1050 South Cedar Crest Boulevard
Allentown 18103 (Lehigh County)

MI-12-13-15-16-22-25-29-31-41-42-44-45-49 51-52-53-54-56-65-71
Phone 610-770-9346 **FAX** 610-770-9361
EIN 23-6207356 **Year Created** 1957

AMV $9,560,080 **FYE** 12-01 **(Gifts Received** $0) 57 **Grants totaling** $421,000

All giving to the Lehigh Valley; some grants comprise multiple awards. High grant of **$75,000** to CACLV/Community Action Committee of the Lehigh Valley (Forte building project). **$60,000** to Old Allentown Preservation Assn. (building campaign). **$55,000** to Allentown Art Museum (technology capacity-initiatives). **$52,500** to Discovery Center of Science & Technology (capital campaign/school programs). **$50,000** each to Allentown School District Community Council and Lehigh County Historical Society (capital campaign). **$45,000** to Civic Theatre of Allentown (capital campaign). **$40,000** to Girls' Club of Allentown (learning club/summer program). **$30,000** to Wildlands Conservancy (Trexler Environmental Education Center). **$25,000** to Community Services for Children (children's campus campaign). **$20,000** each to Alliance for Building Communities (lease-purchase initiative), Lafayette College (community-based visual arts teaching program), Salvation Army/Allentown (capital campaign), and Valley Youth House (client tracking system). **$15,000** each to Baum School of Art (inner-city scholarships), Red Cross/LV Chapter (Lifeline), and St. Joseph's Evangelical Lutheran Church (community development corp.). **$10,000** each to Bach Choir of Bethlehem (Christmas concerts) and Parkettes (capital grant). **$8,000** to Congregations United for Neighborhood Action (community organizations). **$7,500** to National Museum of Industrial History (Preview Center). **$5,000-$6,000** each to Communities in Schools of the Lehigh Valley (alternative learning center), Community Bike Works (Earn a Bike program), Lehigh Valley Arts Council (arts integration school program), Muhlenberg College (Central Elementary School partnership), The National Learning Club (operating support), Pa. Shakespeare Festival/DeSales U. (scholarship program), Repertory Dance Theatre (school district programs/Nutcracker performance), and Touchstone Theatre (community programs). **$3,000-$4,000** to Ballet Guild of the Lehigh Valley (outreach program/performance), Lehigh Valley Conference of Churches (justice-advocacy etc. programs), Mock Turtle Marionette Theater (field trips program), and Moravian College (artists series). **$1,000-$2,500** each to Allentown Symphony Assn. (youth-family concerts), Camelot for Children (computer research learning center-library), Community Music School (general support), Fund to Benefit Children & Youth (family needs program), Interfaith Coalition on Poverty (sponsorship program), Junior Achievment of Lehigh Valley (elementary school program), Junior League of the Lehigh Valley (Dinosaurs Alive program), Lehigh Valley Chamber Orchestra (educational program), Lehigh Valley Child Care (capital campaign), Leonardo DaVinci's Horse (develop study units), Lexie's Dream (assistice technology purchase), Little Pond Retreat (summer programs), Open Space Gallery (regional scholastic art awards), Pa. Ballet (Zoellner performances), Pa. Youth Theatre (arts initiative), Satori (concert series), Penn State Berks-Lehigh Valley (Mosser Village Family Center Program), WDIY (program underwriting), and Wildlife Information Center (young ecologists summer camp). ■**PUBLICATIONS:** Annual Report; Grant Application Guidelines brochure ■**WEBSITE:** www.pooltrust.com ■**E-MAIL:** drpool@ptd.net ■**APPLICATION POLICIES & PROCEDURES:** The Foundation reports that giving is generally restricted to the Lehigh Valley for general support, special projects, and capital drives for educational, health/welfare, and arts/cultural activities; multi-year grants are awarded. No support is awarded to/for: individuals, hospitals, United Way member agencies, sectarian organizations which primarily propagate religion, benefit dinners, fund-raising events, advertising, subsidization of books, mailings or articles in professional journals, legislative or lobbying efforts, political or fraternal groups, or organizations located outside the United States. Grant requests may be submitted in a concise proposal with cover letter at any time—deadlines are April 1st and August 15th; include a description of need; specific objectives; work plan for accomplishing the objectives and a time schedule; proposed method of evaluating effectiveness; a fully-defined budget; list of all funding sources, committed or pending; current list of Board members, and IRS tax-exempt status documentation. Site visits sometimes are made to organizations being considered for a grant. Grants are awarded at Trustee meetings in May and October and funds disbursed on June 1st and November 1st.

O+D+T Edward F. Meehan, MPH (Executive Director+Con) — Edward Donley (C+T) — Leon C. Holt, Jr. (T) — John P. Jones, III (T) — PNC Bank N.A. (Corporate Trustee)

NE-120 Rifkin (Sandy & Arnold) Charitable Foundation
46 East Walnut Street
Kingston 18704 (Luzerne County)

MI-13-22-44-55-57-62-72
Phone 570-288-3345 **FAX** None
EIN 23-6869676 **Year Created** 1986

AMV $659,374 **FYE** 12-00 **(Gifts Received** $10,100) 13 **Grants totaling** $110,290

Mostly local giving. High grant of **$42,000** to Jewish Federation of Greater Wilkes-Barre. **$35,790** to Wilkes U. **$14,000** to Jewish Community Center. **$6,000** to Kirby Center for the Performing Arts. **$4,000** to Luzerne County SPCA. **$2,000** to YMCA of Wilkes-Barre. **$1,700** to Temple B'nai B'rith. **$1,000** each to Osterhout Library and WVIA. Other smaller local contributions. **Out-of-state** giving includes **$1,000** each to Jewish National Fund and Union of American Hebrew Congregations Foundation [NY]. ■**PUBLICATIONS:** None ■**WEBSITE:** None ■**E-MAIL:** None ■**APPLICATION POLICIES & PROCEDURES:** The Foundation reports giving if generally limited to the Wilkes-Barre area. Grant requests may be submitted in writing at any time; describe the intended use of the funding requested.

O+D+T Allan M Kluger, Esq. (T+Con) — Joseph E. Kluger, Esq. (T) — Arnold Rifkin (Donor) — Harriett Rifkin (Donor) — Sandy Rifkin (Donor) — Corporate donor: Damon Corp.

NE-121 RJ Foundation
2278 Bobby Court
Orefield 18069 (Lehigh County)

MI-13-22-41-42-45-53-54-65
Phone 610-395-0499 **FAX** None
EIN 23-7824343 **Year Created** 1995

AMV $2,447,237 **FYE** 12-00 **(Gifts Received** $1,510,464) 7 **Grants totaling** $15,000

All local/Pa. giving. High grant of **$5,000** to Academy of Natural Sciences [Philadelphia]. **$2,000** each to Allentown Art Museum, Allentown Jewish Family Service, The Clay Studio [Philadelphia], and Moravian Academy (Summerbridge). **$1,000** each to Adult Literacy Center of the Lehigh Valley and Moravian Academy (interfaith awareness). — Grants awarded the prior year included **$10,000** each to Allentown Art Museum and Muhlenberg College (Institute for Jewish-Christian Understanding) and **$5,000** each to Academy of Natural Sciences [Philadelphia] and Massachusetts Institute of Technology (alumni fund and secondary school fund). ■**PUBLICATIONS:** None ■**WEBSITE:** None ■**E-MAIL:** None ■**APPLICATION POLICIES & PROCEDURES:** Information not available. — Also called the Joseph B. & Rita P. Scheller Foundation.

O+D+T Joseph B. Scheller (C+T+Donor+Con) — Susan Scheller Arsht [Fogelsville] (T+Donor) — Nancy Scheller Hays [Broomall] (T) — Michael H. Scheller [Bethlehem] (T+Donor) — Rita P. Scheller (T)

NE-122 Rodale (Robert & Ardath) Family Foundation
2098 South Cedar Crest Blvd.
Allentown 18103 (Lehigh County)

MI-11-41-71-84
Phone 610-967-7582 **FAX** None
EIN 23-2715042 **Year Created** 1993

AMV $234,384 **FYE** 12-00 **(Gifts Received** $0) 8 **Grants totaling** $16,000

About half local giving. High Pa. grant of **$3,000** to Rodale Institute. $2,000 each to Robert Rodale Aquatic Center and United Way of the Greater Lehigh Valley. $1,000 each to Moravian Academy and Wildlands Conservancy. **Out-of-state** grants: $4,000 to Bob Scrowcroft Organic Farming Foundation [CA]; $2,000 to Pole to Pole [Canada]; and $1,000 to American Horticulture Society [VA]. ■**PUBLICATIONS:** None ■**WEBSITE:** None ■**E-MAIL:** None ■**APPLICATION POLICIES & PROCEDURES:** Grant requests may be submitted in a letter during January-February; deadline is March 1st.

O+D+T Heather Rodale Stoneback (Con) — Ardath H. Rodale [Allentown] (P) — Heidi Rodale [Allentown] (VP) — Anthony Rodale (S)

NE-123 Roman-Mason Foundation, The
c/o Fleet Bank, Trust Dept.
1 Bethlehem Plaza
Bethlehem 18018 (Lehigh County)

MI-22-42-62
Phone 610-997-7740 **FAX** 610-865-8636
EIN 23-6298763 **Year Created** 1958

AMV $525,016 **FYE** 1-01 **(Gifts Received** $0) 17 **Grants totaling** $36,600

All local giving. High grant of **$27,250** to Beth Israel Temple. **$3,500** to Hazleton Federated Jewish Charities. **$1,000** to Penn State U./Hazleton. **$750** to Camp Cadet Troop N. **$650** to Jewish Community Center. Other contributions **$100-$500** for various local charities and organizations. ■**PUBLICATIONS:** None ■**WEBSITE:** None ■**E-MAIL:** None ■**APPLICATION POLICIES & PROCEDURES:** Grant requests may be submitted in a letter at any time.

O+D+T Charles J. Mason (Co-T+Con) — Fleet Bank (Corporate Co-Trustee)

NE-124 Rose Garden Foundation
315 North 27th Street
Allentown 18104 (Lehigh County)

MI-13-22-31-34-42-62
Phone 610-435-1905 **FAX** None
EIN 22-2776754 **Year Created** 1986

AMV $326,502 **FYE** 12-00 **(Gifts Received** $223,627) 15 **Grants totaling** $154,378

Limited local/Pa. giving; all grants are for general support: **$4,218** to Lehigh Valley Hospital, and **$1,000** each to Jefferson Medical College [Philadelphia] and U. of Pa. **Out-of-state** giving, all to New York City or Long Island, includes **$40,000** to Zionist Organization of America; **$25,000** to V.I.S.A.; **$24,500** to U. Shenantown; **$11,000** to Yeshiva U.; and **$10,000** each to Chabad House and One Israel Fund Ltd. ■**PUBLICATIONS:** None ■**WEBSITE:** None ■**E-MAIL:** None ■**APPLICATION POLICIES & PROCEDURES:** No grants awarded to individuals. — Also called Stanley Benzel Charitable Foundation.

O+D+T Stanley Benzel, M.D. (P+T+Donor+Con)

NE-125 Ross Family Foundation, The
5 Overlook Road
Clarks Green 18411 (Lackawanna County)

MI-11-13-18-29-31-41-42-44-52-54-55-57-63-71
Phone 570-587-1365 **FAX** None
EIN 24-6017499 **Year Created** 1956

AMV $3,867,989 **FYE** 12-00 **(Gifts Received** $171,401) 82 **Grants totaling** $168,562

Mostly local or Philadelphia-area giving. High grant of **$28,500** to Keystone College. **$20,300** to First United Church of Germantown [Philadelphia]. **$16,000** to United Way of Lackawanna County. **$15,000** to Abington Community Library. **$10,550** to Covenant Presbyterian Church. **$7,500** to Johnson Technical Institute. **$6,500** to Greater Scranton YMCA. **$4,000** to Scranton Cultural Center. **$3,200** to Endless Mountain Medical Care Foundation. **$3,000** to U. of Scranton. **$2,000-$2,500** each to Community Concerts Assn., Scranton Tomorrow, United Way of SE Pa., and Wyoming Seminary. **$1,000-$1,500** each to Allied Services Foundation, Boy Scouts/NE Pa. Council, Everhart Museum, The Nature Conservancy, Philharmonic Society of NE Pa., Planned Parenthood, WHYY, Women's Resource Center, and WVIA. Other local contributions **$100-$700** for similar purposes. **Out-of-state** giving includes **$10,500** to Massachusetts Institute of Technology; **$2,500** to The Tannenwald Foundation [DC]; and **$1,800** to Society of Women Engineers [DE]. ■**PUBLICATIONS:** None ■**WEBSITE:** None ■**E-MAIL:** None ■**APPLICATION POLICIES & PROCEDURES:** The Foundation reports that giving focuses on Scranton-area organizations with most grants for annual campaigns, capital campaigns, or endowment. Grant requests may be submitted in a letter at any time. — Formerly called James A. Ross Foundation.

O+D+T Adrian E. Ross (P+T+Donor+Con) — James A. Ross [Clarks Summit] (VP+T+Donor) — Daniel R. Ross, Esq. [Philadelphia] (S+F+T+Donor) — Holly Ross [NJ] (AS+AF+T) — Faye Z. Ross [Philadelphia] (Donor)

NE-126 Ryan Family Foundation, The
2875 Country Club Road
Allentown 18103   (Lehigh County)

MI-11-41-42-54-61
Phone 610-966-4811 **FAX** None
EIN 23-2901049   **Year Created** 1997

AMV $1,994,713   **FYE** 12-00   **(Gifts Received** $1,456,800)   9 **Grants totaling** $102,000

All local/SE Pa. giving. High grant of **$50,000** to LaSalle College High School [Montgomery County]. **$15,000** to Villanova U. **$10,250** each to Mt. St. Joseph Academy [Montgomery County] and St. Thomas More Church. **$10,000** to Diocese of Allentown/Bishop's Annual Appeal. **$3,000** to United Way of Greater Lehigh Valley. **$2,500** to DeSales U. **$1,000** to Allentown Art Museum. Other smaller contributions. ■**PUBLICATIONS:** None ■**WEBSITE:** None ■**E-MAIL:** None ■**APPLICATION POLICIES & PROCEDURES:** Information not available.

O+D+T Frank Ryan (D+T+Donor+Con) — Jane Ryan (D) — Carolyn Healey [NJ] (D+T)

NE-127 Salvaggio FamilyFoundation
c/o Computer Aid, Inc.
1390 Ridgeview Drive
Allentown 18104   (Lehigh County)

MI-11-13-14-22-41-42-51-61

Phone 610-530-5000 **FAX** None
EIN 25-6614812   **Year Created** 1998

AMV $5,541,182   **FYE** 12-00   **(Gifts Received** $335,594)   38 **Grants totaling** $188,780

Mostly local/Pa. giving. High grant of **$50,000** to Diocese of Allentown/Bishop's Annual Appeal. **$30,000** to United Way of Greater Lehigh Valley. **$25,500** to St. Thomas More Church. **$20,000** each to Easter Seals of Eastern Pa. and The Second Mile [State College]. **$10,000** to Holy Child School. **$6,600** to Penn State U. **$6,250** to Pa. Shakespeare Festival. **$4,500** to DeSales U. **$3,450** to Boys & Girls Club of Allentown. **$2,000** to Communities in Schools of the Lehigh Valley. **$1,500** to Lily Guild of Easter. Other local and out-of-state contributions **$20-$500** for health, educational, civic, and other various purposes. ■**PUBLI-CATIONS:** ■**WEBSITE:** None ■**E-MAIL:** None ■**APPLICATION POLICIES & PROCEDURES:** Information not available.

O+D+T Anthony J. Salvaggio (Con) — Norene L. Salvaggio (T+Donor) — Christy A. Salvaggio (T) — Suzie A. Salvaggio (T) — Thomas A. Salvaggio (T)

NE-128 Samuels Family Foundation
c/o Automatic Devices Company
2121 South 12th Street
Allentown 18103   (Lehigh County)

MI-11-12-14-15-31-41-42-44-52-54-55-56-62

Phone 610-797-6000 **FAX** 610-797-4088
EIN 23-6259595   **Year Created** 1959

AMV $1,802,873   **FYE** 9-01   **(Gifts Received** $0)   40 **Grants totaling** $120,391

Mostly local/NE Pa. giving. High grant of **$56,500** to Cedar Crest College. **$7,150** to Lehigh County Historical Society. **$6,000** to Lehigh Valley Hospital. **$5,000** each to Lehigh U. and Wyoming County Cultural Center. **$4,000** each to Fund to Benefit Children & Youth and Good Shepherd Home. **$3,670** to Congregation Keneseth Israel. **$3,000** to Muhlenberg College. **$2,500** each to Allentown Symphony Orchestra and Swain School. **$1,000** each to Allentown Art Museum, Ashland Public Library, Easter Seals, Leonard Pool Society, Sacred Heart Foundation, United Way of Greater Lehigh Valley, and Zoellner Arts Center. Other local contributions **$100-$600** for various purposes. **Out-of-state** giving includes **$4,000** to Friends of the Ocean City Pops [NJ]; and **$1,000** each to New York Sheet Music Society and Ocean City Free Public Library [NJ]. ■**PUBLICATIONS:** None ■**WEBSITE:** None ■**E-MAIL:** None ■**APPLICATION POLICIES & PROCEDURES:** Grant requests may be submitted in any form at any time; include an annual report, Board member list, and IRS tax-exempt status documentation. — Formerly called A. Samuels Foundation.

O+D+T Abram Samuels (P+Con) — John A. Samuels [Bethlehem] (VP) — Harriet Samuels (S) — Corporate donor: Automatic Devices, Inc.

NE-129 Schautz (Walter L.) Foundation
c/o Grove Silk Company
150 East Grove Street
Scranton 18510   (Lackawanna County)

MI-11-12-13-14-15-17-20-22-24-25-29-32-33-
35-41-42-44-52-55-63-71-72-89
Phone 570-344-1174 **FAX** 570-344-1177
EIN 24-6018362   **Year Created** 1948

AMV $6,433,121   **FYE** 1-02   **(Gifts Received** $0)   82 **Grants totaling** $307,180

Mostly local/Pa. giving; grants are for general purposes except as noted. High grant of **$15,000** to Habitat for Humanity/Lackawanna County. **$10,000-$10,100** each to Abington Community Library, Northeastern Philharmonic, Penn State U./Scranton Campus, Red Cross/Scranton, Salvation Army/Scranton, Scranton Area Foundation, and United Way of Lackawanna County. **$6,000-$7,000** each to Bach & Handel Chorale, Boys & Girls Clubs of NE Pa., MS Self-Help Group/Scranton Chapter, and Scranton Counseling Center. **$5,000-$5,500** each to Animal Care Assn., Camphill Foundation-Kimberton Hills [Chester County], Catholic Social Services of Lackawanna County, Countryside Conservancy, Community Medical Center (neonatal clinic), Friendship House, Humane Society of Lackawanna County, Johnson Technical Institute, Keystone College, Lackawanna Neighbors, Lackawanna Pro Bono, NE Child Care Service, Project Hope/United Neighborhood Center, Safety Net, Simpson Park United Methodist Church, St. Michael's School of Tunkhannock, and Women's Resource Center/Catherine McAuley Center of Scranton. **$4,000** each to NE Regional Cancer Institute and Scranton Preparatory School. **$2,000-$3,300** each to Abington Ministerium (Renaissance Youth Program), Agency for Animal Welfare, Boy Scouts [Moosic], The Bread Basket, Choral Society of NE Pa., Family Service of Lackawanna County, First Presbyterian Church of Clarks Summit, Greater Scranton YMCA, International Assn. of Firefighters/Dunmore Fire Dept., Jim Thorpe Lions Club (Community Nurse Fund), Jim Thorpe Ministerium, Lake Ariel United Methodist Church, Lupus Foundation/NE Pa. Chapter, Make-A-Wish Foundation of NE Pa., Marywood U., Masonic Homes of Pa. [Elizabethtown], Mercy Hospice, Muscular Dystrophy Assn./Clarks Summit, The Nature Conservancy [Long Pond], Pa. Assn. for the Blind/Scranton, Robert Dale Chorale, Sts. Peter & Paul School, Scranton Cultural Center, Scranton-Pocono Girl Scout Council, Scranton-Lackawanna Human Development Agency, Scranton Tomorrow, Serving Seniors, Inc., TAIG Development Services Corp.

[Philadelphia], and VNA Hospice of Lackawanna County. Other grants/contributions, **$50-$1,500** for various community organizations. ■**PUBLICATIONS:** None ■**WEBSITE:** None ■**E-MAIL:** None ■**APPLICATION POLICIES & PROCEDURES:** Grant requests may be submitted in any form at any time; include IRS tax-exempt status documentation.

O+D+T Walter L. Schautz, Jr. (P+F+Donor+Con) — Nancy Miles [Scranton] (S) — John Cherb, CPA [Jim Thorpe] — James Reid, Esq. [Clarks Summit] — Corporate donor: Grove Silk Company

---

NE-130 **Schiowitz Family Foundation**
  c/o General Supply & Paper Company
  1 George Avenue
  Wilkes-Barre 18705   (Luzerne County)
AMV $608,326   **FYE** 12-00   **(Gifts Received** $0)

MI-22-62

Phone 570-823-1194 **FAX** 570-822-6065
EIN 23-2672420   **Year Created** 1992
  17 **Grants totaling** $27,220

Mostly local giving. High grant of **$20,220** to Jewish Federation of Greater Wilkes-Barre. **$5,000** to United Hebrew Institute. Other local and out-of-state contributions **$100-$200** various purposes. ■**PUBLICATIONS:** None ■**WEBSITE:** None ■**E-MAIL:** None ■**APPLICATION POLICIES & PROCEDURES:** No grants awarded to individuals.

O+D+T Nathan N. Schiowitz (P+F+Donor+Con) — Dr. Albert Schiowitz (VP+Donor) — Bernice Schiowitz Mager (S+Donor)

NE-131 **Schultz (Wilmer R. & Evelyn M.) Family Foundation**
  1540 Chestnut Street, P.O. Box 449
  Emmaus 18049   (Lehigh County)
AMV $337,974   **FYE** 12-00   **(Gifts Received** $0)

MI-22-31-32-44-63

Phone 610-967-2141 **FAX** None
EIN 23-2902342   **Year Created** 1998
  13 **Grants totaling** $19,283

Mostly local/Pa. giving. High grant of **$8,333** to Schwenkfelder Library. **$2,500** to Palm Schwenkfelder Church. **$1,000-$1,500** each to American Cancer Society, Arthritis Foundation, Lutheran Services Northeast, and Shriners Hospital-Philadelphia. Other smaller contributions for various purposes. ■**PUBLICATIONS:** None ■**WEBSITE:** None ■**E-MAIL:** None ■**APPLICATION POLICIES & PROCEDURES:** Grant requests in any form may be submitted at any time.

O+D+T Wilmer R. Schultz (P+Donor+Con) — Evelyn M. Schultz (S+AF) — Scott R. Schultz [Macungie] (F) — Kevin R. Schultz [Zionsville] (AS) — Karen E. Schultz [Zionsville] — Karla R. Schultz [Macungie]

NE-132 **Schuylkill Area Community Foundation**
  101 North Centre Street, 2nd Floor
  Pottsville 17901   (Schuylkill County)
AMV $4,964,046   **FYE** 4-01   **(Gifts Received** $342,926)

MI-13-35-39-43-44-52-55-71-84-89

Phone 570-624-1580 **FAX** 570-624-1581
EIN 23-6422789   **Year Created** 1967
  175+ **Grants totaling** $220,783

As a Community Foundation all discretionary giving (10% of the total) is limited to organizations serving the Schuylkill County area (including adjacent counties); this includes scholarships for local high school graduates and support for arts/culture, education, environment, youth, health/human services, youth, volunteer programs, and other purposes. No details on grants available. About 90% of the giving is from restricted or donor-advised funds. ■**PUBLICATIONS:** None ■**WEBSITE:** www.schuylkillacfoundation.org [limited information] ■**E-MAIL:** tsadusky@uplink.net ■**APPLICATION POLICIES & PROCEDURES:** Grant requests from Schuylkill County organizations only should be submitted by May 1st; include IRS tax-exempt status documentation. Scholarship recipients must be local residents or graduates of area high schools; a scholarship application form, available from the Trust, must be submitted in April; deadline is May 1st. The Board of Directors meets in February, June, September, and December, but awards grants only at the June meeting. — Formerly called Ashland Trusts.

O+D+T Therese Sadusky, Esq. (Director+Con) — Jean S. Baglin (P+D) — Carl D. Edling (VP+D) — Harry Strouse, Esq. (S+D) — Keith Strouse, Esq. (D) — Richard L. Berger (D) — Gary R. Glessner (D) — Charles Heizenroth, III (D) — Carl J. Reidler (D) — Catherine H. Schilling (D) — G. Fred Schilling (D) — Ann F. Snyder (D) — Frank Staudenmeier (D) — Frank J. Toole, Esq. [ME] (D)

NE-133 **Scranton Area Foundation**
  Bank Towers, Suite 608
  321 Spruce Street
  Scranton 18503   (Lackawanna County)
AMV $18,197,000   **FYE** 12-01   **(Gifts Received** $318,661)

MI-11-12-13-17-20-22-24-25-29-31-32-35-41-42-44-52-55-56-57-89

Phone 570-347-6203 **FAX** 570-347-7587
EIN 23-2890364   **Year Created** 1954
  108 **Grants totaling** $530,758

As a Community Foundation all discretionary giving is limited to organizations serving the Greater Scranton/Lackawanna County area. Grants from unrestricted funds included **$65,000** to Housing Services Collaborative; **$60,000** to United Way of Lackawanna County; **$23,750** to Northeastern Pa. Philharmonic; **$20,000** to Scranton Tomorrow; **$15,000** to Countryside Conservancy; **$5,000** to September 11th Fund; **$4,000** to Lackawanna County Child Care Consortium; and **$2,000** to Emergency Defibrillator Project. — In the prior year, over 40 discretionary grants were awarded, including: **$100,000** to Scranton Primary Health Care Center (dental clinic development); **$75,000** to United Way of Lackawanna County (programs/services); **$40,000** to Nonprofit Resource Center (Collaborative Community Program); **$34,106** to Scranton Tomorrow (Fire Safety House); **$25,000** to Scranton Tomorrow (educational programming); **$20,000** each to Boys & Girls Club of Scranton (Teen Supreme Program), Employment Opportunity & Training Center (Neighborhood Outreach Program), and Teen Mercy (outreach programs/services); and others **$500-$15,000** for a wide variety of purposes. ■**PUBLICATIONS:** Annual Report; newsletter; application guidelines; Grant Application Form ■**WEBSITE:** www.safdn.org ■**E-MAIL:** safinfo@safdn.org ■**APPLICATION POLICIES & PROCEDURES:** Grants from unrestricted funds are limited to the Greater Scranton-Lackawanna County area. Most grants are for special projects, special needs of qualifying organizations, research, seed money, and matching funds. No grants generally are awarded to/for individuals, annual campaigns, routine operating expenses, special events, building campaigns (unless vital to program meeting priority community needs), equipment (unless an integral part of a qualifying project), endowments (except for those within the Foundation), or existing obligations or to replenish resources used to pay for such purposes. The Foundation seeks to support projects/programs which: (a) facilitate cooperation/collaboration among people/organizations; (b) demonstrate the opportunity for positive and significant results; (c) improve the range/effectiveness of charitable programs/services in the community; and (d) approach existing and emerging community issues in a well-planned and timely manner. Prospective applicants should submit an initial Letter of Intent (2 pages maximum); the Foundation will provide an immediate response as to the potential for project support and, if appropriate, will provide the required formal Grant Application Form. Grant applications may be submitted at any time; decisions on grants are made quarterly. Site visits sometimes are made to organizations being considered for a grant.

O+D+T Board of Governors members: Jeanne A. Bovard (Executive Director+Con) — James W. Reid, Esq. (C) — Austin J. Burke (VC) — William J. Calpin (S) — Kathleen Graff (F) — Warren T. Acker — Dorrance R. Belin, Esq. — Richard S. Bishop, Esq. — Edward G. Boehm, Ed.D. — Thomas C. Capezio — Karen Clifford — Eugene F. Cosgrove — Sr. Jean Coughlin, IHM — L. Peter Frieder, Jr. — Carlene R. Gallo, Esq. — Judith O. Graziano — Robert N. Lettieri — George V. Lynett, Esq. — Thomas R. Nealon, Esq. — Carlon E. Preate, CPA — Letha Reinheimer — Walter L. Schautz, Jr. — Murray Weinberger — Trustee banks: Penn Security Bank; PNC Bank N.A.

NE-134   Seruga (Ruth P.) Lehigh County Charities
c/o First Union/Wachovia - PA 2106
640 Hamilton Street
Allentown 18101   (Lehigh County)

MI-11-12-13-14-15-17-25-29-31-41-42-71-51
52-54-55-56-65
Phone 610-439-4686 **FAX** 610-740-1207
EIN 23-6908392   **Year Created** 1988

AMV $904,810   **FYE** 12-00   **(Gifts Received** $0)   31 **Grants totaling** $67,063

All giving limited to Lehigh County. High grant of **$5,000** to Wildlands Conservancy. **$3,000** to Boys & Girls Club of Allentown. **$2,000-$2,500** each to Lehigh Valley Child Care, Pa. Shakespeare Festival, Special Learning Center, The Program for Women & Families, and Valley Youth House. **$1,000-$1,250** each to Allentown Art Museum, Allentown Symphony, Assn. for the Blind & Visually Impaired, Bike Works, Community Music School, Fund to Benefit Children & Youth, Girls' Club of Allentown, Good Shepherd, Habitat for Humanity, Lehigh County Conference of Churches, Lehigh County Historical Society, Lehigh County Senior Citizen's Center, Lehigh Valley Arts Council, Muhlenberg College, Parkettes, Phoebe-Devitt Homes, St. Luke's Hospital, St. Michael the Archangel School, United Way of Greater Lehigh Valley, and Volunteer Center of the Lehigh Valley. Other smaller contributions for similar purposes. ■**PUBLICATIONS:** application guidelines ■**WEBSITE:** None ■**E-MAIL:** None ■**APPLICATION POLICIES & PROCEDURES:** The Foundation reports that giving is limited to well-managed, non-profit Lehigh County organizations which are making substantial efforts to improve the quality of life in the county; most grants are for special projects or scholarships. Prospective applicants initially should make a telephone inquiry about the feasibility of submitting a request. Grant requests must be on a formal application form—available from the Bank—and submitted in April or October (deadlines are May 1st and November 1st). The form requires information on an organization's purpose/objectives, project description/purpose and budget, grant amount requested, total dollars solicited from business and community, geographical areas and populations covered by the proposed service/project, and the proposed method of project evaluation; also include an annual report, most recent audited financial statement, Board member list, and IRS tax-exempt status documentation. Site visits sometimes are made to organizations being considered for a grant. The Trust Review Committee recommends grant awards at meetings in June-July and November-December; these recommendations are forwarded to the Bank's Board of Directors for final approval. — **Note:** In Fall 2002, administration of this Trust will move to a First Union office in Reading; call 610-655-3148 for updated information. — Formerly called Ruth A. Seruga Trust.

O+D+T Bank's Trust Review Committee members: James A. Kressler (VP at Bank+Con) — Jan Armfield (Regional President at Bank) — Gilbert Stauffer (VP at Bank) — Kathryn Stephanoff — First Union/Wachovia (Trustee)

NE-135   Shafer Family Charitable Trust
c/o Nazareth National Bank
76 South Main Street
Nazareth   18064   (Northampton County)

MI-12-13-14-15-17-21-22-29-35-52-55-63

Phone 610-746-7318 **FAX** None
EIN 23-6952392   **Year Created** 1989

AMV $1,484,298   **FYE** 12-01   **(Gifts Received** $0)   28 **Grants totaling** $37,000

All local/Pa. giving. High grant of **$5,000** to Epworth United Methodist Church. **$2,000-$2,500** each to Children's Home of Easton, Hope Lutheran Church [Cherryville], Masonic Charities Fund [Elizabethtown], Meals on Wheels/Bethlehem, Pa. Special Olympics, ProJeCt of Easton, St. John's Lutheran Church of Nazareth, and The State Theatre. **$1,000-$1,500** each to Fund to Benefit Children & Youth, Jenn's House, Miller Memorial Blood Center, Rajah Temple Complex (Children's Hospital Fund), Safe Harbor/Community Action Committee of Lehigh Valley, Salvation Army/Easton, Valley Youth House, and Visiting Nurse Assn. of Bethlehem & Vicinity. Other local contributions **$300-$500** for civic, cultural, health/human services, and other purposes. ■ **PUBLICATIONS:** None ■**WEBSITE:** None ■**E-MAIL:** None ■**APPLICATION POLICIES & PROCEDURES:** The Foundation reports that local area charities are favored. Grant requests may be submitted in a full proposal with cover letter during January-August (deadline is September 1st) include an annual report, organization and project budgets, board member list, list of major funding sources, audited financial statement, and IRS tax-exempt status documentation. Site visits sometimes are made to organizations being considered for a grant. Grants are awarded at a September meeting.

O+D+T Sally F. Jablonski (Trust Officer at Bank+Con) — Susan Bartholomew (D) — Bertram Shafer (D) — Bruce Shafer (D) — Linda Shafer (D) — Lester B. Shafer (Donor) — Nazareth National Bank (Trustee)

NE-136 Shaffer Family Charitable Trust
3548 Bingen Road
Bethlehem   18015
(Northampton County)

MI-11-12-13-14-15-18-21-22-29-31-44-51-52
61-62-72
Phone 610-867-7568 **FAX** 610-317-0587
EIN 23-2502319   **Year Created** 1987

AMV $13,672,895   **FYE** 12-00   **(Gifts Received** $522,435)   31 **Grants totaling** $749,400

All local giving; all grants are unrestricted support. High grant of **$200,000** to St. Luke's Hospital. **$150,000** to United Way of Greater Lehigh Valley. **$125,000** to Jewish Federation of the Lehigh Valley. **$25,000** each to Banana Factory, Burn Prevention Foundation, and Trexler-Lehigh County Game Preserve. **$20,000** each to CACLV/Community Action Committee of the Lehigh Valley, Bridges Foundation, and Holy Infancy Church. **$15,000** each to Community Bike Works, Lehigh Valley Child Care, Lehigh Valley Summerbridge, and ProJeCt of Easton. **$12,500** to ARC of Lehigh & Northampton Counties. **$10,000** to Allentown Art Museum. **$7,700** to Community Music School. **$7,500** to Diocese of Allentown/Bishop's Annual Appeal. **$5,000-$5,400** each to Communities in Schools, Meals on Wheels of Lehigh County, Pa. Special Olympics, and Phoebe-Devitt Homes Foundation. **$2,500-$4,000** each to Fund to Benefit Children & Youth, Mercy Special Learning Center, Parkettes, Pa. Youth Theatre, and VI-ABL Services. **$1,000-$1,500** each to Hellertown Area Library, Mock Turtle Marionette Theatre, Planned Parenthood of NE Pa., ShareCare, and Volunteer Center of the Lehigh Valley. ■**PUBLICATIONS:** None ■**WEBSITE:** None ■**E-MAIL:** None ■**APPLICATION POLICIES & PROCEDURES:** The Foundation reports that giving is limited to the Lehigh Valley; most grants are for general support, special projects, building funds, capital drives or endowment not funded through normal funding sources. Prospective applicants initially should make a telephone inquiry about the feasibility of submitting a request. Grant requests may be submitted in a letter (2 pages maximum) at any time; include an annual report, organization and project budgets, list of major funding sources, audited financial statement, Board member list, and IRS tax-exempt status documentation. Site visits sometimes are made to organizations being considered for a grant. Grants are awarded at meetings in March, June, September, and December.
O+D+T David N. Shaffer (T+Donor+Con) — Cecile Shaffer (T+Donor) — Rose B. Shaffer [Rosemont] (T+Donor) — Susan T. Shaffer (T+Donor)

NE-137 Sigal (Roland & Doris) Foundation
313 North Main Street
Allentown   18104
(Lehigh County)

MI-12-14-22-62
Phone 610-433-0851 **FAX** 610-433-6280
EIN 23-2433373   **Year Created** 1986

AMV $99,400   **FYE** 9-01   **(Gifts Received** $110,048)   28 **Grants totaling** $65,394

Mostly local giving. High grant of **$28,000** to Lehigh Valley Jewish Federation. **$5,000** to Lehigh U. **$3,444** to American Jewish Committee. **$1,705** to Jewish Community Center. **$1,000-$1,390** each to Fund to Benefit Children, Jewish Family Service, and Temple Beth El. Other smaller local contributions, primarily for educational or human services organizations. ■**PUBLICATIONS:** None ■**WEBSITE:** None ■**E-MAIL:** sigrolly@aol.com ■**APPLICATION POLICIES & PROCEDURES:** The Foundation reports that giving focuses on the Lehigh Valley for educational, cultural, health, or Jewish-related purposes; most grants are for continuing/annual support or capital campaigns. No grants are awarded to individuals. Grant requests may be submitted in a letter at any time; include an annual report, organization and project budgets, list of major funding sources, audited financial statement, and Board member list. Site visits sometimes are made to organizations being considered for a grant.
O+D+T Roland Sigal (P+Donor+Con) — Doris Sigal (S+F+Donor)

NE-138 Skier Foundation, The
c/o A.M. Skier Insurance
209 Main Ave.
Hawley   18428
(Wayne County)

MI-13-22-31-32-52-56-62-71-84-85
Phone 570-226-4571 **FAX** 570-226-1105
EIN 23-2186639   **Year Created** 1982

AMV $105,728   **FYE** 12-00   **(Gifts Received** $62,475)   35 **Grants totaling** $40,835

Limited local giving. High local grant of **$2,000** to Wildflower Music Festival. **$1,300** to Dorflinger-Suydam Wildlife Sanctuary. **$1,000** each to Congregation Beth Israel, MS Society, and United Jewish Communities. **$500** each to Golden Slipper Camp, Wayne County Community Foundation, Wayne County Historical Society, and Wayne Memorial Health Foundation. Other smaller contributions. **Out-of-state** giving includes high grant of **$15,000** to American Camping Assn. [NY]; **$10,000** to The Ben Appelbaum Foundation [NJ] (business entrepreneurships); and **$2,000** to Happiness is Camping [NJ]. ■**PUBLICATIONS:** None ■**WEBSITE:** None ■**E-MAIL:** None ■**APPLICATION POLICIES & PROCEDURES:** No grants awarded to individuals. — Formerly called Abram & Mabel Skier Foundation.
O+D+T Henry M. Skier [Honesdale] (T+Donor+Con)

NE-139 Snayberger (Harry E. & Florence W.) Foundation
c/o M&T Bank
1 South Centre Street
Pottsville   17901
(Schuylkill County)

MI-12-13-14-19-43-44-63-84
Phone 570-628-9309 **FAX** 570-622-1306
EIN 23-7446492   **Year Created** 1976

AMV $4,585,173   **FYE** 3-01   **(Gifts Received** $0)   300+ **Grants totaling** $225,017

All giving restricted to Schuylkill County for scholarships, children's programs, child welfare activities, and youth agencies. Sixty-five organizational grants totaled **$28,680** with high grant of **$2,500** to Boy Scouts/Hawk Mountain Council. **$1,000** each to Big Brothers Big Sisters, Friendship House, Pottsville Lions Charities, St. John's Evangelical Lutheran Church, Trinity Lutheran Church. Other local contributions mostly **$200-$500** for Boy Scout/Girl Scout troops, Brownie troops, public libraries, sports teams, churches, day care centers, cultural and performing arts organizations and others serving children. All remaining awards were scholarships for Schuylkill County students, mostly **$250** with a few up to **$2,500**. ■**PUBLICATIONS:** application form ■ **WEBSITE:** None ■**E-MAIL:** None ■**APPLICATION POLICIES & PROCEDURES:** The Foundation reports that giving is restricted to Schuylkill County residents or organizations benefiting children in the county. Prospective applicants must request a formal application form from the Bank; completed applications must be submitted between mid-December and the last business day of February; organizations must provide IRS tax-exempt status documentation. The Board makes awards at May and September meetings.

O+D+T Joseph Popson (VP at Bank+Con) — M&T Bank (Trustee)

NE-140   Sordoni Foundation, Inc.
c/o Sordoni Construction Services, Inc.
45 Owen Street
Forty Fort   18704   (Luzerne County)

MI-11-12-13-15-22-29-41-42-44-54-55-56-57
71-85
Phone 570-283-1211   **FAX** 570-288-3663
EIN 24-6017505   **Year Created** 1946

AMV $14,729,203   **FYE** 12-00   **(Gifts Received** $2,325)   52 **Grants totaling** $941,165

Mostly local giving. High grant of **$140,000** to U. of Scranton. **$102,500** to Marywood College. **$100,000** to Wyoming Valley United Way. **$75,250** to Catholic Youth Center. **$70,000** to Wilkes U. **$53,688** to King's College. **$50,000** each to Committee on Economic Growth and Mt. Laurel Center for the Performing Arts. **$40,000** to St. Joseph's Center. **$33,332** to United Way of Lackawanna County. **$30,000** to Scranton Tomorrow. **$20,000** each to Hazleton YMCA and Pa. Environmental Council. **$18,500** to Misericordia College. **$11,985** to Wyoming Seminary. **$10,000** each to Collegiate Museum on Art, The Kirby Center for the Performing Arts, and WVIA. **$8,000** to YMCA of Wilkes-Barre. **$7,000** to Elan Gardens. **$6,000** each to Lackawanna Junior College and Tunkhannock Library. **$5,000-$5,250** each to Back Mountain Recreation, Lacawac Sanctuary, Greater Wilkes-Barre Assn. for the Blind, and VNA Hospice of Lackawanna County. **$4,000** to Red Cross/Wilkes-Barre. **$3,000** to Osterhout Free Library. **$2,000-$2,500** each to Greater Hazleton Health Alliance, Mercy Health Partners, Northeast Pa. Philharmonic, Ruffed Grouse Society, United Jewish Appeal, and United Rehabilitation Services. **$1,000-$1,250** each to Allied Services for the Handicapped, ARC of Luzerne County, Back Mountain Land Trust, Child Development Council, Endless Mountain Health, Fine Arts Fiesta, Jazz Gallery, Johnson Technical School, Keystone College, Leadership Wilkes-Barre, Pa. Special Olympics, and Wyoming Historical Society. Other local contributions **$250-$500** for various purposes. **Out-of-state** grant: **$14,000** to The Nature Conservancy [VA]. — Major grants approved for future payment include **$290,570** to Collegiate Museum of Art; **$280,000** to U. of Scranton; **$50,000** each to Catholic Youth Center, Marywood U., and United Way of Wyoming Valley; **$45,000** to Back Mountain Recreation; **$40,000** to St. Joseph Center; and **$30,000** each to Committee on Economic Growth and North Branch Land Trust. ■ **PUBLICATIONS:** statement of program policy; application guidelines ■ **WEBSITE:** None ■ **E-MAIL:** None ■ **APPLICATION POLICIES & PROCEDURES:** The Foundation reports that giving is limited to Northeastern Pa., in particular Wilkes-Barre/Scranton area; priority interests are arts/culture, economic development, education, health/human services, and the environment. As the Foundation conceives and develops its own programs at certain qualified host institutions it seldom supports ongoing programs at those particular institutions. Capital campaign requests are considered but are limited to 1% of funds raised for the project. No grants are awarded to individuals or for scholarships, or programs supported by (or required to be supported by) Federal, state, or local government agencies. Grant requests may be submitted in a letter (3 pages maximum) at any time and should contain the following: a brief description of proposed project with a specific amount requested; a brief description of the problem to be addressed, the project's principal objectives, the proposed intervention, and anticipated results/outcome. Also provide a project timetable, detailed budget, expected sources of funding, plans for project evaluation and continuation of the project after grant funds expire, Board member list, annual report, a statement indicating the organization's structure, purpose and history, IRS tax-exempt status documentation, and most recent IRS Form 990. Site visits sometimes are made to organizations being considered for a grant. The Board of Directors meets as necessary. — Formerly called Andrew J. Sordoni Foundation.

O+D+T Benjamin Badman, Jr. (Executive VP+AS+AF+D+Con) — Andrew J. Sordoni, III [Harveys Lake] (P+Donor) — William B. Sordoni [Harveys Lake] (S+F+D+Donor) — Richard Allen [Dallas] (D) — A. William Kelly [Pittston] (D) — John J. Menapace [Clarks Summit] (D) — Patrick Solano [Pittston] (D) — Stephen Sordoni [Newtown] (D+Donor) — Susan F. Sordoni [Harveys Lake] (D) — Ruth Hitchener [West Pittston] (AS) — Corporate donor: Sordoni Enterprises, Inc.

NE-141   Spring Hill Foundation
c/o Spring Hill Aviation, Inc.
Spring Hill Road, P.O. Box 55
Sterling   18463   (Wayne County)

MI-14-22-42-31-43

Phone 570-689-2696   **FAX** None
EIN 23-2217537   **Year Created** 1983

AMV $331,598   **FYE** 3-01   **(Gifts Received** $74,030)   6 **Grants totaling** $17,600

All local giving; all grants are unrestricted support. High grant of **$10,000** to St. Vincent College. **$5,000** to Geisinger Medical Center Scholarship Fund. **$1,500** to Salvation Army/Scranton. **$500** to Pa. Special Olympics. Other small contributions for Scranton organizations. ■ **PUBLICATIONS:** None ■ **WEBSITE:** None ■ **E-MAIL:** None ■ **APPLICATION POLICIES & PROCEDURES:** No grants awarded to individuals.

O+D+T Michael Caputo (P+Donor+Con)

NE-142   Trexler Trust
Suite 205
33 South 7th Street
Allentown   18101   (Lehigh County)

MI-12-13-14-15-17-22-25-29-35-41-42-43-44
45-51-52-53-55-56-57-71-84-85-89
Phone 610-434-9645   **FAX** 610-437-5721
EIN 23-1162215   **Year Created** 1934

AMV $119,632,864   **FYE** 3-01   **(Gifts Received** $0)   94 **Grants totaling** $4,924,674

All giving restricted to Lehigh County; grants are for budgetary/operating/general program support except as noted, and some grants comprise multiple payments. High grant of **$1,639,720** to City of Allentown (maintenance/improvement of city parks). **$370,000** to Lehigh Valley Hospital (expanded services for ambulatory adults). **$170,200** to Catholic Diocese of Allentown (youth programs/indigent care/school building projects/special learning center). **$150,000** to DeSales U. (science center). **$125,000** to County of Lehigh (6th Street Shelter/game preserve exhibits). **$110,000** to Allentown Symphony (building renovations/conductor salary). **$100,000** each to Cedar Crest College (science center addition) and Muhlenberg College (arts center expansion). **$90,000** to Allentown Public Library (family reading program). **$75,000** each to Allentown Art Museum, Baum

School of Art (building addition/scholarships/operating support), and Boy Scouts/Minsi Trails Council (urban scouting program). **$70,000** to Salvation Army (family shelter/program support). **$65,000** to Girls Club of Allentown (education program/building improvements/equipment). **$60,000** each to Hispanic American Organization (building renovations) and Phoebe Home (indigent care). **$50,000** each to Allentown YMCA/YWCA (building improvements), America on Wheels, Inc., Boys & Girls Club of Allentown (mortgage reduction), CEO America/Lehigh Valley (scholarships), Civic Theatre (capital campaign), Good Shepherd Home (building renovation), Lehigh County Historical Society (new museum construction), Lehigh County Senior Citizens Center (program support/building improvements), Lehigh Valley Chamber Orchestra (guest soloist underwriting/concerts), and St. Joseph's Evangelical Lutheran Church (building improvements/community programs). **$40,000** each to Pa. Shakespeare Festival (new stage/budgetary support) and Presbyterian Homes (facility improvements). **$38,000** to Red Cross (emergency response vehicle). **$35,000** to Program for Women & Families (building renovations/operating support). **$30,000-$33,335** each to Allentown School District (Standard Works program), Allentown Downtown Improvement District Authority (downtown trolley trial), Community Music School (operating support/scholarships/chamber music program/), Valley Youth House (computer system upgrade), and Wildlands Conservancy (education center). **$25,000-$25,720** each to Adult Literacy Center, Allentown Jewish Community Center (scholarship programs), Casa Guadalupe (youth programs), Habitat for Humanity, Lehigh County Council of Churches (Daybreak), Lynn Township (land acquisition), Mayfair (festival), Parkette National Gymnastic Team (special needs support/scholarships), Pa. Assn. for the Blind/Lehigh County Branch (prevention education/radio reading), Pa. Sinfonia Orchestra (concert underwriting), and Suburban North YMCA (building improvements). **$20,000** each to Allentown YMCA (youth programs), Allentown YWCA (youth programs), Family & Counseling Services of Lehigh Valley (computer equipment), Junior Achievement of Lehigh Valley (Allentown schools program), Lehigh Valley Christian High School (building improvements), Municipal Opera Company (building improvements/tickets), Repertory Dance Theatre, Theatre Outlet, and VIA of the Lehigh Valley. **$15,000** each to Burn Prevention Foundation (fire safety education), Communities in Schools (school-to-work program), Crisis Pregnancy Center, Turning Point of Lehigh Valley (office equipment), and WLVT-TV (program underwriting). **$10,000-$12,000** each to Allentown Area Ecumenical Food Bank, Allentown Band, Allentown Rescue Mission (new beds/improvements), Community Bike Works, Lehigh County Meals on Wheels, Lehigh Valley Arts Council, Lehigh Valley Business Education Partnership, Lehigh Valley Center for Independent Living (computer training for disabled), Lehigh Valley Child Care (scholarships), Lehigh Valley Community Broadcasters, Old Allentown Preservation Assn. (building renovation), Southern Lehigh Public Library (automated system), and Whitehall Township Public Library (reference collection expansion). **$7,000-$9,000** each to Emmaus Main Street Program, Emmaus Public Library, Open Space Gallery, and Slatington Public Library. **$5,000-$6,700** each to Assn. for Retarded Citizens (camperships), Camerata Singers (concert underwriting), Cityspace, East Penn School District (playground construction), Fund to Benefit Children, Lehigh County Conservation District (Kids-to-Farms program), Lehigh County 4-H (school enrichment program), Macungie Band, Marine Band, Municipal Band of Allentown, Parkland Community Library (science collection), Public Library of Catasauqua (roof repairs), and Wildlife Information Center. **$3,000** to Masonic Lodges Library (collection enhancement). **$2,500** to Emmaus Historical Society. ■**PUBLICATIONS:** Annual Report with application guidelines ■**WEBSITE:** None ■**E-MAIL:** None ■**APPLICATION POLICIES & PROCEDURES:** The Foundation reports that only organizations serving Lehigh County residents exclusively or substantially so are eligible to apply. Priority areas of interest are human services, education, arts/culture, and youth. Most grants are for general support, special projects, building funds, capital drives, and matching grants; multiyear grants are awarded. No grants are awarded for endowment, research, deficit financing, or loans. First-time applicants are encouraged to telephone or meet with Trust staff to discuss an application and necessary background materials. Grant requests may be submitted in a letter (3 pages maximum) before the December 1st deadline; describe the purpose of the requested grant and its benefit to community, total amount requested and other projected sources of support, if relevant. Also, include client statistics (numbers served in major categories of service and fees received), an organizational operating budget, project budget, list of major funding sources, most recent audited financial statement, list of Board members with addresses and term expiration dates, articles of incorporation, current by-laws, latest Form 990, 1st Quarter Form 941 (for organizations with employees), and IRS tax-exempt status documentation. All grant requests are acknowledged. Site visits sometimes are made to organizations being considered for a grant. Grants are awarded annually at an April or May meeting and payments disbursed in July. — Formerly known as The Harry C. & Mary W. Trexler Foundation or The Harry C. Trexler Estate.
O+D+T Thomas H. Christman (PO+Con) — Malcolm J. Gross (C+T) — Dexter F. Baker (T) — Daniel G. Gambet (T) — Kathryn Stephanoff (T) — Robert C. Wood (T)

NE-143   Trumbower Hospital Foundation
c/o Pierce & Dally
124 Belvidere Street, P.O. Box 57
Nazareth   18064   (Northampton County)
MI-12-14-29-32-35-39-41-44

Phone 610-759-1420 **FAX** None
EIN 23-7377310   **Year Created** 1978

AMV $1,461,139   **FYE** 10-00   **(Gifts Received** $0)   16 **Grants totaling** $72,385
All giving limited to organizations serving the Nazareth Area School District area with support for medical supplies/equipment or health education activities. High grant of **$10,000** to YMCA of Nazareth. **$9,912** to Nazareth Area School District. **$5,400** to Nazareth Ambulance Corps. **$5,000** each to ARC Family Resource Center, Valley Youth House, and Weller Center for Health Education. **$4,000-$4,935** each to American Lung Assn., Hecktown Volunteer Ambulance Corps., Memorial Library of Nazareth, Red Cross, and Visiting Nurse Assn. **$2,800** to Good Shepherd Home. **$1,000-$2,000** each to American Heart Assn., Burn Prevention Foundation, Lehigh Valley Child Care, and Northeast Pa. Lions Eye Bank. ■**PUBLICATIONS:** statement of program policy; application guidelines ■**WEBSITE:** None ■**E-MAIL:** None ■**APPLICATION POLICIES & PROCEDURES:** The Foundation reports that only agencies providing health care services/programs which benefit the residents of the Nazareth Area School District are eligible to apply. Priority is given to new, improved, or expanded primary health care programs; most grants for general support, special projects, building funds, or capital drives. Prospective applicants should first consult a detailed statement of program policy (available from the Foundation) and may request an informal consultation prior to applying. Grant requests should be submitted in writing (seven copies required) during November-January (the deadline is February 1st); include background in-

formation and descriptive materials, demographic data on intended beneficiaries, annual report, project budget, audited financial statement, and IRS tax-exempt status documentation. The Board awards grants at meetings in May and June.

O+D+T Lillian Knecht (AS+AF+Con) — Richard W. Kraemer (P) — Helen Ziegler (S) — Susan Rundle, Esq. (F)

NE-144 Updegrove (Ruby & John H.) Family Trust
4430 Fairview Drive
Easton 18045   (Northampton County)

MI-11-15-22-29-35-42-63
Phone 610-253-8641 **FAX** None
EIN 23-6869477   **Year Created** 1987

AMV $318,514   **FYE** 12-00   **(Gifts Received** $577)   31 **Grants totaling** $18,717

Mostly local/Pa. giving. High grant of **$4,175** to College Hill Presbyterian Church. **$2,350** to Lafayette College. **$2,000** to ProJeCt Easton. **$1,000-$1,320** each to Lehigh Valley Community Foundation, Presbyterian Homes [Camp Hill], and United Way of Greater Lehigh Valley. **$500** each to Northampton Community College and Weller Center for Health Education. Other local contributions **$25-$250** for various purposes. **Out-of-state** giving includes **$1,250** to Cornell U. [NY] and **$1,000** to United Negro College Fund [VA]. ■**PUBLICATIONS:** None ■**WEBSITE:** None ■**E-MAIL:** None ■**APPLICATION POLICIES & PROCEDURES:** The Foundation reports that giving focuses on health and education; most grants are for general support, special projects, building funds, and capital drives. Prospective applicants initially should make a telephone inquiry about the feasibility of submitting a request. Grant requests may be submitted in any form at any time; include IRS tax-exempt status documentation.

O+D+T John H. Updegrove, M.D. (P+T+Donor+Con) — Ruby H. Updegrove (VP+T+Donor) — Stephen Updegrove (T) — Andrew S. Updegrove (T)

NE-145 Wagner (Harold A. & Marcia K.) Family Foundation
1306 Prospect Ave.
Bethlehem 18018   (Lehigh County)

MI-11-12-13-31-41-42-54-55-56
Phone 610-865-6735 **FAX** None
EIN 23-7886100   **Year Created** 1997

AMV $777,626   **FYE** 12-00   **(Gifts Received** $1,160)   18 **Grants totaling** $101,500

Mostly local/Pa. giving; all grants are general contributions. High grant of **$25,000** to United Way of Greater Lehigh Valley. **$15,000** to Lehigh U. **$10,000** to Discovery Center. **$7,500** to Penn State U. **$5,000** each to Lehigh Valley Child Care, Lehigh Valley Hospital, Northampton Community College, and Zoellner Arts Center. **$4,000** to Boys & Girls Club of Allentown. **$3,500** to S.T.A.R. Academies. **$2,000-$2,500** each to Historic Bethlehem, KidsPeace, and Valley Youth House. **$1,500** to Game Preserve. **$1,000** to Communities in Schools-Lehigh Valley. **Out-of-state** giving includes **$5,000** to Historic Delaware Corp. and **$1,000** to United Negro College Fund [VA]. ■**PUBLICATIONS:** None ■**WEBSITE:** None ■**E-MAIL:** None ■**APPLICATION POLICIES & PROCEDURES:** Information not available.

O+D+T Harold A. Wagner (T+Donor+Con) — Sandra Boyce [CA] (T) — Kristi Wagner [CA] (T) — Tracey Wagner [CO] (T) — Harold E. Wagner [NJ] (T) — Marcia K. Wagner (T)

NE-146 Waldman Family Charitable Trust
900 West Fairfield Ave.
Easton 18040   (Northampton County)

MI-12-13-14-17-18-22-29-31-32-35-41-42-51-56
Phone 610-253-8093 **FAX** None
EIN 23-6869549   **Year Created** 1987

AMV $2,360,001   **FYE** 12-00   **(Gifts Received** $12,660)   31 **Grants totaling** $125,000

Mostly local/Pa. giving. High grant of **$25,000** to Easton Cemetery. **$12,000** to Northampton Community College Foundation. **$5,000** each to Moravian Academy, ProJeCt of Easton, Temple Covenant of Peace, Valley Health Foundation of Easton Hospital, VIA Foundation, and Weller Center for Health Education. **$3,000** each to Children's Home of Easton, Easton Boys & Girls Club, Spring Garden Children's School, and United Negro College Fund. **$2,000-$2,500** each to Buckingham Friends School, Hillside School, Lehigh Valley Summerbridge, Planned Parenthood of NE Pa., St. Anthony's Youth Center, State Theatre, and Third Street Alliance for Women & Children. **$1,000-$1,500** each to AIDS Service Center, Children's Hospital of Philadelphia, Communities in School-Lehigh Valley, Community Services for Children, Lehigh Valley Child Care, Red Cross, and Salvation Army. Other smaller local contributions for various purposes. **Out-of-state** giving includes **$5,000** to Hunterdon Regional Cancer Program [NJ] and **$2,500** each to Lawrenceville School [NJ] and Mayo Clinic-Jacksonville [FL]. ■**PUBLICATIONS:** None ■**WEBSITE:** None ■**E-MAIL:** None ■**APPLICATION POLICIES & PROCEDURES:** The Foundation reports that most giving is to Pa.; no grants are awarded to individuals.

O+D+T Herman B. Waldman (Manager+Donor+Con) — Mark Waldman [NJ] (Manager) — Bruce Waldman [Hellertown] (Manager) — Corporate donors: A&H Sportswear Company; Metric Products, Inc. [CA] — First Union/Wachovia (Trustee)

NE-147 Wayne County Community Foundation
214 Ninth Street, Suite 201
Honesdale 18431   (Wayne County)

MI-24-41-43-45-54-56-71
Phone 570-251-9993 **FAX** 570-251-9904
EIN 23-2656896   **Year Created** 1993

AMV $1,105,542   **FYE** 6-01   **(Gifts Received** $69,923)   **Grants totaling** $57,318

As a Community Foundation all discretionary giving is limited to organizations serving Wayne County. Recent community projects supported include Historic White Mills, Prompton State Park, Vision Unlimited, and Wayne County Historical Society but grant amounts not reported. Three local school teachers each received **$500** grants for an after-school reading program, science fair, and humanities program materials. Also, 18 scholarships for local students totaled **$24,868.** ■**PUBLICATIONS:** Annual   Report ■**WEBSITE:** None ■**E-MAIL:** wccf@ezaccess.net ■**APPLICATION POLICIES & PROCEDURES:** Only organizations serving Wayne County residents are eligible to apply. Prospective applicants initially should make a telephone inquiry about the feasibility of submitting a request. Grant requests may be submitted in a letter/proposal at any time; include a project budget and IRS tax-exempt status documentation. Site visits sometimes are made to organizations being considered for a grant. Grants are awarded at meetings in March, June, September, December.

O+D+T Warren Schloesser (P+D+Con) — Vicki Lamberton (1st VP+D) — Joseph Murray (2nd VP+D) — P.R. Monaghan (S+D) — Thomas Sheridan (F+D) — and 19 additional directors

NE-148   Weber (Jacques) Foundation
c/o Bloomsburg Mills, Inc.
6th & West Streets, P.O. Box 420
Bloomsburg   17815   (Columbia County)

MI-11-12-13-14-15-31-32-43-44-51-71-89

Phone 570-784-4262 **FAX** 570-784-8098
EIN 13-6101161   **Year Created** 1948

AMV $3,752,900   **FYE** 9-01   (**Gifts Received** $900)   61 **Grants totaling** $213,350

Limited Pa. giving to organizations. High Pa. grant of **$15,000** to Philadelphia U. **$1,000** to Bloomsburg Town Park. Also, college scholarships (**$1,250-$5,000** each totaled **$110,250**) were awarded to 32 dependents of Bloomsburg Mills employees, both local and other states. **Out-of-state** giving to organizations in other corporate locations, primarily NJ, NC, or SC, including **$10,000** each to New York Firefighter 9/11 Disaster Fund, Red Cross Disaster Relief Fund, and United Way/September 11th Fund. — Local giving in the previous year included **$2,000** each to Bloomsburg Fire Dept., Camp Victory; and Red Cross; **$1,000-$1,250** each to American Cancer Society, American Heart Assn., Bloomsburg Town Park, Columbia/Montour Home Hospice, Ronald McDonald House, and Suncom Industries; and other smaller contributions. ■**PUBLICATIONS:** None   ■**WEBSITE:** None ■**E-MAIL:** None ■**APPLICATION POLICIES & PROCEDURES:** College scholarships are restricted to children of employees of Bloomsburg Mills, Inc. who are interested in studying textiles; applicants must apply by letter and provide a transcript copy. Application information for organizations submitting grant requests is unavailable.

O+D+T Sandra Grasley (AS+TCon) — James P. Marion, III [CT] (P+T) — Robert McCoy [Millville] (VP+T) — Michael Spruyt [NJ] (F+T) — Fred F. Evans [SC] (AF+T) — Joan McCarty [Orangeville] (T+Chair, Scholarship Committee) — William Parker [NC] (T) — Corporate donor: Bloomsburg Mills, Inc.

NE-149   Weiler Family Foundation, The
c/o Weiler Corporation
1 Wildwood Drive
Cresco   18326   (Monroe County)

MI-22-31-42-71

Phone 570-595-7495 **FAX** 570-595-2002
EIN 23-2962255   **Year Created** 1998

AMV $435,447   **FYE** 12-00   (**Gifts Received** $50,672)   5 **Grants totaling** $36,700

All local giving. High grant of **$30,000** to Pocono Mountain Medical Center. **$5,000** to Northampton Community College Foundation. **$1,000** to Salvation Army (capital campaign). **$500** to Buck Hill Conservation Fund. **$200** to Junior Achievement.
■**PUBLICATIONS:** None. ■**WEBSITE:** None ■**E-MAIL:** None ■**APPLICATION POLICIES & PROCEDURES:** Information not available.

O+D+T Karl M. Weiler (P+D+Donor+Con) — Ann Weiler (VP+D+Donor) — Richard Weiler (S+D) — Christopher Weiler (D) — James Weiler (D) — Jennifer Weiler (D)

NE-150   White (Gerald A. & Mary Alice) Foundation
3714 Laurel Lane
Center Valley   18034   (Lehigh County)

MI-22-52-54-61

Phone 610-797-5370 **FAX** None
EIN 23-7877903   **Year Created** 1997

AMV $415,969   **FYE** 12-00   (**Gifts Received** $0)   4 **Grants totaling** $8,000

All local/Pa. giving; all grants are for general support. High grant of **$5,000** to Allentown Art Museum. **$1,000** each to DeSales Theatre (Angels), Diocese of Allentown/Bishop's Annual Appeal, and Pa. Shakespeare Festival. — Major support in prior years to St. Joseph's Church [Limeport]. ■**PUBLICATIONS:** None ■**WEBSITE:** None ■**E-MAIL:** None ■**APPLICATION POLICIES & PROCEDURES:** No grants are awarded to individuals.

O+D+T Gerald A. White (T+Donor+Con) — Mary Alice White (T+Donor)

NE-151   Willary Foundation
P.O. Box 283
Scranton   18501   (Lackawanna County)

MI-31-35-41-42-55-71-85
Phone 570-961-6952 **FAX** 570-961-7269
EIN 23-7014785   **Year Created** 1969

AMV $5,810,799   **FYE** 12-00   (**Gifts Received** $0)   8 **Grants totaling** $279,719

All local giving. High grant of **$125,000** to Scranton Cultural Center (master plan campaign and film support). **$35,000** to Northeastern Pa. Diversity Education Consortium (multicultural, diversity curriculum initiative) **$30,000** to Employment Opportunity Training Center (workforce development for unemployed/underemployed). **$25,000** to Countryside Conservancy (walking trail land acquisition). **$24,719** to Keystone College/Water Discovery Center (equipment for educational activities). **$20,000** to Mountain Laurel Center for the Performing Arts (Unity House planning expenses). **$10,000** each to Neighborhood Development Trust (Great Valley Technology Alliance startup) and Scranton Tomorrow (expand CATV coverage of local programming). — Grants approved for future payment include **$35,000** to Employment Opportunity Training Center (grant development specialist salary) and **$10,000** to Northeast Regional Cancer Institute (cancer prevention outreach initiative). ■**PUBLICATIONS:** application form ■**WEBSITE:** www.willary.org [comprehensive, current information] ■**E-MAIL:** info@willary.org ■**APPLICATION POLICIES & PROCEDURES:** The Foundation reports giving primarily to Northeastern Pa. for (1) development of imaginative ideas and projects that benefit communities in Northeastern Pa.. (2) support of projects which will help to leverage other sources of funding, (3) projects that promote the special qualities of Northeastern Pennsylvanians; and (4) regional projects that support leadership and the development of leadership in business, the economy, education, human services, government, the arts, media and research. No grants awarded to individuals or for capital campaigns or annual drives. Grant requests must be submitted on an application form available from the Foundation or on its website—deadlines are March 25th and September 10th; include IRS tax-exempt status documentation. The Board awards grants at meeting in June and November.

O+D+T William W. Scranton (T+Donor+Con) — Susan Scranton Dawson (T) — Joseph C. Scranton [KS] (T) — Mary L. Scranton (T+Donor) — Peter K. Scranton [CA] (T) — William W. Scranton, III (T) — PNC Bank/Northeast Pa. (Corporate Trustee)

NE-152   Yudacufski (Herman) Charitable Foundation
c/o Stoudt's Ferry Preparation Co.
Mill Creek Manor, P.O. Box 279
St. Clair   17970   (Schuylkill County)
AMV $2,466,998   **FYE** 11-00   **(Gifts Received** $0)

MI-14-31-32-42-61-62-64-84-89

Phone 570-429-1575 **FAX** None
EIN 23-2906569   **Year Created** 1997
21 **Grants totaling** $42,355

All local/Pa. giving. High grant of **$20,000** to Penn State U. **$5,000** each to County of Schuylkill and Mahanoy Township. **$3,000** to the Simon Kramer Institute. **$1,000-$1,500** each to Our Lady of Mt. Carmel Church, St. Joseph's Center for Special Learning, Sts. Peter & Paul Church, and a summer camp scholarship. Other smaller local contributions for youth, medical, and other purposes. — In the prior year, major grants included **$20,000** to Penn State U.; **$15,000** to Pottsville Hospital; and **$10,000** each to Ner Israel Rabbinical College [MD], Jewish Community Foundation, and Ryan Township Parks & Recreation. ■ **PUBLICATIONS:** None. ■ **WEBSITE:** None ■ **E-MAIL:** None ■ **APPLICATION POLICIES & PROCEDURES:** Submit written requests before the September 30th deadline; provide details on how the requested funds will be used, the amount requested, and include an annual report, audited financial statement, and IRS tax-exempt status documentation.
O+D+T Kenneth J. Huebner (Con) — Steve Cotler (P) — Allan Yudacufski [FL] (VP) — Marjorie Cotler (S) — Alvin B. Marshall (D) — Herman Yudacufski (Donor)

NE-153   Yuengling (Richard L.), Jr. Charitable Foundation
c/o Jones & Company
110 North 2nd Street
Pottsville   17901   (Schuylkill County)
AMV $690,121   **FYE** 12-00   **(Gifts Received** $100,000)

MI-11-12-13-14-21-22-31-32-44-52-56

Phone 570-622-5010 **FAX** 570-622-3283
EIN 23-2790830   **Year Created** 1995
19 **Grants totaling** $30,000

All local giving. High grant of **$5,600** to Schuylkill United Way. **$5,000** to Historical Society of Schuylkill County. **$2,000** each to Pottsville Cancer Clinic, Pottsville Free Public Library, Pottsville Hospital, and Salvation Army. **$1,000** each to Big Brothers/Big Sisters of Schuylkill County, Make-A-Wish Foundation of Mideastern Pa., Rotary Charities, St. Joseph Center for Special Learning, Schuylkill County Society for Crippled Children, Schuylkill Symphony Orchestra, Schuylkill YMCA, Third Brigade Band, UCP of Schuylkill/Carbon/Northumberland Counties, and YWCA of Pottsville. **$700** to Port Carbon Library. Other local contributions **$200-$500.** ■ **PUBLICATIONS:** None ■ **WEBSITE:** None ■ **E-MAIL:** None ■ **APPLICATION POLICIES & PROCEDURES:** The Foundation reports that giving is primarily to Schuylkill County organizations. No grants are awarded to individuals. Grant requests in any form may be submitted at any time.
O+D+T William L. Jones, III (T+Con)

NE-154   Zimmerman (Floyd & Arlene) Charitable Trust
RR #1, Box 1130
Tamaqua   18252   (Schuylkill County)
AMV $616,882   **FYE** 5-01   **(Gifts Received** $0)

MI-22-41-63

Phone 570-668-2519 **FAX** None
EIN 23-7848279   **Year Created** 1996
3 **Grants totaling** $32,500

Mostly local giving. High grant of **$25,000** to Salvation Army/Tamaqua. **$2,500** to Tamaqua Area School District. **Out-of-state grant: $5,000** to Blue Mountain Christian Retreat [GA]. ■ **PUBLICATIONS:** application guidelines ■ **WEBSITE:** None ■ **E-MAIL:** None ■ **APPLICATION POLICIES & PROCEDURES:** The Foundation reports that giving is limited to furthering Christian education/support. Prospective applicants should make an initial telephone inquiry regarding the feasibility of submitting a request. Grant requests may be submitted in any form at any time.
O+D+T Floyd Zimmerman (Co-T+Donor+Con) — Lynn D. Zimmerman (Co-T) — Peggy L. Strack (Co-T) — First Union/Wachovia (Co-Trustee)

NE-155   Zimmerman Heimbach Foundation
56 East Wall Street
Bethlehem   18018   (Northampton County)
AMV $1,768,795   **FYE** 12-00   **(Gifts Received** $0)

MI-13-22-41-42-43-44-52-54-55-57-63-71-84

Phone 610-691-5306 **FAX** None
EIN 22-2493652   **Year Created** 1984
15 **Grants totaling** $112,500

Mostly local/Pa. giving; grants are unrestricted/operating support except as noted. High grant of **$50,000** to Cedar Crest College (scholarships). **$10,000** to Zion United Church of Christ. **$5,000** each to Bach Choir, Boy Scouts, Central Moravian Church (campground improvements), Moravian Museum, Morris Arboretum (research), and WLVT-TV. **$3,000** each to Chamber Music Society (memorial education fund) and Saucon Valley Fine Arts. **$2,500** to Elizabethtown College (book fund). **$2,000** each to Gateway School and Liberty Bell Shrine of Allentown. **Out-of-state** giving: **$5,000** each to The Citadel [SC] (scholarships) and Fairfax Opportunities United [VA]. ■ **PUBLICATIONS:** None ■ **WEBSITE:** None ■ **E-MAIL:** None ■ **APPLICATION POLICIES & PROCEDURES:** The Foundation reports that grants are made only to preselected organizations and unsolicited requests are not accepted.
O+D+T George Z. Heimbach (C+Con) — Elizabeth W. Heimbach (VC) — John E. Freund, Esq. (D) — Daniel E. Heimbach (D) — David G. Heimbach (D)

Northeastern Region / NE
Non-profiled Foundations

*NE Region foundations which did **not** meet the criteria for profiling are listed here; the letter code in parentheses after the foundation name indicates its status, per the following key:*

L — **Limited Assets/Giving**: The market value of assets was $250,000 or under and the total of grants awarded was less than $12,500 in the last year of record. If information about grants is available, up to three Major Interest (MI) Codes are listed; if no information on giving interests is available, the notation "N/R" (Not Reported) is shown.

O — **Operating Foundation**: This special designation by IRS is for a foundation that operates its own program or institution and, generally, does not award grants to other organizations.

R — **Restricted Trust/Foundation**: Grants are awarded only to designated organizations or beneficiaries, typically under the terms of a Will or Trust Instrument.

I — **Inactive**: The assets, generally, are nominal (typically under $5,000) and there has been little or no grants activity within the last year or more.

NP — **Non-Pennsylvania Foundation**: The foundation's connection to Pennsylvania is only incidental; typically these are trusts or foundations managed by a bank trust department or a lawyer located in Pennsylvania, but there are no Pennsylvania-based trustees/directors and no grants are awarded to Pennsylvania.

T — **Terminated**: A final IRS Form 990-PF has been filed, or the foundation has provided notice of intended liquidation/termination.

U — **Undetermined Status**: There is no record of Form 990-PFs being filed for the last three or more years and no other evidence of grant-making activity. In many cases the foundation may have terminated without giving formal notice or has been reclassified by IRS as a "public charity."

AAA Scholarship Fund of L.V. Automobile Club (R)
1020 Hamilton Street, Allentown 18101

Abrams (Carry & Rudolf) Charitable Trust (U)

Agnew Foundation of New York (NP)
c/o Rubin, 2605 Houghton Lane, Macungie 18062

Air Products Foundation, The (T)

Allentown Housing Finance Corporation (R)
215 South 22nd Street, Allentown 18104

Allentown South Whitehall Civic Assn. (R)
918 Dorset Road, Allentown 18104

American Truck Foundation
(Formerly of Allentown; now located in FL).

Animal Care Fund, Inc. (O)
c/o Animal Care Sanctuary, P.O. Box A, East Smithfield 18817

Aquarium Foundation (R)
22 South 18th Street, Allentown 18104

Ashland Trusts
(New name: Schuylkill Area Community Foundation)

Ballard Angels, Inc. (L) MI-11-63-99
14 Sidehill Trail, Sugarloaf 18249

Barbetti (Orlando & Jennie) Scholarship Fund (R)
1421 East Drinker Street, Dunmore 18512

Basila (G.) Scholarship Fund (R)
P.O. Box 1383, Scranton 18501

Becker (Thomas F.) Memorial Scholarship Fund (R)
c/o Heritage National Bank, Pottsville 17901

Bennett (Annabelle) Trust for Five Rivers Council (R)
c/o Citizens & Northern Bank, Towanda 18848

Bennett (Robert L.), Sr. Trust for Five Rivers Council (R)
c/o Citizens & Northern Bank, Towanda 18848

Bennett (Robert L.), Sr. Trust for Packer School of Nursing (R)
c/o Citizens & Northern Bank, Towanda 18848

Bennett (Robert L.), Sr. Trust for Towanda High School Scholarships (R)
c/o Citizens & Northern Bank, Towanda 18848

Boyle (Bernard F.) Memorial Scholarship Fund (R)
c/o Mellon Bank N.A., Wilkes-Barre 18711

Campbell (Harold S.) Foundation (I)
c/o Beth Westgate, Inc. 2285 Schoenersville Road, Bethlehem 18017

Cardon (Bruce & Charlotte) Memorial Scholarship (R)
c/o Mellon Bank N.A., Wilkes-Barre 18711

Carey (Raymond B.) Foundation (NP)
c/o McQueen Ball, 214 North 8th Street, Allentown 18102

Catawissa Lumber & Specialty Trust/College Educ. Fund (R)
c/o First Columbia Bank & Trust Co., Bloomsburg 17815

Chakrabarti Foundation (R)
100 Station Ave., Stockertown 18083

Chappell (Corabelle) Memorial Fund (R)
c/o First Union/Wachovia, Scranton 18501

Cherry Lane Foundation (L) MI-42-63-71
711 Sarah Street, Stroudsburg 18360

Chowdary Family Foundation (L) MI-12-13-14
   4115 Pheasant Court, Allentown 18103

Christ (Elmer & Frances R.) Scholarship Fund (R)
   c/o Union Bank & Trust Co., Pottsville 17901

Christiansbrunn die Families der Erde (R)
   RR 1, Box 140, Pitman 17965

Clements (H. Loren) Scholarship Fund (R)
   c/o First Union/Wachovia, Scranton 18501

Cohen Family Foundation, The (U)

Cornell (Milton Keen) Charitable Trust (L) MI-71
   North Shore Road, Pocono Lake Reserve 18348

Curtis (T. Manning) Athletic Trust (R)
   c/o Stroudsburg Area School District, Stroudsburg 18360

Dee (Raymond C. & Maureen K.) Foundation (U)

Dessin (Olga & Dorothea) Trust for S.P.C.A. (R)
   c/o Wayne Bank, Honesdale 18431

Dex Family Foundation (L) MI-18-29-99
   3890 Larkspur Drive, Allentown 18103

Dick (Alexander W.) Foundation (R)
   c/o Mellon Bank N.A., Wilkes-Barre 18711

Dorflinger Suydam Wildlife Sanctuary, Inc. (R)
   c/o Wayne Bank, Honesdale 18431

Easton Home, The (O)
   1700 Northampton Street, Suite A, Easton 18042

Ecumenical-Honesdale, Inc. (R)
   1075 Memorial Highway, Dallas 18612

Eureka Foundation (R)
   1221 West Grove Street, Clarks Summit 18411

Evangelism International, Inc. (O)
   c/o Smith, Box 1261, Bethlehem 18016

Eyer (George S.) Trust (R)
   P.O. Box 240, Bloomsburg 17815

Gaines Family Foundation (L) MI-11-42
   1441 North 40th Street, Allentown 18104

Garrity (Jane Forsyth) Scholarship Trust (R)
   RD 1, Box 108A, Pleasant Mount 18453

Genetti Private Charitable Foundation (I) MI-99
   77 East Market Street, Wilkes-Barre 18701

Glassman Family Foundation (I)
   637 Clay Ave., Scranton 18510

Greater Carbondale Community Development Corp. (L) MI-56
   1 North Main Street, Carbondale 18407

Guthrie Home Care (R)
   Guthrie Square, Sayre 18840

Harley (Sylvia M.) Scholarship Fund (R)
   c/o Heritage National Bank, Pottsville 17901

Hill (David & Edith E.) Scholarship Fund (R)
   c/o PNC Bank N.A., Scranton 18501

Hoffman (Harvey F. & Raymond F.) Trust (R)
   c/o Fogelson, 850 Pine Street, Catasauqua 18032

Home for Homeless Women (R)
   c/o Heritage House, 80 E. Northampton St., Wilkes-Barre 18701

Horvat (Dr. Arthur J. & Helen M.) Foundation (R)
   c/o First Union/Wachovia, Scranton 18501

Hull (Herbert J. & Geneva S.) Scholarship Fund (R)
   85 Laurel Lane, Box 863, Greentown 18426

JEM Classic Car Museum, Inc. (R)
   RR #1, Box 120C, Andreas 18211

Jenkins (Melvin H. & Thelma N.) Scholarship Fund (R)
   c/o Pa. National Bank & Trust Company, Pottsville 17901

Kanjorski (Paul E.) Foundation (R)
   c/o Mellon Bank N.A., Wilkes-Barre 18711

Kaplan (Harold & Nancy) Foundation (L) MI-22-62
   102 Windmere Circle, Dalton 18414

Kautz (Jessie B.) Trust (R)
   c/o Mellon Bank N.A., Wilkes-Barre 18711

Keblish (Peter & Ruth) Foundation, The (L) MI-N/R
   1243 South Cedar Crest, Suite 2500, Allentown 18103

Keefer (Elinor R.) Trust (R)
   c/o PNC Bank N.A., Scranton 18501

Kelly (Thomas L.), Jr. Foundation (NP)
   Old Windmill Road, Clarks Green 18411

Kensington Associates, Inc. (R)
   529 South Main Street, Nazareth 18064

Kerling (Teddie) Scholarship Fund (R)
   c/o PNC Bank N.A., Scranton 18501

King's Daughters & King's Sons of Bethlehem (O)
   61 West Market Street, Bethlehem 18018

Kirby (Angeline Elizabeth) Memorial Health Center (O)
   c/o Mellon Bank N.A., Wilkes-Barre 18711

Kirby (Fred M. & Jessie A.) Episcopal House, Inc. (O)
   P.O. Box 2862, Wilkes-Barre 18703

Kirtland (David L. & Marijo M.) Foundation (L) MI-N/R
   c/o Tellie & Coleman, 310 East Drinker Street, Dunmore 18512

Kriss Foundation (O)
   c/o PNC Bank N.A., Scranton 18501

Lacawac Sanctuary Foundation (R)
   R.D. 1, Box 518, Lake Ariel 18436

Lackawanna Institute, Inc. (O)
   1117 Richmont Street, Scranton 18509

LARC Residential Services, Inc. (R)
   336 West Spruce Street, Bethlehem 18018

Larkin (Matthew P. & Barbara J.) Scholarship Fund (U)

Lehigh Valley Coalition Against Addiction (R)
   c/o Carlin, 3687 Lanark Road, Coopersburg 18036

Lehigh Valley Helping Hand Foundation (T)

Lehigh Valley Housing Development Corporation (R)
   215 South 22nd Street, Allentown 18104

Lehigh Valley Workers Memorial Scholarship Fund (L) MI-43
   P.O. Box 20226, Lehigh Valley 18002

Leonardo DaVinci's Horse, Inc. (R)
   P.O. Box 396, Fogelsville 18051

Lesaius Memorial Fund for Muhlenberg College (R)
   c/o PNC Bank N.A., Scranton 18501

Levy (Leon M.) Trust (R)
   c/o Scranton School District, Secondary Ed. Director, Scranton 18503

Liberty Chevrolet & Cadillac Inc. Educational Trust (R)
   420 Central Road, Bloomsburg 17815

Lippert Scholarship Trust (R)
   P.O. Box 85, Factoryville 18419

Love Foundation, The (L) MI-14-63
   c/o Dinger, 102 East Main Street, Schuylkill Haven 17972

Lower Nazareth Teachers (R)
   Lower Nazareth Elementary School, Nazareth 18064

Mack (Harry & Helen) Foundation
   (New name: Schwartz-Mack Foundation)

Malone (Mary A.) Trust (L) MI-63-72-99
   c/o M&T Bank, 1 South Centre Street, Pottsville 17901

Malone (Mary Alice Dorrance) Foundation
   (New name: The Roemer Foundation)

MAPS/The Micrographic Preservation Service, Inc. (O)
   9 South Commerce Way, Bethlehem 18017

Marcon (Frank L.) Foundation (L) MI-42-56
   c/o First Union/Wachovia, Bethlehem 18018

McLaughlin (Edward & Alice) Scholarship Fund (R)
   c/o Pa. National Bank, Pottsville 17901

McNulty (Revs. Raymond & Terrence) Memorial Endowment Fund (R)
   c/o PNC Bank N.A., Scranton 18501

Meske Foundation, The (T)

Misty Foundation (I)
17 Little Street, Canton 17724

Moravian Union of the King's Daughters & Sons (R)
61 West Market Street, Bethlehem 18018

Morgan (Leslie E.) Charitable Trust (R)
c/o PNC Bank N.A., Scranton 18501

Morgan (Russell E. & Elizabeth W.) Foundation
(Formerly of Bethlehem, now located in MD)

Morrison (Betty R.) Scholarship Fund (R)
c/o First Columbia Bank & Trust Co., Bloomsburg 17815

Morrison (Betty R.) Trust (R)
c/o First Columbia Bank & Trust Co., Bloomsburg 17815

Mount Laurel Pools, Inc. (R)
271 South Pine Street, Hazleton 18201

Murphy (M. Catherine) Scholarship Fund (R)
c/o First Columbia Bank & Trust Co., Bloomsburg 17815

Myers (Wilbur A. & Ruth M.) Trust (R)
c/o PNC Bank N.A., Wilkes-Barre 18701

National Men's Health Foundation (O)
14 East Minor Street, Emmaus 18098

Nesbitt (Abram G.) Trust #1 for Nesbitt Memorial Hospital (R)
c/o PNC Bank N.A., Wilkes-Barre 18701

Nesbitt (Abram G.) Trust #2 for Nesbitt Memorial Hospital (R)
c/o PNC Bank N.A., Wilkes-Barre 18701

Orlando Foundation (I)
1 South Church Street, Hazleton 18201

Orwigsburg Boys Club Home Association (R)
c/o Klemkosky, R. D. #2, Box 2056, Orwigsburg 17961

Ostheimer (Rev. Joseph J.) Memorial Scholarship Fund (R)
c/o Vechte, 31 East Centre Street, Shenandoah 17976

Paragon Foundation, Inc. (NP)
c/o Sheff, 714 Coleman Street, Easton 18042

Peckitt (Leonard Carlton) Scholarship Fund (R)
650 Pine Street, Catasauqua 18032

Pennsylvania Human Performance Foundation (L) MI-N/R
2775 Schoenersville Road, Bethlehem 18017

Philos Foundation, The (L) MI-43
33 South Kennedy Drive, McAdoo 18237

Pollock (Ken L.) Scholarship Fund of Northwest H. S. (R)
c/o Northwest Area High School, Shickshinny 18655

Purrfect Love Haven for Homeless Cats Trust (O)
RR1, Box 1965D, Nescopeck 18635

Risa Charitable Trust (L) MI-82
c/o Folin, RR #1, Box 172A, Uniondale 18470

Roaring Creek Valley Scholarship Fund (R)
R.D. #1, P.O. Box 71, Catawissa 17820

Roberts (Warren R.) Trust (R)
c/o Summit Bank, Bethlehem 18018

Rodale Working Tree Arboretum Society (O)
2098 South Cedar Crest Blvd., Allentown 18103

Rodale Working Tree Arboretum Society, The (R)
2098 South Cedar Crest Boulevard, Allentown 18103

Rose Foundation for Leprosy (R)
c/o Ziobro, 601 North Main Street, Wilkes-Barre 18705

Rosenn (Max & Tillie) Foundation (L) MI-11-22-62
177 James Street, Kingston 18704

Roth (David Rubinow) Foundation (I)
436 Jefferson Ave., Scranton 18510

Roth (Linda Lutz) Education Fund (L) MI-N/R
22 Walden Drive, Mountaintop 18707

Rothrock (Bruce L.) Charitable Foundation (L) MI-42-84-99
c/o Rothrock Motor Sales, Route 22 & 15th Street, Allentown 18104

Samuels (A.) Foundation
(New name: Samuels Family Foundation)

Schafer (Stephen A. & Nina B.) Foundation (L) MI-99
826 North Muhlenberg Street, Allentown 18104

Scheller (Joseph J. & Rita P.) Foundation.
(New name: RJ Foundation)

Schuylkill County Bar Assn. Scholarship Fund (L) MI-43
c/o Courthouse-Law Library, Pottsville 17901

Schuylkill County Vietnam Veterans Memorial Fund (O)
c/o First United Church of Christ, Route 61 South, Schuylkill Haven 17972

Schuylkill Haven H.S. Class of '32 Memorial Fund (R)
114 West Mifflin Street, Orwigsburg 17961

Schwartz-Mack Foundation (L) MI-11-99
1730 Monroe Ave., Dunmore 18509

Scott Foundation (I)
315 Pennsylvania Ave., Pen Argyl 18072

Shaner (Brian R.) Memorial Scholarship Fund (R)
R.D. #1, Towanda 18848

Simmons (Donald M.) Family Foundation (L) MI-99
c/o Sayre Lingerie, Inc., 807 West Lockhart Street, Sayre 18840

Skier (Abram M. & Mabel B.) Foundation
(New name: The Skier Foundation)

Smith (Paul H. & Ann E.) Community Foundation (I)
717 Washington Street, Easton 18042

Smithfield Township College Assistance Fund (R)
c/o Mellon Bank N.A., Wilkes-Barre 18711

Sonshine Family TV Corporation (U)

Stancato Family Foundation (L) MI-11-13-61
15 Coventry Road, Drums 18222

Sumneytown Yoga Fellowship (R)
P.O. Box 250, Sumneytown 18084

Sunrise Christian Ministries (O)
RR #2, Box 469, Hawley 18428

Suraci (Henry & Janet) Charitable Trust (L) MI-41-42-61
c/o First Union/Wachovia, Scranton 18501

Sutton (James) Home for Aged/Infirm Men Trust (R)
39 Public Square, Suite 400, Wilkes-Barre 18701

Tellie (Nicholas D.) Charitable Foundation (I)
310 East Drinker Street, Dunmore 18512

Tranguch/Shonkwiler Foundation (NP)
RR #1, Box 13, Valley View, Weatherly 18255

Turnbach (S.P.) Scholarship Fund (R)
c/o PNC Bank N.A., Wilkes-Barre 18701

Urban (Joseph & Margaret) Scholarship Fund (R)
c/o Mahanoy Area School District, Mahanoy City 17948

Van Horn (Mae Cooper) Trust (R)
c/o Mellon Bank N.A., Wilkes-Barre 18711

Wagner (C.R. & E.J.M.) Charitable Trust (R)
c/o Lafayette Bank, P.O. Box 25091, Lehigh Valley 18002

Well Spring Ministries (R)
P.O. Box 832, Whitehall 18052

Weller (Carl E. & Emily) Foundation (R)
P.O. Box 2467, Lehigh Valley 18002

Wesel Foundation (L) MI-11-99
1141 North Washington Ave., Scranton 18509

Williams (Gwilym T.) Scholarship Fund (R)
c/o PNC Bank N.A., Scranton 18501

Williams (Richard D.) Trust for Slatington Library et al (R)
650 Main Street, Slatington 18080

Willman (H.A.) Trust for Battenberg Scholarship Fund (R)
c/o PNC Bank N.A., Scranton 18501

Wolf (Louis) Foundation (R)
c/o Mardo, Monroe & Gibson Streets, Scranton 18510

Wyoming Monument Fund (R)
c/o PNC Bank N.A., Wilkes-Barre 18701

Young (Dorris H.) Home Economics Fund (R)
c/o Liberty High School, Bethlehem 18018

Your Loving Choices (R)
260 Riverview Drive, Bloomsburg 17815

Zaberer (Frances M.) Foundation (R)
HCI, Box 1070, Blakeslee 18610

Ziegler (Isaac) Charitable Trust
(Formerly of Scranton; now located in CA)

Northwestern Region / NW

covers the following 12 counties

Cameron - Clarion - Clearfield - Crawford - Elk - Erie
Forest - Jefferson - McKean - Mercer - Venango - Warren

NW-001 Anderson (Dorotha A.) Charitable Foundation
1 Anderson Plaza
Greenville   16125   (Mercer County)

MI-12-42-44-52-54-63-89
Phone 724-588-8310 **FAX** None
EIN 23-7885028   **Year Created** 1996

AMV $273,826   **FYE** 12-00   **(Gifts Received** $97,343)   10 **Grants totaling** $23,500

All local/Pa. giving. High grant of **$6,500** to Zion's Reformed Church. **$5,500** to Greenville Area Public Library. **$5,000** to Museum of Bus Transportation [Lemoyne]. **$1,000-$1,500** to Allegheny College, Children's Aid Society of Mercer County, Hempfield Fire Company, Slippery Rock U., and Thiel College. **$500** each to Greenville Symphony and Shenango Valley Chorale.
■ **PUBLICATIONS:** None ■ **WEBSITE:** None ■ **E-MAIL:** None ■ **APPLICATION POLICIES & PROCEDURES:** Information not available.

O+D+T Members of the Advisory Committee: Douglas D. Anderson (Con) — Lyle Anderson — Karen Jones — Sue Ann Nicklin

---

NW-002 Armstrong County Community Foundation
101 Market Street, Suite 120
Kittanning   16201   (Armstrong County)

MI-12-29-41-44
Phone 724-548-5897 **FAX** 724-548-4720
EIN 31-1625798   **Year Created** 1998

AMV $450,570   **FYE** 12-01   **(Gifts Received** $159,638)   5 **Grants totaling** $14,500

(*Editor's note/apology: This entry should have been listed in the SW Region!*) As a Community Foundation all discretionary giving is limited to organizations serving Armstrong County. High grants of **$3,500** each to Armstrong Educational Trust (Crooked Creek Environmental Center) and Family Resource Network (skilled care workers for disabled children). **$2,500** each to Apollo Memorial Library (books), Armstrong County Memorial Hospital (digital thermometers for newborns), and Worthington/West Franklin Community Library (children's reading room renovations). — In the prior year, four grants awarded: **$6,050** to Armstrong County YMCA (swimming pool handicapped lift); **$5,000** each to Armstrong Heritage Park and Armstrong County Fireman's Assn. (Fire Safety House); and **$3,000** to Armstrong County Safe Kids Coalition (car seats). ■ **PUBLICATIONS:** Annual Report, statement of program policy; application guidelines ■ **WEBSITE:** None ■ **E-MAIL:** kgreen@tribweb.com ■ **APPLICATION POLICIES & PROCEDURES:** Only organizations serving Armstrong County are eligible to apply for grants from discretionary funds; grants are awarded in the areas of arts/culture, economic/community development, education, health/human services, recreation, and the environment. Priority support is given to specific programs which will directly benefit Armstrong County residents. No grants are awarded to individuals or for operational funding. Prospective applicants should submit a Letter of Intent (2 pages maximum) during June-July (check with the Foundation or the local newspaper for the deadline); describe the organization, describe the proposed project and its benefits, and state the amount of funding requested as well as the project's total cost; include a project budget, list of major funding sources, and IRS tax-exempt status documentation. Upon review, the organizations which most closely fit the Foundation's mission will be required to submit documentation as eligibility for grant consideration. Site visits sometimes are made to organizations being considered for a grant. Decisions on grants are announced in the fall.

O+D+T Kristy L. Green (P+D+Con) — Jerry Arbaugh, CPA (F+D) — Frank Baker [Elderton] (D) — Donna Blose (D) — Robert A. Cinpinski, Esq. (D) — Joseph Cippel [Ford City] (D) — Joseph R. Dannels [Cowansville] (D) — Philip Dunmire (D) — Robert Hallman, Sr. (D) — Patricia Kirkpatrick (D) — Ralph Knepshield (D) — Jeffrey A. Mantini [Ford City] (D) — John Shoop (D) — Jack Steiner, Esq. (D)

NW-003 Bean (Calvin Z.) Community Service
c/o John M. Read Temple Assn.
25 North 4th Street, P.O. Box 213
Reynoldsville   15851   (Elk County)

MI-44-89

Phone 814-653-2455 **FAX** None
EIN 25-6341398   **Year Created** 1990

AMV $388,907   **FYE** 6-00   **(Gifts Received** $0)   2 **Grants totaling** $21,000

All local giving. High grant of **$20,000** to Reynoldsville Public Library. **$1,000** to Reynoldsville Fire Dept. ■ **PUBLICATIONS:** None
■ **WEBSITE:** None ■ **E-MAIL:** None ■ **APPLICATION POLICIES & PROCEDURES:** No grants awarded to individuals.

O+D+T Richard R. Gordon, CPA (F+Con) — Robert L. Vizza (P) — Melvin Uplinger (VP) — Frank B. Bussard (S)

NW-004 Betts Foundation, The
c/o Betts Industries, Inc.
1800 Pennsylvania Ave. West, P.O. Box 88
Warren   16365   (Warren County)

MI-11-13-15-19-20-25-31-42-43-71-89

Phone 814-723-1250 **FAX** None
EIN 25-6035169   **Year Created** 1957

AMV $3,537,328   **FYE** 12-00   **(Gifts Received** $75,000)   45 **Grants totaling** $206,616

Mostly local/Pa. giving. High grant of **$50,000** to Warren Sports Boosters. **$34,575** to City of Warren. **$25,500** to Salvation Army/Warren. **$20,000** to Warren County YMCA. **$13,825** to United Fund of Warren County. **$12,500** to The Rouse Home. **$5,000** to Warren Senior Center. **$3,500** to Warren County Commissioners. **$3,116** to Warren County School District. **$2,696** to

Betts Foundation Drug Education Program. **$2,000** to Assn. of Independent College of Pa. [Harrisburg]. **$1,000-$1,500** each to Cherry Grove Volunteer Fire Dept., George Junior Republic, Lacy Community Park Foundation, North Warren Volunteer Fire Dept., Soccer Assn. of Warren, Starbrick Volunteer Fire Dept., Wrightsville Volunteer Fire Dept. Other smaller contributions. In addition, scholarships of **$500** each were disbursed to 21 Pa. and NY colleges/universities for 47 local students. ■**PUBLICATIONS:** None ■**WEBSITE:** None ■**E-MAIL:** None ■**APPLICATION POLICIES & PROCEDURES:** Grant requests may be submitted in any form at any time; telephone requests/inquiries also are accepted. Scholarships are awarded principally to Warren County residents; contact local high schools for more information.

O+D+T Richard T. Betts (T+Con) — Clifford R. - Betts (T) — R.E. Betts (T) — M. Dennis Hedges, Jr. (T) — Corporate donor: Betts Industries, Inc.

NW-005 **Black Family Foundation, The**
    c/o Black & Associates Insurance
    400 French Street
    Erie 16507   (Erie County)

MI-11-12-13-14-25-35-49-51-52-54-55-57

Phone 814-453-6746 **FAX** None
EIN 25-1705824   **Year Created** 1993

AMV $1,085,433   **FYE** 12-00   **(Gifts Received** $180,000)   30 **Grants totaling** $158,050

All local giving. High grant of **$100,000** to Gertrude Barber Foundation. **$14,000** to United Way of Erie. **$8,000** to Erie Philharmonic. **$3,400** to Make-A-Wish Foundation. **$3,000** each to ACES, Pa. Free Enterprise Week, and United Arts Fund. **$2,500** to House of Healing. **$2,000** to Community Shelter Services. **$1,000-$1,600** each to Erie Dawn, Erie Art Museum, Gifts for Kids, Glinodo Center, Lake Erie Ballet, Morningstar Baptist Church, Neighborhood Art House, Special Olympics, Sara Reed Children's Center, St. Paul's Free Clinic, WQLN, Woman's Club of Erie, and YMCA of Greater Erie. Other contributions **$300-$800** for various purposes. ■**PUBLICATIONS:** None ■**WEBSITE:** None ■**E-MAIL:** None ■**APPLICATION POLICIES & PROCEDURES:** The Foundation reports that giving is limited to local organizations. No grants awarded to individuals. Submit grant requests in a letter during October-November; provide details on the charitable organization's purpose and include an annual report and IRS tax-exempt status documentation. Site visits sometimes are made to organizations being considered for a grant. Grants are awarded at a December meeting.

O+D+T Samuel P. Black, III (P+Con) — James D. Cullen (S+F) — Robert L. Wagner (AS+AF)

NW-006 **Blaisdell (Philo & Sarah) Foundation**
    410 Seneca Building
    2 Main Street
    Bradford 16701   (McKean County)

MI-12-13-14-23-29-31-41-42-44-51-52-55-72-84-89

Phone 814-362-6340 **FAX** None
EIN 25-6035748   **Year Created** 1950

AMV $4,808,629   **FYE** 12-00   **(Gifts Received** $609)   71 **Grants totaling** $466,381

All giving limited to/for McKean County. High grant of **$200,000** Bradford Family YMCA (building fund). **$50,000** Bach to Bradford Educational Foundation (for scholarships) and Bradford Regional Medical Center (cardiology center). **$35,000** to Bradford Marching Owls Boosters (uniforms/equipment). **$13,750** to Futures Rehabilitation Center (mentally handicapped programs). **$12,300** to Bradford Family YMCA (swim program). **$10,000-$10,600** each to Bradford Area Creative & Performing Arts (programs), Bradford Township Volunteer Fire Dept. (thermal imaging equipment), Bradford YWCA (building repairs), and McKean County SPCA (building repairs). **$8,000** to Beacon Light Behavioral Systems (reading systems). **$6,500** to Bradford Area Public Library (new compressor). **$6,000** to Western Pa. Caring for Children (children's hospitalization insurance). **$5,812** to Bradford Area School District (program equipment). **$4,100** to U. of Pittsburgh at Bradford (foreign study program). **$3,400** each to Make-A-Wish Foundation of Western Pa. (transportation). **$2,500** to First Night Bradford (community events). **$2,000** to Friendship Table (meals program). **$1,000-$1,048** each to ATA Transport, Bradford Family Center (programs), Lewis Run Borough (playground equipment), and Move Over Boys Sports (programs). Other organizational contributions **$100-$700** for various purposes. Also, 15 donations **$100-$2,895** to individuals for medical or special personal needs. ■**PUBLICATIONS:** None ■**WEBSITE:** None ■**E-MAIL:** None ■**APPLICATION POLICIES & PROCEDURES:** The Foundation reports that giving is generally limited to McKean County organizations and residents. Prospective applicants initially should make a telephone inquiry about the feasibility of submitting a request. Grant requests may be submitted in a letter (2 pages maximum) at any time; include both organizational and project budgets. The scholarship awards (for McKean County residents only) are administered by the Office of Financial Aid, University of Pittsburgh at Bradford, telephone 814-362-7500.

O+D+T Howard L. Fesenmyer (Executive Secretary+Con) — Sarah B. Dorn (T) — George B. Duke (T) — Paul C. Duke (T) — Richard McDowell (T) — Corporate donor: Zippo Manufacturing Company

---

NW-007 **Blake (Charles I.) Family Foundation**
    c/o First Commonwealth Trust Company
    Shaffer Road, P.O. Box 1046
    DuBois 15801   (Clearfield County)

MI-13-42-43

Phone 814-371-0660 **FAX** 814-375-5449
EIN 25-6311914   **Year Created** 1988

AMV $622,979   **FYE** 12-00   **(Gifts Received** $0)   3 **Grants totaling** $34,000

All giving to Erie. High grant of **$13,000** to YMCA of Greater Erie (unrestricted). **$10,500** each to Mercyhurst College (4th of July celebration) and Wolves Club of Erie/Den VIII (scholarship program at Mercyhurst College). **Note:** These three grantees have been the only grant recipients for some years. ■**PUBLICATIONS:** None ■**WEBSITE:** None ■**E-MAIL:** None ■**APPLICATION POLICIES & PROCEDURES:** Information not available.

O+D+T D. Edward Chaplin (Executive VP at Bank+Con) — Charles I. Blake (Donor) — First Commonwealth Trust Company (Trustee)

NW-008 Britton Family Foundation, The
c/o MacDonald, Illig, Jones & Britton
100 State Street, Suite 700
Erie 16507 (Erie County)

MI-11-13-22-32-41-56

Phone 814-870-7600 **FAX** None
EIN 25-1618532 **Year Created** 1989

AMV $3,624,345 **FYE** 11-00 **(Gifts Received** $0) 7 **Grants totaling** $190,350

All local giving; all grants are for unrestricted support. high grant of **$175,000** to Dr. Gertrude A. Barber Foundation. **$10,000** to Greater Erie Charity Golf Classic. **$2,000** to City Mission New Life Center. **$12,50** to Boy Scouts/French Creek Council. **$1,000** to Muscular Dystrophy Foundation. Other smaller contributions. — Grants awarded in the prior year included **$100,000** each to Boys & Girls Club of Erie and Erie Day School; **$75,000** to Warner Theater Preservation Trust; and **$25,000** to United Way of Erie County. ■**PUBLICATIONS:** None ■**WEBSITE:** None ■**E-MAIL:** None ■**APPLICATION POLICIES & PROCE-DURES:** The Foundation reports that most grants are for special projects or capital drives. Grant requests may be submitted in any form at any time; include a project budget, Board member list, list of major funding sources, and IRS tax-exempt status documentation. No grants are awarded to individuals.
O+D+T John E. Britton, Esq. (P+D+Donor+Con) — Suzanne E. Britton (VP+S+D) — John W. Britton [Waterford] (VP+F+D)

NW-009 Community Foundation of Warren County
P.O. Box 691
Warren 16365
(Warren County)

MI-11-12-13-14-15-20-22-29-31-32-42-43-44
54-55-56-63-71-83-84-85-89
Phone 814-726-9553 **FAX** 814-726-5302
EIN 25-1380549 **Year Created** 1949

AMV $35,322,721 **FYE** 12-00 **(Gifts Received** $676,656) 430+ **Grants totaling** $1,172,800

As a Community Foundation all discretionary giving is limited to organizations serving Warren County and vicinity; about 50 grants totaling **$803,050** were awarded—some from discretionary funds. High grant of **$155,763** to Struthers Library Building. **$145,795** to United Fund of Warren County. **$97,014** to Warren Library Assn. **$49,994** to First United Methodist Church of Warren. **$49,328** to Donald H. Mills Center. **$39,167** to Salvation Army of Warren. **$36,015** to Warren County Senior Center. **$17,000** to Penn Lakes Girl Scout Council. **$15,695** to Warren County Assn. for Retarded Children. **$14,120** each to Warren County Chamber of Commerce and YMCA of Warren County. **$9,800-$12,750** each to Boy Scouts/Chief Cornplanter Council, Jefferson DeFrees Family Center, Pa. Economy League, Rouse Warren County Home, Warren Concert Assn., Warren County Probation Assn., and Warren/Forest Higher Education Council. **$5,000-$7,500** each to American Cancer Society/Warren County Unit, American Heart Assn./Warren County Chapter, First Presbyterian Church of Warren, Lacy Playground Assn., Ophelia Project of Warren, Sheffield Parks & Recreation Committee, Ruth M. Smith Center, and Warren Main Street Manager Program. **$2,000-$4,400** each to ARC Enterprises of Warren, Bethlehem Covenant Church, Northern Allegheny Conservation Assn., Red Cross, U.S. Marine Corps/General Pendleton Detachment, Warren Baseball Boosters, Warren County Historical Society, and Warren County School District. **$1,000-$1,611** each to Cherry Grove Volunteer Fire Dept., Grace Methodist Church of Warren, Interfaith Center of Warren State Hospital, Pa. Special Olympics, Warren Civic Orchestra, Warren General Hospital (pediatrics), Warren Jaycees, and Wesbury United Methodist Community. Other smaller contributions for various purposes including many churches. In addition, scholarships totaling **$370,750** were awarded to about 380 local students. ■**PUBLICATIONS:** annual report ■**WEBSITE:** None ■**E-MAIL:** warrenfoundation@westpa.net ■**APPLICATION POLICIES & PROCEDURES:** The Foundation reports that all discretionary giving is restricted to Warren County; most grants are for special projects, building funds, capital drives, scholarships, and matching grants. Grant requests from Warren County organizations may be submitted at any time in a formal, full proposal with cover letter; include organization and project budgets, list of major funding sources, and IRS tax-exempt status documentation. Site visits sometimes are made to organizations being considered for a grant. The Distribution Committee meets monthly to award organizational grants. Scholarship applications must be received in the Spring before an early May deadline (call for exact date). — Formerly called Warren Foundation.
O+D+T Distribution Committee members: Charles E. MacKenzie, M.D. (Director+S+Con) — John O. Hanna (Chairman, Distribution Committee) — Bernard J. Hessley — Gerald A. Huber — Edward A. Kavanaugh — Murray K. McComas — Trustee banks: PNC Bank N.A.; National City Bank of Pa., Northwest Savings Bank

NW-010 Conarro Family Foundation
105 East Street
Warren 16365 (Warren County)

MI-11-22-25-32-41-42-44-72
Phone 814-723-8160 **FAX** None
EIN 25-6612120 **Year Created** 1998

AMV $594,537 **FYE** 12-00 **(Gifts Received** $180,000) 12 **Grants totaling** $31,100

Mostly local/Pa. giving. High grant of **$11,000** to Struthers Library (building fund/theatre). **$5,000** each to The Hill School [Montgomery County] and Warren YMCA. **$2,000** each to Salvation Army and Warren County Humane Society. **$1,500** to Faith in Action Housing Coalition [Russell]. **$1,100** to Crohn's & Colitis Foundation of Western Pa. **$1,000** to United Fund of Warren. Other smaller local contributions. **Out-of-state** grant: **$1,500** to Dartmouth College [NH]. ■**PUBLICATIONS:** None ■**WEBSITE:** None ■**E-MAIL:** None ■**APPLICATION POLICIES & PROCEDURES:** The Foundation reports that giving is restricted to the Warren area; only local organizations are eligible to apply.
O+D+T Harry W. Conarro, Esq. (T+Donor+Con) — Mary E. Conarro (Donor)

NW-011 Crawford Heritage Foundation, The
c/o Seco/Warwick Corp. - Attn. Paul Huber
180 Mercer Street
Meadville 16335 (Crawford County)

MI-11-13-18-31-43-56-63
Phone 814-336-5206 **FAX** None
EIN 25-1813245 **Year Created** 1998

AMV $1,118,388 **FYE** 12-00 **(Gifts Received** $861,923) 16 **Grants totaling** $28,913

As a Community Foundation all discretionary giving is limited to organizations serving Crawford County. High grant of **$4,558** to Titusville Area Health Center. **$3,516** to United Way of Crawford County. **$3,200** to Crawford County Historical Society. **$2,550** each to Centerville Baptist Church, Centerville Methodist Church. and YMCA of Titusville. **$1,000-$1,500** each to Titusville Leisure Services and five college scholarships for local students. **$916** to Meadville YMCA. **$800** to Family Planning Services. Other smaller contributions for Methodist churches. ■**PUBLICATIONS:** scholarship application form ■**WEBSITE:** www.sideroads.com/crawfordheritage/ ■**E-MAIL:** youngs@toolcity.net ■**APPLICATION POLICIES & PROCEDURES:** Only Crawford County nonprofit organizations are eligible to apply. The Grantmaking Committee screens applications using a needs-based approach. Scholarships for Crawford County students are based on need and a formal application form must be completed; awards are sent directly to the colleges/universities.

O+D+T Lisa Pepicelli-Youngs, Esq. [Cochranton] (P+Con) — Paul Huber (1st VP) — Christine Lang (2nd VP) — Marnie Kirkpatrick (3rd VP) — Melissa Mencotti (Corporate Secretary) — Kenneth Montag (Recording Secretary) — John Hodges (F+D) — Dwight Haas (AF+D) — Rev. Susan Buell (D) — Harold W. Coleman (D) — Rev. Barry Cressman [Titusville] (D) — Christopher Junker, Esq. (D) — Milosh Mamula [Cambridge Springs] (D) — Kathi Miller (D) — Stephen Mizner (D) — Dr. John Nesbit (D) — Rev. William Smith (D) — Mark Strausbaugh (D) — Earl Yingling (D)

NW-012 **D'Angelo (George J. & Mary T.) Foundation**

3232 Westwood Estates Drive

Erie 16506 (Erie County)

AMV $368,995 **FYE** 12-00 (**Gifts Received** $160,000)

MI-13-31-41-42-52

Phone 814-833-9065 **FAX** None

EIN 25-1661862 **Year Created** 1991

25 **Grants totaling** $97,250

About three-fourths local/Pa. giving. High grant of **$30,000** to Erie Boys & Girls Club. **$10,000** each to Erie Youth Symphony Orchestra, Hamot Second Century Fund, and Lehigh U. **$3,000** to Millcreek Educational Fund. **$2,500** to Warner Theatre Restoration. **$2,000** to Our Lady of Peace School. **$1,000** each to Community Country Day School, Discovery Square, Erie Community Foundation, Erie Philharmonic, Marilyn Horne Foundation, and Palmer Fund. Other smaller local contributions for various purposes. **Out-of-state** giving includes **$15,000** to Metropolitan Opera [NY] and **$2,500** to U. of Rochester Medical Center [NY]. ■**PUBLICATIONS:** None ■**WEBSITE:** None ■**E-MAIL:** None ■**APPLICATION POLICIES & PROCEDURES:** The Foundation reports that giving is limited to Northwestern Pa. with a preference for musical or educational organizations; grants are awarded for special projects or musical/arts scholarships. Grant requests may be submitted in a letter (2 pages maximum) during September-October (deadline is November 15th)—provide two copies; include an annual report, organization and project budgets, and IRS tax-exempt status documentation. Grants are awarded at a November meeting.

O+D+T Mary T. D'Angelo (P+T+Con) — Josephine D'Angelo [MA] (VP+T) — Gina D'Angelo [FL] (S+F+T) — George J. D'Angelo, M.D. (T+Donor)

NW-013 **Dailey (Charles A.) Foundation**

5127 Wolf Run Village Lane

Erie 16505 (Erie County)

AMV $1,202,729 **FYE** 11-00 (**Gifts Received** $0)

MI-11-32-42-61

Phone 814-838-4619 **FAX** 814-838-4619

EIN 25-6035686 **Year Created** 1952

15 **Grants totaling** $55,200

Mostly local giving. High grant of **$30,000** to Mercyhurst College. **$10,000** to St. Peter's Cathedral. **$7,600** to YMCA of Greater Erie. **$5,000** to Dr. Gertrude Barber Foundation. **$1,000** to United Way of Erie. Other contributions **$100-$500** for various charities. ■**PUBLICATIONS:** None ■**WEBSITE:** None ■**E-MAIL:** None ■**APPLICATION POLICIES & PROCEDURES:** Information not available.

O+D+T Charles A. Dailey (P+D+Donor+Con) — Ellen G. Dailey (D) — Deborah Dailey Currie (D) — William C. Sennett (D)

NW-014 **DeFrees Family Foundation**

c/o Allegheny Coupling Company

419 Third Ave., P.O. Box 708

Warren 16365 (Warren County)

AMV $10,316,399 **FYE** 12-00 (**Gifts Received** $0)

MI-12-13-15-22-33-41-42-43-49-51-52-55-56 65-72-84-89

Phone 814-723-8150 **FAX** 814-723-8400

EIN 25-1320042 **Year Created** 1978

53 **Grants totaling** $328,909

Mostly local/Western Pa. giving; grants are for general program support except as noted. High grants of **$25,000** each to Penn Lakes Girl Scout Council (capital campaign) and YMCA of Warren (capital campaign). **$12,500** each to Warren County School District (SMARTS program) and Warren Senior Center (elevator). **$12,000** to Boy Scouts/Chief Cornplanter Council (Learning for Life/program). **$10,000** each to Library Summer Theater, Mental Health of Warren (hospice), The Ophelia Project [Erie] (seed money), Penn State U. (scholarships), Pa. Free Enterprise Week [Erie] (scholarships), Rouse Home (Alzheimer's unit), U. of Pa. (endowment), U. of Pittsburgh-Titusville (scholarships/technology), Warren-Forest Higher Education Council (scholarships), Woman's Club of Warren (historical preservation group), and Youth Baseball/Softball. **$5,000** to City of Warren (playground rehabilitation), Friends Hospital [Philadelphia] (Scattergood Fund), Jefferson Elementary School (playground), Pa. Economy League [Harrisburg], Russell Volunteer Fire Dept. (new truck), Salvation Army, Warren County Soccer Assn., and Western Pa. Caring Foundation [Pittsburgh]. **$3,000** each to Warren Civic Orchestra, Warren County Humane Society, Scandia Volunteer Fire Dept. (handicapped rest rooms), and Warren Concert Assn. **$2,000-$2,500** each to American Cancer Society, Community Support Services (respite program), Pa. Special Olympics (Warren summer games), and Warren County Jail Ministry. **$1,000** each to Brother's Brother Foundation [Pittsburgh], RSVP (volunteer recognition), Warren County 4-H, and Youth Connection of Warren. Other local contributions **$150-$500** for various purposes. **Out-of-state** giving includes **$11,609** to Jamestown Audubon Society [NY] (tractor); **$6,000** to Fund for Human Possibility [NC]; **$5,000** to Cumberland College [KY] (scholarships); and **$1,000** to U.S. English Foundation. ■**PUBLICATIONS:** Guidelines for Grants and Applications for Grants memoranda ■**WEBSITE:** www.alleghenycoupling.com [corporate info only] ■**E-MAIL:** acc@alleghenycoupling.com ■**APPLICATION POLICIES & PROCEDURES:** The Foundation reports that it assists efforts to solve problems in Warren and Warren County through one-time grants, and to improve the quality of life of the area's residents through continuing aid to worthy organizations. Most grants are for special projects, research, or scholarships. Support for construction is limited to exceptional circumstances when related to a larger program which the Foundation wishes to support. Grants normally are for one year only. No grants are awarded to/for relief projects, individuals, or loans. Grant requests in the form of a proposal should include (1) a brief description of the organization's purposes, activities and leadership; (2) a detailed description of the purpose for which a grants is sought and the plan/timetable for accomplishing that; (3) copy of annual budget and project budget, (4) particulars on person(s) administering the proposed project or program, (5) list of Board members, and (6) IRS tax-exempt status documentation. Deadlines for requests are March 1st, July 1st, and October 1st; all applications are acknowledged. Grants are awarded at meetings in April, August and November.

O+D+T Harold A. Johnson (P+F+Con) — David E. Martin (VP+S) — Mary Garvey [Russell] (AF) — William M. Hill, Jr. [North Warren] (D) — Susan J. Merritt (D)

NW-015 **Eccles (Ralph M. & Ella M.) Foundation**   MI-13-31-41-44-63-84
    213 Seneca Street, 3rd Floor
    P.O. Box 374   **Phone** 814-677-5085   **FAX** 814-677-3404
    Oil City   16301   (Venango County)   **EIN** 23-7261807   **Year Created** 1972
AMV $4,643,329   **FYE** 12-00   (Gifts Received $0)   5 **Grants totaling** $272,779

All giving restricted to organizations serving Clarion County with the Rimersburg area receiving priority. High grant of **$192,261** to Eccles-Lesher Memorial Library. **$43,830** to Union School District. **$19,150** to Rimersburg Little League. **$14,798** to Rimersburg Medical Center. **$3,000** to United Methodist Church of Rimersburg. — In prior years support were awarded to other local organizations, school districts, and local governments. ■**PUBLICATIONS:** application guidelines ■**WEBSITE:** None ■**E-MAIL:** None ■**APPLICATION POLICIES & PROCEDURES:** Only organizations serving Clarion County are eligible to apply; most grants are for operating budgets, special projects, capital purchases, matching funds, seed money and emergency funds; multi-year grants are awarded. No grants for research, endowment, or to individuals. Prospective applicants initially should make a telephone inquiry about the feasibility of submitting a request. A formal application form, available from the foundation, will be provided and should be submitted in duplicate, preferably in April, August or November; include an annual report, organizational budget, project budget, audited financial statement, list of other funding sources, Board member list, and IRS tax-exempt status documentation. Site visits sometimes are made to organizations being considered for a grant. Grants are awarded in May, September, and December.

O+D+T Stephen P. Kosak (Consultant+Con) — National City Bank of Pa. (Trustee)

NW-016 **Eldred (Ruby Marsh) Scholarship Fund**   MI-43
    Old Post Office Building
    941 Federal Court   **Phone** 814-337-7662   **FAX** None
    Meadville   16335   (Crawford County)   **EIN** 25-6114997   **Year Created** 1969
AMV $315,061   **FYE** 6-01   (Gifts Received $0)   20 **Grants totaling** $16,700

All giving restricted to college scholarship grants for needy students residing in parts of central or western Crawford County; awards were **$600, $900** or **$1,000**. ■**PUBLICATIONS:** General Information Sheet, Application Form ■**WEBSITE:** None ■**E-MAIL:** None ■**APPLICATION POLICIES & PROCEDURES:** Only residents of central or western Crawford County—for at least one year—are eligible to apply. An applicant must rank in the top quartile of one's high school graduating class and must enroll (or be enrolled) in a regionally accredited 2-year or 4-year institution. A formal application form which details procedures and documentation is available from the Trust and should be submitted during January-March; the deadline is April 1st. Recipients will be notified in late April. Awards can be renewed up to five consecutive years, depending upon need and academic record.

O+D+T Mary Ann Kirkpatrick, Esq. (Con) — PNC Bank N.A. (Trustee)

NW-017 **Elk County Community Foundation**   MI-29-43-44-85
    111 Erie Ave.   **Phone** 814-834-2125   **FAX** 814-834-2126
    St. Marys   15857   (Elk County)   **EIN** 25-1859637   **Year Created** 2000
AMV $793,000   **FYE** 12-01   (Gifts Received $720,000)   17 **Grants totaling** $96,000

As a Community Foundation all discretionary giving is limited to organizations serving Elk County; in 2001 all giving was from donor-advised or from restricted funds with grants for libraries, economic development, civic/community organizations, or scholarships. ■**PUBLICATIONS:** Grant Application form ■**WEBSITE:** None ■**E-MAIL:** eccf@penn.com ■**APPLICATION POLICIES & PROCEDURES:** The Foundation reports that all discretionary giving must benefit Elk County residents; grants are awarded to nonprofit organizations in the fields of The Arts, The Environment, Health & Social Services, Education, and Economic Development. Scholarships for local students are also awarded. Normally, no grants are awarded for operating purposes or budget deficits. Grant requests must be submitted on a Grant Application form available from the Foundation; completed applications must attach the following: operating budget for the previous, current and next fiscal years, including income statement and balance sheet; the two most recent year-end financial statements, audited if possible; names/addresses of Board members and administrative staff; and IRS tax-exempt status documentation.

O+D+T Martha A. Engel (Executive Director+S+Con) — Richard Masson (P+T) — Bea Terbovich [Ridgway] (VP+T) — J.M. Hamlin Johnson (F+T) — Paul Brazinski, Jr. [Ridgway] (T) — William C. Conrad (T) — Charles Constable [Johnsonburg] (T) — Douglas Dobson [Ridgway] (T) — Judy Manno-Stager [Ridgway] (T) — Jake Meyer (T) — Lou Radowski (T) — Daniel Straub (T) — Larry Thorwart (T) — Larry Whiteman (T)

NW-018 **Emporium Foundation**   MI-12-13-15-20-21-31-35-41-55-71-84-85-89
    c/o Sun Bank, 2 East Fourth Street   **Phone** 814-486-3333   **FAX** 814-486-2081
    Emporium   15834   (Cameron County)   **EIN** 25-0995760   **Year Created** 1929
AMV $4,846,835   **FYE** 12-00   (Gifts Received $0)   33 **Grants totaling** $155,244

As a Community Foundation all discretionary giving is limited to organizations serving Cameron County; some grants comprise multiple awards. High grant of **$47,158** to Cameron County Recreation Board (general budget/playgrounds). **$20,000** to Emporium Volunteer Fire Dept. (tanker truck). **$16,000** to Sinnemahoning Volunteer Fire Dept. (truck purchase). **$13,950** to Emporium-Cameron County Chamber of Commerce (new computers/other purposes). **$13,625** to Cameron County High School (Honor Society/Music Boosters/other projects). **$11,220** to Cameron County Little League. **$4,000** to Cameron County Tourist Promotion Agency. **$1,000-$3,100** each to Boy Scout Troop #551, Bucktail Rod & Gun Club, Cameron County Arts, Cameron County Fair Assn., Cub Scouts Pack #591, Drum & Henry Kids Fishing Derby Committee, Emporium Alle-Cat Baseball Assn., Emporium Shade Tree Commission, Fourth of July Celebration Committee, Mountain Country Archery, Mountain Country Search & Rescue, Scan Pep & Family Center, Woodland Elementary School, and Young Art Makers. Other smaller local contributions. ■**PUBLICATIONS:** None ■**WEBSITE:** None ■**E-MAIL:** None ■**APPLICATION POLICIES & PROCEDURES:** Only Cameron County organizations or those serving county residents are eligible to apply. Grant requests may be submitted in a letter at any time; include the organization name and contact person, purpose of the requested grant, and the date when funds are needed.

O+D+T L. William Smith (F+Con) — James B. Miller (P) — Edward B. Lundberg (VP) — Edwin W. Tompkins, III (S) — David E. Guloien (AS) — John T. Rogers (AF)

NW-019 **Erie Community Foundation, The**
  127 West 6th Street
  Erie   16501
  (Erie County)

MI-11-12-13-14-15-17-20-22-29-31-32-35-41
42-44-49-51-52-54-55-56-57-72-81-84-85
Phone 814-454-0843 **FAX** 814-456-4965
EIN 25-6032032   **Year Created** 1935

AMV $100,900,000 est.   **FYE** 12-01   (**Gifts Received** $14,490,174)   500+ **Grants totaling** $6,933,853

As a Community Foundation all discretionary giving is limited to organizations serving Erie County; over 90 grants from discretionary funds were awarded in five major interest area with some grants comprising multiple payments. **I. ARTS & CULTURE GRANTS: $56,500** to Arts Council of Erie. **$50,000** to Asbury Woods (capital campaign). **$29,000** to Erie Civic Ballet/Lake Erie Ballet (annual support/building renovations). **$25,000** each to Erie County Historical Society & Museums (documentation continuation) and Erie Philharmonic (concert series sponsorship/instruments/etc.). **$21,000** to Lake Erie Arboretum at Frontier Park (electrical system). **$16,000** to Roadhouse Theater (performance support/facility repairs). **$10,000** each to Erie Youth Symphony Orchestra (office equipment), Erie Zoological Society (museum guide), Humane Society of NW Pa. (equipment), and WQLN (public service announcements). **$7,500** to Harry T. Burleigh Society (documentary/teacher guide). **$6,000** each to Erie Art Museum (dance festival), Erie Opera Theatre (production support), and expERIEence Children's Museum (office equipment). **$5,000** to Lake Erie Fanfare (office equipment upgrade). **$2,200** to Presque Isle Chorale (summer performances). **II. ECONOMIC OPPORTUNITY/CIVIC ENGAGEMENT GRANTS: $13,500** to Chamber of Commerce (technology upgrade/promotional program/special event). **$13,000** to Center for Nonprofit Services (general support). **$12,100** to Foundation for Free Enterprise Education (Free Enterprise Week). **$10,000** to Economic Research Institute of Erie (website). **$8,000** each to ACES, Inc. (business management experience program) and Erie Conference on Community Development (forums). **$3,000** to Mercy Center for Women (Ladies Economic Advancement Program). **III. EDUCATION GRANTS: $224,000** to Gannon U. (Information into Action program/capital campaign). **$85,000** to Gertrude A. Barber Center (commitment payment). **$65,000** to Penn State U./Behrend (commitment payment/4-H Agent/youth development program). **$50,000** to Bayfront Center for Maritime Studies (new educational facility). **$40,000** to Community Country Day School (school-family program/Community 2001 program). **$23,250** to Sarah Reed Children's Center (therapeutic classrooms). **$20,000** each to Ophelia Project (offices/volunteer training) and Western Pa. Caring Foundation (staff training). **$10,000** each to Fellowship of Christian Athletes (school assembly program), Northwestern Legal Services (technology upgrade), Presque Isle Partnership (Perry Monument exhibit), Quality of Life Learning Center (merger expenses). **$7,500** to Leadership Erie (Nonprofit Leadership Day). **$4,000-$4,200** each to Glinodo Center (educators training) and KIDco/TADco (anti-drug training). **$2,500-$3,000** each to Edinboro U. (astronomy education program), Gannon U. (Fish Commish), and Union City Public Library (community support project). Other smaller contributions. **IV. HEALTH GRANTS: $90,000** to Community Health Net (community-based clinic services/dental equipment). **$40,000** to Healthcare Ventures Alliance (wellness equipment). **$30,000** to Vision & Blindness Resources-Erie Center (facility expansion/name change). **$20,000** each to Achievement Center (dictation system/summer day camp program), Case Management Support Services (Kids connection), Gannon U. (psychology services clinic), and Protection for Abuse (victim services). **$18,000** to Erie County WIC Program (East Erie County program). **$15,000** each to Gaudenzia Crossroads (building renovations) and Stairways (safety-security project). **$10,000** each to American Respiratory Alliance (facility repairs), MECA/UCP (home ramp building), and Northwestern Pa. Optical Clinic (liaison officer-coordinator). **$5,000-$7,000** each to Erie Independence House (automatic door), Hamot Diabetes Care Center (camp for diabetic children), Sisters of Mercy (infirmary equipment), and St. Paul's Neighborhood Clinic (storage area). **$2,000-$4,000** each to Forresters' Harbor (respite care), Lutheran Home (residents' property ID), and Maryvale Apartments (defibrillator). **V. FAMILIES & NEIGHBORHOODS GRANTS: $74,509** to Erie YWCA (Heinz Child Care Project). **$32,000** to SafeNet (roof repairs). **$30,000** each to Bayfront NATO/MLK Center (boiler repairs) and Perseus House (technology/HVAC). **$29,000** to St. Martin Center (school bus/walk-in freezer). **$21,000** to United Way of Erie County (computers). **$26,000** to Maria House Projects (truck and van). **$24,000** to Boys & Girls Clubs of Erie (communications infrastructure). **$20,000** each to First Presbyterian Church of North East (handicapped accessible addition). Lower Eastside Sports Center (building purchase). **$15,000** to Joel II Ministries (facility repairs). **$12,000** each to Edinboro Chamber of Commerce (baseball field) and International Institute (interior repairs/office equipment). **$11,000** to Habitat for Humanity (delivery truck). **$10,000** each to Christian Institute of Human Relations (sound system), Community of Caring (facilities renovations), and Erie-Western Pa. Port Authority (free ferry program). **$7,000-$8,000** each to Bayfront East Side Taskforce (master plan development), Camp Notre Dame (sponsorships/youth festival), Erie Silent Club (restoration), Gifts for Kids (sprinkler system), and House of Healing (handicap accessibility-playground). **$5,000** each to Bethany House II (shelter repairs) and CARE/Citizens Against Racism in Erie (research study). **$5,000** each to Holy Trinity Lutheran Church (community center) and Make-A-Wish Foundation (display unit). **$3,500** to Community Shelter Services (voice mail system). **$1,500** to Pa. Special Olympics (summer games). **$1,000** to Card Table Connection (seniors information access). All other grants and scholarship awards from restricted funds. — Also, discretionary grants are awarded from two affiliated funds. **CORRY COMMUNITY FOUNDATION: $102,000** to YMCA of Corry; **$5,000** to United Fund of Corry; **$4,800** to Corry Memorial Hospital; **$4,000** to Corry Community Development Corp.; and **$430-$2,000** to seven other Corry organizations. **THE NORTH EAST COMMUNITY FOUNDATION: $3,900** to North East Arts Council and **$564-$1,547** to other North East community organizations. ■**PUBLICATIONS:** Annual Report; Guidelines for Grant Seekers pamphlet; Grant Summary Sheet ■**WEBSITE:** www.cferie.org ■**E-MAIL:** ecf@team.org ■ **APPLICATION POLICIES & PROCEDURES:** The Foundation reports that only Erie County nonprofit organizations are eligible to apply. When grant requests from discretionary/unrestricted funds are being considered, preference will be given to applications that: (a) propose practical solutions to community problems; (b) promote cooperation among existing agencies without duplicating services—joint proposals from multiple agencies addressing a single community issue are given priority; (c) utilize volunteers effectively; (d) leverage additional resources; (e) have broad-based appeal (as measured by support from other sources); (f) are one-time expenses with a realistic plan for sustainability; and (g) primarily address preventive measures—a hand up, not a hand out. Most grants are for one year only and are for building funds, capital needs, equipment, matching grants, special projects, seed money, and emergency needs. Grants are not normally awarded to/for operations, budget deficits, seed money, or political or religious purposes; and no direct assistance is given to individuals. Prospective applicants are encouraged to discuss with Foundation staff a proposed project prior to submission of a full application; also consult the website for application guidelines and the required Grant Summary Sheet (downloadable). Deadlines for completed applications are February 1st, May 1st, August 1st, and November 1st in order for consideration at meetings in March, June, September, and December. Site visits sometimes are made to organizations being considered for a grant.

O+D+T Michael L. Batchelor (P+Con) — Raymond L. McGarvey (C+T) — M. Peter Scibetta, M.D. (VC+T) — James D. McDonald, Jr. Esq. (S+T) — Edward P. Junker, III (F+T) — Joan F. Bert (T) — Sister Joan D. Chittister, O.S.B. (T) — Thomas L. Doolin (T) — William M. Hilbert, Sr. (T) — William J. Hill (T) — Trustee Banks: Mellon Bank N.A.; National City Bank of Pa.; PNC Bank N.A.

NW-020 Fish (Henry E. & Laurana S.) Foundation

2802 Zuck Road
Erie 16506   (Erie County)

MI-11-13-41-42-84
Phone 814-833-9072 **FAX** None
EIN 25-1567601   **Year Created** 1987

AMV $576,464   **FYE** 12-00   (**Gifts Received** $0)   19 **Grants totaling** $24,300

About half local giving. High Pa. grant of **$4,500** to Erie Day School. **$3,000** to United Way of Erie County. **$2,000** to The Ophelia Project. **$1,000** to Allegheny College. Other local contributions **$100-$500** for various purposes. **Out-of-state** grant: **$10,100** to National Sports Academy [NY]. ■**PUBLICATIONS:** None ■**WEBSITE:** None ■**E-MAIL:** None ■**APPLICATION POLICIES & PROCEDURES:** The Foundation reports that Pa. charities receive priority. Submit grant requests in any form at any time; include a recent financial statement and IRS tax-exempt status documentation.

O+D+T Henry E. Fish (T+Donor+Con) — Laurana S. Fish (T+Donor)

NW-021 Glendorn Foundation, The

Forest Oil Building, 78 Main Street
Bradford 16701   (McKean County)

MI-13-31-32-42
Phone 814-368-7171 **FAX** 814-362-8113
EIN 25-1024349   **Year Created** 1953

AMV $3,407,529   **FYE** 12-01   (**Gifts Received** $100)   9 **Grants totaling** $214,500

One local grant: **$20,000** to U. of Pittsburgh/Bradford Campus. **Out-of-state** giving includes high grant of **$50,000** to New York Presbyterian Hospital; **$40,000** to Midland Memorial Foundation [TX]; **$37,500** to U. of Colorado Health Sciences Center (medical research); **$25,000** to Johns Hopkins U. (medical research); and other smaller grants for medical research purposes. — Local giving in the prior year included **$25,000** to YMCA of Bradford (education/endowment). ■**PUBLICATIONS:** None ■ **WEBSITE:** None ■**E-MAIL:** None ■**APPLICATION POLICIES & PROCEDURES:** The Foundation reports that only Trustee-initiated requests are considered. The Board meets in August and October.

O+D+T William F. Higie (Foundation Manager+S+Con) — Clayton D. Coburn [TX] (T) — David F. Dorn [CO] (T) — John C. Dorn [TX] (T) — Dale Bird Grubb [MN] (T) — Jeffrey W. Miller [CA] (T) — Carolyn Dorn Warner [CO] (T) — Leslie Dorn Young [CO] (T)

NW-022 Gray Family Foundation of DuBois

c/o First Commonwealth Trust Company
Shaffer Road, P.O. Box 1046
DuBois 15801   (Clearfield County)

MI-11-13-15-22-29-31-41-43-44-55-57-61-63
Phone 814-371-0660 **FAX** 814-375-5449
EIN 25-6311915   **Year Created** 1988

AMV $869,239   **FYE** 12-00   (**Gifts Received** $0)   35 **Grants totaling** $49,100

Mostly local giving; grants are for general purposes except as noted. High grant of **$6,000** to DuBois Area United Way. **$4,000** each to DuBois Area YMCA (capital campaign), Penn State Public Broadcasting, and St. Catherine of Siena Church (sister parish program). **$3,000** each to Catholic Social Services (emergency pregnancy services program), DuBois Area Catholic Schools (development/expansion), and Free Medical Clinic of DuBois. **$2,000-$2,500** each to Agape Community Services (outreach programs), Boy Scouts/Bucktail Council (Hallstrom Lodge), Cultural Resources, Inc. (performances), DuBois Educational Foundation (scholarships), DuBois Public Library (acquisitions), DuBois Regional Medical Center Auxiliary, (holiday ball), First United Presbyterian Church (pastoral care), Red Cross, and Salvation Army. **$1,500** each to DuBois Regional Medical Center (Hugs for Kids program) and DuBois Senior & Community Center (materials/improvements). Other local contributions, mostly **$500** each, for community organizations. **Out-of-state** grant: **$1,000** to Wooster College [OH]. ■**PUBLICATIONS:** None ■**WEBSITE:** None ■ **E-MAIL:** None ■**APPLICATION POLICIES & PROCEDURES:** The Foundation reports that only DuBois area organizations with specific projects or needs should apply. No grants awarded to individuals. Submit written requests in a letter by the November 1st deadline. Include the following: (1) a brief description of the organization, its legal name, history, and governing board members; (2) purpose for which the grant is requested; (3) itemized budget for the project/program and, if appropriate, a time schedule; (4) amount of money requested; (5) list of other sources of financial support, either committed or pending; (6) recent audited financial statement; (7) annual organizational budget; and (8) IRS tax-exempt status documentation. Organizational representatives may be asked to meet with a foundation trustee.

O+D+T D. Edward Chaplin (Executive VP at Bank+Con) — Jason S. Gray, Jr. (C+T+Donor) — Kathleen Gray Braun [MD] (T) — Elizabeth S. Gray (T) — Catherine E. Gray (T) — First Commonwealth Trust Company (Corporate Trustee)

NW-023 Grove City Foundation
c/o McNickle & Bonner
209 West Pine Street
Grove City   16127   (Mercer County)
AMV $1,056,643   **FYE** 12-00   (**Gifts Received** $10,141)

MI-31-43-44

Phone 724-458-9550 **FAX** None
EIN 25-6065759   **Year Created** 1948
10 **Grants totaling** $16,381

As a Community Foundation all discretionary giving is restricted to organizations the Grove City area. High grant of **$5,821** to Health & Oncology Services (pay medical bills). **$3,890** to Grove City Community Library (purchase books). **$2,040** to Porter Memorial Hospital (pay medical bills). Two scholarships of **$1,000** awarded, and three awards **$360-$900** each. Other smaller payments for various purposes. ■**PUBLICATIONS:** Annual Report; statement of program policy ■**WEBSITE:** None ■**E-MAIL:** gmccomb007@aol.com ■**APPLICATION POLICIES & PROCEDURES:** Only Grove City area organizations are eligible to apply. Prospective applicants should make a preliminary telephone inquiry to discuss the possible submission of an application. Grant requests may be submitted by letter (or orally) at any time.

O+D+T Timothy Bonner (S+Con) — Ernest D. May (C) — Norman S. Crill (D) — Joy R. Gallagher (D) — Dolores Rodgers (D) — Richard R. Stevenson (D) — Mellon Bank N.A. (Corporate Trustee)

NW-024 Hamlin (Hannah L.) Memorial Fund
c/o Hamlin Bank & Trust Company
333 West Main Street
Smethport   16749   (McKean County)
AMV $366,953   **FYE** 12-00   (**Gifts Received** $0)

MI-11-13-31-63-84

Phone 814-887-5555 **FAX** None
EIN 25-6001645   **Year Created** 1943
4 **Grants totaling** $18,000

All local giving; grants are for general purposes. High grant of **$8,000** to Bradford Hospital Foundation. **$6,000** to St. Luke's Episcopal Church. **$3,000** to Smethport Area United Way. **$1,000** to Smethport Area Youth Soccer. ■**PUBLICATIONS:** None ■ **WEBSITE:** None ■**E-MAIL:** None ■**APPLICATION POLICIES & PROCEDURES:** The Foundation reports that grants are restricted to McKean County charitable organizations. Prospective applicants initially should make a telephone inquiry about the feasibility of submitting a request.

O+D+T Robert A. Digel, Jr. (P+Con) — Martin Digel [Bradford] (D)

NW-025 Heindl (Dennis & Rose) Family Foundation
602 Hyde Ave, P.O. Box 146
Ridgway   15853   (Elk County)
AMV $7,823   **FYE** 12-00   (**Gifts Received** $12,917)

MI-13-21-63-71-84-89
Phone 814-375-0938 **FAX** None
EIN 52-6468833   **Year Created** 1990
9 **Grants totaling** $23,760

All local giving. High grant of **$9,750** to Ridgway Fire Dept. **$5,000** to Vision 2000 Church. **$2,500** each to Boy Scouts/Bucktail Council, Elks BPO Lodge, and Ridgway Park Redevelopment. **$1,000** to Ridgway Area High School Wrestling Team. Other smaller local contributions. ■**PUBLICATIONS:** None ■**WEBSITE:** None ■**E-MAIL:** None ■**APPLICATION POLICIES & PROCEDURES:** Grant requests may be submitted in a letter at any time; describe the purpose of the request and include IRS tax-exempt status documentation.

O+D+T Dennis D. Heindl (T+Donor+Con)

NW-026 Henne (John K.) Charitable Trust
c/o National City Bank of Pa.
248 Seneca Street, 3rd Floor
Oil City   (Venango County)
AMV $2,271,401   **FYE** 12-00   (**Gifts Received** $6,367)

MI-11-13-29-31-41-42-63-54-71

Phone 814-678-3543 **FAX** None
EIN 25-6261354   **Year Created** 1985
42 **Grants totaling** $94,141

Mostly local/Pa. giving; all grants are for general support. High grant of **$40,000** to Penn State/Behrend Center. **$9,490** to Titusville Area Schools. **$7,000** to First Presbyterian Church of Titusville. **$3,000-$3,500** each to Drake Well Museum, Titusville Area Health Center Foundation, and U. of Pittsburgh/Titusville. **$2,000** each to Titusville Area United Way and YMCA of Titusville. **$1,000** each to Associated Charities of Titusville, Lancaster Country Day School, Titusville Leisure Services, and Western Pa. Conservancy. **$750** each to Galloway United Methodist Church [Pittsburgh], Haverford College, Red Cross, and Titusville Woodlawn Cemetery. Other local contributions **$100-$650** each for various community purposes. **Out-of-state** giving includes **$5,000** to Lynchburg College [VA]; and **$1,000-$1,500** each to Loomis Chaffee School [CT], Memorial Sloan Kettering Cancer Center [NY], and Moore Regional Hospital Foundation [NC]. ■**PUBLICATIONS:** None ■**WEBSITE:** None ■ **E-MAIL:** None ■**APPLICATION POLICIES & PROCEDURES:** Grant requests may be submitted in a letter at any time; include IRS tax-exempt status documentation.

O+D+T Lynette Pedensky (AVP at Bank+Con) — Todd L. Olsen [VA] (Co-T) — National City Bank of Pa. (Co-Trustee)

NW-027 Hirtzel (Orris C. & Beatrice Dewey) Memorial Foundation
c/o Bryan & Bryan
11 Park Street
North East   16428   (Erie County)
AMV $25,322,284   **FYE** 12-00   (**Gifts Received** $0)

MI-31-34-42-43-44-57-71-89
Phone 814-725-8691 **FAX** None
EIN 25-6018933   **Year Created** 1956
135 **Grants totaling** $1,572,074

Mostly local/Western Pa. giving; some grants are payments on multiyear pledges. High grant of **$250,000** to Children's Hospital of Pittsburgh. **$225,000** to Borough of North East (school purchase). **$150,000** to Mercyhurst College (capital campaign). **$144,678** to Borough of North East (general operating support). **$160,273** to Borough of North East (Heard Memorial Park Project). **$70,000** to Children's Hospital of Pittsburgh (capital campaign). **$40,000** to Greenfield Township (Greenfield Park). **$30,000** to Fuller Hose Company. **$20,000** to Lake Erie College of Osteopathic Medicine. **$5,000** each to Crescent Hose Company, Foundation for Independent Colleges [Harrisburg], Greenfield Fire Company, McCord Memorial Library, North East Community Chest, and WQLN. Also, 116 scholarships awarded to local students, mostly **$1,500**. **Out-of-state** giving includes **$167,000** to Cleveland Clinic Foundation [OH] (capital campaign); **$100,000** to Virginia Tech Foundation (medical); and **$5,000** each to Ripley Hose Company [NY] and Ripley Public Library [NY]. ■**PUBLICATIONS:** None ■**WEBSITE:** None ■**E-MAIL:** None ■**APPLICATION POLICIES & PROCEDURES:** The Foundation reports that most grants are for general operating support, capital campaigns/needs, building/renovations, or scholarships. Grant requests may be submitted in any form at any time; grants are awarded at meetings in May and September. — Formerly called The Electric Materials—Hirtzel Memorial Foundation. **O+D+T** James S. Bryan, Esq. (S+T+Con) — Robert E. Galbraith [NY] (C+T) — James L. Johnson (T) — Douglas P. Moorhead (T) — Mellon Bank N.A. (Corporate Trustee)

NW-028 **Howes-Nelson Charitable Trust**
    c/o Mellon Bank N.A., Trust Dept.
    1128 State Street, P.O. Box 300
    Erie 16512   (Erie County)

MI-11-15-22-63

Phone 814-453-7247 **FAX** None
EIN 25-6159365   **Year Created** 1972

AMV $228,607   **FYE** 12-00   (**Gifts Received** $47,192)   6 **Grants totaling** $12,000

Most giving to Venango County. High grant of **$5,000** to Venango Youth for Christ. **$2,500** to YMCA of Oil City. **$2,000** to Second Presbyterian Church of Oil City (local mission project). **$1,000** each to Salvation Army of Oil City and United Way of Venango County. **$500** to Presbyterian Homes [Erie]. ■**PUBLICATIONS:** None ■**WEBSITE:** None ■**E-MAIL:** None ■**APPLICATION POLICIES & PROCEDURES:** Grant requests may be submitted in a letter during August-early September (deadline is September 15th); include IRS tax-exempt status documentation.
O+D+T Marilyn King (Trust Officer at Bank+Con) — Mellon Bank N.A. (Trustee)

NW-029 **Ideal Foundation, The**
    c/o Ideal Products, Inc.
    101 West DuBois Ave., P.O. Box 1006
    DuBois 15801   (Clearfield County)

MI-11-13-41-42-44-54-57-63

Phone 814-371-8616 **FAX** None
EIN 23-7046799   **Year Created** 1969

AMV $1,831,456   **FYE** 6-01   (**Gifts Received** $0)   15 **Grants totaling** $48,729

About half local giving. High Pa. grant of **$6,000** to St. Peter's United Church. **$5,195** to DuBois Central Christian High School. **$5,000** to DuBois YMCA (building campaign). **$4,000** to Grace Methodist Church of Sykesville. **$2,500** to DuBois Area United Way. **$1,000** to WPSX [University Park]. Other smaller local contributions. **Out-of-state** giving includes high grant of **$9,700** to Ringling Museum [FL]; **$5,500** to U. of Arizona; and **$5,000** to New College Library Assn. [FL]. ■**PUBLICATIONS:** None ■**WEBSITE:** None ■**E-MAIL:** None ■**APPLICATION POLICIES & PROCEDURES:** The Foundation reports that giving focuses on Jefferson and contiguous counties. Grant requests may be submitted in a letter (2 pages maximum) at any time; include an annual report, organizational budget, project budget, Board member list, and IRS tax-exempt status documentation. Site visits sometimes are made to organizations being considered for a grant.
O+D+T John W. Bean (T+Donor+Con)

NW-030 **Jones (Harold D.) Charitable Trust**
    c/o National City Bank of Pa./Trust Division
    801 State Street
    Erie 16538   (Erie County)

MI-12-13-11-31-56-57

Phone 814-871-1279 **FAX** 814-454-7831
EIN 25-6119452   **Year Created** 1970

AMV $1,576,354   **FYE** 12-00   (**Gifts Received** $0)   8 **Grants totaling** $67,000

All giving restricted to Crawford County; all grants are for general support. High grant of **$25,000** to Titusville Hospital Foundation. **$18,000** to Titusville Area United Way. **$10,000** Titusville Leisure Service. **$8,000** to Drake Well Museum. **$3,000** to WQLN-TV54. **$1,000** each to Genesis, Titusville YMCA, and Titusville YWCA. ■**PUBLICATIONS:** None ■**WEBSITE:** None ■**E-MAIL:** christopher.junker@nationalcity.com ■**APPLICATION POLICIES & PROCEDURES:** The Trust reports that only organizations serving Titusville are eligible to apply. Most grants are for general support, special projects, building funds, capital drives, and publications. No grants awarded to individuals. Grant requests should be submitted in April in a letter (2 pages maximum) before the June 1st deadline; include an annual report, organization and project budgets, audited financial statement, list of major funding sources, and IRS tax-exempt status documentation. Site visits sometimes are made to organizations being considered for a grant.
O+D+T Christopher A. Junker (VP at Bank+Con) — National City Bank of Pa. (Trustee)

NW-031 **Justus (Edith C.) Trust**
    213 Seneca Street, 3rd Floor
    P.O. Box 374
    Oil City 16301   (Venango County)

MI-11-12-13-15-29-31-41-44-54-55-56-63-71 84-85

Phone 814-677-5085 **FAX** 814-677-3404
EIN 25-6031057   **Year Created** 1931

AMV $7,170,766   **FYE** 12-00   (**Gifts Received** $0)   38 **Grants totaling** $216,293

All giving restricted to/for Venango County; grants are for general support/operations except as noted. High grant of **$66,539** to City of Oil City (Justus Trail/Justus Park). **$24,500** to United Way of Venango County (challenge grant). **$20,000** to Clarion U. (childcare center). **$12,688** to Faith in Action. **$8,900-$10,000** each to Northwest Imminent Community Institute, Oil City Community Development, Oil City Library, and Oil City YMCA (cycling program). **$7,000** to Community Services of Venango County. **$6,000** to Family Service & Children's Aid Society. **$5,000** each to Franklin YMCA (capital improvements) and Parks Unlimited (infrastructure improvements). **$2,000-$3,300** each to Belles Letres Club, Oil City Area School District (RIF program), Oil City Civic Center (operations/capital improvements), Oil Valley Center for the Arts (youth art classes), Venango Area Community Foundation (fathers' workshop program), and Venango Christian High School (music/theatre program). **$1,000-$1,668** each to Allegheny Valley Trails Assn. (safety patrol), Calvary Baptist Church (multimedia program), Child Development Center, Clarion U. (community service fair), County of Venango (Kids 'n K9s program), First United Methodist Church (nursery/pre-school), Franklin Fine Arts Council (youths' arts festival), Free Methodist Church of Oil City, Grove Hill Cemetery Assn. (preservation program), Oil Heritage Region, Inc. Venango County Area Agency on Aging (workshop), and YWCA of Oil City (girls softball league). Other local contributions **$25-$500** each. ■**PUBLICATIONS:** application guidelines ■**WEBSITE:** None ■**E-MAIL:** None ■**APPLICATION POLICIES & PROCEDURES:** Only Venango County organizations are eligible to apply. Most grants are for operating budgets, endowment, special projects, building funds, capital needs, publications, matching funds; multi-year grants are awarded. Prospective applicants initially should make a telephone inquiry about the feasibility of submitting a request. A formal application form, available from the foundation, should be submitted in April, August or November; include an annual report, organizational budget, project budget, audited financial statement, list of other funding sources, Board member list, and IRS tax-exempt status documentation. Interviews to discuss preliminary proposal drafts are conducted by appointment with the Trust's consultant or site visits sometimes are arranged. Decisions on grants are made at meetings in May, September, and December.

O+D+T Discretionary Committee members: Stephen P. Kosak (Consultant+Con) — Rodney L. Campbell — R. Grant Carner — Emily P. Eisenman — National City Bank of Pa. (Trustee)

NW-032 Justus (Samuel) Charitable Trust
213 Seneca Street, 3rd Floor
P.O. Box 374
Oil City   16301   (Venango County)
AMV $22,000,000 est.   **FYE** 12-00   **(Gifts Received** $0)

MI-11-12-13-14-19-20-22-25-29-35-41-42-44
54-55-71-84
Phone 814-677-5085 **FAX** 814-677-3404
EIN 25-6031058   **Year Created** 1967
31 **Grants totaling** $563,934

All giving restricted to Venango County to benefit children, youth and their families; some grants comprise multiple awards. High grant of **$91,250** to Community Services of Venango County (operating support/children's programs). **$89,315** to Salvation Army/Oil City (capital campaign/youth volunteering/other). **$42,800** to Child Development Centers (infirmary/programs). **$38,336** to Family Service & Children's Aid Society (operations/renovations). **$34,812** to Youth Alternatives, Inc. (fellows program/operating support/other). **$20,000-$24,165** each to Grace Learning Center (after-school program), Oil City Area School District (family literacy/reading program/other), YMCA of Oil City (operating subsidy), and YWCA of Oil City (playground program/salary). **$15,000-$15,492** each to Parks Unlimited, Inc. (juvenile justice program), Venango County Children & Youth Services (lice task force), and Venango County Court Supervision Services (parenting classes). **$10,000-$14,000** each to City of Franklin (CREATE program), Franklin YMCA (youth programs), United Way of Venango County (campaign challenge grant), Venango County 4-H Fair (activity center), Venango County Human Services (community caring program), and Venango Museum of Art Science & Industry (exhibit). **$8,000-$8,850** each to Venango Area Community Foundation (education/arts festival), Venango Christian High School (learning disability program). **$4,565-$7,500** each to Christ Episcopal Church (teen center), De-Bence Antique Music World (building improvements), Emlenton Borough (recreation improvements), Galloway United Methodist Church (Catacombe Jam House), Girl Scouts/Keystone Tall Trees Council (day camp/camperships), Oil City Arts Council (youth programming), and St. Stephen School (technology program). **$1,400-$2,500** each to ABC Crisis Pregnancy Center (client expenses/education), Oil City Civic Center ((operations/improvements), Pa. Free Enterprise Week (scholarships), and Titusville Area Hospital (obstetrics dept. renovations). ■**PUBLICATIONS:** Annual Report; application guidelines ■**WEBSITE:** None ■**E-MAIL:** None ■**APPLICATION POLICIES & PROCEDURES:** The Trust reports that all giving must benefit Venango County children/youth and requests from outside the county will not be considered. Most grants are for operating budgets, special projects, building funds, capital needs, endowment, matching funds; multi-year grants are awarded. Generally no grants are awarded for scholarships, research, publications, conferences, loans, or to individuals. Prospective applicants initially should make a telephone inquiry about the feasibility of submitting a request; interviews to discuss preliminary proposal drafts are conducted by appointment with the Trust's Consultant. A formal application form, available from the Trust, should be submitted during January, March-April, June-July, or September-October; the deadlines are February 1st, May 1st, August 1st, and November 1st. The application must include an annual report, organizational/project budgets, audited financial statement, list of other funding sources, Board member list, and IRS tax-exempt status documentation. Site visits sometimes are made to organizations being considered for a grant. The Trustees award grants at meetings in March, June, September, and December.

O+D+T Committee Members: Stephen P. Kosak (Consultant+Con) — Hon. William E. Breene — Rodney L. Campbell — Joseph S. Harvey — Hon. H. William White — National City Bank of Pa. (Trustee)

NW-033 Kaul (Andrew) Foundation
c/o National City Bank of Pa.
248 Seneca Street, 3rd Floor
Oil City   16301   (Venango County)
AMV $574,090   **FYE** 12-00   **(Gifts Received** $0)

MI-13-44-56-84
Phone 814-678-3649 **FAX** None
EIN 25-1112032   **Year Created** 1970
1 **Grant of** $13,100

All giving to Elk County. Sole grant to Boys Club Holding Corp. [St. Marys]. — Grants in prior years included **$10,000** to Berwind Park Stadium Fund (new bleachers); **$7,500** to Boys Club Holding Corp.; **$5,000** to Bucksgahuda & Western Railroad; and **$3,000** to St. Marys Public Library. ■**PUBLICATIONS:** None ■**WEBSITE:** None ■**E-MAIL:** None ■**APPLICATION POLICIES & PROCEDURES:** Only Elk County organizations are eligible to apply; health, medical, and religious organizations receive priority. Most grants are for special projects, building funds, or capital needs. Prospective applicants initially should make a telephone inquiry about the feasibility of submitting a request. Grant requests in any form should be submitted in October (deadline is November 15th); describe the purpose of the requested fund and include a project budget and IRS tax-exempt status documentation. Site visits sometimes are made to organizations being considered for a grant. Grants are awarded at a December meeting.

O+D+T David G. Anderton (VP/Trust Officer at Bank+S+F+D+Con) — Andrew Kaul, IV (P+D) — Frank Kaul [NC] (D) — William Keating (D) — Edward H. Kuntz (D) — Heidi Kaul Krutek [FL] (D) — Jane Kaul Wilson [AL] (D) — National City Bank of Pa. (Trustee)

NW-034 **Kavanagh (Edward J.) Foundation**
c/o Melvin Bandzak
1340 Yahres Road
Sharon 16146 (Mercer County)
AMV $2,115,559 **FYE** 7-00 (**Gifts Received** $0)

MI-13-14-22-31-32-41-42-44-55-61-63-85-89

Phone 724-347-5215 **FAX** None
EIN 23-7023865 **Year Created** 1969
37 **Grants totaling** $109,200

Mostly Mercer County/Pa. giving. High grant of **$16,600** to Prince of Peace Center. **$11,000** to Church of Notre Dame. **$6,000** to Penn Lakes Girl Scout Council. **$5,000-$5,500** each to Buhl Farm Trust, Fredonia Methodist Church, Kennedy Christian High School, Shenango Valley Initiative, and Shenango Valley Performing Arts Council. **$4,000** each to St. Joseph's School and St. Michael's School. **$3,000** to The Good Shepherd Center. **$2,000-$2,500** each to American Cancer Society, F.H. Buhl Club, John XIII Home, Keystone Blind Assn., St. Thomas the Apostle Church [Delaware County], Shenango Valley Community Library, United Way of Mercer County, and Valley Arts Guild. **$1,000-$1,500** each to American Heart Assn., Carlow College, Delaware Valley College of Science & Agriculture [Bucks County], Epilepsy Foundation of Western Pa., Fredonia-Delaware Youth Baseball League, George Jr. Republic, Mercer County Education & Habilitation Center, Mercyhurst College, O'Brien Children Memorial Fund, Pa. Special Olympics, Shenango Conservancy, and Shenango Valley YMCA. Other smaller local contributions. **Out-of-state** giving includes **$2,000** each to Daemen College [NY] and Kevin Guest House [NY]. ■**PUBLICATIONS:** None ■**WEBSITE:** None ■**E-MAIL:** None ■**APPLICATION POLICIES & PROCEDURES:** Grant requests may be submitted in a letter at any time; describe the organization, the proposed project and its objectives, and state the amount of funding requested.

O+D+T Kevin E. Kavanagh (P+T+Con) — Thomas E. Kavanagh [Hermitage] (VP+T) — Eileen Buchanan [Fredonia] (VP+T) — Katherine Kavanagh Hammer [Lansdowne] (VP+T) — Joan Kavanagh Feeney (S+F+T)

NW-035 **Kavanagh (T. James) Foundation**
234 East State Street
Sharon 16146 (Mercer County)
AMV $15,529,312 **FYE** 12-00 (**Gifts Received** $0)

MI-13-14-15-22-25-31-41-42-44-49-52-61-71-89

Phone 724-981-2911 **FAX** None
EIN 23-6442981 **Year Created** 1968
96 **Grants totaling** $303,101

Mostly Pa. giving to Mercer, Erie, and Potter counties and Philadelphia area; grants are for operating/annual support except as noted. **MERCER & ERIE COUNTY GRANTS: $25,000** to Notre Dame Church [Hermitage] (church school library). **$20,000** to Prince of Peace Center (housing project). **$15,000** to St. Joseph's School [Sharon] (learning assistance program). **$5,000** to Catholic Rural Ministries [Roulette] (travel costs). **$3,000** each to Buhl Farm Trust (golf course improvements), George Junior Republic (buildings), John XIII Home, and United Way of Mercer County. **$2,000** to Hermitage Volunteer Fire Co. (pumper), Mercer County 4H Development Committee (show costs), Shenango Valley YMCA (sports field improvements), and Valley Arts Guild (after-school/summer programs). **$1,000** each to Boy Scouts/St. Joseph's Troop 1 (equipment), Columbia Theatre for the Arts (children's programs), Fredonia Volunteer Fire Co. (new tanker), Good Shepherd Church, Kennedy Christian High School, Keystone Blind Assn., Mercyhurst College, St. John's Romanian Catholic Church, and St. Michael's School (athletic uniforms). **PHILADELPHIA-AREA GRANTS: $10,000** each to Camilla Hall Nursing Home (special equipment) and Glaucoma Service Foundation. **$7,500** to Cabrini College (endowment). **$6,000** to Nehemiah's Way (temporary housing costs). **$5,000** each to Newtown Square Fire Company, Philadelphia College of Osteopathic Medicine (student grants), and St. Maron's Church (renovations). **$2,000-$3,000** each to Aid for Friends (homebound program), Academy of Vocal Arts (opera season), Casa Enrico Fermi (furniture), Church Farm School (tuition assistance), Country Day School of the Sacred Heart (sound system), Darlington Fine Arts Center (musical scholarships), Delaware County Youth Orchestra, Delaware Valley College of Agriculture & Science (scholarship fund), Discalced Carmelite Monastery (renovations), Drexel Hill School of the Holy Child (tuition support), George Washington Carver Science Fair, Hallahan Catholic Girls High School (text books), Immaculata College, LaSalle College High School (tuition assistance), Merion Mercy Academy (tuition assistance), Monastery at St. Clare (supplies), Monastery of the Visitation (heating costs), Old St. Joseph's Outreach Center (food for needy), Opera Company of Philadelphia (parochial student program), Philadelphia Art Alliance, Queen Village Neighborhood Assn. (capital improvements), Redemptorist Volunteer Ministries (homeless clothes), Rock School of the Pa. Ballet, St. Charles Boromeo Church (exterior lighting), St. Francis Xavier Church School (student materials), St. Ignatius Nursing Home (renovations), St. Joseph's Preparatory School (scholarship fund), St. Malachy Church (equipment), St. Monica's Church (day care center), St. Nicholas Church (assistance to needy), St. Paul's Church, St. Rita's Church (renovations), St. Thomas the Apostle Church (school library), Sisters of St. Francis Convent (housewares), South Philadelphia Lions Club (party for blind), and Tolentine Community Center & Development Co. (salary). Other Philadelphia-area grants **$1,000-$1,500** each for other Catholic churches, schools, and organizations. **POTTER COUNTY GRANTS: $5,000** to St. Eulalia's Church (window replacements). **$1,000** each to Coudersport Public Library (book purchases), Coudersport Volunteer Fire Co. (equipment), and St. Augustine Mission (exterior painting). **OUT-OF-STATE** giving includes **$8,200** to Convent at Sea Isle City [NJ]; **$5,000** to First United Methodist Church of Cape May (furnace system); and other grants **$1,500-$3,000** to Catholic churches or schools in NJ and NY. ■**PUBLICATIONS:** application guidelines ■**WEBSITE:** None ■**E-MAIL:** None ■**APPLICATION POLICIES & PROCEDURES:** The Foundation reports that at least 51% of giving is restricted to the Roman Catholic Church and affiliated organizations. Most grants are for specific projects in Pa. and Southern NJ. Initial grants generally do not exceed $1,000. No grants are awarded to/for programs/organizations outside the U.S., endowment, seed money, publications, conferences, land acquisition, or individuals. The Foundation suggests an initial Letter of Inquiry; include IRS tax-exempt status documentation or, if a Roman Catholic organization, a copy of the U.S. Catholic Conference's group ruling letter from IRS. If the Foundation is interested in the proposed project a formal Grant Application Form will be provided; this form must be submitted with a proposal which briefly describes the organization's history, purpose, goals, and significant past projects; details the project for which funding is sought; states the amount requested and total amount needed for the project; and includes an annual report, list of other funding sources solicited for the project, and IRS tax-exempt status documentation. Personal interviews are discouraged but site visits sometimes are made to organizations being considered for a grant. The board meets in March, August and November.

O+D+T Thomas E. Kavanagh [Hermitage] (T+Con) — Melvin Bandzak [Sharon] (T) — Louis J. Esposito [Philadelphia] (T)

NW-036 Kelly Family Charitable Foundation
504 Cherokee Drive
Erie 16505   (Erie County)

MI-32-42-52-57-61
Phone 814-459-1296 **FAX** None
EIN 25-1810962   **Year Created** 1998

AMV $278,087   **FYE** 12-00   **(Gifts Received** $0)   11 **Grants totaling** $12,570

All local giving. High grant of **$7,625** to WQLN. **$1,000** each to Edward Frederick Society, Erie Youth Symphony, and Juvenile Diabetes Foundation. Other smaller contributions for civic and Catholic purposes. ■**PUBLICATIONS:** None ■**WEBSITE:** None ■ **E-MAIL:** None ■**APPLICATION POLICIES & PROCEDURES:** Prospective applicants should make an initial telephone inquiry about the feasbility of submitting a request. Grant requests may be submitted in a letter before the September 1st deadline; provide details on the purpose of the charitable organization.

O+D+T William J. Kelly, Sr. (T+Con) — William J. Kelly, Jr. (T) — Elizabeth Kelly Witchcoff (T)

NW-037 Khalaf Foundation, The
122 Aspen Road
Punxsutawney 15767   (Jefferson County)

MI-16-31-82
Phone 814-938-1836 **FAX** None
EIN 25-1736562   **Year Created** 1994

AMV $67,358   **FYE** 12-00   **(Gifts Received** $68,000)   5 **Grants totaling** $108,200

One Pa. grant: **$6,000** to Punxsutawney Area Hospital. **Out-of-state** giving includes **$100,000** to Palestine Red Crescent Society [Palestine] and **$1,000** each to American-Arab Anti-Discrimination Committee Research Institute [DC] and Arab-American Medical Assn. [NJ] ■**PUBLICATIONS:** None ■**WEBSITE:** None ■**E-MAIL:** None ■**APPLICATION POLICIES & PROCEDURES:** Information not available.

O+D+T Kamal Khalaf, M.D. (P+S+Donor+Con) — Maysoun Khalaf (VP) — Aman Khalaf (F)

NW-038 Kostkan (Paul) Foundation
c/o Community National Bank
53 East State Street
Albion 16401   (Erie County)

MI-29-44-89

Phone 814-756-4138 **FAX** None
EIN 25-1564430   **Year Created** 1988

AMV $245,314   **FYE** 12-00   **(Gifts Received** $0)   5 **Grants totaling** $12,778

All giving limited the Albion area. High grant of **$4,500** to Albion Area Public Library (new shelving). **$2,300** to NEED, Inc. (building repairs). **$2,034** each to Albion Volunteer Fire Dept. (equipment) and Cranesville Volunteer Fire Dept. (equipment) **$1,910** to Northwestern Veterans Memorial (repair doors). ■**PUBLICATIONS:** None ■**WEBSITE:** None ■**E-MAIL:** None ■**APPLICATION POLICIES & PROCEDURES:** The Foundation reports that giving is restricted to organizations in the Albion-area: Albion Borough, Conneaut Township, Cranesville Borough, and Elk Creek Township. Grant requests may be submitted on a formal application form, available from the Bank, before the December 15th deadline.

O+D+T Edward J. Kempf, Jr. (S+F+Con) — James F. Mikovich [Cranesville] (P) — William B. Tucker (VP)

NW-039 Lancy (Alice & Leslie) Foundation
c/o National City Bank of Pa.
66 East State Street
Sharon 16146   (Mercer County)

MI-41-42

Phone 724-982-1125 **FAX** None
EIN 25-1371367   **Year Created** 1972

AMV $4,020,282   **FYE** 12-00   **(Gifts Received** $11,783)   1 **Grant of** $265,000

Sole grant to National Conference of Undergraduate Research [CA] (summer undergraduate research fellowship program). — In the prior year **$250,000** awarded to the same grantee. In 1998 three grants were awarded, all for general support: **$75,000** to the above grantee; **$60,000** to Berea College [KY]; and **$17,074** to Carnegie Mellon U. ■**PUBLICATIONS:** None   ■**WEBSITE:** None ■**E-MAIL:** craig.kelsey@nationalcity.com ■**APPLICATION POLICIES & PROCEDURES:** The Foundation reports that only educational institutions serving deprived populations/areas are eligible to apply. Grant requests may be submitted in a letter at any time; include descriptive literature about the organization.

O+D+T Craig Kelsey (VP at Bank+Con) — Donor: Estate of Leslie E. Lancy — National City Bank of Pa. (Trustee)

NW-040 Leslie Family Foundation
291 Avonia Road
Fairview 16415   (Erie County)

MI-11-13-17-29-31-42-43-49-52-53-54-55-57-63
Phone 814-474-1126 **FAX** None
EIN 31-1484689   **Year Created** 1996

AMV $589,162   **FYE** 12-00   **(Gifts Received** $0)   30 **Grants totaling** $117,900

Mostly local giving; all grants are for general support. High grant of **$40,000** to Discovery Square. **$14,000** to United Way of Erie County. **$10,000** each to Erie Arts Endowment (Children's Fund) and The Ophelia Project. **$4,000-$5,000** each to Gertrude Barber Center, Hamot Second Century Fund, Penn State U. (Erie Duval Scholarship), and WQLN. **$2,500** each to Erie Youth Symphony and Wayside Presbyterian Church. **$1,000-$1,500** each to ACES/Americans for the Competitive Economic System, Erie Art Museum, Erie Philharmonic Fund, Flagship Niagara League, Neighborhood Art House, Sara Reed Children's Center, and United Arts Fund. Other local contributions **$200-$500** for similar purposes. **Out-of-state** giving includes **$5,000** to Boston U. [MA] (Excellence in Philosophical Studies) and **$2,500** to Aspen Music Festival & School [CO]. ■**PUBLICATIONS:** None ■**WEBSITE:** None ■**E-MAIL:** None ■**APPLICATION POLICIES & PROCEDURES:** Information not available.

O+D+T Miriam B. Leslie (P+D+Donor+Con) — Donald S. Leslie, Jr. (S+F+D+Donor) — PNC Advisors (Trustee)

NW-041 Lindquist (Walter J.) Foundation MI-12-13-22-35-41-63
c/o First National Trust Company
1 FNB Boulevard   **Phone** 724-983-3607 **FAX** None
Hermitage 16148   (Mercer County)   **EIN** 23-7950549   **Year Created** 1997
AMV $368,277   **FYE** 12-00   (**Gifts Received** $0)   10 **Grants totaling** $22,000

Most giving to Oil City/NW Pa. High grant of **$5,000** to Zion Evangelical Lutheran Church of Oil City. **$3,000** to Family Service & Children's Aid Society. **$2,000** each to Sugarcreek Station [Franklin], St. Joseph's School, Salvation Army of Oil City, and Visiting Nurses Assn. of Venango County. **$1,000** each to Boy Scouts/French Creek Council and YMCA of Oil City. **Out-of-state** grants to FL and NC for child welfare purposes. ■**PUBLICATIONS:** None ■**WEBSITE:** None ■**E-MAIL:** None ■**APPLICATION POLICIES & PROCEDURES:** Information not available.

O+D+T Gary C. Rauschenberger (VP at Bank+Con) — Robert W. McFate, Esq. [Oil City] (Co-T) — William J. McFate, Esq. [Oil City] (Co-T) — First National Trust Company (Co-Trustee)

NW-042 Lindsey Charity Fund MI-11-12-13-14-22-32-43-44-56
c/o Mellon Bank N.A., Trust Dept.
1128 State Street, P.O. Box 300   **Phone** 814-453-7247 **FAX** None
Erie 16512   (Erie County)   **EIN** 25-1404227   **Year Created** 1991
AMV $1,085,880   **FYE** 12-00   (**Gifts Received** $0)   22 **Grants totaling** $60,900

Most giving to Mercer County. High grants of **$8,500** to Mercer Area Library and Mercer County Historical Society. **$6,000** to Children's Aid Society. **$4,200-$4,400** each to American Cancer Society, Keystone Blind Assn., Mercer County Education & Rehabilitation Center, Salvation Army, and United Way of Mercer County. **$3,000** each to Boy Scouts/Troop 35, Boy Scouts of Mercer/Troop 83, and Girl Scouts of Mercer. **$2,000** to Brandy Springs Park Assn. Other smaller contributions. Also, seven scholarships, two **$1,000** and five **$500,** for graduating seniors of Mercer High School. ■**PUBLICATIONS:** application guidelines ■**WEBSITE:** None ■**E-MAIL:** None ■**APPLICATION POLICIES & PROCEDURES:** Grant requests from organizations may be submitted in a letter before the September 15th deadline; scholarship are awarded only to graduating seniors of Mercer High School and must be received by the May 13th deadline.

O+D+T Marilyn King (Trust Officer at Bank+Con) — John G. Johnson [Mercer] (Co-T) — Mellon Bank N.A. (Co-Trustee)

NW-043 Logan (Harry A.), Jr. Foundation MI-41-42-52-55
c/o National City Bank of Pa.
315 - 2nd Ave.   **Phone** 814-726-5781 **FAX** 814-726-7235
Warren 16365   (Warren County)   **EIN** 25-1514648   **Year Created** 1986
AMV $316,002   **FYE** 12-00   (**Gifts Received** $0)   3 **Grants totaling** $84,719

Mostly Northwest Pa. giving. High grant of **$50,494** to Penn State-Erie (Logan Music Series). **$30,650** to Warren County School District (music programs). **Out-of-state** grant of **$3,750** to Cleveland Institute of Music [OH]. ■**PUBLICATIONS:** application guidelines ■**WEBSITE:** None ■**E-MAIL:** None ■**APPLICATION POLICIES & PROCEDURES:** The Foundation reports that preference is given to Western Pa. charitable organizations; most grants are for special projects or scholarships. Grant requests may be submitted in any form during January-April, before the June 30th deadline; include organization and project budgets, Board member list, list of major funding sources, and IRS tax-exempt status documentation. Grants are awarded at a July meeting.

O+D+T Edward A. Kavanaugh (VP at Bank+Con) — Kay H. Logan (Co-T+Donor) — Marty Merkley (Co-T) — National City Bank of Pa. (Co-Trustee)

NW-044 Lord (Thomas) Charitable Trust, The MI-13-29-31-32-41-42-44-55-56-71
c/o National City Bank of Pa.
801 State Street   **Phone** 814-871-1279 **FAX** 814-454-7831
Erie 16538   (Erie County)   **EIN** 25-6028793   **Year Created** 1955
AMV $3,313,856   **FYE** 12-00   (**Gifts Received** $0)   6 **Grants totaling** $145,000

Mostly local giving; grants were for general support except as noted. High grants of **$50,000** each to Arts Council of Erie and Hamot Medical Center (research). **$10,000** each to Erie County Library Foundation and Penn Lakes Girl Scout Council. **$5,000** to Allegheny College. **Out-of-state** grant: **$20,000** to Virginia Polytechnic Institute. — Giving in recent years included **$50,000** to Allegheny College; **$25,000** to Asbury Woods Nature Center; and **$20,000** each to Dr. Gertrude Barber Center, Erie Day School, Warner Theatre Preservation Trust (restoration & modernization). ■**PUBLICATIONS:** None ■**WEBSITE:** None ■ **E-MAIL:** christopher.junker@nationalcity.com ■**APPLICATION POLICIES & PROCEDURES:** The Trust reports that giving is geographically restricted to the Erie area for three purposes: education (preferably technical education), medical/health, and historic preservation. Grant requests may be submitted at any time in a letter which describes the purpose of the requested funds; include IRS tax-exempt status documentation.

O+D+T Christopher A. Junker (VP at Bank+Con) — Daniel R. Miller, Esq. (Co-T) — Donald Alstadt (Co-T) — National City Bank of Pa. (Co-Trustee)

NW-045 Luce (Eileen Jean) Charitable Trust MI-11-12-55-56-71-84
213 Seneca Street, 3rd Floor
P.O. Box 374   **Phone** 814-677-5085 **FAX** 814-677-3404
Oil City 16301   (Venango County)   **EIN** 25-6394192   **Year Created** 1992
AMV $468,178   **FYE** 10-00   (**Gifts Received** $0)   3 **Grants totaling** $10,715

All local giving. **$5,000** each to Family Services & Children and Salvation Army. **$715** to Youth Alternatives. — Giving in prior years for cultural, environmental, sports, and health/human services. ■**PUBLICATIONS:** None ■**WEBSITE:** None ■**E-MAIL:**

None ■**APPLICATION POLICIES & PROCEDURES:** The Trust reports that Venango County organizations receive preference. Submit grant requests in a letter any time; describe how funds will be used and include IRS tax-exempt status documentation.

O+D+T Discretionary Committee members: Stephen P. Kosak (Consultant+Con) — Rodney L. Campbell — R. Grant Carner — Emily P. Eisenman — National City Bank of Pa. (Trustee)

NW-046 Maier Family Foundation   MI-14-22-29-31-35-42-63-71
    c/o Omni Plastics, Inc.
    6100 West Ridge Road   **Phone** 814-838-6664 **FAX** 818-838-9379
    Erie 16506   (Erie County)   **EIN** 25-6397893   **Year Created** 1992
AMV $1,228,875   **FYE** 12-00   **(Gifts Received** $325,014)   8 **Grants totaling** $212,009

About half local giving. High Pa. grant of **$70,000** to Dr. Gertrude A. Barber Center Foundation. **$17,459** to Westminster Presbyterian Church. **$13,000** to St. Paul's Neighborhood Free Clinic. **$7,000** to Red Cross. **$2,000** to House of Healing. **$1,300** to Church World Service/Westminister Presbyterian Church. **$1,250** to Glinodo Center. **Out-of-state** grant: **$100,000** to Sterling College [KS]. ■**PUBLICATIONS:** None ■**WEBSITE:** None ■**E-MAIL:** None ■**APPLICATION POLICIES & PROCEDURES:** The Foundation reports that giving is generally limited to the Erie area. Grant requests may be submitted in a letter at any time; state the amount/purpose of the request and include organizational/project budgets, audited financial statement, list of major funding sources, Board member list, and IRS tax-exempt status documentation. No grants awarded to individuals. Site visits sometimes are made to organizations being considered for a grant.

O+D+T Peggy J. Maier (C+T+Donor+Con) — Wilhelm Maier (VC+T+Donor) — Alan F. Woolslare (S+F+T) — Mark W. Maier (T+Donor) — Daniel L.R. Miller (T) — Stephen E. Morse (T) — Hunter Pugh [NC] (T) — Corporate donor: Omni Plastics, Inc.

NW-047 McCain Foundation   MI-12-14-43-52-55-57-71
    c/o Erie Concrete & Steel Supply Co.
    1301 Cranberry Street, P.O. Box 10336   **Phone** 814-453-5641 **FAX** None
    Erie 16514   (Erie County)   **EIN** 25-6049931   **Year Created** 1952
AMV $867,630   **FYE** 11-00   **(Gifts Received** $54,500)   9 **Grants totaling** $16,500

All local giving. High grant of **$6,000** to Dr. Gertrude A. Barber Center. **$1,500** to WQLN. **$1,000** to Erie Homes for Children & Youth. Also, six employee-related scholarships, **$500** or **$1,750,** awarded. — Grants approved for future payment include **$15,000** to Lake Erie Arboretum at Frontier Park (endowment fund); **$7,500** to Erie Youth Symphony at Mercyhurst; **$2,000** to WQLN; and other grants/scholarships. ■**PUBLICATIONS:** None ■**WEBSITE:** None ■**E-MAIL:** None ■**APPLICATION POLICIES & PROCEDURES:** The Foundation reports that Erie County organizations are favored, and employee-related scholarships; multiyear grants are awarded. Grant requests may be submitted in a letter at any time. Site visits sometimes are made to organizations being considered for support. Grants are awarded at a March meeting.

O+D+T Donald P. McCain, Jr. (P+D+Con) — Julie McCain Schirmer [MA] (S+D) — J. Scott McCain (F+D) — Corporate donors: Dobi Plumbing & Heating Supply Co.; Melac Enterprises; Perry Mill Supply Co.

NW-048 McCormick (John J.) Foundation   MI-15-22-42-61
    c/o Joseph McCormick Construction Co.
    P.O. Box 176   **Phone** 814-899-3111 **FAX** None
    Erie 16512   (Erie County)   **EIN** 25-6071598   **Year Created** 1966
AMV $117,069   **FYE** 12-00   **(Gifts Received** $0)   2 **Grants totaling** $15,500

No Pa. giving. **Out-of-state** grants: **$13,000** to U. of Notre Dame [IN] and **$2,500** to Canisius College [NY]. — Local giving in prior years included **$5,000** to Mercyhurst College; **$1,600** to St. Mary's Home of Erie; and **$1,000** each to Gannon U., Holy Family Monastery, and St. Peter's Cathedral. ■**PUBLICATIONS:** None ■**WEBSITE:** None ■**E-MAIL:** None ■**APPLICATION POLICIES & PROCEDURES:** The Foundation reports that educational and religious organizations receive priority. No grants awarded to individuals. Grant requests may be submitted in any form at any time. The Board meets in October.

O+D+T John J. McCormick, Jr. (Manager+Donor+Con) — Richard T. McCormick (P+D) — Mary McCormick Riley (S+D) — Corporate donor: Joseph McCormick Construction Company

---

NW-049 McCormick (Timothy J.) Foundation   MI-15-22-42-61
    c/o Construction Management, Inc.
    1819 German Street   **Phone** 814-455-5075 **FAX** None
    Erie 16503   (Erie County)   **EIN** 25-1290613   **Year Created** 1975
AMV $103,656   **FYE** 11-00   **(Gifts Received** $0)   14 **Grants totaling** $10,280

Mostly local giving; all grants are general support. High grant of **$2,980** to St. Peter's Cathedral. **$1,000-$1,200** each to Gannon U., Mercyhurst College, and St. Mary's Home of Erie. Other smaller contributions, mostly for Catholic purposes. **Out-of-state** grants: **$1,000** each to U. of Notre Dame [IN] and a Catholic church in NY. ■**PUBLICATIONS:** None ■**WEBSITE:** None ■ **E-MAIL:** None ■**APPLICATION POLICIES & PROCEDURES:** No grants awarded to individuals.

O+D+T Timothy J. McCormick (P+Donor+Con) — Ann S. McCormick (VP+Donor) — Kathleen McCormick Klebanski (VP) — Timothy J. McCormick, Jr. (VP)

NW-050 McMannis (William J. & A. Haskell) Educational Trust Fund   MI-43
c/o PNC Advisors
901 State Street, P.O. Box 8480   **Phone** 814-871-9204 **FAX** None
Erie 16553   (Erie County)   **EIN** 25-6164183   **Year Created** 1974
AMV $6,813,503   **FYE** 8-00   **(Gifts Received** $0)   198 **Grants totaling** $305,093

All grants are scholarships for U.S. citizens (mostly from Western Pa.) who are enrolled and in good standing at an institution of higher education. Awards range from **$500-$5,000**, but more typically are **$1,000-$3,000;** continuing support is given to complete one degree only, either undergraduate or graduate. ■**PUBLICATIONS:** informational brochure with application guidelines ■**WEBSITE:** None ■**E-MAIL:** None ■**APPLICATION POLICIES & PROCEDURES:** The Fund reports any U.S. citizen is eligible to apply; academic achievement is the primary selection criterion, and students must be pursuing a baccalaureate or graduate degree at selected institutions. Applications must be submitted on a formal application form, available from the participating colleges, before the May 1st deadline; also include information on student costs. The Executive Board awards scholarships at a June meeting.

O+D+T Bank Trust Officer (Con) — Fred B. Sieber [ME] (Co-T) — plus an Executive Board comprised of four local college representatives and an attorney — PNC Advisors (Co-Trustee)

NW-051 Mengle (Glenn & Ruth) Foundation   MI-11-13-14-15-17-21-22-25-31-35-41-42-43
c/o First Commonwealth Trust Company   44-45-57-61-63-71
Shaffer Road, P.O. Box 1046   **Phone** 814-371-0660 **FAX** 814-375-5449
DuBois 15801   (Clearfield County)   **EIN** 25-6067616   **Year Created** 1956
AMV $14,155,592   **FYE** 12-00   **(Gifts Received** $0)   46 **Grants totaling** $605,094

Most giving limited to the DuBois, Brockway, and Erie areas; grants are unrestricted or operating support except as noted; some comprise multiple payments. High grant of **$78,000** to Boy Scouts/Bucktail Council (challenge grant/lodge construction/general support). **$73,694** to DuBois Area YMCA (pool operations/endowment/unrestricted). **$50,500** to Free Medical Clinic of DuBois. **$36,500** to American Legion Post #95 of Brockway (matching grant). **$35,000** to Mengle Memorial Library (operations/depreciation fund). **$30,000** to DuBois Area United Way. **$23,000** to DuBois Regional Medical Center (hospice care/general support). **$22,000** to YMCA of Greater Erie (camp improvements). **$18,000** to Salvation Army of DuBois. **$16,500** to Central Christian Junior-Senior High School. **$16,300** to Christ the King Manor. **$15,000** to WPSX-TV [University Park]. **$12,500** to Penn State/DuBois (building renovation). **$10,000-$10,100** each to Keystone Tall Tree Girl Scout Council (Camp Curry Creek), Moorhead United Methodist Church, and Shriners Hospital for Crippled Children [Erie] (wheelchair seating program). **$8,000** to Marian House Women's Shelter. **$6,000-$7,000** each to Agape Community Services, Catholic Charities, DuBois Ministerium Food Pantry, and DuBois Public Library. **$5,000** each to DuBois Area Catholic School System (capital campaign), DuBois Senior & Community Center (renovations), Good Samaritan Center, Headwaters Charitable Trust (Rails to Trails project), Mid-State Literacy Council [State College], Pa. Assn. for the Blind [Harrisburg], and Penn State U. (ceramic science scholarship). **$4,000** each to Goodwill Industries of DuBois and Habitat for Humanity of Clearfield County. **$2,000-$3,000** each to Achievement Center (Christmas party), Make-A-Wish Foundation, Teen Court of Clearfield County, St. Vincent DePaul Food Pantry, and Western Pa. Conservancy (Lake Pleasant project). **$1,000-$1,500** each to Clearfield YMCA/Bigler Division, Cultural Resources, and St. Catherine of Siena Church Food Pantry. **Out-of-state** giving includes **$25,000** to Alfred U. [NY] (building restoration); **$10,000** each to Notre Dame U. [IN] (business administration scholarship) and Ohio U. (Sheesley Endowed Scholarship Fund); and **$5,000** to Hurricane Island Outward Bound School [ME]. ■**PUBLICATIONS:** None ■**WEBSITE:** None ■**E-MAIL:** None ■**APPLICATION POLICIES & PROCEDURES:** The Foundation reports that giving is limited to Brockway, DuBois and Erie areas with most grants for capital capaigns or gneral operating support. No grants awarded to individuals. Grant requests may be submitted in a letter before the September 1st deadline; include a recent annual report, organizational budget, project budget, and the last three years' financial statements.

O+D+T D. Edward Chaplin (Executive VP at Bank+Con) — DeVere L. Sheesley (T) — First Commonwealth Trust Company (Trustee)

NW-052 Merwin Foundation, The   MI-13-14-29-31-41-42-49-51-52
c/o Eriez Magnetics Federal Credit Union
2200 Asbury Road   **Phone** 814-833-9881 **FAX** None
Erie 16506   (Erie County)   **EIN** 25-6060860   **Year Created** 1955
AMV $4,341,649   **FYE** 12-00   **(Gifts Received** $0)   12 **Grants totaling** $79,450

Mostly local/Pa. giving. High grant of **$55,000** to Penn State U. **$10,000** to Dr. Gertrude A. Barber Center. **$8,000** to Boys & Girls Club of Erie. **$1,000** each to ACES/Americans for the Competitive Enterprise System, Erie Playhouse, Hamot Second Century Foundation, and Millcreek Services Center. **$700** to Free Youth Symphony. Other smaller contributions. **Out-of-state** grant: **$1,000** to Lawrenceville School [NJ]. ■**PUBLICATIONS:** None ■**WEBSITE:** None ■**E-MAIL:** None ■**APPLICATION POLICIES & PROCEDURES:** Information not available.

O+D+T Richard A. Merwin (P+F+D+Donor+Con) — John E. Britton (S+D) — James E. Spoden, Esq. (AS+D)

NW-053 Miller (Henry C.) Foundation   MI-11-12-13-14-22-29-31-42-63-84
56 Smedley Street, P.O. Box 432   **Phone** 814-725-8973 **FAX** None
North East 16428   (Erie County)   **EIN** 25-1649974   **Year Created** 1991
AMV $2,656,832   **FYE** 12-00   **(Gifts Received** $0)   20+ **Grants totaling** $127,100

Mostly local/nearby NY giving. High grant of **$20,400** to Make-A-Wish Foundation. **$16,000** to United Way of Erie County. **$13,000** to Salvation Army. **$10,000** each to Hamot Second Century Fund, Penn State U./Urban-4H Youth Development, and Skating Association for the Blind and Handicapped/Erie Chapter. **$8,200** to Red Cross/Erie County Chapter. **$2,000** to First Baptist Church of North East. **Out-of-state** giving includes **$10,000** to Northern Chautauqua Community Foundation [NY]; **$8,200** to Red Cross/Chautauqua County [NY]; and **$5,400** to United Way of Chautauqua County [NY]. ■**PUBLICATIONS:**

None ■**WEBSITE:** None ■**E-MAIL:** hcmiller@verizon.net ■**APPLICATION POLICIES & PROCEDURES:** The Foundation reports that giving is restricted to Pa. counties of Erie and Warren, and to Chautauqua County, NY. No grants awarded to individuals. Grant requests may be submitted in any form at any time; describe the purpose of the requested funds and include IRS tax-exempt status documentation.

O+D+T Richard S. Steele (T+Con) — Robert S. Miller (T+Donor) — Janet L. Miller (Donor) — Fleet Bank N.A. [MA] (Agent)

NW-054 Mukaiyama-Rice Foundation, The MI-41-52
c/o KOA Speer Electronics, Inc.
Bolivar Drive, P.O. Box 547 **Phone** 814-362-5536 **FAX** 814-362-8883
Bradford 16701 (McKean County) **EIN** 23-2949160 **Year Created** 1998
AMV $3,505,846 **FYE** 12-00 **(Gifts Received** $133,542) 2 **Grants totaling** $124,008

All local giving. High grant of **$123,508** to Bradford Educational Foundation. **$500** to Bradford Contemporary Christian Choir. ■**PUBLICATIONS:** None ■**WEBSITE:** None ■**E-MAIL:** None ■**APPLICATION POLICIES & PROCEDURES:** Information not available.

O+D+T Lance E. Eastman (P+D+Con) — Lester Rice (VP+S+D) — Howard L. Fesenmyer (D) — Timothy D. Rice [NY] (D) — Corporate donor: KOA Speer Electronics, Inc.

NW-055 Nelson (Eleanor & Rudolph) Charitable Trust MI-11-12-13-15-22-35-56-63
c/o Mellon Bank N.A., Trust Dept.
1128 State Street, P.O. Box 300 **Phone** 814-453-7247 **FAX** None
Erie 16512 (Erie County) **EIN** 25-6128716 **Year Created** 1970
AMV $409,721 **FYE** 12-00 **(Gifts Received** $108,204) 12 **Grants totaling** $21,000

All giving limited to the Oil City area. High grant of **$5,000** to Venango Youth for Christ (building purchase). **$3,000** to Grace Lutheran Church of Franklin (Learning Center). **$2,000** each to Second Presbyterian Church of Oil City (local mission projects), YMCA of Oil City (youth coordinator position), and YWCA of Oil City (door replacement). **$1,000** each to Family Services & Children's Aid Society, Presbyterian Homes [Erie] (Oil City computer-based training), United Way of Venango County, Venango County Historical Society (archival collection), Venango Museum of Art Science & Industry, Venango Video (furniture), and Visiting Nurse Assn. of Venango County. ■**PUBLICATIONS:** None ■**WEBSITE:** None ■**E-MAIL:** None ■**APPLICATION POLICIES & PROCEDURES:** Only Oil City area organizations are eligible to apply. No grants awarded to individuals. Grant requests may be submitted in a letter in August — the deadline is September 1st; include IRS tax-exempt status documentation.

O+D+T Marilyn King (Trust Officer at Bank+Con) — Mellon Bank N.A. (Trustee)

NW-056 Northwest Bancorp, Inc. Charitable Foundation MI-31-42
c/o Northwest Bancorp, Inc.
301 - 2nd Ave. **Phone** 814-726-2140 **FAX** 814-727-1980
Warren 16365 (Warren County) **EIN** 25-1819537 **Year Created** 1998
AMV $747,821 **FYE** 6-00 **(Gifts Received** $200,000) 2 **Grants totaling** $17,500

All NW Pa. giving. High grant of **$10,000** to Corry Higher Education Council (general operations). **$7,500** to Corry Memorial Hospital (facility improvements). ■**PUBLICATIONS:** application form and instructions ■**WEBSITE:** www.northwestsavingsbank.com [corporate information only] ■**E-MAIL:** None ■**APPLICATION POLICIES & PROCEDURES:** The Foundation reports that grants are limited to 501(c)(3) organizations; scholarship awards are restricted to Bank employees or their dependents. Grant requests must be submitted on an application form, provided by the Bank; applications received by the deadlines of March 31st, June 30th, September 30th and December 31st will be considered during the following quarter.

O+D+T Vicki Stec (S+Con) — John O. Hanna (P) — William J. Wagner (VP) — Gregory C. LaRocca (F) — Corporate donor: Northwest Bancorp, Inc.

NW-057 PFC Bank Charitable Foundation MI-11-13-31-42-44-85
c/o New Bethlehem Bank
363 Broad Street **Phone** 814-275-3133 **FAX** None
New Bethlehem 16242 (Clarion County) **EIN** 25-6383224 **Year Created** 1992
AMV $2,268 **FYE** 12-00 **(Gifts Received** $0) 15 **Grants totaling** $21,575

All local giving. High grant of **$9,500** to Clarion U. Foundation. **$2,500** to United Way of Clarion County. **$1,000-$1,500** each to Boy Scouts/Moraine Trails Council, Clarion County Economic Development, Clarion Hospital Foundation, New Bethlehem Free Library, United Way of Armstrong County and United Way of Indiana County. Other contributions **$50-$525** for various purposes. ■**PUBLICATIONS:** None ■**WEBSITE:** None ■**E-MAIL:** None ■**APPLICATION POLICIES & PROCEDURES:** Information not available. — Formerly known as New Bethlehem Bank Charitable Foundation.

O+D+T R.B. Robertson (P+T+Con) — Darl Hetrick (T) — Corporate donor: PFC Bank

---

NW-058 Phillips (Dr. & Mrs. Arthur William) Charitable Trust MI-12-13-14-22-29-32-41-42-43-44-51-61-63
c/o McFate, McFate & McFate 84-89
229 Elm Street, P.O. Box 316 **Phone** 814-676-2736 **FAX** None
Oil City 16301 (Venango County) **EIN** 25-6201015 **Year Created** 1978
AMV $16,551,801 **FYE** 9-00 **(Gifts Received** $0) 31 **Grants totaling** $695,623

All giving to/for Northwestern Pa. with emphasis on Venango County. High grants of **$100,000** each to Grove City College (classroom building construction) and Westminster College (building renovations). **$76,148** to Sugar Valley Lodge (support for low-income residents). **$50,000** each to Emlenton Presbyterian Church (upgrades/improvements), Penn State U./Erie-Behrend Campus (scholarship funds), Salvation Army of Oil City (capital improvements), and Slippery Rock U. (scholarship funds). **$25,000** each to Clarion U. (building renovations) and Thiel College (multimedia and language lab). **$20,000** to Oil City YMCA (fitness center renovation). **$17,539** to St. Michael Church of Fryburg (church/school improvements). **$15,000** each to American Cancer Society/Oil City (new copier/supplies) and George Junior Republic (multimedia center/library). **$10,000** each to American Heart Assn./Erie, Oil City YWCA (new roof), and Venango Christian High School (property improvements). **$7,500-$7,870** each to Barrow Civic Theatre (heating/AC system), Clarion Free Library (copier), and North Washington Volunteer Fire Dept. & Rescue (equipment). **$6,000-$6,800** each to Big Bend United Methodist Church (handicapped access improvements), Grace Learning Center (computer upgrades), and Make-A-Wish Foundation of Western Pa. (wishes for Franklin or Venango County children). **$5,000** each to Keystone Tall Tree Girl Scout Council (summer day camperships), St. Joseph Church of Oil City (steeple refurbishing), St. Stephen School (kitchen improvements), and YMCA Camps Kon-o-wee & Spencer (capital improvements). **$1,000-$2,765** each to Calvary/St. Joseph Cemetery (repaving), Pa. Special Olympics (funding for local athletes), Salvation Army of Franklin (annual fund), Salvation Army of Oil City (annual fund), and YWCA of Titusville (new phone system). ■**PUBLICATIONS:** descriptive brochure; application guidelines ■**WEBSITE:** None ■**E-MAIL:** None ■**APPLICATION POLICIES & PROCEDURES:** The Foundation reports that preference is given to Northwestern Pa. organizations for capital projects, particularly ones concerned with health care, medical research, higher education, young people, or religion. As a rule, funding for capital purposes will cover only part of the total project cost and grantees must furnish satisfactory evidence of the ability to raise remaining funds. Grant requests (three copies) may be submitted in any form at any time; include a brief organizational history, annual budget, and IRS tax-exempt status documentation.

O+D+T William J. McFate, Esq. (T+Con) — Hon. William E. Breene [Franklin] (T) — Edith Gilmore Letcher [Wallingford] (T)

NW-059 Proper (J. Bowman) Charitable Trust   MI-12-19-25-29-39-41-43-56-63-84-89
213 Seneca Street, 3rd Floor
P.O. Box 374   **Phone** 814-677-5085 **FAX** 814-677-3404
Oil City 16301   (Venango County)   **EIN** 25-1670828 **Year Created** 1991
AMV $2,871,108   **FYE** 9-00   (**Gifts Received** $0)   15 **Grants totaling** $147,697

All local giving, primarily to Tionesta; grants are for general support except as noted. High grant of **$16,573** to Tionesta Borough Volunteer Fire Dept. (exterior improvements). **$16,573** Tionesta Recreation Board. **$14,000** to Venango County Community Foundation (scholarships). **$12,500** to Tionesta Ambulance Service (new equipment). **$10,000** to United Methodist Church of Tionesta (building). **$8,210** to Tionesta Borough (public projects). **$6,000** to Forest-Warren Dept. of Human Services. **$5,000** to Focus on Forest's Future. **$4,265** to Forest County Historical Society (property improvement). **$3,000** to Daffy-Forest County Drug & Alcohol Free. **$875-$2,000** each to Children's Camping Services of West Pa., Forest Area School District, North Clarion-Marienville Area Food Bank, Riverside Cemetery Associates, and West Forest Area Youth Sports Assn. ■**PUBLICATIONS:** None ■ **WEBSITE:** None ■**E-MAIL:** None ■**APPLICATION POLICIES & PROCEDURES:** Giving is restricted to organizations in Forest County or those serving county residents; highest priority is given to matching grants for construction, equipment or one-time maintenance expenses. Requests for operating expenses or recurring costs are considered low priority. Prospective applicants should first submit a brief letter which explains the envisioned program or project, amount of funding requested, and when the funding is needed. The Trust will then send the proposal format for use as a guide in drafting a full proposal. Subsequently it will be discussed with the Trust's consultant who also is available for assistance in preparing the proposal.

O+D+T Administrative Committee members: Stephen P. Kosak (Consultant+Con) — Frank Blum — Paul Blum — Steve Gilford, Esq. — Donald Hall, Jr. — Bruce Johnson — National City Bank of Pa. (Trustee)

NW-060 Rabild (Helmer) Charitable Trust   MI-11-12-31-42-44-51-55-56
c/o National City Bank of Pa./Trust Division
801 State Street   **Phone** 814-871-1279 **FAX** 814-454-7831
Erie 16538   (Erie County)   **EIN** 25-6013302 **Year Created** 1953
AMV $1,101,830   **FYE** 12-00   (**Gifts Received** $0)   7 **Grants totaling** $48,500

Details on 2000 grants are unavailable. — In prior years, giving to the Titusville area included **$10,000** each to Titusville Area Hospital and Titusville Area United Way; **$7,500** to Drake Well Foundation; **$7,000** to Titusville Summer Theater; **$5,000** each to Titusville Leisure Services Board and Titusville Toy Shop (toys for needy children); and also for the library and higher education. ■**PUBLICATIONS:** None ■**WEBSITE:** None ■**E-MAIL:** christopher.junker@nationalcity.com ■**APPLICATION POLICIES & PROCEDURES:** The Trust reports that giving is generally limited to the Titusville area; most grants are for general support, special projects, building funds, capital drives, and publications. All grants are for one year only. Prospective applicants should make an initial telephone inquiry about the feasibility of submitting a request. Grant requests should be submitted in April in a letter (2 pages maximum) before the June 1st deadline; include organization and project budgets, list of major funding sources, audited financial statement, and IRS tax-exempt status documentation. Site visits sometimes are made to organizations being considered for a grant.

O+D+T Christopher A. Junker (VP at Bank+Con) — National City Bank of Pa. (Trustee)

NW-061 Rees (John Nesbit & Sarah Henne) Charitable Foundation MI-11-13-15-22-34-41-42-43-51-52-54-55-56
c/o Roeder & Rothschild   57-71
314 South Franklin St. #B, P.O. Box 325   **Phone** 814-827-1844 **FAX** 814-827-6620
Titusville 16354   (Crawford County)   **EIN** 25-6264847 **Year Created** 1988
AMV $14,412,134   **FYE** 12-00   (**Gifts Received** $0)   42 **Grants totaling** $720,090

Mostly local/NW Pa. giving; grants are for program/operating support except as noted—some comprise multiple payments. High grant of **$100,000** to U. of Pittsburgh School of Medicine (scholarship fund). **$71,150** to Erie Fund for the Arts. **$70,000** to WQLN. **$60,000** to Penn State U./Behrend Center (speaker program/study abroad program). **$52.230** to Titusville Area Hospital (obstetrics building/annual fund). **$35,000** to The Colonel, Inc. Drake Well (museum education program). **$28,700** to Oil Creek Railway Historical Society. **$26,500** to Titusville Leisure Services Board (pavilion). **$25,000** to George Junior Republic. **$24,320** to Titusville YMCA. **$19,600-$21,500** each to Academy Theatre, Keystone Tall Trees Girl Scout Council, Titusville Area United Way, U. of Pittsburgh at Titusville (scholarship fund), and Venango Vo-Tech (young women's counseling). **$17,000** to Clarion U./Venango Campus (scholarship fund). **$15,000** to Titusville Council on the Arts. **$9,000-$10,000** each to Benson Memorial Library, St. Titus School (reconstruction), Struthers Library Theatre (capital campaign), and Victims Resource Center (rape crisis counseling). **$5,000-$7,000** each to Cook Forest Sawmill Center, Hospice of Crawford County, and Titusville Shade Tree Commission. **$4,000-$4,600** each to Benedictine Sisters of Erie, Lacy Community Park, Oil Valley Center for the Arts, Titusville Summer Theatre, Titusville Toy Shop, and Titusville YWCA. **$2,000-$2,500** each to Erie Playhouse, Mt. Aloysius College (music programs), and Titusville Area Schools (performance funds). Other local and out-of-state grants/contributions, **$100-$1,500,** for similar purposes. ■ **PUBLICATIONS:** Annual Report; Application & Grant Procedures brochure ■ **WEBSITE:** None ■ **E-MAIL:** jn&shrees@stargate.net ■ **APPLICATION POLICIES & PROCEDURES:** The Foundation reports that giving is limited to NW Pa., near or relevant to Titusville, and focused on community/civic causes, performing arts, medical education, and the physical/biological science education. Priority is given projects/programs which directly impact the Titusville area. Most grants are for general support, special projects, program development, and matching grants; no grants are awarded directly to individuals or for scholarships. Prospective applicants should make an initial telephone inquiry about the feasibility of submitting a request. Grant requests may be submitted in a letter (two copies), preferably in November; include an annual report, organization and project budgets, Board member list, and IRS tax-exempt status documentation. The letter must state that the proposal has been approved by the organization's CEO or Board. If a more formal proposal is required, the Foundation will request it. Site visits sometimes are made to organizations being considered for a grant. Grants are awarded at monthly meetings.

O+D+T Richard W. Roeder, Esq. (T+Con) — Barbara L. Smith, Esq. [Thornhurst] (T)

NW-062 Saint Marys Catholic Foundation   MI-41-42-61
c/o Keystone Carbon Company
1935 State Street   **Phone** 814-781-4222 **FAX** None
St. Marys   15857   (Elk County)   **EIN** 25-6036961   **Year Created** 1960
AMV $12,252,696   **FYE** 11-00   (**Gifts Received** $7,440)   11 **Grants totaling** $568,502

Mostly local/NW Pa. giving; grants are for general support except as noted. High grant of **$227,732** to Elk County Christian High School. **$99,693** to St. Marys Catholic Elementary School System. **$73,639** to Opportunity for Parochial Education Network [Erie] (scholarships). **$18,938** to St. Leo's Parochial School [Ridgway]. **$16,000** to Diocese of Erie (youth ministry/vocations). **$11,875** to Holy Rosary Parochial School [Johnsonburg]. **$10,500** to St. Boniface Parochial School [Kersey]. **Out-of-state** giving includes **$25,000** to Morality in Media [NY]; **$12,500** to Foundations & Donors Interested in Catholic Activities [DC]; and **$5,000** to National Catholic Educational Assn. [DC] (symposium). ■ **PUBLICATIONS:** None ■ **WEBSITE:** None ■ **E-MAIL:** None ■ **APPLICATION POLICIES & PROCEDURES:** The Foundation reports that grants are made primarily to Erie Diocese (especially Catholic schools) with emphasis on Elk County and the St. Marys area. Most grants are for operating budgets or special projects; no grants are awarded for endowment or to individuals. Prospective applicants initially should make a telephone inquiry about the feasibility of submitting a request. Grant requests may be submitted in any form at any time; state the need for the grant and give essential background information; include organizational/project budgets, audited financial statement, list of other funding sources, and IRS tax-exempt status documentation. Site visits sometimes are made to organizations being considered for a grant. The Board meets in February and October.

O+D+T Richard J. Reuscher (S+F+T+Donor+Con) — Bishop Donald Trautman [Erie] (C) — E.H. Reuscher (P+T+Donor) — W.E. Reuscher (VP+T+Donor) — R.B. Reuscher (T+Donor) — Conrad J. Kogovsek, III (T) — Corporate donors: Keystone Carbon Company; Keystone Thermistor Corporation; Keystone Investment Corporation [DE]; EB & Associates

---

NW-063 Scholarship Foundation/Erie Scottish Rite   MI-43
4611 Sunnydale Blvd., P.O. Box 1364   **Phone** 814-866-5382 **FAX** None
Erie   16512   (Erie County)   **EIN** 25-1710223   **Year Created** 1992
AMV $1,326,055   **FYE** 7-01   (**Gifts Received** $63,795)   36 **Grants totaling** $53,000

All grants are scholarship awards for high school graduates in Northwestern Pa.; awards ranged from **$500** to **$2,500** and were paid directly to the colleges/universities. ■ **PUBLICATIONS:** annual report; statement of program policy; application guidelines; application form ■ **WEBSITE:** None ■ **E-MAIL:** None ■ **APPLICATION POLICIES & PROCEDURES:** Scholarships are restricted to high school students resident in Northwestern Pa. during June-July of the year prior to application. Applications must be submitted before the April 15th deadline on a designated application form, available from Erie Scottish Rite, and signed by a member of that organization; include a copy of high school transcripts. Decisions are based on a student's grades, financial need, interests, civic involvement and work history; scholarships awarded at a June ceremony.

O+D+T Harold A. Durst (F+T+Con) — Merle E. Wood [Fairview] (P+T) — Robert W. Lawson (S+T) — G. William Blakeslee [Union City] (T) — Kim W. Jeffreys (T) — Herbert J. Johnson, Esq. (T) — Harvey D. McClure, Esq. (T) — Raymond L. McGarvey (T) — R. Perrin Baker, Esq. (T+Counsel)

NW-064 Sharonsteel Foundation   MI-11-12-13-22-41-42-43-49
c/o Precision Steel Services
P.O. Box 6   **Phone** 724-347-5041 **FAX** 724-347-5965
Farrell   16121   (Mercer County)   **EIN** 25-6063133   **Year Created** 1953
AMV $5,672,228   **FYE** 12-00   (**Gifts Received** $0)   21 **Grants totaling** $278,272

About four-fifths local giving. High grant of **$31,836** to St. Michael School [Greenville] (upgrade computer lab). **$30,000** each to Kennedy Christian High School (wireless computer lab) and Sharon Christian Academy (scholarships for needy students). **$27,636** to Penn State U. (scholarship tuition). **$25,000** to Penn Lakes Girl Scouts Council (Camp Trefoil Trails programs). **$20,000** to United Way of Mercer County. **$15,000** each to Villa Education Center (STAR program) and Westminster College (scholarship tuition). **$10,000** each to Junior Achievement of Mercer County and Prince of Peace (emergency services for low-income persons). **$7,500** to Salvation Army/Sharon. **$6,900** to The Bair Foundation (scholarships for foster children). **$5,000** to Shenango Valley YMCA (improvements). **$3,400** to Make-A-Wish Foundation of Western Pa. (fulfill children's wishes). **Out-of-state** giving includes **$20,000** to Phillips Exeter Academy [NH] (scholarships) and **$10,000** to Greenwich Country Day School [CT] (programs). ■**PUBLICATIONS:** None ■**WEBSITE:** None ■**E-MAIL:** None ■**APPLICATION POLICIES & PROCEDURES:** Grant requests may be submitted in any form at any time; describe the organization and purpose of funds requested, state a specific amount, an include an audited financial statement (if possible) and IRS tax-exempt status documentation. No grants awarded to individuals.

O+D+T Lori Darby (Administrator+Con) — Christian L. Overbeck [NY] (T) — Malvin G. Sandler (T) — Hume R. Styer, Esq. [NY] (T)

NW-065 Shenango Valley Foundation

41 Chestnut Street
Sharon 16146   (Mercer County)

MI-11-12-13-14-16-22-23-34-35-41-55
Phone 724-981-5882 **FAX** 724-981-5480
EIN 25-1407396   **Year Created** 1981

AMV $14,952,727   **FYE** 12-00   **(Gifts Received** $478,073)   500+ **Grants totaling** $1,048,997

As a Community Foundation all discretionary giving is limited to organizations serving Mercer and Lawrence counties and nearby OH. Pa. grants awarded from discretionary/unrestricted funds totaled about **$68,000.** High grant of **$8,500** to Camp Middlesex (for underprivileged children). **$5,000-$5,500** each to Assn. for Children with Learning Disabilities (scholarships), Sharon Regional Health System/School of Nursing, Shenango Valley Foundation (Humanitarian Award-shared by three individuals), Shenango Valley Initiative (work camp), and Young Life/Penn-Ohio. **$3,000-$3,500** each to Sharon City School District (adult computer training), Sharon Regional Health Agency (bereavement program for children), United Way of Mercer County, and West Hill Ministries. **$2,000-$2,500** to Horizon Foundation (training materials), Mercer County 4-H Playground, Minority Health Advisory Committee (Grandparents Support Program), Prince of Peace, Shenango Valley Initiative, and United Way of Northern Mercer County. **$1,000-$1,750** to Black Men for Progress, City Rescue Mission, Columbia Theatre, E.R.A.S.E., Farrell Midget Cheerleading (uniforms), Shenango Valley YMCA, and Valley Art Guild (summer program). Other smaller contributions to local organizations and grants to 43 needy individuals totaled about **$35,000.** All other grants/contributions from donor-advised/restricted funds for many other organizations and individuals for scholarships. ■**PUBLICATIONS:** Annual Report; informational brochure; application guidelines; application form ■**WEBSITE:** None ■**E-MAIL:** svf@svol.net ■**APPLICATION POLICIES & PROCEDURES:** The Foundation reports that only organizations in Mercer or Lawrence counties (or Trumbull and Mahoning counties in OH) are eligible to apply. Most grants are for special projects, matching grants, individuals, or scholarships; multi-year grants are made. Prospective applicants should make an initial telephone inquiry about the feasibility of submitting a request. Organizational requests (accepted at any time) should be submitted on a formal application form available from the Foundation; indicate how many persons will benefit from the project/program, and include organization/project budgets, list of major funding sources, audited financial statement, Board member list, and IRS tax-exempt status documentation. Site visits sometimes are made to organizations being considered for a grant. Grants are awarded at meetings in March, June, September, and December. Individual/scholarship requests should be submitted in the form of a letter; contact the foundation regarding necessary supporting documentation.

O+D+T Lawrence E. Haynes (Executive Director+Con) — James A. O'Brien (P+D) — Robert C. Jazwinski (Executive VP+D) — Karen Winner Hale (VP+D) — Ronald R. Anderson (S+D) — James E. Feeney (F+D) — Carol Gamble (D) — Mel Grata (D) — Lynda Holm (D) — Paul E. O'Brien (D) — Albert T. Puntureri (D) — William J. Strimbu (D) — Kenneth Turcic (D) — James T Weller, Sr. (D) — James E. Winner, Jr. (D)

NW-066 Siebert (Kate) Trust

c/o National City Bank of Pa./Trust Division
801 State Street
Erie 16538   (Erie County)

MI-11-12-21-29-31-41
Phone 814-871-1279 **FAX** 814-454-7831
EIN 25-6013317   **Year Created** 1953

AMV $956,513   **FYE** 12-99   **(Gifts Received** $0)   6 **Grants totaling** $41,838

All giving restricted to Crawford County organizations serving blind, crippled or destitute children; all grants are for general support. **$8,368** each to Associated Charities, Red Cross, Shriners Hospital [Erie], and Titusville School District. **$4,184** each to Bethesda Children's Home and Titusville Lions Club. ■**PUBLICATIONS:** None ■**WEBSITE:** None ■**E-MAIL:** christopher.junker@nationalcity.com ■**APPLICATION POLICIES & PROCEDURES:** The Trust reports that preference is given to Titusville-area organizations serving children, especially blind, crippled or destitute. Most grants are for general support or special projects; only annual grants are awarded. Prospective applicants should make an initial telephone inquiry about the feasibility of submitting a request. Grant requests may be submitted, preferably in April, in a letter (2 pages maximum) before the June 1st deadline; include organization and project budgets, a list of major funding sources, and IRS tax-exempt status documentation. Grants can be renewed annually upon evidence of proper use of grant funds.

O+D+T Christopher A. Junker (VP at Bank+Con) — National City Bank of Pa. (Trustee)

NW-067 Smith (Arlene H.) Charitable Foundation

c/o McInnes Steel Company
441 East Main Street
Corry 16407   (Erie County)

MI-13-17-21-22-25-33-31-32-41-44-89
Phone 814-664-9664 **FAX** None
EIN 25-1515142   **Year Created** 1982

AMV $4,879,626   **FYE** 12-00   **(Gifts Received** $0)   13 **Grants totaling** $270,450

Giving limited to the Corry area; all grants are unrestricted gifts. High grant of **$150,000** to YMCA of Corry. **$30,000** to Corry Memorial Hospital. **$22,500** to Corry Higher Education Council. **$20,000** to Corry Ambulance Service. **$10,150** to American Cancer Society/Corry Area Unit. **$8,000** to Safe Horizons Services for Women. **$6,800** to Make-A-Wish Foundation of Western

Pa. [Erie]. **$5,000** each to Corry Community Development Corp. and Salvation Army/Corry. **$2,500-$4,000** each to Corry Area Food Pantry, Corry Rotary Club, and Spring Creek Volunteer Fire Dept. ■ **PUBLICATIONS:** Application Guidelines and Request for Funding form ■ **WEBSITE:** None ■ **E-MAIL:** None ■ **APPLICATION POLICIES & PROCEDURES:** The Foundation reports that giving is restricted to the Corry area. No grants awarded to individuals. Grant requests may be submitted at any time in duplicate on a Request for Funding form, available from the Foundation; include a Board list and IRS tax-exempt status documentation. If the request is for a special project also provide an annual report, if available, audited financial statement for the most recent year, and program and agency budgets.

O+D+T Timothy M. Hunter (F+Con) — Stephen J. Mahoney (P+D) — Frank K. Smith (VP+D) — James D. Cullen, Esq. [Erie] (S+D) — John E. Britton, Esq. [Erie] (D)

NW-068 Sokolski Family Foundation
204 Pamela Drive
Warren 16365   (Warren County)
AMV $944,566   **FYE** 12-00   (**Gifts Received** $379,920)

MI-11-51-56-89
Phone 814-723-4234 **FAX** None
EIN 25-6612279   **Year Created** 1998
12 **Grants totaling** $23,625

Mostly local giving. High grants of **$10,000** each to Struthers Library Theatre and Warren County United Fund. **$1,000** to Warren Fire Fighters Assn. Other local and out-of-state contributions **$100-$500** for various purposes. ■ **PUBLICATIONS:** None ■ **WEBSITE:** None ■ **E-MAIL:** None ■ **APPLICATION POLICIES & PROCEDURES:** Information not available.

O+D+T Robert D. Sokolski (T+Donor+Con) — Sara P. Sokolski (Donor)

NW-069 Stackpole (Muriel Dauer) Foundation
699 Maurus Street
St. Marys 15857   (Elk County)
AMV $323,265   **FYE** 10-00   (**Gifts Received** $0)

MI-12-13-14-15-44-55
Phone 814-834-1417 **FAX** None
EIN 25-1723753   **Year Created** 1994
3 **Grants totaling** $14,000

All local giving; grants are for general purposes. High grant of **$9,000** to Marienstadt Corp. **$3,000** to Christian Food Bank. **$2,000** to Elk County Council on the Arts. ■ **PUBLICATIONS:** None ■ **WEBSITE:** None ■ **E-MAIL:** None ■ **APPLICATION POLICIES & PROCEDURES:** The Foundation reports that all giving is to benefit St. Marys and residents. No grants are awarded to individuals. Grant requests should be submitted during December-August in a letter (4 pages maximum) which clearly states the purpose of the request; include organization and project budgets and IRS tax-exempt status documentation. Grants are awarded at an October Trustees' meeting.

O+D+T T. Scott Stackpole (S+T+Con) — Sara-Jane Stackpole (P+T) — County National Bank (Custodian)

NW-070 Stackpole-Hall Foundation, The
44 South St. Marys Street
St. Marys 15857
   (Elk County)
AMV $27,154,326   **FYE** 12-00   (**Gifts Received** $0)

MI-12-13-14-17-19-31-32-33-35-41-44-55-56 84-89
Phone 814-834-1845 **FAX** 814-834-1869
EIN 25-6006650   **Year Created** 1951
90+ **Grants totaling** $1,454,463

Most giving limited to Elk County and surrounding area; grants are unrestricted support except as noted. High grant of **$300,000** to Elk County Christian High School (capital campaign). **$100,000** each to Erie County Community Foundation (Elk County Community Foundation operations) and Ridgway Borough (fire dept. ladder truck). **$50,000** to Elk Regional Health System (information/technology systems). **$33,400** to Jay Township (fire truck). **$30,333** to Bradford Educational Foundation (classroom technology/faculty training). **$30,000** to St. Marys Public Library (children's library). **$27,579** to Dickinson Mental Health Center (children's partial hospitalization program/drop-in center cultural programs). **$23,000** to Kane Community Center (handicapped accessibility). **$20,000** each to Jay Township (playground project), Johnsonburg Borough (fire dept. building), and Wilcox Volunteer Fire Dept. (fire station addition). **$17,573** to City of St. Marys (softball field improvements). **$15,500** to Charles Cole Memorial Hospital (outpatient cancer treatment center). **$15,000** each to Boy Scouts/Bucktail Council (programming/administrative center) and Elk County Christian High School (career mentoring). **$13,340** to CAPSEA/Citizens Against Physical, Sexual, and Emotional Abuse (shelter improvements). **$12,631** to Community Nurses of Elk & Cameron County (managed care information system). **$11,466** to Life & Independence for Today (counselor). **$10,000** to American Heart Assn. (equipment/training). **$9,500** to Elk County Historical Society (equipment/publication/renovation). **$8,000** to Cook County Sawmill Center for the Arts (refurbishment). **$6,156** to City of St. Marys (DARE training). **$5,000** to Ridgway Heritage Council (historical registry application). **$3,400** to Make-A-Wish Foundation (staff). **$4,500** to Western Pa. Caring Foundation [Pittsburgh] (health insurance for needy children). **$3,000** to Elk County Council on the Art (kids summer art program). **$2,500** each (all for minority student grants/projects) to Allegheny College, Edinboro U., and Gannon U. and Boys & Girls Club of St. Marys. **$1,000-$1,225** each to Community Education Council (scholarship funds), Johnsonburg United Methodist Church (youth mission project), Penn State U./WPSX, Tri-County Rails to Trails, and Western Pa. Conservancy. Twenty-eight local municipalities, government agencies, public and private schools, and nonprofit organizations were awarded grants, mostly **$1,000-$10,000** (a few higher), for the Summer Jobs Program. Also, **$307,577** in Restricted Grants disbursed to seven local and out-of-state organizations/institutions. Other smaller local contributions **$500-$750** for various purposes. ■ **PUBLICATIONS:** Annual Report (with application guidelines); newsletter; informational brochure ■ **WEBSITE:** None ■ **E-MAIL:** None ■ **APPLICATION POLICIES & PROCEDURES:** The Foundation reports that organizations located in or serving Elk County receive first priority, as well as to communities in which the donors, donors' families and Trustees reside. Most grants are for special projects but also awards matching grants, seed money grants, and partnership grants, as well as general operating support under certain circumstances. Support for endowments has a low priority unless very unusual circumstances exist. No grants are awarded to individuals. Prospective applicants should initially telephone the Foundation to inquire about the feasibility of submitting a request. Grant requests should be submitted at least 30 days prior to the quarterly meetings (see months below) and must include: (1) brief background on the organization; (2) a detailed description of the project for which support is requested, why it is necessary, how it will benefit the organization, how it will work, and who it will serve; (3) the specific amount being requested; (4) information about the person/s responsible for carrying out the project and his/her qualifications; (5) the projected budget, including all sources of support and how the project will be financed upon expiration of the proposed grant; (6) a recent financial statement, preferably audited; (7) a list of current officers, directors and administrative staff; and (8) IRS tax-exempt status documentation. Two copies of the complete application are required. Site visits sometimes are made to organizations being considered for a grant. Grants are awarded at meetings in February, May, August, and November.

O+D+T William C. Conrad (Executive Secretary+Con) — Lyle G. Hall [MA] (C+T) — Douglas R. Dobson (VC+T) — Helen Hall Drew [SC] (T) — Megan Hall [MA] (T) — J.M. Hamlin Johnson (T) — Alexander G. Sheble-Hall [MA] (T) — R. Dauer Stackpole [SC] (T) — Sara-Jane Stackpole [Ridgway] (T) — Laurey Turner [Langhorne] (T) — Heather Conrad [KY] (Board Member) — Jeff Drew [AZ] (Board Member) — Laurey Nixon [GA] (Board Member) — Charlotte Hall Perkins [MA] (Board Member)

NW-071 Suhr (Charles L.) Charitable Trust
213 Seneca Street, 3rd Floor
P.O. Box 374
Oil City   16301   (Venango County)
MI-11-12-22-29-31-56-63-89

Phone 814-677-5085 **FAX** 814-677-3404
EIN 25-6063178   **Year Created** 1953

AMV $760,910   **FYE** 12-00   **(Gifts Received** $0)   **Grants totaling** $50,355

All giving restricted to Venango County. High grant of **$27,855** to Good Hope Lutheran Church—as designated by Trust instrument. **$10,000** to Venango County Human Services (Communities that Care program). **$5,000** to Salvation Army of Oil City (capital campaign). **$2,500** each to Oil City Civic Center (operations), Oil Heritage Region, Inc. (bicentennial celebration), and Titusville Area Hospital (renovations). ■**PUBLICATIONS:** application guidelines ■**WEBSITE:** None ■**E-MAIL:** None ■**APPLICATION POLICIES & PROCEDURES:** The Trust reports that half of annual income must be awarded to Good Hope Lutheran Church; the remaining funds are restricted first to organizations in Oil City and, secondly, to Venango County. Most grants are for operating budgets, special projects, building funds, capital needs, endowment, and matching funds; multiyear grants are awarded. Prospective applicants initially should make a telephone inquiry about the feasibility of submitting a request. A formal application form, available from the Trust, must be submitted together with an annual report, organizational budget, project budget, audited financial statement, list of other funding sources, Board member list, and IRS tax-exempt status documentation; requests should be submitted in April, August, or November (deadlines are April 30th, August 31st, and November 30th). Decisions on grants are made at meetings in May, September, and December.

O+D+T Discretionary Committee members: Stephen P. Kosak (Consultant+Con) — Rodney L. Campbell — R. Grant Carner — Emily P. Eisenman — National City Bank of Pa. (Trustee)

NW-072 Symmco Foundation, The
c/o Symmco, Inc.
5 Park Street
Sykesville   15865   (Jefferson County)
MI-11-13-21-22-29-31-39-41-42-44-63-89

Phone 814-894-2461 **FAX** 814-894-5272
EIN 25-1480507   **Year Created** 1984

AMV $1,394,279   **FYE** 12-00   **(Gifts Received** $50,000)   21 **Grants totaling** $66,509

All local/Pa. giving. High grant of **$18,014** to Sykesville Public Library. **$7,500** each to Penn State U./DuBois and Sykesville Lions Club. **$3,500** to DuBois Area United Way. **$5,000** each to DuBois Area Catholic Schools and Punxsutawney Area Hospital. **$3,195** to Sykesville Ambulance. **$2,500** each to Boy Scouts/DuBois and Sykesville Fire Dept. **$1,000-$1,500** each to DuBois Public Library, Fox Chase Cancer Center [Philadelphia], Grace Methodist Church, Leopards Midget Football, Red Cross/DuBois, Salvation Army/DuBois, Salvation Army/Punxsutawney, and Stump Creek Residents. Other smaller contributions. ■**PUBLICATIONS:** None ■**WEBSITE:** www.symmco.com [corporate info only] ■**E-MAIL:** betty@symmco.com ■**APPLICATION POLICIES & PROCEDURES:** The Foundation reports giving restricted to Jefferson County and contiguous counties. No grants are awarded to individuals. Grant requests may be submitted in a letter (2 pages maximum) at any time.

O+D+T Betty Hoare (Con) — John W. Bean [DuBois] (T) — Corporate donor: Symmco, Inc.

NW-073 Venango Area Community Foundation
213 Seneca Street, 3rd Floor
P.O. Box 374
Oil City   16301   (Venango County)
MI-13-29-41-43-55-85-89

Phone 814-677-8687 **FAX** 814-677-3404
EIN 25-1292553   **Year Created** 1975

AMV $2,975,849   **FYE** 8-00   **(Gifts Received** $793,000)   90+ **Grants totaling** $318,825

As a Community Foundation all discretionary giving is limited to organizations serving Venango County. High grants of **$15,000** each to Conneaut Lake Institute, Edinboro U. (Rural Youth Leadership Team), Forest County Industrial Development Corp. (Enterprise Center), Northwest Eminent Community Institute, Oil City Arts Council, and Venango Economic Development Corp. Other smaller grants/contributions awarded to schools. About **$51,000** awarded in 80+ scholarships to local high school graduates under the Baum, Bear, Cranberry, Daniels, Feldman Essay, Forker Memorial, Lamey, Locke, Loeffler, Proper, Russell, Venango Education Foundation, and Venus scholarship programs; awards usually range from **$250** to **$2,000**. ■**PUBLICATIONS:** Annual Report; application guidelines ■**WEBSITE:** None ■**E-MAIL:** vacoffice@usachoice.net ■**APPLICATION POLICIES & PROCEDURES:** As a 'Community Foundation,' all giving is limited to enhancing the quality of life of Venango County residents. Prospective applicants initially should make a telephone inquiry about the feasibility of submitting a request. Scholarship applicants must complete a formal scholarship application form, available from the Foundation, and submit it with financial data and scholastic record information.

O+D+T Stephen P. Kosak (Executive Director+Con) — Diane E. Hasek, Esq. [Seneca] (P+VP+T) — William Bowen (S+T) — Charles Stubler (F+T) — Robin D. Hart (F+T) — James Alexander, Esq. (T) — Dan Brockett [Franklin] (T) — Bridgett Davis, M.D. [Franklin] (T) — Emily P. Eisenman (T) — Brandon Hammond [Clintonville] (T) — Lois McElwee (T) — Denise Parisi [Franklin] (T) — Donald G. Pfohl (T) — Dan Roessner (T) — Ed Scurry [Franklin] (T) — Loretta Strawbridge (T) — Ted Welch, Esq. (T)

NW-074 Vicary Foundation, The
3919 State Street
Erie 16508
Erie 16508 (Erie County)

MI-11-12-13-14-17-29-31-32-41-43-44-51-52
54-55-56-57
Phone 814-868-9347 **FAX** 814-868-0574
EIN 25-6035971 **Year Created** 1958

AMV $2,357,423 **FYE** 12-00 **(Gifts Received** $0) 39 **Grants totaling** $183,796

Mostly local giving; grants are unrestricted/operational support except as noted. High grant of **$23,816** to Erie Philharmonic. **$17,500** to United Way of Erie County. **$14,300** to ExpERIEnce Children's Museum. **$11,353** to Erie County Historical Society. **$11,074** to Warner Theatre Preservation Trust. **$7,500-$8,925** each to Community Country Day School, Erie Area Fund for the Arts and Erie Summer Festival of the Arts, and Make-A-Wish Foundation/Erie (operations/endowment). **$5,000-$6,600** each to Erie Bayfront Playground (capital campaign), Erie County Library (capital campaign), Mercy Center for Women (computer lab), MS Society of NW Pa., Penn State U./Behrend Campus (PEPP program), and SafeNet (capital campaign). **$4,500** to WQLN (building/operations). **$2,300-$3,000** each to Erie Art Museum, Erie Day School (scholarship fund), March of Dimes of NW Pa., and Neighborhood Art House. **$1,000-$1,869** each to ACES/Americans for Competitive Economic System, Cathedral Preparatory School (scholarship), Dafmark Dance Theatre & School, Edinboro U. Juvenile Diabetes Foundation, Red Cross, St. Vincent's Health Center, Villa Maria (operations/building), West Ridge Fire Company, and Westtown School [Chester County]. Other smaller local contributions. **Out-of-state** giving includes **$5,000** to Southern Poverty Law Center [AL]; **$2,500** to Northfield League for Women [OH]; and **$1,690** to American Symphony Orchestra League [VA]. ■**PUBLICATIONS:** None ■**WEBSITE:** None ■**E-MAIL:** None ■**APPLICATION POLICIES & PROCEDURES:** The Foundation reports that giving is generally limited to Erie County organizations. Multiyear grants are awarded. Grant requests may be submitted in a letter at any time; describe the program goals/objectives and include organizational and project budgets, list of major funding sources, audited financial statement, and IRS tax-exempt status documentation. Site visits sometimes are made to organizations being considered for a grant. Grants generally are awarded at a December meeting but requests are considered at other times.

O+D+T Thomas C. Vicary (P+F+D+Con) — Cheryl G. Vicary (S+D) — Arthur Curtze [State College] (D) — Charles A. Curtze (D) — Louise Vicary Curtze (D)

NW-075 Walker Foundation Trust
2512 Meadow Road, P.O. Box 171
Clearfield 16830 (Clearfield County)

MI-13-41-43-44
Phone 814-765-7605 **FAX** None
EIN 25-6253677 **Year Created** 1984

AMV $379,361 **FYE** 6-01 **(Gifts Received** $23,600) 11 **Grants totaling** $39,300

All local giving. High grant of **$18,000** Clearfield YMCA. **$5,000** to Clearfield Education Foundation. **$2,000** to Friends of the Philipsburg Library. **$1,800** to Bigler Boy Scout Troop. Also, seven scholarships (**$1,000-$3,500**) awarded to local students. ■**PUBLICATIONS:** None ■**WEBSITE:** None ■**E-MAIL:** None ■**APPLICATION POLICIES & PROCEDURES:** The Foundation reports that most giving is restricted to educational institutions, municipalities, churches, and other charitable organizations which benefit residents of the Clearfield County area.

O+D+T Susan Walker Kriner (Co-T+Con) — Ray S. Walker [Bigler] (P+Co-T+Donor) — William R. Owens (Co-T) — Anne Walker Macko [State College] (Co-T+Donor) — Gloria Thomas [Bigler] (S) — Charles Alan Walker [Bigler] (Co-T+Donor) — Louise S. Walker [Bigler] (Co-T) — Clearfield Bank & Trust Co. (Corporate Co-Trustee)

NW-076 Walker (Margaret M.) Charitable Foundation
c/o Butler Wick Trust Company
First Federal Building, 1 East State Street
Sharon 16146 (Mercer County)

MI-11-12-13-14-15-18-22-25-29-32-41
Phone 724-346-4175 **FAX** 724-346-1620
EIN 25-1790413 **Year Created** 1996

AMV $61 **FYE** 12-00 **(Gifts Received** $77,519) 21 **Grants totaling** $78,200

All local or nearby Ohio giving. High grant of **$20,000** to Penn Lakes Girl Scout Council. **$15,000** to Buhl Farm Trust. **$8,500** to United Way of Mercer County. **$4,500** each to Meals on Wheels and West Hill Ministries. **$3,000** each City Rescue Mission, Family Planning Services of Mercer County, Red Cross, and Salvation Army. **$2,600** to Children's Aid Society. **$2,000** each to American Cancer Society and Assn. for Children with Learning Disabilities. **$1,000-$1,500** each to Almira Home for Independent Women, Community Food Warehouse, George Junior Republic, Keystone Blind Assn., and Prince of Peace Center. Other local contributions **$300-$500** for various purposes. ■**PUBLICATIONS:** None ■**WEBSITE:** None ■**E-MAIL:** None ■**APPLICATION POLICIES & PROCEDURES:** Information not available.

O+D+T David Levine (Advisor+Con) — Richard W. Epstein, Esq. (Advisor) — Joseph J. Evans (Advisor) — Butler Wick Trust Company (Trustee)

NW-077 Werner (Donald M. & Barbara L.) Family Foundation
770 Woodlawn Drive
Hermitage 16148 (Mercer County)

MI-13-22-62
Phone 724-981-1250 **FAX** None
EIN 23-7933631 **Year Created** 1997

AMV $175,801 **FYE** 12-00 **(Gifts Received** $19,889) 40 **Grants totaling** $88,438

About two-thirds local/nearby OH giving. High area grant of **$25,050** to Youngstown Area Jewish Federation [OH]. **$25,000** to Jewish Appeal of Youngstown. **$10,280** to Temple Beth Israel. **$500** each to Donald Werner First Tee Endowment and Penn Lakes Girl Scout Council. Other smaller local contributions. **Out-of-state** grant: **$20,000** to Jewish Federation of Palm Beach County [FL] ■**PUBLICATIONS:** None ■**WEBSITE:** None ■**E-MAIL:** None ■**APPLICATION POLICIES & PROCEDURES:** Grant requests may be submitted in any form at any time.

O+D+T Donald M. Werner (T+Donor+Con) — Barbara L. Werner (T+Donor)

***NW-078* Werner (Richard L. & Lois S.) Family Foundation**
561 Richmond Drive
Sharon 16146   (Mercer County)

MI-11-13-22-25-31-32-41-42-44-54-62
Phone 724-981-1251 **FAX** None
EIN 23-7911213   **Year Created** 1997

AMV $3,221,573   **FYE** 12-00   (**Gifts Received** $0)   78 **Grants totaling** $223,165

About half local/nearby OH giving. High area grant of **$50,000** to Youngstown Area Jewish Federation. **$20,000** to Temple Beth Israel. **$10,000** to Buhl Farm Trust. **$2,000-$2,500** each to American Cancer Society, Buhl Farm Trust (First Tee program), Thiel College, Union of American Hebrew Congregations/Camp Harlam [Lehigh County], and United Way of Mercer County. **$1,000-$1,500** each to American Heart Assn., Butler Museum of American Art [OH], Community Food Warehouse, Penn Lakes Girl Scout Council, Sharon Regional Health System, Sharon Sr. High School (temporary assistance program), Shenango Valley Community Library, and U. of Pittsburgh Medical Center/Horizon Foundation. Other local/area contributions **$100-$300** for various purposes. **Out-of-state** giving includes **$31,000** to U. of Miami Medical School (cardiac simulation/diabetes research); **$15,000** to Cleveland Clinic [OH]; **$12,500** to Rensselaer Polytechnic Institute [NY]; **$5,000** to Israel Children's Tennis Center Assn. [FL]; and smaller grants/contributions, many to IL and NY where Trustees reside. ■**PUBLICATIONS:** None ■**WEBSITE:** None ■**E-MAIL:** None ■**APPLICATION POLICIES & PROCEDURES:** Grant requests may be submitted in a letter before the January 1st deadline.
O+D+T Richard L. Werner (T+Donor+Con) — Elise Werner Frost [IL] (T) — Bruce D. Werner [IL] (T) — Lois S. Werner (T+Donor) — Mindy H. Werner [NY] (T)

***NW-079* Winslow (Harry C.) Foundation, The**
c/o PNC Advisors
928 Park Ave.
Meadville 16335   (Crawford County)

MI-12-13-14-15-29-31-41-55-56-85

Phone 814-337-1420 **FAX** 814-337-1410
EIN 25-6184815   **Year Created** 1976

AMV $638,442   **FYE** 12-01   (**Gifts Received** $0)   11 **Grants totaling** $30,051

All giving restricted to the Meadville area. High grants of **$4,000** each to Big Brothers & Big Sisters of Crawford County (mentoring program) and Meadville Area Free Clinic (medications). **$3,929** to Academy Theatre Foundation (sound equipment). **$3,122** to Seton School (fire alarm system). **$3,000** each to Community Health Services (electrical upgrades). **$2,600** to Crawford County Historical Society (facilities improvements). **$2,000-$2,500** each to Center for Family Services (laptops), Keystone Blind Assn. (local children's program), and YWCA of Meadville (pool maintenance). **$1,500** to YMCA of Meadville (stair unit). **$1,000** to Fairview/Fairmont Outreach (computer). — Grants awarded in the prior year included **$10,000** to Meadville Market House Authority; **$7,500** to Crawford County Historical Society; and **$3,000-$3,500** each to Center for Family Services, Hospice of Crawford County, and Meadville Council on the Arts. ■**PUBLICATIONS:** annual report; statement of program policy; application guidelines; application form ■**WEBSITE:** None ■**E-MAIL:** None ■**APPLICATION POLICIES & PROCEDURES:** The Foundation reports that giving is restricted to the Meadville area with priority given to programs which improve residents' health/well-being, advance educational/enrichment opportunities, encourage higher moral/spiritual values, engender civic improvement and economic development, and promote patriotism, respect for law and order, and our constitutional government. No grants are awarded to individuals. Grant requests must be submitted on a formal application form (available from the Bank) during August-September (deadline is October 1st); include an project budget, list of major funding sources, Board member list, and IRS tax-exempt status documentation. Site visits sometimes are made to organizations being considered for a grant. The Board meets in November; grants are disbursed in December.
O+D+T Program Committee members: Michele A. Burke (Asst. VP+Trust Officer at Bank+Con) — Hon. Gordon R. Miller — Rev. Richard E. Butryn — PNC Advisors (Trustee)

Northwestern Region / NW
Non-profiled Foundations

*NW Region foundations which did **not** meet the criteria for profiling are listed here; the letter code in parentheses after the foundation name indicates its status, per the following key:*

L   **Limited Assets/Giving**: The market value of assets was $250,000 or under and the total of grants awarded was less than $12,500 in the last year of record. If information about grants is available, up to three Major Interest (MI) Codes are listed; if no information on giving interests is available, the notation "N/R" (Not Reported) is shown.

O   **Operating Foundation**: This special designation by IRS is for a foundation that operates its own program or institution and, generally, does not award grants to other organizations.

R   **Restricted Trust/Foundation**: Grants are awarded only to designated organizations or beneficiaries, typically under the terms of a Will or Trust Instrument.

I   **Inactive**: The assets, generally, are nominal (typically under $5,000) and there has been little or no grants activity within the last year or more.

NP   **Non-Pennsylvania Foundation**: The foundation's connection to Pennsylvania is only incidental; typically these are trusts or foundations managed by a bank trust department or a lawyer located in Pennsylvania, but there are no Pennsylvania-based trustees/directors and no grants are awarded to Pennsylvania.

T   **Terminated**: A final IRS Form 990-PF has been filed, or the foundation has provided notice of intended liquidation/termination.

U   **Undetermined Status**: There is no record of Form 990-PFs being filed for the last three or more years and no other evidence of grant-making activity. In many cases the foundation may have terminated without giving formal notice or has been reclassified by IRS as a "public charity."

Anderson (Liddy K.) Foundation (U)

Baird (Gladys) Trust (R)
c/o PNC Bank N.A., Erie 16553

Barco Scholarship Trust (R)
c/o PNC Bank N.A., Erie 16501

Barco-Duratz Foundation, The (T)

Black (Ferdinand F.) Trust (R)
c/o National City Bank of Pa., Oil City 16301

Blair (M.H.) Trust for Bethesda Memorial Hospital (R)
c/o PNC Bank N.A., Erie 16553

Blair (M.H.) Trust for St. John's Hospital (R)
c/o PNC Bank N.A., Erie 16553

Blair (M.H.) Trust for Warren General Hospital (R)
c/o PNC Bank N.A., Erie 16553

Bliley Electric Foundation (I) MI-29
2545 West Grandview Blvd., P.O. Box 3428, Erie 16508

Bonadei (Joseph) Trust (R)
c/o PNC Bank N.A., Erie 16553

Bowers Foundation (T)

Brevillier Village Foundation (R)
5416 East Lake Road, Erie 16511

Brundred (W.J.) Charitable Fund (R)
c/o Mellon Bank N.A., P.O. Box 300, Erie 16512

Budd Orphans' Home (R)
c/o First Western Bank, Sharon 16146

Bulen (Dexter A.) Trust (R)
c/o PNC Bank N.A., Erie 16512

Butler (Emanuel C.), Jr. Memorial Scholarship Fund (R)
c/o Naddeo, P.O. Box 552, Clearfield 16830

Campbell (John Russell) Memorial Fund (R)
c/o National City Bank of Pa., Oil City 16301

Charitable Fund, Trustees of The (R)
730 Forker Boulevard, Sharon 16146

Clarion Area Presbyterian Homes (R)
7th Ave. & Wood Street, Clarion 16214

Clark Foundation (L) MI-N/R
601 Rouse Ave., Youngsville 16371

Cohen (Harold H.) Foundation Charitable Trust ()
(Formerly of Erie, now located in FL)

Cohen (Irene) Foundation (L) MI-22-62
P.O. Box 1819, Erie 16507

Conner (Jim) Foundation, The (R)
3230 West Lake Road, Erie 16505

Corry Community Foundation ()
(Refer to Erie Community Foundation)

Crary (Clare) Trust for The Crary Home (R)
c/o PNC Bank N.A., Erie 16553

Crary Art Gallery, The (R)
511 Market Street, Warren 16365

Crary Home, The (R)
c/o First United Methodist Church, Warren 16365

Crary Trust for Crary Art Gallery (R)
c/o PNC Bank N.A., Erie 16501

Crawford (H.J.) Trust for Crawford Hall-Grove City College (R)
c/o Mellon Bank N.A., P.O. Box 300, Erie 16512

Crawford (H.J.) Trust for Eliz. Crawford Memorial School (R)
c/o Mellon Bank N.A., P.O. Box 300, Erie 16512

Crawford (H.J.) Trust for Oil City Hospital (R)
c/o Mellon Bank N.A., P.O. Box 300, Erie 16512

Cross (Alton & Mildred) Scholarship Fund (R)
P.O. Box 66, Union City 16438

Curry (May) Trust for Roman Catholic Diocese of Erie (R)
c/o PNC Bank N.A., Erie 16553

Curry (May) Trust for St. Leo's Church (R)
c/o PNC Bank N.A., Erie 16553

Defelice Scholarship Trust (R)
RD #1, Box 116, Punxsutawney 15767

Dillon Foundation, The (R)
c/o National City Bank of Pa., Warren 16365

Donald (Jeffrey A.) Memorial Scholarship Trust (R)
63 Grove Road, Mercer 16137

Eccles (Ralph) Trust for Rimersburg Medical Center (R)
c/o National City Bank of Pa., Oil City 16301

Eccles-Lesher Memorial Library Assn., Inc. (R)
P.O. Box 359, Rimersburg 16248

Eldred World War II Museum (O)
210 Main Street, Eldred 16731

Elk County Development Foundation (T)

Epstein (Samuel) Foundation Trust (R)
c/o National City Bank of Pa., Warren 16365

Erichson Scholarship Fund (R)
c/o National City Bank of Pa., Bradford 16701

Erie Sand Charitable Trust (L) MI-72-99
c/o Erie Sand & Gravel Company, P.O. Box 179, Erie 16512

Erskine (George B. & Helen M.) Memorial Scholarship (R)
c/o Sunbank, P.O. Box 108, Emporium 15834

Flick (Loretta) Trust for Erie Center for the Blind (R)
c/o PNC Bank N.A., Erie 16553

Founders Memorial Fund of American Sterilizer Co. (R)
2424 West 23rd Street, Erie 16506

Frangakis Family Charitable Foundation, The (I) MI-N/R
68 Oak Tree Court, West Middlesex 16159

Gates (John B.) Memorial Scholarship Fund (R)
P.O. Box 846, Clearfield 16830

Gerow (James B.) Trust (R)
c/o PNC Bank N.A., Erie 16553

Gnade (Maude F.) Trust for Charities (R)
c/o National City Bank of Pa., Oil City 16301

Gnade (Maude F.) Trust for Oil City Library (R)
c/o National City Bank of Pa., Oil City 16301

Gnade (Maude F.) Trust for Presbyterian Church (R)
c/o National City Bank of Pa., Oil City 16301

Gnade (Maude F.) Trust for Women's Federation (R)
c/o National City Bank of Pa., Oil City 16301

Gnade (Maude F.) Trust for YMCA & YWCA (R)
c/o National City Bank of Pa., Oil City 16301

Goldstein (J.B.) Family Fund (U)

Good (William), Jr. Memorial Fund - L. Strayer Trust (R)
c/o Mellon Bank N.A., P.O. Box 300, Erie 16512

Goodman (Dallas & Samuel 'Shy') Educational Trust (R)
c/o National City Bank of Pa., Oil City 16301

Gospel Crusade Ministries, Inc. (O)
P.O. Box 1026, Erie 16512

Grandview Institution Trust Estate (R)
c/o National City Bank of Pa., Oil City 16301

Grice Clearfield Community Museum (O)
RR2, Box 47A, Clearfield 16830

Harris (Paul Hyland) Trust (R)
c/o National City Bank of Pa., Titusville 16354

Hendricks (Luther V.) Memorial Fund (R)
Edinboro U., 132 Hendricks Hall, Edinboro 16444

Henretta (James E.) Trusts (R)
c/o Mellon Bank N.A., P.O. Box 300, Erie 16512

Hill (Ruth A.) Trust (R)
c/o Mellon Bank N.A., P.O. Box 300, Erie 16512

Himes (Marian) Trust for Wesbury (R)
c/o PNC Bank N.A., Erie 16553

Hoehn Scholarship Fund for Elk County Christian High School (R)
c/o Elk County Christian High School, St. Marys 15857

Hoffman Fund for Warren County (O)
c/o County Commissioners, Courthouse, Warren 16365

Huber (Naomi E.) Trust (R)
c/o PNC Bank N.A., Erie 16553

Hummer (Elias & Mae) Memorial Foundation (R)
c/o Superintendent, Titusville School District, Titusville 16354

Ingraham (Marjorie B.) Trust (R)
c/o PNC Bank N.A., Erie 16553

Irene (Rudy M.) Trust (T)

Irvin (Mary Ann) Scholarship Foundation (R)
c/o Punxsutawney High School, Punxsutawney 15767

Jackson (E.) Family Char. Fdn. for Greenville Area Schools (R)
1 FNB Boulevard, Hermitage 16148

Jackson (E.) Family Char. Fdn. for Reynolds Area School District (R)
1 FNB Boulevard, Hermitage 16148

Jenks (John W.) Memorial Foundation (R)
c/o Fait, North Jefferson Street, Punxsutawney 15767

Jones (Elias & Blanche) Memorial Trust (R)
c/o PNC Bank N.A., Erie 16553

Jones (Joseph) Scholarship Fund (R)
c/o National City Bank of Pa., Oil City 16301

Kane Community Development Corp. (R)
67 Fraley Street, Kane 16735

Kanhofer (L.) Trust for Lee McKinney Scholarship (R)
c/o National City Bank of Pa., Titusville 16354

Keller (Melvin G. & Mary F.) Scholarship Fund (R)
c/o National City Bank of Pa., Warren 16365

Kempel (A.B.) Memorial Fund (R)
c/o Mellon Bank N.A., P.O. Box 300, Erie 16512

Kerr (Friend & B.) Trust for Scholarships (R)
c/o Titusville Area High School, Titusville 16354

Kerr (Mary Jane Weir) Trust (R)
c/o Mellon Bank N.A., P.O. Box 300, Erie 16512

Kirk (Ella B.) Trust (R)
c/o Mellon Bank N.A., P.O. Box 300, Erie 16512

Kiser (Clara Louise) Memorial Fund (R)
c/o National City Bank of Pa., Oil City 16301

Kiwanis Club of Erie Foundation (L) MI-99
P.O. Box 3715, Erie 16508

Lamberton (Chess) Public Charity Trust Fund (R)
c/o National City Bank of Pa., Franklin 16323

Landis (Mildred R.) Foundation (L) MI-32-42-63
341 East Jamestown Road, Greenville 16125

Langdale (Edith A.) Scholarship Fund (R)
c/o National City Bank of Pa., Warren 16365

Lesher (Margaret & Irvin) Foundation (R)
c/o National City Bank of Pa., Oil City 16301

Levine (Alice & Eli) Memorial Trust (R)
c/o National City Bank of Pa., Oil City 16301

Lewis (George & Kathlyn) Charitable Trust (R)
c/o National City Bank of Pa., Oil City 16301

Lezzer (Kenneth L.) Foundation (R)
P.O. Box 217, Curwensville 16833

Liberty Towers, Inc. of Clarion (R)
720 Liberty Street, Clarion 16214

Little Leo Club of Punxsutawney (O)
P.O. Box 472, Punxsutawney 15767

Lynn (Arthur M. & Lillian M.) Charity Trust (R)
c/o Mellon Bank N.A., P.O. Box 300, Erie 16512

MacDonald (Henry A. & Mary J.) Foundation (NP)
100 State Street, Suite 700, Erie 16507

Martin (Jay) Memorial Scholarship Trust (R)
c/o National City Bank of Pa., Titusville 16354

May (Gail Keys) Trust (R)
c/o PNC Bank N.A., Erie 16501

Mayberry Memorial Scholarship Trust of Cameron Co. (R)
c/o Bucktail Bank & Trust Company, Emporium 15834

McBrier Foundation, The (L) MI-99
6721 Brierhill Road, Fairview 16415

McCready (Alexander P.) Trust for Darby Library (R)
c/o National City Bank of Pa., Oil City 16301

McFate (Benjamin G.) Memorial Scholarship Fund (R)
c/o Mellon Bank N.A., P.O. Box 300, Erie 16512

McMillen (Wendell W.) Foundation, The (R)
203 Center Street, Sheffield 16347

Mitchell (Ruth A.) Trust for Charities (R)
c/o PNC Bank N.A., Erie 16501

Moore (Gertrude L.) Trust (R)
c/o National City Bank of Pa., Oil City 16301

Moore (M. Robert) Charitable Scholarship Trust (R)
c/o S&T Bank, P.O. Box 247, DuBois 15801

Myers Foundation (L) MI-99
1401 Lexington Ave., P.O. Box 931, Warren 16365

New Bethlehem Bank Charitable Foundation
(New name: PFC Bank Charitable Foundation)

Nordine (Wayne G. & Barbara L.) Foundation
(Formerly of Ridgway, now located in OH)

North East Community Foundation
(Refer to Erie Community Foundation)

Northwest Pa. Eminent Community Institute (I)
679 Colbert Ave., Oil City 16301

Olszewski (Joseph G.) Scholarship Fund (L) MI-43
c/o Colussi, 925 French Street, Erie 16501

Painter (Jacob K.) Scholarship Fund (R)
c/o National City Bank of Pa., Oil City 16301

Parker (Hyman & Lillyanne) Foundation (L) MI-12-31
801 Pasadena Drive, Erie 16505

Peters (Edward V. & Jessie L.) Foundation (L) MI-13-44-55
c/o National City Bank of Pa., P.O. Box 318, Oil City 16301

Peterson (Catherine C.) Trust (L) MI-20-22-29
c/o Thomas Peterson, 226 California Drive, Erie 16505

Phi Delta Theta Educational Foundation (R)
681 The Terrace, Meadville 16335

Phillips (V. E. & Betty) Scholarship Fund (R)
c/o Corry High School, Corry 16407

Pleasantville High School Student Fund (R)
c/o National City Bank of Pa., Titusville 16354

Porter (Margaret K.) Trust (R)
c/o First National Bank of Pa., Hermitage 16148

Proper (Sharp & Mary) Scholarship Trust (R)
c/o Titusville Area High School, Titusville 16354

Quist (Edna M.) Trust (R)
c/o PNC Bank N.A., Erie 16553

Relihan (Dr. M.J.) Educational Trust Fund (T)
(Refer to Erie Community Foundation)

Reno (Amy E.) Trust (R)
c/o Clearfield Bank & Trust Co., Clearfield 16830

Rickert (Gladys & Evelyn) Memorial Scholarship Fund (R)
c/o Principal, Greenville Area High School, Greenville 16125

Roberts (Victoria) Scholarship Fund (R)
c/o National City Bank of Pa., Sharon 16146

Rose (A. H.) Trust for United Methodist Church (R)
c/o National City Bank of Pa., Oil City 16301

Ross (Helen N.) Charity Trust (R)
c/o Mellon Bank N.A., Erie 16512

Saint Francis Educational Endowment Fund (R)
211 South Second Street, Clearfield 16830

Schwab (John) Foundation (R)
c/o Bucktail Bank & Trust Company, Emporium 15834

Scofield (Hetty Sherwin) Scholarship Fund (U)

Selle (Martha) Memorial Scholarship Trust (R)
c/o Principal, St. Marys High School, St. Marys 15857

Sheen (Howard J. & Ruth) Scholarship Fund (R)
c/o PNC Bank N.A., Erie 16553

Sheil (Edward J. & Lavalette) Memorial Fund (NP)
c/o National City Bank of Pa., Warren 16365

Sibley (Ida Rew) Charitable Trust (R)
c/o National City Bank of Pa., Franklin 16323

Snyder (Melanie) Trust (R)
c/o Titusville High School, Titusville 16354

Spaulding (Leslie & Greta) Education Fund (I)
c/o Ochs, P.O. Box 949, Sharon 16146

Stow Charitable Trust (R)
c/o PNC Bank N.A., Erie 16553

Strattan (Judith Peale) Memorial Educational Trust (R)
c/o CNB Bank, Trust Dept., Clearfield 16830

Union City Elderly & Handicapped Assn. (R)
122 North Main Street, P.O. Box 272, Union City 16438

Valley Grove School District Scholarship Fund (R)
429 Wiley Ave., Franklin 16323

Warren Foundation
(New name: Community Foundation of Warren County)

Watson Memorial Home (O)
1200 Conewango Ave., Warren 16365

Weaver (Rick) Memorial Scholarship Trust (R)
c/o Clarion-Limestone Area High School, Strattanville 16258

Wein (Charles & Dorothy) Foundation (R)
c/o National City Bank of Pa., Clarion 16214

Weis Library (O)
2222 West Grandview Blvd., Erie 16506

Williams (Frank O. & Clara R.) Scholarship Fund (R)
c/o Kosak & Associates, P.O. Box 74, Oil City 16301

Williams (Joseph A.) Medical Foundation (R)
c/o National City Bank of Pa., St. Marys 15857

Winner Family Foundation (L)
32 West State Street, Sharon 16146

Womans Club of Warren Education Scholarship & Historical Preservation Group (L) MI-43-56
c/o Elizabeth Jones, 310 Market Street, Warren 16365

Wright (R.R.) Educational Fund (R)
c/o Mellon Bank N.A., P.O. Box 300, Erie 16512

Youth Tennis Foundation of Erie (R)
300 State Street, Suite 300, Erie 16501

Zacks (E.A.) Charitable Foundation (L) MI-22-62-99
4910 Sunnydale Boulevard, Erie 16509

Southeastern Region / SE

covers the following 5 counties
Bucks - Chester - Delaware - Montgomery - Philadelphia

SE-001   1957 Charity Foundation
P.O. Box 540
Plymouth Meeting   19462
(Montgomery County)

AMV $20,502,961   **FYE** 6-01   **(Gifts Received** $0)

MI-12-13-14-15-16-17-18-22-25-25-29-31-35
41-43-45-54-55-56-71-72-84
Phone 610-828-8145 **FAX** 610-834-8175
EIN 23-3051552   **Year Created** 1957
245 **Grants totaling** $1,325,562

Mostly local giving; grants are for general operating support except as noted and some are payments on two- or three-year grant commitments. High grant of **$85,000** to Upland Country Day School. **$50,000** each to Chester County Community Foundation and Westtown School (Bicentennial Fund/athletic facility). **$30,000** to Fairville Friends School (Open Window Program/general support). **$28,000** to Community Action Agency of Delaware County (summer career exploration program). **$25,000** each to Brandywine Conservancy (Morris Dixon Purse), Camphill Special School-Beaver Run (renovation/expansion), and Consortium to Prevent Homelessness [Spring City]. **$20,000** each to Episcopal Community Services (family empowerment program/homeless program), National Constitution Center, and St. David's Episcopal Church of Wayne. **$15,000** each to Calcutta House (housing-support services), St. Malachy School, and Temple U./Bridging the Gaps (community health internship program). **$14,000** to Impact Services Corp. (summer career exploration program). **$12,000-$12,500** each to County Corrections Gospel Mission, Inner City House (holiday cheer/summer jobs program), and Philadelphia Education Fund (college prep/guidance services). **$11,000** to Harcum College (summer health careers program). **$10,000** each to Bernardine Center in Chester, Bryn Mawr Hospital (nursing excellence program), Coatesville Area Partners in Progress (building construction), Easter Seals (Bright Beginnings program), The Foundation at Paoli (Hospital Cancer Center), French & Pickering Creeks Conservation Trust (salary/Coventry House improvements)), Habitat for Humanity-Delaware Valley, Maternal & Child Health Consortium of Chester County, Maternity Care Coalition of Philadelphia (holiday cheer/MomMobile), Montgomery School, Philadelphia Health Management Corp. (holiday cheer), St. Barnabas Mission, St. Peter's Church in the Great Valley Surrey Services for Seniors (capital campaign), and Woodlynde School (Project Fast Forward). **$6,700-$8,000** each to Adult Care of Chester County, Big Brothers/Big Sisters of Chester County, Crime Prevention Assn. (intergenerational park-play space), Eastern Philadelphia Organizing Project, Good Works, Inc. (building materials/supplies), Homeless Advocacy Project, Jubilee School (mortgage payment), Philadelphia Society for Services to Children (Head Start parent services), School District of Philadelphia (school trip), Support Center for Child Advocates (child victim assistance project), Visiting Nurse Assn. of Greater Philadelphia (pediatric nurse recruitment/training), West Chester Community Center (building improvements), and West Chester School District (FCD educational services). **$6,000** each to Bridge of Hope (at-risk families initiative), Delaware Valley Grantmakers (membership),Greater Philadelphia Urban Affairs Coalition (homelessness program), Help Philadelphia (home furnishings fund), Interfaith of Ambler Senior Community Services (delivered meals), Thresholds in Delaware County, and Travelers Aid Society of Philadelphia. **$4,000-$5,000** each to ActionAIDS (family program), Aid for Friends (retire mortgage), AIDS Alive, Allegheny West Foundation (public schools programs), American Institute of Social Justice (neighborhood parents' organization), Asian Americans United, Asian American Youth Assn., Baker Industries, Catholic Social Services (MR Services), Chester County SPCA Children's Aid Society of Montgomery County (temporary housing), Children's Aid Society of Pa. (teens/tots program), Children's Village Child Care Center (early intervention program), Coatesville Cultural Society College Settlement of Philadelphia (summer camperships), Committee for Dignity & Fairness in Housing (holiday cheer), Community Gardens of Chester County, Community Learning Center, Community Women's Education Project, Cosacosa Art at Large (healing art project), Creative Artists Network (youth classes), Delaware Valley Friends School (athletic field), Domestic Violence Center of Chester County (children's services), Frederick Douglass Elementary School (North Star Outreach), Education Law Center (foster care education), The Enterprise Center (entrepreneurial youth program), Exodus to Excellence (math-science program), Family Service of Chester County (Coatesville services), Friends Assn. for Care & Protection of Children, Germantown YWCA, Habitat of Humanity of Chester County Handmaids of the Sacred Heart of Jesus, Greater Philadelphia Food Bank (supermarket products program), Greensgrow (greenhouse improvements),Health Corner at Larchwood Gardens (after school program), Impact Services Corporation (summer career exploration program), Interfaith Hospitality Network of the Main Line, Thomas Jefferson U. (Reach Out & Read Program), Jewish Federation of Greater Philadelphia (self-sufficiency program), Legal Aid of Chester County, Lighthouse (youth services program), Little Brothers Friends of the Elderly, Malvern Preparatory School, MANNA/Metropolitan AIDS Neighborhood Nutrition Alliance (expansion), Natural Lands Trust, National Constitution Center, Neighbor to Neighbor Community Development Corp., Neighborhood Gardens Assn., Neighborhood Parenting Program (preschool project), Nelson Network Coalition, NetworkArts Philadelphia (ecology arts program), North Light Community Center (Kid Zone project), Overington House (after school childcare), Pa. Home of the Sparrow (affordable housing program), People's Emergency Center, People's Light & Theatre Company (New Voice Ensemble), Philadelphia City Sail (outreach project), Philadelphia Friends of Outward Bound (public school programs), Philadelphia Museum of Art (young people's programs), Philadelphia Physicians for Social Responsibility, Philadelphia Training Program, Philadelphians Concerned About Housing (family self-sufficiency program), Phoenixville Area Economic Development Corp. (Schuylkill Valley Visitors Center), Phoenixville Homes, Police Athletic League of Philadelphia, Potter's House Mission, Recording for the Blind & Dyslexic (Frankford outreach program), Royer-Greaves School for the Blind (non-school year program), Safe Harbor of West Chester, St. Philip's United Methodist Church (youth services initiative), Shalom, Inc. (Adult in Making program), Sisters of St. Joseph, Southwest Community Enrichment Program (senior club/home visitation), Taller Puertorriqueno (youth programs), Wagner Free Institute of Science (GeoKid program), West Chester Area Senior Center, Women's Assn. for Women's Alternatives (renovate facility), Women's Business Development Center, Women's Community Revitalization Project, and Woodlynde School.**$2,500-$3,500** each to 1812 Productions (disabled students outreach), Ad Hoc Committee for Logan/Youth Project, Agape Improvement & Development Corp. (youth jobs training program), Angel Flight East, Asian Arts Initiative (capacity building), Bainbridge House (mentoring-cultural arts program), Camphill Village-Kimberton Hills, Children's Literacy Initiative (summer reading coalition), CHOICE (teen pregnancy prevention program), Community Coalition, Community Learning Center (holiday cheer), Community Legal Services (homeowners loan awareness education) County Corrections Gospel Mission (holiday cheer), Creative Access (salary), Crime Victims Center of Chester County, Delaware County AIDS Network (peer counseling/youth advisory board), Delaware County Children's Camp Assn., Delaware County Literacy Council (satellite centers in Chester), Eastern U. (summer theatre camp), HERO/Helping Energize & Rebuild Ourselves (after school program), Hunter Elementary School (holiday cheer), International Ballet Exchange (program development), Kennett Area Senior Center (expanded programs), Little Flower High School for Girls (scholarship), Living Beyond Breast Cancer (Project Connect), Mid-County Senior Services (stroke survivor services), New World Assn. of Emigrants from Eastern Europe (literacy services), Nonprofit Technology Resources (computers/training for children-parents), Norristown Initiative Philadelphia Wooden Boat Factory (marine education initiative), Police-Barrio Relations Project, Project Forward Leap (Olney Cluster program), Radnor ABC (refurbish/maintain house), Religious Committee for Community Justice, Summerbridge Germantown, SOWN/Supportive Older Women's Network (telegroup project), Upper Darby Educational & Cultural Foundation, Urban Bridges at St. Gabriel's (arts-academic program), Whosoever Gospel Mission (career track learning program), Women's Law Project (telephone counseling project), and The Working Wardrobe (clothing purchase). Other smaller local grants for similar purposes. **Out-of-state** giving includes **$29,000** to Kieve Effective Education [ME]; **$25,000** each to Food & Friends [DC] and Living Classrooms Foundation [MD] (scholarships for Philadelphia & Chester County youth); **$15,000** to Buffalo Bill Memorial Assn. [WY]; **$10,000** to Hole in the Wall Gang [CT]; and others. ■**PUBLICATIONS:** statement of program policy; application guidelines; Proposal Cover Sheet ■**WEBSITE:** None ■**E-MAIL:** judy1@aol.com ■**APPLICATION POLICIES & PROCEDURES:** The Foundation reports that giving is generally limited to the five-county Philadelphia area for human services or social welfare programs; other interests are community development and education for disadvantaged people. No grants are awarded to individuals or to organizations which practice discrimination. Grant requests may be submitted at any time in a brief but full proposal (10 pages maximum) together with a Proposal Cover Sheet, available from the Foundation. The proposal should clearly and succinctly cover the following: (a) Agency Description: history, mission, current programs and accomplishments, recent highlights, and overall plans for the coming year; (b) Funding Request: how the project fits into overall organizational mission, project goals/objectives, planned activities/events, constituency served/target population, key staff/volunteers involved and their roles, implementation timetable, and interaction with other organizations, if relevant; and (c) Evaluation: what accomplishments/results are expected, the definition of a successful project (including how it might be measured, if applicable), and anticipated consequences of eliminating or not undertaking the project. Required attachments are: (1) a Board of Directors list with addresses and occupations (indicate if minority, low-income, consumer and/or neighborhood representatives); (2) Financial Documentation: current annual operating budget, project budget, if applicable, and a recent audited financial statement; (3) Organizational Funding: past major contributors and amounts, recent applications with amounts requested, and anticipated future sources of funds, if different from the above; (4) Project Funding: other requests submitted, if applicable, and current status; (4) Personnel: resumes of top staff and relevant key staff/volunteers involved in the specific project; (5) Annual Report, if available; (6) IRS tax-exempt status documentation; and (7) Other Background Materials: a few recent newspaper/magazine articles about the organization or program. Submit one complete, collated copy of the Proposal Cover Sheet and proposal and attachments. Deadlines are January 15th, May 15th and September 15; only one request may be submitted within a 12-month period. All requests are acknowledged. Distribution Committee meeting are held in February, June, and October; applicants are notified soon after the meetings. — Formerly called 1957 Charity Trust.

O+D+T Judith L. Bardes (Executive Director+Con) — Elizabeth R. Moran (P+D) — James M. Moran, Jr. (VP+D) — Frances Moran Abbott (S+D) — Elizabeth Moran Legnini (F+D) — Caroline Moran Abbott (D) — Michael J. Moran (D) — Ranney Robert Moran (D) — Daphne Chase Rowe (Program Associate)

SE-002   1976 Foundation   MI-12-35-41-53-55
c/o Two Eighteen Enterprises
200 Eagle Road, Suite 316   **Phone** 610-293-0960 **FAX** 610-293-0967
Wayne   19087   (Delaware County)   **EIN** 23-2495676   **Year Created** 1987

AMV $1,052,448   **FYE** 12-00   **(Gifts Received** $0)   7 **Grants totaling** $47,000

About two-thirds local giving. High grant of **$8,000** to Delaware Valley Friends School (annual giving). **$7,000** each to Agnes Irwin School (art department), Benchmark School (art department), and Visiting Nurse Assn. of Greater Philadelphia (annual giving). **Out-of-state** grants: **$5,000-$7,000** each to Avon Old Farms School [CT] (art department), Rectory School [CT] (art department), and Navajo Nation Health Foundation [AZ] (pediatrics department). ■**PUBLICATIONS:** None ■**WEBSITE:** None ■ **E-MAIL:** None ■**APPLICATION POLICIES & PROCEDURES:** The Foundation reports that priority interests are (1) secondary schools teaching American art and artists, and (2) rural hospitals; most grants are for special projects. Prospective applicants initially should make a telephone inquiry about the feasibility of submitting a request. Submit grant requests in a letter (2 pages maximum) during February-June (deadline is June 30th); include an annual report, project budget, and list of major funding sources.

O+D+T Nathaniel Peter Hamilton (S+F+D+Donor+Con) — E. McGregor Strauss [RI] (P+D) — James Sands, Jr. (VP+D)

SE-003   1984 Foundation   **MI**-43-54-56
    c/o Mellon Private Wealth Management
    1735 Market Street, Room 193-0370   **Phone** 215-553-1204 **FAX** 215-553-4542
    Philadelphia   19103   (Philadelphia County)   **EIN** 23-6758319   **Year Created** 1984
AMV $15,782   **FYE** 11-00   **(Gifts Received** $133,000)   11 **Grants totaling** $205,650

All giving is restricted to post-graduate fellowships for scientific archaeological studies. High grant of **$42,550** to a U. of Pa. (History of Art project). **$40,000** to University Museum (Roman-Corinth Computer Project). **$34,500** to a New York U. student (Aphrodias Excavations). **$25,000** to American School of Classical Studies [Greece]. Other grants **$2,800-18,850** awarded for similar purposes. — In prior years, individual fellowships were awarded to many persons affiliated with the American School of Classical Studies and major institutional giving to the U. of Pa. for the University Museum (excavation projects), Arts & Science Department, and various archaeological projects. ■**PUBLICATIONS:** None ■**WEBSITE:** None ■**E-MAIL:** None ■**APPLICATION POLICIES & PROCEDURES:** The Foundation reports that only persons engaged in scientific archaeology scholarship are eligible to apply. Individual Fellowship applicants must submit a full proposal which outlines a dissertation research project and an itemized budget showing living/other expenses related to the research. Requests should be submitted in January or September. — Formerly called the Charles K. Williams II Trust.

O+D+T   Kathleen M. Rock (VP at Bank+Con) — Charles K. Williams [NJ] (D+Donor) Mellon Bank N.A. (Trustee)

SE-004   25th Century Foundation, The   **MI**-Not Reported
    c/o Calibre (First Union/Wachovia)
    2000 Centre Square West, 1500 Market Street   **Phone** 215-973-3143 **FAX** 215-973-3191
    Philadelphia   19102   (Philadelphia County)   **EIN** 31-1738216   **Year Created** 2000
AMV $4,428,736   **FYE** 3-01   **(Gifts Received** $4,642,500)   **Grants totaling** $0

No grants were awarded during the Foundation's first year of operation. ■**PUBLICATIONS:** None ■**WEBSITE:** None ■**E-MAIL:** robert.gallagher@calibreonline.com ■**APPLICATION POLICIES & PROCEDURES:** The Foundation reports major areas of giving interest as human services, health/medical, arts/culture, and the environment, but that unsolicited requests are not accepted.

O+D+T   Robert J. Gallagher (VP at Bank+Con) — J. Mahlon Buck [Haverford] (C+D) — Caroline Buck Rogers [Bryn Mawr] (P+D) — James Buck, III [Bryn Mawr (VP+D) — Marilyn C. Sanborne, Esq. [Philadelphia] (S+D) — Elia Buck [Haverford] (AS+AF+D) — Elinor Buck [Bryn Mawr] (D) — Joseph W. Rogers, Jr. [Bryn Mawr] (D) First Union/Wachovia (Corporate Trustee)

SE-005   Aaron (Dan) Parkinson's Disease Foundation   **MI**-14-32-35
    2401 Pennsylvania Avenue, Apt. 5B24   **Phone** 215-232-5670 **FAX** None
    Philadelphia   19130   (Philadelphia County)   **EIN** 23-2657926   **Year Created** 1991
AMV $319,771   **FYE** 12-00   **(Gifts Received** $78,442)   2 **Grants totaling** $337,000

All local giving. High grant of **$252,000** to Pa. Hospital (Dan Aaron's Parkinson's Rehab Center). **$85,000** to Parkinson's Disease & Movement Disorders Center. ■**PUBLICATIONS:** None ■**WEBSITE:** None ■**E-MAIL:** None ■**APPLICATION POLICIES & PROCEDURES:** Only Philadelphia-area institutions or programs serving persons with Parkinson's Disease are eligible to apply. Grant requests may be submitted in any form at any time.

O+D+T   Daniel Aaron (P+D+Donor+Manager+Con) — Erika Fliegelman Aaron (VP+D) — Marie Molchen (S+D) — Abram E. Patlove (F+D) — Ralph J. Roberts (D+Donor) — Howard L. Hurtig, M.D. (D) — Ralph S. Roberts (D) — Robert Sandler (D) — Matthew B. Stern, M.D. (D) — Gwyn Vernon [Wallingford] (D) — Jane Wright, MSS (D) — Geraldine Aaron (Donor) Corporate donors: Bank of New York, Chase Manhattan Bank [NY], Goldman Sachs [NY], MTV Networks [NY], Time Warner Entertainment Co. [NY]. — Foundation donors: Comcast Foundation, Ralph & Suzanne Roberts Foundation.

SE-006   Aaron Family Foundation, The   **MI**-13-22-32-41-42-54-55-62
    2401 Pennsylvania Ave., Apt. 5B24   **Phone** 215-981-7507 **FAX** None
    Philadelphia   19130   (Philadelphia County)   **EIN** 23-7996346   **Year Created** 1998
AMV $1,788,754   **FYE** 12-00   **(Gifts Received** $0)   48 **Grants totaling** $71,288

Mostly local giving. High grant of **$20,100** to Woodrock. **$10,000** to Greene Street Friends School. **$7,118** to Jewish Federation of Greater Philadelphia. **$5,000** each to IAABO Foundation and Philadelphia Foundation for Parkinson's Disease. **$3,000** to Arcadia U. **$600** to National Liberty Museum. Other local contributions **$25-$500** for various purposes. **Out-of-state** giving includes **$10,500** to Sarasota Arts Council [FL] and **$2,000** each to Longboat Key Center for the Arts [FL] and Sarasota-Manatee Jewish Federation [FL]. ■**PUBLICATIONS:** None ■**WEBSITE:** None ■**E-MAIL:** None ■**APPLICATION POLICIES & PROCEDURES:** Information not available.

O+D+T   Daniel Aaron (T+Donor+Con) — Geraldine Aaron (T+Donor)

SE-007   Abelson (Stanley E. & Dorothy Y.) Charitable Foundation   **MI**-11-22-44-52
    233 South 6th Street, Apt. 2304P   **Phone** 215-574-9595 **FAX** None
    Philadelphia   19106   (Philadelphia County)   **EIN** 23-6764145   **Year Created** 1985
AMV $18,332   **FYE** 12-00   **(Gifts Received** $15,260)   32 **Grants totaling** $12,210

Mostly local giving. High grant of **$2,500** to Opera Company of Philadelphia. **$1,000-$1,545** each to Free Library of Philadelphia, Philadelphia Orchestra, Philadelphia Opera Guild, Seamen's Church Institute, and United Way of SE Pa. Many other local and out-of-state contributions, **$25-$500,** for various purposes. ■**PUBLICATIONS:** None ■**WEBSITE:** None ■**E-MAIL:** None ■ **APPLICATION POLICIES & PROCEDURES:** Grant requests may be submitted in a letter at any time; describe in detail the proposed project, specify the amount of funding requested, and include IRS tax-exempt status documentation. Grants are awarded throughout the year.

O+D+T Stanley E. Abelson (T+Donor+Con) — Dorothy Y. Abelson (T)

SE-008   Abrahamson (Harry & Julia) Fund, The
      186 Springlawn Road
      Glen Mills   19342   (Delaware County)

MI-18-82
Phone 610-358-1832 **FAX** None
EIN 23-2747364   **Year Created** 1993

AMV $778,532   **FYE** 6-00   (**Gifts Received** $507,302)   5 **Grants totaling** $50,000

One Pa. grant: **$5,000** to American Friends Service Committee (Vietnam Program). **Out-of-state** grants: **$20,000** to Planned Parenthood Federation [NY]; **$10,000** each to Assn. for Voluntary Surgical Contraception [NY], and Pathfinder International [MA]; **$5,000** to Population Communication [NY]. — Most giving in prior years has been for to population control organizations in NY and DC. ■**PUBLICATIONS:** None ■**WEBSITE:** None ■**E-MAIL:** hjafund@aol.com ■**APPLICATION POLICIES & PROCEDURES:** The Foundation reports that most grants are for general support or special projects. Grant requests may be submitted in any form at any time; include an annual report, organization and project budgets, and IRS tax-exempt status documentation. Grants are awarded at a September meeting.

O+D+T Marjorie Barnard (T+Con) — Anne Tyler Modarressi [MD] (T) — Adaline P. Satterthwaite, M.D [Newtown] (T)

SE-009   ADCO Foundation
      c/o American Atlantic Company
      900 East 8th Ave., Suite 300
      King of Prussia   19406   (Montgomery County)

MI-15-22-32-54-62

Phone 610-768-8020 **FAX** None
EIN 23-6278135   **Year Created** 1953

AMV $911,407   **FYE** 12-00   (**Gifts Received** $0)   8 **Grants totaling** $40,000

No Pa. giving. **Out-of-state** giving, all to New York, includes **$10,000** each to Jewish Communal Fund and Museum of Television & Radio; **$5,000** to Yadoo Foundation; **$4,000** each to Salvation Army-Central Division and Salvation Army-Eastern Division; and **$3,000-$3,500** each to Anti-Defamation League and NYC Alzheimer's Assn. ■**PUBLICATIONS:** None ■**WEBSITE:** None ■**E-MAIL:** None ■**APPLICATION POLICIES & PROCEDURES:** Grant requests may be submitted in a letter at any time.

O+D+T   Christopher H. Browne (T+Con) — Bruce A. Beal (T) — James M. Clark, Jr. (T)

SE-010   Addams (Frances Jean) Charitable Trust
      518 Edann Road
      Glenside   19038   (Montgomery County)

MI-12-15-52-56-71
Phone 215-886-1940 **FAX** None
EIN 23-7721716   Year Created 1993

AMV $52,025   **FYE** 12-99   (**Gifts Received** $0)   20+ **Grants totaling** $19,906

Mostly local giving. High grant of **$6,150** to Pa. Horticultural Society. **$2,500** to Academy of Music. **$1,720** to Meals on Wheels [Ardmore]. **$1,000** to Philadelphia Horticultural Society. **$930** to Wyck House Assn. **$585** to Philadelphia Orchestra. Other contributions **$100-$495** for various purposes. **Out-of-state** grant: **$3,200** to Protect A Child Foundation. ■**PUBLICATIONS:** None ■**WEBSITE:** None ■**E-MAIL:** None ■**APPLICATION POLICIES & PROCEDURES:** Grant requests may be submitted in a letter at any time; include appropriate supporting materials.

O+D+T J. Howard Brosius (Manager+T+Con) — Frances Jean Addams [NY] (Donor)

SE-011   Affordable Housing Foundation
      c/o Wolf, Block, Schorr & Solis-Cohen
      1650 Arch Street, 22nd Floor
      Philadelphia   19103   (Philadelphia County)

MI-25

Phone 215-977-2026 **FAX** 215-977-2346
EIN 23-2667249   **Year Created** 1992

AMV $1,293,968   **FYE** 12-00   (**Gifts Received** $4,067)   1 **Grant of** $150,000

Sole grant to Point Breeze Federation (low-income housing). — For several years Point Breeze Federation has been the only grant recipient. ■**PUBLICATIONS:** None ■**WEBSITE:** None ■**E-MAIL:** None ■**APPLICATION POLICIES & PROCEDURES:** The Foundation reports that "all income is...to assist in funding the development and/or operation of those public charities that directly or indirectly own, operate, and/or develop government-assisted low-income housing."

O+D+T Robert C. Jacobs, Esq. (P+F+Con) — Graysha Harris [Tunkhannock] (VP) — Brock Vinton [DE] (S) — Richard Barnhart (Donor) — John Rosenthal (Donor)

SE-012   Albert Trust, The
      c/o M. Janowski, Asher & Company Ltd.
      1845 Walnut Street
      Philadelphia   19103   (Philadelphia County)

MI-12-13-25-29-41-42-44-54-56-57-63-71

Phone 215-564-1900 **FAX** None
EIN 23-7709316   **Year Created** 1992

AMV $3,098,693   **FYE** 12-00   (**Gifts Received** $0)   53+ **Grants totaling** $266,575

Mostly local giving. High grant of **$83,000** to Germantown Friends School. **$72,000** to Franklin Institute. **$43,000** to Drexel U. **$6,000** to WHYY-TV12. **$5,000** each to Pastorius Parents Assn. and Summerbridge Germantown. **$3,000** to Philadelphia Museum of Art. **$2,300** to Morris Arboretum. **$2,000** to St. Paul's Episcopal Church. **$1,000-$1,500** each to Chestnut Hill Community Fund, Chestnut Hill Garden District Fund, Chestnut Hill Historical Society, Educating Children for Parenting, Free Library of Philadelphia/Chestnut Hill Branch, Friends of John Paul II Foundation of Philadelphia, Friends of Philadelphia Parks, Friends of the Wissahickon, Philabundance, White-Williams Scholars, World Affairs Council of Philadelphia, WXPN, and Wyck Assn. Other smaller local contributions for various purposes. **Out-of-state** giving includes **$10,000** each to Hobart & William Smith Colleges [NY] and William Eliot Society [MA]; and **$1,000** to White House Project Education Fund [NY]. ■**PUBLICA-**

TIONS: None ■ **WEBSITE:** None ■ **E-MAIL:** None ■ **APPLICATION POLICIES & PROCEDURES:** No grants to individuals; no other information available.

O+D+T Margaret A. Greenawalt (T+Donor+Con) — Richard A. Greenawalt (T+Donor)

SE-013   Albert (William & Nina) Foundation
210 West Rittenhouse Square, Apt. 2807
Philadelphia 19103   (Philadelphia County)
AMV $616,704   **FYE** 12-00   (**Gifts Received** $63,800)

MI-22-31-32-52-54-55-62-65
Phone 215-735-2808 **FAX** 215-732-2807
EIN 22-2766314   **Year Created** 1986
30+ **Grants totaling** $83,471

Mostly local giving. High grant of **$54,500** to Federation Allied Jewish Appeal. **$6,000** to National Liberty Museum. **$4,310** to Jewish Community Centers of Greater Philadelphia. **$3,510** to Philadelphia Orchestra. **$2,710** to Temple Beth Hillel. **$2,000** to Temple Shalom. **$1,147** to Cancer Research Fund. Other smaller local contributions for cultural, arts and Jewish organizations. **Out-of-state** giving includes **$2,600** to Long Beach Island Arts Foundation [NJ] and **$1,000** to South Ocean County Hospital [NJ]. ■ **PUBLICATIONS:** None ■ **WEBSITE:** None ■ **E-MAIL:** None ■ **APPLICATION POLICIES & PROCEDURES:** No grants awarded to individuals.

O+D+T William Albert (T+Donor+Con) — Nina Albert (T+Donor)

SE-014   Alchon Family Foundation, The
7 Hoopes Drive
Landenberg 19350   (Chester County)
AMV $478,112   **FYE** 12-99   (**Gifts Received** $0)

MI-41-42
Phone 610-274-0401 **FAX** None
EIN 36-3677300   **Year Created** 1990
2 **Grants totaling** $41,000

No Pa. giving. High grant of **$40,000** to Tulane U. [LA] and **$1,000** to a Chicago-area high school. ■ **PUBLICATIONS:** None ■ **WEBSITE:** None ■ **E-MAIL:** None ■ **APPLICATION POLICIES & PROCEDURES:** Information not available.

O+D+T Guy Alchon (D+Donor+Con) — Suzanne A. Alchon (D+Donor)

SE-015   Alderbaugh Foundation
c/o Burton & Browse, CPAs
444 South State Street
Newtown 18940   (Bucks County)
AMV $5,363,894   **FYE** 12-00   (**Gifts Received** $0)

MI-18-41-71
Phone 215-968-4224 **FAX** None
EIN 23-2173929   **Year Created** 1981
2 **Grants totaling** $300,000

All local giving. High grant of **$200,000** to Buckingham Friends School (library construction). **$100,000** to Quaker School at Horsham (construction). — In prior years major giving to The Heritage Conservancy (open space) and Planned Parenthood of Bucks County. ■ **PUBLICATIONS:** None ■ **WEBSITE:** None ■ **E-MAIL:** None ■ **APPLICATION POLICIES & PROCEDURES:** Written grant requests may be submitted at any time. No grants awarded to individuals.

O+D+T Ashby Denoon (D+Manager+Con) — David B.H. Denoon (D) — Clarence E. Denoon, Jr. (Donor)

SE-016   Allen-Toebe Foundation
19 Forest Road, P.O. Box 444
Wayne 19087   (Delaware County)
AMV $102,453   **FYE** 12-00   (**Gifts Received** $10,000)

MI-13-22-61
Phone 610-825-5390 **FAX** 610-825-0218
EIN 23-6871066   **Year Created** 1986
5 **Grants totaling** $27,514

Mostly local giving. High grant of **$26,614** to St. Francis De Sales Society [Philadelphia] (general support/refugee program). Other small contributions for various purposes. — Giving in prior years included support for the Educational Advancement Center [Philadelphia]. ■ **PUBLICATIONS:** None ■ **WEBSITE:** None ■ **E-MAIL:** None ■ **APPLICATION POLICIES & PROCEDURES:** Information not available.

O+D+T John W. Toebe (P+T+Donor+Con) — John M. Toebe (T+Donor) — Elizabeth Allen (T) — C. Barry Buckley (T) — Patricia M. Toebe (T) — Sherene Toebe (Donor)

SE-017   Allerton Foundation, The
Five Tower Bridge, Suite 450
300 Barr Harbor Drive
West Conshohocken 19428   (Montgomery County)
AMV $55,058,475   **FYE** 6-01   (**Gifts Received** $50,000,155)

MI-71-72
Phone 610-828-4510 **FAX** 610-828-0390
EIN 23-3035225   **Year Created** 2000
6 **Grants totaling** $596,985

Mostly local giving; grants are unrestricted operating support except as noted. High grant of **$500,000** to U. of Pa. School of Veterinary Medicine; **$5,000** to AARK Wildlife Rehabilitation & Education Center [Newtown]; and **$1,000** to Sebastian Riding Associates [Collegeville]. **Out-of-state** grants: **$75,000** to Becker College [MA] (computer lab renovation); **$13,485** to Delaware Museum of Natural History (Headstart Museum Visit Program); and **$2,500** to Marine Mammal Stranding Center [NJ]. ■ **PUBLICATIONS:** None ■ **WEBSITE:** None ■ **E-MAIL:** lenfestfoundation@lenfestfoundation.org ■ **APPLICATION POLICIES & PROCEDURES:** The Foundation reports that at present giving concentrates on supporting organizations that work to benefit animal welfare and conservation. Grant requests may be submitted (by mail or e-mail) at any time in a Letter of Inquiry which states a specific amount requested; describes the program which the funds would support; describes the expected outcomes and how the results of the program will be evaluated; and explains how the program furthers the Foundation's mission. Also include the budget of the total program for which support is requested; a list of other funding received, requested or expected from foundations, corporations, government or other sources; the most recent audited financial statement; and IRS tax-exempt status documentation showing Federal EIN. All Letters of Inquiry will be acknowledged. Foundation staff and/or board members will review Letters of Inquiry for consistency with the Foundation's current priorities, and if interested, staff will follow up with questions, request a more detailed proposal, and/or arrange a site visit. — Formerly called The Diane Lenfest Myer Foundation.

O+D+T L. Bruce Melgary (F+D+Con) — Diane Lenfest Meyer [Jamison] (P+D+Donor) — Marguerite Lenfest (D) — Grahame P. Richards (S)

SE-018   Alter Family Foundation, The   MI-51-52-54
c/o Advanta Corporation
Welsh & McKean Roads, P.O. Box 844   **Phone** 215-657-4000 **FAX** 215-444-6161
Spring House   19477   (Montgomery County)   **EIN** 23-2951283   **Year Created** 1998
AMV $6,026,653   **FYE** 12-00   **(Gifts Received** $0)   3 **Grants totaling** $530,429

All local giving; all grants are unrestricted support. High grant of **$253,693** to Opera Company of Philadelphia. **$201,736** to Prince Music Theatre/American Music Theater Festival. **$75,000** to Philadelphia Museum of Art. — Grants in prior year: **$246,548** to Opera Company of Philadelphia and **$200,000** to Prince Music Theatre. ■**PUBLICATIONS:** None ■**WEBSITE:** None ■**E-MAIL:** None ■**APPLICATION POLICIES & PROCEDURES:** Information not available.
O+D+T Dennis Alter (P+F+D+Donor+Con) — Gisela Alter (VP+S+Donor+D) — William A. Rosoff (VP+AS+D) — Helen Alter (Donor)

SE-019   Ameche (Alan) Memorial Foundation   MI-41-43
P.O. Box 978   **Phone** 610-664-8477 **FAX** None
Narberth   19072   (Montgomery County)   **EIN** 23-2550681   **Year Created** 1989
AMV $60,469   **FYE** 12-00   **(Gifts Received** $35,900)   14 **Grants totaling** $18,189

All giving is limited to assist students at private, parochial/religious and vocational schools in the Delaware Valley; awards of **$750** to **$3,000** are designated for individual students who also receive mentoring support through the Foundation's program. ■**PUBLICATIONS:** statement of program policy; application guidelines ■**WEBSITE:** None ■**E-MAIL:** None ■**APPLICATION POLICIES & PROCEDURES:** Only students in the Greater Delaware Valley are eligible for support; applicants must be highly motivated but economically disadvantaged. Prospective applicants initially should telephone to inquire about the feasibility of submitting a request. Students in the 5th, 6th or 7th grade are nominated by teachers or school administrators. Applications must be submitted on a formal application form supplied by the Foundation; completed applications should be submitted during April-May; call about the deadline which changes each year. Awards are made at a June meeting.
O+D+T Susan Thal (Executive Director+F+Con) — Louis C. Fischer [Media] (C+D) — Alan M. Ameche [West Chester] (P+D) — Yvonne K. Ameche-Davis [Berwyn] (D) — JoAnne S. Bagnell [Gladwyne] (D) — Henry S. Belber [Devon] (D) — Thomas A. Bruder [Broomall] (D) — Barbara J. Fischer [Media] (D) — Stephen Paolantonio [Wayne] (D) — J. Michael Riordan [NJ] (D) — Richard Scott [Conshohocken] (D) — Hon. Robert J. Shenkin [West Chester] (D) — Glenn Davis [Berwyn] (D) — Corporate donor: Union Pacific Corporation — Foundation donors: The Claneil Foundation, Elizabeth S. Hooper Foundation

---

SE-020   American Foodservice Charitable Trust   MI-12-13-14-15-42-43-56-63
c/o American Foodservice
400 Drew Court   **Phone** 610-277-5010 **FAX** 610-277-8474
King of Prussia   19406   (Montgomery County)   **EIN** 23-7933778   **Year Created** 1997
AMV $22,588   **FYE** 12-00   **(Gifts Received** $0)   29 **Grants totaling** $50,840

About three-fourths local giving. High grant of **$20,000** to Delaware County Community College (Chester County Campus). **$2,000-$2,500** each to Bridge of Hope [Coatesville], Community College of Philadelphia Foundation, King of Prussia Inn, and Young Life. **$1,000-$1,500** each to Birthright [West Chester], Mount Olive Baptist Church [Pottstown] (building program),Multiple Sclerosis Society, Ursinus College (scholarship), and West Chester U. Other local contributions **$50-$850** each for community organizations, youth programs, educational needs, and other civic purposes. **Out-of-state** grant: **$10,000** to BK/McLamore Youth Foundation [FL]. ■**PUBLICATIONS:** None ■**WEBSITE:** None ■**E-MAIL:** None ■**APPLICATION POLICIES & PROCEDURES:** The Foundation reports that giving focuses on Eastern Pa. and mid-Texas. Grant requests may be submitted at any time in a letter which details the organization's need; include a financial statement and IRS tax-exempt status documentation.
O+D+T Richard S. Downs [Phoenixville] (T+Con) — Ronald G. Allen (T)

SE-021   Ametek Foundation   MI-11-13-31-41-42-43-44-45-49-52-54-71-81-89
c/o Ametek, Inc.
37 North Valley Road, Bldg. 4, P.O. Box 1764   **Phone** 610-647-2121 **FAX** None
Paoli   19301   (Chester County)   **EIN** 13-6095939   **Year Created** 1960
AMV $7,801,846   **FYE** 12-00   **(Gifts Received** $0)   88 **Grants totaling** $984,155

About one-third local/Pa. giving. Three grants totaling **$114,000** to The Free Library of Philadelphia (general support/summer reading program/foundation). **$45,000** to Eagles Youth Partnership. **$35,000** to Paoli Memorial Hospital. **$35,025** to United Way of SE Pa. **$15,000** each to Arcadia U./Beaver College and World Affairs Council of Philadelphia. **$10,000** each to Franklin Institute Science Museum (corporate partner program) and Sellersville Volunteer Fire Dept. **$6,000** to Philadelphia Hospitality, Inc. **$5,000** to St. Luke's Quakertown Hospital. **$3,000-$4,100** each to Immaculata College, Junior Achievement of Delaware Valley, Pa. Institute of Technology, and United Way of SW Pa. **$1,000-$2,000** each to Gnaden Huetten Memorial Hospital, Life's Work of Western Pa., Pittsburgh Symphony, and Red Clay Valley Assn. [Chester County]. **Out-of-state** giving includes **$50,000** to New Visions Public School [NY] (neighborhood literacy program); **$30,500** to National Merit Scholarship Corp. [IL]; **$25,000** each to Central Park Conservancy [NY], Cornell Cooperative Extension [NY] and Memorial Sloan-Kettering Cancer Center [NY]; **$20,970** to Youth for Understanding International Exchange [DC]; **$15,000** each to Natural Resources Defense Council [NY] and Proyecto Azteca [TX]; and other grants to corporate operating locations: NY City, Upstate NY, DE, NC, FL, OH, WI and elsewhere. ■**PUBLICATIONS:** None ■**WEBSITE:** www.ametek.com [corporate info only] ■**E-MAIL:** None ■**APPLICATION POLICIES & PROCEDURES:** The Foundation reports priority interests as Education, Health & Welfare, Culture & The Arts, and Civic & Social Programs with preference given to organizations where AMETEK employees volunteer. Most giving is for annual campaigns, building/renovations, endowment, equipment, general support, matching/challenge grants, research, scholarship funds, technical assistance, and exchange programs. No grants to individuals or for matching funds except for United Way. Submit grant requests in a one-page letter in February (February 28th deadline) or in (September 30th deadline); supporting documentation should include a mission statement, project summary and purpose/objective of the grant, description of the benefits to be achieved and the population served, amount requested and rationale, financial analysis of the project, implementation schedule, name of person in charge of the project, and copy of IRS tax-exempt status documentation. When appropriate, site visits are made to organizations being considered for a grant. Grants are awarded at meetings in April and November.

O+D+T Kathryn E. Londra (S+F+Con) — Frank S. Hermance (C+P) — Elizabeth R. Varet [NY] (VP+D) — Lewis G. Cole [NY] (AS+AF+D) — Helmut N. Friedlaender [NY] (D) — Corporate donor: Ametek, Inc.

SE-022 Annenberg Foundation, The
St. Davids Center, Suite A-200
150 Radnor-Chester Road
St. Davids 19087   (Delaware County)

MI-11-13-22-31-41-42-44-52-53-54-55-56-57 62-81
Phone 610-341-9270 **FAX** 610-964-8688
EIN 23-6257083   **Year Created** 1989

AMV $2,932,205,767   **FYE** 6-01   **(Gifts Received** $0)   262 **Grants totaling** $136,895,959

Nationwide giving with particular emphasis on pre-collegiate educational programs/school reform. About **$17,000,000** (13%) awarded to Pa. institutions, primarily in the Philadelphia area. **EDUCATION GRANTS TO PA**: High Pa. grant of **$3,765,000** to U. of Pa. **$2,300,000** to U. of Pa. (public education program). **$1,500,000** to Temple U. **$1,000,000** to School District of Philadelphia (Challenge Program). **$400,000** to Valley Forge Military Academy Foundation. **$200,000** each to Episcopal Academy, Friends' Central School, and Haverford College. **$100,000** each to Greater Philadelphia Urban Affairs Coalition (public education program) and Philadelphia Futures. **$83,000** to Elizabethtown College. **$75,000** to Children's Literacy Initiative. **$66,100** to Monell Chemical Senses Center (public education program). **$50,000** each to Executive Service Corps of the Delaware Valley (public education program), White-Williams Foundation, and YWCA of Germantown (public education program). **$49,500** to The Shipley School. **$20,000** to West Philadelphia Catholic High School. **$10,000** each to Assn. of Independent Colleges & Universities of Pa. [Harrisburg], Eisenhower Exchange Fellowships, Germantown Friends School, Sisters of Mercy (private education) and Williamson Free School of Mechanical Trades. **$7,000** to Central High School. **$5,000** each to Home of the Merciful Saviour for Crippled Children (education program) and RSVP of Montgomery County (public education program). **$2,500** to Hero Scholarship Fund of Philadelphia. **$1,000** each to Junior Achievement of the Delaware Valley and Please Touch Museum (education program). **$500** each to Ardmore Free Library and Elwyn Institute. **$350** to Church Farm School. **ARTS-CULTURAL-HISTORICAL GRANTS TO PA** (some for education-related programs). **$2,673,475** to Philadelphia Museum of Art. **$1,666,666** to Gateway Visitor Center Corp. (Independence National Historical Park). **$263,000** to Independence Seaport Museum. **$250,000** to National Constitution Center. **$33,000** to Pa. Heritage Society [Harrisburg]. **$25,800** to Regional Performing Arts Center. **$21,500** to Pa. Academy of the Fine Arts. **$21,204** to Philadelphia Orchestra. **$9,622** to Academy of Music. **$7,000** to American Philosophical Society. **$5,000** each to Academy of Community Music, Brandywine Conservancy, and Community Arts Center. **$3,000-$4,500** each to Creative Artists Network, Philadelphia Hospitality, and Royal Heritage Society of Delaware Valley. **$1,000-$2,500** each to Cliveden of the National Trust, Historical Society of Pa., Pa. Horticultural Society, Philadelphia Society for the Preservation of Landmarks, University City Science Center, and Wyck Assn. **$500** each to American Swedish Historical Foundation and Friends of Independence National Historical Park. **$250** each to America-Italy Society of Philadelphia and Fleisher Art Memorial. **HEALTH-HUMAN SERVICES GRANTS TO PA**: **$500,000** to Lankenau Hospital Foundation. **$450,000** to United Way of SE Pa. **$200,000** to Albert Einstein Medical Center. **$100,000** each to Fox Chase Cancer Center and Thomas Jefferson U. **$33,100** to Volunteer Medical Service Corps of Narberth. **$30,000** to Caron Foundation [Wernersville]. **$26,000** to Children's Hospital of Philadelphia. **$22,650** to Boy Scouts/Cradle of Liberty Council. **$10,000** to Planned Parenthood of SE Pa. **$5,000-$5,500** each to Jewish Community Centers of Greater Philadelphia and U. of Pa. **$1,000-$2,500** each to American Cancer Society, American Heart Assn., Boys & Girls Clubs of Metropolitan Philadelphia, High Oaks, Inc., Red Cross, Wistar Institute, and YMCA of Philadelphia & Vicinity. **$500** each to Big Brother & Big Sister Assn. of Philadelphia, Burn Foundation, Inglis House Foundation, and Police Athletic League of Philadelphia. **$250** each to Blind Relief Fund of Philadelphia and U.S. Committee for Sports in Israel. **$150** to Mental Health Assn. of SE Pa. **$100** to Bryn Mawr Hospital. **CIVIC-COMMUNITY & OTHER GRANTS TO PA:** **$500,000** to Jewish Federation of Greater Philadelphia. **$10,000** to Community Coalition [Chester Springs]. **$1,000-$1,500** each to International House of Philadelphia, Lower Merion Township Police Pension Fund, Merion Fire Company, Radnor Fire Company of Wayne, and World Affairs Council of Philadelphia. **$500** to Grey Nuns of the Sacred Heart. **$100** to Montgomery County SPCA. **MAJOR OUT-OF-STATE GRANTS** (primarily for education) include high grant of **$10,210,000** to U. of Southern California; **$10,181,700** to South Florida Annenberg Challenge; **$6,701,501** to Schools of the 21st Century [MI]; **$6,685,200** to Chicago Annenberg Challenge [IL]; **$5,950,736** to California Community Foundation (challenge program); **$5,480,000** to Rural School & Community Trust [DC]; **$5,002,000** to Eisenhower Medical Center [CA]; **$4,956,868** to Houston Annenberg Challenge [TX]; **$4,500,000** to Corporation for Public Broadcasting [DC]; **$3,978,000** to Center for Arts Education [NY]; **$3,000,000** each to Colonial Williamsburg Foundation [VA] and Northwestern U. [IL]; **$2,022,918** to Boston Plan for Excellence in the Public Schools Foundation [MA]; **$2,000,000** each to Rancho Mirage Public Library [CA] and United Negro College Fund [VA]; **$1,919,000** to American Friends of the British Museum [NY]; **$1,502,500** to American Associates of the Royal Academy Trust [NY]; **$1,477,241** to Minnesota Center for Arts Education; **$1,411,202** to New Visions for Public Schools [NY]; **$1,500,000** to California State U.-San Bernardino Foundation; **$1,300,000** to Brandeis U. [MA]; **$1,031,000** to Metropolitan Museum of Art [NY]; **$1,000,000** each to George Bush Presidential Library [TX], Chapin School [NY], Mayo Foundation [MN], Museum Associates [CA], and U. of Michigan; and many smaller grants/contributions for various purposes. — **MAJOR UNPAID PA GRANT COMMITMENTS**: **$51,350,000** to U. of Pa. **$10,000,000** each to National Constitution Center and Philadelphia Orchestra. **$2,500,000** each to Philadelphia Museum of Art and Temple U. **$2,000,000** to Valley Forge Military Academy Foundation. **$1,400,000** to Episcopal Academy. **$1,000,000** each to Caron Foundation [Wernersville], Jewish Federation of Greater Philadelphia, Lankenau Hospital Foundation, and The Shipley School. **$940,000** to Independence Seaport Museum. **$667,000** to Devereux Foundation. **$500,000** to

Pa. Academy of the Fine Arts. **$400,000** to Friends' Central School. **$300,000** to Greater Philadelphia Urban Affairs Coalition. **$200,000** to Albert Einstein Medical Center. ■**PUBLICATIONS:** Application Guidelines sheet; The Annenberg Challenge: Lessons and Reflections on Public School Reform; and many other reports/publications ■**WEBSITE:** www.whannenberg.org ■**E-MAIL:** info@whannenberg.org ■**APPLICATION POLICIES & PROCEDURES:** The Foundation reports its primary grantmaking interests as Public K-12 Education, Culture and The Arts, and Community & Civic Life, with significant grants generally limited to programs likely to produce beneficent change on a large scale. Other than the major challenge grant awards, grants typically range from $1,000-$300,000 and are for special projects of one year only. No grants are awarded to individuals, or for charter schools, scholarships, general operating expenses, capital construction, political activities or attempts to influence specific legislation, projects focused exclusively on research, for-profit organizations, or organizations outside the U.S. Prospective applicants should submit an initial Letter of Inquiry (2 pages maximum, single-spaced) at any time; the letter should describe the organization; the purpose of the project for which funds are requested; the problems the project will address; an estimated overall project budget; time period for which funds are requested; qualifications of key project personnel; and contact information—name and title, address, phone, fax, and e-mail. Do not include any additional supporting information, e.g. videotapes, financial reports, annual reports, etc. Letters of Inquiry also may be submitted by e-mail; state the request in the message as no e-mail attachments will be opened. All Letters of Inquiry are acknowledged within four to six weeks; if the Foundation responds favorably, a formal proposal will be requested comprising the following: (1) Cover Letter: brief description of the organization and proposed program; amount of funding requested; organization's legal name as it appears on the IRS exemption letter; and contact name, title, address, and telephone number. (2) Background Information: History and charitable purpose of the organization; primary constituency served by the organization. (3) Program description: Detailed description of the proposed program including its goals and objectives; evidence of the program's need and value; an outline of the method to be used for carrying out the program; and evaluation plan. (4) Personnel information: Biographical information/qualifications of the staff who will implement program; names/principal affiliations of directors or trustees. (5) Financial Information: Detailed program budget and narrative explaining the proposed use of funds, other sources of funding, and total amount requested from the Foundation; organization's financial statement for the prior fiscal year (preferably audited); and projected organizational budget covering years during which proposed program will be carried out. (6) Other: A statement concerning plans for continuing support after the conclusion of Annenberg funding; documentation that the proposal is supported by the organization's board of directors or trustees; and IRS tax-exempt status documentation. Review of an proposal may take up to six months. Grants are approved at a annual meeting, generally in May. — **NOTE:** The Foundation's major program, the Annenberg Challenge for School Reform, provided $500 million for improving public schools by uniting the resources/ideas of those committed to increasing public schooling's effectiveness; it operated through 18 locally-designed initiatives across the country (including Philadelphia), and a report on the program is available on the website.

O+D+T Dr. Gail C. Levin (Executive Director+Con) — Walter H. Annenberg [Wynnewood & CA] (C+T) — Leonore A. Annenberg [Wynnewood & CA] (VC+P+CEO+T) — Wallis Annenberg [CA] (VP+T) — William J. Henrich, Jr., Esq. [Philadelphia] (S+T) — Jennifer H. Pedroni (F)

SE-023   **AO North America, Inc.**   MI-32-34
   c/o AO North America
   1690 Russell Road, P.O. Box 308   **Phone** 610-251-9007 **FAX** 610-251-9059
   Devon 19333   (Chester County)   **EIN** 23-2701788   **Year Created** 1992
AMV $1,821,809   **FYE** 6-00   (**Gifts Received** $449,525)   59 **Grants totaling** $260,482

All giving restricted to scientific research or education in orthopaedic medicine. High grant of **$64,235** to Orthopaedic Trauma Assn. [IL]. **$20,250** to The University of Medicine and Dentistry of New Jersey (research).**$12,000** to Data Harbor [IL] (research). **$10,120** to Maxillofacial Education & Research Fund [NM] (research). **$10,000** to Coalition for American Trauma Care [VA] (research). Other smaller grants/contributions to similar organizations or research professionals in many states, Canada, and Germany. ■**PUBLICATIONS:** application guidelines; application form ■**WEBSITE:** www.aona.com [organizational information only] ■**E-MAIL:** None ■**APPLICATION POLICIES & PROCEDURES:** The Foundation reports that national/international giving is restricted to orthopaedic medicine research, specifically for trauma research projects and the teaching of orthopaedic, maxillofacial, spine or veterinary trauma treatment. Recipients will be chosen based on knowledge of orthopaedic medicine and their research ability. Prospective applicants should contact the Foundation for a formal application form and guidelines.

O+D+T James E. Gerry (F+Con) — Eric Johnson [CA] (P) — Larry Bone [NY] (VP) — Foundation donor: AO/ASIF Foundation

---

SE-024   **Apter (Helene & Allen) Foundation**   MI-22-29-31-42-54-62
   7131 Sheaff Lane   **Phone** 215-699-8701 **FAX** None
   Fort Washington 19034   (Montgomery County)   **EIN** 23-2724364   **Year Created** 1993
AMV $1,122,767   **FYE** 12-00   (**Gifts Received** $272,493)   13 **Grants totaling** $73,950

Mostly local/Pa. giving. High grant of **$60,000** to Bux-Mont Jewish Appeal. **$5,000** to Lehigh U. **$1,700** to Congregation Beth Or. **$1,000** each to Deborah Hospital, Franklin Institute, Phillies Charities, and Sharing is Caring. Other smaller local contributions for various purposes. **Out-of-state** grant: **$1,000** to Museum of Modern Art [NY]. ■**PUBLICATIONS:** None ■**WEBSITE:** None ■**E-MAIL:** None ■**APPLICATION POLICIES & PROCEDURES:** The Foundation reports that grant requests are not accepted.

O+D+T Allen B. Apter (S+F+D+Donor+Con) — Helene Apter (P+D+Donor) — Joshua Apter [NY] (VP+D) — Sherri Apter Wexler [Bala Cynwyd] (VP+D)

SE-025   Arcadia Foundation, The
105 East Logan Street
Norristown   19401
(Montgomery County)

AMV $49,733,968   FYE 9-01   **(Gifts Received** $0)

MI-12-13-14-15-16-25-29-31-32-35-39-41-42-
44-45-51-52-54-55-56-57-63-71-72-84-89
Phone 610-275-8460 **FAX** None
EIN 23-6399772   **Year Created** 1964
258 **Grants totaling** $7,955,744

Mostly Pa. giving within 75 miles of Philadelphia; all grants are unrestricted support. *EDUCATION & LIBRARY GRANTS:* **$500,000** each to Cedar Crest College and Ursinus College. **$250,000** each to Arcadia U. and Drexel U. **$150,000** to Library Company of Philadelphia. **$100,000** to Northampton Community College. **$50,000** each to DeSales U., Immaculata College, and Muhlenberg College. **$40,000** to Temple U. **$25,000** each to Alvernia College, EANA Scholarship Trust [Norristown], East-town Library, and Philadelphia U. **$15,000** each to Compeer of Suburban Philadelphia, Free Library of Philadelphia, and Immaculate Conception School [Levittown]. **$12,730** to Gwynedd Mercy Academy. **$10,000** each to East Stroudsburg U., Institute for the Arts in Education, Jenkintown Library, Kraybill Mennonite School [Mount Joy], Lansdowne Public Library, Literacy Council of Norristown, Plumstead Christian School, and The School in Rose Valley. **$5,000-$5,600** each to Harcum College, Holy Trinity Catholic School [Bridgeport], Literacy Council of Reading, Montgomery County-Norristown Public Library, Norristown Area School District, Research for Better Schools, Southern Lehigh Public Library, West End Computer Lab [Norristown], and Woodlynde School. **$4,000** to William Jeanes Memorial Library. Other smaller grants for similar purposes. *HEALTH & MEDI-CAL GRANTS*: **$50,000** to MCP-Hahnemann U. **$30,000** each to College of Physicians of Philadelphia, Foundation for Melanoma Research, and National Organization for Hearing Research. **$25,000** each to Eagles Fly for Leukemia Foundation, Montgomery Hospital Auxiliary, St. Luke's Hospital [Allentown], The Weller Center [Easton], and Wistar Institute. **$20,000** each to Montgomery County Emergency Services and Wills Eye Hospital. **$18,000** to Magee Rehabilitation Hospital. **$15,000** each to Arthritis Foundation, U. of Pa. Health System, and Valley Health Foundation [Easton]. **$10,000** each to ALS Assn., Fox Chase Cancer Center, and Freedom Valley Disability Center. **$6,000** to Consortium for Health Information & Library Services. **$5,000** to Emergency Care Research Institute. *HUMAN SERVICES & YOUTH GRANTS:* **$500,000** to Red Cross/SE Pa. **$200,000** to Philadelphia Geriatric Center. **$50,000** to Phoenixville Area YMCA. **$32,000** to Norristown Habitat for Humanity. **$30,000** to VNA-Community Services. **$29,000** to Norristown Borough (child recreation). **$25,000** each to Blind Relief Fund, Camp Men-O-Lan, Hayes Manor, and Kelly Ann Dolan Memorial Fund. **$22,000** to Old Kensington Redevelopment Corp. **$20,000** each to ACLAMO [Norristown], Bethanna, Easter Seals [Media], Community Day Care Assn. [Norristown], Independence Dogs [Chadds Ford], MBF Center, Nueva Esperanza, Philabundance, SCAN/Supportive Child-Adult Network, and YMCA of Germantown. **$18,750** to Big Brothers/Big Sisters of Montgomery County. **$15,000** each to Camilla Hall Nursing Home, Camp Rainbow, Inter-community Action, Montgomery County Legal Aid Services, Montgomery County O.I.C., and The Shepherds in Monroe County. **$12,000** each to Kearsley Retirement Community and Universal Community Homes. **$10,000** each to ARC of Chester County, Ardmore Ave. Community Center, ASSETS Montgomery County, BASES, Chestnut Hill Senior Services Center, Colonial Neighborhood Council [Conshohocken], Devereux Foundation [Malvern], Family Services of Chester County, Girl Scouts of SE Pa. [Allentown], Guiding Light for the Blind, Habitat for Humanity-Chester County, Indian Valley Opportunity Center, Overington House, Pa. Home of the Sparrow, Pa. Special Olympics/Montgomery County, Red Cross/Schuylkill Valley, Special Equestrians [Warrington], St. Mary's Family Respite Center, Third Street Alliance [Easton], Unity Center [Media], Variety Club, Volunteer Medical Corps of Lower Merion/Narberth, and Working Wardrobe. **$7,000-$8,000** each to Fellowship Farm, Northwest Interfaith Movement, Philadelphia Committee for the Homeless, and Religious Committee for Community Justice. **$4,800-$6,000** each to Camphill Soltane, Centro Pedro Claver, Contact-Bucks County, Deaf-Hearing Communication Center, Domestic Violence Center of Chester County, Haitian Community Center, Hope Springs Equestrian Therapy, Interagency Council of Norristown, Lakeside Youth Services, Mom's House [Phoenixville], Neighborhood Bike Works, Network of Victim Assistance [Doylestown], New Life Youth & Family Services [Harleysville], Polish-American Social Services, and Women Organized Against Rape. **$3,000-$4,000** each to Assn. for the Blind & Visually Handicapped [Allentown], Central Montgomery County Veterans Council, Christian Network Outreach, Christmas in April, Inn Dwelling, Institute for the Development of African-American Youth, Nonprofit Technology Resources, and Phillips Mill Community Assn. [New Hope]. Other smaller grants for similar purposes. *ARTS-CULTURAL & HISTORICAL GRANTS:* **$395,000** to Franklin Institute. **$300,000** to Philadelphia Museum of Art. **$250,000** each to People's Light & Theatre Company, Please Touch Museum, Prince Music Theater, and Regional Performing Arts Center. **$100,000** each to Discovery Center [Bethlehem], International Institute for Theatre Research [Malvern], and Philadelphia Orchestra. **$75,000** to Arden Theatre Company. **$50,000** to The Wilma Theatre. **$35,000** to Historical Society of Montgomery County. **$30,000** to Settlement Music School. **$24,000-$25,000** each to 1812 Productions, The Fabric Workshop, Montgomery County Cultural Society, Pa. Academy of the Fine Arts, Pa. Academy of Music [Lancaster], Philadelphia Sketch Club, Theatre Alliance of Greater Philadelphia, and Wayne Art Center. **$18,000-$20,000** to The Clay Studio, The Dramateurs, Institute for Contemporary Art, Mennonite Historians of Eastern Pa., Mum Puppet Theatre, and Wagner Free Institute of Science. **$15,000** each to Academy of Community Music, Academy of Natural Sciences, Chester Springs Studio, Ebenezer Maxwell Mansion, Harriton Assn., Philadelphia Theatre Company, Rosenbach Museum & Library, and Wood Turning Center. **$13,100** to Highlands Historical Society. **$12,500** to Philomel Concerts. **$10,000** each to Art Sanctuary, Colonial Theatre [Phoenixville], Conservation Center for Art & Historic Artifacts, Evangelical & Reformed Historical Society/United Church of Christ, Friends to Save Beechwood, Historic Philadelphia, Independence Seaport Museum, King of Prussia Inn, Main Line Art Center, Strings for Schools, Village of Arts & Humanities, and Wood to Wonderful [Bernville]. **$9,500** to Woodland's Trust for Historic Preservation. **$7,500-$8,700** each to Act II Playhouse, Balch Institute for Ethnic Studies, Lehigh County Historical Society, Plymouth Meeting Historical Society, Singing City, and WLVT-TV. **$6,900** to Fairmount Park Preservation Trust. **$4,000-$5,150** each to 1807 & Friends, Allens Lane Art Center, Cliveden of the National Trust, Creative Artists Network, Fireman's Hall, Glen Foerd on the Delaware, Greater Norristown Art League, Pike County Historic Preservation Trust, and Young Audiences of Eastern Pa. **$3,000** to Music Group of Philadelphia. Other smaller arts/cultural grants. *ENVIRONMENT GRANTS:* **$100,000** to Morris Arboretum. **$75,000** each to Pa. Horticultural Society and Philadelphia Zoo. **$50,000** to The Nature Conservancy/Pa. Chapter. **$25,000** to Elmwood Park Zoo. **$15,800** to Schuylkill Center for Environmental Education. **$15,000** to Greensgrow Philadelphia Project. **$10,000** each to Friends of Jenkins Arboretum, Hawk Mountain Sanctuary Assn., Montgomery County Lands Trust, Penn-PIRG Education Fund, Pa. Environ-

mental Council, and Perkiomen Valley Watershed Assn. **$8,000** to Clean Air Council. **$5,000** each to Clean Water Fund, Schuylkill River Development [St. Peters], and Upper Merion Park. Religion GRANTS: **$50,000** to Parish Resource Center [Lancaster]. **$35,000** each to Phoebe Ministries [Allentown] and United Church of Christ of East Goshen. **$25,000** to St. Paul's United Church of Christ [Douglassvile]. **$20,000** to Tabernacle United Church [Philadelphia]. **$15,000** to Peaceable Kingdom [Allentown]. **$12,000** to Mennonite Resources Network. **$11,445** to St. Patrick Church [Norristown]. **$10,000** each to Fair Hill Burial Ground [Kennett Square] and Mt. Pleasant Baptist Church [Philadelphia]. **$5,000** each to Jones Tabernacle A.M.E. Church, Norristown Ministries, Inc., Seaman's Church Institute, and Wo-man 2 Woman Ministries. **$2,000** to Church of the Loving Shepherd [West Chester]. *OTHER & OUT-OF-STATE GRANTS*: **$20,000** to New Observations [NY]. **$15,000** to Chester County Community Foundation. **$10,000** each to Pennsburg Volunteer Fire Company and Philadelphia Dept. of Recreation. ■
PUBLICATIONS: Application Guidelines ■**WEBSITE:** None ■**E-MAIL:** None ■**APPLICATION POLICIES & PROCEDURES:** The Foundation reports that only Pa. organizations with ZIP codes beginning with 18.. or 19.. will be considered as new grantees. Only one-year grants are awarded, mostly for general operating support, special projects, building funds, and endowment. No grants are awarded for publications, conferences, land acquisition, fellowships, demonstration projects, deficit financing, or to individuals. Grant requests may be submitted in a brief letter (2 pages maximum—longer submissions will be discarded!) only between September 1st and November 1st; provide a brief history and purpose of the organization, state what funding is requested and how it will be spent, and include only IRS tax-exempt status documentation—no other enclosures! The Board makes awards at a December meeting; grants are disbursed the following year.
O+D+T Marilyn Lee Steinbright (P+D+Donor+Con) — Tanya Hashorva [NJ] (VP+D) — David P. Sandler [East Norriton] (S+D) — Harvey S.S. Miller [Fort Washington] (F+D) — Edward L. Jones, Jr. (D) — Kathleen Shelllington (D)

SE-026	**Archer Foundation**		**MI**-63-64	
	Roberts Road & Bethel Lane		**Phone** 610-525-4985 **FAX** None	
	Bryn Mawr 19010	(Montgomery County)	**EIN** 23-6442014 **Year Created** 1968	
AMV $1,699,405	**FYE** 12-00	(**Gifts Received** $17,525)	14 **Grants totaling** $250,000	

About three-fourths local/Pa. giving. High grant of **$55,000** to Philadelphia College of Bible. **$50,000** to International Service Fellowship [Upper Darby]. **$20,000** to Scripture Union [Wayne]. **$10,000** each to Agape World Ministries [Berks County], BCM Ministries [Upper Darby], Church Without Walls [Abington], Eastern Mennonite Board of Missions & Charities, Prison Fellowship Ministries [Mechanicsburg], and UFM International [Bala Cynwyd]. **Out-of-state** giving includes **$35,000** to High Adventure Ministries [CO]; and **$10,000** to evangelical ministries in Australia, FL, ME and VA. ■**PUBLICATIONS:** None ■**WEBSITE:** None ■**E-MAIL:** None ■**APPLICATION POLICIES & PROCEDURES:** The Foundation reports that all giving is restricted to Evangelical Christian organizations. Grant requests may be submitted in any form at any time.
O+D+T George W. Moffitt, Jr. [Bryn Mawr] (P+Donor+Con) — H. Eugene Vickers [Newtown] (S) — Robert F. Dolan [West Chester] (F)

SE-027	**Arete Foundation**		**MI**-22-31-41-42-51-52-53-54-57-62-64-85	
	c/o Resource America, Inc.			
	1845 Walnut Street, 10th Floor		**Phone** 215-546-5005 **FAX** 215-546-5388	
	Philadelphia 19103	(Philadelphia County)	**EIN** 23-6779271 **Year Created** 1986	
AMV $5,674,537	**FYE** 11-00	(**Gifts Received** $1,529,375)	24 **Grants totaling** $481,416	

About three-fourths local giving. High grant of **$106,500** to American Music Theater Festival/Prince Music Theater. **$101,500** to Philadelphia Museum of Art. **$50,800** to Rosenbach Museum & Library. **$25,000** to Jewish Publication Society. **$18,500** to Perelman Jewish Day School. **$16,916** to WHYY-TV12. **$5,100** to U. of Pa. **$5,000** to National Museum of American Jewish History. **$3,500** to Jewish National Fund. **$1,000-$2,000** each to Curtis Institute of Music, Greater Philadelphia Chamber of Commerce, Jewish Community Centers of Greater Philadelphia, Pa. Hospital, and Samuel D. Cozen Memorial Fund. Other smaller local contributions for similar purposes. **Out-of-state** giving includes **$60,000** to Metropolitan Opera [NY]; **$40,000** to Jewish Theological Seminary of America [NY]; **$25,000** to U. of Texas Press; **$10,000** to National Humanities Center [NC]; and **$5,000** to Cooper Union School of Art [NY]. ■**PUBLICATIONS:** None ■**WEBSITE:** None ■**E-MAIL:** None ■**APPLICATION POLICIES & PROCEDURES:** Grant requests may be submitted in a letter at any time; include organizational information and IRS tax-exempt status documentation. The Board meets annually.
O+D+T Sue Ann Taylor (Executive Director+Con) — Betsy Z. Cohen (T+Donor) — Edward E. Cohen (T+Donor)

SE-028	**Armstrong Foundation, The**		**MI**-13-31-32-41-42-56-63-71-72	
	612 Shipton Lane		**Phone** 610-648-6000 **FAX** None	
	Bryn Mawr 19010	(Montgomery County)	**EIN** 23-2642354 **Year Created** 1991	
AMV $4,358,865	**FYE** 12-00	(**Gifts Received** $1,000,000)	8 **Grants totaling** $150,000	

About two-thirds local giving. High Pa. grant of **$40,000** to Bryn Mawr Presbyterian Church. **$20,000** to Lower Merion Conservancy. **$10,000** each to Boy Scouts/Cradle of Liberty Council and Shipley School. **$5,000** to Philadelphia Zoo. **Out-of-state** giving includes **$50,000** to American Indian College Fund [CO]; **$10,000** to Nassau Presbyterian Church/Westminster Foundation [NJ]; and **$5,000** to National Trust for Historic Preservation [DC]. — Major grants awarded in the prior year include **$50,000** to American Indian College Fund; **$25,000** each to Johns Hopkins Medicine Cardiovascular Institute and U. of Arizona Foundation (Arrhythmogenic Right Ventricular Dysphasia Forum); and **$15,000** to Princeton U. '51 Foundation. ■**PUBLICATIONS:** None ■**WEBSITE:** None ■**E-MAIL:** None ■**APPLICATION POLICIES & PROCEDURES:** No grants are awarded to individuals. — Formerly called the John C. & Eve S. Bogle Foundation.
O+D+T John C. Bogle (T+Donor+Con) — Eve S. Bogle (T)

SE-029

SE-029 Arpajian (Jack) Armenian Educational Foundation
P.O. Box 1090
Exton 19341   (Chester County)
AMV $1,543,376   FYE 12-00   (Gifts Received $0)

MI-43
Phone 610-344-0909 **FAX** None
EIN 23-2761002 **Year Created** 1996
14 **Grants totaling** $59,167

All grants are scholarships, primarily **$2,500** or **$5,000** each, awarded to students of Amenian descent resident in many states. ■**PUBLICATIONS:** scholarship application form ■**WEBSITE:** None ■**E-MAIL:** None ■**APPLICATION POLICIES & PROCEDURES:** Only persons of Armenian heritage are eligible to apply for scholarships; prospective applicants must request in writing a formal application form. Selection criteria include one's grade point average, extracurricular activities, and financial need. The deadline for Fall Semester applications in August 1st; deadline for Spring Semester is December 1st.

O+D+T Marguerite Parkinson (Executive Director+P+D+Con) — Laurel Connelly [MD] (S+F+D) — Kevin Connelly [MD] (D) — Joan Gallagher [Malvern] (D) — Dante W. Renzulli, Jr. (D) — Donor: Estate of Jack Arpajian

---

SE-030 Arronson Foundation
c/o Kohn, Swift & Graf, P.C.
1 South Broad Street, Suite 2100
Philadelphia 19107   (Philadelphia County)
AMV $7,408,291   FYE 10-00   (Gifts Received $0)

MI-11-12-13-14-15-17-18-22-31-41-42-44-51
52-54-55-62-71
Phone 215-238-1700 **FAX** 215-238-1968
EIN 23-6259604 **Year Created** 1957
42 **Grants totaling** $847,140

Mostly local giving; some grants comprise multiple payments and others are payments on multiyear pledges. High grant of **$100,000** to Federation Allied Jewish Appeal. **$60,000** to Wilma Theater. **$50,000** each to Easttown Library Foundation, MossRehab Hospital, Planned Parenthood of SE Pa., and Regional Performing Arts Center. **$30,000** to Philadelphia Geriatric Center. **$25,000** each to Academy of Vocal Arts, Jewish Community Centers of Greater Philadelphia, and St. Joseph's Preparatory School. **$20,000** each to American Swedish Historical Museum, Concerto Soloists, and U. of Pa. Law School. **$18,530** to Haverford College. **$15,900** to Delius Society of Philadelphia. **$14,000** to National Liberty Museum. **$10,000-$11,000** each to Arden Theatre Company, Awbury Arboretum Assn., Community College of Philadelphia, Gershman 'Y', Settlement Music School, and United Way of SE Pa. **$4,000-$5,000** each to Astral Artistic Services, Community Women's Education Project., Philadelphia Art Alliance, Philadelphia Youth Tennis, Wagner Free Institute of Science, Walnut Street Theatre, and White-Williams Scholars. **$1,000-$2,500** each to American Revolution Patriots Fund, Pa. School for the Deaf, Philadelphia Youth Orchestra, Philadelphia Zoo, and Young Audiences of Eastern Pa. **Out-of-state** giving includes **$100,000** to Cumberland College [KY]; **$25,000** to Israel Children's Center [FL]; and **$15,000** each to National Partnership for Women & Families [DC] and St. Andrew's Episcopal School [MD]. ■**PUBLICATIONS:** None ■**WEBSITE:** None ■**E-MAIL:** info@kohnswift.com ■**APPLICATION POLICIES & PROCEDURES:** Grant requests may be submitted at any time in a letter; briefly state the nature of the organization's work, the amount requested, and how it will be used; include an annual report, list of Board members, audited financial statement for the last fiscal year, and IRS tax-exempt status documentation. The Board meets in March, June, September and December.

O+D+T Joseph C. Kohn, Esq. (P+F+D+Con) — Edith A. Kohn (VP+S+D) — Amy D. Goldberg (VP+D) — Ellen Kohn (VP+D)

SE-031 Ash Family Foundation, The
990 Lafayette Road
Bryn Mawr 19010   (Montgomery County)
AMV $623,910   FYE 10-00   (Gifts Received $26,250)

MI-11-14-22-32-42-51-52-62-71
Phone 610-525-1722 **FAX** None
EIN 23-2225051 **Year Created** 1982
24 **Grants totaling** $49,800

Mostly local/Pa. giving. High grant of **$26,000** to Federation Allied Jewish Appeal. **$5,000** each to HIAS/Hebrew Immigrant Aid Society & Council Migration Service of Philadelphia, Jewish Employment & Vocational Service, and Penn State U. **$1,000-$1,250** each to Pa. Special Olympics, Riverbend Environmental Center, Settlement Music School, United Way of SE Pa., and Walnut Street Theatre. Other contributions **$100-$450** for medical, educational, and Jewish purposes. ■**PUBLICATIONS:** None ■**WEBSITE:** None ■**E-MAIL:** None ■**APPLICATION POLICIES & PROCEDURES:** No grants are awarded to individuals.

O+D+T Franklin C. Ash (F+T+Donor+Con) — Larry Ash [AZ] (T+Donor) Corporate donors: Active Amusement Machines Company; Galaxy Amusement of Pa.

SE-032 Asplundh (Edward & Gwendolyn) Family Foundation
450 Tomlinson Road
Huntingdon Valley 19006   (Montgomery County)
AMV $236,526   FYE 12-00   (Gifts Received $0)

MI-22-31-32-41-42-54-71
Phone 215-938-7909 **FAX** None
EIN 23-7921981 **Year Created** 1997
41 **Grants totaling** $17,900

Limited local giving. High local grant of **$1,100** to Loving Arms Mission. **$1,000** each to Fox Chase Cancer Center and Pennypack Ecological Restoration Trust. **$600** to Kimberton Waldorf School. Other smaller local contributions for cultural, environmental and other purposes. **Out-of-state** giving includes **$1,000** to Princeton Day School [NJ], Trigeminal Neuralgia Assn. [NJ, Wellesley College [MA], and others; and other smaller contributions to several states. ■**PUBLICATIONS:** None ■**WEBSITE:** None ■**E-MAIL:** None ■**APPLICATION POLICIES & PROCEDURES:** Grant requests may be submitted in a letter at any time.

O+D+T Edward K. Asplundh (P+T+Donor+Con) — Gwendolyn Asplundh (S+F+Donor)

SE-033 Asplundh Foundation
c/o Asplundh Tree Expert Company
708 Blair Mill Road
Willow Grove 19090   (Montgomery County)
AMV $12,478,746   FYE 12-00   (Gifts Received $100,500)

MI-12-22-29-31-41-44-52-54-56-63-71-89
Phone 215-784-4200 **FAX** None
EIN 23-6297246 **Year Created** 1953
150+ **Grants totaling** $610,025

About four-fifths local/Pa. giving; most grants reported below comprise multiple payments. Grants totaling about **$350,000** awarded to Swedenborgian churches and related schools/organizations in Bryn Athyn and other locations in Pa. **$36,500** to

159

Doylestown Hospital. **$36,000** to Holy Redeemer Hospital Foundation. **$17,525** to Pennypack Ecological Restoration Trust. **$13,475** to Abington Memorial Hospital. **$8,000** to Make-a-Wish Foundation of Philadelphia/SE Pa. **$7,500** to Germantown Academy. **$5,000** to Loving Arms Mission. **$3,000-$3,500** each to The Heritage Conservancy, Philadelphia Museum of Art, and Swedenborg Foundation Publishers [West Chester]. **$2,000-$2,500** each to Fox Chase Cancer Center, Huntingdon Valley Grange, Red Cross, St. Martin's Church [New Hope], and Western Pa. School for Blind Children [Pittsburgh]. **$1,000-$1,500** each to A Woman's Place, Bryn Athyn Arts Center, Carnegie Mellon U./School of Drama, Children's Hospital of Philadelphia, Developmental Enterprises Corp., Marine Corps Heritage 2000 Foundation, Morris Arboretum, Pa. Horticultural Society, Philadelphia Orchestra, Point Pleasant-Plumstead EMS, The Nature Conservancy, Point Pleasant Volunteer Fire Company, Three Rivers Rowing Assn. [Pittsburgh], U. of Pa. Other smaller contributions to local police and fire departments, libraries, health organizations, and others. **Out-of-state** giving includes **$20,000** to ISA Research Trust [IL], **$9,000** to Colonial Williamsburg Foundation; **$5,000** to National Arbor Day Foundation [NE]; numerous grants to Swedenborgian churches and organizations in many states; and other contributions. ■**PUBLICATIONS:** None ■**WEBSITE:** www.asplundh.com [corporate info only] ■**E-MAIL:** None ■**APPLICATION POLICIES & PROCEDURES:** Grant requests in any form may be submitted at any time; describe the nature of the organization, and the amount/purpose of requested funding.

O+D+T Christopher B. Asplundh (P+D+Con) — Barr E. Asplundh (VP+D) — E. Boyd Asplundh (S+F+D) — Brent D. Asplundh (D) — Carl Hj. Asplundh, Jr. (D) — Carl Hj. Asplundh, III (D) — Gregg G. Asplundh (D) — Paul S. Asplundh (D) — Robert H. Asplundh (D) — Scott M. Asplundh (D) — Steven G. Asplundh (D) — Stewart L. Asplundh (D) — George E. Graham (D) — James E. Graham (D)

SE-034 **Atofina Chemical Foundation**
c/o Atofina Chemical, Inc.
2000 Market Street
Philadelphia 19103   (Philadelphia County)

MI-11-13-41-42-52-51-52-54-56-57-72-81-88

Phone 215-419-7614 **FAX** 215-419-5494
EIN 23-6256818   **Year Created** 1957

AMV $5,129   **FYE** 12-00   **(Gifts Received** $600,000)   240 **Grants totaling** $678,059

About half local/Pa. giving; some grants represent multiple payments. High grant of **$200,000** to School District of Philadelphia. **$135,435** to Science Teacher Program (a foundation-sponsored program). **$100,000** to WHYY. **$43,000** to Philadelphia Orchestra. **$20,000** to Chemical Heritage Foundation. **$15,000** to Philadelphia Museum of Art. **$12,500** to Opera Company of Philadelphia. **$10,000** to International House of Philadelphia. **$9,500** to United Way of Bucks County. **$7,500** to Franklin Institute. **$6,500** to Academy of Natural Sciences. **$5,000** each to Arden Theatre Company, Philadelphia Zoo, Philadelphia Police Federation, and YMCA of Philadelphia & Vicinity. **$2,500** to United Way of Berks County. **Out-of-state** giving mostly for United Ways/community organizations in corporate operating locations in AL, CT, KY, MI, NY, OH, OK, SC, TN, and TX. In addition, 203 matching gifts totaling **$44,224** were disbursed to colleges/universities, art museums, performing arts groups, history and science museums, public radio/TV, and hospitals. — Major Pa. grants approved for future payment include **$100,000** to WHYY; **$67,000** to Philadelphia Museum of Art; **$50,000** each to Regional Performing Arts Center and YMCA of Philadelphia & Vicinity; and **$25,000** to Philadelphia Orchestra. ■**PUBLICATIONS:** None ■**WEBSITE:** None ■**E-MAIL:** None ■**APPLICATION POLICIES & PROCEDURES:** Most giving is limited to corporate operating locations with most grants for general support, capital drives, matching grants, matching gifts, and scholarships for employee dependents; multiple-year grants are awarded. Grant requests may be submitted by organizations who: (1) have an active and responsible governing body which serves without compensation, (2) have a program that benefits the community at large which does not substantially duplicate the work of other organizations receiving Atofina Chemical Foundation support, (3) operate a program with reasonable efficiency and adequate resources, and (4) conduct its fundraising activities in an ethical manner. No grants are awarded outside the United States, or for endowment, research, publications, conferences, courtesy advertising, entertainment, promotions, or to individuals; also no support to/for public education or veterans, fraternal, labor, sectarian or religious organizations. Submit grant requests at any time in a letter or a brief proposal; include an audited financial statement and IRS tax-exempt status documentation. Applications are acknowledged but no interviews are granted. Matching gifts for colleges/universities, art museums, performing arts groups, history and science museums, public radio/TV, and hospitals have a $15 minimum; maximum matching gifts are $1,000/employee/institution/year for educational institutions and $500 for other organizations; the first $100 is matched 2:1; other conditions also apply. The Trustees award grants at meetings in March, June, September and December. — Formerly called ELF Atochem North America Foundation.

O+D+T Jane Crawford (Director+Con) — Bernard Azoulay (T) — Francis Lauchert, Jr. (T) — Peter J. McCarthy (T) — Robert F. Pellicari (T) — Corporate donor: Atofina Chemicals, Inc.

SE-035 **Auldridge Fund, The**
1225 Farview Road
Villanova 19085   (Montgomery County)

MI-11-112-3-22-32-41-42-55-62

Phone 610-525-3986 **FAX** None
EIN 23-2900851   **Year Created** 1997

AMV $1,532,238   **FYE** 12-00   **(Gifts Received** $549,923)   9 **Grants totaling** $348,000

About three-fourths local giving. High grant of **$148,000** to Jewish Federation of Greater Philadelphia. **$50,000** to Regional Performing Arts Center. **$25,000** each to United Way of SE Pa. (One to One/Mentoring Partnership) and U. of Pa. Wharton School. **$10,000** each to Haverford School and Jewish Family & Children's Service. **Out-of-state** grants: **$50,000** to Brown U. [RI]; **$20,000** to Johns Hopkins Oncology Center [MD]; and **$10,000** to Massachusetts Institute of Technology. ■**PUBLICATIONS:** None ■**WEBSITE:** None ■**E-MAIL:** None ■**APPLICATION POLICIES & PROCEDURES:** Information not available.

O+D+T Roy S. Neff (P+D+Donor+Con) — Rosalind S. Neff (S+D+Donor)

SE-036   **Avery Foundation**   MI-13-31-22-32-33-41-42-61
c/o Bil-Mar
110 Commerce Drive   **Phone** 215-855-4336 **FAX** None
Montgomeryville 18936   (Bucks County)   **EIN** 23-2647387   **Year Created** 1991
AMV $125,872   **FYE** 12-00   **(Gifts Received** $0)   20 **Grants totaling** $35,525

About two-thirds local giving. High grant of **$10,500** to YMCA of Philadelphia & Vicinity. **$9,000** to Friends Hospital. **$6,000** to Holy Family College. **$2,000-$2,500** to each Fox Chase Cancer Center, Gwynedd Mercy Academy, and PhAME/Philadelphia Area Accelerated Manufacturing Education, Inc. **$1,000** each to Catholic Social Services, Little Flower Catholic High School, Rosemont College, and St. Bridget Church. Other local contributions, **$25-$500. Out-of-state** giving includes **$10,000** to Pope John Paul II Foundation [Italy]. ■**PUBLICATIONS:** None ■**WEBSITE:** None ■**E-MAIL:** None ■**APPLICATION POLICIES & PROCEDURES:** Grant requests may be submitted in a letter at any time; include IRS tax-exempt status documentation. No grants awarded to individuals.

O+D+T William J. Avery (T+Donor+Con) — Sharon L. Avery (T) — Michele L. Clark (T)

SE-037   **Backe Foundation, Inc.**   MI-12-22-32-41-61
232 Walnut Road   **Phone** 610-688-3063 **FAX** None
Strafford 19087   (Chester County)   **EIN** 23-2876140   **Year Created** 1996
AMV $3,400,112   **FYE** 12-00   **(Gifts Received** $1,048,169)   7 **Grants totaling** $152,000

About two-thirds local giving. High grant of **$50,000** to Gesu School. **$30,000** to Make-A-Wish Foundation of Philadelphia & SE Pa. **$1,000** each to Catholic Charities and St. Paul's Church. **Out-of-state** giving includes **$30,000** each to Guadalupe Center [FL] and Ara Parseghian Medical Research Foundation [AZ]; and **$10,000** to Beta Theta Pi [OH]. ■**PUBLICATIONS:** None ■**WEBSITE:** None ■**E-MAIL:** None ■**APPLICATION POLICIES & PROCEDURES:** Information not available.

O+D+T John E. Backe (D+Con) — John D. Backe [NJ] (P+Donor+D) — Katherine A. Backe [NJ] (F+D) — Kimberly A. Marr [NJ] (S+D)

SE-038   **Bader (Michelle H. & David) Family Foundation**   MI-41-42-56-62
165 Geigel Hill Road, P.O. Box 242   **Phone** 610-294-9951 **FAX** None
Erwinna 18920   (Bucks County)   **EIN** 31-1496075   **Year Created** 1997
AMV $16,789   **FYE** 6-00   **(Gifts Received** $904)   6 **Grants totaling** $177,000

Mostly local giving. High grant of **$115,000** to Friends of Bridgeton School. **$30,000** to Kehilat Hanahar [New Hope]. **$10,000** each to Emunah of America [Philadelphia] and WSADRV [New Hope]. **$2,000** to Elfreth's Alley Assn. **Out-of-state** grant: **$10,000** to U. of Wisconsin-Milwaukee. ■**PUBLICATIONS:** None ■**WEBSITE:** None ■**E-MAIL:** None ■**APPLICATION POLICIES & PROCEDURES:** Information not available.

O+D+T Michelle Henkin Bader (T+Donor+Con) — David Bader (T+Donor)

SE-039   **Baker (Margaret) Memorial Fund**   MI-12-14-23-29
44 Galicia Drive   **Phone** 610-933-7548 **FAX** None
Phoenixville 19460   (Chester County)   **EIN** 23-6227403   **Year Created** 1957
AMV $593,873   **FYE** 12-00   **(Gifts Received** $2,548)   30+ **Grants totaling** $44,324

All giving is restricted to Phoenixville and immediate vicinity; no details on recent grants are available. — In prior years many grants of **$500** or smaller were awarded to day care centers, youth organizations, visiting nurse agencies, and other human service agencies, as well as modest stipends to individuals/families in distress, as stipulated below. ■**PUBLICATIONS:** None ■**WEBSITE:** None ■**E-MAIL:** None ■**APPLICATION POLICIES & PROCEDURES:** The Fund reports that giving is strictly limited to Phoenixville and immediate vicinity. Its primary purpose is to assist widows or single women over 30 years of age, and children under 14; other individuals or handicapped persons in financial distress are also considered. The Fund's secondary purpose is to support organizations in Phoenixville or immediate vicinity. Grant requests may be submitted in a letter at any time. Requests from individuals must include the age of the person(s) requesting assistance, disability or infirmity (if applicable), annual income, and supporting information such as the name of a social worker, doctor, minister, etc. who can verify the need for support, except when the Fund Committee is already familiar with the situation. Most grants are made in July and November, but interim emergency grants are considered.

O+D+T Gerald F. Moore (S+F+Con) — Mellon Bank N.A. (Trustee)

SE-040   **Ball Family Foundation**   MI-11-12-14-41-35-52-72-84
c/o American Manufacturing Corp.
555 Croton Road, Suite 300   **Phone** 610-962-3770 **FAX** None
King of Prussia 19406   (Montgomery County) **EIN** 51-6017780   **Year Created** 1965
AMV $678,890   **FYE** 12-00   **(Gifts Received** $0)   18 **Grants totaling** $200,950

Mostly local giving. High grant of **$113,500** to Haverford School. **$20,000** to Philadelphia Health Management Corp. (Resources for Children's Health). **$10,000** to United Way of SE Pa. **$5,250** to Baker Industries. **$3,000** to U.S. Squash Racquets Assn. **$2,000-$2,500** each to Academy of Music, American Cancer Society, and Philadelphia Zoo (zoobilee). **$1,500** to Philadelphia Orchestra. **$1,000** to Philadelphia Ronald McDonald House. Other smaller contributions. **Out-of-state** giving includes **$25,000** to Squashbusters, Inc. [MA](clubhouse campaign) and **$11,000** to Jewish Community Foundation of Baltimore [MD] (AIDS Outreach Fund). ■**PUBLICATIONS:** None ■**WEBSITE:** None ■**E-MAIL:** None ■**APPLICATION POLICIES & PROCEDURES:** Submit grant requests in a letter at any time; include IRS tax-exempt status documentation. — Formerly called the Russell C. Ball Foundation.

O+D+T Russell C. Ball, III (P+F+D+Con) — Andrew L. Ball (VP+D) — Gregory J. Kelemen (S+Administrator) — Robert H. Strouse (D) Corporate donors: Philadelphia Gear Corp.; American Manufacturing Corp.

SE-041 Ball (Wilbur) Foundation, The

c/o Herr, Potts & Herr
175 Strafford Ave., Suite 314
Wayne 19087 (Delaware County)

MI-11-31-41-42-56

Phone 610-254-0114 **FAX** None
EIN 23-7965324 **Year Created** 1998

AMV $1,337,326 **FYE** 12-00 **(Gifts Received** $0) 7 **Grants totaling** $65,134

About one-third local giving. High grant of **$25,000** to United Way of SE Pa. **$1,000** each to Academy of Music and Bryn Mawr Hospital. **$750** to Drexel U. Other smaller contributions. **Out-of-state** grants: **$21,000** to Vanderbilt U. [TN] and **$16,134** to Culver Academy Educational Foundation [IN]. — In prior year, **$35,000** to Harvard Business School [MA]. ■**PUBLICATIONS:** None ■**WEBSITE:** None ■**E-MAIL:** None ■**APPLICATION POLICIES & PROCEDURES:** Information not available.

O+D+T Alexander E. Wilson (T+Con) — Barbara B. Wilson [FL] (T+Donor) — J. Lawrence Wilson [FL] (T+Donor) — Lawrence B. Wilson [GA] (T)

SE-042 Balzereit (Betty & Leo) Foundation

c/o The Glenmede Trust Company
1650 Market Street, Suite 1200
Philadelphia 19103 (Philadelphia County)

MI-12-25-43-63

Phone 215-419-6000 **FAX** 215-419-6196
EIN 25-6655172 **Year Created** 1999

AMV $1,156,952 **FYE** 12-00 **(Gifts Received** $0) 4 **Grants totaling** $11,000

Two local grants: **$2,500** to White-Williams Scholars and **$1,500** to People's Emergency Center. **Out-of-state** grants: **$6,000** to First Presbyterian Church of Tequesta [FL] and **$1,000** to Prevent Child Abuse America [IL]. ■**PUBLICATIONS:** None ■ **WEBSITE:** None ■**E-MAIL:** None ■**APPLICATION POLICIES & PROCEDURES:** Information not available.

O+D+T Joseph J. Rink (1st VP at Trust Company+Con) — Leo G. Balzereit [Mount Joy] (T) — George C. Balzereit [FL] (T) — Jane Balzereit Gruson [CT] (T) The Glenmede Trust Company (Corporate Trustee)

SE-043 Bar-Nir Bergreen Foundation

896 Brushtown Road, P.O. Box 488
Gwynedd Valley 19437 (Montgomery County)

MI-22-31-42-62

Phone 215-619-4732 **FAX** None
EIN 23-3024104 **Year Created** 1999

AMV $384,243 **FYE** 12-00 **(Gifts Received** $0) 9 **Grants totaling** $30,666

All local giving. High grant of **$15,231** to Congregation Beth Or. **$12,800** to American Society for the Technion. **$1,000** to Abington Memorial Hospital. **$500** to Sharing is Caring. Other smaller local contributions. ■**PUBLICATIONS:** None ■**WEBSITE:** None ■**E-MAIL:** None ■**APPLICATION POLICIES & PROCEDURES:** Information not available.

O+D+T Zahava Bar-Nir (P+D+Donor+Con) — Karen Bar-Nir [NY] (S+D) — Anat B. Dubin [NC] (F+D) — Zvi Bergreen (D+Donor)

SE-044 Bard (Robert) Foundation

c/o Mellon Private Wealth Management
1735 Market Street, Room 193-0370
Philadelphia 19103 (Philadelphia County)

MI-11-12-13-14-15-39-41-44-52-55-56-72-84

Phone 215-553-2596 **FAX** 215-553-4542
EIN 23-6806099 **Year Created** 1989

AMV $4,689,968 **FYE** 6-00 **(Gifts Received** $0) 27 **Grants totaling** $472,007

All giving generally is limited to the area around Royersford [Montgomery County]. High grant of **$50,000** to Spring-Ford Historical Society (property purchase). **$15,000** to Spring City Legion Baseball Committee (lighting/seating). **$11,000** to YMCA of Phoenixville (CPR training equipment). **$10,000** each to Family Services of Montgomery County (Project Hearth), Pottstown Symphony Orchestra (program series), Royersford Community Chest (for redistribution), and Spring Ford Counseling Services (program support). **$9,000** to RSVP of Montgomery County (general support). **$7,500** to Project Outreach (emergency aid funds). **$5,000** each to Camphill Village-Kimberton (building maintenance), Freedom House (disabled facilities), Open Hearth, Sacred Heart Home & School Assn. (music books/equipment), Spring City Free Public Library (catalog replacement), and Spring-Ford Rescue (protective gear). **$4,500** to Make-A-Wish Foundation (underwrite local child). **$4,000** each to Easter Seal Society, and Royersford Public Library (collection improvements). **$3,000** each to Limerick Township Historical Society (bake house restoration) and St. Pius X High School (AV equipment purchase). **$2,000** each to Elmwood Park Zoo (signage), Frederick Mennonite Community (benevolent care fund), Spring-Ford Recreational Commission (concerts), and Schuylkill Canal Assn. (house restoration). **$1,000** each to Citizen Advocacy of Chester County (training expenses) and Community Music School (student assistance). ■**PUBLICATIONS:** None ■**WEBSITE:** None ■**E-MAIL:** smith.ft@mellon.com ■**APPLICATION POLICIES & PROCEDURES:** Giving is restricted first to organizations in Royersford, Montgomery County, Pa., then to any worthy area charity serving Royersford residents. Most grants are for general support, special projects, building funds and, on occasion, matching grants or multiple-year grants. No grants are awarded to individuals, or for scholarships, endowment, research, or publications. Grant requests may be submitted in a full proposal with cover letter during January-March (deadline is April 15th); briefly describe the organization and proposed project, and include project budget, audited financial statement, and IRS tax-exempt status documentation. Grants are awarded at a June meeting.

O+D+T Frances T. Smith (Portfolio Officer at Bank+Con) — Norman E. Donoghue, II, Esq. (T) Mellon Bank N.A. (Corporate Trustee)

SE-045 Barra Foundation, The
Suite 12
8200 Flourtown Ave.
Wyndmoor 19038 (Montgomery County)

MI-11-12-13-14-15-22-25-29-31-34-41-42-44
52-53-54-55-56-57-63-71-72-85
Phone 215-233-5115 **FAX** 215-836-1033
EIN 23-6277885 **Year Created** 1963

AMV $54,500,983 **FYE** 12-00 **(Gifts Received** $1,003) 286 **Grants totaling** $3,966,213

Mostly local giving; grants are for general purposes except as noted, and some grants comprise multiple awards. ***HEALTH-HU-MAN SERVICES GRANTS:*** **$202,500** to Chestnut Hill HealthCare (mostly for Emergency Room). **$74,233** to College of Physicians (computer installation). **$53,500** to Metropolitan Career Center (employment project). **$23,000** to Overington House (business plan). **$17,500** to Greater Philadelphia Urban Affairs Coalition (Blueprint Project). **$16,675** to ASPIRA of Philadelphia (summer youth education project). **$14,000-$15,000** to American Street Financial Services Center (manual), Executive Services Corps of the Delaware Valley (health care projects/general support), and Greater Philadelphia Federation of Settlements (summer youth education project). **$13,000** to Impact Services Corp. (summer youth education project). **$12,500** to United Way of SE Pa. **$10,000** to U. of Pa. Medical Center (Cancer Center/Bridging the Gap). **$7,500** to 18th Street Development Corp. **$5,000-$6,500** each to Baker Industries, Children's Country Week Assn., Episcopal Community Services, Make-A-Wish Foundation, People's Emergency Center, Red Cross (Chestnut Hill Division/youth program), Salvation Army, Travelers Aid Society, and Youth Services, Inc. (crisis nursery evaluation). **$2,000-$3,500** each to Bethesda Project, Big Brothers/Big Sisters Assn., Big Sisters of Philadelphia, Boys & Girls Clubs of Metropolitan Philadelphia, Camp Dreamcatcher, Center in the Park, Chestnut Hill Community Fund, Children's Hospital of Philadelphia Foundation, City Year Philadelphia, Contact CareLine Philadelphia, Domestic Abuse Project, Fellowship Farm, Fox Chase Cancer Center, Inn Dwelling, Institute on Aging (acute elderly care), Kelly Anne Dolan Memorial Fund, Lankenau Hospital Foundation, Living Beyond Breast Cancer, MANNA/Metropolitan AIDS Neighborhood Nutrition Alliance, North Light Community Center, One Day At A Time, Pa. Special Olympics, Philadelphia Citizens for Children & Youth, The Philadelphia Foundation, Philadelphia Senior Center, Polish American Social Services, Project H.O.M.E., Project Rainbow, Recording for the Blind & Dyslexic, Royer-Greaves School for the Blind, St. Christopher's Hospital for Children Foundation, SCAN/Supportive Child-Adult Network, Therapeutic Horseback Riding, Universal Center for Employment Training, Voyage House, Whosoever Gospel Mission, Wills Eye Hospital, Wissahickon Hospice, Wistar Institute, Wissinoming Presbyterian Church, YMCA of Germantown, and Youth Work Foundation of Union League. ***ARTS-CULTURE-ENVIRONMENT GRANTS:*** High grant of **$1,000,000** to Woodmere Art Museum (endowment for Curator of Education). **$552,500** to Library Company of Philadelphia (acquisition of early American imprints/retrospective conversion). **$512,500** to Philadelphia Museum of Art (mostly for Houdon bust of Benj. Franklin). **$87,925** to U. of Pa. Press (publications on Philadelphia Navy Yard, Historic Places of Worship, and Christ Church). **$71,873** to Academy of Natural Sciences (historic pamphlets/electronic data delivery/general support). **$57,500** to Athenaeum of Philadelphia (mostly for retroconversion project). **$45,000** to American Revolution Patriots Fund (Washington Square signage). **$29,932** to Temple U. Press (Philadelphia's Cultural Landscape publication). **$25,000** to Balch Institute for Ethnic Studies (mostly for Chautauqua Conferences). **$20,000** to Wissahickon Valley Watershed Assn. (land acquisition). **$12,500** each to Brandywine Valley Assn. (Watershed Learning Center), and Brandywine Workshop (Master Printer Education). **$9,600-$10,000** each to Moore College of Art (Sartain introduction/multicultural intern), Philadelphia Orchestra, and Philadelphia Zoo (Leadership Fund). **$7,500** each to Academy of Music, Opera Company of Philadelphia, Pa. Academy of the Fine Arts, Pa. Ballet, Philadanco, and WHYY. **$5,000-$6,000** each to Astral Artistic Services, Concerto Soloists, Philadelphia Chamber Music Society, Philadelphia Museum of Art/Women's Committee (Crafts Show), Please Touch Museum, and Settlement Music School. **$4,000** to Philadelphia Society for Preservation of Landmarks. **$2,000-$3,500** each to African American Museum of Philadelphia, American Theater Arts for Youth, Archives of American Art, Arden Theatre Company, Atwater Kent Museum, Awbury Arboretum Assn., Bach Festival of Philadelphia, The Clay Studio, Conservation Center for Art & Historic Artifacts, Creative Artists Network, Fabric Workshop, Fort Mifflin on the Delaware, Franklin Institute, Historic Bartram's Garden, Historical Society of Pa., Independence Seaport Museum, Main Line Art Center, Morris Arboretum, National Museum of American Jewish History, Opera North, Painted Bride Art Center, Pa. Horticultural Society, Philadelphia Singers, Philomel Concerts, Point Breeze Performing Arts Center, Prince Music Theater, The Print Center, Rosenbach Museum & Library, Singing City, Society Hill Playhouse (school programs), Strawberry Banke, Taller Puertorriqueno, University City Science Center (Esther Klein Gallery), University Museum of Archaeology & Anthropology, Village of Arts & Humanities, Walnut Street Theatre, Wilma Theatre, and Young Audiences of Eastern Pa. ***EDUCATION-CIVIC GRANTS:*** **$250,000** to National Constitution Center (educational exhibits). **$52,500** to American Philosophical Society (mostly for Fellowship). **$31,000** to Community College of Philadelphia (mostly for biotech development). **$30,000** to Temple U. (human services internship). **$22,500** to Germantown Academy (distance learning/general support). **$15,000** to Phillies Charities, Inc. (Phillies Phundamentals Education). **$13,092** to U. of Pa. (McNeil Center for Early American Studies-Publications/Student Conference). **$10,000** to Free Library of Philadelphia Foundation. **$7,500** to U. of the Sciences. **$5,000** each to Agnes Irwin School, Committee of Seventy, East Stroudsburg U. (American Revolution War Dept. papers), Springside School, and Stroud Water Research Center. **$3,750** to Gladwyne Montessori School. **$2,000-$2,500** each to Episcopal Academy, Foundation of St. Andrews Society of Philadelphia, Haverford School, Philadelphia Education Fund (College Access Program), Schuylkill Center for Environmental Education, Shipley School, Thomas Jefferson U., U. of the Arts, and William Penn Charter School. Also, 80+ grants of **$1,000-$1,500** awarded in the above categories. ***OUT-OF-STATE GRANTS*** include **$49,500** to Society of Architectural Historians [IL] (Buildings of Pa. publication); **$7,500** to Winterthur Museum [DE]; **$5,000** each to National Gallery of Art [DC], United Negro College Fund [VA], and U.S. Department of State (diplomatic reception rooms); and smaller grants for various purposes. ■**PUBLICATIONS:** statement of program policy; application form ■**WEBSITE:** None ■**E-MAIL:** None ■**APPLICATION POLICIES & PROCEDURES:** The Foundation reports most giving is restricted to Greater Philadelphia for human services (particularly inner-city problems), arts/culture, health, and education. In addition, projects in 18th Century American art and material culture are of special interest. In general, no support is given for budget deficits, endowment, capital campaigns (construction, equipment, renovation/repairs), exhibitions or catalogues, international programs or institutions, or individual scholarships/fellowships. Only single-year grants are awarded. Preliminary grant requests may be submitted at any time in a letter (two-page maximum) at any time; briefly describe the organization, its history, the proposed project and funding requested; include organizational/project budgets, Board member list, list of other funding sources, and IRS tax-exempt status documentation. If the Foundation is interested, a formal application form will be provided for completion. Grant applications are acknowledged but interviews are not arranged. The Board meets in November and as necessary; the usual waiting period for a decision on a grant request is three to six months.

O+D+T William Harral, III (P+D+Con) — Robert L. McNeil, Jr. (C+F+D) — Herman R. Hutchinson (VP+D) — Frank R. Donahue, Jr., Esq. (S+D) — Harry E. Cerino (D) — Robert P. Hauptfuhrer (D) — Joanna M. Lewis (D) — Victoria M. Le Vine (D) — Collin F. McNeil (D) — Robert L. McNeil, III (D) — Seymour S. Preston, III (D) — Lowell S. Thomas, Jr. Esq. (D)

SE-046   Barrack Foundation, The
930 Rock Creek Road
Bryn Mawr   19010   (Montgomery County)
AMV $934,350   **FYE** 11-00   **(Gifts Received** $350,156)

MI-11-22-32-42-62
Phone 215-963-0600 **FAX** None
EIN 23-2084461   **Year Created** 1978
33 **Grants totaling** $306,287

About two-thirds local giving. High grant of **$129,162** to Temple Beth Israel. **$30,678** to Jewish Federation of Greater Philadelphia. **$10,000** to United Way of SE Pa. **$8,222** to Har Zion Temple. **$5,000** each to American Friends of Hebrew U. and Gerda & Kurt Klein Foundation. **$3,500** to Champions of Caring. **$3,000** to Jewish Community Centers of Greater Philadelphia. **$1,000-$1,500** each to Abrahamson Family Cancer Research Institute, Beth Solomon, Camp Gan Israel, Golden Yarmulka Youth Campaign, and Temple U. Law School (Reinstein Scholarship). Other smaller local contributions. **Out-of-state** giving includes **$100,000** to William J. Clinton Presidential Foundation [AR]. ■**PUBLICATIONS:** None ■**WEBSITE:** None ■**E-MAIL:** None ■ **APPLICATION POLICIES & PROCEDURES:** Submit grant requests in a letter at any time. No grants awarded to individuals.

O+D+T Leonard Barrack, Esq. (Manager+Donor+Con)

SE-047   Bartol (Stockton Rush) Foundation, The
The Belgravia, Suite 301
1811 Chestnut Street
Philadelphia   19103   (Philadelphia County)
AMV $5,805,190   **FYE** 9-01   **(Gifts Received** $30,000)

MI-51-52-53-54-55-56-57
Phone 215-557-7225 **FAX** 215-557-7316
EIN 23-2318470   **Year Created** 1984
41 **Grants totaling** $243,000

All giving for arts/cultural purposes in Philadelphia; grants are for general operating support except as noted. High grants of **$10,000** each to Clay Studio (outreach program), Mural Arts Program/Recreation Dept., Philadelphia Dance Company, Philadelphia Fringe Festival (festival), Southwest Community Enrichment Center (community art project/Bartol Award), and Taller Puertorriqueno (education program). **$8,000** each to Sedgwick Music School (children-youth programs), Settlement Music School (preschool enrichment program). **$7,000** each to Asian Arts Initiative, Headlong Dance Theatre (dance camp/seasonal support), Philadelphia Folklore Project (multicultural education project, Philadelphia Young Playwrights Festival, Prince Music Theater (educational programs), Rosenbach Museum & Library (young adults 'Zine publication), and Tyler School of Art (Artworks in Different Places). **$6,000** each to Eastern College (Germantown summer theatre camp), Philadelphia Museum of Art (Art2002 Collaboration), and SCRAP Performance Group (The Collaboratory Project). **$5,000** each to American Composers Forum (residencies), Arden Theatre Company (children's theatre), Big Picture Alliance, Fabric Workshop & Museum (education programs), Freedom Theatre (performing arts training program), Institute of Contemporary Art (collaborative exhibition), Network for New Music (new works/educational outreach), Nexus/Foundation for Today's Art, Painted Bride Art Center (educational-community programs), Pa. Academy of the Fine Arts (school visits), Pa. Ballet (dance education program), Philadelphia Arts in Education Partnership (public school mini-grants), Philadelphia Volunteer Lawyers for the Arts, Singing City (director salary), Spiral Q Puppet Theatre (education initiative), Temple U. Music Preparatory Division (Center for Gifted Young Musicians), Theatre Catalyst, Wilma Theatre (in school program), and YWCA of Germantown (children's art program). **$1,000** each to American Ballet Competition/Dance Affiliates, Jeanne Ruddy Dance, Moore College of Art Gallery, The Philadelphia Foundation (conference), and Print Center. — In the prior year, larger grants included **$10,000** each to Fleisher Art Memorial (public school artist residencies) and Point Breeze Performing Arts Center (community access project); and **$7,500** each to Asociacion de Musicos Latino Americanos (develop 3-year plan), Opera Company of Philadelphia (Sound of Learning program), Philadelphia Theatre Company (outreach programs), and Village of Arts & Humanities (outreach programs). ■**PUBLICATIONS:** statement of program policy; application guidelines; Proposal Summary Form ■**WEBSITE:** www.bartol.org ■**E-MAIL:** info@bartol.org ■**APPLICATION POLICIES & PROCEDURES:** The Foundation reports that giving focuses on supporting exemplary arts/cultural organizations (both new and emerging) in Philadelphia to help ensure a vibrant cultural life for all of its citizens. Grants are made for general operating support or special projects. Higher priority is given to organizations or projects that: (1) serve children through arts education programs that promote social and educational development; and/or (2) serve communities by providing broader access at the neighborhood level to high-quality arts experiences; and/or (3) serve the arts community by supporting cultural organizations at critical junctures in their artistic or organizational development. In addition, support is given to expand or diversify audiences; support individual artists in the production, exhibition or distribution of their work; support the creation of new work; or, provide services to the broad cultural community. No support is given for programs presented outside of the City of Philadelphia; requests by organizations located outside of the five-county Philadelphia area; capital requests—except as part of historic preservation efforts; grants to individuals; or grants to organizations for religious or political purposes. Prospective applicants should first obtain the detailed application guidelines and the required Proposal Summary Form—available on the website, or contact the Foundation. Grant requests should be submitted during March-April; deadline is May 1st. Grants are awarded at a June meeting and grantees notified in July.

O+D+T Beth Feldman Brandt (Executive Director+Con) — Lise Yasui (C+T) — Jo-Anna Moore (S+T) — Margaret Sager (F+T) — Abigail Adams (T) — Joan Myers Brown (T) — Valerie Clayton (T) — Dana Hall (T) — Roko Kawai (T) — Cheryl McClenney-Brooker (T) — June O'Neill (T) — Susan Terrell Saunders (T) — Blair MacInnes (Advisor)

SE-048 **Baruch (Richard F.) Private Foundation, The**
25 North Buck Lane, Unit 1
Haverford   19041   (Montgomery County)

MI-41-42-57-84
Phone 215-665-6604 **FAX** None
EIN 23-2903488   **Year Created** 1997

AMV $332,339   **FYE** 12-00   **(Gifts Received** $840)   2 **Grants totaling** $10,439

All local giving: **$7,439** to Camp Tecumseh (Blue-Grey Fund) and **$3,000** to The Crossroads School. — Other giving in prior years included **$9,548** to U. of VA and **$3,405** to WHYY-TV12. ■**PUBLICATIONS:** None ■**WEBSITE:** None ■**E-MAIL:** None ■ **APPLICATION POLICIES & PROCEDURES:** Information not available.

O+D+T   Richard F. Baruch (P+S+F+D+Donor+Con) — David G. Baruch (VP+D) — Mary C. Baruch (VP+D) — Richard F. Baruch, Jr. (VP+D) — Rodney G. Day (VP+D)

SE-049 **Basic Cutaneous Research, The Foundation for**
210 West Rittenhouse Square, #3302
Philadelphia   19103   (Philadelphia County)

MI-11-32-34-42-54-55-57
Phone 215-898-3234 **FAX** None
EIN 23-2439001   **Year Created** 1986

AMV $2,194,955   **FYE** 7-00   **(Gifts Received** $463,000)   26 **Grants totaling** $97,775

About two-thirds local/Pa. giving. High grant of **$56,000** to College of Physicians of Philadelphia (mostly for library fund). **$7,500** to United Way. **$5,000** to Regional Performing Arts Center. **$1,000** each to Penn State U./Friends of Palmer Museum and WHYY-TV12. Other smaller local contributions for various purposes. **Out-of-state** giving includes **$8,500** to U. of Arizona; **$5,000** each to Cutaneous Biological Fund and Photobiological Foundation [DC]; and **$1,000** to Business Leaders for Sensible Priorities [NY]. ■**PUBLICATIONS:** None ■**WEBSITE:** None ■**E-MAIL:** None ■**APPLICATION POLICIES & PROCEDURES:** The Foundation reports that only requests for dermatological research will be accepted. Submit written proposals at any time which detail the specific nature of the research and funding requested. Site visits sometimes are made to organizations being considered for a grant.

O+D+T   Lorraine H. Kligman, Ph.D. (P+S+Donor+Con) — Albert M. Kligman, M.D. (Donor) Corporate donors: Ajinmoto U.S.A., Clairol-Gelb Foundation; Hoechst Company; Johnson & Johnson Baby Products; Lever Brothers; Medicis; Ortho Pharmaceutical/Dermatologic Division; The Upjohn Co.

SE-050 **Bass (William) Charitable Foundation**
101 Cheswold Lane, #4D
Haverford   19041   (Montgomery County)

MI-22-51-56-62
Phone 610-649-1663 **FAX** None
EIN 23-2339056   **Year Created** 1984

AMV $455,998   **FYE** 11-00   **(Gifts Received** $0)   7 **Grants totaling** $25,500

About one-third local giving. High Pa. grant of **$6,000** to Jewish Federation of Greater Philadelphia. **$2,500** to Farmers' Market Trust. **$1,000** to The Irish Memorial. **$500** to National Organization on Hearing. **Out-of-state** giving include **$8,000** to Jewish Fund for Justice [NY]; **$5,000** to Carolina Ballet [NC]; and **$2,500** to School of American Ballet [NY]. ■**PUBLICATIONS:** None ■**WEBSITE:** None ■**E-MAIL:** None ■**APPLICATION POLICIES & PROCEDURES:** Information not available.

O+D+T   Rosalind B. Bass (P+Donor+Con) — Robert S. Bass, Esq. [Philadelphia] (VP) — Jerome Bass, M.D. [MA] (S)

SE-051 **Baxter (Harold) Foundation**
P.O. Box 916
Bryn Mawr   19010   (Montgomery County)

MI-63-72
Phone 610-525-1013 **FAX** None
EIN 23-1628244   **Year Created** 1955

AMV $434,411   **FYE** 12-00   **(Gifts Received** $0)   24 **Grants totaling** $22,600

About one-quarter local giving. High grant of **$3,500** to St. Martin's Church of Radnor. **$1,000** to Arboretum of Barnes Foundation. Other smaller local contributions. **Out-of-state** giving, primarily to Palm Beach, FL and Hilton Head, SC, for cultural, human services and other purposes. ■**PUBLICATIONS:** None ■**WEBSITE:** None ■**E-MAIL:** None ■**APPLICATION POLICIES & PROCEDURES:** Information not available.

O+D+T   Elizabeth Baxter Michell [Radnor] (S+Con) — Samuel B. Wheeler [Devon] (P) — Henry F. Michell [Radnor] (VP) — Martha D. Baxter [FL] (F)

SE-052 **Beach Foundation, The**
c/o Beach Investment Counsel, Inc.
3 Radnor Corporate Center, Suite 410
Radnor   19087   (Delaware County)

MI-11-29-31-52-71-84-86
Phone 610-225-1100 **FAX** None
EIN 23-2897351   **Year Created** 1997

AMV $2,261,655   **FYE** 12-00   **(Gifts Received** $0)   17 **Grants totaling** $89,990

About one-fifth local giving. High local grant of **$10,000** to United Way of SE Pa. **$5,000** to Bryn Mawr Rehab Hospital. **$500** each to Academy of Vocal Arts and Red Cross. **Out-of-state** giving includes **$51,715** to Squam Lakes Assn. [NH]; **$10,000** to International Lawn Tennis Club [NY]; **$5,000** to AmeriCares [CT]; **$1,000** to Manhattan Institute for Policy Research [NY]; and other grants/contributions, many to NH. ■**PUBLICATIONS:** None ■**WEBSITE:** None ■**E-MAIL:** None ■**APPLICATION POLICIES & PROCEDURES:** Grant requests may be submitted in a letter at any time; describe the nature of the charitable organization and include IRS tax-exempt status documentation.

O+D+T   Thomas E. Beach (P+D+Donor+Con) — Walter T. Beach (VP+D) — Jonathan T. Beach (S+D) — Theodore T. Beach (F+D)

SE-053 Beans (Fred W.) Charitable Foundation   MI-13-25-29-54-55-56-63-84
c/o Fred Beans Ford
3960 Airport Boulevard   **Phone** 215-345-8270 **FAX** None
Doylestown 18901   (Bucks County)   **EIN** 23-2670159   **Year Created** 1992
AMV $1,703   **FYE** 12-00   (**Gifts Received** $97,550)   81 **Grants totaling** $110,426

All local giving; grants are for general purposes except as noted. High grant of **$40,000** to Central Bucks Family YMCA. **$17,956** to Michener Art Museum. **$11,816** to Doylestown Township First Night Committee (cultural event). **$7,000-$7,205** each to Central Bucks Chamber of Commerce and Doylestown Presbyterian Church. **$2,600** to Boy Scouts/Bucks County Council. **$1,000-$1,500** each to Buckingham Township (Hansel Park renovations), Bucks County Historical Society, Doylestown Township Oktoberfest Committee (cultural event), and Habitat for Humanity of Greater Bucks. **$750-$952** each to Bucks County Intermediate Unit, Children's Hospital of Philadelphia Foundation, Our Lady of the Sacred Heart Church, Robert Winters Fund, and Tinicum Polo Club. Other contributions **$25-$600** for many types of local community organizations/activities. ■ **PUBLICATIONS:** None ■ **WEBSITE:** None ■ **E-MAIL:** None ■ **APPLICATION POLICIES & PROCEDURES:** No grants awarded to individuals.
O+D+T Fred W. Beans (P+D+Donor+Con) — Patrick Clayton (D) — Mark Donahue (D) — Elizabeth Beans Gilbert (D) — Jennifer B. Keiser (D) — Brian Nesbitt (D)

SE-054 Beatty (Helen D. Groome) Trust   MI-12-13-14-15-16-17-18-22-25-29-31-32-41
c/o Mellon Private Wealth Management   42-49-51-52-53-53-54-55-71-85
1735 Market Street, Room 193-0314   **Phone** 215-553-2517 **FAX** 215-553-2054
Philadelphia 19103   (Philadelphia County)   **EIN** 23-6224798   **Year Created** 1948
AMV $13,530,406   **FYE** 9-00   (**Gifts Received** $0)   90 **Grants totaling** $557,812

All giving restricted to the five-county Philadelphia area for specific capital projects. High grants of **$25,000** each to Congreso de Latinos Unidos and University City District. **$20,000** each to Jewish Federation of Greater Philadelphia, Regional Performing Arts Center, and Secretariat for Catholic Human Services. **$15,000** each to James Michener Art Museum, Natural Lands Trust, and Philadanco. **$12,500** to Gwynedd Mercy College. **$10,000** each to Atwater-Kent Museum, Bala Presbyterian Home, Boy Scouts/Cradle of Liberty Council, Curtis Institute of Music, Holy Family College, Opera Company of Philadelphia, Ophthalmic Research Associates, Philadelphia OIC, Wagner Free Institute of Science, and Westtown School. **$7,000-$7,500** each to Abington YMCA, African-American Museum of Philadelphia, American Swedish Historical Museum, Junior Achievement of Delaware Valley, Main Line Art Center, Mount Pleasant-Four Counties Garden Club, and White-Williams Scholars. **$6,012** to Brandywine Conservancy. **$5,000** each to Academy of Vocal Arts, Children's Seashore House, College of Physicians of Philadelphia, Crime Prevention Assn., Delco Blind/Sight Center, Domestic Violence Center of Chester County, Drexel U., Easter Seals, Fair Hill Burial Ground, Fox Chase Cancer Center, Friends Rehabilitation Program, Greater Philadelphia Food Bank, Habitat for Humanity-Germantown, Institute for Cancer Research, Melmark, Norris Square Neighborhood Project, Overbrook School for the Blind, Painted Bride Art Center, Philadelphia Boys Choir & Chorale, Philadelphia Shakespeare Festival, Planned Parenthood of Chester County, Planned Parenthood of SE Pa., Point Breeze Federation, Rosenbach Museum & Library, Sleighton School, SOWN/Supportive Older Women's Network, Woods Services Foundation, and WYBE-TV. **$4,000** each to Carr School/Mt. Pleasant Chapel, Eastern College, and St. Joseph's Villa. **$3,000-$3,600** each to Awbury Arboretum, Bryn Mawr Rehab, Colonial Theatre, Episcopal Community Services, Kearsley Retirement Community, Manor Junior College, North Light Community Center, RSVP of Montgomery County, Sedgwick Cultural Center, VNA-Community Services of Montgomery County, and Williamson Free School of Mechanical Trades. **$2,000-$2,500** each to Chestnut Hill Hospital, Community Music School, Congregation Or Shalom, Don Guanella Village, Goshen Friends School, Great Valley Nature Center, Jubilee School, Ken-Crest Services, Kids' Smiles, Lakeside Youth Service, Plymouth Meeting Friends School, PEP/Programs Employing People, Royer-Greaves School for the Blind, Sebastian Riding Associates, Silver Springs-Martin Luther School, Stagecrafters, Warwick Township Historical Society (Moland House), and YWCA of Chester. **$1,500** to Nexus. Also, a special and recurring annual grant—an exception to established guidelines—of **$25,000** is disbursed to the Student Welfare Council. ■ **PUBLICATIONS:** Information & Proposal Guidelines memorandum ■ **WEBSITE:** None ■ **E-MAIL:** morse.g@mellon.com ■ **APPLICATION POLICIES & PROCEDURES:** Only nonprofit organizations located in Philadelphia, or in Bucks, Chester, Delaware, or Montgomery county are eligible to apply. Grants are awarded for health, social concerns, education, and the arts—generally in that order of priority. Grants are awarded only for Capital Projects, usually for building purchase/construction, major/minor renovations, and some types of equipment. However, only rarely are grants awarded for general office equipment, recording equipment, recreational equipment, musical instruments, or office furnishings. Support for vehicles/vans is considered only if transportation is an organization's primary function. No grants are awarded to individuals. Ordinarily, grants of up to $10,000 only are considered, although grants up to $25,000 will be considered if is a two-tier plan with a project request under $10,000 is proposed. Grant requests must be submitted in a full proposal during May-September (deadline is September 15th) which includes a summary sheet briefly describing the request; total cost of project; name/address of contact person; detailed explanation of project with breakdown of costs and reason for undertaking the project at this time; and a brief statement of organizational purpose and history. Also include an annual report; board member list; organization budget; most recent audited financial statement; list of all major funding sources, not just those related to the current project; and IRS tax-exempt status documentation issued since 1969. Grants are awarded by the Charitable Trust Committee at a meeting in November-December. Within a year of receipt of a grant, the project must be completed and a report submitted indicating that the funds were used for the purpose granted. Organizations cannot submit a new proposal until two years after the date of a grant, or until two years after the report is received, if not submitted within the year.
O+D+T Gail Curtis Morse (VP at Bank+Con) — Mellon Bank N.A. (Trustee)

SE-055   Bell (Vincent & Elaine) Foundation
7007 Lafayette Ave.
Fort Washington   19034
                                (Montgomery County)

MI-12-13-14-17-22-25-29-31-32-35-41-42-54
71-72
Phone 215-643-7205 **FAX** None
EIN 23-2384942   **Year Created** 1985

AMV $3,410,195   **FYE** 12-00   **(Gifts Received** $0)   73 **Grants totaling** $222,650

Mostly local giving. High grant of **$26,000** to Community Volunteers in Medicine. **$25,000** each to Anti-Defamation League and The Philadelphia Foundations (Health Advocates for the Uninsured Fund). **$20,500** to MANNA/Metropolitan AIDS Neighborhood Nutrition Alliance. **$10,000** to Paoli Memorial Hospital. **$5,000-$5,500** each to City Year of Greater Philadelphia, George School, Hepatitis B Foundation, Maternity Care Coalition, National MS Society, University Museum, and Wistar Institute (Taxin Brain Tumor Research Center). **$3,000** each to American Friends Service Committee, Education for Parenting, Lehigh U., National Organization for Hearing Research, and Philadelphia Museum of Art. **$2,000-$2,900** each to Baker Industries, The Baldwin School, Boy Scouts/Cradle of Liberty Council, Episcopal Academy, Fox Chase Cancer Center, Nightingale Awards of Pa., Ryerss Farm for Aged Equines, Upper Darby High School, and Wissahickon Valley Watershed Assn. **$1,000-$1,500** each to Academy of Natural Sciences, Charter High School for Architecture & Design, Chester Community Center, Endow-A-Home, Franklin Institute, Free Library of Philadelphia, Leukemia & Lymphoma Society, Main Line Art Center, Metropolitan Career Center, Montgomery County SPCA, National Conference on Community & Justice, Natural Lands Trust, The Nature Conservancy/Pa., Philadelphia Orchestra, Philadelphia Zoo, Recording for the Blind & Dyslexic, and Wheels, Inc. Other smaller local contributions for similar purposes. **Out-of-state** giving includes **$3,000** to World Wildlife Fund [DC] and smaller grants, primarily to AK, for human service organizations. ■**PUBLICATIONS:** Informational brochure; grants list ■**WEBSITE:** None ■**E-MAIL:** EVBfoundation@aol.com ■ **APPLICATION POLICIES & PROCEDURES:** The Foundation reports that most grants are for building/renovation, capital campaigns, general support, land acquisition, and research. No grants awarded to individuals. The Board meets in June and November.
O+D+T Marguerite Bell Knysh (Executive Director+T+Con) — Vincent G. Bell, Jr. [Radnor] (P+T+Donor) — Elaine V. Bell [Radnor] (F+Donor+T) — Scott Bell (T) — Amy Bell Brody (T)

SE-056   Beneficia Foundation
c/o Pitcairn Trust Company
3000 Pitcairn Place, 165 Township Line Road
Jenkintown   19046   (Montgomery County)

MI-12-35-51-52-54-55-56-71-72-79-83

Phone 215-887-6700 **FAX** 215-881-6092
EIN 24-6015630   **Year Created** 1953

AMV $18,197,264   **FYE** 4-00   **(Gifts Received** $0)   43 **Grants totaling** $1,377,000

About two-thirds local giving. High grant of **$475,000** to Philadelphia Society of the Lord's New Church (Swedenborgian). **$40,000** to Philadelphia Museum of Art. **$35,000** to Academy of Vocal Arts. **$30,000** each to Clean Air Council of Philadelphia and Visiting Nurses Assn. of Greater Philadelphia. **$28,000** to Academy of the New Church (Swedenborgian). **$25,000** each to Opera Company of Philadelphia and Regional Performing Arts Center. **$20,000** to Wildlife Preservation International Trust. **$15,000** each to 10,000 Friends of Pa., Abington Art Center, Kardon Institute of the Arts, Philadelphia Chamber Music Society, and The Wilma Theatre. **$10,000** each to Bucks County Symphony, Lenape Chamber Ensemble, The Nature Conservancy/Pa., Pa. Horticultural Society, Rosenbach Museum & Library, and Settlement Music School. **$7,000** to Hawk Mountain Sanctuary. **Out-of-state** giving includes **$75,000** to Center to Prevent Handgun Violence [DC]; **$56,000** to Southern Poverty Law Center [AL]; **$55,000** to NY Botanical Garden; **$51,000** to Oxfam America [MA]; **$30,000** to Center for Marine Conservation [DC]; and **$10,000-$25,000** for environmental, conservation, zoos, and Native American organizations in many states. ■**PUBLICA-TIONS:** informational brochure with application guidelines ■**WEBSITE:** None ■**E-MAIL:** None ■**APPLICATION POLICIES & PROCEDURES:** The Foundation reports that it favors small, innovative projects with limited alternative sources of support in two programmatic areas: (1) Conservation of the environment through inventory, protection, and stewardship of high priority ecosystems (especially tropical and marine); creation of economic incentives for the conservation of biodiversity; and policy/legislation. (2) Promotion of the performing arts (especially classical music, theatre and opera) and the visual arts (especially museums and art centers). Specific project support is favored over general support; no scholarships or grants are awarded to individuals. Submit requests which focus on one of the two stated programmatic areas during the August-January period (deadline is January 31st) and directed to either the Arts Committee or Environment Committee. A completed application (10 pages maximum) should include a one-page project summary; a brief proposal covering project description/objectives, expected outcomes, and timetable; a complete budget showing project expenses, committed sources of funding, and a specific amount requested; qualifications of key personnel involved with the project; and IRS tax-exempt status documentation. The Board of Directors meets in May and grantees are notified by May 31st; no response is sent if an organization is not approved for a grant.
O+D+T Feodor U. Pitcairn (Executive Secretary+D+Donor) — Laren Pitcairn (P+D+Donor+Chair, Arts Committee) — J. Daniel Mitchell, Jr. (VP+D+Chair, Environment Committee) — Mark J. Pennink (F+D) — Diene Pitcairn Duncan (D+Donor) — Mirian Pitcairn Mitchell (D+Donor) — Eshowe P. Pennink (D) — Kirstin O. Pitcairn (D) — Mary Eleanor Pitcairn (D) — Sharon R. Pitcairn (D) — Heather C. Reynolds (D)

SE-057   Bentley Foundation
c/o Bentley Developers, Inc.
1595 Paoli Road
West Chester   19380   (Chester County)

MI-12-13-21-22-25-32-72

Phone 610-436-5500 **FAX** 610-431-3813
EIN 23-2792411   **Year Created** 1994

AMV $18,165   **FYE** 12-00   **(Gifts Received** $0)   38 **Grants totaling** $21,395

Mostly local giving. High grant of **$3,200** to Habitat for Humanity of North Central Philadelphia. **$2,000** to Kiwanis Foundation of Philadelphia. **$1,000-$1,200** each to Make-A-Wish Foundation of Philadelphia, Maternal & Child Health Consortium, and Philadelphia Zoo. **$750** each to Adoption Center of Delaware Valley and Greater Philadelphia Food Bank. Other local contributions **$25-$500** for health/human services, education, environmental and other purposes. **Out-of-state** grant: **$1,000** to Covenant House [NY]. ■**PUBLICATIONS:** None ■**WEBSITE:** www.bentleyhomes.com [corporate info only] ■**E-MAIL:** None ■**APPLICATION POLICIES & PROCEDURES:** Grant requests may be submitted in any form at any time.

O+D+T Thomas G.M. Bentley (T+Donor+Con) — Mitchell Reddy [Wayne] (T)

SE-058	**Berdan Support Fund**		**MI**-61-43-64
	2 Cedarwood Lane		**Phone** 610-388-1667 **FAX** None
	Mendenhall 19357	(Chester County)	**EIN** 23-2746616 **Year Created** 1995

AMV $325,264 **FYE** 12-99 (**Gifts Received** $30,500) 26 **Grants totaling** $13,000

Most grants are for seminarians who primarily attend major Roman Catholic seminaries, e.g., St. Charles Borromeo Seminary [Wynnewood]; awards are **$300** or **$600. Out-of-state** grant: **$3,000** to Mopkin Abbey [SC]. ■**PUBLICATIONS:** None ■**WEBSITE:** None ■**E-MAIL:** None ■**APPLICATION POLICIES & PROCEDURES:** Grant requests may be submitted in a letter at any time; explain the requested amount and its intended purpose.

O+D+T John D. Sheridan (P+Donor+Con) — Annamae Sheridan (S+F+Donor) — Daniel P. Dougherty (D) — Theresa Venello (D)

SE-059	**Berger (David) Foundation**		**MI**-42-54-55-82-84
	c/o Berger & Montague, P.C.		
	1622 Locust Street		**Phone** 215-875-3030 **FAX** None
	Philadelphia 19103	(Philadelphia County)	**EIN** 23-6424659 **Year Created** 1967

AMV $2,058,301 **FYE** 12-00 (**Gifts Received** $500,000) 23 **Grants totaling** $248,615

One Pa. grant: **$20,000** to U. of Pa. **Out-of-state** giving includes **$100,000** to The Duke of Edinburgh's Award International Foundation [England]; **$35,790** to International Tennis Hall of Fame [RI]; **$15,000** each to Society of the Four Arts [FL] and U.S. Holocaust Memorial Museum [DC]; and smaller grants/contributions, many to Palm Beach, FL area. ■**PUBLICATIONS:** None ■**WEBSITE:** None ■**E-MAIL:** None ■**APPLICATION POLICIES & PROCEDURES:** Submit grant requests in a letter at any time. No grants awarded to individuals. — Formerly called the David & Harriet Berger Foundation.

O+D+T David Berger, Esq. (P+Donor+Con)

SE-060	**Berger (Harold & Renee) Foundation**		**MI**-22-42-52-54-62
	1703 Rittenhouse Square		**Phone** 215-875-3000 **FAX** None
	Philadelphia 19103	(Philadelphia County)	**EIN** 23-2439490 **Year Created** 1986

AMV $823,388 **FYE** 12-00 (**Gifts Received** $0) 62 **Grants totaling** $163,095

Mostly local giving. High grant of **$70,900** to U. of Pa. **$27,000** to Federation Allied Jewish Appeal. **$25,000** to Germantown Jewish Center. **$12,000** to National Museum of American Jewish History. **$10,193** to Jewish Federation of Greater Philadelphia. **$7,305** to HIAS & Council Migration Services of Philadelphia. **$5,198** to Congregation Beth Am Israel. **$1,082** to Philadelphia Orchestra. **$1,000** to Philadelphia Bar Foundation. Other smaller local and out-of-state contributions for various purposes. ■**PUBLICATIONS:** None ■**WEBSITE:** None ■**E-MAIL:** None ■**APPLICATION POLICIES & PROCEDURES:** Grant requests may be submitted in a letter at any time. No grants awarded to individuals.

O+D+T Harold Berger, Esq. [FL] (P+Donor+Con) — Renee Berger [FL] (VP)

SE-061	**Bergson-Kook (Betty) Memorial Foundation**		**MI**-12-31-32-82
	c/o Yampolsky Mandeloff Silver & Co.		
	1420 Walnut Street, Suite 200		**Phone** 215-545-4800 **FAX** 215-545-4810
	Philadelphia 19102	(Philadelphia County)	**EIN** 23-7000127 **Year Created** 1968

AMV $680,250 **FYE** 12-00 (**Gifts Received** $0) 20 **Grants totaling** $26,300

No Pa. giving. **Out-of-state** giving includes **$10,000** to Institute for Mediterranean Affairs [NY]; **$5,000** each to Beilenson Hospital (Dept. of Neurology) [Israel] and Hadassah U. Hospital [Israel]; and **$3,000** to Kupat Holim Leumit [Israel]. ■**PUBLICATIONS:** None ■**WEBSITE:** None ■**E-MAIL:** None ■**APPLICATION POLICIES & PROCEDURES:** The Foundation reports that grants are awarded for research and medical & family assistance to established agencies. Grant requests in any form may be submitted at any time. Grants are awarded at a June meeting.

O+D+T Jack Yampolsky (T+Con) — Astra Bergson-Kook (T) — Rebecca Bergson-Kook (T) — Nili Kook (T) — Philip Yampolsky (T)

SE-062	**Berkowitz (Edwin J. & Barbara R.) Family Foundation**		**MI**-22-31-41-42-62-64-82
	506 Oak Terrace		**Phone** 610-664-8335 **FAX** None
	Merion Station 19066	(Montgomery County)	**EIN** 23-7978506 **Year Created** 1998

AMV $276,902 **FYE** 12-99 (**Gifts Received** $353,853) 17 **Grants totaling** $154,375

About two-thirds local/Pa. giving. High grant of **$53,000** to Har Zion Temple. **$25,000** to The Ellis School [Pittsburgh] (capital campaign). **$10,000** to U. of Pa. **$5,000** to Center for Judaic Studies. **$2,500** to Perelman Jewish Day School. **$1,000-$1,275** each to American Committee for Shaare Zedek Hospital, American-Israel Chamber of Commerce Foundation, and MossRehab Hospital. **Out-of-state** giving includes **$25,000** to American Friends of Aish Hatorah [NJ]; **$10,000** to P.E.F. Israel Endowment Funds; **$9,600** to American Friends of WUJS Institute [NJ]; and **$5,000** to Jewish Theological Seminary of America [NY].■ **PUBLICATIONS:** None ■**WEBSITE:** None ■**E-MAIL:** None ■**APPLICATION POLICIES & PROCEDURES:** Written grant requests may be submitted to a Managing Trustee at any time; describe the organization and purpose of the requested funds and include IRS tax-exempt status documentation.

O+D+T Edwin J. Berkowitz (Managing Trustee+Con) — Barbara R. Berkowitz (Managing Trustee) — Alan Berkowitz (T) — Arthur M. Berkowitz (T) — Daniel M. Berkowitz (T) — Pnina B. Siegler (T)

SE-063 **Berman Charitable Foundation**
 3277 West Ridge Pike, P.O. Box 957
 Pottstown   19464   (Montgomery County)

MI-41-43-62
Phone 610-495-7166 **FAX** None
EIN 23-6239058   **Year Created** 1952

AMV $370,839   **FYE** 3-00   **(Gifts Received** $0)   2 **Grants totaling** $1,500

$1,000 to Temple Brith Achim (building fund). **$500** to St. Timothy's School [MD] (annual giving). — Giving in the prior year included **$11,000** to The Hill School (mostly scholarship fund); **$3,000** to Temple Brith Achim (building fund); and **$1,000** to St. Timothy's School [MD]; and smaller contributions. ■ **PUBLICATIONS:** None ■ **WEBSITE:** None ■ **E-MAIL:** None ■ **APPLICATION POLICIES & PROCEDURES:** The Foundation reports that most grants are for annual or capital campaigns, general support and scholarship funds.

O+D+T Jay S. Berman (P+D+Con) — Jennifer Berman Scotese (VP+F+D) — Susan C. Berman (S+D)

SE-064 **Bernard (Viola W.) Foundation**
 210 West Washington Square, Suite 750
 Philadelphia   19106   (Philadelphia County)

MI-12-20-31
Phone 215-829-7886 **FAX** 215-829-7887
EIN 13-2621140   **Year Created** 1968

AMV $287,642   **FYE** 12-00   **(Gifts Received** $57,162)   5 **Grants totaling** $95,000

Nationwide giving; no recent Pa. grants. High grant of **$35,000** to Children's Hospital at Yale U. [CT] (children at risk report). **$20,000** each to Children's Rights Initiative [NY] (general support) and Howard Center for Human Services [VT] (Baird Center for Children & Families). **$10,000** each to Louise Wise Services [NY] (general support) and Welfare Law Center [NY] (general support). ■ **PUBLICATIONS:** statement of program policy; application guidelines ■ **WEBSITE:** None ■ **E-MAIL:** None ■ **APPLICATION POLICIES & PROCEDURES:** The Foundation reports that funding is limited to projects having a psychiatric component with social impact. Prospective applicants should make an initial telephone call regarding the feasibility of submitting a request. Grant requests may be submitted at any time in a proposal with cover letter; include organization/project budgets, Board members list, list of major funding sources, and IRS tax-exempt status documentation.

O+D+T Perry Ottenberg, M.D. (P+D+Con) — Stephen Tulin [VT] (S+F+D) — Cary Koplin [NY] (D) — Peter Neubauer, M.D. [NY] (D) — Cary Wofford [DC] (D) — Joan Wofford [MA] (D)

SE-065 **Berry (Archie W. & Grace) Foundation**
 c/o U.S. Liability Insurance Company
 1030 Continental Drive, P.O. Box 1551
 King of Prussia   19406   (Montgomery County)

MI-13-14-15-22-32-54-71-72-82

Phone 610-688-2535 **FAX** None
EIN 23-6951678   **Year Created** 1988

AMV $9,961,727   **FYE** 6-01   **(Gifts Received** $0)   29 **Grants totaling** $572,000

About one-quarter local/Pa. giving. High Pa. grant of **$50,000** to Howard Steel Orthopedic Foundation. **$40,000** to Philadelphia Senior Center. **$25,000** to Philadelphia Museum of Art. **$10,000** each to American Friends Service Committee, Earthspan [York County], and Super Kids of Montgomery County. **$3,000** to Church Farm School. **$2,000** to Cabrini College. **Out-of-state** giving includes high grants of **$100,000** each to Peregrine Fund [ID] and Sandy River & Rangeley Lake's [ME]; **$25,000** each to Cornell Laboratory of Ornithology [NY], The Nature Conservancy [WY], and Piedmont Environmental Council [VA]; **$15,000** to Raptor Center [MN]; and **$10,000** each to American Tinnitus Assn. [OR], AmeriCares [CT]. Church World Service [IN], Heifer Project International [AR], Holt International Children's Services [OR], Oxfam America [MA], Project Hope [VA], Roger Tory Peterson Institute [NY], World Vision [WA], and Wyoming Audubon Society; and other smaller grants, mostly to WY. ■ **PUBLICATIONS:** None ■ **WEBSITE:** None ■ **E-MAIL:** None ■ **APPLICATION POLICIES & PROCEDURES:** The Foundation reports that grants are awarded for special projects. Grant requests may be submitted in any form at any time. Grant decisions are made at a June meeting.

O+D+T Louis F. Rivituso [West Chester] (T+Con) — Archie W. Berry, Jr. [ME] (T) — Robert B. Berry [WY] (T)

SE-066 **Betz (Theodora B.) Foundation**
 c/o Bishop & Associates
 1617 JFK Boulevard, Suite 1610
 Philadelphia   19103   (Philadelphia County)

MI-31-32

Phone 215-568-5450 **FAX** None
EIN 23-6965187   **Year Created** 1989

AMV $14,029,867   **FYE** 4-01   **(Gifts Received** $0)   3 **Grants totaling** $1,279,615

One local grant: **$200,000** to Pa. Hospital (Joan Karnell Cancer Center). Two grants totaling **$1,079,216** to U. of California/San Francisco Foundation (colo-rectal research and ENC research). — In the prior year the same grantees received all grants. ■ **PUBLICATIONS:** None ■ **WEBSITE:** None ■ **E-MAIL:** None ■ **APPLICATION POLICIES & PROCEDURES:** The Foundation reports that giving is restricted to medical research with most awards initiated by the Trustees. Prospective applicants initially should make a telephone inquiry about the feasibility of submitting a request.

O+D+T Henry Kwiecinski (Co-T+Con) — George H. Nofer, J.D. (Co-T)

SE-067 **Binswanger Foundation**
 c/o The Binswanger Company
 Two Logan Square
 Philadelphia   19103   (Philadelphia County)

MI-11-13-22-31-32-34-41-44-52-54-55-56-62
71-83
Phone 215-448-6000 **FAX** None
EIN 23-6296506   **Year Created** 1942

AMV $1,230,006   **FYE** 12-00   **(Gifts Received** $175,000)   95 **Grants totaling** $468,263

Mostly local/Pa. giving. High grant of **$77,500** to Jewish Federation of Greater Philadelphia. **$75,100** to Fox Chase Cancer Center. **$34,000** to United Way of SE Pa. **$40,000** to Children's Hospital of Philadelphia. **$12,500** to Thomas Jefferson U. **$11,050** to Academy of Music. **$11,000** to Germantown Friends School. **$10,000** to National Liberty Museum. **$9,500** to Police Athletic League. **$9,195** to Fairmount Park Commission. **$7,000** to Franklin Institute. **$6,500** to Girard College. **$6,000** to

Regional Performing Arts Center. **$5,000** each to Fund for the Waterworks, League of Women Voters-Citizen Education Fund [Harrisburg], Philadelphia 2000, Philadelphia Fashion for Parkinson's, and Philadelphia Jewish Archives Center. **$2,000-$3,200** each to 2000 Fantasy Auction, Abington Memorial Hospital Foundation, BUILD [Conshohocken], Celebrity Golf for Parkinson's, City Year-Philadelphia, Free Library of Philadelphia, Giving of Self Partnership, Greater Philadelphia Urban Affairs Coalition, Prince Music Theater, and Wistar Institute. Also, 41 grants/contributions **$250-$1,775** for arts, cultural, conservation, historic, educational, human services, youth and other purposes. **Out-of-state** giving includes **$18,500** to American Jewish Committee [NY]; **$17,750** to Wesleyan U. [CT]; and other smaller grants, many for higher education. ■**PUBLICATIONS:** None ■**WEBSITE:** None ■**E-MAIL:** None ■**APPLICATION POLICIES & PROCEDURES:** Grant requests may be submitted in a one-page letter at any time; include all pertinent information. No grants awarded to individuals. — Formerly called the Frank G. Binswanger Foundation.

O+D+T John K. Binswanger (P+Donor+Con) — Frank G. Binswanger, Jr. (C+Donor) — Robert B. Binswanger (VC) — Frank G. Binswanger, III (S) — David G. Binswanger (F) — Donor: Estate of Elizabeth Binswanger

---

SE-068   Birnhak (Marilyn & J. Robert) Foundation
c/o Weight Watchers
245 New York Drive, P.O. Box 2300
Fort Washington   19034   (Montgomery County)
AMV $209,618   **FYE** 6-00   **(Gifts Received** $100,000)

MI-15-22-42-62-64-82
Phone 215-643-6363   **FAX** None
EIN 22-2779210   **Year Created** 1986
5 **Grants totaling** $141,000

Mostly local giving. High grant of **$75,000** to Jewish Federation of Greater Philadelphia. **$50,000** to Philadelphia Geriatric Center. **$10,000** to American Associates of Ben-Gurion U. of the Negev [Jenkintown]. **Out-of-state** giving includes **$5,000** to Jewish Theological Seminary of America [NY]. ■**PUBLICATIONS:** None ■**WEBSITE:** None ■**E-MAIL:** None ■**APPLICATION POLICIES & PROCEDURES:** No grants awarded to individuals.

O+D+T J. Robert Birnhak (T+Donor+Con) — Marilyn J. Birnhak (T+Donor) Corporate donor: Weight Watchers of Philadelphia, Inc.

SE-069   BJNB Foundation
1265 South Avignon Drive
Gladwyne   19035   (Montgomery County)
AMV $243,852   **FYE** 12-00   **(Gifts Received** $38,307)

MI-12-17-22-41-51-62-84
Phone 610-520-1844   **FAX** 610-520-1916
EIN 23-2865970   **Year Created** 1996
15 **Grants totaling** $18,100

About two-thirds local giving. High grants of **$3,000** each to Philadelphia Youth Tennis and Woodlynde School. **$2,500** to Laurel House. **$1,000** each to Bryn Mawr Hospital Foundation, Prince Music Theatre, and Support Center for Child Advocates. **$700** to Fox Chase Cancer Center. Other smaller local donations. **Out-of-state** giving includes **$2,500** to Juvenile Diabetes Foundation [NY] and **$1,200** to Hadassah [NY]. ■**PUBLICATIONS:** None ■**WEBSITE:** None ■**E-MAIL:** bjnb@comcast.net ■**APPLICATION POLICIES & PROCEDURES:** Grant requests may be submitted in a letter (3 pages maximum) at any time; describe the organization's charitable activities and include an annual report, organization and project budgets, audited financial statement, and IRS tax-exempt status documentation. No grants are awarded to individuals.

O+D+T Jacqueline L. Bergman (P+Donor+Con) — Barry D. Bergman (S+F+Donor)

SE-070   Bloomer (Caroline D.) Charitable Trust
c/o PNC Advisors
1600 Market Street, 6th Floor
Philadelphia   19103   (Philadelphia County)
AMV $1,456,659   **FYE** 6-01   **(Gifts Received** $0)

MI-15-22-25-32-33-41-43-61-63-65
Phone 215-585-5921   **FAX** None
EIN 23-2120151   **Year Created** 1972
23 **Grants totaling** $29,500

About one-quarter local/Pa. giving. High Pa grants of **$2,000** each to Scholarship Foundation of the Union League of Philadelphia and University City Hospitality Coalition. **$1,000** to Berks Counseling Center [Reading]. **$600** to Episcopal Academy. **$500** each to Exeter Friends Meeting [Berks County] and Salvation Army/Philadelphia. Other smaller local contributions. **Out-of-state** giving includes **$5,000** each to Chesapeake Center [MD] and Sts. Peter & Paul Church and Family Life Center [MD]; **$4,000** to Berkshire School [MA]; and **$2,500** to Moorestown Friends School [NJ]. — In the prior year, local/Pa. grants included **$10,000** to Proclamation Presbyterian Church [Bryn Mawr]; and **$3,000-$3,666** to Chautauquans for a Christian Focus [Pittsburgh], Parkinson's Disease & Movement Research Center, and St. Ignatius Nursing Home. ■**PUBLICATIONS:** None. ■**WEBSITE:** None ■**E-MAIL:** None ■**APPLICATION POLICIES & PROCEDURES:** Grant requests may be submitted in a full proposal with cover letter during January-March. Grants are usually awarded at a Trustees meeting in April-May. — Formerly called the Asahel & Caroline Bloomer Charitable Trust

O+D+T Margaret Linette Gallagher (Assistant VP at Bank+Con) — John A. Keeley [MD] (T) — John Van Roden, Jr. [Radnor] (T) — Eleanor McKnight Haupt [Wayne] (T) PNC Advisors (Managing Trustee)

SE-071   Board of City Trusts, City of Philadelphia
21 South 12th Street, 5th Floor
Philadelphia   19107   (Philadelphia County)
AMV $733,997,000   **FYE** 12-01   **(Gifts Received** $0)

MI-12-15-22-23-41-43
Phone 215-568-0440   **FAX** 215-568-0347
EIN 23-6000204   **Year Created** 1869
Grants totaling $72,060,000

Giving by this City-related entity comprises 120+ Charitable Trusts bequeathed to the City, some over 200 years ago, and is largely restricted to Philadelphia institutions as designated by the Trusts' donors. Primary beneficiaries are Girard College which received about **$37,000,000** in support (also Girard College graduates who received **$232,900** in scholarships) and Wills Eye Hospital which altogether receive over 90% of the total annual support. Other designated beneficiaries of smaller amounts include Independence Hall, Penn Treaty Park, The Free Library of Philadelphia, Philadelphia organizations caring for the aged, infirm or imprisoned persons, special scholarships/awards for Philadelphia public school students (**$87,100** total), mummers parade prizes, certain groups of retired City employees, widows, and others. Some income from the Collective Legal Investment Fund for **SUNDRY TRUSTS** (**$1,490,000** in income) was awarded on a partly discretionary basis to Philadelphia organizations assisting children or the needy—specific grant information available in the annual report, and the FUEL FUNDS provided **$244,000** on a discretionary basis to needy Philadelphia residents for purchasing heating oil, gas or coal. Also, the Alexander G. **MERCER FUND** (est. 1884) provided housing opportunities on a discretionary basis to laboring, worthy poor residents of Philadelphia—further details are unavailable. ■**PUBLICATIONS:** Annual Report ■**WEBSITE:** www.citytrusts.com ■**E-MAIL:** info@citytrusts.com ■**APPLICATION POLICIES & PROCEDURES:** Prospective applicants for Fuel Fund assistance should telephone the Fuel Funds Office (Telephone 215-665-1811) to make an appointment after mid-October; applicants are eligible to request up to 150 gallons of fuel oil, up to $70 for gas, or an unlimited amount of coal; the Fuel Season begins December 1st. Prospective applicants for housing support under The Mercer Fund should contact the Real Estate Department (Telephone 215-568-0440) for information on available rental properties and to request an application. The Board of Directors meets monthly (except August) on the second Friday of each month and meetings are open to the public. — Note: The Annual Report is available for inspection only at the Board of City Trust offices and The Free Library of Philadelphia's Central Library [Logan Square on the Parkway], Government Publications Department.

O+D+T Marlene Brenner (S+Con) — Louis J. Esposito (P) — M.W. Baehr, Sr. (VP) — John J. Egan, Jr. (VP) — Isadore A. Shrager, Esq. (VP) — Hon. Dominic M. Cermele (D) — Hon. Ronald R. Donatucci (D) — Ann G. Eisman (D) — Hon. Vincent J. Fumo (D) — Hon. Michael A. Nutter (D) — Bernard W. Smalley, Esq. (D) — Hon. Anna C. Verna (D) — Stephen R. Wojdak, Esq. (D) — Hon. John F. Street (Ex-Officio Director) — Richard W. Burcik (General Manager, Girard Estate & Chief Investment Officer)

SE-072 **Bogash (Richard & Bernice) Family Foundation, The**
101 Cheswold Lane, Suite 4F
Haverford   19041   (Montgomery County)
AMV $64,367   **FYE** 10-00   (**Gifts Received** $0)

MI-15-22-31-41-42-62-64
Phone 610-642-5591 **FAX** None
EIN 23-7996185   **Year Created** 1998
11 **Grants totaling** $37,990

Mostly local giving. High grant of **$10,790** to Temple Adath Israel. **$10,000** to Jewish Federation of Greater Philadelphia. **$5,000** to Gerdora Kent Klein Foundation [Narberth]. **$1,000-$2,500** each to Benchmark School [Media], Crohn's & Colitis Foundation, Friends of Lankenau Hospital, Gratz College, Saunders House, and U. of Pa. Other smaller contributions. **Out-of-state** grant: **$1,800** to Jewish Theological Society [NY]. ■**PUBLICATIONS:** None ■**WEBSITE:** None ■**E-MAIL:** None ■**APPLICATION POLICIES & PROCEDURES:** Grant requests in any form may be submitted at any time.

O+D+T Bernice Bogash (T+Donor+Con)

SE-073 **Bogutz Foundation, The**
c/o Christie, Pabarue, Mortensen & Young
1880 JFK Boulevard, 10th Floor
Philadelphia   19103   (Philadelphia County)
AMV $66,194   **FYE** 9-00   (**Gifts Received** $0)

MI-22-42-62

Phone 215-587-1692 **FAX** 215-587-1699
EIN 22-2424113   **Year Created** 1983
5+ **Grants totaling** $11,747

Mostly local giving. High grant of **$10,000** to Federation Allied Jewish Appeal. **$2,000** to Villanova U. Law School. Other contributions **$125** or smaller. ■**PUBLICATIONS:** None ■**WEBSITE:** None ■**E-MAIL:** cpmy@cpmy.com ■**APPLICATION POLICIES & PROCEDURES:** Grant requests may be submitted in a letter at any time; detail the purpose of the requested funds. No grants awarded to individuals.

O+D+T Jerome E. Bogutz, Esq. (P+Donor+Con) — Helen R. Bogutz (VP)

SE-074 **Boiron Research Foundation**
c/o Boiron, Inc.
6 Campus Boulevard, Building A
Newtown Square   19073   (Delaware County)
AMV $206,412   **FYE** 12-00   (**Gifts Received** $115,309)

MI-32

Phone 610-325-0918 **FAX** None
EIN 52-1268329   **Year Created** 1988
2 **Grants totaling** $45,000

Nationwide giving restricted to homeopathic medical-clinical research. High grant of **$40,000** to Henry M. Jackson Foundation for the Advancement of Military Medicine [MD] (Protocol 28 research). **$5,000** to an individual researcher for Dengue Fever research. — Grants approved for future payment include **$225,000** for Protocol 29 research and **$85,000** for Dengue Fever research. ■**PUBLICATIONS:** None ■**WEBSITE:** None ■**E-MAIL:** None ■**APPLICATION POLICIES & PROCEDURES:** The Foundation reports that only high-level homeopathic medical researchers at universities are eligible to apply. Prospective applicants initially should make a telephone inquiry about the feasibility of submitting a research funding proposal with detailed research protocol and budget; the deadline for proposals is September 30th.

O+D+T Thierry Boiron (P+S+F+D+Con) — Christian Boiron [France] (Honorary P+D) — Jacky Abecassis [France] (VP+D) — Daniel Cohen [France] (Asst. VP+D) — Phillipe Belon [France] (D) — Didier Maillot [France] (AF) Corporate donor: Boiron-Borneman Company

---

SE-075 **Borowsky Family Foundation**
220 Society Hill Towers, Suite 31B
Philadelphia   19106   (Philadelphia County)
AMV $2,042,143   **FYE** 12-00   (**Gifts Received** $565,625)

MI-13-22-31-41-42-52-54-55-57-62-82
Phone 215-574-0206 **FAX** 215-925-2800
EIN 23-2949444   **Year Created** 1998
89 **Grants totaling** $134,320

About three-fourths local giving. High grant of **$18,250** to Jewish Federation of Greater Philadelphia. **$15,000** to United Way of SE Pa. **$10,250** to Academy of Music. **$8,900** to Opera Company of Philadelphia. **$8,400** to Jewish Community Centers of Greater Philadelphia. **$6,000** to American Friends of Ben Gurion U. **$5,000-$5,600** each to Mann Center for Performing Arts, Philadelphia Orchestra, and U. of the Arts. **$4,175** to Temple Beth Zion. **$3,600-$3,900** each to Boys Town [Jenkintown] and Police Athletic League. **$2,500** to Beth Am Israel Congregation. **$1,000-$1,250** each to American Israel Public Affairs Committee, Epilepsy Foundation, Gerda & Kurt Klein Foundation [Narberth], NLM Endowment Fund, Perelman Jewish Day School, Philadelphia Museum of Art (Women's Committee), and WHYY-TV12. Other smaller local contributions, mostly for Jewish or cultural organizations. **Out-of-state** giving includes **$5,000** to Stern High School [NY]; **$2,500** to Hillel U. [NM]; **$1,800** to Yemin Orde [Israel]; and smaller grants to Israel and elsewhere. ■**PUBLICATIONS:** None ■**WEBSITE:** None ■**E-MAIL:** None ■**APPLICATION POLICIES & PROCEDURES:** Information not available.

O+D+T Irvin J. Borowsky (P+Con) — Gwen Borowsky Camp [Narberth] (S) — Ned Borowsky [Conshohocken] (F)

SE-076 Botstiber (Dietrich W.) Foundation, The
27 East Front Street, P.O. Box 1819
Media   19063   (Delaware County)

MI-31-41-42-43-49
Phone 610-566-3330 **FAX** None
EIN 23-7807828   **Year Created** 1995

AMV $2,863,032   **FYE** 8-00   **(Gifts Received** $233,792)   11 **Grants totaling** $193,795

About two-thirds local giving. High local grant of **$26,250** to Drexel U. (fellowship for inventors). **$25,000** each to Delaware County Education Foundation (programs/facility improvements) and Villanova U. (engineering building lab). **$16,000** to Delaware Valley Science Fair (general support/endowment). **$12,500** to Philadelphia Community Academy (science lab). **$11,570** to Garnet Valley School District (advanced placement program). **$3,500** to National Conference for Community & Justice (conference). **$2,400** to Riddle Memorial Hospital (operating support). **Out-of-state** giving includes high grant of **$50,000** to Science Service [DC] (enhance science awareness); **$12,000** to Camden County College [NJ] (science education program); and **$9,575** to Today's Science [NY] (science teacher education enrichment). ■**PUBLICATIONS:** Annual Report; Application Guidelines/Policies flyer ■**WEBSITE:** None ■**E-MAIL:** None ■**APPLICATION POLICIES & PROCEDURES:** The Foundation reports priority interests as (1) supporting reform of educational systems that will make the U.S. paramount in the fields of technology, science and commerce; (2) promoting an understanding of the historical Austria-U.S. relationship and fostering this relationship; and (3) preventing, in general, cruelty to human beings and animals. Prospective applicants should make an initial telephone inquiry about the feasibility of submitting a request. Grant proposals may be submitted at any time (deadlines are June 30th and December 31st); include information about the organization's purpose and specific activities, a description of the program (and expected outcome) of the program for which funding is sought, the amount requested, a program budget, most recent audited financial statement, list of major funding sources, and IRS tax-exempt status documentation. Site visits sometimes are made to organizations being considered for a grant. Grants are awarded at meetings in August and February.

O+D+T Terrance A. Kline, Esq. (T+Con) — Dietrich W. Botstiber (T+Donor) — Dorothy Boylan [Glen Mills] (T)

SE-077 Bradburd Family Foundation
1880 Hemlock Circle
Abington   19001   (Montgomery County)

MI-22-52-63
Phone 267-757-1080 **FAX** None
EIN 23-7978514   **Year Created** 1999

AMV $11,810   **FYE** 5-00   **(Gifts Received** $45,000)   17 **Grants totaling** $32,400

About two-thirds local giving. High grant of **$18,000** to Church of the Restoration. **$500** each to Philadelphia Classical Symphony and U. of Pa. Other smaller local contributions. **Out-of-state** giving primarily to the Unitarian-Universalist Church/Service Committee [MA]. ■**PUBLICATIONS:** None ■**WEBSITE:** None ■**E-MAIL:** None ■**APPLICATION POLICIES & PROCEDURES:** The Foundation reports that giving is limited to certain communities and religious groups. Grant requests may be submitted in any form at any time; include IRS tax-exempt status documentation.

O+D+T Arnold W. Bradburd (T+Donor+Con) — Julia A. Bradburd (T+Donor)

SE-078 Bradley (Joseph G.) Charitable Trust
c/o Nehrbas, 101 Fairview Road
Penn Valley   19072   (Montgomery County)

MI-52-53
Phone 610-664-1593 **FAX** None
EIN 23-7647762   **Year Created** 1990

AMV $9,188,940   **FYE** 11-00   **(Gifts Received** $0)   1 **Grant of** $460,000

Sole grant to Fine Arts Museum of San Francisco [CA] (general fund). — In six prior years this institution received the Foundation's only annual grant. ■**PUBLICATIONS:** None ■**WEBSITE:** None ■**E-MAIL:** None ■**APPLICATION POLICIES & PROCEDURES:** The Foundation reports that while the Fine Arts Museum of San Francisco has been on the only organization supported for some years, other projects involving organs or organ music are eligible for available funds. Grant requests may be submitted in any form at any time.

O+D+T Andrew R. Nehrbas (T+Con)

SE-079 Brady (William & Kathleen) Foundation
1680 Hunters Circle
West Chester   19380   (Chester County)

MI-12-14-22-25-41-43
Phone 610-644-2272 **FAX** None
EIN 23-2938437   **Year Created** 1997

AMV $389,505   **FYE** 12-00   **(Gifts Received** $0)   4 **Grants totaling** $20,500

All local giving. High grant of **$8,000** to West Catholic High School. **$7,500** to The Bridge of Hope. **$4,000** to Archbishop Prendergast High School. **$1,000** to St. Mary's Franciscan Shelter. — Giving in the prior year included **$3,000-$4,000** each to ARC Chester County, Greater Philadelphia Food Bank, Project Children, and the donees listed above. ■**PUBLICATIONS:** None ■**WEBSITE:** None ■**E-MAIL:** None ■**APPLICATION POLICIES & PROCEDURES:** The Foundation reports that scholarships will be awarded to individuals attending approved educational institutions, and applications must be submitted on a Scholarship Application Form provided by the Foundation.

O+D+T Kathleen G. Brady (P+Donor+Con) — William P. Brady (F+S+Donor) — Michael P. Brady [Downingtown] (AF)

SE-080 Bray Family Foundation

2826 Mount Carmel Ave.
Glenside 19038 (Montgomery County)

AMV $562,435 **FYE** 11-00 **(Gifts Received** $0)

MI-12-13-14-21-22-35-41-43-61
Phone 215-885-9900 **FAX** 215-851-0214
EIN 23-2791988 **Year Created** 1994
15 **Grants totaling** $18,800

Mostly local giving; grants are unrestricted except as noted. High local grant of **$2,500** to St. Basil Academy (tuition assistance). **$2,000** to Western Delaware Valley Lions (family assistance). **$1,000-$1,500** each to BLOCS/Business Leaders Organized for Catholic Schools (study tour tuition), Camphill Village/Kimberton Hills (healthcare subsidy fund), Christ Lutheran Church of Upper Darby (summer day camp), The Christian Academy [Media] (scholarship aid), Crossing the Finish Line [Doylestown] (cancer care support), Liberty Resources (managed care coalition), Maysie's Farm Conservation Center [Glenmoore] (intern support), Roman Catholic High School (graduation fees), and The Wellness Place [Lansdale] (cancer care support). Other smaller contributions for similar purposes. **Out-of-state** grant: **$3,200** to Friends of St. Malachy [NJ] (scholarship opportunities). ■**PUBLICATIONS:** None ■**WEBSITE:** None ■**E-MAIL:** None ■**APPLICATION POLICIES & PROCEDURES:** Grant requests may be submitted in any form at any time.

O+D+T Susan H. Bray, M.D. [Wyndmoor] (P+Co-T+Donor+Con) — Robert J. Bray, Esq. [Wyndmoor] (VP+S+Co-T) — Molly E. O'Neill [King of Prussia] (F) — Brian J. Bray [Wyndmoor] (D) — Joanne M. Kyle [Oreland] (D) — Anne S. Muir [Norristown] (D) — Janice C. Muir [Newtown Square] (D)

SE-081 Bread and Roses Community Fund

1500 Walnut Street, Suite 1305
Philadelphia 19102 (Philadelphia County)

AMV $1,757,868 **FYE** 6-01 **(Gifts Received** $769,953)

MI-14-15-16-17-18-20-35-39-43-55-79-81-83
Phone 215-731-1107 **FAX** 215-731-0453
EIN 23-2047297 **Year Created** 1977
42+ **Grants totaling** $282,422

All giving generally limited to the five-county Philadelphia area and Camden County, NJ for community-based, social-change-oriented organizations/projects in eight interest areas—see below. High grant of **$40,092** to New Society Educational Foundation. **$17,920** to Philadelphia Fight. **$12,000** each to Police-Barrio Relations Project (community education workshops)and Resources for Human Development. **$9,100** to Empty the Shelters. **$7,000** to Disabled in Action (general operating support). **$6,000** each to CATA Farmworker Support Committee (worker organizing), Graterfriends, Inc., and Mobilization Against AIDS International [CA]. **$5,000-$5,750** each to ActionAIDS, Center for Creative Activities, Decade of Human Rights [NY], Human-RightsTech (general support), Mountain Meadow Summer Camp (general support), Pa. Prison Society, San Carlos Educational Foundation [CA], and Spiral Q Puppet Theater (social change demonstrations). **$4,000-$4,650** each to Art Sanctuary (African/African-American arts programming), Center for Responsible Funding, Scribe Video Center (community organization training/screening series), WAVE/Women's Anti-Violence Education (Outreach to Young Women project), and Women's Institute for Family Health (self-help/advocacy training). **$3,000-$3,810** each to American Institute for Social Justice [DC], Asian Arts Initiative (GenerAsian Next teen theater project), Center for Fair Employment, Childspace Cooperative Development Concerned Citizens of North Camden [NJ] (general support), Moonstone Inc. (Cuban Arts Festival), New Liberty Productions (general support for post-production services to community groups), Pa. Institutional Law Project, Planned Parenthood of SE Pa., William Way Community Center (project coalition building). **$2,000** each to Grands As Parents, Incarnation of Our Lord Church, and National Coalition Against the Death Penalty. Seven Lax Scholarship grants totaled **$65,000**. Other smaller contributions/emergency grants totaled **$350**. ■**PUBLICATIONS:** Annual Report; application guidelines for different grant programs ■**WEBSITE:** www.breadrosesfund.org ■**E-MAIL:** info@breadrosesfund.org ■**APPLICATION POLICIES & PROCEDURES:** Only organizations in Bucks, Chester, Delaware, Montgomery, Philadelphia, and Camden counties are eligible to apply, and must be working to redistribute wealth, power, and resources, and eliminate the barriers that keep people from participating fully in society. Priority is given to small, community-based groups (budgets under $100,000) without access to traditional funding sources, particularly those working in poor, working class or minority communities. Grants are awarded for the following purposes: Arts & Social Change, Community Organizing, Human Rights/Civil Liberties, International/Peace, Lesbian/Gay/Bisexual/Transgender Activism, Resources for Organizing, Women's Rights, and Workers' Rights. The Fund can legally support not-yet-incorporated or not-yet tax-exempt organizations, provided the activities for which funding is requested are consistent with IRS regulations defining eligibility for tax-exempt funding. The Fund has four grant programs: (1) The General Fund awards grants ranging from $3,000-$7,000 to organizations whose main objective is taking collective action against a problem affecting the community—to work for social change; application deadlines are January 15th and September 20th. (2) Emergency/Discretionary Grants (usually $50-$500 each), awarded monthly, are offered for special projects or emergencies not part of an organization's ongoing work; deadlines are the second Tuesday every month, except August. (3) Phoebus Criminal Justice Initiative grants ($2,500-$6,000) are for organizations dealing with preventing violence against women; application deadline is September 14th. (4) Lax Scholarship Fund grants (up to $20,000) are available for gay men currently seeking education; application deadline is January 15th. Prospective applicants for any of the grant programs should make an initial telephone call to inquire about the feasibility of submitting an application, or to arrange for an interview. If appropriate, a formal application form and other information will be provided.

O+D+T Christie Balka (Executive Director+Con) — Adina Abramowitz (D) — Cathy Coate (D) — Carrie Dupree (D) — Cynthia Fowler (D) — Molly Frantz [Flourtown] (D) — Debbie Friedman (D) — Greg Jones (D) — Jeri Nutter (D) — Angie Pabon (D) — Allyson Randolph (D) — Aissa Richardson (D) — Terry Rumsey [Media] (D) — Ellen Somekowa (D) — Wayne Wynn (D)

SE-082 Brent (Lillian & Robert) Fund

1543 Ulster Court
West Chester 19380 (Chester County)

AMV $316,692 **FYE** 12-00 **(Gifts Received** $75,800)

MI-22-34-62
Phone 610-719-1996 **FAX** None
EIN 23-2735247 **Year Created** 1993
46 **Grants totaling** $24,418

About half local/Pa. giving. High grant of **$7,786** to Temple Beth Am Israel. **$2,800** to Poale Zedeck Sisterhood [Pittsburgh]. Other local contributions **$35-$250** for various purposes. **Out-of-state** giving includes **$5,060** to U. of Rochester Medical

School [NY]; **$2,500** to National Council of Radiation Protection [MD]; and **$1,536** to Sarasota Manatee Jewish Federation [FL]. ■**PUBLICATIONS:** None ■**WEBSITE:** None ■**E-MAIL:** None ■**APPLICATION POLICIES & PROCEDURES:** Information not available.

O+D+T Robert L. Brent (P+Donor+Con) — Lillian Brent (F+Donor)

SE-083 **Brickman Foundation**		**MI**-12-22-25-31-51-54-57-63
3219 Buck Road		**Phone** 215-938-0416 **FAX** None
Huntingdon Valley 19006	(Montgomery County)	**EIN** 23-7790986 **Year Created** 1994
AMV $5,284,419 **FYE** 12-00	**(Gifts Received** $0)	26 **Grants totaling** $6,878,701

Mostly local giving. High grant of **$6,500,000** to National Philanthropic Trust [Jenkintown]. **$60,000** to Ivyland New Church/Swedenborgian. **$54,911** to General Church of New Jerusalem (Swedenborgian). **$23,000** to Project H.O.M.E. **$19,000** to Academy of the New Church. **$16,200** to Red Cross of Bucks County. **$5,000** each to Abington Memorial Hospital, St. Mary's Medical Center, and WXPN-FM. **$2,500** to Stepping Stones. **$1,000** to Children's Hospital of Philadelphia Foundation. **Out-of-state** giving, much for Swedenborgian institutions, includes **$75,000** to Oak Arbor Church of New Jerusalem [MI]; **$30,000** to Immanuel Church of New Jerusalem [IL]; **$20,000** to Peace Lutheran Church [MI]; **$15,000** to Washington Church of New Jerusalem; **$10,000** each to Baptist Home for Children [MD] and Metropolitan Museum of Art [NY]; and **$5,000** to National Theatre Workshop of the Handicapped [NY] and San Diego New Church [CA]. ■**PUBLICATIONS:** None ■**WEBSITE:** None ■**E-MAIL:** None ■**APPLICATION POLICIES & PROCEDURES:** Information not available.

O+D+T Theodore W. Brickman (T+Donor+Con) — Sally Brickman (T+Donor) — Scott W. Brickman (T) — Steven G. Brickman [FL] (T) — Julie Brickman Carr [Bethlehem] (T) — Susan Brickman McGrath [Langhorne] (T) Pitcairn Trust Co. (Trustee)

SE-084 **Brind (Ira & Myrna) Foundation**		**MI**-13-31-32-41-42-44-51-52-53-54-55
c/o Brind Lindsay & Company		
1926 Arch Street		**Phone** 215-569-3031 **FAX** None
Philadelphia 19103	(Philadelphia County)	**EIN** 23-7978519 **Year Created** 1998
AMV $387,213 **FYE** 12-00	**(Gifts Received** $0)	84 **Grants totaling** $60,020

Mostly local giving; some grants represent multiple payments. High grants of **$5,000** each to Friends Central School, Suzanne Morgan Memorial Fund, and Wistar Institute (honor gift). **$3,500** to Prince Music Theater. **$3,000** each to Educating Children for Parenting and Wellness Community of Philadelphia. **$1,500-$2,500** each to Institute for Contemporary Art, Macular Vision Research Foundation, Philadelphia Museum of Art, Solomon Schechter Day School (capital campaign), and U. of Pa. Law School. **$1,000** each to Free Library of Philadelphia, Jefferson Digestive Disease Institute, National Organization for Hearing Research, Philadelphia Orchestra, Philadelphia Theater Company, Thos. Jefferson U./Women's Board, University Museum, and U. of Pa. Class of 1963. Other local contributions **$25-$500** for various purposes. **Out-of-state** giving includes **$2,600** to Anti-Defamation League [NY] and **$2,500** to Manhattan Theatre Club [NY]. — In prior years, major giving included **$10,000** to Thos. Jefferson U. Hospital (Center for Integrative Medicine); **$10,000** to U. of the Arts; and **$6,000** to Educating Children for Parenting. ■**PUBLICATIONS:** None ■**WEBSITE:** None ■**E-MAIL:** None ■**APPLICATION POLICIES & PROCEDURES:** Grant requests may be submitted at any time in a letter; describe the purpose of the request and include IRS tax-exempt status documentation.

O+D+T Ira Brind (Managing Trustee+Donor+Con) — Myrna Brind (Managing Trustee+Donor) — David Brind (T)

SE-085 **Bristol Fund, The**		**MI**-22-29-31-41-42-54-57-63-71-72
Saw Mill Road, P.O. Box 206		**Phone** 215-297-0639 **FAX** None
Carversville 18913	(Bucks County)	**EIN** 23-7209712 **Year Created** 1961
AMV $2,150,054 **FYE** 12-00	**(Gifts Received** $1,006,110)	140 **Grants totaling** $742,200

About one-fifth local giving; some grants represent multiple payments. High Pa. grant of **$64,500** to George School. **$26,300** to Red Cross [Doylestown]. **$25,000** to Salvation Army [Levittown]. **$8,000** to Lingohocken Fire Dept. **$2,000-$2,500** each to Doylestown Hospital, Thomas Jefferson Hospital, Newtown Ambulance Squad, St. Mary Hospital, and Wrightstown Friends Meeting. **$1,000** each to Artist in Rural Ireland [Philadelphia], Chestnut Hill Academy, Crossroads School, Episcopal School, Love the Children, Michener Art Museum, Shipley School, U. of Pa. Veterinary Hospital, WHYY, and Woodmere Art Museum. Other local contributions **$250-$750** for various purposes. **Out-of-state** giving includes **$82,000** to Groton School [CT]; **$70,500** to Hamilton College [NY]; **$60,000** to Pennington School [NJ]; **$47,000** to The Nature Conservancy [VA]; **$32,650** to Madeline Island Music Camp [WI]; **$27,000** to Pingry School [NJ]; **$25,500** each to CPMC Fund [NY] and U. of Virginia; **$23,000** to Northland College [WI]; **$20,000** to San Domenico School [CA]; and other smaller grants, rimarily in areas where Fund directors/donors reside or attended school/college. ■**PUBLICATIONS:** None ■**WEBSITE:** None ■**E-MAIL:** None ■**APPLICATION POLICIES & PROCEDURES:** The Foundation reports that grants are for special projects, capital needs, or matching grants; no grants are awarded to individuals. Only requests recommended/sponsored by a Fund director/donor are considered; unsolicited requests/proposals are not accepted. The Board meets in November.

O+D+T Michal W. Bristol (F+Donor+Con) — Pamela W. Bristol [NJ] (P+Donor) — Sanford A. Bristol [NJ] (VP+Donor) — Susannah B. Bristol [NY] (VP+Donor) — James D. Bristol [IL] (S+Donor) — Atherton Bristol [MN] (Donor) — Brian T. Bristol [NY] (Donor) — Edith Wells Bristol [Carversville] (Donor) — Gerald R. Bristol [NJ] (Donor) — Jane C. Bristol (Donor) — Karyn P. Bristol (Donor) — Steven Bristol (Donor) — William M. Bristol, III [Newtown] (Donor) — George M. Kunkel (Donor) — Madeline B. Kunkel (Donor) — Sara G. Ritchie (Donor)

SE-086   Brodsky (Julian A. & Lois G.) Foundation

c/o Comcast Corporation
1500 Market Street, 35th Floor
Philadelphia   19102   (Philadelphia County)

MI-13-14-17-18-32-35-41-51-52-54-55-56-57
72-81-82
Phone 215-665-1700 **FAX** None
EIN 23-2785280   **Year Created** 1995

AMV $2,822,393   **FYE** 12-00   **(Gifts Received** $0)   92 **Grants totaling** $165,148

About half local giving. High grant of **$30,000** to Philadelphia Museum of Art. **$10,000** to Settlement Music School. **$5,000** each to National Liberty Museum and Philadelphia Fashion for Parkinson's. **$3,000** each to Philadelphia Orchestra and WRTI-FM. **$2,000-$2,500** each to Arden Theatre Company, Curtis Institute of Music, Philadelphia Arts in Education Partnership, White-Williams Scholars, WHYY, and Working Wardrobe. **$1,000-$1,500** each to Academy of Music, Elizabeth Blackwell Health Center, Fleisher Art Memorial, Franklin Institute Science Museum, Juvenile Diabetes Foundation, Library Company of Philadelphia, National Organization for Hearing Research, Philadelphia Geriatric Center, Philadelphia Museum of Art/Women's Committee, Philadelphia Zoo, Planned Parenthood, Radnor ABC, Red Cross, United Negro College Fund, Wilma Theatre, and WXPN. Other local contributions **$100-$600** for various purposes. **Out-of-state** giving includes **$25,000** to American Institute of Physics [MD]; **$7,500** to National Peace Corps Assn. [DC]; **$5,000** to Doctors Without Borders [NY]; and smaller grants/contributions, many to southern NJ, NY, and New England. ■**PUBLICATIONS:** None ■**WEBSITE:** None ■**E-MAIL:** None ■**APPLICATION POLICIES & PROCEDURES:** Grant requests may be submitted in any form at any time; include organization and project budgets, audited financial statement, a Board member list, and IRS tax-exempt status documentation. No grants awarded to individuals. Site visits sometimes are made to organizations being considered for a grant. Grants are awarded at meetings in April and November.

O+D+T   Julian A. Brodsky (D+Manager+Donor+Con) — Lois G. Brodsky (D+Manager) — Debra G. Brodsky (D) — Ellen G. Brodsky [MA] (D) — Laura G. Brodsky (D)

SE-087   Bronstein (Solomon & Sylvia) Foundation, The

c/o Blank, Rome, Comisky & McCauley
One Logan Square
Philadelphia   19103   (Philadelphia County)

MI-12-14-15-22-31-34-41-42-52-54-62-64-82

Phone 215-569-5500 **FAX** None
EIN 22-2656339   **Year Created** 1985

AMV $2,829,909   **FYE** 6-00   **(Gifts Received** $0)   22 **Grants totaling** $125,100

About two-thirds local giving; all grants are for general purposes. High grant of **$15,000** to Central High School Music Assn. **$10,000** each to Jewish Community Centers of Greater Philadelphia and U. of Pa. School of Nursing. **$5,000** each to Federation Day Care Services, Federation of Jewish Agencies, Jewish National Fund, MossRehab Hospital (Aphasia Center), Philadelphia Geriatric Center, and U. of Pa. Center for Bioethics. **$4,000** to Har Zion Temple (Bronstein Scholarship & Pastoral Fund). **$2,500** each to American Friends of Tel Aviv U., Boys Town Jerusalem Foundation, and National Museum of American Jewish History. **$1,300-$1,500** each to Bread Upon the Waters Scholarship Fund, Breast Health Institute, and Center for Literacy. **Out-of-state** giving includes **$20,000** each to Jewish Theological Seminary [NY] (Louis Finkelstein Institute and general support), and smaller grants for other Jewish charities/organizations. — Grants approved for future payment: **$20,000** to Philadelphia Geriatric Center; **$1-0,000** to U.S. Holocaust Memorial Museum [DC]; and **$5,000** to U. of Pa. School of Nursing (Bronstein Scholarship Fund). ■**PUBLICATIONS:** None ■**WEBSITE:** None ■**E-MAIL:** None ■**APPLICATION POLICIES & PROCEDURES:** Grant requests may be submitted in any form at any time.

O+D+T   Marvin Comisky, Esq. (T+Con) — Gerald Broker, Esq. [Narberth] (T) — Rabbi Gerald I. Wolpe (T)

SE-088   Brookmead Trust

431 Glyn Wynne Road
Haverford   19041   (Montgomery County)

MI-15-18-71-72
Phone 610-649-8964 **FAX** None
EIN 23-7787805   **Year Created** 1994

AMV $1,169,128   **FYE** 12-00   **(Gifts Received** $0)   9 **Grants totaling** $63,500

About two-thirds local giving. High Pa. grant of **$13,000** to Philadelphia Zoo. **$10,000** to Planned Parenthood of SE Pa. **$5,000** each to Brandywine Conservancy, Pa. Horticultural Society, and The Nature Conservancy. **$2,500** to Endow-A-Home. **$2,000** to Morris Animal Rescue. **Out-of-state** giving includes **$20,000** to Wildlife Conservation Society [NY]. ■**PUBLICATIONS:** None ■ **WEBSITE:** None ■**E-MAIL:** None ■**APPLICATION POLICIES & PROCEDURES:** No grants awarded to individuals.

O+D+T   Wendy C. Fritz (T+Con) — Charles A. Fritz, IV [CA] (Co-T) — Jennifer C. Fritz [MD] (Co-T)

SE-089   Brooks Foundation, The

c/o Dechert, Price & Rhoads
4000 Bell Atlantic Tower, 1717 Arch St.
Philadelphia   19103   (Philadelphia County)

MI-12-42-45-55

Phone 215-994-2838 **FAX** 215-994-2222
EIN 23-2410692   **Year Created** 1986

AMV $1,061,054   **FYE** 12-00   **(Gifts Received** $0)   20 **Grants totaling** $66,266

One Pa. grant: **$1,100** to The Baldwin School. **Out-of-state** giving includes **$13,000** to Vermont State Craft Center; **$10,000** each to Kent State U. Foundation [OH], Prevent Child Abuse/Vermont, and Rhode Island Foundation; **$9,141** to South Burlington Community Education Fund [VT]; and smaller grants/contributions to New England, DC, OH. ■**PUBLICATIONS:** None ■**WEBSITE:** None ■**E-MAIL:** None ■**APPLICATION POLICIES & PROCEDURES:** The Foundation reports priority interests are human services, education, arts/culture, religion and environment. No grants awarded to individuals.

O+D+T   F.J. Gerhart, Esq. (Con) — Robert T. Brooks [RI] (P+F+T+Donor) — Rhea A. Brooks [RI] (S+T)

SE-090   Broughton Foundation   MI-12-13-14-15-22-25-32-35-41-55-65
5030 State Road, Suite 2-600
P.O. Box 397   **Phone** 610-284-9944 **FAX** None
Drexel Hill 19026   (Delaware County)   **EIN** 23-2792113   **Year Created** 1994
AMV $2,456,278   **FYE** 12-00   **(Gifts Received** $1,974,771)   16 **Grants totaling** $78,068

Mostly local giving. High grant of **$53,000** to Penn Home. **$10,000** to Upper Darby Educational & Cultural Foundation. **$2,000** to ActionAIDS. **$1,000** each to Associated Services for the Blind, CityTeam Ministries [Chester], Community Arts Center, Fox Chase Cancer Center, Northwest Interfaith Movement, Philadelphia Ronald McDonald House, St. John's Hospice, Salvation Army, Sunday Breakfast Assn., Whosoever Gospel Mission, and William Penn School District. **Out-of-state** grants: **$1,000** each to Guiding Eyes for the Blind [NJ] and Peale Center for Christian Living [NY]. ■**PUBLICATIONS:** None ■ **WEBSITE:** None ■ **E-MAIL:** None ■**APPLICATION POLICIES & PROCEDURES:** Grant requests may be submitted in a letter which describes the purpose of the proposed project and amount of funding requested; include a financial statement and IRS tax-exempt status documentation.
O+D+T Douglas E. Cook, Esq. (T+Con) — Delbert E. Broughton, Jr. [Philadelphia] (T) — Frank C. Wilhelm, Esq. [Philadelphia] (T) — Donor: Estate of Minerva B. Stanford

SE-091   Brown (Jack A.) Foundation   MI-41
c/o Penn Warehousing & Distribution Corp.
2147 South Columbus Blvd.   **Phone** 215-218-3000 **FAX** None
Philadelphia 19148   (Philadelphia County)   **EIN** 23-6088706   **Year Created** 1987
AMV $195,486   **FYE** 12-00   **(Gifts Received** $0)   2 **Grants totaling** $20,550

All local giving. High grant of **$20,000** to St. Aloysius Academy [Bryn Mawr]. **$550** to Ancient Order of Hibernians. ■**PUBLICATIONS:** None ■**WEBSITE:** None ■**E-MAIL:** None ■**APPLICATION POLICIES & PROCEDURES:** Submit grant requests at any time on organizational letterhead; state a specific amount requested and describe the intended use of funds. No grants awarded to individuals.
O+D+T Jack M. Brown, Sr. (T+Donor+Con)

SE-092   Brown (T. Wistar) Teachers' Fund   MI-43
1315 Arrowmink Road   **Phone** 610-520-0147 **FAX** None
Villanova 19085   (Montgomery County)   **EIN** 23-6200741   **Year Created** 1916
AMV $2,339,144   **FYE** 9-00   **(Gifts Received** $0)   **Grants totaling** $25,588

All giving is restricted to teacher training, scholarships, and fellowships for members of the Philadelphia Yearly Meeting/Religious Society of Friends (Quakers). Details on number/sizes of awards were not reported. ■**PUBLICATIONS:** Annual Report ■ **WEBSITE:** None ■**E-MAIL:** None ■**APPLICATION POLICIES & PROCEDURES:** The Fund reports that all scholarship awards are restricted to members of the Philadelphia Yearly Meeting/Religious Society of Friends (Quakers), 21 years or older and teaching below college level; this includes school librarians, reading specialists, and counselors. Support is given to/for (a) a one-year course of study in a university to prepare for the teaching profession, or (b) those already teaching who wish to attend a summer school or other place of instruction during a vacation period, or (c) those already teaching who could benefit by a summer at Woodbrooke College [England]. Prospective applicants must request a copy of the Fund's Application for a Grant form which must submitted with letters of reference. Application deadlines depend upon the period for which support is requested.
O+D+T Kay M. Edstene (Executive Director+T+Con) — Eleanor M. Elkinton [Philadelphia] (T) — William D. Ravdin [Philadelphia] (T) — PNC Bank N.A. (Corporate Trustee)

SE-093   Bruder (Michael A.) Foundation   MI-41-42-43-72
c/o M.A. Bruder & Sons
600 Reed Road, P.O. Box 600   **Phone** 610-353-5100 **FAX** None
Broomall 19008   (Delaware County)   **EIN** 23-6298481   **Year Created** 1956
AMV $592,986   **FYE** 12-00   **(Gifts Received** $0)   21 **Grants totaling** $50,250

One Pa. organization grant: **$1,000** to Allentown College. **Out-of-state** giving included high grant of **$25,000** to Human Society of Broward County [Fl.]. Eighteen scholarships, usually **$1,250** each, for dependents of company employees awarded to students at five Pa. institutions and six out-of-of-state. — In prior years, major local grants included **$25,000** to MBF Computer Center and **$10,000** to Malvern Preparatory School. ■**PUBLICATIONS:** None ■**WEBSITE:** www.mabpaints.com [corporate info only] ■**E-MAIL:** None ■**APPLICATION POLICIES & PROCEDURES:** The Foundation reports that organizations in company operating areas receive preference. Grant requests in any form may be submitted at any time; decision on grants are usually within two months. Scholarship awards are restricted to dependents of company employees.
O+D+T Thomas A. Bruder, Jr. (T+Con) — William R. Sasso, Esq. [Philadelphia] (T) — Andrew B. Young, Esq. [Philadelphia] (T) — Corporate donor: M.A. Bruder & Sons

SE-094   Brunswick (Edward B.) Foundation   MI-31-42-44-52-62-71
c/o Sardinsky, Braunstein & Co., CPAs
Ten Penn Center, Suite 617   **Phone** 215-563-6222 **FAX** None
Philadelphia 19103   (Philadelphia County)   **EIN** 13-3401549   **Year Created** 1986
AMV $273,211   **FYE** 9-00   **(Gifts Received** $93,657)   25 **Grants totaling** $163,660

Three Pa. grants: **$25,000** to Lafayette College; **$7,500** to American Jewish Committee; and **$1,500** to Philadelphia Orchestra. **Out-of-state** giving includes high grant of **$101,000** to Rangeley Region Health Center [ME]; **$11,000** to Rangeley Lakes Heritage Trust [ME]; and **$10,000** to Rangeley Library [ME]; with smaller grants/contributions to NY, FL and elsewhere. ■**PUB-**

LICATIONS: None ■**WEBSITE:** None ■**E-MAIL:** None ■**APPLICATION POLICIES & PROCEDURES:** Grant requests may be submitted in any form at any time to Edward B. Brunswick, 3900 Pine Shadow Court, Bonita Springs, FL 34139; provide complete details on the proposed project and funding requested.

O+D+T Edward B. Brunswick [FL] (P+D+Donor+Con) — Beth Brunswick [NY] (F+D) — Joseph Sedlacek, Esq. (D)

SE-095 **Buck (Caroline Alexander) Foundation**
c/o Schnader Harrison Segal & Lewis
1600 Market Street, Suite 3600
Philadelphia 19103 (Philadelphia County)
AMV $12,906,552 **FYE** 12-00 **(Gifts Received** $0)

MI-12-13-14-17-22-25-29-41-42-52-54-63-65 84-86
Phone 215-751-2080 **FAX** 215-246-9018
EIN 23-6257115 **Year Created** 1960
32 **Grants totaling** $456,000

All local giving; all grants are for general purposes and some grants comprise multiple payments. High grant of **$60,000** to Jubilee School. **$57,000** to MicroSociety, Inc. (school reform). **$50,000** to Settlement Music School. **$45,000** to The Lighthouse. **$25,000** each to Planned Parenthood of SE Pa. and Rosemont College. **$16,000** to Lincoln Center for Family & Youth. **$15,000** each to Chester County Futures and Philadelphia Community Academy. **$12,000** to Southern Home Services. **$10,000** each to Church of the Advocate, Kensington Area Ministry, Lakeside Educational Network, Norris Square Neighborhood Project, Philadelphia Youth Tennis, and Providence Center. **$7,500** to Community Women's Education Project. **$5,000** each to Allegheny West Foundation, Asociacion de Musicos Latino Americanos, CASA/Youth Advocates, Congreso de Latinos Unidos, Episcopal Community Services, Face to Face/Camp St. Vincent, Frankford Group Ministry, Inn Dwelling, Lutheran Settlement House, Maternity Care Coalition, Neighbor to Neighbor Community Development, and Wagner Free Institute of Science. **$3,500** to Hosanna Ministries. **$2,500** to Northern Home for Children. **$1,500** to Franklin Institute Science Museum. **$1,000** to Philadelphia Zoo. ■**PUBLICATIONS:** application guidelines ■**WEBSITE:** None ■**E-MAIL:** None ■**APPLICATION POLICIES & PROCEDURES:** The Foundation reports that most grants are limited to Greater Philadelphia for special projects, capital needs, endowment, research, or scholarships; no grants are awarded to individuals. Grant requests may be submitted in any form at any time; include an annual report, organizational budget, Board member list, and IRS tax-exempt status documentation. The Board meets in the spring and fall.

O+D+T Bruce A. Rosenfield, Esq. (Managing Director+Con) — J. Alexander Churchman (D) — Leidy McIlvaine Churchman (D) — Leigh Stirling Churchman (D) — W. Morgan Churchman, III (D) — George Connell (D) — George L. Keen, Jr. Esq. (D) — Binney H.C. Wietlisbach

---

SE-096 **Buckingham Mountain Foundation**
Dept. of Surgery, Hospital of U. of Pa.
Silverstein-4th Floor, 3400 Spruce Street
Philadelphia 19104 (Philadelphia County)
AMV $3,026,335 **FYE** 12-00 **(Gifts Received** $69,743)

MI-31-32-34-56-72
Phone 215-662-2024 **FAX** 215-349-5849
EIN 23-6254714 **Year Created** 1952
11 **Grants totaling** $121,500

Mostly local giving. High grant of **$100,000** to U. of Pa. (J.R. Barton Fellowship). **$5,000** to Fox Chase Cancer Center. **$2,500** to Philadelphia Zoo. **$2,000** to American Philosophical Society. **$1,000** each to American Surgical Assn., Elizabeth Blackwell Health Center, and Miraj Medical Center. **Out-of-state** giving includes **$7,500** to U. of Medicine & Dentistry of NJ and contributions to other medical schools. ■**PUBLICATIONS:** annual report ■**WEBSITE:** None ■**E-MAIL:** None ■**APPLICATION POLICIES & PROCEDURES:** The Foundation reports health/medical and education are priority interests; most grants are for general support, endowment, or research and are limited to institutions well known to the Foundation's directors. No grants are awarded to individuals. Prospective applicants should make an initial telephone inquiry about the feasibility of submitting a request. Grant requests may be submitted in a letter, preferably in May or November; include IRS tax-exempt status documentation. The Board awards grants at meetings in July and December.

O+D+T Jonathan E. Rhoads, Jr. M.D. [York] (S+F+D+Donor+Con) — George G. Rhoads, M.D. [NJ] (P+D+Donor) — Frances Rhoads [NJ] (VP+D+Donor) — Julia Rhoads (D)

SE-097 **Bucks County Foundation**
c/o Eastburn & Gray
60 East Court Street
Doylestown 18901 (Bucks County)
AMV $2,895,100 **FYE** 12-00 **(Gifts Received** $0)

MI-41-43-72
Phone 215-345-7000 **FAX** None
EIN 23-9031005 **Year Created** 1980
2 **Grants totaling** $93,440

All giving by this Community Foundation presently is restricted to scholarship awards at Delaware Valley College of Science & Agriculture and Bucks County Community College for needy/deserving students resident in Central Bucks School District. — In prior years some grants awarded for education of abused children and care/shelter of animals in Bucks County, but details are unavailable. ■**PUBLICATIONS:** application guidelines ■**WEBSITE:** None ■**E-MAIL:** gdeon@eastburngray.com ■**APPLICATION POLICIES & PROCEDURES:** The Foundation reports that application guidelines are in the process of being formulated; prospective applicants should request a copy. Scholarships are restricted to needy/deserving students from Central Bucks School District attending Bucks County Community College or Delaware Valley College, and applicants should get guidelines/forms from the financial aid offices at the two colleges. Applicants must apply directly to the colleges which in turn make the selection and notify the Foundation; all disbursements are made to the colleges.

O+D+T Distribution Committee members: Grace Deon, Esq. (P) — Ronald Bolig, Esq. (F) — Enrico J. DiRienzo, M.D. — Roy R. Hager — Jennifer Schumeyer — Jeffrey A. Sprowles — Peter VanDine, J.D. — J. Lawrence Grim, Esq. (Adviser) PNC Advisors (Trustee)

SE-098   Bucks County Medical Society Foundation   MI-12-25-29-31-35
c/o Bucks County Medical Society
200 Apple Street, Suite 3   **Phone** 215-536-8665 **FAX** 215-536-3234
Quakertown 18953   (Bucks County)   **EIN** 23-6563688   **Year Created** 1991
AMV $195,614   **FYE** 12-00   **(Gifts Received** $0)   8 **Grants totaling** $11,330

All giving is limited to Bucks County; grants are for general operations. High grants of **$2,000** each to Big Brothers/Big Sisters of Bucks County, Bucks County Health Improvement Project, and Child Home & Community. **$1,500** each to Interfaith Housing Development, Philabundance, and Red Cross. Other smaller contributions. ■**PUBLICATIONS:** None ■**WEBSITE:** www.bcms-pa.org [Society information only] ■**E-MAIL:** info@bcms-pa.org ■**APPLICATION POLICIES & PROCEDURES:** Only organizations serving the health and well-being of Bucks County residents are eligible to apply; most grants are for general support or special projects. Grant requests may be submitted in a letter during June-August; deadline is September 1st. Grant decisions are made at the Medical Society's Board of Directors meeting in October.

O+D+T John Detweiler (Executive Director+Con)

SE-099   Bucks County Women's Fund, The   MI-12-13-15-16-17-18
P.O. Box 1617   **Phone** 215-345-5440 **FAX** None
Doylestown 18901   (Bucks County)   **EIN** 23-2595505   **Year Created** 1989
AMV $120,000 est.   **FYE** 6-02   **(Gifts Received** $70,000)   5 **Grants totaling** $19,601

All giving restricted to assisting Bucks County organizations serving women and girls. High grant of **$6,200** to Planned Parenthood of Bucks County (Russian outreach worker). **$5,000** to Planned Parenthood of Bucks County (Carolyn Marks Social Justice Fund for advocacy with youth program). **$3,000** each to Bucks County Community College (Women's Center startup) and Sister to Sister Teen Conference. **$1,706** to VITA/Volunteers in Teaching Alternatives. — Grants in prior years awarded to Libertae, Inc., Today, Inc., Upper Bucks YMCA, YWCA of Bucks County, and others. ■**PUBLICATIONS:** application guidelines ■**WEBSITE:** None ■**E-MAIL:** None ■**APPLICATION POLICIES & PROCEDURES:** Only organizations serving women/girls in Bucks County are eligible to apply. The Foundation reports that priority is given to organizations which (a) develop creative/non-traditional services for women; (b) create improvements in delivery of services to women; (c) have limited access to other funding sources; (d) have a majority of women as Board members; (e) hold a feminist philosophy dedicated to empowering women; and (f) fill an identified gap in services to women. No support awarded to/for government agencies, sectarian religious purposes, endowment, capital drives, or political campaigns. Prospective applicants should submit a preliminary letter early in the Fall to the Allocations Committee outlining a request for funding/technical assistance; after Committee review, applicant organizations may be provided with detailed guidelines for submission of a full proposal; the deadline for proposals is late November. Site visits sometimes are made to organizations whose proposals are under consideration. Final decisions on grants/technical assistance are made by the full Board of Directors at meetings in January-February. NOTE: Non-tax-exempt organizations should first contact the Allocations Committee for clarification of status.

O+D+T Mary Jane Kirkpatrick, Ph.D (P+D+Con) — Meredith Betz (VP+D) — Sallie Fabian (S+D) — Dianne Magee, Esq. (F+D) — Elizabeth Fritsch, Esq. (D) — Maggie Leigh Groff (D) — Barbara Katz (D) — Tina Paugh-Greenwood (D)

SE-100   Burket-Plack Foundation   MI-71-72
c/o The Glenmede Trust Company
1650 Market Street, Suite 1200   **Phone** 215-419-6000 **FAX** 215-419-6196
Philadelphia 19103   (Philadelphia County)   **EIN** 23-2735643   **Year Created** 1993
AMV $659,080   **FYE** 12-00   **(Gifts Received** $320,184)   14 **Grants totaling** $25,300

Mostly local giving. High grant of **$5,400** to CARE/Compassionate Animal Relief Effort. **$3,000** to MAC Animal Welfare Fund. **$2,000-$2,500** each to Animal Adoption Center, Mobilization for Animals, Bunny's Animal Shelter, and Greene for Pets. **$1,200** each to Academy of Natural Sciences, Schuylkill Wildlife Rehabilitation, Spayed Club [Frazer], and Spay & Save [Lafayette Hills]. Other smaller contributions for animal welfare purposes. **Out-of-state** giving includes **$1,000** to Fund for Animals [MD]. ■ **PUBLICATIONS:** None ■**WEBSITE:** None ■**E-MAIL:** None ■**APPLICATION POLICIES & PROCEDURES:** The Foundation reports that giving focuses on the Delaware Valley, primarily for rescuing/preventing cruelty to animals and preserving the environment. Grants are for one year and mostly for general support or special projects. Grant requests may be submitted in a letter (3 pages maximum) during October-November (deadline is November 30th); include a Board member list and IRS tax-exempt status documentation. Site visits sometimes are made to organizations being considered for a grant. Grants are awarded at a December meeting.

O+D+T Francis X. Mehaffey (VP+Trust Offfcer at Trust Company+Con) — Carmen W. Burket (C+S+F+Donor)

SE-101   Butterer (M. Verna) Educational Trust   MI-43
P.O. Box 273   **Phone** 215-249-0503 **FAX** None
Fountainville 18923   (Bucks County)   **EIN** 23-7751390   **Year Created** 1995
AMV $4,267,804   **FYE** 1-01   **(Gifts Received** $0)   33 **Grants totaling** $234,124

All grants are college scholarships restricted to Bucks County residents; scholarships typically range from **$2,500** to **$8,000** with some higher and lower. ■**PUBLICATIONS:** Scholarship Application Form ■**WEBSITE:** None ■**E-MAIL:** None ■**APPLICATION POLICIES & PROCEDURES:** Scholarship awards restricted to residents of Bucks County. Application Forms are available at the Guidance Departments of all public/private high schools, colleges and universities in Bucks County, or on request from the Trust Administrator.

O+D+T Elissa J. Kirkegard (Administrator+T+Con) — Dudley W. Saurman (Foundation Manager) — Carol A. Baumhauer [Ottsville] (T) — Elizabeth Boudreau [Doylestown] (T) — Robert W. Butterer [Holland] (T)

SE-102   Butwel Family Foundation
1536 Blueberry Court
Jamison 18929   (Bucks County)

MI-22-31-32-61
Phone 215-491-9227 **FAX** None
EIN 23-7770589   **Year Created** 1994

AMV $336,664   **FYE** 12-00   (**Gifts Received** $0)   8 **Grants totaling** $14,000

Over half local giving. High grant of **$3,000** to St. Cyril Church. **$2,000** to Our Lady of the Lake Church [Pocono Pines]. **$1,000** each to Children's Hospital of Philadelphia, Fox Chase Cancer Center, and Salvation Army. **Out-of-state** giving to Catholic church/organizations in FL and MD. ■**PUBLICATIONS:** None ■**WEBSITE:** None ■**E-MAIL:** None ■**APPLICATION POLICIES & PROCEDURES:** Grant requests may be submitted in a letter at any time; describe the organization and purpose of the request, and include IRS tax-exempt status documentation.

O+D+T Nancy C. Devlin (Administrator+T+Con) — Susan Goetter [Pipersville] (T+S) — Henry E. Butwel (T+Donor) — Catherine M. Butwel (T+Donor)

SE-103   Byers Foundation, The
c/o Byers' Choice Ltd.
4355 County Line Road, P.O. Box 158
Chalfont 18914   (Bucks County)

MI-13-15-22-25-29-31-32-41-42-52-54-56-63
64-82-85
Phone 215-822-6700 **FAX** 215-822-7665
EIN 23-2406657   **Year Created** 1986

AMV $3,333,657   **FYE** 12-00   (**Gifts Received** $2,800,000)   47 **Grants totaling** $1,414,705

Mostly local giving. High grant of **$150,000** to Doylestown Hospital. **$100,000** each to City Center Academy, Biblical Theological Seminary, and Williamson Free School of Mechanical Trades. **$50,000** each to Christ's Home Retirement Community. Fox Chase Cancer Center, and Souderton Mennonite Homes. **$35,000** to Central Bucks YMCA. **$30,000** to Academy of Vocal Arts. **$25,000** each to Delaware Valley College, Haycock Camping Ministries, The Heritage Conservancy, National Liberty Museum, and Plumsteadville Christian School. **$12,500** to SAT7 North America [Wayne]. **$11,000** each to Please Touch Museum and YMCA of Philadelphia & Vicinity. **$10,000** each to City Team Ministries, Eastern College, Healthlink Medical Center, International Health Services, Life Abundant, Inc., and Philadelphia Leadership Fund. **$5,000** to Christ Lutheran Church of Upper Darby, Neighbor to Neighbor, The Irish Memorial, and Willow Grove Community Development Corp. **$3,000** to Philabundance. **$2,500** each to Opera Company of Philadelphia. **Out-of-state** giving includes **$114,555** to Salvation Army [NY]; **$100,000** to Caring Institute [DC]; **$50,000** each to Advancing Churches in Missions Committee [GA] and World Vision [WA]; **$30,000** to Interdev [WA]; **$25,000** to CBMC International [TN]; **$20,000** to Opportunity International [IL]; **$17,150** to Bengali Evangelical Assn. [CA]; and smaller grants **$3,000-$15,000**, mostly for Christian activities. ■**PUBLICATIONS:** None ■**WEBSITE:** www.byerschoice.com [corporate info only] ■**E-MAIL:** None ■**APPLICATION POLICIES & PROCEDURES:** The Foundation reports that giving focuses on Bucks and Montgomery counties where Byers' Choice Ltd. employees are active in community. Grant requests may be submitted at any time in a one-page letter which gives the name of the company employee who is involved; include organizational and project budgets, list of major funding sources, a Board member list, and IRS tax-exempt status documentation. The Delaware Valley Grantmakers Common Grant Application Form also may be used. Site visits sometimes are made to organizations being considered for a grant. Grants are awarded at an annual meeting in the fall.

O+D+T Robert L. Byers (P+D+Donor+Con) — Robert L. Byers, Jr. (Executive VP+D) — Jeffrey D. Byers (VP+D) — Joyce F. Byers (S+F+D+Donor) — Alex J. Mandl [VA] (Donor) — Corporate donor: Byers' Choice Ltd.

SE-104   Cades (Ralph E.) Family Foundation, The
191 Presidential Boulevard, Suite 924
Bala Cynwyd 19004   (Montgomery County)

MI-12-20-53-55
Phone 215-546-0404 **FAX** None
EIN 23-2164662   **Year Created** 1979

AMV $159,123   **FYE** 11-00   (**Gifts Received** $16,250)   31 **Grants totaling** $15,280

Mostly local giving. High grant of **$10,000** to Pa. Academy of the Fine Arts. **$1,000** each to Juvenile Law Center and The Print Center. Other local and out-of-state contributions **$25-$400** each for various purposes. ■**PUBLICATIONS:** None ■**WEBSITE:** None ■**E-MAIL:** None ■**APPLICATION POLICIES & PROCEDURES:** The Foundation reports priority giving interests are animal welfare, scholarship aid for operatic and music students, the arts, and medical research, preferably in the Miami and Philadelphia areas. No grants awarded to individuals. Submit grant requests at any time on letterhead stationery; describe the proposed program/project and include a list of staff and Board members, a financial statement, and IRS tax-exempt status documentation. Grants are usually awarded at meetings in early June and December.

O+D+T Stewart R. Cades, Esq. (F+Manager+Donor+Con) — Lilian G. Cades [FL] (P+S+Donor)

SE-105   Cain Foundation, The
c/o General Doors Corporation
1 Monroe Street, P.O. Box 205
Bristol 19007   (Bucks County)

MI-22-41-43-61
Phone 215-788-9277 **FAX** None
EIN 23-2494912   **Year Created** 1987

AMV $517,059   **FYE** 11-00   (**Gifts Received** $100,000)   10 **Grants totaling** $73,000

All local or NJ giving. High grant of **$50,000** to St. Catherine of Siena (building fund). **$8,000** to Catholic Charities. **$3,000** each to Ancillae Assumpta, St. Charles Borromeo, and St. Mary's Academy. **$1,500** each to Father McCafferty Scholarship Fund, Christ the King Catholic Church, Christ the King Catholic School, and St. Ignatius Catholic Church. ■**PUBLICATIONS:** None ■**WEBSITE:** None ■**E-MAIL:** None ■**APPLICATION POLICIES & PROCEDURES:** The Foundation reports that grants are made to organizations as determined by the trustees in their sole discretion; applications are not solicited.

O+D+T George P. Cain, Sr. [NJ] (T+Donor+Con) — Mary J. Cain [NJ] (T+Donor)

SE-106   **Cairns (Ernestine Bacon) Trust**   **MI**-42-43-52
c/o Mellon Private Wealth Management
1735 Market Street, Room 193-0370   **Phone** 215-553-2596 **FAX** 215-553-4542
Philadelphia   19103   (Philadelphia County)   **EIN** 23-6745014   **Year Created** 1982
AMV $2,928,945   **FYE** 9-00   **(Gifts Received** $0)   **Grants totaling** $0

All giving restricted to scholarship funds for Philadelphia-area schools of music. No grants awarded in 2000; in the the prior year **$100,000** was awarded: **$50,000** to Curtis Institute of Music; **$20,000** to Settlement Music School; and **$15,000** each to Academy of Vocal Arts and U. of the Arts. ■**PUBLICATIONS:** None ■**WEBSITE:** None ■**E-MAIL:** smith.ft@mellon.com ■**APPLICATION POLICIES & PROCEDURES:** Only Philadelphia-area accredited schools of music are eligible to apply for scholarship funds; grantee institutions award scholarships to worthy students, preferably those studying voice. Grants are awarded directly to the schools, not the students.

O+D+T Frances T. Smith (Portfolio Officer at Bank+Con) — Thomas J. Burke, Esq. (Co-T) Mellon Bank N.A. (Trustee)

SE-107   **Cameron (Alpin J. & Alpin W.) Memorial Trust**   **MI**-12-13-14-15-17-18-22-25-31-32-33-41-42
c/o Ehmann, Van Denbergh & Trainor   52-54-57-71-79-81-83
Two Penn Center Plaza, Suite 725   **Phone** 215-851-9800 **FAX** 215-851-9820
Philadelphia   19102   (Philadelphia County)   **EIN** 23-6213225   **Year Created** 1957
AMV $5,541,146   **FYE** 9-00   **(Gifts Received** $0)   98 **Grants totaling** $238,800

Mostly local/Pa. giving; all grants are for general support. High grants of **$10,000** each Glaucoma Service Foundation to Prevent Blindness and Red Cross. **$9,000** to Bethesda Mission. **$6,000** to Friends Hospital. **$5,000** each to Assn. of Independent Colleges & Universities-Pa. [Mechanicsburg], Franklin Institute, Gesu Catholic School, Mercy Suburban Hospital, Opera Company of Philadelphia, Planned Parenthood of Southeastern Pa., Salvation Army, and Visiting Nurse Assn. of Greater Philadelphia. **$4,000** each to Friends School-Haverford, Independence Seaport Museum, Inglis House, Pa. Academy of the Fine Arts, and Philadelphia Orchestra. **$3,000-$3,500** each to Academy of Natural Sciences, The Baldwin School, Center School, MANNA/Metropolitan AIDS Neighborhood Nutrition Alliance, North Philadelphia Health System, Northern Home for Children, School of Rose Valley, Southern Home Services, Wheels, Inc., and William Penn Charter School. **$2,000-$2,500** each to American Bird Conservancy, Chester-Swarthmore College Community Coalition, Children's Seashore House, Choral Arts Society of Philadelphia, Domestic Abuse Project of Delaware County, Family & Community Service of Delaware County, Gwynedd Friends Meeting, Pa. School for the Deaf, Penn State U., Philabundance, Philadelphia Museum of Art, Planned Parenthood of Susquehanna Valley [Harrisburg], Providence Center, Public Interest Law Center of Philadelphia, Riverbend Environmental Education Center, School at Rose Valley, Temple U., U. of the Arts, University Museum, WHYY-TV12, Woodmere Art Gallery, Young Audiences of Eastern Pa., and Young Scholars Charter School. **$1,000-$1,500** each to Big Brother/Big Sister Assn. of Philadelphia, Boys & Girls Clubs of Metropolitan Philadelphia, Carson Valley School, City Team Ministries, Friends Central School, Greater Philadelphia Urban Affairs Council, Greater Philadelphia Urban League, Greentree School, Haverford College, International House of Philadelphia, Pa. Pro Musica, Philadelphia Citizens for Children & Youth, Philadelphia College of Textiles & Science, Philadelphia High School for Girls, Police Athletic League, Providence Friends Meeting, Shalom, Inc., U. of Pa., U. of Pa. Law School, Voyage House, White-Williams Scholars, and YWCA of Philadelphia. Other smaller contributions for similar purposes. **Out-of-state** grants, mostly **$1,000-$2,500,** for environmental or educational purposes with a focus on the Adirondacks. ■**PUBLICATIONS:** None ■**WEBSITE:** None ■ **E-MAIL:** mpastuszek@evt.net ■**APPLICATION POLICIES & PROCEDURES:** The Trust reports that giving is generally restricted to the Philadelphia area with grants typically $1,000-$5,000. No grants are awarded for lobbying/advocacy activities. Grant requests may be submitted in a letter at any time; include an annual report, organization and project budgets, list of Board members, list of major funding sources, audited financial statement, and IRS tax-exempt status documentation. Grants are awarded at Board of Overseers meetings held in March, June, September, and December.

O+D+T Members of the Board of Overseers: Ross Van Denbergh, Esq. [Wallingford] (Con) — Jonathan H. Sprogell [Rose Valley] — Frederick A. Van Denbergh, Jr. [Gwynedd] — Margaret Anne Van Denbergh [Villanova] PNC Advisors (Trustee)

SE-108   **Camp Council, Inc.**   **MI**-12-14-22-62-84
961 Frog Hollow Terrace   **Phone** Unlisted **FAX** None
Rydal   19406   (Montgomery County)   **EIN** 23-6000790   **Year Created** 1995
AMV $1,206,028   **FYE** 12-00   **(Gifts Received** $0)   10 **Grants totaling** $100,000

All local giving. High grant of **$35,000** to Golden Slipper Camp. **$20,000** to Jewish Federation of Philadelphia. **$12,000** to Jewish Community Center/Klein Branch Day Camp. **$4,000-$6,000** each to Camp Galil, Easter Seal Society, Female Hebrew Benevolent Society, Gan Israel Day Camp, Jewish Family & Children's Service, Pinemere Camp, and Variety Club. ■**PUBLICATIONS:** None ■**WEBSITE:** None ■**E-MAIL:** None ■**APPLICATION POLICIES & PROCEDURES:** Information not available.

O+D+T Herbert Sachs (F+Con) — Judy Kramer [Jenkintown] (P) — Tracy Kauffman-Wood [Ardmore] (S)

SE-109   **Camp Foundation**   **MI**-22-62
1611 Gerson Drive   **Phone** 610-668-7394 **FAX** None
Penn Valley   19072   (Montgomery County)   **EIN** 23-6478899   **Year Created** 1069
AMV $126,029   **FYE** 12-99   **(Gifts Received** $0)   **Grants totaling** $21,748

Most giving is for religious purposes. High grant of **$4,500** to Beth Am Israel. No details available on **$17,248** in other grants/contributions. — In prior year **$5,950** to Beth Am Israel. ■**PUBLICATIONS:** None ■**WEBSITE:** None ■**E-MAIL:** None ■ **APPLICATION POLICIES & PROCEDURES:** Grant requests in any form may be submitted at any time.

O+D+T David I. Camp (T+Con) — Jonathon C. Camp [MD] (T)

SE-110   Campbell-Oxholm Foundation, The

622 South Bowman Ave.
Merion Station   19066   (Montgomery County)

MI-12-13-17-18-25-29-35-41-42
Phone 610-687-4856 **FAX** None
EIN 23-2790496   **Year Created** 1995

AMV $2,981,012   **FYE** 12-00   **(Gifts Received** $0)   28 **Grants totaling** $129,300

About half local giving; all grants are for general operating support. High grant of **$25,000** to Planned Parenthood of SE Pa. **$10,000** each to Norris Square Civic Assn. and Project H.O.M.E. **$8,000** to Philadelphia Futures. **$5,500** to U. of Pa. Graduate School of Education (Partners Program). **$5,000** each to Bread & Roses Community Fund and Greater Philadelphia Women's Medical Fund. **$3,000** to White-Williams Scholars. **$2,500** to Philadelphia Citizens for Children & Youth. **$1,000** each to Philabundance and Support Center for Child Advocates. **$800** to One Love. **Out-of-state** giving, mostly to OR, includes **$10,000** each to Community Outreach of Corvallis and Benton County Youth Shelter; and smaller grants, many for child welfare purposes. ■ **PUBLICATIONS:** None ■ **WEBSITE:** None ■ **E-MAIL:** kcoxholm@comcast.net ■ **APPLICATION POLICIES & PROCEDURES:** Grant requests may be submitted in proposals which follow Delaware Valley Grantmakers' Common Grant Application Form (see Appendix or www.dvg.org).

O+D+T Kimberly C. Oxholm (P+Con) — C. Duncan Campbell [OR] (Senior VP) — Janet L. Campbell [OR] (VP) — Carl Oxholm, III (S)

SE-111   Caplan Family Charitable Trust

P.O. Box 14
Bryn Mawr   19010   (Montgomery County)

MI-14-17-35-43-81
Phone 610-527-1812 **FAX** None
EIN 23-7749795   **Year Created** 1993

AMV $204,646   **FYE** 12-00   **(Gifts Received** $0)   37 **Grants totaling** $11,200

About half local giving. High Pa. grants of **$1,000** each to Greater Philadelphia Women's Medical Fund and Lower Merion Township Scholarship Fund. **$500** to Overbrook School for the Blind. **$400** to Planned Parenthood Advocates of Chester County. Other smaller local contributions for various purposes. **Out-of-state** giving includes **$2,000** to Middle East Forum [DC] (the Investigating Project) and **$1,000** to FLAME [CA]. ■ **PUBLICATIONS:** None ■ **WEBSITE:** None ■ **E-MAIL:** None ■ **APPLICATION POLICIES & PROCEDURES:** Grant requests may be submitted in an informal letter at any time.

O+D+T James A. Caplan (T+Donor+Con)

SE-112   Cardone (Michael) Foundation

c/o Cardone Industries, Inc.
5670 Rising Sun Avenue
Philadelphia   19120   (Philadelphia County)

MI-12-22-25-32-41-63-64
Phone 215-722-9700 **FAX** None
EIN 23-6652761   **Year Created** 1977

AMV $4,915,356   **FYE** 12-00   **(Gifts Received** $0)   308 **Grants totaling** $765,750

About half local/Pa. giving; all grants are for general support. High grant of **$200,000** to Christian Life Center [Bensalem]. **$25,000** to Spirit & Truth Fellowship. **$20,000** to Center for Urban Resources. **$18,000** to Lighthouse Family Center. **$15,000** to Philadelphia Committee to End Homelessness. **$10,000-$10,500** each each to American Cancer Society, Delaware Valley Habitat for Humanity, and Salvation Army. **$9,750** to Calvary Chapel of Philadelphia. **$6,500** to St. Mary's Orthodox Church of Philadelphia. **$5,000-$5,500** each to Bethel Deliverance Church, Bethel Fellowship Community Church, and Oasis Tabernacle Assembly of God. **$3,500** to Marantha Assembly of God. **$2,500** to Philadelphia Full Gospel Assembly. **$2,000** to Calvary Assembly of God of Wyncote. **$1,000-$1,500** each to Bensalem Baseball of Lower Bucks, Biblical Theological Seminary, Calvary Christian Academy, and Coalition for Christian Outreach [Pittsburgh]. Also, **$300-$1,500** each for 75 other churches, schools or organizations in Pa. **Out-of-state** giving includes **$20,500** to South Jersey Vietnamese Alliance Church [NJ]; **$16.500** to Kingsway Assembly of God [NJ]; **$14,000** to Calvary Temple Assembly of God [NJ]; **$12,250** to Oral Roberts U. [OK]; **$10,000** to Lifeline Chaplaincy [TX]; and numerous other grants/contributions **$500-$5,000** for churches and religious organizations nationwide. ■ **PUBLICATIONS:** special request form ■ **WEBSITE:** None ■ **E-MAIL:** None ■ **APPLICATION POLICIES & PROCEDURES:** Grant requests may be submitted at any time on a special request form available from the Foundation. No grants awarded to individuals.

O+D+T Jacqueline Cardone [Cheltenham] (C+T+Con) — Michael Cardone, Jr. [Cheltenham] Corporate donor: Cardone Industries, Inc.

SE-113   Caritas Foundation, The

700 Hobbs Road
Wayne   19087   (Montgomery County)

MI-22-41-42-61-64-84
Phone 610-687-1753 **FAX** None
EIN 23-6802982   **Year Created** 1984

AMV $2,166,883   **FYE** 9-00   **(Gifts Received** $53,261)   **Grants totaling** $38,662

About three-fourths local/Pa. giving. High Pa. grants of **$5,000** each to Villanova Block V Club (sports program) and Society of St. John [Pike County]. **$2,000** to Catholic Charities. **$1,700** to The Second Mile [State College]. **$1,000** each to Bedesen Scholarship Foundation [Bucks County], Our Lady of Hope [Philadelphia], Priestley Fraternity of St. Peter [Lackawanna County], and St. Gregory's Academy [Lackawanna County]. **$763** to Villanova U. Other smaller contributions, many for Catholic churches, institutions or organizations. **Out-of-state** giving includes **$2,500** to College of St. Thomas More [TX]; **$2,000** to Augustinian Peruvian Missions [Peru]; and **$1,100** to Caasa Balthasar [Italy]. ■ **PUBLICATIONS:** None ■ **WEBSITE:** None ■ **E-MAIL:** None ■ **APPLICATION POLICIES & PROCEDURES:** The Foundation reports priority interests are Roman Catholic institutions, human services, education, aiding special-needs children, and programs dealing with the free market system and personal liberty. No grants awarded to individuals.

O+D+T Marybeth Toscani (Con) — Patrice A. McGinley [Malvern] (T) — Dominic P. Toscani, Jr. [NJ] (T+Donor) — Gerard M. Toscani [NJ] (T+Donor) — Lisa Toscani [Phoenixville] (T) — Corporate donors: Lindenmeyr Paper Company; Peck, Young & Van Sant; Technicarbon

SE-114 Carlson Cultural Trust MI-41-42-44-53-54-55
c/o Ediene's
3 South 3rd Street **Phone** 610-932-0366 **FAX** None
Oxford 19363 (Chester County) **EIN** 23-7752835 **Year Created** 1994
AMV $491,006 **FYE** 12-00 (**Gifts Received** $0) 15 **Grants totaling** $32,152

Mostly local/Lancaster County giving. High grant of **$10,000** to Quarryville Library. **$5,000** to Ware Presbyterian Church. **$2,300** to Solanco School District. **$2,000** each to Clermont Elementary School, Lancaster Museum of Art, and Temple U./Tyler School of Art. **$1,000-$1,100** each to Art Show, Art Institute of Philadelphia, Elizabethtown College, Kutztown U., Millersville U., The Restaurant School, and West Chester U. **$750** to Antonelli Institute of Photography [Philadelphia]. **Out-of-state** grant: **$1,000** to Cedarville College [OH]. ■**PUBLICATIONS:** None ■**WEBSITE:** None ■**E-MAIL:** None ■**APPLICATION POLICIES & PROCEDURES:** The Foundation's primary focus is enhancing the artistic/cultural understanding and awareness of southern Chester County and Lancaster County residents. No grants are awarded to individuals.

O+D+T John W. Roberts (T+Con) — Judith A. Bergdoll [Peach Bottom] (T) — Richard Humphreys [Kirkwood] (T) — Ediene Ringler (T) — Stephen Roka [Holtwood] (T)

SE-115 Carlson (Gunard Berry) Memorial Foundation, The MI-13-14-22-29-31-34-41-42-44-56-61-63
c/o G.O. Carlson, Inc.
352 Thorndale-Marshallton Road, P.O. Box 526 **Phone** 610-384-2800 **FAX** 610-383-6032
Thorndale 19372 (Chester County) **EIN** 23-6261693 **Year Created** 1957
AMV $1,795,614 **FYE** 12-00 (**Gifts Received** $7,500) 28 **Grants totaling** $72,075

Mostly local/Pa. giving. High grant of **$10,000** to St. Joseph's Church of Downingtown. **$6,625** to Bishop Shanahan High School (building fund/tuition fund). **$5,000** each to Brandywine Hospital Auxiliary. Downingtown Good Neighbor Community Center, Jefferson Medical College & U., Lafayette College (leadership campaign), and Villa Maria Lower School. **$2,500** to Catholic Charities. **$2,000** to Assn. of Independent Colleges [Harrisburg]. **$1,000-$1,600** each to Coatesville Area Public Library, Coatesville Cultural Society, Friends Central School, Lafayette College (annual giving), Muhlenberg College, Philabundance, Perkiomen School (annual fund), Red Cross/Greater Brandywine, St. Aloysius Academy, St. Francis College [Blair County] (writing contest), and St. Martha Manor. **Out-of-state** grant: **$4,000** to Community Presbyterian Church of Brigantine [NJ] and **$2,000** to Bacharach Rehabilitation Hospital [NJ]. ■**PUBLICATIONS:** None ■**WEBSITE:** None ■**E-MAIL:** None ■**APPLICATION POLICIES & PROCEDURES:** Most grants are awarded for capital projects, scholarship funds, or special programs in the fields of religion, health, community efforts, and education; no grants are awarded to individuals. Submit grant requests in a letter (2 pages maximum) that describes the nature of the project and states the amount requested; include a project budget and IRS tax-exempt status documentation. Requests should be submitted in, preferably, May-June or October-November, but at least two weeks before semi-annual Distribution Meetings held the last Friday in July and the first Friday in December.

O+D+T Barbara C. Travaglini (D+Con) — Benjamin Bacharach [NJ] (D) — Rev. Vincent Negherbon (D) — A. Frederick Travaglini (D)

SE-116 Carpenter (E. Rhodes & Leona B.) Foundation, The MI-15-22-31-34-35-39-42-53-54-64
c/o Morgan Lewis & Bockius
1701 Market Street, P.O. Box 58880 **Phone** 215-963-5212 **FAX** 215-963-5299
Philadelphia 19102 (Philadelphia County) **EIN** 51-0155772 **Year Created** 1975
AMV $237,865,221 **FYE** 12-00 (**Gifts Received** $0) 150+ **Grants totaling** $10,626,224

Limited Pa. giving. High Pa. grant of **$150,000** to Washington Hospital Foundation [Washington County] (new residential hospice facility). **$85,000** to Lancaster Theological Seminary (international scholar expenses). **$60,000** to Children's Hospital of Philadelphia (supportive nursing care salary). **$50,000** to Keystone Hospice [Wyncote] (residential facility purchase). **$47,700** to Moravian Theological Seminary [Bethlehem] (international student scholarships). **$25,000** to The Mattress Factory [Pittsburgh] (exhibition). **$20,724** to Board of Rabbis of Greater Philadelphia (Jewish Hospice Chaplaincy Program). **$17,500** to Visiting Nurse Assn. of Pottstown & Vicinity (home health/hospice care). **$15,000** to Wissahickon Hospice (needy patient fund). **$11,440** to U. of Pa. Health System (Rabbinic Externship position). **$10,000** to Delco Memorial Foundation (volunteer program support). **$7,500** to The Fabric Workshop (Artists-in-Residence program). **$5,000** to Citizen Advocacy of Chester County (general support). **$2,000** to Old First Reformed Church (renovations). **Out-of-state** giving includes high grant of **$1,080,000** to Johns Hopkins U. [MD] (mostly community Health Nursing Program endowment); **$1,000,000** to Virginia Museum of Fine Arts Foundation (Asian art galleries/collection care); **$537,** 570 to Art Institute of Chicago [IL] (Chinese exhibit); **$500,000** to Science Museum of Virginia Foundation (programs/equipment); **$380,000** to Pacific School of Religion [CA] (Center for Lesbian & Gay Studies in Religion and Ministries); **$340,000** to Princeton U. Center for Study of Religion (visiting theological scholars program); **$313,365** to Richmond Ballet [VA] (new building/operations); **$229,325** to Nelson-Atkins Museum of Art [MO] (exhibition catalogue); **$200,000** to Virginia Opera (seasonal support); and other grants mostly **$5,000-$150,000** for similar purposes nationwide, with major giving concentrations to Richmond, VA, northwestern NC, and Temple, TX areas. ■**PUBLICATIONS:** None ■**WEBSITE:** None ■**E-MAIL:** None ■**APPLICATION POLICIES & PROCEDURES:** The Foundation reports that grants are awarded only for specific projects/programs at the following: (1) public institutions which had direct relationships with Leona or Rhodes Carpenter during their lifetimes; (2) graduate theological educational institutions; (3) museums—including those associated with colleges or universities—for purchase, restoration, and conservation of Asian art; (4) organizations relating to education in the field of Asian art; (5) organizations involved in providing hospice care; or (6) public charities in communities where E.R. Carpenter Co. had longtime manufacturing or business facilities—presently this refers only to the Richmond, VA area and only from arts organizations there. Generally, no grants will be awarded to/for endowment, private secondary education, or large public charities such as the American Cancer Society, Red Cross, United Ways, etc. Submit requests in an informal letter before the March 15th or September 15th deadlines which includes (a) a brief organizational history, (b) description of the project/program for which the support is requested, (c) a detailed project/program budget, (e) a specific amount being requested, and (e) IRS tax-exempt status documentation. Note: No decisions on grant awards are made by the Philadelphia-based Contact Person; all grant requests are redirected to Board members resident in MA or VA.

O+D+T Joseph A. O'Connor, Jr. Esq. (Con) — Ann B. Day [MA] (P+D) — Paul B. Day, Jr. [VA] (VP+S+F+D) — M.H. Reinhart [VA] (D)

SE-117   **Carter Memorial Foundation, The**   MI-14-22-32-34-41-42-43-56-71
      74 Pasture Lane, Apt. 120   **Phone** 610-527-3303   **FAX** None
      Bryn Mawr   19010   (Montgomery County)   **EIN** 23-6395203   **Year Created** 1963
AMV $1,130,647   **FYE** 12-00   **(Gifts Received** $15)   23 **Grants totaling** $25,550

About two-thirds local giving; grants are for general support except as noted. High Pa. grant of **$3,000** to Great Valley Nature Center. **$2,500** to Community Gardens of Chester County. **$2,000** to College of Physicians of Philadelphia. **$1,000** each to Fox Chase Cancer Center, Missions Unlimited [Wallingford], Peter Wentz Farmstead Society [Worcester], Recording for the Blind, and Riverbend Environmental Education Center. Other smaller local contributions for private schools, human services, and cultural organizations. **Out-of-state** giving includes high grant of **$5,000** for a scholarship [MA]; **$1,500** to Wells College [NY]; and **$1,000** to U. of Michigan (graduate-level ecological research). ■**PUBLICATIONS:** application guidelines letter ■**WEBSITE:** None ■**E-MAIL:** None ■**APPLICATION POLICIES & PROCEDURES:** The Foundation's primary interests are (1) promoting/protecting the welfare of children/young adults, (2) advancing medical research in diseases affecting children/young adults, and (3) supporting higher education scholarships. Of particular interest is support for fresh, innovative approaches to pressing educational, societal, or medical problems. Most grants are for special projects or scholarships. Prospective applicants initially should make a telephone inquiry about the feasibility of submitting a request. Grant requests may be submitted in a letter (3 pages maximum)— deadline is November 30th; includes (a) a one-sentence summary of the request; (b) the amount of funding requested; (c) a description of what the funds will be used for, including how the requested amount was determined, how the grant would affect the program/project, and a timetable for expending the grant; (d) how the requested grant relates to the organization's mission and current activities; (e) plans for funding the program/project when the Foundation's funding expires, and (f) a copy of IRS tax-exempt status documentation. If kept to a minimum, other supporting documentation (letters, information, etc.) may be submitted. Site visits sometimes are made to organizations being considered for a grant. The Board awards grants at June and December meetings. — Formerly called the Charles Carter Wentz Foundation.

O+D+T Eleanor B. Wentz (P+D+Con) — Harriet B. Wentz [West Chester] (VP+D) — Helen Wentz Panitt [VA] (S+D) — Charles R. Wentz, III [MA] (D) — Bess Wentz Woodworth [MA] (D)

SE-118   **Casper (Doris S.) Foundation**   MI-22-41-51-52-54-62
      Society Hill Towers, #17A
      200 Locust Street   **Phone** 215-627-4271   **FAX** None
      Philadelphia   19106   (Philadelphia County)   **EIN** 23-2441111   **Year Created** 1986
AMV $6,989   **FYE** 9-00   **(Gifts Received** $18,000)   120 **Grants totaling** $16,905

Mostly local giving. High grant of **$1,425** to Society Hill Synagogue. **$1,250** to Opera Company of Philadelphia. **$1,000** to Federation Allied Jewish Appeal. **$700** to Pa. Ballet. **$650** to Philadelphia Museum of Art. Many smaller local contributions for cultural, Jewish and other purposes. **Out-of-state** grant: **$1,300** to Close-Up Foundation for Oakland Technical High School [CA]. ■**PUBLICATIONS:** None ■**WEBSITE:** None ■**E-MAIL:** None ■**APPLICATION POLICIES & PROCEDURES:** The Foundation reports that unsolicited grant requests are not accepted. — Formerly called the Lee A. Casper Foundation.

O+D+T Doris S. Casper (P+F+Donor+Con) — Stanley J. Casper (S)

SE-119   **Cassett (Louis N.) Foundation**   MI-11-12-13-14-15-17-22-25-31-32-41-42-51
      c/o Gerstley Estates   52-54-55-56-62-63-71
      335 One Penn Center, 1617 JFK Boulevard   **Phone** 215-563-8886   **FAX** 215-972-0295
      Philadelphia   19103   (Philadelphia County)   **EIN** 23-6274038   **Year Created** 1946
AMV $12,255,521   **FYE** 12-00   **(Gifts Received** $0)   195 **Grants totaling** $636,350

About two-thirds local/Pa. giving; some grants comprise multiple payments. High grant of **$50,000** to Regional Performing Arts Center. **$25,000** to Philadelphia Geriatric Center. **$15,000** each to Abington Art Center, Federation Allied Jewish Appeal, Philadelphia Orchestra, and United Way of SE Pa. **$10,000** to Academy of Music Restoration Fund. **$7,500** to Abington Memorial Hospital. **$6,000** to Cystic Fibrosis Foundation of Delaware Valley. **$4,000-$5,000** each to Baldwin School, Mann Center for the Performing Arts, Philadelphia Museum of Art, Settlement Music School, and Temple U./Music Preparatory Dept. **$3,000-$3,600** each to Camp Rainbow, Crime Prevention Assn., Developmental Enterprises Corp., Executive Service Corps of the Delaware Valley, Jewish Employment Vocational Service, Kelly Ann Dolan Memorial Fund, MANNA/Metropolitan AIDS Neighborhood Nutrition Alliance, Montgomery County Assn. for the Blind, Opera Company of Philadelphia, Pa. Ballet, Philadanco, Philadelphia Ronald McDonald House, Planned Parenthood of SE Pa., Southern Home Services, Pa. Special Olympics, Philadelphia Orchestra, Wilma Theatre, and Young Audiences of SE Pa. **$2,000-$2,750** each to Academy of Natural Sciences, Artreach, Carelift International, Brian's House, CARIE/Center for Advocacy for the Rights & Interests of the Elderly, Carnegie Mellon U. [Pittsburgh], Carson Valley School, Children's Aid Society, Christmas in April, Committee of Seventy, Creative Artists Network, Curtis Institute of Music, Diversified Community Services, Drexel U. (student support), Elmwood Park Zoo, Frankford Group Ministry, Franklin Institute, Free Library of Philadelphia, From The Heart, Gateway Employment Resources, Jewish Family & Children's Service, Kardon Institute of the Arts, Main Line Art Center, March of Dimes, MBF Center, Moore College of Art & Design, Operation Understanding, Opportunities Industrialization Center, Ophthalmic Research Associates, Painted Bride Art Center, Penn State Dance Marathon, Philabundance, Philadelphia Senior Center, Please Touch Museum, Police Athletic League of Philadelphia, Recording for the Blind & Dyslexic, Rock School of Pa. Ballet, Royer-Greaves School for the Blind, RSVP of Montgomery County, Salvation Army, United Westmont Soccer Assn., Urban Bridges at St. Gabriel, Urban Tree Connection, Variety Club, Wheels, White-Williams Scholars, Wissahickon Hospice, Women's Assn. for Women's Alternatives, and Women in Transition. About 50 other grants **$1,000-$1,750** for various local purposes: arboreta, art/cultural centers, children, day care, disabled, ethnic, health care, museums, music, schools, senior centers, women, and youth. **Out-of-state** giving includes **$50,000** to United Cerebral Palsy [NY]; **$25,000** to First Unitarian Church of North Palm Beach [FL]; **$20,000** to Fairfield U. [CT]; **$10,000** each to Children's Hospital Trust [FL], Friends of the Unitarian-Universalist Church [MA], and Raymond Kravis Center [FL]; and smaller grants, many to FL. ■ **PUBLICATIONS:** None ■ **WEBSITE:** None ■ **E-MAIL:** None ■ **APPLICATION POLICIES & PROCEDURES:** The Foundation reports that giving is largely limited to the Northeastern U.S., mostly for special projects, building funds, research, and matching grants. No grants are awarded to individuals or for endowment. Prospective applicants should initially telephone the Foundation to inquire about the feasibility of submitting a request. Grant requests may be submitted in a letter during September-December; specify the amount/purpose of requested grant and provide organizational background information. The Trustees meet as necessary to award grants.

O+D+T Malcolm B. Jacobson (T+Con) — Albert J. Elias (T) — Carol K. Gerstley (T)

SE-120 **Catherwood Foundation, The**
P.O. Box 80
Bryn Mawr 19010 (Montgomery County)
AMV $378,972 **FYE** 12-00 **(Gifts Received** $0)

MI-12-14-17-29-35-41-42-72
Phone 610-525-3720 **FAX** None
EIN 23-6235334 **Year Created** 1948
22 **Grants totaling** $32,000

Mostly local/Pa. giving; grants are for general operating support except as noted. High grant of **$15,000** to Philadelphia Zoo (conservation program for neotropical primates). **$5,000** each to U. of Pa. and Red Cross (disaster relief fund). **$1,000** each to Easter Seals (president's council) and Pa. Partnerships for Children [Harrisburg] (child advocacy program). **$500** each to Greater Philadelphia Women's Medical Fund and Shipley School. Other smaller local contributions for various purposes. **Out-of-state** giving includes **$1,000** each to U. of Virginia/Colgate-Darden Graduate School and Longyear Museum [MA]. ■ **PUBLICATIONS:** None ■ **WEBSITE:** None ■ **E-MAIL:** None ■ **APPLICATION POLICIES & PROCEDURES:** The Foundation reports that giving focuses primarily on the fine arts or scientific research in Metropolitan Philadelphia. No grants are awarded to individuals. Grant requests may be submitted in a letter (2 pages maximum) before the November 30th deadline; describe the proposed project, state the amount of funding requested, and include an annual report, organization and project budgets, Board member list, list of major funding sources, audited financial statement, and IRS tax-exempt status documentation. Site visits sometimes are made to organizations being considered for a grant. The Board awards grants at a December meeting.

O+D+T Cummins Catherwood, Jr. (P+D+Donor+Con) — W. Perry Gresh (VP+D) — Tucker C. Gresh (S+F+D) — Susan W. Catherwood (D)

SE-121 **Cavitolo (Andrea) Foundation, The**
c/o ACF Holding Company
303 West Lancaster Ave., #265
Wayne 19087 (Delaware County)
AMV $923,156 **FYE** 5-01 **(Gifts Received** $483,223)

MI-14-31-22-32-41-54
Phone 610-656-4301 **FAX** None
EIN 23-2818544 **Year Created** 1995
19 **Grants totaling** $67,235

All local giving. High grant of **$40,000** to Children's Hospital of Philadelphia Foundation. **$10,000** to Wills Eye Hospital. **$3,380** to The Shipley School. **$2,400** to Philadelphia Museum of Art. **$2,000** to Philadelphia Charity Ball. **$1,000** to The Center for Loss and Bereavement [Skippack]. **$840** to Academy of Music. Other local contributions **$100-$650** for health, human services, and cultural organizations. **Out-of-state** grant: **$3,640** to Helen Diller Vacation Home for Blind Children [NJ]. — Major grants awarded the prior year include **$20,000** to The Shipley School; **$13,100** to St. Christopher's Hospital for Children; and **$10,000** to Wills Eye Hospital. ■ **PUBLICATIONS:** application form ■ **WEBSITE:** None ■ **E-MAIL:** None ■ **APPLICATION POLICIES & PROCEDURES:** The Foundation reports that giving is restricted to children's medical or educational causes in the Philadelphia area with most grants for special projects, building funds, capital drives, and matching grants. Grant requests may be submitted at any time on an application form available from the Foundation; include an annual report, organization and project budgets, list of Board members, list of major funding sources, audited financial statement, and IRS tax-exempt status documentation.

O+D+T Andrea C. Cavitolo (C, Grants Committee+Con) — Donna Caulfield (P+S) — John Calamari (VP+F) — Warren Kantor (Donor) Corporate donor: ACF Holding Company; Kantor Associates [DE]

SE-122 **Central Soup Society of Philadelphia**
964 Locust Grove Terrace
Rosemont 19010 (Montgomery County)
AMV $251,841 **FYE** 12-00 **(Gifts Received** $0)

MI-18-22-25-63
Phone Unlisted **FAX** None
EIN 23-6238324 **Year Created** 1861
11 **Grants totaling** $14,300

Mostly two-thirds local giving. High grant of **$2,000** to People's Emergency Center. **$1,900** each to Greater Philadelphia Food Bank and Philabundance. **$1,500** each to A Better Chance/Lower Merion and Endow-A-Home. **$500** each to Mission of Hope and Planned Parenthood of SE Pa. **Out-of-state** giving includes **$2,000** to Task Force for the Hungry [MO] and **$1,000** each to Martha's Table [DC] and So Others Might Eat [DC]. ■ **PUBLICATIONS:** None ■ **WEBSITE:** None ■ **E-MAIL:** None ■ **APPLICATION POLICIES & PROCEDURES:** Information not available.

O+D+T Robert M. Howard (S+D+Con) — Michael G. Mercer [NJ] (P+D) — Helen Mercer Coyne [VA] (F+D) — Susan MacInnes Howard [Bryn Mawr] (D) — Richard C. Paullin [MD] (D) — Catherine C. Warner [VA] (D)

SE-123 **Cervelli Charitable Trust**
2123 Fox Creek Road
Berwyn 19312 (Chester County)
AMV $741,786 **FYE** 3-01 **(Gifts Received** $0)

MI-31-41-42-52-54-61
Phone 610-296-0865 **FAX** None
EIN 23-2118559 **Year Created** 1979
31 **Grants totaling** $55,700

Mostly local giving. High grant of **$11,000** to Agnes Irwin School. **$9,000** to Doylestown Hospital. **$6,000** to Free Clinic of Doylestown. **$4,000** to Haverford School. **$3,000** to Our Lady of Mount Carmel [Doylestown]. **$1,000-$1,500** each to Academy of Vocal Arts, Church of the Sacred Heart [Philadelphia], Delaware Valley College, Jubilee School, Michener Art Museum, Rosemont College, and St. Norbert's Roman Catholic Church. Other smaller Philadelphia-area contributions for various purposes. **Out-of-state** giving includes **$3,500** to Cornell U. [NY]; **$2,500** to Bates College [ME]; and smaller grants to other colleges. ■ **PUBLICATIONS:** None ■ **WEBSITE:** None ■ **E-MAIL:** None ■ **APPLICATION POLICIES & PROCEDURES:** The Trust reports that giving is generally limited to Southeastern Pa., mostly for general support, special projects, and building funds. Submit grant requests in any form at any time; include IRS tax-exempt status documentation. Site visits sometimes are made to organizations being considered for a grant. The Trustees meet in February, June and October to award grants.

O+D+T Joyce L. Rehorst (T+Con) — Brian Bernhardt [VA] (T) — Levia Cervelli [Doylestown] (T)

SE-124   Charlestein (Julius & Ray) Foundation, Inc.
    c/o Premier Dental Products Company
    1710 Romano Drive, P.O. Box 4500
    Plymouth Meeting 19462   (Montgomery County)

MI-11-13-14-15-22-31-32-41-54-62-64-82-84

Phone 610-239-6000 **FAX** 610-239-6171
EIN 23-2310090   **Year Created** 1963

AMV $2,100,814   **FYE** 6-00   **(Gifts Received** $93,994)   69 **Grants totaling** $1,682,711

Mostly local giving. High grant of **$144,167** to Jewish Federation of Greater Philadelphia (general support/endowment/hunger relief). **$77,000** to ALS Assn. (mostly for operations/research). **$21,000** to Akiba Hebrew Academy. **$20,000** to Camp Ramah in the Poconos. **$15,000** to Har Zion Temple (mostly for Tikun Olam Fund). **$13,180** to United Way of SE Pa. **$10,500** to National Liberty Museum. **$8,600** to Perelman Jewish Day School. **$7,500** to Jewish National Fund. **$6,000** each to Philadelphia Geriatric Center and Woodrock. **$5,000** each to Adath Jeshurun and Jewish Theological Seminary. **$1,000-$2,500** each to Albert Einstein Medical Center, American Assn. for Ben-Gurion U., American Friends of Weizmann Institute, Crohn's & Colitis Foundation of America, Drexel U. (Judaic studies program), Germantown Jewish Center, Gratz College, Har Zion Religious School, Israel Guide Dog Center for the Blind, Jewish Community Centers of Greater Philadelphia, Rabbinical Assembly/Philadelphia Branch, Salvation Army, U. of Pa. Health System (pastoral care/education). Other local contributions, **$100-$750,** for various purposes. **Out-of-state** grants/contributions primarily for Jewish purposes. In addition, **$1,263,314** was transferred to the new Frezel Family Foundation (see separate profile). ■ **PUBLICATIONS:** None ■ **WEBSITE:** www.premusa.com [corporate info only] ■ **E-MAIL:** None ■ **APPLICATION POLICIES & PROCEDURES:** The Foundation reports that giving is generally, but not specifically, limited to the Philadelphia area for social services/educational purposes. Grant requests may be submitted at any time in a letter (2 pages maximum); include a project budget, list of Board members, and IRS tax-exempt status documentation.

O+D+T Ellyn Phillips (Executive Director+Con) — Morton L. Charlestein [Narberth] (P+Donor) — Jerrold A. Frezel [Philadelphia] (VP) — Gary Charlestein (S+F) Corporate donors: Premier Dental Products Company; Premier Medical Company

---

SE-125   Chester County Community Foundation, The
    The Lincoln Building
    28 West Market Street
    West Chester 19382   (Chester County)

MI-11-12-13-15-17-22-25-29-35-41-42-43-44-55-85-89

Phone 610-696-8211 **FAX** 610-696-8213
EIN 23-2773822   **Year Created** 1993

AMV $15,600,000 est.   **FYE** 6-02   **(Gifts Received** $3,800,000)   238 **Grants totaling** $1,100,000

As a Community Foundation comprising 125+ trusts/funds, established by individuals and families, grants are awarded to local organizations from discretionary and semi-discretionary funds; high grants of **$10,000-$20,000** each to Chester County Art Assn., Chester Springs Studio, Coatesville Center for Community Health, Community Volunteers in Medicine, Downingtown Main Street, GoodWorks, Habitat for Humanity of Chester County, Maternal & Child Health Consortium of Chester County. **$2,000-$9,999** each to Bridge of Hope, Children's Country Week, Community Gardens of Chester County, The Hickman, Maysie's Farm Conservation Center, Oxford Area Neighborhood Services, Phoenixville Area Positive Alternatives, Safe Harbor, Sheltering Arms, and West Chester Community Center. **$1,000** each to Chester County Bar Foundation, Citizen Advocacy of Chester County, People's Light & Theatre, Project Salud, St. Mary's Shelter, and Thorncroft Equestrian Center. In addition, many other grants, contributions and scholarships awarded from non-discretionary funds. ■ **PUBLICATIONS:** Annual Report; application guidelines; Grant Proposal Summary Cover Page ■ **WEBSITE:** www.chescocf.org ■ **E-MAIL:** info@chescocf.org ■ **APPLICATION POLICIES & PROCEDURES:** Only Chester County nonprofit organizations are eligible to apply for support. Grants may be awarded either (1) From the Fund for Chester County, an unrestricted but highly competitive fund awarding grants of $1,000-$2,500 once a year, or (2) From one of many donor-advised or field-of-interest funds in which case the Foundation staff consuls on decision-making with the funds' benefactors; these grants, awarded throughout the year, are typically $1,000-$10,000. Grants from the Fund for Chester County are not awarded to individuals or organizations not providing services in Chester County, or for endowment, event fundraising, or annual meetings. Grant requests may be submitted in a full proposal at any time, except for requests to the The Fund for Chester County which have an August 1st deadline. A complete application comprises the following: *Grant Proposal Summary Cover Page* (available on the website or from the Foundation); Proposal Narrative (4 pages total/maximum) which includes (a) Organization history, goals, key achievements and distinctiveness (1 page); (b) Funding Request (up to 2 pages) with project description (or for general operating requests, description of organizational impact); How the program addresses specific Chester County needs and issues; Overall strategies for implementing the project; and Why it is important the request be funded at this time; (c) Timetable for project with expected outcomes and their relevance to the organization's mission (up to 1 page); and (d) Explanation of how project effectiveness and impact will be determined, describing criteria for project success and anticipated results (1 or 2 paragraphs). Required attachments include an operating budget for the current fiscal year, the most recent financial statement—audited, if possible, Board member list with affiliations, and IRS tax-exempt status documentation. E-mail proposals are strongly encouraged, and electronic submission forms are available on the website. Proposals following the Delaware Valley Grantmakers Common Grant Application Format also are accepted but must be accompanied by the Foundation's Grant Proposal Summary Cover Page. Site visits are frequently arranged to organizations being considered for a grant. Board meetings are held quarterly. Final decisions on proposals usually take several months. Note: The Foundation staff provides technical support and endowment management services to nonprofit organizations, and facilitates research/discussion of important public policy issues affecting Chester County.

O+D+T Karen A. Simmons [Kennett Square] (P+D+Con) — Eva L. Verplanck, Ph.D. [Kennett Square] (C+D) — John Ceili, Jr. [Chadds Ford] (VC+D) — Elizabeth R. Moran [Paoli] (VC+D) — Kenneth W. Tunnell [West Chester] (VC+D) — John A. Henry [Malvern] (S+F+D) — Kenneth D. Hill [Wayne] (Co-Chair, Distribution Committee+D) — Rita S. Jones, Ed.D. [Malvern] (Co-Chair, Distribution Committee+D) — Madeleine Wing Adler, Ph.D. [West Chester] (D) — Jeremy C. Allen [Malvern] (D) — Frank J. Brewer [Douglassville] (D) — Anne M. Congdon [Malvern] (D) — John A. Featherman, III, Esq. [West Chester] (D) — David M. Frees, III, Esq. [Phoenixville] (D) — Richard J. Hutton [West Grove] (D) — Mary MacKinnon [Coatesville] (D) — Moira Mumma [Chester Springs] (D) — Thomas Paulus [Chester Springs] (D) — Mary Ann Rossi, Esq. [Exton] (D) — Burton Rothenberger [Kennett Square] (D) — Langhorne B. Smith [Newtown Square] (D) — L. Peter Temple, Esq. [Kennett Square] (D) — Dr. Henry A. Jordan [Chester Springs] (Chairman Emeritus)

SE-126   Chester County Evergreen Foundation, The
c/o Everfast, Inc.
203 Gale Lane
Kennett Square   19348   (Chester County)

MI-41-71-79

Phone 610-444-9700 **FAX** 610-444-1221
EIN 23-2605977   **Year Created** 1990

AMV $1,107   **FYE** 12-00   **(Gifts Received** $31,500)   4 **Grants totaling** $30,700

All local giving. High grant of **$10,000** each to Natural Lands Trust (general operations). **$5,450** to Chester County Intermediate Unit (Academy of Environmental Studies). **$5,250** to World Information Transfer (sponsor student to UN conference). **Out-of-state** grant: **$10,000** to Terralumina [DE] (environmental film). ■**PUBLICATIONS:** None ■**WEBSITE:** None ■**E-MAIL:** None ■**APPLICATION POLICIES & PROCEDURES:** The Foundation reports that generally giving is limited to Chester County for land conservation and environmental educational purposes. No grants awarded to individuals. Submit grant requests in a letter at any time; describe in detail the proposed project, state the amount of funding requested, and give a brief history of the organization and its mission.

O+D+T Bert G. Kerstetter (P+Executive Director+Donor+Con) — Diane M. Maguire [DE] (S) — Lynne Dewson [DE] (F)

SE-127   Child Development Foundation
1605 West Main Street
Norristown   19403   (Montgomery County)

MI-12-13-14-22-29-33-41-52

Phone 610-539-6600 **FAX** 610-539-6033
EIN 23-1539361   **Year Created** 1987

AMV $8,770,789   **FYE** 6-01   **(Gifts Received** $57,332)   37 **Grants totaling** $363,527

All giving restricted to organizations serving handicapped Montgomery County children/youth. High grant of **$45,000** to Gateway Employment Resources. **$42,000** to Pathway School. **$25,000** to Variety Club Camp. **$20,000** each to Developmental Enterprises Corp. and MARC Advocacy Services. **$17,000** each to Center School and Easter Seals. **$15,000** each to Central Montgomery MH/MR Center, Children's Aid Society, and Sebastian Riding Associates. **$12,000** to Family Services of Montgomery County. **$11,000** to Carson Valley School. **$10,000** each to Indian Creek Foundation and Kelly Anne Dolan Memorial Fund. **$8,000** to RSVP of Montgomery County. **$6,000-$7,263** each to Access Services, Baptist Children's Services, Montgomery County Assn. for the Blind, Ken-Crest Services, MBF Center, and Philadelphia Rowing Program for the Disabled [Philadelphia]. **$4,000-$5,000** each to Brian's House [West Chester], Flying High Equestrian Therapy, Gwynedd Mercy College, Make-A-Wish Foundation, National Hemophilia Foundation, and Recording for the Blind & Dyslexic. **$2,000-$3,000** each to St. Joseph's Home for Children [Philadelphia] Norristown Zoo, Our Lady of Confessions Church, Quaker School at Horsham, and St. Katherine Day School. Other grants/contributions $50-$1,500. ■**PUBLICATIONS:** Informational Brochure with statement of program policy, application guidelines, and financial statement; Grant Application Cover Sheet. ■**WEBSITE:** www.childdevelopmentfoundation.org ■**E-MAIL:** childdevelop@earthlink.net ■**APPLICATION POLICIES & PROCEDURES:** The Foundation reports that all giving is restricted to Montgomery County, Pa. organizations providing direct services to physically, mentally and/or emotionally handicapped children—birth to 21 years—who reside in Montgomery County. Support is awarded to (a) promote the general welfare of handicapped children in Montgomery County; (b) develop a better understanding of the program and needs of handicapped children by the public, and (c) promote the optimum integration between handicapped children of all backgrounds and their environments in order to promote their welfare through treatment, care, education, research, vocational training, and employment. Grants of one-year only are awarded for special projects, general support, equipment or program development. No support is given presently for capital campaigns, debt service, or multiyear commitments. Prospective applicants initially should make an inquiry about the feasibility of submitting a request. If appropriate, the Foundation will provide detailed application instructions and a copy of the Foundation's Grant Application cover sheet which must be submitted with required attachments. Completed applications are accepted only between January 1st and March 31st, the deadline. An organization may submit only one application annually. Site visits sometimes are made to organizations being considered for support as well as to most agencies receiving grants. Preliminary grant decisions are made in April and final decisions at a June meeting; grants are disbursed in late June. — Also called Montgomery County Foundation for Handicapped Children.

O+D+T Wendy A. Flango (Manager+Con) — James J. Oliver, Esq. (P+D) — Raymond L. Butera (VP+D) — Anthony Grasso [Harleysville] (S+F+D) — Joanne E. Bryers [Horsham] (D) — Marie B. Constable (D) — Carrie Darden (D) — Francis L. Genuardi (D) — Carole Haas Gravagno [Philadelphia] (D) — R. Kurtz Holloway, Esq. [Pottstown] (D) — Harry Mirabile [Plymouth Meeting] (D)

SE-128   Churchill Foundation, The
c/o CIP Capital Management
435 Devon Park Drive, Bldg. 300
Wayne   19087   (Delaware County)

MI-11-12-22-41-42-43-51-53-55

Phone 610-964-7860 **FAX** None
EIN 23-2904826   **Year Created** 1997

AMV $2,782,428   **FYE** 4-01   **(Gifts Received** $2,734,199)   18 **Grants totaling** $321,485

About three-fourths local giving; all grants are for general operating support. High grant of **$155,000** to Gesu School. **$35,000** to Warren V. Musser Young Scholars Fund [Philadelphia]. **$15,250** to St. Joseph's Preparatory School. **$10,000** each to The Hill

School [Pottstown], Pa. Academy of the Fine Arts, Perelman Jewish Day School [Richboro], Regional Performing Arts Center, and Young Scholars Charter School [Philadelphia]. **$5,000** to First Service Children [Devon]. Other local contributions **$100-$250** for various purposes. **Out-of-state** giving includes **$50,000** to Georgetown U. [DC]; **$5,000** to Yale Law School [CT]; and **$4,000** to Chai Lifeline [NY]. ■**PUBLICATIONS:** Scholarship Guidelines & Application ■**WEBSITE:** None ■**E-MAIL:** None ■ **APPLICATION POLICIES & PROCEDURES:** Scholarships are awarded only to deserving, full-time students; prospective applicants should initially request a copy of the detailed guidelines and application form.

O+D+T Winston J. Churchill, Jr. (C+Donor+Con) — Barbara G. Churchill (D)

SE-129	**CIGNA Foundation**	**MI**-11-12-13-14-29-31-32-35-41-42-45-51-52
	c/o CIGNA Corporation	54-55-56-72-81-83-85-86-88
	One Liberty Place, 1650 Market Street, OL54C	**Phone** 215-761-6054 **FAX** 215-761-5515
	Philadelphia 19192 (Philadelphia County)	**EIN** 23-6261726 **Year Created** 1982

AMV $1,121,024 **FYE** 12-00 **(Gifts Received** $6,445,287) 2000+ **Grants totaling** $5,799,574

Nationwide giving allocated to Health/Human Services-45%, Education-28%, Community & Civic Affairs-14% and Culture/The Arts-13%. About one-third giving to Philadelphia-area. High Pa. grant of **$400,000** to United Way of SE Pa. **$107,500** to Breast Health Institute. **$70,000** to Franklin Institute Science Museum. **$62,850** to Greater Philadelphia Chamber of Commerce Foundation. **$60,000** to Maternity Care Coalition of Greater Philadelphia. **$37,500** to Philadelphia High School Academies. **$34,000** (5 grants) to U. of Pa. (Institute for Law & Economics/Huebner Foundation for Insurance Education/The Wharton School/Other support). **$30,000** each to Eisenhower Exchange Fellowships and WHYY. **$28,000** to Academy of Natural Sciences. **$25,000** each to BLOCS/Business Leaders Organized for Catholic Schools, Fox Chase Cancer Center, Philadelphia Health Management Corp., Philadelphia Museum of Art, Resources for Human Development, Temple U. School of Nursing, and Urban Genesis. **$22,500-$23,000** each to 1807 & Friends and Philadelphia Opera Company. **$20,000** each to Drexel U., Focus on Women's Health: Living Beyond Breast Cancer, and Pa. Ballet. **$16,500-$18,000** each to Central Philadelphia Development Corp., Children's Hospital of Philadelphia, Penn State U., and Temple U. **$15,000** each to U. of Pa. School of Nursing and Village of Arts & Humanities. **$13,500** to Womens Way. **$11,500** to Operation Understanding. **$10,000** each to Academy of Community Music, Committee of Seventy, Freedom Theatre, Greater Philadelphia Urban Affairs Coalition, International Visitors Center of Philadelphia, Jewish Federation of Greater Philadelphia, March of Dimes/Eastern Pa. Chapter, Moore College of Art & Design, People's Light & Theatre Company, and Philadelphia Fun Fit & Free Program. **$7,500-$9,000** each to Children's Literacy Initiative, Citizens Crime Commission of the Delaware Valley, Delaware Valley Grantmakers, and Philadelphia Zoo. **$5,000-$6,000** each to Brandywine Workshop, Friends of Independence National Historical Park, Gesu School, Philadelphia Hospitality, Inc., Philadelphia Youth Tennis, Please Touch Museum, Police Athletic League of Philadelphia, Rena Rowan Foundation, and Walnut Street Theatre. Other smaller grants but details unavailable. **Out-of-state** giving primarily focused on Hartford, CT; for national public policy organizations or university-level projects related to the insurance/financial services industry or actuarial sciences; and for a highly select group of cultural institutions of national/international renown. Matching grants nationwide for educational or arts/culture organizations totaled **$1.56** million. — CIGNA Corporation's Direct Corporate Giving Program also awarded two grants to Pa. in 2000: **$961,080** to Philadelphia Orchestra and **$25,000** to Historical Society-U.S. District Court of Eastern Pa. ■**PUBLICATIONS:** annual Contributions Report (lists grants of $5,000 or more) and application guidelines ■**WEBSITE:** www.cigna.com/general/about/community/ [mostly corporate info] ■**E-MAIL:** - see CIGNA website, select Customer Service ■ **APPLICATION POLICIES & PROCEDURES:** The Foundation reports that Philadelphia-area giving focuses on four priority areas: (1) Health & Human Services—primary support for women's health and infant & maternal care; (2) Education—preference for Philadelphia's elementary/secondary schools; (3) Community & Civic Affairs—primarily for projects addressing core community problems in Center City Philadelphia; and (4) Culture and The Arts—preference given Philadelphia-based organizations serving a significant local population or in which CIGNA employees have expressed interest. No support is awarded to individuals, or for sectarian/denominational religious programs/activities, fraternal organizations, political campaigns/organizations, or organizations whose prime purpose is influencing legislation or litigation. Generally no support will be given to organizations substantially supported by United Way or other CIGNA-supported federated funding agencies; hospital capital improvement or expansion; or research, treatment or prevention of specific diseases. In addition, requests for capital campaigns or endowment are discouraged and are not considered as part of the Foundation's regular operating budget. Grant requests may be submitted in a one- or two-page letter any time before September (grants will be disbursed the following year); describe the proposed program, its objectives, and suggested methods for evaluation; also include a brief description of the organization; its history, purpose, and activities; board of directors list; the most recent audited financial statement and IRS Form 990; and IRS tax-exempt status documentation. Also, proposals which follow Delaware Valley Grantmakers' Common Grant Application Form are accepted. Site visits sometimes are made to organizations being considered for a grant. Note: Contact the Foundation for more specific information on the National Grants Program and the Matching Gift program.

O+D+T Arnold W. Wright, Jr. (VP+Executive Director+Con) — H. Edward Hanway (D) — Donald M. Levinson (D) — Judith E. Soltz (D) — Carol J. Ward (S) — David B. Gerges (F) Corporate donor: CIGNA Corp.

SE-130	**Claneil Foundation, The**	**MI**-12-13-14-15-17-18-20-22-29-31-35-41-42
	c/o Claneil Enterprises	45-51-52-54-55-56-57-71-79-82-83
	630 West Germantown Pike, Suite 400	**Phone** 610-828-6331 **FAX** 610-828-6405
	Plymouth Meeting 19462 (Montgomery County)	**EIN** 23-6445450 **Year Created** 1968

AMV $51,265,949 **FYE** 12-01 **(Gifts Received** $13,078,940) 233 **Grants totaling** $3,718,604

About two-thirds local/Pa. giving. ***HEALTH/HUMAN SERVICES GRANTS:*** **$130,000** to Chester County Community Foundation (general funds/human service programs). **$59,700** to United Way (September 11th Fund). **$55,000** to Red Cross (Disaster Fund/Lower Bucks Chapter). **$50,000** to Boy Scouts/Chester County Council. **$40,000** each to Coatesville Center for Community Health and Hope Springs Equestrian Therapy. **$29,267** each to Living Beyond Breast Cancer and Planned Parenthood of

Chester County. **$26,707** to Educating Children for Parenting. **$25,000** each to Virtual Breast Cancer Organization and Women's Assn. for Women's Alternatives. **$23,000-$23,500** each to Baker Industries, Center in the Park. Kelly Anne Dolan Memorial Fund, Pa. Home of the Sparrow, and Surrey Services for Seniors. **$21,600-$22,000** to Domestic Violence Center of Chester County, Good Works, Inc. [Coatesville], Open Hearth, Inc. [Spring City], and Wissahickon Hospice. **$20,000** to Pocono Services for Families & Children [East Stroudsburg]. **$17,560** to Freedom Valley Girl Scout Council. **$17,343** to North Penn Valley Boys & Girls Club. **$14,000-$14,650** each to ActionAIDS, Adoption Center of the Delaware Valley, Children's Aid Society, Crime Victims Center of Chester County, Juvenile Law Center of Philadelphia, Little Brothers-Friends of the Elderly, Montgomery County Big Brothers/Big Sisters Assn., RSVP, and Women in Transition. **$10,000-$11,700** each to Angel Flight Pa., Calcutta House, Weller Center for Health Education [Easton], Community Volunteers in Medicine, Interfaith of Ambler, Maternal & Child Health Consortium, NARAL-PA. Foundation, National Transplant Assistance Fund, Need in Deed, Philabundance, Phoenixville Homes, Spring City Elderly Housing Corp., U. of Pa. Cancer Center, Unity Center [Media], VNA Community Services, West Chester Area Senior Center, Working Wardrobe, and YMCA of Central Chester County. **$7,000-$8,700** to Episcopal Community Services, MANNA/Metropolitan AIDS Neighborhood Nutrition Alliance, Montgomery County Assn. for the Blind, Pearl S. Buck International, and Safe Harbor of Greater West Chester. **$6,000** each to Bryn Mawr Rehab Hospital, Family Service of Chester County, Girls Star, Mother's Home, Inc., Pegasus Riding Academy, Therapeutic Center at Fox Chase, and Women's Community Revitalization Project. **$5,000** each to AIDS Law Project of Pa., Alzheimer's Assn./SE Pa. Chapter, American Lung Assn./SE Pa. Region, Camp Soltane, Chestnut Hill Healthcare, Children's Hospital of Philadelphia (poison control center), Childspace Cooperative Development, Contact USA, Delaware County AIDS Network, Elizabeth Blackwell Health Center for Women, Endow-A-Home, Free Health Clinic of Montgomery County, Montgomery County MH/MR Emergency Service, Neighborhood Bike Works, Northwest Interfaith Movement, Pa. Coalition to Prevent Teen Pregnancy, Pa. Special Olympics, Philadelphia Senior Center, Philadelphia Youth for Change, Planned Parenthood of SE Pa., PEP/Programs Employing People, United Communities SE Philadelphia, and United Way of SE Pa. **$3,800-$4,000** to Associated Services for the Blind, Camphill Village Kimberton Hills, Committee for Dignity & Fairness for the Homeless Housing Development, Daemion House, Ghebre Michael Inn, Homeless Advocacy Project, March of Dimes/Pa. State, Upper Perkiomen Senior Citizen Center, and WINGS for Success. **$2,000-$3,000** each to Bethany Christian Services, Brian's House, Central Pa. Health Education Center, Child Home & Community, College Settlement of Philadelphia, Friends Rehabilitation Program, Inn Dwelling, Liberty Resources, Wheels, Inc., and Women's Resource Center. **ARTS-CULTURE-HISTORY GRANTS: $54,267** to People's Light & Theatre Company. **$35,000** to Partners for Sacred Places. **$30,000** to Brandywine Conservancy (Young Friends). **$25,000** to Friends of The Mill at Anselma [Chester County]. **$20,000** each to Assn. for The Colonial Theatre and The Circus Barn. **$17,300-$17,600** each to Academy of Natural Sciences, The Fabric Workshop, Franklin Institute Science Museum, and Strings for Schools. **$14,452** each to Independence Seaport Museum, Philadelphia Society for Preservation of Landmarks, Philadelphia Volunteer Lawyers for the Arts, and TOVA. **$11,562** to Whitemarsh Community Art Center. **$10,000** to Village of Arts & Humanities. **$8,780** to WHYY. **$8,000** to Valley Forge Historical Society. **$7,500** to Philadelphia Wooden Boat Factory. **$5,000** each to Act II Playhouse, Chester Springs Studio, and Choral Arts Society of Philadelphia. **$6,000** each to Academy of Community Music, Johnson House Historic House, and Wagner Free Institute of Science. **$5,000** each to Arden Theatre Company, Astral Artistic Services, The Athenaeum of Philadelphia, Conservation Center for Art & Historic Artifacts, Historic Rittenhousetown, Historical Society of Montgomery County, National Liberty Museum, NetworkArts Philadelphia, New World Assn. of Emigrants from Russia in Pa., Schuylkill Canal Assn., Sedgwick Cultural Center, and Suburban Music School. **$2,500-$4,000** to Atwater Kent Museum, Main Line Art Center, National Exhibits by Blind Artists, and Singing City. **EDUCATION GRANTS: $75,000** to Westtown School. **$40,000** to Architecture & Design Charter High School. **$25,000** to Williamson Free School for Mechanical Trades. **$21,072** to White-Williams Scholars. **$19,997** to Penn State U. (Hamer Center for Community Design Assistance). **$14,633** to Alan Ameche Memorial Foundation (tuition assistance). **$14,452** to United Negro College Fund. **$10,000** to Greater Philadelphia Urban Affairs Coalition (Philadelphia Reads!), Literacy Council of Norristown, and Villanova U. **$6,000** to Harcum College. **$5,000** each to Community Women's Education Project, Delaware Valley Friends School, IHM Center for Literacy & GED Programs, Jubilee School, Philadelphia Community Academy, and West End Computer Lab. Other smaller grants. **CIVIC-COMMUNITY-ENVIRONMENT GRANTS: $50,000** to Farmers' Market Trust. **$40,000** each to Maysie's Farm Conservation Center [Glenmoore] and Pa. Partnership on Economic Education [Selinsgrove]. **$25,000** to Kennett Square Revitalization Task Force. **$20,000** to Natural Lands Trust [Media]. **$14,000-$15,000** each to Awbury Arboretum Cochranville Fire Company, Patrician Society of Central Norristown, and Women's Law Project. **$10,000** each to 10,000 Friends of Pa., Norristown Zoo, Perkiomen Valley Watershed Assn., and Wissahickon Valley Watershed Assn. **$7,000-$8,000** each to American Civil Liberties Foundation, and Ogontz Ave. Revitalization Corp. **$5,000** each to ASSETS Montco, Community Gardens of Chester County, Interagency Council of Norristown, Montgomery County Lands Trust, Pa. Horticultural Society, St. Philip's United Methodist Church, Tyler Arboretum, and Urban Tree Connection. **$3,000-$4,000** each to Executive Service Corps of the Delaware Valley, Greater Philadelphia Chamber of Commerce Regional Foundation, Neighborhood Gardens Assn., and Philadelphia Assn. of Community DevelopmentCorporations. **OUT-OF-STATE GRANTS** include high grant of **$600,345** to King's College Long/St. Thomas Hospital [U.K.]; **$100,000** to Glynwood Center [NY]; **$50,000** each to Pilot School [DE], Nature Conservancy/Massachusetts Chapter, Sanford School [DE], and Wellesley College [MA] (Center for Research on Women); **$30,000** each to Boston Medical Center [MA] and Women Express, Inc. [MA]; **$25,000** each to Cape Eleuthera Marine Conservation Project [Bahamas] and Wildlife Trust, Inc. [NY]; **$20,000** each to Circus Barn, Inc. [VT], Massachusetts Audubon Society, and National Trust for Historic Preservation [DC]; and smaller grants for similar purposes. ■**PUBLICATIONS:** application guidelines; Grant Application Summary sheet ■**WEBSITE:** None ■**E-MAIL:** None ■**APPLICATION POLICIES & PROCEDURES:** The Foundation reports that giving focuses on organizations located in and serving communities within the greater Philadelphia region in five programmatic areas: The Arts & Humanities, Community Development, Education, the Built and Natural Environment, and Health & Human Services. No grants are awarded to religious organizations for sectarian purposes, to organizations outside the Foundation's grantmaking area (unless invited by a Foundation Board Member), to other private foundations or individuals. Grants are awarded in two categories: (1) Small Grants—generally between $3,000 and $10,000—are available for programs/projects and general operating support; multiyear grants also are considered; and (2) Large Grants—greater than $10,000—which are *by invitation only* and, generally, are reserved for organizations with which the Foundation has an existing relationship. Organizations which have never applied to the Foundation, or have applied within the past three years and *not* received a grant, must first submit a Letter of Intent prior submitting a full proposal. In addition, any organization wanting to apply for a Large Grant must submit a Letter of Intent . All Letters of Intent (deadlines are June 30th and December 15th) must be brief; describe your organization and the purpose for requesting funding. After review, the applicant will be notified whether or not a full proposal will be invited for further consideration. Only one Letter of Intent may be submitted per calendar year. If an organization is invited to submit a full proposal it must be received before the March 1st and August 15th deadlines and must include the following: (a) a completed Claneil Foundation Application Summary (available from the Foundation); (b) a description of the organization and its mission; (c) a description of the project for which funds are requested including the problem to be addressed, the need, the objectives, the personnel involved in the project and their qualifications, and a project timetable; (d) a project budget and organization budget showing both income sources and expenses; and (e) the methods for evaluating the successful attainment of the project's objectives. Also include a list of current officers, trustees or directors and their affiliations; copy of the latest IRS tax-exempt status documentation, including the determination that the organization is not classified as a private foundation; the most recently completed audit or IRS form 990; the current registration statement from the Pa. Bureau of Charitable Organizations; and any pertinent documentation that might be used to support the request; such as planning documents, contracts, letters of support, etc. Note that if the organization implementing the program is submitting a proposal under a fiscal agent, a cover letter from the fiscal agent also must be included with the proposal; and all of the documentation that is requested herein must be submitted for the fiscal agent. Grants are awarded at Board Meetings in June and November. — **Note**: The Foundation also reports that since application guidelines are undergoing transition, prospective applicants are advised to check with Foundation prior to submission of any request. As of October 1, 2002, however, the above guidelines were in effect.

O+D+T Cathy M. Weiss (Executive Director+Con) — Henry A. Jordan, M.D. [Chester Springs] (C+D) — Marjorie M. Findlay [MA] (VC+D) — Langhorne B. Smith [Newtown] (F+D) — Geoff Freeman [MA] (D) — Gretchen Jordan [NY] (D) — Jennifer McNeil [Coatesville] (D) — Robert D. McNeil [Coatesville] (D) Corporate donor: Claneil Enterprises, Inc.

SE-131 **Clayman Family Foundation, The**   MI-12-14-22-32-33-62
    c/o Jules Jurgensen Corp.
    101 West City Line Ave.   **Phone** 610-667-3500 **FAX** 610-667-3522
    Bala Cynwyd 19004   (Montgomery County)   **EIN** 23-8993816   **Year Created** 1997
AMV $2,288,347   **FYE** 12-00   **(Gifts Received** $0)   400+ **Grants totaling** $117,955

About half local giving. High local grant of **$10,000** to Federation Allied Jewish Appeal. **$5,000** each to Akiba Hebrew Academy, Friends of Samuel Paley, Jewish Family & Children's Services, and Philadelphia Police Foundation. **$3,000** to Advocates for the Jewish Mentally Ill. **$2,000** each to Fanconi Anemia Research Foundation and Samuel Paley Day Care Center. **$1,000-$1,500** each to Family & Children's Services, John Paul Jones Middle School, Open Hearts/Open Doors, Philadelphia Ronald McDonald House, St. Christopher's Foundation, St. Gabriel's Hall, St. Monica Day Care Center, and Tinley Temple (food for poor). Many local and out-of-state contributions of **$100-$300**, mostly **$25** each. **Out-of-state** grants include **$40,000** to Rutgers U. Foundation [NJ]; **$5,000** to Haifa Foundation [Israel]; and **$3,500** to National Hemophilia Foundation [NY]. ■**PUBLICATIONS:** None ■ **WEBSITE:** None ■**E-MAIL:** None ■**APPLICATION POLICIES & PROCEDURES:** Grant request may be submitted in any form at any time; describe the charitable activity and its purpose. No grants awarded to individuals.

O+D+T Morton Clayman (P+D+Donor+Con) — Deborah Clayman (S+F+D) — Roberta Clayman (D)

SE-132 **Clemens Foundation**   MI-11-12-13-14-15-22-31-42-43-63-64-65-89
    c/o Clemens Markets, Inc.
    1 Towamencin Corp. Center, P.O. Box 1555   **Phone** 215-361-9000 **FAX** None
    Kulpsville 19443   (Montgomery County)   **EIN** 23-1675035   **Year Created** 1966
AMV $878,561   **FYE** 8-00   **(Gifts Received** $108,411)   113 **Grants totaling** $111,300

Mostly local/Pa. giving; grants generally are for general operating support except as noted. High grant of **$14,400** to North Penn United Way. **$5,000** to Gideons International [Flourtown] (free bibles distribution). **$5,000** to St. Joseph's U. **$4,000** to Juniata College (scholarship fund). **$3,800** to Eastern College (student aid). **$3,000** each to North Penn Valley Girls & Boys Club (facility expansion). **$2,000-$2,200** each to Bucks County United Way, Calvary Baptist Theological Seminary (scholarships), Dock Woods Community Foundation (chapel fund), Elizabethtown College (building fund), Faith Baptist Church-Haiti of Lansdale, and Harleysville Community Fire Company. **$1,000-$1,500** each to Biblical Theological Seminary, Calvary Baptist Church, Calvary Church of Souderton (building fund), Children's Hospital of Philadelphia (uncompensated care fund), Church of the Brethren of Ambler (renovations), COBY's Family Services [Leola], Doylestown Hospital (rehab unit), EAPE (ministry work), Faith Baptist Church of Lansdale (building fund), Freedom Community Church, Grandview Hospital (renovations), Greater Philadelphia Food Bank, Indian Creek Church of the Brethren (new room), Integrity Mission, Interfaith Community Service (medical needs), Interfaith of Ambler (homeless program), Lancaster Bible College (scholarships), Lansdale Catholic High School (software), North Penn Hospital (partnership program), Penn View Christian School (school supplies/tuition), Peter Becker Memorial Home (benevolent fund), Philadelphia College of Bible, Plumstead Christian School (financial aid), St. Mary's Medical Foundation (community clinic), Samaritan Counseling Clinic (client support), Schwenkfelder Library & Heritage (expansion/renovation), Senior Adult Activity Center, Soldiers & Sailors Memorial Hospital [Tioga County] (equipment), Souderton Mennonite Church (building fund), Volunteer Medical Service Corps (ambulance fund), and Wycliffe Bible Translators [Lancaster] (new regional office). Other local contributions **$200-$500** for similar purposes. **Out-of-state** giving includes **$1,000** each to Moody Bible Institute [IL] and smaller contributions for religious purposes.— Major grants approved for future payment: **$10,000** to St. Joseph's U. (tuition/grants) and **$4,000** to Dock Woods Community Chapel Fund. ■**PUBLICATIONS:** None ■**WEBSITE:** None ■**E-MAIL:** None

APPLICATION POLICIES & PROCEDURES: Grant requests may be submitted at any time on a Donee Organization Information Form, available from the Foundation; applications deadline is September 30th.

O+D+T Jack S. Clemens [Lansdale] (F+T+Donor+Con) — Abram S. Clemens [Lansdale] (P+T+Donor) — Cheryl Mehl [Harleysville] (VP+T) — Janice Clemens Tyson [Mainland] (S+T) — Jill Clemens [Lansdale] (AS+T) — Suzanne Clemens Harris [Lansdale] (AF+T) — Lillian H. Clemens [Lansdale] (T+Donor) — Jules Pearlstine [Jenkintown] (T) — Marilyn Clemens Rohrbach [Telford] (T) — Corporate donor: Clemens Markets, Inc.

SE-133 **Clinical Nutrition Foundation**　　　　　　　　　　　　　　MI-31-32
　　　c/o The Glenmede Trust Company
　　　1650 Market Street, Suite 1200　　　　　　　　　　　　　　　**Phone** 215-419-6000　**FAX** 215-419-6196
　　　Philadelphia　19103　　　　　　(Philadelphia County)　　　**EIN** 23-2507225　　**Year Created** 1988
AMV $53,017　　　　**FYE** 12-00　　　**(Gifts Received** $600)　　1　**Grant of** $10,000

Sole grant to Hospital of the U. of Pa. (Bioethics Center). ■**PUBLICATIONS:** statement of program policy ■**WEBSITE:** None ■**E-MAIL:** None ■**APPLICATION POLICIES & PROCEDURES:** Only requests relevant to clinical nutrition are eligible for consideration; national activities are supported; a statement of program policy is published. No grants awarded to individuals. Prospective applicants initially should make a telephone inquiry about the feasibility of submitting a request. Submit grant requests in a letter (2 pages maximum) at any time; include an annual report, project budget, list of Board members, and IRS tax-exempt status documentation. Site visits sometimes are made to organizations being considered for a grant. Grants are awarded at meetings in February, May, August, and November.

O+D+T Estelle R. Soppe (D+Donor+Con) — James L. Mullen, M.D. (P+D) — William H. Pope, Jr. (S+F+D) — George T. Atwood [Lansdale] (D) — John J. Lombard, Jr. , Esq. (D) — Steven B. Soppe [NJ] (D) The Glenmede Trust Company (Trustee)

SE-134 **CMS Endowment Foundation**　　　　　　　　　MI-11-12-13-14-15-22-32-41-42-52-53-54-55-62
　　　c/o CMS Companies
　　　1926 Arch Street　　　　　　　　　　　　　　　　　　**Phone** 215-246-3000　**FAX** None
　　　Philadelphia　19103　　　　　　(Philadelphia County)　　　**EIN** 23-7819212　　**Year Created** 1995
AMV $662,204　　　　**FYE** 9-00　　　**(Gifts Received** $1,159,329)　　150+　**Grants totaling** $730,238

About two-thirds local giving. High grant of **$115,000** to Jewish Federation of Greater Philadelphia. **$101,718** to Foundations, Inc. (for Leeds Middle School). **$62,600** to Regional Performing Arts Center. **$55,500** to United Way of SE Pa. **$29,220** to Germantown Jewish Center. **$16,610** to Perelman Jewish Day School. **$10,000** to National Liberty Museum. **$7,500** to Boys Town-Jerusalem [Jenkintown]. **$5,000** each to Camphill Special School-Beaver Run and Philadelphia Ronald McDonald House. **$2,000-$2,500** each to Camp Gan-Israel, Gesu School, Gwynedd-Mercy College, Institute for Contemporary Art, Jewish Community Center of Reading (building fund), Make-A-Wish Foundation, Pa. Ballet, Temple U./Fox School of Business & Management, and Walnut Street Theatre. **$1,000-$1,900** each to ALS Assn., American Cancer Society, Anti-Defamation League, Arts & Business Council, Jefferson Center for Integrated Medicine, Jewish Family & Children's Service, Philadelphia Boys Choir, Police Athletic League of Philadelphia, Temple Beth Hillel-Beth El, Thomas Jefferson U. Hospital, Torah Academy of Greater Philadelphia, and Wellness Community of Philadelphia. Other smaller local contributions for various purposes. **Out-of-state** giving includes **$100,300** to Friends of Yemin Orde [DC]; **$30,000** to United Nations Assn./USA (Adopt a Minefield); **$20,000** to Jaffa Institute [Israel]; **$15,000** to WIZO [NY]; **$10,000** each to American Israel Education Foundation, Brandeis U. [MA], Rutgers U. [NJ], and UNICEF; and smaller grants/contributions to several states. ■**PUBLICATIONS:** None ■**WEBSITE:** None ■**E-MAIL:** None ■**APPLICATION POLICIES & PROCEDURES:** No grants awarded to individuals.

O+D+T Mark I. Solomon (T+Donor+Con) — Paul Silberberg (T+Donor+Con) — and 16 individual donors — Corporate donor: Parkway Corp.

SE-135 **CMS Foundation**　　　　　　　　　　　　　MI-11-13-15-22-41-42-49-54-62-64-82-86
　　　c/o CMS Companies
　　　1926 Arch Street　　　　　　　　　　　　　　　　　　**Phone** 215-246-3000　**FAX** None
　　　Philadelphia　19103　　　　　　(Philadelphia County)　　　**EIN** 23-7819211　　**Year Created** 1995
AMV $872,327　　　　**FYE** 12-00　　　**(Gifts Received** $1,624,548)　　85+　**Grants totaling** $823,575

Nearly half local giving; all grants are unrestricted support. High Pa. grant of **$113,200** to United Way of SE Pa. **$33,500** to Perelman Schechter Jewish Day School. **$25,000** each to Westtown School and Young Scholars Charter School. **$19,050** to Federation Allied Jewish Appeal. **$17,666** to Temple Beth Hillel-Beth El. **$14,270** to Germantown Jewish Center. **$11,000** to Franklin Institute. **$10,000** to Jewish Heritage Programs. **$8,800** to Jewish Federation of Greater Philadelphia (CMS Friday Night Alive). **$5,000-$5,300** each to Gesu School, Gratz College, One Israel Fund [Huntington Valley], Stern Hebrew High School, and U.S. Committee/Sports for Israel. **$4,000** to Anti-Defamation League. **$3,500** to Police Athletic League of Philadelphia. **$2,000-$2,500** each to Akiba Hebrew Academy, Big City Dinner, Israel Guide Dog Center [Warrington], Jewish Federation of Greater Philadelphia, St. Andrew's Church, and Walnut Street Theatre. **$1,000-$1,500** each to ALS Assn., Delaware County Christian School, Foster America (Martin Pollack Project), Germantown Friends School, Jewish Community Centers of Greater Philadelphia, Jewish Relief Agency, National Organization for Hearing Research, Philadelphia Race for a Cure, U. of Pa., and Waldron Mercy Academy. Other smaller local contributions. **Out-of-state** giving includes **$128,250** to Friends of Yemin Orde [DC]; **$125,000** to UJA Federation Charitable Common Foundation [NY]; **$33,400** to Yemin Orde Youth Village [DC]; **$20,000** to WIZO [NY]; **$15,200** to New York City Ballet; **$15,000** to American Israel Education Foundation [NY]; and **$10,000-$10,500** each to Business Executives for National Security [DC]; Charleston Education Network [SC]; Institute for

Education-Jaffa [Israel], Institute for the Advancement of Education [Israel], International Center for Residential Education [DC], International Rescue Committee [DC], and United Ways of America [VA] (deToqueville Society); and other smaller grants. ■ **PUBLICA-TIONS:** None ■ **WEBSITE:** None ■ **E-MAIL:** None ■ **APPLICATION POLICIES & PROCEDURES:** No grants awarded to individuals.

O+D+T Mark I. Solomon (T+Con) — Paul Silberberg (T+Con) — Morey Goldberg [NJ] (Donor) — William Landman (Donor) — Peter Miller (Donor) — Corporate donor: Security Life of Denver

---

SE-136 Cohen (Abram & D. Walter) Foundation
210 West Rittenhouse Square, #2045
Philadelphia 19103 (Philadelphia County)

MI-11-22-34-42-54-56-62-64
Phone 215-732-4541 **FAX** 215-732-4542
EIN 23-6413811 **Year Created** 1966

AMV $703,604 **FYE** 12-00 (**Gifts Received** $0) 15 **Grants totaling** $35,627

Mostly local giving. High local grant of **$9,127** to Jewish Federation of Greater Philadelphia. **$7,000** to National Museum of American Jewish History. **$5,000** to United Way of SE Pa. **$1,000-$1,500** each to American Friends of Hebrew U., Foundation for the History of Women in Medicine, Gratz College, Jewish Publication Society, and Medical College of Pa. (special trust fund). Other smaller contributions. **Out-of-state** giving includes **$1,000** each to American Academy of Periodontology Foundation [IL] and Research America [VA]. ■ **PUBLICATIONS:** None ■ **WEBSITE:** None ■ **E-MAIL:** None ■ **APPLICATION POLICIES & PROCEDURES:** Grant requests may be submitted in a letter (2 pages maximum) at any time. Grants are awarded at meetings scheduled as necessary. — Formerly called the Abram Cohen Foundation.

O+D+T D. Walter Cohen, DDS (P+T+Donor+Con) — Jane Millner (S+T) — Joanne Cohen (T) — Josephine Cohen (T)

SE-137 Colehower (H. Howard) Foundation
518 Cresheim Valley Road
Wyndmoor 19038 (Montgomery County)

MI-12-22-31-32-41-43-63
Phone 215-836-5307 **FAX** None
EIN 22-2849506 **Year Created** 1987

AMV $226,126 **FYE** 6-01 (**Gifts Received** $0) 10 **Grants totaling** $15,000

About two-thirds local giving. High Pa. grants of **$2,000** each to William Penn Charter School (Colehower Scholarship Fund) and Fox Chase Cancer Center. **$1,000-$1,500** each to Abington Memorial Hospital, Catholic Charities, Free Clinic of Doylestown, and Philadelphia Ronald McDonald House. Other local contributions of **$500** for various purposes. **Out-of-state** giving includes high grant of **$5,000** to Holy Innocents Episcopal Church of Beach Haven [NJ]. ■ **PUBLICATIONS:** None ■ **WEBSITE:** None ■ **E-MAIL:** None ■ **APPLICATION POLICIES & PROCEDURES:** Information not available.

O+D+T William S. Colehower (P+Con) — William J. Grundy (VP) — Thomas M. Hyndman, Jr. Esq.

SE-138 Coleman Foundation, The
c/o Pitcairn Trust Company
3000 Pitcairn Place, 165 Township Line Road
Jenkintown 19046 (Montgomery County)

MI-11-12-31-41-42-44-53-54-55-56-63
Phone 215-881-6147 **FAX** 215-881-6090
EIN 23-6214964 **Year Created** 1935

AMV $1,726,916 **FYE** 12-00 (**Gifts Received** $0) 29 **Grants totaling** $106,000

Mostly Philadelphia or Easton area giving. High grant of **$10,000** to West Philadelphia Cultural Alliance. **$6,000** to Spring Garden Children's Center [Easton]. **$7,000** to Easton Area Public Library. **$6,000** to Lafayette College. **$5,000-$5,500** each to National Canal Museum [Easton], St. Francis de Sales School [47th Street, Philadelphia], University City Arts League, University City Historical Assn., and Valley Health Foundation [Easton]. **$3,000** each to Friends of Skillman Library [Easton], Hugh Moore Historical Park & Museum [Easton], Spruce Hill Community Assn., Third Street Alliance for Women & Children [Easton], and University Lutheran Church of the Resurrection. **$2,000-$2,500** each to Arts West Charitable, Church of the Resurrection, St. Francis de Sales School [Springfield Ave., Philadelphia], and United Way of Greater Lehigh Valley. **$1,000** each to Fresh Start Community Development Corp. [Philadelphia] and University City District. Other smaller contributions. **Out-of-state** giving, all to NY, includes **$5,000** each to Friends of Rye Nature Center and Rye Presbyterian Church; and **$4,250** to Jane Addams Peace Assn. ■ **PUBLICATIONS:** None ■ **WEBSITE:** None ■ **E-MAIL:** pi6147@pitcairn.com ■ **APPLICATION POLICIES & PROCEDURES:** Prospective applicants should make an initial telephone inquiry regarding the feasibility of submitting a request. Grant requests may be submitted in any form at any time; include an annual report and IRS tax-exempt status documentation. Site visits sometimes are made to organizations being considered for a grant. Grants are awarded at Trustee meetings in March, June, September, and December.

O+D+T Paul Irwin (Executive VP at Bank+Con) — Agnes Coleman [Easton] (T) — Samuel Coleman [NY] (T) — William S. Coleman [Philadelphia] (T) — Parke H. Hess [Exton] (T) — Pitcairn Trust Company (Corporate Trustee)

SE-139 Coleman (Helen W.) Residuary Trust
c/o Pitcairn Trust Company
3000 Pitcairn Place, 165 Township Line Road
Jenkintown 19046 (Montgomery County)

MI-41-42-63
Phone 215-881-6147 **FAX** 215-881-6090
EIN 23-6439502 **Year Created** 1968

AMV $1,092,068 **FYE** 12-00 (**Gifts Received** $0) 11 **Grants totaling** $38,750

One Pa. grant: **$6,750** to First Presbyterian Church of Easton. **Out-of-state** giving includes high grant of **$8,500** to Greenwich Academy [CT]; **$5,000** to Dartmouth College/Tuck School of Business [NH]; and smaller grants to NY and New England. ■ **PUBLICATIONS:** None ■ **WEBSITE:** None ■ **E-MAIL:** pi6147@pitcairn.com ■ **APPLICATION POLICIES & PROCEDURES:** Prospective applicants should make an initial telephone inquiry regarding the feasibility of submitting a request. Grant requests may be submitted in any form at any time; include an annual report and IRS tax-exempt status documentation. Site visits sometimes are made to organizations being considered for a grant. Grants are awarded at Trustee meetings in March, June, September, and December.

O+D+T Paul Irwin (Executive VP at Bank+Con) — Agnes Coleman [Easton] (T) — Samuel Coleman [NY] (T) — William S. Coleman [Philadelphia] (T) — Parke H. Hess [Exton] (T) — Pitcairn Trust Company (Corporate Trustee)

SE-140 Colket (Ethel D.) Foundation
c/o PNC Advisors
1600 Market Street, 29th Floor
Philadelphia 19103   (Philadelphia County)
AMV $5,795,497   **FYE** 8-01   **(Gifts Received** $0)

MI-11-14-18-22-29-31-35-41-42-52-54-55-72
Phone 215-585-5666 **FAX** None
EIN 23-6292917   **Year Created** 1964
20 **Grants totaling** $351,676

About three-fourths local giving; all grants are for general purposes. High grant of **$100,338** to Children's Hospital of Philadelphia. **$50,169** each to Academy of Music and Regional Performing Arts Center. **$15,000** each to Paoli Memorial Hospital and Red Cross. **$10,000** each to Bryn Mawr Hospital and Philadelphia Museum of Art. **$7,500** to U. of Pa. **$5,000** each to Easter Seals, Philadelphia Orchestra, Philadelphia Zoo, United Way of SE Pa., and Visiting Nurse Assn. of Philadelphia. **$2,500** to Planned Parenthood of Chester County. **Out-of-state** giving includes **$25,000** to Acadia Waldorf Assn. [ME]; **$12,000** to United Ways of America [VA] (de Tocqueville Society); **$10,000** to Mt. Desert Island Hospital [ME]; and other grants mostly to Bar Harbor, ME area. ■**PUBLICATIONS:** None ■**WEBSITE:** None ■**E-MAIL:** None ■**APPLICATION POLICIES & PROCEDURES:** The Foundation reports that Delaware Valley organizations receive preference. Prospective applicants should make an initial telephone inquiry about the feasibility of submitting a request. Grant requests should be submitted in March or October; include IRS tax-exempt status documentation. Grants are awarded at Trustee meetings in June and December.

O+D+T Alice C. Cory (VP at Bank+Con) — Ruth M. Colket [Malvern] (Co-T) — Tristram C. Colket, Jr. [Malvern] (Co-T+Donor) — PNC Advisors (Co-Trustee)

SE-141 Coltman Family Foundation, The
211 Wisteria Lane
Media 19063   (Delaware County)
AMV $3,937,953   **FYE** 1-01   **(Gifts Received** $0)

MI-11-25-29-41-42-44-53-55-56-61-71
Phone 610-565-1770 **FAX** None
EIN 23-2954759   **Year Created** 1998
49 **Grants totaling** $175,910

Nearly half local/Pa. giving. High local grant of **$30,000** to Peoples Emergency Center. **$12,000** to United Way of SE Pa. **$5,000** each to Academy of Music (restoration), Society for the Performing Arts/Media Theatre, and Temple Teammates. **$3,000-$3,500** each to Church of the Assumption BVM [Bethlehem] and Pa. Horticultural Society. **$1,000-$1,500** each to Benchmark School and Pa. Academy of the Fine Arts. Other local contributions **$100-$500** for education, cultural, civic, historical, and other purposes. **Out-of-state** giving includes high grant of **$100,000** to Lewes Library [DE] (building fund); and **$1,500** to Tufts U. [MA]. — In the prior year, major local giving included **$40,500** to Peoples Emergency Center; **$22,000** to United Way of SE Pa.; **$20,400** to Fort Mifflin on the Delaware; **$15,000** to Benchmark School; and **$12,400** to Westtown School. ■**PUBLICATIONS:** None ■**WEBSITE:** None ■**E-MAIL:** None ■**APPLICATION POLICIES & PROCEDURES:** Information not available.

O+D+T Charles L. Coltman, III (P+D+Donor+Con) — Joann F. Coltman (VP+D) — Clayton F. Coltman (S+D) — Charles L. Coltman, IV (F+D)

SE-142 Comcast Foundation, The
c/o Comcast Corporation
1500 Market Street, East Tower, 35th Floor
Philadelphia 19102   (Philadelphia County)
AMV $33,632,347   **FYE** 12-00   **(Gifts Received** $0)

MI-11-13-14-16-25-29-35-41-42-43-44-51-52
53-54-55-72-84-89
Phone 215-665-1700 **FAX** None
EIN 51-0390132   **Year Created** 1999
101 **Grants totaling** $1,925,198

About two-thirds local/Pa. giving. High grant of **$250,000** to Project H.O.M.E (learning/technology center). **$140,000** to United Way of SE Pa. (annual campaigns). **$125,000** to Delaware County Community College (Workforce Training/Videoconferencing Center). **$70,440** to Police Athletic League of Philadelphia (computers/cable modem access for youth centers and after-school homework/recreation programs). **$50,000** each to National Constitution Center (educational programs) and Universal Community Homes (teacher training/internet integration). **$40,000** to Big Picture Alliance (Pixillation Animation Workshop and Bartram High School Communications Academy Satellite program) and Philadelphia Cares (youth volunteerism promotion). **$35,000** to Philadelphia Dept. of Recreation/Mural Arts Program (digital technology center). **$28,500** Prince Music Theater (Rainbow Connection arts education and programs). **$25,000** each to Methodist Hospital Foundation (breast cancer early detection/treatment), School District of Philadelphia (Service Learning Scholarships), Settlement Music School (Teacher Training Institute for the Arts), Please Touch Museum (Community Partners program), and Philadelphia Women's Basketball 2000 (NCAA Youth Education through Sports clinics). **$20,000** to White-Williams Scholars (academic achievement website). **$15,000** to Philadelphia Museum of Art (Distance Learning Program). **$10,000** each to Dan Aaron Parkinson's Disease Foundation (rehab center), Montgomery County Fire & Rescue Service (bicycle helmet safety initiative), National Liberty Museum (educational programs), Olney Theater Center for the Arts (Holocaust Collaborative Project), Pennsylvania Ballet (outreach/education youth programs), Philadelphia 2000 (Convention Appreciation Day), Philadelphia Foundation/Good Neighbor Partnership Fund (pairing corporations with nonprofit arts organizations), and YMCA of Philadelphia and Vicinity (annual support). **$9,000** to Operation Understanding (youth leadership programs for local African-American and Jewish communities). **$7,500** to Avenue of the Arts (arts/culture revitalization). **$7,150** to Arts & Business Council (programs support). **$6,440** to Police Athletic League of Philadelphia (after-school homework/recreation). **$4,900-$5,250** each to Academy of Music (restoration program), Anti-Defamation League (programs), Arden Theater Company (tickets for disadvantaged youth), Easter Seals of Delaware County (Assistive Technology Lab), Greater Philadelphia Food Bank (hunger relief/nutrition education programs), Philadelphia Zoo (conservation/science/education programs) and YWCA of Carlisle (CyberSpace program). **$4,000** each to Atwater Kent Museum (education programs), Boy Scouts/Cradle of Liberty Council (Learning for Life program). **$3,250-$3,705** each to Franklin Institute Science Museum (technology education programs), National Conference for Community & Justice (community programs), and Prince Music Theatre (educational programs). **$2,000-$2,750** each to Boys & Girls Club of Philadelphia (inner-city youth program), City Year Greater Philadelphia (youth mentoring), Concerto Soloists (general support), Grand Lodge of Pa. (benefit event), Diagnostic & Rehabilitation Center/Philadelphia (substance abuse treatment programs), Martin Luther King, Jr. Assn. for Nonviolence (education programs), National MS Society (research/programs), Philadelphia Hospitality (general support), and Wills Eye Hospital (research/education). **$1,000-$1,750** each to Morris Arboretum, Red Cross (weather emergency info), Rena Rowan Foundation for the Homeless (welfare-to-employment transitional support), Terri Lynn Lokoff Child Care Foundation (child care availability), and Youth Leadership Foundation (scholarship fund). **Out-of-state** giving (mostly in corporate operating locations) includes **$400,000** to National Cable Television Center & Museum (develop distance learning programs); **$200,000** to District of Columbia College Access Program (counseling/financial aid initiates); **$100,000** each to Health Sciences Foundation of the Medical U. of South Carolina (cancer center programs), Kennedy Krieger Institute [MD] (educational opportunities for special needs students); **$59,500** to Cable in the Classroom [VA] (internet education training); **$50,000** to Boys & Girls Club of Camden County [NJ] (education/leadership training for youth); and other smaller grants to CT, NJ, NY, MD, VA, SC, TN, AZ, NM, CO, and CA. ■**PUBLICATIONS:** detailed application guidelines—available on website ■**WEBSITE:** www.comcast.com/in_the_community/ ■**E-MAIL:** None ■**APPLICATION POLICIES & PROCEDURES:** The Foundation focuses on enhancing the quality of life in communities where Comcast operates or employees live. A primary interest is supporting organizations/programs using communications technology to effectively address community needs in the fields of education, literacy, arts/culture, and community service/volunteerism; refer to the Foundation's website for more detail on programmatic interests in the the these interest areas. No grants are awarded for sporting events, capital campaigns, political candidates/organizations, organizations that discriminate by race, color, sex or national origin, or to individuals. Prospective applicants are urged to carefully review giving guidelines to determine whether the program reflects the Foundation's community funding goals; although the Foundation accepts unsolicited proposals, grants are awarded typically to nonprofit organizations that Comcast has proactively engaged in partnership. National or Philadelphia organizations should submit a preliminary letter of inquiry (2 pages maximum) directly to the Philadelphia address; organizations or programs located elsewhere should submit requests to their local Comcast community office. Submit the preliminary letter on organization letterhead and include the following: purpose of organization; brief description with a project summary which clearly outlines the purpose of the request; how the project relates to the Foundation's goals and objectives; a specific grant amount requested; the program evaluation process; and IRS tax-exempt status documentation. If the Foundation determines that the preliminary request is eligible for further consideration a formal application will be requested. Faxed or e-mailed grant requests will not be considered, and due to the volume of grant requests received follow-up phone calls are strongly discouraged.

O+D+T Diane Tuppeny-Hess (VP+D+Executive Director+Con) — Ralph J. Roberts (C+D) — Joseph W. Waz, Jr. (P+D) — William E. Dordelman (VP+D) — C. Stephen Backstrom (S+D) — Aileen K. Roberts (D) — Holly Rutkowski (D) — Michael Tallent (D) — Judie Dionglay [DE] (F) — Rosemarie Teta [DE] (AS)

SE-143 Comisky Family Foundation Trust
1109 Orleans Road
Cheltenham 19012   (Montgomery County)
AMV $29,136   **FYE** 12-00   **(Gifts Received** $0)

MI-22-62
Phone 215-635-6965 **FAX** None
EIN 23-7747091   **Year Created** 1994
11 **Grants totaling** $11,325

Mostly local giving. High Pa. grant of **$2,500** to Women of Vision. **$1,800** to Federation Allied Jewish Appeal. **$1,250** to Congregation Beth Shalom. **$1,000** to Jewish National Fund. Other local contributions **$25-$300** mostly for Jewish organizations. **Out-of-state** grant: **$3,000** to U.S. Friends of Akim [NY]. ■**PUBLICATIONS:** None. ■**WEBSITE:** None ■**E-MAIL:** None ■**APPLICATION POLICIES & PROCEDURES:** Information not available.

O+D+T Marvin Comisky (T+Donor+Con) — Goldye Comisky (T+Donor)

SE-144 Community Service Society, Inc.
P.O. Box A
Wayne 19087   (Delaware County)
AMV $32   **FYE** 9-00   **(Gifts Received** $61,300)

MI-14-15-31-41-42-63
Phone 610-393-0910 **FAX** None
EIN 23-7264528   **Year Created** 1963
9 **Grants totaling** $53,110

Two Pa. grants: **$2,460** to Melmark Home. **$925** to Frederick Erdman Assn. [Havertown]. **Out-of-state** giving includes **$36,818** to South Shore Community Service Assn. [Nova Scotia]; **$2,500** to Chester United Baptist Church [Nova Scotia]; **$2,500** to Shoreham Village Senior Citizens Assn.; and **$2,460** each to Sweet Briar College [VA] and St. Mary's U. [Nova Scotia]. — Note: The same giving pattern has been in effect for many years. ■**PUBLICATIONS:** None ■**WEBSITE:** None ■**E-MAIL:** None ■**APPLICATION POLICIES & PROCEDURES:** Grant requests in any form may be submitted at any time.

O+D+T Alberta Pew Baker [Canada] (P+Donor+Con) — Dr. David W. Baker [Canada] (VP) — Edward McL. Watters, III Esq. [Berwyn] (S) — Joseph W. Roskos [Wayne] (F)

SE-145 Connelly Foundation
One Tower Bridge, Suite 1450
100 Front Street
West Conshohocken 19428   (Montgomery County)
AMV $263,595,333   **FYE** 12-00   **(Gifts Received** $0)

MI-12-13-14-15-16-17-22-24-25-29-31-35-41
42-43-45-51-52-53-54-55-56-61-64-71
Phone 610-834-3222 **FAX** 610-834-0866
EIN 23-6296825   **Year Created** 1955
465 **Grants totaling** $14,008,662

Mostly local/Delaware Valley giving with heavy emphasis on support for Roman Catholic institutions; grants are for general support except as noted. ***EDUCATION GRANTS***-63%; grants designated as PACT (Proficiency & Access in Computer Technology) are for computer labs at eligible Philadelphia and suburban parish elementary schools; grants designated AEP (Academic Enrichment Program) are for Archdiocesan high schools; and grants designated FFF (Foundation for the Future) are for tuition assistance, faculty/curricula support at parochial elementary schools. High grant of **$1,101,133** to Archdiocese of Philadelphia (Josephine C. Connelly Achievement Awards and Neumann Scholars Program awards). **$819,200** to Gwynedd-Mercy College (Connelly Scholarships/capital campaign/technology enhancements). **$813,824** to Chestnut Hill College (capital construction). **$500,000** to Country Day School of the Sacred Heart (building renovation/expansion). **$465,965** to Holy Ghost Preparatory School (capital campaign). **$250,000** each to Cabrini College (capital grant/renovations), Settlement Music School (capital support/scholarships), and Waldron Mercy Academy (capital campaign). **$117,000-$120,000** each to Monsignor Bonner High

School (AEP), Roman Catholic High School (AEP), and St. Hubert Catholic High School (AEP). **$102,298** to Academy of Notre Dame (capital campaign/improvements). **$81,000** to Archbishop Prendergast High School (AEP). **$75,000-$78,000** to Friends School-Haverford (capital campaign), Overbrook School for the Blind (building renovation), and Rosemont College (Connelly Scholarships/other programs). **$70,413** to Sisters of St. Joseph-Chestnut Hill (field counselors for Connelly Scholars). **$68,120** to Incarnation of Our Lord School (FFF/transport costs). **$66,000** to Conwell-Egan Catholic High School (AEP). **$60,000** each to St. Pius X High School (AEP) and West Catholic High School (AEP). **$50,000-$52,200** to Annunciation BVM School [Havertown] (PACT), Benchmark School (capital construction), Our Lady of Good Counsel School (PACT), Presentation BVM School (PACT), Sacred Heart of Jesus School (PACT), Shipley School (capital campaign), St. Joseph's U. (John Connelly Scholarship Fund). **$49,144** to St. Martin de Porres School (PACT). **$48,000** to Little Flower Catholic High School for Girls (AEP). **$46,560** to St. Veronica School (FFF/transportation costs). **$45,000** to Cardinal Dougherty High School (AEP). **$40,000-$42,000** each to Hallahan Catholic Girls' High School (AEP), Mercy Vocational High School (AEP), Northeast Catholic High School (AEP), St. Colman-John Neumann School (PACT), St. Catherine of Siena Church-Wayne (PACT), and Visitation BVM School (FFF/transportation costs). **$35,000-$36,000** each to Kennedy-Kenrick Catholic High School (AEP), St. Boniface School (FFF), St. Francis de Sales School (FFF), St. Francis Xavier (FFF), St. Gabriel Church & School/Our Lady of Angels (FFF),St. Ignatius of Loyola School (FFF), and St. John the Baptist School (FFF). **$30,000** to St. Peter the Apostle School (FFF). **$23,000-$25,000** each to Church of the Sacred Heart School [Oxford] (capital campaign), Philadelphia U. (PACT), St. Catherine Day School (special ed computers), and Sts. Philip & James School (PACT). **$20,000-$21,000** each to Gladwyne Montessori School (capital campaign), IHM Center for Literacy & GED Programs (non-English-speaking programs), Nativity BVM Parish & School (PACT), Our Lady of Peace School (PACT), St. Maria Goretti High School for Girls (AEP), Temple U. (LEAP-Law Education and Participation Project). **$18,000** each to Sisters Servants of the Immaculate Heart of Mary (counselors for Connelly Scholars) and St. Peter's School (computer lab). **$15,500-$16,000** each to Eastern U. (Urban Studies Multicultural Education Project), St. Agnes-Sacred Heart School (science lab construction), and U. of Pa. (Law School/general support). **$12,500** to World Affairs Council of Philadelphia (Schools of Excellence program). **$10,000-$11,000** each to Brandywine Workshop (Visual Technology Center work-study program), Conshohocken Catholic School (PACT), Easttown Library & Information Center (capital support), Episcopal Academy, Our Lady of Charity School (PACT), Rosemont School of the Holy Child, St. Christopher School (PACT), St. Martin of Tours School (PACT), Stella Maris School (PACT), and Valley Forge Military Academy. **$6,000-$8,000** each to St. Malachy Church & School, Thomas Jefferson U., U. of the Arts, and White-Williams Scholars (Peer Academic Development Program).**$3,000-$5,000** each to The Center School (scholarship endowment fund), Community Arts Center (Chester outreach program), Educating Children for Parenting (Overbrook demonstration site), Eisenhower Exchange Fellowship (Philadelphia International Leadership Initiative), Holy Redeemer Church & School, Police Athletic League of Philadelphia, Quaker School at Horsham (computer equipment), and St. Barnabas School. Other smaller local grants/contributions. **Out-of-state** education grants include **$1,000,000** to Georgetown U. [DC] (capital campaign); **$405,093** to St. Elizabeth High School [DE] (capital campaign); **$70,000** to Church of the Sacred Heart [NJ]; **$40,000** each to San Miguel School [NJ] and St. Joseph's Pro-Cathedral (enrichment programs); Rutgers-Camden Center for the Arts [NJ] (Arts Education Enrichment Program for parochial schools); and **$10,000** to Pope John Paul II Foundation [Italy]. Other smaller, local education grants/contributions. *HEALTH & HUMAN SERVICES GRANTS-25%:* **$657,975** to Holy Redeemer Health System (capital campaign-elderly care facility). **$263,331** to Project H.O.M.E. (mostly for Rowan Homes). **$200,500** to Aid for Friends (capital campaign). **$100,000** each to Congreso de Latinos Unidos (capital campaign), Jewish Federation of Greater Philadelphia (capital campaign), Phoenixville Homes (construction/operating support), and Rocky Run YMCA [Media] (capital campaign). **$62,000** to Episcopal Community Services (home care services program/endowment). **$58,000** to North Light Community Center (capital campaign/program development).each to Cathedral Church of St. Catherine of Siena [Allentown] (Parish Revitalization Project-capital grant), CityTeam Ministries (homeless shelter renovation), U. of Pa. Hospital (Philadelphia Community Health Internship program). **$46,000-$46,500** each to St. John's Hospice (refrigeration truck) and Thomas Jefferson U. (Digestive Disease Institute/general support). **$40,000-$42,000** each to Maternity Care Coalition of Greater Philadelphia (Einstein Healthcare Network partnership), Partnership Community Development Corp. (development collaborative with Mercy Hospital), Philadelphia Senior Center (interior renovations), Simpson House (renovations), and Society of Holy Child Jesus-Drexel Hill (capital campaign). **$30,000** each to Hospitality House of Philadelphia (ex-offenders services), Surrey Services for Seniors (Chester County facility computers), and WHYY (documentary on Katherine Drexel canonization). **$24,000-$25,000** each to Anti-Violence Partnership of Philadelphia (schools program), ARC of Chester County (capital support), Chester Community Improvement Project (West End Initiative), Domestic Violence Center of Chester County (office renovations), National Shrine of St. Rita of Cascia, Philadelphia Police Foundation, SE Pa. Area Health Education (diabetes education-outreach program), and St. Thomas of Villanova (handicapped accessibility). **$20,000** each to Farmers' Market Trust (fresh produce for inner-city neighborhoods), Medical Mission Sisters, and St. Mary's Franciscan Shelter. **$18,000** to Support Center for Child Advocates (Child Victim Assistance Project). **$16,000** to YWCA of Bucks County (after-school program).**$15,000** each to Allegheny West Foundation (summer career exploration program), Bernardine Franciscan Sisters (La Communidad Hispana (new program initiatives), HIAS & Council Migration Service of Philadelphia (Regional Immigration & Citizenship Coalition), Jones Tabernacle A.M.E. Church (building restoration), Philadelphia Immigration Resource Center, Philadelphia Physicians for Social Responsibility (Peaceful Posse), Polish American Social Services (radio outreach/technology upgrades), Red Cross/SE Pa. (service learning program), Sisters of the Blessed Sacrament (radio series on Katherine Drexel), United Way of SE Pa., and Woodrock (Youth Development Program). **$14,000** to Southwest Community Enrichment Center (senior citizens-home visitation program). **$10,000-$12,000** each to Bridge of Hope (budgeting skills program), Camphill Village-Kimberton Hills (Aging in Community Program), Campus Boulevard Corp. (job training programs), Center for Urban Resources (Community Impact Institute), Chester Education Foundation (social work consulting services), Community Learning Center, Good Shepherd Home [Allentown] (equipment), Greensgrow Philadelphia Project (general-capital support), Homeless Advocacy Project, Network for Congregational Development (pilot entrepreneurship program), Old First Reformed Church (interior renovations), Overington House (new staff), Philadelphia Corp. for Aging (Emergency Fund Coalition), Red Cross/Lower Bucks (homeless shelter repairs), St. Patrick Church of Norristown (chair glide), Sisters of Mercy of the Americas, Tenants' Action Group of Philadelphia (Senior Assistance Program), and Ukrainian Catholic Archeparchy of Philadelphia (religious education). **$6,000-$8,000** each to Advocate Community Development Corp. (playground), AIDS Alive, Archdiocese of Philadelphia (Camp Overbrook/Cardinal's event), Blind Relief Fund of Philadelphia, Care Center for Christ, Devereux Foundation, Fair Housing Council of Suburban Philadelphia (educational initiative), HELP Philadelphia, Inner City House (food-shelter for young adults), North Penn Valley Boys & Girls Club (program-services expansion), SOWN/Supportive Older Women's Network (telegroup program), and Whosoever Gospel Mission (Career Track Learning Program computers). **$3,000-$5,000** each to Alpha Pregnancy Services (Life Skills program), Association for Developmental Disabilities (staff support), Bainbridge House (mentoring-reading program), Big Brothers Big Sisters of Chester County (school-based mentoring program), Center for Growth & Development (scholarship fund), Center on Hearing & Deafness (hospice volunteer project), Chester County Hospital Foundation (interpreter training), Child Home & Community (high school program), Christmas in April of Philadelphia (house rehab outreach program), Community Outreach Partnership (volunteer programs), Cradle of Hope (salary support), Deaf-Hearing Communication Center (emergency interpreting service), Diversified Community Services (counseling staff support), Episcopal Church of the Advocate (afterschool-summer programs), Family Service Assn. of Bucks County (teen center), Fellowship Farm (leadership training), Girl Scouts of SE Pa. (middle-school students program), Greater Philadelphia Coalition Against Hunger (Roundtable Discussions), Little Brothers Friends of the Elderly (capacity building), Mercy Collaborative Ministries, Montgomery County Mediation Center, Mother's Home-Darby (OASIS program), New Directions for Women (counseling services), New Kensington Community Development Corp. (community improvements), Our Mother of Good Counsel (Parish Nurse Ministry), Partners for English as a Second Language, Penn Home (air conditioning), Pa. Home of the Sparrow, Pa. Special Olympics (Philadelphia-area delegation support), Philadelphia City Sail, Philadelphia Friends of Outward Bound School (program expansion), Reformation Lutheran Church (playground), RSVP of Montgomery County (Eldercare program), St. Charles Borromeo Seminary (memorial donation), St. Gertrude Church, Sebastian Riding Associates, Security on Campus, Siloam Ministries, Stop Child Abuse Now, Street Clothes Project (start-up costs), Teams Mentoring Teens (pilot program), Unity Center, Urban Bridges at St. Gabriel's (literacy-computer program), Vietnamese Assn. for the Aging in Philadelphia/Suburbs, VNA Community Services (home care project), Wissahickon Hospice (volunteer recruitment-support), Women's Business Development Center, Working Wardrobe, and YMCA of Philadelphia/Vicinity. Other smaller, local health/human services grants/contributions. **Out-of-state** giving includes **$200,000** to Oblates of St. Francis de Sales [DE] (capital campaign); **$40,000** to Cooper Health System [NJ] (Geriatric Home Visitation Program); **$20,000** to Bayard House [DE] (programs for at-risk persons); **$15,000** each to Camden County Council on Economic Opportunity [NJ] (summer career exploration program) and Children's Beach House [DE] (capital campaign); and **$10,000** each to Atlantic City Rescue Mission (preschool program) and St. Joseph's Carpenter Society [NJ]. *CIVIC & CULTURE GRANTS*-12%; grants designated as (CAP)—Connelly Access Program—are for elementary-level arts/cultural activities, in-school and field trips to area cultural institutions, for selected Philadelphia Catholic schools, grades 4-8. **$500,000** to Gateway Visitor Center Corp./Independence National Historical Park (payment on **$2MM** pledge). **$150,000** to Rosenbach Museum & Library (building restoration). **$100,000** each to Irish Famine Memorial (sculpture/construction), Mann Music Center (Arts in the Park program), and Wagner Free Institute of Science (capital improvements). **$75,000** to Fund for the Water Works (restoration). **$50,000** to Upland Country Day School (skating rink renovation). **$40,000** to Library Company of Philadelphia (capital campaign). **$37,100** to Stages of Imagination (CAP). **$28,835** to Old Philadelphia Congregations (visitor brochure). **$24,000-$25,345** each to Academy of Natural Sciences (mostly CAP), Balch Institute for Ethnic Studies (marketing program), and Point Breeze Performing Arts Center. **$21,730** to Opera Company of Philadelphia (CAP). **$20,380** to Arden Theatre Company (CAP). **$13,500-$16,330** to Abington Art Center (mostly renovations), Freedoms Foundation at Valley Forge (mostly CAP), Philadanco (CAP), Philadelphia Civic Ballet Company (CAP), and Taller Puertorriqueno (CAP/other youth programs). **$9,800-$12,000** each to Academy of Vocal Arts (educational enrichment program), Art Sanctuary, Fort Mifflin on the Delaware (CAP), Historic Bartram's Garden (educational initiatives), Institute for the Study of Civic Values (Neighborhood Builders Online project), National Liberty Museum (CAP), Old Christ Church Preservation Trust (capital campaign), Philadelphia Orchestra (mostly CAP), Phoenixville Public Library (children's library renovation), Strings for Schools (pilot schools program), and Wilma Theatre (educational-community outreach programs). **$7,500-$8,300** each to Asociacion de Musicos Latino Americanos (CAP), Chestnut Brass Company (CAP), FrankfordStyle (arts programming), Mum Puppettheatre (CAP), National Museum of American Jewish History (educational programs), Philadelphia Art Alliance (free program series), and Walnut Street Theatre (educational programs). **$5,000-$6,500** each to 1807 & Friends Chamber Music Ensemble (CAP), Historic Rittenhouse Town (educational paper making program), International House of Philadelphia (CAP), Pa. Academy of Ballet Society (productions for underprivileged groups), Philadelphia Chamber Music Society (educational activities), Philadelphia Classical Symphony (family concert series), Philadelphia Mural Arts Advocates (CAP), Philadelphia Museum of Art (CAP), Philadelphia Theatre Company (youth outreach programs), and Po-Mar-Lin Fire Company (capital campaign). **$2,500-$4,000** each to Artreach, Inc., Cheltenham Center for the Arts (children's programs), Chester Springs Studio (Coatesville area art students program), Community Gardens of Chester County, Darlington Fine Arts Center (outreach program in Chester), Hedgerow Theatre, InterAct Theatre Company (seasonal support/school residencies), International Ballet Exchange (school residencies/performances), Lantern Theater Company (educational outreach programming), Philadelphia Society for the Preservation of Landmarks (Grumblethorpe/School Partnership), Sedgwick Cultural Center (children's programs), Singing City (schools program), Society for Performing Arts of the Media Theatre (empowerment program), Storybook Musical Theatre (student programs), U. of Pa./Arthur Ross Gallery (interactive arts program), and Wharton Esherick Museum (marketing materials). Other smaller local arts/cultural/civic grants/contributions. ■**PUBLICATIONS:** application guidelines ■**WEBSITE:** www.connellyfdn.org ■**E-MAIL:** info@connellyfdn.org ■**APPLICATION POLICIES & PROCEDURES:** The Foundation reports that giving focuses on Philadelphia and the surrounding Delaware Valley region in the areas of Education, Health/Human Services, and Civic/Culture. The Trustees have specified that at least 60% of giving be to organizations affiliated with the Roman Catholic Church or toward programs that impact its members; consult the website for details on programmatic initiatives. No grants are awarded to individuals, political or national organizations, other foundations, or in response to annual appeals or solicitation letters; also, guidelines restrict funding of an organization to once within a 12-month period. Preference is given to projects receiving support from several sources as evidence of broad community interest. Grant requests may be submitted at any time in a proposal which includes the following: (a) an executive project summary, its goals, financial requirements—state a specific amount requested, and status; (b) a brief history of the organization, annual report, two years of the most recent audited financial statements, and current list of Board members; (c) a detailed description of the project, including its objectives, budget (document all capital expenses), implementation timetable, and target population, (d) committed and prospective funding sources for the project with names and amounts; (e) plans for evaluating and funding the project in the future; (f) resume of project director and a list of key staff; and (g) IRS tax-exempt status documentation. In the absence of audited financial statements, copies of the past two years' IRS Form 990 with all schedules are required. Proposals which follow Delaware Valley Grantmakers Common Grant Application Format are accepted. Applications are acknowledged usually within two weeks and a response given within about three months; however, applicants may be contacted earlier for a telephone conference, site visit, or presentation. Visits to the Foundation or contacts with Foundation staff during the proposal review process are discouraged. The Trustees meet in January, March, May, August and November.

O+D+T Josephine Connelly Mandeville [Villanova] (C+P+T+Con) — Emily Connelly Riley (Executive VP, Programs+T) — Lewis W. Bluemle, Jr., M.D. [Bryn Mawr] (Senior VP+T) — Victoria 'Kim' Flaville (VP, Administration+S) — Lawrence T. Mangan (VP, Finance) — William J. Avery [Gwynedd Valley] (T) — Andrew J. Bozzelli [Ardmore] (T) — Ira Brind [Philadelphia] (T) — Christine C. Connelly [NJ] (T) — Danielle M. Connelly (T) — Thomas S. Connelly [Gladwyne] (T) — Kurt R. Crowley, M.D. [Berwyn] (T) — Eleanor L. Davis (T) — Philippe Delouvrier [NY] (T) — Thomas F. Donovan (T) — Barbara W. Riley [DC] (T) — Thomas A. Riley [DC] (T) — Andrew P. Willis (T)

SE-146 Connolly (Christine & John) Foundation, the
P.O. Box 219
Gwynedd   19436   (Montgomery County)
AMV $741,605   **FYE** 5-00   **(Gifts Received** $0)

MI-12-22-31-41-61
Phone 215-542-0945 **FAX** None
EIN 23-7890525   **Year Created** 1998
9 **Grants totaling** $39,457

All local giving. High grant of **$12,000** to Epiphany of our Lord Church. **$10,000** to St. Edmonds Home for Children. **$7,257** to Mount St. Joseph Academy. **$4,000** to Catholic Charities. **$2,500** to Catholic Leadership Assn. **$1,400** to Holy Redeemer Hospital. Other smaller grants. ■PUBLICATIONS: None ■WEBSITE: None ■E-MAIL: None ■APPLICATION POLICIES & PROCEDURES: Information not available.

O+D+T Christine A. Connolly (T+Donor+Con) — John L. Connolly (T+Donor)

SE-147 Conston Foundation, The
The Fairmount, Apt. 612
41 Conshohocken State Road
Bala Cynwyd   19004   (Montgomery County)
AMV $2,107,510   **FYE** 12-00   **(Gifts Received** $0)

MI-11-12-22-41-54-62
Phone 610-664-7898 **FAX** None
EIN 23-6297587   **Year Created** 1959
8 **Grants totaling** $44,000

Mostly local giving. High grants of **$10,000** each to Jewish Community Centers of Greater Philadelphia, National Liberty Museum, and United Way of SE Pa. **$6,500** to Mishkan Shalom. **$5,000** to Akiba Hebrew Academy. **$1,000** to Heart of Variety Fund. **$500** to Foundation for Independent Colleges [Harrisburg]. **Out-of-state** grant: **$1,000** to Children's Inn at National Institutes of Health [MD]. ■PUBLICATIONS: None ■WEBSITE: None ■E-MAIL: None ■APPLICATION POLICIES & PROCEDURES: Prospective applicants initially should make a telephone inquiry about the feasibility of submitting a request. Grant requests in letter form (2 pages maximum) may be submitted at any time; include an organizational budget and IRS tax-exempt status documentation.

O+D+T Charles S. Conston (T+Con) — Corporate donor: Conston, Inc.

SE-148 Copernicus Society of America
2001 Pennsylvania Ave., P.O. Box 385
Fort Washington   19034   (Montgomery County)
AMV $5,712,561   **FYE** 6-01   **(Gifts Received** $200)

MI-13-15-22-41-42-49-55-61-65-72-82-84
Phone 215-646-4101 **FAX** 215-646-1026
EIN 23-7184731   **Year Created** 1972
23 **Grants totaling** $292,672

About half local/Pa. giving. High Pa. grant of **$100,000** to The Papal Foundation [Philadelphia]. **$20,000** to Penn State U. **$3,900** to Germantown Academy. **$2,500** each to Polish American Cultural Center and Thaddeus Kosciuszko National Memorial. **$2,200** to Little League Foundation [Lycoming County] (capital campaign). **$1,000** to Lower Merion Symphony Orchestra. **$900** to Police Athletic League. **$750** to Gettysburg College. Other local/Pa. contributions **$100-$500** for various purposes. **Out-of-state** giving includes **$111,902** to Copernicus Foundation of Poland; **$23,750** to U. of Iowa (James Michener-Copernicus Society Writers' Award Endowment); **$10,000** to Center for Christian-Jewish understanding [CT]; and **$5,000** each to The American Center for Polish Culture [DC] and National Poetry Series [NJ]. ■PUBLICATIONS: statement of program policy; application guidelines ■WEBSITE: None ■E-MAIL: None ■APPLICATION POLICIES & PROCEDURES: The Society reports that priority interests include supporting Polish culture/heritage projects and advancing literature/language arts. Most grants are for continuing support, special endowments, publications, or conferences/seminars. No grants are awarded to individuals or for scholarships. Submit full proposals at any time together with a project budget, list of other funding sources, and IRS tax-exempt status documentation. The Board meets monthly and decisions on applications are usually made within six weeks.

O+D+T P. Erik Nelson (Executive Director+Con) — Edward J. Piszek (P+D+Donor) — Helen P. Nelson (VP+D) — Edward J. Piszek, Jr. [Gwynedd Valley] (VP+D) — George W. Piszek [Lafayette Hill] (VP+D) — William P. Piszek [Ambler] (VP+D) — Ann Piszek Reitenbaugh [Gwynedd Valley] (VP+D) — Francis Keenan [Chalfont] (VP)

SE-149 Corad Foundation
1122 Walters Road
Pennsburg   18073   (Montgomery County)
AMV $407,908   **FYE** 10-00   **(Gifts Received** $422,500)

MI-41-63-64
Phone 215-679-6117 **FAX** None
EIN 23-2443194   **Year Created** 1986
8 **Grants totaling** $44,400

Mostly local giving. High grant of **$14,000** Student Life Center, Inc. **$10,000** to Calvary Church of Souderton. **$6,300** to Christopher Dock Mennonite High School. **$5,000** to Philadelphia College of Bible. **$4,000** to Morning Star Ministries of the North

Penn Area. **$1,800** to Lehigh Valley Youth for Christ. **$300** to Hilltown Baptist Church. **Out-of-state** grant: **$3,000** to HCJB World Radio Missionary Fellowship [CO]. ■**PUBLICATIONS:** None ■**WEBSITE:** None ■**E-MAIL:** None ■**APPLICATION POLICIES & PROCEDURES:** The Foundation reports that grants are awarded to preselected charitable organizations only.

O+D+T Clare M. Moyer (T+Donor+Con) — Marvin Torgan, CPA [Bala Cynwyd] (T) — Chad Moyer [East Greenville] (Donor) — Christine Moyer (Donor) — Trina Moyer [East Greenville] (Donor)

SE-150 **Corbman (Morriss & Myrtle) Foundation**
2001 Stone Ridge Lane
Villanova   19085   (Montgomery County)

MI-12-13-17-22-29-31-32-41-62
Phone 610-525-2757 **FAX** None
EIN 23-2701894   **Year Created** 1992

AMV $196,483   **FYE** 12-00   (**Gifts Received** $0)   7 **Grants totaling** $19,000

All giving to Lehigh and Northampton counties except as noted. High grant of **$5,500** to Lehigh Valley Hospital. **$2,750** to Jewish Day School. **$2,000-$2,500** each to Community Action Committee of the Lehigh Valley, Crohn's & Colitis Foundation [Bucks County], Jewish Family Services, The Program for Women & Families, and Turning Point of Lehigh Valley. ■**PUBLICATIONS:** None ■**WEBSITE:** None ■**E-MAIL:** None ■**APPLICATION POLICIES & PROCEDURES:** Grant requests may may be submitted in a letter at any time; describe the charitable purpose of the request. Grants are awarded at a December meeting.

O+D+T Ellen S. Varenhorst (P+Con) — Gregory C. Hartman [Reading] (VP) — Donald Senderowitz [Allentown] (S+F) — Morris Corbman (Donor) — Myrtle Corbman (Donor)

SE-151 **Cornerstone Foundation**
c/o CF Capital
4020 Main Street
Elverson   19520   (Chester County)

MI-63-64
Phone 610-286-2946 **FAX** 610-286-2872
EIN 23-2593411   **Year Created** 1989

AMV $19,605,844   **FYE** 12-00   (**Gifts Received** $0)   14 **Grants totaling** $1,182,120

Nearly half local/Pa. giving. High grant of **$270,120** to High Point Baptist Chapel [Berks County] (general fund, missionary/special projects, camp scholarships). **$150,000** to Calvary Baptist Seminary [Lansdale] (library). **$65,000** to Association of Baptists for World Evangelism [Harrisburg] (South Africa Camp Ministry). **$25,000** to Northeast Baptist School of Theology [Downingtown] (building fund). **Out-of-state** grants mostly **$20,000-$200,000** for evangelical seminaries or churches in CA, GA, HI, NC, TN, and WI. ■**PUBLICATIONS:** None ■**WEBSITE:** None ■**E-MAIL:** None ■**APPLICATION POLICIES & PROCEDURES:** No grants awarded to individuals. — Formerly called the GCP Foundation.

O+D+T Edward H. Cone (P+F+Donor+Con) — Robert L. Cone (VP+S+Donor) — Stephen Cone (D) — Derial H. Sanders [Chester Springs] (D) — Julie E. Zuber [Reading] (D) — Corporate donors: Graco Children's Products; Graco Metal Products

---

SE-152 **Corson Foundation, The**
c/o Corson Investment Company
P.O. Box 710
Plymouth Meeting   19462   (Montgomery County)

MI-13-22-29-31-41-42-43-61-63-71
Phone 610-825-2000 **FAX** None
EIN 23-6390878   **Year Created** 1957

AMV $2,978,481   **FYE** 12-00   (**Gifts Received** $0)   46 **Grants totaling** $149,280

Mostly local/Pa. giving. High grant of **$30,000** to Plymouth Friends School. **$25,100** to Montgomery Health Foundation/Montgomery Hospital. **$25,000** to Ursinus College. **$7,600** to Children's Hospital of Philadelphia. **$6,000** to Mercersburg Academy. **$5,000** to George School (alumni fund). **$2,000-$2,600** each to Eastern U., Germantown Friends School, and Scantastic Foundation [Gladwyne]. **$1,000-$1,500** each to Ambler YMCA, Catholic Charities, and William Penn Charter School. Also, ten scholarships ranging from **$500** to **$7,400** awarded (mostly) to graduates of schools in the Plymouth-Whitemarsh area. Other local contributions **$100-$750** for various purposes. **Out-of-state** giving includes **$10,000** to Adelphi U. [NY] and **$1,500** to Williams College (alumni fund). ■**PUBLICATIONS:** Application for Scholarship form ■**WEBSITE:** None ■**E-MAIL:** None ■**APPLICATION POLICIES & PROCEDURES:** Scholarships are generally restricted to graduates of schools in the Plymouth-Whitemarsh area; applicants must complete an Application for Scholarship form which is available from the Foundation.

O+D+T John E.F. Corson (Manager+T+Con) — Harry Murphy (T) — Carol Posse (T)

SE-153 **Coslett Foundation, The**
c/o Wallingford Arms Apartments
27 Wallingford Ave.
Wallingford   19087   (Delaware County)

MI-13-18-22-31-41-42-53-54-63-71-72
Phone 610-566-8071 **FAX** None
EIN 23-6231832   **Year Created** 1957

AMV $925,376   **FYE** 12-00   (**Gifts Received** $0)   35 **Grants totaling** $30,000

Mostly local giving. High grant of **$2,500** to Academy of Natural Sciences. **$2,200** to Christ Church. **$2,000** to Crozer-Chester Foundation. **$1,000-$1,600** each to Chester YMCA, Church Farm School, Philadelphia Museum of Art, Philadelphia Zoo, Planned Parenthood of SE Pa., Salvation Army, Swarthmore College/Scott Arboretum, Seamen's Church Institute, United Negro College Fund, and U. of Pa. School of Fine Arts (Coslett Traveling Fellowship). Other local contributions **$100-$600** for various purposes. **Out-of-state** giving includes **$2,000** to St. Mary Ann Episcopal Church of Northeast [MD]; and **$1,000** each to three colleges in VA and NC. ■**PUBLICATIONS:** None ■**WEBSITE:** None ■**E-MAIL:** None ■**APPLICATION POLICIES & PROCEDURES:** Prospective applicants should initially telephone the foundation to inquire about the feasibility of submitting a request. Grant requests may be submitted in a letter at any time; provide details of the project and the funding requested. Site visits sometimes are made to organizations being considered for a grant.

O+D+T Edward W. Coslett, Jr. [Media] (T+Con) — Edward W. Coslett, III [Media] (T) — Harry W. Coslett [Swarthmore] (T)

SE-154 Cotswold Foundation, The
c/o John Dowds, 2997 Pennview Ave.
Broomall 19008   (Delaware County)

MI-13-22-41-42-63-64-71-81
Phone 610-353-3022 **FAX** None
EIN 23-7767257   **Year Created** 1994

AMV $3,496,541   **FYE** 12-00   **(Gifts Received** $355,777)   18 **Grants totaling** $125,625

Limited local giving. High Pa. grants of **$3,000** each to Academy of Notre Dame de Namur and Gesu School. **$2,000** to Main Line Unitarian Church. **$1,000** each to A Better Chance/Main Line and A Better Chance/Radnor. **Out-of-state** giving includes **$42,125** to Seminario Evangelico Presbilteriano de Guatemala [Guatemala] (grant through Bryn Mawr Presbyterian Church); **$25,000** to Northminster Presbyterian Church [CA]; **$10,000** each to Bruckner Nature Center [OH] and Center for Global Education [MN]; **$8,000** to Annunciation House [TX]; and **$5,000** each to Augsburg College [MN] and Casa Allanza [FL]. ■ **PUBLICATIONS:** None ■ **WEBSITE:** None ■ **E-MAIL:** None ■ **APPLICATION POLICIES & PROCEDURES:** The Foundation reports that grants are awarded only to donor-initiated projects.

O+D+T I. Wistar Morris, III [Villanova] (Co-T+Donor+Con) — Martha H. Morris [Villanova] (Co-T+Donor) — Eleanor Morris [Villanova] (Donor) — Lydia Morris [Villanova] (Donor) — Melissa Morris [Villanova] (Donor)

SE-155 Covenant Foundation, The
723 Clovelly Lane
Devon 19333   (Chester County)

MI-22-63
Phone 610-688-3418 **FAX** None
EIN 23-7451873   **Year Created** 1990

AMV $2,764,439   **FYE** 12-00   **(Gifts Received** $127,133)   23 **Grants totaling** $127,140

About two-thirds local/Pa. giving; grants are for general operations except as noted. **$19,250** to WBEB-FM [Bala Cynwyd] (religious messages). **$14,000** each to Salvation Army and Trinity School for Ministry [Beaver County]. **$12,000** to Good Samaritan Church of Paoli. **$4,000** to John Guest Evangelist Team [Allegheny County]. **$3,750** to WEEU-AM [Reading] (religious messages).**$2,500** to South American Missions Society [Beaver County]. **$2,440** to WNPV-AM [Lansdale] (religious messages). **$1,000** to Episcopal Community Services. Other local contributions **$500-$750** for other religious activities. **Out-of-state** giving includes **$14,850** to Campus Crusade for Christ [FL]; **$13,050** to Jesus Film Project [CA]; and **$6,000** to Young Life [CO]. ■ **PUBLICATIONS:** None ■ **WEBSITE:** None ■ **E-MAIL:** None ■ **APPLICATION POLICIES & PROCEDURES:** The Foundation reports that no unsolicited requests are being accepted at this time.

O+D+T Arnold C. Schneider, Jr. (T+Donor+Con) — Dorothy H. Schneider (T+Donor) — Arnold C. Schneider, III [Wayne] (Donor) — Gregory Schneider [DE] (Donor) — John Schneider (Donor)

SE-156 Craig Foundation, The
P.O. Box 817
Spring House 19477   (Montgomery County)

MI-32-51-54-61
Phone Unlisted **FAX** None
EIN 23-2984311   **Year Created** 1998

AMV $713,306   **FYE** 12-00   **(Gifts Received** $461,295)   17 **Grants totaling** $17,600

Mostly local giving. High grant of **$5,025** to Friends of St. Maria Goretti. **$5,000** to Philadelphia Theatre Company. **$4,250** to St. Joseph's Church. **$1,000** to National Liberty Museum. Other smaller contributions, mostly for health purposes. ■ **PUBLICATIONS:** None ■ **WEBSITE:** None ■ **E-MAIL:** None ■ **APPLICATION POLICIES & PROCEDURES:** Information not available.

O+D+T Barbara M. Osinski (P+Donor+Con) — Frank Osinski (Donor) Foundation donor: Christian Community Foundation [CO]

SE-157 Creative Financial Group, Ltd. Charitable Foundation
c/o Creative Financial Group, Ltd.
16 Campus Boulevard, Suite 200
Newtown Square 19073   (Delaware County)

MI-12-14-22-31-32-35-41-42-61-63-84
Phone 610-325-6100 **FAX** 610-325-6220
EIN 23-2705803   **Year Created** 1993

AMV $9,590   **FYE** 12-00   **(Gifts Received** $134,995)   43 **Grants totaling** $126,218

Mostly local giving; grants are for general purposes except as noted. High grant of **$60,464** to Variety Club. **$10,000** to Crozer-Chester Medical Center. **$5,035** to St. John Neumann High School (Millay Club). **$5,000** to St. Patrick's Church [Malvern]. **$2,000-$2,500** each to Community Volunteers in Medicine [West Chester], Easter Seals, Greater Philadelphia Scholastic Golf Assn., Paoli Presbyterian Church, and Villa Maria Academy. **$1,000-$1,500** each to MBF Center (work placement for disabled persons), St. Mary's Villa, and a local minister. **$800** to Bucks Assn. for Retarded Citizens. Other local contributions **$100-$700** for various purposes. **Out-of-state** giving includes **$12,000** to Wesley College [DE] (athletic program); **$6,000** to Wings Foundation [CO]; and **$1,475** to Children's Hope Foundation [NY]. ■ **PUBLICATIONS:** None ■ **WEBSITE:** None ■ **E-MAIL:** None ■ **APPLICATION POLICIES & PROCEDURES:** The Foundation reports that giving is nationwide. Grant requests may be submitted at any time in a full proposal; include IRS tax-exempt status documentation.

O+D+T Gary E. Daniels (P+Con) — Joseph V. Naselli (S+F) — Claire Daniels (T) — Diana Naselli (T) Corporate donor: Creative Financial Group, Ltd.

SE-158 Cushman (Charlotte) Foundation
P.O. Box 40037
Philadelphia 19106   (Philadelphia County)

MI-43-51
Phone 215-735-4676 **FAX** 856-854-7092
EIN 23-1280780   **Year Created** 2001

AMV $1,110,111   **FYE** 8-01   **(Gifts Received** $300,000)   4 **Grants totaling** $7,250

All local giving. Four scholarships **$750** to **$2,500** each awarded to students enrolled in four-year performing arts programs in Philadelphia-area colleges/universities. Grants also awarded now for theatre-related purposes to qualified groups/organizations in the Greater Philadelphia area. ■ **PUBLICATIONS:** application guidelines flyer ■ **WEBSITE:** None ■ **E-MAIL:** CushmanFdn@aol.com ■ **APPLICATION POLICIES & PROCEDURES:** All giving is restricted to theatre-related activities in the five-county Philadelphia area and Southern NJ. Cushman Scholarships are awarded by audition to students enrolled in four-year Performing Arts curricula in local colleges/universities. Grants for artistic/creative theatre-related projects are awarded to qualified Philadelphia-area theatre-related groups/organizations. Grant requests may be submitted at any time in a concise letter-proposal (four copies required) which includes: (1) narrative description of the project with project goals and timetable; (2) project budget; (3) list of other funders with grant sizes; (4) list of current Board members and staff; (5) brief organizational history; (6) Pa. Bureau of Charitable Organization form; and (7) IRS tax-exempt status documentation. Omission of any of the required materials will preclude consideration of grant support. Site visits sometimes are made to organizations being considered for a grant.

O+D+T Carol Nitzberg (Administrator+Con) — Donna Thomas (P+T) — Audrey Walters (VP+T) — Cirel Magen (S+T) — Lois Flook (F+T) — Betty Burke (T) — Margaret Chimples (T) — Anne Elder (T) — Ann Kalbach (T) — Virginia Maloney (T) — Norma Pomerantz (T) — Jeanne Wrobleski, Esq. (T) Donor: Charlotte Cushman Club

---

SE-159 D&CN Trust
334 Grays Lane
Haverford 19041   (Montgomery County)
AMV $946,339   FYE 12-00   (Gifts Received $683,848)

MI-41-42-63
Phone 610-649-9580 **FAX** None
EIN 23-6427949   **Year Created** 1966
27 **Grants totaling** $28,775

About three-fourths Pa. giving. High grant of **$21,000** to Penn State U. **$750** to The Baldwin School. Other smaller local contributions. **Out-of-state** giving includes **$2,500** to First Congregational Church of Houston [TX]; **$1,500** to First Congregational Church of Camden [ME]; and other smaller contributions to many states. ■**PUBLICATIONS:** None ■**WEBSITE:** None ■**E-MAIL:** None ■**APPLICATION POLICIES & PROCEDURES:** No grants awarded to individuals.

O+D+T Charles P. Neidig (T+Donor+Con) — Dorothy A. Neidig (T) — Catherine P. Lewis (T+Donor) — Patricia N. Lewis (T+Donor) — Richard N. Lewis (T+Donor)

SE-160 Daniels (Robert C.) Foundation, The
625 Creighton Road
Villanova 19085   (Montgomery County)
AMV $518,931   FYE 12-99   (Gifts Received $37,500)

MI-12-15-22-32-42-62
Phone 610-527-8080 **FAX** None
EIN 22-2773507   **Year Created** 1987
16 **Grants totaling** $62,353

Mostly local/Pa. giving; all grants are unrestricted. High grant of **$25,000** to Penn State U. **$12,518** each to Federation Allied Jewish Appeal **$10,000** to Temple U. Law School. **$6,680** to Philadelphia Ronald McDonald House. **$3,955** to Har Zion Temple. **$1,000** each to Hospice Program and Linda Creed Breast Cancer Foundation. Other local and out-of-state contributions **$100-$500** for various purposes. ■**PUBLICATIONS:** None ■**WEBSITE:** None ■**E-MAIL:** None ■**APPLICATION POLICIES & PROCEDURES:** Grant requests may be submitted in a letter at any time; describe the purpose of the requested funds, state the amount sought, and include pertinent information and IRS tax-exempt status documentation.

O+D+T Robert C. Daniels (T+Donor+Con)

SE-161 Davenport Family Foundation, The
1000 Lakeview Drive (West Chester)
P.O. Box 178
Pocopson 19366   (Chester County)
AMV $61,905,075   FYE 12-00   (Gifts Received $0)

MI-12-13-14-15-41-42-45-51-52-54-71-84
Phone 610-793-2025 **FAX** None
EIN 23-7871419   **Year Created** 1997
18 **Grants totaling** $2,600,729

Mostly local/Pa. giving. High grant of **$1,644,000** to Mercersburg Academy (scholarships/physics labs). **$105,000** to Jenkins Arboretum (collections conservation/improvements). **$84,289** to Brandywine Conservancy (publications). **$41,500** to William Penn Charter School (college prep program). **$40,000** to Center for Growth & Development [Philadelphia] (renovations/computers/publications). **$37,250** to Stroud Water Research Center (publications). **$28,575** to Tick-Tock Early Learning Center [Avondale] (wish list). **$20,000** to Children's Home of Easton (education center). **$15,000** to Family Services of Chester County (flower show). **$14,000** to Pa. Ballet (equipment/Nutcracker production). **$13,372** to Pa. Home of the Sparrow (facility improvements). **$10,000** to American Helicopter Museum (video). **$8,510** to Volunteer English Program in Chester County (publications/videos). **$6,000** to College Settlement of Philadelphia (general support/camp project). **$5,000** to Chester County Community Foundation (scholarship fund). **$4,860** to Brian's House (program support). **$2,500** to Security on Campus, Inc. (video). **$2,000** to Kennett Symphony. **Out-of-state** giving includes **$348,500** to San Miguel School of Camden [NJ] (mostly matching grant); **$75,000** to Trinity College [CT] (urban leadership program); **$46,694** to Kent County Adult Education Center [MD]; **$35,679** to Skating Assn. for the Blind & Handicapped [NY] (newsletter/program activities); **$13,000** to The Paper Bag Players [NY] (project); ■**PUBLICATIONS:** None ■**WEBSITE:** None ■**E-MAIL:** None ■**APPLICATION POLICIES & PROCEDURES:** No grants awarded to individuals.

O+D+T Peter D. Davenport [West Chester] (Executive Trustee+Con) — Sharon A. Byrne [Wynnewood] (T) — Sylvia Davenport [West Chester] (T) — William C. Pickett, III [Chadds Ford] (T) — Edna Marion Davenport [FL] (Donor)

SE-162 David Library of the American Revolution
1201 River Road, P.O. Box 748
Washington Crossing 18977   (Bucks County)
AMV $9,065,822   FYE 12-00   (Gifts Received $350)

MI-43-44-56-89
Phone 215-493-6776 **FAX** 215-493-9276
EIN 23-7289047   **Year Created** 1974
Grants totaling $9,620

This operating foundation also awards a few grants, mostly related to the Library's purpose of research and study of the American Revolution and the Revolutionary War Period. In 2000, **$9,620** was awarded in fellowships, grants and honoraria, but no details available. — In prior years, grants included **$1,125** to Bucks County Historical Society; **$1,000** to American Philosophical Society; and other contributions **$20-$500** for historical societies/libraries, historic sites, American studies programs at universities, local fire departments/rescue squads, and other organizations. ■**PUBLICATIONS:** descriptive brochure ■**WEBSITE:** www.dlar.org ■**E-MAIL:** dlar@libertynet.org ■**APPLICATION POLICIES & PROCEDURES:** Prospective applicants should initially telephone the foundation to inquire about the feasibility of submitting a grant request; consult the website for details on

Academic Fellowships and the Library's holdings. Fellowship applicants, pre- or post-doctoral candidates, must submit a curriculum vitae, at least two letters of recommendation, a 3-5 page statement of purpose, a sample of work, and project budget. Submit requests during September-March; deadline is March 31st.

O+D+T Marjorie E. Torongo (Director+Con) — James Sullivan [York] (P) — David Kimball [NJ] (VP) — Christine Jochem]NJ] (S) — Dr. David Fowler (Librarian)

SE-163   De La Cour Family Foundation
77 Middle Road, Apt 169
Bryn Mawr   19010   (Montgomery County)
AMV $10,184,872   **FYE** 12-00   **(Gifts Received** $0)

MI-29-35-41-42-56-63-82
Phone Unlisted **FAX** None
EIN 23-3025610   **Year Created** 1999
22 **Grants totaling** $400,000

About one-quarter local/Pa. giving. High Pa. grant of **$75,000** to The Hill School [Pottstown]. **$10,000** to Eagles Mere Conservancy [Sullivan County]. **$7,500** to Bryn Mawr Presbyterian Church. **Out-of-state** giving includes **$100,000** to Hillside School [MA]; **$40,000** to The Learning Tree Education; **$30,000** to Partners in Health [MA]; **$25,000** each to Community Service Society [NY] and Poly Prep Country Day School [NY]; and other smaller grants, mostly to NY and MA, for health, education and civic purposes. ■**PUBLICATIONS:** None ■**WEBSITE:** None ■**E-MAIL:** None ■**APPLICATION POLICIES & PROCEDURES:** Information not available.

O+D+T Willis S. De La Cour (P+D+Donor+Con) — Willis S. De La Cour, Jr. [NY] (VP+S+F) — Edmund P. De La Cour [MA] (D) — Eleanore P. De La Cour (D) — Lea De La Cour [MA] (D)

SE-164   de Mazia (Violette) Trust
P.O. Box 413
Bryn Mawr   19010   (Montgomery County)
AMV $15,147,312   **FYE** 6-00   **(Gifts Received** $0)

MI-53-54
Phone 610-668-6406 **FAX** 610-527-5248
EIN 23-6954824   **Year Created** 1991
7 **Grants totaling** $1,074,764

All giving limited to/for activities relating to the art theories, methods and approaches of the the late Dr. Albert Barnes. Six grants totaling **$1,032,554** to Barnes Foundation (general support, art education program, classroom access, and student support). **$31,680** to Pa. Academy of the Fine Arts (Barnesian art course support). **$530** to Lincoln U. (student visits to Barnes). **Out-of-state** grant: **$10,000** to Delaware Art Museum (Barnes documentary underwriting). — In the prior year **$200,000** awarded to Barnes Foundation (Barnesian art education program). ■**PUBLICATIONS:** application guidelines; application form ■**WEBSITE:** www.demazia.org ■**E-MAIL:** info@demazia.org ■**APPLICATION POLICIES & PROCEDURES:** The Trust develops and underwrites programs, projects and activities that are consistent with its mission of advancing, teaching, studying, promoting and supporting the aesthetics and appreciation of art, based on the theories, methods and approaches of the late Dr. Albert C. Barnes. Prospective grant applicants should write or e-mail for grant request instructions and an application form. **Note:** The Trust is *not* an affiliate of The Barnes Foundation—the Trust and The Barnes Foundation are independent organizations with separate trustees and directors. The Barnes Foundation is not involved in the presentation or content of the educational program of the de Mazia Trust or in the selection of the students that attend the educational programs supported by the de Mazia Trust.

O+D+T Sharon Hicks (Administrator+Con) — Ernest J. Pick, M.D. [Devon] (Co-T) — Marcelle Pick [Devon] (Co-T) — Esther Van Sant [Philadelphia] (Co-T) PNC Bank N.A. (Agent)

SE-165   Debemac Foundation, The
c/o Drinker, Biddle and Reath
One Logan Square, 18th Floor
Philadelphia   19103   (Philadelphia County)
AMV $138,014   **FYE** 9-01   **(Gifts Received** $0)

MI-11-15-41-42-44-54-56-63-71-83
Phone 215-988- 2869 **FAX** 215-988-2757
EIN 23-6222789   **Year Created** 1958
15 **Grants totaling** $94,499

About four-fifths local giving. High grant of **$24,649** to 10,000 Friends of Pa. **$18,000** to United Way of SE Pa. **$12,500** to Hayes Manor. **$10,000** to Rosenbach Museum & Library. **$5,000** to Bryn Mawr Presbyterian Church. **$3,000** to Andalusia Foundation. **$1,500** to U. of Pa. **$1,000** to New Society Education Foundation. Other smaller local contributions. **Out-of-state** giving includes **$10,000** to Wesleyan U. [CT]; **$5,500** to Fund for Justice & Education [IL]; and **$2,000** to Lawrenceville School. ■**PUBLICATIONS:** None ■**WEBSITE:** None ■**E-MAIL:** bullitwc@dbr.com ■**APPLICATION POLICIES & PROCEDURES:** Information not available.

O+D+T Lewis H. Van Dusen, Jr. Esq. (T+Donor+Con) — William C. Bullitt, Esq. (T) — Nora E Pomerantz, Esq. (T) — Maria P.W. Van Dusen (Donor) — Marian A. Boyer (Donor)

SE-166   Dee (Elise Galman) Foundation
c/o The Galman Group
P.O. Box 646
Jenkintown   19046   (Montgomery County)
AMV $243,597   **FYE** 11-00   **(Gifts Received** $0)

MI-22-32-52-62
Phone 215-886-2000 **FAX** None
EIN 23-2938431   **Year Created** 1997
4 **Grants totaling** $21,500

All local giving. High grant of **$10,000** to Anti-Defamation League. **$6,000** to Jewish National Fund. **$5,000** to Federation Allied Jewish Appeal. **$500** to an individual. — Giving in the prior year included **$12,000** to Concerto Soloists; **$10,000** to Anti-Defamation League; and **$2,000** to Linda Creed Breast Cancer Foundation. ■**PUBLICATIONS:** None ■**WEBSITE:** None ■**E-MAIL:** None ■**APPLICATION POLICIES & PROCEDURES:** Information not available.

O+D+T Arnold Galman (P+Donor+Con) — Robert J. Dee (VP+Donor)

SE-167 Delaware County Medical Society Public Health Fund
P.O. Box 449
Wayne 19087 (Delaware County)
AMV $553,942 **FYE** 12-00 **(Gifts Received** $0)

MI-12-13-14-15-17-22-25-29-31-35-84
Phone 610-687-7906 **FAX** None
EIN 23-6436006 **Year Created** 1964
28 **Grants totaling** $12,250

All giving restricted to/for Delaware County. High grants of **$1,000** each to Camp Sunshine, Marple Dental Clinic, Meals on Wheels of Media, and Recording for the Blind & Dyslexic. **$500** each to Delaware County AIDS Network, Delco Memorial Foundation, Domestic Abuse Project of Delaware County, Family & Community Services of Delaware County, Philabundance, Planned Lifetime Assistance Network, Surrey Services for Seniors, Salvation Army, Wayne Senior Center, Women's Assn. for Women's Alternatives, Women's Resource Center of Wayne, and Volunteers in Action. Other local contributions **$100-$250** for similar purposes. ■**PUBLICATIONS:** None ■**WEBSITE:** None ■**E-MAIL:** None ■**APPLICATION POLICIES & PROCEDURES:** Only organizations which provide health/human services in Delaware County are eligible to apply. Grant requests should be submitted in a letter (4 pages maxiumum) in September or early October; the deadline is October 31st. Grants are awarded at a November meeting and mailed in December.
O+D+T John Rosecky [Wayne] (P+D+Con) — David M. Smilk, Esq. [Broomall] (S+D+Member, Examination Committee) — Robert F. Plotkin, M.D. (D+Chair, Examination Committee) — Graham D. Andrews [Wayne (D+Member, Examination Committee) — Kenneth Kirkpatrick [East Norriton] (D) — David McKeighan (D) — Richard C. Nelson, D.D.S. [West Chester] (D) — Deana Smith [King of Prussia] (D) — Rehka P. Yagnik, M.D. [Media] (D)

SE-168 DeLong (Benjamin F.) Trust
c/o First Union/Wachovia
123 South Broad Street, PA1279
Philadelphia 19109 (Philadelphia County)
AMV $611,675 **FYE** 8-99 **(Gifts Received** $0)

MI-14-15-31
Phone 215-670-4226 **FAX** 215-670-4236
EIN 23-6221391 **Year Created** 1940
4 **Grants totaling** $82,876

One-quarter of giving is awarded on a discretionary basis to Philadelphia-area agencies assisting needy persons suffering from lung disease: One grant of **$17,500** to American Lung Assn. of SE Pa. All remaining giving for three designated institutions: Fox Chase Cancer Center, Inglis House, and Salvation Army. ■**PUBLICATIONS:** None ■**WEBSITE:** None ■**E-MAIL:** reginald.middleton@wachovia.com ■**APPLICATION POLICIES & PROCEDURES:** Only social service agencies in the Philadelphia area which assist needy persons suffering from lung diseases are eligible to apply; some preference is given agencies serving the inner city. Grant requests may be submitted at any time in a proposal signed by an officer on behalf of the governing board.
O+D+T Reginald J. Middleton (VP at Bank+Con) — First Union/Wachovia (Trustee)

SE-169 Delphi Project Foundation, The
c/o Reliance Standard Life Insurance Co.
2001 Market Street, Suite 1500
Philadelphia 19103 (Philadelphia County)
AMV $6,836 **FYE** 12-00 **(Gifts Received** $500,000)

MI-41-51-52-54-55-72
Phone 215-256-4214 **FAX** 215-256-3531
EIN 23-2711230 **Year Created** 1992
5 **Grants totaling** $464,568

All giving limited to organizations providing educational programs in Philadelphia. High grant of **$331,000** to Philadelphia Museum of Art. **$57,000** to Pa. Ballet. **$40,500** to Philadelphia Zoo. **$20,068** to School District of Philadelphia. **$16,000** to The Wilma Theater. ■**PUBLICATIONS:** None ■**WEBSITE:** www.rsli.com [corporate info only] ■**E-MAIL:** None ■**APPLICATION POLICIES & PROCEDURES:** The Foundation reports that all giving is restricted to supporting educational programs in Philadelphia public schools through an innovative educational choice program for children and adolescents. No grants are awarded to individuals and unsolicited grant applications are not accepted. However, prospective applicants may make an initial telephone inquiry regarding the possibility of submitting a request.
O+D+T Tammy E. Salvatore (Foundation Manager+Con) — Lawrence E. Daurelle (P+D) — Charles T. Denaro (S+D) — Olivia C. Niemczuk (F+D) — Amy L. Jared (D) — Charles P. O'Brien (D) — Tessi Varthas (D)

SE-170 Denenberg Foundation
c/o Adelphia Lamps and Shades, Inc.
5000 Paschall Ave.
Philadelphia 19143 (Philadelphia County)
AMV $149,149 **FYE** 12-00 **(Gifts Received** $0)

MI-11-22-25-62-82
Phone 215-729-2600 **FAX** 215-729-8077
EIN 23-6431888 **Year Created** 1968
47 **Grants totaling** $32,819

About three-fourths local giving. High grant of **$12,000** to United Way of SE Pa. **$8,000** to Federation Allied Jewish Appeal. **$2,000** to Project H.O.M.E. **$1,000** to UNICEF/Philadelphia. Other local contributions **$15-$500** for various purposes. **Out-of-state** giving includes **$1,500** to CARE [NY] and **$1,000** each to Mercy Corps [OR] and Oxfam America [MA]. ■**PUBLICATIONS:** None ■**WEBSITE:** None ■**E-MAIL:** None ■**APPLICATION POLICIES & PROCEDURES:** Information not available. — Formerly called the Gertrude Deneberg Charitable Trust.
O+D+T Alfred Denenberg (T+Con) — Robert Denenberg [CA] (T)

SE-171 DeValpine (Newell) Foundation, The
c/o Eizen Fineburg & McCarthy
2001 Market Street, Suite 3410
Philadelphia 19103 (Philadelphia County)
AMV $4,189,187 **FYE** 12-00 **(Gifts Received** $26)

MI-12-22-31-32-34-42-54-62-81
Phone 215-751-9666 **FAX** 215-751-9310
EIN 23-7821726 **Year Created** 1995
27 **Grants totaling** $130,650

Mostly local giving; all grants are for general purposes. High grant of **$40,000** to Old York Road Temple-Beth Am. **$14,500** to Gratz College. **$10,000** each to Laurel House and Temple U. Medical School. **$5,000** each to Children's Hospital of Philadelphia and Hillel of Greater Philadelphia. **$1,800-$2,500** each to Arthritis Foundation, Foreign Policy Research Institute, Golden Slipper Charities, Jewish Community Centers of Greater Philadelphia, Jewish Federation of Greater Philadelphia, and Kesher Israel Congregation [West Chester]. **$1,000** each to Franklin Institute, Greater Philadelphia Food Bank, Kardon Institute of the Arts, and Pa. Horticultural Society. Other smaller local contributions for various purposes. **Out-of-state** giving includes **$15,000** to Brooklyn Law School [NY] and **$5,000** each to All Stars Project [NY] and Friends of Bezalel [NY]. ■**PUBLICATIONS:** None ■ **WEBSITE:** None ■**E-MAIL:** None ■**APPLICATION POLICIES & PROCEDURES:** No grants are awarded to individuals.

O+D+T Bernard Eizen, Esq. (T+Con) — Brown Brothers Harriman Trust Co.]NY] (Trustee)

SE-172 **Devlin (Agnes L.) Memorial Fund**   MI-43
            c/o Philadelphia Corp. for Investment Services
            1650 Market Street, Suite 3050   **Phone** 215-419-6400 **FAX** None
            Philadelphia   19103   (Philadelphia County)   **EIN** 52-1932531   **Year Created** 1995
AMV $1,039,252   **FYE** 12-00   **(Gifts Received** $0)   1 **Grant of** $44,500

Sole grant to Montgomery County Community College (scholarship fund). ■**PUBLICATIONS:** None ■**WEBSITE:** None ■ **E-MAIL:** None ■**APPLICATION POLICIES & PROCEDURES:** The Foundation reports that scholarships will be awarded to underprivileged young people who demonstrate strong academic and/or vocational potential; there are no geographical restrictions for applicants. Submit a scholarship application at any time together with a high school transcript, parents' tax return, a reference letter from a teacher/faculty member, and information on activities, etc.

O+D+T A. Louis Denton (Con) — Edith Rubin [FL] (T) — Eunice Rubel [FL] (T)

SE-173 **DiBona (G. Fred & Sylvia) Family Foundation**   MI-11-13-14-15-29-32-41-42-55
            1211 Mount Pleasant Road   **Phone** Unlisted **FAX** None
            Villanova   19085   (Montgomery County)   **EIN** 23-2867497   **Year Created** 1996
AMV $163,325   **FYE** 12-00   **(Gifts Received** $50,000)   22 **Grants totaling** $65,200

Mostly local/Pa. giving. High grant of **$15,000** to United Way of SE Pa. **$10,000** to Villanova U. **$5,000** each to Encore Series, Inc., Lehigh U., Malvern Preparatory School, and Widener U. **$2,500** each to Academy of Notre Dame de Namur, Caron Foundation [Wernersville], Jefferson Hospice, Rena Rowan Breast Cancer Fund, and YMCA of Philadelphia. **$1,000** each to Devereux Foundation, Msgr. Walmsley Scholarship Fund, and Peoples Energy Fund. Other smaller local contributions. **Out-of-state** grant: **$2,500** to Juvenile Diabetes Foundation [NY]. ■**PUBLICATIONS:** None ■**WEBSITE:** None ■**E-MAIL:** None ■**APPLICATION POLICIES & PROCEDURES:** Grant requests may be submitted in a letter at any time.

O+D+T Sylvia M. DiBona (S+F+Donor+Con) — G. Fred DiBona, Jr. (P+Donor)

SE-174 **Dickey (Clarence E. & Marie W.) Foundation**   MI-22-63-72
            332 Joy Lane   **Phone** 610-696-5924 **FAX** None
            West Chester   19380   (Chester County)   **EIN** 25-1563520   **Year Created** 1987
AMV $632,129   **FYE** 12-00   **(Gifts Received** $1,000)   1 **Grant of** $12,000

Sole grant to Westminster Presbyterian Church. — Giving in prior years included **$10,500** to Chester County Community Foundation; **$9,000** to Westminster Presbyterian Church; **$2,000** to Care Center for Christ; and for child welfare and animal humane purposes. ■**PUBLICATIONS:** None ■**WEBSITE:** None ■**E-MAIL:** None ■**APPLICATION POLICIES & PROCEDURES:** Brief written requests may be submitted at any time; include IRS tax-exempt status documentation.

O+D+T David W. Dickey (T+Donor+Con) — Marie Warren Dickey (T+Donor)

SE-175 **Dietrich Foundation, Inc.**   MI-42-51-52-53-54-55-57
            P.O. Box 649   **Phone** 215-988-0778 **FAX** None
            Gladwyne   19035   (Montgomery County)   **EIN** 23-6255134   **Year Created** 1953
AMV $10,424,273   **FYE** 12-00   **(Gifts Received** $0)   30 **Grants totaling** $512,290

About half local giving. High Pa. grants of **$40,000** each to Orchestra 2001 (CD/concert), Painted Bride Art Center (program/theater), and Wharton Esherick Museum (mission support). **$30,000** to Institute for Contemporary Art (operations). **$22,000** to Chester Springs Studio (project/program). **$20,000** each to American Poetry Review (operations/program) and Susan Hess Modern Dance (project). **$15,000** each to Network for New Music (CD support) and Philadelphia Theatre Company (program). **$12,000** to Church of the Advocate/Art Sanctuary (program support/scholarship fund). **$10,000** each to Philadelphia Museum of Art (program) and WHYY(operations/program). **$5,000** each to Arcadia U. (art exhibit), Paoli Memorial Hospital Foundation (nursing program). **$3,000** to Project H.O.M.E. (operations/program). **$2,000** to Chestnut Brass Company (tour). **Out-of-state** giving includes high grant of **$45,000** to World Music Institute [NY] (film); **$40,000** to Hamilton College [NY] (art galley/music/drama); **$30,000** each to Theater for the New City [NY] (operations/program) and Unified Buddhist Church [VT] (land fund/program); and smaller grants for similar arts/cultural purposes in NY and AZ. ■**PUBLICATIONS:** None ■**WEBSITE:** None ■**E-MAIL:** None ■**APPLICATION POLICIES & PROCEDURES:** The Foundation reports major giving interests as performing arts, music, visual arts, museums, and cultural programs; most grants are for special projects, research, publications, or matching grants. Multi-year grants are awarded; no grants are awarded to individuals. Unsolicited grant requests are not encouraged. The Board usually meets in January and July to award grants. — Formerly called the Daniel B. Dietrich Foundation.

O+D+T Daniel W. Dietrich, II [Chester Springs] (P+F+D) — Joseph G.J. Connolly, Esq. (S+D) Foundation donor: The Dietrich American Foundation

SE-176   Dietrich (William B.) Foundation, The   MI-12-15-32-41-44-53-54-56
1811 Chestnut Street, Suite 304
P.O. Box 58177   **Phone** 215-979-1919 **FAX** None
Philadelphia   19102   (Philadelphia County) **EIN** 23-1515616   **Year Created** 1936
AMV $19,382,601   **FYE** 12-00   (**Gifts Received** $0)   12 **Grants totaling** $1,038,135

Mostly local giving. High grant of **$350,500** to The Shipley School (Beechwood restoration). **$319,750** to Fairmount Park Historic Preservation Trust (Sheep Barn restoration/Sedgley Porter House improvements). **$229,885** to Rosenbach Museum & Library (historic preservation). **$100,000** to University Museum of Archaeology & Anthropology (gallery renovations). **$6,000** each to Church Farm School (annual support) and Options in Aging (hot lunch program). **$5,000** to Make-A-Wish Foundation of Philadelphia/SE Pa. (program support). Other small contributions for local fire companies. **Out-of-state** giving: **$10,000** each to AIDS Project [CA] and U. of Southern California School of Medicine (AIDS research). — Major grants in the prior year include **$200,000** to Woodmere Art Museum; **$100,000** to Wellness Community of Philadelphia (barn restoration); and **$93,860** to Philadelphia Art Alliance (building renovations). ■**PUBLICATIONS:** None ■**WEBSITE:** None ■**E-MAIL:** None ■**APPLICATION POLICIES & PROCEDURES:** The Foundation reports that 'local needs' receive priority in giving with most grants for special projects, building funds, or matching grants; multi-year grants are awarded. Submit grant requests in a letter at any time; describe the organization, intended use of the funds, amount of funding requested, and include descriptive literature and IRS tax-exempt status documentation. Site visits sometimes are made to organizations being considered for a grant. The Board meets in January, April, July and October. — Formerly called The Dietrich Foundation.
O+D+T   William B. Dietrich [Villanova] (P+F+D) — Frank G. Cooper, Esq. [Narberth] (S+AF+D) The Dietrich American Foundation (Donor)

SE-177   DiLoreto Foundation   MI-22-31-61
1031 Old Cassatt Road (Berwyn)
P.O. Box 784   **Phone** 610-647-1280 **FAX** None
Southeastern   19399   (Chester County)   **EIN** 11-6036781   **Year Created** 1954
AMV $5,958   **FYE** 12-00   (**Gifts Received** $60,000)   24 **Grants totaling** $60,250

Three local/Pa. grants: **$15,000** to Archdiocese of Philadelphia. **$1,000** each to Oblates of Mary [Scranton] and Paoli Memorial Hospital. **Out-of-state** giving includes **$5,000** each to Christendom College [VA], Legionaires of Christ [CT], St. Gregory the Great Seminary [NE], and Thomas Aquinas College [CA]; and other smaller grants/contributions to Catholic churches and organizations in AL, CA, CO, FL, MN, NY, OH, and WI. ■**PUBLICATIONS:** None ■**WEBSITE:** None ■**E-MAIL:** None ■**APPLICATION POLICIES & PROCEDURES:** Grant requests may be submitted in any form at any time.
O+D+T   Richard DiLoreto (P+Donor+Con)

SE-178   Dinnocenti (David) Memorial Foundation   MI-18-22-31-52-61
c/o Twin County Construction Company
324 Limerick Center Road   **Phone** 610-495-7001 **FAX** 610-495-7004
Pottstown   19464   (Montgomery County)   **EIN** 23-2576371   **Year Created** 1989
AMV $227,108   **FYE** 2-01   (**Gifts Received** $5,200)   32 **Grants totaling** $15,900

About two-thirds local giving. High grant of **$4,910** to St. Aloysius Church of Pottstown. **$700** to Birthright of Pottstown. Other local contributions **$100-$500** for health/medical, cultural, civic, and Catholic church purposes. **Out-of-state** giving includes **$2,000** to Johns Hopkins Medicine [MD] and other smaller contributions, mostly to FL. ■**PUBLICATIONS:** None   ■**WEBSITE:** None ■**E-MAIL:** None ■**APPLICATION POLICIES & PROCEDURES:** Grant requests may be submitted in any form at any time.
O+D+T   Richard G. Roesler (Con) — Eugene Dinnocenti (T+Donor) — Anthony Dinnocenti (Donor) — Ronald Dinnocenti (Donor) — Marie Dooner (Donor) — Peter S. Dooner (Donor) — John Orgill (Donor) — Nancy Orgill (Donor) Corporate donor: Twin County Construction Co.

SE-179   Djerassi Foundation   MI-22-52-54-62
1820 Rittenhouse Square, Apt. 14A   **Phone** 215-732-5638 **FAX** None
Philadelphia   19103   (Philadelphia County) **EIN** 23-2224978   **Year Created** 1982
AMV $1,050,419   **FYE** 6-00   (**Gifts Received** $0)   9 **Grants totaling** $11,953

Mostly local giving. High grant of **$4,050** to Philadelphia Orchestra. **$2,410** to Main Line Reform Temple Beth Elohim. **$1,943** to Temple Beth Zion-Beth Israel. **$1,550** to Opera Company of Philadelphia. **$1,500** to Philadelphia Museum of Art. Other smaller contributions. ■**PUBLICATIONS:** None ■**WEBSITE:** None ■**E-MAIL:** None ■**APPLICATION POLICIES & PROCEDURES:** The Foundation reports that trustees seek out prospective grantees and unsolicited requests are not accepted. — Formerly called the Djerassi Cancer Research Foundation.
O+D+T   Isaac Djerassi, M.D. (T+Donor+Con) — Ady Lynn Djerassi, M.D. (T) — Niza Djerassi (T+Donor) — Ramy I. Djerassi, Esq. (T)

SE-180 Dolfinger-McMahon Foundation
c/o Duane Morris LLP
One Liberty Place, Suite 4200
Philadelphia 19103   (Philadelphia County)

MI-12-13-14-15-16-17-18-19-20-22-25-29-35-39
41-44-45-51-52-54-55-56-71-79-81-83-84
Phone 215-979-1768 **FAX** 215-979-1020
EIN See below   **Year Created** 1957

AMV $16,903,144   **FYE** 9-01   **(Gifts Received** $0)   201 **Grants totaling** $1,026,187

All giving generally restricted to/for the Greater Philadelphia area (including the City of Camden); grants are for general support except as noted. *HUMAN SERVICES GRANTS*: **$20,000** to Public Interest Law Center of Philadelphia (legal services for disabled children). **$13,000** to Salvation Army (Spark of Hope program). **$12,000** to Women Against Abuse **$11,500** to People & Stories/Gente y Cuentos (adult reading-discussion program). **$10,000** each to American Alliance for Rights & Responsibilities (Philadelphia school violence/safety program), American Street Financial Services Center (technical assistance to entrepreneurs), Center in the Park (Creative Arts & Aging Network), Corporate Alliance for Drug Education (grade school program), Hosts for Hospitals (outreach coordinator), MARC Advocacy Services (parent advocates program), and Women of Excellence (services/transitional housing for homeless women). **$9,000** to Institute for the Development of African-American Youth (gun safety campaign). **$8,000** to YouthBuild Philadelphia Charter School (services to graduates). **$7,500** each to Adult Day Care of Chester County (program assessment), Cornerstone Center for Training & Development (counseling ministry from children), Devereux Foundation (Picture Exchange Community System), LaSalle U. (technical assistance for nonprofits), Metropolitan Camden Habitat for Humanity [NJ] (Shalom House project), Metropolitan Career Center (job retention/career advancement training), Pa. Assn. for the Blind/Delaware County Branch (medical transcription service), Surrey Services for Seniors (Community Cares Program), Thomas Jefferson U. Hospital (pediatric weight management program), and YWCA of Germantown (program marketing). **$7,000** to Providence Center (after-school program coordinator). **$6,000** each to Camden County Council on Economic Opportunity [NJ] (summer career exploration program), Hurricane Island Outward Bound School [ME] (Philadelphia educators course), Korean Community Development Services Center (summer career exploration program), and Manor College (community service learning program). **$5,000** each to Aid for Friends (inner-city breakfast bag project), Bernardine Franciscan Sisters (low-income single parents program), Calcutta House (safety net program), Camphill Village Kimberton Hills (site plan development), Elwyn (transitional services model for young adults), Family Support Line of Delaware County (child abuse services), Ghebre Michel Inn (training curriculum), Horizons Unlimited Geriatric Education Corp. (school intergenerational program), Lower Merion Counseling Services (fundraising capacity), MBF Center (employer partnership project), NARAL-PA Foundation (campaign for contraceptive coverage), New Frankford Community 'Y' (out-of-school enrichment programs), Overington House (financial counseling program), Presbyterian Children's Village Foundation (needy families assistance), Thresholds in Delaware County (volunteer training/teaching materials), Unity Center (Chester summer youth program), Villanova U. School of Law (legal symposium re war on drugs), and Wo-Man 2 Woman Ministries (emergency shelter/transitional housing program). **$3,000-$4,000** each to Allens Lane Art Center (children's summer day camp), Montgomery County Assn. for the Blind (blind children summer day camp), Philabundance (food-rescue expansion initiative), Philadelphia Society for the Preservation of Landmarks (Grumblethorpe/school partnership), and SOWN/Supportive Older Women's Network (telegroup service project).Also, 26 grants **$1,000-$2,500** for similar purposes/programs. *HEALTH GRANTS*: **$50,000** (3 grants) to Delaware Valley Health Education & Research Foundation (develop region-wide medication safety goals/improved implementation of First Steps program/domestic violence project conference. **$7,500-$8,000** each to Exceptional Care, Inc. (pediatric hospice program), Focus on Women's Health/Living Beyond Breast Cancer (develop resource materials for Latinas). Planned Parenthood of Bucks County (new clinic management system), and Planned Parenthood of SE Pa. (public outreach activities). **$5,000** each to Bryn Mawr Hospital (stroke awareness program), Elizabeth Blackwell Health Center for Women (special needs program), Paoli Memorial Hospital (stroke awareness program), Planned Parenthood of Chester County (college students information program), and Visiting Nurse Assn. of Greater Philadelphia (hospice services in poor neighborhoods). **$3,500** to Philadelphia Community Health Alternatives (HIV prevention services for young adults). **$1,800-$2,500** each to AIDS Coalition of Southern NJ (life skills program), Children's Hospital of Philadelphia/Craig Dalsimer Division, and Women's Therapy Center (Feminist Therapy Collective). *ARTS & CULTURE*: **$14,000** (2 grants) to Conservation Center for Art & Historic Artifacts (cooperative collections storage facility planning/business expansion plan development). **$12,500** to Please Touch Museum (Penn's Landing project). **$10,000** each to American Philosophical Society (public exhibitions program), Fairmount Park Historic Preservation Trust (internship program), Greater Philadelphia Cultural Alliance (member services expansion), Philadelphia Orchestra (children's educational TV series), Regional Performing Arts Center (Legacy Club), and The Wilma Theatre (premiere performance). **$8,000** each to Moxie Dance Collective/Painted Bride Art Center (create movement theater piece) and WHYY (gay-lesbian documentary). **$6,500-$7,500** each to Arden Theatre Company (world-premiere musical), Atwater Kent Museum (students program/website), Bryn Mawr Rehab Hospital (Art Ability), Philadelphia Museum of Art (teen docents program), Point Breeze Performing Arts Center (after-school youth classes), Rosenbach Museum & Library (photographic exhibition), Settlement Music School (therapeutic arts program), and Wagner Free Institute of Science (history exhibit).**$5,000** each to American Composers Forum (Community Partners program), Prince Music Theater (composer/educator residency), Bach Festival of Philadelphia (high school Bach weekend), Brandywine Graphic Workshop (printmaking/arts schools collaborative), The Clay Studio (international exhibition), Creative Artists Network (at-risk youth program), Germantown Historical Society (community history preservation), Jeanne Ruddy & Dancers (production-presentation support), National Museum of American Jewish History (klezmer music family program), NetworkArts Philadelphia (education/art-making program), New Freedom Theatre (youth programs), Orchestra 2001 (guest artist appearances), Painted Bride Art Center (multidisciplinary Latino festival), Philadelphia Dance Company (youth training program), Philadelphia U. (promotional billboard), Philadelphia Volunteer Lawyers for the Arts (Cultural Entrepreneurship Center), Sedgwick Cultural Center (teen jazz workshop), Storybook Musical Theatre (subsidized tickets), and Strings for Schools (Great Music Education Headstart Series). **$3,500-$4,000** each to Philadelphia Society for the Preservation of Landmarks (Grumblethorpe School Partnership), and Philomel Concerts (arts education consultant. **$2,000-$3,500** each to 1812 Productions (in-school theatre-education program), Academy of Community Music (Head Start centers programs),African American Museum in Philadelphia, Anne-Marie Mulgrew & Dancers Company (premiere performance), Asian Arts Initiative, Celebration Theater (seed money), Chester Springs Studio (Studio Days program), Cliveden, Delaware Valley Arts Institute (school tickets support), District One Community Education Center (community group productions), Group Motion multimedia Dance Theatre (premiere performance), Interact, Inc., J.R. Lowell School, Kardon Institute of Music for the Handicapped (Community Connections program), LaSalle U., National Liberty Museum (student tours/training), Moonstone, The Philadelphia Company (closed captioning services), Philadelphia Festival Chorus (seasonal support), Philadelphia Shakespeare Festival/Red Heel Theatre Company, Philadelphia Sketch Club, Time to Share Foundation, TOVA, Tri-County Assn. (emergency grant), University Museum of Archaeology & Anthropology (theatrical performance), Village of Arts & Humanities (Graterford Prison project), Urban Bridges at St. Gabriel's (artist residency), Whitemarsh Community Art Center (community outreach programs), and Young Audiences/Philadelphia Chapter. Also, 15 grants **$1,000-$1,500** for similar arts/cultural purposes. ***EDUCATION GRANTS:*** **$10,000** each to Philadelphia Education Fund (Principals Leadership Development) and Temple U./College of Education (after-school academic enrichment program). **$7,500** to First United Methodist Church of Germantown (after-school program) and Summerbridge Germantown (academic enrichment program). **$5,000** each to Greene Towne School (professional development program), IHM Center for Literacy & GED Programs (ESL program), and Need in Deed (annotated social issues bibliography). **$2,000-$3,000** each to Boys & Girls Clubs of Philadelphia (education career development program), The Christian Academy (staff development), Exodus to Excellence Inc., Jubilee School (computer curriculum), and Project Forward Leap Foundation. Two other smaller grants. ***ENVIRONMENT GRANTS:*** **$6,500** to Community Gardens of Chester County (low-income residents gardens). **$3,000** to Awbury Arboretum (children's environmental education program). **$2,000** each to Pa. Horticultural Society (Greensource program) and Peopling of Philadelphia Collaborative. ***PUBLIC-SOCIETY BENEFIT GRANTS:*** **$15,000** to Committee of Seventy (emergency grant). **$10,000** each to Academy of Natural Sciences (emergency evacuation notification system), Chatham College [Pittsburgh] (civic involvement program for Philadelphia women), and United Way of SE Pa. (Initiative for Early Childhood). ■**PUBLICATIONS:** Annual Report with application guidelines ■**WEBSITE:** None ■**E-MAIL:** valcich@duanemorris.com■**APPLICATION POLICIES & PROCEDURES:** The Foundation reports that most grants are for (1) experimental, demonstration, seed-money projects; or (2) projects likely to be accomplished within a relatively short period of time; or (3) emergency grants or loans to cover a period of temporary funds shortage or help in starting a new agency. As a general policy, multi-year grants are not awarded; if funds are required for one to three years, the Trustees will make a first (or second) year grant with renewal possible for a second (or third) year, provided progress reports and the grant expenditure breakdown merit continued support. Grants are not awarded, except in the rarest instances, to projects beyond the greater Philadelphia area; individuals for scholarship or research purposes; ordinary operating expenses; endowment; medical/scientific research; construction, renovation, or acquisition of physical facilities; equipment or supplies (except when merely incidental to a project's primary purpose); or projects requiring Foundation support beyond 3 years and unlikely to become self-supporting. Also, only rarely will grants close to or exceeding $20,000 be awarded in any one year for a single project/program. Prospective applicants should initially telephone the Foundation to request a copy of the guidelines. If after reviewing the guidelines, the organization feels it is eligible for support, a full proposal should be prepared and received in the Foundation's office on/before the April 1st or October 1st deadlines. The first six pages of the proposal must be prepared exactly as follows: (Page 1) Name and address of applicant organization; amount of grant requested and the term if for more than one year; and a concise one paragraph description of the program. (Page 2) A one-page statement about the need to be met and the method by which the program will be carried out. Also, state whether the project will completed by the end of the grant term, or if it will be self-supporting or supported by other funding sources. (Page 3) List of Board members and officers. (Page 4) A copy of the IRS tax-exempt status documentation, including the ruling that the applicant organization is not a private foundation. (Page 5) Information about whether support has been received or requested from other foundations or funding sources, and if so, the amount committed or requested. (Page 6) An itemized budget. Any additional information supplied should be attached as appendices to the above six pages. Most grants are awarded at meetings in April and October, but under special, unusual circumstances requests for emergency support will be considered outside the normal grant-making timetable. Note: The Foundation's assets are comprised of several trusts with the following EINs: 23-6207346, 23-6232909, 23-6232910.

O+D+T Marlene Valcich (Executive Secretary+Con) — Roland Morris, Esq. (T) — David E. Loder, Esq. (T)

SE-181   **Donley Foundation**
   P.O. Box 540
   Plymouth Meeting 19462   (Montgomery County)

MI-11-12-13-17-42-44-45-51
Phone 610-828-8145 **FAX** 610-834-8175
EIN 23-6859909   **Year Created** 1987

AMV $17,106,068   **FYE** 12-00   **(Gifts Received** $1,835,148)   30 **Grants totaling** $1,071,300

Mostly NE and CP region giving; grants are for general support except as noted and many are payments on multiyear pledges. Allentown-Bethlehem-Easton Area Grants: **$500,000** to Community Services for Children (new facility capital campaign). **$100,000** each to Allentown Public Library (children's services), KidsPeace (facility construction), and Lehigh Carbon Community College Foundation. **$85,000** to Lehigh Valley Community Foundation (CEO America program). **$10,000** to The Program for Women & Families (day reporting program). **$7,000** to The Caring Place (education program). **$5,000** each to Communities in School of the Lehigh Valley, Lehigh Valley Child Care (scholarship assistance), Northeastern Regional Adult Literacy Conference, Pa. Shakespeare Festival (school presentations), ProJeCt of Easton (summer literacy camp), and West End Youth Center. **$4,000** to Girls Club of Allentown (Just the Facts program). **$2,500** to Fund to Benefit Children & Youth. **$1,500** to Community Music School (financial aid). Dauphin & York County Grants: **$30,000** to Pa. Partnership for Children. **$14,400** to Foundation of York County Chamber of Commerce (student matching service). **$10,000** to York County Literacy Council. **$5,000** to United Way of York County (early childhood careers initiative). **Out-of-state** giving includes **$12,000** to Children's Literacy Foundation [NH]; **$10,000** each Cabrini Mission Foundation [IL] (bilingual parenting newsletter), Vermont Institute of Natural Sciences (program); and other smaller grants to New England and IL. ■**PUBLICATIONS:** Annual Report; application guidelines; Proposal Cover Sheet; Check-Off List ■**WEBSITE:** None ■**E-MAIL:** judy1@aol.com ■**APPLICATION POLICIES & PROCEDURES:** The Foundation reports that giving favors organizations in the Greater Lehigh Valley; York County; as well as parts of VT, NH, and IL. Priority interests are education, human services, and other projects that benefit young persons or disadvantaged people, particularly those which encourage community leadership or require only seed money. Grants for capital expenditures, endowments are a low priority. No grants are awarded for religious, political purposes, promotion (marketing, development, publications, fundraising event sponsorship, etc.), or to individuals. Grant applications must include a Proposal Cover Sheet and a Check-Off List (both available from the Foundation) and a proposal narrative (8 pages maximum) which includes the following: name and mission/purpose of the organization; purpose of the grant; special nature of the project emphasizing its innovative qualities and potential impact; constituency to be served; key staff/volunteer leadership involved in the project and their roles; and the amount of funding needed and funding requested including what other funds are available or anticipated. Also include a project budget, annual organization budget, balance sheet, list of the Board members, and the most recent audited financial statement. Grant requests may be submitted at any time (deadlines are April 1st and October 1st); submit seven collated copies of the Proposal Cover Sheet/Proposal Narrative, and one copy each of the Check-Off List and IRS tax-exempt status documentation. Receipt of proposals will be acknowledged. Site visits sometimes are made to organizations being considered for a grant.

O+D+T Judith L. Bardes (Grants Coordinator+Con) — Edward J. Donley (T+Donor) — Inez C. Donley (T+Donor) — John W. Donley , Esq. [IL] (T) — Thomas E. Donley , Esq. (T) — Martha Donley Robb , Ph.D. [NH] (T) Mellon Bank N.A. (Custodian)

SE-182   Douty Foundation, The
P.O. Box 540
Plymouth Meeting   19462
(Montgomery County)

MI-12-13-14-15-16-17-18-22-24-25-35-41-45 55-71-81-84
Phone 610-828-8145 **FAX** 610-834-8175
EIN 23-6463709   **Year Created** 1968

AMV $7,742,068   **FYE** 12-00   **(Gifts Received** $0)   91 **Grants totaling** $292,450

All local/Pa. giving; grants are for operating support except as noted. High grants of **$10,000** to Children's Hospital of Philadelphia (Summer Community Internships) and Delaware Valley Habitat for Humanity. **$6,000** each to Greater Philadelphia Federation of Settlements (Summer Career Exploration Program), Korean Community Development Services Center (Summer Career Exploration Program), The Philadelphia Foundation (Emma Lazarus Partnership), and Respond (Summer Career Exploration Program). **$5,000** each Asian Arts Initiative (youth workshop), ASSETS Montco, Community Learning Center, Domestic Violence Center of Chester County (bilingual project), Eastern Philadelphia Organizing Project, Family Care Solutions, Montessori Genesis II School, Point Breeze Performing Arts Center (academy program), and Taller Puertorriqueno (cultural education project). **$4,000** each to AIDS Law Project of Pa. (immigration advocacy project), Asociacion de Musicos Latino Americanos (Latin Music School), Asian American Youth Assn. (educational programs), College Settlements of Philadelphia (camperships), Delaware County Family Centers (Chester after-school program), Frankford Group Ministry (parenting program), HELP Philadelphia (homeless families support), Maternal & Child Health Consortium of Chester County (Healthy Start Program), and YWCA of Chester (childcare project). **$3,000-$3,500** each to Ad Hoc Committee for Logan/Youth Project, Allegheny West Foundation (elementary school program), Anti-Violence Partnership of Philadelphia (SAVE program), Center for Urban Resources (Hispanic training program), Coatesville Cultural Society, Community Housing Services of Lansdale (Project Self-Sufficiency), Community Women's Education Project (program), Germantown Women's Educational Project, Greater Philadelphia Urban Affairs Coalition (mural arts program), Greensgrow (urban agriculture center), Independence Media Of Philadelphia/WYBE-TV (educational programming), Jeanes Memorial Library (children's dept.), Jubilee School, Main Line Art Center (summer residencies for children), Neighborhood Gardens Assn., NetworkArts Philadelphia (ecology/arts program), North Light Community Center (Youth Encouragement Program), North Philadelphia Health System (Reboot Philadelphia), Philadelphia Physicians for Social Responsibility (violence prevention program), Planned Parenthood of Chester County (healthy moms/babies program), Police-Barrio Relations Project, Potter's House Mission, Providence Center (after school program), St. Mary's Church/Hamilton Village (neighborhood bikes program), St. Philip's United Methodist Church (Youth Services Initiative), Salvation Army (female offender initiative), Sisters of St. Joseph (literacy project), Southwest Community Enrichment Center (family school program), Thresholds, TOVA (children's substance abuse prevention program), Travelers Aid Society of Philadelphia (summer camp for kids in transitional housing), Urban Bridges at St. Gabriel's, Urban Retrievers, Village of Arts & Humanities (summer camp), Whosoever Gospel Mission & Rescue Home (career track learning program), and Working Wardrobe. **$2,000-$2,500** each to 1812 Productions (in-school theatre education), Aid for Friends (Breakfast Bag project), All Saints Church of Norristown (computer lab), American Institute for Social Justice (predatory lending education), CASA Youth Advocates, Children's Aid Society of Pa. (teens/tots program), Children's Village Child Care Center (early intervention/parent support), Committee for Dignity & Fairness in Housing (summer program), Darlington Fine Arts Center (Chester City Youth Initiative), Endow-A-Home Program (case management), First United Methodist Church of Germantown (academic after-school program), Ghebre Michael Inn, Institute for the Development of African-American Youth (learning center), John Bartram Assn. (children's educational programs), Juvenile Law Center, NARAL-PA Foundation (Campaign for Contraceptive Coverage), Nelson Network Coalition (adolescents program), Norristown Zoo, Old First Reformed Church (summer camp program), Resources for Human Development (street clothes project), RSVP of Montgomery County (family literacy volunteers), Sedgwick Cultural Center (children's program), Wagner Free Institute of Science (children's programs), Ward AME Church (summer enrichment program), and West Mt. Airy Neighbors (school focus). **$1,000-$1,500** to Eastern College (summer theatre camp), IHM Center for Literacy & GED Programs, and Mountain Meadow Summer Camp (scholarships). ■**PUBLICATIONS:** Annual Report (grantees listed, not grant sizes) with application guidelines ■**WEBSITE:** None ■**E-MAIL:** judy1@aol.com ■**APPLICATION POLICIES & PROCEDURES:** The Foundation reports that giving focuses on the Greater Philadelphia area, with preference for Philadelphia and Montgomery County organizations, especially educational or other projects with potential for social change and to benefit disadvantaged people. General operating support is sometimes given to small organizations; organizations with annual budgets exceeding $2 million are discouraged from applying. Grants for capital expenditures or endowments are not a priority, nor for agency promotion (marketing, development, publications, fundraising events). No grants are awarded for religious/political purposes. Grants usually are awarded on a one-year basis with a five year limit on continuous funding. Grant requests must include an *Application Form* cover sheet (available from the Foundation) and a proposal narrative (10 pages maximum) which includes the following: (1) Organizational Description: mission, services provided, and leadership, including officers, directors and Board members; and (2) Project Description: describe the project and who (how many?) will be served directly and how they will benefit, expected outcome/s, geographic area served; explain how the project's success/outcome will be measured; the project leader's name with qualifications and experience—give evidence that involved staff are able to work with and understand the needs of the persons to be served; describe how the project meets the Foundation's priorities; and a detailed project budget (costs for staff, supplies and other specific costs) and project funding—include actual/anticipated sources of income. Applications may be submitted at any time (deadlines are February 15th, April 15th, and October 15th. Submit one copy of the proposal narrative and any supporting materials together with seven copies of Page 1 of the *Application Form* Cover Sheet, and one copy of IRS tax-exempt status documentation. Proposals will be acknowledged if an addressed envelope or label is enclosed. Only one funding request may be submitted by an organization in one calendar year, except under special circumstances. Site visits sometimes are made to organizations being considered for a grant. The Board of Directors awards grants at meetings in April, June, and November.

O+D+T Judith L. Bardes (Executive Director+T+Con) — Richard G. Alexander [Dresher] (T) — Lynette E. Campbell [Philadelphia] (T) — Carrolle Perry Devonish [Philadelphia] (T) — Norma Elias [Lafayette Hill] (T) — Nancy J. Kirby, MSW [Bryn Mawr] (T) PNC Advisors (Custodian)

SE-183 Downs Foundation, The
    c/o Downs Carpet Company
    Davisville Road, P.O.Box 475
    Willow Grove 19090   (Montgomery County)
AMV $1,582,715   **FYE** 12-00   **(Gifts Received** $0)

MI-15-31-32-41-42-71-72

Phone 215-672-1100 **FAX** None
EIN 23-6257328   **Year Created** 1960
   10 Grants totaling $90,000

About three-quarters local giving. High grant of **$40,000** to Philadelphia U./School of Textiles & Science. **$20,000** to Abington Memorial Hospital. **$1,000** each to ALS Assn., Penn Treaty Middle School, Pennypack Ecological Restoration Trust, and SPCA/Montgomery County Chapter. Other smaller local contributions. **Out-of-state** giving includes **$15,000** to Duke U. [NC] (brain tumor center) and **$10,000** to Cedars-Sinai Medical Center [CA]. ■**PUBLICATIONS:** None ■**WEBSITE:** None ■**E-MAIL:** None ■**APPLICATION POLICIES & PROCEDURES:** The Foundation reports that most giving is for general support, special projects, building funds, capital drives, endowment, research, and scholarships for dependents of company employees; also, multiple-year grants are awarded. Grant requests may be submitted in a letter at any time; include organizational and project budgets and IRS tax-exempt status documentation. The Board meets in September and December.

O+D+T George T. Downs, III (T+Con) — Joan Downs Brehm (T)

SE-184 Dozor (Harry T. & Shirley W.) Foundation
    191 Presidential Boulevard, PH12
    Bala Cynwyd 19004   (Montgomery County)
AMV $1,010,251   **FYE** 5-00   **(Gifts Received** $0)

MI-11-22-42-52-62-82

Phone 610-667-4016 **FAX** None
EIN 23-7033771   **Year Created** 1955
   Grants totaling $0

No grants awarded in 2000. — Local grants in prior years, **$2,000** or smaller, to Federation Allied Jewish Appeal, Friends of the Mann Music Center, Temple Adath Israel, and United Way of SE Pa. **Out-of-state** giving to NY and FL. In 1996, a major grant of **$75,000** to American Associates of Ben Gurion U. [Israel] ■**PUBLICATIONS:** None ■**WEBSITE:** None ■**E-MAIL:** None ■**APPLICATION POLICIES & PROCEDURES:** Grant requests may be submitted in a letter at any time.

O+D+T Harry T. Dozor (T+Donor+Con) — Richard J. Dozor (T) — Robert B. Dozor (T) — Shirley W. Dozor (T) — Allison Lit (T)

SE-185 Driscoll Family Foundation
    615 St. Andrews Road
    Philadelphia 19118   (Philadelphia County)
AMV $491,523   **FYE** 12-00   **(Gifts Received** $40,000)

MI-11-22-32-41-42-54-56-61-71

Phone 610-668-0950 **FAX** None
EIN 23-2897985   **Year Created** 1997
   150 Grants totaling $103,600

Mostly local giving; some grants comprise multiple payments. High grant of **$50,000** to U. of Pa. **$8,750** to Our Mother of Consolation. **$7,750** to Alzheimer's Assn./SE Pa. **$5,000** to Anti-Defamation League. **$3,500** to William Penn Charter School. **$3,000** to Chestnut Hill HealthCare. **$2,500** each to Catholic Charities and United Way of SE Pa. **$1,000-$1,500** each to Mount St. Joseph Academy, Philadelphia Museum of Art, St. Joseph's U., and Wissahickon Valley Watershed Assn. Other smaller local contributions for various purposes, especially cultural, educational, and Catholic organizations. — Giving in the prior year included **$25,000** to U. of Pa./Center for Neuro Degenerative Disease Research; **$11,000** to American Academy of the Sacred Arts; **$4,650** to Alzheimer's Assn.; and **$3,000** to Chestnut Hill Historical Society. ■**PUBLICATIONS:** None ■**WEBSITE:** None ■**E-MAIL:** None ■**APPLICATION POLICIES & PROCEDURES:** Information not available.

O+D+T Edward C. Driscoll (AF+Donor+Con) — David B. Driscoll [NY] (P) — Edward C. Driscoll, Jr. [CA] (S+F)

SE-186 Driscoll (Lee F. & Phoebe A.) Family Foundation
    720 Swedesford Road
    Ambler 19002   (Montgomery County)
AMV $431,889   **FYE** 6-01   **(Gifts Received** $0)

MI-11-20-22-42-54-63-56-71

Phone 215-699-9648 **FAX** None
EIN 23-2982380   **Year Created** 1998
   86 Grants totaling $15,192

Mostly local giving. High grant of **$2,000** to Wissahickon Valley Watershed. **$1,500** to Montgomery County Lands Trust. **$1,050** to Church of the Messiah. **$1,000** to Natural Lands Trust. **$500** each to Academy of Natural Sciences, Catholic Charities, and Philadelphia Museum of Art. Other local contributions **$25-$250** for conservation and other purposes. **Out-of-state** grant: **$1,000** to Natural Resources Defense Council [NY]. — In the prior year, local grants included **$6,000** to The Nature Conservancy; **$2,500** to United Way of SE Pa.; and **$2,000** each to Bryn Mawr College and Public Interest Law Center of Philadelphia. ■**PUBLICATIONS:** None ■**WEBSITE:** None ■**E-MAIL:** None ■**APPLICATION POLICIES & PROCEDURES:** Prospective applicants should make an initial telephone inquiry about the feasibility of submitting a request. Grant requests may be submitted in any form at any time; include any appropriate background information about the organization.

O+D+T Lee F. Driscoll (P+F+Donor+Con) — Phoebe A. Driscoll (VP+S+Con)

SE-187 Drueding Foundation
669 Dodds Lane
Gladwyne 19035 (Montgomery County)
AMV $7,437,891 **FYE** 6-01 (**Gifts Received** $0)

MI-12-13-15-18-22-25-31-32
Phone 610-649-0203 **FAX** None
EIN 23-2418214 **Year Created** 1986
28 **Grants totaling** $378,000

Mostly local/Pa. giving; all grants are for general purposes. High grant of **$173,000** to Project Rainbow Drueding Center. **$20,000** to Abington Memorial Hospital. **$16,000** to Ambler Community Cupboard. **$15,000** to Fox Chase Cancer Center. **$13,000** to Cystic Fibrosis Foundation. **$12,000** to Chestnut Hill Healthcare. **$10,000** to Alzheimer's Assn./SE Pa. **$9,000** each to Make-A-Wish Foundation of SE Pa. and MANNA/Metropolitan AIDS Neighborhood Nutrition Alliance. **$8,000** each to Aid for Friends and Kelly Ann Dolan Fund. **$5,000** each to Grey Nuns of the Sacred Heart, Nehemiah's Way, St. Edmund's Home for Children, St. Mary's Villa for Children. and Sunshine Foundation. **$4,000** to Orton Dyslexia Society. **$3,000** to Richland Monthly Meeting (Food for Friends). **$2,000** to Pa. Pro-Life Federation [Harrisburg] and St. John's Hospice. **Out-of-state** giving includes **$15,000** to Community Partners [ME]; **$10,000** to U. of Washington Medical Center (neurological research); **$8,000** to Making Memories Breast Cancer [OR]; **$5,000** to Twelve Step Education Program of New England [MA]; and other smaller grants, mostly to MA. ■**PUBLICATIONS:** None ■**WEBSITE:** None ■**E-MAIL:** None ■**APPLICATION POLICIES & PROCEDURES:** No grants awarded to individuals.

O+D+T Patricia Drueding Stokes (F+T+Con) — Elizabeth Snyder Michener [Philadelphia] (P+T) — Bernard J. Drueding, Jr. [Radnor] (VP+T) — James A. Drueding [MA] (S+T) — Albert J. Drueding, Jr. [Wyndmoor] (T) — Frank J. Drueding [Blue Bell] (T) — Diana S. Gifford [Lower Gwynedd] (T) — Mary Grace Snyder [Glenside] (T) — Diana D. Stewart [Fort Washington] (T)

SE-188 Drumcliff Foundation, The

1021 West Hortter Street
Philadelphia 19119 (Philadelphia County)
AMV $2,227,777 **FYE** 12-00 (**Gifts Received** $0)

MI-12-13-14-15-31-41-42-44-51-52-55-56-57
61-71-84-85
Phone 215-844-1163 **FAX** None
EIN 23-6957302 **Year Created** 1988
43 **Grants totaling** $726,388

About two-thirds local/Pa. giving. High grant of **$215,000** to Philadelphia School District. **$62,298** to Philadelphia Youth Tennis Assn. **$25,000** to Hospital of the U. of Pa./Institute on Aging. **$20,000** to University City District. **$15,000** to Outward Bound. **$12,500** each to Bryn Mawr Rehab and Settlement Music School. **$10,000** each to NetworkArts Alliance, Oak Lane Charter School, Summerbridge, and Transfiguration School. **$9,000** to Library Company of Philadelphia. **$7,000** to Awbury Arboretum. **$5,000** each to Arden Theatre, Farmers Market Trust, Freedom Theatre, Philadelphia Art Alliance, Philadelphia Starlings, Pocono Services for Family & Children [Monroe County], and Sisters of the Immaculate Heart. **$3,000** to West Philadelphia Catholic High School. **$2,000-$2,500** each to Need in Deed, Nueva Esperanza, and Wissahickon Wanderers. **$1,000** each to Blind Relief Fund, Free Library of Philadelphia, Germantown YMCA, New Music Network, Nonprofit Technology Resources, Philadanco, U. of Pa., and WVIA-TV [Luzerne County]. Other smaller local contributions for various purposes. **Out-of-state** giving includes **$100,000** each to Greater Boston Legal Service [MA] and Harvard U. [MA]; **$15,000** to Vassar College [NY]; and **$10,000** each to Mill Street Loft [NY], Roxbury Latin School [MA], and Yale Law School [CT]. ■**PUBLICATIONS:** None ■**WEBSITE:** None ■**E-MAIL:** None ■**APPLICATION POLICIES & PROCEDURES:** The Foundation reports that giving generally focuses on Philadelphia; most grants are for general support or special projects. No grants to individuals. Grant requests may be submitted in a proposal at any time; outline the purpose of the requested funds and include an organization budget, project budget, list of major funding sources, audited financial statement, list of Board members, and IRS tax-exempt status documentation. Site visits sometimes are made to organizations being considered for a grant.

O+D+T Daniel F. Gordon (T+Donor+Con) — Albert W. Gordon [NY] (Donor)

SE-189 DuPont (John E.) Foundation
13 Paoli Court
Paoli 19301 (Chester County)
AMV $449,493 **FYE** 12-00 (**Gifts Received** $206,000)

MI-84
Phone 610-296-9900 **FAX** None
EIN 23-2499540 **Year Created** 1988
1 **Grant of** $26,500

Sole grant to FILA/International Federation of Associated Wrestling Styles [Switzerland]. ■**PUBLICATIONS:** None ■**WEBSITE:** None ■**E-MAIL:** None ■**APPLICATION POLICIES & PROCEDURES:** Grant requests may be submitted in a proposal at any time; describe in detail organizational activities and proposed use of requested funds. No grants awarded to individuals.

O+D+T Taras M. Wochok, Esq. (T+Con) — John E. DuPont (P+T+Donor)

SE-190 Eastwood Family Foundation, The
705 Sturbridge Drive
Bryn Mawr 19010 (Montgomery County)
AMV $242,219 **FYE** 12-00 (**Gifts Received** $220,000)

MI-31-32-35-39-41-54-56-63
Phone 610-519-9664 **FAX** None
EIN 31-1587433 **Year Created** 1998
30+ **Grants totaling** $225,745

About half local/Pa. giving. High Pa. grant of **$19,000** to Wills Eye Hospital. **$8,600** to The Renfrew Center. **$5,000** to Jefferson Health System. **$4,500** to Mercy Health System. **$3,000** to St. John Neumann High School. **$2,500** each to The Carpenter's Company, Please Touch Museum. **$1,000-$1,800** each to The Alliance [Chester Springs], LaSalle Academy [Lackawanna County], Leukemia & Lymphoma Society, The Millay Club, North Philadelphia Health System, PinnacleHealth System [Harrisburg], Riddle Memorial Hospital, St. Katherine of Siena Parish, University City District, U. of the Sciences in Philadelphia Women's Club, and Wellness Community of Philadelphia. Other smaller contributions totaled **$7,345** but no details available. **Out-of-state** giving includes high grant of **$57,500** to Montefiore Medical Center [NY]; **$37,500** to Robert Wood Johnson Foundation [NJ]; and **$5,000** to Meridian Health System [NJ]. ■**PUBLICATIONS:** None ■**WEBSITE:** None ■**E-MAIL:** None ■**APPLICATION POLICIES & PROCEDURES:** Information not available.

O+D+T James W. Eastwood (P+Donor+Con) — Linda D. Eastwood (S+F+Donor) Corporate donor: Granary Associates, Inc.

SE-191 Eden Charitable Foundation
Strafford Building Two, Suite 204
200 Eagle Road
Wayne 19087 (Delaware County)

MI-11-13-14-15-22-31-32-41-42-56-63-64-72

Phone 610-687-9422 **FAX** 610-687-9423
EIN 23-2706163 **Year Created** 1955

AMV $10,985,560 **FYE** 12-00 (**Gifts Received** $676,895) 102 **Grants totaling** $552,750

Mostly local/Pa. giving. High grant of **$35,000** to Wilson College [Franklin County]. **$20,000** to Ebenezer Maxwell Mansion. **$15,000** each to Church of the Good Samaritan, Drexel U., Ursinus College, Wayne Presbyterian Church (general support/Kapp Memorial Fund), and Wynnefield Presbyterian Church. **$10,000** each to Alzheimer's Assn./SE Pa., Bala Presbyterian Home, Boy Scouts/Cradle of Liberty Council, Bryn Mawr Hospital, Doylestown Hospital, Eastern Baptist Theological Seminary, Eastern College, Fox Chase Cancer Center, Girl Scouts of SE Pa., Grand View Hospital (general support/children's center/hospice program), Lankenau Hospital, Malvern Public American Legion, Paoli Memorial Hospital (Cancer Center), Partners in Ministry of Swarthmore, Pa. Bible Society, Red Cross, Royer-Greaves School for the Blind, Salvation Army, St. Joseph's U. (Academy of Food Marketing), USO of Philadelphia, Valley Forge Military Academy, and Williamson Free School of Mechanical Trades. **$8,000** to New Goshenhoppen Reformed United. **$7,500** each to Big Brothers/Big Sisters and Doylestown Presbyterian Church. **$5,000** each to Bryn Mawr Rehab, Bucks County Audubon Society, Franklin Institute, Harcum College, Moravian College, New Hanover United Methodist Church, Philadelphia College of Bible, Philadelphia Zoo, and St. Hubert's Catholic High School for Girls. **$4,000** to Chapel of Four Chaplains. **$2,000-$2,500** each to Aark Wildlife Rehabilitation, Central Bucks Family YMCA, Crohn's & Colitis Foundation, Doylestown Area FISH, Freedoms Foundation of Valley Forge, Historic St. Peter Church Preservation Corp., Jewish Federation of Greater Philadelphia, Junior Service Board, Kearsley, Lakeside Youth Service, Lehigh U., Lupus Foundation of Delaware Valley, Pa. School for the Deaf, Philadelphia OIC, Philadelphia Presbytery Homes Foundation, Philadelphia High School for Girls, Roman Catholic High School, Southern Home Services, St. Mary Magdalen Church, and United Way of SE Pa. Other local contributions **$500-$1,500** for arts/cultural, civic, human service, and other purposes. **Out-of-state** giving includes **$15,000** to San Francisco I Have A Dream Foundation; **$7,500** to Northwestern U. [IL]; and smaller grants in FL and NJ. ■**PUBLICATIONS:** None ■**WEBSITE:** None ■**E-MAIL:** None ■**APPLICATION POLICIES & PROCEDURES:** No grants are awarded to individuals. — Formerly called the Eden Foundation.
O+D+T John M. Kapp (P+F+Con) — Earl M. Eden [Paoli] (T) — Donald E. Parlee, M.D. [Doylestown] (T) — Kim S.P. Eble [Green Lane] (Associate Trustee) — Brooks D. Eden [Paoli] (Associate Trustee)

SE-192 Eglin (Meyer & Stephanie) Foundation
c/o Eglin Square Garage
15th & Sansom Streets
Philadelphia 19102 (Philadelphia County)

MI-11-22-31-32-52-53-54-62-56-72

Phone 215-564-4242 **FAX** None
EIN 23-2832453 **Year Created** 1995

AMV $3,266,430 **FYE** 12-00 (**Gifts Received** $0) 18 **Grants totaling** $1,798,000

All local/Pa. giving; grants are for general use unless otherwise noted. High grant of **$1,365,000** to Philadelphia Museum of Art (mostly general support). **$102,500** to Thomas Jefferson U. (surgical dept./urology dept./Deans' Funds). **$80,000** each to Jewish Federation of Greater Philadelphia and Pa. Hospital (various funds). **$35,000** each to Congregation Rodef Shalom and Wistar Institute (cancer research). **$20,000** to United Way of SE Pa. **$17,000** to Curtis Institute of Music. **$15,000** each to National Museum of American Jewish History and Philadelphia Zoo (primate house). **$10,000** each to Mann Music Center and Pa. Heritage Society (Governor's Mansion). **$5,000** to Linda Creed Breast Cancer Foundation. **$3,000** to Polish American Cultural Center. **$2,500** to Female Hebrew Benevolent Society. **$1,000** each to Montgomery County SPCA, Ryerss Farm for Aged Equines [Pottstown], and Women's Humane Society [Bensalem]. ■**PUBLICATIONS:** None ■**WEBSITE:** None ■**E-MAIL:** None ■**APPLICATION POLICIES & PROCEDURES:** Grant requests may be submitted in a letter at any time; provide a detailed project description, state the amount of funding requested, and include an annual report, audited financial statement (or copy of most recent Form 990), and IRS tax-exempt status documentation.
O+D+T Stephanie S. Eglin (P+Donor+Con) — Loretta Zeiger (S)

SE-193 Elias Family Charitable Trust
509 Spring Avenue
Elkins Park 19027 (Montgomery County)

MI-22-29-62

Phone 215-635-0305 **FAX** None
EIN 23-6749244 **Year Created** 1980

AMV $2,703,390 **FYE** 11-00 (**Gifts Received** $0) 125+ **Grants totaling** $49,000

Mostly local giving. High local grant of **$20,000** to Anti-Defamation League Foundation. **$3,696** to Congregation Beth Hillel Beth El. **$1,000-$1,500** each to Congregation Adath Jeshurun, Consumer Education & Protection Assn., Jewish Federation of Greater Philadelphia, and Lower Merion Synagogue. **$805** to Hadassah. Other local contributions **$10-$500** for a wide variety of organizations. **Out-of-state** giving includes support for synagogues and small contributions for Jewish, humanitarian, and other purposes in many states. ■**PUBLICATIONS:** None ■**WEBSITE:** None ■**E-MAIL:** None ■**APPLICATION POLICIES & PROCEDURES:** The Foundation reports a priority interest in Delaware Valley institutions which engender the American ideals of universal egalitarian humanism and rationalism. No grants for capital expenditures or to individuals. Grant requests may be submitted at any time in a proposal which details the proposed project and states the amount of funding requested.
O+D+T Alma Elias (T+Manager+Con) — Gabriel Elias (T+Donor)

SE-194 Elkman (Stanley & Lois) Foundation
7360 Huron Lane
Philadelphia 19119 (Philadelphia County)

MI-22-31-32-62-69-82

Phone 215-247-9580 **FAX** None
EIN 65-0372014 **Year Created** 1992

AMV $2,199 **FYE** 12-00 (**Gifts Received** $117,938) 29 **Grants totaling** $135,350

Limited local giving. High local grant of **$5,000** to Jewish Federation of Greater Philadelphia. **$2,500** each to Boys Town Jersusalem Foundation of America [Jenkintown] and National Liberty Museum. **$1,000** to Wistar Institute. Other smaller local contributions for medical and Jewish purposes. **Out-of-state** giving includes high grant of **$45,000** to Vedanta Center of Greater Washington [DC]; **$38,500** to Jewish Federation of South Palm Beach County [FL]; and Jaffa Institute for Social Advancement [NY]. ■**PUBLICATIONS:** None ■**WEBSITE:** None ■**E-MAIL:** None ■**APPLICATION POLICIES & PROCEDURES:** Information not available.

O+D+T Carol A. Schwartz (S+D+Con) — Stanley Elkman [FL] (P+D) — Lois D. Elkman [FL] (VP+D) — Stuart M. Elkman [CA] (F+D)

SE-195 Ellis (Abraham & Rose) Foundation
552 Fulwell Court
Ambler 19002 (Montgomery County)
AMV $1,842,693 **FYE** 12-00 **(Gifts Received** $0)

MI-11-12-22-31-34-42-52-55-62-72
Phone Unlisted **FAX** None
EIN 23-7442471 **Year Created** 1952
45 **Grants totaling** $88,500

Mostly local giving. High grant of **$25,000** to Jefferson Medical College. **$20,000** to U. of Pa. **$5,000** each to Jewish Federation of Greater Philadelphia, Philadelphia Ronald McDonald House, Regional Performing Arts Center, and United Way of SE Pa. **$1,000** each to Congregation Mikveh Israel, Lankenau Hospital, Medical College of Pa., Red Cross, Ryerss Farm for Aged Equines, and Settlement Music School. **Out-of-state** giving includes **$2,500** each to Sarasota-Manatee Jewish Federation [FL] and University Medical Center [AZ]; **$2,000** to Arizona-Sonora Desert Museum [AZ]; and smaller grants/contributions to AZ, CA, FL, NY and Israel. ■**PUBLICATIONS:** None ■**WEBSITE:** None ■**E-MAIL:** None ■**APPLICATION POLICIES & PROCEDURES:** No grants awarded to individuals.

O+D+T Michael D. Ellis, M.D. (T+Con) — Carol Ellis (T) — Jeffrey B. Ellis (T) — Robert Ellis (T) — Syliva M. Ellis (T) — Anne Lieberman (T) — Donald Lieberman (T) — Glenmede Trust Company (Corporate Trustee)

SE-196 Ellis (Charles E.) Grant & Scholarship Fund
c/o White-Williams Scholars/Foundation
215 South Broad Street, 5th Floor
Philadelphia 19107 (Philadelphia County)
AMV $40,380,930 **FYE** 6-01 **(Gifts Received** $0)

MI-43

Phone 215-735-4483 **FAX** 215-735-4485
EIN 23-6725618 **Year Created** 1981
3000+ **Grants totaling** $1,815,869

Support is available to Philadelphia girls (grades 9 through 12) for the following: (a) tuition at Archdiocesan or Independent schools, and (b) grants to female public school students for pre-college preparation, music, theater, sports, special school supplies, tutoring, college application fees, college admission test fees, college visits, college courses, and other opportunities. The annual support for Archdiocesan, Independent, or Public School students is roughly divided into thirds. ■**PUBLICATIONS:** brochure; statement of program policy; application guidelines ■**WEBSITE:** www.wwscholars.org/ellis/ ■**E-MAIL:** info@wwscholars.org ■**APPLICATION POLICIES & PROCEDURES:** The Fund reports that only those who meeting the following criteria are eligible to apply: (1) female; (2) resident of City of Philadelphia; (3) enrolled and in good academic standing in a public, parochial, or private high school; (4) living in a household where one or both parents are absent; and (5) cannot afford the educational advantages sought because of financial hardship. The financial support may be used as described above. All awards are for one year but recipients may reapply. A formal application form, available from the Fund, must be completed and submitted together with transcripts and income verification; deadlines for receipt of tuition support applications are first week of April for study the following academic year. Disbursements are made directly to the students' schools/programs.

O+D+T Patricia Blakely (Program Director+Con) — PNC Bank N.A. (Corporate Trustee)

SE-197 Ellis (Elizabeth B.) Foundation Trust
c/o Sosnov & Sosnov
540 Swede Street, P.O. Box 70
Norristown 19401 (Montgomery County)
AMV $5,362,639 **FYE** 5-01 **(Gifts Received** $0)

MI-13-22-25-42-43-53-54-55-63

Phone 610-279-8700 **FAX** 610-277-9490
EIN 23-6851809 **Year Created** 1986
18 **Grants totaling** $220,156

About three-fourths local giving; grants are for general operating support except as noted. High grant of **$150,000** to American Swedish Historical Museum (salaries/award/musical presentation). **$5,000** to Gloria Dei (Old Swedes) Church. **$2,500** to Haws Ave. United Methodist Church (scholarship fund/soup kitchen). **$2,000** to St. John's Church (general support/soup kitchen). **$1,500** to Barnes Foundation. **$1,000** to Norristown Cultural Center. **$750** to Philadelphia Court Appointed Special Advocate. **$500** to The Lincoln Center (Move Ahead program). **Out-of-state** giving includes four grants totaling **$39,406** to Rutgers U. (Center for Innovative Print & Paper/library fund/graduate arts scholarship/minority arts scholarship); and **$10,000** to Boys & Girls Clubs of America [NJ]. ■**PUBLICATIONS:** None ■**WEBSITE:** None ■**E-MAIL:** None ■**APPLICATION POLICIES & PROCEDURES:** Grant requests may be submitted in a letter at any time.

O+D+T Amy W. Sosnov, Esq. (T+Con) — William Allen [Doylestown] (T) — Lynne Allen Tsvetkov (T)

SE-198 Ellis Eye Foundation
109 Clwyd Road
Bala Cynwyd 19004 (Montgomery County)
AMV $4,021 **FYE** 12-00 **(Gifts Received** $2,042)

MI-12-22-31-34-41-54-62

Phone 610-664-7977 **FAX** None
EIN 23-6291178 **Year Created** 1951
80 **Grants totaling** $27,104

Mostly local giving. High grant **$5,000** to Federation Allied Jewish Appeal. **$3,025** to Har Zion Temple. **$2,800** to Rosenbach Museum & Library. **$1,500** to Friends Select School. **$2,000** to National Liberty Museum. **$1,000** each to Jefferson Medical College (alumni fund) and Wills Eye Hospital. Other local contributions **$10-$500** for various purposes. **Out-of-state** giving includes **$2,652** to Israel Children's Centers [FL] and other contributions under **$200**. ■**PUBLICATIONS:** None ■**WEBSITE:** None ■**E-MAIL:** None ■**APPLICATION POLICIES & PROCEDURES:** No grants awarded to individuals.

O+D+T Richard A. Ellis, M.D. (P+Donor+Con) — Aaron Ellis (VP) — Gilda Ellis (S+Donor+Con)

SE-199 **Emergency Aid of Pennsylvania Foundation, The**   MI-12-13-14-15-17-19-22-25-29-41
221 Conestoga Road, Suite 300   **Phone** 610-225-0944 **FAX** 610-225-0945
Wayne   19087   (Delaware County)   **EIN** 23-2321913   **Year Created** 1984
AMV $3,031,182   **FYE** 6-01   (**Gifts Received** $31,900)   62 **Grants totaling** $94,316

All giving restricted to the five-county Philadelphia area. High grant of **$5,000** to United Communities of SE Philadelphia. **$4,000** to La Communidad Hispana. **$3,000-$3,500** each to Cradle of Hope, Home of the Sparrow, Little Brothers/Friends of the Elderly, and RSVP of Montgomery County. **$2,000-$2,500** each to Allegheny West Foundation, Bridge of Hope, Christ Lutheran Church, Community Women's Education Project, CONTACT-Careline for Greater Philadelphia, Darlington Fine Arts Center, Delaware County Childrens Camp Assn., Episcopal Church of the Advocate, Episcopal Community Services, Girl Scouts of SE Pa., Harcum College, Hospitality House of Philadelphia, IHM Center for Literacy & GED Programs, Mother's Home, North Light Community Center, Old First Reformed Church, Philadelphia Senior Center, Philadelphia Society for Preservation of Landmarks, Point Breeze Performing Arts Center, Safe Harbor of Greater West Chester, and Urban Bridges at St. Gabriel's. **$1,000-$1,500** each to ARC of Chester County, Cora Services, Fort Mifflin on the Delaware, Jewish Family & Children's Service, Lights of the World, Taller Puertorriqueno, and Urban Tree Connection. Also, 28 scholarships, mostly **$500-$750** each and totaling **$15,750,** were awarded to prior recipients of Emergency Aid's Founders Awards (see below). ■**PUBLICATIONS:** Annual Report; application guidelines & form ■**WEBSITE:** www.eafoundation.org ■**E-MAIL:** eapa@erols.com ■**APPLICATION POLICIES & PROCEDURES:** The Foundation reports that only organizations in Philadelphia, Bucks, Chester, Delaware and Montgomery counties are eligible to apply; principal consideration is given to agencies providing services to/for women & children, the elderly, disabled youth, youth, and education; an organization's use of volunteers is also given consideration. Most grants are for general support, special projects, building funds, research, publications, and scholarships. Prospective applicants initially should make a telephone inquiry about the feasibility of submitting a request. Grant requests are accepted throughout the year. Grant requests must be submitted on a formal Emergency Aid Application Form, available from the Foundation, or on Delaware Valley Grantmakers Common Grant Application form—if the latter is used additional information may be required; please inquire. Applications must be accompanied by an annual report, organizational budget, project budget (if applicable), audited financial statement, Board member list, list of present and applied-for funding, IRS tax-exempt status documentation, and the most recent Form 990. Also, the organization must be registered with the Pa. Bureau of Charitable Organizations. Site visits sometimes are made to organizations being considered for a grant. The Distribution Committee regularly reviews requests and makes recommendations to the Board of Directors; grants are awarded at meetings in January, April, July, and October. Scholarships are restricted to prior recipients of Emergency Aid's Founders Awards. These awards are given to 9th grade Philadelphia-area girls for outstanding school and community service/leadership who were nominated by recreation program leaders or school administrators. When these Founders Award recipients enter their senior year in high school they become eligible to compete for the scholarships.
O+D+T Joanne Platt (Office Manager+Con) — Judith Huffaker (Chair, Distribution Committee) — Michele Howard (C) — Mrs. Charles E. Dagit (1st VC) — Mrs. Mark M. Bridge (S) — Mrs. James A. Lynch (F) — Mrs. Stowe B. Milhous (AS) — Anne B. Haegele (AF) — Mrs. Arlin Adams (D) — Mrs. Albert E. Bailey (D) — Joann D. Baumgarten (D) — Mrs. Robert P. Moran (D) — Kathleen C. Murphy (D) — Sonia N. Naus (D) — Sandra S. Pfaff (D) — Mrs. Peter A. Theodos (D) — Mrs. Robert J. Thomas (D) — Mrs. A. Whitten Vogel (D) — Mrs. Arnold H. Winicov (D)

SE-200 **Engle Foundation, The**   MI-12-13-14-17-18-25-29-32-41-51
c/o Engle Family Office
Four Tower Bridge, #400, 200 Barr Harbor Drive   **Phone** 610-941-2928 **FAX** None
West Conshohocken 19428   (Montgomery County)   **EIN** 23-2440499   **Year Created** 1986
AMV $1,202,094   **FYE** 12-00   (**Gifts Received** $0)   20 **Grants totaling** $59,450

Mostly local giving. High grant of **$23,500** to Gesu School. **$10,000** to Kelly Anne Dolan Memorial Fund. **$5,000** to Bethesda Project. **$2,000-$2,500** each to Boy Scouts/Cradle of Liberty Council, Children's Country Week Assn., Make-A-Wish Foundation of Philadelphia/SE Pa., Philadelphia Hospitality, and Project H.O.M.E. **$1,000-$1,500** each to Germantown Academy, J. Wood Platt Caddie Scholarship Trust, Leukemia Society of America, Planned Parenthood of SE Pa., Red Cross, and Women's Resource Center [Wayne]. **$500** each to Arden Theatre Company and RSVP of Montgomery County. Other local contributions **$250** each. **Out-of-state** grant: **$1,000** to Epilepsy Foundation [DC]. ■**PUBLICATIONS:** None ■**WEBSITE:** None ■**E-MAIL:** None ■**APPLICATION POLICIES & PROCEDURES:** The Foundation reports that giving is limited to Philadelphia and Montgomery County. Grant requests may be submitted in a letter (2 pages maximum) at any time; describe the proposed use of the funding, state the amount requested, and indicate the percentage of support used for programs/services vs. overhead/fundraising costs; include organization and project budgets, audited financial statement, and IRS tax-exempt status documentation. Site visits sometimes are made to organizations being considered for a grant. Grants are awarded at quarterly meetings.
O+D+T Stanley H. Engle (T+Donor+Con) — Scott F. Engle [West Chester] (T+Donor) — Kimberley Engle Forbes [Lower Gwynedd] (T+Donor)

SE-201 **Epstein (Maxine P. & Martin) Family Foundation**   MI-17-22-29-31-34-42-62
c/o First Union/Wachovia - Personal Trusts
123 South Broad Street   **Phone** 215-670-4063 **FAX** None
Philadelphia   19109   (Philadelphia County)   **EIN** 22-2815417   **Year Created** 1986
AMV $635,745   **FYE** 12-00   (**Gifts Received** $0)   22 **Grants totaling** $29,500

Mostly local and Trenton, NJ giving; grants are for general purposes except as noted. High grant of **$5,000** to Thomas Jefferson U. **$3,000** to Greenwood House. **$1,000-$1,500** each to Adath Israel (capital fund), Albright College, Bucks County Opportunity Council, and Planned Parenthood of Bucks County. Other smaller local contributions. **Out-of-state** giving, mostly to Trenton, NJ, includes **$3,500** to United Jewish Federation of Trenton; **$2,000** to Capital Health System Foundation; and **$1,000-$1,500** each to Case Western Reserve U./School of Medicine [OH], Jewish Community Center of Trenton, Jewish Family

Service [NJ], Planned Parenthood of Mercer County, Trenton Rescue Mission, Trenton Soup Kitchen, and United Way of Mercer County. ■**PUBLICATIONS:** None ■**WEBSITE:** None ■**E-MAIL:** None ■**APPLICATION POLICIES & PROCEDURES:** The Bank reports that all grant decisions are made by Epstein Family members. No grants are awarded to individuals.

O+D+T Brenda Kincaid (VP at Bank+Con) — Dr. Martin Epstein (T) — Maxine P. Epstein (T) — First Union/Wachovia (Corporate Trustee)

SE-202 **Erichson (Bright & Christella) Charitable Trust**   MI-15-17-22-31
    c/o Schnader Harrison Segal & Lewis
    1735 Market Street, Suite 3800   **Phone** 215-751-2324 **FAX** None
    Philadelphia 19103   (Philadelphia County)   **EIN** 23-6697739   **Year Created** 1980
AMV $1,970,420   **FYE** 10-00   **(Gifts Received** $0)   8 **Grants totaling** $98,500

All local giving. High grants of **$15,000** each to Golden Slipper Uptown Home, Holy Redeemer Medical Center, and Philadelphia Geriatric Center. **$12,500** to St. Ignatius Nursing Home. **$12,000** each to Holy Family Home, Immaculate Mary Home, and SOWN/Supportive Older Women's Network. **$5,000** to Jewish Family & Children's Services. ■**PUBLICATIONS:** None ■**WEBSITE:** None ■**E-MAIL:** None ■**APPLICATION POLICIES & PROCEDURES:** The Foundation reports that all giving is restricted to Philadelphia-area charitable organizations assisting the needy and elderly, principally nursing homes. No grants awarded to individuals. Grant requests in any form should be submitted during May-July. Site visits sometimes are made to organizations being considered for a grant. Grants are awarded at a September meeting.

O+D+T Harvey N. Shapiro, Esq. (Co-T+Con) — Rev. Gonzalo Correa Santa Cruz [Broomall] (Co-T)

SE-203 **Erlbaum Family Foundation**   MI-13-15-22-32-54-62
    c/o Commercial Abstract Corp.
    44 West Lancaster Ave., Suite 110   **Phone** 610-896-7700 **FAX** None
    Ardmore 19003   (Montgomery County)   **EIN** 23-2962563   **Year Created** 1998
AMV $1,200,296   **FYE** 12-00   **(Gifts Received** $277,288)   49 **Grants totaling** $84,951

About two-thirds local giving; all grants are unrestricted donations. High grant of **$13,000** to Lubavitch House/Guideline Services. **$10,000** each to Chasdei Eliyahu, Etz Chaim Center for Jewish Studies, and Kaiserman Jewish Community Center (Aish Ha Torah). **$5,000** to Congregation Beth HaMedrash. **$1,500** to Temple Beth Hillel-Beth El. **$1,000** each to Beth David, Delaware Valley Center/NGF, Juvenile Diabetes Foundation, Kevin Boyle Memorial, National Liberty Museum, and Philadelphia Geriatric Center. Smaller local contributions for similar purposes. **Out-of-state** giving includes **$5,000** each to Boys Club of New York and Yeshiva Gedolah of Paterson [NJ]; **$4,850** to Congregation Binei Yakov [NJ]; and **$2,000** each to Franciscan Sisters of the Poor [NY] and Ken's Kids [NY]. ■**PUBLICATIONS:** None ■**WEBSITE:** None ■**E-MAIL:** None ■**APPLICATION POLICIES & PROCEDURES:** Grant requests may be submitted in writing at any time.

O+D+T Gary E. Erlbaum (P+Donor+Con) — Dan Erlbaum (D) — Jon Erlbaum (D) — Marc Erlbaum (D) — Vicki Erlbaum (D)

SE-204 **Eustace Foundation, The**   MI-11-13-15-22-25-41-42-61
    c/o Cabrini Asset Management, Inc.
    700 South Henderson Road, #202   **Phone** 610-992-5889 **FAX** 610-945-1662
    King of Prussia 19406   (Montgomery County)   **EIN** 22-2664349   **Year Created** 1985
AMV $20,106,487   **FYE** 9-01   **(Gifts Received** $0)   63 **Grants totaling** $1,436,350

Mostly local giving. High grant of **$505,000** to St. Joseph's U. **$200,000** to Cabrini College. **$129,245** to Country Day School of the Sacred Heart. **$127,000** to The Papal Foundation [Philadelphia]. **$98,634** to Malvern Preparatory School (general support/benefit event). **$75,000** to AIDS Alive. **$50,000** to Archdiocese of Philadelphia (Cardinal Bevilacqua). **$24,000** to United Way of SE Pa. (deToqueville Society). **$20,000** to Archdiocese of Philadelphia. **$15,000** to St. Vincent's. **$13,750** to Family Life Educational Foundation. **$12,503** to St. Joseph's U. (Father Rashford). **$10,000** each to Catholic Youth Organization, Inn Dwelling, J. Wood Platt Scholarship Trust, MBF Center, and St. Ignatius Nursing Home. **$8,000** to Guadalupe Guild. **$6,968** to Sisters of St. Joseph's U. **$5,000** each to Catholic Leadership Conference, Face to Face Corp., Holy Family Home, and M-Able. **$3,000** to Prayer Power [Wynnewood]. **$1,000-$2,800** each to American Catholic Historical Society, Boy Scouts/Cradle of Liberty Council, Don Guanella Villa, Friends of the Philadelphia Zoo, Hansen Charitable Foundation, Philadelphia Museum of Art, Project Children, Riverbend Environmental Center, St. Edmund's Cup Day, St. Francis DeSales Parish (renovation fund), St. Gertrude Church, Vanguard School, and Wellness Community of Philadelphia. Other local contributions **$200-$500** for similar purposes. **Out-of-state** giving includes **$9,500** to Sun Up of Indian River [FL]; **$5,000** to Detroit Institute for Children [MI] and **$5,000** each to Georgetown U./Woodstock Theological Center [DC], Holy Cross High School [NY], and Oblates of St. Francis DeSales [DE]. ■**PUBLICATIONS:** None ■**WEBSITE:** None ■**E-MAIL:** None ■**APPLICATION POLICIES & PROCEDURES:** Information not available.

O+D+T Mimi Heany (Executive Director+Con) — J. Eustace Wolfington (T+Donor) — Marjorie Wolfington (Donor)

SE-205 **Evans Foundation**   MI-12-13-14-22-31-41-42-51-54-55-71-84
    c/o Rankin, Brennan & Donaldson
    225 North Olive Street, P.O. Box 258   **Phone** 610-566-5800 **FAX** 610-566-8197
    Media 19063   (Delaware County)   **EIN** 13-3178754   **Year Created** 1983
AMV $2,130,415   **FYE** 1-01   **(Gifts Received** $0)   26 **Grants totaling** $98,614

Mostly local giving; grants are for general purposes except as noted. High grant of **$25,000** to Crozer-Keystone Health System. **$7,500** to Discovery Day School [West Chester] (sign/playground). **$6,500** to Franklin Institute Science Museum (Access Program). **$5,794** to Pa. Ballet. **$5,000** each to Baldwin School (camp), DELARC, Delco Blind/Sight Center, and Haverford School (soccer program). **$4,000** to City Team Ministries [Chester]. **$3,000** each to Cabrini College and Darlington Fire Arts Center.

$2,000-$2,500 to Camp Sunshine, Easter Seals, Gettysburg College (golf classic/sports club), Hedgerow Theatre, and Thornbury Township Park. **$1,000-$1,500** each to Family Forum, Inc. [Wayne] (Single Mom Solution), Rosemont School of the Holy Child, and West Hill School (playground). **Out-of-state** giving, all to NJ, includes **$3,820** to Avalon Recreation Dept.; and **$2,000** each to Cape May County Zoo and Stone Harbor Lions Home for the Blind. ■**PUBLICATIONS:** None ■**WEBSITE:** None ■**E-MAIL:** None ■**APPLICATION POLICIES & PROCEDURES:** The Foundation reports that giving is generally limited to Delaware and Montgomery counties. No grants are awarded to individuals. Prospective applicants should make an initial telephone inquiry regarding the feasibility of submitting a request. Grant requests should be submitted in a letter during April-May—deadline is May 31st; include IRS tax-exempt status documentation. Site visits sometimes are made to organizations being considered for a grant. Grants are awarded at a June meeting.

O+D+T Megan E. Zavawski (S+F+Con) — Anita Seits [FL] (P+Principal Manager) — Kevin P. Seits [Haverford] (VP) — Joy M. Brennan (D)

SE-206 Evergreen Foundation, The
250 Beechwood Drive
Rosemont   19010   (Delaware County)
AMV $339,432   **FYE** 12-00   (**Gifts Received** $0)

MI-29-32-71-79-82-83
Phone 610-527-8572 **FAX** None
EIN 23-6919877   **Year Created** 1988
23 **Grants totaling** $28,285

About two-thirds local giving. High grant of **$7,210** to Training for Change. **$4,200** to The Shefa Fund. **$2,500** to Delaware Highland Conservancy [Wayne County]. **$1,000** each to National MS Society and Peace Action Delaware Valley. **$500** to Bryn Mawr Stakeholder. Other smaller local contributions. **Out-of-state** giving includes **$5,000** to Gandhian Foundation [NJ]; and **$1,000-$1,500** each to Earth Defense Education Project [OR], Heifer Project International [AR], and Southern Utah Wilderness Alliance. ■**PUBLICATIONS:** None ■**WEBSITE:** None ■**E-MAIL:** None ■**APPLICATION POLICIES & PROCEDURES:** Information not available.

O+D+T Viki Laura List (T+Donor+Con)

SE-207 Ewing Cole Cherry Charitable Foundation
c/o Ewing Cole Cherry Brott
100 North 6th Street
Philadelphia   19106   (Philadelphia County)
AMV $158,668   **FYE** 11-00   (**Gifts Received** $153,100)

MI-13-15-31-42-72
Phone 215-923-2020 **FAX** 215-574-9163
EIN 23-2706727   **Year Created** 1992
30 **Grants totaling** $173,600

About two-thirds local/Pa. giving. High grant of **$26,000** to Fox Chase Cancer Center. **$10,000** each to Architecture & Design Charter High School of Philadelphia, Chestnut Hill Hospital Foundation, Lehigh Valley Hospital, and Philadelphia Zoo. **$6,000** to U. of Pa. **$5,000** each to Geisinger Foundation [Montour County], Lancaster General Hospital Foundation, Riddle Hospital Foundation [Media], and Thomas Jefferson U. Hospital. **$3,000** to Inglis House. **$2,000** to Bryn Mawr College. **$1,500** to Holy Redeemer Hospital. **$1,000** to LaSalle U. **Out-of-state** giving includes **$25,000** to NY Presbyterian Hospital for Babies & Children; **$7,500** to Boys Club of NY; **$6,000** each to Cooper Hospital Foundation [NJ] and Deborah Hospital Foundation [NJ]; and other smaller grants to NJ and NY. ■**PUBLICATIONS:** None ■**WEBSITE:** None ■**E-MAIL:** None ■**APPLICATION POLICIES & PROCEDURES:** No grants awarded to individuals.

O+D+T Joseph T. Kelly [Broomall] (F+Con) — J. Andrew Jarvis (C) — James A. Wilson [West Chester] (P) — Pradeep R. Patel [Berwyn] (Senior VP) Corporate donor: Ewing Cole Cherry Brott

---

SE-208 Faith Foundation
c/o Griffith, Inc.
458 Pike Road
Huntingdon Valley   19006   (Montgomery County)
AMV $221,821   **FYE** 9-00   (**Gifts Received** $210,000)

MI-15-22-63
Phone 215-322-8100 **FAX** None
EIN 23-7794551   **Year Created** 1994
3 **Grants totaling** $42,000

Mostly local/Pa. giving. High grant of **$36,000** to Calvary Chapel. **$1,000** to Wycliffe Bible Translators [Lancaster]. **Out-of-state** grant: **$5,000** to Harvest Christian Fellowship [NJ]. — Grants awarded in the prior year include **$15,000** to Somers Point United Methodist Church [NJ]; **$7,000** to Mercy Corps [OR]; and **$5,000** to Christ's Home Retirement Community. Also, scholarships have been awarded in earlier years. ■**PUBLICATIONS:** scholarship application form ■**WEBSITE:** None ■**E-MAIL:** None ■**APPLICATION POLICIES & PROCEDURES:** The Foundation reports that scholarship preference is given to disadvantaged students attending theology school; submit requests on a Scholarship Application Form available from the Foundation six months prior to beginning studies.

O+D+T Brett R. Griffith [Newtown] (T+Donor+Con) — Richard S. Griffith [Newtown] (T+Donor) — Helga L. Griffith [Newtown] (T+Donor) — Scott M. Griffith [Ivyland] (T+Donor) — Barbara L. Baldwin [Newtown] (T) — Richard S. Griffith, Jr. [FL] (T) Corporate Donor: Griffith, Inc.

SE-209 Family Foundation
500 Telner Street
Philadelphia   19118   (Philadelphia County)
AMV $287,208   **FYE** 12-00   (**Gifts Received** $0)

MI-44-71-81
Phone 215-242-6529 **FAX** None
EIN 23-7061681   **Year Created** 1968
2 **Grants totaling** $14,940

All local giving. High grant of **$10,000** to Morris Arboretum. **$4,940** to Free Library of Philadelphia. — Local grants awarded in the prior year include **$50,000** to Morris Arboretum and **$6,800** to Foreign Policy Research Institute. ■**PUBLICATIONS:** None ■**WEBSITE:** None ■**E-MAIL:** None ■**APPLICATION POLICIES & PROCEDURES:** No grants awarded to individuals. — Formerly called the W.W. Keen & Madeleine Butcher Family Foundation

O+D+T W.W. Keen Butcher (D+Con)

SE-210   Farber Family Foundation   MI-11-22-30-32-42-54-62
c/o CSS Industries, Inc.
1845 Walnut Street, Suite 800   **Phone** 215-569-9900 **FAX** 215-569-9979
Philadelphia   19103   (Philadelphia County)   **EIN** 65-0336266   **Year Created** 1992
AMV $7,003,619   **FYE** 12-00   (**Gifts Received** $0)   20 **Grants totaling** $361,350

About three-quarters local/Pa. giving. High grant of **$105,000** to National Liberty Museum. **$77,000** to Federation Allied Jewish Appeal. **$50,000** to ALS Assn./NE Pa. Region. **$27,000** to United Way of SE Pa. **$5,000** each to Security on Campus [King of Prussia] and U. of Pa. (Penn Fund). **$2,500** to Camp Lee Mar. **$1,100** to Middle Atlantic Blind Golfers Assn. **$1,000** to Vanguard School. Other smaller local contributions. **Out-of-state** giving includes **$60,000** to Jewish Federation of Palm Beach [FL]; and **$10,000** each to Jewish Foundation for the Righteous [NY] and Jewish Family Services of Ulster County [NY]. ■**PUBLICATIONS:** None ■**WEBSITE:** None ■**E-MAIL:** None ■**APPLICATION POLICIES & PROCEDURES:** Information not available.
O+D+T David M. Farber [Rydal] (VP+D+Con) — Jack Farber [FL] (P+D+Donor) — Vivian Farber [FL] (VP+S+D) — Ellen B. Kurtzman [Penn Valley] (F+D)

SE-211   Farber Foundation   MI-11-13-15-22-32-34-43-52-54-55-57-62-81
c/o CSS Industries, Inc.   83-84
1845 Walnut Street, Suite 800   **Phone** 215-569-9900 **FAX** 215-569-9979
Philadelphia   19103   (Philadelphia County)   **EIN** 23-6254221   **Year Created** 1951
AMV $2,667,768   **FYE** 12-00   (**Gifts Received** $0)   44+ **Grants totaling** $338,680

Mostly local/Pa. giving; all grants are for general purposes except as noted. High grant of **$75,000** to Thomas Jefferson U. (Farber Foundation Health Professions Scholars Program). **$25,000** to Regional Performing Arts Center. **$20,000** to United Way of SE Pa. **$5,000** each to Eisenhower Exchange Fellowship, Jefferson Digestive Disease Institute, and Jefferson U. Physicians. **$4,500** to Greater Philadelphia Urban Affairs Coalition. **$3,000** each to Boy Scouts/Cradle of Liberty Council, Philadelphia Museum of Art, and WHYY. **$2,000-$2,500** each to American Heart Assn., Camp Lee Mar, Committee of Seventy, Eagles Fly for Leukemia, Eagles Youth Partnership, Philadelphia Senior Center, and The Music Group. **$1,000-$1,500** each to American Cancer Society, Anti-Defamation League, Franklin Institute, Muhlenberg College, NTSAD-Delaware Valley, Operation Understanding, Pa. Economy League, and Phillies Charities. Other smaller local contributions for various purposes. In addition, 29 scholarships totaling **$111,000** were awarded to children of employees of CSS Industries and subsidiaries. **Out-of-state** giving includes **$37,000** to American Jewish Committee [NY] and **$5,000** to South Kent School [CT]. ■**PUBLICATIONS:** application guidelines ■**WEBSITE:** None ■**E-MAIL:** None ■**APPLICATION POLICIES & PROCEDURES:** Applicants for the Health Professions Scholars program should request guidelines from the Program Coordinator at Thomas Jefferson U. (215-955-2867); applications must be submitted before the June 15th deadline. — Formerly called the PII Foundation -or- Philadelphia Industries, Inc. Foundation.
O+D+T Jack Farber (P+Con) — Stephen V. Dubin (VP+S) — Clifford E. Pietrafitta (VP) — Paul Delaney (F) Corporate donor: Philadelphia Industries, Inc.

SE-212   Feiner (Eugene) Foundation, The   MI-13-15-22-25-31-55-62-82
c/o Pepper Hamilton LLP
3000 Two Logan Square, 18th & Arch Sts.   **Phone** 215-981-4768 **FAX** 215-981-4750
Philadelphia   19103   (Philadelphia County)   **EIN** 23-2775300   **Year Created** 1994
AMV $130,457   **FYE** 12-00   (**Gifts Received** $252,000)   12 **Grants totaling** $459,700

About half local giving. High local grant of **$115,000** to Federation Allied Jewish Appeal. **$62,500** to Regional Performing Arts Center. **$50,000** to Variety Club. **$5,000** each to Maccabi USA/Sports for Israel and Wills Eye Hospital/Women's Committee. **$3,750** to Boy Scouts/Cradle of Liberty Council. **$2,500** each to Jewish Federation of Greater Philadelphia, Philadelphia Committee to End Homelessness, and Philadelphia Geriatric Center-Horsham. Other smaller local contributions. **Out-of-state** giving includes high grant of **$209,700** to Haifa Foundation [NY]. ■**PUBLICATIONS:** None ■**WEBSITE:** None ■**E-MAIL:** None ■**APPLICATION POLICIES & PROCEDURES:** Information not available.
O+D+T Bennett L. Aaron, Esq. (S+F+D+Con) — Eugene Feiner (P+D+Donor) — Martin A. Coopersmith, CPA (D) — Arthur D. Kapelow [Bensalem] (D)

SE-213   Feinstein (Myer & Rosaline) Foundation   MI-11-14-22-41-54-62
1009 Delene Road   **Phone** Unlisted **FAX** None
Rydal   19046   (Montgomery County)   **EIN** 23-6235232   **Year Created** 1945
AMV $3,720,043   **FYE** 12-00   (**Gifts Received** $0)   18 **Grants totaling** $623,500

About one-third local giving. High local grant of **$100,000** to Federation Allied Jewish Appeal. **$50,000** to Temple U. (Feinstein Center). **$25,000** to United Way of SE Pa. **$12,500** to National Museum of American Jewish History. **$7,000** to Raymond & Ruth Perelman Jewish Day School. **$2,000** each to Abrams Hebrew Academy, Akiba Hebrew Academy, Politz Hebrew Academy, Rimon Jewish Day School, Stern Hebrew High School, and Torah Academy. **Out-of-state** giving, all to Israel, includes high grants of **$150,000** each to Institute for Advancement of Education in Jaffa and Israel Elwyn; **$85,000** to Yemin Orde; and **$10,000** each to AKIM, Joint Distribution Committee, and New Jerusalem Foundation. ■**PUBLICATIONS:** None ■**WEBSITE:** None ■**E-MAIL:** None ■**APPLICATION POLICIES & PROCEDURES:** The Foundation reports that support is restricted generally to special projects or operating support for cultural, educational and religious organizations in the Philadelphia area or Israel; unsolicited requests for funds are not encouraged.
O+D+T Peggy F. Freedman (P+D+Con) — Samuel Feinstein [Lumberville] (VP+D) — Saul Freedman (F+D) — Elisa Feinstein [Lumberville] (D) — Myra Freedman [Feasterville] (D)

SE-214 **Felgoise (Judith & Marc) Charitable Foundation**
120 Belle Circle
Blue Bell   19422   (Montgomery County)

MI-15-41-62-82
Phone Unlisted **FAX** None
EIN 23-7857249   **Year Created** 1997

AMV $299,470   **FYE** 12-00   **(Gifts Received** $0)   5 **Grants totaling** $19,690

Mostly local giving. **$10,000** to Stiffed Senior Center. **$5,190** to Tiferet Bet Israel. **$2,500** to Germantown Academy. **$1,000** to Gerda & Kurt Klein Foundation [Narberth]. **Out-of-state** grant: **$1,000** to OROT [Israel]. ■**PUBLICATIONS:** None ■**WEBSITE:** None ■**E-MAIL:** None ■**APPLICATION POLICIES & PROCEDURES:** Grant requests may be submitted in a letter at any time. No grants awarded to individuals.

O+D+T Marc Felgoise (T+Donor+Con) — Judith Felgoise (T+Donor)

SE-215 **Fels (Samuel S.) Fund**
Suite 800
1616 Walnut Street
Philadelphia   19103   (Philadelphia County)

MI-12-13-14-15-16-17-18-20-25-29-35-41-45
51-52-53-54-55-56-71-79-81-83-86
Phone 215-731-9455 **FAX** 215-731-9457
EIN 23-1365325   **Year Created** 1935

AMV $47,114,633   **FYE** 12-01   **(Gifts Received** $0)   185 **Grants totaling** $2,368,036

All giving is restricted to Philadelphia in five areas of interest—see below. ***COMMUNITY PROJECT GRANTS***-56%; grants are for general support except as noted: **$200,000** to Regional Performing Arts Center (new orchestra hall). **$170,000** to Franklin Institute (Fels Planetarium modernization). **$50,000** to Hispanics in Philanthropy (funders collaborative for Latino communities). **$38,400** to Asociacion de Musicos Latino (booking agent salary). **$34,800** to Moore College of Art (Neighborhood Art Partnerships). **$33,821** to Philadelphia Health Management Corp. (evaluation tools for agencies serving homeless). **$30,000** each to Crime Prevention Assn. of Philadelphia (Summer Career Exploration Program), Southeast Philadelphia Community Technology Collaborative/Evangelical Lutheran Church, and Universal Community Homes (staff support). **$25,000** each to Center for Lesbian & Gay Civil Rights, Philadelphia Citizens for Children & Youth, The Reinvestment Fund (predatory lending project), Support Center for Child Advocates (new building planning), United Way of SE Pa. (advocacy salary support), and Youth Service (West Philadelphia initiative). **$22,000** to Community Legal Services (welfare advocacy). **$20,000** each to Church of the Advocate (Centennial campaign coordinator), Drueding Center (youth services expansion), Philabundance (information systems upgrade), Philadelphians Concerned About Housing (family self-sufficiency program), Tabernacle United Church (mural/garden), and Taller Puertorriqueno (cultural programming). **$18,000** each to Christ & St. Ambrose Episcopal Church (Open Borders project) and Trinity Memorial Center (master plan). **$15,000** each to Advocate Community Development Corp. (Diamond St. Corridor Plan), Arab-American Community Development Corp. (start-up support), Cambodian Assn. of Greater Philadelphia, Committee for Dignity & Fairness for the Homeless (Work Options Now program), Greater Philadelphia Cultural Alliance (Director's grant), Joseph J. Peters Institute (Stop It Now), LaSalle Nonprofit Management Center (capacity building), New Kensington Community Development Corp. (development project), Pa. Low Income Housing Corp. (outreach/education), Philadelphia Assn. of Community Development Corporations, Philadelphia Interfaith Action (organizing internships), and Women's Opportunities Resource Center. **$12,000** each to Northwest Interfaith Movement (Neighbor to Neighbor project), Women's Community Revitalization Project (affordablehousing advocacy), and The Working Wardrobe (salary support). **$10,000** each to Community Women's Education Project (family literacy program startup), Consumer Bankruptcy Assistance Project, Delaware Valley Child Care Council (preschool programs advocacy), Greater Philadelphia Urban Affairs Coalition (mural artists training), Greensgrow Philadelphia Project (Neighborhood Urban Agriculture Cooperative), HIAS & Council Migration Service of Philadelphia (elderly immigrants citizenship program), I-LEAD, Leadership, Inc. (diversity building project), New Frankford Community Y (youth programs), New World Assn. of Emigrants from Eastern Europe, Pan Asia Radio (local programming), Preschool Project (new family day care enterprises), Scribe Video Center (Community Visions & Street Movies), Tradeswomen of Philadelphia (home repair/maintenance course), United Labor Center for Unemployment Information (advocacy), and Women's Assn. for Women's Alternatives (family self-sufficiency project). **$6,000-$8,000** each to Community Education Center, Delaware Valley Habitat for Humanity (organizations merger), Greater Philadelphia Urban Affairs Coalition (ending homelessness plan), and Sedgwick Cultural Center (staff support). **$5,000** each to The Clay Studio (Claymobile program), Community Design Collaborative of AIA-Philadelphia (strategic planning), Neighborhood Bike Works (scholarcycles), Pa. Assn. for Sustainable Agriculture, and Vietnamese Assn. for the Aging. **$4,615** to Evangelical Lutheran Church in America (church cemetery restoration). **$3,000** to Gay Community Center of Philadelphia (space use study). ***EDUCATION GRANTS***-19%; grants are for general support except as noted. **$250,000** to U. of Pa./Fels Center of Government (graduate student support/Fels House renovations). **$50,000** to Public Education Network (Startup Good Schools Pa.). **$25,000** to Public Interest Law Center of Philadelphia (public education funding advocacy). **$15,000** each to Education Law Center (advocacy for English language learners), Philadelphia Education Fund (literacy action project), and Philadelphia Folklore Project (multicultural education program). **$12,000** to Academy of Music (crescendo program). **$10,000-$11,000** each to Brandywine Graphic Workshop, Center for Literacy (learning disabilities initiative), IHM Center for Literacy & GED Programs, and Philadelphia Public School Notebook. **$7,500** each to Need in Deed, Philadelphia City Sail, and Urban Retrievers. **$5,000** each to Philadelphia Wooden Boat and Teachers for Democratic Culture/New City Press (prison workshops project). **$2,000** to Summer Reading Coalition. ***ARTS & HUMANITIES GRANTS***-10%; grants are for general or seasonal support except as noted: **$12,000** each to Concerto Soloists of Philadelphia and Opera Company of Philadelphia (production). **$7,500-$8,000** each to American Music Theater Festival (Silver River), Art Sanctuary/Church of the Advocate, Painted Bride Art Center, Philadelphia Chamber Music Society, Philadelphia Dance Company, Philadelphia Fringe Festival, and Theatre Communications Group [NY] (Philadelphia conference registration support). **$6,000** each to Arden Theatre Company, Asian Arts Initiative, Philadelphia Theatre Company, and The Wilma Theatre. **$4,000-$5,000** each to Academy of Vocal Arts, American Ballet Competition (NextMove Series), Mann Center for the Performing Arts (young people's free concerts), Moonstone (Festival Cubano/Black Writing Celebration), and Settlement Music School (contemporary music series). **$2,000-$3,000** each to 1812 Productions, Amaryllis Theatre Company, Artreach, Astral Artistic Services, Azuka Theatre Collective (marketing/outreach), Brat

Productions, Catholic Heritage Center, Choral Art Society of Philadelphia, Creative Access (program director salary), Elfreth's Alley Assn. (develop educational plan), Friends of the Japanese House, Headlong Dance Theatre, Institute of Contemporary Art (exhibit), Interact Theatre, Jeanne Ruddy & Dancers (new work), Koresh Dance Company, Lantern Theatre Company, Mendelssohn Club, Network for New Music (premieres), Orchestra 2001 (one-act operas), Philadelphia Dance Alliance, Philadelphia Independent Film & Video Assn., Philadelphia Photo Review (publication), Philadelphia Renaissance Wind Band, Philadelphia Volunteer Lawyers for the Arts (expansion), Philomel Concerts, Pig Iron Theatre Company, The Print Center, Singing City (concert series), Spiral Q Puppet Theater, Spoken Hand, Theater Catalyst (salary support), Theatre Alliance of Greater Philadelphia, Vox Populi, and Walnut Street Theatre (school program). **$1,000** each to 11 other arts/cultural organizations. ***INTERNSHIPS IN COMMUNITY SERVICE***-8%: 28 grants of **$6,000** each awarded to many types of nonprofit organizations for Graduate Students employed in a variety of community service projects, community betterment initiatives, community arts programs, etc. ***HEALTH GRANTS***-7%: **$125,000** to Temple U./Fels Research Institute for Cancer & Molecular Biology (new faculty support). **$20,000** to Regional Nursing Centers Consortium (education-advocacy). **$15,000** to Maternity Care Coalition of Greater Philadelphia (policy/research/education). ■**PUBLICATIONS:** Annual Report; Guidelines for Applicants flyer; Proposal Cover Sheet ■ •
WEBSITE: www.samfels.org ■**E-MAIL:** helenc@samfels.org ■**APPLICATION POLICIES & PROCEDURES:** The Foundation reports that giving is restricted to organizations in the City of Philadelphia or those focused on local issues, and focus on Community Programs, Education, Arts & Humanities, and Health. Also, Internships in Community Service grants ($6,000 each) support full-time employment by Graduate Students at nonprofit organizations in Philadelphia for ten weeks during the May 1st - August 31st period. A Graduate Student is defined as one who is beginning, is enrolled in, or has graduated from a graduate or professional program (law, medicine, etc.) that year; graduate students should apply directly to the community agency with which they are interested in working. No grants are awarded to/for the following: national, umbrella or re-granting organizations; scholarships, fellowships, grants-in-aid for travel/research; endowment; deficit funding or emergency aid; benefit events, tickets, sponsorships, parties, conferences, fairs, or festivals; publications or university presses; disease research; hospitals; routine social services or counseling; drug/alcohol addiction programs; litigation; programs for animals; summer recreation programs; religious education or private schools; individual daycare or after-school care; or studies lacking action plans for utilization. Prospective applicants should initially contact the Fund to inquire about the feasibility of submitting a request. Grant requests must include both a completed Proposal Cover Sheet—available on the website or from the Fund, and a proposal that follows Delaware Valley Grantmakers Common Grant Application Format (see www. dvg.org); other required documentation include an annual report, organizational/project budgets, list of major funding sources, audited financial statement, list of Board members, and IRS tax-exempt status documentation. Proposal-applications may be submitted at any time except for arts proposals which have January 15th and May 15th deadlines—no later than 5 p.m. those days. In general, an organization may submit only one proposal a year, regardless of the agency's size. Site visits are made to organizations being considered for a grant. Grants are awarded at meetings in February, April, May, June, September, October, November, and December, excepting arts grants which are awarded only twice yearly. Organizations whose grant requests have been declined must wait a year before submitting another proposal.
O+D+T Helen Cunningham (Executive Director+S+D+Con) — Hon. Ida K. Chen, Esq. (P+D) — Dr. Sandra Featherman (VP+D) — David H. Wice, Esq. (F+D) — Iso Briselli (D) — Bro. Daniel Burke, FSC (D) — Christine L. James-Brown (D) — David Melnicoff (D) — Emanuel Ortiz (D)

SE-216   Female Association of Philadelphia, The
    c/o 1420 Creek Road
    Huntingdon Valley   19006   (Montgomery County)

MI-15-17
Phone Unlisted **FAX** None
EIN 23-6214961   **Year Created** 1810

AMV $3,657,252   **FYE** 9-01   **(Gifts Received** $0)   450+ **Grants totaling** $226,600
Grants of mostly **$400-$600** each awarded to Philadelphia-area agencies serving disadvantaged women, as defined below.
■**PUBLICATIONS:** None ■**WEBSITE:** None ■**E-MAIL:** None ■**APPLICATION POLICIES & PROCEDURES:** Only Philadelphia-area health/human service organizations or church social assistance agencies are eligible to apply on behalf of older, needy Philadelphia-area women 60 years or older with annual incomes under $10,000 and not receiving SSI. No direct requests from individuals will be accepted. Grant requests should be submitted in March and September. The Board makes awards at meetings in April and October.
O+D+T Attn: Grants Administrator (Con) Mrs. Robert B. Hobbs, Jr. (P) — Mrs. Rodney D. Day, III (F) and a 20-member Board of Trustees — PNC Advisors (Agent/Custodian)

SE-217   Ferst Foundation, The
    10 Tall Trees Drive
    Bala Cynwyd   19004   (Montgomery County)

MI-15-22-52-62
Phone 610-664-7774 **FAX** None
EIN 23-6297112   **Year Created** 1963

AMV $225,460   **FYE** 12-00   **(Gifts Received** $0)   4 **Grants totaling** $13,250
Mostly local giving. High grant of **$11,250** to Jewish Federation of Greater Philadelphia. **$500** each to Central High School Music Assn. and Martin's Run. **Out-of-state** grant: **$1,000** to Women's Resource Center [FL]. — Grant approved for future payment: **$30,000** to Jewish Federation of Greater Philadelphia. ■**PUBLICATIONS:** None ■**WEBSITE:** None ■**E-MAIL:** None ■
APPLICATION POLICIES & PROCEDURES: Grant requests may be submitted in any form at any time; include IRS tax-exempt status documentation.
O+D+T Richard J. Ferst (T+Donor+Con) — Barton E. Ferst, Esq. (T) — Robert L. Ferst [FL] (T+Donor) — Stanley L. Ferst (T+Donor) — Walter B. Ferst (T) — Carol Baer Mott [DC] (T) — Susan Ferst Shapiro [MD] (T)

SE-218   Field (Joseph & Marie) Foundation
c/o Entercom Communications Corp.
401 City Ave., Suite 409
Bala Cynwyd   19004   (Montgomery County)
MI-12-32-41-42-45-49-52-54-82

Phone 610-660-5610 **FAX** None
EIN 23-3009586   **Year Created** 1999

AMV $10,478,636   **FYE** 7-00   (**Gifts Received** $11,981,250)   8 **Grants totaling** $760,000

Mostly local giving; grants are for operating support except as noted. High grants of **$200,000** each to Curtis Institute of Music (concert hall renovation/endowment) and National Liberty Museum. **$100,000** each to Settlement Music School (chamber music center construction) and Thos. Jefferson U. (research). **$50,000** each to Project Forward Leap and U. of Pa. (Center for Children's Policy, Practice & Research). **Out-of-state** grants: **$50,000** to International Rescue Committee [NY] and **$10,000** to Ovarian Cancer Research Fund [NY]. — Grants approved for future payment: **$1,800,000** to Curtis Institute of Music (chamber music center construction); **$900,000** to Thos. Jefferson U. (medical research); **$800,000** to National Liberty Museum (operating support); and **$400,000** to Settlement Music School (chamber music center construction). ■**PUBLICATIONS:** None ■**WEBSITE:** None ■**E-MAIL:** None ■**APPLICATION POLICIES & PROCEDURES:** Information not available.
O+D+T Joseph M. Field (P+F+D+Donor+Con) — Marie H. Field (VP+D+Donor) — S. Gordon Elkins [Melrose Park] (S+D) — John C. Donlevie (AS)

SE-219   Fields (Harry A.) Foundation, The
c/o First Keystone Federal Savings
22 West State Street
Media   19063   (Delaware County)
MI-42-43-62

Phone 610-565-6210 **FAX** 610-892-5150
EIN 34-0892632   **Year Created** 1997

AMV $571,047   **FYE** 8-00   (**Gifts Received** $13,575)   3 **Grants totaling** $34,100

One Pa. grant: **$13,100** to Automotive Training Center [Exton] (training van). **Out-of-state** grants: **$15,000** to Career Training Foundation [DC] (scholarships). **$6,000** to Rodef Sholom Congregation of Atlantic City [NJ]. — Giving in prior years included **$10,000** to Harvard U. [MA] and scholarships for students in SE Pa. ■**PUBLICATIONS:** None ■**WEBSITE:** None ■ **E-MAIL:** None ■**APPLICATION POLICIES & PROCEDURES:** Information not available.
O+D+T Terry D. Crain, Esq. (S+Con) — Richard A. Fields [MD] (P+F) — John B. Crain [NJ] (VP) — Louise M. Fields [NJ] (T)

SE-220   Finkelstein (Herman & Jerry) Foundation
c/o Blank, Rome, Comisky & McCauley
One Logan Square
Philadelphia   19103   (Philadelphia County)
MI-22-15-42-54-62-64-82

Phone 215-569-5500 **FAX** None
EIN 23-7690111   **Year Created** 1992

AMV $1,800,102   **FYE** 2-00   (**Gifts Received** $0)   15 **Grants totaling** $88,500

Mostly local/Pa. giving; all grants are for general support. High grant of **$25,000** to Jewish Community Centers of Greater Philadelphia. **$10,000** to Har Zion Temple. **$5,000** each to Gratz College, Jewish Community Centers/Kaiserman Branch, Penn State U. (Chair in Jewish Studies), Philadelphia Geriatric Center, Prince Music Theater, Temple U. School of Medicine, and U. of Pa. Law School. **$2,000-$2,500** each to American Friends of Israel-Elwyn, National Liberty Museum, and U. of Pa. Graduate School of Arts & Sciences. **$1,000** each to American Friends of Ben Gurion U. and American Friends of the Hebrew U. **Out-of-state** grant: **$10,000** to Haifa Foundation of North America. ■**PUBLICATIONS:** None ■**WEBSITE:** None ■**E-MAIL:** None ■**APPLICATION POLICIES & PROCEDURES:** Information not available.
O+D+T Samuel N. Rabinowitz, Esq. (T+Con) — Paul Auerbach, Esq. [Merion] (T) Donor: Estate of Herman Finkelstein

SE-221   Fire Streak Ministry
34 Longview Road
East Fallowfield   19320   (Chester County)
MI-63

Phone 610-384-6240 **FAX** None
EIN 23-2663299   **Year Created** 1995

AMV $101,374   **FYE** 12-99   (**Gifts Received** $75,250)   5 **Grants totaling** $53,950

Three Pa. grants: **$10,000** to Pilgrim's Progress [Downingtown]. **$5,000** to County Corrections Gospel Mission. **$500** to Praise Fellowship Church. **Out-of-state** grants: high grant of **$28,450** to Jesus Brethren Ministries [Nigeria] and **$10,000** to Cornerstone Ministries [NJ]. ■**PUBLICATIONS:** None ■**WEBSITE:** None ■**E-MAIL:** None ■**APPLICATION POLICIES & PROCEDURES:** No grants awarded to individuals.
O+D+T Robert G. Watkins (P+Donor+Con)

SE-222   First Hospital Foundation
117 South 17th Street, Suite 2300
Philadelphia   19103   (Philadelphia County)
MI-12-14-17-22-25-31-32-34-35
Phone 215-568-2225 **FAX** 215-563-2204
EIN 23-2904262   **Year Created** 1997

AMV $29,782,462   **FYE** 12-01   (**Gifts Received** $0)   19 **Grants totaling** $682,123

All local giving, all for direct health service programs. Five grants totaling **$246,346** to Pennsylvania Hospital units/centers, as follows: **$69,300—Women's** & Children's Health Services, Inc.; **$60,000—Hall** Mercer Community MH/MR Center; **$57,000—Joan** Karnell Cancer Center; **$49,446—Hospital** Archivist; and **$10,600—J.E.** Wood Clinic. **$60,000** to Delaware Valley Health Services. **$50,000** to Horizon House. **$45,000** to Spectrum Health Services. **$38,000** to Catholic Social Services/Northeast Family Service Center. **$31,000** to Women Organized Against Rape. **$28,600** to ALS Foundation/Greater Philadelphia Chapter. **$24,712** to U. of Pa. School of Nursing. **$22,430** to Women Against Abuse. **$20,000** each to MANNA/Metropolitan AIDS Neighborhood Nutrition Alliance and UCP Assn. of Philadelphia. **$17,000** to Center for Autistic Children. **$10,000** each to Calcutta House and Children's Crisis Treatment Center. **$5,035** to Bethesda Project. ■**PUBLICATIONS:** Funding Guidelines & Application Packet (with Application Cover Sheet) ■**WEBSITE:** None ■**E-MAIL:** walker@10000friends.org ■**APPLICATION POLICIES & PROCEDURES:** The Foundation reports that giving is restricted to Greater Philadelphia region organizations (preference given to agencies serving City of Philadelphia residents) for programs which address one or more of the following health issues: (a) access to health care by the uninsured/underinsured; (b) behavioral health needs, especially those of children/families; (c) perinatal health care; (d) services to children at risk; and (e) populations with special needs. Grants are awarded in these interest areas for direct service programs, as well as for education, research, public policy, and advocacy initiatives. Most grants are for one year, although a limited number of multiyear grants will be considered. Applicant organizations must demonstrate experience in serving the health needs of the poor or underserved. No grants are awarded to individuals or for general operating support, capital campaigns, major building projects, scholarships, or fellowships. Prospective applicants must request a copy of the Funding Guidelines Packet which includes detailed instructions and the required Application Cover Sheet. Completed grant proposals (hardcopy only) must be received by the October 15th deadline; incomplete applications will not be considered. The proposal review process generally takes about two months; applicants not meeting the guidelines will be notified promptly.

O+D+T Joanne R. Denworth, Esq. (C+D+Con) — Jane G. Pepper (S+D) — Louis J. Mayer, CPA (F+D) — Suzanne Sheehan Becker (D) — Rev. Ralph E. Blanks (D) — Bernard Borislow, Ph.D. (D) — Morris Cheston, Jr., Esq. (D) — Peter L. DeAngelis, Jr. (D) — Gail W. Hearn, Ph.D. (D) — Bruce W. Herdman, Ph.D. (D) — Natalie Levkovich (D) — Morris J. Lloyd, Jr. (D) — Alan N. Rosenberg, Esq. (D) — Donor: Funding from sale of Pennsylvania Hospital.

SE-223   First Savings Community Foundation   MI-13-15-31-39-85-89
　　　　c/o First Savings Bank of Perkasie
　　　　1211 North 5th Street, P.O. Box 176   **Phone** 215-257-5035 **FAX** None
　　　　Perkasie 18944   (Bucks County)   **EIN** 23-2984663   **Year Created** 1998
AMV $698,523   **FYE** 12-00   **(Gifts Received** $250,000)   24 **Grants totaling** $23,971

All local giving. High grant of **$5,000** to Pennridge Senior Center. **$3,000** to Grandview Hospital Foundation. **$2,500** to Main Street Program. **$2,000** each to The Jolly Roger Society and Sellersville Fire Company Trust Fund. **$1,000** each to Dublin Fire Company, Milford Fire Company, Pa. Assn. of Community Bankers Foundation, Perkasie Fire Company, Richlandtown Fire Company, Riegelsville Fire Company, and Upper Bucks YMCA. Other contributions **$100-$250** for health services, fire departments, youth and other purposes. ■**PUBLICATIONS:** None ■**WEBSITE:** www.fsbperkasie.com/comm_foundation.htm ■**E-MAIL:** jhollenbach@fsbperkasie.com ■**APPLICATION POLICIES & PROCEDURES:** The Foundation reports that support focuses on charitable organizations in the bank's service area. Grant requests may be submitted in any form at any time; describe the specific need for which support is requested and include IRS tax-exempt status documentation. All requests will be considered at regularly scheduled meetings.

O+D+T John D. Hollenbach (T+Con) — Claude H. Buerhle (T) — Walter Cressman (T) — Edward Gana, Jr. (T) — Robert Heacock (T) — Jeffrey Naugle (T) — Bernard Suess (T) — Vernon Wehrung (T) Corporate donor: First Savings Bank of Perkasie

---

SE-224   First Union Foundation   MI-11-12-13-14-16-17-22-25-31-35-41-42-45
　　　　c/o First Union/Wachovia - PA4360   49-51-52-53-54-55-85-88
　　　　1339 Chestnut Street   **Phone** 267-321-7664 **FAX** 267-321-7662
　　　　Philadelphia 19107   (Philadelphia County)   **EIN** 56-6288589   **Year Created** 1988
AMV $892,746   **FYE** 12-00   **(Gifts Received** $13,170,918)   1500+ **Grants totaling** $23,933,599

About one-fifth giving to Pa. in the Bank's trading area: SE, CP and NE Regions—28 Pa. counties only (see list below); some grants comprise multiple awards/payments. ***SE REGION GRANTS:*** High Pa. grant of **$1,706,077** to United Way of SE Pa. **$975,000** to Regional Performing Arts Center. **$780,000** to Lights of Liberty, Inc. **$400,000** to Philadelphia Festival of the Arts. **$385,000** to Philadelphia 2000. **$300,000** to National Constitution Center. **$250,000** to Avenue of the Arts. **$325,000** to School District of Philadelphia (Children Achieving). **$180,000** to U. of Pa./Wharton School. **$175,000** each to Academy of Natural Sciences and New Freedom Theatre. **$150,000** to Please Touch Museum. **$125,000** to The Reinvestment Fund. **$120,000** to Jewish Federation of Greater Philadelphia. **$110,000** to Greater Philadelphia Urban Affairs Coalition. **$100,000** each to People's Emergency Center and Villanova U. **$85,000** each to Free Library of Philadelphia and United Community Services of Bucks County. **$80,000** to Pa. Ballet. **$73,000-$75,000** each to Anti-Defamation League, Community Ventures, Inc., Greater Philadelphia First Foundation, and Philadelphia Zoo. **$65,000** each to Lincoln U. and Philadelphia Museum of Art. **$55,000** to ASPIRA of Pa. **$50,000** each to The Enterprise Center, People's Light & Theatre Company, Philadelphia Dance Company, WHYY, and Woodrock. **$45,000** to Philadelphia Futures. **$35,000** to Central Bucks Family YMCA. **$29,450-$30,000** each to Heritage Conservancy, Schuylkill River Development Council, and YMCA of Philadelphia & Vicinity. **$25,000** each to Bushfire Theatre of Performing Arts, Crozer Chester Foundation, Darlington Fine Arts Center, German Society of Pa., James Michener Art Museum, Junior Achievement of Delaware Valley, Nueva Esperanza, Paoli Battlefield Preservation Trust, Philadelphia Bar Foundation, Philadelphia Cares, Philadelphia City Sail, Sonny Hill Community Involvement League, and Universal Community Homes. **$21,800** to Wistar Institute. **$20,000** each to Associated Services for the Blind, Big Brother/Big Sister Assn. of Philadelphia, Boy Scouts/Cradle of Liberty Council, Central Philadelphia Development Corp., Chester County Community Foundation, Public/Private Ventures, Village of Arts & Humanities, and YMCA of Central Chester County. **$16,000-$18,000** each to Academy of Notre Dame de Namur, Arden Theatre Company, Franklin Institute, Pa. Academy of the Fine Arts, and Settlement Music School. **$14,000-$15,000** each to Friends of Brian, Gwynedd Mercy College, Independence Seaport Museum, Society for the Performing Arts of Media Theatre, White-Williams Scholars, and Womens Way. **$10,000-$13,000** each to Boy Scouts/Bucks County Council, Coatesville Regional Development Corp., Greater Philadelphia Chamber of Commerce Regional Foundation, Institute for the Study of Civic Values, International House of Philadelphia, Montgomery County Community College Foundation, Montgomery County OIC, Prince Music Theater, North Penn United Fund, Opera Company of Philadelphia, Partnership Community Development Corp., Philadelphia Youth Tennis, St. Mary Hospital of Langhorne Foundation, United Way of Chester County, U. of the Arts, Upper Bucks YMCA, Ursinus College, and Wilma Theatre. **$9,000** to Creative Artists Network. **$6,600-$7,500** each to Bucks County Historical Society, Farmers' Market Trust, Fort Mifflin on the Delaware, Greater Plymouth Community Center Fund, United Negro College Fund, and Young Audiences of Eastern Pa. **$4,000-$5,000** each to Abington Art Center, Academy of Vocal Arts,

Accion Communal Latino Americano de Montgomery County, African American Interdenominational Ministries, Balch Institute, Big Brothers Big Sisters of Bucks County, Boy Scouts/Unity District, Chester County Historical Society, Executive Service Corps of the Delaware Valley, Family YMCA of Lower Bucks County,Indochinese-American Council, Main Line Art Center, Norristown Zoo, Philabundance, Philadelphia Hospitality, Inc., Philadelphia Martin Luther King Jr. Assn. for Nonviolence, Second Macedonia Baptist Church, and Women's Resource Center. **$2,000-$3,700** each to American Heart Assn., Atwater Kent Museum, Housing Consortium for Disabled Individuals, Philadelphia Dance Alliance, Pa. Special Olympics, Philadelphia Health Management Corp., Roman Catholic High School, Roxborough YMCA, and Women's Opportunities Resource Center. ***CP REGION GRANTS:*** **$246,000** to Fund for the Advancement of the System of Higher Education. **$200,720** to United Way of Berks County. **$135,000** to United Way of Lancaster County. **$95,000** to United Way of the Capital Region. **$78,300** to Foundation for Reading Public Museum. **$62,000** to United Way of Lebanon County. **$50,000** to Lancaster Alliance. **$48,000** to United Way of York County. **$35,000** each to Pa. Downtown Center, Inc. and Penn State/Berks-Lehigh Valley. **$22,000** to Neighborhood Housing Services of Reading. **$20,000** to Penn State/Harrisburg Campus. **$18,000-$18,500** each to Jewish Federation of Reading, Millersville U. **$14,000-$15,000** each to Berks County Community Foundation, Bethany Home, Hispanic Center of the Spanish Speaking Council of Reading-Berks, and Wyomissing Institute of Fine Arts. **$10,000-$10,500** each to Boy Scouts/Hawk Mountain Council, Fulton Opera House Foundation, Lancaster Housing Opportunity Partnership, Pinnacle Health Foundation, Rainbow Home of Berks County, Reading Emergency Shelter, Reading Symphony Orchestra, and South Central Pa. Housing Development Foundation.**$7,500-$8,500** each to Allied Arts Fund, Red Cross/Berks County, Berks Community Television, Community First Fund of Lancaster, Crispus Attucks Community Development Corp., Hemlock Girl Scout Council, Junior Achievement of Central Pa., Lancaster Symphony Orchestra, Salvation Army/Lancaster, South George Street Community Partnership, and WITF. **$6,500** each to Adams-Hanover Counseling Services and Alliance for Young Artists & Writers. **$4,000-$5,250** each to Berks Business Education Coalition, Berks County Conservancy, Crispus Attucks Community Center, Foundation for Reading Area Community College, Harrisburg Area Community College, Kaltreider Memorial Library, Kutztown U. Foundation, Long Park Amphitheater Foundation, Pa. School of Art & Design, Visiting Nurse Assn. of Harrisburg, York County Cerebral Palsy Home, and York Symphony Orchestra. **$2,000-$3,700** each to Boy Scouts/Keystone Council, Boy Scouts/Pa. Dutch Council, Caron Foundation, Cultural Alliance of York County, Easter Seals/Berks & Schuylkill Counties, Goodwill Industries of Central Pa., Habitat for Humanity/Reading-Berks, HARB-Adult, Harrisburg Community Theatre, John Paul II Center for Special Learning, Junior Achievement of Berks County, Martin Library Assn., MetroArts of the Capital Region, Penn Laurel Girl Scout Council, Quarryville Library Center, Reading Hospital Auxiliary, Red Cross/York County, School District of Lancaster, United Jewish Community of Harrisburg, and Wildcat Foundation. ***NE REGION GRANTS:*** **$175,000** to United Way of Greater Lehigh Valley. **$52,000** to United Way of Wyoming Valley. **$45,000** to Lehigh U. **$36,000** to Schuylkill United Way. **$33,000** to United Way of Lackawanna County. **$30,000** to CACLV/Community Action Committee of the Lehigh Valley. **$25,000** each to Committee for Economic Growth, Smart Discovery Center, and Wilkes U. **$23,000** to Historic Bethlehem Partnership. **$20,000-$22,000** each to College Misericordia, Lehigh Valley Hospital, Penn State/Schuylkill Campus, and Wilkes-Barre Family YMCA. **$15,000-$17,600** each to Allentown Art Museum, Can Do Community Foundation, DeSales U., Friends of the State Theatre,and Game Preserve Fund. **$10,000** each to Allentown Economic Development Corp., Allentown Symphony, Bethlehem Economic Development Corp., King's College, Lehigh Valley Community Foundation, Sacred Heart Foundation, Scranton Tomorrow, and U. of Scranton. **$8,000-$9,600** each to Catholic Youth Center of Wyoming Valley, Neighborhood Development Trust Fund of Scranton, Northampton Community College Foundation, and Schuylkill County Volunteer Fireman's Assn. **$6,000-$7,600** each to Bach Choir of Bethlehem, Baum School of Art, Bethlehem Musikfest Assn., Boy Scouts/NE Pa. Council, Easter Seals of NE Pa., Good Shepherd Rehabilitation Hospital, Great Valley Girl Scout Council, HCSC/Miller Blood Center, Hillside School, Jewish Community Center of Allentown, Jewish Federation of the Lehigh Valley, Salvation Army/Allentown, and Valley Youth House. **$4,000-$5,400** each to Adult Literacy Center of Lehigh Valley, Albright College, Allentown Neighborhood Housing Services, Allentown Rescue Mission, Alvernia College, American Cancer Society/Wyoming Valley Unit, Boys & Girls Club of Allentown, Celtic Fest, Community Bike Works, Danville Child Development Center, Ecumenical Enterprises, F.M. Kirby Center for the Performing Arts, Lehigh County Conference of Churches, Lehigh County Senior Citizens, Moravian College, Muhlenberg College, NAACP-Allentown Branch Scholarship Fund, Pittston Memorial Library, Repertory Dance Theatre, Sacred Heart Foundation, Salvation Army/East Stroudsburg, Schuylkill County Council for the Arts, Schuylkill County Orchestra, United Way of Monroe County, West End Youth Center, Wyoming Seminary, YMCA & YWCA Council of Allentown, and YMCA of Greater Scranton. **$2,000-$3,500** each Arthritis Foundation/Eastern Pa., Boys & Girls Club of Scranton, Burn Prevention Foundation, Civic Theatre of Allentown, Community Music School, Community Services for Children, Easton Heritage Alliance, Girls Club of Allentown, Hugh Moore Historical Park & Museums, Housing Assn. & Development Corp., Junior Achievement of Lehigh Valley, Korean Vietnam Memorial, Lehigh-Carbon Community College Foundation, Lehigh Valley Business Education Partnership, Lehigh Valley Chamber Orchestra, March of Dimes/Eastern Pa., Pa. Shakespeare Festival, Philharmonic Society of NE Pa., Phoebe Home, Red Cross/Scranton Chapter, Volunteer Center of the Lehigh Valley, Wildlands Conservancy, and Wyoming County United Fund. In addition, many smaller grants contributions to local organizations for similar purposes. Most other giving to the other states where the Bank operates. ■**PUBLICATIONS:** Community Annual Report; application guidelines ■**WEBSITE:** www.firstunion.com ■**E-MAIL:** kevin.dow@wachovia.com ■**APPLICATION POLICIES & PROCEDURES:** Giving focuses on states where the bank operates: NC, SC, FL, GA, VA, MD, DE, NJ, NY, CT, as well as Philadelphia and 27 Pa. counties—Adams, Berks, Bradford, Bucks, Centre, Chester, Clinton, Cumberland, Dauphin, Delaware, Lackawanna, Lancaster, Lebanon, Lehigh, Luzerne, Lycoming, Montgomery, Montour, Northampton, Northumberland, Pike, Potter, Schuylkill, Susquehanna, Tioga, Union, and York. Grants are awarded in four priority areas: **(1) Education:** early childhood literacy/school readiness, K-12 mentoring, after school enrichment, school-to-work programs, drop-out prevention, financial literacy, technology training, higher education scholarships focused on minority students, enhanced teacher preparation/training, adult education—job skills training, financial literacy; and technology training. **(2) Community Development:** affordable housing—single and multifamily housing, and shelters; small business ownership—assisting individuals in start-up/management; economic development—promoting economic vitality and job creation; financial literacy for individuals with homeownership counseling and budgeting. **(3) Health/Human Services:** United Ways; Hospitals/Medical Centers promoting health education and outreach program; Disaster relief efforts for physical, emotional and economic recovery. **(4) Arts/Culture:** Programs that expand arts/cultural experiences with a focus on education and outreach. Special consideration is given to programs that (a) have a high level of First Union employee involvement, (b) help build inclusive and diverse communities, and (c) foster collaborative efforts that leverage the Bank's community investment. No grants are awarded to individuals or for organizations already receiving First Union support through the United Way or united arts drives—except for approved community-wide capital campaigns; intermediary or pass-through organizations; precollege level private schools (except through the Employees' Educational Matching Gift program); programs/projects of a national scope; political causes/candidates whose primary purpose is influencing legislation; veterans organizations; fraternal groups; religious organizations unless engaged in significant projects benefiting a broad-based community; books, research papers/articles in professional journals; travel; conferences; international organizations; and sponsorships, events or projects for which First Union receives benefits/privileges. Grant requests may be submitted at any time in a letter (2 pages maximum) covering the following: organizational objectives/background; demonstration of the need; specific plans and timetable; budget with sources of funding; description of funding plans—current and long-term; and qualifications of the organization and personnel involved. Also include the name/address/phone number of the program's contact person; list of Board members and key management personnel; a current operating budget; most recent audit; IRS tax-exempt status documentation; and information on First Union's relationship with the organization including contributions and First Union employee volunteer involvement. Organizations currently receiving multiyear funding from the Foundation must wait one year from the completion of the grant period before seeking additional support. — **Notes:** (1) While the Foundation is headquartered in Charlotte, NC all grant requests from Pa. and the State of Delaware must be submitted to the Philadelphia office. (2) In late 2003, the Foundation's name, reportedly, will change to Wachovia Foundation.

O+D+T Kevin Dow (VP & Community Affairs Manager for Pa./Del. at Bank+Con) — and a Board of about 25, mostly out-of-state residents — Corporate donor: First Union/Wachovia

---

SE-225 **First Union Regional Foundation**
c/o First Union/Wachovia - PA4360
1339 Chestnut Street
Philadelphia 19107 (Philadelphia County)

MI-12-16-17-22-24-25-29-34-35-45-57-85

Phone 267-321-7658 **FAX** 267-321-7656
EIN 22-2625990 **Year Created** 1998

AMV $87,823,863 **FYE** 12-01 **(Gifts Received** $0) 10 **Grants totaling** $4,575,000

All giving is limited to the Bank's trading areas in PA, NJ and DE (see below); six multiyear grants awarded to Pa. High grant of **$725,000** (over 3 years) to Our City Reading/Community Initiative Development Corp. [Berks County] (purchase/rehabilitate inner-city homes for subsidized resale/educational greenhouse program). **$650,000** (over 3 years) to Schuylkill Community Action [Pottsville] (Schuylkill County Neighborhood Revitalization Initiative start-up funding, providing multidisciplinary services in selected communities). **$400,000** (over 3 years) to Community Action Commission/Capital Region [Harrisburg] (Success Academy start-up costs including staff, equipment, materials—primarily for Harrisburg's south side residents). Also, commitments on three other major grants (**$300,000** to **$525,000**) were made to Philadelphia and Lehigh County organizations, but details have not been released. **Out-of-state** grants included **$700,000** (over 3 years) to YWCA of New Castle County [DE] (Stepping Stones to Self-Sufficiency project for neighborhood-based financial empowerment); and **$300,000** (over 3 years) to Cumberland County College [NJ] (seed money for Cumberland County Literacy Institute). — Grants awarded in 2000 to Pa. organizations included **$750,000** (over 3 years) to Resources for Human Development (Capital to People regional expansion program, providing venture capital to small businesses employing low-income persons). **$448,000** (over 2 years) to Philadelphia Housing Authority/Tenant Support Services (training/placement of public housing residents in a pre-apprenticeship program run with local building trade unions). **$550,000** (over 3 years) to United Way of Berks County/United Way of SE Pa. (resource sharing/collaboration re improving affordable childcare). **$450,000** (over 3 years) to Inner City Group [Lancaster] (comprehensive rebuilding initiative in South Duke Street corridor). **$300,000** (over 2 years) to Philadelphia Safe & Sound (Philadelphia Coalition for Kids—research to improve health/safety of city's children). **$230,000** (over 3 years) to West Philadelphia Partnership (transition of two public schools into a university-assisted comprehensive model community school). **$150,000** (over 2 years) to Campus Boulevard Corp. (Incubator Without Walls program—provide business assistance to community based entrepreneurs in targeted city neighborhoods). ■**PUBLICATIONS:** Informational Folder with grants list and application guidelines ■**WEBSITE:** www.firstunion.com ■**E-MAIL:** kimberly.allen@wachovia.com ■**APPLICATION POLICIES & PROCEDURES:** The Foundation reports that Pa. giving is restricted to the Bank's trading area which includes the 5-county Philadelphia area plus Adams, Berks, Bradford, Centre, Clinton, Cumberland, Dauphin, Lackawanna, Lancaster, Lebanon, Lehigh, Luzerne, Lycoming, Montour, Northampton, Northumberland, Pike, Potter, Schuylkill, Susquehanna, Tioga, Union, and York counties, as well as NJ and DE. Grantmaking focuses on a limited number of targeted community development initiatives, some proactively solicited, with the potential to improve community residents' quality of life, connecting them to the region's economic vitality. Projects are selected based on their potential to significantly contribute to systemic community change, especially those suitable as replicable models for rebuilding communities. Priority is given to major initiatives which (a) contribute to long-term, sustainable improvements in our communities; (b) provide tools to enable low- and moderate-income persons to access the social/economic mainstream; (c) elevate disadvantaged youth and adults through innovative education programs, e.g. linking education to job/workforce development; (d) revitalize neighborhoods through comprehensive development plans; (e) utilize effective strategic partnerships; and (f) incorporate accountability and evaluation measures. No requests are considered for direct grants to individuals, political causes, candidates or organizations whose primary purpose is influencing legislation, or national or international organizations. As a special project fund, the Foundation normally does not support endowment, annual operating funds, capital campaigns, debt reduction, or special events. Also, no support generally is awarded to/for precollege level private schools, colleges/universities; veteran or fraternal organizations; religious programs/activities; arts/cultural organizations; hospital/medical centers; and health or disease-related organizations. Exceptions may be considered on a case-by-case basis if the project is part of a comprehensive, strategic community development plan. Grant requests should be submitted in a preliminary letter (3 pages maximum) which covers the following: demonstrate how the organization or proposed project addresses the Foundation's giving objectives (see above); describe the organization/its work and summarize the organization's achievements, particularly in relation to the problem/issue being addressed; state the problem/need being addressed, explain how it will be addressed, and describe anticipated results; outline the project's time frame; and estimate the project's total cost including the amount requested from the Foundation. Preliminary request letters may be submitted at any time and are acknowledged, pro or con. If Foundation staff determines that the request fits the Foundation's mission/guidelines, a full proposal will be requested and details on preparing a proposal will be provided. Site visits are made to organizations being considered for a grant. Final decisions on grants are made by the Board of Directors at Board meetings in January, April, July and October. — **Note:** The Foundation reports that mission and guidelines are currently under review, to be released June 2003. — Formerly called Corestates Foundation.

O+D+T Denise McGregor Armbrister (Executive Director +S+F+Con) — Stephanie W. Naidoff, Esq. (C+D) — Robert L. Reid [NJ] (P+D) — Reginald E. Davis (VP+D) — Lillian Escobar Haskins (D) — Eleanor V. Horne [NJ] (D) — Carlton E. Hughes (D) — Ernest E. Jones, Esq. (D) — George V. Lynett, Esq. (D) — Dr. Patricia A. McFate (D) — Marlin Miller, Jr. (D) — Malcolm D. Pryor (D) — Peter S. Strawbridge (D) — John D. Wallace [NJ] (D) Corporate donor: First Union/Wachovia

---

SE-226   FirstFruits Foundation   MI-63-64
c/o Conetex, Inc.
102 South Pine Street, P.O. Box 239   **Phone** 610-286-1936 **FAX** None
Elverson   19520   (Chester County)   **EIN** 23-2808624   **Year Created** 1995
AMV $14,506,787   **FYE** 12-00   **(Gifts Received** $0)   16 **Grants totaling** $1,007,500

About one-third Pa. giving; grants are for general support except as noted. High Pa. grant of **$205,000** to High Point Baptist Chapel [Berks County]. **$75,000** to Assn. of Baptists for World Evangelism [Harrisburg] (training center/conference center). **$60,000** to Calvary Baptist Seminary [Lansdale] (building fund). **$20,000** to Baptist Bible Seminary [Lackawanna County] (Project Jerusalem). **$10,000** to Dover Bible Church [York County]. **Out-of-state** giving includes high grant of **$350,000** to Northland Baptist Bible College [WI] (building fund); **$60,000** each to Tri-State Ministries [MO] (camp scholarships/missions) and Woodlands Camp & Conference Center [GA]; **$40,000** to Christian Liberty School [HI]; and other grants **$7,500** to **$25,000** for similar purposes in NH, OH, MO, TX and CA. ■**PUBLICATIONS:** None ■**WEBSITE:** None ■**E-MAIL:** None ■**AP-PLICATION POLICIES & PROCEDURES:** Information not available.

O+D+T Robert L. Cone (P+F+D+Donor+Con) — Edward H. Cone (VP+S+D) — Derial H. Sanders [Chester Springs] (D) — Dawn M. Cone (Donor)

SE-227   Fischer Foundation, The   MI-13-22-32-42-54-62
c/o Legg Mason
1735 Market Street, 10th Floor   **Phone** 215-988-0700 **FAX** None
Philadelphia   19103   (Philadelphia County)   **EIN** 22-6104376   **Year Created** 1964
AMV $291,447   **FYE** 12-00   **(Gifts Received** $0)   58 **Grants totaling** $49,083

Mostly local giving. High grant of **$10,000** to Anti-Defamation League. **$5,000** each to City Year-Philadelphia and Federation Allied Jewish Appeal. **$4,000** to Boy Scouts/Cradle of Liberty Council. **$2,800** to National MS Society. **$2,550** to National Museum of American Jewish History. **$1,000-$1,500** each to Center for the Advancement of Cancer Education [Newtown], Drexel U., The Fund, Susan B. Komen Foundation/Philadelphia Race for the Cure, Main Line Reform Temple, Philadelphia Museum of Art, and Widener U. **$700** to People's Emergency Center. Other contributions **$12-$500** for various purposes. **Out-of-state** giving includes **$3,100** to American Parkinson Disease Assn. [NY] and smaller grants/contributions. ■**PUBLICATIONS:** Annual Report ■**WEBSITE:** None ■**E-MAIL:** None ■**APPLICATION POLICIES & PROCEDURES:** Grant requests may be submitted in a letter at any time; include an audited financial statement, Board member list, and IRS tax-exempt status documentation. No grants are awarded to individuals. Site visits sometimes are made to organizations being considered for a grant.

O+D+T Bruce Fischer [Wynnewood] (P+T+Donor+Con) — Nedra Fischer [Wynnewood] (T+Donor) — Marc Fischer [IL] (T) — Stephanie Fischer [CA] (T) — Margelle Liss [Narberth] (T)

SE-228   Fisher Family Foundation   MI-15-22-29-41-42-62
c/o PEI-Genesis
2180 Hornig Road   **Phone** 215-673-0400 **FAX** None
Philadelphia   19116   (Philadelphia County)   **EIN** 22-2473752   **Year Created** 1983
AMV $1,106,250   **FYE** 12-00   **(Gifts Received** $117,477)   20 **Grants totaling** $90,268

Mostly local giving. High grant of **$40,100** to Gratz College. **$22,500** to Jewish Family & Children's Service. **$6,000** to Temple Sinai. **$5,000** to Congregation Beth El. **$3,000** to American Jewish Congregation. **$2,500** to Kosher Meals on Wheels. **$1,000-$1,500** each to Philadelphia Geriatric Center, Red Cross, and School District of Philadelphia. Other smaller local contributions for various purposes. **Out-of-state** giving includes **$2,500** to American Committee for Shaare Zedek [NY] and **$1,000** each to Masorti Movement Scholarship Program [Israel], U. of Chicago [IL], and World War II Memorial Fund [DC]. ■**PUBLICATIONS:** None ■**WEBSITE:** None ■**E-MAIL:** None ■**APPLICATION POLICIES & PROCEDURES:** The Foundation reports a primary interest is Jewish causes. No grants are awarded to individuals. Prospective applicants should make an initial telephone inquiry about the feasibility of submitting a request. Grant requests may be submitted in any form at any time.

O+D+T Murray Fisher [Wyncote] (T+Donor+Con) — Mildred Fisher [Wyncote] (T) — Stephen Fisher [Rydal] (T+Donor) — Carol Ruth Rosenthal [Yardley] (T+Donor) — Ricki Fisher (Donor) — Corporate donor: PEI-Genesis

SE-229 Fishman (Bernard & Annabelle) Family Foundation
The Fairmont, #409
41 Conshohocken State Road
Bala Cynwyd   19004   (Montgomery County)

MI-14-15-22-32-62

Phone 610-667-4626 **FAX** None
EIN 23-2921665   **Year Created** 1997

AMV $504,291   **FYE** 12-00   **(Gifts Received** $430,000)   6 **Grants totaling** $69,400

Mostly local giving; all grants are for general operating support. High grant of **$50,000** to Philadelphia Geriatric Center. **$5,000** to National Organization for Hearing Research [Narberth]. **$3,000** to ALS Foundation/Philadelphia Chapter. **$1,000** to Associated Services for the Blind. **Out-of-state** grant: **$10,000** to Jewish Federation of Southern Palm Beach County [FL]. ■**PUBLICATIONS:** None ■**WEBSITE:** None ■**E-MAIL:** None ■**APPLICATION POLICIES & PROCEDURES:** Grant requests in any form may be submitted at any time.

O+D+T   Bernard Fishman (P+Con) — Corporate donor: Fishman & Tobin, Inc.

SE-230 Fleisher (Robert H. & Janet S.) Foundation
c/o Duane Morris LLP
One Liberty Place, Suite 4200
Philadelphia   19103   (Philadelphia County)

MI-12-25-41-43-51-53-55

Phone 215-979-1972 **FAX** 215-979-1020
EIN 23-6758238   **Year Created** 1983

AMV $1,224,896   **FYE** 5-01   **(Gifts Received** $0)   26 **Grants totaling** $73,000

About two-thirds local giving; all grants are for general support. High grant of **$10,000** to Creative Artists Network. **$7,000** to Peoples' Emergency Center. **$6,000** to William Penn Exemplary Senior High School. **$4,500** to The Fabric Workshop. **$3,000** to Endow-A-Home. **$2,000** each to Abington Art Center and Clay Studio. **$1,000** each to ArtReach, Gesu School, Jeanne Ruddy Dance Co., Moore College of Art, and Philadelphia Futures. Other contributions **$50-$500** for various purposes. **Out-of-state** giving includes **$9,300** to Take Stock in Children [FL]; **$4,900** to Cunningham Dance Foundation [NY]; and **$4,650** to Sufi Order International [WA]. ■**PUBLICATIONS:** None ■**WEBSITE:** None ■**E-MAIL:** smbonovitz@duanemorris.com ■**APPLICATION POLICIES & PROCEDURES:** Grant requests in any form may be submitted at any time; include organizational information and purpose/amount of requested funds. No grants awarded to individuals.

O+D+T   Sheldon M. Bonovitz, Esq. (Con) — Nancy F. Blood [Wyncote] (T) — Jill F. Bonovitz (T) — Janet S. Fleisher [Elkins Park] (T)

SE-231 Foreman-Fleisher (Ida) Trust
c/o Federation of Jewish Agencies
2100 Arch Street, 6th Floor
Philadelphia   19103   (Philadelphia County)

MI-43

Phone 215-832-0500 **FAX** 267-256-2133
EIN 23-6201637   **Year Created** 1929

AMV $564,647   **FYE** 9-00   **(Gifts Received** $0)   5 **Grants totaling** $32,000

All giving restricted to scholarships for young, Jewish women pursuing higher education in a professional field; all awards were **$6,400** each. ■**PUBLICATIONS:** statement of program policy; application guidelines ■**WEBSITE:** None ■**E-MAIL:** None ■**APPLICATION POLICIES & PROCEDURES:** Only young female Jewish graduate students who reside in the Philadelphia area or attend local institutions are eligible to apply. Prospective applicants initially should make a telephone inquiry about the feasibility of submitting a request. A formal application form, available from Federation of Jewish Agencies, must be completed and submitted during May-June (deadline is June 30th); also provide income information. Decisions on awards are made in August.

O+D+T   Richard Nassau (Con) — PNC Advisors (Trustee)

SE-232 Forney Family Foundation
P.O. Box 549
Unionville   19375   (Chester County)

MI-11-13-41-52-54-56-63-71-89

Phone 610-486-6566 **FAX** None
EIN 23-7079172   **Year Created** 1970

AMV $3,293,304   **FYE** 12-00   **(Gifts Received** $665,000)   66 **Grants totaling** $85,715

About half local giving. High grant of **$22,000** to St. Michael Lutheran Church of Unionville. **$2,700** to United Way of Kennett Square. **$2,000** each to Stroud Water Research Center and Po-Mar-Lin Fire Company. **$1,000** each to Academy of Natural Sciences, Camp Dreamcatcher, Chemical Heritage Foundation, and Chester County Community Foundation. Other local contributions **$250-$500** for educational, religious, cultural/arts, human services, and environmental purposes. **Out-of-state** giving includes **$6,000** to Tau Beta Pi [TN]; **$4,000** to Kalmar Nyckel Foundation [DE]; **$3,540** to Delaware Theatre Company; **$3,000** to Centreville School [DE]; and smaller grants for similar purposes to many states, especially DE, DC and CO. ■**PUBLICATIONS:** None ■**WEBSITE:** None ■**E-MAIL:** None ■**APPLICATION POLICIES & PROCEDURES:** Information not available.

O+D+T   Robert C. Forney (P+F+Donor+Con) — Marilyn G. Forney (VP+S) — Barbara D. Forney [Coatesville] (T)

SE-233 Forst Foundation, The
145 Blake Ave.
Rockledge   19046   (Montgomery County)

MI-12-13-14-22-25-32-41-43-61-84
Phone 215-663-9543 **FAX** None
EIN 23-7685957   **Year Created** 1991

AMV $974,877   **FYE** 12-00   **(Gifts Received** $193,044)   50 **Grants totaling** $120,240

Mostly local/Pa. giving. High grant of **$15,000** to Diocese of Allentown. **$14,200** to Incarnation Elementary School [Philadelphia]. **$9,000** to Little Flower Catholic High School for Girls. **$7,500** to FRSC. **$6,000** to Face to Face/St. Vincent's. **$5,000** each to Associated Services for the Blind and United Cerebral Palsy. **$4,500** to Philadelphia Futures. **$3,500** to LaSalle College High School. **$3,000** to CORA Services. **$2,000-$2,500** each to Center for Literacy at Incarnation, Family Relations Council, Foundations, Inc. (Beyond School Hours), McDevitt High School, Mercy Vocational High School, Philabundance, Rho Chapter Education Foundation, St. John's Hospice, St. Madeleine Parish [Ridley Park], and Second Harvest. **$1,000-$1,500** each to Boy Scouts, Frontiers International [Allegheny County], Lupus Foundation of America, The Pathway School, St. Francis Inn, and St.

Vincent's Church (soup kitchen). Other smaller local contributions for similar purposes. **Out-of-state** giving includes **$1,500** to Women's Sports Foundation [NY] and **$1,000** to Canine Companions for Independence [CA]. ■**PUBLICATIONS:** None ■ **WEBSITE:** None ■**E-MAIL:** None ■**APPLICATION POLICIES & PROCEDURES:** Information not available.

O+D+T Mariellen Forst Paulus (T+Con) — Thomas Forst [North Wales] (T) — Edward S. Forst (Donor)

SE-234 Foster Foundation, The
Stonybrook Road, P.O. Box 390
Newtown   18940   (Bucks County)
AMV $57,408   **FYE** 11-00   **(Gifts Received** $55,000)

MI-12-13-14-22-32-42-52-63
Phone 215-968-5031 **FAX** None
EIN 23-2807767   **Year Created** 1995
41 **Grants totaling** $77,430

About one-quarter local giving. High Pa. grant of **$8,100** to Church of God's Love. **$3,575** to Boy Scouts/Bucks County Council. **$2,000** each to Pa. Special Olympics and Philadelphia Orchestra. **$1,200** to Family Services of Bucks County. **$1,150** to Lutheran Charities. **$500** each to Bucks County Assn. for the Blind and Salvation Army/Levittown. Other local contributions **$100-$400** for various purposes. **Out-of-state** giving includes high grant of **$30,000** to Good Shepherd Lutheran Church [NJ]; **$5,000** each to The Jackson Laboratory [ME] and Massachusetts Institute of Technology; **$2,500** to Parkinson's Disease Foundation [NY]; and other grants/contributions, many to CO. ■**PUBLICATIONS:** None ■**WEBSITE:** None ■**E-MAIL:** None ■**APPLICATION POLICIES & PROCEDURES:** Information not available.

O+D+T Richard L. Foster (P+F+T+Donor+Con) — Marilyn E. Foster (VP+S)

SE-235 Foster (John H.) Foundation, The
c/o Foster Management Company, Inc.
P.O. Box 767
King of Prussia   19406   (Montgomery County)
AMV $8,749,092   **FYE** 12-00   **(Gifts Received** $0)

MI-31-34-35-42-52-54-56-63-72

Phone 610-935-4673 **FAX** None
EIN 13-3249353   **Year Created** 1984
15 **Grants totaling** $1,441,000

No Pa. giving in 2000. **Out-of-state** grants include **$1,010,000** to Hospital for Special Surgery [NY]; **$210,000** to World Wildlife Fund [DC]; **$100,000** to Island Health Project [NY]; **$40,000** to Metropolitan Museum of Art; and **$25,000** each to Harvard School of Public Health and Dartmouth College/Tuck School of Business. — Local giving in prior years included **$50,000** to Academy of Music; **$10,100** to Philadelphia Orchestra; **$4,000** to St. Christopher's Church [Gladwyne]; and **$2,500** to WHYY. ■**PUBLICATIONS:** None ■**WEBSITE:** None ■**E-MAIL:** None ■**APPLICATION POLICIES & PROCEDURES:** No grants awarded to individuals.

O+D+T John H. Foster (P+D+Donor+Con) — Nathan Hale, Esq. [NY] (S+D) — Stephen C. Curley, Esq. [NY] (F+D) — John Butler, Esq. [NY] (AS)

SE-236 Fourjay Foundation, The
Building G, Suite 1
2300 Computer Ave.
Willow Grove   19090   (Montgomery County)
AMV $22,584,306   **FYE** 12-00   **(Gifts Received** $250,000)

MI-12-13-14-15-16-17-18-19-25-31-32-33-35
42-45-52-65-84
Phone 215-830-1437 **FAX** 215-830-0157
EIN 23-2537126   **Year Created** 1988
115 **Grants totaling** $1,257,270

Mostly local/Pa. giving; some grants comprise multiple awards. High grant of **$200,000** to Abington Memorial Hospital. **$60,960** to Gettysburg College. **$50,000** each to Children's Hospital of Philadelphia Foundation (cardiovascular research) and Lankenau Hospital (cardiovascular research). **$30,000** to HealthLink Medical Center. **$20,000** to Aid for Friends (mostly capital). **$15,000** to Arcadia U. **$10,650** to New Directions for Women. **$10,000** each to The Beck Institute, Best Nest, Inc., Bethanna, Bethesda Project, Bridging the Gaps, Burn Foundation, Center on Hearing & Deafness, Christmas in April of Philadelphia, Community Volunteers in Medicine, Community Women's Education Project, Deaf-Hearing Communication Center, Elizabeth Blackwell Health Center for Women, Family Service Assn. of Bucks County, Free Clinic of Doylestown, Greater Philadelphia Food Bank, The Growing Center [Frederick], Habitat for Humanity/West Philadelphia, Interfaith Development Corp. of Bucks County, Keystone Hospice, The Lamb Foundation [North Wales], Manor College, Network of Victim Assistance, North Penn Valley Boys & Girls Club, Overington House, Philadelphia Senior Center, Philadelphia Training Program, Wissahickon Hospice, Wo-man 2 Woman Ministries, Women of Excellence, and Youth & Family Services of Upper Perkiomen Valley. **$9,600** to Gwynedd Mercy Academy. **$8,000** to Farmers Market Trust. **$7,000-$7,500** each to Center for Advancement in Cancer Education, Center in the Park, Compeer, Developmental Enterprises Corp., Institute for the Advancement of African-American Youth, MBF Center, National Assn. of the Mentally Ill of Pa., Philadelphians Concerned About Housing, Recording for the Blind & Dyslexic, Trevor's Campaign for the Homeless, and Working Wardrobe. **$6,000** each to Easter Seals and Living Beyond Breast Cancer. **$5,000-$5,500** each to Adoption Center of Delaware Valley, Anti-Violence Partnership of Philadelphia, Brian's House, Children's Village Child Care Center, Community Outreach Partnership, CONTACT Careline for Greater Philadelphia, Corporate Alliance for Drug Education, Daemion House, Endow-A-Home, Friends Rehabilitation Program, Greater Philadelphia Coalition Against Hunger, Haitian Community Center of Philadelphia, Haven of Hope, hireAbility, Indian Creek Foundation, Inn Dwelling, Kailo Mantua Art Center, Little Brothers Friends of the Elderly, Make-A-Wish Foundation of Philadelphia/SE Pa., MANNA/Mantua AIDS Neighborhood Nutrition Alliance, Maternity Care Coalition, North Light Community Center, North Philadelphia Visions, The Partnership Community Development Corp., Pa. Assistive Technology Foundation, Philabundance, Philadelphia Committee to End Homelessness, Philadelphia Community Academy, Phoenix Horizons, Polish American Social Services, RSVP of Montgomery County, Second Alarmers' Assn. & Rescue Squad, Siloam Ministries, Street Clothes Project, Variety Club, VNA Community Services, VNA of Pottstown & Vicinity, VITA Education Services, Wheels, Inc., and Woodrock. **$3,000-$4,500** each to Assets Montco, Caring About Sharing, Lutheran Children & Family Service, Pals for Life, and Philadelphia Physicians for Social Responsibility. Other smaller local grants for similar purposes. **Out-of-state** giving, all under the Foundation's Cardiovascular Research Grant Program, includes **$50,000** each to Baylor College of Medicine [TX], Ohio State U. Medical Center, and Washington U. School of Medicine [MO]; and **$19,200** to Johnson O'Connor Research Foundation [TX]. ■**PUBLICATIONS:** Grant Application Guidelines brochure ■

WEBSITE: www.fourjay.org ∎ **E-MAIL:** info@fourjay.org ∎ **APPLICATION POLICIES & PROCEDURES:** The Foundation focuses on education and human services, primarily in the City of Philadelphia, and Bucks & Montgomery counties, and reports a particular interest in organizations where staff members exhibit ingenuity, commitment, and motivation. Most grants are for general support, special projects, capital/building funds, research, and scholarship funds. No support is awarded to/for arts/cultural, alumni, athletic, civic, elementary/secondary schools, foreign, religious, political, public broadcasting, individuals, libraries, local chapters of national organizations, United Ways, or to individuals. The Foundation also funds a Cardiovascular Research Grant Program (see full details on the Foundation website). Grant proposals may be submitted at any time; deadlines are March 1st, June 1st, September 1st, and December 1st; submit one complete proposal (and seven copies of the proposal cover letter on letterhead paper); describe a well-defined need; state a plan of action and request a specific amount; and include an annual report, audited financial statement, organization and project budgets, Board member list with affiliations, list of major funding sources, and IRS tax-exempt status documentation. Proposals submitted without audited financial information will be returned or rejected. An organization may submit only one request per year. Review of applications takes about four months and site visits may be initiated by the Board to organizations being considered for a grant; applicants, however, should not make unsolicited visits to the Foundation's office. Grants are awarded at mid-month meetings in March, June, September and December.

O+D+T Geoffrey W. Jackson (Executive Director+D+Con) — Eugene W. Jackson (P+T+Donor) — Mary Louise Jackson (VP+T) — Thomas Lynch (D) — Daniel O'Connell (D)

SE-237   **Fox (Geraldine Dietz) Foundation, The**   MI-32
     c/o The Fox Companies
     955 Chesterbrook Blvd., Suite 125
     Wayne   19087   (Delaware County)   **Phone** 610-640-1400   **FAX** None
                                              EIN 23-2542904   **Year Created** 1988
AMV $1,297,828   **FYE** 12-00   **(Gifts Received** $0)   3   **Grants totaling** $177,000

All giving restricted to auditory research. High grant of **$175,000** to National Organization for Hearing Research (a family-affiliated foundation). **$1,000** each to Bertha Abess Children's Center [FL] and Security on Campus, Inc. — In prior years grants have been awarded nationally to hospitals, medical centers and universities engaged in auditory research. ∎ **PUBLICATIONS:** None ∎ **WEBSITE:** None ∎ **E-MAIL:** None ∎ **APPLICATION POLICIES & PROCEDURES:** The Foundation reports that only auditory research-related grant requests are accepted. No grants awarded to individuals.

O+D+T Geraldine Dietz Fox (T+Donor+Con) — Richard J. Fox (T)

SE-238   **Fox (Richard J.) Foundation, The**   MI-11-12-22-31-32-34-41-42-49-53-54-56-62
     c/o The Fox Companies   82
     955 Chesterbrook Blvd., Suite 125
     Wayne   19087   (Delaware County)   **Phone** 610-640-1400   **FAX** None
                                            EIN 23-2267786   **Year Created** 1983
AMV $2,098,809   **FYE** 12-00   **(Gifts Received** $0)   22   **Grants totaling** $1,069,350

Mostly local giving. High grant of **$475,000** to Temple U. (Center for Biomedical Physics). **$150,000** to Temple U. (Center for Frontier Sciences). **$100,000** to Perelman Jewish Day School. **$75,000** to National Organization for Hearing Research (a family-affiliated foundation). **$50,000** to Lubavitcher Center. **$40,000** to United Way of SE Pa. **$20,000** to Temple U. (Vital Difference Fund). **$12,200** to National Liberty Museum. **$10,000** to Feinstein Center for American Jewish History. **$8,800** to Montessori Genesis. **$7,750** American Jewish Committee. **$7,500** to Chabad Chester County. **$5,000** to Wistar Institute. **$1,000** each to Albert Einstein Healthcare Network and Institute for Contemporary Art. Other smaller contributions. **Out-of-state** giving includes **$65,000** to Friends of Israel [Israel]; **$20,000** to American Jewish Committee [NY] (Commentary); and **$14,000** to Jewish Policy Center [DC]. ∎ **PUBLICATIONS:** None ∎ **WEBSITE:** None ∎ **E-MAIL:** None ∎ **APPLICATION POLICIES & PROCEDURES:** Information not available.

O+D+T Richard J. Fox (P+T+Donor+Con) — Harry D. Fox (T)

SE-239   **Free Quaker Society**   MI-12-15-22-35-56-63
     233 East Meade Street
     Philadelphia   19118   (Philadelphia County)   **Phone** 215-242-3872   **FAX** None
                                              EIN 23-7336758   **Year Created** 1774
AMV $258,558   **FYE** 12-00   **(Gifts Received** $0)   7   **Grants totaling** $9,500

All local/nearby New Jersey giving. High grant of **$3,500** to Independence National Historical Park. **$1,000-$1,500** each to Little Brothers Friends of the Elderly, St. Paul's Memorial Church [Oaks], and Sunday Breakfast Assn. **$750** each to Child Guidance Resource Center, Old Union Church [Audubon], and Moorestown Visiting Nurse Assn. [NJ]. ∎ **PUBLICATIONS:** None ∎ **WEBSITE:** None ∎ **E-MAIL:** None ∎ **APPLICATION POLICIES & PROCEDURES:** The Foundation reports that only requests from members of the Free Quaker Society will be considered; submit requests during September/early October. The Board meets in October to award grants.

O+D+T Elkins Wetherill, Jr. (Stated Clerk+D+Con) — Radclyffe F. Thomson [Rosemont] (F) — John H. Hallock [Flourtown] (D) — Mrs. Philip Heizer [DE] (D) — George Stout Hundt [Malvern] (D) — Lester Thomas Hundt, Jr. [Newtown Square] (D) — Christopher W. Parker (D) — Mrs. Lawrence L. Stevens [NJ] (D) — Mrs. Wirt L. Thompson, Jr. [Media] (D) — Francis D. Wetherill (D) — David Wetherill Wood, Jr. [West Chester] (D) — Frederick L. Wood [Wawa] (D)

SE-240   **French Benevolent Society of Philadelphia**   MI-23-43-81
     (Contact the Society by telephone)
                                        (Chester County)   **Phone** 610-935-6995   **FAX** None
                                              EIN 23-1401532   **Year Created** 1793
AMV $1,461,312   **FYE** 10-00   **(Gifts Received** $0)   15+   **Grants totaling** $44,377

Details on scholarships/financial assistance given in 2000 are unavailable, but in the prior year three scholarships (**$3,000, $5,000** and **$11,685**) were awarded, and nine individuals received financial assistance ranging from **$250** to **$5,900**. ∎ **PUBLICATIONS:** Annual Report; application guidelines ∎ **WEBSITE:** None ∎ **E-MAIL:** None ∎ **APPLICATION POLICIES & PROCE-**

DURES: Only French citizens or French immigrants (or their descendants) who reside in Metropolitan Philadelphia area are eligible to apply for (a) financial assistance because of misfortune, age or illness, or (b) higher education scholarships to study in the U.S. or France. Preference is giving in the following order: persons of French birth, those with French-born parents, or of French extraction. Make initial contact with the Society by telephone. Scholarship applicants must prove financial need above and beyond any private/government support. A formal scholarship application form must be requested from the Society and submitted during March-June. The Board meets monthly except August.
O+D+T Christiane L. Aubry (Administrator+Con) — Pierre T. Ravacon [Fort Washington] (P) — Yves P. Quintin [Philadelphia] (VP) — Sonya Dehon Driscoll [Plymouth Meeting] (S) — John W. Nilon [Media] (F) — Carlos J. Alvare [Valley Forge] (D) — Robert E. Chatot [Bensalem] (D) — Rene A. Des Jardins [FL] (D) — K. Patricia Haley [Devon] (D) — Alison Douglas Knox [Philadelphia] (D) First Union/Wachovia (Trustee)

SE-241   Frezel Family Foundation
233 South 6th Street, #1302
Philadelphia   19106   (Philadelphia County)
MI-11-13-14-22-32-41-42-52-62
Phone 215-972-6005 **FAX** None
EIN 25-6693450   Year Created 2000
AMV $1,502,079   **FYE** 12-00   (**Gifts Received** $1,803,128)   24 **Grants totaling** $123,592
Mostly local giving. High grant of **$84,167** to Jewish Federation of Greater Philadelphia. **$13,000** to Akiba Hebrew Academy. **$5,000** to Temple U. **$2,000-$2,500** each to ALS Assn./Phillies Charities, Crohn's & Colitis Foundation of America/Philadelphia Chapter, Gerda & Kurt Klein Foundation, Jewish Community Centers of Greater Philadelphia, United Way of SE Pa. and Woodrock. **$1,000** each to Maccabi Games, Philadelphia Geriatric Center, Philadelphia Orchestra, and Temple Beth Zion-Beth Israel.
■ **PUBLICATIONS:** None ■ **WEBSITE:** None ■ **E-MAIL:** None ■ **APPLICATION POLICIES & PROCEDURES:** Information not available.
O+D+T Jerrold A. Frezel (P+Donor+Con) — Foundation donor: Julius & Ray Charlestein Foundation

---

SE-242   Friedland (Harold & Elaine) Family Foundation
210 West Rittenhouse Square, Suite 2901
Philadelphia   19103   (Philadelphia County)
MI-12-13-22-24-31-32-54-56-62-65-84
Phone 215-546-7774 **FAX** None
EIN 23-2841007   **Year Created** 1997
AMV $3,613,057   **FYE** 12-00   (**Gifts Received** $0)   33 **Grants totaling** $119,500
Mostly local giving. High grant of **$55,600** to National Liberty Museum. **$21,150** to Philadelphia Ronald McDonald House. **$5,000** to Philadelphia Museum of Art. **$2,750** to Rittenhouse Row Society. **$2,000** to Hadassah. **$1,000-$1,800** each to Arthur Ashe Youth Tennis Center, Flyers Wives Fight for Lives, Friends of Rittenhouse Square, Living Beyond Breast Cancer, National Museum of American Jewish History, Philadelphia Festival Arts, and Philadelphia Pediatric Center. Other smaller contributions for similar purposes. **Out-of-state** grants: **$10,800** to Jewish Federation of Palm Beach County [FL] and **$4,100** to Addison Reserve Cancer Unit [FL]. — In the prior year, major local grants included **$15,000** to American Cancer Society; **$11,695** to Philadelphia Ronald McDonald House; and **$10,000** each to American Interfaith Institute and Children's Hospital of Philadelphia Foundation. ■ **PUBLICATIONS:** None ■ **WEBSITE:** None ■ **E-MAIL:** None ■ **APPLICATION POLICIES & PROCEDURES:** Grant requests may be submitted in any form at any time; explain the organization's objectives and how the requested funds will be used. Alternatively, requests may be sent to: 16420 Maddalena Place, Delray Beach, FL 33446; telephone 561-638-8072.
O+D+T Elaine Friedland (T+Donor+Don) — Harold Friedland (T+Donor)

SE-243   Friendly Sons of St. Patrick, Society of
P.O. Box 969
Dublin   18917   (Bucks County)
MI-22-23-25-31-43-56-61
Phone 215-249-9337 **FAX** 215-249-9331
EIN 23-1445675   **Year Created** 1752
AMV $1,024,139   **FYE** 6-00   (**Gifts Received** $0)   17 **Grants totaling** $62,200
All giving restricted to Irish or Irish-related concerns/interests. High grant of **$25,000** for Irish Famine Memorial. **$5,000** to Jeanie Johnston Ship Program. **$1,000-$1,500** each to Assn. of Celtic Societies/CCC-Committee for Education Literature & Theater, Civil War Enactment, Irish Emigration Program, and Philadelphia Ceili Group. **$500-$700** each to Irish American Cultural Institution and four local agencies feeding the hungry on St. Patrick's Day. Also, three scholarships (**$600, $7,500** and **$16,000**) for Irish students attending Pa. colleges. — In some years giving also to Ireland for humanitarian assistance purposes. ■ **PUBLICATIONS:** None ■ **WEBSITE:** www.friendlysons.com ■ **E-MAIL:** info@friendlysons.com ■ **APPLICATION POLICIES & PROCEDURES:** Only requests dealing with Irish-related issues in the Greater Delaware Valley are accepted; most giving is for community service, research or scholarships/fellowships. Prospective applicants initially should make a telephone inquiry about the feasibility of submitting a request. Submit grant requests in a letter in April or October (deadlines are April 30th and October 31st); provide a project budget, list of major funding sources, Board member list, and IRS tax-exempt status documentation. The Board awards grants at January and June meetings.
O+D+T Elizabeth Donovan (Con) — Thomas P. O'Malley (P+F+D) — J. Thomas Showler (VP+D) — Timothy P. Dunigan, Jr. (S+D) — Thomas O. Peterman (D) — Thomas P. Coyne, Jr. (D) — John F. Donovan (D) — George J. Flannery (D) — John E. Kane (D) — John F. Kull (D) — Edward P. Last (D) — Thomas J. Lynch (D)

SE-244   Fuller (Lawrence C.), Jr. Memorial Diabetic Fund
c/o First Union/Wachovia
123 South Broad Street, PA1279
Philadelphia   19109   (Philadelphia County)
MI-31-32-35

Phone 215-670-4230 **FAX** 215-670-4236
EIN 23-2663503   **Year Created** 1991
AMV $1,085,416   **FYE** 12-00   (**Gifts Received** $0)   7 **Grants totaling** $40,000
All giving restricted to diabetes-related activities/programs. High grant of **$10,000** to Lions Club of Pa. (Diabetes Awareness Committee). **$5,000** each to Bryn Mawr Rehab, Children's Hospital of Philadelphia, Crozer-Keystone Health System, MCP-Hahnemann U, Pottstown Memorial Medical Center, and Thomas Jefferson U. ■ **PUBLICATIONS:** Grant Proposal Guidelines; application form ■ **WEBSITE:** None ■ **E-MAIL:** eugene.williams1@wachovia.com ■ **APPLICATION POLICIES & PROCEDURES:** Only institutions dealing with diabetes/hypoglycemia are eligible to apply for special support or research grants for the following: (1)

creation of consultation clinics for diabetics/hypoglycemics and families; (2) educational programs regarding diabetes/hypoglycemia; (3) advertising of highly qualified diabetic/hypoglycemic centers; and (4) promotion/support of research into the cause/management of diabetes/hypoglycemia. Grant requests must be submitted in early November on a formal application form available from the Bank (the deadline is November 15th); the application specifies required attachments. Site visits sometimes are made to organizations being considered for a grant. The Trustee Committee awards grants at a December meeting.

O+D+T Eugene J. Williams (VP at Bank+Con) — First Union/Wachovia (Trustee)

SE-245   Fund for Education
    537 Avonwood Road
    Haverford   19041   (Montgomery County)

MI-34-41-42-62
Phone 610-658-2471 **FAX** None
EIN 23-6849172 **Year Created** 1984

AMV $3,201,570 **FYE** 12-99 **(Gifts Received** $0) 4 **Grants totaling** $131,500

Two Pa. grants: **$18,000** to Beth Am Israel Discretionary Fund; **$10,500** to Perelman Day School (scholarship fund). **Out-of-state** grants; High grant of **$98,000** to Harvard Medical School and **$5,000** to Brandeis U. ■**PUBLICATIONS:** None ■ **WEBSITE:** None ■**E-MAIL:** None ■**APPLICATION POLICIES & PROCEDURES:** Grant requests may be submitted in a letter (2 pages maximum) in April—deadline is April 30th. Site visits sometimes are made to organizations being considered for a grant. The Trustees award grants at a May meeting. — Formerly called the Fund for Medical Education

O+D+T Paul M. Prusky, M.D. (T+Donor+Con) — Susan M. Prusky (T)

SE-246   Gabriele Family Foundation
    62 Bridle Way
    Newtown Square   19073   (Delaware County)

MI-14-41-45
Phone 610-355-9850 **FAX** None
EIN 23-2870613 **Year Created** 1996

AMV $244,953 **FYE** 12-99 **(Gifts Received** $0) 3 **Grants totaling** $15,666

All local giving. High grant of **$6,500** to Center School. **$6,166** to M-Able, Inc. **$3,000** to Literacy Council of Norristown. — Giving in the prior two years included **$8,500** to Community of Hope [DC] and **$4,800** to Ions, Inc. ■**PUBLICATIONS:** None ■ **WEBSITE:** None ■**E-MAIL:** None ■**APPLICATION POLICIES & PROCEDURES:** Information not available.

O+D+T Alfonse Gabriele (T+Donor+Con) — Barbara Gabriele (T+Donor)

SE-247   Garbose Family Foundation
    c/o Harriet Carter Gifts
    425 Stump Road, P.O. Box 427
    Montgomeryville   18936   (Montgomery County)

MI-12-22-31-41-42-62
Phone 215-361-5100 **FAX** None
EIN 23-7818372 **Year Created** 1995

AMV $579,225 **FYE** 11-00 **(Gifts Received** $167,974) 32 **Grants totaling** $91,054

About three-fourths local giving. High grant of **$34,007** to Jewish Federation of Greater Philadelphia. **$10,385** to Germantown Academy. **$10,100** to Children's Hospital of Philadelphia. **$3,986** to Congregation Beth Or. **$1,852** to Friends of Philadelphia Ronald McDonald House. **$1,000** each Jewish Family & Children's Service and Living Beyond Breast Cancer. **$3,270** to Philadelphia Ronald McDonald House. **$1,000-$2,400** each to Abramson Family Cancer Research Center, Academy of Music, The Wellness Community, and Wordsworth Academy. Other smaller local contributions for various purposes. **Out-of-state** giving includes **$5,000** each to Tufts U. [MA] and U. of Michigan; **$2,675** to Children's National Medical Center [DC]; and **$1,000** to Planned Parenthood Federation of America [NY]. ■**PUBLICATIONS:** None ■**WEBSITE:** None ■**E-MAIL:** None ■**APPLICATION POLICIES & PROCEDURES:** No grants awarded to individuals.

O+D+T William Garbose [Gwynedd Valley] (T+Donor+Con) — Lynne Garbose [Gwynedd Valley] (T+Donor)

SE-248   Garfield (Eugene) Foundation, The
    1031 Barberry Road
    Bryn Mawr   19010
        (Montgomery County)

MI-12-13-15-31-32-41-42-44-49-52-54-56-63
64-81
Phone Unlisted **FAX** None
EIN 23-2553258 **Year Created** 1988

AMV $9,912,479 **FYE** 11-00 **(Gifts Received** $0) 59 **Grants totaling** $1,098,909

About half/Pa. local giving. High Pa. grant of **$101,150** to Chemical Heritage Foundation. **$100,000** to Temple U. Children's Medical Center. **$42,000** to U. of Pa. **$30,000** to Drexel U. **$25,000** each to Free Library of Philadelphia, Institute for Cancer Research, and Philadelphia Orchestra. **$22,000** each to Monell Chemical Senses Center and Shipley School. **$20,000** to National Liberty Museum. **$15,000** each to Opera Company of Philadelphia and Summerbridge of Germantown. **$12,500** to Old First Reformed Church. **$11,000** to Institute for Experimental Psychiatry Research Foundation. **$10,000** to Friends of Health [Centre County]. **$9,000** to Little Flower Catholic High School for Girls. **$6,200** to University City New School. **$5,000** each to Children's Project 2000, Gratz College and INCLEN/International Clinical Epidemiology Network. **$1,000-$2,500** each to Bryn Mawr Rehab Hospital, International Arts-Medicine Assn., International House of Philadelphia, Options in Aging/Lower Merion Senior Center, University Museum of Archaeology & Anthropology, and U. of Pittsburgh. **Out-of-state** giving includes high grant of **$150,000** to National Academy of Sciences [DC]; **$50,000** each to ACLU Foundation [NY], Committee for the Scientific Investigation of Claims of the Paranormal [NY], Research America [VA], UCLA [CA], and U. of California-San Francisco; **$25,000** to U. of California-Davis; **$20,000** each to Center for Academic & Social Advancement [CA] and Rockefeller U. [NY]; **$15,000** to Minot State U. [ND]; **$11,000** to Assn. for Library & Information Science Education [VA]; and other smaller grants for various purposes. ■**PUBLICATIONS:** None ■**WEBSITE:** None ■**E-MAIL:** None ■**APPLICATION POLICIES & PROCEDURES:** Grant requests may be submitted in a letter at any time; describe the purpose of the organization. No grants awarded to individuals.

O+D+T Catheryn Stout (VP+S+Donor+Con) — Dr. Eugene Garfield (C+P+F+Donor) — Robert S. Bramson [Conshohocken] (D)

SE-249 Garrigues (Edwin B.) Trust, The MI-52
c/o Duane Morris LLP
One Liberty Place, Suite 4200 **Phone** 215-979-1779 **FAX** 215-979-1020
Philadelphia   19103 (Philadelphia County) **EIN** 23-6220616 **Year Created** 1922
AMV $5,357,377 **FYE** 12-99 **(Gifts Received** $0) 5 **Grants totaling** $200,000

Mostly local giving to accredited music schools for scholarship assistance. High grants of **$35,000** each to Swarthmore College and Temple U. **$25,000** to Curtis Institute of Music. **$18,000** to Settlement Music School. **Out-of-state** grant: **$22,000** to Westminster Choir College [NJ]. ■**PUBLICATIONS:** None ■**WEBSITE:** None ■**E-MAIL:** sdwagner@duanemorris.com ■**APPLI-CATION POLICIES & PROCEDURES:** Only accredited schools of music in the U.S. are eligible to apply on behalf of individual students. A formal application form, available from the Trust, must be completed and submitted with student data; requests may be submitted at any time; the deadline is June 1st. Site visits sometimes are made to organizations being considered for a grant. The Grant Committee meets in June-July to award grants.

O+D+T Seymour C. Wagner, Esq. (Con) — Robert W. Denious, Esq. (Co-T) First Union/Wachovia (Co-Trustee)

SE-250 Garrison Family Foundation, The MI-15-17-29-35-42
220 North Jackson Street, 2nd Floor **Phone** 610-565-2626 **FAX** 610-565-3684
Media   19063 (Delaware County) **EIN** 23-7650510 **Year Created** 1990
AMV $706,994 **FYE** 12-00 **(Gifts Received** $0) 4 **Grants totaling** $48,500

All local giving. High grant to The Center Foundation [Media] (a family-affiliated operating foundation, for a womencare program). **$17,500** to Pa. Institute of Technology (Winning Ways Project). **$6,000** to Women's Assn. for Women's Alternatives (education project). **$5,000** to RSVP of Montgomery County (Project Protégé). — Grants approved for future payment: **$40,000** to The Center Foundation and **$2,500** to RSVP of Montgomery County. ■**PUBLICATIONS:** application guidelines ■ **WEBSITE:** None ■**E-MAIL:** swankgar@aol.com ■**APPLICATION POLICIES & PROCEDURES:** The Foundation reports that giving is restricted to Southeastern Pa. and focuses on organizations which help people overcome adverse social/economic disadvantages and/or increase their access to training/education to build independence/self-sufficiency. Most grants are for special projects or general support. Generally, no grants are given to organizations with budgets exceeding $1 million, religious organizations, umbrella-funding agencies, affiliates of national/international organizations, government agencies, or for capital campaigns, conferences, deficit financing, endowment, publications, recreation, research projects, tours, trips, or special events. No grants are ever awarded to individuals. Prospective first-time applicants may submit at any time a brief letter or make a telephone inquiry about the feasibility of submitting a request. The Foundation will advise if a full proposal should be submitted and will provide detailed application information and copies of the Foundation's Proposal Cover Sheet and Constituency Information Form which must accompany any proposal; the Common Grant Application Format of Delaware Valley Grantmakers may be used in preparing a proposal. Site visits sometimes are made to organizations being considered for a grant.

O+D+T Susan K. Garrison (Executive Trustee+T+Con) — Walter R. Garrison (T+Donor) — Michael J.J. Campbell (T) — Ann-Michelle Garrison [NY] (T) — Bruce Garrison [Australia] (T) — C. Jeffrey Garrison [NY] (T) — Heather Garrison [Jenkintown] (T) — Jayne B. Garrison (T) — Jennifer Garrison [Australia] (T) — Mark R. Garrison [Jenkintown] (T) — Lawrence T. Phelan [Wynnewood] (T) — Pamela Garrison Phelan [Wynnewood]

SE-251 Garthwaite (Elsie Lee) Memorial Foundation, The MI-12-13-14-15-16-17-18-19-20-22-25-29-31
c/o Algar Enterprises, Inc. 35-45-51-52-54-55-57-71-72
1234 East Lancaster Ave., P.O. Box 709 **Phone** 610-527-8101 **FAX** 610-527-7808
Bryn Mawr   19010 (Montgomery County) **EIN** 23-6290877 **Year Created** 1943
AMV $5,548,151 **FYE** 12-00 **(Gifts Received** $121,839) 95 **Grants totaling** $373,907

Mostly local giving. High local grant of **$6,000** to Wheels, Inc. **$5,000** each to Academy of Community Music, Aid for Friends, Baker Industries, Bryn Mawr Rehab (Crusin' not Boozin' Program), Daemion House, Dignity Housing, Inc., Drueding Center-Project Rainbow, Fellowship House of Conshohocken, Historic Bartram's Garden, Kardon Institute of the Arts for People with Disabilities, Lower Merion Township Scholarship Fund, Mommy's Light Lives On Fund, Mural Arts Program, Need in Deed, Norristown Zoo, Pa. Ballet, People's Light & Theatre Company, Philadelphia Orchestra, Philadelphia Zoo, Please Touch Museum, Recording for the Blind & Dyslexic, Riverbend Environmental Education Center, Senior Adult Activities Center of Montco, Settlement Music School, Urban Bridges at St. Gabriel's, Voyage House, WHYY-TV12, and Working Wardrobe. **$4,000** each to 1812 Productions, Academy of Vocal Arts, Big Sisters of Philadelphia, CASA/Youth Advocates, Darlington Fine Arts Center, Delco Memorial Foundation, ECS/Advocate L.I.F.E. Program, Kelly Anne Dolan Memorial Fund, Lakeside Educational Network, Philabundance, Philadelphia Community Academy, Suburban Music School, Surrey Services for Seniors, VNA-Community Services, Wayne Art Center, White-Williams Scholars, Williamson Free School of Mechanical Trades, Wilma Theatre, and Woodrock. **$2,000-$3,500** each to Adoption Center of Delaware Valley, Art Sanctuary, Astral Art Services, Bethel-Bryn Mawr Child Care & Development Center, Camp Dreamcatcher, Camp Sunshine, Care Center for Christ, Chester County Cares for Kids, Children's Aid Society of Montco, Community Action Agency of Delco, Corporate Alliance for Drug Education, Episcopal Community Services, First United Church of Germantown, Hedgerow Theatre, Hope Springs Equestrian Therapy, Horizons Unlimited, The Lighthouse, Main Line Art Center, Main Line YMCA, Montgomery County Assn. for the Blind, Mt. Zion African Methodist Episcopal Church, NetworkArts, Nonprofit Technology Resources, North Light Community Center, Old First Reformed Church, Pals for Life, The PARTNERS Program, Pa. Home of the Sparrow, Philadelphia Citizens for Children & Youth, Philadelphia City Sail, Philadelphia Physicians for Social Responsibility, Philadelphia Young Playwrights Festival, Philadelphians Concerned About Housing, Point Breeze Performing Arts Center, Resources for Children's Health, RSVP of Montgomery County, Taller Puertorriqueno, Wissahickon Hospice, and Young Audiences of Eastern Pa. Other smaller local grants. **Out-of-state** giving includes high grant of **$20,000** to Jewish Board of Family & Children's Services [NY]; **$7,500** to Life Experience School [MA]; and **$5,000** each to CRC Recovery Program [FL] and Little Sisters of the Assumption Family Health Service [NY]. ■**PUBLICATIONS:** application guidelines ■**WEBSITE:** None ■**E-MAIL:** tk8101@aol.com ■**APPLICATION POLICIES & PROCEDURES:** The Foundation reports that support focuses on the Greater Philadelphia area. Most giving is for programs which (1) provide for the physical/emotional well-being of children and young people, or (2) seek to enable young people, particularly the needy, to reach their full potential through education, empowerment, and exposure to the arts. Most grants are awarded to smaller organizations with annual or project budgets not exceeding $1 Million. No grants are awarded to public, private, or parochial schools, colleges and universities, or to individuals. Prospective applicants should first submit a letter requesting permission to submit a grant request; if the Foundation responds favorably, guidelines and a Grant Request Cover Sheet will be provided. Deadlines for completed applications are March 31st and August 31st. Site visits sometimes are made to organizations being considered for a grant. The Board awards grants at Spring and Fall meetings. — Formerly called The Leeland Foundation.

O+D+T Thomas M. Kaneda (S+T+Con) — Diane Garthwaite [MA] (P+T) — John A. Acuff (VP+T) — A. Alexander Ridley (F+T) — Bettina Buschel [NY] (T+Donor) — Wendy Garthwaite DeMarco (T) — Ann Bennett Garthwaite (T) — Kirsten A. Kling (T) — Paul C. Lowerre [NY] (T) — June A. Stack (T) — Bruce Buschel [NY] (Donor) — Bettina Lowerre [VT] (Donor)

SE-252   **Gatter Foundation**   MI-13-22-29-32-42-43-61
           c/o Public Mortgage Company
           2300 Computer Ave., Suite H-42
           Willow Grove   19090   (Montgomery County)   **Phone** 215-830-8900 **FAX** None
AMV $261,227   **FYE** 12-00   (**Gifts Received** $106,887)   **EIN** 23-6243026   **Year Created** 1952
                                                                    33 **Grants totaling** $121,236

Limited local giving. High Pa. grant of **$1,000** to American Cancer Society. **$100-$500** each for many health/human services, youth agencies, educational institutions, religious organizations, and others. **Out-of-state** giving includes high grant of **$107,336** to Holy Spirit High School [NJ] (scholarship fund) and small contributions for various purposes, mostly in NJ or NY. ■**PUBLICATIONS:** None ■**WEBSITE:** None ■**E-MAIL:** None ■**APPLICATION POLICIES & PROCEDURES:** No grants awarded to individuals.

O+D+T L. Gene Gatter (C+T+Donor+Con) — Joseph Livezey (S+F+T) Donor: Estate of Joseph Formica

---

SE-253   **Gentle (James C.) Foundation**   MI-42
           c/o Morgan Lewis & Bockius
           1701 Market Street
           Philadelphia   19103   (Philadelphia County)   **Phone** 215-963-5212 **FAX** 215-963-5299
AMV $4,177,197   **FYE** 12-00   (**Gifts Received** $0)   **EIN** 23-2612150   **Year Created** 1990
                                                                    2 **Grants totaling** $160,510

Both grants to U. of Pa. (for Penn-in-Washington program and underwriting a Burke Symposium); all grants awarded since the Foundation's inception have been to U. of Pa. ■**PUBLICATIONS:** None ■**WEBSITE:** None ■**E-MAIL:** None ■**APPLICATION POLICIES & PROCEDURES:** The Foundation reports that grants for charitable, scientific, literary, or educational purposes must be for the purpose of fostering conservative political philosophy and thought; the U. of Pa. receives special consideration in awarding grants but the co-trustees are not required to limited awards to Penn. No grants awarded to individuals.

O+D+T Joseph A. O'Connor, Jr. Esq. (Co-T+Con) — William E. Lingelbach, Jr. Esq. (Co-T)

SE-254   **Genuardi (Charles & Anne S.) Family Foundation**   MI-41-56-61
           c/o McCabe, 307 Thomas Drive
           King of Prussia   19406   (Montgomery County)   **Phone** 610-279-2480 **FAX** None
AMV $2,131,828   **FYE** 12-01   (**Gifts Received** $2,020,000) **EIN** 23-2984191   **Year Created** 1998
                                                                    2 **Grants totaling** $15,000

All local giving. **$10,000** to Kennedy-Kendrick Catholic High School. **$5,000** to Catholic Heritage Center. ■**PUBLICATIONS:** None ■**WEBSITE:** None ■**E-MAIL:** None ■**APPLICATION POLICIES & PROCEDURES:** Information not available.

O+D+T Josephine Genuardi McCabe (F+D+Con) — Gasper A. Genuardi [Conshohocken] (P+D+Donor) — Charles A. Genuardi [Norristown] (VP+D) — Antoinette Genuardi Deever [Collegeville] (S+D+Donor) — Paula Genuardi Molnar (D)

SE-255   **Genuardi Family Foundation**   MI-12-13-14-15-16-17-19-25-29-31-33-35-39
           c/o Blue Bell Executive Campus   43-44-45-49-51-52-53-54-55
           470 Norristown Road, Suite 300   **Phone** 610-834-2030 **FAX** 610-834-5786
           Blue Bell   19422   (Montgomery County)   **EIN** 23-3041300   **Year Created** 2000
AMV $18,667,825   **FYE** 12-01   (**Gifts Received** $12,973,753) 66 **Grants totaling** $72,500

All local giving; information on grant sizes was unavailable. **CULTURE GRANTS:** Academy of Community Music, Arden Theatre Company, Artreach, Community Conservatory of Music, Old York Road Symphony Society, Philadelphia Museum of Art, Settlement Music School, Ursinus College, and Woodmere Art Museum. **EDUCATION GRANTS:** Ancillae-Assumpta Academy, Center School, Conshohocken Catholic School, The Crossroads School, Gwynedd Mercy Academy, Kennedy-Kenrick Catholic High School, Literacy Council of Norristown, Lower Providence Community Library, Mercy Vocational High School, Norristown Education Fund, St. Joseph's Preparatory School, Timothy School Development Fund, Vanguard School, and Woodlynde School. **HEALTH/WELLNESS GRANTS:** Advance Lane Training & Employment Corp., ALS Association/Greater Philadelphia Chapter, Center for Autistic Children, Children's Hospital of Philadelphia, Community Housing Services, Community Volunteers in Medicine, HealthLink Medical Center, Living Beyond Breast Cancer, Montgomery County Emergency Services, and Montgomery Hospital. **HUMAN SERVICES GRANTS:** Bucks ARC, Baptist Children's Services, Big Brothers/Big Sisters of Montgomery County, Camp Rainbow, Central Montgomery Mental Health/Mental Retardation Center, Cradle of Hope, Developmental Enterprises Corp., Devereux Foundation, Family Services, Gateway Employment Resources, Greater Philadelphia Food Bank, Habitat for Humanity/Montgomery County, hireAbility, Hospitality House of Philadelphia, Make-A-Wish Foundation of Philadelphia & SE Pa., Mom's House, Montgomery County OIC, Network of Victim Assistance, Norristown Ministries, Norristown Police Athletic League, Patrician Society of Central Norristown, Philadelphia Ronald McDonald House, Resources for Human Development, Saunders House, Silver Springs-Martin Luther School, Society of St. Vincent DePaul, Southwest Community Enrichment Center, St. Mary's

Villa for Children, Superkids of Montgomery County, Support Center for Child Advocates, Ambler Area YMCA, Variety Club, and Volunteers in Action. ■**PUBLICATIONS:** brochure with statement of program policy and application guidelines ■**WEBSITE:** www.genuardifamilyfoundation.org ■**E-MAIL:** info@genuardifamilyfoundation.org ■**APPLICATION POLICIES & PROCEDURES:** The Foundation reports that giving focuses on the Delaware Valley for specific projects/programs in five areas: (1) Education—programs that foster innovative approaches to learning and providing access for persons with low income or special needs; (2) Health—care for persons with mental or physical disabilities or those not receiving appropriate care; (3) Human Services—programs assisting persons who are economically, mentally or physically challenged); and (4) Cultural—events, programs, or organizations which enhance community life. Preference is given to projects receiving broad-based community support. Grant requests may include some funding for general operating support. On a limited basis, requests for capital campaigns (facilities or equipment) will be considered, and for organizational capacity building. No grants are awarded to individuals, or for annual appeals/solicitation letters, fraternal/civic organizations, political candidates, lobbying, endowment, general funding appeals, debt reduction, environmental issues/initiatives, or other foundations. Prospective applicants must first submit a brief letter which includes contact information, organizational background, a brief project description, and the specific funding being requested. After review, applicants will receive either a denial, a request for more information, or an invitation to submit a proposal at which time the proposal requirements will be provided. Proposals should be submitted only after being requested to do so; if a proposal is requested, it must be during September-October (deadline is October 31st). Site visits sometimes are made to organizations being considered for a grant. Grants are awarded by May 1st of the following year. — **Note:** The Foundation no longer is associated with Genuardi's Family Markets.

O+D+T Robert C. Fernandez, Esq. (Executive Director+Con) — James V. Genuardi [West Conshohocken] (P+D+Donor) — Michael A. Genuardi [Gwynedd Valley] (VP+D+Donor) — Laurence P. Genuardi [North Wales] (S+D+Donor) — Dominic S. Genuardi, Jr. [Gwynedd Valley] (F+D+Donor) — Anthony D. Genuardi [Lansdale] (D+Donor) — Charles A. Genuardi [Wayne] (D+Donor) — David T. Genuardi [Norristown] (D+Donor) — Francis L. Genuardi [Valley Forge] (D+Donor) — Gasper A. Genuardi [Conshohocken] (D+Donor)

SE-256 **Genuardi (Frank O.) Family Foundation**
1906 Brandon Road
Norristown 19403 (Montgomery County)

MI-14-41-61
Phone 610-834-8100 **FAX** None
EIN 23-2828488 **Year Created** 1995

AMV $449,548 **FYE** 9-01 **(Gifts Received** $0) 4 **Grants totaling** $25,000

About half local giving. **$5,000** each to Devereux Foundation, The Gesu School, and Mercy Vocational High School. **Out-of-state** grant: **$10,000** to Pope John II Foundation [Italy]. ■**PUBLICATIONS:** None ■**WEBSITE:** None ■**E-MAIL:** None ■**APPLICATION POLICIES & PROCEDURES:** No grants awarded to individuals.

O+D+T Frank O. Genuardi (VP+D+Donor+Con) — Lawrence P. Genuardi (P+D) — Francis L. Genuardi (S+F+D+Donor)

SE-257 **Germantown Relief Society Foundation**
c/o First Union/Wachovia
123 South Broad Street, PA1279
Philadelphia 19109 (Philadelphia County)

MI-13-15-17-22-25-31-35-41-43-65
Phone 215-670-4228 **FAX** 215-670-4236
EIN 23-6215778 **Year Created** 1873

AMV $1,207,597 **FYE** 9-00 **(Gifts Received** $0) 17 **Grants totaling** $60,000

All giving restricted to organizations that provide direct relief to residents of Philadelphia's Germantown area; all grants are for general support. High grant of **$8,000** to White-Williams Scholars. **$5,000** each to Center in the Park, First Presbyterian Church of Philadelphia, Northwest Meals on Wheels, St. Vincent's Inn Dwelling, and Whosoever Gospel Mission. **$4,000** to Ghebre Michael Inn. **$3,000-$3,500** each to Germantown Hospital & Community Health, Interfaith Hospitality Network, Jeanes Community Outreach, Tabor Children's Service, and Wisdom YMCA. **$2,000** each to Metropolitan Career Center, Pastorius School, and Pickett Middle School. **$1,000** to Germantown Friends School. **$500** to Philabundance. ■**PUBLICATIONS:** None ■**WEBSITE:** None ■**E-MAIL:** diane.stables@wachovia.com ■**APPLICATION POLICIES & PROCEDURES:** Only organizations providing direct emergency relief to residents of Philadelphia's Germantown area are eligible to apply; no other requests will be considered. Submit grant requests in any form in September-October (deadline is October 31st); include an annual report, organizational/project budgets, and IRS tax-exempt status documentation. The Dispensing Committee awards grants at a November meeting.

O+D+T Diane O. Stables (VP at Bank+Con) — and a 15-member Dispensing Committee — First Union/Wachovia (Trustee)

SE-258 **Gershman (Joel & Elaine) Foundation**
250 South 18th Street
Philadelphia 19103 (Philadelphia County)

MI-15-22-31-32-42-52-53-54-62
Phone 215-546-3262 **FAX** 215-546-5343
EIN 22-2529629 **Year Created** 1984

AMV $4,034,235 **FYE** 11-00 **(Gifts Received** $0) 51 **Grants totaling** $151,234

About four-fifths local giving; some grants comprise multiple payments. High grant of **$21,600** to Philadelphia Museum of Art. **$16,000** to U. of the Arts. **$13,500** to Franklin Institute. **$10,000** to Wills Eye Hospital Women's Committee. **$5,000-$5,500** each to Fox Chase Cancer Center, Friends of Rittenhouse Square, Jewish Community Centers of Greater Philadelphia, National Museum of American Jewish History, and Philadelphia Geriatric Center. **$3,944** to The Rittenhouse Benefit. **$3,805** to Congregation Rodeph Shalom. **$2,800** to Philadelphia Orchestra. **$2,000** to Heart of Variety Club. **$1,000** each to Dance Celebration-Annenberg, For the Love of Life, National Organization for Hearing Research, Thomas Jefferson U. Hospital, and Wistar Institute. Other smaller local contributions for various purposes. **Out-of-state** giving includes **$20,000** to Smith College [MA]; **$10,000** to Glaucoma Foundation of NY; and **$5,000** each to Aspen Music Festival [CO] and Cornell U. [NY]. ■**PUBLICATIONS:** None ■**WEBSITE:** None ■**E-MAIL:** None ■**APPLICATION POLICIES & PROCEDURES:** Grant requests may be submitted in any form at any time. — Formerly called the Joel Gershman Foundation.

O+D+T Joel Gershman (P+D+Donor+Con) — Sylvan M. Cohen, Esq. (VP+D) — Elaine Levitt Gershman (S+F+D) — J. David Levitt (D) — William Levitt, III (D)

SE-259 Gerstley (William), II Foundation
c/o Gerstley Estates
335 One Penn Center, 1617 JFK Boulevard
Philadelphia 19103   (Philadelphia County)

MI-11-12-19-22-42-51-52-55-56-57-62

Phone 215-563-8886 **FAX** 215-972-0295
EIN 23-6275982   **Year Created** 1954

AMV $643,306   **FYE** 12-00   **(Gifts Received** $0)   37 **Grants totaling** $72,005

Mostly local giving. High grant of **$15,000** to United Way of SE Pa. **$12,500** to Regional Performing Arts Center. **$6,350** to Philadelphia Orchestra. **$5,000** each to Academy of Music and Jewish Family & Children's Agency. **$4,200** to Federation Allied Jewish Appeal. **$3,000** to Pa. Ballet. **$1,000** each to Federation Day Care Services, Temple U. (music dept.), and WHYY. Other local contributions **$100-$500** for various purposes. **Out-of-state** giving includes **$10,000** to Crossroads Club [FL] and **$2,000** to Friends of the Children [NY]. ■**PUBLICATIONS:** None ■**WEBSITE:** None ■**E-MAIL:** None ■**APPLICATION POLICIES & PROCEDURES:** The Foundation reports that grants generally are limited to special projects, building funds, and research. Grant requests may be submitted in a letter at any time.

O+D+T Carol K. Gerstley (T+Con) — Leon C. Sunstein, Jr. (T)

SE-260 Gibb Foundation, The
c/o Wolf, Block, Schorr & Solis-Cohen
1650 Arch Street, 22nd Floor
Philadelphia 19103   (Philadelphia County)

MI-41-42

Phone 215-977-2090 **FAX** 215-977-2990
EIN 23-6766810   **Year Created** 1984

AMV $1,135,200   **FYE** 7-00   **(Gifts Received** $0)   8 **Grants totaling** $46,500

About four-fifths Pa. giving; all grants are for general fund support. High grants of **$7,000** each to Bloomsburg U., Dickinson College, Lehigh U., and Ursinus College. **$5,000** each to Gettysburg College and Lebanon Valley U. **Out-of-state** grants: **$4,500** to Pennsauken High School [NJ] and **$4,000** to Deptford High School [NJ]. ■**PUBLICATIONS:** None ■**WEBSITE:** None ■**E-MAIL:** rfriedman@wolfblock.com ■**APPLICATION POLICIES & PROCEDURES:** Grant requests may be submitted in any form at any time.

O+D+T Edwina A. Robb [NJ] (T+Con) — Robert I. Friedman, Esq. (D) — Matthew H. Kamens, Esq. (D) — F. Richard Robb [NJ] (D) — Ronald W. Robb [NJ] (D)

SE-261 Gilbert Foundation, The
c/o Alfred A. Gilbert Realtors
135 South 19th Street, Suite 503
Philadelphia 19103   (Philadelphia County)

MI-22-32-41-52-62-64

Phone 215-563-2728 **FAX** None
EIN 23-2155419   **Year Created** 1982

AMV $570,810   **FYE** 12-00   **(Gifts Received** $0)   8 **Grants totaling** $69,065

Mostly local giving. High grant of **$30,250** to Federation Allied Jewish Appeal. **$18,000** to Jewish Federation of Greater Philadelphia. **$10,000** to Crohn's & Colitis Foundation. **$7,000** to Reconstructionist Rabbinical College. **$1,000-$1,500** each to National Liberty Museum, Penncrest High School [Media], and Prince Music Theater. ■**PUBLICATIONS:** None ■**WEBSITE:** None ■ **E-MAIL:** None ■**APPLICATION POLICIES & PROCEDURES:** No grants awarded to individuals.

O+D+T Alfred A. Gilbert (T+Con) — Louise Gilbert (T)

SE-262 Giliberti (Michael A.) Foundation, The
c/o St. Philip's Catholic Church
437 Ridge Pike
Lafayette Hill 19444   (Montgomery County)

MI-22-41-61

Phone 610-834-1975 **FAX** None
EIN 25-1599451   **Year Created** 1989

AMV $234,800   **FYE** 12-00   **(Gifts Received** $0)   2 **Grants totaling** $4,500

All local giving. **$2,500** to The Oratory/St. Francis Xavier Rectory [Philadelphia]. **$2,000** to Nativity Blessed Virgin Mary School [Media]. — Giving in the prior year included **$6,000** to Catholic Charities and other grants to the above institutions. ■**PUBLICATIONS:** None ■**WEBSITE:** None ■**E-MAIL:** None ■**APPLICATION POLICIES & PROCEDURES:** Grant requests may be submitted in a letter at any time.

O+D+T Rev. Charles R. Vance (T+Con) — Rev. Robert Vogen [Aston] (T)

SE-263 Gimbel (Ellis A.) Charitable Trust
c/o Wolf, Block, Schorr & Solis-Cohen
1650 Arch Street, 22nd Floor
Philadelphia 19103   (Philadelphia County)

MI-22-44-52-53-55-62-84

Phone 215-977-2106 **FAX** 215-405-3706
EIN 23-6503956   **Year Created** 1952

AMV $1,477,847   **FYE** 12-00   **(Gifts Received** $0)   14 **Grants totaling** $77,400

About one-third local giving. High Pa. grant of **$8,000** to Esther M. Klein Art Gallery/University City Science Center. **$5,100** to Old York Road Little League. **$5,000** to West Chester Pop Warner Football League. **$2,500** to West Chester Chamber Orchestra. **Out-of-state** giving includes high grant of **$12,000** to Charlestown Lacrosse [MA]; **$10,500** to American Jewish Committee [NY]; **$10,000** to Rangeley Library Assn. [ME]; and smaller grants for educational and cultural purposes, many to New England. ■**PUBLICATIONS:** None ■**WEBSITE:** None ■ **E-MAIL:** dglyn@wolfblock.com ■**APPLICATION POLICIES & PROCEDURES:** The Foundation reports that a major interest is to provide entertainment for underprivileged children. Grant requests may be submitted in a letter at any time; include a project budget.

O+D+T David R. Glyn, Esq. (Con) — Paul A. Gimbel [CT] (T) — Doris Gimbel Simon [NY] (T) — Sally Gimbel Taussig (T)

SE-264 **Ginsberg (James & Arlene) Foundation, The**
1496 Hampton Road
Rydal 19046 (Montgomery County)
AMV $25,983 **FYE** 12-00 **(Gifts Received** $0)

MI-22-32-62
Phone 215-887-4343 **FAX** None
EIN 23-6697761 **Year Created** 1981
25 **Grants totaling** $11,095

Mostly local giving. High grant of **$6,000** to Federation Allied Jewish Appeal. **$1,590** to Congregation Rodeph Shalom. Other local contributions **$35-$250** for various purposes. **Out-of-state** giving includes **$971** to Lyme Disease Assn. of NJ and other smaller contributions. ■**PUBLICATIONS:** None ■**WEBSITE:** None ■**E-MAIL:** None ■**APPLICATION POLICIES & PROCEDURES:** Grant requests may be submitted in a letter at any time; provide a detailed project description, amount of funding requested, and include IRS tax-exempt status documentation.

O+D+T James J. Ginsberg (T+Donor+Con) — Arlene Ginsberg (T) — Morris A. Wilensky, CPA (T)

SE-265 **Ginsburg Family Foundation, The**
1016 Sutton Terrace, 50 Belmont Ave.
Bala Cynwyd 19004 (Montgomery County)
AMV $12,623 **FYE** 12-00 **(Gifts Received** $46,185)

MI-15-22-35-42-43-81-82
Phone 610-660-0370 **FAX** None
EIN 23-2980572 **Year Created** 1998
22 **Grants totaling** $59,285

Mostly local giving; grants are for scholarship programs except as noted. High grant of **$25,000** to American Assn. for Ben-Gurion U. [Jenkintown]. **$5,000** to World Affairs Council of Philadelphia (general support). **$3,831** to LaSalle U. **$3,000** to Temple U. **$1,500-$2,500** each, all for general support, to Linda Creed Breast Cancer Foundation, Middle East Forum, and Philadelphia Geriatric Center. **$1,000** to Anti-Defamation League (general support). **$904** to LaSalle U. Other smaller local contributions for various charitable purposes. **Out-of-state** giving includes **$4,000** to Syracuse U. [NY]; **$2,870** to Bob Jones U. [SC]; and **$2,700** to Brigham Young U. [UT]. ■**PUBLICATIONS:** None ■**WEBSITE:** None ■**E-MAIL:** None ■**APPLICATION POLICIES & PROCEDURES:** Information not available.

O+D+T Stanley D. Ginsburg (C+Con) — Arlene Ginsburg (D)

SE-266 **Gitlin Family Foundation**
c/o Equipment Systems & Devices, Inc.
270 New Jersey Drive
Fort Washington 19034 (Montgomery County)
AMV $978,166 **FYE** 11-00 **(Gifts Received** $0)

MI-12-14-15-17-22-25-29-31-32-52-62
Phone 215-628-0860 **FAX** None
EIN 22-2770930 **Year Created** 1986
30 **Grants totaling** $63,350

Mostly local giving. High grant of **$25,000** to Jewish Federation of Greater Philadelphia. **$5,000** to Abington Memorial Hospital. **$3,500** to Congregation Beth Or. **$3,000** to Red Cross. **$2,000** each to ALS Hope Foundation and Jewish Family & Children's Service. **$1,000-$1,500** each to Children's Hospital of Philadelphia, Curtis Institute of Music, Fox Chase Cancer Center, Interfaith of Ambler, Laurel Home Shelter, Montgomery County Assn. for the Blind, Pa. School for the Deaf, Philabundance, Philadelphia Geriatric Center, Philadelphia Orchestra, Philadelphia Ronald McDonald House, Women's Center of Montgomery County, and several Jewish and health/human services agencies. **Out-of-state** grants/contributions for health and human service purposes. ■**PUBLICATIONS:** None ■**WEBSITE:** None ■**E-MAIL:** None ■**APPLICATION POLICIES & PROCEDURES:** Grant requests may be submitted in any form at any time.

O+D+T Harvey S. Gitlin [Maple Glen] (T+Donor+Con) — Phyllis S. Gitlin [Maple Glen] (T+Donor)

SE-267 **Giving Productively, Inc.**
c/o Radnor Financial Advisors, Inc.
485 Devon Park Drive, Suite 119
Wayne 19087 (Chester County)
AMV $703,141 **FYE** 12-00 **(Gifts Received** $0)

MI-22-41-61
Phone 610-975-0280 **FAX** None
EIN 23-2931801 **Year Created** 1997
1 **Grant of** $27,220

Sole grant to The Gesu School [Philadelphia] — Giving in prior years include **$14,000** each to Old St. Joseph's Church and Salvation Army. ■**PUBLICATIONS:** None ■**WEBSITE:** None ■**E-MAIL:** None ■**APPLICATION POLICIES & PROCEDURES:** Information not available.

O+D+T C. Ian Sym-Smith (P+S+F+D+Donor+Con) — Alexandra Smith (D) — Andrea Claudia Sym-Smith (D) — Andrew James Sym-Smith (D) — David Bruce Sym-Smith (D)

SE-268 **Gizzio (John A.), Sr. Charitable Foundation**
c/o American Computer Estimating, Inc.
1155 Phoenixville Pike, Suite 109
West Chester 19380 (Chester County)
AMV $95,509 **FYE** 6-01 **(Gifts Received** $213,958)

MI-22-41-63
Phone 610-429-5200 **FAX** None
EIN 23-2900098 **Year Created** 1997
17 **Grants totaling** $213,802

High grant of **$30,000** to Christ's Presbyterian Church [Philadelphia]. **$25,000** to Stepping Stone Education Center [West Chester]. **$5,000** to Greentree Ministries [Bryn Mawr]. **$2,000** to Upper Bucks Christian School. **Out-of-state** giving—location unknown except as noted—includes **$23,492** to New Castle Baptist Academy [DE]; **$23,000** to World Reach, Inc.; **$20,000** each to Concord Christian Academy [DE] and Mount Hope Church; and **$15,000** to Castlewood Baptist Church. ■**PUBLICATIONS:** None ■**WEBSITE:** None ■**E-MAIL:** None ■**APPLICATION POLICIES & PROCEDURES:** Grant requests may be submitted in a letter at any time. Site visits sometimes are made to organizations being considered for a grant.

O+D+T John A. Gizzio, Jr. [Aston (D+Con) — Joyce Gizzio (D) — Robert Gizzio (D) — Janet Peterkin [Thornbury] (D) Corporate donor: American Computer Estimating, Inc.

SE-269   Glaberson (Sandra) Foundation, The   MI-17-22-42-54-57-62-71-83-84
c/o Rome & Glaberson
One South Broad Street, Suite 1630   **Phone** 215-751-9700 **FAX** None
Philadelphia 19107   (Philadelphia County)   **EIN** 23-2774133   **Year Created** 1994
AMV $769,079   **FYE** 12-00   **(Gifts Received** $0)   21 **Grants totaling** $38,400

Mostly local giving. High grant of **$10,000** to Temple U. Law School. **$5,490** to National Liberty Museum. **$5,000** to Women's Law Project. **$4,000** to Temple U. (Owls Athletic Fund). **$1,900** to Beth Sholom. **$1,000-$1,500** each to Closely Watched Films [Doylestown], Federation Allied Jewish Appeal, Golden Slipper Club, James Michener Museum, Pennypack Ecological Restoration Trust, and WHYY. Other smaller local contributions. **Out-of-state** grant: **$2,750** to American Craft Museum [NY]. ■ **PUBLICATIONS:** None ■**WEBSITE:** None ■**E-MAIL:** None ■**APPLICATION POLICIES & PROCEDURES:** Information not available.

O+D+T Arnold Glaberson, Esq. [Huntingdon Valley] (P+D+Donor+Con) — Amy Glaberson [CA] (VP+Donor)

SE-270   GlaxoSmithKline Foundation   MI-88
c/o GlaxoSmithKline
One Franklin Plaza, P.O. Box 7929   **Phone** 215-751-7024 **FAX** None
Philadelphia 19101   (Philadelphia County)   **EIN** 23-2120418   **Year Created** 1967
AMV $3,401,675   **FYE** 12-00   **(Gifts Received** $3,598,675)   2500+ **Grants totaling** $3,525,509

All Foundation giving is presently limited to Matching Gifts for various types of nonprofit organizations and institututions in the United States and its possessions; see details below. ■**PUBLICATIONS:** Matching Gift Program brochure ■**WEBSITE:** None ■**E-MAIL:** None ■**APPLICATION POLICIES & PROCEDURES:** Matching gifts (to those of employees/retirees) have a $25 minimum, $10,000 maximum/employee/year and are limited to (1) Educational Institutions: accredited, degree-granting, public and private, two- and four-year colleges/universities, graduate and professional schools; private elementary/secondary schools; and education-funding conduit foundations/organizations like United Negro College Fund; (2) Healthcare Organizations: accredited nonprofit hospitals; nonprofit medical research, healthcare education, or healthcare delivery agencies—like VNA; (3) Human Service Organizations: all types of nonprofit human services agencies; and (4) Arts/Cultural Organizations: performing arts companies, performing art centers, arts councils, cultural centers, museums, arboreta/botanical gardens, zoos, historical associations, public libraries, and public broadcasting stations. Other restrictions may apply. — Note: Most of GlaxoSmithKline's philanthropic giving is through 'Community Partnership,' a corporate-giving program which allocates about 95% for community-based healthcare initiatives worldwide and 5% for Science Education or Community Betterment. Detailed information on the Community Partnership program is on the websites: www.gsk.com/community/gcp_criteria.htm -and- www.gsk.com/community/namerica.htm. Alternatively, contact the Director, North American Community Partnerships, c/o the Foundation. — Formerly called SmithKline Beecham Foundation.

O+D+T Emily Gerasimoff (Program Officer, Matching Gifts+Con) — Jean Glenn (Director, North American Community Partnerships) — Robert W. Carr, M.P.H. (P+D) — Corporate donor: Glaxo SmithKline

---

SE-271   Glencairn Foundation   MI-41-63
c/o Pitcairn Trust Company
3000 Pitcairn Place, 165 Township Line Road   **Phone** 215-887-6700 **FAX** 215-881-6092
Jenkintown 19046   (Montgomery County)   **EIN** 23-1429828   **Year Created** 1950
AMV $17,412,426   **FYE** 12-00   **(Gifts Received** $0)   13 **Grants totaling** $882,265

All local giving for Swedenborgian purposes. Nine grants totaling **$570,265** to General Church of New Jerusalem. Three grants totaling **$310,000** to Academy of the New Church. **$2,000** to Bryn Athyn Church of New Jerusalem. ■**PUBLICATIONS:** None ■**WEBSITE:** None ■**E-MAIL:** None ■**APPLICATION POLICIES & PROCEDURES:** Grant requests in any form may be submitted at any time.

O+D+T Clark Pitcairn (P+D+Con) — Gary Pitcairn (VP+Investment Manager+Donor) — Dirk Junge (S+D) — Laird Pendleton (F+D) — Emily Bau-Madsen (D) — Brandon Junge (D) — Kim Junge (D) — Charles S. Cole, Jr. (Donor) — James F. Junge (Donor) — Garthowen Pitcairn (Donor) — Lachlan Pitcairn (Donor) — Michael Pitcairn

---

SE-272   Gold Family Foundation   MI-22-31-41-42-43-45-52-54-62-64-82
252 Ironwood Circle   **Phone** 215-572-5520 **FAX** None
Elkins Park 19027   (Montgomery County)   **EIN** 22-2783283   **Year Created** 1986
AMV $1,680,157   **FYE** 11-00   **(Gifts Received** $0)   32 **Grants totaling** $265,517

About four-fifths local giving. High grant of **$50,000** to Thomas Jefferson U. Hospital. **$34,465** to Congregation Adath Jeshurun. **$25,000** each to Central Agency for Jewish Education and U. of Pa./Penn Literacy Network. **$20,000** to Perelman Jewish Day School. **$12,500** to Presbyterian Hospital. **$10,100** to Medowbrook School. **$5,000** to Miquon School (scholarship fund). **$4000-$4,817** each to Central High School (Music Dept.), Congregation Beth Or, and National Liberty Museum. **$1,000** each to Gratz College and Montgomery County Emergency Services. Other smaller local contributions for various purposes. **Out-of-state** giving includes **$25,000** to American Technion Society [NY]; **$20,000** to Masorti Foundation [MD]; **$10,000** to Megiddo Expedition [NY]; and **$6,000** to Jewish Theological Seminary of America [NY]. ■**PUBLICATIONS:** None ■**WEBSITE:** None ■**E-MAIL:** None ■**APPLICATION POLICIES & PROCEDURES:** No grants awarded to individuals.

O+D+T Claire Gold (D+Manager+Con) — Joshua Gold [Wyncote] (D) — Julie Gold-Goldenberg [Philadelphia] (D) — R. Michael Gold [Gwynedd Valley] (T)

SE-273 Goldberg (Raymond & Ellen) Foundation
c/o Penn Maid Foods, Inc.
2701 Red Lion Road
Philadelphia 19154   (Philadelphia County)

MI-12-15-22-31-32-41-42-62
Phone 215-934-6000 **FAX** 215-969-4387
EIN 22-2787780   **Year Created** 1987

AMV $450,334   **FYE** 11-00   **(Gifts Received** $0)   96 **Grants totaling** $61,332

Mostly local giving; some grants comprise multiple payments. High grant of **$18,000** to Federation Allied Jewish Appeal. **$12,730** to Har Zion Temple. **$3,000** to Conquer Fragile X Foundation. **$2,500** to Jewish National Fund. **$2,000** to St. Joseph's U. **$1,000-$1,500** each to Food Marketing Education Foundation, Haverford School, and Philadelphia Geriatric Center. **$800** to Children's Hospital of Philadelphia Foundation. Other local contributions **$15-$700** for various purposes. **Out-of-state** includes **$5,000** to U.S. Holocaust Memorial Museum [DC] and various smaller contributions. ■**PUBLICATIONS:** None ■**WEBSITE:** None ■**E-MAIL:** None ■**APPLICATION POLICIES & PROCEDURES:** The Foundation reports that unsolicited applications are not accepted.

O+D+T Raymond Goldberg (T+Donor+Con) — Rick Goldberg (T) — Ellen Goldberg (Donor)

SE-274 Golden Rule Foundation, The
P.O. Box 540
Plymouth Meeting 19462   (Montgomery County)

MI-13-29-51-53-55-56-57-71-79-82
Phone 610-828-8145 **FAX** 610-834-8175
EIN 59-9207701   **Year Created** 1981

AMV $7,622,090   **FYE** 10-00   **(Gifts Received** $0)   41 **Grants totaling** $322,000

Two Pa. grants: **$20,000** to U. of Pa. (arts administrator scholarships). **$5,000** to Point Breeze Federation (community beautification). **Out-of-state** giving includes **$30,000** to Tenants & Workers Support Committee [VA]; **$20,000** each to Billiard Education Fund, Millinocket Regional Hospital [ME] and Royal Institute of International Affairs [England]; **$16,000** to Big Brothers/Big Sisters of Richmond [VA]; **$15,000** each to Belfast Arts Council [ME], Biblioteca Publica de San Miguel de Allende [Mexico], For The Children International [Mexico], and Haystack Mountain School of Crafts [ME]; and other grants **$2,000-$10,000**, mostly to ME, NYC area, and VA. — In the prior year, Philadelphia-area grants included **$18,000** Bicycle Coalition of Philadelphia (bike safety/information); **$15,000** to WYBE-TV (arts initiative); **$10,000** each to Pedals for Progress (general support) and Philadelphia Community Access Coalition (publicity campaign); **$8,000** to Philadelphia Folklore Project (services expansion); **$7,000** to Vox Populi (general support); **$6,500** to Eastern Philadelphia Organizing Project (The Democracy Project); and **$2,000** to Storybook Musical Theatre (general support). ■**PUBLICATIONS:** informational brochure with application guidelines ■**WEBSITE:** www.goldrule.org ■**E-MAIL:** judy1@aol.com ■**APPLICATION POLICIES & PROCEDURES:** The Foundation reports that while unsolicited grant applications are not accepted, the deadline for other applications is July 15th. Most grants are for capital campaigns, operating support, and program development. Site visits sometimes are made to organizations being considered for a grant. Grants are awarded at a Board meeting in late August.

O+D+T Judith L. Bardes (Manager+Con) — Jean Evans [ME] (P) — Tegan Evans-Stephen [VA] (S) — Gareth Evans [Philadelphia] (F) — Trevor Evans [NY] (Board Member) — Sian Evans [ME] (Advisory Board Member)

SE-275 Golder (Ruth B. & Mervyn M.) Foundation, The
1001 Hunters Lane
Wynnewood 19096   (Montgomery County)

MI-15-22-32-54-62
Phone 610-642-7976 **FAX** None
EIN 23-6861840   **Year Created** 1986

AMV $88,382   **FYE** 6-01   **(Gifts Received** $140,000)   95 **Grants totaling** $103,463

About two-thirds local giving; some grants comprise multiple payments. **$20,000** to Jewish Federation of Greater Philadelphia. **$11,000** to Philadelphia Geriatric Center. **$6,000** to Suburban Jewish Community Center. **$5,000** each to Jewish Community Centers of Greater Philadelphia (Stiffel Senior Center) and Kosher Food Bank. **$4,700** to Living Beyond Breast Cancer. **$3,500** to HIAS and Council Migration Service of Philadelphia. **$2,500** to Terri Lynn Lokoff Foundation. **$1,000** each to Passover League and Philadelphia Museum of Art. Other local contributions **$35-$500** for various purposes. **Out-of-state** giving includes **$20,000** to Jewish Federation of South Palm Beach [FL] and **$4,800** to American Assn. for Ben Gurion U. [FL]. ■**PUBLICATIONS:** None ■**WEBSITE:** None ■**E-MAIL:** None ■**APPLICATION POLICIES & PROCEDURES:** No grants awarded to individuals.

O+D+T Ruth B. Golder (T+Donor+Con) — Mervyn M. Golder (T+Donor)

SE-276 Goldman (Myer H.) Foundation
c/o Schachtel, Gerstley, Levine & Koplin
1600 Market Street, Suite 3450
Philadelphia 19103   (Philadelphia County)

MI-15-17-22-42-62
Phone 215-981-0630 **FAX** 215-981-0652
EIN 23-7243855   **Year Created** 1972

AMV $545,060   **FYE** 12-00   **(Gifts Received** $0)   5 **Grants totaling** $30,000

All local giving. High grant of **$10,000** to Myer H. Goldman Religious School. **$6,000** each to U. of Pa. Graduate School of Education (Partners Program) and Women's Center of Montgomery County. **$5,000** to J/CHAI - Jewish Community Home for Adult Independence. **$3,000** to Jewish Community Centers of Greater Philadelphia (Stiffel Senior Center). ■**PUBLICATIONS:** None ■**WEBSITE:** None ■**E-MAIL:** None ■**APPLICATION POLICIES & PROCEDURES:** The Foundation reports giving limited to Pa.; no grants awarded to individuals.

O+D+T Bernice J. Koplin, Esq. (D+Con) — Charles G. Blumstein, M.D. [Erdenheim] (D) — Michael D. Fishbein, Esq. (D) — Charlotte W. Levin [Wynnewood] (D)

SE-277   Goldman (William) Foundation

Suite 1116,
42 South 15th Street
Philadelphia 19102   (Philadelphia County)

MI-13-14-15-17-18-20-22-32-33-34-35-41-42
43-54-55-57-62
Phone 215-568-0411   **FAX** None
EIN 23-6266261   **Year Created** 1952

AMV $3,596,437   **FYE** 12-00   **(Gifts Received** $0)   53 **Grants totaling** $139,500

Mostly local giving. A total of **$79,000** is for scholarships at designated Philadelphia-area graduate schools or medical schools, as follows: **$23,000** to U. of Pa. Dental School; **$13,000** to Philadelphia College of Osteopathic Medicine; **$12,000** to MCP/Hahnemann School of Medicine; **$11,500** to U. of Pa. School of Veterinary Medicine; **$8,500** to Thomas Jefferson U.; **$7,000** to Temple U. Dental School; and **$4,000** to U. of Pa. Medical School. — Other grants, all unrestricted support, totaled **$60,500**, as follows: **$8,000** to Federation Allied Jewish Appeal. **$3,000** to Community Hebrew Schools. **$2,000-$2,500** each to Gratz College, National Assn. for the Mentally Ill of Pa., Politz Hebrew Academy, and WHYY. **$1,000-$1,500** each to Alzheimer's Assn., American Heart Assn., Auerbach Central Agency, Congregation Beth Solomon, Diagnostic Rehabilitation Center, Fox Chase Cancer Center, Golden Slipper Uptown Home, Hadassah-Philadelphia Chapter, Jewish Employment & Vocational Service, Jewish Family & Children's Service, Institute for the Arts in Education, Juvenile Diabetes Foundation, National Museum of American Jewish History, Pa. Special Olympics, Philabundance, Philadelphia Geriatric Center, Pierce Junior College, Planned Lifetime Assistance Network, Planned Parenthood of SE Pa., Police Athletic League, Red Cross, and Talmudical Yeshiva of Philadelphia. Other local contributions, **$250-$500**, for various purposes. **Out-of-state** giving includes **$3,000** to Simon Wiesenthal Center [NY]; **$2,000** to National Institute for Trial Advocacy [IN]; and **$1,000** each to National Criminal Defense College [GA] and Southern Poverty Law Center [AL]. ■**PUBLICATIONS:** statement of program policy ■**WEBSITE:** None ■**E-MAIL:** None ■**APPLICATION POLICIES & PROCEDURES:** The Foundation reports that most organizational grants are for general operating support, special projects, or research; multi-year grants are awarded. No grants are awarded for endowment or matching grants. Grant requests from organizations may be submitted at any time in a letter or proposal; describe the purpose of requested funding and enclose a project budget, list of other funding sources, and IRS tax-exempt status documentation. Grants are awarded at a November-December meeting. — Scholarship grants (tuition only) are restricted to Metropolitan Philadelphia residents attending graduate or medical school on a full-time matriculated basis at one of eight designated Philadelphia-area institutions: Bryn Mawr College, Drexel U., MCP/Hahnemann, Pa. College of Osteopathic Medicine, Temple U., Thomas Jefferson U., U. of Pa., and Villanova U. Awards are based upon financial need, good academic achievement, and one's potential to contribute to the Philadelphia community in the future. Scholarship applicants must request a formal application form from a designated institution or the Foundation; the deadline is March 15th for fall semester scholarships; awards are announced mid-summer.

O+D+T William R. Goldman [Havertown] (C+F+Con) — Randolph L. Goldman, Esq. [Wynnewood] (VC+F+T) — Barbara Goldman Susman [NJ] (S+T) — Lowell H. Dubrow, Esq. (T) — Anne Goldman [Havertown] (T) — Jeffrey L. Susman [OH] (T) — Ronald M. Weiner, Esq. (T)

SE-278   Goldsmith-Weiss Foundation

8302 Old York Road, Suite A33
Elkins Park 19027   (Montgomery County)

MI-29-42-52-54-55-56
Phone 215-884-1276   **FAX** None
EIN 23-7913889   **Year Created** 1998

AMV $750,309   **FYE** 12-00   **(Gifts Received** $0)   9 **Grants totaling** $25,150

Mostly local/Pa. giving; all grants are for general purposes. High grant of **$10,000** to American Philosophical Society. **$5,500** to Regional Center for the Performing Arts. **$5,000** to Emergency Aid Fund. **$2,500** to the Pa. Fund. Other smaller contributions, mostly for higher education. — Major grants in the prior year included **$7,000** to American Philosophical Society, **$6,000** to Philadelphia Museum of Art, and **$5,000** to U. of Pa. ■**PUBLICATIONS:** None ■**WEBSITE:** None ■**E-MAIL:** None ■**APPLICATION POLICIES & PROCEDURES:** Grant requests in any form may be submitted at any time; include all pertinent information.

O+D+T Arlin M. Adams, Esq. (T+Con) — Judith A. Adams (T) — Neysa C. Adams (T) — Olga Goldsmith Weiss (Donor)

SE-279   Goodman (Edward J. & Myrna K.) Foundation

930 Meetinghouse Road
Rydal 19046   (Montgomery County)

MI-22-41-55-62
Phone 215-884-4460   **FAX** None
EIN 22-2770994   **Year Created** 1986

AMV $1,088,544   **FYE** 10-00   **(Gifts Received** $0)   11 **Grants totaling** $56,367

All local giving. High grant of **$25,000** to U. of Pa. **$9,580** to Congregation Rodeph Shalom. **$7,700** to Federation Allied Jewish Appeal. **$5,000** each to Abington Friends School and Hillel of Greater Philadelphia. **$2,750** to Abington Art Center. Other local contributions **$60-$540** for various purposes. ■**PUBLICATIONS:** None ■**WEBSITE:** None ■**E-MAIL:** None ■**APPLICATION POLICIES & PROCEDURES:** Grant requests may be submitted in a letter at any time. No grants awarded to individuals.

O+D+T Myrna K. Goodman (D+Con)

SE-280   Gorson (Joseph N.) Foundation, The

c/o Eagle National Bank
8045 West Chester Pike
Upper Darby 19082   (Delaware County)

MI-11-22-31-32-62
Phone 610-853-4800   **FAX** None
EIN 23-6297463   **Year Created** 1957

AMV $495,122   **FYE** 11-00   **(Gifts Received** $0)   25 **Grants totaling** $35,855

Mostly local giving. High grant of **$30,000** to Federation Allied Jewish Appeal. **$1,000** each to Albert Albert Einstein Healthcare Network (Albert Einstein Society), Delaware County Regional Cancer Center, United Way of SE Pa., and Wills Eye Hospital (Corneal Research Fund). Other local and out-of-state contributions **$25-$250 for various purposes.** ■**PUBLICATIONS:** None ■**WEBSITE:** None ■**E-MAIL:** None ■**APPLICATION POLICIES & PROCEDURES:** Grant requests may be submitted in a letter at any time; describe the organization's charitable activities and state the funding requested. No grants awarded to individuals.

O+D+T Murray S. Gorson (T+Con) — S. Marshall Gorson (T) — Janice W. Gorson [Merion] (T)

SE-281 Gottlieb Family Foundation
c/o Multi-Flow Dispensers
1434 County Line Road
Huntingdon Valley 19006   (Montgomery County)

MI-15-22-32-35-62

Phone 215-322-1800 **FAX** None
EIN 23-6870692   **Year Created** 1986

AMV $175,697   **FYE** 11-00   **(Gifts Received** $6,000)   15+ **Grants totaling** $20,968

Mostly local giving. High grant of **$12,350** to Philadelphia Geriatric Center. **$3,600** to Temple Beth Torah. **$1,318** to Federation Allied Jewish Appeal. **$1,000** to Living Beyond Breast Cancer [Ardmore]. Other smaller local contributions. **Out-of-state** grant: **$1,000** to Memorial Sloan Kettering Cancer Center [NY]. ■**PUBLICATIONS:** None ■**WEBSITE:** None ■**E-MAIL:** None ■ **APPLICATION POLICIES & PROCEDURES:** Grant requests may be submitted in a letter at any time; describe the project and the problem it will address, state the amount of funding requested, and provide organization and project budgets. For a research grant, an individual should submit a brief resume of academic qualifications and an outline of the proposed investigation, and a budget.
O+D+T Samuel Gottlieb (T+Donor+Con) — Bernard Gottlieb (T+Donor)

SE-282 Grandom Institution
366 Roumfort Road
Philadelphia 19119   (Philadelphia County)

MI-13-14-15-17-22-29-63

Phone 215-248-1465 **FAX** None
EIN 23-0640770   **Year Created** 1841

AMV $1,707,024   **FYE** 7-01   **(Gifts Received** $0)   15 **Grants totaling** $92,308

All giving to Philadelphia-area organizations providing fuel distribution to needy persons. High grant of **$29,398** to G.R.A.C.E./Germantown Residents Acting to Conserve Energy. **$7,500-$8,300** each to Bellmont Improvement Assn., Diversified Community Services, Germantown Settlement, New Kensington Community Development Corp., and Southwest Community Development Corp. **$4,200** each to Friends Neighborhood Guild and Northwest Counseling Service. **$2,100-$2,520** each to Germantown YMCA, Interfaith of Ambler, and St. Barnabas Mission, Whosoever Gospel Mission, and Women Against Abuse/Sojourner House. **$1,175** each to St. Asaph Limited Partners and Stapeley in Germantown. ■**PUBLICATIONS:** informational brochure ■**WEBSITE:** None ■**E-MAIL:** None ■**APPLICATION POLICIES & PROCEDURES:** Only Delaware Valley organizations providing fuel assistance to needy persons are eligible to apply; organizations serving Germantown residents receive preference. The Board awards grants at a meeting in October.
O+D+T Board of Managers members: John N. Childs, Jr. (S+F+Con) — F. Preston Buckman [Blue Bell] (P) — Robert C. Bodine [Wayne] — Mary L. Buckman [Blue Bell] — Thomas O. Ely [Ambler] — Carolyn Moon [Ambler] — Robert Neff [Gwynedd] — Louise W. Senopoulos [NJ] — Gerald van Arkel [Wayne]

SE-283 Greater Pottstown Foundation, The
c/o Prince & Prince P.C.
934 High Street, P.O. Box 696
Pottstown 19464   (Montgomery County)

MI-16-20-29-43-56-89

Phone 610-718-0708 **FAX** 610-327-0373
EIN 23-2568998   **Year Created** 1989

AMV $2,014,218   **FYE** 12-00   **(Gifts Received** $1,832)   3 **Grants totaling** $14,775

Mostly local giving. Two scholarships, **$6,000+** each, awarded to local students and **$2,400** to St. Aloysius Church (discretionary use). — Grants in recent years other than scholarships included support of Boyertown Area Unity Coalition (anti-bigotry campaign), Hate Watch (discretionary use), Pottstown Library, St. Aloysius Church, St. Pius High School (discretionary use), renewal of local landmarks, and creating/support programs promoting tolerance and understanding in the U.S. ■**PUBLICATIONS:** scholarship application form ■**WEBSITE:** www.toleranceunlimited.com ■**E-MAIL:** pprince@toleranceunlimited.com ■**APPLICATION POLICIES & PROCEDURES:** The Foundation reports that giving at this time focuses on the greater Pottstown area in Montgomery, Chester or Berks counties, or as determined by the Board of Directors; most grants are for special projects, publications, or scholarships. Prospective applicants should make an initial telephone inquiry regarding the feasibility of submitting a request. Grant requests from organizations may be submitted in a letter at any time. Scholarship applicants must be seniors in one of the following schools: The Hill School, Owen J. Roberts High School, Pottsgrove High School, Pottstown High School, or St. Pius X High School; students must apply before the May 1st deadline on a scholarship application form which includes an essay on their perception of some aspect of life and progress in the greater Pottstown area. Scholarship for students attending Montgomery County Community College were selected by college officials.
O+D+T Harold H. Prince, Esq. (S+D+Con) — Paul A. Prince, Esq. (P+D) — Patricia Crossen (D) — Anthony Giamo (D) — Chris Webb Heidenreich (D) — Harleysville National Bank (Trustee)

SE-284 Greenberg (Seymour & Doris) Foundation
8470 Limekiln Pike
Wyncote 19095   (Montgomery County)

MI-22-25-31-54-62-72

Phone 215-687-0997 **FAX** None
EIN 23-2820633   **Year Created** 1995

AMV $264,667   **FYE** 12-00   **(Gifts Received** $0)   34 **Grants totaling** $59,120

About three-fourths local giving. High grant of **$40,000** to Abington Memorial Hospital. **$1,000** to Greater Philadelphia Food Bank. **$500** to Philadelphia Zoo. Other local contributions **$100-$350** for various purpose. **Out-of-state** giving includes **$6,000** to Jewish Federation of South Palm Beach County; **$5,000** to AMHF Roediger Endowment [NY]; and **$2,000** to National Museum of Women in the Arts [NY]. ■**PUBLICATIONS:** None ■**WEBSITE:** None ■**E-MAIL:** None ■**APPLICATION POLICIES & PROCEDURES:** No grants awarded to individuals.
O+D+T Seymour Greenberg (T+Donor+Con) — Doris Greenberg (T+Donor)

SE-285 Greenberg (Victoria R.) Memorial Scholarship Fund   **MI**-22-42-43-82

c/o Epstein, Shapiro & Epstein
1515 Market Street, 15th Floor   **Phone** 215-563-1200 **FAX** None
Philadelphia 19102   (Philadelphia County)   **EIN** 23-6676705   **Year Created** 1981
AMV $601,362   **FYE** 9-00   (**Gifts Received** $0)   7 **Grants totaling** $40,000

About half Pa. giving. High grant of **$20,000** to Penn State (Sheal College of Business Administration). **$2,000** to Hadassah/Philadelphia. **Out-of-state** grants include **$10,000** to Duke U. [NC] and four for Israeli institutions: **$2,000** each to American Friends of Hebrew U., American Technion Society, Ben Gurion U. of the Negev, and Friends of Bezalel Academy of Arts & Sciences. ■**PUBLICATIONS:** None ■**WEBSITE:** None ■**E-MAIL:** None ■**APPLICATION POLICIES & PROCEDURES:** The Fund reports that all grants are initiated by the Trustee; no unsolicited requests are accepted.

O+D+T J. Earl Epstein, Esq. (T+Con) — Mellon Bank N.A. (Corporate Trustee)

SE-286 Greenfield (Albert M.) Foundation, The   **MI**-12-13-22-25-41-42-44-51-54-56-62-71-84

P.O. Box 30267   **Phone** 215-333-8949 **FAX** None
Philadelphia 19103   (Philadelphia County)   **EIN** 23-6050816   **Year Created** 1953
AMV $11,083,193   **FYE** 8-00   (**Gifts Received** $0)   15 **Grants totaling** $371,650

All local giving. High grant of **$51,650** to Interfaith Council on the Holocaust (Facing History & Ourselves - Philadelphia program). **$50,000** each to Arden Theatre Company (children's theatre programs) and Franklin Institute (Cutting Edge Gallery/cyberzone). **$44,500** to Fairmount Park Commission (summer beautification project). **$29,000** to Philadelphia Committee to End Homelessness (best practices research). **$25,000** to The Wilma Theatre (Camp Wilma). **$20,000** each to Richie Ashburn Baseball Foundation (free clinics for underprivileged children) and U. of Pa. School of Graduate Education (Partners Program for outdoor team-building). **$18,500** each, all for summer beautification projects, to Abraham Lincoln High School, W.B. Saul High School, and Swenson Arts & Technology High School. **$10,000** each to The Athenaeum of Philadelphia (book fund) and Support Center for Child Advocates (general support). **$5,000** to Federation Allied Jewish Appeal (general support). **$1,000** to Philabundance. — Grants approved for future payment: **$100,000** to Arden Theatre Company (children's theatre programs) and **$10,000** to The Athenaeum of Philadelphia (book fund). ■**PUBLICATIONS:** None ■**WEBSITE:** None ■**E-MAIL:** None ■**APPLICATION POLICIES & PROCEDURES:** The Foundation reports that giving is generally limited to Philadelphia-area projects with an educational component; multiple-year grants are awarded. No grants are awarded to/for general operating support, individuals, or loans. Grant requests may be submitted in a letter at any time; provide supporting documentation.

O+D+T Priscilla M. Luce [OH (P+Con) — Debra Greenfield DeLauro [CA] (S+T) — Juliet Greenfield Six [DC] (F+T) — Albert M. Greenfield, III (T) — Bruce H. Greenfield [Huntingdon Valley] (T) — Bernard M. Guth [Andalusia] (T) — Janet H. Guth (T) — Derek G. Howard [CA] (T) — Sarah E. Mark [MD] (T)

SE-287 Groff (Mary E.) Surgical, Medical Research . . . Char. Trust   **MI**-31-34-42

One Graduate Plaza, Suite 1004   **Phone** 856-566-2700 **FAX** None
Philadelphia 19146   (Philadelphia County)   **EIN** 23-2725113   **Year Created** 1995
AMV $5,804,115   **FYE** 12-00   (**Gifts Received** $275,957)   6 **Grants totaling** $158,477

About four-fifths local giving; all grants are for general purposes. High local grant of **$30,000** to Thomas Jefferson U. **$29,444** to U. of Pa. **$26,700** to Temple U. **$22,500** to Presbyterian/U. of Pa. Medical Center. **$16,500** to U. of the Sciences in Philadelphia. **Out-of-state** grant: **$33,333** to Washington U. [MO]. ■**PUBLICATIONS:** None ■**WEBSITE:** None ■**E-MAIL:** None ■ **APPLICATION POLICIES & PROCEDURES:** No grants awarded to individuals.

O+D+T Manucher Fellahnejad, M.D. [NJ] (Co-T+Manager+Con) — Anne M. Cusack, M.D. [Gladwyne] (Co-T) — Herbert W. Wallace, M.D. [Penn Wynn] (Co-T)

SE-288 Gross (Rose) Charitable Foundation   **MI**-32

c/o Feldman & Feldman
1500 JFK Boulevard, Suite 526   **Phone** 215-985-1200 **FAX** None
Philadelphia 19102   (Philadelphia County)   **EIN** 23-7894843   **Year Created** 1997
AMV $847,656   **FYE** 12-00   (**Gifts Received** $0)   **Grants totaling** $0

No grants awarded during 2000, but in the prior year three grants totaling **$184,375** awarded to Tenet Healthcare [TX] (medical research). ■**PUBLICATIONS:** None ■**WEBSITE:** None ■**E-MAIL:** None ■**APPLICATION POLICIES & PROCEDURES:** The Foundation reports that giving is limited to education, medical research, and Jewish causes. Grant requests may be submitted in a letter at any time; include a brief history and description of the organization.

O+D+T Paul L. Feldman, Esq. (Con) — Leon S. Gross (T+Donor) — Lawrence M. Miller [DC] (T)

SE-289 Grundy Foundation, The   **MI**-11-12-13-15-17-18-25-29-32-39-41-42-44

680 Radcliffe Street   51-52-54-55-56-71-72-84-89
P.O. Box 701   **Phone** 215-788-5460 **FAX** 215-788-0915
Bristol 19007   (Bucks County)   **EIN** 23-1609243   **Year Created** 1961
AMV $52,783,731   **FYE** 12-01   (**Gifts Received** $0)   64 **Grants totaling** $1,275,915

Mostly local giving, primarily Bucks County; some grants comprise multiple payments; grants are for general purposes except as noted. High grant of **$320,000** to Bristol Riverside Theater Company (operating-seasonal support/endowment). **$125,000** to Bristol Borough School District (athletic field construction/mini-grant program/school publicity/activity fund). **$105,000** to Bristol Borough Recreation Authority (debt service subsidy/skating rink promotion). **$82,500** to and United Way of Bucks County (annual campaign/affordable housing program). **$50,000** to Pennsbury Society (new visitors' center) and Please Touch Museum (capital campaign). **$25,000** each to American Cancer Society (new Bucks/Montco office), Family Service Assn. of Bucks County (Lower Bucks office), Friends of Southampton Free Library (lighting replacement), Historic Delaware Canal Improvement Corp. (restoration), Pa. Guild of Craftsmen (craft center renovation), and Philadelphia U. (Bucks County campus laboratory). **$21,000** to Andalusia Foundation (building remodeling). **$20,000** each to Bucks County Audubon Society (new tractor), Bucks County Health Improvement Project (health/human services assessment), Indian Valley Opportunity Committee (office renovations), Newtown Historic Assn. (Thornton/Hicks House restoration), and Red Cross/Lower Bucks (information technology). **$16,000** to Bowman's Hill Wildflower Preserve Assn. (interpretive signage). **$15,000** to Network of Victim Assistance (equipment development). **$13,000** to Langhorne Players (new parking lot). **$11,000-$11,990** each to Big Brothers/Big Sisters of Bucks County (mentoring institute), Community Conservatory of Music (facility expansion), Heritage Conservancy (Aldie Mansion restoration/general support), Philabundance (Bucks County distributions), and Planned Parenthood of Bucks County (building-phone improvements). **$10,000-$10,200** each to Bristol Borough Community Action Group, Closely Watched Films (construction), Friends of Silver Lake Nature Center (new tractor), and Tabor Children's Services (parking lot repairs). **$8,500** to YWCA of Bucks County (Child Development Education program). **$5,000-$5,500** each to Bristol Cultural & Historical Foundation (First Night expenses), Bucks County Symphony Orchestra (staff), Pennsbury School District (art scholarships), Pa. Economy League, and Senior Adult Activity Center of Indian Valley (auditorium chairs). **$3,000-$3,500** each to Boy Scouts/Cradle of Liberty Council, Global Interdependence Center (conference/general support), and Washington Square West Trust [Philadelphia] (tree planting). **$2,000-$2,800** each to Lower Makefield Society for the Performing Arts (dance residence in school), No Longer Bound (summer camp), Philomel Concerts (Bucks County concerts), Simpson House [Philadelphia], and Urban League of Philadelphia (youth programs). **$1,000** each to ABC/Strath Haven [Swarthmore] (building maintenance), American Philosophical Society (research), Boy Scouts/Paoli Troop #1, Bucks County Historical Society, Executive Service Corps [Ardmore], Franklin Institute, Friends of Louis Kahn Park, James A. Michener Art Museum (video documentary), Meadowbrook Retirement Community, Morris Animal Refuge, Neighbor to Neighbor [Sharon Hill] (summer camperships), NLNA Playground Fund [Philadelphia], Penn Home [Philadelphia], Pa. Prison Society, Swarthmore Public Library (outdoor projector), Wyck Assn. [Philadelphia], and Youth Service, Inc. [Philadelphia]. **Out-of-state** grants included **$25,000** to Red Cross [DC] (9/11 Disaster Relief) and **$14,000** to Friends of the Middle Border [SD] (replication of a Bucks County artist's studio). ■**PUBLICATIONS:** Applying for a Grant brochure (with application guidelines); foundation history brochure ■**WEBSITE:** None ■**E-MAIL:** grundyf@voicenet.com ■**APPLICATION POLICIES & PROCEDURES:** The Foundation reports that giving focuses on Bucks County or agencies serving Bucks County. Most grants are for building/renovations, equipment, program development, land acquisition, or seed money; multi-year grants are made. No grants are awarded for endowment, fellowships, loans, research, religious organizations, or to individuals. Grant requests may be submitted in a letter at any time; include an annual report, organizational/project budgets, Board member list, audited financial statement, list of major funding sources, and IRS tax-exempt status documentation. In addition, grant requests which follow Delaware Valley Grantmakers Common Grant Application Form (see www.dvg.org) are accepted. Site visits or interviews are arranged as necessary. Decisions on grants are made on an on-going basis; the Trustees meet monthly except in August.

O+D+T Roland H. Johnson (Executive Director+S+Con) — Frederick J.M. LaValley, Esq. [Philadelphia] (C+T) — John E. Knoell [New Britain] (T) — James M. Gassaway [Swarthmore] (T) — Leonard N. Snyder (T) — First Union/Wachovia (Corporate Trustee)

SE-290 **GT Foundation**
c/o Greene, Tweed & Company
2075 Detwiler Road, P.O. Box 305
Kulpsville   19443   (Montgomery County)

MI-12-31-42-62

Phone 215-256-9521 **FAX** 215-256-0189
EIN 23-7927474   **Year Created** 1998

AMV $1,596,154   **FYE** 12-00   **(Gifts Received** $540,000)   4 **Grants totaling** $56,600

One Pa. grant: **$21,600** to Shriners Hospital. **Out-of-state** grants: **$15,000** each to Canine Companions [NY] and U. of Miami [FL], and **$5,000** to Hadassah [NY]. ■**PUBLICATIONS:** None ■**WEBSITE:** None ■**E-MAIL:** None ■**APPLICATION POLICIES & PROCEDURES:** Information not available.

O+D+T Kenneth Stanley (T+Con) — Hannah Delfiner (T) — Michael Delfiner (T) — Ruth Delfiner (T) — Joan Stanley (T) — Nancy Stanley (T) Corporate donor: Greene, Tweed & Company

---

SE-291 **Gulack Foundation**
c/o Byron Shoemaker, CPA
5 South Sunnybrook Road, Suite 100
Pottstown   19464   (Montgomery County)

MI-11-13-15-31-43-39-89

Phone 610-323-4900 **FAX** 610-323-5650
EIN 23-6432037   **Year Created** 1966

AMV $922,816   **FYE** 12-00   **(Gifts Received** $0)   16 **Grants totaling** $41,600

All giving limited to the Perkiomen Valley. High grants of **$7,500** each to Boyertown Area School District and Upper Perkiomen School District (both for scholarship funds). **$5,000** each to Bally Ambulance and Upper Perkiomen Ambulance. **$3,200** each to Goodwill Fire Co. and Red Hill Fire Co. **$1,500** each to Bally Senior Center, Boyertown Area United Way, Upper Perkiomen Senior Center, and Upper Perkiomen United Way.**$1,000** each to Grandview Hospital (capital improvements), Pottstown Memorial Medical Center (capital improvements), and Upper Perkiomen Valley Youth. Other smaller contributions for Boy Scouts. ■**PUBLICATIONS:** None ■**WEBSITE:** None ■**E-MAIL:** None ■**APPLICATION POLICIES & PROCEDURES:** The Foundation reports that giving is primarily for the Perkiomen Valley; most grants are for capital campaigns, general/operating support, or scholarship funds. Grant requests may be submitted in any form, preferably in October but before the October 31st deadline; include IRS tax-exempt status documentation. Grants are awarded at a December meeting.

O+D+T Byron L. Shoemaker, CPA (F+D+Con) — Robert Mumbauer [Red Hill] (P+D) — Richard Quigley [Bally] (VP+D) — Ronald J. Psaris, Esq. [Red Hill] (S+D) — Thomas Eddinger [Bally] (D) — Peter Reigner [Palm] (D)

SE-292   Gushner (Alexander) Family Foundation
c/o Gushner Brothers, Inc.
1818 Chestnut Street
Philadelphia 19103   (Philadelphia County)

MI-22-62

Phone 215-564-9000 **FAX** None
EIN 23-6393631   **Year Created** 1965

AMV $66,072   **FYE** 12-00   **(Gifts Received** $75,000)   1 **Grant of** $75,000

Sole grant to Jewish Federation of Greater Philadelphia. — Grants in prior years were to Jewish Federation of Greater Philadelphia and Jewish Employment & Vocational Services. ■**PUBLICATIONS:** None ■**WEBSITE:** None ■**E-MAIL:** None ■**APPLICATION POLICIES & PROCEDURES:** Grant requests may be submitted on letterhead stationery at any time; describe the intended use of the funds requested.

O+D+T Mark L. Gushner (T+Donor+Con) — Gerald L. Gushner (T+Donor)

SE-293   Gutman (Mary B. & Alvin P.) Fund
c/o CMS Companies
1926 Arch Street
Philadelphia 19103   (Philadelphia County)

MI-12-22-31-42-44-45-52-54-62

Phone 215-246-3000 **FAX** None
EIN 23-6391200   **Year Created** 1961

AMV $1,268,797   **FYE** 11-00   **(Gifts Received** $0)   114 **Grants totaling** $139,247

Mostly local giving. High grant of **$52,525** to Pa. Ballet. **$27,500** to Federation Day Care Services. **$12,500** to U. of Pa. **$5,000** to Philadelphia Museum of Jewish Art. **$3,000-$3,500** to Albert Einstein Medical Center (Bannett Transplant Society), Free Library of Philadelphia, and Philadelphia Museum of Art. **$1,000-$2,900** each to Children's Literacy Initiative, Congregation Rodeph Shalom, Fox Chase Cancer Center, Jewish Employment & Vocational Service, Jewish Family & Children's Service, National Liberty Museum, and Philadelphia Orchestra. Many other local smaller contributions for arts/cultural, Jewish, human services, and other purposes. **Out-of-state** grant: **$1,769** to Dartmouth College Alumni Fund [NH]. ■**PUBLICATIONS:** None ■ **WEBSITE:** None ■**E-MAIL:** None ■**APPLICATION POLICIES & PROCEDURES:** Grant requests may be submitted in any form at any time. No grants awarded to individuals.

O+D+T Alvin P. Gutman [Elkins Park] (T+Donor+Con) — Mary B. Gutman [Elkins Park] (T) — Helen J. Gutman [CA] (T) — James C. Gutman [NY] (T)

SE-294   Guzzardi (Tina) Memorial Foundation
c/o First Union/Wachovia
123 South Broad Street, PA1279
Philadelphia 19109   (Philadelphia County)

MI-29-32-41-55-81-62-85

Phone 215-670-4228 **FAX** 215-670-4236
EIN 22-6453591   **Year Created** 1988

AMV $899,037   **FYE** 12-00   **(Gifts Received** $0)   15 **Grants totaling** $531,500

Mostly local/Pa. giving. High grant of **$145,000** to York Catholic High School [York] (building improvements). **$100,000** to Toward Tradition/Philadelphia Chapter. **$50,000** to REACH Alliance/Road to Educational Achievement through CHoice. **$45,000** to East of Broad Improvement Assn. **$25,000** to Middle East Forum. **$15,000** each to BLOCS/Business Leaders Organized for Catholic Schools and St. Patrick School. **$10,000** each to Abington Friends School and Friends Central School. **$5,000** to American Jewish Congress. **$3,000** to Nonprofit Technology Resources. **$2,500** to Bucks County Mikveh Assn. **$1,000** each to Crohn's & Colitis Foundation and Red Cross. **Out-of-state** grant: **$75,000** to NY Foundation for the Arts. ■**PUBLICATIONS:** None ■**WEBSITE:** None ■**E-MAIL:** diane.stables@wachovia.com ■**APPLICATION POLICIES & PROCEDURES:** The Foundation reports that requests for funds are not being accepted at this time.

O+D+T Diane O. Stables (VP at Bank+Con) — Lawrence J. Guzzardi, M.D. (Co-T) — Michael Guzzardi (Co-T) — First Union/Wachovia (Corporate Trustee)

SE-295   H & H Charitable Trust
c/o Wynnewood, Inc.
300 East Lancaster Ave., Suite 104
Wynnewood 19096   (Montgomery County)

MI-11-13-22-31-51-52-54-57-62-64-71

Phone 610-642-0188 **FAX** None
EIN 22-2924281   **Year Created** 1990

AMV $3,461,701   **FYE** 12-00   **(Gifts Received** $0)   21 **Grants totaling** $149,750

About two-thirds local giving. High local grant of **$25,000** to Philadelphia Museum of Art. **$20,000** to Federation Allied Jewish Appeal. **$12,500** to United Way of SE Pa. (deToqueville Society). **$10,000** each to French & Pickering Creeks Conservation Trust and Lankenau Hospital. **$5,000** each to Big Brothers/Big Sisters of America, Gratz College, and Pa. Ballet. **$2,500** each to Great Philadelphia First and WHYY-TV12. **$2,000** to Philadelphia Geriatric Center. **$1,000** each to Special Olympics and Visiting Nurses Assn. Other local contributions **$50-$600** each. **Out-of-state** grants include high grant of **$35,000** to Manhattan School of Music [NY] and **$5,000** each to Natural Lands Trust [NY] and New York City Ballet. ■**PUBLICATIONS:** None ■**WEBSITE:** None ■**E-MAIL:** None ■**APPLICATION POLICIES & PROCEDURES:** Information not available.

O+D+T Harriett B. Kravitz (T+Donor+Con)

SE-296   Haas (John C. & Chara C.) Charitable Trust, The
c/o Herr, Potts & Herr
175 Strafford Ave., Suite 314
Wayne 19087   (Delaware County)

MI-12-13-14-15-17-22-25-29-31-32-35-41-42
51-52-53-55-56-63-71-72-82

Phone 610-254-0114 **FAX** None
EIN 23-2587109   **Year Created** 1989

AMV $12,163,915   **FYE** 6-01   **(Gifts Received** $3,000,000)   54 **Grants totaling** $514,000

Mostly local giving; grants are general support except as noted. High grants of **$50,000** each to Bryn Mawr Presbyterian Church (building preservation fund) and Chemical Heritage Foundation (John Haas Fellowship). **$35,000** to Children's Hospital of Philadelphia (neuroblastoma research fund). **$30,000** to Academy of the New Church (capital campaign). **$25,000** to National Constitution Center (center completion). **$15,000** each to Focus on Women's Health (benefit event) and Lower Merion Conservancy (Cottage campaign). **$10,000** each to Dauphin Street Baptist Church (summer day camp), Friends Rehabilitation Program, Keystone Hospice, Pennypack Ecological Restoration Trust (Bethayres Wood challenge), St. Francis Inn, and Williamson Free School of Mechanical Trades. **$8,000** each to Moore College of Art (capital campaign) and Wayne Art Center (capital campaign). **$5,000** each to Asociacion de Musicos Latino Americanos, Bethesda Project, The Boarders & Stewards of The Monastery (capital improvements), Carelift International, Chestnut Hill Healthcare, Children & Their Families Fund, City Team Ministries, Darlington Fine Arts Center, Delaware County AIDS Network, Elmwood Park Zoo, Energy Coordinating Agency of Philadelphia (Cool Aid program), Fair Hill Burial Ground (project completion), Freedom Theatre, Greater Philadelphia Food Bank (at-risk teen nutrition education), Harcum College (PACT Program), Interfaith Housing Development Corp. of Bucks County, Jenkins Arboretum, Kennett Area YMCA (community pool), Montgomery County Assn. for the Blind, Nehemiah's Way, New Directions for Women, Norristown Zoo (restoration/expansion), Philadelphia READS (100 Book Challenge), Presbyterian Children's Village Foundation (capital campaign), Prince Music Theater (capital campaign), Rail-Trail Council of NE Pa., RSVP of Montgomery County, (prolege program), The Rittenhouse Coalition (lighting project), Salvation Army (Rebuilding Lives program), School District of Philadelphia, Tyler Arboretum (exhibit), Trevor's Campaign for the Homeless, United American Indians of the Delaware Valley, Urban Tree Connection (Wright School project), and The Wilma Theatre. **$4,000** each to Ghebre Michael Inn (entrepreneurial training project) and Surrey Services of Seniors (capital campaign). **$3,500** to King of Prussia Chamber of Commerce (Inn restoration). **$3,000** to Rosemont School of the Holy Child (capital campaign). **Out-of-state** giving: **$20,000** to Medical Benevolence Foundation [TX] (nursing school project/maternal child health project) and **$8,500** to Bossey-The Ecumenical Institute [NY] (scholarship). ■**PUBLICATIONS:** None ■**WEBSITE:** None ■**E-MAIL:** None ■**APPLICATION POLICIES & PROCEDURES:** The Trust reports that giving is usually limited to the Delaware Valley. No grants awarded to individuals. Prospective applicants initially should make a telephone inquiry about the feasibility of submitting a request. Grant requests may be submitted in a letter (3 pages maximum) at any time; include IRS tax-exempt status documentation. Site visits only occasionally are made to organizations being considered for a grant.

O+D+T Philip C. Herr, II Esq. [Radnor] (Co-T+Con) — Chara C. Haas [Villanova] (Co-T+Donor) — John C. Haas [Villanova] (Co-T+Donor)

SE-297 **Haeseler (Louise H.) Memorial Fund**
c/o Girls High School of Philadelphia
Broad Street & Olney Ave.
Philadelphia 19141 (Philadelphia County)
AMV $922,043 **FYE** 12-00 **(Gifts Received** $0)

MI-23

Phone 215-364-4257 **FAX** None
EIN 23-6428035 **Year Created** 1935
Grants totaling $24,735

All giving to present/past professional employees of the Philadelphia School District who are in need because of extended illness or old age; assistance is limited to helping meet basic needs. ■**PUBLICATIONS:** None ■**WEBSITE:** None ■**E-MAIL:** None ■**APPLICATION POLICIES & PROCEDURES:** Only present/past professional employees of the Philadelphia School District are eligible to apply. Prospective applicants initially should make a telephone inquiry about the feasibility of applying. Requests for support are accepted at any time and must be submitted on a formal application form, available from the Fund; include income and expense information such as receipted bills, bank statements, credit card statements, tax bills, physician and hospital statements, etc. Visits sometimes are made to persons being considered for assistance. The Trustees meet monthly except in July, August, and October.

O+D+T Eva F. Fidler (C+T+Con) — Fannie Kendall (Recording Secretary+T) — Cora Robinson (Corresponding Secretary+T) — Mervin Krimins (F+T) — Judith Brindle (T) — Frances Conway (T) — Doris T. Johnson (T) — Edward Magliocca (T) — Dr. Mary H. Wright (T)

SE-298 **Hafter (Martin & Florence D.) Foundation, The**
751 Lantern Lane, Pennlyn
Blue Bell 19422 (Montgomery County)
AMV $732,216 **FYE** 12-00 **(Gifts Received** $493)

MI-22-34-62
Phone 215-923-6050 **FAX** None
EIN 23-2548688 **Year Created** 1989
1 **Grant of** $7,000

Sole grant to Jewish Federation of Greater Philadelphia. — Grants awarded the prior year: **$200,000** to Pa. College of Optometry and **$6,7289** to Jewish Federation of Greater Philadelphia. ■**PUBLICATIONS:** None ■**WEBSITE:** None ■**E-MAIL:** None ■ **APPLICATION POLICIES & PROCEDURES:** Grant requests may be submitted in any form at any time; describe the purpose of the funds requested and include IRS tax-exempt status documentation. Decisions on grants are usually made with two months.

O+D+T Robert Hafter (T+Con) — Florence D. Hafter [FL] (T) — Martin Hafter, O.D. [FL] (T+Donor)

SE-299 **Haley Foundation, The**
Post Office Box 205
New Hope 18938 (Bucks County)
AMV $509,570 **FYE** 12-00 **(Gifts Received** $113,670)

MI-12-45-51-52-56-72
Phone 215-862-5670 **FAX** None
EIN 23-2869076 **Year Created** 1996
9 **Grants totaling** $17,000

About half local/Pa. giving. High grant of **$4,000** to Philips Mill Community Assn. (theatre workshop). **$1,300** to New Hope Solebury Free Library (summer reading program). **$1,000** each to Bucks County Children, Inc. (operating support) and Philadelphia Revels (program development). **$500** to Images of the Motherland Theater [Philadelphia]. **Out-of-state** giving includes **$3,700** to McCarter Theater [NJ] (capital fund); **$3,500** to Friends of Rockingham Church [Ontario] (building restoration); and **$1,500** to Friends of Dag Hammarskjold Plaza [NY] (summer children's program). ■**PUBLICATIONS:** None ■**WEBSITE:** None ■**E-MAIL:** None ■**APPLICATION POLICIES & PROCEDURES:** The Foundation reports that the majority of grants are to the Upper Delaware Valley for projects or programs in: (a) Arts/Cultural (theatre and music); (b) Education (arts, cultural and historic); (c) Human Services (women/children in need and promotion of individual/family self-sufficiency); and (d) Animal Welfare (animals in need and prevention activities). Particular consideration is given to less established or less sophisticated organizations having few secure or traditional sources of funding. Grant requests may be submitted at any time in a letter (3-5 pages maximum) which includes a brief description of the organization's history, purposes and activities and give a one-page statement of the problem, project, need or issue to be addressed, including how the program fits into the purposes of the organization and expected outcomes; a specific amount requested and other expected funding; and a short statement of how project success/failure will be evaluated. Also provide an annual report, list of Board members/officers, financial statement, and IRS tax-exempt status documentation.

O+D+T Robert Huxley (Executive Director+T+Donor+Con) — Sally Huxley (T+Donor)

SE-300 Hall (Edwin), 2nd Charitable Trust MI-14-31
c/o Luskus & Tinucci
212 Sovereign Bank Building, P.O. Box 81 **Phone** 610-565-6677 **FAX** None
Media 19063 (Delaware County) **EIN** 23-7892195 **Year Created** 1996
AMV $21,078,824 **FYE** 12-00 **(Gifts Received** $0) 2 **Grants totaling** $795,981

All local giving. High grant of **$557,187** to University of Pennsylvania Medical Center/Center for Human Appearance. **$238,794** to Baker Industries [Paoli]. — All grants since the Foundation's inception have been awarded to the same organizations. ■ **PUBLICATIONS:** None ■ **WEBSITE:** None ■ **E-MAIL:** None ■ **APPLICATION POLICIES & PROCEDURES:** Information not available.

O+D+T William T. Luskus, Esq. (Co-T+Con) — Robert E.J. Curran, Esq. (Co-T) — Richard B. Goldbeck [Devon] (Co-T) — Donor: Estate of Edwin Hall 2nd.

SE-301 Hallowell Foundation, The MI-13-31-32-33-41-42-63
c/o First Union/Wachovia
123 South Broad Street, PA4394 **Phone** 215-670-4223 **FAX** 215-670-4236
Philadelphia 19109 (Philadelphia County) **EIN** 23-6234545 **Year Created** 1956
AMV $12,912,223 **FYE** 12-00 **(Gifts Received** $0) **Grants totaling** $650,000

The last available grants information dates from 1998 when **$500,000** in grants was awarded; about half local giving. High Pa. grant of **$63,100** to Church of Jesus Christ of Latter Day Saints/Jarrettown Ward (Mormons). **$52,500** to St. John's Episcopal Church [Huntingdon Valley]. **$42,500** to Jeanes Hospital. **$25,000** each to Swarthmore College (Class of '61 Fund) and U. of Pa./Wharton School (Class of '63 Fund). **$20,000** to Penn State U./College of Liberal Arts. **$12,500** to Fox Chase Cancer Center. **$10,000** to Abington YMCA. **$5,000** to Historic Fort Mifflin. **$2,000** to Abington Memorial Hospital. **$1,000-$1,500** each to Abington Friends School, Abington YMCA, Holy Redeemer Health Foundation, and William Penn Charter School. Other local contributions **$200-$500** for various purposes. **Out-of-state** giving includes high grant of **$114,000** to Rochester Area Community Foundation [NY]; **$23,000** to Salvation Army [MD]; **$17,500** to Mount Holyoke College [MA]; **$15,000** to Salisbury Zoo [MD]; **$7,500** to Colonial Williamsburg [VA]; and other grants to MD, FL, and CA where trustees/family members reside. ■ **PUBLICATIONS:** None ■ **WEBSITE:** None ■ **E-MAIL:** vicki.hills@wachovia.com ■ **APPLICATION POLICIES & PROCEDURES:** No grants are awarded to individuals.

O+D+T Vicki Hills (Assistant VP at Bank+Con) — Dorothy W. Hallowell [Rydal] (T) — Howard T. Hallowell, III [NY] (T) — Merritt W. Hallowell [Rydal] (T) — Anne Hallowell Miller [MD] (T) — First Union/Wachovia (Manager+Agent)

SE-302 Hamilton Family Foundation MI-11-12-13-17-18-22-29-31-32-35-41-42-44
c/o Two Eighteen Enterprises 51-54-56-57-71-72-84
200 Eagle Road, Suite 316 **Phone** 610-975-0517 **FAX** 610-293-0967
Wayne 19087 (Delaware County) **EIN** 23-2684976 **Year Created** 1992
AMV $48,999,555 **FYE** 12-00 **(Gifts Received** $0) 270+ **Grants totaling** $4,247,185

Mostly local giving; grants are for annual giving-support except as noted, and many grants comprise multiple payments. **$1,011,400** to Franklin Institute (mostly trains exhibit revitalization). **$1,000,000** to Williamson Free School of Mechanical Trades (horticulture program). **$250,000** to Cabrini College (Founder's Hall renovations). **$200,000** to People's Light & Theatre Company (Project Discovery). **$100,000** each to Arden Theatre Company (children's theatre project) and Delaware Valley Friends School (library/media center). **$75,000** to United Way of SE Pa. **$53,000** to St. Frances de Sale School [Philadelphia] (salaries/art program). **$40,000** to Main Line Center for the Arts (capital campaign). **$31,000** to Red Cross (mostly for Partner for Youth program). **$25,000** each to Fox Chase Cancer Center, Freedom Theatre (training program), and Main Line Health System. **$20,000-$22,500** each to Brandywine Conservancy, Church of the Advocate/Art Sanctuary (inner city program), Jenkins Arboretum (educational fellowship program), Philadelphia Community Academy (science program), and Visiting Nurse Assn. Community Services (preschool screening program). **$16,000** to Easttown Township Library (library expansion). **$15,000** to Philadelphia Museum of Art (annual support and acquisitions) and Southwest Community Enrichment Center (community-based employment training program for teens). **$13,000** to Benchmark School. **$10,000-$11,500** each to Academy of Natural Sciences (mostly for summer scholars program), Dauphin Street Baptist Street (summer camp program), Evangelical Lutheran Church in America (Upper Darby summer day camp), First African Presbyterian Church (computer technology program), Jubilee School (computer technology program), Overbrook School for the Blind (technology training for teachers), and Planned Parenthood of SE Pa. **$7,000-$7,500** each to Philadelphia Theatre Company (young people's outreach program) and Women's Resource Center of Wayne. **$5,000-$6,000** each to Academy of Music, Canine Partners for Life, Chester-Swarthmore College Community Coalition (summer learning program), Easter Seal Society, Germantown YWCA (children's arts program), Morris Arboretum, Pa. Home of the Sparrow (life skills program), Philadelphia City Sail (inner-city youth program), Philadelphia Zoo Project Forward Leap (summer program expansion), Thos. Jefferson U. (Digestive Disease Institute), Walnut Hill Community Development Corp. (tutorial and other youth programs), and WHYY-TV12. **$3,000-$4,500** each to Abrahamson Foundation/U. of Pa. Medical Center, Care Center for Christ, Educating Children for Parenting (teacher training), IHM Center for Literacy & GED Programs (immigrants program), Please Touch Museum, St. Davids Church, and U. of the Arts. **$2,000-$2,500** each to Agnes Irwin School, Episcopal Community Services, Germantown YMCA (teens enrichment program), Haverford School, Middleton Center for Pastoral Care (office equipment), National Trust for Historic Preservation (Heritage Society), Paoli Presbyterian Church (Basic Needs program), Police Athletic Program of Philadelphia (computer/homework programs), Salvation Army, Visiting Nurse Assn. of Philadelphia, and West Hill School. **$1,000-$1,500** each to American Helicopter Museum & Education Center, Atwater Kent Museum, Chester County Community Foundation, Community Volunteers in Medicine, Daemion House Community Counseling Center (programs), Free Library of Philadelphia, Friends of Philadelphia Parks, Inglis House Foundation, Landmarks Society, Montgomery County Big Brothers & Big Sisters Assn. (adult recruitment), National Liberty Museum, Nonprofit Technology Resources (program for low-income parents/students), Old Christ Church Preservation Fund, Paoli Memorial Hospital Auxiliary, Pa. Ballet, Pa. Horticultural Society, Planned Parenthood of Chester County, Radnor Educational Foundation, SCAN, Surrey Services for Seniors, Wayne Art Center, Wayne Senior Center, White-Williams Foundation, Willistown Conservation Trust, and World Affairs Council of Philadelphia. Other local contributions **$50-$500** for various purposes. **Out-of-state** giving includes **$503,000** to Westminster School [CT]; **$203,000** to The Rectory School [CT] (new dorm); **$50,000** to Aquidneck Island Land Trust [RI] (preservation project); **$41,000** to Winterthur Museum [DE]; **$25,000** to Institute for Global Ethics [ME]; **$10,000** to National Audubon Society [FL]; **$10,500** to Cardigan Mountain School [NH]; **$5,000** to Princeton U.; and other smaller grants, particularly to RI and New England. ■**PUBLICATIONS:** application guidelines; grant application form ■**WEBSITE:** None ■**E-MAIL:** None ■**APPLICATION POLICIES & PROCEDURES:** The Foundation reports that most giving is for capital and operating needs primarily in Philadelphia and surrounding counties; its principal interest is supporting organizations with educational matters in the areas of schooling, conservation, historic preservation, medicine, and the arts. No grants are awarded to individuals or for endowment, and generally not for bricks & mortar projects. Prospective applicants must complete a Grant Application Form, available from the Foundation, and the stipulated additional information and attachments/documentation. Grant requests may be submitted at any time—check with the Foundation regarding deadlines, but only one request may be submitted by an organization in a 12-month period. Applications are reviewed at least semiannually.

O+D+T Cynthia Smith (Administrator+Con) — Dorrance Hill Hamilton (P+D+Donor) — Barbara R. Cobb (D) — Margaret Hamilton Duprey (D) — S. Matthews V. Hamilton, Jr. (D) — Nathaniel Peter Hamilton (D) — Francis J. Mirabello (D)

SE-303 **Hamilton (Frank & Marie) Charitable Trust**
c/o Abrahams, Loewenstein, Bushman et al
1650 Market Street, Suite 3100
Philadelphia 19103   (Philadelphia County)
AMV $888,807   **FYE** 12-00   **(Gifts Received** $0)

MI-12-22-25-41-44-51-52-53-55-56-62-81-83
Phone 215-587-0818 **FAX** 215-587-0888
EIN 23-7667824   **Year Created** 1991
61 **Grants totaling** $38,740

Mostly local giving. High grant of **$6,250** to Moore College of Art & Design. **$5,000** to American Jewish Congress. **$4,500** to Committee of Seventy. **$3,000** to Philadelphia Futures. **$1,000-$1,850** each to Astral Artistic Services, Curtis Institute of Music, Federation Day Care Services, Jewish Community Relations Council, Judicare Project, Middle East Forum, Philabundance, and Philadelphia Volunteer Lawyers for the Arts. **$625-$850** each to Friends of Rittenhouse Square, Library Company of Philadelphia, and Pa. Ballet. Other local and out-of-state contributions **$10-$500** for various purposes. **Out-of-state** grant: **$1,000** to U. of Michigan. ■**PUBLICATIONS:** None ■**WEBSITE:** None ■**E-MAIL:** jkaplan@e-alb.com ■**APPLICATION POLICIES & PROCEDURES:** Grant requests may be submitted in an informal letter at any time; include an organization budget, list of major sources, Board member list, and IRS tax-exempt status documentation. Site visits sometimes are made to organizations being considered for a grant.

O+D+T Jerome Kaplan, Esq. (T+Con) — Marie Hamilton (Donor)

SE-304 **Hankin Foundation**
c/o The Hankin Group
717 Constitution Drive, P.O. Box 562
Exton 19341   (Chester County)
AMV $106,453   **FYE** 11-00   **(Gifts Received** $0)

MI-11-13-14-18-25-31-44-71-84
Phone 610-458-1900 **FAX** None
EIN 25-1479501   **Year Created** 1984
93 **Grants totaling** $140,699

Mostly local/Pa. giving. High grant of **$49,528** to Upper Main Line YMCA. **$17,590** to Camp Soltane. **$12,000** to United Way of Chester County. **$10,000** each to Chester County Hospital and Housing Partnership of Chester County. **$3,300** to Planned Parenthood of Chester County. **$3,000** to Christmas in April. **$2,500** each to Pa. Environmental Council and The Second Mile. **$2,000** to Angels Without Wings [Bucks County]. **$1,000-$1,700** each to Brandywine YMCA, Chester County Library, Community Service Council, Devereux Foundation, HBA Charitable Foundation, Ludwig's Corner Horse Show Assn., Pa. Special Olympics, and Uwchlan Township Community Days. **$750** to Chester County Futures. Other local contributions **$50-$500** for various purposes. **Out-of-state** giving includes **$1,900** to Tides/Social Venture Network [CA] and **$1,000** to Tibet House [NY]. ■**PUBLICATIONS:** None ■**WEBSITE:** None ■**E-MAIL:** None ■**APPLICATION POLICIES & PROCEDURES:** Grant requests may be submitted in any form at any time. No grants awarded to individuals. — Formerly called the Bernard & Henrietta Hankin Foundation.

O+D+T Robert S. Hankin [Downingtown] (P+Con) — Henrietta Hankin [West Chester] (S+F+Donor)

SE-305 **Harrison (Thomas Skelton) Foundation**
c/o Drinker Biddle & Reath LLP
One Logan Square, 18th & Cherry Sts.
Philadelphia 19103   (Philadelphia County)
AMV $2,959,607   **FYE** 12-01   **(Gifts Received** $0)

MI-12-20-56-57-83-86
Phone 215-988-2503 **FAX** 215-988-2757
EIN 23-1489839   **Year Created** 1924
8 **Grants totaling** $88,500

All giving is restricted to projects in the City of Philadelphia which promote sound municipal government/finance or general welfare of the public. High grant of **$20,000** to Women's Law Project (improvements in Police Dept. handling of sex crime victims). **$15,000** to WHYY-FM (reporting on distressed neighborhoods/citizen rehabilitation efforts). **$10,000** each to ACLU Foundation of Pa. (monitoring improvements in foster care system), Center City District (information technology coordinator for Community Court), Committee of Seventy (assist in procurement of electronic voting machines), and Pennsylvanians for Modern Courts

(Philadelphia Jury Improvement project). **$9,500** to Foundation for Architecture (virtual tour website of historic Philadelphia sites). **$4,000** to Working Wardrobe (employment-related support for economically disadvantaged women entering the workforce). — Selected grants awarded in 2000 include **$10,000** each to Greater Philadelphia Chamber of Commerce (study on tourism/development initiatives) and Support Center for Child Advocates (Model Courtroom project participation re juvenile dependency proceedings); **$8,000** to 21st Century League (report on improvements to Pa. welfare law); **$7,500** to an individual (to underwrite research/writing of Benjamin Franklin biography); and **$6,000** to Pennsylvanians for Modern Courts (increase participation in jury system). ■**PUBLICATIONS:** annual report with grant application guidelines ■**WEBSITE:** None ■**E-MAIL:** david.abernethy@dbr.com ■**APPLICATION POLICIES & PROCEDURES:** The Foundation reports that all giving is restricted to specific projects or publications which exclusively impact upon the City of Philadelphia, as follows: (a) promotion of municipal reform, (b) investigations of public corruption, (c) studies of governmental activities, and if funds are available, (d) efforts which promote the General Welfare of Philadelphia residents. General operating support grants are awarded only in very rare circumstances. Prospective applicants may make an initial telephone inquiry regarding the feasibility of submitting a request. Grant requests preferably should be submitted during August-early September in a concise letter (deadline is September 15th) which covers the following: a description of the proposed project; how the project will fulfill one of the Foundation's specific purposes (as stated above); how the project's impact on community will be evaluated; and if a study or report is contemplated, how that information will be disseminated. Also include a project budget; information on any project funding sought or received from other sources; and IRS tax-exempt status documentation including a determination that it is not a private foundation. Some applicants are invited to meet with the Trustees. Trustee meetings are held during November-December and grants are paid in installments the following calendar year as Trust income permits.

O+D+T David F. Abernethy, Esq. (S+Con) — Stephen J. Harmelin, Esq. (C+T) — Angell A. Keene (VC+T) — George L. Spaeth, M.D. (F+T) — Susan W. Catherwood [Bryn Mawr] (T) — J. David Davis (T) — Naomi M. Post, Esq. (T) — Stanley C. Tuttleman [Bala Cynwyd] (T) Mellon Bank N.A. (Corporate Trustee)

SE-306   Hartman (Frank & Amanda) Educational Foundation   MI-43
           c/o Mellon Private Wealth Management
           1735 Market Street, Room 193-0370   **Phone** 215-553-2596 **FAX** 215-553-4542
           Philadelphia   19103   (Philadelphia County)   **EIN** 23-6810792   **Year Created** 1986
AMV $1,169,436   **FYE** 9-00   **(Gifts Received** $0)   50+ **Grants totaling** $57,700

All grants are restricted to college scholarships for students from Boyertown, Montgomery County or vicinity; awards ranging from **$800** to to **$1,500** were paid directly to the colleges/universities. ■**PUBLICATIONS:** None ■**WEBSITE:** None ■**E-MAIL:** smith.ft@mellon.com ■**APPLICATION POLICIES & PROCEDURES:** Only undergraduate students in Boyertown and the surrounding area are eligible to apply. Applications are available at the Superintendent's Office, Boyertown School District. Applications must include details on academic performance and of financial need; the deadline for applications is May 1st. — Formerly called the Russell L. Hartman Trust.

O+D+T Frances T. Smith (Portfolio Officer at Bank+Con) — Mellon Bank N.A. (Trustee)

SE-307   Hassel Foundation, The   MI-12-13-14-15-22-25-32-41-42-43-45-51-52
           c/o Fineman & Bach   54-55-62-72-81
           1608 Walnut Street, 19th Floor   **Phone** 215-893-9300 **FAX** 215-893-8719
           Philadelphia   19103   (Philadelphia County)   **EIN** 23-6251862   **Year Created** 1961
AMV $9,342,228   **FYE** 12-00   **(Gifts Received** $0)   47 **Grants totaling** $468,200

Mostly local giving; grants are for general purposes except as noted. High grant of **$100,000** to Regional Performing Arts Center. **$30,000** each to Philadelphia Geriatric Center (caregiving project), Philadelphia Orchestra, and Wistar Institute. **$17,500** each to Board of Rabbis of Philadelphia and Friends Central School. **$15,000** to Wagner Free Institute for Science. **$12,500** to Philadelphia READS. **$10,000** each to A Better Chance of Lower Merion, Avenue of the Arts, Federation Allied Jewish Appeal, HIAS & Council Migration Service, The Middle East Forum, Philadelphia Community College (scholarships), Philadelphia Zoo, Sylvan Opera, and U. of Pa. (Tzedek Hillel). **$7,200-$7,500** each to Philadelphia Futures, Summerbridge Germantown, and White-Williams Scholars. **$5,000** each to Astral Artistic Services, Children's Aid Society of Pa., Franklin Institute, Greater Philadelphians Food Bank, The Harriton Assn., Lantern Theatre, Pa. Ballet, Philabundance, Settlement Music School, U. of the Arts, and Woodrock. **$1,000-$2,500** each to Chester County Art Assn., Jewish Community Centers of Greater Philadelphians, Pa. School for the Deaf, and Recording for the Blind & Dyslexic. Also, eight scholarships, **$1,500** each, awarded to individuals. **Out-of-state** giving includes **$15,000** to Bread for the City & Zacchaeus Free Clinic [DC]; and **$5,000** each to Alzheimer's Assn. [IL] and The Solomon Project [DC] ■**PUBLICATIONS:** None ■**WEBSITE:** None ■**E-MAIL:** None ■**APPLICATION POLICIES & PROCEDURES:** Grant requests may be submitted in any form may at any time. Most grants are for general/operating support, building/renovations, or scholarships to individuals. Site visits sometimes are made to institutions being considered for a grant. Scholarships are awarded without restrictions or limitation; scholarship applications are available from high school principals The Executive Committee meets frequently to award grants; the Board meets in June and as needed.

O+D+T Michael H. Krekstein, Esq. (S+T+Con) — Andrea Cohen [DC] (T) — Barbara Cohen [Wynnewood] (T) — Elizabeth Cohen [NC] (T) — Ellen Cohen [NY] (T) — Dr. Sarle H. Cohen [Wynnewood] (T) — Andrew Goldberg (T) — Jay L. Goldberg, Esq. [Bala Cynwyd] (T) — Maxine Goldberg [Bala Cynwyd] (T) — Michael Goldberg [CA] (T) — David Khoury [CA] (T) — Lisa Khoury (T) — Marilyn Khoury [MD] (T) — Dr. Ephrain Royfe [Villanova] (T) — Merle A. Wolfson, Esq. [Bala Cynwyd]

SE-308 Hassman Family Foundation
2123 Inverness Lane
Berwyn 19312   (Chester County)

MI-14-41-62
Phone 610-240-0180 **FAX** None
EIN 33-0777149 **Year Created** 1998

AMV $97,250   **FYE** 12-00   (**Gifts Received** $0)   10+ **Grants totaling** $15,962

Limited local giving. **$945** to Hill Top Preparatory School. **$746** to Devereux Foundation. Other smaller local contributions. **Out-of-state** grants include high grant of **$10,000** to Congregation Beth Am [CA] and others in southern CA. ■**PUBLICATIONS:** None ■**WEBSITE:** None ■**E-MAIL:** None ■**APPLICATION POLICIES & PROCEDURES:** Information not available.

O+D+T Cheryl Hassman (P+D+Con) — Howard Hassman (S+D) — Allyson Davis [MI] (D) — Mark Simowitz [CA] (D)

SE-309 Hayne Foundation, The
c/o Urban Outfitters, Inc.
1809 Walnut Street
Philadelphia 19103   (Philadelphia County)

MI-42

Phone 215-564-2313 **FAX** None
EIN 23-2870131 **Year Created** 1996

AMV $406,400   **FYE** 11-00   (**Gifts Received** $0)   **Grants totaling** $0

Most recent grants (1998) awarded: **$21,519** each to Drexel U. and Trinity College [CT]. ■**PUBLICATIONS:** None ■**WEBSITE:** None ■**E-MAIL:** None ■**APPLICATION POLICIES & PROCEDURES:** Information not available.

O+D+T Richard A. Hayne (C+P+Donor+Con) — Margaret Hayne (VP) — Freeman Zausner (S+F)

SE-310 HBE Foundation, The
350 Pond View
Devon 19333   (Chester County)

MI-12-15-22-25-29-41-42-44-53-56-71
Phone 610-688-0143 **FAX** None
EIN 23-6910944 **Year Created** 1988

AMV $1,464,217   **FYE** 6-01   (**Gifts Received** $50,300)   21 **Grants totaling** $62,080

About half local giving; grants are for general support except as noted. High Pa. grant of **$7,900** to Resources for Human Development (homeless children education). **$5,000** each to Aid for Friends (building fund), The Irish Memorial (sculpture), and Kearsley (Continuum of Care construction). **$2,500** to Eastern College (nonprofit lecture series). **$2,000** to Southeastern Pa. Intergroup Assn. **$1,000-$1,500** each to Center School (Kids Help Fund), Free Library of Philadelphia (Regional Foundation Center), Pa. Horticultural Society (The 1827 Society), Peter's Place [Berwyn], and World Harvest Mission [Jenkintown] (India evangelists). **$580** for National Philanthropy Day. **Out-of-state** giving includes **$10,000** to National Arbor Day Foundation [NE] (greenhouse construction); **$5,000** each to Bay Head Historical Society [NJ] (museum renovations) and World Vision [WA] (international pastors' conferences/Vision Appalachia); **$2,000** each to Lawrence U. [WI] (sciences building fund) and National Sculpture Society [NY]; **$1,000** to Camden City Garden Club [NJ]; and other grants to NJ, DC, and TX. ■**PUBLICATIONS:** Ten-Year Report (1987-1998) with giving priorities and application guidelines ■**WEBSITE:** None ■**E-MAIL:** None ■**APPLICATION POLICIES & PROCEDURES:** The Foundation reports a priority interest is meeting human needs in the City of Chester; in addition, the Foundation has a broad interest in cultural, religious, scientific, literary, and educational concerns, especially in the Delaware Valley; a Ten-Year Report details the particular interests. Operating support usually is limited to new or small organizations, to facilitate essential expansion, or to supplement insurance in emergencies. No grants are awarded for deficit funding or, generally, to organizations making 'Payments In Lieu Of Taxes' (PILOT) to any government. The Foundation suggests that first-time, prospective applicants initially should telephone the Foundation to discuss a possible proposal; unsolicited proposals are not acknowledged unless there is Trustee interest. If a proposal is submitted, the Delaware Valley Grantmakers' Common Grant Application may be used; it should be brief and must include a complete audited financial statement, current fiscal year operating budget, Board list with addresses/telephone numbers, staff list, statement of anticipated sources of other funding, most recent IRS Form 990, and current IRS tax-exempt status documentation. Site visits are mandatory prior to initial grants as the Foundation wishes to assist organizations in securing other sources of support.

O+D+T Bruce M. Brown (T+Donor+Con)

SE-311 Heck (Eileen M.) Foundation
1170 Grandview Terrace
Radnor 19087   (Montgomery County)

MI-41-42-52
Phone Unlisted **FAX** None
EIN 23-7788354 **Year Created** 1994

AMV $526,692   **FYE** 12-00   (**Gifts Received** $20,000)   **Grants totaling** $0

No recent grants; grants awarded in prior years included **$7,000** to LaSalle U. and **$5,000** each to Gwynedd Mercy Academy, Mount St. Joseph Academy, and Polish American String Band. ■**PUBLICATIONS:** None ■**WEBSITE:** None ■**E-MAIL:** None ■**APPLICATION POLICIES & PROCEDURES:** Information not available.

O+D+T Eileen Heck Slawek (T+Donor+Con) — Kellyann Heck [Lansdale] (T) — Kimberly Cilio (T) — Corporate donor: Accupac, Inc.

SE-312 Hedgebrook Foundation, The
808 Warren Ave.
Malvern 19355   (Chester County)

MI-12-13-16-18-22-25-29-31-35-44-63-86
Phone 610-644-4125 **FAX** None
EIN 23-6964253 **Year Created** 1991

AMV $2,524,632   **FYE** 3-01   (**Gifts Received** $2,433,750)   21 **Grants totaling** $674,595

About two-thirds local giving. High Pa. grant of **$65,000** to Habitat for Humanity/North Central Philadelphia. **$55,000** each to Habitat for Humanity/Chester County and Planned Parenthood of Chester County. **$41,985** to Friends Assn. for Care & Protection of the Child. **$26,700** to Eagleville Hospital. **$25,000** each to Camp Dreamcatcher [Kennett Square], Episcopal Church of the Advocate, and La Comunidad Hispana [Kennett Square]. **$23,500** to West Chester Community Center. **$15,000** to Community Volunteers in Medicine [Frazer]. **$10,000** each to Coatesville Emergency Food Cupboard and Family Service of Chester County. **$5,000** to Exchange Club Family Center for Child Abuse. **$2,500** each to Downingtown Public Library, Good Works of

Chester County, and Kelly Ann Dolan Foundation. **$1,000** to Lord's Pantry [Downingtown]. **Out-of-state** giving: **$100,000** each to American Indian College Fund [CO] and Amnesty International [NY]; **$44,000** to Massachusetts General Hospital (resident fellowship); and **$40,000** to Equality State Policy Center [WY]. ■**PUBLICATIONS:** None ■**WEBSITE:** None ■**E-MAIL:** None ■**APPLICATION POLICIES & PROCEDURES:** No grants awarded to individuals.

O+D+T Michael A. Wall (T+Donor+Con) — Sandra A. O'Haire [Downingtown] (F)

SE-313 **Heerdt (Mary J.) Charitable Trust**
600 Lindley Road
Glenside 19038 (Montgomery County)
AMV $218,103 **FYE** 2-00 **(Gifts Received** $23,444)

MI-22-41-63
Phone 215-886-4798 **FAX** None
EIN 23-7798748 **Year Created** 1995
5 **Grants totaling** $14,500

About half local giving. High local grant of **$4,000** to Bethan Christian Services. **$2,000** to Spruce Hill Christian School. **$1,000** to Philmont Academy. **Out-of-state** giving: **$5,000** to a church in Uganda, East Africa, and **$2,500** to The Bible League [IL]. ■**PUBLICATIONS:** None ■**WEBSITE:** None ■**E-MAIL:** None ■**APPLICATION POLICIES & PROCEDURES:** Information not available.

O+D+T Robert J. Heerdt (T+Donor+Con) — Charlotte J. Homan (T) — Catherine J. Struck (T)

SE-314 **Heidmann (George B.), Jr. Foundation**
1454 Scrope Road, P.O. Box 185
Jenkintown 19046 (Montgomery County)
AMV $374,643 **FYE** 12-00 **(Gifts Received** $0)

MI-22-31-32-41-42-71-72-84-89
Phone 215-886-4300 **FAX** None
EIN 23-2191012 **Year Created** 1982
19 **Grants totaling** $18,220

Mostly local giving. High grant of **$3,500** to Abington Memorial Hospital. **$2,000-$2,500** each to Bishop McDevitt High School, Meadowbrook School, and St. Hilary of Poitiers School. **$1,000** each to Abington Township Parks & Recreation Dept., Chestnut Hill Academy, Fox Chase Cancer Center, Salvation Army, SPCA of Montgomery County, and Temple U. Baseball. Other smaller local and out-of-state contributions for various purposes. ■**PUBLICATIONS:** None ■**WEBSITE:** None ■**E-MAIL:** None ■**APPLICATION POLICIES & PROCEDURES:** The Foundation reports that all giving is limited to Philadelphia and surrounding counties. Grant requests may be submitted in a letter at any time; describe what services the organization provides and who it helps. Scholarship awards are limited to baseball players; provide information on one's major field of study and the coach's name.

O+D+T Barbara R. Heidmann (T+Con) — Ruth E. Heidmann (T)

SE-315 **Hellendall Family Foundation, The**
8119 Heacock Lane
Wyncote 19095 (Montgomery County)
AMV $284,412 **FYE** 12-00 **(Gifts Received** $98,844)

MI-12-31-35-41-42-52-54-81-82
Phone 215-884-4115 **FAX** None
EIN 23-2798144 **Year Created** 1995
20+ **Grants totaling** $50,817

Mostly local giving. High grant of **$14,867** to Arcadia U./Beaver College. **$5,000-$5,750** each to Germantown Friends School, Opera Company of Philadelphia, Philadelphia Orchestra, and World Affairs Council of Philadelphia. **$3,750** to Academy of Music. **$3,000** to Nursing Mothers Advisory Council [Abington]. **$2,550** to Abington Memorial Hospital. Other local contributions **$500** or smaller for various purposes. **Out-of-state** giving includes **$1,000-$1,100** each to Doctors Without Borders [NY], Save the Children [CT], and Smithsonian Institution [DC]. ■**PUBLICATIONS:** None ■**WEBSITE:** None ■**E-MAIL:** None ■**APPLICATION POLICIES & PROCEDURES:** No grants awarded to individuals.

O+D+T Walter Hellendall (T+Donor+Con) — Gretel Hellendall (T) — Kenneth C. Hellendall [Melrose Park] (T) — Ronald D. Hellendall [NC] (T)

SE-316 **Henkels Foundation**
c/o Henkels & McCoy, Inc.
985 Jolly Road
Blue Bell 19422 (Montgomery County)
AMV $46,658 **FYE** 12-00 **(Gifts Received** $66,000)

MI-11-13-22-41-42-52-61

Phone 215-283-7600 **FAX** None
EIN 23-6235239 **Year Created** 1956
34 **Grants totaling** $74,125

About two-thirds local giving. High grant of **$24,875** to St. Genevieve's Church [Flourtown]. **$6,000** to Philadelphia Orchestra. **$5,000** to St. Joseph's U. **$1,000** each to Archdiocese of Philadelphia/Propagation of the Faith, Assn. of Missionaries of the Assumption, Boy Scouts/Cradle of Liberty Council, St. Malachy School, United Way of SE Pa. Other local contributions, **$100-$500,** many for Catholic churches. **Out-of-state** giving includes **$20,000** to The Moreley Institute [DC] and **$1,750** to Sovereign Military Order of Malta/Federal Assn. [VA]. ■**PUBLICATIONS:** None ■**WEBSITE:** None ■**E-MAIL:** None ■**APPLICATION POLICIES & PROCEDURES:** No grants awarded to individuals.

O+D+T Paul M. Henkels (P+D+Donor+Con) — Barbara B. Henkels [Plymouth Meeting] (S+F+D) — Christopher B. Henkels (D) — Paul M. Henkels, Jr. [HI] (D) Corporate donor: Henkels & McCoy, Inc.

SE-317 **Herr (James S.) Foundation**
c/o Herr Foods, Inc.
P.O. Box 300
Nottingham 19362 (Chester County)
AMV $2,797,385 **FYE** 12-00 **(Gifts Received** $93,335)

MI-11-12-13-14-18-22-25-29-44-52-63-64-85

Phone 610-932-9330 **FAX** None
EIN 23-2531170 **Year Created** 1988
77 **Grants totaling** $703,800

About half Delaware Valley/Central Pa. giving. High Pa. grant of **$80,000** to Southern Chester County YMCA. **$35,000** to Habitat for Humanity of the Delaware Valley. **$26,000** to Lancaster Bible College. **$25,000** to Evangelical Anabaptist Fellowship [Lancaster County]. **$16,000** to Golden Slipper Camp [Bala Cynwyd]. **$12,000** to Pa. Family Institute [Harrisburg]. **$10,000** each to MEDA-Economic Development [Lancaster] and Mission Year [Philadelphia]. **$8,500** to Urban Family Council [Philadelphia]. **$7,000** to Friendship Community [Lititz]. **$6,000** to Neighborhood Services Center [Oxford]. **$5,000** each to Friendship

Ministries Foundation [Devon], Front Line Ministries [Blair County], Kennett Symphony, Pa. Pro-Life Federation, and Song for the Nations [Landisville]. **$4,000** each to Cornerstone Pregnancy Care Services [Gap] and InterVarsity Christian Fellowship [Wayne]. **$3,000** each to Bethany Christian Services [Lancaster] and Onesimus Prison Ministry. **$2,000-$2,500** each to Biblical Theological Seminary, Brandywine River Museum, Center for Parent/Youth Understanding [Elizabethtown], Chester County Christian Chorale, Cornerstone Presbyterian Church [Kemblesville], Naaman Center [Elizabethtown], Quarryville Library, Teen Challenge Training Center [Berks County], and United Way of Oxford. **$1,000-$1,500** each to American Family Ministry [Westtown], Campus Crusade for Christ, Christar/Jets, Community Accountants, Good Neighbors/Koinonia Christian Ministries, Good Works [Coatesville], Hanover YMCA, Neffsville Mennonite Church [Lancaster], Oxford Education Foundation, Phil Haven, Philadelphia Leadership Foundation, Philadelphia Zoo, Spruce Hill Christian School [Philadelphia], Teen Haven, UCP of Lancaster, and United Negro College Fund. **Out-of-state** giving includes high grant of **$131,500** to Marketplace Ministries [TX]; **$30,000** each to Back to the Bible [NE] and New York City Relief [NJ]; **$27,300** to Haggai Institute [GA]; **$25,000** each to Focus on the Family [CO] and Global Action [CO]; **$19,000** to Young Life [CO]; **$15,000** to Steve Wingfield Ministries [VA]; and smaller grants for similar purposes. ■**PUBLICATIONS:** None ■**WEBSITE:** None ■**E-MAIL:** None ■**APPLICATION POLICIES & PROCEDURES:** Grant requests may be submitted in a letter at any time; include IRS tax-exempt status documentation. No grants awarded to individuals.

O+D+T James S. Herr (P+Donor+T+Con) — Miriam Herr (S+T) — Gene Herr (F+T) — June Gunden [GA] (T) — Edwin H. Herr (T) — James M. Herr (T+Donor) — Martha Thomas [Oxford] (T) — Corporate donor: Herr Foods, Inc.

SE-318   **Herrin (Melvin & Melva) Charitable Foundation**
1156 Mill Road Circle
Rydal   19046   (Montgomery County)

MI-15-22-32-35-62
Phone 215-886-1277 **FAX** None
EIN 23-2954135   **Year Created** 1998

AMV $170,968   **FYE** 12-00   **(Gifts Received** $0)   5 **Grants totaling** $118,962

All local giving; all grants are general support. High grant of **$50,000** to Philadelphia Geriatric Center. **$29,000** to Yeshivah Chofetz 3. **$25,000** to Jewish Federation of Greater Philadelphia. **$10,000** to Macula Vision Research Foundation. **$3,000** to Living Beyond Breast Cancer. **$1,762** to Reform Congregation Keneseth Israel. One smaller contribution. ■**PUBLICATIONS:** None ■**WEBSITE:** None ■**E-MAIL:** None ■**APPLICATION POLICIES & PROCEDURES:** Information not available.

O+D+T Melvin B. Herrin (T+Donor+Con) — Melva Herrin (T+Donor)

SE-319   **Hewitt (Robert H. & Mary Gamble) Memorial Fund**
3382 Brae Bourn Drive
Huntingdon Valley   19006   (Montgomery County)

MI-12-13-22-63
Phone 215-947-0704 **FAX** None
EIN 23-2618765   **Year Created** 1991

AMV $1,066,507   **FYE** 12-00   **(Gifts Received** $0)   16 **Grants totaling** $50,100

About three-fourths local/Pa. giving. High grant of **$18,500** to Cornerstone Community Church [Philadelphia]. **$3,000** each to Bethanna, Child Evangelism Fellowship of Bucks County, Mission Projects Fellowship [Willow Grove], Salvation Army, and Teen Challenge of Philadelphia. **$2,000** each to Pilgrim Fellowship [Lebanon] and Transport for Christ [Lancaster County]. Other smaller Pa. contributions. **Out-of-state** giving, **$1,000-$3,000** for similar purposes in several states. ■**PUBLICATIONS:** None ■**WEBSITE:** None ■**E-MAIL:** None ■**APPLICATION POLICIES & PROCEDURES:** No grants awarded to individuals.

O+D+T Elizabeth H. Hewitt (P+F+Con) — Robert W. Hewitt [Hilltown] (VP) — Ruth Scofield [FL] (S)

SE-320   **Hilles (Allen) Fund, The**
P.O. Box 8777
Philadelphia   19101   (Philadelphia County)

MI-12-13-17-18-22-25-29-41-54-63-65-71-85
Phone 610-828-8145 **FAX** 610-834-8175
EIN 51-6154986   **Year Created** 1983

AMV $6,012,889   **FYE** 12-00   **(Gifts Received** $0)   56 **Grants totaling** $219,000

Mostly local giving; grants are for operating support except as noted. High grants of **$10,000** to Children's Hospital of Philadelphia (community health internship) and Education Law Center (Partnership for Fair Chance Schools). **$7,500** to Community Action Agency of Delaware County (summer career exploration project). **$6,000** to North Light Community Center (youth encouragement program) and The Philadelphia Foundation (Emma Lazarus Partnership). **$5,000** each to American Institute for Social Justice (predatory lending outreach program), Business Leaders for Sensible Priorities (Philadelphia priorities project), Clay Studio (community outreach), First United Methodist Church of Germantown (academic after school program), Norris Square Neighborhood Project (summer day camp), North Philadelphia Health System (Reboot Philadelphia project), Our Lord Catholic Church/Philadelphia Dominican Grocers Assn., Philadelphia Public School Network, Philadelphians Concerned About Housing (family self-sufficiency program), Planned Parenthood of Chester County (healthy moms/babies program), Police-Barrio Relations Project, and Women's Law Project. **$4,000** each to Asian Arts Initiative (youth workshop), CASA Youth Advocates [Media], Community Learning Center, Episcopal Church of the Advocate (L.I.F.E. programs), Greater Philadelphia Women's Medical Fund, Jubilee School, NetworkArts Philadelphia (ecology/arts program in public schools), Newtown Yearly Meeting (peace project), Urban Bridges of St. Gabriel's (artist residence program), and Wagner Free Institute of Science (children's programs). **$3,000-$3,500** each to 1812 Productions (in-school theatre performances), Bainbridge House (mentoring/cultural arts program), Center for Lesbian & Gay Civil Rights, Fair Hill Burial Corp. (restoration), Farmer's Market Trust, Frankford Group Ministry (parenting program), Greater Philadelphia Urban Affairs Coalition (for Asian-American Youth Assn.), Juvenile Law Center, Montessori Genesis II, Nueva Esperanza (summer camp scholarships), Philadelphia Physicians for Social Responsibility (violence prevention program), Philadelphia Training Program Philadelphia Youth Tennis Assn. (after school programs), Philabundance (community kitchens collaborative), Point Breeze Performing Arts Center (Freedom School), Project Synergy, Sisters of St. Joseph (literacy project), Taller Puertorriqueno (cultural education project), White-Williams Scholars (peer academic development program), and Working Wardrobe (clothing). **$1,000-$2,500** each to Community Gardens of Chester County, Congregation Keneseth Israel (Spring Garden School tutoring program), Friends Journal (survey/website), and Green Circle Program (elementary school program). Out of state grants: **$3,000** to Latin American Community Center [DE] (domestic violence program) and **$2,000** to Delaware Center for Justice (read-in/read-out). ■**PUBLICATIONS:** Annual Report (lists grantees but not grant sizes) with grant application guidelines ■

WEBSITE: www.dvg.org/hilles/ ■**E-MAIL:** judy1@aol.com ■**APPLICATION POLICIES & PROCEDURES:** The Fund reports that support focuses on education, health, counseling, or activities of the Religious Society of Friends in Philadelphia; grants usually are awarded on a one-year basis. The Fund prefers to support specific programs or provide seed money, but occasionally will support general operations. Preference is given to organizations with annual budgets under $2 million and to specific projects that provide opportunities to make positive change. No grants are awarded for capital projects, endowments, agency promotion (marketing, development, publication of annual reports, or fundraising events), or to individuals. Grant requests may be submitted at any time (deadlines are February 1st, May 1st, and October 1st) in a full proposal together with the Application Form, available from the Fund. The proposal must include the following: (a) name and purpose of the organization; (b) purpose of the grant and special nature of the project; (c) leadership involved in the project and Board of Directors list; (d) funding requested, total funding needed, other funding available or anticipated and, if applicable, a detailed project budget including expected sources of income; and (e) an annual budget and most recent audited financial statement. Other background materials about the project may be included. Five complete, collated sets (proposal, Application Form, and supporting materials) must be submitted with one copy of the IRS tax-exempt status documentation. Except under special circumstances, only one application may be submitted by an organization within a one-year period. Receipt of proposals will be acknowledged if a self-addressed envelope or label is included. The Fund also accepts the Common Grant Application Form of Delaware Valley Grantmakers (see Appendix)—but applications still must include the aforementioned Application Form—and five collated sets of all materials.

O+D+T Judith L. Bardes (Manager+S+Con) — Robert L. Dewees , Jr. [MA] (P+D) — Edward D. Dewees [NY] (D) — Stephen L. Honeyman [Philadelphia] (D) — Stephanie D. Judson [NJ] (D) — Bryn Mawr Trust Company (Corporate Trustee)

SE-321	**Hoffman (Arnold & Bette) Family Foundation**		**MI**-15-22-42-62	
	1464 Hunter Road		**Phone** 215-572-7780 **FAX** None	
	Rydal 19046	(Montgomery County)	**EIN** 22-2702299 **Year Created** 1986	
AMV $268,759	**FYE** 7-00	(**Gifts Received** $300,530)	25+ **Grants totaling** $186,637	

Mostly local/Pa. giving. High grant of **$101,000** to Penn State U. **$34,500** to Philadelphia Geriatric Center. **$25,000** to Federation Allied Jewish Appeal. **$16,137** to Congregation Adath Jeshurun. **Out-of-state** grant: **$3,000** to Sarasota Jewish Federation [FL]. Other contributions total **$7,000** but no details available. ■**PUBLICATIONS:** None ■**WEBSITE:** None ■**E-MAIL:** None ■**APPLICATION POLICIES & PROCEDURES:** No grants are awarded to individuals.

O+D+T Arnold S. Hoffman (T+Donor+Con) — Bette G. Hoffman (T+Donor) — Louis W. Fryman, Esq. [Philadelphia] (T)

SE-322	**Holstrom-Kineke Foundation**		**MI**-29-41-42-52-55-63	
	112 Mount Airy Road		**Phone** 610-294-9057 **FAX** None	
	Pipersville 18947	(Bucks County)	**EIN** 22-2611162 **Year Created** 1984	
AMV $204,098	**FYE** 11-00	(**Gifts Received** $0)	15 **Grants totaling** $84,895	

Mostly local giving. High grant of **$42,095** to Trinity Episcopal Church of Solebury. **$10,000** each to Buckingham Friends School and National Philanthropic Trust [Jenkintown]. **$5,000** to Closely Watched Films [Doylestown]. **$800** to Red Cross. Other local contributions **$250-$500** for various purposes. **Out-of-state giving includes $5,250 to Rutgers U. [NJ]; $5,000 to Public Education Assn. [NY]; and $2,000** to State Theatre/New Brunswick Cultural Center [NJ]. ■**PUBLICATIONS:** None ■**WEBSITE:** None ■**E-MAIL:** None ■**APPLICATION POLICIES & PROCEDURES:** No grants awarded to individuals. — Formerly called The Holstrom Family Foundation.

O+D+T Mary Beth Kineke (P+Con) — Christina L. Holstrom (VP) — Margaret Kineke (S) — Carleton A. Holstrom (F+Donor)

SE-323	**Honickman Foundation, The**		**MI**-12-17-32-42-44-45-52-53-54-55	
	210 West Rittenhouse Square, Suite 3303		**Phone** 215-790-1710 **FAX** None	
	Philadelphia 19103	(Philadelphia County)	**EIN** 23-2513138 **Year Created** 1988	
AMV $8,115,584	**FYE** 12-00	(**Gifts Received** $254,904)	24 **Grants totaling** $164,325	

Mostly local giving; grants are for general support except as noted. High grant of **$25,000** to Thomas Jefferson U. Hospital (medical research). **$20,000** to St. Joseph's U. (campaign). **$13,000** to Philadelphia Mural Arts (book design fees). **$12,500** to Institute of Contemporary Art (Architectural Unconscious). **$10,000** each to American Poetry Review (book award) and Philadelphia Museum of Art. **$7,000** to Philadelphia Art Alliance (photography project). **$6,500** to The Print Center (photography collectors series). **$5,000** each to Church of the Advocate/The Art Sanctuary (Project H.O.M.E. collaboration) and MANNA/Metropolitan AIDS Neighborhood Nutrition Alliance (benefit auction). **$3,000** to Curtis Institute of Music (student assistance fund). **$2,500** each to Free Library of Philadelphia and Women's Way. **$1,000-$1,200** each to The Fabric Workshop, Contexts Books Through Bars, Franklin Institute (science award projects), Pa. Academy of the Fine Arts/U.S. Artists (special needs program), St. Mary's Family Respite Center. Other smaller local contributions. **Out-of-state** giving includes **$21,000** to Aperture Foundation (projects); and **$15,000** to Duke U./Center for Documentary Studies (photography project). ■**PUBLICATIONS:** None ■**WEBSITE:** None ■**E-MAIL:** None ■**APPLICATION POLICIES & PROCEDURES:** The Foundation reports that giving is limited to the five-county Philadelphia area but that requests are by invitation only. Most grants are for endowment, publications, seed money, program development, and for individuals. Requests submitted it may be in any form and should include an annual report, organization and project budgets, list of Board members, and a list of major funding sources. Site visits sometimes are made to organizations being considered for a grant. Grants are awarded primarily in December. — Formerly called the Lynne & Harold Honickman Foundation.

O+D+T Lynne Honickman (T+Donor+Con)

SE-324 Hood (Esther Gowen) Music Fund
c/o Mellon Private Wealth Management
1735 Market Street, Room 193-0370
Philadelphia 19103 (Philadelphia County)
MI-43-52
Phone 215-553-2596 **FAX** 215-553-4542
EIN 23-6223620 **Year Created** 1927
AMV $270,220 **FYE** 9-00 **(Gifts Received** $0) 4 **Grants totaling** $11,000

All grants are restricted to scholarships for Philadelphia-area students to study music in the United States or abroad. Annually up to four awards—limited to two years' support and usually **$2,000-$4,000** per student per year—are made. Three **$3,000** grants for students attending Julliard School [NY], Temple U., and U. of the Arts. **$2,000** for student at U. of the Arts. ■**PUBLICATIONS:** application guidelines ■**WEBSITE:** None ■**E-MAIL:** smith.ft@mellon.com ■**APPLICATION POLICIES & PROCEDURES:** The Fund reports that only talented Philadelphia-area music students whose financial resources preclude receiving proper musical instruction are eligible to apply. Applications must be submitted on a formal application form (available from the Fund) during January-March (deadline is April 15th) with grade reports and a statement of financial need.

O+D+T Frances T. Smith (Portfolio Officer at Bank+Con) — Mellon Bank N.A. (Trustee)

SE-325 Hood (Esther Gowen) Trust
c/o Mellon Private Wealth Management
1735 Market Street, Room 193-0314
Philadelphia 19103 (Philadelphia County)
MI-12-13-14-15-16-17-19-22-25-29-31-33-35
Phone 215-553-2517 **FAX** 215-553-2054
EIN 23-6223619 **Year Created** 1927
AMV $2,919,357 **FYE** 9-00 **(Gifts Received** $0) 38 **Grants totaling** $153,000

All grants restricted to organizations in the City of Philadelphia which provide direct physical assistance (food, fuel, clothing, shelter, etc.) to needy persons in the city; grants are for operating support except as noted. High grant of **$16,000** to Secretariat for Catholic Human Services (children & family services). **$7,000** to Frankford Group Ministry (food/direct assistance programs). **$6,000** each to Calcutta House. **$5,000** each to Drueding Center/Project Rainbow (child care center), 18th Street Development Corp. (Point Breeze area stabilization), Energy Coordinating Agency of Philadelphia, Ghebre Michael Inn, Greater Philadelphia Food Bank (food transportation support), Kearsley (special needs resident support), Metropolitan Career Center (Link Program), Philadelphia Senior Center (fuel/clothing/medical support), Red Cross (local disaster relief), Women's Community Revitalization Program (low-income women's program), and Working Wardrobe. **$4,000** each to North Light Community Center (utilities/fuel cutoff support), Special Equestrians, and Wissahickon Hospice. **$3,000-$3,500** each to Aid for Friends, CARIE/Center for Advocacy for the Rights & Interests of the Elderly (outreach/advocacy), Center for Advancement on Cancer Education (counseling/referral services), Chestnut Hill Healthcare (women's community education/prevention programs), Episcopal Community Services (home-delivered meals to elderly), Jeanes Vital Age (adult day health services), MANNA/Metropolitan AIDS Neighborhood Nutrition Alliance, Philabundance, Point Breeze Performing Arts Center (Christmas food baskets), Southwest Community Enrichment Center (nutrition program), and White-Williams Scholars. **$2,000-$2,500** each to Center in the Park (transportation subsidies), Episcopal Church of the Advocate (support for needy/homeless), Federation Day Care Services (scholarships for low-income children), Intercommunity Action (multi-service aging program), Lutheran Settlement House, Northwest Philadelphia Interfaith Hospitality Network (food/temporary shelter), Old First Reformed Church (Southwark area support), Polish American Social Services (emergency food/fuel), Wheels, Inc. (medical appointment transport), and Whosoever Gospel Mission (homeless men services). ■**PUBLICATIONS:** Information & Proposal Guidelines memorandum ■**WEBSITE:** None ■**E-MAIL:** morse.g@mellon.com ■**APPLICATION POLICIES & PROCEDURES:** Only organizations in the City of Philadelphia which directly assist needy persons are eligible to apply. Grant requests may be submitted in a full proposal with cover letter at any time (deadline is April 15th); provide a summary sheet with a brief description of the request, total costs of the project, detailed explanation of the project with breakdown of costs, statement of purpose and brief organizational history, and name/address of contact person; include an annual report, organization and project budgets, list of board members, list of major funding sources, audited financial statement, and IRS tax-exempt status documentation. Grants are awarded at a June meeting.

O+D+T Gail Curtis Morse (VP at Bank+Con) — Mellon Bank N.A. (Trustee)

SE-326 Hooker (Janet Annenberg) Charitable Trust
c/o Hawthorn/PNC Advisors
1600 Market Street, 29th Floor
Philadelphia 19103 (Philadelphia County)
MI-42-52-53-54-82
Phone 215-585-3958 **FAX** None
EIN 23-6286762 **Year Created** 1952
AMV $4,639,358 **FYE** 12-00 **(Gifts Received** $0) 23 **Grants totaling** $5,455,500

Two Pa. grants: **$800,000** to Somerset House Art History Foundation [Merion Station—institution is in U.K.]. **$25,000** to U. of Pa. (Deubler Fund-Charing Cross Research). **Out-of-state** giving includes **$2,375,000** to Charities Aid Foundation [VA—grantee is in U.K]; **$656,000** to American Friends of the Monteverdi Choir & Orchestra [DC]; **$624,000** to American Friends of the British Museum [NY] (Cobbe Collection Trust); **$300,000** to Florida Grand Opera; **$165,000** to International Festival Society [CA]; **$100,000** each to Florida Philharmonic Orchestra and Metropolitan Opera Assn. [NY]; and other grants **$5,000-$65,000** for similar purposes in NY, DC, FL, CA, and MO. — In prior years, the only Pa. giving was to U. of Pa. ■**PUBLICATIONS:** None ■**WEBSITE:** None ■**E-MAIL:** None ■**APPLICATION POLICIES & PROCEDURES:** Information not available.

O+D+T Lynn A. Brickman (Trust Administrator+Con)

SE-327   Hooper (Elizabeth S.) Foundation
489 Devon Park Drive, Suite 300-B
P.O. Box 7453
St. Davids   19087   (Chester County)

MI-12-13-14-15-18-22-25-29-31-32-41-52-53
54-56-62-71-72-89
Phone 610-688-3551 **FAX** None
EIN 23-6434997   **Year Created** 1967

AMV $3,547,861   **FYE** 6-00   **(Gifts Received** $561,951)   148 **Grants totaling** $761,100

About two-thirds local giving; some grants comprise multiple payments. High grant of **$65,000** to Bryn Mawr Presbyterian Church. **$55,000** to Pa. Horticultural Society. **$50,000** to Presbyterian Children's Village. **$40,000** to Curtis Institute of Music. **$20,000** to Philabundance. **$13,000** to Academy of Natural Sciences. **$10,000** each to American Cancer Society, Inglis House, and Red Cross. **$7,000** each to Agnes Irwin School and American Helicopter Museum & Education Center. **$6,000** each to Franklin Institute, Hilltop Preparatory School, Valley Forge Military Academy, and Williamson Free School of Mechanical Trades. **$5,000** each to ALS Assn., Freedoms Foundation at Valley Forge, Philadelphia Society for Preservation of Landmarks, Philadelphia Museum of Art, Philadelphia Zoo, and USO of Philadelphia. **$4,000** each to Baker Industries, Boy Scouts/Cradle of Liberty Council, Elwyn Institute, Friends of Penn Nursing, Gesu School, Pa. Academy of the Fine Arts, Please Touch Museum, and Wharton Esherick Museum. **$3,000** each to Adoption Center of the Delaware Valley, Delco Blind/Sight Center, Eldernet of Lower Merion, Fort Mifflin on the Delaware, Historical Society of Pa., Jubilee School, MBF Center, Newtown Public Library, Planned Parenthood of SE Pa., Simpson House (renewal fund), St. David Episcopal Church, and Salvation Army. **$2,000-$2,500** each to Academy of Music, Brandywine Conservancy, Children's Country Week Assn., Children's Hospital of Philadelphia, Conshohocken Veterans' Memorial Fund, Daemion House, Freedom Valley Girl Scout Council, Lankenau Hospital, Need in Deed, Newtown Square Fire Company, Police Athletic League of Philadelphia, Royer-Greaves School for the Blind, Seamen's Church Institute, St. Christopher's Hospital for Children, St. Stephen's Episcopal Church, Thorncroft Therapeutic Horseback Riding, Wheels, Inc., and YMCA of Philadelphia. Also, about 25 local grants **$500-$1,500** for arts/cultural, educational, child welfare, human services, animal welfare, and other purposes. **Out-of-state** giving includes **$40,000** to Congressional Medal of Honor Society [DC]; **$20,000** each to Center for the Study of Popular Culture [CA] and Penobscot Marine Museum [ME]; **$15,000** to Autism Society of America Foundation [MD]; **$10,000** each to Hoover Institution [CA], Independent Women's Forum [VA], and Marine Corps Heritage Foundation [VA]; and other grants to Chesapeake Bay area, ME, and for maritime-related organizations. ■**PUBLICATIONS:** None ■**WEBSITE:** None ■**E-MAIL:** None ■**APPLICATION POLICIES & PROCEDURES:** Grant requests may be submitted in a letter at any time; requests must be received at least several weeks prior to the semi-annual meetings held in early June and December; describe the organization and its programs, and state the amount requested and specific purpose of the funding requested. No grants are awarded to individuals.
O+D+T Bruce H. Hooper [Villanova] (S+D+Con) — Adrian S. Hooper [Chester Springs] (P+D+Donor) — Thomas Hooper [Bryn Mawr] (VP+Donor) — Ralph W. Hooper [Newtown Square] (F+D+Donor) Corporate donors: Interstate Marine Transport Co. and related companies

---

SE-328   Horsham Lions Foundation
c/o 200 Oakland Place
North Wales   19454   (Bucks County)

MI-14-29-41
Phone 215-699-3328 **FAX** None
EIN 23-2826356   **Year Created** 1996

AMV $27,249   **FYE** 12-99   **(Gifts Received** $13,500)   5 **Grants totaling** $13,000

All local giving. High grant of **$5,300** to Lions Club Charities. **$5,000** to Hatboro-Horsham School District (scholarships). **$2,500** to Blair Mill Home & School Assn. (handicap needs). Other small contributions. ■**PUBLICATIONS:** None ■**WEBSITE:** None ■**E-MAIL:** None ■**APPLICATION POLICIES & PROCEDURES:** Information not available.
O+D+T James R. Faber (P+D+Con) — Salvatore Calise (VP+D) — Thomas H. Burgess (S+F+D) — John R. Bill (D) — Theodore L. Truver (D)

SE-329   Hostvedt (Erik T.) Foundation
Dark Hollow Road, P.O. Box 285
Pipersville   18947   (Bucks County)

MI-18-22-63-64
Phone 215-766-2236 **FAX** None
EIN 23-6847270   **Year Created** 1985

AMV $290,427   **FYE** 12-00   **(Gifts Received** $120,000)   19 **Grants totaling** $89,720

About two-thirds local giving. High grant of **$41,000** to Covenant Presbyterian Church. **$3,000** each to Alpha Pregnancy Services and Gospel Friendships [Hatfield]. **$2,000-$2,500** each to Alliance of Confessing Evangelicals, Arab World Ministries, Bethany Christian Services, Center for Urban Theological Studies, HOPE, Philadelphia Presbytery PCA, SeeJesus.Net, and The Simple Way. **$1,000** to World Harvest Mission [Jenkintown]. **Out-of-state** giving includes **$13,000** to Bethel Seminary of the East [MN] and **$2,000-$3,000** to Evangelical Christian organizations in CA, NC, NJ, WA, and WI. ■**PUBLICATIONS:** None ■ **WEBSITE:** None ■**E-MAIL:** None ■**APPLICATION POLICIES & PROCEDURES:** Information not available.
O+D+T Erik T. Hostvedt (T+Donor+Con) — Jill C. Hostvedt (T)

SE-330   Houghton Carpenter Foundation, The
c/o Houghton International
Madison & Van Buren Aves., P.O. Box 930
Valley Forge   19482   (Chester County)

MI-13-14-15-42-51-54-55-57-71-81-84
Phone 610-666-4049 **FAX** 610-666-5689
EIN 23-6230874   **Year Created** 1951

AMV $3,473,902   **FYE** 6-01   **(Gifts Received** $0)   45 **Grants totaling** $153,634

Mostly local giving; grants are unrestricted support or annual giving except as noted. High grant of **$30,000** to Eisenhower Exchange Fellowships. **$20,000** to WHYY. **$13,000** to World Affairs Council of Philadelphia (annual support/50th anniversary campaign). **$5,000** each to Camphill Village, Kearsley Retirement Community, and Philadelphia Museum of Art. **$3,334** to Need in Deed. **$3,000** each to Independent Colleges of Pa. **$2,000-$2,750** each to Boys & Girls Clubs of Philadelphia, College Settlement of Philadelphia (summer camp), Easter Seals (adaptive summer camp), Franklin Institute, Great Valley Nature Center (children's programs), Hope Springs Equestrian, Kardon Institute of the Arts (creative arts therapy), MBF Center (training for disabled adults), The Nature Conservancy, Nueva Esperanza (summer camp scholarships), Old First Reformed Church (summer camp/employment skills program), Pa. Ballet, Pa. Free Enterprise Week, Pa. Special Olympics (Fall Festival), Philadelphia Zoo, Planned Parenthood of SE Pa., Please Touch Museum, (exhibits/community programs), Police Athletic League of Philadelphia, Programs Employing People (summer program), Radnor ABC (group home), RSVP of Montgomery County, Upper Merion Township Concerts, White-Williams Scholars (stipends), and Woodrock (youth development program). Other smaller grants/contributions for similar purposes. **Out-of-state** giving includes **$5,000** to Yale U. [CT] (squash court renovation) and **$2,500** to American Foundation for the Blind [NY]. — Major grants approved for future payment: **$90,000** to Eisenhower Exchange Fellowships and **$20,000** each to Camphill Village and WHYY. ■**PUBLICATIONS:** application guidelines ■**WEBSITE:** None ■**E-MAIL:** None ■ **APPLICATION POLICIES & PROCEDURES:** Grant requests may be submitted in a letter at any time; include a project budget and IRS tax-exempt status documentation. No grants are awarded to individuals.

O+D+T William F. MacDonald, Jr. (T+Con) — Stephen B. Harris (T)

SE-331 Hovey Foundation, The
955 Chesterbrook Blvd., Suite 125
Chesterbrook 19087 (Chester County)
AMV $226,306 **FYE** 12-99 (**Gifts Received** $27,939)
MI-13-32-41-42-71-81
Phone 215-233-2983 **FAX** None
EIN 23-2544450 **Year Created** 1988
13 **Grants totaling** $67,250

Mostly local giving. High grant of **$35,000** to U. of Pa. **$20,000** to Eisenhower Exchange Fellowships. **$2,500** to National Organization for Hearing Research [Wayne]. **$1,000** each to Chestnut Hill Academy, Children's Oncology Services, The Hill School [Pottstown], Morris Arboretum, Need in Deed, and Springside School. **Out-of-state** giving includes **$2,500** to Boy Scouts [NY] and **$1,000** to Hollins College [VA]. ■**PUBLICATIONS:** None ■**WEBSITE:** None ■**E-MAIL:** None ■**APPLICATION POLICIES & PROCEDURES:** Information not available. — Formerly called the James W. & Carol A. Hovey Foundation.

O+D+T James W. Hovey (T+Donor+Con) — Carol A. Hovey (T+Donor)

SE-332 Huston Foundation, The
Two Tower Bridge, Suite 190
One Fayette Street
West Conshohocken 19428 (Montgomery County)
AMV $41,303,651 **FYE** 12-00 (**Gifts Received** $0)
MI-12-13-14-15-17-18-22-29-31-35-41-42-44
45-51-52-54-55-57-63-64-65-72-84-86
Phone 610-832-4949 **FAX** 610-832-4960
EIN 23-6284125 **Year Created** 1957
230+ **Grants totaling** $2,059,741

Nearly two-thirds local/Pa. giving with emphasis on Chester County; grants are for general support except as and some grants comprise multiple payments. *HEALTH/HUMAN SERVICES GRANTS*: **$40,000** to Pa. Assn. of Nonprofit Organizations [Harrisburg]. **$30,000** to Chester County Community Foundation. **$20,000** to Urban Family Council [Philadelphia] (programs support). **$18,000** to Neighbor to Neighbor Community Development Corp. [Sharon Hill] (van). **$15,000** to Resources for Better Families (planning consultant). **$13,000** to Center for Parent/Youth Understanding [Elizabethtown] (training). **$12,500** to YMCA of Central Chester County (capital campaign). **$10,000** each to Camp Cadet of Chester County, Chester County Chamber of Business & Industry (job mentoring) , Chester County Fund for Women & Girls, Children's Hospital of Philadelphia (story hour sessions), Children's Seashore House (disability awareness in schools), Community Foundations for Pa. (planned giving design center), Community Service Council of Chester County, Episcopal Community Services (Coatesville children's programs), Family Service of Chester County (Coatesville services), Hosts for Hospitals (outreach activities), Kelly Ann Dolan Memorial Fund, Ophthalmic Research Associates [Flourtown] (physicians collaborative project), Pa. Home of the Sparrow (housing for homeless women), Philadelphia Cares, Safe Harbor of Greater West Chester (homeless shelter), Summer Medical Institute [Philadelphia], Surrey Services for Seniors (Community Cares Program), and U. of Scranton Nonprofit Resource Center (community collaboration program). **$9,000** to International Health Services (planning). **$7,000-$7,500** each to Amnion Crisis Pregnancy Center (new center), Christ's Home, and Wheels Medical Transportation (Chester County operations). **$6,000-$6,500** each to Baker Industries, Crippled Children's United Rehabilitation Effort [Harrisburg] (Kenya program), Good Neighbor's Home Repair Ministry [Kennett Square], and Good Works, Inc. (Coatesville housing improvements). **$5,000** each to ALS Foundation (assistive technology program), Bridge of Hope (homeless assistance), Children's Country Week Assn. (camping program), Contact Careline of Greater Philadelphia (reassurance program), Crime Victims' Center of Chester County, Delaware County Pregnancy Center, Exceptional Care, Inc., Maternal & Child Health Consortium of Chester County (Healthy Start Program), Montgomery Early Learning Center, Pa. Right to Work Defense & Education Foundation (legal assistance), Phoenixville Area Positive Alternatives (after school program), RSVP of Montgomery County, Special Equestrians Therapeutic Riding & Driving Program, U. of Pa. School of Medicine (wilderness medicine course), and YWCA of Chester (youth program). **$3,000-$4,000** each to Burn Foundation (prevention-treatment programs), Care Center for Christ Foundation (West Chester programs), Lafiya Family Services Center (reading-books awards program), Montgomery County Assn. for the Blind (summer day camp), Simpson Meadows (Eden Alternative Program), and Sterling Housekeeping (training program). *ARTS, CULTURE & CONSERVATION GRANTS*: **$20,000** to Primitive Hall Foundation [Coatesville] (new kitchen). **$15,000** to Norristown Zoo. **$11,000** to Graystone Society (various programs). **$10,000** each to Kailo Mantua Art Center (emergency funding), The Lukens Band, Mann Music Center (programs/concerts), Nightingale Productions [Philadelphia] (documentary on Rebecca Lukens), Philadelphia Museum of Art (special family events), and WHYY. **$9,150** to Williamson Free School of Mechanical Trades (development office). **$7,000-$8,000** each to Amaryllis Theater Company (sign language theatre production), National Liberty Museum (Freedom Tours), The Nature Conservancy (vehicle), and Tyler Arboretum (signage). **$5,000-$6,125** each to Chester Springs Studio (Coatesville programs), Main Line Art Center (children's art program), Strings for Schools (Great Music Programs), and Wilma Theatre (schools outreach program). **$3,000** each to Chester County Christian Chorale (sing-a-long), Philadelphia Theatre Company (youth outreach), and Sylvan Opera. *EDUCATION GRANTS*: **$38,000** to Episcopal Academy (chapel stained-glass windows). **$10,000** each to Community of Bosnia Foundation [Philadelphia], Eastern College (student emergency aid), Pa. School for the Deaf (technology initiative), and Reboot Philadelphia (computer training for low-income persons). **$7,000-$8,000** each to Delaware Valley Friends School (outward bound program), Hill Top Preparatory School (nonreaders tutoring), Maysie's Farm Conservation Center [Glenmoore] (college-age interns program), and Owen J. Roberts School District (camp program). **$5,000-$6,000** each to Bethany Christian School (social studies curriculum), Charter School Resource Center (electronic library), Coatesville Cultural Society, Fellowship House of Conshohocken (children's programs), Quaker School of Horsham (reading software), Upper Octorara Presbyterian Church Preschool, Volunteer English Program of Chester County (Coatesville classes), and White-Williams Scholars. **$3,000** each to FrankfordStyle (summer neighborhood programs) and Plymouth-Whitemarsh High School (educational trip). *EVANGELICAL CHRISTIAN MINISTRIES/SERVICE ORGANIZATION GRANTS*: High grant of **$125,000** to Coatesville Bible Fellowship (building renovations). **$20,000** to Biblical Theological Seminary (graduate program) and Life Transforming Ministries [Coatesville] (community workshops). **$15,000-$15,500** each to International Renewal Ministries/Greater Philadelphia (pastors prayer summits), InterVarsity Christian Fellowship (staff support), and Tel-A-Village International [Pittsburgh] (Indonesian radio programs). **$14,000** to Adelaide College of Ministries [Doylestown] (field education officer). **$12,000** each to Magee Rehabilitation Hospital (pastoral care program) and World Mission Associates [Lancaster] (local leadership development). **$10,000** each to Scholarship Soley d'Haiti [Rosemont] (school in Haiti) and Watchman Fellowship [Westmoreland County] (cult awareness program). **$7,500** to UFM International [Bala Cynwyd] (seminary professors in Haiti). **$6,000** to Cornerstone Family Ministries [Waverly] (youth training). **$4,000-$5,000** each to Awake America! (Philadelphia crusade), Campus Crusade for Christ (military outreach), Central Pa. Youth for Christ [Shamokin Dam], Kensington Area Ministry (Youth Corps), Northside Christian Health Center [Pittsburgh], Prayer Evangelism Network [New Hope] (Lighthouses of Prayer), Scripture Union [Wayne] (summer children's mission project), Temple Brotherhood Mission [Philadelphia] (program for homeless men), Transport for Christ [Lancaster County] (chaplain recruiting, etc.), Try God Ministries [Pennsburg], WEC International [Fort Washington] (Christian youth literature), Wilkey Church [Philadelphia] (leadership development), Young Life/Western Philadelphia Suburbs (high schools program), and Youth Outreach International [Lancaster] (West Africa hospital project). **$3,000** to Life Abundant, Inc. (volunteer recruitment, etc.) *OTHER Pa. GRANTS*: **$20,000** to Lincoln Institute of Public Opinion Research [Harrisburg] and other smaller local/Pa. grants, **$2,500** or less. **Out-of-state** grants mostly ranged from **$3,000-$10,000** (a few higher) and were primarily for Christian evangelical programs/ministries in AZ, CA, CO, DC, DE, FL, GA, IL, KY, MA, MD, MI, MN, MO, MT, NC, NJ, NY, OH, OK, SC, TN, TX, VA, WA. ■ **PUBLICATIONS:** Annual Report; booklet with a statement of program policy and application guidelines ■ **WEBSITE:** None ■ **E-MAIL:** hustonfndn@aol.com ■ **APPLICATION POLICIES & PROCEDURES:** The Foundation reports that at least half of giving annually is for Evangelical Christian purposes worldwide. All other giving is national (though focused on Chester County, Pa.) and is for Health/Human Services, Education, Civic, Arts & Culture, Science, or the Environment. Most grants are for general support or special projects. No grants are awarded to individuals or for travel, endowment, benefit advertising/tickets, fraternal groups, political candidates/parties, lobbying, veterans organizations, labor groups, social clubs, budget deficits, or to intermediate organizations (except United Ways) which redistribute funds. Prospective applicants initially should make a telephone inquiry about the feasibility of submitting a request. First-time applicants should submit a one-page Letter of Intent describing a proposed program/project. If appropriate, the Foundation will send a complete information packet with an Applicant Information Form; completed forms should be submitted in January-February or July-August (deadlines are March 15th and September 15th) together with organizational/project budgets, list of major funding sources, audited financial statement, the latest IRS Form 990, and IRS tax-exempt status documentation. In addition, requests from Evangelical Christian organizations must include a doctrinal Statement of Faith in conformance with that detailed in the guidelines. Site visits sometimes are made to organizations being considered for a grant. Grants are awarded at meetings in May and November.

O+D+T Susan B. Heilman (Contact, Secular Relations) — Nancy Huston Hansen [Malvern] (VP+Contact, Evangelical Relations) — Charles Lukens Huston, III [Chester Springs] (VP, Community Relations & Director of Operations) — Elinor Huston Lashley [VA] (VP, Arts & Cultural Relations & Education) — Rebecca Lukens Huston (S+D) — Charles Lukens Huston, IV [Coatesville] (F+D) — Charles Chadwick (D) — Gardiner Hansen (D) — Scott G. Huston (D)

SE-333   Huston (Stewart) Charitable Trust, The
Lukens Historic District
50 South First Ave., 2nd Floor
Coatesville   19320   (Chester County)

MI-12-13-14-15-18-20-22-25-29-31-35-41-42
51-52-53-54-55-56-63-64-65-86
Phone 610-384-2666 **FAX** 610-384-3396
EIN 23-2612599   **Year Created** 1990

AMV $23,940,213   **FYE** 12-00   **(Gifts Received** $0)   133 **Grants totaling** $1,989,454

Over half local/Pa. giving; grants are for operating support except as noted and some comprise multiple awards. **SECULAR GRANTS: $88,000** to Graystone Society, Inc. (capital projects/various programs). **$35,000** to Pa. Assn. of Nonprofit Organizations [Harrisburg] (operating support/leadership programs). **$30,000** to Nightingale Productions [Philadelphia] (Rebecca Lukens documentary). **$25,000** each to Chester County Community Foundation (pledge payments/benefit events), Chester Springs Studio (Coatesville studio/programs), and Primitive Hall Foundation (facility expansion). **$20,000** each to Champions of Caring [Villanova], City of Coatesville (neighborhood park), and Ophthalmic Research Associates (minority health care in Chester County). **$15,000** each to Handi-Crafters [Thorndale], Lincoln Institute of Public Opinion Research [Harrisburg], and Theatre Ariel [Merion]. **$14,000** to Lukens Band. **$10,000-$11,000** each to Chester County Assn. for the Blind (employment workshop materials), Cheyney U. (historic house restoration), Coatesville Center for Community Health (building renovation), Coatesville Cultural Society, Family Service of Chester County (Coatesville operations), Freedoms Foundation of Valley Forge (teacher scholarships/internet project), Friends to Save Beechwood [Bryn Mawr] (restoration), Pa. State Police Camp Cadet (camperships for local children), and Planned Parenthood of Chester County (Coatesville center relocation). **$9,000** to W.C. Atkinson Memorial Community Services. **$6,500** each to Maternal & Child Health Consortium and Natural Lands Trust [Media] (Sadsbury Wood stewardship project). **$5,000** each to Big Brothers/Big Sisters of Chester County (Coatesville outreach program), Chester County Healthy Communities Partnership (Dental Network expansion), Coatesville Parent's Music Club (concert series), Crime Victims' Center of Chester County (Coatesville programs), Kelly Anne Dolan Memorial Fund [Ambler], Easter Seals [Philadelphia] (adaptive summer camp), LaSalle U. Nonprofit Management Development Center (Chester County programs), National Liberty Museum (Freedom Tours), People's Light & Theatre Company (Coatesville school project), Philabundance (Chester County operations), Phoenixville Area Economic Development Corp. (Foundry visitors center), Upattinas School [Glenmoore] (Appalachian Trail project), Valley Forge Historical Society (house-catalog collection evaluation), and Whitaker Center for Science & the Arts [Harrisburg] (science exhibits). **$2,500-$4,000** each to Center on Hearing & Deafness (volunteers for hospice patients), Coatesville Christmas Parade, Human Services, Inc. (Coatesville School District consultant), Norristown Zoo (winter animal care), and Strings for Schools (Coatesville school programs). Other smaller local/Pa. contributions for similar secular purposes. **Out-of-state** giving includes **$30,000** to Denison U. [OH] (Organizational Studies Program) and **$15,000** to National Trust for Historic Preservation [DC] (stabilize six Revolutionary War buildings). ***TRINITARIAN EVANGELICAL GRANTS***—for religious, educational and social outreach purposes: High grant of **$125,000** to Coatesville Bible Fellowship (building repair). **$50,000** to Greater Deliverance Church [Coatesville] (elevator construction). **$37,500** to Pine Forge Academy [Berks County] (building renovation). **$35,000** each to Lan-Chester Christian School (programs/capital needs) and Life Transforming Ministries [Coatesville]. **$25,000** to Eastern U. (Emergency Aid Fund/Nonprofit Excellence Award/scholarship benefit). **$22,500** to Frederick Mennonite Community (chapel renovation). **$20,000** to New Life in Christ (building maintenance/equipment). **$17,500** to Good Works, Inc. (building materials). **$15,000** to Episcopal Church of the Trinity (capital improvements). **$12,000** each to Bridge of Hope (homelessness program) and Friends Boarding Home (new roof). **$10,000** each to American Baptist Historical Society [Valley Forge] (curator salary), Brandywine YMCA (challenge course project), Center for Parent/Youth Understanding (radio-audio equipment), Church of the Ascension [Parkesburg] (building renovation), County Corrections Gospel Mission (renovations/staff), Kearsley Retirement Community (stained glass window restoration), Olivet United Methodist Church (emergency food cupboard), Safe Harbor of Greater West Chester (lunch program), Scripture Union [Wayne] (Chester Children's Mission), and Working Wardrobe. **$7,500** each to Bethany Christian Services [Fort Washington] (foster-adoptive family recruitment) and YMCA of Philadelphia & Vicinity (child care/summer camp/scholarship support). **$3,000-$5,000** each to Chester County Christian Chorale (sing-a-long), Phoenixville Area YMCA (pool renovations), and Upper Octorara Presbyterian Church (preschool scholarships/computers). **Out-of-state** Trinitarian/Evangelical grants include **$86,500** to Bridges for Peace [OK] (building renovations/food bank outreach); **$45,000** to Christian Friends of Israel [Israel] (Russian immigrant assistance); **$30,000** to Project Light [VA] (Bible-based literacy programs); **$20,000** each to International Christian Embassy Jerusalem-USA [DC] and Urban Promise [NJ] (building purchase/programs/salaries); and 34 grants to GA (mostly Savannah) totaling $651,384.■ **PUBLICATIONS:** Annual Report; Distribution Guidelines booklet and Grant Request Attachments sheet; Request for Contribution Form; informational brochure ■ **WEBSITE:** www.stewarthuston.org ■ **E-MAIL:** admin@stewarthuston.org ■ **APPLICATION POLICIES & PROCEDURES:** The Foundation reports that Pa. giving support focuses on Chester County (particularly Coatesville) and Georgia (especially Savannah). Priority areas of interest are Religion—particularly Trinitarian/Evangelical activities, as well as Health & Human Services, Education, Civic Affairs, and Arts & Culture. Overall, at least of 60% of giving must be for Trinitarian/Evangelical activities—defined to include all Protestant churches (except Unitarian churches) and affiliated/related organizations which follow and exemplify the Christian Gospel or charitable endeavors such as preaching/conducting services, offering religious instruction, distributing religious literature, providing food/shelter to the homeless, maintaining orphanages, operating hospices, and conducting drug/alcohol abuse prevention and rehabilitation programs. Most grants are for specific projects, capital projects, general operations, or equipment purchases/upgrades; requests must address a particular community need/issue. The Trust seeks to support organizations which encourage commitments of human resources, i.e. community volunteers, and prefers not to be the major source of an organization's funding. Generally, no grants are awarded to/for individuals; endowment; benefit tickets/advertising; operating deficits; document publications; pass-through funds; fraternal, veteran, labor, or local civic organizations, volunteer fire companies; political parties/candidates, and groups involved in influencing legislation. Prospective applicants initially should make a telephone inquiry about the feasibility of submitting an application and to request the Request for Contribution Form -and- the 15-page Distribution Guidelines booklet (both available on the website). In brief, applicants for Secular grants must submit an initial Letter of Intent (6 pages maximum—see Distribution Guidelines booklet) before a January 15th deadline; Trinitarian/Evangelical grant applicants must submit a full proposal (refer to the Distributions Guidelines booklet for details) before the March 1st or September 1st deadlines. Site visits usually are made to organizations being considered for a grant. The Trustees award grants at June and December meetings.

O+D+T Scott G. Huston (Executive Director+Con) — Charles Lukens Huston, III [Chester Springs] (T) — Samuel A. Cann, Esq. [GA] (T) — Louis N. Seltzer [Bryn Mawr] (T)

SE-334 Idyll Development Foundation, The MI-25-85
c/o Idyll, Ltd.
415 East Jasper Street, P.O. Box 405 **Phone** 610-565-5242 **FAX** 610-565-5142
Media 19063 (Delaware County) **EIN** 23-2703497 **Year Created** 1992
AMV $2,162,324 **FYE** 12-01 **(Gifts Received** $629,264) 25 **Grants totaling** $19,985

About half local giving/philanthropic activity, primarily through entrepreneurship loans. Major local loans include **$275,000** to Homecare Associates [Philadelphia] (to build an employee-owned home nursing care agency); **$100,000** for CitySort [Philadelphia] (to build a mail-sorting business in an Empowerment Zone); and **$40,000** to Chester Community Improvement Project (rehabilitation of affordable home ownership opportunities for low-income families). Other local support included **$5,000** each to Opera Company of Philadelphia and Social Venture Network-Philadelphia; and **$2,400-$2,585** each to Domestic Abuse Project, Family & Community Service Agency [Media], Habitat for Humanity/Philadelphia, and Maloca Project. **Out-of-state** loans to organizations in IL, Mexico, Brazil, and other locations. ■ **PUBLICATIONS:** Informational brochure with statement of program priorities and application guidelines ■ **WEBSITE:** www.untours.com ■ **E-MAIL:** kate.duncan@untours.com ■ **APPLICATION POLICIES & PROCEDURES:** The Foundation reports that it makes capital available to economically disenfranchised, low-income people (local, national and global) to encourage an expansive entrepreneurship, primarily through low-interest loans to individuals, groups and organizations dealing with the issues of job creation, living wage, low-cost housing, and fair trade. Special consideration is given to projects that are innovative and replicable; are environmentally sustainable; have potential to help revitalize a community; foster a humane workplace, including living wages and good benefits; and have a feasibility based on interviews, evaluation of financial data, management team strength, and the length/terms of the loan. To request a loan, submit at any time a budget and letter (3 pages maximum) with a Business Plan which includes a brief history/description of the project; the number of people to be employed by the project and at what wage; what community will benefit from the project, and in what way; how the project will be self-sustaining; the amount and terms of the requested loan, including a repayment schedule; very brief resumes of the project's principal directors; and other details deemed relevant to the request. Site visits sometimes are made to organizations under consideration for support.

O+D+T Kate Duncan (Assistant Director+Con) — Harold E. Taussig (P+D+Donor) — Norma L. Taussig (VP+D+Donor) — Lee DeWoody (D) — Rev. David Funkhouser (D) — Robert Johnson (D) — Mary LeFever (D) — Alix Rabin (D) — Bob Seiwell, Esq. (D) — Brian Taussig-Lux (D) Corporate donor: Idyll, Ltd.

SE-335   IGN Foundation
c/o Mass Marketing Insurance Group
300 Berwyn Park, Suite 100
Berwyn   19312   (Chester County)

MI-15-22-25-43-61

Phone 610-408-8600 **FAX** None
EIN 23-7653516   **Year Created** 1990

AMV $6,488,007   **FYE** 6-01   **(Gifts Received** $0)   7 **Grants totaling** $450,767

About one-fifth local giving. High Pa. grant of **$50,000** to Immaculate Conception Catholic Church [Levittown]. **$10,000** each to Divine Providence Village [Delaware County] and St. Mary's Franciscan Shelter [Phoenixville]. **$5,000** to Chestnut Hill Senior Service Center. **Out-of-state** grants: **$355,767** to Evans Scholars Foundation [IL] (scholarships for caddies) and **$20,000** to a Catholic church [IL]. ■**PUBLICATIONS:** None ■**WEBSITE:** None ■**E-MAIL:** None ■**APPLICATION POLICIES & PROCEDURES:** Grant requests may be submitted in a letter at any time; briefly describe the organization, state the amount and purpose of the funding needed, and include IRS tax-exempt status documentation. No grants awarded to individuals.

O+D+T Frank S. Polizzi (T+Donor+Con)

SE-336   Ikon Office Solutions Foundation
c/o Ikon Office Solutions, Inc.
70 Valley Stream Parkway
Malvern   19355   (Chester County)

MI-12-13-32-41-72

Phone 610-296-8000 **FAX** 610-296-3248
EIN 23-7378726   **Year Created** 1974

AMV $4,451,702   **FYE** 12-00   **(Gifts Received** $0)   400+ **Grants totaling** $297,268

Limited local/Pa. giving. **$10,000** to Police Athletic League. **$7,714** to American Cancer Society. **$2,950** to Juvenile Diabetes Foundation. **$1,000** to Children's Miracle Network. Other Pa. giving mostly matching gifts to institutions as defined below. **Out-of-state** giving in corporate operating locations nationwide. — In the prior year, Philadelphia-area grants included **$12,500** to Philadelphia Zoo and **$1,000** to Delaware Valley Science Fair. ■**PUBLICATIONS:** None ■**WEBSITE:** www.ikon.com [corporate info only] ■**E-MAIL:** None ■**APPLICATION POLICIES & PROCEDURES:** Grant requests may be submitted in a brief letter at any time to the Foundation or to an Ikon subsidiary company; but, all grants are disbursed by the Foundation. The Contributions Committee meets quarterly or as needed. Matching gifts are restricted to colleges, universities, private secondary schools or public radio/TV stations and have a $1,500 maximum/employee/year. — Formerly called Alco Standard Foundation.

O+D+T Robin Mitchell (Administrator+Con) — William Urkiel (P+D) — J.F. Quinn (F+D) — Don Liu (S+D) — Michael T. Rush (AS) — Arlen Shenkman (AS) Corporate donor: Ikon Office Solutions Inc.

SE-337   Independence Foundation
Offices at The Bellevue, Suite 1101
200 South Broad Street
Philadelphia   19102   (Philadelphia County)

MI-12-13-14-15-16-17-18-20-25-29-31-33-34
35-39-42-43-5-1-52-53-54-55-56-57-83
Phone 215-985-4009 **FAX** 215-985-3989
EIN 23-1352110   **Year Created** 1945

AMV $131,761,086   **FYE** 12-01   **(Gifts Received** $0)   382 **Grants totaling** $8,973,778

Most giving limited to Greater Philadelphia area to support organizations providing services to people who do not ordinarily have access to them. Note: The above Grants Totaling figure refers to funds disbursed in 2001; the 216 grants reported below $6,521,821 total) were approved/appropriated in 2001—some were paid in full, others in part if multiyear awards. Grants are for general support except as noted. ***ARTS-CULTURE GRANTS*** ($2,070,200 approved): **$325,000** to Opera Company of Philadelphia (general support-3 years/challenge grant-2 years). **$215,000** to Arden Theatre Company (project /challenge grants-2 years). **$199,000** to Mural Arts Advocates (project/challenge grants). **$150,000** to Philadelphia Fringe Festival (general support/challenge grant-3 years). **$145,000** to Philadelphia Zoo (challenge grant-2 years/general support-3 years). **$115,000** to Please Touch Museum (mostly challenge grant-3 years). **$100,000** each to Mann Center for the Performing Arts (challenge grant-2 years) and WHYY (challenge grant-2 years). **$60,000** to Asociacion de Musicos Latino Americanos (project/general support-2 years). **$45,000** each to Painted Bride Art Center (3 years) and Southwest Community Enrichment Center (project-3 years). **$50,000** to Free Library of Philadelphia (mostly project-3 years). **$30,000** each to American Ballet Competition/Dance Affiliates (3 years), American Swedish Historical Foundation (3 years), Scribe Video Center (3 years), and Warwick Township Historical Society (project-3 years). **$25,000** each to Academy of Children's Music (project), The Irish Memorial (project), and Theatre Communications Group [NY] (project). **$20,000** to Greater Philadelphia Cultural Alliance (grant). **$17,500** to Pa. Ballet (general support/project). **$15,000** to SCRAP Performance Group. **$10,000** each to Astral Artistic Services (challenge grant), Greater Philadelphia Tourism Marketing Corp., and Orchestra 2001 (challenge grant). **$7,500-$7,700** each to Mum Puppettheatre (project/general support), Prince Music Theater (project), and Theatre Alliance of Greater Philadelphia. **$5,000** each to Act II Playhouse, Amaryllis Theatre Company (project), Bushfire Theatre of Performing Arts, Jeanne Ruddy Dance, Landis & Company, NetworkArts Philadelphia, Network for New Music, Philadelphia Classical Symphony (project), Spiral Q Puppet Theater (project), and Theatre Exile (project). **$2,500** each to Eastern State Penitentiary Historic Site and Fleisher Art Memorial (children's scholarships). Also, **Performing Arts Fellowships/Visual Arts Fellowships** (mostly **$5,000-$7,500** each) awarded to 26 sponsoring organizations. ***HEALTH-HUMAN SERVICES & EDUCATION GRANTS*** ($1,505,045 approved): **$200,000** to Planned Parenthood of SE Pa. (2 years). **$194,825** to Foundation for Cognitive Therapy & Research (project/Fellows-2 years). **$190,000** to Planned Parenthood of Bucks County (general support-2 years/project/challenge grant). **$150,000** to Planned Parenthood of

Chester County (2 years). **$50,000** to YWCA of Bucks County (2 years). **$30,000** each to Bridging the Gaps (project-2 years), Congreso de Latinos Unidos (capital campaign-2 years), Elizabeth Blackwell Health Center for Women (special needs program-2 years), Greater Philadelphia Food Bank, Human Rights Watch [NY] (Children's Rights Project), MANNA/Metropolitan AIDS Neighborhood Nutrition Alliance (2 years), Overbrook School for the Blind (TEAMS program-2 years), Philabundance (2 years), and Philadelphians Concerned About Housing (2 years). **$24,000-$25,000** each to Cambodian Assn. of Greater Philadelphia (project), Community College of Philadelphia (project), Lebanon Valley College (Eugene Fish Professorship in Business-endowed chair), and Red Cross/SE Pa. Chapter (project). **$20,000** each to CHOICE (2 years), Committee for Dignity & Fairness for the Homeless Housing (2 years), Domestic Violence Center of Chester County (project-2 years), Inn Dwelling (2 years), Liberty Resources (2 years), Little Brothers-Friends of the Elderly (project-2 years), Northwest Interfaith Movement (project-2 years), Philadelphia READS (2 years), Recording for the Blind & Dyslexic (2 years), SOWN/Supportive Older Women's Network (project-2 years), Wheels Medical Transportation (2 years), and Women's Center of Montgomery County (2 years). **$15,000** each to Howard U. School of Law [DC] (scholarships), Royer-Greaves School for the Blind, and U. of New Mexico Health Sciences Center (project). **$12,000** to Philadelphia Health Management Corp. (project). **$10,000** each to Cheyney U. (scholarships), Chi Eta Phi Sorority/Theta Chapter (scholarship fund), Eagles Fly for Leukemia (family support fund), and U. of Rhode Island College of Nursing (Dean's Fund). **$5,000** to Verde Valley Sanctuary [AZ]. **$1,000** each to Children's Hospital of Philadelphia (project), National Transplant Assistance Fund, Woodlynde School (project), and World Affairs Council of Philadelphia. ***NURSE MANAGED PRIMARY CARE INITIATIVE*** (**$2,245,500** approved). **$455,000** to National Nursing Centers Consortium (general support/project). **$340,000** to Philadelphia Health Management Corp. (Mary Howard Health Center-2 years/project). **$250,000** to La Comunidad Hispana [Kennett Square] (project-2 years). **$225,000** to LaSalle U. (project). **$160,000** each to Abington Memorial Hospital (mostly scholarships/project support) and Visiting Nurses Assn. of Greater Philadelphia (House Calls Project-2 years). **$158,000** to U. of Pa. (Francis J. Myers Youth Access Center). **$150,000** to Wellness Community of Philadelphia (general support/challenge grant). **$97,500** to APM Community Health Centers (projects). **$60,000** each to Face to Face (St. Vincent Health Center-2 years) and Resources for Human Development (project). **$50,000** each to Community College of Philadelphia (nursing interns project) and MCP/Hahnemann U.(urban primary care project). **$30,000** to VNA Community Services (Children's Health Centers). ***PUBLIC INTEREST LAW FELLOWSHIPS*** (**$362,576** approved): **$58,758** to Nationalities Service Center. **$56,367** to Women Against Abuse Legal Center. **$48,741** to Pa. Health Law Project **$44,103** to AIDS Law Project of Pa. **$22,045-$28,224** each to Education Law Center of Pa., HIAS & Council Migration Service of Philadelphia, Homeless Advocacy Project, Philadelphia Legal Assistance Center, Senior Citizen Judicare Project, and Women's Law Project. LEGAL AID GRANTS (**$286,000** approved): **$120,000** to Legal Aid of SE Pa. (2 years). **$50,000** to Community Legal Services (challenge grant). **$40,000** each to Community Impact Legal Services [West Chester] (2 years) and Defender Assn. of Philadelphia (capital representation project). **$10,000** each to Committee of Seventy (challenge grant), MidPenn Legal Services [Harrisburg] (Education for Life project), and Public Interest Law Center of Philadelphia. **$5,000** to National Senior Citizen Law Center [DC]. ***ADVISORY COMMITTEE GRANTS*** (**$52,500** approved): The Foundation's six Advisory Committees awarded 47 discretionary grants (**$500-$2,500**) to various organizations of their choice, mostly in Greater Philadelphia. ■**PUBLICATIONS:** Annual Report; grant application guidelines ■**WEBSITE:** www.independencefoundation.org ■**E-MAIL:** ssherman@independencefoundation.org ■**APPLICATION POLICIES & PROCEDURES:** The Foundation reports that giving is restricted to nonprofit organizations in Philadelphia, and Bucks, Chester, Delaware and Montgomery counties, and that unsolicited proposals are not considered. The Foundation usually sends out Requests For Proposals (RFP's) under six giving categories: Culture & the Arts; Health & Human Services; Public Interest Legal Aid; Nurse Managed Health Care Initiative; Public Interest Law Fellowships; and Fellowships in the Arts. Organizations that wish to become eligible to receive an RFP may submit a Letter of Inquiry (2 pages maximum); include organizational background, the amount being requested, and a description of the program/services for which funds would be used. Letters of Inquiry may be submitted at any time, but grant cycles (and deadlines) for each program category are established annually and all decisions are made within that cycle; consult the website or contact the Foundation for proposal submission deadlines. After a Letter of Inquiry is received and reviewed for consistency with current funding priorities, the applicant is notified of eligibility to receive an RFP, or not. Generally, no grants are awarded directly to individuals, or for building and development funds, travel, research, or publications. — Note: Detailed application procedures (and application forms) for the Public Interest Law Fellowships and Fellowships in the Arts are available on the website. Applicants must be nominated by an official local, nonprofit organization (i.e. an arts/cultural organization -or- an organization providing public interest legal services) which is a current grantee of the Foundation and has elected to participate in a Fellowships program.

O+D+T Susan E. Sherman, R.N. (P+D+Con) — Hon. Phyllis W. Beck (C+D) — Eugene C. Fish, Esq. (VP+D) — Theodore K. Warner, Jr., Esq. (S+F+D) — Andre L. Dennis, Esq. (D) — Andrea Mengel, Ph.D., R.N. (D)

SE-338   Ingerman Family Foundation, The
1320 Centennial Road
Narberth   19072   (Montgomery County)

MI-22-32-35-42-62-81-82
Phone 215-732-9010 **FAX** None
EIN 23-2278199   **Year Created** 1983

AMV $47,828   **FYE** 11-00   **(Gifts Received** $39,339)   46 **Grants totaling** $10,169

Mostly local giving. High grants of **$2,000** each to American Committee for Ben Gurion U. [Jenkintown] and Wistar Institute. **$1,000** to Taxin 5K Run. **$500** each to Living Beyond Breast Cancer and Middle East Forum. Other local and out-of-state contributions, **$18-$350**, for various purposes. — Major grants in the prior year included **$24,000** to Jewish Community Centers of Greater Philadelphia (Jewish Fed-Israel Programs); **$23,000** to Ben-Gurion U. of the Negev [Israel] (overseas student scholarships); **$10,000** to Hillel of Greater Philadelphia; and **$5,000** to Congregation Adath Israel. ■**PUBLICATIONS:** None ■**WEBSITE:** None ■**E-MAIL:** None ■**APPLICATION POLICIES & PROCEDURES:** Information not available. — Formerly called Ingerman-Ginsberg Israeli Fellowship Foundation.

O+D+T Ira Ingerman (C+Donor+Con) — Eileen Ingerman (D)

SE-339 **Innisfree Foundation of Bryn Mawr**
c/o Center Bridge Group, Inc.
234 Mall Boulevard, Suite 105
King of Prussia 19406 (Montgomery County)
MI-34-41-42-43-56
Phone 610-992-5022 **FAX** None
EIN 23-6950379 **Year Created** 1989
AMV $317,677 **FYE** 9-00 (**Gifts Received** $100,000) 4 **Grants totaling** $186,000
Mostly local giving; all grants are general support. High grant of **$100,000** to Temple U. **$80,500** to Gwynedd-Mercy College. **$3,000** to Academy of Music. **Out-of-state** grant: **$2,500** to Somerset Hills Learning Center [NJ]. — Grants awarded the prior year include **$22,500** to Gwynedd-Mercy College (Health Care Opportunity Program) and **$1,000** to Shipley School (scholarship fund). ■**PUBLICATIONS:** None ■**WEBSITE:** None ■**E-MAIL:** None ■**APPLICATION POLICIES & PROCEDURES:** No grants awarded to individuals.
O+D+T Harold G. Schaeffer (T+Donor+Con) — Adele K. Schaeffer (T) — Anthony L. Schaeffer (T) — James R. Schaeffer (T) — Robert D. Schaeffer (T)

SE-340 **Inverso-Baglivo Foundation, The**
824 Hood Road
Swarthmore 19081 (Delaware County)
MI-14-82
Phone 610-544-5960 **FAX** 610-544-5665
EIN 23-2775468 **Year Created** 1994
AMV $468,452 **FYE** 12-00 (**Gifts Received** $987,873) 15 **Grants totaling** $182,311
One U.S. grant: **$43,720** to ARC of Delaware. All other grants support various human services programs in Indonesia: low vision, hearing aids, community development, vocational training for disabled, and others. ■**PUBLICATIONS:** None ■**WEBSITE:** None ■**E-MAIL:** ibfound@icdc.com ■**APPLICATION POLICIES & PROCEDURES:** Grant requests may be submitted in a letter at any time; include IRS tax-exempt status documentation.
O+D+T Anthony W. Inverso (VP+S+F+D+Con) — Daniel A. Inverso [Indonesia] (C+P+D+Donor) — Carmella Adams [NY] (D) — Daniel Baglivo [Jamison] (D) — Jessie B. Barbuto [NJ] (D) — Angelo J. Inverso [Pipersville] (D) — Gloria C. Melloni [Philadelphia] (D) — Antoinette Sgro [NJ] (D+Donor) — Rina A. Sukartawidjaja [Indonesia] (Donor)

SE-341 **Ithan Foundation, The**
615 Newtown Road
Villanova 19085 (Delaware County)
MI-15-31-55
Phone 610-688-8779 **FAX** 610-688-2923
EIN 23-2896573 **Year Created** 1997
AMV $591,990 **FYE** 12-01 (**Gifts Received** $0) 4 **Grants totaling** $30,000
All local giving. High grants of **$10,000** each to Children's Hospital of Philadelphia Foundation and Surrey Services for Seniors. **$5,000** each to Wayne Art Center and Wayne Senior Center. ■**PUBLICATIONS:** None ■**WEBSITE:** None ■**E-MAIL:** None ■**APPLICATION POLICIES & PROCEDURES:** Information not available.
O+D+T George R. Atterbury (P+F+Donor+Con) — Moira Atterbury (VP) — Susannah Atterbury Gardner (S)

SE-342 **Jacobs (Margaret G.) Charitable Trust**
6114 Ensley Drive
Flourtown 19031 (Montgomery County)
MI-12-13-14-15-18-22-25-29-31-32-33-41-44 62-71
Phone 215-419-6152 **FAX** None
EIN 23-2743317 **Year Created** 1992
AMV $3,236,821 **FYE** 6-00 (**Gifts Received** $0) 44 **Grants totaling** $155,400
Mostly local/nearby NJ giving. High grant of **$15,000** to Red Cross (international response fund). **$12,500** to The Green Tree School. **$8,000** to Elwyn Institute. **$7,500** each to Greater Philadelphia Food Bank and Special Olympics of Pa. **$5,000-$5,500** each to Arthritis Foundation, Carson Valley School, Congregation Kol Ami, Germantown Friends School, Juvenile Diabetes Foundation, Salvation Army/Philadelphia, and YWCA of Germantown. **$3,000-$3,500** each to Academy of Notre Dame de Namur, Adoption Center of Delaware Valley, and Wissahickon Hospice [needy patient fund]. **$2,000-$2,500** each to ALS Assn., Awbury Arboretum, Children's Miracle Network of Greater Philadelphia, Crime Prevention Assn. of Philadelphia, Crossroad School, Delaware Valley Friends School, Girl Scouts-Troop 996, Jubilee School, Kelly Ann Dolan Memorial Fund, Philabundance, Philadelphia Committee to End Homelessness, Philadelphia Ronald McDonald House, Philadelphia Senior Center, Plymouth Meeting Friends School, Salvation Army/Norristown, Surrey Services for Seniors, Trevor's Campaign for the Homeless, and Women in Transition. **$1,000-$1,500** each to American Cancer Society, Deaf-Hearing Communication Center, Jeanes Memorial Library, Paws With a Cause, Pa. School for the Deaf, Sunday Breakfast Rescue Mission, and Tamaqua Public Library [Schuylkill County]. **$900** to SCAN Foundation. **Out-of-state** giving includes **$5,000** to The Toddy Pond School [ME] and **$2,500** each to Deborah Hospital Foundation [NJ] and The Parents Assn. [NJ]. ■**PUBLICATIONS:** None ■**WEBSITE:** None ■**E-MAIL:** None ■**APPLICATION POLICIES & PROCEDURES:** Grant requests in any form may be submitted at any time.
O+D+T William R. Levy (Co-T+Con) — Philip H. Brown, II [Springfield] (Co-T)

SE-343 **JDB Fund, The**
404 South Swedesford Road
P.O. Box 157
Gwynedd 19436 (Montgomery County)
MI-11-14-15-17-22-25-31-32-41-42-52-54-56 57-61-71
Phone 215-699-2233 **FAX** 215-699-5998
EIN 23-6418867 **Year Created** 1966
AMV $3,135,223 **FYE** 12-00 (**Gifts Received** $21,434) 60 **Grants totaling** $367,950
Mostly local giving; grants are for annual giving/general purposes except as noted. High grant of **$212,500** to Mount St. Joseph Academy (building renovations). **$41,000** to St. Rose of Lima [North Wales] (building improvements). **$20,000** each to North Penn United Way and Wissahickon Valley Watershed Assn. (capital campaign). **$15,000** to Schuylkill Center for Environmental Education. **$10,000** each to Catholic Charities Appeal and St. John Neumann. **$2,500** to Historical Society of Montgomery County (building improvements). **$1,500** to U. of Pa. Medical Center. **$1,000** each to Academy of Natural Sciences, Angel Flight

East, Chestnut Hill Healthcare (women's health programs), Dignity Housing, Holy Redeemer Foundation (homeless mothers-children program), MBF Center, Montgomery County Assn. for the Blind, National MS Society, The Nature Conservancy, Philadelphia Orchestra, St. Joseph's U. (commemorative book), WHYY-TV12, and Wissahickon Hospice. Other local contributions, mostly **$250** or **$500**, for various types of organizations. **Out-of-state** giving includes **$5,000** to Ocean Reef Cultural Center [FL] and **$500-$1,000** for health, civic, Catholic and other purposes. — Grants approved for future payment: **$137,500** to Mount St. Joseph Academy (building renovations); **$80,000** to Wissahickon Valley Watershed Assn. (capital campaign pledge payment); and **$15,000** to Ocean Reef Cultural Center [FL] (capital campaign pledge payment). ■**PUBLICATIONS:** None ■**WEBSITE:** None ■**E-MAIL:** None ■**APPLICATION POLICIES & PROCEDURES:** The Foundation reports that most grants are for general/operating support, building/renovation, equipment, land acquisition, and challenge grants. No grants awarded to individuals. The Board meets monthly.

O+D+T Paul J. Corr, CPA (Manager+Con) — Claire S. Betz (T+Donor)

SE-344 **Jefferson (Ethel) Scholarship Fund**   **MI**-43
c/o First National Bank & Trust of Newtown
34 South State Street, P.O. Box 158   **Phone** 215-968-4872 **FAX** None
Newtown   18940   (Bucks County)   **EIN** 23-7749232   **Year Created** 1993
AMV $1,513,757   **FYE** 12-00   **(Gifts Received** $0)   29 **Grants totaling** $58,000

All awards are scholarships for Bucks County students attending state or state-related institutions of higher education in several states; scholarships generally range from **$1,500** to **$2,500.** ■**PUBLICATIONS:** None ■**WEBSITE:** None ■**E-MAIL:** None ■ **APPLICATION POLICIES & PROCEDURES:** The Fund reports that scholarships are generally restricted to Bucks County students. Applications must be submitted before fhte April 15th deadline on a form available from the Bank.

O+D+T Foundation Managers: Barry L. Pflueger, Jr. (Senior VP at Bank+Con) — Richard Danese, Esq. (Co-T) — Joseph Colacicco — Richard Fusco First National Bank & Trust of Newtown (Corporate Trustee)

SE-345 **Jerrehian Foundation**   **MI**-31-34-41-42-54
c/o Harvey Pennington Cabot et al
26 South Bryn Mawr Ave.   **Phone** 610-527-9200 **FAX** None
Bryn Mawr   19010   (Montgomery County)   **EIN** 23-6261005   **Year Created** 1951
AMV $1,023,515   **FYE** 12-00   **(Gifts Received** $0)   71 **Grants totaling** $30,770

About half local giving. High local grant of **$1,500** to The Baldwin School. **$1,250** to U. of Pa. **$1,000** each to Chester County Hospital and Habitat for Humanity. **$810** to Philadelphia Museum of Art. Other local contributions **$50-$500** for community, cultural and other purposes. **Out-of-state** giving includes high grant of **$5,000** to Frank A. Oski Pediatrics Scholars Program and **$1,000** to Wellesley College [MA]. ■**PUBLICATIONS:** None ■**WEBSITE:** None ■**E-MAIL:** None ■**APPLICATION POLICIES & PROCEDURES:** Grant requests may be submitted in a letter at any time.

O+D+T Aram K. Jerrehian, Jr. Esq. (T+Con)

SE-346 **JGA Foundation**   **MI**-31-41-42-56-63-72
c/o Saul, Ewing, Remick & Saul
3800 Centre Square West, 1500 Market Street   **Phone** 215-972-7828 **FAX** None
Philadelphia   19102   (Philadelphia County)   **EIN** 23-2326454   **Year Created** 1984
AMV $2,352,883   **FYE** 10-00   **(Gifts Received** $0)   13 **Grants totaling** $120,000

Two Pa. grants: **$5,000** to Philadelphia Zoo. **$3,000** to Academy of Music. **Out-of-state** giving includes **$75,000** to Babson College [MA]; **$7,000** to Red Cross [DC]; **$5,000** each to Lord of Life Lutheran Church [NJ], Memorial Hospital Foundation [NJ], and The Taft School [CT]; and smaller grants, many to NJ. ■**PUBLICATIONS:** None ■**WEBSITE:** None ■**E-MAIL:** None ■ **APPLICATION POLICIES & PROCEDURES:** Grant requests may be submitted in any form at any time; include IRS tax-exempt status documentation.

O+D+T Richard T. Frazier, Esq. (Con) — John R. Dougherty [NJ] (T) — John C. Merritt [NJ] (Donor)

SE-347 **Johnson (Alice L.) Charity Trust**   **MI**-12-14-21-19-23-29-43
c/o First Union/Wachovia
123 South Broad Street, PA1279   **Phone** 215-670-4228 **FAX** 215-670-4236
Philadelphia   19109   (Philadelphia County)   **EIN** 23-6222364   **Year Created** 1935
AMV $625,763   **FYE** 8-99   **(Gifts Received** $0)   7 **Grants totaling** $27,234

All giving restricted to assisting needy/deserving poor persons residing in Bristol Borough, Bucks County. High grant of **$6,034** to Bucks Council Council on Alcoholism & Drug Dependence (Quality Time Program). **$5,000** each to Bristol Lioness Club (clothes for children), Bucks County Assn. for Retired Senior Citizens (Meals on Wheels), and Bucks County Peace Centers (Ventures in Peace program). **$2,500** each for two scholarships of local students. **$1,200** to Home & Community (teen parenting support group). ■**PUBLICATIONS:** None ■**WEBSITE:** None ■**E-MAIL:** diane.stables@wachovia.com ■**APPLICATION POLICIES & PROCEDURES:** Only social service agencies or local government agencies in Bristol Borough, Bucks County are eligible to apply, either for relevant program support or on behalf of eligible individuals. Requests may be submitted at any time in a letter; requests on behalf of individuals should detail the person's case history. Disbursements are made monthly.

O+D+T Diane O. Stables (VP at Bank+Con) — First Union/Wachovia (Trustee)

SE-348 Johnson (Edwin T. & Cynthia S.) Foundation
Spring Lane Farm, 3 Jefferson Court
Newtown 18940 (Bucks County)
AMV $809,869 **FYE** 4-01 (**Gifts Received** $5,900)

MI-12-22-32-42-63-71
Phone 215-968-6284 **FAX** None
EIN 22-2777060 **Year Created** 1986
17 **Grants totaling** $32,655

About three-fourths local/Pa. giving. High grant of **$10,000** to Family Services Assn. of Bucks County. **$5,585** to Gettysburg College. **$4,000** to Newtown Presbyterian Church. **$1,000** each to Anchor Presbyterian Church [Penns Park], Huntington's Disease Society/Delaware Valley Chapter, and Old First Reformed Church. Other smaller local contributions for cultural and human service purposes. **Out-of-state** giving includes **$5,000** to The Jackson Laboratory [ME] (medical research) and **$1,000** to The Conservation Fund [VA]. ■**PUBLICATIONS:** None ■**WEBSITE:** None ■**E-MAIL:** None ■**APPLICATION POLICIES & PROCEDURES:** The Foundation reports that giving focuses on the Delaware Valley, with a special interest in children-related concerns, especially if addressed by church organizations, and in basic science. No grants are awarded to individuals. Prospective applicants initially should make a brief written inquiry about the feasibility of submitting a formal request. Grant requests may be submitted in January-February in any form; include an annual report, organizational budget, and Board member list.

O+D+T Edwin T. Johnson (T+Donor+Con) — Cynthia S. Johnson (T+Donor) — E. Thomas Johnson, Jr. [MA] (T) — Rebecca J. Johnson (T) Corporate donor: The Johnson Companies

SE-349 Jomar Foundation
c/o Fountainhead Publishing
19 Short Road
Doylestown 18901 (Bucks County)
AMV $2,155 **FYE** 12-00 (**Gifts Received** $0)

MI-41-61

Phone 215-348-8775 **FAX** 215-348-4882
EIN 23-2920775 **Year Created** 1997
1 **Grant of** $2,714,704

Sole grant to St. Martin of Tours Catholic Church (for religious school). ■**PUBLICATIONS:** None ■**WEBSITE:** None ■**E-MAIL:** None ■**APPLICATION POLICIES & PROCEDURES:** No grants awarded to individuals.

O+D+T Joseph A. Murphy (P+Donor+Con) — Jerrold A. Walton (VP+F) — Nancy A. Garvey (S)

SE-350 Jones (Donald P.) Foundation
P.O. Box 58910
Philadelphia 19102 (Philadelphia County)
AMV $2,211,299 **FYE** 12-00 (**Gifts Received** $0)

MI-12-13-14-15-25-29-32-41-42-44-54-55-57
Phone 610-565-6944 **FAX** None
EIN 23-6259820 **Year Created** 1953
112 **Grants totaling** $126,300

About three-fourths Delaware Valley giving. High grant of **$6,500** to Benchmark School [Media]. **$3,000-$3,800** each to Aid for Friends, Franklin Institute, Philadelphia Zoo, Presbyterian Children's Village, and YMCA of Philadelphia & Vicinity. **$2,200** each to Community Arts Center [Wallingford] and Horizons Unlimited/Geriatric Education Corp. **$2,000** each to Alzheimer's Assn. of SE Pa. and WHYY. **$1,000-$1,800** each to American Cancer Society, Big Brothers/Big Sisters of America, Boy Scouts/Cradle of Liberty Council, CASA/Youth Advocates, Church Farm School, Delaware County Children's Camp Assn., Delaware County Community College Foundation, Delco Blind/Sight Center, Girl Scouts of SE Pa., Inn Dwelling, Lakeside Youth Services, Lansdowne Public Library, Pa. Right to Work Defense & Education Foundation [Harrisburg], RSVP of Delaware County, Rose Tree-Media Education Foundation, Voyage House, and Woodmere Art Museum. Other local contributions mostly **$500-$700** for health/human services, educational, cultural and other purposes. **Out-of-state** giving includes **$5,000** to Cystic Fibrosis Foundation [MD]; **$4,400** to The Reason Foundation [CA]; **$2,000** to American U. of Paris Foundation [NY]; and **$1,200-$1,600** each for Accuracy in Media [DC], Alice Lloyd College [KY], Alzheimer's Assn. [IL], Center on National Labor Policy [VA], Citizens for a Sound Economy Foundation [DC], Cumberland College [KY], Hillsdale College [MI], and Institute for Justice [DC]. — Major grants awarded in 2001 included **$10,000** to Cystic Fibrosis Foundation [MD]; **$6,600** to Benchmark School; and **$3,300** to Franklin Institute. ■**PUBLICATIONS:** None ■**WEBSITE:** None ■**E-MAIL:** None ■**APPLICATION POLICIES & PROCEDURES:** The Foundation reports that giving focuses on the Philadelphia area, particularly Delaware County. No grants are awarded to individuals. Grant requests may be submitted in a letter at any time; include an annual report, audited financial statement and IRS tax-exempt status documentation.

O+D+T Arthur W. Jones (Co-T+Con) — Elizabeth Jones Gilson [FL] (Co-T) — Lawrence T. Jones [WI] (Co-T)

SE-351 Kahaner (Charles A.) Foundation
c/o Hanover Fire & Casualty Insurance Co.
220 West Germantown Pike, P.O. Box 4000
Plymouth Meeting 19462 (Montgomery County)
AMV $695,174 **FYE** 12-00 (**Gifts Received** $62,920)

MI-15-22-31-52-54-62-82-84

Phone 610-940-1477 **FAX** None
EIN 23-6296585 **Year Created** 1952
33 **Grants totaling** $57,022

About four-fifths local giving. High grant of **$14,500** to Albert Einstein Healthcare Network. **$10,000** to National Liberty Museum. **$6,820** to Boys Town Jerusalem Foundation of America [Jenkintown]. **$5,000** to Prince Music Theater. **$1,000-$2,500** each to Federation Allied Jewish Appeal, Golden Slipper Club & Charities, Philadelphia Geriatric Center, and Philadelphia Youth Tennis. Other smaller local contributions for various purposes. **Out-of-state** giving includes **$2,500** to Women's International Zionist Organization [NY]; **$2,017** to Jewish Theological Seminary [NY]; and **$1,000** to Mitey Riders [NC]. ■**PUBLICATIONS:** None ■**WEBSITE:** None ■**E-MAIL:** None ■**APPLICATION POLICIES & PROCEDURES:** The Foundation reports that most grants are for general operating support. Prospective applicants should submit a brief letter outlining a proposed grant request, and if the Foundation is interested a full proposal may be requested. No grants are awarded to individuals. The Trustees meet in March, June, September and December.

O+D+T Ross D. Miller (T+Manager+Con) — Herbert Brill [Wyndmoor] (T) — Joyce Brill [Wyndmoor] (T) — Susan Kater [Philadelphia] (T) — Ilene R. Miller [Villanova] (T) — Jonathan S. Miller [Philadelphia] (T) — Melvyn K. Miller [Villanova] (T) — Karen Venus [Philadelphia] (T) — Minerva Miller (Donor) — Corporate donors: Life & Health Insurance Co. of America; Hanover Fire & Casualty Insurance Co.

SE-352   Kahn (Barbara R. & Charles, Jr.) Foundation
1147 Rydal Road
Rydal   19046   (Montgomery County)

MI-13-14-22-31-41-42-54-62
Phone Unlisted **FAX** None
EIN 23-2898465   **Year Created** 1997

AMV $881,056   **FYE** 6-01   (**Gifts Received** $10,953)   11 **Grants totaling** $70,600

All local/Pa. giving. High grant of **$28,000** to Federation Allied Jewish Appeal. **$20,000** to Holy Redeemer Health Systems. **$9,000** to American Jewish Committee. **$5,000** to St. Joseph's Preparatory School. **$2,000** each to Jaffa Institute and St. Joseph's U. **$1,000** each to Franklin & Marshall College, TAIG/The Assn. for Independent Growth, YMCA of Abington, and YMCA of Philadelphia. **$600** to National Liberty Museum. ■**PUBLICATIONS:** None ■**WEBSITE:** None ■**E-MAIL:** None ■**APPLICA-TION POLICIES & PROCEDURES:** The Foundation reports that unsolicited grant requests are not accepted; all grants are made to organizations in which the Trustees have a personal interest.

O+D+T   Charles Kahn, Jr. (P+D+Donor+Con) — Barbara R. Kahn (S+F+D+Donor)

SE-353   Kahn (Robert J.) Lifetime Charitable Foundation
c/o Kleinbard, Bell & Brecker LLP
1900 Market Street, Suite 700
Philadelphia   19103   (Philadelphia County)

MI-12-15-22-54-62-81-83

Phone 215-568-2000 **FAX** 215-568-0140
EIN 23-7787340   **Year Created** 1994

AMV $506,654   **FYE** 12-00   (**Gifts Received** $0)   18 **Grants totaling** $29,300

About three-fourths local giving. High grant of **$5,000** to Federation Allied Jewish Appeal. **$3,500** to U. of Pa. Law School. **$2,000-$2,500** each to America On Wheels [Allentown], Make-A-Wish Foundation of Philadelphia/SE Pa., and Philadelphia Geriatric Center. **$1,000** each to Atwater Kent Museum, Sacred Heart Church [Bridgeport], and Support Center for Child Advo-cates. Other smaller local contributions for various purposes. **Out-of-state** giving includes **$5,000** to International League for Hu-man Rights [NY]; **$2,000** to American Jewish Committee [NY]; and **$1,250** to Guggenheim Museum. ■**PUBLICATIONS:** None ■ **WEBSITE:** None ■**E-MAIL:** mblackman@kleinbard.com ■**APPLICATION POLICIES & PROCEDURES:** Information not available.

O+D+T   Murray I. Blackman, Esq. (T+Con)

SE-354   Kaiserman (Kevy K. & Hortense M.) Foundation
c/o Kaiserman Enterprises
201 South 18th Street, Suite 300
Philadelphia   19103   (Philadelphia County)

MI-11-22-42-41-42-51-52-62-71

Phone 215-546-2665 **FAX** 215-546-6828
EIN 23-2299921   **Year Created** 1980

AMV $5,473,999   **FYE** 6-00   (**Gifts Received** $979,172)   22 **Grants totaling** $698,500

About four-fifths local giving. High grant of **$195,000** to Jewish Federation of Greater Philadelphia. **$155,000** to Federation Al-lied Jewish Appeal. **$100,000** to Philadelphia Theatre Company. **$40,000** to Prince Music Theater. **$22,000** to United Way of SE Pa. **$20,000** to Temple U. **$15,000** to Jewish Community Centers of Greater Philadelphia. **$14,000** to Akiba Hebrew Acad-emy. **$10,000** to Perelman Jewish Day School/Solomon Schechter. **$5,000** each to Aish Hatorah, HIAS & Council Migration Services and Pa. Horticultural Society. **$2,000** to Central High School. **$1,000** to Franciscan Ministries. **Out-of-state** giving in-cludes **$50,000** to Brandeis U. [MA]; **$24,000** each to American Jewish Committee [NY] and NYC Acting Society; and **$5,000** each to Jewish Federation of South Jersey and North American Conference on Ethiopian Jewry [NY]. — Major grants approved for future payment include **$100,000** each to Jewish Federation of Greater Philadelphia and Philadelphia Theatre Company; **$33,000** to American Jewish Committee (Partners in Education); and **$20,000** to Prince Music Theater. ■**PUBLICATIONS:** None ■**WEBSITE:** None ■**E-MAIL:** kaiser@voicenet.com ■**APPLICATION POLICIES & PROCEDURES:** The Foundation re-ports most major giving is to Philadelphia-area organizations—largely educational, arts, and Jewish social service agencies—with which the Trustees have had long-standing relationships. Because of several long-term commitments the Foundation reports that unsolicited requests will not be accepted for several years, through about 2005.

O+D+T   Ronald L. Kaiserman (T+Donor+Con) — Kenneth S. Kaiserman (T+Donor) — Constance Kaiserman Robinson (T+Donor) — Corporate donor: Kaiserman Enterprises L.P.

SE-355   Kanev (Charles & Miriam) Foundation, The
210 West Rittenhouse Square, Apt. 2702
Philadelphia   19103   (Philadelphia County)

MI-12-52
Phone 215-735-8704 **FAX** None
EIN 23-7750570   **Year Created** 1993

AMV $157,754   **FYE** 6-00   (**Gifts Received** $0)   2 **Grants totaling** $13,000

All local giving. **$10,000** to Curtis Institute of Music. **$3,000** to Adoption Resource Center. — Giving in the prior year: **$10,000** each to Curtis Institute of Music and Holistic Learning Center, and **$5,000** to ArtGrowth 2000. ■**PUBLICATIONS:** None ■**WEBSITE:** None ■**E-MAIL:** None ■**APPLICATION POLICIES & PROCEDURES:** Information not available.

O+D+T   Miriam Kanev (T+Donor+Con) — Carl Kanev [NY] (T) — Charles Kanev (Donor)

SE-356   Kaplan (Shirley R.) Charitable Fund
c/o Larson Allen & Weishair Co., LLP
16 Sentry Parkway West, Suite 310
Blue Bell   19422   (Montgomery County)

MI-22-41-62
Phone 215-643-3900 **FAX** None
EIN 23-2712805   **Year Created** 1992

AMV $324,212   **FYE** 12-00   (**Gifts Received** $0)   5 **Grants totaling** $202,025

Mostly local giving. High grant of **$100,000** to Stern Hebrew High School. **$75,000** to Torah Academy. **$12,000** to Etz Chaim Center for Jewish Studies. **Out-of-state** grant: **$15,000** to Nachal Novea [NY]. — Grants awarded the prior year: **$126,000** to Lower Merion Synagogue and **$5,000** to Congregation Khal Torath Chaim [NY]. ■**PUBLICATIONS:** None ■**WEBSITE:** None ■ **E-MAIL:** None ■**APPLICATION POLICIES & PROCEDURES:** Information not available.

O+D+T   Seymour Kaplan (T+Donor+Con) — Elizabeth Kaplan Davis [England] (T)

SE-357 Kaplin (Elmer & Gertrude) Foundation
70 Portland Road
West Conshohocken 19428   (Montgomery County)
AMV $1,183,760   **FYE** 12-00   **(Gifts Received** $37,200)

MI-14-22-62
Phone 215-487-1652 **FAX** None
EIN 23-2791482   **Year Created** 1994
27 **Grants totaling** $68,875

Mostly local giving. High grant of **$35,000** to Jewish Federation of Greater Philadelphia. **$20,000** to Philadelphia Geriatric Center. **$5,000** to Anti-Defamation League. **$1,000** each to Carelink Community Support Services and Hillel Foundation. Other local contributions **$50-$500** for various purposes. **Out-of-state** grant: **$2,000** to Jewish Federation of Broward County [FL]. ■ **PUBLICATIONS:** None ■**WEBSITE:** None ■**E-MAIL:** None ■**APPLICATION POLICIES & PROCEDURES:** Grant requests may be submitted in any form at any time.

O+D+T Elmer L. Kaplin (D+Donor+Con) — Gertrude R. Kaplin (D+Donor) — Marc B. Kaplin (D) — Ned J. Kaplin (D)

SE-358 Karabots Foundation, The
6107 Sheaff Lane, P.O. Box 736
Fort Washington 19034   (Montgomery County)
AMV $1,028,505   **FYE** 6-00   **(Gifts Received** $500,000)

MI-32-41
Phone 215-643-5800 **FAX** None
EIN 23-2939856   **Year Created** 1998
2 **Grants totaling** $26,000

One Pa. grant: **$1,000** to Fox Chase Cancer Center. **Out-of-state** grant: **$25,000** to St. Anselm's School [NY] (computers). ■ **PUBLICATIONS:** None ■**WEBSITE:** None ■**E-MAIL:** None ■**APPLICATION POLICIES & PROCEDURES:** Information not available.

O+D+T Nicholas G. Karabots (P+F+Donor+Con) — Athena Karabots (VP+S+Donor)

SE-359 Kardon (Morris & Sophie) Foundation
c/o Kardon Industries, Inc.
1201 Chestnut Street, Suite 1002
Philadelphia 19107   (Philadelphia County)
AMV $70,941   **FYE** 10-00   **(Gifts Received** $12,444)

MI-22-53-54-62-72

Phone 215-665-9600 **FAX** 215-564-0529
EIN 23-6251918   **Year Created** 1946
27 **Grants totaling** $49,275

About 15% local giving. High local grant of **$3,000** to Federation Allied Jewish Appeal. **$1,000** to Philadelphia Museum of Art. **$600** to National Liberty Museum. **$500** to Fabric Workshop. Other smaller contributions for educational or cultural purposes. **Out-of-state** giving includes **$30,000** to Humane Society of Boulder Valley [CO]; and **$1,000-$1,600** each to American Craft Museum [NY], American School of Tangier [NY], Boca Raton Museum of Art [FL, Collegiate Chorale [NY], and Independent Curators International [NY]. ■**PUBLICATIONS:** None ■**WEBSITE:** None ■**E-MAIL:** None ■**APPLICATION POLICIES & PROCEDURES:** Written grant requests may be submitted in a letter at any time; detailed how the requested funds will be used; include IRS tax-exempt status documentation.

O+D+T Leroy Kardon (T+Con) — Lawrence Kardon [CO] (T) — Linda Kardon [CO] (T) — Richard Kardon [CO] (T) — Robert Kardon (T+Donor) — Corporate donor: Kardon Industries, Inc.

SE-360 Kardon (Samuel & Rebecca) Foundation
c/o Larson, Allen & Weishair & Co., CPAs
18 Sentry Park West, Suite 300
Blue Bell 19422   (Montgomery County)
AMV $9,020,471   **FYE** 12-00   **(Gifts Received** $0)

MI-11-12-13-14-15-22-31-41-42-52-53-54-55
62-65
Phone 215-643-3900 **FAX** 215-646-1937
EIN 23-6278123   **Year Created** 1952
56 **Grants totaling** $551,430

Nearly two-thirds local giving. High local grant of **$83,000** to Jewish Federation of Greater Philadelphia. **$56,000** to Kardon Institute of the Arts. **$38,500** to Settlement Music School. **$25,000** to Philadelphia Chamber Music Society. **$18,500** to Holy Family College. **$15,000** to Philadelphia Museum of Art. **$10,000** each to Federation Allied Jewish Appeal, Inglis House, and United Way of SE Pa. **$7,200** to Albert Einstein Healthcare Network. **$5,000** each to American Interfaith Institute and William Penn Charter School. **$3,000** to Congregation Rodeph Shalom. **$2,000-$2,500** each to American Associates of Ben-Gurion U., Curtis Institute of Music, Hand Rehabilitation Foundation, Pathway School, Pa. Ballet, Philadelphia Orchestra, and U. of Pa. Law School. **$1,000-$1,500** each to Art Growth 2000, Leo Baech Education Center Foundation, Boys Town Jerusalem [Jenkintown], Drexel U., Executive Service Corps of the Delaware Valley, Jewish Community Centers of Greater Philadelphia, Living Beyond Breast Cancer, Mann Center for Performing Arts, MossRehab, Opera Company of Philadelphia, Philadelphia Art Alliance, Philadelphia Geriatric Center, and Philadelphia Zoo. Other smaller local contributions for health, cultural or community purposes. **Out-of-state** giving includes high grant of **$100,500** to Alzheimer's Assn. [IL]; **$65,000** to Museum of American Folk Art [NY]; **$10,000** each to The Goodspeed Foundation [CT], Kayne-ERA Center [CA], U. of North Carolina, Temple Sinai [FL], and Yale U. [CT]; and smaller grants for various purposes. ■**PUBLICATIONS:** None ■**WEBSITE:** None ■**E-MAIL:** None ■**APPLICATION POLICIES & PROCEDURES:** Grant requests may be submitted in a letter at any time; describe the applicant organization and project for which funds are requested. No grants are awarded to individuals.

O+D+T David Kittner, Esq. (Executive Director+T+Con) — Emanuel S. Kardon (T+Donor) — Corporate donor: American Bag & Paper Company

---

SE-361 Karr Foundation
c/o Quaker Group Developers
5 Cambridge Lane
Newtown 18940   (Bucks County)
AMV $151,151   **FYE** 12-00   **(Gifts Received** $80,000)

MI-22-25-41

Phone 215-504-9720 **FAX** None
EIN 23-7011973   **Year Created** 1969
8 **Grants totaling** $61,875

All local/nearby NJ giving. High Pa. grants of **$2,500** each to Germantown Academy and William Penn Charter School. **$1,000** to Salvation Army/Norristown. **$500** to Interfaith of Ambler. Other smaller contributions. **Out-of-state** grants: high grant of **$50,000** to Metro Camden Habitat for Humanity [NJ] and **$5,000** to Katz Jewish Community Center [NJ]. ■**PUBLICATIONS:** None ■**WEBSITE:** None ■**E-MAIL:** quakergroup@aol.com ■**APPLICATION POLICIES & PROCEDURES:** The Foundation reports that giving focuses on local organizations, mostly for building funds or capital drives. Prospective applicants should make an initial telephone inquiry about the feasibility of submitting a request. Grant requests may be submitted in a typed letter at any time; provide a background summary of the proposed project. Site visits sometimes are made to organizations being considered for a grant.

O+D+T Susan Nydick (Con) — Thelma Karr (P)

SE-362 Karr (George W., Jr. & Barbara M.) Foundation

c/o Karr Barth Associates
40 Monument Road, Suite 205
Bala Cynwyd 19004 (Montgomery County)

MI-13-29-31-41-42-44-55

Phone 610-660-4203 **FAX** 610-668-2076
EIN 22-2773554 **Year Created** 1986

AMV $387,027 **FYE** 8-01 **(Gifts Received** $0) 3 **Grants totaling** $28,500

All local giving. High grant of **$25,000** to Regional Performing Arts Center. **$2,500** to Free Library of Philadelphia Foundation. **$1,000** to Gesu School. — Major giving in prior years to Abington Memorial Hospital, Boy Scouts/Cradle of Liberty Council; Lehigh U.; and Red Cross. ■**PUBLICATIONS:** None ■**WEBSITE:** None ■**E-MAIL:** None ■**APPLICATION POLICIES & PROCEDURES:** Grant requests may be submitted in a letter at any time; the deadline is May 31st.

O+D+T George W. Karr, Jr. [Kintnersville] (P+D+Donor+Con) — Barbara M. Karr [Kintnersville] (S+F) — Kimberly Karr Dunham [Kintnersville] (AS+AF)

SE-363 Katz (Harold) Family Foundation, The

c/o G. Daniel Jones
283 Second Street Pike, Suite 150
Southampton 18966 (Bucks County)

MI-12-22-32-62

Phone 215-364-0400 **FAX** None
EIN 23-2439844 **Year Created** 1986

AMV $14,679 **FYE** 12-00 **(Gifts Received** $71,282) 22 **Grants totaling** $421,833

Limited local giving. High Pa. grant of **$3,000** to Jerry Segal Classic. **$2,500** to Commonwealth National Foundation. **$1,000-$1,350** to Golden Slipper Club & Charities, Jewish Federation of Greater Philadelphia, MECA/Mission for Educating Children with Autism, and The Wistar Institute. Other smaller contributions. **Out-of-state** giving includes **$402,733** to Polycystic Kidney Research Foundation [MO] and grants/contributions **$2,500** or smaller, mostly to FL. ■**PUBLICATIONS:** None ■**WEBSITE:** None ■**E-MAIL:** None ■**APPLICATION POLICIES & PROCEDURES:** The Foundation reports that Philadelphia-area health-related organizations receive priority. Submit written requests in any form at any time; describe the organization's health-related activities/research and specific needs and include financial information. Decision on grants are made with within three months.

O+D+T Harold Katz [FL] (P+Donor+Con) — Diane Feinstein [Richboro] (D) — David Katz [Ambler] (D) — Marlene Katz [FL] (D) — Peggy Katz [FL] (D) — Corporate donor: Creative Investors Limited Partnership [NV]

SE-364 Kaufman (Cora & Saul) Memorial Foundation

1521 Morstein Road
Frazer 19355 (Chester County)

MI-42-51

Phone 610-251-2270 **FAX** None
EIN 52-6041716 **Year Created** 1942

AMV $375,104 **FYE** 12-00 **(Gifts Received** $0) 3 **Grants totaling** $18,000

Mostly local giving. High grant of **$10,000** to Drexel U. **$7,000** to Movement Theatre International. **Out-of-state** grant: **$1,000** to Stephen F. Austin U. [TX]. — Pa. Grants awarded in the prior year: **$10,000** each to Drexel U. and Movement Theatre International; and **$2,000** to Golden Slipper Charities. ■**PUBLICATIONS:** None ■**WEBSITE:** None ■**E-MAIL:** None ■**APPLICATION POLICIES & PROCEDURES:** Grant requests may be submitted in a letter at any time; provide a brief organization history, describe its mission and details of the project; state the amount of funding requested.

O+D+T Gary R. Gross (T+Con)

SE-365 Keller Charitable Foundation

662 Keller Road
Telford 18969 (Bucks County)

MI-14-15-22-31-33-63-84-89

Phone 215-723-4852 **FAX** 215-723-7799
EIN 23-2703552 **Year Created** 1993

AMV $531,038 **FYE** 12-00 **(Gifts Received** $0) 11 **Grants totaling** $19,000

Mostly local/Pa. giving. High grant of **$5,000** to Senior Adult Activity Center of Souderton. **$1,000-$1,500** each to Grand View Hospital, Have Christ Will Travel, Indian Creek Foundation, MEDA-Economic Development [Lancaster], Mennonite Disaster Service, Penn Foundation for Mental Health, Pennridge Little League, and Sellersville Fire Dept. **Out-of-state** grants: **$4,500** to Victory Ministries [AK] and **$1,000** to Mennonite Board of Missions [IN]. ■**PUBLICATIONS:** None ■**WEBSITE:** None ■**E-MAIL:** None ■**APPLICATION POLICIES & PROCEDURES:** The Foundation reports that giving focuses on tax-exempt religious organizations that help the needy, spread the Christian faith, and raise the level of religious awareness. Grant requests may be submitted in a letter at any time; give a brief organization history and description of mission, detailed project description and amount of funding requested; include an annual report, audited financial statement, and most recent Form 990.

O+D+T Arden L. Keller (P+D+Donor+Con) — Shirley G. Keller (S+F+D) — Claire Keller [Souderton] (D) — Donna Keller [Souderton] (D) Corporate donor: Indian Valley Camping Center

---

SE-366 Kellmer (Jack) Company Foundation

c/o Jack Kellmer Company
717 Chestnut Street
Philadelphia 19107 (Philadelphia County)

MI-12-15-22-55-62

Phone 215-727-8350 **FAX** None
EIN 23-6701981 **Year Created** 1982

AMV $329,075 **FYE** 7-00 **(Gifts Received** $0) 18 **Grants totaling** $21,750

About one-quarter local giving. High Pa. grant of **$3,000** to Golden Slipper Club. **$500-$650** each to Chapel of Four Chaplains, Friends of Philadelphia Ronald McDonald House, and Inglis Foundation. Other smaller contributions. **Out-of-state** giving, mostly to NJ, includes **$5,000** to Jewish Federation of Southern NJ; **$4,500** to Ronald McDonald House of Camden; and **$2,800** to Katz Jewish Community Center (Festival of Arts, Books & Culture). ■**PUBLICATIONS:** None ■**WEBSITE:** None ■**E-MAIL:** None ■**APPLICATION POLICIES & PROCEDURES:** Grant requests may be submitted in a letter at any time.

O+D+T James Kellmer (T+Con) — Marjorie Kellmer (T+Donor) — Diane Young (T) — Corporate donor: Jack Kellmer Co.

SE-367 Kelly (Paul E.) Foundation
109 Forrest Ave.
Narberth 19072 (Montgomery County)
AMV $21,357,108 **FYE** 12-00 (**Gifts Received** $0)

MI-22-41-42-43-51-54-61
Phone 610-664-9890 **FAX** 610-664-9892
EIN 23-6298237 **Year Created** 1952
82 **Grants totaling** $795,850

Mostly local giving. High grant of **$250,000** to St. Joseph's Preparatory School. **$50,000** each to Academy of Vocal Arts and Waldron Mercy Academy. **$25,000** each to Catholic Charities, Gesu School, Merion Mercy Academy, and St. Joseph's U. **$20,000** each to Immaculate Conception Catholic Church [Philadelphia] and St. Francis Inn/Order of Friars Minor. **$10,000** each to BLOCS/Business Leaders Organized for Catholic Schools, Immaculata College, LaSalle U., and St. Francis of Assisi Parish [Philadelphia]. **$7,500** each to Special Olympics of Montgomery County and World Affairs Council of Philadelphia. **$6,500** to Mercy Vocational High School. **$5,000** each to Boy Scouts/Cradle of Liberty Council, Devon Preparatory School, Drexel Hill School of the Holy Child, Family Life Educational Foundation, Global Interdependence Center, Our Lady of Lourdes School [Philadelphia], Project H.O.M.E., Ursinus College, and Wentz's United Church of Christ [Worcester]. **$4,000** to St. Edmond's Home. **$2,000-$3,000** each to Ambler Olympic Club, Free Library of Philadelphia, Gilbert & Sullivan Society of Chester County, Hallahan Catholic Girls High School, Inglis House, Partners for Healthy Babies, Pa. Economy League, Philadelphia Museum of Art, Philadelphia Zoo, St. Charles Borromeo Seminary, Salvation Army, and WHYY. Also, 19 local grants/contributions **$500-$1,500** each for arts/cultural, educational, health, human services, and other purposes, and 10 scholarships of **$1,000-$2,500** for area students. **Out-of-state** giving includes **$25,000** each to Cornelia Connelly School [CA], Georgetown U. [DC], and IESA Foundation [NY]; **$20,000** to College of Holy Cross [MA]; and **$5,000** to Rider U. Science Scholarship Fund [NJ]. ■**PUBLICATIONS:** None ■**WEBSITE:** None ■**E-MAIL:** PEKF@comcast..net ■**APPLICATION POLICIES & PROCEDURES:** The Foundation reports that grants are awarded generally only to Delaware Valley organizations. Most grants are for general support, building/renovation, capital campaigns, continuing support, or endowment. Grant requests may be submitted in a letter (2 pages maximum) at any time; describe the project and amount of funding requested, and include an annual report, organization and/or project budgets, list of Board members, list of major funding sources, an audited financial statement, and IRS tax-exempt status documentation. Note: The scholarship awards program for dependents of Superior Tube Company employees has been discontinued. — Formerly called the Superior-Pacific Fund, Inc.

O+D+T Paul E. Kelly, Jr. (P+D+Con) — Janet F. Kelly (VP+D) — Christine Kelly Kiernan (VP+D) — Judith Kelly Shea (VP+D)

SE-368 Kent Foundation, The
205 Glenn Road
Ardmore 19003 (Montgomery County)
AMV $3,967,269 **FYE** 12-00 (**Gifts Received** $3,091,115)

MI-12-18-22-25-41-42-54-55
Phone 610-995-9760 **FAX** None
EIN 51-0382152 **Year Created** 1999
3 **Grants totaling** $73,810

All local giving. High grants of **$25,000** each to Millennium Philadelphia Celebration and Philadelphia Museum of Art. **$23,810** to Hireability. — Grants awarded the prior year include **$177,000** to Rosemont School of the Holy Child; **$30,000** to Drueding Center/Project Rainbow; **$20,000** to Salvation Army; **$15,000** each to Adoptions from the Heart, Golden Cradle [NJ]; Haverford School, and Melmark; **$10,000** to U. of St. Thomas [MN]; and **$7,500** to Holy Family Services [CA]. ■**PUBLICATIONS:** None ■**WEBSITE:** None ■**E-MAIL:** None ■**APPLICATION POLICIES & PROCEDURES:** Information not available.

O+D+T Lawrence J. Kent (P+Donor+Con) — Mary A. Kent (VP) — Lawrence A. Palmer (S)

SE-369 Kessler Fund
c/o Wolf, Block, Schorr & Solis-Cohen
1650 Arch Street, 22nd Floor
Philadelphia 19103 (Philadelphia County)
AMV $911,998 **FYE** 5-01 (**Gifts Received** $20,924)

MI-20-41-52
Phone 215-977-2062 **FAX** 215-405-2962
EIN 23-7839028 **Year Created** 1996
5 **Grants totaling** $46,273

Two Pa. grants: **$15,000** to Organized Anti-Crime Community Network. **$1,500** to The Philadelphia School. **Out-of-state** giving includes **$14,753** to Jacksonville Symphony Orchestra [FL] and **$10,000** to Lucius Burch Center for Western Tradition [WY]. — In the prior year, two local grants: **$30,000** to The Philadelphia School and **$1,500** to Diagnostic & Rehabiliation Center. ■**PUBLICATIONS:** None ■**WEBSITE:** None ■**E-MAIL:** mdean@wolfblock.com ■**APPLICATION POLICIES & PROCEDURES:** Grant requests may be submitted in a letter at any time.

O+D+T Michael M. Dean, Esq. (T+Con) — Donor: Estate of Lillie A. Kessler

---

SE-370 Kim (James & Agnes) Foundation
c/o Amkor Technology, Inc.
1345 Enterprise Drive
West Chester 19380 (Chester County)
AMV $4,988,114 **FYE** 12-00 (**Gifts Received** $924,538)

MI-16-17-41-42-52-61
Phone 610-431-9600 **FAX** 610-431-9967
EIN 23-2899799 **Year Created** 1997
5 **Grants totaling** $472,667

Mostly Eastern Pa. giving. High grants of **$200,000** each to Precious Blood Convent [Reading] (general support) and U. of Pa. (Wharton School Building Fund). **$66,667** to The Shipley School (resources campaign). **$5,000** to Asian American Women's Coalition [Philadelphia]. **Out-of-state** grant: **$1,000** to Hamilton College [NY] (annual campaign). — Major Pa. grants in the prior year: **$1,500,000** to U. of Pa. (professorship/Huntsman Hall Fund); **$36,000** to Philadelphia Orchestra (annual support); **$33,333** to The Shipley School (resources campaign); and **$25,000** to Musser Young Scholars Fund (general support). ■**PUBLICATIONS:** None ■**WEBSITE:** None ■**E-MAIL:** jkim@amkor.com ■**APPLICATION POLICIES & PROCE-DURES:** The Foundation reports that giving focuses on highly respected educational institutions in the Philadelphia region to improve the quality of secondary and post-secondary education. No grants are awarded to individuals.

O+D+T Agnes C. Kim (P+Donor+Con) — James J. Kim (F+Donor) — Susan Y. Kim (S)

SE-371 Kimmel (Sidney) Foundation
c/o Wolf, Block, Schorr & Solis-Cohen
1650 Arch Street, Attn. Matthew H. Kamens, Esq.
Philadelphia 19103 (Philadelphia County)

MI-15-31-32-41-52-54-56-62-72-81

Phone 215-977-2538 **FAX** 215-977-2644
EIN 23-2698492 **Year Created** 1993

AMV $23,273,641 **FYE** 7-00 (**Gifts Received** $3,897,325) 25+ **Grants totaling** $5,134,100

Mostly local giving. High grant of **$1,900,000** to Kimmel Scholar Awards Program (awards made nationwide to cancer researchers). **$1,500,000** to Foundation for Cancer Research (a division of the Sidney Kimmel Foundation). **$1,000,000** to Thomas Jefferson U./Kimmel Cancer Center. **$200,000** to U. of Pa. Medical Center/Rena Rowan Breast Cancer Center. **$50,000** to Solomon Schechter Day School. **$35,000** to Philadelphia Museum of Art. **$26,000** to Philadelphia Orchestra. **$25,000** to Marian Anderson Award. **$6,000** to Academy of Music. **$5,000** each to Congregation Rodeph Shalom (Rabbi's Fund) and Philadelphia Geriatric Center. **$2,500** each to St. Ignatius Nursing Home and SPCA. **$1,500** each to Adath Tikvah Montefiore Synagogue and Philadelphia Futures. **$1,000** to Institute for Contemporary Art. **Out-of-state** giving includes **$250,000** to National Coalition for Cancer Survivorship [MD] (Rays of Hope program) ; **$50,000** to Memorial Sloan Kettering Cancer Center [NY]; **$45,000** to National Prostate Cancer Coalition Fund [DC]; **$15,000** to World Federation of United Nations Assns. [NY]; and **$10,000** to Food Allergy Initiative [NY]. — In the prior year, major grants included **$1,900,00** for Kimmel Scholar Awards; **$1,000,000** each to Sidney Kimmel Cancer Center [CA], Thomas Jefferson U./Kimmel Cancel Center and U.S. Holocaust Memorial Council [DC]; **$250,000** to Survivors of the Shoah [CA]; **$200,000** each to Beth Israel Deaconess Medical Center [MA], U. of Pa. Medical Center/Rena Rowan Breast Cancer Center, and Temple U. Health Sciences Center; **$166,000** to Federation Allied Jewish Appeal; **$100,000** each to Association for the Cure of Cancer of the Prostate/CAP Cure [CA] and Memorial Sloan-Kettering Cancer Center [NY]; **$50,000** each to American Cancer Society and Solomon Schechter Day School; and **$35,000** to Philadelphia Museum of Art. ■**PUBLICATIONS:** application guidelines for cancer research grants ■**WEBSITE:** www.kimmel.org [cancer research info only] ■**E-MAIL:** mkamens@wolfblock.com ■**APPLICATION POLICIES & PROCEDURES:** The Foundation reports that giving focuses primarily on cancer research; detailed application guidelines/forms for the Kimmel Scholar Awards (for cancer researchers) are available on the website. Application guidelines/policies for grants to educational and cultural organizatins are unavailable. **Note:** The Sidney Kimmel Foundation for Cancer Research, a division of the Sidney Kimmel Foundation, has its own Board of Directors and Medical Advisory Board, as listed on the website.

O+D+T Sidney Kimmel (P+D+Donor+Con) — Matthew H. Kamens, Esq.

SE-372 Kind (Patricia) Family Foundation
7707 Pine Road
Wyndmoor 19038
(Montgomery County)

MI-12-13-14-15-16-17-18-19-20-22-25-33-35
41-45-54
Phone Unlisted **FAX** 215-233-2569
EIN 23-7839035 **Year Created** 1996

AMV $29,628,164 **FYE** 12-01 (**Gifts Received** $0) 93 **Grants totaling** $2,427,600

Mostly Philadelphia-area giving—most grants are multiyear awards; *the following are one-third payments on three-year grants:* **$50,000** each to Baker Industries (operating support), Bethesda Project (long-term housing program staff-Bethesda Bainbridge), Big Brother Big Sister Assn. of Philadelphia (school-based mentoring/Unassigned Littles program), Calcutta House (housing, direct care and supportive services for persons with AIDS), Carson Valley School (residential facility for at-risk children/adolescents), Delaware Valley Child Care Council (improved child care quality through adequate training, compensation, and resources), Greater Philadelphia Food Bank (collection, storage, and distribution of wholesome food to needy), Health Annex at Francis J. Myers Youth Access Center (nurse managed health center), LaSalle Neighborhood Nursing Center (CHIPLINK Program), and Planned Parenthood of SE PA (Youth First program), VNA Community Services (primary health care services for uninsured Montco children), The Wellness Community (support for cancer patients/families), and White-Williams Scholars (Peer Academic Development Program). **$46,000** to Chestnut Place Clubhouse (full-time Deaf Services Coordinator/Interpreter). **$45,000** to NetworkArts (programs for middle-school students). **$40,000** each to Aid for Friends (home cooked/delivered meals for homebound disabled) and Face to Face (St. Vincent De Paul Community Center services to needy). **$38,000** to Women Organized Against Rape (counseling services for adults/children in Latino community). **$35,000** each to Bucks County Housing Group (housing continuum programs for homeless/low-income families), Center for Grieving Children, Teens & Families (grief support services), Dignity Housing (Enhanced Service Program), and MANNA/Metropolitan AIDS Neighborhood Nutrition Alliance (direct food assistance to individuals/families living with HIV/AIDS). **$32,000** to Children's Advocacy Center (Forensic Child Interviewer/Clinical Specialist staff position). **$30,000** each to Germantown Women's Y (general operating support), Jubilee School (Special Education Program), Philabundance (Delaware Valley Community Kitchen Collaborative), and Taller Puertorriqueno (expanded youth outreach). **$28,000** to Delaware Valley Community Health (program integrating mental health care/primary health care of low-income Latino and African-American patients). **$25,000-$26,000** each to Auerbach Central Agency for Jewish Education (Moral Education Programs), Children's Literacy Initiative (Philadelphia Model Classrooms Project), Children's Village Child Care Center (Early Intervention-Parent Support Program), Childspace Cooperative Development (direct delivery of financial education/counseling services to low-wage child care workers), Congreso de Latinos Unidos (youth services programs), Crime Prevention Assn. of Philadelphia (Pregnancy Prevention Program at R.W. Brown Community Center, Drueding Center/Project Rainbow (day care services for children of homeless families), Endow A Home (youth programs), Frankford Group Ministry

(Neighborhood Parenting Program), LaSalle University (community service/youth outreach initiative), Philadelphia Dept. of Recreation Mural Arts Program (Job Shadowing program), Project H.O.M.E. (residence for chronically homeless, mentally disabled single women), SILOAM Ministries (pastoral care/spiritual direction for HIV-positive persons), Women's Community Revitalization Project (Tenant Supportive Services), Women's Law Project (Telephone Counseling & Consumer Education Service), and Woodrock (Youth Development Program). **$20,000-$21,000** each to Community Women's Education Project (community-based educational/support services), Homeless Advocacy Project (operating support), and Summerbridge of Greater Philadelphia (college prep programs for NW Philadelphia middle school students). **$15,000** each to Academy of Natural Sciences (Women in Natural Sciences program), Bethanna (parent education program), Central Bucks Forty Assets Project (decreased children's' drug-alcohol use through community involvement), Family Services (Families and Schools Together Program), First United Methodist Church of Germantown (community-based, academic after school high school program), Mt. Airy Schools Committee (improve Mt. Airy's public elementary schools/programs), North Hills Health Center (nurse-managed community health center), Outward Bound (educational programs for public middle/high school students), Penn Council for Relationships (family-marriage counseling/establish regional counseling centers in African-American churches), and Senior Citizen Judicare Project (legal representation/outreach to low-income seniors). **$16,400** to Woods Services Foundation (Family Support Project). **$16,000** to Lenape Valley Foundation (rental housing for homeless with mental illness). **$15,000** to Episcopal Community Services (Supportive Therapy to AIDS Affected Relatives Program). **$12,000** to People and Stories/Gente y Cuentos [NJ] (expanded reading comprehension programs at several Philadelphia organizations). **$10,000** each to Chestnut Hill Meals on Wheels (delivered home cooked meals), Chestnut Hill Senior Center (educational-recreational programs), North Penn Valley Boys & Girls Club (After School Activities Program), Pa. Home of the Sparrow (operating support), Sedgwick Cultural Center (Teen Art Partners/Youth programs), and Urban Bridges at St. Gabriel's (operating support). *The following are one-half payments on two-year grants:* **$50,000** to Anti-Violence Partnership of Philadelphia (counseling services for children exposed to violence, and training mental health/school-based professionals). **$35,000** each to New Directions for Women (counseling services to women from the Philadelphia County prison system and families) and St. Francis de Sales School (Fine Arts Program). **$25,000** each to Women's Therapy Center (low-cost mental health services to Philadelphia women) and Youth Services, Inc. (West Philly Supports program). **$10,000** to Montgomery County Assn. for the Blind (expanded training programs for visually impaired). *The following are one-year grants:* **$35,000** to Delaware County Family Centers (Positive Parenting Course/Parent Education Group for at-risk families). **$30,000** to Olde Kensington Redevelopment Corp.(GrandPALS project). **$25,000** to Elizabeth Blackwell Health Center For Women (support services to women with developmental, mental health & physical disabilities) and Please Touch Museum (Parent Education Program). **$17,500** to Artists for Recovery (expanded programs for people with psychiatric histories). **$10,000** to Urban Family Council (sexual abstinence programs at Roosevelt High School, Norristown). In addition, 14 Trustee Discretionary Grants of **$1,000-$25,000** each ($179,900 in total) were awarded to local and out-of-state organizations for various purposes. ■**PUBLICATIONS:** Annual Report with application guidelines; informational brochure ■**WEBSITE:** None ■**E-MAIL:** PKFFoundation@comcast.net ■**APPLICATION POLICIES & PROCEDURES:** The Foundation supports Philadelphia-area organizations that help children, adults and seniors in need, to obtain physical or mental health care and related human services; the foundation encourages practical, innovative and creative solutions to community problems and supports preventive and direct services in these fields. Many multiyear grants are awarded, but subsequent second- or third-year payments are contingent on satisfactory progress reports. Priority is given to smaller organizations with the potential to make a difference. Support for arts/cultural projects is only occasional and highly selective. No grants are awarded to individuals (scholarships or fellowships) or for endowment, capital projects, annual fundraising appeals, international activities or organizations, or research. Grant requests may be submitted at any time in a cover letter+proposal. The cover letter (2 pages maximum) should cover the objectives/significance of the proposed project/program and state a specific amount of funding requested. The proposal (5 pages maximum) must include (a) a detailed description of the project/program design and proposed accomplishments during the grant period; (b) a statement of qualifications of personnel and organizational capabilities to carry out the project/program; (c) a budget detailing all planned expenditures, anticipated income, and sources of income; and (d) future fundraising plans for the project/program, if necessary. In addition, include the most recent financial statement, current operating budget, list of directors/officers, and IRS tax-exempt status documentation. Also, proposals which follow Delaware Valley Grantmakers' Common Grant Application Form are accepted (see Appendix or www.dvg.org). The Board awards grants at meetings in January, April and August.

O+D+T Laura Kind McKenna (Managing Trustee+Con) — Patricia van Ameringen Kind [Huntingdon Valley] (C+T) — Christina Kind Baiocchi [Glenside] (T) — Andrew Kind-Fuller [NJ] (T) — Kenneth A. Kind [[Huntingdon Valley] (T) — Philip Kind [Huntingdon Valley] (T) — Valerie Kind-Rubin [Doylestown] (T) — Foundation Donor: Arnold L. Van Ameringen Trust

---

SE-373 King (William M.) Charitable Foundation
4110 Apalogen Road
Philadelphia 19144   (Philadelphia County)

MI-12-13-16-29-34-41-42-43-54-57-63-84
Phone 215-844-3500 **FAX** None
EIN 23-7788220   **Year Created** 1994

AMV $508,524   **FYE** 12-00   **(Gifts Received** $10,000)   23 **Grants totaling** $140,850

Mostly local giving. High grant of **$50,000** to Central High School Alumni Assn. **$30,000** to Franklin Institute. **$20,000** to Philadelphia College of Osteopathic Medicine (Mission Minority Scholarship). **$7,500** to Concerned Black Men. **$3,800** to John Story Jenks School. **$3,500** to Philadelphia Museum of Art. **$3,000** to Medical Society of Eastern Pa. **$1,900-$2,000** each to Anigiduawa Intertribal [Berks County], Champs Gym, Christian Tabernacle Church of God in Christ, and Student National Medical Assn. **$1,000-$1,500** each to Deliverance Evangelistic Church, Kids-N-Hope Foundation, Olney High School Alumni Assn., Philadelphia Ronald McDonald House, Southwest Belmont Community Assn., and WHYY. Other smaller local contributions. **Out-of-state** giving includes **$2,500** to U.S. Japan Institute (ATO Yero Hand) [CO]; **$2,000** to Morris Brown College [GA]; and **$1,000** to Phi Beta Kappa [DC]. ■**PUBLICATIONS:** None ■**WEBSITE:** None ■**E-MAIL:** None ■**APPLICATION POLICIES & PROCEDURES:** Grant requests may be submitted in a letter at any time.

O+D+T William M. King, D.O. (P+Donor+Con)

SE-374 Kirschner Family Foundation
   c/o Kirschner Brothers Oil Company
   518 West Lancaster Ave.
   Haverford 19041   (Montgomery County)

MI-14-22-62

Phone 610-527-4200 **FAX** None
EIN 23-6299767   **Year Created** 1964

AMV $101,959   **FYE** 12-99   **(Gifts Received** $39,432)   10+ **Grants totaling** $39,221

Mostly local/Pa. giving. High grant of **$20,000** to Jewish Federation of Greater Philadelphia. **$11,150** to Anti-Defamation League. **$5,236** to Har Zion Temple. **$1,250** to Pa. Special Olympics. Other contributions totaled **$1,585** but no details available. ■**PUBLICATIONS:** None ■**WEBSITE:** None ■**E-MAIL:** None ■**APPLICATION POLICIES & PROCEDURES:** Grant requests may be submitted in a letter at any time. No grants awarded to individuals. Site visits sometimes are made to organizations being considered for a grant.

O+D+T Michael Kirschner (T+Con) — Fred Kirschner (T+Donor) — Helen Kirschner (Donor) — Corporate donor: Kirschner Investments, Inc.

SE-375 Klein (Raymond) Charitable Foundation, The
   c/o Klein Realty Company
   1700 Market Street, Suite 2600
   Philadelphia 19103   (Philadelphia County)

MI-22-31-32-53-54-55-62

Phone 215-751-9600 **FAX** None
EIN 23-2535513   **Year Created** 1989

AMV $6,247,350   **FYE** 10-00   **(Gifts Received** $0)   21 **Grants totaling** $318,095

Mostly local giving; all grants are unrestricted donations. High grant of **$200,000** to Regional Performing Arts Center. **$67,750** to Congregation Adath Jeshurun. **$20,000** to Thomas Jefferson Hospital. **$12,500** to National Liberty Museum. **$2,500** each to Anti-Defamation League and National Museum of American Jewish History. **$1,000-$1,500** each to American Cancer Society, Philadelphia Art Alliance, and Philadelphia Museum of Art. **$750** to Philadelphia Geriatric Center and United Way of SE Pa. Other smaller local contributions for various purposes. **Out-of-state** giving to Boca Raton, FL area. ■**PUBLICATIONS:** None ■ **WEBSITE:** None ■**E-MAIL:** None ■**APPLICATION POLICIES & PROCEDURES:** Grant requests may be submitted in any form at any time. No grants awarded to individuals.

O+D+T Stephen B. Klein (P+T+Con) — Miriam K. Klein (T) — Raymond Klein (Donor)

SE-376 Kligman (Albert M.) Foundation
   210 West Rittenhouse Square, #3302
   Philadelphia 19103   (Philadelphia County)

MI-32-34

Phone 215-898-3234 **FAX** None
EIN 23-2812009   **Year Created** 1995

AMV $611,622   **FYE** 5-01   **(Gifts Received** $0)   1 **Grant of** $90,000

Sole grant to Society for Investigative Dermatology [OH] (fellowships). — For several years, the Society has been the sole grantee. ■**PUBLICATIONS:** None ■**WEBSITE:** None ■**E-MAIL:** None ■**APPLICATION POLICIES & PROCEDURES:** The reports its major interest is skin disorders. No grants are awarded to individuals.

O+D+T Albert M. Kligman, M.D. (P+Donor+Con) — Lorraine H. Kligman, M.D. (VP) — Elliott P. Footer (S+F)

SE-377 Klorfine Foundation
   Post Office Box 128
   Gladwyne 19035   (Montgomery County)

MI-12-32-53-54-55-86

Phone 610-525-5115 **FAX** None
EIN 22-7743385   **Year Created** 1993

AMV $10,018,176   **FYE** 11-01   **(Gifts Received** $3,023,044)   21 **Grants totaling** $302,650

Mostly local giving. High grant of **$89,300** to Regional Performing Arts Center. **$50,000** to Main Line Art Center. **$36,500** to Woodmere Art Museum. **$32,500** to Red Cross. **$15,500** to Philadelphia Museum of Art. **$10,000** to Pa. Academy of the Fine Arts. **$7,000** to Corneal Research Fund. **$2,000** to Philadelphia Ronald McDonald House. Other smaller local grants/contributions. Out-of-state giving includes **$22,000** to Pilchuck Glass School [WA]; **$10,000** to The Heritage Foundation [DC]; and **$5,000** each to American Craft Museum [NY] and Museum of Glass [WA]. ■**PUBLICATIONS:** None ■**WEBSITE:** None ■**E-MAIL:** nklorfine@netreach.net ■**APPLICATION POLICIES & PROCEDURES:** The Foundation reports that most grants are for special projects, endowment, or matching grants. Grant requests may be submitted in a letter (3 pages maximum) at any time; include an annual report, organization budget, Board member list, and IRS tax-exempt status documentation. Site visits sometimes are made to organizations being considered for a grant.

O+D+T Leonard Klorfine (T+Donor+Con) — Norma E. Klorfine (T+Con) Corporate donor: Klorfine Interests, Inc.

SE-378 Knoppel (E. Roy) Charitable Trust
   121 Putney Lane
   Malvern 19355   (Chester County)

MI-14-32-53-55-61

Phone 610-651-0156 **FAX** None
EIN 23-6963605   **Year Created** 1989

AMV $235,674   **FYE** 12-00   **(Gifts Received** $0)   4 **Grants totaling** $27,500

About two-thirds local giving. **$10,000** to Woodmere Art Gallery. **$5,000** to Sisters of Mercy of Merion. **$2,500** to Chester County Art Assn. **Out-of-state** grant: **$10,000** to Memorial Sloan Kettering Cancer Center [NY]. — In the prior year, local grants included **$35,000** to Fox Chase Cancer Center; **$15,000** to Chester County Community Foundation; **$7,000** to Recording for the Blind & Dyslexic; and **$5,000** to Wissahickon Hospice. ■**PUBLICATIONS:** None ■**WEBSITE:** None ■**E-MAIL:** None ■**APPLICATION POLICIES & PROCEDURES:** Grant requests may be submitted in a letter at any time; describe in detail the proposed use of funds and organizational history, and include a financial statement.

O+D+T Joseph E. Greene, Jr. (T+Con)

SE-379 **Knorr (John K. & Elizabeth W.) Foundation, The**
901 Stony Lane
Gladwyne 19035   (Montgomery County)
AMV $1,386,516   FYE 12-00   **(Gifts Received** $250,000)

MI-12-13-16-18-25-32-41-42-52-57-63-71-79-82
Phone 610-525-6467 **FAX** None
EIN 23-7876318   **Year Created** 1997
28 **Grants totaling** $66,000

About half local giving. High grant of **$6,000** to CARE International. **$5,000** to Bryn Mawr Presbyterian Church. **$4,000** to Pa. Horticultural Society. **$3,000** each to Pa. Environmental Council and Temple U./Esther Boyer College of Music. **$2,000-$2,500** each to Fox Chase Cancer Center, Maternity Care Coalition, Philabundance, and Planned Parenthood of SE Pa. **$1,000** each to Police Athletic League of Philadelphia, Silver Spring Martin Luther School, and WHYY. Other smaller local contributions. **Out-of-state** giving includes **$6,500** to United Negro College Fund [VA]; **$5,000** each to Dartmouth College [NH], Mt. Holyoke College [MA], and Trailblazers [NY]; and smaller grants, several for international child/family welfare purposes. ■ **PUBLICA-TIONS:** None ■ **WEBSITE:** None ■ **E-MAIL:** None ■ **APPLICATION POLICIES & PROCEDURES:** No grants awarded to individuals.
O+D+T John K. Knorr, 3rd, M.D. (T+Donor+Con) — Jeffrey Brillhart [Philadelphia] (T) — W. Stephen Jeffrey [CT] (T) — Sandra F. Kirch [Philadelphia] (T) — Elizabeth W. Knorr (T+Donor) — Elizabeth Knorr Payne [MA} (T) The Glenmede Trust Company (Corporate Trustee)

SE-380 **Knox Family Foundation, The**
2113 Delancey Street
Philadelphia 19103   (Philadelphia County)
AMV $11,174,486   FYE 12-00   **(Gifts Received** $0)

MI-22-25-31-41-42-51-71-72-81
Phone 215-732-9931 **FAX** None
EIN 14-6017797   **Year Created** 1970
237 **Grants totaling** $551,500

Nationwide giving for civic, educational, medical and religious purposes with some recipients receiving multiple grants. Limited local/Pa. giving: high Pa. grant of **$28,000** to The Grier School/Foundation [Blair County]. **$8,000** to American Friends Service Committee. **$3,000** to Rehabilitation & Industrial Training Center of York County. **$2,500** each to Pa. Ballet. **$2,000** to Schuylkill River Development Council. **$1,500** to Friends Select School. **$1,000** each to Friends of Schuylkill River Park and Pa. Hospital. **$500** each to Angel Flight Pa., Bread & Roses Fund, Greater Philadelphia Food Bank, and Philabundance. **Out-of-state** grants, many to states/regions where Board members reside, include **$55,000** to Historic Saranac Lake [NY]; **$20,000** to U. of South Florida Foundation; **$18,000** to Cornell College [IA]; **$15,500** to Dartmouth College [NH]; **$15,000** to African Wildlife Foundation [DC]; and numerous grants/contributions **$250** to **$10,000** for various purposes nationwide. ■ **PUBLICATIONS:** None ■ **WEBSITE:** None ■ **E-MAIL:** None ■ **APPLICATION POLICIES & PROCEDURES:** The Foundation reports that no unsolicited applications or inquiries are accepted; contributions are made only to pre-selected charitable organizations. The Foundation's official address is P.O. Box 387, Johnstown, NY 12095.
O+D+T Eleanor G. Nalle (P+F+Con) — John K. Graham [MA] (VP+S) — Rose Ann Armstrong [FL] (VP) — Roseann K. Beaudoin [CT] (VP) — Rosemary Birchard [MD] (VP) — Amy Brumley [MD] (VP) — Peter Foe [FL] (VP) — Richard Hallock [CT] (VP) Corporate donor: Knox Gelatine, Inc.

SE-381 **Kohn Foundation**
c/o Kohn, Swift & Graf, P.C.
1 South Broad Street, Suite 2100
Philadelphia 19107   (Philadelphia County)
AMV $1,843,091   FYE 12-00   **(Gifts Received** $1,561,372)

MI-18-22-32-41-42-56-62

Phone 215-238-1700 **FAX** 215-238-1968
EIN 23-6398546   **Year Created** 1965
17 **Grants totaling** $52,895

Mostly local giving. High grant of **$10,000** to Cardiovascular Institute of Philadelphia. **$8,500** to The Baldwin School. **$6,500** to Haverford School. **$3,000** to Temple U. (music preparatory). **$2,500** to American Swedish Historical Museum. **$1,000-$1,500** each to B'nai B'rith, The Irish Memorial, Planned Parenthood of SE Pa., and Variety Club. Other local contributions **$100-$750** for various purposes. **Out-of-state** giving includes **$10,000** to St. Andrews Episcopal School [MD] and **$5,000** to Wheaton College [MA]. ■ **PUBLICATIONS:** None ■ **WEBSITE:** None ■ **E-MAIL:** info@kohnswift.com ■ **APPLICATION POLI-CIES & PROCEDURES:** The Foundation reports that most grants are for endowment, scholarships, or matching grants; no building funds are supported. Grant requests may be submitted in any form and preferably in March, June, September and December; briefly state the nature of the organization's work, the amount requested, and how it will be used. Also include an annual report, list of Board members, audited financial statement for the last fiscal year, and IRS tax-exempt status documentation. Site visits sometimes are made to organizations being considered for a grant.
O+D+T Joseph C. Kohn, Esq. (P+F+D+Con) — Edith A. Kohn (VP+S+D) — Amy Kohn Goldberg (VP) — Ellen Kohn (VP)

SE-382 **Koncurat (Pierre) Foundation Charitable Trust**
411 South Waterloo Road
Devon 19333   (Chester County)
AMV $121,077   FYE 12-00   **(Gifts Received** $21,000)

MI-42-63

Phone 610-688-8899 **FAX** None
EIN 22-2783294   **Year Created** 1986
2 **Grants totaling** $18,715

No Pa. giving. **$18,515** to Church of Jesus Christ of Latter Day Saints/Mormons [UT]. **$200** to Brigham Young U. [UT]. — All giving in prior years has been for the Mormons. ■ **PUBLICATIONS:** None ■ **WEBSITE:** None ■ **E-MAIL:** None ■ **APPLICATION POLICIES & PROCEDURES:** No grants awarded to individuals.
O+D+T Pierre J. Koncurat (T+Donor+Con) — Sharon Koncurat (T)

SE-383   Korman (Hyman) Family Foundation   MI-11-22-31-32-34-41-55-62-64
c/o The Korman Corporation
Two Neshaminy Interplex, Suite 307   **Phone** 215-244-5179 **FAX** None
Trevose 19053   (Bucks County)   **EIN** 23-6297326   **Year Created** 1947
AMV $9,699,953   **FYE** 12-00   **(Gifts Received** $0)   12 **Grants totaling** $506,200
All local giving. High grant of **$133,000** to Federation Allied Jewish Appeal. **$100,000** to Temple Sholom. **$100,000** to Albert Einstein Medical Center. **$50,000** to Regional Performing Arts Center. **$40,000** to Germantown Academy. **$25,000** to Girard College Alumni Assn., **$15,000** to Talmudical Yeshiva of Philadelphia and Thomas Jefferson U. **$10,000** to Reform Congregation Keneseth Israel. **$5,000** each to Cystic Fibrosis Foundation and United Way of Bucks County. **$2,200** to Albert Einstein Medical Center (benefit event). ■**PUBLICATIONS:** None ■**WEBSITE:** None ■**E-MAIL:** None ■**APPLICATION POLICIES & PROCEDURES:** Information not available.
O+D+T Diane Casey (Administrator+Con) — Berton E. Korman (T+Donor) — Leonard I. Korman (T+Donor) — Steven H. Korman (T+Donor) — I. Barney Moss (T+Donor) — Sarah R. Moss (Donor)

SE-384   Kraftsow (Edward & Minnie) Foundation   MI-22-62
c/o Craftmatic Industries, Inc.
2500 Interplex Drive   **Phone** 215-639-1310 **FAX** 215-639-9941
Trevose 19053   (Bucks County)   **EIN** 22-2676211   **Year Created** 1985
AMV $278,518   **FYE** 12-00   **(Gifts Received** $0)   1 **Grant of** $25,000
Sole grant to Greater Miami Jewish Federation. — Giving in prior years to Philadelphia organizations. ■**PUBLICATIONS:** None ■
WEBSITE: None ■**E-MAIL:** None ■**APPLICATION POLICIES & PROCEDURES:** Information not available.
O+D+T Stanley Kraftsow (T+Con) — Carolyn Kraftsow (T)

SE-385   Kramer Family Fund   MI-22-41-62
c/o Trimfit, Inc.
1900 Frost Road, Suite 111   **Phone** 215-781-0600 **FAX** None
Bristol 19007   (Bucks County)   **EIN** 13-6117359   **Year Created** 1953
AMV $197,705   **FYE** 9-00   **(Gifts Received** $0)   77 **Grants totaling** $30,633
Limited local giving. High Pa. grant of **$1,645** to Congregation Rodeph Shalom. **$750** to The Hill School [Pottstown]. Other smaller local contributions for various purposes. **Out-of-state** giving, mostly to NY/Long Island and Southern CA where trustees live, was for educational, cultural, religious and other purposes. — In prior years major local giving to Federation Allied Jewish Appeal. ■**PUBLICATIONS:** None ■**WEBSITE:** None ■**E-MAIL:** None ■**APPLICATION POLICIES & PROCEDURES:** Grant requests may be submitted in a letter at any time. — Formerly called the Julia Adler Kramer Foundation.
O+D+T Arnold A. Kramer, Jr. (T+Con) — Martin B. Kramer [NY] (T) — Robert M. Kramer [CA] (T)

SE-386   Kroiz (Harvey & Barbara) Family Foundation, The   MI-22-32-52-54-62-81
815 Roscommon Road   **Phone** 610-940-4305 **FAX** None
Bryn Mawr 19010   (Montgomery County)   **EIN** 23-7883529   **Year Created** 1997
AMV $676,558   **FYE** 12-00   **(Gifts Received** $0)   9 **Grants totaling** $132,000
Mostly local giving. High grant of **$76,000** to U. of Pa. **$20,000** to Federation Allied Jewish Appeal. **$10,000** to Opera Company of Philadelphia. **$3,500** to Middle East Forum. **$1,500** to Etz Chaim Center for Jewish Studies. **$1,000** to Crohn's & Colitis Foundation. **Out-of-state** grants: **$10,000** to American Associates of Ben Gurion U. [NY] and **$5,000** each to Berkshire Center [MA] and Massachusetts SPCA. — In the prior year **$10,000** awarded to Philadelphia Museum of Art. ■**PUBLICATIONS:** None ■**WEBSITE:** None ■**E-MAIL:** None ■**APPLICATION POLICIES & PROCEDURES:** Information not available.
O+D+T Harvey Kroiz (T+Donor+Con) — Barbara Kroiz (T+Donor) — Karen Kroiz (T) — Michelle Kroiz (T) — Nicole Kroiz (T)

SE-387   Krzyzanowski Foundation   MI-12-13-22-29-42-53-61
c/o Crown Cork & Seal Company
1 Crown Way   **Phone** 215-698-5208 **FAX** 215-698-7751
Philadelphia 19154   (Philadelphia County)   **EIN** 23-2501529   **Year Created** 1988
AMV $770,842   **FYE** 12-00   **(Gifts Received** $0)   **Grants totaling** $54,000
Details on 2000 grants are unavailable. — In the prior year, 27 grants totaling **$38,300** awarded; about one-fourth Pa. giving. High Pa. grant of **$2,650** to DeSales U./Allentown College. **$2,000** to Gwynedd Mercy College. **$1,000** each to Pauline Fathers/National Shrine of our Lady of Czestochowa, Polish American Social Services, Samuel D. Cozen Police Athletic League Center, and U. of Pa. Law School. Other local contributions **$100-$500** for various purposes. **Out-of-state** giving includes **$20,000** to John Paul II Foundation [Italy]; **$1,000** each to ABC XXI-Child Awareness Program in Poland [VA], American Center of Polish Culture [DC], and Patrons of the Arts in the Vatican Museum [Italy]. ■**PUBLICATIONS:** None ■**WEBSITE:** None ■**E-MAIL:** None ■**APPLICATION POLICIES & PROCEDURES:** Grant requests may be submitted in any form at any time. No grants are awarded to individuals. Site visits sometimes are made to organizations being considered for a grant.
O+D+T Richard L. Krzyzanowski (P+T+Donor+Con) — Taiko A. Krzyzanowski (VP+T) — Christine A. Krzyzanowski (T) — Peter R. Krzyzanowski (T) — Suzanne I. Krzyzanowski (T)

SE-388 Kucker (Edward G.) Charitable Foundation
c/o M.A. Bruder & Sons
600 Reed Road, P.O. Box 600
Broomall   19008   (Delaware County)

MI-14-22-31-32-41-61

Phone 610-353-5100 **FAX** None
EIN 23-7772284   **Year Created** 1994

AMV $431,790   **FYE** 12-00   **(Gifts Received** $0)   1 **Grant of** $500

Sole grant to Cardinal Krol Center. — In the prior year, 17 grants totaled **$25,000;** mostly local giving. High grants of **$5,000** each to Mt. St. Joseph Academy and Riddle Memorial Hospital Foundation. **$2,000** each to Chestnut Hill Hospital, Cystic Fibrosis Foundation, MBF Center, and Neumann League. **$1,000** each to American Cancer Society, National MS Society, Order of St. Augustine, and Our Lady of Confidence Day School. Other smaller local and out-of-state contributions. ■**PUBLICATIONS:** None ■**WEBSITE:** None ■**E-MAIL:** None ■**APPLICATION POLICIES & PROCEDURES:** Grant requests may be submitted in a letter at any time; describe the purpose and intended use.

O+D+T Thomas A. Bruder, Jr. (T+Con) — Martin L. Longstreth (T) Donor: Estate of E.G. Kucker

---

SE-389 Kulicke Fund, The
537 Rolling Glen Drive
Horsham   19044   (Montgomery County)

MI-12-13-14-84

Phone 215-643-1346 **FAX** None
EIN 23-7094864   **Year Created** 1971

AMV $893,590   **FYE** 12-00   **(Gifts Received** $0)   5 **Grants totaling** $44,004

Mostly local giving; all grants are for general operations. High grants of **$10,000** each to Angel Flight Pa., Bethanna, and Northern Home for Children. **$4,004** to Special Equestrians [Warrington]. **Out-of-state** grant: **$10,000** to National Sports Center for the Disabled [CO]. ■**PUBLICATIONS:** None ■**WEBSITE:** None ■**E-MAIL:** None ■**APPLICATION POLICIES & PROCEDURES:** No grants awarded to individuals. — Formerly called the Lt. Frederick W. Kulicke, III Fund.

O+D+T Frederick W. Kulicke, Jr. (T+Donor+Con) — Harry S. Cherken, Jr. , Esq. [Philadelphia] (T) — C. Scott Kulicke [Willow Grove] (T) — Danielle Kulicke [Willow Grove] (T) — Allison F. Page, Esq. [CO] (T)

SE-390 Kurz Foundation
c/o Keystone Shipping Company
P.O. Box 1134
Bala Cynwyd   19004   (Montgomery County)

MI-13-14-22-29-32-41-42-63

Phone 610-617-6834 **FAX** None
EIN 23-6235374   **Year Created** 1962

AMV $392,520   **FYE** 12-00   **(Gifts Received** $20,657)   30 **Grants totaling** $35,000

About three-thirds local giving. High grants of **$2,000** each to Academy of Notre Dame de Namur, Episcopal Academy, Haverford School, and Upper Dublin Lutheran Church. **$1,000-$1,500** each to American Cancer Society, American Heart Assn., Blind Relief Fund of Philadelphia, CARE International, City Team Ministries, Eastern College, Interfaith of Ambler, LaSalle U., Old Pine Community Center, St. John Neumann High School, Seaman's Church Institute, U. of Pa. and Villanova U. **Out-of-state** giving includes **$1,000** each to American Merchant Marine Museum [NY], Trinity College [CT], U. of Notre Dame [IN], U.S. Coast Guard Foundation [NY], maritime academies in several states, and other merchant-marine related institutions. ■**PUBLICATIONS:** None ■**WEBSITE:** None ■**E-MAIL:** None ■**APPLICATION POLICIES & PROCEDURES:** Grant requests may be submitted in any form at any time; the annual review period begins November 30th.

O+D+T Charles Kurz, II (P+D+Con) — G.H. Kurz (VP+D) — R. Kurz (S+D) — P.W. Fisher (F+D)

SE-391 Kynett (Edna G.) Memorial Foundation
P.O. Box 8228
Philadelphia   19101   (Philadelphia County)

MI-31-34-35

Phone 610-828-8145 **FAX** 610-834-8175
EIN 23-6296592   **Year Created** 1954

AMV $11,117,531   **FYE** 12-00   **(Gifts Received** $0)   10 **Grants totaling** $595,647

All giving to Greater Philadelphia for specific healthcare purposes under the Kynett Cardiovascular Education Program. High grant of **$165,997** to U. of Pa.**$75,000** to Children's Hospital of Philadelphia. **$59,000** to Abington Memorial Hospital. **$51,400** to Chestnut Hill Healthcare. **$50,000** each to Foundation of Hahnemann & Medical College of Pa., Jefferson Medical College, and Villa Vincent-St. Catherine LaBoure Medical Clinic. **$47,000** to Bryn Mawr Hospital. **$42,000** to Visiting Nurses Assn. of Greater Philadelphia. **$5,250** to Riddle Memorial Hospital. ■**PUBLICATIONS:** statement of program policy; application guidelines ■ **WEBSITE:** None ■**E-MAIL:** judy1@aol.com ■**APPLICATION POLICIES & PROCEDURES:** The Foundation reports that giving is focused on Delaware Valley's community hospitals and teaching hospitals for educating students, primary care physicians, and specialists about cardiovascular disease. Activities supported include conferences, seminars, lectures, and assisting professorships or training sessions; innovative proposals are encouraged. No grants are awarded for endowment. Prospective applicants initially should make a telephone inquiry about the feasibility of submitting a request. Submit brief proposals with cover letter (original plus 10 copies required) at any time (deadline is December 1st). Proposals must include (1) Summary: briefly describe the program and how it will improve cardiovascular healthcare in the community; (2) Details of Proposed Program: purpose and objective of the program; description, names/qualifications of key personnel and attendees/presenters; start/completion dates, project budget, and (3) A plan for evaluating the program. Grants are awarded at a May meeting.

O+D+T Judith L. Bardes [Plymouth Meeting] (Manager+Con) — Norman Makous, M.D. [West Brandywine] (P+D) — John Urban Doherty, M.D. (VP+D) — Susan C. Day, M.D. (S+D) — Michael A. Walsh (F+D) — Oliver Bullock, D.O. (D) — Elmer H. Funk, Jr., M.D. [Haverford] (D) — Ann L. O'Sullivan, M.S.N., Ph.D. (D) — Donald F. Schwartz, M.D. (D) — Thomas M. Vernon, M.D. [West Point] (D) — D. Stratton Woodruff, Jr. M.D. [Bryn Mawr] (D) — Mellon Bank (custodian)

SE-392 Lake (William B.) Foundation MI-23
c/o First Union/Wachovia
123 South Broad Street, PA1279
Philadelphia 19109 (Philadelphia County) **Phone** 215-670-4224 **FAX** 215-670-4236
EIN 23-6266137 **Year Created** 1948
AMV $1,079,663 **FYE** 5-01 **(Gifts Received** $0) 30 **Grants totaling** $49,388

All giving is restricted to individuals in the Delaware Valley who suffer from pulmonary health problems. Typical support is about **$500** annually, although a few recipients receive considerably more assistance. ■**PUBLICATIONS:** None ■**WEBSITE:** None ■ **E-MAIL:** robert.prischak@wachovia.com ■**APPLICATION POLICIES & PROCEDURES:** Only pulmonary specialists may apply on behalf of Delaware Valley residents suffering with pulmonary health problems. A letter-request must be submitted by the specialist which describes the individual's medical diagnosis and need for financial assistance. If eligible for consideration, a Social Worker will arrange for an interview to document the case and then will make a recommendation to the Review Committee that meets in June and December. Payments are disbursed monthly and recipients are reviewed every six months over a two-year period.

O+D+T Robert Prischak (Assistant VP at Bank+Con) — Elizabeth K. Deegan (Social Worker/Consultant) — Baido Carnecchia, Esq. (Committee Member) — Thomas Prestal, M.D. (Committee Member) — Susan Sink, R.N. (Committee Member) — Linda Smith, L.S.W. (Committee Member) — (Committee Member) — First Union/Wachovia (Manager)

SE-393 Lamm Family Foundation MI-22-32-41-52-54-62-84
508 Waldron Park Drive **Phone** 610-642-5185 **FAX** None
Haverford 19041 (Montgomery County) **EIN** 23-2699481 **Year Created** 1992
AMV $98,813 **FYE** 12-00 **(Gifts Received** $9,222) 28 **Grants totaling** $33,325

Mostly local giving. High grant of **$11,500** to Federation Allied Jewish Appeal. **$5,000** to The Gesu School. **$2,500** to Conquer Fragile X Foundation [Blue Bell]. **$1,000-$1,500** each to Perelman Jewish Day School, Philadelphia Museum of Art, Philadelphia Orchestra, and Wistar Institute. Other local contributions **$100-$500** for various purposes. **Out-of-state** grant: **$5,000** to U.S. Ski Team Foundation [UT]. ■**PUBLICATIONS:** None ■**WEBSITE:** None ■**E-MAIL:** None ■**APPLICATION POLICIES & PROCEDURES:** No grants awarded to individuals.

O+D+T Harvey Lamm (D+Donor+Con) — Sandra Lamm (D+Donor)

SE-394 Landon Family Foundation MI-14-41-42-54-71
1404 Anvil Court **Phone** 610-269-4232 **FAX** None
Downingtown 19335 (Chester County) **EIN** 23-2868535 **Year Created** 1997
AMV $600,646 **FYE** 12-00 **(Gifts Received** $41,237) 10+ **Grants totaling** $76,020

Mostly local/Pa. giving. High grant of **$20,000** to Penn State U. **$17,200** to Camphill-Beaver Run. **$5,000** each to Franklin Institute and Gesu School. Other grants/contributions **$3,000** or smaller totaled **$21,320,** but not details available. **Out-of-state** grant: **$7,500** to Chesapeake Bay Foundation [MD]. — Major giving in prior years to Penn State U. ■**PUBLICATIONS:** None ■ **WEBSITE:** None ■**E-MAIL:** None ■**APPLICATION POLICIES & PROCEDURES:** Grant requests may be submitted in any form at any time. Site visits sometimes are made to organizations being considered for a grant. Grants are awarded at meetings in April and November.

O+D+T Ronald A. Landon (P+D+Donor+Con) — Joyce S. Landon (VP+F+D+Donor) — Katherine McGrath (D) — Harry Norton [Lancaster] (D) — Nancy Norton [Lancaster] (D)

SE-395 Larking Hill Foundation MI-41-42-84
330 Thornbrook Ave. **Phone** 610-527-5634 **FAX** None
Rosemont 19010 (Montgomery County) **EIN** 23-7978393 **Year Created** 1998
AMV $1,004,851 **FYE** 5-00 **(Gifts Received** $335,896) 2 **Grants totaling** $13,500

One local grant: **$12,500** to The Haverford School. **Out-of-state** grant: **$1,000** to Duke U. (men's crew). ■**PUBLICATIONS:** None ■**WEBSITE:** None ■**E-MAIL:** None ■**APPLICATION POLICIES & PROCEDURES:** Grant requests may be submitted in a letter at any time; describe the organization and include IRS tax-exempt status documentation.

O+D+T Thomas L. Bennett (T+Donor+Con) — Carolyn E. Bennett (T) — Christopher F. Bennett (T) — Geoffrey T. Bennett (T)

SE-396 Lasko Charitable Trust MI-18-22-29-41-42-62
c/o Eizen Fineburg & McCarthy
2001 Market Street, Suite 3410
Philadelphia 19103 (Philadelphia County) **Phone** 215-751-9666 **FAX** 215-751-9310
EIN 23-2856376 **Year Created** 1996
AMV $5,325,184 **FYE** 6-00 **(Gifts Received** $40,000) 5 **Grants totaling** $69,250

All local giving; all grants are for general purposes. High grants of **$25,000** each to Planned Parenthood of SE Pa. and West Chester U. **$10,000** to Politz Hebrew Academy. **$7,500** to Champions of Caring [Villanova]. **$1,750** to Albert Einstein Academy. — Grants awarded in the prior year included **$200,000** each to Associated Beth Rivka School for Girls [NY] and Machne Israel; **$23,000** to Bishop Shanahan High School (building fund); **$7,500** to Champions of Caring; and **$5,000** each to Abrams Hebrew Academy, Albert Einstein Academy, and Planned Parenthood. ■**PUBLICATIONS:** None ■**WEBSITE:** None ■**E-MAIL:** None ■**APPLICATION POLICIES & PROCEDURES:** Grant requests may be submitted in any form at any time; provide complete information about the project.

O+D+T Bernard Eizen, Esq. (P+D+Con) — Dr. Maury Huberman (D) — Vivian Simkins Lasko (D) — Organizational donor: RealTemp, Inc.

SE-397 Lasko Family Foundation
c/o Lasko Metal Products, Inc.
820 Lincoln Avenue
West Chester 19380   (Chester County)

MI-11-13-22-41-42-43-49-62-64-82

Phone 610-692-7400 **FAX** None
EIN 23-2307053   **Year Created** 1984

AMV $5,149,741   **FYE** 6-00   **(Gifts Received** $0)   23 **Grants totaling** $181,719

Mostly local/Pa. giving. High grant of **$53,750** to Jewish Federation of Greater Philadelphia. **$20,000** to Torah Academy of Greater Philadelphia. **$18,591** to Gratz College. **$10,000** each to Auerbach Central Agency for Jewish Education. **$8,333** to Boy Scouts/Chester County Council. **$7,500** to Abrams Hebrew Academy [Yardley]. **$5,000** each to United Way of Lancaster County and West Chester U. **$2,500** each to Aid for Friends and Abrams Scholarship Fund. Other local contributions **$500** or smaller for various purposes. **Out-of-state** giving includes **$15,000** to Students in Free Enterprise [MO]; **$10,000** to Israel Free Loan Society; **$9,085** to Albert Einstein Academy [DE]; **$6,500** to United Way of Williamson County [TN]; and **$5,500** to United Way of Tarrant County [TX]. ■**PUBLICATIONS:** None ■**WEBSITE:** None ■**E-MAIL:** None ■**APPLICATION POLICIES & PROCEDURES:** No grants awarded to individuals.

O+D+T Vivian Simkins Lasko (D+Con) — Bernard Eizen, Esq. [Philadelphia] (P+D) — Dr. Maury Huberman (D) — Oscar Lasko (Donor) Corporate donor: Lasko Metal Products, Inc.

SE-398 Lassin Family Foundation, The
7135 Sheaff Lane
Fort Washington 19034   (Montgomery County)

MI-12-15-22-41-42-54-62

Phone Unlisted **FAX** None
EIN 23-2070532   **Year Created** 1978

AMV $955,803   **FYE** 11-00   **(Gifts Received** $108,470)   33 **Grants totaling** $220,963

Mostly local giving. High grant of **$110,050** to Federation Allied Jewish Appeal. **$51,675** to Philadelphia Geriatric Center. **$10,110** to Philadelphia Museum of Art. **$10,000** to Germantown Academy. **$3,045** to Congregation Rodeph Shalom. **$2,700** to Federation Day Care Services. **$2,000** to Congregation Beth Or. **$1,000-$1,650** each to Boys Town Jerusalem Foundation of America, Living Beyond Breast Cancer, and National Museum of American Jewish History. Other local contributions **$50-$550** for various purposes. **Out-of-state** giving includes **$11,070** to Florida International U. and **$10,700** to Fisher Island Philanthropic Fund [FL]. ■**PUBLICATIONS:** None ■**WEBSITE:** None ■**E-MAIL:** None ■**APPLICATION POLICIES & PROCEDURES:** No grants awarded to individuals.

O+D+T Ronald P. Lassin (T+Donor+Con) — Harriet J. Lassin (T)

SE-399 Lassin Philanthropic Foundation, The
c/o Harriet Carter Gifts
425 Stump Road, P.O. Box 427
Montgomeryville 18936   (Montgomery County)

MI-12-22-29-41-42-62

Phone 215-361-5100 **FAX** None
EIN 23-7862354   **Year Created** 1996

AMV $585,776   **FYE** 11-00   **(Gifts Received** $185,000)   7 **Grants totaling** $39,500

About two-thirds local giving; all grants are unrestricted support. High Pa. grant of **$10,000** to U. of Pa./The Wharton Fund. **$5,000** to Germantown Academy. **$4,500** to Congregation Beth Or. **$2,500** to Federation Day Care Services. **$1,500** to Friends of Philadelphia Ronald McDonald House. **$1,000** to Red Cross. **Out-of-state** grant: **$15,000** to Brandeis U. [MA]. ■**PUBLICATIONS:** None ■**WEBSITE:** None ■**E-MAIL:** None ■**APPLICATION POLICIES & PROCEDURES:** No grants awarded to individuals.

O+D+T Gary D. Lassin (T+Donor+Con) — Robin Lassin (T)

SE-400 Laurel Charitable Trust
230 Laurel Lane
Haverford 19041   (Montgomery County)

MI-11-13-17-18-31-41-52-63-83-84-85

Phone 610-649-9860 **FAX** None
EIN 23-7453139   **Year Created** 1990

AMV $171,365   **FYE** 12-00   **(Gifts Received** $0)   62 **Grants totaling** $98,773

About half local giving. High Pa. grant of **$10,000** to Community Academy of Philadelphia. **$8,000** to Philadelphia Physicians for Social Responsibility (Peaceful Posse program). **$7,600** to Bryn Mawr Presbyterian Church. **$5,000** to Philadelphia Youth Tennis. **$3,000** to Youthbuild Philadelphia Charter School. **$2,250** to Church of the Advocate. **$2,000** to Planned Parenthood of SE Pa. **$1,000-$1,750** each to Bryn Mawr Hospital Foundation, Children's Hospital of Philadelphia Foundation, Gesu School, Greater Philadelphia Chamber of Commerce, Philadelphia Futures, Philadelphia Orchestra, United Way of SE Pa., White-Williams Scholars, and Women's Way. Other local contributions **$100-$500** for various purposes. **Out-of-state** giving includes high grant of **$25,052** to North Carolina Outward Bound School; **$10,000** to Girls on the Move [NY]; and smaller grants/contributions to many states. ■**PUBLICATIONS:** None ■**WEBSITE:** None ■**E-MAIL:** None ■**APPLICATION POLICIES & PROCEDURES:** The Trust reports that unsolicited grant applications are not accepted. No grants awarded to individuals.

O+D+T Ann R. Baruch (T+Donor+Con)

SE-401 Lazarich (John) Foundation, The
c/o ECS, Inc.
520 Eagleview Boulevard
Exton 19341   (Chester County)

MI-13-14-17-41-56-71-82

Phone 610-458-0570 **FAX** 610-458-8667
EIN 23-7918137   **Year Created** 1997

AMV $4,952,930   **FYE** 11-00   **(Gifts Received** $0)   6 **Grants totaling** $132,650

All local giving. High grant of **$125,000** to Camp Soltane. **$5,000** to Phoenixville Police Athletic League. **$1,000** each to Historic Yellow Springs and Special Olympics of Pa. **$500** to Chester County Futures. Other smaller contributions. — Major giving in prior years included **$275,000** to Camp Soltane; **$50,000** to Domestic Violence Center of West Chester; **$25,000** each to Malvern Preparatory School and Stroud Water Foundation Trust; **$10,000** to Pilot School [DE]; and **$5,000** each to Heifer Project [AR], Hurricane Island Outward Bound School [ME], and Croatian Franciscan Emergency Fund [NY]. ■**PUBLICATIONS:** None ■**WEBSITE:** www.ecsinc.com ■**E-MAIL:** None ■**APPLICATION POLICIES & PROCEDURES:** Grant requests may be submitted in writing at any time; include IRS tax-exempt status documentation.

O+D+T William Kronenberger, III (Manager+T+Donor+Con) — Julie I. Blank (T+Con)

SE-402 Lee (Jerry) Foundation
c/o WBEB-FM Radio, Inc.
10 Presidential Boulevard
Bala Cynwyd 19004 (Montgomery County)
AMV $245,918 **FYE** 12-01 **(Gifts Received** $807,000)

MI-20-22-41-42-43
Phone 610-667-8400 **FAX** 610-667-6795
EIN 23-2867684 **Year Created** 1996
7 **Grants totaling** $644,000

About four-fifths local giving; grants are unrestricted support except as noted. High grant of **$500,000** to U. of Pa. (Jerry Lee Center of Criminology). **$10,000** each to Gesu School and Girard College. **$2,000** each to Broadcast Pioneers Educational Fund and Philadelphia Police Foundation. **Out-of-state** grants: **$120,000** to U. of Maryland (Jerry Lee Crime Scholarship Fund) and **$10,000** to Broadcast Industry Council [DC] (crime/prevention project). — Grants awarded in the prior year included **$17,000** to Fels Center of Government and **$12,500** to Salvation Army (Block by Block program). ■**PUBLICATIONS:** None ■**WEBSITE:** None ■**E-MAIL:** jerry1@101-fm.com ■**APPLICATION POLICIES & PROCEDURES:** Grant requests may be submitted in proposals which follow Delaware Valley Grantmakers' Common Grant Application Form (see Appendix or www.dvg.org). No grants are awarded to individuals.

O+D+T Gloria Dreon (Adminstrator+Con) — Gerald Lee (D+Donor) — David Kurtz (D+Donor) — Corporate donor: Clear Channel Communications

---

SE-403 Leeway Foundation, The
123 South Broad Street, Suite 2040
Philadelphia 19109 (Philadelphia County)
AMV $10,350,127 **FYE** 12-01 **(Gifts Received** $33,323)

MI-17-53-55
Phone 215-545-4078 **FAX** 215-545-4021
EIN 23-2727140 **Year Created** 1993
47 **Grants totaling** $237,089

Mostly Philadelphia-area giving, to recognize excellence and achievement of local women artists and writers, primarily through annual, competitive awards in a single and different artistic discipline each year. In 2003, the selected discipline is Fiction & Creative Non-fiction; other disciplines will be selected for future years—check the website for updates. The **Established Artists Awards** include the The Bessie Berman Award (one **$35,000** award) for a woman artist 50 years or older; The Leeway Award for Excellence (one **$30,000** award); and The Leeway Awards for Achievement (several **$20,000** awards). The **Emerging Artists Awards** include The Edna Andrade Award (one **$15,000** award); The Inspiration Awards (several **$7,500** awards), and Seedling Awards (several **$2,500** awards). In addition, **Window of Opportunity Grants** (several dozen, up to **$2,000** each) support specific projects of women artists working in any discipline, enabling them to take advantage of unique, time-limited opportunities that could significantly benefit their work or increase its recognition. The Foundation publicizes the work of the award recipients in its annual awards catalogue. ■**PUBLICATIONS:** annual Awards for Artists Catalog; application guidelines ■**WEBSITE:** www.leeway.org ■**E-MAIL:** info@leeway.org ■**APPLICATION POLICIES & PROCEDURES:** The Foundation's primary mission is supporting individual women artists in the five-county Philadelphia area, to promote their representation and increased recognition in the arts community, through annual competitive grants under two programs: **I. Awards to Emerging Artists and to Established Artists** (juried separately and anonymously) are for demonstrating outstanding creativity and vision in a body of work in a selected visual or literary discipline. A different discipline is selected annually and artists at all stages of development are encouraged to apply. Application guidelines are available annually—check website for availability. Eligible applicants must be (a) female; (b) age 20 or older by application deadline; (c) have resided continuously in the five-county Philadelphia area for at least two years by application deadline and intend to be in residence until notification of the grants; (d) have exhibited one's work in at least one juried show (visual artists) or had work published at least once (writers); (e) not be enrolled full-time in an undergraduate, degree-granting program; and (f) not be officially connected with The Leeway Foundation or related family members. For additional application information and jurying criteria, consult the website. **II. Window of Opportunity Grants** are project-specific grants for women artists working in any discipline, to support such activities as an exceptional chance for advanced study with a significant mentor (not degree related); travel associated with an imminent, concrete opportunity (book tour, artist's exhibition, commission, performance, residency, etc.); rental of equipment, purchase of materials, or other expenses needed for an arts project (e.g. an exhibition, performance, etc.) Grants will not support self-produced activities/materials related to ongoing work; tuition, entry fees or registration fees; living expenses; expenses to establish/maintain an organization or company; costs involved in real estate, e.g. purchase, renovations); medical, legal, accounting or marketing fees; and publications, documentation or finishing costs without a specific opportunity. An eligible applicant must (a) be a woman artist residing in the 5-county Philadelphia area and 20 years or older; (b) have a commitment from a recognized institution, organization or mentor for a specific date or dates; (c) not be a full-time matriculated student; and (d) not be a Leeway Emerging or Established Artist Award recipient in the past 2 years. Application deadlines for these grants are quarterly, usually in January, April, June, and November. Prospective applicants should consult the website, or telephone/e-mail the Foundation for detailed application guidelines (including current deadlines) and grant selection criteria, and/or to discuss a prospective application. Also, prospective applicants may attend one of the grant program workshops held by the Foundation. Note: Unsolicited grant requests from arts organizations are not accepted—all grants to organizations are initiated by the Foundation.

O+D+T Barbara J. Silzle (Executive Director+Con) — Sara Becker (P+D) — Linda Lee Alter (Founder+Donor+D) — Suzanne M. Cunningham (D) — Charlene S. Longnecker (D) — Virginia P. Sikes, Esq. (D) — Helen Berman Alter (Donor)

SE-404   Lefton (Al Paul) Company Foundation   MI-11-53-54-55
c/o Al Paul Lefton Company, Inc.
100 Independence Mall West, 4th Floor   **Phone** 215-923-9600 **FAX** 215-351-4298
Philadelphia 19106   (Philadelphia County)   **EIN** 23-6298693   **Year Created** 1946

AMV $39,486   **FYE** 12-00   **(Gifts Received** $20,000)   18 **Grants totaling** $22,270

About three-fourths local giving. High grant of **$5,300** to U. of the Arts. **$4,600** to Institute of Contemporary Art. **$2,000** to Main Line Art Center. **$1,700** to United Way of SE Pa. **$840** to Academy of Music. Other local contributions **$100-$500** for various purposes. **Out-of-state** grant: **$5,050** to Yale U. [CT] ■**PUBLICATIONS:** None ■**WEBSITE:** www.lefton.com [corporate info only] ■**E-MAIL:** None ■**APPLICATION POLICIES & PROCEDURES:** The Foundation reports that most support is for cultural/arts organizations which the Trustees personally select. Grant requests may be submitted in a letter at any time.

O+D+T   Al Paul Lefton, Jr. (P+T+Con) — Raymond D. Scanlon (F+T)

SE-405   Lenfest (Brook J.) Foundation, The   MI-20-29-41-43-45-49-51-54-55-56-85
Five Tower Bridge, Suite 450
300 Barr Harbor Drive   **Phone** 610-828-4510 **FAX** 610-828-0390
West Conshohocken 19428   (Montgomery County)   **EIN** 23-3031338   **Year Created** 2000

AMV $24,862,046   **FYE** 6-01   **(Gifts Received** $25,043,424)   5 **Grants totaling** $95,000

All local giving. High grants of **$25,000** each to Koresh Dance Company (operating support) and National Liberty Museum (Freedom Tours program). **$20,000** to Philadelphia Futures (Class of 2004). **$15,000** to Southwest Community Enrichment Center (computer training program). **$10,000** to White-Williams Scholars (general operations/programs). ■**PUBLICATIONS:** mission statement; application guidelines ■**WEBSITE:** www.brookjlenfestfoundation.org ■**E-MAIL:** lenfestfoundation@lenfestfoundation.org ■**APPLICATION POLICIES & PROCEDURES:** The Foundation reports that it primarily supports programs/organizations in urban areas of SE PA (especially Philadelphia), South Central PA (especially Franklin County and Harrisburg), Southern NJ, and Northern DE. Most grants are for general support, special projects, building funds, and capital drives, and range from $10,000 to $100,000; multiyear requests are considered. Major programmatic interests are: (a) educational programs that enable children/adults to learn skills and improve their lives, (b) scholarships and other programs that help people take advantage of educational opportunities, (c) programs to help former inmates and their families lead productive lives, and (d) programs to help people improve their employment opportunities through education in technology. The Foundation may work independently or in partnership with other foundations, government and nonprofit organizations to initiate programs that address a particular problem. The Foundation will consider support for programs/organizations where its contribution will have a significant impact, and is interested in supporting small and entrepreneurial organizations, especially those with an educational component. No grants are awarded to individuals, or for health issues, litigation, medical research/treatment, religious programs/activities, publications, research/academic studies lacking action plans, political or quasi-political organizations, and university presses. Grant requests should be submitted in a Letter of Inquiry (4 pages maximum) which (1) describes how the program will further the Foundation's stated mission/interests; (2) describes the program for which the funds will be used; (3) states an amount of funding requested; (4) for existing programs, describes both short and long-term outcomes; and (5) for new programs, describes expected outcomes and how program results will be evaluated. Also include a complete program budget for the proposed project; a list other funding received, requested or expected from foundations, corporations, government or other revenue sources; the organization's current year budget; the most recent audited financial statement; titles and annual salaries of the five highest paid staff members; and IRS tax-exempt status documentation showing Federal EIN. Letters of Inquiry may mailed or submitted by e-mail. Foundation staff and/or board members will review Letters of Inquiry for the potential to advance the Foundation's objectives. If interested, the Foundation will seek additional information, request a more detailed proposal, or arrange for a site visit. — Note: Because of existing commitments and budget limitations, no new Letters of Inquiry should be submitted until after January 1, 2003; final decisions on these grant requests will be made at a May/June 2003 Board meeting.

O+D+T   L. Bruce Melgary (Con) — Brook J. Lenfest (P+D+Donor) — Dawn Lenfest (S+D) — Marguerite B. Lenfest (F+D)

SE-406   Lenfest Foundation, The   MI-12-13-22-25-41-43-44-45-52-53-54-56-84
Five Tower Bridge, Suite 450
300 Barr Harbor Drive   **Phone** 610-828-4510 **FAX** 610-828-0390
West Conshohocken 19428   (Montgomery County)   **EIN** 23-3031350   **Year Created** 1987

AMV $157,410,225   **FYE** 6-01   **(Gifts Received** $153,408,184)   36 **Grants totaling** $6,635,656

About half local/Pa. giving. High grant of **$2,000,000** to Pa. Academy of the Fine Arts (special exhibition gallery renovations). **$500,000** to Williamson Free School of Mechanical Trades (endowment). **$60,000** to Pa. Heritage Society [Harrisburg] (Governor's Residence Gardens renovation). **$50,000** to YWCA of Bucks County (summer camp). **$45,000** to Schwenkfelder Library [Pennsburg] (Heritage Center). **$25,000** each to Delaware Valley Friends School (library/media center) and Wharton Esherick Museum (endowment). **$20,000** each to Philadelphia Museum of Art (125th anniversary) and West Chester Community Center (office skills & after-school enrichment programs). **$18,000** to White-Williams Scholars (student stipends). **$12,600** to West Chester U. (outward bound training partnership). **$10,000** each to Baker Industries (work rehabilitation program), Children's Country Week Assn. (Paradise Farm Camp), Crime Prevention Assn. of Philadelphia (summer camp program), and Easter Seals (summer camp program). **$7,000** to Woodmere Art Gallery (expansion). **$5,000** each to Abington Free Library (lecture series), ARC of Chester County (Camp Safari), Boy Scouts/Cradle of Liberty Council (luncheon event), Committee for Dignity & Fairness for the Homeless Housing Development (youth programs), Interfaith Housing Development Corp. of Bucks County (Project Fresh Start), Philadelphia Art Alliance (endowment), and Urban Bridges at St. Gabriel's (partnering program). **$4,911** to Salvation Army/Norristown (emergency housing program). **$4,525** to Quaker School at Horsham (25 Bell School Set). **$3,620** to The Christian Academy (two scholarships). **$3,000** to Old First Reformed Church (day camp/YES program). **$2,000** to Summer Reading Coalition (summer reading project). **Out-of-state** giving includes **$2,000,000** to National Cable Television Center &

Museum [CO] (cable programming archives); **$1,000,000** to Foundations, Inc. [NJ] (after-school program in Franklin County, PA); **$500,000** to Teach for America [NY] (general operations); **$100,000** each to Chesapeake Bay Maritime Museum [MD] (lecture series endowment) and Greater Kanawha Valley Foundation [WV] (memorial fund trust); **$25,000** each to Kennedy Krieger Foundation [MD] (Downs Syndrome research) and NetDay [CA] (digital day initiative/NetDay Compass); and **$10,000** to Trenton Community Music School [NJ] (preschool program). ■**PUBLICATIONS:** mission statement; application guidelines; brochures on the two scholarship programs. ■**WEBSITE:** www.lenfestfoundation.org ■**E-MAIL:** lenfestfoundation@lenfestfoundation.org ■**APPLICATION POLICIES & PROCEDURES:** The Foundation reports most giving focuses on SE Pa., South Central Pa., Southern NJ, and Northern DE with significant support for the Lenfest Achievement Scholarship Program (college prep boarding schools), the Lenfest College Scholarship Program (primarily for students in rural areas), and an after school enrichment programs in Franklin County, Pa. and Cumberland County, NJ. The Foundation awards a limited number of grants in response to unsolicited proposals from nonprofits working within its mission and located in the designated geographic areas. Also, proposals may be invited from specific nonprofit organizations. Grants will be awarded for specific programs and general operating support. Generally, no grants are awarded to individuals or scholarship programs (other than the Lenfest-sponsored programs); after school enrichment programs (other than the two listed above); disease research; organizations/programs that deal with health/physical disabilities; political or quasi-political organizations; litigation; studies or publications; conferences, fairs or festivals; or purchase of tickets, tables, ads or sponsorships. Grant requests may be submitted (by mail or e-mail) at any time in a Letter of Inquiry (3 pages maximum) which (a) briefly describes the organization and its mission; (b) states the amount of support requested and, if requesting funds for a specific program/project, the total amount needed; (c) the organization's total revenue and expenses for the most recent fiscal year (not a copy of the budget—just the totals); and (d) IRS tax-exempt status documentation with the Federal EIN. Do not enclose any other materials. All Letters of Inquiry will be acknowledged and reviewed by Foundation staff and/or board members to determine the Foundation's level of interest based on current priorities and availability of funds. If interested, Foundation staff will follow up with questions, request a more detailed proposal, and/or arrange a site visit. — Formerly called the H.F. Lenfest Foundation.

O+D+T L. Bruce Melgary (Executive Director+Con) — H.F. 'Gerry' Lenfest (C+D+Donor) — Marguerite B. Lenfest (P+D+Donor) — Albert C. Bellas (D) — T. Douglas Hale (D) — John Strassburger (D) — Grahame P. Richards (S)

SE-407   Levee (Polly Annenberg) Charitable Trust / Krancer Trust   MI-11-22-31-32-62-71
844 Harriton Road   **Phone** 215-569-5500 **FAX** None
Bryn Mawr 19010   (Montgomery County)   **EIN** 23-2735661   **Year Created** 1993
AMV $5,047,252   **FYE** 12-00   (**Gifts Received** $0)   8 **Grants totaling** $289,500

All local giving. High grant of **$200,000** to Jewish Federation of Greater Philadelphia. **$25,000** to Crohn's & Colitis Foundation of America. **$20,000** each to Albert Einstein Medical Society and Jewish Community Centers of Greater Philadelphia. **$10,000** each to Children's Hospital of Philadelphia Foundation and United Way of SE Pa. **$2,500** to Albert Einstein Healthcare Network. **$2,000** to Riverbend Environmental Education Center. ■**PUBLICATIONS:** None ■**WEBSITE:** None ■**E-MAIL:** None ■**APPLICATION POLICIES & PROCEDURES:** Information not available.

O+D+T Michael L. Krancer, Esq. (Con) — Walter H. Annenberg (T) — William J. Henrich, Jr., Esq. (T) — PNC Advisors (Corporate Trustee)

SE-408   Levine (Joseph & Bessie) Fund, The   MI-22-31-54-56-62
4737 Street Road   **Phone** 215-927-2700 **FAX** None
Trevose 19053   (Bucks County)   **EIN** 23-6296625   **Year Created** 1962
AMV $62,296   **FYE** 12-00   (**Gifts Received** $0)   25 **Grants totaling** $57,310

Mostly local giving. High grant of **$11,000** to Jewish Federation of Greater Philadelphia. **$10,000** to National Museum of American Jewish History. **$7,500** to Temple Sinai. **$5,200** to Congregation Tifereth Israel. **$5,000** to Jewish Archives of Philadelphia. **$2,500-$3,000** each to Albert Einstein Healthcare Foundation, Golden Slipper Club/Charities, Jewish Employment & Vocational Services, and Greater Philadelphia Rabbinical Assembly. **$1,000-$1,200** each to Congregation B'nai Jacob [Phoenixville], Flyers Wives Fight for Lives, Gratz College, and Kehilat Reim. Other smaller contributions, mostly for Jewish purposes. ■**PUBLICATIONS:** None ■**WEBSITE:** None ■**E-MAIL:** None ■**APPLICATION POLICIES & PROCEDURES:** Information not available.

O+D+T Joseph H. Levine (T+Con) — Corporate donor: Joseph Levine & Son, Inc.

SE-409   Levit (J.H.) Foundation   MI-22-62-82
c/o Simon Miller Sales Company
1218 Chestnut Street, Suite 802   **Phone** 215-923-3600 **FAX** 215-923-1173
Philadelphia 19107   (Philadelphia County)   **EIN** 23-7408956   **Year Created** 1974
AMV $132,188   **FYE** 12-00   (**Gifts Received** $0)   5 **Grants totaling** $31,200

About two-thirds local giving. High grant of **$15,500** to Drexel U. **$4,500** to Suburban Jewish Community Center/B'nai Aaron. Other smaller local contributions. **Out-of-state** giving includes **$10,000** to Boys Town Jerusalem [Israel]. ■**PUBLICATIONS:** None ■**WEBSITE:** None ■**E-MAIL:** None ■**APPLICATION POLICIES & PROCEDURES:** Grant requests may be submitted in a letter in January; describe the purpose of the funding requested and include IRS tax-exempt status documentation. No grants are awarded to individuals. Site visits sometimes are made to organizations being considered for a grant.

O+D+T Henri C. Levit [Bryn Mawr] (VP+S+T+Con) — Joseph Levit [Wynnewood] (P+T+Con)

SE-410   Levitties Foundation, The
280 Brookway Road
Merion   19066   (Montgomery County)

MI-11-14-22-29-31-41-42-54-56-62-64-71
Phone 610-664-0404 **FAX** None
EIN 23-6200022   **Year Created** 1953

AMV $1,986,587   **FYE** 12-00   **(Gifts Received** $0)   37 **Grants totaling** $94,465

Mostly local giving. High grant of **$30,850** to Albert Einstein Healthcare Foundation. **$10,150** to Philadelphia Museum of Art. **$8,405** to Harcum Junior College. **$6,945** to MossRehab. **$5,208** to Har Zion Temple. **$4,000** to U. of Pa. **$3,210** to Morris Arboretum. **$2,500** to Philadelphia Cares. **$2,000** to United Way of SE Pa. **$1,000** to Chestnut Hill Historical Society. **$800** to Friends' Central School. Other smaller contributions **$15-$500** for various purposes. **Out-of-state** giving includes **$12,500** to Jewish Theological Seminary of America [NY]. ■**PUBLICATIONS:** None ■**WEBSITE:** None ■**E-MAIL:** None ■**APPLICATION POLICIES & PROCEDURES:** Prospective applicants should initially telephone the Foundation to inquire about the feasibility of submitting a request. No grants awarded to individuals.

O+D+T Marvin B. Levitties (T+Donor+Con)

SE-411   Lida Foundation. The
504 West Mermaid Lane
Philadelphia   19118   (Philadelphia County)

MI-18-22-29-51-52-54-55-57-62-71
Phone 215-247-5578 **FAX** None
EIN 23-2706456   **Year Created** 1993

AMV $2,478,145   **FYE** 12-00   **(Gifts Received** $0)   32 **Grants totaling** $50,270

About three-fourths local giving; all grants are general support. High grant of **$12,000** to WHYY-91FM. **$6,200** to Planned Parenthood of SE Pa. **$5,500** to Partners Program. **$1,000** each to Jewish Federation of Greater Philadelphia, Morris Arboretum, Painted Bride Art Center (Hunger Theatre), and The Wilma Theater. **$600** to Philadelphia Museum of Art. Other local contributions **$250-$500**, primarily for arts/cultural and human services purposes. **Out-of-state** giving includes **$5,000** each to Career Connection [MA] and Greater Hartford Jewish Federation [CT]; and **$1,500** to Metropolitan Opera [NY]. ■**PUBLICATIONS:** None ■**WEBSITE:** None ■**E-MAIL:** None ■**APPLICATION POLICIES & PROCEDURES:** Grant requests may be submitted in any form at any time; describe the problem that the project will address and include IRS tax-exempt status documentation.

O+D+T Linda S. Glickstein (T+Con) — David L. Glickstein (T)

SE-412   Lieberman (Harry A.) Foundation, The
101 Cheswold Lane, Apt. 3C
Haverford   19041   (Montgomery County)

MI-22-32-42-54-62-64
Phone 610-896-6925 **FAX** None
EIN 23-2328740   **Year Created** 1986

AMV $1,458,910   **FYE** 12-00   **(Gifts Received** $3,476)   21 **Grants totaling** $58,700

About two-thirds local giving. High grant of **$7,500** to Huntington's Disease Society of America/Delaware Valley Chapter. **$6,000** to Susan G. Komen Breast Cancer Foundation. **$5,000** each to Federation Allied Jewish Appeal and Jewish Community Centers of Greater Philadelphia. **$4,000** to American Cancer Society. **$3,000** each to Catholic Charities, Gratz College, and Wistar Institute. **$1,000-$1,200** each to Hadassah of Greater Philadelphia, Philadelphia Museum of Art, and U. of Pa. **$500** to Israel Guide Dog Center for the Blind [Warrington]. **Out-of-state** giving includes **$6,000** to Jewish Theological Seminary of America [NY] and **$5,000** to Jewish National Fund [NY]. ■**PUBLICATIONS:** None ■**WEBSITE:** None ■**E-MAIL:** None ■**APPLICATION POLICIES & PROCEDURES:** The Foundation reports that grantees are selected only on the Trustee's invitation. No grants awarded to individuals.

O+D+T Harry A. Lieberman (T+Donor+Con)

SE-413   Lilliput Foundation
P.O. Box 70
Lederach   19450   (Montgomery County)

MI-14-25-31-41-44-51-54-55-56-63-71-72-86
Phone 610-287-0100 **FAX** None
EIN 23-2385383   **Year Created** 1985

AMV $1,877,531   **FYE** 12-00   **(Gifts Received** $700,103)   54 **Grants totaling** $620,727

Mostly local/Pa. giving; all grants are for general charitable purposes. High Pa. grant of **$110,000** to Perkiomen School. **$50,000** each to Fox Chase Cancer Center, Grand View Hospital, and North Penn Abstract. **$30,000** to Academy of Natural Sciences. **$25,000** each to Elmwood Park Zoo, Habitat for Humanity/Norristown, and Montgomery County Theatre Project. **$20,000** to Montgomery County Lands Trust. **$10,000** each to Albert Einstein Healthcare Foundation (Albert Einstein Society), Baker Industries, Goshenhoppen Historian, Inc. [Barto], Moravian Academy [Bethlehem], Palm Schwenkfelder Church, and Perkiomen Valley Watershed Assn. **$5,000-$5,500** each to Academy of Music, Bryn Mawr Presbyterian Church, Mountain Laurel Center for the Performing Arts [Pike County], Need in Deed, and Schwenkfelder Library [Pennsburg]. **$4,650** to Boyertown Antiques. **$3,526** to Massey Powell Enterprises [Plymouth Meeting]. **$1,000-$2,000** each to Allied Arts Fund [Harrisburg], Central Schwenkfelder Church, Central Pa. Youth Ballet [Carlisle], Chester County SPCA, Full Circle Health & Fitness Services [Blue Bell], Haverford College, National Organization for Hearing, Norristown Ministries, WLVT [Allentown], and YWCA. Other smaller local contributions for various purposes. **Out-of-state** giving includes **$68,276** to Mountainside [CT]; **$25,000** to Center for Security Policy [DC]; and **$5,000** each to America Responds With Love [KS], Deerfield Academy [MA], Lollipop Foundation [TX], and St. George's Church [NY]. ■**PUBLICATIONS:** None ■**WEBSITE:** None ■**E-MAIL:** None ■**APPLICATION POLICIES & PROCEDURES:** Grant requests may be submitted at any time in a letter (2 pages maximum); include IRS tax-exempt status documentation. The Board meets annually.

O+D+T Drew Lewis (S+F+T+Donor+Con) — Marilyn S. Lewis (P+Donor) — Andrew L. Lewis, IV [Haverford] (T) — Russell S. Lewis [Harrisburg] (T)

SE-414 Lily Foundation, The
245 Abrahams Lane
Villanova   19085   (Delaware County)
AMV $1,569,831   **FYE** 12-00   **(Gifts Received** $0)

MI-12-13-17-41-55-71-84
Phone Unlisted **FAX** None
EIN 52-6854621   **Year Created** 1998
10 **Grants totaling** $33,952

Mostly local giving. High grant of **$11,500** to Domestic Abuse Project of Delaware County (continuing legal education/licensing). **$3,500** to Camp Dreamcatcher (camper program sponsorship). **$3,000** to Carson Village School. **$2,500** to Schuylkill Center for Environmental Education. **$1,000-$1,500** each to Camphill Village-Kimberton, Children's Country Day Camp, Children's Country Week Assn., and Cultural Heritage Alliance. **Out-of-state** giving includes **$5,000** to The Island School [Bahamas] and **$3,000** to World War II Memorial [DC].■**PUBLICATIONS:** None ■**WEBSITE:** None ■**E-MAIL:** None ■
APPLICATION POLICIES & PROCEDURES: Information not available.

O+D+T   Robert L. McNeil, III (T+Donor+Con) — Jane McNeil (T+Donor)

SE-415 Limaye (Sharon H.) Foundation
16 Andover Road
Haverford   19041   (Montgomery County)
AMV $274,981   **FYE** 12-00   **(Gifts Received** $50,888)

MI-11-12-14-32
Phone 610-658-2989 **FAX** None
EIN 23-2738735   **Year Created** 1993
6 **Grants totaling** $15,172

Mostly local giving; grants are for general expenses except as noted. High grant of **$10,000** to Emergency Care Research Institute (diabetes center). **$1,000** to Elwyn Institute. **Out-of-state** giving includes **$2,000** to United Way of San Francisco [CA]; **$1,122** to Childreach [RI]; and **$1,000** to Student Sponsor Partnership [NY]. ■**PUBLICATIONS:** None ■**WEBSITE:** None ■**E-MAIL:** None ■**APPLICATION POLICIES & PROCEDURES:** Grant requests may be submitted in a letter at any time.

O+D+T   Dilip R. Limaye (T+Donor+Con) — Ryan D. Limaye [CA] (T+Donor) — Kris N. Limaye [CA] (T)

SE-416 Lindback Foundation, The
c/o Duane Morris LLP
One Liberty Place, Suite 4200
Philadelphia   19103   (Philadelphia County)
AMV $23,190,175   **FYE** 12-01   **(Gifts Received** $0)

MI-11-13-18-22-31-34-35-41-42-43-44-52-53
54-55-72-81
Phone 215-979-1076 **FAX** 215-979-1020
EIN 23-6290348   **Year Created** 1955
104 **Grants totaling** $1,255,804

Mostly Eastern Pa./Southern NJ giving—some grants comprise multiple payments. High grant of **$100,000** to Regional Performing Arts Center (construction). **$90,000** each to Philadelphia Museum of Art (Friday Nights Program/operating support) and Philadelphia Orchestra (neighborhood access concerts/operating support). **$75,000** to Salvation Army (emergency aid/capital campaign). **$65,000** to Philadelphia Zoo (junior zoo apprentice program/operating support). **$55,000** to Academy of Natural Sciences (operating support). **$45,000** to Franklin Institute (operating support). **$40,000** to Prince Music Theater (Youth Arts Education Program). **$25,000** to Bucknell U. (endowment). **$20,000** each to National Constitution Center (exhibits), Russell Byers Charter School, and United Way of SE Pa. **$15,000** each to Archdiocese of Philadelphia (needy students tuition), Fund for the Water Works (restoration), Rosenbach Museum & Library (operating support), and Settlement Music School (scholarship aid). **$5,000** to Planned Parenthood of SE Pa. (sex education program). **$2,500** to WHYY (community service program). ***MINORITY JUNIOR FACULTY AWARDS*** (**$15,000-$17,000** each) given to faculty at 13 institutions: Bryn Mawr College, Bucknell U., Cabrini College, Haverford College, Lehigh U., Philadelphia U., Swarthmore College, U. of the Sciences in Philadelphia, U. of Pa., West Chester U., and three NJ institutions. ***DISTINGUISHED TEACHING AWARDS*** (**$4,000** each) awarded to professors at about 60 Pa. and NJ colleges/universities: Albright College, Alvernia College, Arcadia U., Bryn Mawr College, Bucknell U., Bucks County Community College, Cabrini College, Chestnut Hill College, Cheyney U., Community College of Philadelphia, Delaware County Community College, Drexel U., Eastern U, Franklin & Marshall College, Gwynedd-Mercy College, Harcum College, Haverford College, Holy Family College, Immaculata College, Thomas Jefferson U., Jefferson College of Allied Health Sciences, Lafayette College, LaSalle U., Lehigh U., Lincoln U., Montgomery County Community College, Moore College of Art, Moravian College, Muhlenberg College, Neumann College, Philadelphia College of Osteopathic Medicine, Philadelphia Health & Education Corp., Philadelphia U., Rosemont College, St. Joseph's U., Swarthmore College, Temple U. (6 awards), U. of the Arts, U. of the Sciences, Ursinus College, Villanova U., U. of Pa. (8 awards), West Chester U., and Widener U. — and the following in NJ: Atlantic Cape Community College, Burlington County Community College, Camden County Community College, Gloucester County Community College, Rowan College, Rutgers/Camden, and U. of Medicine & Dentistry of NJ. Other out-of-state grants, all to NJ: **$50,933** to New Jersey State Aquarium (urban enrichment program/operating support); **$20,000** each to Appel Farm Arts & Music Center and United Way of Atlantic County; **$15,000** to Archdiocese of Camden (needy students tuition); **$10,000** each to Glassboro Center for the Arts (Family Arts Adventure program) and Princeton Project (intern program expansion); and **$5,000** to Walt Whitman Cultural Arts Center. ■**PUBLICATIONS:** Teaching/Minority Faculty Awards Announcement Memorandum ■ **WEBSITE:** None ■**E-MAIL:** morris@duanemorris.com ■**APPLICATION POLICIES & PROCEDURES:** The Foundation reports that giving focuses on Eastern Pa. and Southern NJ for (1) educational or charitable purposes; (2) Distinguished Teaching Awards for a faculty member at about 60 preselected Pa. colleges/universities; and (3) Minority Junior Faculty Awards for full-time, untenured, junior, minority faculty at the same institutions to support scholarly opportunities, e.g. summer/sabbatical leave, special research projects, special equipment purchases, and other purposes; each institution may submit up to three nominations in a year for awards that generally range from $5,000-$15,000. In December, each eligible higher education institution is sent announcements about the two award programs which further clarify eligibility criteria. No grants are awarded directly to individuals or for endowment. Grant requests are not encouraged unless an organization is specifically requested to do so. The Trustees meet in March, June, and November. — Also called the Christian R. & Mary F. Lindback Foundation.

O+D+T   Roland Morris, Esq. (T+Con) — Martin A. Heckscher, Esq. [West Conshohocken] (T) First Union/Wachovia (Corporate Trustee)

SE-417 Lindberg (Carl M.) Family Foundation, The
P.O. Box 811
Wayne   19087   (Delaware County)

MI-12-15-25-41-42-53-56-63-71-72
Phone Unlisted **FAX** None
EIN 23-2966581   **Year Created** 1998

AMV $1,024,275   **FYE** 12-00   **(Gifts Received** $0)   21 **Grants totaling** $36,200

About half local giving. High grant of **$4,000** to Valley Forge REACT. **$2,000** each to Habitat for Humanity, Natural Lands Trust, Pa. Academy of the Fine Arts, and The Shipley School. **$1,000-$1,100** each to Chester County SPCA, Philabundance, St. David Episcopal Church, and Surrey Services for Seniors. **Out-of-state** giving includes **$1,000** to Colonial Williamsburg Foundation with other grants to several Bridgton, ME organizations, and universities in RI and MT. ■**PUBLICATIONS:** None ■**WEBSITE:** None ■**E-MAIL:** None ■**APPLICATION POLICIES & PROCEDURES:** Information not available.

O+D+T Carl M. Lindberg (P+Donor+Con) — Brooks L. Kellogg (VP) — Julienne K. Lindberg (S+F)

SE-418 Lipsett (Phyllis & Norman) Foundation
c/o Bennett L. Aaron, Esq., Pepper Hamilton LLP
3300 Two Logan Square, 18th & Arch Streets
Philadelphia   19103   (Philadelphia County)

MI-15-22-31-41-52-55-57-62
Phone 215-981-4768 **FAX** 215-981-4750
EIN 23-2185093   **Year Created** 1981

AMV $2,862,320   **FYE** 8-00   **(Gifts Received** $336,961)   120+ **Grants totaling** $63,305

About half giving to Harrisburg area; some grants comprise multiple payments. High Pa. grant of **$8,086** to Beth El Temple. **$1,000-$1,500** each to Hospice of Central Pa., WITF, and Yeshiva Academy. **$750** to Allied Arts Fund. **$500** each to Harrisburg Symphony, Jake Gittlen Memorial Fund, and Pinnacle Health Foundation. Other local contributions **$25-$300,** many for Jewish organizations. **Out-of-state** giving includes **$20,000** to Hadassah [NY] and smaller grants/contributions to many states. ■**PUBLICATIONS:** None ■**WEBSITE:** None ■**E-MAIL:** aaronb@pepperlaw.com ■**APPLICATION POLICIES & PROCEDURES:** Grant requests may be submitted in any form at any time; include organizational and project budgets. No grants are awarded to individuals.

O+D+T Bennett L. Aaron, Esq. (S+F+Con) — Norman B. Lipsett [NJ] (P+Donor) — Phyllis Lipsett [NJ] (VP) — Beth Bernan (Donor) — Jane Javitch (Donor) — Yale Lipsett (Donor) — Julie Lipsett Singer [RI] (Donor)

SE-419 Liss Family Charitable Trust
c/o Michel's Bakery, Inc.
5698 Rising Sun Ave.
Philadelphia   19120   (Philadelphia County)

MI-22-31-32-62
Phone 215-742-3900 **FAX** None
EIN 23-6868703   **Year Created** 1987

AMV $174,437   **FYE** 4-01   **(Gifts Received** $325)   130+ **Grants totaling** $36,556

Mostly local giving. High grant of **$10,000** to Jewish Federation of Greater Philadelphia. **$5,575** to Temple Adath Israel. **$2,500** to Congregation Beth Am Israel. **$2,000** to Temple Beth Hillel-Beth El. **$1,000** to Congregation B'nai Jacob [Phoenixville]. Other local and out-of-state grants/contributions, mostly for health-medical or Jewish purposes. ■**PUBLICATIONS:** None ■**WEBSITE:** None ■**E-MAIL:** None ■**APPLICATION POLICIES & PROCEDURES:** Information not available.

O+D+T Joseph R. Liss (T+Donor+Con) — Betty J. Liss (T+Donor)

SE-420 Live Oak Foundation
c/o Calibre (First Union/Wachovia)
2000 Centre Square West, 1500 Market Street
Philadelphia   19102   (Philadelphia County)

MI-17-31-32-41-42-53-54
Phone 215-973-3143 **FAX** 215-973-3191
EIN 23-6424637   **Year Created** 1966

AMV $1,294,019   **FYE** 8-00   **(Gifts Received** $15,000)   27 **Grants totaling** $438,253

Limited local giving; grants are for general purposes except as noted. High Pa. grant of **$33,753** to Fox Chase Cancer Center. **$1,250** to U. of the Arts. **$1,000** to Children's Hospital of Philadelphia. **Out-of-state** giving includes high grant of **$296,129** to Metropolitan Museum of Art [NY]; **$51,630** to Blair Academy [NJ]; **$38,816** to U. of Chicago [IL]; **$5,000** to New York Women's Foundation (celebration). ■**PUBLICATIONS:** None ■**WEBSITE:** None ■**E-MAIL:** robert.gallagher@calibreonline.com ■**APPLICATION POLICIES & PROCEDURES:** The Foundation reports funding interests as (1) hospitals and medical research projects; (2) art museums and collections of paintings, sculptures, antiques and other art objects; (3) churches and other religious institutions; (4) theatre, opera, ballet, and similar activities; and (5) such other religious, charitable, scientific, literary or educational activities, including the protection of animals and the preservation of wildlife, as the Trustees may deem appropriate. Submit grant requests in a one-page letter during January-February (deadline is February 28th) which describes organizational background and the purpose of the requested funds. Awards are made in July.

O+D+T Robert J. Gallagher (VP at Bank+Con) — Charlotte Colket Weber [FL] (Co-T+Donor) First Union/Wachovia (Co-Trustee)

SE-421 Locks Family Foundation
c/o Locks Gallery
600 Washington Square South
Philadelphia   19106   (Philadelphia County)

MI-32-41-42-53
Phone 215-629-1000 **FAX** 215-629-3868
EIN 22-2707744   **Year Created** 1985

AMV $7,742,359   **FYE** 6-00   **(Gifts Received** $1,200,000)   **Grants totaling** $0

No grants awarded in 1999 or 2000. In 1998, three grants awarded: **$25,000** to Baldwin School (general support). **$15,000** to Moore College of Art (general support). **$10,000** to Allegheny U. (ophthalmology development). ■**PUBLICATIONS:** None ■**WEBSITE:** www.locksgallery.com ■**E-MAIL:** slocks@locksgallery.com ■**APPLICATION POLICIES & PROCEDURES:** The Foundation reports that prospective applicants should call or write for application guidelines. — Formerly called the Marian Locks Foundation.

O+D+T Gene Locks [NJ] (P+Donor+Con) — Sueyun Locks [NJ] (S+F)

SE-422 Logan (Maria Dickinson) Trust
c/o Mellon Private Wealth Management
1735 Market Street, Room 193-0314
Philadelphia 19103 (Philadelphia County)

MI-12-13-14-15-17-22-25-41-43-45-52-55-56 71
Phone 215-553-2517 **FAX** 215-553-2054
EIN 23-6225776 **Year Created** 1940

AMV $595,419 **FYE** 6-00 (**Gifts Received** $0) 33 **Grants totaling** $57,300

All giving restricted to Germantown-based organizations or institutions except those designated in the donor's will. Most support ranges from **$1,000** to **$4,000,** mostly for general operations, with some organizations receiving two grants: Awbury Arboretum (environmental education program), Center for Literacy, Chestnut Hill Healthcare (women's center education/prevention program), Easter Seals (summer camping), Germantown Ecumenical Ministries (GEMS program), Germantown Friends School (Summerbridge program), Germantown Historical Society (educational programs), Historic Rittenhousetown, Inn Dwelling (job training), International Ballet Exchange (school residency program), Metropolitan Career Center (computer technology), Northwest Philadelphia Interfaith Hospitality Network, Philabundance, Philadelphia Society for the Preservation of Landmarks (Grumblethorpe School partnership), Police Athletic League (after-school programs), Resources for Human Development, Settlement Music School (summer arts camp), United Methodist Church of Germantown (tutoring/homework assistance), White-Williams Scholars, Whosoever Gospel Mission (job readiness program), Wissahickon Hospice (needy patient fund), and YMCA of Germantown (day camp). ■**PUBLICATIONS:** Information & Proposal Guidelines memorandum ■**WEBSITE:** None ■**E-MAIL:** morse.g@mellon.com ■**APPLICATION POLICIES & PROCEDURES:** Only organizations located in the Germantown section of Philadelphia are eligible to apply; no grants are awarded to individuals. Grant requests may be submitted in a full proposal with cover letter at any time (deadline is April 15th); provide a summary sheet with a brief description of the request, total costs of the project, detailed explanation of the project with breakdown of costs, statement of purpose and brief organizational history, and name/address of contact person; include an annual report, organization and project budgets, list of board members, list of major funding sources, audited financial statement, and IRS tax-exempt status documentation. Grants are awarded at a June meeting.

O+D+T Gail Curtis Morse (VP at Bank+Con) — Mellon Bank N.A. (Trustee)

SE-423 Long (Sara) Charity Fund
c/o First Union/Wachovia
123 South Broad Street, PA1279
Philadelphia 19109 (Philadelphia County)

MI-14-15-22-25
Phone 215-670-4224 **FAX** 215-670-4236
EIN 23-6296713 **Year Created** 1902

AMV $399,299 **FYE** 12-00 (**Gifts Received** $0) 12 **Grants totaling** $38,350

All giving restricted to Philadelphia-area social service agencies assisting needy individuals. High grant of **$6,000** to Philadelphia Corp. on Aging (low-income client assistance). **$3,000** each to Center on Hearing & Deafness (hospice volunteer project), Frederick Mennonite Community (benevolent care fund), Kearsley Retirement Community (emergency assistance program), Philadelphia Senior Center (community dining collaborative), Presbyterian Home at 58th Street (resident assistance), Senior Adult Activities Center (meals program), and Surrey Services for Seniors (home care client assistance). **$2,350** to Presbyhomes Foundation (residents financial aid). **$2,000** each to CARIE/Center for Advocacy for the Rights & Interests of the Elderly (emergency security fund) and OIC's of America (housing/healthcare services program). **$1,000** to Royer-Greaves School for Blind (scholarship fund). ■**PUBLICATIONS:** statement of program policy; application guidelines ■**WEBSITE:** None ■**E-MAIL:** robert.prischak@wachovia.com ■**APPLICATION POLICIES & PROCEDURES:** Only Philadelphia-area social service agencies are eligible to apply on behalf of needy individuals unable to be self-supporting because of accident, disease, or old age, and have no other means of support. No grants are awarded directly to individuals or for endowment or political purposes. Grant requests may be submitted at any time on an organization's letterhead and signed by an officer on behalf of the governing board (deadlines for receipt are February 15th, May 15th, August 15th, and November 15th). Include the following: names of individuals who will receive benefits and a brief description of their circumstances, or if the grant is part of a project, describe how it fits into the Foundation's purpose; amount of funding requested; organization/project budgets; a bound, audited financial statement; organizational background information; list of major past/present funding sources; and IRS tax-exempt status documentation. Only complete applications will be considered. Decisions on grants are made at meetings in March, June, September and December.

O+D+T Robert Prischak (Assistant VP at Bank+Con) — First Union/Wachovia (Trustee)

SE-424 Longstreth (Peter & Betsy) Foundation, The
301 West Gravers Lane
Philadelphia 19118 (Philadelphia County)

MI-31-41-71-84
Phone 215-568-5050 **FAX** None
EIN 23-2974092 **Year Created** 1998

AMV $247,283 **FYE** 12-00 (**Gifts Received** $109,279) 11 **Grants totaling** $16,200

Mostly local giving. High grants of **$5,000** each to Chestnut Hill Academy and Chestnut Hill Hospital/Healthcare. **$1,000** each to Fairmount Park Commission, Friends of Philadelphia Parks, and Roman Catholic High School. Other smaller contributions for civic, cultural, educational and religious purposes. **Out-of-state** giving includes **$1,000** each to the New Jersey Aquarium and Camp Tecumseh [NJ]. ■**PUBLICATIONS:** None ■**WEBSITE:** None ■**E-MAIL:** None ■**APPLICATION POLICIES & PROCEDURES:** Information not available.

O+D+T Peter Longstreth (D+Donor+Con) — Elizabeth Longstreth (D+Donor)

SE-425 Lotman (Karen & Herbert) Foundation, The
c/o Keystone Foods Corp.
300 Barr Harbor Drive, Suite 600
West Conshohocken 19428 (Montgomery County)

MI-12-14-15-29-31-32-35-42-52-55
Phone 610-668-6700 **FAX** None
EIN 22-2429821 **Year Created** 1982

AMV $3,882,822 **FYE** 11-00 (**Gifts Received** $177,000) 24 **Grants totaling** $559,120

About one-fourth local giving. High Pa. grant of **$40,000** to U. of Pa. **$25,000** each to Prince Music Theatre and Jeffrey Jay Weinberg Memorial Foundation [Blue Bell]. **$10,000** each to Juvenile Diabetes Foundation and Thomas Jefferson U. Hospital.

$6,000 to Wistar Institute. $5,000 each to Assn. for Developmental Disabilities [Jenkintown], Chris W. Davis Memorial Fund, Main Line Art Center, Rowan House, Scheie Eye Institute, and The Wellness Community of Philadelphia. $3,000 to American Cancer Society. $2,520 to Macular Vision Research Foundation. $1,000 each to European Immigrant Benevolent Fund [Philadelphia] and Holy Family College. $500 to Samuel Cozen Memorial Fund. ■PUBLICATIONS: None ■WEBSITE: None ■E-MAIL: None ■APPLICATION POLICIES & PROCEDURES: Grant requests may be submitted in a letter at any time (deadline is August 31st); describe in detail the proposed project/program and state an amount of funding requested.

O+D+T Herbert Lotman (VP+Donor+Con) — Karen Lotman [Haverford] (P+Donor) — Shelly Lotman Fisher [Villanova] (S+Donor) — Jeffrey Lotman [CA] (F+Donor) Corporate donor: Keystone Foods Corp.

SE-426 Loualan Foundation, The
1106 Spring Mill Road
Villanova   19085   (Montgomery County)
AMV $1,639,588   **FYE** 11-00   **(Gifts Received** $639,676)

MI-11-22-41-42-51-52-54-55-72
Phone 610-525-2890 **FAX** None
EIN 22-2779310   **Year Created** 1986
10 **Grants totaling** $160,500

Mostly local giving; all grants are for general operations/program support. High grant of $60,000 to Philadelphia Orchestra. $45,000 to Franklin Institute. $12,500 to Regional Performing Arts Center. $10,000 each to Academy of Music, United Way of SE Pa., and The Vanguard School. $3,000 to Philadelphia Zoo. **Out-of-state** giving: $5,000 to Williams College [MA] and $2,500 each to Bread for the Journey [NM] and Milton Mountain School [VT]. — In the prior year, $25,000 to Pa. Ballet. ■ PUBLICATIONS: None ■WEBSITE: None ■E-MAIL: None ■APPLICATION POLICIES & PROCEDURES: The Foundation reports that unsolicited grant requests are not accepted.

O+D+T Alan L. Reed, Esq. (P+F+Donor+Con) — Louise H. Reed (VP+S)

SE-427 Ludwick (Christopher) Foundation
c/o The Athenaeum of Philadelphia
219 South Sixth Street
Philadelphia   19106   (Philadelphia County)
AMV $5,541,736   **FYE** 4-01   **(Gifts Received** $0)

MI-12-13-16-22-41-42-45-51-52-53-54-55-56-71-72
Phone 215-925-2688 **FAX** 215-925-3755
EIN 23-6256408   **Year Created** 1799
28 **Grants totaling** $250,000

All giving restricted to Philadelphia to assist economically disadvantaged children. High grant of $50,000 to School District of Philadelphia (Voyager Program). $15,000 to Academy of Natural Sciences. $12,500 to School District of Philadelphia. $9,000 to Philadelphia Zoo. $7,500 each to Episcopal Community Services, Historic Bartram's Garden, Wagner Free Institute of Science, and William Penn Charter School. $6,500 to First United Methodist Church of Germantown. $6,000 to University Museum of Archaeology & Anthropology. $5,000 each to Astral Artistic Services, Congreso de Latinos Unidos, The Fabric Workshop, Freedom Theatre, Impact Services Corp., NetworkArts, The Partners Program, Point Breeze Performing Arts Center, Settlement Music School, Taller Puertorriqueno, and Urban League of Philadelphia. $4,000 each to Executive Service Corps of the Delaware Valley and Southwest Community Enrichment Center. $3,000-$3,500 each to Awbury Arboretum, Cliveden of the National Trust, Shirley Rock School of the Pa. Ballet, and World Affairs Council of Philadelphia. $2,500 to Philadelphia Young Playwrights Festival. ■ PUBLICATIONS: Annual Report; statement of program policy; application guidelines; Grant Application Form ■WEBSITE: www.ludwickfoundation.org ■E-MAIL: rwmoss@philaathenaeum.org ■APPLICATION POLICIES & PROCEDURES: The Foundation's charter restricts all support to projects that advance the education of poor children in the City of Philadelphia; the current funding priority is secondary school students. Most grants are for special projects; multiyear grants are awarded. No grants are given for programs not specifically targeted at children resident within city limits; also no support for programs serving after-school or elementary school age children, or for programs targeted at children with disabilities for which other funding sources exists. Also excluded from funding are building campaigns, endowment drives, equipment purchases, general operating support, and direct grants to individuals. Grant requests (15 complete sets) must be submitted during January-March (deadline is March 31st) on a Grant Application Form (available on the website or from the Foundation); include an annual report, organization budget, project budget, list of major funding sources, audited financial statement, a listing of (with affiliations) Board members and other key people, organizational charter/by-laws, and IRS tax-exempt status documentation. Site visits sometimes are made to organizations being considered for a grant. Grants are awarded at May and October meetings. — Formerly called The Ludwick Institute.

O+D+T Board of Managers: Dr. Roger W. Moss (S+Con) — Hugh A.A. Sargent, Esq. (P) — Susan W. Catherwood [Bryn Mawr] (VP) — William M. Davison, 4th [Blue Bell] (F) — Rhonda R. Cohen — Lee F. Driscoll, Jr. — Bruce C. Gill — Christine L. James-Brown — Philip Price, Jr. — Lea Carson Sherk — Robert W. Sorrell — Trina Vaux — L. Wilbur Zimmerman — First Union/Wachovia (Trustee)

SE-428 M&S Foundation, The
c/o Buckeye Partners L.P.
5 Radnor Corporate Center, Suite 500
Radnor   19087   (Delaware County)
AMV $1,690,421   **FYE** 12-00   **(Gifts Received** $1,012,273)

MI-12-13-14-22-32-34-39-41-61-63-72-84
Phone 484-232-4000 **FAX** None
EIN 31-1478148   **Year Created** 1996
33 **Grants totaling** $433,010

About four-fifths local giving. High grant of $297,000 to Juvenile Diabetes Foundation. $30,000 to Haverford School. $4,500 to Agnes Irwin School. $3,100 to St. Edmond's Home for Children. $3,000 to Gesu School. $2,000-$2,500 each to Cardiovascular Institute of Philadelphia, MCP-Hahnemann U., Pa. Special Olympics, Philadelphia Zoo, and Wheels, Inc. $1,000-$1,500 each to Catholic Charities, Conestoga High School Gridiron Club, Magee Rehab, The MBF Center, Men of Malvern, Philadelphia Orchestra, and St. David's Church of Wayne. $840 to Academy of Music. Other local contributions $250-$500 for various purposes. **Out-of-state** giving includes **$50,000** to Boston College [MA] and **$5,000** each to Big Brothers Big Sisters of Houston [TX] and Parents Against Cancer [TX]. ■**PUBLICATIONS:** None ■**WEBSITE:** None ■**E-MAIL:** None ■**APPLICATION POLICIES & PROCEDURES:** No grants awarded to individuals.

O+D+T Alfred W. Martinelli (D+Donor+Manager+Con) — Aline Martinelli (D+Donor) — Christine Martinelli (D) — David Martinelli (D) — Bill Shea (D) — Susan Shea (D)

SE-429 Malfer Foundation
716 West Mount Airy Ave.
Philadelphia 19119 (Philadelphia County)
AMV $2,208,348 **FYE** 12-00 (**Gifts Received** $0)

MI-13-17-18-25-29-31-32-41-42-44-51-56-71-55
Phone 215-753-0353 **FAX** None
EIN 23-2791318 **Year Created** 1994
70 **Grants totaling** $94,150

About three-fourths local giving. High grants of **$12,000** each to Morris Arboretum and Mural Arts Advocates. **$11,500** to Pa. Horticultural Society. **$8,500** to Chestnut Hill Healthcare. **$2,000** each to Free Library of Philadelphia Foundation and Neighborhood Gardens Assn. **$1,000-$1,500** each to Arden Theatre Company, Fox Chase Cancer Center, Friends of Philadelphia Parks, Fund for the Water Works, Greater Philadelphia Food Bank, Metropolitan Career Center, Natural Lands Trust, Philabundance, Philadelphia Futures, Planned Parenthood of SE Pa., and Womens Way. Other local contributions **$100-$500** for similar purposes. **Out-of-state** giving includes **$5,000** each to Amherst College Alumni Fund [MA] and Smith College Alumnae Fund [MA]; and smaller grants contributions, primarily to New England where Trustees reside. ■**PUBLICATIONS:** None ■**WEBSITE:** None ■**E-MAIL:** None ■**APPLICATION POLICIES & PROCEDURES:** No grants awarded to individuals.

O+D+T Frank E. Reed (Executive Trustee+Donor+Con) — Ann L. Reed (T) — Jeffrey L. Reed [MA] (T) — Timothy G. Reed [NH] (T) First Union/Wachovia (Agent)

SE-430 Maltby (Frederick & Mildred) Charitable Trust
780 Glen Road
Jenkintown 19046 (Montgomery County)
AMV $29,024 **FYE** 12-00 (**Gifts Received** $0)

MI-11-22-31-63
Phone 215-884-5296 **FAX** None
EIN 23-7723088 **Year Created** 1993
30 **Grants totaling** $36,040

Mostly local giving. High grant of **$15,000** to Olney Baptist Church. **$7,500** to Abington Memorial Hospital. **$4,000** each to Salvation Army and United Way of SE Pa. **$2,200** to Abington Presbyterian Church. Other local and out-of-state contributions **$50-$200** for various purposes. ■**PUBLICATIONS:** None ■**WEBSITE:** None ■**E-MAIL:** None ■**APPLICATION POLICIES & PROCEDURES:** The Foundation reports that unsolicited requests are not accepted.

O+D+T Frederick L. Maltby (T+Donor+Con) — Mildred N. Maltby (T+Donor)

SE-431 Mandell (Samuel P.) Foundation
1735 Market Street, Suite 3410
Philadelphia 19103 (Philadelphia County)
AMV $17,255,427 **FYE** 12-00 (**Gifts Received** $0)

MI-11-13-14-15-25-31-42-54-52-53-54-55-62
Phone 215-979-3404 **FAX** 215-979-3410
EIN 23-6274709 **Year Created** 1955
235 **Grants totaling** $1,574,635

Mostly local giving. High grant of **$322,400** to National Museum of American Jewish History. **$205,375** to Philadelphia Geriatric Center. **$165,014** to Drexel U. **$128,100** to Federation Allied Jewish Appeal. **$50,000** each to Chestnut Hill College and Regional Performing Arts Center. **$46,050** to Opera Company of Philadelphia. **$40,000** to Main Line Art Center. **$33,525** to Delaware Valley College. **$30,300** to Temple Adath Israel. **$25,200** to Jewish Federation of Greater Philadelphia. **$24,000** to United Way of SE Pa. **$22,200** to Gratz College. **$20,000** to Academy of Music. **$17,666** to LaSalle U. **$14,700** to U. of Pa. **$12,500** to Franklin Institute. **$9,600-$10,865** each to Albert Einstein Medical Center/Health Network/Auxiliary, American Friends of Israel Elwyn, Mann Center for the Performing Arts, and West Chester U. **$7,407** to Philadelphia Orchestra. **$7,000** to Philadelphia Committee to End Homelessness. **$6,880** to American Friends of Hebrew U. **$6,000** each to Police Athletic League, Rowan House, and U. of the Arts. **$5,000-$5,500** each to Ben Gurion U. of the Negev [Jenkintown], Boy Scouts/Cradle of Liberty Council, Haverford College, Prince Music Theater, Temple Judea Museum of Keneseth Israel, and U. of Pa. Law School. **$3,000** each to Philadelphia Craft Show and Philadelphia Museum of Art . **$2,000-$2,500** each to American Red Magen David for Israel, Congregation Beit Harambam, College of Physicians of Philadelphia, Flyers Wives Fight for Lives, Middle East Forum, and Torah Academy of Greater Philadelphia. **$100-$1,900** each for 118 local arts/cultural organizations, museums, health/human service agencies, schools/literacy programs, youth organizations, religious orders, synagogues, and churches. **Out-of-state** giving includes **$28,500** to Chabad Lubavitch of Delaware; **$20,000** to Centreville School [DE]; **$14,000** to Jewish Federation of Palm Beach [FL]; **$10,800** to Whitney Museum for American Art [NY]; **$10,000** to Delaware Guidance Services for Children; **$5,000** each to Conservation Alliance of Palm Beach County [FL], Jewish Theological Seminary of America [NY], and Maimon World Center [NY]; and other smaller grants/contributions, mostly to NY, MA, FL and CA. ■**PUBLICATIONS:** None ■**WEBSITE:** None ■**E-MAIL:** None ■**APPLICATION POLICIES & PROCEDURES:** The Foundation reports that giving focuses on the Philadelphia area. No grants are awarded to individuals or other foundations. Grant requests may be submitted in a letter at any time—the deadline is two weeks prior to the Trustees' quarterly Board meetings; include IRS tax-exempt status documentation.

O+D+T Seymour G. Mandell (T+Con) — Gerald Mandell, M.D. [AZ] (T) — Judith Mandell [Narberth] (T) — Morton Mandell, M.D. [Wynnewood] (T) — Ronald Mandell [FL] (T)

SE-432 Maple Hill Foundation
115 Maple Hill Road
Gladwyne 19035 (Montgomery County)
AMV $7,591,198 **FYE** 7-01 (**Gifts Received** $0)

MI-14-18-31-32-34-42-43-57-71-72-81
Phone 610-642-5167 **FAX** None
EIN 22-2751182 **Year Created** 1986
32 **Grants totaling** $1,275,100

About one-third local/Pa. giving; grants are for general fund purposes except as noted; some grants comprise multiple awards. High Pa. grant of **$301,000** to U. of Pa. (Wharton Building Fund/Scholarship Funds). **$22,000** to Planned Parenthood of SE Pa.

$20,000 to U. of Pa. (Bondi & Sparkman Medical Education Funds). $14,000 to WHYY (capital campaign). $10,000 to International House of Philadelphia. $5,000 each to Neighborhood Gardens Assn. and U. of Pa. Medical Center. $1,000 each to Chalutzim Academy [Philadelphia], Kesher Ministries [Havertown], and UCP of Philadelphia & Vicinity. **Out-of-state** giving includes high grant of $350,000 to Lakes Region Conservation Trust [NH] (Kasumpe Pond/Red Hill project); $181,000 to Appalachian Mountain Club [MA] (capital campaign/general fund); $135,000 to Squam Lakes Natural Science Center [NH] (capital campaign/education project/general fund); $120,000 to World Wildlife Fund [DC] (capital campaign); and $50,000 to Colonial Williamsburg Foundation (capital campaign). ■**PUBLICATIONS:** None ■**WEBSITE:** None ■**E-MAIL:** None ■**APPLICATION POLICIES & PROCEDURES:** Prospective applicants initially should make a telephone inquiry about the feasibility of submitting a request. Grant requests may be submitted in a letter (2 pages maximum) at any time; detail the nature of the organization and include an annual report, organizational and project budgets, list of major funding sources, audited financial statement, Board member list, and IRS tax-exempt status documentation.

O+D+T Ella Warren Miller (C+AS+D+Donor+Con) — Ella Warren Merrill [MA] (P+D) — Katherine S. Miller [CA] (VP+S+D) — Paul F. Miller, III [Newtown Square] (VP+F+D) — Paul F. Miller, Jr. (D+Donor)

SE-433   Marcus Family Foundation
915 Exeter Court
Villanova   19085
(Montgomery County)

MI-12-13-14-15-18-22-31-32-41-42-45-52-53
55-62-72-84
Phone 610-519-1123 **FAX** None
EIN 23-2769110   **Year Created** 1994

AMV $6,206,408   **FYE** 9-00   (**Gifts Received** $180,000)   74 **Grants totaling** $422,970

Mostly local giving. High grant of $75,250 to Federation Allied Jewish Appeal. $65,000 to Friends' Central School. $42,405 to Temple Adath Israel. $25,000 each to Encore Series, Inc./Peter Nero & Philly Pops and Philadelphia Geriatric Center. $15,000-$15,300 each to Children's Hospital of Philadelphia, Jewish Community Centers of Greater Philadelphia, and National MS Society. $13,450 to American Cancer Society. $10,500 to Leukemia Society of America. $10,000 each to National Adoption Center and U. of Pa. $5,000 to Elmwood Park Zoo. $1,000-$2,500 each to Big Brothers, Bryn Mawr Hospital, Camphill Village/Kimberton Hills, Crohn's & Colitis Foundation of America, Congregation Beth Tovim, Crime Prevention Assn., Esther M. Kim Gallery, Har Zion Temple, IHM Center for Literacy, Pa. Academy of the Fine Arts, Philadelphia Casa, Philadelphia Ronald McDonald House, Philadelphia Sports Hall of Fame, Planned Parenthood of SE Pa., Variety Club, and Wetherill School. Other smaller local contributions for various purposes. **Out-of-state** giving includes $20,000 to Brad Kimmiley Medical Fund; $10,000 to National Tay-Sachs & Allied Diseases Foundation [MA]; $7,500 each to Fox House and Kids Place; and other smaller grants/contributions. ■ **PUBLICATIONS:** None ■**WEBSITE:** None ■**E-MAIL:** None ■**APPLICATION POLICIES & PROCEDURES:** The Foundation reports that giving is generally to local organizations, especially for child-related, needy, etc. purposes. Grant requests may be submitted in a letter (2 pages maximum) at any time; include an annual report, Board member list, and IRS tax-exempt status documentation.

O+D+T Stephen C. Marcus (P+Donor+Con) — Jonathan H. Newman, Esq. (VP) — Nancy Marcus Newman, Esq. (VP) — Julie Marcus Paul, M.F.T. (VP) — Russell D. Paul, Esq. (VP) — Lois Simon Marcus (S+F)

SE-434   Martin Foundation, The
c/o MME, Inc.
3993 Huntingdon Pike, Suite 110
Huntingdon Valley   19006   (Montgomery County)

MI-12-13-14-32-41-42-61

Phone 215-947-1783 **FAX** None
EIN 23-2182719   **Year Created** 1981

AMV $2,937,503   **FYE** 3-01   (**Gifts Received** $0)   49 **Grants totaling** $147,000

Limited local/Pa. giving. High Pa. grant of $6,000 to Holy Cross Church [Philadelphia]. $1,000-$2,500 each to Abington Friends School, Boy Scouts/Bucks County Council, College Misericordia [Luzerne County], Huntington's Disease Society, Main Line YMCA, National Shrine of St. Anthony, National Transplant Assistance Fund (spinal injury fund), Pa. Special Olympics, J. Wood Platt Caddie Scholarship Fund, S.A.F.E./Supporting Autism & Families Everywhere [Wilkes-Barre], and Support Center for Child Advocates. **Out-of-state** giving includes $11,000 to Lupus Foundation/MA Chapter; $8,000 each to Abbe Museum [ME] and Santa Fe Rape Crisis Center [NM]; $7,500 each to Doane College [NE] and U. of Iowa; and other smaller grants, many to New England and Penobscot Bay, ME area, for various purposes. ■**PUBLICATIONS:** None ■**WEBSITE:** None ■**E-MAIL:** None ■ **APPLICATION POLICIES & PROCEDURES:** Submit grant requests in a letter at any time; describe how the requested funding will be used, state the amount requested, and include IRS tax-exempt status documentation. No grants awarded to individuals or for scholarships.

O+D+T Jovina Armente (Con) — Dr. Alfred S. Martin (PO+T+Donor) — George J. Hartnett [Philadelphia] (T) — Mary M. Martin (T) — Zachary S. Martin (T) — W. James Quigley (T)

SE-435   Martin (George & Miriam) Foundation
c/o Martin, Banks, Pond, Lehocky & Wilson
1818 Market Street, 35th Floor
Philadelphia   19103   (Philadelphia County)

MI-71-79

Phone 215-587-8400 **FAX** 215-587-8417
EIN 23-2828201   **Year Created** 1995

AMV $2,133,900   **FYE** 12-00   (**Gifts Received** $383,630)   23 **Grants totaling** $99,350

About three-fourths local giving. High grant of $20,000 to Green Valleys Assn. (watershed advocacy). $10,000 each to Delaware Riverkeeper Network (protect/restore/dam removal), French & Pickering Creeks Conservation Trust (obtain conservation trail easements), and Natural Lands Trust (legal defense initiative for watershed). $5,000 each to Brandywine Valley Assn. (watershed watch program), Patrick Center for Environmental Research (watershed research), and Schuylkill Riverkeeper (protection/restoration). $4,000 to Schuylkill River Greenway Assn. (establish trails). $2,000-$2,500 each to Camphill Village/Kimberton Hill (stream bank restoration), Green Valleys Assn. (film), and Greater Pottstown Watershed Alliance (remove Manatawny Creek dam). $1,000 to Wissahickon Valley Watershed Assn. (networking equipment). $500 to Riverbend Environmental Education Center. **Out-of-state** giving for similar purposes, mostly $1,000-$3,000, to organizations in NY, DC, ID, TX, WV and other states. — In 2001, major Pa. grants awarded included $50,000 to Delaware River Network (attorney salary);

$15,000 to Camphill Village Kimberton; and $10,000 each to French & Pickering Creeks Conservation Trust (partly challenge grant), Green Valleys Assn. (challenge grant), Natural Lands Trust, and Schuylkill River Greenway Assn. (challenge grant). ■**PUBLICATIONS:** None ■**WEBSITE:** www.themartinfoundation.org ■**E-MAIL:** gmartin@paworkinjury.com ■**APPLICATION POLICIES & PROCEDURES:** The Foundation reports that giving focuses on Eastern Pa. for the protection/preservation of rivers and watersheds, particularly the improvement of water quality and public access to rivers. Grant requests may be submitted in a brief letter at any time; describe the organization's activities and include an annual report, list of Board members, and IRS tax-exempt status documentation. Site visits sometimes are made to organizations being considered for a grant. Grants are awarded at July and November meetings.

O+D+T George Martin, Esq. (T+Donor+Con) — Glenn Emery [IN] (T) — M. Christine Martin [Coventryville] (T) — Rebecca Martin [Cheltenham] (T) — Regis A. McCann [NY] (T) — Carol Martin Strange [Huntingdon Valley] (T) — H. Lawrence Strange, Jr. [DE] (T)

SE-436 Martino (Rocco & Barbara) Foundation
512 Watch Hill Road
Villanova 19085 (Delaware County)
AMV $3,561,795 FYE 12-00 (Gifts Received $0)

MI-11-13-15-22-41-42-43-61
Phone 610-687-1933 **FAX** None
EIN 23-2834739 **Year Created** 1996
20 **Grants totaling** $245,025

Mostly local giving. High grant of $81,000 to Papal Foundation (c/o Archdiocese of Philadelphia). $51,000 to St. Joseph's U. $50,325 to Chestnut Hill College. $15,000 to Friends of Little Flower Manor. $12,000 to Archdiocese of Philadelphia. $10,000 to United Way of SE Pa. $2,000-$2,500 each to Cardinal O'Hara High School Scholarship Fund, Jesuit Center for Spiritual Growth [Berks County], and Office of Youth & Young Adults. $1,000 each to St. Aloysius Academy and St. Joseph's Preparatory School. Other smaller local contributions. **Out-of-state** giving includes $8,500 to Sovereign Military Order [DC]; $2,350 to Path to Peace Foundation [NY]; $1,400 to The Pontifical North American College [Italy]; $1,000 to Archdiocese of St. Louis [MO]; and other contributions, primarily for Catholic purposes. ■**PUBLICATIONS:** None ■**WEBSITE:** None ■**E-MAIL:** None ■**APPLICATION POLICIES & PROCEDURES:** No grants awarded to individuals.

O+D+T Dr. Rocco L. Martino (P+D+Donor+Con) — Barbara I. Martino (VP+F+S+D) — John F. Martino [MD] (VP+D) — Joseph A. Martino [Wayne] (VP+D) — Paul G. Martino [CA] (VP+D) — Peter D. Martino [Phoenixville] (VP) — Father Milton E. Jordan [Philadelphia] (D)

SE-437 Masel Family Charitable Trust
1680 Huntingdon Pike, P.O. Box 513
Huntingdon Valley 19006 (Montgomery County)
AMV $195,037 FYE 12-00 (Gifts Received $35,000)

MI-22-32-62
Phone 215-947-1546 **FAX** None
EIN 23-7452541 **Year Created** 1990
58 **Grants totaling** $18,332

About two-thirds local giving. High grant of $5,000 to Federation Allied Jewish Appeal. $670 to Lady of Good Council Church. Other local contributions $10-$500, mostly for health agencies or Jewish charities. **Out-of-state** giving includes $2,061 to Congregation Beth Emeth [DE], $1,500 to Jewish Community Center of Margate [NJ], and small contributions to several states. ■**PUBLICATIONS:** None ■**WEBSITE:** None ■**E-MAIL:** None ■**APPLICATION POLICIES & PROCEDURES:** Grant requests may be submitted in any form at any time.

O+D+T Edythe J. Masel (T+Donor+Con) — Theresa Masel-Auerbach (T+Donor)

SE-438 Matzkin Foundation
230 Maple Hill Road
Gladwyne 19035 (Montgomery County)
AMV $129,477 FYE 12-00 (Gifts Received $0)

MI-15-22-41-52-54-57-62
Phone 610-896-5088 **FAX** None
EIN 22-2659502 **Year Created** 1986
78 **Grants totaling** $17,575

Mostly local giving. High grant of $4,800 to Federation Allied Jewish Appeal. $2,720 to Beth Sholom Congregation. $2,000 to National Liberty Museum. $1,667 to Prince Music Theater. $500-$550 each to Opera Company of Philadelphia, Philadelphia Geriatric Center, Perelman Jewish Day School, and WHYY. Other local and out-of-state contributions, $10-$400 for various purposes. ■**PUBLICATIONS:** None ■**WEBSITE:** None ■**E-MAIL:** None ■**APPLICATION POLICIES & PROCEDURES:** Grant requests should be submitted during January-March (deadline is July 31st) in a letter; include a project budget and IRS tax-exempt status documentation. No grants awarded to individuals.

O+D+T Stanley Matzkin (P+Donor+Con)

SE-439 Mayer Family Foundation, The
8620 Prospect Ave.
Philadelphia 19118 (Philadelphia County)
AMV $225,704 FYE 12-00 (Gifts Received $21,107)

MI-11-41-42-52-54-63-72
Phone 215-649-5630 **FAX** None
EIN 23-2407011 **Year Created** 1986
10 **Grants totaling** $16,919

All local giving. High grant of $7,000 to United Way of SE Pa. $2,273 to Philadelphia Orchestra. $2,000 to St. Martins in the Field. $1,500 to Philadelphia Museum of Art. $1,000 each to Friends Select School and U. of Pa. $896 to Philadelphia Zoo. Other smaller contributions. ■**PUBLICATIONS:** None ■**WEBSITE:** None ■**E-MAIL:** None ■**APPLICATION POLICIES & PROCEDURES:** Grant requests may be submitted in any form at any time.

O+D+T Lester R. Mayer, Jr. (T+Donor+Con) — Lester R. Mayer, III [NJ] (Donor) — Thomas N. Mayer [NJ] (Donor)

SE-440   McCausland Foundation, The   MI-15-18-31-32-41-54-71-81
  c/o Airgas, Inc.
  259 North Radnor-Chester Road, P.O. Box 6675   **Phone** 610-687-5253 **FAX** None
  Radnor   19087   (Delaware County)   **EIN** 23-2776475   **Year Created** 1994
AMV $79,603   **FYE** 12-00   (**Gifts Received** $0)   23 **Grants totaling** $101,000

Mostly local giving; grants are for annual support/program support except as noted. High grants of **$25,000** each to Fox Chase Cancer Center and Independence Seaport Museum. **$15,000** to Eisenhower Exchange Fellowships. **$10,000** to Springside School. **$3,000** each to Chestnut Hill HealthCare, Fairmount Park Foundation, and Morris Arboretum. **$1,000** to Inglis Foundation. Other local contributions **$200-$500** for arts/culture, education, disabled, and other purposes. **Out-of-state** giving includes **$5,000** to National Council for Adoption [DC] (computer system) and smaller grants, many to Nantucket, MA. ■ **PUBLICATIONS:** None ■ **WEBSITE:** None ■ **E-MAIL:** None ■ **APPLICATION POLICIES & PROCEDURES:** Grant requests may be submitted in a letter at any time; describe in detail the proposed project and state the amount of funding requested. No grants awarded to individuals.

O+D+T   Bonnie McCausland [Wyndmoor] (P+D+Donor+Con) — Peter McCausland [Wyndmoor] (VP+D+Donor) — Cornelia B. Gross [Phoenixville] (S+F+D) — Gordon L. Keen, Jr. [Strafford] (D)

SE-441   McConnell-Willits Charitable Trust   MI-12-22-32-41-42-43
  c/o McConnell & Associates P.C.
  353 West Lancaster Ave., Suite 120   **Phone** 610-687-1600 **FAX** None
  Wayne   19087   (Delaware County)   **EIN** 23-7867442   **Year Created** 1998
AMV $272,023   **FYE** 12-00   (**Gifts Received** $264,062)   5 **Grants totaling** $65,000

One Pa. grant: **$25,000** to Episcopal Academy (annual fund). **Out-of-state** grants: **$20,000** to CFM Bright Star Scholarship Program [NJ]; **$10,000** to Dartmouth College [NH] (annual fund); and **$5,000** each to Duke U. [NC] (annual fund) Harvard Business School [MA] (annual fund). — Local giving in prior years included **$2,877** to American Cancer Society; **$2,500** each to Friends Assn. for Care & Protection of Children and United Way of Chester County; and **$1,000** to Germantown Academy. ■ **PUBLICATIONS:** None ■ **WEBSITE:** None ■ **E-MAIL:** None ■ **APPLICATION POLICIES & PROCEDURES:** Grant requests may be submitted in any form at any time; include IRS tax-exempt status documentation.

O+D+T   Merritt N. Willits, IV [Fort Washington] (Co-T+Con) — William McCoy [Bala Cynwyd] (Co-T)

SE-442   McCormick Family Charitable Trust   MI-12-14-22-41-42-61
  958 Netherwood Drive, P.O. Box 964   **Phone** 610-279-8473 **FAX** None
  Blue Bell   19422   (Montgomery County)   **EIN** 23-7688160   **Year Created** 1992
AMV $1,024,473   **FYE** 12-00   (**Gifts Received** $0)   9 **Grants totaling** $51,000

Mostly local/Pa. giving. High grants of **$10,000** each to LaSalle U. and Men of Malvern. **$8,000** each to House of Friendship Foundation/Malvern Retreat House and Malvern Preparatory School. **$5,000** each to Cora Services (visioning fund) and Patrician Society of Norristown. **$1,000** each to Good Shepherd [Allentown] and West Philadelphia Catholic High School. **Out-of-state** grant: **$3,000** to St. Gabriel's [NY]. ■ **PUBLICATIONS:** None ■ **WEBSITE:** None ■ **E-MAIL:** None ■ **APPLICATION POLICIES & PROCEDURES:** Grant requests may be submitted in a letter at any time—deadline is March 31st; describe the organization's purpose and state the percentage of expenses used for overhead.

O+D+T   William J. McCormick, Jr. (T+Donor+Con)

SE-443   McGinley (Edward F.), III Foundation   MI-17-19-32-42-84
  741 Newtown Road   **Phone** 610-687-2731 **FAX** None
  Villanova   19085   (Delaware County)   **EIN** 23-1984830   **Year Created** 1975
AMV $321,943   **FYE** 12-00   (**Gifts Received** $0)   12 **Grants totaling** $16,060

Two Pa. grants: **$2,000** to U. of Pa. (Weightman Gym). **$200** to Livingrin Foundation [Bensalem]. **Out-of-state** giving includes **$5,000** to National Football Foundation [NY]; **$3,000** to Cancer Research Foundation [VA]; and **$2,000** to Woman In Need [NY]. ■ **PUBLICATIONS:** None ■ **WEBSITE:** None ■ **E-MAIL:** None ■ **APPLICATION POLICIES & PROCEDURES:** No grants awarded to individuals.

O+D+T   Edward F. McGinley, III (T+Donor+Con) — Helga Hammarskjold (Donor)

SE-444   McKee (Jeffrey P.) Foundation, The   MI-12-29-32-42-55-72
  2032-B Arch Street   **Phone** 215-496-0741 **FAX** None
  Philadelphia   19103   (Philadelphia County)   **EIN** 23-2484718   **Year Created** 1988
AMV $259,242   **FYE** 12-99   (**Gifts Received** $15,000)   17 **Grants totaling** $8,800

About two-thirds local/Pa. giving. High Pa. grant of **$1,590** to Red Cross [Allentown]. **$1,000** to Allied Arts Fund [Harrisburg]. **$650** to Scartache (medical research). **$450** to Philadelphia Zoo (zoobilee). Other contributions **$60-300** to many parts of Pa. for children's services, medical research, and other purposes. **Out-of-state** grant: **$2,000** to to Dartmouth College [NH]. — In prior years major support to Dartmouth College. ■ **PUBLICATIONS:** None ■ **WEBSITE:** None ■ **E-MAIL:** None ■ **APPLICATION POLICIES & PROCEDURES:** Grant requests in any form may be submitted at any time; describe the purpose of the requested funds

O+D+T   Jeffrey P. McKee (T+Donor+Con) — Pierce McKee (T)

SE-445   McKenna Family Foundation, The
247 Magnolia Drive
Churchville   18966   (Bucks County)
AMV $354,246   **FYE** 12-00   **(Gifts Received** $0)

MI-22-31-41-42-61
Phone 215-357-5354   **FAX** None
EIN 22-6609294   **Year Created** 1993
18 **Grants totaling** $38,871

Mostly local giving. High Pa. grant of **$10,000** to Friends of John Paul II Foundation. **$5,200** to LaSalle U. **$5,000** to St. Joseph's U. **$1,000-$1,631** each to Nazareth Hospital, Northeast Catholic High School, and Sisters of the Holy Family of Nazareth. Other local contributions **$25-$200** for various purposes. **Out-of-state** grant: **$12,850** to Our Lady of Good Counsel [NJ]. ■**PUBLICATIONS:** None ■**WEBSITE:** None ■**E-MAIL:** None ■**APPLICATION POLICIES & PROCEDURES:** The Foundation reports that most giving is for capital drives and scholarships. Grant requests may be submitted in a letter (3 pages maximum), preferably in September; include organizational/project budgets, audited financial statement, list of major funding sources, Board member list, and IRS tax-exempt status documentation. Site visits sometimes are made to organizations being considered for a grant. Grants are awarded at an October meeting. — The Foundation's alternative address is 8650 South Ocean Drive, Jensen Beach, FL 34957; phone 561-229-5296.

O+D+T   Michael J. McKenna [FL] (T+Donor+Con) — Letitia W. McKenna [FL] (T+Donor) — Letitia Palumbo (T) — Carol Steinke (T) — Suzanne Karcher (T) — Kathleen Doyle (T) — Jane Dorey (T) — Margaret Herman (T)

SE-446   McLean Contributionship, The
c/o Independent Publications
945 Haverford Road, Suite A
Bryn Mawr   19010   (Montgomery County)
AMV $47,200,000 est.   **FYE** 12-01   **(Gifts Received** $88,517)

MI-11-12-13-14-15-17-25-29-31-32-34-41-42
43-44-52-54-55-56-71-72-89
Phone 610-527-6330   **FAX** 610-527-9733
EIN 23-6396940   **Year Created** 1951
92 **Grants totaling** $2,269,240

Mostly local or NW Pa. giving; grants are for general support excepts as noted; some grants are payments on multiyear awards. **$150,000** each to The Library Company of Philadelphia (conservation endowment), The Nature Conservancy (science/stewardship endowment), and Williamson Free School of Mechanical Trades (student residence renovation). **$100,000** each to Lankenau Hospital (emergency room renovations/services), Morris Arboretum (natural areas land management endowment), and National Constitution Center (endowment). **$75,000** each to Jenkins Arboretum (endowment) and Regional Performing Arts Center (building campaign). **$57,900** to Lower Merion Library Foundation (collection development). **$55,000** to Philadelphia Protestant Home (Midway Manor renovation). **$50,000** each to Bryn Mawr Rehab Hospital (stroke unit construction), Historic Bartram's Garden (building design/construction), Project H.O.M.E. (learning center library), and Wissahickon Valley Watershed Assn. (endowment). **$36,000** to Germantown Women's YMCA (heating system/interior renovations). **$30,000** each to Jubilee School (building repairs), Lower Merion Historical Society (archives center), Northeast Community Center (building expansion), and U. of Pa. Press (electronic publishing initiative). **$27,000-$28,000** each to Awbury Arboretum Assn. (tree maintenance equipment), Baker Industries (roof repairs), and Recording for the Blind & Dyslexic (recording booths conversions). **$25,000** each to Community Women's Education Project (exterior improvements), Franklin Institute (Train Factory exhibit), Fund for the Water Works (maintenance endowment), Hope Springs Equestrian Therapy (arena/stables construction), Lower Merion Conservancy (endowment), Schuylkill Center for Environmental Education (trailhead pavilion construction), and United Way of SE Pa. **$20,000-$21,500** each to ARC of Chester County (new classroom facility), Delco Blind/Sight Center (vehicle), Elmwood Park Zoo (animal exhibit), Family Service Assn. of Bucks County (building purchase), Philadelphia Senior Center (information technology software), Prince Music Theater (renovations), and Royer-Greaves School for the Blind (automobile). **$15,000** each to Fair Hill Burial Ground Corp. (capital campaign), Friends School-Haverford (endowment), Harcum College (dental clinical teaching facility expansion), Philadelphia PresbyHomes & Services (Rosemont Presbyterian Village dining room improvements)Ralston House (therapy gardens construction), and Taylor Hospice (building renovations). **$13,090** to Philadelphia Wooden Boat Factory (tools/equipment purchase). **$12,000** each to Assn. of Independent Colleges & Universities of Pa. [Harrisburg] (nursing/physician assistant scholarship fund), and DuBois Area Catholic School System [Clearfield County] (property purchase/building fund). **$9,000-$10,000** each to Abington Township Public Library (children's library renovations), American Heart Assn. (defibrillators purchase), Arthritis Foundation/Eastern Pa. Chapter (services capacity expansion), DuBois Area YMCA [Clearfield County] (facility expansion), Elwyn (residence renovation), Jefferson County Area Agency on Aging (Brockwayville Depot renovation), Morris Animal Refuge (computer network/database), New Bethlehem Area Free Public Library [Clarion County] (new building), Penn Home (endowment), Perkiomen Watershed Conservancy (education project capital needs), Philadelphia Outward Bound (outdoors equipment), and Youth Service, Inc. (crisis nurseries renovations). **$4,500-$5,000** each to Associated Services for the Blind (Braille embosser/printer), Center for Literacy, J. Lewis Crozer Library [Chester] (interior improvements), Jefferson County Fair Authority (show arena construction), Philadelphia Museum of Art, Philadelphia Orchestra, Philadelphia Youth Tennis (tennis center construction), St. Peter's School (financial aid endowment), and WHYY. **$3,000-$4,000** each to Academy of Natural Sciences, Daemion House, Greater Philadelphia Urban Affairs Coalition, Opera Company of Philadelphia, Options in Aging (lunch program), Pa. Ballet, Philadelphia Zoo, Surrey Services for Seniors, White-Williams Scholars, and World Affairs Council of Philadelphia. Other smaller local grants/contributions for similar purposes. **Out-of-state** giving includes **$75,000** to Delaware Nature Center (capital campaign); **$25,000** each to Adult Learning Center [NH] (endowment), DeSales High School [NY] (gymnasium), Keuka College [NY] (environmental sciences lab); and **$10,000c** to Natural Heritage Trust [NY] (playground construction). ■**PUBLICATIONS:** Brochure with statement of purpose, policies, and application procedures ■**WEBSITE:** http://fdncenter.org/grantmaker/mclean ■**E-MAIL:** None ■**APPLICATION POLICIES & PROCEDURES:** The Contributionship reports that giving focuses on Delaware Valley organizations or institutions; current priority interests are programs/projects which (1) stimulate a better understanding of the natural environment and its preservation; (2) encourage compassionate and cost-effective health care for the ill or aged; or (3) promote education, medical or scientific advancements or, on occasion, cultural developments which enhance the quality of life. In addition, occasional projects are supported that motivate youth to assess their talents realistically and develop them despite social/economic obstacles, as well as to efforts that encourage persons in newspaper (or related information/communications) work to be more effective and responsible in responding to the needs of people to know and understand how world happenings affect them. Most grants are for capital projects, endowment or seed money for priority programmatic interests; multiyear grants are awarded. Requests for operating support, as a general rule, receive low priority; also The Contributionship does not support the costs/expenses of existing staff allocated to the proposed project. Prospective applicants are encouraged to make an initial telephone inquiry regarding the feasibility of submitting a request. Grant requests may be submitted using Delaware Valley Grantmakers Common Grant Application Form (see Appendix) or in a letter which describes or justifies the proposed project; the application must include a project budget and timetable; a financial statement for the latest year; interim operating statements/budgets for future periods, if appropriate; a Board member list; and IRS tax-exempt status documentation. Applications are carefully reviewed by the Trustees and if the project falls with the framework of current priorities, more detailed information may be requested. Grant requests should be submitted at least six weeks before the Board meetings held in March, June, September and December; see the website for exact dates of upcoming deadlines. Site visits sometimes are made to organizations being considered for a grant. — Formerly called The Bulletin Contributionship.

O+D+T Sandra L. McLean (Executive Director+S+Advisory Trustee+Donor+Con) — William L. McLean, III (C+T+Donor) — William L. McLean, IV (VC+T+Donor) — Jean G. Bodine (T) — Joseph K. Gordon (T) — Carolyn M. Raymond (T) — Leila Gordon Dyer (Advisory Trustee) — Hunter R. Gordon (Advisory Trustee) — John H. Buhsmer (Emeritus Trustee) — Elizabeth McLean (Donor) Corporate donor: Independent Communications, Inc.

SE-447   Means Charitable Trust
P.O. Box 829
Washington Crossing   18977   (Bucks County)

MI-42-49
Phone 215-369-8165 **FAX** None
EIN 23-7743238   **Year Created** 1994

AMV $263,375   **FYE** 12-00   **(Gifts Received** $0)   4 **Grants totaling** $307,895

Mostly local giving. High grant of **$274,000** to Bristol Riverside Theatre. **$25,000** to Temple U. (Critical Languages Center). **$3,895** to National Association of Self-Instructional Language Programs (handbook printing). **Out-of-state** grant: **$5,000** to Arts for Anyone [NJ]. ■**PUBLICATIONS:** None ■**WEBSITE:** None ■**E-MAIL:** means@compuserve.com ■**APPLICATION POLICIES & PROCEDURES:** The Foundation reports that giving is generally limited to the Delaware Valley for higher education. Grant requests may be submitted in a letter at any time; include a list of major funding sources and a Board member list. Site visits sometimes may be made to organizations being considered for a grant.

O+D+T Dr. John B. Means (T+Con) — Walker Means [AR] (Donor) — Rosetta Means [AR] (Donor)

SE-448   Measey (Benjamin & Mary Siddons) Foundation
c/o Rankin, Brennan & Donaldson
225 North Olive Street, P.O. Box 258
Media   19063   (Delaware County)

MI-32-34-42

Phone 610-566-5800 **FAX** None
EIN 23-6298781   **Year Created** 1958

AMV $70,609,602   **FYE** 12-00   **(Gifts Received** $0)   12 **Grants totaling** $2,910,094

All giving restricted to supporting medical/dental education in the Delaware Valley. High grant of **$740,094** to U. of Pa. (departmental chairs and other purposes). **$700,000** to Temple U. (cardiothoracic chair). **$400,000** to Hospital of the U. of Pa. (fellowships). **$300,000** to U. of Pa. School of Medicine (tuition grant). **$225,000** to Jefferson Medical College (tuition grant). **$200,000** to Temple U. School of Medicine (tuition grant). **$175,000** to MCP/Hahnemann School of Medicine (tuition grant). **$75,000** to Thomas Jefferson U. (fellowships). **$30,000** to Bryn Mawr College (post-baccalaureate pre-med program). **$25,000** each to U. of Pa. School of Dental Medicine (tuition grant) and Fox Chase Cancer Center (operating support). **$15,000** to Philadelphia College of Osteopathic Medicine (tuition grant). ■**PUBLICATIONS:** Informational Brochure about the Foundation's history ■**WEBSITE:** None ■**E-MAIL:** None ■**APPLICATION POLICIES & PROCEDURES:** The Foundation reports that giving is restricted the Greater Philadelphia area for professorships at local medical schools and physician education (scholarships); no awards are made directly to individuals. Prospective institutional applicants should make an initial telephone inquiry about the feasibility of submitting a request and to request application details. Grant requests are due by mid-month February, May, August and November. Site visits sometimes are made to institutions being considered for a grant. Grants/awards are made at meetings held the second Tuesday in March, June, September, and December.

O+D+T Board of Managers members: James C. Brennan, Esq. (Con) — Matthew S. Donaldson, Esq. (S) — Clyde F. Barker, M.D. [Haverford] — Marshall E. Blume, Ph.D. [Villanova] — Brooke Roberts, M.D. [Bryn Mawr] — Truman G. Schnabel, M.D. [Bryn Mawr] PNC Bank N.A. (Agent)

SE-449   Medleycott Family Foundation, The
1120 Bristol Road
Churchville   18966   (Bucks County)

MI-12-15-22-31-44-63-72
Phone 215-355-1943 **FAX** None
EIN 23-7683693   **Year Created** 1991

AMV $562,949   **FYE** 12-00   **(Gifts Received** $520,000)   19 **Grants totaling** $601,000

About three-fourths local giving. High grant of **$70,000** to Aid for Friends. **$60,000** to Life Abundant, Inc. **$50,000** each to Christ's Home and Healthlink Medical Center. **$35,000** each to Doylestown Hospital and Holy Redeemer Health System. **$30,000** each to NGA, Inc./Needlework Guild of America and Spirit & Truth Fellowship [Philadelphia]. **$25,000** to Bethanna. **$20,000** to Memorial Baptist Church of Huntingdon Valley. **$15,000** to Aark Wildlife Education & Rehabilitation Center. **$10,000** to Jesus Focus Ministry. **$1,000** to Southampton Free Library. **Out-of-state** giving includes **$55,000** to Precept Ministries [TN]; **$30,000** to Family Radio [CA]; and **$25,000** each to Berean Call [OR, New Hope Ministries [FL], and Menna Church [NC]. ■**PUBLICATIONS:** None ■**WEBSITE:** None ■**E-MAIL:** None ■**APPLICATION POLICIES & PROCEDURES:** No grants awarded to individuals.

O+D+T Alice E. Medleycott (T+Donor+Con) — James E. Medleycott [FL] (T) — Mary E. Medleycott (T) — Lee Marchetti [Chalfont] (T) — Clyde Medleycott (Donor) — Corporate donor: Superpac, Inc.

SE-450 Medveckis (J.J.) Foundation
c/o Cooke & Bieler, Inc.
1700 Market Street, Suite 3222
Philadelphia 19103 (Philadelphia County)
AMV $98,331 **FYE** 11-00 **(Gifts Received** $0)

MI-42-51-52-53-54-55
Phone 215-567-1101 **FAX** None
EIN 23-6838439 **Year Created** 1986
8 **Grants totaling** $63,700

Mostly local giving; all grants are for general purposes. High grant of **$24,000** to Curtis Institute of Music. **$17,200** to Philadelphia Museum of Art. **$10,000** to U. of Pa. **$2,000** to Annenberg Center. **$1,000** to Eagles Youth Program. **$500** to Philadelphia Boys Choir. **Out-of-state** grants: **$6,000** to Metropolitan Museum of Art [NY] and **$3,000** to Cunningham Dance Foundation [NY]. ■**PUBLICATIONS:** None ■**WEBSITE:** None ■**E-MAIL:** None ■**APPLICATION POLICIES & PROCEDURES:** Prospective applicants initially should make a telephone inquiry about the feasibility of submitting a request. No grants awarded to individuals. Grant requests may be submitted in a letter (2 pages maximum) at any time; include an annual report, organization budget, list of major funding sources, list of Board members, and IRS tax-exempt status documentation. Site visits sometimes are made to organizations being considered for a grant.
O+D+T John J. Medveckis (T+Donor+Con)

SE-451 Merchants Fund of Philadelphia
P.O. Box 408
Bryn Mawr 19010 (Montgomery County)
AMV $9,382,722 **FYE** 12-00 **(Gifts Received** $255,389)

MI-23
Phone 610-949-9270 **FAX** None
EIN 23-1548975 **Year Created** 1854
90 **Grants totaling** $505,655

All giving is restricted to assisting current or former Philadelphia-area business owners and/or their widows. Beneficiaries receive stipends of **$200-$500** per month. ■**PUBLICATIONS:** Information Sheet & Guidelines and application form ■**WEBSITE:** None ■**E-MAIL:** None ■**APPLICATION POLICIES & PROCEDURES:** Only current or former business owners/merchants in the Philadelphia area (or their widows) who encounter financial hardships due to age, disability, or business failure are eligible to apply. The businesses must be/have been located in the Greater Philadelphia area, but it is not necessary for a beneficiary to be a current resident of the area. Assistance is based on an assessment of need and is annually reviewed. Support may continue for life as long as the assistance is deemed necessary. Applicants must first request from the Fund a copy of the formal Application Form; applications may be submitted at any time.
O+D+T Dot Darragh (Con) — Henry Winsor [Bryn Mawr] (P+D) — Peter Wilmerding [Haverford] (VP+D) — C. Joyce Kaufmann [Point Pleasant] (S+F+D) — John S. Carter [Philadelphia] (D) — Frederic Dittman [Radnor] (D) — Hugh McBirney Johnston [Philadelphia] (D) — Bruce Lipa [Bryn Mawr] (D) — J. Stephen Peake [Penllyn] (D) — John A. Philbrick [Bryn Mawr] (D) — George M. Riter [Philadelphia] (D) — G. Stephen Voorhees [Blue Bell]

SE-452 Meyers Foundation of Philadelphia, The
c/o Wolf, Block, Schorr & Solis-Cohen
1650 Arch Street, 22nd Floor
Philadelphia 19103 (Philadelphia County)
AMV $879,126 **FYE** 12-00 **(Gifts Received** $1,500)

MI-11-22-62
Phone 215-977-2099 **FAX** None
EIN 23-6243367 **Year Created** 1951
2 **Grants totaling** $56,000

All local giving. High grant of **$52,500** to United Way of SE Pa. **$3,500** to Jewish Federation of Greater Philadelphia. ■**PUBLICATIONS:** None ■**WEBSITE:** None ■**E-MAIL:** None ■**APPLICATION POLICIES & PROCEDURES:** Grant requests may be submitted in any form at any time. No grants awarded to individuals.
O+D+T Peter E. Meyers [King of Prussia] (F+T+Con) — Helen Spigel Sax [NM] (S+T) — Joan E. Myers [FL] (T+Donor)

SE-453 Meyers (Lillian F. & Edward B.) Family Foundation
237 Fairview Road, Penn Valley
Narberth 19072 (Montgomery County)
AMV $14,785 **FYE** 10-99 **(Gifts Received** $20,000)

MI-15-22-32-62
Phone 610-667-0168 **FAX** None
EIN 23-7918138 **Year Created** 1997
21 **Grants totaling** $12,105

Mostly local giving. High grant of **$2,500** to Main Line Reform Temple (celebratory journal). **$1,850** to Jewish Defense Fund. **$1,000** to St. Sharbel Church. **$700** to Wissahickon Hospice. **$600** to Breast Cancer Foundation. Other contributions **$100-$500** for Jewish charities and other purposes. — Grants awarded in 2000 include **$11,500** to Juvenile Diabetes Foundation; **$10,000** to Auschwitz Jewish Center Foundation [NY]; **$5,000** to Police Pension Assn.; **$2,000** each to City of Hope [CA], Linda Creed Breast Cancer Foundation, and National Parkinson Foundation; and **$1,500** to Wissahickon Hospice. ■**PUBLICATIONS:** None. ■**WEBSITE:** None ■**E-MAIL:** None ■**APPLICATION POLICIES & PROCEDURES:** Grant requests may be submitted in any form at any time.
O+D+T Lillian Meyers (T+Donor+Con)

SE-454 Meyerson Family Foundation, The
2016 Spruce Street
Philadelphia 19103 (Philadelphia County)
AMV $554,710 **FYE** 11-00 **(Gifts Received** $17,789)

MI-42-56-81
Phone 215-732-6116 **FAX** None
EIN 23-7743081 **Year Created** 1994
10 **Grants totaling** $19,112

About one-fourth local giving; all grants are for general fund purposes. High Pa. grant of **$2,150** to American Philosophical Society. **$1,700** to World Affairs Council of Philadelphia. **$1,500** to International House of Philadelphia. **$750** to Jewish Publication Society. **Out-of-state** giving includes **$10,912** to Columbia U. [NY] and **$1,000** to Massachusetts Institute of Technology. ■**PUBLICATIONS:** None ■**WEBSITE:** None ■**E-MAIL:** None ■**APPLICATION POLICIES & PROCEDURES:** The Foundation reports that unsolicited requests for support are not considered.
O+D+T Martin Meyerson (T+Donor+Con) — Margy Ellin Meyerson (T+Donor+Con)

SE-455 Michael Foundation, The
3 MacBride Drive
Spring City 19475   (Chester County)
AMV $2,533,867   **FYE** 6-01   **(Gifts Received** $0)

MI-41
Phone 610-948-7876 **FAX** 610-917-0800
EIN 58-1992204   **Year Created** 1991
34 **Grants totaling** $177,495

All giving restricted to Waldorf Schools in North America. Grants to Pa. include **$6,000** to Kimberton Waldorf School [Chester County], **$4,000** to Susquehanna Waldorf School [Lancaster County], and **$2,000** to Kimberton Foundation Studies. **Out-of-state** grants $1,400-$10,000 to schools and individuals in many states to promote the Waldorf method of education. ■ **PUBLICATIONS:** Grant Information brochure with application guidelines ■ **WEBSITE:** None ■ **E-MAIL:** None ■ **APPLICATION POLICIES & PROCEDURES:** The Foundation reports that only North American (including Mexican) Waldorf schools, training centers, initiatives, organizations, or individuals supporting Waldorf education are eligible to apply; grants are awarded to/for teachers, students, scholarships, school programs, special projects, training, publications, and research. Also, matching grants and multiyear awards are made. Grant requests may be submitted in a letter during December-January (deadline is February 1st) which describes the proposed project, verifies the financial need and worthiness of the project, and how it will be funded in the future; include organizational and project budgets, list of major funding sources, and IRS tax-exempt status documentation. Site visits sometimes are made to organizations being considered for a grant. Grants are awarded at meetings in March-April and announced in early June.

O+D+T Edward R. Hill (P+D+Con) — Marsha Hill (VP+S+D) — Stuart O.R. Mays (F+D)

SE-456 Millard Foundation
c/o Intervention Associates
P.O. Box 572
Wayne 19087   (Delaware County)
AMV $500,000 est.   **FYE** 12-01   **(Gifts Received** $250,000)

MI-14-15-41

Phone 610-254-9001 **FAX** None
EIN 23-2452507   **Year Created** 1987
28 **Grants totaling** $52,000

All local giving, primarily for care management of the elderly and disabled. Grants for care management assistance averaged about **$2,000** per person but ranged from **$150** to about **$5,000**. — In prior years, **$7,500** grants awarded to Aid for Friends, Baker Industries, Delaware Valley Friends School, Hill Top Preparatory School, Spirit of Gheel, Surrey Services for Seniors, and Thorncroft Therapeutic Riding Center; and other smaller grants. ■ **PUBLICATIONS:** None ■ **WEBSITE:** None ■ **E-MAIL:** None ■ **APPLICATION POLICIES & PROCEDURES:** The Foundation reports that giving is primarily for care management services for the elderly or disabled in the Delaware Valley; occasional special projects serving the disabled/elderly are supported. No cash assistance is given to individuals. Most referrals for assistance come from the Foundation's social work contacts. Grant requests may be submitted in a letter at any time; describe the program/purpose for the requested funding.

O+D+T Marion M. Thompson (Manager+Con) — John N. Irwin [Radnor] (P) — Marsha Solmssen [Bryn Mawr] (S) — Klaus Naude [Lafayette Hill] (F)

SE-457 Miller (Alan) Family Foundation, The
57 Crosby Brown Road
Gladwyne 19035   (Montgomery County)
AMV $6,885,533   **FYE** 1-01   **(Gifts Received** $2,010,938)

MI-11-12-15-31-32-42-55-62-84
Phone 610-896-6955 **FAX** None
EIN 23-2899896   **Year Created** 1998
17 **Grants totaling** $223,000

About three-fourths local giving. High grant of **$100,000** to U. of Pa. Wellness Center. **$25,000** each to Regional Performing Arts Center and U. of Pa. Wharton School. **$8,000** to Wistar Institute. **$5,000** each to Anti-Defamation League, Philadelphia Ronald McDonald House, and Rowan House. **$1,000** to United Way of SE Pa. **Out-of-state** giving includes **$25,000** to William & Mary College Athletic Educational Fund [VA] and **$17,000** to U. of South Carolina. ■ **PUBLICATIONS:** None ■ **WEBSITE:** None ■ **E-MAIL:** None ■ **APPLICATION POLICIES & PROCEDURES:** Grant requests may be submitted in any form at any time. No grants awarded to individuals.

O+D+T Alan B. Miller (P+F+D+Donor+Con) — Jill S. Miller (S+D) — Abby D. Miller [NY] (D) — Marc D. Miller [FL] (D) — Marni E. Miller [IL] (D)

SE-458 Miller (Melvin & Eunice) Foundation
475 Warick Road
Wynnewood 19096   (Montgomery County)
AMV $809,702   **FYE** 12-00   **(Gifts Received** $52,251)

MI-22-35-42-62
Phone 610-896-8697 **FAX** None
EIN 23-7705908   **Year Created** 1995
28 **Grants totaling** $284,465

About two-thirds local giving. High grant of **$100,000** to Congregation Beth HaMredrash. **$50,000** to America Friends of Lubavitch. **$16,280** to Jewish Employment & Vocational Services. **$11,267** to Haverford College. **$8,100** to Jewish Community Relations Council. **$6,927** to Jewish Federation of Greater Philadelphia. **$6,440** to AIDS Fund. **$1,450** to Lubavitcher of Montgomery County. **$1,000** each to Etz Chaim Center for Jewish Studies. Other smaller local contributions. **Out-of-state** giving includes **$33,000** to American Friends of Open U. of Israel [NY]; **$13,580** to Jewish Funders Network [NY]; and **$10,000** each to Hampton Synagogue [NY] and United Synagogue of Conservative Judaism [NY]. ■ **PUBLICATIONS:** application guidelines, Grant Application Form ■ **WEBSITE:** None ■ **E-MAIL:** None ■ **APPLICATION POLICIES & PROCEDURES:** The Foundation reports the following receive priority support: small-budget, special projects of fiscally sound organizations, especially (1) projects helping families access their cultural heritage and contribute to family functioning/community cohesiveness, or (2) creative projects that help children and their families make responsible life choices and become productive citizens. Generally not considered for support are projects with budgets over $1 million, private schools, individuals, capital campaigns, deficit financing, organizations that discriminate in hiring, organizations without a Board, or organizations employing the founder or his/her family as paid staff. Grant requests must be submitted on the designated Grant Application Form (available from the Foundation) before the December 1st deadline.

O+D+T Eunice A. Miller (P+Donor+Con) — Deborah J. Miller [NY] (S) — Rachel S. Miller [NY] (F) — Emily N. Miller [Philadelphia] (T) — Melvin N. Miller (T)

SE-459   Miller (Walter J.) Trust
c/o First Union/Wachovia
123 South Broad Street, PA1279
Philadelphia   19109   (Philadelphia County)

MI-12-14-15-31-41-42-44-51-52-54-55-56-57
71-72
Phone 215-670-4224 **FAX** 215-670-4236
EIN 23-6878958   **Year Created** 1987

AMV $3,696,292   **FYE** 7-00   **(Gifts Received** $0)   40 **Grants totaling** $153,666

Mostly local giving; grants are for general operating support except as noted. High grant of **$10,000** to Wildlife Preservation Trust International (office communications). **$8,333** each to Japanese House & Garden (new gate) and WHYY-91FM (Campaign for Independence). **$7,500** to Rosenbach Museum & Library. **$5,000** each to The Athenaeum of Philadelphia (Miller Book Fund), Balch Institute (library acquisitions), Bryn Mawr Hospital (heart patient study), Camphill Village-Kimberton Hills (renovations), Delaware Valley Friends School (library/media center), Eastern College (library book fund), Lankenau Hospital (ER renovations), Opera Company of Philadelphia (educational program), Philadelphia Museum of Art (Leaves of Gold), Presbyterian Children's Village (computerization), Prince Music Theatre (renovations), and Ralston House (medical services). **$3,000** to Historic Philadelphia (Betsy Ross House project). **$2,000-$2,500** each to Fort Mifflin on the Delaware (renovations), Maternity Care Coalition (MOMobile), Nature Conservancy of Pa. (urban youth partnership), Philadelphia Young Playwrights Festival (programs/productions), Please Touch Museum (local artists' performance fees), Recording for the Blind & Dyslexic (educational outreach), Settlement Music School, Taller Puertorriqueno, Tyler Arboretum (education program), U. of the Arts (activities), Williamson Free School of Mechanical Trades (student assistance fund), and Wilma Theatre (Leeds School project). **$1,000** each to Elmwood Park Zoo (signs/exhibits), Historic Bartram Garden (educational programs), Kearsley Retirement Community (new roof), Philadelphia Art Alliance (visual/literary arts program), Sylvan Opera (festival), and Wayne Art Center (renovations). **Out-of-state** giving includes **$5,000** each to Colonial Williamsburg [VA], Hotchkiss School [CT], and Marion Foundation [MA] (rain forest preservation). ■**PUBLICATIONS:** statement of program policy; application guidelines ■**WEBSITE:** None ■**E-MAIL:** robert.prischak@wachovia.com■**APPLICATION POLICIES & PROCEDURES:** The Foundation reports that strongest consideration is given to organizations offering the broadest benefit to community; capital improvements are supported when a specific project and a clear need are demonstrated. No grants are awarded to/for endowment, political activities, benefit events, individuals, or loans. Submit grant requests in a full proposal with cover letter (signed by an officer on behalf of the governing board) during June-early August (deadline is August 15th); indicate the project title, describe the purpose/duration of the proposed project (needs/problems to be met and solved) and expected outcomes, and outline a plan of action. Also provide an annual report and background information; organizational and project budgets; a list of current major funding sources and, if applicable, anticipated future resources for the project; a bound audited financial statement; Board member list; and IRS tax-exempt status documentation. Site visits sometimes are made to organizations being considered for a grant. Grants are awarded at meetings in September and December.

O+D+T   Robert Prischak (Assistant VP at Bank+Con) — John C. Tuten, Jr. [Villanova] (T) First Union/Wachovia (Trustee)

SE-460   Miller-Plummer Foundation
7036 Sheaff Lane
Fort Washington 19034   (Montgomery County)

MI-53-55
Phone 215-646-1300 **FAX** None
EIN 23-2373703   **Year Created** 1986

AMV $84,221   **FYE** 4-01   **(Gifts Received** $40,525)   2 **Grants totaling** $99,000

All local giving. High grant of **$62,000** to Philadelphia Museum of Art. **$37,000** to The Fabric Workshop. ■**PUBLICATIONS:** None ■**WEBSITE:** None ■**E-MAIL:** None ■**APPLICATION POLICIES & PROCEDURES:** The Foundation reports that giving is restricted to art institutions and individuals. Grant requests may be submitted in a one-page letter before the April 30th deadline; additional information will be requested.

O+D+T   J. Randall Plummer (P+Con) — Harvey S.S. Miller (S+F+Donor) — Marion Boulton Stroud (Donor) — Corporate donor: Pars Manufacturing Co.

SE-461   Millett (Albert B.) Memorial Fund
c/o Mellon Private Wealth Management
1735 Market Street, Room 193-0314
Philadelphia 19103   (Philadelphia County)

MI-14-15-34

Phone 215-553-2517 **FAX** 215-553-2054
EIN 23-6225988   **Year Created** 1956

AMV $2,015,329   **FYE** 6-00   **(Gifts Received** $0)   26 **Grants totaling** $185,500

All giving restricted to organizations assisting blind persons in Pa., New Jersey, and New York; grants are for general support except as noted. Two grants totaling **$50,000** to Pa. College of Optometry (rehabilitation center and support for visually impaired Pa. and NJ clients). Two grants totaling **$35,000** to Lighthouse International [NY] (vision services in NY and vision rehab services). **$10,000** each to The Associated Blind [NY] (internet service for visually impaired), Glaucoma Service Foundation to Prevent Blindness, and Overbrook School for the Blind (teams program for infants/toddlers). **$8,000** to Recording for the Blind & Dyslexic [NJ] (general support and library for NJ residents). **$7,000** to Delco Blind/Sight Center (dictaphones/spellers and Braille computer). **$5,000** each to Aperture Foundation [NY] (photography project), Associated Services for the Blind, Easter Seals (camping/recreational programs), Montgomery County Assn. for the Blind (summer camp), Presbyhomes Foundation (large-print books), and Royer-Greaves School for the Blind. **$2,000-$4,500** each to Catholic Guild for the Blind [NY] (adaptive language lab), Opthalmic Research Associates (blindness prevention), Dog Guide Users' Network, Guiding Light for the Blind (electronic travel aids), Greater Philadelphia Urban Affairs Coalition (Work Stream program), Kardon Institute for the Arts (Community Connections program and scholarship fund), Recording for the Blind & Dyslexic [Bryn Mawr] (recording studio), and Seeing Eye (puppy raising clubs in Pa.). ■**PUBLICATIONS:** Information & Proposal Guidelines memorandum ■**WEBSITE:** None ■ **E-MAIL:** morse.g@mellon.com ■**APPLICATION POLICIES & PROCEDURES:** Only Pennsylvania, New Jersey, and New York organizations which assist blind persons (or work to prevent or cure blindness) are eligible to apply; no grants are awarded to individuals. Grant requests may be submitted in a full proposal with cover letter at any time (deadline is April 15th); provide a summary sheet with a brief description of the request, total costs of the project, detailed explanation of the project with breakdown of costs, statement of purpose and brief organizational history, and name/address of contact person; include an annual report, organization budget, list of board members, list of major funding sources, audited financial statement, and IRS tax-exempt status documentation. Grants are awarded at a June meeting.

O+D+T Gail Curtis Morse (VP at Bank+Con) — Mellon Bank N.A. (Trustee)

SE-462 **MKM Foundation**
c/o The Glenmede Trust Company
One Liberty Place, 1650 Market St., Suite 1200
Philadelphia 19103 (Philadelphia County)
AMV $2,297,837 **FYE** 12-00 **(Gifts Received** $0)

MI-12-25-29-32-41-71-82

Phone 215-419-6000 **FAX** 215-419-6196
EIN 23-7966478 **Year Created** 1998
13 **Grants totaling** $100,300

About two-thirds local giving; all grants are for general purposes except as noted. High grant of **$25,000** to St. Joseph's Preparatory School. **$9,000** each to Greater Philadelphia Food Bank, Linda Creed Breast Cancer Foundation, Red Cross, and Salvation Army (For the Kids campaign). **$3,000** to Friends' Central School. **$2,000** to The Shipley School. **Out-of-state** giving includes **$9,000** each to Doctors Without Borders [NY], The Nature Conservancy of NJ, and Red Cross (disaster fund) [DC]; and **$5,000** to San Miguel School of Camden [NJ]. ■**PUBLICATIONS:** None ■**WEBSITE:** None ■**E-MAIL:** None ■**APPLICATION POLICIES & PROCEDURES:** No grants are awarded to individuals.

O+D+T John J. Cunningham, Jr. Esq. (Con) — James E. O'Donnell [NJ] (T+Donor) — Elizabeth O'Donnell [Havertown] (T) — Marie O'Donnell [NJ] (T)

SE-463 **Molle (Frank) Foundation**
704 Haywood Drive
Exton 19341 (Chester County)
AMV $155,178 **FYE** 12-00 **(Gifts Received** $0)

MI-13-41

Phone 610-458-1090 **FAX** None
EIN 23-2941216 **Year Created** 1998
11 **Grants totaling** $13,525

Mostly local giving. High grant of **$10,000** to Malvern Preparatory School. **$2,500** to Upper Main Line YMCA. Other local and out-of-state contributions **$50-$250** for various purposes. ■**PUBLICATIONS:** None ■**WEBSITE:** None ■**E-MAIL:** None ■**APPLICATION POLICIES & PROCEDURES:** Grant requests may be submitted in a letter at any time. No grants awarded to individuals.

O+D+T Frank A. Piliero (T+Donor+Con) — Sandra L. Piliero (T+Donor+Con)

SE-464 **Montgomery County Foundation, The**
Commonwealth Bank Plaza
2 West Lafayette Street, Suite 250
Norristown 19401 (Montgomery County)
AMV $10,931,002 **FYE** 12-01 **(Gifts Received** $65,740)

MI-12-13-14-15-16-17-18-19-21-22-23-25-29-31
33-35-39-41-42-43-44-45-49-53-55-56-71-84
Phone 610-313-9836 **FAX** 610-313-9839
EIN 23-6298550 **Year Created** 1960
200+ **Grants totaling** $339,896

As a Community Foundation all discretionary giving is restricted to organizations servingMontgomery County; 94 discretionary grants totaling **$226,060** were awarded as follows: **$5,000** each to ACLAMO, Central Montgomery Mental Health/Mental Retardation Center, Developmental Enterprises, Montgomery County Legal Aid Service, Norristown Initiative, and Open Line. **$3,000-$3,500** each to B.I.S.P.P, Boyertown YMCA, Children's Aid Society, Community Day Care Assn., Creative Health Services, Family Services, Gwynedd-Mercy College, Habitat for Humanity-Montgomery County, Interagency Council of Norristown, Keystone Hospice, Literacy Council of Norristown, North Penn Valley Boys & Girls Club, Phoenixville Area YMCA, RSVP of Montgomery County, Senior Adult Activities Center of Montgomery County. **$2,000-$2,500** each to Ambler YMCA, Ardmore Avenue Community Center, ASSETS Montco, Carson Valley School, Federation Day Care Services, Fellowship House of Conshohocken, Freedom Valley Girl Scout Council, Gateway Employment Resources, Genesis Housing Corp., Harcum College, Indian Valley Housing Corp., Indian Creek Foundation, Jewish Community Homes, Kelly Anne Dolan Memorial Fund, Living Beyond Breast Cancer, MARC Advocacy Services, Maternity Care Coalition, Montgomery County Assn. for the Blind, Montgomery County Cultural Center, Montgomery County Drug Awareness Coalition, Montgomery County Farm Home and 4-H, Montgomery County Mediation Center, Montgomery Hospital Foundation, Neighborhood Meals on Wheels, New Life Youth & Family Services, North Penn Senior Center, Options in Aging, Pathway School, Philabundance, Philadelphia Geriatric Center, Pottstown Symphony Orchestra, Senior Adult Activities Center of Indian Valley, Senior Citizens Center of Ardmore, Silver Springs-Martin Luther School, St. John's Episcopal Church-Soup Kitchen, and Willow Grove Community Development Corp. **$ 1,000-$1,500** each to Abington Art Center, ARTREACH, Bel Canto Children's Chorus, Bridge of Hope BuxMont, Care Consortium of the Main Line, Center School, Child, Home & Community, Christian Network Outreach Church-UCC, Delaware Valley Planned Giving Council, Diakon Lutheran Social Ministries, Executive Service Corps of the Delaware Valley, Forteniters Club, Greater Norristown Art League, Historical Society of Montgomery County, Interfaith HospitalityNetwork-Main Line, Main Line Art Center, Manor College, Montgomery County-Norristown Public Library, Norristown Chorale, Norristown Family Center, Nursing Mothers Advisory Council, Perkiomen Valley Art Center, Perkiomen Watershed Conservancy, Quaker School at Horsham, Sebastian Riding Associates, Storybook Musical Theatre, Strings for Schools, Upper Merion Township, Upper Merion Township Library, Volunteers in Action, West End Preschool, Wissahickon Valley Public Library. Other smaller local contributions. In addition, 79 grants totaling **$35,548** were awarded to students from the Norristown area for post-secondary education,13 grants totaling **$13,836** for specific assistance, and one donor-advised grant of **$100,000.** ■**PUBLICATIONS:** Brochure; application guidelines ■**WEBSITE:** www.mcfoundationinc.org ■**E-MAIL:** execoffice@mcfoundationinc.org ■**APPLICATION POLICIES & PROCEDURES:** The Foundation reports that only agencies serving Montgomery County are eligible to apply; requests from ineligible organizations will not be acknowledged. All grants are project-oriented; generally no grants are awarded for general operating support, capital fund drives, or major physical development/improvements. Prospective organizational applicants must make an initial telephone inquiry to discuss with the Executive Director the feasibility of submitting a request. Proposals must be submitted in duplicate with the following five items each on a separate sheet of paper: (1) description of agency history, services, programs, and clientele served; (2) an organizational budget and description of current funding sources; (3) full description of the program/project for which funding is sought with a detailed budget; an explanation of whether the proposed project is a new, innovative one, an expansion of an existing one, or the continuation of one currently operating; and rationale for selecting this particular project at this time; (4) a brief statement agreeing to provide a follow-up report; and (5) IRS tax-exempt status documentation. Application deadlines are June 30th and December 31st for consideration at Board meetings in June and December. Site visits sometimes are made to organizations being considered for a grant. — Scholarship awards are restricted to graduating seniors or graduates in the Norristown area; contact the Foundation for more details. — Financial assistance (daily living expenses) is available from the Shannon Cassel Fund to low-income individuals and families residing in the Lower Providence area; contact the Foundation for more details.

O+D+T John C. Webber [Gilbertsville] (P+Con) — Payson W. Burt [East Norriton] (C+D) — Muriel H. Anderson [Hendricks] (VC+D) — Bettie A. Palombo [West Norriton] (S+D) — Thurman D. Booker [Norristown] (F+D) — Marsha B. Bolden [Gladwyne] (D) — Clark E. Bromberg [Ambler] (D) — Walter Camenisch, Jr. [Lansdale] (D) — John E.F. Corson [Blue Bell] (D) — William L. Landsburg, Esq. [Merion] (D) — Linda A. Mackey [Lansdale] (D) — James L. Hollinger, Esq. [Norristown] (Counsel) Corporate Trustees: First Union/Wachovia; Harleysville National Bank; PNC Bank

---

SE-465 Morgan (Eleanor & Howard) Family Foundation

764 Mount Moro Road
Villanova 19085 (Montgomery County)

MI-42-51-54-62
Phone 610-667-4262 **FAX** None
EIN 23-2868322 **Year Created** 1996

AMV $89,871 **FYE** 12-00 **(Gifts Received** $0) 6 **Grants totaling** $79,600

About half local giving. High grant of **$25,000** to Prince Music Theatre. **$20,800** to Temple Beth Hillel. **Out-of-state** giving includes **$18,000** to Jewish Children's Museum [NY]; **$10,000** to SUNY/Stony Brook Foundation; and **$4,300** to Bruce Museum [CT]. ■**PUBLICATIONS:** None ■**WEBSITE:** www.morganfamily.org ■**E-MAIL:** hmorgan@arcagroup.com ■**APPLICATION POLICIES & PROCEDURES:** The Foundation reports that most grants are for special projects or capital campaigns. Grant requests may be submitted in any form at any time; include a project budget, Board member list, and IRS tax-exempt status documentation. Site visits sometimes are made to organizations being considered for a grant.

O+D+T Howard L. Morgan (T+Donor+Con) — Danielle A. Morgan (T) — Eleanor K. Morgan (T) — Elizabeth S. Morgan [NY] (T) — Kimberly Morgan [NY] (T)

SE-466 Morganroth-Morrison Foundation

1040 Stony Lane
Gladwyne 19035 (Montgomery County)

MI-22-41-62
Phone 610-527-0973 **FAX** None
EIN 23-2244767 **Year Created** 1983

AMV $303,488 **FYE** 12-00 **(Gifts Received** $0) 5 **Grants totaling** $51,750

All local giving; all grants are unrestricted support. High grant of **$22,000** to The Baldwin School. **$18,000** to Haverford School. **$7,500** to Federation Allied Jewish Appeal. **$4,000** to Main Line Reform Temple. **$250** to Golden Slipper Charities. ■**PUBLICATIONS:** None ■**WEBSITE:** None ■**E-MAIL:** None ■**APPLICATION POLICIES & PROCEDURES:** Information not available.

O+D+T Joel Morganroth, M.D. (D+Donor+Con) — Gail Morrison Morganroth, M.D. (D+Donor)

SE-467 Moriuchi (Takashi & Yuriko) Charitable Foundation

c/o The Glenmede Trust Company
1650 Market Street, Suite 1200
Philadelphia 19103 (Philadelphia County)

MI-22-54-63-65-81
Phone 215-419-6000 **FAX** 215-419-6196
EIN 22-6471255 **Year Created** 1989

AMV $193,638 **FYE** 12-00 **(Gifts Received** $0) 10 **Grants totaling** $12,000

One-third local giving: **$1,000** each to American Friends Service Committee, Friends of the Japanese House & Garden, Pendle Hill [Wallingford], and Philadelphia Yearly Meeting-Society of Friends. **Out-of-state** giving includes high grant of **$3,000** to Japanese American Naitonal Museum [CA], and **$1,000** to Quaker organizations/institutions in NJ and other states. ■**PUBLICATIONS:** None ■**WEBSITE:** None ■**E-MAIL:** None ■**APPLICATION POLICIES & PROCEDURES:** The Foundation reports that preference is given to Japanese-American organizations. No grants are awarded to individuals Grant requests may be submitted in a letter at any time to Mr. Takashi Moriuchi, 667 Bridlington South, Medford Leas, Medford, NJ 08055.

O+D+T Takashi Moriuchi [NJ] (T+Donor+Con) — Yuriko Moriuchi [NJ] (T+Donor) — Norman D. Col [NJ] (T)

SE-468 MorningStar Foundation, The

6154 Stoney Hill Road
New Hope 18938 (Bucks County)

MI-12-25-41
Phone 215-862-3963 **FAX** None
EIN 23-2855899 **Year Created** 1996

AMV $289,607 **FYE** 12-00 **(Gifts Received** $0) 3 **Grants totaling** $14,000

All local giving for aiding abuse, hungry or needy children. High grants of **$5,000** each to Adoption Center of the Delaware Valley and Greater Philadelphia Food Bank. **$4,000** to The Pathway School. ■**PUBLICATIONS:** None ■**WEBSITE:** None ■**E-MAIL:** None ■**APPLICATION POLICIES & PROCEDURES:** The Foundation reports that organizations in Bucks County and the surrounding area receive preference, especially those which alleviate the suffering of abused and disadvantaged children. Grant requests may be submitted in a letter at any time; provide a brief history, reason for grant, amount requested, and include IRS tax-exempt status documentation. Site visits sometimes are made to organizations being considered for a grant. Grants are awarded at a December meeting.

O+D+T Katherine N. Murphy (P+F+T+Con) — Martha J. Murphy (VP+T) — Joseph A. Murphy (T+Donor)

SE-469   Morris Charitable Trust, The
440 Parkview Drive
Wynnewood   19096   (Montgomery County)
AMV $1,748,350   **FYE** 12-00   **(Gifts Received** $175,000)

MI-14-31-41-42-61-89
Phone 610-896-8513 **FAX** None
EIN 22-2798233   **Year Created** 1986
14 **Grants totaling** $157,715

Mostly local giving. High grant of **$78,550** to Gwynedd-Mercy College. **$60,220** to St. Joseph's U. **$5,000** to St. Charles Borromeo School. **$1,920** to St. Margaret's School/Church. **$1,000-$1,025** each to Lower Merion Township, Magee Rehab, and Mercy Health System. Other local contributions **$100-$500** for various purposes. **Out-of-state** grant: **$7,500** to Walsingham Academy [VA]. ■**PUBLICATIONS:** None ■**WEBSITE:** None ■**E-MAIL:** None ■**APPLICATION POLICIES & PROCEDURES:** The Foundation reports that giving is generally to the Philadelphia area, particularly for educational purposes. Grant requests may be submitted in a letter at any time. Site visits sometimes are made to organizations being considered for a grant.

O+D+T   Michael J. Morris (T+Donor+Con) — Rose M. Morris (T)

SE-470   Morrissey Family Foundation
c/o F.J. Morrissey & Company
1700 Market Street, Suite 1420
Philadelphia   19103   (Philadelphia County)
AMV $669,426   **FYE** 12-00   **(Gifts Received** $0)

MI-31-42-43-53-61

Phone 215-563-8500 **FAX** None
EIN 23-2870762   **Year Created** 1996
16 **Grants totaling** $43,230

About two-thirds local giving. High grant of **$10,000** to Chester County Hospital (open heart program). **$8,450** to Cabrini College (scholarship fund). **$5,000** to Sts. Peter & Paul Church [West Chester]. **$4,000** to U. of the Arts. Other smaller local contributions. **Out-of-state** giving includes **$7,500** to Boston U. [MA] (scholarship fund) and **$6,580** to St. Patrick's Church [FL] (building fund). — Giving in prior years for scholarship funds at other colleges/universities. ■**PUBLICATIONS:** None ■**WEBSITE:** None ■**E-MAIL:** None ■**APPLICATION POLICIES & PROCEDURES:** Information not available.

O+D+T   Maryanne D. Morrissey (P+Con) — Joseph C. Morrissey (VP) — Jane M. Morrissey (S)

SE-471   Moyer (A. Marlyn) Scholarship Foundation
c/o Lower Bucks County Chamber of Commerce
409 Hood Boulevard
Fairless Hills   19030   (Bucks County)
AMV $678,984   **FYE** 12-00   **(Gifts Received** $0)

MI-43

Phone 215-943-7400 **FAX** 215-943-7404
EIN 23-2037282   Year Created 1978
8 **Grants totaling** $27,750

All awards (seven of **$3,750**, one of **$1,500**) are scholarships for Bucks County high school graduates. ■**PUBLICATIONS:** None ■**WEBSITE:** None ■**E-MAIL:** None ■**APPLICATION POLICIES & PROCEDURES:** Scholarships are restricted to Bucks County residents who are graduating high school seniors who will enroll full time in post-secondary schools for the first time; awards are based on academic achievement and financial need. A formal application form, available from the Foundation or guidance departments at Bucks County high schools, must be submitted before the April deadline (call for exact date).

O+D+T   Susan M. Harkins (Recording Secretary+AF+Con) — Edward G. Biester, Jr. Esq. (P+D) — Sidney T Yates (VP+D) — Dirk Dulap (S+D) — Peter J. Farmer (F+D) and six other directors

---

SE-472   Mozino (Peter S.) Foundation
c/o Drexeline Shopping Center, Inc.
5100 State Road, Suite E-500
Drexel Hill   19026   (Delaware County)
AMV $2,095,383   **FYE** 12-00   **(Gifts Received** $0)

MI-12-31-42-52-54-55-72

Phone 610-259-1460 **FAX** 610-259-2711
EIN 23-7642668   **Year Created** 1990
47 **Grants totaling** $112,500

Almost half local giving. High Pa. grant of **$15,000** to Franklin Institute. **$5,000-$5,500** each to Academy of Music, Cabrini College, Children's Hospital of Philadelphia, Pa. Ballet, and Supportive Child/Adult Network. **$4,000** to Philadelphia Ronald McDonald House. **$2,500** each to Philadelphia Museum of Art and Philadelphia Orchestra. **$1,000** each to Delco Memorial Foundation (cancer care) and First Serve Children. **$500** to Morris Animal Refuge. **Out-of-state** giving, mostly to Fort Lauderdale, FL area, includes **$10,000** to Gold Coast Opera [FL]; **$6,000** to Florida Grand Opera; and **$5,000** to Broward Performing Arts Foundation [FL]. ■**PUBLICATIONS:** None ■**WEBSITE:** None ■**E-MAIL:** None ■**APPLICATION POLICIES & PROCEDURES:** No grants awarded to individuals.

O+D+T   H. David Seegul (T+Con) — Catherine Mozino [Havertown] (T)

SE-473   Mullen Foundation, The
c/o Apple Vacations
7 Campus Boulevard
Newtown Square   19072   (Delaware County)
AMV $978,328   **FYE** 9-00   **(Gifts Received** $0)

MI-15-22-41-42-61-71

Phone 610-359-8999 **FAX** 610-359-8998
EIN 23-2125388   **Year Created** 1976
9 **Grants totaling** $75,100

Mostly local giving. High grants of **$20,000** each to Neumann College and Project H.O.M.E. [Media]. **$10,000** to West Catholic Alumni Assn. **$8,000** to Willistown Conservation Trust. **$5,000** to Franciscan Monastery [Montgomery County]. **Out-of-state** giving includes **$5,000** each to Greek Orthodox Church [NC] (radio pulpit) and Christian Brothers [MD]; and **$2,000** to Brothers of the Christian Schools [MD]. — Local grants in prior years included **$10,000** each to Catholic Charities and Catholic Standard & Times; **$8,000** to Willistown Conservation Trust; **$2,750** to Siloam Ministries; **$2,000** to De La Salle Christian Brothers [Philadelphia] and Neumann College; and **$1,000** each to Brandywine Conservancy, Holy Family Home, St. Francis Inn, and Village of Divine Providence. ■**PUBLICATIONS:** None ■**WEBSITE:** www.applevactions.com [corporate info only] ■**E-MAIL:** None ■**APPLICATION POLICIES & PROCEDURES:** The Foundation reports that giving generally favors Philadelphia-area Catholic charities but other charitable causes are considered. Submit grant requests in a letter (4 pages maximum) in October; include an audited financial statement, Board member list, and IRS tax-exempt status documentation. Site visits sometimes are made to organizations being considered for a grant. The Trustees meet in November. — Formerly called The Mullen Family Foundation.

O+D+T Joan A. Mullen (T+Donor+Con) — John J. Mullen (T+Donor)

SE-474 Muller (C. John & Josephine) Foundation
c/o Muller, Inc.
2800 Grant Ave.
Philadelphia 19114 (Philadelphia County)
AMV $910,531 **FYE** 12-00 **(Gifts Received** $0)

MI-20-29-31-41-56-89

Phone 215-676-7575 **FAX** None
EIN 23-2324413 **Year Created** 1984
5 **Grants totaling** $171,000

All local/Pa. giving. High grant of **$100,000** to Abington Memorial Hospital. **$50,000** to German Society of Pa. **$10,000** each to Philadelphia Police Foundation and School District of Philadelphia. **$1,000** to Mount Carmel Human Development Corp. [Northumberland County]. — In the prior year grants included **$50,000** to German Society of Pa. and **$25,000** to Abington Friends School. ■**PUBLICATIONS:** None ■**WEBSITE:** None ■**E-MAIL:** None ■**APPLICATION POLICIES & PROCEDURES:** The Foundation reports giving focuses on the Philadelphia area with most support for building/renovations. No grants awarded to individuals.

O+D+T C. John Muller [Huntingdon Valley] (P+D+Donor+Con) — Ellen Gusman, Esq. (T) — Frederick T. Miller (T) — Joel Shaffer (T) Corporate donor: Clement & Muller, Inc.

SE-475 Murphy Charitable Foundation
c/o Pepper Hamilton LLP
400 Berwyn Park, 899 Cassatt Road
Berwyn 19312 (Chester County)
AMV $1,744,463 **FYE** 12-00 **(Gifts Received** $0)

MI-13-31-35-41-42-52-54-63-72-84

Phone 610-640-7832 **FAX** 610-640-7835
EIN 23-2747488 **Year Created** 1993
81 **Grants totaling** $100,000

About one-third local giving. High local grant of **$7,000** to Episcopal Academy. **$5,000** to Agnes Irwin School. **$2,000** to The Shipley School. **$1,000** each to Academy of Natural Sciences, Angel Flight East, Bryn Mawr Hospital Foundation, Bryn Mawr Presbyterian Church, The Center School, Chestnut Hill Presbyterian Nursery School, Community Health Affiliates, Franklin Institute, Philadelphia Museum of Art, Philadelphia Orchestra, Philadelphia Youth Tennis, Philadelphia Zoo, Valley Forge Military Academy, and White-Williams Scholars. Other local contributions **$500** for various purposes. **Out-of-state** giving includes high grants of **$8,000** each to Ellsworth Congregation of Jehovah's Witnesses [ME] and Watchtower Bible & Tract Society of NY; **$4,000** to First Congregational Church of Blue Hill [ME]; **$3,000** each to Christ Episcopal Church [CT] and Yale U. [CT]; and smaller grants/contributions, mostly to ME - Penobscot Bay area ■**PUBLICATIONS:** None ■**WEBSITE:** None ■**E-MAIL:** None ■ **APPLICATION POLICIES & PROCEDURES:** No grants awarded to individuals.

O+D+T John B. Huffaker, Esq. (AS+AF+Con) — R. Blair Murphy [CT] (P+D) — Eleanor K. Richard [Bryn Mawr] (S+D) — Ann M. Zabel [Bryn Mawr] (F+D) — Eric S. Murphy [CA] (D) — John H. Murphy [ME] (D) Donor: Estate of W. Beverly Murphy

---

SE-476 Musser (Warren V.) Foundation
c/o Safeguard Scientifics, Inc.
500 Safeguard Building, 435 Devon Park Drive
Wayne 19087 (Chester County)
AMV $1,511,070 **FYE** 11-01 **(Gifts Received** $366,563)

MI-11-13-22-25-29-31-35-41-49-56-84

Phone 610-293-0600 **FAX** 610-293-0601
EIN 23-2162497 **Year Created** 1980
23 **Grants totaling** $193,188

About two-thirds local/Pa. giving. High grant of **$25,000** to Philadelphia Youth Tennis. **$15,000** to Red Cross. **$10,000-$10,400** each to Boy Scouts/Cradle of Liberty Council, Jewish Federation of Greater Philadelphia, and United Way of SE Pa. **$5,000** each to Boy Scouts/Chester County Council, City Year of Philadelphia, Eagles Youth Partnership, Gesu School, Greater Philadelphia Food Bank, Pa. Partnership for Economic Education [Harrisburg], Temple U., and Valley Forge Historical Society. **$4,000** to The Vanguard School. **$3,788** to Community Volunteers in Medicine. **$1,000** to Alan Ameche Foundation. Other smaller local contributions. **Out-of-state** giving includes **$25,000** to Nantucket AIDS Network [MA]; **$20,000** to Henry H. Kessler Foundation [NJ]; and **$11,500** to Nantucket Cottage Hospital [MA]. ■**PUBLICATIONS:** None ■**WEBSITE:** None ■**E-MAIL:** None ■**APPLICATION POLICIES & PROCEDURES:** Grant requests may be submitted in a letter at any time; include all pertinent information necessary to evaluate a request.

O+D+T Diane Swiggart (Administrator+Con) — Warren V. Musser (P+F+T+Donor) — Carl Sempier (T)

SE-477 National Organization for Hearing Research Foundation
225 Haverford Ave., Suite 1
Narberth 19072 (Montgomery County)
AMV $1,234,366 **FYE** 12-00 **(Gifts Received** $428,995)

MI-32

Phone 610-664-3135 **FAX** 610-668-1428
EIN 23-2528578 **Year Created** 1988
38 **Grants totaling** $557,020

Nationwide and international giving restricted to auditory research; one Pa. contribution: **$520** to Temple U. School of Medicine (infant testing program). High grant of **$230,360** to Washington U. [MO] (gene expression profiling of hair cell regeneration research). Most other awards were **$10,000** each (seed money grants) for university or medical school auditory research projects in many states and overseas. ■**PUBLICATIONS:** annual report; informational brochure; application form & guidelines ■ **WEBSITE:** www.nohrfoundation.org ■**E-MAIL:** peggyatnohr@worldnet.att.net ■**APPLICATION POLICIES & PROCEDURES:** All giving is restricted to innovative biomedical research into the prevention, causes, and cures and treatments of hearing loss and deafness; high-risk and contemporary project or experiments are encouraged so as to promote significant new advances. Most grants are in the form of seed money for one-year projects although multiple-year grants are awarded. Grant requests must be submitted during June-September on a detailed Application Form (available from the Foundation); the deadline is the 1st Friday in October. A national scientific review committee of recognized auditory scientists reviews applications and advises on grant awards. Grants are awarded at a January meeting.

O+D+T Geraldine Dietz Fox (P+Donor+Con) — Richard J. Fox (S+F+Donor) — other donors include many individuals, foundations, corporations and businesses

SE-478 Nayovitz (Louis) Foundation

Briar House, Suite A33
8302 Old York Road
Elkins Park 19027   (Montgomery County)

MI-11-22-31-42-44-56-62

Phone 215-884-1276 **FAX** None
EIN 23-2142539   Year Created 1980

AMV $1,494,700   **FYE** 12-00   **(Gifts Received** $0)   58 **Grants totaling** $48,740

All local giving. High grant of **$10,520** to Jewish Federation of Greater Philadelphia. **$7,500** to American Philosophical Society. **$5,345** to Reform Congregation Keneseth Israel. **$5,000** to Albert Einstein Medical Center. **$4,500** to Federation Allied Jewish Appeal. **$1,750** to United Way of SE Pa. **$1,500** to U. of Pa. School of Social Work. **$1,000** each to Free Library of Philadelphia, and Philadelphia Bar Foundation. Other local contributions **$20-$500** for various purposes. ■**PUBLICATIONS:** None ■**WEBSITE:** None ■**E-MAIL:** None ■**APPLICATION POLICIES & PROCEDURES:** The Foundation reports that only Philadelphia-area organizations are eligible to apply. Most grants are for general support, special projects, or building funds. No grants awarded to individuals. Prospective applicants initially should make a telephone inquiry about the feasibility of submitting a request. Grant requests may be submitted in any form at any time. The Trustees award grants at meeting in November and December.

O+D+T Neysa C. Adams (T+Con) — Margaret D. Nayovitz (T) — Judith A. Adams (T) — Ralph S. Snyder (T)

SE-479 Neducsin Foundation, The

c/o Neducsin Properties
161 Leverington Ave.
Philadelphia 19127   (Philadelphia County)

MI-11-24-29-34

Phone 215-483-5435 **FAX** None
EIN 23-2938583   **Year Created** 1997

AMV $532,964   **FYE** 6-00   **(Gifts Received** $675,126)   4 **Grants totaling** $83,093

All local giving. High grant of **$74,593** to North Light Community Center. **$5,000** to United Way of SE Pa. **$2,500** to Philadelphia College of Osteopathic Medicine. **$1,000** to Intercommunity Action. ■**PUBLICATIONS:** None ■**WEBSITE:** None ■**E-MAIL:** None ■**APPLICATION POLICIES & PROCEDURES:** Grant requests in any form may be submitted at any time.

O+D+T Daniel R. Neducsin [nJ] (P+Donor+Con) — Luana Neducsin [NJ] (S+Donor)

SE-480 Nelson (Grace S. & W. Linton) Foundation, The

940 West Valley Road, Suite 1601
Wayne 19087   (Chester County)

MI-11-12-13-14-16-17-19-22-24-35-41-42-43
Phone 610-975-9169 **FAX** 610-975-9170
EIN 22-2583922   **Year Created** 1984

AMV $28,057,800   **FYE** 12-00   **(Gifts Received** $0)   107 **Grants totaling** $1,435,055

All local giving for children/youth programs. **CHILD ADVOCACY PROGRAM GRANTS:** **$10,000** to Support Center for Child Advocates. **$5,760** to Northwest Interfaith Movement. **$5,000** each to CASA/Youth Advocates and Juvenile Law Center. **ADOPTION/FOSTER CARE/SHELTER PROGRAM GRANTS:** **$15,000** to Family & Community Services of Delaware County. **$10,000** to 18th Street Development Corp. **$5,000** to Voyage House. **DAY CARE PRESCHOOL PROGRAM GRANTS:** **$50,000** to United Way of SE Pa. (Child Care Matters). **$40,000** to Philadelphia Early Childhood Collaborative. **$25,000** to Foundations, Inc. **$20,000** to Delaware Valley Child Care Council. **$10,000** each to Community Women's Education Project (day care center), and Delaware Valley Assn. for the Education of Young Children. **$5,000** each to Childspace Cooperative Development (day care center), Children's Village Child Care Center, and Women's Community Revitalization Project. **$3,000** to Main Line YMCA. **$2,500** to Settlement Music School (early childhood education initiative). **AFTER SCHOOL PROGRAM GRANTS:** **$57,619** to Police Athletic League. **$25,000** to Foundations, Inc. **$15,000** to Drexel U. (precollege engineering/science program). **$10,000** each to Chester YWCA, Providence Center, and Germantown YWCA. **$7,500** each to Episcopal Community Services, Red Cross (Partners for Youth), and Village of Arts & Humanities. **$6,000** to First United Church of Germantown. **$5,000** each to Childspace Cooperative Development (day care center), Inn Dwelling's Learning Institute, Neighbor to Neighbor Community Development Corp., and North Penn Boys & Girls Club. **$3,500** to Northeast Community Center. **$2,500** each to Institute for the Development of African-American Youth and Settlement Music School. **SUMMER RECREATION PROGRAM GRANTS:** **$7,500** each to Episcopal Community Services and Woodrock. **$4,000** to Christ Lutheran Church of Upper Darby. **$3,000** each to Patrician Society of Central Norristown and Supportive Child/Adult Network. **$2,000** to Old First Reformed Church. **PARENT TRAINING PROGRAM GRANTS:** **$20,000** to Frankford Group Ministry (Neighborhood Parenting Project). **$5,700** to Child, Home & Community. **$5,000** to Children's Aid Society of Pa. and Homeless Advocacy Project. **$3,500** to Interfaith Hospitality Network of the Main Line. **LEADERSHIP/CITIZENSHIP FOR YOUNG CHILDREN PROGRAM GRANTS:** **$60,000** to Boy Scouts/Cradle of Liberty Council (Learning for Life program). **$25,000** to Big Brothers/Big Sisters of Philadelphia. **$15,000** to Big Brothers/Big Sisters of Bucks County. **$7,500** each to Red Cross (Partners for Youth) and Village of Arts & Humanities (education through arts program). **$5,000** each to Girl Scouts of SE Pa. (scouting in schools), LaSalle U. (Project Teamwork), and Philadelphia Physicians for Social Responsibility (Peaceful Posse). **$2,500** to RSVP of Montgomery County. **EDUCATION AID FOR ELEMENTARY, SECONDARY & VOCATIONAL PROGRAMS:** **$35,000** to Philadelphia Futures (Sponsor A Scholar). **$30,000** to Philadelphia High School Academies. **$25,000** to Chester County Futures (Sponsor A Scholar). **$20,000** to Philadelphia Education Fund (college access program). **$15,000** to Academy of Natural Sciences (women in sciences program). **$10,000** each to Allegheny West Foundation (One Giant Step program), Community Action Agency of Delaware County (summer career exploration program), and White-Williams Scholars. **$5,000** each to Neighbor to Neighbor Community Development Program and Warren Musser Young Scholars Program at Gesu School. **$3,500** to Bainbridge House (mentoring program). **$2,500** to RSVP of Montgomery County. **COLLEGE AID FOR NEEDY CHILDREN GRANT:** **$40,000** to Police Athletic League. **HEALTH CARE PROGRAM GRANTS:** **$71,000** to VNA-Community Services [Abington]. **$10,000** each to Boy Scouts/Chester County Council (health service center) and Children's Hospital of Philadelphia (Bridging the Gaps). **$7,500** to Maternity Care Coalition. **$5,000** each to Community Medical & Dental Center, Maternal & Child Health Consortium of Chester County, Mother's Home of Darby, and Women's Community Revitalization Project. **$2,000** to Paoli Presbyterian Church/Basic Needs Fund. **CHILD ABUSE/DRUG ABUSE PREVENTION PROGRAM GRANTS:** **$30,000** to Corporate Alliance for Drug Education. **$10,000** to Exchange Club Family Center. **$5,000** each to Crime Victim's Center of Chester County and Domestic Violence Center of Chester County. **MISCELLANEOUS GRANTS:** **$10,000** each to Inglis House and Mercy Vocational High

School. **$5,000** each to Blind Relief Fund and Philadelphia Museum of Art. **$1,000** each to American Cancer Society, American Heart Assn., Philadelphia Orchestra, Philadelphia Zoo, Red Cross, and United Way of Chester County. Also, under the **Nelson Scholarship Program** a total of **$402,976** in scholarships (tuition and books) were awarded to 16 undergraduate students attending the U. of Pa. Wharton School. ■**PUBLICATIONS:** None ■**WEBSITE:** None ■**E-MAIL:** None ■**APPLICATION POLICIES & PROCEDURES:** The Foundation reports that grantmaking is limited to Philadelphia and surrounding suburbs for two priority interests: (1) the unmet needs of young children (includes shelter, daycare, preschool, education, preventive healthcare, child abuse prevention, drug abuse prevention, after-school and summer programs, child advocacy, parenting, foster care, and adoption); and (2) fostering leadership and citizenship in youth. Most grants are for program development, seed money, equipment grants, and for general operating support; multiyear requests are considered. No grants are awarded directly to individuals. Prospective applicants initially should make a telephone inquiry about the feasibility of submitting a request. Grant requests in any form may be submitted at any time six weeks before the quarterly meeting (see below); include a narrative describing the program, an organization budget, project budget, list of major funding sources and amounts, list of Board members with Board responsibilities and committee assignments, resumes or job descriptions of key program/project personnel, most recent audited financial statement, and IRS tax-exempt status documentation. Site visits sometimes are made to organizations being considered for a grant. The Board of Directors awards grants at meetings held the first week of January, April, July, and October. Note: Awards under The Nelson Scholarship Program are restricted to graduates of preselected secondary schools entering the Wharton School/U. of Pa. as a first year undergraduate; no unsolicited requests for these scholarships are accepted.

O+D+T Fred C. Aldridge, Jr. Esq. [Haverford] (P+F+D+Con) — James P. Schellenger [Berwyn] (VP+S+D) — William P. Brady [West Chester] (VP+AS+AF+D) — Delaware Management Company (Donor)

SE-481   Neubauer Foundation, The
210 Rittenhouse Square West, #3106
Philadelphia 19103   (Philadelphia County)

MI-22-42-52-54-56-62-82
Phone 215-238-3880 **FAX** None
EIN 25-6627704   **Year Created** 1993

AMV $17,377,122   **FYE** 11-00   **(Gifts Received** $1,301,269)   12 **Grants totaling** $704,800

Limited Pa. giving; all grants are for program support. High Pa. grant of **$50,000** to Jewish Heritage Program. **$25,000** to American Friends of Interdisciplinary Center [Philadelphia/Israel]. **$15,000** to Philadelphia Museum of Art. **$5,000** to Academy of Music. **Out-of-state** giving includes **$312,500** to Brandeis U. [MA]; **$93,000** to The Jewish Museum [NY]; **$87,000** to U. of Chicago [IL]; **$58,750** to Metropolitan Opera [NY]; **$21,000** to Princeton U. [NJ]; and **$20,000** to Horatio Alger Assn. [VA]. ■**PUBLICATIONS:** None ■**WEBSITE:** None ■**E-MAIL:** None ■**APPLICATION POLICIES & PROCEDURES:** Grant requests may be submitted in a proposal at any time; describe in detail the project and funding requested, and include background information and IRS tax-exempt status documentation. — Formerly called the Neubauer Family Foundation.

O+D+T Joseph Neubauer (T+Donor+Con) — Melissa Neubauer Anderson (T) — Lawrence Neubauer (T)

SE-482   Neuman-Publicker Trust
1518 Willowbrook Lane
Villanova 19085   (Montgomery County)

MI-41-42-72-81-82
Phone 215-525-2957 **FAX** None
EIN 23-6232559   **Year Created** 1946

AMV $627,034   **FYE** 12-99   **(Gifts Received** $0)   5 **Grants totaling** $143,000

Mostly local giving. High grant of **$75,000** to PNC Corporation (a family-related foundation supporting animal rights). **$30,000** to Josep Maria Ferrater Mora Foundation (a family-related foundation). **$25,000** to Global Learning [Bryn Mawr]. **$10,000** to Wessex Fund [Bryn Mawr]. **Out-of-state** grant: **$3,000** to Trickle-Up Program [NY]. — Most giving in prior years to animal rights organizations, universities, and preparatory schools. ■**PUBLICATIONS:** None ■**WEBSITE:** None ■**E-MAIL:** None ■**APPLICATION POLICIES & PROCEDURES:** Grant requests in any form may be submitted at any time; include IRS tax-exempt status documentation. — Also known as Harry & Rose Publicker Trust.

O+D+T Priscilla Cohn Ferrator-Mora (T+Con) — A. Bruce Neuman (T) — Harry Publicker (Donor) — Rose Publicker (Donor)

SE-483   Newman (Paul L.) Foundation
117 Raynham Road
Merion Station 19066   (Montgomery County)

MI-22-41-62
Phone 610-617-0482 **FAX** None
EIN 31-1287223   **Year Created** 1990

AMV $554,190   **FYE** 12-00   **(Gifts Received** $0)   10+ **Grants totaling** $16,175

Mostly local giving. High grant of **$6,570** to Lower Merion Synagogue. **$1,370** to Bikur Cholim Philadelphia. **$1,000** to Stern Hebrew High School. **$820** to Hillel of Greater Philadelphia. Other smaller local and out-of-state contributions, mostly for Jewish purposes. ■**PUBLICATIONS:** None ■**WEBSITE:** None ■**E-MAIL:** None ■**APPLICATION POLICIES & PROCEDURES:** The Foundation reports that unsolicited requests are not accepted.

O+D+T Paul L. Newman (P+Donor+Con) — Nancy Helwig [OH] (T)

SE-484   Newport Foundation, The
1119 Ashbourne Road
Cheltenham 19012   (Montgomery County)

MI-12-14-17-25-32-41
Phone Unlisted **FAX** None
EIN 23-2438116   **Year Created** 1986

AMV $1,603,821   **FYE** 12-00   **(Gifts Received** $30,174)   6 **Grants totaling** $46,500

All giving to Philadelphia; all grants are for operating support. High grant of **$20,000** to St. Williams School. **$10,000** to Arthritis Foundation/Eastern Pa. Chapter. **$7,000** to Easter Seals. **$5,000** to Drueding Center/Project Rainbow. **$2,500** to Pa. School for the Deaf. **$2,000** to Associated Services for the Blind. ■**PUBLICATIONS:** None ■**WEBSITE:** None ■**E-MAIL:** None ■**APPLICATION POLICIES & PROCEDURES:** No grants awarded to individuals.

O+D+T William W. Moyer, III (P+D+Donor+Con) — Jacalyn Moyer (VP+S+F+D+Donor) — Daniel J. Paci [Silverdale] (VP+AS+D) — Donor: Estate of Arthur Sidewater

SE-485 Niessen (Leo), Jr. Charitable Foundation   MI-13-17-22-41-42-43-54-71
c/o First Union/Wachovia
123 South Broad Street, PA1279   **Phone** 215-670-4230 **FAX** 215-670-4236
Philadelphia 19109   (Philadelphia County)   **EIN** 23-7723097 **Year Created** 1994
AMV $4,970,139   **FYE** 6-00   **(Gifts Received** $0)   14 **Grants totaling** $102,490

Mostly local giving. High grants of **$15,000** each to LaSalle U. (annual fund) and Philadelphia Chamber of Commerce (scholarships for working women). **$7,000** to Please Touch Museum (general support). **$6,000** to Acadia U. (scholarships for Philadelphia public school graduates). **$5,490** to Archdiocese of Philadelphia/Office of Catholic Education (special ed students). **$5,000** each to Chestnut Hill College (information technology complex), Conwell-Egan Catholic High School [Bucks County] (tuition assistance), Delaware Valley Friends School (inner-city student tuition assistance), Drexel U. (prescience/engineering program), Mercy Vocational High School (nursing assistant/home health aide program), Pa. Horticultural Society (JFK Blvd. project), and West Philadelphia Catholic High School (technology director position). **Out-of-state** grants: **$$15,000** to Red Cloud Indian School [SD] (literacy initiative) and **$10,000** to St. Mary's College & Seminary (S.PI.C.E. program). — Note: Under the donor's Will, three organizations receive preference: Holy Redeemer Hospital & Medical Center, Society for Propagation of the Faith, and Red Cloud Indian School [SD]. ■**PUBLICATIONS:** Grant Proposal Guidelines; application form ■**WEBSITE:** None ■**E-MAIL:** eugene.williams1@wachovia.com ■**APPLICATION POLICIES & PROCEDURES:** The Foundation reports that support focuses on the Philadelphia area for (1) health services for all ages, (2) education of the needy and educable at all academic levels, without regard to age, (3) youth, (4) religious organizations providing spiritual and emotional guidance, and (5) social service agencies providing assistance and care to the homeless, elderly, and economically disadvantaged. Most grants are for special projects, building funds, and scholarships. No grants are awarded to individuals or for endowment, political purposes, or loans and no support, generally, is awarded for capital improvements. Grant requests should be submitted in January or July on a formal application form available from the Bank (the deadlines are January 31st and July 31st); the application specifies required attachments. If any documentation is missing, the proposal will not be considered. Site visits sometimes are made to organizations being considered for a grant. The Trustee Committee awards grants at meetings twice annually.

O+D+T Eugene J. Williams (VP at Bank+Con) — William R. Sasso, Esq. (Co-Trustee) First Union/Wachovia (Co-Trustee)

SE-486 Nobadeer Foundation   MI-18-56-72
c/o Thomas Travel Services
123 South Main Street   **Phone** 215-348-1770 **FAX** 215-340-9390
Doylestown 18901   (Bucks County)   **EIN** 23-2870056 **Year Created** 1996
AMV $179,870   **FYE** 12-00   **(Gifts Received** $0)   4 **Grants totaling** $13,000

Mostly local giving. Two grants totaling **$7,500** to Bucks County Historical Society (master plan update and planned giving seminar). **$3,000** to Planned Parenthood of Bucks County (medical equipment). **Out-of-state** grant: **$2,500** to Nantucket Maria Mitchell [MA] (bird walk program). — Giving in the prior year: **$6,000** each to Central Bucks Family YMCA (public relations program) and Planned Parenthood of Bucks County (development office support). ■**PUBLICATIONS:** None ■**WEBSITE:** www.thomas-travel.com [corporate info only] ■**E-MAIL:** None ■**APPLICATION POLICIES & PROCEDURES:** No grants awarded to individuals.

O+D+T Thomas McKean Thomas (P+Donor+Con) — Rebecca R. Thomas (S) — Patricia R. Thomas (F) — Corporate donor: Thomas Travel Services

---

SE-487 Norris (Nancy & Norman) Private Foundation   MI-11-63-71-72
P.O. Box 29   **Phone** 610-827-9306 **FAX** None
Birchrunville 19421   (Montgomery County)   **EIN** 23-2707519 **Year Created** 1992
AMV $195,367   **FYE** 12-00   **(Gifts Received** $0)   25+ **Grants totaling** $10,940

Mostly local giving. High grant of **$4,500** to St. Peter's United Church of Christ. **$1,100** to French & Pickering Creeks Conservation Trust. Other local contributions **$250** or smaller for environmental, animal humane, human services, civic and other purposes. **Out-of-state** giving includes **$1,200** to United Way of Lee County [FL] and smaller contributions. ■**PUBLICATIONS:** None ■**WEBSITE:** None ■**E-MAIL:** None ■**APPLICATION POLICIES & PROCEDURES:** Information not available.

O+D+T Norman L. Norris (T+Donor+Con) — Nancy Norris (T+Donor)

SE-488 North Penn Charitable Foundation   MI-63-64
562 Constitution Road   **Phone** 215-368-5379 **FAX** None
Lansdale 19446   (Montgomery County)   **EIN** 23-6802678 **Year Created** 1984
AMV $612,681   **FYE** 11-00   **(Gifts Received** $25,000)   75 **Grants totaling** $165,185

About two-thirds local giving. High grant of **$118,600** to Calvary Baptist Church. Other grants/contributions to Pa. any many other states ranged from **$200** to **$2,600,** for Baptist churches, seminaries, Evangelical mission activities, and Bible organizations. ■**PUBLICATIONS:** None ■**WEBSITE:** None ■**E-MAIL:** None ■**APPLICATION POLICIES & PROCEDURES:** The Foundation reports that giving is generally limited to general support/building funds for churches/seminaries and to individual missionaries to promote the Christian faith; most support is for seminary graduates of Calvary Baptist Church, Lansdale. Unsolicited requests for funds are not accepted.

O+D+T Lorraine Edmonds (T+Donor+Con)

SE-489 Novotny (Yetta Deitch) Charitable Trust
255 Meetinghouse Lane
Merion Station 19066 (Montgomery County)
AMV $11,488,354 **FYE** 8-00 **(Gifts Received** $0)

MI-15-22-31-35-41-62-64-82
Phone 610-664-1323 **FAX** None
EIN 23-7642807 **Year Created** 1990
20+ **Grants totaling** $690,000

About half local giving. High Pa. grant of **$125,000** to U. of Pa. Hospital. **$100,000** to Federation Allied Jewish Appeal. **$50,000** to Philadelphia Geriatric Center. **$25,000** to Perelman Jewish Day School. **$10,000** to Gratz College. **$5,000** each to Jewish Family & Children's Services and Yad Sarah Organization. **$2,000** to Living Beyond Breast Cancer. **Out-of-state** giving includes **$315,000** to Hadassah Medical Relief Assn. [NY]; **$20,000** to ORT [NY]; and **$15,000** to Westchester Fairfield Hebrew Academy [NY]. ■**PUBLICATIONS:** None ■**WEBSITE:** None ■**E-MAIL:** None ■**APPLICATION POLICIES & PROCEDURES:** No grants awarded to individuals.

O+D+T Stanley L. Zolot (T+Con) — Andrew Zolot [Bryn Mawr] (T) Donor: Estate of Yetta Deitch Novotny

---

SE-490 O'Connor Family Foundation, The
442 Inverary Road
Villanova 19085 (Delaware County)
AMV $453,023 **FYE** 12-00 **(Gifts Received** $110,000)

MI-12-14-22-31-41-42-61
Phone 610-254-0464 **FAX** None
EIN 23-7927963 **Year Created** 1997
29 **Grants totaling** $53,975

Mostly local giving. High grant of **$16,500** to St. Joseph's Preparatory School. **$10,725** to St. Joseph's U. **$5,000** to Academy of Notre Dame de Namur. **$3,000** to The MBF Center. **$2,000** to Catholic Charities, **$1,000** each to Grey Nuns of the Sacred Heart, Sisters of St. Joseph, and Trevor's Endeavors. Other smaller local contributions, many for Catholic purposes. **Out-of-state** giving includes **$2,500** to Food for Poor; **$2,000** each to Covenant House [NY] and St. Jude Children's Research Hospital [TN]; and **$1,000** to Holy Name of Camden [NJ]. ■**PUBLICATIONS:** None ■**WEBSITE:** None ■**E-MAIL:** None ■**APPLICATION POLICIES & PROCEDURES:** Information not available.

O+D+T Gerald J. O'Connor, Sr. (Co-T+Donor+Con) — Sheila T. O'Connor (Co-T)

SE-491 O'Grady Family Foundation
1160 Norsam Road
Gladwyne 19035 (Montgomery County)
AMV $527,814 **FYE** 12-00 **(Gifts Received** $0)

MI-13-14-22-25-41-42-52-61-84
Phone 610-527-3604 **FAX** None
EIN 23-7770587 **Year Created** 1994
25 **Grants totaling** $112,250

About half local giving. High Pa. grant of **$28,500** to Philadelphia Orchestra. **$6,600** to Pa. Ballet. **$5,850** to St. John the Baptist Church. **$5,000** each to Opera Company of Philadelphia and Project H.O.M.E. **$2,500** to Philadelphia Youth Tennis. **$2,000** to MBF Center. **$1,000-$1,500** each to Academy of Music, Friends of Erik, Gesu School, St. Joseph U., and Vanguard School. Other local contributions **$500-$700** for education. **Out-of-state** giving includes **$30,000** to U. of Notre Dame [IN]; **$5,000** to Holy Cross Order/Moreau Seminary [IN]; and **$3,500** to Metropolitan Opera [NY]. ■**PUBLICATIONS:** None ■ **WEBSITE:** None ■**E-MAIL:** None ■**APPLICATION POLICIES & PROCEDURES:** No grants awarded to individuals.

O+D+T Jeremiah Patrick O'Grady (T+Donor+Con) — Kathleen A. O'Grady (T)

SE-492 O'Neill Foundation, The
980 Stoke Road
Villanova 19085 (Montgomery County)
AMV $124,260 **FYE** 12-99 **(Gifts Received** $87,344)

MI-41-43
Phone Unlisted **FAX** None
EIN 31-1496748 **Year Created** 1996
1 **Grant of** $12,500

Sole grant to Rosemont School of the Holy Child (scholarship fund). ■**PUBLICATIONS:** None ■**WEBSITE:** None ■**E-MAIL:** None ■**APPLICATION POLICIES & PROCEDURES:** Grant requests may be submitted in a letter at any time.

O+D+T Miriam O'Neill (P+Donor+Con) — Michael P. Haney, Esq. (S+F+D) — J. Brian O'Neill (Donor)

SE-493 Oberkotter Foundation
c/o Schnader Harrison Segal & Lewis
1600 Market Street, Suite 3600
Philadelphia 19103 (Philadelphia County)
AMV $195,278,685 **FYE** 11-00 **(Gifts Received** $31,505,476)

MI-14-15-31-32-41
Phone 215-751-2601 **FAX** 215-751-2678
EIN 23-2686151 **Year Created** 1985
56 **Grants totaling** $21,334,724

Nationwide giving primarily for oral deaf education, deafness research, or diabetes research/clinical purposes; ten Pa. grants. High Pa. grant of **$292,000** to American Institute for Voice & Ear Research [Philadelphia] (tinnitus/research). **$966,658** to Children's Hospital of Philadelphia (community-based program/childhood communication center). **$300,000** to Juvenile Diabetes Foundation [Bala Cynwyd] (general support). **$250,000** to MCP/Hahnemann U. (gene therapy research). **$215,000** to Temple U. Hospital (child hearing intervention initiative). **$156,150** to Diabetes Education & Research Center [Philadelphia] (patient guidance program). **$100,000** to Helen Beebe Speech & Hearing Center [Easton] (matching grant). **$75,000** to Main Line Academy (general support). **$67,000** to DePaul Institute [Pittsburgh] (speech pathologist). **$50,000** to Alzheimer's Disease & Related Disorders Assn. [Philadelphia] (general support). **Out-of-state** giving, mostly for multiple purposes, includes high grant of **$4,586,054** to Clarke School for the Deaf [MA]; **$1,285,000** to Foundation for Hearing Research [CA]; **$1,222,000** to The Moog Center for Deaf Education [MO]; **$1,017,658** to Advanced Education Services/Children's Choice for Hearing & Talking [CA]; **$806,909** to St. Joseph Institute for the Deaf [MO]; **$737,000** to Alexander Graham Bell Assn. for the Deaf [DC]; and other grants **$45,000-$521,000** to hearing/deafness organizations in AZ, CA, CO, DC, IL, LA, MA, ME, MI, MN, MO, MS, MT, NC, NE, NH, NJ, NM, NY, OH, OR, TN, WA, Canada, and England. — In addition, the Foundation supports an extensive public relations program on deaf education (videos, brochures, etc.) and sponsors a website, www.oraldeafed.org. ■**PUBLICATIONS:** None ■**WEBSITE:** None ■**E-MAIL:** gnofer@schnader.com ■**APPLICATION POLICIES & PROCEDURES:** The Foundation reports that nationwide giving is generally limited to oral deafness education, deafness research, and diabetes research/clinical programs; most grants are for general support, special projects, or matching grants; multiyear grants are awarded. In most instances grants are made on the initiative of the Trustees. Grant requests may be submitted in a letter (2 pages maximum) at any time; include organization and project budgets, list of major funding sources, Board member list, appropriate background information, and IRS tax-exempt status documentation. Site visits sometimes are made to organizations being considered for a grant.

O+D+T George H. Nofer, J.D. (Executive Director+Co-T+Con) — Mildred L. Oberkotter [CA] (Co-T+Donor) — Bruce A. Rosenfield, Esq. (Associate Executive Director) — Donors: Louise Oberkotter Trust and Estate of Paul Oberkotter

---

SE-494 Oiseaux (Les) Foundation
323 Llandrillo Road
Bala Cynwyd   19004   (Montgomery County)
AMV $4,061,231   **FYE** 12-01   **(Gifts Received** $0)

MI-52-63
Phone 610-668-8856 **FAX** None
EIN 25-6642155   **Year Created** 1999
4 **Grants totaling** $13,650

About two-thirds local/Pa. giving. High grant of **$8,000** to Vox Ama Deus. **$600** to Ardmore United Methodist Church. One small local contribution. **Out-of-state** grant: **$5,000** to a Methodist church in OH. — In the prior year, grants included **$17,850** to Ardmore United Methodist Church and **$1,250** to Opera Company of Philadelphia. ■**PUBLICATIONS:** None ■**WEBSITE:** None ■**E-MAIL:** None ■**APPLICATION POLICIES & PROCEDURES:** Information not available.

O+D+T Kenneth B. Dunn (P+T+Con) — Amy Dunn (T) — Brett Dunn (T) — Pamela R. Dunn (T) — Chester Spatt (T)

SE-495 Orange Foundation
P.O. Box 175
Hatboro   19040   (Montgomery County)
AMV $501,475   **FYE** 6-01   **(Gifts Received** $455)

MI-12-15-31-32-43-54
Phone 215-887-6299 **FAX** None
EIN 23-1261147   **Year Created** 1996
10 **Grants totaling** $19,500

Mostly local giving. High grant of **$10,000** to Maple Village. **$3,000** to American Cancer Society. **$2,000** to American Heart Assn. **$1,000** to Balch Institute for Ethnic Studies. Five scholarships, **$500-$4,000,** awarded to local college students. **Out-of-state** grant: **$2,000** to Shriners Hospital for Children [FL]. ■**PUBLICATIONS:** None ■**WEBSITE:** None ■**E-MAIL:** None ■**APPLICATION POLICIES & PROCEDURES:** The Foundation reports that giving primarily focuses on the Hatboro area.

O+D+T Howard M. Gaul [Oreland] (P+D+Con) — Frederick E. Stewart [Trappe] (VP+D) — Walter C. Wilson [DE] (S+D) — William E. Orr [Ambler] (F+D) — and 11 additional directors

---

SE-496 Orleans Family Charitable Foundation
c/o Orleans Construction Company
3333 Street Road, Suite 101
Bensalem   19020   (Bucks County)
AMV $151,353   **FYE** 12-00   **(Gifts Received** $0)

MI-12-22-32-41-42-54-62
Phone 215-245-7500 **FAX** 215-533-2352
EIN 23-2868577   **Year Created** 1997
40+ **Grants totaling** $42,475

About three-fourths local giving; some grants comprise multiple payments. High grant of **$11,250** to Philadelphia Museum of Art. **$8,000** to Jewish Federation of Greater Philadelphia. **$4,210** to Beth Sholom Congregation. **$1,000-$1,500** each to Benchmark School, Drexel U., Friends of Samuel Paley Day Care Center, Jewish Community Centers of Greater Philadelphia, and Linda Creed Breast Cancer Foundation. **$800** to The Baldwin School. Other local contributions **$25-$500** for various purposes. **Out-of-state** giving includes **$5,000** to Jewish Federation of Palm Beach [FL] and **$1,000** to Simon Wiesenthal Center [CA]. ■**PUBLICATIONS:** None. ■**WEBSITE:** None ■**E-MAIL:** None ■**APPLICATION POLICIES & PROCEDURES:** Information not available.

O+D+T Jeffrey P. Orleans [Bryn Mawr] (T+Donor+Con) — Selma H. Orleans [FL] (T+Donor)

SE-497 Orleans (Jeffrey P.) Charitable Foundation
c/o Orleans Construction Company
3333 Street Road, Suite 101
Bensalem   19020   (Bucks County)
AMV $79,824   **FYE** 12-00   **(Gifts Received** $98,716)

MI-11-22-25-31-32-41-42-52-53-54-62-72-82
Phone 215-245-7500 **FAX** 215-533-2352
EIN 23-2870134   **Year Created** 1997
100+ **Grants totaling** $230,571

Mostly local giving. High grant of **$52,000** to Jewish Federation of Philadelphia. **$50,000** to Federation Allied Jewish Appeal. **$20,000** each to Jewish Employment & Vocational Services and Pa. Academy of the Fine Arts. **$10,200** to United Way of SE Pa. **$7,000-$7,500** each to Baldwin School, Main Line Reform Temple Beth Elohim. **$5,000-$5,500** each to Jewish Community Centers of Greater Philadelphia, Philadelphia Police Museum, and Prince Music Theatre. **$2,000-$2,800** each to Albert Einstein Healthcare, Anti-Defamation League, National Liberty Museum, and Philadelphia Museum of Art. **$1,000** each to City of Hope, National Organization on Hearing Research, Philadelphia Committee to End Homelessness, Philadelphia Zoo, and U. of Pa. Smaller local contributions for cultural, educational, medical, Jewish and other purposes. **Out-of-state** giving includes **$16,667** to Weizmann Institute of Science [Israel] and many smaller contributions. ■**PUBLICATIONS:** None ■**WEBSITE:** None ■**E-MAIL:** None ■**APPLICATION POLICIES & PROCEDURES:** Information not available.

O+D+T Jeffrey P. Orleans [Bryn Mawr] (T+Donor+Con)

SE-498 Otto Company, The
9006 Crefeld Street
Philadelphia   19118   (Philadelphia County)
AMV $380,490   **FYE** 12-00   **(Gifts Received** $0)

MI-12-23-41-42-43-52-53
Phone 215-247-3113 **FAX** None
EIN 23-6296932   **Year Created** 1931
15 **Grants totaling** $19,943

Mostly local giving. High grant of **$3,000** to Barnes Foundation. **$1,000** each to Friends of the Fountain, Germantown Friends School, Haverford College, Pa. Ballet, Settlement Music School/Germantown, and White-Williams Scholars. Two grants for relief of indigent/distressed persons. Other smaller local contributions. **Out-of-state** giving includes **$3,000** to Children of Bedford [CT] and **$1,000** to Southern Poverty Law Center [AL]. ■**PUBLICATIONS:** None ■**WEBSITE:** None ■**E-MAIL:** None ■**APPLICATION POLICIES & PROCEDURES:** The Foundation reports that unsolicited requests for funds are not encouraged.

O+D+T David Mallery (P+D+Donor+Con) — Judith P. Mallery (VP+D) — Robert L. Bast, Esq. [Ambler] (AS+F+D)

SE-499 Pacifico Family Foundation
c/o Pacifico Ford, Inc.
6701 Essington Ave.
Philadelphia 19153 (Philadelphia County)
AMV $234,883 **FYE** 12-00 (**Gifts Received** $50,000)

MI-22-31-41-42-43-61
Phone 215-492-1700 **FAX** 215-492-1656
EIN 22-2782890 **Year Created** 1988
38 **Grants totaling** $15,875

All local giving; all grants are for general purposes. High grant of **$2,500** to Drexel U. **$1,000-$1,500** each to Furness High School, Lower Merion Scholarship Fund, St. John Neumann Scholarship, St. Maria Goretti High School, South Philadelphia High School, and Thomas Jefferson Hospital. Other contributions **$100-$500** for Catholic churches/organizations/schools and various purposes. ■**PUBLICATIONS:** None ■**WEBSITE:** None ■**E-MAIL:** None ■**APPLICATION POLICIES & PROCEDURES:** Grant requests may be submitted in a letter at any time; describe the project in detail and state the funding requested. No grants awarded to individuals.

O+D+T Kerry T. Pacifico, Sr. (D+Con) — Joseph R. Pacifico (D+Donor) Corporate donor: Pacifico Airport Valet Partnership

---

SE-500 Packman Family Foundation
214 Sycamore Avenue
Merion 19066 (Montgomery County)
AMV $425,320 **FYE** 12-00 (**Gifts Received** $0)

MI-11-15-22-29-31-41-42-54-62
Phone 610-623-2100 **FAX** 610-667-7883
EIN 22-2781594 **Year Created** 1986
154 **Grants totaling** $64,678

Mostly local giving. High grant of **$18,000** to Federation Allied Jewish Appeal. **$17,932** to Har Zion Temple. **$5,000** to Lankenau Hospital Foundation. **$4,000** to Philadelphia Geriatric Center. **$3,500** to Perelman Jewish Day School. **$1,000-$1,600** each to Akiba Hebrew Academy, Philadelphia Futures, Philadelphia Museum of Art, Red Cross, United Way of SE Pa., and University of the Sciences in Philadelphia. Other local and out-of-state contributions **$25-$550** for various purposes. ■**PUBLICATIONS:** None ■**WEBSITE:** None ■**E-MAIL:** None ■**APPLICATION POLICIES & PROCEDURES:** Grant requests may be submitted in an informal letter at any time; include IRS tax-exempt status documentation; only one request per year will be accepted. No grants are awarded to individuals.

O+D+T Dr. Elias W. Packman (T+Donor+Con)

SE-501 Patman (Maxine) Charitable Trust
820 Pine Hill Road
King of Prussia 19406 (Montgomery County)
AMV $427,920 **FYE** 12-00 (**Gifts Received** $0)

MI-33-42-52
Phone 610-687-2941 **FAX** None
EIN 31-1578453 **Year Created** 1998
4 **Grants totaling** $15,600

Mostly local giving. High grant of **$5,400** to Curtis Institute of Music (education program). **$5,000** to Psycholegal Institute (research). **$3,000** to Cabrini College (education program). **Out-of-state** grant: **$2,200** to Wild Ginger Philharmonic [NY] (education program). ■**PUBLICATIONS:** None ■**WEBSITE:** None ■**E-MAIL:** None ■**APPLICATION POLICIES & PROCEDURES:** Grant requests may be submitted in writing at any time; detail the proposed program, including estimates of time, material, and technical support needed.

O+D+T Wilhelmina M. Hardee (T+Donor+Con) — Wayne Hardee (T+Donor)

SE-502 Paul Family Foundation
c/o Queen Village Animal Hospital
323 Bainbridge Street
Philadelphia 19147 (Philadelphia County)
AMV $773,995 **FYE** 12-98 (**Gifts Received** $0)

MI-72
Phone 215-925-5753 **FAX** 215-925-6414
EIN 23-2893913 **Year Created** 1997
43 **Grants totaling** $24,689

All giving for animal humane purposes. High grant of **$5,500** to CARE/Compassionate Animal Relief Effort. **$800** to The Spayed Club. **$750** to Philly PAWS. Other local and out-of-state contributions **$150-$1,000** for same purposes. ■**PUBLICATIONS:** None ■**WEBSITE:** None ■**E-MAIL:** hwvmd@aol.com ■**APPLICATION POLICIES & PROCEDURES:** Information not available.

O+D+T Howard Wellens, DVM (T+Con) — John H.L. Paul (T)

SE-503 Pavoni (Louis G. & Karen A.) Foundation
960 Catfish Lane
Pottstown 19464 (Montgomery County)
AMV $155,982 **FYE** 12-00 (**Gifts Received** $30,000)

MI-22-63
Phone 610-705-5779 **FAX** None
EIN 23-2432421 **Year Created** 1986
6 **Grants totaling** $44,550

About one-third local giving; all grants are for general operations. High local grant of **$8,350** to Morning Star Fellowship [Bechtelsville]. **$6,000** to Good Works, Inc. [Coatesville]. Other small contributions. **Out-of-state** grant: **$30,000** to Marriage Ministries International [CO]. ■**PUBLICATIONS:** None ■**WEBSITE:** None ■**E-MAIL:** None ■**APPLICATION POLICIES & PROCEDURES:** No grants awarded to individuals.

O+D+T Karen A. Pavoni (P+T+Donor+Con)

SE-504 Pearl (Regina) Foundation, The
560 South Bryn Mawr Ave.
Bryn Mawr 19010   (Delaware County)

MI-22-62
Phone 610-525-7373 **FAX** None
EIN 23-7787120   **Year Created** 1994

AMV $421   **FYE** 11-00   (**Gifts Received** $25,863)   1 **Grant of** $26,063

Sole grant to Golden Slipper Club & Charities which has been the only grantee in recent years. ■**PUBLICATIONS:** None ■**WEBSITE:** None ■**E-MAIL:** None ■**APPLICATION POLICIES & PROCEDURES:** Information not available.

O+D+T Michael S. Haber (D+Donor+Con) — Lois S. Haber (D+Donor)

SE-505 Penn (William) Foundation
Two Logan Square, 11th Floor
100 North 18th Street
Philadelphia 19103
           (Philadelphia County)

MI-12-13-14-15-16-17-18-20-24-25-29-35-41
44-45-51-52-53-54-55-56-57-71-79-81-83
84-85
Phone 215-988-1830 **FAX**|215-988-1823
EIN 23-1503488   **Year Created** 1945

AMV $1,047,720,982   **FYE** 12-01   (**Gifts Received** $17,260)   244 **Grants totaling** $64,193,032

Most giving focuses on the Philadelphia area and Camden County, NJ, excepting environmental grants which are awarded to eastern Pa. and NJ. *Note: The Grants Totaling figure above refers to total grants payments in 2001; the following were newly appropriated grants in 2001.* Grants are for one year or less, except as noted. ***CHILDREN, YOUTH & FAMILY GRANTS ($23,343,995—46%):*** **$1,298,603** to United Way of SE Pa. (Center for Youth Development-2 years). **$1,115,954** to Temple U. (Healthcare Connection Cluster/violence intervention system-3+ years). **$985,000** to U. of Pa./Center for Greater Philadelphia (advocacy with corporations-unions re school reform-3 years). **$984,500** to The Reinvestment Fund (Workforce Connections program-2 years). **$755,093** to Children's Hospital of Philadelphia Foundation (Healthcare Connection Cluster/violence intervention system-3 years). **$746,946** to Thomas Jefferson U. (Healthcare Connection Cluster/violence intervention system-3 years). **$601,928** to Temple U. (Pathways to Desistance project-3 years). **$598,400-$600,000** each to Children's Hospital of Philadelphia Foundation (impaired infants intervention program-3 years), Philadelphia High School Academies (transition-to-work program support), and U. of Pa. (develop database on Philadelphia children re improving school readiness-14 mos.). **$552,242** to Albert Einstein Healthcare Network (Healthcare Connection Cluster/violence intervention system-3 years). **$541,256** to Philadelphia Health Management Corp. (Healthcare Connection Cluster/violence intervention system-3 years). **$495,000** to YMCA of Philadelphia & Vicinity (West Philadelphia branch capital campaign). **$487,245** to Education Law Center-Pa. (expanded Pa. School Reform Network-3 years). **$400,000** to People's Emergency Center (Families First Center). **$396,000** to Planned Parenthood of Chester County (Coatesville Center for Community Health construction). **$387,568** to Greater Philadelphia Urban Affairs Coalition (Work-Stream/Twilight Program expansion). **$385,000** to Philadelphia Education Fund (strategic planning re School District changes). **$351,890** to Maternity Care Coalition (Women's Health/Children's Future program-2 years). **$346,500** to City Year, Inc. (improved recruitment-retention-3 years). **$338,247** to Philadelphia Physicians for Social Responsibility (family violence prevention-intervention policies re city agencies-3 years). **$330,000** each to The Attic Youth Center (expanded services) and Evangelical Lutheran Church in America (SE Philadelphia youth program network expansion-3 years). **$323,070** to Greater Philadelphia Urban Affairs Coalition (Anti-Drug/Anti-Violence Network strategic planning-2 years). **$300,000** to U. of Pa./Dept. of Sociology (Philadelphia Educational Longitudinal Study-2 years). **$293,700** to Harold Oliver Davis Memorial Baptist Church (youth development initiative-3 years). **$275,000** to Philadelphia Physicians forSocial Responsibility (Peaceful Posse program-3 years). **$260,000-$267,300** each to Children's Village (Chinatown child care renovation-expansion), and Norris Square Neighborhood Assn. (Children's Center construction/startup). **$260,000** to Institute for the Development of African American Youth (capacity building-2 years). **$249,700** to Philadelphia Youth Tennis (youth tennis center construction). **$247,500** to Big Picture Alliance (after school teen enrichment program). **$220,000** each to The Enterprise Center (enhance organizational operations-2 years) and the School District of Philadelphia (Freedom Summer School program). **$178,805** to Philadelphia Education Fund (School Leadership Collaborative). **$150,183** to Temple U. (delinquent youth re court-mandated programs-2 years). **$148,500** to Philadelphia Student Union (student leadership training in three high schools). **$110,306** to Planned Parenthood Assn. of Bucks County (sexuality education for youths-2 years). **$80,000-$82,500** each to African-American Interdenominational Ministries (volunteer mentors program), AIDS Law Project of Pa. (Standby Guardianship Initiative), Alliance Organizing Project for Education Reform (parental involvement in schools/teacher unions), Domestic Violence Center of Chester County (expanded counseling services), Educating Children for Parenting (capacity building), Empowerment Group (strengthen Empowerment Painters-2 years), Greater Philadelphia Urban Affairs Coalition (expanded mural painting program), La Comunidad Hispana (program support), MANNA/Metropolitan AIDS Neighborhood Nutrition Alliance(technology upgrade), OICs of America (develop strategic fundraising plan), Public/Private Ventures (Youth Violence Reduction Project support), Tenants Action Group (lead poisoning prevention program), Unemployment Information Center (Mothers on the Move project), Wistar Institute (biomedical technician training for disadvantaged students), Women's Assn. for Women's Alternatives (welfare reform impact study), Youth Empowerment Services (school-leavers program planning), and Youth Service, Inc. (West Philadelphia crisis nurseries support). **$71,500-$74,685** each to Greater Philadelphia Urban Affairs Coalition (Delaware Valley Financial Literacy Coalition), Resources for Human Development (Philadelphia Public School Network coordinator position), and U. of Pa./Center for the Study of Youth Policy (assessment of statewide juvenile justice advocacy projects-18 mos.). **$62,000-$66,000** each to Crime Prevention Assn. of Philadelphia (improved youth-serving operations), Frankford Group Ministry Community Development Corp. (career services program), Research for Action (research on preschool children), Terry Lynne Lokoff Foundation (Mobile Children's Safety Center), and Training for Change (young activists leadership training). **$45,650** to Kennett Square MainStreet Assn. (Kennett Square Center construction). **$41,250** to Greater Philadelphia Urban Affairs Coalition (leadership training for parents re school reform). **$33,000** to Greater Philadelphia Urban Affairs Coalition (charter school formula analysis). **$27,500-$28,050** each to First United Methodist Church of Germantown (after school program for 9th graders-3 years), and Philadelphia Health Management Corp. (Women's Death Row Review Team). **$9,900-$10,000** each to Big Brothers/Big Sisters of Chester County (Phoenixville outreach program) and U.S. Catholic Conference (North Philadelphia ESL/after school programs). — *Summer Youth Career Exploration Program* grants, all for 6 months: **$381,042** to Greater Philadelphia Urban Affairs Coalition; **$300,203** to Greater Philadelphia Federation of Settlements; **$159,667** to The Philadelphia Foundation (SYCP administration); **$132,962** to Boys & Girls Clubs of Metropolitan Philadelphia; **$68,169** to Community Action Agency of Delaware County; **$64,228** to Crime Prevention Assn. of Philadelphia; **$56,500** to Impact Services Corp.; **$39,061** to Korean Community Development Services Center; **$34,941** to Allegheny West Foundation; **$29,130** to Mt. Airy USA; **$21,097** to Centro Nueva Creacion/New Creation Community Center; and **$2,702** to Cambodian Assn. of Greater Philadelphia. **Out-of-state** grants included **$1,350,000** to Public Education Fund Network [DC] (statewide campaign re comprehensive school reform); **$500,000** to Manpower Demonstration Research Corp. [NY] (Project on Devolution & Urban Change—Philadelphia component); **$255,310** to Brady Center to Prevent Gun Violence [DC] (developing the Pa. Million Mom March State Council); **$202,400** to Cross City Campaign for Urban School Reform [IL] (Indicators Project on Education—Philadelphia portion); and other grants under **$50,000** to Camden, NJ and other locations. ***ENVIRONMENT & COMMUNITIES GRANTS*** **($19,603,695—26%):** **$5,000,000** to The Reinvestment Fund (loans-finance products for targeted development in Philadelphia/Camden-10 years). **$2,000,000** to United Way of SE Pa. (Philadelphia Neighborhood Development Collaborative-3 years). **$1,650,000** to Natural Lands Trust (enhanced stewardship of Delaware River watershed/Pa. Highlands-3 years). **$482,790** to Stroud Water Research Center (Schuylkill River watershed research/training-technical assistance-3 years). **$407,000** to National Audubon Society [Harrisburg] (expanded Bird Area program/Kittatinny Conservation Planning Project-2 years). **$374,000** to Central Philadelphia Development Corp. (neighborhood marketing initiative demonstration-2 years). **$308,330** to Alliance for the Chesapeake Bay (technical assistance for local watershed organizations-2 years). **$300,000** each to Pa. Horticultural Society (vacant/open land management pilot program-18 mos.) and U. of Pa./School of Social Work (enhanced usage of Neighborhood Information System-3 years). **$253,000** to Temple U. (Center for Public Policy re developing a regional immigration agenda/strategy-2 years). **$165,000** each to Citizens for Pennsylvania's Future [Harrisburg] (initiative re environmental impact of factory farming-2 years), Philadelphia Interfaith Action (coalition building of congregations/organizations re smart growth issues-2 years), and Phoenix Land Recycling Company [Harrisburg] (brownfield proprieties redevelopment). **$154,000** to Philadelphia Assn. of Community Development Corporations (expanded neighborhood stabilizing/revitalizing programs-2 years). **$150,700** to Green Valleys Assn. (Sustainable Watershed Management program-2 years). **$121,000** to Montgomery County LandsTrust (capacity building re smart growth/watershed protection-2 years). **$110,000** to Village of Arts & Humanities (Germantown Ave. green corridor). **$81,400-$82,500** each to Academy of Natural Sciences (Patrick Center for Environmental Research-2 years), Awbury Arboretum (enhanced communications/marketing), Fairmount Park Foundation (strategic planning), Frankford Group Ministry (neighborhood greening projects), French & Pickering Creeks Conservation Trust (development director support-3 years), Hawk Mountain Sanctuary Assn. (land acquisition), and The Reinvestment Fund (feasibility studies re private sector investment products).**$77,000** each to Enterprising Environmental Solutions [Pittsburgh] (web-based database of sustainable development investors), Greater Philadelphia Chamber of Commerce Regional Foundation (Parkside neighborhood redevelopment plan), and PIDC/Regional Development Corp. (industry-CDCs partnership in two North Philadelphia neighborhoods). **$72,600** to Chester County Community Foundation (community attitudes study re smart growth). **$68,200** to Cobbs Creek Community Environmental Education Center (organizational capacity building-2 years). **$55,000** each to Clean Water Fund (grassroots advocacy re recycling), Greater Philadelphia First Corp. (comparative analysis of knowledge-based economies), Pa. Environmental Council (promote Delaware Riverfront landscape remediation/sustainable development), Pottstown Area Industrial Development (develop-promote smart growth ordinances), SEDA-Council of Governments [Union County] (Susquehanna Greenway concept plan), and Women's Health & Environmental Network (medical waste-incineration demonstration project in four hospitals). **$47,850-$49,225** each to Berks County Conservancy (Kittatinny Ridge preservation), New Manayunk Corp. (Lower Venice Island park feasibility study), and RFK Riverfront Community Development Corp. (Clean & Green Corps in Richmond, Fishtown & Kensington). **$44,000** to Jewish Employment & Vocational Service (pilot home maintenace training project). **$33,000** each to Camphill Village Kimberton Hills (watershed stewardship program) and Greensgrow Philadelphia Project (hydroponic farm model). **$27,500** each to Bicycle Coalition of the Delaware Valley (regional bicycle map), Fair Hill Burial Group Corp. (physical improvements/organize community support), and The Nature Conservancy/Pa. Chapter (Piedmont landscape conservation area plan). **Out-of-state Environment & Communities grants** included **$1,650,000** to The Nature Conservancy/NJ Chapter (land acquistion-management in threatened natural areas); **$1,200,000** to Trust for Public Land [NJ] (develop greenway corridor DelawareRiver to Barnegat Bay-2 years); **$660,000** to NJ Conservation Foundation (land preservation efforts in Delaware Bay Watershed/Delaware River Corridor-2 years); **$341,000** each to Delaware & Raritan Greenway [NJ] (develop greenway corridors-2 years) and Housing & Community Development Network of NJ (expanded technical assistance in Camden-2 years); **$330,000** to Delaware River Basin Commission (public participation re Delaware River Basin water resource plan-2 years); **$292,600** to Project for Public Spaces [NY] (Vine Street Expressway planning-18 months); **$250,250** to Assn. of NJ Environmental Commissions (technical assistance to South Jersey environmental commissions); and other smaller grants to NJ, DC, MN, and RI , mostly for environmental grants related to the Delaware Valley or NJ. ***ARTS & CULTURE GRANTS*** **($13,630,106—16%):** **$1,306,514** to U. of the Arts (Center for Professional Development & Community Education-3 years). **$887,095** to Greater Philadelphia Tourism Marketing Corp.(regional cultural marketing-3 years). **$811,234** to Greater Philadelphia Cultural Alliance (regional cultural planning/data collection-3 years). **$777,299** to Franklin Institute (emergency fire stairwell construction-2 years). **$706,262** to Rosenbach Museum & Library (renovations/structural upgrading-3 years). **$639,640** to College of Physicians of Philadelphia (historical library conservation, etc.-3 years). **$550,000** each to Philadelphia Orchestra (increased marketing/PR-3 years) and Settlement Music School (technology upgrade-2 years). **$519,750** to American Ballet Competition (Dance Celebration/festival/holiday production-3 years). **$500,869** to The Wilma Theatre (guest artist housing-renovation/capital needs-2 years). **$449,790** to Philadelphia Fringe Festival (capacity building-3 years).**$378,393** to People's Light & Theatre Company (Main Stage Lobby expansion-3 years). **$348,661** to Asociacion de Musicos Latino Americanos (Latin School of the Arts salaries-3 years). **$330,000** each to Curtis Institute of Music (Curtis Hall redesign-construction) and Scribe Video Center (capacity building-3 years). **$302,500** to Village of Arts & Humanities (adjacent properties renovations). **$247,500** to Philadelphia Chamber Music Society (Kimmel Center performances/expanded programming-3 years). **$220,000** to Chester County Historical Society (Underground Railroad exhibition-2 years). **$200,000** to Philadelphia Singers (operating support). **$192,500** to

Abington Art Center (capacity building-3 years). **$183,599** to Philadelphia Folklore Project (Community Projects program-3 years). **$176,550** to Bucks County Historical Society (expanded education program-3 years). **$165,000** each to Bristol Riverside Theater (marketing consultant-2 years) and Taller Puertorriqueno (capacity building-3 years). **$144,100** to WITF [Harrisburg] (collaboration program with WHYY re regional historical markers).**$115,500-$115,610** each to Brandywine Graphic Workshop (salaries-2 years), Clay Studio (development/PR positions-3 years), and Greater Philadelphia Chamber of Commerce Regional Foundation (Arts & Business Council services-3 years). **$81,502-$82,500** each to Academy of Vocal Arts (replace lighting),Creative Artists Network (exhibitions of local emerging artists-3 years), Mann Music Center (anniversary concert), Old Christ Church Preservation Trust (Neighborhood House design), Philadelphia Sketch Club (safety-related repairs), Red Heel Theater Company (designer fees), and U. of the Arts (Arts in Education Partnership expansion). **$77,000** to National Liberty Museum (expanded families' program-2 years). **$75,460** to Drexel U. (research on public funding for arts). **$66,000** to Mill at Anselma Preservation & Educational Trust (water wheel restoration-3 years). **$64,405** to Historic Rittenhousetown (exterior restoration). **$61,875** to Moore College of Art (local artists exhibition/curatorial assistantship). **$55,000** to Chester Springs Studio (salary support-2 years). **$38,500** to ArtReach (guide for people with disabilities-2 years). **$37,950** to Fairmount Park Historic Preservation Trust (interpretive signage). **$33,000** each to Friends of Lemon Hill (mansion repairs) and Pottstown Symphony Orchestra (school concerts expansion). **$27,500** each to BushfireTheatre of Performing Arts (production expense-2 years) and Hatboro-Horsham Educational Foundation (K-12 performing arts curriculum-2 years). **$22,000** each to Art Sanctuary (North Philadelphia programming-outreach), Closely Watched Films (accessible restroom construction), and Moonstone (Latin American arts festival). **$19,800** to Schwenkfelder Library. **$15,000-$16,500** each to Act II Playhouse (capacity building), Philadelphia Dance Company (conference-festival in Poland), and Pig Iron Theatre Company (salary support). **$10,000-$11,000** each to 1812 Productions (theater salaries), Headlong Dance Theater (salaries/marketing), Hedgerow Theatre (general operating support), Lantern Theater Company (automated ticketing system), Mum Puppettheatre (master puppet builder), Regional Performing Arts Center (student transportation to performance), and Theatre Double Repertory Company (salary support). **$5,000-$6,600** each to Creative Artists Network (printmaking exhibit), Philadelphia Gay Men's Chorus (training/marketing), and Theater Catalyst, Inc. (operating support). Two smaller local grants. **Out-of-state arts/cultural grants** include **$$750,930** to Nonprofit Finance Fund [NY] (Arts Comprehensive Capitalization Program re Philadelphia-area cultural groups capacity building) and **$78,210** to Theatre Communications Group [NY] (membership/conference attendance of Philadelphia theatre groups). *INTERDISCIPLI-NARY GRANTS* **($12,750,452-10%): $3,300,000** to Eastern National (Independence National Historic Park education facility-3 years). **$1,210,000** to United Way of SE Pa. (general operating support re-grants to children/family/youth nonprofits-2 years). **$803,000** to The Philadelphia Foundation (support for re-grants to emerging/other local nonprofits-2 years). **$384,977** to WHYY (demonstration project to develop community service model re news/public affairs). **$322,300** to LaSalle U./Nonprofit Management Development Center (expanded/subsidized technical service/consulting). **$257,435** to Bread & Roses Community Fund (grassroots leadership training program-3 years). **$250,000** to United Way of SE Pa. (September 11th Fund). **$220,000** to The Philadelphia Foundation (planning/development re National Center for the American Revolution, Valley Forge). **$146,652** to Womens Way (general operation support re-grants to member organizations-2 years). **$110,000** each to Community Design Collaboration of AIA Philadelphia (expanded services to nonprofits-2 years) and Philadelphia Bar Foundation (support for re-grants to local nonprofits-2 years). **$82,500** to WHYY (independent study re community's need for WHYY's Learning Center). **$75,000** to Chester County Community Foundation (leadership transition support). **$66,000** to Executive Service Corps of the Delaware Valley (recruit/train additional volunteers-2 years). **$60,500** to Ben Franklin Technology Center of SE Pa. (Collegetown Project website). **$57,200** to Environmental Fund for Pa. (increased re-grants to environmental/conservation organizations-2 years). **$31,592** to Bread & Roses Community Fund (operating support-2 years). **$10,000** to Free Library of Philadelphia/Regional Foundation Center (operating support). **$6,600** to AIDS Fund (AIDS Walk sponsorship). **$5,060** to Black United Fund of Pa. (expand re-grant program). **Out-of-state** Interdisciplinary grants include **$753,000** to Nonprofit Finance Fund [NY] (expanded planning services to additional Philadelphia-area nonprofits); **$550,000** to Rockefeller Family Fund [CA] (expanded TechRocks technical assistance services to Philadelphia-area nonprofits); **$404,600** to Hispanics in Philanthropy [CA] (establish Philadelphia site re local Latino nonprofits-3 years); and **$55,000** to Rutgers U. Foundation [NJ] (technical assistance/training for Camden nonprofits). ■**PUBLICATIONS:** Annual Report with application guidelines; informational brochure ■**WEBSITE:** www.williampennfoundation.org ■**E-MAIL:** moreinfo@williampennfoundation.org ■**APPLICATION POLICIES & PROCE-DURES:** The Foundation reports that virtually all giving is limited to organizations located in and serving constituents within the Delaware Valley (five-county Philadelphia area and Camden County, NJ) in three grantmaking categories: **I. Arts & Culture**—giving priorities are to (a) enable the creation/presentation of high-quality artistic work; (b) provide support for artists in advancing their careers; (c) encourage active participation in the cultural life of the region; (d) preserve/promote the region's cultural assets; (e) create new cultural opportunities in/for a particular neighborhood/community; and (f) strengthen arts and cultural organizations in their core programs and administration. **II. Children, Youth & Families**—giving priorities are to promote (a) School Readiness (the physical, social, emotional, and cognitive well being of children, from prenatal to age six) to facilitate learning and a successful transition to school/academic success, and (b) Youth Development, to increase the ability of young people to make an effective transition to higher education and/or the work force. **III. Environment & Communities** grants are made throughout a larger geographic region (see web site for map) and giving priorities are to (a) protect/restore watersheds and related ecosystems; (b) stabilize/revitalize communities around existing infrastructure; and (c) promote smart growth and livable communities within the region. Prospective applicants should note that many 2001 grants were awarded before the Foundation's current strategic priorities were fully in place; consult the website for a current, in-depth description of Goals, Philosophy, Priorities, Objectives and Strategies for the three grantmaking categories, and for steps to take before submitting a proposal. The Foundation gives preference to proposed projects which will be (or are) supported by more than one funding source, as a demonstration of broad interest in the project. No grants are awarded to individuals or for scholarships/fellowships, nonpublic schools, sectarian religious activities, recreational programs, political lobbying or legislative activities, pass-through organizations, profit-making enterprises, medical research, mental health/mental retardation treatment programs, programs concerned with a particular disease or treatment of addictions, hospital capital projects, housing construction/rehabilitation, loans, program-related investments, debt reduction, or organizations which discriminate by race, creed, or sex. Prospective applicants are encouraged to visit the website's *Grant Center* to take the brief *Eligibility Quiz*, review the *Our Approach to Grantmaking* sections, and if eligible, register for a program-specific *Information Session* (scheduled every few weeks). In all cases, a Letter of Inquiry and/or conversation with a Foundation staff member is/are required before any proposal is submitted. Once an organization has been invited to submit a proposal, an applicant should download (copy+paste) the entire four-section proposal outline from the Foundation's website into a word processor and prepare the proposal following the outline. Proposals may be submitted at any time; mail one copy only together with the stipulated attachments. **Note:** Proposals following Delaware Valley Grantmakers Common Grant Application Form are *no* longer accepted.

O+D+T Kathryn J. Engebretson, Ph.D. (P+Con) — David W. Haas (C+D) — Frederick R. Haas (VC+S+D) — Carol A. Collier (D) — Joseph A. Dworetzky, Esq. (D) — Robert E. Hanrahan, Jr. (D) — Nancy B. Haas (D) — Ernest E. Jones, Esq. (D) — Thomas M. McKenna (D) — John P. Mulroney (D) — Terrie S. Rouse (D) — Gary Walker (D) — Lise Yasui (D)

SE-506 **Pennsylvania Fund, The**   MI-13-14-18-22-29-31-32-41-51-54-57-71-86
c/o Morse Partners Ltd.
100 Four Falls Corporate Center, Suite 205   **Phone** 610-397-0880 **FAX** None
West Conshohocken 19428   (Montgomery County)   **EIN** 23-2222176   **Year Created** 1982
AMV $2,037,539   **FYE** 6-01   **(Gifts Received** $0)   50 **Grants totaling** $640,250

About three-fourths local/Pa. giving. High grant of **$300,000** to Children's Hospital of Philadelphia. **$105,000** to The Shipley School. **$7,000** each to Gesu School and Planned Parenthood of Pa. **$6,000** to Paoli Memorial Hospital Foundation. **$5,000** each to Brandywine Conservancy, Fox Chase Cancer Center, WHYY, and Young Scholars Charter School. **$3,000** each to Franklin Institute and Philadelphia Museum of Art. **$2,000-$2,500** each to Boys & Girls Club of Philadelphia, Crossroads School, Teddy Sezna Memorial Foundation, and Willistown Conservation Trust. **$1,000-$1,500** each to Baker Industries, Commonwealth Foundation for Public Policy Alternatives, Pa. Ballet, People's Light & Theatre Company, Red Cross, and Salvation Army. Other local contributions **$500-$750** for similar purposes. **Out-of-state** giving includes **$75,000** to Boys & Girls Clubs of America [GA]; **$50,000** to Salisbury School [CT]; **$7,000** to National Center for Policy Analyses [TX]; and smaller grants/contributions to many states for similar purposes. ■**PUBLICATIONS:** None ■**WEBSITE:** None ■**E-MAIL:** None ■**APPLICATION POLICIES & PROCEDURES:** The Fund reports that giving is generally limited to charitable organizations already known to and of interest to the Trustees. No grants are awarded to individuals. Grant requests may be submitted in a brief letter at any time; include a financial statement and IRS tax-exempt status documentation.

O+D+T Peter C. Morse (T+Donor+Con) — Martha F. Morse (T+Donor)

SE-507 **Pepper Hollow Fund, The**   MI-13-41-42-43-52-55-62
1779 Oak Hill Drive   **Phone** 215-638-3500 **FAX** None
Huntingdon Valley 19066   (Montgomery County)   **EIN** 23-6411419   **Year Created** 1960
AMV $107,108   **FYE** 11-00   **(Gifts Received** $10,000)   33 **Grants totaling** $13,925

Mostly local giving. High grant of **$3,350** to Opera Company of Philadelphia. **$1,000-$1,250** each to Philadelphia Orchestra, Cheltenham Center for the Arts, and Community College of Philadelphia (scholarship fund). **$500-$700** each to Flyers Wives Fight for Lives, Big Brother/Big Sister Assn. of Philadelphia, Curtis Institute of Music, Friends Select School, and Reform Congregation of Keneseth Israel. Other smaller local and out-of-state contributions. ■**PUBLICATIONS:** None ■**WEBSITE:** None ■**E-MAIL:** None ■**APPLICATION POLICIES & PROCEDURES:** Grant requests may be submitted in writing at any time; include IRS tax-exempt status documentation.

O+D+T Benjamin Alexander, Jr. (T+Donor+Con) — Foundation donor: Fred J. Rosenau Foundation

---

SE-508 **Perelman (Jennie) Foundation**   MI-12-13-31-32-53-54
c/o Michael J. Cull, CPA
225 City Line Ave., Suite 14   **Phone** 610-660-8824 **FAX** None
Bala Cynwyd 19004   (Montgomery County)   **EIN** 23-6251650   **Year Created** 1952
AMV $5,216,995   **FYE** 2-00   **(Gifts Received** $0)   **Grants totaling** $17,248

No details available on grants. — In the prior year, 41 grants totaling **$27,120** were awarded; about half Pa. giving. High Pa. grant of **$3,300** to American Cancer Society. **$500-$600** each to Friends of Philadelphia Ronald McDonald House, Pa. Hospital, Philadelphia Art Alliance, Philadelphia Museum of Art, Urban Bridges at St. Gabriel's, and YJUH-Women's Board. Other smaller contributions. **Out-of-state** giving primarily to Palm Beach, FL for arts, cultural, health, Jewish, and other purposes. ■**PUBLICATIONS:** None ■**WEBSITE:** None ■**E-MAIL:** None ■**APPLICATION POLICIES & PROCEDURES:** Grant requests may be submitted in a letter or full proposal at any time; include a project budget and IRS tax-exempt status documentation.

O+D+T Raymond G. Perelman (T+Donor+Con) — Ruth Perelman (T) — Michael J. Cull, CPA (F) — Corporate donor: General Refractories Co.

SE-509 **Perelman (Raymond & Ruth) Community Foundation**   MI-15-18-22-31-32-51-52-53-54-55-62-81
c/o Michael J. Cull, CPA
225 City Line Ave., Suite 14   **Phone** 610-660-8824 **FAX** None
Bala Cynwyd 19004   (Montgomery County)   **EIN** 23-2820843   **Year Created** 1995
AMV $16,529,137   **FYE** 4-00   **(Gifts Received** $0)   28 **Grants totaling** $826,350

Mostly local giving; grants are for operating support except as noted. High grant of **$400,000** to Regional Performing Arts Center (building fund). **$100,000** to Lubavitcher Center. **$75,000** to National MS Society (research). **$50,000** to Philadelphia 2000 (cultural activities). **$25,000** each to Academy of Music and National Museum of American Jewish History. **$7,500** to American Cancer Society. **$1,000-$2,500** each to Albert Einstein Medical Center (renovations), Breast Health Institute, Foreign Policy Research Institute, Friends of Rittenhouse Square, Pa. Ballet, Pa. Hospital (renovations), Opera Guild of Philadelphia, Philadelphia Art Alliance, Philadelphia Geriatric Institute, Philadelphia Museum of Art, and Planned Parenthood of SE Pa. **Out-of-state** giving includes **$35,000** to Intercoastal Health Foundation [FL]; **$25,000** each to Ballet Florida and Red Cross; and **$10,000** each to Anti-Defamation League [NY], Palm Beach Community Chest [FL], Society of the Four Arts [FL], and Washington Institute [DC]. ■**PUBLICATIONS:** None ■**WEBSITE:** None ■**E-MAIL:** None ■**APPLICATION POLICIES & PROCEDURES:** Grant requests may be submitted in a letter or full proposal at any time; include a project budget and IRS tax-exempt status documentation.

O+D+T Raymond G. Perelman (T+Donor+Con) — Ruth Perelman (T) — Michael J. Cull, CPA (F)

SE-510 Perelman (Raymond & Ruth) Education Foundation   MI-31-51-52-53-54-55
c/o Michael J. Cull, CPA
225 City Line Ave., Suite 14   **Phone** 610-660-8824 **FAX** None
Bala Cynwyd 19004   (Montgomery County)   **EIN** 23-2819735   **Year Created** 1995
AMV $52,209,245   **FYE** 4-00   **(Gifts Received** $0)   12 **Grants totaling** $2,056,200

Mostly local giving. High grant of **$1,481,000** to Philadelphia Museum of Art. **$500,000** to Regional Performing Arts Center (building fund). **$25,000** to Children's Hospital of Philadelphia. **$5,000** to Pa. Ballet. **$2,500** to Albert Einstein Society. **$1,000** to Institute of Contemporary Art. **Out-of-state** giving includes **$25,000** to Good Samaritan & St. Mary's Medical Center [FL] and **$10,000** to Norton Museum of Art [FL]. ■**PUBLICATIONS:** None ■**WEBSITE:** None ■**E-MAIL:** None ■**APPLICA-TION POLICIES & PROCEDURES:** Grant requests may be submitted in a letter or full proposal at any time; include a project budget and IRS tax-exempt status documentation.

O+D+T Raymond G. Perelman (T+Donor+Con) — Ruth Perelman (T) — Michael J. Cull, CPA (F)

SE-511 Perelman (Raymond & Ruth) Judaica Foundation   MI-12-22-54-55-56-62-64-82
c/o Michael J. Cull, CPA
225 City Line Ave., Suite 14   **Phone** 610-660-8824 **FAX** None
Bala Cynwyd 19004   (Montgomery County)   **EIN** 23-2820841   **Year Created** 1995
AMV $36,066,807   **FYE** 4-00   **(Gifts Received** $0)   11 **Grants totaling** $1,556,980

Mostly local giving; grants are for operating support except as noted. High grant of **$550,000** to Philadelphia Museum of Art. **$500,000** to Gratz College. **$210,000** to Federation Allied Jewish Appeal. **$100,000** each to Lubavitcher Center and Regional Performing Arts Center (building fund). **$50,000** to Jewish Family & Children's Service. **$26,500** to National Museum of American Jewish History. **$12,980** to Beth Sholom Congregation (capital improvements). **Out-of-state** giving to FL and NY. ■**PUBLI-CATIONS:** None ■**WEBSITE:** None ■**E-MAIL:** None ■**APPLICATION POLICIES & PROCEDURES:** Grant requests may be submitted in a letter or full proposal at any time; include a project budget and IRS tax-exempt status documentation.

O+D+T Raymond G. Perelman (T+Donor+Con) — Ruth Perelman (T) — Michael J. Cull, CPA (F)

SE-512 Perilstein Foundation   MI-12-15-22-62
1001 City Ave., Apt. 1107WA   **Phone** 610-642-1196 **FAX** None
Wynnewood 19096   (Montgomery County)   **EIN** 23-6276160   **Year Created** 1971
AMV $210,846   **FYE** 10-00   **(Gifts Received** $0)   23 **Grants totaling** $12,215

Mostly local giving. High grant of **$2,000** to Jewish Federation of Greater Philadelphia. **$1,000-$1,100** each to Akiba Hebrew Academy, Federation Day Care Services, Har Zion Temple, and Philadelphia Geriatric Center. Other local and out-of-state giving, **$100-$850** for various purposes. ■**PUBLICATIONS:** None ■**WEBSITE:** None ■**E-MAIL:** None ■**APPLICATION POLICIES & PROCEDURES:** Grant requests may be submitted in a letter at any time before the October 15th deadline; provide a detailed project description, state the funding requested, and include an organizational budget and IRS tax-exempt status documentation. The Board awards grants at a November meeting.

O+D+T Betty Perilstein Krestal (T+Con) — Charlotte Kirschner (T) — Kenneth Kirschner (T) — Joel Perilstein, Esq. (T) — William Perilstein (T)

SE-513 Pew Charitable Trusts, The   MI-11-12-13-14-15-16-17-18-19-22-25-29-31-32
One Commerce Square, Suite 1700   35-41-42-49-51-52-53-54-55-56-57-64-71-72
2005 Market Street   79-83-85-86
Philadelphia 19103   **Phone** 215-575-9050 **FAX** 215-575-4939
                          (Philadelphia County)   **EIN** See below   **Year Created** 1947
AMV $4,338,580,605   **FYE** 12-01   **(Gifts Received** $0)   222 **Grants totaling** $230,135,400

Nationwide giving in 2001 was allocated to Environment (18%, 37 grants, $42,066,400); Venture Fund (15%, 20 grants, $34,221,000); Special Distribution Funding (14%, 8 grants, $32,430,000); Health & Human Services (14%, 76 grants, $31,705,000); Public Policy (13%, 23 grants, $30,141,900); Culture (11%, 31 grants, $24,564,000); Religion (9%, 12 grants, $20,254,500); and Education (6%, 15 grants, $13,754,000). (Note: The Grants Totaling figure above is for grants authorized in 2001—the total of grants disbursed in 2001 was $192,291,755. About 30% of giving was to the five-county Philadelphia area listed below; grants are for one year except as noted. *CULTURE GRANTS* (23 Pa. grants totaled $19,264,000). *The Philadelphia Program* grants: **$3,379,000** to Settlement Music School of Philadelphia (artistic development program for local music organization-3 years). **$2,000,000** to Franklin Institute (capital campaign for Science Museum exhibits). **$1,850,000** to Drexel U. (Philadelphia Cultural Management Initiative-2 years). **$750,000** to Nonprofit Finance Fund [NY] (Comprehensive Capitalization Initiative re SE Pa. arts institutions-2 years). **$357,000** to Greater Philadelphia Cultural Alliance (public relations campaign for local arts institutions). **$300,000** to Preservation Pa. (Philadelphia Intervention Fund re preservation of historic sites-3 years). **$250,000** to WHYY (Thomas Eakins program/arts reports on radio). *Philadelphia Cultural Leadership Program* grants (all for operating support, to recognize/reward artistic excellence and strong governance/management): **$2,400,000** to Philadelphia Museum of Art. **$1,200,000** to Philadelphia Orchestra. **$900,000** to Franklin Institute. **$825,000** to Philadelphia Zoo. **$675,000** to University Museum of Archaeology & Anthropology. **$405,000** to Please Touch Museum. **$315,000** to U. of Pa./Morris Arboretum. **$345,000** to Brandywine Conservancy. **$225,000** to Fabric Workshop. **$180,000** to The Clay Studio. **$150,000** to Taller Puertorriqueno. **$105,000** to Philadelphia Dance Alliance. **$54,000** each to Greater Philadelphia Chamber of Commerce Regional Foundation/Arts & Business Council of Greater Philadelphia, and Philadelphia La/wyers for the Arts. **$45,000** to The Print Center. **_HEALTH & HUMAN SERVICES GRANTS_** (61 Pa. grants totaled $7,258,000). **_Pew Fund for Health & Human Services in Philadelphia grants:_** **$1,022,000** to U. of Pa./Institute of Aging (assistance to Pew Fund grantees serving the elderly). **$345,000** to OMG Center for Collaborative Learning (educational series for local nonprofit health/human service providers-2 years). **$215,000** to Abrahamson Center for Jewish Life (Counseling for Caregivers Program-2 years; develop service effectiveness plan-1 year). **$208,000** to Mid-County Senior Services (Continuum of Independent Living Program-2 years). **$191,000** to Center in the Park (operating support/strengthen financial position-2 years). **$180,000** to Jewish Family & Children's Service of Philadelphia (Enhanced Home Services Project for frail elderly-2 years). **$175,000** each to St. Agnes Medical Center (Living Independently for Elders program/computer software-2 years) and U. of Pa. (Living Independently for Elders program/second site-2 years; computer software-1 year). **$155,000** to CARIE/Center for the Advocacy for the Rights & Interests of the Elderly (telephone support system for elderly-2 years). **$152,000** to Lincoln Center for Family & Youth (counseling services for elderly-2 years; develop long-range funding plan for Montco elderly service providers-1 year). **$130,000** each to COM-HAR (outreach mental health assessment/treatment services-2 years) and Temple U. (program to train/place college students to provide respite care for elderly infirm elderly and caregivers). **$125,000** to Thomas Jefferson U. (Senior Health Independence Program program-2 years). **$120,000-$122,000** each to American Cancer Society/Pa. Division (home health services-2 years), Family Service of Montgomery County (in-home MH counseling for elderly-2 years), and VNA Community Services (in-home personal care/homemaker support services-2 years; communications enhancements-1 year). **$113,000-$115,000** each to Delco Memorial Hospital (Senior Advocate Program-2 years), Health Promotion Council of SE Pa. (Healthy Living for Asian Elders project-2 years), Little Brothers—Friends of the Elderly (homebound visiting services/computer enhancements-2 years), Senior Citizen Judicare Project of Philadelphia (homeowners assistance program-2 years), and Senior Community Services (in-home recreational program for homebound elderly-2 years). **$108,000-$110,000** each to Aid for Friends (operating support-2 years), Community Legal Services (Elderly Law Project-2 years), Elwyn, Inc. (deaf elderly project-2 years), and Jewish Community Centers of Greater Philadelphia (home-delivered meals/services to seniors-2 years). **$103,000-$104,000** each to Central Montgomery MH/MR Center (senior outreach services program-2 years) and Golden Slipper Center for Seniors (operating support-2 years). **$100,000** each to Family Service Assn. of Bucks County (outreach to isolated seniors-2 years), North Penn Visiting Nurse Assn. (adult day care operating support), and Tenant Action Group (Senior Assistance Program-2 years). **$90,000** to Energy Coordinating Agency of Philadelphia (Cool Homes project for elderly-2 years). **$80,000** each to ACLAMO/Accion Comunal Latino American de Montgomery County (Latino Senior Linkages program-2 years) and Korean Community Development Services Center (services to Asian elderly-2 years). **$73,000** to Adult Care of Chester County (operating support-2 years; information system improvements-1 year). **$70,000** each to Cambodian Assn. of Greater Philadelphia (elderly services program-2 years), Kennett Area Senior Center (Assisted Senior Program-2 years), and Supportive Older Women's Network (establish/maintain support groups-2 years). **$65,000** to Pa. Assn. for the Blind/Delaware County Branch (Homebound Rehabilitation Program for elderly-2 years). **$60,000** to Montgomery County Assn. for the Blind (blind-visually impaired elderly program support). **$52,000** each to Eldernet of Lower Merion/Narberth (operating support/fundraising system-2 years) and Philadelphia Corp. for Aging (collaborative resource development plan for senior center programs-1 year). **$47,000** to Intercommunity Action, Inc. (client database management system-2 years). **$44,000** to Horizons Unlimited/Geriatric Education Corp. (operating support-2 years). **$41,000** to Alzheimer's Disease & Related Disorders Assn./SE Pa. Chapter (new software/toll-free helpline). **$30,000** each to CONTACT Bucks County (telephone contact program for elderly-2 years) and Senior Adult Activities Center of Montgomery County (adult day care support)-2 years). **$20,000** to Senior Adult Activity Center of Lansdale & Vicinity (computer upgrade). **$13,000** to Oxford Area Neighborhood Services (outreach-links to isolated elderly-2 years). **_Community Development Grants:_** **$450,000** to Regional Housing Legal Services (operating support for community development intermediary-2 years). **$400,000** to The Reinvestment Fund (operating support for a community development intermediary-2 years). **$200,000** to Pa. Low Income Housing Corp. (Philadelphia Acquisition Project re blighted land-2 years). **_Other Project Grants:_** **$1,540,000** to United Way of SE Pa. (annual campaign support/enhanced communication capabilities). **$1,000,000** to Wistar Institute (recruit biomedical investigators/equip laboratories). **$150,000** to Ralston House (new kitchen). **$120,000** to United Way of SE Delaware County (annual campaign support). **_VENTURE FUND GRANTS-including Special Distribution Funding:_** (Nine Pa. grants totaled $25,790,000): **$17,000,000** to The Philadelphia Foundation (challenge grant for Regional Performing Arts Center, resident arts companies, and Academy of Music renovation-5 years). **$5,000,000** to Philadelphia Museum of Art (installation of outdoor Calder sculptures along The Parkway-12 years). **$3,500,000** to Pa. Academy of the Fine Arts (acquisition of 'The Dream Garden'). **$3,980,000** to The Franklin Institute (consortium exhibition on Benjamin Franklin, and related conservation activities-8 years). **$3,000,000** to Central Philadelphia Development Corp. (design/implement new lighting along The Parkway-2 years). **$2,000,000** to Independence Visitor Center Corp. (new Liberty Bell Center-18 mos.) **$2,000,000** to Declaration of Independence, Inc. [CA] (Philadelphia launch of the Declaration of Independence Road Trip). **$750,000** to Red Cross/SE Pa. Chapter (disaster relief funds for El Salvador, Peru and U.S.) **$640,000** to Pa. Economy League (Choices for Pennsylvania's Future project). **_RELIGION GRANTS_** (Four Pa. grants totaled $7,150,000): **$4,000,000** to Public/Private Ventures (Philadelphia Community Serving Ministry initiative/faith-based social services-2 years). **$2,600,000** to U. of Pa./Center for Research on Religion & Urban Civil Society (research activities/fellows programs/curricular offering/public lectures—3 years). **$500,000** to U. of Pa. (longitudinal study of religion-religious activities of new immigrants to the U.S.—5 years). **$50,000** to St. Peter's Church in the Great Valley (new pipe organ). Out-of-state grants ranging from **$350,000** to **$6,300,00** awarded in the programmatic areas of Religion & Academic Life, Religion & Public Life, and Urban & Hispanic Ministry. **_EDUCATION GRANTS_** (Two Pa. grants totaled **$2,485,000** which reflect historical interests of the Trusts): **$2,100,000** to U. of Pa. (construction of new life sciences building and laboratories-4 years). **$385,000** to Kimberton Waldorf School (enhanced high school activiities/expanded garden program-3 years). ***ENVIRONMENT GRANTS:*** (No Pa. grants). Out-of-state grants, ranging from **$150,000** to **$5,035,000,** addressed issues under the programmatic areas of Conservation of Living Marine Resources, Global Warming & Climate Change, Old Growth Forests and Wilderness Protection. ***PUBLIC POLICY GRANTS:*** (No Pa. grants). **Out-of-state** grants, ranging from **$100,000** to **$2,482,000** addressed issues under the programmatic areas of Civic Engagement, Government Performance, and Improving Elections.— For full details on out-of-state/national grants in all program areas, consult the website or the Program Resource Guide. ■**PUBLICATIONS:** *Program Resource Guide* (published annually) with grant listings and application guidelines; Philadelphia Cultural Leadership Program booklet; many other reports and white papers. ■**WEBSITE:** www.pewtrusts.com ■**E-MAIL:** info@pewtrusts.com (for general information only; also see Program Office e-mail addresses below) ■**APPLICATION POLICIES & PROCEDURES:** The Pew Charitable Trusts comprise seven charitable trusts (listed below) which were established between 1948 and 1979 by Pew family members. The Trusts award grants in six program areas, and grantseekers should note that grantmaking within each program area is increasingly focused and strategic, making support unlikely for activities that are not closely aligned with the Trusts' current program goals/objectives. Seeking a grant from the Trusts is a rigorously competitive process and only about 10% of the 3,000-4,000 proposals received annually are ultimately funded. Grant sizes vary from program to program, but in 2001 the median grant size was $300,000 with smaller ones, generally, for programs working closely with community-based and direct-service organizations, and the larger ones for programs at research, academic and health institutions. The Trusts do not award grants to individuals or for capital campaigns, unsolicited construction requests, endowments, debt reduction, or scholarships/fellowships that are not part of a Trusts-initiated program. About 70% of the Trusts' grantmaking is national in scope, but the **Pew Fund for Health & Human Services** and **The Philadelphia Program** (for local cultural institutions) only accept applications from the five-county Philadelphia area. Prospective applicant organizations should first secure a copy of the current ***Program Resource Guide*** (available on the website, or on request) which includes very detailed policies/guidelines for each program—too detailed to be summarized here, as well as goals/objectives and the kinds of activities that will/will not be considered. In addition, prospective applicants with questions about eligibility or the proposal review process are encouraged to contact the appropriate Program Office: *Culture* (culturemail@pewtrusts.com, 215-575-4870); *Education* (edumail@pewtrusts.com, ***215-575-4755); Environment*** (envimail@pewtrusts.com, 215-575-4740); *Health & Human Services* (hhsmail@pewtrusts.com, 215-575-4860); *Public Policy* (pubpolmail@pewtrusts.com, 215-575-4720); *Religion* (religmail@pewtrusts.com, 215-575-4730); and *Venture Fund* (vfmail@pewtrusts.com, 215-575-4848). If, after review of the guidelines, other information or consultation with Trusts staff, you feel your project/activity is a match, you may submit at any time (no deadlines) a brief Letter of Inquiry (three pages maximum) that: (a) describes your organization and the nature of its work, and summarize the organization's achievements, particularly as they relate to the problem/issue to be addressed; (b) states the problem/need you plan to address and explain how it will be addressed, including a brief description of anticipated achievements or outcomes; (c) lays out the time frame for the proposed activities; and (d) provides an estimated cost for the project/activity and the amount to be requested from the Trusts. Do ***not*** include examples of articles, reports, videos or other material with a Letter of Inquiry. After the Letter of Inquiry is reviewed by the Trusts' staff, applicants are notified (usually within 4-6 weeks) by telephone or letter whether the request meets current funding criteria and program guidelines. *Applicants should note that an organization may submit multiple Letters of Inquiry, but if an organization's full proposal has been declined it must wait a minimum of 12 months before submitting a new proposal.*) If the Letter of Inquiry request appears to qualify, the organization may be sent a detailed Application Package and asked to develop a full proposal. Proposals in all program areas are accepted for review throughout the year (no specific application deadlines) but Board agendas are closed usually several months before the Board meetings held in March, June, September, and December at which all final grant decisions are made. If a proposal/application is approved for funding, a formal letter is sent within 4-6 weeks after the board meeting. — The individual Trusts' Federal ID's (EIN's) are: The Pew Memorial Trust/23-6234669; The J. Howard Pew Freedom Trust/23-6234671; The Mabel Pew Myrin Trust/23-6234666; The J.N. Pew, Jr. Charitable Trust/23-6299309; The Medical Trust/23-2131641; The Mary Anderson Trust/23-6234670; and The Knollbrook Trust/23-6407577.

O+D+T Rebecca W. Rimel (P+D+Con) — J. Howard Pew, II [Nova Scotia] (C+D)— Robert H. Campbell (D) — Susan W. Catherwood [Bryn Mawr] (D) — Thomas W. Langfitt, M.D. [Ardmore] (D) — Arthur E. Pew, III [MN] (D) — Mary Catherine Pew, M.D. (D) — J.N. Pew, 3rd [Gladwyne] (D) — J.N. Pew, IV, M.D. [Reading] (D) — R. Anderson Pew [Bryn Mawr] (D) — Sandy Pew [MT] (D) — Robert G. Williams (D) The Glenmede Trust Company (Trustee)

SE-514 **Pfundt Foundation**
　　　　c/o General Machine Products Co., Inc.
　　　　3111 Old Lincoln Highway
　　　　Trevose　19053　　　　　　　(Bucks County)

MI-12-13-18-25-29-31-42-44-52-53-54-56-57-84
Phone 215-357-5500 **FAX** 215-357-6216
EIN 23-6442007　　**Year Created** 1968

AMV $2,671,371　　　　**FYE** 9-00　　**(Gifts Received** $315,000)　　38 **Grants totaling** $141,060

Mostly local giving; grants are annual gifts except as noted. High grant of **$32,000** to Michener Arts Center (capital campaign). **$30,000** to Doylestown Hospital (capital campaign). **$18,750** to Newtown Borough (playground). **$10,000** to Newtown Library Company. **$5,000** each to Family Service Assn., Habitat for Humanity/Bucks County, U. of Pa., and WHYY-TV12. **$2,000-$2,500** each to Choral Arts Society, Contact Bucks County, Franklin Institute, Pearl S. Buck Foundation, and Presbyterian Children's Village. **$1,000-$1,500** each to Bucks County Historical Society, Make-A-Wish Foundation, Pa. Ballet, Philadelphia Orchestra, and Planned Parenthood of Bucks County. Other local contributions **$25-$500** for various purposes. **Out-of-state** giving includes **$3,500** to Metropolitan Opera [NY] and **$1,000** to Institute of the American Indian [NM]. ■**PUBLICATIONS:** None ■**WEBSITE:** None ■**E-MAIL:** None ■**APPLICATION POLICIES & PROCEDURES:** Grant requests may be submitted in a letter or proposal at any time. Site visits sometimes are made to organizations being considered for a grant.

O+D+T Lauren Pfundt Meyer (D+Con) — G. Nelson Pfundt (Manager+Donor+D) — Scott R. Pfundt (D) — William N. Pfundt (D) Corporate donor: General Machine Products Company, Inc.

SE-515 Philadelphia Foundation, The
Suite 1800
1234 Market Street
Philadelphia 19107   (Philadelphia County)
AMV $195,134,000   **FYE** 12-01   **(Gifts Received** $7,559,111)   801 **Grants totaling** $18,605,408

MI-12-13-14-15-16-17-18-19-20-22-24-25-29
33-35-39-41-45-51-52-53-54-55-79-81-83
Phone 215-563-6417 **FAX** 215-563-6882
EIN 23-1581832   **Year Created** 1918

As a Community Foundation all discretionary giving is restricted to organizations serving the 5-county Philadelphia area (plus Camden area); grants are awarded in six categories: Arts, Culture & the Humanities; Education; Environment; Health; Human Services; and Public & Community Development. About one-third of total giving was discretionary, awarded from unrestricted or field-of-interest funds. Grants are for general operating support except as noted. High grant of **$348,000** to Please Touch Museum (project support). **$185,000** to Resources for Human Development (New Beginnings Programs/RHD Initiatives/Neighborhood Yellow Pages). **$154,000** to Emergency Services Fund of Philadelphia. **$125,000** to Red Cross (Local Disaster & Sept. 11th Relief Funds). **$120,600** to Energy Coordinating Agency of Philadelphia (emergency heating assistance). **$120,000** to Children's Hospital ofPhiladelphia (mental health research). **$100,000** each to Annenberg Center for the Performing Arts, Health Promotion Council of Philadelphia (Allies Against Asthma Coalition), and Hispanics in Philanthropy (Funders' Collaborative for Strong Latino Communities). **$65,000** to Bridging the Gaps. **$61,000** to Center for Responsible Funding (Academy for Fundraising Training/four other programs). **$50,000** each to Philadelphia AIDS Consortium (emergency food vouchers) and School District of Philadelphia (musical program-equipment). **$39,720** to Philadelphia High School Academies (support scholarships/supplies). **$37,000** to Community Foundations for Pa. (membership/operating support). **$35,000** each to Philadelphia Fight, Ken-Crest Centers (Toward Self-Determination Project), and Metropolitan Career Center (STRIVE program/office software). **$30,000-$33,061** each to Delaware Valley Health Education & Research Foundation (Life Sciences program), The Enterprise Center (Youth Entrepreneurship Success program), Family Service of Chester County, Livengrin Foundation (community outreach services), Philabundance, Philadelphia Fight, Philadelphia Health Management Corp. (Interim House West Children's Services), and Public Interest Law Center of Philadelphia (disabilities project enforcement). **$28,822** to Asian Arts Initiative (Williams Award/operating support). **$24,000-$25,000** each to Adult Care of Chester County, Chester Springs Studio (Art Partners Studio), Delaware Valley Child Care Council, Fellowship Farm, MANNA/Metropolitan AIDS Neighborhood Nutrition Alliance (operating support/conference), Maternity Care Coalition of Greater Philadelphia (staff training), Philadelphia Corporation on Aging (emergency funds for seniors), Philadelphia Youth Orchestra, Reboot Philadelphia, Red Cross (Partners for Youth program), Speaking for Ourselves, Taller Puertorriqueno, and Women's Business Development Center. **$20,000-$23,000** each to Asian Americans United, Alzheimer's Assn. of SE Pa., The Attic, Big Sisters of Philadelphia, Calcutta House, Centro Nueva Creacion (Summer Career Exploration Program/general support), Coatesville Center for Community Health, Disabilities Law Project, Domestic Abuse Project of Delaware County, Eastern Pa. Organizing Project, Education Law Center, Frankford Group Ministry (general support/emergency heating assistance), Gay Community Center of Philadelphia, Interfaith Coalition of Food Centers/Delaware County, Juvenile Law Center of Philadelphia, Montgomery County OIC, Octorara Community Recreation Commission (preschool/after school programs), Point Breeze Performing Art Center, St. Mary's Franciscan Shelter for Homes Families (Consortium to Prevent Homelessness), Scribe Video Center, Senior Citizen Judicare Project, and YWCA of Chester. **$17,000-$18,000** each to AIDS Law Project of Pa., Delco Memorial Foundation (Asian Diversity Outreach Project), Disabled in Action of Pa., Housing Consortium for Disabled Individuals (relocation costs/operating support), Indochinese American Council (youth-technology program), Kids' Smiles, Montgomery County Big Brothers/Big Sisters (volunteer recruitment), New Freedom Theatre, and Painted Bride Art Center. **$15,000-$16,500** each to ASPIRA (Summer Career Exploration Program), W.C. Atkinson Memorial Community Services Center, Chester Education Foundation (Social Work Consultation Services), Children's Country Week Assn., Children's Village,Inc. (early intervention/parent support program), City Year, Inc., (public school scholarships), Comite de Apoyo a Los Trabajadores Agricolas (migrant-immigrants workers organizing), Community Learning Center, Congreso de Latinos Unidos (capacity building), Living Beyond Breast Cancer (Project Connect), Mountain Meadow Country Experience, Mural Arts Program, New Liberty Productions, New World Assn. of Emigrants from Eastern Europe, Pa. Environmental Council (brownfields redevelopment program), Pa. Low-Income Housing Coalition (resource development strategy), Philadelphia Health & Education Corp. (MCP-HU Health Center's BEST Program), Please Touch Museum, Police-Barrio Relations Project, Resources for Children's Health (Focus on Fathers program), St. Mary's Family Respite Center, Southwest Community Enrichment Center, Terry Lynne Lokoff Child Care Foundation (mobile children's safety center), Urban Retrievers, Volunteer English Program in Chester County, Women in Transition, Women's Assn. for Women's Alternatives (advocacy program), Women's Center of Montgomery County, and Women's Law Project. **$13,000-$13,830** each to Adoption Center of Delaware Valley (African-American children initiative), Delaware Valley Health Education & Research Foundation (research report), Fellowship Farm, Free Health Clinic of Montgomery County, Kardon Institute of the Arts for People with Disabilities, and Overington House. **$10,000-$12,500** each to 21st Century Foundation for Photography (field trips), ACORN (predatory lending education project), American Heart Assn. of SE Pa. (public access defibrillation), Arden Theatre Company (stagebill), Art Sanctuary, Arts & Spirituality Center, Asian Arts Initiative, ASSETS-Montco, Baker Industries, Big Brothers/Big Sisters of Chester County, Blueprint to End Homelessness, Boys & Girls Clubs of Metropolitan Philadelphia (Summer Career Exploration Program), Brandywine Graphic Workshop, Bushfire Theatre of the Performing Arts, Cambodian Assn. of Greater Philadelphia, Caring About Sharing, CASA/Youth Advocates, CARIE (ombudsman program), Carroll Park Community Council, Cerebral Palsy Assn. of Chester County, Chester Community Improvement Project, Chester County Interlink, Chestnut Hill Hospital Health Care Center (geriatric resource center), CHOICE/Concern for Health Options, The Clay Studio (Claymobile), Clean Water Fund (Environmental Health Organizing Project), Cobbs Creek Community Environmental Education Center, Community Care Center of Northeast, Community Conservatory of Music, Community Design Collaborative of AIA Philadelphia, Community Dispute Settlement Program of Delaware County, Community Service Council of Chester County, Creative Access, Crime Prevention Assn. of Philadelphia (Summer Career Exploration Program), Crime Victims' Center of Chester County, Delaware Riverkeeper Network (program implementation), Delaware Valley Assn. for the Education of Childcare Workers (worthy wage campaign), District One Community Education Center, Domestic Violence Center of Chester County, Downingtown Senior Center, Eastern U. (Nonprofit Leadership Institute), Exodus to Excellence, The Fabric Workshop (youth education project), Family Care Solutions, Inc., First United Methodist Church of Germantown (after school program), Frankford Group Ministry

Community Development Corp. (career services), The GALAEI Project, Ghebre Michael Inn, Good Works, Inc., Greater Philadelphia Cultural Alliance, Greater Philadelphia Overseas Chinese Assn., Greater Philadelphia Urban Affairs Coalition (Tavis Smiley Foundation/youth leadership), HERO/Helping Energize & Rebuild Ourselves, Homeless Advocacy Project, Hospitality House of Philadelphia, Immaculata College (art show/scholarship), Inn Dwelling, Inner City Scholarship Fund (Careers-Success Program), Institute for the Study of Civic Values (Neighborhood Builders Online), InterAct, Inc. (outreach), International Foundation for Education & Self-Help (education programs in Philadelphia & Chester), Jewish Employment & Vocational Service (advisory committee for emigres), Joseph J. Peters Institute (Philadelphia Project), Legal Clinic for the Disabled, Literacy Assistance Center, Little Brothers Friends of the Elderly, Maysie's Farm Conservation Center, Montgomery County Assn. for the Blind (service provision database), NARAL-PA Foundation, National Liberty Museum (tours/workshops), Need in Deed, Neighbor to Neighbor Community Development Corp., Norris Square Neighborhood Project, North Light Community Center, North Penn Valley Boys & Girls Club (homework-tutoring help), North Philadelphia Health System (AIDS Care Clinic), Paoli Memorial Hospital (teens-bereavement program), Pegasus Riding Academy, Peniel Recovery Center, Penn Asylum for Indigent Widows, Pa. Young Playwrights Program, Philadelphia Cares, Philadelphia Chinatown Development Corp. (bilingual support services), Philadelphia Education Fund (humanities course), Philadelphia Futures for Youth (emergency fund for youth/families), Philadelphia Geriatric Center (caregivers counseling program), Philadelphia Interfaith Action, Philadelphia READS, Philadelphia Urban Finance Corp., Philadelphia Youth Orchestra (technical assistance), Philadelphians Concerned About Housing (family self-sufficiency program), Philip Jaisohn Memorial Foundation, Phoenixville Homes, Physicians for Social Responsibility/Philadelphia, Planned Parenthood Assn. of SE Pa. (public affairs dept.), Planned Parenthood of Chester County (HIV Street Outreach Program), Police-Barrio Relations Project, Preschool Project, Prevention Point-Philadelphia, PrideFest Philadelphia, Prince Music Theater (The Rainbow Connection), Raices Culturales Latinoamericanas, Recording for the Blind & Dyslexic, Rosenbach Museum & Library (storytelling program), RSVP of Montgomery County, Safe Harbor of Greater West Chester, Sedgwick Cultural Center, Settlement Music School (early childhood education initiative), Spiral Q Puppet Theater, Sylvan Opera (educational program), Travelers Aid Society (community voice mail program), Unemployment Information Center, Urban Tree Connection (Strawberry Mansion area project), Valley Forge Military Academy & College (scholarship), The Wellness Community - Philadelphia (cancer support program), Women's Opportunity Resources Center, Woodmere Art Museum (exhibit), Work-Stream Project of GPUAC, Youth Service, Inc. (West Philadelphia parenting project), YWCA of Greater West Chester (Mothers' Center), and YWCA of Germantown. **$7,000-$9,900** each to Abington Art Center (Youth Empowerment Initiative), Act II Playhouse, Advocates for Jewish Mentally Ill (Tikvah Program), Aid for Friends, ACLU Foundation of Pa. (reproduction freedom project), John Bartram Assn. (Gardening the Garden Program), Bridge of Hope (Family Building Program), Bridge of Hope-Buxont, Camp Soltane (job placement program), Chester County Housing Development Corp. (conference participation), Church of St. Martin-in-the-Fields (Germantown Ave. Crisis Ministry), Community Women's Education Project, Congregational Nursing Service, CONTACT Careline for Greater Philadelphia (recruitment/outreach), Delaware County AIDS Network, Delaware County Women Against Rape (crime victims services), Farmers' Market Trust, FrankfordStyle, Germantown Academy (speakers' series), Give A Smile/Pa. Smiles, Grace Temple Community Services (summer reading program), Jewish Community Centers of Greater Philadelphia (RSVP Program), Koresh Dance Company (Kids Dance program), The MBF Center, Mercy Vocational High School (scholarships/special resources), Network of Victim Assistance of Bucks County (supervised visitation project), NetworkArts Philadelphia (ecology-arts program), New Frankford Community Y (out-of-school enrichment program), No Longer Bound, Inc., Operation Understanding, Pa. Coalition of AIDS Service Organizations, Philadelphia Black Women's Health Project, Philadelphia Children's Alliance, Philadelphia Community Health Alternatives, Philadelphia Council for Community Advancement, Philadelphia Orchestra (educational concerts), Police Athletic League of Greater West Chester, Seaman's Church Institute, St. Philips' United Methodist Church (summer activities program), Stenton (education coordinator salary), Transgender Health Action Coalition, United Families, University City Hospitality Coalition, Vita Education Services, West Chester Area Senior Center, Willow Grove Community Development Corp. (home buyers program), Youth Project, and YWCA of Bucks County (teen mothers program). **$5,000-$6,500** each to ActionAIDS for Washington West Project, Allegheny West Foundation (neighborhood youth cultural program), American Helicopter Museum & Education Center (preschool science project), Andalusia Foundation (summer interns), Anna Crusis Women's Choir, ArtReach (in-facility program), Black Women in Sport Foundation, Buildabridge International (cultural exchange program), Camphill Village Kimberton Hills (environmental initiative), Care Center Foundation, Central Bucks Healthier Community Team, Child Home & Community, Chinese Christian Church & Center (community programs), Community Legal Services (child care business legal guide), Dawn Staley Foundation, Easter Seals (camp-recreational programs), Entourage Community Development (summer enrichment program), Evangelical Lutheran Church of the Reformation (tutoring services), Fair Hill Burial Ground, Foundation for Today's Art/NEXUS, Free Library of Philadelphia (Regional Foundation Center), Friends Rehabilitation Program (homeless initiative), German Society of Pa. (strategic planning), Germantown Historical Society, Haitian Community Center of Philadelphia, Harvard Business School Club of Philadelphia (nonprofit intern support), Historic Philadelphia, Inc., Humanrightstech.org (internet empowerment training), Kearsley (emergency assistance program), Logan Learning Club, Media Fellowship House, Moonstone (Cuban festival), MulticulturalResource Center, Mum Puppettheatre, National Conference for Community & Justice, Neighborhood Bike Works, One House at a Time (Beds for Kids project), Paoli Presbyterian Church (emergency services), Pa. Assn. for the Blind/Delaware County, Philadelphia City Sail, Philadelphia Dance Alliance, Philadelphia Museum of Art (community outreach programs), Presbyterian Home at 58th Street (residents' assistance program), Saunders House, Springside School (neighborhood scholar's fund), Tolentine Community Center & Development Corp. (family literacy program), U. of Pa. Health System (conference), Victim/Witness Services of South Philadelphia (Asian outreach project), The Working Wardrobe, World Affairs Council of Philadelphia (middle school initiative), and YMCA of Philadelphia & Vicinity (capital campaign). In addition, 60+ smaller local discretionary grants/contributions **$300-$4,500** awarded for similar purposes and the SAGE/Securing Assets for Grassroots Empowerment program. All other local giving was from restricted funds. ■ **PUBLICATIONS:** Annual Report; Competitive Grant Guidelines & Application; detailed instructions sheet ■ **WEBSITE:** www.philafound.org ■ **E-MAIL:** parkow@philafound.org ■ **APPLICATION POLICIES & PROCEDURES:** Only Pa. organizations located in Philadelphia or Bucks, Chester, Delaware, or Montgomery counties are eligible to apply. Most grants are for specific projects or general operating support to organizations which are: (1) responding to the existing and emerging needs of the community and diverse populations; (2) promoting social justice and equity across diverse population groups; and/or (3) building bridges across different population groups, organizations and communities that will result in mutually beneficial outcomes. High priority is given to requests from nonprofit organizations with operating budgets under $1.5 million that work to empower people and groups within the community. Priority is also given to (a) nonprofit organizations that build community assets as they seek to cultivate communities' human, financial and material resources—through the arts, the environment and education, in community centers and after-school programs, and by promoting intergenerational volunteerism and civic responsibility; (b) organizations that manage current issues by providing direct services that counteract domestic violence, hunger, lack of shelter, or illiteracy that pervade many low-income or multicultural communities; and (c) programs that help communities prepare for meeting future trends. Generally, no support is given to individuals or for capital campaigns, deficit financing, endowment, government agencies, affiliates of national or international organizations, private schools, publications, research projects, tours and trips, umbrella-funding organizations, or organizations outside the 5-county Philadelphia area. Prospective applicants initially should contact the Foundation to discuss the feasibility of submitting a request and/or to request copies of Competitive Grant Guidelines & Application and detailed instructions. Proposals which follow Delaware Valley Grantmakers' Common Grant Application Form are accepted, but the mandatory attachments are still required. To allow for any necessary consultation with Foundation staff, proposals should be submitted well in advance of the May 1st or November 1st deadlines—proposals must be received in the Foundation office by 5 p.m. on those dates. Only one request per year per organization is accepted. Site visits usually are made to organizations being considered for a grant, especially new applicants or requests above $10,000. Grants are awarded at Board of Managers meetings in April and October, and applicants are notified within a month of the meetings.

O+D+T R. Andrew Swinney (P+Con) — Board of Managers members: H. Craig Lewis, Esq. (C) — Ignatius C. Wang, A.I.A. (VC) — Herman Mattleman, Esq. (F) — Lawrence J. Beaser, Esq. — Ellen P. Foster — Eric Fraint, CPA — Oliver S. Franklin — Gene Locks, Esq. — Eliana Papadakis — Stanley A. Simpkins — Judith A.W. Thomas, Ed.D. — Mark C. Twyman, MBA — Cuyler H. Walker, Esq. — Andrew N. Yao — Trustees: Bryn Mawr Trust Company, First Union/Wachovia, First National Bank & Trust Company, The Glenmede Trust Company, Mellon/PSFS N.A., The Philadelphia Foundation, Inc., Pitcairn Trust Company, PNC Bank N.A., Wilmington Trust of Pa.

SE-516 Philadelphia Health Care Trust   MI-31-32-34-35
    c/o The Weightman Group
    2129 Chestnut Street   **Phone** 215-977-1705 **FAX** None
    Philadelphia 19103   (Philadelphia County)   **EIN** 23-1985544   **Year Created** 1997
AMV $118,790,818   **FYE** 6-00   (**Gifts Received** $0)   9 **Grants totaling** $4,300,000

All local/nearby NJ giving; all grants are for special projects or research. High grant of **$2,000,000** to Thomas Jefferson U. **$550,000** to U. of Pa. **$500,000** to American Medical Foundation for Peer Review & Education. **$375,000** to Philadelphia Health Management Corp. **$250,000** to Coriel Institute for Medical Research [NJ]. **$175,000** to HCA: The Healthcare Company (Para Professionals). **$150,000** each to Gwynedd Mercy, Philadelphia FIGHT (AIDS services), and The Philadelphia Foundation. ■**PUBLICATIONS:** None ■**WEBSITE:** None ■**E-MAIL:** None ■**APPLICATION POLICIES & PROCEDURES:** Information not available. — Formerly called Graduate Health System, Inc.

O+D+T Bernard J. Korman, Esq. (C+Con) — Peter D. Carlino [Wyncote] (Member) — Harold Cramer, Esq. (Member) — Russell Kunkel [Reading] (Member) — Janice L. Richter, Esq. [NJ] (Member)

SE-517 Philadelphia Stock Exchange Foundation   MI-11-13-14-22-25-31-32-42-52-54-62-81
    c/o Philadelphia Stock Exchange, Inc.
    1900 Market Street   **Phone** 215-496-5199 **FAX** None
    Philadelphia 19103   (Philadelphia County)   **EIN** 22-2437173   **Year Created** 1982
AMV $1,140,893   **FYE** 12-00   (**Gifts Received** $0)   21 **Grants totaling** $78,500

Mostly local giving. High grant of **$10,000** to Eisenhower Exchange Fellowships. **$7,500** to Federation Allied Jewish Appeal. **$6,000** to Philadelphia Museum of Art/Women's Committee. **$5,000** each to American Cancer Society, Catholic Charities Appeal, Leukemia & Lymphoma Society/Eastern Pa. Chapter, Police Athletic League, and U. of Pa./Graduate School of Education (Partners Program). **$3,500** to Special Olympics of Philadelphia. **$2,500** each to Franklin Institute (Family Funfest), One-to-One/The Greater Philadelphia Mentoring Partnership, Project H.O.M.E., United Way of SE Pa. **$1,000** each to Easter Seals, Freedom Theatre, and Richard Allen Classic. Other smaller local contributions. **Out-of-state** giving includes **$5,000** each to United Service Organization [NJ] and Street Care Foundation [NJ]; and **$2,500** to St. Jude's Children's Research Hospital [NY]. ■**PUBLICATIONS:** None ■**WEBSITE:** None ■**E-MAIL:** None ■**APPLICATION POLICIES & PROCEDURES:** Grant requests may be submitted in a letter at any time.

O+D+T William N. Briggs (Administrator+Con) — Meyer S. Frucher (C+T) — John F. Wallace (VC+T) — Michael J. Curcio (T) — Lawrence N. Gage (T) — Kevin J. Kennedy (T) — Eleanor W. Myers, Esq. (T) — Christopher Nagy (T) — Constantine Papadakis, Ph.D. (T) — Thomas W. Wynn (T) Corporate donor: Philadelphia Stock Exchange, Inc.

SE-518 Phoenixville Community Health Foundation   MI-12-13-14-15-17-22-29-31-35-39-41-43-55
    Valley Forge Professional Center   88-89
    1260 Valley Forge Road, Suite 102   **Phone** 610-917-9890 **FAX** 610-917-9861
    Phoenixville 19460   (Chester County)   **EIN** 23-2912035   **Year Created** 1998
AMV $33,133,071   **FYE** 6-01   (**Gifts Received** $4,000)   100+ **Grants totaling** $1,723,337

All giving limited to organizations/programs serving the Greater Phoenixville Area (delineated below); grants are for general operating support except as noted and some comprise multiple awards. Six grants totaling **$708,852** to Phoenixville Hospital (cancer center/departmental upgrades and other purposes). **$150,000** to Phoenixville Area YMCA (family wellness center construction). **$83,920** to Community Service Council of Chester County (healthcare referral services). **$77,400** to Lincoln Center for Family & Youth [Bridgeport] (at-risk youth programs). **$63,000** to Montgomery County Emergency Medical Services (equipment for local services). **$43,000** to Chester County Office of Human Services (Barkley School family outreach center). **$35,000** each to Open Hearth and Phoenixville Homes. **$30,000** each to Community Volunteers in Medicine, Family Service of Chester County (counseling for low-income residents), and Schuylkill Canal Assn. (construction-related services). **$25,000** each to Big Brothers/Big Sisters of Chester County (local outreach), Easter Seals (local Bright Beginnings program), Pa. Assn. for the Blind/Chester County Branch (clinic equipment), Phoenixville Area Community Services (respite care training), Ridge Volunteer Firefighters Relief (special equipment), and St. Mary's Franciscan Shelter (staff salary). **$22,000-$22,310** each to Open Hearth (homeless alliance), Orion Communities, and Phoenixville Area Community Services (emergency fund operations). **$20,544** to Pa. Assn. for Nonprofit Organizations [Harrisburg] (local program services). **$19,500** to Phoenixville Area School District (elementary school programs/Operation FOCUS). **$15,000** each to Boy Scouts/Chester County Council (health care facility improvements) and Mom's House (day care support). **$13,015** to Creative Health Services (Park Springs School program). **$12,000** to LaSalle Nonprofit Management Development Center [Philadelphia] (local program services). **$9,000-$12,000** each to Camphill Village-Kimberton Hills (health oversight program), Chester County Community Foundation (local technical assistance programs), Chester County Healthy Communities Partnership Crime Victims Center of Chester County, **$11,410** to Phoenixville Area Children's Learning Center (staff training/respite care), Phoenixville Area Community Services (violence prevention services), and Spring Ford Counseling Services (program expansion). **$5,000** each to First United Church of Christ of Royersford (Project Outreach) and Pa. Home of the Sparrow (transitional housing). **$4,450** to Kimberton Fire Company (fire prevention education). **$2,000-$3,000** each to 202 Housing, Astral Artistic Services [Philadelphia] (local programs), First Presbyterian Church, Phoenixville Homes, and Phoenixville Youth. Other smaller grants/contributions for similar purposes. Also, 27 Academic Scholarship Grants, **$1,000** each, awarded to Phoenixville-area students pursuing careers in health care, and **$9,700** (19 grants) awarded to match Board of Directors personal contributions. ■**PUBLICATIONS:** Annual Report and Statement of Program Policy; application guidelines; application form ■**WEBSITE:** www.pchf1.org ■**E-MAIL:** pchf1@juno.com ■**APPLICATION POLICIES & PROCEDURES:** All giving is restricted to the improving the personal health, community health, and quality of life in the 19 townships/boroughs comprising the Greater Phoenixville Area; this includes the boroughs of Phoenixville and Spring City; Chester County townships of Charlestown, East Coventry, East Nantmeal, East Pikeland, West Pikeland, East Vincent, North Coventry, Schuylkill, South Coventry, West Vincent; Montgomery County townships of Limerick, Lower Pottsgrove, Lower Providence, and Upper Providence, and the boroughs of Collegeville, Royersford, and Trappe. Most grants are for general support, special projects, building funds, and matching grants—in partnership with local community organizations. No support is awarded to/for fraternal organizations, political parties, veterans groups, labor organizations, civic groups, benefit events, operating deficits, or publications. Prospective applicants should make an initial telephone inquiry about the feasibility of submitting a request. Grant requests may be submitted at any time on a formal application form (available from the Foundation or the website); include an annual report, organizational/project budgets, audited financial statement, list of major funding sources, Board member list, By-laws, IRS tax-exempt status documentation, and other documentation which the Foundation will stipulate. Site visits sometimes are made to organizations being considered for a grant. Grants are awarded at meetings in January, March, May, July, September and November.

O+D+T Louis J. Beccaria, Ph.D. (P+D+Con) — Richard A. Kunsch, Sr. (C+D) — James G. Reading (VC+D) — Debbie Mitchell (S+D) — Ronald F. Brien, Esq. (F+D) — Daniel Baer (D) — Augustus A. Boova (D) — Richard S. Downs (D) — David M. Frees, Jr. (D) — Samuel A. Jervis (Director Emeritus) — Raymond Kovalski, M.D. (Ex-officio/Medical Staff Representative) — Kevin Mahoney (D) — Edward H. McDaniel (D) — Walter J. McDonald (D) — John J. Sedlacek (Director Emeritus) — Joseph R. Zikmund, Jr. (Director Emeritus) Foundation corpus from sale of Phoenixville Hospital.

SE-519   Piasecki Foundation   MI-54-56-81
          c/o Kania, Lindner, Lasak & Feeney
          Two Bala Plaza, Suite 525   **Phone** 610-667-3240   **FAX** None
          Bala Cynwyd   19004   (Montgomery County)   **EIN** 23-7006412   **Year Created** 1958
AMV $683,150   **FYE** 12-00   (**Gifts Received** $0)   5 **Grants totaling** $19,850

Two Pa. grants: **$2,900** to American Helicopter Museum & Education Center [West Chester] (general support). **$1,000** to Foreign Policy Research Institute (research on foreign policy's effect on history). **Out-of-state** giving includes **$14,900** to Foundation for the Promotion of the Art of Navigation [MD] (educational support for navigation teaching) and **$1,000** to National Air & Space Museum [DC] (educational activities). ■**PUBLICATIONS:** None ■**WEBSITE:** None ■**E-MAIL:** None ■**APPLICATION POLICIES & PROCEDURES:** The Foundation's mission is to enhance public understanding of Navigation as an Art, as well as generating public interest in Aviation as a Business Art. Grant requests may be submitted in any form at any time (deadline is December 31st); describe the organization's scope, objectives, activities, proposed activity, and how public education interestsa are served.

O+D+T   Arthur J. Kania, Esq. (Manager+Con) — Frank N. Piasecki (Donor)

SE-520   Pilgrim Foundation, The   MI-12-18-43
          121 Mine Road   **Phone** 610-647-4100   **FAX** None
          Malvern   19355   (Chester County)   **EIN** 23-2955610   **Year Created** 1998
AMV $2,952,203   **FYE** 6-00   (**Gifts Received** $3,250,000)   3 **Grants totaling** $45,000

All local giving; all grants are for general support. **$15,000** each to Birthright of West Chester, Mom's House [Phoenixville], and Urban Student Scholarship Assistance Fund [St. Davids]. ■**PUBLICATIONS:** None ■**WEBSITE:** None ■**E-MAIL:** None ■**APPLICATION POLICIES & PROCEDURES:** The Foundation reports its mission as supporting Christian organizations in Chester County with an emphasis on children's welfare. Grant requests may be submitted in a full proposal letter before the January 31st deadline; include an annual report, list of Board members, list of major funding sources, organization and project budgets, an audited financial statement, most recent Form 990, and IRS tax-exempt status documentation. Site visits sometimes are made to organizations being considered for a grant.

O+D+T   Gary L. Pilgrim (P+Donor+Con) — Suzanne T. Daniel (S) — Ruth E. Pilgrim (Donor)

SE-521   Pincus Charitable Fund, The
c/o Pincus Brothers Company
Independence Mall East
Philadelphia   19106   (Philadelphia County)
AMV $38,425   FYE 11-00   (Gifts Received $96,925)

MI-13-22-32-43-44-53-54-62-72-82

Phone 215-922-4900 **FAX** 215-922-1140
EIN 22-2781261   **Year Created** 1986
44 **Grants totaling** $145,150

About two-thirds local/Pa. giving; grants are for general purposes except as noted. High grant of **$61,000** to Temple Beth Hillel. **$5,000** to Philadelphia Museum of Art. **$3,500** to Philadelphia Scholars Fund. **$1,000-$2,100** each to Brother's Brother Foundation [Pittsburgh], Free Library of Philadelphia, National MS Society, Pa. Academy of the Fine Arts, Philadelphia Zoo, and Woodrock. Other local contributions **$750** each to Old First Reformed Church and U. of Pa. **$100-$500** for arts/cultural, educational, and human services purposes. **Out-of-state** giving includes **$30,000** to Israel Sports Center for the Disabled [Israel]; **$12,000** to International Rescue Committee [NY]; and **$5,000** each to Anti-Defamation League [NY] and Friends of Incarnation Children's Center [NY]. ■**PUBLICATIONS:** None ■**WEBSITE:** None ■**E-MAIL:** None ■**APPLICATION POLICIES & PROCEDURES:** Prospective applicants initially should telephone the foundation to inquire about the feasibility of submitting a request. No grants awarded to individuals. Grant requests may be submitted in any form at any time. Site visits sometimes are made to organizations being considered for a grant. Grants are awarded at a November Board meeting.

O+D+T   David N. Pincus [Wynnewood] (P+D+Donor+Con) — Gerry Pincus [Wynnewood] (S+D) — Bruce Fishberg [Huntingdon Valley] (F+D) — Alvin H. Dorsky, Esq. [Norristown] (D) — Andrew Epstein [MA] (D) — Daniel J. Kachelein, CPA [NJ] (D) — Nathan Pincus [Bryn Mawr] (D) — Wendy Pincus [Wynnewood] (D) Corporate donor: Pincus Brothers Company

SE-522   Pine Tree Foundation
120 Righters Mill Road
Gladwyne   19035   (Montgomery County)
AMV $26,060,615   FYE 7-01   (Gifts Received $640,000)

MI-22-25-41-42-43-44-45-51-52-71-72-82

Phone 610-649-4601 **FAX** None
EIN 22-2751187   **Year Created** 1986
22 **Grants totaling** $1,255,000

About half local giving; all grants are for general support purposes. High Pa. grants of **$100,000** each to Free Library of Philadelphia, Philadelphia Orchestra, Philadelphia Scholars Fund, and Salvation Army. **$50,000** to Pa. Ballet. **$25,000** to Gesu School. **$20,000** to Vox Ama Deus. **$15,000** each to Gateway School and Riverbend Environmental Center. **$10,000** each to Children's Literacy Initiative and Project Forward Leap [Lancaster]. **Out-of-state** giving includes **$300,000** to CARE USA [GA]; **$150,000** to Habitat for Humanity [GA]; **$100,000** each to College of Wooster [OH] and Duke U. [NC]; **$10,000** to NY Foundation for the Arts and several CO organizations; and **$5,000** to Heifer Project International [AR]. ■**PUBLICATIONS:** None ■ **WEBSITE:** None ■**E-MAIL:** None ■**APPLICATION POLICIES & PROCEDURES:** Grant requests may be submitted in a letter at any time; describe the organization's activities and include IRS tax-exempt status documentation. No grants awarded to individuals.

O+D+T   A. Morris Williams, Jr. (C+F+D+Donor+Con) — Ruth W. Williams (P+S+D+Donor) — Susan Williams Beltz [CO] (D) — Joanne Williams Markman [Wynnewood] (D)

SE-523   Plotkin-Katz Foundation
1340 Brighton Way
Newtown Square   19073   (Delaware County)
AMV $378,096   FYE 12-00   (Gifts Received $0)

MI-22-29-32-42-62-83

Phone 610-358-5366 **FAX** None
EIN 23-7866034   **Year Created** 1996
21 **Grants totaling** $27,287

Mostly local giving; grants are for general purposes except as noted. High grant of **$11,552** to Congregation Beth Israel [Media] (building fund). **$5,000** to Drexel U. (biology dept. cancer research). **$3,500** to Jewish Employment & Vocational Services. **$2,200** to Federation Allied Jewish Appeal. **$1,000** each to Philadelphia Physicians for Social Responsibility and Temple Sholom [Broomall]. Other local and out-of-state contributions **$25-$500** for various purposes. ■**PUBLICATIONS:** None ■**WEBSITE:** None ■**E-MAIL:** None ■**APPLICATION POLICIES & PROCEDURES:** The Foundation reports that most grants are for special projects or research; multiyear grants are awarded. Prospective applicants initially should make a telephone inquiry about the feasibility of submitting a request. Grant requests may be submitted in a letter; describe a specific proposed project and include an annual report, project budget, and IRS tax-exempt status documentation. Site visits sometimes are made to organizations being considered for a grant. Grants are awarded at meetings in January, May, and September.

O+D+T   Stephen G. Plotkin (T+Con) — Marcia J. Plotkin (T+Con)

SE-524   PMC Foundation
c/o PMA Reinsurance Corp.
Mellon Center, 1735 Market Street
Philadelphia   19103   (Philadelphia County)
AMV $38,680   FYE 12-00   (Gifts Received $150,000)

MI-11-14-31-32-35-51-54-84-88

Phone 215-665-5070 **FAX** 215-665-5099
EIN 23-2159233   **Year Created** 1981
100+ **Grants totaling** $187,164

About three-fourths local/Pa. giving. High grant of **$70,000** to United Way of SE Pa. **$22,129** to Arden Theatre Company. **$20,000** to St. Mary Medical Center Foundation (outpatient facility). **$10,000** to The Philadelphia Foundation (outreach program). **$5,430** to Academy of Music. **$5,000** to Philadelphia Museum of Art. **$4,000** to Independence Gala (benefit event). **$1,000-$1,500** each to Elwyn, Juvenile Diabetes Foundation, Living Beyond Breast Cancer, Red Cross, Thomas E. Starzl Transplantation Institute [Pittsburgh], and U.S. Olympic Committee/Philadelphia. **$750** to Harrisburg Shakespeare Festival. Other smaller contributions for various purposes. **Out-of-state** giving includes **$7,200** to Atlantic City LPG Benefit Assn. [NJ] and **$5,000** each to Irish American Endowment [CT], School for Special Children [NJ], and Wellness Community [NJ]. Also, educational matching gifts disbursed to 42 colleges/universities in many states. ■**PUBLICATIONS:** None ■**WEBSITE:** None ■**E-MAIL:** None ■**APPLICATION POLICIES & PROCEDURES:** The Foundation reports that support focuses on Pa. and that all grants are initiated through employee requests. No grants awarded to individuals. — Formerly called the PMA Foundation.

O+D+T   William E. Hitselberger (CFO+Con) — Frederick W. Anton, III (C+T) Corporate donor: PMA Group

SE-525   Poor Richard's Charitable Trust
618 South 8th Street, Suite 306
Philadelphia   19147   (Philadelphia County)

MI-12-17-41-53-54-56
Phone Unlisted **FAX** None
EIN 23-7909451   **Year Created** 1997

AMV $1,056,295   **FYE** 12-00   (**Gifts Received** $0)   18 **Grants totaling** $71,000

Over three-fourths local giving. High grants of **$10,000** each to Architecture & Design Charter High School of Philadelphia, Children's Crisis Treatment Center, St. Peter's School, and The Shipley School. **$5,000** each to Atwater Kent Museum and Greater Philadelphia Women's Medical Fund. **$1,000-$1,500** each to The Free Library of Philadelphia, Lutheran Children & Family Service, Philabundance, Philadelphia Committee to End Homelessness, and U. of Pa. **Out-of-state** giving includes **$1,000** each to Corporate Design Foundation [NY], Jewish National Fund [NY], and Trinity College [CT]; and several grants **$1,000-$5,500** to Crested Butte, CO organizations. ■**PUBLICATIONS:** None ■**WEBSITE:** None ■**E-MAIL:** None ■**APPLICATION POLICIES & PROCEDURES:** The Foundation reports giving primarily to Philadelphia organizations identified by the Trustees; applications are not solicited. Site visits sometimes are made to organizations being considered for a grant. — Formerly called the Lisa Roberts & David Seltzer Charitable Trust.

O+D+T   Lisa S. Roberts (T+Donor+Con) — David Seltzer (T)

SE-526   Popkin (Susan & Ivan) Foundation
8317 Fairview Road
Elkins Park   19027   (Montgomery County)

MI-11-22-32-54-56-62
Phone 215-886-1136 **FAX** None
EIN 23-2824452   **Year Created** 1996

AMV $35,924   **FYE** 12-00   (**Gifts Received** $25,800)   7 **Grants totaling** $29,800

Mostly local giving. High grant of **$10,000** to Philadelphia Jewish Archives Center. **$8,700** to National Multiple Sclerosis Society. **$6,500** to Federation Allied Jewish Appeal. **$2,000** to Please Touch Museum. **$1,100** to United Way of SE Pa. **$500** to Balch Institute for Ethnic Studies. **Out-of-state** grant: **$1,000** to National Alliance for Autism Research [NJ]. ■**PUBLICATIONS:** None ■**WEBSITE:** None ■**E-MAIL:** None ■**APPLICATION POLICIES & PROCEDURES:** Information not available.

O+D+T   Susan Popkin (P+Donor+Con) — Ivan Popkin (S+F+Donor) — Ruth S. Alexander (Donor)

SE-527   Posel Foundation
c/o Posel Management Company
212 Walnut Street
Philadelphia   19106   (Philadelphia County)

MI-11-12-15-18-22-29-41-42-51-55-62-71-83
Phone 215-627-0900 **FAX** 215-627-3295
EIN 23-2581520   **Year Created** 1989

AMV $2,733,648   **FYE** 8-00   (**Gifts Received** $114,409)   105 **Grants totaling** $150,975

About one-third local giving. High grant of **$13,000** to Swarthmore College. **$12,000** to United Way of SE Pa. **$6,500** to Federation Allied Jewish Appeal. **$5,000** each to Gesu School and Philadelphia Museum of Art. **$1,000-$1,850** each to American Friends Service Committee, Briar Bush Nature Center, Children's Country Week Assn., Green Tree School, Inglis Foundation, Kearsley Retirement, Philadelphia Young Playwrights, and Public Interest Law Center of Philadelphia. **$750** to Southwest Community Enrichment Center. Other local contributions **$50-$500** for various community organizations. **Out-of-state** giving includes **$10,000** to American Civil Liberties Union Foundation of Florida, First Place School Competition [WA], Planned Parenthood of Seattle [WA], and Seattle Youth Garden Works [WA]; **$5,000** each to Harvard Law School [MA] and Make The Road by Walking, Inc. [NY]; and **$2,000** each to The Nature Conservancy [VA], Planned Parenthood of New York City, Sarasota Day Nursery [FL]; and other smaller grants/contributions mostly to NY. ■**PUBLICATIONS:** None ■**WEBSITE:** None ■**E-MAIL:** None ■**APPLICATION POLICIES & PROCEDURES:** No grants awarded to individuals.

O+D+T   Ramon L. Posel [FL] (D+Donor+Con) — Sidney L. Posel [NY] (D+Donor)

SE-528   Potamkin (Vivian O. & Meyer P.) Foundation
The Barclay, 237 South 18th Street, Apt. 20-B
Philadelphia   19103   (Philadelphia County)

MI-12-13-22-32-41-42-53-54-55-56-62-81-83
Phone 215-732-1781 **FAX** 215-636-0913
EIN 23-2197860   **Year Created** 1982

AMV $212,637   **FYE** 12-00   (**Gifts Received** $5,000)   73 **Grants totaling** $83,697

Mostly local giving. High grant of **$25,000** to U. of Pa. Cancer Center. **$10,000** to Federation Allied Jewish Appeal. **$3,750** to Foreign Policy Research Institute. **$2,000** to Philadelphia Museum of Art (Women's Committee). **$1,000-$1,500** each to Cliveden of the National Trust, CORA Services, Encore Series, Historical Society of Pa., Jacob & Gwendolyn Lawrence Foundation, LaSalle U., Perkiomen School, Philadelphia Antiques Show, Ron Patel Scholarship Fund, The Print Center, Southwest Community Enrichment Center, Temple U. (endowed chair), Union League of Philadelphia/Abraham Lincoln Foundation, and U.S. Artists. Other local contributions **$50-$500** for various purposes. **Out-of-state** giving includes **$6,000** to Archives of American Art [NY]; **$2,500** to The Wilson Quarterly [DC]; **$1,750** to Southern Poverty Law Center [AL]; and **$1,000-$1,500** each to The American Spectator Educational Foundation [DC], International League for Human Rights [NY], Museum of Modern Art [NY], and U. S. Holocaust Memorial Museum [DC]. ■**PUBLICATIONS:** None ■**WEBSITE:** None ■**E-MAIL:** None ■**APPLICATION POLICIES & PROCEDURES:** The Foundation reports that giving focuses on the Middle Atlantic States with general support for the arts, special projects, research and scholarships. Grant requests may be submitted at any time in a typewritten letter; include a project budget and IRS tax-exempt status documentation. Site visits sometimes are made to organizations being considered for a grant. Grants are awarded at an April meeting. — Formerly called VIPA Foundation.

O+D+T   Vivian O. Potamkin (T+Donor+Con)

SE-529 Pottstown Mercury Foundation
c/o The Pottstown Mercury/Peerless Publications
24 North Hanover Street
Pottstown 19464   (Montgomery County)

MI-22-23

Phone 610-323-3000 **FAX** None
EIN 23-6256419   **Year Created** 1960

AMV $29,431   **FYE** 11-00   **(Gifts Received** $58,558)   200+ **Grants totaling** $43,473

All giving assists needy Pottstown community residents/families/children through the Operation Holiday program; food and toys are distributed through various agencies: Arbor Career Center, Creative Health Services, Obelisk Head Start, Montgomery County Housing Authority/Bright Hope Residential Community, Park Spring Apartments, Project Outreach, Pottstown Cluster of Religious Communities, Women's Center of Montgomery County, and others. — In prior years, grants have been awarded to local organizations and camperships for needy children. ■**PUBLICATIONS:** None ■**WEBSITE:** www.pottstownmercury.com■**E-MAIL:** None ■ **APPLICATION POLICIES & PROCEDURES:** The names of indigent/needy families in the Pottstown community are provided by the Salvation Army/Boyertown, United Way of Pottstown & Vicinity, and Pottstown Cluster of Religious Communities. After review by the Foundation's administrative staff, food/toys are distributed during the holidays.

O+D+T Dennis Pfeiffer (D+Con) — Corporate donor: Peerless Publications, Inc. and other local businesses/individuals.

SE-530 Powell (Alice, Debra & Donna) Trust Foundation, The
313 Linden Drive
Elkins Park 19027   (Montgomery County)

MI-19-21-41-61-72

Phone 215-884-8146 **FAX** None
EIN 232762647   **Year Created** 1994

AMV $327,494   **FYE** 12-00   **(Gifts Received** $6,769)   9 **Grants totaling** $16,300

About two-thirds local giving. High Pa. grant of **$3,000** to Sisters of St. Basil. **$2,500** to Caron Foundation. **$1,800** to Germantown Academy. **$1,300** to American Legion-Christmas Fund [Bucks County]. **$700** to Hope for the Animals. **$500** each to Montgomery County SPCA and Ukrainian Educational & Cultural Center. **Out-of-state** grant: **$5,000** to Chalice of Repose Project [MT]. ■**PUBLICATIONS:** None ■**WEBSITE:** None ■**E-MAIL:** None ■**APPLICATION POLICIES & PROCEDURES:** No grants are awarded to individuals.

O+D+T Alice E. Powell (T+Donor+Con) — Donna Powell Abel [North Wales] (T) — Debra Powell [OR] (T)

SE-531 Powell (Arthur L. & Lea R.) Foundation, The
c/o Wolf, Block, Schorr & Solis-Cohen
1650 Arch Street, 22nd Floor
Philadelphia   (Philadelphia County)

MI-21-31-41-42-43-44-56-62-71-72-89

Phone 215-977-2106 **FAX** 215-405-3706
EIN 23-2769441   **Year Created** 1988

AMV $1,644,181   **FYE** 2-01   **(Gifts Received** $187,500)   13 **Grants totaling** $252,715

Mostly local giving; grants are for general support except as noted. Three grants totaling **$91,000** to Upper Merion Township (community service projects/park program/employee scholarship fund). **$75,000** to Montgomery Hospital (general support/van purchase). **$22,500** to King of Prussia Rotary Foundation. **$20,000** to Norristown Zoo. **$10,715** to Temple B'rith Achim. **$10,000** each to King of Prussia Historical Society and Upper Merion Township Library. **$2,500** to Upper Merion School District (scholarship fund). **$1,000** to Middletown Township, Bucks County (parks & recreation). **Out-of-state** grant: **$10,000** to Alfred U. 21st Century Group [NY]. ■**PUBLICATIONS:** None ■**WEBSITE:** None ■**E-MAIL:** dglyn@wolfblock.com ■**APPLICATION POLICIES & PROCEDURES:** No grants are awarded to individuals.

O+D+T David R. Glyn, Esq. (Con) — Arthur L. Powell [Phoenixville] (P+Donor) — Lea R. Powell [Phoenixville] (VP) — David J. Kaufman, Esq. (S)

SE-532 Presser Foundation, The
385 Lancaster Ave., Suite 205
Haverford 19041   (Montgomery County)

MI-15-42-43-51-52-55

Phone 610-658-9030 **FAX** None
EIN 23-2164013   **Year Created** 1916

AMV $58,243,872   **FYE** 6-01   **(Gifts Received** $1,203,569)   300+ **Grants totaling** $2,180,348

Nationwide giving for music education, advancement of music, aid to needy music teachers, and other musical purposes; about 40% giving to Pa. **MUSIC ADVANCEMENT GRANTS** (60 grants totaling $436,700): **$30,000** each to Concerto Soloists Chamber Orchestra and Philadelphia Chamber Music Society. **$25,000** to Philadelphia Singers. **$20,000** each to Academy of Vocal Arts and Philadelphia Orchestra. **$15,000** each to Annenberg Center, Astral Artistic Services, Mendelssohn Club of Philadelphia, Opera Company of Philadelphia, Settlement Music School, and Singing City. **$12,500** to Temple U. (Music Prep). **$10,000** each to Network for New Music and Sylvan Opera. **$7,000-$7,500** each to Bach Choir of Bethlehem, Darlington Fine Arts Center, Pa. Ballet, and Salvation Army. **$6,000** to Bach Festival of Philadelphia. **$5,000** each to Academy of Community Music, Choral Arts Society of Philadelphia, Philadelphia Youth Orchestra, Saunders House, Strings for Schools, and Young Audiences of Eastern Pa. **$4,000** each to Community Music School of Collegeville, Philomel Concerts, and Recording for the Blind & Dyslexic. **$1,000-$3,000** each to 1807 & Friends, Delaware County Orchestra, German Society of Pa., King's College, Main Line Symphony Orchestra, Mozart Society of Philadelphia, Music Group of Philadelphia, Pa. Academy of Music, Pa. Pro Music, Philadelphia Art Alliance, Philadelphia Boys Choir & Chorale, Philadelphia Senior Center, Relache, Suburban Music School, Susquehanna Chorale, Tri-County Concerts Assn., and Voices Novae et Antiquae. **Out-of-state** grants, **$1,000-$10,000**, to 15 musical organizations/festivals in many states. **SPECIAL GRANTS/CAPITAL SUPPORT PROJECTS** (15 grants totaling $647,045): **$200,000** to Curtis Institute of Music. **$62,500** to Philadelphia Orchestra. **$50,000** to Philadelphia Chamber Music Society. **$30,000** to Astral Artistic Services. **$25,000** to Moravian College. **$20,000** to Mansfield U. **$10,000** to Orchestra 2001. **$7,500** to Salvation Army. **$6,545** to Darlington Fine Arts Center. **$5,000** each to Community Music School. **$3,500** to Philadelphia Classical Guitar Society. **$2,000** to Delaware County Youth Orchestra. **Out-of-state** giving includes **$100,000** to Stetson U. [SC]; **$75,000** to Randolph-Macon Woman's College; and **$50,000** to Houston Symphony [TX]. **PRESSER MUSIC AWARDS** for Music Schools (209 grants totaling $880,500): **$4,000** scholarship awards to 190 colleges/universities nationwide including 12 in Pa., and Presser

Music Awards of **$7,500** each to Curtis Institute of Music, Temple U. and 17 others out of state. ***Assistance to Needy Music Teachers***: **$216,103** including support for Presser residents at Cathedral Village Retirement Home. ■**PUBLICATIONS:** statement of program policy ■**WEBSITE:** None ■**E-MAIL:** None ■**APPLICATION POLICIES & PROCEDURES:** Nationwide giving is restricted to (a) charitable or educational organizations for the advancement of music, or (b) established educational institutions for music scholarship aid, or (c) assisting needy music teachers. Most grants are for special projects, building funds, scholarships, or matching grants; multiyear grants are awarded. No grants are awarded to/for salaries, travel, publications, or organizations outside the United States; no scholarships are awarded directly to music students. Scholarship aid requests from schools of music must be submitted on a Scholarship Aid Application form available from the Foundation. Grant requests for 'Advancement of Music' or 'Special Musical Project' awards may be submitted at any time in a full proposal together with a cover letter; include a project budget and IRS tax-exempt status documentation. Site visits sometimes are made to organizations being considered for a grant. The Board of Trustees awards grants at meetings held monthly except March, July and August.

O+D+T Edith A. Reinhardt [Swarthmore] (P+T+Con) — Thomas M. Hyndman, Jr. Esq. (VP+T) — Bruce Montgomery (S+T) — William M. Davison, 4th (F+T) — Leon Bates (T) — Robert Capanna (T) — Anthony P. Checchia (T) — Robert W. Denious (T) — Herbert T. Evert (T) — Martin A. Heckscher, Esq. (T) — Helen Laird (T) — Wendell Pritchett (T) — Michael Stairs (T) — Henderson Supplee, III (T) — Vera Wilson (T) — David Boe (T)

SE-533   Pressman (Roy) Foundation

The Pennsylvanian, Apt. 9A5
2401 Pennsylvania Ave.
Philadelphia 19130   (Philadelphia County)

MI-15-20-52-53

Phone 215-684-0500 **FAX** None
EIN 23-2690562   **Year Created** 1992

AMV $742,551   **FYE** 5-01   (**Gifts Received** $0)   4 **Grants totaling** $46,200

All local giving. High grant of **$15,700** to Curtis Institute of Music (scholarships). **$15,000** each to Clay Studio (Claymobile Project) and Senior Citizen Judicare (general support). **$500** to Academy of Vocal Arts (scholarships). ■**PUBLICATIONS:** None ■ **WEBSITE:** None ■**E-MAIL:** None ■**APPLICATION POLICIES & PROCEDURES:** Grant requests may be submitted in a letter at any time; detail the proposed project with a budget, and include financial data and IRS tax-exempt status documentation.

O+D+T Sylvan H. Savadove, Esq. (P+F+S+D+Con) — Paul L. Feldman, Esq. (D)

SE-534   Pritchard Foundation

115 Aarons Ave.
Doylestown 18901   (Bucks County)

MI-13-84

Phone 215-345-9450 **FAX** None
EIN 23-7982138   **Year Created** 1998

AMV $1,306,663   **FYE** 12-99   (**Gifts Received** $0)   2 **Grants totaling** $65,000

No Pa. giving. High grant of **$50,000** to Outward Bound [NY]. **$15,000** to Thompson Island Outward Bound Education Center [NY]. — Grant in 1998: **$50,000** to Outward Bound [NY]. ■**PUBLICATIONS:** None ■**WEBSITE:** None ■**E-MAIL:** None ■**APPLICATION POLICIES & PROCEDURES:** Information not available.

O+D+T Douglas M. Newton (Con) — Peter L. Buttenwieser [Philadelphia] (T) — Allen Grossman [Philadelphia (T) — Lee P. Klingenstein [NY] (T)

SE-535   Professional Underwriters Foundation

c/o Professional Underwriters, Inc.
V.F. Corp. Center, 820 Adams Ave., Suite 200
Trooper 19403   (Montgomery County)

MI-12-13-35-41-63

Phone 610-631-8700 **FAX** 610-631-8686
EIN 23-2746886   **Year Created** 1993

AMV $70,732   **FYE** 12-00   (**Gifts Received** $0)   8 **Grants totaling** $24,350

Mostly local giving. High grant of **$15,000** to Germantown Boys & Girls Club. **$3,350** to Children's Dental Center of Greater Philadelphia. **$2,000** to Agnes Irwin School. **Out-of-state** giving includes **$2,000** to Big Laurel Learning Center [WV] and **$1,000** to Orthodox Christian Mission Center [FL]. ■**PUBLICATIONS:** None ■**WEBSITE:** www.professionalunderwriters.com [corporate info only] ■**E-MAIL:** None ■**APPLICATION POLICIES & PROCEDURES:** No grants awarded to individuals.

O+D+T Michael P. Miles (T+Donor+Con) — Robert B. Hill (T) — S. Alan Pcsolyar (T)

SE-536   Progress Foundation

c/o Progress Bank / Progress Financial Group
4 Sentry Parkway, Suite 200
Blue Bell 19422   (Montgomery County)

MI-13-14-15-29-41-43-84

Phone 610-940-1395 **FAX** 610-238-0231
EIN 23-2421995   **Year Created** 1986

AMV $151,644   **FYE** 12-00   (**Gifts Received** $61,819)   12 **Grants totaling** $21,500

All local giving in the Bank's trading area. High grant of **$5,600** for a scholarship. **$5,000** to Camp Rainbow. **$3,500** to A Home for the Inn. **$2,000** to Plymouth Meeting Friends School. **$1,000-$1,500** each to Camphill Soltane, Gateway Employee Resources, and Wissahickon Hospice. **$500** each to Montgomery County Big Brothers/Big Sisters and Recording for the Blind & Dyslexic. Other smaller contributions. ■**PUBLICATIONS:** None ■**WEBSITE:** www.progressbank.com [corporate info only] ■ **E-MAIL:** None ■**APPLICATION POLICIES & PROCEDURES:** The Foundation reports that all giving is for education or children in the Bank's trading area (see website for Bank branch office locations); most grants are for special projects or scholarships. No grants are awarded to individuals. Prospective applicants should make an initial telephone inquiry about the feasibility of submitting a grant request. Grant requests may be submitted in a letter at any time; include an annual report, organizational budget, audited financial statement, and IRS tax-exempt documentation. Site visits sometimes are made to organizations being considered for a grant.

O+D+T George E. Gunning, Jr. (P+D+Con) — W. Kirk Wycoff (Executive VP+D) — Georgann McKenna (VP+D) — Eric Morgan (F+D) — Dr. Joseph DiMino (D) — Fran Fusco (D) — John Ondik (D) — Thomas Speers, Esq. (D)

SE-537   **Progressive Business Publications Charitable Trust**   MI-13-41-42-51-81
c/o Progressive Business Publications
370 Technology Drive   **Phone** 610-695-8600 **FAX** 610-647-8089
Malvern 19355   (Chester County)   **EIN** 23-7835073   **Year Created** 1996
AMV $490,153   **FYE** 12-00   **(Gifts Received** $204,744)   8 **Grants totaling** $56,100
All local giving; all grants are for general purposes. High grant of **$22,250** to U. of Pa. **$10,000** to United Way of SE Pa.
$8,500 to World Affairs Council of Philadelphia. **$6,250** to International House. **$5,000** to Walnut Street Theatre. **$2,500** to
Boy Scouts/Cradle of Liberty Council. **$1,500** to Philadelphia Futures. Also, the Foundation sponsored an after-school enrich-
ment program, grades K-5, at Cook-Wissahickon Elementary School [Philadelphia]. ■**PUBLICATIONS:** None ■**WEBSITE:** None
■**E-MAIL:** None ■**APPLICATION POLICIES & PROCEDURES:** No grants are awarded to individuals.
O+D+T   Edward M. Satell (T+Donor+Con) — Corporate donor: American Future Systems, Inc.

SE-538   **Psalm 103 Foundation, The**   MI-22-34-41-63
601 Pembroke Road   **Phone** 610-525-6879 **FAX** None
Bryn Mawr 19010   (Montgomery County)   **EIN** 23-2500843   **Year Created** 1987
AMV $4,329,717   **FYE** 9-00   **(Gifts Received** $304,537)   9 **Grants totaling** $278,890
Mostly local giving. High grant of **$200,000** to Delaware County Christian School (Advancing the Kingdom Campaign). **$8,000**
to Salvation Army/Philadelphia (Christmas gift/program support). **$2,500** to Salvation Army/Norristown (capital campaign).
Out-of-state giving includes **$46,390** to American Trauma Society [MD] (program support); **$12,000** to Impact America
Foundation (Servant Leadership Project); and **$6,000** to Advancing Churches in Missions Commitment [GA] (program support);
and **$4,000** to Young Life. ■**PUBLICATIONS:** None ■**WEBSITE:** None ■**E-MAIL:** None ■**APPLICATION POLICIES & PROCE-
DURES:** Grant requests may be submitted in any form at any time. No grants awarded to individuals.
O+D+T   John M. Templeton, Jr. ,M.D. (P+F+Donor+Con) — Josephine J. Templeton (VP+S)

SE-539   **PTS Foundation**   MI-17-31-41-42-43-54
c/o Glenville Group
580 West Germantown Pike, Suite 202   **Phone** 610-825-4300 **FAX** None
Plymouth Meeting 19462   (Montgomery County)   **EIN** 23-2930670   **Year Created** 1998
AMV $10,149,573   **FYE** 12-00   **(Gifts Received** $0)   8 **Grants totaling** $362,375
Two local grants: **$65,000** to Shipley School and **$25,000** to LaSalle U. **Out-of-state** grants, all to OH, include **$100,000** to
Cleveland Museum of Art (fund restoration project); **$59,875** to HRH Scholarship Fund (scholarships for dependents of former
employees of family businesses in OH and NY); **$37,500** each to Case Western Reserve U. (program for family business execu-
tives) and Horvitz Newspapers Charity Fund (support to organizations in OH and NY); **$25,000** to United Jewish Cemeteries;
and **$12,500** to Cleveland Clinic (Horvitz Palliative Care Center). — In 1998, one local grant awarded: **$4,250** to U. of Pa./An-
nenberg School of Communications (monitor/evaluate domestic violence program). ■**PUBLICATIONS:** None ■**WEBSITE:** None
■**E-MAIL:** None ■**APPLICATION POLICIES & PROCEDURES:** Grant requests may be submitted at any time; outline the specifics of the proposed project.
O+D+T   Pam Horvitz Schneider (C+D+Con) — Milton S. Schneider (P+S+F+D) — Thomas H. Oden [OH] (AF) — Leo M.
Krulitz [OH] (AS) Foundation donor: Lois U. Horvitz Foundation

---

SE-540   **Quaker Chemical Foundation, The**   MI-12-13-14-15-17-24-25-29-31-35-41-42-43
c/o Quaker Chemical Corporation   44-45-51-52-53-54-55-72-81-88
Elm & Lee Streets   **Phone** 610-832-4127 **FAX** 610-832-4494
Conshohocken 19428   (Montgomery County)   **EIN** 23-6245803   **Year Created** 1959
AMV $610,241   **FYE** 6-00   **(Gifts Received** $307,000)   122+ **Grants totaling** $300,558
Mostly local giving; all grants are for general support. ***ARTS/CULTURE GRANTS*** totaling $50,500: **$3,500** to Young Audiences
of Eastern Pa. **$3,000** each to Opera Company of Philadelphia and Philadelphia Orchestra. **$2,500** each to Bach Festival of
Philadelphia, International House of Philadelphia, and Philadelphia Museum of Art. **$2,000** each to Academy of Natural Sciences
and University Museum of Archaeology & Anthropology. **$1,000-$1,500** each to Academy of Vocal Arts, Arden Theatre Company, Astral Artistic Services, Atwater Kent Museum, Franklin Institute, Independence Seaport Museum, International Visitors
Council of Philadelphia, Library Company of Philadelphia, Mann Center for the Performing Arts, Pa. Ballet, Philadelphia Chamber
Music Society, Philadelphia Theatre Company, Philadelphia Young Playwrights, Philadelphia Zoo, Please Touch Museum, Point
Breeze Performing Arts Center, Rock School of Pa. Ballet, Rosenbach Museum & Library, and Storybook Musical Theatre. Other
smaller contributions. ***HEALTH/WELFARE GRANTS*** totaling $42,100: **$2,000** each to Recording for the Blind & Dyslexic,
RSVP of Montgomery County, and Women's Assn. for Women's Alternatives. **$1,000-$1,500** each to AHEDD [Cumberland
County], Corporate Alliance for Drug Education, Child Home & Community, Children's Aid Society of Montgomery County, Crime
Victim's Center of Chester County, Family Services, Focus on Women's Health, Fox Chase Cancer Center, Jeanes Vital Age, Kearsley
Retirement Community, Lakeside Youth Service, MANNA/Metropolitan AIDS Neighborhood Nutrition Alliance, Melmark, National
Transplant Assistance Fund, Philabundance, Philadelphians Concerned About Housing, Senior Adult Activities Center, Southern
Home Services, STRIVE/Metropolitan Career Center, Voyage House, Wissahickon Hospice, and Youth Service, Inc. Other smaller
local contributions. ***EDUCATION GRANTS*** totaling $47,068: **$12,000** to Free Library of Philadelphia (special project grant).
$2,000-$2,500 each to Academy of Notre Dame deNamur, Bryn Mawr College, Cabrini College, Haverford College, Metropolitan Career Center, Overbrook School for the Blind, and Pathway School. **$1,000-$1,500** each to Abington School District, Abraham Lincoln High School, Center for Greater Philadelphia, Delaware Valley College, Manor Junior College, MBF Center,
NetworkArts, Pa. Free Enterprise Week, Pa. School for the Deaf, Philadelphia U., Royer-Greaves School for the Blind, Settlement

Music School, Villanova U., and White-Williams Scholars. Other smaller local contributions. Also, 21 college scholarships Goodling **$59,000** awarded to company employee dependents. ***CIVIC/COMMUNITY GRANTS*** totaling **$33,580: $2,500** each to Colonial Meals on Wheels and Colonial Neighborhood Council. **$2,000** each to Conshohocken AMBUCS and William Jeanes Memorial Library. **$1,000-$1,500** each to Central Philadelphia Development Corp., Conshohocken Historical Society, Committee of Seventy, Elmwood Park Zoo, Executive Service Corps, Forteniters Club, Freedom Valley Girl Scout Council, Historic Bartram's Garden, Norris Square Neighborhood Project, North Penn Valley Boys & Girls Club, Old First Reformed Church, Patrician Society of Central Norristown, Pa. Special Olympics, Perkiomen Valley Watershed Assn. Plymouth Meeting Historical Society, Schuylkill Center for Environmental Education, Whitemarsh Community Art Center, and Willow Grove Community Development Center. Other smaller local contributions. **Out-of-state** giving in all above areas of interest was limited to corporate operating locations in MI, OK, CA, and South Africa. In addition, about 365 matching gifts totaling **$67,490** were disbursed to all types of nonprofit organizations.
■**PUBLICATIONS:** application guidelines ■**WEBSITE:** None ■**E-MAIL:** None ■**APPLICATION POLICIES & PROCEDURES:** The Foundation reports that giving focuses on arts/cultural, educational (especially related to chemistry or the physical sciences), health/welfare, and civic/community organizations in corporate operating locations. Most grants are for special projects, research, or matching gifts. Generally, no grants are awarded for bricks & mortar projects or to national organizations; scholarships are awarded only to dependents of Quaker Chemical employees. Prospective applicants initially should request a copy of the application guidelines. Grant requests should be submitted in a full proposal before the April 30th deadline; include a project description with pro forma budget, current organizational budget, audited financial statement, list of major past/current/anticipated funding sources, Board member/officer list, and IRS tax-exempt status documentation. The Board of Directors meets in May or June. Matching gifts for all types of nonprofit organizations have a $10 minimum, $1,000 maximum/employee/year; gifts up to $250 are matched 2:1.
O+D+T Kathleen A. Lasota (S+Con) — Karl H. Spaeth (C+T) — Katherine N. Coughenour (T) — Dr. Edwin J. Delattre (T) — Alan G. Keyser (T) — Jane L. Williams (T) — J. Everett Wick (T) — Corporate donor: Quaker Chemical Corporation

---

SE-541   Quaker City Fund
c/o Schumacker & Lunkenheimer
825 Duportail Road, Suite 103
Wayne   19087   (Chester County)

MI-12-22-29-31-33-41-42-63-71-89

Phone 610-651-4900 **FAX** None
EIN 51-0200152   **Year Created** 1976

AMV $1,836,686   **FYE** 12-00   (**Gifts Received** $0)   36 **Grants totaling** $87,500

Mostly local giving; grants are for general support except as noted. High grant of **$25,000** to Paoli Memorial Hospital. **$20,000** to St. John's Presbyterian Church of Devon (retirement/housing fund/general support). **$4,000** to Old First Reformed Church. **$2,000-$2,500** each to The Baldwin School, Daemion House, Pierce Junior College, Presbyterian Children's Village, and Wills Eye Hospital. **$1,000** each to Berwyn Fire Company, Easttown Township Police Dept., Jenkins Arboretum, and Main Line Community Services (Junior Service Board). Other smaller local/Pa. contributions for various purposes. **Out-of-state** giving includes **$5,000** to Ocean Reef Medical Center [FL]; **$2,500** each to Massachusetts Institute of Technology and Winterthur Museum [DE]; **$1,000** each to Burdette Tomlin Memorial Hospital [NJ] and Helen Diller Home for the Blind [NJ]; and other grants/contributions to DE, NJ and FL. ■**PUBLICATIONS:** None ■**WEBSITE:** None ■**E-MAIL:** None ■**APPLICATION POLICIES & PROCEDURES:** Information not available.
O+D+T Scott F. Schumacker, Esq. (P+Con) — John C. Voss, Esq. (VP+F)

SE-542   Raab (Norman) Foundation
Buckingham II, Suite 2CC
P.O. Box 657
Holicong   18928   (Bucks County)

MI-15-22-32-62

Phone 215-794-5640 **FAX** None
EIN 23-7006390   **Year Created** 1968

AMV $172,432   **FYE** 9-00   (**Gifts Received** $0)   22 **Grants totaling** $19,585

About half local giving. High grant of **$10,000** to Jewish Federation of Greater Philadelphia. Other local contributions **$100** or smaller. **Out-of-state** giving includes **$5,500** to Wilmer Ophthalmological Institute [MD] and **$1,500** to Hospice Care of Broward County [FL]. ■**PUBLICATIONS:** None ■**WEBSITE:** None ■**E-MAIL:** None ■**APPLICATION POLICIES & PROCEDURES:** Grant requests may be submitted in a letter at any time; describe the organization, state the amount requested and a person to contact for further information, and include the prior year's financial statement (or Form 990). No grants awarded to individuals.
O+D+T Stephen Raab (T+Donor+Con) — Norman Raab [FL] (T+Donor) — Whitney Raab [CA] (T+Donor)

SE-543   Rabbis' Fund of Philadelphia, The
c/o Wolf, Block, Schorr & Solis-Cohen
1650 Arch Street, 22nd Floor
Philadelphia   19103   (Philadelphia County)

MI-15-17-22-25-29

Phone 215-977-2114 **FAX** 215-977-2346
EIN 23-2260986   **Year Created** 1983

AMV $105,582   **FYE** 8-00   (**Gifts Received** $1,339)   22 **Grants totaling** $10,700

All giving limited to Philadelphia-area organizations providing food for the needy. High grant of **$800** to Mercy Hospice-Catholic Social Services. **$750** to Red Cross/Lower Bucks Chapter. **$650** to Christ Church Home-Kearsley Retirement Home. Other local contributions **$300-$500** for 19 religious service organizations, churches, community groups, and social service agencies providing food for the needy. ■**PUBLICATIONS:** None ■**WEBSITE:** None ■**E-MAIL:** jgoldberg@wolfblock.com ■**APPLICATION POLICIES & PROCEDURES:** Only Philadelphia-area organizations providing food for the needy are eligible to apply. Prospective applicants initially should make a telephone inquiry about the feasibility of submitting a request. Grant requests may be submitted in a letter at any time; include IRS tax-exempt status documentation. Site visits sometimes are made to organizations being considered for a grant.
O+D+T Jay L. Goldberg, Esq. (F+D+Con) — Rabbi Robert Layman (S+D) — Alvin H. Dorsky, Esq. (D) — Rabbi Sanford Hahn (D) — David N. Pincus (D) — Elizabeth Pincus [Wallingford] (D)

SE-544 RAF Foundation, The
One Pitcairn Place, Suite 2100
165 Township Line Road
Jenkintown 19046   (Montgomery County)

MI-11-13-14-15-31-32-42-52-53-54-56-81

Phone 215-572-0738 **FAX** None
EIN 23-2331199 **Year Created** 1985

AMV $9,050,954   **FYE** 11-00   (**Gifts Received** $4,671,657)   21 **Grants totaling** $3,680,000

Mostly local giving; grants are for general purposes except as noted. High grant of **$2,763,500** to U. of Pa. **$262,000** to Moore College of Art (building fund). **$200,000** to United Way of SE Pa. **$100,000** each to National Organization for Hearing Research and Wistar Institute. **$33,000** to National Constitution Center. **$30,000** to Temple U. (Center for American Jewish History/Friedman Chair). **$17,500** to Foreign Policy Research Institute. **$15,000** to Macula Vision Research Foundation. **$5,000** each to Academy of Music Restoration Fund/Philadelphia Orchestra, Fox Chase Cancer Center, Friends' Central School (building construction), National Museum of American Jewish History, and Police Athletic League of Philadelphia (scholarships). **$1,500-$2,500** each to Philadelphia Geriatric Center, United Negro College Fund, U. of Pa. Medical Center, and Woodlynde School. **Out-of-state** grants: **$100,000** to Nantucket Cottage Hospital [MA] and **$25,000** to American Friends of Israel Democracy Institute [GA]. ■**PUBLICATIONS:** None ■**WEBSITE:** None ■**E-MAIL:** None ■**APPLICATION POLICIES & PROCEDURES:** Grant requests may be submitted in a letter at any time; describe the organization's charitable activities. No grants awarded to individuals.
O+D+T Robert A. Fox (T+Donor+Con) — Esther G. Fox (T) Corporate donors: RAF Industries; Bar Plate Manufacturing; Ferche Millwork; Hardware Supply Co.; Vinyl Building Products [NJ]

SE-545 Rafalin (Mario & Sara) Foundation, The
606 Ballytore Road
Wynnewood 19096   (Montgomery County)

MI-14-32-42-54-81

Phone 610-642-3190 **FAX** None
EIN 23-2489543 **Year Created** 1987

AMV $182,172   **FYE** 11-00   (**Gifts Received** $0)   13 **Grants totaling** $13,450

About one-third local giving. High grant of **$3,000** to World Affairs Council of Philadelphia. **$1,000** each to American Friends of Jerusalem Elwyn and National Museum of American Jewish History. **Out-of-state** giving includes **$2,000** to American Committee for the Weizmann Institute of Science [NY] and **$1,000-$1,500** each to American Academy of Periodontology Foundation [IL], American Red Magen David [NY], Brandeis U. [MA], Israel Cancer Research Fund [NY], and Jewish Braille Institute of America [NY]. ■**PUBLICATIONS:** None ■**WEBSITE:** None ■**E-MAIL:** None ■**APPLICATION POLICIES & PROCEDURES:** No grants awarded to individuals.
O+D+T Dr. Mario Rafalin (P+Donor+Con)

SE-546 Rankin Family Foundation, The
501 Schoolhouse Road
Telford 18969   (Bucks County)

MI-22-42-63-64

Phone 215-721-1721 **FAX** None
EIN 23-2867283 **Year Created** 1996

AMV $1,024,736   **FYE** 12-00   (**Gifts Received** $0)   12 **Grants totaling** $268,000

Mostly local/Pa. giving. High grant of **$130,000** to Hilltown Baptist Church. **$60,000** to Salvation Army/Philadelphia. **$25,000** to Seminary of the East. **$10,000** to Mission Projects Fellowship [Telford]. **$5,000** each to Child Evangelism Fellowship [Dublin] and Pocket Testament League [Lititz]. **Out-of-state** giving includes **$20,000** to Focus on the Family [CO] and **$10,000** to Billy Graham Evangelistic Assn. [MN]. — Major giving in prior years to U. of Illinois/Champaign-Urbana. ■**PUBLICATIONS:** None ■**WEBSITE:** None ■**E-MAIL:** None ■**APPLICATION POLICIES & PROCEDURES:** Grant requests may be submitted in a letter at any time.
O+D+T Alexander Rankin, V (P+Donor+Con) — Joanne S. Rankin (S+F)

SE-547 Rappolt Charitable Foundation, The
1156 Eleni Lane
West Chester 19382   (Chester County)

MI-17-31

Phone 610-793-3751 **FAX** None
EIN 25-1823899 **Year Created** 1998

AMV $569,469   **FYE** 12-00   (**Gifts Received** $0)   1 **Grant of** $50,000

Sole grant to Children's Hospital Boston [MA]. — In the prior year, **$500** to Calvary Women's Shelter [DC]. ■**PUBLICATIONS:** None ■**WEBSITE:** None ■**E-MAIL:** None ■**APPLICATION POLICIES & PROCEDURES:** Information not available.
O+D+T William G. Rappolt (T+Donor+Con) — Pamela H. Rappolt (T+Donor)

SE-548 Redmond (John Charles & Kathryn S.) Foundation
1602 Sylvan Drive, P.O. Box 1146
Blue Bell 19422   (Montgomery County)

MI-222-42-42-61

Phone 610-279-4090 **FAX** None
EIN 23-6279089 **Year Created** 1955

AMV $1,509,784   **FYE** 12-00   (**Gifts Received** $0)   24 **Grants totaling** $63,700

Mostly local or NE Pa. giving. High grant of **$20,000** to Chestnut Hill College. **$6,500** to Seton Catholic High School [Luzerne County]. **$5,000** to U. of Scranton. **$4,000** to St. Helena's Church [Center Square]. **$3,000** to St. Helena's School. **$2,000** each to St. Mary Help of Christians Church [Luzerne County], Mt. St. Joseph Academy, LaSalle College High School, and Norwood-Fontbonne Academy. **$1,000-$1,500** each to 11 Catholic churches/schools locally and in NE Pa. **Out-of-state** giving to MD and NJ for the same purposes. ■**PUBLICATIONS:** None ■**WEBSITE:** None ■**E-MAIL:** None ■**APPLICATION POLICIES & PROCEDURES:** The Foundation reports that unsolicited grant requests are not accepted. No grants awarded to individuals.
O+D+T John Charles Redmond, III (P+Con) — Maree Redmond (VP) — Barbara Redmond (S+F) — Dorothy H. Roche (F)

SE-549 Reichlin Family Foundation, The
Fairmont Apartments #604
41 Conshohocken State Road
Bala Cynwyd 19004   (Montgomery County)

MI-11-22-31-32-53-54-62

Phone 610-962-0100 **FAX** 610-962-1080
EIN 23-2815231   **Year Created** 1995

AMV $867,080   **FYE** 12-00   **(Gifts Received** $0)   40 **Grants totaling** $43,050

Mostly local giving; all grants are for general use purposes except as noted. High grant of **$7,438** to Federation Allied Jewish Appeal. **$6,692** to Har Zion Temple. **$5,000-$5,100** each to Anti-Defamation League, Jefferson Digestive Disease Institute, and U. of Pa. Medical Center. **$3,000** to Institute of Contemporary Art (endowment fund). **$2,650** to Albert Einstein Healthcare. **$1,000-$1,700** each to Children's Hospital of Philadelphia, Greater Philadelphia Rabbinical Assembly, National Museum of American Jewish History, and United Way of SE Pa. Other local and out-of-state contributions **$10-$600** for similar purposes. ■
PUBLICATIONS: None ■**WEBSITE:** None ■**E-MAIL:** None ■**APPLICATION POLICIES & PROCEDURES:** Prospective applicants initially should make a telephone inquiry about the feasibility of submitting a request. No grants awarded to individuals.
O+D+T Robert J. Reichlin (P+Donor+Con)

SE-550 Rentschler (George W.) Foundation, The
c/o Obermayer Rebmann Maxwell & Hippel
One Penn Center, 1617 JFK Boulevard, 19th Floor
Philadelphia 19103   (Philadelphia County)

MI-12-13-14-15-22-25-35-41-43-54-61-81-83

Phone 215-665-3096 **FAX** 215-665-3165
EIN 23-6627872   **Year Created** 1975

AMV $2,146,713   **FYE** 1-01   **(Gifts Received** $0)   20 **Grants totaling** $49,500

Mostly local giving; grants are for general operating support except as noted. High Pa. grant of **$5,000** to Sisters of the Holy Family of Nazareth (stained glass windows/wheelchair lift). **$4,000** to Jewish Community Centers of Greater Philadelphia (latchkey program). **$3,500** to Boy Scouts/Cradle of Liberty Council (Learning for Life program). **$2,000-$2,500** each to American Cancer Society (school mini-grants), Elwyn (transitional services), Friends' Central School (basketball/reading/math clinics), Phelps School (scholarship), St. Edmond's Home for Children, and U. of the Arts. **$1,000-$1,500** each to American Educational Film & Video Center (expanded video distribution), Big Brother/Big Sister Assn. of Philadelphia, Center in the Park (intergenerational programs), Please Touch Museum, Salvation Army (shelter for homeless), To Our Children's Future With Health (teen program), and Woods Services Foundation (computer equipment/software). **Out-of-state** grants: **$6,000** to Lawyers Committee for Human Rights [NY]; **$4,000** to National Coalition for Haitian Rights [NY]; and **$3,000** to Pregnancy Aid Center [MD]. ■**PUBLICATIONS:** application form ■**WEBSITE:** None ■**E-MAIL:** hugh.sutherland@obermayer.com ■**APPLICATION POLICIES & PROCEDURES:** The Foundation reports that giving focuses on the Philadelphia-area with most support for operating budgets, special projects, building funds, and scholarships; multiyear grants are awarded. No grants are awarded to individuals. An annual report and statement of program policy are available for review in the Foundation's office. Prospective applicants initially should make a telephone inquiry about the feasibility of submitting a request. Grant requests must be submitted on a formal application form, available from the Foundation, from February to October (deadlines are August 31st and October 15th); include an organization budget, audited financial statement, Board member list, articles of incorporation, most recent IRS Form 990, and IRS tax-exempt status documentation. No site visits are made and no personal interviews are granted. Grants are awarded at a January meeting.
O+D+T Hugh C. Sutherland, Esq. (S+F+Con) — William G. O'Neill, Esq. [Plymouth Meeting] (P) — Samuel Evans, III [Malvern] (VP)

SE-551 Respiratory Distress Syndrome Foundation
24 Wilson Avenue
Chalfont 18914   (Bucks County)

MI-32

Phone 215-822-3585 **FAX** None
EIN 23-2526029   **Year Created** 1989

AMV $3,564   **FYE** 7-01   **(Gifts Received** $16,948)   1 **Grant of** $15,000

Sole grant to U. of Washington (respiratory disease syndrome research). ■**PUBLICATIONS:** None ■**WEBSITE:** None ■**E-MAIL:** None ■**APPLICATION POLICIES & PROCEDURES:** All giving restricted to medical research. Grant requests may be submitted in a letter at any time.
O+D+T Francis X. Cannon (C+Con) — E.F. Hansen, Jr. (VC) — R.T Hansen (P)

SE-552 Ressler Family Foundation, The
1124 Berwind Road
Wynnewood 19096   (Montgomery County)

MI-15-41-82

Phone 215-425-9400 **FAX** 215-425-9414
EIN 23-2797835   **Year Created** 1994

AMV $1,516,680   **FYE** 12-00   **(Gifts Received** $134,438)   2 **Grants totaling** $110,000

One Pa. grant: **$10,000** to Akiba Hebrew Academy. **Out-of-state** grant: **$100,000** to Haifa Foundation [Israel] (day care center for elderly). — Grant approved for future payment: **$400,000** to Haifa Foundation (day care center for elderly). ■**PUBLICATIONS:** None ■**WEBSITE:** None ■**E-MAIL:** None ■**APPLICATION POLICIES & PROCEDURES:** No grants are awarded to individuals.
O+D+T Emerich Ressler (P+D+Donor+Con) — Edith Ressler (S+F+D+Donor) — David Israeli [Bryn Mawr] (D) — Katherine Israeli [Bryn Mawr] (D) — Liga G. Israeli [Bryn Mawr] (D)

SE-553 Rhoads (Jonathan E.) Trust
131 West Walnut Lane
Philadelphia 19144   (Philadelphia County)

MI-15-18-22-31-33-34-41-42-43-56-63

Phone 610-395-8000 **FAX** 610-395-9444
EIN 23-6385682   **Year Created** 1963

AMV $3,070,495   **FYE** 12-00   **(Gifts Received** $20,701)   64 **Grants totaling** $121,750

About three-fourths local giving; grants are unrestricted except as noted. High grant of **$31,300** to Westtown School (mostly capital fund). **$16,000** to Haverford College (building fund / unrestricted / scholarship fund). **$7,000** to Germantown Monthly Meeting. **$4,100** to Philadelphia Yearly Meeting. **$2,000-$2,500** each American Friends Service Committee, American Philosophical Society, College of Physicians, Delaware Valley Friends School (capital fund), Germantown Friends School (library/reading program), and Planned Parenthood Assn. of Delaware Valley. **$1,500** to Stapeley in Germantown. **$1,000** each to Stratford Friends School, and U. of Pa. Other local contributions **$250-$800** for health/human service agencies, schools, Quaker organizations, and others. **Out-of-state** giving includes **$10,000** to Mullica Hill School [NJ]; **$5,000** to U. of Medicine & Dentistry [NJ]; **$4,000** to Hospital Albert Schweitzer [Haiti]; **$2,600** to Earlham College [IN]; and other smaller grants/contributions. ■ **PUBLICATIONS:** None ■ **WEBSITE:** None ■ **E-MAIL:** None ■ **APPLICATION POLICIES & PROCEDURES:** The Foundation reports that giving focuses principally on Society of Friends/Quaker institutions. Submit grant requests in a letter at any time (deadlines are June 1st and November 15th); provide pertinent information and IRS tax-exempt status documentation. The Board meets in June and December.

O+D+T Edward O.F. Rhoads [Macungie] (S+F+T+Donor+Con) — George G. Rhoads, M.D. [NJ] (T+Donor) — Jonathan E. Rhoads, Jr. M.D. [York] (Donor) — Patricia A. Rhoads (Donor)

SE-554 **Rittenhouse Foundation**
2034 Lewis Tower Building
225 South 15th Street
Philadelphia 19102 (Philadelphia County)

MI-11-13-15-22-31-34-41-42-51-52-53-54-56 62-71-72-81-83-89
Phone 215-735-3863 **FAX** None
EIN 23-6005622 **Year Created** 1952

AMV $2,478,156 **FYE** 12-00 **(Gifts Received** $0) 91 **Grants totaling** $101,120

Mostly local giving. High grant of **$10,750** to Walnut Street Theatre. **$6,000** each to Academy of Music and Temple Beth Zion-Beth Israel. **$5,000** each to Free Library of Philadelphia and Philadelphia Dept. of Recreation. **$4,000-$4,500** each to Opera Company of Philadelphia, Philadelphia Orchestra, and United Way of SE Pa. **$3,200** to Historical Society of Pa. **$3,000** to Theatre Alliance of Greater Philadelphia. **$2,000-$2,300** each to Arden Theatre, ASPIRA, Pa. Horticultural Society, Philadelphia Art Alliance, and Philadelphia Senior Center. **$1,000-$1,500** each to Academy of Natural Sciences, Committee of Seventy, Haverford College, Philadelphia Zoo, Plays & Plays, Please Touch Museum, Scheie Eye Institute, Temple U. School of Podiatric Medicine, University City Science Center, U. of Pa. Medical Center, and Valley Forge Military Academy. **$700-$800** each to American Cancer Society, Golden Slipper Club & Charities, International House of Philadelphia, Mikveh Israel Cemetery, Philadelphia Museum of Art, and U. of Pa. Other local contributions **$200-$600** for similar purposes. **Out-of-state** giving includes **$1,000** each to Jerusalem Foundation [NY] and St. Matthias Church [NJ]. ■ **PUBLICATIONS:** Annual Report (lists grantees but not grant sizes) with application procedures ■ **WEBSITE:** None ■ **E-MAIL:** None ■ **APPLICATION POLICIES & PROCEDURES:** The Foundation reports that giving focuses on the Philadelphia area with most grants for operating budgets or special projects; no grants are awarded for endowment or to individuals. Grant requests may be submitted at any time in a letter (2 pages maximum) which describes project goals, objectives, budget, anticipated duration, names of project personnel, and states an amount requested. Supporting materials should include a brief organizational history, Board member list, audited financial statement, IRS tax-exempt status documentation, and a statement that an accounting will be provided upon project completion. Also, proposals which follow Delaware Valley Grantmakers' Common Grant Application Form are accepted (see Appendix or www.dvg.org). An organization may submit only one request per year. Site visits sometimes are made to organizations being considered for a grant. Grants are awarded throughout the year on an unscheduled basis; the Trustees meet in January, April, July, and September.

O+D+T Judith Klein Francis (VP+T+Con) — Arthur Klein (C+T) — Joshua Klein (P+F+T) — Rebecca Klein Clark (T) — Alexander Klein (T) — Esther M. Klein (T)

SE-555 **Robbins (John A.) Foundation**
c/o John A. Robbins Companies, Inc.
555 City Line Ave., Suite 1130
Bala Cynwyd 19004 (Montgomery County)

MI-41-52-63-71
Phone 610-668-6200 **FAX** 610-668-1810
EIN 22-2840041 **Year Created** 1987

AMV $65,589 **FYE** 12-00 **(Gifts Received** $0) 32 **Grants totaling** $15,020

Mostly local/Pa. giving. High grant of **$2,270** to Philadelphia Orchestra. **$2,000** to Phelps School. **$1,872** to Buck Hill Conservation [Monroe County]. **$1,308** to Opera Company of Philadelphia. **$1,000** to Overbrook Church. Other local and out-of-state contributions **$50-$830** for various purposes. ■ **PUBLICATIONS:** None ■ **WEBSITE:** None ■ **E-MAIL:** None ■ **APPLICATION POLICIES & PROCEDURES:** No grants awarded to individuals.

O+D+T Faith Robbins (T+Con) — Ann Cimini (Manager)

SE-556 **Roberts (Aileen K. & Brian L.) Foundation, The**
c/o Comcast Corporation
1500 Market Street, 35th Floor
Philadelphia 19102 (Philadelphia County)

MI-11-21-22-32-41-42-54-56-62-71-84
Phone 215-665-1700 **FAX** None
EIN 23-2787654 **Year Created** 1994

AMV $1,737,751 **FYE** 12-00 **(Gifts Received** $0) 38 **Grants totaling** $194,574

About three-fourths local giving. High grant of **$100,000** to U. of Pa. **$6,666** to Jewish Federation of Greater Philadelphia. **$5,000** each to Brandywine Conservancy, National Liberty Museum, Philadelphia Fashion for Parkinson, Franklin Institute, and United Way of SE Pa. **$3,734** to Academy of Music. **$3,705** to All-American Billiard & Spas [Bucks County]. **$2,000** to Chestnut Hill Rotary Club. **$1,759** to Germantown Academy/Highland Historical Society. **$1,000** to Pa. Horticultural Society. Other local contributions **$$100-$500** for various purposes. **Out-of-state** giving includes **$25,000** to National Cable Television Museum [CO]; **$10,000** to Squashbusters [MA]; and **$2,000** to National Alliance for Autism Research [NJ]. ■ **PUBLICATIONS:** None ■ **WEBSITE:** None ■ **E-MAIL:** None ■ **APPLICATION POLICIES & PROCEDURES:** No grants awarded to individuals.

O+D+T Aileen K. Roberts (P+Donor+Con) — Brian L. Roberts (VP)

SE-557 Roberts (Gilroy & Lillian P.) Charitable Foundation
c/o St. Clair Easton CPAs
10 Presidential Blvd., Suite 250
Bala Cynwyd 19004 (Montgomery County)
AMV $11,140,423 FYE 6-01 (Gifts Received $0)

MI-11-12-13-15-22-29-31-32-42-52-53-54-56
62-84
Phone 610-668-1998 **FAX** 610-668-3479
EIN 23-2219044 **Year Created** 1982
97 **Grants totaling** $537,480

Mostly local giving. High grant of **$156,000** to Temple U. (Merves Professorship in Accounting). **$55,000** to Philadelphia Geriatric Center. **$53,800** to Temple U. (Athletics Dept.). **$40,000** to Temple U. (Jewish Studies program). **$25,000** each to Bryn Mawr Hospital and Red Cross. **$20,000** to Pa. Academy of the Fine Arts. **$13,000** to Harriton Assn. **$10,000** each to Lankenau Hospital and United Way of SE Pa. **$8,550** to U. of Pa. (various purposes). **$8,000** to Temple U./Tyler School of Art. **$6,900** to Philadelphia Folk Song Society. **$5,000** each to Hillel of Greater Philadelphia, Jewish Community Center, Jewish Federation of Greater Philadelphia, and Thomas Jefferson U. Hospital. **$2,000-$2,700** each to Chapel of Four Chaplains, Female Hebrew Benevolent Society, Franklin Institute, Hebrew Immigrant Aid Society, Jewish Employment & Vocational Service, Jewish Publications Society, Philadelphia Jewish Archives Center, Scheie Eye Institute, Settlement Music School, Stiffel Senior Center, and Voyage House. **$1,000-$1,500** each to Abraham Lincoln Foundation, American Cancer Society, American Heart Assn., American Philosophical Society, Boy Scouts/Cradle of Liberty Council, Eldernet of Lower Merion, Gratz College, Library Company of Philadelphia, MANNA/Metropolitan AIDS Neighborhood Nutrition Alliance, RSVP of Montgomery County, and Temple Adath Israel. Other local contributions **$10-$500** for various purposes. **Out-of-state** giving includes **$25,000** to American Numismatic Assn. [CO] and **$10,000** to U. of New England [ME]. ■**PUBLICATIONS:** None ■**WEBSITE:** None ■**E-MAIL:** None ■**APPLICATION POLICIES & PROCEDURES:** The Foundation reports that giving focuses on Montgomery and Delaware counties. No grants awarded to individuals. Prospective applicants initially should make a telephone inquiry about the feasibility of submitting a request. Grant requests may be submitted in a letter (2 pages maximum) at any time; describe the organization's purpose, the proposed project, and amount of funding requested; include an audited financial statement, IRS tax-exempt status documentation, and a statement that 100% of Board members have contributed financial (cash) support to the organization. Site visits sometimes are made to organizations being considered for a grant.

O+D+T Stanley Merves [Haverford] (T+PO+Con) — Walter G. Arader [Radnor] (T) — Audrey Stein Merves [Haverford] (T) — Jennifer Merves [Haverford] (T) — John Taylor Roberts [Newtown Square] (T) — Donor: Estate of Gilroy Roberts

---

SE-558 Roberts (Ralph & Suzanne) Foundation, The
c/o Comcast Corporation
1500 Market Street, 35th Floor
Philadelphia 19102 (Philadelphia County)
AMV $20,391,968 FYE 11-00 (Gifts Received $0)

MI-11-12-22-29-31-32-44-49-51-52-53-54-55
57-62-71-82
Phone 215-665-1700 **FAX** None
EIN 23-7015984 **Year Created** 1969
125+ **Grants totaling** $1,018,349

Mostly local giving; some grants represent multiple awards. **$202,500** to Albert Einstein Healthcare Foundation. **$100,000** to National Liberty Museum. **$95,000** to Hedgerow Theatre. **$70,250** to Brandywine Conservancy. **$30,000** to Federation Allied Jewish Appeal. **$25,000** each to Thomas Jefferson U. Hospital, and U. of Pa. Cancer Center. **$20,000** to Susan Hess Modern Dance, Headlong Dance Theatre, Moxie Dance Collective, SCRAP Performance Group, and U. of the Arts. **$11,000** each to Inter-Act Theatre Company and Pa. Ballet. **$10,500** to Wilma Theatre. **$10,000** each to 1812 Productions, Anti-Defamation League, Arden Theatre Company, Dan Aaron's Parkinson's Disease Foundation, Big Picture Alliance, Brat Productions, Hunger Theatre, Koresh Dance Company, New Paradise Laboratories, Philadelphia Folklore Project, Red Cross, Spiral Q Puppet Theater, The Theatre Catalyst, Inc., Theatre Exile, and Vox Theatre Company. **$7,704** to Philadelphia Orchestra. **$6,000** to Fleisher Art Memorial. **$5,000** each to Academy of Music, Academy of Natural Sciences, Franklin Institute, Free Library of Philadelphia, Opera Company of Philadelphia, Philadelphia Futures, Philadelphia Theatre Company, Prince Music Theater, United Way of SE Pa., and WHYY-91FM. **$3,000** to Executive Service Corps of the Delaware Valley, and Pa. Partnership for Economic Education. **$2,500** to Urban Genesis. **$2,000** to Children's Crisis Treatment Center. **$1,000-$1,600** each to Congregation Rodeph Shalom, Fox Chase Cancer Center, National MS Society, Philadelphia Museum of Art, Rock School of Pa. Ballet (scholarship fund), Walnut Street Theatre, and West Chester Holocaust Commission. Other local contributions **$100-$500** for arts/cultural and health/welfare purposes. **Out-of-state** giving includes **$15,000** to CARE Foundation; **$10,000** each to UNICEF [NY], U.S. Holocaust Memorial Museum [DC], and Simon Wiesenthal Center [CA]; and **$5,000** each to CAP Cure [CA], Doctors Without Borders [NY], Polycystic Kidney Research Foundation [MO], and Starkey Foundation [MN]. ■**PUBLICATIONS:** None ■**WEBSITE:** None ■**E-MAIL:** None ■**APPLICATION POLICIES & PROCEDURES:** Grant requests may be submitted in any form at any time. No grants are awarded to individuals.

O+D+T Ralph J. Roberts (T+Donor+Con) — Suzanne Roberts (T+Donor)

SE-559 Robinson Foundation, The
c/o PNC Advisors
1600 Market Street, 6th Floor
Philadelphia 19103 (Philadelphia County)
AMV $2,061,494 FYE 12-00 (Gifts Received $0)

MI-12-15-18-22-52-85

Phone 215-585-8184 **FAX** 609-722-9218
EIN 23-6207354 **Year Created** 1952
20 **Grants totaling** $117,000

About one-third local giving. High Pa. grants of **$8,000** each to Presbyhomes Foundation and Presbyterian Children's Village Foundation. **$7,000** to Philadelphia Orchestra. **$3,000** each to 18th Street Development Corp. and Planned Parenthood of SE Pa. **Out-of-state** giving, primarily where the Trustees live, includes high grant of **$13,500** to United Way of Orange County [CA]; **$9,750** each to Nursing Clinic of Battle Creek [MI] and St. Paul's School [MD]; and **$2,000-$6,000** each for arts/cultural and human services organizations in ME, GA, TN, and CA. ■**PUBLICATIONS:** application guidelines ■**WEBSITE:** None ■ **E-MAIL:** None ■**APPLICATION POLICIES & PROCEDURES:** The Foundation reports that funds are for relief of poverty, education, health, scientific medical research, and civic affairs purposes. Grant requests should be submitted in a letter during June-August (deadline is September 1st); include a project budget and IRS tax-exempt status documentation. The Trustees award grants at a November meeting.

O+D+T Diane D. Bakley [NJ] (VP at Bank+Con) — Margaret R. Bailey [CA] (T) — Anne B. Nutt [CA] (T) — Kelsey P. Robinson [OH] (T) — Mary R. Talbot [Bryn Mawr] (T) — William R. Talbot [NM] (T) — Sarah R. Wyeth [MD] (T) — PNC Advisors (Corporate Trustee)

SE-560   Rock (Milton L. & Shirley) Foundation   MI-51-52
c/o MLR Holdings LLC / Metroweek Publishing
1845 Walnut Street, Suite 900   **Phone** 215-567-3200 **FAX** 215-405-6078
Philadelphia 19103   (Philadelphia County)   **EIN** 22-2670382   **Year Created** 1985
AMV $2,602,725   **FYE** 12-00   **(Gifts Received** $0)   7 **Grants totaling** $1,067,208

All local giving. High grant of **$1,062,913** to Shirley Rock School of Pa. Ballet. **$1,500** to Dance Affiliates. **$1,000** to Temple U./Esther Boyer College of Music. **$805** to Jeanne Ruddy Dance. Other smaller local contributions for dance or theatre organizations. ■**PUBLICATIONS:** None ■**WEBSITE:** None ■ **E-MAIL:** None ■**APPLICATION POLICIES & PROCEDURES:** The Foundation reports giving is limited to Philadelphia-area arts and related educational institutions; grants are for general support and special projects; multiyear grants are awarded. No grants are awarded to individuals. Grants generally are awarded only to preselected charitable organizations and unsolicited applications are not encouraged.

O+D+T Milton L. Rock [Pocono Pines] (P+D+Donor+Con) — Robert H. Rock [Gladwyne] (VP+F+D) — Susan Mae Rock [Pocono Pines] (VP+S+D)

SE-561   Roemer Foundation, The   MI-14-17-18-32-34-41-56-71-72-84-89
75 Old Stottsville Road   **Phone** 610-857-3595 **FAX** None
Coatesville 19320   (Chester County)   **EIN** 23-2870277   **Year Created** 1996
AMV $8,082,752   **FYE** 6-00   **(Gifts Received** $0)   27 **Grants totaling** $500,000

About three-fourths local giving. High grant of **$115,000** to U. of Pa School of Veterinary Medicine. **$100,000** to Brandywine Conservancy. **$50,000** to Fox Chase Cancer Center. **$30,000** to Planned Parenthood of Chester County. **$25,000** to Thomas Jefferson U./Rothman Institute Research Foundation. **$10,000** each to Brandywine Hospital Foundation and Philadelphia Zoo. **$5,000** each to Canine Partners for Life, Cochranville Fire Co., Parkesburg Fire Co., Stroud Water Research Center, and Thorncroft Therapeutic Horseback Riding. **$2,000** to Chester County Fund for Women & Girls. **$1,000** each to Chester County SPCA, Primitive Hall Foundation, and Upland Country Day School. **Out-of-state** giving included **$55,000** to Sanford School [DE]; **$20,000** each to Arabian Horse Owners Assn. [AZ] and Coriell Institute for Medical Research [NJ]. **$10,000** each to United States Equestrian Team [NJ] and U. of Kentucky. **$5,000** each to Freedom Hills Therapeutic Riding Program [MD] and The Dressage Foundation [NE]. Other smaller grants for similar purposes to several states. ■**PUBLICATIONS:** None ■**WEBSITE:** None ■ **E-MAIL:** None ■**APPLICATION POLICIES & PROCEDURES:** The Foundation reports that in most instances grants are awarded on the initiative of the directors. However, grant requests in any form may be submitted at any time; describe the intended use of the requested funds and include the IRS tax-exempt status determination letter. — Formerly called the Mary Alice Dorrance Malone Foundation.

O+D+T Mary Alice Dorrance Malone (D+Donor+Con) — Margaret M. Duprey (D)

SE-562   Rogers (Martha W.) Charitable Trust   MI-32-33
c/o Mellon Private Wealth Management
1735 Market Street, Room 193-0370   **Phone** 215-553-2596 **FAX** 215-553-4542
Philadelphia 19103   (Philadelphia County)   **EIN** 25-6412239   **Year Created** 1966
AMV $1,531,342   **FYE** 12-99   **(Gifts Received** $0)   3 **Grants totaling** $90,000

All local giving restricted to cancer research, eye research, and mental health research. High grants of **$35,000** each to Friends Hospital and Wills Eye Hospital. **$20,000** to Fox Chase Cancer Center. ■**PUBLICATIONS:** None ■**WEBSITE:** None ■**E-MAIL:** smith.ft@mellon.com ■**APPLICATION POLICIES & PROCEDURES:** Only institutions involved in cancer research, eye research, or mental health research are eligible to apply with Philadelphia-area institutions receiving preference. Grant requests may be submitted in a proposal with an audited financial statement and IRS tax-exempt status documentation.

O+D+T Frances T. Smith (Portfolio Officer at Bank+Con) — Thomas M. Hyndman, Jr., Esq. (T) Mellon Bank N.A. (Trustee)

SE-563   Rokacz (Marian & Eva) Family Foundation   MI-22-62
Academy House, #K-34
1420 Locust Street   **Phone** 215-985-9412 **FAX** None
Philadelphia 19102   (Philadelphia County)   **EIN** 23-6887255   **Year Created** 1986
AMV $80,798   **FYE** 11-00   **(Gifts Received** $10,000)   39 **Grants totaling** $19,368

Limited Pa. giving. **$2,000** to Federation Allied Jewish Appeal. Small local contributions to Community Design Collaboration and Congregation Ner Zedekl Ezrath-Beth Israel. **Out-of-state** giving includes **$1,500** to Volunteers of America [VA]; **$1,000** to UJA-Federation of New York; and other contributions **$800** or smaller, many for arts purposes in New York. ■**PUBLICATIONS:** None ■**WEBSITE:** None ■**E-MAIL:** None ■**APPLICATION POLICIES & PROCEDURES:** Grant requests may be submitted in any form at any time; include IRS tax-exempt status documentation. No grants awarded to individuals. Requests may also be sent to Joseph Rokacz, 440 West 24th Street, New York, NY 10011.

O+D+T Eva Rokacz (T+Donor+Con) — Joseph Rokacz [NY] (T+Donor) — John Rokacz [IL] (T)

SE-564 **Rome (Bonnie) Memorial Foundation, The**   MI-15-22-41-54-62
c/o Rome & Glaberson
1 South Broad Street, Suite 1630   **Phone** 215-751-9700 **FAX** None
Philadelphia 19103   (Philadelphia County)   **EIN** 22-2776756   **Year Created** 1986
AMV $53,400   **FYE** 12-00   (**Gifts Received** $492)   5 **Grants totaling** $20,620

All local giving; all grants are for general purposes. High grant of **$10,000** to Gesu School. **$6,820** to Temple Adath Israel. **$2,000** to Jewish Federation of Greater Philadelphia. **$1,200** to Philadelphia Museum of Art. **$600** to Rowan House. ■ **PUBLI-CATIONS:** None ■ **WEBSITE:** None ■ **E-MAIL:** None ■ **APPLICATION POLICIES & PROCEDURES:** Grant requests may be submitted in any form at any time. No grants awarded to individuals.
O+D+T Joel E. Rome, Esq. (T+Donor+Con) — Jonathan M. Rome, Esq. (T) — Allan B. Schneirov, Esq. (T)

SE-565 **Rorer Foundation, The**   MI-11-12-15-17-22-25-29-31-32-35-41-42-52
761 Newtown Road   54-56-63-71-72
Villanova 19085   **Phone** 610-688-4626 **FAX** 610-688-2291
          (Delaware County)   **EIN** 51-6017981   **Year Created** 1963
AMV $12,436,968   **FYE** 11-00   (**Gifts Received** $0)   55 **Grants totaling** $480,002

About four-fifths local/Pa. giving; grants are unrestricted support/annual giving except as noted. High Pa. grant of **$50,000** to U. of Pa. Wharton School (Campaign for Sustained Leadership). **$33,710** to Chestnut Hill Academy. **$33,333** to U. of Pa./Institute on Aging. **$29,005** to Arcadia U. **$25,000** to Academy of Natural Sciences. **$24,000** to United Way of SE Pa. **$20,000** each to Greater Philadelphia Food Bank and Salvation Army. **$18,000** to Wistar Institute. **$17,000** to Episcopal Community Services. **$15,000** each to Main Line/Delaware Community Orchestra and Red Cross. **$12,000** to St. Davids Church [Wayne]. **$10,000** each to Philabundance and Philadelphia Museum of Art. **$9,184** to The Nature Conservancy/Pa. Chapter. **$7,000** to Academy of Music (restoration fund). **$5,000** each to Agnes Irwin School, Philadelphia Zoo, and Women's Assn. for Women's Alternatives. **$3,000** to Presbyterian Children's Village (capital campaign). **$1,000-$1,650** each to ActionAIDS, Bryn Mawr Hospital Foundation, Corinthian Historical Foundation, Franklin Institute, Philadelphia Orchestra, Voyage House, and Woodlynde School. **$750** to Wildlands Conservancy [Emmaus]. Other local contributions **$200-$500** for various purposes. **Out-of-state** giving includes high grant of **$55,000** to Trinity College [CT]; **$10,000** each to Campus Crusade for Christ [FL] (Jesus Film Project-India) and Food for the Poor [FL]; **$5,000** each to Duke U. [NC], Vassar College [NY], and Yale U. [CT]; and **$4,100** to Sea Education Foundation [MA]. ■ **PUBLICATIONS:** None ■ **WEBSITE:** None ■ **E-MAIL:** None ■ **APPLICATION POLICIES & PROCEDURES:** The Foundation reports that unsolicited grant requests are not accepted.
O+D+T Gerald B. Rorer [Villanova] (P+Donor+Con) — Edward C. Rorer [Villanova] (VP+Donor) — Herbert T. Rorer [Gladwyne] (S+F+Donor)

SE-566 **Rosato (Dr. Donald J.) Charitable Foundation**   MI-14-34-42-52-55-56-57-63-71-72-
176 East Conestoga Road   **Phone** 610-688-1184 **FAX** None
Devon 19333   (Chester County)   **EIN** 23-2746893   **Year Created** 1993
AMV $896,440   **FYE** 12-00   (**Gifts Received** $0)   56 **Grants totaling** $42,120

About two-thirds local giving. High Pa. grant of **$7,000** to Historic Yellow Springs. **$2,500** each to French & Pickering Creeks Foundation and Historical Society of Phoenixville Area. **$1,500** to Ludwigs Corners Horse Show. **$1,000** each to Brandywine Conservancy, Temple U. School of Medicine, Villanova U., West Vincent Land Trust. and WHYY. **$650** to Philadelphia Orchestra. Other local contributions **$250-$500** for many arts, cultural, educational, environmental, historical, and human services organizations. **Out-of-state** giving includes high grant of **$7,500** to Bethesda Episcopal Church [NY]; and **$1,000** each to An Evening in Old Saratoga [NY] and Harvard School of Public Health [MA]. ■ **PUBLICATIONS:** None ■ **WEBSITE:** None ■ **E-MAIL:** None ■ **APPLICATION POLICIES & PROCEDURES:** No grants awarded to individuals.
O+D+T Donald J. Rosato, M.D. (T+Donor+Con) — Joseph F. Parella, Jr. [Malvern] (T) — Judith M. Rosato (T) — Robert Rosato (T)

SE-567 **Rosefsky (Sue Perel) Foundation**   MI-42-51-54
2 Thatcher Court   **Phone** 610-649-9211 **FAX** None
Haverford 19041   (Montgomery County)   **EIN** 23-2675269   **Year Created** 1992
AMV $307,708   **FYE** 12-00   (**Gifts Received** $0)   7 **Grants totaling** $3,812

Mostly local giving. High grant of **$2,137** to Philadelphia Theater Company. **$500** to Philadelphia Museum of Art. **$450** each to Congregation Rodeph Shalom and U. of Pa. Other smaller local and out-of-state contributions. ■ **PUBLICATIONS:** None ■ **WEBSITE:** None ■ **E-MAIL:** None ■ **APPLICATION POLICIES & PROCEDURES:** No grants are awarded to individuals.
O+D+T Sue Perel Rosefsky (P+F+D+Con) — Robert L. Gorman, Esq. [Philadelphia] (S+D) Foundation donor: Ruth & Milton Perel Foundation

---

SE-568 **Rosenau (Fred J.) Foundation**   MI-13-32-42-52-54-56
1100 Shadeland Avenue   **Phone** 610-446-4153 **FAX** None
Drexel Hill 19026   (Delaware County)   **EIN** 23-6251768   **Year Created** 1943
AMV $1,500,000   **FYE** 12-00   (**Gifts Received** $0)   60 **Grants totaling** $75,875

About half local giving; some grants comprise multiple payments. High local grants of **$10,000** each to Pepper Hollow Fund and Gary Rosenau Foundation. **$7,500** to Philadelphia Orchestra. **$3,500** to Opera Company of Philadelphia. **$1,500** to Philadelphia Opera Guild. **$1,000** each to Academy of Music (restoration fund), Fox Chase Cancer Center, National Liberty Museum, Police Athletic League, Temple U., and University Museum of Archaeology & Anthropology. Other smaller local contributions, mostly for cultural purposes. **Out-of-state** giving mostly to Aspen, CO and the NY Adirondacks region, primarily for cultural or environmental purposes. ■**PUBLICATIONS:** None ■**WEBSITE:** None ■**E-MAIL:** None ■**APPLICATION POLICIES & PROCEDURES:** Grant requests may be submitted in a letter at any time to Gary Rosenau, 424 Sinclair Road, P.O. Box 5667, Snowmass, CO 81615; telephone 970-923-4215. No grants are awarded to individuals.

O+D+T Francis X. Connell, CPA (Con) — Gary Rosenau [CO] (Manager+T) — Donald Bean, Esq. (T)

SE-569 **Rosenau (Sidney R.) Foundation**
1100 Shadeland Avenue
Drexel Hill   19026   (Delaware County)
AMV $687,000   **FYE** 12-00   (**Gifts Received** $0)

MI-13-14-18-22-41-42-52-53-54-55-56-57-62-84
Phone 610-446-4153 **FAX** None
EIN 23-6259121   **Year Created** 1941
67 **Grants totaling** $97,350

Nearly half local giving; some grants comprise multiple payments. High Pa. grant of **$7,000** to Philadelphia Museum of Art. **$6,800** to Philadelphia Orchestra. **$4,500** to Opera Company of Philadelphia. **$3,000** to Philadelphia Opera Guild. **$2,000** to Jewish Family & Children's Agency. **$1,500** to Planned Parenthood of SE Pa. **$1,000** each to Abington Art Center, Congregation Rodeph Shalom, Devereux Foundation, Mann Center for Performing Arts, Msgr. Bonner High School, Pa. Academy of the Fine Arts, Police Athletic League, Society for the Preservation of Landmarks, Temple U. (music prep), WHYY-TV12, and Wistar Institute. Other smaller local contributions, mostly for cultural purposes. **Out-of-state** giving includes high grant of **$20,000** to U.S. Ski & Snowboard Foundation [UT]; **$5,000** to Aspen Music Festival [CO]; and **$2,000** to Smith College [MA]. ■**PUBLICATIONS:** None ■**WEBSITE:** None ■**E-MAIL:** None ■**APPLICATION POLICIES & PROCEDURES:** Grant requests may be submitted in a letter at any time to Gary Rosenau, 424 Sinclair Road, P.O. Box 5667, Snowmass, CO 81615; telephone 970-923-4215. No grants are awarded to individuals.

O+D+T Francis X. Connell, CPA (Con) — Gary Rosenau [CO] (Manager+T) — Donald Bean, Esq. (T)

SE-570 **Rosenberg (Alexis) Foundation**
P.O. Box 540
Plymouth Meeting   19462
                                     (Montgomery County)
AMV $4,705,470   **FYE** 6-00   (**Gifts Received** $0)

MI-12-13-14-16-17-18-19-22-25-35-41-43-45
51-52-84
Phone 610-828-8145 **FAX** 610-834-8175
EIN 23-2222722   **Year Created** 1983
66 **Grants totaling** $199,000

All giving limited to Philadelphia-area organizations serving children/youth; grants are for general operating support except as noted. High grants of **$5,000** each to Abington YMCA (salary), Germantown Friends School (community scholarships), Greater Philadelphia Urban Affairs Coalition (summer career exploration program), Juvenile Law Center, Pa. Special Olympics (Fall Festival), Southern Home Services (indigent children care), Temple U. Music Preparatory Division (Center for Gifted Musicians), and West Philadelphia Partnership (Partners Program). **$4,000** each to Allegheny West Foundation (elementary school program), College Settlement (campership subsidies), Drueding Center/Project Rainbow (program expansion), Educating Children for Parenting (parent involvement program), Maternity Care Coalition of Greater Philadelphia (MOMobile at Overbrook High School), Summerbridge Germantown, and Voyage House (youth project). **$3,500** each to Easter Seals (Bright Beginnings Program) and Philadelphia Society for Services to Children (Head Start parent support project). **$3,000** each to Adoption Center of Delaware Valley (newspaper columns), Asian American Youth Assn., Church of the Advocate (after-school/summer programs), Clay Studio (community outreach), Community Women's Education Project (child care program), Douglass Elementary School (Northstar-Teen Development program), Frankford Human Relations Coalition (community organizing), Greater Philadelphia Urban Affairs Coalition (Philadelphia Reads!), Jubilee School, Moore College of Art & Design (young artist workshop scholarships), Neighborhood Bike Works, Northwest Interfaith Movement (school age ministry program), Philadelphia Youth Tennis (after-school programs), Philadelphians Concerned About Housing (Project El-Tec), Police Athletic League of Philadelphia, Schuylkill Center for Environmental Education (service land restoration camps), Settlement Music School (after-school arts program), Support Center for Child Advocates (child victim assistance project), Taller Puertorriqueno (cultural exploration program), Village of Arts & Humanities (North Philadelphia arts-youth program), White-Williams Foundation (student stipends), and Woodrow Wilson National Fellowship Foundation (MLK Day of Service). **$2,500** each to Awbury Arboretum Assn. (children's environmental program), Greater Philadelphia Urban Affairs Coalition (mural arts program), Kelly Ann Dolan Memorial Foundation, NetworkArts Philadelphia (ecology-arts program at four schools), Old First Reformed Church (summer camp/YES program), and Planned Parenthood of SE Pa. (sex education for at-risk youth). **$2,000** each to Ad-hoc Committee for Logan/Youth Project, ACLU Foundation of Pa. (Know Your Rights program), Arden Theatre (free tickets for special play), Asian Arts Initiative (youth arts workshop), Center in the Park (intergenerational programs at two schools), Episcopal Community Services (after-school program for at-risk children), Kardon Institute of Arts for People with Disabilities (financial assistance for disabled youth), Montessori Genesis II School, Norris Square Neighborhood Project (summer program), North Light (youth encouragement program), Nueva Esperanza (summer camp scholarships), Philadelphia Home & School Assn. (create associations at low-income schools), Philadelphia Physicians for Social Responsibility (violence prevention program), Preschool Project (neighborhood parenting project), Providence Center (after-school program), Urban Retrievers (Philadelphia Student Union), Wagner Free Institute of Science (children's education program), and West Mt. Airy Neighbors (schools committee). Other smaller grants for similar purposes. ■**PUBLICATIONS:** informational brochure with application guidelines ■**WEBSITE:** None ■ **E-MAIL:** judy1@aol.com ■**APPLICATION POLICIES & PROCEDURES:** The Foundation reports that all grants must exclusively benefit American youth and only organizations in Greater Philadelphia are eligible to apply; requests from national organizations are not considered. No grants are awarded for construction, equipment, or isolated, non-recurring programs. Applicants must demonstrate successful history and financial development abilities. Prospective applicants initially should make a telephone inquiry about the feasibility of submitting a request. Applications must include one copy of the Foundation's Grant Application Form—available from the Foundation—and four sets of a Grant Proposal which must include: I. Proposal Summary, maximum one-half page; II. Narrative (3 pages maximum) with (a) background, history, and mission; (b) current program, activities and accomplishments; (c) description of current need or why you believe need exists, program objectives addressing the need, constituency and number served, events and activities planned with implementation timetables, and interaction with other agencies, if applicable; and (d) how will the program be evaluated, success defined, and measured in the short-term and long-term. III. One copy each of the following must be attached to the original of the Grant Proposal: last annual report or financial statement (audited if available); copy of most recent IRS tax-exempt status exemption letter; program budget and expected sources of revenue; list of Officers and Board members with addresses and telephone numbers; and assurance that the organization is registered under the Pa. Solicitation for Charitable Purposes Act. Deadlines for submission of applications are March 1, June 1, September 1, and December 1; do not sent applications by Express, Certified or Registered Mail. Only one application from an organization within a 12-month period will be considered. The Trustees award grants at meetings in the latter half of March, June, September, and December. Only rarely are site visits made to organizations.

O+D+T Judith L. Bardes (Administrator+Con) — William S. Greenfield, M.D. [Philadelphia] (P+Co-T) — Charles Kahn, Jr. [Philadelphia] (S+Co-T) — William Epstein [Philadelphia] (Co-T)

SE-571 Rosenberg (David M. & Marjorie D.) Foundation
893 Parkes Run Lane
Villanova 19085 (Delaware County)
AMV $2,750,142 **FYE** 12-00 **(Gifts Received** $140,000)

MI-12-14-22-25-31-41-42-62
Phone 610-458-1090 **FAX** None
EIN 23-7715847 **Year Created** 1993
41 **Grants totaling** $291,820

Mostly local/Pa. giving. High grant of **$99,682** to Champions of Caring (Philadelphia schools program). **$87,500** to Penn State U. **$59,400** to Camp Soltane [Glenmoore]. **$8,000** to MossRehab Hospital. **$13,750** to Chester County Futures. **$2,608** to Children's Hospital of Philadelphia. **$2,330** to Bryn Mawr Rehabilitation Hospital. **$2,000** to Federation Allied Jewish Appeal. **$1,000** each to Montessori Children's House [Wayne] and Philabundance. **$800** to Abrahamson Family Cancer Research. Other local contributions **$50-$500** for various community organizations and purposes. **Out-of-state** grants: **$5,000** to Josephson Institute of Ethics [CA] and **$1,000** to E. Glaser Pediatric AIDS Foundation [CA]. ■**PUBLICATIONS:** None ■**WEBSITE:** None ■**E-MAIL:** None ■**APPLICATION POLICIES & PROCEDURES:** Grant requests may be submitted in writing at any time before the September 30th deadline; include IRS tax-exempt status documentation. Also, proposals which follow Delaware Valley Grantmakers' Common Grant Application Form are accepted (see Appendix or www.dvg.org).

O+D+T David M. Rosenberg (P+T+Donor+Con) — Marjorie D. Rosenberg (T+Donor+Con)

SE-572 Rosenberg (Gail & Michael) Foundation
522 Red Oak Drive
Elkins Park 19027 (Montgomery County)
AMV $146,092 **FYE** 12-00 **(Gifts Received** $0)

MI-11-12-22-42-62
Phone 215-886-8756 **FAX** 215-885-6478
EIN 23-2753387 **Year Created** 1996
22 **Grants totaling** $27,264

Mostly local giving. High grant of **$18,061** to Federation Day Care. **$3,750** to Jewish Federation of Greater Philadelphia. **$2,301** to Congregation Rodeph Shalom. **$500** to United Way of SE Pa. Other local contributions **$10-$300** for various purposes. **Out-of-state** giving includes **$500** to Yale U. [CT]. ■**PUBLICATIONS:** None ■**WEBSITE:** None ■**E-MAIL:** None ■**APPLICATION POLICIES & PROCEDURES:** The Foundation reports that all giving is to organizations in which Trustees are active. No grants are awarded to individuals.

O+D+T Michael J. Rosenberg (T+Con) — Gail Rosenberg (T)

SE-573 Rosenberger Family Charitable Trust
640 Sentry Parkway, Suite 104
Blue Bell 19422 (Montgomery County)
AMV $810,335 **FYE** 12-00 **(Gifts Received** $181,955)

MI-12-15-42-44-52-63-64
Phone 610-834-9810 **FAX** None
EIN 23-2583927 **Year Created** 1990
18 **Grants totaling** $47,000

About half Pa. giving—all Central Pa.; grants are for general purposes except as noted. High grant of **$10,000** to Juniata College [Huntingdon County] (capital campaign/general support). **$6,500** to Children's Aid Society [Adams County]. **$1,500** each to Brethren Village [Lancaster], Elizabethtown Public Library, and Lititz Church of the Brethren. **$1,000** to Hershey Symphony Orchestra. **$750** to Elizabethtown Church of the Brethren. **Out-of-state** giving includes **$10,000** to Bethany Theological Seminary [IN] (general support/memorial recital fund); **$2,000** each to Church of the Brethren General Board [IL] and The Hymn Society of America [MA]; and smaller grants for various purposes. ■**PUBLICATIONS:** None ■**WEBSITE:** None ■**E-MAIL:** None ■**APPLICATION POLICIES & PROCEDURES:** Grant requests may be submitted in a letter at any time.

O+D+T Samuel T. Swansen, Esq. (Con) — Rev. Nancy Rosenberger Faus [IN] (T) — Cynthia A. Markham [Elizabethtown] (T) — Rev. W. Clemens Rosenberger [Lancaster] (T)

SE-574 Rosenblum (Samuel) Foundation
1361 Drayton Lane
Wynnewood 19096 (Montgomery County)
AMV $467,320 **FYE** 12-00 **(Gifts Received** $0)

MI-22-31-62
Phone 215-642-7227 **FAX** None
EIN 23-6295709 **Year Created** 1964
75 **Grants totaling** $31,645

Mostly local giving. High grant of **$8,300** to Federation Allied Jewish Appeal. **$8,070** to Har Zion Temple. **$1,000-$1,200** each to Children's Hospital of Philadelphia, Lankenau Hospital, Magee Rehab, and U. of Pa. Medical Center. **$800** to Temple Beth Torah. Other local contributions **$50-$500** for various purposes. **Out-of-state** giving includes **$2,500** to Tamarac Jewish Center [FL] and **$1,000** to Dartmouth Hitchcock Medical Center [NH]. ■**PUBLICATIONS:** None ■**WEBSITE:** None ■**E-MAIL:** None ■**APPLICATION POLICIES & PROCEDURES:** No grants awarded to individuals.

O+D+T Zena Rosenblum Wolfe (S+F+Con) — David Rosenblum [VT] (P) — Donald Jay Wolfe (VP)

SE-575   Rosenfeld (Mary & Emmanuel) Foundation Trust
c/o First Union/Wachovia
123 South Broad Street, PA1279
Philadelphia   19109   (Philadelphia County)

MI-11-12-13-14-22-31-32-42-51-52-54-62

Phone 215-670-4226   **FAX** 215-670-4236
EIN 23-6220061   **Year Created** 1960

AMV $2,421,077   **FYE** 12-00   **(Gifts Received** $0)   40+   **Grants totaling** $308,711

Details on 2000 grants are unavailable. — In the prior year, 50+ grants totaling **$511,200** was awarded, about half local/Pa. High Pa. grant of **$40,000** each to Abington Memorial Hospital and Wistar Institute. **$25,000** to Congregation Beth Or. **$12,000** to Make-A-Wish Foundation. **$10,000** each to Anti-Defamation League and Children's Hospital of Philadelphia. **$7,000** to School of the Pa. Ballet. **$6,500** each to Fox Chase Cancer Center, Franklin & Marshall College, and Juvenile Diabetes Foundation. **$5,700** to Physicians for Social Responsibility. **$5,000** each to American Cancer Society, Cystic Fibrosis Fund, Friends of Moss Rehab, Jewish Community Centers of Greater Philadelphia, Lankenau Hospital, and Pa. Tourette Syndrome Assn. **$3,500-$4,000** each to Congregation Adath Israel, Federation Day Care Services, UCP Foundation, and United Way. **$1,000-$2,000** each to Big Brother/Big Sister of Philadelphia, Friends of Paley Day Care, Gratz College, Philadelphia Museum of Art, Red Cross, Ronald McDonald House, and Temple Emmanuel. Other smaller local contributions. **Out-of-state** giving includes **$95,000** to Miami City Ballet [FL]; **$40,000** to Mazon [CA]; **$55,000** to Florida Philharmonic Orchestra; **$20,000** to Allied Jewish Appeal [NJ];and **$10,000** to St. Judes Children's Hospital [TN]. ■**PUBLICATIONS:** Grant Proposal Guidelines; application form ■**WEBSITE:** None ■**E-MAIL:** reginald.middleton@wachovia.com■**APPLICATION POLICIES & PROCEDURES:** The Foundation reports that most grants are for general support, special projects, endowment, research and scholarships. Athough unsolicited applications are not encouraged, grant requests may be submitted in September on a formal application form available from the Bank (deadline is October 1st); the form specifies the required attachments. Decisions on grants are made by the three individual co-trustees before the end of the year.

O+D+T   Reginald J. Middleton (VP at Bank+Con) — Lester Rosenfeld (T) — Robert Rosenfeld [NJ] (T) — Rita E. Stein [FL] (T) First Union/Wachovia (Corporate Trustee)

SE-576   Rosenlund Family Foundation, The
Post Office Box 297
Haverford   19041
                                           (Montgomery County)

MI-12-13-14-15-22-25-29-35-51-54-56-57-61
63-71

Phone Unlisted **FAX** None
EIN 23-6243642   **Year Created** 1962

AMV $3,146,395   **FYE** 6-01   **(Gifts Received** $29,684)   53 **Grants totaling** $184,500

About half local giving. High Pa. grant of **$25,000** to Salvation Army/Philadelphia. **$10,000** to The Nature Conservancy/Pa. Chapter. **$5,000** each to People's Light & Theatre Company, Philadelphia Society for Services to Children, and WHYY. **$3,000** to Old St. Joseph's Church (outreach program). **$2,000-$2,500** each to Angel Flight East, American Swedish Historical Museum, Clay Studio, and Pa. Ballet. **$1,000-$1,500** each to 18th Street Community Development Corp., ActionAIDS, Arden Theatre Company, Boys & Girls Club of Metropolitan Philadelphia, Center for Advancement in Cancer Education [Wynnewood], Christ Lutheran Church of Upper Darby, Contact Careline for Greater Philadelphia, Crime Prevention Assn., Daemion House, Eldernet of Lower Merion/Narberth, Episcopal Community Services, Franklin Institute, Greater Philadelphia Food Bank, Historic Rittenhousetown, Kelly Anne Dolan Memorial Fund, Little Brothers-Friends of the Elderly, Mother's Home [Darby], Neighborhood Gardens Assn., Nonprofit Technology Resources, Old First Reformed Church, Partners for Sacred Places, Pa. School for the Deaf, Pa. SPCA, Pa. Special Olympics, Philadelphia Hospitality, Inc., Philadelphia Museum of Art, Philadelphia Senior Center, Police Athletic League of Philadelphia, RSVP of Montgomery County, Sts. Sahag & Mesrob Armenian Church (youth group), Taylor Hospice, Urban Tree Connection, Wilma Theatre, YMCA of Germantown, and YMCA of Philadelphia & Vicinity. **Out-of-state** giving includes high grant of **$50,000** to Promisek, Inc. [CT] and **$10,000** each to Catholic Charities [NY], Catholic Relief Services [MD], and Project H.O.P.E. [DC]. ■**PUBLICATIONS:** None ■**WEBSITE:** None ■**E-MAIL:** None ■**APPLICATION POLICIES & PROCEDURES:** The Foundation reports that giving focuses on Philadelphia-area organizations with grants for general support, special projects, and endowment. No grants awarded to individuals or to political organizations. Grant requests may be submitted from February through early May in a letter (2 pages maximum)—the deadline is May 15th; include organization and project budgets, list of major funding sources, list of Board members, and IRS tax-exempt status documentation. Also, proposals which follow Delaware Valley Grantmakers' Common Grant Application Form are accepted (see Appendix or www.dvg.org). Site visits occasionally are made to organizations being considered for a grant. Decisions on grants are made by the Board on an irregular basis.

O+D+T   Hope Rosenlund (Managing Trustee+Con) — April Rosenlund Ford (T) — Alarik A. Rosenlund (T) — Arthur O. Rosenlund, Jr. (T) — David E. Rosenlund (T) — Mary L. Rosenlund (T+Donor) — Stephanie Rosenlund (T) — Kristen Rosenlund Turrill (T)

SE-577   Rosewater Fund, The
8207 Cedar Road
Elkins Park   19027   (Montgomery County)

MI-11-22-31-42-62

Phone 215-635-0110 **FAX** None
EIN 23-6261858   **Year Created** 1960

AMV $2,494,741   **FYE** 5-01   **(Gifts Received** $0)   20 **Grants totaling** $27,250

Mostly local giving. High grant fo **$11,275** to Congregation Rodeph Shalom. **$10,000** to Haverford College. **$3,000** to Federation Allied Jewish Appeal. **$1,000** to United Way of SE Pa. **$500** to Abington Memorial Hospital. Other local and out-of-state contributions **$25-$400** for various purposes. ■**PUBLICATIONS:** None ■**WEBSITE:** None ■**E-MAIL:** None ■**APPLICATION POLICIES & PROCEDURES:** The Fund reports that all giving represents personal annual charitable contributions; no grants as such are awarded.

O+D+T   Edward Rosewater (C+T+Donor+Con) — Ann Rosewater [GA] (S+T) — Lewis Rosewater [NY] (F+T) — Elizabeth Snyder [MA] (AS+T)

SE-578 Ross Family Fund
c/o Goldman Sachs & Company
1735 Market Street, 26th Floor
Philadelphia   19103   (Philadelphia County)

MI-11-22-29-41-42-51-52-53-54-55-56-57
62-65
Phone 215-656-7800 **FAX** 215-656-7854
EIN 23-2049592   **Year Created** 1977

AMV $11,965,729   **FYE** 2-01   **(Gifts Received** $6,985)   144 **Grants totaling** $405,194

About three-fourths local/Pa. giving; some grants comprise multiple payments. High grant of **$38,905** to National Museum of American Jewish History. **$34,000** to Regional Performing Arts Center. **$25,000** to Kimmel Center for the Performing Arts. **$22,000** to Philadelphia Orchestra. **$15,000** each to Philadelphia Museum of Art and United Way of SE Pa. **$11,000** to American Jewish Committee. **$10,000** each to Chestnut Hill College, Drexel U., One to One/The Greater Philadelphia Mentoring Project, and WHYY. **$7,000** to Operation Understanding. **$5,000** each to BLOCS/Business Leaders Organized for Catholic Schools and U. of Pittsburgh. **$3,748** to Academy of Music. **$3,500** to Prince Music Theater and U. of Pa./The Wharton Fund. **$2,000-$2,500** each to Episcopal Academy, Hillel of Philadelphia, Jewish Family & Children's Service, and Philadelphia Festival of the Arts. **$1,000-$1,950** each to Albert Einstein Society, American Cancer Society, Anti-Defamation League, Bread Upon the Water Scholarship Fund, The Carpenters Company, Free Library of Philadelphia, JCC-Stiffel Center, Jewish Community Centers of Greater Philadelphia, Jewish Federation of Greater Philadelphia, Living Beyond Breast Cancer, Main Line Art Center, Main Line Reform Temple, Mann Center for the Performing Arts, National Organization for Hearing Research, Philadelphia Development Partnership, Philadelphia Scholars, Red Cross/Harrisburg, and Resources for Human Development. Other local contributions **$100-$700** for various purposes. **Out-of-state** giving includes **$36,000** to National Jewish Center for Learning Leadership [NY]; **$25,000** to Jewish Federation of Palm Beach [FL]; **$10,000** to Jewish Women Archives [MA], Living Arts Counseling Center [CA], and The Washington Institute [DC]; and **$9,710** to Solomon Guggenheim Museum [NY]. ■ **PUBLICATIONS:** None ■ **WEBSITE:** None ■ **E-MAIL:** None ■ **APPLICATION POLICIES & PROCEDURES:** No grants are awarded to individuals.

O+D+T George M. Ross [Bryn Mawr] (P+T+Donor+Con) — Lyn M. Ross [Bryn Mawr] (T) — Michael Ross [NY] (Donor) — Merry Beth Ross [NY] (Donor)

SE-579 Rotenberger Foundation, The
240 South 9th Street
Quakertown   18951   (Bucks County)

MI-18-22-63
Phone 215-536-3294 **FAX** None
EIN 22-2846655   **Year Created** 1987

AMV $216,745   **FYE** 12-00   **(Gifts Received** $0)   50 **Grants totaling** $41,150

About two-thirds local/Pa. giving. High grant of **$8,000** to Brethren Revival Fellowship [York]. **$6,200** to Springfield Church of the Brethren [Coopersburg]. **$4,500** to Grace Bible Fellowship Church [Quakertown]. **$1,000** each to Brethren Evangelical Leadership Foundation [Lancaster], Brethren Mission Fund [Lititz], Evangelical Congregational Church/Board of Missions [Myerstown], Quakertown Christian School, and Seibert Evangelical Congregational Church [Allentown].**$800** to Crossroad Pregnancy Care Center [Quakertown]. Other local/Pa. contributions **$75-$500** for similar purposes. **Out-of-state** giving includes **$1,700** to Prison Fellowship Ministries [DC]; **$1,200** to Samaritan's Purse [NC]; and **$1,000** to Back to the Bible [NE]. ■ **PUBLICATIONS:** None ■ **WEBSITE:** None ■ **E-MAIL:** None ■ **APPLICATION POLICIES & PROCEDURES:** The Foundation reports that grants are awarded to preselected charitable organizations only; unsolicited applications are not accepted. No grants awarded to individuals.

O+D+T Kathy Rotenberger Pickering (T+Con) — Donna Roberts (T) — Nancy Zintak (T) — Linford J. Rotenberger (Donor)

SE-580 Roth Foundation, The
1182 Wrack Road
Meadowbrook   19046   (Montgomery County)

MI-34
Phone 215-886-6459 **FAX** None
EIN 23-6271428   **Year Created** 1953

AMV $453,505   **FYE** 10-00   **(Gifts Received** $0)   1 **Grant of** $75,000

Sole grant to Columbia U. Medical School [NY]. — Grants in the two prior years awarded to the same grantee. ■ **PUBLICATIONS:** None ■ **WEBSITE:** None ■ **E-MAIL:** None ■ **APPLICATION POLICIES & PROCEDURES:** Information not available.

O+D+T Henry I. Boreen (T+Con) — Roland Roth [Ambler] (T) — Linda Schwartz [Jenkintown] (T)

SE-581 Rotko Family Foundation
c/o Schnader Harrison Segal & Lewis
1600 Market Street, Suite 3600
Philadelphia   19103   (Philadelphia County)

MI-11-12-13-18-22-34-41-42-44-62-84-89

Phone 215-751-2338 **FAX** 215-246-9018
EIN 23-2200115   **Year Created** 1982

AMV $1,228,957   **FYE** 12-00   **(Gifts Received** $0)   29 **Grants totaling** $134,500

Mostly local giving. High grant of **$35,000** to Jefferson Medical College. **$25,000** to U. of Pa. Law School. **$12,000** to Planned Parenthood of Chester County. **$10,000** to American Associates of Ben-Gurion U. of the Negev [Jenkintown]. **$5,000** each to Pro-Mar-Lin Fire Company [Unionville], U. of Pa., and U. of Pa. School of Veterinary Medicine. **$3,500** to Beth Sholom Congregation. **$3,000** to Philadelphia Ronald McDonald House. **$2,000-$2,500** each to AIDS Law Project of Pa., Federation Allied Jewish Appeal, Gesu School, Philadelphia Hispanic Chamber of Commerce Services, Philadelphia Tennis Patrons Assn., United Way of SE Pa., U. of Pa. Women's Athletic Board, and Villanova U. **$1,000** each to Abington Friends School, Free Library of Philadelphia, U. of Pa. School of Nursing, and William Penn Charter School. Other local contributions **$500** for education and health/human services. **Out-of-state** giving includes **$5,000** to Wilmington Youth Rowing Assn. [DE] and **$1,000** to Chicago College of Osteopathic Medicine [IL]. ■ **PUBLICATIONS:** None ■ **WEBSITE:** None ■ **E-MAIL:** None ■ **APPLICATION POLICIES & PROCEDURES:** Grant requests may be submitted in a letter at any time; describe the purpose of the request and include appropriate organizational information and IRS tax-exempt status documentation. No grants are awarded to individuals.

O+D+T John D. Iskrant, Esq. (Con) — Lionel Felzer [Elkins Park] (T) — Bessie Rotko [Elkins Park] (T) — Michael J. Rotko [Unionville] (T) — Judith M. Shipon [Rydal] (T)

SE-582   Rowan (Rena) Foundation
210 West Rittenhouse Square, Suite 1102
Philadelphia   19103   (Philadelphia County)

MI-22-25-29-41-52-54-55-61
Phone 215-985-9989 **FAX** 215-985-9969
EIN 23-2745464   **Year Created** 1993

AMV $1,313,910   **FYE** 12-00   **(Gifts Received** $2,098)   14 **Grants totaling** $609,000

Mostly local giving. High grant of **$500,000** to Project H.O.M.E. **$12,000** to Rena Rowan Foundation for the Homeless (benefit event). **$10,000** each to Red Cross, St. Matthias Church [Bala Cynwyd], and Waldron Mercy Academy. **$5,000** to Prince Music Theatre. **$2,000** to Sisters of Mercy. Other smaller local contributions. **Out-of-state** giving includes **$35,000** to Vatican Museum [Italy] (Patron of the Arts); **$10,000** to American Center of Polish Culture [DC]; **$6,000** to Missionaries of the Poor [FL]; and **$5,000** to The Lord's Place [FL]. ■**PUBLICATIONS:** None ■**WEBSITE:** None ■**E-MAIL:** None ■**APPLICATION POLICIES & PROCEDURES:** The Foundation reports that grant requests are not being accepted at this time [Summer 2002]. No grants are awarded to individuals.

O+D+T   Dianna Lubbe (Adminstrator+Con) — Rena Rowan [FL] (P+Donor)

SE-583   Rubenstein (Bernice & Jerry G.) Foundation, The
223 Glenmoor Road
Gladwyne   19035   (Montgomery County)

MI-22-52-54-62-81
Phone 610-649-5155 **FAX** None
EIN 23-2045912   **Year Created** 1977

AMV $350,930   **FYE** 12-00   **(Gifts Received** $0)   50+ **Grants totaling** $27,155

About four-fifths local giving. High grants of **$3,000** each to Curtis Institute of Music and Philadelphia Chamber Music Society. **$2,500** to Beth David Reform Congregation. **$1,500** to Philadelphia Museum of Art. **$1,000** each to Beth David Tree of Life, Federation Allied Jewish Appeal, and Settlement Music School. **$500-$750** each to Anti-Defamation League, Foreign Policy Research Institute, Martin's Run, and Philadelphia Orchestra. Other local contributions **$100-$400** for arts, cultural, educational, Jewish and other purposes. **Out-of-state** grant: **$4,000** to Marlboro School of Music [VT]. ■**PUBLICATIONS:** None ■ **WEBSITE:** None ■**E-MAIL:** None ■**APPLICATION POLICIES & PROCEDURES:** Grant requests may be submitted in a letter at any time; describe the organization's charitable purpose and state the amount of funding requested. No grants awarded to individuals.

O+D+T   Jerry G. Rubenstein (T+Donor+Con) — Laura M. Barzilai [NY] (T) — Bernice G. Rubenstein (T) — Daniel A. Rubenstein [NJ] (T) — Karen B. Rubenstein [Penn Valley] (T)

SE-584   Rubin (Seymore & Helen Ann) Foundation
c/o Seymore Rubin & Associates
430 North 4th Street
Philadelphia   19123   (Philadelphia County)

MI-22-32-62-63
Phone 215-923-3456 **FAX** 215-923-8802
EIN 23-2586851   **Year Created** 1989

AMV $535,258   **FYE** 12-00   **(Gifts Received** $0)   27 **Grants totaling** $35,166

Mostly local giving; some grants comprise multiple awards. High grant of **$18,300** to Temple Adath Israel. **$5,000** to Federation Allied Jewish Appeal. **$3,000** each to Christian Baptist Church and Sisterhood Gift Shop [Merion]. **$1,000** to a doctor. **$500** each to Ivy Cultural & Educational Foundation and Macular Vision Research Foundation. Other local and out-of-state contributions **$25-$300** for various purposes. ■**PUBLICATIONS:** None ■**WEBSITE:** None ■**E-MAIL:** None ■**APPLICATION POLICIES & PROCEDURES:** Grant requests may be submitted in a letter at any time; include an organizational budget, audited financial statement, and IRS tax-exempt status documentation.

O+D+T   Seymore Rubin (P+Donor) — Mark Rubin [Wynnewood] (VP+Donor) — Karen Spewak [Bryn Mawr] (S) — Helen Ann Rubin [Bala Cynwyd (F+Donor)

SE-585   Rudman (Kal & Lucille) Foundation
c/o Asher & Company
1845 Walnut Street, Suite 1300
Philadelphia   19103   (Philadelphia County)

MI-13-20-22-31-41-51-52-53-62
Phone 215-564-1900 **FAX** 215-564-3940
EIN 22-3237107   **Year Created** 1993

AMV $6,628,562   **FYE** 12-00   **(Gifts Received** $274,062)   25+ **Grants totaling** $250,751

Mostly local giving; most grants comprise multiple payments. High grant of **$100,000** to Jewish Federation of Greater Philadelphia. **$25,000** each to Prince Music Theater/American Music Theater Festival and St. Christopher's Hospital for Children. **$23,214** to Citizens Crime Commission. **$13,560** to U. of the Arts. **$11,628** to various vendors on behalf of Philadelphia Police. **$11,000** to Montgomery County District Law Enforcement. **$10,000** to Jewish Community Center. **$3,790** to Police Athletic League. **$3,000** to Shomrin Society of Philadelphia (Jewish Police). **$2,280** to Anti-Defamation League. **$1,000** each to Central High School Alumni Assn., Roman Catholic High School, and Variety Club. **$750** to St. John Neumann High School. Other local contributions **$200-$250** for various purposes. **Out-of-state** giving includes **$11,129** to Camden County [NJ]; **$5,000** to Force One; and **$850** to National Organization of Black Law Enforcement Executives [VA]. ■**PUBLICATIONS:** None ■**WEBSITE:** None ■**E-MAIL:** None ■**APPLICATION POLICIES & PROCEDURES:** Information not available.

O+D+T   Solomon 'Kal' Rudman [NJ] (T+Donor+Con) — Lucille Rudman [NJ] (T+Donor)

SE-586   Safeguard Scientifics Foundation
c/o Safeguard Scientifics, Inc.
800 Safeguard Building, 435 Devon Park Drive
Wayne   19087   (Chester County)

MI-13-14-16-25-29-32-35-41-42-49-51-52-53-55-56-71-72-84-85-88
Phone 610-293-0600 **FAX** 610-293-0601
EIN 23-2571278   **Year Created** 1989

AMV $59,661   **FYE** 12-00   **(Gifts Received** $2,546,000)   170+ **Grants totaling** $2,929,806

Mostly local giving; some grants represent multiple payments. High grant of **$500,000** to Philadelphia 2000 (for Republican Convention). **$238,150** to City Year Philadelphia. **$200,000** each to Boy Scouts/Cradle of Liberty Council and Penn State/Great

Valley. **$132,500** to Red Cross. **$125,000** to Valley Forge Historical Society. **$100,000** each to Drexel U., Philadelphia O.I.C., and Philadelphia Youth Tennis. **$62,500** to Regional Performing Arts Center. **$55,000** to American Cancer Society. **$50,000** each to FIRST, Philadelphia Zoo, RSVP, and Temple U./Safeguard Scientifics Center for Economic Education. **$35,000** to Anti-Defamation League. **$24,000-$25,000** each to Community Volunteers in Medicine, Eagles Youth Partnership, Laboratory School of Communication & Languages [Philadelphia], Main Line Academy, Mural Arts Advocates [Philadelphia], Sylvan Opera, UCP of Philadelphia (auction), and Team Pa. Foundation. **$20,000-$21,000** each to Bournelyf Special Camp, Juvenile Diabetes Foundation, National MS Society, Settlement Music School, and Special Olympics. **$15,000** each to Jack & Jill of America and Philadelphia Orchestra. **$12,500** each to Arden Theatre Company, Pa. Partnership for Economic Education, and Prince Music Theater. **$10,000-$10,800** each to ALS Assn., American Heart Assn., Boy Scouts/Pa. Dutch Council, Dick Vermeil Invitational/Boy Scouts, Fund for the Water Works, Greater Philadelphia Food Bank, Huntington's Disease of America, Philadelphia Friends of Outward Bound School, and U.S. Artists. **$9,000** to Great Valley Nature Center (educational programs). **$6,795** to West Chester U. (mostly challenge grant match). **$4,000-$5,000** each to Aid for Friends, American Associates of Ben-Gurion U., Ben Franklin Technology Partners, Carousel House, Delco Blind/Sight Center, Eastern U., Habitat for Humanity/Delaware Valley Branch, Ludwig's Corner Horse Show, Old First Reformed Church (homeless shelter), Paoli Memorial Hospital, Pa. Chamber of Business & Industry Educational Foundation [Harrisburg], Philadelphia Academies, Inc., Police Athletic League of Philadelphia, Radnor Hunt Three Day, Southwest Community Enrichment Center, Stratford Friends School, United Way of SE Pa., U. of Pa./Institute for Law & Economics, and Vanguard School. **$2,000-$3,500** each to Adoption Center of Delaware Valley, American Lung Assn., Community Accountants, Eagles Fly for Leukemia, Foreign Policy Research Institute, League of Women Voters of Pa. Citizen Education Fund, Main Line Chamber of Commerce, Marine Fore Scholarship Program, National Liberty Museum, Operation Understanding, Penjerdel Regional Foundation, Pa. Ballet, UNICEF, and Women's Resource Center. Other local smaller grants/contributions for similar purposes. **Out-of-state** giving includes **$100,000** to Nantucket Cottage Hospital [MA]; **$50,000** to Santa Clara U. [CA]; **$20,000** to National Business Incubation Assn.; **$10,000** each to Princess Grace Foundation-USA [NY] and Progressive Policy Institute [DC]; **$5,000** to Cristiana Care Foundation [DE]. In addition, 52 matching gifts for educational institutions and nonprofit organizations. ■**PUBLICATIONS:** None ■**WEBSITE:** www.safeguard.com [corporate info only] ■**E-MAIL:** None ■**APPLICATION POLICIES & PROCEDURES:** The Foundation reports that most grants are for building funds, capital drives, or endowment. Grant requests may be submitted in any form at any time. Site visits sometimes are made to organizations being considered for a grant.

O+D+T Warren V. Musser (P+D+Con) — Harry Wallaesa (VP+D) — Deirdre Blackburn (S+D) — Gerald A. Blitstein (F+D) Corporate donor: Safeguard Scientifics, Inc.

SE-587 Saint Benedict's Charitable Society
1663 Bristol Pike
Bensalem 19020 (Bucks County)

MI-23-43-61
Phone 215-244-9900 **FAX** None
EIN 23-6256990 **Year Created** 1935

AMV $456,639 **FYE** 12-00 **(Gifts Received** $1,250) 52 **Grants totaling** $17,050

Limited Pa. giving: seven **$100-$300** contributions for Christmas charities at local Roman Catholic parishes, and **$1,200** for an individual's medical needs. **Out-of-state** giving includes 39 Christmas charities, **$50-$300,** at Roman Catholic parishes in many states, two **$2,000** scholarship aid grants to Catholic or Native American schools in AZ and LA. and emergency aid grants to Native American reservations in LA, NM, and TX. ■**PUBLICATIONS:** None ■**WEBSITE:** None ■**E-MAIL:** None ■**APPLICATION POLICIES & PROCEDURES:** The Society reports that most grants are for scholarships or to individuals. Grant requests may be submitted in any form at any time. Site visits sometimes are made to organizations being considered for a grant. Grants are awarded in December.

O+D+T Margaret Kuehmstedt (F+Con) — Sr. Monica Loughlin (P) — Roger A. Johnsen [Philadelphia] (VP) — Sr. Beatrice Jeffries (S) — Sr. Donna Breslin (AF)

SE-588 Saint Martha Foundation, The
114 Cove Lane
Media 19063 (Delaware County)

MI-22-61
Phone 610-566-8094 **FAX** None
EIN 23-2982957 **Year Created** 1998

AMV $42,668 **FYE** 12-00 **(Gifts Received** $95,967) 3 **Grants totaling** $56,000

All local giving. High grant of **$50,000** to U. of Pa. (Dr. John Mikulba Fund). **$5,000** to Augustinian Foreign Missions [Villanova]. **$1,000** to Grace United Methodist Church. — In the prior year **$189,900** in grants (**$1,000-$15,000** mostly) were awarded primarily to local Catholic churches, orders, and agencies. ■**PUBLICATIONS:** None ■**WEBSITE:** None ■**E-MAIL:** None ■**APPLICATION POLICIES & PROCEDURES:** Information not available.

O+D+T Jerry Francesco (P+Donor+Con) — Lucille Francesco (S+F)

SE-589 Saint-Gobain Corporation Foundation
c/o CertainTeed Corporation
750 Swedesford Road, P.O. Box 860
Valley Forge 19482 (Chester County)

MI-11-14-25-29-31-32-41-45-51-54-55-57-81 83-88
Phone 610-341-7428 **FAX** 610-341-7777
EIN 23-6242991 **Year Created** 1955

AMV $160,937 **FYE** 12-00 **(Gifts Received** $346,807) 680+ **Grants totaling** $412,152

About half local/Pa. giving. High grant of **$60,000** to Regional Performing Arts Center. **$15,000** to Philadelphia Museum of Art. **$10,000** each to French International School of Philadelphia and United Way of Chester County. **$5,000** each to Baker Industries, Committee for Economic Growth [Wilkes-Barre], Penn State Educational Partnership Program [State College], Red Cross/Philadelphia, U. of Pa./Graduate School of Education (Penn Literacy Network), and WHYY. **$3,000** to Main Line Health System. **$2,000-$2,500** each to IHM Center for Literacy & GED Programs, Interfaith Hospitality Network [Norristown], The

MBF Center, Mountaintop Hose Company #1 [Luzerne County], People's Light & Theatre Company, and Sedgwick Cultural Center. **$1,000-$1,100** each to Chester Community Improvement Project, Energy Coordinating Agency of Philadelphia, and International House of Philadelphia. **Out-of-state** giving mostly to plant locations in CA, GA, IA, IN, KS, LA, MD, MI, MN, NC, NJ, WV, and TX. Also, over 500 matching gifts totaling about **$155,000** were disbursed to all types of educational institutions and nonprofit organizations in Pa. and other states. ■**PUBLICATIONS:** grant application form ■**WEBSITE:** www.certainteed.com [corporate info only] ■**E-MAIL:** corporate@certainteed.com ■**APPLICATION POLICIES & PROCEDURES:** The Foundation reports that giving ordinarily is limited to communities with CertainTeed plants/facilities with support given, listed in order of priority, to education, arts/culture, community, and health/human services. No grants are awarded to organizations that receive significant United Way or government support, or to individuals. Grant requests may be submitted at any time on a formal grant application form available from the Foundation; include an annual report, organization/project budgets, an audited financial statement, list of major funding sources, Board member list, and IRS tax-exempt 501(c)(3) status documentation. Grants are awarded at April and September meetings. Matching gifts for all types of nonprofit organizations have a $25 minimum; maximum gifts are $2,000/employee/year for educational institutions and $1,000/employee/year for non-educational organizations. — Note: In early 2002, the CertainTeed Corp. Foundation and the Norton Company Foundation combined to form this foundation. — Formerly called CertainTeed Corp. Foundation

O+D+T Dorothy C. Wackerman (VP+S+D+Con) — Jean-Francois Phelison (P+D) — D. Chris Altmansberger (VP+D) — Robert C. Ayotte (VP+D) — Dennis J. Baker (VP+D) — David Boivin (VP+D) — F. Lee Faust (VP+D) — James E. Hilyard (VP+D) — Mark E. Mathisen (VP+D) — Mark J. Scott (VP+D) — George B. Amoss (VP-Finance) — James F. Harkins, Jr. (F) Corporate donor: Certainteed Corporation

---

SE-590   **Saligman (Robert) Charitable Trust**
c/o Cynwyd Investments
261 Old York Road, Suite 613
Jenkintown   19046   (Montgomery County)
AMV $17,992,785   **FYE** 12-00   (**Gifts Received** $0)

MI-14-15-18-22-31-32-34-42-54-56-62

Phone 215-886-7260 **FAX** 215-886-7261
EIN 23-6875203   **Year Created** 1987
41 **Grants totaling** $879,685

About four-fifths local giving; some grants comprise multiple payments. High grant of **$238,100** to National Museum of American Jewish History. **$200,000** to American Friends of Hebrew U. [Philadelphia]. **$150,000** to Federation of Jewish Agencies. **$56,000** to Temple Adath Israel. **$50,000** to Jewish Family & Children's Services. **$40,000** to U. of Pa. School of Nursing. **$20,000** to Golden Slipper Charities. **$10,000** to Philadelphia Jewish Archives. **$5,000** each to RSVP of Delaware County, Society Hill Synagogue, and Stiffel Community Center. **$1,000-$2,000** each to ALS Foundation, Friends of Lynn Saligman, Hyman Gratz Society, Jewish Community Centers of Greater Philadelphia, Moss Rehab, Philadelphia Museum of Art, and Planned Parenthood of SE Pa. Other smaller local contributions. **Out-of-state** giving includes **$120,000** to American Friends of Israel Museum [NY]; **$25,000** to Juvenile Diabetes Foundation [NY]; **$12,000** to Pritikin Research Foundation [CA]; and **$7,860** to Solomon S. Guggenheim Foundation [NY]. ■**PUBLICATIONS:** None ■**WEBSITE:** None ■**E-MAIL:** None ■**APPLICATION POLICIES & PROCEDURES:** Grant requests may be submitted in any form at any time, to the Bala Cynwyd address -or- to Alice Saligman, 830 Park Ave., Suite 7B, New York, NY 10021.

O+D+T Herschel Cravitz, Esq. [Rydal] (T+Con) — Alice Saligman [NY] (T+Donor+Con) — Carolyn Saligman [Philadelphia] (T+Donor)

SE-591   **Saligman (Samuel & Irene) Charitable Fund**
407 Timber Lane
Newtown Square   19073   (Delaware County)
AMV $206,952   **FYE** 12-00   (**Gifts Received** $0)

MI-22-31-62

Phone 610-353-4434 **FAX** None
EIN 23-2810084   **Year Created** 1995
3 **Grants totaling** $11,500

High grants of **$5,000** each to Jewish Federation of Greater Philadelphia and Ocean Reef Medical Center [FL]. **$1,500** to Temple Adath Israel. ■**PUBLICATIONS:** None ■**WEBSITE:** None ■**E-MAIL:** None ■**APPLICATION POLICIES & PROCEDURES:** Grant requests may be submitted in a letter at any time.

O+D+T Irene Saligman (T+Con) — Herschel Cravitz, Esq. [Rydal] (T) — Herbert Kurtz [Melrose Park] (T) — Lynn C. Saligman

---

SE-592   **Salt & Light Foundation**
c/o Conetex, Inc.
102 South Pine Street, P.O. Box 237
Elverson   19520   (Chester County)
AMV $5,617,780   **FYE** 12-00   (**Gifts Received** $0)

MI-41-42-43-63-86

Phone 610-286-1936 **FAX** None
EIN 23-2808631   **Year Created** 1995
9 **Grants totaling** $402,000

One Pa. grant: **$2,000** to Commonwealth Foundation for Public Policy Alternatives [Harrisburg] (student scholarships). **Out-of-state** giving, all for general fund support except as noted, includes high grant of **$150,000** to Heidi Group [TX]; **$100,000** to The Heritage Foundation [DC]; **$50,000** to National Institute of Family & Life Advocacy [VA] (sonogram program); **$25,000** each to Baptists for Life [MI], Children's Education Opportunity Foundation [AR] (scholarships), and Patrick Henry College [VA]; **$15,000** to American Assn. for Christian Schools [MO] (building fund); and **$10,000** to National Heritage Foundation [VA]. ■**PUBLICATIONS:** None ■**WEBSITE:** None ■**E-MAIL:** None ■**APPLICATION POLICIES & PROCEDURES:** No grants are awarded to individuals.

O+D+T Robert L. Cone (P+F+Donor+Con) — Edward H. Cone (VP+S) — Derial H. Sanders [Chester Springs] (D)

SE-593 **Saltzman (Irvin & Marion-Louise) Family Foundation** **MI**-13-17-31-41-62
c/o Penn-America Group, Inc.
420 South York Road **Phone** 215-443-3600 **FAX** 215-443-3603
Hatboro 19040 (Montgomery County) **EIN** 23-2827744 **Year Created** 1995
AMV $739,486 **FYE** 11-00 (**Gifts Received** $108,883) 7 **Grants totaling** $141,500

All local giving. Three grants totaling **$107,000** to Albert Einstein Medical Center (mostly for Marion-Louise Saltzman Women's Center). **$30,000** to Meadowbrook School. **$2,000** each to Hatboro YMCA and Silver Springs-Martin Luther School. **$500** to OYRT Beth Am. ■**PUBLICATIONS:** None ■**WEBSITE:** www.penn-america.com [corporate info only] ■**E-MAIL:** None ■**APPLICATION POLICIES & PROCEDURES:** No grants are awarded to individuals; unsolicited grants are not encouraged.

O+D+T Jami Saltzman-Levy [Newtown] (S+F+Con) — Irvin Saltzman (P+Donor) Corporate donors: Penn-America Insurance Co.

SE-594 **Salzer (Jane & Robert) Foundation** **MI**-31-34-42
5 Averstone Drive East **Phone** 215-321-9804 **FAX** None
Washington Crossing 18977 (Bucks County) **EIN** 23-6856148 **Year Created** 1987
AMV $1,615,220 **FYE** 12-00 (**Gifts Received** $0) 34 **Grants totaling** $121,065

Limited local/Pa. giving. High local grant of **$10,000** to Abington Memorial Hospital. **$$4,560** to Penn State U. **$1,900** to Hahnemann U. Other smaller local contributions. **Out-of-state** giving includes high grant of **$40,290** to U. of North Dakota; **$30,000** to George Mason U. [VA]; and other smaller grants, mostly for higher education. ■**PUBLICATIONS:** None ■**WEBSITE:** None ■**E-MAIL:** None ■**APPLICATION POLICIES & PROCEDURES:** Grant requests may be submitted in any form at any time.

O+D+T Thomas B. Salzer (F+Con) — Jane Salzer [VA] (P)

SE-595 **Sam & Charles Foundation, The** **MI**-25-54-57-72-81-82
121 Pine Street **Phone** 215-928-9226 **FAX** None
Philadelphia 19106 (Philadelphia County) **EIN** 23-7919005 **Year Created** 1997
AMV $169,852 **FYE** 12-00 (**Gifts Received** $20,003) 29 **Grants totaling** $16,069

Limited local giving. High local grant of **$950** to WHYY-TV12; other smaller local contributions for the arts, cultural institutions, museums, public broadcasting, and other purposes. **Out-of-state** giving includes **$3,000** each to Doctors Without Borders [NY] and Habitat for Humanity [GA]; and **$2,500** to The Carter Center [GA]. — In the prior year, high grant of **$14,200** to Yucatan Animal Rescue Foundation [CO]. ■**PUBLICATIONS:** None ■**WEBSITE:** None ■**E-MAIL:** None ■**APPLICATION POLICIES & PROCEDURES:** Grant requests in any form may be submitted at any time.

O+D+T David U'Prichard (T+Donor+Con) — Alissa U'Prichard (T+Donor)

SE-596 **Sanders (Caroline J.S.) Charitable Trust #1** **MI**-14-15-22-25-35-41-43-45-54-56-71
c/o First Union/Wachovia
123 South Broad Street, PA1279 **Phone** 215-670-4226 **FAX** 215-670-4236
Philadelphia 19109 (Philadelphia County) **EIN** 23-6781822 **Year Created** 1984
AMV $1,207,214 **FYE** 9-00 (**Gifts Received** $0) 21 **Grants totaling** $54,000

All local giving. High grant of **$4,000** to Central High School. **$3,500** to Dignity Housing. **$3,000** each to CARIE/Center for Advocacy for the Rights & Interests of the Elderly, Metropolitan Career Center, Montgomery County Assn. for the Blind, Northwest Interfaith Movement, Philabundance, Polish American Social Services, RSVP Program of Montgomery County, Surrey Services for Seniors, and White-Williams Scholars. **$2,000-$2,500** each to City Team Ministries, Community Gardens of Chester County, Episcopal Community Services, Franklin Institute, Germantown Historical Society, IHM Center for Literacy & GED Programs, MANNA/Metropolitan AIDS Neighborhood Nutrition Alliance, and Philadelphia Visions. **$1,000** each to MBF Center and Strings for Schools. ■**PUBLICATIONS:** Grant Proposal Guidelines; application form ■**WEBSITE:** None ■**E-MAIL:** reginald.middleton@wachovia.com ■**APPLICATION POLICIES & PROCEDURES:** The Bank reports that giving focuses on small or medium-sized organizations, listed in priority order: (1) educational institutions, including scholarship funds and libraries; (2) social welfare agencies providing broad-based services to the elderly, youth, indigent and the homeless; (3) training/education of the handicapped; and (4) religious organizations for education and capital improvements. Most grants are for general support. special projects, or scholarships; multiyear grants are awarded. Large-budget organizations with significant funding sources will not receive priority consideration. Grants for capital improvement will be considered only if for a specific project and a clear need is demonstrated. No grants will be awarded to/for individuals, loans, endowment, general operations, political purposes, churches, benefit dinners, or athletic events. Grant requests must be submitted on a formal application form (available from the Bank), preferably in January, April, July, and October; the deadlines are February 1st, May 1st, August 1st, and November 1st. The application form will specify the required attachments, and requests will be considered until all required documentation is received. Site visits sometimes are made to organizations being considered for a grant. The Trustee Committee awards grants at meetings in March, June, September, and December.

O+D+T Reginald J. Middleton (VP at Bank+Con) — First Union/Wachovia (Trustee)

SE-597 **Sanders (Caroline J.S.) Charitable Trust #2** **MI**-12-13-14-15-17-22-25-32-42-43-51-54-71-72
c/o First Union/Wachovia
123 South Broad Street, PA1279 **Phone** 215-670-4226 **FAX** 215-670-4236
Philadelphia 19109 (Philadelphia County) **EIN** 23-2676889 **Year Created** 1990
AMV $4,896,549 **FYE** 9-00 (**Gifts Received** $0) 35 **Grants totaling** $197,000

About three-fourths local giving. High Pa. grant **$8,000** to Wissahickon Hospice. **$6,000** each to Easter Seals, Greater Philadelphia Food Bank, Habitat for Humanity/West Philadelphia, Potter's House Mission, and Recording for the Blind & Dyslexic.

$5,000 each to John Bartram Assn., Boy Scouts/Cradle of Liberty Council, Brian's House, Community Women's Education Project, Kelly Anne Dolan Memorial Fund, Philadelphia Senior Center, Planned Lifetime Assistance Network of Pa., Pa. Special Olympics, Radnor ABC (scholarship aid program), Southern Home Services, Voyage House, Wagner Free Institute of Science, and Wilma Theatre. $4,000 to Deaf-Hearing Community Center, Elwyn, Inc., Little Brothers/Friends of the Elderly, and Senior Community Service. $3,000 each to HELP Philadelphia, Kensington Area Ministry, Senior Adult Activities Center, Special Equestrians, and Woods Services Foundation. $2,000 to Advocate Community Development Corp. **Out-of-state** giving includes high grant of $20,000 to Sweet Briar College [VA] (natural areas/ecological studies endowment); $15,000 to Boys Homes, Inc. [NC]; $10,000 to Barter Theatre [VA]; and $6,000 to New Jersey Aquarium. ■**PUBLICATIONS:** Grant Proposal Guidelines; application form ■**WEBSITE:** None ■**E-MAIL:** reginald.middleton@wachovia.com■**APPLICATION POLICIES & PROCEDURES:** Refer to application guidelines above for Caroline J.S. Sanders Charitable Trust #1.

O+D+T Reginald J. Middleton (VP at Bank+Con) — Thomas A. Brown [TN] (Co-T) First Union/Wachovia (Co-Trustee)

SE-598 Sanford Foundation, The
c/o The Brinton Group
1653 Brinton's Bridge Road
Chadds Ford 19317 (Chester County)
AMV $549,552 **FYE** 11-00 **(Gifts Received** $0)

MI-11-13-21-41-71-82

Phone 610-388-2500 **FAX** None
EIN 23-6971120 **Year Created** 1989
4 **Grants totaling** $46,920

All local/Pa. giving. High grant of $25,000 to Kennett Area YMCA (general support). $16,000 to VOSH/Pennsylvania (medical program in Guatemala). $5,000 to Kennett After School Assn. $920 to Kennett Rotary Club. — In the prior year, giving included $25,000 to Brandywine Conservancy, $10,000 to United Way of Kennett Square, and $5,000 to Kennett After School Assn. ■**PUBLICATIONS:** informational brochure ■**WEBSITE:** None ■**E-MAIL:** None ■**APPLICATION POLICIES & PROCEDURES:** The Foundation reports that giving is limited to educational purposes. Typically the Foundation collaborates with other concerned foundations, corporations, philanthropic organizations, or individuals, often using foundation funds as venture capital to initiate new approaches that are preventive in nature. No grants are awarded to individuals. Grant requests must be submitted on a formal grant application form available from the Foundation; the completed application must include a current financial statement, most recent audited financial report, appropriate background materials, and IRS tax-exempt status documentation.

O+D+T Richard D. Sanford (T+Donor+Con) — Sheila Sanford (T+Donor) — Barry W. Abelson, Esq. [Philadelphia] (T)

SE-599 Satell Family Foundation
c/o Progressive Business Publications
370 Technology Drive
Malvern 19355 (Chester County)
AMV $600,762 **FYE** 12-00 **(Gifts Received** $200,000)

MI-11-22-41-52-62-82

Phone 610-695-8600 **FAX** 610-647-8089
EIN 23-7769039 **Year Created** 1994
30+ **Grants totaling** $92,762

About one-third local giving. High Pa. grant of $10,000 to United Way of SE Pa. $6,000 to Jewish Federation of Greater Philadelphia. $5,000 each to Episcopal Academy and The Founders Society. $1,000 each to Curtis Institute of Music, EAPE/Kingdomworks, Jewish Family & Children's Service, Mendelssohn Club of Philadelphia, and U. of Pa. Other local contributions $50-$500 for various purposes. **Out-of-state** giving includes $25,000 to American Friends of Israel Democracy Institute [GA]; $15,032 to Union of American Hebrew Congregations [NY]; $9,000 to Friends of Yemin Orde [DC]; and $5,200 to The Jaffa Institute [Israel]. ■**PUBLICATIONS:** None ■**WEBSITE:** None ■**E-MAIL:** None ■**APPLICATION POLICIES & PROCEDURES:** No grants are awarded to individuals.

O+D+T Edward M. Satell (T+Donor+Con) — Corporate donor: American Future Systems, Inc.

SE-600 Saunders (Lawrence) Fund
c/o First Union/Wachovia
123 South Broad Street, PA1279
Philadelphia 19109 (Philadelphia County)
AMV $2,269,252 **FYE** 12-00 **(Gifts Received** $0)

MI-12-13-14-15-16-18-22-25-35-41-52-55
71-84
Phone 215-670-4226 **FAX** 215-670-4236
EIN 23-6488524 **Year Created** 1970
38 **Grants totaling** $121,800

All local giving; grants are for general operating support except as noted. High local grants of $5,000 each to Mural Arts Program, Philadelphia Senior Center (delivered meals), and Taller Puertorriqueno (after school/summer program). $4,000-$4,500 each to Episcopal Church of the Advocate, Nueva Esperanza (summer camp), and Senior Community Services (delivered meals). $3,000-$3,500 each to Asian Arts Initiative (youth workshop), Awbury Arboretum (education center), Carson Valley School (new facilities), Episcopal Community Services (after school program), Habitat for Humanity-West Philadelphia, Historic Bartram's Gardens (educational program), Jenkins Arboretum (brochure), Jubilee School, Kardon Institute for the Arts (financial assistance), Kearsley Retirement Community (low-income resident support), MANNA/Metropolitan AIDS Neighborhood Nutrition Alliance (free services), Mantua-Haverford Community Center (youth leadership program), Pa. Horticultural Society (community gardens), Philabundance (food rescue program), Philadelphia Fight (medicine/treatment for AIDS patients), Royer-Greaves School for the Blind (non-school year program), Suburban Music School (music ed program), City Team Ministries (homeless program), and Wood Services Foundation. $2,000-$2,500 each to Associated Services for the Blind (rehabilitation services), Brian's House (arts program), Children's Aid Society of Pa. (interactive teens-tots program), Creative Artists Network (youth art classes), Deaf-Hearing Communication Center (signing training), H.E.R.O. (teen program), North Light Community Center (teens social program), Pa. Home of the Sparrow Planned Parenthood of Chester County (books), and Walnut Street Theatre (adopt a school program). $1,500 to Child Home & Community (support group). $1,000 to Wings for Success. **Out-of-state** grant: $12,000 to Stratton Mountain School [VT] (building fund). ■**PUBLICATIONS:** statement of program policy; application guidelines ■ **WEBSITE:** None ■**E-MAIL:** reginald.middleton@wachovia.com■**APPLICATION POLICIES & PROCEDURES:** The Foundation reports that giving focuses on small Philadelphia-area organizations for programs dealing with education, youth, women, senior citizens, health services, religious organizations providing human services, arts, historical preservation, and environment. Most grants are for special projects or general support; capital improvements are supported only when a specific project and a clear need are demonstrated. No grants are awarded to/for individuals, endowment, political activities, or loans. Grant requests should be submitted in a proposal with cover letter (signed by an officer on behalf of the governing board) during March-May (deadline is June 15th). The proposal must include the following: the project title, purpose of the grant request, and expected project outcome; a problem statement documenting the needs to be met/problems to be solved; a plan of action; a project budget outlining program elements; and a statement about the project's duration including, if applicable, anticipated long-term funding requirements. Also provide a current Board list, a list of immediate past/present major funding sources, current organization budget, a bound audited financial statement, and IRS tax-exempt status documentation. Incomplete proposals will not be considered. Site visits sometimes are made to organizations being considered for a grant. Grants are awarded at a December meeting.

O+D+T Reginald J. Middleton (VP at Bank+Con) — Isaac H. Clothier, IV Esq. (T) — Kenneth W. Gemmill, Esq. [VA] (T) — Anne B. Kellett [Villanova] (T) First Union/Wachovia (Corporate Trustee)

SE-601 Savadove (Patricia & Lionel) Fund, The   MI-52
    6 Old Mill Lane   **Phone** 215-862-5598 **FAX** None
    New Hope 18938   (Bucks County)   **EIN** 23-2442430   **Year Created** 1987
AMV $101,006   **FYE** 12-00   **(Gifts Received** $0)   12 **Grants totaling** $13,400

Mostly local giving. High grant of **$6,420** to Opera Company of Philadelphia. **$3,020** to Orchestra 2001. **$900** to Academy of Vocal Arts. **$750** to Philadelphia Opera Guild. Other local and out-of-state giving **$50-$550** all for musical purposes. ■**PUBLICATIONS:** None ■**WEBSITE:** None ■**E-MAIL:** None ■**APPLICATION POLICIES & PROCEDURES:** No grants awarded to individuals.
O+D+T Lionel Savadove (P+D+Donor+Con) — Patricia Savadove (VP+S+F+D) — Lane J. Savadove (D) — Lorin M. Savadove (D)

SE-602 Scheller (Roberta & Ernest, Jr.) Family Foundation   MI-11-22-32-42-54-55-62
    730 Canterbury Lane   **Phone** 610-527-2557 **FAX** None
    Villanova 19085   (Montgomery County)   **EIN** 23-7828732   **Year Created** 1995
AMV $1,419,364   **FYE** 12-99   **(Gifts Received** $0)   17 **Grants totaling** $58,300

Limited local giving. High Pa. grant of **$5,000** to Franklin Institute. **$1,000** to Main Line Art Center. **$600** to United Way of SE Pa. Other smaller local contributions. **Out-of-state** giving includes **$21,300** to B'nai Vail Congregation [CO]; **$21,000** to Georgia Tech; **$2,000** to American Liver Foundation [NY]; and smaller grants to Israel, NY, and other states. ■**PUBLICATIONS:** None ■**WEBSITE:** None ■**E-MAIL:** None ■**APPLICATION POLICIES & PROCEDURES:** No grants awarded to individuals.
O+D+T Ernest Scheller, Jr. (C+T+Donor+Con) — Roberta Scheller (T+Donor) — Lisa Jane Peretz [Schnecksville] (T)

SE-603 Schiel Foundation   MI-17-25-41-56
    P.O. Box 150   **Phone** Unlisted **FAX** None
    Doylestown 18901   (Bucks County)   **EIN** 23-3022575   **Year Created** 2000
AMV $587,492   **FYE** 4-01   **(Gifts Received** $0)   5 **Grants totaling** $31,000

Mostly local giving. High grant of **$10,000** to A Woman's Place. **$6,000** to Bethesda Project [Philadelphia]. **$5,000** each to Bucks County Women's Fund and Wordsworth Academy. **Out-of-state** grant: **$5,000** to Avalon Museum & Historical Society [NJ]. ■**PUBLICATIONS:** None ■**WEBSITE:** None ■**E-MAIL:** None ■**APPLICATION POLICIES & PROCEDURES:** The Foundation reports it is not soliciting grant applications at this time.
O+D+T Mary Jane Kirkpatrick (S+Con) — George L. Schiel [Lansdale] (P) — Jane B. Schiel [Lansdale] (VP) — Arthur L. Schiel [Wayne] (F)

SE-604 Schiff (Mortimer S. & Vera M.) Foundation   MI-22-62
    c/o Lawrence Schiff Silk Mills, Inc.
    590 California Road   **Phone** 215-538-2880 **FAX** None
    Quakertown 18951   (Bucks County)   **EIN** 22-2450589   **Year Created** 1984
AMV $257,602   **FYE** 12-00   **(Gifts Received** $725)   13 **Grants totaling** $16,808

About three-fourths giving to Allentown area. High grant of **$10,000** to Jewish Federation of the Lehigh Valley. **$1,558** to Temple Beth El. **$675** to Jewish Community Center of Allentown. Other smaller local contributions. **Out-of-state** giving includes **$2,000** to United Jewish Appeal of Key West [FL]. ■**PUBLICATIONS:** None ■**WEBSITE:** None ■**E-MAIL:** None ■**APPLICATION POLICIES & PROCEDURES:** Grant requests may be submitted in a letter at any time. — Formerly called the Lawrence & Mortimer S. Schiff Foundation.
O+D+T Richard J. Schiff (S+D+Con) — Vera M. Schiff [FL] (P+F+D) Corporate donor: Lawrence Schiff Silk Mills, Inc.

SE-605 Scholler Foundation, The   MI-12-14-15-22-31-32-35-43
    c/o Hepburn, Willcox, Hamilton & Putnam
    1100 One Penn Center, 1617 JFK Boulevard   **Phone** 215-568-7500 **FAX** 215-751-9044
    Philadelphia 19103   (Philadelphia County)   **EIN** 23-6245158   **Year Created** 1939
AMV $17,423,906   **FYE** 12-00   **(Gifts Received** $0)   48 **Grants totaling** $766,762

All local/Pa. or nearby NJ giving; grants are for general operating support except as noted. High grant of **$50,000** to Pa. Hospital (new incubator). **$40,000** to Jeanes Hospital (new anesthesia system). **$35,000** each to Fox Chase Cancer Center (new spectrometer) and Glaucoma Service Foundation (educational newsletter). **$30,000** each to Center in the Park. **$27,500** to Surrey Services for Seniors (patient transportation van). **$25,000** each to Philadelphia U. (scientific equipment purchase) and Wheels, Inc. **$20,000-$20,300** each to Delco Blind/Sight Center (blindness prevention services), Doylestown Hospital (Heart Center equipment), Exceptional Care, Inc. (rehabilitation/hospice care services for children), Institutes for the Achievement of Human

Potential (diagnostic equipment for brain-injured children), Junior Service Board (nursing scholarship fund), Philadelphia Senior Center (social service/health independence program), Temple U. School of Podiatric Medicine (prevention fund), and U. of Pa. School of Nursing (equipment for frail elderly). **$17,000** each to Lankenau Institute for Medical Research (osteoporosis research equipment) and Montgomery County Emergency Service (defibrillator and other equipment). **$15,000-$15,200** each to Chestnut Hill Healthcare (maternity/ICU dept. equipment), Delaware Valley Friends School (health education program), Guiding Light for the Blind (laser canes/mobility devices), Kearsley Retirement Community, Magee Rehab (wheelchairs for needy patients), MCP/Hahnemann U. (medical students' homeless outreach program), Wissahickon Hospice (working capital), and Wistar Institute (research equipment). **$9,500-$10,000** each to Baker Industries, Episcopal Community Services (home care program equipment), Northwest Interfaith Movement (long-term care program), Pa. College of Optometry (services for low-income patients), Valley Health Foundation [Easton] (pediatric care monitors), and Woodlynde School (curriculum for auditory impaired). **$8,000** to Children's Hospital of Philadelphia Foundation (transport monitor). **$5,000-$5,700** each to CONTACT CareLine for Greater Philadelphia (program expansion), Fore Kids Campaign (benefit event), Grand View Health Foundation (capital improvement project), Melmark (community resource center expansion), Pa. School for the Deaf (technology program), Philadelphia Presbytery Homes (special transportation equipment), and St. Luke's Quakertown Hospital (renovations/upgrading). **$2,500-$3,530** each to Elwyn, Inc. (dental equipment purchase), Penn Home (patient security system), and Roman Catholic High School (academic enrichment program). **Out-of-state** grants, all to NJ: **$25,000** to Deborah Hospital Foundation (equipment); **$22,325** to Atlantic City Day Nursery (play structure); **$20,000** to Somerset Health Care Foundation (new construction); and **$5,000** to Underwood Memorial Hospital (renovations). ■**PUBLICATIONS:** None ■**WEBSITE:** None ■**E-MAIL:** None ■**APPLICATION POLICIES & PROCEDURES:** The Foundation reports priority giving to Delaware Valley for healthcare delivery organizations; most grants are for special projects or matching grants, and multiyear grants are awarded. Some emphasis is given to supporting small community hospitals for equipment purchases. No grants are awarded to/for general support, endowment, scholarships, fellowships, or individuals. Prospective applicants initially should make a telephone inquiry about the feasibility of submitting a request. Grant requests may be submitted in a letter/proposal in March or September (deadlines are April 1st and October 1st); include organizational and project budgets, audited financial statement, a statement certifying the application organization is not a private foundation, and IRS tax-exempt status documentation. Site visits sometimes are made to organizations being considered for a grant. Grants are awarded at meetings in May and November.
O+D+T E. Brooks Keffer, Jr., Esq. (P+T+Con) — Frederick L. Fuges, Esq. (S+T) — Edwin C. Dreby, III (T)

SE-606 Schrenk (C.W. & Marjorie J.) Family Foundation
c/o Holland Enterprises, Inc.
130 Buck Road, Suite 201
Holland 18966 (Bucks County)

MI-12-13-14-22-23-63-84

Phone 215-357-6195 **FAX** 215-357-8160
EIN 23-6906450 **Year Created** 1988

AMV $1,887,919 **FYE** 12-00 **(Gifts Received** $81,886) 32 **Grants totaling** $93,550

Mostly local giving. High grant of **$20,663** to Boy Scouts/Camp Kirby (camp repairs). **$17,611** to a local family/children with rare illnesses (residential renovations). **$13,781** to a disabled/quadriplegic individual (van purchase). **$5,589** to a disabled individual (wheelchair accessible van purchase). **$4,308** to DARE Program (drug/alcohol abuse education). **$3,500** to Grace Bible Chapel (van to transport handicapped to church). **$1,000-$2,700** each to American Legion (renovations), Bensalem Township Police (Christmas presents for needy children), Camp Discovery (summer camp supplies), Camp Dreamcatcher (children with AIDS), Children's Aid Society (daycare for underprivileged), Episcopal Community Services (after-school programs for underprivileged children), Family Services Assn. of Bucks County (baby items for needy families), Nonprofit Technology Resources (computer training for low-income families), Pa. Special Olympics (festival sponsorships), Pegasus Riding Academy (horse for handicapped children), United Church of Christ (inner-city youth skills employment program), and support to needy families struggling with illnesses. Other smaller local and out-of-state contributions for similar purposes. ■**PUBLICATIONS:** annual report ■**WEBSITE:** None ■**E-MAIL:** None ■**APPLICATION POLICIES & PROCEDURES:** The Foundation reports that all giving is restricted to organizations within Pennsylvania, New Jersey, or Delaware which (1) better the lives of children/families who are physically, mentally, socially, financially or religiously deprived for reasons beyond their control, -or- (2) further the lives of individuals who have subjected to abuse, -or- (3) foster Christian religious chaplaincies in educational institutions, -or- (4) perpetuate the family unit in American society. Most grants are for special projects, building funds, or capital needs. Grant requests may be submitted in a letter or proposal at any time; describe the organization's purpose, its history, and how the requested funds will be used; include an annual report, organizational/project budgets, list of Board members, and IRS tax-exempt status documentation. Site visits sometimes are arranged to organizations being considered for a grant. Grants are awarded at meetings in January, March, June, September and December.
O+D+T Clarence W. Schrenk (P+T+Donor+Con) — Marjorie Schrenk (C+T+Donor) — Michael Piotrowitcz [Wayne] (VC+T+Donor) — Bonnie Schrenk Stellwagon [Churchville] (S+T+Donor) — Robert F. Pritz [Perkasie] (F+T+Donor) — Beverly Schrenk Gormley [Jamison] (T+Donor) — Susan Marquiss (T+Donor) — Jean Schrenk Traub [Doylestown] (T+Donor)

SE-607 Schumacker (Lloyd J.) Fund
c/o Schumacker & Lunkenheimer
825 Duportail Road, Suite 103
Wayne 19087 (Chester County)

MI-41-44-79

Phone 610-651-4900 **FAX** None
EIN 23-6251929 **Year Created** 1956

AMV $869,741 **FYE** 12-00 **(Gifts Received** $0) 2 **Grants totaling** $45,000

High grant of **$25,000** to Easttown Library. **Out-of-state** grant: **$20,000** to U. of Virginia Fund. — In the prior year, one grant of **$75,000** to National Resources Defense Council [NY]. ■**PUBLICATIONS:** None ■**WEBSITE:** None ■**E-MAIL:** None ■**APPLICATION POLICIES & PROCEDURES:** No grants awarded to individuals.
O+D+T Scott F. Schumacker, Esq. (T+Con) — Betsy Schumacker

SE-608   Schusler Foundation, The
c/o Devland Associates
161 West Lancaster Ave., P.O. Box 935
Paoli 19301   (Chester County)

MI-12-13-22-25-29-32-41-83

Phone 610-296-3012 **FAX** None
EIN 23-2191242   **Year Created** 1982

AMV $191,414   **FYE** 12-00   **(Gifts Received** $0)   18 **Grants totaling** $20,000

Mostly local giving; all grants are for general support. High grant of **$4,000** to Red Cross. **$3,000** to Salvation Army. **$1,000-$1,500** each to American Heart Assn., Big Brothers/Big Sisters, Boys & Girls Club of Metropolitan Philadelphia, Philabundance, Episcopal Academy, Family Services of Chester County, Agnes Irwin School, and Phoenixville Area YMCA. Other local contributions **$500** for various purposes. **Out-of-state** grant: **$1,000** to Concord Coalition [DC]. ■**PUBLICATIONS:** None ■**WEBSITE:** None ■**E-MAIL:** None ■**APPLICATION POLICIES & PROCEDURES:** Grant requests may be submitted in any form during October-December. Site visits sometimes are made to organizations being considered for a grant. — Formerly called the David W. Schusler Foundation.

O+D+T David W. Schusler [Villanova] (P+D+Donor+Con) — Linda K. Schusler [Villanova] (S+D)

SE-609   Schwartz Foundation, The
700 Merion Square Road
Gladwyne 19035   (Montgomery County)

MI-11-12-13-14-15-22-41-44-54-57-62-82-85

Phone 610-896-4444 **FAX** None
EIN 23-2267403   **Year Created** 1983

AMV $22,277,793   **FYE** 8-00   **(Gifts Received** $80,418)   38 **Grants totaling** $2,674,780

Limited local giving. High Pa. grant of **$96,000** to Jewish Community Centers of Greater Philadelphia. **$30,000** to Raymond & Ruth Perelman Jewish Center. **$22,100** to Politz Hebrew Academy. **$20,000** to Guidelines Services. **$15,000** to Police Athletic League of Philadelphia. **$11,700** to Free Library of Philadelphia. **$10,000** each to ARC of Delaware County and United Way of SE Pa. **$5,000** to Federation Day Care Services. **$2,500** each to Delaware Valley Friends School, Ogontz Avenue Revitalization Corporation, and Temple Adath Israel. **$1,800** to American Friends of the Jaffa Institute. **$1,000-$1,500** each to The Baldwin School, Crossroads, Delaware Valley Grantmakers, Gesu School, Haddington Multi-Services for Older Adults, Jewish Federation of Greater Philadelphia, Please Touch Museum, United Negro College Fund, and WHYY. Other local contributions **$150-$500** for various purposes. **Out-of-state** giving includes high grant of **$2,300,000** to Foundations, Inc. [NJ] (before/after-school enrichment programs); **$100,000** to Institute for Advanced Education [Israel]; **$15,000** to Camden County ARC [NJ]; and **$10,000** to Horatio Alger Assn. [VA]. ■**PUBLICATIONS:** None ■**WEBSITE:** None ■**E-MAIL:** None ■**APPLICATION POLICIES & PROCEDURES:** Grant requests may be submitted in a letter at any time. — Formerly called The Bernard & Robert Schwarz Foundation.

O+D+T Robert S. Schwartz (C+F+D+Donor+Con) — Bernard Schwartz [Bala Cynwyd] (P+D+Donor) — Carol Auerbach [NY] (D) — David N. Bressler, Esq. [Blue Bell] (D) — Rhonda H. Lauer [NJ] (D) — Erika Schwartz (D) — Lois Schwartz [Bala Cynwyd] (D) — Michael Schwartz (D) Corporate donor: Food Sciences Corp. [NJ]

SE-610   Schwartz (Ira) Foundation, The
122 Naudain Street
Philadelphia 19147   (Philadelphia County)

MI-12-17-22-62-82

Phone Unlisted **FAX** None
EIN 23-2787036   **Year Created** 1994

AMV $124,970   **FYE** 6-01   **(Gifts Received** $3,000)   4 **Grants totaling** $20,105

All local giving. High grant of **$15,995** to Kesher Israel Preschool. **$2,000** to Girlstown Jerusalem [Jenkintown]. **$1,100** to Kesher Israel Synagogue. **$1,000** to Laurel House. ■**PUBLICATIONS:** None ■**WEBSITE:** None ■**E-MAIL:** None ■**APPLICATION POLICIES & PROCEDURES:** No grants awarded to individuals.

O+D+T Ira Schwartz (T+Donor+Con) — John T. Kehner, Esq. [West Chester] (T) — Sol Sardinsky, CPA (T)

SE-611   Schweiker (Malcolm A.), Jr. Memorial Foundation
c/o PNC Advisors
1600 Market Street, 6th Floor
Philadelphia 19103   (Philadelphia County)

MI-13-41-44-63

Phone 215-585-5564 **FAX** None
EIN 23-6207352   **Year Created** 1949

AMV $755,169   **FYE** 12-00   **(Gifts Received** $0)   4 **Grants totaling** $14,500

All giving limited to Lansdale, Montgomery County area. High grant of **$11,500** to Garden of Memories. **$2,000** to Central Schwenkfelder Church. **$500** each to Calvary Methodist Church and St. Paul's Lutheran Church. — Other giving in prior years to Schwenkfelder Library, youth organizations, and local private schools. ■**PUBLICATIONS:** None ■**WEBSITE:** None ■**E-MAIL:** None ■**APPLICATION POLICIES & PROCEDURES:** The Foundation reports that grants are primarily for religious or educational purposes in the Lansdale, Montgomery County area. Prospective applicants initially should make a telephone inquiry about the feasibility of submitting a request. Site visits sometimes are made to organizations being considered for a grant. Grant decisions are made semi-annually by Schweiker family trustees, not Bank representatives.

O+D+T Beverly J. Rowan (VP at Bank+Con) — Claire C. Schweiker [VA] (T) — Richard S. Schweiker, Jr. [VA] (T) — Sylvia Schweiker Strasburg (T) — William E. Strasburg (T)

SE-612   Scott (Ruth & Earl) Charitable Trust
813 Mount Pleasant Road
Bryn Mawr 19010   (Montgomery County)

MI-22-42-62

Phone 215-525-1958 **FAX** None
EIN 23-2629692   **Year Created** 1992

AMV $1,047,933   **FYE** 12-00   **(Gifts Received** $0)   **Grants totaling** $0

No grants awarded in 1999 or 2000. — In 1998, grants totaling **$169,500** were awarded, including **$85,500** to U. of Pa.; **$25,000** each to Jewish Federation of Greater Philadelphia and United Way of SE Pa; and local grants/contributions **$500-**

$2,500 for art/culture, education, and human services. ■**PUBLICATIONS:** None ■**WEBSITE:** None ■**E-MAIL:** None ■**APPLICATION POLICIES & PROCEDURES:** No grants awarded to individuals.

O+D+T Samuel R. Scott (T+Con) — Ruth R. Scott (P+Donor)

SE-613 Sedlacek Family Foundation
17 Painter's Lane, Chesterbrook
Wayne 19087 (Chester County)
AMV $309,353 **FYE** 12-00 (**Gifts Received** $0)

MI-13-41-42-55-63
Phone 610-644-5158 **FAX** None
EIN 23-2615234 **Year Created** 1990
9 **Grants totaling** $19,000

About half local giving. High grant of **$4,500** to First Presbyterian Church of Phoenixville. **$3,000** to Colonial Theatre. **$2,500** to Bethel Baptist church. **$2,000** to Phoenixville YMCA. **$250** to PAEDCO. **Out-of-state** giving includes **$2,500** to Moorestown Friends School [NJ] and **$2,000** to U. of Nebraska. ■**PUBLICATIONS:** None ■**WEBSITE:** None ■**E-MAIL:** None ■**APPLICATION POLICIES & PROCEDURES:** No grants awarded to individuals.

O+D+T John J. Sedlacek (P+F+Donor+Con) — Vivian Sedlacek (VP+S)

SE-614 Segal (Bernard G.) Foundation, The
c/o Schnader Harrison Segal & Lewis
1600 Market Street, Suite 3600
Philadelphia 19103 (Philadelphia County)
AMV $979,495 **FYE** 6-01 (**Gifts Received** $462,828)

MI-12-25-41

Phone 215-751-2080 **FAX** 215-246-9018
EIN 23-6232487 **Year Created** 1955
4 **Grants totaling** $50,000

One Pa. grant: **$5,000** to Jubilee School. **Out-of-state** grants: **$25,000** to National Foundation on Counseling; and **$10,000** each to Children's Relief Network [CA] and Table to Table [NJ]. ■**PUBLICATIONS:** None ■**WEBSITE:** None ■**E-MAIL:** None ■**APPLICATION POLICIES & PROCEDURES:** The Foundation reports that Trustees self-select all charitable recipients.

O+D+T Bruce A. Rosenfield, Esq. (T+Con) — Geraldine R. Segal (T+Donor) — Marc Cohen [NJ] (T) — Thomas P. Glassmoyer, Esq. (T)

SE-615 Segal (Patricia & Stephen) Family Foundation
722 Westview Street
Philadelphia 19119 (Philadelphia County)
AMV $132,822 **FYE** 12-00 (**Gifts Received** $89,000)

MI-22-41-55-62
Phone 215-843-2442 **FAX** None
EIN 23-7880724 **Year Created** 1997
3 **Grants totaling** $31,000

All local giving. High grant of **$25,000** to Federation Allied Jewish Appeal. **$5,000** to Sedgwick Cultural Center. **$1,000** to The Miquon School. — In the prior year, major grants included **$22,756** to Federation Allied Jewish Appeal; **$10,000** to Germantown Jewish Center; and **$9,500** to Joint Distribution Committee [NY]. ■**PUBLICATIONS:** None. ■**WEBSITE:** None ■**E-MAIL:** None ■**APPLICATION POLICIES & PROCEDURES:** Grant requests may be submitted in any form at any time.

O+D+T Stephen P. Segal (T+Donor+Con) — Patricia Segal (T+Donor)

SE-616 Segel Foundation
c/o St. Clair Easton CPAs
10 Presidential Blvd., Suite 250
Bala Cynwyd 19004 (Montgomery County)
AMV $1,284,035 **FYE** 12-00 (**Gifts Received** $0)

MI-11-22-35-41-42-62

Phone 610-668-1998 **FAX** 610-668-3479
EIN 23-7014746 **Year Created** 1969
30 **Grants totaling** $28,020

Mostly local giving. High grant of **$10,000** to United Way of Chester County. **$4,000** to West Philadelphia High School. **$2,500** to Drexel U. **$1,000-$1,500** each to Breast Health Institute, Jewish Family & Children's Services, and Temple Adath Israel. **$720** to Muhlenberg College (Hillel House). Other local contributions **$100-$500** for health, educational, and Jewish purposes. **Out-of-state** giving includes **$1,000** to Anti-Defamation League [NY] and smaller contributions. ■**PUBLICATIONS:** None ■**WEBSITE:** None ■**E-MAIL:** None ■**APPLICATION POLICIES & PROCEDURES:** Grant requests may be submitted in a letter (2 pages maximum) at any time; include appropriate background information, an audited financial statement, and IRS tax-exempt status documentation. No grants awarded to individuals. The Board meets as needed. — Formerly called the Franklin Foundation.

O+D+T Stanley Merves [Haverford] (T+Donor+Con) — Joseph M. Segel [FL] (T+Donor) — Doris Segel [FL] (T) — Rickey Bogdanoff [AZ] (Manager)

SE-617 Seltzer Family Foundation
1019 Morris Ave.
Bryn Mawr 19010 (Montgomery County)
AMV $868,940 **FYE** 12-00 (**Gifts Received** $0)

MI-14-16-51-62-82
Phone 610-527-8960 **FAX** None
EIN 23-2829071 **Year Created** 1996
31 **Grants totaling** $13,921

About one-fourth local giving. High Pa. grants of **$1,000** each to Theatre Ariel and Zionist Organization of America. Other local contributions **$15-$325** for Jewish and other purposes. **Out-of-state** giving includes **$1,000** each to American Red Magen David in Israel [NY], Friends of Israel Disabled Vets [NY], Jewish National Fund [NY], Southern Poverty Law Center [AL], and Yemin Orde [DC]. ■**PUBLICATIONS:** None ■**WEBSITE:** None ■**E-MAIL:** None ■**APPLICATION POLICIES & PROCEDURES:** No grants awarded to individuals.

O+D+T Stephanie Seltzer (P+T+Donor+Con) — Stephen Zlotowski [Danville] (VP+T) — David Zlotowski [Malvern] (S+T) — Louis N. Seltzer (F+T+Donor) — Debra Seltzer [CA] (T)

SE-618 **Seybert Institution for Poor Boys & Girls**
P.O. Box 8228
Philadelphia 19101 (Philadelphia County)

MI-12-13-14-16-17-19-20-22-29-41-55-84
Phone 610-828-8145 **FAX** 610-834-8175
EIN 23-6260105 **Year Created** 1914

AMV $8,202,452 **FYE** 12-00 **(Gifts Received** $0) 48 **Grants totaling** $279,500

All giving restricted to programs serving poor, deprived, or abused children in the City of Philadelphia. High grant of **$50,000** to Greater Philadelphia First Foundation (Children Achieving/Parent Involvement Initiative). **$13,000** to Greater Philadelphia Urban Affairs Coalition (summer career exploration program). **$12,500** to School District of Philadelphia (Douglas Elementary School/North Star Outreach). **$7,000** each to Hunter Elementary School (parent partnership program) and Southwest community Enrichment Center (teen enrichment program). **$6,000** to Academy of Community Music (Head Start program in Philadelphia). **$5,000** each to Asian Arts Initiative (youth workshop), Children's Aid Society (teens-tots program), Community Women's Education Project (staff training), Congreso de Latinos Unidos (START program for youth), Crime Prevention Assn. (intergenerational program), Episcopal Church of the Advocate (after-school/summer programs), Frankford Group Ministry (parenting program), Greater Philadelphia Urban Affairs Coalition (Asian-American youth programs), Greater Philadelphia Women's Medical Fund, Hannah House (mother-children programs), International Ballet Exchange (school residencies/children's performances), Ludlow Youth Community Center (youth programs), NetworkArts Philadelphia (mural project), Norris Square Neighborhood Project (summer program), North Light Community Center (after-school/summer programs), Philadelphia Fight (youth health project), Philadelphia Society for Services to Children (parenting programs), Philadelphia Training Program (youth programs), Philadelphia Young Playwrights Festival (school anti-volence project), Settlement Music School (early childhood initiative), Taller Puertorriqueno (cultural awareness program), Urban Bridges at St. Gabriel's (enrichment program), and YWCA of Germantown (Saturday arts programs). **$4,000-$4,500** each to College Settlement of Philadelphia (summer camp for Philadelphia kids), Committee for Dignity & Fairness in Housing (youth program), Face to Face (Camp St. Vincent), and Montessori Genesis II School (summer program). **$3,000-$3,500** each to Allens Lane Art Center (summer day camp), Awbury Arboretum (environmental education program), Children's Country Week Assn. (summer programs for disadvantaged children), Children's Village Child Care (early intervention/parent support program), COSACOSA Art At Large (healing art project), MANNA/Metropolitan AIDS Neighborhood Nutrition Alliance (table-talk program for children/mothers), Philadelphia Physicians for Social Responsibility (violence prevention program), Philadelphia Wooden Boat Factory (marine education program), Potter's House Mission (youth programs), and Urban Retrievers (Philadelphia Student Union). **$2,000-$2,500** each to 1812 Productions (in-school/outreach programs), Episcopal Community Services (West Philadelphia programs), First United Church of Germantown (after-school program), and Old First Reformed Church (summer day camp). ■ **PUBLICATIONS:** Annual Report (grantees only listed) with application guidelines ■ **WEBSITE:** None ■ **E-MAIL:** judy1@aol.com ■ **APPLICATION POLICIES & PROCEDURES:** The Foundation reports that only organizations serving disadvantaged or needy children (birth to high school age) in the City of Philadelphia are eligible to apply. Priority interests are innovative teaching methods; cultural, artistic and craft programs; and counseling services re child abuse, drugs, dropouts and runaways. Most grants are for special projects and are for only one year. Grants for capital expenditures are a low priority, and no grants are awarded to/for endowment, individuals, or organizations which discriminate on the basis of race, ethnic origin, sexual or religious preference, age, or gender. Grant requests may be submitted at any time in the form of a proposal narrative together with a Proposal Cover Sheet (available from the foundation). The proposal narrative (6 pages maximum) should clearly and succinctly state: (a) name and purpose of the organization; (b) purpose of the requested grant and special nature of the project and how it will benefit low-income young persons in Philadelphia; (c) funding requested, total funding needed, and other funding available or expected; (d) leadership involved in the project; (e) list of Board members and key staff; and (f) an annual budget. Submit an original plus nine complete, collated copies of the proposal narrative with Proposal Cover Sheets, two copies of the most recent audited financial statement, one copy of IRS tax-exempt status documentation, and up to three supporting items (e.g. press clipping, pamphlets, endorsements). No more than one request will be considered in one calendar year except under special circumstances. Also, the Common Grant Application of Delaware Valley Grantmakers (see Appendix) may be used, but the Proposal Cover Sheet must be attached. Deadlines for receipt of applications are January 2nd, April 1st, and October 1st. Board meetings are held in late January, April, and October; decisions on grants for summer program are made at the April meeting.

O+D+T Judith L. Bardes [Plymouth Meeting] (Executive Secretary+Con) — William C. Bullitt, Esq. (P+F+D) — Susan C. Day, M.D. (VP+D) — Kevin T. Green (S+D) — Graham S. Finney (D) — Rev. David I. Hagan, OSFS (D) — Dee Hillas [Gwynedd Valley] (D) — Sara S. Moran (D) — Carver A. Portlock (D) — Lucy Wolf Tuton, Ph.D. (D)

SE-619 **Shade Tree Foundation**
c/o Tru-Brew Coffee Service
387 Springdale Ave.
Hatboro 19040 (Montgomery County)

MI-14-35

Phone 215-441-0110 **FAX** None
EIN 23-2869030 **Year Created** 1997

AMV $0 **FYE** 9-00 **(Gifts Received** $27,875) 1 **Grant of** $31,597

Sole grant to Volunteer Optometric Services to Humanity [Richboro] (assistance with cataract surgeries and eye exams). ■ **PUBLICATIONS:** None ■ **WEBSITE:** None ■ **E-MAIL:** None ■ **APPLICATION POLICIES & PROCEDURES:** Information not available.

O+D+T Christian J. Wurst, Jr. [Warminster] (P+Donor+Con) — Craig J. Wurst [Doylestown] (S+F) — Rev. Stephen P. McHenry [Ambler] (D) — M.D. McHenry [Willow Grove] (Donor)

SE-620 **Sheerr Foundation**
800 Edwin Lane
Bryn Mawr 19010 (Montgomery County)

MI-11-18-22-41-42-62

Phone 610-527-4073 **FAX** None
EIN 23-6298319 **Year Created** 1949

AMV $319,256 **FYE** 12-00 **(Gifts Received** $0) 37 **Grants totaling** $19,350

Mostly local giving; some grants comprise multiple payments. High grant of **$8,100** to The Baldwin School. **$1,500** to Beth Sholom Congregation. Other local contributions **$100-$525** for civic, cultural, educational, health/human services, Jewish, and other purposes. **Out-of-state** grant: **$800** to Planned Parenthood Federation of America. ■ **PUBLICATIONS:** None ■ **WEBSITE:** None ■ **E-MAIL:** None ■ **APPLICATION POLICIES & PROCEDURES:** No grants to individuals. Grant requests in any form may be submitted at any time.

O+D+T Richard C. Sheerr (T+Con) — Constance F. Kittner [Philadelphia] (T) — Betsy R. Sheerr (T) — Melanie Sheerr (T)

SE-621 Sherrerd Foundation
c/o Sherrerd & Company
One Tower Bridge, 9th Floor
West Conshohocken 19428 (Montgomery County)
AMV $16,699,340 **FYE** 7-01 **(Gifts Received** $199,605)

MI-13-14-31-32-41-42-45-54-63-72-84
Phone 610-940-5020 **FAX** None
EIN 22-2751186 **Year Created** 1986
43 **Grants totaling** $780,124

About four-fifths local giving; some grants comprise multiple payments. High grant of **$327,938** to U. of Pa. Wharton School (building fund). **$50,000** each to Arthur Ashe Youth Tennis Center, Philadelphia Youth Tennis, and Young Scholars Charter School. **$35,000** to Franklin Institute. **$30,000** each to Bryn Mawr Presbyterian Church and Philadelphia Museum of Art. **$15,000** each to Gesu School and U. of Pa. Wharton School. **$5,000** each to Bryn Mawr Hospital Foundation, Camp Soltane (endowment), The Philadelphia Scholars, and The Shipley School. **$3,286** to The Hill School. **$3,000** to UCP of Philadelphia. **$1,000** each to Friends of the Philadelphia Zoo, National Constitution Center, and YouthBuild Philadelphia Charter School. Other local contributions **$150-$500** for various purposes. **Out-of-state** giving includes **$50,000** to Princeton Charter Foundation [NJ]; **$25,000** to Fleur de Lis Camp for Girls [NH]; **$24,250** to Princeton U. [NJ]; **$14,000** to Friends of Princeton Athletics [NJ]; **$5,000** to Teach for America [NY]; and **$2,500** to National Humanities Center [NC]. ■ **PUBLICATIONS:** None ■ **WEBSITE:** None ■ **E-MAIL:** None ■ **APPLICATION POLICIES & PROCEDURES:** The Foundation reports that grants are awarded primarily to organizations with which the officers are personally involved or have personal knowledge; unsolicited requests are not encouraged. No grants are awarded to individuals. — Formerly called Muirfield Foundation.

O+D+T John J.F. Sherrerd [Bryn Mawr] (P+F+Donor+Con) — Kathleen C. Sherrerd [Bryn Mawr] (VP+S+Donor)

SE-622 Shickman Family Foundation
c/o Sardinsky Braunstein & Co.
10 Ten Center, Suite 617
Philadelphia 19103 (Philadelphia County)
AMV $533,952 **FYE** 12-00 **(Gifts Received** $99,967)

MI-22-52-55-62
Phone 215-563-6222 **FAX** None
EIN 23-2902143 **Year Created** 1997
38 **Grants totaling** $29,185

Two local grants: **$3,000** to Kardon Institute of the Arts and **$500** to Philadelphia Youth Orchestra. **Out-of-state** giving, primarily to NY, includes **$5,000** to American Friends of Israel; **$3,000** to United Jewish Appeal; **$2,000** to Fifth Ave. Synagogue; and **$100-$1,500** for many Jewish organizations and others. ■ **PUBLICATIONS:** None. ■ **WEBSITE:** None ■ **E-MAIL:** None ■ **APPLICATION POLICIES & PROCEDURES:** Information not available.

O+D+T Sol Sardinsky, CPA (AS+AF+Con) — Lila Schickman [NY] (P+F) — Herman Schickman [NY] (VP+S) — Barbara Kaye [Wayne] (VP+D) — Howard Kaye [Wayne] (VP+D)

SE-623 Shoemaker (Thomas H. & Mary Williams) Fund
c/o Carolyn Moon
1120 Hagues Mill Road
Ambler 19002 (Montgomery County)
AMV $7,387,687 **FYE** 9-01 **(Gifts Received** $0)

MI-12-13-14-15-16-19-22-41-42-56-63-65-71
81-83
Phone 215-542-1340 **FAX** 215-542-1340
EIN 23-6209783 **Year Created** 1953
105 **Grants totaling** $464,105

About three-fourths local/Pa. giving; some grants comprise multiple payments. High grant of **$24,000** to Friends Journal. **$21,000** to Friends General Conference. **$16,000** to Haverford College. **$5,000** each to Friends Education Fund and Stapeley in Germantown. **$13,000** to Pendle Hill. **$11,000** to George School. **$10,000** each to George Fox Friends School [Cochranville], Germantown YWCA, and The School in Rose Valley. **$8,000** to Jubilee School. **$7,500** to Abington Quarterly Meeting. **$7,000** to Nueva Esperanza. **$6,000-$6,500** each to Providence Monthly Meeting, Stratford Friends School, and Swarthmore College. **$5,000** each to Barclay Friends, Community of Bosnia [Philadelphia], Delaware Valley Friends School, Friends Center Corporation, Friends School-Haverford, Greene Street Friends School, Global Education Motivators, John Bartram Assn., Lansdowne Friends School, Media-Providence Friends School, Newtown Monthly Meeting, Pendle Hill (scholarship fund), Pa. Program for Justice, Philabundance, Quaker Inner City School (endowment), We The People/GEM, West Chester Friends School, and Westtown School. **$4,000-$4,100** each to A Better Chance/Strath Haven, Fellowship Farm, Interfaith of Ambler, and Philadelphia Yearly Meeting (school). **$3,000-$3,540** each to Community Gardens of Chester County, Freire Charter School [Philadelphia], Olney Friends School, Philadelphia Senior Center, Green Circle, Quaker School at Horsham, and Wyck Assn. **$2,000** each to Awbury Arboretum, Carpenters Company of Philadelphia, C.C. Morris Cricket Library Assn., Lansdowne Friends School, Maternal & Child Health Consortium of Chester County, Philadelphia Physicians for Social Responsibility, Summerbridge Germantown, Union League of Philadelphia (Abraham Lincoln Foundation), and Wissahickon Valley Watershed Assn. **$1,000-$1,500** each to Kearsley Retirement Community, Media Monthly Meeting, and Swarthmore College (Morris Bowie Fund). Other local contributions **$500** each for similar purposes. **Out-of-state** giving includes **$20,000** to Virginia Beach Friends School [VA]; **$16,000** to Moorestown Friends School [NJ]; **$15,000** to Mercer Street Friends [NJ]; **$9,000** to Friends Committee on National Legislation [DC]; and smaller grants, primarily for Quaker schools and Friends-related concerns in many states. ■ **PUBLICATIONS:** application guidelines brochure ■ **WEBSITE:** None ■ **E-MAIL:** None ■ **APPLICATION POLICIES & PROCEDURES:** The Fund reports that beyond its historic support of Quaker organizations/institutions in the Greater Philadelphia area, there is special interest in environmental awareness programs, innovative educational projects tackling nuclear age issues, and assisting with the problems of homelessness. Most grants are for general support, special projects, capital needs, endowment or scholarship funds, seed money, or publications. No grants are awarded to individuals or as matching funds. Grant requests may be submitted in full proposal with cover letter (original plus five copies) during March-early April or September-early October (deadlines are April 15th and October 15th); clearly state the need for the grant and amount requested, and include organizational and project budgets, Board member list, audited financial statement, and IRS tax-exempt status documentation. Site visits sometimes are made to organizations being considered for a grant. Grants are awarded at May and November meetings; applicants are notified within three weeks after the meetings.

O+D+T Samuel D. Caldwell, IV (S+T+Con) — H. Mather Lippincott, Jr. (C+T) — Martha Brown Bryans (T) — Alan Reeve Hunt, Esq. (T) — Regina Hallowell Peasley (T) — The Glenmede Trust Company (Corporate Trustee)

SE-624 **Shuster (Herman) Memorial Foundation**   MI-82
830 Oxford Crest   **Phone** 610-527-1773 **FAX** None
Villanova 19085   (Montgomery County)   **EIN** 23-6875505   **Year Created** 1987
AMV $2,042,003   **FYE** 2-01   (**Gifts Received** $0)   **Grants totaling** $0

No grants awarded in 2001; in the prior year, **$250,000** awarded to State of Israel/Joint Services Command & Staff College. ■ **PUBLICATIONS:** None ■ **WEBSITE:** None ■ **E-MAIL:** None ■ **APPLICATION POLICIES & PROCEDURES:** The Trust reports that grants are made only to organizations selected by the Trustees; unsolicited requests for funds are not accepted.

O+D+T Warren Rubin (T+Con) — Walter Shuster [Bala Cynwyd] (T) — Bernard Glassman, Esq. [Philadelphia]

SE-625 **Shusterman Foundation, The**   MI-12-15-22-41-42-52-54-62-64-81-82-86
c/o Fox, Rothschild, O'Brien & Frankel
2000 Market Street, 10th Floor   **Phone** 215-299-2026 **FAX** 215-299-2150
Philadelphia 19103   (Philadelphia County)   **EIN** 23-2187215   **Year Created** 1981
AMV $1,942,128   **FYE** 6-01   (**Gifts Received** $0)   49 **Grants totaling** $63,792

Mostly local giving. High grant of **$14,033** to American Friends of Ben Gurion U. [Jenkintown]. **$8,037** to Philadelphia Geriatric Center. **$7,500** to Federation Allied Jewish Appeal. **$6,000** to Temple U. **$5,000** to Gratz College. **$3,195** to Beth Sholom Congregation. **$1,000-$2,500** each to American Interfaith Institute, Anti-Defamation League, Curtis Institute of Music, Foreign Policy Research Institute, Jewish Family & Children's Service, Middle East Forum, Oak Lane Day School, Congregation Or Ami, and Partners for Sacred Places. Other local and out-of-state giving **$100-$1,000** for Jewish and other purposes. ■ **PUBLICATIONS:** None ■ **WEBSITE:** None ■ **E-MAIL:** None ■ **APPLICATION POLICIES & PROCEDURES:** The Foundation reports that most giving is for general support, capital drives and research. Grant requests may be submitted in a letter at any time; describe the services provided and include a list of Board members and IRS tax-exempt status documentation.

O+D+T Murray H. Shusterman, Esq. [Bala Cynwyd] (T+Manager+Donor+Con) — Robert J. Shusterman, Esq. (T+Manager) — Judith W. Shusterman [Bala Cynwyd] (T)

SE-626 **Sickler Foundation**   MI-13-41-42-54-55-61-85
250 Mine Road   **Phone** Unlisted **FAX** None
Malvern 19355   (Chester County)   **EIN** 23-2926508   **Year Created** 1997
AMV $364,192   **FYE** 12-00   (**Gifts Received** $401)   3 **Grants totaling** $17,000

About half local giving. High grant of **$8,000** to St. Isaac Jogues Church. **$1,000** to Phoenixville YMCA. **Out-of-state** grant: **$8,000** to George Washington U. [DC]. — Giving in the prior year included **$7,500** to St. Isaac Jogues Church; **$3,000** to Phoenixville YMCA; **$2,500** each to Colonial Theatre and Phoenixville Economic Development Corp.; and **$1,000** each to East Stroudsburg U., Franklin Institute, and The Shipley School. ■ **PUBLICATIONS:** None ■ **WEBSITE:** None ■ **E-MAIL:** None ■ **APPLICATION POLICIES & PROCEDURES:** Information not available.

O+D+T John J. Sickler (P+D+Donor+Con) — Doris E. Sickler (S+F+D) — Beth A. Sickler (D) — Donna M. Sickler (D) — John J. Sickler, Jr. (D)

SE-627 **Sickles Charitable Foundation**   MI-11-14-32-41-44-54
1625 Amity Road   **Phone** 215-887-0372 **FAX** None
Rydal 19046   (Montgomery County)   **EIN** 23-7250391   **Year Created** 1972
AMV $699,324   **FYE** 11-00   (**Gifts Received** $0)   20 **Grants totaling** $53,650

Mostly local giving; all grants are for general purposes. High grant of **$20,000** to Wistar Institute. **$10,000** to United Way of SE Pa. **$5,000** each to Carson Valley School and Macular Vision Research. **$2,000-$2,500** each to Abington Township Library, National Organization for Hearing Research, and Philadelphia Museum of Art. Other local and out-of-state contributions **$500-$650** for various purposes. ■ **PUBLICATIONS:** None ■ **WEBSITE:** None ■ **E-MAIL:** None ■ **APPLICATION POLICIES & PROCEDURES:** The Foundation reports that priority giving is for medical research, diseases, and local community organizations; the only educational institutions supported are those which family members attended. Grant requests in any form may be submitted at any time. — Formerly called Sickles Charitable Trust.

O+D+T Edward Sickles (PO+T+Donor) — Anne Greenwald Sickles (T+Donor)

SE-628 Sidewater (Arthur & Estelle) Foundation
c/o Lafayette Financial Services Corp.
215 West Church Road, Suite 108
King of Prussia 19406 (Montgomery County)

MI-12-14-17-22-25-32-72

Phone 610-992-0149 **FAX** None
EIN 23-2582882 **Year Created** 1989

AMV $2,703,416 **FYE** 12-00 **(Gifts Received** $131) 7 **Grants totaling** $82,500

Mostly local giving; all grants are general contributions. High grant of **$60,000** to Federation Housing, Inc. **$10,000** to Laurel House. **$2,500** each to American Lung Assn., Greater Philadelphia Coalition Against Hunger (Food Share Program), and Maternity Care Coalition. **Out-of-state** grants: **$2,500** each to Canine Assistants [GA] and Jane Goodall Institute [MD]. ■**PUBLICA-TIONS:** None ■**WEBSITE:** None ■**E-MAIL:** None ■**APPLICATION POLICIES & PROCEDURES:** The Foundation reports that grants are awarded to preselected charitable organizations only; unsolicited requests are not accepted.

O+D+T June Wolfson (P+Con) — Stephen Wolfson (VP+S+F)

SE-629 Sidewater (Morris & Evelyn) Foundation
51 Crosby Brown Road
Gladwyne 19035 (Montgomery County)

MI-15-17-22-42-54-62

Phone Unlisted **FAX** None
EIN 23-2573603 **Year Created** 1989

AMV $4,625,606 **FYE** 12-00 **(Gifts Received** $0) 42 **Grants totaling** $118,722

About two-thirds local giving. High grant of **$25,000** to Federation Allied Jewish Appeal. **$21,275** to Har Zion Temple. **$5,000** each to B'rith Shalom Foundation and Cystic Fibrosis Foundation. **$2,000** each to Middle East Forum and U. of Pa. (Ben Franklin Society). **$1,000-$1,500** each to Camp Gan Israel, Heritage House, Jewish Family & Children's Service, Lankenau Hospital, Laurel House, Macular Vision Foundation, Melrose B'nai Israel Emanuel, National Liberty Museum, Philadelphia Committee to End Homelessness, Philadelphia Geriatric Center, and Talmudical Yeshiva Philadelphia. Other smaller local contributions, many for Jewish charities. **Out-of-state** giving includes **$11,048** to Aventura Turnberry Jewish [FL]; **$10,000** to Jewish Federation of South Broward County [FL]; and **$5,000** each to Jewish Theological Seminary [NY] and Yeshiva of Spring Valley [NY]. ■**PUBLICATIONS:** None ■**WEBSITE:** None ■**E-MAIL:** None ■**APPLICATION POLICIES & PROCEDURES:** No grants awarded to individuals.

O+D+T Steven J. Sidewater (VP+S+Con) — Morris Sidewater [FL] (P+Donor) — Samuel Sidewater [NJ] (VP+F) — Kenneth R. Asher, Esq. [CT] (AS) — Evelyn Sidewater [FL] (Donor)

SE-630 Sidewater (Samuel) Foundation
c/o Schnader Harrison Segal & Lewis
1600 Market Street, Suite 3600
Philadelphia 19103 (Philadelphia County)

MI-12-15-22-25-32-41-44-51-52-62

Phone 215-751-2080 **FAX** 215-246-9018
EIN 23-2673126 **Year Created** 1992

AMV $347,797 **FYE** 11-00 **(Gifts Received** $0) 27 **Grants totaling** $36,995

Mostly local giving. High grant of **$5,500** to Federation of Jewish Agencies. **$4,250** to Philadelphia Committee to End Homelessness. **$2,000-$2,500** each American Music Theater Festival, American Jewish Committee, and Jewish Community Homes for Adult Independence. **$1,000-$1,500** each to Children's Treatment Center, Congregation B'nai Israel Ohev Zedek, Free Library of Philadelphia, Friends of Rittenhouse Square, Habitat for Humanity, John Hallahan Catholic Girls High School, Jewish Family & Children's Service, Jewish Federation of Greater Philadelphia, Linda Creed Breast Cancer Foundation, Lymphoma Foundation, National Tay-Sachs & Allied Diseases Foundation, Philadelphia Orchestra, Philadelphia Geriatric Center, and Wissahickon Hospice. Other smaller contributions for various purposes. ■**PUBLICATIONS:** None ■**WEBSITE:** None ■**E-MAIL:** None ■**APPLICATION POLICIES & PROCEDURES:** Grant requests may be submitted in any form at any time. No grants are awarded to individuals.

O+D+T Bruce A. Rosenfield, Esq. (Con) — Samuel Sidewater [FL] (T+Donor)

SE-631 Sidewater (Samuel) Foundation
c/o Schnader Harrison Segal & Lewis
1600 Market Street, Suite 3600
Philadelphia 19103 (Philadelphia County)

MI-12-15-22-25-32-41-44-51-52-62

Phone 215-751-2080 **FAX** 215-246-9018
EIN 23-2673126 **Year Created** 1992

AMV $347,797 **FYE** 11-00 **(Gifts Received** $0) 27 **Grants totaling** $36,995

Mostly local giving. High grant of **$5,500** to Federation of Jewish Agencies. **$4,250** to Philadelphia Committee to End Homelessness. **$2,000-$2,500** each American Music Theater Festival, American Jewish Committee, and Jewish Community Homes for Adult Independence. **$1,000-$1,500** each to Children's Treatment Center, Congregation B'nai Israel Ohev Zedek, Free Library of Philadelphia, Friends of Rittenhouse Square, Habitat for Humanity, John Hallahan Catholic Girls High School, Jewish Family & Children's Service, Jewish Federation of Greater Philadelphia, Linda Creed Breast Cancer Foundation, Lymphoma Foundation, National Tay-Sachs & Allied Diseases Foundation, Philadelphia Orchestra, Philadelphia Geriatric Center, and Wissahickon Hospice. Other smaller contributions for various purposes. ■**PUBLICATIONS:** None ■**WEBSITE:** None ■**E-MAIL:** None ■**APPLICATION POLICIES & PROCEDURES:** Grant requests may be submitted in any form at any time. No grants are awarded to individuals.

O+D+T Bruce A. Rosenfield, Esq. (Con) — Samuel Sidewater [FL] (T+Donor)

SE-632 Siegel (Stuart & Jill) Charitable Trust
166 Tinari Drive
Richboro 18954 (Bucks County)

MI-29-31-32-42-84

Phone 215-659-8800 **FAX** None
EIN 11-3297021 **Year Created** 1996

AMV $622,914 **FYE** 12-00 **(Gifts Received** $0) 25 **Grants totaling** $29,635

About one-third local giving. High grant of **$5,000** to Abington Memorial Hospital. **$2,700** to U. of Pa. **$1,000** to Cure for Lymphoma Foundation. **$500** each to Richie Ashburn Baseball Foundation and Philadelphia Academies. Other smaller local contribution **$25-$300** for various purposes. **Out-of-state** giving includes **$5,095** to Juvenile Diabetes Foundation [NY]; and **$2,500** each to Christmas Angels/CCOJ, Oral Lee Brown Foundation [CA], Rancho Feliz Charitable Foundation [AZ], and Red Cross [AZ]. ■**PUBLICATIONS:** None ■**WEBSITE:** None ■**E-MAIL:** None ■**APPLICATION POLICIES & PROCEDURES:** Grant requests in any form may be submitted at any time.

O+D+T Stuart Siegel (T+Donor+Con) — Jill Siegel (T+Donor)

SE-633 **Silver Levine Charitable Trust**		**MI**-11-22-62
1844 Meadowbrook Road, P.O. Box 1		**Phone** 215-884-8093 **FAX** None
Abington 19001	(Montgomery County)	**EIN** 23-2188614 **Year Created** 1981
AMV $269,924 **FYE** 12-00	**(Gifts Received** $25,000)	58 **Grants totaling** $25,114

Mostly local giving. High grant of **$7,992** to Old York Road Temple Beth Am. **$6,260** to Hadassah/Greater Philadelphia. **$3,900** to Federation Allied Jewish Appeal. **$900** to United Way of SE Pa. **$650** to Wood Turning Center. Other local contributions **$10-$500** for various purposes. **Out-of-state** grant: **$1,000** to Mazon [CA]. ■**PUBLICATIONS:** None ■**WEBSITE:** None ■**E-MAIL:** None ■**APPLICATION POLICIES & PROCEDURES:** Grant requests in any form may be submitted at any time. No grants awarded to individuals.

O+D+T Evelyn Silver (T+Donor+Con) — Harry Silver (T+Donor)

SE-634 **Silverstein (Louis & Hilda) Charitable Foundation**		**MI**-22-32-52-54-62
c/o PNC Advisors		
1600 Market Street, 6th Floor		**Phone** 215-585-8174 **FAX** 215-585-7689
Philadelphia 19103	(Philadelphia County)	**EIN** 23-6220071 **Year Created** 1976
AMV $403,136 **FYE** 1-02	**(Gifts Received** $0)	8 **Grants totaling** $148,500

About half local giving. High grants of **$25,000** to Anti-Defamation League Foundation and Congregation Beth Or. **$12,000** to Rodeph Shalom Congregation. **$5,000** each to Jewish Federation of Greater Philadelphia and Juvenile Diabetes Foundation. **Out-of-state** giving includes **$50,000** to Boca Raton Museum of Art [FL] and **$25,000** to Philharmonic Orchestra of Boca Raton [FL]. ■**PUBLICATIONS:** None ■**WEBSITE:** None ■**E-MAIL:** None ■**APPLICATION POLICIES & PROCEDURES:** The Trust reports that most grants are for special projects, research, or scholarships. No grants awarded for political or lobbying purposes. Submit grant requests in a full proposal with cover letter at any time; include an organizational budget, project budget, list of other funding sources, and IRS tax-exempt status documentation. Site visits sometimes are made to organizations being considered for a grant. — Note: All decisions on grants are made by the individual co-trustees, not by bank personnel.

O+D+T S. Brooke Cheston (VP at Bank+Con) — Bernice S. Lewis [FL] (PO+Co-T) — Irene Cooper Beer [Glenside] (Co-T) — Charles Kofsky, CPA (Co-T) — Rebecca Cooper Waldman [NY] (Co-T) — PNC Advisors (Trustee)

SE-635 **Skilling (Joseph Kennard) Foundation**		**MI**-12-13-14-15-16-17-18-22-24-25-29-41-44
c/o First Union/Wachovia		45-54-55-71-72
123 South Broad Street, PA1279		**Phone** 215-670-4226 **FAX** 215-670-4236
Philadelphia 19109	(Philadelphia County)	**EIN** 23-6419739 **Year Created** 1975
AMV $7,774,313 **FYE** 12-00	**(Gifts Received** $0)	87 **Grants totaling** $280,500

Giving focuses on the Philadelphia area. High grant of **$10,000** to Baker Industries. **$8,000** each to Wheels and White-Williams Scholars. **$7,000** to Jenkintown Day Nursery. **$6,000** to Recording for the Blind & Dyslexic. **$5,000** each to Academy of Natural Sciences, Associated Services for the Blind, Center in the Park, Elwyn Inc., Free Library of Philadelphia, Kearsley Retirement Community, Ludlow Community Center, MANNA/Metropolitan AIDS Neighborhood Nutrition Alliance, Need in Deed, Overbrook School for the Blind, Pa. Horticultural Society, Philadelphia Senior Center, Philadelphia Zoo, Philadelphians Concerned About Housing, RSVP-Retired Senior Volunteers Program, Silver Springs-Martin Luther School, Urban Bridges at St. Gabriel's, and Wissahickon Hospice. **$4,000** each to Boys & Girls Club of Metropolitan Philadelphia, CARIE/ Coalition of Advocates for Infirm Elderly, Deaf-Hearing Communication Center, Delaware Valley Friends School, Franklin Institute, Habitat for Humanity-West Philadelphia, Landmarks Society, Pa. School for the Deaf, Philadelphia Museum of Art, Simpson House, and Whosoever Gospel Mission. **$3,000-$3,500** each to Awbury Arboretum, Episcopal Church of the Advocate, Episcopal Community Services, Girl Scouts of SE Pa., Little Brothers Friends of the Elderly, Montgomery Early Learning Center, Northwest Interfaith Movement, Philadelphia Community Academy, Philadelphia Training Program, SOWN/Supportive Older Women's Network, Williamson Free School of Mechanical Trades, and Working Wardrobe. **$2,000-$2,500** each to Bethanna, Burn Foundation, City Team Ministries, College Settlement of Philadelphia, Community Gardens of Chester County, Community Women's Education Project, Congreso de Latinos Unidos, Contact Care Line, Developmental Enterprises, Federation Day Care, First United Methodist Church of Germantown, Frankford Human Relations Coalition, Help-USA, IHM Center for Literacy & GED Programs, Inn Dwelling, Institute for Development of African-American Youth, Kailo Mantua Art Center, Kardon Institute of Arts, Logan Learning Club, Philadelphia City Sail, Philadelphia Committee to End Homelessness, Planned Parenthood, St. Matthew Baptist Church, St. Vincent's Tacony, Summerbridge Germantown, Taller Puertorriqueno, Women Organized Against Rape, and Youth Service. **$1,000** each to Ghebre Michael House, Hospitality House, Montgomery Early Learning Center, Nonprofit Technology Resources, North Philadelphia Visions, Overington House, Point Breeze Performing Arts, Wings for Success, and Women's Community Revitalization Project. ■**PUBLICATIONS:** Grant Guidelines; application guidelines ■**WEBSITE:** None ■**E-MAIL:** reginald.middleton@wachovia.com ■**APPLICATION POLICIES & PROCEDURES:** Only Philadelphia-area agencies are eligible to apply; current priority areas of giving are (a) care/support of the elderly, (b) children/youth at risk, (c) spousal or child abuse, (d) rehabilitation of the homeless, (e) care/help for the physically or mentally impaired, (f) education programs for disadvantaged youth/adults, and (g) family support/education/counseling. No support is generally awarded for building, construction, renovations, equipment (except for education of disadvantaged youth), most hospital/healthcare institutions, private school scholarships (except those serving a large percentage at-risk youth), physical therapy programs (unless dealing with the permanently handicapped), national organizations and their local affiliates, and religious organizations (except for education of disadvantaged youth, elderly, or homeless programs). Grant requests must be submitted on a formal application form, available from the Bank, preferably during March and September; deadlines are April 1st and October 1st; the form specifies the required attachments. Site visits sometimes are made to organizations being considered for a grant. Grants are awarded at meetings in May and November.

O+D+T Reginald J. Middleton (VP at Bank+Con) — Mary Louise Mann [Ambler] (T) — Christina A. McKinley [Wyndmoor] (T) — Roger Spaulding, Esq. (T) First Union/Wachovia (Corporate Trustee)

SE-636 Sley Foundation
c/o Wolf, Block, Schorr & Solis-Cohen
1650 Arch Street, 22nd Floor
Philadelphia   19103   (Philadelphia County)
AMV $51,330   **FYE** 12-00   **(Gifts Received** $0)

MI-11-22-31-62-64

Phone 215-977-2104   **FAX** 215-405-3704
EIN 23-6298329   **Year Created** 1954
        14 **Grants totaling** $19,900

Mostly local giving; all grants are general fund support. High grant of **$10,000** to Jewish Federation of Greater Philadelphia. **$3,000** to United Way of SE Pa. **$1,000** each to Gratz College and Friends of MossRehab Hospital. Other local contributions **$200-$600** for Jewish and other charities. **Out-of-state** grants: **$1,000** each to Alzheimer's Assn. [IL] and American Friends of Jaffe Institute [NY]. ■**PUBLICATIONS:** None ■**WEBSITE:** None ■**E-MAIL:** eglickman@wolfblock.com ■**APPLICATION POLICIES & PROCEDURES:** Grant requests may be submitted in any form at any time. No grants are awarded to individuals.

O+D+T Edward M. Glickman, Esq. (T+Con)

SE-637 Sloane Family Foundation, The
c/o Sloane Automotive Group
527 North Easton Road
Glenside   19038   (Montgomery County)
AMV $154,399   **FYE** 12-00   **(Gifts Received** $0)

MI-22-41-62-84

Phone 215-885-5400   **FAX** 215-887-1168
EIN 22-2779195   **Year Created** 1986
        4 **Grants totaling** $18,500

All local giving. High grant of **$10,000** to Jewish Federation of Greater Philadelphia. **$5,000** to Congregation Rodeph Shalom. **$2,500** to Germantown Academy. **$1,000** to Team Philadelphia. ■**PUBLICATIONS:** None ■**WEBSITE:** None ■**E-MAIL:** None ■**APPLICATION POLICIES & PROCEDURES:** Information not available.

O+D+T Robert Sloane [Ambler] (P+Con) — Donor: Estate of Florane Sloane

---

SE-638 Sloane (Manuel & Beatrice) Foundation
1001 City Ave., #EC-1106
Wynnewood   19096   (Montgomery County)
AMV $593,476   **FYE** 11-00   **(Gifts Received** $44,282)

MI-22-29-42-62-82

Phone Unlisted **FAX** None
EIN 23-7818373   **Year Created** 1995
        3 **Grants totaling** $18,000

All local giving; all grants are for general purposes. High grant of **$10,000** to Drexel U. **$5,000** to Carelift International. **$3,000** to Federation of Jewish Agencies. — Grants awarded in the prior year: **$10,000** to Cornell U. [NY] and **$2,000** to Joint Distribution Committee [NY] (Kosovo relief). ■**PUBLICATIONS:** None ■**WEBSITE:** None ■**E-MAIL:** None ■**APPLICATION POLICIES & PROCEDURES:** No grants are awarded to individuals.

O+D+T Manuel Sloane (T+Donor+Con) — Beatrice Sloane (T+Donor)

SE-639 Smith (E. Newbold & Margaret DuPont) Foundation
Station Square One, Suite 205
Paoli   19301   (Chester County)
AMV $698,353   **FYE** 11-00   **(Gifts Received** $595,136)

MI-16-31-42-44-54

Phone 610-647-5577   **FAX** None
EIN 51-6015711   **Year Created** 1996
        7 **Grants totaling** $8,000

Three local grants: **$1,000** each to Academy of Natural Sciences, Bryn Mawr Hospital, and Ludington Library. **Out-of-state** giving includes **$2,000** to St. Mary's & St. Jude's by the Sea [FL]] and **$1,000** each to Bonnell Cove Foundation [FL], Congress of Racial Equality [NY], and the U.S. Naval Academy [MD]. ■**PUBLICATIONS:** None ■**WEBSITE:** None ■**E-MAIL:** None ■**APPLICATION POLICIES & PROCEDURES:** The Foundation reports giving primarily limited to the Greater Philadelphia area. Submit requests in a two-page letter describing the reason for the request; include financial statements and IRS tax-exempt status documentation.

O+D+T E. Newbold Smith (T+Donor+Con) — Henry B. DuPont Smith (T) — Margaret DuPont Smith (T+Donor)

SE-640 Smith (Ethel Sergeant Clark) Memorial Fund
c/o First Union/Wachovia
123 South Broad Street, PA1279
Philadelphia   19109   (Philadelphia County)
AMV $17,532,231   **FYE** 5-01   **(Gifts Received** $0)

MI-12-13-14-15-16-17-22-25-29-31-35-41-42
44-45-49-52-55-71-84-85
Phone 215-670-4228   **FAX** 215-670-4236
EIN 23-6648857   **Year Created** 1977
        66 **Grants totaling** $938,299

Most giving to Delaware County; grants are for general operating support except as noted. High grants of **$100,000** to Rocky Run YMCA (capital campaign/naming rights). **$58,500** to Community Arts Center (children's room/play area). **$50,000** each to Crozer-Chester Medical Center and Wayne Art Center (annex renovation). **$40,000** to Upper Darby Educational Foundation (early literacy initiative) and YMCA of Chester (fire/safety improvements). **$25,000** each to Chester Police Activities League (cultural programs for youth), Riddle Memorial Hospital (cancer education center), Tyler Arboretum (signage), and The Williamson Free School of Mechanical Trades (Smith Cottage support). **$20,000** each to Delaware County Children's Camp Assn. (capital projects), Delaware County Literacy Council (program expansion), Delco Memorial Hospital Foundation, Junior Achievement of Delaware Valley (exchange city initiative), and Pa. Institute of Technology (handicapped accessible ramp). **$18,299** to Delco Tennis Assn. (amateur tennis competition). **$16,000** to Penn State U./Delaware County (Chester Youth Tennis Camp). **$15,000** each to Be Proud Foundation [Sharon Hill] (van), Chester-Upland School District (Participate & Learn program), Chester Youth-Build, Community Action Agency of Delaware County (transitional housing rehabilitation), Delco Blind/Sight Center (computer network system), Family Support Line of Delaware County (sexual abuse treatment program), and Sleighton libraries/cottages). **$12,000** to Presbyterian Children's Village (kitchen/dining renovations). **$11,000** to Big Brothers/Big Sisters of Philadelphia (expanded services in Delaware County). **$10,000** each to Aston Public Library (reference books), Consortium on Health Information & Library (long-term care education), Delaware County Family Centers (parenting program in Chester), Delaware County Education Foundation (leadership program), Delaware County Legal Assistance Assn. (office building restoration), Family & Community Service of Delaware County (budget counseling), Media Fellowship House (writing skills program), Mercy-care Mobile Health, Philadelphia Development Partnership (Chester Microenterprise Partnership), and U.S. Veterans Legacy Project (legacy/sponsorship programs). **$8,000** to Mt. Pleasant Baptist Church [Philadelphia] (outreach program). **$7,500** to Opera Company of Philadelphia (Sound of Learning program). **$6,000** each to Delaware County Symphony (youth concert), Philabundance (Delaware County services), and Red Cross (supplies/leadership development scholarships). **$5,000** each to Aid for Friends (homebound meals), ARC of Delaware County (advocacy), Boy Scouts/Cradle of Liberty Council (Learning for Life program), Darlington Fine Arts Center (educational arts program), Delaware County Flag Foundation, Delaware County Health Dept. (community health outreach), Easter Seals (Bright Beginning Program in Delaware County), Farmers Market Trust (seasonal market in Chester), Habitat for Humanity, Horizon Unlimited Geriatric Education Corp (intergenerational program), MANNA/Metropolitan Neighborhood Nutrition Alliance (Delaware County services/program), Neighbor-to-Neighbor Community (afterschool enrichment), Philadelphia Revels, and St. Michael's Nursery (hot lunch program). **$4,000** each to Drexel Hill School of the Holy Child (collaborative multicultural project), People's Light & Theatre Company (programs for at-risk Delaware County children), and RSVP of Delaware County (program expansion/seminar). **$1,000-$3,500** each to Astral Artistic Services (Inward-Bound program), Joseph J. Barrett Memorial Scholarship Fund (Garrett endowment), Delaware County Youth Orchestra (concerts), Executive Service Corps of the Delaware Valley (Delaware County consultancies), Pig Iron Theatre Company, Rose Tree Pops (senior citizen tickets), and Women's Business Development Center (entrepreneurial training in Delaware County).■**PUBLICATIONS:** Grant Application Form with Guidelines ■**WEBSITE:** None ■**E-MAIL:** diane.stables@wachovia.com ■**APPLICATION POLICIES & PROCEDURES:** The Foundation reports that giving is generally limited to Delaware County organizations or those serving substantial numbers of Delaware County residents. Proposals from grassroots organizations benefiting City of Chester residents are of special interest. Grants are awarded for capital projects, operating expenses, and special programs in amounts meaningful to success; however, operating support is typically awarded only to organizations without capital requirements and when continuing funding is not expected. Multiyear grants are awarded. No requests will be considered for deficit financing, construction or renovations to property not owned by the organization, salaries, or professional fund-raiser fees. Other restrictions are: (1) no organization may receive more than one grant in a given year; (2) no single proposal requesting funding for more than three years will be accepted; (3) funding will not be provided more than three years—either one 3-year grant or three 1-year grants; and (4) any organization receiving support over a 3-year period will be ineligible for additional support until two years have elapsed. Proposals from organizations without a broad fundraising plan or prior development activity will not be reviewed favorably. Prospective applicants initially should contact the Fund to request a formal Grant Application Form which must be submitted together with a letter which describes (a) the purpose/general activities of the organization; (b) description of the proposed project and its justification; (c) project budget; (d) project timetable; and (e) a statement of other anticipated funding sources. Also include the current operating budget and future budgets, as appropriate; an audited financial statement (or if not audited, the IRS Form 990); a Board member list; and IRS tax-exempt status documentation. Requests in the Delaware Valley Grantmakers' Common Grant Application Format are accepted. Deadlines for complete Grant Application Form/Letter-Proposal with documentation are March 1st and September 1st. Personal visits prior to submission of a written proposal are discouraged. Site visits to organizations being considered for a grant are initiated, if appropriate, by Fund staff. The Advisory Board makes grant recommendations to the Trustee at meetings in May and November.

O+D+T Diane O. Stables (VP at Bank+Con) — Diane R. Bricker (Advisory Board member) — Jack Holefelder (Advisory Board member) — Hon. Stephen J. McEwen, Jr., Esq. (Advisory Board member) — Joseph E. Pappano, Jr., M.D. (Advisory Board member) — Alice W. Strine, Esq. (Advisory Board member) First Union/Wachovia (Trustee)

SE-641 Smith (Hoxie Harrison) Foundation
350 Pond View
Devon 19333
(Chester County)

MI-12-13-14-15-22-25-31-32-35-39-41-42-43
52-54-55-57
Phone 610-688-0143 **FAX** None
EIN 23-6238148 **Year Created** 1920

AMV $9,152,569 **FYE** 12-01 **(Gifts Received** $0) 40 **Grants totaling** $279,000

All giving restricted to Southeastern Pa.; grants are for general operating support except as noted. High grant of **$35,000** to Williamson Free School of Mechanical Trades (building renovations). **$15,000** to Police Athletic League. **$12,500** to Philabundance. **$10,000** each to Bethesda Project, USO of Philadelphia, and YWCA of Chester. **$8,000** to Presbyterian Children's Village (school renovations). **$7,000-$7,500** each to Adult Care of Chester County (subsidize client fees), ARC of Chester County (teaching kitchen construction), Crozer-Chester Medical Center (burn center renovations), Handi-Crafters (personal work adjustment program), Kelly Anne Dolan Memorial Fund, Pa. College of Optometry (vision evaluations of disabled), Horizons Unlimited (intergenerational school program), Melmark (school renovations), Pa. School for the Deaf (early childhood center), Philadelphia Wooden Boat Factory (marine education initiative), and Wagner Free Institute of Science. **$6,000-$6,800** each to Chester County Hospital (bilingual assistance), Family Service of Chester County (child abuse prevention staff), Military Order of the World Wars (ROTC scholarships), and White-Williams Scholars (student merit stipends). **$5,000-$5,700** each to Amerikids, Boy Scouts/Chester County Council (lodge renovations), Drexel U. (ROTC scholarships), Fort Mifflin on the Delaware (house restoration), Greater Philadelphia Food Bank (teen nutrition education), The Hickman (building renovations), and Wayne Art Center (building renovations). **$4,000** each to Baker Industries, Care Center for Christ, Darlington Fine Arts Center (new center), Hope Springs Equestrian Therapy (new facility construction), Please Touch Museum (school traveling trunks), and Visiting Nurse Assn. of Montgomery County (child health screenings). **$3,000** each to American Educational Film & Video Center and Fleisher Art Memorial (building renovations). **$2,500** to Montgomery County Emergency Service (management information system). **$2,000** to YWCA of Greater West Chester (mothers' center programs). — Major grants awarded in the prior year include

$25,000 each to Aid for Friends (building purchase), Wagner Free Institute of Science (building renovations), and Wistar Institute (research equipment); **$22,000** to Kearsley Retirement Community (continuum of care program); **$20,000** to Independence Dogs (expansion construction); and **$15,000** each to Boy Scouts/Paoli Troop #1 (camp health center), CityTeam Ministries/Chester (building renovations), Philadelphia Community Academy (daycare support), Police Athletic League, and University Museum (teacher exhibit materials). ■**PUBLICATIONS:** Annual Report (with grantees & grant amounts) and application guidelines ■**WEBSITE:** None ■**E-MAIL:** None ■**APPLICATION POLICIES & PROCEDURES:** The Foundation reports that only organizations in the five-county SE Pa. area are eligible for support and, in general, requests should benefit children, the handicapped, the elderly, education, hospitals, or encourage American patriotism. Multiyear grant requests are discouraged. No grants are awarded to individuals or for endowment, emergency needs, purchase of benefit tickets, special event sponsorship, or donation of tables. An organization may submit only one grant application per year, and all prior grantees must reapply annually to be considered for continuing support. Organizations not previously supported are encouraged initially to telephone the Foundation to discuss the prospect of grant support. Grant requests should be submitted in a letter-proposal and must be received by the September 1st deadline; include a list of Board members and other key persons with their affiliations; most recent annual report, an audited financial statement, and IRS tax-exempt status documentation. Proposals following Delaware Valley Grantmakers Common Grant Application format are accepted. Site visits generally are made to organizations being considered for a grant, but not on a regular schedule. The Board meets semiannually although most grants are awarded at a November meeting; grants are disbursed in December. — Formerly called Smith Foundation.

O+D+T Bruce M. Brown (S+F+D+Con) — Howard W. Busch (P+D) — Charles P. Barber (VP+D) — Robert L. Strayer (VP+D) — Joseph H. Barber (D) — Philip C. Burnham, Jr. (D) — Lee E. Daney (D) — William W. Heilig (D) — Mark T. Ledger (D) — Jack T. Tomarchio (D) — Roger P. Hollingsworth (Director Emeritus) — First Union/Wachovia (Trustee)

SE-642   Smith (W.W.) Charitable Trust, The
200 Four Falls Corporate Center, Suite 300
West Conshohocken   19428   (Montgomery County)
AMV $159,631,581   **FYE** 6-01   (**Gifts Received** $0)

MI-12-13-15-17-19-24-25-32-41-43-45
Phone 610-397-1844 **FAX** 610-397-1680
EIN 23-6648841   **Year Created** 1977
112 **Grants totaling** $7,606,465

Most giving is limited to Bucks, Chester, Delaware, Montgomery, and Philadelphia counties and Camden County, NJ for three specific purposes. **I. FOOD, CLOTHING & SHELTER FOR CHILDREN/THE AGED**—54 grants totaling $1,607,900. High grant of **$75,000** to Melmark (school building renovations). **$65,000** to Trevor's Campaign for the Homeless (transitional housing renovations/furnishings). **$60,000** each to Kearsley Retirement Community (independent living units for low-income elderly) and The Pathway School (cottage renovations). **$55,000** to Chester Community Improvement Project (new homes funding gap). **$50,000** each to Allegheny West Foundation (low-income homes rehabilitation), Carson Valley School (residential cottage repairs), Dignity Housing (housing renovations for single mother families), Energy Coordinating Agency of Philadelphia (Cool Aid program), Philadelphia Geriatric Center (geriatric nursing care center), Resources for Human Development/Family House Norristown (emergency shelter renovations), Rosemont Presbyterian Village (dining room renovations), and United Communities of Southeast Philadelphia (homes rehabilitation for low-income families). **$45,000** to MANNA/Metropolitan AIDS Neighborhood Nutrition Alliance (meals for families with HIV/AIDS children). **$40,000** to Interfaith Housing Development Corp. of Bucks County (housing rehab challenge grant). **$35,000** to Aid for Friends (kitchen), Bethanna Christian Home for Boys & Girls (residential treatment program), Community Ventures (multigenerational housing community), and Sunday Breakfast Rescue Mission (transitional housing upgrades). **$30,000** to A Better Chance/Strath Haven (residential improvements), Blind Relief Fund of Philadelphia (food certificate program), Good Works, Inc. (home repair materials/supplies), Phoenixville Home (home renovations for low-income families), and Women's Community Revitalization Project (affordable housing unit construction). **$25,000** to Bethesda Project (interior renovations), Greater Philadelphia Food Bank (agency delivery costs), Jewish Family & Children's Service (rent relief project), Kelly Ann Dolan Memorial Fund (non-medical needs of critically ill children), Penn Home (elderly home elevator), and Royer-Greaves School for the Blind (residents non-school year support). **$23,500** to Children's Aid Society of Montgomery County (community homes furnishings). **$20,000** each to Delco Blind/Sight Center (seniors program), Eighteenth Street Development Corp. (housing/renovation supplies), One House At A Time (furnishings/challenge grant), Philadelphia Senior Center (community dining collaborative), Taylor Hospice (renovations), and Yorktown Community Development Center (food program for frail elderly). **$15,000** each to Bernardine Franciscan Sister (Bernardine Center), Circle of Care (families emergency needs), Delaware County AIDS Network (food purchases fund), Philadelphia Corp. for Aging (Emergency Fund Coalition), and SCAN/Supportive Child-Adult Network (emergency client fund). **$14,400** to Philabundance (fresh foods transportation). **$12,500** each to Bridge of Hope (homeless families rental assistance) and NOVA/Network of Victim Assistance (senior citizens' home modifications). **$10,000** each to Episcopal Church of the Advocate (emergency food program), Episcopal Community Services (home-delivered meals for elderly), Frankford Group Ministries (emergency assistance program), Friendship House (boys group home supplies/furnishings), Maternal & Child Health Consortium (Healthy Start program), Neighbor to Neighbor (emergency food program), North Light Community Center (emergency assistance program), Walnut Hill Community Development Corp. (emergency food/clothing), and Willow Grove Community Development Corp. (home construction for low-income families). **$9,000** to Friends Rehabilitation Program (apartment renovations for homeless families). **$6,000** First United Methodist Church of Germantown (food program). **$5,000** to Caring About Sharing (new kitchen equipment). **II. MEDICAL RESEARCH DEALING WITH CANCER, HEART DISEASE, AIDS, or JUVENILE DIABETES**—12 grants, $65,000-$296,000 totaling $2,117,000 with multiple grants noted: Children's Hospital of Philadelphia (2 grants), Fox Chase Cancer Center, Johns Hopkins U. [MD] (3 grants), Lankenau Institute for Medical Research, Temple U., Temple U. School of Medicine, U. of Pa. Medical Center, Wistar Institute (2 grants). **III. FINANCIAL AID PROGRAMS FOR QUALIFIED NEEDY UNDERGRADUATE STUDENTS**: *Scholars Program grants* totaling **$2,575,000** (**$188,000** down to **$55,000**) awarded to 29 Delaware Valley colleges/universities for scholarship aid funds; listed by descending grant size: Temple U., Drexel U., U. of Pa., Villanova U., West Chester U., St. Joseph's U., LaSalle U., Widener U., Philadelphia U., U. of the Sciences in Philadelphia, Ursinus College, Arcadia U., U. of the Arts, Cabrini College, Delaware Valley College, Eastern U., Neumann College, Bryn Mawr College, Haverford College, Swarthmore College, Gwynedd-Mercy College, Chestnut Hill College, Immaculata College, Rosemont College, Holy Family College, Moore College of Art & Design, Philadelphia Biblical U., Cheyney U., and Penn State U./Delaware County. Also, 16 Program Prize grants, **$10,000** each, totaling **$160,000** were awarded to many of the same institutions; and **$16,910** for Sea Education Program support. ■**PUBLICATIONS:** Triennial Report with application guidelines ■**WEBSITE:** None ■**E-MAIL:** None ■**APPLICATION POLICIES & PROCEDURES:** The Trust awards grants in three specific areas of interest (see below) with each area having its own specific guidelines/deadlines. Grants are awarded only for specific programs of organizations with proven performance records; evidence of project collaboration with other organizations is favorably viewed. Most grants are for capital projects, special programs, operating support, or medical research. Generally no grants are awarded for deficit financing and never to individuals; also grant funds may not be used to pay a commission to fundraising counsel, nor to purchase/support benefit events, program advertisements, golf tournaments, or similar fundraising activities. Preliminary telephone calls from prospective applicants are encouraged, but personal visits prior to submitting a written request are discouraged. *Guidelines for Food, Clothing and Shelter for Children & the Aged Grants*: Grant requests are accepted only from the five-county Philadelphia area and Camden County, NJ; requests must be for at least $5,000 and of one to three years' duration. As a general rule, the further away a request is from direct provision of literal food or clothing or shelter, the less likely funding will be approved. No requests in this category are accepted from single churches/congregations, summer camps, Y's, or childcare or adult daycare programs. Also, requests for purchase or enhancement of computer systems are almost always denied. Requests may be submitted using Delaware Valley Grantmakers Common Grant Application Form (see www.dvg.org). Alternatively, a letter application should state the amount requested, summarize the request, describe and justify the proposed project, and state the purposes and general activities of the organization; required enclosures are (a) a project budget and timetable, (b) current fiscal year operating organizational budget, (c) list of other anticipated funding, (d) list of officers and Board members, (e) audited financial statement for most recent fiscal year, or, if not audited, most recently filed Federal Form 990. If the organization is too small to file a Form 990, contact the Trust for guidance. Under a 'rolling admissions' policy, the first-completed applications—which must include a site visit by Trust staff—will receive first consideration, regardless of original date of submission. Support may be requested for up to three consecutive years only, after which at least two years must elapse before another request will be considered. Except for emergencies, no retroactive funding is granted. Grant applicants are restricted to one request within a 12-month period. *Guidelines for Basic Research in Cancer, Heart Disease or AIDS Grants:* Projects in this category should have a duration of one to three years and cannot be for purchase of equipment only. Requests must be for the work of individual investigators, not for the general work of research centers. Cancer or AIDS research proposals are due by June 15th and heart research proposals by September 15th. Applicants must use a special application form available from the Trust; a cover letter from the institution's senior official for medical research must endorse the application. Provide four copies of the proposal describing the need, purpose and justification for the project, and a proposed budget, timetable, and an audited financial statement. No more than one application per institution per year may be submitted in each of the three research fields. *Guidelines for Student Financial Aid Program Grants*: Proposals from local 4-year colleges and universities in the 5-county Philadelphia area are by invitation only of the Trust and are due May 1st. No requests from individuals are ever accepted.

O+D+T Fran Pemberton Tyler (Trust Administrator for Food, Clothing & Shelter and Scholarship Programs) — Louise A. Havens (Grant Administrator for Medical Research Program) — Mary L. Smith (Co-T) — First Union/Wachovia (Co-Trustee)

SE-643 **Smukler Lasch Family Foundation**
210 West Rittenhouse Square, Apt. 2906
Philadelphia 19103 (Philadelphia County)
MI-15-22-52-54-55-62
Phone 215-875-9260 **FAX** None
EIN 23-2829857 **Year Created** 1995
AMV $46,609 **FYE** 12-01 (**Gifts Received** $0) 5 **Grants totaling** $65,900

All local giving. High grants of **$25,000** each to Philadelphia Geriatric Center and Prince Music Theater. **$6,900** to National Museum of American Jewish History. **$5,000** to Project H.O.M.E. **$4,000** to Jewish Federation of Greater Philadelphia. ■**PUBLICATIONS:** None ■**WEBSITE:** None ■**E-MAIL:** None ■**APPLICATION POLICIES & PROCEDURES:** The Foundation reports that a major area of interest is Jewish charities providing benefits in the U.S. and Israel; in the Philadelphia area, arts/culture, education and youth are also supported. Grant requests may be submitted in any form at any time. No grants are awarded to individuals. Site visits sometimes are made to organizations being considered for a grant. — Formerly called Lasch-Smukler Family Charitable Foundation

O+D+T Constance Smukler (T+Donor+Con) — Mildred Lasch (T+Donor) — Joseph Smukler (Donor)

SE-644 **SNAVE Foundation**
1106 Foulkeways
Gwynedd Valley 19436 (Montgomery County)
MI-12-13-15-41-42
Phone 215-646-7581 **FAX** None
EIN 23-6928009 **Year Created** 1988
AMV $2,069,310 **FYE** 12-00 (**Gifts Received** $181,311) 8 **Grants totaling** $80,000

About three-fourths local giving. High grant of **$17,000** to Germantown Friends School (community scholarship endowment fund). **$14,000** to Haverford College (endowment). **$10,000** to Newtown Friends School (library/media center). **$8,700** to Aid for Friends (orange juice project). **$7,000** to Friends School-Haverford (community scholarship endowment fund). **$5,800** to William Penn Charter School (college prep summer program). **Out-of-state** grants: **$10,000** to The Food Project [MA] and **$7,500** to Life Haven, Inc. [CT]. ■**PUBLICATIONS:** None ■**WEBSITE:** None ■**E-MAIL:** None ■**APPLICATION POLICIES & PROCEDURES:** No grants awarded to individuals.

O+D+T J. Morris Evans (T+Donor+Con) — Anne T. Evans (T+Donor) — Joseph M. Evans, Jr. [Newtown] (T) — Walter C. Evans [Lafayette Hill] (T) — Wendy Evans Kravitz [CT] (T)

SE-645 **Snider Foundation, The**
c/o Spectacor, Inc.
One First Union Complex
Philadelphia 19148   (Philadelphia County)

MI-11-12-13-14-22-31-32-41-42-44-52-54-56
62-84
Phone 215-389-9480 **FAX** None
EIN 23-2047668   **Year Created** 1977

AMV $13,236,055   **FYE** 4-00   (**Gifts Received** $4,787,500)   64 **Grants totaling** $1,364,350

About two-thirds local giving. High grant of **$400,000** to U. of Pa. (Sol C. Snider Entrepreneurial Center). **$166,600** to Federation Allied Jewish Appeal. **$100,000** to Anti-Defamation League. **$30,000** to Rosemont College. **$27,000** to National Museum of American Jewish History. **$25,000** to Children's Crisis Treatment Center. **$21,000** to Philadelphia Orchestra. **$20,000** to Library Company of Philadelphia. **$17,000** to United Way of SE Pa. **$10,000-$11,750** each to American Interfaith Institute, The Baldwin School, Philadelphia Museum of Art, and The Shipley School. **$5,000** each to Lehigh U. (Project Holocaust), National Organization on Hearing, and Waterloo Gardens. **$1,000-$3,000** each to Academy of Music, Beth David Reform Congregation, Bryn Mawr Hospital Foundation, Carelift International, Friends of Penn Tennis, Jewish Community Centers of Greater Philadelphia, Philadelphia Jewish Archives Center, Police Athletic League of Philadelphia, Susquehanna Art Museum [Harrisburg], U. of Pa. (Levy Pavilion/Women's Tennis), U. of Pa. (Wharton Annual Fund), Volunteer Medical Service Corps of Lower Merion/Narberth, and Wistar Institute. Other smaller local contributions. **Out-of-state** giving includes **$250,000** to Simon Wiesenthal Center [CA]; **$126,000** to CapCure [CA]; **$25,000** each to Institute for Objectivist Studies [NY] and Santa Barbara Jewish Federation [CA]; and **$10,000** each to Cato Institute [DC] and Yeshiva U. High School of Los Angeles [CA]. ■**PUBLICATIONS:** None ■**WEBSITE:** None ■**E-MAIL:** None ■**APPLICATION POLICIES & PROCEDURES:** No grants awarded to individuals.

O+D+T Edward M. Snider (P+Donor+Con) — Sanford Lipstein (S+F+T) — Fred A. Shabel (T) — Jay T. Snider (Donor) — Frances E. Tobin (Donor) — Sylvan M. Tobin (Donor) Corporate donor: Spectacor, Inc.

SE-646 **Snider (Jay & Terry) Foundation, The**
c/o Snider Capital
200 West Montgomery Ave.
Ardmore 19003   (Montgomery County)

MI-39-41-44-56-62-71

Phone 610-645-4513 **FAX** 610-645-5821
EIN 23-2815880   **Year Created** 1995

AMV $852,708   **FYE** 12-00   (**Gifts Received** $0)   35 **Grants totaling** $114,725

Mostly local giving. High grant of **$41,000** to Library Company of Philadelphia. **$27,500** to The Shipley School. **$12,500** to The West Hill School. **$10,000** to Anti-Defamation League. **$4,000** to Volunteer Medical Service Corps of Lower Merion/Narberth. **$1,000** each to Camp Gan Israel. Other local contributions **$100-$625** for arts/cultural, health/human services, and Jewish purposes. **Out-of-state** giving includes **$5,000** to Cobbossee Watershed District [ME] and **$2,500** to Kennebec Historical Society [ME]. ■**PUBLICATIONS:** None ■**WEBSITE:** None ■**E-MAIL:** None ■**APPLICATION POLICIES & PROCEDURES:** Information not available.

O+D+T Jay T. Snider (P+F+Donor+Con) — Terry Snider (S)

SE-647 **Society of the Sons of St. George, Foundation of the**
625 South Bethlehem Pike
Ambler 19002   (Montgomery County)

MI-23-43-82

Phone 215-628-2349 **FAX** None
EIN 22-2774346   **Year Created** 1987

AMV $390,081   **FYE** 12-00   (**Gifts Received** $5,045)   2 **Grants totaling** $12,000

All giving restricted specific English-related activities in the Philadelphia area as detailed below. High grant of **$10,000** to Beaver College Center for Education Abroad (assistance to American students studying in England). **$2,000** to Upper Dublin High School (transportation assistance for English students in the U.S.) ■**PUBLICATIONS:** None ■**WEBSITE:** None ■**E-MAIL:** None ■**APPLICATION POLICIES & PROCEDURES:** All giving restricted to the greater Philadelphia-area for (a) American students of English descent from the eight-county Southeastern Pa./Southern NJ region who are enrolled at an accredited English university, have a good scholastic standing, and need financial assistance; -or- (b) Englishmen enrolled in a British university with good scholastic standing who wish to study for a limited time at a Philadelphia-area college/university and need financial assistance, -or- (c) assistance to distressed persons of English birth—or their dependents—who live within 50 miles of Philadelphia City Hall; Distress Case Assistance Requests should be submitted to 2 East Main Street, #A, Collegeville, PA 19426.

O+D+T G. Tully Vaughan (P+Scholarship Aid Contact) — Robert J. Bateman [Paoli] (VP) — David B. Ermine [Wallingford (S) — David W. Coates [Villanova] (F)

SE-648 **Speare Foundation**
c/o Spearc & Hughey
22 West 2nd Street
Media 19063   (Delaware County)

MI-13-19-31-32-35-41-42-43-55

Phone 610-566-8000 **FAX** 610-566-9460
EIN 23-6245505   **Year Created** 1952

AMV $5,603,760   **FYE** 12-00   (**Gifts Received** $0)   41+ **Grants totaling** $363,520

Mostly local/Pa. giving; grants are for general operating support except as noted. High grants of **$100,000** each to Crozer-Chester Foundation (cancer center construction) and Widener U./School of Business Administration (construction). **$22,500** to Community Arts Center (renovations/community outreach). **$15,000** each to Christ Lutheran Church of Upper Darby (summer day camp/office expenses) and Tyler Arboretum (renovations). **$10,000** to First Tee [Glen Mills]. **$8,000** to Living Beyond Breast Cancer. **$6,000** to American Cancer Society. **$5,000** to Rose Tree-Media DARE. **$3,500** to Reformation Lutheran Church (anniversary celebration). **$2,500** to Leukemia Society of America. **$1,000-$1,675** each to Delaware County Sheriff's Office (drug awareness-resistance program), Media Fellowship House (storytelling festival), National MS Society, Pa. Special Olympics, and Wallingford-Swarthmore School District (athletic programs). Other smaller local contributions to organizations for various purposes. In addition, 25+ scholarships, mostly **$1,000-$3,000** (some larger), were awarded primarily to Delaware County students attending schools in many states. ■**PUBLICATIONS:** None ■**WEBSITE:** None ■**E-MAIL:** None ■**APPLICATION POLICIES & PROCEDURES:** Grant requests may be submitted at any time in a letter or proposal. Site visits sometimes are made to organizations being considered for a grant. Scholarships, primarily for Delaware County residents, are awarded based in part on the student's character; applicants are interviewed personally by the Trustees. — Formerly called Nathan Speare Foundation

O+D+T Robert N. Speare, Esq. [Wallingford] (T+Con) — Jon K. Speare [CT] (T)

SE-649 **Spellissy Foundation, The**
c/o Arthur E. Spellissy & Associates
308 West Lancaster Ave.
Wayne   19087   (Delaware County)
MI-41-52-71-72
Phone 610-293-0700 **FAX** 610-293-0744
EIN 23-6414775   **Year Created** 1966
AMV $643,496   **FYE** 12-00   **(Gifts Received** $0)   17 **Grants totaling** $44,000

Two Pa. grants: **$1,000** each to Germantown Friends School and Strings for Schools. **Out-of-state** giving includes **$5,000** each to Megunticook Watershed Assn. [ME], National Audubon Society [NY], and Owl's Head Transportation Museum [ME]; **$4,000** to Maine Audubon Society and Royal River [ME]; and other smaller grants, mostly to New England. ■**PUBLICATIONS:** None ■**WEBSITE:** None ■**E-MAIL:** spellissy@aol.com ■**APPLICATION POLICIES & PROCEDURES:** The Foundation reports that Maine organizations receive preference. Grant requests may be submitted in a letter at any time to Amy Spellissy Campbell, P.O. Box 659, Rockport, ME 04856; Telephone 206-236-0775.

O+D+T Amy Spellissy Campbell [ME] (T+Con) — Arthur E. Spellissy, Jr. [ME] (T) — Donald W. Weaver (T)

SE-650 **Spiegel Charitable Foundation**
500 Philip Road
Huntingdon Valley   19006   (Montgomery County)
MI-11-15-22-41-42-54-62-64-82
Phone 215-938-0447 **FAX** None
EIN 23-2649352   **Year Created** 1991
AMV $217,388   **FYE** 12-00   **(Gifts Received** $0)   41 **Grants totaling** $86,057

About three fourths local giving. High grant of **$20,000** to Jewish Federation of Greater Philadelphia. **$11,500** to Philadelphia Geriatric Center. **$10,232** to Congregation Adath Jeshurun. **$5,250** to Boys Town Jerusalem/America. **$2,500** to Perelman/Schechter Jewish Day School. **$2,000** to Golden Slipper Club & Charities. **$1,000** each to Beaver College/Arcadia U., Golden Slipper Uptown Home, and United Way of SE Pa. Other contributions, mostly **$150-$500** for cultural, health, or Jewish purposes. **Out-of-state** giving includes **$7,500** each to Jewish Federation of Palm Beach County [FL] and U.S. Holocaust Memorial Museum [DC]; **$5,000** to Jewish Theological Seminary of America [NY]; and **$2,000** to American Committee for the Weizmann Institute of Science [NY]. ■**PUBLICATIONS:** None ■**WEBSITE:** None ■**E-MAIL:** None ■**APPLICATION POLICIES & PROCEDURES:** The Foundation reports that most giving is for general support or capital drives. Grant requests may be submitted in a one-page letter during May-June; include organizational/project budgets and IRS tax-exempt status documentation. Site visits sometimes are made to organizations being considered for a grant. — An alternate contact address is 124 Clipper Lane, Jupiter, FL 33477; telephone 561-743-7211. — Formerly called the William & Sulamita Spiegel Charitable Foundation.

O+D+T William J. Spiegel [FL] (T+Donor+Con) — Sulamita Spiegel [FL] (T+Donor)

SE-651 **Spring Garden Soup Society**
5030 State Road, Suite 2-600
P.O. Box 397
Drexel Hill   19026   (Delaware County)
MI-22-25
Phone 610-284-9944 **FAX** None
EIN 23-2838394   **Year Created** 1997
AMV $1,123,427   **FYE** 10-00   **(Gifts Received** $617)   14 **Grants totaling** $53,000

All local giving. High grants of **$4,000** each to Janes Memorial United Methodist Church, Kensington Soup Society, Norris Square Senior Citizens Center, Penn Home, St. Francis Inn, St. John's Hospice, St. Vincent's Soup Kitchen, Sherwood Presbyterian Church, Spruce Hill Christian School, Sunday Breakfast Assn., Tindley Temple, Trevor's Place, and Whosoever Gospel Mission. **$1,000** to Helping Hand Rescue Mission. ■**PUBLICATIONS:** None ■**WEBSITE:** None ■**E-MAIL:** None ■**APPLICATION POLICIES & PROCEDURES:** No grants awarded to individuals.

O+D+T Board of Managers: Douglas E. Cook, Esq. (S+Con) — Philip H. Peterson, Jr. Esq. [Wayne] (P) — Theodore L. Ricker, Jr. [Philadelphia] (VP) — Kenneth L. Gibb [Wayne] (F) — John Dallas Bowers Radnor — Richard K. Brown [King of Prussia] — C.P. Brucker [Ambler] — Robert J. Gill, M.D. [Philadelphia] — R. Brooke Porche [Swarthmore] — William Z. Suplee, III [Malvern] — J. Jon Veloski [Rose Valley]

SE-652 **Sproul Foundation**
c/o Harris & Harris
1760 Bristol Road, P.O. Box 160
Warrington   18976   (Bucks County)
MI-56-71-89
Phone 215-343-9000 **FAX** None
EIN 22-2725129   **Year Created** 1984
AMV $263,161   **FYE** 10-00   **(Gifts Received** $0)   10 **Grants totaling** $16,000

Mostly Chester County or Lancaster County giving; all grants are annual contributions. High grant of **$4,000** to Brandywine Conservancy. **$2,000** to Nottingham Presbyterian Church. **$1,000** each to Colerain Township, Homeville Meeting House, Lower Oxford Township, Sadsbury Township, Upper Oxford Township, and West Fallowfield Township. **Out-of-state** grant: **$4,000** to Chesapeake Bay Foundation [MD]. ■**PUBLICATIONS:** None ■**WEBSITE:** None ■**E-MAIL:** None ■**APPLICATION POLICIES & PROCEDURES:** The Foundation reports most giving is restricted to southern Chester County and Lancaster County. No grants awarded to individuals. Grant requests may be submitted in a letter at any time; deadline is August 31st. Site visits sometimes are made to organizations being considered for a grant.

O+D+T Stephen B. Harris, Esq. (T+Con) — John D. Jeffords [WY] (T) — Kathleen Jeffords [NY] (T)

SE-653   SPS Foundation, The

c/o SPS Technologies, Inc.
165 Township Line Road, Suite 200
Jenkintown 19046   (Montgomery County)

MI-88

Phone 215-517-2014 **FAX** 215-517-2032
EIN 23-6294553   **Year Created** 1955

AMV $85,234   **FYE** 12-00   **(Gifts Received** $0)   110 **Grants totaling** $45,586

All giving is limited to educational matching gifts for secondary schools and higher education institutions without geographical restriction. ■**PUBLICATIONS:** None ■**WEBSITE:** None ■**E-MAIL:** None ■**APPLICATION POLICIES & PROCEDURES:** Matching gifts (to those of employees, retirees and spouses) are disbursed to secondary schools, colleges, and universities and have a $25 minimum, $10,000 maximum/year.

O+D+T William Scher (Con) — Margaret B. Zminda (F) Corporate donor: SPS Technologies, Inc.

SE-654   Steel (Howard H.) Orthopaedic Foundation

c/o Steel's Sauces
D175 Continental Bus. Center, 55 Front Street
Bridgeport 19405   (Montgomery County)

MI-14-31-34

Phone 610-277-1230 **FAX** 610-277-1228
EIN 23-2192892   **Year Created** 1982

AMV $148,738   **FYE** 9-00   **(Gifts Received** $100,000)   9 **Grants totaling** $91,900

All giving restricted to orthopaedic medicine purposes. High Pa. grants of **$1,200** each to Broad Head Home & Family Assn. and Shriners Hospital for Crippled Children [Philadelphia]. **$500** to Philadelphia Orthopedic Society. **Out-of-state** giving includes high grants of **$25,000** each, all for lectureship endowments, to Mid-American Orthopaedic Society [IL], Scoliosis Research Society [IL], and Western Orthopaedic Society [CA]; and **$5,000** to Foundation for Physically Disabled. ■**PUBLICATIONS:** None ■**WEBSITE:** None ■**E-MAIL:** None ■**APPLICATION POLICIES & PROCEDURES:** The Foundation reports that only applicants with a professional interest in orthopaedic medicine are eligible to apply. Grant requests may be submitted in a letter at any time; provide complete details on one's professional orthopaedic medicine interests.

O+D+T Howard H. Steel, M.D. (S+D+Con) — Betty Jo Steel (P+D) — Townsend Smith (F+D) — Joseph S. Binder, Esq. (D) — Brian Carroll (D) — David Clack (D) — Turner C. Smith (D) — Foundation donor: Archie W. & Grace Berry Foundation

---

SE-655   Stein (Louis & Bessie) Foundation

111 Presidential Blvd., Box 369
Bala Cynwyd 19004   (Montgomery County)

MI-12-14-15-22-31-32-35-41-42-54-56-62-82

Phone 610-667-4050 **FAX** 610-667-1346
EIN 23-6395253   **Year Created** 1952

AMV $22,752,064   **FYE** 12-00   **(Gifts Received** $1,591,374)   113 **Grants totaling** $1,199,817

About half local giving; many grants comprise multiple payments. High Pa. grant of **$100,000** to Drexel U. **$60,000** to Penn State U. **$59,000** to Jewish Family & Children's Service. **$53,795** to Greater Philadelphia Parkinson's Council. **$52,000** to American Cancer Society. **$50,000** each to Children's Hospital of Philadelphia Foundation, Elwyn Israel, Jewish Federation of Greater Philadelphia, and Perelman Jewish Day School. **$25,000** each to Jewish Archives and U. of Pa. (Judaic Studies Program). **$10,000** each to Action AIDS, Israel Guide Dog Center for the Blind [Warrington], and U. of Pa. **$8,500** to Har Zion Temple. **$5,000** to Prince Music Theater. **$2,500** to Congregation Beth Am. **$2,000** to Cystic Fibrosis Foundation. **$1,000-$1,300** each to Congregation Rodeph Shalom, Golden Slipper Camp, National Museum of American Jewish History, Old York Road Temple, and Philadelphia Geriatric Center. Other local contributions **$25-$500** for various purposes. **Out-of-state** giving includes high grant of **$149,000** to Hadassah [NY]; **$75,000** to New Jerusalem Foundation [NY]; **$100,000** to Fordham School of Law [NY]; **$55,645** to American Society for Technion [NY]; **$50,000** to Rona Stern Stout Foundation; and **$25,000** to Lautenberg Center at Hebrew U. [NY]. **$10,000** each to Friends of Karen [NY], Jewish Theological Seminary of America [NY] and Mt. Sinai Medical Center [NY]; and smaller grants/contributions, mostly to NY, MA, and SC. ■**PUBLICATIONS:** None ■**WEBSITE:** None ■**E-MAIL:** None ■**APPLICATION POLICIES & PROCEDURES:** The Foundation reports a preference for nominally sized grant requests. No grants are awarded to individuals. Grant requests may be submitted in a letter (2 pages maximum) at any time. Site visits sometimes are made to organizations being considered for a grant. Grants are awarded at a September meeting. — Formerly called The Louis Stein Foundation.

O+D+T Ruth Leventhal Nathanson (P+Donor+Con) — Sally Bellet (VP) — Marilyn Bellet Stein (S) — Susan Wenger (F) — Amy Breslow (Donor) — Felix Frankel (Donor) — Richard Kessler (Donor) — Ira Leventhal (Donor) — Walter Leventhal (Donor) — Jennifer Merves (Donor) — Stanley Merves (Donor) — Bessie Siegel Stein (Donor) Donor: Louis Stein estate

---

SE-656   Stein (Sidney J.) Foundation

c/o ESL International Corporation
416 East Church Road, P.O. Box 1533
King of Prussia 19406   (Montgomery County)

MI-11-22-41-42-51-53-54-62-82

Phone 610-272-8000 **FAX** 610-272-6759
EIN 22-2315982   **Year Created** 1981

AMV $2,222,532   **FYE** 3-01   **(Gifts Received** $0)   91 **Grants totaling** $108,105

About four-fifths local giving; some grants comprise multiple payments. High grant of **$20,000** to National Liberty Museum. **$13,000** to Germantown Jewish Center. **$10,000** to Jewish Federation of Greater Philadelphia. **$3,000** to Beth Am Israel. **$2,000-$2,750** each to Hadassah/Philadelphia Chapter, National Museum of American Jewish History, Pa. Ballet, and United Way of SE Pa. **$1,000-$1,700** each to American Associates of Ben-Gurion U. [Jenkintown], American Technion Society, The Baldwin School, Federation Allied Jewish Appeal, Muhlenberg College Hillel, Pa. Academy of the Fine Arts, Philadelphia Museum of Art, Temple Sinai, and U. of Pa. Other local contributions **$100-$700** for arts/cultural, health, Jewish, and other purposes. **Out-of-state** giving includes **$10,000** to Brooklyn Polytechnic U. [NY]; **$5,000** to IMAPS/International Microelectronics & Packaging Society Educational Foundation; **$4,000** to Congregation Tiferes Yisrael [MD]; and **$2,000** to Brooklyn College [NY]. ■**PUBLICATIONS:** None ■**WEBSITE:** None ■**E-MAIL:** None ■**APPLICATION POLICIES & PROCEDURES:** Information not available.

O+D+T Dr. Sidney J. Stein [Bryn Mawr] (T+Donor+Con) — Bertha Stein [Bryn Mawr] (T+Donor) — Michael Alan Stein [Radnor] (T) — Corporate donors: Electro-Science Laboratories, Inc.; ESL International Corp.

SE-657 Steinebach (Paula) Trust   MI-12-13-14-22
c/o First Union/Wachovia
123 South Broad Street, PA1279   **Phone** 215-670-4224 **FAX** 215-670-4236
Philadelphia 19109   (Philadelphia County)   **EIN** 23-6574129   **Year Created** 1987
AMV $1,055,640   **FYE** 12-01   **(Gifts Received** $0)   11 **Grants totaling** $61,500

All local giving. High grants of **$10,000** each to Bethanna, Federation Day Care Services, Jewish Family Services, and Melmark Home. **$5,000** each to College Settlement of Philadelphia and Special Olympics (Greater Philadelphia Festival). ■**PUBLICATIONS:** application guidelines ■**WEBSITE:** None ■**E-MAIL:** robert.prischak@wachovia.com ■**APPLICATION POLICIES & PROCEDURES:** The Trust reports that giving is generally restricted to Philadelphia-area organizations providing care, maintenance, support, education, recreation or training to poor, underprivileged, needy, handicapped and/or deserving children, especially orphans. Prospective applicants should make an initial telephone inquiry regarding the feasibility of submitting a request. Grant requests should be submitted in a full proposal with cover letter before the September 1st deadline; include an annual report, organization and project budgets, list of board members, list of major funding sources, audited financial statement, and IRS tax-exempt status documentation. Site visits sometimes are made to organizations being considered for a grant.

O+D+T Robert Prischak (Assistant VP at Bank+Con) — First Union/Wachovia (Trustee)

SE-658 Steiner (Rudolf) Charitable Trust   MI-12-41-42-51
Post Office Box 472   **Phone** 610-783-7293 **FAX** None
Valley Forge 19481   (Chester County)   **EIN** 23-6298220   **Year Created** 1955
AMV $3,013,766   **FYE** 12-00   **(Gifts Received** $0)   20 **Grants totaling** $191,000

Nationwide giving limited to organizations that foster/promote the philosophy of 'Anthroposophy.' Limited Pa. giving. High Pa. grant of **$8,000** to Camphill Village/Kimberton Hills (Anthroposophical research). **$6,000** to Kimberton Waldorf School (scholarship fund). **$5,000** to Camphill Special Schools (capital campaign). **$4,000** to Philadelphia Children's School (scholarship fund). **$3,000** to Sheltering Arms, Inc. [Kimberton] (relocation fund). **$1,000** to Christian Community [Devon] (operations). **Out-of-state** giving includes high grant of **$30,000** to Eurythmy Spring Valley [NY] (scholarship fund); **$28,000** to Anthroposophical Society in America [MI] (national-international societies support) ; **$25,000** to Association of Waldorf Schools of North America [CA] (research); and **$15,000** each to Rudolf Steiner Foundation [CA] (special projects) and Sunbridge College [NY] (endowment/scholarship fund). ■**PUBLICATIONS:** None ■**WEBSITE:** None ■**E-MAIL:** None ■**APPLICATION POLICIES & PROCEDURES:** The Foundation reports that all giving is made exclusively to organizations that work on the basis of Rudolf Steiner's philosophy of Anthroposophy in the fields of medicine, science, art, education, philosophy, and religion. Most giving is for general support, special projects, building funds, capital drives, endowment, research, publications, and scholarships. No grants are awarded to individuals and no multi-year grants. Grant requests should be submitted in a letter (2 pages maximum) during September-October (deadline is October 15th); include an annual report, organization and project budgets, Board member list, list of major funding sources, audited financial statement, and IRS tax-exempt status documentation. Site visits sometimes are made to organizations being considered for a grant. Grants are awarded at a November meeting. — For more information about Anthroposophy and Rudolf Steiner, visit the website: www.anthroposophy.org.

O+D+T Dr. Erika V. Asten (Manager+T+Con) — Gerald T. Chapman [SC] (T) — Janet S. Crossen, Esq. [MD] (T) — Dr. Stephen E. Usher [NY] (T)

SE-659 Stern Charities   MI-12-22-31-42-52-53-62
1411 June Lane   **Phone** 215-667-7533 **FAX** None
Penn Valley 19072   (Montgomery County)   **EIN** 23-6298222   **Year Created** 1942
AMV $4,127   **FYE** 11-00   **(Gifts Received** $15,000)   7 **Grants totaling** $11,200

All local giving. High grant of **$4,100** to Philadelphia Art Alliance. **$2,000** to Federation Allied Jewish Appeal. **$1,000-$1,400** each to Albert Einstein Medical Center, Haverford College, Philadelphia Orchestra, and U. of Pa. Medical Center. **$500** to Philadelphia Ronald McDonald House. ■**PUBLICATIONS:** None ■**WEBSITE:** None ■**E-MAIL:** None ■**APPLICATION POLICIES & PROCEDURES:** The Foundation reports giving primarily to Philadelphia. No grants awarded to individuals. Grant requests may be submitted in a proposal with cover letter before the June 1st deadline; describe purpose/use of requested funds, state the amount requested, and include an audited financial statement and IRS 990 tax-exempt status documentation.

O+D+T Harris I. Stern (P+Con) — Joseph Shanis [Philadelphia] (S+F)

SE-660 Stern (Harry) Family Foundation, The   MI-11-15-22-31-32-41-42-54-55-62-64-65-81
The Colonade, 100 Old York Road, Suite 1-124   **Phone** 215-886-3893 **FAX** 215-886-4013
Jenkintown 19046   (Montgomery County)   **EIN** 23-6806751   **Year Created** 1985
AMV $3,982,526   **FYE** 12-00   **(Gifts Received** $0)   213 **Grants totaling** $226,973

About one-third local giving. High Pa. grant of **$12,000** to Guideline Services. **$6,343** to Federation of Jewish Agencies. **$4,000** to Temple U. **$3,000-$3,430** each to Abrams Hebrew Academy, Aish Hatorah, and Young Israel of the Main Line. **$2,000-$2,800** each to Jewish Family & Children's Service, Torah Academy of Greater Philadelphia, and United Way of SE Pa. **$1,000-$1,700** each to Albert Einstein Medical Center, Arcadia U., Congregation B'nai Israel Ohev Zedek, Congregation Beth Tovim, Congregation Melrose B'nai Israel Emanu-el, Etz Chaim Center for Jewish Studies, Franklin Institute, Jewish Community Centers of Greater Philadelphia, Lower Merion Synagogue, Lubavitch of the Main Line, and Middle East Forum. **$800** each to Auerbach Central Agency for Jewish Education and National Museum of American Jewish History. Many other local contributions **$100-$680** for Jewish and other purposes. **Out-of-state** giving includes high grant of **$25,000** to Ramaz School [NY]; **$13,650** to Zionist Organization of America [NY]; **$8,825** to P.E.F. Israel Endowment Funds [NY]; **$5,320** to Drisah Institute of Jewish Education [NY]; and **$5,000** to Torah Ohr Seminary [NY]; and many smaller grants/contributions for similar purposes. ■**PUBLICATIONS:** None ■**WEBSITE:** None ■**E-MAIL:** None ■**APPLICATION POLICIES & PROCEDURES:** The Foundation reports that giving is limited to educational, health/medical, or religious organizations based in the United States only. No grants are awarded to individuals. Prospective applicants initially should make a telephone inquiry about the feasibility of submitting a request. Grant requests may be submitted at any time on a formal application form available from the Foundation; include a project budget and IRS tax-exempt status documentation. Site visits sometimes are made to organizations being considered for a grant.

O+D+T Jerome Stern [Merion Station] (F+D+Donor+Con) — Harry Stern [Wyncote] (P+D+Donor) — Rebecca Stern Herschkopf [NY] (D+Donor) — Sheva Stern Mann [NY] (D+Donor) — Sareva Stern Naor [Blue Bell] (D+Donor) — Amram Stern [Philadelphia] (D+Donor) — Zelda Stern [NY] (D+Donor)

SE-661   Stern-Wolf Fund, The
1787 Oak Hill Road
Huntingdon Valley   19006   (Montgomery County)
AMV $78,650   **FYE** 9-00   **(Gifts Received** $3,000)

MI-31-51-52-54-55
Phone 215-947-7052 **FAX** None
EIN 23-6243376   **Year Created** 1958
51 **Grants totaling** $14,006

Mostly local giving. High grant of **$2,000** to Philadelphia Orchestra. **$1,800** to Philadelphia Museum of Art. **$1,000** each to Abington Memorial Hospital and Pa. Ballet. **$650** to Abington Art Center. **$625** to Jewish Community Centers of Greater Philadelphia. Other local and out-of-state contributions **$20-$500** for various purposes. ■**PUBLICATIONS:** None ■**WEBSITE:** None ■**E-MAIL:** None ■**APPLICATION POLICIES & PROCEDURES:** The Foundation reports that most giving is for general support, special projects, building funds, or scholarships. No grants are awarded to individuals. Grant requests may be submitted in any form at any time; include a project budget and IRS tax-exempt status documentation.

O+D+T Margery S. Wolf (F+T+Donor+Con) — Fred Wolf, III [MD] (T+Donor) — John S. Wolf [MD] (T)

SE-662   Sternberg (Samuel & Barbara) Charitable Foundation
765 John Barry Drive
Bryn Mawr   19010   (Montgomery County)
AMV $863,229   **FYE** 8-01   **(Gifts Received** $0)

MI-12-22-41-42-62-89
Phone 610-526-9503 **FAX** None
EIN 23-6765536   **Year Created** 1983
34 **Grants totaling** $48,775

About two-thirds local giving. High grant of **$11,400** to Temple Adath Israel. **$9,370** to The Shipley School. **$5,500** to Jewish Federation of Greater Philadelphia. **$850-$1,100** each to Haverford School, Middletown Township Police and U. of Pa. Other local contributions **$25-$500** for child welfare and various purposes. **Out-of-state** giving includes **$5,000** each to Keren Hayosed [NY] and United Israel Appeal [NY] and **$2,250** to Anti-Defamation League [NY]. ■**PUBLICATIONS:** None ■**WEBSITE:** None ■**E-MAIL:** None ■**APPLICATION POLICIES & PROCEDURES:** The Foundation reports that grant requests from Philadelphia-area charitable organizations may be submitted in any form at any time.

O+D+T Harvey J. Sternberg (T+Con) — Cora N. Sternberg [Italy] (T) Corporate donor: Hi-Craft Clothing Company.

SE-663   Stewart (Alexander), M.D. Foundation Trust
c/o Mellon Private Wealth Management
1735 Market Street, Room 193-0370
Philadelphia   19103   (Philadelphia County)
AMV $8,343,280   **FYE** 6-00   **(Gifts Received** $0)

MI-13-14-15-17-20-22-25-29-31-33-41-44-55
56-71-72-84-89
Phone 215-553-8636 **FAX** 215-553-4542
EIN 23-6732616   **Year Created** 1982
49 **Grants totaling** $371,774

All giving restricted to organizations located in or benefiting residents of Cumberland, Franklin, Fulton, or Perry counties in South Central Pa. High grant of **$50,000** to Franklin County Library System. **$20,000** each to Friends of Dykman Hatch House, Lutheran Home & Care Services, Salvation Army-Shippensburg, and Shippensburg Area Recreation. **$15,000** to Central Pa. Conservancy. **$13,000** to Pa. Audubon Society. **$12,000** to Quincy United Methodist Home. **$11,450** to Cumberland Valley Mental Health Center. **$10,000** each to Buchanan Valley Volunteer Fire Company, Legal Services of Chambersburg, The Nature Conservancy [Montgomery County], Rural Opportunities, Shippensburg Housing Non-Profit, Shook Home, and Upper Frankford Township Fire Company. **$8,688** to Shippensburg Historical Society. **$7,500-$8,000** each to Kings Kettle, Pleasant Hall Volunteer Fire Company, and Women in Need. **$6,000-$6,500** each to Chambersburg YMCA and South Central Community Action. **$5,000** each to American Cancer Society, Caledonia Theatre Company, Catholic Charities, CROSS, Cumberland Valley Hose Company, Fulton County Friends of the Library, Penn Laurel Girl Scouts, Vigilant Hose Company, and Westend Fire & Rescue Company. **$3,000-$4,500** each to Chambersburg Council for the Arts, Easter Seals of Franklin County, Franklin & Fulton Mental Health Assn., Kittochtinny Historical Society, and Waynesboro Human Services Council. **$975-$2,000** each to Carlisle Family YMCA, Children's Aid Society, Community Environmental Legal Defense Fund, Cumberland Valley Animal Shelter, D.O.I.T., Franklin County 4-H, Franklin County Therapeutic Riding Program, Franklin-Fulton Assn. for Retarded Citizens, Humane Society of Harrisburg, Mercersburg Area Community Chorus, Newburg Hopewell Fire Dept., and Red Cross. ■**PUBLICATIONS:** None ■**WEBSITE:** None ■**E-MAIL:** None ■**APPLICATION POLICIES & PROCEDURES:** Only organizations located in or benefiting residents of Cumberland, Franklin, Fulton, or Perry counties are eligible to apply; preference is given Shippensburg-area organizations. Prospective applicants should make an initial telephone inquiry regarding the feasibility of submitting a request. Grant requests may be submitted in any form during November-February—the deadline is the February 28th; describe a specific program or capital project, and include a organization and project budgets, audited financial statement, and IRS tax-exempt status documentation. Grants are awarded at a June meeting.

O+D+T Adelina Martorelli (VP at Bank+Con) — Stewart family members comprise the Distribution Committee — Mellon Bank N.A. (Corporate Trustee)

SE-664   Stewart (William K.), Sr. Foundation
428 Inveraray Road
Villanova   19085   (Delaware County)
AMV $484,020   **FYE** 12-00   **(Gifts Received** $7,000)

MI-12-15-42-61
Phone 610-688-3874 **FAX** None
EIN 23-2441723   **Year Created** 1986
3 **Grants totaling** $28,000

One Pa. grant: **$1,000** to St. Edmond's Home (women's auxiliary). **Out-of-state** grants: **$25,000** to Lourdes-Noreen McKeen Residence [FL] and **$2,000** to St. Mary's Church of Gloucester City [NJ]. — One grant in prior year: **$10,000** to U.of Pa. ■ **PUBLI-CATIONS:** None ■ **WEBSITE:** None ■ **E-MAIL:** None ■ **APPLICATION POLICIES & PROCEDURES:** Information not available.

O+D+T William K. Stewart, Jr. (S+Con) — William K. Stewart, Sr. [FL] (P+Donor) — Mary Harmer [Clifton Heights] (F)

SE-665   Stine (James M. & Margaret V.) Foundation
c/o Pepper Hamilton & Scheetz
3000 Two Logan Square, 18th & Arch Sts.
Philadelphia   19103   (Philadelphia County)
AMV $25,463,758   **FYE** 12-00   **(Gifts Received** $0)

MI-22-29-31-32-42-61-71

Phone 215-981-4444 **FAX** 215-981-4750
EIN 23-2834787   **Year Created** 1996
13 **Grants totaling** $724,800

About one-third local/Pa. giving; grants are for general operating support except as noted. High Pa. grants of **$100,000** each to Catholic Medical Foundation [Bethlehem] and Penn State U. **$5,000** each to Covenant House [Philadelphia] and Hanover Charities [Hanover]. **$1,000** to Hawk Mountain Sanctuary. **Out-of-state** giving includes high grants of **$200,000** each to Archdiocese of Baltimore [MD] (Heritage Hope campaign) and Johns Hopkins U. [MD] (prostate cancer research); **$100,000** to Good Samaritan Foundation [DC] (mammography unit); and **$10,00** to Tryall Fund [NY]. ■ **PUBLICATIONS:** None ■ **WEBSITE:** None ■ **E-MAIL:** weinbergr@pepperlaw.com ■ **APPLICATION POLICIES & PROCEDURES:** No grants are awarded to individuals.

O+D+T Robert J. Weinberg, Esq. (D+Con) — Margaret V. Stine [MD] (P+F+D+Donor) — Sarah Igler [MD] (VP+D) — Martha Lee Boyd (S+D) — David J. Stine (D) — James M. Stine (Donor)

SE-666   Stratton Foundation
535 Skippack Pike
Blue Bell   19422   (Montgomery County)
AMV $452,760   **FYE** 12-00   **(Gifts Received** $97,031)

MI-12-18-32-35-41-42-56-63-71-72
Phone 610-941-0889 **FAX** None
EIN 23-2508658   **Year Created** 1988
20 **Grants totaling** $22,550

Mostly local giving. High grant of **$3,250** to Wissahickon Valley Watershed Assn. **$2,500** to Penn State U. **$2,000** to Elmwood Park Zoo. **$1,000-$1,500** each to Carson Valley School, Central Schwenkfelder Church, Germantown Academy, Hawk Mountain Sanctuary, Highlands Historical Society, Planned Parenthood of SE Pa., Silver Springs-Martin Luther School, Wissahickon Community Parenting Center, and Wissahickon Garden Club. **$800** to Juvenile Diabetes Foundation. Other local contributions **$150-$500** for various purposes. **Out-of-state** grant: **$1,500** to The Herring Foundation of Hope [GA]. ■ **PUBLICATIONS:** None ■ **WEBSITE:** None ■ **E-MAIL:** None ■ **APPLICATION POLICIES & PROCEDURES:** The Foundation reports that projects Board members are familiar with receive preference; giving focuses on Central Montgomery County.

O+D+T James W. Stratton (P+Donor+Con) — Arlene E. Stratton (S+F+Donor)

SE-667   Strauss Foundation
231 Cheswold Hill Road
Haverford   19041   (Montgomery County)
AMV $29,226,273   **FYE** 12-00   **(Gifts Received** $0)

MI-13-22-25-32-41-42-51-52-54-55-56-62-72-81
Phone 610-649-0351 **FAX** None
EIN 23-6219939   **Year Created** 1951
300+ **Grants totaling** $1,607,325

About one-fourth local giving; most grants comprise multiple payments. High Pa. grant of **$90,000** to Federation Allied Jewish Appeal. **$50,000** to Regional Performing Arts Center. **$40,000** to Philadelphia Zoo. **$30,200** to Pa. Ballet. **$27,500** to Episcopal Academy. **$25,000** each to Temple U. and U. of Pa. **$15,000** to Eagles Youth Partnership. **$14,700** to Franklin Institute. **$12,000** to National Museum of American Jewish History. **$10,000-$11,000** each to Academy of Music, The Baldwin School, Gesu School, Jewish Community Centers of Greater Philadelphia, and World Affairs Council of Philadelphia. **$7,500** each to Juvenile Diabetes Foundation and Philadelphia Museum of Art. **$6,500** to Philadelphia Committee to End Homelessness. **$5,000** each to SCAN/Supportive Child-Adult Network and Wellness Community of Philadelphia. **$3,500** to Friends of Rittenhouse Square. **$2,500-$3,000** each to Agnes Irwin School, Camp Sunshine, and Philadelphia Orchestra. **$1,000-$2,000** each to CARE, Children's Crisis Treatment Center, Fox Chase Cancer Center, Golden Slipper Club & Charities, Lansdowne Friends School, Leukemia & Lymphoma Society, Police Athletic League, and Rowan House. Other local contributions **$100-$700** for similar purposes. **Out-of-state** giving, primarily to CA, FL, and NY (where Trustees reside) and other states for arts/cultural, health/human services, and educational purposes. ■ **PUBLICATIONS:** None ■ **WEBSITE:** None ■ **E-MAIL:** None ■ **APPLICATION POLICIES & PROCEDURES:** Grant requests may be submittted in a letter at any time; include full supporting materials and IRS tax-exempt status documentation. No grants are awarded to individuals.

O+D+T Benjamin Strauss, Esq. (T+Con) — Henry A. Gladstone, Esq. [Philadelphia] (T) — Scott Rosen Isdaner [NJ] (T) — Sandra Strauss Krause [CA] (T) — Robert Perry Strauss [FL] (T) — First Union/Wachovia (Corporate Trustee)

SE-668   Strauss (Rose & Bernard) Foundation, The
c/o Ellis Coffee Company
2835 Bridge Street
Philadelphia   19137   (Philadelphia County)
AMV $270,100   **FYE** 12-00   **(Gifts Received** $141)

MI-22-32-62-82

Phone 215-537-9500 **FAX** None
EIN 23-2742581   **Year Created** 1993
7 **Grants totaling** $13,348

All local giving. High grant of **$6,950** to Crohn's & Colitis Foundation. **$2,000** to Leukemia Society of America. **$1,575** to Jewish Federation of Greater Philadelphia. **$1,000** each to Beth Shalom Congregation and Boys Town Jerusalem [Jenkintown]. Other smaller local contributions. ■ **PUBLICATIONS:** None ■ **WEBSITE:** None ■ **E-MAIL:** None ■ **APPLICATION POLICIES & PROCEDURES:** Information not available.

O+D+T Bernard N. Strauss [Wyncote] (P+F+D+Donor+Con) — Rose Strauss [Wyncote] (VP+S+D+Donor)

SE-669   Strawbridge (Margaret Dorrance) Foundation of Pa. I
196 Greenlawn Road
Cochranville   19330   (Chester County)

MI-25-32-41-42-71-72-86-89
Phone 610-869-8253 **FAX** None
EIN 23-2373081   **Year Created** 1958

AMV $14,462,911   **FYE** 12-00   (**Gifts Received** $1,000,000)   14 **Grants totaling** $612,181

About one-third local giving. High grant of **$120,981** to Brandywine Conservancy. **$50,000** to Upland Country Day School. **$25,000** to Chester County 2020 Trust. **$5,000** to Po Mar Lin Fire Co. **Out-of-state** giving includes **$120,000** to Marion Foundation [MA]; **$100,000** to Friends of Arcadia [ME]; **$50,000** each to Neighborhood House [ME] and Trinity College [CT]; **$25,000** to Samaritan Inns [DC]; and **$19,700** to International Steeplechase Group [TN]. — Grants awarded in the prior year included **$165,982** to Brandywine River Museum; **$50,000** to Natural Resources Council of Maine; **$20,000** to Ophthalmic Research Associates [Flourtown]; and **$5,000** to Widener U. ■**PUBLICATIONS:** None ■**WEBSITE:** None ■**E-MAIL:** None ■**APPLICATION POLICIES & PROCEDURES:** No grants are awarded to/for endowment or individuals; unsolicited applications are not encouraged. The Board of Directors awards grants at meetings in April, July, and November.

O+D+T George Strawbridge, Jr. (P+S+Donor+Con) — Nina S. Strawbridge (VP) — Diana Strawbridge Norris [FL] (Donor)

SE-670   Strawbridge (Maxwell) Charitable Trust
c/o Wolf, Block, Schorr & Solis-Cohen
1650 Arch Street, 22nd Floor
Philadelphia   19103   (Philadelphia County)

MI-11-12-13-14-15-22-25-32-34-35-41-42-44
51-53-54-56-62-64-82-83-84
Phone 215-977-2104 **FAX** 215-405-3704
EIN 23-2703172   **Year Created** 1992

AMV $9,244,598   **FYE** 12-00   (**Gifts Received** $135)   180+ **Grants totaling** $1,096,400

About four-fifths local/Pa. giving; all grants are general fund support. High grant of **$200,000** to Thomas Jefferson U. **$175,000** to Federation Allied Jewish Appeal. **$25,000** each to American Music Theater Festival, Gerda & Kurt Klein Foundation, Philadelphia Women's Basketball 2000, and Welcome America. **$17,500** to United Way of SE Pa. **$15,000** each to Jewish Family & Children's Service and National Museum of American Jewish History. **$10,000** each to Anti-Defamation League, BLOCS/Business Leadership Organized for Catholic Schools, Fox Chase Cancer Center, Perelman Jewish Day School (capital campaign), Jewish Federation of Greater Philadelphia, The Lantern Theatre, Metropolitan Career Center, Pals for Life, Pa. Academy of the Fine Arts, Philadelphia Geriatric Center, Public Interest Law Center of Philadelphia, Rosenbach Museum & Library, Temple U. Hospital Auxiliary, U. of Pittsburgh, and The Wilma Theatre. **$9,000** to Children's Crisis Treatment Center. **$5,000-$5,600** to Easttown Township Library, Gratz College, Greater Philadelphia Food Bank, Jewish Community Centers of Greater Philadelphia, Jewish Heritage Program, National Coalition for Cancer Survivorship, National Tay-Sachs & Allied Diseases Assn., Northwest Philadelphia Interfaith Hospitality Network, Philadelphia Committee to End Homelessness, Temple Beth Hillel, Terri Lynne Lokoff Child Care Foundation, and Woodrock. **$4,000** each to Akiba Hebrew Academy and Focus on Women's Health: Living Beyond Breast Cancer. **$2,000-$3,000** each to American Diabetes Assn., American Interfaith Institute, Congregation Adath Jeshurun, Crohn's & Colitis Foundation, Golden Slipper Club & Charities, Israel Guide Dog Center for the Blind, Jewish National Fund, Make-A-Wish Foundation of Philadelphia/SE Pa., MossRehab, Options in Aging, Philabundance, Prince Music Theater, Red Cross, Temple Shalom Mitzvah Food Pantry, Trevor's Campaign for the Homeless, Wellness Community of Philadelphia, U. of Pa., and U. of Pa. Law School, and YMCA of Harrisburg. About 55 local grants/contributions, **$250-$1,500** each for similar purposes. **Out-of-state** giving includes **$25,000** each to John Boroughs School [MO] and Jaffa Institute [NY]; **$20,000** each to American Jewish Committee [NY] and National MS Society [NY]; **$17,500** to Jewish National Fund [NY]; **$10,000** each to Alzheimer's Assn. [IL], Amherst College [MA], Cure Autism Now [CA], and National Alliance for Research on Schizophrenia & Depression [NY]; **$7,500** each to American Associates of Ben-Gurion U. [NY] and Yivo Institute for Jewish Research [NY]; **$5,000** each to B'nai B'rith Youth Organization [DC], Children of Chernobyl [NY], Entertainment Industry Foundation [CA], U.S. Holocaust Memorial Museum [DC], and World Hunger Year [NY]. ■**PUBLICATIONS:** None ■**WEBSITE:** None ■**E-MAIL:** eglickman@wolfblock.com ■**APPLICATION POLICIES & PROCEDURES:** Grant requests may be submitted in any form at any time. No grants are awarded to individuals.

O+D+T Edward M. Glickman, Esq. (T+Con) — Charles G. Kopp, Esq. (T)

SE-671   Strick (Frank) Foundation, The
765 Moredon Road
Meadowbrook   19046   (Montgomery County)

MI-18-32-52-55-44-81-83
Phone 215-887-1601 **FAX** None
EIN 23-2484958   **Year Created** 1950

AMV $2,029,644   **FYE** 12-00   (**Gifts Received** $0)   17 **Grants totaling** $80,000

Mostly local giving; grants are for general support except as noted. High grant of **$50,000** to Fox Chase Cancer Center (cancer therapy research). **$5,000** to Wistar Institute (research). **$3,000** to ACLU Foundation of Pa. **$1,000** each to Abington Library Society (bicentennial program), Abington Memorial Hospital (chairman's forum), Abington Township Public Library, Amnesty International, and Artgrowth 2000 (classical music education). **Out-of-state** giving includes **$5,000** to Diabetes Research Institute [FL] (equipment); **$3,000** to Planned Parenthood Federation of America [NY] (Campaign for Responsible Choices); and **$1,000** each for arts/cultural, educational and international institutions in NY and CA. ■**PUBLICATIONS:** None ■**WEBSITE:** None ■**E-MAIL:** None ■**APPLICATION POLICIES & PROCEDURES:** Grant requests may be submitted in a letter or proposal in September (deadline is October 1st): include an annual report, project budget, and IRS tax-exempt status documentation. Site visits sometimes are made to organizations being considered for a grant. The Trustees meet in November. No grants are awarded to individuals.

O+D+T Edith Sheppard, M.D. (S+F+Con) — Maida Gordon [FL] (C+T) — Brad Sheppard, Jr. [Huntingdon Valley] (D) — Jacob B. Strick [FL] (D) — Joseph Strick [France] (D)

SE-672 Strine Foundation, The
c/o Media Real Estate Company
321 West State Street
Media 19063   (Delaware County)

MI-21-41-52-63

Phone 610-565-9000 **FAX** None
EIN 23-2140514   **Year Created** 1980

AMV $93,537   **FYE** 11-00   (**Gifts Received** $25,000)   4 **Grants totaling** $22,700

Mostly local giving. High grant of **$21,000** to Williamson Free Trade School. **$1,000** to Media Rotary Club. **$500** to Christian Academy. **$200** to Cumberland College [KY]. — In the prior year grants included **$2,2025** to Media Presbyterian Church and **$1,025** each to Delaware County Orchestra and Media Rotary Club. ■**PUBLICATIONS:** None ■**WEBSITE:** None ■**E-MAIL:** None ■**APPLICATION POLICIES & PROCEDURES:** Grant requests may be submitted in any form at any time.

O+D+T Alice W. Strine, Esq. (Con) — Walter M. Strine, Sr. (C+Donor+P) — William B. Strine, Sr. (VC) — Walter M. Strine, Jr. (S+Donor)

SE-673 Stroud Foundation, The
Landhope, 254 Stroud Lane
West Grove 19390   (Chester County)

MI-54-71-79

Phone 610-869-9897 **FAX** None
EIN 23-6255701   **Year Created** 1961

AMV $4,919,414   **FYE** 12-00   (**Gifts Received** $16,866)   2 **Grants totaling** $215,088

All local giving; all grants are for general purposes. High grant of **$156,000** to Academy of Natural Sciences. **$59,088** to Stroud Water Research Foundation. ■**PUBLICATIONS:** None ■**WEBSITE:** None ■**E-MAIL:** None ■**APPLICATION POLICIES & PROCEDURES:** The Foundation reports priority interests are environmental research dealing with fresh water streams, rivers, and estuaries. Most grants are for general support, capital needs, endowment, emergency needs, research, or scholarship funds; no awards are made to/for individuals or matching funds. Grant requests may be submitted in any form at any time; include IRS tax-exempt status documentation. The Board of Managers meets semi-annually.

O+D+T Board of Managers members: W.B. Dixon Stroud (PO+Con) — Joan Stroud Blaine [Kennett Square] — Dr. Morris W. Stroud [West Chester] — T. Sam Means, Esq. [SC] — Truman Welling [Kennett Square]

SE-674 Sukonik Foundation
c/o Peggy Sue Associates
1250 Germantown Pike, Suite 100
Plymouth Meeting 19426   (Montgomery County)

MI-12-14-15-31-22-62

Phone 610-239-7333 **FAX** None
EIN 23-2439850   **Year Created** 1986

AMV $287,827   **FYE** 9-00   (**Gifts Received** $90,000)   7 **Grants totaling** $25,100

All local giving. High grant of **$16,000** to Jewish Family & Children's Service. **$5,000** to Thomas Jefferson U. (Women's Board). **$1,000** each to Associated Services for the Blind, Federation Allied Jewish Appeal, Keystone Hospice, and St. Gabriel's Hall. ■**PUBLICATIONS:** None ■**WEBSITE:** None ■**E-MAIL:** None ■**APPLICATION POLICIES & PROCEDURES:** Information not available.

O+D+T Harold A. Sukonik (P+Donor+Con) — Neil Sukonik [Royersford] (S) — Jonathan Sukonik [Devon] (F)

SE-675 Sullivan (Emily O'Neill) Foundation
1329 Beaumont Drive
Gladwyne 19035   (Montgomery County)

MI-12-15-41

Phone 610-642-0123 **FAX** None
EIN 23-2808366   **Year Created** 1995

AMV $238,928   **FYE** 12-00   (**Gifts Received** $0)   34 **Grants totaling** $18,071

About half local giving. High grant of **$4,824** to Academy of Notre Dame de Namur (piano). **$750-$885** each to Benchmark School, Children's Aid Society of Montgomery County, and Sacred Heart Home for Incurable Cancer. Other local contributions **$250-$500** for various purposes. **Out-of-state** giving includes **$1,400** to St. Aquinas High School [NH] and smaller contributions, many to NH. ■**PUBLICATIONS:** None ■**WEBSITE:** None ■**E-MAIL:** None ■**APPLICATION POLICIES & PROCEDURES:** Grant requests may be submitted in any form at any time; deadline is November 30th.

O+D+T Philip A. Sullivan (T+Con) — Paula S. Snyder [NH] (T) — Stephen J. Sullivan [Berwyn] (T)

SE-676 Susquehanna Foundation
c/o Susquehanna Investment Group
401 City Line Ave., Suite 220
Bala Cynwyd 19004   (Montgomery County)

MI-12-14-17-22-25-32-35-41-42-54-55-62-82
84-86

Phone 610-617-2635 **FAX** 610-963-7508
EIN 23-2732477   **Year Created** 1994

AMV $1,909,221   **FYE** 12-00   (**Gifts Received** $3,589,750)   67 **Grants totaling** $1,790,585

Limited local giving. High Pa. grants of **$50,000** each to Community Academy of Philadelphia and Gladwyne Montessori School. **$25,000** to Franklin Institute. **$15,000** to Philabundance. **$13,000** to Children's Crisis Treatment Center. **$11,000** to Jewish Family & Children's Service. **$10,000** each to Female Hebrew Benevolent Society and Jewish Federation of Greater Philadelphia. **$8,000** to Women in Transition. **$5,000-$5,500** each to Easter Seals, Haverford School, Living Beyond Breast Cancer, Philadelphia Museum of Art, U. of Pa. Athletics, and YMCA Camp Ockanickon. **$4,500** to ActionAIDS. **$3,900** to Gesu School. **$1,000-$2,500** each to American Lung Assn., Anti-Defamation League, Beth Am Israel, Educating Children for Parenting, Operation Understanding, Philadelphia Youth Tennis, Project H.O.M.E., and Womens Way. Other smaller local contributions. **Out-of-state** giving includes high grant of **$332,500** to Institute for Justice [DC]; **$295,00** to Cato Institute [DC]; **$250,000** to Memorial Sloan Kettering Cancer Center [NY]; **$215,000** to Save The Children [CT]; **$75,000** to Project Rush [IL]; **$45,000** to 52nd Street Project [NY]; **$30,000** to Coalition of Urban Renewal & Education [CA]; and other smaller grants for similar purposes. ■ **PUBLICATIONS:** None ■**WEBSITE:** None ■**E-MAIL:** None ■**APPLICATION POLICIES & PROCEDURES:** Grant requests in any form may be submitted at any time. No grants are awarded to individuals.

O+D+T Brian P. Sullivan [West Chester] (F+Con) — Arthur Dantchik [Gladwyne] (P+Donor) — Eric Brooks [Bryn Mawr] (VP+Donor) — Andrew Frost [CA] (VP+Donor) — Jeffrey Yass [Haverford] (VP+Donor) — Joel Greenberg [Gladwyne] (S+Donor)

SE-677 Sylk Charitable Trust
350 North Highland Ave.
Merion 19066 (Montgomery County)
AMV $1,205,000 **FYE** 12-01 (**Gifts Received** $203,000)

MI-11-22-32-41-52-53-54-56-62-89
Phone 610-741-1111 **FAX** None
EIN 23-7809130 **Year Created** 1995
29 **Grants totaling** $211,000

Mostly local/nearby NJ giving. High grant of **$100,000** to United Way. **$10,000** each to Friends' Central School, Jewish Federation of Philadelphia, Pa. Academy of the Fine Arts, and St. Christopher's Hospital for Children. **$5,000** to U. of Pa. Hospital/Cancer Center. **$2,500** to Union League of Philadelphia/Abraham Lincoln Foundation and Young Scholars Charter School. **$2,000** each to Linda Creed Breast Cancer Fund and Har Zion Temple. **$1,000-$1,500** each to Franklin Institute, Middle East Forum, Pa. Horticultural Society, Philadelphia Orchestra, and Philadelphia Ronald McDonald House. **$750** to Philadelphia Museum of Art. Other local/Pa. contributions **$100-$600** for various purposes. ■**PUBLICATIONS:** None ■**WEBSITE:** None ■**E-MAIL:** None ■**APPLICATION POLICIES & PROCEDURES:** The Foundation reports that giving is primarily to SE Pa. and Southern NJ performing/visual arts organizations and for the medical field; most grants are for general support, special projects, building funds, capital drives, endowment, or research. Grant requests may be submitted at any time in a letter (2 pages maximum). Site visits sometimes are made to organizations being considered for a grant.

O+D+T Leonard A. Sylk (T+Donor+Con) — Barbara A. Sylk (T+Donor) — Gertrude Sylk (Donor)

SE-678 Sylvan Foundation, The
231 Atlee Road
Wayne 19087 (Delaware County)
AMV $5,321,168 **FYE** 4-01 (**Gifts Received** $0)

MI-15-29-41-42-51-53-54-71-72
Phone 610-688-7674 **FAX** None
EIN 23-2908169 **Year Created** 1997
9 **Grants totaling** $1,155,000

All local/Pa. giving. High grant of **$500,000** to The Nature Conservancy. **$250,000** to People's Light & Theatre Company. **$200,000** to Wayne Arts Center. **$100,000** to Pa. Ballet. **$50,000** to Red Cross. **$30,000** to Philadelphia Senior Center. **$10,000** each to The School in Rose Valley and Schuylkill Center for Environmental Education. **$5,000** to Berman Museum of Art [Allentown]. — Grants awarded in the prior year included **$750,000** to People's Light & Theatre Company; **$400,000** each to Pa. Ballet and Surrey Services for Seniors; **$260,000** to Ursinus College; and **$250,000** to Philadelphia Zoo. ■**PUBLICATIONS:** None ■**WEBSITE:** None ■**E-MAIL:** None ■**APPLICATION POLICIES & PROCEDURES:** No grants are awarded to individuals.

O+D+T Betty U. Musser (T+Donor+Manager+Con) — Francis R. Grebe, Esq. [Devon] (T)

SE-679 Tabas (Daniel M.) Family Foundation
c/o Tabas Enterprises
915 Montgomery Ave., Suite 401
Narberth 19072 (Montgomery County)
AMV $4,230,852 **FYE** 12-00 (**Gifts Received** $1,144,129)

MI-13-31-32-62-81
Phone 610-664-5100 **FAX** None
EIN 23-6934594 **Year Created** 1988
24 **Grants totaling** $31,720

About two-thirds local/Pa. giving. High Pa. grant of **$5,000** to Children's Hospital of Pittsburgh. **$4,750** to Big Brothers/Big Sisters of America. **$3,900** to an individual. **$2,500** to Wills Eye Hospital. **$1,750** to UCP Assn. **$1,200** to Temple Adath Israel. Other local contributions **$25-$250** for various purposes. **Out-of-state** giving includes **$5,000** to Irish Education Development [NY] and **$2,500** each to Kennedy Health System [NJ] and National Pritikin Research Foundation [CA]. ■**PUBLICATIONS:** None ■**WEBSITE:** None ■**E-MAIL:** None ■**APPLICATION POLICIES & PROCEDURES:** Grant requests may submitted in writing at any time; provide full details on how funds will be utilized and include IRS tax-exempt status documentation.

O+D+T Daniel M. Tabas [Haverford] (T+Con) — Murray Stempel, III [Haverford] (T) — Evelyn R. Tabas [Haverford] (T) — Lee E. Tabas [Haverford] (T) — Susan Tabas Tepper [Villanova] (T) — James J. McSwiggan, Jr. [Conshohocken] (T) — Jo Ann Tabas Wurzak [Haverford] (T) — Nicholas Randazzo [Clifton Heights] (Manager) Corporate donors: Acorn Iron & Supply Company; Toll Brothers

SE-680 Tabas (Harriette Steelman & Charles L.) Foundation
737 Montgomery Ave.
Narberth 19072 (Montgomery County)
AMV $4,721,638 **FYE** 3-01 (**Gifts Received** $3,927,151)

MI-11-15-18-22-29-31-32-42-51-62-82
Phone 610-667-9924 **FAX** None
EIN 22-2630429 **Year Created** 1984
59 **Grants totaling** $58,621

About three-fourths local/Pa. giving. High grant of **$10,000** to Philadelphia Geriatric Center. **$6,521** to Abington Memorial Hospital. **$2,000-$2,500** each to Drexel U., Lower Merion AED, and National MS Society. **$1,000-$1,800** each to Boys Town Jerusalem Foundation of America [Jenkintown], Flyers Wives Fight for Lives, Friends of Lankenau Hospital, National Conference for Community & Justice, Pa. Ballet, Planned Parenthood of SE Pa., Reform Congregation Keneseth Israel [Allentown], and United Way of SE Pa., Widener U. School of Law, and Wills Eye Hospital. **$750** each to Buckingham Land Preservation Fund and Jewish National Fund. Other local contributions **$100-$600** for various purposes. **Out-of-state** giving includes **$5,000** to Red Cross [TX] (India Earthquake Relief Fund); **$2,000** to Locomotive Restoration Fund [WI]; and **$1,000** to Golden Cradle Adoption Services [NJ]. ■**PUBLICATIONS:** None ■**WEBSITE:** None ■**E-MAIL:** None ■**APPLICATION POLICIES & PROCEDURES:** Grant requests may be submitted in a letter at any time; include IRS tax-exempt status documentation. — Formerly called the Charles L. Tabas Foundation.

O+D+T Gerald Levinson (Executive Director+Con) — Harriette S. Tabas [Bala Cynwyd] (P+Donor) — Nancy C. Fleming [Honesdale] (VP) — Andrew R. Tabas [Philadelphia] (VP) — Richard S. Tabas [Gladwyne] (S) — Donor: Estate of Charles Tabas

SE-681   Tabas (Samuel) Family Foundation   MI-14-22-31-32-41-62-82
c/o Tabas Enterprises
915 Montgomery Ave., Suite 401   **Phone** 610-664-5100 **FAX** None
Narberth 19072   (Montgomery County)   **EIN** 23-6254348   **Year Created** 1951
AMV $1,456,634   **FYE** 5-01   (**Gifts Received** $0)   98 **Grants totaling** $65,278

About half local/Pa. giving. High Pa. grant of **$6,000** to Temple Adath Israel. **$5,000** to Wills Eye Hospital. **$2,500** to The Wetherill School. **$2,200** to Federation Allied Jewish Appeal. **$1,000** each to Jewish National Fund, Ohr Somayach Institutions, Overbrook School for the Blind, and U. of Pa. Health System (pastoral education office). Other local contributions **$25-$600** for various community organizations. **Out-of-state** giving includes **$5,000** each to Irish Educational Development Foundation [NY] and Rodef Shalom Cemetery [NJ]; and **$2,500** each to Deborah Hospital Foundation [NJ] and National Pritikin Research Foundation [CA]. ■**PUBLICATIONS:** None ■**WEBSITE:** None ■**E-MAIL:** None ■**APPLICATION POLICIES & PROCEDURES:** Grant requests may submitted in writing at any time; provide full details on how funds will be utilized and include IRS tax-exempt status documentation.

O+D+T Daniel M. Tabas [Haverford] (T+Donor+Con) — Richard S. Tabas [Gladwyne] (T) — Nicholas Randazzo [Clifton Heights] (Manager) — Corporate donors: Bowling Palace Corp.; Tabas Brothers Partnership

---

SE-682   Tabitha Foundation, The   MI-12-13-14-17-20-21-22-29-41-52-55-84
PMB 128, 12 West Willow Grove Ave.   **Phone** 215-247-6075 **FAX** None
Philadelphia 19118   (Philadelphia County)   **EIN** 23-2867456   **Year Created** 1996
AMV $977,609   **FYE** 12-00   (**Gifts Received** $247,739)   24 **Grants totaling** $54,850

About three-fourths local giving; most grants are to benefit inner-city or low-income children. High grants of **$5,000** each to Urban Tree Connection (inner-city kids environmental program), and YWCA of Germantown (after-school/Saturday programs for school-age children). **$3,000-$3,500** each to Ad Hoc Committee for Logan (after-school program), Center in the Park (intergenerational arts program), Community Women's Education Project (summer computer program), and NetworkArts Philadelphia (art-environmental program). **$2,000-$2,500** each to First United Methodist Church of Germantown (after-school tutoring/computer program), North Light Community Center (after-school program), Philadelphia Citizens for Children & Youth (advocacy program), and Settlement Music School (preschool program). **$1,000-$1,500** each to Abraham Lincoln High School (deaf students program), Care Center Foundation (preschool programs), Christ Lutheran Church of Upper Darby (summer camp), Crime Victims' Center of Chester County (advocacy program), Frankford Group Ministry (parents support group), Inn Dwelling (after-school program), Neighborhood Bike Works (bike work/academic learning program), Northwest Interfaith Movement (after-school caregivers training program), Police Athletic League of Philadelphia (after-school computer program), The Preschool Project (Head Start supplies), and YWCA of Chester (after-school computer education program). **Out-of-state** giving includes **$5,000** to Adirondack Ensemble [NY] (children's summer music camp) and **$3,000** each to Silver Bay Assn. [NY] (day care program equipment) and Starlings Volleyball Clubs USA [CA] (girls training). ■**PUBLICATIONS:** Annual Report; statement of program policy; application guidelines; application form ■**WEBSITE:** None ■**E-MAIL:** None ■**APPLICATION POLICIES & PROCEDURES:** The Foundation reports that a preference for Philadelphia-area organizations working to improve the quality of life for children by and contributing to their educational, cultural, social, and emotional well-being or health. Most grants are for special projects or general support, and are for one year. Grant requests must be submitted on a formal application form available from the Foundation, preferably during March-early May (deadline May 15th) or September-early November (deadline November 15th); completed requests must include an annual report, organizational/project budgets, list of major funding sources, and IRS tax-exempt status documentation. Site visits sometimes are made to organizations being considered for a grant. Grants are awarded at June and December meetings.

O+D+T Patricia L. Squire (P+Donor+Con) — Edith Giese (VP) — Carol A. Weir [Hatboro] (S) — Elizabeth J. Walker (F) — W.F. Hurlburt [FL] (Donor) — Marjorie H. Squire (Donor)

SE-683   Tanker Family Charitable Foundation   MI-15-22-42-62
336 Sinkler Road   **Phone** 215-572-6267 **FAX** None
Wyncote 19095   (Montgomery County)   **EIN** 23-2868987   **Year Created** 1996
AMV $418,206   **FYE** 12-00   (**Gifts Received** $13,914)   22 **Grants totaling** $19,635

Mostly local/Pa. giving. High grant of **$6,000** to Federation Allied Jewish Appeal. **$5,000** to Penn State U. **$3,325** to Beth Shalom Synagogue/Congregation. **$2,000** to Farmer Jermil DNG School. Other local contributions **$100-$250** for various purposes. **Out-of-state** grant: **$1,000** to Seashore Gardens Home [NJ]. ■**PUBLICATIONS:** None ■**WEBSITE:** None ■**E-MAIL:** None ■ **APPLICATION POLICIES & PROCEDURES:** Grant requests may be submitted in any form at any time.

O+D+T Paul Tanker (T+Con) — Joanne G. Tanker (T) — Mark S. Tanker [Bryn Mawr] (T)

SE-684   Tasty Baking Foundation, The   MI-11-13-14-15-22-31-32-41-42-51-52-54-56
c/o Tastykake, Inc.   57-72-84
2801 Hunting Park Avenue   **Phone** 215-221-8519 **FAX** 215-223-3288
Philadelphia 19129   (Philadelphia County)   **EIN** 23-6271018   **Year Created** 1955
AMV $451,118   **FYE** 12-00   (**Gifts Received** $85,000)   53 **Grants totaling** $88,450

Mostly local/Pa. giving; all grants are for general support. High grant of **$10,000** to Juvenile Diabetes Foundation. **$7,000** to WHYY. **$5,000** each to Blind Relief Fund, Philadelphia Orchestra, Rocky Run YMCA [Media], Salvation Army, and Wills Eye Hospital. **$3,000** each to Academy of Music, Friends of Franklin Institute, Pa. Ballet, Philadelphia Museum of Art, and Philadelphia Zoo. **$2,000-$2,500** each to Academy of Natural Sciences, Carelift International, United Negro College Fund, and Variety Club. **$1,750** to Mercy Vocational High School. **$1,000-$1,500** each to Alzheimer's Assn., Assn. of Independent Colleges & Universities [Harrisburg], Chester County Community Foundation, Fellowship of Christian Athletes, Historical Society of Pa., Pa. School for the Deaf, Penn State-Geisinger [Danville], Please Touch Museum, Philadelphia OIC, St. Joseph's U., Settlement Music School, Summerbridge-Germantown, and YMCA of Philadelphia & Vicinity. Other local/Pa. and out-of-state contributions **$100-$800**, mostly for educational institutions or United Ways. ■**PUBLICATIONS:** None ■**WEBSITE:** None ■**E-MAIL:** None ■**APPLICA-TION POLICIES & PROCEDURES:** The Foundation reports that only organizations in the immediate Philadelphia area are eligible to apply. Grant requests may be submitted in a letter (2 pages maximum) at any time; deadlines are two days before monthly Trustee meetings; describe the nature/purpose of the organization and include an annual report, complete budget, audited financial statement, list of major contributors, list of Board members with affiliations, and IRS tax-exempt status documentation.

O+D+T Patricia Curcio (Foundation Manager+Con) — Philip J. Baur, Jr. (C+T) — John M. Pettine (S+F+T) — Nelson G. Harris (T) — Carl S. Watts (T) — Corporate donor: Tasty Baking Company

---

SE-685 **Taylor Community Foundation**
300 Johnson Ave., P.O. Box 227
Ridley Park 19078   (Delaware County)
AMV $13,142,255   **FYE** 6-01   (**Gifts Received** $172,239)

MI-31-35-43-45
Phone 610-461-6571 **FAX** 610-521-6057
EIN 23-2354770   **Year Created** 1997
16 **Grants totaling** $333,208

All giving restricted to designated Delaware County communities (see list below). High grant of **$150,000** to Taylor Hospital (emergency room). **$6,000** to Barrier Awareness of Delaware County. **$5,000** to Crozer Foundation (gala benefit). **$2,906** to Artcraft (Ridley Health Awareness Day). **$2,000** to Ridley School District (war memorial). **$1,600** to Ridley Park Police Dept. (bullet proof vests). Other smaller contributions. In addition, the Foundation operates/supports Taylor Hospice on a continuing basis. — Grants awarded since June 2001 include **$150,000** to Taylor Hospital (emergency room); **$25,621** to Delaware County Fire & Life Safety (firefighter training); **$20,000** to Maternity Care Coalition (MOMobile in Eastern Delaware County); **$15,000** to Neighbor to Neighbor Community Development Corporation (educational grant); **$6,000** to Barrier Awareness of Delaware County (rent); **$5,000** each to Ridley Community Action Group (health awareness day) and Ridley School District (Reading Achievement Program); **$2,500** to Ridley Park Borough (tot lot); **$1,000** each to Prospect Park Police (vest fund) and Ridley High School (memorial scholarships); 17 Allied Health Profession scholarships totaling **$42,500**; and smaller contributions for various purposes. ■**PUBLICATIONS:** Guidelines for Evaluation of Grant Requests and preliminary application; Scholarship Application Form ■**WEBSITE:** www.taylorcommfdn.org ■**E-MAIL:** info@taylorcommfdn.org ■**APPLICATION POLICIES & PROCEDURES:** The Foundation's current mission is to support nonprofit organizations whose chief purpose is to improve health and/or promote education in 17 designated Delaware County communities: Collingdale, Darby Township, Eddystone, Folcroft, Glenolden, Morton, Nether Providence, Norwood, Prospect Park, Ridley Park, Ridley Township, Rose Valley, Rutledge, Sharon Hill, Springfield, Swarthmore, and Tinicum Township. Grants to Community Organizations in the 17 designated communities are awarded for: (a) providing direct services; (b) new construction, (c) repair/rehabilitation at organizations serving community residents; and (d) those providing educational services to the community. In addition, the Foundation awards Allied Health Profession scholarships to local individuals and continues to support/preserve Taylor Hospital as a community hospital. Generally, no grants are awarded to/for core operating expenses; pass-through grants; individuals; deficit funding; endowment; for-profit enterprises; churches/religious organizations; services duplicated by other area organizations; athletic, recreational, alumni or political groups; public broadcasting; libraries; private or public elementary/secondary schools; yearbook/program advertising; team or individual sponsorships; civic organizations, or United Ways. Also, the Foundation will not support projects for which it is the only funding source or organizations which have applied/funded within the current year. Prospective applicants should first contact the Foundation in writing (or by e-mail) to request the Guidelines for Evaluation of Grant Requests and preliminary application. Requests are reviewed on a case-by-case basis and can be multiyear in nature. Completed applications must be received before the May 1st and November 1st deadlines, and grants are awarded, respectively, at October and April meetings. Scholarships are awarded to selected individuals interested in pursuing an undergraduate degree and who (1) major in the Allied Health Professions (e.g. nursing; social work; health and wellness; or physical, occupational or speech therapy; etc.); (2) upon graduation, will return to Delaware County to work, and (3) live in one of the 17 designated communities. Scholarships will generally be from one to four years and cover only part of a student's total cost. Scholarship awards may vary from one individual to another. Scholarship applicants must request a formal Application Form from the Foundation and submit it before the deadline of the last workday in November. — Formerly called Taylor Hospital Foundation.

O+D+T William T. Skinner (P+CEO+Con) — Horace B. Griffith, III (C+D) — William H. Erb, Jr. M.D. [Wallingford] (VC+D+Donor) — Elizabeth Signor (S+D) — Robert Barbacane (F+D) — John H. Clark, Jr. (D) — Dolores DiSciullo (D) — Henry A. Eberle, Jr. (D) — Thomas P. Gannon (D (Emeritus)) — James M. Gassaway [Swarthmore] (D+Donor) — Steven E. Gilman, M.D. (D) — Anne E. Howanski (D) — Rev. David Krewson (D) — Kurt J. Slenn (D)

SE-686 **Taylor Family Foundation**
c/o Taylor & Ochroch, Inc.
132 Ivy Lane, P.O. Box 62407
King of Prussia 19406   (Montgomery County)
AMV $47,437   **FYE** 12-00   (**Gifts Received** $0)

MI-22-42-56-62
Phone 610-992-1000 **FAX** 610-265-9384
EIN 23-7875149   **Year Created** 1997
3 **Grants totaling** $22,500

All local/Pa. giving. High grant of **$10,500** to King of Prussia Chamber of Commerce (A Home for the Inn). **$7,000** to Federation Allied Jewish Appeal. **$5,000** to Franklin & Marshall College. ■**PUBLICATIONS:** None ■**WEBSITE:** None ■**E-MAIL:** None ■**APPLICATION POLICIES & PROCEDURES:** No grants are awarded to individuals.

O+D+T Cathy L. Taylor [Gladwyne] (T+Con) — Susan E. Bell [MD] (T) — Arthur S. Taylor (T+Donor) — Kenneth R. Taylor [Gladwyne] (Donor)

SE-687 **Teleflex Foundation**
c/o Teleflex, Inc.
630 West Germantown Pike, Suite 461
Plymouth Meeting 19462   (Montgomery County)

MI-12-13-14-15-17-19-25-29-32-35-49-52-54-71-72-88
Phone 610-834-6378 **FAX** 610-834-0248
EIN 23-2104782   **Year Created** 1979

AMV $3,638,116   **FYE** 12-00   **(Gifts Received** $772,500)   85 **Grants totaling** $184,934

Mostly local giving. High grant of **$15,000** to Philadelphia Zoo. **$6,000** to Foundation for Free Enterprise Education. **$5,000-$5,500** each to ALS Assn., Fellowship Farm, Junior Achievement, and Womens Way. **$4,000** each to Easter Seals, North Penn Valley Boys & Girls Club, and Wissahickon Hospice. **$3,000-$3,500** each to Burn Foundation, Camphill Village-Kimberton Hills, Elmwood Park Zoo, Metropolitan Career Center, Pa. Special Olympics, Perkiomen Valley Watershed Assn., Philadelphia Senior Center, Philomel Concerts, Please Touch Museum, Poison Control Center, and RSVP of Montgomery County. **$2,000-$2,500** each to Child Home & Community, Corporate Alliance for Drug Education, Greater Philadelphia Food Bank, and Montgomery County Big Brother. Other local contributions and matching gifts **$100-$1,200** for various purposes. **Out-of-state** giving includes **$15,000** to Safety Sense Institute [Canada]; **$10,000** to Monadnock Community Foundation [NH]; and other smaller grants/contributions, many matching gifts, to many states. ■PUBLICATIONS: statement of program policy; application guidelines ■WEBSITE: www.teleflex.com/foundation/ ■E-MAIL: foundation@teleflex.com ■APPLICATION POLICIES & PROCEDURES: The Foundation supports programs/projects in education, health/human services, arts/culture, civic and and community development in locations with Teleflex facilities. Most grants are for special projects, program development, seed money, technical assistance, and matching gifts. Seldom are grants awarded for general operating support or capital campaigns. Grants are never awarded for technology (phones, computers); endowment; scholarships to individuals; religious organizations; fraternal, veteran or sectarian groups; advertising; benefits or fundraising events; or trips/tours. Prospective applicants initially should make a telephone inquiry about the feasibility of submitting a request. Grant requests may be submitted in a letter (2 pages maximum) before the early March or early September deadlines (call for exact dates); describe the organization's primary mission, objectives and goals as well as the program/project for which funds are sought (show evidence of need, number of people to be served, and how it will be measured); and state a specific amount requested. Also, include both an annual operating budget and a project budget (showing income and expenses for both), a list of Board members, list of current funding sources and amounts, an audited financial statement, and IRS tax-exempt status documentation. Also, proposals which follow Delaware Valley Grantmakers' Common Grant Application Form (see Appendix or www.dvg.org) are accepted. Site visits sometimes are made to organizations being considered for a grant. Grants are awarded at Board meetings in May and November.
O+D+T Thelma A. Fretz (Executive Director+VP+Con) — Lennox K. Black (P) — John H. Remer (F) — Christopher Black (D) — Thomas Byrne (D) — Matthew C. Chisholm (D) — Janine Dusossoit (D) — Diane Fukuda (D) — William Haussmann (D) — Stephen Holland (D) — Anita Piacentino (D) — Palmer Retzlaff (D) Corporate donor: Teleflex Corp.

SE-688 **Templeton (John) Foundation**
5 Radnor Corporate Center, #100
P.O. Box 8322
Radnor 19087   (Delaware County)

MI-49-63-64-65
Phone 610-687-8942 **FAX** 610-687-8961
EIN 62-1322826   **Year Created** 1996

AMV $298,126,612   **FYE** 12-00   **(Gifts Received** $2,775,911)   **Grants totaling** $13,417,578

Most giving is for Foundation-initiated projects, studies, award programs and publications programs worldwide which (1) explore the link between science and religion, (2) encourage character development, or (3) encourage the appreciation of freedom. Among Foundation-initiated activities are the Templeton Prize for Progress in Religion, The Freedom Project, Laws of Life Essay Contest, and Humble Approach Initiative. Some grants are awarded on a discretionary basis. Grants to Pa. included **$665,000** to Philadelphia Center for Religion & Science (Meta Expansion); **$199.500** to U. of Pa. (Templeton Young Scholars in Positive Psychology); **$101,177** to Pittsburgh Theological Seminary (Science & Religion Web Portal Targeted to Church Audience/Web-based Who's Who in Science & Religion); **$69,000** to Drexel U. (Tests of Cosmological Timing & Tuning from Galaxy Formation in Cosmic Voids); **$56,000** to Eastern Baptist Theological Seminary (Congregations, Community & Leadership Development Project); **$22,925** to Grove City College (Religious Community Outreach Project); **$20,000** to Foundation for Individual Rights in Education [Philadelphia] (general donation); **$16,891** to Philadelphia Center for Religion & Science (Webcasting of the Extended Life, Eternal Life Symposium); and **$5,000** to Executive Service Corps of Delaware Valley (general donation). **Out-of-state** and international grants—many/most related to Foundation-initiated projects—included support for: American Assn. for the Advancement of Science [DC], American Psychological Assn. [DC], American Scientific Affiliation [MA], Assn. of Unity Churches [MO], Center for Theology & the Natural Sciences [CA], Character Education Partnership [DC], Christian Education Movement [England], Council of Christian Colleges & Universities [DC], Duke U. [NC], Florida State U. Foundation, Gordon College [MA], History & Economics Research Institute [VA], National Institute for Healthcare Research [MD], Science & Spirit Resources, Inc. [NH], Stanford U. [CA], Students Taking A Right Stand [TN], U. of California-Davis, and U. of Ulster [Ireland].■PUBLICATIONS: None ■WEBSITE: www.templeton.org ■E-MAIL: info@templeton.org ■APPLICATION POLICIES & PROCEDURES: The Foundation reports that it primarily designs large-scale, cost-effective and high-impact projects, and then determines the best organization/individual to administer and implement the initiatives, sometimes soliciting RFP's (Requests for Proposals). In general, the Foundation neither encourages nor considers unsolicited proposals. No grants are awarded for building, capital improvements, endowment, scholarships, or to individuals. However, if an organization has a possible project/program that deals with (1) Spiritual Information Through Science, (2) Spirituality & Health, (3) Free Enterprise, or (4) Character Development, and feels it might be of interest to the Foundation, it first should consult the website to fully explore information on these programmatic areas and to review recent grants. If, subsequently, a proposal is submitted (four complete copies required) it must include: (a) a cover letter on institutional letterhead which briefly describes the proposal and purpose of the request; (b) a full proposal detailing the project and how it will contribute significantly to the progress of scholarly understanding of the issues in one of the four programmatic areas listed above, with a clear focus on supporting highly productive, high-level work; (c) anticipated grant start-date and end-date; (d) requested amount of funding, with budget; (e) cost-effective analysis and strategic impact of the proposed program; (f) curriculum vitae of project director/administrator/principal investigator and other key persons; (g) IRS tax-exempt status documentation; and (h) any relevant documents useful for expert review.

O+D+T Dr. Charles L. Harper, Jr. (Executive Director+Con) — Sir John Marks Templeton [Bahamas] (C+T+Donor) — John M. Templeton, Jr., M.D. (P+T) — Ann Templeton Cameron [TN] (F+T+AS) — John Barrow (T) — Dr. Paul Davies [Australia] (T) — Heather Templeton Dill (T) — Robert Hermann, M.D. [MA] (T) — Rev. Bryant Kirkland (T) — Rev. Dr. Glenn Mosely [MO] (T) — Dr. David G. Myers [MI] (T) — Prof. F. Russell Stannard [England] (T) — Dr. Anne Zimmerman [WY] (T) — Frances D. Schapperle (VP) — Harvey M. Templeton, III, Esq. [TN] (S+AF)

SE-689 **Teoc Foundation, The**
c/o R.A. Industries, Inc.
P.O. Box 247
Lansdale 19446   (Montgomery County)
AMV $220,306   **FYE** 10-00   **(Gifts Received** $0)

MI-22-25-29-41-52-57-62
Phone 215-699-8701 **FAX** None
EIN 23-6849939   **Year Created** 1986
Grants totaling $38,075

Mostly local/Pa. giving. High grant of **$10,000** to Oak Lane Day School. **$9,700** to Sing Out, Inc. [Bethlehem]. **$5,500** to WXPN-FM. **$5,000** to Buxmont Jewish Appeal. **$2,000** to Philabundance. **$1,675** to Congregation Beth Organization. **$1,000** to All Walks of Life. Other smaller local contributions. **Out-of-state** grant: **$2,000** to Grassroots Leadership [NC]. ■**PUBLICATIONS:** None ■**WEBSITE:** None ■**E-MAIL:** None ■**APPLICATION POLICIES & PROCEDURES:** Grant requests may be submitted in any form at any time. — Formerly called The Carl & Beth Apter Foundation.

O+D+T Carl P. Apter (P+D+Donor+Con) — Beth Apter (S+F+D+Donor) — Allen B. Apter (Donor) — Molly Apter (Donor) Corporate donor: R.A. Industries

---

SE-690 **Thayer Corporation**
10 Brettagne, Arbordeau
Devon 19333   (Chester County)
AMV $1,428,217   **FYE** 12-00   **(Gifts Received** $0)

MI-12-14-15-18-31-34-41-42-52-55-72
Phone 610-725-0473 **FAX** None
EIN 23-6266383   **Year Created** 1951
25 **Grants totaling** $54,000

Mostly local/Pa. giving. High Pa. grant of **$4,000** to Penn Home. **$3,000** each to Community Arts Center, Delaware County SPCA, and Ethel Mason Day Care Center. **$2,000** each to Abington Memorial Hospital Foundation, Associated Services for the Blind, Artman Foundation, Church Farm School, Crozer-Chester Medical Center Foundation, Darlington Fine Arts Center, Drexel U., Grove City College, Lafayette College, Philadelphia Orchestra, Philadelphia Youth Orchestra, Royer-Greaves School for the Blind, U. of Pa. Medical School, Widener U., and Williamson Free School of Mechanical Trades. **$1,000** each to College of Physicians of Philadelphia, Germantown Friends School, Philomel Concerts, and Planned Parenthood of SE Pa. **Out-of-state** grants, both to DE: **$5,000** to 4-H Riding and **$2,000** to Mary Campbell Center. ■**PUBLICATIONS:** None ■**WEBSITE:** None ■**E-MAIL:** None ■**APPLICATION POLICIES & PROCEDURES:** The Foundation reports that most grants are for special projects or general operating support. Grant requests in letter form (2 pages maximum) should preferably be submitted in April or September; describe the project or specific need, state the name/telephone number of a contact person, and include an annual report, organizational budget, project budget, and IRS tax-exempt status documentation. Site visits sometimes are made to organizations being considered for a grant. The Board awards grants at a November meeting.

O+D+T Paul E. Macht (P+D+Con) — Alice T. Macht [Haverford] (VP+D) — Elmer L. Macht [Blue Bell] (VP+D) — Albert L. Doering, III [Philadelphia] (S+D) — James T. Macht [GA] (F+D) — Patricia Macht Bulat [DE] (D) — Thomas F. Bulat [DE] (D) — Debra Macht [GA] (D)

SE-691 **Thomas (Harvey) Student Aid Fund**
c/o First Union/Wachovia
123 South Broad Street, PA1279
Philadelphia 19109   (Philadelphia County)
AMV $801,339   **FYE** 9-99   **(Gifts Received** $0)

MI-43
Phone 215-670-4224 **FAX** 215-670-4236
EIN 23-6215693   **Year Created** 1951
14 **Grants totaling** $24,000

All grants are restricted to interest-free loans for students from Chester County; loans ranged from **$1,000** to **$4,000**. ■**PUBLICATIONS:** None ■**WEBSITE:** None ■**E-MAIL:** robert.prischak@wachovia.com ■**APPLICATION POLICIES & PROCEDURES:** The Fund reports that only Chester County residents are eligible to apply for interest-free student loans, starting six months after graduation or departure from college/university. Submit requests at any time on an application form available from Eileen White, Chester County Intermediate Unit, telephone: 610-524-5100. Decisions are made by the Intermediate Unit's Executive Director.

O+D+T Robert Prischak (Assistant VP at Bank+Con) — First Union/Wachovia (Trustee)

SE-692 **Thomson Family Foundation, The**
54 South Whitehorse Road
Phoenixville 19460   (Chester County)
AMV $442,488   **FYE** 12-00   **(Gifts Received** $195,808)

MI-13-42
Phone 610-935-2334 **FAX** None
EIN 06-6480460   **Year Created** 1999
7 **Grants totaling** $16,890

Limited local giving. **$1,500** to Phoenixville Area YMCA. Other small local contributions. **Out-of-state** giving includes high grant of **$10,000** to SUNY-Morrisville [NY] and **$5,000** to Transylvania U. [KY]. ■**PUBLICATIONS:** None. ■**WEBSITE:** None ■**E-MAIL:** None ■**APPLICATION POLICIES & PROCEDURES:** Information not available.

O+D+T Joe M. Thomson (T+Donor+Con) — Joann M. Thomson (T+Donor)

SE-693   Tioga Foundation   MI-22-62
c/o Tioga Pipe Supply Company
2450 Wheatsheaf Lane   **Phone** 215-831-0701 **FAX** 215-533-1645
Philadelphia 19137   (Philadelphia County)   **EIN** 22-2809250   **Year Created** 1986
AMV $1,070,847   **FYE** 12-00   (**Gifts Received** $0)   110 **Grants totaling** $147,394

Mostly local giving. High grant of **$117,474** to Federation Allied Jewish Appeal. **$1,000** to Jewish Community Centers of Greater Philadelphia. Other local contributions **$25-$500** for cultural, health, welfare, youth, Jewish and other purposes. **Out-of-state** grant: **$10,000** to Jewish Federation of Palm Beach County [FL]. ■**PUBLICATIONS:** None ■**WEBSITE:** www.tiogapipe.com [corporate info only] ■**E-MAIL:** None ■**APPLICATION POLICIES & PROCEDURES:** Grant requests may be submitted in any form at any time.

O+D+T Morton Keiser (T+Donor+Con) — Andrew Keiser (T) — Bennett Keiser (T+Donor) — David Keiser (T+Donor) — Eleanor Keiser (T+Donor)

SE-694   Tobin Family Foundation, The   MI-11-12-14-15-22-31-32-41-42-53-62-64
101 Cheswold Lane, Unit 5D   **Phone** 610-828-8400 **FAX** 610-828-4426
Haverford 19041   (Montgomery County)   **EIN** 23-6420013   **Year Created** 1967
AMV $456,668   **FYE** 12-00   (**Gifts Received** $15,910)   43 **Grants totaling** $168,675

Mostly local giving. High grants of **$20,000** each to Har Zion Temple and Philadelphia Geriatric Center. **$18,000** to Jewish Federation of Greater Philadelphia. **$15,000** to United Way of SE Pa. **$11,000** to Perelman Jewish Day School/Stern Center. **$5,000** each to Auerbach Center Agency for Jewish Education, National Organization for Hearing Research, and U. of Pa. (50th Reunion Gift.) **$2,500** each to Anti-Defamation League and Children's Crisis Treatment Center. **$1,000-$1,500** each to Aish Hatorah, Akiba Hebrew Academy, Crohn's & Colitis Foundation, Inglis Foundation, Jewish Community Centers of Greater Philadelphia (Maccabi Games), Magee Rehab, Moore College of Art/Paley Galleries, Philadelphia Friends of ALS, Philadelphia Orchestra, Rabbinical Assembly, and United Negro College Fund. **$875** to Philadelphia Museum of Art/Crafts Show. **$700** to Church of God in Christ (Youth Dept.). Other local contributions **$200-$500** for various purposes. **Out-of-state** giving includes **$20,000** to Jewish Theological Seminary of America [NY]; **$10,000** to Mt. Sinai Hospital [NY] (breast cancer research); **$7,000** to Ahavath Achim Synagogue [MA]; and **$3,000** to Friends of India [MA] (Handcraft project). ■**PUBLICATIONS:** None ■**WEBSITE:** None ■**E-MAIL:** None ■**APPLICATION POLICIES & PROCEDURES:** Information not available. — Formerly called the Sylvan M. & Frances E. Tobin Foundation.

O+D+T Sylvan M. Tobin (P+T+Donor+Con) — Frances E. Tobin (S+T+Donor) Corporate donor: Philadelphia Flyers

---

SE-695   Todi Foundation, The   MI-29-69-82
424 Gwynedd Valley Drive   **Phone** 215-362-1217 **FAX** 215-362-3918
Gwynedd Valley 19437   (Montgomery County)   **EIN** 23-2744913   **Year Created** 1993
AMV $3,750,976   **FYE** 9-00   (**Gifts Received** $0)   2 **Grants totaling** $133,500

High grant of **$128,500** to Bharatiya Temple [Gwynedd Valley]. **$5,000** to Humane Foundation. — Grants awarded in prior years include **$5,000** each to Akhil Bharativa Vanrasi [India], and Mamraj Agarwal Foundation [India]; **$3,500** to Manav Sera Trust [India]. ■**PUBLICATIONS:** None ■**WEBSITE:** None ■**E-MAIL:** None ■**APPLICATION POLICIES & PROCEDURES:** Grant requests may be submitted at any time on a special form available from the Foundation.

O+D+T Nand K. Todi (P+Donor+Con)

SE-696   Toll (Bruce E. & Robbi S.) Foundation, The   MI-22-31-41-42-53-54-62-71-82
c/o Toll Brothers, Inc.
3103 Philmont Avenue   **Phone** 215-938-8024 **FAX** 215-938-8019
Huntingdon Valley 19006   (Montgomery County)   **EIN** 23-2667935   **Year Created** 1991
AMV $3,267,549   **FYE** 1-00   (**Gifts Received** $0)   48 **Grants totaling** $154,260

Over four-fifths local giving. High grant of **$55,000** to Federation Allied Jewish Appeal. **$26,150** to Philadelphia Museum of Art. **$14,925** to Incarnation of Our Lord School. **$6,280** to Rodeph Shalom Congregation. **$5,000** to Abington Memorial Hospital. **$3,690** to National Museum of American Jewish History. **$2,000** to American Associates for Ben-Gurion U. **$1,000-$1,700** each to Albert Einstein Healthcare Network, American Friends of Israel Democracy Institute, Beth Sholom Congregation, Friends of Moss Rehab, Friends Select School, Gwynedd Mercy College, Montgomery County Lands Trust, and Pa. Academy of the Fine Arts. Other local contributions **$40-$600** for various purposes. **Out-of-state** giving includes **$5,000** each to American Enterprise Institute [DC], Nantucket Cottage Hospital [MA], and U.S. Holocaust Memorial Council; and **$2,000** to U. of Miami [FL]. ■**PUBLICATIONS:** None ■**WEBSITE:** www.tollbrothers.com [corporate info only] ■**E-MAIL:** None ■**APPLICATION POLICIES & PROCEDURES:** Grant requests may be submitted in any form at any time. Site visits sometimes are made to organizations being considered for a grant. — Formerly called The Bruce E. Toll Foundation.

O+D+T Bruce E. Toll [Rydal] (Executive Director+P+F+Donor+Con)

SE-697   Toll (Robert & Jane) Foundation, The   MI-17-18-20-25-29-31-22-42-52-62-83
c/o Toll Brothers, Inc.
3103 Philmont Avenue   **Phone** 215-938-8000 **FAX** 215-938-8023
Huntingdon Valley 19006   (Montgomery County)   **EIN** 23-2654322   **Year Created** 1991
AMV $5,075,742   **FYE** 12-00   (**Gifts Received** $5,000,000)   70 **Grants totaling** $202,175

About three-fourths local giving. High grant of **$50,000** to Federation Allied Jewish Appeal. **$31,400** to U. of Pa. (Say Yes to Education). **$30,000** to U. of Pa. Law School. **$7,500** to Womens Way. **$5,000** each to Jefferson Heart Institute and Planned Parenthood Assn. of Bucks County. **$4,500** to Beth Sholom Congregation. **$3,500** to Red Cross. **$1,500** to Bucks County Housing Group. **$650** to Philadelphia Orchestra. Other local contributions **$35-$600** for various purposes. **Out-of-state** giving includes **$15,000** to Metropolitan Opera [NY]; **$11,675** to Seeds of Peace [NY]; **$8,000** to Cornell U. [NY]; and **$5,000-$5,500** each to Amnesty International [NY], Bowdoin Summer Music Festival [ME], and Legal Aid Society [NY]. ■ **PUBLICATIONS:** None ■ **WEBSITE:** www.tollbrothers.com [corporate info only] ■ **E-MAIL:** None ■ **APPLICATION POLICIES & PROCEDURES:** Information not available.

O+D+T Robert I. Toll [Solebury] (Executive Director+P+F+Donor+Con)

SE-698   Tozour (Douglas O. & Gail S.) Foundation   MI-11-22-25-29-31-41-42-61-82
    c/o Tozour Energy Systems
    741 First Avenue, P.O. Box 1549   **Phone** 610-962-1600 **FAX** 610-962-0230
    King of Prussia 19406   (Montgomery County)   **EIN** 22-2779208   **Year Created** 1986
AMV $997,198   **FYE** 12-00   (**Gifts Received** $219,527)   57 **Grants totaling** $78,395

About three-fourths local giving; some grants comprise multiple payments. High grant of **$15,000** to United Way of SE Pa. **$13,808** to Malvern Preparatory School (mostly for Annual Fund). **$6,560** to Family Services of Chester County. **$5,215** to MBF Center (benefit events). **$4,000** to Eastern College. **$3,100** to Gesu School (Children Succeeding Fund). **$1,000** each to Abraham Lincoln High School (recognition gift), Pathway School, and St. Norbert Church (inner-city school computers). **$750** to Volunteers of America of Delaware Valley. Other local contributions **$50-$600** for various purposes. **Out-of-state** giving includes **$10,000** to Georgetown U. Hospital [DC] (Child Life Fund); **$2,000-$2,500** each to Doctors Without Borders [NY], U.S. Naval Academy [MD], and World Vision [WA]; and **$1,500** to Habitat for Humanity [GA] (President's Circle). ■ **PUBLICATIONS:** None ■ **WEBSITE:** None ■ **E-MAIL:** None ■ **APPLICATION POLICIES & PROCEDURES:** Information not available.

O+D+T Douglas O. Tozour (P+T+Donor+Con) — Gail S. Tozour (T)

SE-699   Turner Family Foundation   MI-13-18-22-31-35-41-42-54-57-63
    9 Horseshoe Lane   **Phone** 610-696-1802 **FAX** None
    Paoli 19301   (Chester County)   **EIN** 23-2792012   **Year Created** 1994
AMV $4,708,687   **FYE** 12-99   (**Gifts Received** $978,622)   26 **Grants totaling** $200,290

About half local giving. High grant of **$42,000** to Paoli Presbyterian Church. **$17,500** to United Way of SE Pa. **$15,000** to Episcopal Academy. **$5,000** each to Campus Crusade for Christ and Center for the Advancement of Cancer Education. **$2,500** to WHYY. **$1,000** each to Academy of Natural Sciences, City Team Ministries, Cornerstone Christian Academy, and Upper Main Line YMCA. **$500** each to Amnion Crisis Pregnancy Center, Fox Chase Circle of Hope, and Friends of Paoli Memorial Hospital. Other smaller local contributions. **Out-of-state** giving includes high grant of **$100,000** to Bradley U. [IL] and **$2,040** to Crystal Cathedral Ministries [CA]. ■ **PUBLICATIONS:** None ■ **WEBSITE:** None ■ **E-MAIL:** None ■ **APPLICATION POLICIES & PROCEDURES:** Information not available.

O+D+T Robert E. Turner, Jr. (P+Donor+Con) — Carolyn Turner (F+Donor)

SE-700   Tuttleman Family Foundation, The   MI-15-22-31-32-41-62-53-54-55-56-64
    c/o Tuttsons, Inc.
    349 Montgomery Ave., P.O. Box 2405   **Phone** 610-667-2520 **FAX** 610-667-2525
    Bala Cynwyd 19004   (Montgomery County)   **EIN** 23-7715836   **Year Created** 1993
AMV $6,381,897   **FYE** 12-00   (**Gifts Received** $25,740)   80+ **Grants totaling** $228,968

About three-fourths local giving; some grants comprise multiple payments. High grant of **$48,000** to Jewish Federation of Greater Philadelphia. **$26,000** to Gratz College. **$15,500** to Institute of Contemporary Art. **$13,226** to Temple Adath Israel. **$12,000** to The Shefa Fund. **$10,000** to Wills Eye Hospital. **$5,000** each to City of Philadelphia/Mural Arts Program, Historic Philadelphia, Inc. and Philadelphia Museum of Art. **$2,300** to Academy of Music. **$2,000** to Philadelphia Corporation on Aging (Philly Meals). **$1,500** to Fox Chase Cancer Center. **$1,000** to Perelman Jewish Day School. Other local contributions **$25-$500** for various purposes. **Out-of-state** giving includes **$30,000** to United Jewish Federation of San Diego [CA]; **$5,000** each to Half The Sky Foundation [CA] and OROT [Israel]; and other smaller grants/contributions, many to NY, VT and CA. ■ **PUBLICATIONS:** None ■ **WEBSITE:** None ■ **E-MAIL:** stantut@aol.com ■ **APPLICATION POLICIES & PROCEDURES:** Grant requests may be submitted in a letter at any time. Also, proposals which follow Delaware Valley Grantmakers' Common Grant Application Form (see Appendix or www.dvg.org) are accepted.

O+D+T Stanley C. Tuttleman (T+Con) — Edna S. Tuttleman (T+Donor) — David Z. Tuttleman (T+Donor) — Jan S. Tuttleman (T+Donor) — Steven M. Tuttleman (T+Donor)

SE-701   Uber (Rae S.) Trust   MI-12-13-14-15-25-31-32-33
    c/o Mellon Private Wealth Management
    1735 Market Street, Room 193-0314   **Phone** 215-553-2517 **FAX** 215-553-2054
    Philadelphia 19103   (Philadelphia County)   **EIN** 23-6578512   **Year Created** 1970
AMV $1,286,165   **FYE** 6-00   (**Gifts Received** $0)   33 **Grants totaling** $71,000

All giving limited to Philadelphia-area organizations which work in the following areas of concern: (1) aged persons, (2) blind persons, (3) cancer research, (4) crippled children, and (5) relief of mentally disturbed; grants are for general program support except as noted. High grants of **$5,000** each to Center in the Park (cooperative program with Einstein Healthcare), Crozer-Chester Foundation (Regional Cancer Center), Delco Blind Center, Fox Chase Cancer Center (research equipment upgrades), and

Housing Partnership of Chester County (Project Self-Sufficiency). **$3,000** each to Abington YMCA (swimming pool lift), Easter Seals, Friends Hospital (Scattergood Fund), NAMI-Pa. (Philadelphia area program), and Salvation Army. **$2,000-$2,500** each to Aid for Friends, Artreach, Lower Merion Counseling Services, Options in Aging, Planned Lifetime Assistance Network of Pa., Royer-Greaves School for the Blind, and Silver Springs-Martin Luther School (family resource services). **$1,000-$1,500** each to Associated Services for the Blind (rehabilitation services), Brian's House (vocational equipment), CORP Community Outreach Project (Communicare Program), Friends Rehabilitation Services (social service activities), Guiding Light for the Blind (purchase electronic travel guide devices), Holy Redeemer Foundation (movable bed trapeze), Overbrook School for the Blind (building renovations), Philadelphia Senior Center (independent homemaker services program), Polish American Social Services, RSVP of Montgomery County, Southwest Community Enrichment Center (senior club/home visitation program), Special Olympics-PA, Supportive Older Women's Network, Surrey Services for Seniors, and Wissahickon Hospice. ■**PUBLICATIONS:** Information & Proposal Guidelines memorandum ■**WEBSITE:** None ■**E-MAIL:** morse.g@mellon.com ■**APPLICATION POLICIES & PROCEDURES:** Only Philadelphia-area organizations dealing with aged or blind persons, crippled children, relief of the mentally disturbed, or cancer research are eligible to apply; several grants are awarded annually in each of these areas of concern. Most grants are for special projects, capital drives, or operating budgets. Grant requests may be submitted in a full proposal with cover letter at any time (deadline is November 15th); provide a summary sheet with a brief description of the request, total costs of the project, detailed explanation of the project with breakdown of costs, statement of purpose and brief organizational history, and name/address of contact person; include an annual report, organization and project budgets, list of board members, list of major funding sources, audited financial statement, and IRS tax-exempt status documentation. An organization may submit more than one proposal in a year if the requests fall under different areas of concern as designated above. Grants are awarded at a December meeting.

O+D+T Gail Curtis Morse (VP at Bank+Con) — Mellon Bank N.A. (Trustee)

SE-702 **Union Benevolent Association**
1510 Cecil B. Moore Ave., Suite 300
Philadelphia 19121

(Philadelphia County)

MI-12-13-14-15-16-17-18-19-20-22-24-25-29 35-41-45-49-51-53-55-56-71-79-84-85
Phone 215-232-2975 **FAX** None
EIN 23-1360861 **Year Created** 1831

AMV $4,436,228 **FYE** 12-01 **(Gifts Received** $0) 85 **Grants totaling** $230,550

All giving is exclusively for Philadelphia organizations serving needy residents. High grants of **$5,000** each to ASPIRA, Inc., Fair Hill Burial Ground Corp., The Philadelphia Scholars, and Resource Initiatives Giving Hope Through Training. **$4,000-$4,500** each to Art Sanctuary, Asian Arts Initiative, Boys & Girls Clubs of Philadelphia, Homeless Advocacy Project, Neighborhood Gardens Assn., Overington House, Southwest-Belmont Community Assn., and Women's Community Revitalization Project. **$3,000-$3,500** each to AIDS Law Project of Pennsylvania, Anti-Violence Partnership of Philadelphia, Awbury Arboretum Assn., Calcutta House, CARIE, Christ Church in Philadelphia, Community Planning Associates, Harriet Tubman Group Home, Dignity Housing, Ghebre Michael Inn, Greater Philadelphia Food Bank, Holy Redeemer Health System, Neighborhood Bike Works, Philadelphia Children's Alliance, Philadelphia Senate on Aging, Philadelphia Training Program, Inc., Potter's House Mission, Sisters of St. Joseph, Urban Tree Connection, William Way Lesbian Gay Bisexual Transgender Community Center, and Women Organized Against Rape. **$2,000-$2,500** each to Adoption Center of Delaware Valley, Arden Theatre Company, Baker Industries, Children's Village Child Care Center, The Clay Studio, Community Development Corp. of Frankford Group Ministries, CONTACT Careline of Greater Philadelphia, Evangelical Lutheran Church of the Redeemer, Executive Service Corps, First United Methodist Church of Germantown, Germantown Settlement, Greater Philadelphia Women's Medical Fund, Historic Bartram's Garden, Junior Achievement of Delaware Valley, Inc., Kardon Institute of the Arts, Koresh Dance Company, Landmarks Society, Little Brothers Friends of the Elderly, Manayunk Community Center for the Arts, New Threads, New World Assn. of Emigrants from Eastern Europe, Nonprofit Technology Resources, North Light Community Center, Olney Touchdown Club, Our Lady of Angels School, Painted Bride Art Center, The Partnership CDC, Pa. Environmental Council, Philadelphia Friends of Outward Bound, Philadelphia Wooden Boat Factory, Planned Parenthood of SE Pa., Public Interest Law Center of Philadelphia, Reboot Philadelphia, St. Joseph's Preparatory School, Settlement Music School, SILOAM Ministries, Sisters of Mercy of the Americas, SOWN/Supportive Older Women's Network, Travelers Aid Philadelphia, Urban Bridges at Saint Gabriel's, Visiting Nurse Assn. of Greater Philadelphia, WHEELS, Women's Association for Women's Alternatives, Inc., Working Wardrobe, and YMCA of Germantown. **$1,000-$1,500** each to Atwater Kent Museum, Childspace Cooperative Development, City of Philadelphia Mural Arts Program, Community Education Center, The Filled Cup, Mental Health Association, Metropolitan Career Center, Philadelphia Youth Tennis, Programs Employing People, Recording for the Blind and Dyslexic, Sedgwick Cultural Center, Timothy Academy, United Communities Southeast Philadelphia, and White-Williams Scholars. ■**PUBLICATIONS:** Annual Report & Guidelines booklet ■**WEBSITE:** None ■**E-MAIL:** None ■**APPLICATION POLICIES & PROCEDURES:** The Foundation reports that only organizations serving disadvantaged or needy residents in Philadelphia are eligible to apply. Most grants are for general support, special projects, or matching grants. No grants are awarded for sectarian religious purposes. Grants to any one organization are limited to three out of five years. Prospective applicants initially should make a telephone inquiry about the feasibility of submitting a request. Submit requests in a letter or proposal 30 days before Board meetings; deadlines are January 31st, April 30th, and September 30th. Describe the project and the problem it addresses, state the specific amount needed, and include an annual report, organizational and project budgets, list of major funding sources, Board member list with affiliations, and IRS tax-exempt status documentation. Also, proposals which follow Delaware Valley Grantmakers' Common Grant Application Form (see Appendix or www.dvg.org) are accepted. Site visits sometimes are made to organizations being considered for a grant. The Board of Managers awards grants at meetings in February, May, and October.

O+D+T Members of the Board of Managers: Craig E.F. Alston, Esq. (P+Con) — Lorene E. Cary (Chair, Allocations Committee) — Roberta Griffin Torian, Esq. (VP) — David M. Coates, Jr. [Narberth] (S+F) — William J. Burke, Jr. — Joanne R. Denworth, Esq. — Daniel Gerber — William J. Lee [Newtown Square] — Phyllis Martino — Theodore T. Newbold

SE-703   Union League, The Scholarship Foundation of the   MI-43
c/o The Union League of Philadelphia
140 South Broad Street   **Phone** 215-587-5568 **FAX** 215-587-5562
Philadelphia 19102   (Philadelphia County)   **EIN** 23-6427434   **Year Created** 1967
AMV $2,082,765   **FYE** 6-00   (**Gifts Received** $111,755)   84 **Grants totaling** $82,980

All giving is restricted to scholarships of **$1,000** each for boys and girls from the greater Philadelphia area (including nearby NJ counties) to attend any accredited postsecondary institution in the United States. About 25 new scholarships are awarded each year and are renewable for full-time study for a total of four years or **$4,000**. ■**PUBLICATIONS:** None ■**WEBSITE:** www.unionleague.org/guestframeset.html ■**E-MAIL:** foundations@unionleague.org ■**APPLICATION POLICIES & PROCEDURES:** Scholarship applications are accepted only from boys/girls who reside in Philadelphia, its suburbs, or nearby NJ, and who previously received The Union League of Philadelphia Good Citizenship Award; students are sponsored by 45 youth organizations which participate in The Union League's Youth Work Foundation Program—e.g. Boy Scouts, Police Athletic League, Boys/Girls Clubs, Catholic Youth Organization, Jewish Community Centers, YMCA and others (complete list available on website: www.unionleague.org — select foundations). A formal application form, available from the Union League, must be completed and submitted with an agency certificate before the December 31st deadline. All applicants are interviewed by the Selection Committee which makes the awards at a June reception.
O+D+T Joseph A. Dubee (Foundations Director+Con) — George G. Hawke (C+T) — JoAnne S. Bagnell [Gladwyne] (T) — Robert J. Daly [NJ] (T) — Robert J. Daniels (T) — Linda R. Knox (T) — Leonard Mellman (T) — Richard A. Mulford [Malvern] (T) — J. Permar Richards, Jr. [Bryn Mawr] (T) — George E. Robinette [Haverford] (T) and a 15-member Selection Committee

SE-704   Up East, Inc.   MI-71-72-79
P.O. Box 155   **Phone** 610-793-1356 **FAX** None
Chadds Ford 19317   (Delaware County)   **EIN** 51-0367586   **Year Created** 1997
AMV $12,270,516   **FYE** 6-01   (**Gifts Received** $0)   4 **Grants totaling** $153,385

All giving to Maine; all grants are for operating support. High grant of **$63,048** to U. of Maine. **$53,837** to Island Institute. **$26,500** to Lobster Conservancy. **$10,000** to Natural Resources Council of Maine. ■**PUBLICATIONS:** None ■**WEBSITE:** None ■**E-MAIL:** None ■**APPLICATION POLICIES & PROCEDURES:** The Foundation reports that giving focuses on developing/improving techniques to sustain/improve healthy wild and cultivated marine species/habitats of practical value to Maine's island and coastal areas. Grant requests may be submitted in a letter (2 pages maximum) at any time.
O+D+T Betsy James Wyeth (P+T+Donor+Con) — Andrew N. Wyeth (T+Donor) — Gail A. Graham (S+F) — William Prickett [DE] (T) — J. Robinson West [DC] (T) — Prof. John Wilmerding [ME] (T) — James Browning Wyeth [DE] (T) — Nicholas Wyeth [NY] (T)

SE-705   Valentine Foundation   MI-12-13-16-17-18-20-25-35-45
300 Quarry Lane   **Phone** 610-642-4887 **FAX** 610-642-4887
Haverford 19041   (Montgomery County)   **EIN** 23-6806061   **Year Created** 1985
AMV $2,773,336   **FYE** 11-01   (**Gifts Received** $0)   29 **Grants totaling** $283,700

Mostly local giving; grants are for general operating support except as noted. ***GRANTS FOR GIRLS***: **$15,000** each to Alice Paul Centennial Foundation [NJ] (Leadership Program for middle school students in Camden) and Delaware County Family Centers (Always Sisters program). **$12,000** to Girls Celebrate Science (Girls Celebrate Science! and Institute for Girls' Leadership & Environmental Science programs). **$10,000** each to Academy of Natural Sciences (Women in Natural Sciences program), The Center Foundation (teen girls projects at Chester High School), Maternity Care Coalition (Latina MOMobile), Philadelphia Black Women's Health Project (teen after-school program), Philadelphia YouthBuild Charter School (Young Women Achieving workshops), and YWCA of Bucks County (emergency needs for teen mothers program). **$7,500-$8,000** each to ACLU Foundation Clara Bell Duvall Project (Pa. Minor's Rights to Reproductive Health Care project), Casa del Carmen (teen girls group), Lombard Central Presbyterian Church (adolescent girls empowerment program), and Women's Anti-Violence Education (directory of service agencies for girls in Philadelphia). **$5,000** each to HERO, Inc. (teen girls group) and Montgomery County Community College (Girls Exploring Math & Science project). **$4,000** to The Empowerment Group (Higher Ground teen mentoring project). ***GRANTS FOR WOMEN***: **$15,000** each to Center for Lesbian & Gay Civil Rights (Custody Action for Lesbian Mothers project) and Community Legal Services (Childcare Access/Advocacy Project). **$12,000** each to CHOICE, Delaware Valley Assn. for the Education of Young Children (Worthy Wage Campaign), and National Clearinghouse for the Defense of Battered Women. **$10,000** each to AIDS Law Project of Pa. (Standby Guardianship Initiative), ChildSpace Cooperative Development, Inc. (individual workers development accounts program), Older Women's League [DC] (Caring for Caregivers Campaign), Women's Anti-Violence Education, and Women's Community Revitalization Project (leadership/advocacy skills project). **$7,200-$7,500** each to Planned Parenthood of Chester County (Young Advocates Program), Sabbath of Domestic Peace, and Women in Transition (family violence summit). ■**PUBLICATIONS:** Annual Report with application guidelines ■**WEBSITE:** www.valentinefoundation.org ■**E-MAIL:** valentin@comcast.com ■**APPLICATION POLICIES & PROCEDURES:** The Foundation reports that giving focuses on Philadelphia-area or national organizations/programs which (1) empower women and girls to recognize and develop their full potential or (2) which work to change established attitudes that discourage them from recognizing that potential. Grants will be given for endeavors to effect fundamental change—to change attitudes, policies, or social patterns. At least half of the support is to programs for girls, the remainder for women's programs. The Trustees have particular interest in supporting: (1) programs for women/girls of color who are economically disadvantaged, (2) programs working to sustain healthy development of girls through their adolescence, (3) programs with a mentoring component, and (4) programs incorporating reproductive/physical health education. Grants to programs serving women must provide for social change advocacy. Most grants are for special projects or general support. No grants are awarded for scholarships, endowments or capital expenditures. Prospective applicants must initially submit a letter (2 pages maximum), preferably in June, describing their project or organization—the deadline is June 30th; if the Foundation is interested, a full proposal will be requested and detailed guidelines provided. Site visits sometimes are made to organizations being considered for a grant. The Trustees award grants at a November meeting.

O+D+T Alexandra V.A. Frazier (Director+Con) — Cynthia A. Jetter (C+T) — Lisa Gilden (T) — Jocelyn A. Jones (T) — Mary T. McTernan (T) — Dainette M. Mintz (T) — M. Ann Ricksecker (T) — Daphne Chase Rowe (T) — Frances Vilella-Velez (T) — Donor: Estate of Phoebe Valentine

---

SE-706 **Vanguard Group Foundation, The**		**MI**-11-12-13-14-17-25-29-32-35-41-42-44-49
c/o The Vanguard Group (V29)		51-52-54-55-56-57-71-72-81-82-85-89
P.O. Box 2600		**Phone** 610-669-6331 **FAX** None
Valley Forge 19482	(Chester County)	**EIN** 23-2699769 **Year Created** 1993

AMV $3,846,048 **FYE** 12-00 (**Gifts Received** $3,007,326) 600+ **Grants totaling** $2,322,504

About three-fourths local/Pa. giving; some educational and arts/cultural grants include employee matching gifts. High grant of **$1,302,000** to United Way of SE Pa. **$150,000** to National Constitution Center. **$100,000** to Regional Performing Arts Center. **$57,150** to Junior Achievement of Delaware Valley. **$28,750** to Free Library of Philadelphia Foundation. **$25,000** each to American Heart Assn. and Delaware County Community College. **$20,000** to The Philadelphia Foundation. **$16,400** to Philadelphia Orchestra. **$16,050** to Philadelphia Museum of Art. **$15,260** to The Baldwin School. **$15,000** to West Philadelphia Corporation (Partners program). **$14,205** to Penn State U. **$10,000** each to Philadelphia Zoo and Red Cross/Philadelphia. **$9,285** to The Haverford School. **$8,000** to Women's Community Revitalization Project. **$7,000-$7,600** each to Academy of Natural Sciences, Chester County Historical Society, Community Volunteers in Medicine, Franklin Institute, Greater Philadelphia Urban Affairs Coalition, White-Williams Scholars, and World Affairs Council of Philadelphia. **$5,000-$5,650** each to Aid for Friends, Berwyn Fire Company, Big Brothers/Big Sisters Assn. of Philadelphia, Bryn Mawr Rehab, Camp Soltane, Habitat for Humanity/Philadelphia, John Bartram Assn., East Whiteland Fire Company, Easttown Township Library Foundation, The Enterprise Center, Friends of Jenkins Arboretum, Friends School-Haverford, Fund for the Water Works, Metropolitan Career Center, The Nature Conservancy/Pa. Chapter, Paoli Fire Company, Pa. Academy of the Fine Arts, Pa. Ballet, Philadelphia High School Academies, Recording for the Blind & Dyslexic, and Settlement Music School. **$4,000-$4,150** each to Children's Country Week Assn., League of Women Voters of Pa. [Harrisburg], Phoenixville Public Library, and WHYY. **$3,000-$3,750** each to Academy of Notre Dame de Namur, Baker Industries, Community Accountants, Crime Prevention Assn., Darlington Fine Arts Center, Executive Service Corps of Delaware Valley, Friends of the Japanese House, Our Lady of Assumption School [Strafford], People's Light & Theatre Company, Philadelphia Wooden Boat Factory, and St. Joseph's U. **$2,000-$2,800** each to Balch Institute for Ethnic Studies, Central Philadelphia Development Corp., Centro Pedro Claver, Corporate Alliance for Drug Education, Curtis Institute of Music, Delaware Valley Project/hireAbility, Foundation for Architecture, Fox Chase Cancer Center, Independence Seaport Museum, New Kensington Community Development Corp., Norristown Zoo, Philabundance, Philadelphia Senior Center, RSVP of Montgomery County, St. Maximillian Kolbe School Fund [West Chester], St. Basil the Great School [Kimberton], St. Charles Borromeo Seminary, Temple U., Walnut Street Theatre, Wilma Theatre, Windsor Christian Academy [Eagle], and WXPN. Other local grants/contributions **$25-$1,900** for similar purposes, many as matching gifts. **Out-of-state** giving includes **$125,000** to Valley of the Sun United Way [AZ]; **$80,000** to United Way of the Central Carolinas [NC]; **$37,500** to National Council on Economic Education [NY]; **$25,000** to American Battle Monuments Commission [DC]; **$19,065** to The Nature Conservancy [VA]; **$15,975** to Junior Achievement of Central Carolinas [NC]; **$12,750** to Harvard U. [MA]; **$5,000** to Committee for Economic Development [NY]; and other grants for various purposes. ■**PUBLICATIONS:** Summary of Request form ■**WEBSITE:** www.vanguard.com [corporate info only] ■**E-MAIL:** None ■**APPLICATION POLICIES & PROCEDURES:** The Foundation reports that giving priorities are Health/Human Services, Culture & The Arts, Civic & Community Affairs, The Environment, and Education (primarily matching gifts). Serious consideration is given to requests that (a) are located in the Delaware Valley); (b) address a well-defined and important community concern/need; (c) develop and implement long-term solutions rather than short-term relief; and (d) do not duplicate existing programs. Prospective applicants initially should request a copy of the Vanguard Foundation's Summary of Request form. Grant requests may be submitted at any time and should include the following: (1) a completed Summary of Request form; (2) a letter/proposal with a brief description of the organization (goals, history, past projects, staff and those it serves); a specific amount requested; a detailed statement about how the funding will be used (including the amount used for administrative expenses); and a project timetable; (3) a list of Vanguard employees, if applicable, who are active in the applicant organization; and (4) an annual report, Board list with affiliations, list of other funding sources, audited financial statement, and IRS tax-exempt status documentation. Also, proposals which follow Delaware Valley Grantmakers' Common Grant Application Form (see Appendix or www.dvg.org) are accepted. Applicants are notified within four to six weeks about the status of a request. Grants are awarded on a quarterly basis. — Matching gifts ($25 minimum) are given to secondary schools, most colleges/universities, libraries, arts and cultural organizations, and public broadcasting.

O+D+T Tami Wise (Con) — John J. Brennan (P+D) — Raymond J. Klapinsky [Media] (S+D) — Ralph K. Packard [Wayne] (F+D) — James H. Gately (D) — F. William McNabb (D)

SE-707 **Vernekoff Zuritsky Foundation, The**		**MI**-11-22-41-52-54-62-72-82
c/o Parkway Corporation		
150 North Broad Street		**Phone** 215-569-8400 **FAX** None
Philadelphia 19102	(Philadelphia County)	**EIN** 22-2734623 **Year Created** 1986

AMV $1,252,891 **FYE** 12-00 (**Gifts Received** $0) 17 **Grants totaling** $140,228

About three-fourths local giving. High grant of **$39,812** to Federation Allied Jewish Appeal. **$25,000** to National Museum of American Jewish History. **$10,000** each to Tech New Materials Science Project [Bala Cynwyd] and United Way of SE Pa. **$8,250** to National Liberty Museum. **$5,000** to Aish Hatorah. **$3,000** to Anti-Defamation League. **$2,500** to Jewish Federation of Greater Philadelphia. **$1,000-$1,666** each to Israel Guide Dog Center [Warrington], Jewish National Fund, Perelman Jewish Day School,

Philadelphia Zoo, and Prince Music Theater. **Out-of-state** giving includes **$20,000** to Jaffa Institute [NY]; and **$5,000** each to Haifa Foundation [Israel] and Weizmann Institute of Science [Israel]. ■**PUBLICATIONS:** None ■**WEBSITE:** None ■**E-MAIL:** None ■**APPLICATION POLICIES & PROCEDURES:** Grant requests may be submitted in writing at any time; describe the purpose of the requested grant and include IRS tax-exempt status documentation.

O+D+T Herman Zuritsky (T+Donor+Con) — Etta Winigrad (T+Donor)

SE-708 **Vincent (Anna M.) Scholarship Fund Trust**   MI-43
c/o Mellon Private Wealth Management
1735 Market Street, Room 193-0370   **Phone** 215-553-2596 **FAX** 215-553-4542
Philadelphia 19103   (Philadelphia County)   **EIN** 23-6422666   **Year Created** 1967
AMV $8,499,017   **FYE** 6-00   (**Gifts Received** $0)   100 **Grants totaling** $215,500

All grants are restricted to scholarships for Philadelphia-area undergraduate or graduate students. Each year about 25 new scholarships are awarded, generally ranging from **$2,000** to **$4,000**; scholarship grantees may receive up to five years' support. ■ **PUBLICATIONS:** Brochure ■**WEBSITE:** None ■**E-MAIL:** smith.ft@mellon.com ■**APPLICATION POLICIES & PROCEDURES:** Only Philadelphia-area/Delaware Valley undergraduate or graduate students who are 'worthy of financial assistance, of high scholastic standing and good character, citizens of the USA, residents of the City of Philadelphia or surrounding area, and of caucasian race' — under the Deed of Trust's terms — are eligible to apply. A formal application form, available from Philadelphia-area high schools, must be completed and submitted by March 1st; applicants must show evidence of having been employed part-time while attending high school.

O+D+T Frances T. Smith (Portfolio Officer at Bank+Con) — Robert I. Whitelaw, Esq. (Co-T) Mellon Bank N.A. (Co-Trustee)

SE-709 **Vital Spark Foundation**   MI-18-35-51-71-72-79-83
708 West Mt. Airy Ave.   **Phone** 215-242-5227 **FAX** None
Philadelphia 19119   (Philadelphia County)   **EIN** 13-3537545   **Year Created** 1985
AMV $1,938,474   **FYE** 11-00   (**Gifts Received** $0)   8 **Grants totaling** $95,000

One Pa. grant; **$5,000** to Health Promotion Council of SE Pa. (Project TEACH). **Out-of-state** giving includes **$15,000** each to American Nonsmokers' Rights Foundation [CA], National Labor Committee [NY], Pacific Repertory Theatre [CA], and Population Media Center [VT]; and **$10,000** each to Planned Parenthood Federation of America [NY] and Sierra Club Foundation [CA]. ■ **PUBLICATIONS:** None ■**WEBSITE:** None ■**E-MAIL:** None ■**APPLICATION POLICIES & PROCEDURES:** Alternatively, grant requests may be submitted in any form at any time to Bruce Mitteldorf, 7280 Giovanetti Rd., Forestville, CA 95436; Telephone 408-373-3694.

O+D+T Joshua J. Mitteldorf (F+D+Con) — Bruce Mitteldorf (S+D+Con) — Harriet M. Mitteldorf [FL] (P+D+Donor)

SE-710 **Vogt (William T. & Lorine E.) Charitable Foundation**   MI-31-42-54-55-63-71-84
c/o William T. Vogt Investments
558 West Montgomery Ave.   **Phone** 610-527-1650 **FAX** None
Haverford 19041   (Delaware County)   **EIN** 23-2339924   **Year Created** 1984
AMV $3,847,867   **FYE** 12-00   (**Gifts Received** $988)   29 **Grants totaling** $214,210

Mostly local giving. High grant of **$150,000** to Philadelphia Museum of Art. **$20,000** to National Constitution Center. **$10,000** to Church of the Advocate [Philadelphia]. **$5,250** to Church of the Redeemer. **$5,000** to Friends of Bryn Mawr Hospital. **$2,000** to U. of Pa. **$1,000-$1,500** each to Arcadia U., Brandywine Conservancy, Children's Hospital of Philadelphia Foundation, Main Line Art Center, and U.S. Court Tennis Preservation Foundation. Other local contributions **$35-$500** for various purposes. **Out-of-state** giving includes **$5,500** to Princeton U. [NJ] and **$5,000** to Westerly Hospital [RI]. ■**PUBLICATIONS:** application guidelines ■**WEBSITE:** None ■**E-MAIL:** None ■**APPLICATION POLICIES & PROCEDURES:** Prospective applicants initially should make a telephone inquiry about the feasibility of submitting a request. The Trustees award grants at monthly meetings.

O+D+T William T. Vogt (T+Donor+Con) — Lorine E. Vogt (T+Donor)

SE-711 **Waber Fund, The**   MI-14-17-22-25-31-44-55-62-81-82
7 Wynnewood Road, P.O. Box 323   **Phone** 610-649-6260 **FAX** None
Wynnewood 19096   (Montgomery County)   **EIN** 23-6281585   **Year Created** 1963
AMV $1,003,403   **FYE** 12-00   (**Gifts Received** $0)   24 **Grants totaling** $107,500

About one-third local giving. High Pa. grants of **$10,000** each to Jewish Federation of Greater Philadelphia and Philadelphia Friends of Lubavitch. **$7,500** to American Associates of Ben-Gurion U. of the Negev and Lubavitch House. **$2,000** to Big Picture Alliance. **$1,000** each to Middle East Forum, Philabundance, Salvation Army, and Womens Way. **$500** to Children's Hospital of Philadelphia Foundation. **Out-of-state** giving includes high grant of **$30,000** to Yivo Institute for Jewish Research [NY]; **$10,000** to Jewish Institute for National Security Affairs [DC]; **$8,000** to Central Synagogue Restoration Fund [NY]; **$4,000** to CAMERA [MA]; and **$2,000-$2,500** each to American Film Institute [CA], Foundation Fighting Blindness [MD], and New York Public Library. ■**PUBLICATIONS:** None ■**WEBSITE:** None ■**E-MAIL:** None ■**APPLICATION POLICIES & PROCEDURES:** Grant requests in letter form may be submitted at any time. No grants or loans are awarded to individuals. — Formerly called The Morris Waber Fund.

O+D+T Harry Waber (T+Donor+Con) — Tanya Corbin [NY] (T) — Irwin Jacobs [NY] (T)

SE-712 Wachs (Judith & David) Family Foundation   MI-14-22-32-33-41-54-62-81
c/o Dam Management Corp.
215 West Church Road, Suite 108
King of Prussia 19406   (Montgomery County)   **Phone** 610-768-5885 **FAX** 610-768-9476
                                                             EIN 22-2682604   **Year Created** 1985
AMV $53,353   **FYE** 9-00   (**Gifts Received** $129,400)   27 **Grants totaling** $196,047

About two-thirds local giving; grants are for general fund purposes except as noted. High grant of **$110,546** to Perelman Jewish Day School/Stern Center (scholarship fund). **$18,761** to Jewish Federation of Greater Philadelphia. **$13,452** to Hadassah/Philadelphia Chapter. **$11,700** to Cystic Fibrosis Foundation. **$8,737** to Har Zion Temple. **$6,100** to Akiba Hebrew Academy. **$5,000** to Beck Institute for Cognitive Therapy & Research. **$3,000** to National Organization for Hearing Research. **$2,500** to National Museum of American Jewish History. **$1,000** each to ALS Assn./Greater Philadelphia Chapter, Living Beyond Breast Cancer, and Philadelphia Museum of Art/Craft Show. **$750** to Crohn's & Colitis Foundation. Other local contributions **$25-$500** for various purposes. **Out-of-state** giving includes **$3,000** to Seeds of Peace [NY] and **$1,000** to Washington Institute for Near East Policy [DC]. ■**PUBLICATIONS:** None ■**WEBSITE:** None ■**E-MAIL:** None ■**APPLICATION POLICIES & PROCEDURES:** Grant requests may be submitted in any form at any time. No grants are awarded to individuals.
O+D+T Rachel A. Wachs, Esq. (S+Con) — David V. Wachs (P+Donor) — Judith Wachs (VP+F) — Martin Wachs (VP) — Michael Wachs (VP) — Philip Wachs (VP)

SE-713 Wachs (Peggy & Ellis) Family Foundation   MI-12-15-22-25-31-42-43-44-52-53-54-62
The Barclay - #8B, 237 South 18th Street
Philadelphia 19103   (Philadelphia County)   **Phone** Unlisted **FAX** None
                                                             EIN 23-6802696   **Year Created** 1985
AMV $2,277,170   **FYE** 12-00   (**Gifts Received** $0)   55 **Grants totaling** $87,505

Mostly local giving. High grant of **$25,300** to Free Library of Philadelphia. **$25,100** to U. of Pa. **$10,000** to Federation Allied Jewish Appeal. **$3,000** to Rowan House. **$2,760** to White-Williams Scholars. **$1,000-$1,500** each to Beth David Reform Congregation, Jewish Family & Children's Agency, People's Emergency Center, Philadelphia Committee to End Homelessness, Philadelphia Geriatric Center, Philadelphia Museum of Art, Philadelphia Orchestra, and The Print Club. Other local contributions **$25-$500** for various purposes. **Out-of-state** giving includes **$2,000** to Columbia Presbyterian Medical Center [NY]; **$1,500** to World Jewish Congress [NY]; and **$1,000** to Hospital Albert Schweitzer [FL]. ■**PUBLICATIONS:** None ■**WEBSITE:** None ■ **E-MAIL:** None ■**APPLICATION POLICIES & PROCEDURES:** Grant requests may be submitted in any form at any time; describe the organization and intended purpose of funds; state the amount requested and include IRS tax-exempt status documentation. No grants are awarded to individuals.
O+D+T Ellis G. Wachs (T+Donor+Con) — Peggy B. Wachs (T)

SE-714 Wachs-Weingarten Charitable Trust   MI-41-44-62
210 Glenn Road
Ardmore 19003   (Montgomery County)   **Phone** 610-896-5481 **FAX** None
                                                      EIN 23-7922107   **Year Created** 1997
AMV $291,497   **FYE** 10-00   (**Gifts Received** $250)   11 **Grants totaling** $18,854

Mostly local giving. High grant of **$9,433** to Free Library of Philadelphia. **$3,535** to Beth David Reform Congregation. **$2,500** to Friends Central School. **$500** to Friends School Haverford. Other local contributions **$100-$200**. **Out-of-state** giving includes **$1,500** to Anti-Defamation League [NY]. ■**PUBLICATIONS:** None. ■**WEBSITE:** None ■**E-MAIL:** None ■**APPLICATION POLICIES & PROCEDURES:** Grant requests in any form may be submitted at any time.
O+D+T Brian Weingarten (T+Con) — Marjorie Wachs Weingarten (T+Donor)

SE-715 Wagman (Nancy) Foundation   MI-22-25-32-52-55-62
c/o Harold Sampson, CPA
2508 Grant Road
Broomall 19008   (Delaware County)   **Phone** 610-356-7822 **FAX** None
                                                     EIN 23-2709851   **Year Created** 1993
AMV $413,525   **FYE** 11-00   (**Gifts Received** $0)   19 **Grants totaling** $60,700

Mostly local giving. High grant of **$20,000** to National Disease Research Interchange. **$15,925** to Project H.O.M.E. **$10,000** to Jewish Federation of Greater Philadelphia. **$1,000-$1,075** each to American Poetry Review, Anti-Defamation League, Bottomless Closet, Curtis Institute of Music, and Thomas Jefferson U. Other local contributions **$50-$500** for various purposes. **Out-of-state** giving includes **$5,000** to Jewish Defense Fund [NY] and **$1,075** to PEN American Center [NY]. ■**PUBLICATIONS:** None ■**WEBSITE:** None ■**E-MAIL:** None ■**APPLICATION POLICIES & PROCEDURES:** Grant requests may be submitted in any form at any time. No grants are awarded to individuals.
O+D+T Howard Wagman [NY] (C+T+Con) — Lowell Dubrow, Esq. [Bala Cynwyd] (T) — James Wagman [NY] (T) — Joel Wagman [NH] (T) — Mary Wagman [NY] (T) — Nela Wagman [NY] (T) — Rita Wagman (T)

SE-716 Waldorf Educational Foundation, The   MI-41-42
c/o The Glenmede Trust Company
1 Liberty Place, 1650 Market Street, Suite 1200
Philadelphia 19103   (Philadelphia County)   **Phone** 215-419-6000 **FAX** 215-419-6196
                                                             EIN 23-6254206   **Year Created** 1951
AMV $11,734,563   **FYE** 12-00   (**Gifts Received** $0)   17 **Grants totaling** $587,538

Nationwide giving restricted to Waldorf schools/teacher training colleges. No Pa. grants. **Out-of-state** giving includes **$190,000** to Assn. of Waldorf School of North America [CA]; **$65,038** to Rudolf Steiner Institute [MD]; **$62,000** each to New England Waldorf Teacher Training [MA], Rudolf Steiner College [CA], and Sunbridge College [NY]; **$35,000** to Rudolph Steiner Founda-

tion [CA]; **$21,000** to Artemsia [MI]; and other smaller grants for similar purposes. — Pa. grants in prior years to Kimberton Waldorf School [Chester County]. ■**PUBLICATIONS:** application guidelines ■**WEBSITE:** None ■**E-MAIL:** None ■**APPLICA-TION POLICIES & PROCEDURES:** The Foundation reports that only schools which follow Rudolph Steiner's philosophy/teachings (Waldorf schools) are eligible to apply. Prospective applicants initially should request a copy of the application guidelines; grant requests may be submitted at any time. Grant decisions are made by the Waldorf Schools Assn. of North America, usually at a fall meeting.
O+D+T Stephen R. Starr (VP at Trust Co.+Con) — Dr. Erika V. Asten [Valley Forge] (T) — Mark Finser [CA] (T) — Karen E. Myrin [Valley Forge] (T) — Clemens Pietzner [Kimberton] (T) — The Glenmede Trust Company (Corporate Trustee)

SE-717 Wallace (Rasheed A.) Foundation, The
c/o RAW Consultants, Inc.
2207 Chestnut Street
Philadelphia 19103 (Philadelphia County)
AMV $6,120 **FYE** 12-00 (**Gifts Received** $287,561)

MI-13-29-41-84
Phone 215-563-8007 **FAX** 215-563-4803
EIN 23-2913768 **Year Created** 1997
14 **Grants totaling** $58,275

All local giving. High grant of **$27,715** to Hunting Park All Stars. **$15,000** to International Student Athletic Assn. **$5,400** to Sonny Hill League. **$5,000** to Panther Youth Development. **$1,250** to Police Athletic League. **$750** to Philadelphia Youth Athletic Assn. **$100-$500** each for other local athletic programs and youth organizations. ■**PUBLICATIONS:** None. ■**WEBSITE:** www.rawallacefoundation.com ■**E-MAIL:** see website ■**APPLICATION POLICIES & PROCEDURES:** The Foundation reports that giving focuses on youth programs in Philadelphia, Portland [OR], Durham [NC] and other selected communities in four areas of interest: (1) Recreation—grants to recreation centers and private recreation programs to assist in the funding of basketball leagues, tournaments, cultural events, activities, trips, special events and other programs; (2) Athletics—direct support to the Hunting Park/Rasheed A. Wallace All Star Program to sponsor players' travel to national basketball tournament competitions for players' exposure to college coaches/recruiters; (3) Education—grants to inner city schools for supplies, materials and equipment for enhanced student learning; and (4) Social—sponsor an annual coat drive in Philadelphia to provide families and individuals coats and other outerwear for winter. See the website for more details. Submit grant requests in a clear and brief letter-proposal at any time (deadline November 30th) which includes the following: organization's mission statement; project summary and purpose/objectives of the requested funds; amount requested and rationale; schedule of implementation; description of the benefits to be achieved and population served; plan to evaluate/report results; financial analysis of the project; name and qualifications of the person in charge of the project; names/affiliations of trustees or board of directors; latest audited financial report; and IRS tax-exempt status documentation. Applicants will be contacted the organization if more information is needed. Grants are awarded at a January meeting.
O+D+T Jacqueline Wallace (Executive Director+Con) — Rasheed A. Wallace [OR] (P+Donor) — Tennis Young [FL] (F) — Joe Watson [OR] (Managing Director) — Malcom Wallace [NC] (Senior Director) — Muhammed Wallace [NC] (D)

SE-718 Warner (Lydia Fisher) Trust
c/o First Union/Wachovia
123 South Broad Street, PA1279
Philadelphia 19109 (Philadelphia County)
AMV $2,638,030 **FYE** 12-99 (**Gifts Received** $0)

MI-15-31
Phone 215-670-4223 **FAX** 215-670-4236
EIN 23-6219706 **Year Created** 1955
4 **Grants totaling** $78,190

All discretionary giving restricted to the 5-county Philadelphia-area hospitals. High grant of **$24,260** to Episcopal Diocese of Pa. **$20,000** to Children's Hospital of Philadelphia Foundation (Reach Out & Read Program). **$17,280** to Thomas Jefferson U. (Yes Shelter Outreach Program). **$6,650** to Bryn Mawr Rehab (falls prevention program for elderly). ■**PUBLICATIONS:** None ■**WEBSITE:** None ■**E-MAIL:** vicki.hills@wachovia.com ■**APPLICATION POLICIES & PROCEDURES:** The Trust reports that giving is restricted to the Bucks, Chester, Delaware, Montgomery and Philadelphia counties for hospital contruction or additions. Grant requests may be submitted in a full proposal at any time, preferably well before the September 30th deadline; provide complete construction costs, budget, funding information, and IRS tax-exempt status documentation.
O+D+T Vicki Hills (Assistant VP at Bank+Con) — First Union/Wachovia (Trustee)

SE-719 Warwick Foundation, The
c/o The Glenmede Trust Company
One Liberty Place, 1650 Market Street, Suite 1200
Philadelphia 19103 (Philadelphia County)
AMV $22,929,184 **FYE** 12-00 (**Gifts Received** $9,210)

MI-11-22-31-41-42-43-44-52-53-54-56-57-63
71-72
Phone 215-419-6000 **FAX** 215-419-6196
EIN 23-6230662 **Year Created** 1961
46 **Grants totaling** $1,220,000

Mostly local/Pa. giving focused on Bucks County. High grant of **$900,000** to Bucks County Nature Conservancy. **$75,000** to Heritage Conservancy. **$60,000** to Doylestown Hospital. **$12,000** each to Bryn Mawr College (Helen Gemmill Scholarship) and U. of Pa. Law School (Kenneth Gemmill Scholarship). **$10,000** each to Bucks County Historical Society and Neshaminy Warwick Presbyterian Church. **$7,000** each to United Way of Bucks County and United Way of SE Pa. **$6,000** to Salvation Army/Philadelphia (memorial gift). **$5,000** each to Doylestown Hospital Fund for the Poor (memorial gift), Mercersburg Academy (scholarship), Moland Park, and Wilson College (Charlotte Gemmill Scholarship). **$4,000** each to Delaware Valley College (scholarship) and Lancaster County Day School (scholarship). **$3,000** each to Free Library of Philadelphia, Historical Fallsington, Michener Art Museum, Pa. Academy of the Fine Arts, Pa. Horticultural Society, and Philadelphia Zoo. **$2,000** each to Academy of Natural Sciences, Franklin Institute, Historical Society of Pa., Independence Seaport Museum, Opera Company of Philadelphia, Philadelphia Museum of Art, Philadelphia Orchestra, Please Touch Museum, U. of Pa. Law School (prizes), and WHYY-TV12. **$1,000-$1,500** each to Academy of Vocal Arts, The Athenaeum of Philadelphia, Bowman's Hill Wildflower Preserve, Bucks County Community College (scholarship), Bucks County Symphony, Central Bucks YMCA, Curtis Institute of Music, Overbrook School for the Blind, and Pa. School for the Deaf. **Out-of-state** giving includes **$24,000** to Princeton U. [NJ] (two scholarships) and **$12,000** to Princeton Theological Seminary [NJ] (scholarship). ■**PUBLICATIONS:** None ■**WEBSITE:** None ■**E-MAIL:** None ■**APPLICA-**

TION POLICIES & PROCEDURES: The Foundation reports that giving is generally restricted to Bucks County and SE Pa. No grants are awarded to individuals. Grant requests may be submitted in a letter at any time; include a project budget, audited financial statement, and IRS tax-exempt status documentation; requests are not acknowledged. The Trustees award grants at a March meeting.

O+D+T Mimi Stauffer (VP at Trust Company+Con) — Elizabeth H. Gemmill, Esq. [Conshohocken] (T) — Helen J. Gemmill [NH] (T+Donor) — Lisa M. Gemmill [Flourtown] (T) — Kenneth Norris [Bryn Mawr] (T)

SE-720   Weintraub (Thomas E.) Foundation, The
c/o Weintraub Brothers Company
2695 Philmont Avenue
Huntingdon Valley   19006   (Montgomery County)

MI-13-14-42-44-52

Phone 215-938-7540 **FAX** 215-938-7630
EIN 22-6404320   **Year Created** 1985

AMV $225,128   **FYE** 6-00   **(Gifts Received** $0)   4 **Grants totaling** $30,334

All local giving. High grant of **$25,000** to TAIG/The Assn. for Independent Growth. **$5,000** to Abington YMCA. **$750** to Temple U. (Music Preparatory Division). **$500** to Friends of Abington Library. ■**PUBLICATIONS:** None ■**WEBSITE:** None ■**E-MAIL:** None ■**APPLICATION POLICIES & PROCEDURES:** Grant requests may be submitted in writing at any time; describe the purpose of the requested fund and include IRS tax-exempt status documentation.

O+D+T Thomas E. Weintraub (T+Donor+Con) — Thomas E. Weintraub, Jr. (T) Corporate donor: Weintraub Brothers Co.

SE-721   Weiss (A.H. & Helen L.) Foundation, The
c/o Cozen & O'Connor (Burton K. Stein, Esq.)
200 Four Falls Corporate Center, Suite 400
West Conshohocken   19428   (Montgomery County)

MI-11-12-15-22-31-32-41-42-62

Phone 610-941-2349 **FAX** None
EIN 23-6298302   **Year Created** 1956

AMV $454,723   **FYE** 9-00   **(Gifts Received** $176,230)   20+ **Grants totaling** $69,590

All local giving. High grant of **$42,100** to Philadelphia Geriatric Center. **$7,000** to Jewish Federation of Greater Philadelphia. **$4,000** to United Way of SE Pa. **$2,810** to Temple Adath Israel. **$2,500** each to Children's Hospital of Philadelphia and St. Christopher's Hospital for Children. **$1,000** each to Epilepsy Foundation, Jewish Community Centers of Greater Philadelphia, Perelman Jewish Day School, Torah Academy, and U. of Pa. Other smaller contributions for various purposes. ■**PUBLICATIONS:** None ■**WEBSITE:** None ■**E-MAIL:** None ■**APPLICATION POLICIES & PROCEDURES:** Grant requests may be submitted in a letter at any time. No grants are awarded to individuals.

O+D+T Helen L. Weiss [Bala Cynwyd] (P+T+Donor+Con) — Stephen A. Cozen, Esq. [Philadelphia] (T) — Linda J. Saltz [Bala Cynwyd] (T)

SE-722   Wert (Michael L. & Susan K.) Foundation, The
341 Pineville Road
Newtown   18940   (Bucks County)

MI-12-25-32-34-42-43-63
Phone 215-598-7410 **FAX** None
EIN 23-2901015   **Year Created** 1997

AMV $340,488   **FYE** 12-00   **(Gifts Received** $0)   8 **Grants totaling** $59,550

About three-fourths local giving. High grant of **$19,000** to U. of Pa. (scholarship fund). **$14,500** to Newtown Presbyterian Church. **$5,000** to Family Service Assn. **$3,500** to U. of Pa. School of Nursing. **$1,000** each to Interfaith Housing Development and Philadelphia Ronald McDonald House. **Out-of-state** grant: **$15,000** to The Jackson Laboratory [ME]. ■**PUBLICATIONS:** None ■**WEBSITE:** None ■**E-MAIL:** None ■**APPLICATION POLICIES & PROCEDURES:** Information not available.

O+D+T Michael L. Wert (T+Donor+Con) — Susan K. Wert (T+Donor)

SE-723   West Family Foundation, The
12 Greenbriar Lane
Paoli   19301   (Chester County)

MI-19-33-55
Phone 610-644-0198 **FAX** None
EIN 23-2870271   **Year Created** 1996

AMV $19,302,601   **FYE** 6-01   **(Gifts Received** $1,179,063)   2 **Grants totaling** $332,212

No current Pa. giving. High grant to West Central Services [NH] (mental health research center). **$15,804** to Westbridge, Inc. [NH] (research/rehabilitation center). — Grants awarded in three prior years included **$25,110** to Main Line Art Center (building improvements) and **$181,000** to West Central Services [NH] (research center) and **$55,296** to Dulaney Station, Inc. [MD] (mental health research). ■**PUBLICATIONS:** None ■**WEBSITE:** None ■**E-MAIL:** None ■**APPLICATION POLICIES & PROCEDURES:** No grants are awarded to individuals.

O+D+T Alfred P. West, Jr. (P+D+Donor+Con) — Angela Paige West (S+F+D) — Alfred Paul West, III (D) — A. Palmer West (D) — Loralee West (D)

SE-724   West (H. O.) Foundation, The
c/o West Pharmaceutical Services, Inc.
101 Gordon Drive (Exton), P.O. Box 645
Lionville   19341   (Chester County)

MI-11-13-18-25-29-32-42-43-44-52-54-72-88

Phone 610-594-2945 **FAX** 610-594-3011
EIN 23-7173901   **Year Created** 1972

AMV $573,833   **FYE** 12-00   **(Gifts Received** $4,000)   123 **Grants totaling** $278,106

Mostly local/Pa. giving in company operating areas, including Philadelphia, and Lycoming, Lancaster, Erie, and Clinton counties. High grant of **$34,750** to United Way of Chester County. **$26,000** to U. of the Sciences in Philadelphia. **$25,000** to Fox Chase Cancer Center. **$17,042** to United Way of Lancaster County. **$5,000** each to Phoenixville Public Library and Planned Parenthood of Chester County. **$4,000** to Philadelphia Museum of Art. **$2,000** to Philadelphia Orchestra. **$3,000** to Philadelphia Zoo. **$2,500** to St. Joseph's U. **$1,731** to United Way of SE Pa. **$1,500** to Siloam Golf Classic. **$1,000** each to Children's Country Week Assn., Jersey Shore Area YMCA [Lycoming County], and Philabundance. **$821** to United Way of Erie County. **$700** to Pa. Free Enterprise Week. Other Pa. contributions **$500-$575** for various purposes. **Out-of-state** giving focuses on corporate operating locations in NJ, FL, NC, NE and IN. In addition, 24 scholarships (**$51,507**) were awarded to dependents of company employees and 62 matching gifts (**$15,335**) disbursed to prep schools, colleges, and universities. ■ **PUBLICATIONS:** application guidelines ■ **WEBSITE:** www.westpharma.com [corporate info only] ■ **E-MAIL:** None ■ **APPLICATION POLICIES & PROCEDURES:** The Foundation reports that giving focuses on supporting cultural, health, and public service needs in areas/communities where the company maintains operations; most grants are for general support, specific projects, building funds, and capital drives; multi-year grants are awarded. In addition a matching gift program supports secondary schools and colleges/universities. Scholarships are awarded only to dependents of company employees. Grant requests may be submitted in a letter-proposal at any time; describe the extent of services being provided and the needs/services of the program over the next few years; also provide an audited financial statement and IRS tax-exempt status documentation. Grants are awarded at meetings in April-May and October-November. — Formerly called The Herman O. West Foundation

O+D+T Maureen Goebel (Administrator+Con) — Richard D. Luzzi (C+T) — William G. Little (T) — Dr. Franklin H. West [Narberth] (T+Donor) Corporate donor: West Pharmaceutical Services, Inc.

SE-725 **Western Assn. of Ladies for the Relief of the Poor**
240 Chatham Way
West Chester 19380 (Chester County)
AMV $3,428,827 **FYE** 12-00 (**Gifts Received** $5,300)

MI-12-14-15-17-22-23-25
Phone 610-692-7962 **FAX** None
EIN 23-1353393 **Year Created** 1847
Grants totaling $143,942

All grants/support restricted to the City of Philadelphia for nonprofit service organizations or to vendors (providing services to needy persons) for rent, home repairs, furniture, appliances, utility bills and other necessary goods/services; no further details are available. — In the prior year, organizations supported included Aid for Friends, Community Women's Education Project, MANNA/Metropolitan AIDS Neighborhood Nutrition Alliance, Philadelphia Committee to End Homelessness, Philadelphia Senior Center, and White-Williams Foundation. ■ **PUBLICATIONS:** None ■ **WEBSITE:** None ■ **E-MAIL:** None ■ **APPLICATION POLICIES & PROCEDURES:** The Foundation reports all giving restricted to the City of Philadelphia; requests accepted only from health/human service agencies or churches providing supplemental aid/relief to poor, homeless or needy persons not covered by governmental assistance. Grant requests may be submitted in a letter at any time. Also, proposals which follow Delaware Valley Grantmakers' Common Grant Application Form (see Appendix or www.dvg.org) are accepted. The Board meets monthly except for July, August, and September.

O+D+T Marlene G. Bohon (Executive Secretary+Con) — Abby Ryan (P+D) — Kurt R. Anderson (VP+D) — Jean P. Barr (D) — Luis Cortes (D) — John Frost (D) — Anne B. Hagele (D) — Rev. Deborah A. McKinley (D) — Judith P. Prendergast (D) — Rev. Paul M. Washington (D) First Union/Wachovia (Corporate Trustee)

SE-726 **Whitaker Fund**
c/o Schumacker & Lunkenheimer
825 Duportail Road, Suite 103
Wayne 19087 (Chester County)
AMV $1,292,387 **FYE** 12-00 (**Gifts Received** $0)

MI-13-15-31-42
Phone 610-651-9400 **FAX** None
EIN 23-7289515 **Year Created** 1953
22 **Grants totaling** $63,600

About one-fifth local giving. High Pa. grant of **$5,000** to Philadelphia U./College of Textiles & Science. **$4,000** to YMCA of Germantown. **$1,000** each to Inglis House and Lankenau Hospital. Other local contributions **$500** each for various purposes. **Out-of-state** giving includes **$13,000** to United Way of Roanoke Valley [VA]; **$10,000** to LaGrange Academy [GA]; **$7,000** to VA Foundation for Independent Colleges; and other smaller grants/contributions to VA and GA. ■ **PUBLICATIONS:** None ■ **WEBSITE:** None ■ **E-MAIL:** None ■ **APPLICATION POLICIES & PROCEDURES:** Information not available.

O+D+T Scott F. Schumacker, Esq. (S+F+Con) — Fred L. Firing, Jr. [VA] (P+D) — Fred C. Whitaker, Jr. [VA] (D)

SE-727 **White (Dr. Robert C.) Trust for School Boy Rowing**
c/o First Union/Wachovia
123 South Broad Street, PA1279
Philadelphia 19109 (Philadelphia County)
AMV $885,716 **FYE** 8-01 (**Gifts Received** $0)

MI-41-84
Phone 215-670-4228 **FAX** 215-670-4236
EIN 23-6878917 **Year Created** 1987
15 **Grants totaling** $50,200

All giving restricted to pre-collegiate-level institutions which promote rowing on the Schuylkill River. High grant of **$5,800** to Bonner Rowing Assn. **$5,600** to The Shipley School. **$4,000** to Philadelphia Scholastic Rowing Assn. **$2,900** each to Agnes Irwin School, The Baldwin School, Chestnut Hill Academy, Episcopal Academy, Father Judge High School, Friends of Harriton Crew. Haverford School, LaSalle College High School, Lower Merion High School Crew Assn., Malvern Preparatory School, Northeast Catholic Crew Team, St. Joseph's Preparatory School, and Upper Merion Crew Boosters. ■ **PUBLICATIONS:** Grant Proposal Guidelines, Application for Funding ■ **WEBSITE:** None ■ **E-MAIL:** diane.stables@wachovia.com ■ **APPLICATION POLICIES & PROCEDURES:** Only pre-collegiate institutions that promote rowing on the Schuylkill River are eligible to apply; also, a program must have been in existence for at least five years and competed in the Manny Flicks for the last five consecutiv years, be viable, and committed to promoting youth participation. No grants are awarded to individuals. Grant requests must be submitted in duplicate on a formal Application for Funding, available from the Bank, before the June 30th deadline; it must be signed by a headmaster, principa, vice president for development, the rowing coach, or a parent representative. Include organizational background information, organization and rowing program budgets, a bound audited financial statement, list of present major funding sources, IRS tax-exempt status documentation, and a statement that the requested funds—if granted—will not alter the organization's status as a publicly supported charity, nor be offset against funds otherwise going to the rowing program.

O+D+T Diane O. Stables (VP at Bank+Con) — First Union/Wachovia (Trustee)

SE-728 **Widener Memorial Foundation in Aid of Handicapped Children** MI-12-13-14-41-42-55
665 Thomas Road, P.O. Box 178 — **Phone** 215-836-7500 **FAX** None
Lafayette Hill 19444 (Montgomery County) — **EIN** 23-6267223 **Year Created** 1912
AMV $8,300,476 **FYE** 12-00 (**Gifts Received** $562,543) 17 **Grants totaling** $832,495

All giving restricted to the Delaware Valley for serving orthopedically-handicapped children. Five grants totaling **$227,500** to School District of Philadelphia/Widener Memorial School for Handicapped Children (operating support, summer program, transportation/food costs, and student activities). **$100,000** to Cheyney U. (ADA-compliant elevator). **$95,000** to Moore College of Art & Design (ADA-related improvements). **$72,000** to Canine Partners for Life (canine training re disabled children). **$70,000** to Easter Seals (wheelchair-accessible bus). **$50,000** each to Melmark Home (cottage refurbishing) and Overbrook School for the Blind (handicapped-accessible renovations). **$34,425** to Plymouth Meeting Friends School (handicapped-accessible building/art studio). **$29,000** to Variety Club (Carousel House program for Widener Memorial School students). **$25,000** each to Elwyn, Inc. (handicapped-accessible renovations) and Kardon Institute of the Arts (programs for Widener Memorial School). **$22,320** to Pegasus Riding Academy (participant support). **$17250** to Woods Service Foundation (equipment/therapeutic treatments). **$10,000** to Hope Springs Equestrian Therapy (operating support). **$5,000** to Boy Scouts/Chester County Council (camp-health center construction). ■**PUBLICATIONS:** None ■**WEBSITE:** None ■**E-MAIL:** None ■**APPLICATION POLICIES & PROCEDURES:** Only Delaware Valley organizations (including nearby New Jersey and Delaware areas) which serve orthopedically-disabled children are eligible to apply; most giving is for special projects, building funds, capital improvements, equipment, seed money, or research. No grants are awarded for endowment, scholarships, matching grants, or to individuals. Prospective applicants initially should make a telephone inquiry about the feasibility of submitting a request. Grant requests may be submitted in a full proposal (with cover letter) in April or October (deadlines are April 15th and October 15th); describe the purpose of the proposed project and the intended beneficiaries, and include IRS tax-exempt status documentation. The Trustees normally award grants at May and November meetings.
O+D+T F. Eugene Dixon, Jr. (P+T+Con) — Peter M. Mattoon [Flourtown] (VP+T) — Edith Robb Dixon (S+F+T) — Bruce L. Castor [Philadelphia] (T) — Michael Clancy, M.D. [Philadelphia] (T)

SE-729 **Williams (C.K.) Foundation, The** MI-41-42-54-55
c/o Mellon Private Wealth Management
1735 Market Street, Room 193-0370 — **Phone** 215-553-1204 **FAX** 215-553-4542
Philadelphia 19103 (Philadelphia County) — **EIN** 23-6292772 **Year Created** 1963
AMV $17,669,254 **FYE** 12-00 (**Gifts Received** $0) 6 **Grants totaling** $546,100

About two-thirds Pa. giving. Two grants totaling **$341,484** to Lafayette College (mostly for Street Art project). **$200,000** to University Museum. **Out-of-state** grants: **$299,585** to St. George's School [RI]; **$10,000** to Dexter School [MA]; and **$1,100** to Fargo Methodist Church [GA]. — In prior years, most giving to the same grantees. ■**PUBLICATIONS:** None ■**WEBSITE:** None ■**E-MAIL:** None ■**APPLICATION POLICIES & PROCEDURES:** Grant requests in any form should be submitted in September (deadline is October 1st); grants are awarded at an October meeting.
O+D+T Kathleen M. Rock (VP at Bank+Con) — Joan Williams Rhame [CT] (P+S+D) — Josephine C. Williams [NJ] (VP+D) — Charles K. Williams [NJ] (D+Donor) Mellon Bank N.A. (Agent)

SE-730 **Williams Family Foundation, The** MI-14-22-63
646 Clovelly Lane — **Phone** 610-688-5253 **FAX** None
Devon 19333 (Chester County) — **EIN** 23-6978816 **Year Created** 1989
AMV $128,118 **FYE** 6-01 (**Gifts Received** $45,500) 10+ **Grants totaling** $23,743

About two-thirds local giving. High grant of **$10,273** to Devereux Foundation. **$4,500** to St. David's Church. **$500** to Episcopal Community Services. Other local contributions for various purposes. **Out-of-state** giving includes **$3,000** to 1794 Meetinghouse of New Salem [MA]; **$2,500** to Central Congregational Church [MA]; and **$1,200** to South Boston/Halifax County Hall of Fame Scholarship Fund [VA]. — Grants approved for future payment include **$7,000** to St. David's Church and **$5,000** to Devereux Foundation. ■**PUBLICATIONS:** None ■**WEBSITE:** None ■**E-MAIL:** None ■**APPLICATION POLICIES & PROCEDURES:** The Foundation reports that most giving is for capital drives or scholarships; multiple-year grants are awarded. Grant requests may be submitted in any form at any time. Site visits sometimes are made to organizations being considered for a grant.
O+D+T William L. Williams (T+Donor+Con) — Dorothy L. Williams (T+Donor)

SE-731 **Wind (Dina & Jerry) Foundation, The** MI-42-52-53-54-55
1041 Waverly Road — **Phone** 610-642-2120 **FAX** None
Gladwyne 19035 (Montgomery County) — **EIN** 23-2745202 **Year Created** 1993
AMV $1,288,363 **FYE** 12-00 (**Gifts Received** $800,888) 13 **Grants totaling** $23,500

Mostly local giving; all grants are for general purposes. High grant of **$7,000** to Fleisher Art Memorial. **$5,000** to Philadelphia Museum of Art. **$2,500** to U. of Pa. (Penn's Way Campaign). **$1,000-$1,500** each to Institute of Contemporary Art, Nexus Foundation, and Philadelphia Orchestra. Other local contributions **$500** for similar purposes. **Out-of-state** grant: **$2,500** to American Marketing Assn. Foundation [NY]. ■**PUBLICATIONS:** None ■**WEBSITE:** None ■**E-MAIL:** None ■**APPLICATION POLICIES & PROCEDURES:** Grant requests may be submitted in any form at any time. No grants are awarded to individuals.
O+D+T Yoram J. Wind, Ph.D. (T+Donor+Con) — Vardina Wind (T+Donor+Con)

SE-732 **Winokur Foundation, The**
    c/o Dechert, Price & Rhoads
    4000 Bell Atlantic Tower, 1717 Arch St.
    Philadelphia 19103   (Philadelphia County)
AMV $382,836   **FYE** 7-00   (**Gifts Received** $0)

MI-22-42-62

Phone 215-994-2505 **FAX** 215-994-2222
EIN 23-6856163   **Year Created** 1986
10 **Grants totaling** $8,415

About half local giving. High Pa. grant of **$2,885** to Temple Beth Hillel-Beth El. Other local contributions **$60** or smaller for various charities. **Out-of-state** giving includes **$4,500** to Brandeis U. [MA] and **$500** to Aspen Music Festival [CO]. ■ **PUBLICATIONS:** None ■ **WEBSITE:** None ■ **E-MAIL:** None ■ **APPLICATION POLICIES & PROCEDURES:** No grants are awarded to individuals.

O+D+T Barton J. Winokur, Esq. (T+Donor+Con) — Corporate donor: The Bibb Company [GA]

SE-733 **Wolf (Alfred L. & Constance) Aviation Fund**
    c/o Wolf, Block, Schorr & Solis-Cohen
    1650 Arch Street, 22nd Floor
    Philadelphia 19103   (Philadelphia County)
AMV $2,109,029   **FYE** 4-01   (**Gifts Received** $0)

MI-29-41-42-56-85

Phone 215-977-2387 **FAX** 215-977-2346
EIN 23-2494508   **Year Created** 1984
Grants totaling $108,000

Nationwide giving for projects which foster and promote general aviation and its value to society—grants reportedly range from **$500-$10,000;** details about representative projects are described on the website but specific grant sizes are not reported. Examples of grants awarded in recent years include the following: aviation safety research projects; lectures/presentations on aviation or historic aviators; museum and school curriculum units on the history of aviation and development of airplanes; Eagle Scout project to build an aviation-oriented playscape for children waiting for flights in an airline terminal; a resource publication on aviation scholarships; events honoring disaster-assistance pilots; a security manual for airport operators; a video highlighting the community service of volunteer pilot groups and their missions of service; a seed grant to help develop the National Center for Aircraft Technicians; supporting a team of university students developing a new open-source virtual reality flight simulation program; and assistance to a high school student to build her own airplane! ■ **PUBLICATIONS:** None ■ **WEBSITE:** www.wolf-aviation.org ■ **E-MAIL:** mail@wolf-aviation.org ■ **APPLICATION POLICIES & PROCEDURES:** All giving is limited to organizations and individuals who promote, advance, or support general aviation, or perform research/education in the field of aviation. The Fund encourages prospective applicants to visit the website and review the grants pages and/or discuss their proposal with William R. Murrow, Grants Administrator, Wolf Aviation Fund, 33 Holly Drive, Storrs, CT 06268; telephone 860-429-2972; e-mail: mail@wolf-aviation.org. See the website for detailed instructions on preparation of grant applications. Grant requests (4 pages maximum) may be submitted at any time in any form—preferably in an e-mail or on floppy diskette—or mailed in hardcopy to the CT or Philadelphia address.

O+D+T Leonard J. Cooper, Esq. (T+Con) — Albert E. Wolf (T) — William R. Murrow [CT] (Grants Administrator) — Donor: Estate of Constance Wolf

---

SE-734 **Wolf (Benjamin & Fredora K.) Memorial Foundation**
    Park Towne Place N-1205
    2200 Benjamin Franklin Parkway
    Philadelphia 19130   (Philadelphia County)
AMV $3,188,696   **FYE** 5-00   (**Gifts Received** $0)

MI-43

Phone 215-569-8321 **FAX** None
EIN 23-6207344   **Year Created** 1955
140+ **Grants totaling** $141,000

All grants are scholarships, usually **$1,000** each, for male and female Philadelphia-area students pursuing undergraduate studies. ■ **PUBLICATIONS:** None ■ **WEBSITE:** None ■ **E-MAIL:** None ■ **APPLICATION POLICIES & PROCEDURES:** The Foundation reports that Philadelphia-area students only are eligible to apply; selection criteria include scholastic record, financial need, extracurricular involvement, and ambition. Awards may be renewed annually until completing undergraduate studies, provided a satisfactory academic record is maintained. Prospective applicants should request from the Administrator a formal application form and information about the selection procedure; the application deadline is May 15th. The Trustees meet in June and December.

O+D+T Dr. David A. Horowitz (Administrator+Con) — Mary Wolf Hurtig (P+T) — Flora Barth Wolf (VP+T) — Jean Gray [Doylestown] (S+T) — John Tuton (F+T) — Richard L. Abrahams [Elkins Park] (T) — Virginia Wolf Briscoe (T) — PNC Advisors (Custodian)

SE-735 **Wolf (Howard A. & Martha R.) Fund**
    c/o Wolf, Block, Schorr & Solis-Cohen
    1650 Arch Street, 22nd Floor
    Philadelphia 19103   (Philadelphia County)
AMV $688,351   **FYE** 12-00   (**Gifts Received** $0)

MI-12-42-43-51

Phone 215-977-2106 **FAX** 215-405-3706
EIN 23-6207349   **Year Created** 1951
5 **Grants totaling** $32,500

About half local giving. High Pa. grant of **$12,500** to U. of the Arts (scholarship fund). **$3,000** to Pa. Ballet (general support). **$375** to Jewish Federation of Greater Philadelphia. **Out-of-state** grant: **$16,000** to George & Irene Walker Home for Children [MA] (family counseling center). ■ **PUBLICATIONS:** None ■ **WEBSITE:** None ■ **E-MAIL:** dglyn@wolfblock.com ■ **APPLICATION POLICIES & PROCEDURES:** Grant requests may be submitted in a letter at any time. No grants are awarded to/for endowment, capital campaigns, or individuals.

O+D+T David R. Glyn, Esq. (T+Con) — Pauline Wolf Frankel [MA] (T) — Albert E. Wolf (T) — Anne A. Wolf [MA] (T) — Stephanie G. Wolf (T)

SE-736 **Wolfe (Stanley R.) Foundation, The**
7303 Emlen Street
Philadelphia 19119 (Philadelphia County)

MI-11-22-41-62
Phone 215-248-1799 **FAX** None
EIN 23-2829995 **Year Created** 1995

AMV $494,727 **FYE** 12-00 (**Gifts Received** $47,525) 22 **Grants totaling** $95,443

Mostly local giving. High grant of **$68,720** to Germantown Jewish Center. **$5,000** to Perelman Jewish Day School. **$2,500** to Germantown Jewish Center (religious professional fund). **$2,200** to Gesu School. **$1,000** to Philadelphia Bar Foundation. **$500** to United Way of SE Pa. Other smaller local contributions. **Out-of-state** giving includes **$9,220** to Pardes Institute for Jewish Studies [NY] and **$5,000** to Yale Law School [CT]. ■**PUBLICATIONS:** None ■**WEBSITE:** None ■**E-MAIL:** None ■**APPLICATION POLICIES & PROCEDURES:** Grant requests may be submitted in a letter at any time.

O+D+T Stanley R. Wolfe, Esq. (P+Con)

SE-737 **Wolfson (Nancy & Richard) Charitable Foundation**
560 Leslie Lane, P.O. Box 685
Blue Bell 19422 (Montgomery County)

MI-12-15-22-31-32-41-62
Phone 215-563-6222 **FAX** None
EIN 23-7716735 **Year Created** 1992

AMV $1,350,794 **FYE** 6-00 (**Gifts Received** $1,594) 16 **Grants totaling** $162,204

Mostly local giving. High grant of **$72,000** to Federation Allied Jewish Appeal. **$56,654** to Children's Hospital of Philadelphia. **$10,000** to Germantown Academy. **$5,000** each to Congregation Beth Or and Twin Spring Farm Education Impressions. **$3,400** to Eagles Fly for Leukemia. **$2,900** to Philadelphia Geriatric Center. **$2,500** to Friends of the Children. **$1,000** each to From the Heart and Ronald McDonald House. Other smaller local contributions for various purposes. **Out-of-state** grant: **$1,000** to U.S. Holocaust Memorial Museum [DC]. ■**PUBLICATIONS:** None ■**WEBSITE:** None ■**E-MAIL:** None ■**APPLICATION POLICIES & PROCEDURES:** Information not available.

O+D+T Nancy Wolfson (T+Donor+Con) — Richard Wolfson (T+Donor)

SE-738 **Wood (Peter J.) Foundation**
55 Crosby Brown Road
Gladwyne 19035 (Montgomery County)

MI-11-14-22-31-32-34-62-72
Phone 610-649-3776 **FAX** None
EIN 23-2868525 **Year Created** 1996

AMV $409,595 **FYE** 10-00 (**Gifts Received** $0) 15 **Grants totaling** $97,100

Mostly local giving. High grant of **$55,000** to Jewish Federation of Greater Philadelphia. **$15,000** to United Way of SE Pa. **$10,000** to Philadelphia College of Osteopathic Medicine Foundation. **$5,000** to Children's Hospital of Philadelphia Foundation. **$2,000** to Francisville Home for Smaller Animals. **$1,400** to Wistar Institute. **$1,000** to Magee Rehab. Other smaller local contributions. **Out-of-state** grant: **$5,000** to Dana Farber Cancer Institute [MA]. ■**PUBLICATIONS:** None. ■**WEBSITE:** None ■**E-MAIL:** None ■**APPLICATION POLICIES & PROCEDURES:** No grants are awarded to individuals.

O+D+T Peter J. Wood (P+Donor+Con) — Michael H. Krekstein, Esq. [Philadelphia] (S)

SE-739 **Woodstock Foundation, The**
109 Jem Drive
Ambler 19002 (Montgomery County)

MI-42
Phone 215-628-3773 **FAX** None
EIN 23-2121983 **Year Created** 1982

AMV $35,258 **FYE** 11-00 (**Gifts Received** $0) 2 **Grants totaling** $22,000

Mostly Pa. giving. High grant of **$20,000** to Penn State U. **$2,000** to Mount Holyoke College [MA](memorial fund). ■**PUBLICATIONS:** None ■**WEBSITE:** None ■**E-MAIL:** None ■**APPLICATION POLICIES & PROCEDURES:** The Foundation reports that unsolicited applications are not accepted.

O+D+T Craig Stein (P+Donor+Con)

SE-740 **Woosnam Family Foundation**
c/o Innovest Group, Inc.
2000 Market Street, Suite 1400
Philadelphia 19103 (Philadelphia County)

MI-42-44-51-54-55-57-71-72
Phone 215-564-3960 **FAX** 215-569-3272
EIN 23-6870650 **Year Created** 1986

AMV $1,025,674 **FYE** 12-00 (**Gifts Received** $0) 48 **Grants totaling** $57,075

Mostly local giving. High grant of **$30,000** to Regional Performing Arts Center. **$4,500** to Franklin Institute. **$3,000** to Philadelphia Museum of Art. **$2,500** to Philadelphia Festival of the Arts. **$1,000** each to Dance Alliance, Fairmount Park Foundation, Free Library of Philadelphia, Philadelphia Zoo, and WHYY. Other local contributions **$45-$500,** mostly for arts/cultural organizations. **Out-of-state** giving includes **$4,900** to White Star Endowment [IN] and **$1,950** to Indiana U. Foundation. ■**PUBLICATIONS:** None ■**WEBSITE:** None ■**E-MAIL:** None ■**APPLICATION POLICIES & PROCEDURES:** Grant requests may be submitted in any form at any time. No grants are awarded to individuals. — Formerly called the Richard E. Woosnam Charitable Trust.

O+D+T Richard E. Woosnam (T+Donor+Con)

SE-741 **Worley (Richard B.) & Leslie A. Miller Charitable Trust**
1111 Barberry Road
Bryn Mawr 19010 (Montgomery County)

MI-42-51-52-56-71-72
Phone 610-525-3778 **FAX** None
EIN 23-7862650 **Year Created** 1996

AMV $5,111,239 **FYE** 12-00 (**Gifts Received** $0) 56 **Grants totaling** $213,380

About two-thirds local giving. High grant of **$70,000** to Pa. Ballet. **$60,000** to U. of Pa. (Challenge Trust). **$25,000** to Opera Company of Philadelphia. **$5,000** to The Nature Conservancy. **$2,000** to Academy of Music. **$1,300** to Pa. SPCA. **$1,000** each to Natural Lands Trust and Philadelphia Bar Foundation. Other local contributions **$100-$200** for various purposes. **Out-of-state** giving includes **$20,000** to Colonial Williamsburg [VA]; **$15,000** to Metropolitan Opera [NY]; and **$1,000** each to

PETA/People for Ethical Treatment of Animals [VA] and World Society for the Protection of Animals [MA]. ■**PUBLICATIONS:** None ■**WEBSITE:** None ■**E-MAIL:** None ■**APPLICATION POLICIES & PROCEDURES:** Grant requests may be submitted in a letter at any time; describe the nature of the charitable organization, and include descriptive literature about the organization and IRS tax-exempt status documentation. No grants are awarded to individuals.

O+D+T Richard B. Worley (T+Donor+Con) — Leslie A. Miller, Esq. (T+Con)

SE-742 Wright-Cook Foundation
c/o The Glenmede Trust Company
One Liberty Place, 1650 Market Street, Suite 1200
Philadelphia 19103 (Philadelphia County)

MI-15-32-41-42-56-71

Phone 215-419-6000 **FAX** 215-419-6196
EIN 23-6962132 **Year Created** 1990

AMV $1,832,013 **FYE** 12-00 **(Gifts Received** $0) 12 **Grants totaling** $84,000

About three-fourths local/Pa. giving. High grant of **$12,000** to Surrey Services for Seniors. **$10,000** each to The Quadrangle [Haverford], Riverbend Environmental Education Center, Schuylkill Center for Environmental Education, and Wright's Ferry Mansion [Lancaster County]. **$5,000** each to Academy of Notre Dame de Namur and Fox Chase Cancer Center. **$1,000** each to Episcopal Academy and Westtown School. **Out-of-state** giving includes **$7,500** each to Amherst College [MA] and Smith College [MA]. ■**PUBLICATIONS:** None ■**WEBSITE:** None ■**E-MAIL:** None ■**APPLICATION POLICIES & PROCEDURES:** Grant requests may be submitted in any form at any time.

O+D+T Diana S. Deane (VP at Trust Company+Con) — John W. Church [Villanova] (T) — Susanna Wright Cook (T+Donor) — The Glenmede Trust Company (Corporate Trustee)

SE-743 Wright-Hayre Foundation
3900 Ford Road, Apt. 9A
Philadelphia 19131 (Philadelphia County)

MI-13-16-33-41-43-52-84

Phone 215-878-6023 **FAX** None
EIN 23-2980038 **Year Created** 1998

AMV $609,773 **FYE** 12-00 **(Gifts Received** $276,158) 17 **Grants totaling** $31,500

All local giving. High grant of **$6,000** to People for People. **$5,000** to Philadelphia Youth Tennis Assn. **$4,000** each to Lil' Men of Philadelphia. **$3,500** to Fellowship of Christian Athletes. **$3,000** to The Martin Pollak Project. **$2,500** to Richard Allen Football Classic. **$2,000** to Wayne Smith Fund. **$1,000-$1,500** each to Bill Pickett Riding Academy, Eastern College (scholarship), John Phillip Ford Memorial Foundation, Lincoln U., and Shippensburg U. ■**PUBLICATIONS:** None ■**WEBSITE:** None ■**E-MAIL:** None ■**APPLICATION POLICIES & PROCEDURES:** The Foundation reports that most grants are for general support, special projects, and scholarships; multiyear grants are awarded. Grant requests may be submitted in a letter (2 pages maximum) at any time; include an organization budget and IRS tax-exempt status documentation. Site visits sometimes are made to organizations being considered for a grant.

O+D+T Sylvia Hayre (D+Con) — Coree Cuff (T) — Lee Harrison (T) — Luther Randolph (T) — Estate of Ruth Wright-Hayre (Donor)

SE-744 Wurster Family Foundation
c/o Wurster Group
940 Haverford Road, Suite 103
Bryn Mawr 19010 (Montgomery County)

MI-12-13-22-31-32-42-71-81-84

Phone 610-527-1900 **FAX** None
EIN 23-7880440 **Year Created** 1998

AMV $3,845,908 **FYE** 12-00 **(Gifts Received** $0) 9 **Grants totaling** $225,000

Mostly local giving; grants are for general operating expenses except as noted. High grant of **$65,000** to Foreign Policy Research Institute (special projects). **$50,000** each to Boy Scouts/Cradle of Liberty Council (capital improvements), Bryn Mawr Hospital (capital improvements). **$20,000** to Make-A-Wish Foundation. **$15,000** to Salvation Army. **$10,000** to The Children's Project 2000 [Norristown]. **$5,000** to Fox Chase Cancer Center. **Out-of-state** grants: **$5,000** each to Vermont Law School and Woodstock Ski Runners [VT]. — Grants approved for future payment: **$120,000** to Foreign Policy Research Institute (Merion Special Projects) and **$50,000** to Boy Scouts/Cradle of Liberty Council (capital improvement project). ■**PUBLICATIONS:** None. ■**WEBSITE:** None ■**E-MAIL:** None ■**APPLICATION POLICIES & PROCEDURES:** No grants are awarded to individuals.

O+D+T William H. Wurster (P+T+Donor+Con) — Janine Wurster Putnam (VP+T) — William Glendon Wurster (VP+T) — Jeanne D. Wurster (AS+T) — Donna Ellis (S) — Anthony Melvin (F)

SE-745 Wurts (Henrietta Tower) Memorial
c/o First Union/Wachovia
123 South Broad Street, PA1279
Philadelphia 19109 (Philadelphia County)

MI-12-13-14-15-16-17-18-19-20-22-24-25-29
35-41-49-52-55-84
Phone 215-670-4228 **FAX** 215-670-4236
EIN 23-6297977 **Year Created** 1934

AMV $6,688,623 **FYE** 12-00 **(Gifts Received** $0) 72 **Grants totaling** $329,600

All giving restricted to aiding needy/disadvantaged persons in Philadelphia; grants are for general support except as noted. High grant of **$18,500** to Christmas in April of Philadelphia. **$15,000** to Dignity Housing. **$10,000** to Philadelphia Urban Finance Corp. **$14,000** to MANNA/Metropolitan Neighborhood Nutrition Alliance. **$7,000** each to Center in the Park (Fulton School program), Common Bond Caregivers, HELP Philadelphia (assistance to needy families), Old Kensington Redevelopment Corp (healthy senior program), Little Brothers-Friends of the Elderly (holiday programs for isolated elderly), Philadelphia Children's Alliance (parent information sessions/children's group), Providence Center (after-school program), Recording for the Blind & Dyslexic (educational outreach), Street Clothes Project/Kids Closet, and Working Wardrobe. **$6,000** each to Endow-A-Home (youth consultant/group counselor), Philadelphia Physicians for Social Responsibility (Peaceful Posse). **$5,000** each to Dignity Housing (scholarship fund), Drueding Center/Project Rainbow (child care program), First United Church of Germantown (after-school program), Homeless Advocacy Project (children's educational outreach), Hospitality House of Philadelphia (elder offenders services project), Jubilee School, Little People's Music, Mt. Carmel Human Development Corp., North Light Community Center (Youth Encouragement Program), Philadelphia Society for Services to Children (Head Start Learning Tree), Sisters of St. Joseph Literacy Project (Dreamcatcher Literacy Project), Southwest Community Enrichment Center (senior center/home visitations), Taller Puertorriqueno (cultural awareness program), Urban Tree Connection (West Philadelphia beautification), Women Organized Against Rape (play therapy equipment), and Women's Community Revitalization Project. **$4,000-$4,500** each to Habitat for Humanity-West Philadelphia (staff position), International Ballet Exchange (audience development), Philadelphia Citizens for Children & Youth (Campaign for Kids), Philadelphia Wooden Boat Factory (marine education initiative), Voyage House (counseling program), and Youth Health Empowerment Project (access program). **$3,000-$3,600** each to 18th Street Community Development Corp. (Raising Others Children program), Astral Artistic Services (programs), Careline (volunteer recruitment), Need in Deed, NetworkArts (ecology-arts program), Northwest Victim Services (Living a Victim Free Life Program), St. Mary's Family Respite Center (outdoor play area), SOWN/Supportive Older Women's Network, TOVA (Yes! Theatre), Wheels, Inc., White-Williams Scholars (student stipends), and Women's Law Project (consumer education). **$2,000-$2,500** each to Ad-Hoc Committee for Logan (Youth Project), AIDS Law Project of Pa. (Family Project), Bethesda Project (community activities program), Brandywine Graphic Workshop (summer training program), CARIE/Center for Advocacy for the Rights & Interests of the Elderly, Center for Autistic Children (occupational therapy project), College Settlement of Philadelphia, Community Women's Education Project (Child Care Matters), Easter Seals (summer camp), Frankford Group Ministry (emergency assistance program), Kelly Anne Dolan Memorial Fund (family assistance), Logan Learning Club, Nelson Network Coalition, Northeast Community Center (aquatic equipment), Old First Reformed Church (summer program), Philadelphia Dance Alliance (neighborhood dance exchange program), Philadelphia Senior Center (financial management service), Potter's House Mission, and SCAN/Supportive Child/Adult Network (client fund). **$1,500** each to Big Sisters of Philadelphia (Project Self), Children's Country Week Assn. (summer camp scholarships), and Penn Home. ■**PUBLICATIONS:** Annual Report with statement of program policy and application guidelines ■**WEBSITE:** None ■**E-MAIL:** diane.stables@wachovia.com ■**APPLICATION POLICIES & PROCEDURES:** The Memorial reports that only organizations directly serving or improving the welfare of disadvantaged children/youth or the elderly living within the City of Philadelphia are eligible to apply. National, state and regional organizations are not considered except those with a significant and defined impact on Philadelphia. No grants are awarded to individuals, for religious or political purposes, nor to organizations with annual budgets exceeding $3 Million. Generally, no grants are made for capital expenditures or endowments, but applications for equipment, furnishings and limited renovations connected with specific programs will be considered. All grants are for one year and generally are $7,000 or smaller; the Memorial prefers to support specific programs/projects in which a modest grant can play a significant part and which have meaningful goals in relation to the total resources committed to them. Any organization which has received grants for three successive years must wait a year before reapplying. Prospective applicants initially should make a telephone inquiry about the feasibility of submitting a request. Submit one original and nine copies of the Bank's Common Grant Application Form, available from the Bank, together with one copy each of an audited financial statement including an annual report, balance sheet, and project budget; and IRS tax-exempt status documentation. Deadlines for requests are January 1st, May 1st, and September 30th. The Board meets in February, June and October to award grants; applicants are notified within two weeks after the meetings.

O+D+T Diane O. Stables (VP at Bank+S+Con) — S. Stoney Simons (P+D) — Alison Anderson, Ph.D. (F+D) — Ellen Hass (D) — Sarah Laughlin (D) — Althris W. Shirdan, Ph.D. (D) — Richard Ferree Smith (D) — Nan Wallace (D) First Union/Wachovia (Agent)

SE-746 **Wyncote Foundation**
    1001 City Ave., Apt. WB513
    Wynnewood 19096   (Montgomery County)

MI-12-14-20-22-32-51
Phone 610-642-5927 **FAX** None
EIN 65-0087209 **Year Created** 1990

AMV $181,611   **FYE** 12-00   **(Gifts Received** $0)   4 **Grants totaling** $15,000

No Pa. giving. **Out-of-state** grants; **$5,000** to The Seeing Eye [NJ] (memorial gift); **$4,000** to Hear Now [CO]; and **$3,000** each to Harid Conservatory/Dance Division [FL] and Insight for the Blind [FL] (memorial gift). — In the prior year, local grants included **$4,000** to Philadelphia Ronald McDonald House (Share-A-Night Program); **$3,000** to American Cancer Society; **$2,000** to Salvation Army/Norristown; and **$1,800** to Montgomery County Legal Aid Service. ■**PUBLICATIONS:** None ■ **WEBSITE:** None ■**E-MAIL:** None ■**APPLICATION POLICIES & PROCEDURES:** Grant requests may be submitted in writing at any time; describe the organization's objectives and purpose of the requested funding. No grants are awarded to individuals.

O+D+T Patricia Kofsky (T+Con) — Charles Kofsky (T) — M. Miller, Esq. [Norristown] (T)

SE-747 **Wyss Foundation, The**
    c/o Synthes USA
    1690 Russell Road, P.O. Box 1766
    Paoli 19301   (Chester County)

MI-13-15-17-18-22-29-44-57-71-72-73-84-89
Phone 610-647-9700, Ext. 7246 **FAX** None
EIN 23-1823874 **Year Created** 1990

AMV $46,340,891   **FYE** 12-00   **(Gifts Received** $0)   66 **Grants totaling** $2,225,732

Limited local giving. High local grants of **$10,000** each to Berwyn Fire Co., Planned Parenthood of SE Pa., Upper Main Line YMCA, and Women's Resource Center. **$6,000** to Daemion House. **$5,000** each to Salvation Army, Tredyffrin Public Library, Vesper Boat Club, and WHYY. **$3,000** each to Meals on Wheels of Coatesville and Philabundance. Other smaller local contributions. **Out-of-state** giving includes high grant of **$249,180** to Grand Canyon Trust [AZ]; **$185,000** to New Mexico Conservation Education Fund; **$152,500** to Earthjustice Legal Defense Fund [DC]; **$150,000** each to Americans for Our Heritage [DC] and Idaho Conservation League; **$100,000** each to Alaska Conservation Foundation and League of Conservation Voters DC]; **$79,500** to Colorado Environmental Coalition; **$78,000** to Wilderness Society [DC]; **$75,000** each to Sonoran Institute [AZ],

Rocky Mountain Youth Corps, and San Juan Citizens Alliance [DC]; **$50,000** each to Center for Biological Diversity [AZ], Friends of Nevada Wilderness, Mineral Policy Center [DC], Nevada Wilderness Project; and other grants **$1,000-$40,000** for environmental organizations, food banks, public broadcasting, and other purposes. ■**PUBLICATIONS:** None ■**WEBSITE:** None ■**E-MAIL:** None ■**APPLICATION POLICIES & PROCEDURES:** Grant requests from Philadelphia-area organizations may be submitted in a letter at any time. However, the major support focuses on the Western U.S., specifically on grassroots organizations working to protect open spaces on public and private lands from the Rocky Mountains to the West Coast, and Alaska. Prospective applicants in the Western states initially must discuss project ideas with the New Mexico-based Executive Director (505-466-4616) before submitting any formal proposal.

O+D+T Joseph M. Fisher (S+Con for Philadelphia area) — Hansjoerg Wyss (C+Donor) — Geoff Webb [NM] (Executive Director+Con for Western States)

SE-748   Wyss (Hansjoerg) AO Medical Foundation   MI-31-32-34
c/o Synthes USA
1690 Russell Road, P.O. Box 1766   **Phone** 610-647-9700 **FAX** None
Paoli   19301   (Chester County)   **EIN** 23-3012622   **Year Created** 1999
AMV $29,078,518   **FYE** 12-00   (**Gifts Received** $0)   6 **Grants totaling** $4,132,010

One local grant: **$1,000** to Paoli Memorial Hospital. **Out-of-state** grants: **$2,000,000** each to Johns Hopkins U. [MD] and U. of Mississippi Foundation; **$85,000** to Biomedical Research of Southern Arizona; **$40,000** to Brown U. [RI]; and **$6,010** to Orthopaedics Overseas [NY]. ■**PUBLICATIONS:** None ■**WEBSITE:** None ■**E-MAIL:** None ■**APPLICATION POLICIES & PROCEDURES:** The Foundation reports that primary giving is for education and research in orthopaedics.

O+D+T Hansjoerg Wyss (C+Donor+Con) — Joseph M. Fisher (S)

SE-749   Zeelander Foundation, The   MI-22-31-42-62-82
230 Mathers Lane   **Phone** 215-643-7197 **FAX** None
Ambler   19002   (Montgomery County)   **EIN** 23-2866230   **Year Created** 1996
AMV $946,658   **FYE** 12-00   (**Gifts Received** $0)   23 **Grants totaling** $59,506

Mostly local giving; grants are for annual/general support except as noted. High grant of **$26,889** to Tiferet Bet Israel. **$15,000** to Greater Philadelphia Rabbinical Assembly (day school fund). **$2,000** to Federation Allied Jewish Appeal. **$1,000** each to Anti-Defamation League, Federation Housing, Inc., Jefferson Center of Integrative Medicine, and U. of Pa. Other local giving **$54-$250** for various purposes. **Out-of-state** grant: **$10,000** to This Land is Mine/Olim Fund [Israel] (educational purposes). ■**PUBLICATIONS:** None ■**WEBSITE:** None ■**E-MAIL:** None ■**APPLICATION POLICIES & PROCEDURES:** Grant requests may be submitted in a letter before September 30th deadline; describe the proposed project and state the funding requested; include the current year's organizational budget and/or project budget and copies of the last five years of Form 990s.

O+D+T Norbert J. Zeelander (VP+Donor+Con) — Susan Zeelander (P+Donor) — Elliot Zeelander (VP) — Jeffrey Zeelander, Esq. (VP) — Julie Zeelander (VP)

SE-750   Zeldin Family Foundation   MI-12-22-32-41-42-43-51-52-53-54-55-56
c/o Martex Fiber Corporation   57-62
325-341 Chestnut Street, Suite 1320   **Phone** 215-928-1767 **FAX** 215-928-0195
Philadelphia   19106   (Philadelphia County)   **EIN** 23-6861835   **Year Created** 1987
AMV $2,746,778   **FYE** 11-00   (**Gifts Received** $0)   85 **Grants totaling** $137,680

About three-fourths local giving. High grant of **$20,000** each to Federation Allied Jewish Appeal and Philadelphia U. **$19,000** to Friends Central School. **$7,000** to The Clay Studio. **$3,000** to Philadelphia Museum of Art. **$2,000-$2,500** each to Bread Upon the Waters Scholarship Fund, National Museum of American Jewish History, Philadelphia Futures, Philadelphia Orchestra, and William Sigal Memorial Scholarship Fund [Easton]. **$1,000** each to Catholic Charities, Educating Children for Parenting, Golden Slipper Club, Lupus Foundation of Philadelphia, Third Path Institute, WHYY, and The Wilma Theatre. Other local contributions **$100-$500** for various community organizations and charities. **Out-of-state** giving includes **$10,630** to Harlem RBI [NY]; **$5,000** to National Kidney Foundation of NY; **$4,500** to Temple Rodeph Shalom [VA]; and other smaller grants/contributions to MA, NY, DE, DC, MD, VA, GA, LA, TN, IL, MO, CA, and Mexico. ■**PUBLICATIONS:** None ■**WEBSITE:** None ■**E-MAIL:** None ■**APPLICATION POLICIES & PROCEDURES:** The Foundation reports that most grants are for annual/capital campaigns, general support, program/curriculum development, internship/scholarship/fellowship funds, and matching/challenge support. Grant requests may be submitted in a letter before the September 30th deadline; include an annual report, organizational/project budgets, Board member list, list of major funding sources, audited financial statement, and IRS tax-exempt status documentation. The Board meets in May and November, and grants announced in December.

O+D+T Claudia Zeldin (T+Con) — Martin J. Zeldin (T+Donor) — Jessica Zeldin (T) — Stephanie Zeldin (T) — Sybille Zeldin (T) — Corporate donor: Martex Fiber Corp.

Southeastern Region / SE
Non-profiled Foundations

*SE Region foundations which did **not** meet the criteria for profiling are listed here; the letter code in parentheses after the foundation name indicates its status, per the following key:*

L   **Limited Assets/Giving**: The market value of assets was $250,000 or under and the total of grants awarded was less than $12,500 in the last year of record. If information about grants is available, up to three Major Interest (MI) Codes are listed; if no information on giving interests is available, the notation "N/R" (Not Reported) is shown.

O   **Operating Foundation**: This special designation by IRS is for a foundation that operates its own program or institution and, generally, does not award grants to other organizations.

R   **Restricted Trust/Foundation**: Grants are awarded only to designated organizations or beneficiaries, typically under the terms of a Will or Trust Instrument.

I   **Inactive**: The assets, generally, are nominal (typically under $5,000) and there has been little or no grants activity within the last year or more.

NP   **Non-Pennsylvania Foundation**: The foundation's connection to Pennsylvania is only incidental; typically these are trusts or foundations managed by a bank trust department or a lawyer located in Pennsylvania, but there are no Pennsylvania-based trustees/directors and no grants are awarded to Pennsylvania.

T   **Terminated**: A final IRS Form 990-PF has been filed, or the foundation has provided notice of intended liquidation/termination.

U   **Undetermined Status**: There is no record of Form 990-PFs being filed for the last three or more years and no other evidence of grant-making activity. In many cases the foundation may have terminated without giving formal notice or has been reclassified by IRS as a "public charity."

1957 Charity Trust, The
(New Name: 1957 Charity Foundation)

1st District Adopt-A-Rec Center (I) MI-
532 Fitzwater Street, Philadelphia 19142

Abrams (Howard & Terri) Foundation (R
c/o Finkel, 12002 Panrail Place, Philadelphia 19116

Abramson (Joseph & Lena) Foundation (U)

Abramson (Madlyn & Leonard) Charitable Foundation
(Formerly of Blue Bell; now located in FL)

Acheson (Stuart) Foundation (NP)
c/o PNC Bank N.A., Philadelphia 19103

Ackerman (A. Bernard) Foundation (U)

Adams (May Wilson) Charitable Foundation (R) MI-64
c/o Mellon Bank N.A., Philadelphia 19101

Affordable Housing Opportunities, Inc. (R)
P.O. Box 107, Chester 19016

Aged Women's Home of Montgomery County (R)
c/o PNC Bank N.A., Philadelphia 19103

Allabach (Earl & Mildred) Trust (R)
c/o Mellon Bank N.A., Philadelphia 19101

Allen (Viola) Trust (NP)
c/o PNC Bank N.A., Philadelphia 19103

Allen Family Foundation (NP)

Alper Foundation, The
(Formerly of Pipersville, now located in NY)

AMDT-Stardancers, Inc. (R)
c/o George Stevenson, 108 North Main Street, Yardley 19067

American Federation of Investors & Consumers (R)
c/o Chimicles, 361 West Lancaster Ave., Haverford 19041

American Legion Scholarship Fund (R)
c/o Downingtown Area Senior High School, Downingtown 19335

American Lorinae Conservancy (U)

Ames (Harriett) Charitable Trust
(Formerly of St. Davids, now located in NY)

Andalusia Foundation (O)
P.O. Box 158, Andalusia 19020

Anderson (E. Clive) Foundation, The (I)
8012 Seminole Ave., Philadelphia 19118

Anderson (Mary) Trust, The
(Refer to Pew Charitable Trusts, The)

Andrews (Leonard E.B.) Foundation (R)
4649 West Chester Pike, Newtown Square 19073

Angelo Bros. Co. Founders Scholarship Fdn. (R)
12401 McNulty Road, Philadelphia 19154

Anti-Trust Institute (U)

Antibiotic Research Institute (O)
720 Benjamin Fox Pavilion, Jenkintown 19046

Applebaum Family Foundation, The (L) MI-22-62
8714 Autumn Road, Philadelphia 19115

Applegarth Foundation (T)

Apter (Carl & Beth) Foundation, The
(New name: The Teoc Foundation)

Aronimink Home & School Assn. (R)
Bond Ave. & Burmont Road, Drexel Hill 19026

Asplundh (Christopher B.) Foundation, The (L) MI-99
3700 Buck Road, Huntingdon Valley 19006

Assn. of Pharmaceutical Technologists (R)
c/o J. Zimmerman, Merck & Co., P.O. Box 4, West Point 19486

Associated Production Services, Inc. (R)
325 Andrews Road, Trevose 19047

Associated Services for the Blind, Trust for (R)
1500 East Lancaster Ave., Suite 202, Paoli 19301

Athletes for Affordable Housing (R)
c/o Dandridge, 1735 Market Street, 38th Floor, Philadelphia 19103

Athletic Trauma Research Foundation, The (O)
c/o Isdaner & Co., 100 Presidential Blvd.,, Bala Cynwyd 19004

Atkins (Edward) #4 Trust (R)
c/o PNC Bank N.A., Philadelphia 19103

Atwell (Louise S.) Memorial Music Scholarship Trust (L) MI-43-52
3141 Pelham Place, Doylestown 18901

Auerbach (Isaac & Carol) Family Foundation (M)
(Now located in New York City)

Auerbach Foundation (L) MI-32
c/o N. Auerbach, 210 West Rittenhouse Square, Philadelphia 19103

Aurora Institute, The (R)
436 Williamson Road, Gladwyne 19035

Ayer (N.W.) Foundation (R)
c/o Garber, 1401 Walnut Street, Philadelphia 19102

Bachove Family Fund (L) MI-22-62
c/o Hartman, 123 S. Broad Street, 25th Floor, Philadelphia 19109

Bacon (Elizabeth M.) Trust (NP)
c/o PNC Bank N.A., Philadelphia 19103

Bader (David & Michelle) 1993 Charitable Trust (I)
165 Geigel Hill Road, Erwinna 18920

Baer (Jay R.) Fund (L) MI-62
1650 Arch Street, 22nd Floor, Philadelphia 19103

Bailey (Crawford & Mary) Trust/Greenwood School District (R)
c/o Mellon Bank N.A., Philadelphia 19101

Bailey (Mary H.) Trust #1/Greenwood School District.. (R)
c/o Mellon Bank N.A., Philadelphia 19101

Baird (Edith L.) Trust (R)
c/o First Union/Wachovia, Philadelphia 19109

Baird Foundation (U)

Baird Memorial Trust (R)
c/o First Union/Wachovia, Philadelphia 19109

Baker (Charles J.) Trust (R)
c/o Mellon Bank N.A., Philadelphia 19101

Ball (Russell C.) Foundation.
(New name: Ball Family Foundation)

Bank (David & Celia) Foundation (U)

Bank (Francine & Richard) Foundation (L) MI-22-62
1247 Dundee Drive, Dresher 19025

Baratta (Anthony P.) Foundation (L) MI-N/R
2661 Huntingdon Pike, Huntingdon Valley 19006

Barbieri (Andrea Mills) Foundation (L) MI-41-42-99
501 West Mermaid Lane, Philadelphia 19118

Barclay (Marie M.) Educational Endowment (R)
c/o PNC Bank N.A., Philadelphia 19103

Barclay (Marie M.) Hospital Endowment (R)
c/o PNC Bank N.A., Philadelphia 19103

Barnes (Anna J.) Trust (R)
c/o Mellon Bank N.A., Philadelphia 19101

Barnes (Reba F.) Memorial Foundation (R)
c/o PNC Bank N.A., Philadelphia 19103

Bartash Foundation (I) MI-N/R
1919 Chestnut Street, #2224, Philadelphia 19103

Bartenslager (Clarence) Trust (R) MI-22-63
c/o Mellon Bank N.A., Philadelphia 19101

Barthold (Kathryn H.) Trust (R)
c/o First Union/Wachovia, Philadelphia 19109

Bartschi Foundation
(New name: Swiss Pines)

Batroff (Warren C.) #7 Residuary Trust (R)
c/o PNC Bank N.A., Philadelphia 19103

Baumeister Reichard Trust Fund (R)
c/o PNC Bank N.A., Philadelphia 19103

Baxter Foundation, The
(Formerly of Radnor, now located in CT)

Beck (Bright W. & Lucille) Scholarship Fund (R)
c/o First Union/Wachovia, Philadelphia 19101

Beck (Bright W. & Lucille) Trust (R)
c/o First Union/Wachovia, Philadelphia 19101

Beck (Bright W.) Trust for St. Barnabas (R)
c/o First Union/Wachovia, Philadelphia 19101

Beech Corporation/Interplex (O)
1510 Cecil B. Moore Ave., Suite 300, Philadelphia 19121

Beers/Urice Charitable Trust (U)

Beideman (Dr. & Mrs. Joseph) Trust (R)
c/o PNC Bank N.A., Philadelphia 19103

Beifield (Elaine & Bernard P.) Family Foundation (NP)
c/o Blank, Rome, Comiskey & McCauley, Philadelphia 19103

Bel Canto Lyric Opera Company (R)
P.O. Box 341, Lafayette Hill 19444

Bellows (Adelaide Cole) Scholarship Fund (R)
c/o First National Bank of West Chester, West Chester 19380

Berenato (Anthony F. & Dena M.) Charitable Trust (I)
P.O. Box 178, Springfield 19064

Berger Family Foundation (L) MI-22-54-62
c/o Berger & Co., 2701 East Luzerne Street, Philadelphia 19137

Berky Benvolent Foundation Trust, The (L) MI-22-42-99
c/o Dechert, Price & Rhoads, 1717 Arch Street, #4000, Philadelphia 19103

Berman (Kermit & Annette) Charitable Foundation (L) MI-41
421 North 7th Street, Suite 700, Philadelphia 19123

Berman (Sol & Naomi) Charitable Foundation (L) MI-22-62
1036 Wilson Street, Pottstown 19464

Bernstein (Frank) Memorial Scholarship Fund (R)
1508 Sweetbrier Road, Gladwyne 19035

Berwind (Charles G.) Foundation (R)
3000 Center Square, West Tower, Philadelphia 19102

Besson Foundation, The (L)
c/o Ledwith, 3000 Two Logan Square, Philadelphia 19103

BetzDearborn Foundation, The (T)

Bignell (Lynn Tendler) Foundation (T)

BillIrene Fund (T)

Bilyeu (William H.) Trust (R)
c/o Mellon Bank N.A., Philadelphia 19101

Binenstock (Philip) Foundation (U)

Binnion Foundation, The (NP)
c/o Halbert, Katz & Co., 121 South Broad Street, Philadelphia 19107

Black (Max & Bella) Foundation (NP)
c/o Allia & Associates, 3257 Disston Street, Philadelphia 19149

Blades (Charles G.) Trust (R)
c/o Mellon Bank N.A., Philadelphia 19101

Blair (Joseph W. & Helene E.) Fund (R)
c/o First Union/Wachovia, Philadelphia 19103

Blair (William D.) Charitable Foundation (NP)
c/o Pepper, Hamilton & Scheetz, 1235 Westlakes Drive, Berwyn 19312

Blank (Ruth & Samuel) Foundation (L) MI-22-62
c/o J. Blank & Associates, 300 Jenkintown Commons, Jenkintown 19046

Blank (Samuel A.) Scholarship Foundation (R)
c/o J. Blank & Associates, 300 Jenkintown Commons, Jenkintown 19046

Blazakis (Chris) Foundation, The (L) MI-42-63
650 Palmer Lane, Yardley 19067

Blewitt (John F.) Trust (R)
c/o PNC Bank N.A., Philadelphia 19103

Block (Alice) Foundation (T)

Block (B.E.) #4 Memorial Children's Fund (R)
c/o PNC Bank N.A., Philadelphia 19103

Bloom Staloff Foundation (L) MI-29
c/o Bloom, 2000 Market Street, 18th Floor, Philadelphia 19103

Bloomer (Asahel P.H.) & Caroline D. Bloomer Charitable Trust
(New name: Caroline D. Bloomer Charitable Trust)

Bluestone Trust, The (NP)
127 West Chestnut Hill Ave., Philadelphia 19118

Bobb (C.) Trust for Nason Hospital (R)
c/o Mellon Bank N.A., Philadelphia 19101

Bogle (John C. & Eve S.) Foundation
(New name: Armstrong Foundation)

Bohen Foundation, The
(Formerly of Chester Springs; now located in CO)

Boni's Angel Foundation (L) MI-22-63
6013 Split Log Drive, Pipersville 18947

Bonner (Monsignor John J.) Foundation (R)
c/o Roman Catholic High School Alumni Assn., Philadelphia 19107

Bonsall Village, Inc. (R)
1110 Serrill Ave., Yeadon 19050

Borgel (Charles F.) for Charities (R)
c/o Mellon Bank N.A., Philadelphia 19101

Boyd (Stephanie J.) Charitable Trust (R)
c/o Mellon Bank N.A., Philadelphia 19101

Boyer First Troop, Phila. City Cavalry Memorial Fund (R)
c/o Mellon Bank N.A., Philadelphia 19101

Bragar (Norman H.) Fund (NP)
c/o PNC Bank N.A., Philadelphia 19103

Bridge Foundation, The (R)
52 East Georgianna Drive, Richboro 18954

Bringing the Outside World Inside Foundation (I)
755 Bryn Mawr Ave., Bryn Mawr 19010

Brodie (Jacob) Foundation, The (T)

Brodsky (Samuel B.) Foundation, The (L) MI-22-62
6812 Verbena Ave., Philadelphia 19126

Bryan (Kirke) Trust (R)
c/o PNC Bank N.A., Philadelphia 19103

Buck (Helen R.) Foundation (NP)
c/o The Glenmede Trust Company, Philadelphia 19103

Buck (Pearl S.) Foundation (R)
520 Dublin Road, Hilltown 18927

Bucks-Montgomery Home Builders Charitable Fdn. (O)
275 Commerce Drive, Suite 325, Fort Washington 19034

Bureau of Municipal Research of Philadelphia (U)

Burgess (C.H.) Charitable Trust (R)
c/o Mellon Bank N.A., Philadelphia 19103

Bushkill Reformed Church Trust (R)
c/o First Union/Wachovia, Philadelphia 19109

Bushman Fund, The (R)
c/o Mellon Bank N.A., Philadelphia 19101

Butcher (Margaret) Foundation (I)
c/o PNC Bank N.A., Philadelphia 19103

Byer (Hope Lubin) Foundation (NP)
c/o Isadaner & Co., 3 Bala Plaza, #501W, Bala Cynwyd 19004

Cafaro (William M. & A.) Family Foundation (U)

Callahan McKenna Educational Foundation (L) MI-43
31 South Eagle Road, Suite 202, Havertown 19083

Calvert (Stephen G.) Memorial Merit Fund (R)
c/o Keystone Foods, 401 City Ave., Suite 800, Bala Cynwyd 19004

Camden Trust Foundation (T)

Campbell (Judy & Frank) Foundation (L) MI-99
1045 Sentry Lane, Gladwyne 19035

Campers Bible Ministries (O)
P.O. Box 731, Souderton 18964

Cannon (John) Charitable Foundation (NP)
c/o Glenmede Trust Company, Philadelphia 19103

Capuzzi (Domenico) Foundation (R)
c/o Mellon Bank N.A., Philadelphia 19101

Carley (Joseph L. Foundation (NP)
c/o Yamaguchi, 910 Twyckenham Road, Media 19063

Carnell (Althea J.) Residuary Trust (R) MI-10,614
c/o PNC Advisors, 1600 Market Street, 7th Floor, Philadelphia 19103

Carter (Charles Wentz) Memorial Foundation
(New name: Carter Memorial Foundation)

Casper (Howard M. & Nancy R.) Foundation (T)

Catt Family Foundation
(Formerly of Newtown Square; now located in FL)

Center for Sexuality & Religion (O)
12 Driftwood Road, Audubon 19403

Center Foundation, The (O)
c/o Susan K. Garrison, 339 West State Street, Media 19063

Central Perkiomen Opportunity Committee (R)
524 Main Street, Schwenksville 19473

CertainTeed Corp. Foundation
(New name: Saint-Gobain Corporation Foundation)

Championship Sports, Inc. (R)
25 East Parkway Ave., Chester 19013

Chanticleer Charitable Trust, The (R)
c/o First Union/Wachovia, Philadelphia 19109

Chanticleer Foundation, The (O)
786 Church Road, Wayne 19087

Chase (Ella B.) Memorial Fund (NP)
c/o PNC Bank N.A., Philadelphia 19103

Chauveau (Jeanne) Trust (R)
c/o First Union/Wachovia, Philadelphia 19109

Chelonia Institute (O)
123 South Broad Street, Philadelphia 19109

Cherry Foundation, The (L) MI-17-42-43
P.O. Box 408, Wynnewood 19096

Chester Education Foundation (R)
2201 Providence Ave., Chester 19013

Chester Towers Resident Management Tenant Council (R)
1001 Ave. of the States, Apt. 1204, Chester 19013

Childrens Hospital of Philadelphia, Trust for (R)
1500 East Lancaster Ave., Suite 202, Paoli 19301

Christman (Dewald & Mary Ann) Memorial Fund (R)
c/o Mellon Bank N.A., Philadelphia 19101

Christman (Edward) Trust (R)
c/o First Union/Wachovia, Philadelphia 19109

Ciarco Family Foundation, The (NP)
c/o Glenmede Trust Company, Philadelphia 19103

Clamer (Guilliam H.) Foundation, The (R)
c/o First Union/Wachovia, Philadelphia 19109

Clareth Fund: Philadelphia Assn. of Zeta Psi (R)
c/o Duane Morris & Heckscher, One Liberty Place, Philadelphia 19103

Clark (Horace N.) Educational Fund (R)
c/o PNC Bank N.A., Philadelphia 19103

Clarke-Aff-League Memorial Fund (R)
c/o Mellon Bank N.A., Philadelphia 19101

Clayton Foundation, The (L) MI-21-99
1631 Stony Road, Hartsville 18974

Clendenen (B.) for Clinton County Community Fdn. (R)
c/o First Union/Wachovia, Philadelphia 19109

Clevenger (Kate) Trust for Fountain Fund (R)
c/o Mellon Bank N.A., Philadelphia 19101

Clune (V.) Trust for ACS & AHA (R)
c/o Mellon Bank N.A., Philadelphia 19101

Cocca Family Foundation (U)

Cochran (Josephine) Trust for Chester Poor (T)

Cole (Lloyd) Memorial Fund (L) MI-43
c/o First Union/Wachovia, Philadelphia 19109

Colker Family Foundation (NP)
c/o Grodinsky, 1 South Penn Square, Mezzanine, Philadelphia 19107

Collier (Earl & Catherine) Memorial Fund (R)
c/o First Union/Wachovia, Philadelphia 19101

Colonial Flying Corps Museum, Inc. (O)
P.O. Box 484, Toughkenamon 19374

Columbus Quincentennial Foundation (R)
c/o Sileo, 8D West Brookhaven Road, Brookhaven 19015

Coming Together to Help Promotions (R)
384 Upsal Street, Suite 1B, Philadelphia 19119

Community Services Systems, Inc. (R)
954 Montgomery Ave., Suite 6, Narberth 19072

Comstock Foundation, The (T)

Concord Foundation, The (R)
c/o Berman, 18 Willits Way, Glen Mills 19342

Conill Institute for Chronic Illness (O)
655 Marsten Green Court, Ambler 19002

Connelly (John F.) Scholarship Fund (R)
c/o Crown Cork & Seal Company, Philadelphia 19136

Conwell (H. Ernest) Trust for Masonic Home (NP)
c/o Mellon Bank N.A., Philadelphia 19101

Cook (Dorothy) Fund (NP)
c/o PNC Bank N.A., Philadelphia 19103

Cook (Harry) Foundation, The (U)

Cooke-Kitchen (R.) Corporation (R)
4845 Pulaski Ave., Philadelphia 19144

Corson (Nancy I.) Foundation (I)
4006 Butler Pike, P.O. Box 156, Plymouth Meeting 19462

Council on Compulsive Gambling of Pa. (R)
c/o Salvatore, 1002 Longspur Road, Audubon 19403

Cozen (Samuel D.) Memorial Fund (U)

Craig Foundation, The (I)
P.O. Box 817, Spring House 19477

Craig-Dalsimer Foundation (R)
c/o Kaufman, Packard Building, 12th Floor, Philadelphia 19102

Cramer (Louise A.) Foundation (L) MI-53
220 Locust Street, Apt. 298, Philadelphia 19106

Cranaleith Foundation, Inc. (NP)
c/o Vidgerman, 2000 One Logan Square, Philadelphia 19103

Cranaleith Spiritual Center (O)
13475 Proctor Road, Philadelphia 19116

Crane (Doris I.) Charitable Trust (R)
c/o Mellon Bank N.A., Philadelphia 19101

Crawford Memorial Trust (R)
616 DeKalb Street, Norristown 19401

Croll (Mary A.) Educational Trust (L) MI-43
c/o First Union/Wachovia, Philadelphia 19109

Crozer (Robert H.) Trust #2 (R)
c/o First Union/Wachovia, Philadelphia 19109

Crozer (Robert) Trust for Upland Poor (R)
c/o First Union/Wachovia, Philadelphia 19109

Crozer (Sallie) Trust for Upland Poor (R)
c/o First Union/Wachovia, Philadelphia 19109

Culbertson Family Charitable Foundation, The (NP)
c/o Glenmede Trust Company, Philadelphia 19103

Cunningham (Irene D.) Trust (R)
c/o First Union/Wachovia, Philadelphia 19109

Curry Foundation, The (L) MI-61
1055 West Strasburg Road, West Chester 19382

Cutler Foundation, The (T)

CYJO Foundation, The
(Formerly of West Chester, now located in FL)

d'Aquili (Eugene) Fdn. for Spirituality & MH Research (I)
1004 Bottom Lane, West Chester 19382

Damico (Sam) Foundation (L) MI-99
31 Adrian Road, Glen Mills 19342

Davidson (James B.) Foundation (T)

Davis (Dorothy) Church Fund (NP)
c/o PNC Bank N.A., Philadelphia 19103

Davis (Dorothy) Scholarship Fund (NP)
c/o PNC Bank N.A., Philadelphia 19103

Davis (Hilda & Preston) Foundation, The (NP)
c/o Iskrant, 1600 Market Street, #3600, Philadelphia 19103

Davis (Mildred R.) Charitable Foundation (NP)
c/o PNC Bank N.A., Philadelphia 19103

Deaver (Delema G.) Fund (R)
c/o First Union/Wachovia, Philadelphia 19109

Deaver (Elmer R.) Fund (R)
c/o First Union/Wachovia, Philadelphia 19109

Decker (Charlotte M.) Trust (R)
c/o PNC Bank N.A., Philadelphia 19103

Deckter (Albert E.) Foundation (L) MI-22-29-62
57 Roberts Road, Newtown Square 19073

Decrano (Mary G.) Trust (R)
c/o Mellon Bank N.A., Philadelphia 19101

DeForest (Willard P.) Trust for U. of PA (R)
c/o Mellon Bank N.A., Philadelphia 19101

Delaware Valley Christian Conciliation Service (R)
212 Cricket Ave., Ardmore 19003

Delaware Valley Rainforest Action Group (R)
P.O. Box 134, Newtown Square 19073

Delfiner (Max) Memorial Foundation (NP)
c/o Greene Tweed & Company, P.O. Box 305, Kulpsville 19443

Delmont Research Foundation Trust (R)
P.O. Box 269, Swarthmore 19081

DeMoss (Arthur S.) Foundation
(Formerly of St. Davids; now located in FL)

Deneberg Charitable Trust (L) MI-25-81
616 Addison Street, Philadelphia 19147

Deo Foundation (L) MI-65
c/o D.T. Peer Co., 9701 Bustleton Ave., Philadelphia 19115

DePorres (Martin) Foundation, The (R)
502 South 12th Street, Philadelphia 19147

DeTrampe (Countess) Home for Unwanted Dogs (R)
801 East Lancaster Ave., Villanova 19085

Dicerbo Foundation, The (NP)
c/o The Pennsylvania Trust Company, Radnor 19087

Dickson (Kenneth H.) Charitable Trust (NP)
c/o PNC Bank N.A., Philadelphia 19103

Dietrich American Foundation, The (O)
1311 Art School Road, Chester Springs 19425

Dillman (Julia A.) Fund (NP)
c/o PNC Bank N.A., Philadelphia 19103

DiMarco Family Foundation, The (L) MI-18-63-99
63 Yale Drive, Richboro 18954

DiMiglio (George) Football Scholarship (R)
1311 Jacksonville Road, Ivyland 18974

Diocese of Pennsylvania, Trust for the (R)
c/o Newlin, P.O. Box 357, Paoli 19401

Dobransky (Joseph W.) Foundation (NP)
c/o Iskrant, 1600 Market Street, Suite 3600, Philadelphia 19103

Dogole (Irving M.) Foundation (U)

Donglomur Foundation (O)
220 Trianon Lane, Villanova 19085

Dotson (John), M.D. Fund (NP)
c/o PNC Bank N.A., Philadelphia 19103

Douglas (Dr. Albert & Felice) Memorial Research Foundation (L) MI-15-32-51
2122 Delancey Street, Philadelphia 19103

Douglas (Joyce & Bryce) Foundation (L) MI-42-99
P.O. Box 672, Kimberton 19442

Downingtown Band Parents Scholarship Trust (R)
c/o Downingtown National Bank, Downingtown 19335

Dubrow Foundation (U)

Dunleavy (Albina H. & Francis J.) Corp. (O)
553 Beale Road, Blue Bell 19422

Dunning (Elizabeth Roe) Club (L) MI-14-23
P.O. Box 54016, Philadelphia 19105

Duportail House, Inc. (O)
297 Adams Drive, Wayne 19087

Easby (George Gordon Meade) Foundation (U)

Eastern Scientific & Educational Foundation (R)
c/o First Union/Wachovia, Philadelphia 19109

Eberhard Foundation
(formerly of Malvern; now located in FL)

Eckel (Fred J. & Florence J.) Memorial Foundation (L)
MI-22-63
2209 Mt. Carmel Avenue, Glenside 19038

Eckstein (William) Nurses Relief Fund (L) MI-23
c/o First Union/Wachovia, Philadelphia 19109

ECOG Research & Education Foundation (R)
1025 Walnut Street, 1014 College, Philadelphia 19107

Edward (Elwell G.), Jr. Trust (R)
c/o Mellon Bank N.A., Philadelphia 19101

Edwards (Edith H.) Trust #2 (R)
c/o First Union/Wachovia, Philadelphia 19109

Edwards (J.) & Company Trust for TBF (O)
c/o Mellon Bank N.A., Philadelphia 19101

Ehrenreich (Josiah & Amelia) Foundation (NP)
c/o Iskrant, Suite 3600, 1600 Market Street, Philadelphia 19103

Ehrlich (Abraham & Hinda) Charitable Trust (L) MI-22-62
c/o Brossky Berk, 1653 The Fairway, #214, Jenkintown 19046

Ehrlich (Jack) Foundation (L) MI-99
c/o Kendall, 231 Brydon Road, Philadelphia 19151

ELF Acquitaine International Foundation (O)
2000 Market Street, 27th Floor, Philadelphia 19103

Elf Atochem North America Foundation
(New name: Atofina Chemical Foundation)

Elkin (Lewis) Fund (R)
c/o First Union/Wachovia, Philadelphia 19109

Ellis (Rudulph) Gratuity Fund (R)
c/o First Union/Wachovia, Philadelphia 19109

England (Elizabeth R.) Trust (R)
c/o Mellon Bank N.A., Philadelphia 19101

Entrekin (Paul B.) Foundation Trust (R)
c/o Mellon Bank N.A., Philadelphia 19101

Erdman (Florence W.) Trust (O)
c/o Mellon Bank N.A., Philadelphia 19101

Erdman (Henry P.) Trust (R)
c/o First Union/Wachovia, Philadelphia 19109

ERM Group Foundation (U)

Eschenmann (Jack B.) Charitable Trust (R)
c/o Mellon Bank N.A., Philadelphia 19101

Esherick (Wharton) Museum (R)
Horseshoe Trail, P.O. Box 1026, Paoli 19301

Everitt (S.L.) Charitable Foundation (NP)
c/o PNC Bank N.A., Philadelphia 19103

Fagan (William & Florence) Charitable Trust (T)

Fairhaven Foundation (I)
c/o Brown, 8111 Winston Road, Philadelphia 19118

Faith Community Development Corp. (R)
108 East Price Street, Philadelphia 19144

Farese (Joseph) Education Fund (R)
c/o Bucks County Technical School, 610 Wistar Road, Fairless Hills 19030

Fawley (J. Russell) Trust (R)
c/o PNC Bank N.A., Philadelphia 19103

Federation Foundation of Greater Philadelphia (R)
226 South 16th Street, Philadelphia 19102

Feig Family Foundation (R)
c/o The Glenmede Trust Company, One Liberty Place, Philadelphia 19103

Feinstein (Lionel) Memorial Fund (L) MI-41-62
614 GSB Building, 1 Belmont Ave., Bala Cynwyd 19004

Fenstermacher Foundation, The (R)
1500 Walnut St., 13th Floor, Philadelphia 19102

Ferrater-Mora (Josep Maria) Foundation (I)
1518 Willowbrook Lane, Villanova 19085

Fertell (Paul & Pearl) Foundation (L) MI-99
1459 Yellow Springs Road, Chester Springs 19425

Filippone (Edward J.), M.D. Foundation (L) MI-54-99
2228 South Broad Street, Philadelphia 19145

Fine (Annette & Ira W.) Family Foundation (NP)
c/o Glenmede Trust Company, Philadelphia 19103

Fiorelli (Michael L.), Sr. Foundation, The (L) MI-41-63
284 Glen Mills Road, Glen Mills 19342

Fischer Memorial Burial Park (R)
1420 Walnut Street, Suite 200, Philadelphia 19102

Fixter (R. Douglas) Memorial Trust (R)
646 Malin Road, Newtown Square 19073

Flying Warbirds Foundation (O)
1710 Locust Street, Philadelphia 19103

Focht (George B.), M.D. Trust (R)
c/o Mellon Bank N.A., Philadelphia 19101

Fonthill Trust (R)
c/o Mellon Bank N.A., Philadelphia 19101

Forer (Morris L. & Lois G.) Foundation (L) MI-41-54-99
2401 Pennsylvania Ave., #10A2, Philadelphia 19130

Forman Foundation, The (U)

Forrest (Ella Mae) Fund (NP)
c/o Mellon Bank N.A., Philadelphia 19101

Forrest (Elmer W.) Trust (R)
c/o PNC Bank N.A., Philadelphia 19103

Foseid (Virginia Ann) Foundation (L) MI-31-32
601 Beatty Road, Media 19063

Foster (Benjamin) #15 Charitable Trust (T)

Foster (Mark) Family Foundation, The (NP)
c/o Pitcairn Trust Company, Jenkintown 19046

Foundation for Islamic Education, The (R)
1860 Montgomery Ave., Villanova 19085

Fox (James Frederick) Foundation (R)
Breyer Office Park Building, Suite 401, Elkins Park 19117

Fox (Stuart A. & Claire E.) Charitable Trust (U)

Franks (Betty W.) Charitable Foundation (T)

Fredericks (Harriet G.) Foundation (NP)
c/o First Union/Wachovia, Philadelphia 19109

Friday Night Lights Foundation (U)

Friends of Chinese Dermatology (U)

Friends of Douai (T)

From Greg Fund (L) MI-22-42-61
241 South 7th Street, Philadelphia 19106

Fronheiser (W.G.) Trust (R)
c/o First Union/Wachovia, Philadelphia 19109

Fubini Family Foundation (T)

Fund for Medical Education
(New name: Fund for Education)

Fusfeld (Muriel) Foundation, The (NP)
c/o Mandelbaum, 1600 Market Street, Suite 3600, Philadelphia 19103

Gallagher (Patrick J.) Memorial Foundation (L) MI-43
P.O. Box 790, Kennett Square 19348

Gandhian Foundation (U)
4719 Springfield Ave., Philadelphia 19143

Garrahan (Mary F.) Scholarship Fund (R)
c/o Mellon Bank N.A., Philadelphia 19101

Garrett-Williamson Foundation (O)
P.O. Box 67, Newtown Square 19073

GCP Foundation
(New name: Cornerstone Foundation)

Geetter (Philip & Helene) Charitable Fund (I)
P.O. Box 49, Sellersville 18960

Geiling (J.F.) Trust for J&C Hosfeld Memorial Fund (R)
c/o Mellon Bank N.A., Philadelphia 19101

Gelbach Foundation, The (L) MI-31-42-99
6029 Joshua Road, Fort Washington 19034

General Refractories Matching Gift Program Fund (I)
225 City Line Ave., Bala Cynwyd 19004

Geraghty (Ethel Dinneen) Charitable Trust (R)
c/o First Union/Wachovia, Philadelphia 19109

Gibbons Home (O)
938 Lincoln Ave., Springfield 19064

Gibstein (R.) Trust for Congregation Beth Shalom (NP)
c/o Mellon Bank N.A., Philadelphia 19101

Gift of Life Foundation (T)

Gilberg (Edwin M.) Family Foundation (L) MI-22-62-99
1122 Gainsboro Road, Bala Cynwyd 19004

Gilbertson (Esther) Trust (R)
c/o Mellon Bank N.A., Philadelphia 19101

Ginkinger Memorial Trust (R)
c/o First Union/Wachovia, Philadelphia 19109

Giop (Sandra Kaiziss) Charitable Foundation (R)
c/o Mellon Bank N.A., Philadelphia 19101

Girard-DiCarlo (Constance B. & David F.) Trust (I)
7 Ithan Woods Lane, Villanova 19085

Glatfelter (Philip H.) #21 Trust (R)
c/o PNC Bank N.A., Philadelphia 19103

Glatfelter (William L. & Philip H.) Memorial Foundation (R)
c/o PNC Bank N.A., Philadelphia 19103

Glauser (Anna B.) Trust #3 (R)
c/o First Union/Wachovia, Philadelphia 19109

Glenmede Trust Company, The
(Refer to Pew Charitable Trusts, The)

Global Education Motivators, Inc. (R)
c/o Chestnut Hill College, Philadelphia 19118

Goldberg Family Fund (L) MI-99
22 West Levering Mill Road, Bala Cynwyd 19004

Golder (Cynthia B. & Robert B.) Foundation (U)

Goodman (David H.) Foundation (T)

Goodman (Murray H.) Foundation (U)

Goodrich (B.F.) Foundation (NP)
c/o PNC Bank N.A., Philadelphia 19103

Gordon (Manuel) Foundation (L) MI-99
c/o Myrna G. Snider, P.O. Box 113, Wallingford 19086

Gordon (Reuben & Mollie) Foundation
(Formerly of Philadelphia, now located in FL)

Gornish Charity Foundation (T)

Gorsuch (Edith A. & C.M.) Trust (R)
c/o First Union/Wachovia, Philadelphia 19109

Grace Brothers Foundation (T)

Graduate Hospital System, Inc.
(New name: Philadelphia Health Care Trust)

Gray (Martha G.) Trust #2 (R)
c/o First Union/Wachovia, Philadelphia 19109

Gray (Sidney H. & Mary L.) Family Scholarship Fund (NP)
c/o PNC Bank N.A., Philadelphia 19103

Graybill (Mildred & Winey) Memorial Fund (R)
c/o First Union/Wachovia, Philadelphia 19109

Graystone Society, Inc. (O)
53 South 1st Avenue, Coatesville 19320

Green (Irvin) Family Foundation (L) MI-99
1530 Chestnut Street, Suite 200, Philadelphia 19102

Green (Marcella) Scholarship Trust (NP)
c/o PNC Bank N.A., Philadelphia 19103

Greenberg (Frank) Foundation (L) MI-42-43
c/o Stutman, 2001 Market Street, Suite 3100, Philadelphia 19103

Greene (Michael A.) Foundation (L) MI-29
1985 Bridgetown Pike, Feasterville 19053

Greenfield (Bruce & Adele) Foundation (L) MI-22-62-99
1845 Walnut Street, Suite 800, Philadelphia 19103

Greenfield (William & Joan Rockower) Foundation (L)
MI-41-42-99
1451 Broad Street, Dresher 19025

Grig Fund, The (L) MI-22-62-99
c/o Wolf, Block et al, 1650 Arch Street, 22nd Floor, Philadelphia 191034

Grissinger (Charles R.) Fund (R)
c/o President, Girard College, Philadelphia 19121

Gross (Linda & Irwin) Foundation (U)

Guggenheim (Simon) Scholarship Fund (R)
c/o Principal, Central High School, Philadelphia 19122

Gulf Atlantic Island Corp. (R)
P.O. Box 21392, Philadelphia 19141

Hadley (Theodore & Elizabeth) Fund (L) MI-41-55
P.O. Box 370, Kennett Square 19348

Haigh (Cheston W.) Trust (R)
c/o Mellon Bank N.A., Philadelphia 19101

Hamalkah (Esther) Foundation (L) MI-32-62-99
20324 Valley Forge Circle, King of Prussia 19406

Hand (Morgan & Mary G.) Scholarship Fund (R)
c/o First Union/Wachovia, Philadelphia 19109

Hand (Morgan) II Scholarship Fund (NP)
c/o First Union/Wachovia, Philadelphia 19109

Hankin (Bernard & Henrietta) Foundation
(New name: Hankin Foundation)

Hansen (Fritz) Scholarship Trust (R)
c/o PNC Bank N.A., Philadelphia 19103

Harms (Arthur G. & Helene K.) Foundation (R)
813 Plymouth Road, Gwynedd Valley 19437

Harrington (J.S.) Trust for Masonic Home (R)
c/o Mellon Bank N.A., Philadelphia 19101

Harrington (J.S.) Trust for United Methodist Church (R)
c/o Mellon Bank N.A., Philadelphia 19101

Harris (Raymond J.) Trust (R)
c/o Mellon Bank N.A., Philadelphia 19101

Harris (Walter P.) Foundation (L) MI-41
216 David Drive, Havertown 19083

Harris Scholarship Fund (NP)
c/o PNC Bank N.A., Philadelphia 19103

Harrison (Marie C.) Charitable Trust (L) MI-42
c/o Winokur, 1717 Arch Street, Suite 4000, Philadelphia 19103

Hartman (John H.) Trust (R)
c/o Mellon Bank N.A., Philadelphia 19101

Hartman (Russell L.) Trust
(New name: Frank & Amanda Hartman Educational Fdn.)

Hatfield (Henry Reed) Nicetown Playground (R)
c/o Swansen, 4000 Bell Atlantic Tower, Philadelphia 19103

Hayman (Gray Bradley) Foundation II (L) MI-63
310 Old Lancaster Road, Devon 19333

Haythornthwaite (Robert H. & Mary) Foundation (O)
313 Wellington Terrace, Jenkintown 19046

Hazen (Lita Annenberg) Charitable Trust
(Formerly of St. Davids; now located in NY)

Head (Howard & Martha) Foundation (NP)
c/o Glenmede Trust Company, Philadelphia 19103

Heaton (Ralph S.) Trust (R)
c/o Berger, 1515 Market Street, Suite 300, Philadelphia 19102

Hedgeabout, Inc. (O)
P.O. Box 37, Gladwyne 19035

Heilweil (Jerome P. & Flora P.) Foundation, The (NP)
c/o Elko, Fischer, et al, 524 North Providence Rd., Media 19063

Hellyer (Newlin A.) Trust (R)
c/o PNC Bank N.A., Philadelphia 19103

Henry Foundation for Botanical Research (O)
801 Stony Lane, Gladwyne 19035

Heppe (Florence J.) Memorial Fund (R)
c/o Mellon Bank N.A., Philadelphia 19101

Herrin (Edith Fitton) Trust (R)
c/o Mellon Bank N.A., Philadelphia 19101

Herriott-Granger Foundation, Inc. (R)
c/o Nurney, 70 West Oakland Ave., Doylestown 18901

Hessick Foundation (NP)
c/o Rosenfelt, Siegel & Goldberg, 33 Rock Hill Road, Bala Cynwyd 19004

HFO Foundation (NP)
c/o Rosenfeld, Suite 3600, 1600 Market Street, Philadelphia 19103

Higbee (David Downes) Trust (NP)
c/o PNC Bank N.A., Philadelphia 19103

Hightop Scholarship Foundation (T)

Hilbush Foundation, The (L) MI-43
1408 Favonius Way, West Chester 19382

Hill (E.) Trust for William C. Hill Library (R)
c/o First Union/Wachovia, Philadelphia 19109

Hill (Harold & Ida) Charitable Fund (T)

Hill (Harold Newlin) Foundation (R)
c/o Mellon Bank N.A., Philadelphia 19101

Hill (Sonny) Foundation (L) MI-13-16-99
429 South 50th Street, Philadelphia 19143

Hill (William Collins) Horticultural Library (R)
c/o First Union/Wachovia, Philadelphia 19109

Hinman Family Foundation, The (NP)
c/o Iskrant, 1600 Market Street, #3600, Philadelphia 19103

Historic Sugartown, Inc. (O)
697 Sugartown Road, Malvern 19355

Historical Society of Frankford (O)
1507 Orthodox Street, Philadelphia 19124

Hoechst Foundation, The (L) MI-61-71-99
340 Barren Road, Media 19063

Hoffman (William G. & Helen) Foundation (NP)
c/o First Union/Wachovia, Philadelphia 19109

Hollender (Betty Jane & Marc H.) Foundation (NP)
1845 Walnut Street, Suite 1300, Philadelphia 19103

Holloway (Harry D.) Foundation (R)
c/o Erisman, 1650 Market Street, Suite 1300, Philadelphia 19103

Holstrom Family Foundation, The
(New name: Holstrom-Kineke Foundation)

Home-Free (I)
36 Ardmore Ave., P.O. Box 21, Ardmore 19003

Honickman (Lynne & Harold) Foundation
(New name: Honickman Foundation)

Hoopes (Mildred B. & Lida Y.) Scholarship Fund (R)
c/o First Union/Wachovia, Philadelphia 19109

Hopewell Educational Fund (R)
241 South Third Street, Philadelphia 19106

Hopkins (Joseph J.) Scholarship Foundation (R)
500 Craig Lane, Villanova 19085

Horowitz Foundation (I)
900 Lenmar Drive, Blue Bell 19422

Horvitz (Selwyn A.) Foundation, The (L) MI-99
c/o Reed, Smith et al, 2500 One Liberty Place, Philadelphia 19103

Hovey (James W. & Carol A.) Foundation
(New name: The Hovey Foundation)

Howell (Samuel L.) #4 Trust (R)
c/o PNC Bank N.A., Philadelphia 19103

Hoyle (James E.) Charitable Trust (NP)
c/o First Union/Wachovia, Philadelphia 19109

Huber (Caroline M.) Memorial Scholarship Fund (U)

Huffman (Susan M.) Foundation, The (L) MI-32-41-71
P.O. Box 193, Wayne 19087

Hughes (R.C.) Spelling Bee Fund (R)
c/o Mellon Bank N.A., Philadelphia 19101

Huhn (Harry K.) Trust (R)
c/o Mellon Bank N.A., Philadelphia 19101

Hunsinger (Ralph) Trust (R)
c/o PNC Bank N.A., Philadelphia 19103

Huplits (Myrtle V.C. & Woodman E.) Foundation Trust (R)
c/o Peskin, 2 Davis Drive, Washington Crossing 18977

Huston (Charles Lukens) Fellowship Foundation (R)
c/o Lukens, Inc., 50 South First Ave., Coatesville 19320

Hutchinson (Jane) Trust (R)
c/o PNC Bank N.A., Philadelphia 19103

Hyman Family Charitable Foundation (NP)
c/o Gazer, Kohn et al, 6 Neshaminy Interplex, Trevose 19053

I Have a Dream - Camden, Inc. (O)
1 International Plaza, Suite 300, Philadelphia 19113

I.H.M. Center for Literacy & G.E.D. Programs (O)
425 West Lindley Ave., Philadelphia 19129

IA Construction Foundation, The (L) MI-42-88
P.O. Box 8, Concordville 19331

Ihle (Joseph Fred) Estate (L) MI-43
1101 Market Street, #2820, Philadelphia 19107

Illman (George Morton) Trust (R)
c/o Mellon Bank N.A., Philadelphia 19101

Ingerman-Ginsberg Israeli Fellowship Foundation
(New name: The Ingerman Family Foundation)

Inman (Sidney A. & Margaret C.) Foundation (NP)
c/o PNC Bank N.A., Philadelphia 19103

Institute for Behavior Change, The (O)
848 West Kings Highway, Coatesville 19320

Institute for Bio-Information Research (O)
1325 Morris Drive, Suite 201, Wayne 19087

Institute for Psychoanalytic Psychotherapy (O)
26 Summit Grove Avenue, Bryn Mawr 19010

Institute of Social Medicine & Health (R)
206 North 35th Street, Philadelphia 19104

Integrity Foundation (L) MI-99
1801 Susquehanna Road, Abington 19001

International Society of Angle-Saxonists (R)
c/o Pulsiano, 800 Lancaster Ave., Villanova 19085

Irrevocable Charitable Trust (R)
1201 Conestoga Road, Chester Springs 19425

Irwin (Agnes & Sophie D.) Memorial Fund (R)
c/o PNC Bank N.A., Philadelphia 19103

Irwin (Agnes) School Trust (R)
1500 East Lancaster Ave., Paoli 19401

Isaacs (Harry Z.) Foundation (NP)
c/o The Glenmede Trust Company, Philadelphia 19103

Isen (Nathan D.) Foundation (I)
c/o Gravco, 111 Presidential Blvd., Bala Cynwyd 19004

Isenberg/Sarkisian Foundation (L) MI-32-41
c/o Duane, Morris & Heckscher, 4200 One Liberty Place,
Philadelphia 19103

Iverson (Helen St. John) Trust (NP)
c/o PNC Bank N.A., Philadelphia 19103

Jackson (Lloyd S.) Charitable Trust (R)
549 Locust Street, P.O. Box 164, Oxford 19363

Jacobs (Mary) Memorial Library (O)
c/o Watson, 2600 One Commerce Square, Philadelphia 19103

Jacquelin Foundation (NP)
c/o Coombs, 451 Atkinson Lane, Langhorne 19047

James (Frank) Grand Lodge Residuary Trust (R)
c/o First Union/Wachovia, Philadelphia 19109

Javitch Foundation (NP)
c/o Drucker & Scaccetti, 1845 Walnut Street, #1400,
Philadelphia 19103

Jenkins (H. Lawrence) Trust (O)
c/o First Union/Wachovia, Philadelphia 19109

Jewish Media Workshop (R)
c/o Lacks, 3220 Tillman Drive, Bensalem 19020

JMM Foundation (U)

Johnson (Nicholas R.) Trust for Palmer Home (R)
c/o Mellon Bank N.A., Philadelphia 19101

Johnson (Susan Patrizio) Scholarship Fund (R)
c/o Downington National Bank, Downingtown 19335

Jones (Edmund A.) Scholarship Fund (R)
10 Beatty Road, PO Box 566, Media 19063

Jones (Thomas Roy & Lura) Foundation (NP)
c/o PNC Bank N.A., Philadelphia 19103

Junge (Robert) Trust (R)
3400 Centre Square West, Philadelphia 19102

Junge (Vera P.) Foundation (R)
c/o PNC Bank N.A., Philadelphia 19103

Kahn (Richard P.) Foundation (L) MI-32-42-99
1515 Locust Street, #301, Philadelphia 19102

Kahn Foundation, The (L) MI-12
c/o Jonns, Inc., 765 Bethlehem Pike, Montgomeryville 18936

Kaji Charitable Trust (R) MI-43
1900 Yardley Road, Yardley 19067

Kambin (Parviz) Foundation, The (U)

Kanter Foundation, The (I)
1042 Gypsy Hill Road, Gwynedd Valley 19437

Kaplan Family Charitable Trust (L) MI-22-62
3100 One Liberty Place, 1650 Market Street, Philadelphia 19103

Kaplan Foundation, The (NP)
919 Conestoga Road, Suite 200, Rosemont 19010

Kaplan-Cooke-Snyder Foundation
(Formerly of Huntingdon Valley, now located in FL)

Kardas (Temi Olga) Charitable Trust (L) MI-12-13
1415 Brierwood Road, Havertown 19083

Kassner (Fred E.) Family Foundation (R)
c/o First Union/Wachovia, Philadelphia 19109

Katar (Felix M.) Trust (R)
c/o PNC Bank N.A., Philadelphia 19103

Katila (Neal J.) Scholarship Fund (R)
1247 Forsythe Drive, Fort Washington 19034

Katz (J. Jerome & Clara G.) Scholarship Trust (R)
c/o First Union/Wachovia, Philadelphia 19109

Kean Family Charitable Foundation, The (I)
241 South 6th Street, Philadelphia 19107

Keasbey (H.G. & A.G.) Memorial Fund (R)
c/o First Union/Wachovia, Philadelphia 19109

Keck (Stelletta W.) Trust (R)
c/o PNC Bank N.A., Philadelphia 19103

Kedson (Jeffrey S.) Foundation (R)
20 Sugar Maple Lane, Lafayette Hill 19444

Keith (Ruth) Scholarship Fund (R)
c/o First National Bank of Newtown, Newtown 18940

Kelley (Malcolm S.) Trust (R)
c/o Mellon Bank N.A., Philadelphia 19101

Kellis (George G.) Trust for Kipparissi (R)
c/o PNC Bank N.A., Philadelphia 19103

Kellis (George G.) Trust for Piraieus (R)
c/o PNC Bank N.A., Philadelphia 19103

Kelly (John) Foundation (L) MI-41
P.O. Box 125, Devon 19333

Kensington Soup Society (O)
1036 East Crease Street, Philadelphia 19125

Kentucky School Reform Corporation (NP)
c/o Mandelbaum, 1600 Market Street, #3600, Philadelphia 19103

Kenworthy (Ben) Trust (R)
c/o Mellon Bank N.A., Philadelphia 19101

Kenworthy (J. Howard) Trust (R)
c/o Mellon Bank N.A., Philadelphia 19101

Kenworthy (J. Howard) Trust #2 for Skerett Lodge (R)
c/o Mellon Bank N.A., Philadelphia 19101

Kerr (Charles) Foundation (L) MI-52-89-99
127 North Main Street, New Hope 18938

Kil Chung Hee Fellowship Fund (R)
7818 Oak Lane Road, Cheltenham 19012

Kimmel (Sidney) Foundation for Cancer Research
(Refer to Sidney Kimmel Foundation)

King (Elizabeth C.) Trust (R)
c/o Mellon Bank N.A., Philadelphia 19101

Kirkwood Foundation (L) MI-42-72
546 Street Road, West Grove 19390

Kister (Marie J.) Trust (R)
c/o First Union/Wachovia, Philadelphia 19109

KJB Foundation (I)
c/o MAJ, 16 Sentry Park West, Blue Bell 19422

Klein (Raymond & Miriam) Foundation (R)
1700 Market Street, Suite 2600, Philadelphia 19103

Kleinert's Inc. Scholarship Fund (R)
120 West Germantown Pike, Plymouth Meeting 19462

Kline (Hess & Helyn) Foundation (NP)
c/o Wolf, Block, Schorr & Solis Cohen, Philadelphia 19102

Kline (J. Alexander & Reba C.) Foundation (I)
316 Fawn Hill Lane, Penn Valley 19072

Kline (Leona B. & Sidney D.) Trust #1 (L) MI-42
c/o First Union/Wachovia, Philadelphia 19109

Kline (Leona B. & Sidney D.) Trust #2 (L) MI-42
c/o First Union/Wachovia, Philadelphia 19109

Klopsch (Paul L. & Berta) Trust Fund (NP)
c/o PNC Bank N.A., Philadelphia 19103

Klugh (Thelma F.) Trust (R)
c/o PNC Bank N.A., Philadelphia 19103

Knauer Foundation for Historic Preservation (O)
127 Spruce Street, Philadelphia 19106

Knollbrook Trust, The
(Refer to The Pew Charitable Trusts)

Knox (Charles C.) Home (O)
718 Sussex Road, Wynnewood 19096

Knox (Charles) Trust (R)
c/o Mellon Bank N.A., Philadelphia 19101

Koppelman Family Foundation (NP)
c/o WBSS-C, 1650 Arch Street, #2000, Philadelphia 19103

Kress (John J.)/Jessie L. Kress Memorial Fund (R)
c/o Mellon Bank N.A., Philadelphia 19101

Kress (Samuel & Eva) Memorial Scholarship Fund (R)
c/o PNC Bank N.A., Philadelphia 19103

Krishnarpan Foundation, The (L) MI-82
965 Hunt Drive, Yardley 19067

Kuhn (Henry J. & Willemina B.) Day Camp (O)
600 Witmer Road, Horsham 19044

Kurios Foundation
c/o Engstrom, 743 Woodleave Road, Bryn Mawr 19010

Kurtz (Richard & Jacqueline) Foundation, The (L)
MI-63-99
380 Keller Road, Berwyn 19312

Labar (Frank S.) Memorial Fund (R)
c/o Mellon Bank N.A., Philadelphia 19101

Lamb Foundation (NP)

Lambert Foundation, The (R)
1027 Valley Forge Road, #357, Devon 19333

Land (Maurice & Sara) Foundation (R)
c/o Wissahickon Spring Water, Inc., 10447 Drummond Road,
Philadelphia 19154

Lane (A.W. & Jane C.) Trust for U. of Vermont (NP)
c/o PNC Bank N.A., Philadelphia 19103

Lane (Gertrude S.) Foundation (L) MI-N/R
c/o Omega Group, 937 Haverford Road, Bryn Mawr 19010

Lane (Jane C.) Trust for Wesleyan U. (NP)
c/o PNC Bank N.A., Philadelphia 19103

Langworthy Foundation (NP)
c/o PNC Bank, Charitable-Endowment Group, Philadelphia 19103

Lasch-Smukler Family Charitable Foundation
(New name: Smukler Lasch Family Foundation)

Lasko (Vivian Simkins) Foundation, The (L) MI-53-55
101 Clarke Street, West Chester 19380

Latter Rains Charitable Foundation (T)

Laub (Richard M.) Foundation, The
(Formerly of Rydale, now located in FL)

Laurel Foundation (NP)
c/o Glenmede Trust Company, Philadelphia 19103

Lavino (Edwin M.) Foundation Trust (R)
c/o Mellon Bank N.A., Philadelphia 19101

Leaf (Natalie A.W.) Charitable Trust (T)
(Refer to Chester County Community Foundation)

League (Mary Clarke) Trust (R)
c/o Mellon Bank N.A., Philadelphia 19101

Ledward (Carol J.) Memorial Scholarship Trust (R)
c/o Admissions, University of Pennsylvania, Philadelphia 19104

Ledward (J. Dehaven) Memorial Scholarship Fund
(New name: Carol J. Ledward Memorial Scholarship Trust

Lee (Jannette E.) Memorial Fund for Evanston Twp. H.S. (NP)
c/o PNC Bank N.A., Philadelphia 19103

Lee (Margery P. & B. Herbert) Foundation (L) MI-N/R
305 Gatcombe Lane, P.O. Box 568, Bryn Mawr 19010

Leesona Charitable Foundation (L) MI-42
c/o Peter Jerome, 2005 Market Street, 30th Floor,
Philadelphia 19103

LEFCO Foundation (L) MI-52-55-99
100 Breyer Drive, Elkins Park 19027

LeFevre (Walter R.) Trust for St. John Lutheran Church (R)
c/o PNC Bank N.A., Philadelphia 19103

Lehigh County Prison & Women's Annex Char. Fdn. Trust (R)
c/o Dennis, 2600 One Commerce Square, Philadelphia 19103

Lenfest (H. Chase) Foundation, The (I)
5 Tower Bridge, 300 Barr Harbor Drive., #450, West Chester 19380

Lenfest Education Foundation, The (T)

Lesnick (George & Rosalia) Foundation (L) MI-15-81
21 South 12th Street, Suite 401, Philadelphia 19107

**Lessig (Brooke & Inge) Trust for American Cancer
Society** (R)
c/o First Union/Wachovia, Philadelphia 19109

Lessig (Brooke & Inge) Trust for American Heart Assn. (R)
c/o First Union/Wachovia, Philadelphia 19109

Levee (Polly Annenberg) Charitable Trust/Levee Trust (NP)

Levin (Barbara Silver) Foundation (L) MI-32-62
162 Gramercy Road, Bala Cynwyd 19004

Levin (Simon & Lyna P.) Charitable Foundation (T)

Levine (Leonard & Ruth) Skin Research Fund (L) MI-32
c/o Broderick, P.O. Box 389, Norristown 19404

Levis (Adolph & Rose) Family Foundation (L) MI-22-62
c/o Mellon Bank N.A., Philadelphia 19101

Levy (Charles) Foundation (NP)
1 Alton Road, Yardley 19067

Levy (Leon) Foundation, The (I)
Two Logan Square, Suite 2450, Philadelphia 19103

Light Charitable Trust, The (L) MI-63
c/o Chung, 615 Creek Lane, Flourtown 19036

Lind (Flora) Trust (R)
c/o Mellon Bank N.A., Philadelphia 19101

Lindback (Christian & Mary) Foundation
(New name: The Lindback Foundation)

Lindermann (J.) for Notre Dame High School Trust (R)
c/o Mellon Bank N.A., Philadelphia 19101

Little Guys Football Conference (U)

Little Quakers, Inc. (O)
2680 Tremont Street, Philadelphia 19152

LMS Family Fund
(Formerly of Bala Cynwyd, now located in MD)

Loeb (Bernard & Bernadette) Charitable Foundation (L)
MI-22-42
c/o Alderfer, 935 South Trooper Road, Norristown 19401

Longstreth (M.L. & J.H.) Foundation (L) MI-13-41-61
8502 Elliston Drive, Wyndmoor 19038

Longwood Gardens, Inc. (O)
P.O. Box 501, Kennett Square 19348

Lotsch-Zelman Foundation, The
(Formerly of Audubon, now located in CA)

Lower Merion Academy (R)
510 Bryn Mawr Ave., Bala Cynwyd 19004

Lower Merion Development Corp. (R)
915 Montgomery Ave., Suite 304, Narberth 19072

Lukens Foundation, The
(Refer to Bethlehem Steel Foundation)

Luongo Family Foundation (L) MI-42
c/o Blank, Rome et al, 1 Logan Square, Philadelphia 19103

Luria (A.L. & Jennie L.) Foundation (NP)
c/o Kaufman, 1650 Arch Street, 22nd Floor, Philadelphia 19103

Luria (Herbert B.) Foundation (NP)
c/o Packard Building, 12th Floor, Philadelphia 19102

Lycoming House (R)
c/o Bardes, P.O. Box 8228, Philadelphia 19101

Machmer (R.R. & C.M.) Charitable Trust (R)
c/o First Union/Wachovia, Philadelphia 19109

Macula Vision Research Foundation (L) MI-32
401 City Ave., Suite 400, Bala Cynwyd 19004

Madway Foundation (T)

Making America Beautiful, Inc. (O)
c/o M.A. Bruder & Sons, P.O. Box 600, Broomall 19008

Manderfield (Charles J.) Trust (R)
c/o First Union/Wachovia, Philadelphia 19109

March (Florence) Fund (T)

March (William A.) Education Fund (R)
c/o PNC Bank N.A., Philadelphia 19103

Marino Foundation, The (L) MI-15-22-25
5330 North Sydenham Street, Philadelphia 19141

Mariton Wildlife Sanctuary & Wilderness Trust (O)
c/o Sax, Packard Building/12th Floor, Philadelphia 19102

Markus (Moe B.) Trust (R)
c/o Mellon Bank N.A., Philadelphia 19101

Marriott Business Travel Institute (R)
260 South Broad Street, 12th Floor, Philadelphia 19102

Martin (William F.) Charitable Foundation (L) MI-41
200 Tower Road, Villanova 19085

Masland (Maurice H.) Trust #1
(Formerly of Rosemont, now located in KY)

Masland (Maurice H.) Trust #2
(Formerly of Rosemont, now located in KY)

Massachusetts Institute of Technology, Trust for (R)
1500 Lancaster Ave., Suite 202, Paoli 19301

Matthews Fund, The (L) MI-14-31-99
c/o Hughes, 33 Wistar Road, Paoli 19401

Mattleman Family Foundation, The (L) MI-22-41-99
2226 Land Title Building, Philadelphia 19110

May (William Lyster) Foundation (I) MI-42-52-63
c/o R. K. May, 217 East Washington Street, West Chester 19380

Mayers (Edward C.) Charitable Trust (NP)
c/o Mellon Bank N.A., Philadelphia 19101

McAllen Medical Center Foundation (NP)
P.O. Box 61558, King of Prussia 19406

McCahan (William F.) Trust (R)
c/o Mellon Bank N.A., Philadelphia 19101

McCance Foundation, The (NP)
c/o Keith Jennings, 1531 Walnut Street, Philadelphia 19102

McCann (William F.) Trust (R)
c/o Mellon Bank N.A., Philadelphia 19101

McCarty (Delphine L.) #2 Trust (R)
c/o First Union/Wachovia, Philadelphia 19109

McCombes (Eugene J.) Trust (R)
c/o Mellon Bank N.A., Philadelphia 19101

McCormick (John R.) Trust (R)
c/o First Union/Wachovia, Philadelphia 19109

McCullough (H.F.) Memorial Scholarship Fund (R)
c/o Mellon Bank N.A., Philadelphia 19101

McDonald (Charles F. & Genevieve) Foundation (R)
P.O. Box 2228, West Chester 19380

McDonald (E.) Trust (R)
c/o First Union/Wachovia, Philadelphia 19103

McDonald's Kids Charities (R)
401 City Ave., Suite 800, Bala Cynwyd 19004

McGinley Family Foundation (L) MI-32-33
P.O. Box 312, Bala Cynwyd 19004

McGrew (Hattie T.) Scholarship Trust (NP)
c/o PNC Bank N.A., Philadelphia 19103

McKnight (Sumner T.) Foundation (NP)
c/o Glenmede Trust Company, Philadelphia 19103

McLean (Don) Foundation (L) MI-22-43
261 Old York Road, Suite 720, Jenkintown 19046

McLean (MacLean W.) Trust for World Federalist Assn. (R)
c/o PNC Bank N.A., Philadelphia 19103

McNeil (Robert L.), Jr. 1986 Charitable Trust (T)

McShain (John) Charities (T)

Meade Foundation, The (L) MI-41-42-44
374 Circle of Progress, Pottstown 19464

Meagher (Cecile E.) Charitable Trust (R)
c/o First Union/Wachovia, Philadelphia 19109

Medical Trust, The
(Refer to Pew Charitable Trusts, The)

Medway (Jessica) Memorial Foundation (I)
506 Hobby Horse Hill, Lower Gwynedd 19002

Mende Foundation (L) MI-N/R
85 Hidden Woods Lane, Warminster 18974

Mercer-Fonthill Museum, Trustees of the (R)
East Court Street, Doylestown 18901

Merck Genome Research Institute, The (R)
c/o Merck & Co., WP441-206, P.O. Box 4, West Point 19486

Mercy Douglass Primary Health Care Center (R)
4508 Chestnut Street, Philadelphia 19139

Merion Community Association (O)
625 Hazelhurst Ave., Merion 19066

Merit Gasoline Foundation (T)

Merkel Memorial Scholarship Endowment (R)
c/o Episcopal Diocese, 240 South 4th Street, Philadelphia 19106

Meshewa Farm Foundation (R)
c/o Mellon Bank N.A., Philadelphia 19101

Metcalf (Dorothy A.) Charitable Foundation (NP)
c/o PNC Bank N.A., Philadelphia 19103

Michaels (Frank J.) Scholarship Fund (R)
c/o First Union/Wachovia, Philadelphia 19109

Milani (Ulderico & Anna C.) Charitable Foundation (L)
MI-31-41-61
c/o Crescent Iron Works, 4901 Grays Ave., Philadelphia 19143

Miles (Eric J. & Effie Lu) Memorial Fund (R)
c/o Mellon Bank N.A., Philadelphia 19101

Milewski (Pauline) Scholarship Fund (R)
c/o Mellon Bank N.A., Philadelphia 19101

Miller (Gail E. Gass) Trust (R)
c/o First Union/Wachovia, Philadelphia 19109

Miller Family Foundation (L) MI-N/R
5921 Atkinson Road, New Hope 18938

Mirabile Foundation (L) MI-42-43-61
735 Palmer Place, Blue Bell 19422

Mitchell (Samuel Notman) Foundation (L) MI-43
51 Crestline Road, Wayne 19087

Montemayor (Victor J.) Scholarship Fund (R)
120 West Germantown Pike, Suite 100, Plymouth Meeting 19462

Montgomery (Mildred) Trust (R)
c/o Mellon Bank N.A., Philadelphia 19101

Montgomery Bar Foundation (L) MI-12-13-17
100 West Airy Street, Norristown 19404

Montgomery County Medical Society Foundation (L) MI-12-17-29
491 Allendale Road, #323, King of Prussia 19406

Montgomery County Private Industry Foundation (R)
2605 Egypt Road, Trooper 19403

Mooney Charitable Trust (I)
105 Spencer Road, Devon 19333

Moore (William J.) Trust (R)
c/o Mellon Bank N.A., Philadelphia 19101

Moran (Julia) Trust (R)
c/o Dr. Moore, Temple U., 3233 N. Broad St., Philadelphia 19140

Morris (Joseph M.) Trust (R)
c/o Mellon Bank N.A., Philadelphia 19101

Morris (Joshua) Trust (R)
c/o Buck, 720 Hartranft Ave., Fort Washington 19034

Morris (M. Edward) Foundation (I)
c/o First Union/Wachovia, Philadelphia 19109

Morris Wheeler Foundation, The (L) MI-56-63
8315 St. Martins Lane, Philadelphia 19118

Muirfield Foundation
(New name: Sherrerd Foundation)

Myerley (Carl Hubert) Trust (R)
c/o First Union/Wachovia, Philadelphia 19109

Myrin (Mabel Pew) Trust
(Refer to Pew Charitable Trusts, The)

NADC Charitable Foundation (R)
c/o Taylor, 16 North Franklin Street, Doylestown 18901

Nathan Charitable Foundation (L) MI-82
c/o Nathan, Two Penn Boulevard, #103, Philadelphia 19144

Nature's Educational Yves Rocher Foundation (T)

Neale (Katherine H.) Trust (R)
c/o Mellon Bank N.A., Philadelphia 19101

Neeson (Elsie T.) Trust for SPCA (R)
c/o Mellon Bank N.A., Philadelphia 19101

Neinken (Maurice A.) Scholarship Grant & Loan Fdn. (R)
P.O. Box 193, Souderton 18964

Nelson (James O. & Anna May) Foundation (U)
50 West Welsh Pool Road, Exton 19341

Nemroff (Arthur & Phyllis) Family Foundation (L) MI-12-22
515 Stahr Road, Suite 100, Elkins Park 19027

Nestler Scholarship Foundation (R)
c/o Union National Bank, Souderton 18964

Neubauer Family Foundation
(New name: The Neubauer Foundation)

Nevyas (Jacob) Teaching & Research Foundation, The (L) MI-N/R
1120 Tower Lane, East, Narberth 19072

Newlin (Nicholas) Foundation (O)
P.O. Box 357, Paoli 19301

Nextlevel Systems Foundation, The (I)
101 Tournament Drive, Horsham 19044

Niblo (George W.) Trust (R)
c/o PNC Bank N.A., Philadelphia 19103

North American Renewal Service Committee (R)
P.O. Box 320, Sassamansville 19472

Northeast Harbor Library, et al Trust (R)
1500 Lancaster Ave., Suite 202, Paoli 19301

Northeast High School 131st Class (R)
1601 Kenmare Drive, Dresher 19025

Northeast High School Alumni Foundation (R)
c/o Northeast High School, Cottman & Algon Aves., Philadelphia 19111

Northern Children Network, Inc. (R)
3109 West Coulter Street, Philadelphia 19129

Novak Family Foundation (L) MI-12-14-22
c/o Unique Industries, Inc., 2400 S. Weccacoe Ave., Philadelphia 19148

Open Land Conservancy of Chester County (O)
P.O. Box 1031, Paoli 19301

Orlowitz (Louis B. & Ida K.) Variety Club Fund (R)
c/o First Union/Wachovia, Philadelphia 19109

Ostroff (Isinore) School Fund (R)
c/o First Union/Wachovia, Philadelphia 19109

Ottinger (Harry P.) & A. Viola Woerner Scholarship Fund (R)
c/o High, Swartz et al, 40 East Airy Street, Norristown 19404

Panagos (Nick & Paris N.) Charitable Trust (R)
c/o Midouhas, 1012 Wood Street, Bristol 19007

Panaro (Maria Grazia) Foundation (NP)
c/o Saile, 405 Executive Drive, Langhorne 19047

Panizza Family Foundation (R) MI-43
921 Briarwood Circle, West Chester 19380

Parker (Oscar J.) for C.M. Parker Trust (L) MI-13-42-61
c/o Mellon Bank N.A., Philadelphia 19101

Parkhill (Helon A.) Trust (NP)
c/o PNC Bank N.A., Philadelphia 19103

Parklands Foundation (T)

Pauline-Morton Foundation (L) MI-12-41-71
38 Balmoral Drive, Chadds Ford 19317

PCH Foundation (NP)
2320 Faunce Street, Philadelphia 19152

Pearl Software Educational Foundation (O)
767 Champlain Drive, King of Prussia 19406

Pearson (Eric & Virginia) Foundation, The (T)

Pelson Foundation, The (NP)
c/o Iskrant, 1600 Market Street, #3600, Philadelphia 19103

Pennewill (James) Trust (NP)
c/o Mellon Bank N.A., Philadelphia 19101

Pennsylvania Cincinnati Charitable Trust (R)
128 Ashwood Road, Villanova 19085

Pennsylvania Industrial Chemical Corp./Chester H.S. Fund (R)
c/o First Union/Wachovia, Philadelphia 19109

Pennsylvania Knitted Outerwear Foundation (L) MI-43
c/o Shils, 123 South Broad Street, Suite 2030, Philadelphia 19109

Pennsylvania Metalcasting Environmental Research Fdn. (L) MI-71
412 One Plymouth Meeting, Plymouth Meeting 19462

Pennsylvania Society of Sons of the Revolution (O)
c/o The Racquet Club, 215 South 16th Street, Philadelphia 19102

Percy Fund, The (NP)
591 Skippack Pike, Suite 306, Blue Bell 19422

Perelman (Morris) Foundation (L) MI-62
c/o American Paper Products Co., 2113 E. Rush Street, Philadelphia 19134

Pestcoe (Sally) Trust (R)
c/o First Union/Wachovia, Philadelphia 19109

Peterson (Edna R.) Trust (R)
c/o Mellon Bank N.A., Philadelphia 19101

Peterson Foundation (NP)
1600 Market Street, Suite 3600, Philadelphia 19103

Pew (J. Howard) Freedom Trust, The
(Refer to Pew Charitable Trusts, The)

Pew (J.N.), Jr. Charitable Trust
(Refer to Pew Charitable Trusts, The)

Pew Memorial Trust, The
(Refer to Pew Charitable Trusts, The)

Pfeiffer (G.W.) for E.K. Kohn-WHSPCA Trust (R)
c/o Mellon Bank N.A., Philadelphia 19101

Philadelphia Anti-Graffiti Network, Inc. (R)
1220 Sansom Street, 3rd Floor, Philadelphia 19107

Philadelphia Athletics Historical Society (O)
6 North York Road, Hatboro 19040

Philadelphia Award, The (R)
c/o Newbold, 239 Arch Street, Philadelphia 19106

Philadelphia Bar Assn./International Human Rights Fund (I)
1101 Market Street, 11th Floor, Philadelphia 19107

Philadelphia Biomedical Research Institute, Inc. (O)
502 King of Prussia Road, Radnor 19087

Philadelphia Community Foundation (L) MI-99
1735 Market Street, Suite 3200, Philadelphia 19103

Philadelphia Constitution Foundation (R)
537 Avonwood Road, Haverford 19041

Philadelphia Mens & Boys Apparel Assn. Endowed Scholarships (R)
133 Heathwood Road, Bala Cynwyd 19004

Philadelphia Soup House, The (L) MI-22-25
c/o Childs, 336 Roumfort Road, Philadelphia 19119

Philadelphia Urological Teaching & Research Fdn. (R)
3401 North Broad Street, Philadelphia 19140

Philippian Foundation (L) MI-22-63
1323 Horsham Road, Ambler 19002

Phillips Agency Foundation, The (U)

Phillips Family Foundation (L) MI-89
1243 Lombard Street, Philadelphia 19147

Phoebus Fund (R)
c/o Bread & Roses Community Fund,
1500 Walnut Street, Philadelphia 19102

Picard (Lucie) Trust (R)
c/o PNC Bank N.A., Philadelphia 19103

Pincus (Marjorie & Nat Irwin) Fund, The (R)
1200 Packard Building, 15th & Chestnut Sts., Philadelphia 19102

Pirret Foundation (NP)
c/o Dilworth, Paxson; 1739 Market Street, #3200, Philadelphia 19103

Pitt Buchanan Charitable Trust (T)

Platte (Edward H.), M.D. Pre-Medical Foundation (R)
c/o Harleysville National Bank & Trust Co., Harleysville 19438

Pleet (David H.) Foundation (L) MI-29-51
c/o WBS&S-C,1650 Arch Street, 22nd Floor, Philadelphia 19103

PMA Foundation
(New name: PMC Foundation)

PNC Corporation (L) MI-72
1518 Willowbrook Lane, Villanova 19085

Pollak (Otto & Gertrude K.) Scholarship Fund (R)
c/o Iskrant, 1600 Market Street, #3600, Philadelphia 19103

Potamkin (Vivian O. & Meyer P.) Operating Fdn (L) MI-53
237 South 18th Street, Suite 20B, Philadelphia 19103

Potter (Edna G.) Charities Charitable Trust (R)
c/o Mellon Bank N.A., Philadelphia 19101

Poulson (Susanna Angue) Fund (R)
c/o First Union/Wachovia, Philadelphia 19109

Poulson (William Wilson) Trust
(New name: Susanna Angue Poulson Fund

Presser (Theodore) Foundation (R)
c/o Presser Place, Bryn Mawr 19010

Presser (Theodore) Foundation Trust (R)
c/o First Union/Wachovia, Philadelphia 19109

Presser Foundation (Trust) (R)
c/o First Union/Wachovia, Philadelphia 19109

Primary Health Systems Health Foundation (U)

Primitive Hall Foundation (O)
76 South First Street, Coatesville 19320

Professional Management Principles Foundation (R)
10 Presidential Boulevard, Bala Cynwyd 19004

Psychological Foundation (R)
1235 Bridgetown Pike, Feasterville 19047

Publicker (Harry & Rose) Charitable Trust
(Refer to Neuman Publicker Trust)

Questar Library of Science & Art (O)
P.O. Box 157, New Hope 18938

Quinn (Joseph T.) Memorial Football Scholarship Fund (R)
c/o Strath Haven High School, Wallingford 19086

Radnor Children's Foundation Trust (R)
303 West Lancaster Ave., Box 130, Wayne 19087

Radnor Enhancement Community Trust (R)
c/o McCoy, 1600 Market Street, Suite 3600, Philadelphia 19103

Railroad Museum, The (O)
P.O. Box 102, Telford 18969

Ransome Foundation, The (T)

Raphael Heights Homes, Inc. (R)
3210 North Fifth Street, Philadelphia 19140

Rappaport (Samuel) Family Foundation (I)
117 South 17th Street, 5th Floor, Philadelphia 19103

READS, Inc. (O)
500 North Sixth Street, Philadelphia 19123

Real Light Foundation, The (R)
225 Jamestown Street, Philadelphia 19128

Realen Homes Charitable Foundation (T)

RealTemp, Inc. (T)

Reese (Fannie M.) Trust for Salvation Army (R)
c/o Mellon Bank N.A., Philadelphia 19101

Reeves (Sophia K.) Foundation (R)
c/o Mellon Bank N.A., Philadelphia 19101

Relieve Pain America (O)
1211 Locust Street, Philadelphia 19107

Renfrew Foundation, The (R)
475 Spring Lane, Philadelphia 19128

Rennoc Corporation Foundation (NP)
c/o Hass & Company, 565 East Swedesford Road, Wayne 19087

Repp (Alfred H. & Ada O.) Scholarship Fund (R)
c/o Mellon Bank N.A., Philadelphia 19101

Research Fund for Cystic Fibrosis, Inc (R)
42 Llanberris Road, Bala Cynwyd 19004

Resnick Family Foundation (I)
P.O. Box 1150, Oaks 19456

Ressler (W. Franklin) Trust (R)
c/o Mellon Bank N.A., Philadelphia 19101

Reyenthaler (E.G. & A.L.) Memorial Home Fdn. (R)
c/o PNC Bank N.A., Philadelphia 19103

Reynolds (Lorine L.) Foundation (R) MI-63
2101 Walnut Street, Apt. 1215, Philadelphia 19103

Richland Library Company (O)
c/o Henry, P.O. Box 499, Quakertown 18951

Rickards (Joseph T.) Memorial Scholarship (R)
255 Fox Road, Media 19063

Ridgely (Elizabeth F.) Fund (NP)
c/o Mellon Bank N.A., Philadelphia 19101

Ridgely (Sarah B.) #1 Trust (NP)
c/o Mellon Bank N.A., Philadelphia 19101

Riebman Family Fund, The (L) MI-99
1170 St. Andrews Road, Bryn Mawr 19010

Rieder (Miriam & Robert M.) for Center Park House (O)
8900 Roosevelt Boulevard, Philadelphia 19115

Rieders (Frederic) Family Renaissance Foundation (O)
2850 Rushland Road, Rushland 18956

Riggs (Adelaide C.) Charitable Trust (NP)
c/o Glenmede Trust Company, Philadelphia 19103

Rigterink Foundation, The (L) MI-N/R
356 Pondview Drive, Devon 19333

Ringing Rocks Foundation (O)
1617 JFK Boulevard, Suite 1500, Philadelphia 19103

Risser (E.F.) Trust for Stauffers Mennonite Church (R)
c/o Mellon Bank N.A., Philadelphia 19101

Rixstine (Mary Amanda Hawke) Trust (R)
c/o First Union/Wachovia, Philadelphia 19109

RJM Foundation, The (U)

Roberts (Lisa) & David Seltzer Charitable Trust
(New name: Poor Richard's Charitable Trust)

Robinson (Harry A.) Foundation (L) MI-22-62-99
c/o Moskoff, 44 Greenfield Ave., Ardmore 19003

Rogers (T.P.) Trust for C.M. Rogers Memorial Fund (R)
c/o Mellon Bank N.A., Philadelphia 19101

Rohrer (William C.), Jr. Educational Foundation (NP)
c/o PNC Bank N.A., Philadelphia 19103

Rohrer (William G.) Charitable Foundation (NP)
c/o PNC Bank N.A., Philadelphia 19103

Rolling Ridge Foundation (O)
c/o Hunt, 300 West State Street, Media 19063

Roman (Jessie G.) Charitable Trust (R)
c/o Mellon Bank N.A., Philadelphia 19101

Roseman (Anna & Isidore) Foundation, The (R)
c/o First Union/Wachovia, Philadelphia 19101

Rosen (Paul) Family Foundation (L) MI-22-32-62
c/o First Union/Wachovia, Philadelphia 19109

Rosenau (Gary) Foundation (NP)
c/o Connell, 1100 Shadeland Ave., Drexel Hill 19026

Rosenau (Leo M. & Jeremy A.) Foundation (L) MI-22-31-62
1764 Oak Hill Drive, Huntingdon Valley 19006

Rosenberger (Clarence & Miriam) Scholarship Fund (R)
4259 West Swamp Road, Suite 310, Doylestown 18901

Rosenberger (William & Marcus) Foundation (L) MI-N/R
847 Forty Foot Road, Hatfield 19440

Rosenlund (Sister Dorcas) Trust (NP)
c/o Glenmede Trust Company, Philadelphia 19103

Rotfeld (Cathy) Foundation (R)
109 Forest Ave., 2nd Floor, Narberth 19072

Rothermel Foundation, The (T)

Roxborough Home for Indigent Women (O)
601 East Leverington Ave., Philadelphia 19128

Royston Foundation, The (L) MI-99
570 Colebrook Road, Exton 19341

RSN Foundation (L) MI-71-99
411 Wister Road, Wynnewood 19096

Ru Shi Buddhist Foundation, Inc. (O)
5128 North 2nd Street, Philadelphia 19120

Rubert (William & Theresa) Memorial Trust (R)
919 Conestoga Road, Building 1, #303, Rosemont 19010

Rubin (Lee Scott) Memorial Fund (R)
c/o PNC Bank N.A., Philadelphia 19103

Rubin (Ronald & Marcia J.) Charitable Foundation (I)
200 South Broad Street, 3rd Floor, Philadelphia 19102

Rubinoff (Morris & Dorothy) Foundation (L) MI-22-62-71
Greenhill Apts., 1001 City Avenue, # WA-605, Wynnewood 19096

Rumbaugh (J.H. & R.H.) Foundation (R)
c/o First Union/Wachovia, Philadelphia 19109

Rumsey (George A.) Trust for Cornell Club of Philadelphia (R)
c/o PNC Bank N.A., Philadelphia 19103

Ryan (Helen & Katherine) County Scholarship Fund (L) MI-43
c/o Schleicher, 5915 Worthington Road, Doylestown 18901

Ryerss' Farm for Aged Equines (O)
c/o Donahue, Ridge Road, R.D. #2, Pottstown 19464

Saint Davids Radnor Church, Trust for (R)
c/o Mellon Bank N.A., Philadelphia 19101

Saint Paul's School Trust (NP)
c/o Mellon Bank N.A., Philadelphia 19101

Salzgeber (Gustave A. & Katherine C.) Charitable Fund (NP)
c/o PNC Bank N.A., Philadelphia 19103

Samson (Mary Eaches) Trust #1 (R)
c/o PNC Bank N.A., Philadelphia 19103

Samson (Mary Eaches) Trust #2 (R)
c/o PNC Bank N.A., Philadelphia 19103

Sanatoga Ridge Community, Inc. (O)
2461 East High Street, Pottstown 19464

Sassafras Corporation, The (O)
123 South Broad Street, Suite 2126, Philadelphia 19109

Satyaram Health Clinic, Inc. (R)
1707 Scott Drive, P.O. Box 1625, Newtown 18940

Saunders (Sally Love) Poetry & Arts Foundation (L) MI-41-53-55
c/o Arnold, 639 Timber Lane, Devon 19333

Schafer (Catherine C.) Trust (R)
c/o PNC Bank N.A., Philadelphia 19103

Schapiro (Morris) & Family Foundation (NP)
c/o Glenmede Trust Company, Philadelphia 19103

Schenck (L.P.) Charitable Trust (NP)
c/o PNC Bank N.A., Philadelphia 19101

Schiff (Lawrence & Mortimer S.) Foundation
(New name: Mortimer s. & Vera M. Schiff Foundation

Schimmel (Rose & Joseph H.) Foundation (I)
c/o Royal Electric, 3233 Hunting Park Ave., Philadelphia 19132

Schinault (Fannie) Foundation (T)

Schmidt (Mike) Foundation (L) MI-32-63
610 Old York Road, #230, Jenkintown 19046

Schmitz (Joseph), Jr. Trust (R)
c/o Mellon Bank N.A., Philadelphia 19101

Schneeberg (Arthur & Geraldine C.) Foundation (L) MI-22-62-99
7900 Old York Road, Suite 712A, Elkins Park 19027

Schoch Foundation (L) MI-53
c/o Bowden, 641 Black Rock Road, Bryn Mawr 19010

Schoonmaker (James M.), II Foundation (NP)
c/o PNC Bank N.A., Philadelphia 19103

Schramm Foundation (L) MI-11-43
c/o Schramm, Inc., 800 East Virginia Ave., West Chester 19381

Schulman Foundation, The (L) MI-N/R
c/o Feldman, 1253 Ridgewood Road, Bryn Mawr 19010

Schumm (Charles A. & Cora H.) Trust Fund (R)
c/o First Union/Wachovia, Philadelphia 19109

Schwab Foundation, The (L) MI-42
407 Atwater Road, Broomall 19008

Schwaiger (Wilhemina M.) Memorial Fund (R)
c/o PNC Bank N.A., Philadelphia 19103

Schwartz (Bernard & Robert) Foundation
(New name: The Schwartz Foundation)

Schwartz (Ernest D.) Trust (R)
c/o PNC Bank N.A., Philadelphia 19103

Schwartz (Jane & Martin) Family Foundation (NP)
1600 Market Street, Suite 3600, Philadelphia 19103

Science Research Foundation for the New Church (R)
c/o Durham, 40 East Airy Street, Norristown 19404

Security on Campus, Inc. (R)
c/o Clery, 618 Shoemaker Road, King of Prussia 19406

Segui (Bernardo J.) Trust (R)
c/o Mellon Bank N.A., Philadelphia 19101

Seligsohn Foundation (L) MI-22-62-99
1221 Centennial Road, Narberth 19072

Seltzer (Maurice) Publishing Trust (R)
c/o First Union/Wachovia, Philadelphia 19109

Senseman (Clarence D.) Fund (R)
c/o First Union/Wachovia, Philadelphia 19109

Serenbetz Charitable Foundation, The (L) MI-42-99
P.O. Box 1127, Newtown 18940

Shafer (Catherine C.) Charitable Trust (R)
c/o PNC Bank N.A., Philadelphia 19103

Shannon-Cassel Fund (R)
c/o PNC Bank N.A., Philadelphia 19103

Shapiro (Evelyn) Foundation, The (L) MI-53
204 Rhyl Lane, Bala Cynwyd 19004

Sharp Foundation, The (NP)
c/o Coopers & Lybrand, 2400 Eleven Penn Center, Philadelphia 19103

Shartzer (Helen B.) Scholarship Fund (R)
c/o Norristown High School, Norristown 19401

Shoemaker (Dr. A.C. & S.A.) Trust (R)
c/o Mellon Bank N.A., Philadelphia 19101

Shull (J.) Trust for First Presbyterian Church (R)
c/o Mellon Bank N.A., Philadelphia 19101

Sickles Charitable Trust
(New name: Sickles Charitable Foundation)

Siegal (Edward I.) Private Foundation (L) MI-22-62
2200 The Parkway, Park Towne Plaza, #S-911, Philadelphia 19130

Silverman (Cheryl Beth) Memorial Fund (L)
224 Susan Drive, Elkins Park 19117

Silverman, Flomen, Cohen Charitable Trust (L) MI-N/R
9868 Bridle Road, Philadelphia 19115

Simeone (Frederick A.), M.D. Foundation, The (O)
8700 Seminole Drive, Philadelphia 19118

Simon (Esther) Charitable Trust
(Formerly of St. Davids, now located in DC)

Sinden (Dr. James W.) Scholarship Fund (R)
c/o American Mushroom Institute, Kennett Square 19348

Singer (Michael) Foundation (L)
1117 Spruce Street, Philadelphia 19107

Singh (K. Paul & Virginia M.) Private Foundation (NP)
c/o Aaron, 3000 Two Logan Square, Philadelphia 19103

Sithong Bounsawat Foundation (R)
c/o Kline, 340 Media Station Road, Media 19063

Sivitz (Frank H.) Foundation (R)
P.O. Box 4087, Rydal 19046

Sleeper (Josiah) & Lottie Sleeper Hill Fund (R)
c/o Taylor Hospital, Ridley Park 19078

Smith (Ann C. & Raymond W.) Charitable Trust
(Formerly of Narberth, now located in VA)

Smith (Elizabeth W.) Trust for Ody et al (R)
c/o Mellon Bank N.A., Philadelphia 19101

Smith (Herchel) Charitable Foundation (L) MI-31
1701 Market Street, Philadelphia 19103

Smith (Jim) Memorial Fund (R)
182 Strawberry Circle, Langhorne 19047

Smith (Martha S.) Trust for Grace U.C.C. (R)
c/o Mellon Bank, Philadelphia 19101

Smith (Mary L.) Charitable Lead Trust (T)

Smith (Mary Ulmer) Char. Trust for Bryn Mawr Hospital (R)
c/o First Union/Wachovia, Philadelphia 19109

Smith (Robert E. & Marie Orr) Foundation (NP)
c/o Glenmede Trust Company, Philadelphia 19103

Smith Memorial Scholarship Fund (L) MI-43
5760 Michael Drive, Bensalem 19020

SmithKline Beecham Foundation
(New name: GlaxoSmithKline Foundation)

Society for Learning Disabled Children (I)
1197 Killarney Lane, West Chester 19382

Society of Friendly Sons of St. Patrick
(see Friendly Sons of St. Patrick, Society of)

Sokol Family Foundation, The (L) MI-12-22-57
1312 Wrenfield Way, Villanova 19085

Solomon (Daniel D.) Foundation (L) MI-22-62
451 Copper Beech Circle, Elkins Park 19027

Somarindyck (George A. & Lillian L.) Charitable Trust (R)
c/o Mellon Bank N.A., Philadelphia 19101

Somarindyck (George A. & Lillian L.) Trust (R)
c/o Mellon Bank N.A., Philadelphia 19101

Sonnenberg Foundation, The
(Formerly of Southampton, now located in FL)

Soref (Samuel M. & Helene K.) Foundation (NP)

Spear (Janice Dana) Scholarship (R)
c/o First Union/Wachovia, Philadelphia 19109

Speare (Nathan) Foundation
(New name: Speare Foundation)

Spirit of Gheel, The (O)
P.O. Box 610, Kimberton 19442

Sporkin (Lillian) Trust (R)
c/o First Union/Wachovia, Philadelphia 19103

Spurgeon (Dorsett L. & Mary D.) Charitable Trust (NP)
c/o PNC Bank N.A., Philadelphia 19103

Staats Foundation (T)

Stager (Matt) Memorial Scholarship Fund (R)
c/o Holly Chapman, 1900 Arch Street, Philadelphia 19103

Start (Raymond R.) Memorial Fund (R)
c/o Mellon Bank N.A., Philadelphia 19101

Steele (Margaret S. & Franklin A.) Foundation (L) MI-29-63
7901 Froebel Road, Laverock 19038

Steensma (Jessie) Endowment for El Camino College (NP)
c/o PNC Bank N.A., Philadelphia 19103

Steidler (Evelyn Lennon) Trust for Notre Dame Home
c/o PNC Bank, Philadelphia 19103

Steinig Family Foundation, The
(Formerly of Elkins Park; now located in MA)

Stewart (Gertrude A.) Charitable Foundation (R)
c/o McDonough-Betz, 114 Park Road, Havertown 19083

Stimmel (Margaret B.) Trust (R)
c/o Mellon Bank N.A., Philadelphia 19101

Stimmel (Margaret B.) Trust for Stimmel Scholarship Fund (R)
c/o Mellon Bank N.A., Philadelphia 19101

Stoddart (Harry T.) Trust (R)
c/o Mellon Bank N.A., Philadelphia 19101

Stork Charitable Trust, The (NP)
5727 Twin Silo Road, Doylestown 18901

Straus (Joseph & Gwendolyn) Foundation, The (NP)
101 East State Street, Kennett Square 19348

Strawbridge (Anne West) Trust (O)
c/o First Union/Wachovia, Philadelphia 19109

Strawbridge (Margaret Dorrance) Foundation of Pa. II
(Formerly of Coatesville, now located in FL)

Streitwieser Foundation/Historical Trumpet Collection (O)
Fairway Farm, Vaughn Road, Pottstown 19464

Stroud (Hazel C.) Educational Trust (T)

Strumia Foundation Lab of Clinical Pathology (U)

Stuart (J. William & Helen D.) Foundation (R)
c/o The Glenmede Trust Company, Philadelphia 19103

Sullivan (Francis W.) Fund (R)
c/o The Glenmede Trust Company, Philadelphia 19103

Sunderman (F. William) Foundation (U)

Superior-Pacific Fund, Inc.
(New name: Paul E. Kelly Foundation)

Swartz (John & Jacqueline) Foundation (T)

Swartzlander (R.H.) Trust for Community High School (R)
c/o First Union/Wachovia, Philadelphia 19109

Swartzlander Charitable Trust (R)
c/o PNC Bank N.A., Philadelphia 19103

Sweet Charity, Inc. (I)
c/o Patterson, 1209 Villanova Ave., Folsom 19033

Sweet Water Trust (NP)

Swiss Pines/Bartschi Foundation (O)
Charlestown Road, RD1, Box 127, Malvern 19355

Swope (Charles S.) Memorial Scholarship Trust (R)
c/o First National Bank of West Chester, West Chester 19380

Sycamore Foundation, The (NP)
c/o Glenmede Trust Company, Philadelphia 19103

T&D Foundation
(Formerly of West Chester; now located in Florida)

Talone (Leonard A. & Dorothy E.) Foundation (L) MI-22-61
825 Fayette Street, Conshohocken 19428

Tatem (J. Fithian) Scholarship Fund (NP)
c/o PNC Bank N.A., Philadelphia 19103

Taunton Public Library Trust (NP)
c/o PNC Bank N.A., Philadelphia 19103

Taylor (Joshua C.) Foundation Trust (R)
c/o Mellon Bank N.A., Philadelphia 19101

Taylor (Thomas) Poor Fund (R)
c/o PNC Bank N.A., Philadelphia 19103

Taylor Memorial Arboretum Trust (R)
c/o Mellon Bank N.A., Philadelphia 19101

Teamsters Local 830 Scholarship Fund (R)
12298 Townsend Road, Philadelphia 19154

Teck Fund (L) MI-52-71-81
314 Avon Road, Bryn Mawr 19010

Tecovas Foundation (NP)
c/o Glenmede Trust Company, Philadelphia 19103

Teitelman (Nathan & May B.) Charitable Foundation (L)
MI-22-31-62
625 Ridge Pike, #C101, Conshohocken 19428

Templeton Foundation, Inc. (R)
5 Radnor Corporate Center, Suite 120, Radnor 19087

Tessler Family Foundation, The (I)
41 Conshohocken State Road, Bala Cynwyd 19004

TFA Recordings, Inc. (O)
P.O. Box 368, Bala Cynwyd 19004

Themian Charitable Center/Educational Charitable Trust (R)
c/o Jacobs, 2000 Market Street, 10th Floor, Philadelphia 19103

Thinnes (Michele) Memorial Scholarship Fund (R)
2235 Hedgewood Road, Hatfield 19440

Thoma Family Foundation, The (L) MI-52-61
1481 East Bristol Road, Churchville 18966

Thomas (Morgan H. & Aimee K.) Foundation (NP)
c/o Stockton Bates & Co., 42 South 15th Street, #600,
Philadelphia 19102

Thomas Memorial Foundation (NP)
c/o PNC Bank N.A., Philadelphia 19103

Thompson (Beatrice & Francis) Scholarship Trust (R)
510 Walnut Street, Suite 1100, Philadelphia 19106

Thompson (Paul), III Charitable Foundation (L)
MI-13-41-55
667 Dodds Lane, Gladwyne 19035

Thompson (Regina B. & Walter E.) Charitable Trust (R)
c/o Mellon Bank N.A., Philadelphia 19101

Thompson (Robert & Mimi) Charitable Foundation (I)
2000 Papermill Road, Huntingdon Valley 19006

Thomson (Frank) Scholarship Trust (R)
c/o First Union/Wachovia, Philadelphia 19109

Thomson (John Edgar) Foundation, The (O)
318 Rittenhouse Claridge, 18th & Walnut Street, Philadelphia 19103

Tippett (E.) for United Methodist Homes (R)
c/o Mellon Bank N.A., Philadelphia 19101

Titman (Eloise Frantz) Memorial Fund (R)
c/o Mellon Bank N.A., Philadelphia 19101

Tobin Foundation (NP)
c/o The Glenmede Trust Company, Philadelphia 19103

Toll (Evelyn) Family Foundation, The (NP)
c/o Ballard, Spahr, 1735 Market St., 51st Floor, Philadelphia 19103

Toll Charitable Foundation (NP)
Two Logan Square, Suite 1565, Philadelphia 19103

Tomlin (Charles I.) Trust (R)
c/o Mellon Bank N.A., Philadelphia 19101

Townsend (Laura A.) Trust for Philadelphia PSREA (R)
c/o Mellon Bank N.A., Philadelphia 19101

Tracy-Sandford Foundation (L) MI-41-99
c/o Landreth, 731 Spruce Street, Philadelphia 19106

Trainer (Mary W.) Scholarship Fund (R)
Widener University/Development Office, Chester 19013

Tredennick (William & Helen) Foundation
(Formerly of Norristown; now located in FL)

Tree of Concern International Foundation (R)
3600 Conshohocken Ave., #705, Philadelphia 19131

Treen (Henrietta S.) Trust (R)
c/o First Union/Wachovia, Philadelphia 19109

Tulin (Josephine, Jessar & Morris) Foundation (NP)
c/o Isadaner & Co., 3 Bala Plaza, Bala Cynwyd 19004

Turbo Research Foundation (R)
1442 Phoenixville Pike, West Chester 19380

Tuten (Margaret Evans) Foundation (L) MI-12-14-99
128 Ashwood Road, Villanova 19085

Twersky (Sigmund & Lea) Foundation (T)

Two Charitable Institutions Trust (R)
c/o Mellon Bank N.A., Philadelphia 19101

Tyndale (John) Scholarship Fund (R)
c/o Mellon Bank N.A., Philadelphia 19101

U.S. Healthcare Foundation, The (I)
980 Jolly Road, Blue Bell 19422

Ukrainian Information Bureau (O)
P.O. Box 52739, Philadelphia 19115

Uncommon Individual Foundation, The (O)
290 King of Prussia Road, Suite 314, Radnor 19087

Unger (Pearl) Charitable Trust (NP)
c/o PNC Bank N.A., Philadelphia 19103

Unisource Foundation, The (T)

Unity Club (I)
6312 Vine Street, Philadelphia 19139

Universal Institute, Inc. (R)
814 South 15th Street, Philadelphia 19146

University of Vermont/Lane Scholarship Fund (NP)
c/o PNC Bank N.A., Philadelphia 19103

Urban Research, Foundation for (L) MI-41
910 Hill House, 201 West Evergreen Road, Philadelphia 19118

Urology Research Association (R)
5 Silverstein Pavilion, H.U.P., Philadelphia 19104

Valergakis (Frederick E.G.) Charitable Trust (NP)
c/o Thompson, 1600 Market Street, #1600, Philadelphia 19103

Van Name Charitable Trust, The (NP)
c/o The Glenmede Trust Company, Philadelphia 19103

Van Wynen (J.A., Jr. & W.F.) Trust 'A' (NP)
c/o PNC Bank N.A., Philadelphia 19103

Van Wynen (J.A., Jr. & W.F.) Trust 'B' (NP)
c/o PNC Bank N.A., Philadelphia 19103

Verizon Foundation
(Formerly of Philadelphia; now located in NYC).

Vets Haven, Inc. (R)
3120 Dixon Ave., Bristol 19007

Vox Populi (I)
322 Bryn Mawr Ave., Bala Cynwyd 19004

Waber (Morris) Fund, The
(New name: The Waber Fund)

Wachs (Philip) & Juliet Spitzer Foundation (I)
464 Conshohocken State Road, Bala Cynwyd 19004

Wagman Foundation (NP)
c/o Sampson, 2508 Grant Road, Broomall 19008

Walton (Frank S.) Foundation (NP)
c/o PNC Bank N.A., Philadelphia 19103

Ward (John M. E.) Trust (R)
c/o Mellon Bank N.A., Philadelphia 19101

Waters (Asa Wilson) Trust (NP)
c/o Mellon Bank N.A., Philadelphia 19101

Waters (Thomas P.) Foundation (NP)
c/o Iskrant, 1600 Market Street, #2600, Philadelphia 19103

Wawriw (Rose) Trust for Manor College (R)
c/o First Union/Wachovia, Philadelphia 19109

Way (Anna L.) Trust (R)
c/o First Union/Wachovia, Philadelphia 19109

Wayne Baseball, Inc. (R)
124 Cornell Lane, St. Davids 19087

Weamer (H.C.) Charitable Trust (R)
c/o First Union/Wachovia, Philadelphia 19109

Webster (Ruth) Memorial Fund Trust (NP)
c/o PNC Bank N.A., Philadelphia 19103

Weinberg (Jeffrey Jay) Memorial Foundation (R)
c/o Coombs, 490 Norristown Road, #250, Blue Bell 19422

Weinberg (Jeffrey Jay) Memorial Foundation (R)
c/o 490 Norristown Road, Suite 250, Blue Bell 19422

Welcome Society of Pennsylvania (R)
c/o Strauss, 1600 Market Street, Suite 3600, Philadelphia 19103

Welsh (Edward R.) Scholarship Trust (U)

Welsh Valley Preservation Society (O)
P.O. Box 261, Kulpsville 19443

West (Helen A.) Trust for Lutheran Home for the Aged (R)
c/o Mellon Bank N.A., Philadelphia 19101

West (Herman O.) Foundation, The
(New name: The H.O. West Foundation)

West (Sarah E.T.) Trust #3 (R)
c/o PNC Bank N.A., Philadelphia 19103

West Norriton Little League (R)
57 Carlton Lane, Norristown 19403

Western Soup Society (R)
c/o Stevens, 640 Sentry Parkway, #104, Blue Bell 19422

Westmoreland Coal Co./Penn Virginia Corp. Foundation (NP)
700 The Bellevue, 200 South Broad Street, Philadelphia 19102

Whalesback Foundation
(Formerly of Philadelphia, now located in NY)

Wharton (William W.) Trust for Palmer House (NP)
c/o Mellon Bank N.A., Philadelphia 19101

White-Williams Foundation (R)
Admin. Building, 21st Street & The Parkway, Philadelphia 19130

Whiteley (Purdon) Trust (R)
c/o Mellon Bank N.A., Philadelphia 19101

Whole Cloth Foundation (I)
c/o Milton Feldman, 1735 Market Street, Philadelphia 19103

Widener Memorial School Endowment Foundation (R)
c/o PNC Bank N.A., Philadelphia 19103

Widgeon Foundation
(Formerly of Blue Bell; now located in MD)

Willard (Margaretta) Trust (R)
c/o Mellon Bank N.A., Philadelphia 19101

Williams (Charles C.) Trust/Scholarship Fund (L) MI-43
c/o Bellwoar, 1400 Two Penn Center, Philadelphia 19102

Willits Trust for Central Park United Methodist Church (R)
c/o First Union/Wachovia, Philadelphia 19109

Wilson (Geraldine Diehl) Foundation of Delanco (NP)
c/o Fuhrman, 1900 Market Street, #706, Philadelphia 19103

Wilson Family Memorial Scholarship (R)
c/o First Union/Wachovia, Philadelphia 19109

Wilson Fund, The (NP)
c/o The Glenmede Trust Company, Philadelphia 19103

Winokur Family Foundation, The (L) MI-22-62
40 Trent Road, Wynnewood 19096

Winston (Dr. Lee) & Herman Silver Charitable Fund (T)

Wismer (Russell) Trust for Christ Church (R)
c/o First Union/Wachovia, Philadelphia 19109

Wistar (Isaac J.) Institution (U)

Witkin (Maurice) Hospital Trust (R)
c/o Mellon Bank N.A., Philadelphia 19101

WLG Foundation (R)
c/o PNC Advisors, 1600 Market Street, 6th Floor, Philadelphia 19103

Woelpper (George G.) Trust (I)
c/o First Union/Wachovia, Philadelphia 19109

Wolf (Alice K.) Memorial Scholarship (NP)
c/o PNC Bank N.A., Philadelphia 19103

Wolf (Frances E. & Elias) Fund (T)

Wolf (Walter J.) Trust (R)
c/o PNC Bank N.A., Philadelphia 19103

Wolf Creek Charitable Foundation, The (NP)
c/o PNC Bank N.A., Philadelphia 19103

Wolfer (Alfred) Educational Trust (R)
c/o PNC Bank N.A., Philadelphia 19103

Woloschuk (John) Trust/St. Vladmir's Greek Catholic Church (R)
c/o First Union/Wachovia, Philadelphia 19109

Women's Aid/Penn Central Scholarship Fund (R)
c/o Conrail, 6 Penn Center, Room 1010, Philadelphia 19102

Wood (A.J.) Foundation, The (T)

Wood (Alice) for Haddon Fortnightly (NP)
c/o PNC Bank N.A., Philadelphia 19103

Wood (Alice) for Historical Society of Haddonfield (NP)
c/o PNC Bank N.A., Philadelphia 19103

Wood (J.S.), Jr. for Haddon Fortnightly (NP)
c/o PNC Bank N.A., Philadelphia 19103

Wood (J.S.), Jr. for Historical Society of Haddonfield (NP)
c/o PNC Bank N.A., Philadelphia 19103

Woodward (Harry C.) Trust (R)
c/o First Union/Wachovia, Philadelphia 19109

World Academy of Art & Science, American Division (O)
c/o Palmer, 432 Montgomery Ave., Suite 401, Haverford 19041

World Peace Association, Inc. (O)
615 Ashbourne Road, Elkins Park 19117

World-Wide Book Fdn. of Souderton-Telford Rotary (R)
P.O. Box 1277, Souderton 18964

Wright (Annie) Trust (R)
c/o Mellon Bank N.A., Philadelphia 19101

Wurzel (Lillian) Memorial Foundation (I)
c/o Malis, 329 Sinkler Road, Wyncote 19095

Wychgel (Scott Archer) Memorial Scholarship Trust (R)
701 East Lancaster Ave., Downingtown 19335

Wyck Charitable Trust (R)
c/o First Union/Wachovia, Philadelphia 19109

Yampolsky Foundation, The (L) MI-22-32-62
1420 Walnut Street, Philadelphia 19102

Yarway Foundation (R)
c/o Yarway Corp., 480 Norristown Road, Blue Bell 19422

Yentis Foundation (L) MI-22-62-99
7300 City Line Avenue, Suite 120, Philadelphia 19151

Yerkes (Martha E.) Scholarship Foundation (R)
c/o First Union/Wachovia, Philadelphia 19109

Yoskin Family Foundation, The (I)
1606 Pine Street, 2nd Floor, Philadelphia 19103

Young (Dorothy W.) Trust (NP)
c/o PNC Bank N.A., Philadelphia 19103

Young (Horace L.) Trust (R)
c/o First Union/Wachovia, Philadelphia 19109

Young (John U.) Scholarship Fund (R)
c/o Masonic Temple, 1 North Broad Street, Philadelphia 19107

Young American Preserves, Inc. (R)
c/o Dewey, 44 Papermill Road, Newtown Square 19073

Young People's Church of the Air (R)
P.O. Box 3003, Blue Bell 19422

YPI Charitable Trust (R)
c/o Morgan Lewis & Bockius, 2000 One Logan Square, Philadelphia 19103

Zabriskie (Abram J.F.) for First Presbyterian Church of Stroudsburg (R)
c/o Mellon Bank N.A., Philadelphia 19101

Zambak (Garabed) Memorial Fund (L) MI-N/R
5 Lakeshore Drive, Newtown Square 19073

Zimmerman (Cyrus B.) Fund (R)
c/o Mellon Bank N.A., Philadelphia 19101

Zimmerman (Martin H.) Scholarship Fund (R)
c/o First Union/Wachovia, Philadelphia 19109

Southwestern Region / SW

covers the following 14 counties

Allegheny - Armstrong - Beaver - Bedford - Blair - Butler - Cambria
Fayette - Greene - Indiana - Lawrence - Somerset - Washington - Westmoreland

---

SW-001 Acomb Foundation, The
817 - 8th Street, P.O. Box 499
Colver   15927   (Cambria County)

MI-41-42-84-89
Phone 814-748-7991 **FAX** None
EIN 23-7455794   **Year Created** 1992

AMV $876,131   **FYE** 12-00   (**Gifts Received** $349,321)   5 **Grants totaling** $26,000

One local grant: **$6,000** to Cambria Township Volunteer Fire Dept. **Out-of-state** giving includes **$10,000** to Augustana College [IL]; and **$5,000** each to Camp Berea [NH] and The Master's School [CT]. ■**PUBLICATIONS:** None ■**WEBSITE:** None ■**E-MAIL:** None ■**APPLICATION POLICIES & PROCEDURES:** Information not available.

O+D+T   Dolores F. Ingianni (T+Con) — Guy B. Maxfield [NY] (T) — Estate of Geraldine deM. G. Acomb (Donor)

SW-002 Adams Foundation
c/o Abarta, Inc.
1000 RIDC Plaza, Suite 404
Pittsburgh   15238   (Allegheny County)

MI-11-12-15-32-25-35-44-51
Phone 412-963-3163 **FAX** None
EIN 24-0866511   **Year Created** 1955

AMV $753,191   **FYE** 12-00   (**Gifts Received** $90,500)   9 **Grants totaling** $65,000

All local or Lehigh County giving. High grants of **$15,000** each to Pittsburgh Community Food Bank, United Way of the Greater Lehigh Valley [Bethlehem], and Vintage (capital campaign). **$10,000** to Arthritis Foundation/Western Pa. Chapter. **$5,000** to Bethlehem Area Public Library. **$2,500** to Pittsburgh Ballet Theatre. **$1,000** to Family House. **$500** to Family Health Council. ■**PUBLICATIONS:** None ■**WEBSITE:** None ■**E-MAIL:** None ■**APPLICATION POLICIES & PROCEDURES:** The Foundation reports that most grants are for annual campaigns, building/renovation, capital campaigns, endowment, operating support, matching/challenge grants, program development, research, seed money, or program-related investments/loans. No grants awarded to individuals. Submit grant requests at any time in a proposal (three copies required); provide financial statements stating the need and include IRS tax-exempt status documentation. Site visits sometimes are made to organizations being considered for support. Grants are awarded at meetings in February and August.

O+D+T   Shelley M. Taylor (P+T+Con) — Mary R. Hudson (S+T) — James A. Taylor (F+T) — Nelson C. Romero (T) — Corporate donor: Abarta, Inc.

SW-003 Aircast Foundation, The
5840 Ellsworth Ave., Suite 304
Pittsburgh   15232   (Allegheny County)

MI-32
Phone 412-661-7538 **FAX** 412-661-7539
EIN 22-2784475   **Year Created** 1996

AMV $9,480,019   **FYE** 12-00   (**Gifts Received** $0)   11 **Grants totaling** $748,293

Grants awarded nationally for orthopaedic research and education. Grants ranging from **$50,000** to **$150,000** were awarded during 2000-2001 to U. of Pa. [Philadelphia] and U. of Pittsburgh, as well as to Cleveland Clinic/Lerner Research Institute [OH], Duke U. Medical Center [NC], Massachusetts General Hospital, Mayo Clinic Foundation [MN], Mt. Sinai School of Medicine [NY], National Public Radio (for educational purposes) [DC], Orthopaedic Research & Education Foundation [IL], Rhode Island Hospital, SUNY at Stonybrook [NY], U. of Nebraska Medical Center, U. of North Carolina, and U. of Utah. ■**PUBLICATIONS:** Annual Report; Program Announcement & Preliminary Application Guidelines ■**WEBSITE:** www.aircastfoundation.org ■**E-MAIL:** slephart@aircastfoundation.org ■**APPLICATION POLICIES & PROCEDURES:** The Foundation's giving is restricted to scientific research/education in orthopaedic medicine and science, especially (a) for optimizing function and improving medical outcomes, and (b) for biomedical research that exhibits creative and innovative solutions to complex medical problems. Orthopaedic Medicine Research Grant applications are encouraged from young investigators holding faculty positions at eligible higher education institutions: universities, colleges, and medical, dental, pharmacy and veterinary schools, as well as U.S. research institutions/hospitals affiliated with higher education institutions. Preference in grants is given to Principal Investigators who have not received NIH grant support in their current field of investigation; initial awards are $100,000 over two years. Prospective applicants should initially secure a copy of Program Announcement and Preliminary Application Guidelines, available from the Foundation or on the website. Grants are awarded in August and December

O+D+T   Susan Pressly Lephart, Ph.D. (Administrative Director+Con) — Glenn W. Johnson, III [NJ] (P+F+T) — Henry J. McVicker [NJ] (VP+S+T) — Kristina Flanagan [NJ] (T) — Mark E. Bolander, M.D. [MN] (Advisory Board Member) — Freddie H. Wu, M.D. (Advisory Board Member) — Savio L-Y Woo, Ph.D. (Advisory Board Member) — Corporate donor: Aircast Corporation [NJ]

SW-004   Alcoa Foundation
c/o Alcoa Corporate Center
201 Isabella Street, 2nd Floor
Pittsburgh   15212   (Allegheny County)

MI-11-12-13-14-15-16-17-19-29-31-32-35-39
42-43-49-51-52-54-55-56-57-81-88
Phone 412-553-2348 **FAX** 412-553-4498
EIN 25-1128857   **Year Created** 1952

AMV $410,121,949   **FYE** 12-01   **(Gifts Received** $500,000)   2500+ **Grants totaling** $21,284,785

Nationwide giving, primarily to corporate operating locations or national organizations; about one-third giving to Pa. focused on Pittsburgh with limited support to Armstrong, Columbia, Lancaster, Lebanon, Lehigh, Schuylkill and Westmoreland counties; grant size details are unavailable. **HUMAN SERVICES & HEALTH GRANTS:** Action-Housing (Family Empowerment Project), Allegheny County CASA-Court Appointed Special Advocates, Armstrong County Council on Alcohol & Other Drugs (Life Skills training project/Parents Who Care program), Bethlehem Haven, Big Brothers & Sisters of Greater Pittsburgh (At-Risk Program), Boys & Girls Clubs of Western Pa. (Outlet Connection-Teen Retail Venture/Youth Enterprise Zone project), Boys Club & Girls Club of Lancaster (Vision of the 21st Century Campaign), Brother's Brother Foundation, Burger King Cancer Caring Center, Children's Home of Pittsburgh (Infant Adoption program), Columbia County United Fund, CACLV/Community Action Committee of the Lehigh Valley (Sixth Street Shelter support), DePaul Institute (Second Century campaign), East Liberty Family Health Care Center (The Every Child Protocol-preschool program), Family Guidance (staff-mentor training), Family House, Family Organization Resource Center of Excellence (Bridge Project), Girl Scouts of SW Pa. (Women & Girls Initiative project), Global Links (suture program/transportation equipment), Good Samaritan Health Corp. [Schuylkill County] (diagnostic cardiac catheterization program), Greater Pittsburgh Community Food Bank, Hill House Assn. (capital campaign), Housing Opportunities [McKeesport], Jubilee Assn. (John Heinz Child Development Center), Kidspeace National Centers for Kids in Crisis [Lehigh County], Lehigh Carbon Community College Foundation [Lehigh County] (Employment Retraining Opportunities program), Leukemia & Lymphoma Society [Whitehall], Life's Work (Social Ventures Fund), Louise Child Care Centers, Make-A-Wish Foundation of Western Pa., Mom's House Inc. of Pittsburgh, Mt. Nazareth Center (playground renovation), North Side Christian Health Center, Northside Common Ministries (Black Men Rising computer project), One to One—The Mentoring Partnership of SW Pa. (strategic plan initiatives), Outreach Teen & Family Services, Persad Center, Pittsburgh Action Against Rape (Building Healthy Relationships K-12 program), Pittsburgh AIDS Task Force, Pittsburgh Cares, The Pittsburgh Foundation (Allegheny County Department of Human Services Integration Fund/Regional Healthcare Initiative), Pittsburgh Leadership Foundation (Cross-Trainers summer camp), Pittsburgh Vision Services, Program for Female Offenders (Adult Basic Educational Component), Providence Connections (Family Support Center), Rainbow Kitchen Community Services [Homestead] (Kids Cafe program), Red Cross/Pittsburgh (emergency services fund), Salvation Army/Pittsburgh (capital campaign/Help Wanted & Resource Center/Partners In Service campaign), Schuylkill County United Way, Schuylkill Women in Crisis [Schuylkill County] (children's programs), Shadyside Hospital Foundation (Center for Cancer Information/Referral and Education Facility/Hillman Center), Society of St. Vincent de Paul [Pittsburgh], Three Rivers Center for Independent Living (new headquarters facility), Three Rivers Employment Service, Three Rivers Youth (career learning project), Travelers Aid Society of Pittsburgh (transportation expenses), Trinity Episcopal Church [Schuylkill County] (Trinity Center for Children), UCP Assn./Pittsburgh District (Creating Opportunities. Changing Lives. campaign), United Fund of Middle Armstrong County, United Jewish Federation of Pittsburgh, United Methodist Church Union (Northview Heights training programs), United Way of Lancaster County, United Way of Lebanon County, United Way of SW Pa., United Way of the Greater Lehigh Valley, United Way of WestmorelandCounty, Wesley Institute (building renovations), Western Pa. Caring Foundation, Westmoreland Human Services (Head Start Centers development), Whale's Tale (Allegheny County Juvenile Court Snack program), Women's Center and Shelter of Greater Pittsburgh (Children's Counseling Center), YMCA-McKeesport (Youth Guidance, Development and Teen LEAD programs), Young Men & Women's Hebrew Assn. & Irene Kaufmann Centers, YMCA of Pittsburgh (capital campaign/East End Youth Outreach program/Youth Employment Service project), and YouthWorks. **ARTS & CULTURE GRANTS:** Afro-American Music Institute, Artists Image Resource, Bach Choir of Pittsburgh, Carnegie Institute (Aluminum by Design exhibition/Awards of Excellence program/Math & Science Collaborative Youth Explorers program), Chatham Baroque (WQED-FM residency program), Children's Center for Theater Arts, City Theatre Company (Young Playwrights project), Civic Light Opera (Creative Vision program), Gateway to the Arts (Educator Advisory Panel), Greater Pittsburgh Arts Alliance, Historical Society of Western Pa. (Business Innovation Initiatives), Manchester Craftsmen's Guild (Arts Leadership and Public Service program/Tones of Nature program), Mattress Factory (education department programs), Mendelssohn Choir of Pittsburgh, New Kensington Chamber Foundation (Aluminum Heritage Museum), Philadelphia Museum of Art (architecture-design exhibit), Pittsburgh Ballet Theatre (arts education/outreach activities), Pittsburgh Center for the Arts (Art Tales program), Pittsburgh Children's Museum (YouthALIVE! program), Pittsburgh Dance Alloy, Pittsburgh Dance Council (Class Act educational program), Pittsburgh Filmmakers (Community & Environment initiative), Pittsburgh Glass Center, Pittsburgh International Children's Theater, Pittsburgh Irish and Classical Theatre, Pittsburgh Opera (education programs), Pittsburgh Opera Theater, Pittsburgh Public Theater (planned giving program), Pittsburgh Symphony (Early Childhood Pilot Program/South American Tour), Pittsburgh Trust for Cultural Resources (Carol R. Brown Programming Fund), Pittsburgh Voyager (education programs/Northside programs), Pittsburgh Zoo, Prime Stage, Quantum Theatre, Renaissance City Wind Music Society, River City Brass Band (student Solo competition), Saltworks Theatre Company, Schuylkill County Council for the Arts (Arts & Ethnic Center), Society for Contemporary Craft, Sweetwater Art Center (Celebration of Cultures), Umoja African Arts Company, U. of Pittsburgh (Kuntu Repertory Theatre/Shakespeare-in-the-Schools program), and Western Pa. Professionals for the Arts. **EDUCATION & EDUCATION-RELATED GRANTS:** Allegheny Intermediate Unit, Allegheny Valley School for Exceptional Children (capital campaign), Allegheny Youth Development (Jump Start program), Breachmenders (School-to-Career program), Burrell Education Foundation (Read to Succeed program), Carnegie Mellon University (Children's School program), Center for Creative Play (new building renovations), Central Northside Reading is Fundamental (R.E.A.D. program/Sharry Everett Scholarship fund), Chatham College (Pittsburgh Teachers Institute), Community College of Allegheny County (distance learning program), Dickinson School of Law [Cumberland County] (scholarship program), Duquesne University (law student scholarship/residential summer science camp), Eagle Foundation [Schuylkill County] (Blue Mountain School District programs), Education Policy & Issues Center (Achieving Educational Excellence in the Region program), Episcopal Diocese of Pittsburgh (Urban Program for Reading), Extra Mile Education Foundation (Success Of All in Reading program), Family Communications (Girls, Math and Science Initiative), Foundation for Free Enterprise

Education [Erie] (Pa. Free Enterprise Week), FAME/Fund For The Advancement Of Minorities Through Education (independent school scholarships), Hightower Scholars [Lower Burrell] (Summer Academy), Holy Family Institute (job training readiness program, Columbus Middle School), Kiski Area School District (supplemental instructional materials), La Roche College (Challenge and Scholar programs), Lebanon Valley Family YMCA [Lebanon County] (after school programs), Mon Valley Education Consortium (The Future is Mine initiative), NEED/Negro Educational Emergency Drive, Pace School (capital campaign), Pa. Engineering Foundation [Harrisburg] (MATHCOUNTS program), Pa. Partnership for Economic Education [Snyder County], Pittsburgh Project (B.A.S.I.C. Academy and Day Camp/Literacy Plus training), Pittsburgh Public Schools (Literacy Plus training/Urban Systemic program), Pittsburgh Regional Center for Science Teachers (Lewis & Clark Discover Expedition project), Point Park College (Project Early Start), Pressley Ridge Schools (Pittsburgh International Children & Families Institute), Schuylkill Community Education Council [Schuylkill County] (Schuylkillbotics program), Seton Hill College (National Education Center for Women in Business), Shady Lane School, Slippery Rock University (safety curriculum), St. Ambrose Catholic Church and School [Schuylkill County] (reading program), Thaddeus Stevens Foundation [Lancaster County] (Summer Experience Technology Camp), U. of Pittsburgh (Jumpstart Pittsburgh programs/Young Writers Institute), Urban Impact Foundation (after school program), and Western Pa. School for Blind Children (Early Childhood Center garden). ***CIVIC-COMMUNITY-ENVIRONMENT GRANTS:*** Allegheny Conference on Community Development, Allegheny County Bar Foundation (Center for Volunteer Legal Resources), Alle-Kiski Valley Senior Citizens Center (equipment/yard improvements), Boy Scouts (Scouts in Housing initiative), Carnegie Mellon University (Air Quality Laboratory/Cyert Center program/National Robotics Engineering Consortium), Church Army, Community Design Center of Pittsburgh (Renovation Information Network), Community Media, Cressona [Schuylkill County] (recreation area improvements), Cressona Area Little League [Schuylkill County] (baseball fields lighting), East End Cooperative Ministry (Joblink/Employment Education program), Executive Service Corps of Western Pa. (legal referral services), Focus on Renewal Sto Rox Neighborhood Corp. (McKees Rocks Transportation program), Foundation for Agriculture & Resource Management [Schuylkill County] (Fair), Foundation of the Lancaster Chamber of Commerce [Lancaster County] (leadership program), Friends to Friends [Export] (NCNB Leadership Forum attendance), Garfield Jubilee Assn. (Micrographic training program), Golden Triangle Radio Information Center (outreach program), Grantmakers of Western Pa. (Corporate Citizenship seminar), Greater Pittsburgh Charitable Trust, SW Pa. Workforce Summit Initiative, Hawk Mountain Sanctuary Assn. [Berks County] (land purchase), Hosanna House [Wilkinsburg] (workforce development program), Indiana University of Pa. (Promoting Traffic Safety Through Safe Community Notion), Junior Achievement of Central Pa. [Lancaster County] (Lebanon County programs), Junior Achievement of Southwest Pa. (Impact 2005), Leadership Pittsburgh, League of Women Voters of Greater Pittsburgh, Manchester Youth Development Center (New Millennium Business Skills), Minority Enterprise Corp. of SW PA. (Micro Business Advisory program), Mount Ararat Community Activity Center (Science & Technology project), National Foundation for Teaching Entrepreneurship (BizTech program), Neighborhood Legal Services Assn. (Equal Justice Under Law campaign), New Hope for Neighborhood Renewal (renewal program), North Side Civic Development Council (Business Plan Competition program), Pennsylvanians for Effective Government-Education Committee [Harrisburg] (college intern program), Sports and Exhibition Authority of Pittsburgh/Allegheny County (North Shore Riverfront Park project), Pittsburgh Council for International Visitors, Pittsburgh Digital Greenhouse, Pittsburgh Parks Conservancy (BioBlitz 2001), Pittsburgh Regional Alliance, Riverlife Task Force, Robert Morris University (Bayer Center for Nonprofit Management), Schuylkill Leadership Assn. [Schuylkill County], Tamaqua Area 2004 Partnership [Schuylkill County] (Everhart Care program/Southern Anthracite Community Regional Exhibits), U. of Pittsburgh/School of Law-Community & Economic Development Legal Clinic Initiative), Upper Burrell Township Volunteer Fire #1 (emergency response vehicle), Urban League of Pittsburgh (Director of Research and Public Policy funding), Veterans Place of Washington Blvd. [Monroeville], Wildlands Conservancy [Lehigh County], and World Affairs Council of Pittsburgh. ***OUT-OF-STATE GIVING*** to corporate operating locations in many states and countries, and many national organizations and institutions. Educational matching gifts were disbursed nationwide to many hundreds of colleges/universities. ■**PUBLICATIONS:** Annual Report (lists selected grantees—not amounts) with application guidelines. ■**WEBSITE:** www.alcoa.com/global/en/community/foundation.asp ■**E-MAIL:** alcoa.foundation@alcoa.com ■**APPLICATION POLICIES & PROCEDURES:** The Foundation reports that priority is given to programs/organizations in or near communities with Alcoa plants/offices; visit www.alcoa.com for a complete list of operating locations. A majority of grants awarded are in one of five categories: (a) Conservation & Sustainability—demonstrating a commitment to conservation by educating young leaders, protecting our forests, promoting sound public policy research, and understanding the linkages between business and the environment; (b) Safe & Healthy Children and Families—ensuring that children and their families have the tools, the knowledge, and the services to remain healthy and safe at home, in the community, and in the workplace; (c) Global Education in Business, Science, Engineering & Technology—broadening student participation in areas central to the corporation to ensure that a diverse cross-section of our communities is prepared for a global workplace; (d) Business and Community Partnerships—seeding notions of corporate citizenship, community by community, to strengthen the nonprofit sector and to develop meaningful partnerships among nonprofits, the private sector and local government; and (e) Workforce Skills Today for Tomorrow—providing individuals with critical skills and services to be economically connected, workplace-ready, and productive in a changing economy. Most grants are for general operations, program support, building and capital funds, seed money, emergency funds, conferences, seminars, research, challenge grants, and employee matching gifts. Grants generally are for one year but support for capital or long-term projects may extend over several years. Generally, no grants generally are awarded for local projects except those near plant locations. Also, no grants are given for endowment; deficit reduction; operating reserves; benefit dinners/events, tickets, tables, golf outings, souvenir programs, advertising, trips, tours; documentaries or videos; political or lobbying purposes; hospital capital campaigns except under specific circumstances—contact the Foundation; sectarian religious purposes; or to individuals. Scholarships are awarded only to company employees' dependents. The Foundation generally will not award operating support and capital campaign support at the same time. Prospective applicants may contact at any time the local Alcoa facility as local management makes recommendations on grant awards; submit a one-page letter which describes the organization's mission, the purpose of the request, the request's connection to the Foundation's Areas of Excellence (see above) and contact information. If interested, the local Alcoa official will respond to invite submission of additional information; Local Alcoa community officials will then make recommendations to the Foundation for grant awards. Grants are made throughout the year. Also, a new employee program ACTION (Alcoans Coming Together In Our Neighborhoods) recognizes and rewards employee involvement with nonprofit organizations; grants of $3,000 are made to nonprofit organizations where ten Alcoa employees provide a day of service. Educational matching gifts for universities and two- or four-year colleges have a $25 minimum, $5,000 maximum/employee/year, and are matched 2:1. **Note:** In certain instances, a corporate contribution (not a grant from the Alcoa Foundation) may be available; contact the nearest Alcoa location.

O+D+T All officers/directors are Alcoa employees/retirees: Kathleen W. Buechel (P+F+D+Con) — Richardo E. Belda (D) — Earnest J. Edwards (D) — Richard B. Kelson (D) — William E. Leahey, Jr. (D) — Renata Camargo Nascimento (D) — Barry C. Owens (D) — G. John Pizzey (D) — Richard L. 'Jake' Siewert (D) — Mellon Bank N.A. (Corporate Trustee) — Corporate donor: Aluminum Company of America

---

SW-005 **Alcoa-Alumax Foundation**
c/o Alcoa Corporate Center
201 Isabella Street, 2nd Floor
Pittsburgh   15212   (Allegheny County)

MI-11-13-31-42-43-88-89

Phone 412-553-2779 **FAX** 412-553-4498
EIN 58-2166783   **Year Created** 1997

AMV $3,383,804   **FYE** 12-01   **(Gifts Received** $0)   44 **Grants totaling** $197,251

Limited Pa. giving, primarily to Schuylkill, Columbia, Lancaster and Lebanon counties. High grant of **$15,000** to Schuylkill County Volunteer Firemen's Assn. **$10,000** to Pottsville Hospital/Warne Clinic [Schuylkill County]. **$3,334** to Penn Laurel Girl Scout Council [Adams County]. Other Pa. awards are scholarships, **$2,000-$4,000,** for company employees' children. — In the prior year, Pa. giving included **$65,253** to United Way of Lancaster County; **$30,000** to Schuylkill United Way; **$20,000** each to Cressona [Schuylkill County] and Thaddeus Stevens College of Technology; **$13,000** to United Way of Columbia County; and smaller grants for similar purposes. ■**PUBLICATIONS:** scholarship application form; matching gift form ■**WEBSITE:** www.alcoa.com/global/en/community/foundation.asp ■**E-MAIL:** alcoa.foundation@alcoa.com ■**APPLICATION POLICIES & PROCEDURES:** The Foundation reports that Pa. giving focuses on communities with Alcoa-Alumax facilities in Columbia, Lancaster, Lebanon and Schuylkill counties. Scholarships are restricted to children of company employees. Prospective applicants should contact their local Alcoa-Alumax facility to inquire about submitting a grant request; do not send unsolicited requests to the Pittsburgh address. — **Note:** The Foundation will be terminating sometime before December 2004.

O+D+T Kathleen W. Buechel (P+Con) — Grace A. Smith (S) — Robert F. Slagle (D)

SW-006 **Allegheny Foundation**
One Oxford Center, Suite 3900
301 Grant Street
Pittsburgh   15219   (Allegheny County)

MI-13-22-25-29-31-41-42-44-52-56-61-71-72
83-86-89
Phone 412-392-2900 **FAX** 412-392-2922
EIN 25-6012303   **Year Created** 1953

AMV $42,098,138   **FYE** 12-00   **(Gifts Received** $0)   45 **Grants totaling** $1,582,500

Mostly local/Pa. giving; grants are for general support except as noted. High grants of **$100,000** each to Catholic Diocese of Pittsburgh Foundation/Bishop's Education Fund (tuition assistance endowment), Pittsburgh Parks Conservancy, and Pittsburgh Symphony (challenge grant). **$75,000** to Greater Pittsburgh Community Food Bank (capital support). **$68,000** to Extra Mile Education Foundation (scholarship fund/capital support). **$57,500** to Brownsville Area Revitalization Corp. (Newspapers in Education program/capital support). **$55,000** to Carnegie Library of Homestead (capital support). **$50,000** each to Allegheny Institute for Public Policy, Epiphany Catholic Church (capital support), and River City Brass Band. **$40,000** to Boys & Girls Clubs of Western Pa. (summer program). **$25,000** each to Braddock's Field Historical Society (archive project/capital support), Light of Life Rescue Mission (general/capital support), Ligonier Borough Volunteer Hose Co. (capital support), PHASE/Perry Hilltop Assn. for Successful Enterprise (capital support), PANO/Pa. Assn. of Nonprofit Organizations [Harrisburg], and Pa. Economy League (Allegheny County Transition Project). **$20,000** each to Mel Blount Youth Home of Washington (program support) and Pittsburgh Civic Garden Center (program support). **$16,000** to Penn State U. (forest decline research). **$15,000** to Allegheny Youth Development. **$10,000** to Community Foundation of Westmoreland County (one-room schoolhouse project), Holy Family Foundation, Ligonier Township Volunteer Fire Dept., Lincoln Institute of Public Opinion Research [Harrisburg], Midway Boys Club (capital support), Operation Dig (capital support), and Pittsburgh Mercy Foundation (Operation Safety Net). **$6,000** each to Pittsburgh History & Landmarks Foundation (project support) and Ryerss Farm for Aged Equines [Montgomery County]. **$5,000** each to Duquesne U. (trustee leadership institute) and Mon-Yough Riverfront Entertainment & Cultural Council (program support). **$2,500** each to Garden Club of McKeesport (capital support) and Ligonier Assn. of Churches (food bank). **Out-of-state** giving includes **$100,000** to Intercollegiate Studies Institute [DE] (prep school lecture program); **$75,000** each to American Legislative Exchange Council [DC] and Children Requiring a Caring Kommunity [CA]; **$52,000** to Nantucket Athenaeum [MA]; **$50,000** to Nantucket Boys & Girls Club [MA] (capital support); **$25,000** each to Aquidneck Island Land Trust [RI], Center for the Study of Popular Culture [CA] (civil rights project), Historic Red Clay Valley [DE] (capital support); and smaller grants for similar purposes. ■**PUBLICATIONS:** Annual Report and application guidelines; also available on Foundation's website. ■**WEBSITE:** www.scaife.com ■**E-MAIL:** None ■**APPLICATION POLICIES & PROCEDURES:** The Foundation reports that giving focuses on Western Pa., especially for historic preservation, civic development, education, youth development, and animal welfare. Most grants are for general support or special projects; multiyear grants are awarded. No grants are awarded to individuals or for scholarships/fellowships, nor generally for sponsorships, endowment, renovations or government agencies. Grant requests may be submitted at any time in a brief letter (2 pages maximum) signed by the organization's CEO or authorized representative and approved by the organization's Board of Directors; describe the specific program for which funds are requested and include organizational/project budgets, audited financial statement, list of major funding sources, Board member list, and IRS tax-exempt status documentation. Site visits sometimes are made to organizations being considered for a grant. Grants generally are awarded at a December meeting.

O+D+T Joanne B. Beyer (P+Con) — Richard M. Scaife (C+T+Donor) — Ralph H. Goettler [OH] (F) — Doris O'Donnell [OH] (T) — Margaret R. Scaife (T) — Nathan J. Stark [DC] (T) — George A. Weymouth [Chadds Ford] (T) — Arthur P. Ziegler, Jr. (T)

SW-007 Allegheny Technologies Charitable Trust
c/o Allegheny Technologies, Inc.
1000 Six PPG Place
Pittsburgh 15222   (Allegheny County)

MI-11-13-14-22-29-31-35-41-42-44-49-52-54
55-56-57-71-81-85-88-89
Phone 412-394-2800 **FAX** 412-394-3010
EIN 23-7873055   **Year Created** 1996

AMV $2,934,548   **FYE** 12-00   **(Gifts Received** $2,500,000)   102 **Grants totaling** $1,475,840

Mostly local/regional giving. High grant of **$463,596** to United Way of SW Pa. **$250,000** to Carnegie Mellon U. **$120,000** to Early Childhood Initiative. **$55,000** to Pittsburgh Symphony. **$42,238** to WQED. **$41,524** to United Way of Kiski Valley [Greensburg]. **$33,813** to United Way of Washington County. **$33,600** to Allegheny Conference on Community Development. **$30,000** each to Boy Scouts/Moraine Trails Council [Butler] and Pittsburgh Public Theater. **$25,000** to Penn State U./New Kensington. **$20,000** each to Carnegie Science Center (robotics exhibit) and Children's Hospital of Pittsburgh (free care fund). **$15,000** to Extra Mile Education Foundation. **$10,000** each to Civic Light Opera, Duquesne U., Holy Family Institute, Kiski Valley YMCA, St. Joseph High School [Natrona Heights], and Westmoreland Museum of American Art. **$7,500** to Pittsburgh Children's Museum. **$5,000** each to Girl Scouts of SW Pa., National Parkinson Foundation/Greater Pittsburgh Chapter, Team Pennsylvania Foundation [Harrisburg], and Three Rivers Arts Festival. **$4,000** to Community Library of Allegheny Valley. **$3,000** each to Catholic Charities, Pittsburgh Vintage Grand Prix, and YMCA of Allegheny Valley. **$1,000-$2,500** each for American Heart Assn., ARC-Allegheny Foundation, Big Brothers Big Sisters of Greater Pittsburgh, Boy Scouts/Greater Pittsburgh Council, Boy Scouts/Catawba Council, Carnegie Museum of Pittsburgh, Coalition for Christian Outreach, Contact Pittsburgh, Epilepsy Foundation of Western Pa., Family Guidance Center, Family Resources, First Night Pittsburgh, Gateway Rehabilitation Center, Greater Pittsburgh Community Food Bank, Historical Society of Western Pa., Jewish National Fund, Juvenile Diabetes Foundation, League of Women Voters/Allegheny County Council, Make A Wish Foundation of Western Pa., Mendelssohn Choir of Pittsburgh, National Council of Jewish Women (race for the cure), Opera Theatre of Pittsburgh, Pauline Auberle Foundation, Phipps Conservatory & Botanical Garden, Pittsburgh Center for the Arts, Pittsburgh Dance Council, Pittsburgh Vision Services, Pittsburgh Zoo, Poise Foundation, Pressley Ridge School, Saltworks Theatre Company, Strongland Chamber of Commerce, Three Rivers Young Peoples Orchestra, Urban League of Pittsburgh, Visiting Nurse Assn., Vocational Rehabilitation Center, World Affairs Council of Pittsburgh, and YMCA of Pittsburgh. Other smaller local contributions. **Out-of-state** giving includes **$30,000** to United Way of Wallingford [CT] ; **$10,082** to United Way of Greater New Bedford [MA]; **$10,000** each to Economic Strategy Institute [DC] and North Alabama Science Center;**$9,000** to Junior Achievement of SE Connecticut; **$6,500** to Rensselaer Polytechnic Institute [NY]; **$5,000** to International Women's Democracy Center [DC]; and other grants to United Ways in corporate locations in CT, IN and NY, and several national organizations. — Major grants approved for future payment include: **$640,000** to Early Childhood Initiative; **$90,000** to Pittsburgh Public Theater (lobby staircase); **$71,400** to Allegheny Conference on Community Development; **$70,000** to St. Joseph High School; **$60,000** each to Boy Scouts/Moraine Trails Council and Children's Hospital of Pittsburgh; **$50,000** each to Penn State/New Kensington and Westminster College; **$40,000** to Chatham College; and **$30,000** to Washington Hospital Foundation. ■**PUBLICATIONS:** None ■**WEBSITE:** www.alleghenytechnologies.com [corporate info only] ■**E-MAIL:** None ■**APPLICATION POLICIES & PROCEDURES:** The Trust reports that giving focuses on corporate operating areas—Allegheny, Westmoreland, Washington, and Chester counties in Pa. and CT, IN, MA and OH—with most grants for special projects, building funds, capital needs, publications, and scholarships; no grants are awarded to individuals or to other private foundations. Grant requests may be submitted in a letter (2 pages maximum) at any time; include IRS tax-exempt status documentation. The trustees generally, but not always, meet in January, April, July and October to award grants. **Note:** An educational matching gift program ($25 minimum, $2,000 maximum/employee/institution/year) for secondary schools and most types of higher education institutions is administered directly by the Corporation, not the Charitable Trust. — Formerly called the Allegheny Ludlum Foundation -or- Allegheny Teledyne Inc. Charitable Trust.
O+D+T Jon D. Walton, Esq. (Chair, Contributions Committee+Con) — T.A. Corcoran (T) — J.L. Murdy (T) — PNC Bank N.A. (Corporate Trustee) — Corporate donor: Allegheny Technologies, Inc.

SW-008 Aloe (William & Frances) Charitable Foundation
c/o United Pittsburgh Coal Sales
200 Neville Road, Neville Island
Pittsburgh 15225   (Allegheny County)

MI-12-14-25-32-45-61-71

Phone 412-777-6641 **FAX** None
EIN 25-1540814   **Year Created** 1986

AMV $356,496   **FYE** 12-00   **(Gifts Received** $0)   5 **Grants totaling** $10,000

All local giving. **$2,000** each to Greater Pittsburgh Community Food Bank, Greater Pittsburgh Literacy Council, Make-A-Wish Foundation of Western Pa., Muscular Dystrophy Assn. and Serra Club of Pittsburgh. — Grants awarded in the prior year: **$5,000** each to Chartiers Valley Partnership and Stream Restoration [Rochester]. ■**PUBLICATIONS:** None ■**WEBSITE:** None ■**E-MAIL:** None ■**APPLICATION POLICIES & PROCEDURES:** Grant requests may be submitted in any form at any time.
O+D+T Daniel Aloe (D+Donor+Con) — Frances Aloe (P+Donor+D) — Andrew Aloe (S+F+D) — David Aloe (D) — Joesph Aloe (D+Donor) — Mark Aloe (D) — Kathryn Aloe Cashman (D)

SW-009 Armstrong-McKay Foundation
c/o Henry H. Armstrong Associates, Inc.
1706 Allegheny Towers, 625 Stanwix Street
Pittsburgh 15222   (Allegheny County)

MI-12-13-31-41-57-63-71

Phone 412-471-1551 **FAX** None
EIN 25-1754629   **Year Created** 1994

AMV $756,902   **FYE** 12-00   **(Gifts Received** $17,100)   26 **Grants totaling** $57,375

About two-thirds local giving. High grant of **$6,000** to Calvary Episcopal Church. **$5,000** to Pittsburgh Parks Conservancy. **$3,695** to Fox Chapel Country Day School. **$2,500** to The Ellis School. **$2,145** to Ligonier Valley YMCA. **$1,000-$1,500** each to Children's Home of Pittsburgh, Children's Hospital of Pittsburgh, Children's Institute of Pittsburgh, Loyalhanna Watershed

Assn., Pittsburgh/Muskoka Foundation, and WQED. Other smaller local contributions for similar purposes. **Out-of-state** giving includes **$5,000** to Bay Area Girls Center [CA]; **$2,860** to Atlantic Salmon Federation [ME]; **$2,500** to South Muskoka Hospital Foundation [Canada]; and smaller grants for private schools/colleges or environmental organizations in New England and elsewhere. ■**PUBLICATIONS:** None ■**WEBSITE:** None ■**E-MAIL:** None ■**APPLICATION POLICIES & PROCEDURES:** No grants awarded to individuals.

O+D+T   James McKay Armstrong (T+Con)

SW-010   **Aspire Foundation, The**   MI-11-43
   c/o Equitable Resources, Inc.
   One Oxford Center, 301 Grant Street, Suite 3300   **Phone** 412-553-5700 **FAX** None
   Pittsburgh   15219   (Allegheny County)   **EIN** 25-1759917   **Year Created** 1995
AMV $250,965   **FYE** 12-00   **(Gifts Received** $0)   11 **Grants totaling** $55,250

All local giving. Ten ASPIRE Scholarships, **$2,500** to **$7,500** each, awarded to local high school seniors. Also, **$15,000** to United Way of SW Pa. ■**PUBLICATIONS:** Scholarship application policies/guidelines ■**WEBSITE:** None ■**E-MAIL:** None ■**APPLICATION POLICIES & PROCEDURES:** The Foundation reports its primary interest is mentorship programs for junior/senior high schools in Western Pa. and college scholarships for graduating seniors of this mentoring program. Submit applications on a formal application form (available from the Foundation) in January-February (deadline is February 28th) for participation the following academic year.

O+D+T   Carol B. Gras (Manager+Con) — Clifford W. Baker (P+D) — Babatunde Fapohunda (VP+D) — Cheryl O'Malley (S+D) — Greg Mrozek (F+D) — Holly Hudson (D) — Greg Spencer (D) — Corporate donors: Equitable Resources, Inc., Energy Technology Corp.

SW-011   **Avner (Michael Bill) Memorial Foundation**   MI-29-41
   c/o Citron Alex & Zionts
   429 Forbes Ave., Suite 1700   **Phone** 412-765-2720 **FAX** None
   Pittsburgh   15219   (Allegheny County)   **EIN** 25-6074647   **Year Created** 1965
AMV $345,595   **FYE** 12-00   **(Gifts Received** $0)   9 **Grants totaling** $19,940

About three-fourths local giving. High grant of **$13,000** to Shady Side Academy. **$1,000** to Fox Chapel Country Day School. **Out-of-state** giving incluces **$2,000** to Wesley House Community Center [FL] and **$1,000** to Walker School [GA].■**PUBLICATIONS:** Application Form ■**WEBSITE:** None ■**E-MAIL:** None ■**APPLICATION POLICIES & PROCEDURES:** Prospective applicants should contact the Foundation in a letter requesting an application form. Submit grant requests on the application form at any time include IRS tax-exempt status documentation.

O+D+T   Howard M. Alex, Esq. ' (Co-T+Con) — Louis L. Avner [FL] (Co-T+Donor) — Helen L. Avner [FL] (Co-T+Donor) — Robin Avner [CA] (Co-T) — Constance Buchanan [NC] (Co-T)

SW-012   **Babcock Charitable Trust**   MI-11-14-31-32-41-42-72
   c/o Babcock Lumber Company
   2220 Palmer Street   **Phone** 412-351-3515 **FAX** None
   Pittsburgh   15218   (Allegheny County)   **EIN** 25-6035161   **Year Created** 1957
AMV $4,473,453   **FYE** 12-00   **(Gifts Received** $3,750)   31 **Grants totaling** $57,865

Nearly half local giving. High local grant of **$6,250** to United Way of SW Pa. **$5,000** each to Allegheny Valley School, Duquesne U. (Beard Center for Leadership in Ethics), and Pittsburgh Zoo. **$1,000** to Shady Side Academy. Other smaller local contributions. **Out-of-state** giving includes **$8,000** to U. of Florida; **$7,300** to City of Hope [CA]; **$5,000** to Kingswood-Oxford School [CT]; and other smaller grants, mostly to AL , FL, or CT. ■**PUBLICATIONS:** None ■**WEBSITE:** None ■**E-MAIL:** None ■**APPLICATION POLICIES & PROCEDURES:** The Trust reports that most giving is for organizations in Babcock company locations or those in which family members are involved, especially educational institutions and arts/cultural organizations. Most giving is for special projects, building funds, publications, scholarships, or matching grants. No grants are awarded to politically oriented/motivated organizations or individuals. Grant requests may be submitted in a letter (4 pages maximum) at any time; describe the project and amount of funding requested, and include a list of other funding sources, Board member list, and IRS tax-exempt status documentation. Site visits sometimes are made to organizations being considered for a grant.

O+D+T   Courtney Babcock Borntraeger (T+Con) — Richard S. Cuda (T) — Carl P. Stillitano (T) — Corporate donor: Babcock Lumber Company

---

SW-013   **Bailey (Helen L.) Foundation**   MI-29-42-43
   c/o Mellon Private Wealth Management
   One Mellon Center, P.O. Box 185   **Phone** 412-234-0023 **FAX** 412-234-1073
   Pittsburgh   15230   (Allegheny County)   **EIN** 25-6018937   **Year Created** 1958
AMV $1,907,521   **FYE** 12-00   **(Gifts Received** $0)   6 **Grants totaling** $85,000

High grant of **$64,500** to Grove City College (John Bailey Memorial Scholarship Fund). **$3,000** to Training, Inc. **$2,500** to Shady Side Academy. **Out-of-state** grants include **$10,000** to John Stott Ministries [IL] and **$2,500** each to Regent U. [VA] and The Heights School [MD]. ■**PUBLICATIONS:** application form ■**WEBSITE:** None ■**E-MAIL:** None ■**APPLICATION POLICIES & PROCEDURES:** The Foundation reports that unsolicited grant requests are not accepted.

O+D+T   Laurie A. Moritz (VP at Bank+Con) — Frank R. Bailey, Jr. (T) — Helen L. Bailey (Donor)

SW-014 Bane (Joella P.) Trust
Refer to PNC Advisors Charitable Trust Committee entry.
(Allegheny County)

MI-41-51-52-81

EIN 25-6229084   **Year Created** 1982

AMV $501,671   **FYE** 6-00   (**Gifts Received** $0)   4 **Grants totaling** $23,440

All local giving. High grants of **$8,000** each to Bulgarian-Macedonian National Center [West Homestead] (multimedia station/sound system) and Gristmill Productions [Jennerstown] (maintenance/renovations). **$4,282** to Community Foundation of Murrysville/Export/Delmont (fiber optic cabling to schools, etc.) **$3,158** to Pittsburgh Piano Teachers Assn. (scholarship program). ■**PUBLICATIONS:** None ■**APPLICATION POLICIES & PROCEDURES:** Refer to the PNC Advisors Charitable Trust Committee entry for a statement on giving priorities and full application guidelines.

O+D+T Refer to PNC Advisors Charitable Trust Committee entry. — PNC Advisors (Corporate Trustee)

SW-015 Bannerot-Lappe Foundation
c/o Mellon Private Wealth Management
One Mellon Center, P.O. Box 185
Pittsburgh   15230   (Allegheny County)

MI-14

Phone 412-234-0023 **FAX** 412-234-1073
EIN 25-6440597   **Year Created** 1994

AMV $7,880,930   **FYE** 5-00   (**Gifts Received** $0)   2 **Grants totaling** $65,000

High grant of **$60,000** to Guiding Eyes for the Blind [NY]. **$5,000** to Freedom Guide Dogs [NY]. — One local grant awarded the prior year: **$50,000** to Western Pa. School for Blind Children (early intervention program). ■**PUBLICATIONS:** None ■**WEBSITE:** None ■**E-MAIL:** None ■**APPLICATION POLICIES & PROCEDURES:** The Foundation reports that giving is limited to helping the visually impaired with an emphasis on organizations which train seeing-eye dogs. There are no geographical restrictions, but no grants are awarded to individuals. Prospective applicants should make an initial telephone inquiry regarding the feasibility of submitting a request. Grant requests may be submitted in a letter (2 pages maximum) at any time (deadline is December 31st); include a annual report, a project budget, audited financial statement, and IRS tax-exempt documentation. Site visits sometimes are made to organizations being considered for a grant. Grants are awarded at a January meeting.

O+D+T Laurie A. Moritz (VP at Bank+Con) — Mellon Bank N.A. (Corporate Trustee)

SW-016 Baronner-Chatfield Foundation
3117 Washington Pike
Bridgeville   15017   (Allegheny County)

MI-13-22-25-32-41-42-43-57-61-63
Phone 412-257-9060 **FAX** None
EIN 52-1739290   **Year Created** 1991

AMV $1,601,093   **FYE** 12-00   (**Gifts Received** $0)   26 **Grants totaling** $116,350

Limited local giving. High local grant of **$10,605** to St. Alphonsus Church [Wexford]. **$1,000-$1,300** each to Extra Mile Education Foundation, Greater Pittsburgh Community Food Bank, Light of Life Ministries, Manchester Craftsmen's Guild, North Hills Community Church, Salvation Army, Spina Bifida Assn., and WQED. Other smaller local contributions. **Out-of-state** giving includes high grant of **$100,000** to Friends of Queen's [DC] and **$2,000** to International Institute for Effective Communication [MN]. ■**PUBLICATIONS:** None ■**WEBSITE:** None ■**E-MAIL:** None ■**APPLICATION POLICIES & PROCEDURES:** The Foundation reports that generally grants are awarded only to organizations dealing with higher education. Submit grant requests in any form at any time.

O+D+T Susan H. Earley (Con) — Glen F. Chatfield [Bradfordwoods] (P+Donor) — Elizabeth Chatfield [Bradfordwoods] (S+F+Donor)

SW-017 Baskin (Graham S. & Anna Mae Sweeney) Foundation
131 Cambridge Street
Indiana   15701   (Indiana County)

MI-34-43
Phone 412-288-3008 **FAX** None
EIN 25-1777790   **Year Created** 1995

AMV $1,090,523   **FYE** 12-00   (**Gifts Received** $0)   24 **Grants totaling** $46,433

All giving restricted to scholarships for Indiana County students pursuing a nursing or physical education degree. Most scholarships were **$2,000** to **$3,500**, a few higher, and students attended colleges/universities in several states.   ■**PUBLICATIONS:** application form ■**WEBSITE:** None ■**E-MAIL:** None ■**APPLICATION POLICIES & PROCEDURES:** Only Indiana County high school students/graduates who are pursuing (or intend to pursue) a degree in nursing or physical education are eligible to apply. Applications must be submitted on an official application form available from the Foundation; deadline for applications is March 1st.

O+D+T Edward E. Mackey (T+Con) — Loren C. Alico [Lewisburg] (T) — Cecelia A. Mackey (T) — Donor: Estate of Anna Mae Sweeney Baskin

---

SW-018 Bayer Foundation
c/o Bayer Corporation
100 Bayer Road, Building 4
Pittsburgh   15205   (Allegheny County)

MI-11-41-42-51-52-54-55-57-72
Phone 412-777-5791 **FAX** 412-778-4432
EIN 25-1508079   **Year Created** 1985

AMV $54,459,134   **FYE** 12-00   (**Gifts Received** $1,727,600)   375+ **Grants totaling** $4,573,274

About one-half local/Pa. giving. High grant of **$395,000** to United Way of SW Pa. **$360,000** to Duquesne U./Bayer School of Natural & Environmental Sciences. **$150,000** to U. of Pittsburgh/Chancellor's Office. **$145,000** to ASSET/Allegheny County School Science Education & Technology Partnership. **$125,000** to Carnegie Mellon U./Dept. of Chemical Engineering. **$100,000** to Carnegie Museum of Art. **$80,000** to WQED. **$75,000** to Pittsburgh Cultural Trust. **$50,000** to Pittsburgh Zoo.

$48,850 to Carlow College. **$43,000** to Pittsburgh Symphony. **$40,000** to Holocaust Center/United Jewish Federation. **$33,600** to Allegheny Conference on Community Development. **$30,000** each to Carnegie Mellon U./Dept. of Chemistry and Chemical Heritage Foundation [Philadelphia]. **$25,000** each to American Friends of Action Reconciliation-Service for Peace/United Jewish Federation, First Night Pittsburgh, and Pittsburgh Ballet Theatre. **$20,000** to U. of Pittsburgh/Depts. of Chemistry and Petro Engineering. **$15,000** each to Penn State U./Depts. of Chemistry & Chemical Engineering, Polymers Science Program) and Pittsburgh Dance Council. **$9,000-$11,000** each to Carnegie Science Center, Crossroads Program, U. of Pa./Dept. of Chemistry [Philadelphia], Girls Hope of Pittsburgh, Greater Pittsburgh Community Food Bank, LaRoche College, Manchester Craftsmen's Guild, and Pittsburgh Regional Alliance. **$7,000-$7,500** each to Creative Nonfiction, Drue Heinz Lectures, and Pittsburgh Center for the Arts. **$6,000** each to Pittsburgh Opera and Western Pa. Conservancy. **$3,500-$5,000** each to Carnegie Mellon U./Environmental Institute, City Theatre Company, Dance Alloy, Eastern Lebanon County High School (Science Dept.), Family Resources, Junior Achievement of SW Pa., Mendelssohn Choir of Pittsburgh, Persad Center, Pittsburgh Public Theater, River City Brass Band, Umoja African Arts Company, Vocational Rehabilitation Center, and World Affairs Council of Pittsburgh. **$1,000-$3,000** each to Annville Cleona School District [Lebanon County], Camp Kon-O-Wee/Spencer, Duquesne U. (Graduate Student Symposium), Frick Art & Historical Center, Greater Pittsburgh Commission for Women, McKeesport Symphony, Myerstown Community Library [Lebanon County], NEED/Negro Emergency Educational Drive, Neurofibromatosis Clinics Assn., Penn State U.-Beaver, Pittsburgh AIDS Task Force, Pittsburgh Council for International Visitors, and Pittsburgh Children's Museum. **Out-of-state** giving primarily to corporate operating locations in CA, CT, IN, MA, MO, OH, NC, NJ, NY, and RI and other states for similar purposes, as well as science programs at colleges/universities. ■**PUBLICATIONS:** Application Guidelines booklet ■ **WEBSITE:** www.bayerus.com/about/community/i_foundation.html ■**E-MAIL:** None ■**APPLICATION POLICIES & PROCEDURES:** The Foundation reports giving focuses on locations with a major Bayer Corp. presence. Priority giving interests are: (1) Civic and Social Service Programs which meet a community's basic needs; (2) Science Education & Workforce Development; and (3) The Arts, Arts Education & Culture, including program which integrate science and the arts. Most grants are for general support, special projects, or endowment; multiyear grants are awarded. No grants are awarded to individuals or organizations without 501(c)(3) status, or for charitable events/dinners/sponsorships, community or event advertising, lobbying/politicking, endowment funds, deficit reduction/operating reserves, telephone solicitations, religious organizations, student trips/exchange programs, athletic sponsorships/scholarships, religious organizations, operating support for United Way agencies (only special projects are considered), telephone solicitations, organizations outside the U.S., organizations which practice discrimination. Grant requests which focus on one of the three areas cited above may be submitted in a full proposal (12 pages maximum) before the March 15th and September 15th deadlines; the proposal must include the following: (1) a Cover Sheet with the organization's name, contact person/title, address, phone number, and Federal ID number; (2) a one-page letter outlining the proposal, including the project/program name and total amount requested. (3) in six pages (or less) provide (a) a brief history and purpose of the organization, including the services it provides and the people/geographic area served; (b) the purpose of the grant and the specific funding requested; (c) the benefits to the Bayer Foundation for this partnership; (d) brief plan for achieving the goals and how results will be measured; and (e) total budget for the project. Supporting documentation must include a list of other funding sources for the particular project and/or organization for the past two years, and IRS tax-exempt status documentation. Do not submit books, binders, video/cassette tapes, programs, brochures, or other collateral materials. Proposals which follow the Grantmakers of Western Pa. Common Grant Application Format are accepted. The total application should not exceed 12 pages. Grants are awarded at meetings in June and November. — Formerly called Miles, Inc. Foundation -or- Bayer-Mobay Foundation.

O+D+T Rebecca Lucore (Executive Director+Con) — Joseph A. Akers [Wexford] (P+D) — Margo L. Barnes [Wexford] (VP+D) — Thomas E. Kerr (S+D) — Jon R. Wyne [Sewickley] (F+D) — Nicholas T. Cullen, Jr. (D) — Helge H. Wehmeier [Sewickley] (D) — Corporate donor: Bayer Corporation

---

SW-019 Beaver County Foundation
P.O. Box 569
Beaver   15009   (Beaver County)

MI-13-19-32-42-43
Phone 724-728-1331 **FAX** 724-728-0965
EIN 25-1660309   **Year Created** 1992

AMV $871,671   **FYE** 12-00   **(Gifts Received** $161,176)   **Grants totaling** $30,300

As a Community Foundation all discretionary giving is limited to organizations serving Beaver County, and presently the only discretionary giving is from the Benjamin Franklin Fund which supports and encourages entrepreneurship. Grants from restricted or donor-advised funds are to/for (1) scholarships for high school graduates of Ambridge, Aliquippa, Beaver Falls, Hopewell, and Western Beaver high schools; (2) innovative research into pharmacological cures for drug/alcohol dependency; (3) and for education, healthcare, community, and business development in Beaver County. No additional grant details are available. ■**PUBLICATIONS:** Annual Report ■**WEBSITE:** None ■**E-MAIL:** None ■**APPLICATION POLICIES & PROCEDURES:** The Foundation reports that only Beaver County organizations are eligible to apply for grants from discretionary funds; most grants are for special projects, research, or scholarships. Other grants from some designated/donor-advised funds, e.g. the pharmacological cures for drug/alcohol dependency research fund, are accepted from outside Beaver County. Prospective applicants for discretionary grants (or scholarships) should first telephone the Foundation. Grant requests may be submitted in a letter (2 pages maximum) during March or October; include a project budget; applicants also may use the Grantmakers of Western Pa. Common Grant Application Format.

O+D+T Robert A. Smith (Executive Director+Con) — Charles N. O'Data (P+D) — Jean Macaluso (S+D) — Joseph N. Tosh, II (F+D) — Irving Bennett, O.D. (D) — W. Scott Bliss [Beaver Falls] (D) — Vince Dioguardi [Rochester] (D) — Sally Erath [Beaver Falls] (D) — Delmar E. Goedeker [Aliquippa] (D) — David J. Kuder [Beaver Falls] (D) — Celeste LeBate [Beaver Falls] (D) — Claire Mervis [Beaver Falls] (D) — Beverly O'Leary (D) — Robert Rimbey (D) — Michael I. Roman (D) — John F. Salopek, Esq. [Aliquippa] (D) — Phyllis Snedden (D) — Paul R. Vochko, Ph.D. [Ambridge] (D) — James P. Wetzel, Jr. [Beaver Falls] (D) — Thomas P. Woolaway [Sewickley] (D)

SW-020 **Beckwith Family Foundation, The**
    c/o Beckwith Machinery Company
    4565 Wm. Penn Highway, P.O. Box 435
    Murrysville 15668   (Westmoreland County)

MI-13-17-22-31-34-41-42-44-51-55-71

Phone 724-325-9205 **FAX** 724-325-9269
EIN 31-1607888   **Year Created** 1998

AMV $7,970,416   **FYE** 9-01   (**Gifts Received** $0)   10 **Grants totaling** $291,500

All local/Pittsburgh giving. High grant of **$125,000** to Shadyside Hospital Foundation. **$112,500** to YMCA of Pittsburgh. **$15,000** to Phipps Conservatory & Botanical Garden. **$10,000** each to Robert Morris College and St. Edmund's Academy. **$5,000** each to Bethlehem Haven, Pittsburgh Public Theater, and U. of Pittsburgh School of Nursing. **$2,500** to Ligonier Public Library. **$1,000** to Pittsburgh Trust for Cultural Resources. **$500** to Grantmakers of Western Pa. ◼**PUBLICATIONS:** None ◼**WEBSITE:** None ◼**E-MAIL:** None ◼**APPLICATION POLICIES & PROCEDURES:** Grant requests may be submitted in any form at any time. Describe the organization and request, and include IRS tax-exempt status documentation. Proposals following Grantmakers of Western Pa. Common Grant Application Format are accepted.
O+D+T John E. Trabucco (S+Con) — G. Nicholas Beckwith, III [Fox Chapel] (P+T+Donor) — James S. Beckwith, III [Fox Chapel] (F+T)

SW-021 **Benedum (Claude Worthington) Foundation**
    1400 Benedum-Trees Building
    223 Fourth Avenue
    Pittsburgh 15222   (Allegheny County)

MI-11-25-35-39-41-42-51-52-55-85-86

Phone 412-288-0360 **FAX** 412-288-0366
EIN 25-1086799   **Year Created** 1944

AMV $346,406,822   **FYE** 12-00   (**Gifts Received** $0)   160+ **Grants totaling** $16,668,604

About one-third giving to SW Pa.; some grants comprise funding for multiple projects and multiyear awards are designated. Note: The above 'Grants Totaling' figure refers to funds disbursed in 2000 whereas the grants detailed below (totaling **$19,135,860)** were those approved in 2000. High grant of **$400,000** to Pittsburgh Digital Greenhouse (electronic chip design development-3 years). **$300,000** to Southwestern Pa. Corporation (regional technical assistance program-3 years; develop integrated regional resources database to attract business). **$250,000** each to Allegheny Conference on Community Development (Agenda Development Fund/minority contractor initiative) and Community Foundation of Fayette County (seed funding). **$225,000** each to The Pittsburgh Foundation (regional healthcare cost containment-3 years; social entrepreneurship training program-3 years) and Robert Morris College (manufacturing engineering curriculum). **$200,000** each to Greater Pittsburgh Convention & Visitors Bureau Education Foundation (Office of Cultural Tourism; RiverPoint Tradeshows) and Pittsburgh Regional Alliance (economic development initiatives). **$185,000** to United Way of SW Pa. (annual campaign). **$164,000** to Community College of Allegheny County Educational Foundation (Washington County technology curriculum-2 years). **$150,000** each to Carnegie Mellon U. (technology-based economic development research) and New Century Careers (manufacturing training in Washington, Greene & Fayette counties). **$138,000** to Pittsburgh Children's Museum (mostly for exhibit planning at new children's center). **$120,000** each to Fay-Penn Economic Development Corp. (Fort Necessity educational program-3 years), Pittsburgh Trust for Cultural Resources (Cultural District collaboration-5 years; diverse presentations in Cultural District; conference support). **$100,000** each to ElderHostel (startup funding-2 years), Penn State U. (service learning program at Fayette & McKeesport campuses-3 years), and Pittsburgh Symphony (season support). **$75,000** each to Historical Society of Western Pa. (exhibit/gallery renovations), Pittsburgh Ballet Theatre (season support), Pittsburgh Opera (season support), and Pittsburgh Public Theater (season support). **$60,000** to Mon Valley Education Consortium (develop employer-responsive curricula). **$55,000** to Assn. for Retarded Citizens/Washington County (marketing employment services-3 years). **$50,000** each to Allegheny County Commission on Workforce Excellence (economic development agency networking), Fayette County Community Action Agency (job training for low-income adults) and Pa. Economy League (Allegheny County Government Transition Assistance project). **$35,000** to Technology Development & Education Corp. (research for improved workforce development). **$30,000** each to Mon Valley Progress Council (regional economic development plan), Pittsburgh Dance Council (season support), and Science Matters (math/science curriculum enhancement in Fayette/Greene counties). **$20,000** each to Greater Uniontown Heritage Consortium (community foundation planning) and Touchstone Center for Crafts (arts enhancement program in Pittsburgh/Uniontown elementary schools). **$15,000** to Carnegie Institute (Three Rivers Arts Festival). **$13,232** to Grantmakers of Western Pa. (operating support). **Out-of-state** grants, primarily to WV, included **$3,000,000** to Center for the Arts & Sciences of WV (Clay Center development); **$665,00** to U. of Charleston; and other smaller grants for many economic development initiatives and arts/cultural organizations; see full listing of grants on website. ◼**PUBLICATIONS:** annual report; statement of program policy; application guidelines ◼**WEBSITE:** www.fdncenter.org/grantmaker/benedum ◼**E-MAIL:** None ◼**APPLICATION POLICIES & PROCEDURES:** All giving focuses on West Virginia and selected SW Pa. counties: Allegheny, Fayette, Greene, and Washington; SW Pa. usually receives about one-third of giving. The Foundation's newly redesigned SW Pa. grants program focuses on Regional Economic Development: through six interest areas: (1) Education: preparing a qualified workforce through school improvement (K-12), private sector involvement in public education, literacy, post-secondary technical education and customized job training; (2) Business Development: encouraging entrepreneurial activity, attracting new businesses to the region, retaining and growing existing businesses, increasing the aggregate number of jobs, raising the level of spendable income and generating local tax revenues; (3) Special Initiatives: supporting institutions whose collaborative projects contribute to regional economic vitality, preferably through program and not capital grants; (4) Capacity Building: growing the social assets of rural communities by strengthening the nonprofit sector and cultivating leadership, an example of which may be the establishment of community foundations; (5) Support for the Pittsburgh Cultural District will focus on the operating needs of the major performing arts institutions in the Downtown Cultural District; and (6) Support for United Way of SW Pa. with annual campaign support. Local initiatives and voluntary support are encouraged. No grants are generally awarded to individuals; to organizations outside SW Pa. or WV; for student aid, fellowships, or travel; ongoing operating expenses; national organizations; biomedical research; religious activities; individual elementary or secondary schools; annual appeals or membership drives; or conferences, films, books, and audiovisual productions unless an integral part of a Foundation-supported project. Prospective applicants may submit by mail at any time a

Preliminary Proposal (3 pages maximum) covering the following: brief description of organization; name of contact person, address, telephone, fax and e-mail address; one-sentence summary of the project; a clear and concise description of the project and expected outcomes for which funding is sought; total project costs, other funding sources, and a specific amount requested from Benedum; the plan for project continuance or self-sufficiency upon the grant's conclusion; a specific start date and expected project duration; and a copy of IRS tax-exempt status documentation. The Foundation also accepts proposals following the Grantmakers of Western Pa. Common Grant Application Format. After review by staff, the applicant will be notified within 60 days if the request will be considered by the Foundation, or if additional information is required. Grants are awarded at Board of Directors meetings in March, June, September and December.

O+D+T William P. Getty (P+T+Con) — Beverly Railey Walter (VP for Programs) — Paul G. Benedum, Jr. (C+T) — Ralph J. Bean, Jr. [WV] (T) — G. Nicholas Beckwith (T) — Hon. Gaston Caperton [WV] (T) — Paul R. Jenkins (T) — G. Randolph Worls [WV] (T) — Hon. Robert E. Maxwell [WV] (Honorary Trustee) — Hon. Hulett C. Smith [WV] (EmeritusTrustee) — L. Newton Thomas [WV] (Emeritus Trustee)

SW-022 **Benedum (Paul G.), Jr. Foundation**   MI-13-17-22-41-43-65-72
             1500 Benedum Trees Building
             223 Fourth Avenue   **Phone** 412-288-0280 **FAX** None
             Pittsburgh 15222   (Allegheny County)   **EIN** 23-2887993   **Year Created** 1997
AMV $3,748,564   **FYE** 12-00   **(Gifts Received** $0)   10 **Grants totaling** $164,000

Mostly local giving. High grants of **$20,000** each to Crossroads Foundation, Girls Hope of Pittsburgh, Glade Run Foundation, Kiskiminetas Springs School, and Shady Side Academy. **$14,000** to I Have A Dream Foundation. **$10,000** each to Christian Fellowship Center, Extra Mile Education Foundation, and Pittsburgh Urban Christian Academy. **Out-of-state** grant: **$20,000** to The Linsly School [WV]. ■**PUBLICATIONS:** None ■**WEBSITE:** None ■**E-MAIL:** None ■**APPLICATION POLICIES & PROCEDURES:** Grant requests may be submitted in any form at any time.

O+D+T Paul G. Benedum, Jr. (C+T+Donor+Con) — Henry A. Bergstrom, Jr. (VP+T) — Thomas L. Myron, Jr. (S+F+T) — Richard F. Bumer [FL] (T+Chief Investment Officer) — Michael S. Higgins (T) — John C. Harmon (T) — John McClay (T) — Edwin F. Scheetz, Jr.

SW-023 **Bergstrom Foundation**   MI-12-13-14-22-41-42-63-71-84
             c/o PNC Advisors, M.S. P2-PTPP-25-1
             Two PNC Plaza, 620 Liberty Ave.   **Phone** 412-762-3502 **FAX** 412-762-5439
             Pittsburgh 15222   (Allegheny County)   **EIN** 25-1112093   **Year Created** 1960
AMV $7,860,346   **FYE** 12-00   **(Gifts Received** $0)   14 **Grants totaling** $299,620

About two-thirds local giving. High local grant of **$40,000** to Coalition for Christian Outreach. **$20,000** each to Christian Camps of Pittsburgh and Western Pa. Conservancy. **$19,620** to Homeless Children & Families Emergency Fund. **$17,000** to Young Life of the Steel Valley. **$15,000** each to Pittsburgh Coalition Against Pornography, The Pittsburgh Project, and Verland Foundation. **$11,000** to YMCA of Pittsburgh. **$8,000** to Pittsburgh Leadership Foundation. **$5,000** each to Children's Institute and Kiskiminetas Springs School. **Out-of-state** grant:: **$109,000** to U. of Michigan Law School. ■**PUBLICATIONS:** None ■**WEBSITE:** None ■**E-MAIL:** bruce.bickel@pncadvisors.com ■**APPLICATION POLICIES & PROCEDURES:** The Foundation reports that unsolicited requests for funds are not accepted; grants are made to preselected charitable organizations.

O+D+T R. Bruce Bickel (Senior VP at Bank+Con) — Henry A. Bergstrom, Jr. (P) — Dr. Robert E. Long (VP) — Larry E. Phillips, Esq. (VP)

SW-024 **Berkman (Allen H. & Selma W.) Charitable Trust**   MI-11-22-25-41-42-43-52-54-55-56-57-62-64-81
             5000 Fifth Avenue, Apt. 207   **Phone** 412-355-8640 **FAX** None
             Pittsburgh 15232   (Allegheny County)   **EIN** 25-6144060   **Year Created** 1972
AMV $5,006,529   **FYE** 10-00   **(Gifts Received** $0)   35 **Grants totaling** $424,879

About three-fourths local giving; most grants are for general purposes/annual giving except as noted. High grant of **$200,000** to Congregation Rodef Shalom (capital campaign). **$25,000** to American Friends of the Union of Progressive Congregations in Germany, Austria & Switzerland (Geiger College). **$22,500** to United Jewish Federation of Pittsburgh. **$17,500** to Pittsburgh Symphony. **$10,000** to United Way of SW Pa. **$7,500** each to Pittsburgh Cultural Trust (Designs on Downtown/annual campaign) and Winchester Thurston School. **$2,500** each to Life's Work of Western Pa. (benefit dinner). **$2,000** to Greater Pittsburgh Community Food Bank. **$1,879** to Historical Society of Western Pa. (benefit dinner). **$1,000** each to Carnegie Museum of Art (Fellows), Shady Side Academy, World Affairs Council of Pittsburgh, and WQED. Other smaller contributions for various purposes. **Out-of-state** giving include **$50,000** to Hawken School [OH] (swimming pool/annual fund); **$25,000** to Jewish National Fund [IL]; and **$10,000** each Harvard Law School [MA] (scholarship fund), Hebrew Union College [OH] (academic programs), and National Conference for Community & Justice [NY] (diversity programs in Pittsburgh area). ■**PUBLICATIONS:** Annual Report ■**WEBSITE:** None ■**E-MAIL:** None ■**APPLICATION POLICIES & PROCEDURES:** Most giving is for annual campaigns, building/renovations, capital campaigns, general support, emergency funds, endowment, fellowships, scholarship funds, program development, research, and technical assistance. Prospective applicants initially should make a telephone inquiry about the feasibility of submitting a request. Submit grant requests in a letter before the September 1st deadline; include a list of Board members and IRS tax-exempt status documentation.

O+D+T Allen H. Berkman, Esq. (T+Donor+Con) — Barbara Berkman Ackerman (T) — Richard L. Berkman, Esq. [Philadelphia] (T) — James S. Berkman [OH] (T) — Helen Berkman Habbert [OH] (T) — Susan Berkman Rahm [NY] (T)

SW-025 Berkman (Carol E. & Myles P.) Foundation
1224 Shady Ave.
Pittsburgh 15222 (Allegheny County)
AMV $1,546,068 **FYE** 12-00 **(Gifts Received** $0)

MI-12-15-22-41-54-62
Phone 412-281-1907 **FAX** None
EIN 25-1754310 **Year Created** 1994
25 **Grants totaling** $82,450

Mostly local giving. High grant of **$30,000** to United Jewish Federation of Pittsburgh. **$27,000** to Rodef Shalom Congregation. **$7,500** to Pittsburgh Children's Museum. **$3,500** to Carnegie Museums of Pittsburgh. **$2,500** to Shady Side Academy. **$2,000** to Tree of Life Congregation. **$1,500** to Jewish Family & Children's Service of Pittsburgh. **$1,000** to Jewish Residential Services. Other local contributions **$100-$500. Out-of-state** giving includes **$2,000** to Deerfield Academy [MA] and **$1,000** to Harvard Hillel [MA]. ■**PUBLICATIONS:** None ■**WEBSITE:** None ■**E-MAIL:** None ■**APPLICATION POLICIES & PROCEDURES:** Information not available.

O+D+T Myles P. Berkman (P+S+Donor+Con) — Carol E. Berkman (VP+Donor) — David J. Berkman (VP) — Pamela T. Berkman (VP) — William H. Berkman (VP) — Mara Berkman Landis (VP)

SW-026 Berkman (Sybiel B.) Foundation
1224 Shady Ave.
Pittsburgh 15222 (Allegheny County)
AMV $12,415,464 **FYE** 12-00 **(Gifts Received** $752,520)

MI-11-22-31-32-34-41-42-52-53-54-55-62-64
Phone 412-281-1907 **FAX** None
EIN 34-6566801 **Year Created** 1965
43 **Grants totaling** $1,078,220

The Foundation giving included **$395,700** in grants and **$682,520** in artwork. About one-quarter giving to Pa. High grant of **$100,000** to Carnegie Mellon U. **$7,500** to National Museum of American Jewish History [Philadelphia]. **$3,000** to Reconstructionist Rabbinical College [Montgomery County]. **$2,500** to North Allegheny Center of Excellence. **$1,000** to Battin' for Betsy Charities. Also, artwork worth **$158,425** was donated to Pittsburgh Children's Museum. **Out-of-state** giving, primarily where trustees live, included **$50,000** each to Memorial Sloan-Kettering Cancer Center, Metropolitan Opera [NY], and Mt. Sinai Medical Center Foundation [NY]; **$16,000** to Whitney Museum of American Art [NY]; **$20,000** to Museum of Television & Radio [NY]; **$10,000** each to Prep for Prep [NY], The ALS Assn. [NY], New York Weill Cornell Medical Center [NY], The Allen Stevenson School [NY], and Internet Policy Institute [DC]; and other smaller grants mostly for arts or cultural purposes in FL or NY. — Pa. grants in the prior year included **$200,000** to United Jewish Federation of Greater Pittsburgh, **$112,500** to U. of Pa. and **$10,000** to United Way of Southeastern Pa. [Philadelphia]. ■**PUBLICATIONS:** None ■**WEBSITE:** None ■**E-MAIL:** None ■**APPLICATION POLICIES & PROCEDURES:** Information not available.

O+D+T Myles P. Berkman (P+F+T+Donor+Con) — Stephen L. Berkman [FL] (S+T) — Lillian R. Berkman [NY] (T) — Monroe E. Berkman [FL] (T) — Corporate donor: Associated American Artists [CO]

SW-027 Bernstein (Marci Lynn) Private Foundation
144 North Woodland Road
Pittsburgh 15232 (Allegheny County)
AMV $356,397 **FYE** 4-00 **(Gifts Received** $0)

MI-22-54-55-62
Phone 412-441-1347 **FAX** None
EIN 65-6235943 **Year Created** 1997
50 **Grants totaling** $37,920

Mostly local giving. High grant of **$20,000** to United Jewish Federation of Greater Pittsburgh. **$5,744** to Temple Beth Shalom. **$5,000** to Tickets for Kids. Other local contributions **$20-$425** for various purposes. **Out-of-state** giving includes **$1,000** each to Sarasota International Cricket Club [FL] and U.S. Holocaust Museum [DC]. ■**PUBLICATIONS:** None. ■**WEBSITE:** None ■**E-MAIL:** None ■**APPLICATION POLICIES & PROCEDURES:** Grant requests may be submitted in a proposal at any time; describe the purpose of the requested funds. No grants awarded to individuals.

O+D+T Thomas E. Bernstein (T+Donor+Con) — Karen Bernstein (Donor) — Corporate donor: Bernstein Family Ltd.

SW-028 Bethany Foundation
5220 Fifth Ave., Apt. 3G
Pittsburgh 15232 (Allegheny County)
AMV $1,803,999 **FYE** 12-00 **(Gifts Received** $500)

MI-22-52-61-82
Phone 412-681-1789 **FAX** None
EIN 25-1718608 **Year Created** 1993
6 **Grants totaling** $40,500

Mostly local giving; all grants are for general support. High grant of **$20,000** to Jubilee Assn. **$10,800** to The Oratory. **$4,200** to Pro Papa Missions America [Johnstown]. **$1,000** to St. Sebastian Church. **Out-of-state** giving includes **$2,500** to Mi Refugio [MD] and **$2,000** to Spiritan Refugee Center [Tanzania]. ■**PUBLICATIONS:** None ■**WEBSITE:** None ■**E-MAIL:** None ■**APPLICATION POLICIES & PROCEDURES:** Information not available.

O+D+T Harold S. Evans (P+F+T+Donor+Con) — Elizabeth W. Evans [Wilkinsburg] (VP+S+T) — Rev. Drew Morgan (T)

SW-029 Bethel Park Community Foundation
5311 Brightwood Road
Bethel Park 15102 (Allegheny County)
AMV $63,563 **FYE** 12-00 **(Gifts Received** $17,859)

MI-13-29-55-71-89
Phone 412-854-8820 **FAX** None
EIN 25-1749936 **Year Created** 1994
5 **Grants totaling** $40,950

As a Community Foundation all discretionary giving is limited to Bethel Park. High grant of **$29,073** for Bethel Park Community Center (interior improvements). **$5,198** to Bethel Park Recreation Dept. (PRIDE program). **$3,179** to Bethel Park Heritage Players (community center lighting). **$3,000** to Trolley Beautification Committee (holiday banners). **$500** to Municipal Bicycle Patrol Unit. — Major giving in prior years to the Community Center (interior improvements, furnishings, playground equipment) with smaller grants for local schools, trolley beautification committee, parks revitalization, and other community purposes. ■**PUBLICATIONS:** Grant Application Guidelines; Grant Application Cover Sheet ■**WEBSITE:** www.bpcf.com/ ■**E-MAIL:** info@bpcf.org ■**APPLICATION POLICIES & PROCEDURES:** The Foundation's mission is limited to enhancing residents' quality of life in Bethel Park; current priority interests are to provide needed community facilities, opportunities in education, expanded recreational/leisure time activities, and greater exposure to the fine/performing arts. Prospective applicants should make an initial phone call to discuss the feasibility of submitting an application and/or to request a copy of the application guidelines and Grant Application Cover Sheet (also available on the website).

O+D+T Susan J. Hughes (P+T) — James D. Kling (VP+T) — Henry J. Szymanski, Jr., CPA (S+T) — David H. Ross (F+T) — David A. Allison, Ph.D. (T) — David Amaditz (T) — Diane L. Doyle (T) — Ronald J. Fees (T) — Robert Fragasso (T) — Fred Green, Jr. (T) — Jane S. Lupia (T) — Charles T. Manion (T) — Samuel A. Moore (T) — David L. Peet (T) — Richard N. Rose (T) — Lisa P. Sbei (T) — Timothy G. Shack (T) — C. Dean Streator (T) — Richard W. Talarico (T)

SW-030 Biddle (Margaret J.) Charitable Trust MI-31-42-63

Refer to PNC Advisors Charitable Trust Committee entry.

(Allegheny County) **EIN** 25-6021765 **Year Created** 1954

AMV $343,770 **FYE** 9-00 **(Gifts Received** $0) 4 **Grants totaling** $16,038

One-fourth of yearly income awarded on a discretionary basis to Protestant charities in the City of Pittsburgh: **$8,035** to U. of Pittsburgh (women's & dental depts.). **$3,962** to Soli DeoGloria Ministries (Christian Ministry program). **$2,433** to Allegheny General Hospital (dental dept.). **$1,607** to Mercy Hospital (dental dept.) ■**APPLICATION POLICIES & PROCEDURES:** Refer to the PNC Advisors Charitable Trust Committee entry for a statement on giving priorities and full application guidelines.

O+D+T Refer to PNC Advisors Charitable Trust Committee entry. — PNC Advisors (Corporate Trustee)

SW-031 Biddle (Mary L.C.) Fund for Ladies in Reduced Circumstances MI-15-17-23

c/o PNC Advisors Service Center, P2-PTPP-05-1

Two PNC Plaza, 620 Liberty Ave., 5th Floor **Phone** 800-762-2272 **FAX** None

Pittsburgh 15222 (Allegheny County) **EIN** 23-6205851 **Year Created** 1891

AMV $409,878 **FYE** 12-00 **(Gifts Received** $0) 11 **Grants totaling** $21,615

All giving restricted to aiding needy, older women resident in the City of Philadelphia; typical support was about **$1,900** per person per year. ■**PUBLICATIONS:** None ■**WEBSITE:** None ■**E-MAIL:** pncadvisors@pncbank.com ■**APPLICATION POLICIES & PROCEDURES:** Only social assistance agencies in Philadelphia are eligible to apply on behalf of needy, older women living in Philadelphia; agency requests should be submitted in a one-page letter detailing a woman's financial background and needs.

O+D+T Dawn Thomas (Trust Officer at Bank+Con) — PNC Advisors (Trustee)

SW-032 Birmingham Foundation, The MI-12-13-14-15-16-17-19-20-22-24-25-29-31

Roesch-Taylor Building 33-35-39-45-49-55-71

2100 Jane Street, 4th Floor **Phone** 412-481-2777 **FAX** 412-481-2727

Pittsburgh 15203 (Allegheny County) **EIN** 25-0965572 **Year Created** 1996

AMV $21,564,546 **FYE** 6-01 **(Gifts Received** $0) 43 **Grants totaling** $1,035,175

All giving restricted to services/programs benefiting South Pittsburgh residents; some grants are payments on multiyear awards. High grant of **$255,000** to Beltzhoover Citizen's Community Development Corp. (community-based health center). **$100,000** to YouthWorks (summer/year-round employment). **$60,000** to Nazareth Housing Services (senior/family services). **$50,000** each to Pittsburgh Action Against Rape (enhanced local safety) and YouthPlaces/Pittsburgh Council on Public Education (local community program). **$40,400** to Interfaith Volunteer Caregivers (volunteer training/support). **$38,000** to ARC Allegheny (planning for long-term care). **$31,000** to Hilltop Health Ministerium/Mercy Health (expanded health ministry). **$30,000** each to Christmas in April (South Pittsburgh project), Kuntu Repertory Theatre (cultural outreach to seniors), Domestic Abuse Counseling Center (program for men), and Goodwill Industries (facility renovation). **$26,950** to Vintage (parenting-grandparent support program). **$25,000** each to Girl Scouts of SW Pa. (local program) and U. of Pittsburgh School of Pharmacy (Birmingham Clinic pharmaceutical care). **$20,000** each to Arthritis Foundation (seniors' exercise program) and U. of Pittsburgh Medical Center/South Side (diabetes self-management education program). **$19,000** to Consumer Health Coalition (children's health insurance campaign-2 years). **$18,000** to Habit-Tat for Youth Education/All of Us (Prospect Elementary/Middle School program). **$17,000** to Conservation Consultants (energy surveys/referrals for low-income households). **$16,000** to Allegheny County Health Dept. (dental sealant program in schools). **$14,125** to Red Cross (Senior Safety/Lifeline program). **$12,200** to Brashear Assn. (student programs in St. Clair Village). **$12,000** to Program for Healthcare to the Underserved Population (program expansion). **$10,000** each to Boy Scouts (St. Clair program), Carrick High School (community center planning), and South Side Local Development Co. (senior home repair program). **$6,500** to Executive Service Corps (strengthen South Pittsburgh nonprofits). **$5,000** each to American Cancer Society (Tell a Friend program) and University Center for Social & Urban Research (health reports). **$3,700** to Pittsburgh Fire Bureau (smoke detector program). **$3,000** each to U. of Pittsburgh Health Policy Institute (funding partnership) and Mt. Oliver Borough (cardiac defibrillator program). **$1,000-$1,500** each to Beltzhoover Citizen's Community Development Corp. (anti-violence program), Mental Health Assn. of Allegheny County (depression project), and South Pittsburgh Housing Services Coalition (community outreach). Other smaller contributions. ■**PUBLICATIONS:** annual report; Initial Grant Guidelines brochure ■**WEBSITE:** www.birminghamfoundation.org ■**E-MAIL:** info@ birminghamfoundation.org ■**APPLICATION POLICIES & PROCEDURES:** The Foundation's grantmaking focuses on enhancing the quality of life in the South Pittsburgh communities: Allentown, Arlington and Arlington Heights, Beltzhoover, Bon Air, Carrick, Duquesne Heights, Knoxville, Mt. Oliver, Mt. Washington, St. Clair Village, and South Side. Priority interests are children's well-being, health access/promotion, senior safety/wellness, organizational capacity building, and community life (violence, substance abuse, and mental health). One to three year grants are awarded. No grants are awarded to/for individuals, private foundations, sectarian religious purposes, or for the influencing of legislation unless grant-related. Normally, no support is given for operating budgets, deficits, fundraising campaigns, general research, overhead costs, scholarships, political campaigns, or loans. Prospective applicants should submit a Letter of Intent (1-3 pages) at any time which succinctly describes the organization, the program to be funded and its objectives, how the program responds to the Foundation's mission, amount of the request and other sources of support, and IRS tax-exempt status documentation. Interviews and requests for additional information may follow and a formal proposal may be requested; the Grantmakers of Western Pa. Common Grant Application Format is suggested. Deadlines for submission of proposals are March 15th, July 15th, and November 15th. Decision on grants are made at meetings in June, November, and March.

O+D+T Mary Phan-Gruber (Executive Director+Con) — Daniel A. Goetz (C+D) — Floyd R. Ganassi (VC+D) — Mihai Marcu (VC+D) — Judith M. Davenport, D.M.D. (S+D) — H. Don Gordon (F+D) — Mark S. Bibro (D) — Louise R. Brown (D (ex-officio)) — Hugo M. Churchill (D) — Cyril F. Esser (D) — Jane H. Roesch (D) — Judge William T. Simmons (D) — Eileen O. Smith (D) — Duane Swager, II (D) — Terrence L. Wirginis (D) — Roberta F. Smith (Emeritus Director) — Foundation corpus from sale of South Side Hospital.

SW-033 Bitner (H.M.) Charitable Trust
c/o Mellon Private Wealth Management
One Mellon Center, Room 3825
Pittsburgh 15258   (Allegheny County)

MI-14-17-41-42-44-51-52-53-54-55-56-57-71
Phone 412-234-1634 **FAX** 412-234-1073
EIN 25-6018931   **Year Created** 1955

AMV $2,552,975   **FYE** 12-00   **(Gifts Received** $0)   76 **Grants totaling** $151,650

Nearly half local giving. High Pa. grants of **$5,000** each to Carnegie Mellon U. (mural project), Chatham College, and Pittsburgh History & Landmarks Foundation. **$4,000-$4,500** each to Carnegie Institute, The Children's Institute, and Washington & Jefferson College. **$3,000-$3,500** each to Brother's Brother Foundation, Carnegie Library of Braddock, Western Pa. Conservancy, Winchester-Thurston School, and WQED. **$2,000-$2,500** each to Goodwill Industries of Pittsburgh, Pittsburgh Ballet Theatre, Pittsburgh Dance Council, Pittsburgh Parks Conservancy, and Pittsburgh Symphony. **$1,000** each to Beginning With Books, Shady Lane School, Three Rivers Arts Festival, Western Pa. Caring Foundation, Western Pa. Family Center, WDUQ-FM, Women's Center & Shelter of Greater Pittsburgh, WQED-FM, and WYEP-FM. Other local contributions **$500**, mostly for cultural purposes. **Out-of-state** giving includes high grant of **$20,000** to St. Gregory Choir School/Church of the Epiphany [IL]; **$15,000** to Columbia Law School [NY]; and other grants/contributions **$500-$3,000, mostly where Trustees lived or attended college.** ■**PUBLICATIONS:** statement of program policy ■**WEBSITE:** None ■**E-MAIL:** None ■**APPLICATION POLICIES & PROCEDURES:** The Trust reports that giving is primarily to areas where Trustees reside, presently Pittsburgh, Chicago, and San Francisco, and that very few unsolicited grant requests are funded. Grant requests may be submitted in a letter during January-October; include IRS tax-exempt status documentation.

O+D+T Annette Calgaro (VP at Bank+Con) — John Bitner [IL] (T) — Kerry BItner [GA] (T) — Evelyn Bitner Pearson (T) — Priscilla Pearson [CA] (T) — Mellon Bank N.A. (Corporate Trustee)

SW-034 Bitz Foundation
1640 Pleasant Hill Road
Baden 15005   (Beaver County)

MI-31-32-35-41-51-52-55-72
Phone 724-933-5504 **FAX** None
EIN 23-2901971   **Year Created** 1997

AMV $10,694,682   **FYE** 12-00   **(Gifts Received** $345,750)   10 **Grants totaling** $936,524

Moslty local giving. High grant of **$815,235** to Pittsburgh Board of Education. **$61,204** to Pittsburgh Opera. **$39,560** to Children's Hospital of Pittsburgh. **$9,025** to Cystic Fibrosis Foundation. **$5,000** to Pittsburgh Public Theater. **$2,200** to Heinz Hall. **$1,600** to Pittsburgh Zoo. **$1,000** each to Mario Lemieux Foundation and Pittsburgh AIDS Task Force. — In the prior year, major giving included **$200,000** to Pittsburgh Cultural Trust; **$36,000** to Mario Lemieux Foundation; and **$32,480** to Cystic Fibrosis Foundation. ■**PUBLICATIONS:** None ■**WEBSITE:** None ■**E-MAIL:** None ■**APPLICATION POLICIES & PROCEDURES:** Information not available.

O+D+T Francois Bitz (P+Donor+Con) — Graziella Pruiti [NY] (S)

SW-035 Blair County Community Endowment
1216 - 11th Ave., Suite 315
Altoona 16601   (Blair County)

MI-13-14-15-22-44-51-52-54-55-56-72-85
Phone 814-944-6102 **FAX** None
EIN 25-1761379   **Year Created** 1995

AMV $2,012,622   **FYE** 12-01   **(Gifts Received** $942,860)   **Grants totaling** $99,434

As a Community Foundation all discretionary giving is limited to organizations serving Blair County. In 2001, discretionary giving was limited to **$300** or smaller contributions to ARC of Blair County, Celebrate Diversity!, and Respiratory Disease Society. — Recent grants from (primarily) discretionary funds awarded during January-June 2002: **$20,000** to Altoona Railroaders Memorial Museum; **$5,858** to Leap the Dips Preservation Foundation; **$3,600** to Home Nursing Agency; **$2,900** to Blair County Arts Foundation; **$2,500** each to Altoona Area Public Library and Blair Senior Services; **$1,500** to Hollidaysburg Area YMCA; **$1,000** each to Allegheny Lutheran Social Ministries, Altoona Community Theatre, ARC of Blair County, Central PA Humane Society, Easter Seals/Central Pa., Greater Altoona Economic Development Corp., Make-A-Wish Foundation, Roaring Spring Community Library, St. Leonard's Home, and Tyrone-Snyder Township Public Library; and **$500-$750** each to African American Heritage Project of Blair County, Allegheny Ballet Company, Allegheny Ridge Corp., Altoona Symphony Society, Big Brothers/Big Sisters, Blair County Historical Society, and Diocese of Altoona-Johnstown. ■**PUBLICATIONS:** Grant Application Form ■**WEBSITE:** www.bcce.org ■**E-MAIL:** cessna@bcce.org ■**APPLICATION POLICIES & PROCEDURES:** Only nonprofit organizations located in or serving Blair County are eligible for grants from unrestricted or donor-advised funds; no grants are awarded to individuals. An organization may apply for only one grant in a 12-month period. Prospective applicants must initially contact the Endowment to request a Grant Application Form; applicants also are advised to consult the Endowment's website for current information. Completed applications (an original and eight copies) must be submitted before the last business day in April. After review by the Grants Committee in May, final decisions on grants are made at a June Board meeting. — Formerly called the Greater Altoona-Blair County Community Endowment

O+D+T Jodi L. Cessna (Executive Director+Con) — Gerald P. Wolf [Hollidaysburg] (C+D) — Allan G. Hancock [East Freedom] (P+D) — Nancy Devorris (VP+D) — Len Whiting [Hollidaysburg] (S+D) — John P. Kazmaier [Hollidaysburg] (F+D+Chair, Grants Committee) — John E. Eberhardt, Jr. Esq. (D) — Merle Evey (D) — Joseph Gildea (D) — Tera Herman (D) — Rex Hershberger (D) — Ray Hess (D) — Fred Imler, Sr. (D) — Gail H. Irwin (D) — Stephen J. Katcher (D) — Craig Kilmer (D) — Neil M. Port (D) — Sylvia Schraff (D) — Dr. James Scott (D) — Maureer Smithe (D) — Randy Tarpey (D) — Andrea Ward Zupon (D)

SW-036 Bloch (Raymond & Elizabeth) Educ. & Charitable Fdn.
830 Frick Building, 437 Grant Street
Pittsburgh   15219   (Allegheny County)

MI-12-32-81-83-86
Phone 412-281-5457 **FAX** None
EIN 25-1561204   **Year Created** 1989

AMV $4,029,531   **FYE** 12-00   **(Gifts Received** $0)   10 **Grants totaling** $215,000

About two-thirds local/Pa. giving. High grant of **$80,500** to World Federalist Assn. of Pittsburgh. **$47,000** to University Anesthesiology and Critical Care Medical Foundation. **$6,500** to American Friends Service Committee [Philadelphia]. **$1,000** to Jewish Community Center of Pittsburgh. **Out-of-state** giving includes **$40,500** to World Federalist Assn. [DC]; **$15,000** to National Gaucher Foundation [MD]; **$6,500** each to Parliamentarians for Global Action [NY], ChildReach [RI], and Save the Children Federation [CT]; and **$5,000** to Center for Defense Information [DC]. — Note: These same organizations have been the only grantees for several years. ■**PUBLICATIONS:** None ■**WEBSITE:** None ■**E-MAIL:** None ■**APPLICATION POLICIES & PROCEDURES:** Grant requests in any form may be submitted at any time; include IRS tax-exempt status documentation.

O+D+T Bernard L. Bloch (P+Con)

SW-037 Bluestone (Max L. & Charlotte C.) Charitable Trust
220 North Dithridge Street, #1100
Pittsburgh   15213   (Allegheny County)

MI-22-62
Phone 412-682-7676 **FAX** None
EIN 25-1430964   **Year Created** 1982

AMV $570,595   **FYE** 11-00   **(Gifts Received** $68,938)   34 **Grants totaling** $38,533

Mostly local giving. High grant of **$14,600** to United Jewish Federation of Greater Pittsburgh. **$12,125** to Congregation Rodef Shalom. **$1,000-$1,435** each to Jewish Community Center, Jewish Residential Services, and Jewish University Center. Other contributions **$100-$300** each. **Out-of-state** grant: **$4,365** to Jewish Federation of Palm Beach [FL]. ■**PUBLICATIONS:** None ■**WEBSITE:** None ■**E-MAIL:** None ■**APPLICATION POLICIES & PROCEDURES:** Submit grant requests in any form at any time. No grants awarded to individuals.

O+D+T Max L. Bluestone (T+Donor+Manager+Con) — Charlotte C. Bluestone (T+Manager) — Burton L. Bluestone (T) — Joan S. Bluestone (T) — Stuart Bluestone [NM] (T)

SW-038 Bowen (Franklin W. & Helen S.) Charitable Trust
1127 Arrowood Drive
Pittsburgh   15243   (Allegheny County)

MI-15-22-43-63
Phone 412-281-5472 **FAX** None
EIN 25-6091907   **Year Created** 1966

AMV $251,283   **FYE** 12-00   **(Gifts Received** $16,578)   19 **Grants totaling** $17,164

Mostly local giving. High grant of **$3,504** to Mt. Lebanon Baptist Church. **$1,000-$1,572** each to Baptist Homes of Western Pa., Christ Church of Grove Farm, and Christian East Africa & Equatorial Development [Baden]. Other contributions **$75-$500** for various purposes or individuals, and scholarships, **$500-$2,500** each, to students in PA, VA, WV, and FL. ■**PUBLICATIONS:** Annual Report ■**WEBSITE:** None ■**E-MAIL:** None ■**APPLICATION POLICIES & PROCEDURES:** The Foundation reports that most grants are for special projects, scholarships, or individuals. Grant requests may be submitted in any form at any time; decisions on requests usually are made within two months. Site visits sometimes are made to organizations being considered for a grant.

O+D+T Franklin W. Bowen (P+T+Donor+Con) — Violet Bowen Hugh (Donor)

SW-039 Bozzone Family Foundation
311 Hillcrest Drive
Lower Burrell   15068
                                    (Westmoreland County)

MI-11-12-13-14-22-25-29-41-42-43-51-54-55
61-71-72
Phone 724-335-4741 **FAX** None
EIN 25-6277066   **Year Created** 1986

AMV $14,757,262   **FYE** 12-00   **(Gifts Received** $0)   100+ **Grants totaling** $1,330,242

Mostly local/western Pa. giving; grants are for general fund purposes except as noted. High grant of **$300,000** to Diocese of Greensburg (Catholic schools endowment). **$75,000** to Carnegie Mellon U. (professorship). **$60,000** to St. Joseph High School [Natrona Heights]. **$58,000** to United Way of SW Pa. **$30,000** to The Early Childhood Initiative. **$28,600** to Pittsburgh Habitat for Humanity. **$25,000** to Penn State U. (capital campaign). **$17,900** to Boyd Community Center (building improvements). **$15,000** each to Catholic Charities and Pittsburgh Children's Museum. **$13,000** each to Carnegie Institute and St. Margaret Mary Church. **$11,600** to Pittsburgh Leadership Foundation (golf classic/contribution fund). **$11,000** to Sisters of Charity of Seton Hill (anniversary campaign). **$10,000** to Boy Scouts/Moraine Trails Council (Campaign for Character), Carnegie Science Center (exhibit), Communities in Schools of Pittsburgh/Allegheny County (Westinghouse High School), Kiski Valley YMCA, Keystone Tall Tree Girl Scout Council, Life's Work of Western Pa., National Flag Foundation, St. Mary's of the Assumption Catholic Church (John Neumann Fund), St. Scholastica Church (renovation project), and YMCA of Pittsburgh. **$7,000** to Make-A-Wish Foundation of Western Pa. **$6,500** to Saltworks Theatre Company (summer camping program). **$6,250** to WQED (Leadership Circle). **$5,000** to Pauline Auberle Foundation (Back to the Family campaign), Benefactors of Allegheny Township (Finnin Park), The Chimbote Foundation (Circle of Mission), The Cultural Trust Campaign for a Dynamic Downtown, Extra Mile Education Foundation, and Westmoreland ARC Foundation (People First Project). **$4,200** to Summerbridge Pittsburgh. **$3,000-$3,500** each to Family Resources (Family Retreat Center), Indiana U. of Pa. (scholarship fund), Leadership Alle-Kiski Valley (leadership/development fund), Mom's House, Pittsburgh Zoo (membership), and The Watson Institute (Autism Center). **$2,000-$2,500** each to Allegheny Valley YMCA, Carnegie Museums of Pittsburgh, Family House, Fox Hill Preschool, National Parkinson Foundation/Greater Pittsburgh Chapter, Junior Achievement of SW Pa., Pittsburgh Public Theater, Salvation Army (cadet scholarship fund), and UCP Foundation (capital campaign). **$1,000-$1,900** each to Animal Protectors of Allegheny Valley, ARC-Allegheny Foundation (living-learning campaign), Beechwood Farms Nature Reserve, Beginning With Books, Duquesne U. Society, Fox Chapel School District, Freeport Area Community Center, Girl Scouts of SW Pa., Goodwill Industries of Pittsburgh (awards fund), Girls Hope of Pittsburgh, Historical Society of Western Pa., Library Society of New Kensington, Leukemia Society of America/Western Pa. Chapter (school program), New Kensington Youth Programs, Opera Theatre of Pittsburgh, Pittsburgh Symphony, Special

Olympics of Pa. (winter games), Spina Bifida Assn. of Western Pa., VNA Services & Foundation, and YMCA of New Kensington. Also, **$75,000** for 'sundry donees charities, anonymous gifts' but details unavailable, and other local contributions **$200-$500** for various purposes. **Out-of-state** giving includes **$200,000** to Rensselaer Polytechnic Institute [NY]; **$100,000** to Archdiocese of Detroit (Cultural Center); **$25,000** to U. of Notre Dame [IN]; **$20,000** to Missionaries of Charity [NY]; and **$5,000** to Holy Family Hospital Foundation [DC]. ■**PUBLICATIONS:** None ■**WEBSITE:** None ■**E-MAIL:** None ■**APPLICATION POLICIES & PROCEDURES:** Grant requests may be submitted in any form at any time; include IRS tax-exempt status documentation. No grants awarded to individuals.

O+D+T   Robert P. Bozzone (T+Donor+Con)

SW-040   Bramowitz (Alan D. & Marsha W.) Charitable Trust
        5430 Forbes Avenue
        Pittsburgh   15217   (Allegheny County)

MI-41-42-62
Phone 412-521-0240 **FAX** 412-521-0244
EIN 25-6232163   **Year Created** 1985

AMV $492,060   **FYE** 12-00   (**Gifts Received** $5,200)   8 **Grants totaling** $45,278

One Pa. grant: **$5,000** to Rodef Shalom Congregation (restoration fund). **Out-of-state** giving includes **$17,778** to Duke U. [NC] (Annual Fund/Bramowitz Family Endowment/Freeman Center for Jewish Life); **$15,000** to Phillips Academy-Andover [MA] (Annual Fund/Bramowitz Family Endowment); and **$5,000** to The Fay School [MA] (endowment). ■**PUBLICATIONS:** None ■**WEBSITE:** None ■**E-MAIL:** mwb331@aol.com ■**APPLICATION POLICIES & PROCEDURES:** The Foundation reports that most grants are for building funds, capital drives, endowment, research, or scholarships. Grant requests may be submitted in any form at any time. Grants are awarded at a December meeting. — Formerly called the Alan & Marsha Bramowitz Family Foundation.

O+D+T   Marsha W. Bramowitz (T+Donor+Con) — Alan D. Bramowitz, M.D. (T+Donor) — Emily A. Bramowitz (T) — Melissa Bramowitz (T) — Craig Koryak, CPA (T)

SW-041   Breedlove (Howell A. & Ann M.) Charitable Foundation
        2015 Blairmont Drive
        Pittsburgh   15241   (Allegheny County)

MI-11-13-22-31-32-41-43-44-54-61-71
Phone 412-378-6490 **FAX** None
EIN 25-1661386   **Year Created** 1991

AMV $2,860,260   **FYE** 12-00   (**Gifts Received** $430,803)   34 **Grants totaling** $143,240

About half local giving. High Pa. grant of **$20,000** to United Way of SW Pa. **$12,850** to St. John Capistran Church. **$5,000** each to Beaver County YMCA, Bishop's Education Fund, Extra Mile Education Foundation, and B.F. Jones Memorial Library. **$3,000** to YMCA of Pittsburgh. **$2,000** to Western Pa. Conservancy. **$1,000-$1,500** each to Boy Scouts/Greater Pittsburgh Council, Catholic Charities, Developmental Disabilities, Juvenile Diabetes Foundation, Little Sisters of the Poor, and St. John's Hospital. Other smaller local contributions. **Out-of-state** giving includes high grant of **$32,400** to National Museum of Wildlife [WY]; **$26,000** to Community Foundation of Jackson Hole [WY]; and other grants to WY. ■**PUBLICATIONS:** None ■**WEBSITE:** None ■**E-MAIL:** None ■**APPLICATION POLICIES & PROCEDURES:** No grants awarded to individuals.

O+D+T   Howell A. Breedlove (T+Donor+Con) — Ann M. Breedlove (T+Donor) — Alan Merkle Breedlove (T) — John Adams Breedlove (T) — Mark Howell Breedlove (T) — William Parker Breedlove (T) — Ann Marie Garbin (T)

SW-042   BridgeBuilders Foundation
        560 Epsilon Drive—RIDC Park
        Pittsburgh   15238   (Allegheny County)

MI-12-16-17-25-39-41-55-79-81-83
Phone 412-963-0232 **FAX** 412-963-0240
EIN 25-6074470   **Year Created** 1957

AMV $1,410,405   **FYE** 12-00   (**Gifts Received** $75,000)   13 **Grants totaling** $41,000

About half local/Pa. giving. High grant of **$6,500** to The Heartwood Institute (on-line book/video library on multicultural teaching materials). **$4,000** to Impact Services Corp. [Philadelphia] (computer center for inner-city youth program). **$3,000** each to Global Link (Pittsburgh-Matanzas, Cuba Sister City Project on HIV/AIDS) and Nego Gato, Inc. (African-Brazilian cultural program for youths). **$2,000** to Sun Crumbs, Inc. (poetry outreach program). **$1,000** to Thomas Merton Center (Pittsburgh-Matanzas Sister City Project). **Out-of-state** grants, **$2,500-$4,000** each to AK, CA, GA, IL, ME, NC, and SC, for culturally diverse projects involving/addressing the needs of minority and low-income youth. — In 2001, Pa. grants awarded include **$4,000** to Pa. Peace Links (Family Treasures program for low-income families); **$3,500** to The Heartwood Institute (video on building teacher-student respect); and **$2,500** to Family Health Council (youth attendance at international health conference). ■**PUBLICATIONS:** Annual Report with statement of giving interests and application guidelines ■**WEBSITE:** None ■**E-MAIL:** ktwilson@hotmail.com ■**APPLICATION POLICIES & PROCEDURES:** The Foundation reports a priority interest in small, community-based organizations in Western Pa. which work to build bridges between groups differing in race, ethnicity, age, gender, economic resources, and physical/mental ability. Projects which promote social, economic and environmental justice, especially those which address the needs of and/or broaden the experience of minority and low-income children are favored. No grants are awarded to/for individuals, colleges/universities, hospitals, endowments, or capital campaigns. Grant requests should be thorough and specific and include a one-page proposal summary, full description of the organization and proposed project, and a project timeline, as well as an annual report, organization and project budgets, audited financial statement, list of other project funding sources, IRS tax-exempt status documentation, and descriptive materials (brochures, newspaper stories, etc.) Requests following the Grantmakers of Western Pa. Common Grant Application Format are also accepted. Submit requests before the June 1st and November 1st deadlines. Site visits sometimes are made to organizations being considered for a grant. Grants are awarded at meetings in the summer and December. — Formerly called Pittsburgh Bridge & Iron Works Charitable Trust.

O+D+T   Katie Klingelhofer Wilson [NH] (Executive Director+T+Con) — George E. Klingelhofer (S+Donor+Advisor) — Kristan Klingelhofer [ID] (T) — Ned Klingelhofer [CA] (T) — Eleanore Childs, Esq. [Zelienople] (Advisor) — Joseph L. Fey (F) — Corporate donor: Bitterroot Enterprises [DE]

SW-043 Brooks Family Foundation

3465 Treeline Drive
Murrysville 15668 (Westmoreland County)

MI-15-32-42-43
Phone 724-325-4490 **FAX** None
EIN 23-2753021 **Year Created** 1995

AMV $961,993 **FYE** 12-00 **(Gifts Received** $35,000) 11 **Grants totaling** $46,600

All local/Pa. giving. High grant of **$35,000** to Washington & Jefferson College. **$3,000** to Franklin & Marshall College. **$1,300-$2,000** each to Cystic Fibrosis Foundation, Roberto Clemento Foundation (scholarships), Redstone Highlands (Woodside Program), Pete Henry Society of Washington & Jefferson College. Other smaller local contributions for various purposes. ■**PUBLICATIONS:** None ■**WEBSITE:** None ■**E-MAIL:** None ■**APPLICATION POLICIES & PROCEDURES:** Information not available.

O+D+T Robert J. Brooks (D+Donor+Con) — Susan C. Brooks (D)

SW-044 Brooks Foundation

c/o PNC Advisors, M.S. P1-POPP-02-1
One PNC Plaza, 249 Fifth Ave., 2nd Floor
Pittsburgh 15222 (Allegheny County)

MI-12-13-14-15-17-22-31-32-41-42-52-53-54-56-61-63-71
Phone 412-762-3808 **FAX** 412-705-1183
EIN 25-6026627 **Year Created** 1961

AMV $5,846,389 **FYE** 12-00 **(Gifts Received** $0) 64 **Grants totaling** $358,785

All SW Pa. giving; all grants are for general operations. High grant of **$20,000** to Pittsburgh Parks Conservancy. **$19,425** to Concordia Lutheran Church. **$15,000** each to St. Margaret Memorial Hospital and Seton Hill College. **$12,500** to Pittsburgh History & Landmarks Foundation. **$11,760** to Frick Art & Historical Society. **$10,000** each to Bethlehem Haven, Boy Scouts of SW Pa., Extra Mile Education Foundation, and The Watson Institute. **$7,500** to Children's Home of Pittsburgh. **$5,000** each to Allegheny Valley School, Carnegie Museum of Art, The Corporate Foundation, The Ellis School, FAME/Foundation for Advancement of Minorities through Education, Grace Memorial Church, Lutheran Foundation, Lydia's Place, Mom's House, Northside Common Ministries, Phipps Conservatory & Botanical Garden, Pittsburgh Children's Museum, Pittsburgh Leadership Council, Pittsburgh Symphony, Red Cross, St. Paul of the Cross, St. Vincent's Seminary, Sisters of St. Francis, Society of St. John, Sisters of St. Joseph, U. of Pittsburgh., Western Pa. Historical Society, and Yeshiva Schools. **$3,700** to Girls Hope of Pittsburgh. **$3,000** to Verland Foundation. **$2,000-$2,500** each to Laughlin Children's Home, Lupus Foundation, Mattress Factory, Pittsburgh Ballet Theatre, Pittsburgh Center for the Arts, Pittsburgh Cultural Trust, Pittsburgh Dance Council, Pittsburgh Opera, River City Brass Band, St. Bartholomew School, Sewickley Valley Historical Society, and Society for Contemporary Crafts. **$1,000-$1,750** each to Campus Life, Catholic Youth Ministries, Family Resources, Girl Scouts of Western Pa., Greater Pittsburgh Community Chest, Louise Child Care Center, Mt. Calvary Baptist Church, Myasthenia Gravis Foundation, Neville House Associates, New Life Community Church, Shady Side Academy, Tickets for Kids, and Women's Center & Shelter of Greater Pittsburgh. ■**PUBLICATIONS:** None ■**WEBSITE:** None ■**E-MAIL:** j.ferguson@pncadvisors.com ■**APPLICATION POLICIES & PROCEDURES:** Grant requests may be submitted in a letter at any time; include IRS tax-exempt status documentation.

O+D+T James M. Ferguson, III (Executive VP at Bank+Con) — PNC Advisors (Corporate Trustee)

SW-045 Brubaker (Fred & Janet) Foundation

607 Tayman Ave.
Somerset 15501 (Somerset County)

MI-14-15-22-31-51-56
Phone 814-445-6650 **FAX** None
EIN 25-6401741 **Year Created** 1992

AMV $339,172 **FYE** 12-99 **(Gifts Received** $24,675) 5 **Grants totaling** $14,000

Mostly local giving. High grant of **$8,000** to Somerset Hospital Foundation. **$2,500** to Somerset County Blind Center. **$2,000** to Agape Residential Ministries & Services [Mechanicsburg]. **$500** to Grist Mill Productions. **Out-of-state** grant: **$1,000** to Colonial Williamsburg Fund. ■**PUBLICATIONS:** None ■**WEBSITE:** None ■**E-MAIL:** None ■**APPLICATION POLICIES & PROCEDURES:** Information not available.

O+D+T I. Fred Brubaker (T+Donor+Con) — Janet M. Brubaker (T+Donor) — Somerset Trust Company (Corporate Trustee)

SW-046 Bruce Family Foundation

c/o Bruce & Merrilees Electric Co.
930 Cass Street
New Castle 16101 (Lawrence County)

MI-11-13-42-51-53-56-63
Phone 724-652-5566 **FAX** 724-652-8290
EIN 23-2892817 **Year Created** 1997

AMV $1,520,397 **FYE** 12-00 **(Gifts Received** $160,901) 17 **Grants totaling** $28,670

Mostly local giving; all grants are fellowships except as noted. High grant of **$11,900** to Third Presbyterian Church of New Castle. **$7,200** to Westminster College. **$2,700** to Boy Scouts/Moraine Trails Council. **$1,000-$1,500** each to Hoyt Institute of Fine Arts, Lawrence County Historical Society (general support), New Castle Playhouse (general support) United Way of Lawrence County (general support). Other local contributions **$10-$500** for various purposes. **Out-of-state** grant: **$1,000** to Robert Schuller Ministries [CA]. ■**PUBLICATIONS:** None ■**WEBSITE:** None ■**E-MAIL:** None ■**APPLICATION POLICIES & PROCEDURES:** No grants awarded to individuals.

O+D+T Robert J. Bruce (P+Donor+Con) — M. Joyce Bruce (S+F+Donor)

SW-047 Buhl Foundation, The

Suite 2300
650 Smithfield Street
Pittsburgh 15222 (Allegheny County)

MI-12-13-14-15-17-22-24-25-41-42-44-52-54-55-56-57-86
Phone 412-566-2711 **FAX** 412-566-2714
EIN 25-0378910 **Year Created** 1927

AMV $80,664,699 **FYE** 6-01 **(Gifts Received** $100) 70+ **Grants totaling** $4,396,118

Most giving to/for Pittsburgh/Western Pa. Note: The 'Grants Totaling' figure above refers to funding disbursed in 2000-01; the following covers the 71 grants (**$3,541,506** total) appropriated that year, whether or not payments were made on those commitments—some are multiyear awards. *LEARNING & TEACHING GRANTS*: High grant of **$651,300** to U. of Pittsburgh/School of Education ('Bringing Learning Technologies Completely Into Education' program). **$180,000** to Pace School (computer network). **$150,000** each to Allegheny Valley School (computer-science linkages) and Life'sWork of Western Pa. (employment program for disabled clients). **$100,000** to Family Communications, Inc. (childhood training materials development). **$85,000** to Pauline Auberle Foundation (computer laboratory). **$82,860** to CMU/Studio for Creative Inquiry (Mars project). **$52,500** to All of Us, Inc./Habi-Tat for Youth & Education [Zelienople] (caring habit of the month program). **$42,385** to Quaker Valley School District (curriculum accountable teacher training). **$39,000** to The Heartwood Institute (teacher support). **$20,000** each to Boys & Girls Clubs of Western Pa. (BizTech program), U. of Pittsburgh/Dept. of Theatre Arts (Shakespeare-in-the-Schools program), and Urban Youth Action (youth development/education programs). **$15,000** to Society for Contemporary Crafts (Teacher Training Institute). **$12,000** to Mon Valley Education Consortium (professional education experience). 10,000-**$10,500** each to Carnegie Museum of Art (exhibition support), Pittsburgh Ballet Theatre (residence program/student matinees), Prime Stage (educational outreach productions), and Three Rivers Urban Youth Corps (startup). **$8,300** to Gateway to the Arts (integrating arts in the curriculum institutes). **$6,700** to Pittsburgh Chamber Music Society (middle school/high school programs). **$6,150** to McKeesport Symphony Society (educational concert series). **$4,000-$5,100** each to Chatham Baroque (jam sessions), Children's Festival Chorus (music library system/consultant), CMU/Institute for Talented Elementary Students (C-MITES program), Extra Mile Education Foundation (computer enhancement at St. JamesSchool), Grantmakers of Western Pa., Human Services Center Corporation (Youth LIFE/K.O.O.L. prgram curriculum), Japan-America Society of Pa. (Japan Bowl/classroom presentations), Minority Enterprise Corp. of SW Pa. (PowerConference 2000), Pittsburgh Musical Theater (educational programs), Renaissance & Baroque Society of Pittsburgh (outreach/education projects), River City Youth Chorale (concert/program), Saltworks Theatre Company (educational plays in public schools), School District of Pittsburgh (summer chemistry workshop), Society of Women Engineers (workshop), Sun Crumbs (poetry programming/workshops), U.of Pittsburgh School of Social Work (educational forum), Upper St. Clair School District (Middle School Institute), and World Affairs Council of Pittsburgh (teachers summer institute). **$2,500-$3,750** each to Engineers Society of Western Pa. (Future City competition), Family Health Council (professional development for youth), Sci-Tech Festival (Edinburgh festival attendance), and Starlight Productions (seminars/workshops). **$1,000** to Tuesday Musical Club (international artists/school). *SERVICES TO COMMUNITY GRANTS*: **$178,000** to WQED (Pittsburgh A to Z). **$150,000** to Southwestern Pa. Corporation (Regional Enterprise Tower information hub). **$100,000** each to Robert Morris College (Center for Nonprofit Management technology initiative), UCP of Pittsburgh (computer laboratory), and YMCA of McKeesport integrated technology project). **$70,000** to Allegheny Conference on Community Development (agenda development fund). **$68,000** to Peoples Oakland (information systems). **$57,500** to Coro Center for Civic Leadership (transitional initiatives support). **$53,350** to Pittsburgh Regional Alliance (occupation/workforce link project). **$50,000** to Northside Leadership Conference (Allegheny Commons plan). **$30,000** to Allegheny County Dept. of Human Services (data warehouse). **$25,000** each to Artists & Cities, Inc. (Ice House Artists Studios project) and Urban League of Pittsburgh (Freedom Corner Memorial construction). **$17,900** to Greater Pittsburgh Community Food Bank. **$15,000** to Pittsburgh Mercy Foundation (Northside services directory). **$10,000** each to Pittsburgh Downtown Partnership (planning support), Pittsburgh Filmmakers (exhibit support), and Pittsburgh Cultural Trust (Carol Brown Fund). **$5,000** each to First Night Pittsburgh (Children's Celebration), Gateway to the Arts (long-range planning), and WITF [Harrisburg] (Stephen Foster project). **$1,000** to Community Involvement Foundation/Tickets for Kids (Phipps Conservatory tickets for disadvantaged children). *DEMONSTRATION PROGRAM GRANTS*: Three grants totaling **$500,000** to Carnegie Science Center (signage/building expansion planning/SciTech Festival). **$100,000** to Technology Development & Education Corp. (EnterPrize program). **$50,000** to NEED/Negro Educational Emergency Drive (Career School Program startup). In addition, **$23,336** awarded under employee matching gift program. ■**PUBLICATIONS:** Annual Report with application guidelines ■**WEBSITE:** None ■**E-MAIL:** buhl@buhlfoundation.org ■**APPLICATION POLICIES & PROCEDURES:** The Foundation reports giving focuses on the Pittsburgh area; priority interests as: (1) educational programs; (2) programs for young people; (3) studies to produce practical applications and which contribute to basic theory; (4) attempts which relate specialists in a common approach to problems or which call for cooperative efforts among separate agencies; (5) institutional, experimental, or demonstration approaches to innovative problem resolution; and (6) continuing support for previously supported and promising programs. Grants are awarded for periods of one to three years. Normally no grants are awarded to/for individuals, building funds, overhead costs, accumulated deficits, ordinary operating budgets, general fund raising campaigns, loans, other foundations, scholarships or fellowships, or nationally funded organizations. Also, no grants are awarded for conferences/seminars unless grant-related, support of propaganda, sectarian religious activities, or efforts to influence legislation. Prospective applicants should initially submit a letter of inquiry regarding the feasibility of submitting an grant request. If the Foundation responds favorably, a full proposal must be submitted; the proposal may follow the Grantmakers of Western Pa. Common Grant Application Format (see Appendix) or as detailed in the Foundation's annual report. Decisions on proposals generally are made within two months; the Board of Directors meets bimonthly.

O+D+T Dr. Doreen E. Boyce (P+Con) — Francis B. Nimick, Jr. (C+D) — Helen S. Faison (VC+D) — Jean A. Robinson (VC+D) — Albert C. Van Dusen (VC+D) — Marsha Zahumensky (S+F)

SW-048 Buncher Family Foundation
c/o The Buncher Company
5600 Forward Avenue
Pittsburgh 15217   (Allegheny County)

MI-11-22-41-52-53-54-55-62

Phone 412-422-9900 **FAX** 412-422-1298
EIN 23-7366998   **Year Created** 1974

AMV $10,383,872   **FYE** 11-00   **(Gifts Received** $1,450,000)   93 **Grants totaling** $808,055

Mostly local giving. High grant to **$504,000** to United Jewish Federation of Greater Pittsburgh (Buncher Family Leadership Program/general support). **$204,969** to Rodef Shalom Congregation (mostly capital campaign). **$27,175** to Jewish Community Center of Pittsburgh. **$10,000** to United Way of Allegheny County. **$5,100** to Carnegie Museum of Art. **$3,968** to Society for Contemporary Crafts. **$3,150** to Beth David Reform Congregation. **$2,000** each to Historical Society of Western Pa. (Italian-American Collection) and Pittsburgh Opera. **$1,000-$1,250** each to Allegheny Valley School, American Jewish Committee, Anti-Defamation League, Associated Artists of Pittsburgh, Carnegie Museum of Art Women's Committee, Community College of Allegheny County (Foerster Scholarship Endowment), Ladies Hospital Aid Society, National Aviary in Pittsburgh, National Conference for Community & Justice, National Council of Jewish Women, North Side Friends & Neighbors Education Fund, Pittsburgh Cultural Trust, Pittsburgh Parks Conservancy, and RSC Amyloidosis Research Fund. Other smaller contributions **$25-$500** for various purposes. **Out-of-state** giving includes **$10,000** to Intracoastal Health Foundation [FL]; **$4,000** to American Friends of the Israel Museum [NY]; and smaller grants/contributions, mostly to NY and FL. ■**PUBLICATIONS:** application guidelines ■**WEBSITE:** None ■**E-MAIL:** None ■**APPLICATION POLICIES & PROCEDURES:** Grant requests may be submitted at any time in a letter or in Grantmakers of Western Pa. Common Grant Application Format; state the organizational purpose and the amount/purpose of funds being requested. No grants are awarded to individuals. Site visits sometimes are made to organizations being considered for a grant.

O+D+T Bernita Buncher (P+Con) — Thomas J. Balestrieri (VP) — Herbert S. Green (VP) — Joseph M. Jackovic (S) — H. William Doring (F) — Ruth H. Neff (AS) — Corporate donors: The Buncher Company; Buncher Management Agency; Buncher Rail Car Service Co.

SW-049 Burke Family Foundation, The
c/o The Grable Foundation
650 Smithfield Street, Suite 250
Pittsburgh 15222   (Allegheny County)

MI-11-12-41-42-54-55-56-57-63-71

Phone 412-471-4550 **FAX** None
EIN 31-1583757   **Year Created** 1998

AMV $448,264   **FYE** 12-00   (**Gifts Received** $379,411)   60+ **Grants totaling** $124,024

See entry for The Burke Foundation below. ■**PUBLICATIONS:** None ■**WEBSITE:** None ■**E-MAIL:** None ■**APPLICATION POLICIES & PROCEDURES:** Refer to The Burke Foundation entry.

O+D+T Charles R. Burke, Jr. (P+Donor+Con) — Patricia Grable Burke [FL] (VP+F) — Steven E. Burke (T)

SW-050 Burke Foundation, The
c/o The Grable Foundation
650 Smithfield Street, Suite 250
Pittsburgh 15222   (Allegheny County)

MI-11-12-41-42-54-55-56-57-63-71

Phone 412-471-4550 **FAX** None
EIN 25-1407410   **Year Created** 1982

AMV $447,975   **FYE** 12-00   (**Gifts Received** $379,410)   60+ **Grants totaling** $124,025

The grants reported are funded 50-50 with The Burke Family Foundation; see prior entry. Mostly local giving; all grants are for general operating support. High grant of **$100,000** to Pace School. **$26,000** each to The Ellis School and Westminster College. **$25,000** to United Way of Allegheny County. **$10,000** to Fox Chapel Presbyterian Church. **$2,725 $5,450** to Audubon Society of Western Pa./Beechwood Farms Nature Center. **$1,800-$2,000** each to Historical Society of Western Pa., Winchester-Thurston School, and WQED. **$1,000-$1,100** each to Carnegie Museums of Pittsburgh, Exccutive Service Corps, Extra Mile Education Foundation, Fox Chapel Country Day School, Pittsburgh Cultural Trust, and Shady Side Academy. Other local contributions **$100-$500** for varied civic purposes. **Out-of-state** giving includes **$26,000** to Connecticut College and grants/contributions **$100-$3,000** to organizations in FL, OH, and VA. ■**PUBLICATIONS:** None ■**WEBSITE:** None ■**E-MAIL:** None ■**APPLICATION POLICIES & PROCEDURES:** This Foundation and Burke Family Foundation report that giving focuses on the Pittsburgh area; no grants are awarded to individuals. Grant requests may be submitted at any time in letter or a proposal following the Grantmakers of Western Pa. Common Grant Application Format (see www.gwpa.org); the application must include a one-page summary; information about the applicant organization; statement of need for the proposed project; description of the project; the project supervisor and staff; project budget showing committed and anticipated funds; organization's current operating budget; description of how the project will be sustained after the grant has ended; description of anticipated outcomes from the project; list of Board members; letters of support from the applicant's board and collaborating organizations; and IRS tax-exempt status documentation.

O+D+T Steven E. Burke (P+Donor+Con) — Patricia Grable Burke [FL] (VP+F) — Charles R. Burke, Jr. (T)

SW-051 Burki (Albert H.) Foundation
c/o Pittsburgh Cut Flower Company
1901 Liberty Avenue
Pittsburgh 15222   (Allegheny County)

MI-Not Reported

Phone 412-355-7000 **FAX** None
EIN 25-1402862   **Year Created** 1981

AMV $275,645   **FYE** 12-00   (**Gifts Received** $0)   **Grants totaling** $0

No grants awarded since 1993. ■**PUBLICATIONS:** None ■**WEBSITE:** None ■**E-MAIL:** None ■**APPLICATION POLICIES & PROCEDURES:** Information not available.

O+D+T Donald E. Hook (T+Donor+Con) — Corporate donor: Pittsburgh Cut Flower Company

---

SW-052 Byham Charitable Foundation
c/o Development Dimensions International
1225 Washington Pike
Bridgeville 15017   (Allegheny County)

MI-11-13-32-42-51-52-54-55-57

Phone 412-257-3890 **FAX** 412-257-0614
EIN 25-1739254   **Year Created** 1994

AMV $896,478   **FYE** 12-00   (**Gifts Received** $605,000)   22 **Grants totaling** $53,740

Mostly local giving. High grant of **$20,000** to Pittsburgh Ballet Theatre. **$12,600** to Pittsburgh Public Theater. **$10,000** to United Way of SW Pa. **$1,875-$2,000** each to Arthritis Foundation, The Carnegie, and WQED-FM. **$1,000** to Pittsburgh Musical Theater. **$750** to Manchester Craftsmen's Guild. Other smaller local and out-of-state contributions, many for educational purposes. ■**PUBLICATIONS:** None ■**WEBSITE:** www.ddiworld.com [corporate info only] ■**E-MAIL:** None ■**APPLICATION POLICIES & PROCEDURES:** Grant requests may be submitted in a letter at any time; describe the organization's charitable purpose and intended use of the funds.

O+D+T Karen Ann Krauss (Manager+Con) — William C. Byham [Pittsburgh] (D+T+Donor) — Carolyn M. Byham [Pittsburgh] (D+T+Donor) — Carter W. Byham [Pittsburgh] (D) — Tacy Byham Lehman [Pittsburgh] (D)

SW-053 Calihan Foundation, The
c/o Bradford Capital Partners
600 Grant Street, Suite 4606
Pittsburgh 15219   (Allegheny County)

MI-11-17-31-41-42-43-44-52-54-55-56-57-61

Phone 412-227-6900 **FAX** None
EIN 25-1560562   **Year Created** 1987

AMV $957,255   **FYE** 12-00   (**Gifts Received** $0)   93 **Grants totaling** $682,443

About two-thirds local/Pa. giving; grants are for operating support/annual giving except as noted; some larger grants comprise multiple awards. Seven grants totaling **$166,872** to Extra Mile Education Foundation (Elizabeth Seton/Good Shepherd/endowment/annual support). **$59,250** to Diocese of Pittsburgh/Crossroads Foundation (development salary/scholarships). **$32,972** to Oakland Catholic High School (scholarships/annual support). **$30,879** to Historical Society of Western Pa. (endowment/capital campaign). **$26,150** to Our Lady of Mercy High School (mostly capital campaign). **$25,000** to United Way of SW Pa. **$16,667** to Carlow College Campus School (capital campaign). **$10,000** to Carnegie Institute. **$7,500** each to Pittsburgh Center for the Arts, Shady Side Academy (capital campaign/annual support), and Women's Center & Shelter of Greater Pittsburgh. **$6,050** to St. Scholastica Church (capital campaign/annual support). **$5,560** to American Ireland Fund. **$5,000** each to Diocese of Pittsburgh Foundation (Bishop's Education Fund), Holy Family Hospital Foundation, and St. Vincent College (capital campaign). **$3,500** to Children's Hospital of Pittsburgh. **$2,000-$2,400** each to Cardinal Wright Regional School, Pittsburgh Cultural Trust (mostly capital campaign), Pittsburgh Symphony, and U. of Pa. Graduate School of Education [Philadelphia]. **$1,000-$1,500** each to Carnegie Library of Pittsburgh, National Flag Foundation, NEED, Parental Stress Center, Sacred Heart Church (memorial gift), U. of Pittsburgh Cancer Center (research fund), Wesley Institute (program), and WQED-FM/TV. Other smaller local contributions for various purposes. **Out-of-state** giving includes **$85,000** to Summer Search [CA and MA]; **$80,000** to Acton Institute [MI]; and **$40,000** to Lyford Cay Foundation [FL] (scholarship fund). ■**PUBLICATIONS:** None ■**WEBSITE:** None ■**E-MAIL:** None ■**APPLICATION POLICIES & PROCEDURES:** The Foundation reports that most giving is restricted to the Pittsburgh area and that unsolicted requests are not accepted.
O+D+T Victoria L. Pacoe (S+Con) — Brenda S. Calihan (P+Donor) — Joseph L. Calihan (VP+Donor) — David H. Kropp (F) — Katherine R. Calihan (Donor) — Martin J. Calihan [MN] (Donor)

SW-054 Calvary Foundation
104 Trenton Circle
McMurray 15317   (Washington County)

MI-12-22-63-64
Phone 724-941-1414 **FAX** None
EIN 25-1633965   **Year Created** 1990

AMV $992,806   **FYE** 12-00   (**Gifts Received** $100)   17 **Grants totaling** $47,164

About half local giving. High Pa. grant of **$4,000** to Washington City Mission. **$3,000** each to Family Guidance, Inc., New Day, Inc., and Youth for Christ. **$2,000** each to Salvation Army, Sheldon Calvary Camp, South Hills Crisis Pregnancy Center, and Trinity Episcopal School for Ministry. **$1,000** to South American Mission Society [Ambridge]. **$800** to Interfacing [Sewickley]. **Out-of-state** giving include **$5,000** each to Alliance Defense Fund [AZ] and Gospel Missionary Union [MO]; and smaller grants for similar purposes in several states. ■**PUBLICATIONS:** None ■**WEBSITE:** None ■**E-MAIL:** None ■**APPLICATION POLICIES & PROCEDURES:** The Foundation reports that all grants usually involve spreading the Christian Gospel and are mostly for special projects, building funds, seed money, capital drives, or scholarships. Prospective applicants initially should make a telephone inquiry about the feasibility of submitting a request. Submit grant requests in a proposal at any time; state the purpose of the organization, a clear statement of the need, and the means for measuring the success; include an organization budget, project budget, Board member list, list of major funding sources, and IRS tax-exempt status documentation. Site visits sometimes are made to organizations being considered for a grant. Grant requests usually are reviewed at the end of March, June, September, and December.
O+D+T Schuyler L. Brooks (D+Donor+Con) — Joan G. Brooks (D+Donor) — Peter S. Brooks (D) — Stephen G. Brooks [CO] (D) — Margaret E. Schmitt [Pittsburgh] (D)

SW-055 Campbell (Charles Talbot) Foundation
c/o National City Bank of Pa.
National City Center, 20 Stanwix Street
Pittsburgh 15222   (Allegheny County)

MI-13-14-15-31-32-41-42-56-52-55
Phone 412-644-8332 **FAX** 412-261-6252
EIN 25-1287221   **Year Created** 1975

AMV $9,439,819   **FYE** 1-01   (**Gifts Received** $0)   19 **Grants totaling** $317,000

About four-fifths local giving. High grant of **$70,000** to Western Pa. School for the Deaf. **$50,000** each to Goodwill Industries of Pittsburgh and Shadyside Hospital Foundation. **$25,000** each to Boys & Girls Club of Western Pa. **$12,000** to Pittsburgh Vision Service. **$10,000** each to Children's Festival Chorus, Extra Mile Education Foundation, Family Hospice, Radio Information Service, and D.T. Watson Rehabilitation Service. **$5,000** each to National Society of Arts & Letters, Pittsburgh Youth Symphony, and Three Rivers Young People's Orchestra. **Out-of-state** giving includes **$10,000** each to Alice Lloyd College [KY], College of the Ozarks [MO], and Pima Community College [AZ]; and **$5,000** each to Foundation of the American Academy of Ophthalmology [CA], International Eye Foundation [MD], and Joint Commission on Allied Health Personnel in Ophthalmology Education & Research Fund [MN]. ■**PUBLICATIONS:** None ■**WEBSITE:** None ■**E-MAIL:** None ■**APPLICATION POLICIES & PROCEDURES:** The Foundation reports that giving focuses on Western Pa.; no support is awarded to/for United Ways, Community Chests, individuals, or scholarships. Prospective applicants should make an initial telephone inquiry about the feasibility of submitting a request. Grant requests should be submitted using the Grantmakers of Western Pa. Common Grant Application Format (original plus 4 copies), preferably during February-March or July-August (deadlines are March 31st and August 31st); include an annual report, organization and project budgets, Board member list, list of major funding sources, audited financial statement, and IRS tax-exempt status documentation. Site visits sometimes are made to organizations being considered for a grant. The Distribution Committee awards grants at April and September meetings.
O+D+T Distribution Committee members: — William M. Schmidt (VP at Bank+Con) — Robert P. Cornell — Robert S. Foltz — Dr. Joseph F. Novak — John N. Wilson, Jr. — National City Bank of Pa. (Trustee)

SW-056 Carnegie Hero Fund Commission
425 - 6th Ave., Suite 1640
Pittsburgh 15219   (Allegheny County)

MI-23-43
Phone 412-281-1302 **FAX** 412-281-5751
EIN 25-1062730   **Year Created** 1904

AMV $33,667,953   **FYE** 12-00   **(Gifts Received** $0)   200+ **Grants totaling** $685,312

All grants are Carnegie Hero Awards to civilians who performed acts of heroism (in the United States, Canada, or their waters) in which they saved or attempted to save the lives of others. Awardees receive a medal and a financial grant of **$3,000,** as well as educational aid and financial assistance to disabled Carnegie Hero awardees or dependents of deceased awardees. ■**PUBLICA-TIONS:** Annual Report (with statement of program policy and application guidelines) ■**WEBSITE:** www.carnegiehero.org/ ■**E-MAIL:** carnegiehero@carnegiehero.org ■**APPLICATION POLICIES & PROCEDURES:** Nominations or recommendations for recognition of an outstanding act of civilian heroism should be submitted on an application form available from the Commission; the application must provide the name of the hero, date and time of the heroic act, names/addresses of any witnesses, and must be received within two years of the heroic act. The Trustees meet five times annually to make awards.

O+D+T Walter F. Rutkowski (Executive Director+S+Con) — Robert W. Off (P+T) — Priscilla J. McCrady (VP+T) — James M. Walton (F+T) — and 17 other Trustees

---

SW-057 Carthage Foundation, The
One Oxford Center, Suite 3900
301 Grant Street
Pittsburgh 15219   (Allegheny County)

MI-42-49-81-86

Phone 412-392-2900 **FAX** 412-392-2922
EIN 25-6067979   **Year Created** 1964

AMV $24,565,077   **FYE** 12-00   **(Gifts Received** $0)   17 **Grants totaling** $627,500

Nationwide giving for programs addressing national or international public policy issues; grants are for general support except as noted. One Pa. grant: **$200,000** to Allegheny Institute for Public Policy. **Out-of-state** giving includes **$100,000** to U. of VA Law School (Center for National Security Law Education Project); **$62,500** to Stanford U./Hoover Institution on War, Revolution & Peace Stanford U. [CA] (fellowship fund); **$30,000** each to Capital Research Project [DC] (Mandate for Charity project) and Defense Forum Foundation [VA]; **$25,000** each to American Studies Center [DC] (Radio America), Committee for Constructive Tomorrow [DC], Foundation for the Advancement of Monetary Education Ltd. [NY], Mountain States Legal Foundation [CO], and Women's Freedom Network [DC]; and other grants **$5,000-$15,000** for similar purposes in several states. ■**PUBLICATIONS:** Annual Report available on the Foundation's website. ■**WEBSITE:** www.scaife.com ■**E-MAIL:** None ■**APPLICATION POLICIES & PROCEDURES:** The Foundation's reports that giving focuses on U.S. organizations addressing national or international public policy issues; most grants are for general support/operating budgets, special projects, research, publications, or matching grants. No grants awarded for building funds, endowment, or to individuals. Prospective applicants should initially telephone the foundation to inquire about the feasibility of submitting an application. Grant requests may be submitted at any time in a two-page letter signed by the organization's chief executive officer or an authorized representative which indicates Board approval of the application; include a concise description of the specific program for which funding is requested, organizational and project budgets, an audited financial statement, annual report, Board member list, a list of other funding sources, and IRS tax-exempt status documentation. Site visits sometimes are made to organizations being considered for a grant. Grants normally are awarded at quarterly meetings.

O+D+T Michael W. Gleba (F+T+Con) — Richard M. Scaife (C+T+Donor) — R. Daniel McMichael (S+T) — W. McCook Miller, Jr. (T) — Alexis J. Konkol (AS) — Roger W. Robinson (AF)

SW-058 Castelli (Deno) Charitable Scholarship Fund
Law & Finance Bldg., 35 West Pittsburgh Street
Greensburg 15601   (Westmoreland County)

MI-43
Phone 724-837-1910 **FAX** 724-837-7868
EIN 25-6242226   **Year Created** 1984

AMV $2,635,353   **FYE** 6-00   **(Gifts Received** $0)   150+ **Grants totaling** $104,750

All grants are scholarship awards for Westmoreland County residents/high school graduates who are pursuing (or will be entering) a four-year bachelor's degree program anywhere in the U.S.; awards are paid directly to colleges/universities. ■**PUBLICA-TIONS:** statement of program policy; application guidelines ■**WEBSITE:** None ■**E-MAIL:** None ■**APPLICATION POLICIES & PROCEDURES:** Only graduates of Westmoreland County high schools and residents of the county are eligible to apply for scholarships. A formal application form, available from the Fund or high school guidance counselors in the county, must be completed and submitted before the May 1st deadline; provide evidence of acceptance from a college/university, and income tax returns for applicant and parents. Scholarships are awarded at a July meeting. — Formerly called Castelli Charitable Trust.

O+D+T Gregory T. Nichols (Executive Director+Con) — Hon. Gilfert M. Mihalich (Chairman, Scholarship Committee) — Louis J. Kober — Jerry Roy — PNC Bank N.A. (Trustee)

SW-059 Childs (Otis H.) Trust
Refer to PNC Advisors Charitable Trust Committee entry.
                                     (Allegheny County)

MI-31-32

EIN 25-6024249   **Year Created** 1910

AMV $1,739,614   **FYE** 12-00   **(Gifts Received** $0)   3 **Grants totaling** $82,408

All giving restricted to organizations involved in caring for persons suffering from tuberculosis or in TB research. Two Pa. grants: **$27,408** to Children's Hospital of Pittsburgh (TB research/treatment). **$20,000** to Pittsburgh Mercy Foundation (Operation Safety Net/TB Testing). **Out-of-state** grant: **$35,000** to National Jewish Medical & Research Center [CO] (TB research/treatment). ■**APPLICATION POLICIES & PROCEDURES:** Refer to the PNC Advisors Charitable Trust Committee entry for a statement on giving priorities and full application guidelines.

O+D+T Refer to PNC Advisors Charitable Trust Committee entry. — PNC Advisors (Corporate Trustee)

SW-060 Chosky (Philip) Charitable & Educational Foundation, The MI-22-29-31-41-42-51-52-54-62
c/o Electronic Institutes, Inc.
4634 Browns Hill Road   **Phone** 412-521-8686 **FAX** None
Pittsburgh 15217   (Allegheny County)   **EIN** 23-2932969   **Year Created** 1998
AMV $9,902,808   **FYE** 12-00   (**Gifts Received** $648,655)   17 **Grants totaling** $745,142

Mostly local giving; grants are discretionary except as noted. High grant of **$374,142** to Electronic Institutes (scholarship and educational programs). **$204,000** to Carnegie Mellon U. **$57,000** to Rosedale Technical Institutes (scholarship and educational programs). **$35,000** each to United Jewish Federation of Greater Pittsburgh and U. of Pittsburgh. **$25,000** to Yeshiva Archie 2100. **$3,800** to Oasis. **$1,000-$2,000** each to Andy Warhol Museum, Kollel Bais Yitzchok, Pittsburgh Irish & Classical Theater, Pittsburgh Opera, Pittsburgh Symphony, Quantum Theater, and Travelers Aid Society. Other smaller contributions. **Out-of-state** grant: **$1,000** to Cleveland Clinic [OH]. ■**PUBLICATIONS:** None ■**WEBSITE:** None ■**E-MAIL:** None ■**APPLICATION POLICIES & PROCEDURES:** Information not available.

O+D+T Philip Chosky (Executive Director+Con) — Stanley Barg [West Conshohocken] (D) — Charles Kirshner (D) — Michael O'Malley (D) — Corporate donors: Electronic Institutes, Inc. Foundation donor: Electronic Institutes Foundation.

SW-061 Citizens Bank Foundation   MI-11-13-33-42-43-44-71-85
c/o Citizens National Bank of Evans City
108 East Diamond Street, P.O. Box 1550   **Phone** 724-214-5805 **FAX** None
Butler 16003   (Butler County)   **EIN** 31-1631195   **Year Created** 1998
AMV $92,200   **FYE** 12-00   (**Gifts Received** $0)   26 **Grants totaling** $77,434

All local giving; grants are for capital campaigns except as noted — many grants are payments on multiyear commitments. High grant of **$20,000** to Butler County YMCA. **$15,000** to Butler County Community College Education Foundation. **$10,734** to United Way of Butler County (annual campaign). **$7,000** to Mental Health Assn. of Butler County. **$5,000** each to Boy Scouts/Moraine Trails Council and Cranberry Township Community Park. **$3,000** to Butler Area Public Library (departmental upgrades). **$1,000** each to Allegheny-Clarion Valley Development Industrial Park, Evans City Public Library (annual campaign), Slippery Rock U. Foundation (annual campaign), and four scholarships for local students. Other local contributions **$100-$750** for scholarships and community organizations. ■**PUBLICATIONS:** None ■**WEBSITE:** www.citizensnatl.com [corporate info only] ■**E-MAIL:** None ■**APPLICATION POLICIES & PROCEDURES:** Information not available.

O+D+T Brenda Lemmon (Corporate Secretary+Con)

SW-062 Clapp (Anne L. & George H.) Charitable & Educ. Trust   MI-12-13-14-15-16-17-18-22-25-29-31-32-35
c/o Mellon Private Wealth Management   41-42-43-44-51-52-53-54-55-56-71-72
One Mellon Center, Room 3825   **Phone** 412-234-1634 **FAX** 412-234-1073
Pittsburgh 15258   (Allegheny County)   **EIN** 25-6018976   **Year Created** 1949
AMV $24,509,682   **FYE** 9-00   (**Gifts Received** $0)   106 **Grants totaling** $1,244,000

Most giving limited to SW Pa.; grants are for general purposes/operating support except as noted, and some are payments on multiyear pledges. High grant of **$50,000** to The Carnegie ('Aluminum by Design'). **$25,000** each to Carnegie Institute and Sewickley YMCA. **$20,000** each to Children's Hospital of Pittsburgh, Laughlin Children's Center, Sewickley Public Library, Sewickley Valley Hospital, U. of Pittsburgh (Clapp Scholarship Fund), Valley Care Assn., Watson Institute (rehab services), and Western Pa. Conservancy. **$15,000** each to American Cancer Society, Audubon Society of Western Pa., Boys & Girls Club of Western Pa., Chatham College (student-faculty research program), The Ellis School (capital campaign), FAME/Fund for Advancement of Minorities through Education, Frontier Nursing Service, Gateway Rehabilitation Service, Habitat for Humanity of Greene County, Historical Society of Western Pa., Marion Manor, National MS Society, Pittsburgh History & Landmarks Foundation, Pittsburgh Opera, Pittsburgh Symphony, Pittsburgh Zoo, Rainbow Kitchen [Homestead] (anti-hunger programs), Salvation Army, Sewickley Academy, Sewickley Community Center, Western Pa. School for Blind Children, and WQED. **$12,500** each to Little Sisters of the Poor (capital campaign), NEED/Negro Educational Emergency Drive, Pa. Special Olympics (support for Western Pa. athletes), Planned Parenthood of Western Pa., Sewickley Valley Historical Society, and Union Aid Society. **$10,000** each to Beaver County CSC (preschool-daycare programs), Boy Scouts/Pittsburgh Council (programs for MR youth), Bridge to Independence [Braddock] (capital campaign), Carnegie Mellon U. (library books purchase), Children's Hospital of Pittsburgh (Family Care Connection Center), Clelian Heights School for Exceptional Children, Duquesne U. (law school renovations), Extra Mile Education Foundation, Family Resources (family retreat center), Jane Holmes Residence (patient monitoring system), Lupus Foundation, March of Dimes, Marion Hall Home (renovations), Mars Home for Youth (capital campaign), McGuire Home (community residence program), Mercy Hospital (Child's Place), Mom's House (SOS program), National Aviary in Pittsburgh, Pace School (student services), Pittsburgh Action Against Rape (school programs), Pittsburgh Ballet Theatre, Pittsburgh Civic Light Opera (Creative Vision program), Pittsburgh Public Theater, The Program for Female Offenders, Southwinds (staff training), and Wilkinsburg Community Ministry (social services). **$7,000-$7,500** each to Butler YMCA (health-wellness center), City Mission (homeless youths shelter), Daybreak Adult Day Care (medical resale facility), Emanuel Episcopal Church (reading program), I Have A Dream Foundation (Dreamers Hall), Interfaith Volunteer Caregivers (recruitment-training), Lydia's Place, McKeesport YMCA (youth guidance program), Pittsburgh Youth Symphony, Saltworks (student performances), and Wings for Children (airlifts). **$6,000** to Greater Pittsburgh Literacy Council (ESL program). **$5,000-$5,500** each to Northside Common Ministries (food bank), Phillips School (technology program), Pine Valley Camp [Ellwood City] (septic system), Reading is Fundamental (after school program), River City Brass Band, Rx Council of Pittsburgh, Sisters Place [Clairton] (women's shelter), and Women's Center/Rape Crisis Center [New Castle] (capital campaign). **$3,500** each to Derry Area School District (reading programs) and,Mendelssohn Choir of Pittsburgh. **$2,000** each to Northside Christian Health Center, First Charities (facility upgrade), and Youngwood Public Library (books purchase). **Out-of-state** giving includes **$27,500** to Morris Museum of Arts &

Sciences [NJ]; **$20,000** to Hotchkiss School [CT]; and other grants, mostly to Northern NJ or New England for schools/colleges. ■**PUBLICATIONS:** Application Guidelines memorandum ■**WEBSITE:** None ■**E-MAIL:** None ■**APPLICATION POLICIES & PROCEDURES:** Only SW Pa. organizations are eligible to apply. Primary fields of interest are education, social services, youth/child welfare programs, and aging; limited support to cultural programs, historic preservation, and conservation. Only rarely is support given to community development organizations or to educational institutions not previously supported. No grants are awarded to/for medical research, research projects, filmmaking, conferences, camping programs, field trips, or individuals. Most grants are for general support, special projects, building funds, capital drives, endowment, scholarships, and matching grants; multiyear grants are awarded. Grant requests must be submitted during January-April; deadline is May 31st but applications at deadline are strongly discouraged. Submit requests in a letter (10 pages maximum) or in Grantmakers of Western Pa. Common Grant Application Format. Provide a brief background on the organization/its mission; clearly describe the proposed project and its objectives; state the specific amount requested and total project cost; and include an annual report, project budget, Board member list, and IRS tax-exempt status documentation. Three complete sets of the application must be submitted; do not include videocassettes. The Trustees award grants at an August-September meeting.

O+D+T Annette Calgaro (VP at Bank+Con) — William E. Collin [NC] (T) — William A. Galbraith, Jr. [FL] (T) — Mellon Bank N.A. (Corporate Trustee)

SW-063   CMS Realize Your Dream Foundation   MI-21-31-32-35-41-43-49
  c/o CMS Mid-Atlantic, Inc.
  235 Alpha Drive, Suite 300   **Phone** 412-967-6200 **FAX** None
  Pittsburgh   15238   (Allegheny County)   **EIN** 23-2884514   **Year Created** 1997
AMV $792,726   **FYE** 12-00   (**Gifts Received** $750)   26 **Grants totaling** $86,702

All local giving. Organizational grants included **$20,000** to National Foundation for Teaching Entrepreneurship-Pittsburgh; **$10,000** to The Ellis School (annual fund/annual pledge); **$5,000** each to Juvenile Diabetes Education Foundation (Walk for Cure) and St. Margaret Memorial Hospital (Fall Face-off); **$2,500** to Rotary District 7300 (Gold Medal Education); and **$1,000** to Pittsburgh Rotary Club (international education). Eighteen scholarships, **$600-$5,000** each, awarded to Pittsburgh-area students attending colleges in many states. ■**PUBLICATIONS:** application guidelines; scholarship application form ■**WEBSITE:** None ■**E-MAIL:** None ■**APPLICATION POLICIES & PROCEDURES:** Scholarship awards are restricted to graduates of a public, private or parochial high schools in the City of Pittsburgh or within the following geographical area: east to Lower Burrell, west to Sewickley, north to Butler, and south to the Allegheny & Ohio rivers; a listing of all eligible high schools is available. A formal scholarship application form, available from the Foundation, must be submitted by the February 28th deadline. In addition, other grants are awarded to organizations for community or educational purposes.

O+D+T Bernard E. Stocklein, Jr. (T+Donor+Con (Organizational Grants)) — Kathleen A. Santelli (Coordinator+Con (Scholarship Awards)) — Dr. Ronald Bowes (Member, Scholarship Committee) — Sister Clarice Carlson (Member, Scholarship Committee) — Linda W. Ebel (Member, Scholarship Committee) — John Novey (Member, Scholarship Committee) — Louis Shook (Member, Scholarship Committee) — Rosalie P. Wisotzki (Member, Scholarship Committee)

SW-064   CNS Health & Education Foundation   MI-34-43
  c/o Community Nursing Services in Greensburg
  P.O. Box 98   **Phone** 724-837-6827 **FAX** None
  Greensburg   15601   (Westmoreland County)   **EIN** 25-0967471   **Year Created** 1951
AMV $1,249,217   **FYE** 4-00   (**Gifts Received** $29,306)   **Grants totaling** $53,000

All grants are for students pursuing studies aimed at the community health care professions; no details were reported on the number or sizes of awards. ■**PUBLICATIONS:** application form ■**WEBSITE:** None ■**E-MAIL:** None ■**APPLICATION POLICIES & PROCEDURES:** All grants are restricted to scholarships for persons who are pursuing studies aimed at the community health care professions, and who are a two-year (or more) resident of: City of Greensburg; -or- borough of South Greensburg, Southwest Greensburg, Youngwood or West Newton; -or- township of Hempfield, North Huntingdon, Salem, Sewickley, or Unity. Applicants must complete a formal application form, available from the Foundation.

O+D+T Members of the Scholarship Committee: — Edward Benson (P+Con) — Ronald Silvis (VP) — Anita Leonard (S) — Mark Zagar (F)

SW-065   Cochrane (Andrew R. & Dorothy L.) Foundation   MI-11-12-13-15-22-29-31-32-41-63-82-84
  121 South Drive   **Phone** 412-967-9778 **FAX** None
  Pittsburgh   15238   (Allegheny County)   **EIN** 25-6093648   **Year Created** 1968
AMV $2,085,310   **FYE** 12-00   (**Gifts Received** $150,877)   30+ **Grants totaling** $90,370

About three-fourths local/Pa. giving; all grants are for annual, unrestricted support. High grant of **$11,500** to Red Cross. **$10,100** to Coalition for Christian Outreach. **$10,000** to Salvation Army. **$7,500** to YMCA of Pittsburgh. **$3,000** to United Way of SW Pa. **$2,500** to Family Guidance. **$2,000** to Camp Kon-O-Wee [Fombell]. **$1,000-$1,600** each to American Cancer Society, Aspinwall Presbyterian Church, Jane Holmes Residence, Mercersburg Academy [Franklin County], Shadyside Presbyterian Church, St. Barnabas Charitable Foundation, and Stenser Camps & Conference Center [Fombell]. Other smaller local contributions. **Out-of-state** giving includes **$10,000** each to American Bible Society [NY] and UNICEF [NY]. ■**PUBLICATIONS:** None ■**WEBSITE:** None ■**E-MAIL:** None ■**APPLICATION POLICIES & PROCEDURES:** The Foundation reports that Pittsburgh-area organizations receive priority. Prospective applicants should initially telephone the Foundation to inquire about the feasibility of submitting an request. Submit grant requests in a letter (2 pages maximum) at any time.

O+D+T Christine Cochrane Yukevich (T+Con) — Andrew R. Cochrane (T+Donor) — Corporate donors: Arch Engineering Company; Wise Machine Company

SW-066 Coen (Charles S. & Mary) Family Foundation
Post Office Box 34
Washington 15301
(Washington County)

MI-11-12-13-14-15-25-29-31-32-41-42-44-45
56-63-71-84
Phone 724-223-5503 **FAX** None
EIN 25-6033877 **Year Created** 1959

AMV $7,889,299 **FYE** 2-01 (**Gifts Received** $76,000) 94 **Grants totaling** $598,000

Mostly local/Western Pa. giving. High grant of **$95,000** to Presbyterian SeniorCare. **$70,000** to Washington & Jefferson College. **$65,000** to Wilson College [Chambersburg]. **$45,000** to Waynesburg College. **$40,000** to Washington Hospital Foundation. **$36,000** to Church of the Covenant. **$26,000** to United Cerebral Palsy. **$11,000** each to Foundation for California U. of Pa. and LeMoyne Multi-Cultural Community Center. **$10,000** each to Westminster College and Youth for Christ. **$8,750** to Pine Springs Camp [Jennerstown]. **$6,000** to Washington High School. **$5,000** to Pa. Trolley Museum. **$4,500** to United Way of Washington County. **$3,000-$3,500** each to Citizens Library of Washington, Make-A-Wish Foundation of Western Pa., and Try-Again Homes. **$2,000** each to Amwell Township Volunteer Fire Company, ARC Washington Foundation, Center in the Woods, East Buffalo Presbyterian Church, First United Methodist Church of Washington, Washington County Community Foundation, Washington Literacy Council, and Western Pa. Conservancy. **$1,000** each to Abernathy Black Community Development & Education Fund, Boy Scouts, Bradford House Historical Society, Children's Hospital of Pittsburgh, Girl Scouts of SW Pa., Greene County Habitat for Humanity, Holy Rosary Church [Muse], John Wesley United Methodist Church, Junior Achievement of SW Pa., Leukemia Society of America, Meadowcroft Museum of Rural Life, Mel Blount Youth Home, Mt. Pleasant Township Community Center, National Road Heritage Park, Neighborhood Drug Awareness, Pittsburgh Symphony, Pony Baseball, St. Paul AME Church, Washington County Habitat for Humanity, Washington County Historical Society, Washington Area Humane Society, Washington YMCA, and Washington YWCA. Other local contributions **$100-$500** for various purposes. **Out-of-state** giving includes **$25,000** each to Colonial Williamsburg Foundation [VA] and West Virginia Wesleyan College; **$20,000** to Ohio State U.; **$5,000** each to Boys & Girls Club of Pleasants County [WV], Pleasants County Public Library, and Pleasants County Habitat for Humanity; and other smaller grants, many to WV. ■**PUBLICATIONS:** None ■**WEBSITE:** None ■**E-MAIL:** None ■**APPLICATION POLICIES & PROCEDURES:** Submit grant requests in any form at any time; fully describe the organization's need/purpose and include IRS tax-exempt status documentation. No grants awarded to individuals.

O+D+T Mona L. Thompson (T+Con) — Lawrence A. Withum, Jr. (T) — Corporate donor: C.S. Coen Land Co.

SW-067 Colcom Foundation
c/o Laurel Assets Group
Two Gateway Center, Suite 1800
Pittsburgh 15222
(Allegheny County)

MI-18-41-49-54-71-79-81-86

Phone 412-765-2400 **FAX** 412-765-2407
EIN 31-1479839 **Year Created** 1996

AMV $25,013,090 **FYE** 12-00 (**Gifts Received** $2,510,750) 15 **Grants totaling** $882,000

Two Pa. grants: **$100,000** to Pa. Environmental Council [Philadelphia] (Alleghenies Watershed Network/WPA Watershed Protection). **$50,000** to Montour Trail Council (land acquisition). **Out-of-state** giving includes **$152,000** to Californians for Population Stabilization (membership development); **$150,000** each to Federation for American Immigration Reform [DC] (general support/program grants) and U.S., Inc. [MI] (program support and NumbersUSA.com website); **$100,000** to Parents Television Council [CA] (Steve Allen honor). **$50,000** each to Center for Immigration Studies [DC] (research) and Negative Population Growth [DC] (restricted program grants). **$30,000** each to American Alliance for Rights & Responsibilities [NY], **$30,000** to Intercollegiate Studies Institute [DE], and New York U. (Margaret Sanger Papers project); **$20,000** to International Services Assistance Fund [CA] (population & security research); and **$10,000** each to Migration Dialogue [CA] and Research in English Acquisition & Development [DC] (READ Perspectives). — Pa. grants approved for future payment: **$70,000** to Three Rivers Employment Service (high school diploma program). **$50,000** to Carnegie Museum of Natural History (photographic exhibit). ■**PUBLICATIONS:** None ■**WEBSITE:** None ■**E-MAIL:** None ■**APPLICATION POLICIES & PROCEDURES:** The Foundation reports a priority interest in immigration reform. No grants are awarded to individuals. Grant requests may be submitted in a letter describing the program, its objectives and justification, a statement of funds needed, and the total proposed budget.

O+D+T Donna M. Panazzi (S+Program Officer+Con) — Cordelia Scaife May (C+Managing Director+Donor+Con) — Roger F. Meyer (P+D) — E. Saxman (D) — Timothy M. Inglis (D)

SW-068 Colonna Family Foundation, The
Foster Plaza #11
790 Holiday Drive
Pittsburgh 15220
(Allegheny County)

MI-11-41-42-43-63

Phone 412-937-7677 **FAX** 412-937-9144
EIN 25-1481851 **Year Created** 1984

AMV $2,040,762 **FYE** 9-00 (**Gifts Received** $0) 31 **Grants totaling** $85,725

About three-fourths local giving. High grant of **$34,035** to St. Edmund's Academy (scholarship program/annual giving). **$9,004** to Chatham College (scholarship program). **$8,392** to Winchester Thurston School (scholarship program). **$5,500** to Calvary Episcopal Church (annual gift). **$2,125** to United Way of Allegheny County. Other local contributions **$45-$250** for various purposes. **Out-of-state** giving includes **$12,100** to Archbishop Spalding High School [MD] (scholarships) and **$10,000** to Colby College [ME] (scholarships). ■**PUBLICATIONS:** None ■**WEBSITE:** None ■**E-MAIL:** None ■**APPLICATION POLICIES & PROCEDURES:** Grant requests may be submitted in a letter at any time; provide a brief history of the organization and its mission, a detailed project description, and the amount of funding requested. No grants awarded to individuals.

O+D+T Robert J. Colonna (P+Donor+Con) — Richard C. Colonna (VP+S) — Audrey N. Ballentine (F)

SW-069 **Community Foundation for the Alleghenies, The**   **MI**-14-21-25-29-32-43-44-45-51-55-56-85

606 AmeriServ Financial Building
216 Franklin Street   **Phone** 814-536-7741   **FAX** 814-536-5859
Johnstown   15901   (Cambria County)   **EIN** 25-1637373   **Year Created** 1990

AMV $16,357,483   **FYE** 6-01   **(Gifts Received** $1,311,242)   214 **Grants totaling** $1,179,225

As a Community Foundation all discretionary giving is restricted to organizations serving Bedford, Cambria, Indiana, and Somerset counties; 22 grants totaling **$26,248** awarded from unrestricted funds: high grant of **$3,500** to Johnstown Area Heritage Assn. **$3,000** each to First United Methodist Church (pipe organ restoration) and Memorial Baptist Church (pipe organ repairs). **$2,500** to Moxham Renaissance Assn. **$2,000** for one scholarship. **$1,500** to Meyersdale Public Library. **$1,000** each to Habitat for Humanity for Bedford County, Habitat for Humanity of Cambria County, St. John Gualbert Cathedral Parish (cathedral restoration), Somerset Blind Center, South Central Blind Assn., and UCP of Southern Alleghenies. **$500-$750** each to Bedford County Arts Council, Cambria County Literacy Council, Everett Free Library, Pa. Consort Guest Artist Series, Pa. Special Olympics, Somerset County Habitat for Humanity, and Theater Classics for Students. All other grants/contributions awarded from non-discretionary, restricted funds. ■ **PUBLICATIONS:** Annual Report ■ **WEBSITE:** www.cfalleghenies.org ■ **E-MAIL:** cfalleghenies@charter.net ■ **APPLICATION POLICIES & PROCEDURES:** The Foundation reports that giving focuses on The Arts, Children & Youth, Civic Affairs, Community Development, Education, Environment, Health & Human Services, Heritage, and Religion. Only organizations serving Bedford, Cambria, Indiana or Somerset counties are eligible to apply for grants from discretionary/unrestricted funds. Preference is given to grant requests for a specific program or project. Typically, only a percentage of a project's total cost is awarded and those with matching funds identified are viewed favorably. Grant requests should be submitted in a a proposal following the Grantmakers of Western Pa. Common Grant Application Format; deadlines are last Friday in January and August; be concise—bulleted lists and outlines are acceptable, and use bold/italics only for headings and identifying key points. Submit one signed original of the completed Common Grant Application Format and two copies of the entire packet. The Distribution Committee reviews requests and makes recommendations to the Board of Directors which awards grants at meetings in late February and September. — Formerly called Community Foundation of Greater Johnstown.

O+D+T Michael Kane (Executive Director+Con) — Daniel Glosser (C+D) — Gary C. Horner, Esq. (S+D) — Kim Craig (F+D) — Abe Beerman (D) — G. Henry Cook (D) — Terry K. Dunkle (D) — Albert L. Etheridge, Ph.D. (D) — Robert J. Eyer, CPA (D) — William L. Glosser, Esq. (D) — John M. Kriak (D) — Richard H. Mayer (D) — Mark E. Pasquerilla (D) — Michael Sahlaney, Esq. (D) — James V. Saly, CPA (D) — Sara Ann Sargent (D) — Thomas C. Slater (D) — Rev. Dr. Robert Swanson (D) — Robert D. Sweet, Jr. (D) — Dr. Donato Zucco (D)

SW-070 **Community Foundation of Fayette County**   **MI**-12-13-14-15-20-21-22-25-29-31-35-41-52

c/o Greater Uniontown Heritage Consortium   56-71-84-85-89
65 West Main Street   **Phone** 724-437-8600   **FAX** 724-438-3304
Uniontown   15401   (Fayette County)   **EIN** 25-1851158   **Year Created** 2000

AMV $1,260,205   **FYE** 12-00   **(Gifts Received** $1,317,300)   **Grants totaling** $0

As a Community Foundation all discretionary giving is restricted to organizations serving Fayette County; no grants were awarded during the Foundation's first year of operation. — In 2001, 35 grants totaling **$99,009** were awarded. Systemic Change grant of **$20,000** to Fayette County Community Action-Dental Clinic. Also, Project grants awarded to All Saints School, Appalachian Community Center, ARC-Fayette, Big Brothers and Big Sisters, Brownsville Area Revitalization Corp., Brownsville General Hospital, Christian Family and Children's Center, Community in Schools, Connellsville Community Ministries, Curfew Grange, East End United Community Center, Fayette County Assn. for the Blind, Fayette County Children & Youth Services, Fayette County Crime Stoppers, Fayette County Fair, Fayette County Youth Soccer Club, Georges Creek Clearwater Co-op, Greater Uniontown Chorale & Children's Chorus, Greater Uniontown Heritage Consortium, Habitat for Humanity-Fayette County, Healthy Start, Holy Trinity Orthodox Church/New Salem, Izaak Walton League/Brownsville Chapter, Marklysburg-Henry Clay Ladies Auxiliary, Midway Boys' Club/Connellsville, Ohiopyle-Stewart Community Center, Penn State/Fayette, Redstone Township Recreation Committee, Rendu Services, Inc., Shakespeare in the Schools-U. of Pittsburgh, Smithfield Borough, Spectrum Family Network, The Second Mile, and Try-Again Homes. ■ **PUBLICATIONS:** Annual Report; application guidelines; application/proposal form ■ **WEBSITE:** None ■ **E-MAIL:** bgarrett@hhs.net ■ **APPLICATION POLICIES & PROCEDURES:** Only Fayette County organizations are eligible to apply for grants from discretionary funds which are awarded in two categories: (1) Project Support—up to $5,000, for innovative programs/projects, and (2) Systemic Change—up to $50,000, for projects/initiatives advancing systemic change to improve the long-term structural, social and economic challenges. Grants are awarded for education; health/human services; arts/culture; economic development; environmental awareness, conservation and improvement; community leadership development; and community/neighborhood revitalization. Prospective applicants should make an initial telephone inquiry regarding the feasibility of submitting a request. **Project Support** requests should be submitted in a letter (3 pages maximum) during February or August (deadlines are March 1st and September 1st); describe the organization; provide information on the lead contact—name, affiliation, address, telephone number, fax, and e-mail; describe the proposed project and estimated cost; list any partners who will be collaborating on the project (including funders); describe how the project meets the Foundation's grantmaking criteria. Also include a project budget and IRS tax-exempt status documentation. **Systemic Change** grant requests should be submitted in a Letter of Interest (2-3 pages) before the January 10th or July 10th deadlines; describe the applicant organization, the proposed project and how it meets the Foundation's criteria for promoting systemic change. After review of the Letter of Interest, and if the Foundation is interested, an application based on the Grantmakers of Western Pa. Common Grant Application Format will be provided for completion. Site visits sometimes are made to organizations being considered for a grant. Grants are awarded at meetings in May and December. An applicant may receive funding only once per calendar year in each grant category.

O+D+T Robert Garrett (Marketing Director+Con) — Charles B. Cluss (C+D) — Lee Frankhouser (VC+D) — Albert N. Skomra, Ph.D. (S+D) — David R. Hughes (F+D) — Jess C. Ball (D) — George A. Bashour, Esq. (D) — James T. Davis, Esq. (D) — John A. Fiesta (D) — Joan Graziano (D) — William Jackson (D) — Samuel F. Sheehan (D) — Jean H. Smith (D) — Lynda S. Waggoner (D) — H. Scott Whyel (D)

SW-071 **Community Foundation of Greene County**

157 East High Street, P.O. Box 768
Waynesburg   15370   (Greene County)

MI-Not reported
Phone 724-627-2010 **FAX** 724-627-3187
EIN 25-1881899   **Year Created** 2001

AMV $325,196   **FYE** 12-01   (**Gifts Received** $138,936)   **Grants totaling** $0

As a Community Foundation all discretionary giving is limited to organizations serving Greene County. No grants were awarded during the Foundation's first year of operation. ■**PUBLICATIONS:** None ■**WEBSITE:** www.cfgcpa.org ■**E-MAIL:** info@cfgcpa.org ■**APPLICA-TION POLICIES & PROCEDURES:** The Foundation reports that application guidelines will be available sometime before early 2003.

O+D+T   John McCall (Executive Director+Con) — Sally S. Cameron (C+D) — Rev. Dr. Richard E. Visser (VC+D) — David J. Cumberledge (P+D) — Dolly Throckmorton (S+D) — Thomas G. Milinovich, CPA (F+D) — Marcia M. Biddle (D) — Forrest Cottle (D) — Nancy I. Davis, Ed.D. (D) — Janet R. Matteucci (D) — Jack McCracken (D) — Margaret E. Rock (D)

SW-072 **Community Foundation of Upper St. Clair**

2585 Washington Road, Suite 131A
Upper St. Clair   15241   (Allegheny County)

MI-29-41-44-45-51-52-55
Phone 412-831-1107 **FAX** 412-257-4160
EIN 25-1699881   **Year Created** 1993

AMV $334,143   **FYE** 12-00   (**Gifts Received** $208,273)   10+ **Grants totaling** $132,940

As a Community Foundation all discretionary giving is limited to organizations serving Upper St. Clair. High grant of **$96,337** to Upper St. Clair School District (technology initiative). **$18,870** for video cameras/equipment for teleconferencing among schools and community organizations. **$3,299** to Boyce School (courtyard improvements). The Foundation also sponsored other various local educational and arts/cultural events/performances; see website for more details. ■**PUBLICATIONS:** Grant Funding Guidelines; Grant Application Form ■**WEBSITE:** www.mainstreetusc.com/cfusc ■**E-MAIL:** LHSerene@aol.com ■**APPLICATION POLICIES & PROCEDURES:** As a 'Community Foundation' all discretionary giving is limited to projects serving the Upper St. Clair community, specifically those which: (1) promote educational enrichment opportunities for educators, students and community residents; (2) provide residents with opportunities to experience life-long enrichment and enjoyment of the arts; (3) enhance life-long physical fitness and wellness activities that promote individual well-being and community spirit; and (5) promote/sustain use up-to-date technologies by students and residents. The Foundation encourages new and creative projects which enhance A Sense of Community, reach a broad section of Upper St. Clair residents, have complementary/matching funding, and have long-term impact potential. No grants are awarded for salaries. Grant requests must be submitted on a Grant Application Form, available from the Foundation or its website.

O+D+T   Linda H. Serene (Executive Director+Con) — James M. Bennett (C+T) — Angela B. Petersen (VC+T) — Pamela C. Batz (S+T) — Abraham L. Nader (F+T) — Robert L. Allman, II (T) — William N. Andrews (T) — David E. Bluey (T) — James E. Davison (T) — Raymond D. Gergich (T) — Girish G. Godbole (T) — Terry J. Himes (T) — Robin G. Johnson (T) — Roy T. Johnston (T) — Julie M. Klym (T) — Catherine L. Luke (T) — Richard W. Purnell (T) — Mariam T. Richardson (T) — Margaret B. Snavely (T) — Sandra L.R. Thomas (T)

SW-073 **Community Foundation of Westmoreland County, The**

111 Station Place, Train Station at Greensburg
101 Ehalt Street
Greensburg   15601   (Westmoreland County)

MI-12-13-14-15-31-32-35-39-41-42-43-44-49
52-55-71-72-84-85
Phone 724-836-4400 **FAX** 724-837-5571
EIN 25-1776105   **Year Created** 1995

AMV $9,061,280   **FYE** 6-01   (**Gifts Received** $1,133,101)   98 **Grants totaling** $945,990

As a Community Foundation all discretionary giving is limited to Westmoreland County, some to Greensburg specifically. Local organizations supported from unrestricted or restricted funds—grant sizes not reported—included Adelphoi, Alle-Kiski Learning Center, Alzheimer's Assn., Bethlehem Project, Big Brothers/Big Sisters of Laurel Region, Center Against Domestic & Sexual Violence, Clelian Heights, Community Nursing Service in Greensburg, Courthouse Square Heritage Conservancy, Girl Scout Council of Westmoreland, Greensburg Art Center, Greensburg Community Development Corp., Greensburg Garden Center, Greensburg-Hempfield Area Library, Greensburg Recreation Board, Greensburg Volunteer Fire Assn., Homes Build Hope, Junior Achievement of SW Pa., Latrobe Area Hospital Charitable Foundation, Laurel Valley Roller Hockey League, local high schools and school districts, McKenna Senior Community Center, Meals on Wheels, Midway Boys Club, Mom's House of Greensburg, Pa. Clean-Ways/Westmoreland County, ParentWise, Plum Creek Chamber Orchestra, Redstone Highlands, Rotary After School Program, St. Anne Home, Seton Hill Child Services, Seton Hill College, Sheltered Lives, Inc., Sisters of Charity of Seton Hill, Society of St. Vincent de Paul, Special Olympics/Westmoreland County, Spectrum Family Network, Toys for Tots, Union Mission, Westmoreland AIDS Service Organization, Westmoreland ARC Foundation, Westmoreland Arts & Heritage Festival, Westmoreland County Blind Assn., Westmoreland County Camp Cadet Assn., Westmoreland County Children's Bureau, Westmoreland County Community College, Westmoreland Manor, Westmoreland Museum of American Art, Westmoreland Regional Hospital Foundation, Westmoreland Symphony, Westmoreland Youth Symphony Orchestra, Wildlife Works, YMCA of New Kensington, YMCA of Greensburg, YWCA of Westmoreland County, as well as animal humane organizations, county agencies/departments, major health/human service organizations, and others. Also, 10 scholarship awarded to local students. ■**PUBLICATIONS:** Annual Report; informational brochure; application guidelines; Grant Application Form ■**WEBSITE:** www.cfwestmoreland.org ■**E-MAIL:** bgeer@cfwestmoreland.org ■**APPLICATION POLICIES & PROCEDURES:** Only charitable organizations located in or serving Westmoreland County are eligible to apply. Grant requests are accepted for projects/programs dealing with education, health, human services, arts/culture, and civic/community development. Also, organizations in the Greensburg-15601 Zip Code are eligible for particular consideration under The Greensburg Foundation Fund. Prospective applicants should make an initial telephone call regarding the feasibility of applying for a grant and/or consult the website for current application guidelines and required forms. Grant requests may be submitted at any time; deadlines are January 1st and July 1st. Grants are awarded at February and August Board meetings.

O+D+T   Bobbi Watt Geer (P+Con) — T. Terrance Reese (C+D) — J. Robert Stemler [Export] (VC+D) — Mark B. Robertshaw [Ligonier] (S+D) — Scott A. Gongaware [Ligonier] (F+D) — John Andrighetti (D) — Esther Glasser (D) — Edwin R. Hogan

[West Newton] (D) — Daniel Joseph, Esq. [New Kensington] (D) — A. Richard Kacin [Plum] (D) — Nancy Kukovich [Harrison City] (D) — Jay R. Mangold [Export] (D) — Arthur McMullen [Ligonier] (D) — Judith O'Toole (D) — Vincent J. Quatrini, Jr., Esq. (D) — Myles D. Sampson [Murrysville] (D) — Rev. Timothy W. Sawyer (D) — Irvin Tantlinger [Bolivar] (D) — Tina Thoburn, Ed.D. [Ligonier] (D) — Thomas C. Wilkinson, Ph.D. [Monessen] (D)

SW-074 Compton (Beatrice) Memorial Fund

21 St. Andrews Drive
Beaver Falls 15010   (Beaver County)

MI-13-42-63
Phone 724-843-4961 **FAX** None
EIN 25-1676211   **Year Created** 1992

AMV $482,446   **FYE** 12-00   (**Gifts Received** $0)   4 **Grants totaling** $11,100

About one-third local giving. **$2,500** to St. Marys Church. **$500** to Girl Scouts of Beaver County. **Out-of-state** grant: **$8,000** to Baldwin Wallace College [OH]. ■**PUBLICATIONS:** None ■**WEBSITE:** None ■**E-MAIL:** None ■**APPLICATION POLICIES & PROCEDURES:** Grant requests may be submitted in a letter at any time.

O+D+T Richard A. Rocereto (T+Con)

SW-075 Conrad (R.J.) Charitable Foundation

Portersville Commons, Suite 209
1244 Perry Highway
Portersville 16051   (Butler County)

MI-41-43-89
Phone 724-368-3331 **FAX** None
EIN 23-7863991   **Year Created** 1996

AMV $349,041   **FYE** 12-00   (**Gifts Received** $0)   13 **Grants totaling** $44,365

Mostly local/Pa. giving. High grant of **$15,000** to Pitcairn High School Alumni/RJC Scholarship Fund [Allegheny County]. **$4,000** each to Burrell Township Volunteer Fire Dept., Burrell Township Volunteer Fire Dept. Auxiliary, and Burrell Township Volunteer Fire Dept. Relief Fund. All other grants are scholarships, **$1,000** to **$2,000** each. ■**PUBLICATIONS:** None ■**WEBSITE:** None ■**E-MAIL:** None ■**APPLICATION POLICIES & PROCEDURES:** Information not available.

O+D+T Jeffrey M. Thompson, Esq. (T+Con) — Robert J. Conrad [Ford City] (C+Donor) — David J. Caruso, CPA [Oakmont] (T)

SW-076 Cooper (Reldon & Hattie) Charitable Foundation

c/o Du Co Ceramics Company
145 State Street, P.O. Box 149
Saxonburg 16056   (Butler County)

MI-13-43-44-56-63
Phone 724-352-1511 **FAX** None
EIN 25-1515561   **Year Created** 1985

AMV $1,367,045   **FYE** 12-00   (**Gifts Received** $100,000)   4 **Grants totaling** $58,530

All local giving. High grant of **$25,000** to Saxonburg Public Library. **$13,350** to St. Luke's Lutheran Church. **$10,000** each to Boy Scouts and Knoch High School (scholarship fund). — In the prior year grants included **$10,000** to Saxonburg Historical Commission and Saxonburg Memorial Church, and **$7,500** to Lutheran Church of America/SW Pa. Synod. ■**PUBLICATIONS:** None ■**WEBSITE:** None ■**E-MAIL:** None ■**APPLICATION POLICIES & PROCEDURES:** Grant requests should be submitted in written narrative form before the November 1st deadline.

O+D+T Reldon W. Cooper (C+P+Donor+Con) — Linda Knapp (S) — Lora Saiber (F)

SW-077 Cooper-Siegel Family Foundation, The

c/o Reed Smith, LLP
435 Sixth Ave.
Pittsburgh 15219   (Allegheny County)

MI-12-13-14-18-22-25-31-32-41-42-44-45-54
57-71-72-82
Phone 412-288-7252 **FAX** 412-288-3063
EIN 31-1537177   **Year Created** 1996

AMV $1,154,927   **FYE** 4-01   (**Gifts Received** $895,862)   28 **Grants totaling** $485,000

About two-thirds local giving. High grants of **$100,000** each to Beginning with Books and Juvenile Diabetes Foundation. **$25,000** each to Carnegie Mellon U. and Children's Hospital of Pittsburgh. **$15,000** to Greater Pittsburgh Community Food Bank. **$10,000** each to Anti-Defamation League, The Ellis School, and Planned Parenthood of Western Pa. **$5,000** each to to Holocaust Center of Pittsburgh and The Whale's Tale/FamilyLink. **$1,000** each to Children's Home of Pittsburgh, Friends of the Lauri Ann West Memorial Library, National Aviary in Pittsburgh, WDUQ-FM, WQED-FM, WQED-TV, and WYEP-FM. **Out-of-state** grants include **$100,000** to Harvard College [MA]; **$20,000** to U.S. Committee for UNICEF [NY]; **$10,000** each to Susan G. Komen Breast Cancer Foundation [TX], Simon Wiesenthal Center [CA], Radcliffe Institute (Schlesinger Library), and U.S. Holocaust Memorial Museum [DC]; and **$5,000** each to The Nature Conservancy [DC] and New York Times Neediest Cases Fund [NY]. ■**PUBLICATIONS:** None ■**WEBSITE:** None ■**E-MAIL:** emargolis@reedsmith.com ■**APPLICATION POLICIES & PROCEDURES:** Grant requests may be submitted in any form at any time. No grants are awarded to individuals.

O+D+T E. David Margolis, Esq. (Con) — Eric C. Cooper (T+Donor) — Naomi L. Siegel (T) — Mellon Bank (Corporate Trustee)

SW-078 Copperweld Foundation

c/o Copperweld Corporation
2200 Four Gateway Center
Pittsburgh 15222   (Allegheny County)

MI-11-12-13-14-15-21-22-29-42-51-52-54-55
65-84
Phone 412-263-3216 **FAX** None
EIN 25-6035603   **Year Created** 1941

AMV $1,408,612   **FYE** 6-01   (**Gifts Received** $0)   84 **Grants totaling** $252,440

About two-thirds local giving. High grant of **$25,000** to Pittsburgh Leadership Foundation. **$20,000** each to Fellowship of Christian Athletes [Irwin] and U. of Pittsburgh/Katz School of Business. **$15,000** to Keystone Christian Academy. **$13,000** to Coalition for Christian Outreach. **$10,000** to Pittsburgh Symphony. **$7,000** each to Family Hospice and YMCA of Pittsburgh. **$5,000** each to Carnegie Mellon U. and Glassport American Legion Post #443. **$4,000** to Boy Scouts/Greater Pittsburgh Council. **$2,000-$2,500** each to Carnegie Museums of Pittsburgh, Mom's House, North Hills Youth Ministry, Pa. Special Olympics, Robert Morris College, and YMCA of Pittsburgh. **$1,000-$1,500** each to City Theatre of the South Side, Girl Scouts of SW Pa., Make-A-Wish Foundation of Western Pa., National Flag Foundation, Pittsburgh Ballet Theatre, Pittsburgh Cultural Trust, Salvation Army, River City Brass Band, and United Negro College Fund. Other smaller local contributions for various purposes. **Out-of-state** giving, primarily in plant locations, includes **$18,500** to United Way of Shelby [OH]; **$15,000** to Motlow Foundation [TN]; **$10,000** to Ashland U. [OH]; **$5,000** to Red Cross [DC] (relief fund); and other smaller grants/contributions to GA, OH, MI, KY, and TN. — Note: Copperweld also operates a corporate giving program. ■**PUBLICATIONS:** application guidelines ■ **WEBSITE:** www.cwwire.com [corporate info only] ■**E-MAIL:** None ■**APPLICATION POLICIES & PROCEDURES:** The Foundation reports that giving focuses on locations where corporate employees work/live with a preference for SW Pa. organizations. Grant requests in any form should be submitted in April-early May or October-early November (deadlines are May 15th and November 15th); state the amount being requested and include an annual report, organization budget, project budget, audited financial statement, Board member list, and IRS tax-exempt status documentation. Site visits sometimes are made to organizations being considered for a grant. Grants are awarded at meetings in June and December.

O+D+T Douglas E. Young (T+Con) — Eugene R. Pocci (T) — John D. Turner (T) — Corporate donor: Copperweld Corporation

---

SW-079 **Cost (Charles L.) Foundation, The**　　　　　　　　　　　　MI-17-31-42
　　　　　c/o Cost Company, Inc.
　　　　　2400 Ardmore Boulevard　　　　　　　　　　　　　　　　　**Phone** 412-271-0420　**FAX** None
　　　　　Pittsburgh　15221　　　　　　　(Allegheny County)　　　**EIN** 25-1588998　　**Year Created** 1988
AMV $1,855　　　　　　**FYE** 12-00　　　　(**Gifts Received** $262,800)　　**7 Grants totaling** $262,800

All local giving; all grants are for general purposes. Two grants totaling **$166,800** to Carnegie Mellon U. **$50,000** to Children's Hospital of Pittsburgh. **$25,000** to Duquesne U. **$10,000** each to Penn State U. and U. of Pittsburgh. **$1,000** to Women's Center & Shelter of Greater Pittsburgh. ■**PUBLICATIONS:** None ■**WEBSITE:** None ■**E-MAIL:** None ■**APPLICATION POLICIES & PROCEDURES:** Information not available.

O+D+T Charles L. Cost (P+T+Donor+Con) — Corporate donors: Cost Company, Inc.; Franco

---

SW-080 **Crawford (Edwin R.) Estate Trust Fund**　　　　　　MI-12-13-14-15-22-23-25-29-31-32-41-42-43
　　　　　214 Masonic Building　　　　　　　　　　　　　　　　　44-45-51-52-56-61-63-71-84
　　　　　522 Walnut Street, P.O. Box 487　　　　　　　　　　　　**Phone** 412-672-6770　**FAX** None
　　　　　McKeesport　15134　　　　　　　(Allegheny County)　　　**EIN** 25-6031554　　**Year Created** 1936
AMV $7,754,069　　　　**FYE** 12-00　　　　(**Gifts Received** $0)　　　**103+ Grants totaling** $370,674

Most giving limited to Allegheny County. High grant of **$45,000** to McKeesport Heritage Center. **$35,000** to YMCA of McKeesport. **$30,000** to Carnegie Free Library of McKeesport. **$25,000** to South Hills Health System Foundation. **$20,000** each to McKeesport Hospital Foundation and Salvation Army. **$20,000** to McKeesport Area Meals on Wheels. **$10,000** each to Auberle Foundation, Community Food Bank [Elizabeth], Kane Foundation, and YWCA of McKeesport. **$7,000-$7,500** each to Boys & Girls Club of McKeesport and Boys & Girls Club of Western Pa./Duquesne & West Mifflin, Long Run Learning Center, and McKeesport Symphony Society. **$5,000** each to City of McKeesport (Recreation Dept.), McKeesport Hospital, Penn State U./McKeesport, and The Intersection, Inc. **$4,000** to Multiple Sclerosis Service Society [Clairton]. **$3,000-$3,500** each to Garden Club of McKeesport. **$3,000** each to American Cancer Society, Western Pa. Humane Society, and Woman's Place. **$2,500** each to Community College of Allegheny County, Crescentia's Circle, and National Steelworkers Oldtimer's Foundation. **$1,000-$1,500** each to Elizabeth Township Historical Society, Human Services of Western Pa., Make-A-Wish Foundation of Western Pa., McKeesport Choraliers, McKeesport Little Theater, Mon-Yough Chamber Foundation, Mon-Yough Riverfront Entertainment & Cultural Council, Red Cross, Ventures in People, and White Oak Athletic Assn. Other smaller contributions for various local organizations. Also, 59 Protestant, Catholic, or Orthodox churches and Jewish synagogues located in McKeesport, Duquesne, North Versailles, Elizabeth, Blythdale, White Oak, Boston, Greenock, or Dravosburg received grants of **$500** or **$1,000-higher** in a few cases. Also, disbursements totaling **$2,424** given to indigent persons, all former employees of McKeesport Tin Plate Co. ■ **PUBLICATIONS:** statement of program policy; application guidelines ■**WEBSITE:** None ■**E-MAIL:** None ■**APPLICATION POLICIES & PROCEDURES:** The Foundation reports that giving is primarily restricted to McKeesport, Duquesne, Southern Allegheny County; most grants are for general support, special projects, building funds, capital drives, scholarships, and matching grants; multiple-year grants are awarded. Prospective applicants initially should make a telephone inquiry about the feasibility of submitting a request. Written requests from organizations may be submitted in any form at any time—except in June or December; describe the purpose/nature of the organization and intended use of the funds; include an annual report, organizational/project budgets, list of major funding sources, Board member list, audited financial statement, and IRS tax-exempt status documentation. Proposals which follow Grantmakers of Western Pa. Common Grant Application Format are accepted. The Foundation may request additional information. Site visits sometimes are made to organizations being considered for a grant. The Trustees award grants at meeting in June and December. — Scholarship assistance is available only to qualified McKeesport Area High School and Duquesne High School seniors to attend U. of Pittsburgh, Community College of Allegheny County, or Penn State-McKeesport Campus. — Individual assistance grants are limited to former, needy employees of McKeesport Tin Plate Co.; a formal application form, available from the Foundation, must be submitted.

O+D+T George F. Young, Jr. (T+Con) — William H. Johnson [White Oak] (T) — Edward T. Phillips [Irwin] (T)

SW-081   Danforth (Douglas & Janet) Foundation. The

2210 One PPG Place
Pittsburgh   15222   (Allegheny County)

MI-11-12-25-32-41-42-51-52-55
Phone 724-941-9119 **FAX** None
EIN 25-1540430   **Year Created** 1986

AMV $256,551   **FYE** 12-00   **(Gifts Received** $331,868)   14 **Grants totaling** $70,700

Mostly local giving; all grants are for general purposes. High grant of **$16,000** to Sewickley Academy. **$15,000** to Washington County Habitat for Humanity. **$10,000** to United Way of SW Pa. (deToqueville Society). **$5,000** to River City Brass Band. **$3,200** to Extra Mile Education Foundation. **$3,000** to Pittsburgh Public Theater. **$2,500** each to Juvenile Diabetes Foundation and National Flag Foundation. **$1,000** to Pittsburgh Cultural Trust. **$500** each to Allegheny Conference for Community Development and Parental Stress Center. **Out-of-state** giving includes **$10,000** to Syracuse U. [NY] and **$1,000** to Founders Fund [FL]. ■**PUBLICATIONS:** None ■**WEBSITE:** None ■**E-MAIL:** None ■**APPLICATION POLICIES & PROCEDURES:** Grant requests may be submitted in any form at any time; include general information about the organization and its purposes.

O+D+T   Douglas D. Danforth (P+C+Donor+Con) — Janet P. Danforth (S+F)

SW-082   DeGol (Bruno & Lena) Family Foundation

c/o The DeGol Organization
3229 Pleasant Valley Blvd.
Altoona   16602   (Blair County)

MI-12-14-41-42-61-89
Phone 814-941-7777 **FAX** None
EIN 25-1753903   **Year Created** 1994

AMV $1,885,720   **FYE** 12-00   **(Gifts Received** $2,000)   20 **Grants totaling** $251,462

All local/Pa. giving. High grant of **$174,562** to St. Francis College. **$35,000** to Gallitzin Borough General Fund. **$10,000** to St. Patrick's Church of Gallitzin. **$5,000** each to Diocese of Altoona, Foreman Foundation [Lancaster County], and Mt. Aloysius College. **$4,800** to Easter Seals. **$4,000** to Providence Academy. **$3,400** to Make-A-Wish Foundation of Altoona. **$1,400** to Trinity Lutheran Church of Altoona. Other local contributions **$100-$750** for various purposes. ■**PUBLICATIONS:** None ■**WEBSITE:** None ■**E-MAIL:** None ■**APPLICATION POLICIES & PROCEDURES:** Grant requests may be submitted in any form at any time; provide details on the organization's activities and the purpose of the requested funds. No grants awarded to individuals. The Board meets quarterly.

O+D+T   Donald A. DeGol, Sr. [Hollidaysburg] (VP+D+Con) — Bruno A. DeGol, Sr. [Tyrone] (P+D+Donor) — Joseph T. Adams [Hollidaysburg] (F+D) — Gloria DeGol Burgan [Cresson] (D) — Richard Burgan [Ebensburg] (D) — Bruno A. DeGol, Jr. [Tyrone] (D) — Donald A. DeGol, Jr. [Cresson] (D) — David A. DeGol [Hollidaysurg] (D) — Dennis W. DeGol [Hollidaysburg] (D) — Lena DeGol [Tyrone] (D+Donor) — Edward McGowan [Hollidaysburg] (D) — Corporate donors: Laurel Insurance Management, Inc., MAFG Services, Inc., Stover Financial Services.

SW-083   Delligatti Charitable Foundation

c/o McDonald's Restaurant
147 Delta Drive
Pittsburgh   15238   (Allegheny County)

MI-13-22-42-61
Phone 412-963-6550 **FAX** None
EIN 25-6289193   **Year Created** 1986

AMV $352,899   **FYE** 12-00   **(Gifts Received** $1,000)   8 **Grants totaling** $23,025

Mostly local giving; all grants are general contributions. High grant of **$10,000** to Fombell YMCA. **$5,000** each to LaRoche College and St. Mary's Church of Sewickley. Other local contributions **$75-$200**. **Out-of-state** giving includes **$2,000** to Food for the Poor [FL] and smaller grants/contributions to FL. ■**PUBLICATIONS:** None ■**WEBSITE:** None ■**E-MAIL:** None ■**APPLICATION POLICIES & PROCEDURES:** Grant requests may be submitted in a letter at any time.

O+D+T   James A. Delligatti (P+D+Donor+Con)

SW-084   Demarest (Eben) Trust, The

c/o Mellon Private Wealth Management
One Mellon Center, P.O. Box 185
Pittsburgh   15230   (Allegheny County)

MI-51-52-53-54-55-56
Phone 412-234-0023 **FAX** 412-234-1073
EIN 25-6108821   **Year Created** 1938

AMV $367,189   **FYE** 12-00   **(Gifts Received** $0)   1 **Grant of** $16,000

Sole grant awarded to Rob Evans [Wrightsville], an artist. — In the prior year, the awardee was Melissa Tubbs [AL], an artist. ■ **PUBLICATIONS:** application guidelines ■**WEBSITE:** None ■**E-MAIL:** None ■**APPLICATION POLICIES & PROCEDURES:** The Trust reports that one grant annually is awarded to either an archeologist or a person gifted in literature, music, visual arts, performing arts, or other arts discipline. Only applicants recommended by a member of the Demarest Advisory Council -or- by an organization on behalf of an exceptionally gifted individual will be considered; self-nominations are not accepted and will not be acknowledged. Completed applications and supporting documents should be received well before the June 1st deadline; the decision on the award is made at a late June meeting. Note: A grantee must devote full time to one's field and not depend upon public sale of one's work for support.

O+D+T   Laurie A. Moritz (VP at Bank+Con) — Anne Shiras (Secretary, Demarest Council) — and a 5-member Advisory Council - Mellon Bank N.A. (Trustee)

SW-085   dePalma (Robert A.) Family Charitable Foundation

70 Woodland Drive
Pittsburgh   15228   (Allegheny County)

MI-31-32-41-52-61
Phone 412-338-7740 **FAX** None
EIN 25-1546487   **Year Created** 1986

AMV $326,061   **FYE** 12-00   **(Gifts Received** $0)   9 **Grants totaling** $55,118

Mostly local giving. High grant of **$21,768** to Pittsburgh Opera. **$12,000** to St. Anne's Church of Pittsburgh. **$5,000** each to Allegheny Heart Assn., Allegheny Heart Institute, and Clelian Heights School. **$2,500** each to Catholic Charities and Diocese of Pittsburgh. **$1,250** to Pittsburgh Symphony. One small contribution. ■**PUBLICATIONS:** None ■**WEBSITE:** None ■**E-MAIL:**

None ■**APPLICATION POLICIES & PROCEDURES:** Grant requests may be submitted in a letter at any time; describe the project and state an amount of funding requested. — Formerly called Robert A. & Maryann A. dePalma Charitable Foundation.

O+D+T Maryann dePalma Burnett (T+Donor+Con) — Robert M. dePalma [CT] (T) — Diane D. Lange (T)

SW-086 **Dollar Bank Foundation**
    c/o Dollar Bank, Public Affairs Dept.
    3 Gateway Center, 8 North
    Pittsburgh 15222   (Allegheny County)

MI-11-12-13-24-25-29-41-43-52-54-85

Phone 412-261-8109 **FAX** None
EIN 25-1822243   **Year Created** 1998

AMV $3,333,515   **FYE** 11-00   **(Gifts Received** $0)   26 **Grants totaling** $229,550

About four-fifths local/Western Pa. giving. High grant of **$50,000** to United Way of SW Pa. **$35,000** to Pittsburgh Partnership for Neighborhood Development. **$19,550** to Parental Stress Center. **$10,000** each to Bloomfield-Garfield Corp., Garfield-Jubilee Assn., Pittsburgh Regional Healthcare Initiative, and Pittsburgh Symphony. **$5,000** each to Carnegie Museums of Pittsburgh, CTAC/Community Technical Assistance Center, FAME/Fund for Advancement of Minorities through Education, National Medal of Honor Foundation, and Northside Leadership Conference. **$1,000-$3,000** each to Boy Scouts/Greater Pittsburgh Council, Extra Mile Education Foundation, Greater Pittsburgh Community Food Bank, Pa. Assn. of Community Bankers Foundation [Harrisburg], and Sisters of Charity of Seton Hill/DePaul Center [Greensburg]. **Out-of-state** grants, all to OH, included **$25,000** to Working for Empowerment through Community Organizing; and **$5,000-$5,500** each to Cleveland Housing Network, United Way of Cuyahoga County, and Clark Metro Development Corp. ■**PUBLICATIONS:** Annual Report ■**WEBSITE:** www.dollarbank.com [corporate info only] ■**E-MAIL:** None ■**APPLICATION POLICIES & PROCEDURES:** All giving is generally restricted to the area served by the Bank and its subsidiaries, specifically Pittsburgh and Cleveland, OH. Grants are awarded on an annual basis. No grants are awarded to individuals; political, labor, fraternal or veteran's organizations; religious activities or programs; hospitals or other healthcare delivery facilities; nonacademic elementary/secondary programs; or organizations without nonprofit status. Grant requests may be submitted at any time in letter (2 pages maximum) which describes the organization and the specific project/program seeking funding, itemizes the project/program budget, states a specific amount requested, and indicates if the Bank or a subsidiary has been a prior donor; also include a list of Board members and IRS tax-exempt status documentation. Site visits sometimes are made to organizations being considered for a grant.

O+D+T Thomas A. Kobus (P+Con) — James Carroll (VP) — Robert T. Messner (S) — James T. Jurcic (F)

SW-087 **Dominion Foundation**
    c/o Dominion
    Dominion Tower, 625 Liberty Ave., 21st Floor
    Pittsburgh 15222   (Allegheny County)

MI-11-12-13-14-15-21-22-25-29-31-41-42-45
51-52-54-55-56-57-71-84-85-88

Phone 412-690-1430 **FAX** 412-690-7608
EIN 13-6077762   **Year Created** 1985

AMV $8,048,954   **FYE** 12-00   **(Gifts Received** $0)   538+ **Grants totaling** $4,084,563

About one-sixth giving to Pa. in counties with corporate operations: Armstrong, Allegheny, Armstrong, Blair, Butler, Cambria, Clinton, Crawford, Fayette, Franklin, Indiana, Potter, Tioga, and Westmoreland. Grants are for general operating support except as noted, and some grants represent multiple payments. High Pa. grant of **$109,354** to United Way of SW Pa. **$102,500** to U. of Pittsburgh. **$70,000** to Dollar Energy Fund. **$64,000** to WQED. **$46,500** to Pittsburgh Ballet Theatre. **$43,000** to Pittsburgh Opera. **$42,900** to Allegheny Conference on Community Development. **$39,700** to Western Pa. Conservancy. **$34,000** to Early Childhood Initiative. **$32,500** to Pittsburgh Public Theater. **$25,000** each to Armstrong County Conservancy Charitable Trust and Pittsburgh Symphony. **$20,000** each to Chatham College and Historical Society of Western Pa. **$17,000** to United Way of Laurel Highlands [Johnstown]. **$16,900** to Community Builders, Inc. **$15,000** each to Conservation Consultants and Westmoreland Trust. **$13,000** to Pittsburgh Cultural Trust. **$12,900** to United Way of Westmoreland County. **$10,000** each to Civic Light Opera, Community Foundation of Westmoreland County, Laurel Health System [Tioga County], The National Aviary, Pittsburgh Children's Museum, Salvation Army/Greensburg, and Westmoreland Museum of American Art. **$9,000** to United Way of Blair County. **$8,000** each to Airport Area Development Corp., Armstrong County Community Action Agency, and Human Services Center Corp. [Turtle Creek]. **$7,000-$7,500** each to Beginning With Books, Hosanna Industries [Beaver County], National Foundation for Teaching Entrepreneurship-Pittsburgh, and Phipps Conservatory & Botanical Garden. **$6,000-$6,250** each to Butler County Bicentennial Celebration, Carnegie Institute, Junior Achievement of SW Pa., and Tour de 'Toona [Altoona]. **$5,000-$5,300** each to African American Chamber of Commerce, Altoona Railroaders Memorial Museum, Armstrong County Community Foundation, Carlow College, City Theatre, First Night Pittsburgh, Greater Pittsburgh Literacy Council, Katz Business Alliance, Louise Child Care, Mon Valley Initiative, Pa. CleanWays [Greensburg], Pittsburgh Cares, Pittsburgh Regional SciTech Festival, Pittsburgh Zoo & Aquarium, Regional Trail Corp. [Westmoreland County], Slippery Rock U., Three Rivers Arts Festival, Tioga County Development Corp. (capital campaign), United Negro College Fund, United Way of Allegheny County, Urban League of Pittsburgh, D.T. Watson Institute, and YouthBuild Pittsburgh. **$3,000-$4,500** each to Artists in Cities, Big Brothers Big Sisters of Greater Pittsburgh, Cambria County Area Community College, Community College of Allegheny County, Extra Mile Education Foundation, Gateway to the Arts, Kuntu Repertory Theatre, Red Cross/Greensburg, Red Cross/Westmoreland County, United Way of Armstrong County, Ursuline Center, and Western Pa. Professionals for the Arts. **$1,500-$2,500** each to Audubon Society of Western Pa., Big Brothers Big Sisters of Beaver County, Boy Scouts/Greater Pittsburgh Council, Carlow College Women of Spirit, Civic Senior Citizens [Aliquippa], Greensburg Area Cultural Council, Habitat of Humanity of Cambria County, Habitat for Humanity/Allegheny Valley, Hazelwood Outreach Center, Homeless Children & Family Emergency Fund, Johnstown Symphony Orchestra, Kiski Valley Habitat for Humanity, Magee-Women's Health Foundation, Mendelssohn Choir of Pittsburgh, Mom's House of Johnstown, New Day, Inc. [Johnstown], Pittsburgh Dance Council, Pittsburgh New Music Ensemble, Pittsburgh Parks Conservancy, Pittsburgh Voyager, Renovo Area Public Library, Seton Hill College/National Education Center for Women In Business, United Way of Indiana County, Urban Youth Action, YMCA of Pittsburgh, and YWCA of Greater Pittsburgh. Other local/Pa. contributions **$300-$1,200** for similar purposes. **Out-of-state** giving to corporate operating locations in CT, LA, NC, NY, OH, VA, WV and other states with business interests. In addition, about 875 matching gifts totaling

$335,403 were disbursed to educational institutions, art/cultural organizations, health/human service agencies, and environmental groups. ■**PUBLICATIONS:** informational brochure with application guidelines ■**WEBSITE:** www.dom.com/about/community/foundation ■**E-MAIL:** frances_c._toohill@dom.com■**APPLICATION POLICIES & PROCEDURES:** The Foundation supports nonprofit organizations dedicated to improving the economic, physical and social health of the communities served by Dominion's gas companies; giving focuses on Health/Human Services, including United Ways; Education; Arts/Culture; Economic & Community Development; and the Environment. No grants are awarded to individuals or for operating funds to United Way-supported agencies, religious/sectarian purposes, courtesy advertising in program booklets, etc., or benefit/fundraising events. Grant requests may be submitted at any time, using either a letter or Grantmakers of Western Pa. Common Grant Application Format; organizations requesting renewal of support should submit applications no later than the September 1st deadline. All requests must include a brief description of the organization including its legal name, history, activities, and governing board; purpose for which the grant is requested; amount of the request and a list of other sources of financial support committed or pending; narrative statement describing the project's objectives, need/s to be addressed, impact on community, and method of accomplishing the objectives; most recent audited financial statement; and IRS tax-exempt status documentation. Matching gifts have a $50 minimum, $2,500 maximum/employee/year. — Formerly called Consolidated Natural Gas Co. Foundation.

O+D+T James C. Mesloh (Executive Director+D+Con) — W.C. Hall, Jr. [VA] (P+D) — M.N. Grier [VA] (VP+D) — T.F. Farrell [VA] (D) — E.S. Teig Hardy [VA] (D) — D. Radtke [LA] (D) — E.M. Roach, Jr. (D) — Mellon Bank (Corporate Trustee) — Corporate donors: Dominion

---

SW-088 Donahue Family Foundation
c/o Beechwood Company
1001 Liberty Ave., Suite 850
Pittsburgh 15222   (Allegheny County)

MI-22-29-41-42-61-86

Phone 412-471-9047 **FAX** 412-471-9011
EIN 25-1619351   **Year Created** 1990

AMV $3,654,550   **FYE** 12-00   (**Gifts Received** $214,280)   31 **Grants totaling** $2,664,836

About one-fifth local giving. High local grant of **$270,836** to Catholic Diocese of Pittsburgh. **$25,000** to Epiphany Assn. **$20,000** to Central Catholic High School. **$15,500** to Oakland Catholic High School. **$10,000** each to Catholic Youth Assn., Extra Mile Education Foundation, and Mom's House. **$3,000** each to Holy Family Foundation and U. of Pittsburgh. **Out-of-state** giving includes high grant of **$1,000,000** to Royal Palm International Academy [FL]; **$500,000** to American Ireland Fund [MA]; **$200,000** to Pope John Paul II Cultural Trust [DC]; **$150,000** to John Carroll U. [OH]; **$100,000** each to The Becket Fund for Religious Liberty [DC]; **$50,000** each to Boston College [MA], Religion & Public Life, and The Papal Foundation; **$30,000** to Youngstown Catholic Diocese [OH]; **$25,000** each to Acton Institute for the Study of Religion & Liberty [MI], Children's Scholarship Fund [NY], and Prison Fellowship; **$15,000** to PGA of Collier County [FL]; and other grants **$5,000-$10,000** for Catholic, conservative, literacy, and other purposes. ■**PUBLICATIONS:** None ■**WEBSITE:** None ■**E-MAIL:** None ■ **APPLICATION POLICIES & PROCEDURES:** Prospective applicants should make an initial telephone inquiry about the feasibility of submitting a request. Grant requests may be submitted in a letter (2 pages maximum) during January-May; include an annual report, organization budget, project budget, audited financial statement and IRS tax-exempt status documentation. Site visits sometimes are made to organizations being considered for a grant. Grants are awarded at a June meeting.

O+D+T William J. Donahue (P+D+Con) — John F. Donahue [FL] (C+D+Donor) — Daniel J. McGrogan (S+F) — Kim Donahue (D) — Rhodora J. Donahue [FL] (D+Donor) — Maribeth Donley (D) — Carol Moore (D) — Maureen Murphy (D) — Bishop Donald W. Wuerl (D)

SW-089 Donnell (Richard H.) Foundation
P.O. Box 1340
McMurray 15317   (Washington County)

MI-11-12-15-22-31-72
Phone 724-746-3253 **FAX** 724-746-2309
EIN 23-2900282   **Year Created** 1997

AMV $1,383,359   **FYE** 12-00   (**Gifts Received** $250)   2 **Grants totaling** $775,137

All local giving. High grant of **$750,137** to Washington Hospital Foundation (hospice construction). **$25,000** to United Way of Washington County (Christian Outreach). — Giving in the prior year included **$27,500** to Cornerstone Care (medical equipment/improvements); **$25,000** to United Way of Washington County (outreach programs); **$15,000** each to Washington Christian Outreach (matching funds) and Washington Hospital Foundation (hospice construction); **$10,000** to Neighborhood Drug Awareness Corps (summer playground program); and **$5,000** to PETA/People for Ethical Treatment of Animals [VA]. ■**PUBLICATIONS:** annual report; brochure ■**WEBSITE:** None ■**E-MAIL:** rdonn8249@gateway.net ■**APPLICATION POLICIES & PROCEDURES:** The Foundation reports that most giving is for general support, special projects, or matching grants. Grant requests may be submitted in a full proposal with cover letter during January-April (deadline is April 30th deadline; describe the organization's history and who it serves, and include a project budget, list of major funding sources, and IRS tax-exempt status documentation. Grants are awarded in October.

O+D+T Richard H. Donnell [Canonsburg] (P+F+D+Donor+Con) — Shana M. Donnell [Canonsburg] (VP+S+D) — Christopher Donnell [Canonsburg] (D) — Edwin E. Edwards, III [OH] (D) — Catherine E. Kresh [Washington] (D)

SW-090 Donnelly (Mary J.) Foundation
650 Smithfield Street, Suite 1810
Pittsburgh 15222   (Allegheny County)

MI-12-22-25-29-31-41-42-55-61-64
Phone 412-471-5828 **FAX** 412-471-0736
EIN 25-6037469   **Year Created** 1951

AMV $5,604,872   **FYE** 6-01   (**Gifts Received** $0)   50 **Grants totaling** $1,454,500

About one-fifth local/Pa. giving; some grants comprise multiple payments. High local grant of **$55,000** to Carlow College. **$30,000** each to Central Catholic High School, and Epiphany Assn. **$25,000** to Institute for Advanced Catholic Studies [Greensburg]. **$20,000** each to Little Sisters of the Poor, Rosemont College [Montgomery County], and Society for Propagation of the Faith. **$10,000** each to Allegheny County/Assn. for Children with Learning Disabilities, Diocese of Pittsburgh, Oakland Catholic High School, Waldron Mercy Academy [Montgomery County], and The Pittsburgh Foundation. **$5,000** to Center for Life

& Family, Diocese of Greensburg, Greater Pittsburgh Community Food Bank, Pittsburgh Cultural Trust, St. Anthony School, and Shadyside Hospital Foundation. **$2,000-$2,500** each to Focus on Renewal, St. Paul Cathedral, and Salvation Army. **$1,000-$1,500** each to Capuchin-Franciscan Fathers, Contact Pittsburgh, The de Paul Institute, International Poetry Forum, Marian Manor, St. Paul of the Cross Retreat Center, Society of St. Vincent de Paul, Vincentian Home, and Whale's Tale Foundation/FamilyLink. **Out-of-state** giving includes high grant of **$530,000** to Morality in Media [NY]; **$500,000** to St. Mary Student Parish [MI]; **$20,000** to Bread for the World Institute [MD] and Maryknoll Mission Assn. of the Faithful [NY]; **$15,000** to National Catholic Community Foundation [MD]; **$12,000** to Catholic Charities USA [VA]; **$10,000** each to Adelante Project [NY] and Catholic Theological Union [IL]; and smaller grants, mostly for Catholic purposes. ■**PUBLICATIONS:** None ■**WEBSITE:** None ■ **E-MAIL:** None ■**APPLICATION POLICIES & PROCEDURES:** Prospective applicants should make an initial telephone inquiry about the feasibility of submitting a request. No grants are awarded for endowment, matching gifts, or to individuals. Grant requests may be submitted in a letter at any time; include necessary supporting documentation. Grants are awarded at June and December meetings.

O+D+T Thomas J. Donnelly, Esq. (T+Con) — Elizabeth A. Donnelly (T) — Frederick N. Egler, Jr. (T) — Ruth D. Egler (T) — C. Holmes Wolfe, Jr., Esq. (T)

SW-091 **Doverspike (J&R) Charitable Foundation**
P.O. Box 1034
Punxsutawney   15767   (Indiana County)
AMV $1,552,360   **FYE** 12-00   (**Gifts Received** $1)

MI-12-13-23-29-31-32-41-43-63
Phone Unlisted **FAX** None
EIN 25-6571881   **Year Created** 1997
35 **Grants totaling** $57,300

All local giving; all grants are for general support except as noted. High grant of **$10,000** to Punxsutawney Area Hospital. **$5,000** to Punxsutawney Christian School. **$4,700** to Make-A-Wish Foundation of Punxsutawney. **$1,000-$1,500** each to American Cancer Society, Cub Scouts/Ringgold, and Red Cross. Sixteen scholarships ranging from **$500** to **$5,000** awarded to local students. Other local contributions **$200-$500** for Protestant churches and needy individuals. ■**PUBLICATIONS:** Grant Application Procedures ■**WEBSITE:** None ■**E-MAIL:** None ■**APPLICATION POLICIES & PROCEDURES:** Prospective applicants should send an initial Letter of Inquiry (2 pages maximum—provide an original and 2 copies) which includes (a) organization name, address, telephone number, principal contact name; (b) a brief project description detailing the intended result, and the project's expected duration; (c) total amount budgeted for the entire project; (d) amount sought from the Foundation; and (e) a one-sentence statement certifying its status as a 501(c)(3) tax-exempt organization which is not classified as a private foundation—do not attach the IRS determination letter. An organization may submit only one Letter of Inquiry annually, but more than one project may be described as long as the 2-page limit is not exceeded. After review by the Distribution Committee an applicant will be notified whether to submit a full proposal or not.

O+D+T Distribution Committee (Con) — (Chair, Selection Committee (Con)) — S&T Bank (Corporate Trustee)

SW-092 **Dozzi (Peter C.) Charitable Foundation**
c/o Jendoco Construction Corporation
2000 Lincoln Road
Pittsburgh   15235   (Allegheny County)
AMV $1,923,002   **FYE** 4-01   (**Gifts Received** $270,000)

MI-12-22-25-31-32-42-53-55-61-63
Phone 412-361-4500 **FAX** None
EIN 23-7023479   **Year Created** 1969
26 **Grants totaling** $81,773

All local/regional giving. High grant of **$23,500** to Carnegie Mellon U. **$11,500** to Pittsburgh Cultural Trust. **$10,300** to United Cerebral Palsy of Pittsburgh. **$10,000** to Children's Hospital of Pittsburgh. **$5,500** to Geneva College. **$5,000** to Society for Contemporary Crafts. **$3,600** to Jewish Assn. on Aging. **$1,000-$2,100** each to Community Design Center (Pedal Pittsburgh), First Lutheran Church of Johnstown, Ladies Hospital Aid Society, Pauline Auberle Foundation, Pittsburgh Habitat for Humanity, and Western Pa. Hospital Foundation. Other contributions **$40-$833** for civic, educational, environmental, health, Catholic and other purposes. ■**PUBLICATIONS:** None ■**WEBSITE:** None ■**E-MAIL:** None ■**APPLICATION POLICIES & PROCEDURES:** The Foundation reports that contributions are given to local charities but not for financial aid for schooling or scholarships. — Formerly called the Eugene Dozzi Charitable Foundation.

O+D+T Petrina A. Lloyd (T+Manager+Con) — Peter C. Dozzi (T+Donor) — Domenic P. Dozzi [Oakmont] (T) — Dwight E. Kuhn [New Kensington] (T) — Thomas J. Murphy (T) — Corporate donors: Epic Metals Corp. and Jendoco Construction Corp.

SW-093 **Dunlap (Edward B.), Jr. Foundation**
12 Grandview Circle
Canonsburg   15317   (Washington County)
AMV $246,032   **FYE** 12-00   (**Gifts Received** $0)

MI-22-61
Phone 724-743-7747 **FAX** None
EIN 25-6361678   **Year Created** 1991
1 **Grant of** $11,300

Sole grant to St. Vincent DePaul Society. — In prior two years, all giving to same grantee. ■**PUBLICATIONS:** None ■**WEBSITE:** None ■**E-MAIL:** None ■**APPLICATION POLICIES & PROCEDURES:** Information not available.

O+D+T Edward B. Dunlap, Jr. (T+Donor+Con) — Anna B. Dunlap (T) — Timothy Dunlap [McMurray] (T)

SW-094 **Dupre (Philip K.) Family Foundation**
R.R. #1, Seven Springs
Champion   15622   (Somerset County)
AMV $269,164   **FYE** 12-00   (**Gifts Received** $6,363)

MI-12-22-41-42-61-63-71
Phone Unlisted **FAX** None
EIN 23-7895524   **Year Created** 1997
5 **Grants totaling** $7,050

About one-third local giving. High Pa. grant of **$1,000** to Seven Springs Ski Patrol. **$400** each to St. Children's Aid Home of Somerset and Peter's Roman Catholic Church. **$250** to St. Raymond's Catholic Church. **Out-of-state** grant: **$5,000** to National Council of State Garden Clubs [MO]. — Local/Pa. giving in the prior year included **$6,000** each to Franciscan Fathers [Loretto] and Light of Life Ministries [Pittsburgh]; **$5,000** to Indianhead Church of God; and **$600** each to Carnegie Mellon U., Mercersburg Academy, St. Vincent College, Shady Side Academy, and U. of Pittsburgh (Semester at Sea program). ■**PUBLICATIONS:**

None ■**WEBSITE:** None ■**E-MAIL:** loisdds@compuserve.com ■**APPLICATION POLICIES & PROCEDURES:** The Foundation reports giving focuses on culture, museums, youth development, medical research, and education. Grant requests may be submitted in a letter at any time.

O+D+T Lois Dupre Shuster (Foundation Manager+Donor+Con) — PNC Advisors [Trustee]

SW-095 Eberly Foundation, The
610 National City Bank Building
2 West Main Street
Uniontown 15401   (Fayette County)

MI-13-29-31-34-41-42-43-44-52-54-55-56-71-84-85-86
Phone 724-438-3789 **FAX** 724-438-3856
EIN 23-7070246 **Year Created** 1963

AMV $21,167,233   **FYE** 12-00   **(Gifts Received** $0)   105 **Grants totaling** $18,799,868

Mostly local/Western Pa. giving; grants are for general operating/program support except as noted, and many grants comprise multiple payments/awards. High grant of **$9,300,000** to Penn State U. (Hershey Medical Center Innovation Fund/Eberly Building renovations/Fayette Business School professorship & scholarship endowment)/Hobby-Eberly Telescope). **$1,482,666** to Greater Uniontown Heritage Consortium (operations/renovations/piano/event support). **$1,267,000** to California U. of Pa. (mostly Science & Technology Building). **$1,000,000** to Western Pa. Conservancy (Fallingwater restoration). **$921,071** to Fay-Penn Economic Development Council. **$622,000** to Touchstone Center for Crafts (Activity Center/Blacksmith Studio Maintenance Endowment/general endowment). **$600,000** to Children's Hospital of Pittsburgh (Pediatric Otolaryngology Chair endowment). **$500,550** to Indiana U. of Pa. (Business School technology initiatives). **$500,000** each to Community Foundation of Fayette County (challenge/matching grants) and Girl Scouts of Western Pa. (Eberly Family Learning Center endowment). **$250,000** each to National Park Foundation [Farmington] (Fort Necessity interpretive center) and Waynesburg College (Library). **$200,000** to Fayette County Agricultural Improvement Assn. (outdoor arena project). **$100,000** to Edinboro U. of Pa. (honors scholarship fund). **$76,000** to Connellsville Area School District (school programs). **$65,000** each to Penn State U./Fayette Campus (mostly for Fayette Business Adventure and County Fair) and Redstone Foundation. **$60,000** to Boy Scouts/Greensburg (Lodges construction). **$57,795** to Albert Gallitin School District (mostly supplemental education programs). **$56,227** to Laurel Highlands School District (supplemental education programs). **$54,750** to YMCA of Uniontown Area (mostly Eberly Family Fitness Center expansion). **$50,000** to National Pike Water Assn. [Markleysburg] (water distribution system). **$45,000** to Westmoreland-Fayette Historical Society (Overholt House renovations). **$43,000** to Brownsville Area School District (supplemental education programs). **$40,000** to Fayette County Community Action Agency (Family Service Center). **$32,202** to Uniontown Area School District (school programs). **$27,000** to Diocese of Greensburg (school programs). **$25,000** each to East End United Community Center (executive director support) and Regional Family YMCA of Laurel Highlands. **$21,000** to National Flag Foundation [Pittsburgh] (flagpole installation). **$20,000** each to Grantmakers of Western Pa. (dues), Habitat for Humanity/Uniontown (housing project), and Uniontown Public Library (challenge grant). **$17,016** to Frazier School District (supplemental education programs). **$15,000** to Wharton Township (sports programs). **$12,000** to Uniontown Hospital Foundation (golf tournament sponsorship). **$10,000** each to Brownsville Area Revitalization Corp. (Melaga Art Museum upgrades), Carnegie Free Library of Connellsville (waterproofing), Duquesne U. (outdoor tourism project), and Regional Trail Corp. (hiking/biking trail marketing). **$8,900** to Perryopolis Area Heritage Society (landscaping). **$5,000** each to Chestnut Ridge Christian Academy (art/science supplies), Commonwealth Foundation for Public Policy Alternatives [Harrisburg], Johnstown Area Heritage Assn. (Discovery Center), The Lincoln Institute for Public Opinion Research [Harrisburg], Pittsburgh Symphony, Point Marion Public Library, and The Second Mile. Other local grants/contributions **$500-$2,900** for various arts/cultural, civic, environmental, health/human services, historical, and other purposes. **Out-of-state** giving includes **$305,000** to West Virginia Public Theatre (Streets of Gold project) and **$50,000** to Oklahoma City Community Foundation (YMCA Camp scholarships endowment). ■**PUBLICATIONS:** None ■**WEBSITE:** None ■**E-MAIL:** None ■**APPLICATION POLICIES & PROCEDURES:** The Foundation reports that giving is generally limited to PA, WV and OK and is focused on (1) education, particularly at the university level; (2) local economic development and redevelopment, and (3) The Arts. Requests relating to other areas, however, are considered; most grants are for capital improvements, endowed chairs, acquisitions, research, scholarships, or publications. No grants are awarded to individuals for any purpose or to nationally organized fundraising groups. Grant requests may be submitted in a letter before the August 1st deadline; provide a concise description of the purpose for which funds are requested and a related budget. The letter must be signed by the organization's chief executive officer and approved by its Board of Directors, and must include the following: current organizational operating budget; projected operating budget for the years funding is requested; audited financial statements for the most recent two years; list of Board members; latest Form 990 filed (if required); IRS tax-exempt status documentation under Sections 501(c)(3) and 509(a); and available printed materials such as annual reports, pamphlets, or catalogs. Additional information may be requested for further evaluation. Request submitted without the required documentation will not be considered. The Trustees meet periodically to consider requests.

O+D+T Robert E. Eberly, Sr. (P+F+T+Con) — Patricia H. Miller (VP+S+T) — Carolyn Eberly Blaney [Chalk Hill] (T) — Ruth Ann Carter [Chalk Hill] (T) — Carolyn Jill Drost [Farmington] (T) — Paul O. Eberly [NM] (T) — Robert E. Eberly, Jr. [SC] (T)

SW-096 Eberly (Robert E. & Elouise R.) Foundation
610 National City Bank Building
2 West Main Street
Uniontown 15401   (Fayette County)

MI-12-13-21-31-32-41-55-56-82-85-89
Phone 724-438-3789 **FAX** 724-438-3856
EIN 25-1723010 **Year Created** 1993

AMV $955,640   **FYE** 12-00   **(Gifts Received** $175,034)   29 **Grants totaling** $127,648

Mostly local/Pa. giving; grants are for general purposes except as noted. High grant of **$35,000** to Friends of George C. Marshall (sculpture). **$20,000** to Penn State Dance Marathon (children's cancer fund). **$13,500** to Uniontown Area YMCA (property purchase). **$10,00** to Boy Scouts/Westmoreland-Fayette Council. **$5,000** each to Brother's Brother Foundation [Pittsburgh],

Johnstown Area Heritage Assn. (Discovery Center), North Union Township Fire Dept., and Uniontown Hospital Foundation. **$3,362** to Uniontown Downtown Business District Authority (summer lunch series). **$3,500** to Pittsburgh Tissue Engineering Initiative (local intern). **$2,000-$2,500** each to Fayette County Airport Authority (air show sponsor), National Flag Foundation/Fayette County (fundraising campaign), Operation Santa Claus (Fayette County families), and Vietnam Children's Fund (elementary schools program). **$1,000-$1,100** each to Albert Gallatin Planning & Development (benefit event), American Cancer Society, Fay-Penn Economic Development Council (video), Geibel Catholic High School, Hematology-Oncology Associates (TV fund), Perryopolis Area Heritage Society, State Theatre Center for the Arts, Tub Mill Arts Assn., and Youngwood Historical & Railroad Museum (building fund). Other smaller local and out-of-state contributions for various purposes. ■ **PUBLICATIONS:** annual report ■ **WEBSITE:** None ■ **E-MAIL:** None ■ **APPLICATION POLICIES & PROCEDURES:** Grant requests may be submitted in a letter before the August 1st deadline; detail the proposed use of the grant and include an audited financial statement, Federal ID Number, copy of latest IRS Form 990 (if filed), and IRS tax-exempt status documentation. Grants are disbursed in the following year. — Formerly called the Robert E. Eberly Foundation.

O+D+T Robert E. Eberly, Sr. (P+D+Donor+Con) — Elouise R. Eberly (S+F+D) — Patricia H. Miller (AS+AF) — Paul O. Eberly [NM] (D)

SW-097 **Eden Hall Foundation**
USX Tower, Suite 3232
600 Grant Street
Pittsburgh 15219   (Allegheny County)
AMV $194,219,827   **FYE** 12-00   **(Gifts Received** $0)

MI-11-12-13-14-15-16-17-22-29-31-35-41-42
43-44-45-51-52-55-71-72-84
Phone 412-642-6697 **FAX** 412-642-6698
EIN 25-1384468   **Year Created** 1980
76 **Grants totaling** $9,765,730

Most giving limited to SW Pa. High grant of **$800,000** to Holy Family Institute (Family Life Center). **$670,000** to St. Vincent College (Pathways program). **$500,000** each to Point Park College (property purchase) and Wilson College [Franklin County] (fitness/health facility). **$400,000** each to Carlow College (lab equipment/furnishings) and YWCA of Greater Pittsburgh (headquarters renovation). **$359,600** to Carnegie Mellon U. (science van). **$300,000** each to Duquesne U. (reading clinic/computer camp), United Way of Allegheny County (annual campaign), and YWCA of Greater Pittsburgh (adolescent girls programs). **$294,000** to Seton Hill College (science program). **$270,545** to National Aviary in Pittsburgh (Red Siskin program). **$250,000** to Miryam's (new facility purchase). **$240,000** to Women's Center & Shelter of Pittsburgh (violence prevention program). **$225,000** to Pittsburgh Voyager (educational program). **$200,000-$210,000** each to Allegheny College (lab equipment), Bradley Center South (building purchase/renovation), Family House (new facility renovation), Three Rivers Adoption Council (program services), Three Rivers Center for Independent Living (facility purchase/renovation), and West Penn Hospital Foundation (conference center construction). **$174,000** to Urban League of Pittsburgh (children/youth programs/services). **$150,000** each to I Have A Dream Foundation of Pittsburgh (programming), National Fatherhood Initiative (establish Pittsburgh chapter/office), and Pace School (facility purchase/renovation). **$130,000** to Vocational Rehabilitation/Life's Work (update samples). **$112,000** to Greensburg Community Development Corp. (park project). **$111,000** to Seton Hill Child Services (scholarship program). **$103,000** to Mom's House (windows replacement). **$100,000** each to Emmaus Community of Pittsburgh (facility purchase/renovation) and Salvation Army (disaster fund). **$90,000** to Family Pathways (generations program). **$80,000** each to Bethlehem Haven (employment project) and East Liberty Health Care (dental care center). **$75,000** to Family Health Council (house renovations). **$68,000** to Holy Family Institute (summer camps). **$60,000** to Sister's Place (renovations). **$52,000** to Rankin Christian Center (renovations/upgrades). **$50,000** each to Chartiers Nature Conservancy (property purchase), Mon Valley Youth & Teen Assn. (facility renovation), North Hill Community Outreach (family assistance), Plum Borough Community Library (facility purchase/renovation), St. Mary's of Lawrenceville Art Program (school/summer programs), YMCA of Kiski Valley (renovations/upgrades), and YWCA of Greensburg (programming). **$45,000** to Allegheny Conference on Community Development (agenda development fund). **$30,000-$36,300** each to LaRoche College (computer equipment), Mt. Ararat Community Activity Center (summer camp), NEED /Negro Education Emergency Drive (scholarships), Pittsburgh Children's Museum (planning process), Pittsburgh Communications Foundation (journalism workshop), and United Negro College Fund (scholarships). **$20,000-$26,000** each to Carnegie Mellon U. (vocal coach project), The Corporate Collection (women's life skills center), Hillel Academy (asbestos abatement), Lupus Foundation of America (outreach programs), Pa. Environmental council (summer program), Pittsburgh Foundation (Cultural Trust endowment), Pittsburgh Musical Theater (operating support), Radio Information Services (programming), Rx Council (prescription program), SIDS Alliance (safe cribs program), and Valley Players of Ligonier (renovation). **$18,000** to Circle C Youth & Family Services (window replacement). **$10,000-$13,685** each to Allegheny County Literacy Program (summer reading camps), Emmanuel Episcopal Church (reading program), First Night Pittsburgh (programs), Ligonier Valley Memorial Foundation (chapel construction), and Pittsburgh Zoo (programs/computer). **$3,500-$6,500** each to Latrobe Area Hospital Charitable Foundation (therapeutic summer camp), Pittsburgh Cultural Trust (Designs on Downtown), Pittsburgh Tissue Engineering Initiative (summer interns), and Travelers Aid Society of Western Pa. (sports benefit events). ■ **PUBLICATIONS:** Guidelines & Application Procedures brochure ■ **WEBSITE:** None ■ **E-MAIL:** None ■ **APPLICATION POLICIES & PROCEDURES:** The Foundation reports that giving is primarily to SW Pa. organizations for special projects, capital drives, building funds, and matching grants; multiple-year grants are awarded. Requests for support of operating expenses, general fund raising campaigns, or to cover accumulated deficits are discouraged; no grants are awarded to individuals. Primary areas of interest are (1) social welfare and improvement of the poor and needy; (2) educational programs dedicated to the advancement and dissemination of useful knowledge, support and maintenance or private colleges, universities and other educational institutions; (3) advancement of better health through support of organizations whose primary purpose is prevention and alleviation of sickness/disease; and (4) advancement of good morals. Grant requests may be submitted in a letter (5 pages maximum) at any time; describe the organizations's purpose and the intended purposes of the requested funding; include organizational/project budgets, list of major funding sources, a current audited financial statement, Board member list, project evaluation plan, and a IRS tax-exempt status documentation. Proposals which follow the Grantmakers of Western Pa. Common Grant Application Format area accepted. Requests should be submitted in January, April, July or October; all applications are acknowledged and Interviews or site visits sometimes are arranged with organizations being considered for support. Grants are awarded at Board meetings in April, June, September, and December.

O+D+T Sylvia V. Fields (Program Director+Con) — George C. Greer (C+D) — E.H. Shifler (VP+D) — Debora S. Foster (S+D) — John M. Mazur (F+D)

SW-098 **Edwards (Lillian) Foundation**   MI-15-22-52-63
c/o Mellon Private Wealth Management
One Mellon Center, P.O. Box 185   **Phone** 412-234-0023 **FAX** 412-234-1073
Pittsburgh 15230   (Allegheny County)   **EIN** 25-6365074   **Year Created** 1991
AMV $3,393,702   **FYE** 12-00   (**Gifts Received** $0)   7 **Grants totaling** $170,947

Five local grants of **$24,421** each to Episcopal Diocese of Pittsburgh, Lutheran Service Society of Western Pa., Pittsburgh Opera, Pittsburgh Symphony, and Salvation Army. **Out-of-state** grants: **$24,421** each to Meals on Wheels/Lexington [KY] and St. John's Lutheran Church [KY]. — This giving pattern has been in effect since 1991. ■**PUBLICATIONS:** None ■**WEBSITE:** None ■ **E-MAIL:** None ■**APPLICATION POLICIES & PROCEDURES:** The Bank reports that under the Deed of Trust, the seven listed donee organizations are designated as (only) the preferred grantees.
O+D+T Laurie A. Moritz (VP at Bank+Con) — and a Trust Administrative Committee of Mellon Bank employees — Mellon Bank N.A. (Trustee)

SW-099 **Eichleay Foundation**   MI-41-42-52-53-54-56-82
c/o Eichleay Engineers, Inc.
6585 Penn Avenue   **Phone** 412-363-9000 **FAX** None
Pittsburgh 15206   (Allegheny County)   **EIN** 25-6065754   **Year Created** 1954
AMV $2,058,112   **FYE** 12-00   (**Gifts Received** $0)   12 **Grants totaling** $81,000

About three-quarters local giving. High grant of **$50,000** to Carnegie Institute. **$10,000** to CARE International [Philadelphia]. **$2,500** to Frick Art & Historical Center. **$1,000** each to Historical Society of Western Pa. and Pittsburgh Symphony. Other smaller contributions. **Out-of-state** giving includes **$10,000** to Cornell U. [NY] and **$2,000** to Hotchkiss School [CT]. ■**PUBLICATIONS:** None ■**WEBSITE:** None ■**E-MAIL:** None ■**APPLICATION POLICIES & PROCEDURES:** The Foundation suggests making initial contact in a brief letter which outlines a proposed project; if the Foundation is interested, a full proposal will be requested. Grant requests should be submitted during October-November. The Trustees meet in December.
O+D+T George F. Eichleay (T+Con) — John W. Eichleay, Jr. Esq. (T)

SW-100 **Elder Foundation, The**   MI-12-14-29-31-55-56-57-63-81
c/o Somerset Trust Company
151 West Main Street, P.O. Box 777   **Phone** 814-443-9201 **FAX** None
Somerset 15501   (Somerset County)   **EIN** 23-7749572   **Year Created** 1993
AMV $640,272   **FYE** 12-00   (**Gifts Received** $0)   18 **Grants totaling** $33,000

About half local/Pa. giving. Local grants **$1,000-$1,395** each to Asbury United Methodist Church, Clarion Historical Society, Children's Aid Home & Society, Children's Hospital of Pittsburgh, Cook Forest Sawmill Center, Hillcrest United Presbyterian Church, Pa. Elks Legacy Trust, Pa. Elks Home Service Program, Pittsburgh Blind Assn., Presbyterian Church of Mt. Washington, River City Brass Band, Presbyterian Assn. on Aging, and WQED. **Out-of-state** grant of **$15,620** to The Rotary Foundation [IL] (international understanding). ■**PUBLICATIONS:** None ■**WEBSITE:** None ■**E-MAIL:** None ■**APPLICATION POLICIES & PROCEDURES:** Information not available.
O+D+T Ann Persun (VP & Trust Officer at Bank+Con) — Georgianna Petrilla (T) — Somerset Trust Co. (Trustee)

SW-101 **Elias (Joseph) Charitable Trust, The**   MI-12-22-62
c/o Elias Industries
Epsilon Drive/RIDC Park, P.O. Box 2812   **Phone** 412-782-4300 **FAX** None
Pittsburgh 15230   (Allegheny County)   **EIN** 25-6284538   **Year Created** 1987
AMV $38,520   **FYE** 12-00   (**Gifts Received** $24,000)   29 **Grants totaling** $43,383

Mostly local giving. High grant of **$30,000** to United Jewish Federation of Greater Pittsburgh. **$3,010** to Congregation Beth Shalom. **$1,500** to Jewish Family Assistance Fund. **$1,000** each to Charles Morris Center, The Children's Institute, Jewish Family & Children's Service, and Jewish National Fund. Other local contributions **$25-$500** for various purposes. **Out-of-state** giving includes **$750** to Jewish Solidarity [FL]. ■**PUBLICATIONS:** None ■**WEBSITE:** None ■**E-MAIL:** None ■**APPLICATION POLICIES & PROCEDURES:** No grants awarded to individuals.
O+D+T Norman Elias (T+Donor+Con) — Sylvia M. Elias (T) — Corporate donors: Elias Industries; Tap South, Inc.

SW-102 **Elish (Herbert & Eloise Hirst) Charitable Foundation**   MI-22-41-42-44-51-52-62
108 Woodland Road   **Phone** 412-661-2753 **FAX** None
Pittsburgh 15232   (Allegheny County)   **EIN** 25-1779189   **Year Created** 1995
AMV $60,686   **FYE** 11-00   (**Gifts Received** $810)   7 **Grants totaling** $44,450

Mostly local giving. High grant of **$16,000** to The Ellis School. **$11,000** to United Jewish Federation of Greater Pittsburgh. **$6,200** to City Theatre Company. **$5,000** to Carnegie Library of Pittsburgh. **$1,000** to Pittsburgh Chamber Music Society. **Out-of-state** grant: **$5,000** to Williams College [MA]. ■**PUBLICATIONS:** None ■**WEBSITE:** None ■**E-MAIL:** None ■**APPLICA-

TION POLICIES & PROCEDURES: Grant requests may be submitted in any from at any time; include the most recent financial statement and IRS tax-exempt status documentation. No grants awarded to individuals.

O+D+T Herbert Elish (T+Donor+Con) — Eloise H. Elish (T+Donor)

SW-103 Environmental Trust, An, Inc.
    412 Washington Trust Building
    6 South Main Street
    Washington 15301   (Washington County)

MI-25-42-71-72-79-83

Phone 724-225-8655 **FAX** 724-228-5888
EIN 25-1608399 **Year Created** 1989

AMV $2,373,441   **FYE** 12-00   (**Gifts Received** $125,934)   13 **Grants totaling** $110,336

Mostly local giving, but see below re new geographic emphasis. High grant of **$19,500** to Allegheny College. **$10,000** each to Chartiers Nature Conservancy, Greater Pittsburgh Community Food Bank, Pa. Cleanways, Penn Energy Project-Tides Center [Harrisburg], and Wildlife Habitat Council. **$7,650** to Washington & Jefferson College/Science Matters, Inc. **$6,000** to Raymond Proffitt Foundation [Bucks County]. **$5,000** to Conemaugh Valley Conservation. **$4,000** to Group Against Smog & Pollution. **$1,185** to League of Women Voters/Washington County Conservation District. **Out-of-state** grants: **$12,000** to U. of Massachusetts and **$5,000** to Elm Research Institute [NH]. ■**PUBLICATIONS:** Proposal Submittal Guidelines ■**WEBSITE:** None ■**E-MAIL:** None ■**APPLICATION POLICIES & PROCEDURES:** The Foundation reports that beginning in 2002, the Trust will give precedence to New England, especially ME and NH, and only proposals dealing with environmental or energy issues will be considered. Most grants are for special projects, endowment, or research, and Program Related Investments are considered; only rarely are multiyear requests funded. Prospective applicants initially should make a telephone inquiry regarding the feasibility of submitting a request. Grant requests may be submitted in a specific proposal which states the exact funding requested; proposals should be submitted as early in as possible each year, preferably in the first quarter, although no later than October 31st. The proposal must include organization and project budgets, list of major funding sources, Board member list, audited financial statement, and IRS tax-exempt status documentation. Site visits sometimes are made to organizations being considered for a grant.

O+D+T Rebecca A. Ramsey (S+F+Con) — William T. Hopwood [ME] (P+D+Donor) — Jane T. Hopwood [ME] (VP+D) — Taite W. Hopwood [Pittsburgh] (D)

SW-104 Fair Oaks Foundation
    c/o Ampco-Pittsburgh Corporation
    600 Grant Street, Suite 4600
    Pittsburgh 15219   (Allegheny County)

MI-11-13-22-29-32-41-42-44-51-52-54-55-56
57-62-65

Phone 412-456-4418 **FAX** None
EIN 25-1576560 **Year Created** 1988

AMV $5,539,621   **FYE** 12-00   (**Gifts Received** $0)   100 **Grants totaling** $452,675

About one-quarter SW Pa. giving; all grants are for program support. High Pa. grant of **$50,000** to United Jewish Federation of Greater Pittsburgh. **$20,000** each to Hillman Cancer Center and United Way of Allegheny County. **$10,000** to Lauri Ann West Memorial Library. **$1,000-$1,250** each to The Carnegie, Chartiers Boys & Girls Club, Civic Light Opera, Family House, Hillel Jewish University Center, Historical Society of Western Pa., Japan-America Society of Pa., National Conference for Community & Justice, Pittsburgh Ballet Theatre, Pittsburgh Opera, Pittsburgh Public Theater, Pittsburgh Symphony, Pittsburgh Youth Golf Foundation, Shadyside Hospital Foundation, United Way of Lawrence County, WQED, and Women's Board of Pittsburgh. Other local contributions **$40-$500** for various purposes. **Out-of-state** giving includes **$200,000** to Harvard U. [MA]; **$100,000** to Cornell U. [NY]; and many grants/contributions **$50-$3,000** to corporate operating locations in NY, IN and VA. ■**PUBLICATIONS:** None ■**WEBSITE:** None ■**E-MAIL:** None ■**APPLICATION POLICIES & PROCEDURES:** Grant requests may be submitted in a brief letter during September-October; deadline is October 31st. Grants are awarded at a mid-November meeting. — Formerly called Ampco-Pittsburgh Foundation II, Inc. -or- Pittsburgh Forgings Foundation.

O+D+T Rose Ann Hoover (S+Con) — Louis Berkman (C+T) — Robert A. Paul (P+T)

SW-105 Fairbanks-Horix Foundation
    c/o National City Bank of Pa. - Loc. 25-162
    National City Center, 20 Stanwix Street, 16th Floor
    Pittsburgh 15222   (Allegheny County)

MI-22-43-52-54-56-71

Phone 412-644-8002 **FAX** 412-261-6252
EIN 25-6084211 **Year Created** 1965

AMV $828,225   **FYE** 12-00   (**Gifts Received** $0)   12 **Grants totaling** $43,427

Mostly local giving. High grant of **$24,882** to Pa. Trolley Museum (matching grant). **$4,000** to Robert Morris College (engineering scholarship fund). **$2,000-$2,500** each to Pittsburgh Symphony, Salvation Army, and U.S. Term Limits Foundation [DC]. **$500** to Western Pa. Conservancy. Also, five scholarships of **$600-$1,800** awarded to dependents of company employees. ■**PUBLICATIONS:** None ■**WEBSITE:** None ■**E-MAIL:** joanna.mayo@nationalcity.com ■**APPLICATION POLICIES & PROCEDURES:** The Foundation reports that priority is given to Western Pa. organizations Prospective applicants initially should make a telephone inquiry about the feasibility of submitting a request. Grant requests from organizations may be submitted in any form at any time; include IRS tax-exempt status documentation. Site visits sometimes are arranged to organizations being considered for a grant. Horix Scholarship awards are restricted to Horix Manufacturing Company employees' children. — Formerly called Fairbanks-Horis Charitable Trust

O+D+T Joanna M. Mayo (VP at Bank+Con) — Bryan H. Fairbanks (Co-T) — Frank Fairbanks (Co-T) — National City Bank of Pa. (Corporate Trustee)

SW-106 **Falk (Leon) Family Trust**
3315 Grant Building
310 Grant Street
Pittsburgh   15219   (Allegheny County)

MI-11-25-31-42-52-56-57

Phone 412-261-5533 **FAX** 412-471-7739
EIN 25-6065756   **Year Created** 1952

AMV $3,849,745   **FYE** 12-01   **(Gifts Received** $0)   18 **Grants totaling** $175,200

Mostly local giving; grants are unrestricted support except as noted. High grant of **$74,000** to Chatham College (capital campaign & unrestricted support). **$35,000** to Shadyside Hospital Foundation (capital campaign & unrestricted support). **$15,000** to Pittsburgh Symphony. **$12,000** to United Way of Allegheny County. **$10,000** to Historical Society of Western Pa. **$5,000** to Sewickley Academy (capital campaign). **$3,000** to Greater Pittsburgh Community Food Bank. **$2,000** to WQED. **$1,000** to Jubilee Assn. Other local contributions **$200-$500. Out-of-state** giving includes **$8,000** to Chautauqua Foundation [NY] (capital campaign) and **$5,000** to American Jewish Committee [NY]. — Major grants approved for future payment include **$251,000** to Chatham College (capital campaign & unrestricted support); **$40,000** each to Historical Society of Western Pa. (capital campaign & unrestricted support) and Shadyside Hospital Foundation (capital campaign); and **$15,000** to Pittsburgh Symphony. ■**PUBLICATIONS:** None ■**WEBSITE:** None ■**E-MAIL:** sigofalk@falkfund.org ■**APPLICATION POLICIES & PROCEDURES:** The Foundation reports that giving focuses on cultural, mental health, and service organizations in Western Pa., particularly Allegheny County. Most grants are for general support, special projects, building funds, capital drives, and endowment. Prospective applicants should make an initial telephone inquiry about the feasibility of submitting a request. Grant requests may be submitted in an informal letter (3 pages maximum), preferably in September-October; describe the organization's need/purpose of the requested funding and include a project budget, list of Board members, and IRS tax-exempt status documentation. The Trustees award grants at a meeting in November-December.

O+D+T   Sigo Falk (C+T+Con) — Andrew D. Falk (T) — Margaret F. Steckel [OH] (T)

SW-107   **Falk (Maurice) Medical Fund**
3315 Grant Building
310 Grant Street
Pittsburgh   15219   (Allegheny County)

MI-12-13-14-16-17-29-31-32-33-34-35-42-43
45-49-54-55-86

Phone 412-261-2485 **FAX** 412-471-7739
EIN 25-1099658   **Year Created** 1960

AMV $17,559,288   **FYE** 8-01   **(Gifts Received** $37,663)   13 **Grants totaling** $520,578

Nationwide giving (with an emphasis on Pittsburgh) focusing on racism, mental health and minority affairs. High grant of **$500,000** to U. of Pittsburgh/School of Social Work & Graduate School of Public Health (final payment on pledge creating the Philip Hallen Chair in Community Health & Social Justice). Six grants were from the Innovation & Development Fund, **$1,750-$2,500** each, awarded for a program startup, award/benefit event underwriting, leadership program sponsorship, and educational forum support. — During the September 2001-June 2002 period, 26 project grants totaling **$580,675** were awarded: high grants of **$50,000** each to Carnegie Mellon U. (summer internship program for minority students in biostatistics), Chatham College (Center for Women in Politics in Pa. leadership program), and U. of Pittsburgh Medical Center Health System (HEP Stress Coping Program evaluation). **$40,000** to Carnegie Mellon U. (postdoctoral fellowship at Center for Africanamerican Urban Studies & The Economy). **$37,530** to Mon Valley Initiative (community outreach services). **$37,000** to Midwife Center (free clinic). **$35,000** each to Good Schools Pa. (Pittsburgh office support) and Persad Center (community needs assessment). **$30,000** each to Domestic Abuse Counseling Center (treatment program research) and Lupus Foundation of America (minority outreach program). **$25,000** to Point Park College (pilot education project with Women's Center & Shelter of Greater Pittsburgh) and U. of Pittsburgh/Center for Social & Urban Research (comparative benchmark study on female-male quality of life). **$20,000** to FAME/Fund for the Advancement of Minorities through Education (scholarship program). **$15,000** to Prevention Point Pittsburgh (needle exchange program). **$10,025** to The Tides Center (minority communities project). **$10,000** each to Artists & Cities, Inc. (video on a civil rights photographer), California U. of Pa. (female/minority scholarships for Science & Technology Leadership Academy) and Carnegie Institute/Andy Warhol Museum (exhibit/programs re lynching). **$3,000-$5,000** each to Big Brothers/Big Sisters of Greater Pittsburgh (African-American mentor recruitment), Copeland Fund (strategy re sustaining community-based mental health service providers), Pittsburgh AIDS Task Force (strategic planning process), Pittsburgh Filmmakers (film on an African-American foreign correspondent), U. of Pittsburgh Center for Minority Health (leadership summit), and U. of Pittsburgh Institute of Politics (public policy forum re eliminating health disparities). Also, 22 grants (**$300-$2,500** each and totaling **$36,410**) awarded from the Innovation & Development Fund for purposes similar to listed above. **Out-of-state** grants: **$30,000** to Worldwide Documentaries, Inc. [NY] (film on global AIDS and planetary responsibilities) and **$5,000** to National Video Resources [NY] (philanthropy video). ■**PUBLICATIONS:** statement of program policies/application procedures ■**WEBSITE:** www.falkfund.org ■**E-MAIL:** kerryo@falkfund.org ■**APPLICATION POLICIES & PROCEDURES:** The Fund's primary interest areas are healthcare, education, workforce development, mental health, housing, and criminal justice; long-term priorities include training of professionals and publication of research and field trial results. The Fund will support proposals for the following: (a) to examine through academic research the root causes of injustice, (b) to educate the public and policymakers about equity issues, (c) to design approaches for preventing injustice, and (d) to implement practices which promote equal access and opportunity. In particular, the Fund seeks innovative, creative or imaginative projects that address injustice and which may have a high degree of risk. Most grants are for special projects, publication, research, and partnering projects; multiyear grants are awarded. No grants are awarded to individuals. Prospective applicants should submit an initial letter of inquiry (2 pages maximum) that describes the project's purpose and states an amount requested; these may be submitted at any time. Within three weeks the Fund will respond with either an invitation to submit a full proposal, a request for a site visit, or a declination. If a proposal is solicited, the Grantmakers of Western Pa. Common Grant Application may be used. Major grants are awarded at spring and fall Board meetings, and grants of $2,500 or smaller from the Fund's Innovation & Development Fund are awarded throughout the year.

O+D+T   (Ms.) Kerry J. O'Donnell (P+Con) — Sigo Falk (C+T) — Estelle F. Comay (S+F+T) — Bertram S. Brown, M.D. [MD] (T) — Michele Rone Cooper (T) — Eric W. Springer (T)

SW-108 Farmerie (Wilson J. & Karen A.) Charitable Foundation

1173 Grouse Run Road, Bethel Park

Pittsburgh 15102 (Allegheny County)

MI-12-17-42

Phone 412-833-9853 **FAX** None

EIN 23-7931543 **Year Created** 1997

AMV $760,552 **FYE** 9-01 **(Gifts Received** $0) 2 **Grants totaling** $50,000

All local giving. High grant of **$40,000** to Mom's House of Pittsburgh. **$10,000** to U. of Pittsburgh. — In the prior year, the same grants awarded. ■**PUBLICATIONS:** None ■**WEBSITE:** None ■**E-MAIL:** None ■**APPLICATION POLICIES & PROCEDURES:** Information not available.

O+D+T Wilson J. Farmerie (Donor+Con) — Karen A. Farmerie (Donor) — Smithfield Trust Company (T)

SW-109 Farrell Family Charitable Foundation

c/o Farrell & Company

1200 Reedsdale Street

Pittsburgh 15233 (Allegheny County)

MI-11-42-43-61

Phone 412-237-2260 **FAX** 412-321-0111

EIN 23-7940677 **Year Created** 1998

AMV $490,185 **FYE** 12-00 **(Gifts Received** $0) 2 **Grants totaling** $51,250

All Pa. giving. High grant of **$50,000** to Penn State U. (Michael Farrell Center). **$1,250** for a scholarship. — Grants awarded in prior years included **$25,000** to United Way of Allegheny County; **$9,750** to Catholic Diocese of Pittsburgh; **$1,065** to Seton Hill College; and two scholarships. ■**PUBLICATIONS:** None ■**WEBSITE:** None ■**E-MAIL:** None ■**APPLICATION POLICIES & PROCEDURES:** Grant requests may be submitted in a letter at any time.

O+D+T Michael J. Farrell (P+Con) — Corporate donor: Farrell & Company

---

SW-110 Federated Investors Foundation, Inc.

c/o Federated Investors, Inc.

Federated Investors Tower, 1001 Liberty Ave.

Pittsburgh 15222 (Allegheny County)

MI-11-12-13-14-15-22-25-29-32-35-41-42-43

41-42-43-45-49-52-56-61-71-85

Phone 412-288-1900 **FAX** None

EIN 23-2913182 **Year Created** 1997

AMV $1,689,790 **FYE** 4-01 **(Gifts Received** $275,000) 61 **Grants totaling** $500,350

Mostly local/Pa. giving; grants are for general purposes except as noted. High grant of **$100,000** to Winnie Palmer Nature Reserve [Youngstown]. **$60,000** to United Way of SW Pa. **$25,000** to Oakland Catholic High School (capital improvements). **$20,000** each to Pittsburgh Regional Alliance (economic development) and St. Vincent College (scholarships/capital improvements). **$15,500** to Allegheny Conference on Community Development (regional education, workforce & civic development). **$15,000** each to Little Sisters of the Poor and National Flag Foundation (educational programs). **$10,000** each to Carnegie Mellon U. (professorship endowments), Extra Mile Education Fund, Pittsburgh Leadership Foundation (religious education programs), Pittsburgh Opera, and Sisters of Charity of Seton Hill (building fund). **$7,000-$7,500** each to Carlow College (capital improvements/scholarships), Historical Society of Western Pa. (educational programming), and YMCA of Pittsburgh. **$6,000** each to Greater Pittsburgh Community Food Bank, Holy Family Institute/Foundation (girls' home). **$5,000** each to A Hand to Hold (baby abandonment program), Auberle Foundation, Cardinal Wright Regional School (renovations), Central Catholic High School (tuition assistance), Diocesan Judicial Center (building fund), Foundation for Indiana U. of Pa. (scholarship fund), Marion Manor (Alzheimer's care), One to One Mentoring Program (youth program), Opera Theatre of Pittsburgh, Pa. Economy League, Philadelphia Foundation's Good Neighbor Partnership Fund (support poor families), River City Brass Band (regional concerts), and Travelers Aid Society (emergency assistance). **$1,000-$3,000** each to Allegheny Valley School, Beginning With Books, Birthright, Children's Institute (free pediatric care), Executive Service Corps of Western Pa., Girl Scouts of Western Pa., Junior Achievement of SW Pa. (youth development), Life's Work of Western Pa. (program for disabled), Salvation Army, Thiel College (capital improvements), U. of Pittsburgh Cancer Institute (research), and Visiting Nurses Assn. Foundation. **Out-of-state** giving includes **$20,000** to American United for Life [IL] (public interest law/education); **$15,000** to Morality in Media [NY] (anti-pornography campaign); **$5,000** each to Foundation for Student Communication [NJ] (business leader-student communications), Prison Fellowship Ministries [VA] (inmate family support) and Youth Defence of Ireland [Ireland](mother/child campaign); and **$4,000** to Royal Palm International Academy [FL] (tuition assistance). ■**PUBLICATIONS:** None ■**WEBSITE:** www.federatedinvestors.com [corporate info only] ■**E-MAIL:** None ■**APPLICATION POLICIES & PROCEDURES:** Information not available.

O+D+T J. Christopher Donahue (P+D+Con) — John W. McGonigle (S) — Thomas R. Donahue (F) — John F. Donahue [FL] (D) — Thomas J. Donnelly (D) — Corporate donor: Federated Investors, Inc.

SW-111 Feeney (John M.) Foundation, The

872 Canterbury Lane

Pittsburgh 15232 (Allegheny County)

MI-12-18-22-42-51-52-55-83

Phone 412-687-6499 **FAX** None

EIN 25-1416510 **Year Created** 1981

AMV $87,595 **FYE** 11-00 **(Gifts Received** $1,000) 20 **Grants totaling** $23,264

Mostly local giving; all grants are unrestricted support. High grant of **$4,484** to Pittsburgh Public Theater. **$3,600** to Civic Light Opera. **$3,500** to Parental Stress Center. **$2,000** each to Little Sisters of the Poor and Providence Family Support Center. **$1,000-$1,050** each to ACLU Foundation of Pa., Planned Parenthood of Western Pa., and Point Park College. **$800** each to Pittsburgh Cultural Trust and Pittsburgh Symphony. Other smaller local and out-of-state contributions. ■**PUBLICATIONS:** None ■**WEBSITE:** None ■**E-MAIL:** None ■**APPLICATION POLICIES & PROCEDURES:** No grants awarded to individuals.

O+D+T John M. Feeney (P+S+F+Con) — Erin Feeney (D) — Patrick J. Feeney (D) — Terrance Feeney (D)

SW-112 **Fend (Jacob) Foundation, The**
551 Main Street, P.O. Box 98
Johnstown 15907 (Cambria County)

MI-12-13-22-43-55-84
Phone 814-532-3801 **FAX** 814-536-2278
EIN 25-1371934 **Year Created** 1978

AMV $0 **FYE** 12-00 **(Gifts Received** $46,543) 7 **Grants totaling** $45,063

All giving restricted to the Greater Johnstown Area for projects benefiting needy children. High grant of **$28,563** to Community Arts Center of Cambria County (mostly for mortgage on art education building for needy children). **$12,000** to St. Francis College (scholarships for needy children). **$1,000-$1,500** each, all for summer camp scholarships, to Boy Scouts/Penn Woods Council, Cambria City Mission, New Day, Inc., and Talus Rock Girl Scout Council. ■**PUBLICATIONS:** annual report; Rules & Regulations memorandum ■**WEBSITE:** None ■**E-MAIL:** None ■**APPLICATION POLICIES & PROCEDURES:** Only organizations in the Greater Johnstown Area which provide assistance, care, direction and support for needy children (3 to 18 years) may apply for special project funds. Educational organizations in the same area may request funding for the tuition expenses of students who quality as needy, as set forth by the institution requesting the funds. Submit requests in a letter in February, May or August; include a project description and budget, audited financial statement, and IRS tax-exempt status documentation. The Board awards grants at March, June, and September meetings.

O+D+T Laura L. Roth (S+F+D+Con) — John H. Anderson (C+D) — Carl J. Motter, Jr. (VC+D) — Martin Goldhaber (D) — Ethel J. Otrosina (D) — Charles S. Price (D) — Gerald W. Swatsworth (D)

SW-113 **Fenstermacher (Martha) Trust**
c/o PNC Advisors Service Center, P2-PTPP-05-1
Two PNC Plaza, 620 Liberty Ave., 5th Floor
Pittsburgh 15222 (Allegheny County)

MI-11-12-13-14-17-22-29-44-65-84

Phone 800-762-2272 **FAX** None
EIN 23-6249671 **Year Created** 1973

AMV $790,575 **FYE** 12-00 **(Gifts Received** $0) 8 **Grants totaling** $45,000

All giving is restricted to aiding poor/needy residents of Pottstown [Montgomery County; grants are for general support except as noted. High grants of **$7,000** each to Pottstown Area United Way Foundation (Court of Last Resort Program) and Salvation Army. **$6,000** each to ACLAMO, Developmental Enterprises Corp., and Women's Center of Montgomery County. **$5,000** each to Pottstown Cluster of Religious Communities and Pottstown Public Library (summer reading program). **$3,000** to Campership Panel/United Way (campership program). ■**PUBLICATIONS:** None ■**WEBSITE:** None ■**E-MAIL:** pncadvisors@pncbank.com ■ **APPLICATION POLICIES & PROCEDURES:** The Trust reports that only those agencies assisting poor/needy residents of Pottstown are eligible to apply; some preference is given to grantees named in the governing Will. Grant requests may be submitted in any form at any time.

O+D+T Brenda Harris (Trust Officer at Bank+Con) — PNC Advisors (Trustee)

SW-114 **Fetterolf Family Foundation**
Glen Mitchell Road
Sewickley 15143 (Allegheny County)

MI-11-12-13-16-17-22-25-35-41-51-63

Phone 412-741-8398 **FAX** None
EIN 25-1630949 **Year Created** 1990

AMV $715,816 **FYE** 12-00 **(Gifts Received** $92,326) 23 **Grants totaling** $34,200

Mostly local giving; all grants are for general support. High grant of **$10,000** to Eden Christian Academy. **$3,500** to The Pittsburgh Project. **$3,000** to Saltworks Theatre Company. **$1,000-$1,500** each to Bidwell Training Center, Church Army, East End Cooperative Ministry, FAME/Foundation for Advancement of Minorities through Education, Family Guidance, Inc., Focus on the Family, Light of Life Ministries, Greater Pittsburgh Community Food Bank, North Side Christian Health Center, United Way of Allegheny County, and Women's Center & Shelter of Greater Pittsburgh. Other smaller local contributions for similar purposes. **Out-of-state** grants: **$1,000** each to National Coalition for Protection of Children [OH] and World Vision [WA]. ■**PUBLICATIONS:** None ■**WEBSITE:** None ■**E-MAIL:** None ■**APPLICATION POLICIES & PROCEDURES:** Information not available.

O+D+T C. Frederick Fetterolf (P+Donor+Con) — Frances S. Fetterolf (VP) — Regan J. Fetterolf [Pittsburgh] (S+Donor) — Scott F. Fetterolf (F)

SW-115 **Fine Family Charitable Foundation, The**
c/o FFC Capital Corporation
Foster Plaza Ten, 680 Andersen Drive, 4th Floor
Pittsburgh 15220 (Allegheny County)

MI-22-25-34-41-52-56-62-71-82

Phone 412-937-3512 **FAX** None
EIN 25-6335329 **Year Created** 1996

AMV $774,717 **FYE** 6-00 **(Gifts Received** $362,422) 25 **Grants totaling** $391,256

Nearly half local giving. High grant of **$150,000** to United Jewish Federation of Greater Pittsburgh. **$8,334** to Jewish Education Institute (capital campaign). **$6,667** to Historical Society of Western Pa. (capital campaign). **$5,000** each to Greater Pittsburgh Community Food Bank (capital campaign), Pittsburgh Opera, and Pittsburgh Symphony. **$2,000** each to Jewish Community Center of the South Hills (capital campaign) and U. of Pittsburgh School of Medicine (Eugene Myers Chair). **Out-of-state** giving includes **$76,255** to Charities Aid Foundation [England]; **$28,000** to Solomon Schechter Day School [MA]; **$25,000** to Nature Conservancy of Maine; **$15,000** to Combined Jewish Philanthropies of Greater Boston; **$10,000** each to Jewish Fund for Justice [NY], Newton 2000 [MA], and Southeastern Massachusetts Wildlands Trust; and smaller grants, mostly to the Boston area. ■ **PUBLICATIONS:** None ■**WEBSITE:** None ■**E-MAIL:** None ■**APPLICATION POLICIES & PROCEDURES:** Grant requests in any form may be submitted at any time. — Formerly called Milton Fine Family Charitable Foundation.

O+D+T Milton Fine (P+S+F+D+Donor+Con) — David J. Fine (D) — Sheila Reicher Fine (D) — Carolyn Fine (D) — Sibyl Fine King (D)

SW-116 Finley (J.B.) Charitable Trust

Refer to PNC Advisors Charitable Trust Committee entry.

(Allegheny County)

MI-12-13-14-15-17-22-31-42-52-61-65-84

EIN 25-6024443 **Year Created** 1919

AMV $3,127,500 **FYE** 9-00 **(Gifts Received** $0) 20 **Grants totaling** $165,000

Mostly local giving for advancement of Christian religion, education and other charitable purposes; grants are for special projects except as noted. High grant of **$13,500** to Waynesburg College (summer day camp). **$12,000** each to Athletes in Action (pro athlete involvement), Center in the Woods (furnishings/equipment), Pittsburgh Jazz Society (scholarship fund), and Rock the World Youth (office equipment). **$11,250** to Christian Life Skills, Harvest Evangelism (program expansion), and Young Life. **$11,000** to Clelian Heights School for Exceptional Children (capital expenditure). **$10,000** to Somerset Hospital Foundation (capital expenditure). **$8,000** to Ronald McDonald House (capital expenditure). **$7,500** to Samaritan Counseling of Western Pa. **$5,000** each to Center Against Domestic & Sexual Violence (capital expenditure), Catholic Youth Assn. (general contribution), and Theotherapy Seminars (conflict resolution program). **$2,000-$2,789** each to Christian Camps of Pittsburgh (van), Conflict Resolution Center International (special project), and Sisters of Mercy of the Americas (special project). **$711** to Day Break Adult Day Care (new shop). **Out-of-state** grant: **$10,000** to Luther Rice Seminary [GA] (matching grant). ■**APPLICATION POLICIES & PROCEDURES:** Refer to the PNC Advisors Charitable Trust Committee entry for a statement on giving priorities and full application guidelines.

O+D+T Refer to PNC Advisors Charitable Trust Committee entry. — PNC Advisors (Trustee)

SW-117 FISA Foundation

1001 Liberty Ave., Suite 650

Pittsburgh 15222

(Allegheny County)

MI-14-17-35

Phone 412-456-5550 **FAX** 412-456-5551

EIN 25-0965388 **Year Created** 1996

AMV $38,400,376 **FYE** 6-01 **(Gifts Received** $11,020) 49 **Grants totaling** $1,557,330

All giving restricted to SW Pa. organizations serving persons with disabilities. High grant of **$250,000** to U. of Pittsburgh/School of Health & Rehabilitation Sciences (endowment of chair in Dept. of Rehabilitation Science & Technology). **$192,340** to Magee-Womens Hospital/UPMC Medical Center (study health needs of women with disabilities). **$100,000** to U. of Pittsburgh/Dept. of Physical Medicine & Rehabilitation (develop website on healthcare resources guide for women with disabilities). **$89,942** to RAND (analyze financing re healthcare for women with disabilities & disseminate results). **$68,497** to U. of Pittsburgh/Center for Injury Research & Control (evaluation/support for brain & spinal cord injury prevention program). **$60,000** to Life'sWork of Western Pa. (paid internships for students with disabilities). **$55,782** to Carlow College (collaborative pre-service training with Children's Institute of Pittsburgh). **$50,000** each to Center Against Domestic & Sexual Violence (office renovations), National MS Society (gynecologic screening program for women with MS), and Passavant Memorial Homes (training equipment for adults with MR). **$40,000** to Hope Network (recreational therapist salary support). **$35,000-$38,000** each to Mainstay Life Services (capital needs/development consulting), McGuire Memorial Foundation (residential beds replacement), The Program for Female Offenders (therapist salary support), U. of Pittsburgh Cancer Institute (breast cancer vaccine clinical trials), and YMCA Camps Kon-O-Wee & Spencer (nature trail for people with disabilities). **$25,000-$30,000** each to Emmaus Community of Pittsburgh (respite care program), Interfaith Hospitality Network (Homeless Families Program van), Lydia's Place (family reunification program for female offenders), Sto-Rox Family Health Center (perinatal nurse salary support), Three Rivers Center for Independent Living (headquarters capital campaign), Victim Outreach Intervention Center (mental health advocate salary). **$20,000** each to Domestic Abuse Counseling Center (expanded services), Every Child, Inc. (Children's Trust Fund), and North Hills Community Outreach (training/support for volunteers with disabilities). **$15,000** each to Pittsburgh CLO/Civic Light Opera (musical theatre training for people with disabilities), United Mitochondrial Disease Foundation (educational video), and Variety the Children's Charity (mobility equipment for children with disabilities). **$12,262** to North Side Christian Health Center (expanded Colposcopy Biopsy system). **$8,000-$10,000** each to Health Policy Institute (operating support), Lupus Foundation of America (educational awareness campaign), Southwinds (computers for supervisors), and YWCA of McKeesport (computer lab for homeless women). **$4,000-$5,500** each to Burger King Cancer Caring Center (breast cancer support group for African-American women), The Corporate Collection (health-wellness special in Women's Life Skills Center), Mon Valley Providers Council (vision screening program), National Council of Jewish Women (Komen Race for the Cure), Parental Stress Center (operating support), Tech-Link Program of Pittsburgh (student collaboration on robotics team), and Three Rivers Rowing Assn. (adaptive rowing equipment for people with disabilities). **$1,000-$2,500** each to organizations for an award, coalition memberships, event sponsorship, benefit table support, educational outreach, and special performances, all related to programs for persons with disabilities. ■**PUBLICATIONS:** Annual Report; Grant Application Guidelines booklet; Application Form ■**WEBSITE:** www.fisafoundation.org ■**E-MAIL:** lori@fisafoundation.org■**APPLICATION POLICIES & PROCEDURES:** The Foundation reports that giving is restricted to SW Pa. organizations addressing the following: (1) Quality of Life Issues for Adults and Children with Physical & Sensory Disabilities. Priority is given to organizations fostering inclusion and enabling people with disabilities (acquired or developmental) to reach their potential; these include head/spinal cord injury, hearing or visual impairment, mental retardation, and neurological diseases. Grants are made for disability prevention, employment programs, adaptive leisure activities, respite care programs, durable medical equipment, and other needs. (2) Health Needs of Women & Girls. Programs supported include domestic and sexual violence, homelessness, parenting, prenatal care, substance abuse, teen pregnancy, wellness, and diseases primarily affecting women. Also, the Foundation occasionally funds programs, initiatives or conferences which intersect the primary funding areas, as well as building funds and capital drives. No grants are awarded to individuals; organizations outside the 10-county SW Pa. region; political campaigns or lobbying; religious organizations for religious purposes; travel; study; scholarships; or organizations without 501(c)(3) status. Prospective applicants should first request a copy of the Grant Application Guidelines booklet with detailed guidelines and policies. In brief, grant requests may be submitted at any time in a two-step process: (1) Submit a formal Application Form, available from the Foundation, together with a Letter of Inquiry (2 pages maximum) which describes the project and its objectives; this will be acknowledged within two weeks. (2) If the Grant Review Committee determines the request falls within the Foundation's guidelines, the organization will be contacted to discuss its scope and specifications, and asked to submit a full proposal, preferably one that follows the Grantmakers of Western Pa. Common Grant Application Format (see www.gwpa.org). Site visits sometimes are made to organizations being considered for a grant. Final decisions on grants are made at Board meetings in February, June, and October. — Formerly called Federation of Independent School Alumnae

O+D+T M. Dee Delaney (Executive Director+Con) — Karen F. Dajani, Ph.D. (P+D) — Louise Ketchum (VP+D) — Patricia M. Duggan (S+D) — Molly Y. Sauereisen (F+D) — Ann W. Austin (D) — Lois Blaufeld (D) — Sheila F. Fisher (D) — Christine Fulton (D) — Carol K. Henderson (D) — Mary Ellen Leigh (D) — Angela Maher (D) — Hetsy McCoy (D) — Laura Meaden, Esq. (D) — Patti Michaud (D) — Amy Mindlin (D) — Connie Mockenhaupt (D) — Jane Owens, D.P.H. (D) — Laurel Roberts, Ph.D. (D) — Marcia B. Roque, Esq. (D) — Ellen Srodes (D) — Donor: Proceeds from sale of Harmarville Rehabilitation Center

---

SW-118 **Fisher (Audrey Hillman) Foundation, Inc., The**
2000 Grant Building
310 Grant Street
Pittsburgh 15219 (Allegheny County)
MI-12-13-14-17-31-32-41-42-51-52-54-55-57 63-71
Phone 412-338-3466 **FAX** 412-338-3463
EIN 25-1536655 **Year Created** 1986

AMV $8,558,295 **FYE** 12-00 **(Gifts Received** $0) 81 **Grants totaling** $315,250

Nearly half local giving; grants are unrestricted support or annual giving except as noted; some grants represent multiple awards. **$26,000** to City Theatre Company (anniversary gift). **$25,000** to The Ellis School (mostly faculty endowment). **$20,000** to Pittsburgh Parks Conservancy (benefit luncheon). **$15,000** to Women's Center & Shelter of Greater Pittsburgh (legal advocacy services/annual support). **$11,500** to Pittsburgh Cultural Trust (mostly for Carol Brown Recognition). **$10,000** each to Allegheny Valley School (capital campaign) and Shadyside Hospital Foundation (Hillman Cancer Center). **$6,000** to Carnegie Institute (partly for Warhol Museum). **$5,000** each to Phipps Conservatory & Botanical Gardens (capital campaign), Pittsburgh Symphony, U. of Pittsburgh Cancer Institute (research fund), and U. of Pittsburgh Medical Center. **$3,000-$3,500** each to Ladies Hospital Aid Society (gala for Hillman Cancer Center), Make-A-Wish Foundation of Western Pa., and WQED (Elsie Awards program). **$2,000-$2,500** each to Calvary Episcopal Church, Chatham College, Historical Society of Western Pa., Magee-Women's Health Foundation (neonatal research), Penn State U., and U. of Pittsburgh (Cameos of Caring). **$1,000-$1,500** each to Children's Home of Pittsburgh, Children's Institute (free care fund), Family House (renovations), Gateway Rehabilitation Center (benefit event), Light of Life Ministries, Parental Stress Center, PERSAD Center, Pittsburgh Concert Chorale (equipment), Pittsburgh Foundation (memorial scholarship fund), Pittsburgh Musical Theatre, Pittsburgh Public Theater, U. of Pittsburgh Dental School (memorial gift), Western Pa. School for Blind Children, and YWCA of Greater Pittsburgh (care programming). Other smaller local contributions for similar purposes. **Out-of-state** giving includes **$50,000** each to Holderness School [NH] (endowment) and Squam Lakes Natural Science Center [NH] (memorial gift); **$30,500** to Squam Lakes Assn.; **$26,000** to Lakes Region Conservation Trust [NH] (property purchase); and **$25,000** to Colgate U. [NY]. ■**PUBLICATIONS:** application guidelines ■**WEBSITE:** None ■**E-MAIL:** foundation@hillmanfo.com ■**APPLICATION POLICIES & PROCEDURES:** The Foundation reports that most grants are for annual giving, capital/renovation campaigns, operating support, program development, endowment, equipment, land acquisition, and seed money. No grants are awarded to individuals or organizations outside the U.S. Grant requests may be submitted at any time in a letter signed by a fully authorized official; describe/justify the program/project and its objectives, specify the amount of funding needed, and include an annual budget, list of officers/directors, detailed project cost information, a time schedule (if appropriate), other significant background information, and IRS tax-exempt status documentation. The Board meets in May and December.

O+D+T Ronald W. Wertz (S+D+Con) — Audrey Hillman Fisher (P+D+Donor) — Lawrence M. Wagner (VP+D) — Maurice J. White (F+D) — Lisa R. Johns (AF) — Donors: Henry L. Hillman Trust; Henry L. Hillman Charitable Lead Trust

---

SW-119 **Fisher (Justin Brooks) Foundation, Inc., The**
2000 Grant Building, 310 Grant Street
Pittsburgh 15219 (Allegheny County)
MI-22-25-31-32-35-41-42-63-71
Phone 412-338-3466 **FAX** 412-338-3463
EIN 25-1752992 **Year Created** 1995

AMV $1,196,437 **FYE** 12-00 **(Gifts Received** $0) 26 **Grants totaling** $62,000

Limited local giving; grants are unrestricted support or annual giving except as noted. High local grant of **$2,500** to Pittsburgh Parks Conservancy (benefit luncheon). **$2,000** to U. of Pittsburgh Cancer Institute (research fund). **$1,000** each to The Ellis School (Hillman Family Building) and Greater Pittsburgh Community Food Bank (table program). **$500** each to Northside Christian Health Center, Northside Common Ministries, and Pittsburgh Mercy Foundation (Operation Safety Net). **Out-of-state** giving includes **$11,000** to Squam Lakes Assn. [NH] (endowment); **$10,000** to Students of Human Ecology [VT]; and other smaller grants, mostly to NH, VT, and CO. ■**PUBLICATIONS:** None ■**WEBSITE:** None ■**E-MAIL:** foundation@hillmanfo.com ■**APPLICATION POLICIES & PROCEDURES:** No grants are awarded to individuals or to organizations outside the U.S. Grant requests may be submitted at any time in a letter signed by a fully authorized official; describe/justify the program/project and its objectives, specify the amount of funding needed, and include an annual budget, list of officers/directors, detailed project cost information, a time schedule (if appropriate), other significant background information, and IRS tax-exempt status documentation. The Board meets in May and December.

O+D+T Ronald W. Wertz (S+D+Con) — Justin Brooks Fisher (P+D) — Lawrence M. Wagner (VP+D) — Maurice J. White (F+D) — Audrey Hillman Fisher (D) — Lisa R. Johns (AF) — Donor: Henry L. Hillman Trust

---

SW-120 **Fisher (Lilah Hilliard) Foundation Inc., The**
2000 Grant Building, 310 Grant Street
Pittsburgh 15219 (Allegheny County)
MI-12-13-14-17-32-35-41-51-55-71
Phone 412-338-3466 **FAX** 412-338-3463
EIN 25-1752994 **Year Created** 1995

AMV $1,192,231 **FYE** 12-00 **(Gifts Received** $0) 37 **Grants totaling** $70,000

About two-thirds local giving; grants are unrestricted support or annual giving except as noted. High local grant of **$6,000** to The Ellis School (Hillman Family Building/annual fund). **$5,000** to Pittsburgh Public Schools (antismoking curriculum/programs).

$3,000 to Variety Club of Pittsburgh (children's program equipment) and Women's Center & Shelter of Western Pa. (legal advocacy services). **$2,000-$2,500** each to Pittsburgh Parks Conservancy (benefit luncheon), Prime Stage (school programs), U. of Pittsburgh Cancer Center (memorial gift), and YouthWorks (job creation program). **$1,000-$1,500** each to Big Brothers/Big Sisters of Greater Pittsburgh (mentoring programs), Center for Creative Play (programs), Early Learning Institute (playground improvements), Gateway to the Arts (arts in education program), Mattress Factory (education programs), Pittsburgh Musical Theatre (productions/programs), St. Mary's Lawrenceville Arts Program (school arts programs), Ronald McDonald House Charities of Pittsburgh (Share-a-Night program), Spina Bifida Assn. of Western Pa. (weekend retreats), and The Worksmith Institute (job market training for low-income women). Other smaller local contributions for similar purposes. **Out-of-state** giving includes **$11,000** to Squam Lakes Assn. [NH] (capital campaign); **$5,000** to Lakes Region Conservation Trust [NH] (land purchase); and smaller grants to NH, MA and NY. ■**PUBLICATIONS:** None ■**WEBSITE:** None ■**E-MAIL:** foundation@hillmanfo.com ■**APPLICATION POLICIES & PROCEDURES:** No grants are awarded to individuals or to organizations outside the U.S. Grant requests may be submitted at any time in a letter signed by a fully authorized official; describe/justify the program/project and its objectives, specify the amount of funding needed, and include an annual budget, list of officers/directors, detailed project cost information, a time schedule (if appropriate), other significant background information, and IRS tax-exempt status documentation. The Board meets in May and December.

O+D+T Ronald W. Wertz (S+D+Con) — Lilah H. Fisher (P+D) — Lawrence M. Wagner (VP+D) — Maurice J. White (F+D) — Audrey Hillman Fisher (D) — Lisa R. Johns (AF) — Donor: Henry L. Hillman Trust

---

SW-121 Fisher (Matthew Hillman) Foundation, Inc., The
2000 Grant Building, 310 Grant Street
Pittsburgh 15219   (Allegheny County)
AMV $1,197,894   **FYE** 12-00   (**Gifts Received** $0)

MI-13-31-32-41-51-52-55-57-71
Phone 412-338-3466 **FAX** 412-338-3463
EIN 25-1752985   **Year Created** 1995
34 **Grants totaling** $59,000

About one-third local giving; grants are for general support/annual giving except as noted. High local grant of **$2,500** to Pittsburgh Parks Conservancy (benefit luncheon). **$2,000** each to Shadyside Hospital Foundation, St. Mary's Lawrenceville Arts Program (after school/summer programs), and Youthworks (employment opportunities for at-risk youth). **$1,000-$1,500** each to City Theatre Company, Gateway to the Arts (arts-in-education program), Pittsburgh Foundation (scholarship fund), Pittsburgh Musical Theater, Prime Stage (educational programs), Saltworks Theatre Company (programs), St. Edmund's Academy, U. of Pittsburgh Cancer Institute, and WQED. **Out-of-state** giving includes **$11,000** to Squam Lakes Assn. [NH] (endowment); **$5,000** to Lakes Region Conservation Trust [NH] (property purchase); and **$3,000** each to Adirondacks Theatre Festival [NY] (writers residency program), The Field [NY] (fairy tale festival), and Boys Harbor [NY] (music class teachers). ■**PUBLICATIONS:** None ■**WEBSITE:** None ■**E-MAIL:** foundation@hillmanfo.com ■**APPLICATION POLICIES & PROCEDURES:** No grants are awarded to individuals or to organizations outside the U.S. Grant requests may be submitted at any time in a letter signed by a fully authorized official; describe/justify the program/project and its objectives, specify the amount of funding needed, and include an annual budget, list of officers/directors, detailed project cost information, a time schedule (if appropriate), other significant background information, and IRS tax-exempt status documentation. The Board meets in May and December.

O+D+T Ronald W. Wertz (S+D+Con) — Matthew H. Fisher (P+D) — Lawrence M. Wagner (VP+D) — Maurice J. White (F+D) — Audrey Hillman Fisher (D) — Lisa R. Johns (AF) — Donor: Henry L. Hillman Trust

---

SW-122 Fisher (Nina Baldwin) Foundation Inc., The
2000 Grant Building, 310 Grant Street
Pittsburgh 15219   (Allegheny County)
AMV $1,197,630   **FYE** 12-00   (**Gifts Received** $0)

MI-12-13-14-17-22-25-31-41-71
Phone 412-338-3466 **FAX** 412-338-3463
EIN 25-1752991   **Year Created** 1994
39 **Grants totaling** $56,000

About three-fourths local/Pa. giving; grants are unrestricted support/annual giving except as noted. High local grant of **$5,000** to Pittsburgh Public Schools (teacher training for children with exceptionalities). **$3,500** to Riverview Children's Center (facility improvements). **$2,000-$2,500** each to Legal Aid for Children (services to abused/neglected children), Northside Common Ministries (community food pantry), Pittsburgh Parks Conservancy (benefit luncheon), and Variety Club of Pittsburgh (children's program equipment). **$1,000-$1,500** each to A Second Chance, Center for Creative Play (special needs children programs), Children's Home of Pittsburgh (special campaign), Children's Hospital of Pittsburgh (free care fund), Children's Institute (pediatric free care fund), Early Learning Institute (playground improvements), The Ellis School, KidsPeace National Centers for Kids Overcoming Crisis [Lehigh County], Greater Pittsburgh Community Food Bank, Hosanna Industries (home repair program), Pittsburgh Mercy Foundation (Operation Safety Net), Shadyside Hospital Foundation, The Whale's Tale/FamilyLink (emergency shelter/counseling), Women's Center & Shelter of Greater Pittsburgh, and YWCA of Greater Pittsburgh. Other local contributions **$500** each for similar purposes. **Out-of-state** giving includes **$11,000** to Squam Lakes Assn. [NH] (endowment) and **$5,000** to Lakes Region Conservation Trust [NH] (property purchase). ■**PUBLICATIONS:** None ■**WEBSITE:** None ■**E-MAIL:** foundation@hillmanfo.com ■**APPLICATION POLICIES & PROCEDURES:** No grants are awarded to individuals or to organizations outside the U.S. Grant requests may be submitted at any time in a letter signed by a fully authorized official; describe/justify the program/project and its objectives, specify the amount of funding needed, and include an annual budget, list of officers/directors, detailed project cost information, a time schedule (if appropriate), other significant background information, and IRS tax-exempt status documentation. The Board meets in May and December.

O+D+T Ronald W. Wertz (S+D+Con) — Nina Baldwin Fisher (P+D) — Lawrence M. Wagner (P+D) — Maurice J. White (VP+D) — Audrey Hillman Fisher (D) — Lisa R. Johns (AF) — Donor: Henry L. Hillman Trust

SW-123 Fisher-Hess Foundation
3003 North Mercer Street Extension
New Castle 16105   (Lawrence County)

MI-22-51-52-55-62
Phone 724-658-3335 **FAX** None
EIN 25-1267981   **Year Created** 1976

AMV $144,804   **FYE** 12-00   **(Gifts Received** $0)   21 **Grants totaling** $32,100

Limited local/Pa. giving. High Pa. grants of **$1,000** each to New Castle Community YMCA and U. of Pa. **$800** to Temple Hadar Israel. **$500** to New Castle Playhouse (endowment fund). Other smaller local contributions. **Out-of-state** giving includes **$15,000** to Jewish Federation of Palm Beach [FL]; **$5,150** to Kravis Center for Performing Arts [FL]; and other smaller grants/contributions. ■**PUBLICATIONS:** None ■**WEBSITE:** None ■**E-MAIL:** None ■**APPLICATION POLICIES & PROCEDURES:** Written grant requests in any form may be submitted at any time; describe the proposed use funds.

O+D+T Marianne Hess (P+Donor+Con) — Marshall Hess (VP) — First Western Trust Services Co. (Trustee)

SW-124 Foster Charitable Trust
c/o Foster Industries, Inc.
681 Anderson Drive, Suite 300
Pittsburgh 15220   (Allegheny County)

MI-11-18-22-31-32-41-42-44-51-52-54-55-62
71-72-84
Phone 412-928-8900 **FAX** None
EIN 25-6064791   **Year Created** 1962

AMV $4,840,761   **FYE** 12-00   **(Gifts Received** $0)   71 **Grants totaling** $413,940

About two-thirds local giving. High grant of **$50,000** to United Jewish Federation of Greater Pittsburgh. **$48,240** to YMCA Camp Kon-O-Kwee/Spencer [Beaver County]. **$38,500** to Congregation Rodef Shalom. **$29,000** to Society for Contemporary Crafts. **$21,000** to United Way of Allegheny County. **$12,000** to Carnegie Museum of Art. **$10,000** each to American Jewish Committee and Congregation Beth Shalom. **$7,000** to Tree of Life Congregation. **$6,000** to Jewish National Fund. **$5,000** each to Hillel Jewish U. Center of Pittsburgh and Jewish Education Institute. **$3,000-$3,500** each to The Ellis School, Pittsburgh Cultural Trust, Rodef, and U. of Pittsburgh Cancer Institute. **$2,500** to Pittsburgh Symphony. **$2,000** to Planned Parenthood of Western Pa. **$1,000-$1,875** each to Alzheimer Disease Research Center, American Cancer Society, Children's Hospital of Pittsburgh, Green Tree Public Library, Magee-Women's Health Foundation, Mattress Factory, Persad Center, Pittsburgh Opera, Pittsburgh Public Theater, Pittsburgh Zoo, Shady Side Academy, and Western Pa. Conservancy. **Out-of-state** giving includes **$36,000** to Temple Jeremiah [IL]; **$20,000** to Trinity College [CT]; **$12,000** to Sarasota-Manatee Jewish Federation [FL]; **$10,000** to Museum of Modern Art [NY]; **$5,000** to Lyric Opera of Chicago [IL]; and other smaller grants for similar purposes to the Chicago area, southern CA, FL, and NY. ■**PUBLICATIONS:** None ■**WEBSITE:** None ■**E-MAIL:** None ■**APPLICATION POLICIES & PROCEDURES:** No grants are awarded for endowment or to individuals. Grants requests (typewritten) may be submitted at any time in any form; provide information on the organization, describe the intended purpose of the requested funds and include IRS tax-exempt status documentation. The Trustees meet as necessary.

O+D+T Bernard S. Mars (T+Con) — Penny F. Alpern (T) — James R. Foster [IL] (T) — Lee B. Foster, II (T) — Peter F. Mars (T) — Kim Petracca [IL] (T) — Corporate donors: Foster Industries, Inc.; Fostin Securities, Inc. [DE]

SW-125 Fountainhead Foundation
c/o Abarta, Inc.
1000 RIDC Plaza, Suite 404
Pittsburgh 15238   (Allegheny County)

MI-13-15-32-41-63
Phone 412-963-3163 **FAX** None
EIN 25-1605441   **Year Created** 1989

AMV $156,081   **FYE** 12-00   **(Gifts Received** $90,500)   5 **Grants totaling** $15,350

About one-third local giving. High Pa. grant of **$3,000** to Arthritis Foundation of Western Pa. **$850** to Fox Chapel Episcopal Church. **$500** to Big Brothers & Big Sisters of Greater Pittsburgh. **Out-of-state** grants: **$10,000** to Grace Episcopal Church of Windsor [CT] and **$1,000** to Pine Cay Project [OH]. — In the prior year Pa. grants included **$24,000** to Arthritis Foundation of Western Pa.; **$15,000** each to Vintage, Inc. and Swain School [Lehigh County]; and **$5,000** to Shady Side Academy (Middle School). ■**PUBLICATIONS:** application guidelines ■**WEBSITE:** None ■**E-MAIL:** None ■**APPLICATION POLICIES & PROCEDURES:** Application guidelines are available on request. No grants awarded to individuals.

O+D+T Charles W. Bitzer (P+Con) — Michelle R. Bitzer (VP+S) — Astrid S. Bitzer (F) — Henrietta G. Lelis (AS) — Corporate donor: Abarta, Inc.

SW-126 Frazer Family Foundation, The
c/o Lowe, Blackburn Road, P.O. Box 372
Sewickley 15143   (Allegheny County)

MI-11-18-31-35-54-63-71
Phone 412-471-3042 **FAX** None
EIN 25-6479935   **Year Created** 1994

AMV $374,608   **FYE** 12-00   **(Gifts Received** $0)   25 **Grants totaling** $17,800

About two-thirds local giving; grants are for general support except as noted. High grant of **$5,000** to West Penn Hospital Foundation (education center). **$1,000** to Phipps Conservancy and Western Pa. Nature Conservancy. **$500** each to Frick Art & Historical Center, Planned Parenthood of Western Pa., Trinity Cathedral, and United Way of SW Pa. Other smaller contributions for various purposes. **Out-of-state** giving to MT and VA where trustees reside. ■**PUBLICATIONS:** None ■**WEBSITE:** None ■**E-MAIL:** None ■**APPLICATION POLICIES & PROCEDURES:** The Foundation reports that giving focuses on family planning, libraries/literacy, and conservation/ecology, but that unsolicited requests are not accepted.

O+D+T Eliza H. Frazer [MT] (T+Con) — Barbara R. Franks [VA] (T) — Barbara Frazer Lowe (T+Donor)

SW-127   Freeport Brick Company Charitable Trust, The
c/o Freeport Brick Company
P.O. Box F
Freeport   16229   (Armstrong County)

MI-11-13-15-44-71-84-89

Phone 725-295-2111 **FAX** None
EIN 25-6074334   **Year Created** 1964

AMV $695,443   **FYE** 12-00   (**Gifts Received** $0)   9 **Grants totaling** $33,000

All local giving. High grant of **$27,000** to Freeport Community Park Corp. **$1,000** each to Freeport Area Library Assn. (endowment), Freeport Area Meals on Wheels, Freeport Volunteer Fire Dept., and Pa. State Police Camp Cadet. **$500** each to Boy Scouts, Pittsburgh Youth Golf Foundation, South Buffalo Volunteer Fire Dept., and United Way of Armstrong County. ■**PUBLICATIONS:** None ■**WEBSITE:** None ■**E-MAIL:** None ■**APPLICATION POLICIES & PROCEDURES:** The Trust reports that preference is given to organizations near corporate facilities in Freeport and Kittanning, and to local chapters of national charities. Submit grant requests in a letter early in the year; describe the project and amount of funding requested.
O+D+T   Francis H. Laube, III (S+T+Con) — Donald P. Thiry [Apollo] (C+T) — J.C. Overholt (VC+T) — J. Terry Medovitch [Sarver] (F+T) — Harry R. Laube [Meadville] (AS+AF+T) — Corporate donor: Freeport Brick Company

---

SW-128   Frick (Helen Clay) Foundation, The
c/o Mellon Private Wealth Management
525 William Penn Way, Room 4000
Pittsburgh   15259   (Allegheny County)

MI-41-42-54-56-71

Phone 412-234-5784 **FAX** 412-234-1073
EIN 25-6018983   **Year Created** 1947

AMV $29,306,760   **FYE** 12-00   (**Gifts Received** $0)   65+ **Grants totaling** $943,719

Limited local/Pa. giving. High Pa. grant of **$60,000** to Westmoreland Fayette Historical Society.**$35,000** to West Overton Museums [Scottsdale]. **$30,000** to U. of Pa. **$10,000** to Pittsburgh Parks Conservancy. **Out-of-state** giving, largely where Trustees reside, includes high grant of **$150,000** to the Frick Collection [NY] (preservation of Frick family archives); **$50,000** each to American Museum of Natural History [NY], The Frick Collection [NY], Gonzaga Eastern Point Retreat House [MA], Old Westbury Gardens [NY], and University Preparatory Academy [WA]; **$25,000** each to Nature Conservancy of Alaska, Telluride Society for the Performing Arts [CO], and Fauquier & Loudoun Garden Club [VA]; and other grants **$2,000-$20,000** to AZ, CA, DC, GA, ID, NH, NY, MD, ME, MT, OH, VA, mostly for preparatory schools, environmental or conservation organizations, and art/musical purposes. ■**PUBLICATIONS:** None ■**WEBSITE:** None ■**E-MAIL:** robinson.bk@mellon.com ■**APPLICATION POLICIES & PROCEDURES:** The Foundation reports that priority is given to arts/cultural organizations in Pittsburgh and New York and grant requests must be sponsored by a Trustee. Most giving for annual/operating support, special projects, capital campaigns, or publications. No grants are awarded to individuals. The Trustees meet in January, May, September and November.
O+D+T   Barbara K. Robinson (First VP at Bank+Con) — I. Townsend Burden, III [DC] (VC+T) — Peter P. Blanchard, III [NY] (T) — Dixon Frick Burden [CO] (T) — Frances D. Burden, [MA] (T) — Helen Clay Chace [NY] (T) — Arabelle S. Dane [NH] (T) — Emily T. Frick [NJ] (T) — H. Clay Frick, III [AK] (T) — J. Fife Symington, III [AZ] (T) — Adelaide Frick Trafton [ME] (T) — Mellon Bank N.A. (Corporate Trustee)

SW-129   Friend (Kennedy T.) Educational Fund
c/o PNC Advisors, M.S. P2-PTPP-25-1
Two PNC Plaza, 620 Liberty Ave.
Pittsburgh   15222   (Allegheny County)

MI-43

Phone 412-762-3390 **FAX** 412-762-5439
EIN 25-6026198   **Year Created** 1929

AMV $7,230,365   **FYE** 12-00   (**Gifts Received** $0)   1 **Grant of** $122,713

Sole grant to Yale U. [CT] for scholarships for students qualifying under the selection criteria below. — In prior years, scholarships to attend U. of Paris [France] have also been awarded. ■**PUBLICATIONS:** None ■**WEBSITE:** None ■**E-MAIL:** None ■**APPLICATION POLICIES & PROCEDURES:** Only children of lawyers practicing in Allegheny County (must have principal office in the county) are eligible to apply for scholarships to attend either Yale U. [CT] or the University of Paris [France]. Prospective applicants initially should make a telephone inquiry about the feasibility of submitting a request. A formal application form, available from the Bank, should be submitted during January-April; the deadline is May 1st and awards made at a June meeting.
O+D+T   John D. Culbertson (VP at Bank+Con) — James Darby (Co-T) — President, Allegheny County Bar Assn. (Co-T) — President, Yale Club of Pittsburgh (Co-T) — PNC Advisors (Co-Trustee)

SW-130   Froelich (Dorothy M.) Charitable Trust
8041 Brittany Place
Pittsburgh   15237   (Allegheny County)

MI-42-52

Phone 412-635-6550 **FAX** None
EIN 25-6507209   **Year Created** 1995

AMV $515,551   **FYE** 6-01   (**Gifts Received** $0)   4 **Grants totaling** $25,250

Limited local giving. **$2,800** to Pittsburgh Opera. **$1,000** to Pittsburgh Concert Society. **$300** to Mendelssohn Choir of Pittsburgh. **Out-of-state** grant: **$21,150** to Metropolitan Opera [NY]. — In prior years local giving included **$10,000** to Duquesne U. and **$1,000** to Carnegie Mellon U./School of Music. ■**PUBLICATIONS:** None ■**WEBSITE:** None ■**E-MAIL:** None ■**APPLICATION POLICIES & PROCEDURES:** Information not available.
O+D+T   Ross F. Dacal (T+Con) — Donor: Estate of Dorothy M. Froelich

---

SW-131   Fugh (Clarence S. & Margaret F.) Foundation
c/o National City Bank of Pa. - Loc. 25-162
National City Center, 20 Stanwix Street, 16th Floor
Pittsburgh   15222   (Allegheny County)

MI-13-22-25-29-39-41-43-63-89

Phone 412-644-8002 **FAX** 412-261-6252
EIN 25-6062524   **Year Created** 1966

AMV $3,517,771   **FYE** 6-01   (**Gifts Received** $0)   14 **Grants totaling** $130,760

All local giving; grants are for general support except as noted. High grant of **$39,000** to Etna Borough. **$20,000** each to Fox Chapel Area Excellence for Education Fund (scholarships) and Shaler Area School District (scholarships). **$19,250** to Sharpsburg

Borough. **$7,500** to Aspinwall Borough. **$5,000** each to All of Us Care and First Evangelical Lutheran Church of Pittsburgh. **$2,000-$2,500** each to Bread of Life Food Pantry, Northern Area Multi-Service Center, Northern Area Boys & Girls Club, North Hills Community Outreach, and St. Vincent DePaul Society. ■**PUBLICATIONS:** None ■**WEBSITE:** None ■**E-MAIL:** joanna.mayo@nationalcity.com ■**APPLICATION POLICIES & PROCEDURES:** The Foundation reports that giving is limited to local charities, particularly in Etna & Sharpsburg, Pa. Prospective applicants initially should make a telephone inquiry about the feasibility of submitting a request. Grant requests may be submitted in a letter in November-December; state the purpose of the requested funds and include IRS tax-exempt status documentation. Grants are awarded at a January meeting.

O+D+T Joanna M. Mayo (VP at Bank+Con) — Lee A. Donaldson, Jr. Esq. (Co-T) — National City Bank of Pa. (Co-Trustee)

SW-132 **Gabriel (Arthur & Millicent) Family Trust, The**
132 Heritage Hills Road
Uniontown 15401 (Fayette County)
AMV $224,003 **FYE** 12-00 **(Gifts Received** $0)

MI-63
Phone 724-437-2731 **FAX** None
EIN 23-7895352 **Year Created** 1997
1 **Grant of** $40,000

Sole grant to Eparchy of St. Maron of Brooklyn [NY] (Maronite Church). ■**PUBLICATIONS:** None ■**WEBSITE:** None ■**E-MAIL:** None ■**APPLICATION POLICIES & PROCEDURES:** Grant requests may be submitted in a letter at any time.

O+D+T Arthur Gabriel, Sr. (T+Donor+Con) — Arthur Gabriel, Jr. [Washington] (T) — Ronald Gabriel (T) — Millicent Gabriel (Donor)

SW-133 **Gailliot Family Foundation**
5734 West Woodland Road
Pittsburgh 15232 (Allegheny County)
AMV $606,586 **FYE** 12-00 **(Gifts Received** $0)

MI-22-42-54-51-52-56-61-71
Phone 412-521-2570 **FAX** None
EIN 25-1754605 **Year Created** 1994
10 **Grants totaling** $30,500

Mostly local giving. High grants of **$5,000** each to Horticultural Society of Western Pa. (botanic garden), Pittsburgh Children's Museum, and Pittsburgh History & Landmarks Foundation. **$3,000** to Bethlehem Haven of Pittsburgh. **$2,000-$2,500** each to Franciscan Friars, The Oratory, Pittsburgh Civic Garden Center, and Pittsburgh Opera Theater. **$1,500** to U. of Pittsburgh/School of Library & Information Science. ■**PUBLICATIONS:** None ■**WEBSITE:** None ■**E-MAIL:** None ■**APPLICATION POLICIES & PROCEDURES:** The Foundation reports that giving is generally but not exclusively to the Pittsburgh area. Grant requests may be submitted in a letter (2 pages maximum) at any time.

O+D+T Henry J. Gailliot (T+Donor+Con) — Anne L. Gailliot (T) — Charles H. Gailliot (T) — Mary Louise Gailliot (T+Donor) — Peter C. Gailliot (T)

SW-134 **Gailliot Foundation, The**
5734 West Woodland Road
Pittsburgh 15232 (Allegheny County)
AMV $2,912,510 **FYE** 12-00 **(Gifts Received** $2,803,135)

MI-Not Reported
Phone 412-261-6470 **FAX** None
EIN 25-1754605 **Year Created** 2000
Grants totaling $0

No grants awarded during the Foundation's first year of operation. ■**PUBLICATIONS:** None ■**WEBSITE:** None ■**E-MAIL:** None ■**APPLICATION POLICIES & PROCEDURES:** Information not available.

O+D+T Henry J. Gailliot (T+Donor+Con) — W. Lee Hoskins [NV] (T) — Allan H. Meltzer (T)

SW-135 **Ganassi Foundation**
c/o FRG Group
1000 RIDC Plaza, Suite 106
Pittsburgh 15238 (Allegheny County)
AMV $335,568 **FYE** 11-00 **(Gifts Received** $0)

MI-12-22-43-54-63
Phone 412-967-5600 **FAX** 412-967-5607
EIN 25-1591687 **Year Created** 1988
7 **Grants totaling** $16,235

All local giving; grants are for general support except as noted. High grant of **$10,000** to Alexis deToqueville Society (scholarship endowment). **$2,500** to Family House (capital campaign). **$1,000** each to Fox Chapel Presbyterian Church and Sisters of Charity. Other smaller local contributions for various purposes. — Giving in the prior year include **$5,000** each to Duquesne U. (scholarship endowment) and U. of Pittsburgh/Katz School of Business (scholarships endowment). ■**PUBLICATIONS:** None ■**WEBSITE:** None ■**E-MAIL:** None ■**APPLICATION POLICIES & PROCEDURES:** The Foundation reports that all giving is limited to local organizations. No grants are awarded to individuals. Grant requests may be submitted in any form during September-October; include IRS tax-exempt status documentation. Site visits sometimes are to organizations being considered for a grant. Grants are awarded at a November meeting.

O+D+T Annette D. Ganassi (P+T+Con) — Floyd R. Ganassi [Pittsburgh] (T+Donor) — Edward W. Seifert [Pittsburgh] (T) — Manor Asset Corporation (Trustee)

SW-136 **Gander (Helen Forde) & Mary A. Baldwin Trust**
c/o Aufman Associates, Inc.
2200 Georgetown Drive, Suite 401
Sewickley 15143 (Allegheny County)
AMV $1,117,108 **FYE** 12-00 **(Gifts Received** $0)

MI-12-13-14-41-56-72
Phone 724-934-5600 **FAX** None
EIN 25-6405906 **Year Created** 1993
2 **Grants totaling** $51,000

One Pa. grant: **$48,000** to Sewickley Academy (capital campaign). **Out-of-state** grant: **$5,000** to Guide Dog Foundation for the Blind [NY] (dog sponsorship program). — Giving in prior years included **$54,000** to Sewickley Academy (capital campaign); and **$6,000-$8,500** each to Animal Friends, Inc. (birth control program), Historical Society of Western Pa. (general support), Ligonier Valley YMCA (equipment/supplies), Pa. Special Olympics (program underwriting), and Ronald McDonald House Charities (secret garden). ■**PUBLICATIONS:** None ■**WEBSITE:** None ■**E-MAIL:** None ■**APPLICATION POLICIES & PROCEDURES:** No grants awarded to individuals.

O+D+T Edward J. Aufman (T+Con)

SW-137 **Giant Eagle Foundation**
    c/o Giant Eagle Markets, Inc.
    101 Kappa Drive
    Pittsburgh 15238   (Allegheny County)

MI-12-13-14-17-19-22-25-29-31-32-41-42-43
44-51-52-54-55-56-62-71-72-81-86
Phone 412-963-6200 **FAX** None
EIN 25-6033905   **Year Created** 1955

AMV $19,482,390   **FYE** 8-00   (**Gifts Received** $3,887,036)   290 **Grants totaling** $2,624,913

Mostly local/Western Pa. giving; some grants are payments on multiyear pledges. High grant of **$1,000,500** to United Jewish Federation of Greater Pittsburgh. **$190,000** to Carnegie Mellon U. **$72,000** to United Way of Allegheny County (Early Childhood Initiative). **$41,000** to U. of Pittsburgh. **$35,000** to Pittsburgh Symphony. **$32,250** to Allegheny Conference on Community Development. **$25,000-$26,666** each to Community Day School, Education & Policy Issues Center, Extra Mile Education Foundation, Hillel Academy of Pittsburgh, Jewish National Fund, Pittsburgh Cultural Trust, Pittsburgh Zoo, and Yeshiva Schools. **$20,000-$22,500** each to B'nai B'rith Hillel Foundation, Pittsburgh Public Theater, and Pittsburgh Regional Alliance. **$15,000-$15,833** each to Jewish Community Center of Pittsburgh, Kollel Bais Yitzchok, Magee Women's Health Foundation, Pittsburgh AIDS Task Force, Pittsburgh Ballet Theatre, and Pittsburgh Opera. **$12,000** to YWCA of Greater Pittsburgh. **$10,000-$10,250** each to American Cancer Society, B'nai Zion, Carnegie Museums of Pittsburgh, Crohn's & Colitis Foundation, Foundation for the Rehabilitation of Prisoners, Greater Pittsburgh Community Food Bank, Persad Center, P.O.W.E.R., and Tides Center. **$8,000-$9,400** each to Carnegie Library of Pittsburgh, Pittsburgh Dance Council, River City Brass Band, Seton Hill College, and Technology Development. **$7,500-$7,600** each to City Theatre Company, National Council of Jewish Women, Pa. Economy League, and U. of Pittsburgh Cancer Institute. **$6,000-$6,666** each to Conservation Consultants, UCP of Pittsburgh, and Vintage. **$5,000** each to Audubon Society of Western Pa., D.T. Watson Institute, Family House, Gannon U., Gateway Rehabilitation Center, Historical Society of Western Pa., Horticultural Society of Western Pa., Interfaith Volunteer Caregivers, International Assistance Group, Jewish Residential Services, Leukemia & Lymphoma Society, Manchester Youth Development Center, The Mattress Factory, National Aviary in Pittsburgh, Outreach Teen & Family Services, Pittsburgh Action Against Rape, Pittsburgh Center for the Arts, Pittsburgh Children's Museum, Pittsburgh Civic Light Opera, Radio Information Service, Shady Lane School, Whale's Tale Foundation/FamilyLink, and Women's Shelter & Rape Crisis Center. **$4,000** each to Artists & Cities, Bethlehem Haven and Carlow College. **$3,000-$3,333** each to Anti-Defamation League, ARC-Allegheny Foundation, Hill House Assn., Ladies Hospital Aid Society, National Conference for Community & Justice, NEED/Negro Education Emergency Drive, Robert Morris College, and U. of Pittsburgh Medical Center. **$2,000-$2,500** each to American Parkinson Disease Foundation, Big Brothers & Big Sisters of Greater Pittsburgh, Bradley Center, Easter Seals, Friends of the New Park, Goodwill Industries of Pittsburgh, Hunger Services Network, Leadership Pittsburgh, United Negro College Fund, United Way of Lawrence County, and WQED. Other Western Pa. grants/contributions **$500-$1,500** for various purposes. Also, 44 scholarships of **$1,000** each awarded to dependents of company employees. **Out-of-state** giving, mostly to OH except as noted includes **$50,000** to American Pardes Foundation [NY]; **$20,000** to Catholic Diocese of Cleveland; **$15,000** to MetroHealth Foundation; **$12,500** to Make-A-Wish Foundation of Cleveland, **$10,000** each to Case Western Reserve U., Cleveland Museum of Art, Cleveland Orchestra, St. Malachi Center, Urban Community School and YWCA of Cleveland; and many other smaller grants/contributions for similar purposes. ■**PUBLICATIONS:** None ■**WEBSITE:** None ■**E-MAIL:** None ■**APPLICATION POLICIES & PROCEDURES:** Grant requests in any form may be submitted at any time. Scholarships are restricted to dependents of company employees. — Formerly called Beacon Foundation.

O+D+T Charles Porter (Con) — Gerald Chait — Edward Moravitz — Donald S. Plung, CPA — David S. Shapira — Norman Weizenbaum — Corporate donor: Giant Eagle Markets

---

SW-138 **Gibson (Addison H.) Foundation**
    One PPG Place, Suite 2230
    Pittsburgh 15222   (Allegheny County)

MI-23-43
Phone 412-261-1611 **FAX** 412-261-5733
EIN 25-0965379   **Year Created** 1936

AMV $29,326,754   **FYE** 12-01   (**Gifts Received** $13,106)   256 **Grants totaling** $1,720,092

All giving to Western Pa. for two specific purposes: (1) Medical Assistance payments totaling **$818,447** to health service providers on behalf of 92 Western Pa. residents with correctable dental/medical/surgical problems, but unable to pay for treatment; and (2) Educational loans totaling **$901,645** for 164 college/university students—all residents of Western Pa.—who had completed at least one year in good academic standing at an accredited institution. ■**PUBLICATIONS:** brochures on the Medical Trust and Education Trust; application forms ■**WEBSITE:** www.gibson-fnd.org ■**E-MAIL:** rwallace@gibson-fnd.org -or- ldunbar@gibson-fnd.org ■**APPLICATION POLICIES & PROCEDURES:** The Foundation reports that only Western Pa. residents are eligible to apply for grants/loans. No support is awarded for building funds, endowments, operating budgets, or special projects, and no medical funds are available for programs, projects, or capital needs. *Medical Assistance Applicant Guidelines:* Individuals must be referred by one's attending physician or social service agent, and must have correctable medical problems, be uninsured, and unable to pay for them. *Student Loan Applicant Guidelines:* Loans are available to Western Pa. students who have completed at least one year of undergraduate or graduate studies; first year students are ineligible. Eligibility criteria include character, reputation, moral responsibility, academic record, personality, and the likelihood that support will lead to making one a more useful person who will benefit society. Prospective applicants must e-mail Lynn Dunbar (see above) or call the Foundation to arrange for a personal interview at which time the necessary application forms and instructions will be provided. The education loans are low interest and the principal must be repaid beginning one year after completing studies. Grants/loans are approved at monthly Trustee meetings.

O+D+T Rebecca Wallace (Director+CON for Medical Trust) — Lynn Streator Dunbar (Assistant Director+CON for Education Loan Program) — Douglas Gilbert, Esq. (Co-T) — Timothy Slavish, Esq. (Co-T) — National City Bank of Pa. (Corporate Trustee)

SW-139   Gibson (Roger C.) Family Foundation
1304 Regency Drive
Pittsburgh   15237   (Allegheny County)

MI-31-42-49-69
Phone 412-369-9925 **FAX** None
EIN 25-6297679   **Year Created** 1993

AMV $40,807   **FYE** 12-00   (**Gifts Received** $14,530)   11 **Grants totaling** $22,876

About one-third local giving. High local grant of **$4,200** to LaRoche College. **$1,000** to Carnegie Mellon U. Other local contributions **$26-$300** for various purposes. **Out-of-state** giving includes high grant of **$11,000** to Tara Mandala Foundation/Buddhist Meditation Retreat [CO] and **$5,000** to Foundation for Financial Planning [GA]. — Local giving in the prior year included **$1,700** to Butler Symphony Assn. and **$1,000** each to Holy Family Hospital and R. Beddow Foundation [McKeesport]. ■ **PUBLICATIONS:** None ■ **WEBSITE:** None ■ **E-MAIL:** None ■ **APPLICATION POLICIES & PROCEDURES:** Grant requests may be submitted in a letter at any time. No grants awarded to individuals.

O+D+T   Roger C. Gibson (T+Donor+Con)

SW-140   Glasser Family Foundation
1419 Highview Drive
Greensburg   15601   (Westmoreland County)

MI-32-34-35-42
Phone 724-837-1338 **FAX** None
EIN 25-1496445   **Year Created** 1986

AMV $522,937   **FYE** 12-00   (**Gifts Received** $0)   15 **Grants totaling** $43,200

Mostly local/Pa. giving. High grant of **$11,000** to Spina Bifida Assn. **$10,000** each to Hempfield Emergency Assn. and U. of the Sciences in Philadelphia. **$5,000** to Friends of Hepatitis Assn. **$2,500** to Community Foundation of Westmoreland. **$1,000** to Seton Hill College. Other local contributions **$100-$500** each. **Out-of-state** giving includes **$1,000** each to Anti-Defamation League [FL] and Finch U. of Health Science [IL]. ■ **PUBLICATIONS:** None ■ **WEBSITE:** None ■ **E-MAIL:** None ■ **APPLICATION POLICIES & PROCEDURES:** The Foundation reports that giving focuses on the Greensburg area; health/medical needs and religion are priority interests. Submit grant requests in a letter at any time to 5742 NW 24th Ave., Boca Raton, FL 33496, telephone 561-241-5632; describe the organization's charitable needs and include IRS tax-exempt status documentation. — Formerly called Abe & Gloria Glasser Foundation -or- Stuarts Foundation.

O+D+T   Gloria Glasser [FL] (S+F+D+Con) — Abe Glasser [FL] (P+D) — Corporate donor: Stuart Drug & Surgical Supply

---

SW-141   Glosser (David A.) Foundation
c/o M. Glosser & Sons, Inc.
72 Messenger Street
Johnstown   15902   (Cambria County)

MI-11-12-13-22-32-41-44-52-62
Phone 814-535-7521 **FAX** None
EIN 25-6066913   **Year Created** 1962

AMV $3,068,271   **FYE** 6-01   (**Gifts Received** $0)   38 **Grants totaling** $103,800

Mostly local giving. High grant of **$65,000** to United Jewish Appeal of Johnstown. **$5,000** to Beth Sholom Congregation. **$4,000** to Johnstown Central High School. **$2,000-$2,500** each to Community Foundation of Johnstown, Johnstown Symphony Orchestra, and Salvation Army. **$1,000-$1,500** each to Beaverdale Public Library, Friends of Hospice, Sandyvale Memorial Gardens, United Cerebral Palsy, United Way of Greater Johnstown, Windber Public Library, and YMCA of Johnstown. Other local contributions **$100-$500** for civic, educational, and health/human services purposes. **Out-of-state** grant: **$8,400** to Abraham Geiger College [Germany]. ■ **PUBLICATIONS:** None ■ **WEBSITE:** None ■ **E-MAIL:** None ■ **APPLICATION POLICIES & PROCEDURES:** The Foundation reports that preference is given to Pa. organizations; no grants are awarded to/for endowment or individuals. Grant requests may be submitted in a letter at any time; decisions on grants are made within two months.

O+D+T   Robert Krantzler (P+Con) — Lester Goldstein (VP) — Robert Lux (S+F) — Robert Horowitz (D)

SW-142   Goedeker Foundation, The
c/o GAIN - Group Against Intellectual Neglect
200 Geneva Drive
Aliquippa   15001   (Beaver County)

MI-13-41-43-61
Phone 724-375-1171 **FAX** None
EIN 25-6565140   **Year Created** 1996

AMV $1,047,582   **FYE** 12-00   (**Gifts Received** $138,178)   12 **Grants totaling** $45,400

Mostly local giving. High grant of **$15,950** to Beaver County YMCA. **$11,000** to Geneva College. **$1,550** to Church of Notre Dame. **$1,000** to St. Francis Cabrini Church. Most other grants are scholarships for graduates of Beaver County high schools attending colleges in Pa., OH and NY. ■ **PUBLICATIONS:** Scholarship Application Form ■ **WEBSITE:** None ■ **E-MAIL:** None ■ **APPLICATION POLICIES & PROCEDURES:** Only graduates of Beaver County high schools are eligible to apply for scholarships; priority is given to students planning to attend either Geneva College or St. Bonaventure U. [NY]. Applicants must complete a detailed application form available from the Foundation.

O+D+T   Michelle M. Reichert (T+Con) — Delmar E. Goedeker (T+Donor) — Margaret J. Goedeker (T+Donor) — Melanie Rubocki [ID] (T) — Mary Beth Stuver [Coraopolis] (T)

SW-143   Gordon Foundation, The
c/o General American Corporation
700 Fifth Avenue
Pittsburgh   15219   (Allegheny County)

MI-14-17-18-22-33-41-44-51-53-54-56-62-72
Phone 412-765-0505 **FAX** 412-281-7548
EIN 25-6036563   **Year Created** 1958

AMV $338,377   **FYE** 12-00   (**Gifts Received** $0)   50 **Grants totaling** $112,385

Mostly local/Pa. giving. High grant of **$53,300** to City Theatre. **$20,100** to Allegheny Valley School. **$10,000** to United Jewish Federation of Greater Pittsburgh. **$5,000** to The Grier School [Blair County]. **$2,000-$2,500** each to Carnegie Museum of Natural History, Life'sWork of Western Pa., and Winchester Thurston School. **$1,000-$1,650** each to Carnegie Library of Pittsburgh, Carnegie Museum of Art, Historical Society of Western Pa., Jewish Community Center, Pittsburgh Public Theater, and Pittsburgh Zoo. **$750** to Planned Parenthood of Western Pa. Other local contributions **$10-$680** for various purposes. **Out-of-state** giving includes **$1,100** to Jewish National Fund [NY] and smaller contributions. ■**PUBLICATIONS:** None ■**WEBSITE:** None ■ **E-MAIL:** None ■**APPLICATION POLICIES & PROCEDURES:** Grant requests may be submitted in a letter at any time; include a descriptive brochure about the organization.

O+D+T Ira H. Gordon (T+Donor+Con) — Peter I. Gordon (T) — Corporate donor: General American Corporation

---

SW-144 Gospel Evangelism Foundation   MI-63
c/o PNC Advisors, M.S. P2-PTPP-25-1
Two PNC Plaza, 620 Liberty Ave.   **Phone** 412-762-3502 **FAX** 412-762-5439
Pittsburgh 15222   (Allegheny County)   **EIN** 25-6502637   **Year Created** 1999
AMV $3,474,314   **FYE** 12-00   **(Gifts Received** $0)   5 **Grants totaling** $187,976

All giving for Evangelical Christian purposes; one Pa. grant: **$30,000** to Assn. of Baptists for World Evangelism [Harrisburg]. **Out-of-state** grants: **$54,008** to Wycliffe Bible Translators [FL]; **$53,968** to Trans World Radio [NC]; **$30,000** to Word of Life [NY]; and **$20,000** to New Tribes Missions [FL]. ■**PUBLICATIONS:** None ■**WEBSITE:** None ■**E-MAIL:** bruce.bickel@pncadvisors.com ■**AP-PLICATION POLICIES & PROCEDURES:** The Foundation reports that unsolicited requests for funds are not accepted; no grants are awarded to individuals.

O+D+T R. Bruce Bickel (Senior VP at Bank+Con) — Joseph F. Sprankle, III [VA] (Co-T+Donor) — PNC Advisors (Co-Trustee)

SW-145 Grable Foundation, The   MI-11-12-13-14-15-16-17-18-22-29-33-35-41
240 Centre City Tower   42-44-45-49-55-56-85-86
650 Smithfield Street   **Phone** 412-471-4550 **FAX** 412-471-2267
Pittsburgh 15222   (Allegheny County)   **EIN** 25-1309888   **Year Created** 1976
AMV $234,656,940   **FYE** 12-01   **(Gifts Received** $0)   275 **Grants totaling** $10,984,014

Mostly SW Pa. giving focused on programs critical to the successful development of children/youth. High grant of **$385,000** to Pittsburgh Public Schools (Literacy Plus planning-support). **$350,000** to Sports & Exhibition Authority (North Shore Riverfront Park). **$300,000** to Carnegie Science Center (SciQuest Exhibition). **$200,000** to Allegheny County Library System (eiNetwork). **$158,100** to Beginning With Books (Project Beacon). **$150,000** each to DePaul Institute (transition program), Family Communications (The Challenging Child), Western Pa. Conservancy (school garden initiative), and YMCA of Pittsburgh (capital campaign). **$140,000** to Pittsburgh Zoo (aquarium project). **$133,000** to Pittsburgh Center for the Arts (comprehensive school partnership). **$125,000** to United Way of Allegheny County (capacity building). **$115,000** to Carnegie Mellon U. (Grable Symposia). **$107,061** to Pittsburgh Public Schools (Extended Year Program). **$104,500** to U. of Pittsburgh (principals' academy). **$100,000** each to 3 Rivers Connect (regional education technology initiative), ASSET, Inc. (bridge funding), Center for Creative Play (capital campaign), Education Policy & Issues Center [Harrisburg] (student improvement plan), Education Policy & Leadership (operating support), Executive Service Corps of Western Pa. (volunteer development), Family Resources (planning position), National Board for Professional Teaching Standards [VA] (Pittsburgh initiative), Pa. Economy League (Wilkinsburg empowerment plan), Pittsburgh Council on Public Education (community involvement), Pittsburgh Public Schools (CAPA strategic planning), U. of Pittsburgh (Starting Points), and YouthWorks (youth employment program). **$90,000** to Fox Chapel School District (professional/staff development program). **$80,000** each to Chatham College (teacher training), Pittsburgh Council on Public Education (YouthPlaces), and Pittsburgh Public Schools (information technology program). **$75,000** each to Allegheny Conference on Community Development (agenda development center), Carnegie Mellon U. (RoboticsAcademy), Child Development Center [Franklin] (quality improvement efforts), Historical Society of Western Pa. (educational programs), Pa. Economy League (Workforce Connection), and Riverlife Task Force (Pittsburgh Riverfronts). **$67,000** to Point Park College (Project Teach). **$60,000** each to Derry Area School District (after school program), Hill House Assn. (technology coordinator), Mentoring Partnership of SW Pa. (expanded programming), Northside Urban Pathways (transitional costs), Pittsburgh Parks Conservancy (education-outreach programs), Pittsburgh Voyager (education programs), and United Way of Westmoreland County (volunteer services initiative). **$55,000-$56,500** each to Allegheny Youth Development (after school program), Penn Hills School District (professional development), and U. of Pittsburgh (Western Pa. writing projects). **$50,000-$53,000** each to 3 Rivers Connect (connected learners class), APEX/Duquesne U. (professional development), Carnegie Mellon U. (Infolink Program), Carnegie Institute (arts-eduction collaborative), Carnegie Mellon U. (Role Models Program), Carnegie Museum of Art (teacher programs), City Theatre Company (Young Playwrights), Duquesne U. (charter school project), EDSYS (technology charter schools), Hilltop Community Children's Center (quality improvement plan), National Aviary (education staff-program), Pa. Economy League (Empowerment Schools), Pa. Partnership for Children [Harrisburg] (educational policy program), The Pittsburgh Foundation (Human Services Integration Program), Pittsburgh Mercy Foundation (adolescent care center), Pittsburgh Public Schools (planning grant), Pittsburgh Public Schools (Urban Systematic Program), Planned Parenthood of Western Pa. (peer education program), Robert Morris College (executive transition program), Schenley Heights Community Development Program (after school enrichment program), Student Conservation Assn./Three Rivers, Summerbridge Pittsburgh (teacher support), U. of Pittsburgh (McGowan Center support), Andy Warhol Museum (education outreach), Women Center & Shelter (anti-violence program), and YMCA ofPittsburgh (Camp Kon-o-Wee). **$45,000-$47,500** each to Allegheny County Dept. of Human Services (Safe Start), Carnegie Mellon U./College of Fine Arts (Keyboard Lessons), Gateway to the Arts (teacher professional development), Pa. Resources Council (environmental education training), Quaker Valley School District (CAT2 training), and U. of Pittsburgh (Superintendent's Forum). **$40,000-$42,000** each to Aliquippa Alliance for Unity (educational outreach program), Civic Light Opera (Creative Vision), Crossroads Foundation (summer enrichment program), Heartwood Institute (operating support), Magee Women's Health Foundation (Girls on the Run), One Small Step (after school program), The Open Door (community outreach), Pittsburgh Assn. for the Education of Young Children, Pittsburgh Glass Center (high school students program), Pittsburgh Opera (Steel Valley Partnership), Pittsburgh Public Schools (Miller Elementary School Program), Pittsburgh Shade Tree Commission (urban forest-tree steward program), Shadyside Hospital Foundation (sex education program), Three Rivers Youth (family partnership program), and Tides Center (youth standards project). **$35,000** each to Allegheny County CASA (operating support), Jewish Family & Children's Service (high school career program), and YMCA of Beaver County (Dreams Alive Program). **$28,500-$33,500** each to Ambridge Area School District (community learning center), Audubon Society of Western Pa. (schoolground habitat enhancement), Beginning With Books (Books for Kids project), Big Brothers Big Sisters of Greater Pittsburgh (BUK's program), Breachmenders (school-to-career program), Community Involvement Foundation (Tickets for Kids), Dance Alloy (dance education programming), East End Cooperative (summer day camp), East Liberty Presbyterian Church (music-arts academy), Fayette County Community Action Agency (Links to Learning), Grantmakers of Western Pa. (implement strategic plan), Information Renaissance (after school computer club), Mt. Ararat Community Activity Center (Creative Arts Education Initiative), NAMI of SW Pa. (children's coordinator), New Hope for Neighborhood Renewal(after school program), The OASIS Institute (intergenerational tutoring program), Pittsburgh History & Landmarks Foundation (education programs), Pittsburgh Musical Theatre (education/outreach programs), The Pittsburgh Project (student development programs), Pittsburgh Public Schools (Carrick after school program), Program for Female Offenders (Saturday sessions), Providence Family Support Center (children's liaison specialist), U. of Pittsburgh (Institute of Politics), YMCA-Homewood/Brushton (tutorial assistance program), and YMCA of McKeesport (Teen LEAD Program). **$23,000-$25,000** each to Adelphoi, Inc. (Riverview Academy Charter School), Allegheny Intermediate Unit (Smart Start), Boy Scouts/Greater Pittsburgh Council (work-based mentoring project), Braddock's Field (after school-summer program), Carnegie Mellon U. (C-Mites Program), Carnegie Museum of Art (ARTventures), The Corporate Collection, The Mattress Factory (education coordinator), Operation Better Block (virtual learning center), Pittsburgh International Children's Theater (staff position), Pittsburgh Public Theater (education outreach), POWER/Pa. Organization for Women in Recovery (creative writing-education program), Three Rivers Rowing Assn. (All City Crew), Young Life of the Steel Valley (expansion project), and Youth Enrichment Services (in-home peer mentoring). **$18,000-$21,000** each to Allegheny Conference on Community Development (War for Empire program), Boys & Girls Club of Western Pa. (organizational merger), Butler County Community College (summer environmental program), Carnegie Mellon U. (community connection program), Central Northside Reading Is Fundamental, Christian Literacy Associates (Project L.A.S.T.), Citizens to Abolish Domestic Apartheid [North Versailles] (after school-summer programs), Duquesne U. (City Music Center), East End United Community Center [Uniontown] (Operation Growth), Extra Mile Education Foundation (after schoolprogram), Family Tyes (school-based fishing program), Focus on Renewal (administration), Greater Pittsburgh Community Food Bank (job shadowing/mentoring project), Human Services Center/Turtle Creek (youth learning program), Keystone Oaks School District (Project Succeed), Mom's House (operating support), Parental Stress Center (volunteer program), Pa. Economy League (Wilkinsburg early childhood transition plan), Pa. Environmental Council (youth outdoor adventure program), Pa. Hoop Stars (operating support), Pittsburgh Urban Magnet Project (operating support), Riverview Children's Center (Family Support children's center), Soldiers & Sailors Memorial (education department), Solid Rock Foundation (community enrichment center), Upper St. Clair School District (middle school institute), and Vietnam Veterans Leadership (Achieving Dad Program). **$14,000-$15,000** each to 3 Rivers Connect (summer program fund), Amani Christian Community (nurture clubs), Associated Artists of Pittsburgh (educational coordinator), Baldwin-Whitehall School District (S.T.A.I.R.S. program), Better Business Bureau (upgrade automated system), Brown AME Church (children's program), Chatham Baroque (Peanut Butter & Jam Sessions), Children's Festival Chorus (education outreach), Duquesne U. (nonprofit leadership institute), EPI Center (video project), Guitar Society of the Fine Art (guitar lessons), John Wesley Cern Project (hi-tech program), Keystone Oaks School District (student overtime support project), LABCO/Laboratory Company Dance (Attach Theatre/education-outreach programs), Latrobe Area Hospital (Camp Focus), Pittsburgh Arts & Lectures (Family Author Series), Pittsburgh Ballet Theatre (arts education-outreach), Pittsburgh Chamber Music Society (Beethoven Project), Pittsburgh Chess Club (public schools program), Pittsburgh Dance Council (Minds in Motion), Prime State Theatre (education program), Saltworks Theatre Company (substance prevention program), Sewickley Valley YMCA (Black Achievers program), Silver Eye Center for Photography (educational outreach), Society for Contemporary Craft (museum-school partnership), U. of Pittsburgh (Falk School training), U. of Pittsburgh (Literacy Plus planning-support) U. ofPittsburgh (Shakespeare in the Schools), West Mifflin Area School District (Homeville school), Wilkinsburg School District (Random Acts of Kindness program), and World Affairs Council of Pittsburgh (understanding global conflict). **$10,000-$12,500** to Big Brothers Big Sisters of Beaver County (PSU-Beaver campus mentoring project), Bloomfield-Garfield FACES (after school program), Carnegie Mellon U. (summer program fund), Christian Sports International (demo program), Citizens to Abolish Domestic Apartheid (S.A.I.L.S program), Cornell School District (middle school concept-program), Grantmakers of Western Pa. (operating support), International Poetry Forum (Poets in Person program), National Fatherhood Initiative (Allegheny County program), National Flag Foundation (youth civic action center), Neighborhood Academy (summer program fund), Pittsburgh Cultural Trust (Carol Brown Fund), Pittsburgh Irish & Classical Theatre (education outreach), Pittsburgh Public Schools (Westinghouse girls basketball program), Pittsburgh Tissue Engineering Initiative (summer program fund), Slippery Rock U. (summer creative-arts program), Sun Crumbs (Pittsburgh Youth Poetry Slam Project), Tiger Pause Youth Ministry [Beaver Falls] (after school program), Umoja Arts Company (African Heritage School Initiative), U. of Pittsburgh/Greensburg (high school science teacher workshops), Urban Impact Foundation (summer day camp), D.T. Watson Rehabilitation Service (day-overnight respite program), Western Pa. Professionals (Artsource), Youth Enhancement Support (summer program fund), and YWCA of Butler (preschool-youth programs). **$8,000-$9,700** each to Brashear Assn. (summer youth program), Magee Women's Health Foundation (summer student-teacher program), and Providence Connections (summer program fund). **$5,000-$7,000** each to Brashear Assn. (homework assistance program), Brew House Assn. (children's workshop), Carnegie Mellon U. (physics concepts program), Collaboratives for Learning (TIMSS presentation), Hosanna Industries (summer staff program), Mon Yough Riverfront (summer arts festival), Pittsburgh Downtown Partnership (Park Easy Guide), Pittsburgh Magazine (Raising Readers), Pittsburgh Technology Council (business plan competition), Presbyterian Church of Mt. Washington (reading-tutoring program), River City Youth Chorale (outreach program), Rodef Shalom Congregation (summer program), Steel Valley School District (arts education program), U. of Pittsburgh (model assisted reasoning), Western Pa. Conservancy (student volunteers), WQED (Raising Readers), and Zion Christian Church (Solid Rock Cafe). Ten other smaller local grants for cultural educational, and other purposes. **Major out-of-state** grants include **$270,000** to National Alliance for Research on Schizophrenia & Depression [NY]; **$125,000** to Children's Literacy Initiative (Newark, NJ Literacy Project); **$100,000** to Manpower Demonstration Corp.[NY] (core funding/Project GRAD); **$50,000** each to Harlem Educational Fund [NY] and U. of North Carolina (school outreach programming); **$40,000** to

Smithsonian Institution [DC] (outreach coordinator); and **$30,000** to National Parks Foundation [DC] (visitor-interpretive center). ■**PUBLICATIONS:** Annual Report with statement of program policy and application guidelines ■**WEBSITE:** www.grablefdn.org ■**E-MAIL:** grable@grablefdn.org ■**APPLICATION POLICIES & PROCEDURES:** The Foundation reports five priority areas of grantmaking: (1) Focusing on quality precollegiate education as a key to the ultimate rescue of children/teenagers within a growing underprivileged population; (2) Reaching these young people by strengthening the family unit, supporting family planning, and encouraging viable family structures/formats; (3) Integrating and fostering the arts—particularly the visual arts—to enrich school experiences and provide another avenue for expression/learning; (4) Strengthening the nonprofit sector by encouraging volunteerism as a way of building agencies' capacities; and (5) Supporting promising research on schizophrenia with the objective of understanding the pathology of the illness and finding ways of treatment/containment. Most grants are for general operating/continuing support, program development, seed money, curriculum development, consulting services, conferences/seminars, program evaluation, technical assistance, and research. No grants are awarded to individuals or conduit organizations or for scholarships, endowment, or capital campaigns; unsolicited proposals for programs outside SW Pa. are not accepted. Prospective applicants are encouraged to submit at any time an initial, brief Letter of Inquiry which clearly identifies how the proposed project relates to one of the five priority giving areas and indicates the amount of funding requested. If the Foundation responds favorably, then a full proposal must be submitted which includes: (1) a one-page summary; (2) information about the organization; (3) statement of need for the proposed project; (4) description of the project, the project supervisor and staff; (5) project budget showing committed and anticipated funds; (6) current organizational operating budget; (7) description on how the project will be sustained after the grant ends; (8) description of anticipated outcomes from the project; (9) Board member list; (10) letters of support from applicant's Board and collaborating organizations; and (11) IRS tax-exempt status documentation. Proposals following Grantmakers of Western Pa. Common Grant Application Format are accepted. Site visits sometimes are made to organizations being considered for a grant. The Trustees award grants at meetings in March, July, and November.
O+D+T Susan H. Brownlee (Executive Director+Con) — Charles R. Burke, Esq. (C+T) — Jan Nicholson [NY] (P+T) — Charles R. Burke, Jr. (VP+T+Associate Director) — Patricia Grable Burke (S+T) — Steven E. Burke (F+T) — Barbara Nicholson McFadyen [NC] (T) — Marion Grable Nicholson [NJ] (T) — William B. Nicholson [NJ] (T) — Donor: Minnie K. Grable Trust

---

SW-146 Grasso (Leonard C.) Charitable Foundation   MI-13-17-22-29-52
120 Trotwood Drive, P.O. Box 426   **Phone** 412-372-3968 **FAX** None
Monroeville 15146   (Allegheny County)   **EIN** 25-1778803   **Year Created** 1995
AMV $172,533   **FYE** 12-00   (**Gifts Received** $20,000)   6 **Grants totaling** $10,000
Mostly local giving. High Pa. grant of **$2,000** each to Pittsburgh Piano Teacher's Assn. and Women's Center & Shelter of Greater Pittsburgh. **$1,500** to Salvation Army. **$1,000** to C-Mites. **$500** to South East Area YMCA. **Out-of-state** grant: **$3,000** to National Air Disaster Foundation [DC]. ■**PUBLICATIONS:** None ■**WEBSITE:** None ■**E-MAIL:** None ■**APPLICATION POLICIES & PROCEDURES:** Grant requests may be submitted in a letter (5 pages maximum) at any time; include IRS tax-exempt status documentation. Site visits sometimes are made to organizations being considered for a grant.
O+D+T Alice E. Grasso (P+D+Donor+Con) — Kimberly J. Gallagher [West Newton] (VP+D) — Kemper Arnold [OH] (S+F+D)

SW-147 Gray (Jane & Dan) Charitable Trust   MI-32-35-43-44-52-56
Refer to PNC Advisors Charitable Trust Committee entry.
                                       (Allegheny County)   **EIN** 25-6065758   **Year Created** 1957
AMV $252,524   **FYE** 12-00   (**Gifts Received** $0)   2 **Grants totaling** $11,518
All Western Pa. giving. High grant of **$5,760** to Butler Area Public Library (newspaper preservation project). **$5,758** to Pittsburgh Piano Teachers Assn. (college scholarship awards). — In the prior year, two grants: **$4,680** to American Cancer Society (public school education campaign) and **$1,320** to National Kidney Foundation of Western Pa. (public education campaign). ■ **APPLICATION POLICIES & PROCEDURES:** Refer to the PNC Advisors Charitable Trust Committee entry for a statement on giving priorities and full application guidelines.
O+D+T Refer to PNC Advisors Charitable Trust Committee entry. — PNC Advisors (Corporate Trustee)

SW-148 Green (Mayer A.) Allergy Foundation   MI-22-34-35-62
120 Woodshire Drive   **Phone** 412-471-3818 **FAX** None
Pittsburgh 15215   (Allegheny County)   **EIN** 23-7068003   **Year Created** 1970
AMV $396,781   **FYE** 12-00   (**Gifts Received** $1,121,002)   40 **Grants totaling** $1,173,904
About two-thirds local giving. High grant of **$388,200** to United Jewish Federation of Greater Pittsburgh (Berman Fund). **$375,000** to Richard & Dana Green Philanthropic Foundation (a related family entity). **$20,000** to Rodef Shalom Congregation. **$1,500** to Pa. Allergy & Asthma Assn. [Harrisburg]. **$1,000** to U. of Pittsburgh School of Medicine. Many other local contributions **$25-$200** for various purposes. **Out-of-state** grant: **$385,000** to United Jewish Federation [CA] (Satenberg Fund). ■**PUBLICATIONS:** None ■**WEBSITE:** None ■**E-MAIL:** None ■**APPLICATION POLICIES & PROCEDURES:** Grant requests may be submitted in a proposal at any time; describe the scientific, educational or public benefits of the requested funds.
O+D+T Richard L. Green, M.D. (P+T+Donor+Con) — Dana S. Green (S+T) — Paul K. Rudoy, CPA (F+T)

SW-149   Green (Richard & Dana) Philanthropic Foundation
120 Woodshire Drive
Pittsburgh   15215   (Allegheny County)

MI-22-42-62
Phone 412-471-3818 **FAX** None
EIN 31-1714818   **Year Created** 2000

AMV $328,230   **FYE** 12-00   **(Gifts Received** $375,000)   38 **Grants totaling** $6,495

Mostly local/Pa. giving. High grant of **$3,400** to United Jewish Federation of Greater Pittsburgh. **$750** to Swarthmore College. Other local and out-of-state contributions mostly **$100** or smaller. ■**PUBLICATIONS:** None ■**WEBSITE:** None ■**E-MAIL:** None
■**APPLICATION POLICIES & PROCEDURES:** Grant requests may be submitted in any form at any time.

O+D+T Richard L. Green, M.D. (T+Con) — Dana S. Green (T) — Jessica L. Green [CA] (T) — Jonathon M. Green [CA] (T) — Todd D. Green (T) — Foundation donor: Mayer A. Green Allergy Foundation

---

SW-150   Gurrentz Family Charitable Foundation
c/o Gurrentz International Corporation
2020 Ardmore Boulevard, Suite 250
Pittsburgh   15221   (Allegheny County)

MI-22-54-52-54-62

Phone 412-351-3200 **FAX** 412-351-4051
EIN 25-1790376   **Year Created** 1996

AMV $103,717   **FYE** 12-00   **(Gifts Received** $0)   65 **Grants totaling** $45,857

About one-third local giving. High local grant of **$10,000** to Temple David Congregation. **$1,300** to United Jewish Appeal. **$1,000** each to Anti-Defamation League and Carnegie Institute. Other local giving **$500** or less to a wide variety of organizations. **Out-of-state** giving includes high grant of **$16,335** to Aspen Art Museum [CO]; **$5,000** to Aspen Music Festival; **$3,000** to Jazz Aspen Snowmass; and **$1,000** to U.S. Holocaust Memorial Museum [DC]. ■**PUBLICATIONS:** None ■ **WEBSITE:** None ■**E-MAIL:** None ■**APPLICATION POLICIES & PROCEDURES:** Information not available.

O+D+T Morton E. Gurrentz (P+S+F+D+Donor+Con) — Patrick H. Gurrentz (D) — Rodger B. Gurrentz (D) — Thomas L. Gurrentz (D)

SW-151   Hadley Family Foundation, The
RD #1, Box 160
Latrobe   15650   (Westmoreland County)

MI-18-22-25-29-61-65-82
Phone 724-423-5630 **FAX** None
EIN 25-1783304   **Year Created** 1996

AMV $397,566   **FYE** 12-00   **(Gifts Received** $9,844)   18 **Grants totaling** $21,400

About one-quarter local/Pa. giving. High Pa. grant of **$1,800** to Salvation Army. **$1,000-$1,200** each to Mom's House [Greensburg], Northside Common Ministries, and The Spark of Hope. **$500** each to CARE-International [Philadelphia] and Red Cross/Chestnut Ridge Chapter. **Out-of-state** giving includes **$3,700** each to Catholic Relief Services [MD] and Food for the Poor [FL]; and smaller grants/contributions, mostly for religious organizations. ■**PUBLICATIONS:** None ■**WEBSITE:** None ■**E-MAIL:** None ■**APPLICATION POLICIES & PROCEDURES:** Information not available.

O+D+T Distribution Committee Members: — Jack L. Hadley (P+Con) — Jeanne Hadley — Ken Hadley [TX] — Thomas Hadley [OK] — Susan Ross — Linda Schoenfeldt [MI] — Judy Schaffer [OK] — Carol Vasinko — Corporate donor: The Hadley Family Partnership

---

SW-152   Hafner Charitable Foundation
c/o PNC Advisors, M.S. P2-PTPP-25-1
Two PNC Plaza, 620 Liberty Ave.
Pittsburgh   15222   (Allegheny County)

MI-13-15-22-32

Phone 412-762-3390 **FAX** 412-762-5439
EIN 25-6222970   **Year Created** 1981

AMV $1,225,761   **FYE** 6-00   **(Gifts Received** $0)   1 **Grant of** $65,000

Sole grant to YWCA of Greater Pittsburgh. — In 1999, one grant of **$100,000** to Jewish Assn. on Aging with support in prior years to Alzheimer's Disease Alliance, Council Care Senior Adult Day Care Centers, Riverview Center for Jewish Seniors, and U. of Pittsburgh School of Medicine (Alzheimer's disease research), among others. ■**PUBLICATIONS:** None ■**WEBSITE:** None ■ **E-MAIL:** None ■**APPLICATION POLICIES & PROCEDURES:** No grants awarded to/for scholarships or individuals. Submit grant requests at any time in a letter (5 pages maximum); describe the organizational purpose and intended use of the requested funds; include a project budget and IRS tax-exempt status documentation.

O+D+T Richard S. Crone, Esq. (Co-T+Con) — John D. Culbertson (VP at Bank) — PNC Advisors (Co-Trustee)

SW-153   Hagan (W. Clark) Trust
Refer to PNC Advisors Charitable Trust Committee entry.
                                   (Allegheny County)

MI-12-14-17-19-22-29-33

EIN 25-6070592   **Year Created** 1963

AMV $1,133,675   **FYE** 12-00   **(Gifts Received** $0)   7 **Grants totaling** $55,551

All giving restricted to research projects dealing with alcoholism, both cause/effect and cure/prevention. High grant of **$10,750** to Mon Yough Community Services. **$10,000** each to Domestic Abuse Counseling Center, Gateway Rehabilitation Center, and Salvation Army. **$9,801** to Strength, Inc. **$4,000** to Zoar. **$1,000** to Mental Health Assn. of Allegheny County. ■**APPLICATION POLICIES & PROCEDURES:** Refer to the PNC Advisors Charitable Trust Committee entry for a statement on giving priorities and full application guidelines.

O+D+T Refer to PNC Advisors Charitable Trust Committee entry. — PNC Advisors (Corporate Trustee)

SW-154   Halpern Foundation
c/o Halpern Enterprises
810 Penn Avenue
Pittsburgh   15222   (Allegheny County)

MI-11-12-22-41-42-52-54-62

Phone 412-391-6130 **FAX** None
EIN 25-6060720   **Year Created** 1952

AMV $3,904,470   **FYE** 12-00   (**Gifts Received** $8,000)   34 **Grants totaling** $218,620

Mostly local giving. High grant of **$158,000** to United Jewish Federation of Greater Pittsburgh. **$12,805** to Beth Shalom Congregration. **$8,000** to Pittsburgh Symphony. **$5,000** each to The Ellis School and Rodef Shalom Congregation. **$2,500** to United Way of SW Pa. **$2,000** to U. of Pittsburgh. **$1,000** each to Carnegie Institute, Hillel Jewish University Center, Jewish Archives Endowment, Jewish Family & Children's Service, Jewish Residential Services, National Council of Jewish Women, and Parental Stress Center. Other local contributions **$20-$500** for various purposes. **Out-of-state** giving includes **$10,000** to Jewish Federation of Palm Beach County [FL] and **$3,000** to American Jewish Committee [NY]. ■**PUBLICATIONS:** None ■**WEBSITE:** None ■**E-MAIL:** None ■**APPLICATION POLICIES & PROCEDURES:** No grants awarded to individuals. Prospective applicants initially should make a telephone inquiry about the feasibility of submitting a request. Grant requests may be submitted in a letter at any time. Site visits sometimes are made to organizations being considered for a grant.

O+D+T Bernard M. Halpern (T+Donor+Con) — Irving J. Halpern (T+Donor) — Richard I. Halpern, Esq. (T+Donor) — Stephen F. Halpern (T) — Nicholas D.J. Lane (Donor)

SW-155   Hansen (William Stucki) Foundation
c/o Hansen, Inc.
2600 Neville Road, Neville Island
Pittsburgh   15225   (Allegheny County)

MI-11-12-22-25-29-41-52-63-65

Phone 412-771-7300 **FAX** 412-771-7308
EIN 25-1483674   **Year Created** 1984

AMV $5,500,311   **FYE** 11-00   (**Gifts Received** $3,327,638)   10 **Grants totaling** $674,199

About one-fifth local giving; grants are for general operating support except as noted. High Pa. grants of **$50,000** each to Pittsburgh Leadership Foundation and Pittsburgh Presbytery. **$10,000** to United Way of Allegheny County (Early Childhood Initiative/Salvation Army). **$5,000** each to The Neighborhood Academy [Greensburg] and Northside Common Ministries. **$2,500** each to Greater Pittsburgh Community Food Bank and Pittsburgh Opera Society. **$1,000** to Philanthropy Roundtable. **$500** to Union Aid Society [Sewickley]. **Out-of-state** grant: **$574,699** to New York Initiative [NY]. ■**PUBLICATIONS:** None ■**WEBSITE:** None ■**E-MAIL:** None ■**APPLICATION POLICIES & PROCEDURES:** Grant requests may be submitted in any form. No grants awarded to individuals. Site visits sometimes are made to organizations being considered for a grant. Grants are awarded at regular meetings.

O+D+T William Gregg Hansen (P+D+Con) — Nancy K. Hansen (S+F+D) — Corporate donor: Hansen, Inc.

SW-156   Hauber Foundation
1491 Candlewood Drive
Pittsburgh   15241   (Allegheny County)

MI-11-25-42-41-52-54-61

Phone 412-831-6426 **FAX** None
EIN 23-7887198   **Year Created** 1997

AMV $853,070   **FYE** 12-00   (**Gifts Received** $200,848)   27 **Grants totaling** $40,900

Mostly local giving. High grant of **$10,000** to United Way of Allegheny County. **$5,000** to Extra Mile Education Foundation. **$3,000-$3,500** each to Carnegie Institute, Catholic Charities, North Catholic High School, and St. John Capistran Church. **$1,425** to Vincentian Sisters of Charity. Other local contributions **$100-$500** for various purposes. **Out-of-state** giving includes **$3,500** to United Way of Collier County [FL]; **$1,250** to Habitat for Humanity of Collier County [FL]; and **$1,000** each to Philharmonic Center for the Arts [FL]. ■**PUBLICATIONS:** None ■**WEBSITE:** None ■**E-MAIL:** None ■**APPLICATION POLICIES & PROCEDURES:** Information not available.

O+D+T William M. Hauber (C+Donor+Con) — Gregory A. Harbaugh (S+F) — Jean D. Hauber (T)

SW-157   Hayes Foundation
c/o Hayes School Publishing Company
321 Pennwood Avenue
Wilkinsburg   15221   (Allegheny County)

MI-12-13-15-22-25-41-42-45-54-63-64-65-82

Phone 412-371-2373 **FAX** None
EIN 25-6079804   **Year Created** 1966

AMV $2,819,161   **FYE** 12-00   (**Gifts Received** $7,900)   28 **Grants totaling** $152,300

Mostly local/Pa. giving. High grant of **$30,000** to Hebron United Presbyterian Church. **$15,000** to Youth Guidance/Family Ministries. **$12,500** to Grove City College. **$7,000** each to Light of Life Mission, Salvation Army, and Trinity Christian School. **$5,000** each to Allegheny Youth Development, Carnegie Museums, Coalition for Christian Outreach, Cornerstone TV, and Reformed Theological Seminary. **$3,000-$3,500** each to Allegheny Literacy Council, Hosanna House, Presbyterian Senior Care Center, Shadyside United Presbyterian Church, and Wilkinsburg Community Ministry. **$2,000-$2,500** each to Boys & Girls Club of Western Pa., Habitat for Humanity, and Ladies GAR Home. **$1,000** each to Christian Church of Wilkinsburg, Mars Home for Youth, Masonic Homes of Elizabethtown [Lancaster County], Philadelphia College of Bible, and Safety Kids. **Out-of-state** giving includes **$8,700** to Ghana Evangelical Society [West Africa]; **$7,000** to Young Life [CO]; and **$6,000** to The Gideons International [TN]. ■**PUBLICATIONS:** None ■**WEBSITE:** None ■**E-MAIL:** None ■**APPLICATION POLICIES & PROCEDURES:** Grant requests may be submitted at any time to any Trustee. No grants awarded to individuals.

O+D+T Nellie I. Hayes (T+Donor+Con) — Sallie H. Brinkhoff (T+Donor) — Robert D. Hayes (T+Donor) — Betty H. Bachelder (Donor) — Richard Bachelder (Donor) — C.N. Hayes, Sr. (Donor) — Clair N. Hayes, III (Donor)

SW-158 Heinz Family Foundation
    32 Dominion Tower
    625 Liberty Avenue
    Pittsburgh 15222   (Allegheny County)

MI-11-12-13-14-17-29-32-33-35-39-42-52-53
54-55-57-71-72-79-82-84
Phone 412-497-5775 **FAX** 412-497-5790
EIN 25-1689382   **Year Created** 1992

AMV $76,299,076   **FYE** 12-00   (**Gifts Received** $7,063,955)   150+ **Grants totaling** $6,375,393

About one-fourth local/Pa. giving; grants are for general operating support except as noted. High Pa. grant of **$1,000,000** to Carnegie Mellon U. (endowment). **$175,000** to Pa. Public School Health Care Trust [Mercer County]. **$70,000** to Three Rivers Area Labor Management Committee (healthcare quality-utilization survey). **$65,000** to Pittsburgh Symphony Society (annual fund/Maazel benefit). **$51,000** to Carnegie Institute (museums' annual sustaining fund). **$50,000** to Manchester Craftsmen's Guild (jazz education/technology training programs). **$35,000** to Penn State Geisinger Foundation [Hershey] (health care information for rural/underserved women project). **$25,000** to Philadelphia Museum of Art (Rome exhibition). **$20,000** to Pittsburgh Parks Conservancy (fundraising event). **$15,000** each to Duquesne U./School of Education (multicultural computer academy) and U. of Pittsburgh (archaeological field research in Colombia). **$10,000** each to Chartiers Community MH/MR Center, Pa. Federation of Injured Workers [Philadelphia], and United Way of Allegheny County. **$5,000** each to Catholic Youth Assn. of Pittsburgh, Children's Institute of Pittsburgh, Pa. Special Olympics (winter games), and Women's Commissions Research & Education Fund [Delaware County] (women in politics documentary). **$3,000** to Make-A-Wish Foundation of Western Pa. (benefit carnival). Also, about 20 local/Pa. grants **$2,500** or smaller for education, arts/cultural, health/human service, and environmental purposes. **Out-of-state** giving includes **$510,000** to Harvard U. (mostly for Heinz Challenge Fund); **$340,000** to St. Luke's Regional Medical Center [ID] (EMS study); **$265,000** each to H. John Heinz III Center for Science, Economics and the Environment [DC] (mostly endowment); **$250,000** each to five individuals under the Heinz Awards Program (see below) of which some funds were directed in full or part to nonprofit organization/institutions; **$250,000** to Sun Valley Ski Education Foundation [ID]; **$150,000** each to Environmental Defense Fund [NY] and National Gallery of Art [DC] (endowment); **$100,000** to Maryland Public Broadcasting Foundation (Healthweek production-distribution); **$60,000** to International Center for Journalists [DC] (Heinz Fellowship in Environmental Reporting); **$55,000** to Brookings Institution [DC]; **$50,000** each to American Institute for Public Service [DC] (President's Student Service Awards program), John F. Kennedy Center for the Performing Arts [DC], and Mozambique Education & Health Foundation [VA]; **$35,000** to United Negro College Fund (Heinz Environmental Fellows Fund); **$25,000-$27,500** each to Earth Action Network [CT], Eureka Communities [DC] (Boston-area project), ROSE Fund [MA], Rosie's Place [MA], Save The Children Federation [CT], and Tides Center [DC] (minority women vote project). Other grants/contributions to many states for similar purposes. ■**PUBLICATIONS:** None ■**WEBSITE:** None ■**E-MAIL:** None ■**APPLICATION POLICIES & PROCEDURES:** The Foundation reports three special interests: (1) Awards to individuals for outstanding achievement in the Arts & Humanities, Human Condition, Public Policy, Technology & Employment, and the Environment; (2) Supporting graduate/postgraduate research on emerging environmental issues; and (3) Awarding the Heinz Senate Fellowship to assist the U.S. Senate in identifying/developing new leaders on issues affecting children/seniors. Grant requests may be submitted in a letter (3 pages maximum) at any time; describe the organization's projects/activities and type of funding sought (operating, capital, endowment, etc.); include an annual report, organization and project budgets, an audited financial statement, list of other funding sources, and IRS tax-exempt status documentation.

O+D+T Jeffrey R. Lewis (Executive Director+Con) — Teresa F. Heinz (C+Chief Executive Officer+D+Donor) — Wendy Mackenzie [NY] (S+D) — S. Donald Wiley (F+D) — Andre T. Heinz (D) — Jack E. Kime (Chief Financial Officer)

SW-159 Heinz (H.J.) Company Foundation
    c/o H.J. Heinz Company
    600 Grant Street, P.O. Box 57
    Pittsburgh 15230   (Allegheny County)

MI-11-12-13-14-15-16-17-19-29-31-32-41-42
49-51-52-54-55-83-88
Phone 412-456-5772 **FAX** 412-456-7868
EIN 25-6018924   **Year Created** 1951

AMV $753,778   **FYE** 12-00   (**Gifts Received** $6,000,000)   1200+ **Grants totaling** $6,494,241

Nationwide giving, primarily in corporate operating locations; about half Pa. giving—primarily to Pittsburgh. Grants are for general-operating support except as noted, and some include employee matching gifts. *HUMAN SERVICES GRANTS*: High grant of **$475,000** to United Way of SW Pa. **$55,000** to Brother's Brother Foundation. **$50,000** each to Greater Pittsburgh Community Food Bank and Hill House Assn. **$35,000** to D.T. Watson Rehabilitation Services. **$33,330** to Children's Institute of Pittsburgh. **$25,000** each to Make-A-Wish Foundation of Western Pa., Manchester Youth Development Center, Ronald McDonald House Charities of Pittsburgh, Women's Shelter/Rape Crisis Center of Lawrence County, and YMCA of Pittsburgh. **$20,000** to Women's Center & Shelter of Greater Pittsburgh. **$15,000** each to Pa. Special Olympics and Travelers Aid Society of Pittsburgh. **$12,500** to Bethlehem Haven. **$10,000** to Villa St. Joseph of Baden. **$8,000** to Family Guidance, Inc. **$6,000** to Big Brothers & Big Sisters of Greater Pittsburgh. **$5,000** each to The Bradley Center and Contact Pittsburgh. Other smaller grants/contributions. *HEALTH-MEDICAL GRANTS*: **$150,000** to U. of Pittsburgh Cancer Institute. **$58,000+** to Children's Hospital of Pittsburgh. **$55,000** to Magee-Women's Health Foundation. **$50,000** to Shadyside Hospital Foundation (capital fund). **$30,000** each to American Heart Assn./Western District (research) and Burger King Cancer Caring Center (patient aid). **$26,000** to Holy Family Foundation. **$10,000** each to American Cancer Society, Pittsburgh Mercy Foundation, and Spina Bifida Assn. of Western Pa. (patient aid). **$7,500** to Leukemia Society of America. **$5,000** each to American Cancer Society and Mario Lemieux Foundation. Other smaller grants/contributions and matching gifts. *EDUCATION GRANTS*: **$125,000** to Westminster College. **$115,000** to Robert Morris College (some for scholarships). **$100,000** each to Carnegie Mellon U. and Extra Mile Education Foundation. **$62,000** to Foundation for California U. of Pa. **$50,000** each to Carlow College, Gannon U. [Erie], Manchester Craftsmen's Guild/Bidwell Training Center, and Penn State U. **$25,000** to Pace School. **$20,000+** each to Sewickley Academy and U. of Pittsburgh. **$13,000+** each to The Ellis School and Winchester Thurston School. **$10,000** each to Allegheny Valley School and Incarnation Academy. **$5,000** each to Central Catholic High School, FAME/Fund for the Advancement of Minorities through Education, and U. of Pa. [Philadelphia]. **$4,000** to U. of Pa. Law School. **$3,000+** each to Clelian Heights School and St. Anne School. Other smaller grants/contributions and matching gifts. *ARTS-CULTURE GRANTS*: **$145,000+** to Pittsburgh Symphony. **$118,000+** to Pittsburgh Opera. **$107,000** to Pittsburgh Children's Museum. **$100,000** to Pittsburgh Public Theater. **$97,000+** to Carnegie Institute. **$65,000** each to Historical Society of Western Pa. **$57,000+** to WQED. **$55,000** to Pittsburgh Ballet Theatre. **$50,000** to Civic Light Opera. **$18,000** each to City Theatre Company and River City Brass Band. **$15,000** to Gargaro Productions. **$10,000** to Pittsburgh Cultural Trust. **$9,000** to Pittsburgh Arts & Lectures. **$8,000** to Opera Theatre of Pittsburgh. **$7,500** each to Three Rivers Arts Festival. **$3,000** to Pittsburgh Chamber Music Society. Other smaller grants/contributions and matching gifts. ***CIVIC-COMMUNITY-ENVIRONMENTAL GRANTS***: **$42,900** to Allegheny Conference on Community Development. **$30,000** to Pittsburgh Leadership Foundation. **$25,000** to Ireland Institute of Pittsburgh. **$10,000** to Ligonier Valley Memorial Assn. **$7,000+** each to Pittsburgh Council for International Visitors and Western Pa. Conservancy. **$5,000** to Audubon Society of Western Pa. **$3,000** to Pennsylvanians for Modern Courts. Other smaller grants/contributions. **Out-of-state** giving includes **$500,000** to American Ireland Fund [MA] but mostly focused on corporate operating locations in CA, IA, ID, MI, NC, NY, OH, VA and overseas; support is mostly for United Ways, scholarship programs, food-related courses of study, health/medical facilities, and matching gifts. Note: H.J. Heinz Company also awards grants/contributions through a corporate giving program but details are unavailable. ■**PUBLICATIONS:** Grant Application Information memorandum ■**WEBSITE:** www.heinz.com/jsp/foundation.jsp ■**E-MAIL:** heinz.foundation@hjheinz.com ■**APPLICATION POLICIES & PROCEDURES:** The Foundation reports five priority program areas: Nutrition/Nutritional Education, Youth Services & Education, Diversity, Healthy Children & Families, and Quality of Life. Giving typically focuses on significant corporate operating locations (especially SW Pa.) with grants awarded for general operating support, special projects, building/capital needs, seed money, technical assistance, research, scholarship funds, publications, conferences, seminars, or employee matching gifts. No grants are awarded to individuals or for general scholarships, equipment, conferences, unsolicited research projects, travel, political campaigns, sectarian religious purposes, or loans. Except for major capital or grant campaigns, no multiyear pledges are made. Grant requests which indicate how the proposed project fits one of the five priority program areas may be submitted at any time in a proposal which includes: (1) Executive Summary; (2) Organizational background including the purpose/overall goals for the current year; (3) Project Description—the specific purpose for which funding is sought, i.e. problem to be solved, need to be met, service to be provided; (4) Measurable Goals/Objectives—how the project will be accomplished; (5) Target Demographic—population and/or geographic area to be serviced; (6) Impact—the plan for evaluating the project; (7) Sustainability—how the project will be sustained after the grant ends. Also include an annual report; current operating and project budgets; a recent audited financial statement; list of Board members with affiliations; IRS tax-exempt status documentation; information on any Heinz employees, retirees, or directors involved in the organization; and brief details on volunteer opportunities in your organization. Proposals following the Grantmakers of Western Pa. Common Grant Application Format are accepted. Matching gifts for secondary schools, 2-year and 4-year colleges, universities, art museums, performing arts organizations, libraries, public broadcasting stations, and hospitals have a $25 minimum, $5,000 maximum/employee/year, and are matched 2:1.

O+D+T Tammy Aupperle (Program Director+Con) — Anthony J.F. O'Reilly (C+T) — S. Donald Wiley (VC+T) — Karyll A. Davis (S+T) — David R. Williams (T) — Mellon Bank N.A. (Corporate Trustee) — Corporate donor: H.J. Heinz Company

---

SW-160 **Heinz (Howard) Endowment**	**MI**-11-12-13-15-16-17-29-31-34-35-41-42-43
30 Dominion Tower	44-45-51-52-53-54-55-56-72-81-85-86
625 Liberty Avenue	**Phone** 412-281-5777 **FAX** 412-281-5788
Pittsburgh 15222 (Allegheny County)	**EIN** 25-1064784 **Year Created** 1941
AMV $912,613,000 **FYE** 12-01 (**Gifts Received** $0)	199 **Grants totaling** $41,100,027

Giving focuses on SW Pa. in five major programmatic areas: Arts & Culture; Children, Youth & Families; Economic Opportunity; Education; and Environment. Some grants reflect multiple awards. ***ARTS & CULTURE GRANTS:*** **$1,000,000** to Phipps Conservatory (Campaign 2000). **$970,000** to Pittsburgh Cultural Trust (mostly operating support). **$520,000** to Pittsburgh Symphony (operating support-3 years). **$500,000** each to Greater Pittsburgh Convention & Visitors Bureau Education Foundation (Office of Cultural Tourism), Pittsburgh Ballet Theatre (Nutcracker production), and The Pittsburgh Foundation (Multi-Cultural Arts Initiative). **$438,000** to Brew House Assn. (building renovations/strategic planning/performance-gallery costs). **$265,000** to U. of Pittsburgh (mostly theatre restoration). **$228,500** to Gateway to the Arts (strategic plan implementation). **$225,000** to City Theatre Company (mostly operating support-3 years). **$200,000** each to Pittsburgh Center for the Arts (Arts in Community Division) and Pittsburgh Musical Theater (business plan). **$197,000** to Historical Society of Western Pa. (operating support-3 years). **$150,000** to Society for Arts in Crafts (capital campaign). **$122,500** to Pittsburgh Chapter AIA (mostly bridge barrier project). **$120,000** to Greater Pittsburgh Arts Alliance (operations/awareness plan). **$115,000** to River City Brass Band (operating support-3 years). **$100,000** each to Pittsburgh Board of Public Education (CAPA High School planning) and Pittsburgh New Music Ensemble (develop resident company). **$64,000** to Three Rivers Arts Festival (exhibition/planning). **$60,000** each to Associated Artists of Pittsburgh (debt reduction/financial planning) and Carnegie Mellon U. (regional arts organizations database). **$58,500** to Chatham Baroque (director's salary/guest artists). **$50,000** to Citizens for the Arts in Pa. [Harrisburg] (strategic plan). **$35,000** to Pittsburgh International Children's Theatre (transitional support). **$30,500** to Mon Valley Media (environmental art exhibitions/films). **$25,000** to RIDC SW Pa. Growth Fund (North Shore Park project). **$23,000** to Renaissance & Baroque Society (marketing plan/performances). **$20,000** each to Children's Festival Chorus, Downtown Management Organization (5th & Forbes Quick Fixes), and First Night Pittsburgh (artists' projects). **$17,560** to Mendelssohn Choir of Pittsburgh (long-range plan). **$15,000** to Urban League of Pittsburgh (Freedom Corner). **$12,000-$14,000** each to Artists & Cities (dance/theatre performances), Laboratory Company Dance (dancers' compensation/performance support), and Prime Stage (productions). **$9,000-$11,000** each to Artists Image Resource (artist-in-residence program), Bach Choir of Pittsburgh (concert/summer institute), Nego Gato (performance), Pittsburgh Irish & Classical Theatre (production), SilverEye Center for Photography (exhibitions), Starlight Productions (production), The Unseem'd Shakespeare Company (artistic fees), and Xpressions Contemporary Dance Company (production/guest artists). **$7,200-$7,500** each to McKeesport Symphony Orchestra (string rehearsals support), Srishti Dances of India (production), and Times Project (public art project). **$4,000-$6,000** each to Aliquippa Alliance for Unity & Development (art festival), Autumn House Press (poetry readings/workshops), Bricolage (theatre performance), Bulgarian-Macedonian National Educational & Cultural Center (folk ensemble support), Carnegie Institute, Community Media (Homewood Library programs), New Horizon Theater (production), Open Stage Theatre (production), Pittsburgh Chamber Music Project (Warhol Museum concerts), Pittsburgh Concert Chorale (musical premiere), Pittsburgh Filmmakers (neighborhoods component/film), Pittsburgh Playback Theatre (subscription series), and Renaissance City Choirs (vocal training workshops/concert series). Five other local grants **$1,500-$3,500**. ***CHILDREN, YOUTH & FAMILIES GRANTS:*** **$6,000,000** to U. of Pittsburgh/Office of Child Development (Braddock-Wilkinsburg ECI model demonstration management). **$1,080,000** to United Way of Allegheny County (mostly for annual campaign). **$1,062,000** to U. of Pittsburgh (6 grants—mostly support for family support centers program and Program in Policy & Evaluation). **$977,000** to Sarah Heinz House Assn. **$600,000** to Pittsburgh Board of Public Education (Literacy Plus program). **$380,000** to RAND Corp. (maternal-child health service blueprint). **$300,000** each to The William Copeland Fund (capacity building initiative for faith-based organizations), Lancaster Osteopathic Health Supporting Organization [Lancaster County] (statewide strategy re Early Care & Education model), Pa. Partnerships for Children [Harrisburg] (communications planning re Early Care & Education statewide initiative/school readiness report), and Pittsburgh Assn. for Education of Young Children (capacity building). **$200,000** to YouthWorks (youth training-employment program). **$150,000** to A Second Chance (Saturday program for out-of-home children). **$100,000** each to Family Resources (child abuse prevention initiative) and Pa. Economy League (Wilkinsburg early child care/literacy model). **$80,000** to Hill House Assn. (father-son mentoring/literacy program). **$75,000** each to Magee-Women's Hospital (girls healthy growth project), The Pittsburgh Foundation (Human Services Integration Fund), PittsburghPastoral Institute (adolescents smoking prevention program), and Urban League of Pittsburgh (African-American Leadership Development Program). **$55,000** to Allegheny Youth Development (African-American youth leadership program). **$50,000** each to Family Communications (public space signage), Family Health Council (teen parents program), Greater Pittsburgh Fatherhood Initiative (programming re interfaith church ministries), and YMCA of McKeesport (youth leadership-employment program). **$40,000** to Grantmakers of Western Pa. (enhanced services). **$21,112** to Carlow College (conferences underwriting). **$5,000** to Community Human Services Corp. ***ECONOMIC OPPORTUNITY GRANTS:*** **$1,250,000** to U. of Pittsburgh/McGowan Institute for Regenerative Medicine (expansion). **$1,150,000** to Carnegie Mellon U. (medical robotics-information technology research and Entrepreneurship Education Program). **$1,000,000** to Strategic Investment Fund Partners (Round 2 funding). **$625,000** to Duquesne U. (Community Manufacturing Initiative/recruitment re minority communities skills training). **$750,000** to Pa. Economy League (workforce development initiative/operating support/tax study projects). **$540,000** to Technology Development & Education Corp. (develop industry-learning provider relationships/increased public sector research funding/conferences). **$400,000** to New Century Careers (regional workforce recruiting-training initiative). **$330,000** to Pittsburgh Gateway Corp. (mostly university-based business startup tech assistance). **$300,000** each to Coro Center for Civic Leadership (Civic Leadership Program), Pittsburgh Partnership for Neighborhood Development (neighborhood CDC's/operating support), and U. of Pittsburgh/Office of Technology Management (graduate student internships). **$250,000** to U. of Pittsburgh (bioengineering products incubator/bioengineering jobs creation).**$245,000** to Community College of Allegheny County Education Foundation (mostly inner-city machining/welding employment training). **$200,000** each to Allegheny Intermediate Unit (Steel Center Vo-Tech), El Centro Hispano (recruitment-employment services), and Pittsburgh Council for International Visitors (support-retain international college students/website). **$150,000** each to Pittsburgh Regional Alliance (regional internship initiative) and U. of Pittsburgh/Katz School of Business (entrepreneurial education programs). **$100,000** to Westmoreland County Community College (rural manufacturing workforce training). **$87,500** to Tides Center-Western Pa. (community initiatives fund). **$75,000** to Black Contractors Assn. (Youth Construction Initiative). **$25,000** to Innovation Works (Indian entrepreneurial organization start-up). Out of state grant: **$50,000** to Women's Institute for Secure Retirement [DC] (SW Pa. survey of residents' economic status). ***EDUCATION GRANTS:*** **$1,400,000** to Pittsburgh Board of Public Education (Literacy Plus program). **$250,000** each to Carnegie Mellon U. (high school-based robotics-science program at national consortium) and Community Loan Fund of SW Pa. (working capital fund for alternative schools). **$210,000** to Manchester Craftsmen's Guild (program-operating support). **$200,000** each to Carnegie Mellon U. (science education initiative), Community College of Allegheny County Education Foundation (web-based network supporting school performance efforts), and NEED/Negro Emergency Education Drive (minority scholarships). **$150,000** each to APEX Consortium (performance-based teacher development), ASSET, Inc. (develop elementary school environmental education curricula), Mon Valley Education Consortium (improved quality-funding of Pa. public schools initiative), and Pittsburgh Council on Public Education (program-operating support). **$130,000** to Carnegie Institute (Science & Technology festival). **$100,000-$105,000** each to Education Policy & Issues Center (regional analysis of schoolperformance/policies), Education Policy & Leadership Center (program-operating support), Penn Hills School District (improved school performance initiative), Sharon City School District (elementary-middle schools performance initiative), Steel Valley School District (elementary-middle schools performance initiatives), U. of Pittsburgh (Heinz Memorial Chapel), U. of Pittsburgh (university-school partnerships re teacher preparation), and Woodland Hills School District (secondary schools school performance initiatives). **$90,000** to Highlands School District (early grades school performance initiative). **$75,000** to Spring Cove School District (elementary-middle schools performance initiative). **$50,000** each to Foundation for California U. of Pa. (university-schools teacher preparation initiative), Indiana U. of Pa. (university-schools teacher preparation initiative), Pa. Humanities Council [Philadelphia] (rural education initiative using technology), Slippery Rock U. (university-schools teacher preparation initiative), and U. of Pittsburgh/Institute of Politics (education forum). **$30,000** to Homeless Children & Family Emergency Fund (computer lab program in shelters). **$25,000** to Tech Link Program of Pittsburgh (sponsorship of local F.I.R.S.T./Robotics Team). **$20,000** each to All of Us Care (computer learning center), Carnegie Mellon U. (special-needs students computing workshops), and Citizens to Abolish Domestic Apartheid (summer computer programs). **$15,000** each to Allegheny Intermediate Unit (substitute teacher preparation program), Pittsburgh Chess Club (program support), Pittsburgh Council on Public Education (Peabody High School program), and U. of Pittsburgh/School of Education (LEADERS Project). **$12,000** to East Liberty Development (high speed technology for nonprofits). Other smaller local grants. **Out-of-state** grant: **$200,000** to F.I.R.S.T./For Inspiration and Recognition of Science & Technology [NH] (Pittsburgh participation in robotics competition). ***ENVIRONMENT GRANTS:*** **$1,044,000** to Community Foundation for the Alleghenies [Johnstown] (mostly for Pittsburgh Business Efficiency Partnership and Western Pa. Watershed Protection Program). **$1,000,000** to The Pittsburgh Foundation (Frick Nine Mile Run Trust). **$500,000** to Citizens for Pennsylvania's Future (Western Pa. Environmental Communications Resource Center/renewable energy campaign). **$380,000** to Conservation Consultants, Inc. (Green

Neighborhood Initiative/Pa. Wind Map Project). **$300,000** to Tides Center-Western Pa. (Sustainable Pittsburgh). **$250,000** each to Green Building Alliance (operating support) and Pb X, Inc. (lead safety projects). **$140,000** to The Downtown Management Organization (downtown planning-enhancements). **$130,000** to U. of Pittsburgh/Graduate School of Public Health (chemical toxicity testing program). **$128,000** to Air & Waste Management Assn. (Pittsburgh environmental-business collaboration with targeted Central European cities). **$100,000** to Pittsburgh Community Broadcasting Corp. (environmental radio program). **$75,000** to Friends of the Riverfront (trail development/public education). **$50,000** each to Clean Air Council [Philadelphia] (Clean Air Act monitoring in Pa.), Community Loan Fund of SW Pa. (technical assistance for green business programs), Group Against Smog & Pollution (regional environmental advocacy re air quality), South Side Local Development Company (business district energy efficiency program), and Western Pa. Conservancy (Sideling Hill Creek Watershed Outreach Project). **$45,000** to Community Environmental Legal Defense Fund [Franklin County] (grassroots litigation support program). **$40,000** to Pa. Conservation Voters Education League (voter education programs). **$20,000** to Penn State U../Center for Sustainability (business-strategic plan). **Out-of-state** grants include **$250,000** to Clean Air Task Force [MA] (air quality protection in SW Pa.); **$200,000** to Second Nature [CA] (Western Pa. higher education environmental literacy readiness); **$115,000** to Clean Water Fund [DC] (two SW Pa. projects); **$100,000** each to Clark Atlanta U. [GA] (Pittsburgh transit equity initiative) and The Tides Center [CA] (Chemical Strategies Partnerships with Pa. industries); **$80,000** to National Audubon Society [NY] (white-tailed deer management research); **$50,000** each to Chesapeake Bay Foundation [MD] (nutrient pollution reduction) and Earth Force [VA] (Western Pa. program expansion); **$40,000** to Pinchot Institute for Conservation [DC] (Appalachian Forest Workshop); and others. ■**PUBLICATIONS:** Annual Report; statement of program policy; application guidelines ■**WEBSITE:** www.heinz.org ■**E-MAIL:** info@heinz.org ■**APPLICATION POLICIES & PROCEDURES:** The Endowments report that most grants awarded meet two criteria: (1) the organization is located in SW Pa. or the project clearly benefits the region, and (2) the project must be in one of five focus areas: Arts & Culture; Children, Youth & Families; Economic Opportunity; Education; or Environment. Funding is unlikely unless an application meets these criteria. No grants are awarded to individuals or for-profit organizations. The Endowments seek to support programs that (a) will have a significant and continuing impact; (b) intervene at the appropriate level to address the underlying causes of problems; (c) offer opportunities for leverage by forming partnerships with other grantmakers, organizations, government, or the private sector; (d) are grounded in the community but which may have potential for application elsewhere; (e) and complement—not duplicate—other foundations' efforts. Prospective applicants should review carefully the guidelines for the programmatic area for which funding is sought; see the website. Grant requests may be submitted at any time to the appropriate Program Director of The Heinz Endowments (see the website or telephone the Endowments) and follow a two-step process. **Step 1:** Send a concise Letter of Inquiry, signed by head of the applicant organization or of its board, which answers the following questions: What is the nature of the proposed program, including its objectives, target population/s and specific action plan? What is the need for the proposed program and why is it important? How is it different from existing programs or projects? How does the proposed program advance the goals and strategies of The Heinz Endowments, and how is it consistent with the Foundation's work? What is the nature of your organization and what are its qualifications to carry out the proposed program? How will the program's effectiveness be monitored and evaluated? What are the implications of the program in terms of public policy/public awareness? How will the program's outcomes be communicated to relevant audiences? What is the estimated cost of the overall project and the amount of funding you are requesting? Do not include supporting materials, e.g. videotapes or publications, with the initial Letter of Inquiry. After the Letter of Inquiry is reviewed by the Endowments' program staff, an applicant will be notified by telephone or in writing if the request meets the Endowments' funding criteria. **Step 2:** If further consideration is merited, the Endowment will ask an applicant to submit a formal proposal; proposals which follow the Grantmakers of Western Pa. Common Grant Application Format (see website: www.gwpa.org) are accepted. The Boards of Directors of both Endowments award grants at meetings held twice a year.

O+D+T Maxwell King (Executive Director+Con) — Teresa F. Heinz (C+D) — H. John Heinz, IV [MA] (D) — Carol R. Brown (D) — Frank V. Cahouet (D) — Howard M. Love (D) — Shirley M. Malcom (D) — William H. Rea (D) — Barbara K. Robinson (D) — Frederick W. Thieman (D) — Mallory Walker (D) — Drue Heinz (Director Emeritus) — Mellon Bank N.A. (Corporate Trustee)

SW-161 Heinz (Vira I.) Endowment
30 Dominion Tower
625 Liberty Avenue
Pittsburgh 15222   (Allegheny County)

MI-11-12-13-14-15-17-22-25-29-31-41-42-44
49-51-52-53-54-55-56-71-72-81-85
Phone 412-281-5777 **FAX** 412-281-5788
EIN 25-1762825   **Year Created** 1983

AMV $468,932,000   **FYE** 12-01   **(Gifts Received** $0)   142 **Grants totaling** $18,501,097

Giving focuses on SW Pa. in five major programmatic areas: Arts & Culture; Children, Youth & Families; Economic Opportunity; Education; and Environment. Some grants reflect multiple awards. ***ARTS & CULTURE GRANTS:*** **$1,000,000** to Strategic Regional Developments, Inc. (policy research re creating downtown housing). **$520,000** to Pittsburgh Ballet Theatre (operating support-3 years). **$480,000** to Pittsburgh Opera (operating support-3 years). **$311,500** to Riverlife Task Force (mostly operating support). **$277,500** to Carnegie Institute (mostly for Arts Education Collaborative). **$215,000** to Mattress Factory (operating support/strategic planning-3 years). **$150,000** to Pittsburgh Children's Museum (operating support-3 years). **$91,700** to Western Pa. Professionals for the Arts (Arts Management Enhancement Service/regional artists database). **$52,500** each to Historical Society of Western Pa. (mostly exhibit). **$24,000** to Sweetwater Art Center (fundraising consultant). **$20,000-$22,500** each to Carnegie Museum of Art, Pittsburgh Dance Alloy (director search), and Youth Works (Youth ArtWorks program training). **$16,000** to Pittsburgh Cultural Trust (programming fund/operating support). **$9,000-$10,000** each to Artists & Cities (documentary), Earthome Productions (documentary film), Gateway to the Arts (long-range planning), Northside Leadership Conference (cultural planning), Pittsburgh International Children's Theatre (planning process), and U. of Pittsburgh (Heinz Chapel music). **$3,000-$5,000** each to Civic Light Opera (development consultant). Pa. Art Education Assn. (conference), and Point Park College (summer theatre). Other smaller local grants. **Out-of-state** grants include **$120,000** to Mid-Atlantic Arts Foundation [MD] (program); and **$50,000** each to Friends of Dresden [NY] (documentary) and Grantmakers in the Arts [WA]. ***CHIL-***

DREN, YOUTH & FAMILIES GRANTS: **$300,000** to Shady Lane School (early childhood arts programming). **$250,000** to Education Policy & Issues Center (professional training initiative). **$200,000** each to TidesCenter-Western Pa. (YouthPlaces program improvements) and YouthWorks (youth employment/Youth ArtWorks program). **$175,000** to Hill House Assn. (after school literacy program). **$150,000** to YWCA of Greater Pittsburgh (program re increasing girls' math-science interest). **$125,000** to Pb X, Inc. (environmental health collaborative). **$100,000** each to The Kingsley Assn. (African-American youth leadership program), The Pittsburgh Foundation (9/11 Fund), Program to Aid Citizen Enterprise (African-American youth leadership program), Sarah Heinz House Assn. (youth leadership mini-grants program), and Small Seeds Development, Inc. (faith-based violence prevention program). **$90,000** to Beginning With Books (book drive). **$75,000** to National Conference for Community & Justice (youth leadership mini-grants program). **$70,000** to Gateway to the Arts (Arts-and-Literacy mini-grants program). **$60,000** to The Mentoring Partnership of SW Pa. (expanded faith-based initiative). **$10,000** to United Way of Allegheny County. **$5,000** to Westmoreland-Fayette Work Force Investment Board (career literacy survey). **ECONOMIC OPPORTUNITY GRANTS:** **$1,170,000** to Carnegie Mellon U. (4 grants: information technology skills training initiative/expanded CMU-federal partnerships/Center for Economic Development/tech-transfer initiative). **$1,000,000** to Strategic Investment Fund Partners (Strategic Investment Fund). **$300,000** to Pittsburgh Regional Alliance (regional economic development activities). **$250,000** each to Duquesne U. (labor force research/regional immigration strategies) and Tides Center-Western Pa. (regional employment skills assessment initiative for high school students). **$225,000** to Technology Development & Education Corp. (recruiting initiative/tech transfer practices review). **$200,000** each to Coro Center for Civic Leadership (civic leadership program) and Jewish Family & Children's Service of Pittsburgh (immigration services). **$160,000** to Allegheny Conference on Community Development (Agenda Development Fund). **$150,000** each to Community College of Allegheny County Educational Foundation (bioscience/life sciences workforce training), Education Policy & Issues Center (high school to workforce transition research), Pittsburgh Tissue Engineering Initiative (engineering internships/sectoral initiatives), and World Affairs Council of Pittsburgh (regional initiative re international diversity). **$100,000** each to Mon Valley Education Consortium (vo-tech career recruiting partnership) and Robert Morris College (recruit girls/minorities to science-technology programs). **$50,000** each to African American Chamber Foundation of Western Pa. (business mentoring program) and U. of Pittsburgh (Mini-MBA program for biomedical scientists). **$20,000** to Pa. Economy League (statewide Economic Future project). **$15,000** to The Carnegie (low-income community outreach/National Engineering Week). **Out-of-state** grants include **$75,000** to Manufacturing Institute [DC] (promote SW Pa. manufacturing careers) and **$20,000** to Community Foundation Silicon Valley [CA] (support stewardship conference in Pittsburgh). **EDUCATION GRANTS:** **$1,000,000** to Carnegie Library of Pittsburgh (eiNetwork expansion). **$250,000** each to Community Loan Fund of SW Pa. (working capital fund for alternative schools) and Pace School (school performance initiative re special-needs students). **$200,000** each to FAME/Fund for the Advancement of Minorities through Education (minority student scholarships at local independent schools) and U. of Pittsburgh (church-based technology learning initiative). **$150,000** each to 3 Rivers Connect (technology-assisted learning initiatives), ASSET, Inc. (practice-based K-12 science educational initiative), Carnegie Institute (School Performance Network online support), Duquesne U. (technology training initiative for teachers), and Mon Valley Education Consortium. **$130,000** to Carnegie Mellon U. (special needs students computer training initiative). **$70,000-$75,000** each to Altoona Area School District (school performance initiative), Bedford Area School District (school performance initiative), Communities in School of Pittsburgh-Allegheny County (strengthen alternative models of schools), Duquesne U. (charter school project), and Pittsburgh Board of Public Education (Langley High School health careers academy). **$50,000** each to Allegheny Intermediate Unit (Pa. Educator Net online teacher recruitment), Chatham College (Pittsburgh Teachers Institute), and Pa. Partnership for Economic Education [Snyder County] (K-12 economic principles program). **$42,000** to Extra Mile Education Foundation (Extra Mile elementary schools evaluation). **$30,000** to Monaca School District (school performance initiative). **$4,000** each for Vira Heinz Travel Study Awards to Arcadia U. [Montgomery County], Bethany College [OH], Carnegie Mellon U., Chatham College, Duquesne U., Temple U. [Philadelphia], Thiel College, U. of Pittsburgh, Washington & Jefferson College, and Wilberforce U. [OH]. Other small local grants. **Out-of-state** grants include **$100,000** to National Foundation for Teaching Entrepreneurship to Disadvantaged and Handicapped Youth [DC] (inner-city education program); **$10,000** to The Tides Center [CA] (Funders Forum on Environmental Education); and small grants for philanthropy-related organizations. **ENVIRONMENT GRANTS:** **$292,000** to Pa. Environmental Council (Western Pa. Watershed Protection efforts). **$200,000** each to 3 Rivers Wet Weather, Inc. (storm water management design) and Environmental Defense, Inc. (Pa. TDML Project). **$150,000** each to Dollar Energy Fund (energy conservation programs in low-income communities) andEnterprising Environmental Solutions, Inc. (Interfaith Power & Light Program). **$148,000** to Tides Center-Western Pa. (Pa. Energy Project). **$100,000** each to Pittsburgh Parks Conservancy (membership development re master plan implementation) and Western Pa. Conservancy (Green Neighborhood Initiative). **$75,000** to Pa. Resources Council (regional anti-litter/waste reduction program). **$70,000** to Enterprising Environmental Solutions, Inc. (Pa. Sustainable Investor's Database). **$50,000** each to Carnegie Mellon U./Center for Building Performance & Diagnostics (environmental building projects technical assistance), Penn State U. (Maurice Goddard Chair for natural resources-environment), and U. of Pa. (Pa. Flora Database on the web). **$25,000** to Carnegie Mellon U. (science-technology forum). **$10,000** to EcoLogic Development Fund. Other smaller local grants. **Out-of-state** grants include **$250,000** to Brookings Institution [DC] (smart growth education-assistance in SW Pa.); **$100,000** to The Nature Conservancy [VA] (Pa. Aquatic Community Classification Project); **$25,000** each to National Parks Conservation Assn. (Heinz School participation in National Parks' business initiative) and Resources for the Future [DC] (Millennium Project); **$45,000** to ULI Foundation [DC] (national symposium in Pittsburgh); **$20,000** each to North American Water Trails [DC] (projects in Western Pa.) and Wildlife Habitat Council [MD] (Three Rivers Habitat Partnership); and other smaller grants. ■**PUBLICATIONS:** None ■ **WEBSITE:** www.heinz.org ■**E-MAIL:** info@heinz.org ■**APPLICATION POLICIES & PROCEDURES:** Refer to the application guidelines for the Howard Heinz Endowment.

SW-162 Henry (Margaret L.) Children's Home
Sky Bank Building, Suite 300
14 North Mercer Street
New Castle 16101   (Lawrence County)

MI-12-13-17

Phone 724-658-9068 **FAX** None
EIN 25-6065991   **Year Created** 1921

AMV $308,038   **FYE** 3-01   **(Gifts Received** $0)   11 **Grants totaling** $17,666

All local giving. High grants of **$3,025** each to City Rescue Mission and Cray Youth & Family Services. **$2,420** each to Lawrence County Children & Youth Services (children's gifts), Lawrence County Women's Shelter (children's programs), and New Castle Area YMCA (youth programs). **$1,210** to Elwood Area Family Center (operating support). Other contributions **$726** or smaller for children/youth purposes. ■**PUBLICATIONS:** None ■**WEBSITE:** None ■**E-MAIL:** None ■**APPLICATION POLICIES & PROCEDURES:** The Foundation reports that only organizations providing education or welfare assistance to Lawrence County children are eligible to apply. Grant requests may be submitted in any form at any time prior to the annual meeting in May.
O+D+T Richard E. Flannery, Esq. (P+Con) — Patti Chambers (VP) — Debra McElwain [Ellwood City] (S) — Anna Mary Mooney (F) — and 16 other directors — Sky Bank (Trustee)

SW-163 Highmark Foundation
120 Fifth Ave., Suite 2628
Pittsburgh 15222   (Allegheny County)

MI-31-32-35

Phone 412-544-8800 **FAX** 412-544-5318
EIN 25-1876666   **Year Created** 2000

AMV $8,135,666   **FYE** 12-01   **(Gifts Received** $0)   2 **Grants totaling** $150,000

All giving to Pa. **$75,000** each (both initial payments on **$125,000** grants) to Faith Based Network and Foundation of the Pa. Medical Society/Free Clinic Assn. of Pa. (resource sharing, website development, and public policy development among 70 member clinics). — One grant approved for future payment: **$500,000** to Susan Byrnes Health Education Center [York] (develop a national distance-learning health education network). ■**PUBLICATIONS:** informational brochure ■**WEBSITE:** www.highmark.com/was/hmpr/comm/hmfoundation.jsp ■**E-MAIL:** lynne.marchese@highmark.com ■**APPLICATION POLICIES & PROCEDURES:** The Foundation's mission is improvement in the well-being, health status, and quality of life of individuals living in communities/regions served by Highmark Blue Cross/Blue Shield. Giving focuses on four priority areas: (1) Chronic Diseases—e.g. diabetes, cardiovascular disease, cancer and osteoporosis) as well as nutrition, weight management and physical management; (2) Family Health—e.g. adolescent health, dental health and senior care; (3) Service Delivery Systems—e.g. long-term care, coordination of services, access/availability of dental and primary care services; (4) Communicable Disease—e.g. immunizations, pneumonia, influenza, sexually transmitted diseases. Occasionally the Foundation will invest in health-related projects outside of these four areas. Normally, no grants are awarded for capital campaigns, annual fundraising campaigns, endowments, event sponsorships, clinical research, scholarships, routine operational costs, lobbying, political campaign activities, or direct financial subsidy of health services to individuals or groups. The Foundation reports that most grants are awarded in response to Foundation-initiated RFPs (Requests for Proposals). While unsolicited requests are rarely considered, prospective nonprofit organizations still may submit a one-page Letter of Inquiry which shows that the proposed project will (a) demonstrate broad or strong community impact, (b) create lasting value, (c) demonstrate new and sustainable ways to solve health problems, (d) reach underserved populations, (e) leverage additional financial or volunteer resources, (f) reduce long-term cost or duplication of services and resources, and (g) incorporate sound programmatic methods/evaluations as building blocks for long-term program success.
O+D+T Lynne Marchese (Program Officer+Con) — George F. Grode [Camp Hill] (C+D) — Doris Carson Williams (VC+D) — Aaron A. Walton (P+D) — Elaine B. Krasik (S) — Melissa M. Anderson (F) — Scott Becker (D) — Thomas J. Rohner, Jr. M.D. [Elizabethtown] (D) — Corporate donor: Highmark Blue Cross Blue Shield

---

SW-164 Hillman Foundation, Inc., The
c/o The Hillman Company
2000 Grant Building, 310 Grant Street
Pittsburgh 15219   (Allegheny County)

MI-11-12-13-14-15-16-22-29-41-42-44-45-54
55-57-71-84-85

Phone 412-338-3466 **FAX** 412-338-3463
EIN 25-6011462   **Year Created** 1951

AMV $132,594,674   **FYE** 12-01   **(Gifts Received** $0)   58 **Grants totaling** $6,462,400

Mostly Pittsburgh/Western Pa. giving. Note: The above 'Grants Totaling' figure refers to those disbursed in 2001; the following refers to the 40 grants totaling **$7,869,400** approved in 2001, whether or not any payments were made on those commitments—some are multiyear pledges as indicated. High grant of **$3,000,000** to Pittsburgh Children's Museum (Children's Center development-5 years). **$500,00** to Allegheny Conference on Community Development (strategic investment fund-5 years). **$350,000** to Pittsburgh Public Schools (Literacy Plus Initiative). **$300,000** each to Manchester Craftsmen's Guild (recording studio expansion/equipment-3 years), Riverlife Task Force (master plan development/implementation), Sports & Exhibition Authority (North Shore Riverfront Park development-2 years). **$250,000** each to Allegheny County Library Assn. (information network infrastructure) and DePaul Institute (facility renovation-3 years). **$235,000** to WQED (Elsie Hillman Conference Center). **$225,000** to The Wesley Institute (facility renovation-3 years). **$150,000** each to Life's Work of Western Pa. (job training for disabled), Minority Enterprise Corp. of SW Pa. (business development assistance program), Pittsburgh Regional Alliance (marketing/economic development initiatives), and Washington & Jefferson College (Vilar Technology Center construction/equipment-2 years). **$129,000** to Community College of Allegheny County (biology technician program). **$110,000** to United Way of Allegheny County (annual campaign). **$106,500** to The Pittsburgh Foundation (Human Services Integration Fund). **$100,000** each to FAME/Fund for the Advancement of Minorities through Education (scholarships endowment-2 years), and Pittsburgh Parks Conservancy (Schenley Park visitors center restoration). **$75,000** each to Carriage House Children's Center (building renovation), Center for Creative Play (facility renovation), Family Guidance, Inc. (fathers' program-2 years), Passavant Memorial Homes (resource center construction), Pittsburgh History & Landmarks Foundation (historic municipal building restoration), and Providence Connections (family support center renovations). **$60,000** to Mon Valley Education Consortium (Literacy for Life program). **$54,000** to Carnegie Museum of Natural History (mineral specimen purchases). **$50,000** each to The DoorWay (facility renovation), Ward Youth & Family Services (independent living program for females), Winnie Palmer Nature Reserve (site development/maintenance), and YouthWorks (job creation program for at-risk teens). **$47,000** to Habit-Tat for Youth & Education [Zelienople] (middle school behavioral program. **$40,000** to Hoyt Institute of Fine Arts (children's traveling performing arts series). **$35,000** to Allegheny Land Trust (land purchase). **$30,000** each to Pa. Environmental Council (program expansion/youth programs) and Westmoreland Human Services, Inc. (program facility purchase/renovation). **$25,000** to Bushy Run Battlefield Heritage Society (land acquisition). **$20,000** to Homeless Children & Family Emergency Fund (computer study centers in homeless shelters). **$10,000** to Associated Artists of Pittsburgh (facility renovation). **Out-of-state** grant: **$12,000** to The Foundation Center [NY] (information services/outreach-3 years). ■**PUBLICATIONS:** Annual Report with grant application procedures ■**WEBSITE:** None ■**E-MAIL:** foundation@hillmanfo.com ■**APPLICATION POLICIES & PROCEDURES:** The Foundation reports that preference is given to organizations in the Pittsburgh/SW Pa. region; current priority interests are strengthening family and community, especially youth/youth services and human/social services. Most grants are for capital needs, special projects, seed money, professorships, land acquisition, or equipment. No grants are awarded to/for individuals, conferences/seminars meetings, travel, or organizations outside the U.S. The Foundation reports it prefers to have prospective grant applicants make initial contact in writing or to personally visit the Foundation's office to discuss the possible submission of a request. If a grant request is submitted, the Grantmakers of Western Pa. Common Grant Application Format (see Appendix) should be used as an outline for proposal development and for a list of required supporting documentation; the Foundation subsequently may request additional materials. Grant applications may be submitted at any time. Site visits sometimes are made to organizations being considered for a grant. The Board of Directors awards grants at quarterly meetings (April, June, October, and December) and has an annual meeting in May.

O+D+T Ronald W. Wertz (P+Con) — Henry L. Hillman (C+D) — C.G. Grefenstette (VP+D) — H. Vaughan Blaxter, III (S+D) — Lawrence M. Wagner (F+D) — Elsie H. Hillman (D) — Corporate donors: The Hillman Company; J.H. Hillman & Sons Co.; Hillman Land Company; and family-owned corporations.

SW-165 **Hillman (Henry L.) Foundation, The**		**MI**-12-14-17-31-32-41-42-52-53-54-55-56-57
2000 Grant Building		63-71
310 Grant Street		**Phone** 412-338-3466 **FAX** 412-338-3463
Pittsburgh 15219	(Allegheny County)	**EIN** 25-6065959 **Year Created** 1964
AMV $89,438,347 **FYE** 12-00	(**Gifts Received** $9,875,773)	93 **Grants totaling** $4,098,150

Mostly local giving; grants are for general/unrestricted support except as noted; some grants comprise multiple awards. High grants of **$1,000,000** each to Shady Side Academy (performing arts facility) and U. of Pittsburgh Medical Center/Shadyside (cancer care/research programs). **$300,000** to Phipps Conservatory & Botanical Gardens (horticulture chair endowment). **$250,000** to Magee-Women's Health Foundation (Elsie Hillman Chair in Women's/Infant's Health Research Endowment). **$200,000** to Allegheny Valley School (capital campaign endowment). **$155,650** to Historical Society of Western Pa. (mostly Hillman Gallery endowment). **$57,000** to WQED (mostly local programming). **$36,000** to Calvary Episcopal Church (annual giving/music program). **$35,000** each to Carnegie Institute/Andy Warhol Museum (operating support/audio guide) and Carnegie Museum of Art (acquisitions program). **$33,500** to Carlow College. **$25,000-$26,000** each to Extra Mile Education Foundation (support for four Catholic schools) Pittsburgh Filmmakers (documentary), Pittsburgh Symphony (sustaining fund), and Westmoreland Museum of American Art (mostly photographic exhibit). **$23,000** to The Children's Institute (research study). **$10,000** to Carnegie Institute (Trustee Annual Fund). **$7,000** to Shadyside Hospital Foundation (mostly for cardiology lecture). **$5,000** each to Carnegie Museum of Natural History (gem/mineral show), Children's Hospital of Pittsburgh, Grantmakers of Western Pa. (Social Venture Partnership), Sewickley Valley Hospital Foundation, and U. of Pittsburgh Cancer Institute. **$2,000-$3,000** each to Loyalhanna Watershed Assn. (art auction), St. Edmund's Academy, and Three Rivers Arts Festival. Also, 35 local grants of **$1,000** each for community/economic development, arts/cultural, educational, health/medicine, human/social services, and youth services purposes. **Out-of-state** giving includes **$257,500** to Rider U./Westminster Choir College [NJ] (Elsie Hillman Chair for Artistic Direction endowment); **$134,000** to Princeton U. [NJ] (Class of '41 Fund); **$100,000** each to Masters School [NY] (science building) and Squam Lakes Assn. [NH] (endowment); **$50,000** to International Foundation for Education & Self-Help [AZ] (African development projects); and smaller grants. — Major grants approved for future payment: **$4,000,000** to Shady Side Academy (performing arts facility construction) and **$700,000** to Phipps Conservatory & Botanical Gardens (Horticulture Chair endowment). ■**PUBLICATIONS:** None ■**WEBSITE:** None ■**E-MAIL:** foundation@hillmanfo.com ■**APPLICATION POLICIES & PROCEDURES:** The Foundation reports that requests from Pittsburgh/SW Pa. organizations receive preference, and most grants are for general operating support, special projects, seed money, emergency funds, building funds, equipment, matching funds, and scholarships funds. No grants are awarded to individuals or for deficit financing, publications, conferences, or loans. Grant requests may be submitted at any time in a letter (signed by a fully authorized official of the organization); describe the program and its objectives, specify the funds needed, and justify the request; include an annual organizational budget, list of directors and trustees, detailed information on costs of the project/program to be funded, a time table (if appropriate), and IRS tax-exempt status documentation. The Board of Directors meets in March and December; final notification on requests is within three to four months.

O+D+T Ronald W. Wertz (S+D+Con) — Henry L. Hillman (P+D+Donor) — Lawrence M. Wagner (F+D) — H. Vaughan Blaxter, III [FL] (D) — Lisa R. Johns (AF)

SW-166 **Hillman (William Talbott) Foundation, Inc., The**		**MI**-12-18-19-20-25-31-32-41-51-53-54-55-57
2000 Grant Building		71-72-82
310 Grant Street		**Phone** 412-338-3466 **FAX** 412-338-3463
Pittsburgh 15219	(Allegheny County)	**EIN** 25-1536657 **Year Created** 1986
AMV $11,216,708 **FYE** 12-00	(**Gifts Received** $0)	121 **Grants totaling** $554,000

About one-third local/Pa. giving; grants are unrestricted support/annual giving except as noted and some comprise multiple payments for different purposes. High Pa. grant of **$19,500** to Allegheny Intermediate Unit (visual arts curriculum project).

$11,000 to Carnegie Institute (Museum of Art/Warhol Museum/general support). $10,000 each to ACLU Foundation of Pa./Greater Pittsburgh Chapter (video on police & rights) and U. of Pittsburgh Cancer Institute (research fund/general support). $6,500 to Pittsburgh Filmmakers ((film/general support). $5,000 each to Goods for Guns of Allegheny County, Planned Parenthood of Western Pa., and WQED (Elsie Awards/general support). $2,000-$2,500 each to Brother's Brother Foundation, Clara Bell Duvall Education Fund [Philadelphia] (minors' health care rights), Greater Pittsburgh Community Food Bank, Mattress Factory, PERSAD Center, and Shady Side Academy. $1,000-$1,500 each to Children's Hospital of Pittsburgh, Creative Nonfiction Foundation, Dance Alloy, Domestic Abuse Counseling Center, Life's Work of Western Pa., National Center for Juvenile Justice, National Society of Arts & Letters (sculpture competition), Pittsburgh Center for the Arts, Pittsburgh Cultural Trust, Pittsburgh Dance Council, Pittsburgh Parks Conservancy, Pittsburgh/Muskoka Foundation (for redistribution), Shadyside Hospital Foundation, Silver Eye Center for Photography, Society for Contemporary Craft, Southern Alleghenies Museum of Art, Three Rivers Arts Festival, and Western Pa. Conservancy. Other smaller local contributions for similar purposes. **Out-of-state** giving includes high grant of $176,000 to Lacoste School of the Arts in France [NY] (general operations/scholarships); $50,000 to Center to Prevent Handgun Violence [DC]; $30,000 to Princeton U. [NJ]; $15,000 to Heart of Yoga Assn. [NY] (internet presence); $10,000 each to Comprehensive Community Development Corp. [NY] (housing fund) and The Threshold Foundation [CA] (grant fund); and $5,000-$5,500 each to American Foundation for AIDS Research [NY], Doctors Without Borders [NY], Lincoln Center for the Performing Arts [NY], NARAL Foundation [DC], Organizacao Indigena do Xingu [Brazil] (travel), TriBeCa Partnership [NY] and WideCast [CA] (sea turtle survival); $4,000 to Amnesty International [NY]. ■**PUBLICATIONS:** application guidelines ■ **WEBSITE:** None ■**E-MAIL:** foundation@hillmanfo.com ■**APPLICATION POLICIES & PROCEDURES:** The Foundation reports that requests from Pittsburgh/SW Pa. organizations receive preference. Most grants are for annual/continuing support, building/capital purposes, program development, or seed money. No grants are awarded to individuals. Grant requests may be submitted at any time in a letter, signed by a fully authorized official, which describes and justifies the program/project, its objectives, and specifies the funding needed. Include an annual budget, list of officers/directors, detailed information on project costs, a time schedule, if appropriate, and IRS tax-exempt status documentation; additional significant background information also is welcomed. The Board meets in May and December.

O+D+T Ronald W. Wertz (S+D+Con) — William Talbott Hillman [NY] (P+D+Donor) — Lawrence M. Wagner (VP+D) — Maurice J. White (F+D) — Lisa R. Johns (AF) — Donors: Henry L. Hillman Trust; Henry L. Hillman Charitable Lead Trust

---

SW-167   Hitchcock (Margaret Mellon) Foundation

c/o Mellon Private Wealth Management
525 William Penn Place, Suite 4000
Pittsburgh   15259   (Allegheny County)

MI-12-31-32-41-52-54

Phone 412-234-5892 **FAX** 412-234-1073
EIN 25-6018992   **Year Created** 1961

AMV $4,189,771   **FYE** 12-00   **(Gifts Received** $0)   54 **Grants totaling** $222,700

Limited local giving. $5,000 to Mary & Alexander Laughlin Children's Center. $4,150 to Carnegie Mellon U. $1,000-$2,300 each to The Ellis School, Pittsburgh-Muskoka Foundation, and U. of Pittsburgh Cancer Institute (Knowles Research Fund). **Out-of-state** giving includes high grant of $22,000 to South Muskoka Hospital Foundation [Canada]; $20,000 each to the Grant Foundation [FL] (Hospital Albert Schweitzer) and Metropolitan Opera [NY]; and other grants $1,000-$10,000 for educational, cultural, medical and other purposes, mostly as directed by Trustees (and their dependents) in areas where they reside. ■**PUBLICATIONS:** None ■**WEBSITE:** None ■**E-MAIL:** richards.lb@mellon.com ■**APPLICATION POLICIES & PROCEDURES:** The Foundation reports that grants generally are awarded only to institutions in which the Trustees have a personal interest. No grants are awarded for endowment, building funds, special projects, or to individuals. Contact the Foundation for guidelines, deadlines and an appliction form. The Trustees meet in October or November.

O+D+T Leonard B. Richards, III (S+Con) — Peggy M. Hitchcock (T) — Thomas M. Hitchcock, III [OH] (T) — William M. Hitchcock (T) — Alexander M. Laughlin [NY] (T) — William J. Simpson (T) — Louise Hitchcock Stephaich (T) — Mellon Bank N.A. (Corporate Trustee)

SW-168   Hodge (Emma Clyde) Memorial Fund

c/o PNC Advisors, M.S. P2-PTPP-25-1
Two PNC Plaza, 620 Liberty Ave.
Pittsburgh   15222   (Allegheny County)

MI-13-14-32-41-42-44-54-56-63-71-72

Phone 412-762-5182 **FAX** 412-762-5439
EIN 25-6227653   **Year Created** 1990

AMV $10,963,794   **FYE** 6-00   **(Gifts Received** $0)   44 **Grants totaling** $485,349

About one-half SW Pa. giving; grants are general contributions except as noted. High grant of $90,998 to National Aviairy in Pittsburgh (White Dove Program/bird acquisition). $70,785 to U. of Pittsburgh. $25,000 to Thiel College. $10,000 each to United Cerebral Palsy of Southern Alleghenies Region and Westmoreland Museum of American Art. $5,000 to Ligonier Valley Library. $4,000 to Ligonier Valley Education Trust. $3,000 each to Emmanuel Episcopal Church and Southern Alleghenies Museum of Art (lecture & film series). $2,000-$2,500 each to Historical Society of Western Pa., Ligonier Valley Endowment, Powdermill Nature Reserve, and YMCA of Ligonier Valley. **Out-of-state** giving includes $30,000 to Virginia Hodge Military Institute; $25,000 to Bascom Palmer Eye Institute [FL] (macular degeneration research); $20,000 to Red Cross [DC] (disaster fund); and $10,000 each to The Craig School [NJ], Guadalupe Center [FL], Make-A-Wish Foundation [AZ], Moses Brown School [RI], Planned Parenthood of Collier County [FL], Rhode Island Hospital Foundation, Salvation Army [VA], Save The Bay [RI], Save the Children [CT], and Shelter for Abused Women [FL]. ■**PUBLICATIONS:** None ■**WEBSITE:** None ■**E-MAIL:** None ■**APPLICATION POLICIES & PROCEDURES:** Grant requests may be submitted at any time in a formal letter of introduction which describes the nature and purpose/s of the organization.

O+D+T Beatrice A. Lynch (Trust Officer at Bank+Con) — L. Van Dauler, Jr. (Co-T) — Anne G. Earle [RI] (Co-T) — Emma M. Sarosdy [NC] (Co-T) — PNC Advisors (Corporate Trustee)

SW-169 Hopwood (J.M.) Charitable Trust
c/o PNC Advisors, M.S. P1-POPP-02-1
One PNC Plaza, 249 Fifth Ave., 2nd Floor
Pittsburgh 15222   (Allegheny County)

MI-12-13-14-19-22-29-31-32-41-42-43-51-52
54-56-63-71-72-79
Phone 412-762-3808 **FAX** 412-705-1183
EIN 25-6022634   **Year Created** 1948

AMV $31,585,289   **FYE** 12-00   **(Gifts Received** $0)   73 **Grants totaling** $1,418,354

About three-fourths local/Pa. giving. High grant of **$100,000** to Shadyside Hospital Foundation. **$75,000** to Washington Hospital. **$50,000** each to Allegheny Valley School, National Aviary in Pittsburgh, and Ohio Valley General Hospital. **$40,000** to ARC-Washington County. **$36,000** to St. Clair Hospital Foundation. **$35,000** each to Penn Future [Harrisburg] and Western Pa. Conservancy. **$33,000** to Make-A-Wish Foundation of Western Pa. **$30,000** each to The Carnegie and Duquesne U. **$27,500** to The Watchful Shepherd. **$26,714** to Clean Air Council [Philadelphia]. **$25,000** each to Carnegie Mellon U., Citizen Power, Inc., Pittsburgh Symphony, United Cerebral Palsy of Washington County, and U. of Pittsburgh. **$23,153** to Conservation Consultants. **$20,000** to Family Guidance, Inc. **$15,000** each to Rachel Carson Homestead Assn., Soli Deo Gloria Ministries, and Washington & Jefferson College. **$13,275** to Washington YMCA. **$10,000-$10,700** each to Big Brothers Big Sisters of Greater Pittsburgh, Chartiers Nature Conservancy, Coalition for Christian Outreach, Mental Health Assn. of Allegheny County, Mt. Pleasant Township Community Center, Neighborhood Drug Awareness Corps, Pa. Conservation Voters Education League, Pa. Environmental Council, and Whale's Tale Foundation/FamilyLink. **$7,500** each to Manchester Youth Development Center and Pittsburgh Ballet Theatre. **$6,000** to Civic Light Opera. **$5,000-$5,500** each to Goodwill Industries of Pittsburgh, Pittsburgh Opera, Saltworks Theatre Company, Southern Alleghenies Museum of Art, Washington Cemetery, and Washington Christian Outreach. **$2,000-$3,000** each to Chatham Baroque, Church of the Nativity, Girls Hope, Heartwood Institute, Human Services Center Corp., Junior Achievement of SW Pa., Three Rivers Arts Festival, and United Way of Greene County. **$1,000** each to Contact Pittsburgh and Friends of the Riverfront. Other smaller local contributions. **Out-of-state** giving includes **$155,000** to Citizens Scholarship Foundation [FL]; **$135,000** to Richardson Scholarship Foundation [FL]; **$30,000** each to 12th Street Academy [NY] and New London Hospital [CT]; **$10,000** to Indian River Children's Museum [FL]; and other smaller grants to NY, NC and FL. ■**PUBLICATIONS:** None ■**WEBSITE:** None ■**E-MAIL:** j.ferguson@pncadvisors.com■**APPLICATION POLICIES & PROCEDURES:** Grant requests may be submitted in a letter at any time; include IRS tax-exempt status documentation.

O+D+T James M. Ferguson, III (Executive VP at Bank+Con) — William T. Hopwood [Washington] (Co-T+Donor) — PNC Advisors (Co-Trustee)

SW-170 Horwitz (William & Dora) Endowment Fund, The
148 Haverford Drive
Butler 16001   (Butler County)

MI-13-14-17-22-31-41-42-44-52-56-62-71-82
Phone 724-287-5166 **FAX** None
EIN 25-1151970   **Year Created** 1964

AMV $1,761,101   **FYE** 3-01   **(Gifts Received** $0)   42 **Grants totaling** $94,000

About one-half local/Pittsburgh giving. High Pa. grant of **$6,000** each to B'nai Abraham Congregation. **$5,000** to Butler Jewish Welfare Fund. **$4,000** to Butler Public Library. **$2,000** each to Abraham Geiger College, George Junior Republic, and Hillel Academy of Pittsburgh. **$1,000-$1,500** each to Allegheny Valley School, Boy Scouts/Butler, Butler County Community College, Butler County Historical Society, Butler Symphony, Gateway Rehabilitation Center, Hadassah/Butler Chapter, Jewish Educational Institute of Pittsburgh, Keystone Tall Tree Girl Scout Council, Lifesteps, Inc., Northside Christian Health Center, Pa. Assn. for the Blind, Salvation Army/Butler, Volunteers Against Abuse Center of Butler County, D.T. Watson Rehabilitation Center, Western Pa. Conservancy, WQED-TV, and Yeshiva Achei Tmimim. Other smaller local contributions. **Out-of-state** giving includes high grant of **$12,500** to American ORT Federation [NY]; **$11,500** each to American Technion Society [NY] and Weizmann Institute of Science [Israel]; and **$10,500** to American Friends of Hebrew U. [NY] ■**PUBLICATIONS:** None ■**WEBSITE:** None ■**E-MAIL:** None ■**APPLICATION POLICIES & PROCEDURES:** The Foundation reports that giving focuses on Butler and Pittsburgh with most grants for general operating support, capital campaigns, or building/renovations. Grant requests may be submitted in a letter at any time.

O+D+T Maurice Horwitz (T+Con) — Harriet Cohen [CT] (T) — Dr. Anthony Horwitz [IL] (T) — Samuel B. Horwitz [IL] (T) — Tem Horwitz [IL] (T) — Mellon Bank N.A. (Agent)

SW-171 Hoss Foundation, The
c/o Grimm & Associates
219 Pittsburgh Street
Uniontown 15401   (Fayette County)

MI-41-63

Phone 410-740-3303 **FAX** None
EIN 52-1751819   **Year Created** 1995

AMV $871,556   **FYE** 6-01   **(Gifts Received** $0)   2 **Grants totaling** $50,000

All local giving. **$35,000** to Trinity High School (facility development). **$15,000** to Avery United Methodist Church. ■**PUBLICATIONS:** None ■**WEBSITE:** None ■**E-MAIL:** None ■**APPLICATION POLICIES & PROCEDURES:** The Foundation reports that support focuses on furthering Christian education, adoptions, assisting families with medical needs, and other purposes; there are no geographical restrictions on giving. Grant requests may be submitted in a letter at any time; briefly describe the needs/purpose and include IRS tax-exempt status documentation.

O+D+T N. Douglas Hostetler [MD] (P+Donor+Con) — W. Jeffrey Hostetler [WV] (F+Donor)

SW-172 Hough (Wallace P.) Charitable Trust
Refer to PNC Advisors Charitable Trust Committee entry.
                                        (Allegheny County)

MI-12-14-33-41

EIN 25-6352924   **Year Created** 1993

AMV $1,144,149   **FYE** 12-00   **(Gifts Received** $0)   2 **Grants totaling** $15,347

All giving restricted to Western Pa. organizations supporting mentally/physically challenged persons. High grant of **$8,347** to Allegheny Valley School. **$7,000** to Pace School. — Grants awarded in the prior year: **$13,500** to Western Pa. School for the Blind;

$11,000 to Early Learning Institute; and **$8,105** to Make-A-Wish Foundation of Western Pa. ■**APPLICATION POLICIES & PROCEDURES:** Refer to the PNC Advisors Charitable Trust Committee entry for a statement on giving priorities and full application guidelines.

O+D+T Refer to PNC Advisors Charitable Trust Committee entry. — PNC Advisors (Trustee)

SW-173 Hoyt Foundation, The
    c/o Kopp,
    Newport Road
    Wampum   16157   (Lawrence County)
AMV $13,520,743   **FYE** 10-01   **(Gifts Received** $0)

MI-11-13-14-17-19-22-25-29-31-41-42-43-44
53-54-63-86
Phone 724-535-3255 **FAX** 724-654-3479
EIN 25-6064468   **Year Created** 1962
150+ **Grants totaling** $1,019,021

All giving limited to Lawrence County; all grants are for general support/annual giving unless noted otherwise and some grants are discretionary payments by the Foundation's directors. High grant of **$166,667** to Community YMCA (payment on **$500,000** 3-year pledge).**$162,500** to Hoyt Institute of Fine Arts (payment on **$500,000** 3-year pledge). **$152,716** to Westminster College (payment on **$500,000** 3-year pledge). **$134,000** to Boy Scouts/Moraine Trails Council (payment on **$400,000** 3-year pledge). **$100,000** to City Rescue Mission (matching grant). **$61,667** to Women's Shelter/Rape Crisis Center (payment on **$185,000** 3-year pledge). **$32,000** to Lawrence County United Way. **$30,000** to First Presbyterian Church. **$9,000** to Wilmington Area School District (drug-alcohol training/capital improvement/marching band instruments). **$8,500** to Red Cross/Lawrence County Chapter. **$3,000** each to Big Brothers Big Sisters, Community Outreach, and Friends of the Library. **$1,000-$2,000** each to 4-H, American Legion, City Rescue Mission, Community YMCA, Cray Youth & Family Services, Ellwood City Area Chamber of Commerce, Ellwood City Community Business Assn., Hess Ice Skating Club, Jameson Health Care Foundation, Pa. Special Olympics, Red Cross, St. Paul's Baptist Church, and Special Olympics/Lawrence County. **$500** each to American Cancer Society, Jameson Hospital Aid Society, and Old Timers' Day. Also, a total of **$134,272** in scholarships awarded to Lawrence County students. ■**PUBLICATIONS:** Scholarship Application Form ■**WEBSITE:** None ■**E-MAIL:** mansell@sgi.net ■ **APPLICATION POLICIES & PROCEDURES:** The Foundation reports that giving is restricted to Lawrence County organizations or individuals—priority support is for human services, federated funds, health/medical purposes, and education. Most grants are for special projects, building funds, capital needs, and scholarships; multiyear grants are made. **Organizational Applicants** should initially telephone the Foundation to inquire about the feasibility of submitting a request. Grant requests may be submitted at any time in a full proposal with cover letter; include an annual report, organization and project budgets, audited financial statement, list of other funding sources, and Board member list. Site visits sometimes are made to organizations being considered for a grant. **Scholarship Applicants** must be Lawrence County residents, and must use the 4-page Scholarship Application Form available from the Administrator each year on April 15th. Completed applications must be submitted by the Second Friday in June deadline. Scholarships are awarded based on aptitude, achievement, and need; recipients are selected by a separate, independent Scholarship Committee of three educators (appointed by the Board of Directors) which prepares its own guidelines and application forms. Scholarships are granted for the entire school year, payable in halves; Spring Semester payment is contingent upon receipt of acceptable Fall Semester grades and a tuition invoice for Spring Semester.

O+D+T Jaimie L. Kopp (Administrator+Con) — Stephen R. Sant [New Wilmington] (C+D) — Floyd H. McElwain [Ellwood City] (D) — John W. Sant [New Castle] (D) — Steven C. Warner [New Wilmington] (D) — Charles Y. Mansell, Esq. [New Castle] (Counsel) — Sky Trust (Trustee)

SW-174 Hulme (Milton G.) Charitable Foundation
    c/o Glover & MacGregor, Inc.
    519 Frick Building, 437 Grant Street
    Pittsburgh   15219   (Allegheny County)
AMV $10,112,258   **FYE** 12-00   **(Gifts Received** $0)

MI-11-12-13-14-18-22-25-29-31-41-44-51-52
54-55-56-57-63-65-71-84
Phone 412-281-2007 **FAX** None
EIN 25-6062896   **Year Created** 1960
46 **Grants totaling** $415,000

Mostly local giving. High grant of **$48,000** to Shadyside Hospital Foundation. **$33,000** to Pittsburgh Cultural Trust. **$25,000** to Family Resources. **$20,000** to WQED/TV-FM. **$18,000** to Salvation Army. **$15,000-$15,200** each to Bolton for Christian Outreach, Shadyside Presbyterian Church, and Three Rivers Rowing Assn. **$13,500** each to Shady Side Academy and Winchester Thurston School. **$12,000** each to The Carnegie (Second Century Fund) and Lauri Ann West Memorial Library. **$10,000** each to Carnegie Library of Pittsburgh, Children's Hospital of Pittsburgh, Greater Pittsburgh Community Food Bank, Red Cross, United Way of SW Pa. (Early Childhood Initiative), and Western Pa. School for Blind Children. **$6,000-$8,000** each to Children's Institute, East End Cooperative Ministry, Northern Area Multi-Service Center, and Western Pa. Conservancy. **$5,000** each to Bethlehem Haven, Civic Light Opera, FamilyLink, Family House, Goodwill Industries of Pittsburgh, Pittsburgh Vision Services, Holy Family Institute, Pittsburgh Symphony, Planned Parenthood of Western Pa., Spina Bifida Assn., Travelers Aid Society of Pittsburgh, United Way of SW Pa., and Vintage. **$1,000-$3,000** each to Assn. of Children & Adults with Learning Disabilities, Boys & Girls Club of Western Pa., Children's Home of Pittsburgh, Heinz Hall for the Performing Arts, Opera Theatre of Pittsburgh, Pittsburgh Ballet Theatre, Pittsburgh History & Landmarks Foundation, and Pittsburgh Opera. **Out-of-state** giving includes **$2,000** each to International Dyslexia Assn. [MD] and Presbyterian Lay Committee [NC]. ■**PUBLICATIONS:** None ■**WEBSITE:** None ■**E-MAIL:** None ■**APPLICATION POLICIES & PROCEDURES:** The Foundation reports that special projects receive preference; no grants are awarded for endowment, capital campaigns, scholarships, or to individuals. Grant requests may be submitted in a letter or proposal at any time—the deadline is June 30th; describe the proposed project, state what funding is requested, and include background information and IRS tax-exempt status documentation.

O+D+T Holiday Hulme Shoup (T+Donor+Con) — Natalie Hulme Curry (T) — Aura P. Hulme (T) — Jocelyn Hulme MacConnell [VA] (T) — Corporate donor: Glover & MacGregor, Inc.

SW-175 Hunt (Roy A.) Foundation, The
Suite 630
One Bigelow Square
Pittsburgh 15219 (Allegheny County)

MI-11-12-13-14-29-31-32-41-42-44-51-52-54
55-56-57-63-71-72-81-85
Phone 412-281-8734 **FAX** 412-255-0522
EIN 25-6105162 **Year Created** 1966

AMV $95,065,725 **FYE** 5-01 **(Gifts Received** $0) 500+ **Grants totaling** $3,644,131

About one-third local/Pa. giving; grants are for operating/annual fund support except as noted. High grant of **$76,000** to Carnegie Institute (aluminum exhibit/Warhol Museum/education program/general support/special funds). **$75,000** to Friendship Development Associates. **$50,000** each to East Liberty Development Corp, Inc. (Real Estate Development Program), Southwestern Pa. Corp. (exhibit at Regional Enterprise Tower), and Public Auditorium Authority of Pittsburgh/Allegheny County (North Shore Riverfront Park development). **$35,000** to Phipps Conservatory & Botanical Gardens (capital campaign/general support). **$30,000** to Pittsburgh Public Theater (capital campaign/general support). **$28,000** to Shady Side Academy (mostly for Roy Hunt Computer Center). **$27,500** to Historical Society of Western Pa. (Museum of Rural Life/general support). **$25,000** each to Community Human Services Corp. (South Oakland needs assessment), Elizabeth Glass Workshop, Inc. (East Liberty studio campaign), Pittsburgh Leadership Foundation (summer day camp for inner-city children), and U. of Pittsburgh Cancer Institute (Knowles Research Fund). **$21,666** to Church of the Ascension (Growing to Serve campaign/general support). **$20,000** each to Lawrenceville Development Corp. (website/computer equipment) and Pa. Environmental Council (conservation-water programs/develop air emissions trading policies). **$19,500** to Pittsburgh Zoo (3 grants—capital campaign, river dolphin, general support). **$18,000** to U. of Pittsburgh (3 grants—School of Medicine Surgical Research endowment, Center for Latin American Studies, Nationality Rooms/Exchange Program). **$15,000** each to Eye & Ear Foundation (Chair in Ophthalmology/general support), Pittsburgh Symphony, United Way of Allegheny County (Early Childhood Initiative/general support), and West Penn Hospital Foundation (conference center capital campaign/general support). **$12,500-$13,000** each to Carnegie Mellon U. (3 grants—Architecture Cornerstones initiative, libraries, sports programs), Community Specialists Corp. (documentary), and Horticultural Society of Western Pa. (botanic garden). **$10,000** each to Allegheny Cemetery Historical Assn., Allegheny Valley School (capital campaign), Children's Home of Pittsburgh, Civic Light Opera (Gray Award), Family Tyes/Baldwin High School (Partnership with Youth), Frick Art & Historical Center (Excellence in Teaching award), The Mattress Factory (mostly building-grounds endowment fund), National Aviary (capitalcampaign), Pace School (new facility purchase-renovation), Pittsburgh Cultural Trust (Carol Brown Fund/general support), Pittsburgh Dynamo Youth Soccer Assn. (fields fund), Shadyside Hospital Foundation (Hillman Cancer Center capital campaign), Student Conservation Assn./Three Rivers Regional Office, and WQED. **$7,000-$7,500** each to Audubon Society of Western Pa. (start-up of native plants center), Bloomfield Preservation & Heritage Society (education center), Coalition for Christian Outreach (staff training), Conservation Consultants (capital campaign), and National Foundation for Teaching Entrepreneurship to Handicapped & Disadvantaged Youth (in-school/after-school programs). **$6,000** each to Mt. Ararat Community Activity Center (African American Assistance Project) and Third Path Institute [Philadelphia]. **$5,000** each to Allegheny Conference on Community Development, Allegheny Institute for Public Policy, Animal Rescue League of Western Pa., Big Brothers & Big Sisters of Greater Pittsburgh, Brew House Assn. (puppet festival), CARE Foundation [Philadelphia], Carnegie Library of Pittsburgh (Special Collections Room), Chatham Baroque, Community Design Center, Contact Pittsburgh (volunteer training), Epiphany Catholic Church (capital campaign), Family Guidance, Inc., First Night Pittsburgh, Fort Ligonier Assn. (fort restoration), Greater Pittsburgh Chamber of Commerce Trust (outreach program), Grantmakers of Western Pa., Junior Achievement of Western Pa., Leadership Pittsburgh, Ligonier Valley Historical Society, Ligonier Valley Library, Loyalhanna Watershed Assn., Ned Smith Center for Nature & Art [Dauphin County], People's Library of New Kensington, Pittsburgh Action Against Rape (various program services), Pittsburgh Children's Museum, Pittsburgh Council for International Visitors, Pittsburgh Downtown Partnership, Pittsburgh Filmmakers (Teenie Harris documentary), Pittsburgh Garden Place, Pittsburgh History & Landmarks Foundation (Riverwalk program), Pittsburgh Irish & Classical Theatre (staff salary), Pittsburgh Opera, Program for Female Offenders, Radio Information Service, Red Cross/SW Pa. Chapter, River City Brass Band (capital campaign), Sunshine Foundation [Philadelphia], Sweetwater Art Center, Trinity Cathedral (Dean's Activity Fund), UCP of Pittsburgh (capital campaign), Western Pa. Family Center, Western Pa. Humane Society, Western Pa. School for the Deaf (capital campaign), Westmoreland Museum of American Art (capital campaign), World Affairs Council of Pittsburgh, and YMCA of New Kensington (refurbish Capt. Alfred E. Hunt Room). **$2,000-$4,000** each to Allegheny College, Animal Friends, Inc., Joe Bellante Ministry, Boys & Girls Club of Western Pa., Central Catholic High School, East End Cooperative Ministries, East Liberty Family Health Care Center (capital campaign), Garfield Jubilee Assn., Gateway to the Arts, Greater Pittsburgh Community Food Bank (new warehouse-office building), Leukemia Society of America/Western Pa. Chapter, Mary Miller Dance Company (Peace 2001 project), National Flag Foundation (civics education initiative), Pittsburgh Ballet Theatre, Pittsburgh Dance Alloy, Pittsburgh Dance Council, Pittsburgh Voyager, Planned Parenthood of Western Pa., Preservation Fund of Pa. [Harrisburg], Shadyside Presbyterian Church (outreach ministries), U. of Pittsburgh/Theatre Arts Dept., St. Edmund's Academy, Trinity Christian School, U. of Pa., and Western Pa. Conservancy. Other smaller local grants. **Out-of-state** giving primarily to New England and other states where Trustees reside. ■**PUBLICATIONS:** Annual Report ; application guidelines ■**WEBSITE:** www.rahuntfdn.org ■**E-MAIL:** info@rahuntfdn.org ■**APPLICATION POLICIES & PROCEDURES:** The Foundation reports that giving focuses on the Metro Pittsburgh, Boston, and other areas where Trustees reside. Most grants are for Arts/Culture, Conservation/Environment, Health & Human Services, as well as three Special Program Initiatives: Youth Violence Prevention, Community Development, and the Environment. Most educational support is for institutions in which individual trustees have a particular interest. *First-time Applicants* are advised to submit a preliminary Letter of Inquiry which must be received no later than two weeks before the proposal submission deadlines (see schedule below). E-mailed Letters of Inquiry may be submitted if the inquiry is brief and includes a return mailing address. If the Foundation determines the proposed project to be of potential interest, a full proposal may be requested (see proposal preparation details below). A site visit may be requested as part of the review process. *Previously-funded Applicants* need only submit a full proposal. Deadlines for applications are: April 15th September 15th for General Grants, and March 15th and August 15th for Special Program Initiatives. Grant requests from previously-funded organizations are considered only at a November meeting, but requests from first-time applicants are considered at June and November Board meetings. A complete application must have a General Information Form (available from the Foundation or on the website) and a Full Proposal (concise and simply bound for ease in duplicating) with the following:

Problem Statement, Program Objectives, Methods (3 pages maximum): Discuss, describe and document the proposed program/project, why it is needed, what specific, measurable objectives will be achieved, and the methods/means by which the goals will be achieved, i.e., the implementation plan and timetable. Capital campaign proposals should include evidence of the project's priority in the organization's strategic or long-range plan. Any discussion beyond the three pages considered essential for understanding the proposal must be submitted as an attachment, or, a 3-page summary of the proposal should be submitted. Proposals that do not conform to this particular guideline will not be considered. In addition, required attachments/appendices include: (a) Evaluation—expected results or outcomes of the program or project and how they will be evaluated; priority is given programs/projects with clearly defined evaluation components; (b) Program/project budget,including funding strategy. Capital campaign proposals must include the overall campaign strategy, detailing amounts of funding committed and pending from other sources. Proposals for start-up funding must include a plan for long term funding to sustain the program. If the request is for general operating support, the annual budget should be submitted, including projected aggregate amounts of annual income from all sources, public and private—individuals, foundations, corporations, special events, etc. (c) A brief history of the organization including its mission and purpose, and a description of the targeted populations and/or communities it serves; this may be unnecessary in general operating support requests since it is assumed that organization mission/history would be addressed in the body of the proposal under Problem Statement, Program Objectives, and Methods. (d) List of the Trustees or Board of Directors, unless printed on the applicant's letterhead. (e) Most recent audited annual financial statements; new applicants are asked to send the last two years' audited statements. Organizations without audits should send a Form 990. (f) IRS tax-exempt status documentation. Failure to include any of these attachments may render the proposal ineligible for consideration. Additional materials—such as the most recent annual report, program marketing brochures, newsletters, or published newspaper articles—may optionally be submitted. Note: Grant applications under the Special Program Initiatives (Community Development, Environment, or Youth Violence Prevention) should be sent directly to the Foundation's Program Officer, Beatrice C. Carter. Also, applicants who are invited by a specific Trustee to submit a proposal must send a complete duplicate of the proposal with all attachments to the Foundation's office.

O+D+T Torrence M. Hunt, Jr. (P+Administrative Trustee+Con) — William E. Hunt (T) — Dr. Helen Hunt Bouscaren [MA] (T) — Dr. Susan Hunt Hollingsworth [MA] (T) — Andrew M. Hunt [NH] (T) — A. James Hunt (T) — Caroline H. Hunt (T) — Cathryn J. Hunt (T) — Dr. Christopher M. Hunt [ME] (T) — Daniel K. Hunt [ID] (T) — John B. Hunt [NH] (T) — Dr. Richard M. Hunt [MA] (T) — Dr. Roy A. Hunt, III [MA] (T) — Torrence M. Hunt, Sr. (T) — Marion M. Hunt-Badiner [CA] (T) — Rachel Hunt Knowles [GA] (T) — Joan F. Scott (T) — Mellon Bank N.A. (Corporate Trustee)

SW-176 Hwilc (Nat) Foundation

c/o Cookson, Peirce & Company
535 Smithfield Street
Pittsburgh 15222   (Allegheny County)

MI-31-41-44-54

Phone 412-471-5320 **FAX** None
EIN 22-2899613   **Year Created** 1987

AMV $1,391,912   **FYE** 12-00   **(Gifts Received** $0)   4 **Grants totaling** $36,000

All local giving. High grants of **$15,000** each to Community Library of Allegheny Valley and Westmoreland Museum of American Art. **$5,000** to St. Joseph High School. **$1,000** to Allegheny Kiski Health Foundation. ■**PUBLICATIONS:** None ■**WEBSITE:** None ■**E-MAIL:** None ■**APPLICATION POLICIES & PROCEDURES:** Grant requests may be submitted in a letter at any time; describe the organization's purpose and include IRS tax-exempt status documentation.

O+D+T Robert A. Walsh [Natrona Heights] (T+Donor+Con) — Jean Ann Walsh [Natrona Heights] (T+Donor+Con) — Kevin R. Walsh (T) — Rebecca A. Walsh [WI] (T) — Dr. Susan Walsh [NH] (T)

SW-177 Hyman Family Foundation

6315 Forbes Avenue
Pittsburgh 15217   (Allegheny County)

MI-22-25-32-52-62

Phone 412-521-7200 **FAX** None
EIN 25-6065761   **Year Created** 1957

AMV $1,236,398   **FYE** 8-00   **(Gifts Received** $0)   46 **Grants totaling** $68,850

About three-fourths local giving. High grant of **$21,000** to United Jewish Federation of Greater Pittsburgh. **$7,500** to Jewish Education Institute. **$6,500** to New Light Congregation. **$6,425** to Jewish Community Center. **$2,680** to Aleph Foundation. **$1,000-$1,600** each to Greater Pittsburgh Community Food Bank, Race for the Cure, and YMHA Music Society. Other local contributions **$15-$750** for cultural, Jewish, and other purposes. **Out-of-state** giving mostly to MA and FL. ■**PUBLICATIONS:** None ■**WEBSITE:** None ■**E-MAIL:** None ■**APPLICATION POLICIES & PROCEDURES:** Grant requests may be submitted in a letter or proposal at any time. No grants awarded to individuals.

O+D+T Lois Rubin (T+Manager+Con) — Saul Elinoff (T) — William Elinoff (T) — Yetta Elinoff (T)

SW-178 Industrial Scientific Foundation

c/o Industrial Scientific Corp.
1001 Oakdale Road
Oakdale 15071   (Allegheny County)

MI-12-14-15-29-43-56

Phone 412-788-4353 **FAX** None
EIN 25-1756557   **Year Created** 1994

AMV $440,828   **FYE** 6-01   **(Gifts Received** $20,000)   8 **Grants totaling** $20,200

Mostly local/Pa. giving; grants are for general support. High grant of **$5,000** to Clarion U. (McElhattan Scholarship). **$3,000** each to Family Hospice & Palliative Care, Pittsburgh Hearing Speech & Deaf Services, and Pittsburgh Vision Services. **$2,000** each to Bidwell Training Center and Vocational Rehabilitation Center. **$1,000** to Conservation Consultants. **Out-of-state** grant to ID for scholarship fund. ■**PUBLICATIONS:** None ■**WEBSITE:** None ■**E-MAIL:** None ■**APPLICATION POLICIES & PROCEDURES:** Grant requests may be submitted in a letter at any time. — Formerly called Industrial Scientific/McElhattan Foundation.

O+D+T Kent D. McElhattan (P+D+Donor+Con) — Kenton E. McElhattan (S+D+Donor) — James P. Hart (F+D) — Elaine L. Bonoma (D) — Charles C. Cohen, Esq. [Pittsburgh] (D) — Corporate donor: Industrial Scientific Corp.

SW-179 Isaly Dairy Charitable Trust
c/o PNC Advisors, M.S. P2-PTPP-25-1
Two PNC Plaza, 620 Liberty Ave.
Pittsburgh 15222   (Allegheny County)

MI-41-42-52-53

Phone See below **FAX** None
EIN 25-6024887   **Year Created** 1945

AMV $314,858   **FYE** 12-00   **(Gifts Received** $0)   14 **Grants totaling** $14,050

Two Pa. grants: **$1,000** to Shady Side Academy and **$800** to Assn. of Independent Colleges & Universities of Pa. [Harrisburg]. **Out-of-state** giving includes **$2,500** to Dunedin Fine Art Center [FL], **$2,000** to Florida Craftsmen, **$1,250** to Florida Orchestra, and others to FL and OH. ■**PUBLICATIONS:** None ■**WEBSITE:** None ■**E-MAIL:** None ■**APPLICATION POLICIES & PROCEDURES:** Sumbit requests in a letter at any time which describes the nature and purpose of the organization; send to H. William Isaly, The Isaly Klondike Company, 5400 118th Avenue North, Clearwater, FL 33520; telephone 813-576-8424. Decisions on grants are made by a Committee comprised of board members of the Isaly Co., Inc.

O+D+T Elizabeth Gay (Admin. Officer at Bank+Con) — H. William Isaly [FL] (T) — PNC Advisors (Corporate Trustee) — Corporate donor: Isaly Klondike Co.

SW-180 J&L Specialty Steel, Inc. Charitable Foundation
c/o J&L Specialty Steel, Inc.
1550 Coraopolis Heights Road, P.O. Box 1425
Coraopolis 15108   (Allegheny County)

MI-11-13-29-31-32-41-42-43-49-51-52-54-72-89

Phone 412-375-1600 **FAX** None
EIN 25-6311251   **Year Created** 1988

AMV $2,172,709   **FYE** 12-00   **(Gifts Received** $0)   88 **Grants totaling** $185,498

About half local or Beaver County giving. High Pa. grant of **$19,855** to United Way of Beaver County. **$8,125** to Robert Morris College. **$7,200** to Midland Borough School District [Beaver County]. **$6,000** each to Pittsburgh Zoo and YMCA of Beaver County. **$5,000-$5,675** each to Carnegie Mellon U., Carnegie Museums of Pittsburgh, United Way of Allegheny County, and U. of Pittsburgh/School of Engineering. **$3,700** to Borough of Midland. **$1,960** to Penn State U. **$1,000-$1,500** each to Assn. of Iron & Steel Engineers Scholarships, Advisory Board on Autism & Related Disorders, American Heart Assn., Big Brothers & Big Sisters of Greater Pittsburgh, Boy Scouts/Greater Pittsburgh Council, Boys & Girls Clubs of Western Pa., Children's Hospital of Pittsburgh, City Theatre Company, Communities in Schools, Cystic Fibrosis Foundation, FamilyLink/Whale's Tale Foundation, Greater Pittsburgh Community Food Bank, ISS Foundation, Jubilee Assn., Junior Achievement of Beaver Valley, Junior Achievement of SW Pa., Leukemia Society of America/Western Pa., Make-A-Wish Foundation of Western Pa., McGuire Memorial Home, National Parkinson Foundation/Greater Pittsburgh, Neurofibromatosis Clinics Assn., Pittsburgh Ballet Theatre, Pittsburgh Civic Light Opera, Pittsburgh Public Theater, Pittsburgh Symphony, Red Cross, Salvation Army, South Hills Chorale, UCP of Pittsburgh, and WQED. Other smaller Pa. contributions for various purposes. **Out-of-state** giving includes **$21,725** to United Way of Central Stark County [OH]; **$13,255** to United Way of Southern Columbiana County [OH]; and **$20,000** to Children's Hospital Medical Center of Akron [OH]. ■**PUBLICATIONS:** None ■**WEBSITE:** www.jlspecialty.com [corporate info only] ■**E-MAIL:** None ■**APPLICATION POLICIES & PROCEDURES:** The Foundation reports that giving is limited to Pittsburgh, Beaver County, and to J&L plant facility communities in Louisville, OH and Canton, OH. Prospective applicants initially should make a telephone inquiry about the feasibility of submitting a request. Grant requests may be submitted in a letter at any time; describe the organization and provide organizational and project budgets, audited financial statement, and IRS tax-exempt status documentation. Grants are awarded at meetings in January, March, May, July, September, and November. — Formerly called J&L Specialty Products Charitable Foundation.

O+D+T Daryl K. Fox (Administrator+Con) — Jacques Chabanier (C) — Mellon Bank N.A. (Corporate Trustee) — Corporate donor: J&L Specialty Steel, Inc.

SW-181 Jackson (John E. & Sue M.) Charitable Trust
c/o National City Bank of Pa.
National City Center, 20 Stanwix Street
Pittsburgh 15222   (Allegheny County)

MI-12-13-22-29-31-32-41-42-56-64-71

Phone 412-644-6005 **FAX** 412-644-6176
EIN 25-6019484   **Year Created** 1950

AMV $13,141,502   **FYE** 12-00   **(Gifts Received** $0)   62 **Grants totaling** $450,000

Limited local/Pa. giving. High Pa. grant of **$15,000** to Historical Society of Western Pa. **$8,000** to Pa. Right to Work Defense & Education Foundation. **$4,000** to United Negro College Fund [Philadelphia]. **$3,000** each to Leukemia Society of America and Coalition for Christian Outreach. **$2,000** each to Children's Hospital of Pittsburgh and Pittsburgh Theological Seminary. **$1,000** each to Freedoms Foundation of Valley Forge, Goodwill Industries of Pittsburgh, Masonic Charities [Lancaster County], Mid-Atlantic Career Center [Lancaster], Pittsburgh Leadership Council, and Western Pa. Conservancy. Other smaller local contributions. **Out-of-state** giving includes high grant of **$100,000** to National Right to Work Legal Defense Fund [VA]; **$30,000** each to Coral Ridge Ministries [FL] and The Leadership Institute [VA]; **$25,000** to The Heritage Foundation [DC]; **$22,000** to Hollins U. [VA]; **$20,000** to Eagle Forum Education Foundation; **$10,000** each to Alliance Defence Fund [DC], American Center for Law [VA], Free Congress Foundation [DC], Hillsdale College [MI], Media Research Center [VA], Red Cross [DC], Salvation Army [VA], and Young Americans Foundation [VA]; and smaller grants **$1,000—$6,000,** primarily for Conservative or Fundamentalist Christian causes in VA, FL and other states or organizations in Maryland's Eastern Shore. ■**PUBLICATIONS:** None ■**WEBSITE:** None ■**E-MAIL:** None ■**APPLICATION POLICIES & PROCEDURES:** No grants awarded to individuals. Grant requests may be submitted in a letter during August-October; the deadline is October 31st; include organizational/project budgets, list of major funding sources, and IRS tax-exempt status documentation.

O+D+T John M. Dodson (VP at Bank+Con) — Polly Jackson Townsend [MA] (Co-T) — National City Bank of Pa. (Co-Trustee)

SW-182 **Jackson (Ruth H.) Charitable Trust**
  c/o Pitt-Des Moines, Inc.
  3400 Grand Avenue, Neville Island
  Pittsburgh   15225   (Allegheny County)

MI-13-22-29-63-86

Phone 412-331-3000 **FAX** None
EIN 25-6065763   **Year Created** 1951

AMV $2,531,174   **FYE** 12-00   (**Gifts Received** $0)   51 **Grants totaling** $142,600

Limited local/Pa. giving. High Pa. grants of **$2,000** each to Pa. Right to Work Defense & Education Foundation [Harrisburg], Red Cross, and Salvation Army. **$1,000** to YWCA of Greater Pittsburgh. Other local contributions **$200-$500** for various purposes. **Out-of-state** giving includes **$50,000** to National Right to Work Legal Defense Foundation [VA]; **$12,000** to Media Research Center [VA]; **$10,000** each to Coral Ridge Ministries [FL] and Mount Holyoke College [MA]; **$5,000** to The Heritage Foundation [DC]; and smaller grants for Conservative Christian, health, educational and other organizations. ■**PUBLICATIONS:** None ■**WEBSITE:** None ■**E-MAIL:** None ■**APPLICATION POLICIES & PROCEDURES:** Grant requests should be submitted in a letter in October. Grants are awarded at a November meeting. No grants awarded to individuals.

O+D+T W.R. Jackson (T+Con) — Polly Jackson Townsend [MA] (T)

SW-183 **Jackson (William R. & Lucilla S.) Charitable Trust**
  c/o Mellon Private Wealth Management
  One Mellon Center, Room 3825
  Pittsburgh   15258   (Allegheny County)

MI-22-41-44-63-64-71-86

Phone 412-234-1634 **FAX** 412-234-1073
EIN 25-6018923   **Year Created** 1950

AMV $1,611,152   **FYE** 12-00   (**Gifts Received** $139,124)   86 **Grants totaling** $455,116

About two-thirds local/Pa. giving. High grant of **$300,318** to Pittsburgh Theological Seminary. **$12,500** to Sewickley Public Library. **$8,500** to Sewickley Presbyterian Church. **$2,000** each to Pa. Right to Work Defense & Education Foundation [Harrisburg], Salvation Army, and Sewickley Civic Garden Council (village fund/Riverfront Park). **$1,000-$1,500** each to Coalition for Christian Outreach, John Guest Evangelistic Ministries, Sewickley Academy, and Shady Side Academy. Other smaller local contributions for various purposes. **Out-of-state** giving includes **$50,000** to Legal Defense Foundation [VA]; **$10,000** each to Coral Ridge Ministries [FL], Eagle Forum Education & Legal Defense Foundation [IL], and Leadership Institute [VA]; **$4,000** to Free Congress Foundation [DC]; and other smaller grants/contributions for many conservative Christian organizations. ■**PUBLICATIONS:** None ■**WEBSITE:** None ■**E-MAIL:** None ■**APPLICATION POLICIES & PROCEDURES:** The Trust reports that very few unsolicited requests are funded. No grants are awarded to individuals. Grant requests in any form should be submitted before the October 30th deadline; grants are awarded at a November meeting.

O+D+T Annette Calgaro (VP at Bank+Con) — William R. Jackson, Jr. [ME] (T+Donor) — Mellon Bank N.A. (Corporate Trustee)

SW-184 **Jennings (Mary Hillman) Foundation**
  c/o Lea Company
  2203 Allegheny Tower, 625 Stanwix Street
  Pittsburgh   15222   (Allegheny County)

MI-11-12-13-14-22-25-29-31-32-41-42-44-51
52-54-55-56-71-72
Phone 412-434-5606 **FAX** 412-434-5907
EIN 23-7002091   **Year Created** 1969

AMV $49,843,763   **FYE** 12-00   (**Gifts Received** $0)   166 **Grants totaling** $3,408,000

Mostly local giving, primarily to Allegheny and Westmoreland counties. High grant of **$402,000** to Shadyside Hospital Foundation. **$200,000** each to Allegheny Valley School, Latrobe Area Hospital Foundation, and Shady Side Academy. **$100,000** to Outside in School of Experiential Education. **$50,000** each to Eye & Ear Institute, Juvenile Diabetes Foundation, Manchester Craftsmen's Guild, and Westmoreland Museum of American Art. **$40,000** each to Ligonier Valley YMCA, National Aviary in Pittsburgh, Rodef Shalom Congregation, and Sewickley Public Library. **$35,000** each to Allegheny General Hospital and Historical Society of Western Pa. **$30,000** each to The Ellis School, Gateway Rehabilitation Center, and St. Edmund's Academy. **$25,000** each to Chatham College, The Children's Institute, Family House, Fox Chapel Country School, Greater Pittsburgh Community Foodbank, The Heartwood Institute, McGuire Memorial Home Foundation, St. Barnabas Charitable Foundation, Sewickley Academy, Y.E.S. Kids Tutoring, and YMCA of Greater Pittsburgh. **$22,000** to The Watson Institute. **$20,000** each to Bethlehem Haven, Catholic Charities, East Liberty Family Health Center, Extra Mile Education Foundation, Hill House Associates, Manchester Youth Development Center, Marian Manor, The Mattress Factory, Pace School, Peoples Oakland, Inc., Pittsburgh Public Theater, River City Brass Band, Salvation Army, Seton Hill College, Society for Contemporary Crafts, Three Rivers Youth, Touchstone Center for Crafts, Western Pa. Conservancy, and YMCA of Beaver County. **$15,000** each to Brother's Brother Foundation, Coalition for Christian Outreach, Girl Scout Council of Western Pa., Holy Family Foundation, Mom's House, Pittsburgh Project, St. Vincent College, United Way of Allegheny County, Western Pa. School for the Deaf, and Women's Christian Renewal. **$10,000** each to Beginning With Books, Bridge to Independence, Civic Light Opera, Coalition for Leadership, Community Center/Library Assn., Cross-Trainers, Executive Service Corps of Western Pa., Johnstown Area Heritage Assn., Junior Achievement of SW Pa., Mentoring Partner of SW Pa., Mon Valley Initiative, Pittsburgh Downtown Partnership, Pittsburgh Environmental Council, St. Anne Home, Sewickley Valley YMCA, YMCA of McKeesport, and Youthbuild Pittsburgh. **$7,500** each to Planned Parenthood of Western Pa. and WQED. **$4,000-$5,000** each to 10,000 Friends of Pa., [Philadelphia], Arthritis Foundation/Western Pa. Chapter, The Center Against Violence, Children's Center of Pittsburgh, Conservation Consultants, Contact Pittsburgh, Family Guidance, Family Health Council, Family Resources, I Have A Dream Foundation of Pittsburgh, Jeannette Public Library, Joe Bellante Ministry, Ligonier Valley Learning Center, Lupus Foundation of America, National Hemophilia Foundation, National Kidney Foundation of Western Pa.,Neighborhood Academy, One to One: Citizen Advocates, Pittsburgh Civic Garden Center, Pittsburgh Children's Museum, Pittsburgh Council for International Visitors, Pittsburgh Dance Council, Pittsburgh Habitat for Humanity, Pittsburgh Symphony, Rx Council of Western Pa., Sweetwater Center for the Arts, Susan Komen Cancer Foundation, Tennis Patrons Foundation of Pittsburgh, Travelers Aid Society of Pittsburgh, Western Pa. Family Center, Westmoreland Conservation, and Westmoreland County Historical Society. **$1,000-$3,000** each to Artists & Cities, Children's Home of Pittsburgh, Gateway to the Arts, Greater Pittsburgh Boy Scouts, Homewood Cemetery Historical Society, Leadership Foundation, Loyalhanna Watershed Assn., Make-A-Wish Foundation of Western Pa., Mendelssohn Choir of Pittsburgh, National Assn. of Arts & Letters, National MS Foundation, NEED/Negro Educational Emergency Drive, Northside Common Ministry, Oncology Nursing Society, Opera Theatre of Pittsburgh, Pa. Special Olympics, Persad Center, Pittsburgh Ballet Theatre, Pittsburgh AIDS Task Force, St. Margaret Memorial Hospital, St. Michael of the Valley, Three Rivers Arts Festival, United Negro College Fund, and World Affairs Council of Pittsburgh. **Out-of-state** giving includes **$200,000** each to Baptist Hospital [FL] and Lahey Clinic Foundation [MA]; **$100,000** to George Washington's Mt. Vernon [VA]; **$40,000** to Trigeminal Neuralgia Assn. [NJ]; and **$10,000** to National Fatherhood Initiative [MD]. ■**PUBLICATIONS:** None ■**WEBSITE:** None ■**E-MAIL:** None ■**APPLICATION POLICIES & PROCEDURES:** The Foundation reports that most giving is for general support, special projects, endowment, capital needs, or research; multi-year grants are awarded. No grants are awarded to individuals. Prospective applicants initially should make a telephone inquiry about the feasibility of submitting a request. Grant requests may be submitted in a letter at any time; deadlines are May 31st and October 15th; give a brief history of the organization and its mission, and describe in detail the project and amount of requested fund. Also include an organizational budget, project budget, audited financial statement, list of major funding sources, Board member list, and IRS tax-exempt status documentation. Site visits sometimes are made to organizations being considered for a grant. The Board of Directors awards grants at June and December meetings.

O+D+T Paul Euwer, Jr. (Executive Director+Con) — Evan D. Jennings, II (P+D) — Andrew L. Weil (S+D) — Irving A. Wechsler, CPA (F+D) — Christina W. Jennings (D) — Cynthia B. Jennings (D)

SW-185 Jewish Family Assistance Fund
　　　5743 Bartlett Street
　　　Pittsburgh 15217　　　　　　　　　(Allegheny County)
AMV $146,042　　　**FYE** 12-00　　　**(Gifts Received** $75,354)

MI-22-23-62
Phone 412-521-3237 **FAX** None
EIN 25-1512726　　**Year Created** 1987
300+ **Grants totaling** $114,157

Most disbursements—typically **$200** to **$400,** a few larger—were to individuals for food, shelter, medical/dental services, medical supplies, prescriptions, education, transportation, car repairs, legal assistance, moving costs, etc. In addition, seven organization grants awarded: **$8,000** to Hillel Academy; **$2,500** to Jewish National Fund; **$2,000** to Jewish Education Institute; **$1,000** each to Chabad House (scholarships), Poale Zedeck Congregation (educational), and Zionists of America (scholarships); and **$500** to Aleph Institution. ■**PUBLICATIONS:** None ■**WEBSITE:** None ■**E-MAIL:** None ■**APPLICATION POLICIES & PROCEDURES:** The Foundation reports that giving is limited to Pittsburgh residents. Grant requests from individuals or organizations may be submitted in a letter at any time.

O+D+T Sam Steinberg (F+Con) — James F. Reich (P) — Herman Lipsitz (Donor) — Mrs. Herman Lipsitz (Donor) — Foundation donors: Jewish Healthcare Foundation; Charles Morris Trust

---

SW-186 Jewish Healthcare Foundation
　　　Centre City Tower, Suite 2330
　　　650 Smithfield Street
　　　Pittsburgh 15222　　　　　　　　　(Allegheny County)
AMV $119,803,018　　　**FYE** 12-01　　　**(Gifts Received** $2,000,000 est.)

MI-11-12-13-14-15-16-17-18-19-22-29-31-32
33-34-35-39-71-84-86
Phone 412-594-2550 **FAX** 412-232-6240
EIN 25-1624347　　**Year Created** 1990
100+ **Grants totaling** $6,000,000 est.

Giving focuses on Western Pa. health-related programs/concerns; the Grants Totaling figure above includes payments on prior commitments and grants approved in 2001 (in three programmatic areas), listed here. *(1) INTEGRATING HEALTH GRANTS—Physical, Behavioral, Environmental:* **$900,000** to United Jewish Federation (block grant for agency services). **$150,000** to Riverview Towers (matching grant for PHFA financing). **$95,000** to Allegheny County Dept. of Human Services (mental health court). **$75,000** to Foundation of Jewish Communities (video series on caregivers). **$60,000** each to Elderhostel-Pittsburgh (seniors programs), United Way of Allegheny County (annual & special allocations), and U. of Pittsburgh Center for Biomedical Ethics (physician education on end-of-life planning). **$50,000** to Allegheny Trail Alliance (promoting seniors' recreational trail use). **$43,000** to Allegheny County Parks (comprehensive master plan). **$31,250** to Street Behavior Initiative of the Foundation. **$30,000** to SW Pa. Partnerships for Aging (endowment). **$20,000** to Family House (volunteer programming/recognition). **$10,000** to Jewish Family Assistance Fund (cash assistance for needy families). *(2) FINANCING & DELIVERING HEALTH GRANTS—Strengthening Health Systems and Expanding Insurance Coverage:* **$125,000** to Duquesne U. School of Business (Institute for Economic Transformation Health Careers Factory). **$90,000** to Health & Human Services Public/Private Partnerships—a joint initiative of the United Jewish Federation and the Foundation. **$75,000** to SW Pa. Partnerships for Aging (Healthy Elders-Health Jobs 2005). **$50,000** to CORO Center for Civic Leadership (developing future health sciences leaders). **$21,000** to Consumer Health Coalition (pursuing mental health parity). **$10,000** to National Health Law Program ([promoting the rights of vulnerable populations). *(3) ADVANCING HEALTH GRANTS—Biomedical, Technological and Informatics Discovery:* **$300,000** for a Program Related Investment to the Strategic Investment Fund (to support the local biotechnology and health sciences sector). **$100,000** each to Carnegie Mellon U. Research Institute (cancer screening technologies/Eastern Medicine techniques technology) and U. of Pittsburgh Medical Center/Shadyside - Center for Complementary Medicine (National Research Center building). **$50,000** to BioBridge (commercializing Pittsburgh's biomedical discoveries). **$40,000** to U. of Pittsburgh/Neuromuscular Research Laboratory (orthopaedic injuries prevention project). **$35,000** to The Working Hearts Initiative (sustain women's heart health improvements). *OTHER GRANTS* outside the priority areas: **$140,248** for a Facilities Security Fund (emergency grants for local religious organizations following the 9/11 attacks). Also, 58 Small Grants including **$18,000** to Creative Nonfiction Foundation; **$10,000** each to Carnegie Institute (lynching photography in America), Harvey R. Brown Family Education Fund, and Variety Fund for Handicapped Children; **$7,500** each to Allegheny County Career Connection, Human Services Center Corporation (dental/vision screening project), and Yeshiva Schools; **$6,000** to Allegheny County Court of Common Pleas (Generations Custody Program); **$5,962** to Heritage Media Corporation; **$5,000** each to Beth Israel Medical Center (Prevention Point Pittsburgh) and Pittsburgh Urban Magnet Project; and smaller grants/contributions **$100-$3,760** for various health related issues/projects. In addition, 19 Community Education Grants, **$250-$5,000** each, awarded for health-related programs/services, symposia, conferences, and other purposes. ■**PUBLICATIONS:** Annual Report; application guidelines ■ **WEBSITE:** www.jhf.org ■**E-MAIL:** info@jhf.org ■**APPLICATION POLICIES & PROCEDURES:** Only Western Pa. organizations/institutions dealing healthcare services/issues are eligible to apply for support in one of the Foundation's three priority areas (see above). Special attention will be given to proposed programs if they (a) provide opportunities for new information and fresh perspectives about health problems; (b) improve healthcare systems or utilization of health care; or (c) build partnerships among community institutions and/or contain a community education component. Most grants are for special projects, research, publications, or matching grants; multiyear grants are awarded. No grants are awarded to/for the following: organizations outside Western Pa. or lacking IRS tax-exempt status; programs without a health care component; general operations; capital needs; operating deficits; debt retirement; political campaigns; scholarships; fellowships; individual research grants; or individual travel. Prospective applicants should make an initial telephone inquiry about the feasibility of submitting a request, and if encouraged to apply, should then submit a preliminary Letter of Intent (6 pages maximum; four copies required) with the following: problem description, program objectives, theory of change, outcomes, deliverables and milestones, project principals and partners, communications strategy, consideration for sustainability, and financial requirements/use of the requested Funds. Also, provide the contact person's name/address, institutional and personnel qualifications, list of Board members, organizational budget, most recent financial statement (showing amounts/sources of current income), most recent auditor's report (if available), and IRS tax-exempt status documentation. The Foundation may request additional information and make a site visit to an organization eligible for support. Grants are awarded at meetings in April, September, and December.

O+D+T Karen Wolk Feinstein, Ph.D. (P+Con) — Farrell Rubenstein (C+T) — Patricia Siger (S+T) — Stephen Halpern (F+T) — Leon L. Netzer (Chair, Distribution Committee+T) — and 45 additional Trustees including 18 Life Trustees

---

SW-187   Johns (Roy F.), Jr. Family Foundation   MI-12-14-32-41-42-44-52-55-56-72-89
                c/o Roy F. Johns, Jr. Associates
                200 Marshall Drive   **Phone** 412-264-8383 **FAX** None
                Coraopolis 15108   (Allegheny County)   **EIN** 25-6426447   **Year Created** 1993
AMV $2,131,005   **FYE** 12-00   **(Gifts Received** $0)   19 **Grants totaling** $77,000

About two-thirds local giving. High grants of **$10,000** to Citizen Care, Inc., Robert Morris College, and Pittsburgh Symphony. **$8,000** to Carnegie Mellon U. **$2,000-$2,500** each to Alzheimer's Disease Foundation, B.F. Jones Memorial Library, Coraopolis Memorial Library, Moon Township Library, and Moon Township Volunteer Fire Company. **$1,000** each to Aliquippa High School Fund, ARC-Allegheny Foundation, Associated Artists of Pittsburgh, Old Sewickley Post Office, and Robinson Township Volunteer Fire Dept. Other smaller contributions. **Out-of-state** grants: **$10,000** each to Opera Company of NY, Paws for a Cause [VA], and Pinion Inc. [FL]. ■**PUBLICATIONS:** application guidelines ■**WEBSITE:** None ■**E-MAIL:** None ■**APPLICATION POLICIES & PROCEDURES:** The Foundation reports that priority will be given to Western Pa. organizations for specific projects, programs, or causes. Grants are awarded for general support but applicants must apply annually; however, no organizations should expect automatic, on-going support. No grants are awarded to/for individuals, politics, lobbying, specialized health/medical programs without a specific community impact, welfare or social programs that do not support self-reliance, programs of sectarian or religious organizations limited to members of one particular group, organizations that discriminate, university chairs or professorships, or organizations which support euthanasia or cruelty to animals. Grant requests may be submitted in a letter at any time before the July 1st deadline to be considered that year. Stipulate a specific funding request in the first paragraph and then describe the project/need, its purposes/objectives, and how it will be implemented; include an itemized budget showing income/expenses, a list of other major funding sources, an audited financial statement, and IRS tax-exempt status documentation. The Board meets in October and grantees are notified in December.

O+D+T Thomas W. Weaver (Con) — Roy F. Johns, Jr. (T+D+Donor) — Barbara Johns (T+D)

SW-188   Johnson (Carl J. & Margot A.) Foundation   MI-42-44-52-63
                1211 Minnesota Ave.   **Phone** 724-226-8558 **FAX** None
                Natrona Heights 15065   (Allegheny County)   **EIN** 25-1675809   **Year Created** 1991
AMV $2,158,196   **FYE** 12-00   **(Gifts Received** $202,920)   6 **Grants totaling** $41,862

All local giving; all grants are unrestricted support. High grant of **$20,012** to U. of Pittsburgh (Physics Dept.). **$18,154** to United Church of Christ (Western Pa. Annual Conference). **$1,874** to Carnegie Mellon U. (Material Science & Engineering Dept.). **$1,135** to Community Library of Allegheny Valley. Other small local contributions. — Major giving in prior years for choral music. ■**PUBLICATIONS:** None ■**WEBSITE:** None ■**E-MAIL:** None ■**APPLICATION POLICIES & PROCEDURES:** The Foundation reports that most grants are for general support, special projects, building funds, research, and scholarships. No grants awarded to individuals. Prospective applicants initially should make a telephone inquiry about the feasibility of submitting a request. Grant requests may be submitted in any form, preferably in August-September. Site visits sometimes are made to organizations being considered for a grant. Grants are awarded at an October meeting.

O+D+T Margot A. Johnson (T+F+Donor+Con) — Carl J. Johnson (PO+T+Donor)

SW-189   Johnson (Ernest Q.) for Charity   MI-12-13-14-19-22-33-41-44-51-61-63-84
                c/o Mellon Private Wealth Management
                One Mellon Center, P.O. Box 185   **Phone** 412-234-0023 **FAX** 412-234-1073
                Pittsburgh 15230   (Allegheny County)   **EIN** 25-6103319   **Year Created** 1969
AMV $1,600,496   **FYE** 9-00   **(Gifts Received** $0)   31 **Grants totaling** $65,110

All giving restricted organizations serving youth in the Canonsburg area; all grants are for specific projects/programs/purchases. High grant of **$5,000** to Greater Canonsburg Library (children's/young adult books). **$4,000** to Canon-McMillan Hockey (practice time). **$3,000-$3,800** each to Boy Scout Troop #1365 (Jamboree trips), Boy Scout Troop #1385 (summer camp), Boy Scout Troop #1393 (meeting room/supplies), Canon-McMillan Baseball Assn. (new equipment), Canon-McMillan School District (computer station), Canonsburg Youth Baseball (batting cage), Girl Scouts of SW Pa. (summer camp scholarships), Lil Mac Football Assn. (helmet reconditioning), and South Canonsburg Church (summer camp scholarships). **$1,900-$2,500** each to All Saints Greek Orthodox Church (summer camp/games), Boy Scout Troop #1373 (equipment), Canonsburg United Presbyterian Church (summer camp), Friends of the Park (new carousel), St. Patrick Elementary School (science lab), and Try-Again Homes (youth therapy). **$1,000-$1,500** each to Asset, Inc., Canonsburg Cemetery Pilot Project (after school program), Canonsburg General Hospital (children's health project), Central Assembly of God (children's programs), Chartiers Houston Community Library (summer reading program), Chartiers Houston Girls Softball Assn. (concession stand), Child Evangelism Outreach (local summer camping), Cub Scout Pack #1305 (summer camp scholarships), Greater Canonsburg Girls' Softball Assn. (new bats), Peters Township Library (world history kits), and Recording for the Blind & Dyslexic [NJ] (services to Canonsburg clients). Other smaller contributions for similar purposes. ■**PUBLICATIONS:** None ■**WEBSITE:** None ■ **E-MAIL:** None ■**APPLICATION POLICIES & PROCEDURES:** Only organizations with programs benefiting Canonsburg-area youth are eligible to apply. Grant requests should be submitted in March (the deadline is April 15th); include an organizational budget, project budget, and IRS tax-exempt status documentation. Decisions on grants are made at a May meeting.

O+D+T Laurie A. Moritz (VP at Bank+Con) — Mellon Bank N.A. (Trustee)

SW-190 **Johnson (Thomas Phillips & Jane Moore) Foundation**
535 Smithfield Street, Suite 605
Pittsburgh 15222 (Allegheny County)

MI-16-53-54-56-63-71
Phone 412-261-9008 **FAX** None
EIN 25-6357015 **Year Created** 1990

AMV $3,004,221 **FYE** 12-00 **(Gifts Received** $43,660) 21 **Grants totaling** $223,160

About one-fifth local giving. High local grant of **$25,000** to Frick Art & Historical Center. **$10,000** to Covenant Whosoever Will Church [Wilkinsburg]. **$2,500** to Western Pa. Conservancy. **$2,000** to Historical Society of Western Pa. **Out-of-state** giving includes **$43,660** to Capital Hill Foundation [MD]; **$30,000** to International Film Seminars [NY]; **$30,000** to National Gallery of Art [DC]; and **$12,000** to WestCAP/Western Colorado AIDS Project; **$10,000** each to GLAAD/Gay & Lesbian Alliance Against Defamation [CA], San Miguel County Purchase of Development Rights Program [CO], Telluride Society of the Performing Arts [CO]; and **$7,500** to Teachers & Writers Collaboration [NY]. ■**PUBLICATIONS:** None ■**WEBSITE:** None ■**E-MAIL:** None ■ **APPLICATION POLICIES & PROCEDURES:** The Foundation reports that unsolicited grant requests are not accepted. Site visits sometimes are made to organizations being considered for a grant. Grants are awarded at June and November meetings.

O+D+T William L. Casey (AS+Con) — Thomas P. Johnson, Jr. (C+T) — Asa J. Johnson (T) — James M. Johnson [CO] (T) — Jane T. Johnson (T) — Jesse D. Johnson (T)

SW-191 **Joshowitz (Isadore & Yetta) Charitable Foundation**
c/o Josh Steel Company
46 Sixth Street
Braddock 15104 (Allegheny County)

MI-22-41-62
Phone 412-351-3500 **FAX** None
EIN 25-6381619 **Year Created** 1991

AMV $1,372,502 **FYE** 6-00 **(Gifts Received** $86,835) 120 **Grants totaling** $82,082

Mostly local giving. High grant of **$35,000** to United Jewish Federation of Greater Pittsburgh. **$17,129** to Hillel Academy of Pittsburgh. **$3,500** to Yeshiva Schools of Pittsburgh. **$3,000** to Jewish Educational Institute. **$1,552** to Gemila Chesed Synagogue. **$930** to Kollel Bais Yitzchok. Other local contributions **$15-$500** for Jewish, civic, health and other purposes. **Out-of-state** giving includes **$1,000-$1,500** to Anti-Defamation League [NY], synagogues in OH, NY and Israel, and other smaller contributions. ■**PUBLICATIONS:** None ■**WEBSITE:** None ■**E-MAIL:** None ■**APPLICATION POLICIES & PROCEDURES:** Information not available.

O+D+T Isadore Joshowitz (T+Donor+Con) — James H. Joshowitz [Pittsburgh] (T) — Steven M. Joshowitz [Pittsburgh] (T) — Yetta Joshowitz (Donor)

SW-192 **Juliano Family Foundation**
755 Chestnut Road
Sewickley 15143 (Allegheny County)

MI-41-54
Phone 412-741-3318 **FAX** None
EIN 52-2170559 **Year Created** 1999

AMV $512,312 **FYE** 4-00 **(Gifts Received** $493,732) 2 **Grants totaling** $450

Small contributions to Pittsburgh Children's Museum and Sewickley Academy. ■**PUBLICATIONS:** None ■**WEBSITE:** None ■**E-MAIL:** None ■**APPLICATION POLICIES & PROCEDURES:** Information not available.

O+D+T Mark Juliano (T+Donor+Con) — Lisa Juliano (T+Donor)

SW-193 **Kacin (Alvin) Family Foundation**
1011 Poke Run Church Road
Apollo 15613 (Westmoreland County)

MI-13-41-71
Phone 724-733-7717 **FAX** None
EIN 25-1472340 **Year Created** 1984

AMV $132,409 **FYE** 12-00 **(Gifts Received** $30,000) 12 **Grants totaling** $43,150

All local giving; all grants are for general operating support. High grant of **$33,000** to YMCA of Pittsburgh. **$5,000** to Westmoreland Conservation District. **$3,000** to Mother of Sorrows School. Other contributions **$100-$600** for various purposes. ■**PUBLICATIONS:** None ■**WEBSITE:** None ■**E-MAIL:** None ■**APPLICATION POLICIES & PROCEDURES:** The Foundation reports that giving is generally to/for the Plum Borough area. Grant requests may be submitted in any form at any time; provide specific project details and amount requested; include current organizational and/or project budgets.

O+D+T Alvin R. Kacin (T+Con) — Charmaine Kacin (T) — Timothy Kacin [Pittsburgh] (T) — Todd Kacin [Murrysville] (T) — Corporate donors: Vinor, Inc.; Washington Properties, Inc.

SW-194   Kaplan (Lois) Charitable Fdn. . Prevention of Child Abuse   MI-12
c/o Glimcher Group, Inc.
1 Mellon Center, 500 Grant Street, Suite 2000
Pittsburgh 15219   (Allegheny County)   **Phone** 412-765-3310 **FAX** None
                                                                           EIN 25-6535974   **Year Created** 1997
AMV $39,595   **FYE** 12-00   (**Gifts Received** $11,000)   1 **Grant of** $13,750

Sole grant to Family Resources, Inc. (child abuse prevention education). — Giving for several prior years to Jewish Family & Children's Services (child abuse prevention). ■**PUBLICATIONS:** None ■**WEBSITE:** None ■**E-MAIL:** None ■**APPLICATION POLICIES & PROCEDURES:** Information not available.

O+D+T   Robert Glimcher (T+Con) — Ivan Kaplan [FL] (T+Donor) — Jason Samreny [GA] (T)

SW-195   Karnavas (A.) Foundation   MI-14-15-31-41-43
c/o A. Karnavas Company
240 Merchant Street
Ambridge 15003   (Beaver County)   **Phone** 724-266-4060 **FAX** None
                                                                       EIN 25-1197658   **Year Created** 1968
AMV $294,088   **FYE** 6-01   (**Gifts Received** $0)   11 **Grants totaling** $12,000

All local giving. High organization grant of **$3,300** to Beaver Valley Geriatric Center. **$2,300** to Beaver County Rehabilitation Center. **$700** to Allegheny Valley School. **$500** to D.T. Watson Rehabilitation Hospital. One **$3,750** scholarship awarded. Other local contributions **$100-$250** for various purposes. ■**PUBLICATIONS:** application guidelines; application form ■**WEBSITE:** None ■**E-MAIL:** None ■**APPLICATION POLICIES & PROCEDURES:** Grant requests from organizations must be on a formal application form, available from the Foundation. Individuals requesting post-secondary scholarship assistance must submit a brief resume of academic qualifications. Requests for research grants must include an outline of the proposed investigation and a proposed budget. Grant requests may be submitted at any time; decisions are usually made within a month.

O+D+T   Jack A. Karnavas (VP+S+F+D+Con) — George Karnavas (P+D) — Robert G. Panagulias, Esq. [Pittsburgh] (D) — Sophie Karnavas (Donor)

SW-196   Kassling (William & Patricia) Family Foundation   MI-11-12-15-18-31-32-41-42-52-54-56-63
540 Squaw Run Road, Fox Chapel   **Phone** 412-963-0421 **FAX** None
Pittsburgh 15238   (Allegheny County)   **EIN** 25-1802794   **Year Created** 1996
AMV $930,649   **FYE** 12-00   (**Gifts Received** $0)   25 **Grants totaling** $50,450

All local giving. High grant of **$10,000** each Pittsburgh Symphony and United Way of Allegheny County. **$5,000** to Pittsburgh School of Massage. **$3,500** to St. Margaret's Memorial Hospital. **$3,000** to Mario Lemieux Foundation. **$2,500** to LaRoche College. **$2,000** to Historical Society of Western Pa. **$1,000-$1,500** each to Allegheny Valley School, Alzheimer's Assn., American Cancer Society, Carnegie Museum/Women's Committee, Cystic Fibrosis Foundation, Fox Chapel Presbyterian Church, Planned Parenthood of Pa., Shady Side Academy, and Three Rivers Adoption Council. Other local contributions **$200-$500** for various purposes. ■**PUBLICATIONS:** None ■**WEBSITE:** None ■**E-MAIL:** None ■**APPLICATION POLICIES & PROCEDURES:** Grant requests may be submitted in any form at any time.

O+D+T   Patricia J. Kassling (P+T+Donor+Con) — William E. Kassling (S+F+T+Donor+Con)

SW-197   Kelley (Kate M.) Foundation   MI-13-14-15-22-25-32-41-42-44-61
c/o St. Bernard's Church
311 Washington Road   **Phone** 412-561-3300 **FAX** 412-563-0211
Pittsburgh 15216   (Allegheny County)   **EIN** 25-6090985   **Year Created** 1969
AMV $4,414,934   **FYE** 12-00   (**Gifts Received** $0)   60 **Grants totaling** $263,000

Mostly Greater Pittsburgh giving. High grants of **$10,000** each to Carlow College, Catholic Charities, DePaul Institute, Little Sisters of the Poor, Marian Manor, and Quigley High School. **$7,500-$8,000** each to Gilmary Diocesan Center, Jubilee Soup Kitchen, St. Joseph House of Hospitality, and St. Sebastian/St. Vincent de Paul. **$6,000** each to Bishop's Education Fund, Catholic Crusade for the Future, Chimbote Foundation, Mom's House, Sacred Heart Church, St. Paul Cathedral, and St. Paul Seminary. **$5,000** each to Catholic Youth Assn., Central Catholic High School, Duquesne U., Hope Network, Ladies of Charity, North Catholic High School, Oakland Catholic High School, Pittsburgh Vision Services, St. Bartholomew Church, St. Vincent Seminary, Villa de Marillac, and Vincentian Home for the Chronically Ill. **$4,000** to Leukemia Society. **$2,000-$3,000** each to Auberle Foundation, Bethlehem Haven, Big Brothers & Big Sisters of Greater Pittsburgh, Carnegie Library of Homestead, Crossroads Foundation, Extra Mile Education Foundation, Girls Hope of Pittsburgh, Holy Family Institute, Just-Inn Transition, LaRoche College, Pace School, People Concerned for the Unborn Child, Regency Hall Nursing Home, Seton LaSalle High School, Sisters of Charity/DePaul Center, Sisters of Mercy, St. Bede Church, St. Benedict the Moor, Sts. Cyril & Methodius Seminary, St. Paul of the Cross Retreat Center, St. Titus [Aliquippa], Vincentian Collaborative Services, Western Pa. School for the Blind, and Xavier Guild for the Blind. Other local grants **$1,000-$1,500** for similar purposes. **Out-of-state** grants: **$3,000** to Covenant House [NY] and **$2,000** to Pontifical College Josephinum [OH]. ■**PUBLICATIONS:** None ■**WEBSITE:** None ■**E-MAIL:** None ■**APPLICATION POLICIES & PROCEDURES:** The Foundation reports that most giving is for Catholic churches, organizations, and related schools. Grant requests may be submitted in writing at any time; describe the charitable mission of the organization and reason for requesting support. No grants awarded to individuals.

O+D+T   Rev. Leo V. Vanyo (T+Con) — Rev. Roy G. Getty (T) — Edward C. Ifft (T)

SW-198 Kennametal Foundation, The
c/o Kennametal Inc.
Route 981 South, P.O. Box 231
Latrobe 15650 (Westmoreland County)

MI-11-13-15-31-42-44-49-52-54-57-71-85-88

Phone 724-539-5203 **FAX** None
EIN 25-6036009 **Year Created** 1955

AMV $980,235 **FYE** 6-01 (**Gifts Received** $300,000) 145 **Grants totaling** $397,916

About three-quarters local/Pa. giving; some grants include matching gifts. High grant of **$61,625** to St. Vincent College. **$53,450** to Seton Hill College. **$30,000** to United Way of Westmoreland County. **$25,000** to Westmoreland Trust. **$10,000-$10,875** each to Carnegie Institute, Latrobe Chamber of Commerce, and Ligonier Public Library. **$8,026** to U. of Pittsburgh. **$6,500** to Pittsburgh Opera. **$5,000** each to Derry Area School District and Foundation for Free Enterprise Education [Erie]. **$2,500-$3,600** to Latrobe Foundation (Veterans Plaza Fund), Latrobe Area Hospital Foundation, Penn State U., Regional Federal Advocacy Institute, and Western Pa. Conservancy. **$1,000-$2,000** each to Advisory Board on Autism, American Cancer Society, America Diabetes Assn., Greensburg-Hempfield Area Library, Indiana U. of Pa., Pa. CleanWays, Pa. Veteran's Memorial [Annville], Public Service Scholarship Program, Westmoreland County Camp Cadet, Westmoreland Museum of American Art, Westmoreland Symphony Orchestra, and WQED-TV. Other smaller contributions. **Out-of-state** giving includes **$50,000** to City of Hope [CA]; **$33,325** to National Merit Scholarship Corp [IL] with most other giving to United Ways, colleges/universities, and community organizations in corporate operating locations in OH, VA and NC. ■**PUBLICATIONS:** None ■**WEBSITE:** None ■**E-MAIL:** None ■**APPLICATION POLICIES & PROCEDURES:** The Foundation reports giving primarily to organizations in Kennametal or corporate subsidiary locations. Most grants are for general/continuing support, building/renovations, equipment, endowment, and matching/challenge support; multi-year grants are awarded. No grants awarded to individuals or for scholarships/fellowships. Submit grant requests in a letter at any time; include an annual report, organization budget, project budget, list of major funding sources, audited financial statement, and IRS tax-exempt status documentation. The Trustees set the overall contributions budget in March and award grants at quarterly meetings. Matching grants for most types of higher education institutions, libraries, art & science museums, historical museums or societies, and public broadcasting stations have a $25 minimum, $3,500 maximum/employee/year.

O+D+T Richard P. Gibson (S+F+Con) — Stanley B. Duzy (T) — Derwin R. Gilbreath (T) — William R. Newlin (T) — Markos I. Tambakeras (T) — Corporate donor: Kennametal Inc.

SW-199 Kiefer (Marilyn K.) Foundation
150 Pittsburgh Street
Scottdale 15683 (Westmoreland County)

MI-13-21-31-35-44-54-55-56-63-71-84
Phone 724-887-8330 **FAX** None
EIN 25-1759914 **Year Created** 1995

AMV $626,684 **FYE** 12-00 (**Gifts Received** $75,000) 24 **Grants totaling** $34,250

All local giving. High grant of **$5,000** to Scottdale Community Pool. **$4,000** to Highland Hospital. **$3,500** to Scottdale Showtime. **$3,000** to Yough River Trail Council. **$2,000** to Christ United Methodist Church. **$1,000-$1,500** each to Bullskin Historical Society, Calvin United Methodist Church, Carnegie Free Library of Connellsville, Connellsville Youth Center, DAR of Mt. Pleasant, Mt. Pleasant Free Library, Pleasant Valley Lions Club, Scottdale Public Library, Scottdale Soccer Club, State Theater of Uniontown, Wesley Community Health Center, and West Overton Museum. Other smaller local contributions. ■**PUBLICATIONS:** None ■**WEBSITE:** None ■**E-MAIL:** None ■**APPLICATION POLICIES & PROCEDURES:** The Foundation reports that giving is restricted to Scottdale, Mt. Pleasant, and Connellsville. Grant requests from organizations in those three communities may be submitted in a letter at any time before the December 1st deadline; describe the organization's purpose and financial need.

O+D+T Marilyn K. Kiefer (P+Con) — Donald F. Kiefer (VP) — Marilyn Kiefer Andras [Acme] (S) — Lawrence J. Kiefer [Fairchance] (F)

SW-200 King Foundation
c/o King's Country Shoppes, Inc.
1180 Long Run Road, Suite A
McKeesport 15131 (Allegheny County)

MI-12-13-52-84
Phone 412-751-0700 **FAX** None
EIN 25-1762453 **Year Created** 1995

AMV $17,643 **FYE** 12-00 (**Gifts Received** $0) 10 **Grants totaling** $77,475

All local giving. High grant of **$60,000** to Make-A-Wish Foundation of Western Pa. **$7,700** to River City Brass Band. **$5,000** to Shriners Charity Golf Classic. **$2,500** to Western Pa. Golf Assn. **$1,000** to Women's Board of Pittsburgh (benefit events). Other local contributions **$75-$500** for various purposes. ■**PUBLICATIONS:** None ■**WEBSITE:** None ■**E-MAIL:** None ■**APPLICATION POLICIES & PROCEDURES:** Information not available.

O+D+T Hartley C. King (P+T+Donor+Con) — Corporate donor: King's Country Shoppes, Inc.

SW-201 Kirkwood Charitable Trust
c/o Resource Conservancy, Inc.
3 Gateway Center, Suite 290
Pittsburgh 15222 (Allegheny County)

MI-13-52-54-81
Phone 412-471-9117 **FAX** None
EIN 25-6022200 **Year Created** 1956

AMV $470,186 **FYE** 12-00 (**Gifts Received** $0) 6 **Grants totaling** $11,550

All local giving. High grant of **$3,000** to YMCA of Pittsburgh (Partners with Youth program). **$2,800** to Ireland Institute of Pittsburgh. **$2,000** to Center Band Parents. **$1,000-$1,500** each to Carnegie Institute, Pittsburgh Symphony, and YMCA of Pittsburgh. ■**PUBLICATIONS:** None ■**WEBSITE:** None ■**E-MAIL:** None ■**APPLICATION POLICIES & PROCEDURES:** The Trust reports that most giving is limited to communities with Edgewater Corporation facilities; most grants are for general/operating support. No grants are awarded to/for scholarships or individuals. Grant requests may be submitted in a letter at any time; describe the organization's nature/purposes and intended use of the requested funds. — Formerly called the Edgewater Corp. Charitable Trust.

O+D+T Kathy Shotwell (Con) — John H. Kirkwood (T) — Corporate donor: Edgewater Corporation

SW-202 **Knudsen (Earl) Charitable Foundation**
104 Broadway Ave.
Carnegie 15106
(Allegheny County)

MI-12-13-14-15-22-31-32-41-43-54-51-56-61
63-64-85
Phone 412-278-4118 **FAX** None
EIN 25-6062530 **Year Created** 1964

AMV $6,781,688 **FYE** 12-00 (**Gifts Received** $0) 67 **Grants totaling** $406,000

Mostly local/Pa. giving; all grants are for general support. High grant of **$25,000** to Pittsburgh Leadership Foundation. **$20,000** each to Family Hospice and Trinity Episcopal School for Ministry. **$15,000** each to Extra Mile Education Foundation and Family House, Inc. **$10,000** each to Baptist Homes of Western Pa., Coalition for Christian Outreach, First Baptist Church of Crafton, Focus on Renewal Sto-Rox Neighborhood Corp., Make-A-Wish Foundation of Western Pa., Mt. Lebanon Baptist Church, and St. Winifred Church. **$8,000** to Kephart United Methodist Church. **$7,500** to Outreach Teen & Family Services. **$6,000** to YMCA of Pittsburgh/South Hills Area Branch. **$5,000** each to Allegheny Valley School, Beaver County Historical Research & Landmarks Foundation, Big Brothers & Big Sisters of Greater Pittsburgh, Boy Scouts/Greater Pittsburgh Council, Carnegie Museums of Pittsburgh, Circle C Youth & Family Services, Early Learning Institute, East Liberty Family Health Care Center, Emmanuel Episcopal Church, Girl Scouts of SW Pa., Girls Hope of Pittsburgh, I Have A Dream Foundation of Pittsburgh, Lupus Foundation of America/Western Pa. Chapter, Mom's House, National Center for Juvenile Justice, Parent & Child Guidance Center Foundation, Pittsburgh Ballet Theatre, Pittsburgh Vision Services, Red Cross/SW Pa. Chapter, Red Cross/York County Chapter, Salvation Army, Sisters of St. Joseph [Baden], Southwest Butler County YMCA, YMCA of McKeesport, and YouthWorks. **$4,000** each to Louise Child Care Center, Northside Common Ministries, and YMCA of Pittsburgh/North Boroughs Branch. **$2,000-$3,000** each to American Lung Assn., Auberle Foundation, Children's Home of Pittsburgh, Community Outreach Ministries, Family Resources, Friends of the National Parks at Gettysburg [Adams County], Greater Pittsburgh Community Food Bank, Horticultural Society of Western Pa., Interfaith Volunteer Caregivers of SW Pa., Leukemia Society of America/Western Pa./WV Chapter, Life's Work of Western Pa., NEED/Negro Educational Emergency Drive, United Negro College Fund, and Variety Club of Pittsburgh. Other local grants/contributions **$500-$1,000** for similar purposes. **Out-of-state** grants: **$10,000** each to Arkansas Dept. of Human Services, InterVarsity Christian Fellowship [KY], U. of Arkansas for Medical Sciences, and Wells College [NY]; and **$5,000** to Berea College [KY]. ■**PUBLICATIONS:** None ■**WEBSITE:** None ■**E-MAIL:** None ■**APPLICATION POLICIES & PROCEDURES:** The Foundation reports that giving is primarily focused on Western Pa. with most giving for annual campaigns, capital campaigns, and general operating support. No grants are awarded for endowment, scholarships, fellowships, or matching grants. Prospective applicants initially should make a telephone inquiry about the feasibility of submitting a request. Grant requests may be submitted in a letter (3 pages maximum) at any time; include an annual report, audited financial statement, and IRS tax-exempt status documentation. Site visits sometimes are made to organizations being considered for a grant. Grants are awarded at meetings in January, April, July, and October.
O+D+T Distribution Committee members: — Judith D. Morrison (S+Co-T+Con) — Roy Thomas Clark, Esq. (Co-T) — William M. Schmidt (Bank Representative) — National City Bank of Pa. (Co-Trustee)

SW-203 **Kossman (Curtis I. & Paul) Charity Fund**
c/o Kossman Development Company
11 Parkway Center, Suite 300
Pittsburgh 15220 (Allegheny County)

MI-12-14-17-18-22-25-34-52-62
Phone 412-921-6100 **FAX** 412-921-0913
EIN 25-6066759 **Year Created** 1961

AMV $1,880,018 **FYE** 12-00 (**Gifts Received** $0) 36 **Grants totaling** $79,800

Mostly local giving. High grant of **$40,000** to United Jewish Federation of Greater Pittsburgh. **$10,000** to Greater Pittsburgh Community Food Bank. **$2,500** to Pittsburgh Opera. **$2,000** to Pittsburgh Habitat for Humanity. **$1,000-$1,500** each to Catholic Charities of Pittsburgh, Domestic Abuse Counseling Center, Planned Parenthood of Western Pa., POWER/Pa. Organization for Women in Early Recovery, Rainbow Kitchen, Rehabilitation Institute of Pittsburgh, Salvation Army (Project Bundle Up), U. of Pittsburgh School of Medicine, and Women's Center & Shelter of Greater Pittsburgh. Other smaller local contributions for various purposes. **Out-of-state** giving for Jewish, international and other purposes. ■**PUBLICATIONS:** None ■**WEBSITE:** None ■ **E-MAIL:** None ■**APPLICATION POLICIES & PROCEDURES:** Grant requests may be submitted in a letter (3 pages maximum) at any time. No grants awarded to individuals. Grants are awarded at a December meeting.
O+D+T Paul Kossman (Co-T+Donor+Con) — Carl D. Citron, Esq. (Co-T) — Agnes Gouillon Kossman (Co-T) — Curtis I. Kossman (Co-T) — Deborah Anne Kossman (Donor) — Karen Michelle Kossman (Donor) — Mellon Bank N.A. (Co-Trustee); Corporate donor: Kossman Development Company

SW-204 **Laughlin Memorial, Inc.**
202 Orchard Lane, Edgeworth
Sewickley 15143 (Allegheny County)

MI-12-13-14-15-29-31-41-44-72-85
Phone 412-741-8889 **FAX** None
EIN 25-1072140 **Year Created** 1928

AMV $3,001,884 **FYE** 12-00 (**Gifts Received** $14,513) 15 **Grants totaling** $71,500

All giving restricted to the Ambridge area; all grants are for operating support. High grant of **$20,000** to Mary & Alexander Laughlin Children's Center. **$15,000** to Lifesteps of Beaver County. **$13,000** to Laughlin Memorial Free Library. **$5,000** to Center for C.A.R.I.N.G. of Ambridge. **$3,000** to Quigley High School Library Fund. **$2,000-$2,500** each to Baden Memorial Library, Beaver-Castle Girl Scout Council, Harmonie Associates, and Valley Care Assn. **$1,000** each to Beaver County Humane Society, Sewickley Public Library, Sewickley Valley Hospital, and Trinity Episcopal School for Ministry (Library Fund). **$500** to Beaver County Head Start. ■**PUBLICATIONS:** None ■**WEBSITE:** None ■**E-MAIL:** None ■**APPLICATION POLICIES & PROCEDURES:** Only organizations which benefit residents of the Ambridge-area are eligible to apply. Prospective applicants should initially telephone the Foundation to inquire about the feasibility of submitting a request. Grant requests may be submitted in a letter at any time (deadline is November 30th); describe how the organization's charitable activities benefit the Ambridge area and include an annual report, audited financial statement, and IRS tax-exempt status documentation. The Trustees award grants at a December meeting.
O+D+T Frederick C. Emerick, Jr. (S+F+T+Con) — Alexander M. Laughlin [NY] (P+T) — Carl M. Kerchner [Leetsdale] (T) — David W. Laughlin [NY] (T) — John E. Matter [Erie] (T) — James F. Schell (T) — William J. Simpson [Pittsburgh] (T) — James P. Wetzel (T)

SW-205 Laurel Foundation
c/o Laurel Assets Group
Two Gateway Center, Suite 1800
Pittsburgh 15222   (Allegheny County)

MI-13-15-17-18-29-41-42-44-51-52-53
54-55-56-71-72-79
Phone 412-765-2400 **FAX** 412-765-2407
EIN 25-6008073   **Year Created** 1951

AMV $42,948,724   **FYE** 12-00   **(Gifts Received** $2,510,750)   97 **Grants totaling** $1,895,045

About 90% local/Western Pa. giving; grants are for general/continuing program support except as noted. High grants of **$50,000** each to Conemaugh Valley Conservancy (educational publication and salary), Family Communications, Inc. (The Magic Woods), National Aviary in Pittsburgh, National Flag Foundation (O Say Can You See program), Pa. Environmental Council [Philadelphia] (Clean Air Now project), Pittsburgh Parks Conservancy (park stewards program), Three Rivers Arts Festival, Western Pa. Conservancy (Downtown Greening Initiative), Westmoreland Museum of American Art, and Women's Health Services. **$48,000** to Mountain Watershed Assn. (Indian Creek Watershed restoration). **$45,000** to ASSET Inc. (Westmoreland Co. science program and Science Matters program). **$40,000** each to Keystone Oaks High School (Project Succeed) and Red Cross/SW Pa. & Chestnut Ridge Chapters. **$30,000** each to Big Brothers & Big Sisters of Greater Pittsburgh (at-risk program), Carnegie Mellon U. (Solar System program), Family Planning Services of Snyder, Union & Northumberland Counties [Lewisburg], Hollow Oak Land Trust [Coraopolis], Pittsburgh Arts & Lectures (lecture series and Poem Chase), Pittsburgh Opera (artistic excellence project), Ruffed Grouse Society (new computer system), Westmoreland Symphony Orchestra (educational programs), and Whale's Tale Foundation/FamilyLink. **$25,000** each to Pa. Heritage Society (Bushy Run Battlefield land acquisition), Presbyterian SeniorCare (Alzheimer's' unit), Regional Resources, Inc., Society for Contemporary Crafts (capital campaign), Three Rivers Arts Festival, Westminster College (teaching/learning excellence center), and Women's Shelter of Lawrence County (capital campaign). **$20,000** each to Chatham College (architectural archives), Conservation Consultants, Inc., Day Break Adult Care Center (resale shop), Earth Force [Erie] (community action/problem solving program), National Fatherhood Initiative [Lancaster] (Allegheny County organizing), Pittsburgh Trust for Cultural Resources (creative achievement awards), St. Francis Health Foundation (cardiac assessment risk center), Touchstone Center for Crafts (capital campaign), and Wildlife Habitat Council (Three Rivers Habitat Partnership). **$15,000** each to Bottle Works Ethnic Arts Center (salary), Children's Festival Chorus, Clara Bell Duvall Education Fund (medical training/advocacy), Executive Service Corps of Western Pa., Greater Uniontown Heritage Consortium (State Theatre), Ligonier Valley Memorial Assn. (chapel), Pa. Environmental Network, Pa. Organization for Women in Early Recovery, and Plum BoroughLibrary Friends (new library). **$10,000-$12,500** each to Allegheny Historic Preservation Society (Church Tiffany windows), Animal Rescue League of Western Pa. (pay-to-spay program), Borough of Oakmont (Kerr Memorial Museum), Child's Way, Community Foundation of Westmoreland County (Salem Twp. Recreation initiative), Contact Pittsburgh (volunteer training), Gateway to the Arts, Greater Pittsburgh Literacy Council (tutor recruitment/training), Mendelssohn Choir of Pittsburgh (special performance), Pine-Richland School District (Veterans' Day/Memorial Day activities), Pittsburgh Musical Theater (seasonal support), Valley Players of Ligonier (young people's programs), and World Affairs Council of Pittsburgh (education program). **$8,000** each to Duquesne U. (tourism marketing) and ICW Vocational Services (microfilming business). **$5,000-$6,000** each to Center for Domestic & Sexual Violence (legal advocacy program), Dream Wrights Youth & Family Theatre [York] (program development), Historical Society of Western Pa., Indiana U. of Pa. (History Through Art/Drama program), Pittsburgh Children's Museum, Pittsburgh Savoyards, and Starlight Productions (community outreach programs). **$1,000-$3,500** each to Civil Air Patrol (cadet's program), Garden Club of McKeesport (butterfly garden), Grantmakers of Western Pa., Laurel Arts (children's summer workshop), Leadership Pittsburgh, and Pittsburgh Tissue Engineering Initiative (summer interns), Vintage (annual fund). **Out-of-state** giving includes **$40,000** to Planned Parenthood Federation of American [NY]; **$25,000** each to American Bird Conservancy [DC], American Chestnut Foundation [VT], Population Communications International [NY], and U. of Arizona Foundation; **$20,000** each to Conservancy of Southwest Florida, George Washington's Fredricksburg Foundation [VA], Monongalia Emergency Medical Services [WV], and Scenic America [DC]; and **$10,000** to Elm Research Institute [NH]. — Pa. Grants approved for future payment include: **$100,000** to National Flag Foundation (O Say Can You See program); **$50,000** each to Borough of Thornburg (land acquisition), Chartiers Nature Conservancy (land acquisition), and Phipps Conservatory; **$20,000** each to Derry Area School District (mobile library branch), Neighborhood Academy and Penn-PIRG Education Fund (Clean Air Now project); **$10,000** to NARAL/National Abortion Rights Action League-Pa. Foundation [Philadelphia] (Western Pa. organizing); and **$5,000** to National Right to Work Legal Defense Foundation. ■**PUBLICATIONS:** Annual Report with a statement of program policy and application guidelines ■**WEBSITE:** None ■**E-MAIL:** None ■**APPLICATION POLICIES & PROCEDURES:** The Foundation reports that preference is given to SW Pa. community organizations or programs, particularly smaller, more innovative ones; most grants are for general support, program development, building/renovation, capital campaigns, equipment, conferences, curriculum development, research, publications, matching grants, and seed money. No grants awarded to individuals. Prospective applicants initially should make a telephone inquiry about the feasibility of submitting a request. Grant requests may be submitted at any time on the Common Grant Application of Grantmakers of Western Pa. (deadlines are April 1st and October 1st); describe the program, its objectives and justification, specific amount of funding needed, and how it will be evaluated; include an annual report, organizational/project budgets, audited financial statement, list of major funding sources, Board/staff member list, a project evaluation plan, and IRS tax-exempt status documentation. Grants are awarded at meetings in June and December.

O+D+T Donna M. Panazzi (VP+S+Con) — Cordelia Scaife May (C+T+Donor) — Roger F. Meyer (P+T) — Nancy C. Fales (T) — Curtis S. Scaife (T) — Thomas M. Schmidt (T) — Timothy M. Inglis (F)

SW-206 Lebovitz Foundation
c/o Lebovitz & Lebovitz
2018 Monongahela Avenue
Pittsburgh 15218   (Allegheny County)

MI-14-22-62

Phone 412-351-4422 **FAX** 412-351-4425
EIN 23-7007749   **Year Created** 1966

AMV $1,758,104   **FYE** 12-00   **(Gifts Received** $61,500)   22 **Grants totaling** $100,446

Mostly local giving. High grant of **$55,869** to Goodwill Industries of Pittsburgh. **$13,777** to Rodef Shalom Congregation. **$13,500** to United Jewish Federation of Greater Pittsburgh (general contribution/Renaissance Campaign). **$5,000** to American

Friends of the Union of Progressive Jews. **$1,310** to Jewish Community Center of Pittsburgh. **$1,050** to National Council of Jewish Women. Other smaller local contributions for various purposes. **Out-of-state** giving includes **$2,500** to Victory Living Programs [FL] and **$1,958** to Goodwill Industries of Northern New England [ME]. ■**PUBLICATIONS:** None ■**WEBSITE:** None ■**E-MAIL:** None ■**APPLICATION POLICIES & PROCEDURES:** Grant requests may be submitted in a letter at any time; detail the proposed project and and state the amount of funding requested.

O+D+T Stephen H. Lebovitz, Esq. (VP+T+Con) — Robert A. Lebovitz, Esq. (P+T+Donor) — Charles N. Lebovitz (VP+T) — Carolyn R. Lebovitz (S+T) — Richard D. Lebovitz (F+T)

SW-207 **Lemieux (Mario) Foundation**
  920 Fort Duquesne Blvd.
  Pittsburgh 15222 (Allegheny County)
AMV $1,737,330 **FYE** 12-00 (**Gifts Received** $1,318,973)

MI-31-32
Phone 412-261-1842 **FAX** None
EIN 25-1708231 **Year Created** 1993
Grants totaling $0

No grants awarded in 2000; in the prior year seven grants totaling **$1,038,450** were awarded. High grant of **$515,000** to U. of Pittsburgh Cancer Institute (Mario Lemieux Centers for Patient Care & Research; payment on a **$5,000,000** pledge). **$235,203** each to Magee-Women's Hospital (Division of Neonatology & Developmental Biology) and McGowan Center for Regenerative Medicine. **$41,444** to Leukemia Society. **$5,000** each to ALS Association/Pittsburgh Chapter and Lupus Foundation. **$1,600** to Foley Memorial Fund. ■**PUBLICATIONS:** application form ■**WEBSITE:** www.mariolemieux.org ■**E-MAIL:** None ■**APPLICATION POLICIES & PROCEDURES:** The Foundation's primary objective is to support promising medical research project in the Greater Pittsburgh Region. Grant requests must be submitted on an application form available from the Foundation; submit requests for the form on official hospital/research facility letterhead paper.

O+D+T Tom Grealish (P+D+Executive Director+Con) — Mario Lemieux (C+D+Donor) — Nathalie Lemieux (VP+D) — Charles Greenburg (S+D) — Robert Hofmann (F+D) — Anthony Liberati (D) — Steve Reich (D) — Tom Reich (D)

SW-208 **Leslie (Donald & Dorothy) Foundation**
  c/o Mellon Private Wealth Management
  One Mellon Center, P.O. Box 185
  Pittsburgh 15230 (Allegheny County)
AMV $67,983 **FYE** 12-00 (**Gifts Received** $0)

MI-44-52-54-57-63
Phone 412-234-1101 **FAX** 412-234-0112
EIN 41-6013949 **Year Created** 1959
4 **Grants totaling** $82,000

No Pa. giving. **Out-of-state** giving includes **$69,000** to Church of the Holy Family [FL] (mostly for capital campaign) and **$12,000** to Duke U. [NC] (scholarships). — The last local grants awarded were in 1998, including: **$10,000** to Pittsburgh Symphony; **$6,000** to Fox Chapel Episcopal Church; **$4,000** to WQED; and **$3,600** to Carnegie Institute. ■**PUBLICATIONS:** None ■**WEBSITE:** None ■**E-MAIL:** None ■**APPLICATION POLICIES & PROCEDURES:** Grant requests may be submitted in any form at any time; describe the organization, its goals, and purpose of the requested grant.

O+D+T Robert Lepre (Trust Officer at Bank+Con) — Mellon Bank N.A. (Trustee)

SW-209 **Lewis (Martha Mack) Foundation**
  c/o PNC Advisors, M.S. P2-PTPP-25-1
  Two PNC Plaza, 620 Liberty Ave.
  Pittsburgh 15222 (Allegheny County)
AMV $1,266,470 **FYE** 12-00 (**Gifts Received** $0)

MI-22-51-52-54-56
Phone 412-762-3502 **FAX** 412-762-5439
EIN 23-2936195 **Year Created** 1997
4 **Grants totaling** $31,000

All local giving. High grant of **$15,000** to Historical Society of Western Pa. **$6,500** each to Carnegie Institute and Pittsburgh Symphony. **$3,000** to Coalition for Christian Outreach. — Grants in the prior year included **$25,000** to Pittsburgh Opera; **$15,000** each to Carnegie Institute and Historical Society of Western Pa.; and **$10,000** each to Pittsburgh Ballet Theatre and Pittsburgh Symphony. ■**PUBLICATIONS:** None ■**WEBSITE:** None ■**E-MAIL:** bruce.bickel@pncadvisors.com ■**APPLICATION POLICIES & PROCEDURES:** Grant requests may be submitted at any time in a letter; provide information about the organization's nature and purpose.

O+D+T R. Bruce Bickel (Senior VP at Bank+Con) — John C. Harmon, Esq. (Co-T) — PNC Advisors (Co-Trustee)

SW-210 **Lieber Foundation, The**
  c/o Klett, Lieber, Rooney & Schorling
  One Oxford Center, 40th Floor
  Pittsburgh 15219 (Allegheny County)
AMV $271,658 **FYE** 11-00 (**Gifts Received** $0)

MI-22-62-71
Phone 412-392-2000 **FAX** None
EIN 23-7000487 **Year Created** 1968
73 **Grants totaling** $22,871

Mostly local giving. High grant of **$10,000** to United Jewish Federation of Greater Pittsburgh. **$4,360** to Rodef Shalom Congregation. **$1,500** to National Council of Jewish Women/Pittsburgh Section. Other local contributions **$10-$500** for various purposes. **Out-of-state** giving includes **$1,500** to Theodore Roosevelt Sanctuary [DC] and many small contributions. ■**PUBLICATIONS:** None ■**WEBSITE:** None ■**E-MAIL:** None ■**APPLICATION POLICIES & PROCEDURES:** Grant requests may be submitted in a typewritten letter at any time. No grants awarded to individuals.

O+D+T Jerome B. Lieber, Esq. (C+T+Donor+Con) — Ruth Lieber (T) — Julian Ruslander, Esq. (T)

SW-211 Lil Maur Foundation
116 Valhalla Drive
New Castle 16105   (Lawrence County)

MI-31-41-43-51-84
Phone 724-654-4155 **FAX** None
EIN 25-6066104   **Year Created** 1955

AMV $494,217   **FYE** 9-00   **(Gifts Received** $0)   5 **Grants totaling** $5,000

All local giving. High grant of **$1,500** to New Castle Playhouse. **$1,000** each to Conneaut Labs Aquatic Management, Neshannock Township Education Foundation, and St. Francis Health Foundation. **$500** to Hovencamp Scholarship Foundation. ■ **PUBLICATIONS:** None ■ **WEBSITE:** None ■ **E-MAIL:** None ■ **APPLICATION POLICIES & PROCEDURES:** Grant requests may be submitted in a letter at any time; describe the organization's history and mission, and detail the proposed project and funding requested.

O+D+T Maureen Flaherty Flannery (P+Con) — Harry A. Flannery (S)

SW-212 Lipsitz (Herman & Helen) Charitable Trust
c/o Lipsitz, Nassau, Schwartz & Leckman
1100 Fifth Avenue
Pittsburgh 15219   (Allegheny County)

MI-22-41-62

Phone 412-281-4777 **FAX** 412-338-0728
EIN 25-6134327   **Year Created** 1970

AMV $1,982,589   **FYE** 11-00   **(Gifts Received** $80,438)   20 **Grants totaling** $64,828

Mostly local giving; some grants comprise multiple payments. High grant of **$42,150** to Jewish Family Assistance Fund. **$10,000** to United Jewish Federation of Greater Pittsburgh. **$5,750** to Young People's Synagogue. **$1,000-$1,500** each to Hillel Academy, Jewish Education Institute, Yeshiva Toras, and Zionist Organization of America. Other smaller local and out-of-state contributions. ■ **PUBLICATIONS:** None ■ **WEBSITE:** None ■ **E-MAIL:** None ■ **APPLICATION POLICIES & PROCEDURES:** Grant requests may be submitted in any form at any time.

O+D+T Herman Lipsitz, Esq. (T+Donor+Con) — Helen Lipsitz (T+Donor)

SW-213 Lloyd Foundation
Refer to PNC Advisors Charitable Trust Committee entry.
                    (Allegheny County)

MI-12-13-14-42-51-53-72

EIN 25-6228888   **Year Created** 1983

AMV $2,433,940   **FYE** 6-00   **(Gifts Received** $0)   15 **Grants totaling** $161,486

About two-thirds local giving. High local grant of **$15,000** to Carnegie Mellon U. **$13,500** each to Pittsburgh Public Theater and St. Vincent College. **$12,907** to YMCA of Beaver County. **$10,500** to Best Friends, Inc. **$9,000** to Ruffed Grouse Society. **$7,500** to Harmarville Outreach Programs. **$6,000** each to ARC-Washington Foundation, The Doorway, and Society for Art In Craft. **$4,250** to Pace School. **Out-of-state** grants: **$53,289** to Presbyterian Church USA Foundation [IN]; **$2,000** to Cumberland College [KY]; and **$1,500** to West Virginia U. ■ **APPLICATION POLICIES & PROCEDURES:** Refer to the PNC Advisors Charitable Trust Committee entry for a statement on giving priorities and full application guidelines.

O+D+T Refer to PNC Advisors Charitable Trust Committee entry. — PNC Advisors (Corporate Trustee)

SW-214 Lockard (J. Leon) Charitable Trust
Refer to PNC Advisors Charitable Trust Committee entry.
                    (Allegheny County)

MI-13-14-19-22-29-31-41-85

EIN 23-6836910   **Year Created** 1994

AMV $713,112   **FYE** 12-00   **(Gifts Received** $0)   6 **Grants totaling** $19,500

All giving limited to the Philadelphia area; grants are for general purposes. High grant of **$5,000** to Woodrock, Inc. **$2,500-$3,500** each to Camphill Village-Kimberton Hills, Campus Boulevard Corp., Don Guanella Village, Old First Reformed Church, and Reading Terminal Farmers Market Trust. — In the prior year, 13 grants of **$1,000-$1,500** awarded for health/human service or educational purposes. ■ **APPLICATION POLICIES & PROCEDURES:** Refer to the PNC Advisors Charitable Trust Committee entry for a statement on giving priorities and full application guidelines.

O+D+T Refer to PNC Advisors Charitable Trust Committee entry. — PNC Advisors (Trustee)

SW-215 Longvue Foundation
Scaife Road
Sewickley 15143   (Allegheny County)

MI-12-31-41
Phone 412-749-0891 **FAX** None
EIN 23-7920494   **Year Created** 1997

AMV $85,465   **FYE** 12-00   **(Gifts Received** $81,684)   2 **Grants totaling** $51,000

All local giving. High grant of **$50,000** to Sewickley Academy. **$1,000** to Allegheny Valley Hospital. — Grants awarded in the prior year: **$25,000** to Sewickley Academy and **$2,000** to Women's and Infants' Development. ■ **PUBLICATIONS:** None ■ **WEBSITE:** None ■ **E-MAIL:** None ■ **APPLICATION POLICIES & PROCEDURES:** Information not available.

O+D+T Ronald E. Long (T+Donor+Con) — Mary Owen Long (T)

SW-216 Loughney (Edward D. & Opal C.) Foundation
720 Oliver Building, 535 Smithfield Street
Pittsburgh 15222   (Allegheny County)

MI-11-22-31-32-41-42-52-55-57-61
Phone 412-263-2822 **FAX** None
EIN 25-1487046   **Year Created** 1984

AMV $390,647   **FYE** 11-00   **(Gifts Received** $17,084)   15 **Grants totaling** $48,500

Mostly local giving. High grant of **$10,000** to Pittsburgh Symphony. **$8,000** to St. Mary of Mercy Church [Pittsburgh]. **$5,000** to Holy Family Hospital Foundation. **$4,000** to United Way of Allegheny County. **$3,000** each to Catholic Charities and Pittsburgh Cultural Trust. **$2,000-$2,500** each to Children's Hospital of Pittsburgh, Diocese of Pittsburgh/Bishop's Education Fund, and WQED. **$1,000-$1,500** each to Carlow College, Pittsburgh Opera, and Seton Hill College. **Out-of-state** giving: **$3,000** to

U. of Oklahoma and **$1,000** each to Memorial Sloan Kettering Cancer Center [NY] and St. Mary-of-the-Woods College [IN]. ■ **PUBLICATIONS:** None ■**WEBSITE:** None ■**E-MAIL:** None ■**APPLICATION POLICIES & PROCEDURES:** Grant requests may be submitted in any form at any time.

O+D+T   Edward D. Loughney (T+Donor+Con)

SW-217   **Lucente (Frank S.) Foundation**
413 - 2nd Ave.
Meyersdale   15552   (Somerset County)
AMV $366,637   **FYE** 12-00   (**Gifts Received** $0)

MI-31-39-44-61-89
Phone 814-634-8643 **FAX** None
EIN 23-7949281   **Year Created** 1997
6 **Grants totaling** $20,000

All local giving. High grant of **$12,000** to Meyersdale Medical Center. **$2,000** each to Meyersdale Borough, Meyersdale Public Library, and Sts. Philip & James Catholic Church. **$1,000** each to Meyersdale Area Ambulance and Meyersdale Volunteer Fire Dept. ■**PUBLICATIONS:** None ■**WEBSITE:** None ■**E-MAIL:** None ■**APPLICATION POLICIES & PROCEDURES:** Information not available.

O+D+T   Frank S. Lucente (T+Donor+Con) — Somerset Trust Company (Corporate Trustee)

SW-218   **Mack (J.S.) Foundation, The**
134 South 6th Street, P.O. Box 34
Indiana   15701   (Indiana County)
AMV $3,290,353   **FYE** 12-00   (**Gifts Received** $8,648)

MI-11-13-39-54-56-84
Phone 724-463-7300 **FAX** None
EIN 25-6002036   **Year Created** 1935
2 **Grants totaling** $11,500

The Foundation owns a park located in the Borough of Indiana and White Township where it underwrites various sporting activities as well as programs at the J.S. Mack Community Center. In addition, selected grants are awarded: **$10,000** to Indiana County YMCA and **$1,500** to Southern Allegheny Museum of Art. — In the prior year, four grants awarded: **$5,000** to Beulah Baptist Church; **$2,000** to Citizens Ambulance of Indiana; **$500** to Indiana County United Way; and **$200** to Indiana County Historical Society. ■**PUBLICATIONS:** None ■**WEBSITE:** None ■**E-MAIL:** None ■**APPLICATION POLICIES & PROCEDURES:** Most giving is for general support, building funds, and matching grants; no grants are awarded for scholarships, fellowships, prizes, or to individuals. Grant requests may be submitted in a letter at any time; include an audited financial statement, list of major funding sources, organization budget, project budget, and IRS tax-exempt status documentation. The Board meets in January and as required.

O+D+T   Joseph N. Mack (S+F+T+Con) — L. Blaine Grube (P+T) — Peter Stewart [Armagh] (VP+T) — J. Merle Rife (T) — Jonathan B. Mack (T)

SW-219   **Madia Family Foundation, The**
503 Salem Heights Drive
Gibsonia   15044   (Allegheny County)
AMV $11,565   **FYE** 12-00   (**Gifts Received** $275,945)

MI-63
Phone 724-935-2325 **FAX** None
EIN 31-1490172   **Year Created** 1996
3 **Grants totaling** $445,707

All local giving. High grant of **$443,707** to Victory Christian Fellowship. **$1,000** each to Allison Park Assembly and Light of Life Ministries. — Giving in the prior year included **$166,000** to Victory Christian Fellowship; **$15,000** to Salem Heights Christian Center; and **$2,000** to Evangel Christian Fellowship [CA]. ■**PUBLICATIONS:** None ■**WEBSITE:** None ■**E-MAIL:** None ■**APPLICATION POLICIES & PROCEDURES:** The Foundation reports that preference is given to Pennsylvania charities. Grant requests may be submitted in any form at any time; include the most recent financial statements and IRS tax-exempt status documentation.

O+D+T   Frank Madia (T+Donor+Con) — Jean Madia (T+Donor)

SW-220   **Magovern Family Foundation**
251 Old Mill Road
Pittsburgh   15238   (Allegheny County)
AMV $271,619   **FYE** 12-00   (**Gifts Received** $0)

MI-61-32-64
Phone 412-963-7611 **FAX** None
EIN 25-6282388   **Year Created** 1986
2 **Grants totaling** $24,250

One Pa. grant: **$9,250** to St. Vincent's Seminary [Latrobe]. **Out-of-state** grant: **$15,000** to American Ireland Fund [MA]. — Giving in prior years to other Catholic institutions/organizations and for medical research. ■**PUBLICATIONS:** None ■**WEBSITE:** None ■**E-MAIL:** None ■**APPLICATION POLICIES & PROCEDURES:** No grants awarded to individuals.

O+D+T   George J. Magovern, M.D. (T+Donor+Con) — Margaret A. Magovern (T+Donor)

SW-221   **Mann (Job) #2 Trust**
c/o John B. Koontz, Esq.
Professional Building, P.O. Box 645
Bedford   15522   (Bedford County)
AMV $284,248   **FYE** 9-00   (**Gifts Received** $9,300)

MI-64
Phone 814-623-5114 **FAX** None
EIN 23-6201775   **Year Created** 1877
4 **Grants totaling** $21,000

All grants are restricted to scholarships for Bedford County males pursuing ministerial training; awards ranged from **$3,000** to **$7,000** for students attending seminaries in PA and TX. ■**PUBLICATIONS:** None ■**WEBSITE:** None ■**E-MAIL:** None ■**APPLICATION POLICIES & PROCEDURES:** Under the terms of the Trust only male residents of Bedford County pursuing ministerial training are eligible for consideration. Scholarship applicants may submit a request at any time in a letter.

O+D+T   John B. Koontz, Esq. (Advisory Board Member+Con) — and an Advisory Board of Trustees — PNC Bank (Trustee)

SW-222 Maplewood Foundation
c/o PNC Advisors, M.S. P2-PTPP-25-1
Two PNC Plaza, 620 Liberty Ave.
Pittsburgh 15222   (Allegheny County)

MI-41-42-52-56-63

Phone 412-762-3502 **FAX** 412-762-5439
EIN 25-6502637   **Year Created** 1995

AMV $26,415,852   **FYE** 6-00   **(Gifts Received** $35,253)   5 **Grants totaling** $1,420,312

Mostly local giving. High grant of **$500,000** to Chatham College (campus renewal). **$392,000** to Calvary Episcopal Church (window restoration). **$253,312** to Extra Mile Education Foundation (inner-city endowment fund). **$25,000** to Episcopal Diocese of Pittsburgh (Canterbury Place chaplaincy). **Out-of-state** grant: **$250,000** to American Indian College Fund [CO]. — Grants in the prior three years included **$250,000** each to Historical Society of Western Pa. (endowment) and U. of Pittsburgh (Center for American Music endowment);**$25,000** to Episcopal Diocese of Pittsburgh (Canterbury Place chaplaincy); **$15,000** to Calvary Episcopal Church (general contribution); and **$10,000** to Williams College [MA]. ■**PUBLICATIONS:** None ■**WEBSITE:** None ■**E-MAIL:** bruce.bickel@pncadvisors.com ■**APPLICATION POLICIES & PROCEDURES:** The Foundation reports that applications are not accepted; grants awarded only to preselected organizations. No grants are awarded to individuals.

O+D+T R. Bruce Bickel (Senior VP at Bank+Con) — G. William Bissell, Esq. (Co-T) — PNC Advisors (Co-Trustee)

SW-223 Maria Foundation
c/o PNC Advisors, M.S. P2-PTPP-25-1
Two PNC Plaza, 620 Liberty Ave.
Pittsburgh 15222   (Allegheny County)

MI-15-22-32-35-72

Phone 412-762-3502 **FAX** 412-762-5439
EIN 23-7892071   **Year Created** 1997

AMV $1,338,060   **FYE** 12-00   **(Gifts Received** $0)   14 **Grants totaling** $45,500

About half local giving. High grant of **$20,000** to National Parkinson Foundation/Greater Pittsburgh Chapter. **$3,000** to Asbury Foundation. **$2,500** to Rankin Christian Center. **Out-of-state** giving includes **$3,000** each to Volunteers in Medicine [SC] and Wildlife Waystation [CA]; and **$2,000** each to Pathways [CT], Performing Animal Welfare Society [CA], and Physicians Committee for Responsible Medicine [DC]. ■**PUBLICATIONS:** None ■**WEBSITE:** None ■**E-MAIL:** bruce.bickel@pncadvisors.com ■**APPLICATION POLICIES & PROCEDURES:** Grant requests may be submitted at any time in a letter.

O+D+T R. Bruce Bickel (Senior VP at Bank+Con) — PNC Advisors (Trustee)

SW-224 Marous (John C. & Lucine O.B.) Charitable Foundation
33 Easton Road, Fox Chapel
Pittsburgh 15238   (Allegheny County)

MI-11-41-42-51-52-57-61-64-81

Phone 412-963-8670 **FAX** None
EIN 25-1544612   **Year Created** 1986

AMV $253,696   **FYE** 12-00   **(Gifts Received** $0)   41 **Grants totaling** $151,500

Mostly local giving; all grants are for general support. High grant of **$30,500** to St. Vincent's Seminary [Latrobe]. **$20,000** each to United Way of Allegheny County and U. of Pittsburgh. **$10,000** each to Bishop Bosco Fund [Greensburg] and Carlow College. **$6,000-$6,250** each to Little Sisters of the Poor, River City Brass Band, and St. Scholastica Church. **$5,000** each to National Flag Foundation and Pittsburgh Public Theater. **$2,000** to Cardinal Wright Regional School. **$1,000-$1,500** each to March of Dimes, The Pittsburgh Oratory, World Affairs Council of Pittsburgh, and WQED. Other local contributions **$100-$500** for similar purposes. **Out-of-state** giving includes **$10,000** to Royal Palms International Academy [FL]; **$6,500** to Education for Parish Service [DC]; and **$2,500** to Bishop's Annual Appeal [FL]. ■**PUBLICATIONS:** None ■**WEBSITE:** None ■**E-MAIL:** None ■**APPLICATION POLICIES & PROCEDURES:** The Foundation reports that most giving is for general operating support or endowment. Grant requests may be submitted in any form at any time.

O+D+T John C. Marous, Jr. (P+Donor+Con) — Lucine O.B. Marous (VP+F+Donor) — Edward J. Greene, Esq. (S)

SW-225 Mars Family Charitable Foundation, The
c/o Fostin Capital Corporation
681 Andersen Drive, 3rd Floor
Pittsburgh 15220   (Allegheny County)

MI-14-22-41-51-54-62

Phone 412-928-1400 **FAX** None
EIN 25-6585615   **Year Created** 1998

AMV $962,717   **FYE** 12-00   **(Gifts Received** $500,000)   201 **Grants totaling** $31,718

About two-thirds local giving. High grant of **$3,076** to Zionist Organization of America. **$1,850** to Rodef Shalom Congregation. **$1,000** each to Carnegie Museum of Art, Jewish Residential Services, and Western Pa. School for Blind Children. **$750** to Tree of Life Congregation. **$500** each to City Theatre, Pittsburgh Public Theater, United Jewish Federation of Greater Pittsburgh, Women's American ORT, and Yeshiva Schools. Numerous local and out-of-state contributions **$15-$450** for various purposes. ■**PUBLICATIONS:** None ■**WEBSITE:** None ■**E-MAIL:** None ■**APPLICATION POLICIES & PROCEDURES:** Information not available. — Formerly called The Barbara & Bernard Mars Charitable Foundation.

O+D+T Bernard S. Mars (T+Con) — Andrew F. Mars (T) — Barbara F. Mars (T) — Peter F. Mars (T) — Sally Mars (T) — David M. Martin (Administrative Trustee)

SW-226 Marshall (Thomas) Foundation
USX Tower, Suite 3278
600 Grant Street
Pittsburgh 15219   (Allegheny County)

MI-11-12-13-14-17-18-22-25-32-34-42-71-72

Phone 412-433-7801 **FAX** 412-433-7891
EIN 25-6479933   **Year Created** 1994

AMV $10,629,689   **FYE** 12-00   **(Gifts Received** $769,295)   43 **Grants totaling** $311,300

Mostly local giving; all grants are for general charitable purposes. High grant of **$200,000** to U. of Pittsburgh/Katz Graduate School of Business. **$55,000** to U. of Pittsburgh Medical School. **$50,000** to U. of Pittsburgh (Chancellors Fund). **$25,000** to United Way of SW Pa. **$15,000** to Clelian Heights School for Exceptional Children. **$10,000** each to Girls Hope of Pittsburgh, Holy Family Institute, Mom's House, and Salvation Army. **$5,000** each to Bridge to Independence [Braddock], Emmaus Community of Pittsburgh, Family House, Hill House Associates, National Kidney Foundation, D.T. Watson Rehabilitation Services, and YWCA of Pittsburgh. **$3,000** each to Pittsburgh Planned Parenthood and Youth in Action. **$1,000-$2,000** each to Bethlehem Haven, North Hills Community Research, Pittsburgh Zoo, Union Aid Society, and Western Pa. Conservancy. **Out-of-state** giving includes **$20,000** to Vermont Institute of National Science and smaller grants for various purposes to SW Florida and NH. ■**PUBLICATIONS:** policy statement ■**WEBSITE:** None ■**E-MAIL:** jsharpski@tmfound.org ■**APPLICATION POLICIES & PROCEDURES:** The Foundation reports its principal mission is supporting new and established organizations working to improve the quality of life for children and their families—by assisting individuals to maximize their potential for self-sufficiency and economic independence; educational programs for young people are of particular interest. No grants are awarded for conferences or seminars, support of propaganda, sectarian religious activities, or efforts to influence legislation. Grants are usually for a limited period of time, one to three years. Prospective applicants should first request from the Foundation a Grant Application Form which stipulates the required attachments; submit the completed Form at any time with a full proposal and attachments.

O+D+T Janet L. Sharpski (Executive Director+Con) — Sue Marshall Roberts [TX] (T+D) — Theresa Marshall [VT] (D) — Thomas Marshall [FL] (D+Donor) — Virginia P. Marshall [FL] (D) — PNC Bank N.A. (Agent)

SW-227 Massey Charitable Trust
935 Beaver Grade Road
P.O. Box 1178
Coraopolis 15108   (Allegheny County)
AMV $38,433,065   **FYE** 12-01   **(Gifts Received** $0)

MI-12-13-14-15-17-20-22-25-29-31-32-41-42 45-52-54-56-63-65-71-72
Phone 412-262-5992 **FAX** 412-262-1995
EIN 23-7007897   **Year Created** 1968
140 **Grants totaling** $1,926,580

About three-fourths local giving. High grant of **$125,000** to Robert Morris College. **$75,000** to Carlow College. **$70,000** to Pittsburgh Leadership Foundation. **$40,000** to Carnegie Museums of Pittsburgh. **$35,000** to Manchester Youth Development Center. **$25,000** each to ARC-Allegheny Foundation, Coalition for Christian Outreach, Extra Mile Education Foundation, Grove City College, Pace School, Pittsburgh Civic Light Opera, Pittsburgh Opera, Pittsburgh Vision Services, Salvation Army/Western Pa. Division, Shriners Hospitals for Children, Spina Bifida Assn. of Western Pa., Western Pa. School for Deaf Children, and The Woodlands Foundation. **$20,000** each to Boy Scouts/Greater Pittsburgh Council, Catholic Youth Assn. of Pittsburgh, Cystic Fibrosis Foundation/Western Pa., East Liberty Family Health Care Center, Family Guidance Inc. FamilyLinks, LaRoche College, Pittsburgh Symphony, Three Rivers Center for Independent Living, and Women's Center & Shelter of Greater Pittsburgh. **$15,000** each to Assn. for Children & Adults with Learning Disabilities, Beginning With Books, Bethlehem Haven of Pittsburgh, Big Brothers/Big Sisters of Greater Pittsburgh, Greater Pittsburgh Community Food Bank, Historical Society of Western Pa., Hollow Oak Land Trust, Marian Manor, Pittsburgh Zoo, South Hills Health System Foundation, Visiting Nurse Foundation, and Wesley Institute. **$12,000** to Pittsburgh Children's Museum. **$10,000** each to Allegheny Valley School, Allegheny Youth Development, Arthritis Foundation/Western Pa Chapter, Center Against Domestic & Sexual Violence, Family Hospice, Family House, Family Resources, F.O.R. Sto-Rox, Girl Scouts of Western Pa., Interfaith Volunteer Caregivers of SW Pa., Juvenile Diabetes Foundation /Western Pa., Leukemia Society of America/Western Pa., Life's Work of Western Pa., Mom's House of Pittsburgh, National Kidney Foundation of Western Pa., North Side Christian Health Center, Orr Compassionate Care Center, Parents League for Emotional Adjustment, Pittsburgh Action Against Rape, Pittsburgh Center for the Arts, Pittsburgh Coalition Against Pornography, Pittsburgh Habitat for Humanity, Pittsburgh Irish & Classical Theatre, Pittsburgh Youth Symphony, Point Park College, POWER/Pa. Organization for Women in Early Recovery, Presbyterian Senior Care, Rainbow Kitchen Community Services, Special Olympics of Allegheny County, St. Paul Homes, St. Vincent College/Center for Economic & Policy Education, Syria Temple/Syria Shrine Hospital, UCP of Pittsburgh, Urban ImpactFoundation, Western Pa. Conservancy, Westmoreland ARC Foundation, YMHA & Irene Kaufmann Centers, YMCA of McKeesport, and Young Life-East Hills. **$7,500-$8,000** each to Allegheny County Center for Victims of Violent Crimes, Big Brothers/Big Sisters of Beaver County, Christian Sports International, Oncology Nursing Foundation, Three Rivers Youth, Young Men's & Women's African Heritage Assn. **$4,000-$5,000** each to Adult Resources, Inc., Allegheny County Literacy Council, Boys & Girls Clubs of Western Pa., Civic Light Opera Guild, Greater Pittsburgh Literacy Council, Human Services Center Corp., Lifesteps, Inc., Make-A-Wish Foundation of Western Pa., North Side Common Ministries, One-to-One Citizen Advocacy, St. Mary's Lawrenceville Arts Program, Sewickley Public Library, Soli Deo Gloria, and YMCA of Pittsburgh. **$2,000-$3,000** each to Contact Pittsburgh, Grantmakers of Western Pa., Moon Township Public Library, and YWCA of Butler. **Out-of-state** giving includes **$90,000** to High Museum of Art [GA]; **$60,000** to Atlanta Symphony [GA]; **$50,000** each to Atlanta Historical Society [GA]; **$30,000** to Georgia Justice Project; **$25,000** each to Belmont U. [TN], Museum of Photographic Arts [CA], and Scripps Institution of Oceanography [CA]; and smaller grants, mostly for arts/cultural or educational purposes in GA. ■**PUBLICATIONS:** None ■**WEBSITE:** None ■**E-MAIL:** None ■**APPLICATION POLICIES & PROCEDURES:** The Foundation reports a preference for organizations ministering to the health care, educational and spiritual needs of SW Pa. and Atlanta, GA. Most grants are for general support or capital drives. No grants are awarded to individuals. Prospective applicants should make an initial telephone inquiry about the feasibility of submitting a request. Grant requests may be submitted in a letter (3 pages maximum) at any time; include a project budget, list of major funding sources, audited financial statement, and IRS tax-exempt status documentation. Site visits sometimes are made to organizations being considered for a grant. The Trustees award grants at meetings in June and September.

O+D+T Walter J. Carroll (Executive Director+T+Con) — Joe B. Massey [GA] (T) — Daniel B. Carroll [TX] (T) — Robert M. Connolly, CPA [Monaca] (T) — Robert M. Entwhisle, III, Esq. [Pittsburgh] (T) — Donor: Estates of Doris J. & Harris B. Massey

---

SW-228 Matthews (James H.) & Co. Educational & Charitable Trust **MI**-11-14-42-51-52-54-56-71
c/o Matthews International Corporation
Two North Shore Center, Suite 200
Pittsburgh 15212   (Allegheny County)
AMV $2,258,780   **FYE** 9-00   **(Gifts Received** $90,000)

Phone 412-442-8200 **FAX** None
EIN 25-6028582   **Year Created** 1940
30 **Grants totaling** $86,485

Mostly local giving. High grant of **$55,377** to United Way of SW Pa. **$3,500** to Pittsburgh Symphony. **$1,000-$1,750** each to Allegheny Cemetery Historical Assn., Carnegie Museums of Pittsburgh, First Night Pittsburgh, Goodwill Industries of Pittsburgh,

Kuntu Repertory Theatre, Pittsburgh History & Landmarks Foundation, Pittsburgh Opera, Pittsburgh Public Theater, D.T. Watson Rehabilitation Services, United Negro College Fund, and Western Pa. Conservancy. Other local contributions **$250-$700** for similar purposes. **Out-of-state** giving, mostly for United Ways, in company operating locations: AR, CA, MO, NY, and Canada. ■ **PUBLICATIONS:** None ■**WEBSITE:** None ■**E-MAIL:** None ■**APPLICATION POLICIES & PROCEDURES:** No grants awarded to individuals.

O+D+T David M. Kelly (T+Con) — Edward J. Boyle (T) — Corporate donor: Matthews International Corporation

---

SW-229 McCain (Genevieve B. & John L., Sr.) Foundation
c/o PNC Advisors, M.S. P2-PTPP-33-4
Two PNC Plaza, 620 Liberty Ave.
Pittsburgh 15222 (Allegheny County)

MI-21-31-32-63

Phone 412-762-3617 **FAX** None
EIN 25-1557328 **Year Created** 1986

AMV $390,462 **FYE** 9-00 **(Gifts Received** $20,000) 13 **Grants totaling** $20,472

About half local/Pa. giving. High grant of **$3,000** to Southminster Presbyterian Church. **$1,200-$1,500** each to Grand Chapter Charities Masonic Temple [Philadelphia], Grand Lodge Mason Library & Museum [Philadelphia], Hike Fund [Lancaster County], Mercy Heart Foundation, St. Clair Hospital Foundation, and West Penn Hospital Foundation. **Out-of-state** giving mostly to/for Masonic-related or religious organizations in MA, IL, KY, FL, and MO. ■**PUBLICATIONS:** None ■**WEBSITE:** None ■**E-MAIL:** None ■**APPLICATION POLICIES & PROCEDURES:** Grants requests may be submitted in a letter at any time; describe the nature and purpose of the organization.

O+D+T Michael O'Donnell (Trust Officer at Bank+Con) — Genevieve H. McCain (Co-T+Donor) — John L. McCain, Jr. (Co-T) — PNC Advisors (Co-Trustee)

SW-230 McCandless (James Francis) Charitable Trust
Refer to PNC Advisors Charitable Trust Committee entry.
(Allegheny County)

MI-12-14-17-22-29-31-41-42-51-52-54-61-63-71-89

EIN 25-1347840 **Year Created** 1978

AMV $6,961,385 **FYE** 12-00 **(Gifts Received** $0) 36 **Grants totaling** $336,948

Mostly Western Pa. giving. High grant of **$15,000** to Brandy Springs Park [Mercer]. **$13,500** to Pittsburgh Dance Foundation. **$12,000-$12,750** each to Allegheny County Airport, Covenant Presbyterian Church, Family Communications, The DePaul Institute, Jewish Community Center, Jubilee Christian School, Leadership Pittsburgh, National Fatherhood Initiative, and Pittsburgh Ohio Valley General Hospital. **$10,975-$11,250** each to Assn. for Children & Adults with Learning Disabilities, Garden City Community Outreach, Duquesne U., Hillel Foundation, Pittsburgh Urban Leadership, Southern Alleghenies Museum of Art, and Working Order. **$8,000-$8,850** each to Byzantine Catholic Cemetery, Community Design Center, George Junior Republic, Holy Family Institute, Suburban General Hospital, and Woodard's Educational Services & Scholarship Foundation. **$7,500** each to Learning Disabilities of Pittsburgh, Mendelssohn Choir of Pittsburgh, Pine Richland Youth Center [Richland], and Woman's Shelter [New Castle]. **$6,000** each to Allegheny Intermediate Unit, Bradley Center, and Balmoral School [Greensburg]. **$4,000** to Sisters of St. Francis [Millvale]. **$3,750** to Competitive Employment. **Out-of-state** grants to NY and TX. ■**APPLICATION POLICIES & PROCEDURES:** Refer to the PNC Advisors Charitable Trust Committee entry for a statement on giving priorities and full application guidelines.

O+D+T Refer to PNC Advisors Charitable Trust Committee entry. — PNC Advisors (Trustee)

SW-231 McCune Foundation
Suite 750,
6 PPG Place
Pittsburgh 15222 (Allegheny County)

MI-13-14-15-22-32-41-42-44-51-52-54-55-56-57-84-85

Phone 412-644-8779 **FAX** 412-644-8059
EIN 25-6210269 **Year Created** 1979

AMV $564,173,106 **FYE** 9-01 **(Gifts Received** $0) 185 **Grants totaling** $27,858,921

Mostly SW Pa. giving in four priority categories: Community/Economic Development & Civic, Education/Libraries, Health & Human Services, and Arts/Culture & Humanities. **_COMMUNITY/ECONOMIC DEVELOPMENT & CIVIC GRANTS_**: **$2,000,000** to Strategic Regional Developments (program related investment to develop former LTV Coke Works/Homestead). **$575,000** to Pittsburgh Partnership for Neighborhood Development (operating support/conference underwriting/technical assistance to Hill CDC). **$500,000** each to Local Initiatives Support Corp. (East End Growth Fund) and Westmoreland Trust (James Building renovation). **$475,000** to Greater Pittsburgh Convention & Visitors Bureau Education Foundation (cultural tourism programs/trade shows). **$450,000** to Pittsburgh Regional Alliance (program operations). **$325,000** to Allegheny Conference on Community Development (Agenda Development Fund-2 years). **$300,000** to National Park Foundation [DC] (visitor-interpretive center for Fort Necessity/National Road). **$250,000** each to Pittsburgh Digital Greenhouse (electronic chip design industry cluster development) and Western Pa. Humane Society (new facility construction). **$235,000** to Mon Valley Initiative (mostly Workforce Development Program). **$200,000** each to Corporation for Owner-Operator Projects (rural technology development initiative) and Three Rivers Connect (interactive information system at airport). **$150,000** each to Pa. Audubon Society (Cooperative Deer Management Initiative) and Pa. Economy League (Workforce Connections Career Development Program Network). **$125,000** to Minority Enterprise Corp. of SW Pa. (business assistance programs). **$100,000** to Riverlife Task Force (develop master plan). **$75,000** each to Community Builders (East Liberty low-income housing planning) and Oakland Planning & Development Corp. (western entrance development). **$60,000** to Leadership Pittsburgh (employment-related initiatives). **$50,000** each to 10,000 Friends of Pa. (land use management project), Grantmakers of Western Pa. (3-year strategic plan), and Pittsburgh Downtown Partnership (new conference room). **$45,000** to Northside Leadership Conference (technology-systems upgrades). **$33,000** to Duquesne U. (global awareness project for SW Pa.). **$25,000** to Spring Garden Neighborhood Council (land use study). **$20,000** to City of Pittsburgh (assess East End community development financing needs). **$15,000** to Urban League of Pittsburgh (Freedom Corner Memorial construction). **_EDUCATION-LIBRARY GRANTS_**: **$1,509,500** to Imani Christian Academy (operating support-2 years). **$750,000** each to Chatham College (institutional technology plan), Point Park College (Academic Hall renovations), U. of Pittsburgh/Center for Industry Studies (endowment) and Washington & Jefferson College (Burnett Center construction). **$500,000** to Carnegie Science Center (Sportswork exhibit). **$250,000** each to St. Vincent College (3-year planning initiative) and U. of Pittsburgh/University Library System (Richard Thornburg Archival Collection endowment). **$200,000** to U. of Pittsburgh/School of Engineering (Swanson Center endowment). **$150,000** each to Carnegie Mellon U./School of Computer Science (innovation fund) and Western Pa. School for the Deaf (TV studio equipment). **$120,000** to U. of Pittsburgh/Institute of Politics (program support-3 years). **$113,400** to United Negro College Fund (scholars program). **$80,000** to Heartwood Institute (character education curriculum project). **$50,000** to The Pittsburgh Foundation (Mihail Stolarevsky Fund-music/arts camp scholarship). **$25,000** each to Community Foundation of Westmoreland County (one-room schoolhouse project) and U. of Pittsburgh (science research festival). **$17,500** to U. of Pittsburgh/School of Education (professional development for departmental chairpersons). **$15,000** to Adams Memorial Library (Bookmobile acquisitions). ***HEALTH & HUMAN SERVICES GRANTS***: **$1,250,000** to Hosanna House (Wilkinsburg capital campaign). **$350,000** to Center in the Woods (exterior construction). **$300,000** to UCP of Pittsburgh (capital campaign). **$250,000** each to Community Foundation of Fayette County (endowment), SW Pa. Partnership for Aging (5 year research-demonstration project), Three Rivers Center for Independent Living Foundation (capital campaign), YouthWorks (program support), and YWCA of Greater Pittsburgh (downtown facility renovations). **$200,000** each to Allegheny County Dept. of Human Services (organizational enhancement projects), Family House, Inc. (Shadyside facility renovations), and Life'sWork of Western Pa. (social ventures fund). **$150,000** each to National Fatherhood Initiative [DC] (establish Western Pa. chapter) and Pine Springs Camp (facilities improvement plan). **$125,000** to Golden Triangle Radio Information Service (new business venture). **$120,000** to Pittsburgh Pastoral Institute (free care fund). **$102,350** to Community Foundation for the Alleghenies(Somerset County fund development). **$100,000** each to Allegheny Valley School (Kennedy Township Program Center), Achieva/ARC-Allegheny Foundation (The Family Trust seed money),Pittsburgh Social Venture Partners (startup costs-3 years), Residential Resources, Inc. (properties purchase/renovations), and William J. Copeland Fund (Tropman Nonprofit Research Fund). **$87,000** to Pittsburgh Harlequins Rugby Football Assn. (Indiana Township facility). **$85,000** to City Mission (new Fayette County facility). **$62,200** to Duquesne U. (social entrepreneurship training). **$50,000** each to Grantmakers of Western Pa. (social entrepreneurship conference), Human Services of Western Pa. (downtown building acquisition/renovation), Pittsburgh Mediation Center (office relocation), and YMCA of McKeesport (youth programs). **$43,300** to Share Our Strength [DC] (design Pittsburgh Social Venture Forum). **$40,000** each to Rosedale Block Cluster (business plan/operating support) and Tides Center of Western Pa. (youth-serving organizations standards initiative). **$20,000** to Northside Common Ministries (job readiness curriculum). ***ARTS/CULTURE & HUMANITIES GRANTS***: **$800,000** to Historical Society of Western Pa. (endowment/Museum of Rural Life/new exhibits). **$600,000** to Pa. Historical & Museums Commission (Old Economy Village visitors' center construction). **$427,000** to City Theatre Company (institutional stabilization campaign). **$350,000** to Carnegie Museum of Art (exhibition). **$325,000** to Pittsburgh Glass Center (establish center/youth scholarships). **$300,000** each to Mattress Factory (capital campaign) and WQED (nightly news program/documentary). **$250,000** to Pittsburgh Center for the Arts (business venture with Cinemuse). **$200,000** to Western Pa. Arts Initiative (program operations). **$100,000** to Greater Pittsburgh Arts Alliance (membership development/advocacy). **$75,000** to Artists & Cities (real estate & artists program), Pittsburgh Ballet Theatre (technology upgrade). **$50,000** each to Brew House Assn. (renovations), Opera Theatre of Pittsburgh (productions/education/outreach), and Pittsburgh Chamber Music Society (program enrichment/marketing campaign). **$35,000** to Associated Artists of Pittsburgh (facility renovation). **$25,800** to Bushy Run Battlefield Heritage Society (land purchase). **$25,000** to Soldiers & Sailors Memorial Hall of Allegheny County (educational programs/outreach). **$15,000** to Pittsburgh Filmmakers (Teenie Harris documentary). RELIGION GRANTS: **$250,000** to Church of the Good Shepherd (Raising the Roof campaign). **$34,000** to Epiphany Catholic Church (basement refurbishing). ***MANAGEMENT REVITALIZATION INITIATIVE GRANTS***: Six grants, **$35,900-$54,957** to engage nonprofit leaders in self-directed professional/personal activities awarded to Bethlehem Haven, Mom's House of Pittsburgh, Pittsburgh Filmmakers, Riverview Children's Center, Rosedale Block Cluster, and Westmoreland Museum of American Art. ***OUT-OF-STATE GRANTS*** were primarily to the southwestern U.S. in cooperation with a related McCune family foundation or for other family interests. In addition, 28 grants of **$15,000** or less (totaling **$198,750**) were awarded; also, 12 McCune family matching grants totaled $260,477. ■**PUBLICATIONS:** Annual Report with application guidelines ■**WEBSITE:** www.mccune.org ■**E-MAIL:** info@mccune.org ■**APPLICATION POLICIES & PROCEDURES:** The Foundation reports that giving focuses on SW Pa., especially Pittsburgh, except for McCune family interests elsewhere. Unsolicited proposals from outside SW Pa. are not accepted, and no grants are awarded to individuals. Capital campaign requests (especially for new construction) are broadly reviewed within the context of how they will advance regional change, not just how they may benefit a particular organization/constituency. Priority is given projects that demonstrate the greatest likelihood of achieving measurable results in one of the four priority categories (see above); this includes initiatives creating economic opportunities, preparing young people for the workforce, and building healthy and economically viable communities to attract people to the city/region. Criteria used in screening proposals include: (a) the potential for high impact on the health, growth and prosperity of the region; (b) the organization's capacity for implementation and evidence the project/program can be sustained beyond the grant period; (c) timing/fit of the project/program re related community efforts/initiatives; and (d) the research, development and experimental aspects to influence/improve the operations of individual organizations or clusters of related organizations. Further, high priority is given to proposals that show solid planning, especially in identifying additional/supplementary funding sources; evidence collaboration and creative approaches; demonstrate efficient operations and accountability; leverage resources; avoid duplication; demonstrate realistic expectations; and assure measurable outcomes. The grant application process has two steps: **Step 1**: Submit a Letter of Inquiry (3 pages maximum) describing what the proposed project intends to achieve for the region, as well as for the organization; what activities/actions are planned to meet the stated goals; the project timeline; total cost of the project; anticipated income, including private and public funders; and the funding requested from McCune Foundation. Also include theMcCune Foundation Applicant Information Sheet (available on request or the website) and IRS tax-exempt status documentation. — Note: The Letter of Inquiry now may be submitted electronically from the Foundation's website; click on 'Applicant Information Sheet - Online Interactive' from the Guidelines screen. **Step 2**: If the proposed project is of potential interest, meets current funding priorities, and sufficient resources are available, Foundation staff will contact the applicant to arrange a meeting and provide guidance regarding the possible submission of a formal proposal. Proposals which follow the Grantmakers of Western Pa. Common Grant Application Format are accepted, although additional information may be requested. Decisions on grants may take several months, especially for new projects. The Distribution Committee awards grants at May, September and December meetings—and sometimes other months. Incomplete inquiries/proposals which fall outside the Foundation's stated interests or current priorities will not be considered.

O+D+T Distribution Committee members: Henry S. Beukema (Executive Director+Con) — James M. Edwards (C) — Michael M. Edwards [MA] — John R. McCune, VI [OK] — Richard D. Edwards (Chairman Emeritus) — National City Bank of Pa. (Corporate Trustee)

SW-232 **McCune (John R.) Charitable Trust**	**MI**-12-13-14-15-22-31-32-35-41-42-43-45-56
Six PPG Place, Suite 750,	57-63-64-65-71-72
P.O. Box 1749	**Phone** 412-644-7796 **FAX** 412-644-8059
Pittsburgh 15230 (Allegheny County)	**EIN** 25-6160722 **Year Created** 1972
AMV $180,910,159 **FYE** 11-00 **(Gifts Received** $0)	188 **Grants totaling** $8,563,359

Nearly half local/Western Pa giving.; all grants are listed as general support and some comprise multiple payments. High grant of **$292,000** to The Ellis School. **$125,000** to Winchester Thurston School. **$115,000** each to American Cancer Society and Grove City College. **$105,000** to Children's Hospital of Pittsburgh. **$100,000** each to Carriage House Children's Center, Jubilee Christian School [Grove City], Marian Manor, National Aviary in Pittsburgh, Three Rivers Center for Independent Living, Western Pa. Humane Society, and YMCA of Beaver County. **$95,000** to West Penn Hospital Foundation. **$80,000** to U. of Pittsburgh Medical Center. **$75,000** each to McGuire Memorial Home Foundation [New Brighton], North Side Christian Health Center, Pace School, Shady Side Academy, and U. of Pittsburgh Cancer Center. **$67,000** each to Bucknell U. **$60,000** to Church of the Good Shepherd. **$55,000** to Western Pa. Caring Foundation. **$50,000** each to Auberle Foundation, Beginning With Books, Bethlehem Haven, Crohn's & Colitis Foundation of American/Greater Pittsburgh Chapter, East End Cooperative Ministry, Family Guidance, Inc., Juvenile Diabetes Foundation, Northside Common Ministries, Presbyterian Seniorcare, Southwest Butler County YMCA, Spina Bifida Assn. of Western Pa., St. Barnabas Charitable Foundation, UCP of Pittsburgh, Urban Youth Action, Inc., and Westmoreland ARC Foundation. **$40,000-$46,000** each to Duquesne U., Pittsburgh Theological Seminary, Reformed Presbyterian Theological Seminary, SIDS Alliance, and Western Pa. School for the Deaf. **$30,000-$35,000** each to Chatham College, Crossroads Scholarship Program, East Liberty Family Health Care Center, Global Links, Historical Society of Western Pa., One to One: Citizen Advocacy, Parent & Child Guidance Center, St. Mary's Lawrenceville Arts Program, Westminster College, and YMCA of McKeesport. **$25,000-$26,000** each to Allegheny College, Big Brothers & Big Sisters of Greater Pittsburgh, Cancer Caring Center, Geneva College, Saltworks Theatre Company, Samaritan Counseling Center, and Waynesburg College. **$19,000-$23,675** each to Animal Friends, CONTACT Pittsburgh, Manchester Youth Development Center, Neighborhood Academy Summer School, Pittsburgh Parks Conservancy, South Hills Interfaith Ministries, St. Francis Health Foundation, Washington & Jefferson College, Western Pa. Conservancy, andWhale's Tale Foundation/FamilyLink. **$15,000-$17,000** each to Aquinas Academy [Wildwood], ARC-Allegheny Foundation, Arsenal Family & Children's Center, The Hill School [Montgomery County], Outreach Teen & Family Services, Wesley Institute, and WQED. **$6,000-$12,000** to Hollow Oak Land Trust [Coraopolis], Homestead Unemployed Center, Jane Holmes Residence, Kingsley Assn., Parish of the Word of God School, Pittsburgh Coalition Against Pornography, Sewickley Academy, St. Edmund's Academy, Valley Medical Facilities, Inc., and Western Pa. Family Center. **Out-of-state** giving includes **$156,000** to School of the Plains [OK]; **$125,000** each to Greater Oklahoma Hunter Jumper Assn., Jews for Jesus [CA], Oklahoma Medical Research Foundation, and Project Woman Coalition [OK]; **$116,000** to Sterling College [KS]; **$110,000** to U. of New Haven [CT]; **$105,000** to Sturdy Memorial Foundation [MA]; **$100,000** to Alzheimer's Disease & Related Orders Assn. [IL], Before & After School Enrichment [CO], Community Preparatory School [RI], Ft. Collins Community Foundation [CO], Innovative Media Access Institute [OK], Intercollegiate Studies Assn. [DE], Oklahoma City Art Museum, Oklahoma City Public Schools Foundation, Wednesday's Child Benefit Corp. [TX], and Wheaton College [MA]; **$95,000** to Center for Marine Conservation [DC]; and many other smaller grants to about a dozen states, especially in OK, TX, CO and MA where Trustees are resident. ■**PUBLICATIONS:** None ■**WEBSITE:** None ■**E-MAIL:** None ■**APPLICATION POLICIES & PROCEDURES:** The Foundation reports that major support focuses on Pittsburgh and SW Pa. and is generally limited to health care, educational, or Presbyterian-related institutions; many grantees are ones favored by the late John R. McCune. Grants are awarded for general support, special projects, building funds, capital drives, or endowment. Submit preliminary inquiries in a letter (2 pages maximum) between July and March (deadline is April 1st); enclose an annual report and IRS tax-exempt status documentation. If the proposed project/program interests the Foundation, a proposal will be invited and complete application instructions provided. Site visits sometimes are made to organizations being considered for a grant. Decisions on grants are made at a June meeting and paid out in November.

O+D+T Dispensing Committee members: James M. Edwards (Executive Director+Con) — David L. Edwards [CO] (C) — Molly McCune Cathey [OK] — John H. Edwards [CT] — Michael M. Edwards [MA] — Laurie M. Lewis [OK] — Sarah McCune Losinger [TX] — John R. McCune, VI [OK] — National City Bank of Pa. (Corporate Trustee)

SW-233 **McFeely-Rogers Foundation**	**MI**-11-12-13-14-15-22-29-31-35-41-42-44-49
1100 Ligonier Street, Suite 300	52-54-56-61-63-64-71-84
P.O. Box 110	**Phone** 724-537-5588 **FAX** 724-537-5589
Latrobe 15650 (Westmoreland County)	**EIN** 25-1120947 **Year Created** 1953
AMV $20,910,497 **FYE** 12-01 **(Gifts Received** $0)	89 **Grants totaling** $894,245

Most giving is limited to Westmoreland and Allegheny counties, particularly Latrobe and Pittsburgh; most grants are for general support. High grant of **$217,000** to The Latrobe Foundation. **$71,100** to Greater Latrobe School District. **$59,200** to Adams Memorial Library. **$55,300** to St. Vincent College. **$40,500** to Red Cross/Chestnut Ridge Chapter. **$35,000** to Latrobe Area

Hospital Charitable Foundation. **$30,000** to St. Vincent Archabbey. **$25,000** to Pittsburgh Youth Orchestra Assn. **$20,000** each to Family Communications, Inc. and Sixth Presbyterian Church. **$15,300** to Latrobe Presbyterian Church. **$15,000** to Unon Mission of Latrobe. **$12,500** to U. of Pittsburgh. **$10,000** each to Crossroads Foundation, Latrobe Area Chamber of Commerce Education Foundation, The Neighborhood Academy, Orr Compassionate Care Center, Winchester Thurston School, and Winne Palmer Nature Reserve. **$5,500** Girl Scout Council of Westmoreland. **$5,000** each to Center Against Domestic & Sexual Violence, Loyalhanna Watershed Assn., Pine Springs Camp [Jennerstown], and Pittsburgh Theological Seminary. **$4,600** to Boy Scouts/Westmoreland Fayette Council. **$3,000-$3,900** each to Foundation for Free Enterprise Education [Erie], Pittsburgh Children's Museum, The Pittsburgh Foundation, Presbyterian Media Mission, St. Stephen's A.M.E. Church, and United Way of Westmoreland County. **$2,000-$2,650** each to Assn. of Independent Colleges & Universities of Pa., Children's Home of Pittsburgh, Duquesne U., Manchester Craftsmen's Guild, Pittsburgh Center for the Arts, Salvation Army/Latrobe, Westmoreland Museum of American Art, Westmoreland Symphony Orchestra, and YMCA of Westmoreland County. Other local grants/contributions **$245-$1,500** for community service organizations, arts/culture, independent school, colleges, health/human service, and church-related activities. **Out-of-state** giving includes **$55,000** to Rollins College [FL]; **$25,250** to Roanoke College [VA]; and **$10,000** to The Angiogenesis Foundation [MA]; and **$5,000** each to Brazelton Foundation [MA] and Our Little Brothers & Sisters of Haiti [VA]. ■**PUBLICATIONS:** statement of program policy; application guidelines ■**WEBSITE:** None ■**E-MAIL:** None ■**APPLICATION POLICIES & PROCEDURES:** The Foundation reports that giving focuses primarily on the Latrobe area, and then Pittsburgh. Most grants are for operating/continuing support, program development, annual campaigns, capital campaigns, seed money, building/renovations, equipment, matching funds, challenge grants, emergency support, endowment, or scholarships funds. No grants are awarded to/for individuals, land acquisition, special projects, research, publications, or conferences. Grant requests may be submitted in a letter (2 pages maximum) in April/early May or October (deadlines are May 15th and November 1st) and must include a description of the project's general aims, a concise statement of need/problem, the specific purpose/objective for which funds are sought, who the project will serve, how the project will be operated, and how the project will be financed upon completion of the grant. Also include organization and project budgets, list of Board members, and IRS tax-exempt status documentation. Submit two complete copies of the grant request. Site visits sometimes are made to organizations being considered for a grant. Grants are awarded at Trustee meetings in late May and late November.

O+D+T James R. Okonak (Executive Director+VP+S+T+Con) — Fred M. Rogers (P+T+Donor) — Nancy R. Crozier (F+T) — William P. Barker (T) — Daniel G. Crozier, Jr. (T) — James Brooks Crozier (T) — Douglas R. Nowicki (T) — James B. Rogers (T) — John F. Rogers (T)

SW-234 McGinley (Rita M.) Foundation
c/o Eckert Seamans Cherin & Mellott
600 Grant Street, 44th Floor
Pittsburgh 15219   (Allegheny County)

MI-14-22-25-31-41-43-61

Phone 412-566-1984 **FAX** 412-566-6099
EIN 25-1593336   **Year Created** 1988

AMV $51,509   **FYE** 12-00   (**Gifts Received** $203,584)   23 **Grants totaling** $177,550

Mostly local giving; grants are general donations except as noted. High grants of **$25,000** each to Jubilee Assn. (Sister Ligouri Project), Little Sisters of the Poor (capital campaign), and Pittsburgh Mercy Foundation (pledge payment). **$20,000** to Epiphany Church. **$12,500** to Extra Mile Education Foundation **$15,000** to St. Paul's Cathedral (parish share/Fall campaign). **$10,000** each to American Ireland Fund (youth action), Marian Manor, and Good Samaritan Hospice. **$5,000** each to Legionnaires of Christ and Spark of Hope (St. Sebastian Conference). **$3,000** to Capuchin Development Center (chapel support). **$2,000-$2,500** each to Cancer Caring Center, East End Co-op Ministry, and Northside Common Ministries. **$1,000** to Pittsburgh Vision Services. Other smaller contributions for similar purposes. **Out-of-state** grant: **$2,000** to Alphonsian Academy [Italy]. ■**PUBLICATIONS:** Application Information sheet ■**WEBSITE:** None ■**E-MAIL:** john.mcginley@escm.com■**APPLICATION POLICIES & PROCEDURES:** Grant requests may be submitted in a proposal at any time (by an organization's senior administrative officer) which includes: (a) an executive summary giving an overview of the sponsoring organization, the proposed project, and the problem it seeks to address; (b) background on the organization, including history, purposes and goals, program types it offers, and names/affiliations of board members; (c) information on the proposed project describing clearly its specific purpose/objectives, how it will be operated, population it will serve, qualifications of those undertaking it, how it will be evaluated, project budget, timetable, statement of other sources of project support, and how it will be financed upon completion of the requested grant; (d) copy of the current organizational operating budget and projected operating budgets for the period of the grant; (e) copy of the most recent audited financial statement; (f) readily available descriptive materials (annual report, pamphlet, etc.); and (g) IRS tax-exempt status documentation.

O+D+T John R. McGinley, Jr. Esq. (T+F+Con) — Rita M. McGinley (Donor)

SW-235 McGinnis (Gerald E.) Charitable Foundation
3585 Hills Church Road
Export 15623   (Westmoreland County)

MI-11-31-42-49-52
Phone 724-327-7505 **FAX** None
EIN 25-1671236 **Year Created** 1991

AMV $3,716,343   **FYE** 12-00   (**Gifts Received** $0)   **Grants totaling** $0

No grants awarded in 2000, but in the prior year **$27,000** was awarded locally, all for general support: **$12,000** to Junior Achievement of SW Pa.; **$10,000** to Pittsburgh Symphony; and **$5,000** to Pittsburgh Mercy Foundation. In earlier years, other local support for universities, United Way, and other purposes. ■**PUBLICATIONS:** None ■**WEBSITE:** None ■**E-MAIL:** None ■ **APPLICATION POLICIES & PROCEDURES:** Grant requests may be submitted in any form at any time. No grants are awarded to individuals. Site visits sometimes are made to organizations being considered for a grant.

O+D+T Gerald E. McGinnis (T+Donor+Con) — Audrey McGinnis (Donor)

SW-236   McKaig (Lalitta Nash) Foundation   MI-43
    c/o PNC Advisors, M.S. P2-PTPP-25-1
    Two PNC Plaza, 620 Liberty Ave.   **Phone** 412-762-7941 **FAX** None
    Pittsburgh   15222   (Allegheny County)   **EIN** 25-6071908   **Year Created** 1973
AMV $14,526,858   **FYE** 9-00   **(Gifts Received** $0)   200+ **Grants totaling** $436,203

All awards are college scholarships for students from Bedford or Somerset counties (also certain MD and WV counties—see below); awardees must be full-time students in an undergraduate, graduate, or professional program in a U.S. college or university. The range of awards is typically **$1,500-$2,000** with some larger/smaller. ■**PUBLICATIONS:** None ■**WEBSITE:** None ■**E-MAIL:** None ■**APPLICATION POLICIES & PROCEDURES:** Scholarship applications are accepted only from residents of Bedford or Somerset counties (also West Virginia counties of Mineral and Hampshire, and Maryland counties of Allegany or Garrett) who obtained a high school education or equivalency in those counties; scholarships may be for undergraduate, graduate or professional studies. Vocational or technical school students are ineligible for support. Applicants must complete and submit a formal application form, available from the Foundation, between January 1st and the May 30th deadline; include a transcript, student aid report, and letter of acceptance from a college/university. July interviews are managed by Geppart, McMullen, Paye & Getty, 21 Prospect Square, Cumberland, MD; telephone 301-777-1533. Initial awards are based on financial need; academic performance generally is not a factor. Renewals of scholarships, however, are based in part on academic performance.

O+D+T   Elizabeth Gay (Admin. Officer at Bank+Con) — PNC Advisors (Corporate Trustee)

SW-237   McKee (Virginia A.) Poor Fund   MI-11-12-14-15-22
    Refer to PNC Advisors Charitable Trust Committee entry.
                                  (Allegheny County)   **EIN** 25-6023292   **Year Created** 1929
AMV $4,635,009   **FYE** 9-00   **(Gifts Received** $0)   11 **Grants totaling** $212,894

All giving restricted to organizations in the City of Pittsburgh which provide direct assistance to poor/needy persons. High grant of **$80,000** to Goodwill Industries of Pittsburgh. **$50,000** to Pittsburgh Leadership Foundation. **$30,000** to United Way of Allegheny County. **$13,000** to Pittsburgh Mercy Foundation. **$10,000** to Salvation Army. **$6,500-$6,930** each to Communities in Schools of Pittsburgh-Allegheny County, Gibbs Rest Home, and Jubilee Assn. **$4,000** to East End Cooperative Ministry. **$3,794** to Christmas in April. **$2,500** to Duquesne U. ■**APPLICATION POLICIES & PROCEDURES:** Refer to the PNC Advisors Charitable Trust Committee entry for a statement on giving priorities and full application guidelines.

O+D+T   Refer to PNC Advisors Charitable Trust Committee entry. — PNC Advisors (Corporate Trustee)

SW-238   McKenna (Katherine Mabis) Foundation   MI-11-13-14-29-41-42-44-54-55-56-71-84-85
    P.O. Box 186   87-89
    Latrobe   15650   **Phone** 724-537-6900 **FAX** 724-537-6906
                              (Westmoreland County)   **EIN** 23-7042752   **Year Created** 1969
AMV $85,335,916   **FYE** 12-00   **(Gifts Received** $0)   70 **Grants totaling** $3,717,750

All local/Pa. giving, primarily to Westmoreland County; grants are for general support except as noted and some grants comprise multiple awards. Three grants totaling **$565,000** to The Westmoreland Trust (Palace Theatre/capital campaign/Greensburg Garden & Civic Center). **$525,000** to Seton Hill College (mostly capital campaign). **$500,000** to U. of Pittsburgh at Greensburg (science laboratories). **$325,000** to Philip M. McKenna Foundation (public policy support). **$230,000** to Loyalhanna Watershed Assn. (land acquisition/Monastery Run project/Youth Conservation Corps/general support). **$150,000** to Fay-Penn Economic Development Council (Ft. Necessity Center). **$130,000** to Community Foundation of Westmoreland County (Human Services Task Force/Smart Growth Partnership). **$125,000** to Bushy Run Battlefield Heritage Society (land acquisition). **$100,000** to Greater Uniontown Heritage Consortium (State Theatre restoration). **$63,500** to and Western Pa. Conservancy (land acquisition/Fallingwater internship program). **$73,000** to Latrobe Foundation (Legion Keener Park/Veteran's Plaza Project/Whitney Veteran's Fund/Garden Fund). **$50,000** each to Chartiers Nature Conservancy (land acquisition), Greensburg Central Catholic High School, Johnstown Area Heritage Assn. (Discovery Center), Penn's Corner Resource Conservation & Development Council (farmland preservation program), Pa. Recreation & Park Society, and Westmoreland County Blind Assn. (embroidery project). **$45,000** each to Carnegie Museums of Pittsburgh and Westmoreland County Historical Society (education/outreach programs). **$40,000** to Greensburg YMCA (capital campaign). **$31,400** to Boy Scouts/ Westmoreland-Fayette Council (equipment). **$30,000** to Southern Alleghenies Museum of Art (museum-school partnership/acquisitions). **$27,000** to Regional Trail Corp. (Coal & Coke Trail Chapter/trail operations). **$25,000** each to Assn. of Independent College & Universities of Pa. (technology integration project), Bucknell U. (McKenna Internship Program), Christ the Divine Teacher School (technology integration project), Derry Area Recreation Board (pool reconstruction), Fort Ligonier Assn., Ligonier Valley Library Assn., Pittsburgh History & Landmarks Foundation, and United Way of Westmoreland County. **$21,500** to Carnegie Science Center (Westmoreland County school programming). **$20,000** to Horticultural Society of Western Pa. (botanic garden). **$15,000** each to Penn's Corner Charitable Trust (challenge grant), Washington County Community Foundation (railroad station renovations), and Westmoreland Museum of American Art (acquisitions). **$10,000** each to Gateway to Music & the Performing Arts (Westmoreland County programs), Salvation Army/Latrobe, Talus Rock Girl Scout Council (building), and United Fire Companies of Ligonier. **$9,000** to WDUQ-FM (Sustainable Pittsburgh Project). **$7,500** to Big Brothers/Big Sisters of Westmoreland County (school-based mentoring program). **$5,000** each to Caldwell Memorial Library Committee, Chestnut Ridge Conservancy, Laurel Mountain Ski Patrol (equipment), Theatre Classics for Students, and United Negro College Fund. **$4,050** to Grantmakers of Western Pa. **$1,000-$2,500** each to Botanical Society of Westmoreland County, Carnegie Museum of Nature History (Powdermill History Preserve), Garden Club of McKeesport, Goodwill Industries of Pittsburgh, Latrobe Area Hospital Aid Society (health fair), and Pa. Environmental Council. Other smaller local contributions. **Out-of-state** giving includes **$25,000** to Boy Scouts [TX] and **$5,000** to Cumberland College [KY]. ■**PUBLICATIONS:** application guidelines ■**WEBSITE:** None ■**E-MAIL:** None ■**APPLICATION POLICIES & PROCEDURES:** The Foundation reports that giving focuses on Eastern Westmoreland County; most grants are for general/operating support, special projects, program development, seed money, capital campaigns, building/renovations, equipment, endowment, scholarship funds, or land acquisition. No grants are awarded to individuals. Grant requests may be submitted in a letter (4 pages maximum) before the October 1st deadline; include organization and project budgets, an audited financial statement, and IRS 501(c)(3) tax-exempt status documentation. Site visits sometimes are made to organizations being considered for a grant. Decisions on requests usually are made within three to six months; the Board awards grants at January, April, September and December meetings.

O+D+T Linda McKenna Boxx (C+D+Con) — Wilma F. McKenna (VC+D) — Zan McKenna Rich (S+D) — T. William Boxx (F) — Mellon Bank N.A. (Trustee)

SW-239 McKenna (Philip M.) Foundation

P.O. Box 186

Latrobe   15650   (Westmoreland County)

AMV $19,682,099   **FYE** 12-00   (**Gifts Received** $325,000)

MI-11-22-41-42-43-49-54-71-83-84-86

Phone 724-537-6900 **FAX** 724-537-6906

EIN 25-6082635   **Year Created** 1967

50 **Grants totaling** $1,234,495

Nationwide giving for public policy related issues with about one-third local/Pa. giving; grants are for general operations except as noted. High Pa. grant of **$95,000** to The Commonwealth Foundation for Public Policy Alternatives [Harrisburg]. **$49,800** to Allegheny Institute for Public Policy (urban diversity study). **$49,500** to St. Vincent College/Center for Economic & Policy Education (McKenna Economic Education Series/Fellowship Program). **$38,000** to Pennsylvanians for Effective Government [Harrisburg] (Education Committee/internships). **$25,000** each to Carnegie Mellon U./Graduate School of Industrial Administration (Friends of Allen Meltzer Professorship). **$21,500** to Carnegie Science Center (Westmoreland County school programming). **$20,000** to Pa. Right to Work Defense & Education Foundation (legal program). **$15,000** each to Charter School Resource Center [Philadelphia], Foundation for Free Enterprise Education [Erie] (Westmoreland County scholarships/Patron Fund), and Latrobe Foundation (baseball fund). **$10,000** each to Civil Society Project [Harrisburg] and Lincoln Institute for Public Opinion Research. **$7,000** to Loyalhanna Watershed Assn. **$5,000** to Salvation Army-Latrobe. **$2,500** to Junior Achievement of SW Pa. (Westmoreland County program). **$1,000** to Service Corps of Retired Executives Assn. **Out-of-state** giving includes **$140,000** to Intercollegiate Studies Institute [DE] (general operations/market study); **$100,000** to The Heritage Foundation [DC] (McKenna Senior Fellow/Center for American Studies); **$90,000** to Claremont Institute for the Study of Statesmanship & Political Philosophy [CA] (general operations/publications); **$50,000** to The Morley Institute [DC] (conference/book); **$40,000** to Pacific Research Institute for Public Policy [CA] (Center for School Reform/Center for Enterprise & Opportunity); **$37,000** to Capital Research Center [DC]; **$35,000** to Federalist Society for Law & Public Policy Studies [DC] (Pa. programs/general support); **$33,000** to U. of Dallas/Dept. of Politics (conferences/books); and other grants, mostly **$7,000-$25,000,** for similar public policy related purposes. ■**PUBLICATIONS:** Mission & Guidelines memorandum ■**WEBSITE:** None ■**E-MAIL:** None ■**APPLICATION POLICIES & PROCEDURES:** The Foundation reports that giving is nationwide for public policy research on free market economics, as well as for charitable purposes in the Latrobe area. Multi-year grants are awarded; no grants are awarded to individuals or for overseas programs. Grant requests may be submitted at any time in a letter (3 pages maximum) before the deadlines of April 1st and October 1st; include an annual report, organization and project budgets, Board member list with major affiliations, list of major donors/funding sources, audited financial statement, and IRS tax-exempt status documentation. Site visits sometimes are made to organizations being considered for a grant. Grants are awarded at April and October Board meetings.

O+D+T T. William Boxx (C+D+Con) — Charles R. Kesler (VC+D) — Norbert J. Pail (S+F+D) — Johnathan C. Hall (D) — Zan McKenna Rich (D) — Mellon Bank N.A. (Trustee) — Foundation donor: Katharine M. McKenna Foundation

---

SW-240 McKinney (William V. & Catherine A.) Charitable Fdn.

c/o National City Bank of Pa. - #25-154

National City Center, 20 Stanwix Street

Pittsburgh   15222   (Allegheny County)

AMV $19,047,068   **FYE** 3-00   (**Gifts Received** $0)

MI-12-13-14-15-20-22-24-25-29-32-33-41-42

49-51-52-54-64-84

Phone 412-644-8332 **FAX** 412-261-6252

EIN 25-1641619   **Year Created** 1990

61 **Grants totaling** $591,500

All Western Pa. giving; grants are for general support except as noted. High grant of **$30,000** to Trinity Episcopal School for Ministry. **$25,000** each to The DePaul Institute (programs for hearing impaired), Little Sisters of the Poor, and Salvation Army (Family Crises Center). **$20,000** each to Erie Youth Symphony (music camp), Pittsburgh Leadership Foundation (Coalition for Leadership), and Western Pa. School for the Deaf. **$15,000** each to Family Hospice (Family House capital campaign), Multiple Sclerosis Service Society, Pittsburgh Symphony, and YMCA of Pittsburgh (Kon-o-Wee/Spencer Camps). **$14,000** to Coalition for Christian Outreach (urban ministry). **$10,000** each to Allegheny County Special Olympics, Carnegie Museum of Natural History, Catholic Charities (Senior Connections), Community College of Allegheny County Educational Foundation (internet video conferencing), Comprehensive Service Alliance (Timothy Place facility), Diocese of Pittsburgh (Crossroads program), Extra Mile Education Foundation, Focus on Renewal Neighborhood Corp., I Have A Dream Foundation of Pittsburgh (family education program), Interfaith Volunteer Caregivers (in-home services), Junior Achievement of SW Pa., Make a Wish Foundation of Western Pa., National Center for Juvenile Justice, North Hills Community Outreach (interfaith volunteer program), Pauline Auberle Foundation (capital campaign), Pittsburgh 2000, Pittsburgh CLO/Civic Light Opera (creative vision program), Pittsburgh Youth Symphony Orchestra, Southwinds (client transportation), and YMCA-North Hills/Boroughs Branch (Camp High Hopes). **$7,500** to Life'sWork of Western Pa. **$5,000** each to Alzheimer's Assn./Greater Pittsburgh Chapter (support groups), Alzheimer's Assn./Laurel Mountains Chapter, ARC-Washington Foundation (Camp Laughalot), Arthritis Foundation/Western Pa. Chapter (patient services), Big Brothers Big Sisters of Greater Pittsburgh (at-risk client support), Brashear Assn. (program for disadvantaged), Children's Festival Chorus, Emmanuel Episcopal Church, Family Resources, FAME/Fund for the Advancement of Minorities through Education (endowment), Greater Pittsburgh Community Food Bank (camp construction), Jefferson County Area Agency on Aging, Leukemia Society/Western Pa. Chapter (patient aid), Lutheran Affiliated Services, Mental Health Assn. of Allegheny County, Mom's House (scholarships), New Day [Altoona], Pace School (learning disabled program), Saltworks Theatre Company, Sisters Place, Spina Bifida Assn. of Western Pa., Variety Club of Pittsburgh (Kids on the Go program), Whale's Tale Foundation/FamilyLink (outreach/shelter program), Working Order, and YMCA of McKeesport (youth guidance/counseling). **$2,500** each to Schenley Heights Community Development Program and Transitional Services, Inc. ■**PUBLICATIONS:** None ■**WEBSITE:** None ■**E-MAIL:** None ■**APPLICATION POLICIES & PROCEDURES:** The Foundation reports that giving is restricted to Western Pa. organizations which assist disadvantaged youth, the elderly, the disabled, or encourage/sustain the arts. Religious affiliation is not a prerequisite for support. Most grants are for general/operating support, program development, capital campaigns, matching/challenge grants, or endowment. No grants are awarded to individuals. Prospective applicants should make an initial telephone inquiry about the feasibility of submitting a request. Grant requests may be submitted at any time using the Grantmakers of Western Pa. Common Grant Application Form (original plus 2 copies required) during January, May-June, or October; include an annual report, organization and project budgets, Board member list, listing of major funding sources, audited financial statement, and IRS tax-exempt status documentation. Site visits sometimes are made to organizations being considered for a grant. Grants are awarded at meetings in March, July, and November.

O+D+T Distribution Committee members: William M. Schmidt (VP at Bank+Con) — John M. Dodson (VP at Bank) — Gilbert L. Haag (VP at Bank) — National City Bank of Pa. (Corporate Trustee)

SW-241 **Mellon Financial Corporation Foundation**
　　　　c/o Mellon Financial Corporation
　　　　One Mellon Center, 500 Grant Street, Suite 1830
　　　　Pittsburgh　15258　　　　　　　(Allegheny County)

MI-11-13-14-15-24-25-31-32-39-42-45-51-52 54-55-83-85-88
Phone 412-234-2732　**FAX** 412-234-0831
EIN 23-7423500　　**Year Created** 1974

AMV $65,116,758　　**FYE** 12-00　　**(Gifts Received** $40,655)　　575+　**Grants totaling** $4,300,349

All Pa. giving now limited to Mellon's current corporate operating locations in SW & SE Pa. *PITTSBURGH-REGION GRANTS*: High grant of **$440,000** to United Way of Allegheny County. **$100,000** each to Pittsburgh Regional Alliance and The Pittsburgh Foundation/Pittsburgh Regional Healthcare Initiative. **$70,000** to Pittsburgh Partnership for Neighborhood Development. **$50,000** to U. of Pittsburgh Hillman Cancer Center. **$40,000** to YMCA of Pittsburgh. **$33,000** to UCP of Pittsburgh. **$30,000** each to Manchester Youth Development Center and Pittsburgh Symphony Orchestra. **$25,000** each to American Cancer Society, Pittsburgh Glass Center, and Society for Contemporary Craft. **$20,000** each to Action Housing, Inc., Greater Pittsburgh Literacy Council, and Mon Valley Initiative. **$15,000** each to Boy Scouts/Greater Pittsburgh Council, Community Theater Project Corp., Pa. Economy League/Western Division, Pittsburgh Technology Council, and YWCA of Greater Pittsburgh. **$14,000** to Inroads Pittsburgh, Inc. **$13,650** to Pittsburgh Ballet Theatre. **$10,000** each to Artists & Cities, Inc., Bloomfield-Garfield Corp., City Theatre Company, Family House, Miryam's, Northside Leadership Conference, Pittsburgh Children's Museum, and Pittsburgh Public Theater. **$7,500** each to Civic Light Opera, East Liberty Family Health Care Center, and Working Order. **$6,000-$6,500** each to Butler County Community College, Manchester Craftsmen's Guild, Progressive Workshop of Armstrong County, and United Negro College Fund. **$5,000** each to Community Technical Assistance Corp., East End Neighborhood Forum, Enterprise Zone Corp. of Braddock, Grantmakers of Western Pa., Mom's House, Corporation for Owner-OperatorProjects, Pittsburgh Filmmakers, Pittsburgh Social Venture Partners, U. of Pittsburgh (Center for Latin American Studies), Urban Youth Action, and YMCA of Beaver County. **$1,500-$3,500** each to Airport Area Development Corp., Best Friends, Bridge to Independence, Butler Area Development Corp., Carnegie Institute, Duquesne U., Housing Enterprises & Local Programs, Monessen Community Development Corp., and SW Pa. Area Labor-Management Committee. Other smaller local grants/contributions. *MID-ATLANTIC (PHILADELPHIA)-REGION GRANTS*: **$365,000** to United Way of SE Pa. **$50,000** to Greater Philadelphia First Foundation. **$30,000** to Greater Philadelphia Chamber of Commerce Regional Foundation. **$20,500** to Wilma Theatre. **$15,000** each to Academy of Natural Sciences, and People's Light & Theatre Company. **$13,500** to Philadelphia Museum of Art. **$10,000** each to Chester County Hospital and Philadelphia Police Foundation. **$8,500** to Pa. Economy League/Eastern Division. **$6,500** to Central Philadelphia Community Development Corp. **$4,000-$5,000** each to Painted Bride Art Center, Liberty Resources, and Urban League of Philadelphia. **$1,500-$3,000** each to Curtis Institute of Music, Germantown Settlement, Greater Philadelphia Urban Affairs Coalition, Hedgerow Theatre, Junior Achievement of the Delaware Valley, Overington House, Second Baptist Church of Germantown, Philadelphia Futures, Philadelphia Street Fund for Transition, Philomel Concerts, Red Cross/SE Pa., Society of Choral Arts, YMCA of Eastern Delaware County, and YMCA of Philadelphia & Vicinity. Other smaller local grants/contributions. *OTHER PA GIVING* included **$100,000** to Penn State U. and smaller grants to NW Pa./Erie, Central Pa./Harrisburg , and NE Pa./ Wilkes-Barre where Mellon previously had consumer banking operations in those areas. **Out-of-state** giving focused on corporate operatinglocations in DE, NJ, and New England. — Overall, Mellon's 2000 corporate giving/support exceeded **$36** million and comprised foundation grants (reported in part above), direct corporate support, community programs/activities/events underwriting, indirect and in-kind support, United Way and gift matching contributions, employee/retiree volunteer involvement, and below-market financing. ■**PUBLICATIONS:** Report to the Community (annual) with a statement of program policy, giving restrictions, sampling of grants/sponsorships, and application guidelines ■**WEBSITE:** www.mellon.com/communityaffairs ■**E-MAIL:** None ■**APPLICATION POLICIES & PROCEDURES:** Giving is limited to communities/regions where a majority of Mellon employees live and work—in Pa. giving focuses on the Pittsburgh and Mid-Atlantic (Philadelphia) regions. Support is given to promote economic vitality, develop a qualified workforce, support cultural awareness/diversity, promote employee volunteerism, meet community reinvestment goals and initiatives, and increase capacity between consumers & businesses. No grants given to individuals, religious programs of churches or other sectarian organizations, or to political parties, campaigns or candidates. Usually no support is available for specialized health campaigns, fraternal groups, police/fire organizations, or for endowment, conference/seminar attendance, scholarships, fellowships, or travel. Prospective applicants are encouraged to submit at any time an initial Letter of Inquiry. If a formal grant request is subsequently submitted, it should be a full proposal which follows the Grantmakers of Western Pa. Common Grant Application Format (see www.gwpa.org). Both the organization and the specific proposal are evaluated in reaching a decision, taking into consideration the organization's operational structure, objectives, history and management capability, its relationship to the population to be served, its position relative to organizations providing similar services/functions, its financial position, and sources of funds. — NOTE: In addition to awarding foundation grants and matching gifts, Mellon provides technical expertise and volunteer support to nonprofit organizations, and offers advice to neighborhood groups, economic development organizations and small businesses. — Formerly called Mellon Bank Foundation.

O+D+T James P. McDonald (Director, Community Affairs+P+T+Con) — Rose M. Cotton (C+T) — Steven G. Elliott (S+F) — Paul S. Beideman (T) — Michael E. Bleier (T) — Walter R. Day, III (T) — Jeffrey L. Leininger (T) — Martin G. McGuinn (T) — James P. Palermo (T) — Lisa B. Peters (T) — Corporate donor: Mellon Financial Corp.

SW-242   Mellon (R.K.) Family Foundation   MI-13-29-34-39-41-42-54-55-56-61-63-71-72-89
One Mellon Bank Center
500 Grant Street, Suite 4106   **Phone** 412-392-2800 **FAX** 412-392-2837
Pittsburgh 15219   (Allegheny County)   **EIN** 25-1356145   **Year Created** 1978
AMV $39,571,913   **FYE** 12-01   **(Gifts Received** $0)   71 **Grants totaling** $1,944,550

About half local/Pa. giving; grants are for annual giving or unrestricted/general operating support except as noted and some comprise multiple awards. High grant of **$140,000** to St. Michael's of the Valley Episcopal Church (capital improvements/annual support). **$120,000** to U. of Pittsburgh (Watson Surgical Education Center). **$105,000** to Valley School of Ligonier (scholarship fund/annual support). **$100,000** each to Latrobe Presbyterian Church (Unity Chapel maintenance endowment) and Western Pa. Conservancy (Fallingwater matching grant). **$50,000** each to Allegheny Conference on Community Development (projects planning), Brandywine Conservancy [Delaware County], Loyalhanna Assn., Susquehanna U. [Snyder County] (sport/fitness facility), and Youngstown Volunteer Fire Dept. & Relief Assn. (new tanker truck). **$40,000** to Action for Animals (facility expansion/general support). **$32,000** to Fort Ligonier Assn. (portrait acquisition). **$25,000** each to Laurel Valley Ambulance Service (new ambulance) and Tri-Community Ambulance Assn. (new ambulance). **$10,000** each to Artists & Cities (The Pittsburgh Project), Chestnut Ridge Conservancy (litigation debt reduction), and Epiphany Catholic Church (organ restoration). **$6,000** to The Neighborhood Academy. **$5,000** each to Catholic Diocese of Pittsburgh (Christian Leaders Fellowship) and Valley Youth Network. **$4,000** to Loyalhanna Watershed & Environmental Assn. (park design/bench). **$2,500** to Pittsburgh Trust for Cultural Resources. **$1,000** to Kiskiminetas Springs School. **Out-of-state** giving includes **$100,000** to Yampa Valley Land Trust [CO] (land conservation/general support); **$75,000** each to Pigeon Key Foundation [FL] (marine ecology-environment education center) and Humane Society of Boulder Valley [CO] (capital campaign); **$50,000** each to Healthcare Foundation of Cape Cod [MA] and Weiser Memorial Hospital Foundation [ID]; **$47,500** to Medical Foundation of North Carolina (research); **$45,000** to Auburn U. Foundation [AL] (quail management project); and other smaller grants for similar purposes in many states. — Pa. grants approved for future payment: **$200,000** to Loyalhanna Assn.; **$10,000** to U. of Pittsburgh; and **$6,000** to Ruffed Grouse Society. ■ **PUBLICATIONS:** informational brochure with application guidelines ■ **WEBSITE:** http://fdncenter.org/grantmaker/rkmellon/ ■ **E-MAIL:** None ■ **APPLICATION POLICIES & PROCEDURES:** The Foundation reports that giving focuses on Pittsburgh/Western Pa. for conservation, education, human services, medicine, civic, and culture. Most grants are for operating support, special projects, building funds, endowment, equipment, research, or seed money. No grants generally are awarded to/for conduit organizations, individuals, scholarships, or matching gifts. Grant requests should be submitted in a proposal during January-March or July-September (deadlines are April 1st and October 1st); the request must be signed by an organization's senior administrative officer and must include the following: (1) a two-page executive summary with an organizational overview, the proposed project and the problem it seeks to address; (2) organizational background, including its history, purpose and goals, the types of programs it offers, and names/affiliations of Board members/Trustees; (3) specific information on the proposed project, i.e. (a) the specific purpose and objective for which funds are sought, (b) a clear description of how the project will be operated, (c) the population it will serve, (d) qualifications of persons conducting the project; (e) project budget and timetable, (f) an explanation of how the project will be financed upon expiration of the proposed grant, and (g) an explanation of the plan, criteria, and indicators to be used in evaluating the success of the program; (4) a current operating budget for the organization and a projected operating budget for the year/s in which funding is requested; (5) audited financial statements for the two most recent years; (6) any readily available printed material such as annual reports, pamphlets or catalogs; and (7) a copy of the latest IRS tax-exempt status documentation. Grants are awarded at June and December Trustee meetings. Decisions on applications can take from one to six months.

O+D+T Michael Watson (Director+Con) — Richard P. Mellon (C+T) — Mason Walsh, Jr. (VC+T) — Robert B. Burr, Jr. (F+T) — Seward Prosser Mellon (T+Donor) — Scott D. Izzo (S) — John J. Turcik (Controller) — Ann Marie Helms (AS) — Lawrence S. Busch (AF)

SW-243   Mellon (Richard King) Foundation   MI-11-12-13-14-16-17-18-19-22-25-29-31-35
One Mellon Bank Center   41-42-51-52-55-56-57-71-72-79-85-86-89
500 Grant Street, Suite 4106   **Phone** 412-392-2800 **FAX** 412-392-2837
Pittsburgh 15219   (Allegheny County)   **EIN** 25-1127705   **Year Created** 1947
AMV $1,661,919,000   **FYE** 12-01   **(Gifts Received** $0)   144 **Grants totaling** $77,054,950

About two-thirds Pittsburgh/Western Pa. giving; grants are for general operating/program support except as noted; some grants comprise multiple awards and multiyear grants are indicated. **EDUCATION GRANTS**: **$3,000,000** to Penn State U. (new business school construction-3 years). **$1,000,000** each to Diocese of Greensburg (community center/school construction-2 years) and Duquesne U. (Chancellor's discretionary grant). **$750,000** each to Valley Forge Military Academy & Junior College [Montgomery County] (Mellon Hall refurbishment) and Washington & Jefferson College (capital campaign). **$350,000** to Northside Urban Pathways/Charter School (operating-capital support). **$300,000** each to Extra Mile Education Foundation-3 years and Junior Achievement of Western Pa. (partnership with Diocese of Pittsburgh-3 years). **$200,000** to Westminster College (Campus Center Complex construction). **$150,000** each to ASSET, Inc. (transition to fee-for-service model-3 years) and Sewickley Academy (Summerbridge program-3 years). **$100,000** to Ligonier Valley Library (technology-related upgrades). **$75,000** to Duquesne U. (charter schools project). **$50,000** to U. of Pittsburgh (Institute of Politics-2 years). **$40,000** to The Neighborhood Academy (develop fundraising plan). **$27,000** to Coro Center for Civic Leadership (leadership summit). **$25,000** each to Allegheny College (Center for Economic & Environmental Development strategic plan) and U. of Pittsburgh School of Medicine (scientific symposium). **$20,000** to Armbrust Wesleyan Christian Academy (upgraded students' computer network). ***REGIONAL***

ECONOMIC DEVELOPMENT: **$750,000** to Three Rivers Rowing Assn. (Millvale boathouse-3 years). **$625,000** to Pittsburgh Partnership for Neighborhood Development (operating support/public transportation loop trial). **$600,000** each to Duquesne U. (Institute for Economic Transformation-3 years), Pittsburgh Digital Greenhouse (2 years), and Riverlife Task Force. **$518,500** to Tides Center/Western Pa. (Western Pa. Field Institute/jobs preparation for studentsprogram/mini-grants program for regional growth/outdoor recreation festival). **$500,000** each to City of Pittsburgh (Crescent Park development) and Economic Growth Connection of Westmoreland. **$350,000** to New Century Careers (job training program). **$340,000** to Greater Pittsburgh Convention & Visitors Bureau (Office for Cultural Tourism). **$300,000** each to Coro Center for Civic Leadership (postgraduate internships) and Pittsburgh Opera (marketing/PR initiative-2 years). **$250,000** to Corporation for Owner-Operator Projects (Beaver County economic recovery initiatives). **$230,000** to Carnegie Mellon U. (Technology Transfer Office/Institute for the Universities & The Economy business plan/Maglev Technology summit). **$225,000** to Shadyside Hospital Foundation (operating support/Center for Complementary Medicine evaluation). **$218,000** to Aliquippa Alliance for Unity & Development (employability project/workforce development training). **$200,000** each to Community Foundation of Fayette County (Greene County economic development initiatives), Dollar Energy Fund (new strategic plan), and Three Rivers Connect (web-based regional map of natural resources/amenities). **$175,000** to The Mattress Factory (audience development/capital support). **$170,000** to Phipps Conservatory & Botanical Gardens (new park fencing). **$150,000** each to Pittsburgh Housing Development Corp. (downtown housing), Pittsburgh Public Theater (marketing-audience development), and Society for Contemporary Craft (capital campaign/operating support). **$128,000** to Port Authority of Allegheny County (First Ave. Bike/Blade Station). **$125,000** to Minority Enterprise Corp. of SW Pa. (operating support/program expansion). **$120,000** to Southwestern Pa. Corp. (Farm Market Action Plan). **$115,000** to The Tides Center [CA] (GIS project for Sustainable Pittsburgh). **$100,000-$102,000** each to Human Services Center Corp. (2 years), Opera Theatre of Pittsburgh (regional marketing initiative), and Technology Development & Education Corp. (EnterPrize innovation program). **$69,800** to Allegheny Conference on Community Development. **$55,000** to Steel Industry Heritage Corp. (immigrant housing preservation in Braddock). **$52,000** to Pittsburgh Urban Magnet Project (director search/transition costs). **$50,000** to Johnstown Area Heritage Assn. (exhibit). **$40,000** to Carnegie Institute (art museum audioguides). **$35,000** to Downtown Management Organization. **$25,000** each to Associated Artists of Pittsburgh (capital support), International Poetry Forum (audience development), Neighborhood Housing Services(conference), and RIDC Fund for Economic Development (River Front Park plan). **$20,000** to Renaissance & Baroque Society of Pittsburgh (marketing research/financial planning). **$10,000** each to Chatham Baroque (office relocation), Greensburg Development Corp. (park renovation), Pittsburgh Downtown Partnership (conference), and Squonk Opera (new show). **FAMILIES, YOUTH & CHILD DEVELOPMENT**: **$1,000,000** to United Way of Allegheny County (annual campaign). **$600,000** to U. of Pittsburgh (Office of Child Development-3 years). **$350,000** to Spectrum Family Network Foundation (merger facilitation). **$275,000** to YouthWorks (pre-employment job training/job opportunities). **$250,000** to Red Cross/Chestnut Ridge Chapter (capital campaign). **$200,000** each to Providence Connections (capital campaign) and YMCA of McKeesport (youth development program-2 years). **$150,000** each to One Small Step (school-based intervention program-2 years) and Westmoreland CHODO (emergency shelter for women/families). **$125,000** to Primary Care Health Services/East Side Community Collaborative (transitional housing program). **$100,000** each to Big Brothers Big Sisters of Westmoreland County (Fayette County expansion-3 years), Bridge to Independence (HUD match), North Side Christian Health Center, Rosedale Block Cluster (operating/planning support), and Urban Youth Action (student financial management training-2 years). **$75,000** each to City Mission [Uniontown] (temporary housing capital support) and Young Life of Steel Valley Youth Ministry (program expansion-3 years). **$70,000** to North Hills Community Outreach (program expansion in North boroughs). **$60,000** each to Operation Nehemiah (staff for program expansion) and Vietnam Veterans Leadership Program of Western Pa. (transitional/permanenthousing). **$50,000** each to Derry Area Recreation Board (community pool renovation), Every Child, Inc. (capital support), Ligonier Valley Little League (field improvements), and Talus Rock Girl Scout Council (outdoor education center construction). **$48,000** to Primary Care Health Services (early childhood facility purchase). **$41,600** to Bradford Child Care Services (learning center expansion). **$20,000** to YWCA of Butler (capital improvement project). **$10,000** each to Adams Memorial Library, Sisters Place, and Ventures in People (latchkey children program).**CONSERVATION GRANTS**: **$2,000,000** to Western Pa. Conservancy (Fallingwater refurbishment). **$750,000** to Foundation for California U. of Pa. (cooperative partnership to implement riparian buffer projects). **$600,000** to First Presbyterian Church of Pittsburgh (Ligonier Camp/Conference Center land acquisition). **$300,000** each to Regional Trail Corp. (Allegheny Trail Alliance/bike trail-3 years), National Audubon Society [Harrisburg] (deer management research), and Ruffed Grouse Society (leadership transition costs). **$210,000** to Pa. Assn. for Sustainable Agriculture [Centre County] (Community Farm Initiative in SW Pa.). **$120,000** to Chartiers Nature Conservancy (Thornburg Borough riparian flood plain protection). **$100,000** each to Friends of the Riverfront (2 years) and Western Pa. Conservancy (riparian buffer projects). **$80,000** to Loyalhanna Watershed Conservancy (2 years). **$75,000** to Conemaugh Valley Conservancy. **$70,000** to The Tides Center [CA] (bike racks on Pittsburgh buses). **$25,000** each to Allegheny Land Trust and Northside Leadership Conference (Allegheny Commons master planning process). **$20,000** to Mountain Watershed Assn. (historic Jones Mills grist mill acquisition). **$10,000** to Community Foundation of Westmoreland County (Salem Township Recreation Initiative). **Out-of-state** Conservation Grants included **$2,800,000** to The Conservation Fund [VA] (capital campaign/operating support-3 years); **$750,000** to Chesapeake Bay Foundation [MD] (cooperative partnership to implement riparian buffer projects); **$500,000** to Appalachian Mountain Club [MA] (environmental education center in NH); and **$300,000** each to Trout Unlimited [VA] (Kettle Creek Watershed Project in Pa.) and Wildlife Conservation Society [MT] (Greater Yellowstone Ecosystem research). **SYSTEM REFORM GRANTS**: **$500,000** to The Pittsburgh Foundation (Allegheny County Dept. of Human Services Integration Fund/Data Warehouse Project). **$225,000** to Tides Center/Western Pa. (Youth Standards Project pilot-evaluation). **$150,000** each to Grantmakers of Western Pa. (Pittsburgh Social Venture Partners-2 years/strategic plan implementation) and William J. Copeland Fund (nonprofit sector employment trends study). **$100,000** each to Adopt-A-Pet (animal shelter campaign-2 years). **$60,000** to Robert Morris College (Collaboration Project-2 years). **$57,000** to Greater Pittsburgh Community Food Bank (urban farm stands-2 years). **$50,000** to Executive Service Corps of Western Pa. (expand resources for nonprofit leaders). **$45,000** to Share Our Strength [DC] (for Pittsburgh Social Enterprise Forum). **$20,000** to Hosanna House (comprehensive evaluation). ■**PUBLICATIONS:** Annual Report with application guidelines; Grant Application Form/Cover Sheet ■**WEBSITE:** http://fdncenter.org/grantmaker/rkmellon ■**E-MAIL:** None ■

APPLICATION POLICIES & PROCEDURES: The Foundation reports two distinct areas of interest: (1) Pittsburgh/SW Pa. which includes Regional Economic Development, Education—emphasizing elementary/secondary, System Reform, and Families Youth & Child Development, and (2) Conservation—Regional Focus for Pennsylvania and the American Land Conservation Program. Most grants are for general operating/continuing support, seed money, building/renovation funds, capital campaigns, equipment, matching/challenge support, land acquisition, research, and program-related investments; single and multiyear awards are made. No grants are awarded to individuals, conduit organizations, or outside the United States. Prospective applicants initially should consult the most recent Annual Report (or information on website) to determine the feasibility of submitting a request. Grant requests may be submitted at any time and must include the following: (1) a completed one-page Grant Application Form (available in the Annual Report or on the website), and (2) a full proposal that includes (a) an executive summary with organizational overview, a brief description of the proposed project and the problem it seeks to address, the population it will serve, and how it will be operated; (b) an operating budget and timetable for the proposed project; (c) other sources of funding and an explanation of how the project will be financed upon expiration of the grant period; (d) the method for evaluating the project's success; (e) organizational background (history, purpose, goals, and types of programs offered); (f) list of Board members and officers; (g) audited financial statements for the two most recent years; (h) readily available printed material such as annual reports, pamphlets, catalogs, etc.; and (i) the latest IRS tax-exempt status documentation. Proposals following the Grantmakers of Western Pa. Common Grant Application Format (see www.gwpa.org) are accepted if accompanied by the Foundation's Grant Application Form and other required attachments. Video tapes should not be submitted unless requested. The Board of Trustees meets periodically to review proposals and award grants.

O+D+T Michael Watson (VP+T+Director+Con) — Richard P. Mellon (C+T) — Seward Prosser Mellon (P+Chairman, Executive Committee+T) — Mason Walsh, Jr., Esq. (VC+T) — Robert B. Burr, Jr. (F+T) — Lawrence S. Busch (AF+T) — Arthur D. Miltenberger (VP) — Scott D. Izzo (S+Associate Director) — Ann Marie Helms (AS+Program Officer) — John J. Turcik (Controller)

SW-244 Memorial Hospital of Bedford County Foundation MI-31-34-43
c/o UPMC-Bedford
10455 Lincoln Highway **Phone** 814-623-6161 **FAX** None
Everett 15537 (Bedford County) **EIN** 23-2938090 **Year Created** 1997
AMV $7,750,625 **FYE** 6-00 (**Gifts Received** $29,000) 13 **Grants totaling** $134,548

Most giving restricted to scholarships for Bedford County residents pursuing degrees in selected healthcare professions (which the Foundation defines each year); individual awards range up to **$6,615** per annum. In addition, **$26,257** awarded to UPMC-Bedford Memorial (equipment purchase). ■**PUBLICATIONS:** application form ■**WEBSITE:** www.bedford.org/fndtn.htm ■**E-MAIL:** None ■**APPLICATION POLICIES & PROCEDURES:** The Foundation reports all giving restricted to Health Professions Scholarships for persons who are (1) a resident of Bedford County, (2) officially accepted into an actual health professions program of study, (3) provides verification of financial need, and (4) submits letters of recommendation—refer to the website for details. Scholarship applications must be submitted on an Application Form available from the Foundation. Scholarships may be renewed for up to four years; funds may be used for tuition, books, supplies and/or uniforms. If upon completion of a student's academic program, a position is available at U. of Pittsburgh Medical Center-Bedford, then the graduate must return to work there for three consecutive years; if no position is available, the repayment obligation is waived; check the website for other stipulations.

O+D+T Sherry Obert, R.N. (Director of Education+Con) — John R. Blackburn, Jr. (C+P) — Clyde Morris (Co-Chair) — Tom Bailey (F) — and a Board of Directors with 16 additional members.

SW-245 Miles (Amelia) Foundation MI-12-13-15-20-22-29-32-35-44
Refer to PNC Advisors Charitable Trust Committee entry.
(Allegheny County) **EIN** 25-6092021 **Year Created** 1968
AMV $2,840,260 **FYE** 12-00 (**Gifts Received** $0) 22 **Grants totaling** $204,934

All SW Pa. giving. High grant of **$15,000** to National Parkinson Foundation/Pittsburgh Chapter. **$12,750** each to National Flag Foundation and One to One Citizen Advocacy [Beaver]. **$12,000** to Allegheny County Court Appointed Special Advocate Program. **$11,250-$11,489** each to Alzheimer's Disease & Related Disorders Assn., American Diabetes Assn., Jane Holmes Residence, and U. of Pittsburgh School of Medicine/Office of Research. **$10,000** each to Northside Common Ministries and Prime Stage. **$9,000** to SIDS Alliance/Pa. Affiliate. **$8,000-$8,500** each to Civic Senior Citizens [Aliquippa], The Family Trust, North Hills Community Outreach, and Urban Youth Action, Inc. **$7,500** each to Intersection, Inc. and Visiting Nurse Assn. of Indiana County. **$5,625-$6,700** each to Homeless Children & Family Emergency Fund, RX Council of Western Pa., St. Anne Home [Greensburg], Sewickley Public Library, and Shenango Presbyterian Church [New Wilmington]. ■**APPLICATION POLICIES & PROCEDURES:** Refer to the PNC Advisors Charitable Trust Committee entry for a statement on giving priorities and full application guidelines.

O+D+T Refer to PNC Advisors Charitable Trust Committee entry. — PNC Advisors (Corporate Trustee)

SW-246 Miles Family Foundation, The MI-22-42-61
c/o A.G. Mauro Company
310 Alpha Drive **Phone** 412-782-6600 **FAX** 412-963-6913
Pittsburgh 15238 (Allegheny County) **EIN** 25-6507666 **Year Created** 1995
AMV $144,824 **FYE** 12-00 (**Gifts Received** $24,000) 44 **Grants totaling** $22,994

Limited local giving. High local grant of **$2,700** to St. Mary Mercy Church (Red Door program). **$500** to Extra Mile Education Foundation. Other local contributions **$20** to **$130,** many for Catholic purposes. **Out-of-state** giving includes **$9,599** to U. of Notre Dame [IN] and **$1,600** to a Roman Catholic church in India. ■**PUBLICATIONS:** None ■**WEBSITE:** www.agmauro.com ■ **E-MAIL:** None ■**APPLICATION POLICIES & PROCEDURES:** No grants awarded to individuals.

O+D+T Richard P. Miles (T+Con) — Richard C. Miles (T+Donor) — Virginia E. Miles (T+Donor) — Kathleen Miles Limauro (T) — Jerome A. Miles (T) — Joseph A. Miles (T)

SW-247   Miller (Howard & Nell E.) Foundation
c/o PNC Advisors, M.S. P1-POPP-02-1
One PNC Plaza, 249 Fifth Ave., 2nd Floor
Pittsburgh   15222   (Allegheny County)

MI-12-13-14-17-22-25-29-31-52

Phone 412-762-3808   **FAX** 412-705-1183
EIN 25-6305933   **Year Created** 1988

AMV $9,139,612   **FYE** 5-00   (Gifts Received $0)   19 **Grants totaling** $213,500

All local giving; all grants are for general purposes. High grant of **$50,000** to Pittsburgh Opera. **$15,000** each to Bridge to Independence, Greater Pittsburgh Food Bank, Manchester Youth Development, Mars Home for Youth, and Opera Theatre of Pittsburgh. **$10,000** each to Children's Hospital of Pittsburgh, Coalition for Christian Outreach, Mom's House, Pittsburgh Urban Christian Center, and YMCA of McKeesport. **$5,000** each to Caty Foundation, North Hills Community Center, North Side Christian Health Center, and Pittsburgh Public Theater. **$3,000** to River City Brass Band. **$500** to Contact Pittsburgh. ■**PUBLICATIONS:** None ■**WEBSITE:** None ■**E-MAIL:** j.ferguson@pncadvisors.com ■**APPLICATION POLICIES & PROCEDURES:** Grant requests may be submitted in a letter at any time; include IRS tax-exempt status documentation.

O+D+T   James M. Ferguson, III (Executive VP at Bank+Con) — Thomas M. Mulroy, Esq. (Co-T) — PNC Advisors (Co-Trustee)

SW-248   Miller (Mark & Kimberley) Charitable Foundation
99 Little John Drive
McMurray   15317   (Washington County)

MI-12-15-22-29-41-42-43-63-64

Phone 724-941-1324   **FAX** None
EIN 25-6585614   **Year Created** 1999

AMV $5,122,029   **FYE** 12-00   (Gifts Received $0)   7 **Grants totaling** $280,000

Mostly local giving. High grant of **$192,000** to Westminster Presbyterian Church (missions/ministry). **$30,000** to The Pittsburgh Project. **$10,000** each to Pittsburgh Theological Seminary, and U. of Pittsburgh/Katz School of Business (scholarship). **$3,000** to Family Hospice. **Out-of-state** grants: **$34,000** to Georgia Tech (Alexander Tharpe Scholarship Fund) and **$1,000** to Child Help USA [VA]. ■**PUBLICATIONS:** None ■**WEBSITE:** None ■**E-MAIL:** None ■**APPLICATION POLICIES & PROCEDURES:** Information not available.

O+D+T   Mark G. Miller (T+Donor+Con) — Kimberley R. Miller (T)

SW-249   Millmont Foundation, The
4279 Green Glade Court
Allison Park   15101   (Allegheny County)

MI-42-44-71-82

Phone 412-486-4709   **FAX** None
EIN 06-6051671   **Year Created** 1956

AMV $904,582   **FYE** 7-00   (Gifts Received $0)   29 **Grants totaling** $47,387

Limited Pa. giving. High Pa. grant of **$1,000** to Carnegie Library of Pittsburgh. **$750** to Brother's Brother Foundation. Other smaller local contributions to Extra Mile Education Foundation, Horticultural Society of Western Pa., Pittsburgh Garden Place, and Western Pa. Conservancy. **Out-of-state** giving includes **$16,807** to Harvard U. [MA]; **$6,000** to Stepping Stones Museum [CT]; **$4,000** to Mayo Fund for Medical Education [MN]; and other smaller grants to New England and MT, many for environmental purposes. ■**PUBLICATIONS:** None ■**WEBSITE:** None ■**E-MAIL:** None ■**APPLICATION POLICIES & PROCEDURES:** Grant requests may be submitted in a letter at any time.

O+D+T   Carrie M. Stanny (S+F+D+Con) — Peter Cholnoky [CT] (P+D) — Dorothy Cholnoky [CT] (D) — Richard Montague [Germany] (D) — Theodore G. Montague, Jr. [AZ] (D)

SW-250   Millstein Charitable Foundation
c/o Millstein Industries
Cherry Creek Commons-Building 1, P.O. Box K
Youngwood   15697   (Westmoreland County)

MI-11-13-22-29-31-32-41-42-53-54-56-62-71
83-85

Phone 724-925-1300   **FAX** 724-925-1390
EIN 25-6064981   **Year Created** 1964

AMV $7,829,775   **FYE** 9-00   (Gifts Received $0)   135 **Grants totaling** $355,326

About two-thirds local/Pa. giving. High grant of **$43,334** to American Civil Liberties Foundation/Greater Pittsburgh Chapter. **$20,000** to Western Pa. Conservancy (Fallingwater). **$17,500** to Westmoreland Museum of American Art. **$15,000** to U. of Pa. [Philadelphia]. **$12,585** to U. of Pittsburgh at Greensburg. **$10,000** each to Greensburg Community Development Corp., Mercersburg Academy [Franklin County], and Seton Hill College. **$5,000-$5,350** each to Allegheny Trail Alliance, Human Services Center of Greensburg (Hero Project), United Way of Westmoreland County, Washington & Jefferson College, and Westmoreland County Community College. **$2,000-$3,000** each to ALS Foundation, Congregation Emanu-el Israel, United Jewish Federation of Greater Pittsburgh, and YWCA of Greensburg. **$1,000-$1,500** each to Assn. of Independent Colleges & Universities of Pa., Duquesne U., Jewish Community Center of Greater Pittsburgh, Leukemia & Lymphoma Society, National Catholic Center for Holocaust Education, One Room Schoolhouse Project, Parent Wise, Shriners Hospitals for Children [Cheswick], and Southern Alleghenies Museum of Art. Other local contributions $50-$500 for various purposes. **Out-of-state** giving includes **$34,890** to Temple Beth El [CT]; **$17,460** to Temple Shalom [FL]; **$15,200** to Hadassah [NY]; **$10,000** to United Jewish Federation of Stamford [CT]; **$9,000** to New School U. [NY]; **$6,200** to West Virginia U. Foundation; **$5,000-$5,500** each to B'nai B'rith Foundation International [DC], Community Foundation of Collier County [FL], Fibromyalgia Treatment Center [NY], New Hampton School [NH], Shelter for Abused Women [FL], and U. of Tennessee Health Science Center. ■**PUBLICATIONS:** None ■**WEBSITE:** None ■**E-MAIL:** None ■**APPLICATION POLICIES & PROCEDURES:** The Foundation reports that local organizations only are considered generally for large grants; most grants are for general support, special projects, building funds, or capital drives. Grant requests may be submitted in a letter (2 pages maximum) at any time; describe the proposed project and state the funding requested. Site visits sometimes are made to organizations being considered for a grant. The Board meets annually in September

O+D+T   Jack H. Millstein, Jr. (Executive Secretary+T+Con) — David J. Millstein (T)

SW-251 Mine Safety Appliances Company Charitable Foundation
c/o Mine Safety Appliances Company
121 Gamma Drive, P.O. Box 426
Pittsburgh 15230   (Allegheny County)

MI-11-13-14-15-22-31-32-39-41-42-44-51-52
54-55-71-81-83-85
Phone 412-967-3046 **FAX** 412-967-3367
EIN 25-6023104   **Year Created** 1951

AMV $2,844,350   **FYE** 12-00   (**Gifts Received** $1,706)   110 **Grants totaling** $719,850

Mostly local/Western Pa. giving to Allegheny, Butler and Westmoreland counties in corporate operating locations. High grant of **$235,000** to United Way of SW Pa. **$40,000** to Children's Hospital of Pittsburgh. **$35,000** to United Way of Butler County. **$25,000** to United Way of Westmoreland County. **$21,000** to Pittsburgh Regional Alliance. **$20,000** to U. of Pittsburgh/Center for Latin American Studies. **$16,500** to Pittsburgh Symphony. **$14,900** to Allegheny Conference on Community Development. **$11,000** to Pittsburgh Opera. **$10,000** each to Marian Manor, Phipps Conservatory & Botanical Garden, and Pittsburgh Foundation (Regional Healthcare Initiative Fund). **$8,400** to Pa. Economy League/Western Division. **$8,000** each to Extra Mile Education Foundation and Gargaro Productions. **$7,500** to Pittsburgh Technology Council. **$7,000** to Operation Better Block. **$6,500** to Carnegie Museums of Pittsburgh. **$5,000** each to Allegheny Valley School, Alzheimer's Disease Alliance of Western Pa., Cranberry Public Library, Opera Theater of Pittsburgh, Pittsburgh Ballet Theatre, Pittsburgh Civic Light Opera, Pittsburgh Irish & Classical Theatre, Seton Hill College, and UCP of Pittsburgh. **$4,000-$4,500** each to Carlow College, Friends of the New Park, National Kidney Foundation of Western Pa., and World Affairs Council of Pittsburgh. **$3,000-$3,750** each to Manchester Youth Development Center, Mom's House, Multiple Sclerosis Service Society, Pa. Special Olympics, Radio Information Service, and Society of Women Engineers. **$2,000-$2,500** each to Alternative Program Associates, Assn. of Independent Colleges & Universities of Pa. [Harrisburg], Brother's Brother Foundation, Catholic Charities, The Children's Institute, Cystic Fibrosis Foundations/Western Pa. Chapter, Evans City Public Library, Greater Pittsburgh Community Food Bank, The Mattress Factory, Mercy Foundation, Northside Common Ministries, O'Hara Township Police Athletic Club, Penn State/Behrend Center [Erie] (senior project), Pa. Partnership for Economic Education, Pittsburgh Vision Services, Pittsburgh Zoo, and United Negro College Fund. Other local grants/contributions **$200-$1,500** for similar purposes. **Out-of-state** giving includes **$20,000** to City of Hope [CA]; **$10,000** each to American Industrial Hygiene Assn. Foundation [VA] and United Way of Onslow County [NC]; **$8,500** to American Enterprise Institute [DC]; and **$7,500** to Harvard Business School [MA]. ■**PUBLICATIONS:** None ■**WEBSITE:** www.msanet.com [corporate info only] ■ **E-MAIL:** None ■**APPLICATION POLICIES & PROCEDURES:** The Foundation reports giving focuses on the greater Pittsburgh area and corporate operating locations in RI, NY and NC; most grants are for annual/continuing support, building/renovations, capital campaigns, or emergency support. No grants are awarded to/for individuals, scholarships, or matching gifts; support for United Way member agencies is minimal except for approved capital campaigns. Grant requests may be submitted at any time in a brief letter which describes the nature/purpose of the organization/institution and details the proposed project/program; include a project budget, list of major funding sources, and IRS tax-exempt status documentation. The Board meets as needed. — Formerly called Mine Safety Appliances Co. Charitable Trust.

O+D+T Charitable Contributions Committee members: Dennis L. Zeitler (VP+CFO at Company+Con) — D.H. Cuozzo — B. DeMaria — J.T. Ryan, III — PNC Bank N.A. (Trustee) — Corporate donor: Mine Safety Appliances Company

---

SW-252 Moore (P.M.) Foundation
1531 Second Street
P.O. Box 416
Beaver 15009   (Beaver County)

MI-11-12-13-15-17-22-29-32-35-42-44-53-54
56-63-64-72-83-89
Phone 724-774-4997 **FAX** None
EIN 25-6066268   **Year Created** 1958

AMV $8,128,118   **FYE** 12-00   (**Gifts Received** $0)   31 **Grants totaling** $314,000

Mostly local giving; all grants are for general operations except as noted. High grants of **$25,000** each to Beaver Area Memorial Library, B.F. Jones Memorial Library, and Mars Home for Youth Foundation. **$22,000** to First Presbyterian Church of Monaca. **$23,000** to Salvation Army (general operations/capital fund/special fund). **$20,000** each to Beaver Heritage Museum Foundation, Glade Run Foundation, and YMCA of Beaver County. **$10,000** each to Beaver County Industrial Museum, Contact-New Brighton, Beaver/Castle Girl Scout Council, First Presbyterian Church of Beaver, Homemakers-Home Health Aid Service, and Lutheran Service Society of Western Pa. (Meals on Wheels). **$5,000** each to Beaver County Cancer & Heart, Chippewa Volunteer Fire Dept., Merrick Art Gallery, Red Cross/Beaver County Chapter, and United Way of Beaver County. **$4,000** to Boy Scouts/Explorer Post 488. **$2,000** to Boy Scouts/Greater Pittsburgh Council. **$1,000** each to Beaver County Humane Society, Head Start of Beaver County, League of Women Voters Education Fund, Pittsburgh Theological Seminary, St. Titus Church of Aliquippa, and Woman's Center of Beaver County. **Out-of-state** giving includes **$25,000** to Muskingum College [OH] and **$10,000** to Bloomfield United Presbyterian Church [OH]. ■**PUBLICATIONS:** None ■**WEBSITE:** None ■**E-MAIL:** None ■**APPLICATION POLICIES & PROCEDURES:** The Foundation reports that giving focuses on Beaver County. Grant requests may be submitted in any form at any time. No grants awarded to individuals.

O+D+T Dana L. Duff (F+Con) — Ruth Ann Duff (S) — David M. Duff (T) — Paul W. Duff (T)

SW-253 Morelli (Robert L.) Foundation
2 Lindsay Drive
Beaver Falls 15010   (Beaver County)

MI-15-32-41-54
Phone 724-843-5974 **FAX** None
EIN 23-7319091   **Year Created** 1975

AMV $633,943   **FYE** 10-00   (**Gifts Received** $0)   1 **Grant of** $23,100

Sole grant to Divine Mercy Academy. — In the prior year giving included **$13,600** to Divine Mercy Academy; **$3,000** to McGuire Memorial Home; **$2,700** to Smithsonian Institution/National Air & Space Museum [DC]; and **$1,000** to Beaver County Cancer & Heart Assn. ■**PUBLICATIONS:** None ■**WEBSITE:** None ■**E-MAIL:** None ■**APPLICATION POLICIES & PROCEDURES:** Information not available.

O+D+T Robert L. Morelli (T+Donor+Con) — Norma Jean Morelli (T) — Eleanor T. Morelli (T)

SW-254 Morris (Charles M.) Charitable Trust, The
    c/o National City Bank of Pa. - Loc. 25-162
    National City Center, 20 Stanwix Street, 16th Floor
    Pittsburgh 15222   (Allegheny County)

MI-11-12-13-14-15-18-22-25-29-41-52-54-62

Phone 412-644-8002 **FAX** 412-261-6153
EIN 25-6312920   **Year Created** 1988

AMV $33,935,480   **FYE** 12-01   **(Gifts Received** $0)   32 **Grants totaling** $1,412,854

Mostly Allegheny County giving. High grant of **$725,000** to United Jewish Federation of Greater Pittsburgh. **$50,000** each to Chabad Lubavitch of the South Hills, Hillel Jewish University Center, Jewish Community Center of Pittsburgh/South Hills, Kollel Jewish Learning Center, Pittsburgh Children's Museum, and Rodef Shalom Congregation. **$37,500** to United Way of Allegheny County. **$32,500** to Greater Pittsburgh Community Food Bank. **$25,000** each to DePaul Institute and YMCA of Pittsburgh. **$20,000** each to Emmaus Community of Pittsburgh and St. Mary of Mercy Church (Red Door program). **$15,000** to Big Brothers/Big Sisters of Greater Pittsburgh and B'nai B'rith Youth Organization/Keystone Mountain Region. **$13,600** to Make-A-Wish Foundation of Western Pa., **$10,000** to Allegheny County Literacy Council, Bethlehem Haven, Boys & Girls Clubs of Western Pa., Catholic Youth Assn. of Pittsburgh, Extra Mile Education Foundation, Focus on Renewal, Girls Hope of Pittsburgh, Greater Pittsburgh Literacy Council, Life's Work of Western Pa., Manchester Youth Development Center, Marian Manor, and Spina Bifida Assn. of Western Pa. **$5,000** each to Northside Common Ministries and Providence Connections. **$4,254** to Beginning With Books. **Out-of-state** grant: **$50,000** to North Tahoe Hebrew Congregation [NV]. — Major grants awarded in the prior year included **$700,000** to United Jewish Federation of Greater Pittsburgh; **$100,000** each to City Theatre Company (capital campaign) and Temple Ohev Shalom; **$50,000** each to American Friends of the Union of Progressive Jews in Germany Austria & Switzerland (visiting scholars), Hillel Jewish University Center (capital campaign), Jewish Community Center (capital campaign), Rodef Shalom Congregation (capital campaign), and Zionist Organization of America (Holocaust Museum trips); **$40,000** to Hillel Academy; **$30,000** to Community College of Allegheny County Educational Foundation (scholarship endowment/videoconferencing capabilities); and **$25,000** each to Allegheny Valley School, Family House, Little Sisters of the Poor, Marian Hall, Pittsburgh Children's Museum, Pittsburgh Symphony, Pittsburgh Vision Services (Bridgeville facility), Presbyterian Seniorcare, Western Pa. School for the Deaf, and YMCA of Pittsburgh (capital campaign). ■**PUBLICATIONS:** annual report; statement of program policy; application guidelines ■**WEBSITE:** www.morrisfoundation.org ■**E-MAIL:** joanna.mayo@nationalcity.com ■**APPLICATION POLICIES & PROCEDURES:** The Foundation reports giving primarily to Allegheny County organizations, particularly for Jewish charities, the elderly, educational excellence, poverty alleviation, the arts, and children/families; most grants are for capital projects. No grants are awarded to individuals. Prospective applicants initially should make a telephone inquiry about the feasibility of submitting a request. Grant requests may submitted on-line (see the Foundation's website) or on a formal, detailed application form, available from the Bank (or downloadable from the website) together with the required attachments; an original and three copies are required. If the application is submitted on-line the required attachments still must be mailed (postmarked) by the deadlines, usually about the 1st of February, May, August, or November—see website for definite dates. Site visits sometimes are made to organizations being considered for a grant. Grants are awarded at meetings in March, June, September, and December.
O+D+T Joanna M. Mayo (VP at Bank+Con) — Arthur Fidel (Member, Distribution Committee) — Charles S. Perlow (Member, Distribution Committee) — National City Bank of Pa. (Corporate Trustee)

SW-255 Morrison Foundation, The
    1122 Gulf Tower, 707 Grant Street
    Pittsburgh 15219   (Allegheny County)

MI-22-52-54-57-62

Phone 412-281-5200 **FAX** 412-281-5201
EIN 25-1671840   **Year Created** 1991

AMV $735,559   **FYE** 12-00   **(Gifts Received** $7,200)   8 **Grants totaling** $95,363

About three-fourths local giving. High grant of **$50,363** to Pittsburgh Symphony (mostly for instrument loan fund). **$5,000** to Pittsburgh Opera. **$4,000** each to United Jewish Federation of Greater Pittsburgh and WQED (program underwriting). **Out-of-state** giving includes **$20,000** to Metropolitan Opera Assn. [NY] and **$1,500** to U.S. Holocaust Memorial Museum [DC]. ■ **PUBLICATIONS:** None ■**WEBSITE:** None ■**E-MAIL:** None ■**APPLICATION POLICIES & PROCEDURES:** The Foundation reports that unsolicited requests are not accepted.
O+D+T Perry E. Morrison (T+Donor+Con) — Beatrice E. Morrison (T+Donor)

SW-256 Mudge Foundation
    c/o PNC Advisors Service Center
    Two PNC Plaza, 620 Liberty Ave., 33rd Floor
    Pittsburgh 15222   (Allegheny County)

MI-41-42-54-56

Phone 412-762-4133 **FAX** 412-762-6160
EIN 25-6023150   **Year Created** 1955

AMV $4,457,455   **FYE** 12-00   **(Gifts Received** $0)   15 **Grants totaling** $205,220

Limited local giving; all grants are for general operations. High Pa. grant of **$30,000** to Carnegie Mellon U. **$22,600** to Western Pa. Historical Society. **Out-of-state** giving includes **$25,000** each to Heard Natural Science Museum [TX] and Middlesex School [MA]; **$21,000** to U. of Vermont; and other grants **$500-$12,900** in ME, NY, KY, and TX. — In the prior year, one local grant: **$37,500** to Grace Episcopal Church. ■**PUBLICATIONS:** None ■**WEBSITE:** None ■**E-MAIL:** None ■**APPLICATION POLICIES & PROCEDURES:** The Foundation reports that the family is primarily interested in supporting organizations in PA, ME, and TX. No grants are awarded to individuals. Grant requests may be submitted in a letter at any time; describe the proposed project and include IRS tax-exempt status documentation.
O+D+T M. Bradley Dean (VP at Bank+Con) — Edmund W. Mudge, III (Co-T) — Taylor Mudge (Co-T) — PNC Advisors (Corporate Trustee)

SW-257 **Murphy (Bob) Foundation, The**
514 Justabout Road
Venetia   15367   (Washington County)

MI-12-22-32-84
Phone Unlisted **FAX** None
EIN 25-1608327   **Year Created** 1989

AMV $34   **FYE** 12-00   (**Gifts Received** $12,500)   4 **Grants totaling** $12,550

All local giving. High grant of **$10,000** to Tri-State PGA of America/Professional Golfers Assn. **$975** each to American Cancer Society and Salvation Army. **$600** to Children's Institute of Pittsburgh. ■**PUBLICATIONS:** None ■**WEBSITE:** None ■**E-MAIL:** None ■**APPLICATION POLICIES & PROCEDURES:** No grants awarded to individuals.

O+D+T   Robert W. Murphy, Jr. (P+F+Donor+Con) — Vincent C. DeLuzio, Esq. [Pittsburgh] (S)

SW-258 **Murphy (G.C.) Company Foundation**
211 Oberdick Drive
McKeesport   15135   (Allegheny County)

MI-12-13-14-17-22-25-29-31-43-44-52-55-56-84
Phone 412-751-6649 **FAX** None
EIN 25-6028651   **Year Created** 1952

AMV $4,977,973   **FYE** 12-00   (**Gifts Received** $0)   35 **Grants totaling** $266,000

Mostly local giving; grants are for general purposes/operating support except as noted. High grant of **$30,000** to YMCA of McKeesport. **$20,000** to South Hills Interfaith Ministries. **$15,000** each to Greater Pittsburgh Community Food Bank, McKeesport Heritage Center (building fund/operations), Outreach Teen & Family Services, and U. of Pittsburgh Medical Center-McKeesport (seniors transportation). **$10,000** each to Braddock's Field Historical Society (brochures), Long Run Children's Learning Center, McKeesport Area Meals on Wheels (equipment), McKeesport Symphony Orchestra, Salvation Army/McKeesport, and Womansplace. **$7,500** to Goodwill Industries of Pittsburgh (equipment for McKeesport center). **$5,000** each to Auberle Foundation (building fund), Boy Scouts/Greater Pittsburgh Council (expand program in McKeesport), Carnegie Library of McKeesport (computer lab equipment), Human Services of Western Pa. (MH outpatient clinic), Larosa Boys & Girls Club of McKeesport (program materials), McKeesport Hospital Foundation (graduate medical/patient education programs), McKeesport Little Theater (remodeling), Mon-Yough Chamber Foundation (economic development/education), South Hills Health System Foundation (indigent care), and YWCA of McKeesport. **$4,000** to Allegheny Intermediate Unit/McKeesport Family Center (youth camp sponsorship). **$3,000** each to Mon Valley Providers Council (annual fund), Mothers Against Drunk Drives (victim services), and Radio Information Service. **$2,000** each to Allegheny County Special Olympics (uniforms/equipment), Junior Achievement of SW Pa., and Ventures in People. **$1,000** each to Garden Club of McKeesport (garden maintenance) and McKeesport Area Rotary Charities (millennium clock fund). **Out-of-state** grants: **$10,000** to a hospice in Louisiana and **$6,000** to Otterbein College [OH]. ■**PUBLICATIONS:** None ■**WEBSITE:** None ■**E-MAIL:** None ■**APPLICATION POLICIES & PROCEDURES:** The Foundation reports that most giving is restricted to Southeastern Allegheny County organizations for operating support, special projects, building funds, capital drives, and scholarship funds. No grants are awarded to individuals. Grant requests may be submitted in a letter (2 pages maximum) at any time; describe the organization's program/goals and state the amount of funding requested; include a project budget and IRS tax-exempt status documentation. Grants are awarded at meetings in March, July, and November.

O+D+T   Edwin W. Davis (Administrator+S+D+Con) — Charles W. Breckenridge [Gibsonia] (D) — Clair A. McElhinny [Greensburg] (D) — Alice J. Hajduk (D) — Thomas F. Hajduk [Presto] (D) — Robert T. Messner [Pittsburgh] (D) — Corporate donor: G.C. Murphy Company

---

SW-259 **Muse Foundation**
c/o Crown Coal & Coke Company
200 Nine Parkway Center
Pittsburgh   15220   (Allegheny County)

MI-18-31-32-41-42-52-53-54-55-57-63

Phone 412-921-1950 **FAX** 412-921-2938
EIN 25-6042685   **Year Created** 1959

AMV $808,930   **FYE** 12-00   (**Gifts Received** $0)   37 **Grants totaling** $47,275

Mostly local giving. High grants of **$5,000** each to Carnegie Institute, Ellis School, Shadyside Hospital Foundation, and U. of Pittsburgh Cancer Center. **$1,800-$2,000** each to Eye & Ear Foundation, Loyalhanna Assn., Magee-Womens Health Foundation, and Pittsburgh Cultural Trust. **$1,000** each to Extra Mile Education Foundation, Pittsburgh Opera, Shadyside Presbyterian Church, and WQED. **$750** each to Heartwood Institute and Planned Parenthood of Western Pa. Other local contributions **$50-$500** for arts/cultural, educational and other purposes. Out-of-state giving includes **$1,000** to U. of Southern California; **$750** to Creative Women of the Arts [CA]; and smaller contributions for educational purposes. ■**PUBLICATIONS:** None ■**WEBSITE:** None ■**E-MAIL:** None ■**APPLICATION POLICIES & PROCEDURES:** The Foundation reports that most giving is to charities favored by family members and that unsolicited requests are not given serious consideration. No grants awarded to individuals.

O+D+T   Albert C. Muse (T+Donor+Con) — Charles H. Muse, Jr. (T)

SW-260 **National City Foundation**
c/o National City Bank of Pa. - Public Affairs
20 Stanwix Street, 14th Floor, #46-25-146
Pittsburgh   15222   (Allegheny County)

MI-11-13-14-16-17-22-24-25-29-31-32-41-42
-44-49-51-52-54-55-56-57-72-83-85-88
Phone 412-644-8086 **FAX** 412-644-8099
EIN 34-7050989   **Year Created** 1990

AMV $44,080,889   **FYE** 6-00   (**Gifts Received** $0)   1800+ **Grants totaling** $17,127,194

Giving in Pa. is limited to the Bank's 23-county Western Pa. trading area (counties listed below); about 10% of giving to Pa. including matching gifts. High Pa. grant of **$210,000** to United Way of Allegheny County. **$100,000** to United Jewish Federation of Greater Pittsburgh. **$55,000** to Pittsburgh Community Reinvestment Group. **$51,150-$52,325** each to Penn State U., Point Park College, and Westminster College. **$45,000** each to Pittsburgh Regional Alliance and Pittsburgh Symphony. **$42,050** to Washington & Jefferson College. **$35,000** to Neighborhood Housing Services. **$25,000-$25,500** each to Allegheny Conference on Community Development, Family House, Mon Valley Initiative, and Punxsutawney Area Hospital. **$21,000** to NEED/Negro Educational Emergency Drive. **$20,000** each to Jewish Community Center of Pittsburgh. **$17,500** to Community Lender Credit Program. **$14,900-$15,800** each to Community College of Allegheny County Education Foundation, Pittsburgh Children's Museum, United Way of Erie County, United Way of Washington County United Way of Westmoreland County, and Westmoreland

Economic Development Corp. **$12,500** to The Carnegie. **$10,000-$10,350** each to Civic Light Opera, Indiana U. of Pa./Eberly College of Business, Leukemia & Lymphoma Society, Meadville Medical Center Foundation, Minority Enterprise Corp., Pittsburgh Ballet Theatre, Pittsburgh Leadership Foundation, POWER, Trinity Episcopal School for Ministry [Ambridge], Western Pa. School for the Deaf, Yeshiva Schools, andYMCA of Greensburg. **$7,500-$8,700** each to Holy Family Institute, Hosanna Industries, March of Dimes/Erie, Northside Leadership Conference, Pittsburgh Public Theater, United Way of Butler County, United Way of Venango County, and Western Pa. Humane Society. **$5,000-$6,600** each to Aliquippa Alliance for Unity & Development, American Cancer Society/Erie, B.F. Jones Memorial Library [Aliquippa], Beginning With Books, Bloomfield -Garfield Corp., Boy Scouts/French Creek Council, Boy Scouts/Moraine Trails Council, Butler County Community College Education Fund, Children's Hospital of Pittsburgh, Civic Senior Citizens [Aliquippa], Clearfield Foundation for Health, The Community Builders, Community Technical Assistance Center, DuBois Area Catholic School System, Greater Uniontown Heritage Consortium, Housing Opportunities [McKeesport], Leadership Pittsburgh, Make-A-Wish Foundation of Western Pa., Marian Manor, Pa. Economy League/Western Division, Penn Northwest Development Corp. [Mercer], Pittsburgh Opera, Rainbow Kitchen Community Services [Homestead], Red Cross, Uniontown Hospital Foundation, United Arts Fund Drive [Erie], United Way of Mercer County, United Way of South Fayette County, and Women's Shelter Rape Crisis Center [New Castle]. **$2,000-$4,500** each to Alle-Kiski Literacy Council, Allegheny Policy Council, Allegheny Valley Habitat for Humanity, Allegheny West Civic Council, American Cancer Society/Pittsburgh, Bridge to Independence [Braddock], Child Development Centers [Franklin], Children's International Summer Villages, Columbia Theatre for the Arts [Sharon], Community Design Center of Pittsburgh, Corry YMCA, Domestic Abuse Counseling Center, DuBois Area United Way, Eastern Westmoreland Development Corp., Eastside Neighborhood Employment Center, Erie Insight, Focus on Renewal/Sto-Rox Neighborhood Corp., Free Medical Clinic of DuBois, Friendship Development Associates, Greater Erie Youth Symphony Orchestra, Greater Latrobe School District, Hazelwood Development Corp., Human Services Center Corp. [Turtle Creek], Mon Valley YMCA, NAACP/North Hills Branch, National Foundation for Teaching Entrepreneurship, Neighborhood Art House [Erie], North Side Civic Development, Pittsburgh Cultural Trust, Rankin Christian Center, Redstone Township Recreational Center, Regional Trail Corp., Salvation Army/Pittsburgh, Seton LaSalle High School, South Western Legal Aid Society [Washington], St. Vincent Small Business Development Center [Latrobe], Sto-Ken-Rox Meals on Wheels, Titusville Area United Way, United Way of Beaver County, United Way of Bradford Area, United Way of Clarion County, United Way of the Mon Valley, United Way of Western Crawford County, Westmoreland Columbus 500, Working Order, YMCA of Beaver County, and YMCA of Titusville. Other Pa. grants/contributions **$100-$1,500** for similar purposes. **Out-of-state** giving in bank trading areas in OH, IL, IN, KY, and MI, and selected national or regional programs. ■**PUBLICATIONS:** annual Community Report ■ **WEBSITE:** www.nationalcity.com/communityrelations/pennsylvania ■ **E-MAIL:** angela.longo@nationalcity.com ■**APPLICATION POLICIES & PROCEDURES:** The Foundation reports that giving is generally limited to the Bank's 23-county Western Pa. trading area: Allegheny, Armstrong, Beaver, Bedford, Butler, Clarion, Clearfield, Crawford, Elk, Erie, Fayette, Forest, Greene, Indiana, Jefferson, Lawrence, McKean, Mercer, Somerset, Venango, Warren, Washington, and Westmoreland counties. Giving focuses on Educational Institutions (elementary/secondary, colleges/universities, adult education, special education/training, and libraries); also supported are Health/Human Service Agencies (particularly United Ways—also children/youth, social service agencies, hospitals, and healthcare agencies), Arts/Cultural Organizations (particularly education-related programs), and Community Development (capacity building, nonprofit development, and training). Most grants are for annual campaigns, building/renovations, capital drives, and matching gifts. No multi-year awards are made. When requesting support, prospective applicants are encouraged to work with their local National City Bank of Pa. officials (throughout the 23-county area); participation by bank employees in an organization's activities/programs is viewed favorably in making grant decisions. Grant requests may be submitted at any time using the Grantmakers of Western Pa. Common Grant Application Format (see Appendix); include an annual report, organizational/project budgets, audited financial statement, list of major funding sources, Board member list, and IRS tax-exempt status documentation. Site visits are made to organizations being considered for a grant. Grants are awarded at monthly meetings. Matching gifts for colleges, universities, theological schools, non-public secondary schools, libraries, and public broadcasting stations have a $25 minimum, $5,000 maximum/employee/year. — Note: National City Bank of Pa. is a unit of National City Corporation (Cleveland, OH) where the Foundation is officially headquartered. — Formerly called Integra Foundation.

O+D+T Angela J. Longo (VP for Public Affairs+Con) — Corporate donor: National City Bank of Pa.

SW-261 Neal (Vernon C. & Alvina B.) Fund
653 Arden Road
Washington 15301
(Washington County)

MI-12-13-14-19-22-24-25-32-41-42-43-61-72 84-89

Phone 724-228-7578 **FAX** None
EIN 25-1608371 **Year Created** 1987

AMV $2,594,294 **FYE** 12-00 **(Gifts Received** $0) 26 **Grants totaling** $137,500

All giving to Washington or Allegheny counties; grants are for general program support except as noted. High grant of **$15,000** Holy Family Foundation (abused children housing/services). **$10,000-$10,500** each to Boys & Girls Clubs of Western Pa./Sto-Ken Rox Branch, Bronson House/Neighborhood House Assn. (recreational/educational programs), North Star Kids [Ingomar], St. Malachy Church Angel Fund (tuition for needy families), and Washington Hospital Foundation (women/children programs). **$8,000** to Seton Hill College (institutional advancement). **$6,500** to Pittsburgh Mercy Foundation (infant mortality program). **$6,000** to Washington City Mission/Avis Arbor (shelter for abused women). **$5,000** each to Greater Pittsburgh Community Food Bank, Pittsburgh Civic Light Opera (youth training), Pittsburgh Irish & Classical Theatre (capital campaign), Washington County Habitat for Humanity, and Washington County Humane Society. **$3,000** each to Big Brothers & Big Sisters of Greater Pittsburgh and Clean & Sober Humans Assn. (family member support). **$2,000-$2,500** each to DePaul Institute (hearing-impaired children's education), Kennedy Township Athletic Assn. (field renovation), and YMCA of Pittsburgh (youth programs). **$1,000-$1,500** each to Boy Scouts/Greater Pittsburgh Council, Italian-American War Veterans (recreation for exceptional children), Kennedy Township Independent Volunteer Fire Company (equipment), Parent & Child Guidance Center, Science Matters, Inc. (Washington County science curriculum kits), and Sisters of the Holy Family of Nazareth (Family Festival). ■**PUBLICATIONS:** None ■**WEBSITE:** None ■**E-MAIL:** None ■**APPLICATION POLICIES & PROCEDURES:** The Foundation reports that giving focuses on programs for children and youth in SW Pa. No grants awarded to individuals. Grant requests may be submitted in any form at any time; include IRS tax-exempt documentation. Site visits sometimes are made to organizations being considered for a grant. Grants are awarded at April and October meetings.

O+D+T Margaret L. Johnston (Co-T+S+Con) — Frank L. Corsetti, CPA [Coraopolis] (Co-T) — Rosemary L. Corsetti, Esq. [Coraopolis] (Co-T)

SW-262 Netzer Charitable Foundation
  c/o Federal Alloy Corporation
  2600 Chartiers Ave., P.O. Box 4336
  Pittsburgh 15204   (Allegheny County)
AMV $562,388   **FYE** 1-01   **(Gifts Received** $0)

MI-11-22-32-41-62

Phone 412-331-2100 **FAX** 412-331-8634
EIN 25-6065741   **Year Created** 1962
  32 **Grants totaling** $63,250

Mostly local giving. High grant of **$42,000** to United Jewish Federation of Greater Pittsburgh. **$10,000** to United Way of SW Pa. **$3,500** to Hillman Cancer Center. **$1,750** to Congregation Rodef Shalom. **$1,555** to Winchester Thurston School. Other local contributions **$25-$500** for various purposes. **Out-of-state** grant: **$1,555** to Sarasota Manatee Jewish Foundation [FL]. ■ **PUBLICATIONS:** None ■ **WEBSITE:** None ■ **E-MAIL:** None ■ **APPLICATION POLICIES & PROCEDURES:** Grant requests may be submitted in a letter at any time; describe the purpose of the organization and the requested funds. No grants are awarded to individuals. — Formerly called the Bluestone-Netzer Charitable Foundation.

O+D+T Leon L. Netzer (T+Donor+Con) — Edith S. Netzer (T+Donor) — Nancy Netzer [MA] (T) — Thomas Netzer (T+Donor) — Corporate donors: Federal Alloy Corporation; Nicroloy Corporation

---

SW-263 Nicholas (Nicholas G.) Foundation
  c/o Nicholas Coffee Company
  23 Market Square
  Pittsburgh 15222   (Allegheny County)
AMV $365,026   **FYE** 12-00   **(Gifts Received** $1,140)

MI-12-31-32-42-43-63

Phone 412-471-2208 **FAX** None
EIN 25-1646744   **Year Created** 1990
  13 **Grants totaling** $38,200

About two-thirds local giving; all grants are for general purposes except as noted. High grant of **$10,000** to Children's Hospital of Pittsburgh. **$9,500** to Holy Cross Greek Orthodox Church (building fund). **$1,000-$1,200** each to Duquesne U., National MS Society, and two scholarships. Other smaller local contributions. **Out-of-state** giving includes **$10,000** to Lynn U. [FL] and **$2,950** to Unicorn Children's Foundation [FL]. ■ **PUBLICATIONS:** application guidelines ■ **WEBSITE:** None ■ **E-MAIL:** None ■ **APPLICATION POLICIES & PROCEDURES:** Grant requests from organizations may be submitted at any time on a special form available from the Foundation. Also, the Foundation reports it will award scholarships for study at post-secondary institutions with awards based on need and prior scholastic achievement; individuals must complete a Scholarship Application Form and a Financial Information Form, also available from the Foundation. Decisions on grant applications are usually made within a month. — Formerly called Nicholas G. & Annette Nicholas Foundation

O+D+T Nicholas G. Nicholas (P+Donor+Con) — Robert G. Panagulias, Esq. (VP+S) — Annette M. Nicholas (Donor)

SW-264 Niesen Foundation, The
  c/o United Refractories Company
  264 Valleybrook Road
  McMurray 15317   (Washington County)
AMV $234,494   **FYE** 12-00   **(Gifts Received** $5,000)

MI-12-63

Phone 412-833-3638 **FAX** 412-941-9690
EIN 25-1539242   **Year Created** 1987
  3 **Grants totaling** $20,000

Two Pa. grants: **$5,000** each to Family Guidance, Inc. and South Hills Bible Chapel. **Out-of-state** grant: **$10,000** to Good Friends, Inc. [AZ]. ■ **PUBLICATIONS:** None ■ **WEBSITE:** None ■ **E-MAIL:** None ■ **APPLICATION POLICIES & PROCEDURES:** Grant requests may be submitted in a brief letter at any time. No grants awarded to individuals.

O+D+T Raymond J. Niesen [Upper St. Clair] (Manager+Donor+Con) — Douglas Niesen [Venetia] (Donor)

SW-265 Nimick-Forbesway Foundation
  c/o Buchanan Ingersoll, P.C.
  One Oxford Center, 301 Grant Street, 20th Floor
  Pittsburgh 15219   (Allegheny County)
AMV $1,937,379   **FYE** 6-01   **(Gifts Received** $0)

MI-31-32-35-42-56-63-71

Phone 412-562-8879 **FAX** 412-562-1041
EIN 25-1597437   **Year Created** 1988
  12 **Grants totaling** $120,000

Mostly local giving; some grants comprise multiple payments. Three grants totaling **$65,000** to Shadyside Hospital Foundation (U. of Pittsburgh Cancer Institute/Nimick Family Library/Conference Center, Complimentary Medicine Research Fund, and Cardiopulmonary Rehabilitation Program). **$20,000** to East Liberty Family Health Care Center (reserve fund). **$10,000** each to Carnegie Institute (Powdermill Nature Reserve seminars/education fund) and Phipps Conservatory & Botanical Gardens (capital campaign). **$5,000** to St. Michaels of the Valley Church [Ligonier]. **$4,000** to Loyalhanna Watershed Assn. (scientific program/easement fund). **$1,000** to Society for the Preservation of the Duquesne Heights Incline (reserve fund). **Out-of-state** grant: **$5,000** to Princeton U. [NJ] (Nimick Scholarship Fund). ■ **PUBLICATIONS:** None ■ **WEBSITE:** None ■ **E-MAIL:** kesslerjj@bipc.com ■ **APPLICATION POLICIES & PROCEDURES:** The Foundation reports that grants are awarded only for special projects; no grants awarded to individuals. Grants requests may be submitted at any time in a full proposal with cover letter; include an annual report, organization budget, project budget, Board member list, list of major funding sources, audited financial statement, and IRS tax-exempt status documentation. Site visits sometimes are made to organizations being considered for a grant. — Formerly called Forbesway Foundation.

O+D+T Jack J. Kessler, Esq. (S+F+D+Con) — Thomas H. Nimick, Jr. (P+D+Donor) — Theresa L. Nimick (VP+D) — Victoria Nimick Enright [WI] (D)

SW-266 O'Neill (Paul H.) Charitable Foundation
3 Von Lent Place
Pittsburgh   15232   (Allegheny County)

MI-11-12-14-54-56-85-86
Phone 412-683-6867 **FAX** None
EIN 25-6378671   **Year Created** 1991

AMV $1,649,719   **FYE** 12-00   **(Gifts Received** $3,508)   28 **Grants totaling** $494,700

Limited local giving. High Pa. grant of **$20,000** to United Way of SW Pa. **$5,000** each to Historical Society of Western Pa., Laughlin Center, and Western Pa. School for Blind Children. **$2,500** to Carnegie Museums of Pittsburgh. **$1,000** to South Hills Junior Orchestra. Other local contributions **$250-$500** for education and youth. **Out-of-state** giving includes high grant of **$250,000** to RAND [CA]; **$50,000** each to Heinz Center for Science, Economics & The Environment [DC], Manpower Demonstration Research Corp. [NY], and National Museum of American History [DC]; **$25,000** to West Liberty Heritage Foundation [IA]; and **$20,000** to Gerald R. Ford Foundation [MI]. ■**PUBLICATIONS:** application guidelines ■**WEBSITE:** None ■**E-MAIL:** None ■**APPLICATION POLICIES & PROCEDURES:** The Foundation reports that priority is given to Western Pa. organizations for specific projects, programs, or causes. Grants are awarded for general support but applicants must apply annually, and no organization should expect automatic, on-going support. No grants are awarded to/for individuals, politics, lobbying, specialized health/medical programs without a specific community impact, welfare/social programs that do not support self-reliance, programs of sectarian or religious programs limited to members of one particular group, organizations that discriminate, university chairs or professorships, or organizations which promote/support abortion, euthanasia or cruelty to animals. Submit grant requests in a letter at any time (deadline is September 15th) for consideration that year; state a specific amount requested in the first paragraph, and then describe the project/need with purposes/objectives and means of implementation; include an itemized budget showing income/expenses, a list of other major funding sources, an audited financial statement, and IRS tax-exempt status documentation. The Board awards grants at June and December meetings.

O+D+T Paul H. O'Neill (C+D+Con) — Nancy J. O'Neill (D)

SW-267 Ochiltree Foundation
c/o Mellon Private Wealth Management
One Mellon Center, Room 3810
Pittsburgh   15258   (Allegheny County)

MI-14-16-25-31-32-63-71-72
Phone 412-234-2281 **FAX** None
EIN 23-7883781   **Year Created** 1997

AMV $1,177,716   **FYE** 12-00   **(Gifts Received** $0)   15 **Grants totaling** $142,000

Three Pa. grants: **$12,000** to UFM International [Montgomery County]. **$10,000** each to East Liberty Health Care Center and Western Pa. Humane Society. **Out-of-state** giving includes high grant of **$30,000** to Madison-Oglethorpe Animal Shelter [GA]; **$20,000** to Southern Poverty Law Center [AL]; **$10,000** each to Extra Special People [GA] and Habitat for Humanity [GA]; **$8,000** to Physicians Committee for Responsible Medicine [DC]; **$7,000** to In Defense of Animals [CA]; **$5,000** to American SPCA; and other grants, **$2,000-$4,000** for medical research and other purposes. ■**PUBLICATIONS:** None ■**WEBSITE:** None ■**E-MAIL:** zern.ja@mellon.com ■**APPLICATION POLICIES & PROCEDURES:** The Foundation reports that animal rights, environmental and medical research organizations receive priority in grants. Prospective applicants should first write for application information; requests may be submitted at any time. An external trustee has sole discretion in awarding grants; the bank officer acts only as agent.

O+D+T James Zern (1st VPat Bank+Con) — Mellon Bank N.A. (Corporate Trustee)

SW-268 Palmer (Arnold D. & Winifred W.) Foundation, The
P.O. Box 52
Youngstown   15696   (Westmoreland County)

MI-22-29-32
Phone 724-537-7751 **FAX** None
EIN 31-1536438   **Year Created** 1998

AMV $287,372   **FYE** 12-00   **(Gifts Received** $0)   3 **Grants totaling** $9,695

Mostly local giving. **$4,598** to Red Cross [Latrobe]. **$4,597** to Salvation Army [Latrobe]. **Out-of-state** contribution: **$500** to Leukemia Society of America [TN]. ■**PUBLICATIONS:** None ■**WEBSITE:** None ■**E-MAIL:** None ■**APPLICATION POLICIES & PROCEDURES:** Information not available.

O+D+T Arnold D. Palmer (P+Donor+Con) — Margaret A. Palmer [NC] (D) — Amy L. Saunders [FL] (D)

SW-269 Palumbo (A.J. & Sigismunda) Charitable Trust
c/o Smithfield Trust Company
20 Stanwix Street, Suite 650
Pittsburgh   15222   (Allegheny County)

MI-12-13-14-22-25-31-32-41-42-56-61-63-82
Phone 412-261-0779 **FAX** 412-261-3482
EIN 25-6168159   **Year Created** 1974

AMV $17,372,207   **FYE** 3-01   **(Gifts Received** $1,360,000)   30 **Grants totaling** $934,000

About three-fourths local or Elk County/Clearfield County giving. High grant of **$125,000** to Elk Regional Health Center [St. Marys] (observation suite). **$75,000** to DuBois Area Catholic Schools [Clearfield County] (capital campaign). **$60,000** to St. Marys Church [Elk County]. **$50,000** each to Cystic Fibrosis Foundation (drug recovery/development program), Duquesne U. (cancer research in Nicaragua), and Marion Manor Corp. (outdoor therapeutic Area). **$35,000** each to Elk County Christian High School (curriculum materials) and National Kidney Foundation (education program). **$30,000** to Pressley Ridge Schools Foundation (construction). **$25,000** each to Big Brothers & Big Sisters of Greater Pittsburgh (match up underwriting), Holy Family Institute (furnishings/salaries), Juvenile Diabetes Foundation International (research), Queen of the World Church [Elk County] (renovations), and Salvation Army/Pittsburgh (special project). **$20,000** to Summerbridge Pittsburgh (pipeline college program). **$10,000** each to FamilyLink/Whale's Tale Foundation (emergency shelter/counseling), First Evangelical Lutheran Church of Ridgway [Elk County] (new windows), Global Links (Honduras Project), Historical Society of Western Pa. (Italian-American program), and Jubilee Assn. of Western Pa. (housing project). **$5,000** each to Arthritis Foundation (home assessment program), National Flag Foundation (general support), Northside Common Ministries (food purchase), St. Germaine School (construction), and Watson Institute (autism program). **$4,000** to Cancer Caring Center (support group services). **Out-of-state** giving, mostly

for medical research, includes **$100,000** to Mayo Clinic of Scottsdale [AZ]; and **$50,000** each to Mayo Clinic Children's Hospital [MN] and Rochester Ronald McDonald House [MN]. ■**PUBLICATIONS:** Application Procedure memorandum ■**WEBSITE:** None ■**E-MAIL:** rkopf@smithfieldtrust.com ■**APPLICATION POLICIES & PROCEDURES:** The Foundation reports giving is primarily to Western Pa. organizations; most grants are for general support, special projects, or research. No grants are awarded to individuals or outside the United States. Prospective applicants initially should make a telephone inquiry about the feasibility of submitting a request, and to request a copy of detailed Application Procedure guidelines. Grant requests may be submitted following the prescribed guidelines during April-November; deadline is December 31st. The Trustees award grants at an annual meeting on the first Saturday in March.
O+D+T Robert Y. Kopf, Jr. (Adminstrator+Con) — A.J. Palumbo [St. Marys] (C+T) — E. Rolland Dickson [MN] (VC+T) — Frank W. Knisley (F+T) — Donald W. Meredith (S+T) — John W. Kowach [St. Marys] (T) — Janet F. Palumbo [St. Marys] (T) — P.J. Palumbo [AZ] (T) — Richard L. White [Gibsonia] (T) — PNC Bank N.A. (Corporate Trustee)

SW-270 Papernick Family Foundation, The
146 North Bellefield Ave., Apt. 1201
Pittsburgh 15213   (Allegheny County)
AMV $83,671   **FYE** 11-00   **(Gifts Received** $0)

MI-22-62
Phone 412-765-2212 **FAX** None
EIN 23-7750564   **Year Created** 1993
18 **Grants totaling** $11,618

Mostly local giving. High grant of **$7,500** to United Jewish Federation of Greater Pittsburgh. **$1,513** to Congregation Beth Shalom. Other local and out-of-state contributions **$20-$1,000** for various purposes. ■**PUBLICATIONS:** None ■**WEBSITE:** None ■ **E-MAIL:** None ■**APPLICATION POLICIES & PROCEDURES:** Information not available.
O+D+T Alan Papernick, Esq. (T+Donor+Con) — Judith R. Papernick (T+Donor) — Amy B. Glick [FL] (T) — Lisa G. Glick (T) — Stephen M. Papernick, Esq. (T)

SW-271 Pappafava (Premo J.) Foundation
c/o General Carbide Corporation
G-H Industrial Park, P.O. Box C
Greensburg 15601   (Westmoreland County)
AMV $176,943   **FYE** 12-00   **(Gifts Received** $0)

MI-41-42-61

Phone 724-836-3000 **FAX** 724-836-6274
EIN 25-6277032   **Year Created** 1986
7 **Grants totaling** $46,000

All local giving; all grants are for general support. High grant of **$22,500** to Seton Hill College. **$16,500** to Blessed Sacrament Cathedral. **$5,000** to Carnegie Mellon U. Other local contributions **$500** each for educational purposes. ■**PUBLICATIONS:** None ■**WEBSITE:** None ■**E-MAIL:** None ■**APPLICATION POLICIES & PROCEDURES:** The Foundation reports that giving is limited to educational or religious organizations within 35 miles of Greensburg; most grants are for general support, special projects, building funds, and capital drives; multi-year grants are made. No grants are awarded to individuals. Grant requests should be submitted in a full proposal with cover letter during October-November; deadline is November 30th; include an annual report, project budget, audited financial statement, list of major funding sources, and IRS tax-exempt status documentation. Site visits sometimes are made to organizations being considered for a grant. Grants are awarded at a December meeting.
O+D+T Lorraine B. Pappafava (T+Con)

SW-272 Parker Foundation
c/o Mellon Private Wealth Management
One Mellon Center, Room 3810
Pittsburgh 15258   (Allegheny County)
AMV $2,949,668   **FYE** 12-00   **(Gifts Received** $0)

MI-12-22-29-31-41-42-52-61-71

Phone 412-234-2281 **FAX** None
EIN 23-7883782   **Year Created** 1997
10 **Grants totaling** $270,000

Mostly local giving. High grants of **$50,000** to Phipps Conservatory & Botanical Gardens, The Neighborhood Academy, Pittsburgh Leadership Foundation, and Shadyside Hospital Foundation. **$10,000** each to Bethlehem Haven, East Liberty Family Health Care Center, Glade Run Lutheran Services, and Pittsburgh Oratory. **Out-of-state** grants: **$20,000** to Wheelock College [MA] and **$10,000** to Lahey Clinic [MA]. — Other giving in prior years included **$10,000** each to Christian Children's Fund [VA], Love the Children [Bucks County], and World Vision [CA]. ■**PUBLICATIONS:** None ■**WEBSITE:** None ■**E-MAIL:** zern.ja@mellon.com ■**APPLICATION POLICIES & PROCEDURES:** The Foundation reports that religious charities, children/youth programs, and human rights organizations receive priority in grants. Prospective applicants should first write or telephone the bank for application information. Grant requests may be submitted at any time. The external trustees have sole discretion in awarding grants; the bank officer acts only as agent.
O+D+T James Zern (1st VP at Bank+Con) — John C. Harmon, Esq. (Co-T) — Susan Sharp Dorrance (Co-T+Donor) — Mellon Bank N.A. (Corporate Trustee)

SW-273 Partners Charitable Trust, The
135 West 8th Street
Pittsburgh 15215   (Allegheny County)
AMV $286,324   **FYE** 6-01   **(Gifts Received** $0)

MI-14-29-32-84
Phone 412-781-6473 **FAX** None
EIN 25-6501559   **Year Created** 1995
12 **Grants totaling** $13,620

All local giving; all grants are unrestricted support. High grant of **$5,995** to College Bound Student Alliance (student athlete). **$1,000-$1,800** each to Contact Pittsburgh, Dad's Fund, Gateway Rehabilitation Center, and National MS Society. **$500** each to Lower Valley Little League and St. Edward Church. Other contributions **$100-$300** for various purposes. ■**PUBLICATIONS:** None ■**WEBSITE:** None ■**E-MAIL:** None ■**APPLICATION POLICIES & PROCEDURES:** Information not available.
O+D+T John C. Campbell (P+Con) — James L. Campbell (T)

SW-274 Patterson (W.I.) Charitable Fund

c/o Tener, Van Kirk, Wolf & Moore
920 Oliver Bldg., 535 Smithfield Street
Pittsburgh 15222 (Allegheny County)

MI-12-13-15-25-41-44-45-51-52-56

Phone 412-281-5580 **FAX** 412-281-6115
EIN 25-6028639 **Year Created** 1955

AMV $4,989,029 **FYE** 7-00 **(Gifts Received** $0) 68 **Grants totaling** $259,675

Mostly local/Pa. giving; grants are for general purposes except as noted. High grant of **$51,939** to Carnegie Library of Pittsburgh. **$7,000** to Pittsburgh Symphony. **$6,240** to Society for the Preservation of the Duquesne Heights Incline. **$6,000** each to Goodwill Industries of Pittsburgh and Pace School. **$5,000** each Alzheimer's Assn., Bradley Center, Bridge to Independence (housing for homeless women/children), Children's Home of Pittsburgh, Family Resources (child abuse prevention), Genesis of Pittsburgh (services for pregnant women/adoptive families), Lupus Foundation of America/Western Pa. Chapter, Make-A-Wish Foundation of Western Pa., Salvation Army, West Penn Hospital Foundation, and Variety Clubs of Pittsburgh (mobility equipment for disabled children). **$4,000** each to Assn. for Independent Colleges & Universities in Pa. [Harrisburg], Big Brothers & Big Sisters of Greater Pittsburgh, Children's Hospital of Pittsburgh, North Side Christian Health Center, Pittsburgh Public Theater, Shadyside Hospital Foundation, St. Barnabas Charitable Foundation, D.T. Watson Rehabilitation Hospital, and YMCA of McKeesport. **$3,000-$3,500** each to Allegheny History Preservation Society, Arthritis Foundation /Western Pa. Chapter, The Children's Institute (services for disabled children), Human Services of Western Pa. (rehabilitation programs), Life's Work of Western Pa. (vocational counseling), Northside Common Ministries (emergency shelter/food), Pa. Special Olympics, Pittsburgh Civic Light Opera, and River City Brass Band. **$2,000-$2,500** each to Allegheny County Literacy Council, Brashear Assn. (summer youth program), Bridge Christian Outreach (programs for disabled), Cancer Caring Center, Easter Seals, Extra Mile Education Foundation, Garfield Jubilee Assn. (youth programs), Gateway to The Arts (youth music programs), Greater Pittsburgh Community Food Bank, Historical Society of Western Pa., Junior Achievement of SW Pa., Laughlin Center (children's programs), Leukemia Society of America, Manchester Youth Development Center, National Kidney Foundation of Western Pa., Pittsburgh Leadership Foundation, Presbyterian Seniorcare, Sisters Place (transitional housing for single mothers), Southwestern Pa. Partnership for Aging, Spina Bifida Assn. of Western Pa., United Negro College Fund, Western Pa. Conservancy, WQED, and YWCA of Greater Pittsburgh (youth programs). Other local grants **$1,000-$1,500** for similar purposes. ■**PUBLICATIONS:** None ■**WEBSITE:** None ■**E-MAIL:** rbshust@aol.com ■**APPLICATION POLICIES & PROCEDURES:** The Foundation reports that Allegheny County organizations receive preference. No grants are awarded to individuals or for endowment, scholarships, or fellowships. Prospective applicants should make an initial telephone inquiry regarding the feasibility of submitting a request. Grant requests may be submitted at any time in a letter (4 pages maximum)—deadline is June 30th; briefly describe the proposed project and include a list of major funding sources, Board member list, and IRS tax-exempt status documentation. Site visits sometimes are made to organizations being considered for a grant. The Board meets at least three times annually.

O+D+T Robert B. Shust, Esq. (T+Con) — Timothy F. Burke, Jr. Esq. (T) — Robert B. Wolf, Esq. (T)

SW-275 Patton (Margaret) for Charities

219 North Jefferson Street, #3
Kittanning 16201 (Armstrong County)

MI-11-12-13-14-22-29-31-32-33-42-63

Phone 724-548-1092 **FAX** None
EIN 25-6170579 **Year Created** 1976

AMV $4,129,383 **FYE** 12-00 **(Gifts Received** $1,540) 37 **Grants totaling** $228,000

All giving restricted to local/regional programs serving Armstrong County residents (except as noted in guidelines); grants are for general purposes unless noted otherwise, and some grants comprise multiple payments. High grant of **$22,000** to United Way of Armstrong County. **$16,000** to ARC Manor. **$13,000** to First United Methodist Church of Kittanning. **$10,000** each to Havin, Inc. and Red Cross/Kittanning. **$8,500** to Armstrong County Memorial Hospital. **$8,000** to Indiana U. of Pa./Kittanning Campus. **$7,000** each to Armstrong County YMCA and Young Adult Handicapped, Inc. **$6,000** each to American Cancer Society/SW Pa. Region, American Heart Assn., American Respiratory Alliance of Western Pa., Armstrong County Children & Youth Services, Assn. of Retarded Citizens/Armstrong County Chapter, Boy Scouts/Moraine Trails Council, Evergreen Homes, Family Counseling Center of Armstrong County, Keystone Tall Tree Girl Scout Council, LifeSteps, Progressive Workshop of Armstrong County, Salvation Army/Kittanning, and UCP of Western Pa. **$5,000** each to Armstrong/Indiana Special Olympics, Bethanna [Bucks County], Children's Hospital of Pittsburgh, Leukemia & Lymphoma Society, Make-A-Wish Foundation of Western Pa., Ranch Hope for Girls [NJ], Spina Bifida Assn. of Western Pa., and Whosoever Gospel Mission & Rescue Home [Philadelphia]. **$2,500** each to Philadelphia Men's Teen Challenge Home and Philadelphia Women's Teen Challenge Home. **$1,000-$1,500** each to Camp Cadet, Head Start, and Meals on Wheels/Kittanning. ■**PUBLICATIONS:** application guidelines; Application Form ■**WEBSITE:** None ■**E-MAIL:** None ■**APPLICATION POLICIES & PROCEDURES:** The Foundation reports that only organizations/programs serving Armstrong County residents/children are eligible to apply; grants to the Delaware Valley are special exceptions. Most grants are for general support, special projects, or scholarships. No grants awarded to individuals. Prospective applicants initially should telephone the Foundation to inquire about the feasibility of submitting a request, and to request a required Application Form. Grant requests may be submitted at any time together with an annual report, organizational/project budgets, audited financial statement, and IRS tax-exempt status documentation. Site visits sometimes are made to organizations being considered for a grant.

O+D+T John W. Rohrer, III (Co-T+Con) — Mellon Bank N.A. (Co-Trustee)

SW-276 Pearlman Family Foundation, The

c/o Alpern, Rosenthal & Co.
400 Warner Center, 332 - 5th Ave.
Pittsburgh 15222 (Allegheny County)

MI-22-31-32-42-54-62

Phone 412-281-2501 **FAX** 412-471-1996
EIN 23-2938419 **Year Created** 1997

AMV $239,618 **FYE** 12-00 **(Gifts Received** $56,475) 50 **Grants totaling** $52,500

About one-quarter local giving. High Pa. grant of **$10,000** to U. of Pittsburgh. **$2,000** to Bethlehem Haven. **$1,400** to Rodef Shalom Congregation. Many other local contributions **$50-$500** for various purposes. **Out-of-state** giving includes high grant of **$18,000** to Jewish Federation of Palm Beach County [FL], **$5,000** to Pan Mass Challenge/Jimmy Fund [MA]; **$2,000** to

Dana Farber Cancer Institute [MA]; and **$1,000** to Norton Museum of Art [FL]. — In the prior year, high grant of **$10,000** to U. of Pittsburgh Medical Center. ■**PUBLICATIONS:** None ■**WEBSITE:** None ■**E-MAIL:** None ■**APPLICATION POLICIES & PRO-CEDURES:** Information not available.

O+D+T Emanuel V. DiNatale, CPA (S+F+Con) — Doris M. Pearlman [FL] (P+Donor)

SW-277 Peirce Family Foundation, The
    c/o Peirce, Raimond & Coulter, P.C.
    2500 Gulf Tower, 707 Grant Street
    Pittsburgh 15219   (Allegheny County)

MI-13-14-41-42-43-54-56-71

Phone 412-281-7229 **FAX** 412-281-4229
EIN 23-2903074 **Year Created** 1997

AMV $3,426,249 **FYE** 12-00 (**Gifts Received** $910,787) 35 **Grants totaling** $173,484

Mostly local giving. High grant of **$51,250** to Duquesne U. (scholarship fund). **$45,000** to Geneva College (scholarship fund). **$32,100** to Extra Mile Education Foundation. **$20,000** to Riverfront Parks. **$1,000-$2,500** each to Carnegie Institute, Girls Hope, Historical Society of Western Pa., Pittsburgh Speech Hearing & Deaf Services, Sewickley Academy, and Western Pa. Conservancy. Other local contributions **$35-$500** for various purposes. **Out-of-state** grant: **$5,000** to The Stony Brook School [NY]. ■**PUBLICATIONS:** None. ■**WEBSITE:** None ■**E-MAIL:** rpeircejr@peircelaw.com ■**APPLICATION POLICIES & PROCEDURES:** Grant requests may be submitted in writing at any time; include name/address of proposed recipient, purpose/nature of request, amount requested, organizational background information, and IRS tax-exempt status documentation.

O+D+T Robert N. Peirce, Jr., Esq. [Sewickley] (P+Donor+Con) — Joan Peirce [Sewickley] (S+Donor)

SW-278 Perlow Family Foundation
    c/o Perlow Investment Company
    Foster Plaza X, 680 Andersen Drive
    Pittsburgh 15220   (Allegheny County)

MI-15-22-62-84

Phone 412-937-5400 **FAX** None
EIN 23-2894160 **Year Created** 1997

AMV $375,202 **FYE** 12-00 (**Gifts Received** $306,250) 2 **Grants totaling** $12,250

High grant of **$12,000** to Riverview Towers. **$250** to Jewish Sports Hall of Fame of Western Pa. — In prior years, grants included **$6,500** to United Jewish Federation of New York; **$5,400** to Beth Shalom; and **$895** to Jewish Funders Network [NY]. ■**PUBLICATIONS:** None. ■**WEBSITE:** None ■**E-MAIL:** None ■**APPLICATION POLICIES & PROCEDURES:** The Foundation reports that giving primarily benefits nonprofit organizations in Western Pa.

O+D+T Rodney W. Fink, Esq. (S+F+Con) — Charles S. Perlow (VP+D+Donor) — Ellen Perlow Kessler (VP+D) — Lori Perlow [NY] (VP+D)

SW-279 Peters (Charles F.) Foundation

    923 Fawcett Ave.
    McKeesport 15132   (Allegheny County)

MI-12-13-15-17-22-25-31-39-41-44-52-55-56
61-62-63-71-84

Phone 412-678-6652 **FAX** None
EIN 25-6070765 **Year Created** 1965

AMV $3,746,420 **FYE** 12-00 (**Gifts Received** $0) 82 **Grants totaling** $138,500

All giving restricted to McKeesport-area religious, educational or community organizations—or for services in McKeesport area by Pittsburgh-based agencies; grants are for general support except as noted. High grants of **$5,000** to Auberle Foundation (program center), Greater Pittsburgh Community Food Bank, Human Services of Western Pa. (mental health outpatient clinic), Long Run Children's Learning Center, McKeesport Area Meals on Wheels, McKeesport Hospital Foundation (community health initiatives project), McKeesport Little Theatre, McKeesport Symphony, Salvation Army, and YWCA of McKeesport. **$3,000** to McKeesport Music Club (general support/scholarship). **$2,000-$2,500** each to Boy Scouts/Greater Pittsburgh Council, Coalition for Christian Outreach (staffing at Penn State-McKeesport), Community College of Allegheny County-McKeesport Center (video-conferencing facility), Contact Pittsburgh, Duquesne Food Pantry, LaRosa Boys & Girls Club of McKeesport, McKeesport YMCA, and Mon Yough Riverfront Entertainment & Cultural Council. **$1,000-$1,500** each to Alliance Child Care Center, American Cancer Society, FamilyLink, Family Resources, Garden Club of McKeesport, Housing Opportunities, Junior Achievement of SW Pa., McKeesport Family Center (My Camp Collaborative Committee), Mon Yough ARC, and Mon Yough Community Services. Also, **$1,000-$2,500** each (for general support/specific programs) to 52 Catholic/Protestant churches or Jewish synagogues in Boston, Clairton, Dravosburg, Duquesne, Elizabeth, Glassport, Greenock, McKeesport, North Versailles, West Elizabeth, West Mifflin, or White Oak. ■**PUBLICATIONS:** None ■**WEBSITE:** None ■**E-MAIL:** None ■**APPLICATION POLICIES & PROCEDURES:** The Foundation reports that only organizations in or around McKeesport are eligible to apply; the largest grant awarded any organization is $5,000/year. Most grants are for general support, building/renovation, equipment, and emergency funds. No grants are awarded to individuals. Grant requests may be submitted in a letter at any time; include IRS tax-exempt status documentation. Site visits sometimes are made to organizations being considered for a grant. The Distribution Committee awards grants at monthly meetings.

O+D+T Distribution Committee members: — Robert A. Stone (S+Con) — William H. Balter, Esq. [Pittsburgh] — Herman A. Haase [White Oak] — National City Bank of Pa. (Trustee)

SW-280 Piatt (Jack B.) Foundation
    c/o Millcraft Industries, Inc.
    400 Southpointe Boulevard, Suite 400
    Canonsburg 15317   (Washington County)

MI-14-31-32-35-43

Phone 724-743-3400 **FAX** 724-745-2400
EIN 23-7079264 **Year Created** 1967

AMV $76 **FYE** 10-00 (**Gifts Received** $19,499) 14 **Grants totaling** $19,950

All local giving. High grant of **$10,000** to Italian American Society of Washington County (scholarship fund). **$5,000** to American Heart Assn./Uniontown (Health Walk). **$1,000** each to ARC-Washington (benefit event) and Kelly & Laura Boyd Fund (hospital expenses). **$900** to S&T Bancorp Charitable Foundation. **$500** each to American Diabetes Assn. and Washington Hospital Foundation. Other smaller contributions for various charities. ■**PUBLICATIONS:** None ■**WEBSITE:** None ■**E-MAIL:** None ■ **APPLICATION POLICIES & PROCEDURES:** Grant requests may be submitted in writing (or by telephone) at any time.

O+D+T Jack B. Piatt (T+Con) — Corporate donor: Millcraft Industries, Inc.

SW-281 Pitcairn-Crabbe Foundation
6 PPG Place, Suite 750
Pittsburgh 15222 (Allegheny County)

MI-12-13-14-22-25-29-31-34-41-63-64-65-84
Phone 412-644-8779 **FAX** 412-644-8059
EIN 25-0965459 **Year Created** 1940

AMV $9,451,768 **FYE** 12-01 **(Gifts Received** $0) 15 **Grants totaling** $352,290

All giving restricted to Pa. (largely Western Pa.) with emphasis on Christian education, religious and church projects, and community welfare/assistance programs; the following grants were approved for payment in 2001 but not all were disbursed that year. High grant of **$60,000** to East End Cooperative Ministry (AmeriCorps staff for Children & Youth Program). **$39,000** to Chatham College (spiritual development program). **$35,500** to Christian Literacy Associates (children's edition of Christian literacy series). **$30,000** each to Coalition for Christian Outreach (minority campus ministry positions) and Schenley Heights Community Development Program (tutorial-enrichment programs). **$25,000** each to Allegheny Valley Habitat for Humanity (house renovation for homeless family) and Lighthouse Foundation. **$20,000** to Pine Springs Camp (facilities improvement master plan). **$18,750** to Greater Love Ministry (summer camp scholarships). **$17,500** to Pittsburgh Theological Seminary (program evaluation). **$15,000** to Greater Pittsburgh Community Food Bank (general support). **$14,000** to Contact Pittsburgh (emergency case assistance). **$12,000** to Allegheny County Assistance Office/George Mills Fund (emergency support). **$10,000** to Waynesburg College (parish nurse training). — In the prior year, grants included **$55,000** to Pittsburgh Theological Seminary (pastors continuing education); **$35,000** to North Hills Youth Ministry (planning/development); **$30,000** to Pittsburgh Project (academy/day camp); **$22,684** to Reformed Presbyterian Theological Seminary (online library system); **$20,000** each to Allegheny Valley Assn. of Churches (interfaith hospitality network), Center for Urban Biblical Ministry (Aliquippa site startup), Manchester Youth Development Center (School before School program), Regional Interfaith Chaplaincy Services (pastoral care study), West Penn Allegheny Health System (hospital pastoral care); and 13 smaller grants. ■**PUBLICATIONS:** application guidelines ■**WEBSITE:** www.pitcairn-crabbe.org ■**E-MAIL:** info@mccune.org ■ **APPLICATION POLICIES & PROCEDURES:** The Foundation reports that ordinarily giving is limited to agencies/institutions within a 100-mile radius of Pittsburgh. Priority is given to requests that not only fit at least one of the following categories, but also demonstrate the greatest likelihood of achieving measurable results: (a) religious and church work; (b) Christian education; (c) relief of distress and enhancement of the spiritual/material condition of humanity; (d) community improvement through non-profit agencies sponsored by religious organizations; and (e) the timing of the project/program fits and augments other related community efforts/initiatives. In addition, preference is given to proposals that will significantly effect the grantee's operations; demonstrate a realistic assessment of both external and internal challenges facing successful project implementation; have the potential of attracting other sources of support; and show strong promise of achieving articulated goals. No grants are awarded to/for the medical needs of hospitals or scientific causes, the arts, endowments, or national organizations' annual appeals. Prospective applicants should submit a Letter of Inquiry (3 pages maximum) which includes (1) a description of the proposed efforts to address the problem or opportunity; and (2) the resources required to meet project objectives, including other sources of funding support. Also include the latest audited financial statement and IRS tax-exempt status documentation. The Letter of Inquiry also may be submitted electronically from the Foundation's website; click on Online Project Application. If the request meets the current criteria and funding priorities, a staff member will arrange a meeting and provide guidance regarding the submission of a formal proposal. The Board of Directors normally meets quarterly to review formal proposals and make funding decisions.The Foundation reports three primary areas of giving: (1) annual giving for outreach and social service programs of religious agencies in Greater Pittsburgh; (2) assistance to agencies aiding individuals with emergency medical or other needs; and (3) certain local programs which have received support from the Foundation historically. No grants are awarded to/for operating budgets, capital needs, medical needs of hospitals or scientific causes, research, annual appeals of national organizations, individuals, scholarships, fellowships, or to organizations outside Pa. Prospective applicants should submit a Letter of Inquiry (signed by the organization's president or authorized representative, and indicating Board approval); briefly describe a specific proposed program, and include an annual report, program budget, organizational budget, latest audited financial statement, and IRS tax-exempt status documentation. The Board awards grants at May and November meetings.

O+D+T Henry S. Beukema (Executive Director+Con) — G. Dixon Schrum, Jr. (P+D) — Boyd S. Murray (VP+D) — Jacqui F. Lazo (S+F+D) — Jeffrey S. Craig (D) — Natalie Hulme Curry (D) — Robert Dunkelman (D) — Sheila A. Fisher (D) — Gretchen B. Gockley (D) — Michael P. Martin (D) — W. Duff McCrady (D) — Jo ann Patross (D) — William D. Pettit (D) — Norman R. Smith (D) — PNC Bank N.A. (Custodian)

SW-282 Pitt-Des Moines, Inc. Charitable Trust
c/o Pitt-Des Moines, Inc.
3400 Grand Avenue, Neville Island
Pittsburgh 15225 (Allegheny County)

MI-11-12-13-25-29-31-42-51-52-55-56-63-71
72-86
Phone 412-331-3000 **FAX** None
EIN 25-6032139 **Year Created** 1974

AMV $1,702,763 **FYE** 12-00 **(Gifts Received** $0) 80+ **Grants totaling** $131,260

About half local/Pa. giving. High Pa. grant of **$5,000** to Pa. Right to Work Defense & Education Foundation [Harrisburg]. **$3,000** to SHOUT/Support Helps Others Use Technology. **$2,000** each to Sewickley Civic Garden Council and United Way of SW Pa. **$1,000-$1,500** each to Boy Scouts/Greater Pittsburgh Council, Extra Mile Education Foundation, Family Resources, Foundation for Free Enterprise Education, Greater Pittsburgh Community Food Bank, Historical Society of Western Pa., NEED/Negro Education Emergency Drive, Pittsburgh Cultural Trust, Pittsburgh Opera, Pittsburgh Symphony, Pittsburgh Zoo, St. Margaret Memorial Hospital Foundation, Salvation Army, and United Way of Warren County. Other local contributions **$100-$500** for arts, cultural, civic, health/human service, and other purposes. **Out-of-state** giving includes high grant of **$37,000** to National Right to Work Legal Defense Fund [VA]; **$6,500** to Coral Ridge Ministries [FL]; **$5,000** each to The Heritage Foundation [DC] and Red Cross/Greater Houston [TX]; and other grants/contributions for United Ways and community organizations in corporate operating locations in AL, CA, IA, OK, UT, WI and other states. ■**PUBLICATIONS:** None ■**WEBSITE:** None ■**E-MAIL:** None ■**APPLICATION POLICIES & PROCEDURES:** The Foundation reports that giving is generally limited to special projects, building funds, or capital needs. Grant requests may be submitted in a letter during October-December; include an annual report, organizational/project budgets, audited financial statement, list of major funding sources, Board member list, and IRS tax-exempt status documentation. Grants are awarded at meetings in November and December. — Formerly called Pittsburgh-Des Moines Steel Company Charitable Trust.

O+D+T W.R. Jackson (T+Con) — R.A. Byers [TX] (T) — P.O. Elbert [TX] (T) — Corporate donor: Pitt-Des Moines, Inc.

SW-283 Pittsburgh Child Guidance Foundation
425 Sixth Ave., Suite 2460
Pittsburgh 15219   (Allegheny County)
AMV $5,851,065   **FYE** 12-01   (**Gifts Received** $0)

MI-12-13-14-18-22-35-41-84
Phone 412-434-1665 **FAX** 412-434-0406
EIN 25-0965465   **Year Created** 1982
12 **Grants totaling** $218,864

All giving limited to organizations serving Allegheny County children (birth-12 years). *AREA OF EMPHASIS GRANTS*: **$31,300** to Schenley Heights Community Development Program (after-school tutorial/enrichment program). **$27,270** to Hazelwood Youth Football & Cheerleaders Assn. (football/cheerleading program with mentoring/skill development). **$25,000** to Hosanna House (mentoring/group activities for children having academic/behavioral difficulties). **$15,000** to Centre Ave. YMCA (after-school program/summer day camp). *DISCRETIONARY GRANTS*: **$49,999** (over 2 years) to Citizens to Abolish Domestic Apartheid (staff/equipment for after-school/summer youth programs). **$35,666** (over 2 years) to North Hills Youth Ministry Counseling Center (tutoring pilot project). **$27,000** (over 2 years) to Hosanna House (staff for aquatics/swimming program). **$26,621** (over 2 years) to Greater Pittsburgh Community Food Bank (intensive after-school assistance). **$25,582** (over 2 years) to Zion Christian Church (Carrick after-school/summer programs and other projects). **$21,500** (over 2 years) to Pittsburgh Helmet Coalition (campaign to promote helmet use by children). **$19,356** to Pa. Peace Links (conflict management skills puppet show for children/teachers). JACK'S GRANT: **$75,000** (over 3 years) to Young Men & Women's African Heritage Assn. (support/educate foster/adopted children and their parents). ■**PUBLICATIONS:** Guidelines for Grants brochure; Grant Application Package ■**WEBSITE:** http://trfn.clpgh.org/pcgf/ ■**E-MAIL:** pcgf@smartbuilding.org ■**APPLICATION POLICIES & PROCEDURES:** The Foundation reports that giving is limited to organizations promoting the mental health of children (birth to 12 years) in Allegheny County, including preventive and early intervention programs, and those fostering healthy development. Projects may include services to children, training/support for parents/caregivers, and research. No grants are awarded to individuals or for general operating expenses, capital campaigns, or scholarships. Three kinds of grants are awarded: (1) **Area of Emphasis Program Grants**: Through 2002 at least half of the grant resources will focus on helping children learn coping skills and build competence; grants are directed primarily at grassroots and faith-based organizations; the deadline for proposals is the first Wednesday in March. **Note**: In late December 2002, a new Area of Emphasis will be announced—check the website for details; (2) **Discretionary Grants** include (a) awards for specific projects that support children's development in area such as recreation, education, counseling, mentoring, etc.; (b) requests which include activities that strengthen the organization providing the services, and (c) requests to conduct research in the Foundation's areas of interest. One-year and multiyear grants are considered. Proposal deadlines are the first Wednesday in March and in September. (3) **Jack's Grant** is a single, annual Memorial Award (grant) which addresses the needs of adoptable/adopted children and their families. Proposals are due first Wednesday in September. Prospective applicants may telephone the Foundation to discuss the feasibility of submitting a request. Grant requests should be submitted in a preliminary one- or two-page Letter of Intent which describes, in summary form, the proposed project's purpose, beneficiaries, activities, total costs, a specific amount requested, and the amounts/sources of other revenue (actual and potential). If the proposed project fits the Foundation's mission/requirements, the Foundations' formal application form will be provided. Completed applications must be submitted by the appropriate deadline (see above), and if the request is $10,000 or larger, a site visit will be made to the organization. The Board meets quarterly and decisions on grants are made at April and October meetings.

O+D+T Claire A. Walker, Ph.D. (Executive Director+Con) — Nancy D. Washington, Ph.D. (P+T) — Thelma Lovette Morris (VP+T) — Kelly J. Kelleher, M.D., M.P.H. (S+T) — Lloyd F. Stamy, Jr. (F+T) — Randolph W. Brockington (T) — Jane C. Burger (T) — Carolyn Duronio (T) — Jesse W. Fife, Jr. (T) — David B. Hartmann, M.D. (T) — Claudia L. Hussein (T) — Steven W. Jewell, M.D. (T) — Rev. Ronald Edward Peters (T) — Karen VanderVen, Ph.D. (T)

SW-284 Pittsburgh Foundation, The
30th Floor
One PPG Place
Pittsburgh 15222   (Allegheny County)
AMV $519,616,368   **FYE** 12-01   (**Gifts Received** $22,339,157)

MI-12-13-14-15-16-17-18-19-20-22-25-29-33
39-41-42-44-49-51-52-53-54-55-56-84-85
Phone 412-391-5122 **FAX** 412-391-7259
EIN 25-0965466   **Year Created** 1945
1,917 **Grants totaling** $25,539,949

As a Community Foundation all discretionary giving is limited to organizations serving Pittsburgh/Allegheny County. About 220 discretionary grants from unrestricted, field-of-interest or Special Purpose funds were awarded; grants are for general operating support except as noted and some represent multiple awards. *ARTS/CULTURE & THE HUMANITIES GRANTS:* **$400,000** for the Multi-Cultural Arts Initiative. **$300,000** to Pittsburgh Opera (Artistic Excellence Project). **$225,000** to Pittsburgh Filmmakers (fundraising/artists services/education staff salaries). **$100,000** to Society for Contemporary Craft (national artist-in-residence program). **$75,000** each to Greater Pittsburgh Convention & Visitors Bureau (Marketing Partnership re African-American arts organizations), Pittsburgh Tissue Engineering Initiative (high-tech planetarium show), Quantum Theatre (Producing Director position), Sports and Exhibition Authority of Pittsburgh/Allegheny County (North Shore Riverfront Park artists' fees), and The BJWL Fund for Children's Programs (expanded arts programming). **$70,000** to Western Pa. Professionals for the Arts (Arts Management Enhancement Service). **$50,000** to Pittsburgh Chamber Music Society (The Beethoven Project), Rodef Shalom Congregation (renovate educational facility), and The Pittsburgh Foundation (research in partnership with The Heinz Endowments to create a regional cultural profile). **$40,000** to Historical Society of Western Pa. (exhibition on Western Pa. as an innovation center). **$35,000** to APT Pittsburgh (performances-exhibitions at International Sculpture Conference). **$25,000** each to Artists and Cities (survey re needs of local individual artists) and Pittsburgh Cultural Trust (Carol R. Brown Programming Fund). **$20,000** to Pittsburgh Symphony. **$15,000** each to Associated Artists of Pittsburgh (debt retirement) and Urban League of Pittsburgh (Freedom Corner monument). **$13,600** to Pittsburgh Dance Alloy. **$12,614** to Mon Yough Riverfront Entertainment & Cultural Council. **$11,000** to Gateway to the Arts. **$10,000-$10,500** each to Afrika Wetu (Arts for Aids in Africa awareness program), Associated Artists of Pittsburgh, Bach Choir of Pittsburgh, Calliope/Pittsburgh Folk Music Society, Chatham Baroque (office relocation/rehearsal space), Jewish Community Center of Greater Pittsburgh (American Jewish Museum exhibition),Kenneth Love (documentary re W, Eugene Smith), Mendelssohn Choir of Pittsburgh, Pittsburgh International Children's Theater, Pittsburgh Opera Theater, Pittsburgh Youth Symphony Orchestra, Silver Eye Center for Photography, Society for Contemporary Craft, Umoja African Arts Company (African Voyage program), U. of Pittsburgh Kuntu Repertory Theatre (commissioned work). **$8,000-$9,800** to Chatham Baroque, Children's Festival Chorus, Pittsburgh Concert Chorale, Pittsburgh Chamber Music Society, Pittsburgh New Music Ensemble, Renaissance & Baroque Society of Pittsburgh, Three Rivers Young Peoples Orchestras, and XPRESSIONS Contemporary Dance Company (artist in residency/performance). **$7,000-$7,600** each to Attack Theatre (artist fees/production costs), Bach Choir of Pittsburgh (new commissioned pieces), David Stock (commissioned orchestral piece), Faces of Pittsburgh (Faces of Pittsburgh Project), Photo Antiquities Museum of Photographic History (exhibition), Pittsburgh Cultural Trust (benefit performance), Pittsburgh Irish & Classical Theatre, Renaissance City Wind Music Society, Shona Sharif African Dance & Drum Ensemble (production), Squonk Opera (create-produce original production), Srishti Dances of India (concert), and Tuesday Musical Club (opera premiere). **$6,000-$6,550** each to East Liberty Grassroots Theatre Project (six performances), Graham Shearing (book on Pittsburgh's history of public art), Junction Dance Theatre (Face Off Project), Laboratory Dance Company (Spring/Summer Series), Mary Miller Dance Company (dance creation-presentation), McKeesport Symphony Society (musicians' fees), National Black Programming Consortium (Film-Video Festival), Nego Gato (production), and U. of Pittsburgh Music on the Edge (concert). **$5,000** each to Brew House Assn. (Puppet Festival artists' fees), Bulgarian-Macedonian National Educational & Cultural Center (film showing at Jewish Community Center), Pittsburgh Theological Seminary (special event), SPIC MACAY Carnegie Mellon U. (festival of contemporary Indian cinema), and Western Pa. Model Railroad Museum (historically accurate scenery backdrop). **$4,000** each to David Keberle (collaborative performance installation with sculptor), Latin American Cultural Union (Latino culture project in Pittsburgh schools), Pittsburgh Chamber Music Project (two concerts), and Renaissance CityChoir (two African/African-American music concerts). **$3,000** each to Barbara Bernstein (Brew House installation) and Dean Novotny (new plays at City Theatre's Hamburg Partner Program). ***ECONOMIC/COMMUNITY DEVELOPMENT & THE ENVIRONMENT GRANTS:*** **$250,000** to Pittsburgh Partnership for Neighborhood Development (community-based planning and development by CDC's). **$249,471** to YouthWorks (create/coordinate summer/year-round part-time jobs for African American youth). **$192,500** to Manchester Bidwell Corp. (Information Technology Manager position). **$175,000** each to Coro Center for Civic Leadership (Community Problem Solving Fellowship for African-American college students) and Mon Valley Initiative (develop affordable housing). **$170,000** to Local Initiatives Support Corporation (community development corporation investment in East Liberty commercial projects). **$160,000** to Pittsburgh Gateways Corporation (expand capacity to launch new business ventures). **$150,000** to Pa. Low-Income Housing Corp. (resident empowerment/affordable housing revitalization project in East Liberty). **$140,000** to Allegheny Conference on Community Development (Agenda Development Fund). **$135,000** to Pittsburgh Interfaith Impact Network (start up funding for faith-based organizations). **$135,000** to PowerLink, Inc (executive director position). **$113,500** to Pittsburgh Tissue Engineering Initiative, Inc (develop business support system for new businesses). **$110,000** to Technology Development & Education Corporation (EnterPrize program to grow new technology businesses). **$98,700-$100,000** each to Allegheny Conference on Community Development (develop regional biotechnology strategy), Christmas in April/Pittsburgh (expanded service capacity), Citizens East Community Development Federal Credit Union (start up/marketing support), Nazareth Housing Services/Mount Nazareth Center (expanded Senior Homeowner Assistance Program), Pa. Economy League, Inc (campaign re the Commonwealth's future economic competitiveness), Pittsburgh Downtown Partnership (implement Construction Mitigation Strategic Communications Plan), Pittsburgh Regional Alliance (regional marketing program toward businesses), and Western Pa. Humane Society (strengthen volunteer program). **$95,000** to Hosanna Industries (expanded home rehabilitation in East End). **$74,400-$75,000** each to Borough of Thornburg (acquire open space), The Community Builders (develop revitalization/supportive services master plan), Family Services of Western Pa. (loan loss reserve fund for working poor families), Minority Enterprise Corporation (business programs creation, etc.), Pittsburgh Mediation Center (Assistant Director position), and Rosedale Block Cluster (program site manager/developer position). **$60,000** each to Pa. Economy League, Inc (establish network of career development programs to help low-income entry-level workers) and to Vincentian de Marillac (master plan to develop a continuum of housing and long-term care services). **$56,619** to Chartiers Nature Conservancy (land acquisition). **$55,000** to East Liberty Development (support community-based predevelopment East End activities). **$50,000** each to Community Human Services Corp. (Wilkinsburg Intra-Community Network re CyberCafe) and Scott Conservancy (acquire Kane Woods).**$43,500** to Community Design Center of Pittsburgh (develop in-house staff/board fundraising-marketing capacity). **$40,274** to Central Northside Neighborhood Council (consultant re community planning process). **$35,000** each to Allegheny County Airport Authority (cultural sensitivity/regional awareness training for airport employees) and Highland Park Community Development Corp. (develop community plan). **$30,000** each to Animal Rescue League of Western Pa. (enhance sustainability of Pa. Wildlife Center) and Pittsburgh Film Office (measure the industry's economic impact on SW Pa.) **$25,000** to The UltraViolet Loop Advisory Team (project consultants). **$10,000** each to Partners for Livable Communities (program support) and Partners for Livable Communities (Pittsburgh presence on national website). **$8,500** to Urban League of Pittsburgh, Inc (benefit event). **$6,400** to Pittsburgh Partnership for Neighborhood Development (exploratory technology skill study in the Hill District/Oakland). **$4,800-$5,000** each to Anti-Defamation League (awareness campaign re hate-related activities), National Congress for Community Economic Development (Annual Conference), and Phipps Conservatory & Botanical Gardens (transition assistance for merger with Pittsburgh Garden Place). **$3,790** to Travelers Aid Society of Pittsburgh (partnership with United Way re transportation needs assessment). **$3,000** to City of Pittsburgh (planning for Central Business District redevelopment). **$1,500** to League of Women Voters of GreaterPittsburgh (workshop on running for office). ***EDUCATION GRANTS:*** **$300,000** each to Fair Learning Opportunities for All Children Pa. (campaign re comprehensive school reform/financing) and Pa. Economy League (launch Achieving Academic Success in Western Pa. Empowerment School Districts program). **$242,648** to Pittsburgh Public Schools (student participation in Keys2Work program). **$209,923** to Pittsburgh Public Schools (Creative & Performing Arts High School's Strategic Vision Project). **$200,000** to Pittsburgh Public Schools (implement three-year K-5 Literacy Plus Initiative). **$196,644** to Allegheny CountyLibrary Assn. (pilot the Virtual Student Gateway of eiNetwork). **$196,000** to The Pittsburgh Teachers Institute (assist teachers in revising the District's science/math curricula). **$194,950** to Hosanna House (expand School-Based Services). **$166,500** to Pa. Economy League (strategic revisioning plan re Duquesne City School District into the state's first public Independent School). **$160,000** to Sewickley Community Center (restart after school/summer programs). **$123,504** to Beginning with Books (new executive director). **$100,000** to Education Policy and Leadership Center (policy work on statewide educational reforms re Allegheny County public school districts). **$75,000** to Teacher Excellence Foundation (transition the Academy of Teachers to independent self-sustaining professional development service). **$50,000** to Plum Borough Community Library (children's programming). **$30,690** to Baldwin-Whitehall School District (summer reading-writing program). **$25,000** to Allegheny Intermediate Unit (attract/train pool of substitute teachers). **$10,000** to U. of Pittsburgh/School of Law (scholarships). **$8,356** to Allegheny County Library Assn. (eiNetwork/Duquesne City School District). **$5,000** to U. of Pittsburgh/School of Social Work (activities re Dean Epperson celebration). **$3,500** to Kane Public School & Library (update AV materials). Other smaller grants/contributions. ***FAMILIES, CHILDREN & YOUTH GRANTS:*** **$872,062** for Fund for Children's Programs (a joint initiative of The Pittsburgh Foundation with Allegheny County Dept. of Human Services and the Allegheny County Housing Authority in cooperation with the city's Housing Authority). **$150,000** to Womanspace East, Inc (transitional housing/support services for homeless women/children). **$145,000** to Allegheny County Family Support Policy Board (establish needs funds in Family Support Centers). **$100,000** to United Jewish Federation of Greater Pittsburgh (Teen Counselor position). **$58,500** to Vietnam Veterans Leadership Program of Western Pa. (match HUD grant providing permanent housing/services to disabled homeless male veterans and children). **$54,000** to Jewish Family & Children's Service (basic needs of children). **$28,600** to Program to Aid Citizen Enterprise (design mentoring consultation model for community-based organizations). **$15,000** to Planned Parenthood of Western Pa. (expanded professional training services for social service agencies). **$12,711** to Catholic Charities (winter fuel assistance). **$10,000** to UPMC Health System (initiate Tangible Aid Fund for GAPS II). **$9,250** to Womanspace East (holiday baskets). **$8,000** to Greene County United Way (prenatal-early childhood services). **$7,441** each, all for winter fuel assistance, to East Liberty Presbyterian Church, Highlands Community Action Committee, Northern Area Multi-ServiceCenter, Rankin Christian Center, Salvation Army, and Society of St. Vincent de Paul. Other smaller contributions. ***HEALTH & SPECIAL NEEDS POPULATIONS:*** **$223,981** to St. Margaret Foundation (Community Oriented Primary Care program). **$200,000** to U. of Pittsburgh/Graduate School of Public Health (Minority Health Disparities Scholars Initiative). **$189,450** to Faith-Based Health Initiative of Greater Pittsburgh (start up multi-community-based project to reduce health disparities). **$179,000** to Red Cross/SW Pa. (improve local disaster-related needs of special needs populations). **$155,000** to Dollar Energy Fund (new Management Information System administrator position). **$148,863** to Metro Family Practice (administrative/service positions for increased services). **$137,000** to Allegheny County Dept. of Human Services (establish Mental Health Court providing services to incarcerated mentally ill prisoners). **$125,000** to U. of Pittsburgh/Graduate School of Public Health (Countdown to 2010 Campaign). **$122,771** to Health Agency Coalition (transition costs of relocating four health service agencies). **$117,281** to Domestic Abuse Counseling Center (develop/implement service model to reduce disparities in outcomes among African-American males). **$100,000** each to Advisory Board on Autism & Related Disorders (strengthen organizational capacity), United Way of Allegheny County (assist homeowners impacted by tax reassessments). **$98,565** to Golden Triangle Radio Information Center (improve organizational capacity). **$76,767** to Pittsburgh Vision Services (in-home training). **$75,000** to Emmaus Community of Pittsburgh (respite center for persons with MR/developmental disabilities). **$70,000** each to Consumer Health Coalition (start up of Self-Directed Agenda for System Improvement for Seniors) and North Hills Community Outreach (expanded services to North Boroughs). **$69,822** to East Liberty Family Health Care Center (dental care for the underserved). **$64,992** to East Side Community Collaborative Initiative for Families (implement Transitional Care for Families project). **$30,008** to East Side Community Collaborative Initiative for Families (transitional care project). **$9,250** to Women's Center & Shelter of Greater Pittsburgh (Adopt-a-Family program). **$7,721** to Child's Way (develop/provide vision-related staff training). **$5,000** to Leukemia Society of America/Western Pa. Branch. **$3,000** to Mental Health Assn. of Allegheny County (focus group study on treatment pathways for depressed African Americans). **$2,719** to Domestic Abuse Counseling Center (develop a service model). **$1,500** to U. of Pittsburgh Graduate School of Public Health (Minority Health Leadership Summit). ■**PUBLICATIONS:** Annual Report with policy guidelines and application guidelines ■**WEBSITE:** www.pittsburghfoundation.org ■**E-MAIL:** email@pghfdn.org ■**APPLICATION POLICIES & PROCEDURES:** The Foundation reports that only Allegheny County organizations (or those with a significant service population in Allegheny County) are eligible to apply for grants from discretionary/unrestricted funds which are awarded in five programmatic areas (1) Families, Children and Youth—to strengthen the family unit and help children grow and develop; (2) Economic & Community Development and the Environment—to increase employment, build strong neighborhoods, and promote civic engagement by all segments of the population; (3) Education—to ensure that all children are achieving at least at grade level and, upon completion of high school, are prepared for post-secondary education and/or a career; (4) Arts & Culture and the Humanities—to strengthen the organizational stability of small, mid-sized, and large arts organizations and make the arts accessible to low-income populations; and (5) Health and Special Needs Populations—to maximize functioning of special needs populations in mainstream society and improve health outcomes for all. Within these categories, from unrestricted funds, there is particular interest in proposals that address the critical issues of Persistent Poverty, Economic Vitality of the Region, Racism, and Quality of Life. Preference is given to projects/programs dealing with organizational capacity building, systematic change; improved service delivery, planning and program development, and community building. No grants are awarded (from unrestricted funds) to individuals, nor generally is support given for operating costs, sectarian purposes, private and parochial schools, hospitals, research, endowments, capital costs, equipment, special events,conferences, scholarships, internships, or awards. Prospective applicants are encouraged first to submit a Letter of Inquiry that includes a brief statement about the organization, describes the proposed project and its intended results, and provides a general idea of project costs; deadlines for Letters of Inquiry are February 1st, May 1st, August 1st, and November 1st. Program officers will review each request and contact the organization if additional information (including a proposal) is required. Proposals which follow the Grantmakers of Western Pa. Common Grant Application Format are accepted, but applicants are still encouraged to submit an initial Letter of Inquiry. Grant decisions are based on the quality of planning, the project's potential impact, the financial and management strengths of the organization, the amount of funding requested, and other relevant factors. Grants are awarded at Board meetings in March, June, September and December, and applicants are notified promptly after the meetings. — **Note:** From time to time, the Foundation undertakes special grant initiatives to address critical issues, such as the Fund for Children's Programs, Multi-Cultural Arts Initiative (in cooperation with the Howard Heinz Endowment), and the Medial Research Initiative); the Foundation issues Requests for Proposals for these initiatives.

O+D+T William E. Trueheart, Jr., Ed.D. (P+CEO+Con) — James S. Broadhurst (C+D) — Benjamin R. Fisher, Jr. (VC+D) — Alvin Rogal (S+D) — Aaron A. Walton (F+D) — Estelle F. Comay (AS+D) — Robert P. Bozzone (D) — JoAnne E. Burley (D) — Joseph L. Calihan (D) — Douglas D. Danforth (D) — George A. Davidson (D) — Arthur J. Edmunds (D) — Sherin H. Knowles (D) — David M. Matter (D) — Mary Lou McLaughlin (D) — Samuel Y. Stroh (D) — Nancy D. Washington (D)

SW-285   Platt (Mary Jane & Joseph P., Jr.) Family Foundation
224 Thorn Street
Sewickley   15143   (Allegheny County)
AMV $3,995,219   **FYE** 12-00   **(Gifts Received** $367,911)

MI-11-13-14-22-32-42-54-55-61-71
Phone 412-741-4120 **FAX** None
EIN 25-1815288   **Year Created** 1998
24 **Grants totaling** $187,348

Mostly local giving; all grants are for general purposes. High grant of **$54,500** to Girls Hope of Pittsburgh. **$30,000** to Boys Hope/Girls Hope [Baden]. **$23,298** to Legionnaires of Christ. **$15,000** to Carnegie Mellon U. **$10,500** to Sisters of St. Joseph. **$10,000** to United Way of SW Pa. **$3,500** to Watson Institute. **$2,500** to FAME/Foundation for Advancement of Minorities through Education. **$1,000** each to Leukemia & Lymphoma Society, Riverfront Park, and Salvation Army/Sewickley. **$600** to Pittsburgh Cultural Trust. Other local contributions **$250-$500** for similar purposes. **Out-of-state** giving includes **$20,000** to St. Louis U. Heights [MO]; **$5,000** to Mill Reef Fund [NY]; and **$1,500** to Lower East Side Tenement Museum [NY]. ■ **PUBLICATIONS:** None. ■ **WEBSITE:** None ■ **E-MAIL:** None ■ **APPLICATION POLICIES & PROCEDURES:** Information not available.

O+D+T Mary Jane Platt (P+Donor+Con) — Joseph P. Platt, Jr. (S+Donor)

SW-286   PNC Advisors Charitable Trust Committee
c/o PNC Advisors, M.S. P2-PTPP-25-1
Two PNC Plaza, 620 Liberty Ave., 25th Floor
Pittsburgh   15222   (Allegheny County)

MI-Refer to individual Trusts/Foundations

Phone 412-762-7076 **FAX** 412-705-1043

The Charitable Trust Committee of PNC Advisors is the decision-making group which largely controls discretionary giving by about two dozen foundations/trusts with aggregated assets of about **$55.6** million. In 2000 a total of **$2.7** million in grants from these trusts/foundations was awarded for Social Services, Education, Health, Religion, and The Arts. Of these trusts/foundations, the following are individually profiled in the directory: Joella P. Bane Trust, Margaret J. Biddle Charitable Trust, Otis H. Childs Trust, J.B. Finley Charitable Trust, Jane & Dan Gray Charitable Trust, W. Clark Hagan Trust, Wallace P. Hough Charitable Trust, Lloyd Foundation, J. Leon Lockard Charitable Trust, James F. McCandless Charitable Trust, Virginia A. McKee Poor Fund, Amelia Miles Foundation, W.H. & Althea A. Remmel Foundation, Ovid D. Robinson Charitable Trust, Clarence & Grace Rowell Memorial Fund, Glen Sample, Jr. M.D. Memorial Fund, Elizabeth Shiras Charitable Trust, John C. Williams Charitable Trust, and other smaller trusts. ■ **PUBLICATIONS:** Periodic reports (listing grantees but not amounts) with statement of objectives and application procedures; Charitable Trust Grant Application ■ **WEBSITE:** None ■ **E-MAIL:** foundations@pnc.com ■ **APPLICATION POLICIES & PROCEDURES:** *Requests for grants in any of the areas of giving supported by these trusts/foundations must be directed to the PNC Advisors Charitable Trust Committee, not to a specific Trust/Foundation.* The Charitable Trust Committee reports the following criteria are followed in reviewing grant requests: (1) The requesting organization must be a qualified charity classified under current IRS regulations whose activities emphasize one of the following: art, education, health, religion, social services, children, elderly, or alcoholism cure/prevention. (2) Support is awarded only for projects, matching grants, seed money, or capital expenditures; multiyear grants are not considered. In addition, positive consideration is given to requests that are longer in duration, collaborative in nature, trackable in administration, and measurable in impact. Prospective applicants first must request a Charitable Trust Grant Application which details the required information and documentation. Grant applications may be submitted at any time; decisions on grants are made at quarterly Committee meetings.

O+D+T Charitable Trust Committee members (all PNC Advisors employees): Mia Hallett Bernard (V.P.+Con) — Arlene Yocum (Executive V.P., Managing Executive) — Jennifer Miller (V.P., Managing Director of Administrative Services) — Sharon Gertz (Senior V.P., Director, Trust & Planning) — Diane Blanton (Director, Charitable & Endowment Management) — Martha Zatezalo, Esq. (Senior Counsel)

SW-287   PNC Foundation
c/o PNC Financial Services Group, M.S. P2-PTPP-25-1
Two PNC Plaza, 620 Liberty Ave., 25th Floor
Pittsburgh   15222   (Allegheny County)
AMV $32,129,985   **FYE** 12-00   **(Gifts Received** $0)

MI-11-12-13-14-15-17-24-25-29-31-32-35-41
42-44-49-51-52-54-55-56-57-83-85-88
Phone 412-762-7076 **FAX** 412-705-1043
EIN 25-1202255   **Year Created** 1970
1300+ **Grants totaling** $10,440,079

Giving mostly to PNC's trading areas throughout Pa. and six other states; grants awarded outside the SW Pa. Region are designated by region, e.g. [CP], [NE], etc.) **HEALTH/HUMAN SERVICES GRANTS**: **$606,415** to United Way of SW Pa. **$398,000** to United Way of SE Pa. [SE]. **$70,000** each to United Way of Lackawanna County [NE] and United Way of Wyoming Valley [NE]. **$50,000** each to Children's Hospital of Pittsburgh and People for People [SE]. **$41,930** to Dr. Gertrude Barber Center [NW]. **$34,333-$35,000** each to Greater Pittsburgh Community Food Bank, Salvation Army, and United Way of the Capital Region [CP]. **$30,000** to People's Emergency Center [SE]. **$20,650** to Somerset Community Hospital. **$20,000** each to Project H.O.M.E. [SE], United Communities-SE Philadelphia [SE], and Wilkes-Barre Family YMCA [NE]. **$17,000-$18,500** each to Boy

Scouts/Greater Pittsburgh Council, Grand View Health Foundation [SE], and United Fund of Warren County [NW]. **$15,000** each to Family House, Fox Chase Cancer Center [SE], Friends' Rehabilitation Program [SE], Girl Scouts of SE Pa., Nueva Esperanza [SE], St. Martin Center [NW], and United Way of the Greater Lehigh Valley [NE]. **$10,000-$12,000** each to Bethlehem Haven, Boy Scouts/National Council [SE], Centre County United Way [CP], CACLV/Community Action Committee of the Lehigh Valley [NE], Holy Family Institute, OASIS, United Way of Greater Hazleton [NE], United Way of Indiana County, United Way of Westmoreland County, and Women's Center & Shelter of Greater Pittsburgh. **$9,600** to YWCA of Greater Pittsburgh. **$6,000-$8,000** each to Asbury Heights, Big Brothers Big Sisters of Bucks County [SE], City Mission of the Evangelical Churches of Erie [NW], Congreso de Latinos Unidos [SE], Corry Regional Health System [NW], Delaware Valley Child Care Council [SE], Geisinger Foundation [NE], Hamot Health Foundation [NW], Mental Health Assn. of Butler County, Philadelphia Cares [SE], St. Joseph's Center [NE], United Way of Butler County, and United Way of Western Crawford County [NW]. **$4,500-$5,000** each to ACLAMO/Philadelphia [SE], Case Management Support Services [NW], Catholic Youth Center [NE], East LibertyFamily   Health Care Center, Erie Home for Children & Adults [NW], Harrisburg Area YMCA [CP], Penn Lakes Girl Scout Council [NW], Police Athletic League of Philadelphia [SE], Rouse Home Contributions Fund [NW], St. Barnabas Health System, United Way of Corry Area [NW], Urban Bridges at St. Gabriel's [SE], Volunteers of America of Pa. [NE], and YMCA of Philadelphia & Vicinity [SE]. **$2,000-$3,500** each to Boy Scouts/Bucks County [SE]. Crispus Attucks Community Center [CP], Drueding Center/Project Rainbow [SE], Episcopal Community Services [SE], Glade Run Foundation, Greater Philadelphia Food Bank [SE], Hazleton YMCA/YWCA [NE], House of Umoja [SE], Human Services Center Corp., Lycoming County United Way [CP], Make-A-Wish Foundation of Western Pa., Meals on Wheels of NE Pa., Metropolitan Career Center [SE], Northeast Regional Cancer Institute [NE], Rankin Christian Center, Red Cross [NE], Red Cross [SE], Sharon Regional Health System [NW], Surrey Services for Seniors [SE], Titusville Area United Way [NW], United Way of Columbia County [NE], YWCA of Germantown [SE], and YWCA of Greater Harrisburg [CP]. Other smaller grants/contributions for similar purposes. ***ARTS/CULTURAL GRANTS***: **$700,000** to Pa. Horticultural Society [SE]. **$385,000** to Carnegie Museums of Pittsburgh. **$110,000** to WHYY [SE]. **$75,000** to Philadelphia Orchestra [SE]. **$65,000** to Pittsburgh Symphony. **$60,000** to Regional Performing Arts Center [SE]. **$45,000** each to Civic Light Opera, F.M. Kirby Center for the Performing Arts [NE], and Pittsburgh Public Theater. **$42,500** to Pittsburgh Ballet Theatre. **$35,000** to River City Brass Band. **$20,000-$22,500** each to Franklin Institute, Please Touch Museum, Scranton Cultural Center [NE], Settlement Music School [SE], WITF-TV/FM [CP], and WQED. **$19,000** to Whitaker Center for Science & The Arts [CP]. **$17,500** to Philadelphia Museum of Art [SE]. **$15,000** each to Erie Area Fund for the Arts [NW]. **$12,000-$12,500** each to Allied Arts Fund [CP] and Fund for the Water Works [SE]. **$10,000** each to National Civil War Museum [CP], Philadelphia Zoo [SE], Pittsburgh Children's Museum, Strand-Capitol Performing Arts Center [CP], Village of Arts & Sciences [SE], and Warner Theatre Preservation Trust [NW]. **$7,000-$7,500** each to Academy of Natural Sciences [SE], American Ballet Competition [SE], and Laurel Arts. **$5,000** each to Academy of Community Music [SE], African American Museum in Philadelphia [SE], Community Design Center, Community Theater Project Corp., Greater Philadelphia Cultural Alliance [SE], Mann Music Center [SE], Pittsburgh Center for the Arts, Pittsburgh Cultural Trust, Pittsburgh Zoo, andTheatre Harrisburg [CP]. **$4,000** to Curtis Institute of Music [SE]. **$2,000-$3,500** each to Abington Art Center [SE], Annenberg Center, Astral Artistic Services [SE]. Children's Festival Chorus, Choral Arts Society of Philadelphia [SE], Clarion U., College Misericordia, Community Arts Center [SE], The Corporate Collection, Cranberry Historical Society, Cultural Alliance of York County [CP], Everhart Museum [NE], New Sounds Music, Inc. [SE], Philadelphia Art Alliance [SE], Philadelphia Volunteer Lawyers for the Arts [SE], Philadelphia Young Playwrights Program [SE], Scranton Community Concerts [NE], and Sylvan Opera [SE]. Other smaller grants/contributions for similar purposes. ***EDUCATION-LIBRARY GRANTS***: **$541,000** to U. of Pittsburgh. **$400,000** to Penn State U. [CP] **$100,000** to Duquesne U. **$60,000** to Carnegie Mellon U. **$57,500** to Seton Hill College. **$35,000** to U. of Scranton [NE]. **$30,000** to Free Library of Philadelphia [SE]. **$25,000** each to Robert Morris College and Widener U. [SE]. **$20,000** each to Butler County Community College, Immaculata College [SE], Junior Achievement of the Delaware Valley [SE], and Marywood College [NE]. **$18,000** to NEED/Negro Emergency Educational Drive. **$15,000-$15,209** each to Community Country Day School [NW] and Gwynedd Mercy College [SE]. **$12,000** to Johnston Technical Institute [NE]. **$10,000** each to Arcadia U. [SE], Cardinal Wright Regional School, Delaware County Community College [SE], Keystone College [NE], Muhlenberg College [NE], Temple U. [SE], and U. of Pittsburgh/Katz School of Business. **$9,000** to Carlow College. **$7,500** each to PhAME/Philadelphia Area Accelerated Manufacturing Education [SE] and U. of Pa. [SE]. **$6,000** to Pittston Memorial Library [NE]. **$5,000** each to Cathedral Prep Academic Excellence Fund [NW], Cranberry Public Library, FAME/Fund for the Advancement of Minority Education, Lake Erie College of Osteopathic Medicine [NW], and United Negro College Fund [CP]. **$4,000** to Junior Achievement of SW Pa. **$2,000-$3,000** each to Cedar Crest College [NE], Gannon U. [NW], Junior Achievement of NE Pa., Mercyhurst College [NW], Osterhout Free Library [NE], Pace School, United Negro College Fund [SE], and Wilkes U. [NE]. Other smaller grants/contributions for similar purposes. ***CIVIC, COMMUNITY DEVELOPMENT & HOUSING GRANTS***: **$225,000** to Greater Philadelphia First Corp. [SE]. **$85,000** to Acorn Housing Corp. [SE]. **$70,00** each to Jewish Federation of Greater Philadelphia [SE] and Pittsburgh Partnership for Neighborhood Development. **$35,000** each to Dignity Housing [SE], Neighborhood Housing Services, and Pittsburgh Community Reinvestment Group. **$30,000** to Allegheny West Foundation [SE]. **$25,000-$27,000** each to Committee for Economic Growth [NE], Greater Philadelphia Urban Affairs Coalition [SE], Local Initiatives Support Corp., [SE], Mon Valley Initiative, Mt. Airy USA [SE], Minority Enterprise Corp., and National Flag Foundation. **$20,000** each to Housing Partnership of Chester County [SE] and University City District [SE]. **$18,000** to Can Do Community Foundation [Luzerne County]. **$16,000** to Friendship Development Associates. **$15,000** each to Greater Germantown Housing Development Corp. [SE], Urban League of Pittsburgh, and Women's Community Revitalization Project [SE]. **$12,500** each to Bloomfield-Garfield Corp. and Northside Leadership Conference. **$11,000** to Philadelphia Assn. of Community Development Corporations [SE]. **$10,000** each to Community Ventures [SE], The Enterprise Center [SE], Garfield Jubilee Associates, Leadership Harrisburg Area [CP], Pa. Low-Income Housing Corp. SE], Philadelphia Police Foundation [SE], Philadelphians Concerned About Housing [SE], Regional Housing Legal Services [SE], Spring Garden Neighborhood Council, and Wesbury United Methodist Community [NW]. **$7,000-$8,000** each to Executive Service Corps of Western Pa., Greater Philadelphia Chamber of Commerce Regional Foundation [SE], Partnership Community Development Corp. [SE], and Philadelphia Neighborhood Housing Services [SE]. **$3,800-$5,000** each to Campus Boulevard Corp. [SE], Chester Community Improvement Project [SE], Community Technical Assistance Center, Delaware Valley Habitat for Humanity [SE], East Liberty Development, Inc., Energy Coordinating Agency of Philadelphia [SE], Harrisburg Fair Housing Council [CP], Harrisburg Parks Partnership [CP], Homeownership Counseling Assn. of the Delaware Valley [SE], Horticultural Society of Western Pa., Housing Assn. & Development Corp. [NE], Housing Opportunities, Inc., International Institute of Erie [NW], Lackawanna Neighbors [NE], Mon Valley Progress Council, Neighborhood Housing of Scranton [NE], New Kensington Community Development Corp. [SE], Operation Better Block, Philadelphia Commercial Development Corp. [SE], Philadelphia Chinatown Development Corp. [SE], Sisters of St. Joseph of NW Pa., Susquehanna Housing Initiatives [CP], Urban Erie Community Development Corp. [NW], Urban League of Metropolitan Harrisburg [CP], West Pittsburgh Partnership for Regional Development, and Westmoreland Economic Development Corp. **$2,000-$3,500** each to 21st Century League [SE], Allentown Neighborhood Housing [NE], Alliance for Building Community [NE], ACES/Americans for Competitive Enterprise System [NW], ASSETS Lancaster [CP], Benedictine Sisters of Erie [NW], Borough of Gettysburg [CP], Borough of Oakmont, Central Germantown Council [SE], Chester County Community Foundation [SE], Commission on Economic Opportunity [NE], Committee of Seventy [SE], Community Design Collaborative of AIA [SE], Community Foundation of Westmoreland County, Consumer Credit Counseling Service of NE Pa., County Correction Gospel Mission [SE], Cumberland Valley Habitat for Humanity [CP], Freedom Unlimited, Hispanic Assn. of Contractors & Enterprises [SE], Holy Cross Neighborhood Development, Hurricane Island Outward Bound School [SE], Leadership Wilkes-Barre [NE], Neighbor to Neighbor Community Development Corp. [SE], Philadelphia Council for Community Advancement [SE], Pittsburgh Housing Development Corp., Pittsburgh Leadership Foundation, Pittsburgh Project, Pittsburgh Tissue Engineering Initiative, Scranton-Lackawanna Jewish Federation [NE], South Philadelphia Homes, Inc. [SE], Spanish American Civic Assn. [CP], Technical Assistants [SE], Tri-County Habitat for Humanity [CP], Tri-County Housing Development Corp. [CP], United Jewish Federation of Greater Pittsburgh, Urban Development Authority of Pittsburgh, Women's Business Development Center [SE], and World Affairs Council of Pittsburgh. Other smaller grants/contributions for similar purposes. **OUT-OF-STATE** grants are awarded in for similar purposes in corporate operating locations in DE, IN, NJ, OH, and KY. Also, over 700 matching gifts were made to nonprofit organizations in corporate operating locations and elsewhere. ■**PUBLICATIONS:** Annual Report (selected grants listed, not amounts) ■**WEBSITE:** www.pnc.com/aboutus/pncfoundation.html ■**E-MAIL:** foundations@pnc.com ■**APPLICATION POLICIES & PROCEDURES:** The Foundation reports that giving focuses on the Bank's trading areas in PA, DE, IN, NJ, OH, and KY with an emphasis on organizations/programs which develop or strengthen the economic vitality of these areas, especially education-related activities, youth development, and artistic, cultural, and civic endeavors. Most grants are for operating support, capital improvements, special projects, or employee matching gifts for all types of nonprofit organizations ($2,500 maximum/employee/institution/year). No grants are awarded to organizations that discriminate by race, color, creed, gender, or national origin; religious organizations except for nonsectarian activities; loans or grants to individuals; conferences/seminars; tickets/goodwill ads; or in areas where PNC does not have a meaningful presence. Grant requests may be submitted at any time in a full proposal which includes the following: **(1) Cover Letter-Summary** (1 page only): name, address and e-mail address of the organization's contact person, a brief description the proposed project/program with the requested funding specified and total cost of the project/program. **(2) Proposal Elements**: (a) brief description of the organization and its purpose; (b) statement of the problem or need to be addressed; (c) description of the specific project/program that is the focus of the request, including number of people to be served, recruitment/outreach, management structure, etc.; (c) statement of expected accomplishments and method for evaluating results; (d) a board-approved project budget; (e) project/program schedule, including projected budget; (f) plans to sustain the project/program; and (g) the organization's track record of working with community organizations and civic leadership. (3) **Attachments**: (a) list of board of directors, identified by occupation or organization; (b) a board-approved organization budget for the current year; (c) the fundraising plan for the proposed project/program; (d) an audited financial statement for the previous year; (e) organizational brochures, pamphlets or other descriptive material (if available); (f) IRS tax-exempt 501(c)(3) status documentation; (g) a list of recent contributions with amounts; (h) resumes of key staff members; and (i) a strategic or long-range plan for the organization. If the grant request is for $1,000 or less, the following documentation need not be submitted: (2) e, f, and g; and (3) g, h, and i. — NOTE: The PNC Foundation has four Local Distribution Committees in Pa. (outside Pittsburgh), and prospective applicant organizations may wish to communicate with their local Committee—write to The PNC Foundation, as follows: Central Pa., P.O. Box 8874, Camp Hill 17001; Northeast Pa., 200 Penn Ave., Scranton 18503; Northwest Pa., 901 State Street, Box 8480, Erie 16553; Philadelphia Area, 1600 Market Street, 3rd Floor, Philadelphia 19103. — Formerly called PNC Bank Foundation.

O+D+T Mia Hallett Bernard (VP+Foundation Manager+Con) — Eva T. Blum (C+T) — Thomas R. Moore, Esq. (S) — Samuel R. Patterson (F) — Joseph C. Guyaux (T) — James E. Rohr (T) — Corporate donor: The PNC Financial Services Group

---

SW-288   Poise Foundation   **MI**-16
425 - 6th Ave., Suite 1060   **Phone** 412-281-4967 **FAX** None
Pittsburgh   15219   (Allegheny County)   **EIN** 25-1393426   **Year Created** 1981
AMV $4,162,297   **FYE** 12-99   (**Gifts Received** $728,698)   64 **Grants totaling** $131,723

All giving to Pittsburgh organizations which enhance the participation of African-American Pittsburghers in the city's philanthropic life; details on specific grants are unavailable. ■**PUBLICATIONS:** None ■**WEBSITE:** None ■**E-MAIL:** None ■**APPLICATION POLICIES & PROCEDURES:** Information not available.

O+D+T Benard H. Jones (P+CEO+Con) — Paul G. Patton (C) — Edward E. Guy, Jr. (VC) — Lenny R. Henry (VC) — Annette Cuffee Gillcrese (S) — Mark S. Lewis, Jr. (F) — Dale C. Perdue (Counsel) — Daisy L. Wilson (Counsel)

SW-289   Polk Foundation, Inc., The   **MI**-14-41-31-32
2000 Grant Building, 310 Grant Street   **Phone** 412-338-3466 **FAX** 412-338-3463
Pittsburgh   15219   (Allegheny County)   **EIN** 25-1113733   **Year Created** 1957
AMV $5,481,903   **FYE** 12-00   (**Gifts Received** $0)   2 **Grants totaling** $264,500

High grant of **$262,000** to Allegheny Valley School (capital campaign). **$2,500** to U. of Pittsburgh Medical Center/Shadyside (Hillman Cancer Center). — In recent years, all major giving to Allegheny Valley School. ■**PUBLICATIONS:** None ■**WEBSITE:** None ■**E-MAIL:** foundation@hillmanfo.com ■**APPLICATION POLICIES & PROCEDURES:** The Foundation reports that only organizations in SW Pa. are eligible to apply. Most grants are for building funds, equipment, or seed money. No grants awarded to/for individuals, general operating support, endowment, emergency needs, special projects, land acquisition, scholarships, publications, conferences, matching gifts, or deficit financing. Grant requests may be submitted in a letter at any time. Decisions on applications are made within four to six months; the Board of Directors meets in May and December.

O+D+T Ronald W. Wertz (Executive Director+S+Con) — Henry L. Hillman (P+D) — C.G. Grefenstette (VP+D) — Lawrence M. Wagner (F) — Patricia M. Duggan (D) — Lisa R. Johns (AF)

SW-290 Pollack Family Foundation
5735 Woodmont Street
Pittsburgh 15217   (Allegheny County)

MI-22-41-62
Phone 412-422-6737 **FAX** None
EIN 23-2938840 **Year Created** 1998

AMV $27,767   **FYE** 12-00   **(Gifts Received** $25,000)   102 **Grants totaling** $31,310

Mostly local giving; some grants comprise multiple payments. High grant of **$16,948** to Hillel Academy of Pittsburgh. **$1,903** to Congregation Poale Zedek. Multiple smaller grants/contributions for local and out-of-state Jewish charities and others. ■**PUBLICATIONS:** None ■**WEBSITE:** None ■**E-MAIL:** None ■**APPLICATION POLICIES & PROCEDURES:** Information not available.

O+D+T Dean Pollack (P+T+Donor+Con) — Chaya Pollack (S+F+T) — David Pollack (T)

SW-291 Poorbaugh (Karl W. & Mary Ann) Foundation
690 Clover Hill Road
Somerset 15501   (Somerset County)

MI-13-14-22-25-31-41-42-49-51-55-56-61-63
Phone 814-445-8597 **FAX** None
EIN 25-1647906 **Year Created** 1990

AMV $1,069,985   **FYE** 12-00   **(Gifts Received** $60,056)   20 **Grants totaling** $59,700

Mostly local giving; all grants were for general purposes. High grant of **$10,000** to Somerset Historical Society. **$5,000** each to Laurel Arts, Somerset Blind Center, and Somerset Hospital. **$3,600** to Shanksville School. **$3,000** to St. Paul's United Church of Christ. **$2,000-$2,500** each to Gristmill Productions, Penn West Foundation, Salvation Army, and Somerset County Habitat for Humanity. **$1,000-$1,500** each to Arcadia Theatre, Boy Scouts/Penns Woods Council, Jaffa Shrine Hospital Crusade, Junior Achievement, and New Day, Inc. **Out-of-state** giving includes **$6,000** to Southwest Florida Golf Charities and **$2,500** each to Laity Renewal Foundation [TX] and U. of the Incarnate Word [TX]. ■**PUBLICATIONS:** None ■**WEBSITE:** None ■**E-MAIL:** None ■**APPLICATION POLICIES & PROCEDURES:** Information not available.

O+D+T Karl W. Poorbaugh (T+Donor+Con) — Mary Ann Poorbaugh (T+Donor)

SW-292 Port Family Foundation
RD 2, Box 597
Altoona 16601   (Blair County)

MI-13-22-25-41-42-54-55-62
Phone 814-944-9491 **FAX** None
EIN 23-2777280 **Year Created** 1994

AMV $376,735   **FYE** 12-00   **(Gifts Received** $0)   31 **Grants totaling** $17,720

About half local/Pa. giving; all grants are for general purposes. High grant of **$2,660** to Camp Ramah. **$2,560** to Greater Altoona Jewish Federation. **$850** to Blair County Arts Foundation. **$500** each to Altoona Area Schools Foundation, Big Brothers/Big Sisters of Blair County, Leap-the-Dips Preservation Foundation, Mt. Aloysius College, St. Vincent DePaul Food for Families, and Southern Alleghenies Museum of Art. Other smaller local contributions. **Out-of-state** giving to MA, NY, for Jewish charities and other purposes. ■**PUBLICATIONS:** None ■**WEBSITE:** None ■**E-MAIL:** None ■**APPLICATION POLICIES & PROCEDURES:** Grant requests may be submitted in any form, preferably during June-September (deadline is October 15th); include an annual report, organizational budget, and a list of Board members. Grants are awarded at an October meeting.

O+D+T Neil M. Port (Co-T+Donor+Con) — Marilyn J. Port (Co-T+Donor) — Lawrence Port (Co-T) — Douglas Simon (Co-T) — Susan Port Simon (Co-T) — Lisa Port White [MA] (Co-T) — Malcolm White [MA] (Co-T)

SW-293 Porter (Adrienne & Milton) Charitable Foundation
c/o Fostin Capital Corp.
681 Andersen Drive, 3rd Floor
Pittsburgh 15220   (Allegheny County)

MI-12-13-35-42-52-54-84
Phone 412-928-1406 **FAX** 412-928-9635
EIN 25-6500406 **Year Created** 1996

AMV $2,297,390   **FYE** 12-00   **(Gifts Received** $0)   7 **Grants totaling** $94,260

Mostly local giving. High grants of **$25,000** each to Family House and U. of Pittsburgh/Graduate School for Public Health (payment on 1-year **$250,000** grant for Health Education). **$20,000** to U. of Pittsburgh/Center for Latin Studies. **$15,000** to Pittsburgh Symphony (payment on 5-year **$75,000** grant). **$6,750** to YMCA/Camp Kon-O-Wee. **$500** to Health Education Center. **Out-of-state** grant: **$2,000** to Fund for Children of America. — Giving in prior years to Carnegie Museums. ■**PUBLICATIONS:** None ■**WEBSITE:** None ■**E-MAIL:** None ■**APPLICATION POLICIES & PROCEDURES:** No grants awarded to individuals.

O+D+T Lee B. Foster, II (T+Con) — Donor: Estate of Milton Porter

---

SW-294 Posner Foundation of Pittsburgh
c/o Hawthorne Group, Inc.
500 Greentree Commons, 381 Mansfield Ave.
Pittsburgh 15220   (Allegheny County)

MI-11-12-13-15-22-41-42-62-85
Phone 412-928-7700 **FAX** None
EIN 25-6055022 **Year Created** 1963

AMV $16,416,630   **FYE** 12-00   **(Gifts Received** $7,500,000)   12 **Grants totaling** $169,815

Mostly local/Pa. giving. High grant of **$100,000** to United Way of SW Pa. **$25,000** to American Friends of the Union of Progressive Jews. **$10,000** to Parental Stress Center. **$5,000** each to Shadyside Academy, United Way of Allegheny County, and Winchester Thurston School. **$4,315** to Catholic Charities. **$2,500** to Three Rivers Youth. **$1,000** each to Canterbury Place and U. of Pa. **Out-of-state** grants: **$10,000** to Private Sector Initiatives Foundation [DC] and **$1,000** to Princeton U. [NJ]. ■**PUBLICATIONS:** None ■**WEBSITE:** None ■**E-MAIL:** None ■**APPLICATION POLICIES & PROCEDURES:** Grant requests may be submitted in a brief statement at any time; describe the organization's activities, how the requested funds will be used, and include an annual report, audited financial statement, and IRS tax-exempt status documentation. No grants are awarded to individuals.

O+D+T Henry Posner, Jr. (T+Donor+Con) — Helen M. Posner (T) — Henry Posner, III (T) — James T. Posner (T+Donor) — Corporate donor: Lyndhurst Associates

---

SW-295 PPG Industries Foundation
c/o PPG Industries, Inc.
One PPG Place
Pittsburgh   15272   (Allegheny County)

MI-11-12-13-14-25-31-35-41-42-44-45-49-51
52-54-55-57-71-72-83-88
Phone 412-434-2788 **FAX** 412-434-2545
EIN 25-6037790   **Year Created** 1951

AMV $24,919,606   **FYE** 12-00   (**Gifts Received** $5,179,868)   455 **Grants totaling** $4,896,746

About one-third Pa. giving, primarily to Pittsburgh and corporate locations in Allegheny, Blair, Crawford, and Cumberland counties; most grants are for general operating support except as noted. **HEALTH/HUMAN SERVICES GRANTS**: High grant of **$525,000** to United Way of SW Pa. **$45,000** to Greater Pittsburgh Community Food Bank. **$32,000** to Magee Women's Hospital/Health Foundation. **$30,000** to YMCA of Pittsburgh. **$25,000** each to Hill House Assn. and United Way of Carlisle [Cumberland County]. **$20,000** to United Way of Western Crawford County. **$18,000** to Children's Hospital of Pittsburgh. **$17,000** to United Way of Blair County. **$15,000** each to Allegheny General Hospital (mobile mammography unit), Boys & Girls Club of Western Pa., Easter Seals/Western Pa. (capital campaign), Holy Family Foundation (capital campaign), Three Rivers Center for Independent Living, and Western Pa. Caring Foundation for Children. **$12,500** to Family House. **$10,000** each to Action Housing, Inc., Bethlehem Haven, and Penn Lakes Girl Scout Council. **$6,795** to YMCA of McKeesport. **$5,000** to ARC of Crawford County. **$3,500** to Persad Center. **$2,000** to Carlisle Regional Medical Center/Medical Care Foundation [Cumberland County]. Other smaller local/Pa. grants/contributions. **EDUCATION GRANTS**: **$155,000** to U. of Pittsburgh (campaign campaign/operating support/minority engineering). **$110,000** to Carnegie Mellon U. **$50,000** each to Robert Morris College and Early Childhood Initiative/United Way of SW Pa. **$28,500** to Penn State U. (various colleges/programs). **$25,000** to Langley High School (Project Aspire). **$20,000** each to Carnegie Science Center (Regional Math/Science Fair), NEED/Negro Emergency Education Drive, and YouthWorks. **$17,500** to Junior Achievement of SW Pa. and U. of Pa. **$10,000** each to ASSET Inc., Beginning With Books, Chatham College, Extra Mile Education Foundation, and Indiana U. of Pa. **$9,000** to Pa. Foundation for Free Enterprise [Erie]. **$7,500** to Pa. Partnership for Economic Education. **$5,000** each to Carlow College (capital campaign), Edinboro U., Lehigh U., Manchester Youth Development Center, Pittsburgh Regional Center for Science Teachers, and St. Vincent College (capital campaign). **$2,500** to National Foundation for Teaching Entrepreneurship. Other smaller local/Pa. grants/contributions. **CIVIC, CULTURAL & COMMUNITY ACTIVITIES GRANTS**: **$55,000** to Pittsburgh Public Theater. **$40,000** each to Pittsburgh Cultural Trust and Pittsburgh Opera. **$33,600** to Allegheny Conference on Community Development. **$30,000** each to Carnegie Library of Pittsburgh, Carnegie Science Center, and Pittsburgh Ballet Theatre. **$25,000** to Pittsburgh Symphony. **$20,000** to Pittsburgh Zoo. **$18,000** to Pa. Economy League. **$15,250** to The Carnegie. **$14,000** to WQED-FM. **$10,000** each to City Theatre Company and Civic Light Opera. **$7,500** each to River City Brass Band and Three Rivers Arts Festival. **$5,000-$6,000** each to Cranberry Public Library, Pa. Environmental Council, Pittsburgh Children's Museum, Pittsburgh Dance Council, Pittsburgh Musical Theater, and Plum Borough Community Library (capital campaign). **$2,000-$4,000** to Engineers Society of Western Pa., French Creek Recreation Trails, Grantmakers of Western Pa., League of Women Voters of Pa., Pennsylvanians for Effective Government, Pennsylvanians for Modern Courts, Pittsburgh Arts & Lectures,. Pittsburgh Concert Chorale, Pittsburgh Council for International Visitors, ProArts, and World Affairs Council of Pittsburgh. Other smaller local/Pa. grants/contributions. **GIVE GRANTS**—grants initiated by PPG employees who volunteer at nonprofit organizations—totaled **$171,250** and were awarded to 375 organizations or institutions. MATCHING GIFTS totaling **$1.28MM** were disbursed to 1,040 organizations/institutions: colleges, universities, private secondary schools, special education schools, hospitals, and cultural organizations. OUT-OF-STATE giving for similar purposes to organizations in corporate operating locations in AL, GA. IN, KY, LA, NC, NM, MI, OH, OK, SC, TN, TX, VA, WI and other states. ■ **PUBLICATIONS:** Annual Report with statement of program policy, grant policies/guidelines, and grants of $5,000 and up ■ **WEBSITE:** http://corporate.ppg.com/PPG/Corporate/AboutUs/PPGIndustriesFoundation ■ **E-MAIL:** None ■ **APPLICATION POLICIES & PROCEDURES:** The Foundation reports that giving focuses on organizations in PPG operating locations with most grants for operating support, capital projects, or special projects. No grants are awarded to/for individuals, United Way agencies (for operating funds), endowment, lobbying/political activities, benefit event advertising/support, religious groups for sectarian purposes, organizations outside the U.S., or projects directly benefiting PPG. No requests for less than $100 will be considered. Grant requests may be submitted at any time in a full proposal with cover letter signed by the authorized executive of the organization; to be considered for the following calendar year's budget, requests must be received by the September 1st deadline. Pittsburgh-area or national organizations should write the Foundation directly; organizations located in other communities with PPG facilities should submit requests to the Foundation's local agent. The proposal should include the following: (1) organization's mission statement; (2) purpose/objectives of the grant; (3) summary of the project, amount requested, and rationale; (4) schedule of implementation; (5) description of the benefits to be achieved and the population to be served; (6) plans for evaluating and reporting results; (6) most recent audited financial report; (7) financial analysis of the proposed project; (8) name and qualifications of the person in charge of the project; (9) names/affiliations of Board members; and (10) IRS tax-exempt status documentation. Proposals following Grantmakers of Western Pa. Common Grant Application Format are accepted. Requests that cannot be honored are generally acknowledged within six weeks. Factors considered in reaching a decision include: (a) the consistency of the applicant's goals to the Foundation's priorities/available resources; (b) the organization's financial needs; (c) whether PPG previously awarded support; (d) the organization's capability/reputation; (e) funds available to the applicant from other sources; (f) the extent to which the organization's work duplicates that of others; (g) the public scope/impact of theproposal; and (h) whether other corporate foundations are interested in the organization's proposal. Site visits sometimes are made to organizations being considered for a grant. Applications are reviewed on a quarterly basis by the Screening Committee which makes decisions on grants under $5,000. On larger requests the Screening Committee makes recommendations to the Board which awards grants at June and December meetings. GIVE/Grants are initiated by PPG employees who may submit each year one application for a $250 grant to a nonprofit organization at which they have personally volunteered; each organization/institution may receive a maximum of $2,500/annum through this program. Matching gifts have a $25 minimum, $20,000 maximum/institution/employee/year.

O+D+T Jeffrey R. Gilbert (Executive Director+D+Chair, Screening Committee+Con) — Raymond W.. LeBoeuf (C+D) — Charles E. Bunch (D) — James C. Diggs (D) — William H. Hernandez (D) — Andrew Calabrese (Member, Screening Committee) — Michael A. Ludlow (Member, Screening Committee) — Bernie Ouimette (Member, Screening Committee) — Madelyn A. Reilly (Member, Screening Committee) — Paula D. Shepard (Member, Screening Committee) — Corporate donor: PPG Industries, Inc.

SW-296 **Price Foundation**   MI-12-17-18-35-71-81-82
c/o Schofield Financial Counseling
P.O. Box 369   **Phone** 412-767-7043 **FAX** None
Indianola   15051   (Allegheny County)   **EIN** 25-1701024   **Year Created** 1993
AMV $5,311,998   **FYE** 12-00   **(Gifts Received** $0)   12 **Grants totaling** $325,280

One Pa. grant: **$12,000** to Global Links. **Out-of-state** giving includes **$50,000** to Planned Parenthood Federation [NY]; **$49,280** to National Foundation for the Centers for Disease Control [GA]; **$33,000** each to Pathfinder International [MA] and Save the Children [CT]; **$30,000** to AVSC International/Engender Health [NY]; **$27,000** to The Nature Conservancy [DC]; **$25,000** to Population Communications International [NY]; **$20,000** to New Forests Project [DC]; and other smaller grants for similar purposes. ■**PUBLICATIONS:** None ■**WEBSITE:** None ■**E-MAIL:** None ■**APPLICATION POLICIES & PROCEDURES:** The Foundation reports that no unsolicited grant requests are accepted.

O+D+T Douglas F. Schofield (T+Con) — Wendell Price (T+Donor)

SW-297 **Quail Hill Foundation**   MI-41-42-51-54-55-57-71-72
128 Beaver Creek Court   **Phone** 412-635-7344 **FAX** None
Sewickley   15143   (Allegheny County)   **EIN** 25-1616338   **Year Created** 1989
AMV $327,362   **FYE** 12-00   **(Gifts Received** $0)   70 **Grants totaling** $26,463

About half local/Pa. giving. High grant of **$2,100** to Audubon Society of Western Pa. **$1,000-$1,200** each to Carnegie Institute, Pittsburgh Public Theater, Rolling Rock Club-CIP [Ligonier], Shady Side Academy, WDUQ-FM, and WQED-FM. **$500** to Pittsburgh Cultural Trust. Other contributions, **$30-$300** each, to local and Philadelphia-area organizations for environmental, animal welfare, educational, religious, historical, and other purposes. **Out-of-state** giving includes **$2,000** each to Portuguese Water Dog Foundation [NY] and Skidmore College [NY; and **$1,000** each to Garden Conservancy [NY] and The Nature Conservancy [VA]; and smaller contributions to many states, especially MA. ■**PUBLICATIONS:** None ■**WEBSITE:** None ■**E-MAIL:** None ■**APPLICATION POLICIES & PROCEDURES:** Prospective applicants initially should make a telephone inquiry about the feasibility of submitting a request. Grant requests may be submitted in a letter at any time; indicate the organization's official name, ID number, name/telephone number of a contact person, and describe the organizational purpose.

O+D+T Stuart L. Bell, CPA (S+Con) — Carolyn M. Knutson (C+P) — Sarah G. Flanagan [Chester County] (VP) — Anne K. Hargrave [NJ] (VP) — Todd M. Knutson [GA] (F)

SW-298 **Queequeg Foundation Trust**   MI-41-53-55
c/o Feldstein Grinberg Stein McKee P.C.
428 Boulevard of the Allies   **Phone** 412-471-0677 **FAX** None
Pittsburgh   15219   (Allegheny County)   **EIN** 25-6429739   **Year Created** 1994
AMV $354,004   **FYE** 12-00   **(Gifts Received** $0)   4 **Grants totaling** $22,000

Mostly local giving. High grant of **$20,000** to Mattress Factory (artistic writing and production of visual art). **$500** each to Reading is Fundamental and Westmoreland Museum of American Art. **Out-of-state** grant: **$1,000** to Prendergast Library [NY]. ■**PUBLICATIONS:** None ■**WEBSITE:** None ■**E-MAIL:** None ■**APPLICATION POLICIES & PROCEDURES:** Grant requests may be submitted in any form at any time. No grants awarded to individuals.

O+D+T Edwin I. Grinberg, Esq. (T+Con) — Ralph H. Reese (T+Manager+Donor) — Diane I. Samuels (T+Donor)

SW-299 **Randall (Charity) Foundation**   MI-12-14-29-41-42-43-44-49-51-52-55-56-57
c/o Three Rivers Aluminum Company   71-72
71 Progress Ave.   **Phone** 724-776-7000 **FAX** None
Cranberry Township   16066   (Butler County)   **EIN** 25-1329778   **Year Created** 1978
AMV $4,100,325   **FYE** 6-00   **(Gifts Received** $55)   34 **Grants totaling** $160,500

Mostly local giving; grants are for general purposes except as noted. High grant of **$40,000** to Carnegie Mellon U. **$20,000** to LaRoche College (Presidential Scholarship Fund). **$15,000** to Phipps Conservatory & Botanical Garden. **$10,000** each to Pittsburgh Zoo and Western Pa. Conservancy. **$5,000** each to Civic Light Opera, Cranberry Public Library, International Poetry Forum, Make-a-Wish Foundation of Western Pa., Pa. Partnership for Economic Education, and Pittsburgh Public Theatre. **$1,000-$2,000** each to Animal Friends, Butler County Federated Library System, Central Northside Reading is Fundamental, Contact Pittsburgh, Gateway to the Arts, Historical Society of Western Pa., Mattress Factory, Pittsburgh Aviary, Pittsburgh Ballet Theater, Pittsburgh Center for the Arts, Pittsburgh Symphony, Pittsburgh Dance Council, Pittsburgh Opera, Pittsburgh Playhouse, River City Brass Band, Special Olympics of Pa., Teacher Excellence Foundation, and WQED. **Out-of-state** grants include **$5,000** to Sierra Club [CA]; and **$2,500** each to Greenpeace USA [MD] and National Audubon Society [NY]. ■**PUBLICATIONS:** Statement of Program Policy ■**WEBSITE:** None ■**E-MAIL:** None ■**APPLICATION POLICIES & PROCEDURES:** The Foundation reports that giving is primarily for the environment, the arts, and education. Prospective applicants initially should make a telephone inquiry about the feasibility of submitting a request. Grant requests must be submitted during March-April (deadline is April 30th) on a Application Form available from the Foundation. Site visits sometimes are made to organizations being considered for a grant. Also, scholarships are awarded to college students based on need, prior scholastic achievement, and area of study; those pursuing literary or environmental conservation endeavors receive preference. Grants are awarded at a June meeting.

O+D+T Robert P. Randall (P+T+Donor+Con) — Robin S. Randall (S+T) — Brett R. Randall (F+T) — Robert G. Panagulias, Esq. (AF+T) — Earl R. Randall (Donor) — Corporate donor: Three Rivers Aluminum Company

---

SW-300 Rangos (John G.), Sr. Charitable Foundation, The
1301 Grandview Ave., Suite 230
Pittsburgh 15221   (Allegheny County)
AMV $10,855,972   **FYE** 11-00   **(Gifts Received** $0)

MI-12-22-31-32-42-52-54-63-64-72
Phone 412-871-6120 **FAX** 412-871-6125
EIN 25-1599198   **Year Created** 1987
13 **Grants totaling** $1,633,765

Mostly local giving. High grant of **$1,030,000** to Children's Hospital of Pittsburgh (Rangos Research Center). **$400,000** to Carnegie Mellon U. (Rangos Hall). **$50,000** to International Orthodox Christian Charities. **$38,675** to Children's Museum of Pittsburgh. **$30,000** to Carnegie Institute. **$7,500** to Pittsburgh Opera. **$5,000** each to Heritage Agency and Jewish National Fund. **$2,500** each to Champs for Kids, Ronald McDonald House of Pittsburgh, and Pittsburgh Zoo. **Out-of-state** grants: **$50,000** to Johns Hopkins U. Hospital [MD] and **$10,000** to St. Vladimir's Orthodox Theological Seminary [NY]. ■**PUBLICA-TIONS:** statement of program policy; application guidelines ■**WEBSITE:** www.rangosfoundation.org ■**E-MAIL:** None ■**APPLICATION POLICIES & PROCEDURES:** The Foundation reports its mission as serving children through improved education and health care; most grants are for general support, special projects, capital drives and research. Prospective applicants initially should make a telephone inquiry about the feasibility of submitting a request. Grant requests in the form of a full proposal should be submitted during January-April; include an annual report, organization budget, project budget, list of Board members, list of major funding sources, audited financial statement, and IRS tax-exempt status documentation. Site visits sometimes are made to organizations being considered for a grant. The trustees award grants at meetings in February, April, June, August, October, and December.

O+D+T Nancy Barnhart (Con) — John G. Rangos, Sr. (C+T+Donor) — John G. Rangos, Jr. (S+T) — Alexander W. Rangos (T) — Jenica Anne Rangos (T) — Jill Rangos (T) — Corporate donor: USA Waste Services, Inc.

SW-301 Ray (Norman C.) Trust
c/o Daniels Group, Inc.
Two Oliver Plaza, 609 Penn Ave., Suite 200
Pittsburgh 15219   (Allegheny County)
AMV $1,515,688   **FYE** 12-00   **(Gifts Received** $0)

MI-11-12-13-14-15-22-29-31-32-35-42-49-51
52-56-71-85
Phone 412-355-0780 **FAX** None
EIN 25-6186356   **Year Created** 1977
32 **Grants totaling** $74,373

All local/Pa. giving. High grant of **$10,000** to Pa. Partnership for Economic Education [Snyder County]. **$5,000** each to Mon-Vale Health & Resources Foundation, Mon Valley Initiative, and United Way of Allegheny County. **$3,000** each to Big Brothers & Big Sisters of Greater Pittsburgh and Watson Institute. **$2,500** each to Pittsburgh Vision Services and Travelers Aid Society. **$2,000** each to The Bradley Center, Center in the Woods, Children's Hospital of Pittsburgh, Contact Pittsburgh, Historical Society of Western Pa., Make-A-Wish Foundation of Western Pa., Pa. YMCA [Cumberland County], Phipps Conservancy, Pittsburgh Symphony, and Whale's Tale/FamilyLink. **$1,873** to Carnegie Mellon U./GSIA. **$1,500** each to American Cancer Society, American Heart Assn., Bethlehem Haven, Children's Home of Pittsburgh, National Parkinson Foundation/Pittsburgh Chapter, Northside Common Ministries, Pittsburgh Public Theater, and Salvation Army. Other smaller local contributions. ■**PUBLICATIONS:** None ■**WEBSITE:** None ■**E-MAIL:** None ■**APPLICATION POLICIES & PROCEDURES:** The Foundation reports that Allegheny and Washington county organizations receive priority. No grants awarded to individuals. Prospective applicants initially should make a telephone inquiry about the feasibility of submitting a request. Grant requests may be submitted in any form at any time; deadline is December 15th.

O+D+T J. Edgar Williams, Sr. (T+Con) — Nathan K. Parker, Jr. (T)

SW-302 Reinecke Family Charitable Foundation
c/o Farrell & Company
1200 Reedsdale Street
Pittsburgh 15233   (Allegheny County)
AMV $543,102   **FYE** 12-00   **(Gifts Received** $0)

MI-11-17-42-43
Phone 412-237-2260 **FAX** 412-321-0111
EIN 23-2937856   **Year Created** 1998
3 **Grants totaling** $31,250

All local giving. High grants of **$15,000** each to United Way of Allegheny County and U. of Pittsburgh. **$1,250** for a scholarship. — Giving in the prior year included **$25,000** to United Way of Allegheny County; **$5,000** to U. of Pittsburgh; **$1,000** each to Girls Hope of Pittsburgh and Hope Network; and two scholarships. ■**PUBLICATIONS:** None ■**WEBSITE:** None ■**E-MAIL:** None ■**APPLICATION POLICIES & PROCEDURES:** Grant requests may be submitted in a letter at any time.

O+D+T Thomas J. Reinecke (P+Con) — Corporate donor: Farrell & Company

---

SW-303 Reliance Bank Foundation
c/o Reliance Bank
1119 - 12th Street
Altoona 16601   (Blair County)
AMV $174,368   **FYE** 12-01   **(Gifts Received** $135,600)

MI-13-22-25-32-41-42-49
Phone 814-944-4061 **FAX** 814-949-6294
EIN 31-1675396   **Year Created** 1999
35 **Grants totaling** $72,032

Mostly local giving. High grant of **$25,000** to Local 299-9-11 Disaster Fund. **$4,000** to St. Francis College. **$3,500** each to American Cancer Society, Pa. Free Enterprise Week [Erie], and United Way of Blair County. **$3,000** to Hollidaysburg Area YMCA. **$2,500** each to Greater Altoona Career & Technology Center and Habitat for Humanity-Blair County. **$2,000** to Tri-County Habitat for Humanity. **$1,500** to St. Vincent DePaul Soup Kitchen. **$1,000** to Small Occasional Short-Term Loan Program [State College]. Smaller local contributions for youth, civic and other purposes. ■**PUBLICATIONS:** None ■**WEBSITE:** www.reliancebank.com ■**E-MAIL:** None ■**APPLICATION POLICIES & PROCEDURES:** The Foundation reports giving is limited to the Bank's marketing area (Blair and Centre counties) with most grants for special projects, building funds, capital drives, and scholarships. Grant requests may be submitted in any form at any time; include an annual report, project budget, list of board members, list of major funding sources, and IRS tax-exempt status documentation. Site visits sometimes are made to organizations being considered for a grant.

O+D+T Bruce R. Hostler (C+D+Con) — Timohty P. Sissler (P+D) — John W. Musser (Executive VP) — Dennis E. Doll (VP) — Lisa A. Michelone (VP) — Susan Meier (S) — Brian Lehman (F) — James J. Clarke (D) — James B. Plummer (D) — Ben Stepelfeld (D) — David K. Ward (D) — Corporate donor: Reliance Bank

---

SW-304 Remmel (W.H. & Althea F.) Foundation   **MI**-12-13-17-20-22-29-32-41-63-71-85
Refer to PNC Advisors Charitable Trust Committee entry.
                                    (Allegheny County)   **EIN** 23-7009732   **Year Created** 1951
AMV $4,709,114   **FYE** 12-00   (**Gifts Received** $0)   25 **Grants totaling** $255,651

All SW Pa. giving. High grant of **$15,000** to Horticultural Society of Western Pa. **$13,500** to Communities in Schools. **$12,750** to Pine Valley Bible Camp. **$12,000** each to Community Fitness Center, Manchester Academic Charter School, The Neighborhood Academy, The Pittsburgh Project, and Pittsburgh Urban Christian School. **$11,250** each to Contact Pittsburgh, Kiskiminetas Springs School, Mon-Valley Initiative, Presbyterian Church of Mt. Washington, Schenley Heights Community Development Center, and Veterans Place of Washington Blvd. **$10,000** each to Sickle Cell Society, Mt. Zion Evangelical Lutheran Church, and Orr Compassionate Care Center. **$9,500** to The Lazarus Center. **$7,500-$8,500** each to Freedom Unlimited, Inc., I Have A Dream Foundation, Ligonier Valley Memorial, Lupus Foundation of America/Western Pa. Chapter, and The Program for Female Offenders. **$6,000** to East End Cooperative Ministry. **$2,401** to Woodard's Educational Services. ■**APPLICATION POLICIES & PROCEDURES:** Refer to the PNC Advisors Charitable Trust Committee entry for a statement on giving priorities and full application guidelines.

O+D+T Refer to PNC Advisors Charitable Trust Committee entry. — PNC Advisors (Corporate Trustee)

SW-305 Richman (John W. & Shirley F.) Foundation   **MI**-12-14-25-29-31-32-41-61-62
c/o I. Richman & Company, Inc.
40 Pennsylvania Ave., P.O. Box 232   **Phone** 724-222-5900 **FAX** 724-225-1660
Washington 15301   (Washington County)   **EIN** 25-1753663   **Year Created** 1994
AMV $41,139   **FYE** 9-00   (**Gifts Received** $1,664)   37 **Grants totaling** $26,382

Mostly local giving. High grant **$6,000** to Washington Hospital Foundation. **$3,000** to The Pittsburgh Foundation. **$2,860** to Beth Israel Congregation. **$2,000** to Habitat for Humanity of Washington. **$1,000-$1,500** each to Albert Gallatin School District, American Cancer Society, Community Action Southwest, St. Agnes Church (building fund), Transitional Employment Consultants, Try-Again Homes, and Watchful Shepherd USA. **$650** to American Diabetes Assn. **$596** to Pa. Special Olympics. Other local and out-of-state contributions **$15-$500** for various purposes. ■**PUBLICATIONS:** None ■**WEBSITE:** None ■**E-MAIL:** None ■**APPLICATION POLICIES & PROCEDURES:** Grant requests may be requested at any time, in person or in a letter. No grants awarded to individuals.

O+D+T John W. Richman (T+Donor+Con) — Shirley E. Richman (T+Donor) — Corporate donors: Hotel Auld; Syndicated Equities.

SW-306 Richman (Stephen I. & Audrey G.) Foundation   **MI**-11-12-22-42-52-55-62-71-85-89
c/o Washington Trust Buildings, Inc.
206 Washington Trust Building   **Phone** 724-225-3080 **FAX** None
Washington 15301   (Washington County)   **EIN** 25-1738946   **Year Created** 1994
AMV $505,968   **FYE** 5-01   (**Gifts Received** $0)   11 **Grants totaling** $45,850

All local/Pa. giving. High grant of **$13,100** to Pittsburgh Opera. **$10,000** each to Jewish Family & Children's Service and United Jewish Federation of Greater Pittsburgh. **$5,000** to City of Washington Economic Development Assn. **$3,000** to Pittsburgh Symphony. **$1,000** each to Greater Washington Area Parks & Recreation Commission, National Catholic Center for the Holocaust, United Way of Washington County, and U. of Pa. Law School [Philadelphia]. Other local contributions **$250-$500**. ■**PUBLICATIONS:** None ■**WEBSITE:** None ■**E-MAIL:** None ■**APPLICATION POLICIES & PROCEDURES:** No grants awarded to individuals.

O+D+T Stephen I. Richman, Esq. (T+Donor+Con) — Audrey G. Richman (T+Donor) — Corporate donors: Hotel Auld; Washington Trust Buildings, Inc.; Syndicated Equities. Foundation donor: Ben & Bessie Richman Foundation.

SW-307 Riordan (Robert W.) Charitable Trust   **MI**-13-42-61
29 Blackburn Road   **Phone** Unlisted **FAX** None
Sewickley 15143   (Allegheny County)   **EIN** 23-7913373   **Year Created** 1997
AMV $215,000   **FYE** 9-01   (**Gifts Received** $0)   1 **Grant of** $25,000

Sole grant to U. of Virginia. — Grants awarded in prior years include: **$10,058** to St. James Church and **$5,000** to Girls Hope of Pittsburgh. ■**PUBLICATIONS:** None ■**WEBSITE:** None ■**E-MAIL:** None ■**APPLICATION POLICIES & PROCEDURES:** The Trust reports that giving generally is restricted to Western Pa. organizations with whom relationships are already established. No grants are awarded to individuals.

O+D+T Robert W. Riordan (Donor+Con) — Corporate Trustee: Smithfield Trust Company

---

SW-308 Robertshaw Charitable Foundation   **MI**-12-13-14-22-29-35-41-42-44-52-54-55-56
116 North Main Street   71-72-85
Greensburg 15601   **Phone** 724-832-7576 **FAX** 724-834-5044
                               (Westmoreland County)   **EIN** 25-1622184   **Year Created** 1989
AMV $1,809,690   **FYE** 6-00   (**Gifts Received** $0)   32 **Grants totaling** $103,200

All local giving. High Pa. grant of **$6,000** to Seton Hill College (academic computing lab). **$5,000** each to Action for Animals Humane Society (facility expansion), Greensburg Community Development Corp. (park project), Greensburg Hempfield Area Library (technology upgrades), and The Westmoreland Trust (computer equipment). **$4,165** to St. Emma Monastery & Retreat House (organ repairs). **$4,000** each to Aquinas Academy (gym improvements), Big Brothers Big Sisters of Westmoreland County (special program), Economic Growth Connection of Westmoreland (computer equipment), Ligonier Volunteer Hose Co. #1 (truck fund), Red Cross (disaster equipment, and Westmoreland County Blind Assn. (digital copier). **$3,400** to Make-A-Wish Foundation of Western Pa. (local wish). **$3,000** each to Greensburg Central Catholic High School (calculators), St. Anne Home (shop improvements), Westmoreland ARC Foundation (capital campaign), Westmoreland Arts & Heritage Festival (exhibit), and Westmoreland Symphony (youth symphony concerts). **$2,500** each to Center Against Domestic & Sexual Violence (bully awareness program), East Suburban Citizen Advocacy (computer equipment), Greensburg YWCA (Forward Fund campaign), Mom's House (office equipment), ParentWISE (publication), Special Olympics of Westmoreland County (sports fund/training), Westmoreland County Historical Society (log house kit), and Westmoreland Museum of American Art (portraits exhibition). **$2,000** each to Greensburg Area Cultural Council (art exhibition), Hero Project (prevention program), Pa. CleanWays Westmoreland County (fugitive tire program), and Spina Bifida Assn. of Western Pa. (summer camp program). **$1,635** to Union Mission of Latrobe (lighting equipment). **$1,000** to Junior Achievement of SW Pa. (local high school program). ■**PUBLICATIONS:** program policy statement; application guidelines ■**WEBSITE:** None ■**E-MAIL:** robertshaw@wpa.net ■**APPLICATION POLICIES & PROCEDURES:** The Foundation reports that giving is concentrated in central Westmoreland County (except for special interests of Board members) and are mostly for special projects, building funds, or capital drives; multiyear grants are approved occasionally. No support is awarded to/for individuals; general operating support; politics; lobbying; highly specialized health/medical programs without specific community impact; welfare or social programs not supporting or projecting independence; purely sectarian or religious activities; organizations which discriminate; chairs or professorships; and organizations that promote, research, or support the prevention of life, abortion, the practice of euthanasia or cruelty of animals. Prospective applicants initially should make a telephone inquiry about the feasibility of submitting a request. Grant requests should be submitted in May and November (deadlines are June 1st and December 1st); the first paragraph must specify the amount requested, then describe the project, its purpose and objective, and how it will be implemented; also include a project budget, audited financial statement, and IRS tax-exempt status documentation. Grants are awarded at meetings in mid-June and mid-December.

O+D+T Jane A. Himes (Foundation Manager+Con) — John A. Robertshaw, Jr. (C+D+Donor) — Anne B. Robertshaw (D) — Natalie Robertshaw Kelley [Pittsburgh] (D) — Lisa Robertshaw Moeller [New Florence] (D) — John A. Robertshaw, III [NY] (D) — Marc B. Robertshaw [Ligonier] (D)

SW-309   Robinson (Donald & Sylvia) Family Foundation
6507 Wilkins Avenue
Pittsburgh 15217   (Allegheny County)

MI-11-17-22-31-41-42-51-52-53-54-55-62-71
Phone 412-661-1200 **FAX** 412-661-4645
EIN 23-7062017   **Year Created** 1970

AMV $5,327,096   **FYE** 10-00   **(Gifts Received** $198,278)   190+ **Grants totaling** $235,771

Mostly local giving; some grants comprise multiple payments. High grant of **$41,500** to Southern Alleghenies Museum of Art. **$25,000** to United Jewish Federation of Greater Pittsburgh. **$14,500** to Hillel Academy. **$10,000** to Carnegie Institute. **$4,500** to Phipps Conservancy & Botanical Garden. **$3,000-$3,500** each to American Friends of Israel War Disabled, Family House, Silver Eye Center for Photography, Tree of Life Congregation, and Western Pa. Conservancy. **$2,000-$2,500** each to American Friends of Union of Progressive Jews, Associated Artists of Pittsburgh, I Have A Dream Foundation, Jewish Community Center of Pittsburgh, Pittsburgh Cultural Trust, Pittsburgh Public Theater, Planned Parenthood of Western Pa., and U. of Pittsburgh Medical Center Auxiliary. **$1,000-$1,500** each to Carnegie Mellon U., Crohn's & Colitis Foundation, JCC/American Jewish Museum, Jewish Israeli Film Festival, FamilyLink, Foundation for the Rehabilitation of Prisoners, Leadership Pittsburgh, Loyalhanna Watershed Assn., National Parkinson Foundation/Greater Pittsburgh Chapter, National Society of Arts & Letters, Neighborhood Academy/Penn West Conference, Shadyside Hospital Foundation, Yeshiva Schools, and Zionist Organization of America. Other local contributions **$70-$600** for similar purposes. **Out-of-state** giving includes **$4,500** to Old School Square [FL]; **$2,000** each to Boca Raton Museum of Art and Cleveland Museum of Natural History; and **$1,000** each to Canyonlands Field Institute [UT], Chautauqua Center for the Visual Arts [NY, Jewish Federation of South Palm Beach County [FL], and others. ■ **PUBLICATIONS:** None ■**WEBSITE:** None ■**E-MAIL:** None ■**APPLICATION POLICIES & PROCEDURES:** The Foundation reports that giving is national with most grants for annual/operating support, capital campaigns, and building/renovation. Grant requests may be submitted at any time in a letter (2 pages maximum); include an annual report, organization and project budgets, Board member list, list of major funding sources, and IRS tax-exempt status documentation. Proposals which follow Grantmakers of Western Pa. Common Grant Application Format are accepted. Site visits sometimes are made to organizations being considered for a grant.

O+D+T Donald M. Robinson (P+T+Donor) — Carol L. Robinson (T) — Stephen G. Robinson (T) — Sylvia M. Robinson (T+Donor)

SW-310   Robinson (Ovid D.) Charitable Trust
Refer to PNC Advisors Charitable Trust Committee entry.
                          (Allegheny County)

MI-12-13-14-15-31-42-63-84

EIN 25-6023648   **Year Created** 1957

AMV $5,652,956   **FYE** 12-00   **(Gifts Received** $0)   14 **Grants totaling** $276,722

All SW Pa. giving; all grants are for general support. High grant of **$96,754** to Boys & Girls Club of Western Pa. **$48,377** to The Children's Institute. **$25,608** to The Watson Institute. **$22,769** to D.T. Watson Rehabilitation Services. **$13,500** to Glade Run Foundation [Zelienople]. **$12,000** to Pittsburgh Wrestling Club. **$11,250** to Pittsburgh Voyager and Try-Again Homes [Washington]. **$7,500** each to Boy Scouts/Penn's Wood Council and Duquesne U. **$6,000** to Butler Health System. **$5,562** to Young Life-Steel Valley. **$5,000** to Wagner Family Charities. **$3,653** to Allegheny Valley School. ■**APPLICATION POLICIES & PROCEDURES:** Refer to the PNC Advisors Charitable Trust Committee entry for a statement on giving priorities and full application guidelines.

O+D+T Refer to PNC Advisors Charitable Trust Committee entry. — PNC Advisors (Corporate Trustee)

SW-311 Rockwell Foundation, The
Suite 1A,
1330 Old Freeport Road
Pittsburgh 15238   (Allegheny County)

MI-12-13-14-15-29-32-41-42-44-51-52-54-55
57-63-65-81
Phone 412-967-1140 **FAX** None
EIN 25-6035975   **Year Created** 1956

AMV $16,423,745   **FYE** 12-00   (**Gifts Received** $0)   67 **Grants totaling** $1,001,500

About two-thirds local/Pa. giving. High Pa. grant of **$95,000** to Penn State U. **$60,000** to Kiski School. **$50,000** each to Riverview Children's Center and U. of Pittsburgh. **$40,000** to Carnegie Museum of Natural History. **$25,000** each to Allegheny Valley School, The Ellis School, and Shady Side Academy. **$15,000** each to Epilepsy Foundation of Western Pa., Sweetwater Center for the Arts, and Young Life. **$10,000** each to American Diabetes Assn., Aspinwall Presbyterian Church, Baldwin High School/Family Types, Civic Light Opera, FAME/Fund for the Advancement of Minority Education, Family Guidance, Inc., Jane Holmes Residence, Juvenile Diabetes Foundation, Laurie Ann West Memorial Library, Pittsburgh Leadership Foundation, Society for Contemporary Crafts, Western Pa. School for the Deaf, and WYEP. **$7,500** each to Circle C Youth & Family, Pa. Special Olympics, and Pittsburgh Ballet Theatre. **$5,000** each to Boys & Girls Clubs of Western Pa., Brashear Assn., Caring Foundation for Children, Children's Institute, Commonwealth Education, Contact Pittsburgh, Extra Mile Education Foundation, First Presbyterian Church of Edgewood, Freeport Theatre Festival, Greater Pittsburgh Council, Pressley Ridge School, Prime Stage, Rails to Trails [Harrisburg], Sheldon Calvary Camp, SIDS Alliance, Spina Bifida Assn. of SW Pa., and World Affairs Council of Pittsburgh. **$4,000** to Arthritis Foundation. **$3,000** to Leukemia Society of America. **$1,000-$2,500** each to Foxwall Emergency Medical Service, National Society of Arts & Letters, and Sewickley Valley Historical Society. **Out-of-state** giving includes high grant of **$100,000** to YMCA of Lake Norman [NC]; **$50,000** each to Alden Kindred of America [MA] and Cornerstone Presbyterian Church [FL]; **$25,000** to Sands Montessori School [OH]; **$20,000** to Rollins College [FL]; and smaller grants to NY, DC, VA, NC, SC, OH, and CO, many for cultural organizations or higher education. ■**PUBLICATIONS:** None ■**WEBSITE:** None ■**E-MAIL:** None ■**APPLICATION POLICIES & PROCEDURES:** The Foundation reports that PA, WV and OH organizations receive priority; grants are for general support, special projects, building funds, capital needs, endowment, research, publications, or scholarships; multi-year grants are awarded. No grants are awarded to individuals. Grant requests may be submitted in a letter (3 pages maximum) at any time before the December 10th deadline; describe the intended use of the funds, and include current financial statements and IRS tax-exempt status documentation. The Trustees award grants at a December meeting.

O+D+T H. Campbell Stuckeman (S+T+Con) — George Peter Rockwell (T) — Russell A. Rockwell (T) — PNC Advisors (Corporate Trustee)

SW-312 Rooney Foundation
c/o Klett, Lieber, Rooney & Schorling
One Oxford Center, 40th Floor, 301 Grant Street
Pittsburgh 15219   (Allegheny County)

MI-42

Phone 412-392-2000 **FAX** None
EIN 25-6500407   **Year Created** 1995

AMV $282,190   **FYE** 12-00   (**Gifts Received** $1,383)   1 **Grant of** $5,000

Sole grant to Carlow College. — In the prior year, two grants: **$10,000** to Duquesne U. and **$5,000** to Carlow College. ■**PUBLICATIONS:** None ■**WEBSITE:** None ■**E-MAIL:** None ■**APPLICATION POLICIES & PROCEDURES:** Grant requests may be submitted in a letter at any time.

O+D+T Daniel M. Rooney (T+Con) — Arthur J. Rooney, Jr. (T) — Patrick T. Rooney [FL] (T)

SW-313 Rosario Foundation
c/o Three Rivers Cardiac Institute
100 Broadway Ave.
Carnegie 15106   (Allegheny County)

MI-31-43-56-82

Phone 412-276-7340 **FAX** 412-276-6215
EIN 25-1519395   **Year Created** 1986

AMV $50,462   **FYE** 12-00   (**Gifts Received** $0)   11 **Grants totaling** $16,029

About two-thirds local/Pa. giving. High grant of **$5,500** to Pittsburgh Italian Scholarship Fund. **$1,000-$1,350** each to Pittsburgh Columbus Day Parade, Pittsburgh Mercy Foundation, Washington Hospital Foundation, and one scholarship award. **$600** to Uniontown Hospital Foundation. Other local contributions **$9-$150**. **Out-of-state** grant: **$5,000** to Achimota School [Ghana, West Africa]. ■**PUBLICATIONS:** None ■**WEBSITE:** None ■**E-MAIL:** None ■**APPLICATION POLICIES & PROCEDURES:** The Foundation reports that scholarships are restricted to PA, WV and OH residents, and are based on financial need/academic performance. No information available re organizational grant requests.

O+D+T Susan M. Latella (Manager+Con) — Seth Bekoe, M.D. (D+Donor) — Ross F. DiMarco, Jr. M.D. (D+Donor) — Kathleen J. Grant, M.D. (D+Donor) — Ronald V. Pelligrini, M.D. (D+Donor)

SW-314 Rossin Foundation
c/o Dynamet, Inc.
P.O. Box 1225
McMurray 15317   (Washington County)

MI-11-13-14-15-22-31-32-41-42-52-54-55-56
57-61-63-81
Phone 724-746-3401 **FAX** None
EIN 25-6327217   **Year Created** 1989

AMV $21,166,973   **FYE** 12-00   (**Gifts Received** $0)   44 **Grants totaling** $1,896,470

Mostly local/Pa. giving. High grant of **$1,003,950** to Washington & Jefferson College. **$500,000** to Lehigh U. **$125,000** to Carnegie Mellon U. **$95,000** to Community Foundation of Upper St. Clair. **$30,920** to Washington Hospital Foundation. **$20,000** to Coalition for Christian Outreach (campus ministries). **$10,000** to Carnegie Institute, Pittsburgh Trust for Cultural Resources, and United Way of SW Pa. **$5,000** each to Children's Hospital of Pittsburgh, Pittsburgh Opera, Presbyterian Seniorcare, and Wesley Institute. **$3,500-$4,500** each to U.S. Catholic Conference, World Affairs Council of Pittsburgh, and YMCA of

Pittsburgh. **$2,000-$2,500** each to Allegheny Conference on Community Development, ALS Assn., American Cancer Society, American Society for Metals Foundation, Historical Society of Western Pa., Pa. Special Olympics, Pittsburgh Civic Light Opera, Pittsburgh Vision Services, St. Sebastian (Spark of Hope), Washington County Community Foundation, Western Pa. School for the Blind, Westminster Presbyterian Church, and WQED. **$1,000** each to American Lung Assn., Asbury Health Center, Family House, and Watchful Shepherd. Other local contributions **$500** for similar purposes. **Out-of-state** giving includes **$15,000** to Bay Ridge Christian College [TX] and **$5,000** to Alfred U. [NY]. — Major grants approved for future payment include **$2,742,550** to Washington & Jefferson College; **$1,371,275** to Lehigh U.; and **$481,382** to Coalition for Christian Outreach. ■ **PUBLICA-TIONS:** None ■ **WEBSITE:** None ■ **E-MAIL:** None ■ **APPLICATION POLICIES & PROCEDURES:** The Foundation reports that giving is primarily for educational institutions/purposes. No grants awarded to individuals. Grant requests may be submitted in a letter at any time; describe the proposed project and state the amount of funding requested. — Formerly called Dynamet Foundation.

O+D+T Viola G. Taboni (AS+F+T+Con) — Peter C. Rossin [Pittsburgh] (C+T+Donor+Manager) — Peter N. Stephans [Pittsburgh] (P+T) — J. Robert Van Kirk [Sewickley] (S+T) — Ada E. Rossin [Pittsburgh] (T+Donor+Manager) — Joan R. Stephans [Pittsburgh] (T) — Corporate donor: Dynamet, Inc.

SW-315 Rowell (Clarence A. & Grace R.) Memorial Fund
    Refer to PNC Advisors Charitable Trust Committee entry.

MI-13-14-15-17-22-25-41-51-52-55-56-71

(Allegheny County)   **EIN** 23-7217984   **Year Created** 1953

AMV $1,912,230   **FYE** 1-01   **(Gifts Received** $0)   18 **Grants totaling** $60,000

All giving restricted to organizations/programs serving Philadelphia's Germantown-area residents. High grants of **$5,000** each to Center in the Park, Easter Seals, Germantown Friends School, Germantown Women's Educational Program, Metropolitan Career Center, Partners Program, Wheels, Inc., and Young Audiences of Eastern Pa. **$3,000** to Awbury Arboretum. **$2,000-$2,500** each to Germantown YWCA, International Ballet School, Mum Puppettheatre, Philabundance, Philadelphia Society for Preservation of Landmarks, and Special Olympics/Philadelphia. **$1,000** each to Allens Lane Art Center, Whosoever Gospel Mission, and Young Women's Residence, Inc. ■ **APPLICATION POLICIES & PROCEDURES:** Refer to the PNC Advisors Charitable Trust Committee entry for a statement on giving priorities and full application guidelines. — Also called Clarence A. Rowell Trust #2.

O+D+T Refer to PNC Advisors Charitable Trust Committee entry. — Eleanor O. Dunning (T) — PNC Advisors (Trustee)

SW-316 Rust Foundation, The
    5505 Dunmoyle Street
    Pittsburgh 15217

MI-11-13-14-17-22-25-29-31-32-41-42-54-56 63-71

(Allegheny County)   **Phone** 412-487-6990 **FAX** 412-487-4942
    EIN 25-6049037   **Year Created** 1950

AMV $7,933,286   **FYE** 12-00   **(Gifts Received** $0)   106 **Grants totaling** $393,500

About two-thirds local/Pa. giving; some grants comprise multiple payments reflecting designated gifts of individual trustees; grants are for general purposes except as noted. High grant of **$66,000** to Shadyside Hospital Foundation (patient care services/cancer center construction). **$27,000** to Chatham College (science building construction). **$15,000** to The Ellis School. **$12,100** to Carlow College (capital campaign). **$7,500** to Calvary Episcopal Church (youth camp). **$3,000-$4,000** each to Shadyside Presbyterian Church, United Way of SW Pa., and Western Pa. School for Blind Children. **$2,000-$2,500** each to Carnegie Institute (women's committee), Housing Opportunities (counseling services), Lehigh U., Vectors Pittsburgh Foundation, and Women's Center & Shelter of Greater Pittsburgh. **$1,000-$1,500** each to Allegheny County Bar Foundation, Allegheny Heart Institute, American Cancer Society, Children's Hospital of Pittsburgh, Children's Institute of Pittsburgh, East End Coop Ministry (various programs), Episcopal Diocese of Pittsburgh (Calvary Camp), North Hill Community Outreach, Pittsburgh Mercy Foundation (burn center), Pittsburgh Public Theater, Pittsburgh Symphony, Pittsburgh Vision Services, St. Andrews Episcopal Church, and Western Pa. Conservancy. Other smaller local contributions for similar purposes. **Out-of-state** giving, primarily where Trustees reside, include **$50,000** to Friends of Thomas Balch Library [VA]; **$25,650** to Community Foundation of Cape Cod [MA]; **$20,050** to George C. Marshall Home Preservation Fund [VA]; and other smaller grants/contributions, **$500-$13,500,** to many states. ■ **PUBLICATIONS:** None ■ **WEBSITE:** None ■ **E-MAIL:** None ■ **APPLICATION POLICIES & PROCEDURES:** The Foundation reports that priority is given to institutions in which Trustees are involved. No grants are awarded to individuals, and no multiyear grants. Prospective applicants initially should make a telephone inquiry about the feasibility of submitting a request. Grant requests in any form may be submitted to any individual Trustee at any time—deadlines vary; provide a brief description of the project with budget and timetable, and describe how the success of the project will be evaluated. Include brief organizational background information (history, purpose, mission, programs), current organization and project budgets, and IRS tax-exempt status documentation. All grant requests must be approved by at least one Trustee prior to being submitted to the Foundation office. Site visits sometimes are made to organizations being considered for a grant. Grants are awarded at Trustee meetings in August and December. — Note: An alternative address for submission of grant requests: Jane C. Rust, 373 Old Woodbury Pike, Readyville, TN 37149, Phone: 615-409-6009; FAX: 615-409-6090.

O+D+T S. Murray Rust, III (PO+T+Con) — James O. Rust [TN] (S+T) — Anne S. Gillies [KY] (T) — David C. Gillies [VA] (T) — Mary Rust Gillies (T) — Nancy L. Gillies [VA] (T) — Molly Rust Montgomery (T) — John M. Rust [NY] (T) — S.M. Rust, Jr. [MA] (T) — Alice Rust Scheetz (T)

SW-317 Ryan Memorial Foundation
    5708 Lynn Haven Road, P.O. Box 426
    Pittsburgh 15230   (Allegheny County)

MI-11-12-31-22-41-42-52-57-61-71-81
Phone 412-363-3724 **FAX** None
EIN 25-1781266   **Year Created** 1996

AMV $7,875,195   **FYE** 12-00   **(Gifts Received** $0)   49 **Grants totaling** $413,285

About half local/Pa. giving. High Pa. grant of **$61,102** to United Way of SW Pa. **$42,534** to Word of God School [Swissvale]. **$33,250** to Pittsburgh Oratory. **$25,200** to Penn State Catholic Community [State College]. **$7,905** to Diocese of Pittsburgh.

$5,000 each to Central Catholic High School, Children's Hospital of Pittsburgh, Mount Nittany Conservancy [Centre County], Penn State U., Pittsburgh Mercy Hospital, and Pittsburgh Symphony. **$4,500** to Catholic Charities, **$3,000** to Early Learning Institute. **$2,750** to World Affairs Council of Pittsburgh. **$2,000** each to Carnegie Mellon U. and Duquesne U. **$1,000** each to Children's Home of Pittsburgh, International Poetry Forum, Oakland Catholic High School, and WQED. Other smaller local contributions arts/cultural and other purposes. **Out-of-state** giving includes high grant of **$81,205** to Georgian U. Foundation [NY]; **$41,850** to U. of Notre Dame [IN]; **$15,000** to Northwestern Memorial Hospital [IL]; **$9,375** to Council on Foreign Relations [NY]; and other grants, mostly where trustees are resident. ■**PUBLICATIONS:** None ■**WEBSITE:** None ■**E-MAIL:** None ■**APPLICATION POLICIES & PROCEDURES:** No grants awarded to individuals.
O+D+T John T. Ryan, III (T+Con) — Julia Ryan Parker [CT] (T) — Dr. Daniel H. Ryan [NY] (T) — Mary Irene Ryan (T) — Michael Denis Ryan [WI] (T) — William F. Ryan [State College] (T) — Irene Ryan Shaw [NY] (T)

SW-318 S&T Bancorp Charitable Foundation
c/o S&T Bank
800 Philadelphia Street, P.O. Box 190
Indiana 15701 (Indiana County)
AMV $552,080 **FYE** 12-00 (**Gifts Received** $72,900)

MI-11-13-15-25-29-31-32-39-42-52-54-55-72-87-89
Phone 724-465-1443 **FAX** 724-465-1488
EIN 25-1716950 **Year Created** 1993
90+ **Grants totaling** $246,250

All giving limited to the Bank's marketing area; grants are for general fund purposes except as noted and some comprise multiple payments. High grant of **$26,000** to United Way of Indiana County (mostly general fund). **$25,000** to Punxsutawney Area Hospital (capital campaign). **$12,000** to DuBois Area United Way. **$10,000** each to DASC Building Fund, Jefferson County Fair Assn., and Seton Hill College/National Education Center for Women. **$6,000** to Jefferson County Area Agency on Aging (capital campaign). **$5,000-$5,750** each to Brockway Volunteer Hose Company, Brookville Area United Fund, Citizens Ambulance of Indiana, Community Foundation of Westmoreland County, Indiana U. of Pa. (Nell Jack Classic), Indiana County Memorial to Veterans, Indiana County Memorial Wall Fund, Indiana Symphony Orchestra (concerts), and Westmoreland Hospital Foundation. **$4,000-$4,500** each to Clarion U. Foundation, Indiana Arts Council (mostly arts festival), Indiana Fire Assn., and YMCA of Indiana County. **$3,000-$3,500** each to American Cancer Society/Indiana County, Cystic Fibrosis Foundation, Indiana County Humane Society, Pa. Legacy Trust Fund, United Way of Westmoreland County, and Westmoreland County Museum of Art (capital campaign). **$2,000-$2,500** each to Aging Services, Inc., American Heart Assn., Boy Scouts/Bucktail Council, Boy Scouts/Penns Woods Council, East Communities YMCA, Free Medical Clinic of DuBois, Greater Pittsburgh Community Food Bank, Homer Center Athletic Boosters, ICCAP Back-to-School, Immaculate Conception School (scholarship fund), Indiana County Fair Assn., and Westmoreland Human Services. In addition, 46 other grants **$500-$1,700** for cultural and educational institutions, health care providers, local safety forces, and social services. ■**PUBLICATIONS:** None ■**WEBSITE:** www.stbank.com/community_interest.htm ■**E-MAIL:** None ■**APPLICATION POLICIES & PROCEDURES:** The Foundation reports that only organizations in the Bank's marketing area (Allegheny, Armstrong, Clarion, Clearfield, Indiana, Jefferson, and Westmoreland counties) are eligible to apply. Grant requests may be submitted in writing at any time; state the amount of funding requested and its purpose. No grants are awarded to individuals.
O+D+T James C. Miller (P+Con) — Edward C. Hauck (VP) — H. William Klumpp (F) — S & T Bank (Trustee) — Corporate donor: S & T Bank

---

SW-319 Sachnoff (Bruce D. & Treasure) Charitable Family Fdn.
1223 Bennington Avenue
Pittsburgh 15217 (Allegheny County)
AMV $620,925 **FYE** 4-01 (**Gifts Received** $101)

MI-11-22-29-33-54-57-62
Phone 412-681-7894 **FAX** None
EIN 25-6346205 **Year Created** 1990
42 **Grants totaling** $47,980

Limited local giving. High Pa. grant of **$5,000** to United Jewish Federation of Greater Pittsburgh. **$3,500** to United Way of SW Pa. **$2,500** to Mental Health Assn. of Allegheny County. **$1,000-$1,250** each to Carnegie Institute, Red Cross, and WQED. **$750** to Salvation Army. Other local contributions **$25-$500** for various purposes. **Out-of-state** giving includes high grant of **$20,550** to Recovery, Inc. [IL] and **$8,500** to Abraham Low Institute [IL]. ■**PUBLICATIONS:** None ■**WEBSITE:** None ■**E-MAIL:** None ■**APPLICATION POLICIES & PROCEDURES:** Grant requests in any form may be submitted at any time. Site visits sometimes are made to organizations being considered for a grant. No grants are awarded to individuals.
O+D+T Bruce D. Sachnoff (T+Con) — Treasure A. Sachnoff (T) — Donald S. Plung, CPA (T)

SW-320 Sachs (Murray & Marjorie) Foundation, The
1344 Squirrel Hill Ave.
Pittsburgh 15217 (Allegheny County)
AMV $99,151 **FYE** 11-00 (**Gifts Received** $0)

MI-22-62
Phone 412-621-1200 **FAX** None
EIN 25-1550424 **Year Created** 1987
70+ **Grants totaling** $12,396

Mostly local giving. High grant of **$2,900** to United Jewish Federation of Greater Pittsburgh. **$2,082** to Beth Shalom Congregation. **$696** to Yeshiva School. Other local and out-of-state contributions **$5-$500** for Jewish and other purposes. ■**PUBLICATIONS:** None ■**WEBSITE:** None ■**E-MAIL:** None ■**APPLICATION POLICIES & PROCEDURES:** Grant requests may be submitted in a letter at any time; describe the proposed project and include IRS tax-exempt status documentation. No grants awarded to individuals.
O+D+T Murray Sachs, M.D. (T+Donor+Con) — Marjorie Sachs (T)

SW-321   Salvitti Family Foundation
600 Lemoyne Ave. Extension
Washington   15601
(Washington County)

MI-13-14-15-17-22-25-31-32-34-41-42-43-44
52-61-71
Phone 724-222-2982 **FAX** None
EIN 25-1755617   **Year Created** 1995

AMV $7,031,294   **FYE** 12-00   **(Gifts Received** $0)   38 **Grants totaling** $520,000

Mostly local/Pa. giving; grants are for general purposes except as noted. High grant of **$292,000** to Temple U. Medical School [Philadelphia]. **$50,000** to Washington Hospital Foundation. **$25,000** each to Seton Hill College and Washington & Jefferson College. **$20,000** each to Immaculate Conception Church and Temple U. Medical School (scholarship program). **$10,000** to Greater Washington County Food Bank. **$5,000** each to ARC-Washington Foundation, Bronson House-The Neighborhood, Greater Washington Area Parks, Mario Lemieux Foundation, Washington County City Mission, and Washington Women's Shelter. **$3,000** each to John F. Kennedy School and Presbyterian Senior Care. **$2,000-$2,500** each to American Cancer Society, Big Brothers/Big Sisters of Greater Pittsburgh, Catholic Charities of Washington County, Citizen's Library, Clelian Heights School, Eye & Ear Institute, Greater Pittsburgh Guild for the Blind, Juvenile Diabetes Foundation, Pittsburgh Opera, and Salvation Army/Washington. Other local grants **$1,000** each for various purposes. **Out-of-state** giving includes **$5,000** each to American Academy of Ophthalmology [CA] and The Linsly School [WV]. ■**PUBLICATIONS:** None ■**WEBSITE:** None ■**E-MAIL:** None ■**APPLICATION POLICIES & PROCEDURES:** No grants awarded to individuals.

O+D+T E. Ronald Salvitti, M.D. (P+Donor+Con) — Constance A. Salvitti (VP+Donor) — Mary Moss [FL] (S) — Raymond J. Popeck (F)

SW-322   Sample (H. Glenn, Jr.), M.D. Memorial Fund
Refer to PNC Advisors Charitable Trust Committee entry.
(Allegheny County)

MI-13-14-15-17-20-22-29-34-41-44-45-51-52
54-57-61-63-64-72-84-89
EIN 91-6453143   **Year Created** 1999

AMV $7,049,729   **FYE** 12-00   **(Gifts Received** $0)   71 **Grants totaling** $270,500

All giving to Greater Pittsburgh area. High grants of **$10,000** each to The Corporate Collection, New Life Community Baptist Church, Pine Springs Camp, Sports & Exhibition Authority of Pittsburgh & Allegheny County, Steel Center Area Vo-Tech School, Washington County Literacy Council, Westmoreland Museum of American Art, and WQED. **$9,000** to Trinity Episcopal School for Ministry. **$7,000-$7,500** each to Blessed Sacrament Cathedral [Greensburg], Mendelssohn Choir of Pittsburgh, and Pittsburgh Voyager. **$5,000-$5,500** each to Domestic Abuse Counseling Center, Gateway Rehabilitation Center, Mon Yough Riverfront Entertainment & Cultural Council, and Prince of Peace Catholic Elementary School. **$3,000-$4,025** each to Allegheny County Court Appointed Special Advocate Program, Allegheny County Airport Authority, Allegheny Valley School, Animal Partners of Butler County, Butler Area Public Library, Covenant Presbyterian Church, DePaul Institute, First United Methodist Church, Girl Scouts of SW Pa., Hillel Foundation at the U. of Pittsburgh, Jane Holmes Residence, Jewish Community Center of Greater Pittsburgh, Kiskiminetas Springs School, Manchester Academic Charter School, Mary Miller Dance Company, Mon Valley Initiative, The Neighborhood Academy, The Pittsburgh Project, Pittsburgh Urban Christian School, Pittsburgh Wrestling Club, Schenley Heights Community Development Program, Southern Alleghenies Museum of Art, Sun Crumbs, Inc., U. of Pittsburgh School of Medicine, Veterans Place of Washington Blvd., Woodard's Educational Services, and Young Life-Steel Valley Youth Ministry. **$1,500-$2,870** each to American Heart Assn., Balmoral School of Highland Piping, Byzantine Catholic Seminary of Sts. Cyril & Methodius, Carnegie Institute, Center for Urban Biblical Ministry, Civic Senior Citizens of Aliquippa, Community Design Center, Family Trust, Freedom Unlimited, George Junior Republic, Glade Run Foundation, Ligonier Valley Memorial Assn., North Hills Community Outreach, Northside Common Ministries, Orr Compassionate Care Center, Pittsburgh Dance Council, The Program for Female Offenders, Rx Council of Western Pa., Search Ministries, Suburban General Hospital, Try-Again Homes, Urban Youth Actions, and Women's Shelter & Rape Crisis Center. Other smaller local grants/contributions for similar purposes. ■**APPLICATION POLICIES & PROCEDURES:** Refer to the PNC Advisors Charitable Trust Committee entry for a statement on giving priorities and full application guidelines.

O+D+T Refer to PNC Advisors Charitable Trust Committee entry. — PNC Advisors (Trustee)

SW-323   Sampson (Myles D. & J. Faye) Family Foundation
c/o Bar Development Co., Inc.
772 Pine Valley Road
Pittsburgh   15239
(Allegheny County)

MI-11-13-14-22-31-32-41-42-57-71-63-89
Phone 412-327-5755 **FAX** 412-733-0189
EIN 25-6407379   **Year Created** 1993

AMV $301,700   **FYE** 12-00   **(Gifts Received** $243,960)   38 **Grants totaling** $215,051

Mostly local giving. High grant of **$110,000** to East Suburban YMCA. **$25,000** to Community Foundation of Westmoreland County. **$13,500** to Boy Scouts/Westmoreland-Fayette Council. **$5,000** each to First Presbyterian Church of Murrysville and The Westmoreland Trust. **$4,500** to Children's Hospital of Pittsburgh. **$4,000** each to ARC-Westmoreland Foundation and Holiday Park Volunteer Fire Dept. **$3,700** to Clelian Heights School. **$3,000** to Salvation Army/Pittsburgh. **$1,000-$2,000** each to Bucknell U. [Lewisburg], Leukemia Society, Pittsburgh Vision Services, United Way of Westmoreland County, Westmoreland County Community College, and WQED. Other local contributions **$150-$500** for various purposes. **Out-of-state** giving includes **$10,000** to Rocky Mountain Elk Foundation [MT]; **$5,000** to Project Parent MD [OH]; and **$4,000** to Rotary International Foundation [IL]. ■**PUBLICATIONS:** None ■**WEBSITE:** None ■**E-MAIL:** None ■**APPLICATION POLICIES & PROCEDURES:** No grants awarded to individuals.

O+D+T Myles D. Sampson [Murrysville] (T+Donor+Con) — J. Faye Sampson [Murrysville] (T+Donor) — Corporate donor: Rimdo Properties, Inc.

SW-324   Sampson (Twila) Family Foundation

c/o The Sampson Group
2500 Eldo Road, #1
Monroeville 15146   (Allegheny County)

MI-13-56-63-71-89

Phone 412-374-1060 **FAX** None
EIN 25-1437507   **Year Created** 1983

AMV $47,476   **FYE** 12-00   (**Gifts Received** $0)   5 **Grants totaling** $19,500

All local giving. High grant of **$11,000** to Calvary United Methodist Church. **$5,000** to Homewood Hunting Camp of Westmoreland County. **$1,500** to Allegheny Historic Preservation Society. **$1,000** each to East Suburban YMCA and Holiday Park Volunteer Fire Dept. ■**PUBLICATIONS:** None ■**WEBSITE:** None ■**E-MAIL:** None ■**APPLICATION POLICIES & PROCEDURES:** Grant requests may be submitted in any form at any time; no grants awarded to individuals or for scholarships.

O+D+T Benard A. Sampson (T+Con) — Myles D. Sampson [Murrysville] (T+Donor) — Corporate donors: Rimco Construction; Bearfield Properties; Toro Development Company

---

SW-325   Sanctis (Ernest & Mae) Foundation

2442 North Meadowcroft Ave.
Pittsburgh 15216   (Allegheny County)

MI-31

Phone 412-343-6479 **FAX** None
EIN 25-1519455   **Year Created** 1986

AMV $2,183,097   **FYE** 6-01   (**Gifts Received** $0)   1 **Grant of** $110,060

Sole grant to Children's Hospital of Pittsburgh (for medical services to critically-ill, indigent patients). — Note: The hospital has been the Foundation's sole grantee for some years. ■**PUBLICATIONS:** Annual Report; grant application guidelines ■**WEBSITE:** None ■**E-MAIL:** None ■**APPLICATION POLICIES & PROCEDURES:** The Foundation reports that preference is given to the Greater Pittsburgh area. Grant requests must be submitted directly by the hospital and include a doctor's opinion as to the medical necessity, estimated medical cost, and family financial data.

O+D+T Julius A. Sanctis (Executive Director+Con) — Stuart H. Perilman (T) — Harvey A. Miller, Esq. (T)

SW-326   Sansom-Eligator Foundation

105 Fairway Lane
Pittsburgh 15238   (Allegheny County)

MI-13-41-44-55-71

Phone 412-963-1968 **FAX** None
EIN 23-2870275   **Year Created** 1996

AMV $9,134,695   **FYE** 12-00   (**Gifts Received** $993,713)   2 **Grants totaling** $200,000

All local giving. **$100,000** each to Boyd Community Center & Library Assn. (building improvements) and Western Pa. Conservancy (Lake Pleasant land purchase/other programs). — In the prior year, giving included **$225,000** each to The Ellis School (building improvements) and Shady Lane School; **$5,000** to Meadville Council on the Arts; and **$3,900** to Shenango Valley YMCA. ■**PUBLICATIONS:** None ■**WEBSITE:** None ■**E-MAIL:** None ■**APPLICATION POLICIES & PROCEDURES:** Information not available.

O+D+T Robert D. Sansom (P+D+Donor+Con) — Edith L. Eligator (F+D) — John R. Washlick, Esq. [Philadelphia] (D)

SW-327   Scaife Charitable Foundation

5840 Ellsworth Ave., Suite 200
Pittsburgh 15232   (Allegheny County)

MI-11-12-13-14-17-31-32-41-42-45-54-72-84

Phone 412-362-6000 **FAX** 412-362-6600
EIN 25-1847237   **Year Created** 2000

AMV $93,167,985   **FYE** 12-01   (**Gifts Received** $0)   43 **Grants totaling** $4,319,431

All local giving; the Grants Totaling figure above refers to funds disbursed in 2001 and the **$4,540,829** in grants reported below are those approved in 2001—some were fully paid and others in part as multiyear awards. High grant of **$1,035,000** to Pittsburgh Children's Museum (exhibit development). **$1,000,000** to Carnegie Mellon U. (launch Biomedical & Health Engineering Dept.). **$210,000** to Boy Scouts/Greater Pittsburgh Council (program support). **$200,000** each to Beginning with Books (Project BEACON/Read Together), Holy Family Institute (Institute for Learning Abilities research project), and U. of Pittsburgh/McGowan Institute for Regenerative Medicine (early-stage research). **$120,000** to Junior Achievement of SW Pa. (ImpACT 2005 Initiative). **$113,897** to Hill House Assn. (Youth Fair Chance School-to-Work program). **$104,000** to Every Child (renovation/additional office space). **$100,000** each to Family Guidance (One-to-One Program and Y.E.S. Program), Mentoring Partnership of SW Pa. (general operating support), Big Brothers Big Sisters of Greater Pittsburgh (School-Based Mentoring), Child's Way (charitable care/equipment purchase), and Greater Pittsburgh Literacy Council (Families for Learning Program/Distance Learning Program). **$80,000** to Westmoreland County Blind Assn. (general operating support). **$75,000** to Schenley Heights Community Development Program (support for two programs). **$65,200** to Presbyterian SeniorCare (Timothy Place-capital/operating support). **$50,000** each to YWCA of Greater Pittsburgh (Child Care Partnerships and Bridge Housing programs), Allegheny Youth Development (program support), Pennsylvania Environmental Council (Youth Outdoor Adventure Program), and Providence Connections (family support center). **$48,000** to Paws with a Cause (assistance dogs). **$47,000** to National Aviary (educational website). **$40,000** each to Breachmenders (School-to-Career Program), YouthWorks (marketing campaign), Human Services Center Corp (general operating support), and Pittsburgh Cares (expanded Volunteer Services/Children's Literacy Program). **$38,626** to Jubilee Assn. (Medical Clinic/John Heinz Child Development Center). **$35,000** to One-to-One: Citizen Advocacy (general operating support). **$34,106** Carnegie Mellon U./Role Models Program (minibus acquisition-support). **$30,000** each to Manchester Youth Development Center (program outcome study) and Make-A-Wish Foundation of Western Pa. (wishes for children with life-threatening illnesses). **$15,000** to Good Grief Center for Bereavement Support (general operating support). — In the prior year, major grants included **$1,000,000** to United Way of Allegheny County (internet development plan); **$745,000** to Pittsburgh Zoo & Aquarium (education complex expansion); **$500,000** to UCP of Pittsburgh (capital campaign); **$483,654** to Carnegie Science Center (science outreach programs); **$400,000** each to Manchester Youth Development Center (support for four programs) and U. of Pittsburgh/Neurology Dept. (various programs/staff); **$300,000** to Family House (Shadyside facility); **$290,000** to Western Pa. School for the Deaf (various projects); **$254,577** to Women's Center & Shelter of Greater Pittsburgh (staff support/development); **$215,740** to UPMC

Health System (Theiss Center/child care program); **$200,000** to Pace School (major campaign); **$160,000** to I Have A Dream Foundation of Pittsburgh (program/operating support); and **$120,000** to U. of Pittsburgh/Principals' Academy (general support). ■**PUBLICATIONS:** application guidelines ■**WEBSITE:** None ■**E-MAIL:** nbeldecos@scaifecharitable.org ■**APPLICATION POLICIES & PROCEDURES:** The Foundation reports that giving focuses on SW Pa. organizations with priority for human services, health, or educational purposes. No grants are awarded to individuals. Initial inquiries may be submitted at any time in a letter signed by the organization's Executive Director or authorized representative; provide general information on the organization, a concise description of the proposed project and the funding requested. After review, the Foundation will notify applicants if a full proposal should be submitted; for this the Grantmakers of Western Pa. Common Grant Application may be used and should include a project budget, audited financial statements for the last four years, and IRS tax-exempt status documentation. Grants are awarded at least three times per year. — Formerly called David N. Scaife Charitable Foundation.

O+D+T J. Nicholas Beldecos (Executive Director+Con) — David N. Scaife (C+T) — Sanford B. Ferguson [Champion] (VC+T) — Sara D. Scaife (S+T) — Edward Goncz [Wexford] (F+T) — Donald Collins [DC] (T) — Frances G. Scaife (T) — Joseph C. Walton (T)

SW-328 **Scaife Family Foundation**
One Oxford Center, Suite 3900
301 Grant Street
Pittsburgh 15219   (Allegheny County)

MI-12-13-14-17-18-22-25-29-31-32-42-45-71
72-86
Phone 412-392-2900 **FAX** 412-392-2922
EIN 25-1427015   **Year Created** 1984

AMV $108,063,816   **FYE** 12-00   **(Gifts Received** $0)   76 **Grants totaling** $7,710,135

About two-thirds local/Pa. giving; grants are for program/general support except as noted. The 'Grants Totaling' figure above refers to funds disbursed in 2000; the 72 grants reported below (totaling **$9,301,935**) were approved in 2000—some were fully paid and others multiyear awards paid in part. High grant of **$2,000,000** to Magee-Women's Health Foundation. **$400,000** to Three Rivers Employment Services (satellite child care). **$360,000** to Duquesne U. (mostly for Family Institute). **$350,000** to Beginning With Books (program/capital support). **$250,000** each to Animal Rescue League of Western Pa. (capital support), Mercy Hospital Foundation, and Western Pa. Conservancy. **$225,000** to Western Pa. Family Center (program/capital support). **$100,000** each to Gateway Rehabilitation Center, Hosanna Industries (capital support), The Pittsburgh Project, Planned Parenthood of Western Pa., Women's Center & Shelter of Greater Pittsburgh (program/capital support), and Women's Shelter of Lawrence County (capital support). **$75,000** each to Glade Run Foundation and Louise's Child Care Center (Director's Institute). **$50,000-$50,400** each to Caron Foundation [Berks County] (medical student program in substance dependency), Chartiers Nature Conservancy (land acquisition), Commonwealth Foundation for Public Policy Alternatives [Harrisburg] (education reform), Fayette SPCA (capital support), First Step Recovery Homes (capital support), Make-A-Wish Foundation of Western Pa., North Side Christian Health Center, William & Mildred Orr Compassionate Care Center, and Ryerss Farm for Aged Equines [Montgomery County]. **$40,000** to Institute for Research Education & Training in Addictions. **$36,000** to CONTACT Pittsburgh (volunteer training). **$30,000** each to Big Brothers & Big Sisters of Greater Pittsburgh, The Corporate Collection, Gwen's Montessori School, Neighborhood Housing Services, Pittsburgh Psychoanalytic Foundation, and Strength, Inc. **$25,000** each to Mt. Ararat Community Activity Center and Riverview Children's Center (capital support). **$20,000** each to Bethlehem Haven of Pittsburgh. **$15,000** each to Golden Triangle Radio Information and Westgate Village Resident Council. **$10,000** each to Covenant Presbyterian Church (program/capital support). **$9,500** to Mom's House of Johnstown. **Out-of-state** giving includes **$500,000** to Children of Alcoholics Foundation [NY]; **$357,000** to NYU School of Medicine (fellowships in alcohol/drug abuse); **$288,235** to Susan G. Komen Foundation [TX] (education/research programs); **$250,000** to Johns Hopkins U./School of Advanced International Studies [DC]; **$200,000** each to National Center for Victims of Crime [VA], National Fatherhood Initiative [MD], and Puppies Behind Bars [NY]; **$161,800** to All Creatures Sanctuary [FL]; **$150,000** each to National Foundation for Teaching Entrepreneurship [NY] and North County Humane Society [FL]; **$125,000** to Equal Opportunity Foundation [DC]; **$100,000** each to Education Policy Institute [DC] and Landmark Legal Foundation [MO]; and other grants **$4,000-$75,000** for similar purposes in many states, including a number of grants for the Medical Student Program in Alcohol & Other Drug Dependencies program. ■**PUBLICATIONS:** Annual Report and application guidelines (available on website) ■**WEBSITE:** www.scaife.com ■**E-MAIL:** None ■**APPLICATION POLICIES & PROCEDURES:** The Foundation reports that Pittsburgh/Western Pa. organizations receive special consideration, mostly for general support or special projects. Special interests are programs that (a) strengthen families—specifically the health/welfare of women/children, (b) promote animal welfare, and (c) demonstrate the beneficial interaction between humans and animals. No grants are awarded to individuals and, generally, not for event sponsorships, endowment, capital campaigns, renovations, or to government agencies. Grant requests may be submitted at any time in a letter (2 pages maximum) signed by the organization's CEO or authorized representative and approved by the organization's Board of Directors; include a concise description of the purpose for which funds are requested, organizational/project budgets, audited financial statement, list of major funding sources, Board member list with major affiliations, and IRS tax-exempt status documentation. Additional information may be requested. Grants are awarded at Trustee meetings in February, May, September, and December.

O+D+T Joanne B. Beyer (P+F+Con) — Jennie K. Scaife [FL] (C+T) — Beth H. Genter [NM] (VP) — Mary T. Walton [Sewickley] (VP)

SW-329 **Scaife (Sarah) Foundation**
One Oxford Center, Suite 3900
301 Grant Street
Pittsburgh 15219   (Allegheny County)

MI-41-42-49-71-81-86-89

Phone 412-392-2900 **FAX** 412-392-2922
EIN 25-1113452   **Year Created** 1941

AMV $364,327,000   **FYE** 12-00   **(Gifts Received** $0)   124 **Grants totaling** $25,785,000

Nationwide giving, primarily to organizations dealing with major domestic or international public policy issues; grants are for general operating or program support except as noted. About 10% local/Pa. giving: High Pa. grant of **$1,000,000** to Phipps Conservatory & Botanical Garden. **$140,000** to Catholic Diocese of Pittsburgh Foundation (Bishop's Education Fund). **$110,000** to Carnegie Mellon U. (Allan Meltzer Chair endowment). **$100,000** to Commonwealth Foundation for Public Policy Alternatives [Harrisburg]. **$70,000** to World Affairs Council of Pittsburgh. **$60,000** to Foreign Policy Research Institute [Philadelphia]. **$56,000** to U. of Pittsburgh (Center for Philosophy Science). **$50,000** to Allegheny County District Attorney's Office (child abuse prosecution unit). **$25,000** each to Grove City College (Institute on Economics & Religion) and Pa. Economy League. **$7,500** to Ligonier Valley School District (Christmas gift program). **Out-of-state** giving includes **$1,500,000** to The Heritage Foundation [DC]; **$1,395,000** to Judicial Watch, Inc. [DC]; **$953,000** to Free Congress Research & Education Foundation [DC]; **$885,000** to Center for Strategic & International Studies [DC]; **$600,000** to Social Philosophy & Policy Foundation [OH]; **$595,000** to Institute for Foreign Policy Analysis [MA]; **$550,000** to George Mason U. Foundation [VA]; **$500,000** to Landmark Legal Foundation [MO]; **$400,000** to Accuracy in Media [DC]; **$390,000** to Hudson Institute [IN]; **$375,000** to American Enterprise Institute for Public Policy Research [DC]; **$370,000** to Hoover Institution on War, Revolution & Peace [CA]; **$350,000** to U. of Virginia Law School Foundation; **$325,000** to Center for Security Policy [DC]; **$300,000** each to The Maldon Institute [MD] and Media Research Center [VA]; and other grants **$25,000-$250,000** for similar purposes in many states. ■**PUBLICATIONS:** Annual Report available on the Foundation's website. ■**WEBSITE:** www.scaife.com ■**E-MAIL:** None ■**APPLICATION POLICIES & PROCEDURES:** The Foundation reports that giving is primarily directed toward public policy programs—without geographic restriction—which address major domestic or international issues; most grants are for general operating support, equipment, special projects, seed money, research studies, publications, seminars/conferences, and fellowships; multiyear grants are awarded. No grants are awarded to individuals or to nationally-organized fundraising groups. Initial inquiries may be submitted at any time in a letter signed by an organization's CEO (or authorized representative) and approved by the organization's Board of Directors; provide a concise description of the proposed project/program, a timetable, and related budget; include an annual report, audited financial statement, current organizational budget, list of Board members with their major affiliations, and IRS tax-exempt status documentation. Additional information may be requested or an interview arranged. Grants are awarded by the Trustees at meetings in February, May, September and November.

O+D+T Michael W. Gleba (VP-Programs+Con) — Richard M. Scaife (C+T) — Barbara L. Slaney (VP+F) — R. Daniel McMichael (S+T) — T. Westray Battle, III (T) — Dr. William J. Bennett [DC] (T) — T. Kenneth Cribb, Jr. [DE] (T) — Dr. Edwin J. Feulner, Jr. [DC] (T) — Dr. Allan H. Meltzer (T) — James C. Roddey (T) — James M. Walton (T)

SW-330   Sedwick Foundation   MI-15-22-41-42-63-84
        c/o Armstrong Utilities, Inc.
        1 Armstrong Place   **Phone** 724-283-0925 **FAX** 724-283-9655
        Butler   16001   (Butler County)   **EIN** 25-6284774   **Year Created** 1986
AMV $9,734,607   **FYE** 6-01   (**Gifts Received** $1,600,023)   14 **Grants totaling** $1,830,527

Mostly local/Pa. giving. High grant of **$1,362,237** to U. of Pittsburgh Athletics Dept. **$135,000** to SAT 7 [Delaware County (Christian satellite service to Middle East). **$84,000** to Community Alliance Church of Butler. **$40,000** to Meals on Wheels of Butler. **$20,000** to The Lighthouse Foundation [Bakerstown]. **$15,000** each to Pine Valley Bible Conference [Ellwood City] and Search Ministries, Inc. [Mars]. **$10,000** to Butler County Community College Foundation. **$1,200-$1,667** each to Coalition for Christian Outreach [Pittsburgh], Golden Tornado Scholastic Foundation, and Pine Valley Bible Camp. **Out-of-state** giving includes **$50,023** to Lima Rescue Home [OH]; **$50,000** to Institute for Creation Research [CA]; **$35,000** to Professional Assn. of Christian Educators [TX]; and **$10,000** to Grace Preparatory Academy [TX]. ■**PUBLICATIONS:** None ■**WEBSITE:** www.armstrongonewire.com [corporate info only] ■**E-MAIL:** None ■**APPLICATION POLICIES & PROCEDURES:** No grants awarded to individuals.

O+D+T Kirby J. Campbell (T+Con) — Jay L. Sedwick, Sr. (T+Donor) — William C. Stewart (T) — Mrs. Jay L. Sedwick, Sr. (Donor) — Jay L. Sedwick, Jr. [TX] (Donor) — Mrs. Jay L. Sedwick, Jr. [TX] (Donor) — Dr. Robert Moon [OH] (Donor) — Mrs. Robert Moon [OH] (Donor) — Corporate donors: Armstrong Utilities, Inc.; Armstrong Communications, Inc.; Armstrong Telephone Companies in several states

---

SW-331   Shapira (David S. & Karen A.) Foundation   MI-22-42-52-62
        c/o Giant Eagle Markets, Inc.
        101 Kappa Drive   **Phone** 412-963-6200 **FAX** 412-963-2540
        Pittsburgh   15238   (Allegheny County)   **EIN** 25-1711993   **Year Created** 1990
AMV $1,430,682   **FYE** 12-00   (**Gifts Received** $391,789)   6 **Grants totaling** $125,500

Mostly local giving. High grant of **$105,000** to United Jewish Federation of Greater Pittsburgh. **$10,000** to Pittsburgh Symphony. **$3,000** to Jewish Education Institute. **$2,500** to Carnegie Mellon U. **Out-of-state** grants: **$2,500** each to Oberlin College [OH] and Stanford U. [CA]. ■**PUBLICATIONS:** None ■**WEBSITE:** www.gianteagle.com [corporate info only] ■**E-MAIL:** None ■**APPLICATION POLICIES & PROCEDURES:** Grant requests may be submitted in any form at any time. — Formerly called David & Karen Shapira Charitable Trust.

O+D+T Karen A. Shapira (P+D+Donor+Con) — David S. Shapira (S+F+Donor) — Laura M. Karet (D) — Deborah B. Shapira (D) — Jeremy M. Shapira (D)

SW-332   Shapiro (Zalman & Evelyn) Charitable Trust   MI-22-42-62-81
        1045 Lyndhurst Drive   **Phone** 412-361-3950 **FAX** None
        Pittsburgh   15206   (Allegheny County)   **EIN** 23-7011257   **Year Created** 1969
AMV $119,312   **FYE** 12-00   (**Gifts Received** $41,218)   50+ **Grants totaling** $33,491

About two-thirds local giving. High grant of **$8,412** to Hillel Academy. **$2,491** to Kollel of Pittsburgh. **$2,486** to Young People's Synagogue. **$1,000** to Middle East Forum [Philadelphia]. **$985** to Tree of Life Synagogue. **$765** to Shaare Torah Synagogue. Other smaller local contributions, many for Jewish charities. **Out-of-state** grants includes **$8,000** to Jewish Teachers Training College [NY] and **$2,750** to Zionist Organization of America [NY]. ■**PUBLICATIONS:** None ■**WEBSITE:** None ■**E-MAIL:** None ■**APPLICATION POLICIES & PROCEDURES:** Grant requests may be submitted in a letter at any time; describe the organization's charitable purpose and state the funding requested.

O+D+T Evelyn Shapiro (T+Donor+Con) — Dr. Zalman M. Shapiro (T+Donor)

SW-333 **Shea (Irene C.) Charitable Foundation**   MI-22-31-42
P.O. Box 8050   **Phone** 412-831-1892 **FAX** None
Pittsburgh   15216   (Allegheny County)   **EIN** 25-6410108   **Year Created** 1993
AMV $1,926,238   **FYE** 7-01   **(Gifts Received** $360,000)   6 **Grants totaling** $97,000

About four-fifths local giving. High grant of **$28,000** to Coalition for Christian Outreach. **$23,000** to East Liberty Family Health Care Center. **$15,000** to Shadyside Hospital Foundation. **$10,000** to Carlow College. **Out-of-state** giving includes **$20,000** to Pratt Institute [NY] and **$1,000** to Princeton U. [NJ]. ■**PUBLICATIONS:** None ■**WEBSITE:** None ■**E-MAIL:** None ■**APPLICA-TION POLICIES & PROCEDURES:** Grant requests may be submitted in any form at any time; include IRS tax-exempt status documentation. Grants are awarded at meetings in May and June.

O+D+T Thomas J. Hickey (Co-T+Con) — Irene C. Shea (Donor) — National City Bank of Pa. (Corporate Co-Trustee)

SW-334 **Shiras (Elisabeth) Charitable Trust**   MI-12-13-22-29-41-45
Refer to PNC Advisors Charitable Trust Committee entry.
     (Allegheny County)   **EIN** 25-6347429   **Year Created** 1990
AMV $2,064,973   **FYE** 5-00   **(Gifts Received** $0)   8 **Grants totaling** $64,660

All giving restricted to education, health, or the welfare of children/youth. High grants of **$12,000** each to Beginning With Books and The Wesley Institute. **$11,000** to Big Brothers/Big Sisters of Westmoreland County. **$8,000** each to Christ the Divine Teacher School [Latrobe] and Mt. Ararat Community Activity Center. **$6,000** to Mt. Lebanon Montessori School. **$4,830** to Homeless Children & Family Emergency Fund. **$2,830** to Mary & Alexander Laughlin Children's Home. ■**APPLICATION POLI-CIES & PROCEDURES:** Refer to the PNC Advisors Charitable Trust Committee entry for a statement on giving priorities and full application guidelines.

O+D+T Refer to PNC Advisors Charitable Trust Committee entry. — PNC Advisors (Corporate Trustee)

SW-335 **Shore Fund, The**   MI-12-13-14-25-29-32-41
c/o Mellon Private Wealth Management
One Mellon Center, P.O. Box 185   **Phone** 412-234-0023 **FAX** 412-234-1073
Pittsburgh   15230   (Allegheny County)   **EIN** 25-6220659   **Year Created** 1982
AMV $4,569,472   **FYE** 12-00   **(Gifts Received** $0)   20 **Grants totaling** $207,000

About half local/Pa. giving; grants are for general operating support unless otherwise noted. High Pa. grants of **$25,000** each to American Cancer Society (capital campaign), Hillman Cancer Center (honorary gift), and Pressley Ridge Schools (capital campaign). **$10,000** each to Family House and YWCA of Greater Pittsburgh (van). **$5,000** each to First Night Pittsburgh, Gateway Rehabilitation Center (honorary gift), Greater Pittsburgh Community Food Bank, and Susan G. Komen Breast Cancer Foundation (Race for the Cure). **$2,500** to Sunshine Foundation [Bucks County] (memorial gift). **$1,000** to Contact Pittsburgh. **Out-of-state** giving includes **$25,000** to Hammond-Harwood House [MD] (capital campaign); **$20,000** to The Masters School [NY] (various purposes); **$15,000** to St. Anne's Parish [MD] (restoration); **$10,000** each to Betty Ford Center [CA] (capital campaign) and Phillips Exeter Academy [NH]; and smaller grants to FL and NY. ■**PUBLICATIONS:** None ■**WEBSITE:** None ■**E-MAIL:** None ■**APPLICATION POLICIES & PROCEDURES:** The Fund reports that grants are awarded only to organizations in which individual Trustees are personally involved. Prospective applicants should make an initial telephone call to inquire about the feasibility of submitting a request. Site visits sometimes are made to organizations being considered for a grant.

O+D+T Laurie A. Moritz (VP at Bank+Con) — Christine Fisher Allen [NC] (T) — Benjamin R. Fisher, Jr. (T) — Lillian H. Fisher (T) — Margaret Fisher McKean [MD] (T) — Mellon Bank N.A. (Corporate Trustee)

SW-336 **Simmons (Richard P.) Family Foundation**   MI-11-12-13-14-25-32-41-42-44-45-49-51-52
'Birchmere'   54-57-
Quaker Hollow Road   **Phone** 412-741-7491 **FAX** None
Sewickley   15143   (Allegheny County)   **EIN** 25-6277068   **Year Created** 1987
AMV $11,112,402   **FYE** 12-00   **(Gifts Received** $5,000)   51 **Grants totaling** $6,251,234

About one-fifth local giving; grants are for general purposes except as noted. High Pa. grant of **$300,000** to Sewickley Academy (capital campaign/scholarship fund). **$275,000** to United Way of Allegheny County. **$150,000** to Sewickley Public Library (capital campaign). **$75,000** to Pittsburgh Symphony. **$50,000** to Pa. Partnership for Economic Education [Harrisburg]. **$42,000** to Pittsburgh Public Theater (mostly capital campaign). **$40,000** to Extra Mile Education Foundation. **$25,000** each to Pittsburgh Children's Museum and Sewickley Civic Garden Center. **$20,000** each to Carnegie Science Center, River City Brass Band, and Verland Foundation. **$16,500-$16,667** each to Allegheny Valley School, LaRoche College, and National Flag Foundation. **$15,000** to Summerbridge Pittsburgh. **$10,000** each to Allegheny Valley YMCA (capital campaign), Carnegie Museums, Children's Home of Pittsburgh, Children's Hospital of Pittsburgh, Greater Pittsburgh Community Food Bank, and I Have A Dream Foundation. **$5,000-$6,000** each to Boys & Girls Clubs of SW Pa., Child's Way, Kiski Valley YMCA, Laughlin Children's Center, and WQED. **$6,800** to Make-A-Wish Foundation of Western Pa. **$3,500** to Pittsburgh Tissue Engineering (summer interns). **$1,000-$2,000** each to American Cancer Society, Beginning With Books, Children's Institute, Greater Pittsburgh Literacy Council, Junior Achievement of SW Pa., Mars Home for Youth, Old Sewickley Post Office Corp., Opera Theater of Pittsburgh, Pa. Special Olympics, Pittsburgh Opera, Saltworks Theatre Company, Union Aid Society, and Western Pa. Conservancy. Other local contributions **$100-$500**. **Out-of-state** giving includes high grant of **$5,000,000** to Massachusetts Institute of Technology (capital campaign) and **$10,000** to Economic Strategy Initiative [DC]. — Grants approved for future payment (all multiyear pledges) include **$15,000,000** to Massachusetts Institute of Technology (capital campaign); **$500,000** to Sewickley Academy (capital campaign); **$300,000** to Sewickley Public Library (renovation project); **$275,000** to United Way of Allegheny County; **$250,000** to Carnegie Mellon U. (Queenan Chair); **$150,000** to Pa. Partnership for Economic Education [Harrisburg];

$80,000 each to Hill House Assn. and River City Brass Band; and $60,000 each to Pittsburgh Public Theater and Summerbridge Pittsburgh. ■**PUBLICATIONS:** None ■**WEBSITE:** None ■**E-MAIL:** None ■**APPLICATION POLICIES & PROCEDURES:** No grants are awarded to individuals.

O+D+T Richard P. Simmons (T+Donor+Con) — Amy Simmons Sebastian (Donor) — Brian P. Simmons [IL] (Donor) — Corporate donor: Diamond Investments Corp. [DE]

SW-337 **Simonds (Dylan Todd) Foundation, Inc., The**
2000 Grant Building, 310 Grant Street
Pittsburgh 15219   (Allegheny County)
AMV $1,196,759   **FYE** 12-00   **(Gifts Received** $0)

MI-12-13-25-41-53-54-71-84
Phone 412-338-3466 **FAX** 412-338-3463
EIN 25-1752987   **Year Created** 1995
25 **Grants totaling** $73,000

Nearly half local giving; grants are unrestricted support except as noted. High local grant of **$5,000** to Manchester Craftsmen's Guild (programs). **$4,000** to St. Edmund's Academy (annual fund/scholarship fund). **$3,500** to Pa. Resources Council (Earth Force programs). **$2,000-$2,500** each to Andy Warhol Museum, Big Brothers/Big Sisters of Greater Pittsburgh (mentoring programs), Conservation Consultants (educational programs), Pittsburgh Parks Conservancy, and Western Pa. Conservancy. **$1,000** each to Carnegie Institute, Children's Institute (pediatric free care fund), Greater Pittsburgh Community Food Bank, Loyalhanna Watershed Assn. (outreach programs), Pittsburgh Voyager (environmental education programs), and Regional Trail Corp. Other smaller local contributions. **Out-of-state** giving includes high grant of **$20,000** to Ecotrust [OR] (programs/activities); **$5,000** to Yale U. [CT]; and **$3,000** to S.M.A.R.T./Schools Mentoring and Resource Team [CA] (scholarships). ■**PUBLICATIONS:** None ■**WEBSITE:** None ■**E-MAIL:** foundation@hillmanfo.com■**APPLICATION POLICIES & PROCEDURES:** Grant requests may be submitted at any time in a letter signed by a fully authorized official; describe the program/project, its objectives, and state what funding is requested; include an annual budget, list of officers/directors, detailed information on project costs, time schedule (if appropriate), and other significant background information. Also provide a copy of IRS tax-exempt status documentation. The Board meets in May and December. Periodic written reports are required of all grantees.

O+D+T Ronald W. Wertz (S+D+Con) — Dylan Todd Simonds (P+D) — Lawrence M. Wagner (VP+D) — Maurice J. White (F+D) — Lisa R. Johns (AF) — Donors: Henry L. Hillman Trust

---

SW-338 **Simonds (Henry John) Foundation, Inc., The**
2000 Grant Building, 310 Grant Street
Pittsburgh 15219   (Allegheny County)
AMV $1,192,100   **FYE** 12-00   **(Gifts Received** $0)

MI-12-13-14-22-25-31-32-41-51-53-55-71
Phone 412-338-3466 **FAX** 412-338-3463
EIN 25-1752986   **Year Created** 1995
48 **Grants totaling** $70,000

Over three-fourths local giving; grants are unrestricted support except as noted. High local grant of **$5,000** to Silver Eye Center for Photography (mostly for exhibition). **$3,000-$3,500** each to Allegheny Valley School (capital campaign), Legal Aid for Children (services for abused/neglected children), Pittsburgh Filmmakers (art project/general support), and St. Edmund's Academy (annual fund/scholarship fund). **$2,000-$2,500** each to Brew House Assn. (puppet festival), St. Mary's Lawrenceville Arts Program (after school/summer programs), and U. of Pittsburgh Cancer Institute (research fund). **$1,000-$1,500** each to Conservation Consultants, Greater Pittsburgh Arts Alliance, Greater Pittsburgh Community Food Bank, Manchester Craftsmen's Guild, Northside Common Ministries (food purchases), Pittsburgh Environmental Council (youth program), Pittsburgh Parks Conservancy, The Pittsburgh Project, Quantum Theatre, Schenley Heights Community Development Program (summer enrichment program), Shadyside Hospital Foundation, Three Rivers Employment Service, Western Pa. Conservancy, and YouthWorks (public sector jobs for youth). Other smaller local contributions. **Out-of-state** giving includes **$5,500** to Middlebury College [VT] (equipment); and **$2,000** each to The Field [NY] (fairytale festival) and S.M.A.R.T./Schools Mentoring and Resource Team [CA] (student scholarships). ■**PUBLICATIONS:** None ■**WEBSITE:** None ■**E-MAIL:** foundation@hillmanfo.com ■**APPLICATION POLICIES & PROCEDURES:** Grant requests may be submitted at any time in a letter signed by a fully authorized official; describe the program/project, its objectives, and state what funding is requested; include an annual budget, list of officers/directors, detailed information on project costs, time schedule (if appropriate), and other significant background information. Also provide a copy of IRS tax-exempt status documentation. The Board meets in May and December.

O+D+T Ronald W. Wertz (S+D+Con) — Henry John Simonds (P+D) — Lawrence M. Wagner (VP+D) — Maurice J. White (F+D) — Juliet Lea Hillman Simonds (D) — Lisa R. Johns (AF) — Donors: Henry L. Hillman Trust

---

SW-339 **Simonds (Juliet Lea Hillman) Foundation, Inc., The**
2000 Grant Building, 310 Grant Street
Pittsburgh 15219   (Allegheny County)
AMV $11,038,320   **FYE** 12-00   **(Gifts Received** $0)

MI-12-17-25-31-32-41-45-53-54-55-56-57-63
Phone 412-338-3466 **FAX** 412-338-3463
EIN 25-1536951   **Year Created** 1986
50 **Grants totaling** $334,100

About three-fourths local giving; grants are unrestricted or operating support except as noted and some grants comprise multiple payments. High grant of **$75,000** (2 grants) to Carnegie Institute/Andy Warhol Museum (programming/exhibitions). **$57,200** (five grants) to Carnegie Institute/Museum of Art (acquisitions/Light Show/Architecture Center/ Film-Video Program/Discretionary Fund). **$25,000** to Creative Nonfiction Foundation. **$15,000** to U. of Pittsburgh Cancer Institute (mostly research fund). **$11,000** to The Ellis School (mostly Hillman Family Building). **$10,000** to Carnegie Institute (Trustee Annual Fund). **$7,500** to Pittsburgh Filmmakers (documentary film/general support). **$5,500** to Pittsburgh Arts & Lectures (Poem Chase/lecture underwriting). **$5,000** to International Poetry Forum (Poets-in-Person program). **$3,500** to WQED (Elsie Awards/general support). **$3,000** to Westmoreland Museum of American Art (exhibition). **$2,500** to Mattress Factory (programs). **$1,000-$1,500** each to Calvary Episcopal Church (after school program), Children's Hospital of Pittsburgh (free care fund), Greater Pittsburgh Community Food Bank, Greater Pittsburgh Literacy Council (ESL program), Light of Life Ministries, Pittsburgh/Muskoka Foundation, Pittsburgh Symphony, Preservation Pa. (Meason House project), Ronald McDonald House Charities of Pittsburgh, St. Edmund's Academy, Shadyside Hospital Foundation, and Women's Center & Shelter of Greater Pittsburgh. Other smaller local contributions for similar purposes. **Out-of-state** giving includes **$50,000** to Dia Center for the Arts [NY] (Beacon Museum project); **$10,000** each to Masters School [NY] (science center) and The Taft School [CT]; **$9,900** to Academy of American Poets [NY]; and **$6,000** to S.M.A.R.T./Schools Mentoring and Resource Team [CA] (scholarships). ■**PUBLICATIONS:** None ■**WEBSITE:** None ■ **E-MAIL:** foundation@hillmanfo.com ■**APPLICATION POLICIES & PROCEDURES:** The Foundation reports that requests from Pittsburgh/SW Pa. organizations receive preference. Most grants are for general/operating support, building/capital purposes, endowment, equipment, and program development. No grants are awarded to individuals. Grant requests may be submitted at any time in a letter signed by a fully authorized official which describes/justifies the program/project, its objectives, and states the funding requested; also include an annual budget, list of officers/directors, detailed information on project costs, time schedule (if appropriate), other significant background information, and IRS tax-exempt status documentation. The Board meets in May and December.

O+D+T Ronald W. Wertz (S+D+Con) — Juliet Lea Hillman Simonds (P+D+Donor) — Lawrence M. Wagner (VP+D) — Maurice J. White (F+D) — Lisa R. Johns (AF) — Donors: Henry L. Hillman Trust; Henry L. Hillman Charitable Lead Trust

---

SW-340 Simonds (Talbott Lea) Foundation, Inc., The   MI-13-16-29-41-71
2000 Grant Building, 310 Grant Street   **Phone** 412-338-3466 **FAX** 412-338-3463
Pittsburgh 15219   (Allegheny County)   **EIN** 25-1752984   **Year Created** 1994
AMV $1,198,348   **FYE** 12-00   (**Gifts Received** $0)   36 **Grants totaling** $57,850

Limited local giving; grants are for unrestricted/general support except as noted. High local grant of **$3,500** to St. Edmund's Academy (scholarship fund). **$1,000** each to Big Brothers Big Sisters of Greater Pittsburgh (mentoring programs), FAME/Fund for Advancement of Minorities Through Education (endowment), Manchester Craftsmen's Guild, Pittsburgh Parks Conservancy, and Schenley Heights Community Development Program. Other smaller local contributions for cultural and other purposes. **Out-of-state** giving includes high grant of **$8,500** to S.M.A.R.T./Schools Mentoring and Resource Team [CA] (scholarships/general support); **$6,000** to Environmental Traveling Companions [CA] (mostly for environmental center); **$5,000** to San Francisco Foundation [CA] (Social Venture-Bay Area Partners); and smaller grants/contributions for education, youth, and other purposes, many to CA. ■**PUBLICATIONS:** None ■**WEBSITE:** None ■**E-MAIL:** foundation@hillmanfo.com ■**APPLICATION POLICIES & PROCEDURES:** The Foundation reports that most grants are for general /operating support, building/capital purposes, equipment, land acquisition, program development, or seed money. Grant requests may be submitted at any time in a letter signed by a fully authorized official; describe the program/project, its objectives, and state what funding is requested; include an annual budget, list of officers/directors, detailed information on project costs, time schedule (if appropriate), other significant background information, and IRS tax-exempt status documentation. The Board meets in May and December.

O+D+T Ronald W. Wertz (S+D+Con) — Talbott Lea Simonds (P+D) — Lawrence M. Wagner (VP+D) — Maurice J. White (F+D) — Lisa R. Johns (AF) — Donors: Henry L. Hillman Trust

---

SW-341   Smiy Family Foundation   MI-12-13-22-32-42-43-44-51-52-54-61-71-85
626 Iroquois Street   **Phone** 724-863-5742 **FAX** 724-863-8331
Irwin 15642   (Westmoreland County)   **EIN** 23-2905105   **Year Created** 1996
AMV $2,108,231   **FYE** 6-01   (**Gifts Received** $182,940)   32 **Grants totaling** $236,175

Mostly local giving; some grants comprise multiple payments. High grant of **$145,000** to Immaculate Conception Church (Library-Multimedia Center & Project 2000). **$10,000** to Westmoreland Museum of American Art. **$8,675** to Sisters of Charity of Seton Hill. **$7,000** to Norwin Chamber of Commerce. **$6,000** each to Vet/2000 and Westmoreland Symphony. **$5,000** to Catholic Charities/Pittsburgh, Epilepsy Foundation, Greensburg YMCA (Project Forward), IBEW Local #5 Joint Apprenticeship Training Committee (scholarships), Seton Hill College, and Westmoreland County Community College Foundation. **$3,000** to Westmoreland County Area Labor Management Committee. **$1,000-$2,500** each to Bethlehem Project, Catholic Charities/Greensburg, Irwin Clock Fund, Jeannette Public Library, Laurel Ballet, Loyalhanna Watershed Assn., Mom's House, National Kidney Foundation of Western Pa., and Norwin Public Library. **Out-of-state** giving includes **$2,000** to International Mission Board [FL] and smaller grants to VA. ■**PUBLICATIONS:** None ■**WEBSITE:** None ■**E-MAIL:** None ■**APPLICATION POLICIES & PROCEDURES:** Grant requests may be submitted in a letter at any time.

O+D+T Paul R. Smiy (T+Donor+Con) — PNC Bank N.A. (Agent)

SW-342   Snee-Reinhardt Charitable Foundation   MI-12-13-14-15-16-17-22-31-32-39-41-42-43
c/o River Park Commons Two   45-51-52-54-55-61-71-72-89
2425 Sidney Street   **Phone** 412-390-2690 **FAX** 412-390-2686
Pittsburgh 15203   (Allegheny County)   **EIN** 25-6292908   **Year Created** 1982
AMV $21,761,406   **FYE** 12-01   (**Gifts Received** $11,381,781)   58 **Grants totaling** $831,298

Mostly local/Western Pa. giving. High grant of **$60,000** to Derry Township School District. **$32,000** to Marian Manor. **$30,000** each to Children's Hospital of Pittsburgh, Connect, Inc. and The Watson Institute. **$24,510-$25,500** each to American Heart Assn. /Pa.-DE Affiliate, Every Child, Inc., Gateway Rehabilitation Center, Harmarville Outreach Programs & Education/HOPE Network, McGuire Memorial Home Foundation, Sisters of St. Benedict of Westmoreland County, and South Hills Health System Foundation. **$20,000** each to Pace School, Phipps Conservancy & Botanical Gardens, and Western Pa. Humane Society. **$18,000-$18,524** each to Goodwill Industries of Pittsburgh, Perryopolis Area Ambulance Service, and Salvation Army. **$16,000** to Wings for Charities. **$15,000** each to Alzheimer's Disease Alliance of Western Pa., Pittsburgh Cares, Spectrum Family Network Foundation, Variety the Children's Charity, Western Pa. School for the Deaf, and YMCA of McKeesport. **$14,750** to St. Anthony Church of Monongahela. **$12,500** to Allegheny Land Trust. **$11,050** to St. Anne Home. **$10,000** each to Animal Angels, Auberle Foundation, Beginning With Books, Boy Scouts/Greater Pittsburgh Council, Children's Festival Chorus, Girl Scouts of SW Pa., Highlands Hospital, MADD/Mothers Against Drunk Drivers/Westmoreland-Beaver Chapter, The Magic Woods, National Kidney Foundation of Western Pa., Province of St. Augustine/Capuchin Franciscan Friars, The Nehemiah Project at Pine Valley Bible Camp, and St. Vincent College. **$7,500-$9,000** each to Johnstown Symphony Orchestra, Latrobe Area Hospital Charitable

Foundation, and Pittsburgh Public Theater. **$5,000-$6,500** each to American Cancer Society/SW Region, Cranberry Public Library, Make-A-Wish Foundation of Western Pa., Mom's House of Greensburg, Pa. Special Olympics, Pittsburgh Irish & Classical Theatre, Pittsburgh Musical Theater, Prince of Peace Catholic School, Red Cross/SW Pa. Chapter, and Spina Bifida Assn. of Western Pa. **$3,900** to Emmanuel Episcopal Church (Up for Reading). **$500-$1,145** each to Penn State U., Smithfield Borough Policy Dept., and a school in MD. ■**PUBLICATIONS:** Multi-Year Report; Grant Request Application and Guidelines brochure ■ **WEBSITE:** None ■**E-MAIL:** None ■**APPLICATION POLICIES & PROCEDURES:** The Foundation reports that precedence is given to organizations located (or activities concentrated in), first, SW Pa., then Northern WV, Northern MD, Commonwealth of Pa., and, lastly, the U.S. No support is awarded to individuals or for general capital improvements; general operating expenses (including salaries/benefits); chairs or professorships; endowment funds; lobbying; political contributions or candidates; highly specialized health/medical programs lacking specific community impact; programs that promote, research, or support the prevention of life, abortion, euthanasia, or cruelty to animals; or organizations that discriminate by race, creed, gender, or national origin. Prospective applicants should make an initial telephone inquiry about the feasibility of submitting a request. Grant requests must be submitted on a grant application form (available from the Foundation) together with a formal proposal; deadlines for applications are April 15th and August 15th. The proposal's first paragraph must specify the project and the amount requested, and then describe the project and its purpose, objective and means of implementation. Include an annual report, project budget, a professionally prepared financial statement, list of major funding sources, Board member list, and IRS tax-exempt status documentation. Site visits sometimes are made to organizations being considered for a grant. Grants are awarded at Board meetings in May and September.

O+D+T Joan E. Szymanski (Foundation Manager+Con) — Paul A. Heasley (C+D) — Virginia M. Davis (D) — Christina Heasley (D) — Karen L. Heasley (D) — Richard T. Vail [OH] (D) — Katherine E. Snee (Donor) — PNC Advisors (Corporate Trustee)

SW-343 Snyder Charitable Foundation   MI-11-12-13-14-31-41-42-61-63-64-89
c/o Snyder Associated Companies
409 Butler Road, P.O. Box 1022   **Phone** 724-548-8101 **FAX** None
Kittanning 16201   (Armstrong County)   **EIN** 25-1551808   **Year Created** 1987
AMV $644,244   **FYE** 12-00   (**Gifts Received** $550,000)   88 **Grants totaling** $666,415

Mostly local/regional grants. High local grant of **$18,500** to Union First Presbyterian Church of Cowansville. **$8,000** to United Way of Armstrong County. **$2,000** to Immaculate Conception School [Clarion]. **$2,500** to ACMH Health & Education Foundation. **$1,660** to Children's Hospital of Pittsburgh. **$1,500** to Allegheny River Development Corp. **$1,000** each to Friends of New Park [New Castle], George Junior Republic, Girl Scouts-Keystone Tall Tree, Indiana U. of Pa. Foundation, Kittanning Hose Company #1, Orphans of the Storm, Progressive Workshop, Slippery Rock U., and Washington Township Fire Dept. (building fund). All other giving **$50-$750** each, mostly for local organizations including many churches. High grant of **$600,000** to Fidelity Charitable Gift Fund [MA] (for subsequent disbursement to nonprofit organizations). ■**PUBLICATIONS:** None ■**WEBSITE:** None ■**E-MAIL:** None ■**APPLICATION POLICIES & PROCEDURES:** The Foundation reports that giving is directed to charitable organizations located in the Corporation's trading areas.

O+D+T Elmer A. Snyder (T+Donor+Con) — David E. Snyder (T) — Charles H. Snyder, Jr. (T) — Corporate donors: Allegheny Mineral Corp.; Armstrong Cement & Supply Company; Snyder Brothers, Inc.

SW-344 Snyder (Elmer & Annabelle) Foundation   MI-13-21-31-63
c/o Snyder Associated Companies
409 Butler Road, P.O. Box 1022   **Phone** 724-548-8101 **FAX** None
Kittanning 16201   (Armstrong County)   **EIN** 25-6479936   **Year Created** 1998
AMV $1,006,624   **FYE** 12-00   (**Gifts Received** $0)   49 **Grants totaling** $35,618

Most giving to Armstrong/Butler counties. High grant of **$12,500** to Union First Presbyterian Church of Cowansville (general support and carillon fund). **$2,500** to ACMH Health & Education Foundation. **$2,000** to Boy Scouts-Moraine Trails Council. **$1,000** each to ACMH Richard Laube Cancer Center, B.P.O.E. #203 Renovation Fund, Girl Scouts-Keystone Tall Tree, HAVIN, Inc., Kittanning Lions Club, S.P.A.R.C. [Ford City], and Syria Shrine Hospital (**$100M** Club). Other smaller grants/contributions to various regional and national organizations. ■**PUBLICATIONS:** None ■**WEBSITE:** None ■**E-MAIL:** None ■**APPLICATION POLICIES & PROCEDURES:** Information not available.

O+D+T David E. Snyder (T+Con) — Mark A. Snyder (T) — Thomas C. Snyder (T) — Elmer A. Snyder (Donor) — Annabelle Snyder (Donor)

SW-345 Snyder (G. Whitney) Charitable Trust   MI-14-41-42-44-56-63-84
610 Smithfield Street, Suite 404   **Phone** 412-471-1331 **FAX** None
Pittsburgh 15222   (Allegheny County)   **EIN** 25-1611761   **Year Created** 1990
AMV $6,497,770   **FYE** 12-00   (**Gifts Received** $0)   7 **Grants totaling** $245,000

All local/Pa. giving; grants are unrestricted contributions except as noted. High grant of **$200,000** to Borough of Sewickley Heights History Center. **$10,000** each to Sewickley Academy, Sewickley Public Library, and The Watson Institute. **$5,000** each to Assn. of Independent Colleges & Universities [Harrisburg], Presbyterian Church of Sewickley (memorial gift), and Tennis Patrons Foundation of Greater Pittsburgh. ■**PUBLICATIONS:** None ■**WEBSITE:** None ■**E-MAIL:** None ■**APPLICATION POLICIES & PROCEDURES:** The Foundation reports that most giving is limited to Pa., especially Greater Pittsburgh. Grant requests may be submitted in any form at any time; include IRS tax-exempt status documentation. Site visits sometimes are made to organizations being considered for a grant.

O+D+T Charles E. Ellison (Manager+Con) — G. Whitney Snyder, Jr. (P+T) — Jean Snyder Armstrong [Sewickley] (T) — Linda Snyder Hayes [NJ] (T) — Carolyn Snyder Miltenberger [MD] (T)

SW-346 Snyder (Harrison & Margaret) Charitable Trust
c/o M&T Bank, Trust Dept.
1330 - 11th Ave., P.O. Box 2007
Altoona 16603 (Blair County)

MI-12-13-14-16-22-25-29-41-44-49-52-61-72-89
Phone 814-946-6714 **FAX** None
EIN 25-6436588 **Year Created** 1994

AMV $1,578,684 **FYE** 12-00 (**Gifts Received** $0) 28 **Grants totaling** $77,500

All giving restricted to Blair County. High grant of **$7,532** to Altoona Food Bank. **$5,000** each to Altoona Area Public Library, Bishop Guilfoyle High School, Hollidaysburg Area School, and New Day, Inc. **$4,639** to Hollidaysburg Library. **$4,277** to Church of the Holy Trinity. **$3,000-$3,500** each to Big Brothers/Big Sisters, Central Pa. Humane Society, and NAACP. **$2,000-$2,500** each to American Rescue Workers, Central Pa. Humane Society, Easter Seals, Hollidaysburg Area YMCA, Junior Achievement/Johnstown, Make-A-Wish Foundation, Our Lady of Lourdes School, Phoenix Volunteer Fire Company, Red Cross, and Salvation Army. **$1,000-$1,600** each to Altoona Symphony Orchestra, ARC of Blair County, Blair County Community Endowment, Kittanning Trail Fire Dept., and Pa. Special Olympics. Other smaller local contributions. ■**PUBLICATIONS:** None ■**WEBSITE:** None ■**E-MAIL:** None ■**APPLICATION POLICIES & PROCEDURES:** Only charitable, nonprofit organizations in Blair County are eligible to apply. Grant requests may be submitted in a proposal before the November 1st deadline; describe the proposed project and include IRS tax-exempt status documentation. Grants are awarded the following year.

O+D+T Maria Boyle (Asst. VP+Trust Officer at Bank+Con) — William R. Collins, Jr., CPA [Hollidaysburg] (Co-T) — Daniel J. Ratchford, Esq. [Hollidaysburg] (Co-T) — M&T Bank (Co-Trustee)

SW-347 Snyder (W.P.), III Charitable Trust
610 Smithfield Street, Suite 404
Pittsburgh 15222
(Allegheny County)

MI-11-13-18-22-31-32-34-41-42-44-49-52-53-54-55-57-63-71-72-81-83
Phone 412-471-1331 **FAX** None
EIN 25-1611760 **Year Created** 1990

AMV $6,230,683 **FYE** 12-00 (**Gifts Received** $0) 46 **Grants totaling** $356,795

Mostly local/Pa. giving. Grants are general contributions except as noted and some are payments on pledges. High grants of **$55,000** to Carnegie Mellon U. **$50,000** to Sewickley Academy. **$40,000** to West Penn Allegheny Health System (opal photoactivator laser). **$32,795** to Allegheny General Hospital (ophthalmologic camera). **$25,000** to The Carnegie. **$20,000** to Pittsburgh Symphony. **$15,000** each to Phipps Conservatory/Botanical Garden and Sewickley Public Library (capital campaign). **$10,000** to Pittsburgh Cultural Trust . **$8,000** to Assn. of Independent Colleges & Universities of Pa. [Harrisburg]. **$7,000** to Presbyterian Church of Sewickley. **$6,000** to Allegheny Conference on Community Development. **$5,000** each to Albert Knowles Research Fund, Planned Parenthood of Western Pa., Silver Eye Center for Photography, Tri-State Share, United Way of SW Pa. and WQED. **$4,000** to The Mattress Factory. **$3,000-$3,500** each to Pa. Economy League, Three Rivers Arts Festival, and YMCA of Sewickley Valley. **$2,000-$2,500** each to Allegheny Valley School, Light of Life Ministries, Saltworks, Sewickley Cemetery, and Sweetwater Art Center. **$1,000-$1,500** each to Borough of Sewickley Heights, Greater Pittsburgh Literacy Council, Laughlin Center, Multiple Sclerosis Society, National Audubon Society/Pa. Office, National Aviary, Pittsburgh Downtown Partnership, Pittsburgh Vision Services, Union Aid Society, The Watson Institute, and WDUQ-FM. Other smaller local contributions. **Out-of-state** giving includes **$2,500** to Grant Foundation [FL] (Hospital Albert Schweitzer) and **$1,000** to American Parkinson Disease Assn. [NY] ■**PUBLICATIONS:** None ■**WEBSITE:** None ■**E-MAIL:** None ■**APPLICATION POLICIES & PROCEDURES:** The Foundation reports that most giving is limited to Pa., primarily Greater Pittsburgh; most grants are for general/operating support or annual campaigns. Grant requests in any form may be submitted at any time; include IRS tax-exempt status documentation. Site visits sometimes are made to organizations being considered for a grant.

O+D+T Charles E. Ellison (Manager+S+Con) — William P. Snyder, III (T+Donor) — J. Brandon Snyder [Sewickley] (T) — William P. Snyder, V (T)

SW-348 Snyder (William I. & Patricia S.) Foundation
c/o Rothman Gordon & Foreman
Grant Building, 3rd Floor, 301 Grant Street
Pittsburgh 15219
(Allegheny County)

MI-12-13-22-31-32-35-41-54-55-62-63
Phone 412-338-1108 **FAX** None
EIN 25-1773015 **Year Created** 1996

AMV $3,545,092 **FYE** 8-00 (**Gifts Received** $0) 20 **Grants totaling** $427,582

All local giving. High grant of **$200,000** to Sewickley Valley Hospital (maternity ward renovation). **$102,200** to Beth El Congregation of South Hills (Rabbi's Discretionary Fund). **$41,100** to Sewickley Academy (special gifts). **$36,000** to United Jewish Federation of Greater Pittsburgh. **$15,333** to Jewish Education Institute (Community Scholar in Residence). **$10,000** to YMCA of Pittsburgh (capital campaign). **$6,500** to Children's Hospital of Pittsburgh. **$5,000** to Presbyterian Church of Coraopolis (church restoration fund). **$2,500** to Pittsburgh Cultural Trust. **$1,000-$1,500** each to American Cancer Society, Carnegie Museum of Art, Hillel Foundation, Laughlin Children's Center, Light of Life Ministries, Pittsburgh AIDS Task Force, and Presbyterian Church of Sewickley. Other smaller local contributions. — Grants approved for future payment include **$800,000** to Sewickley Valley Hospital (maternity ward renovation) and **$300,000** to Beth El Congregation of South Hills (building fund). ■**PUBLICATIONS:** None ■**WEBSITE:** None ■**E-MAIL:** None ■**APPLICATION POLICIES & PROCEDURES:** Grant requests may be submitted in a letter (4 pages maximum) at any time; include supporting documentation, organizational and project budgets, an audited financial statement, Board member list, and IRS tax-exempt status documentation.

O+D+T K. Sidney Neuman, Esq. (S+Con) — William I. Snyder (P) — Patricia S. Snyder (VP) — Corporate donor: W.I. Snyder Corp.

SW-349 Society for Analytical Chemists of Pittsburgh, The
300 Penn Center Boulevard, Suite 332
Pittsburgh 15235
(Allegheny County)

MI-41-42-43-44
Phone 412-825-3220 **FAX** 412-825-3224
EIN 25-6072976 **Year Created** 1943

AMV $112,903 **FYE** 6-01 (**Gifts Received** $464,357) 250+ **Grants totaling** $319,059

All giving focuses on advancing analytical chemistry through science education, primarily in the Pittsburgh area. Support includes (1) awards to top students for scientific papers or essays; (2) scholarships for talented chemistry students; (3) funding for research projects; (4) grants for chemistry departments at local colleges/universities; (5) fellowships for summer study; (6) grants for science fairs and lecture series; and (7) science equipment grants for elementary/middle schools. Most support is under **$1,000;** a few grants of **$3,000-$10,000** are awarded to major institutions/programs; check the Society's website for more details. ■**PUBLICATIONS:** Informational brochure; application form ■**WEBSITE:** www.sacp.org ■**E-MAIL:** sacpinfo@pittcon.org ■**APPLICATION POLICIES & PROCEDURES:** The Society reports that giving focuses on Pittsburgh and vicinity (and other areas, depending on the grant) to advance analytical chemistry through science education, educational opportunities, special project grants, and awards for colleges, universities, libraries and community organizations, and scholarships for Society members. Requests must be submitted on a formal Application Form available from the Society; the deadlines vary according to award or program.

O+D+T John A. Varine (C+Con) — James L. Chadwick (S) — Janet K. Pifer (F)

SW-350 **Soffer Foundation**
400 Penn Center Boulevard, Suite 211
Pittsburgh 15235   (Allegheny County)
AMV $5,997,880   **FYE** 12-00   (**Gifts Received** $0)

MI-11-14-22-32-25-51-52-54-55-57-62
Phone 412-824-7400 **FAX** 412-824-2166
EIN 25-1455764   **Year Created** 1984
40+ **Grants totaling** $224,872

Mostly local giving. High grant of **$117,604** to United Jewish Federation of Greater Pittsburgh. **$15,100** to Pittsburgh Symphony. **$12,860** to Carnegie Museums of Pittsburgh. **$10,000-$10,500** each to Greater Pittsburgh Food Bank, Pittsburgh Cultural Trust, and United Way of Allegheny County. **$5,000** each to Pittsburgh Dance Council and Race for the Cure. **$2,500-$3,000** each to Andy Russell Celebrity Golf Benefit, Enzo Piaza for American Singers, Epilepsy Foundation of Western Pa., and Jewish Community Center of Pittsburgh. **$1,000-$1,400** each to American Jewish Committee, Gateway Rehabilitation Center, Hillel Academy, Tree of Life Congregation, Try-Again Homes, and WQED. Other smaller local contributions totaled **$18,780,** but no details available. ■**PUBLICATIONS:** None ■**WEBSITE:** None ■**E-MAIL:** None ■**APPLICATION POLICIES & PROCEDURES:** The Foundation reports that most giving is limited to Pittsburgh. No grants are awarded to individuals. Grant requests in any form may be submitted at any time.

O+D+T Joseph Soffer (D+Donor+Con) — Violet Soffer (D+Donor)

SW-351 **Solomon (Mendel E. & Sylvia G.) Charitable Trust**
c/o PNC Advisors, M.S. P2-PTPP-33-4
Two PNC Plaza, 620 Liberty Ave.
Pittsburgh 15222   (Allegheny County)
AMV $5,208,288   **FYE** 7-00   (**Gifts Received** $0)

MI-14-15-22-31-42-62

Phone 412-762-3617 **FAX** None
EIN 25-6271818   **Year Created** 1984
7 **Grants totaling** $287,500

All local giving; all grants are for general support. High grants of **$47,760** each to Children's Hospital of Pittsburgh, Montefiore Hospital, Riverview Center for Jewish Seniors, U. of Pittsburgh, and Western Pa. School for the Blind. **$15,000** to ARC-Allegheny Foundation. **$5,000** to Beth Hamedresh Hagadol/Beth Jacob Congregation. *Note:* Most of these organizations have been the only grantees for some years. ■**PUBLICATIONS:** None ■**WEBSITE:** None ■**E-MAIL:** None ■**APPLICATION POLICIES & PROCEDURES:** The Foundation reports giving priority to education, scientific research, and social betterment organizations. Grant requests may be submitted in a letter at any time, preferably before early July.

O+D+T Michael O'Donnell (Trust Officer at Bank+Con) — Hon. J. Quint Salmon [Beaver Falls] (Co-T) — PNC Advisors (Co-Trustee)

SW-352 **Spackman (Isabel M.) Trust**
c/o PNC Advisors Service Center, P2-PTPP-05-1
Two PNC Plaza, 620 Liberty Ave.
Pittsburgh 15222   (Allegheny County)
AMV $1,496,511   **FYE** 12-00   (**Gifts Received** $0)

MI-15-22-23-35-63

Phone 800-762-2272 **FAX** None
EIN 23-7226511   **Year Created** 1913
15 **Grants totaling** $77,098

All giving is restricted to assisting needy, older persons in the Philadelphia area. High grant of **$16,610** to Kearsley Home. **$11,467** to Domestic & Foreign Missionary Society of the Episcopal Church. **$8,350** to Church of St. John. **$500** to Visiting Nurse Assn. of Greater Philadelphia. Other local grants, ranging from **$1,355** to **$8,415,** disbursed to individuals, primarily residents in Episcopal facilities, and some for funeral costs. ■**PUBLICATIONS:** None ■**WEBSITE:** None ■**E-MAIL:** pncadvisors@pncbank.com ■**APPLICATION POLICIES & PROCEDURES:** Note: The Trust originally was administered by PNCBank-Philadelphia and most grantees, historically, have been in the Philadelphia-area. The Trust stipulates assistance for "gentlefolk of embarrassed (impoverished) circumstances," with initial preference given to Episcopalians. Only social service agencies may apply on behalf of needy individuals; requests from social service agencies should be submitted in a one-page letter detailing an individual's financial and religious background.

O+D+T Dawn Thomas (Trust Officer at Bank+Con) — PNC Advisors (Trustee)

SW-353 **Spang & Company Charitable Trust**
c/o Spang & Company
100 Brugh Avenue, P.O. Box 751
Butler 16001   (Butler County)
AMV $10,778,129   **FYE** 12-00   (**Gifts Received** $9,864)

MI-11-13-14-17-29-31-32-35-41-42-44-51-52
54-71-72-89
Phone 724-287-8781 **FAX** 724-285-4721
EIN 25-6020192   **Year Created** 1958
52 **Grants totaling** $156,115

About four-fifths local/Western Pa. giving; grants are for general support except as noted. High grant of **$20,000** to United Way of Butler County. **$13,000** to Fox Chapel Country Day School. **$10,000** each to Allegheny Heart Institute and Carnegie Mellon U. **$7,500** to National Conference of Community & Justice. **$5,000-$5,500** each to Boy Scouts/Butler, Butler Public Library, Carnegie Institute, Pittsburgh Symphony, Pittsburgh Zoo, Sandy Lake Volunteer Fire Dept., and West Penn Hospital. **$2,000-$2,500** each to Butler Hospital (Caring Angel Program), Phipps Conservatory & Botanical Garden, and Volunteers Against Abuse [Zelienople]. **$1,000** each to Butler Blind Assn., Butler Humane Society, Children's Hospital of Pittsburgh, Meals on Wheels/Butler, Pittsburgh Ballet Theatre, Pittsburgh Civic Light Opera, Pittsburgh Opera, Pittsburgh Public Theater, and WQED. Other local contributions **$20-$500** for various purposes. **Out-of-state** giving includes **$20,000** to Johns Hopkins U./Brady Institute [MD] and several grants to Booneville, AR—a corporate operating location. ■**PUBLICATIONS:** None ■**WEBSITE:** www.spang.com [corporate info only] ■**E-MAIL:** None ■**APPLICATION POLICIES & PROCEDURES:** The Foundation reports that giving generally focuses on Butler-area organizations. No grants are awarded to individuals. Grant requests may be submitted in any form at any time—deadlines are March 31st, June 30th, September 30th, and December 31st; describe the organization's purpose and state the amount requested. The Trustees award grants at meetings in April, August, and December.

O+D+T K.R. McKnight (Administrator+Con) — David F. Rath (T) — Frank E. Rath, Jr. (T) — Robert A. Rath, Jr. (T) — Corporate donors: Spang & Company and employees; Magnetics, Inc.

SW-354 Speyer (Alexander C. & Tillie S.) Foundation
c/o North Star Coal Company
1202 Benedum-Trees Bldg., 221 4th Ave.
Pittsburgh 15222   (Allegheny County)
MI-11-14-22-29-32-41-42-52-53-54-55-56-57 62-71-72
Phone 412-281-7225 **FAX** None
EIN 25-6051650   **Year Created** 1962
AMV $7,097,195   **FYE** 12-00   **(Gifts Received** $0)   102 **Grants totaling** $299,356

About half local giving. High Pa. grant of **$31,300** to Carnegie Museum of Art. **$22,000** to Carnegie Mellon U. **$16,000** to United Way of SW Pa. **$15,500** to United Jewish Federation of Greater Pittsburgh. **$12,000** to Western Pa. Conservancy. **$11,000** to Phipps Conservatory & Botanical Garden. **$10,000** to Rodef Shalom Congregation. **$7,600** to Pittsburgh Vision Services. **$5,250** to Pittsburgh Parks Conservancy. **$5,000** to Jewish Residential Services. **$4,000** to Pittsburgh Cultural Trust. **$3,350** to Animal Friends. **$2,000-$2,500** each to Frick Architecture & Historical Center, Jewish University Center (capital campaign), and Pittsburgh Symphony. **$1,000-$1,500** each to American Heart Assn., Associated Artists of Pittsburgh, The Mattress Factory, Pittsburgh Center for the Arts, Shady Side Academy, Ursuline Services, and WQED. **$750** to Pittsburgh Ballet Theatre Guild. Other local contributions **$125-$600** for various purposes. **Out-of-state** giving includes **$17,300** to Studio School [NY]; **$15,000** to New York Times Neediest Cases; **$10,000** each to Jesuit Hamshedour Mission [MD], Link Media [France], Provincetown Art Assn. [MA], and Sidwell Friends School [DC]; and other grants/contributions to NY, DC, IL, MT, and WY. ■**PUBLICATIONS:** None ■**WEBSITE:** None ■**E-MAIL:** None ■**APPLICATION POLICIES & PROCEDURES:** Prospective applicants initially should make a telephone inquiry about the feasibility of submitting a request. Grant requests may be submitted in any form, preferably during January-March. Site visits sometimes are made to organizations being considered for a grant. Grants are awarded at meetings in June and December.

O+D+T Alexander C. Speyer, Jr. (T+Foundation Manager+Con) — Darthea Speyer (T+Donor)

SW-355 Standard Steel Specialty Co. Foundation
c/o Standard Steel Specialty Company
Jamison Street, P.O. Box 20
Beaver Falls 15010   (Beaver County)
MI-11-13-42
Phone 724-846-7600 **FAX** 724-846-9814
EIN 25-6038268   **Year Created** 1970
AMV $85,716   **FYE** 12-00   **(Gifts Received** $10,000)   5 **Grants totaling** $12,545

Mostly local giving: **$3,000** each to Geneva College (development fund) and United Way of Beaver County. **$2,000** each to Butler County YMCA (capital fund) and Penn State/Butler Campus. **Out-of-state** grant: **$2,545** to United Way of the Piedmont [SC]. ■**PUBLICATIONS:** None ■**WEBSITE:** None ■**E-MAIL:** None ■**APPLICATION POLICIES & PROCEDURES:** Grant requests may be submitted in a letter at any time; describe the intended use of funds and include IRS tax-exempt status documentation.

O+D+T R.E. Conley (S+F+Con) — National City Bank of Pa. (Trustee) — Corporate donors: Standard Steel Specialty Company; Superior Drawn Steel Company; Duer Spring Manufacturing Company

---

SW-356 Staunton Farm Foundation
210 Centre City Tower
650 Smithfield Street
Pittsburgh 15222   (Allegheny County)
MI-11-12-13-14-15-17-22-31-33-41-42
Phone 412-281-8020 **FAX** 412-232-3115
EIN 25-0965573   **Year Created** 1937
AMV $47,197,631   **FYE** 12-00   **(Gifts Received** $0)   44 **Grants totaling** $1,171,699

All giving restricted to SW Pa. for mental health purposes; some grants comprise multiple awards. High grant of **$75,000** to Vintage, Inc. **$62,000** to Family Services of Western Pa. **$60,000** to Community Empowerment Assn. **$57,200** to Comprehensive Substance Abuse Services of SW Pa. **$51,862** to Bethlehem Haven. **$50,000** to Pa. Health Law Project. **$47,000** to Pittsburgh Pastoral Institute. **$40,000** each to Crossroads Foundation and Pittsburgh Vision Services. **$38,350** to Parents League for Emotional Adjustment. **$37,500** to Geneva College. **$35,000** each to Latrobe Area Hospital Foundation and Turtle Creek Valley Mental Health/Mental Retardation. **$34,200** to U. of Pittsburgh. **$33,510** to Orr Compassionate Care Center. **$30,000** each to East End Cooperative Ministry, I Have A Dream Foundation, National Alliance for the Mentally Ill of SW Pa., Northside Christian Health Center, and Pittsburgh Psychoanalytic Assn. **$28,800** to Mon Yough Community Services. **$27,000** to Circle C Group Homes. **$25,000** each to McKeesport YMCA, Northside Common Ministries, and Pa. Coalition Against Rape. **$23,500** to Early Learning Institute. **$20,500** to Schenley Heights Community Development Program. **$18,100** to Greater Pittsburgh Community Food Bank. **$17,500** to Every Child, Inc. **$12,500** to Butler Memorial Hospital Foundation. **$10,000** each to Clelian Heights School, Latrobe Foundation, and Pressley Ridge Schools. **$6,427** to Outside In School of Experimental Education. **$5,000** each to Bear International, Family Resources, The Pittsburgh Project, and Wilkinsburg Community Ministry. **$1,000-$1,250** each to United Way of Allegheny County and U. of Pittsburgh School of Social Work. Other local contributions **$500** for similar purposes. — In 2001, major grants (mostly multiple-year awards) include **$150,000** to Pace School (classroom support campaign); **$147,000** to U. of Pittsburgh (infant mental health); **$120,000** each to Crossroads Foundation (multicultural student counselor) and Pittsburgh Mercy Foundation (A Child's Place at Mercy); **$115,051** to Parents' League for Emotional Adjustment (after-school project); **$111,650** to Allegheny General Hospital-Singer Research Institute (PTSD screening); **$110,000** to YWCA of Greater Pittsburgh (Bridging the Gap After Bridge Housing); and **$100,000** to Pittsburgh Council on Public Education (Youthreach: Frontline). ■ **PUBLICATIONS:** informational brochure with guidelines ■ **WEBSITE:** www.stauntonfarm.org ■ **E-MAIL:** None ■ **APPLICATION POLICIES & PROCEDURES:** Only organizations in a ten-county region of SW Pa. (Allegheny, Armstrong, Beaver, Butler, Fayette, Greene, Indiana, Lawrence, Washington and Westmoreland counties) which provide mental health treatment, care and support are eligible to apply. The Foundation encourages projects representing new and different approaches to providing direct patient care; most grants are for special projects. With few exceptions, grants are not awarded for general operating support, endowment, building campaigns, conferences, or to individuals. Prospective applicants initially should make a telephone inquiry about the feasibility of submitting a request, or should submit an initial Letter of Intent (2 pages maximum). After initial review, a prospective grantee may be asked to submit a formal application for consideration by the Foundation's Project Committee. Proposals which follow the Grantmakers of Western Pa. Common Grant Application Format are accepted. Deadlines for full, formal applications are early February, early August, and early November; contact the Foundation for exact dates. Site visits sometimes are made to organizations being considered for a grant. Grants are awarded at meetings in February, May, and November.

O+D+T Joni S. Schwager (Foundation Manager+Program Officer+Con) — Andrea Q. Griffiths [VA] (P) — Lee C. Lundback [NY] (VP) — Albert B. Craig, III [NY] (S) — Barbara K. Robinson (F) — Ann W. Austin (D) — Sallie Davis (D) — Joseph W. Dury, Jr. [Sewickley] (D) — John W. Eichleay, Jr. [Sewickley] (D) — Richard L. Frederick, III (D) — Philip G. Gulley (D) — Elizabeth G. Hahl [NY] (D) — Andrea Torres Mahone (D) — Richard W. Reed (D) — Judith S. Sherry [Sewickley] (D) — Mellon Bank N.A. (Trustee)

SW-357 Steinsapir (Julius L. & Libbie B.) Family Foundation
904 Allegheny Building
429 Forbes Avenue
Pittsburgh   15219   (Allegheny County)

MI-11-15-22-29-32-41-42-61-62

Phone 412-261-1505 **FAX** None
EIN 25-6104248   **Year Created** 1969

AMV $3,352,360   **FYE** 1-01   **(Gifts Received** $0)   62 **Grants totaling** $192,225

About three-quarters local giving; all grants are unrestricted support. High Pa. grants of **$22,500** each to Catholic Charities/Franciscan Fathers, Jewish Assn. on Aging, and Yeshiva Achei Tmimim School. **$11,500** to Temple David. **$10,500** to Wightman School (renovations). **$8,500** to Tree of Life Congregation. **$5,000** each to Allegheny County Community College Education Fund, Beth Jacob Congregation & Cemetery, Duquesne U., and United Jewish Federation of Greater Pittsburgh. **$3,000-$4,000** to American Heart Assn., Anti-Defamation League, Holy Angels Church, Red Cross, Salvation Army, St. Nicholas Church [Millvale], United Way of Allegheny County, and U. of Pittsburgh/Graduate School of Business. **$2,000-$2,500** each to American Diabetes Assn., American Lung Assn., American Respiratory Alliance of Western Pa., Arthritis Foundation, Beth Abraham Congregation, Jubilee Assn., Kother Torah Cemetery, National Ovarian Cancer Coalition, and Shaare Torah Cemetery. Other local grants/contributions **$25-$1,500** for various purposes. **Out-of-state** giving includes **$3,000** each to American Cancer Society [DC], Jewish National Fund [NY], and Jewish Residential Services [FL]. ■ **PUBLICATIONS:** None ■ **WEBSITE:** None ■ **E-MAIL:** None ■ **APPLICATION POLICIES & PROCEDURES:** The Foundation reports giving is almost exclusively limited to three locations: Pittsburgh, Atlanta, GA, and Hollywood, FL. No grants are awarded to individuals. Prospective applicants initially should make a telephone inquiry about the feasibility of submitting a request. Grant requests in any form may be submitted during March/April or September/October; include IRS tax-exempt status documentation. Site visits sometimes are made to organizations being considered for a grant. Grants are awarded at May and November meetings.

O+D+T Albert C. Shapira, Esq. (T+Con) — Samuel Horovitz, CPA [FL] (T) — Martin Mallit (T)

SW-358 Stuckeman Foundation, The
1330 Old Freeport Road, Suite 1A
Pittsburgh   15238   (Allegheny County)

MI-15-42-63

Phone 412-967-1141 **FAX** None
EIN 25-1757468   **Year Created** 1994

AMV $1,262,338   **FYE** 12-00   **(Gifts Received** $0)   1 **Grant of** $51,000

Sole grant to Penn State U. — In the prior year, two grants awarded: **$35,000** to Beulah Presbyterian Church and **$8,000** to Forbes Hospice. ■ **PUBLICATIONS:** None ■ **WEBSITE:** None ■ **E-MAIL:** None ■ **APPLICATION POLICIES & PROCEDURES:** The Foundation reports that grants are made to organizations in which the family has a personal interest—in particular Pittsburgh, Racine, WI, and Escondido, CA. Prospective applicants should make an initial telephone inquiry regarding the feasibility of submitting a request. Grant requests may be submitted in a 1-page letter in October (deadline is November 1st) together with IRS tax-exempt status documentation. If the Foundation is interested, additional selected background documentation will be requested. Site visits sometimes are made to organizations being considered for a grant.

O+D+T H. Campbell Stuckeman (T+D+Manager+Donor+Con) — Eleanor R. Stuckeman (T+D) — Ellen Stuckeman Easley (D) — Joyce Stuckeman Biffar [CA] (D) — Alan R. Stuckeman (D)

SW-359 Stuckey Family Foundation
85 Sylvan Drive, P.O. Box 65
Hollidaysburg   16648   (Blair County)

MI-41-42-63

Phone 814-946-8644 **FAX** None
EIN 25-1611905   **Year Created** 1990

AMV $2,320,737   **FYE** 12-00   **(Gifts Received** $84,713)   8 **Grants totaling** $153,750

Mostly local/Pa. giving. High grant of **$85,000** to Young Life. **$18,000** to Williamson Free School [Delaware County]. **$22,500** to Messiah College. **$10,000** each to Girard Alliance Church [Erie County] and Geneva College. **$1,250** to Girard Alliance Academy [Erie County]. **Out-of-state** giving to FL. ■ **PUBLICATIONS:** None ■ **WEBSITE:** None ■ **E-MAIL:** None ■ **APPLICATION POLICIES & PROCEDURES:** No grants are awarded to individuals.

O+D+T Barbara Stuckey (S+Donor+Con) — John Stuckey (P+Donor) — Jennifer Davis [Girard] (F)

SW-360 Swindell (Robert Hunter) Charitable Trust
831 Academy Place
Pittsburgh 15243 (Allegheny County)
AMV $194,370 **FYE** 12-00 **(Gifts Received** $0)

MI-22-63
Phone 412-563-5349 **FAX** None
EIN 23-7188657 **Year Created** 1972
6 **Grants totaling** $13,900

Mostly local giving. High grant of **$7,500** to Mt. Lebanon Presbyterian Church. **$4,500** to Youth Guidance. Other local and out-of-state contributions **$300-$600** for various purposes. ■**PUBLICATIONS:** None ■**WEBSITE:** None ■**E-MAIL:** None ■**APPLICATION POLICIES & PROCEDURES:** The Foundation reports that giving is largely limited to Christian organizations/causes. Grant requests must be submitted on a formal application form, available from the Trust, before the October 30th deadline; grants are awarded in December.

O+D+T Phyllis S. Swindell (T+Donor+Con) — David Durr (Donor) — Robin Durr (Donor) — Corporate donor: Dell Fastener Corp.

SW-361 TAW Scholarship Fund
809 Tener Street
Johnstown 15904 (Cambria County)
AMV $7,000 **FYE** 12-01 **(Gifts Received** $19,050)

MI-43
Phone 814-266-5776 **FAX** None
EIN 25-1869136 **Year Created** 2000
5 **Grants totaling** $19,000

All grants are scholarships, **$1,000-$3,000** each, for students from Eastern Europe; current grantees are from Philadelphia, Michigan, and Oregon. ■**PUBLICATIONS:** application form ■**WEBSITE:** None ■**E-MAIL:** sedlar@pitt.edu ■**APPLICATION POLICIES & PROCEDURES:** The Foundation reports that applicants must be legal immigrants or foreign students from Eastern Europe who have resided for less than five years in the United States, and have been accepted at an accredited US college or university. An application form, available from the Foundation, must be completed and submitted in May-June before the June 30th deadline; include an autobiography, high school transcripts, and two recommendations.

O+D+T Jean W. Sedlar (T+Donor+Con) — Eric V. Sedlar (T+Donor+Con)

SW-362 Thomas (John J.) Foundation
c/o PNC Advisors, M.S. P2-PTPP-26-5
Two PNC Plaza, 620 Liberty Ave.
Pittsburgh 15222 (Allegheny County)
AMV $830,441 **FYE** 9-00 **(Gifts Received** $0)

MI-34-43-64

Phone 412-762-0570 **FAX** None
EIN 25-1381212 **Year Created** 1987
4 **Grants totaling** $30,417

Scholarships for Roman Catholic seminarians or nursing students at Pittsburgh-area institutions typically ranged from **$6,000-$9,000**; recent recipients have attended Carlow College, Duquesne U., Ohio Valley General Hospital School of Nursing, and West Penn Hospital. ■**PUBLICATIONS:** None ■**WEBSITE:** None ■**E-MAIL:** None ■**APPLICATION POLICIES & PROCEDURES:** Only Roman Catholic seminarians or nursing students at Pittsburgh-area institutions are eligible to apply for scholarships; applications may be submitted at any time.

O+D+T Kara Chickson (Administrative Officer at Bank+Con) — PNC Advisors (Trustee)

SW-363 Thompson (Robert M.) Foundation
204 Hawthorne Street, Edgewood
Pittsburgh 15218 (Allegheny County)
AMV $574,976 **FYE** 6-00 **(Gifts Received** $0)

MI-54-83-86
Phone 412-371-8694 **FAX** 412-371-2631
EIN 25-1518805 **Year Created** 1984
3 **Grants totaling** $40,000

All local giving. High grant of **$25,000** to Carnegie Museums of Pittsburgh. **$10,000** to The Reason Foundation. **$5,000** each to American Civil Liberties Union Foundation. ■**PUBLICATIONS:** None ■**WEBSITE:** None ■**E-MAIL:** None ■**APPLICATION POLICIES & PROCEDURES:** The Foundation reports that organizations (or affiliates) that receive government funding (Federal, state or local) or organizations politically involved/active or religiously affiliated will not be considered for support. Most grants are for special projects, research, and matching grants; multi-year grants are awarded. Grant requests may be submitted in a letter (2 pages maximum) at any time; include an annual report, organization budget, project budget, list of major funding sources, and IRS tax-exempt status documentation. Site visits sometimes are made to organizations being considered for a grant.

O+D+T Robert M. Thompson, Jr. (T+Donor+Con)

SW-364 Three Rivers Community Foundation
100 North Braddock Ave., Suite 302
Pittsburgh 15206
  (Allegheny County)
AMV $514,287 **FYE** 6-01 **(Gifts Received** $407,128)

MI-12-13-14-16-17-18-19-20-24-25-29-35-55
  79-83-85
Phone 412-243-9250 **FAX** 412-243-0504
EIN 25-1615511 **Year Created** 1989
25 **Grants totaling** $35,089

All giving focuses on progressive, community-based organizations/groups in the Greater Pittsburgh area. Grants of **$3,000** or smaller (specific grant-size information is unavailable) were awarded to Andy Warhol Museum (Free Tuesdays program), Alliance for Progressive Action (training project), Beaver County AIDS Service Organization (peer-based education/prevention program), Center for Sacred Partnership (lecture/workshop), Community Media (documentary film), Gay & Lesbian Community Center of Pittsburgh (communications equipment), Gay & Lesbian Neighborhood Development Assn. (collaborative community service project), Hamnett Place Neighborhood Assn. (membership development), Mennonite Urban Corps-Pittsburgh (union intern), Midtown Plaza Resident Council (housing rules/regulations education), Mon Valley Media (environment/artists project), People for a Better Community (community empowerment), Pittsburgh Healing Weekend-2001 (networking persons with HIV), Pittsburgh Interfaith Impact Network (leadership training), Prevention Point Pittsburgh (needle-exchange education/advocacy), Renaissance City Choirs/Pittsburgh Gay Chorus (concert/), Women's Resource Center (local resources directory), and Working Women with Disabilities Support Group (information/referral database). Also, seven Special Opportunity Grants, **$500** or smaller, supported meetings, performances, special events, etc. ■**PUBLICATIONS:** Application Guidelines; Application Form ■**WEBSITE:** www.threeriverscommunityfoundation.org ■**E-MAIL:** TRCFPgh@aol.com ■**APPLICATION POLICIES & PROCEDURES:** Only community-based organizations working to eliminate social, economic, and racial barriers to full participation in society, and located in a 10-county SW Pa. region (Allegheny, Armstrong, Beaver, Butler, Fayette, Greene, Indiana, Lawrence, Washington, and Westmoreland counties) are eligible to apply. Grant requests are accepted from: (a) organizations with budgets under $100,000; (b) projects that address persistent divisions in society based on race, color, age, sexual orientation, class, religion, disability, sex, ancestry, or national origin; (c) projects with strong components of community organizing/building, community education, and problem identification/solving; (d) youth-led projects or ones promoting youth activism; (e) projects addressing emerging/cutting-edge issues and/or new approaches to problem solving; (e) new organizations/projects with growth potential; and (f) coalitions that emphasize joint strategies and projects. No support is given for projects whose primary goals/strategies are to provide direct social services, union organizing, lobbying, electoral/legislative activities, or activities benefiting private interests, business or profit-making groups. Grant requests must be submitted on a formal Application Form (available on the Foundation's website or mailed on request) which stipulates the required supporting documentation. Completed grant applications must be received before the early-February deadline; call for exact date. — Formerly called Three Rivers Community Fund.

O+D+T Anne E. Lynch (Office Manager+Con) — Carrie Leana (P+D) — Leo M. Castagnari (S+D) — Mary Reynolds (F+D) — Patricia Murphy (Co-Chair, Grantmaking Committee+D) — Lisa Scales (Co-Chair, Grantmaking Committee+D) — Nancy Bernstein (D) — Herb Clements (D) — Judith E. Donaldson (D) — Tom Hoffman (D) — Bryce Maretzki (D) — Susan Peake (D) — Rhonda Peters (D) — Gary J. Schwager (D) — Giovanni Scolieri (D) — Celeste Taylor (D) — Bill Wekselman (D)

SW-365 Tickets for Kids Foundation/Community Involvement Fdn. MI-12-13-51-52-54-55
139 Freeport Road, Suite 100
Pittsburgh 15215 (Allegheny County) **Phone** 412-781-5437 **FAX** 412-781-5227
EIN 25-1724052 **Year Created** 1994
AMV $3,069,157 **FYE** 11-00 (**Gifts Received** $1,627,426) 111 **Grants totaling** $490,607
All giving to the SW Pa. region, primarily for 180+ organizations to secure tickets for underserved, needy children for them to experience arts/cultural/sports enrichment: music, theater, ballet, professional/collegiate sports, circus, zoo and other public arts/cultural events in the Pittsburgh area. Grants ranged from **$23** to **$28,079** but primarily were under **$8,000**. Organizations and agencies supported included youth organizations, social service centers, literacy programs, shelters, community groups, family centers, and others. ■**PUBLICATIONS:** Tickets Request Form ■**WEBSITE:** www.ticketsforkidspgh.org ■**E-MAIL:** info@ticketsforkidspgh.org ■**APPLICATION POLICIES & PROCEDURES:** The Foundation reports all giving for tickets/field trips involving underprivileged, underserved children/youth as arranged by social service agencies. Organizations wishing to participate should make an initial telephone inquiry about the feasibility of submitting a request. Grant requests (brief letters on letterhead paper) may be submitted at any time; describe the program and children served, and include descriptive literature/mission statement, and IRS tax-exempt status documentation. A Tickets Request Form is also available on the website. Site visits are made to organizations being considered for a grant, and grantees must attend an orientation. Decisions on awards are made weekly. **Note:** In 2003 the Community Involvement Foundation will become a separate foundation with its own grantmaking program.

O+D+T Christopher Smith (Executive Director+Con) — Susan S. Weiner (P) — Bruce B. Weiner (Donor) — Foundation donors: Buhl Foundation, Dapper Dan Charities, Grable Foundation, The Pittsburgh Foundation, Robinson Family Foundation, Marci Lynn Bernstein Private Foundation Trust [FL]; also many in-kind donations of tickets by performance/sports sponsoring organizations/agencies.

SW-366 Tippins Foundation MI-12-13-14-15-17-22-31-32-41-42-49-51-54
c/o Tippins Industries, Inc. 55-56-57-71-72-82-85-89
1090 Freeport Road **Phone** 412-784-8804 **FAX** 412-784-8825
Pittsburgh 15238 (Allegheny County) **EIN** 25-6282382 **Year Created** 1987
AMV $2,186,730 **FYE** 12-00 (**Gifts Received** $1,985,229) 75 **Grants totaling** $484,340
Mostly local/Western Pa. giving. High Pa. grants of **$25,000** each to Alzheimer's Disease Research Center/UPMC, Carnegie Mellon U. (continuing education), Innovation Works, and Salvation Army. **$20,000** to Children's Hospital of Pittsburgh. **$15,000** each to Carnegie Museums of Pittsburgh, Pittsburgh Technology Council Enterprise, and U. of Pittsburgh/Katz School of Business. **$10,000** each to Allegheny College, American Cancer Society, American Heart Assn., Boy Scouts/Greater Pittsburgh Council, Brother's Brother Foundation, The Children's Institute, and WQED. **$8,000** to Duquesne U. **$5,000** each to Animal Friends, ARC-Allegheny, Bethlehem Haven, Fox Chapel Country Day School, Fox Chapel Presbyterian Church, Girl Scouts of SW Pa., Goodwill Industries of Pittsburgh, Historical Society of Western Pa., Juvenile Diabetes Foundation, Lawrenceville Corporation, National Parkinson Foundation, Phipps Conservatory & Botanical Garden, Pittsburgh Children's Museum, Pittsburgh Cultural Trust, Pittsburgh Opera, Pittsburgh Public Theater, Pittsburgh Symphony, Pittsburgh Zoo, Radio Information Service, Red Cross, Shady Side Academy, Whale's Tale/FamilyLink, and Women's Shelter of Greater Pittsburgh. **$2,840** to Loyalhanna Assn. **$2,000-$2,500** each to Animal Rescue League, St. Margaret Memorial Hospital, Three Rivers Adoption Council, The Watson Institute, Western Pa. Conservancy, and Western Pa. Humane Society. **$1,000** each to Audubon Society of Western Pa., The Bradley Center, Fox Chapel Episcopal Church, Junior Achievement of SW Pa., Light of Life Ministries, Loyalhanna Watershed Assn., Mars Home for Youth, Mattress Factory, National Aviary in Pittsburgh, NEED/Negro Emergency Education Drive, Parental Stress Center, Pa. Special Olympics, Pittsburgh Ballet Theatre, UCP of Pittsburgh, United Fire Companies of Ligonier, Valley School of Ligonier, and Westmoreland Museum of American Art. Other local contributions **$500** each. **Out-of-state**

giving includes high grant of **$50,000** to Alzheimer's Assn. [IL] and **$25,000** to Massachusetts General Hospital (Genetics & Aging Unit). ■**PUBLICATIONS:** None ■**WEBSITE:** None ■**E-MAIL:** None ■**APPLICATION POLICIES & PROCEDURES:** Grant requests may be submitted in writing at any time; provide specific information about requested funding. The Board meets during the Fall months.

O+D+T George R. Knapp (Executive Director+T+Con) — Carolyn H. Tippins (T+Donor) — George W. Tippins (T+Donor) — John H. Tippins (T) — William H. Tippins (T) — Corporate donor: Tippins Industries, Inc.; TMC Investment Company [DE]

SW-367 **Tippins (William H. & Karen A.) Foundation** MI-17-35-54-63
   112 Fairway Lane **Phone** 412-355-8692 **FAX** None
   Pittsburgh 15238 (Allegheny County) **EIN** 25-6507667 **Year Created** 1995
AMV $100,816 **FYE** 12-00 **(Gifts Received** $0) 6 **Grants totaling** $29,000

All local giving. High grant of **$20,000** to Fox Chapel Presbyterian Church. **$5,000** to Carnegie Museum of Natural History. **$2,500** to Pregnancy Care Centers. Other local contributions **$500** for various purposes. ■**PUBLICATIONS:** None ■**WEBSITE:** None ■**E-MAIL:** None ■**APPLICATION POLICIES & PROCEDURES:** Information not available.

O+D+T William H. Tippins (T+Donor+Con) — Karen A. Tippins (T+Donor)

SW-368 **Trees (Edith L.) Charitable Trust** MI-12-14-31-33-41-84
   c/o PNC Advisors, M.S. P1-POPP-02-1
   One PNC Plaza, 249 Fifth Ave., 2nd Floor **Phone** 412-762-3808 **FAX** 412-705-1183
   Pittsburgh 15222 (Allegheny County) **EIN** 25-6026443 **Year Created** 1956
AMV $80,438,412 **FYE** 12-00 **(Gifts Received** $1,907,255) 66 **Grants totaling** $4,245,258

Giving limited to aiding mentally retarded persons (especially children) in Western Pa., mainly in Allegheny and surrounding counties; some grants comprise multiple awards. High grant of **$300,000** to Down Syndrome Center of Western Pa. (endowment fund). **$275** to Verland Foundation (endowment fund/debt reduction). **$260,000** to ARC Allegheny Foundation (camping programs). **$200,000** to Allegheny Valley School (facility renovations). **$140,000** to McGuire Memorial Home Foundation (additional residence/renovations). **$136,250** to Sharp Visions, Inc. (camp/internet employment program). **$130,000** to Clelian Heights School for Exceptional Children (endowment fund/tractor). **$126,742** to St. Anthony School Programs (vans). **$125,000** to The Early Learning Institute (endowment fund). **$100,000** to UCP of Pittsburgh (capital campaign). **$99,282** to ARC Enterprises of North Warren (endowment fund/vehicle/staff). **$90,000** to Progressive Workshop of Armstrong County (endowment fund). **$87,477** to Rankin Christian Center (van/reimbursement fund). **$85,000** to The ARC Westmoreland (advocacy efforts). **$80,450** to Citizen Care/Robinson Developmental Center (summer camping/sheltered workshop equipment). **$70,000-$75,000** to The Emmaus Community of Pittsburgh (respite care support/new equipment), Goodwill Industries of Pittsburgh (new heating/air conditioning), Greene ARC (woodworking equipment), Mainstay Life Services (residence upgrading), U. of Pittsburgh (Autism Research Project), and YMCA of McKeesport (enhanced services/facilities). **$62,950** to ARC Butler County (truck/heating system). **$65,000** to John Merck After School Program (multiple disabilities clinic support). **$60,000** each to Family Services of Western Pa. (residence renovations) and Spina Bifida Assn. of Western pa. (summer residential program). **$55,000-$55,800** each to California U. of Pa. Foundation (learning equipment), Camp A.I.M. for Exceptional Children (campership staff support), and Martha Lloyd Community Services [Bradford County] (minivans/building improvements). **$50,000-$50,750** each to ARC Westmoreland Foundation (People First Project), East Suburban Citizens Advocacy (advocacy for transition to community living), Passavant Memorial Homes (communications upgrading), Presbyterian Senior Care (site improvements), Pressley Ridge Schools Foundation (new campus dwellings), Southwinds (minivan/facility improvements), Transitional Services (sprinkler system), The Watson Institute (autism center), and The Woodlands Foundation (sports programs). **$40,000-$44,000** each to Mon Yough Community Services (mailing equipment), Parent & child Guidance Center (home/van adaptations), Turtle Creek Valley MH/MR (vans), TRY/Together for Retarded Youth (camping program/family meeting room), and Western Pa. School for Blind Children (transportation support). **$37,000-$39,900** each to Every Child, Inc. (room refurbishing), Long Run Children's Learning Center (computer/playground improvements), MCAR, Inc. (new van/videos), and Spectrum Charter School (first year operations). **$34,000** to Best Friends of Beaver County (family support-respite care program). **$30,000** each to Boy Scouts/Greater Pittsburgh Council (scouting for youth with MR), Pittsburgh Vision Services (preschool screening), and Variety-The Children's Charity (equipment). **$25,313-$26,335** to ARC of Pa. [Harrisburg] (Parents Educating Parents program), Center for Theater Arts (performing arts classes for MR children), and Transitional Employment Consultants (van). **$20,000-$20,800** each to ARC Indiana County Chapter (patient-mentor program) and Center for Creative Play (free visits by preschool MR children). **$18,500** to Futures Rehabilitation Center (roof repairs). **$15,000** each to Controlled Environment Horticulture, Inc. (greenhouse repairs), and Easter Seals of Western Pa. (employment services marketing). **$10,000-$10,500** each to Carnegie Museum of Natural History (programs for MR children), Lark Enterprises (kitchen equipment/renovations), Pittsburgh Symphony (Allegheny Valley School Concert), and Prader-Willi Syndrome Assn. of Pa. (parents' conference support). **$7,570** to ARC Foundation of York County (Project TRAIN). **$7,500** to Disabilities Law Project (free assistance for mentally retarded). ■**PUBLICATIONS:** None ■**WEBSITE:** None ■**E-MAIL:** j.ferguson@pncadvisors.com ■**APPLICATION POLICIES & PROCEDURES:** The Trust reports that only organizations serving mentally retarded persons (especially children) in Western Pa. are eligible to apply. Grant requests may be submitted in a letter by the October 1st deadline; provide details on services provided to mentally retarded persons, a project budget, financial documentation for prior three years (if available), names of trustees/officers indicating their connections with the community and with mentally retarded persons, and IRS tax-exempt status documentation. Grants are awarded at a December meeting.

O+D+T James M. Ferguson, III (Executive VP at Bank+Con) — J. Murray Egan, Esq. (Co-T) — PNC Advisors (Co-Trustee)

SW-369   Tzedakah Foundation
5851 Phillips Ave.
Pittsburgh   15217   (Allegheny County)

MI-22-62
Phone 412-422-7239 **FAX** None
EIN 25-1752556   **Year Created** 1994

AMV $643,927   **FYE** 12-00   (**Gifts Received** $0)   54 **Grants totaling** $55,930

Mostly local giving. High grant of **$19,750** to Hillel Academy of Pittsburgh. **$5,000** to Jewish National Fund. **$4,600** to Zionist Organization of America. **$4,000** to United Jewish Federation of Greater Pittsburgh. **$3,000** to Poale Zedeck Charity Fund. **$1,000-$1,800** each to Congregation Poale Zedeck, Hebrew Free Loan Assn., Holocaust Center (endowment fund), Jewish Community Center of Greater Pittsburgh, and Kollel Bais Yitzchok. Other local contributions **$18-$750,** mostly for Jewish purposes. **Out-of-state** giving includes **$1,500** to Israel Cancer Research Fund [NY] and **$1,000** to U.S. Holocaust Memorial Museum. ■**PUBLICATIONS:** None ■**WEBSITE:** None ■**E-MAIL:** None ■**APPLICATION POLICIES & PROCEDURES:** Information not available.

O+D+T Philip J. Samson (P+T+Con) — Iris M. Samson (T)

SW-370   Unger-Pfeffer Family Foundation
c/o Freid-El, Inc.
1501 Preble Avenue
Pittsburgh   15233   (Allegheny County)

MI-22-62

Phone 412-322-1363 **FAX** None
EIN 25-6253815   **Year Created** 1986

AMV $129,388   **FYE** 11-00   (**Gifts Received** $64,947)   40+ **Grants totaling** $33,191

Mostly local/Pa. giving. High grant of **$9,000** to Hillel Academy of Pittsburgh. **$4,250** to Yeshiva Tifereth Torah. **$2,090** to Congregation Poale Zedeck. **$2,000** to Prospect Park Yeshiva. **$1,490** to Bnos Chail. Many other smaller local contributions. **Out-of-state** giving includes **$2,080** to Rabbinical Seminary of America [NY] and other contributions to NY, MD, MI and other states. ■**PUBLICATIONS:** None ■**WEBSITE:** None ■**E-MAIL:** None ■**APPLICATION POLICIES & PROCEDURES:** Grant requests may be submitted in a letter at any time; include background information on the organzation.

O+D+T Joel Pfeffer (T+Con) — Elvira Pfeffer (T+Donor) — Murray Pfeffer (T+Donor) — Freda Unger (T+Donor) — Corporate donor: Freid-El, Inc.

SW-371   United States Steel Foundation, Inc.
c/o United States Steel Corporation
600 Grant Street, Room 639
Pittsburgh   15219   (Allegheny County)

MI-11-12-13-14-16-17-22-25-31-32-41-42-43
45-49-51-52-54-55-56-81-88
Phone 412-433-5237 **FAX** 412-433-6847
EIN 13-6093185   **Year Created** 1953

AMV $10,511,365   **FYE** 11-01   (**Gifts Received** $11,113,506)   2113 **Grants totaling** $6,505,023

Nationwide giving focuses on United States Steel corporate operating locations in many states (see below) and allocated to Education-53%, Health/Human Services-31%, and Public, Cultural & Scientific Affairs-16%. About 40% giving to Pa., primarily Pittsburgh; grants are for general operating/program support except as noted. High grant of **$700,000** to United Way of SW Pa. (redistributed in part to 12 Western Pa. organizations). **$500,000** to Braddock's Field Historical Society (Visitors' Center/French & Indian War battle site-capital grant). **$60,000** to Pittsburgh Leadership Foundation (transitional support). **$50,000** each to DePaul Institute (capital campaign) and Pittsburgh Symphony. **$40,000** to United Way of Bucks County. **$35,000** to Carnegie Museums of Pittsburgh. **$25,000** to Robert Morris College (Partnership for Regional Innovation in Manufacturing Education program). **$20,000** each to Coalition for Christian Outreach (Mon Valley services) and Pittsburgh Opera. **$15,000** each to Alvernia College [Berks County] (endowment), Japan-America Society of Pa. (education/research), McGuire Memorial Home (wheelchair-passenger van), National Parkinson Foundation (transitional support), and Verland (dietary dept. equipment). **$10,000** each to Crohn's & Colitis Foundation of America/Pittsburgh Chapter (research), National Kidney Foundation of Western Pa., Pittsburgh Ballet Theatre, Pittsburgh Glass Center (capital campaign), Pittsburgh Leadership Foundation (youth mentor program), Soldiers & Sailors Memorial Hall, and Watson Institute (capital campaign). **$8,400** to Bethlehem Haven (computer hardware/software). **$7,000** to Western Pa. Conservancy (community floral bed program/unrestricted support). **$5,000** each to Allegheny County Literacy Program, City Theatre Company, Glade Run (treatment facility construction), Junior Achievement of SW Pa., Mary Miller Dance Company, Pittsburgh Children's Museum (capital grant), Saltworks Theatre Company, Wilkinsburg Historical Society (Lincoln statue restoration), and YMCA of McKeesport (computer hardware/software). **$2,000-$3,500** each to Allegheny County Bar Assn. (Center for Volunteer Legal Services), Big Brothers Big Sisters of Bucks County (computer system upgrade), Bridge to Independence, Delaware Valley Philharmonic Orchestra [Bucks County], Good Grief Center for Bereavement Support (office renovations), Mendelssohn Choir of Pittsburgh, Pittsburgh Center for the Arts (capital grant), Pittsburgh Council for International Visitors (education), Pittsburgh Dance Council, Society for Contemporary Craft, Tennis Patron's Foundation of Greater Pittsburgh (underprivileged children programs), and World Affairs Council of Pittsburgh (education). Other giving nationally for education, including some to Pa. institutions: **$1,246,619** for 1,640 educational matching gifts to 365 four-year or graduate level educational institutions; **$421,000** to 98 college scholarship funds; and about **$900,000** awarded in individual scholarships, primarily to dependents of employees. Other out-of-state giving was concentrated in corporate operating locations in AL, IN, OH, and TX with lesser amounts to AK, CO, DC, FL, IL, LA, MI, MN, MO, NM, NY, OK, WI, WV, and WY, and emphasized support to United Ways, hospitals, colleges/universities, and selected national organizations. ■**PUBLICATIONS:** Annual Report; Grant Application Guidelines ■**WEBSITE:** www.ussteel.com/corp/ussfoundation/ussfound.htm ■**E-MAIL:** None ■**APPLICATION POLICIES & PROCEDURES:** The Foundation reports that most grants are awarded to nonprofit organizations in major corporate operating locations in three programmatic areas: **Education** (focuses primarily on operating, capital and scholarship fund support at higher education institutions, especially those with strong engineering, science and business programs); **Health/Human Services** (focuses on United Ways with some capital operating support for service providers in corporate operating locations); and **Public, Cultural & Scientific Affairs** (focuses on public policy, legal, business and community organizations, especially those related to corporate business interests). No grants are awarded to individuals for personal needs or scholarships, organizations with programs outside the U.S., organizations receiving operating funds from a United Way, or other grantmaking foundations. Also, no support is given for preschool-grade 12 education, individual research projects; sectarian religious purposes; hospitals or nursing homes; conferences, seminars or symposia; economic development; fundraising or special event sponsorship; travel; publication of papers, books or magazines; or production of films, videotapes or other audiovisual materials. Grant requests may be submitted in a letter/executive summary (2 pages maximum) stating the organization's mission and need; also, the Grantmakers of Western Pa. Common Grant application Format may be used. Deadlines depend on the type of applicant organization: Public, Cultural or Scientific Affairs—January 15th; Education—April 15th; and Health/Human Services—July 15th. Proposals submitted out of sequence are held for review at the appropriate meeting. Supporting documentation that must accompany a request includes: (a) brief history or profile of the organization; (b) a full description of the organization's need and projected outcomes; (c) for capital needs, the campaign goal or total cost of the specific capital need -or- for operating needs, the operating budget for the period for which funding is requested; (d) listing of committed funds and actual amounts -and- listing of prospective contributors that have been (or will be) solicited and amounts requested; (e) copy of most recent audited financial statement; (f) a list of the organization's senior staff members and Board members with affiliations; (g) the signature of an authorized executive of the tax-exempt organization -or- if the request originates in a organization's subdivision, then the signature of the CEO of the parent organization -or- if the request originates in a college/university department or subdivision, then a signed statement by the institution's corporate relations or development officer; and (h) IRS tax-exempt status documentation. Personal interviews or office appointments or site visits are scheduled as needed and appropriate. Decisions on grants depend upon the programmatic area: Public, Cultural & Scientific Affairs— late April, Education—late July, and Health/Human Services—late October. Matching gifts for 4-year or graduate level higher educational institutions have a $100 minimum, $2,000 maximum per employee/year. — Formerly called USX Foundation.

O+D+T Craig D. Mallick (General Manager+Con) — Thomas J. Usher (C+T) — Marilyn A. Harris (P+T) — Dan D. Sandman, Esq. (S+General Counsel+T) — Robert M. Hernandez (CFO+T) — Jerry Howard (T) — John T. Mills (T) — Larry G. Schultz (VP+Comptroller) — Edward F. Guna (VP+F) — Gary A. Glynn (VP-Investments) — Corporate donor: USX Corporation

---

SW-372 USA Waste/Chambers Development Foundation   MI-31-42-52-54-81
c/o USA Waste Services, Inc.
1500 Ardmore Boulevard, Suite 407   **Phone** 412-871-6118 **FAX** None
Pittsburgh 15235   (Allegheny County)   **EIN** 25-6500262   **Year Created** 1995
AMV $1,294,533   **FYE** 6-00   **(Gifts Received** $0)   8 **Grants totaling** $650,000

All local giving. High grant of **$264,417** to Carnegie Science Center. **$162,650** to Children's Hospital of Pittsburgh. **$92,500** to Medal of Honor Foundation. **$85,433** to Duquesne U. **$25,000** to American Hellenic Information & Communications Group. **$19,050** to Pittsburgh Opera. Other smaller local contributions under **$500**. ■**PUBLICATIONS:** None ■**WEBSITE:** None ■**E-MAIL:** None ■**APPLICATION POLICIES & PROCEDURES:** The Foundation reports that all giving is restricted to Pittsburgh charities. Grant requests may be submitted at any time in a formal letter; include IRS tax-exempt status documentation.

O+D+T Nancy Barnhart (Con) — John G. Rangos, Sr. (T) — Corporate donor: USA Waste Services, Inc.

SW-373 Vesuvius Foundation   MI-12-13-14-15-16-17-18-22-29-32-41-42-45
c/o PNC Advisors - M.S. P2-PTPP-25-1   51-52-54-55-56-57-71
Two PNC Plaza, 620 Liberty Ave.   **Phone** 412-762-3390 **FAX** 412-762-5439
Pittsburgh 15222   (Allegheny County)   **EIN** 25-6076182   **Year Created** 1966
AMV $4,100,999   **FYE** 12-00   **(Gifts Received** $0)   45 **Grants totaling** $254,000

Mostly local giving; some grants match individual contributions of co-trustees. High Pa. grants of **$10,000** each to Bradley Center, FAME/Fund for Advancement of Minorities through Education, Family Resources, Kerr Museum Board, Lawrence Citizens Council, Pittsburgh Children's Museum, Pittsburgh Youth Symphony Orchestra, Planned Parenthood of Western Pa., Prime Stages, Saltworks Theatre Company, Pressley Ridge Schools, The Watson Institute, and WQED. **$7,500** to Extra Mile Education Foundation. **$5,300** to Robert Morris College. **$5,000** each to ARC-Allegheny, Big Brothers Big Sisters of Greater Pittsburgh, Children's Home of Pittsburgh, Greater Pittsburgh Literacy Council, Hollow Oak Land Trust [Coraopolis], Life's Work of Western Pa., National Parkinson Foundation/Greater Pittsburgh Chapter, Pittsburgh Ballet Theatre, United Negro College Fund, and The Whale's Tale/FamilyLink. **$3,500** to Pittsburgh Public Theater. **$3,000** to U. of Pittsburgh. **$2,000-$2,500** each to Bethlehem Haven, Contact Pittsburgh, Gateway to the Arts, River City Brass Band, Salvation Army, and YMCA of Pittsburgh. **$1,000-$1,500** each to Carnegie Museums of Pittsburgh, Historical Society of Western Pa., Leukemia Society of Western Pa. and WV, National Center for Juvenile Justice, Penn State U., Pittsburgh Action Against Rape, Shady Side Academy, and Spina Bifida Assn. of Western Pa. **$200** to St. Joseph House of Hospitality. **Out-of-state** giving includes high grant of **$15,000** to Earthwatch Institute [CA]; **$10,000** to Child's Way [AL]; and **$5,000** to Red Cross [DC]. ■**PUBLICATIONS:** None ■**WEBSITE:** None ■**E-MAIL:** None ■ **APPLICATION POLICIES & PROCEDURES:** Grant requests may be submitted in a letter (5 pages maximum) at any time—deadlines are May 15th and November 15th; describe the nature and purpose/s of the organization/institution and the intended use of the requested funds; include a project budget, list of major funding sources, and IRS tax-exempt status documentation. Individual co-trustees' contributions are matched; no grants are awarded for scholarships or to individuals. Grants are awarded at meetings in June and December. NOTE: This Foundation is no longer affiliated with Vesuvius USA.

O+D+T John D. Culbertson (VP at Bank+Con) — Harry A. Thompson (C+Co-T) — Frank L. Arensberg, II [CA] (Co-T) — Robert L. Mayer (Co-T) — Evans Rose, Jr. Esq. (Co-T) — H. Campbell Stuckeman (Co-T) — PNC Advisors (Corporate Trustee)

SW-374 **Vincent (Ethel) Charitable Trust** MI-22-32-34
  c/o Wymard & Dunn
  220 Grant Street **Phone** 412-281-6225 **FAX** None
  Pittsburgh 15219 (Allegheny County) **EIN** 23-7886897 **Year Created** 1997
AMV $2,820,733 **FYE** 9-00 (**Gifts Received** $0) 2 **Grants totaling** $100,000

All local giving. **$50,000** each to U. of Pittsburgh Medical Center (School of Medicine -Surgery Dept.) and U. of Pittsburgh (Dept. of Neurology). — In the prior year, two grants: **$100,000** to U. of Pittsburgh (Dept. of Neurology) and **$20,000** to Salvation Army. ■**PUBLICATIONS:** None ■**WEBSITE:** None ■**E-MAIL:** None ■**APPLICATION POLICIES & PROCEDURES:** The Trust reports giving will focus on Salvation Army, multiple sclerosis, or other similar health issue, research and development. Grant requests may be submitted in any form at any time; describe in detail the purpose of the requested funding.
O+D+T Joseph M. Wymard, Esq. (Co-Fiduciary+Con) — PNC Bank N.A. (Co-Fiduciary)

SW-375 **Walden Trust, The** MI-11-17-22-35-41-42-44-52-54-55-56-57-63
  5057 Fifth Ave. 71-81-83
  P.O. Box 2009 **Phone** 412-621-1159 **FAX** 412-621-2991
  Pittsburgh 15230 (Allegheny County) **EIN** 25-6027635 **Year Created** 1961
AMV $1,585,250 **FYE** 12-00 (**Gifts Received** $0) **Grants totaling** $80,450

Details on 2000 grants are unavailable. — In the prior year, 42 grants totaling **$66,500** were awarded—about two-thirds local giving; grants are unrestricted support except as noted. High grant of **$9,000** to Phipps Conservatory & Botanical Garden (capital campaign). **$8,000** to Pittsburgh History & Landmarks Assn. (unrestricted support/neighborhood grant program) **$3,500** to Carnegie Institute. **$3,000** to Powdermill Nature Preserve. **$2,500** each to Allegheny Cemetery Historical Assn., Northside Common Ministries, Regional Trail Corp., and Shadyside Presbyterian Church. **$1,000-$1,500** each to Pittsburgh Cultural Trust, Valley School of Ligonier, Visiting Nurse Assn. Foundation, Women's Center & Shelter of Greater Pittsburgh, and World Federalist Assn. Other local contributions **$100-$500** for various purposes. **Out-of-state** giving includes **$6,000** to Piedmont Environmental Council [VA]; **$5,000** each to Memorial Church-Harvard [MA] and Summer Opera Theater [DC]; and **$2,500** to Preservation Foundation of Palm Beach [FL]. ■**PUBLICATIONS:** None ■**WEBSITE:** None ■**E-MAIL:** None ■**APPLICATION POLICIES & PROCEDURES:** The Foundation reports priority giving interests as arts/culture, historic preservation, wildlife preservation, and special environmental programs; most grants are for general support, special projects, or building funds. No grants are awarded to individuals. Grant requests may be submitted in any form between March-September; include organizational/project budgets and IRS tax-exempt status documentation. The Trustees award grants at a November meeting.
O+D+T Henry P. Hoffstot, Jr. (T+Donor+Con) — Thayer H. Drew [VA] (T) — H. Phipps Hoffstot, III [Ligonier] (T) — Lora H. Jenkins [VA} (T) — Lorna K. Tahtinen [MD] (T) — Arthur P. Ziegler, Jr. (T)

SW-376 **Walton Family Foundation, The** MI-11-41-54
  c/o Mellon Private Wealth Management
  525 William Penn Way, Room 4000 **Phone** 412-234-5892 **FAX** 412-234-1073
  Pittsburgh 15259 (Allegheny County) **EIN** 25-6568399 **Year Created** 1996
AMV $545,976 **FYE** 12-00 (**Gifts Received** $0) 2 **Grants totaling** $35,000

All local giving; grants are for general support. High grant of **$20,000** to Carnegie Institute. **$15,000** to United Way of Allegheny County. ■**PUBLICATIONS:** Application Guidelines ■**WEBSITE:** None ■**E-MAIL:** richards.lb@mellon.com ■**APPLICATION POLICIES & PROCEDURES:** Grant requests may be submitted in a letter at any time. No grants are awarded to individuals.
O+D+T Leonard B. Richards, III (VP at Bank+Con) — James M. Walton (T) — John F. Walton, II [AZ] (T) — Rachel Mellon Walton (T) — Farley Walton Whetzel (T) — Mellon Bank (Corporate Trustee)

SW-377 **Ward Foundation, The** MI-11-12-13-41-32-42-54-55-61-85
  c/o The Ward Trucking Company
  Ward Tower, P.O. Box 1553 **Phone** 814-944-0803 **FAX** 814-944-5470
  Altoona 16603 (Blair County) **EIN** 25-6059159 **Year Created** 1962
AMV $846,702 **FYE** 9-00 (**Gifts Received** $7,653) 39 **Grants totaling** $49,525

Mostly local/Pa. giving. High grant of **$10,000** to Penn State U./Altoona Campus. **$9,125** to United Way of Blair County. **$4,000** to Annual Catholic Appeal. **$3,000** each to Mount Aloysius College, Partnership for Education, and Southern Alleghenies Museum of Art. **$2,500** to Altoona-Blair County Development Corp. **$2,000** to Blair County Community Endowment. **$1,000** each to Blair County Arts Festival, and Western Pa. Caring Foundation for Children, and Hollidaysburg Area YMCA. Other local/Pa. contributions **$50-$500** for various purposes. **Out-of-state** giving includes **$1,500** to Chautauqua Institution [NY] and **$1,000** to Memorial Sloan Kettering Cancer Center [NY]. — Grants approved for future payment include **$45,000** to Blair County Community Endowment; **$14,125** to United Way of Blair County; and **$7,500** to Altoona-Blair County Development Corp. ■**PUBLICATIONS:** None ■**WEBSITE:** www.wardtrucking.com [corporate info only] ■**E-MAIL:** llweaver@wardtrucking.com ■**APPLICATION POLICIES & PROCEDURES:** The Foundation reports that giving is mostly limited to Pa.
O+D+T G. William Ward [Hollidaysburg] (T+Con) — Michael E. Ward [Hollidaysburg] (T)

SW-378 Washington County Community Foundation
c/o Washington Federal Savings Bank
77 South Main Street
Washington 15301 (Washington County)

MI-14-29-41-42-43-44-55

Phone 724-222-6330 **FAX** 724-223-4167
EIN 25-1726013 **Year Created** 1993

AMV $810,444 **FYE** 12-00 (**Gifts Received** $339,219) 20 **Grants totaling** $13,366

As a Community Foundation all discretionary giving is limited to organizations serving Washington County. High grant of **$2,000** to Washington & Jefferson College. **$700** to Washington Women's Shelter. **$600** each to Bentleyville Public Library and Interfaith Hospitality Network. **$500** each to ARC-Washington, The Artists' Co-op, Burgettstown Elementary School, and Community Action Southwest. Other smaller contributions to local organizations. Also, nine scholarships **$150-$2,000**, awarded. ■**PUBLICA-TIONS:** How To Apply for a Grant memorandum, application form ■ **WEBSITE:** www.wccf.net ■ **E-MAIL:** wccf@cobweb.net ■ **APPLICATION POLICIES & PROCEDURES:** The Foundation reports that all discretionary giving must benefit Washington County. Organizations or projects in the arts, education, environment, health/human services, or religion will be supported with special consideration given to (1) inter-agency proposals which broadly impact/serve the community, (2) projects which leverage (or have received) other funding, and (3) seed money for a new project of an existing organization. Proposals to establish new organizations are discouraged. No grants will be considered for political purposes, lobbying, loans, on-going operating expenses, budget deficits, land acquisition, or endowment—nor to organizations which discriminate by race, color, religious creed, sex, national origin, disability or sexual preference. Prospective applicants should submit an initial one-page Letter of Intent describing the organization, the proposed project/program, and stating the dollar amount requested. All Letters of intent are acknowledged, and if the Foundation is interested in the proposed project, complete application materials will be provided; deadlines are March 15th, May 15th, August 15th, and November 15th for receipt of full applications. Propsosals which follow Grantmakers of Western Pa. Common Grant Application Format are accepted. The Board meets monthly.

O+D+T Betsie Trew (Executive Director) — Dr. Howard Jack (C+T) — Louis E. Waller (VC+T) — Carlyn Belczyk, CPA (F+T) — Janet Abernathy (S+T) — Barry Batusiak, DDS (T) — Martha Berman (T) — John A. Campbell (T) — Dr. Thomas Conner (T) — John R. Duskey (T) — Dennis Dutton (T) — Charles Fife (T) — Shirley Hardy (T) — Robert A. Hillberry (T) — Charles Keller, Esq. (T) — Joseph Marsh (T) — James H. McCune, Esq. (T) — William McMahon, M.D. (T) — John L.S. Northrop (T) — Patrick O'Brien, II (T) — Paul Songer (T) — Frank Tracanna, Jr. (T) — Juliana Uram (T) — Carmina V. Vitullo (T) — Richard L. White (T) — Frank Zerla (T)

SW-379 Washington Federal Charitable Foundation
c/o Washington Federal Savings Bank
190 North Main Street
Washington 15301 (Washington County)

MI-13-22-17-31-41-42-43-54-85-89

Phone 724-222-3120 **FAX** 724-223-4167
EIN 25-6395164 **Year Created** 1991

AMV $517,758 **FYE** 6-00 (**Gifts Received** $139,850) 12 **Grants totaling** $109,000

All local giving. High grant of **$25,000** to Washington Hospital Foundation (construction). **$10,000** each to Boy Scouts/Greater Pittsburgh Council (Scouting in housing), California U. (computer funding), Intermediate Unit #1 (science modules), Washington County Council on Economic Development (community development), Washington & Jefferson College (computer funding), Waynesburg College (campus center), and Youth for Christ (property improvements). **$5,000** each to Mt. Pleasant Township Community Center (improvements) and Pa. Trolley Museum (educational outreach). **$2,000** each to ABCDE Foundation (scholarships) and Watchful Shepherd (abuse prevention). ■**PUBLICATIONS:** application guidelines ■**WEBSITE:** www.washfed.com/Community/community.html ■**E-MAIL:** info@washfed.com ■**APPLICATION POLICIES & PROCEDURES:** The Foundation gives preference to SW Pa. organizations located in the Bank's service area, and which exhibit the following: active board leadership, community involvement, a comprehensive strategic plan for resource development/use, collaboration with other nonprofits, and efficient/effective administration of programs. Multiple year grants are awarded, and the largest grant available is $50,000. No grants are awarded to individuals or for fraternal organizations, conference or seminar attendance, specialized health campaigns, national organizations, religious or sectarian organizations, or political purposes. Grant requests must be submitted on a formal Application Form (available from the Foundation) before the deadlines of February 1st, May 1st, August 1st, or November 1st; include an annual report, organization and project budgets, list of Board members, list of major funding sources, audited financial statement, and IRS tax-exempt status documentation. Site visits sometimes are made to organizations being considered for a grant. Grants are awarded at meetings in March, June, September and December. — The Bank also has a Corporate Giving Program which designates 10% of the Bank's after-tax profits to charitable organizations.

O+D+T Richard L. White (Bank President+T+Con) — William M. Campbell (C+T) — Mary Lyn Drewitz (S+T) — David R. Andrews (T) — Martin P. Beichner, Jr. (T) — James H. Boyland (T) — Joseph M. Jefferson (T) — D. Jackson Milhollan (T) — James R. Proudfit (T) — Telford W. Thomas (T) — Louis E. Waller (T) — Corporate donor: Washington Federal Savings Bank

---

SW-380 Waters (Robert S.) Charitable Trust
c/o Mellon Private Wealth Management
525 William Penn Way, Room 4000
Pittsburgh 15259 (Allegheny County)

MI-11-12-13-14-15-22-29-31-41-42-44-52-54-56-71

Phone 412-234-5784 **FAX** 412-234-1073
EIN 25-6018986 **Year Created** 1952

AMV $9,505,527 **FYE** 12-00 (**Gifts Received** $0) 34 **Grants totaling** $497,000

Mostly local or Cambria County giving; all grants are for operational support. High grant of **$250,000** to Carnegie Institute. **$22,500** to Western Pa. Conservancy. **$15,000** each to Johnstown Area Heritage Assn. and Marian Manor. **$12,500** each to Conemaugh Valley Conservancy and River City Brass Band. **$10,000** each to Carnegie Museum of Art, The Community Foundation for the Alleghenies, The Ellis School, Historical Society of Western Pa., Talus Rock Girl Scout Council, and Winchester Thurston School. **$7,500** each to Allegheny Lutheran Social Ministries, Cambria Free Library, Christian Home of Johnstown, Conemaugh Valley Hospital, Family Social Services, Good Samaritan Hospital, and Shady Side Academy. **$6,000** to Southern Alleghenies Museum. **$5,000** each to Pauline Auberle Foundation, FAME/Foundation for Advancement of Minorities through Education, Family Resources, Historical Society of Pa. [Philadelphia], Laurel Valley Emergency Medical Services,

Shakespeare In The Schools, and U. of Pa. **$2,000-$2,500** each to Foundation for Independent Colleges [Harrisburg], Pittsburgh Children's Museum, United Way of Allegheny County, Whale's Tale Foundation/FamilyLink, and WQED. **$1,500** to United Negro College Fund. **Out-of-state** grant: **$5,000** to Lawrenceville School [NJ]. ■**PUBLICATIONS:** None. ■**WEBSITE:** None ■**E-MAIL:** robinson.bk@mellon.com ■**APPLICATION POLICIES & PROCEDURES:** The Foundation reports that giving is generally limited to Western Pa. No grants are awarded to individuals or for scholarships/fellowships. Grant requests may be submitted in a letter during April or October; provide a detailed project description, organizational/project budgets, Board member list, and IRS tax-exempt status documentation. Site visits sometimes are made to organizations being considered for a grant. Grants are awarded at May and November meetings.

O+D+T Barbara K. Robinson (First VP at Bank+Con) — John P. Davis, Jr. Esq. , Esq. (Co-T) — Mellon Bank N.A. (Co-Trustee)

SW-381 **Wechsler Research Foundation**
c/o Gastroenterology Medical Associates
6301 Forbes Ave., Suite 301
Pittsburgh   15217   (Allegheny County)
AMV $556,186   **FYE** 12-00   **(Gifts Received** $0)

MI-14-22-41-42-62

Phone 412-656-5334 **FAX** None
EIN 25-6038039   **Year Created** 1958
          10 **Grants totaling** $30,261

Mostly local giving; grants are for unrestricted/discretionary support except as noted. High grant of **$21,100** to Jewish Residential Services (residence for mentally impaired). **$2,500** to Winchester-Thurston School. **$2,000** to United Jewish Federation of Greater Pittsburgh. **$1,650** to Shady Side Academy (scholarship fund). Other local contributions **$36-$150**. **Out-of-state** grant: **$2,500** to Harvard College Fund [MA]. ■**PUBLICATIONS:** None ■**WEBSITE:** None ■**E-MAIL:** None ■**APPLICATION POLICIES & PROCEDURES:** Grant requests may be submitted in a letter/proposal at any time.

O+D+T Richard L. Wechsler, M.D. (D+Donor+Con) — Corporate donor: Schering Sales Corp. [NJ]

SW-382 **Weinberg (Alvin & Shirley) Foundation**
c/o Horovitz Rudoy & Roteman, CPAs
436 - 7th Ave., Suite 600
Pittsburgh   15219   (Allegheny County)
AMV $481,998   **FYE** 11-00   **(Gifts Received** $2,500)

MI-22-32-62

Phone 412-391-2920 **FAX** 412-391-4703
EIN 25-1415942   **Year Created** 1982
          30 **Grants totaling** $22,896

Mostly local giving. High grant of **$13,350** to Beth Shalom Congregation. **$1,000** each to Kollel Bais Yitzchok and Yeshiva Licher. **$860** to Na'Amat USA. Other contributions **$25-$500** primarily for health, educational, and Jewish purposes. ■**PUBLICATIONS:** None ■**WEBSITE:** None ■**E-MAIL:** None ■**APPLICATION POLICIES & PROCEDURES:** Grant requests may be submitted in any form at any time before the September 30th deadline.

O+D+T Shirley Weinberg (T+Manager+Donor+Con) — Lisa Antin (T+Donor) — Jeffrey Weinberg (T+Donor) — Alvin Weinberg (Donor) — Ferne Weinberg (Donor)

SW-383 **Weir (Edgar V.) Family Foundation**
345 Brownsdale Road
Butler   16002   (Butler County)
AMV $1,149,057   **FYE** 12-00   **(Gifts Received** $0)

MI-12-13-31-32-44-56-63-89

Phone 724-586-2631 **FAX** None
EIN 25-6070443   **Year Created** 1963
          57 **Grants totaling** $55,100

About one-third local giving. High Pa. grant of **$4,000** to St. Peters Episcopal Church. **$2,000** each to American Cancer Society, Arthritis Foundation, Butler Area Public Library, and Family Guidance, Inc. **$1,000** each to Jameson Health Care Foundation, and YWCA of Butler. **$800** to Penn Township Volunteer Fire Company. Other local contributions **$500** each for various community organizations. **Out-of-state** giving includes high grant of **$5,000** to Foundation for Historic Churches [VA]; **$3,000** to Nolan Catholic High School [TX]; **$2,000** to Arlington Women's Shelter [TX]; and other smaller grants/contributions, mostly to MD/DC, MN, TX where Trustees reside. ■**PUBLICATIONS:** None ■**WEBSITE:** None ■**E-MAIL:** None ■**APPLICATION POLICIES & PROCEDURES:** Grant requests may be submitted in a brief letter at any time; describe the organization and the intended use of requested funds. Decision on grants usually are made within two weeks.

O+D+T Edgar V. Weir, Jr. [TX] (P+D+Con) — Mary Ellen Gallagher [MN] (D) — Rebecca A. Weir [MD] (D)

SW-384 **Weis (Robert J. & Susan K.) Foundation**
1347 Squirrel Hill Ave.
Pittsburgh   15217   (Allegheny County)
AMV $408,647   **FYE** 9-00   **(Gifts Received** $0)

MI-22-32-62

Phone 412-639-3551 **FAX** None
EIN 25-1538895   **Year Created** 1986
          3 **Grants totaling** $18,500

All local giving. High grant of **$11,000** to U. of Pittsburgh Medical Center/Starzl Transplantation Institute (research). **$5,000** to Susan G. Komen Race for the Cure (research). **$2,500** to United Jewish Federation of Greater Pittsburgh. ■**PUBLICATIONS:** None ■**WEBSITE:** None ■**E-MAIL:** None ■**APPLICATION POLICIES & PROCEDURES:** No grants awarded to individuals.

O+D+T Robert J. Weis (P+F+Donor+Con) — Susan K. Weis (VP+S+Donor)

SW-385 **Weisbrod (Robert & Mary) Foundation**
c/o National City Bank of Pa.
National City Center, 20 Stanwix Street
Pittsburgh   15222   (Allegheny County)
AMV $15,985,266   **FYE** 12-00   **(Gifts Received** $0)

MI-11-12-13-14-15-16-22-25-31-41-44-51-52
55-56-72

Phone 412-644-6200 **FAX** 412-261-6252
EIN 25-6105924   **Year Created** 1968
          56 **Grants totaling** $746,818

Most giving to Allegheny County; all grants are for general support. High grant of **$50,000** each to Little Sisters of the Poor, National Aviary in Pittsburgh, Pace School, and The Woodlands Foundation [Wexford]. **$28,000** to Western Pa. School for the Deaf. **$25,000** each to Allegheny Valley School [Coraopolis], Family House, McGuire Memorial Home Foundation [New Brighton],

Manchester Youth Development Center, and Parent & Child Guidance Center Foundation. **$20,000** each to Action-Housing and The DePaul Institute. **$13,000-$18,000** each to FAME/Fund for the Advancement of Minorities through Education, Life'sWork of Western Pa., Mom's House, Passavant Memorial Home, Pittsburgh Symphony, United Cerebral Palsy of Pittsburgh, and United Way of Allegheny County. **$8,000-$10,000** each to Beaver County Civic Senior Citizen, Boy Scouts-Greater Pittsburgh Council, Bridge to Independence [Braddock], Circle C Youth & Family Services, Coalition for Christian Outreach, Extra Mile Education Foundation, Gateway to the Arts, Greater Pittsburgh Literacy Council, Make-A-Wish Foundation of Western Pa., Pittsburgh Ballet Theatre, Plum Borough Community Library, Presbyterian Seniorcare [Washington], Radio Information Service, River City Brass Band, Touchstone [Farmington], Try-Again Homes [Washington], Whale's Tale Foundation/FamilyLink, and YMCA of McKeesport. **$4,000-$5,000** each to Big Brothers Big Sisters of Greater Pittsburgh, Center for Creative Play, The Children's Institute, Family Hospice, Goodwill Industries of Pittsburgh, Light of Life Ministries, Salvation Army, Southwinds, Variety Club of Pittsburgh, and William & Mildred Orr Compassionate Care Center. **$1,000-$3,500** each to Children's Hospital of Pittsburgh, Civic Light Opera, Contact Pittsburgh, Historical Society of Western Pa., Mon Yough Riverfront Entertainment & Culture, Outreach Teen & Family Services, Pittsburgh Opera Society, Vietnam Veterans Leadership Program, and Western Pa. Conservancy. ■**PUBLICATIONS:** None ■**WEBSITE:** None ■**E-MAIL:** None ■**APPLICATION POLICIES & PROCEDURES:** The Foundation reports that giving is primarily to Allegheny County, occasionally to other SW Pa. counties; most grants are for special projects, building funds, and capital drives; multiyear grants are awarded. Prospective applicants initially should make a telephone inquiry about the feasibility of submitting a request. Grant requests may be submitted in a letter (2 pages maximum); describe the purpose of funding sought, amount requested, and the name/address of the individual who can provide additional information; include a project budget, list of major funding sources, and IRS tax-exempt status documentation. Deadlines for requests are two weeks before the Distribution Committee meetings held in May, September, and December. Site visits sometimes are made to organizations being considered for a grant.

O+D+T Distribution Committee Members: — Susan L. Farrell (VP at Bank+Con) — Jack Armstrong — John R. Echement — National City Bank of Pa. (Corporate Trustee)

SW-386 Weyandt (Carl S. & Wanda M.) Foundation
　　c/o Leech, Tishman, Fuscaldo & Lampl
　　1800 Frick Building, 437 Grant Street
　　Pittsburgh　15219　　　　　(Allegheny County)
AMV $774,423　　　**FYE** 12-00　　　(**Gifts Received** $0)

MI-12-13-18-29-13-42-56-72-89

Phone 412-261-1600　**FAX** 412-227-5551
EIN 25-1668618　　**Year Created** 1991
15　**Grants totaling** $34,108

Mostly Indiana County giving. High grant of **$5,000** to Indiana U. of Pa. Foundation. **$4,000** each to Birthright/Indiana County and Red Cross/Indiana. **$3,000** each to Big Brothers/Big Sisters of Indiana County and St. Louis Church [Lucernemines]. **$2,500** each to Alice Paul House and Indiana YMCA. **$1,000** each to Homer City Fire Dept., Humane Society of Indiana County (animal shelter), Indiana Fire Dept. Other local contributions **$250-$610** for various purposes. **Out-of-state** giving includes **$3,748** to Tarahumara Children's Hospital Fund [LA] and Shriners [FL]. ■**PUBLICATIONS:** None ■**WEBSITE:** None ■**E-MAIL:** None ■**APPLICATION POLICIES & PROCEDURES:** The Foundation reports most giving to Indiana County. Grant requests may be submitted in any form at any time; decisions on applications are made within two months.

O+D+T Ted Tishman, Esq. (Con) — John J. Weyandt [IN] (T) — John T. Edelman [AZ] (T) — Kathleen Weyandt [IN] (T)

SW-387 Whalley Charitable Trust
　　1210 Graham Avenue
　　Windber　15963　　　　　(Somerset County)
AMV $4,800,370　　　**FYE** 12-01　　　(**Gifts Received** $0)

MI-13-15-29-31-42-44-52-55-56-63-84-89
Phone 814-467-4000　**FAX** 814-467-6055
EIN 23-7128436　　**Year Created** 1961
62　**Grants totaling** $301,064

All local/Pa. giving; some grants comprise multiple payments. High grant of **$50,500** to Windber Medical Center. **$45,000** to Mt. Aloysius College. **$40,000** to Penn State U. **$25,000** to Windber Public Library. **$20,000** to First Presbyterian Church. **$15,000** to Arcadia Performing Arts. **$14,866** to Windber Community Building. **$10,000-$11,500** each to Laurel Arts, St. Francis U., and Windber Volunteer Fire Company #1. **$7,557** to Windber Area High School. **$6,500** to Johnstown Symphony Orchestra. **$5,000** each to Windber Lutheran Church and Windber Recreational Assn. **$4,500** to Windber Healthcare Foundation. **$3,500** to Windber Club Soccer. **$1,000-$2,500** each to Boy Scouts/Penn's Woods Council, Conemaugh Health Foundation, Foundation for Free Enterprise Education [Erie], Laurel Auto Group Charity Golf Classic, Laurel Highlands Futbol, Pa. Special Olympics, Somerset County Blind Center, Somerset County School to Work, U. of Pittsburgh-Johnstown, Veteran Community Initiatives, Windber Hospice, Windber Little League, Women's Help Center, and YWCA of Greater Johnstown. Other local contributions **$50-$500** for various community organizations. ■**PUBLICATIONS:** annual report ■**WEBSITE:** None ■**E-MAIL:** None ■**APPLICATION POLICIES & PROCEDURES:** The Trust reports that giving generally is limited to the Johnstown-Windber area. Grant requests may be submitted in a one-page letter at any time; include IRS tax-exempt status documentation.

O+D+T David C. Klementik, Esq. (T+Con) — Ruth Whalley Klementik (T)

SW-388 Wheeler Family Charitable Foundation, The
　　415 North Center Ave.
　　Somerset　15501　　　　　(Somerset County)
AMV $2,389,275　　　**FYE** 12-00　　　(**Gifts Received** $1,060,000)

MI-12-13-17-18-44-49-51-55-56
Phone 814-445-7188　**FAX** None
EIN 23-2938580　　**Year Created** 1997
9　**Grants totaling** $295,800

All local/Pa. giving; all grants are unrestricted. High grant of **$278,000** to Children's Aid Home. **$5,000** to Birthright of Somerset. **$3,000** to Gristmill Productions. **$2,500** each to Historical & Genealogical Society of Somerset County and Laurel Arts. **$1,800** to Boy Scouts/Penn's Woods Council. **$1,000** each to Foundation for Free Enterprise Education [Erie], Pennsylvania's Outstanding Young Women, Inc. [Berks County], and Somerset County Federated Library System. — Grant approved for future payment: **$222,000** to Children's Aid Home. ■**PUBLICATIONS:** None ■**WEBSITE:** None ■**E-MAIL:** None ■**APPLICATION POLICIES & PROCEDURES:** The Foundation reports that most grants are for annual campaigns, capital campaigns, general operating support, or emergency funds. No grants are awarded to individuals. Grant requests may be submitted in any form at any time. The Board meets in May and November.

O+D+T Joan M. Wheeler (Manager+D+Donor+Con) — Harold W. Wheeler, Jr. (C+D+Donor) — Barbara Davies (D) — David L. Wheeler (D) — Harold W. Wheeler, III (D) — Paul J. Wheeler (D) — Somerset Trust Company (Trustee) — Corporate donor: Wheeler Brothers, Inc.

SW-389 Whitcomb Charitable Foundation   MI-12-13-18-22-42-49-54-55
    c/o Schofield Financial Counseling
    P.O. Box 369   **Phone** 412-767-7043 **FAX** None
    Indianola 15051   (Allegheny County)   **EIN** 25-1552861   **Year Created** 1986
AMV $1,788,284   **FYE** 11-00   (**Gifts Received** $0)   16 **Grants totaling** $94,000

Nearly half local/Pa. giving. High local grant of **$8,000** to Whale's Tale Foundation/FamilyLink. **$6,000** each to Family Resources and Hill House Assn. **$5,000** each to Chatham College and The Wesley Institute. **$3,000** each to Carnegie Museums (schools program), Coalition for Christian Outreach, and Pa. Partnership for Economic Education [Harrisburg]. **Out-of-state** giving includes high grants of **$10,000** each to Save The Children [CT] and Planned Parenthood Foundation [NY]; **$8,000** to United Negro College Fund [VA]; **$7,000** to Cumberland College [KY]; and smaller grants. ■**PUBLICATIONS:** None ■ **WEBSITE:** None ■**E-MAIL:** None ■**APPLICATION POLICIES & PROCEDURES:** The Foundation reports that unsolicited grant requests are not accepted.

O+D+T Douglas F. Schofield (T+Con) — James S. Whitcomb, Jr. (C+T+Donor) — Dorothy J. Whitcomb (S+T) — Pamela W. Larson (T) — Lisa Capra (T)

SW-390 Williams (John C.) Charitable Trust   MI-15-17-18-22-29-31-41-42-84
    Refer to PNC Advisors Charitable Trust Committee entry.
    (Allegheny County)   **EIN** 25-6024153   **Year Created** 1931
AMV $8,214,348   **FYE** 12-00   (**Gifts Received** $0)   10 **Grants totaling** $364,237

All giving restricted to the Steubenville, OH and Weirton, WV areas. Steubenville grants: **$50,000** each to Martha Cochrance McConville Home for Aged Women (restoration/repairs) and All Saints School (renovations); **$26,000** to Red Cross (van); **$15,337** to Catholic Community Center (refurbishments); **$25,000** to AIM Pregnancy Help Center (improved services); and **$10,000** to Women's Health Center of Jefferson County (medical services). Weirton grants: **$100,000** to Brooke Hancock Family Resource Network (soccer complex construction); **$47,900** to Weirton Regional Campus (computer facilities); **$30,000** to Northern Panhandle Headstart (new building); and **$10,000** to CHANGE, Inc. (renovations). ■**APPLICATION POLICIES & PROCEDURES:** Refer to the PNC Advisors Charitable Trust Committee entry for a statement on giving priorities and full application guidelines.

O+D+T Refer to PNC Advisors Charitable Trust Committee entry. — PNC Advisors (Trustee)

SW-391 Willis (Hilda M.) Foundation #2   MI-12-13-14-22-25-35-41-42-52-84
    c/o Mellon Private Wealth Management
    One Mellon Center, Room 3825   **Phone** 412-234-1634 **FAX** 412-234-1073
    Pittsburgh 15258   (Allegheny County)   **EIN** 25-6371417   **Year Created** 1991
AMV $13,544,203   **FYE** 6-01   (**Gifts Received** $149,598)   21 **Grants totaling** $1,078,264

All local giving; grants are for general support except as noted. High grant of **$600,000** to U. of Pittsburgh (Honors College). **$125,000** to U. of Pittsburgh (academic support center for athletes). **$100,000** to Pittsburgh Symphony (school time concerts). **$31,000** to Pittsburgh Opera. **$30,000** to YES. **$25,000** each to Coalition for Christian Outreach (endowment) and Extra Mile Education Foundation (urban Catholic school support). **$22,264** to Crossroads Foundation (tuition/support services). **$20,000** to Western Pa. School for the Deaf (math-science center). **$15,000** to U. of Pittsburgh (Superintendent's Academy). **$10,000** to Family House (Shadyside facility), Greater Pittsburgh Community Food Bank, Habit-Tat for Youth & Education [Zelienople], Opera Theatre of Pittsburgh Rx Council of Western Pa. (prescriptions for poor). **$5,000** each to Allegheny Valley School (capital campaign), Center for Creative Play (scholarships/maintenance), Civic Light Opera, North Side Christian Health Center (health care for poor), Pa. Special Olympics (Allegheny County games), and Pittsburgh Youth Symphony Orchestra. ■**PUBLICATIONS:** None ■**WEBSITE:** None ■**E-MAIL:** None ■**APPLICATION POLICIES & PROCEDURES:** The Foundation reports giving is limited to Western Pa. with education a priority interest; preference is given to organizations personally supported by Mrs. Willis. No grants are awarded to individuals. Grant requests may be submitted in any form (3 copies required) at any time; include organization background information and IRS tax-exempt status documentation. The Trustees meet in April and November.

O+D+T Annette Calgaro (VP at Bank+Con) — Robert G. Lovett, Esq. (T) — Alexander M. Minno (T) — Mellon Bank N.A. (Corporate Trustee)

SW-392 Wilson (Thomas A.) Foundation   MI-31-41
    c/o National City Bank of Pa. - Loc. 25-162
    National City Center, 20 Stanwix Street, 16th Floor   **Phone** 412-644-8002 **FAX** 412-261-6252
    Pittsburgh 15222   (Allegheny County)   **EIN** 23-7358862   **Year Created** 1974
AMV $7,969,257   **FYE** 12-00   (**Gifts Received** $0)   1 **Grant of** $320,000

Sole grant to Wilson Christian Academy. — In prior years most support has been to the same grantee with occasional smaller grants to McKeesport Hospital and Ventures in People [McKeesport]. ■**PUBLICATIONS:** None ■**WEBSITE:** None ■**E-MAIL:** joanna.mayo@nationalcity.com ■**APPLICATION POLICIES & PROCEDURES:** The Foundation reports that preference is given to Christian education and for health care. Grant requests may be submitted in any form at any time; include IRS tax-exempt status documentation.

O+D+T Joanna M. Mayo (VP at Bank+Con) — National City Bank of Pa. (Corporate Trustee)

SW-393 Window Cleaning & Building Service Foundation   MI-14-22-32-41-61-63
c/o Penn Window Cleaning Company
104 West North Ave.   **Phone** 412-321-4300 **FAX** 412-231-1019
Pittsburgh 15212   (Allegheny County)   **EIN** 25-6033918   **Year Created** 1956
AMV $1,046,905   **FYE** 11-00   (**Gifts Received** $55,000)   **2 Grants totaling** $53,500

All local giving; all grants are general donations. High grant of **$53,000** to Catholic Diocese of Pittsburgh. **$500** to Muscular Dystrophy Assn. — Grants awarded in the prior year included **$7,266** to Western Pa. School for the Blind; **$5,000** each to Allegheny United Methodist Church and Salvation Army; **$3,883** to St. John Capistrano Church; and **$3,683** to St. Mary of Mercy Church. ■**PUBLICATIONS:** None ■**WEBSITE:** www.pennwindow.com [corporate info only] ■**E-MAIL:** None ■**APPLICATION POLICIES & PROCEDURES:** Grant requests may be submitted in a proposal at any time. No grants are awarded to individuals.
O+D+T Steve R. Gaber (T+Con) — Steve R. Gaber, Jr. (T) — Corporate donor: Penn Window Cleaning Company

---

SW-394 Winters (Samuel & Emma) Foundation   MI-32-34-35-42
c/o PNC Advisors - P2-PTPP-10-2
Two PNC Plaza, 620 Liberty Ave.   **Phone** 412-762-5182 **FAX** 412-762-5439
Pittsburgh 15222   (Allegheny County)   **EIN** 25-6024170   **Year Created** 1959
AMV $1,438,297   **FYE** 12-00   (**Gifts Received** $0)   **4 Grants totaling** $48,000

All giving for experimental research in medicine, dentistry, or public health. High grant of **$18,000** to Carnegie Mellon U. **$10,000** each to Duquesne U./School of Natural & Environmental Sciences, U. of Pittsburgh School of Medicine/Division of Infectious Diseases, and U. of Pittsburgh. ■**PUBLICATIONS:** None ■**WEBSITE:** None ■**E-MAIL:** None ■**APPLICATION POLICIES & PROCEDURES:** The Foundation reports that only requests for graduate level research in medicine, dentistry or public health are accepted from institutions; Pittsburgh-area institutions receive preference. No grants are awarded directly to researchers. Grant requests may be submitted in a letter at any time; describe the scientific studies, experimental work or research. Grant decisions are made in January-February and funds disbursed in March.
O+D+T Beatrice A. Lynch (Trust Officer at Bank+Con) — PNC Advisors (Trustee)

SW-395 Wivagg (Blanche & Dewayne) Charitable Foundation   MI-56-63
204 Marshall Drive   **Phone** 412-751-1968 **FAX** None
McKeesport 15132   (Allegheny County)   **EIN** 23-7933106   **Year Created** 1998
AMV $477,533   **FYE** 12-00   (**Gifts Received** $89,858)   **2 Grants totaling** $17,100

All local giving. **$10,000** to McKeesport Heritage Center. **$7,100** to First United Methodist Church of McKeesport. ■**PUBLICATIONS:** None. ■**WEBSITE:** None ■**E-MAIL:** None ■**APPLICATION POLICIES & PROCEDURES:** Grant requests may be submitted in a letter at any time.
O+D+T Dewayne A. Wivagg (T+Donor+Con) — Blanche Wivagg (T+Donor) — PNC Bank (Corporate Trustee)

SW-396 Wolf-Kuhn Foundation   MI-22-41-42-49-51-52-54-55-63
c/o Wolf Furniture Company
1620 North Tuckahoe Street   **Phone** 814-742-4380, x-123 **FAX** None
Bellwood 16617   (Blair County)   **EIN** 25-6064237   **Year Created** 1957
AMV $1,734,242   **FYE** 9-00   (**Gifts Received** $12,800)   **20 Grants totaling** $74,833

All local giving. High grant of **$16,333** to Mr. Aloysius College. **$12,000** to Southern Alleghenies Museum of Art. **$10,000** to Altoona Symphony. **$6,000** to St. Vincent DePaul. **$5,000** to Railroaders Museum. **$5,000** to Greater Altoona Community Endowment. **$4,000** to Penn Mont Academy. **$3,500** to Juniata College. **$3,000** to Bishop Guilfoyle High School. **$2,000** to Altoona-Johnstown Diocesan. **$1,000-$1,500** each to Allegheny Ballet, Blair County Arts Festival, Junior Achievement of Altoona, Pa. Rural Arts Alliance, and Skills Foundation. Smaller contributions for cultural, civic, and Catholic purposes. ■**PUBLICATIONS:** statement of program policy; application guidelines ■**WEBSITE:** None ■**E-MAIL:** None ■**APPLICATION POLICIES & PROCEDURES:** The Foundation reports that giving is restricted to Central Pennsylvania for artistic and educational purposes; project support is preferred over capital improvements. Projects should be visionary, foster institutional cooperation, provide leadership development, and enhance artistic or educational efforts; Prospective applicants initially should make a telephone inquiry about the feasibility of submitting a request. Submit requests in duplicate during October-December on a formal Grant Request Application, available from the Foundation; include an annual report, organizational budget, project budget, audited financial statement, Board member list, and IRS tax-exempt status documentation. The Trustees award grants at meetings in March, June, September, and December.
O+D+T Stephen W. Sloan (T+Con) — Gerald P. Wolf (C+T) — Ann S. Borland (T) — Herbert T. Wolf, II (T) — Corporate donors: Wolf Realty Associates, Wolf Furniture Enterprises

---

SW-397 Woodmere Foundation   MI-11-13-17-29-32-41-44-51-52-53-54-55-56
c/o Education Management Corp.   57-71-86
300 Sixth Ave., Suite 800   **Phone** 412-562-0900 **FAX** 412-562-0934
Pittsburgh 15222   (Allegheny County)   **EIN** 25-1705913   **Year Created** 1993
AMV $1,623,763   **FYE** 12-99   (**Gifts Received** $289,664)   **36 Grants totaling** $132,879

Mostly local giving. High grants of **$25,000** each to Carnegie Institute and Western Pa. Conservancy. **$10,000** to WQED. **$7,500** to Ligonier Valley Library. **$5,000** each to Pittsburgh Opera and Pittsburgh Parks Conservancy. **$3,000** each to City Theatre Company and National Conference for Community & Justice. **$2,000** each to National Parkinson's Foundation/Greater Pittsburgh Chapter and Pittsburgh Cultural Trust. **$1,000-$1,900** each to Associated Artists of Pittsburgh, Extra Mile Education

Foundation, Gateway to the Arts, Historical Society of Western Pa., Phipps Conservatory & Botanical Garden, Southern Allegheny Museum of Art, United Way of Allegheny County, and Women's Center & Shelter of Greater Pittsburgh. **$750** to Boy Scouts/Greater Pittsburgh Council. Other local contributions **$100-$500** for various purposes. **Out-of-state** giving includes **$20,000** to Solomon Guggenheim Museum [NY] and **$5,000** to American Enterprise Institute [DC]. ■**PUBLICATIONS:** None ■**WEBSITE:** www.edumgt.com [corporate info only] ■**E-MAIL:** None ■**APPLICATION POLICIES & PROCEDURES:** Grant requests may be submitted in writing at any time.

O+D+T Kathy Villalpando (Con) — Robert B. Knutson [Ligonier] (P+Donor) — Foundation donor: Quail Hill Foundation

---

SW-398 World Health Foundation
1704 Pittsburgh Street
Cheswick 15024   (Allegheny County)

MI-31-35-82
Phone 724-275-1234 **FAX** None
EIN 25-1347717   **Year Created** 1978

AMV $215,580   **FYE** 9-00   (**Gifts Received** $32,000)   6 **Grants totaling** $34,713

About three-fourths local giving. High grant of **$25,000** to St. Francis Health Foundation (unreimbursed health care costs). Other local contributions under **$400. Out-of-state** giving includes **$7,913** to Friends Stores [India] (purchase anti-TB medicine) and **$600** to two hospitals in India. ■**PUBLICATIONS:** None ■**WEBSITE:** None ■**E-MAIL:** None ■**APPLICATION POLICIES & PROCEDURES:** The Foundation reports that all giving is for health-related services. Grant requests may be submitted in a brief letter at any time; describe the proposed charitable use of funds.

O+D+T Sukhdev S. Grover, M.D. (P+F+Donor+Con) — Jasbir Makar, M.D. [WV] (S) — Joseph Garuccio (D) — Anand Sharma (D) — M. Daniel Splain (D)

SW-399 Yochum (Leo) Family Foundation, The
2024 Blairmont Drive, Upper St. Clair
Pittsburgh 15241   (Allegheny County)

MI-11-22-31-41-61
Phone 412-831-9521 **FAX** None
EIN 25-1551381   **Year Created** 1987

AMV $146,312   **FYE** 12-00   (**Gifts Received** $86,831)   31 **Grants totaling** $122,799

About two-thirds local giving. High grant of **$25,000** to Shadyside Hospital Foundation (Hillman Cancer Center). **$11,667** to Catholic Diocese of Pittsburgh Foundation. **$11,000** to Epiphany Catholic Church. **$10,000** to United Way of Allegheny County. **$7,000** to Our Lady of Grace. **$6,667** to Marian Manor (campaign fund). **$3,000** to St. Mary of Mercy Church. **$2,500** to Extra Mile Education Foundation. **$2,000** each to St. Bernard's Church, St. John Capistran Church, and U. of Pittsburgh Medical Center. **$1,000** each to Catholic Charities, Seton LaSalle High School, Sisters of Charity, and St. Thomas More Church. Other local contributions **$250** for various purposes. **Out-of-state** giving includes **$10,500** to St. Vincent de Paul Church [WV]; **$5,000** to Wheeling Central Catholic High School [WV]; and **$4,000** to Our Lady of Peace Church [NY]. ■**PUBLICATIONS:** None ■**WEBSITE:** None ■**E-MAIL:** None ■**APPLICATION POLICIES & PROCEDURES:** No grants are awarded to individuals.

O+D+T Leo W. Yochum (C+P+Donor+Con) — Mary Jane Yochum (VP)

SW-400 Zappala (Richard A.) Family Foundation
c/o The First City Company
Four Gateway Center, Suite 212
Pittsburgh 15222   (Allegheny County)

MI-11-22-32-41-42-52-61-71
Phone 412-391-9260 **FAX** 412-391-9316
EIN 23-7876878   **Year Created** 1997

AMV $1,980,104   **FYE** 12-00   (**Gifts Received** $398,531)   15 **Grants totaling** $59,283

Mostly local giving. High grant of **$24,000** to Pacem in Terris [Allison Park]. **$10,500** to United Way of SW Pa. **$5,000** each to River City Brass Band and UCP of Pittsburgh. **$3,000-$3,500** each to The Ellis School, Horticultural Society of Western Pa., and Interfaith Volunteer Caregivers. **$1,000** to Sisters of Divine Providence. Other local contributions **$200-$500** for various purposes. **Out-of-state** grants: **$1,000** each to Juvenile Diabetes Foundation [NY] and U. of Notre Dame [IN]. ■**PUBLICATIONS:** None. ■**WEBSITE:** None ■**E-MAIL:** None ■**APPLICATION POLICIES & PROCEDURES:** Information not available.

O+D+T Lori Zappala Hardiman (T+Con) — Nancy B. Zappala (T+Donor) — Richard A. Zappala (T+Donor) — Thomas H. Hardiman (T)

Southwestern Region / SW
Non-profiled Foundations

*SW Region foundations which did **not** meet the criteria for profiling are listed here; the letter code in parentheses after the foundation name indicates its status, per the following key:*

L   **Limited Assets/Giving**: The market value of assets was $250,000 or under and the total of grants awarded was less than $12,500 in the last year of record. If information about grants is available, up to three Major Interest (MI) Codes are listed; if no information on giving interests is available, the notation "N/R" (Not Reported) is shown.

O   **Operating Foundation**: This special designation by IRS is for a foundation that operates its own program or institution and, generally, does not award grants to other organizations.

R   **Restricted Trust/Foundation**: Grants are awarded only to designated organizations or beneficiaries, typically under the terms of a Will or Trust Instrument.

I   **Inactive**: The assets, generally, are nominal (typically under $5,000) and there has been little or no grants activity within the last year or more.

NP   **Non-Pennsylvania Foundation**: The foundation's connection to Pennsylvania is only incidental; typically these are trusts or foundations managed by a bank trust department or a lawyer located in Pennsylvania, but there are no Pennsylvania-based trustees/directors and no grants are awarded to Pennsylvania.

T   **Terminated**: A final IRS Form 990-PF has been filed, or the foundation has provided notice of intended liquidation/termination.

U   **Undetermined Status**: There is no record of Form 990-PFs being filed for the last three or more years and no other evidence of grant-making activity. In many cases the foundation may have terminated without giving formal notice or has been reclassified by IRS as a "public charity."

#1196 Steelworkers Food Bank Trust (U)

Abernathy Black C.D. & Educational Fund (L) MI-43
325 Washington Trust Building, P.O. Box 177, Washington 15301

Academy of Science & Art of Pittsburgh, The (O)
4141 Fifth Ave., P.O. Box 58187, Pittsburgh 15209

Action Industries Charitable Foundation (T)

Adams (R.F.), II Trust for KY United Methodist Home (NP)
c/o PNC Bank N.A., Pittsburgh 15222

Ali (M.I.) Foundation (L) MI-69
50 Valhalla Drive, New Castle 16105

Allegany Environmental Action Coalition (U)

Allegheny Ludlum Foundation
(New name: Allegheny Teledyne Foundation)

Allegheny Widows Home Assn. (O)
1215 Hulton Road, Oakmont 15139

Alliance Foundation (I) MI-N/R
P.O. Box 369, Indianola 15051

Alpha Kappa Psi Fraternity Scholarship Fund (R)
c/o National City Bank of Pa., Pittsburgh 15222

Alpha Upsilon Scholarship Foundation (R)
c/o Yeager, 1500 Oliver Building, Pittsburgh 15222

Alvi Foundation, Inc. (L) MI-41-43-81
600 Munir Road, Elizabeth 15037

Alzheimer's Disease Foundation (O)
1009 Duquesne Boulevard, Pittsburgh 15110

American Indian Council & Cultural Centers, Inc. (R)
c/o Humbles, 123 Turkeyfoot Road, Sewickley 15143

American Institute of Economics (R)
P.O. Box 216, New Wilmington 16142

AP Charitable Trust (T)

Appel (Charles F. & Lillian F.) Charitable Trust
(Formerly of Pittsburgh; now located in IL)

Arch Court, Inc. (U)

Aristech Foundation (T)

ARK Environmental Research, Inc. (O)
3584 Beechwood Boulevard, Pittsburgh 15217

Armco Foundation (T)

Armstrong (Rachel & James) Fund (L) MI-13-31-99
c/o First Commonwealth Trust Co., Greensburg 15601

Aronson (Jacob) Charitable Trust (L)
c/o U.J.F., 234 McKee Place, Pittsburgh 15213

Atkins Family Foundation
(Formerly of Sewickley, now located in NY).

Atlas Foundation, The (U)

August Foundation, The (R)
c/o Lock, 928 Zimmerman Street, Jeannette 15644

Auld (James Alan) Foundation (L) MI-N/R
4499 Mt. Royal Blvd., Allison Park 15101

Automobile Pedestrian Accident Reduction Foundation (R)
28 St. John Street, McKees Rocks 15136

Baird (Nettie & Lillian) Trust (R)
c/o Mellon Bank N.A., Pittsburgh 15230

Bangert (John J.) Trust (R)
c/o National City Bank of Pa., Pittsburgh 15222

Bayer-Mobay Foundation
(New name: Bayer Foundation)

Beck (John A.) Memorial Scholarship Fund (R)
c/o Karns City Area School District, Karns City 16041

Beck Family Memorial Trust (T)

Bedford Elks Youth & Trust Fund (L) MI-43
c/o Elks Lodge, RR #6, Box 480, Bedford 15522

Bellevue Avalon Athletic Assn. (R)
P.O. Box 4171, Pittsburgh 15202

Benford (George H.) Charities (R)
c/o PNC Bank N.A., Pittsburgh 15265

Bennington Foundation (NP)
c/o M. Wasserman, P.O. Box 2256, Pittsburgh 15230

Benz (William L. & Margaret L.) Foundation (R)
c/o Mellon Bank N.A., Pittsburgh 15230

Berger (Michael & Sherle) Foundation (L) MI-N/R
134 West Lyndhurst Drive, Pittsburgh 15206

Bernowski Scholarship Trust Fund (R)
c/o National City Bank of Pa., Pittsburgh 15222

Biederman (Fred) Charitable Trust (NP)
c/o PNC Bank N.A., Pittsburgh 15222

Big Brothers/Big Sisters of Westmoreland County (R)
225 East Otterman Street, Greensburg 15601

Blair Foundation (T)

Bloom (I.H.) Family Charitable Trust (U)

Bloom Foundation, The (U)

Blum (Jerrold S.) Foundation (L) MI-21-22
15 Darlington Court, Pittsburgh 15217

Boehmer (Lucinda V.) Foundation (R)
c/o PNC Bank, Pittsburgh 15222

Bognar Foundation (T)

Borden Baptist Church Trust (R)
c/o PNC Bank N.A., Pittsburgh 15222

Borough & Township Police Assn. (L) MI-23
5241 Brightwood Road, Suite 1, Bethel Park 15102

Bowley (Helen L.) Scholarship Fund (R)
c/o National City Bank of Pa., Pittsburgh 15278

Boyd Foundation, The (L) MI-63-99
1243-1/2 Country Club Road, Monongahela 15063

Boyer (Florence Lamme Feicht) Family Foundation (L)
MI-63-71-72
c/o Daniel, 301 Grant Street, 20th Floor, Pittsburgh 15219

Bradford Area Public Library Endowment Fund (R)
c/o National City Bank of Pa., Pittsburgh 15222

Bradford Ecumenical Home Trust (R)
c/o National City Bank of Pa., Pittsburgh 15222

Brand Foundation (T)

Breisinger (Albert J.) Memorial Scholarship Fund (R)
c/o Mellon Bank N.A., 50 Old Clairton Road, Pittsburgh 15236

Brice (Helen) Scholarship Fund (R)
c/o Mellon Bank N.A., Pittsburgh 15230

Brody (Israel I. & Birdye E.) Foundation (R)
c/o S & T Bank, Indiana 15701

Bromberg (Howard J. & Emily J.) Family Foundation (L)
MI-22-55-62
232 Sheryl Lane, Pittsburgh 15221

Burrell Township Scholarship Fund (R)
c/o PNC Bank N.A., Pittsburgh 15265

Butler Presbyterian Senior Housing, Inc. (O)
1215 Hulton Road, Oakmont 15139

Bycroft (John S.), Jr. Trust (R)
c/o National City Bank of Pa., Pittsburgh 15222

Caputo (Sharon Momeyer) Memorial (R)
c/o Mt. Pleasant Area High School, Mount Pleasant 15646

Carbaugh (Ivan R.), Jr. Scholarship Fund (R)
c/o Supinko, 935 Philadelphia Street, Indiana 15701

Caretti (Joan L.) Memorial Scholarship Trust (R)
c/o St. Mary's Parochial School, Kittanning 16201

Carter (John Lyman & Ruth C.) Trust (T)

Castelli Charitable Trust
(New name: Deno Castelli Charitable Scholarship Fund)

Cat Rescue, Inc. (O)
545 Spang Road, Baden 15005

Central & Southwest Foundation (NP)
c/o Mellon Bank N.A., Pittsburgh 15230

Chamovitz (Robert & Sheila) Family Char. Trust (L) MI-22-62
564 Forbes Ave., #803, Pittsburgh 15219

Charley (Ray T.) Family Foundation (L) MI-42
5440 Centre Ave., 2nd Floor, Pittsburgh 15232

Cherry (Flora & Homer)/Allen County Scholarship (NP)
c/o PNC Bank N.A., Pittsburgh 15222

Churchill Foundation (L) MI-41
P.O. Box 369, Indianola 15051

Cipriani (Brother Victor) Educational Foundation (L) MI-N/R
222 Salem Drive, Pittsburgh 15241

Citizens of Mt. Pleasant, Pa. Fund (R)
c/o First Commonwealth Trust, Greensburg 15601

City of Upton Cemetery Trust (NP)
c/o PNC Bank N.A., Pittsburgh 15222

Clark (Henry H.) Medical Education Foundation (R)
c/o Mellon Bank N.A., Pittsburgh 15230

Clayton Corporation, The (O)
7227 Reynold Street, Pittsburgh 15208

Clister (James D.)/Gilbert A. Carillo Fdn. of Pittsburgh (T)

Clive (Winifred Johnson) Foundation (NP)
1500 Oliver Building, 535 Smithfield Street, Pittsburgh 15222

Cohen (Cecil & Czerna) Foundation (L) MI-99
160 Woodland Road, Greensburg 15601

Colen Family Foundation (L) MI-22-62
4940 Ellsworth Ave., Pittsburgh 15213

Commons Family Charitable Trust (L) MI-22-63-99
109 Bigler Ave., Spangler 15775

Community Involvement Foundation
(Refer to Tickets for Kids Foundation)

Consolidated Natural Gas Co. Foundation
(New name: Dominion Foundation)

Constandy (H.K., V.H. & C.B.) Memorial Fund (R)
c/o Armstrong, 600 Grant Street, 58th Floor, Pittsburgh 15219

Cook (Joseph & Lillian) Foundation (U)

Cooperstown Christian Activities Fund (U)

Coraopolis Economic Revitalization Corp. (R)
P.O. Box 214, Coraopolis 15108

Cord (A.B.) Charitable Foundation (NP)
c/o PNC Bank N.A., Pittsburgh 15222

Cornmesser (E.) Scholarship (R)
c/o Mid-State Bank, Altoona 16603

Cottle (Harold & Betty) Family Foundation (U)

Coulter (W.) for Greensburg et al (R)
c/o Mellon Bank N.A., Pittsburgh 15230

Craig (Edward A. & Sherley F.) Charitable Fdn. (L) MI-17-99
c/o Queenan, 1900 Oliver Building, Pittsburgh 15222

Crawford (G. Kenneth & Margaret B.) Mem'l Scholarship Fund (R)
c/o USBancorp Trust Company, McKeesport 15132

Crossroads Foundation (R)
2901 Webster Ave., Pittsburgh 15219

Curtis (Ford E. & Harriet) Foundation (NP)
c/o PNC Bank N.A., Pittsburgh 15265

Cyert Family Foundation (I)
12 Edgewood Road, Pittsburgh 15215

Czeka (Jake) Memorial Environmental Foundation (L) MI-43
117 Bridgeport Street, Mount Pleasant 15666

Dailey (Emma & Paul P.) Charity Fund (R)
c/o PNC Bank N.A., Pittsburgh 15265

Dallas Morning News Fund/Luther King (NP)
c/o Mellon Bank N.A., Pittsburgh 15230

Daly (Nathan & Harry) Scholarship Fund (R)
c/o Mellon Bank N.A., Pittsburgh 15230

Darlington (Frank G.) Foundation (R)
c/o PNC Bank N.A., Pittsburgh 15265

Darlington Charitable Trust (NP)
c/o PNC Bank N.A., Pittsburgh 15265

Davis (Alan Jay) Memorial Trust (L) MI-12-13
429 Forbes Ave., Suite 1000, Pittsburgh 15219

Davis (William G.) Charitable Trust (R)
c/o PNC Bank N.A., Pittsburgh 15265

De La Torre Foundation (L) MI-42-63
300 Alpha Drive, Pittsburgh 15238

Dendroica Foundation, The (NP)
c/o Mellon Bank N.A., Pittsburgh 15230

dePalma (Robert A. & Maryann A.) Charitable Fdn.
(New name: Robert A. dePalma Family Charitable Foundation)

Dick (Louise & Perry) Foundation (L) MI-12-41-99
c/o Trumbull Corporation, P.O. Box 98100, Pittsburgh 15227

Dickson (Joseph Z. & Agnes F.) Prizes (R)
c/o Mellon Bank N.A., Pittsburgh 15230

Dietrich Foundation, The [Pittsburgh] (L) MI-42
c/o W.S. Dietrich II, 500 Grant Street, #2226, Pittsburgh 15219

Dinardo (Kathryn J.) Fund (I)
c/o F.L. Corsetti, CPA, 68 Herbst Road, Coraopolis 15108

Dinger (Max E. & Maude M.) Scholarship Fund (R)
c/o National City Bank of Pa., Pittsburgh 15222

Doerr (Gertrude B.) Foundation, The (R)
227 Franklin Street, Suite 214, Johnstown 15901

Dudas (Martin W.) Foundation (T)

Duffy Foundation, The (T)

Eberhardt (I.) for Scholarship Fund (R)
c/o Mellon Bank N.A., Pittsburgh 15230

Eckhart (Howard E.) Trust (L) MI-23
c/o Hancher, 101 West Newcastle Street, Zelienople 16063

Eckman Family Foundation (L) MI-63
850 MacArthur Drive, Pittsburgh 15228

Edgewater Corp. Charitable Trust
(New name: Kirkwood Charitable Trust)

Effective Learning Institute (R)
2121 Noblestown Road, Suite 21, Pittsburgh 15205

Engel (Mark) & Jack Seibel Memorial Music Scholarship Fund (R)
P.O. Box 175, Washington 15301

Engelberg (Louis) Charitable Trust (T)

Engelman (Theodore H.) Foundation (T)

Equimark Corp. Merit Scholarship Program (R)
c/o National City Bank of Pa., Pittsburgh 15222

ERI Educational Foundation (R)
420 Boulevard of the Allies, Pittsburgh 15219

Evans (D.A. & J.A.) Memorial Foundation (R)
c/o Ellwood Group, Inc., P.O. Box 31, Ellwood City 16117

Eye & Ear Hospital of Pittsburgh Medical Staff Ed. Fund (R)
c/o V.A. Surgical Services, University Drive C, Pittsburgh 15240

Fair Oaks Charitable Trust (L) MI-11
5219 Kipling Road, Pittsburgh 15217

Fairbanks-Horix Charitable Trust
(New name: Fairbanks-Horix Foundation)

Fallat Family Charitable Foundation (L) MI-99
3115 Deerfield Lane, Monroeville 15148

Family Life Center, Inc. (R)
P.O. Box 100, Aliquippa 15501

Federation of Independent School Alumnae
(New name: The FISA Foundation)

Ferguson (A.B.), Jr. M.D. Orthoped Foundation (T)
(Now part of The Pittsburgh Foundation)

Fine (Milton) Family Charitable Foundation
(New name: Fine Family Charitable Foundation)

Fisher (Wilber E.) Trust (NP)
c/o PNC Bank N.A., Pittsburgh 15265

Fitch (T.S.) Memorial Scholarship Fund (R)
c/o Mellon Bank N.A., Pittsburgh 15230

Fleming (Lloyd L.) Trust for W. Pa. School for the Blind (R)
c/o PNC Bank N.A., Pittsburgh 15265

Forbesway Foundation
(New name: Nimick-Forbesway Foundation)

Ford (John G.) Memorial Hospital Trust (NP)
c/o PNC Bank N.A., Pittsburgh 15222

Fort Pitt Society (R)
909 California Ave, #507,, Pittsburgh 15202

Fortescue (Charles L.) Graduate Scholarship Fund (R)
11 Stanwix Street, Pittsburgh 15222

Foster (L.B.) Charitable Trust (T)

Foster (Solomon) Trust (R)
One Oxford Centre, 40th Floor, Pittsburgh 15219

Foundation in Refractories Education (R)
500 Wood Street, #326, Pittsburgh 15222

Fox (Rubye O.) Trust for Various Charities (R)
c/o National City Bank of Pa., Pittsburgh 15278

Frazier (Mary Fuller) Memorial School/Community Library (O)
P.O. Box 302, Perryopolis 15473

Frick Art & Historical Center, Inc. (O)
7227 Reynolds Street, Pittsburgh 15208

Friedberg (E.B.E.) Memorial Art Scholarship Fdn. (L)
c/o Ouimete, 4240 Greensburg Pike, Pittsburgh 15221

Fullcircle, Inc. (I)
1090 Graham Blvd., Pittsburgh 15222

Gahagen (Zella J.) Charitable Foundation (R)
c/o Mellon Bank N.A., Pittsburgh 15230

Gale (William G.) Foundation (R)
c/o O'Block, 668 Center Road, Pittsburgh 15232

Gatha Studies Trust, The (U)
c/o McIntyre, P.O. Box 461, Glenshaw 15116

Gearhart (J.I.) Trust for West Penn Hosp. Scholarship Fund (R)
c/o Mellon Bank N.A., Pittsburgh 15230

Genesis Twelve Foundation (R)
2200 Georgetown Drive, #401, Sewickley 15143

Geneva Foundation, The (L) MI-N/R
c/o Patterson, 3200 College Ave., Beaver 15010

Gibson (Richard P.) & Rosemark Kirk Charitable Trust (I)
P.O. Box 291, Latrobe 15650

Gilfillian (Alexander B.) Trust (R)
c/o National City Bank of Pa., Pittsburgh 15222

Gilliand (Merle E.) Scholarship Fund (R)
c/o PNC Bank N.A., Pittsburgh 15265

Gladstone Tipton Foundation (L) MI-41
P.O. Box 33, Venetia 15367

Glasgow (Elizabeth Louise) Foundation (L) MI-51-99
914 St. James Street, Pittsburgh 15232

Gleason Family Trust, The (I)
Main Street East, Suite 204, Johnstown 15907

Goldstein (Sarah & Tena) Memorial Fund (R)
c/o JF& CS, 5743 Bartlett Street, Pittsburgh 15217

Good (William), Jr. Memorial Fund (R)
c/o Mellon Bank N.A., Pittsburgh 15230

Goodlin (Jeff) Charitable Trust (U)

Gospa Missions (O)
230 East Main Street, Evans City 16033

Gough (Thomas H.) Memorial Fund (R)
c/o PNC Bank N.A., Pittsburgh 15265

Graves (Catherine) Advanced Educational Fund (R)
c/o PNC Bank N.A., Pittsburgh 15265

Graves (Catherine)—Wheeling, WV Fund (R)
c/o PNC Bank N.A., Pittsburgh 15265

Green (William C.) Charitable Foundation Trust (L) MI-63
12300 Perry Highway, #303, Wexford 15090

Green Family Foundation (L) MI-22-62-99
319 Merchant Street, Ambridge 15003

Greenberger (Marjorie C.) Charitable Trust (L) MI-22-62-99
1232 Murdoch Road, Pittsburgh 15217

Gurrentz (Fay) Charitable Foundation (L) MI-99
c/o Olbum, 1118 South Braddock Ave., Pittsburgh 15218

Hagadus (Henry R.) Memorial Library (R)
522 Indiana Street, Johnstown 15905

Halbritter Foundation, The (L) MI-15- 22
RD #2, Box 582, Altoona 16601

Hamburg (Lester A.) Foundation, The (L) MI-22
2330 One PPG Place, Pittsburgh 15222

Hamm (Angelia) Liver Transplant Fund (R)
823 Washington Drive, Pittsburgh 15229

Handyside (George T.) Memorial Scholarship Fdn. (R)
4121 Washington Road, McMurray 15317

Haney Foundation, The (L) MI-13-22-99
P.O. Box 1429, New Castle 16103

Hanna (Howard) Foundation (L) MI-N/R
119 Gamma Drive, Pittsburgh 15238

Hansen (William Stucki) Foundation
(New name: The Hansen Foundation)

Hardt (Brett A.) Memorial Foundation (L) MI-12- 13-41
1405 Burchfield Road, Allison Park 15101

Hardy (Joe) Foundation, The (I) MI-N/R
/o 84 Lumber Company, P.O. Box 584, Eighty Four 15330

Harris (John H.) Foundation (L) MI-32-63
2445 Old Green Tree Road, Carnegie 15106

Harris (Morris H. & Gertrude M.) Charitable Trust (R)
c/o National City Bank of Pa., Pittsburgh 15222

Hawthornden Literary Institute (O)
535 Smithfield Street, Suite 606, Pittsburgh 15222

Hcinz (Drue) Foundation
(Formerly of Pittsburgh, now located in NYC)

Heinz (Sarah) House Assn. (O)
East Ohio and Heinz Sts., Pittsburgh 15212

Heinz Institute for Nutritional Sciences, Inc. (R)
600 Grant Street, 60th Floor, Pittsburgh 15219

Held (Elizabeth Tuesday) Musical Fund (R)
c/o PNC Bank N.A., Pittsburgh 15265

Hermann #1 Trust for Memorial Art Museum (R)
c/o PNC Bank N.A., Pittsburgh 15265

Hermann #2 Trust for Memorial Art Museum (R)
c/o PNC Bank N.A., Pittsburgh 15265

Hermann (John A.), Jr. Memorial Art Museum (O)
c/o Irvin, 718 Means Ave., Pittsburgh 15202

Hess (Gladys M.) Memorial Scholarship Fund (R)
c/o Siegel, 1240 Lawyers Building, Pittsburgh 15219

Hickman (Flora Paxton) Foundation (R)
c/o Mellon Bank N.A., Pittsburgh 15230

Hillman (Henry L.), Jr. Foundation (NP)
2000 Grant Building, 310 Grant Street, Pittsburgh 15219

Hillman (Juliet Ashby) Foundation (NP)
2000 Grant Building, 310 Grant Street, Pittsburgh 15219

Hillman (Summer Lea) Foundation (NP)
2000 Grant Building, 310 Grant Street, Pittsburgh 15219

Hobar (Anna Korchnak & George, Sr.) Trust (R)
c/o USBancorp Trust Co., Johnstown 15907

Hochheimer (George M. & Anna) Educational Trust (L) MI-43
c/o BT Management Trust Company, 58 W. Main St., Uniontown 15401

Hoehn Scholarship Fund for St. Vincents Seminary (R)
c/o St. Vincents Seminary, Latrobe 15650

Hoffman (Bill & Rita) Family Foundation (L) MI-22-62
5600 Munhall Road, Suite 410, Pittsburgh 15217

Hollingsworth (C.B.) Trust (R)
c/o First Commonwealth Trust Company, Greensburg 15601

Hollingsworth (Lucie F.) Trust (R)
c/o First Commonwealth Trust Company, Greensburg 15601

Holtz Charitable Foundation (L) MI-13-22-61
3200 USX Tower, 600 Grant Street, Pittsburgh 15219

Hoopman (Harold D. & Eleanor G.) Charitable Fdn. (NP)
c/o PNC Bank N.A., Pittsburgh 15222

HRH Foundation
(Formerly of Pittsburgh, now located in DC)

Industrial Scientific/McElhattan Foundation
(New name: Industrial Scientific Foundation)

Integra Foundation
(Refer to National City Foundation)

International Technology Foundation (O)
7125 Saltsburg Road, Pittsburgh 15235

J.D. Charitable Trust (R)
c/o PNC Bank N.A., Pittsburgh 15265

Jaegle (C.), Jr. for Catholic Diocese of Pittsburgh (R)
c/o Mellon Bank N.A., Pittsburgh 15230

Jewish Home for Babies & Children Fund (T)

JP&L Trust Fund (R)
c/o Westmont Hilltop High School, Johnstown 15905

Justice (Jacob) Free Medical Dispensary (R)
P.O. Box 416, Mount Pleasant 15666

Kasey (S.W.) Trust (R)
c/o PNC Bank N.A., Pittsburgh 15222

Kassab (Jacob G. & Helen) Foundation (L) MI-15-42
400 Southpointe Blvd., Plaza A, Canonsburg 15317

Katselas Family Foundation (L) MI-42-55-84
5221 Fifth Ave., Pittsburgh 15232

KDB Ministries (R)
c/o Blank, 208 Frank Court, Irwin 15642

Kelly (J.C.) Trust for McKeesport Hospital Staff Room (R)
c/o National City Bank of Pa., Pittsburgh 15222

Kiefer Charitable Foundation, The (NP)
c/o Mellon Bank N.A., Pittsburgh 15230

Klemstine (G. William) Foundation (L) MI-43
c/o PNC Advisors, Pittsburgh 15265

Krause (Seymoure & Corinne) Family Charitable Trust (U)

Lally Foundation (L) MI-41-61
911 Ligonier Street, #102, Latrobe 15650

Lamme (Benjamin Garver) Scholarship Fund (R)
c/o Westinghouse, 11 Stanwix Street, Pittsburgh 15222

Lane (Winfield Scott) Scholarship Fund (R)
c/o First Commonwealth Trust, Greensburg 15601

Last Generation Ministries (R)
RR 4, Box 209, Berlin 15530

Latchaw (Ren D. & Dorothy M.) Charitable Trust (R)
c/o National City Bank of Pa., Pittsburgh 15222

Lathwood (John A.) Educational Trust (R)
c/o PNC Bank N.A., Pittsburgh 15265

Latrobe (Benjamin Quincy) Fund (R)
c/o PNC Bank N.A., Pittsburgh 15265

Latterman (Bernard & Rachel) Family Foundation (L) MI-22-62
3 Shadyside Lane, Pittsburgh 15232

Laurent (Jules & Paulette Leroy) Scholarship Fund (R)
c/o First Commonwealth Trust, Greensburg 15601

Lee (Bridget) Religious & Charitable Trust (R)
c/o St. Anne's Church, 400 Hoodridge Drive, Pittsburgh 15234

Lee (Cheng) Educational Foundation (L) MI-34-43
1637 Blackburn Heights Drive, Sewickley 15143

Lehman-Epstine Trust (T)

Leisser (Martin B.) Art Fund (R)
c/o PNC Bank N.A., Pittsburgh 15265

Lesbian & Gay Film Festival of Pittsburgh (U)

Levine (Arnold I. & Adelyne Roth) Foundation (L) MI-99
326 Third Ave., 4th Floor, Pittsburgh 15222

Levine Foundation, The (L) MI-62
c/o Alpern, Rosenthal; 332 5th Ave., Pittsburgh 15222

Lewis (Enola M.) for Musicians (L) MI-52
c/o Mellon Bank N.A., Pittsburgh 15230

Lindsey (E.C.) Trust for Lindsey Memorial Char. Fund (R)
c/o Mellon Bank N.A., Pittsburgh 15230

Lintner Scholarship Trust (R)
195 North Walnut Street, Blairsville 15717

Little Sisters of the Poor Trust (NP)
c/o PNC Bank N.A., Pittsburgh 15222

Lords Recovery Ranch, Inc. (R)
c/o Cox, RR2, Scott Wallace Road, Enon Valley 16120

Lorenzen Foundation (NP)
P.O. Box 369, Indianola 15051

Love (George H. & Margaret McClintic) Foundation (T)

Love (Murray S.) Memorial Trust Fund (R)
1537 South Negley Ave., Pittsburgh 15217

Lucostic (Frank) Scholarship Fund (R)
c/o BT Management Trust Company, Uniontown 15401

Lynch (Paul) Foundation (L) MI-31-43
201 North Mercer Street, New Castle 16101

Lynch (T.) for Westmoreland County Art Museum (R)
c/o Mellon Bank N.A., Pittsburgh 15230

Makdad (E. Charles) Memorial Fund (R)
P.O. Box 831, Altoona 16603

Manchester Supportive Housing, Inc. (O)
1215 Hulton Road, Oakmont 15139

Marc & Friends Charitable Trust (R)
c/o Marc Advertising, 500 Four Station Square, Pittsburgh 15219

Maronda Foundation, The (O)
11 Timberglen Drive, Imperial 15126

Mars (Barbara & Bernard) Charitable Foundation
(New name: Mars Family Charitable Foundation)

Marschall-Ferguson Charitable Foundation (L) MI-71
c/o PNC Advisors, Pittsburgh 15265

Mascari (Marion S. & Victoria C.) Charitable Trust (R)
c/o PNC Bank N.A., One Oliver Plaza, Pittsburgh 15265

Mawhinney (Matthew S.) Charitable Trust (O)
P.O. Box 311, Indian Head 15446

McCafferty (B.J.) Trust for St. Charles (R)
c/o National City Bank of Pa., Pittsburgh 15222

McCarl Foundation (L) MI-52-56
c/o McCarl's Inc., 1413 9th Ave., Beaver Falls 15010

McClintock (Grace Wheeler) & David Wheeler Education Fund (R)
c/o National City Bank of Pa., Pittsburgh 15222

McCready (Alexander P.) Trust for Charities (R)
c/o National City Bank of Pa., New Castle 16101

McCune (Marshall L. & Perrine D.) Foundation (NP)
c/o National City Bank of Pa., Pittsburgh 15222

McGillick (Francis Edward) Foundation (R)
100 West Mall Plaza Building, Carnegie 15106

McGinley (John & Mary) Educational Fund (R)
c/o National City Bank of Pa., Pittsburgh 15222

McGinnis (B.B.) Scholarship Fund (L) MI-43
c/o Cromer, 601 Grant Street, #350, Pittsburgh 15219

McKee (Joel & Daisie) Fund (T)

McMaster Foundation, The (L) MI-32-34
490 East North Ave., Suite 500, Pittsburgh 15212

Meadowlake Corporation (I)
1215 Hulton Road, Oakmont 15139

Medovitch (June) Memorial Scholarship (R)
407 Edgewood Drive, Sarver 16055

Mellon (Matthew T.) Foundation (NP)
c/o Simpson, 3901 Three Mellon Bank Center, Pittsburgh 15219

Mellon Bank Foundation
(New name: Mellon Financial Corporation Foundation)

Merrick (Eleanor D.) Foundation (R)
c/o PNC Bank N.A., Pittsburgh 15265

Merrick Free Art Gallery Museum & Library (O)
c/o Standard Horsenail Corp., 1415 Fifth Ave., New Brighton 15066

Miele (Annette) Memorial Scholarship Fund (R)
214 East Washington Street, Mount Pleasant 15666

Miklos Medical Scholarship Trust (I)
1604 Hill Street, White Oak 15131

Miles, Inc. Foundation
(New name: Bayer Foundation)

Millbury Foundation (L) MI-12-22-35
P.O. Box 369, Indianola 15051

Miller (Arch H. & Eula M.) Trust (NP)
c/o PNC Bank N.A., Pittsburgh 15222

Miller (Colin U. & Mary Hay) Charitable Trust/Education (R)
c/o Nelson, USBancorp Trust Company, Johnstown 15907

Miramare Foundation, The (L) MI-41
c/o Kessler, 1 Oxford Centre, 20th Floor, Pittsburgh 15219

Mitchell (R.O.) for Charities (R)
c/o Mellon Bank N.A., Pittsburgh 15230

MLAC, Inc. (R)
P.O. Box 13196, Pittsburgh 15243

Mong (William) Memorial Fund Trust (R)
c/o Mellon Bank N.A., Pittsburgh 15230

Monroe (Anne R.) Foundation (L) MI-12-71-72
1625 Lincoln Way, White Oak 15131

Monroeville Christian Judea Foundation, The (O)
400 Penn Center Boulevard, Suite 733, Pittsburgh 15235

Montefiore History Fund (R)
6425 Beacon Street, Pittsburgh 15217

Moore (Harold E. & M. Jean) Endowment Trust (R)
c/o Citizens National Bank, Butler 16003

Moore (Lee C.) Corp. Charitable Foundation (NP)
c/o National City Bank of Pa., Pittsburgh 15222

Moore (Ruth Danley & William Enoch) Fund (R)
c/o PNC Bank N.A., Pittsburgh 15222

Morby (Andrew & Velda) Education Foundation (R)
116 Woodland Road, Pittsburgh 15232

Morgan (Griffith D.) Memorial Fund (R)
c/o Armstrong Central Senior High School, Kittanning 16201

Morris (J.) For Clark Medical Education Foundation (R)
c/o Mellon Bank N.A., Pittsburgh 15230

Morrison (Marion H.) Trust (NP)
c/o PNC Bank N.A., Pittsburgh 15222

Moses (Joseph Y.) Foundation (L) MI-13-61-99
2016 West State Street, New Castle 16101

Mount Tabor Evangelical Cemetery (R)
c/o National City Bank of Pa., Pittsburgh 15222

Mulhearn-Van Schack Family Foundation (NP)
c/o Beilstein, 1424 Frick Building, Pittsburgh 15219

Mumford (Edwin) Foundation
(New name: Alliance Foundation)

Murray (Ronald) Charitable Fund (R)
c/o Mellon Bank N.A., Pittsburgh 15230

MVP's Retiree Group of Mellon Volunteer Professionals, Inc. (O)
One Mellon Bank Center, Room 151-0572, Pittsburgh 15258

Nailler (Charles R.) Memorial Foundation (NP)
c/o BT Management Trust Co., Johnstown 15901

New Horizons Foundation (O)
R.R. #2, Box 583, Clymer 15728

New Visions For New Castle (R)
138 West Washington Street, New Castle 16101

News and the Bible (O)
6915 Merton Road, Pittsburgh 15202

Nicholas (Nicholas G. & Annette) Foundation
(New name: Nicholas G. Nicholas Foundation)

Nimick (David) Family Foundation (L) MI-44-52-71
P.O. Box 585, Sewickley 15143

Nixon Memorial Education Foundation (R)
c/o PNC Bank N.A., Pittsburgh 15265

North American Air Museum (R)
5465 William Flynn Highway, Gibsonia 15044

O'Brien (Anna Lee Bailey) Trust (NP)
c/o PNC Bank N.A., Pittsburgh 15222

Olmsted (Fayette S.) Foundation (L) MI-99
c/o PNC Advisors/Charitable Trust Committee, Pittsburgh 15265

Otto (Ruth Varner) Trust for Seneca Valley High School (R)
c/o Mellon Bank N.A., Pittsburgh 15230

Ovesen (Henrik & Emile) Foundation (NP)
c/o Mellon Bank N.A., Pittsburgh 15258

Pan-Rhodian Society of America 'Appollon' Inc. (R)
c/o Anthou, 112 Morris Drive, Canonsburg 15312

Panella (Roger C.) Family Charitable Foundation, The
(L) MI-42-61-89
118 Glover Road, New Castle 16105

Papa (Alfred W.) Memorial Scholarship Fund (T)

Paraclete Corporation (NP)
P.O. Box 116, Cheswick 15024

Parks (H.W.) Trust for United Methodist Churches (R)
c/o Mellon Bank N.A., Pittsburgh 15230

Pasquerilla Charitable Trust (T)

Patterson (James A.) Trust (R)
c/o National City Bank of Pa., Pittsburgh 15222

Paul (T.R.) Charitable Trust (L) MI-12-31-99
800 Martha Street, Munhall 15120

Pennsylvania Industrial Chemical Corp./Clairton H.S. Fund (R)
c/o Clairton High School, Clairton 15025

Pennsylvania Medical Staff Education Fund (R)
U.S.V.A. Surgical Service Office, Pittsburgh 15240

Pennsylvania Scouters Museum & Activity Center (U)
939 California Ave., Pittsburgh 15202

Perelman Foundation, The (L) MI-99
c/o Kings, Inc., P.O. Box 630, New Castle 16103

Performing Arts & Education, Foundation for (L) MI-51-52
c/o Rago, 51 Dinsmore Ave., Pittsburgh 15205

Perkins (Jeffrey) Charitable Foundation (L) MI-42
c/o Kopf, 20 Stanwix Street, #650, Pittsburgh 15222

Perrone (John) Memorial Scholarship Fund (R)
c/o Leechburg Area High School, Guidance Office, Leechburg 15656

Peters (Ruth R.) Scholarship (R)
c/o Skybank, New Castle 16103

Petok Charitable Foundation (L) MI-99
2200 Georgetown Drive, Sewickley 15143

Petsonk Foundation (U)

Pfeffer (Murray B.) Trust
(Refer to Unger-Pfeffer Family Foundation)

Pi Sigma Educational Foundation (R)
c/o Scott, 1300 Oliver Building, Pittsburgh 15222

Picco—Clairton High School Fund (R)
c/o Principal, Clairton Senior High School, Clairton 15025

Pittsburgh Allergy Society (O)
c/o Light, 1100 Ligonier Street, Latrobe 15650

Pittsburgh Coalition to Counter Hate Groups (O)
P.O. Box 5294, Pittsburgh 15206

Pittsburgh Research Institute, The (R)
Fifth Avenue Place, Suite 1711, Pittsburgh 15222

Plum Presbyterian Senior Housing Inc. (R)
1215 Hulton Road, Oakmont 15139

PNC Bank Foundation
(New name: PNC Foundation)

PNC Memorial Foundation (R)
c/o PNC Bank N.A., Pittsburgh 15222

Pontious (James C. & Margaret W.) Foundation (L) MI-54-71-99
105 Bella Vista Drive, Murryville 15668

Pool (Lulu A.) Health & Education Fund (L) MI-12-13-14
111 South Main Street, P.O. Box 760, Greensburg 15601

Posner Fine Arts Foundation, The (I) MI-N/R
599 Greentree Commons, 381 Mansfield Ave., Pittsburgh 15220

Poux (Charles A. & Frances M.) Charitable Foundation (R)
c/o National City Bank, Pittsburgh 15278

Power (Howard A.) Scholarship Fund (R)
c/o PNC Bank N.A., Pittsburgh 15265

Preston (Frank K.) Memorial Scholarship Trust (R)
P.O. Box 49, Meridian Station, Butler 16001

Prostejovsky Charitable Trust (L) MI-63
1083 Manor Drive, Ebensburg 15931

Protestant Orphans Relief Fund-Jacoby (L) MI-12-13-22
c/o PNC Advisors/Charitable Trust Committee, Pittsburgh 15265

Quinn (William P.) Scholarship Trust (R)
One Oxford Centre, 36th Floor, Pittsburgh 15219

Rairigh (H.E. & Dorothy) Family Foundation (L) MI-31-42-63
Box 73, Route 286, Hillsdale 15746

Randall Reserve Foundation, The (O)
State Route 711 South, Stahlstown 15687

Rappaport (Earl & Hattie) Foundation (NP)
c/o Lieber, One Oxford Centre, 40th Floor, Pittsburgh 15219

Rappaport (Saul & Edith) Foundation (U)

Rebecca Residence for Protestant Ladies (O)
900 Rebecca Avenue, Pittsburgh 15221

Reed (R.W.) Charitable Foundation (L) MI-22-63
900 Fifth Ave., Suite 500, Pittsburgh 15219

Regional Environmental Monitoring Assn. (U)

Rehmus (Frederick H.) Trust for Chestnut Hill College (R)
c/o PNC Bank N.A., Pittsburgh 15222

Reidbord Foundation (L) MI-22-62-99
c/o Reidbord Realty, 5000 Baum Boulevard, Pittsburgh 15213

Reineman (Adam) Charitable Trust (L) MI-99
c/o PNC Advisors/Charitable Trust Committee, Pittsburgh 15265

Richardson Foundation (NP)
418 Washington Trust Building, Washington 15301

Richland Youth Foundation (R)
c/o PNC Bank N.A., Pittsburgh 15265

Richless Foundation, The (L) MI-63-99
305 Timber Court, Pittsburgh 15238

Robinson (Alex & Leona) Foundation (T)

Robinson (Harold & Shirley) Foundation
(Formerly of Pittsburgh; now located in MD)

Robinson (Sanford N. & Judith) Family Foundation (U)

Rockwell (R.) Memorial Trust (R)
c/o Mellon Bank N.A., Pittsburgh 15230

Rockwell International Corporation Trust
(Formerly of Pittsburgh; now located in WI)

Roesch Family Charitable Trust (I)
c/o DV&W, USX Tower, 58th Floor, Pittsburgh 15219

Rooney (Art) Scholarship Fund (R)
One Oxford Centre, 40th Floor, Pittsburgh 15219

Rose (Norman) Charitable Trust (T)

Rosen (Rose & Harry) Foundation (L) MI-22-54-62
5327 Darlington Road, Pittsburgh 15217

Rosenblum (F.) Trust for Tifereth Cemetery (R)
c/o Mellon Bank N.A., Pittsburgh 15230

Rowland (G.A. & L.G.) Scholarship Trust (R)
c/o Millville Area High School, Millville 17846

Ruscetti (Marshall) Foundation (L) MI-43-61
23 Bristol Lane, New Castle 16105

Ruslander Foundation (T)

Russell Charitable Trust Fund (L) MI-N/R
855 North Meadowcroft, Pittsburgh 15218

Russell Educational Foundation Trust (R)
c/o PNC Bank N.A., Pittsburgh 15265

Safehouse Ministries, Inc. (O)
129 North 3rd Street, Jeannette 15644

Saint Joseph Alter Society et al (NP)
c/o PNC Bank, Pittsburgh 15222

Saint Joseph Parochial School (NP)
c/o PNC Bank, Pittsburgh 15222

Saltsburg Community Memorial Assn. (R)
419 Salt Street, Saltsburg 15681

Samer (Spero) Memorial Fund (R)
c/o First Commonwealth Trust, Greensburg 15601

Saul (Samuel & Esther) Charitable Foundation (L) MI-N/R
2751 Beechwood Boulevard, Pittsburgh 15217

Sayers (Frances M.) Trust for William Sayers Fund (NP)
c/o PNC Bank N.A., Pittsburgh 15222

Scaife (David N.) Charitable Foundation
(New name: Scaife Charitable Foundation)

Schoonmaker (J.& L.) Trust for Sewickley Valley Hospital (R)
c/o Mellon Bank N.A., Pittsburgh 15230

Schwartz (Leonard & Millie) Foundation (R)
5526 Northumberland Street, Pittsburgh 15217

Schwarz (Roberta N.) Charitable Foundation (I)
c/o Conti, 19 North Main Street, Greensburg 15601

Shapira (David S. & Karen A.) Charitable Trust
(New name: David S. & Karen A. Shapira Foundation)

Shapiro (Samuel, Howard & Jason) Charitable Trust (T)

Sharma (D.D.) Charitable Trust (R)
530 Seco Road, Building 3, Monroeville 15146

Sharp (Emma O.) Trust for Ochiltree Foundation
(Refer to Ochiltree Foundation)

Sharp (Emma O.) Trust for Parker Foundation
(Refer to Parker Foundation)

Signs & Wonders Ministry (L) MI-23-63
286 Shafer Road, Moon Township 15108

Silberman-Weinberger Family Foundation (L) MI-35
838 Braddock Ave., Braddock 15104

Simpson (William G. & M. Virginia) Foundation (R)
208 Spencer Court, Moon Township 15108

Sky (David & Sarah) Foundation (L) MI-13-22-62
125 Summit Drive, Hollidaysburg 16648

Smiley (Sandi) Memorial Fund (U)

Smith (Emma Strouse) Memorial Fund (R)
c/o Mellon Bank, Pittsburgh 15230

Smith (L.R.) Trust for Various Charities (R)
c/o Mellon Bank N.A., Pittsburgh 15240

Snee-Reinhardt Foundation
(New name: Snee-Reinhardt Charitable Foundation)

Snyder (Elmer A. & Annabelle C.) Scholarship Fund (L) MI-43
c/o Snyder Associated Companies, P.O. Box 1022, Kittanning 16201

Snyder (Franklin C.)/Longue Vue Club Scholarship Fdn. (R)
c/o Pizzica, 400 Longue Vue Drive, Verona 15147

Society for Advocacy of Victims (U)

Society for Analytical Chemists of Pittsburgh (R)
300 Penn Center Boulevard, Pittsburgh 15235

Soles (Evalyn L.) for Y.W.C.A. (U)

Soos (Louis & Mary) Family Foundation (L) MI-22-31-63
1215 Donald Lane, Johnstown 15907

South Butler County School District Foundation (R)
c/o Knoch Senior High School, Saxonburg 16056

Spatt Family Charitable Foundation (L) MI-22-32-62
1714 Beechwood Blvd., Pittsburgh 15217

Springer (T.) Trust for Washington & Jefferson College (R)
c/o Mellon Bank N.A., Pittsburgh 15230

Stadtlanders Foundation, The (L)
600 Penn Center Boulevard, Pittsburgh 15235

Stalker (John M.) Trust for Borden Baptist Church (NP)
c/o PNC Bank N.A., Pittsburgh 15222

Stannard (Barbara) Residuary Estate (R)
c/o Superintendent, Pittsburgh Public Schools, Pittsburgh 15213

Starck Foundation (U)

Stark Family Foundation (L) MI-22-62
5023 Frew Street, #1A, Pittsburgh 15213

Stein (Gertrude) Foundation (R)
c/o Tyler, 4745 Bayard Street, Pittsburgh 15213

Stenger (R.C.) Scholarship Fund—Rees (R)
c/o PNC Bank N.A., Pittsburgh 15265

Stephenson (Joanne N.) Education Foundation (R)
178 Oak Meadow Drive, Oakmont 15139

Sterling Foundation, The (L) MI-N/R
440 Friday Road, Pittsburgh 15209

Stern (Samuel) Trust for Meadville Assorted Charities (R)
c/o Mellon Bank N.A., Pittsburgh 15230

Stoess (Henry & Martha) Trust Foundation (R)
c/o PNC Bank N.A., Pittsburgh 15222

Sturges Foundation (L) MI-11-22-42
500 Thompson Ave., McKees Rocks 15136

Susquehanna River Arts Center (R)
c/o Hicks, 311 Stone Street, Osceola Mills 16666

Sutton (Gertrude H.) Trust (R)
c/o Mellon Bank N.A., Pittsburgh 15230

Sylvania Foundation, The (O)
c/o Charles White, 317 Mack Road, West Sunbury 16061

Szigethy (Attila) Foundation (R)
c/o Rokop, 400 Old Pond Road, Bridgeville 15017

Teledyne Charitable Trust Foundation (R)
c/o Allegheny Teledyne, 1000 Six PPG Place, Pittsburgh 15222

Tettenborn Memorial Fund A (NP)
c/o PNC Bank N.A., Pittsburgh 15222

Tillow Fund, The (L) MI-23
763 Merchant Street, Ambridge 15003

Titelman Welfare Fund, The (T)

Tomczak (Michael J.) Charitable Trust (T)

Tour-Ed Mine & Museum (O)
P.O. Box 257, Sarver 16055

Transportation & Technology Museum (R)
c/o Snyder, 222 Oliver Building, Pittsburgh 15222

Trauger (L.) for Charities (R)
c/o Mellon Bank N.A., Pittsburgh 15230

Tri-Valley Energy & Services Center (O)
419 Liberty Street, Braddock 15104

Trowbridge (F.B. & O.L.) Memorial Fund (NP)
c/o PNC Bank N.A., Pittsburgh 15222

Twist (William) Trust (R)
c/o PNC Bank N.A., Pittsburgh 15265

Union Area District Education Foundation (R)
P.O. Box 408, New Castle 16101

USX Foundation
(New name: United States Steel Foundation)

Van Horne (Estelle) Scholarship Fund (R)
c/o Mellon Bank N.A., Pittsburgh 15230

Vang Memorial Foundation, The (R)
P.O. Box 11727, Pittsburgh 15228

Vogeley (T.) Memorial Trust (R)
c/o Mellon Bank N.A., Pittsburgh 15230

Wachter (Verneda A. & Leo J., Sr.) Foundation
(Formerly of Hollidaysburg, now located in MO]

Wallace/Ferree Memorial Foundation (L) MI-12-63-72
243 Twin Hills Drive, Pittsburgh 15216

Warburton (Ralph T. & Esther L.) Foundation (NP)
c/o Mellon Bank N.A., Pittsburgh 15258

Washington Presbyterian Senior Housing, Inc. (O)
1215 Hulton Road, Oakmont 15139

Waters (George & Elizabeth) Trust (R)
c/o National City Bank of Pa., Pittsburgh 15222

Weaver (Margaret Craig) Foundation (NP)
c/o Mellon Bank N.A., Pittsburgh 15258

Weinberg (Benjamin B. & Gertrude) Foundation (U)

Weiner (S.L. & Mollie) Family Foundation (L)
c/o Airway Industries, Inc., Airway Park, Ellwood City 16117

Welc (Kerri A.) Memorial Scholarship (R)
51 Vine Street, Mount Pleasant 15666

Wesley Hills of Mount Lebanon (R)
700 Bower Hill Road, Pittsburgh 15243

West Allegheny Physicians Assn. (R)
2101 Law & Finance Building, Pittsburgh 15219

Westinghouse Electric Fund (U)

Westinghouse Foundation (T)

Wheeling (George F.) Athletic & Educational Trust Fund (R)
c/o Wessel & Co., 215 Main Street, Johnstown 15901

Whittaker (William A.) Scholarship Trust (R)
c/o Dean, Altoona Area School District, Altoona 16602

Williams (Howell & Lois) Memorial Fund (R)
c/o National City Bank of Pa., New Castle 16101

Willis (Hilda M.) Foundation #1 (T)

Wimmer (Phillip H. & Betty L.) Family Foundation (L) MI-22-62
1683 Sturbridge Drive, RD#1, Sewickley 15143

Windber Christian Forensic Foundation of St. Anthony's (R)
c/o DiBattista, 1000 Gilda Drive, Windber 15963

Wojdak Foundation (L) MI-11-31-42
c/o Haskell of Pittsburgh, Inc., 231 Haskell Lane, Verona 15147

Wolf Family Foundation (I)
c/o Napco, Inc.,125 McFann Road, Valencia 16059

Woods (M.M.) Trust for Woods-Marchand Foundation (R)
c/o Mellon Bank N.A., Pittsburgh 15230

Woods-Marchand Foundation (O)
c/o Westmoreland Museum of Art, Greensburg 15601

Workable Alternatives Foundation (R)
P.O. Box 369, Indianola 15051

Wright (Charles L.) Foundation (R)
c/o National City Bank of Pa., Pittsburgh 15222

Young (Ralph W.) Family Trust Foundation (I)
c/o Pinebridge Commons, 1580 McLaughlin Run Road, Pittsburgh 15241

Yount (Carl C.) Charitable Trust (R)
c/o PNC Bank N.A., Pittsburgh 15265

Yukevich (Michael Andrew) Foundation
(Formerly of Allison Park, now located in WA)

Zaccheus Daniel Foundation (R)
c/o PNC Bank N.A., Pittsburgh 15265

Zanitsch Charitable Foundation (T)

Appendices
and
Indexes

Delaware Valley Grantmakers
COMMON GRANT APPLICATION FORM

About 30 Philadelphia-area foundations accept proposals which follow Delaware Valley Grantmakers' **COMMON GRANT APPLICATION FORM**, and this is stated in the individual profile-entries' under *Application Policies & Procedures*.

The **COMMON GRANT APPLICATION FORM** is designed to guide applicants through some of the typical questions asked on a grant application, and may be used as a template to organize programmatic thoughts and consider strategies when preparing any grant request. Therefore, Philadelphia-area organizations are strongly encouraged to obtain a copy of DVG's eight-page ***Grant Application Guidelines*** booklet which includes the following:

- ° Grant Proposal Narrative outline
- ° Grant Application Cover Summary sheet (required to accompany a proposal)
- ° Sample Budget Form
- ° Grant Application Checklist
- ° Other forms/information for reporting on a *completed* grant
- ° List of the foundations, corporate giving programs, and other grantmakers which accept the Common Grant Application Form

The booklet is available on DVG's website (see below) in the Adobe Acrobat (PDF) format or may be requested by telephone or e-mail. Get it and use it! It will help you to save time and be more successful in your search for foundation and other philanthropic support.

DELAWARE VALLEY GRANTMAKERS
230 South Broad Street, Suite 4C
Philadelphia, PA 19102
Telephone: 215-790-9700
FAX: 215-790-9704
E-mail: info@dvg.org
Website: www.dvg.org

Grantmakers of Western Pennsylvania
COMMON GRANT APPLICATION FORMAT

Nearly 50 foundations or corporate giving programs in Western Pennsylvania accept proposals using this **COMMON GRANT APPLICATION FORMAT** (CGAF). In addition, the CGAF serves as an excellent model for preparing requests for any funding source. For these reasons, it is strongly recommended that all Western Pa. non-profit organizations who are seeking foundation or corporate support to secure a copy of the free 11-page **COMMON GRANT APPLICATION FORMAT booklet** from Grantmakers of Western Pa.

This valuable publication explains how using the CGAF benefits grantseekers, provides details on how to use the CGAF—for both project grants and capital campaign requests; how not to use the CGAF; offers suggestions on preliminary preparation of a proposal; details the information elements of the application itself; and provides guidance on preparing a project budget. Also, the booklet includes a copy of the mandatory 1-page Common Grant Application Cover Sheet that must be part of every application using CGAF.

The **COMMON GRANT APPLICATION FORMAT booklet** is available on GWPA's website (see below) in the Adobe Acrobat (PDF) format, or by contacting:

GRANTMAKERS OF WESTERN PA
650 Smithfield Street, Suite 210
Pittsburgh, PA 15222
Telephone: 412-471-6488
FAX: 412-232-3115
E-Mail: info@gwpa.org
Website: www.gwpa.org

Application Deadlines Index

The listed foundations have grant application deadlines sometime during the month/s indicated; check the profile-entry for the exact day of the month. Note also that some of the deadlines are for certain types of grants only, e.g. scholarships, arts organizations, summer programs, etc.

» January

CP-002, CP-014, CP-034, CP-036, CP-073, CP-098, CP-115, CP-132, CP-165, NE-053, NE-060, NW-078, SE-001, SE-056, SE-081, SE-215, SE-225, SE-333, SE-403, SE-409, SE-446, SE-485, SE-520, SE-618, SE-659, SE-702, SE-745, SW-069, SW-070, SW-073, SW-371

» February

CP-067, CP-073, CP-074, CP-167, CP-179, CP-193, CP-194, CP-216, NE-111, NE-139, NE-143, NW-019, NW-032, SE-021, SE-182, SE-420, SE-423, SE-448, SE-455, SE-596, SE-597, SE-663, SW-010, SW-063, SW-254, SW-284, SW-356, SW-364, SW-379

» March

CP-033, CP-086, CP-092, CP-159, CP-206, CP-219, CP-221, CP-231, NE-083, NE-113, NE-122, NE-151, NW-014, NW-056, NW-070, SE-127, SE-130, SE-162, SE-216, SE-236, SE-251, SE-277, SE-320, SE-332, SE-333, SE-427, SE-442, SE-480, SE-570, SE-640, SE-708, SW-017, SW-018, SW-032, SW-055, SW-070, SW-175, SW-279, SW-283, SW-353, SW-378

» April

CP-013, CP-034, CP-073, CP-076, CP-088, CP-094, CP-100, CP-123, CP-176, CP-178, CP-189, CP-199, CP-207, CP-208, NE-010, NE-060, NE-061, NE-119, NW-016, NW-063, NW-071, SE-044, SE-180, SE-181, SE-182, SE-196, SE-225, SE-243, SE-245, SE-324, SE-325, SE-344, SE-403, SE-422, SE-446, SE-460, SE-461, SE-471, SE-540, SE-605, SE-618, SE-623, SE-635, SE-702, SE-728, SW-035, SW-089, SW-175, SW-189, SW-205, SW-232, SW-239, SW-242, SW-299, SW-342, SW-371, SW-385

» May

CP-001, CP-023, CP-078, CP-102, CP-116, CP-147, CP-188, NE-070, NE-074, NE-082, NE-100, NE-132, NE-134, NW-009, NW-019, NW-032, NW-042, NW-050, SE-001, SE-019, SE-047, SE-205, SE-215, SE-283, SE-306, SE-320, SE-327, SE-362, SE-423, SE-448, SE-515, SE-576, SE-596, SE-597, SE-682, SE-685, SE-734, SE-745, SW-058, SW-062, SW-078, SW-088, SW-129, SW-184, SW-233, SW-236, SW-254, SW-284, SW-373, SW-378, SW-379

» June

CP-027, CP-032, CP-033, CP-063, CP-069, CP-092, CP-115, CP-187, CP-197, CP-206, CP-221, CP-230, NE-071, NE-079, NE-089, NE-117, NW-030, NW-043, NW-056, NW-060, NW-066, NW-070, SE-002, SE-076, SE-130, SE-211, SE-231, SE-236, SE-249, SE-403, SE-464, SE-480, SE-553, SE-570, SE-600, SE-642, SE-705, SE-727, SW-042, SW-084, SW-173, SW-174, SW-274, SW-279, SW-308, SW-353, SW-361

» July

CP-002, CP-010, CP-014, CP-034, CP-073, CP-189, CP-196, CP-219, NE-005, NE-060, NE-086, NW-014, SE-225, SE-274, SE-438, SE-446, SE-485, SW-032, SW-070, SW-073, SW-187, SW-371

» August

CP-106, CP-132, CP-216, NE-012, NE-113, NE-119, NW-019, NW-032, NW-071, SE-029, SE-125, SE-130, SE-251, SE-423, SE-425, SE-448, SE-459, SE-550, SE-596, SE-597, SE-652, SW-055, SW-069, SW-095, SW-096, SW-175, SW-254, SW-265, SW-284, SW-342, SW-356, SW-378, SW-379, SW-385

» September

CP-029, CP-033, CP-040, CP-054, CP-073, CP-092, CP-139, CP-146, CP-191, CP-199, CP-206, CP-221, CP-231, NE-078, NE-135, NW-028, NW-042, NW-051, NW-055, NW-056, NW-070, SE-001, SE-021, SE-054, SE-074, SE-081, SE-098, SE-132, SE-216, SE-236, SE-305, SE-332, SE-333, SE-480, SE-559, SE-570, SE-571, SE-640, SE-641, SE-642, SE-657, SE-702, SE-718, SE-745, SE-749, SE-750, SW-018, SW-024, SW-070, SW-087, SW-175, SW-266, SW-279, SW-283, SW-295, SW-353, SW-382

» October

CP-034, CP-082, CP-130, CP-147, CP-159, CP-164, CP-177, CP-189, CP-193, CP-194, NE-036, NE-058, NE-060, NE-081, NW-014, NW-079, SE-100, SE-167, SE-180, SE-181, SE-182, SE-222, SE-225, SE-243, SE-257, SE-291, SE-320, SE-446, SE-477, SE-512, SE-550, SE-575, SE-605, SE-618, SE-623, SE-635, SE-658, SE-671, SE-728, SE-729, SW-103, SW-104, SW-181, SW-182, SW-183, SW-184, SW-205, SW-238, SW-239, SW-242, SW-292, SW-360, SW-368

» November

CP-013, CP-073, CP-095, CP-102, CP-173, CP-182, CP-219, NE-043, NE-073, NE-134, NW-012, NW-019, NW-022, NW-032, NW-033, NW-071, SE-025, SE-099, SE-117, SE-120, SE-136, SE-244, SE-327, SE-390, SE-403, SE-423, SE-448, SE-515, SE-553, SE-596, SE-597, SE-675, SE-682, SE-685, SE-701, SE-717, SW-032, SW-042, SW-076, SW-078, SW-204, SW-233, SW-254, SW-284, SW-346, SW-356, SW-358, SW-373, SW-378, SW-379, SW-385

» December

CP-003, CP-004, CP-032, CP-033, CP-081, CP-091, CP-092, CP-206, CP-221, CP-222, NE-142, NW-038, NW-056, NW-070, SE-029, SE-076, SE-130, SE-236, SE-391, SE-458, SE-464, SE-480, SE-519, SE-570, SE-703, SW-015, SW-199, SW-269, SW-279, SW-301, SW-308, SW-311, SW-353

County Location Index

based on a Foundation's mailing address

Adams County

CP-002, CP-119, CP-224

Allegheny County

SW-002, SW-003, SW-004, SW-005, SW-006, SW-007, SW-008, SW-009, SW-010, SW-011, SW-012, SW-013, SW-014, SW-015, SW-016, SW-018, SW-021, SW-022, SW-023, SW-024, SW-025, SW-026, SW-027, SW-028, SW-029, SW-030, SW-031, SW-032, SW-033, SW-036, SW-037, SW-038, SW-040, SW-041, SW-042, SW-044, SW-047, SW-048, SW-049, SW-050, SW-051, SW-052, SW-053, SW-055, SW-056, SW-057, SW-059, SW-060, SW-062, SW-063, SW-065, SW-067, SW-068, SW-072, SW-077, SW-078, SW-079, SW-080, SW-081, SW-083, SW-084, SW-085, SW-086, SW-087, SW-088, SW-090, SW-092, SW-097, SW-098, SW-099, SW-101, SW-102, SW-104, SW-105, SW-106, SW-107, SW-108, SW-109, SW-110, SW-111, SW-113, SW-114, SW-115, SW-116, SW-117, SW-118, SW-119, SW-120, SW-121, SW-122, SW-124, SW-125, SW-126, SW-128, SW-129, SW-130, SW-131, SW-133, SW-134, SW-135, SW-136, SW-137, SW-138, SW-139, SW-143, SW-144, SW-145, SW-146, SW-147, SW-148, SW-149, SW-150, SW-152, SW-153, SW-154, SW-155, SW-156, SW-157, SW-158, SW-159, SW-160, SW-161, SW-163, SW-164, SW-165, SW-166, SW-167, SW-168, SW-169, SW-172, SW-174, SW-175, SW-176, SW-177, SW-178, SW-179, SW-180, SW-181, SW-182, SW-183, SW-184, SW-185, SW-186, SW-187, SW-188, SW-189, SW-190, SW-191, SW-192, SW-194, SW-196, SW-197, SW-200, SW-201, SW-202, SW-203, SW-204, SW-205, SW-206, SW-207, SW-208, SW-209, SW-210, SW-212, SW-213, SW-214, SW-215, SW-216, SW-219, SW-220, SW-222, SW-223, SW-224, SW-225, SW-226, SW-227, SW-228, SW-229, SW-230, SW-231, SW-232, SW-234, SW-236, SW-237, SW-240, SW-241, SW-242, SW-243, SW-245, SW-246, SW-247, SW-249, SW-251, SW-254, SW-255, SW-256, SW-258, SW-259, SW-260, SW-262, SW-263, SW-265, SW-266, SW-267, SW-269, SW-270, SW-272, SW-273, SW-274, SW-276, SW-277, SW-278, SW-279, SW-281, SW-282, SW-283, SW-284, SW-285, SW-286, SW-287, SW-288, SW-289, SW-290, SW-293, SW-294, SW-295, SW-296, SW-297, SW-298, SW-300, SW-301, SW-302, SW-304, SW-307, SW-309, SW-310, SW-311, SW-312, SW-313, SW-315, SW-316, SW-317, SW-319, SW-320, SW-322, SW-323, SW-324, SW-325, SW-326, SW-327, SW-328, SW-329, SW-331, SW-332, SW-333, SW-334, SW-335, SW-336, SW-337, SW-338, SW-339, SW-340, SW-342, SW-345, SW-347, SW-348, SW-349, SW-350, SW-351, SW-352, SW-354, SW-356, SW-357, SW-358, SW-360, SW-362, SW-363, SW-364, SW-365, SW-366, SW-367, SW-368, SW-369, SW-370, SW-371, SW-372, SW-373, SW-374, SW-375, SW-376, SW-380, SW-381, SW-382, SW-384, SW-385, SW-386, SW-389, SW-390, SW-391, SW-392, SW-393, SW-394, SW-395, SW-397, SW-398, SW-399, SW-400

Armstrong County

NW-002, SW-127, SW-275, SW-343, SW-344

Beaver County

SW-019, SW-034, SW-074, SW-142, SW-195, SW-252, SW-253, SW-355

Bedford County

SW-221, SW-244

Berks County

CP-012, CP-013, CP-014, CP-015, CP-016, CP-018, CP-022, CP-024, CP-028, CP-038, CP-048, CP-065, CP-074, CP-093, CP-100, CP-101, CP-102, CP-106, CP-110, CP-134, CP-140, CP-156, CP-160, CP-167, CP-171, CP-181, CP-186, CP-187, CP-227, CP-228

Blair County

SW-035, SW-082, SW-292, SW-303, SW-346, SW-359, SW-377, SW-396

Bradford County

- No profiled foundations

Bucks County

SE-015, SE-036, SE-038, SE-053, SE-085, SE-097, SE-098, SE-099, SE-101, SE-102, SE-103, SE-105, SE-162, SE-223, SE-234, SE-243, SE-289, SE-299, SE-322, SE-328, SE-329, SE-344, SE-348, SE-349, SE-361, SE-363, SE-365, SE-383, SE-384, SE-385, SE-408, SE-445, SE-447, SE-449, SE-468, SE-471, SE-486, SE-496, SE-497, SE-514, SE-534, SE-542, SE-546, SE-551, SE-579, SE-587, SE-594, SE-601, SE-603, SE-604, SE-606, SE-632, SE-652, SE-722

Butler County

SW-061, SW-075, SW-076, SW-170, SW-299, SW-330, SW-353, SW-383

Cambria County

SW-001, SW-069, SW-112, SW-141, SW-361

Cameron County

NW-018

Carbon County

NE-009, NE-036, NE-060

Centre County

CP-033, CP-053, CP-062, CP-080, CP-117, CP-125

Chester County

SE-014, SE-021, SE-023, SE-029, SE-037, SE-039, SE-057, SE-058, SE-079, SE-082, SE-114, SE-115, SE-123, SE-125, SE-126, SE-151, SE-155, SE-161, SE-174, SE-177, SE-189, SE-221, SE-226, SE-232, SE-240, SE-267, SE-268, SE-304, SE-308, SE-310, SE-312, SE-317, SE-327, SE-330, SE-331, SE-333, SE-335, SE-336, SE-364, SE-370, SE-378, SE-382, SE-394, SE-397, SE-401, SE-455, SE-463, SE-475, SE-476, SE-480, SE-518, SE-520, SE-537, SE-541, SE-547, SE-561, SE-566, SE-586, SE-589, SE-592, SE-598, SE-599, SE-607, SE-608, SE-613, SE-626, SE-639, SE-641, SE-658, SE-669, SE-673, SE-690, SE-692, SE-699, SE-706, SE-723, SE-724, SE-725, SE-726, SE-730, SE-747, SE-748

Clarion County

NW-057

Clearfield County
NW-007, NW-022, NW-029, NW-051, NW-075

Clinton County
CP-036, CP-152

Columbia County
NE-004, NE-017, NE-023, NE-070, NE-074, NE-092, NE-099, NE-148

Crawford County
NW-01, NW-016, NW-061, NW-079

Cumberland County
CP-031, CP-035, CP-054, CP-055, CP-078, CP-083, CP-105, CP-112, CP-122, CP-145, CP-148, CP-149, CP-157, CP-159, CP-166, CP-173, CP-175, CP-196, CP-216, CP-219, CP-220

Dauphin County
CP-001, CP-003, CP-004, CP-021, CP-027, CP-034, CP-049, CP-052, CP-060, CP-063, CP-071, CP-072, CP-073, CP-079, CP-084, CP-088, CP-094, CP-096, CP-099, CP-104, CP-109, CP-116, CP-123, CP-126, CP-127, CP-128, CP-129, CP-133, CP-141, CP-142, CP-144, CP-150, CP-154, CP-158, CP-163, CP-168, CP-169, CP-174, CP-176, CP-178, CP-180, CP-189, CP-191, CP-192, CP-204, CP-205, CP-206, CP-207, CP-213

Delaware County
SE-002, SE-008, SE-016, SE-022, SE-041, SE-052, SE-074, SE-076, SE-090, SE-093, SE-121, SE-128, SE-141, SE-144, SE-153, SE-154, SE-157, SE-167, SE-191, SE-199, SE-205, SE-206, SE-219, SE-237, SE-238, SE-246, SE-250, SE-280, SE-296, SE-300, SE-302, SE-334, SE-340, SE-341, SE-388, SE-414, SE-417, SE-428, SE-436, SE-440, SE-441, SE-443, SE-448, SE-456, SE-472, SE-473, SE-490, SE-504, SE-523, SE-565, SE-568, SE-569, SE-571, SE-588, SE-591, SE-648, SE-649, SE-651, SE-664, SE-672, SE-678, SE-685, SE-688, SE-704, SE-710, SE-715

Elk County
NW-003, NW-017, NW-025, NW-062, NW-069, NW-070

Erie County
NW-005, NW-008, NW-012, NW-013, NW-019, NW-020, NW-027, NW-028, NW-030, NW-036, NW-038, NW-040, NW-042, NW-044, NW-046, NW-047, NW-048, NW-049, NW-050, NW-052, NW-053, NW-055, NW-060, NW-063, NW-066, NW-067, NW-074

Fayette County
SW-070, SW-095, SW-096, SW-132, SW-171

Forest County
- No profiled foundations

Franklin County
CP-066, CP-086, CP-089, CP-138, CP-139, CP-143, CP-225, CP-226

Fulton County
- No profiled foundations

Greene County
SW-071

Huntingdon County
- No profiled foundations

Indiana County
SW-017, SW-091, SW-218, SW-318

Jefferson County
NW-037, NW-072

Juniata County
- No profiled foundations

Lackawanna County
NE-027, NE-037, NE-041, NE-048, NE-052, NE-063, NE-079, NE-082, NE-088, NE-094, NE-100, NE-101, NE-104, NE-105, NE-125, NE-129, NE-133, NE-151

Lancaster County
CP-005, CP-007, CP-010, CP-011, CP-020, CP-025, CP-032, CP-039, CP-040, CP-042, CP-050, CP-051, CP-058, CP-059, CP-061, CP-064, CP-068, CP-069, CP-090, CP-091, CP-097, CP-098, CP-111, CP-115, CP-120, CP-124, CP-131, CP-137, CP-146, CP-161, CP-162, CP-165, CP-179, CP-193, CP-194, CP-202, CP-203, CP-209, CP-212, CP-215, CP-222

Lawrence County
SW-046, SW-123, SW-162, SW-173, SW-211

Lebanon County
CP-006, CP-017, CP-030, CP-047, CP-081, CP-118, CP-210

Lehigh County
NE-001, NE-005, NE-008, NE-015, NE-016, NE-018, NE-019, NE-022, NE-025, NE-028, NE-030, NE-031, NE-032, NE-043, NE-044, NE-053, NE-056, NE-057, NE-058, NE-064, NE-067, NE-068, NE-069, NE-075, NE-078, NE-081, NE-085, NE-086, NE-087, NE-090, NE-093, NE-098, NE-111, NE-113, NE-119, NE-121, NE-122, NE-123, NE-124, NE-126, NE-127, NE-128, NE-131, NE-134, NE-137, NE-142, NE-145, NE-150

Luzerne County
NE-002, NE-006, NE-007, NE-011, NE-013, NE-021, NE-026, NE-034, NE-039, NE-040, NE-042, NE-045, NE-050, NE-051, NE-072, NE-077, NE-091, NE-096, NE-097, NE-102, NE-106, NE-107, NE-108, NE-114, NE-116, NE-117, NE-120, NE-130, NE-140

Lycoming County
CP-085, CP-087, CP-113, CP-114, CP-151, CP-153, CP-170, CP-183, CP-184, CP-190, CP-201, CP-221

McKean County
NW-006, NW-021, NW-024, NW-054

Mercer County
NW-001, NW-023, NW-034, NW-035, NW-039, NW-041, NW-064, NW-065, NW-076, NW-077, NW-078

Mifflin County
CP-057, CP-197

Monroe County
NE-003, NE-038, NE-059, NE-061, NE-062, NE-089, NE-149

Montgomery County
SE-001, SE-009, SE-010, SE-017, SE-018, SE-019, SE-020, SE-024, SE-025, SE-026, SE-028, SE-031, SE-032, SE-033, SE-035, SE-040, SE-043, SE-045, SE-046, SE-048, SE-050, SE-051, SE-055, SE-056, SE-062, SE-063, SE-065, SE-068, SE-069, SE-072, SE-077, SE-078, SE-080, SE-083, SE-088, SE-092, SE-104, SE-108, SE-109, SE-110, SE-111, SE-113, SE-117, SE-120, SE-122, SE-124, SE-127, SE-130, SE-131, SE-132, SE-137, SE-138, SE-139, SE-143, SE-145, SE-146, SE-147, SE-148, SE-149, SE-150, SE-152, SE-156, SE-159, SE-160, SE-163, SE-164, SE-166, SE-173, SE-175, SE-178, SE-181, SE-182, SE-183, SE-184, SE-186, SE-187, SE-190, SE-193, SE-195, SE-197, SE-198, SE-200, SE-203, SE-204,

SE-208, SE-213, SE-214, SE-216, SE-217, SE-218, SE-229, SE-233, SE-235, SE-236, SE-245, SE-247, SE-248, SE-251, SE-252, SE-254, SE-255, SE-256, SE-262, SE-264, SE-265, SE-266, SE-271, SE-272, SE-274, SE-275, SE-278, SE-279, SE-281, SE-283, SE-284, SE-290, SE-291, SE-295, SE-298, SE-311, SE-313, SE-314, SE-315, SE-316, SE-318, SE-319, SE-321, SE-332, SE-338, SE-339, SE-342, SE-343, SE-345, SE-351, SE-352, SE-356, SE-357, SE-358, SE-360, SE-362, SE-367, SE-368, SE-372, SE-374, SE-377, SE-379, SE-386, SE-389, SE-390, SE-393, SE-395, SE-398, SE-399, SE-400, SE-402, SE-405, SE-406, SE-407, SE-410, SE-412, SE-413, SE-415, SE-425, SE-426, SE-430, SE-432, SE-433, SE-434, SE-437, SE-438, SE-442, SE-446, SE-451, SE-453, SE-457, SE-458, SE-460, SE-464, SE-465, SE-466, SE-469, SE-477, SE-478, SE-482, SE-483, SE-484, SE-487, SE-488, SE-489, SE-491, SE-492, SE-494, SE-495, SE-500, SE-501, SE-503, SE-506, SE-507, SE-508, SE-509, SE-510, SE-511, SE-512, SE-519, SE-522, SE-526, SE-529, SE-530, SE-532, SE-535, SE-536, SE-538, SE-539, SE-540, SE-544, SE-545, SE-548, SE-549, SE-552, SE-555, SE-557, SE-567, SE-570, SE-572, SE-573, SE-574, SE-576, SE-577, SE-580, SE-583, SE-590, SE-593, SE-602, SE-609, SE-612, SE-616, SE-617, SE-619, SE-620, SE-621, SE-623, SE-624, SE-627, SE-628, SE-629, SE-633, SE-637, SE-638, SE-642, SE-644, SE-646, SE-647, SE-650, SE-653, SE-654, SE-655, SE-656, SE-659, SE-660, SE-661, SE-662, SE-666, SE-667, SE-671, SE-674, SE-675, SE-676, SE-677, SE-679, SE-680, SE-681, SE-683, SE-686, SE-687, SE-689, SE-694, SE-695, SE-696, SE-697, SE-698, SE-700, SE-705, SE-711, SE-712, SE-714, SE-720, SE-721, SE-728, SE-731, SE-737, SE-738, SE-739, SE-741, SE-744, SE-746, SE-749

Montour County

- No profiled foundations

Northampton County

NE-010, NE-014, NE-029, NE-033, NE-047, NE-065, NE-066, NE-073, NE-076, NE-083, NE-084, NE-095, NE-109, NE-110, NE-112, NE-115, NE-118, NE-135, NE-136, NE-143, NE-144, NE-146, NE-155

Northumberland County

CP-008, CP-009, CP-043, CP-044, CP-045, CP-077, CP-121, CP-136, CP-218

Perry County

- No profiled foundations

Philadelphia County

SE-003, SE-004, SE-005, SE-006, SE-007, SE-011, SE-012, SE-013, SE-027, SE-030, SE-034, SE-042, SE-044, SE-047, SE-049, SE-054, SE-059, SE-060, SE-061, SE-064, SE-066, SE-067, SE-070, SE-071, SE-073, SE-075, SE-081, SE-084, SE-086, SE-087, SE-089, SE-091, SE-094, SE-095, SE-096, SE-100, SE-106, SE-107, SE-112, SE-116, SE-118, SE-119, SE-129, SE-133, SE-134, SE-135, SE-136, SE-140, SE-142, SE-158, SE-165, SE-168, SE-169, SE-170, SE-171, SE-172, SE-176, SE-179, SE-180, SE-185, SE-188, SE-192, SE-194, SE-196, SE-201, SE-202, SE-207, SE-209, SE-210, SE-211, SE-212, SE-215, SE-220, SE-222, SE-224, SE-225, SE-227, SE-228, SE-230, SE-231, SE-239, SE-241, SE-242, SE-244, SE-249, SE-253, SE-257, SE-258, SE-259, SE-260, SE-261, SE-263, SE-269, SE-270, SE-273, SE-276, SE-277, SE-282, SE-285, SE-286, SE-287, SE-288, SE-292, SE-293, SE-294, SE-297, SE-301, SE-303, SE-305, SE-306, SE-307, SE-309, SE-320, SE-323, SE-324, SE-325, SE-326, SE-337, SE-346, SE-347, SE-350, SE-353, SE-354, SE-355, SE-359, SE-366, SE-369, SE-371, SE-373, SE-375, SE-376, SE-380, SE-381, SE-387, SE-391, SE-392, SE-396, SE-403, SE-404, SE-409, SE-411, SE-416, SE-418, SE-419, SE-420, SE-421, SE-422, SE-423, SE-424, SE-427, SE-429, SE-431, SE-435, SE-439, SE-444, SE-450, SE-452, SE-454, SE-459, SE-461, SE-462, SE-467, SE-470, SE-474, SE-479, SE-481, SE-485, SE-493,

SE-498, SE-499, SE-502, SE-505, SE-513, SE-515, SE-516, SE-517, SE-521, SE-524, SE-525, SE-527, SE-528, SE-531, SE-533, SE-543, SE-550, SE-553, SE-554, SE-556, SE-558, SE-559, SE-560, SE-562, SE-563, SE-564, SE-575, SE-578, SE-581, SE-582, SE-584, SE-585, SE-595, SE-596, SE-597, SE-600, SE-605, SE-610, SE-611, SE-614, SE-615, SE-618, SE-622, SE-625, SE-630, SE-631, SE-634, SE-635, SE-636, SE-640, SE-643, SE-645, SE-657, SE-663, SE-665, SE-668, SE-670, SE-682, SE-684, SE-691, SE-693, SE-701, SE-702, SE-703, SE-707, SE-708, SE-709, SE-713, SE-716, SE-717, SE-718, SE-719, SE-727, SE-729, SE-732, SE-733, SE-734, SE-735, SE-736, SE-740, SE-742, SE-743, SE-745, SE-750

Pike County

NE-020

Potter County

CP-029, CP-217

Schuylkill County

NE-012, NE-024, NE-035, NE-046, NE-054, NE-055, NE-103, NE-132, NE-139, NE-152, NE-153, NE-154

Snyder County

- No profiled foundations

Somerset County

SW-045, SW-094, SW-100, SW-217, SW-291, SW-387, SW-388

Sullivan County

- No profiled foundations

Susquehanna County

- No profiled foundations

Tioga County

CP-037, CP-147, CP-199, CP-200

Union County

CP-103, CP-208

Venango County

NW-015, NW-026, NW-031, NW-032, NW-033, NW-045, NW-058, NW-059, NW-071, NW-073

Warren County

NW-004, NW-009, NW-010, NW-014, NW-043, NW-056, NW-068

Washington County

SW-054, SW-066, SW-089, SW-093, SW-103, SW-248, SW-257, SW-261, SW-264, SW-280, SW-305, SW-306, SW-314, SW-321, SW-378, SW-379

Wayne County

NE-049, NE-071, NE-080, NE-138, NE-141, NE-147

Westmoreland County

SW-020, SW-039, SW-043, SW-058, SW-064, SW-073, SW-140, SW-151, SW-193, SW-198, SW-199, SW-233, SW-235, SW-238, SW-239, SW-250, SW-268, SW-271, SW-308, SW-341

Wyoming County

- No profiled foundations

York County

CP-019, CP-023, CP-026, CP-041, CP-046, CP-056, CP-067, CP-070, CP-075, CP-076, CP-082, CP-092, CP-095, CP-107, CP-108, CP-130, CP-132, CP-135, CP-155, CP-164, CP-172, CP-177, CP-182, CP-185, CP-188, CP-195, CP-198, CP-211, CP-214, CP-223, CP-229, CP-230, CP-231

Corporate "Connections" Index

The following 490 corporations, businesses, or banks are affiliated with or connected to a profiled foundation. In most cases, the relationship between the foundation and the corporation will be one of the following:

- *A Corporate Foundation whose assets were donated by the corporation, business, etc.*
- *A family foundation funded by the owner (or owners) of a privately-held corporation*
- *A family/independent foundation which is administered from a corporate address*
- *An independent foundation which has received funds from a corporation, business, etc.*

Through careful review of the profile-entry, one can usually determine the relationship/connection between the foundation and the corporation, business, bank etc.

Out-of-Region Giving Index

While most Pennsylvania foundations overwhelmingly focus their grants on their immediate locale or home region, about one in 15 profiled foundations exhibit a pattern of awarding discretionary grants **outside** their home region—elsewhere within Pennsylvania. These foundations are listed below. It should be noted that this listing does **not** include foundations which award grants outside their home region but only to what appear to be an *alma mater* college/university or a "family church," as examples.

Giving to Central/CP Region by . .

- NE-042, NE-018
- NW-035
- SE-070, SE-114, SE-025, SE-022, SE-112, SE-181, SE-132, SE-225, SE-294, SE-317, SE-319, SE-151, SE-224, SE-332, SE-505, SE-405, SE-406, SE-413, SE-418, SE-663, SE-724, SE-573, SE-579
- SW-295, SW-169, SW-239, SW-004, SW-368, SW-287, SW-179, SW-005

Giving to Northeastern/NE Region by . .

- CP-011, CP-019, CP-043, CP-045, CP-083, CP-106, CP-151, CP-186, CP-189, CP-206, CP-219
- SE-021, SE-025, SE-138, SE-139, SE-145, SE-150, SE-181, SE-188, SE-191, SE-224, SE-225, SE-233, SE-332, SE-416, SE-476, SE-505, SE-548, SE-579, SE-589, SE-604, SE-665, SE-729
- SW-002, SW-004, SW-005, SW-125, SW-287

Giving to Northwestern/NW Region . .

- CP-084, CP-175, CP-219
- SE-446
- SW-172, SW-205, SW-230, SW-260, SW-269, SW-287, SW-295, SW-326, SW-368

Giving to Southeastern/SE Region by . .

- CP-019, CP-030, CP-045, CP-083, CP-106, CP-125, CP-146, CP-186, CP-219, CP-222, CP-228
- NE-018, NE-048, NE-058, NE-081, NE-089, NE-125, NE-126
- NW-035
- SW-026, SW-031, SW-103, SW-113, SW-214, SW-239, SW-241, SW-287, SW-297, SW-315, SW-316, SW-328, SW-352

Giving to Southwestern/SW Region by . .

- CP-019, CP-083, CP-084, CP-102, CP-219
- NE-018, NE-054, NE-065, NE-066
- SE-021, SE-022, SE-033, SE-062, SE-112, SE-332, SE-336

Officers+Directors+Trustees
of all profiled foundations

C

D

Dworetzky, Joseph A. SE-505
Dyer, Leila Gordon SE-446
Dyson, David E. CP-159

E

Earle, Anne G. SW-168
Earley, Susan H. SW-016
Easley, Ellen Stuckeman SW-358
Eastman, Lance E. NW-054
Eastwood, James W. SE-190
Eastwood, Linda D. SE-190
Ebel, Linda W. SW-063
Eberhardt, John E., Jr. SW-035
Eberle, Henry A., Jr. SE-685
Eberly, Elouise R. SE-096
Eberly, Paul O. SW-095, SW-096
Eberly, Robert E., Jr. SW-095
Eberly, Robert E., Sr. SW-095, SW-096
Eble, Kim S.P. SE-191
Echement, John R. SW-385
Eddinger, Thomas. SE-291
Eddy, John NE-103
Edelman, John T. SW-386
Edelman, Martin L. CP-224
Eden, Brooks D. SE-191
Eden, Earl M. SE-191
Edling, Carl D. NE-132
Edmonds, Lorraine SE-488
Edmunds, Arthur J. SW-284
Edstene, Kay M. SE-092
Edwards, David L. SW-232
Edwards, Earnest J. SW-004
Edwards, Ed NE-023
Edwards, Edwin E., III SW-089
Edwards, James M. . . . SW-231, SW-232
Edwards, John H. SW-232
Edwards, Michael M. . . . SW-231, SW-232
Edwards, Richard D. SW-231
Egan, J. Murray SW-368
Egan, John J., Jr. SE-071
Egler, Frederick N., Jr. SW-090
Egler, Ruth D. SW-090
Eglin, Stephanie S. SE-192
Eichleay, George F. SW-099
Eichleay, John W., Jr. . . . SW-099, SW-356
Eichler, David F. CP-179
Eichler, Franklin R. CP-179
Eilenberger, Bruce F. CP-037
Eilenberger, Vickie L. CP-037
Eisenhauer, Patricia CP-082
Eisenhauer, Shawn R. CP-082
Eisenman, Emily P. NW-031, NW-045
                           NW-071, NW-073
Eisman, Ann G. SE-071
Eizen, Bernard . . SE-171, SE-396, SE-397
Elbert, P.O. SW-282
Elder, Anne. SE-158
Elfvin, John T. CP-151
Elfvin, Jean Margaret CP-151
Elias, Albert J. SE-119
Elias, Alma SE-193
Elias, Gabriel SE-193
Elias, Norma. SE-182
Elias, Norman. SW-101
Elias, Sylvia M. SW-101
Eligator, Edith L. SW-326
Elinoff, Saul SW-177
Elinoff, William SW-177
Elinoff, Yetta SW-177

Elish, Eloise H. SW-102
Elish, Herbert. SW-102
Elkins, S. Gordon SE-218
Elkinton, Eleanor M. SE-092
Elkman, Lois D. SE-194
Elkman, Stanley. SE-194
Elkman, Stuart M. SE-194
Elliott, Steven G. SW-241
Ellis, Aaron. SE-198
Ellis, Carol SE-195
Ellis, Donna SE-744
Ellis, Gilda SE-198
Ellis, Jeffrey B. SE-195
Ellis, Michael D. SE-195
Ellis, Richard A. SE-198
Ellis, Robert SE-195
Ellis, Syliva M. SE-195
Ellison, Charles E. SW-345, SW-347
Elston, Lloyd L. NE-072
Elston, Richard L. NE-072
Ely, Thomas O. SE-282
Emerick, Frederick C., Jr. SW-204
Emery, Glenn SE-435
Engebretson, Kathryn J. SE-505
Engel, Martha A. NW-017
Engle, Charles A. CP-051
Engle, Dennis L. CP-051
Engle, Fred S. CP-179
Engle, Pauline H. CP-051
Engle, Scott F. SE-200
Engle, Stanley H. SE-200
Enright, Victoria Nimick. SW-265
Entwhisle, Robert M., III SW-227
Epstein, Andrew. SE-521
Epstein, J. Earl SE-285
Epstein, Martin SE-201
Epstein, Maxine P. SE-201
Epstein, Richard W. NW-076
Epstein, William. SE-570
Erath, Sally SW-019
Erb, William H., Jr. SE-685
Erdos, Robert W. CP-214
Erlbaum, Dan. SE-203
Erlbaum, Gary E. SE-203
Erlbaum, Jon SE-203
Erlbaum, Marc SE-203
Erlbaum, Vicki SE-203
Ermine, David B. SE-647
Ertel, Barbara. CP-153
Esbenshade, Lamar R. CP-202
Esbenshade, Nancy Jane CP-202
Eshelman, Glenn CP-120
Eshelman, Shirley R. CP-120
Esposito, Louis J. NW-035, SE-071
Esser, Cyril F. SW-032
Estroff, Belle. NE-041
Etheridge, Albert L. SW-069
Euwer, Paul, Jr. SW-184
Evans, Anne T. SE-644
Evans, Elizabeth W. SW-028
Evans, Fred F. NE-148
Evans, Gareth SE-274
Evans, Harold S. SW-028
Evans, J. Morris SE-644
Evans, James W. CP-001
Evans, Jean SE-274
Evans, Joseph J. NW-076
Evans, Joseph M., Jr. SE-644
Evans, Ronald G. CP-149
Evans, Samuel, III SE-550
Evans, Sian SE-274
Evans, Trevor SE-274

Evans, Walter C. SE-644
Evans, William. NE-098
Evans-Stephen, Tegan SE-274
Evert, Herbert T. SE-532
Evey, Merle SW-035
Eyer, Robert J. SW-069

F

Faber, Eberhard L. NE-040
Faber, James R. SE-328
Faber, Mary Louise NE-040
Fabian, Sallie SE-099
Facini, Deborah L. CP-112
Fairall, Dianne L. CP-004, CP-159
Fairbanks, Bryan H. SW-105
Fairbanks, Frank SW-105
Fairchild, Alvin. NE-076
Faircloth, Karen E. CP-196
Faison, Helen S. SW-047
Falconer, Barbara E. CP-196
Falconer, Keith D. CP-196
Fales, Nancy C. SW-205
Falk, Andrew D. SW-106
Falk, Carol Gundel CP-115
Falk, Sigo SW-106, SW-107
Fallon, Lesley H. NE-086
Fapohunda, Babatunde SW-010
Farber, David M. SE-210
Farber, Fredrick CP-053
Farber, Jack SE-210, SE-211
Farber, Vivian. SE-210
Farmer, Peter J. SE-471
Farmerie, Karen A. SW-108
Farmerie, Wilson J. SW-108
Farrell, Michael J. SW-109
Farrell, Susan L. SW-385
Farrell, T.F. SW-087
Faus, Nancy Rosenberger SE-573
Faust, F. Lee SE-589
Fava, Margaret. CP-210
Fazzolari, Salvatore D. CP-083
Feather, Jeffrey NE-073
Featherman, John A., III SE-125
Featherman, Sandra. SE-215
Fecker, Jill CP-136
Feeney, Erin SW-111
Feeney, James E. NW-065
Feeney, Joan Kavanagh NW-034
Feeney, John M. SW-111
Feeney, Patrick J. SW-111
Feeney, Terrance SW-111
Fees, Ronald J. SW-029
Fegan, Ann B. NE-116
Fegan, Howard D. NE-116
Fegan, John H. NE-116
Fehnel, Sylvia. NE-095
Feiner, Eugene SE-212
Feinstein, Diane SE-363
Feinstein, Elisa SE-213
Feinstein, Karen Wolk SW-186
Feinstein, Samuel. SE-213
Feldman, Paul L. SE-288, SE-533
Felgoise, Judith SE-214
Felgoise, Marc SE-214
Fellahnejad, Manucher. SE-287
Feller, Carol NE-057
Felzer, Lionel SE-581
Ferguson, James M., III . . SW-044, SW-169
                            SW-247, SW-368

G

H

Hanrahan, Robert E., Jr. SE-505	Hayes, Robert D. SW-157	Herschkopf, Rebecca Stern. SE-660
Hansen, E.F., Jr. SE-551	Hayne, Margaret SE-309	Hershberger, Harold D., Jr. CP-147
Hansen, Gardiner. SE-332	Hayne, Richard A. SE-309	Hershberger, Rex SW-035
Hansen, Nancy Huston. SE-332	Haynes, Lawrence E. NW-065	Herzog, John CP-130
Hansen, Nancy K. SW-155	Hayre, Sylvia SE-743	Hess, Anna Ruth CP-050
Hansen, R.T. SE-551	Hays, Nancy Scheller NE-121	Hess, Barbara J. CP-097
Hansen, William Gregg. SW-155	Heacock, Robert. SE-223	Hess, J. Clair CP-090
Hanway, H. Edward SE-129	Healey, Carolyn NE-126	Hess, Kenneth E. CP-090
Harbaugh, Gregory A. SW-156	Heany, Mimi. SE-204	Hess, Marianne SW-123
Hardee, Wayne. SE-501	Hearn, Gail W. SE-222	Hess, Marshall SW-123
Hardee, Wilhelmina M. SE-501	Hearn, Kathryn Watchorn CP-213	Hess, Parke H. SE-138, SE-139
Hardiman, Lori Zappala SW-400	Heasley, Christina. SW-342	Hess, Ray. SW-035
Hardiman, Thomas H. SW-400	Heasley, Karen L. SW-342	Hess-King, A. Tracy CP-089
Harding, Elwood, Jr. NE-023	Heasley, Paul A. SW-342	Hessley, Bernard J. NW-009
Hardy, E.S. Teig SW-087	Heck, Kellyann. SE-311	Hetrick, Darl NW-057
Hardy, Shirley. SW-378	Heckscher, Martin A. SE-416, SE-532	Hewitt, Elizabeth H.. . . . . SE-319
Hargrave, Anne K. SW-297	Hedges, M. Dennis, Jr. NW-004	Hewitt, Robert W.. . . . . SE-319
Harkins, James F., Jr. SE-589	Heerdt, Robert J. SE-313	Hickey, Thomas J. SW-333
Harkins, Susan M. SE-471	Heidenreich, Chris Webb SE-283	Hicks, Linda A.. . . . . CP-073
Harleman, Michael. NE-060	Heidmann, Barbara R. SE-314	Hicks, Sharon SE-164
Harltey, Jocelyn CP-036	Heidmann, Ruth E.. . . . . SE-314	Hieber, Carol O. CP-153
Harmelin, Stephen J. SE-305	Heilig, Richard P. CP-165	Hiestand, Charles. CP-098
Harmer, Mary. SE-664	Heilig, William W. SE-641	Higgins, Michael S. SW-022
Harmon, John C. SW-022	Heilman, Susan B. SE-332	High, Calvin G. CP-091
SW-209, SW-272	Heim, Bruce K.. . . . . CP-033	High, Gregory A. CP-091
Harp, Tom NE-075	Heimbach, Daniel E. NE-155	High, Janet C. CP-091
Harper, Charles L., Jr. SE-688	Heimbach, David G. NE-155	High, Richard L.. . . . . CP-091
Harral, William, III SE-045	Heimbach, Elizabeth W. NE-155	High, S. Dale CP-091, CP-115
Harris, Brenda SW-113	Heimbach, George Z. NE-155	High, Sadie H. CP-091
Harris, Dennis J. NE-014	Heindl, Dennis D. NW-025	High, Steven D. CP-091
Harris, Graysha SE-011	Heintzelman, Scott A. CP-136	Higie, William F. NW-021
Harris, Marilyn A.. . . . . SW-371	Heinz, Andre T. SW-158, SW-161	Hilbert, William M., Sr. NW-019
Harris, Nelson G. SE-684	Heinz, Drue SW-160	Hill, Edward R. SE-455
Harris, Stephen B. SE-330, SE-652	Heinz, H. John, IV SW-160	Hill, Jacquline L. CP-086
Harris, Suzanne Clemens SE-132	Heinz, Teresa F. SW-158	Hill, Kenneth D. SE-125
Harrison, Lee SE-743	SW-160, SW-161	Hill, Marsha. SE-455
Harrison, Ruth J. CP-066	Heitz, Ken CP-019	Hill, Robert B. SE-535
Harrity, Grant E.. . . . . NE-032	Heizenroth, Charles, III NE-132	Hill, William J.. . . . . NW-019
Harrold, Mark A. CP-195	Heizer, Mrs. Philip SE-239	Hill, William M., Jr. NW-014
Hart, James P.. . . . . SW-178	Helbley, John J. CP-036	Hillas, Dee SE-618
Hart, Kenneth. NE-017	Hellendall, Gretel. SE-315	Hillberry, Robert A. SW-378
Hart, Robin D. NW-073	Hellendall, Kenneth C. SE-315	Hillman, Elsie H. SW-164
Hartman, George H. NE-072	Hellendall, Ronald D. SE-315	Hillman, Henry L. SW-164
Hartman, Gerald C. CP-033	Hellendall, Walter SE-315	SW-165, SW-289
Hartman, Gregory C. SE-150	Helms, Ann Marie SW-242, SW-243	Hillman, William Talbott SW-166
Hartman, Larry A. CP-126, CP-127	Helwig, Nancy SE-483	Hills, Vicki SE-301, SE-718
CP-128, CP-129, CP-189	Helwig, Shirley G. CP-204	Hilyard, James E.. . . . . SE-589
Hartmann, David B. SW-283	Henderson, Carol K.. . . . . SW-117	Himes, Jane A.. . . . . SW-308
Hartnett, George J. SE-434	Henkels, Barbara B. SE-316	Himes, Terry J.. . . . . SW-072
Harvey, Joseph S. NW-032	Henkels, Christopher B. SE-316	Hinckley, James L., Jr. NE-017
Hasek, Diane E. NW-073	Henkels, Paul M., Jr.. . . . . SE-316	Hinton, Gregory P. CP-147
Hashorva, Tanya. SE-025	Henkels, Paul M. SE-316	Hitchcock, Peggy M.. . . . . SW-167
Haskins, Lillian Escobar SE-225	Henn, Carol Dean. NE-086	Hitchcock, Thomas M., III SW-167
Hass, Ellen SE-745	Henrich, William J., Jr.. . . SE-022, SE-407	Hitchcock, William M. SW-167
Hass, Hans CP-012, CP-065	Henry, John A.. . . . . SE-125	Hitchener, Ruth NE-140
Hassman, Cheryl SE-308	Henry, Lenny R. SW-288	Hitselberger, William E.. . . . . . . SE-524
Hassman, Howard SE-308	Herdman, Bruce W. SE-222	Hively, Bob. CP-153
Hathaway, Derek C. CP-083, CP-109	Herman, Margaret SE-445	Hoare, Betty. NW-072
Hauber, Jean D. SW-156	Herman, Tera SW-035	Hobbs, Mrs. Robert B., Jr. SE-216
Hauber, William M. SW-156	Hermance, Frank S. SE-021	Hoch, Robert C. NE-010
Hauck, Edward C. SW-318	Hermann, Robert SE-688	Hodges, George W.. . . . . CP-223
Haupt, Eleanor McKnight. SE-070	Hernandez, Robert M. SW-371	Hodges, John. NW-011
Hauptfuhrer, Robert P. SE-045	Hernandez, William H.. . . . . SW-295	Hoffman, Arnold S. SE-321
Haussmann, William SE-687	Herr, Edwin H.. . . . . SE-317	Hoffman, Bette G. SE-321
Havens, Louise A.. . . . . SE-642	Herr, Gene SE-317	Hoffman, Tom SW-364
Hawke, George G. SE-703	Herr, James M.. . . . . SE-317	Hoffstot, H. Phipps, III. SW-375
Hawkins, Susan Lockey CP-005	Herr, James S. SE-317	Hoffstot, Henry P., Jr.. . . . . SW-375
Hayes, C.N., Sr. SW-157	Herr, Miriam SE-317	Hofmann, Bernard M. . . . CP-093, CP-074
Hayes, Clair N., III SW-157	Herr, Philip C., II SE-296	Hofmann, Martin J. CP-093
Hayes, John A. CP-204	Herreda, Leonardo. CP-073	Hofmann, Robert SW-207
Hayes, Linda Snyder. SW-345	Herrin, Melva. SE-318	Hogan, Edwin R. SW-073
Hayes, Nellie I.. . . . . SW-157	Herrin, Melvin B. SE-318	Holcomb, Douglas M. NE-080

I

J

K

M

Moyer, Christine SE-149
Moyer, Clare M. SE-149
Moyer, Glen E. CP-014
Moyer, J. Roger, Jr. CP-115
Moyer, Jacalyn SE-484
Moyer, Sherill T. CP-021
Moyer, Trina SE-149
Moyer, William W., III. SE-484
Mozino, Catherine SE-472
Mrozek, Greg SW-010
Mudge, Edmund W., III. SW-256
Mudge, Taylor SW-256
Mueller, Marnie W. NE-072
Muir, Anne S. SE-080
Muir, Janice C. SE-080
Mulford, Richard A. SE-703
Mullen, James L. SE-133
Mullen, Joan A. SE-473
Mullen, John J. SE-473
Muller, C. John SE-474
Mulroney, John P. SE-505
Mulroy, Thomas M. SW-247
Mumbauer, Robert SE-291
Mumma, Moira SE-125
Murdy, J.L. SW-007
Murphy, Eric S. SE-475
Murphy, Harry SE-152
Murphy, John H. SE-475
Murphy, Joseph A. SE-349, SE-468
Murphy, Katherine N. SE-468
Murphy, Kathleen C. SE-199
Murphy, Kevin K. CP-014
Murphy, Martha J. SE-468
Murphy, Maureen SW-088
Murphy, Patricia SW-364
Murphy, R. Blair SE-475
Murphy, Robert W., Jr. SW-257
Murphy, Thomas J. SW-092
Murphy, William K. NE-086
Murray, Boyd S. SE-281
Murray, Dennis CP-052, CP-192
Murray, Joseph NE-147
Murrow, William R. SE-733
Murry, Emanuel E. CP-137
Murry, William E. CP-137
Muse, Albert C. SW-259
Muse, Charles H., Jr. SW-259
Musser, Betty U. SE-678
Musser, John W. SW-303
Musser, Warren V. SE-476, SE-586
Myers, David G. SE-688
Myers, David NE-048
Myers, Eleanor W. SE-517
Myers, Forest CP-054
Myers, Joan E. SE-452
Myers, Jonathan NE-048
Myers, Leon S. CP-014
Myers, Morey M. NE-048
Myers, Richard J. CP-144
Myers, Sondra Gelb NE-048
Myrin, Karen E. SE-716
Myron, Thomas L., Jr. SW-022

N

Nachtigall, Dean. CP-188
Nader, Abraham L. SW-072
Nagy, Christopher SE-517
Naidoff, Stephanie W. SE-225
Nalle, Eleanor G. SE-380

Naor, Sareva Stern SE-660
Napolitano, Joseph J. NE-113
Nascimento, Renata Camargo . . . SW-004
Naselli, Diana SE-157
Naselli, Joseph V. SE-157
Nassau, Richard SE-231
Nast, Dianne M. CP-032
Nathanson, Ruth Leventhal SE-655
Nation, Robert F. CP-084, CP-109
Naud, Hilary Maslow NE-096
Naude, Klaus SE-456
Naugle, Elmer E. CP-138, CP-139
Naugle, Jeffrey SE-223
Naugle, Nellie I. CP-138
Naus, Sonia N. SE-199
Nayovitz, Margaret D. SE-478
Neag, Ray CP-140
Nealon, Thomas R. NE-133
Neducsin, Daniel R. SE-479
Neducsin, Luana SE-479
Neff, Robert SE-282
Neff, Rosalind S. SE-035
Neff, Roy S. SE-035
Neff, Ruth H. SW-048
Negherbon, Vincent SE-115
Nehrbas, Andrew R. SE-078
Neidig, Charles P. SE-159
Neidig, Dorothy A. SE-159
Neilsen, Anne Fehr CP-016
Nelson, Clarence J. CP-040
Nelson, Helen P. SE-148
Nelson, Joseph M. NE-026
Nelson, Joseph NE-026
Nelson, Louise B. NE-026
Nelson, P. Erik SE-148
Nelson, Richard C. SE-167
Nesbit, John NW-011
Nesbitt, Brian SE-053
Nestor, Donald E. CP-141, CP-142
Nestor, Robin M. CP-141, CP-142
Netzer, Edith S. SW-262
Netzer, Leon L. SW-186, SW-262
Netzer, Nancy. SW-262
Netzer, Thomas SW-262
Neubauer, Joseph SE-481
Neubauer, Lawrence SE-481
Neubauer, Peter SE-064
Neuman, A. Bruce SE-482
Neuman, K. Sidney SW-348
Newbold, Theodore T. SE-702
Newlin, William R. SW-198
Newman, Jonathan H. SE-433
Newman, Nancy Marcus SE-433
Newman, Paul L. SE-483
Newton, Douglas M. SE-534
Nicholas, Annette M. SW-263
Nicholas, Nicholas G. SW-263
Nichols, Gregory T. SW-058
Nicholson, Jan SW-145
Nicholson, Marion Grable SW-145
Nicholson, William B. SW-145
Nicklin, Sue Ann NW-001
Niemczuk, Olivia C. SE-169
Niesen, Douglas SW-264
Niesen, Raymond J. SW-264
Nilon, John W. SE-240
Nimick, Francis B., Jr. SW-047
Nimick, Theresa I. SW-265
Nimick, Thomas H., Jr. SW-265
Nitterhouse, Diane R. CP-143
Nitterhouse, William K. CP-143
Nitzberg, Carol. SE-158

Nixon, Laurey NW-070
Nofer, George H. SE-066, SE-493
Noonan, Charles NE-043
Nork, A. Edward NE-091
Norris, Diana Strawbridge SE-669
Norris, Kenneth SE-719
Norris, Nancy. SE-487
Norris, Norman L. SE-487
Northrop, John L.S. SW-378
Norton, Harry SE-394
Norton, Helen A. CP-198
Norton, Nancy SE-394
Novak, Joseph F. SW-055
Novey, John SW-063
Nowicki, Douglas R. SW-233
Nunan, Caroline Steinman. CP-193
Nunn, Helen CP-044
Nutt, Anne B. SE-559
Nutter, Jeri. SE-081
Nutter, Michael A. SE-071
Nydick, Susan SE-361
Nye, Phyllis CP-054

O

O'Boyle, Michael NE-106
O'Brien, Charles P. SE-169
O'Brien, James A. NW-065
O'Brien, Patrick, II SW-378
O'Brien, Paul E. NW-065
O'Connell, Daniel. SE-236
O'Connor, Gerald J., Sr. SE-490
O'Connor, Joseph A., Jr. SE-116
O'Connor, Joseph A., Jr. SE-253
O'Connor, Michael F. CP-231
O'Connor, Sheila T. SE-490
O'Data, Charles N. SW-019
O'Donnell, Kerry J. SW-107
O'Donnell, Doris SW-006
O'Donnell, Elizabeth SE-462
O'Donnell, James E. SE-462
O'Donnell, Marie SE-462
O'Donnell, Michael SW-229, SW-351
O'Grady, Jeremiah Patrick SE-491
O'Grady, Kathleen A. SE-491
O'Haire, Sandra A. SE-312
O'Leary, Beverly SW-019
O'Malley, Cheryl. SW-010
O'Malley, Michael. SW-060
O'Malley, Thomas P. SE-243
O'Neill, J. Brian SE-492
O'Neill, June SE-047
O'Neill, Miriam SE-492
O'Neill, Molly E. SE-080
O'Neill, Nancy J. SW-266
O'Neill, Paul H. SW-266
O'Neill, William G. SE-550
O'Reilly, Anthony J.F. SW-159
O'Sullivan, Ann L. SE-391
O'Toole, Judith. SW-073
Oberholzer, Rhoda S. CP-186
Oberkotter, Mildred L. SE-493
Obert, Sherry. SW-244
Obrock, John A. CP-109
Oden, Thomas H. SE-539
Off, Robert W. SW-056
Okonak, James R. SW-233
Oliver, James J. SE-127
Olsen, Todd L. NW-026
Ondik, John SE-536

P

T

Thomas, Telford W. SW-379
Thomas, Thomas McKean. SE-486
Thompson, Angela R. CP-094, CP-130
Thompson, Harry A. SW-373
Thompson, Jeffrey M. SW-075
Thompson, John R. NE-023
Thompson, John. NE-070, NE-074
Thompson, Lawrence M., Jr. CP-186
Thompson, Marion M. SE-456
Thompson, Mona L. SW-066
Thompson, Mrs. Wirt L., Jr. SE-239
Thompson, Robert M., Jr. SW-363
Thompson, Terry A. CP-171
Thomson, Joann M. SE-692
Thomson, Joe M. SE-692
Thomson, Radclyffe F. SE-239
Thornton, April L. CP-010
Thorwart, Larry NW-017
Throckmorton, Dolly SW-071
Thun, David L. CP-014, CP-228
Thun, Ferdinand. NE-086
Thun, Peter. CP-228
Thye, Pamela M. CP-194
Tippins, Carolyn H. SW-366
Tippins, George W. SW-366
Tippins, John H. SW-366
Tippins, Karen A. SW-367
Tippins, William H. SW-366, SW-367
Tishman, Ted SW-386
Tobin, Frances E. SE-645, SE-694
Tobin, Sylvan M. SE-645, SE-694
Todi, Nand K. SE-695
Toebe, John M. SE-016
Toebe, John W. SE-016
Toebe, Patricia M. SE-016
Toebe, Sherene. SE-016
Toerper, Delaine A. CP-231
Toll, Bruce E. SE-696
Toll, Robert I. SE-697
Tomarchio, Jack T. SE-641
Tompkins, Edwin W., III NW-018
Toole, Frank J. NE-132
Torgan, Marvin. SE-149
Torian, Roberta Griffin SE-702
Torongo, Marjorie E. SE-162
Torsella, Patricia NE-017
Toscani, Dominic P., Jr. SE-113
Toscani, Gerard M. SE-113
Toscani, Lisa SE-113
Toscani, Marybeth SE-113
Tosh, Joseph N., II SW-019
Towers, James K., III CP-069
Townsend, Polly Jackson SW-181, SW-182
Tozour, Douglas O. SE-698
Tozour, Gail S. SE-698
Trabucco, John E. SW-020
Tracanna, Frank, Jr. SW-378
Trach, John P. CP-021
Trafton, Adelaide Frick. SW-128
Traub, Jean Schrenk SE-606
Trautman, Donald NW-062
Travaglini, A. Frederick SE-115
Travaglini, Barbara C. SE-115
Trew, Betsie SW-378
Trout, David M., Jr. CP-056
Trout, Rebecca Freas CP-056
Troutman, David A. CP-205
Troutman, Dorothy T. CP-205
Trueheart, William E., Jr. SW-284
Truver, Theodore L. SE-328
Tsvetkov, Lynne Allen SE-197
Tucker, William B. NW-038

Tuefel, Mary. CP-183
Tulin, Stephen SE-064
Tunnell, Kenneth W. SE-125
Tuppeny-Hess, Diane SE-142
Turcic, Kenneth NW-065
Turcik, John J. SW-242, SW-243
Turnbach, Beth M. NE-114
Turner, Carolyn SE-699
Turner, John D. SW-078
Turner, Laurey NW-070
Turner, Robert E., Jr. SE-699
Turpin, Ramona D. CP-014
Turrill, Kristen Rosenlund. SE-576
Tuten, John C., Jr. SE-459
Tuton, John SE-734
Tuton, Lucy Wolf SE-618
Tuttleman, David Z. SE-700
Tuttleman, Edna S. SE-700
Tuttleman, Jan S. SE-700
Tuttleman, Stanley C. SE-305, SE-700
Tuttleman, Steven M. SE-700
Twyman, Mark C., MBA. SE-515
Tyler, Fran Pemberton SE-642
Tyson, Janice Clemens SE-132

U

U'Prichard, Alissa SE-595
U'Prichard, David SE-595
Uffelman, Frederick, II CP-231
Ulsh, Keith A. CP-118
Unger, Freda SW-370
Updegrove, Andrew S. NE-144
Updegrove, John H. NE-086, NE-144
Updegrove, Ruby H. NE-144
Updegrove, Stephen. NE-144
Uplinger, Melvin. NW-003
Uram, Juliana SW-378
Urkiel, William. SE-336
Usher, Stephen E. SE-658
Usher, Thomas J. SW-371

V

Vail, Richard T. SW-342
Valcich, Marlene. SE-180
van Arkel, Gerald SE-282
Van Denbergh, Frederick A., Jr. . . . SE-107
Van Denbergh, Margaret Anne SE-107
Van Denbergh, Ross SE-107
Van Dusen, Albert C. SW-047
Van Dusen, Lewis H., Jr. SE-165
Van Dusen, Maria P.W. SE-165
Van Kirk, J. Robert SW-314
Van Roden, John, Jr. SE-070
Van Sant, Esther. SE-164
Vance, Charles R. SE-262
VanderVen, Karen SW-283
VanDine, Peter SE-097
Vanyo, Leo V. SW-197
Varenhorst, Ellen S. SE-150
Varet, Elizabeth R. SE-021
Varine, John A. SW-349
Varthas, Tessi SE-169
Vasinko, Carol SW-151
Vaughan, G. Tully SE-647
Vaux, Trina. SE-427
Veach, Lynn NE-024, NE-035, NE-054
Veloski, J. Jon SE-651

Venello, Theresa. SE-058
Venus, Karen SE-351
Verna, Anna C. SE-071
Vernon, Gwyn SE-005
Vernon, Thomas M. SE-391
Verplanck, Eva L. SE-125
Vicary, Cheryl G. NW-074
Vicary, Thomas C. NW-074
Vickers, H. Eugene. SE-026
Viener, George P. NE-026
Viener, Sue R. NE-026
Vilella-Velez, Frances SE-705
Villalpando, Kathy SW-397
Vinton, Brock SE-011
Vipond, Jonathan, III CP-073
Visser, Richard E. SW-071
Vitullo, Carmina V. SW-378
Vizza, Robert L. NW-003
Vochko, Paul R. SW-019
Vogel, Mrs. A. Whitten SE-199
Vogen, Robert SE-262
Vogt, Lorine E. SE-710
Vogt, William T. SE-710
Volk, James CP-019
Voorhees, G. Stephen. SE-451
Voorheis, Dale C. CP-195
Voss, John C. SE-541
Vowler, Robert C. CP-191

W

Waber, Harry SE-711
Wachs, David V. SE-712
Wachs, Ellis G. SE-713
Wachs, Judith SE-712
Wachs, Martin SE-712
Wachs, Michael SE-712
Wachs, Peggy B. SE-713
Wachs, Philip SE-712
Wachs, Rachel A. SE-712
Wackerman, Dorothy C. SE-589
Waggoner, Lynda S. SW-070
Wagman, Howard SE-715
Wagman, James. SE-715
Wagman, Joel SE-715
Wagman, Mary SE-715
Wagman, Nela SE-715
Wagman, Rita SE-715
Wagner, H.A. NE-113
Wagner, Harold A. NE-145
Wagner, Harold E. NE-145
Wagner, Jay R. NE-103
Wagner, Kristi NE-145
Wagner, Lawrence M. . . . SW-118, SW-119
    SW-120, SW-121, SW-122, SW-164
        SW-165, SW-166, SW-289, SW-337
            SW-338, SW-339, SW-340
Wagner, Marcia C. NE-145
Wagner, Robert L. NW-005
Wagner, Seymour C. SE-249
Wagner, Tracey NE-145
Wagner, William J. NW-056
Waldman, Bruce NE-146
Waldman, Herman B. NE-146
Waldman, Mark NE-146
Waldman, Rebecca Cooper. SE-634
Walizer, Grant W. NE-010
Walker, Charles Alan NW-075
Walker, Claire A. SW-283
Walker, Cuyler H. SE-515

Major Interest Codes Index
for all profiled foundations

MI-11   United Ways   MI-11

CP- 006, 008, 010, 014, 016, 017, 018, 019, 025, 026, 030, 035, 042, 044, 045, 046, 054, 057, 064, 069, 074, 075, 078, 083, 089, 093, 098, 101, 108, 109, 110, 118, 121, 122, 126, 135, 137, 138, 139, 140, 143, 150, 154, 157, 169, 174, 177, 180, 186, 189, 190, 191, 193, 194, 195, 196, 198, 206, 214, 218, 223, 225, 226, 228, 229

NE- 001, 003, 005, 006, 009, 010, 013, 015, 018, 019, 024, 025, 027, 033, 034, 035, 040, 044, 045, 047, 048, 050, 058, 068, 078, 084, 087, 088, 090, 092, 094, 097, 099, 104, 106, 107, 108, 114, 116, 118, 122, 125, 126, 127, 128, 129, 133, 134, 136, 140, 144, 145, 148, 153

NW- 004, 005, 008, 009, 010, 011, 013, 019, 020, 022, 024, 026, 028, 029, 031, 032, 040, 042, 045, 051, 053, 055, 057, 060, 061, 064, 065, 066, 068, 071, 072, 074, 076, 078

SE- 007, 021, 022, 030, 031, 034, 035, 040, 041, 044, 045, 046, 049, 052, 067, 119, 124, 125, 128, 129, 132, 134, 135, 136, 138, 140, 141, 142, 147, 165, 170, 173, 181, 184, 185, 186, 191, 192, 195, 204, 210, 211, 213, 224, 232, 238, 241, 259, 280, 289, 291, 295, 302, 304, 316, 317, 343, 354, 360, 383, 397, 400, 404, 407, 410, 415, 416, 426, 430, 431, 436, 439, 446, 452, 457, 476, 478, 479, 480, 487, 497, 500, 513, 517, 524, 526, 527, 544, 549, 554, 556, 557, 558, 565, 572, 575, 577, 578, 581, 589, 598, 599, 602, 609, 616, 620, 627, 633, 636, 645, 650, 656, 660, 670, 677, 680, 684, 694, 698, 706, 707, 719, 721, 724, 736, 738

SW- 002, 004, 005, 007, 010, 012, 018, 021, 024, 026, 039, 041, 046, 048, 049, 050, 052, 053, 061, 065, 066, 068, 078, 081, 086, 087, 089, 097, 104, 106, 109, 110, 113, 114, 124, 126, 127, 141, 145, 154, 155, 156, 158, 159, 160, 161, 164, 173, 174, 175, 180, 184, 186, 196, 198, 216, 218, 224, 226, 228, 233, 235, 237, 238, 239, 241, 243, 250, 251, 252, 254, 260, 262, 266, 275, 282, 285, 287, 294, 295, 301, 302, 306, 309, 314, 316, 317, 318, 319, 323, 327, 336, 343, 347, 350, 353, 354, 355, 356, 357, 371, 375, 376, 377, 380, 385, 397, 399, 400

MI-12   Child & Family Welfare   MI-12

CP- 002, 004, 007, 013, 014, 015, 016, 018, 019, 028, 032, 033, 034, 036, 038, 042, 043, 044, 045, 046, 047, 048, 049, 051, 053, 055, 056, 061, 062, 064, 067, 073, 075, 078, 079, 080, 082, 084, 095, 102, 103, 115, 117, 126, 130, 134, 135, 136, 137, 146, 147, 151, 153, 154, 159, 162, 164, 165, 168, 176, 177, 181, 184, 186, 191, 193, 194, 195, 198, 200, 208, 209, 214, 216, 221, 226, 228, 231

NE- 001, 003, 005, 006, 008, 010, 011, 012, 013, 014, 017, 024, 025, 027, 028, 029, 031, 032, 033, 035, 038, 042, 047, 048, 052, 053, 054, 057, 060, 064, 065, 068, 071, 073, 075, 076, 081, 083, 084, 085, 086, 089, 091, 092, 101, 103, 110, 111, 113, 114, 119, 128, 129, 133, 134, 135, 136, 137, 139, 140, 142, 143, 145, 146, 148, 153

NW- 001, 002, 005, 006, 009, 014, 018, 019, 030, 031, 032, 041, 042, 045, 047, 053, 055, 058, 059, 060, 064, 065, 066, 069, 070, 071, 074, 076, 079

SE- 001, 002, 010, 012, 020, 025, 030, 033, 035, 037, 039, 040, 042, 044, 045, 054, 055, 056, 057, 061, 064, 069, 071, 079, 080, 083, 087, 089, 090, 095, 098, 099, 104, 107, 108, 110, 112, 119, 120, 125, 127, 128, 129, 130, 131, 132, 134, 137, 138, 145, 146, 147, 150, 157, 160, 161, 167, 171, 176, 180, 181, 182, 187, 188, 195, 198, 199, 200, 205, 215, 218, 222, 224, 225, 230, 233, 234, 236, 238, 239, 242, 247, 248, 251, 255, 259, 266, 273, 286, 289, 290, 293, 296, 299, 302, 303, 305, 307, 310, 312, 315, 317, 319, 320, 323, 325, 327, 332, 333, 336, 337, 342, 347, 348, 350, 353, 355, 360, 363, 366, 368, 372, 373, 377, 379, 387, 389, 398, 399, 406, 414, 415, 417, 422, 425, 427, 428, 433, 434, 441, 442, 444, 446, 449, 457, 459, 462, 464, 468, 472, 480, 484, 490, 495, 496, 498, 505, 508, 511, 512, 513, 514, 515, 518, 520, 525, 527, 528, 535, 540, 541, 550, 557, 558, 559, 565, 570, 571, 572, 573, 575, 576, 581, 597, 600, 605, 606, 608, 609, 610, 614, 618, 623, 625, 628, 630, 631, 635, 640, 641, 642, 644, 645, 655, 657, 658, 659, 662, 664, 666, 670, 674, 675, 676, 682, 687, 690, 694, 701, 702, 705, 706, 713, 721, 722, 725, 728, 735, 737, 744, 745, 746, 750

SW- 002, 004, 008, 009, 023, 025, 032, 036, 039, 042, 044, 047, 049, 050, 054, 062, 065, 066, 070, 073, 077, 078, 080, 081, 082, 086, 087, 089, 090, 091, 092, 094, 096, 097, 100, 101, 107, 108, 110, 111, 112, 113, 114, 116, 118, 120, 122, 135, 136, 137, 141, 145, 153, 154, 155, 157, 158, 159, 160, 161, 162, 164, 165, 166, 167, 169, 172, 174, 175, 178, 181, 184, 186, 187, 189, 194, 196, 200, 202, 203, 204, 213, 215, 226, 227, 230, 232, 233, 237, 240, 243, 245, 247, 248, 252, 254, 257, 258, 261, 263, 264, 266, 269, 272, 274, 275, 279, 281, 282, 283, 284, 287, 293, 294, 295, 296, 299, 300, 301, 304, 305, 306, 308, 310, 311, 317, 327, 328, 334, 335, 336, 337, 338, 339, 341, 342, 343, 346, 348, 356, 364, 365, 366, 368, 371, 373, 377, 380, 383, 385, 386, 388, 389, 391

MI-13   Youth   MI-13

CP-.....002, 006, 007, 009, 010, 013, 014, 017, 018, 019, 021, 022, 025, 026, 030, 033, 034, 036, 038, 042, 043, 044, 045, 048, 053, 056, 057, 058, 062, 067, 069, 070, 073, 074, 075, 076, 077, 078, 079, 080, 081, 082, 083, 085, 086, 089, 091, 092, 093, 094, 098, 101, 102, 103, 108, 109, 110, 112, 114, 115, 117, 118, 119, 121, 122, 125, 126, 129, 130, 132, 134, 136, 137, 141, 145, 146, 147, 151, 152, 153, 155, 157, 158, 159, 161, 164, 165, 169, 172, 173, 175, 177, 180, 182, 184, 186, 187, 189, 190, 191, 193, 194, 195, 198, 199, 200, 204, 205, 206, 208, 209, 214, 215, 218, 223, 226, 228, 229, 231

NE-.....001, 003, 005, 006, 007, 008, 010, 012, 013, 014, 017, 018, 019, 023, 024, 025, 027, 028, 032, 033, 038, 042, 045, 050, 051, 052, 053, 057, 058, 060, 061, 063, 064, 066, 068, 069, 071, 072, 073, 075, 076, 078, 080, 081, 083, 085, 086, 089, 090, 091, 092, 097, 099, 105, 107, 110, 111, 114, 116, 119, 120, 121, 124, 125, 127, 129, 132, 133, 134, 135, 136, 138, 139, 140, 142, 145, 146, 148, 153, 155

NW-....004, 005, 006, 007, 008, 009, 011, 012, 014, 015, 018, 019, 020, 021, 022, 024, 025, 026, 029, 030, 031, 032, 033, 034, 035, 040, 041, 042, 044, 051, 052, 053, 055, 057, 058, 061, 064, 065, 067, 069, 070, 072, 073, 074, 075, 076, 077, 078, 079

SE- 001, 006, 012, 016, 020, 021, 022, 025, 028, 030, 034, 036, 044, 045, 053, 054, 055, 057, 065, 067, 075, 080, 084, 086, 090, 095, 099, 103, 107, 110, 115, 119, 124, 125, 127, 129, 130, 132, 134, 135, 142, 145, 148, 150, 152, 153, 154, 161, 167, 173, 180, 181, 182, 187, 188, 191, 197, 199, 200, 203, 204, 205, 207, 211, 212, 215, 223, 224, 227, 232, 233, 234, 236, 241, 242, 248, 251, 252, 255, 257, 274, 277, 282, 286, 289, 291, 295, 296, 301, 302, 304, 307, 312, 316, 317, 319, 320, 325, 327, 330, 331, 332, 333, 336, 337, 342, 350, 352, 360, 362, 372, 373, 379, 387, 389, 390, 397, 400, 401, 406, 414, 416, 422, 427, 428, 429, 431, 433, 434, 436, 446, 463, 464, 475, 476, 480, 485, 491, 505, 506, 507, 508, 513, 514, 515, 517, 518, 521, 528, 534, 535, 536, 537, 540, 544, 550, 554, 557, 568, 569, 570, 575, 576, 581, 585, 586, 593, 597, 598, 600, 606, 608, 609, 611, 613, 618, 621, 623, 626, 635, 640, 641, 642, 644, 645, 648, 657, 663, 667, 670, 679, 682, 684, 687, 692, 699, 701, 702, 705, 706, 717, 720, 724, 726, 728, 743, 744, 745, 747

SW-....004, 005, 006, 007, 009, 016, 019, 020, 022, 023, 029, 032, 035, 039, 041, 044, 046, 047, 052, 055, 061, 062, 065, 066, 070, 073, 074, 076, 077, 078, 080, 083, 086, 087, 091, 095, 096, 097, 104, 107, 110, 112, 113, 114, 116, 118, 120, 121, 122, 125, 127, 131, 136, 137, 141, 142, 145, 146, 152, 157, 158, 159, 160, 161, 162, 164, 168, 169, 170, 173, 174, 175, 180, 181, 182, 184, 186, 189, 193, 197, 198, 199, 200, 201, 202, 204, 205, 213, 214, 218, 226, 227, 231, 232, 233, 238, 240, 241, 242, 243, 245, 247, 250, 251, 252, 254, 258, 260, 261, 269, 274, 275, 277, 279, 281, 282, 283, 284, 285, 287, 291, 292, 293, 294, 295, 301, 303, 304, 307, 308, 310, 311, 314, 315, 316, 318, 321, 322, 323, 324, 326, 327, 328, 334, 335, 336, 337, 338, 340, 341, 342, 343, 344, 346, 347, 348, 353, 355, 356, 364, 365, 366, 371, 373, 377, 379, 380, 383, 385, 386, 387, 388, 389, 391, 397

MI-14   Disabled/Handicapped   MI-14

CP-.....006, 007, 009, 014, 019, 021, 025, 030, 033, 034, 036, 040, 043, 044, 045, 046, 053, 056, 061, 070, 073, 075, 076, 078, 079, 082, 083, 086, 089, 092, 095, 103, 108, 109, 111, 113, 115, 121, 122, 125, 126, 127, 128, 130, 137, 153, 154, 157, 159, 162, 164, 165, 177, 180, 184, 185, 186, 189, 193, 195, 198, 204, 206, 209, 210, 214, 215, 218, 221, 223, 229, 231

NE-.....005, 008, 009, 010, 012, 013, 014, 017, 020, 025, 027, 032, 038, 042, 044, 045, 052, 053, 057, 061, 064, 067, 073, 075, 076, 078, 081, 083, 093, 096, 102, 104, 109, 110, 111, 127, 128, 129, 134, 135, 136, 137, 139, 141, 142, 143, 146, 148, 152, 153

NW-....005, 006, 009, 019, 032, 034, 035, 042, 046, 047, 051, 052, 053, 058, 065, 069, 070, 074, 076, 079

SE- 001, 005, 020, 025, 030, 031, 039, 040, 044, 045, 054, 055, 065, 079, 080, 081, 086, 087, 090, 095, 107, 108, 111, 115, 117, 119, 120, 121, 124, 127, 129, 130, 131, 132, 134, 140, 142, 144, 145, 157, 161, 167, 168, 173, 180, 182, 188, 191, 199, 200, 205, 213, 215, 222, 224, 229, 233, 234, 236, 241, 246, 251, 255, 256, 266, 277, 282, 296, 300, 304, 307, 308, 317, 325, 327, 328, 330, 332, 333, 337, 340, 342, 343, 347, 350, 352, 357, 360, 365, 372, 374, 378, 388, 389, 390, 394, 401, 410, 413, 415, 422, 423, 425, 428, 431, 432, 433, 434, 442, 446, 456, 459, 461, 464, 469, 480, 484, 490, 491, 493, 505, 506, 513, 515, 517, 518, 524, 536, 540, 544, 545, 550, 561, 566, 569, 570, 571, 575, 576, 586, 589, 590, 596, 597, 600, 605, 606, 609, 617, 618, 619, 621, 623, 627, 628, 635, 640, 641, 645, 654, 655, 657, 663, 670, 674, 676, 681, 682, 684, 687, 690, 694, 701, 702, 706, 711, 712, 720, 725, 728, 730, 738, 745, 746

SW-....004, 007, 008, 012, 015, 023, 032, 033, 035, 039, 044, 045, 047, 055, 062, 066, 069, 070, 073, 077, 078, 080, 082, 087, 097, 100, 107, 110, 113, 116, 117, 118, 120, 122, 136, 137, 143, 145, 153, 158, 159, 161, 164, 165, 168, 169, 170, 172, 173, 174, 175, 178, 184, 186, 187, 189, 195, 197, 202, 203, 204, 206, 213, 214, 225, 226, 227, 228, 230, 231, 232, 233, 234, 237, 238, 240, 241, 243, 247, 251, 254, 258, 260, 261, 266, 267, 269, 273, 275, 277, 280, 281, 283, 284, 285, 287, 289, 291, 295, 299, 301, 305, 308, 310, 311, 314, 315, 316, 321, 322, 323, 327, 328, 335, 336, 338, 342, 343, 345, 346, 350, 351, 353, 354, 356, 364, 366, 368, 371, 373, 378, 380, 381, 385, 391, 393

MI-15   Elderly/Senior Citizens   MI-15

CP-.....034, 046, 067, 073, 076, 080, 102, 107, 111, 115, 135, 157, 186, 193, 194, 209, 214, 223, 228, 231

NE-.....018, 032, 083, 119, 037, 065

SE- 001, 025, 054, 081, 099, 142, 145, 180, 182, 215, 224, 225, 236, 251, 255, 283, 312, 325, 337, 370, 372, 373, 379, 427, 464, 480, 505, 513, 515, 570, 586, 600, 617, 618, 623, 635, 639, 640, 702, 705, 743, 745

SW-....004, 032, 042, 062, 097, 107, 114, 145, 159, 160, 164, 186, 190, 243, 260, 267, 284, 288, 340, 342, 346, 364, 371, 373, 385

MI-16   Minorities/Race Relations   MI-16

CP-.....034, 046, 067, 073, 076, 080, 102, 107, 111, 115, 135, 157, 186, 193, 194, 209, 214, 223, 228, 231

NE-.....018, 032, 083, 119

NW-....037, 065

SE- 001, 025, 054, 081, 099, 142, 145, 180, 182, 215, 224, 225, 236, 251, 255, 283, 312, 325, 337, 370, 372, 373, 379, 427, 464, 480, 505, 513, 515, 570, 586, 600, 617, 618, 623, 635, 639, 640, 702, 705, 743, 745

SW-....004, 032, 042, 062, 097, 107, 114, 145, 159, 160, 164, 186, 190, 243, 260, 267, 284, 288, 340, 342, 346, 364, 371, 373, 385

MI-17   Women/Girls   MI-17

CP-.....013, 015, 018, 026, 027, 037, 038, 067, 068, 073, 077, 079, 080, 091, 102, 103, 115, 137, 147, 151, 152, 157, 159, 162, 186, 210, 221, 226, 231

NE-.....010, 012, 017, 024, 025, 027, 032, 045, 057, 068, 072, 086, 090, 111, 117, 129, 133, 134, 135, 142, 146

NW-....019, 040, 051, 067, 070, 074

SE- 001, 030, 054, 055, 069, 081, 086, 095, 099, 107, 110, 111, 119, 120, 125, 130, 145, 150, 167, 180, 181, 182, 199, 200, 201, 202, 215, 216, 222, 224, 225, 236, 250, 251, 255, 257, 266, 269, 276, 277, 282, 289, 296, 302, 320, 323, 325, 332, 337, 343, 370, 372, 400, 401, 403, 414, 420, 422, 429, 443, 446, 464, 480, 484, 485, 505, 513, 515, 518, 525, 539, 540, 543, 547, 561, 565, 570, 593, 597, 603, 610, 618, 628, 629, 635, 640, 642, 663, 676, 682, 687, 697, 702, 705, 706, 711, 725, 745, 747

SW-....004, 020, 022, 031, 032, 033, 042, 044, 047, 053, 062, 079, 097, 107, 108, 113, 114, 116, 117, 118, 120, 122, 137, 143, 145, 146, 153, 158, 159, 160, 161, 162, 165, 170, 173, 186, 203, 205, 226, 227, 230, 243, 247, 252, 258, 260, 279, 284, 287, 296, 302, 304, 309, 315, 316, 321, 322, 327, 328, 339, 342, 353, 356, 364, 366, 367, 371, 373, 375, 379, 388, 390, 397

MI-18   Family Planning/Adoption   MI-18

CP-.....011, 018, 021, 022, 043, 053, 055, 058, 067, 068, 075, 076, 077, 133, 134, 152, 161, 164, 170, 186, 194, 228, 231

NE-.....010, 025, 032, 052, 084, 086, 111, 116, 125, 136, 146

NW-....011, 076

SE- 001, 008, 015, 030, 054, 081, 086, 088, 099, 107, 110, 122, 130, 140, 153, 178, 180, 182, 187, 200, 215, 236, 251, 277, 289, 302, 304, 312, 317, 320, 327, 329, 332, 333, 337, 342, 368, 372, 379, 381, 396, 400, 411, 416, 429, 432, 433, 440, 464, 486, 505, 506, 509, 513, 514, 515, 520, 527, 553, 559, 561, 569, 570, 579, 581, 590, 600, 620, 635, 666, 671, 680, 690, 697, 699, 702, 705, 709, 724, 745, 747

SW-....062, 067, 077, 111, 124, 126, 143, 145, 151, 166, 174, 186, 196, 203, 205, 226, 243, 254, 259, 283, 284, 296, 328, 347, 364, 373, 386, 388, 389, 390

MI-19   Alcohol/Drug Abuse   MI-19

CP-.....011, 013, 016, 038, 039, 058, 061, 074, 091, 101, 102, 129, 159, 193, 194, 209, 210, 228

NE-.....017, 018, 038, 086, 091, 139

NW-....004, 032, 059, 070

SE- 180, 199, 236, 251, 255, 259, 325, 347, 372, 443, 464, 480, 513, 515, 530, 570, 618, 623, 642, 648, 687, 702, 723, 745

SW-....004, 019, 032, 137, 153, 159, 166, 169, 173, 186, 189, 214, 243, 261, 284, 364

MI-20 Crime/Justice MI-20

CP- 014, 033, 044, 184

NE- 027, 129, 133

NW- 004, 009, 018, 019, 032

SE- 064, 081, 104, 130, 180, 186, 215, 251, 277, 283, 305, 333, 337, 369, 372, 402, 405, 474, 505, 515, 533, 585, 618, 663, 682, 697, 702, 705, 745, 746

SW- 032, 070, 166, 227, 240, 245, 284, 304, 322, 364

MI-21 Community Service Clubs MI-21

CP- 011, 057, 121, 146, 182, 184, 200, 208, 229

NE- 060, 135, 136, 153

NW- 018, 025, 051, 066, 067, 072

SE- 057, 080, 347, 464, 530, 531, 556, 598, 672, 682

SW- 063, 069, 070, 078, 087, 096, 199, 229, 344

MI-22 Religion-related Agencies/Services MI-22

CP- 006, 007, 011, 014, 016, 017, 021, 025, 027, 030, 034, 037, 038, 040, 041, 042, 043, 044, 047, 051, 053, 056, 058, 059, 061, 064, 067, 068, 070, 071, 072, 073, 075, 077, 080, 083, 086, 089, 090, 091, 095, 101, 102, 103, 107, 109, 110, 111, 113, 114, 120, 125, 130, 133, 135, 136, 137, 145, 146, 150, 152, 153, 157, 162, 166, 169, 170, 172, 173, 174, 177, 180, 181, 184, 185, 189, 190, 191, 193, 194, 196, 202, 209, 212, 215, 216, 218, 226, 231

NE- 006, 008, 012, 013, 014, 015, 021, 022, 024, 025, 026, 027, 032, 033, 034, 037, 038, 041, 044, 045, 048, 052, 057, 062, 066, 068, 071, 073, 076, 077, 078, 080, 081, 084, 085, 086, 087, 088, 090, 092, 093, 097, 099, 100, 101, 102, 103, 104, 106, 109, 111, 117, 119, 120, 121, 123, 124, 127, 129, 130, 131, 133, 135, 136, 137, 138, 140, 141, 142, 144, 146, 149, 150, 153, 154, 155

NW- 008, 009, 010, 014, 019, 022, 028, 032, 034, 035, 041, 042, 046, 048, 049, 051, 053, 055, 058, 061, 064, 065, 067, 071, 072, 076, 077, 078

SE- 001, 006, 007, 009, 013, 016, 022, 024, 027, 030, 031, 032, 033, 035, 036, 037, 043, 045, 046, 050, 054, 055, 057, 060, 062, 065, 067, 068, 069, 070, 071, 072, 073, 075, 077, 079, 080, 082, 083, 085, 087, 090, 095, 102, 103, 105, 107, 108, 109, 112, 113, 115, 116, 117, 118, 119, 121, 122, 124, 125, 127, 128, 130, 131, 132, 134, 135, 136, 137, 140, 143, 145, 146, 147, 148, 150, 152, 153, 154, 155, 157, 160, 166, 167, 170, 171, 174, 177, 178, 179, 180, 182, 184, 185, 186, 187, 191, 192, 193, 194, 195, 197, 198, 199, 201, 202, 203, 204, 205, 208, 210, 211, 212, 213, 217, 220, 222, 224, 225, 227, 228, 229, 233, 234, 238, 239, 241, 242, 243, 247, 251, 252, 257, 258, 259, 261, 262, 263, 264, 265, 266, 267, 268, 269, 272, 273, 275, 276, 277, 279, 280, 281, 282, 284, 285, 286, 292, 293, 295, 296, 298, 302, 303, 307, 310, 312, 313, 314, 316, 317, 318, 319, 320, 321, 325, 327, 329, 332, 333, 335, 338, 342, 343, 348, 351, 352, 353, 354, 356, 357, 359, 360, 361, 363, 365, 366, 367, 368, 372, 374, 375, 380, 381, 383, 384, 385, 386, 387, 388, 390, 393, 396, 397, 398, 399, 402, 406, 407, 408, 409, 410, 411, 412, 416, 418, 419, 422, 423, 426, 427, 428, 430, 433, 436, 437, 438, 441, 442, 445, 449, 452, 453, 458, 464, 466, 467, 473, 476, 478, 480, 481, 483, 485, 489, 490, 491, 496, 497, 499, 500, 503, 504, 506, 509, 511, 512, 513, 515, 517, 518, 521, 522, 523, 526, 527, 528, 529, 538, 541, 542, 543, 546, 548, 549, 550, 553, 554, 556, 557, 558, 559, 563, 564, 565, 569, 570, 571, 572, 574, 575, 576, 577, 578, 579, 581, 582, 583, 584, 585, 588, 590, 591, 596, 597, 599, 600, 602, 604, 605, 606, 608, 609, 610, 612, 615, 616, 618, 620, 622, 623, 625, 628, 629, 630, 631, 633, 634, 635, 636, 637, 638, 640, 641, 643, 645, 650, 651, 655, 656, 657, 659, 660, 662, 663, 665, 667, 668, 670, 674, 676, 677, 680, 681, 682, 683, 684, 686, 689, 693, 694, 696, 697, 698, 699, 700, 702, 707, 711, 712, 713, 715, 719, 721, 725, 730, 732, 736, 737, 738, 744, 745, 746, 747, 749, 750

SW- 006, 007, 016, 020, 022, 023, 024, 025, 026, 027, 028, 032, 035, 037, 038, 039, 041, 044, 045, 047, 048, 054, 060, 062, 065, 070, 077, 078, 080, 083, 087, 088, 089, 090, 092, 093, 094, 097, 098, 101, 102, 104, 105, 110, 111, 112, 113, 114, 115, 116, 119, 122, 123, 124, 131, 133, 135, 137, 141, 143, 145, 146, 148, 149, 150, 151, 152, 153, 154, 155, 157, 161, 164, 169, 170, 173, 174, 177, 181, 182, 183, 184, 185, 186, 189, 191, 197, 202, 203, 206, 209, 210, 212, 214, 216, 223, 225, 226, 227, 230, 231, 232, 233, 234, 237, 239, 240, 243, 245, 246, 247, 248, 250, 251, 252, 254, 255, 257, 258, 260, 261, 262, 268, 269, 270, 272, 275, 276, 278, 279, 281, 283, 284, 285, 290, 291, 292, 294, 300, 301, 303, 304, 306, 308, 309, 314, 315, 316, 317, 319, 320, 321, 322, 323, 328, 330, 331, 332, 333, 334, 338, 341, 342, 346, 347, 348, 350, 351, 352, 354, 356, 357, 360, 366, 369, 370, 371, 373, 374, 375, 379, 380, 381, 382, 384, 385, 389, 390, 391, 393, 396, 399, 400

MI-23   Direct Assistance to Needy Individuals   MI-23

CP-.....077, 079, 141, 210

NE-.....004, 020, 036, 049, 114

NW-....006, 065

SE-.....039, 071, 240, 243, 297, 347, 392, 451, 464, 498, 529, 587, 606, 647, 725

SW-....031, 056, 080, 091, 138, 185, 352

MI-24   Neighborhood Organizations   MI-24

CP-.....011, 231

NE-.....032, 129, 133, 147

SE-.....145, 182, 225, 242, 479, 480, 505, 515, 540, 635, 642, 702, 745

SW-....032, 047, 086, 240, 241, 260, 261, 287, 364

MI-25   Housing/Homeless Programs   MI-25

CP-.....002, 010, 013, 014, 015, 018, 019, 021, 025, 030, 033, 034, 038, 042, 045, 046, 056, 058, 061, 068, 072, 073, 077, 078, 080, 083, 095, 101, 102, 103, 107, 108, 109, 110, 115, 119, 134, 135, 136, 137, 146, 153, 157, 162, 164, 180, 181, 184, 186, 189, 193, 194, 198, 204, 209, 212, 216, 221, 223, 226

NE-.....017, 023, 025, 027, 032, 038, 042, 052, 057, 061, 062, 073, 075, 092, 102, 112, 116, 119, 129, 133, 134, 142

NW-....004, 005, 010, 032, 035, 051, 059, 067, 076, 078

SE-.....001, 011, 012, 025, 042, 045, 053, 054, 055, 057, 070, 079, 083, 090, 095, 098, 103, 107, 110, 112, 119, 122, 125, 141, 142, 145, 167, 170, 180, 182, 187, 197, 199, 200, 204, 212, 215, 222, 224, 225, 230, 233, 236, 243, 251, 255, 257, 266, 284, 286, 289, 296, 303, 304, 307, 310, 312, 317, 320, 325, 327, 333, 334, 335, 337, 342, 343, 350, 361, 368, 372, 379, 380, 406, 413, 417, 422, 423, 429, 431, 446, 462, 464, 468, 476, 484, 491, 497, 505, 513, 514, 515, 517, 522, 540, 543, 550, 565, 570, 571, 576, 582, 586, 589, 595, 596, 597, 600, 603, 608, 614, 628, 630, 631, 635, 640, 641, 642, 651, 663, 667, 669, 670, 676, 687, 689, 697, 698, 701, 702, 705, 706, 711, 713, 715, 722, 724, 725, 745

SW-....002, 006, 008, 016, 021, 024, 032, 039, 042, 047, 062, 066, 069, 070, 077, 080, 081, 086, 087, 090, 092, 103, 106, 110, 114, 115, 119, 122, 131, 137, 151, 155, 156, 157, 161, 166, 173, 174, 177, 184, 197, 203, 226, 227, 234, 240, 241, 243, 247, 254, 258, 260, 261, 267, 269, 274, 279, 281, 282, 284, 287, 291, 292, 295, 303, 305, 315, 316, 318, 321, 328, 335, 336, 337, 338, 339, 346, 350, 364, 371, 385, 391

MI-29   Other Human Services   MI-29

CP-.....002, 010, 011, 013, 014, 015, 018, 025, 033, 038, 041, 042, 043, 044, 045, 053, 056, 062, 067, 069, 073, 078, 083, 091, 092, 094, 095, 102, 103, 113, 125, 126, 130, 133, 135, 137, 146, 147, 153, 157, 164, 166, 172, 176, 177, 181, 184, 186, 189, 193, 194, 195, 198, 199, 204, 209, 211, 214, 223, 226, 228, 229, 231

NE-.....001, 008, 009, 010, 012, 013, 017, 019, 027, 029, 032, 033, 034, 042, 045, 046, 048, 050, 052, 060, 066, 071, 076, 080, 086, 091, 092, 094, 097, 104, 112, 116, 119, 125, 129, 133, 134, 135, 136, 140, 142, 143, 144, 146

NW-....002, 006, 009, 017, 019, 022, 026, 031, 032, 038, 040, 044, 046, 052, 053, 058, 059, 066, 071, 072, 073, 074, 076, 079

SE-.....001, 012, 024, 025, 033, 039, 045, 052, 053, 054, 055, 085, 095, 098, 103, 110, 115, 120, 125, 127, 129, 130, 140, 141, 142, 145, 150, 152, 163, 167, 173, 180, 193, 199, 200, 201, 206, 215, 225, 228, 250, 251, 252, 255, 266, 274, 278, 282, 283, 289, 294, 296, 302, 310, 312, 317, 320, 322, 325, 327, 328, 332, 333, 337, 342, 347, 350, 362, 373, 387, 390, 396, 399, 405, 410, 411, 425, 429, 444, 446, 462, 464, 474, 476, 479, 500, 505, 506, 513, 514, 515, 518, 523, 527, 536, 540, 541, 543, 557, 558, 565, 576, 578, 582, 586, 589, 608, 618, 632, 635, 638, 640, 663, 665, 678, 680, 682, 687, 689, 695, 697, 698, 702, 706, 717, 724, 733, 745, 747

SW-....004, 006, 007, 011, 013, 029, 032, 039, 060, 062, 065, 066, 069, 070, 072, 078, 080, 086, 087, 088, 090, 091, 095, 097, 100, 104, 107, 110, 113, 131, 137, 145, 146, 151, 153, 155, 158, 159, 160, 161, 164, 169, 173, 174, 175, 178, 180, 181, 182, 184, 186, 204, 205, 214, 227, 230, 233, 238, 240, 242, 243, 245, 247, 248, 250, 252, 254, 258, 260, 268, 272, 273, 275, 281, 282, 284, 287, 299, 301, 304, 305, 308, 311, 316, 318, 319, 322, 328, 334, 335, 340, 346, 353, 354, 357, 364, 373, 378, 380, 386, 387, 390, 397

MI-31   Hospitals/Medical Centers   MI-31

CP- 005, 007, 012, 015, 017, 019, 021, 028, 029, 030, 032, 035, 037, 038, 040, 043, 045, 048, 053, 056, 057, 065, 068, 070, 074, 076, 077, 078, 080, 084, 086, 093, 099, 101, 103, 111, 112, 113, 115, 116, 118, 125, 126, 128, 130, 132, 135, 139, 146, 147, 159, 161, 164, 169, 172, 174, 180, 189, 193, 194, 196, 206, 210, 216, 221, 223, 224, 226, 229

NE- 003, 005, 008, 009, 014, 017, 018, 019, 024, 030, 038, 044, 045, 050, 051, 058, 059, 060, 062, 064, 066, 067, 071, 073, 078, 081, 084, 086, 093, 101, 102, 103, 109, 110, 112, 113, 116, 117, 118, 119, 124, 125, 128, 131, 133, 134, 136, 138, 141, 145, 146, 148, 149, 151, 152, 153

NW- 004, 006, 009, 011, 012, 015, 018, 019, 021, 022, 023, 024, 026, 027, 030, 031, 034, 035, 037, 040, 044, 046, 051, 052, 053, 056, 057, 060, 066, 067, 070, 071, 072, 074, 078, 079

SE- 001, 013, 021, 022, 024, 025, 027, 028, 030, 032, 033, 036, 041, 043, 045, 052, 054, 055, 061, 062, 064, 066, 067, 072, 075, 076, 083, 084, 085, 087, 094, 096, 098, 102, 103, 107, 115, 116, 119, 121, 123, 124, 129, 130, 132, 133, 137, 138, 140, 144, 145, 146, 150, 152, 153, 157, 167, 168, 171, 177, 178, 183, 187, 188, 190, 191, 192, 194, 195, 198, 201, 202, 205, 207, 212, 222, 223, 224, 235, 236, 238, 242, 243, 244, 247, 248, 251, 255, 257, 258, 266, 272, 273, 280, 284, 287, 290, 291, 293, 295, 296, 300, 301, 302, 304, 312, 314, 315, 325, 327, 332, 333, 337, 341, 342, 343, 345, 346, 351, 352, 360, 362, 365, 371, 375, 380, 383, 388, 391, 400, 407, 408, 410, 413, 416, 418, 419, 420, 424, 425, 429, 430, 431, 432, 433, 440, 445, 446, 449, 457, 459, 464, 469, 470, 472, 474, 475, 476, 478, 489, 490, 493, 495, 497, 499, 500, 506, 508, 509, 510, 513, 514, 516, 517, 518, 524, 531, 539, 540, 541, 544, 547, 549, 553, 554, 557, 558, 565, 571, 574, 575, 577, 585, 589, 590, 591, 593, 594, 605, 621, 632, 636, 639, 640, 641, 645, 648, 654, 655, 659, 660, 661, 663, 665, 674, 679, 680, 681, 684, 685, 690, 694, 696, 697, 698, 699, 700, 701, 710, 711, 713, 718, 719, 721, 726, 737, 738, 744, 748, 749

SW- 004, 005, 006, 007, 009, 012, 020, 026, 030, 032, 034, 041, 044, 045, 053, 055, 059, 060, 062, 063, 065, 066, 070, 073, 077, 079, 080, 085, 087, 089, 090, 091, 092, 095, 096, 097, 100, 106, 107, 116, 118, 119, 121, 122, 124, 126, 137, 139, 159, 160, 161, 163, 165, 166, 167, 169, 170, 173, 174, 175, 176, 180, 181, 184, 186, 195, 196, 198, 199, 202, 204, 207, 211, 214, 215, 216, 217, 227, 229, 230, 232, 233, 234, 235, 241, 243, 244, 247, 250, 251, 258, 259, 260, 263, 265, 267, 269, 272, 275, 276, 279, 280, 281, 282, 287, 289, 291, 295, 300, 301, 305, 309, 310, 313, 314, 316, 317, 318, 321, 323, 325, 327, 328, 333, 338, 339, 342, 343, 344, 347, 348, 351, 353, 356, 366, 368, 371, 372, 379, 380, 383, 385, 387, 390, 392, 398, 399

MI-32   Medical Research   MI-32

CP- 002, 005, 011, 012, 013, 021, 029, 030, 032, 045, 062, 065, 072, 076, 078, 082, 089, 101, 103, 107, 110, 116, 118, 119, 127, 128, 129, 131, 135, 138, 146, 154, 162, 163, 174, 177, 189, 191, 193, 194, 196, 203, 204, 206, 209

NE- 005, 006, 019, 034, 042, 045, 064, 066, 067, 088, 092, 094, 097, 099, 101, 102, 106, 113, 117, 129, 131, 133, 138, 143, 146, 148, 152, 153

NW- 008, 009, 010, 013, 019, 021, 034, 036, 042, 044, 058, 067, 070, 074, 076, 078

SE- 005, 006, 009, 013, 023, 025, 028, 031, 032, 035, 036, 037, 046, 049, 054, 055, 057, 061, 065, 066, 067, 070, 074, 084, 086, 090, 096, 102, 103, 107, 112, 117, 119, 121, 124, 129, 131, 133, 134, 137, 150, 156, 157, 160, 166, 171, 173, 176, 183, 185, 187, 190, 191, 192, 194, 200, 203, 206, 210, 211, 218, 222, 227, 229, 233, 234, 236, 237, 238, 241, 242, 244, 248, 252, 258, 261, 264, 266, 273, 275, 277, 280, 281, 288, 289, 294, 296, 301, 302, 307, 314, 318, 323, 327, 331, 336, 338, 342, 343, 348, 350, 358, 363, 371, 375, 376, 377, 378, 379, 381, 383, 386, 388, 390, 393, 407, 412, 415, 419, 420, 421, 425, 428, 429, 432, 433, 434, 437, 440, 441, 443, 444, 446, 448, 453, 457, 462, 477, 484, 493, 495, 496, 497, 506, 508, 509, 513, 516, 517, 521, 523, 524, 526, 528, 542, 544, 545, 549, 551, 556, 557, 558, 561, 562, 565, 568, 575, 584, 586, 589, 590, 597, 602, 605, 608, 621, 627, 628, 630, 631, 632, 634, 641, 642, 645, 648, 655, 660, 665, 666, 667, 668, 669, 670, 671, 676, 677, 679, 680, 681, 684, 687, 694, 700, 701, 706, 712, 715, 721, 722, 724, 737, 738, 742, 744, 746, 748, 750

SW- 002, 003, 004, 008, 012, 016, 019, 026, 034, 036, 041, 043, 044, 052, 055, 059, 062, 063, 065, 066, 069, 073, 077, 080, 081, 085, 091, 092, 096, 104, 107, 110, 118, 119, 120, 121, 124, 125, 137, 140, 141, 147, 152, 158, 159, 163, 165, 166, 167, 168, 169, 175, 177, 180, 181, 184, 186, 187, 196, 197, 202, 207, 216, 220, 223, 226, 227, 229, 231, 232, 240, 241, 245, 250, 251, 252, 253, 257, 259, 260, 261, 262, 263, 265, 267, 268, 269, 273, 275, 276, 280, 285, 287, 289, 300, 301, 303, 304, 305, 311, 314, 316, 318, 321, 323, 327, 328, 335, 336, 338, 339, 341, 342, 347, 348, 350, 353, 354, 357, 366, 371, 373, 374, 377, 382, 383, 384, 393, 394, 397, 400

MI-33   Mental Health   MI-33

CP- 045, 086, 091, 115, 164, 194, 198, 211, 213, 214

NE- 010, 017, 020, 081, 129

NW- 014, 067, 070

SE- 036, 070, 107, 127, 131, 236, 255, 277, 301, 325, 337, 342, 365, 372, 464, 501, 515, 541, 553, 562, 663, 701, 712, 723, 743

SW- 032, 061, 107, 143, 145, 153, 158, 172, 186, 189, 240, 275, 284, 319, 356, 368

MI-34 Medical Education MI-34

MI-35 Public Health MI-35

MI-39 Other Health MI-39

MI-41 Primary/Secondary Education MI-41

Continuation of MI-41, Primary/Secondary Education

SE- 506, 507, 513, 515, 518, 522, 525, 527, 528, 530, 531, 535, 536, 537, 538, 539, 540, 541, 550, 552, 553, 554, 555, 556, 561, 564, 565, 569, 570, 571, 578, 581, 582, 585, 586, 589, 592, 593, 596, 598, 599, 600, 603, 607, 608, 609, 611, 613, 614, 615, 616, 618, 620, 621, 623, 625, 626, 627, 630, 631, 635, 637, 640, 641, 642, 644, 645, 646, 648, 649, 650, 655, 656, 658, 660, 662, 663, 666, 667, 669, 670, 672, 675, 676, 677, 678, 681, 682, 684, 689, 690, 694, 696, 698, 699, 700, 702, 706, 707, 712, 714, 716, 717, 719, 721, 727, 728, 729, 733, 736, 737, 742, 743, 745, 750

SW- 001, 006, 007, 009, 011, 012, 014, 016, 018, 020, 021, 022, 023, 024, 025, 026, 033, 034, 039, 040, 041, 042, 044, 047, 048, 049, 050, 053, 055, 060, 062, 063, 065, 066, 067, 068, 070, 072, 073, 075, 077, 080, 081, 082, 085, 086, 087, 088, 090, 091, 094, 095, 096, 097, 099, 102, 104, 110, 114, 115, 118, 119, 120, 121, 122, 124, 125, 128, 131, 136, 137, 141, 142, 143, 145, 154, 155, 156, 157, 159, 160, 161, 164, 165, 166, 167, 168, 169, 170, 171, 172, 173, 174, 175, 176, 179, 180, 181, 183, 184, 187, 189, 191, 192, 193, 195, 196, 197, 202, 204, 205, 211, 212, 214, 215, 216, 222, 224, 225, 227, 230, 231, 232, 233, 234, 238, 239, 240, 242, 243, 248, 250, 251, 253, 254, 256, 259, 260, 261, 262, 269, 271, 272, 274, 277, 279, 281, 283, 284, 287, 289, 290, 291, 292, 294, 295, 297, 298, 299, 303, 304, 305, 308, 309, 311, 314, 315, 316, 317, 321, 322, 323, 326, 327, 329, 330, 334, 335, 336, 337, 338, 339, 340, 342, 343, 345, 346, 347, 348, 349, 353, 354, 356, 357, 359, 366, 368, 371, 373, 375, 376, 377, 378, 379, 380, 381, 385, 390, 391, 392, 393, 396, 397, 399, 400

MI-42   Colleges/Universities   MI-42

CP- 004, 010, 014, 015, 016, 017, 018, 020, 025, 030, 035, 038, 040, 042, 045, 046, 047, 048, 054, 056, 064, 067, 069, 070, 073, 074, 075, 076, 077, 078, 080, 083, 091, 092, 093, 098, 101, 102, 103, 107, 109, 111, 113, 114, 118, 122, 125, 126, 128, 132, 134, 135, 136, 138, 139, 140, 141, 143, 145, 146, 147, 148, 150, 152, 154, 158, 160, 161, 165, 166, 169, 171, 174, 175, 176, 179, 180, 186, 189, 190, 193, 194, 198, 200, 206, 213, 214, 216, 221, 222, 223, 224, 225, 226, 227, 228, 229

NE- 002, 003, 005, 006, 007, 008, 011, 013, 015, 016, 018, 019, 021, 024, 027, 030, 032, 033, 035, 038, 040, 042, 045, 046, 047, 048, 050, 052, 053, 054, 055, 057, 058, 061, 062, 063, 065, 066, 072, 075, 078, 080, 083, 085, 086, 088, 089, 090, 092, 094, 095, 096, 097, 099, 102, 103, 104, 105, 106, 107, 108, 109, 110, 111, 112, 116, 118, 119, 121, 123, 124, 125, 126, 127, 128, 129, 133, 134, 140, 141, 142, 144, 145, 146, 149, 151, 152, 155, 001

NW- 004, 006, 007, 009, 010, 012, 013, 014, 019, 020, 021, 026, 027, 029, 032, 034, 035, 036, 039, 040, 043, 044, 046, 048, 049, 051, 052, 053, 056, 057, 058, 060, 061, 062, 064, 072, 078

SE- 006, 012, 014, 020, 021, 022, 024, 025, 027, 028, 030, 031, 032, 034, 035, 036, 038, 041, 043, 045, 046, 048, 049, 054, 055, 059, 060, 062, 068, 072, 073, 075, 076, 084, 085, 087, 089, 093, 094, 095, 103, 106, 107, 110, 113, 114, 115, 116, 117, 119, 120, 123, 125, 128, 129, 130, 132, 134, 135, 136, 138, 139, 140, 141, 142, 144, 145, 148, 152, 153, 154, 157, 159, 160, 161, 163, 165, 171, 173, 175, 181, 183, 184, 185, 186, 188, 191, 195, 197, 201, 204, 205, 207, 210, 218, 219, 220, 224, 227, 228, 234, 235, 236, 238, 241, 245, 247, 248, 250, 252, 253, 258, 259, 260, 265, 269, 272, 273, 276, 277, 278, 285, 286, 287, 289, 290, 293, 296, 301, 302, 307, 309, 310, 311, 314, 315, 316, 321, 322, 323, 326, 330, 331, 332, 333, 337, 338, 339, 343, 345, 346, 348, 350, 352, 354, 360, 362, 364, 367, 368, 370, 373, 379, 380, 381, 382, 387, 390, 394, 395, 396, 397, 398, 399, 402, 410, 412, 416, 417, 420, 421, 425, 426, 427, 429, 431, 432, 433, 434, 436, 439, 441, 442, 443, 444, 445, 446, 447, 448, 450, 454, 457, 458, 459, 464, 465, 469, 470, 472, 473, 475, 478, 480, 481, 482, 485, 490, 491, 496, 497, 498, 499, 500, 501, 505, 507, 513, 514, 517, 522, 523, 527, 528, 531, 532, 537, 539, 540, 541, 544, 545, 546, 548, 553, 554, 556, 557, 565, 566, 567, 568, 569, 571, 572, 573, 575, 577, 578, 581, 586, 590, 592, 594, 597, 602, 612, 613, 616, 620, 621, 623, 625, 626, 629, 632, 638, 639, 640, 641, 644, 645, 648, 650, 655, 656, 658, 659, 660, 662, 664, 665, 666, 667, 669, 670, 676, 678, 680, 683, 684, 686, 690, 692, 694, 696, 697, 698, 699, 706, 710, 713, 716, 719, 720, 721, 722, 724, 726, 728, 729, 731, 732, 733, 735, 739, 740, 741, 742, 744, 749, 750

SW- 001, 004, 005, 006, 007, 012, 013, 016, 018, 019, 020, 021, 023, 024, 026, 030, 033, 039, 040, 043, 044, 046, 047, 049, 050, 052, 053, 055, 057, 060, 061, 062, 066, 068, 073, 074, 077, 078, 079, 080, 081, 082, 083, 087, 088, 090, 092, 094, 095, 097, 099, 102, 103, 104, 106, 107, 108, 109, 110, 111, 116, 118, 119, 124, 128, 130, 133, 137, 139, 140, 145, 149, 154, 156, 157, 158, 159, 160, 161, 164, 165, 168, 169, 170, 173, 175, 179, 180, 181, 184, 187, 188, 196, 197, 198, 205, 213, 216, 222, 224, 226, 227, 228, 230, 231, 232, 233, 235, 238, 239, 240, 241, 242, 243, 246, 248, 249, 250, 251, 252, 256, 259, 260, 261, 263, 265, 269, 271, 272, 275, 276, 277, 282, 284, 285, 287, 291, 292, 293, 294, 295, 297, 299, 300, 301, 302, 303, 306, 307, 308, 309, 310, 311, 312, 314, 316, 317, 318, 321, 323, 327, 328, 329, 330, 331, 332, 333, 336, 341, 342, 343, 345, 347, 349, 351, 353, 354, 355, 356, 357, 358, 359, 366, 371, 372, 373, 375, 377, 378, 379, 380, 381, 386, 387, 389, 390, 391, 394, 396, 400

MI-43   Scholarships/Fellowships   MI-43

CP- 001, 003, 005, 010, 014, 023, 024, 025, 036, 041, 045, 047, 052, 057, 061, 062, 063, 070, 073, 076, 080, 082, 088, 091, 096, 100, 111, 115, 121, 123, 125, 142, 145, 146, 147, 148, 152, 153, 167, 178, 179, 183, 184, 187, 188, 189, 192, 193, 197, 201, 204, 207, 214, 216, 217, 220, 221, 222, 229, 230

NE- 002, 005, 011, 017, 031, 033, 042, 052, 053, 057, 062, 070, 074, 075, 079, 082, 086, 089, 091, 107, 115, 116, 132, 139, 141, 142, 147, 148, 155

NW- 004, 007, 009, 011, 014, 016, 017, 022, 023, 027, 040, 042, 047, 050, 051, 058, 059, 061, 063, 064, 073, 074, 075

Continuation of MI-43, Scholarships/Fellowships

SE- 001, 003, 019, 020, 021, 029, 042, 058, 063, 070, 071, 076, 079, 080, 081, 092, 093, 097, 101, 105, 106, 111, 117, 125, 128, 132, 137, 142, 145, 152, 158, 162, 172, 196, 197, 211, 219, 230, 231, 233, 240, 243, 252, 255, 257, 265, 272, 277, 283, 285, 291, 306, 307, 324, 335, 337, 339, 344, 347, 367, 373, 397, 402, 405, 406, 416, 422, 432, 436, 441, 446, 464, 470, 471, 480, 485, 492, 495, 498, 499, 507, 518, 520, 521, 522, 531, 532, 536, 539, 540, 550, 553, 570, 587, 592, 596, 597, 605, 641, 642, 647, 648, 685, 691, 703, 708, 713, 719, 722, 724, 734, 735, 743, 750

SW- 004, 005, 010, 013, 016, 017, 019, 022, 024, 038, 039, 041, 043, 053, 056, 058, 061, 062, 063, 064, 068, 069, 073, 075, 076, 080, 086, 091, 095, 097, 105, 107, 109, 110, 112, 129, 131, 135, 137, 138, 142, 147, 160, 169, 173, 178, 180, 195, 202, 211, 232, 234, 236, 239, 244, 248, 258, 261, 263, 277, 280, 299, 302, 313, 321, 341, 342, 349, 361, 362, 371, 378, 379

MI-44   Libraries   MI-44

CP- 008, 014, 017, 018, 019, 020, 022, 025, 027, 031, 036, 045, 047, 050, 055, 056, 057, 062, 067, 069, 073, 076, 078, 086, 101, 102, 105, 108, 109, 112, 113, 115, 121, 130, 136, 138, 139, 141, 146, 147, 151, 153, 154, 156, 164, 165, 169, 172, 175, 176, 177, 183, 186, 189, 191, 194, 196, 198, 206, 214, 215, 216, 218, 221, 223, 226, 228, 229

NE- 006, 009, 010, 012, 013, 017, 024, 029, 035, 042, 048, 050, 057, 059, 060, 061, 062, 066, 071, 073, 074, 092, 094, 096, 097, 103, 107, 108, 112, 116, 117, 119, 120, 125, 128, 129, 131, 132, 133, 136, 139, 140, 142, 143, 148, 153, 155

NW- 001, 002, 003, 006, 009, 010, 015, 017, 019, 022, 023, 027, 029, 031, 032, 033, 034, 035, 038, 042, 044, 051, 057, 058, 060, 067, 069, 070, 072, 074, 075, 078

SE- 007, 012, 021, 022, 025, 030, 033, 044, 045, 067, 084, 094, 114, 115, 125, 138, 141, 142, 162, 165, 176, 180, 181, 188, 209, 248, 255, 263, 286, 289, 293, 302, 303, 304, 310, 312, 317, 323, 332, 342, 350, 362, 406, 413, 416, 429, 446, 449, 459, 464, 478, 505, 514, 521, 522, 531, 540, 558, 573, 581, 607, 609, 611, 627, 630, 631, 635, 639, 640, 645, 646, 663, 670, 671, 706, 711, 713, 714, 719, 720, 724, 740, 747

SW- 002, 006, 007, 020, 033, 035, 041, 047, 053, 061, 062, 066, 069, 072, 073, 076, 077, 080, 095, 097, 102, 104, 113, 124, 127, 137, 141, 143, 145, 147, 160, 161, 164, 168, 170, 173, 174, 175, 176, 183, 184, 187, 188, 189, 197, 198, 199, 204, 205, 208, 217, 231, 233, 238, 245, 249, 251, 252, 258, 260, 274, 279, 284, 287, 295, 299, 308, 311, 321, 322, 326, 336, 341, 345, 346, 347, 349, 353, 375, 378, 380, 383, 385, 387, 388, 397

MI-45   Community Education/Literacy   MI-45

CP- 002, 018, 019, 056, 073, 083, 095, 101, 115, 134, 159, 164, 165, 172, 223

NE- 025, 060, 119, 121, 142, 147

NW- 051

SE- 001, 021, 025, 089, 129, 130, 145, 161, 180, 181, 182, 215, 218, 224, 225, 236, 246, 251, 255, 272, 293, 299, 307, 323, 332, 372, 405, 406, 422, 427, 433, 464, 505, 515, 522, 540, 570, 589, 596, 621, 635, 640, 642, 685, 702, 705

SW- 008, 032, 066, 069, 072, 077, 080, 087, 097, 107, 110, 145, 157, 160, 164, 227, 232, 241, 274, 295, 322, 327, 328, 334, 336, 339, 342, 371, 373

MI-49   Other Education   MI-49

CP- 017, 024, 025, 026, 042, 046, 069, 070, 091, 092, 101, 115, 172, 195, 206, 214

NE- 018, 032, 047, 061, 072, 091, 094, 119

NW- 005, 014, 019, 035, 040, 052, 064

SE- 021, 054, 076, 135, 148, 218, 224, 238, 248, 255, 397, 405, 447, 464, 476, 513, 558, 586, 640, 687, 688, 702, 706, 745

SW- 004, 007, 032, 057, 063, 067, 073, 107, 110, 139, 145, 159, 161, 180, 198, 233, 235, 239, 240, 260, 284, 287, 291, 295, 299, 301, 303, 329, 336, 346, 347, 366, 371, 388, 389, 396

MI-51   Theatre/Dance   MI-51

CP- 014, 019, 025, 036, 066, 073, 078, 083, 091, 094, 112, 126, 128, 147, 164, 175, 180, 193, 194, 206, 209, 214, 216, 221, 223, 225, 226, 229

NE- 001, 005, 013, 033, 039, 042, 057, 058, 083, 085, 086, 092, 095, 096, 110, 111, 119, 127, 134, 136, 142, 146, 148

NW- 005, 006, 014, 019, 052, 058, 060, 061, 068, 074

SE- 018, 025, 027, 030, 031, 034, 047, 050, 054, 056, 069, 083, 084, 086, 118, 119, 128, 129, 130, 142, 145, 156, 158, 161, 169, 175, 180, 181, 188, 200, 205, 215, 224, 230, 251, 255, 259, 274, 286, 289, 295, 296, 299, 302, 303, 307, 330, 332, 333, 354, 364, 367, 380, 405, 411, 413, 426, 427, 429, 450, 459, 465, 505, 506, 509, 510, 513, 515, 522, 524, 527, 532, 537, 540, 554, 558, 560, 567, 570, 575, 576, 578, 585, 586, 589, 597, 617, 630, 631, 656, 658, 661, 667, 670, 678, 680, 684, 702, 706, 709, 735, 740, 741, 746, 750

SW- 002, 004, 014, 018, 020, 021, 033, 034, 035, 039, 045, 046, 052, 060, 062, 069, 072, 078, 080, 081, 084, 087, 097, 102, 104, 111, 114, 118, 120, 121, 123, 124, 133, 137, 143, 159, 160, 161, 166, 169, 174, 175, 180, 184, 189, 202, 205, 209, 211, 213, 224, 225, 228, 230, 231, 240, 241, 243, 251, 260, 274, 282, 284, 287, 291, 295, 297, 299, 301, 309, 311, 315, 322, 336, 338, 341, 342, 350, 353, 365, 366, 371, 373, 385, 388, 396, 397

MI-52   Music   MI-52

CP- 004, 008, 010, 017, 018, 019, 025, 026, 028, 033, 036, 045, 057, 062, 066, 070, 071, 072, 073, 078, 083, 094, 101, 102, 106, 109, 115, 126, 127, 128, 129, 146, 147, 152, 160, 161, 165, 171, 172, 174, 177, 180, 189, 191, 193, 194, 206, 215, 216, 219, 221, 226, 228, 229, 231

NE- 001, 005, 008, 013, 015, 018, 024, 025, 027, 032, 033, 034, 038, 039, 042, 043, 046, 047, 053, 057, 058, 068, 073, 075, 085, 086, 088, 090, 094, 095, 097, 099, 103, 104, 107, 108, 111, 112, 115, 117, 119, 125, 128, 129, 132, 133, 134, 135, 136, 138, 142, 150, 153, 155

NW- 001, 005, 006, 012, 014, 019, 035, 036, 040, 043, 047, 052, 054, 061, 074

SE- 007, 010, 013, 018, 021, 022, 025, 027, 030, 031, 033, 034, 040, 044, 045, 047, 052, 054, 056, 060, 067, 075, 077, 078, 084, 086, 087, 094, 095, 103, 106, 107, 118, 119, 123, 127, 129, 130, 134, 140, 142, 145, 161, 166, 169, 175, 178, 179, 180, 184, 188, 192, 195, 211, 215, 217, 218, 224, 232, 234, 235, 236, 241, 248, 249, 251, 255, 258, 259, 261, 263, 266, 272, 278, 289, 293, 295, 296, 299, 303, 307, 311, 315, 316, 317, 322, 323, 324, 326, 327, 332, 333, 337, 343, 351, 354, 355, 360, 369, 370, 371, 379, 386, 393, 400, 406, 411, 416, 418, 422, 425, 426, 427, 431, 433, 438, 439, 446, 450, 459, 472, 475, 481, 491, 494, 497, 498, 501, 505, 507, 509, 510, 513, 514, 515, 517, 522, 532, 533, 540, 544, 554, 555, 557, 558, 559, 560, 565, 566, 568, 569, 570, 573, 575, 578, 582, 583, 585, 586, 599, 600, 601, 622, 625, 630, 631, 634, 640, 641, 643, 645, 649, 659, 661, 667, 671, 672, 677, 682, 684, 687, 689, 690, 697, 706, 707, 713, 715, 719, 720, 724, 731, 741, 743, 745, 750

SW- 004, 006, 007, 014, 018, 021, 024, 026, 028, 033, 034, 035, 044, 047, 048, 052, 053, 055, 060, 062, 070, 072, 073, 078, 080, 081, 084, 085, 086, 087, 095, 097, 098, 099, 102, 104, 105, 106, 110, 111, 115, 116, 118, 121, 123, 124, 130, 133, 137, 141, 146, 147, 150, 154, 155, 156, 158, 159, 160, 161, 165, 167, 169, 170, 174, 175, 177, 179, 180, 184, 187, 188, 196, 198, 200, 201, 203, 205, 208, 209, 216, 222, 224, 227, 228, 230, 231, 233, 235, 240, 241, 243, 247, 251, 254, 255, 258, 259, 260, 272, 274, 279, 282, 284, 287, 293, 295, 299, 300, 301, 306, 308, 309, 311, 314, 315, 317, 318, 321, 322, 331, 336, 341, 342, 346, 347, 350, 353, 354, 365, 371, 372, 373, 375, 380, 385, 387, 391, 396, 397, 400

MI-53   Visual Arts   MI-53

CP- 018, 025, 073, 093, 096, 101, 102, 109, 115, 156, 165, 225

NE- 001, 005, 025, 033, 039, 051, 058, 116, 117, 119, 121, 142

NW- 040

SE- 002, 022, 027, 045, 047, 054, 078, 084, 104, 114, 116, 128, 134, 138, 141, 142, 145, 153, 164, 175, 176, 192, 197, 215, 224, 230, 238, 255, 258, 263, 274, 296, 303, 310, 323, 326, 327, 333, 337, 359, 360, 375, 377, 378, 387, 403, 404, 406, 416, 417, 420, 421, 427, 431, 433, 450, 460, 464, 470, 497, 498, 505, 508, 509, 510, 513, 514, 515, 521, 525, 528, 533, 540, 544, 549, 554, 557, 558, 569, 578, 585, 586, 656, 659, 670, 677, 678, 694, 696, 700, 702, 713, 719, 731, 750

SW- 026, 033, 044, 046, 048, 062, 084, 092, 099, 143, 158, 160, 161, 165, 166, 173, 179, 190, 205, 213, 250, 252, 259, 284, 298, 309, 337, 338, 339, 347, 354, 397

MI-54   Museums   MI-54

CP- 004, 016, 018, 025, 033, 036, 043, 045, 072, 073, 078, 083, 101, 102, 109, 115, 126, 127, 134, 140, 143, 144, 146, 150, 151, 152, 160, 165, 174, 186, 191, 194, 225

NE- 001, 005, 015, 018, 023, 027, 029, 032, 038, 039, 048, 053, 057, 058, 059, 078, 083, 085, 086, 090, 092, 094, 095, 096, 104, 111, 119, 121, 125, 126, 128, 134, 140, 145, 147, 150, 155

NW- 001, 005, 009, 019, 026, 029, 031, 032, 040, 061, 074, 078

SE- 001, 003, 006, 009, 012, 013, 018, 021, 022, 024, 025, 027, 030, 032, 033, 034, 045, 047, 049, 053, 054, 055, 056, 059, 060, 065, 067, 075, 083, 084, 085, 086, 087, 095, 103, 107, 114, 116, 118, 119, 121, 123, 124, 129, 130, 134, 135, 136, 138, 140, 142, 145, 147, 153, 156, 161, 164, 165, 169, 171, 175, 176, 179, 180, 185, 186, 190, 192, 197, 198, 203, 205, 210, 211, 213, 215, 218, 220, 224, 227, 232, 235, 238, 242, 248, 251, 255, 258, 269, 272, 275, 277, 278, 284, 286, 289, 293, 295, 302, 307, 315, 320, 323, 326, 327, 330, 332, 333, 337, 343, 345, 350, 351, 352, 353, 359, 360, 367, 368, 371, 372, 373, 375, 377, 386, 393, 394, 398, 404, 405, 406, 408, 410, 411, 412, 413, 416, 420, 426, 427, 431, 438, 439, 440, 446, 450, 459, 465, 467, 472, 475, 481, 485, 495, 496, 497, 500, 505, 506, 508, 509, 510, 511, 513, 514, 515, 517, 519, 521, 524, 525, 526, 528, 539, 540, 544, 545, 549, 550, 554, 556, 557, 558, 564, 565, 567, 568, 569, 575, 576, 578, 582, 583, 589, 590, 595, 596, 597, 602, 609, 621, 625, 626, 627, 629, 634, 635, 639, 641, 643, 645, 650, 655, 656, 660, 661, 667, 670, 673, 676, 677, 678, 684, 687, 696, 699, 700, 706, 707, 710, 712, 713, 719, 724, 729, 731, 740, 750

SW- 004, 007, 018, 024, 025, 026, 027, 033, 035, 039, 041, 044, 047, 048, 049, 050, 052, 053, 060, 062, 067, 077, 078, 084, 086, 087, 095, 099, 104, 105, 107, 118, 124, 126, 128, 133, 135, 137, 143, 150, 154, 156, 157, 158, 159, 160, 161, 164, 165, 166, 167, 168, 169, 173, 174, 175, 176, 180, 184, 190, 192, 196, 198, 199, 201, 202, 205, 208, 209, 218, 225, 227, 228, 230, 231, 233, 238, 239, 240, 241, 242, 250, 251, 252, 253, 254, 255, 256, 259, 260, 266, 276, 277, 284, 285, 287, 292, 293, 295, 297, 300, 308, 309, 311, 314, 316, 318, 319, 322, 327, 336, 337, 339, 341, 342, 347, 348, 350, 353, 354, 363, 365, 366, 367, 371, 372, 373, 375, 376, 377, 379, 380, 389, 396, 397

MI-55   Community Arts   MI-55

CP- 002, 004, 010, 014, 017, 018, 019, 025, 026, 030, 034, 043, 045, 053, 056, 057, 066, 069, 070, 072, 073, 075, 076, 078, 083, 101, 106, 108, 109, 112, 115, 119, 126, 128, 130, 135, 136, 146, 147, 150, 151, 157, 160, 164, 165, 166, 172, 174, 177, 180, 186, 189, 193, 194, 195, 198, 204, 205, 206, 214, 216, 219, 223, 224, 225, 228, 229, 231

NE- 005, 009, 012, 013, 017, 018, 019, 024, 025, 027, 035, 039, 042, 043, 046, 048, 057, 059, 060, 061, 073, 075, 085, 086, 090, 091, 095, 096, 097, 105, 107, 108, 109, 116, 117, 120, 125, 128, 129, 132, 133, 134, 135, 140, 142, 145, 151, 155

NW- 005, 006, 009, 014, 018, 019, 022, 031, 032, 034, 040, 043, 044, 045, 047, 060, 061, 065, 069, 070, 073, 074, 079

SE- 001, 002, 006, 013, 022, 025, 030, 035, 044, 045, 047, 049, 053, 054, 056, 059, 067, 075, 081, 084, 086, 089, 090, 104, 114, 119, 125, 128, 129, 130, 134, 138, 140, 141, 142, 145, 148, 169, 173, 175, 180, 182, 188, 195, 197, 205, 211, 212, 215, 224, 230, 251, 255, 259, 263, 274, 277, 278, 279, 289, 294, 296, 303, 307, 322, 323, 330, 332, 333, 337, 341, 350, 360, 362, 366, 368, 375, 377, 378, 383, 403, 404, 405, 411, 413, 414, 416, 418, 422, 425, 426, 427, 429, 431, 433, 444, 446, 450, 457, 459, 460, 464, 472, 505, 507, 509, 510, 511, 513, 515, 518, 527, 528, 532, 540, 558, 566, 569, 578, 582, 586, 589, 600, 602, 613, 615, 618, 622, 626, 635, 640, 641, 643, 648, 660, 661, 663, 667, 671, 676, 682, 690, 700, 702, 706, 710, 711, 715, 723, 728, 729, 731, 740, 745, 750

SW- 004, 007, 018, 020, 021, 024, 026, 027, 029, 032, 033, 034, 035, 039, 042, 047, 048, 049, 050, 052, 053, 055, 062, 069, 072, 073, 078, 081, 084, 087, 090, 092, 095, 096, 097, 100, 104, 107, 111, 112, 118, 120, 121, 123, 124, 137, 145, 158, 159, 160, 161, 164, 165, 166, 174, 175, 184, 187, 199, 205, 216, 231, 238, 241, 242, 243, 251, 258, 259, 260, 279, 282, 284, 285, 287, 291, 292, 295, 297, 298, 299, 306, 308, 309, 311, 314, 315, 318, 326, 338, 339, 342, 347, 348, 350, 354, 364, 365, 366, 371, 373, 375, 377, 378, 385, 387, 388, 389, 396, 397

MI-56   Historical   MI-56

CP- 009, 010, 011, 014, 016, 017, 018, 020, 025, 026, 028, 033, 036, 041, 045, 055, 056, 058, 062, 069, 070, 073, 075, 077, 078, 085, 098, 101, 108, 114, 115, 135, 144, 146, 148, 151, 155, 164, 165, 168, 171, 172, 176, 177, 182, 183, 193, 194, 195, 196, 198, 204, 205, 214, 215, 216, 221, 223, 229, 231

NE- 005, 008, 013, 014, 018, 021, 023, 029, 032, 040, 052, 057, 058, 060, 073, 075, 083, 086, 089, 091, 095, 101, 107, 108, 111, 112, 116, 117, 119, 128, 133, 134, 138, 140, 142, 145, 146, 147, 153

NW- 008, 009, 011, 014, 019, 030, 031, 033, 042, 044, 045, 055, 059, 060, 061, 068, 070, 071, 074, 079

SE- 001, 003, 010, 012, 020, 022, 025, 028, 033, 034, 038, 041, 044, 045, 047, 050, 053, 056, 067, 086, 096, 103, 115, 117, 119, 129, 130, 136, 138, 141, 145, 162, 163, 165, 176, 180, 185, 186, 188, 190, 191, 192, 215, 232, 235, 238, 239, 242, 243, 248, 254, 259, 274, 278, 283, 286, 289, 296, 299, 302, 303, 305, 310, 327, 333, 337, 339, 343, 346, 371, 381, 401, 405, 406, 408,

Continuation of MI-56, Historical

SE- 410, 413, 417, 422, 427, 429, 446, 454, 459, 464, 474, 476, 478, 481, 486, 505, 511, 513, 514, 519, 525, 526, 528, 531, 544, 553, 554, 556, 557, 561, 565, 566, 568, 569, 576, 578, 586, 590, 596, 603, 623, 645, 646, 652, 655, 663, 666, 667, 670, 677, 684, 686, 700, 702, 706, 719, 733, 741, 742, 750

SW- 004, 006, 007, 024, 033, 035, 044, 045, 046, 047, 049, 050, 053, 055, 062, 066, 069, 070, 076, 080, 084, 087, 095, 096, 099, 100, 104, 105, 106, 110, 115, 128, 133, 136, 137, 143, 145, 147, 160, 161, 165, 168, 169, 170, 174, 175, 178, 181, 184, 187, 190, 196, 199, 202, 205, 209, 218, 222, 227, 228, 231, 232, 233, 238, 242, 243, 250, 252, 256, 258, 260, 265, 266, 269, 274, 277, 279, 282, 284, 287, 291, 299, 301, 308, 313, 314, 315, 316, 324, 339, 345, 354, 366, 371, 373, 375, 380, 383, 385, 386, 387, 388, 395, 397

MI-57   Public Broadcasting   MI-57

CP- 025, 027, 031, 043, 045, 055, 071, 072, 073, 076, 094, 101, 102, 128, 129, 138, 148, 157, 159, 169, 172, 174, 180, 206, 223, 228

NE- 005, 009, 018, 027, 034, 057, 073, 086, 088, 090, 092, 095, 111, 116, 120, 125, 133, 140, 142, 155

NW- 005, 019, 022, 027, 029, 030, 036, 040, 047, 051, 061, 074, 012

SE- 022, 025, 027, 034, 045, 047, 048, 049, 075, 083, 085, 086, 107, 130, 175, 188, 211, 225, 251, 259, 269, 274, 277, 295, 302, 305, 330, 332, 337, 343, 350, 373, 379, 411, 418, 432, 438, 459, 505, 506, 513, 514, 558, 566, 569, 576, 578, 589, 595, 609, 641, 684, 689, 699, 706, 719, 740, 747, 750

SW- 004, 007, 009, 016, 018, 024, 033, 047, 049, 050, 052, 053, 077, 087, 100, 104, 106, 118, 121, 158, 164, 165, 166, 174, 175, 198, 208, 216, 224, 231, 232, 243, 255, 259, 260, 287, 295, 297, 299, 311, 314, 317, 319, 322, 323, 336, 339, 347, 350, 354, 366, 373, 375, 397

MI-61   Catholic Churches/Missions   MI-61

CP- 011, 017, 021, 038, 074, 093, 104, 121, 141, 145, 156, 189, 227

NE- 002, 003, 007, 013, 018, 056, 063, 064, 065, 080, 088, 097, 098, 102, 126, 127, 136, 150, 152

NW- 013, 022, 034, 035, 036, 048, 049, 051, 058, 062

SE- 016, 036, 037, 058, 070, 080, 102, 105, 113, 115, 123, 141, 145, 146, 148, 152, 156, 157, 177, 178, 185, 188, 204, 233, 243, 252, 254, 256, 262, 267, 316, 335, 343, 349, 367, 370, 378, 387, 388, 428, 434, 436, 442, 445, 469, 470, 473, 490, 491, 499, 530, 548, 550, 576, 582, 587, 588, 626, 664, 665, 698

SW- 006, 008, 016, 028, 039, 041, 044, 053, 080, 082, 083, 085, 088, 090, 092, 093, 094, 109, 110, 116, 133, 142, 151, 156, 189, 197, 202, 216, 217, 220, 224, 230, 233, 234, 242, 246, 261, 269, 271, 272, 279, 285, 291, 305, 307, 314, 317, 321, 322, 341, 342, 343, 346, 357, 377, 393, 399, 400

MI-62   Jewish Synagogues/Charities   MI-62

CP- 030, 071, 072, 075, 107, 110, 150, 166, 169, 174, 190

NE- 006, 013, 015, 016, 022, 024, 025, 026, 033, 034, 035, 037, 041, 045, 046, 048, 052, 071, 077, 078, 084, 085, 087, 088, 093, 099, 100, 104, 106, 111, 120, 123, 124, 128, 130, 136, 137, 138, 152

NW- 077, 078

SE- 006, 009, 013, 022, 024, 027, 030, 031, 035, 038, 043, 046, 050, 060, 062, 063, 067, 068, 069, 072, 073, 075, 082, 087, 094, 108, 109, 118, 119, 124, 131, 134, 135, 136, 143, 147, 150, 160, 166, 170, 171, 179, 184, 192, 193, 194, 195, 198, 201, 203, 210, 211, 212, 213, 214, 217, 219, 220, 227, 228, 229, 238, 241, 242, 245, 247, 258, 259, 261, 263, 264, 266, 269, 272, 273, 275, 276, 277, 279, 280, 281, 284, 286, 290, 292, 293, 294, 295, 298, 303, 307, 308, 318, 321, 327, 338, 342, 351, 352, 353, 354, 356, 357, 359, 360, 363, 366, 371, 374, 375, 381, 383, 384, 385, 386, 393, 396, 397, 398, 399, 407, 408, 409, 410, 411, 412, 418, 419, 431, 433, 437, 438, 452, 453, 457, 458, 465, 466, 478, 481, 483, 489, 496, 497, 500, 504, 507, 509, 511, 512, 517, 521, 523, 526, 527, 528, 531, 542, 549, 554, 556, 557, 558, 563, 564, 569, 571, 572, 574, 575, 577, 578, 581, 583, 584, 585, 590, 591, 593, 599, 602, 604, 609, 610, 612, 615, 616, 617, 620, 622, 625, 629, 630, 631, 633, 634, 636, 637, 638, 643, 645, 646, 650, 655, 656, 659, 660, 662, 667, 668, 670, 674, 676, 677, 679, 680, 681, 683, 686, 689, 693, 694, 696, 697, 700, 707, 711, 712, 713, 714, 715, 721, 732, 736, 737, 738, 749, 750

SW- 024, 025, 026, 027, 037, 040, 048, 060, 101, 102, 104, 115, 123, 124, 137, 141, 143, 148, 149, 150, 154, 170, 177, 185, 191, 203, 206, 210, 212, 225, 250, 254, 255, 262, 270, 276, 278, 279, 290, 292, 294, 305, 306, 309, 319, 320, 331, 332, 348, 350, 351, 354, 357, 369, 370, 381, 382, 384

MI-72   Zoos/Animal Humane/Wildlife   MI-72

MI-79   Other Environmental   MI-79

MI-81   International   MI-81

MI-82   Overseas Institutions/Programs   MI-82

MI-83 Good Government MI-83

CP-.....010, 067, 107, 229

NW-....009

SE-.....056, 067, 081, 107, 129, 130, 165, 180, 206, 211, 215, 269, 303, 305, 337, 353, 400, 505, 513, 515, 523, 527, 528, 550, 554, 589, 608, 623, 670, 671, 697, 709

SW-....006, 036, 042, 103, 111, 159, 239, 241, 250, 251, 252, 260, 287, 295, 347, 363, 364, 375

MI-84 Sports/Camps MI-84

CP-.....008, 033, 036, 043, 044, 045, 062, 074, 078, 085, 092, 098, 109, 114, 117, 119, 136, 138, 139, 141, 147, 148, 151, 153, 176, 177, 182, 187, 199, 200, 204, 209, 221, 223, 224

NE-.....001, 009, 012, 017, 033, 042, 051, 060, 063, 069, 081, 092, 101, 122, 132, 138, 139, 142, 152, 155

NW-....006, 009, 014, 015, 018, 019, 020, 024, 025, 031, 032, 033, 045, 053, 058, 059, 070

SE-.....001, 025, 040, 044, 048, 052, 053, 059, 069, 095, 108, 113, 124, 142, 148, 157, 161, 167, 180, 182, 188, 189, 205, 211, 233, 236, 242, 263, 269, 286, 289, 302, 304, 314, 330, 332, 351, 365, 373, 389, 393, 395, 400, 406, 414, 424, 428, 433, 443, 457, 464, 475, 476, 491, 505, 514, 524, 534, 536, 556, 557, 561, 569, 570, 581, 586, 600, 606, 618, 621, 632, 637, 640, 645, 663, 670, 676, 682, 684, 702, 710, 717, 727, 743, 744, 745, 747

SW-....001, 023, 065, 066, 070, 073, 078, 080, 087, 095, 097, 112, 113, 116, 124, 127, 158, 164, 174, 186, 189, 199, 200, 211, 218, 231, 233, 238, 239, 240, 257, 258, 261, 273, 278, 279, 281, 283, 284, 293, 310, 322, 327, 330, 337, 345, 368, 387, 390, 391

MI-85 Economic Development MI-85

CP-.....010, 014, 050, 054, 057, 115, 119, 124, 138, 143, 144, 164, 166, 168, 186, 194, 198, 199, 214, 221

NE-.....017, 029, 090, 094, 104, 111, 138, 140, 142, 151

NW-....009, 017, 018, 019, 031, 034, 057, 073, 079

SE-.....027, 045, 054, 103, 125, 129, 188, 223, 224, 225, 294, 317, 320, 334, 400, 405, 505, 513, 559, 586, 609, 626, 640, 702, 706, 733

SW-....007, 021, 035, 061, 069, 070, 073, 086, 087, 095, 096, 110, 145, 160, 161, 164, 175, 198, 202, 204, 214, 231, 238, 241, 243, 250, 251, 260, 266, 284, 287, 294, 301, 304, 306, 308, 341, 364, 366, 377, 379

MI-86 Public Policy Research MI-86

CP-.....028, 083, 148, 231

SE-.....052, 095, 129, 135, 215, 305, 312, 332, 333, 377, 413, 506, 513, 592, 625, 669, 676

SW-....006, 021, 036, 047, 057, 067, 088, 095, 107, 137, 145, 160, 173, 182, 183, 186, 239, 243, 266, 282, 328, 329, 363, 397

MI-88 Matching Gift Programs MI-88

CP-.....010, 019, 083, 186, 206

NE-.....018, 034, 129, 224, 270, 518, 524, 540, 586, 589, 653, 687, 724

SW-....004, 005, 007, 087, 159, 198, 241, 260, 287, 295, 371

MI-89 Other Miscellaneous Giving MI-89

CP-.....010, 020, 025, 033, 036, 043, 044, 045, 062, 074, 077, 085, 089, 098, 099, 112, 135, 136, 137, 138, 139, 146, 147, 151, 154, 182, 196, 200, 204, 205, 211, 221, 229

NE-.....003, 009, 014, 024, 031, 038, 046, 055, 060, 064, 067, 081, 090, 092, 099, 103, 129, 132, 133, 142, 148, 152

NW-....001, 003, 004, 006, 009, 014, 018, 025, 027, 034, 035, 038, 058, 059, 067, 068, 070, 071, 072, 073

SE-.....021, 025, 033, 125, 132, 142, 162, 223, 232, 283, 289, 291, 314, 327, 365, 446, 469, 474, 518, 531, 541, 554, 561, 581, 652, 662, 663, 669, 677, 706, 747

SW-....001, 005, 006, 007, 029, 070, 075, 082, 096, 127, 131, 180, 187, 217, 230, 238, 242, 243, 252, 261, 306, 318, 322, 323, 324, 329, 342, 343, 346, 353, 366, 379, 383, 386, 387

Continuation of MI-51, Conservation & Ecology

SE-.....422, 424, 427, 429, 432, 435, 440, 446, 459, 462, 464, 473, 485, 487, 505, 506, 513, 522, 527, 531, 541, 554, 555, 556, 558, 561, 565, 566, 576, 586, 596, 597, 598, 600, 623, 635, 640, 646, 649, 652, 663, 665, 666, 669, 673, 678, 687, 696, 702, 704, 706, 709, 710, 719, 740, 741, 742, 744, 747

SW-....006, 007, 008, 009, 020, 023, 029, 032, 033, 039, 041, 044, 049, 050, 061, 062, 066, 067, 070, 073, 077, 080, 087, 094, 095, 097, 103, 105, 110, 115, 118, 119, 120, 121, 122, 124, 126, 127, 128, 133, 137, 158, 161, 164, 165, 166, 168, 169, 170, 174, 175, 181, 183, 184, 186, 190, 193, 198, 199, 205, 210, 226, 227, 228, 230, 232, 233, 238, 239, 242, 243, 249, 250, 251, 265, 267, 272, 277, 279, 282, 285, 295, 296, 297, 299, 301, 304, 306, 308, 309, 315, 316, 317, 321, 323, 324, 326, 328, 329, 337, 338, 340, 341, 342, 347, 353, 354, 366, 373, 375, 380, 397, 400

MI-72   Zoos/Animal Humane/Wildlife   MI-72

CP-.....013, 025, 057, 078, 082, 089, 109, 133, 138, 151, 156, 177, 221, 226

NE-.....001, 024, 032, 044, 057, 067, 084, 101, 108, 110, 117, 120, 129, 136

NW-....006, 010, 014, 019

SE-.....001, 017, 025, 028, 034, 040, 044, 045, 051, 055, 056, 057, 065, 085, 086, 088, 093, 096, 097, 100, 120, 129, 140, 142, 148, 153, 169, 174, 183, 191, 192, 195, 207, 235, 251, 284, 289, 296, 299, 302, 307, 314, 327, 332, 336, 346, 359, 371, 380, 413, 416, 417, 426, 427, 428, 432, 433, 439, 444, 446, 449, 459, 472, 475, 482, 486, 487, 497, 502, 513, 521, 522, 530, 531, 540, 554, 561, 565, 566, 586, 595, 597, 621, 628, 635, 649, 663, 666, 667, 669, 678, 684, 687, 690, 704, 706, 707, 709, 719, 724, 738, 740, 741, 747

SW-....006, 012, 018, 022, 034, 035, 039, 062, 073, 077, 089, 097, 103, 124, 136, 137, 143, 158, 160, 161, 166, 168, 169, 175, 180, 184, 187, 204, 205, 213, 223, 226, 227, 232, 242, 243, 252, 260, 261, 267, 282, 295, 297, 299, 300, 308, 318, 322, 327, 328, 342, 346, 347, 353, 354, 366, 385, 386

MI-79   Other Environmental   MI-79

CP-.....022, 107, 149

NE-.....071

SE-.....056, 081, 107, 126, 130, 180, 206, 215, 274, 379, 435, 505, 513, 515, 607, 673, 702, 704, 709

SW-....042, 067, 103, 158, 169, 205, 243, 364

MI-81   International   MI-81

CP-.....010, 083, 146, 209

NE-.....019, 068, 088, 090

NW-....019

SE-.....021, 022, 034, 081, 086, 107, 111, 129, 154, 171, 180, 182, 209, 211, 215, 240, 248, 265, 294, 303, 307, 315, 330, 331, 338, 353, 371, 380, 386, 416, 432, 440, 454, 467, 482, 505, 509, 515, 517, 519, 528, 537, 540, 544, 545, 550, 554, 583, 589, 595, 623, 625, 660, 667, 671, 679, 706, 711, 712, 744

SW-....004, 007, 014, 024, 036, 042, 057, 067, 100, 137, 160, 161, 175, 201, 224, 251, 296, 311, 314, 317, 329, 332, 347, 371, 372, 375

MI-82   Overseas Institutions/Programs   MI-82

CP-.....006, 058, 071, 090, 111, 169, 209

NE-.....034, 068, 100, 116

NW-....037

SE-.....008, 059, 061, 062, 065, 068, 075, 086, 087, 103, 124, 130, 135, 148, 163, 170, 184, 194, 206, 212, 214, 218, 220, 238, 265, 272, 274, 285, 296, 315, 326, 338, 340, 351, 379, 397, 401, 409, 462, 481, 482, 489, 497, 511, 521, 522, 552, 558, 595, 598, 599, 609, 610, 617, 624, 625, 638, 647, 650, 655, 656, 668, 670, 676, 680, 681, 695, 696, 698, 706, 707, 711, 749

SW-....028, 065, 077, 096, 099, 115, 151, 157, 158, 166, 170, 249, 269, 296, 313, 366, 398

MI-83   Good Government   MI-83

CP-.....010, 067, 107, 229

NW-....009

SE-.....056, 067, 081, 107, 129, 130, 165, 180, 206, 211, 215, 269, 303, 305, 337, 353, 400, 505, 513, 515, 523, 527, 528, 550, 554, 589, 608, 623, 670, 671, 697, 709

SW-....006, 036, 042, 103, 111, 159, 239, 241, 250, 251, 252, 260, 287, 295, 347, 363, 364, 375

MI-84   Sports/Camps   MI-84

CP-.....008, 033, 036, 043, 044, 045, 062, 074, 078, 085, 092, 098, 109, 114, 117, 119, 136, 138, 139, 141, 147, 148, 151, 153, 176, 177, 182, 187, 199, 200, 204, 209, 221, 223, 224

NE-.....001, 009, 012, 017, 033, 042, 051, 060, 063, 069, 081, 092, 101, 122, 132, 138, 139, 142, 152, 155

NW-....006, 009, 014, 015, 018, 019, 020, 024, 025, 031, 032, 033, 045, 053, 058, 059, 070

SE-.....001, 025, 040, 044, 048, 052, 053, 059, 069, 095, 108, 113, 124, 142, 148, 157, 161, 167, 180, 182, 188, 189, 205, 211, 233, 236, 242, 263, 269, 286, 289, 302, 304, 314, 330, 332, 351, 365, 373, 389, 393, 395, 400, 406, 414, 424, 428, 433, 443, 457, 464, 475, 476, 491, 505, 514, 524, 534, 536, 556, 557, 561, 569, 570, 581, 586, 600, 606, 618, 621, 632, 637, 640, 645, 663, 670, 676, 682, 684, 702, 710, 717, 727, 743, 744, 745, 747

SW-....001, 023, 065, 066, 070, 073, 078, 080, 087, 095, 097, 112, 113, 116, 124, 127, 158, 164, 174, 186, 189, 199, 200, 211, 218, 231, 233, 238, 239, 240, 257, 258, 261, 273, 278, 279, 281, 283, 284, 293, 310, 322, 327, 330, 337, 345, 368, 387, 390, 391

MI-85   Economic Development   MI-85

CP-.....010, 014, 050, 054, 057, 115, 119, 124, 138, 143, 144, 164, 166, 168, 186, 194, 198, 199, 214, 221

NE-.....017, 029, 090, 094, 104, 111, 138, 140, 142, 151

NW-....009, 017, 018, 019, 031, 034, 057, 073, 079

SE-.....027, 045, 054, 103, 125, 129, 188, 223, 224, 225, 294, 317, 320, 334, 400, 405, 505, 513, 559, 586, 609, 626, 640, 702, 706, 733

SW-....007, 021, 035, 061, 069, 070, 073, 086, 087, 095, 096, 110, 145, 160, 161, 164, 175, 198, 202, 204, 214, 231, 238, 241, 243, 250, 251, 260, 266, 284, 287, 294, 301, 304, 306, 308, 341, 364, 366, 377, 379

MI-86   Public Policy Research   MI-86

CP-.....028, 083, 148, 231

SE-.....052, 095, 129, 135, 215, 305, 312, 332, 333, 377, 413, 506, 513, 592, 625, 669, 676

SW-....006, 021, 036, 047, 057, 067, 088, 095, 107, 137, 145, 160, 173, 182, 183, 186, 239, 243, 266, 282, 328, 329, 363, 397

MI-88   Matching Gift Programs   MI-88

CP-.....010, 019, 083, 186, 206

NE-.....018, 034, 129, 224, 270, 518, 524, 540, 586, 589, 653, 687, 724

SW-....004, 005, 007, 087, 159, 198, 241, 260, 287, 295, 371

MI-89   Other Miscellaneous Giving   MI-89

CP-.....010, 020, 025, 033, 036, 043, 044, 045, 062, 074, 077, 085, 089, 098, 099, 112, 135, 136, 137, 138, 139, 146, 147, 151, 154, 182, 196, 200, 204, 205, 211, 221, 229

NE-.....003, 009, 014, 024, 031, 038, 046, 055, 060, 064, 067, 081, 090, 092, 099, 103, 129, 132, 133, 142, 148, 152

NW-....001, 003, 004, 006, 009, 014, 018, 025, 027, 034, 035, 038, 058, 059, 067, 068, 070, 071, 072, 073

SE-.....021, 025, 033, 125, 132, 142, 162, 223, 232, 283, 289, 291, 314, 327, 365, 446, 469, 474, 518, 531, 541, 554, 561, 581, 652, 662, 663, 669, 677, 706, 747

SW-....001, 005, 006, 007, 029, 070, 075, 082, 096, 127, 131, 180, 187, 217, 230, 238, 242, 243, 252, 261, 306, 318, 322, 323, 324, 329, 342, 343, 346, 353, 366, 379, 383, 386, 387

MAIN INDEX
of all foundations in the directory

B

E

F

G

H

I

J

K

L

M

N

O

P

Q

R

T

Y

Z

NOTES